HOYT'S
NEW CYCLOPEDIA
OF
PRACTICAL QUOTATIONS

HOYT'S

New Cyclopedia OF Practical Quotations

DRAWN FROM THE SPEECH AND LITERATURE OF ALL NATIONS, ANCIENT AND MODERN, CLASSIC AND POPULAR, IN ENGLISH AND FOREIGN TEXT. WITH THE NAMES, DATES, AND NATIONALITY OF QUOTED AUTHORS, AND COPIOUS INDEXES

COMPLETELY REVISED AND GREATLY ENLARGED

BY

KATE LOUISE ROBERTS

FUNK & WAGNALLS COMPANY
NEW YORK AND LONDON

Ruhrah Collection

TO

DR. FRANK H. VIZETELLY

IN PRAISE OF THE BRIDGE THAT CARRIED ME OVER,

A BRIDGE OF PATIENT SYMPATHY AND SCHOLARLY HELPFULNESS;

THE KEYSTONE LOYALTY TO THE WORLD OF LETTERS;

THE ARCH BROAD AND GRACIOUS.

K. L. R.

Criticism of our contemporaries is not criticism; it is conversation.

Credited to LEMAÎTRE BY BRANDER MATTHEWS, see *New York Times*, April 2, 1922.

The pressure of public opinion is like the pressure of the atmosphere; you can't see it — but, all the same it is sixteen pounds to the square inch.

LOWELL — In an interview with JULIAN HAWTHORNE; see article by BRANDER MATTHEWS in *New York Times*, April 2, 1922.

PREFACE

To Amalthæa, the nurse of his infancy, Zeus gave a magic horn of plenty, which by his grace was over-brimming no matter what was taken from it. This NEW EDITION of a standard work, like the famous cornucopia, contains a freshened and replenished store. In the garnering of this rich harvest of fruits culled from the vast fields of literature, tribute has been taken from every tree in our literary Eden, so that the reader may share in common with his fellow creatures, not only the kindly fruits of the earth, but also the golden apples plucked from the tree of the knowledge of good and of evil. Since divine discontent is wholesome, we may expect to find some apples of discord as well as of love, the apples of Sodom and of Cain, and a modicum of dead sea fruit. Something there will be of distasteful growth, but the weed's plain heart holds a secret though 'tis shallow rooted. Many a way-side flower in a crannied nook has carried a message to an humble heart, and because its bloom has attracted public attention, it warrants a place among the choicer blossoms in this horn of plenty filled for all sorts and conditions of men.

The effort of the compiler has been to make the collection the most complete that has ever been gathered within the covers of a book. There has been provided

"Fruit of all kinds, in coat
Rough, or smooth rind, or bearded husk, or shell."

of which Milton sang in Paradise Lost.

In seeking enrichment of his own ideas, a speaker or writer is more concerned with the flavor and odor of the flower or fruit than with its progenitor, therefore the compiler, in gathering and preserving the "wisdom of the wise and experience of the ages," labels each specimen according to its quality (Topical arrangement) rather than source (Author arrangement).

The latter need is amply met by a biographical index wherein authors are paged. Thus like is with like, and an index to topics, with cross references, links up combinations of relating attraction.

The phrases which are "the parole of literary men the world over," form the basic value of the work. The compiler's blue pencil has hesitated over the prolific output of the "moderns," for public taste is fickle and what is popular to-day is padding to-morrow.

In these stirring times the press has teemed with utterances of prominent people, but records are inaccurate and unreliable, as has been tested through personal letters.

Locke states: "He that has but ever so little examined the citations of writers cannot doubt how little credit the quotations deserve where the originals are wanting; and consequently, how much less quotations of quotations can be relied on."

Many omissions may be accounted for by the fact that men of action often prefer the gold of silence to the speech of silver, but on the whole, the Biographical Index is a Who's Who of authors of all times.

It has not been easy to follow Dr. Routh's advice, "always to verify your references," for editions, texts and authorities differ. At times only a hint of an authority has been available, but rather than lose an item of value it has been deemed best to retain a meager suggestion in hope of future discovery.

It may be claimed for this work, without fear of contradiction, that no other of its kind contains so full an array of material under topics; none with such a representation of modern writers and speakers; no other includes such a record of modern war phrases, songs and poems; nowhere else are kindred thoughts and expressions so closely connected by cross references that they may be compared, and in no other collection of quotations have the nerves and arteries of the contents been laid open so plainly through so comprehensive and complete a concordance.

Topics have been chosen for their general character, so that similar ideas might not be too widely separated, which is a fault of too detailed subdivision.

The compiler takes comfort in the words of Cotton Mather: "Reader, Carthagena was of the mind that unto those three things which the ancients held to be impossible, there should be added this fourth; to find a book without Erratas. It seems the hands of Briareus and the eyes of Argus will not prevent them."

Whatever degree this work has attained in the achievement of the impossible, it owes to Mr. Leander J. DeBekker, the Briareus and Argus of the printed page and its literary contents. Appreciation and gratitude are but feebly expressed in this tribute to his services.

Acknowledgment is due to Messrs. Harper & Bros. for permission to use the lines written by Peter Newell found on pages 280 and 538.

Kate Louise Roberts.

PLAN OF THE BOOK, AND DIRECTIONS FOR USING IT

The reader is reminded that this work is a book of literary gems selected with a view to their usefulness in suggesting ideas for practical application in literary composition and not a mere collection of familiar quotations to serve as a remembrancer to such as may wish to refresh their memories. Therefore, quotations drawn from standard authors and familiar in our mouths as household words, have not been included because concordances of the works of these authors already exist. Every student of Shakespeare should know of the concordances to Shakespeare, Wordsworth, and other poets.

The quotations are arranged under topics according to their general meaning, sense, or idea. The topics are in alphabetical order, as are the authors under the topics. An Index to Topics, with cross reference to kindred ones, will be found on page **xi**.

The Concordance at the end of the book is a word-index of the text of each quotation. Identifying words are generously indexed, so that the lines may be traced through several channels in case the memory fails in exact reading. Enough of the context is given to identify the lines. After each excerpt the page and numerical order on the page is noted.

The Biographical Index is a record of men and women of all ages and nationalities whose words, thoughts, and visions have been passed along into the minds and speech of the people. Under each author's full name is given his nationality, dates of birth and death (L for living), also a brief character sketch, and the numbers of the pages whereon his lines appear.

To find an appropriate quotation for a definite subject, turn to a topic dealing with such an idea, and consult the Topical Index for related headings.

For the exact text of a quotation, or its authority, consult the Concordance. When exact words are not remembered try synonymous ones, or topics on such subjects. If the author alone is remembered, consult the Biographical Index.

When a topic does not give all that may be sought on a subject, consult the Concordance as quotations may contain, as a whole, ideas which have placed them elsewhere.

When quotations from a special author only are desired, consult the Biographical Index where pages are given on which are found that author's lines.

When modern authors are wanted, choose from the Biographical Index, according to dates given of birth and death.

To find priority of authorship, consult Biographical Index for dates of authors' birth and death.

The plays and poems of Shakespeare and the books of the Bible are given in italics without the names of the authors.

Full names of well-known authors are often omitted.

Popular abbreviations and pen-names are given when established as better known to the public. (Bernard Shaw, Oscar Wilde, George Eliot, Artemus Ward.) The Biographical Index supplies full names and has ample cross references.

Topical Index,

WITH CROSS-REFERENCES.

B

G

H

I

N

S

T

Y

Z

THE NEW CYCLOPEDIA

OF

PRACTICAL QUOTATIONS

A

ABHORRENCE

1
The self-same thing they will abhor
One way, and long another for.
Butler—*Hudibras.* Pt. I. Canto I. L. 219.

2
Boils and plagues
Plaster you o'er, that you may be abhorr'd
Further than seen.
Coriolanus. Act I. Sc. 4. L. 37.

3
How abhorred in my imagination it is!
Hamlet. Act V. Sc. 1. L. 206.

4
* * * few things loves better
Than to abhor himself.
Timon of Athens. Act I. Sc. 1. L. 60.

5
* * * more abhorr'd
Than spotted livers in the sacrifice.
Troilus and Cressida. Act V. Sc. 3. L. 18.

6
* * * make the abhorrent eye
Roll back and close.
Southey—*Curse of Kehama.* VIII. 9.

ABILITY

7
He'll find a way.
Barrie—*Sentimental Tommy.* (Corp's belief in Tommy and Tommy's in himself.)

8
Men who undertake considerable things, even in a regular way, ought to give us ground to presume ability.
Burke—*Reflections on the Revolution in France.*

9
For as our modern wits behold,
Mounted a pick-back on the old,
Much farther off, much further he,
Rais'd on his aged Beast, could see.
Butler—*Hudibras.* Pt. I. Canto II. L. 971. Same idea in Macaulay *Essay on* Sir James Mackintosh. (See also Coleridge, Didacus Stella, Herbert, Seneca.)

10
He could raise scruples dark and nice,
And after solve 'em in a trice:
As if Divinity had catch'd
The itch, on purpose to be scratch'd.
Butler—*Hudibras.* Pt. I. Canto I. L. 163.

11
You are a devil at everything, and there is no kind of thing in the 'versal world but what you can turn your hand to.
Cervantes—*Don Quixote.* Pt. I. Bk. III. Ch. XI.

12
Etiam illud adjungo, sæpius ad laudem atque virtutem naturam sine doctrina, quam sine natura valisse doctrinam.
I add this also, that natural ability without education has oftener raised man to glory and virtue, than education without natural ability.
Cicero—*Oratio Pro Licinio Archia.* VII.

13
The dwarf sees farther than the giant, when he has the giant's shoulders to mount on.
Coleridge—*The Friend.* Sect. I. Essay VIII.
(See also Butler)

14
Pigmies placed on the shoulders of giants see more than the giants themselves.
Didactus Stella—*Lucan.* Vol. II. 10. Quoted by Burton—*Anatomy of Melancholy. Democritus to the Reader.*
(See also Butler)

15
Could swell the soul to rage, or kindle soft desire.
Dryden—*Alexander's Feast.* L. 160.

16
As we advance in life, we learn the limits of our abilities.
Froude—*Short Studies on Great Subjects. Education.*

17
Every person is responsible for all the good within the scope of his abilities, and for no more, and none can tell whose sphere is the largest.
Gail Hamilton—*Country Living and Country Thinking. Men and Women.*

18
A Dwarf on a Giant's shoulder sees farther of the two.
Herbert—*Jacula Prudentum.*
(See also Butler)

19
C'est une grande habileté que de savoir cacher son habileté.
To know how to hide one's ability is great skill.
La Rochefoucauld—*Maximes.* 245.

1
To the very last, he [Napoleon] had a kind of idea; that, namely, of *la carrière ouverte aux talents*—the tools to him that can handle them.
LOCKHART—*Sir Walter Scott* in *London and Westminster Review*, 1838.

2
A Traveller at Sparta, standing long upon one leg, said to a Lacedæmonian, "I do not believe you can do as much." "True," said he, "but every goose can."
PLUTARCH—*Laconic Apothegms. Remarkable Speeches of Some Obscure Men.*

3
Illud tamen in primis testandum est, nihil præcepta atque artes valere nisi adjuvante natura.
One thing, however, I must premise, that without the assistance of natural capacity, rules and precepts are of no efficacy.
QUINTILIAN—*Prooemium.* I. 4.

4
Die Menschen gehen wie Schiesskugeln weiter, wenn sie abgeglättet sind.
Men, like bullets, go farthest when they are smoothest.
JEAN PAUL RICHTER—*Titan.* Zykel 26.

5
Parvus pumilio, licet in monte constiterit; colossus magnitudinem suam servabit, etiam si steterit in puteo.
A dwarf is small even if he stands on a mountain; a colossus keeps his height, even if he stands in a well.
SENECA—*Epistles.* 76.
(See also BUTLER)

6
The world is like a board with holes in it, and the square men have got into the round holes.
SYDNEY SMITH, as quoted in *Punch.*

7
We shall generally find that the triangular person has got into the square hole, the oblong into the triangular, and a square person has squeezed himself into the round hole.
SYDNEY SMITH—*Sketches of Moral Philosophy.*

8
Read my little fable:
He that runs may read.
Most can raise the flowers now,
For all have got the seed.
TENNYSON—*The Flowers.*

9
Les méchants sont toujours surpris de trouver de l'habileté dans les bons.
The wicked are always surprised to find ability in the good.
VAUVENARGUES—*Réflexions.* CIII.

10
Possunt quia posse videntur.
They are able because they think they are able.
VERGIL—*Æneid.* V. 231.

ABSENCE (See also MEMORY)

11
Absence makes the heart grow fonder.
THOMAS HAYNES BAYLY—*Isle of Beauty.*

12
Wives in their husbands' absences grow subtler,
And daughters sometimes run off with the butler.
BYRON—*Don Juan.* Canto III. St. 22.

13
Absent in body, but present in spirit.
I Corinthians. V. 3.

14
Where'er I roam, whatever realms to see,
My heart untravelled, fondly turns to thee;
Still to my brother turns, with ceaseless pain,
And drags at each remove a lengthening chain.
GOLDSMITH—*Traveller.* L. 7.

15
Achilles absent, was Achilles still.
HOMER—*Iliad.* Bk. 22. L. 415. POPE'S trans.

16
In the hope to meet
Shortly again, and make our absence sweet.
BEN JONSON—*Underwoods. Miscellaneous Poems.* LIX.

17
Ever absent, ever near;
Still I see thee, still I hear;
Yet I cannot reach thee, dear!
FRANCIS KAZINCZY—*Separation.*

18
What shall I do with all the days and hours
That must be counted ere I see thy face?
How shall I charm the interval that lowers
Between this time and that sweet time of grace?
FRANCES ANNE KEMBLE—*Absence.*

19
Cum autem sublatus fuerit ab oculis, etiam cito transit a mente.
But when he (man) shall have been taken from sight, he quickly goes also out of mind.
THOMAS À KEMPIS—*Imitation of Christ.* Bk. I. Ch. XXIII. 1.

20
Your absence of mind we have borne, till your presence of body came to be called in question by it.
LAMB—*Amicus Redivivus.*

21
For with G. D., to be absent from the body is sometimes (not to speak it profanely) to be present with the Lord.
LAMB—*Oxford in the Vacation.*

22
L'absence diminue les médiocres passions et augmente les grandes, comme le vent éteint les bougies et allume le feu.
Absence diminishes little passions and increases great ones, as the wind extinguishes candles and fans a fire.
LA ROCHEFOUCAULD—*Maximes.* 276.

23
Oft in the tranquil hour of night,
When stars illume the sky,
I gaze upon each orb of light,
And wish that thou wert by.
GEORGE LINLEY—*Song.*

24
Thou art gone from my gaze like a beautiful dream,
And I seek thee in vain by the meadow and stream.
GEORGE LINLEY—*Thou Art Gone.*

25
For there's nae luck about the house;
There's nae luck at aw;
There's little pleasure in the house
When our gudeman's awa.
Attributed to W. J. MICKLE—*There's Nae*

Luck Aboot the House. Ballad of Cumnor Hall. Claimed for JEAN ADAM. Evidence in favor of MICKLE. Claimed also for MACPHERSON. MS. copy found among his papers after his death.

1
With what a deep devotedness of woe
I wept thy absence—o'er and o'er again
Thinking of thee, still thee, till thought grew pain,
And memory, like a drop that, night and day,
Falls cold and ceaseless, wore my heart away!
MOORE—*Lalla Rookh. The Veiled Prophet of Khorassan.*

2
Condemned whole years in absence to deplore,
And image charms he must behold no more.
POPE—*Eloise to Abelard.* L. 361.

3
Absenti nemo ne nocuisse velit.
Let no one be willing to speak ill of the absent.
PROPERTIUS—*Elegiæ.* II. 19. 32. CHILO in *Life* by DIOGENES LAERTIUS. (Modified by THUCYDIDES. II. 45.)

4
Days of absence, sad and dreary,
Clothed in sorrow's dark array,—
Days of absence, I am weary;
She I love is far away.
ROUSSEAU—*Days of Absence.*

5
Among the defects of the bill [Lord Derby's] which are numerous, one provision is conspicuous by its presence and another by its absence.
LORD JOHN RUSSELL. *Address to the Electors of the City of London,* April 6, 1859. Phrase used by LORD BROUGHAM. Quoted by CHENIER in one of his tragedies. Idea used by HENRY LABOUCHÈRE in *Truth,* Feb. 11, 1886, and by EARL GRANVILLE Feb. 21, 1873. LADY BROWNLOW—*Reminiscences of a Septuagenarian.*
(See also TACITUS)

6
I dote on his very absence, and I wish them a fair departure.
Merchant of Venice. Act I. Sc. 2. L. 120.

7
All days are nights to see till I see thee,
And nights bright days when dreams do show thee me.
Sonnet XLIII.

8
How like a winter hath my absence been
From thee, the pleasure of the fleeting year!
What freezings have I felt, what dark days seen!
What old December's bareness everywhere.
Sonnet XCVII.

9
Præfulgebant Cassius atque Brutus eo ipso, quod effigies eorum non videbantur.
Cassius and Brutus were the more distinguished for that very circumstance that their portraits were absent.
From the funeral of JUNIA, wife of CASSIUS and sister to BRUTUS, when the insignia of twenty illustrious families were carried in the procession.
TACITUS—*Annals.* Bk. III. Ch. 76.
(See also RUSSELL)

10
'Tis said that absence conquers love;
But oh! believe it not.
I've tried, alas! its power to prove,
But thou art not forgot.
FREDERICK W. THOMAS—*Absence Conquers Love.*

11
Since you have waned from us,
Fairest of women!
I am a darkened cage
Songs cannot hymn in.
My songs have followed you,
Like birds the summer;
Ah! bring them back to me,
Swiftly, dear comer!
Seraphim,
Her to hymn,
Might leave their portals;
And at my feet learn
The harping of mortals!
FRANCIS THOMPSON—*A Carrier Song.*

ACACIA

12
A great acacia, with its slender trunk
And overpoise of multitudinous leaves,
(In which a hundred fields might spill their dew
And intense verdure, yet find room enough)
Stood reconciling all the place with green.
E. B. BROWNING—*Aurora Leigh.* Bk. VI.

13
Light-leaved acacias, by the door,
Stood up in balmy air,
Clusters of blossomed moonlight bore.
And breathed a perfume rare.
GEORGE MACDONALD—*Song of the Spring Nights.* Pt. I.

14
Our rocks are rough, but smiling there
Th' acacia waves her yellow hair,
Lonely and sweet, nor loved the less
For flow'ring in a wilderness.
MOORE—*Lalla Rookh. Light of the Harem.*

ACCIDENT

15
Chapter of accidents.
BURKE—*Notes for Speeches.* (Edition 1852) Vol. II. P. 426.
(See also WILKES)

16
Accidents will occur in the best regulated families.
DICKENS—*David Copperfield.* Ch. XXVIII. *Pickwick Papers.* Ch. II. SCOTT—*Peveril of the Peak.* Last Chapter. V. S. LEAN—*Collectanæ.* Vol. III. P. 411.

17
To what happy accident is it that we owe so unexpected a visit?
GOLDSMITH—*Vicar of Wakefield.* Ch. XIX.
(See also MIDDLETON, DE STAËL)

18
Our wanton accidents take root, and grow
To vaunt themselves God's laws.
CHARLES KINGSLEY—*Saint's Tragedy.* Act II. Sc. 4.

19
Nichts unter der Sonne ist Zufall—am wenigsten das wovon die Absicht so klar in die Augen leuchtet.

Nothing under the sun is accidental, least of all that of which the intention is so clearly evident.
LESSING—*Emilia Galotti*. IV. 3.

1
At first laying down, as a fact fundamental,
That nothing with God can be accidental.
LONGFELLOW—*Christus. The Golden Legend.* Pt. VI.

2
By many a happy accident.
THOMAS MIDDLETON—*No Wit, no Help, like a Woman's.* Act IV. Sc. 1.
(See also GOLDSMITH)

3
Was der Ameise Vernunft mühsam zu Haufen schleppt, jagt in einem Hui der Wind des Zufalls zusammen.
What the reason of the ant laboriously drags into a heap, the wind of accident will collect in one breath.
SCHILLER—*Fiesco.* Act II. Sc. 4.

4
I have shot mine arrow o'er the house
And hurt my brother.
Hamlet. Act V. Sc. 2. L. 254.

5
Moving accidents by flood and field.
Othello. Act I. Sc. 3. L. 135.

6
A happy accident.
MADAME DE STAËL—*L'Allemagne.* Ch. XVI.
(See also GOLDSMITH)

7
The accident of an accident.
LORD THURLOW—*Speech in reply to Lord Grafton.*

8
The chapter of accidents is the longest chapter in the book.
Attributed to JOHN WILKES by SOUTHEY—*The Doctor.* Ch. CXVIII.
(See also BURKE)

ACTING; THE STAGE (See also WORLD)

9
Farce follow'd Comedy, and reach'd her prime,
In ever-laughing Foote's fantastic time;
Mad wag! who pardon'd none, nor spared the best,
And turn'd some very serious things to jest.
Nor church nor state escaped his public sneers,
Arms nor the gown, priests, lawyers, volunteers;
"Alas, poor Yorick!" now forever mute!
Whoever loves a laugh must sigh for Foote.
We smile, perforce, when histrionic scenes
Ape the swoln dialogue of kings and queens,
When "Chrononhotonthologos must die,"
And Arthur struts in mimic majesty.
BYRON—*Hints from Horace.* L. 329.

10
As good as a play.
Saying ascribed to CHARLES II. while listening to a debate on Lord Ross's Divorce Bill.

11
But as for all the rest,
There's hardly one (I may say none) who stands the Artist's test.
The Artist is a rare, rare breed. There were but two, forsooth,
In all me time (the stage's prime!) and The Other One was Booth.
EDMUND VANCE COOKE—*The Other One was Booth.*

12
I think I love and reverence all arts equally, only putting my own just above the others; because in it I recognize the union and culmination of my own. To me it seems as if when God conceived the world, that was Poetry; He formed it, and that was Sculpture; He colored it, and that was Painting; He peopled it with living beings, and that was the grand, divine, eternal Drama.
CHARLOTTE CUSHMAN.

13
See, how these rascals use me! They will not let my play run; and yet they steal my thunder.
JOHN DENNIS—See *Biographia Britannica.* Vol. V. P. 103.

14
Like hungry guests, a sitting audience looks:
Plays are like suppers; poets are the cooks.
The founder's you: the table is this place:
The carvers we: the prologue is the grace.
Each act, a course, each scene, a different dish,
Though we're in Lent, I doubt you're still for flesh.
Satire's the sauce, high-season'd, sharp and rough.
Kind masks and beaux, I hope you're pepper-proof?
Wit is the wine; but 'tis so scarce the true
Poets, like vintners, balderdash and brew.
Your surly scenes, where rant and bloodshed join.
Are butcher's meat, a battle's sirloin:
Your scenes of love, so flowing, soft and chaste,
Are water-gruel without salt or taste.
GEORGE FARQUHAR—*The Inconstant; or, The Way to Win Him.* Prologue.

15
Prologues precede the piece in mournful verse,
As undertakers walk before the hearse.
DAVID GARRICK—*Apprentice.* Prologue.

16
Prologues like compliments are loss of time;
'Tis penning bows and making legs in rhyme.
DAVID GARRICK—*Prologue to Crisp's Tragedy of Virginia.*

17
On the stage he was natural, simple, affecting,
'Twas only that when he was off, he was acting.
GOLDSMITH—*Retaliation.* L. 101.

18
Everybody has his own theatre, in which he is manager, actor, prompter, playwright, sceneshifter, boxkeeper, doorkeeper, all in one, and audience into the bargain.
J. C. AND A. W. HARE—*Guesses at Truth.*

19
It's very hard! Oh, Dick, my boy,
It's very hard one can't enjoy
A little private spouting;
But sure as Lear or Hamlet lives,
Up comes our master, Bounce! and gives
The tragic Muse a routing.
HOOD—*The Stage-Struck Hero.*

1
And Tragedy should blush as much to stoop
To the low mimic follies of a farce,
As a grave matron would to dance with girls.
HORACE—*Of the Art of Poetry*. L. 272. WENTWORTH DILLON'S trans.

2
The drama's laws, the drama's patrons give.
For we that live to please, must please to live.
SAMUEL JOHNSON—*Prologue*. Spoken by Mr. Garrick on Opening Drury Lane Theatre. (1747) L. 53.

3
Who teach the mind its proper face to scan,
And hold the faithful mirror up to man.
ROBERT LLOYD—*The Actor*. L. 265.
(See also SPRAGUE)

4
This many-headed monster.
MASSINGER—*Roman Actor*. Act III. Sc. 4.
(See also POPE)

5
A long, exact, and serious comedy;
In every scene some moral let it teach,
And, if it can, at once both please and preach.
POPE—*Epistle to Miss Blount. With the Works of Voiture*. L. 22.

6
This is the Jew that Shakespeare drew.
Attributed to POPE when Macklin was performing the character of Shylock, Feb. 14, 1741.

7
There still remains to mortify a wit
The many-headed monster of the pit.
POPE—*Horace*. Ep. I. Bk. II. L. 30.
(See also MASSINGER. Also CORIOLANUS, SCOTT, under PUBLIC)

8
To wake the soul by tender strokes of art,
To raise the genius, and to mend the heart;
To make mankind, in conscious virtue bold,
Live o'er each scene, and be what they behold—
For this the tragic Muse first trod the stage.
POPE—*Prologue to Addison's Cato*. L. 1.

9
Your scene precariously subsists too long,
On French translation and Italian song.
Dare to have sense yourselves; assert the stage;
Be justly warm'd with your own native rage.
POPE—*Prologue to Addison's Cato*. L. 42.

10
Tom Goodwin was an actor-man,
Old Drury's pride and boast,
In all the light and spritely parts,
Especially the ghost.
J. G. SAXE—*The Ghost Player*.

11
The play bill which is said to have announced the tragedy of Hamlet, the character of the Prince of Denmark being left out.
SCOTT—*The Talisman. Introduction*.

12
If it be true that good wine needs no bush, 'tis true that a good play needs no epilogue.
As You Like It. Epilogue. L. 3.

13
Like a dull actor now,
I have forgot my part, and I am out,
Even to a full disgrace.
Coriolanus. Act V. Sc. 3. L. 40.

14
Good, my lord, will you see the players well bestowed? Do you hear, let them be well used; for they are the abstract and brief chronicles of the time: after your death you were better have a bad epitaph than their ill report while you live.
Hamlet. Act II. Sc. 2. L. 545.

15
Is it not monstrous that this player here,
But in a fiction, in a dream of passion,
Could force his soul so to his own conceit
That from her working all his visage wann'd.
Hamlet. Act II. Sc. 2. L. 577.

16
What's Hecuba to him, or he to Hecuba,
That he should weep for her? What would he do,
Had he the motive and the cue for passion
That I have? He would drown the stage with tears.
Hamlet. Act II. Sc. 2. L. 585.

17
I have heard
That guilty creatures sitting at a play,
Have, by the very cunning of the scene,
Been struck so to the soul that presently
They have proclaim'd their malefactions;
For murder, though it have no tongue, will speak.
With most miraculous organ.
Hamlet. Act II. Sc. 2. L. 617.

18
The play's the thing
Wherein I'll catch the conscience of the king.
Hamlet. Act II. Sc. 2. L. 633.

19
Speak the speech, I pray you, as I pronounced it to you, trippingly on the tongue; but if you mouth it, as many of your players do, I had as lief the town-crier spoke my lines. Nor do not saw the air too much with your hand, thus, but use all gently; for in the very torrent, tempest, and, as I may say, the whirlwind of passion, you must acquire and beget a temperance that may give it smoothness.
Hamlet. Act III. Sc. 2. L. 1.

20
Suit the action to the word, the word to the action, with this special observance, that you o'erstep not the modesty of nature.
Hamlet. Act III. Sc. 2. L. 19.

21
O, there be players that I have seen play, and heard others praise, and that highly, not to speak it profanely, that, neither having the accent of Christians nor the gait of Christian, pagan, nor man, have so strutted and bellowed that I have thought some of nature's journeymen had made men and not made them well, they imitated humanity so abominably.
Hamlet. Act III. Sc. 2. L. 32.

22
A hit, a very palpable hit.
Hamlet. Act V. Sc. 2. L. 294.

23
Come, sit down, every mother's son, and rehearse your parts.
Midsummer Night's Dream. Act III. Sc. 1. L. 74.

1 Is there no play,
To ease the anguish of a torturing hour?
Midsummer Night's Dream. Act V. Sc. 1. L. 36.

2
A play there is, my lord, some ten words long,
Which is as brief as I have known a play;
But by ten words, my lord, it is too long,
Which makes it tedious.
Midsummer Night's Dream. Act V. Sc. 1. L. 61.

3 As in a theatre, the eyes of men,
After a well-grac'd actor leaves the stage,
Are idly bent on him that enters next,
Thinking his prattle to be tedious.
Richard II. Act V. Sc. 2. L. 23.

4
I can counterfeit the deep tragedian;
Speak and look back, and pry on every side,
Tremble and start at wagging of a straw,
Intending deep suspicion.
Richard III. Act III. Sc. 5. L. 5.

5
A beggarly account of empty boxes.
Romeo and Juliet. Act V. Sc. 1. L. 45.

6
And, like a strutting player, whose conceit
Lies in his hamstring, and doth think it rich
To hear the wooden dialogue and sound
'Twixt his stretch'd footing and the scaffoldage.
Troilus and Cressida. Act I. Sc. 3. L. 153.

7
(The) play of limbs succeeds the play of wit.
Horace and James Smith—*Rejected Addresses. By Lord B. Cui Bono.* 11.

8
Lo, where the Stage, the poor, degraded Stage,
Holds its warped mirror to a gaping age!
Charles Sprague—*Curiosity.*
(See also Lloyd)

9
The play is done; the curtain drops,
Slow falling to the prompter's bell:
A moment yet the actor stops,
And looks around, to say farewell.
It is an irksome word and task:
And, when he's laughed and said his say,
He shows, as he removes the mask,
A face that's anything but gay.
Thackeray—*The End of the Play.*

10
In other things the knowing artist may
Judge better than the people; but a play,
(Made for delight, and for no other use)
If you approve it not, has no excuse.
Edmund Waller—*Prologue to the Maid's Tragedy.* L. 35.

ACTION (See also Deeds)

11
Let's meet and either do or die.
Beaumont and Fletcher—*The Island Princess.* Act II. Sc. 2.
(See also Burns)

12
Of every noble action the intent
Is to give worth reward, vice punishment.
Beaumont and Fletcher—*The Captain.* Act V. Sc. 5.

13
That low man seeks a little thing to do,
Sees it and does it;
This high man, with a great thing to pursue,
Dies ere he knows it.
Robert Browning—*A Grammarian's Funeral.*

14
Let us do or die.
Burns—*Bannockburn.*
(See also Beaumont, Campbell)

15
What's done we partly may compute,
But know not what's resisted.
Burns—*Address to the Unco Guid.*

16
Put his shoulder to the wheel.
Burton—*Anatomy of Melancholy.* Pt. II. Sect. I. Memb. 2.

17
To-morrow let us do or die.
Campbell—*Gertrude of Wyoming.* Pt. III. St. 37. (See also Burns)

18
Our grand business undoubtedly is, not to *see* what lies dimly at a distance, but to *do* what lies clearly at hand.
Carlyle—*Essays. Signs of the Times.*

19
The best way to keep good acts in memory is to refresh them with new.
Attributed to Cato by Bacon—*Apothegms.* No. 247.

20
He is at no end of his actions blest
Whose ends will make him greatest and not best.
George Chapman—*Tragedy of Charles, Duke of Byron.* Act V. Sc. 1.

21
Quod est, eo decet uti: et quicquid agas, agere pro viribus.
What one has, one ought to use: and whatever he does he should do with all his might.
Cicero—*De Senectute.* IX.

22
It is better to wear out than to rust out.
Bishop Cumberland. See Horne's *Sermon—On the Duty of Contending for the Truth.*

23
Actions of the last age are like almanacs of the last year.
Sir John Denham—*The Sophy. A Tragedy.*

24
Whatsoever thy hand findeth to do, do it with thy might.
Ecclesiastes. IX. 10.

25 For strong souls
Live like fire-hearted suns; to spend their strength
In furthest striving action.
George Eliot—*Spanish Gypsy.* Bk. IV.

26
Zeus hates busybodies and those who do too much.
Euripides. Quoted by Emerson.

27
Man is his own star, and the soul that can
Render an honest and a perfect man,
Commands all light, all influence, all fate.
Nothing to him falls early or too late.
Our acts, our angels are, or good or ill,
Our fatal shadows that walk by us still.
John Fletcher—*Upon an Honest Man's Fortune.* L. 37.

1
A fiery chariot, borne on buoyant pinions,
Sweeps near me now! I soon shall ready be
To pierce the ether's high, unknown dominions,
To reach new spheres of pure activity!
GOETHE—*Faust.* Bk. I. Sc. 1.

2
Do well and right, and let the world sink.
HERBERT—*Country Parson.* Ch. XXIX.

3
Let thy mind still be bent, still plotting, where,
And when, and how thy business may be done.
Slackness breeds worms; but the sure traveller,
Though he alights sometimes still goeth on.
HERBERT—*Temple. Church Porch.* St. 57.

4
The shortest answer is doing.
HERBERT—*Jacula Prudentum.*

5
Attempt the end, and never stand to doubt;
Nothing's so hard but search will find it out.
HERRICK—*Seek and Find.*

6
A man that's fond precociously of *stirring*
Must be a spoon.
HOOD—*Morning Meditations.*

7
It is not book learning young men need, nor instruction about this and that, but a stiffening of the vertebræ which will cause them to be loyal to a trust, to act promptly, concentrate their energies, do a thing—"carry a message to Garcia."
ELBERT HUBBARD—*Carry a Message to Garcia. Philistine.* March, 1900. (LIEUT. COL. ANDREW S. ROWAN carried the message to Garcia.)

8
Fungar vice cotis, acutum
Reddere quæ ferrum valet, exsors ipsa secandi.
I will perform the function of a whetstone, which is able to restore sharpness to iron, though itself unable to cut.
HORACE—*Ars Poetica.* 304.
(See also PROVERBS. XXVII)

9
In medias res.
Into the midst of things.
HORACE—*Ars Poetica.* 148.

10
That action which appears most conducive to the happiness and virtue of mankind.
FRANCIS HUTCHESON—*A System of Moral Philosophy. The General Notions of Rights, and Laws Explained.* Bk. II. Ch. III.

11
Attack is the reaction; I never think I have hit hard unless it rebounds.
SAMUEL JOHNSON—*Boswell's Life of Johnson.* (1775)

12
Quelque éclatante que soit une action, elle ne doit pas passer pour grande, lorsqu'elle n'est pas l'effet d'un grand dessein.
However resplendent an action may be, it should not be accounted great unless it is the result of a great design.
LA ROCHEFOUCAULD—*Maximes.* 160.

13
No action, whether foul or fair,
Is ever done, but it leaves somewhere
A record, written by fingers ghostly,
As a blessing or a curse, and mostly
In the greater weakness or greater strength
Of the acts which follow it.
LONGFELLOW—*Christus. The Golden Legend.* Pt. II. *A Village Church.*

14
The good one, after every action, closes
His volume, and ascends with it to God.
The other keeps his dreadful day-book open
Till sunset, that we may repent; which doing,
The record of the action fades away,
And leaves a line of white across the page
Now if my act be good, as I believe,
It cannot be recalled. It is already
Sealed up in heaven, as a good deed accomplished.
The rest is yours.
LONGFELLOW—*Christus. The Golden Legend.* Pt. VI.

15
With useless endeavour,
Forever, forever,
Is Sisyphus rolling
His stone up the mountain!
LONGFELLOW—*Masque of Pandora. Chorus of the Eumenides.*
(See also OVID)

16
Trust no future, howe'er pleasant!
Let the dead past bury its dead!
Act,—act in the living Present!
Heart within and God o'erhead.
LONGFELLOW—*Psalm of Life.*

17
Let us then be up and doing,
With a heart for any fate;
Still achieving, still pursuing,
Learn to labor and to wait.
LONGFELLOW—*Psalm of Life.*
(See also BYRON, under FATE)

18
Every man feels instinctively that all the beautiful sentiments in the world weigh less than a single lovely action.
LOWELL—*Among my Books. Rousseau and the Sentimentalists.*
(See also BAILEY, under ADVICE)

19
Nil actum credens dum quid superesset agendum.
Thinking that nothing was done, if anything remained to do.
LUCAN—*Pharsalia.* II. 657.

20
Go, and do thou likewise.
Luke. X. 37.

21
He nothing common did, or mean,
Upon that memorable scene.
ANDREW MARVELL—*Horatian Ode. Upon Cromwell's Return from Ireland.*

22
So much one man can do,
That does both act and know.
ANDREW MARVELL—*Horatian Ode. Upon Cromwell's Return from Ireland.*

23
Therefore all things whatsoever ye would that men should do to you, do ye even so to them: for this is the law and the prophets.
Matthew. VII. 12.

1
Awake, arise, or be forever fall'n!
MILTON—*Paradise Lost.* Bk. I. L. 330.

2
Execute their aery purposes.
MILTON—*Paradise Lost.* Bk. I. L. 430.

3
Those graceful acts,
Those thousand decencies that daily flow
From all her words and actions.
MILTON—*Paradise Lost.* Bk. VIII. L. 600.

4
Ce qui est faict ne se peult desfaire.
What's done can't be undone.
MONTAIGNE—*Essays.* III.
(See also MACBETH)

5
Push on,—keep moving.
THOMAS MORTON—*Cure for the Heartache.* Act II. Sc. 1.

6
Ferreus assiduo consumitur anulus usu.
The iron ring is worn out by constant use.
OVID—*Ars Amatoris.* Bk. I. 473.

7
Aut petis, aut urgues ruiturum, Sisyphe, saxum.
Either you pursue or push, O Sisyphus, the stone destined to keep rolling.
OVID—*Metamorphoses,* 4, 459.
(See also LONGFELLOW)

8
What the Puritans gave the world was not thought, but *action.*
WENDELL PHILLIPS—*Speech. The Pilgrims.* Dec. 21, 1855.

9
Not always actions show the man; we find
Who does a kindness is not therefore kind.
POPE—*Moral Essays.* Epistle I. L. 109.

10
Iron sharpeneth iron.
Proverbs. XXVII. 17.
(See also HORACE)

11
So much to do; so little done.
CECIL RHODES—*Last words.*
(See also TENNYSON)

12
Prius quam incipias consulto, et ubi consulueris mature facto opus est.
Get good counsel before you begin: and when you have decided, act promptly.
SALLUST—*Catilina.* I.

13
Wer gar zu viel bedenkt, wird wenig leisten.
He that is overcautious will accomplish little.
SCHILLER—*Wilhelm Tell.* III. 1. 72.

14
Action is eloquence, and the eyes of the ignorant
More learned than the ears.
Coriolanus. Act III. Sc. 2. L. 75.

15
* * * the blood more stirs
To rouse a lion, than to start a hare.
Henry IV. Pt. I. Act I. Sc. 3. L. 197.

16
I profess not talking: only this,
Let each man do his best.
Henry IV. Pt. I. Act V. Sc. 2. L. 92.

17
We must not stint
Our necessary actions, in the fear
To cope malicious censurers.
Henry VIII. Act I. Sc. 2. L. 76.

18
Things done well,
And with a care, exempt themselves from fear;
Things done without example, in their issue
Are to be fear'd.
Henry VIII. Act I. Sc. 2. L. 88.

19
If it were done, when 'tis done, then 'twere well
It were done quickly.
Macbeth. Act I. Sc. 7. L. 1.

20
From this moment,
The very firstlings of my heart shall be
The firstlings of my hand. And even now,
To crown my thoughts with acts, be it thought and done.
Macbeth. Act IV. Sc. 1. L. 146.

21
But I remember now
I am in this earthly world; where, to do harm,
Is often laudable; to do good, sometime,
Accounted dangerous folly.
Macbeth. Act IV. Sc. 2. L. 74.

22
What's done can't be undone.
Macbeth. Act. V. Sc. 1.
(See also MONTAIGNE)

23
So smile the Heavens upon this holy act
That after hours with sorrow chide us not!
Romeo and Juliet. Act II. Sc. 6. L. 1.

24
How my achievements mock me!
I will go meet them.
Troilus and Cressida. Act IV. Sc. 2. L. 71.

25
Only the actions of the just
Smell sweet and blossom in their dust.
JAMES SHIRLEY—*Contention of Ajax and Ulysses.* Sc. 3. L. 23. ("In the dust" in PERCY'S *Reliques.* Misquoted "Ashes of the dust" on old tombstone at St. Augustine, Florida.)

26
Heaven ne'er helps the men who will not act.
SOPHOCLES—*Fragment.* 288.

27
Rightness expresses of actions, what *straightness* does of lines; and there can no more be two kinds of right action than there can be two kinds of straight line.
HERBERT SPENCER—*Social Statics.* Ch. XXXII. Par. 4.

28
The sweet remembrance of the just
Shall flourish when he sleeps in dust.
TATE and BRADY—*Psalm* 112. (Ed. 1695)

29
So many worlds, so much to do,
So little done, such things to be.
TENNYSON—*In Memoriam.* LXXII. 1.
(See also RHODES)

30
Theirs not to make reply,
Theirs not to reason why,
Theirs but to do and die.
TENNYSON—*Charge of the Light Brigade.* St. 2.

1
Dicta et facta.
Said and done. Done as soon as said.
TERENCE—*Eunuchus*. 5. 4. 19.

2
Actum ne agas.
Do not do what is already done.
TERENCE—*Phormio*. II. 3. 72.

3
A slender acquaintance with the world must convince every man that actions, not words, are the true criterion of the attachment of friends; and that the most liberal professions of good-will are very far from being the surest marks of it.
GEORGE WASHINGTON — *Social Maxims*.

4
Action is transitory, a step, a blow,
The motion of a muscle—this way or that.
WORDSWORTH—*The Borderers*. Act III.

5
And all may do what has by man been done.
YOUNG—*Night Thoughts*. Night VI. L. 611.

ADMIRATION

6
"Not to admire, is all the art I know
(Plain truth, dear Murray, needs few flowers of speech)
To make men happy, or to keep them so,"
(So take it in the very words of Creech)
Thus Horace wrote we all know long ago;
And thus Pope quotes the precept to re-teach
From his translation; but had *none admired*,
Would Pope have sung, or Horace been inspired?
BYRON—*Don Juan*. Canto V. 100. POPE—*First Book of the Epistles of Horace*. Ep. I. L. 1. (See also CREECH)

7
No nobler feeling than this, of admiration for one higher than himself, dwells in the breast of man. It is to this hour, and at all hours, the vivifying influence in man's life.
CARLYLE—*Heroes and Hero Worship*.

8
To admire nothing, (as most are wont to do;)
Is the only method that I know,
To make men happy, and to keep them so.
THOMAS CREECH—*Translation. Horace*. I. Ep. VI. 1. (See also BYRON)

9
Heroes themselves had fallen behind!
—Whene'er he went before.
GOLDSMITH—*A Great Man*.

10
On dit que dans ses amours
Il fut caressé des belles,
Qui le suivirent toujours,
Tant qu'il marcha devant elles.
Chanson sur le fameux La Palisse. Attributed to BERNARD DE LA MONNOYE. (Source of GOLDSMITH's lines.)

11
The king himself has follow'd her
When she has walk'd before.
GOLDSMITH—*Elegy on Mrs. Mary Blaize*.

12
We always love those who admire us, and we do not always love those whom we admire.
LA ROCHEFOUCAULD—*Maxim* 305.

13
For fools admire, but men of sense approve.
POPE—*Essay on Criticism*. L. 391.

14
Season your admiration for awhile.
Hamlet. Act I. Sc. 2. L. 192.

ADVENTURE

15
Some bold adventurers disdain
The limits of their little reign,
And unknown regions dare descry.
GRAY—*Ode on a Distant Prospect of Eton College*.

16
* * * and now expecting
Each hour their great adventurer, from the search
Of foreign worlds.
MILTON—*Paradise Lost*. Bk. X. L. 439.

17
Qui ne s'adventure n'a cheval ny mule, ce dist Salomon.—Qui trop, dist Echephron, s'adventure—perd cheval et mule, respondit Malcon.
He who has not an adventure has not horse or mule, so says Solomon.—Who is too adventurous, said Echephron,—loses horse and mule. replied Malcon.
RABELAIS—*Gargantua*. Bk. I. Ch. 33.

ADVERSITY (See also AFFLICTION)

18
It is hard for thee to kick against the pricks.
Acts. IX. 5.

19
Prosperity is not without many fears and distastes, and Adversity is not without comforts and hopes.
BACON—*Of Adversity*.

20
And these vicissitudes come best in youth;
For when they happen at a riper age,
People are apt to blame the Fates, forsooth,
And wonder Providence is not more sage.
Adversity is the first path to truth:
He who hath proved war, storm or woman's rage,
Whether his winters be eighteen or eighty,
Has won the experience which is deem'd so weighty.
BYRON—*Don Juan*. Canto XII. St. 50.

21
Adversity is sometimes hard upon a man; but for one man who can stand prosperity, there are a hundred that will stand adversity.
CARLYLE—*Heroes and Hero Worship*. Lecture V.

22
In the day of prosperity be joyful, but in the day of adversity consider.
Ecclesiastes. VIII. 14.

23
Aromatic plants bestow
No spicy fragrance while they grow;
But crush'd or trodden to the ground,
Diffuse their balmy sweets around.
GOLDSMITH—*The Captivity*. Act I. (See also ROGERS)

24
Thou tamer of the human breast,
Whose iron scourge and tort'ring hour
The bad affright, afflict the best!
GRAY—*Hymn to Adversity*. St. 1.

1
Dans l'adversité de nos meilleurs amis nous trouvons toujours quelque chose qui ne nous deplaist pas.
In the adversity of our best friends we often find something which does not displease us.
LA ROCHEFOUCAULD—*Maxim* 99. (Ed. 1665. Suppressed in 3rd ed. Quoted as old saying.)

2
Adversæ res admonent religionum.
Adversity reminds men of religion.
LIVY—*Annales.* V. 51.

3
The Good are better made by Ill,
As odours crushed are sweeter still.
SAM'L ROGERS—*Jacqueline.* St. 3.
(See also GOLDSMITH)

4
Ecce spectaculum dignum, ad quod respiciat intentus operi suo Deus. Ecce par Deo dignum, vir fortis cum mala fortuna compositus.
Behold a worthy sight, to which the God, turning his attention to his own work, may direct his gaze. Behold an equal thing, worthy of a God, a brave man matched in conflict with evil fortune.
SENECA—*Lib. de Divina Providentia.*
(See also SYDNEY SMITH)

5
Gaudent magni viri rebus adversis non aliter, quam fortes milites bellis.
Great men rejoice in adversity just as brave soldiers triumph in war.
SENECA—*De Providentia.* IV.

6
Sweet are the uses of adversity;
Which, like the toad, ugly and venomous,
Wears yet a precious jewel in his head.
As You Like It. Act II. Sc. I. L. 12.

7
A wretched soul, bruis'd with adversity,
We bid be quiet when we hear it cry;
But were we burthen'd with like weight of pain,
As much, or more, we should ourselves complain.
Comedy of Errors. Act II. Sc. 1. L. 34.

8
Let me embrace thee, sour adversity,
For wise men say it is the wisest course.
Henry VI. Pt. III. Act III. Sc. 1. L. 24.

9
His overthrow heap'd happiness upon him;
For then, and not till then, he felt himself,
And found the blessedness of being little.
Henry VIII. Act IV. Sc. 2. L. 64.

10
Then know, that I have little wealth to lose;
A man I am cross'd with adversity.
Two Gentlemen of Verona. Act IV. Sc. 1. L. 11.

11
A wise man struggling with adversity is said by some heathen writer to be a spectacle on which the gods might look down with pleasure.
SYDNEY SMITH—*Sermon on the Duties of the Queen.* (1837)
(See also SENECA)

12
In all distresses of our friends
We first consult our private ends.
SWIFT—*On the Death of Dr. Swift.*

ADVERTISEMENT (See JOURNALISM, NEWS)

ADVICE

13
The worst men often give the best advice.
Our deeds are sometimes better than our thoughts.
BAILEY—*Festus.* Sc. *A Village Feast. Evening.* L. 917.
(See LOWELL, under ACTION)

14
Un fat quelquefois ouvre un avis important.
A fop sometimes gives important advice.
BOILEAU—*L'Art Poétique.* IV. 50.

15
Ah, gentle dames! it gars me greet,
To think how mony counsels sweet,
How mony lengthened, sage advices,
The husband frae the wife despises.
BURNS—*Tam o' Shanter.* L. 33.

16
And may you better reck the rede,
Than ever did th' adviser.
BURNS—*Epistle to a Young Friend.*

17
She had a good opinion of advice,
Like all who give and eke receive it gratis.
For which small thanks are still the market price,
Even where the article at highest rate is.
BYRON—*Don Juan.* Canto XV. St. 29.

18
Dicen, que el primer consejo
Ha de ser de la muger.
They say that the best counsel is that of woman.
CALDERON—*El Médico de su Honra.* I. 2.

19
Let no man value at a little price
A virtuous woman's counsel; her wing'd spirit
Is feather'd oftentimes with heavenly words.
GEORGE CHAPMAN—*The Gentleman Usher.* Act IV. Sc. 1.

20
'Twas good advice, and meant,
"My son, be good."
GEORGE CRABBE—*The Learned Boy.* Vol. V. Tale XXI.

21
Know when to speake; for many times it brings
Danger to give the best advice to kings.
HERRICK—*Caution in Councell.*

22
Quidquid præcipies esto brevis.
Whatever advice you give, be short.
HORACE—*Ars Poetica.* CCCXXXV.

23
We give advice, but we do not inspire conduct.
LA ROCHEFOUCAULD—*Maxim.* 403.

24
In rebus asperis et tenui spe fortissima quæque consilia tutissima sunt.
In great straits and when hope is small, the boldest counsels are the safest.
LIVY—*Annales.* XXV. 38.

25
No adventures mucho tu riqueza
Por consejo de hombre que ha pobreza.
Hazard not your wealth on a poor man's advice.
MANUEL—*Conde Lucanor.*

1
Remember Lot's wife.
Luke. XVII. 32.

2
C'est une importune garde, du secret des princes, à qui n'en à que faire.
The secret counsels of princes are a troublesome burden to such as have only to execute them.
MONTAIGNE—*Essays*. III. 1.

3
Primo dede mulieris consilio, secundo noli.
Take the first advice of a woman and not the second.
GILBERTUS COGNATUS NOXERANUS—*Sylloge*. See J. J. GRYNÆUS—*Adagia*. P. 130. LANGIUS—*Polyanthea Col.* (1900) same sentiment. (Prends le premier conseil d'une femme et non le second. French for same.)

4
Consilia qui dant prava cautis hominibus,
Et perdunt operam et deridentur turpiter.
Those who give bad advice to the prudent, both lose their pains and are laughed to scorn.
PHÆDRUS—*Fabulæ*. I. 25.

5
Be niggards of advice on no pretense;
For the worst avarice is that of sense.
POPE—*Essay on Criticism*. L. 578.

6
In the multitude of counsellors there is safety.
Proverbs. XI. 14; XXIV. 6.

7
Vom sichern Port lässt sich's gemächlich rathen.
One can advise comfortably from a safe port.
SCHILLER—*Wilhelm Tell*. I. 1. 146.

8
Bosom up my counsel,
You'll find it wholesome.
Henry VIII. Act I. Sc. 1. L. 112.

9
When a wise man gives thee better counsel, give me mine again.
King Lear. Act II. Sc. 4. L. 76.

10
Here comes a man of comfort, whose advice
Hath often still'd my brawling discontent.
Measure for Measure. Act IV. Sc. 1. L. 8.

11
I pray thee cease thy counsel,
Which falls into mine ears as profitless
As water in a sieve.
Much Ado About Nothing. Act V. Sc. 1. L. 3.

12
Direct not him, whose way himself will choose;
'Tis breath thou lack'st, and that breath wilt thou lose.
Richard II. Act II. Sc. 1. L. 29.

13
Many receive advice, only the wise profit by it.
SYRUS—*Maxim* 152.

14
Che spesso avvien che ne' maggior perigli
Son più audaci gli ottimi consigli.
For when last need to desperation driveth,
Who dareth most he wisest counsel giveth.
TASSO—*Gerusalemme*. VI. 6.

15
A dead father's counsel, a wise son heedeth
TEGNER—*Fridthjof's Saga*. Canto VIII.

16
Facile omnes, quum valemus, recta consilia ægrotis damus.
We all, when we are well, give good advice to the sick.
TERENCE—*Andria*. II. 1. 9.

AERONAUTICS (See also DARWIN, under NAVIGATION)

17
Let brisker youths their active nerves prepare
Fit their light silken wings and skim the buxom air.
RICHARD OWEN CAMBRIDGE, in the *Scriblerad*. (1751)

18
He rode upon a cherub, and did fly: yea, he did fly upon the wings of the wind.
Psalms. XVIII. 10.

19
For I dipt into the future far as human eye could see,
Saw the Vision of the world, and all the wonder that would be;
Saw the heavens fill with commerce, argosies of magic sails,
Pilots of the purple twilight, dropping down with costly bales;
Heard the heavens fill with shouting, and there rain'd a ghastly dew
From the nations' airy navies grappling in the central blue.
TENNYSON—*Locksley Hall*. 117.

20
"Wal, I like flyin' well enough,"
He said, "but the' ain't sich a thundern' sight
O' fun in't when ye come to light."
TROWBRIDGE—*Darius Green and his Flying Machine*.

21
Darius was clearly of the opinion
That the air is also man's dominion
And that with paddle or fin or pinion,
We soon or late shall navigate
The azure as now we sail the sea.
TROWBRIDGE—*Darius Green and his Flying Machine*.

22
"The birds can fly, an' why can't I?
Must we give in," says he with a grin,
"That the bluebird an' phœbe are smarter 'n we be?"
TROWBRIDGE—*Darius Green and his Flying Machine*.

AFFECTATION

23
Affectation is an awkward and forced Imitation of what should be genuine and easy, wanting the Beauty that accompanies what is natural.
LOCKE—*On Education*. Sec. 66. *Affectation*.

24
There Affectation, with a sickly mien,
Shows in her cheek the roses of eighteen.
POPE—*The Rape of the Lock*. Canto 4.

AFFECTION

25
Even children follow'd with endearing wile,
And pluck'd his gown, to share the good man's smile.
GOLDSMITH—*The Deserted Village*. L. 183.

1
The objects that we have known in better days are the main props that sustain the weight of our affections, and give us strength to await our future lot.
WM. HAZLITT—*Table Talk. On the Past and Future.*

2
Who hath not saved some trifling thing
More prized than jewels rare,
A faded flower, a broken ring,
A tress of golden hair.
ELLEN C. HOWARTH—*'Tis but a Little Faded Flower.*

3
Talk not of wasted affection, affection never was wasted.
If it enrich not the heart of another, its waters, returning
Back to their springs, like the rain, shall fill them full of refreshment;
That which the fountain sends forth returns again to the fountain.
LONGFELLOW—*Evangeline.* Pt. II. St. 1.

4
Affection is a coal that must be cool'd;
Else, suffer'd, it will set the heart on fire.
Venus and Adonis. L. 387.

5
Of such affection and unbroken faith
As temper life's worst bitterness.
SHELLEY—*The Cenci.* Act III. Sc. 1.

AFFLICTION (See also ADVERSITY)

6
Afflicted, or distressed, in mind, body, or estate.
Book of Common Prayer. Prayer for all Conditions of Men.

7
Now let us thank th' eternal power, convinc'd
That Heaven but tries our virtue by affliction:
That oft the cloud which wraps the present hour,
Serves but to brighten all our future days!
JOHN BROWN—*Barbarossa.* Act V. Sc. 3.

8
Affliction's sons are brothers in distress;
A brother to relieve, how exquisite the bliss!
BURNS—*A Winter Night.*

9
Damna minus consueta movent.
The afflictions to which we are accustomed, do not disturb us.
CLAUDIANUS—*In Eutropium.* II. 149.

10
Crede mihi, miseris cœlestia numina parcunt;
Nec semper læsos, et sine fine, premunt.
Believe me, the gods spare the afflicted, and do not always oppress those who are unfortunate.
OVID—*Epistolæ Ex Ponto.* III. 6. 21.

11
Henceforth I'll bear
Affliction till it do cry out itself,
Enough, enough, and die.
King Lear. Act IV. Sc. 6. L. 75.

12
Thou art a soul in bliss; but I am bound
Upon a wheel of fire; that mine own tears
Do scald like molten lead.
King Lear. Act IV. Sc. 7. L. 46.

13
Affliction is enamour'd of thy parts,
And thou art wedded to calamity.
Romeo and Juliet. Act III. Sc. 3. L. 2.

14
Affliction is not sent in vain, young man,
From that good God, who chastens whom he loves.
SOUTHEY—*Madoc in Wales.* III. L. 176.

15
The Lord gets his best soldiers out of the highlands of affliction.
SPURGEON—*Gleanings Among the Sheaves. Sorrow's Discipline.*

16
Quæ regio in terris nostri non plena laboris.
What region of the earth is not full of our calamities?
VERGIL—*Æneid.* I. 460.

17
With silence only as their benediction,
God's angels come
Where in the shadow of a great affliction,
The soul sits dumb!
WHITTIER—*To my Friend on the Death of his Sister.*

18
Affliction is the good man's shining scene;
Prosperity conceals his brightest ray;
As night to stars, woe lustre gives to man.
YOUNG—*Night Thoughts.* Night IX. L. 415.

AFTON (RIVER)

19
Flow gently, sweet Afton, among thy green braes,
Flow gently, I'll sing thee a song in thy praise.
BURNS—*Flow Gently, Sweet Afton.*

AGE (See also ANTIQUITY)

20
It is always in season for old men to learn.
ÆSCHYLUS—*Age.*

21
Weak withering age no rigid law forbids,
With frugal nectar, smooth and slow with balm,
The sapless habit daily to bedew,
And give the hesitating wheels of life
Gliblier to play.
JOHN ARMSTRONG—*Art of Preserving Health.* Bk. II. L. 484.

22
What is it to grow old?
Is it to lose the glory of the form,
The lustre of the eye?
Is it for Beauty to forego her wreath?
Yes; but not this alone.
MATTHEW ARNOLD—*Growing Old.*

23
On one occasion some one put a very little wine into a wine cooler, and said that it was sixteen years old. "It is very small for its age," said Gnathæna.
ATHENÆUS—*Deipnosophists.* XIII. 46.

24
Men of age object too much, consult too long, adventure too little, repent too soon, and seldom drive business home to the full period, but content themselves with a mediocrity of success.
BACON—*Essay XLII. Of Youth and Age.*

1
Old wood best to burn, old wine to drink, old friends to trust, and old authors to read.
Quoted by BACON—*Apothegm* 97.
(See also DEUTERONOMY, ECCLESIASTICUS, GENESIS, GOLDSMITH, SHAKERLY-MARMION, MELCHIOR, PSALMS, SELDON, WEBSTER.)

2
Old age comes on apace to ravage all the clime.
BEATTIE—*The Minstrel.* Bk. I. St. 25.

3
An old man in a house is a good sign in a house.
Ascribed to BEN SYRA. (From the Hebrew.)

4
Old age doth in sharp pains abound;
We are belabored by the gout,
Our blindness is a dark profound,
Our deafness each one laughs about.
Then reason's light with falling ray
Doth but a trembling flicker cast.
Honor to age, ye children pay!
Alas! my fifty years are past!
BERANGER—*Cinquante Ans.* C. L. BETTS' trans.

5
By candle-light nobody would have taken you for above five-and-twenty.
BICKERSTAFF—*Maid of the Mill.* Act I. II.
(See also GILBERT)

6
Age shakes Athena's tower, but spares gray Marathon.
BYRON—*Childe Harold.* Canto II. St. 88.

7
What is the worst of woes that wait on age?
What stamps the wrinkle deeper on the brow?
To view each loved one blotted from life's page,
And be alone on earth as I am now.
BYRON—*Childe Harold.* Canto II. St. 98.

8
He has grown aged in this world of woe,
In deeds, not years, piercing the depths of life.
So that no wonder waits him.
BYRON—*Childe Harold.* Canto III. St. 5.

9
* * * Years steal
Fire from the mind, as vigor from the limb;
And life's enchanted cup but sparkles near the brim.
BYRON—*Childe Harold.* Canto III. St. 8.

10
Oh, for one hour of blind old Dandolo,
Th' octogenarian chief, Byzantium's conquering foe!
BYRON—*Childe Harold.* Canto IV. St. 12.

11
Just as old age is creeping on apace,
And clouds come o'er the sunset of our day,
They kindly leave us, though not quite alone,
But in good company—the gout or stone.
BYRON—*Don Juan.* Canto III. St. 59.

12
My days are in the yellow leaf;
The flowers and fruits of love are gone;
The worm, the canker, and the grief
Are mine alone!
BYRON—*On this day I complete my Thirty-sixth Year.*

13
For oute of olde feldys, as men sey,
Comyth al this newe corn from yere to yere;
And out of olde bokis, in good fey,
Comyth al this newe science that men lere.
CHAUCER—*The Parlement of Fowles.* L. 21.

14
I think every man is a fool or a physician at thirty years of age.
DR. CHEYNE.

15
Mature fieri senem, si diu velis esse senex.
You must become an old man in good time if you wish to be an old man long.
CICERO—*De Senectute*, 10. (Quoted as an "honoured proverb.")

16
The spring, like youth, fresh blossoms doth produce,
But autumn makes them ripe and fit for use:
So Age a mature mellowness doth set
On the green promises of youthful heat.
SIR JOHN DENHAM—*Cato Major.* Pt. IV. L. 47.

17
His eye was not dim, nor his natural force abated.
Deuteronomy. XXXIV. 7.

18
Youth is a blunder; Manhood a struggle; Old Age a regret.
BENJ. DISRAELI—*Coningsby.* Bk. III. Ch. I.

19
The Disappointment of Manhood succeeds to the delusion of Youth; let us hope that the heritage of Old Age is not Despair.
BENJ. DISRAELI—*Vivian Grey.* Bk. VIII. Ch. IV.

20
No Spring nor Summer Beauty hath such grace
As I have seen in one Autumnal face.
DONNE—*Ninth Elegy. To Lady Magdalen Herbert.*

21
Fate seem'd to wind him up for fourscore years;
Yet freshly ran he on ten winters more;
Till like a clock worn out with eating time,
The wheels of weary life at last stood still.
DRYDEN—*Œdipus.* Act IV. Sc. 1.

22
His hair just grizzled
As in a green old age.
DRYDEN—*Œdipus.* Act III. Sc. 1.
(See also HOMER)

23
Forsake not an old friend; for the new is not comparable to him: a new friend is as new wine; when it is old, thou shalt drink it with pleasure.
Ecclesiasticus. IX. 10.
(See also BACON)

24
Nature abhors the old.
EMERSON—*Essays. Circles.*

25
We do not count a man's years, until he has nothing else to count.
EMERSON—*Society and Solitude. Old Age.*

26
Remote from cities liv'd a Swain,
Unvex'd with all the cares of gain;
His head was silver'd o'er with age,
And long experience made him sage.
GAY—*Fables.* Part I. *The Shepherd and the Philosopher.*

1
In a good old age.
Genesis. XV. 15.

2
Old and well stricken in age.
Genesis. XVIII. 11.

3
She may very well pass for forty-three,
In the dusk with a light behind her.
W. S. GILBERT—*Trial by Jury*.
(See also BICKERSTAFF)

4
Das Alter macht nicht kindisch, wie man spricht,
Es findet uns nur noch als wahre Kinder.
Age childish makes, they say, but 'tis not true;
We're only genuine children still in Age's season.
GOETHE—*Faust. Vorspiel auf dem Theater*. L. 180.

5
Old age is courteous—no one more:
For time after time he knocks at the door,
But nobody says, "Walk in, sir, pray!"
Yet turns he not from the door away,
But lifts the latch, and enters with speed,
And then they cry, "A cool one, indeed."
GOETHE—*Old Age*.

6
O blest retirement! friend to life's decline—
Retreats from care, that never must be mine
How blest is he who crowns, in shades like these,
A youth of labour with an age of ease!
GOLDSMITH—*Deserted Village*. L. 97.

7
I love everything that's old: old friends, old times, old manners, old books, old wine.
GOLDSMITH—*She Stoops to Conquer*. Act I. Sc. 1. (See also BACON)

8
They say women and music should never be dated.
GOLDSMITH—*She Stoops to Conquer*. Act III.

9
Alike all ages: dames of ancient days
Have led their children thro' the mirthful maze,
And the gay grandsire, skill'd in gestic lore,
Has frisk'd beneath the burthen of threescore.
GOLDSMITH—*The Traveller*. L. 251.

10
Slow-consuming age.
GRAY—*Ode on a Distant Prospect of Eton College*. St. 9.

11
Struggle and turmoil, revel and brawl—
Youth is the sign of them, one and all.
A smoldering hearth and a silent stage—
These are a type of the world of Age.
W. E. HENLEY—*Of Youth and Age. Envoy*.

12
To be seventy years young is sometimes far more cheerful and hopeful than to be forty years old.
O. W. HOLMES—*On the seventieth birthday of Julia Ward Howe*, May 27, 1889.

13
You hear that boy laughing? You think he's all fun;
But the angels laugh, too, at the good he has done.
The children laugh loud as they troop to his call,
And the poor man that knows him laughs loudest of all!
O. W. HOLMES—*The Boys*. St. 9.

14
A green old age, unconscious of decays,
That proves the hero born in better days.
HOMER—*Iliad*. Bk. XXIII. L. 925. POPE'S trans. (See also DRYDEN)

15
When he's forsaken,
Wither'd and shaken,
What can an old man do but die?
HOOD—*Ballad*.

16
Tempus abire tibi est, ne . . .
Rideat et pulset lasciva decentius ætas.
It is time for thee to be gone, lest the age more decent in its wantonness should laugh at thee and drive thee off the stage.
HORACE—*Epistles*. Bk. II. 2. 215.

17
Boys must not have th' ambitious care of men,
Nor men the weak anxieties of age.
HORACE—*Of the Art of Poetry*.
WENTWORTH DILLON'S trans. L. 212.

18
Seu me tranquilla senectus
Exspectat, seu mors atris circumvolat alis.
Either a peaceful old age awaits me, or death flies round me with black wings.
HORACE—*Satires*. Bk. II. 1. 57.

19
Ladies, stock and tend your hive,
Trifle not at thirty-five;
For, howe'er we boast and strive,
Life declines from thirty-five;
He that ever hopes to thrive
Must begin by thirty-five.
SAMUEL JOHNSON—*To Mrs. Thrale, when Thirty-five*. L. 11.

20
Superfluous lags the veteran on the stage,
Till pitying Nature signs the last release,
And bids afflicted worth retire to peace.
SAMUEL JOHNSON—*Vanity of Human Wishes*. L. 308.

21
L'on craint la vieillesse, que l'on n'est pas sûr de pouvoir atteindre.
We dread old age, which we are not sure of being able to attain.
LA BRUYÈRE—*Les Caractères*. XI.

22
L'on espère de vieillir, et l'on craint la vieillesse; c'est-à-dire, l'on aime la vie et l'on fuit la mort.
We hope to grow old and we dread old age; that is to say, we love life and we flee from death.
LA BRUYÈRE—*Les Caractères*. XI.

23
Peu de gens savent être vieux.
Few persons know how to be old.
LA ROCHEFOUCAULD—*Maximes*. 448.

24
La vieillesse est un tyran qui défend, sur peine de la vie, tous les plaisirs de la jeunesse.
Old age is a tyrant who forbids, upon pain of death, all the pleasures of youth.
LA ROCHEFOUCAULD—*Maximes*. 461.

25
The sunshine fails, the shadows grow more dreary,
And I am near to fall, infirm and weary.
LONGFELLOW—*Canzone*.

1
How far the gulf-stream of our youth may flow
Into the arctic regions of our lives,
Where little else than life itself survives.
LONGFELLOW—*Morituri Salutamus.* L. 250.

2
Whatever poet, orator, or sage
May say of it, old age is still old age.
LONGFELLOW—*Morituri Salutamus.* L. 264.

3 For age is opportunity no less
Than youth itself, though in another dress,
And as the evening twilight fades away
The sky is filled with stars, invisible by day.
LONGFELLOW—*Morituri Salutamus.* L. 281.

4
And the bright faces of my young companions
Are wrinkled like my own, or are no more.
LONGFELLOW—*Spanish Student.* Act III. Sc. 3.

5
The course of my long life hath reached at last,
In fragile bark o'er a tempestuous sea,
The common harbor, where must rendered be,
Account of all the actions of the past.
LONGFELLOW—*Old Age.*

6
Age is not all decay; it is the ripening, the swelling, of the fresh life within, that withers and bursts the husk.
GEORGE MACDONALD—*The Marquis of Lossie.* Ch. XL.

7
What find you better or more honorable than age? * * * Take the preeminence of it in everything;—in an old friend, in old wine, in an old pedigree.
SHAKERLEY-MARMION—*Antiquary.* Act II. Sc. 1. (See also BACON)

8
When you try to conceal your wrinkles, Polla, with paste made from beans, you deceive yourself, not me. Let a defect, which is possibly but small, appear undisguised. A fault concealed is presumed to be great.
MARTIAL—*Epigrams.* Bk. III. Ep. 42.

9
Set is the sun of my years;
And over a few poor ashes,
I sit in my darkness and tears.
GERALD MASSEY—*A Wail.*

10
Old wood to burn! Old wine to drink! Old friends to trust! Old authors to read!—Alonso of Aragon was wont to say in commendation of age, that age appeared to be best in these four things.
MELCHIOR—*Floresta Española de Apothegmas o Sentencias,* etc. II. 1. 20.
(See also BACON)

11 The ages roll
Forward; and forward with them, draw my soul
Into time's infinite sea.
And to be glad, or sad, I care no more;
But to have done, and to have been, before I cease to do and be.
OWEN MEREDITH (Lord Lytton)—*The Wanderer.* Bk. IV. *A Confession and Apology.* St. 9.

12
So may'st thou live, till like ripe fruit thou drop
Into thy mother's lap, or be with ease
Gather'd, not harshly pluck'd, for death mature.
MILTON—*Paradise Lost.* Bk. XI. L. 535.

13
So Life's year begins and closes;
Days, though short'ning, still can shine;
What though youth gave love and roses,
Age still leaves us friends and wine.
MOORE—*Spring and Autumn.*

14
We age inevitably:
The old joys fade and are gone:
And at last comes equanimity and the flame burning clear.
JAMES OPPENHEIM—*New Year's Eve.*

15
Thyself no more deceive, thy youth hath fled.
PETRARCH—*To Laura in Death. Sonnet LXXXII.*

16
Senex cum extemplo est, jam nec sentit, nec sapit;
Ajunt solere eum rursum repuerascere.
When a man reaches the last stage of life,—without senses or mentality—they say that he has grown a child again.
PLAUTUS—*Mercator.* II. 2. 24.

17
Why will you break the Sabbath of my days?
Now sick alike of Envy and of Praise.
POPE—*First Book of Horace.* Ep. I. L. 3.

18
Learn to live well, or fairly make your will;
You've played, and loved, and ate, and drank your fill.
Walk sober off, before a sprightlier age
Comes tittering on, and shoves you from the stage.
POPE—*Imitations of Horace.* Bk. II. Ep. 2. L. 322.

19
Me let the tender office long engage
To rock the cradle of reposing age;
With lenient arts extend a mother's breath,
Make languor smile, and smooth the bed of death;
Explore the thought, explain the asking eye!
And keep awhile one parent from the sky.
POPE—*Prologue to the Satires.* L. 408.

20
His leaf also shall not wither.
Psalms I. 3.

21
The days of our years are threescore years and ten; and if by reason of strength they be fourscore years, yet is their strength labour and sorrow; for it is soon cut off, and we fly away.
Psalms XC. 10.

22
So teach us to number our days, that we may apply our hearts unto wisdom.
Psalms XC. 12.

23
Das Alter ist nicht trübe weil darin unsere Freuden, sondern weil unsere Hoffnungen aufhören.
What makes old age so sad is, not that our joys but that our hopes cease.
JEAN PAUL RICHTER—*Titan.* Zykel 34.

1 Age has now
Stamped with its signet that ingenuous brow.
ROGERS—*Human Life*. (1819)
(See also SCOTT)

2
O, roses for the flush of youth,
And laurel for the perfect prime;
But pluck an ivy branch for me,
Grown old before my time.
CHRISTINA G. ROSSETTI—*Song*. St. 1.

3
I'm growing fonder of my staff;
I'm growing dimmer in the eyes;
I'm growing fainter in my laugh;
I'm growing deeper in my sighs;
I'm growing careless of my dress;
I'm growing frugal of my gold;
I'm growing wise; I'm growing,—yes,—
I'm growing old.
SAXE—*I'm Growing Old*.

4
On his bold visage middle age
Had slightly press'd its signet sage.
SCOTT—*Lady of the Lake*. Canto I. Pt. XXI. (1810) (See also ROGERS)

5
Thus pleasures fade away;
Youth, talents, beauty, thus decay,
And leave us dark, forlorn, and gray.
SCOTT—*Marmion*. Introduction to Canto II. St. 7.

6
Thus aged men, full loth and slow,
The vanities of life forego,
And count their youthful follies o'er,
Till Memory lends her light no more.
SCOTT—*Rokeby*. Canto V. St. 1.

7
Old friends are best. King James us'd to call for his Old Shoes, they were easiest for his Feet.
SELDEN—*Table Talk*. *Friends*.
(See also BACON)

8
Nihil turpius est, quam grandis natu senex, qui nullum aliud habet argumentum, quo se probet diu vixisse, præter ætatem.

Nothing is more dishonourable than an old man, heavy with years, who has no other evidence of his having lived long except his age.
SENECA—*De Tranquillitate*. 3. 7.

9
Turpis et ridicula res est elementarius senex: juveni parandum, seni utendum est.

An old man in his rudiments is a disgraceful object. It is for youth to acquire, and for age to apply.
SENECA—*Epistolæ Ad Lucilium*. XXXVI. 4.

10
Senectus insanabilis morbus est.
Old age is an incurable disease.
SENECA—*Epistolæ Ad Lucilium*. CVIII. 29.

11
For we are old, and on our quick'st decrees
The inaudible and noiseless foot of Time
Steals ere we can effect them.
All's Well that Ends Well. Act V. Sc. 3. L. 40.

12
Though I look old, yet I am strong and lusty;
For in my youth I never did apply
Hot and rebellious liquors in my blood;
Nor did not with unbashful forehead woo
The means of weakness and debility;
Therefore my age is as a lusty winter,
Frosty, but kindly.
As You Like It. Act II. Sc. 3. L. 47.

13 All the world's a stage,
And all the men and women merely players:
They have their exits and their entrances;
And one man in his time plays many parts,
His acts being seven ages. At first the infant,
Mewling and puking in the nurse's arms.
And then the whining school-boy, with his satchel
And shining morning face, creeping like snail
Unwillingly to school. And then the lover,
Sighing like furnace, with a woeful ballad
Made to his mistress' eyebrow. Then a soldier,
Full of strange oaths and bearded like the pard,
Jealous in honour, sudden and quick in quarrel,
Seeking the bubble reputation
Even in the cannon's mouth. And then the justice,
In fair round belly with good capon lined,
With eyes severe and beard of formal cut,
Full of wise saws and modern instances;
And so he plays his part. The sixth age shifts
Into the lean and slipper'd pantaloon,
With spectacles on nose and pouch on side,
His youthful hose, well saved, a world too wide
For his shrunk shank; and his big manly voice,
Turning again toward childish treble, pipes
And whistles in his sound. Last scene of all,
That ends this strange eventful history,
Is second childishness and mere oblivion,
Sans teeth, sans eyes, sans taste, sans every thing.
As You Like It. Act II. Sc. 7. L. 139. Same idea in JEAN DE COURCY—*Le Chemin de Vaillance*. Copy in British Museum, KING'S MSS. No. 14. E. II. See also HORACE—*Ars Poetica*. 158. (Ages given as four.) In the *Mishna*, the ages are given as 14, by Jehuda, son of Thema. In PLATO'S (spurious) *Dialog*. *Axiochus*, SOCRATES sums up human life.

14 There is an old poor man
* * * * *
Oppressed with two weak evils, age and hunger.
As You Like It. Act II. Sc. 8. L. 129.

15
Though now this grained face of mine be hid
In sap-consuming winter's drizzled snow,
And all the conduits of my blood froze up,
Yet hath my night of life some memory.
Comedy of Errors. Act V. Sc. 1. L. 311.

16 What should we speak of
When we are old as you? When we shall hear
The rain and wind beat dark December.
Cymbeline. Act III. Sc. 3. L. 36.

17
An old man is twice a child.
Hamlet. Act II. Sc. 2. L. 404.

18 At your age,
The hey-day in the blood is tame, it's humble,
And waits upon the judgment.
Hamlet. Act III. Sc. 4. L. 68.

19
Begin to patch up thine old body for heaven.
Henry IV. Pt. II. Act II. Sc. 4. L. 193.

1
Some smack of age in you, some relish of the saltness of time.
Henry IV. Pt. II. Act I. Sc. 2. L. 91.

2
You are old;
As you are old and reverend, you should be wise.
King Lear. Act I. Sc. 4. L. 261.

3
Nature in you stands on the very verge
Of her confine.
King Lear. Act II. Sc. 4. L. 148.

4
Pray, do not mock me:
I am a very foolish fond old man,
Fourscore and upward; not an hour more nor less,
And, to deal plainly,
I fear I am not in my perfect mind.
King Lear. Act IV. Sc. 7. L. 59.

5
My way of life
Is fallen into the sear, the yellow leaf,
And that which should accompany old age,
As honor, love, obedience, troops of friends,
I must not look to have; but, in their stead,
Curses not loud, but deep, mouth-honor breath,
Which the poor heart would fain deny, and dare not.
Macbeth. Act V. Sc. 3. L. 22.

6
Superfluity comes sooner by white hairs, but competency lives longer.
Merchant of Venice. Act I. Sc. 2. L. 8.

7
Nor age so eat up my invention.
Much Ado About Nothing. Act IV. Sc. 1. L. 192.

8
Give me a staff of honor for mine age,
But not a sceptre to control the world.
Titus Andronicus. Act I. Sc. 1. L. 198.

9
"You are old, Father William," the young man cried,
"The few locks which are left you are gray;
You are hale, Father William,—a hearty old man:
Now tell me the reason, I pray."
SOUTHEY—*The Old Man's Comforts, and how he Gained Them*.

10
When an old gentleman waggles his head and says: "Ah, so I thought when I was your age," it is not thought an answer at all, if the young man retorts: "My venerable sir, so I shall most probably think when I am yours." And yet the one is as good as the other.
R. L. STEVENSON—*Crabbed Age and Youth*.

11
Every man desires to live long; but no man would be old.
SWIFT—*Thoughts on Various Subjects, Moral and Diverting*.

12
I swear she's no chicken; she's on the wrong side of thirty, if she be a day.
SWIFT—*Polite Conversation*. I.

13
Vetera extollimus recentium incuriosi.
We extol ancient things, regardless of our own times.
TACITUS—*Annales*. II. 88.

14
Vetera semper in laude, præsentia in fastidio.
Old things are always in good repute, present things in disfavour.
TACITUS—*Dialogus de Oratoribus*. 18.

15
An old man is twice a child.
JOHN TAYLOR—*The Old, Old, very Old Man*. (Thos. Parr.)

16
O good gray head which all men knew.
TENNYSON—*On the Death of the Duke of Wellington*. St. 4.

17
Age too shines out: and, garrulous, recounts the feats of youth.
THOMSON—*The Seasons. Autumn*. L. 1231.

18
Annus enim octogesimus admonet me, ut sarcinas colligam, antequam proficiscare vita.
For my eightieth year warns me to pack up my baggage before I leave life.
VARRO—*De Re Rustica*. I. 1.

19
For Age with stealing steps
Hath clawed me with his clutch.
THOS. VAUX—*The Aged Lover renounceth Love*. (Quoted in *Hamlet*, Act V. Sc. 1. Not in quartos.)

20
Omnia fert ætas, animum quoque.
Age carries all things away, even the mind.
VERGIL—*Eclogues*. IX. 51.

21
Venerable men! you have come down to us from a former generation. Heaven has bounteously lengthened out your lives, that you might behold this joyous day.
DANIEL WEBSTER—*Address at Laying the Corner-Stone of the Bunker Hill Monument* June 17, 1825.

22
Is not old wine wholesomest, old pippins toothsomest, old wood burn brightest, old linen wash whitest? Old soldiers, sweetheart, are surest, and old lovers are soundest.
JOHN WEBSTER—*Westward Ho*. Act II. Sc. 1.
(See also BACON)

23
Thus fares it still in our decay,
And yet the wiser mind
Mourns less for what age takes away
Than what it leaves behind.
WORDSWORTH—*The Fountain*. St. 9.

24
But an old age serene and bright,
And lovely as a Lapland night,
Shall lead thee to thy grave.
WORDSWORTH—*To a Young Lady*.

25
The monumental pomp of age
Was with this goodly Personage;
A stature undepressed in size,
Unbent, which rather seemed to rise
In open victory o'er the weight
Of seventy years, to loftier height.
WORDSWORTH—*White Doe of Rylstone*. Canto III.

AGRICULTURE

1
"Ten acres and a mule."
American phrase indicating the expectations of emancipated slaves. (1862)

2
Three acres and a cow.
BENTHAM — *Works.* Vol. VIII. P. 448. Quoted from BENTHAM by LORD ROSEBERY. *Monologue on* PITT, in *Twelve English Statesmen.* Referred to by SIR JOHN SINCLAIR *Code of Agriculture, Miscellaneous Essays,* 1802. Same idea in DEFOE'S *Tour through the whole Islands of Britain,* 6th Ed. Phrase made familiar by HON. JESSE COLLINGS in the House of Commons, 1886, "*Small Holdings amendment.*"
(See also MILL)

3
Look up! the wide extended plain
Is billowy with its ripened grain,
And on the summer winds are rolled
Its waves of emerald and gold.
WM. HENRY BURLEIGH—*The Harvest Call.* St. 5.

4
Arbores serit diligens agricola, quarum adspiciet baccam ipse numquam.
The diligent farmer plants trees, of which he himself will never see the fruit.
CICERO—*Tusculanarum Disputationum.* I. 14.

5
He was a very inferior farmer when he first begun, . . . and he is now fast rising from affluence to poverty.
S. L. CLEMENS (Mark Twain)—*Rev.* HENRY WARD BEECHER'S *Farm.*

6
Oculos et vestigia domini, res agro saluberrimas, facilius admittit.
He allows very readily, that the eyes and footsteps of the master are things most salutary to the land.
COLUMELLA—*De Re Rustica.* IV. 18.
(See also PLINY)

7
The first farmer was the first man, and all historic nobility rests on possession and use of land.
EMERSON—*Society and Solitude. Farming.*

8
Oft did the harvest to their sickle yield:
Their furrow oft the stubborn glebe has broke:
How jocund did they drive their team a-field!
How bow'd the woods beneath their sturdy stroke!
GRAY—*Elegy in a Country Churchyard.* St. 7.

9
Beatus ille qui procul negotiis,
Ut prisca gens mortalium,
Paterna rura bobus exercet suis,
Solutus omni fænore.
Happy he who far from business, like the primitive race of mortals, cultivates with his own oxen the fields of his fathers, free from all anxieties of gain.
HORACE—*Epodon.* Bk. II. 1.

10
Ye rigid Ploughmen! bear in mind
Your labor is for future hours.
Advance! spare not! nor look behind!
Plough deep and straight with all your powers!
RICHARD HENGIST HORNE—*The Plough.*

11
Earth is here so kind, that just tickle her with a hoe and she laughs with a harvest.
DOUGLAS JERROLD—*A Land of Plenty.* (Australia.)

12
The life of the husbandman,—a life fed by the bounty of earth and sweetened by the airs of heaven.
DOUGLAS JERROLD—*Jerrold's Wit. The Husbandman's Life.*

13
Cujus est solum, ejus est usque ad cœlum.
He who owns the soil, owns up to the sky.
Law Maxim.

14
When the land is cultivated entirely by the spade, and no horses are kept, a cow is kept for every three acres of land.
JOHN STUART MILL—*Principles of Political Economy.* Bk. II. Ch. VI. Sec. V. (Quoting from a treatise on Flemish husbandry.)
(See also BENTHAM)

15
Adam, well may we labour, still to dress
This garden, still to tend plant, herb, and flower.
MILTON—*Paradise Lost.* Bk. IX. L. 205.

16
Continua messe senescit ager.
A field becomes exhausted by constant tillage.
OVID—*Ars Amatoria.* III. 82.

17
Majores fertilissium in agro oculum domini esse dixerunt.
Our fathers used to say that the master's eye was the best fertilizer.
PLINY the Elder—*Historia Naturalis.* XVIII. 84. (See also COLUMELLA)

18
Where grows?—where grows it not? If vain our toil,
We ought to blame the culture, not the soil.
POPE—*Essay on Man.* Ep. IV. L. 13.

19
Our rural ancestors, with little blest,
Patient of labour when the end was rest,
Indulg'd the day that hous'd their annual grain,
With feasts, and off'rings, and a thankful strain.
POPE—*Second Book of Horace.* Ep. I. L. 241.

20
Here Ceres' gifts in waving prospect stand,
And nodding tempt the joyful reaper's hand.
POPE—*Windsor Forest.* L. 39.

21
And he gave it for his opinion, "that whoever could make two ears of corn, or two blades of grass, to grow upon a spot of ground where only one grew before, would deserve better of mankind, and do more essential service to his country, than the whole race of politicians put together."
SWIFT—*Voyage to Brobdingnag.*

22
In ancient times, the sacred Plough employ'd
The Kings and awful Fathers of mankind:
And some, with whom compared your insect-tribes
Are but the beings of a summer's day,
Have held the Scale of Empire, ruled the Storm
Of mighty War; then, with victorious hand,

Disdaining little delicacies, seized
The Plough, and, greatly independent, scorned
All the vile stores corruption can bestow.
THOMSON—*The Seasons. Spring.* L. 58.

1
Ill husbandry braggeth
To go with the best:
Good husbandry baggeth
Up gold in his chest.
TUSSER—*Five Hundred Points of Good Husbandry.* Ch. LII. *Comparing Good Husbandry.*

2
Ill husbandry lieth
In prison for debt:
Good husbandry spieth
Where profit to get.
TUSSER—*Five Hundred Points of Good Husbandry.* Ch. LII. *Comparing Good Husbandry.*

3
E'en in mid-harvest, while the jocund swain
Pluck'd from the brittle stalk the golden grain,
Oft have I seen the war of winds contend,
And prone on earth th' infuriate storm descend,
Waste far and wide, and by the roots uptorn,
The heavy harvest sweep through ether borne,
As the light straw and rapid stubble fly
In dark'ning whirlwinds round the wintry sky.
VERGIL—*Georgics.* I. L. 351. SOTHEBY's trans.

4
Laudato ingentia rura,
Exiguum colito.
Praise a large domain, cultivate a small state.
VERGIL—*Georgics.* II. 412.

5
Blessed be agriculture! if one does not have too much of it.
CHAS. DUDLEY WARNER—*My Summer in a Garden.* Preliminary.

6
When tillage begins, other arts follow. The farmers, therefore, are the founders of human civilization.
DANIEL WEBSTER—*Remarks on Agriculture,* Jan. 13, 1840. P. 457.

7
But let the good old corn adorn
The hills our fathers trod;
Still let us, for his golden corn,
Send up our thanks to God!
WHITTIER—*The Corn-Song.*

8
Heap high the farmer's wintry hoard!
Heap high the golden corn!
No richer gift has Autumn poured
From out her lavish horn!
WHITTIER—*The Corn-Song.*

AIRSHIPS (See AERONAUTICS)

ALBATROSS

9
And a good south wind sprung up behind,
The Albatross did follow,
And every day, for food or play,
Came to the mariner's hollo!
"God save thee, ancient Mariner!
From the fiends that plague thee thus!—
Why look'st thou so?"—"With my cross-bow
I shot the Albatross."
COLERIDGE—*Ancient Mariner.* Pt. I. St. 18.

10
Great albatross!—the meanest birds
Spring up and flit away,
While thou must toil to gain a flight,
And spread those pinions grey;
But when they once are fairly poised,
Far o'er each chirping thing
Thou sailest wide to other lands,
E'en sleeping on the wing.
CHAS. G. LELAND—*Perseverando.*

ALCHEMY

11
If by fire
Of sooty coal th' empiric alchymist
Can turn, or holds it possible to turn,
Metals of drossiest ore to perfect gold.
MILTON—*Paradise Lost.* Bk. V. L. 439.

12
The starving chemist in his golden views
Supremely blest.
POPE—*Essay on Man.* Ep. II. L. 269.

13
You are an alchemist; make gold of that.
Timon of Athens. Act V. Sc. 1. L. 117.

ALMOND

Amygdalus communis

14
Almond blossom, sent to teach us
That the spring days soon will reach us.
EDWIN ARNOLD—*Almond Blossoms.*

15
Blossom of the almond trees,
April's gift to April's bees.
EDWIN ARNOLD—*Almond Blossoms.*

16
White as the blossoms which the almond tree,
Above its bald and leafless branches bears.
MARGARET J. PRESTON—*The Royal Preacher.* St. 5.

17
Like to an almond tree ymounted hye
On top of greene Selinis all alone,
With blossoms brave bedecked daintily;
Whose tender locks do tremble every one,
At everie little breath, that under heaven is blowne.
SPENSER—*Faerie Queene.* Bk. I. Canto VII. St. 32.

ALPH (RIVER)

18
In Xanadu did Kubla Khan
A stately pleasure-dome decree;
Where Alph, the sacred river ran,
Through caverns measureless to man
Down to a sunless sea.
COLERIDGE—*Kubla Khan.*

AMARANTH

Amarantus

19
Nosegays! leave them for the waking,
Throw them earthward where they grew
Dim are such, beside the breaking
Amaranths he looks unto.
Folded eyes see brighter colors than the open ever do.
E. B. BROWNING—*A Child Asleep.*

1
Bid amaranthus all his beauty shed,
And daffodillies fill their cups with tears,
To strew the laureate hearse where Lycid lies.
MILTON—*Lycidas.* L. 149.

2
Immortal amaranth, a flower which once
In Paradise, fast by the Tree of Life,
Began to bloom, but soon for Man's offence,
To heav'n remov'd, where first it grew, there grows,
And flow'rs aloft shading the fount of life.
MILTON—*Paradise Lost.* Bk. III. L. 353.

3
Amaranths such as crown the maids
That wander through Zamara's shades.
MOORE—*Lalla Rookh. Light of the Harem.* L. 318.

AMARYLLIS

Amaryllis

4
Where, here and there, on sandy beaches
A milky-bell'd amaryllis blew.
TENNYSON—*The Daisy.* St. 4.

AMBITION

5
Nor strive to wind ourselves too high
For sinful man beneath the sky.
CHRISTIAN YEAR—*Morning.*

6
Prima enim sequentem, honestum est in secundis, tertiisque consistere.
When you are aspiring to the highest place, it is honorable to reach the second or even the third rank.
CICERO—*De Oratore.* I.

7
On what strange stuff Ambition feeds!
ELIZA COOK—*Thomas Hood.*

8
By low ambition and the thirst of praise.
COWPER—*Table Talk.* L. 591.

9
On the summit see,
The seals of office glitter in his eyes;
He climbs, he pants, he grasps them! At his heels,
Close at his heels, a demagogue ascends,
And with a dexterous jerk soon twists him down,
And wins them, but to lose them in his turn.
COWPER—*Task.* Bk. IV. L. 58.

10
Il gran rifiuto.
The great refusal.
(Supposed to refer to Celestine V., elected Pope in 1294, who resigned five months later.)
DANTE—*Inferno.* Canto III. LX.

11
But wild Ambition loves to slide, not stand,
And Fortune's ice prefers to Virtue's land.
DRYDEN—*Absalom and Achitophel.* Pt. I. L. 198.
(See also KNOLLES, under GREATNESS)

12
They please, are pleas'd, they give to get esteem
Till, seeming blest, they grow to what they seem.
GOLDSMITH—*The Traveller.* L. 266.

13
For all may have,
If they dare try, a glorious life, or grave.
HERBERT—*The Temple. The Church-Porch.*

14
Sublimi feriam sidera vertice.
I strike the stars with my sublime head.
HORACE—*Carmina.* Bk. I. 1.

15
Nil mortalibus arduum est:
Cœlum ipsum petimus stultitia.
Nothing is too high for the daring of mortals: we would storm heaven itself in our folly.
HORACE—*Carmina.* I. 3. 37.

16
Vestigia nulla retrorsum.
No steps backward.
HORACE—*Epistles.* I. 1. 74.

17
I see, but cannot reach, the height
That lies forever in the light.
LONGFELLOW—*Christus. The Golden Legend.* P. II. *A Village Church.*

18
Most people would succeed in small things if they were not troubled with great ambitions.
LONGFELLOW—*Drift-Wood. Table-Talk.*

19
The shades of night were falling fast,
As through an Alpine village passed
A youth, who bore, 'mid snow and ice
A banner with the strange device,
Excelsior!
LONGFELLOW—*Excelsior.*

20
Ambition has no rest!
BULWER-LYTTON—*Richelieu.* Act III. Sc. 1.

21
He was utterly without ambition [Chas. II.]. He detested business, and would sooner have abdicated his crown than have undergone the trouble of really directing the administration.
MACAULAY—*History of England.* (*Character of Charles II.*) Vol. I. Ch. II.

22
The man who seeks one thing in life, and but one,
May hope to achieve it before life be done;
But he who seeks all things, wherever he goes,
Only reaps from the hopes which around him he sows
A harvest of barren regrets.
OWEN MEREDITH (Lord Lytton)—*Lucile.* Pt. I. Canto II. St. 8.

23
Here may we reign secure, and in my choice
To reign is worth ambition, though in Hell.
Better to reign in hell than serve in heaven.
MILTON—*Paradise Lost.* Bk. I. L. 263.

24
But what will not ambition and revenge
Descend to? who aspires must down as low
As high he soar'd, obnoxious first or last
To basest things.
MILTON—*Paradise Lost.* Bk. IX. L. 168.

25
If at great things thou would'st arrive,
Get riches first, get wealth, and treasure heap,
Not difficult, if thou hearken to me;
Riches are mine, fortune is in my hand,
They whom I favor thrive in wealth amain,
While virtue, valor, wisdom, sit in want.
MILTON—*Paradise Regained.* Bk. II. L. 426.

1
Such joy ambition finds.
MILTON—*Paradise Lost.* Bk. IV. L. 92.

2
Who knows but He, whose hand the lightning forms,
Who heaves old ocean, and who wings the storms,
Pours fierce ambition in a Cæsar's mind.
POPE—*Essay on Man.* Ep. I. L. 157.

3
Oh, sons of earth! attempt ye still to rise,
By mountains pil'd on mountains to the skies?
Heav'n still with laughter the vain toil surveys,
And buries madmen in the heaps they raise.
POPE—*Essay on Man.* Ep. IV. L. 74.

4
But see how oft ambition's aims are cross'd,
And chiefs contend 'til all the prize is lost!
POPE—*Rape of the Lock.* Canto V. L. 108.

5
Be always displeased at what thou art, if thou desire to attain to what thou art not; for where thou hast pleased thyself, there thou abidest.
QUARLES—*Emblems.* Bk. IV. Emblem 3.

6
Licet ipsa vitium sit ambitio, frequenter tamen causa virtutum est.
Though ambition in itself is a vice, yet it is often the parent of virtues.
QUINTILIAN—*De Institutione Oratoria.* II. 22.

7
Ambition is no cure for love!
SCOTT—*Lay of the Last Minstrel.* Canto I. St. 27.

8
O fading honours of the dead!
O high ambition, lowly laid!
SCOTT—*Lay of the Last Minstrel.* Canto II. St. 10.

9
The very substance of the ambitious is merely the shadow of a dream.
Hamlet. Act II. Sc. 2. L. 204.

10
Ill-weav'd ambition, how much art thou shrunk!
When that this body did contain a spirit,
A kingdom for it was too small a bound;
But now, two paces of the vilest earth
Is room enough.
Henry IV. Pt. I. Act V. Sc. 4. L. 88.

11
Virtue is chok'd with foul ambition.
Henry VI. Pt. II. Act III. Sc. 1. L. 143.

12
Mark but my fall, and that that ruin'd me.
Cromwell, I charge thee, fling away ambition.
By that sin fell the angels; how can man then,
The image of his Maker, hope to win by it?
Henry VIII. Act III. Sc. 2. L. 437.

13
'Tis a common proof,
That lowliness is young ambition's ladder,
Whereto the climber upward turns his face;
But when he once attains the upmost round,
He then unto the ladder turns his back,
Looks in the clouds, scorning the base degrees
By which he did ascend.
Julius Cæsar. Act II. Sc. 1. L. 21.

14
Ambition's debt is paid.
Julius Cæsar. Act III. Sc. 1. L. 83.

15
The noble Brutus
Hath told you Cæsar was ambitious;
If it were so, it was a grievous fault;
And grievously hath Cæsar answered it.
Julius Cæsar. Act III. Sc. 2. L. 75.

16
I have no spur
To prick the sides of my intent, but only
Vaulting ambition, which o'erleaps itself,
And falls on the other.
Macbeth. Act I. Sc. 7. L. 25.

17
Ambition is our idol, on whose wings
Great minds are carry'd only to extreme;
To be sublimely great, or to be nothing.
THOS. SOUTHERNE—*The Loyal Brother.* Act I. Sc. 1.

18
Si vis ad summum progredi ab infimo ordire.
If you wish to reach the highest, begin at the lowest.
SYRUS—*Maxims.*

19
Ambition destroys its possessor.
TALMUD—*Yoma* 86.

20
And mad ambition trumpeteth to all.
N. P. WILLIS—*From a Poem delivered at the Departure of the Senior Class of Yale College.* (1827)

21
How like a mounting devil in the heart
Rules the unreined ambition!
N. P. WILLIS—*Parrhasius.*

22
Ambition has but one reward for all:
A little power, a little transient fame,
A grave to rest in, and a fading name!
WILLIAM WINTER—*The Queen's Domain.* L. 90.

23
Too low they build who build beneath the stars.
YOUNG—*Night Thoughts.* Night VIII. L. 225.

AMERICA

24
E pluribus unum.
From many, one.
Motto of the United States of America. First appeared on title page of *Gentleman's Journal,* Jan., 1692. PIERRE ANTOINE (PETER ANTHONY MOTTEAUX) was editor. DR. SIMETIERE affixed it to the American National Seal at time of the Revolution. See HOWARD P. ARNOLD *Historical Side Lights.*

25
Ex pluribus unum facere.
From many to make one.
ST. AUGUSTINE—*Confessions.* Bk. IV. 8. 13.

26
Yet, still, from either beach,
The voice of blood shall reach,
More audible than speech,
"We are one!"
W. ALLSTON—*America to Great Britain.*

1
Asylum of the oppressed of every nation.
Phrase used in the Democratic platform of 1856, referring to the U. S.

2
O, Columbia, the gem of the ocean,
The home of the brave and the free,
The shrine of each patriot's devotion,
A world offers homage to thee.
An adaptation of SHAW's *Britannia*.
(See also under ENGLAND)

3
America! half brother of the world!
With something good and bad of every land.
BAILEY—*Festus*. Sc. *The Surface*. L. 340.

4
A people who are still, as it were, but in the gristle, and not yet hardened into the bone of manhood.
BURKE—*Speech on Conciliation with America*. Works. Vol. II.

5
Young man, there is America—which at this day serves for little more than to amuse you with stories of savage men and uncouth manners; yet shall, before you taste of death, show itself equal to the whole of that commerce which now attracts the envy of the world.
BURKE—*Speech on Conciliation with America*. Works. Vol. II.

6
I called the New World into existence to redress the balance of the Old.
GEORGE CANNING—*The King's Message*. Dec. 12, 1826.

7
The North! the South! the West! the East!
No one the most and none the least,
But each with its own heart and mind,
Each of its own distinctive kind,
Yet each a part and none the whole,
But all together form one soul;
That soul Our Country at its best,
No North, no South, no East, no West,
No yours, no mine, but always Ours,
Merged in one Power our lesser powers,
For no one's favor, great or small,
But all for Each and each for All.
EDMUND VANCE COOKE—*Each for All*, in *The Uncommon Commoner*.

8
Columbia, Columbia, to glory arise,
The queen of the world and the child of the skies!
Thy genius commands thee; with rapture behold,
While ages on ages thy splendors unfold.
TIMOTHY DWIGHT—*Columbia*.

9
Bring me men to match my mountains,
Bring me men to match my plains,
Men with empires in their purpose,
And new eras in their brains.
SAM WALTER FOSS—*The Coming American*.
(See also HOLLAND, under MAN)

10
Wake up America.
AUGUSTUS P. GARDNER—*Speech*, Oct. 16, 1916.

11
The breaking waves dashed high
On a stern and rock-bound coast;
And the woods, against a stormy sky,
Their giant branches tost.
FELICIA D. HEMANS—*Landing of the Pilgrim Fathers*.

12
Hail, Columbia! happy land!
Hail, ye heroes! heavenborn band!
Who fought and bled in Freedom's cause.
JOSEPH HOPKINSON—*Hail Columbia*.

13
America is a tune. It must be sung together.
GERALD STANLEY LEE.—*Crowds*. Bk. V. Pt. III. Ch. XII.

14
Thou, too, sail on, O Ship of State!
Sail on, O Union, strong and great!
Humanity with all its fears,
With all the hopes of future years,
Is hanging breathless on thy fate!
LONGFELLOW—*Building of the Ship*. L. 367.

15
Down to the Plymouth Rock, that had been to their feet as a doorstep
Into a world unknown,—the corner-stone of a nation!
LONGFELLOW—*Courtship of Miles Standish*. Pt. V. St. 2.

16
Earth's biggest Country's gut her soul
An' risen up Earth's Greatest Nation.
LOWELL—*The Biglow Papers*. Second Series. No. 7. St. 21.

17
When asked what State he hails from,
Our sole reply shall be,
He comes from Appomattox
And its famous apple tree.
MILES O'REILLY—*Poem quoted by Roscoe Conkling*. June, 1880.

18
Neither do I acknowledge the right of Plymouth to the whole rock. No, the rock underlies all America: it only crops out here.
WENDELL PHILLIPS—*Speech* at the dinner of the Pilgrim Society at Plymouth, Dec. 21, 1855.

19
Give it only the fulcrum of Plymouth Rock, an idea will upheave the continent.
WENDELL PHILLIPS—*Speech*. New York, Jan. 21, 1863.

20
We have room but for one Language here and that is the English Language, for we intend to see that the crucible turns our people out as Americans of American nationality and not as dwellers in a polyglot boarding-house.
THEODORE ROOSEVELT.

21
My country, 'tis of thee,
Sweet land of liberty,—
Of thee I sing:
Land where my fathers died,
Land of the Pilgrim's pride,
From every mountain side
Let freedom ring.
SAM'L F. SMITH—*America*.

1
In the four quarters of the globe, who reads an American book? or goes to an American play? or looks at an American picture or statue?
SYDNEY SMITH—*Works*. Vol. II. *America*. (*Edinburgh Review*, 1820.)

2
Gigantic daughter of the West
We drink to thee across the flood. . . .
For art not thou of English blood?
TENNYSON—*Hands all Round*. (In the *Oxford* TENNYSON.) (Appeared in the *Examiner*, 1862; *The London Times*, 1880.)

3
So it's home again, and home again, America for me!
My heart is turning home again, and I long to be
In the land of youth and freedom beyond the ocean bars,
Where the air is full of sunshine, and the flag is full of stars.
HENRY VAN DYKE—*America for Me*.
(See also WOODBERRY)

4
The youth of America is their oldest tradition. It has been going on now for three hundred years.
OSCAR WILDE—*A Woman of no Importance*. Act I.

5
Some Americans need hyphens in their names, because only part of them has come over; but when the whole man has come over, heart and thought and all, the hyphen drops of its own weight out of his name.
WOODROW WILSON—*Address*. Unveiling of the Statue to the Memory of Commodore John Barry, Washington, May 16, 1914.

6
Just what is it that America stands for? If she stands for one thing more than another, it is for the sovereignty of self-governing people, and her example, her assistance, her encouragement, has thrilled two continents in this western world with all those fine impulses which have built up human liberty on both sides of the water. She stands, therefore, as an example of independence, as an example of free institutions, and as an example of disinterested international action in the main tenets of justice.
WOODROW WILSON—*Speech*. Pittsburgh, Jan. 29, 1916.

7
We want the spirit of America to be efficient; we want American character to be efficient; we want American character to display itself in what I may, perhaps, be allowed to call spiritual efficiency—clear, disinterested thinking and fearless action along the right lines of thought. America is not anything if it consists of each of us. It is something only if it consists of all of us; and it can consist of all of us only as our spirits are banded together in a common enterprise. That common enterprise is the enterprise of liberty and justice and right. And, therefore, I, for my part, have a great enthusiasm for rendering America spiritually efficient; and that conception lies at the basis of what seems very far removed from it, namely, the plans that have been proposed for the military efficiency of this nation.
WOODROW WILSON—*Speech*. Pittsburgh, Jan. 29, 1916.

8
Home from the lonely cities, time's wreck, and the naked woe,
Home through the clean great waters where freemen's pennants blow,
Home to the land men dream of, where all the nations go.
GEORGE E. WOODBERRY—*Homeward Bound*.
(See also VAN DYKE)

9
We must consult Brother Jonathan.
WASHINGTON'S familiar reference to his secretary and Aide-de-camp, COL. JONATHAN TRUMBULL.

AMUSEMENTS (See also SPORTS)

10
It was an old, old, old, old lady,
And a boy who was half-past three;
And the way they played together
Was beautiful to see.
H. C. BUNNER—*One, Two, Three*.

11
So good things may be abused, and that which was first invented to refresh men's weary spirits.
BURTON—*Anatomy of Melancholy*. Pt. II. Sec. II. Mem. 4.

12
I am a great friend to public amusements; for they keep people from vice.
SAMUEL JOHNSON—*Boswell's Life of Johnson*. (1772)

13
Play up, play up, and play the game.
SIR HENRY NEWBOLT—*Vital Lampada*.

14
Hail, blest Confusion! here are met
All tongues, and times, and faces;
The Lancers flirt with Juliet,
The Brahmin talks of races.
PRAED—*Fancy Ball*. St. 6.

15
Where is our usual manager of mirth?
What revels are in hand? Is there no play,
To ease the anguish of a torturing hour?
Midsummer Night's Dream. Act V. Sc. 1. L. 35.

16
We cry for mercy to the next amusement,
The next amusement mortgages our fields.
YOUNG—*Night Thoughts*. Night II. L. 131.

ANCESTRY (See also POSTERITY)

17
The wisdom of our ancestors.
BACON—(*According to Lord Brougham*).

18
I am a gentleman, though spoiled i' the breeding. The Buzzards are all gentlemen. We came in with the Conqueror.
RICHARD BROME—*The English Moor*. Act II. 4.

19
I look upon you as a gem of the old rock.
SIR THOMAS BROWNE—*Dedication to Urn Burial*.

1
People will not look forward to posterity, who never look backward to their ancestors.

BURKE—*Reflections on the Revolution in France.* Vol. III. P. 274.

2
The power of perpetuating our property in our families is one of the most valuable and interesting circumstances belonging to it, and that which tends the most to the perpetuation of society itself. It makes our weakness subservient to our virtue; it grafts benevolence even upon avarice. The possession of family wealth and of the distinction which attends hereditary possessions (as most concerned in it,) are the natural securities for this transmission.

BURKE—*Reflections on the Revolution in France.* (1790) Vol. III. P. 298.

3
Some decent regulated pre-eminence, some preference (not exclusive appropriation) given to birth, is neither unnatural, nor unjust, nor impolitic.

BURKE—*Reflections on the Revolution in France.* (1790) Vol. III. P. 299.

4
A degenerate nobleman, or one that is proud of his birth, is like a turnip. There is nothing good of him but that which is underground.

SAMUEL BUTLER—"*Characters.*" *A Degenerate Nobleman.*

(See also OVERBURY)

5
Born in the garret, in the kitchen bred.

BYRON—*A Sketch.* L. 1.

(See also CONGREVE, FOOTE)

6
Odiosum est enim, cum a prætereuntibus dicatur:—O domus antiqua, heu, quam dispari dominare domino.

It is disgraceful when the passers-by exclaim, "O ancient house! alas, how unlike is thy present master to thy former one."

CICERO—*De Officiis.* CXXXIX.

7
I came up-stairs into the world; for I was born in a cellar.

CONGREVE—*Love for Love.* Act. II. Sc. 1.

(See also BYRON)

8
D'Adam nous sommes tous enfants,
La preuve en est connue,
Et que tous, nos première parents
Ont mené la charrue.

Mais, las de cultiver enfin
La terre labourée,
L'une a dételé le matin,
L'autre l'après-dinée.

DE COULANGES—*L'Origine de la Noblesse.*

(See also PRIOR for translation. Also GROBIANUS, TENNYSON).

9
Great families of yesterday we show,
And lords whose parents were the Lord knows who.

DANIEL DEFOE—*The True-Born Englishman.* Part I. L. 372.

10
Born in a Cellar, * * * and living in a Garret.

FOOTE—*The Author.* Act II. Sc. 1. L. 375.

(See also BYRON)

11
Primus Adamus duro cum verteret arva ligone,
Pensaque de vili deceret Eva colo:
Ecquis in hoc poterat vir nobilis orbe videri?
Et modo quisquam alios ante locandus erir?
Say, when the ground our father Adam till'd,
And mother Eve the humble distaff held,
Who then his pedigree presumed to trace,
Or challenged the prerogative of place?

GROBIANUS. Bk. I. Ch. IV. (Ed. 1661)

(See also COULANGES and P. 911[1].)

12
No, my friends, I go (always other things being equal) for the man that inherits family traditions and the cumulative humanities of at least four or five generations.

O. W. HOLMES—*Autocrat of the Breakfast Table.* Ch. I.

13
Few sons attain the praise of their great sires, and most their sires disgrace.

HOMER—*Odyssey.* Bk. II. L. 315. POPE'S trans.

14
Fortes creantur fortibus et bonis;
Est in juvencis, est in equibus patrum
Virtus; nec imbellem feroces
Progenerant aquilæ columbam.

The brave are born from the brave and good. In steers and in horses is to be found the excellence of their sires; nor do savage eagles produce a peaceful dove.

HORACE—*Carmina.* Bk. IV. 4.

15
"My nobility," said he, "begins in me, but yours ends in you."

IPHICRATES. See PLUTARCH'S *Morals. Apothegms of Kings and Great Commanders. Iphicrates.*

16
Ah, ma foi, je n'en sais rien; moi je suis mon ancetre.

Faith, I know nothing about it; I am my own ancestor.

JUNOT, DUC D'ABRANTES, when asked as to his ancestry.

(See also NAPOLEON, TIBERIUS)

17
Stemmata quid faciunt, quid prodest, Pontice, longo,
Sanguine censeri pictosque ostendere vultus.

Of what use are pedigrees, or to be thought of noble blood, or the display of family portraits, O Ponticus?

JUVENAL—*Satires.* VIII. 1.

18
Sence I've ben here, I've hired a chap to look about for me
To git me a transplantable an' thrifty fem'ly-tree.

LOWELL—*Biglow Papers. 2d series. No. 3.* III.

19
Sire, I am my own Rudolph of Hapsburg. (*Rudolph was the founder of the Hapsburg family.*)

NAPOLEON to the Emperor of Austria, who hoped to trace the Bonaparte lineage to a prince.

(See also JUNOT)

1
The man who has not anything to boast of but his illustrious ancestors is like a potato,—the only good belonging to him is under ground.
SIR THOMAS OVERBURY—*Characters.*
(See also BURTON)

2
Nam genus et proavos et quæ non fecimus ipsi
Vix ea nostra voco.
Birth and ancestry, and that which we have not ourselves achieved, we can scarcely call our own.
OVID—*Metamorphoses.* XIII. 140.

3
What can ennoble sots, or slaves, or cowards?
Alas! not all the blood of all the Howards.
POPE—*Essay on Man.* Ep. IV. L. 215.

4
If there be no nobility of descent, all the more indispensable is it that there should be nobility of ascent,—a character in them that bear rule so fine and high and pure that as men come within the circle of its influence they involuntarily pay homage to that which is the one pre-eminent distinction,—the royalty of virtue.
BISHOP HENRY C. POTTER—*Address.* Washington Centennial Service in St. Paul's Chapel, New York, Apr. 30, 1889.

5
That all from Adam first begun,
None but ungodly Woolston doubts,
And that his son, and his son's sons
Were all but ploughmen, clowns and louts.

Each when his rustic pains began,
To merit pleaded equal right,
'Twas only who left off at noon,
Or who went on to work till night.
PRIOR—*The Old Gentry.*
(See also COULANGES)

6
On garde toujours la marque de ses origines.
One always retains the traces of one's origin.
JOSEPH ERNEST RENAN—*La Vie de Jésus.*

7
Majorum gloria posteris lumen est, neque bona neque mala in occulto patitur.
The glory of ancestors sheds a light around posterity; it allows neither their good nor bad qualities to remain in obscurity.
SALLUST—*Jugurtha.* LXXXV.

8
Stemma non inspicit. Omnes, si ad primam originem revocentur, a Diis sunt.
It [Philosophy] does not pay attention to pedigree. All, if their first origin be in question, are from the Gods.
SENECA—*Epistles.* XLIV.

9
Qui genus jactat suum
Aliena laudat.
He who boasts of his descent, praises the deeds of another.
SENECA—*Hercules Furens.* Act. II. 340.

10
Our ancestors are very good kind of folks; but they are the last people I should choose to have a visiting acquaintance with.
SHERIDAN—*The Rivals.* Act IV. Sc. 1.

11
I make little account of genealogical trees. Mere family never made a man great. Thought and deed, not pedigree, are the passports to enduring fate.
GENERAL SKOBELEFF—In *Fortnightly Review.* Oct., 1882.

12
The Smiths never had any arms, and have invariably sealed their letters with their thumbs.
SYDNEY SMITH—*Lady Holland's Memoir.* Vol. I. P. 244.

13
Each has his own tree of ancestors, but at the top of all sits Probably Arboreal.
R. L. STEVENSON—*Memories and Portraits.*

14
'Tis happy for him that his father was born before him.
SWIFT—*Polite Conversation.* Dialogue III.

15
From yon blue heavens above us bent,
The gardener Adam and his wife
Smile at the claims of long descent.
Howe'er it be, it seems to me
'Tis only noble to be good.
Kind hearts are more than coronets,
And simple faith than Norman blood.
TENNYSON—*Lady Clara Vere de Vere.* St. 7. ("The Grand Old Gardener" in 1st Ed.)
(See also COULANGES)

16
He seems to be a man sprung from himself.
TIBERIUS. See *Annals* of TACITUS. Bk. XI. Sc. 21. (See also JUNOT)

17
As though there were a tie,
And obligation to posterity!
We get them, bear them, breed and nurse.
What has posterity done for us,
That we, lest they their rights should lose,
Should trust our necks to grip of noose?
JOHN TRUMBULL—*McFingal.* Canto II. L. 121.

18
Bishop Warburton is reported to have said that high birth was a thing which he never knew any one disparage except those who had it not, and he never knew any one make a boast of it who had anything else to be proud of.
WHATELY—*Annot. on Bacon's Essay, Of Nobility.*

19
Rank is a farce: if people Fools will be
A Scavenger and King's the same to *me.*
JOHN WOLCOT—*(Peter Pindar). Title Page. Peter's Prophecy.*

20
He stands for fame on his forefather's feet,
By heraldry, proved valiant or discreet!
YOUNG—*Love of Fame.* Satire I. L. 123.

21
They that on glorious ancestors enlarge,
Produce their debt, instead of their discharge.
YOUNG—*Love of Fame.* Satire I. L. 147.

22
Like lavish ancestors, his earlier years
Have disinherited his future hours,
Which starve on orts, and glean their former field.
YOUNG—*Night Thoughts.* Night III. L. 310.

ANEMONE

1
Within the woods,
Whose young and half transparent leaves scarce cast
A shade, gray circles of anemones
Danced on their stalks.
BRYANT—*The Old Man's Counsel.*

2
Thy subtle charm is strangely given,
My fancy will not let thee be,—
Then poise not thus 'twixt earth and heaven,
O white anemone!
ELAINE GOODALE—*Anemone.*

3
Anemone, so well
Named of the wind, to which thou art all free.
GEORGE MACDONALD—*Wild Flowers.* L. 9.

4
From the soft wing of vernal breezes shed,
Anemones, auritulas, enriched
With shining meal o'er all their velvet leaves.
THOMSON—*The Seasons. Spring.* L. 533.

ANGELS

5
As the moths around a taper,
As the bees around a rose,
As the gnats around a vapour,
So the spirits group and close
Round about a holy childhood, as if drinking its repose.
E. B. BROWNING—*A Child Asleep.*

6
But sad as angels for the good man's sin,
Weep to record, and blush to give it in.
CAMPBELL—*Pleasures of Hope.* Pt. II. L. 357.
(See also STERNE, under OATHS)

7
What though my winged hours of bliss have been
Like angel visits, few and far between.
CAMPBELL—*Pleasures of Hope.* Pt. II. L. 375.
(See also BLAIR, under GOODNESS, NORRIS, under JOY)

8
Hold the fleet angel fast until he bless thee.
NATHANIEL COTTON—*To-morrow.* L. 36.

9
When one that holds communion with the skies
Has fill'd his urn where these pure waters rise,
And once more mingles with us meaner things,
'Tis e'en as if an angel shook his wings.
COWPER—*Charity.* L. 439.

10
What is the question now placed before society with the glib assurance which to me is most astonishing? That question is this: Is man an ape or an angel? I, my lord, I am on the side of the angels. I repudiate with indignation and abhorrence those new fangled theories.
BENJ. DISRAELI—*Speech at Oxford Diocesan Conference.* Nov. 25, 1864.

11
In merest prudence men should teach
* * * * * *
That science ranks as monstrous things
Two pairs of upper limbs; so wings—
E'en Angel's wings!—are fictions.
AUSTIN DOBSON—*A Fairy Tale.*

12
Let old Timotheus yield the prize
Or both divide the crown;
He rais'd a mortal to the skies
She drew an angel down.
DRYDEN—*Alexander's Feast.* Last St.

13
Non Angli, sed Angeli.
Not Angles, but Angels.
Attributed to GREGORY THE GREAT on seeing British captives for sale at Rome.

14
Be not forgetful to entertain strangers, for thereby some have entertained angels unawares.
Hebrews. XIII. 2.

15
Unbless'd thy hand!—if in this low disguise
Wander, perhaps, some inmate of the skies.
HOMER—*Odyssey.* Bk. XVII. L. 570.
POPE'S trans.

16
But all God's angels come to us disguised:
Sorrow and sickness, poverty and death,
One after other lift their frowning masks,
And we behold the Seraph's face beneath,
All radiant with the glory and the calm
Of having looked upon the front of God.
LOWELL—*On the Death of a Friend's Child.* L. 21.

17
In this dim world of clouding cares,
We rarely know, till 'wildered eyes
See white wings lessening up the skies,
The Angels with us unawares.
GERALD MASSEY—*The Ballad of Babe Christabel.*

18
How sweetly did they float upon the wings
Of silence through the empty-vaulted night,
At every fall smoothing the raven down
Of darkness till it smiled!
MILTON—*Comus.* L. 249.

19
The helmed Cherubim,
And sworded Seraphim,
Are seen in glittering ranks with wings display'd.
MILTON—*Hymn on the Nativity.* L. 112.

20
As far as angel's ken.
MILTON—*Paradise Lost.* Bk. I. L. 59.

21
For God will deign
To visit oft the dwellings of just men
Delighted, and with frequent intercourse
Thither will send his winged messengers
On errants of supernal grace.
MILTON—*Paradise Lost.* Bk. VII. L. 569.

22
Then too when angel voices sung
The mercy of their God, and strung
Their harps to hail, with welcome sweet,
That moment watched for by all eyes.
MOORE—*Loves of the Angels. Third Angel's Story.*

23
Men would be angels, angels would be gods.
POPE—*Essay on Man.* Ep. I. L. 126.

24
A guardian angel o'er his life presiding,
Doubling his pleasures, and his cares dividing.
SAM'L ROGERS—*Human Life.* L. 353.

1
All angel now, and little less than all,
While still a pilgrim in this world of ours.
SCOTT—*Lord of the Isles*. (Referring to Harriet, Duchess of Buccleugh.)

2
And flights of angels sing thee to thy rest!
Hamlet. Act V. Sc. 2. L. 371.

3
Angels are bright still, though the brightest fell.
Macbeth. Act IV. Sc. 3. L. 22.

4
How oft do they their silver bowers leave
To come to succour us that succour want!
SPENSER—*Faerie Queene*. Bk. II. Canto VIII. St. 2.

5
Around our pillows golden ladders rise,
And up and down the skies,
With winged sandals shod,
The angels come, and go, the Messengers of God!
Nor, though they fade from us, do they depart—
It is the childly heart
We walk as heretofore,
Adown their shining ranks, but see them nevermore.
R. H. STODDARD—*Hymn to the Beautiful*. St. 3.

6
Sweet souls around us watch us still,
Press nearer to our side;
Into our thoughts, into our prayers,
With gentle helpings glide.
HARRIET BEECHER STOWE—*The Other World*.

7
I have no angels left
Now, Sweet, to pray to:
Where you have made your shrine
They are away to.
They have struck Heaven's tent,
And gone to cover you:
Whereso you keep your state
Heaven is pitched over you.
FRANCIS THOMPSON—*A Carrier Song*. St. 4.

8
For all we know
Of what the Blessèd do above
Is, that they sing, and that they love.
WALLER. (Quoted by WORDSWORTH.)

9
What know we of the Blest above
But that they sing, and that they love?
WORDSWORTH—*Scene on the Lake of Brienz*. (Quoted from WALLER.)

ANGER

10
Anger makes dull men witty, but it keeps them poor.
Certain Apophthegms of LORD BACON. First published in the *Remains*. No. IV. (Remark stated to have been made by Queen Elizabeth to Sir Edward ——)

11
I was angry with my friend:
I told my wrath, my wrath did end.
I was angry with my foe;
I told it not, my wrath did grow.
WM. BLAKE—*Christian Forbearance*.

12
Nursing her wrath to keep it warm.
BURNS—*Tam o' Shanter*. L. 12.

13
Alas! they had been friends in youth;
But whispering tongues can poison truth,
And constancy lives in realms above;
And life is thorny, and youth is vain;
And to be wrothe with one we love
Doth work like madness in the brain.
COLERIDGE—*Christabel*. Pt. II.

14
Beware the fury of a patient man.
DRYDEN—*Absalom and Achitophel*. Pt. I. L. 1005.
(See also FRENCH PROVERB, SYRUS)

15
A man deep-wounded may feel too much pain
To feel much anger.
GEORGE ELIOT—*Spanish Gypsy*. Bk. I.

16
Anger seeks its prey,—
Something to tear with sharp-edged tooth and claw,
Likes not to go off hungry, leaving Love
To feast on milk and honeycomb at will.
GEORGE ELIOT—*Spanish Gypsy*. Bk. I.

17
Be ye angry, and sin not: let not the sun go down upon your wrath.
Ephesians. IV. 26.

18
Craignez la colère de la colombe.
Beware the anger of the dove.
French Proverb. See QUITARD's *Dict. of Proverbs*.
(See also DRYDEN)

19
Anger is one of the sinews of the soul.
FULLER—*The Holy and Profane States*. *Anger*.

20
Anger, which, far sweeter than trickling drops of honey, rises in the bosom of a man like smoke.
HOMER—*Iliad*. XVIII. 108.

21
Ira furor brevis est: animum rege: qui nisi paret imperat.
Anger is momentary madness, so control your passion or it will control you.
HORACE—*Epistles*. I. 2. 62.

22
Fœnum habet in cornu.
He has hay on his horns.
HORACE—*Satires*. I. 4. 34.

23
Trahit ipse furoris
Impetus, et visum est lenti quæsisse nocentem.
They are borne along by the violence of their rage, and think it is a waste of time to ask who are guilty.
LUCAN—*Pharsalia*. II. 109.

24
Nemo me impune lacessit.
No man provokes me with impunity.
Motto of the Order of the Thistle.

25
Quamlibet infirmas adjuvat ira manus.
Anger assists hands however weak.
OVID—*Amorum*. I. 7. 66.

26
Ut fragilis glacies interit ira mora.
Like fragile ice anger passes away in time.
OVID—*Ars Amatoria*. I. 374.

1
Fear not the anger of the wise to raise;
Those best can bear reproof who merit praise.
POPE—*Essay on Criticism.* L. 582.

2
He that is slow to anger is better than the mighty; and he that ruleth his spirit than he that taketh a city.
Proverbs. XVI. 32.

3
Anger wishes that all mankind had only one neck; love, that it had only one heart; grief, two tear-glands; and pride, two bent knees.
RICHTER—*Flower, Fruit and Thorn Pieces.* Ch. VI.

4
Dem tauben Grimm, der keinen Führer hört.
Deaf rage that hears no leader.
SCHILLER—*Wallenstein's Tod.* III. 20. 16.

5
No pale gradations quench his ray,
No twilight dews his wrath allay.
SCOTT—*Rokeby.* Canto VI. St. 21.

6
Quamvis tegatur proditur vultu furor.
Anger, though concealed, is betrayed by the countenance.
SENECA—*Hippolytus.* CCCLXIII.

7
Never anger made good guard for itself.
Antony and Cleopatra. Act IV. Sc. 1. L. 9.

8
If I had a thunderbolt in mine eye,
I can tell who should down.
As You Like It. Act I. Sc. 2. L. 226.

9 Being once chaf'd, he cannot
Be rein'd again to temperance; then he speaks
What's in his heart.
Coriolanus. Act III. Sc. 3. L. 27.

10
Anger's my meat; I sup upon myself,
And so shall starve with feeding.
Coriolanus. Act IV. Sc. 2. L. 50.

11
What, drunk with choler?
Henry IV. Pt. I. Act I. Sc. 3. L. 129.

12 Anger is like
A full-hot horse; who being allowed his way,
Self-mettle tires him.
Henry VIII. Act I. Sc. 1. L. 132.

13
What sudden anger's this? How have I reap'd it?
He parted frowning from me, as if ruin
Leap'd from his eyes: So looks the chafed lion
Upon the daring huntsman that has gall'd him;
Then makes him nothing.
Henry VIII. Act III. Sc. 2. L. 204.

14 You are yoked with a lamb,
That carries anger as the flint bears fire;
Who, much enforced, shows a hasty spark.
And straight is cold again.
Julius Cæsar. Act IV. Sc. 3. L. 109.

15 Touch me with noble anger!
And let not women's weapons, water drops,
Stain my man's cheeks.
King Lear. Act II. Sc. 4. L. 279.

16
The brain may devise laws for the blood; but a hot temper leaps o'er a cold decree: such a hare is madness the youth, to skip o'er the meshes of good counsel, the cripple.
Merchant of Venice. Act. I. Sc. 2. L. 19.

17
It engenders choler, planteth anger;
And better 'twere that both of us did fast,
Since, of ourselves, ourselves are choleric,
Than feed it with such over-roasted flesh.
Taming of the Shrew. Act IV. Sc. 1. L. 175.

18
Come not within the measure of my wrath.
Two Gentlemen of Verona. Act V. Sc. 4. L. 127.

19 Ne frena animo permitte calenti;
Da spatium, tenuemque moram; male cuncta ministrat
Impetus.
Give not reins to your inflamed passions; take time and a little delay; impetuosity manages all things badly.
STATIUS—*Thebais.* X. 703.

20
Not die here in a rage, like a poisoned rat in a hole.
SWIFT—*Letter to Bolingbroke,* March 21, 1729.

21
Furor fit læsa sæpius patientia.
Patience provoked often turns to fury.
SYRUS—*Maxims.* 178.
(See also DRYDEN)

22 Senseless, and deformed,
Convulsive Anger storms at large; or pale,
And silent, settles into fell revenge.
THOMSON—*The Seasons. Spring.* L. 28.

23
Furor arma ministrat.
Their rage supplies them with weapons.
VERGIL—*Æneid.* I. 150.

24
Tantæne animis cœlestibus iræ.
Can heavenly minds such anger entertain?
VERGIL—*Æneid.* I. 11.

ANGLING (See also FISH)

25
A rod twelve feet long and a ring of wire,
A winder and barrel, will help thy desire
In killing a Pike; but the forked stick,
With a slit and a bladder,—and that other fine trick,
Which our artists call snap, with a goose or a duck,—
Will kill two for one, if you have any luck;
The gentry of Shropshire do merrily smile,
To see a goose and a belt the fish to beguile;
When a Pike suns himselfe and a-frogging doth go,
The two-inched hook is better, I know,
Than the ord'nary snaring: but still I must cry,
When the Pike is at home, minde the cookery.
BARKER—*The Art of Angling.* (Reprint of 1820 of the 1657 edition)

26
For angling-rod he took a sturdy oak;
For line, a cable that in storm ne'er broke;
His hook was such as heads the end of pole
To pluck down house ere fire consumes it whole;

This hook was bated with a dragon's tail,—
And then on rock he stood to bob for whale.
SIR WILLIAM DAVENANT—*Brittania Triumphans*. P. 15. Variations of same in *The Mock Romance, Hero and Leander*. London, 1653, 1677. CHAMBER'S *Book of Days*. Vol. 1. P. 173. DANIEL—*Rural Sports, Supplement*. P. 57.
(See also KING)

1
When if or chance or hunger's powerful sway
Directs the roving trout this fatal way,
He greedily sucks in the twining bait,
And tugs and nibbles the fallacious meat.
GAY—*Rural Sports*. Canto I. L. 150.

2
To fish in troubled waters.
MATTHEW HENRY—*Commentaries*. Psalm LX.

3
You must lose a fly to catch a trout.
HERBERT—*Jacula Prudentum*.

4
Canst thou draw out leviathan with an hook?
Job. XLI. 1.

5
A fishing-rod was a stick with a hook at one end and a fool at the other.
SAMUEL JOHNSON, according to HAZLITT—*Essay on Egotism. The Plain Speaker*.

6
Fly fishing is a very pleasant amusement; but angling or float fishing, I can only compare to a stick and a string, with a worm at one end and a fool at the other.
Attributed to JOHNSON by HAWKER—*On Worm Fishing*. (Not found in his works.) See *Notes and Queries*, Dec. 11, 1915.

7
La ligne, avec sa canne, est un long instrument,
Dont le plus mince bout tient un petit reptile,
Et dont l'autre est tenu par un grand imbecile.
A French version of lines attributed to JOHNSON; claimed for GUYET, who lived about 100 years earlier.

8
His angle-rod made of a sturdy oak;
His line, a cable which in storms ne'er broke;
His hook he baited with a dragon's tail,—
And sat upon a rock, and bobb'd for whale.
WILLIAM KING—*Upon a Giant's Angling*. (In CHALMERS's *British Poets*.)
(See also DAVENANT)

9
Down and back at day dawn,
  Tramp from lake to lake,
Washing brain and heart clean
  Every step we take.
Leave to Robert Browning
  Beggars, fleas, and vines;
Leave to mournful Ruskin
  Popish Apennines,
Dirty stones of Venice,
  And his gas lamps seven,
We've the stones of Snowdon
  And the lamps of heaven.
CHARLES KINGSLEY—*Letters and Memories*, Aug., 1856. (Edited by MRS. KINGSLEY.)

10
In a bowl to sea went wise men three,
  On a brilliant night in June:
They carried a net, and their hearts were set
  On fishing up the moon.
THOMAS LOVE PEACOCK—*The Wise Men of Gotham. Paper Money Lyrics*. St. 1.

11
In genial spring, beneath the quivering shade,
Where cooling vapors breathe along the mead,
The patient fisher takes his silent stand,
Intent, his angle trembling in his hand;
With looks unmov'd, he hopes the scaly breed,
And eyes the dancing cork, and bending reed.
POPE—*Windsor Forest*. L. 135.

12
Give me mine angle, we'll to the river; there,
My music playing far off, I will betray
Tawny-finn'd fishes; my bended hook shall pierce
Their slimy jaws.
Antony and Cleopatra. Act II. Sc. 5. L. 10.

13
The pleasant'st angling is to see the fish
Cut with her golden oars the silver stream,
And greedily devour the treacherous bait.
Much Ado About Nothing. Act III. Sc. 1. L. 26.

14
Shrimps and the delicate periwinkle
  Such are the sea-fruits lasses love:
Ho! to your nets till the blue stars twinkle,
  And the shutterless cottages gleam above!
BAYARD TAYLOR — *The Shrimp - Gatherers*. (Parody of Jean Ingelow.)

15
But should you lure
From his dark haunt, beneath the tangled roots
Of pendent trees, the Monarch of the brook,
Behoves you then to ply your finest art.
THOMSON—*The Seasons. Spring*. L. 420.

16
Two honest and good-natured anglers have never met each other by the way without crying out, "What luck?"
HENRY VAN DYKE—*Fisher's Luck*.

17
'Tis an affair of luck.
HENRY VAN DYKE—*Fisher's Luck*.

18
Angling may be said to be so like the mathematics that it can never be fully learnt.
IZAAK WALTON—*The Compleat Angler. Author's Preface*.

19
As no man is born an artist, so no man is born an angler.
IZAAK WALTON—*The Compleat Angler. Author's Preface*.

20
I shall stay him no longer than to wish * * * that if he be an honest angler, the east wind may never blow when he goes a fishing.
IZAAK WALTON—*The Compleat Angler. Author's Preface*.

21
Angling is somewhat like Poetry, men are to be born so.
IZAAK WALTON—*The Compleat Angler*. Pt. I. Ch. I.

22
Doubt not but angling will prove to be so pleasant, that it will prove to be, like virtue, a reward to itself.
IZAAK WALTON—*The Compleat Angler*. Pt. I. Ch. I.

1
I am, Sir, a brother of the angle.
IZAAK WALTON—*The Compleat Angler*. Pt. I. Ch. I.

2
It [angling] deserves commendations; * * * it is an art worthy the knowledge and practice of a wise man.
IZAAK WALTON—*The Compleat Angler*. Pt. I. Ch. I.

3
An excellent angler, and now with God.
IZAAK WALTON—*The Compleat Angler*. Pt. I. Ch. IV.

4
We may say of angling as Dr. Boteler said of strawberries: "Doubtless God could have made a better berry, but doubtless God never did"; and so, (if I might be judge,) God never did make a more calm, quiet, innocent recreation than angling.
IZAAK WALTON—*The Compleat Angler*. Pt. I. Ch. V. (BOTELER was DR. WM. BUTLER. See FULLER'S—*Worthies*. Also ROGER WILLIAMS—*Key into the Language of America*. P. 98.)

5
Thus use your frog: * * * put your hook, I mean the arming wire, through his mouth, and out at his gills, and then with a fine needle and silk sow the upper part of his leg with only one stitch to the arming wire of your hook, or tie the frog's leg above the upper joint to the armed wire; and in so doing use him as though you loved him.
IZAAK WALTON—*The Compleat Angler*. Pt. I. Ch. VIII.

6
O! the gallant fisher's life,
It is the best of any:
'Tis full of pleasure, void of strife,
And 'tis beloved by many.
Other joys
Are but toys;
Only this,
Lawful is;
For our skill
Breeds no ill,
But content and pleasure.
IZAAK WALTON—*The Compleat Angler*. Ch. XVI.

7
And upon all that are lovers of virtue; and dare trust in his providence; and be quiet; and go a-angling.
IZAAK WALTON—*The Compleat Angler*. Pt. I. Ch. XXI.

8
Of recreation there is none
So free as fishing is, alone;
All other pastimes do not less
Than mind and body, both possess:
My hand alone my work can do;
So I can fish and study too.
IZAAK WALTON—*The Compleat Angler*. *The Angler's Song*.

9
The first men that our Saviour dear
Did choose to wait upon Him here,
Blest fishers were; and fish the last
Food was, that He on earth did taste:
I therefore strive to follow those,
Whom He to follow Him hath chose.
IZAAK WALTON—*The Compleat Angler*. *The Angler's Song*.

ANIMALS

10
Cet animal est tres méchant;
Quand on l'attaque il se défend.
This animal is very malicious; when attacked it defends itself.
From a song, La Ménagerie.

11
The cattle upon a thousand hills.
Psalms. L. 10.

12
The cattle are grazing,
Their heads never raising:
There are forty feeding like one!
WORDSWORTH—*The Cock is Crowing*. Written in March while on the bridge.

ANT

13
Ants never sleep.
EMERSON—*Nature*. Ch. IV.

14
Parvula (nam exemplo est) magni formica laboris
Ore trahit, quodcunque potest, atque addit acervo
Quem struit; haud ignara ac non incauta futuri.
For example, the tiny ant, a creature of great industry, drags with its mouth whatever it can, and adds it to the heap which she is piling up, not unaware nor careless of the future.
HORACE—*Satires*. Bk. I. I. 33.

15
While an ant was wandering under the shade of the tree of Phæton, a drop of amber enveloped the tiny insect; thus she, who in life was disregarded, became precious by death.
MARTIAL—*Epigrams*. Bk. VI. Ep. 15.
(See also same idea under BEE, FLY, SPIDER)

16
Go to the ant, thou sluggard; consider her ways, and be wise.
Proverbs. VI. 6.

ANTICIPATION

17
Far off his coming shone.
MILTON—*Paradise Lost*. Bk. VI. L. 768.

18
I would not anticipate the relish of any happiness, nor feel the weight of any misery, before it actually arrives.
Spectator—No. 7.
(See also AGE)

ANTIQUITY (See also AGE)

19
There were giants in the earth in those days.
Genesis. VI. 4.

20
Antiquity, what is it else (God only excepted) but man's authority born some ages before us? Now for the truth of things time makes no alteration; things are still the same they are, let the time be past, present, or to come.
Those things which we reverence for antiquity what were they at their first birth? Were they false?—time cannot make them true. Were they true?—time cannot make them more true.

The circumstances therefore of time in respect of truth and error is merely impertinent.
JOHN HALES ("The Ever Memorable")—*Of Inquiry and Private Judgment in Religion.*

1
The ancient and honorable.
Isaiah. IX. 15.

2
With sharpen'd sight pale Antiquaries pore,
Th' inscription value, but the rust adore.
This the blue varnish, that the green endears;
The sacred rust of twice ten hundred years.
POPE—*Epistle to Mr. Addison.* L. 35.

3
My copper-lamps, at any rate,
For being true antique, I bought;
Yet wisely melted down my plate,
On modern models to be wrought;
And trifles I alike pursue,
Because they're old, because they're new.
PRIOR—*Alma.* Canto III.

4
Remove not the ancient landmark.
Proverbs. XXII. 28; XXIII. 10.

5
There is nothing new except that which has become antiquated.
Motto of the *Revue Rétrospective.*

6
Nor rough, nor barren, are the winding ways
Of hoar Antiquity, but strewn with flowers.
THOMAS WARTON—*Written in a blank Leaf of Dugdale's Monasticon.*

APPAREL (See also FASHION)

7
Che quant' era più ornata, era più brutta.
Who seems most hideous when adorned the most.
ARIOSTO—*Orlando Furioso.* XX. 116.
(See also FLETCHER, MILTON, THOMSON.)

8
Thy clothes are all the soul thou hast.
BEAUMONT AND FLETCHER—*Honest Man's Fortune.* Act V. Sc. 3. L. 170.

9
To a woman, the consciousness of being well dressed gives a sense of tranquillity which religion fails to bestow.
MRS. HELEN BELL. See EMERSON *Letters and Social Aims. II.*

10
To treat a poor wretch with a bottle of Burgundy, and fill his snuff-box, is like giving a pair of laced ruffles to a man that has never a shirt on his back.
TOM BROWN—*Laconics.*

11
Gars auld claes look amaist as weel's the new.
BURNS—*The Cotter's Saturday Night.*

12
His locked, lettered, braw brass collar,
Shewed him the gentleman and scholar.
BURNS—*The Twa Dogs.*

13
And said to myself, as I lit my cigar,
"Supposing a man had the wealth of the Czar
Of the Russias to boot, for the rest of his days,
On the whole do you think he would have much to spare
If he married a woman with nothing to wear?"
WM. ALLEN BUTLER—*Nothing to Wear.*

14
But I do mean to say, I have heard her declare,
When at the same moment she had on a dress
Which cost five hundred dollars, and not a cent less,
And jewelry worth ten times more, I should guess,
That she had not a thing in the wide world to wear!
WM. ALLEN BUTLER—*Nothing to Wear.*

15
Dresses for breakfasts, and dinners, and balls.
Dresses to sit in, and stand in, and walk in;
Dresses to dance in, and flirt in, and talk in,
Dresses in which to do nothing at all;
Dresses for Winter, Spring, Summer, and Fall;
All of them different in color and shape.
Silk, muslin, and lace, velvet, satin, and crape,
Brocade and broadcloth, and other material,
Quite as expensive and much more ethereal.
WM. ALLEN BUTLER—*Nothing to Wear.*

16
Miss Flora McFlimsey of Madison Square,
Has made three separate journeys to Paris,
And her father assures me each time she was there
That she and her friend Mrs. Harris
* * * * * *
Spent six consecutive weeks, without stopping
In one continuous round of shopping,—
* * * * * *
And yet, though scarce three months have passed since the day
This merchandise went on twelve carts, up Broadway,
This same Miss McFlimsey of Madison Square
The last time we met was in utter despair
Because she had nothing whatever to wear.
WM. ALLEN BUTLER—*Nothing to Wear.*

17
Around his form his loose long robe was thrown,
And wrapt a breast bestowed on heaven alone.
BYRON—*Corsair.* Canto II. St. 3.

18
Dress drains our cellar dry,
And keeps our larder lean; puts out our fires
And introduces hunger, frost, and woe,
Where peace and hospitality might reign.
COWPER—*The Task.* Bk. II. L. 614.

19
Beauty when most unclothed is clothed best.
PHINEAS FLETCHER—*Sicelides.* Act II. Sc. 4.
(See also ARIOSTO)

20
He that is proud of the rustling of his silks, like a madman, laughs at the ratling of his fetters. For indeed, Clothes ought to be our remembrancers of our lost innocency.
FULLER—*The Holy and Profane States. Apparel.*

21
They stript Joseph out of his coat, his coat of many colours.
Genesis. XXXVII. 23.

22
A night-cap deck'd his brows instead of bay,
A cap by night,—a stocking all the day.
GOLDSMITH—*Description of an Author's Bedchamber.* In *Citizen of the World,* Letter 30. *The Author's Club.* (1760)

1
It's like sending them ruffles, when wanting a shirt.
GOLDSMITH—*The Haunch of Venison.*

2
The nakedness of the indigent world may be clothed from the trimmings of the vain.
GOLDSMITH—*Vicar of Wakefield.* Ch. IV.

3
Old Grimes is dead, that good old man,
We ne'er shall see him more;
He used to wear a long black coat
All button'd down before.
ALBERT G. GREENE—*Old Grimes.*
(See also SIMMS)

4
Old Rose is dead, that good old man,
We ne'er shall see him more;
He used to wear an old blue coat
All buttoned down before.
Old Rose. Song referred to in WALTON'S *Compleat Angler.* Pt. I. Ch. II.

5
Old Abram Brown is dead and gone,—
You'll never see him more;
He used to wear a long brown coat
That buttoned down before.
HALLIWELL — *Nursery Rhymes of England. Tales.*

6
John Lee is dead, that good old man,—
We ne'er shall see him more:
He used to wear an old drab coat
All buttoned down before.
To the memory of John Lee, who died May 21, 1823. An inscription in Matherne Churchyard.

7
A sweet disorder in the dresse
Kindles in cloathes a wantonnesse.
HERRICK—*Delight in Disorder.*

8
A winning wave, (deserving note,)
In the tempestuous petticote,
A careless shoe-string, in whose tye
I see a wilde civility,—
Doe more bewitch me than when art
Is too precise in every part.
HERRICK—*Delight in Disorder.*

9
It is not linen you're wearing out,
But human creatures' lives.
HOOD—*Song of the Shirt.*

10
A vest as admired Voltiger had on,
Which from this Island's foes his grandsire won,
Whose artful colour pass'd the Tyrian dye,
Obliged to triumph in this legacy.
EDWARD HOWARD—*The British Princes.* (1669) P. 96. See also BOSWELL — *Life of Johnson.* (1769) *European Mag.*, April, 1792. STEELE, in the *Spectator.* The lines are thought to be a forgery of WM. HENRY IRELAND'S.

11
A painted vest Prince Voltiger had on,
Which from a naked Pict his grandsire won.
Attributed to SIR RICHARD BLACKMORE. (Not in Works.) Probably a parody of above.

12
They were attempting to put on
Raiment from naked bodies won.
MATTHEW GREEN—*The Spleen.* Lines called out by Blackmore's parody.

13
After all there is something about a wedding-gown prettier than in any other gown in the world.
DOUGLAS JERROLD—*A Wedding-Gown. Jerrold's Wit.*

14
Fine clothes are good only as they supply the want of other means of procuring respect.
SAMUEL JOHNSON—*Boswell's Life.* (1776)

15
Apes are apes though clothed in scarlet.
BEN JONSON—*Poetaster.* Act V. Sc. 3.

16
Still to be neat, still to be drest,
As you were going to a feast,
Still to be powder'd, still perfum'd.
Lady, it is to be presumed,
Though art's hid causes are not found,
All is not sweet, all is not sound.
BEN JONSON—*Epicœne; or, The Silent Woman.* Act I. Sc. 1. (Song). Trans. from BONNEFONIUS. First part an imitation of PETRONIUS—*Satyricon.*

17
Each Bond-street buck conceits, unhappy elf;
He shows his clothes! alas! he shows himself.
O that they knew, these overdrest self-lovers,
What hides the body oft the mind discovers.
KEATS—*Epigrams. Clothes.*

18
Neat, not gaudy.
CHARLES LAMB—*Letter to Wordsworth.* June 11, 1806. (See also HAMLET)

19
Dwellers in huts and in marble halls—
From Shepherdess up to Queen—
Cared little for bonnets, and less for shawls,
And nothing for crinoline.
But now simplicity's *not* the rage,
And it's funny to think how cold
The dress they wore in the Golden Age
Would seem in the Age of Gold.
HENRY S. LEIGH—*The Two Ages.* St. 4.

20
Not caring, so that sumpter-horse, the back
Be hung with gaudy trappings, in what course
Yea, rags most beggarly, they clothe the soul.
LOWELL—*Fireside Travels.*

21
Let thy attyre bee comely, but not costly.
LYLY—*Euphues.* P. 39. (Ed. 1579)

22
In naked beauty more adorned
More lovely than Pandora.
MILTON—*Paradise Lost.* Bk. IV. L. 713.
(See also ARIOSTO)

23
Be plain in dress, and sober in your diet;
In short, my deary, kiss me! and be quiet.
LADY M. W. MONTAGU—*Summary of Lord Littelton's Advice.*

24
When this old cap was new
'Tis since two hundred years.
Signed with initials M. P. Probably MARTIN PARKER.

1
He was a wight of high renowne,
And thosne but of a low degree:
Itt's pride that putts the countrye downe,
Man, take thine old cloake about thee.
THOMAS PERCY—*Reliques. Take thy Old Cloake about Thee.*

2
My galligaskins, that have long withstood
The winter's fury, and encroaching frosts,
By time subdued (what will not time subdue!)
An horrid chasm disclosed.
JOHN PHILIPS—*The Splendid Shilling.* L. 121.

3
The soul of this man is his clothes.
All's Well That Ends Well. Act II. Sc. 5. L. 45.

4
Thou villain base,
Know'st me not by my clothes?
Cymbeline. Act IV. Sc. 2. L. 80.

5
Costly thy habit as thy purse can buy,
But not express'd in fancy; rich, not gaudy;
For the apparel oft proclaims the man.
Hamlet. Act I. Sc. 3. Line 70.

6
See where she comes, apparell'd like the spring.
Pericles. Act I. Sc. 1. L. 12.

7
So tedious is this day,
As is the night before some festival
To an impatient child, that hath new robes,
And may not wear them.
Romeo and Juliet. Act III. Sc. 2. L. 28.

8
With silken coats, and caps, and golden rings,
With ruffs, and cuffs, and farthingales, and things;
With scarfs, and fans, and double change of bravery,
With amber bracelets, beads, and all this knavery.
Taming of the Shrew. Act IV. Sc. 3. L. 55.

9
He will come to her in yellow stockings, and 'tis a color she abhors; and cross-gartered, a fashion she detests.
Twelfth Night. Act II. Sc. 5. L. 216.

10
Her cap, far whiter than the driven snow,
Emblem right meet of decency does yield.
SHENSTONE—*The Schoolmistress.* St. 6.

11
Now old Tredgortha's dead and gone,
We ne'er shall see him more;
He used to wear an old grey coat,
All buttoned down before.
RUPERT SIMMS, at beginning of list of JOHN TREDGORTHA's works in *Bibliotheca Staffordiensis.* (1894)
(See also GREENE)

12
She wears her clothes as if they were thrown on her with a pitchfork.
SWIFT—*Polite Conversation.* Dialogue I.

13
Attired to please herself: no gems of any kind
She wore, nor aught of borrowed gloss in Nature's stead;
And, then her long, loose hair flung deftly round her head
Fell carelessly behind.
TERENCE—*Self-Tormentor.* Act II. Sc. 2. F. W. RICORD's trans.

14
So for thy spirit did devise
Its Maker seemly garniture,
Of its own essence parcel pure,—
From grave simplicities a dress,
And reticent demureness,
And love encinctured with reserve;
Which the woven vesture would subserve.
For outward robes in their ostents
Should show the soul's habiliments.
Therefore I say,—Thou'rt fair even so,
But better Fair I use to know.
FRANCIS THOMPSON—*Gilded Gold.* St. 2.

15
O fair undress, best dress! it checks no vein,
But every flowing limb in pleasure drowns,
And heightens ease with grace.
THOMSON—*Castle of Indolence.* Canto I. St. 26.

16
Her polish'd limbs,
Veil'd in a simple robe, their best attire;
Beyond the pomp of dress; for Loveliness
Needs not the foreign aid of ornament,
But is, when unadorn'd, adorn'd the most.
THOMSON—*Seasons. Autumn.* L. 202.
(See also ARIOSTO)

17
She's adorned
Amply, that in her husband's eye looks lovely,—
The truest mirror that an honest wife
Can see her beauty in!
JOHN TOBIN—*The Honeymoon.* Act III. Sc. 4.

18
How his eyes languish! how his thoughts adore
That painted coat, which Joseph never wore!
He shows, on holidays, a sacred pin,
That touch'd the ruff, that touched Queen Bess' chin.
YOUNG—*Love of Fame.* Satire IV. L. 119.

19
Their feet through faithless leather met the dirt,
And oftener chang'd their principles than shirt.
YOUNG—*To Mr. Pope.* Epistle I. L. 283.

20
La ropa no da ciencia.
Dress does not give knowledge.
YRIARTE—*Fables.* XXVII.

APPARITIONS

21
Great Pompey's shade complains that we are slow,
And Scipio's ghost walks unavenged amongst us!
ADDISON—*Cato.* Act II. Sc. 1.

22
Who gather round, and wonder at the tale
Of horrid apparition, tall and ghastly,
That walks at dead of night, or takes his stand
O'er some new-open'd grave; and, (strange to tell!)
Evanishes at crowing of the cock.
BLAIR—*The Grave.* L. 67.

1
Where entity and quiddity,
The ghosts of defunct bodies, fly.
BUTLER—*Hudibras.* Pt. I. Canto I. L. 145.

2
The Nightmare Life-in-Death was she.
COLERIDGE—*The Ancient Mariner.* Pt. III.

3
The unexpected disappearance of Mr. Canning from the scene, followed by the transient and embarrassed phantom of Lord Goderich. (Quoted, "He flits across the stage a transient and embarrassed phantom.")
BENJ. DISRAELI—*Endymion.* Ch. III.

4
Thin, airy shoals of visionary ghosts.
HOMER—*Odyssey.* Bk. XI. L. 48. POPE'S trans.

5
So many ghosts, and forms of fright,
Have started from their graves to-night,
They have driven sleep from mine eyes away;
I will go down to the chapel and pray.
LONGFELLOW—*The Golden Legend.* Pt. IV.

6
Of calling shapes, and beck'ning shadows dire,
And airy tongues that syllable men's names.
MILTON—*Comus.* L. 207.

7
For spirits when they please
Can either sex assume, or both.
MILTON—*Paradise Lost.* Bk. I. L. 423.

8
Whence and what are thou, execrable shape?
MILTON—*Paradise Lost.* Bk. II. L. 681.

9
All heart they live, all head, all eye, all ear,
All intellect, all sense, and as they please
They limb themselves, and colour, shape, or size
Assume, as likes them best, condense or rare.
MILTON—*Paradise Lost.* Bk. VI. L. 350.

10
What beck'ning ghost along the moonlight shade
Invites my steps, and points to yonder glade?
POPE—*Elegy to the Memory of an Unfortunate Lady.* L. 1.

11
The graves stood tenantless, and the sheeted dead
Did squeak and gibber in the Roman streets.
Hamlet. Act I. Sc. 1. L. 115.

12
There needs no ghost, my lord, come from the grave.
To tell us this.
Hamlet. Act. I. Sc. 5. L. 126.

13
I can call spirits from the vasty deep.
Why, so can I, or so can any man;
But will they come when you do call for them?
Henry IV. Pt. I. Act III. Sc. 1. L. 52.

14
What are these,
So wither'd, and so wild in their attire;
That look not like the inhabitants o' th' earth,
And yet are on 't?
Macbeth. Act I. Sc. 3. L. 39.

15
Is this a dagger which I see before me,
The handle toward my hand?
Macbeth. Act II. Sc. 1. L. 33.

16
A dagger of the mind, a false creation,
Proceeding from the heat-oppressed brain?
Macbeth. Act. II. Sc. 1. L. 38.

17
Now it is the time of night,
That the graves, all gaping wide,
Every one lets forth his sprite,
In the church-way paths to glide.
Midsummer Night's Dream. Act. V. Sc. 1. L. 386.

18
My people too were scared with eerie sounds,
A footstep, a low throbbing in the walls,
A noise of falling weights that never fell,
Weird whispers, bells that rang without a hand,
Door-handles turn'd when none was at the door,
And bolted doors that open'd of themselves;
And one betwixt the dark and light had seen
Her, bending by the cradle of her babe.
TENNYSON—*The Ring.*

19
I look for ghosts; but none will force
Their way to me; 'tis falsely said
That even there was intercourse
Between the living and the dead.
WORDSWORTH—*Affliction of Margaret.*

APPEARANCES

20
Esse quam videri.
To be rather than to seem.
Latin version of the Greek maxim, found in ÆSCHYLUS—*Siege of Thebes.*

21
Non teneas aurum totum quod splendet ut aurum.
Do not hold everything as gold which shines like gold.
ALANUS DE INSULIS—*Parabolæ.* (In Winchester College Hall-book of 1401–2.)
(See also CERVANTES)

22
O wad some power the giftie gie us
To see oursel's as ithers see us!
It wad fræ monie a blunder free us.
And foolish notion;
What airs in dress and gait wad lea'e us,
And ev'n devotion!
BURNS—*To a Louse.*

23
Think not I am what I appear.
BYRON—*Bride of Abydos.* Canto I. Sc. 12.

24
As large as life, and twice as natural.
LEWIS CARROLL (DODGSON)—*Through the Looking Glass.* Ch. VII.

25
All that glisters is not gold.
CERVANTES—*Don Quixote.* Pt. II. Ch. XXXIII. GOOGE—*Eglogs, etc.* (1563) UDALL—*Ralph Royster Doyster.* (1566) (For variations of same see ALANUS, CHAUCER, CORDELIER, DRYDEN, GRAY, HERBERT, LYDGATE, *Merchant of Venice*, MIDDLETON, SPENSER.)

26
But every thyng which schyneth as the gold,
Nis nat gold, as that I have herd it told.
CHAUCER—*Canterbury Tales. Chanounes Yemanne's Tale. Preamble.* L. 17, 362.

1
Hyt is not al golde that glareth.
CHAUCER—*House of Fame.* Bk. I. L. 272.
(See also CERVANTES)

2
Habit maketh no monke, ne wearing of guilt spurs maketh no knight.
CHAUCER—*Testament of Love.* Bk. II.
(See also ERASMUS)

3
Appearances to save, his only care;
So things seem right, no matter what they are.
CHURCHILL—*Rosciad.* L. 299.

4
Que tout n'est pas or c'on voit luire.
Everything is not gold that one sees shining.
Li Diz de freire Denise Cordelier. (Circa 1300)
(See also CERVANTES)

5
We understood
Her by her sight; her pure and eloquent blood
Spoke in her cheeks, and so distinctly wrought.
That one might almost say her body thought.
DONNE—*Funeral Elegies. Of the Progress of the Soul. By occasion of Religious Death of Mistress Elizabeth Drury.*

6
All, as they say, that glitters is not gold.
DRYDEN—*Hind and the Panther.*
(See also CERVANTES)

7
Cucullus (*or* Cuculla) non facit monachum.
The habit does not make the monk.
Quoted by ERASMUS.
(See also CHAUCER, HENRY VIII., RABELAIS)

8
Handsome is that handsome does.
FIELDING—*Tom Jones.* Bk. IV. Ch. XII.
GOLDSMITH—*Vicar of Wakefield.* Ch. I.

9
He was one of a lean body and visage, as if his eager soul, biting for anger at the clog of his body, desired to fret a passage through it.
THOS. FULLER—*Life of the Duke of Alva.*

10
By outward show let's not be cheated;
An ass should like an ass be treated.
GAY—*Fables. The Packhorse and Carrier.* Pt. II. L. 99.

11
Things are seldom what they seem,
Skim milk masquerades as cream.
W. S. GILBERT—*H. M. S. Pinafore.*

12
Not all that tempts your wandering eyes
And heedless hearts is lawful prize,
Nor all that glisters gold.
GRAY—*Ode on a Favorite Cat.*
(See also CERVANTES)

13
Gloomy as night he stands.
HOMER—*Odyssey.* Bk. XI. L. 744. POPE'S trans.

14
Judge not according to the appearance.
John. VII. 24.
(See also LA FONTAINE)

15
Fronti nulla fides.
Trust not to outward show.
JUVENAL—*Satires.* II. 8.

16
Garde-toi, tant que tu vivras,
De juger des gens sur la mine.
Beware so long as you live, of judging people by appearances.
LA FONTAINE—*Fables.* VI. 5.
(See also JOHN)

17
Même quand l'oiseau marche on sent qu'il a des ailes.
Even when the bird walks one feels that it has wings.
LEMIERRE—*Fastes.* Chant. I.

18
All is not golde that outward shewith bright.
LYDGATE—*On the Mutability of Human Affairs.*

19
All is not golde that shewyth goldishe hewe.
LYDGATE—*Chorle and Byrde.*
(See also CERVANTES)

20
He had a head which statuaries loved to copy, and a foot the deformity of which the beggars in the streets mimicked.
MACAULAY—*On Moore's Life of Lord Byron.* (1831)

21
Whited sepulchres, which indeed appear beautiful outward, but are within full of dead men's bones.
Matthew. XXIII. 27.

22
All is not gold that glisteneth.
MIDDLETON—*A Fair Quarrel.* Act V. Sc. 1.
(See also CERVANTES)

23
Spectatum veniunt, veniunt spectentur ut ipsæ.
They come to see, they come that they themselves may be seen.
OVID—*Ars Amatoria.* 99.

24
Non semper ea sunt, quæ videntur; decipit
Frons prima multos: rara mens intelligit
Quod interiore condidit cura angulo.
Things are not always what they seem; the first appearance deceives many; the intelligence of few perceives what has been carefully hidden in the recesses of the mind.
PHÆDRUS. Bk. IV. Prol. 5.

25
L'habit ne fait le moine.
The dress does not make the monk.
RABELAIS—*Prologue.* I.
(See also ERASMUS)

26
All hoods make not monks.
Henry VIII. Act III. Sc. 1. L. 23.
(See also ERASMUS)

27
All that glisters is not gold;
Often have you heard that told;
Many a man his life hath sold
But my outside to behold.
Merchant of Venice. Act II. Sc. 7. L. 65.

28
Looked as if she had walked straight out of the Ark.
SYDNEY SMITH—*Lady Holland's Memoir.* Vol. I. Ch. 7.

1
Gold all is not that doth golden seem.
SPENSER—*Faerie Queene.* Bk. II. Canto VIII. St. 14.
(See also CERVANTES)

2
Will she pass in a crowd? Will she make a figure in a country church?
SWIFT—*Letter to Stella,* Feb. 9, 1710.

3
She looks as if butter wouldn't melt in her mouth.
SWIFT—*Polite Conversation. Dialogue* I.

4
A fair exterior is a silent recommendation.
SYRUS—*Maxims.*

5
Monstrum horrendum, informe, ingens, cui lumen ademptum.
An immense, misshapen, marvelous monster whose eye is out.
VERGIL—*Æneid.* III. 658.

6
Of the terrible doubt of appearances,
Of the uncertainty after all, that we may-be deluded,
That may-be reliance and hope are but speculations after all,
That may-be identity beyond the grave is a beautiful fable only.
May-be the things I perceive, the animals, plants, men, hills, shining and flowing waters,
The skies of day and night, colors, densities, forms, may-be these are (as doubtless they are) only apparitions, and the real something has yet to be known.
WALT. WHITMAN—*Of the Terrible Doubt of Appearances.*

7
A man of sense can *artifice* disdain,
As men of wealth may venture to go *plain.*
* * * * * *
I find the *fool* when I behold the *screen,*
For 'tis the wise man's interest to be seen.
YOUNG—*Love of Fame. Satire* II. L. 193.

APPETITE (See also COOKERY, EATING, HUNGER)

8
And gazed around them to the left and right
With the prophetic eye of appetite.
BYRON—*Don Juan.* Canto V. St. 50.

9
His thirst he slakes at some pure neighboring brook,
Nor seeks for sauce where Appetite stands cook.
CHURCHILL—*Gotham III.* L. 133.

10
I find no abhorring in my appetite.
DONNE—*Devotion.*

11
L'anima mia gustava di quel cibo,
Che saziando di sè, di sè s'asseta.
My soul tasted that heavenly food, which gives new appetite while it satiates.
DANTE—*Purgatorio.* XXXI. 128.

12
Keen appetite
And quick digestion wait on you and yours.
DRYDEN—*Cleomenes.* Act IV. Sc. 1.
(See also *Macbeth*)

13
Govern well thy appetite, lest Sin
Surprise thee, and her black attendant Death.
MILTON—*Paradise Lost.* Bk. VII. L. 546.

14
My appetite comes to me while eating.
MONTAIGNE—*Essays. Of Vanity.* Bk. III. Ch. IX. Same saying by AMYOT and JEROME. (See also RABELAIS)

15
Put a knife to thy throat, if thou be a man given to appetite.
Proverbs. XXIII. 2.

16
"L'appétit vient en mangeant," disoit Angeston, "mais la soif s'en va en beuvant."
"Appetite comes with eating," says Angeston, "but thirst departs with drinking."
RABELAIS—*Works.* Bk. I. Ch. V. (ANGESTON was JEROME LE HANGESTE, doctor and scholar, who died 1538.)
(See also MONTAIGNE)

17
Wisdom does not show itself so much in precept as in life—a firmness of mind and mastery of appetite.
SENECA—*Epistles.* XX.

18
Epicurean cooks
Sharpen with cloyless sauce his appetite.
Antony and Cleopatra. Act II. Sc. 1. L. 24.

19
Read o'er this;
And after, this; and then to breakfast, with
What appetite you have.
Henry VIII. Act III. Sc. 2. L. 201.

20
Now good digestion wait on appetite,
And health on both!
Macbeth. Act III. Sc. 4. L. 38.
(See also DRYDEN)

21
Who riseth from a feast
With that keen appetite that he sits down?
Merchant of Venice. Act II. Sc. 6. L. 8.

22
Doth not the appetite alter? A man loves the meat in his youth, that he cannot endure in his age.
Much Ado About Nothing. Act II. Sc. 3. L. 250.

23
Or cloy the hungry edge of appetite?
Richard II. Act I. Sc. 3. L. 296.

24
The sweetest honey
Is loathsome in his own deliciousness,
And in the taste confounds the appetite.
Romeo and Juliet. Act II. Sc. 6. L. 11.

25
And through the hall there walked to and fro
A jolly yeoman, marshall of the same,
Whose name was Appetite; he did bestow
Both guestes and meate, whenever in they came,
And knew them how to order without blame.
SPENSER—*Faerie Queene.* Bk. II. Canto IX. St. 28.

26
Young children and chickens would ever be eating.
TUSSER—*Points of Huswifery. Supper Matters.* V.

APPLAUSE

1
Applause is the spur of noble minds, the end and aim of weak ones.
C. C. Colton—*Lacon*. P. 205.

2
O Popular Applause! what heart of man
Is proof against thy sweet, seducing charms?
Cowper—*Task*. Bk. II. L. 431.

3
The silence that accepts merit as the most natural thing in the world, is the highest applause.
Emerson—*An Address*. July 15, 1838.

4
The applause of a single human being is of great consequence.
Samuel Johnson—*Boswell's Life of Johnson*. (1780)

5
Like Cato, give his little senate laws,
And sit attentive to his own applause.
Pope—*Prologue to the Satires*. L. 207.

6
They threw their caps
As they would hang them on the horns o' the moon,
Shouting their emulation.
Coriolanus. Act I. Sc. 1. L. 216.

7
I would applaud thee to the very echo,
That should applaud again.
Macbeth. Act V. Sc. 3. L. 53.

8
I love the people,
But do not like to stage me to their eyes;
Though it do well, I do not relish well
Their loud applause, and Aves vehement;
Nor do I think the man of safe discretion,
That does affect it.
Measure for Measure. Act I. Sc. 1. L. 68.

9
Vos valete et plaudite.
Fare ye well, and give us your applause.
Terence. Last words of several comedies. See his *Eunuchus* V. 9. 64.

APPLE

Pyrus Malus

10
What plant we in this apple tree?
Sweets for a hundred flowery springs
To load the May-wind's restless wings,
When, from the orchard-row, he pours
Its fragrance through our open doors;
A world of blossoms for the bee,
Flowers for the sick girl's silent room,
For the glad infant sprigs of bloom,
We plant with the apple tree.
Bryant—*The Planting of the Apple Tree*.

11
Like to the apples on the Dead Sea's shore,
All ashes to the taste.
Byron—*Childe Harold*. Canto III. St. 34.
(See also Moore)

12
Art thou the topmost apple
The gatherers could reach,
Reddening on the bough?
Shall I not take thee?
Bliss Carman—*Trans. of Sappho*. 53.
(See also Rossetti; also Field under Peach)

13
There's plenty of boys that will come hankering and gruvvelling around when you've got an apple, and beg the core off you; but when *they've* got one, and you beg for the core, and remind them how you give them a core one time, they make a mouth at you, and say thank you 'most to death, but there ain't a-going to *be* no core.
S. L. Clemens (Mark Twain)—*Tom Sawyer Abroad*. Ch. I.

14
Oh! happy are the apples when the south winds blow.
Wm. Wallace Harney—*Adonais*.

15
And what is more melancholy than the old apple-trees that linger about the spot where once stood a homestead, but where there is now only a ruined chimney rising out of a grassy and weed-grown cellar? They offer their fruit to every wayfarer—apples that are bitter-sweet with the moral of time's vicissitude.
Nath. Hawthorne—*Mosses from an Old Manse. The Old Manse*. "Time's vicissitude." See Sterne under Change, Gifford under Song, Bacon under Religion.

16
The Blossoms and leaves in plenty
From the apple tree fall each day;
The merry breezes approach them,
And with them merrily play.
Heine—*Book of Songs. Lyrical Interlude*. No. 63.

17
To satisfy the sharp desire I had
Of tasting those fair apples, I resolv'd
Not to defer; hunger and thirst at once
Powerful persuaders, quicken'd at the scent
Of that alluring fruit, urged me so keen.
Milton—*Paradise Lost*. Bk. IX. L. 584.

18
Like Dead Sea fruit that tempts the eye,
But turns to ashes on the lips!
Moore—*Lalla Rookh. The Fire Worshippers*. L. 1,018.
(See also Byron)

19
Like the sweet apple which reddens upon the topmost bough
A-top on the topmost twig—which the pluckers forgot, somehow—
Forgot it not, nay, but got it not, for none could get it till now.
Rossetti—*Beauty*. A combination from Sappho. (See also Carman)

20
The apples that grew on the fruit-tree of knowledge
By woman were pluck'd, and she still wears the prize
To tempt us in theatre, senate, or college—
I mean the love-apples that bloom in the eyes.
Horace and James Smith—*Rejected Addresses. The Living Lustres, by T. M.* 5.

21
How we apples swim.
Swift—*Brother Protestants*.

22
After the conquest of Afric, Greece, the lesser Asia, and Syria were brought into Italy all the sorts of their Mala, which we interprete apples,

and might signify no more at first; but were afterwards applied to many other foreign fruits.
SIR WM. TEMPLE—*On Gardening.*

APPLE BLOSSOMS

1
Underneath an apple-tree
Sat a maiden and her lover;
And the thoughts within her he
Yearned, in silence, to discover.
Round them danced the sunbeams bright,
Green the grass-lawn stretched before them
While the apple blossoms white
Hung in rich profusion o'er them.
WILL CARLETON—*Apple Blossoms.*

2
The apple blossoms' shower of pearl,
Though blent with rosier hue,
As beautiful as woman's blush,
As evanescent too.
L. E. LANDON—*Apple Blossoms.*

3
All day in the green, sunny orchard,
When May was a marvel of bloom,
I followed the busy bee-lovers
Down paths that were sweet with perfume.
MARGARET E. SANGSTER—*Apple Blossoms.*

APRIL

4
When April winds
Grew soft, the maple burst into a flush
Of scarlet flowers. The tulip tree, high up,
Opened in airs of June her multitude
Of golden chalices to humming birds
And silken-wing'd insects of the sky.
BRYANT—*The Fountain.*

5
Old April wanes, and her last dewy morn
Her death-bed steeps in tears; to hail the May
New blooming blossoms 'neath the sun are born,
And all poor April's charms are swept away.
CLARE—*The Village Minstrel and Other Poems. The Last of April.*

6
Every tear is answered by a blossom,
Every sigh with songs and laughter blent,
Apple-blooms upon the breezes toss them.
April knows her own, and is content.
SUSAN COOLIDGE—*April.*

7
Now the noisy winds are still;
April's coming up the hill!
All the spring is in her train,
Led by shining ranks of rain;
Pit, pat, patter, clatter,
Sudden sun and clatter patter!
* * * * *
All things ready with a will,
April's coming up the hill!
MARY MAPES DODGE—*Now the Noisy Winds are Still.*

8
The April winds are magical,
And thrill our tuneful frames;
The garden-walks are passional
To bachelors and dames.
EMERSON—*April.*

9
Oh, the lovely fickleness of an April day!
W. H. GIBSON—*Pastoral Days. Spring.*

10
Make me over, Mother April,
When the sap begins to stir!
When thy flowery hand delivers
All the mountain-prisoned rivers,
And thy great heart beats and quivers,
To revive the days that were.
RICHARD HOVEY—*April.*

11
For April sobs while these are so glad
April weeps while these are so gay,—
Weeps like a tired child who had,
Playing with flowers, lost its way.
HELEN HUNT JACKSON—*Verses. April.*

12
The children with the streamlets sing,
When April stops at last her weeping;
And every happy growing thing
Laughs like a babe just roused from sleeping.
LUCY LARCOM—*The Sister Months.*

13
I love the season well
When forest glades are teeming with bright forms,
Nor dark and many-folded clouds foretell
The coming on of storms.
LONGFELLOW—*An April Day.* L. 6.

14
Sweet April! many a thought
Is wedded unto thee, as hearts are wed;
Nor shall they fail, till, to its autumn brought,
Life's golden fruit is shed.
LONGFELLOW—*An April Day.* St. 8.

15
Sweet April-time—O cruel April-time!
Year after year returning, with a brow
Of promise, and red lips with longing paled,
And backward-hidden hands that clutch the joys
Of vanished springs, like flowers.
D. M. MULOCK—*April.*

16
The first of April, some do say
Is set apart for All Fools' day;
But why the people call it so,
Nor I, nor they themselves, do know.
Poor Robin's Almanac. (1760) *All Fools' Day.*

17
The lyric sound of laughter
Fills all the April hills,
The joy-song of the crocus,
The mirth of daffodils.
CLINTON SCOLLARD—*April Music.*

18
When well apparell'd April on the heel
Of limping winter treads.
Romeo and Juliet. Act I. Sc. 2. L. 27.

19
When proud-pied April dress'd in all his trim
Hath put a spirit of youth in everything.
Sonnet XCVIII.

20
Spongy April.
Tempest. Act IV. Sc. 1. L. 65.

21
Sweet April's tears,
Dead on the hem of May
ALEX. SMITH—*A Life Drama.* Sc. 8. L. 308.

22
A gush of bird-song, a patter of dew,
A cloud, and a rainbow's warning,

Suddenly sunshine and perfect blue—
An April day in the morning.
HARRIET PRESCOTT SPOFFORD—*April.*

1
Sweet April showers
Do bring May flowers.
TUSSER—*Five Hundred Points of Good Husbandry.* Ch. XXXIX.

2
Again the blackbirds sing; the streams
Wake, laughing, from their winter dreams,
And tremble in the April showers
The tassels of the maple flowers.
WHITTIER—*The Singer.* St. 20.

ARBUTUS, TRAILING

Epigœa repens.

3
Darlings of the forest!
Blossoming alone
When Earth's grief is sorest
For her jewels gone—
Ere the last snow-drift melts your tender buds have blown.
ROSE T. COOKE—*Trailing Arbutus.*

4
Pure and perfect, sweet arbutus
Twines her rosy-tinted wreath.
ELAINE GOODALE—*The First Flowers.*

5
The shy little Mayflower weaves her nest,
But the south wind sighs o'er the fragrant loam,
And betrays the path to her woodland home.
SARAH HELEN WHITMAN—*The Waking of the Heart.*

ARCADIA

6
The Arcadians were chestnut-eaters.
ALCÆUS—*Fragment.* LXXXVI.

7
What, know you not, old man (quoth he)—
Your hair is white, your face is wise—
That Love must kiss that Mortal's eyes
Who hopes to see fair Arcady?
No gold can buy you entrance there;
But beggared Love may go all bare—
No wisdom won with weariness;
But love goes in with Folly's dress—
No fame that wit could ever win;
But only Love may lead Love in.
To Arcady, to Arcady.
H. C. BUNNER—*The Way to Arcady.*

8
Arcades ambo—*id est,* blackguards both.
BYRON—*Don Juan.* Canto IV. St. 93.
(See also VERGIL)

9
Auch ich war in Arkadien geboren.
I, too, was born in Arcadia.
GOETHE. Motto of *Travels in Italy.* SCHILLER—*Resignation.* I.
(See also HEMANS, HOFFMANN, DELILLE, SCHIDONI)

10
I too, Shepherd, in Arcadia dwelt.
FELICIA D. HEMANS—*Song, in Songs for Sunny Hours.*

11
Auch ich war in Arkadien.
E. T. A. HOFFMANN. Motto to *Lebensansichten des Kater Murr.* Vol. I. Ch. II.

12
Les moi aussie je fus pasteur dans l'Arcadie.
DE LILLE—*Les Jardins.*

13
I dwell no more in Arcady,
But when the sky is blue with May,
And birds are blithe and winds are free,
I know what message is for me,
For I have been in Arcady.
LOUISE CHANDLER MOULTON—*Arcady.*

14
In the days when we went gypsying
A long time ago.
EDWIN RANSFORD—*In the Days when We Went Gypsying.*

15
Et in Arcadia ego.
I too was in Arcadia.
BARTOLOMEO SCHIDONI on a painting in the Schiarra-Colonna, Rome. NICHOLAS POUSSIN later used same on a painting in the Louvre. On his monument, San Lorenzo, Rome. WIELAND notes same in PERVOMTE, *Ideen & Erinerung.* HERDER, *Angedenken an Neapel.* Inscription on painting by JOSHUA REYNOLDS. *Portrait of Hariot Fawkener, Mrs. Bouverie and Mrs. Crewe.*
(See also GOETHE)

16
Alas! the road to Anywhere is pitfalled with disaster;
There's hunger, want, and weariness, yet O we loved it so!
As on we tramped exultantly, and no man was our master,
And no man guessed what dreams were ours, as, swinging heel and toe,
We tramped the road to Anywhere, the magic road to Anywhere,
The tragic road to Anywhere, such dear, dim years ago.
ROBERT W. SERVICE—*The Tramps.*

17
Arcades ambo,
Et cantare pares, et respondere parati.
Arcadians both, equal in the song and ready in the response.
VERGIL—*Eclogues.* VII. 4.

18
Tamen cantabitis, Arcades inquit montibus
Hæc vestris: soli cantare periti Arcades.
O mihi tum quam molliter ossa quiescant,
Vestra meos olim si fistula dicat amores.
Arcadians skilled in song will sing my woes upon the hills. Softly shall my bones repose, if you in future sing my loves upon your pipe
VERGIL—*Eclogues.* X. 31.

ARCHITECTURE

19
Houses are built to live in, not to look on; therefore, let use be preferred before uniformity, except where both may be had.
BACON—*Essays. Of Building.*

20
There was King Bradmond's palace,
Was never none richer, the story says:
For all the windows and the walls
Were painted with gold, both towers and halls;
Pillars and doors all were of brass;
Windows of latten were set with glass;

It was so rich in many wise,
That it was like a paradise.
Sir Bevis of Hamptoun. MS. in Caius College.

1
Old houses mended,
Cost little less than new, before they're ended.
COLLEY CIBBER—*Prologue to the Double Gallant.* L. 15.

2
Silently as a dream the fabric rose;
No sound of hammer or of saw was there.
COWPER—*The Task.* Bk. V. L. 144.
(See also *I Kings*)

3
A man who could build a church, as one may say, by squinting at a sheet of paper.
DICKENS—*Martin Chuzzlewit.* Vol. II. Ch. VI.

4
The Gothic cathedral is a blossoming in stone subdued by the insatiable demand of harmony in man. The mountain of granite blooms into an eternal flower, with the lightness and delicate finish, as well as the ærial proportions and perspective of vegetable beauty.
EMERSON—*Essays. Of History.*
(See also SCHELLING)

5
Earth proudly wears the Parthenon
As the best gem upon her zone.
EMERSON—*The Problem.*

6
The hand that rounded Peter's dome
And groined the aisles of Christian Rome,
Wrought in a sad sincerity:
Himself from God he could not free;
He builded better than he knew;
The conscious stone to beauty grew.
EMERSON—*The Problem.*

7
Middle wall of partition.
Ephesians. II. 14.

8
An arch never sleeps.
J. FERGUSSON—*History of Indian and Eastern Architecture.* P. 210. (Referring to the Hindu aphorism of the sleepless arch.) Also the refrain of a novel by J. MEADE FALKNER—*The Nebuly Cloud.*

9
Die Baukunst ist eine erstarrte Musik.
Architecture is frozen music.
GOETHE—*Conversation with Eckermann.* March 23, 1829.
(See also SCHELLING, DE STAËL)

10
Rich windows that exclude the light,
And passages that lead to nothing.
GRAY—*A Long Story.*

11
No hammers fell, no ponderous axes rung,
Like some tall palm the mystic fabric sprung.
Majestic silence.
BISHOP HEBER—*Palestine.* L. 163. ("No workman's steel," as recited by HEBER in *The Sheldonian*, June 15, 1803.)
(See also COWPER, MILTON)

12
When I lately stood with a friend before [the cathedral of] Amiens, . . . he asked me how it happens that we can no longer build such piles? I replied: "Dear Alphonse, men in those days had convictions (Ueberzeugungen), we moderns have opinions (Meinungen) and it requires something more than an opinion to build a Gothic cathedral.
HEINE—*Confidential Letters to August Lewald on the French Stage.* Letter 9. Trans. by C. G. LELAND.

13
So that there was neither hammer nor axe nor any tool of iron heard in the house, while it was in building.
I Kings. VI. 7.
(See also COWPER, HEBER)

14
Grandeur * * * consists in form, and not in size: and to the eye of the philosopher, the curve drawn on a paper two inches long, is just as magnificent, just as symbolic of divine mysteries and melodies, as when embodied in the span of some cathedral roof.
CHARLES KINGSLEY—*Prose Idylls. My Winter Garden.*

15
In the elder days of Art,
Builders wrought with greatest care
Each minute and unseen part;
For the gods see everywhere.
LONGFELLOW—*The Builders.* St. 5.

16
The architect
Built his great heart into these sculptured stones,
And with him toiled his children, and their lives
Were builded, with his own, into the walls,
As offerings unto God.
LONGFELLOW—*Christus. The Golden Legend.* Pt. III. *In the Cathedral.*

17
Ah, to build, to build!
That is the noblest of all the arts.
LONGFELLOW—*Michael Angelo.* Pt. I. II. L. 54.

18
Anon, out of the earth a fabric huge
Rose, like an exhalation.
MILTON—*Paradise Lost.* Bk. I. L. 710.
(See also HEBER)

19
Nor did there want
Cornice or frieze with bossy sculpture graven.
MILTON—*Paradise Lost.* Bk. I. L. 715.

20
The hasty multitude
Admiring enter'd, and the work some praise,
And some the architect: his hand was known
In heaven by many a tower'd structure high,
Where scepter'd angels held their residence,
And sat as princes.
MILTON—*Paradise Lost.* Bk. I. L. 730.

21
Thus when we view some well-proportion'd dome,
* * * * * *
No single parts unequally surprise,
All comes united to th' admiring eyes.
POPE—*Essay on Criticism.* Pt. II. L. 47.

22
The stone which the builders refused is become the head stone of the corner.
Psalms. CXVIII. 22.

1
Better the rudest work that tells a story or records a fact, than the richest without meaning. There should not be a single ornament put upon great civic buildings, without some intellectual intention.

RUSKIN—*Seven Lamps of Architecture. The Lamp of Memory.*

2
It was stated, * * * that the value of architecture depended on two distinct characters:—the one, the impression it receives from human power; the other, the image it bears of the natural creation.

RUSKIN—*Seven Lamps of Architecture. The Lamp of Beauty.*

3
I would have, then, our ordinary dwelling-houses built to last, and built to be lovely; as rich and full of pleasantness as may be within and without: * * * with such differences as might suit and express each man's character and occupation, and partly his history.

RUSKIN—*Seven Lamps of Architecture. The Lamp of Memory.*

4
Therefore when we build, let us think that we build (public edifices) forever. Let it not be for present delight, nor for present use alone, let it be such work as our descendants will thank us for, and let us think, as we lay stone on stone, that a time is to come when those stones will be held sacred because our hands have touched them, and that men will say as they look upon the labor and wrought substance of them, "See! this our fathers did for us."

RUSKIN—*Seven Lamps of Architecture. The Lamp of Memory.*

5
We require from buildings, as from men, two kinds of goodness: first, the doing their practical duty well: then that they be graceful and pleasing in doing it; which last is itself another form of duty.

RUSKIN—*The Stones of Venice.* Vol. I. Ch. II.

6
Architecture is the work of nations.

RUSKIN—*True and Beautiful. Sculpture.*

7
No person who is not a great sculptor or painter, *can* be an architect. If he is not a sculptor or painter, he can only be a *builder*.

RUSKIN—*True and Beautiful. Sculpture.*

8
Ornamentation is the principal part of architecture, considered as a subject of fine art.

RUSKIN—*True and Beautiful. Sculpture.*

9
Since it [architecture] is music in space, as it were a frozen music. . . . If architecture in general is frozen music.

SCHELLING—*Philosophie der Kunst.* Pp. 576, 593.

(See also GOETHE, DE STAËL)

10
When we mean to build,
We first survey the plot, then draw the model;
And when we see the figure of the house,
Then must we rate the cost of the erection.

Henry IV. Pt. II. Act I. Sc. 3. L. 41.

11
'Fore God, you have here a goodly dwelling and a rich.

Henry IV. Pt. II. Act V. Sc. 3. L. 6.

12
He that has a house to put's head in has a good head-piece.

King Lear. Act III. Sc. 2. L. 25.

13
La vue d'un tel monument est comme une musique continuelle et fixée qui vous attend pour vous faire du bien quand vous vous en approchez.

The sight of such a monument is like continual and stationary music which one hears for one's good as one approaches it.

MADAME DE STAËL—*Corinne.* Bk. IV. Ch. III. (See also SCHELLING)

14
Behold, ye builders, demigods who made England's Walhalla [Westminster Abbey].

THEODORE WATTS-DUNTON—*The Silent Voices.* No. 4. *The Minster Spirits.*

ARGUMENT

15
Much might be said on both sides.

ADDISON—*Spectator.* No. 122.

16
Where we desire to be informed 'tis good to contest with men above ourselves; but to confirm and establish our opinions, 'tis best to argue with judgments below our own, that the frequent spoils and victories over their reasons may settle in ourselves an esteem and confirmed opinion of our own.

SIR THOS. BROWNE—*Religio Medici.* Pt. I.VI.

17
And there began a lang digression
About the lords o' the creation.

BURNS—*The Twa Dogs.*

18
He'd undertake to prove, by force
Of argument, a man's no horse.
He'd prove a buzzard is no fowl,
And that a Lord may be an owl,
A calf an Alderman, a goose a Justice,
And rooks, Committee-men or Trustees.

BUTLER—*Hudibras.* Pt. I. Canto I. L. 71.

19
Whatever Sceptic could inquire for,
For every why he had a wherefore.

BUTLER—*Hudibras.* Pt. I. Canto I. L. 131.

20
I've heard old cunning stagers
Say, fools for arguments use wagers.

BUTLER—*Hudibras.* Pt. II. Canto I. L. 297.

21
'Twas blow for blow, disputing inch by inch,
For one would not retreat, nor t'other flinch.

BYRON—*Don Juan.* Canto VIII. St. 77.

22
When Bishop Berkeley said, "there was no matter,"
And proved it—'twas no matter what he said.

BYRON—*Don Juan.* Canto XI. St. 1.

23
I am bound to furnish my antagonists with arguments, but not with comprehension.

BENJ. DISRAELI.

(See also GOLDSMITH)

1
The noble Lord (Stanley) was the Prince Rupert to the Parliamentary army—his valour did not always serve his own cause.
BENJ. DISRAELI—*Speech*, in the House of Commons, April, 1844.
(See also BULWER-LYTTON)

2
A knock-down argument; 'tis but a word and a blow.
DRYDEN—*Amphitryon*. Act I. Sc. 1.

3
How agree the kettle and the earthen pot together?
Ecclesiasticus. XIII. 2.

4
The daughter of debate
That still discord doth sow.
QUEEN ELIZABETH, of MARY QUEEN OF SCOTS. Sonnet in PERCY'S *Reliques*, Vol. I. Bk. V. No. XV. From PUTTENHAM'S *Arte of English Poesie*. London, 1589.

5
Reproachful speech from either side
The want of argument supplied;
They rail, reviled; as often ends
The contests of disputing friends.
GAY—*Fables. Ravens. Sexton and Earth Worm.* Pt. II. L. 117.

6
I always admired Mrs. Grote's saying that politics and theology were the only two really great subjects.
GLADSTONE—*Letter to* LORD ROSEBERY. Sept. 16, 1880. See MORLEY'S *Life of Gladstone*. Bk. VIII. Ch. I.

7
His conduct still right with his argument wrong.
GOLDSMITH—*Retaliation*. L. 46.

8
In arguing, too, the parson own'd his skill,
For even though vanquished he could argue still.
GOLDSMITH—*The Deserted Village*. L. 211.

9
I find you want me to furnish you with argument and intellects too. No, sir, these, I protest you, are too hard for me.
GOLDSMITH—*Vicar of Wakefield*. Ch. VII.
(See also DISRAELI, JOHNSON)

10
Be calm in arguing; for fierceness makes
Error a fault, and truth discourtesy.
HERBERT—*Temple. Church Porch.* St. 52.

11
I have found you an argument; but I am not obliged to find you an understanding.
SAMUEL JOHNSON—*Boswell's Life of Johnson.* (1784)
(See also GOLDSMITH)

12
Nay, if he take you in hand, sir, with an argument,
He'll bray you in a mortar.
BEN JONSON—*The Alchemist.* Act II. Sc. 1.

13
Seria risu risum, seriis discutere.
In arguing one should meet serious pleading with humor, and humor with serious pleading.
GORGIAS LEONTINUS. Endorsed by ARISTOTLE in his *Rhetoric*. Bk. III. Ch. XVIII.
(See also SHAFTSBURY, under RIDICULE)

14
There is no good in arguing with the inevitable. The only argument available with an east wind is to put on your overcoat.
LOWELL—*Democracy and Other Addresses. Democracy.*

15
The brilliant chief, irregularly great,
Frank, haughty, rash—the Rupert of debate.
BULWER-LYTTON—*The New Timon*. Pt. I. (1846)
(See also DISRAELI)

16
In argument with men a woman ever
Goes by the worse, whatever be her cause.
MILTON—*Samson Agonistes*. L. 903.

17
Myself when young did eagerly frequent
Doctor and Saint, and heard great argument
About it and about: but evermore
Came out by the same door wherein I went.
OMAR KHAYYAM—*Rubaiyat*. FITZGERALD'S Trans. St. 27.

18
Discors concordia.
Agreeing to differ.
OVID—*Metamorphoses*. I. 433.
(See also SOUTHEY)

19
Demosthenes, when taunted by Pytheas that all his arguments "smelled of the lamp," replied, "Yes, but your lamp and mine, my friend, do not witness the same labours."
PLUTARCH—*Life of Demosthenes*. See also his *Life of Timoleon*.

20
Like doctors thus, when much dispute has past,
We find our tenets just the same at last.
POPE—*Moral Essays*. Epis. III. L. 15.

21
In some places he draws the thread of his verbosity finer than the staple of his argument.
DR. PORSON, of GIBBON'S *Decline and Fall*, quoted in the *Letters to Travis*.

22
In argument
Similes are like songs in love:
They must describe; they nothing prove.
PRIOR—*Alma*. Canto III.

23
One single positive weighs more,
You know, than negatives a score.
PRIOR—*Epistle to Fleetwood Shepherd*.

24
Soon their crude notions with each other fought;
The adverse sect denied what this had taught;
And he at length the amplest triumph gain'd,
Who contradicted what the last maintain'd.
PRIOR—*Solomon*. Bk. I. L. 717.

25
The first the Retort Courteous; the second the Quip Modest; the third the Reply Churlish; the fourth the Reproof Valiant; the fifth the Countercheck Quarrelsome; the sixth the Lie with Circumstance; the seventh the Lie Direct.
As You Like It. Act V. Sc. 4. L. 96.

1
And sheath'd their swords for lack of argument.
Henry V. Act III. Sc. 1. L. 21.

2
There is occasions and causes why and wherefore in all things.
Henry V. Act V. Sc. 1. L. 3.

3
For they are yet but ear-kissing arguments.
King Lear. Act II. Sc. 1. L. 9.

4
She hath prosperous art
When she will play with reason and discourse,
And well she can persuade.
Measure for Measure. Act I. Sc. 2. L. 189

5
Agreed to differ.
SOUTHEY—*Life of Wesley*.

6
Ah, don't say that you agree with me. When people agree with me I always feel that I must be wrong.
OSCAR WILDE—*The Critic as an Artist*. Pt. II. Also in *Lady Windermere's Fan*. Act II. Founded on a saying of PHOCION.

ARMY (See NAVY, SOLDIERS, WAR)

ARNO (RIVER)

7
At last the Muses rose, * * * And scattered, * * * as they flew,
Their blooming wreaths from fair Valclusa's bowers
To Arno's myrtle border.
AKENSIDE—*Pleasures of the Imagination*. II.

ART (See also PAINTING, SCULPTURE)

8
No work of art is worth the bones of a Pomeranian Grenadier.
Quoted by BISMARCK. Possibly a phrase of FREDERICK THE GREAT.
(See also BISMARCK, under WAR)

9
Now nature is not at variance with art, nor art with nature; they being both the servants of his providence. Art is the perfection of nature. Were the world now as it was the sixth day, there were yet a chaos. Nature hath made one world, and art another. In brief, all things are artificial; for nature is the art of God.
SIR THOMAS BROWNE—*Religio Medici*. Sec. 16.

10
It is the glory and good of Art,
That Art remains the one way possible
Of speaking truth, to mouths like mine at least.
ROBERT BROWNING—*The Ring and the Book. The Book and the Ring*. L. 842.

11
Etenim omnes artes, quæ ad humanitatem pertinent, habent quoddam commune vinculum, et quasi cognatione quadam inter se continentur.
All the arts which belong to polished life have some common tie, and are connected as it were by some relationship.
CICERO—*Oratio Pro Licinio Archia*. I.

12
L'arte vostra quella, quanto puote,
Seque, come il maestro fa il discente;
Si che vostr'arte a Dio quasi è nipote.
Art, as far as it is able, follows nature, as a pupil imitates his master; thus your art must be, as it were, God's grandchild.
DANTE—*Inferno*. XI. 103.

13
There is an art of reading, as well as an art of thinking, and an art of writing.
ISAAC D'ISRAELI—*Literary Character*. Ch. XI.

14
All passes, Art alone
Enduring stays to us;
The Bust out-lasts the throne,—
The coin, Tiberius.
AUSTIN DOBSON—*Ars Victrix*. (Imitated from THÉOPHILE GAUTIER.)
(See also GAUTIER and quotations under TIME)

15
The conscious utterance of thought, by speech or action, to any end, is art.
EMERSON—*Society and Solitude. Art*.

16
L'Art supreme
Seule a l'eternité
Et le buste
Survit la cité.
High art alone is eternal and the bust outlives the city.
THÉOPHILE GAUTIER—*L'Art*.
(See also DOBSON)

17
As all Nature's thousand changes
But one changeless God proclaim;
So in Art's wide kingdom ranges
One sole meaning still the same:
This is Truth, eternal Reason,
Which from Beauty takes its dress,
And serene through time and season
Stands for aye in loveliness.
GOETHE—*Wilhelm Meister's Travels*. Ch. XIV. (Ch. III. 128 of Carlyle's Ed.)

18
His pencil was striking, resistless, and grand;
His manners were gentle, complying, and bland;
Still born to improve us in every part,
His pencil our faces, his manners our heart.
GOLDSMITH—*Retaliation*. L. 139.

19
The canvas glow'd beyond ev'n nature warm;
The pregnant quarry teem'd with human form.
GOLDSMITH—*The Traveller*. L. 137

20
The perfection of an art consists in the employment of a comprehensive system of laws, commensurate to every purpose within its scope, but concealed from the eye of the spectator; and in the production of effects that seem to flow forth spontaneously, as though uncontrolled by their influence, and which are equally excellent, whether regarded individually, or in reference to the proposed result.
JOHN MASON GOOD—*The Book of Nature*. Series 1. Lecture IX.

21
Ars longa, vita brevis est.
Art [of healing] is long, but life is fleeting.
HIPPOCRATES—*Aphorismi*. I. *Nobilissimus*

Medicus. Translated from the Greek.
GOETHE—*Wilhelm Meister* VII. 9.
(See also SENECA, *and quotations under* LIFE, TIME)

1
The temple of art is built of words. Painting and sculpture and music are but the blazon of its windows, borrowing all their significance from the light, and suggestive only of the temple's uses.
J. G. HOLLAND—*Plain Talks on Familiar Subjects. Art and Life.*

2
It is not strength, but art, obtains the prize,
And to be swift is less than to be wise.
'Tis more by art, than force of numerous strokes.
HOMER—*Iliad.* Bk. 23. L. 382. POPE'S trans.

3
Pictoribus atque poetis
Quidlibet audendi semper fuit æqua potestas.
Painters and poets have equal license in regard to everything.
HORACE—*Ars Poetica.* 9.

4
Piety in art—poetry in art—Puseyism in art—let us be careful how we confound them.
MRS. JAMESON—*Memoirs and Essays. The House of Titian.*

5
Art hath an enemy called ignorance.
BEN JONSON—*Every Man Out of his Humour.* Act I. Sc. 1.

6
We have learned to whittle the Eden Tree to the shape of a surplice peg,
We have learned to bottle our parents twain in the yelk of an addled egg.
We know that the tail must wag the dog, for the horse is drawn by the cart,
But the devil whoops, as he whooped of old;
It's clever, but is it art?
RUDYARD KIPLING—*The Conundrum of the Workshops.*

7
Art is Power.
LONGFELLOW—*Hyperion.* Bk. III. Ch. V.

8
The counterfeit and counterpart
Of Nature reproduced in art.
LONGFELLOW—*Keramos.* L. 380.

9
Art is the child of Nature; yes,
Her darling child in whom we trace
The features of the mother's face,
Her aspect and her attitude.
LONGFELLOW—*Keramos.* L. 382.

10
Dead he is not, but departed,—for the artist never dies.
LONGFELLOW—*Nuremburg.* St. 13.

11
For Art is Nature made by Man
To Man the interpreter of God.
OWEN MEREDITH (Lord Lytton)—*The Artist.* St. 26.

12
The heart desires,
The hand refrains,
The Godhead fires,
The soul attains.
WILLIAM MORRIS. Inscribed on the four pictures of Pygmalion and Galatea by BURNE-JONES, in the Grosvenor Gallery, London.

13
Arte citæ veloque rates remoque moventur;
Arte levis currus, arte regendus Amor.
By arts, sails, and oars, ships are rapidly moved; arts move the light chariot, and establish love.
OVID—*Ars Amatoria.* I. 3.

14
The perfection of art is to conceal art.
QUINTILIAN.

15
Die Kunst ist zwar nicht das Brod, aber der Wein des Lebens.
Art is indeed not the bread but the wine of life.
JEAN PAUL RICHTER.

16
Greater completion marks the progress of art, absolute completion usually its decline.
RUSKIN—*The Seven Lamps of Architecture.* Ch. IV. Pt. XXX. *The Lamp of Beauty.*

17
Seraphs share with thee
Knowledge; But Art, O Man, is thine alone!
SCHILLER—*The Artists.* St. 2.

18
Von der Freiheit gesäugt wachsen die Künste der Lust.
All the arts of pleasure grow when suckled by freedom.
SCHILLER—*Der Spaziergang.* L. 122.

19
Kunst ist die rechte Hand der Natur. Diese hat nur Geschöpfe, jene hat Menschen gemacht.
Art is the right hand of Nature. The latter has only given us being, the former has made us men.
SCHILLER—*Fiesco.* II. 17.

20
Schwer ist die Kunst, vergänglich ist ihr Preis.
Art is difficult, transient is her reward.
SCHILLER—*Wallenstein. Prolog.* L. 40.

21
Illa maximi medicorum exclamatio est, Vitam brevem esse, longam artem.
That is the utterance of the greatest of physicians, that life is short and art long.
SENECA—*De Brevitate Vitæ.* I.
(See also HIPPOCRATES)

22
To gild refined gold, to paint the lily,
To throw a perfume on the violet,
To smooth the ice, or add another hue
Unto the rainbow.
King John. Act IV. Sc. 2. L. 11.

23
In framing an artist, art hath thus decreed,
To make some good, but others to exceed.
Pericles. Act II. Sc. 3. L. 15.

24
His art with nature's workmanship at strife,
As if the dead the living should exceed.
Venus and Adonis. L. 291.

25
It was Homer who gave laws to the artist.
FRANCIS WAYLAND—*The Iliad and the Bible.*

1
Around the mighty master came
The marvels which his pencil wrought,
Those miracles of power whose fame
Is wide as human thought.
WHITTIER—*Raphael.* St. 8.

ASH

Fraxinus

2
The ash her purple drops forgivingly
And sadly, breaking not the general hush;
The maple swamps glow like a sunset sea,
Each leaf a ripple with its separate flush;
All round the wood's edge creeps the skirting blaze,
Of bushes low, as when, on cloudy days,
Ere the rain falls, the cautious farmer burns his brush.
LOWELL—*An Indian-Summer Reverie.* St. 11.

ASPEN

Populus Tremuloides

3
What whispers so strange at the hour of midnight,
From the aspen leaves trembling so wildly?
Why in the lone wood sings it sad, when the bright
Full moon beams upon it so mildly?
B. S. INGEMANN—*The Aspen.*

4
At that awful hour of the Passion, when the Saviour of the world felt deserted in His agony, when—
"The sympathizing sun his light withdrew,
And wonder'd how the stars their dying Lord could view"—
when earth, shaking with horror, rung the passing bell for Deity, and universal nature groaned, then from the loftiest tree to the lowliest flower all felt a sudden thrill, and trembling, bowed their heads, all save the proud and obdurate *aspen,* which said, "Why should *we* weep and tremble? we trees, and plants, and flowers are pure and never sinned!" Ere it ceased to speak, an involuntary trembling seized its very leaf, and the word went forth that it should never rest, but tremble on until the day of judgment.
Legend. From *Notes and Queries.* First Series. Vol. VI. No. 161.

5
Beneath a shivering canopy reclined,
Of aspen leaves that wave without a wind,
I love to lie, when lulling breezes stir
The spiry cones that tremble on the fir.
JOHN LEYDEN—*Noontide.*

6
And the wind, full of wantonness, wooes like a lover
The young aspen-trees till they tremble all over.
MOORE—*Lalla Rookh. Light of the Harem.*

7
Do I? yea, in very truth do I,
An 'twere an aspen leaf.
II Henry IV. Act II. Sc. 4. L. 117.

8
O had the monster seen those lily hands
Tremble like aspen-leaves, upon a lute.
Titus Andronicus. Act II. Sc. 5. L. 45.

ASPHODEL

Asphodelus

9
With her ankles sunken in asphodel
She wept for the roses of earth which fell.
E. B. BROWNING—*Calls on the Heart.*

10
By the streams that ever flow,
By the fragrant winds that blow
O'er the Elysian flow'rs;
By those happy souls who dwell
In yellow mead of asphodel.
POPE—*Ode on St. Cecilia's Day.*

ASS

11
John Trott was desired by two witty peers
To tell them the reason why asses had ears.
"An 't please you," quoth John, "I'm not given to letters;
Nor dare I pretend to know more than my betters:
Howe'er, from this time I shall ne'er see your graces,
As I hope to be saved! without thinking on asses."
GOLDSMITH—*The Clown's Reply.*

12
He shall be buried with the burial of an ass.
Jeremiah. XXII. 19.

ASSASSINATION (See MURDER)

ASTER

Aster

13
Chide me not, laborious band!
For the idle flowers I brought;
Every aster in my hand
Goes home loaded with a thought.
EMERSON—*The Apology.*

14
The Autumn wood the aster knows,
The empty nest, the wind that grieves,
The sunlight breaking thro' the shade,
The squirrel chattering overhead,
The timid rabbits lighter tread
Among the rustling leaves.
DORA READ GOODALE—*Asters.*

15
The aster greets us as we pass
With her faint smile.
SARAH HELEN WHITMAN—*A Day of the Indian Summer.* L. 35.

ATHENS

16
Ancient of days! august Athena! where,
Where are thy men of might? thy grand in soul?
Gone—glimmering through the dream of things that were;
First in the race that led to glory's goal,
They won, and pass'd away—Is this the whole?
BYRON—*Childe Harold.* Canto II. St. 2.

17
Athens, the eye of Greece, mother of arts
And eloquence.
MILTON—*Paradise Regained.* Bk. IV. L. 240.

ASTRONOMY (See also Moon, Stars, Sun)

1
It does at first appear that an astronomer rapt in abstraction, while he gazes on a star, must feel more exquisite delight than a farmer who is conducting his team.
Isaac D'Israeli—*Literary Character of Men of Genius. On Habituating Ourselves to an Individual Pursuit.*

2
And God made two great lights, great for their use
To man, the greater to have rule by day,
The less by night, altern.
Milton—*Paradise Lost.* Bk. VII. L. 346.

3
At night astronomers agree.
Prior—*Phillis's Age.* St. 3.

4
My lord, they say five moons were seen tonight:
Four fixed, and the fifth did whirl about
The other four in wondrous motion.
King John. Act IV. Sc. 2. L. 182.

5
These earthly godfathers of heaven's lights
That give a name to every fixed star
Have no more profit of their shining nights
Than those that walk, and wot not what they are.
Love's Labour's Lost. Act I. Sc. 1. L. 88.

6
And teach me how
To name the bigger light, and how the less,
That burn by day and night.
Tempest. Act I. Sc. 2. L. 334.

7
There's some ill planet reigns;
I must be patient till the heavens look
With an aspect more favorable.
Winter's Tale. Act II. Sc. 1. L. 105.

8
O how loud
It calls devotion! genuine growth of night!
Devotion! daughter of Astronomy!
An undevout Astronomer is mad.
Young—*Night Thoughts.* Night IX. L. 774.

AUDACITY (See also Courage)

9
La crainte fit les dieux; l'audace a fait les rois.
Fear made the gods; audacity has made kings.
Crébillon during the French Revolution.

10
Questa lor tracotanza non è nuova.
This audacity of theirs is not new.
Dante—*Inferno.* VIII. 124.

11
De l'audace, encore de l'audace, toujours de l'audace.
Audacity, more audacity, always audacity.
Danton during the French Revolution. (See also Carlyle—*The French Revolution.* Vol. II. 3. 4)

12
Audax omnia perpeti
Gens humana ruit per vetitum nefas.
The human race afraid of nothing, rushes on through every crime.
Horace—*Carmina.* I. 3. 25.

13
Audendo magnus tegitur timor.
By audacity, great fears are concealed.
Lucan—*Pharsalia.* IV. 702.

AUGUST

14
The August cloud * * * suddenly
Melts into streams of rain.
Bryant—*Sella.*

15
In the parching August wind,
Cornfields bow the head,
Sheltered in round valley depths,
On low hills outspread.
Christina G. Rossetti—*A Year's Windfalls.* St. 8.

16
Dead is the air, and still! the leaves of the locust and walnut
Lazily hang from the boughs, inlaying their intricate outlines
Rather on space than the sky,—on a tideless expansion of slumber.
Bayard Taylor—*Home Pastorals. August.*

AURORA

17
Aurora had but newly chased the night,
And purpled o'er the sky with blushing light.
Dryden—*Palamon and Arcite.* Bk. I. L. 186.

18
But when Aurora, daughter of the dawn,
With rosy lustre purpled o'er the lawn.
Homer—*Odyssey.* Bk. III. L. 621. Pope's trans.

19
Night's son was driving
His golden-haired horses up;
Over the eastern firths
High flashed their manes.
Charles Kingsley—*The Longbeards' Saga.*

20
Zephyr, with Aurora playing,
As he met her once a-Maying.
Milton—*L'Allegro.* L. 19.

21
For night's swift dragons cut the clouds full fast,
And yonder shines Aurora's harbinger;
At whose approach ghosts, wandering here and there,
Troop home to churchyards.
Midsummer Night's Dream. Act III. Sc. 2. L. 379.

22
The wolves have prey'd: and look, the gentle day,
Before the wheels of Phœbus, round about,
Dapples the drowsy east with spots of grey.
Much Ado About Nothing. Act V. Sc. 3. L. 25.

23
At last, the golden orientall gate
Of greatest heaven gan to open fayre,
And Phœbus, fresh as brydegrome to his mate,
Came dauncing forth, shaking his dewie hayre;
And hurls his glistring beams through gloomy ayre.
Spenser—*Faerie Queene.* Bk. I. Canto V. St. 2.

24
You cannot rob me of free nature's grace,
You cannot shut the windows of the sky
Through which Aurora shows her brightening face.
Thomson—*Castle of Indolence.* Canto II. St. 3.

AUTHORITY

1
I appeal unto Cæsar.
Acts. XXV. 11.

2
All authority must be out of a man's self, turned * * * either upon an art, or upon a man.
BACON—*Natural History. Century X. Touching emission of immateriate virtues, etc.*

3
Authority intoxicates,
And makes mere sots of magistrates;
The fumes of it invade the brain,
And make men giddy, proud, and vain.
BUTLER—*Miscellaneous Thoughts.* L. 283.

4
There is no fettering of authority.
All's Well That Ends Well. Act II. Sc. 3. L. 248.

5
Shall remain!
Hear you this Triton of the minnows? mark you
His absolute "shall"?
Coriolanus. Act III. Sc. 1. L. 88.

6
Thou hast seen a farmer's dog bark at a beggar,
And the creature run from the cur:
There, thou might'st behold the great image of authority;
A dog's obeyed in office.
King Lear. Act IV. Sc. 6. L. 159.

7
Those he commands, move only in command,
Nothing in love: now does he feel his title
Hang loose about him, like a giant's robe
Upon a dwarfish thief.
Macbeth. Act V. Sc. 2. L. 19.

8
Thus can the demi-god Authority
Make us pay down for our offense by weight.
Measure for Measure. Act I. Sc. 2. L. 124

9
But man, proud man,
Drest in a little brief authority,
Most ignorant of what he's most assur'd,
His glassy essence, like an angry ape,
Plays such fantastic tricks before high heaven,
As make the angels weep.
Measure for Measure. Act II. Sc. 2. L. 117.

10
And though authority be a stubborn bear, yet he is oft led by the nose with gold.
A Winter's Tale. Act IV. Sc. 4. L. 831.

11
Authority forgets a dying king,
Laid widow'd of the power in his eye
That bow'd the will.
TENNYSON—*Morte d'Arthur.* L. 121.

AUTHORSHIP (See also BOOKS, CRITICS, JOURNALISM, PLAGIARISM, PUBLISHERS)

12
The circumstance which gives authors an advantage above all these great masters, is this, that they can multiply their originals; or rather, can make copies of their works, to what number they please, which shall be as valuable as the originals themselves.
ADDISON—*The Spectator.* No. 166.

13
Write to the mind and heart, and let the ear
Glean after what it can.
BAILEY—*Festus.* Sc. *Home.*

14
Indeed, unless a man can link his written thoughts with the everlasting wants of men, so that they shall draw from them as from wells, there is no more immortality to the thoughts and feelings of the soul than to the muscles and the bones.
HENRY WARD BEECHER—*Star Papers. Oxford. Bodleian Library.*

15
There is probably no hell for authors in the next world—they suffer so much from critics and publishers in this.
BOVEE—*Summaries of Thought. Authors.*

16
A man of moderate Understanding, thinks he writes divinely: A man of good Understanding, thinks he writes reasonably.
LA BRUYÈRE—*The Characters or Manners of the Present Age.* Ch. I.

17
A man starts upon a sudden, takes Pen, Ink, and Paper, and without ever having had a thought of it before, resolves within himself he will write a Book; he has no Talent at Writing, but he wants fifty Guineas.
LA BRUYÈRE—*The Characters or Manners of the Present Age.* Ch. XV.

18
And so I penned
It down, until at last it came to be,
For length and breadth, the bigness which you see.
BUNYAN—*Pilgrim's Progress. Apology for his Book.*

19
Writers, especially when they act in a body and with one direction, have great influence on the public mind.
BURKE—*Reflections on the Revolution in France.*

20
The book that he has made renders its author this service in return, that so long as the book survives, its author remains immortal and cannot die.
RICHARD DE BURY—*Philobiblon.* Ch. I. 21. E. C. THOMAS' trans.

21
And force them, though it was in spite
Of Nature and their stars, to write.
BUTLER—*Hudibras.* Pt. I. Canto I. L. 647.

22
But words are things, and a small drop of ink,
Falling, like dew, upon a thought produces
That which makes thousands, perhaps millions think.
BYRON—*Don Juan.* Canto III. St. 88.

23
But every fool describes, in these bright days,
His wondrous journey to some foreign court,
And spawns his quarto, and demands your praise,—
Death to his publisher, to him 'tis sport.
BYRON—*Don Juan.* Canto V. St. 52.

1
And hold up to the sun my little taper.
BYRON—*Don Juan.* Canto XII. St. 21.
(See also CRABBE, FLETCHER, YOUNG)

2
Dear authors! suit your topics to your strength,
And ponder well your subject, and its length;
Nor lift your load, before you're quite aware
What weight your shoulders will, or will not, bear.
BYRON—*Hints from Horace.* L. 59.

3
La pluma es lengua del alma.
The pen is the tongue of the mind.
CERVANTES—*Don Quixote.* V. 16.

4
Apt Alliteration's artful aid.
CHURCHILL—*The Prophecy of Famine.* L. 86.

5
That writer does the most, who gives his reader the *most* knowledge, and takes from him the *least* time.
C. C. COLTON—*Lacon. Preface.*

6
Habits of close attention, thinking heads,
Become more rare as dissipation spreads,
Till authors hear at length one general cry
Tickle and entertain us, or we die!
COWPER—*Retirement.* L. 707.

7
None but an author knows an author's cares,
Or Fancy's fondness for the child she bears.
COWPER—*The Progress of Error.* L. 518.

8
So that the jest is clearly to be seen,
Not in the words—but in the gap between;
Manner is all in all, whate'er is writ,
The substitute for genius, sense, and wit.
COWPER—*Table Talk.* L. 540.

9
Oh! rather give me commentators plain,
Who with no deep researches vex the brain;
Who from the dark and doubtful love to run,
And hold their glimmering tapers to the sun.
CRABBE—*The Parish Register.* Pt. I. *Introduction.*
(See also BYRON)

10
Aucun fiel n'a jamais empoisonné ma plume.
No gall has ever poisoned my pen.
CRÉBILLON—*Discours de Réception.*

11
Smelling of the lamp.
DEMOSTHENES.
(See also PLUTARCH, under ARGUMENT)

12
"Gracious heavens!" he cries out, leaping up and catching hold of his hair, "what's this? Print!"
DICKENS—*Christmas Stories. Somebody's Luggage.* Ch. III.

13
And choose an author as you choose a friend.
WENTWORTH DILLON—*Essay on Translated Verse.* L. 96.

14
The men, who labour and digest things most,
Will be much apter to despond than boast;
For if your author be profoundly good,
'Twill cost you dear before he's understood.
WENTWORTH DILLON—*Essay on Translated Verse.* L. 163.

15
When I want to read a book I write one.
Attributed to BENJ. DISRAELI in a review of *Lothair* in *Blackwood's Magazine.*

16
The author who speaks about his own books is almost as bad as a mother who talks about her own children.
BENJ. DISRAELI—*Speech.* Nov. 19, 1870.

17
The unhappy man, who once has trail'd a pen,
Lives not to please himself, but other men;
Is always drudging, wastes his life and blood,
Yet only eats and drinks what you think good.
DRYDEN—*Prologue to Lee's Cæsar Borgia.*

18
All writing comes by the grace of God, and all doing and having.
EMERSON—*Essays. Of Experience.*

19
For no man can write anything who does not think that what he writes is, for the time, the history of the world.
EMERSON—*Essays. Of Nature.*

20
The lover of letters loves power too.
EMERSON—*Society and Solitude. Clubs.*

21
The writer, like a priest, must be exempted from secular labor. His work needs a frolic health; he must be at the top of his condition.
EMERSON—*Poetry and Imagination. Creation.*

22
Like his that lights a candle to the sun.
FLETCHER—*Letter to Sir Walter Aston.*
(See also BYRON)

23
Les sots font le texte, et les hommes d'esprit les commentaires.
Fools make the text, and men of wit the commentaries.
ABBÉ GALIANI—*Of Politics.*
(See also ROYER-COLLARD)

24
Envy's a sharper spur than pay:
No author ever spar'd a brother;
Wits are gamecocks to one another.
GAY—*The Elephant and the Bookseller.* L. 74.

25
The most original modern authors are not so because they advance what is new, but simply because they know how to put what they have to say, as if it had never been said before.
GOETHE.

26
One writer, for instance, excels at a plan, or a title-page, another works away the body of the book, and a third is a dab at an index.
GOLDSMITH—*The Bee.* No. 1. Oct. 6, 1759.

27
"The Republic of Letters" is a very common expression among the Europeans.
GOLDSMITH—*Citizen of the World.* 20.

28
Their name, their years, spelt by the unlettered Muse.
GRAY—*Elegy.* 20.
(See also WORDSWORTH)

1
His [Burke's] imperial fancy has laid all nature under tribute, and has collected riches from every scene of the creation and every walk of art.

Robert Hall—*Apology for the Freedom of the Press.* Sec. IV.

2
Whatever an author puts between the two covers of his book is public property; whatever of himself he does not put there is his private property, as much as if he had never written a word.

Gail Hamilton—*Country Living and Country Thinking.* Preface.

3
Sumite materiam vestris, qui scribitis, æquam
Viribus.

Ye who write, choose a subject suited to your abilities.

Horace—*Ars Poetica.* 38.

4
Tantum series juncturaque pollet.

Of so much force are system and connection.

Horace—*Ars Poetica.* 242.

5
Scribendi recte sapere est et principium et fons.

Knowledge is the foundation and source of good writing.

Horace—*Ars Poetica.* 309.

6
Nonumque prematur in annum.

Let it (what you have written) be kept back until the ninth year.

Horace—*Ars Poetica.* 388.

7
But every little busy scribbler now
Swells with the praises which he gives himself;
And, taking sanctuary in the crowd,
Brags of his impudence, and scorns to mend.

Horace—*Of the Art of Poetry.* 475. Wentworth Dillon's trans.

8
Deferar in vicum vendentem thus et odores,
Et piper, et quicquid chartis amicitur ineptis.

I (*i.e.* my writings) shall be consigned to that part of the town where they sell incense, and scents, and pepper, and whatever is wrapped up in worthless paper.

Horace—*Epistles.* Bk. II. I. 269.

9
Piger scribendi ferre laborem;
Scribendi recte, nam ut multum nil moror.

Too indolent to bear the toil of writing; I mean of writing well; I say nothing about quantity.

Horace—*Satires.* I. 4. 12.

10
Sæpe stilum vertas, iterum quæ digna legi sint
Scripturus.

Often turn the stile [correct with care], if you expect to write anything worthy of being read twice.

Horace—*Satires.* I. 10. 72.

11
Written with a pen of iron, and with the point of a diamond.

Jeremiah. XVII. 1.

12
He [Milton] was a Phidias that could cut a Colossus out of a rock, but could not cut heads out of cherry stones.

Samuel Johnson, according to Hannah More. (1781)

13
Each change of many-coloured life he drew,
Exhausted worlds and then imagined new:
Existence saw him spurn her bounded reign,
And panting Time toil'd after him in vain.

Samuel Johnson—*Prologue on the Opening of the Drury Lane Theatre.*

14
The chief glory of every people arises from its authors.

Samuel Johnson—*Preface to Dictionary.*

15
There are two things which I am confident I can do very well; one is an introduction to any literary work, stating what it is to contain, and how it should be executed in the most perfect manner.

Samuel Johnson—*Boswell's Life of Johnson.* (1755)

16
A man may write at any time if he set himself doggedly to it.

Samuel Johnson—*Boswell's Life of Johnson.* (1773)

17
No man but a blockhead ever wrote except for money.

Samuel Johnson—*Boswell's Life of Johnson.* (1776)

18
Tenet insanabile multo
Scribendi cacoëthes, et ægro in corde senescit.

An incurable itch for scribbling takes possession of many, and grows inveterate in their insane breasts.

Juvenal—*Satires.* VII. 51.

19
Damn the age; I will write for Antiquity.

Charles Lamb—*Bon Mots by Charles Lamb and Douglas Jerrold.* Ed. by Walter Jerrold.

20
To write much, and to write rapidly, are empty boasts. The world desires to know *what* you have done, and not *how* you did it.

George Henry Lewes—*The Spanish Drama.* Ch. III.

21
If you once understand an author's character, the comprehension of his writings becomes easy.

Longfellow—*Hyperion.* Bk. I. Ch. V.

22
Perhaps the greatest lesson which the lives of literary men teach us is told in a single word: Wait!

Longfellow—*Hyperion.* Bk. I. Ch. VIII.

23
Whatever hath been written shall remain,
Nor be erased nor written o'er again;
The unwritten only still belongs to thee:
Take heed, and ponder well what that shall be.

Longfellow—*Morituri Salutamus.* L. 168.

24
Look, then, into thine heart and write!

Longfellow—*Voices of the Night. Prelude.* St. 19.

1

It may be glorious to write
Thoughts that shall glad the two or three
High souls, like those far stars that come in sight
Once in a century.

LOWELL—*An Incident in a Railroad Car.*

2

He that commeth in print because he woulde be knowen, is like the foole that commeth into the Market because he woulde be seen.

LYLY—*Euphues. The Anatomy of Wit. To the Gentlemen Readers.*

3

He who writes prose builds his temple to Fame in rubble; he who writes verses builds it in granite.

BULWER-LYTTON—*Caxtoniana.* Essay XXVII. *The Spirit of Conservatism.*

4

No author ever drew a character, consistent to human nature, but what he was forced to ascribe to it many inconsistencies.

BULWER-LYTTON—*What Will He Do With It?* Bk. IV. Ch. XIV. Heading.

5

You do not publish your own verses, Lælius; you criticise mine. Pray cease to criticise mine, or else publish your own.

MARTIAL—*Epigrams.* Bk. I. Ep. 91.

6

Jack writes severe lampoons on me, 'tis said—
But he writes nothing, who is never read.

MARTIAL—*Epigrams.* Bk. III. Ep. 9.

7

He who writes distichs, wishes, I suppose, to please by brevity. But, tell me, of what avail is their brevity, when there is a whole book full of them?

MARTIAL—*Epigrams.* Bk. VIII. Ep. 29.

8

The ink of the scholar is more sacred than the blood of the martyr.

MOHAMMED—*Tribute to Reason.*

9

To write upon *all* is an author's sole chance
For attaining, at last, the least knowledge of any.

MOORE—*Humorous and Satirical Poems. Literary Advertisement.*

10

Præbet mihi littera linguam:
Et, si non liceat scribere, mutus ero.

This letter gives me a tongue; and were I not allowed to write, I should be dumb.

OVID—*Epistolæ Ex Ponto.* II. 6. 3.

11

Scripta ferunt annos; scriptis Agamemnona nosti,
Et quisquis contra vel simul arma tulit.

Writings survive the years; it is by writings that you know Agamemnon, and those who fought for or against him.

OVID—*Epistolæ Ex Ponto.* IV. 8. 51.

12

'Tis hard to say if greater want of skill
Appear in writing or in judging ill;
But, of the two less dang'rous is th' offence
To tire our patience than mislead our sense.

POPE—*Essay on Criticism.* L. 1.

13

Authors are partial to their wit, 'tis true,
But are not critics to their judgment too?

POPE—*Essay on Criticism.* L. 17.

14

True ease in writing comes from art, not chance,
As those move easiest who have learn'd to dance.

POPE—*Essay on Criticism.* L. 362. *Epistles of Horace.* II. 178.

15

In every work regard the writer's end,
Since none can compass more than they intend.

POPE—*Essay on Criticism.* Pt. II. L. 55.

16

Why did I write? what sin to me unknown
Dipt me in ink, my parents', or my own?
As yet a child, nor yet a fool to fame,
I lisp'd in numbers, for the numbers came.

POPE—*Proloque to Satires.* L. 125.

17

It is the rust we value, not the gold;
Authors, like coins, grow dear as they grow old.

POPE—*Second Book of Horace.* Ep. I. L. 35.

18

E'en copious Dryden wanted, or forgot,
The last and greatest art—the art to blot.

POPE—*Second Book of Horace.* Ep. I. L. 280.

19

Whether the darken'd room to muse invite,
Or whiten'd wall provoke the skew'r to write;
In durance, exile, Bedlam, or the Mint,
Like Lee or Budgel I will rhyme and print.

POPE—*Second Book of Horace.* Satire I. L. 97.

20

Let him be kept from paper, pen, and ink;
So may he cease to write, and learn to think.

PRIOR—*To a Person who Wrote Ill. On Same Person.*

21

'Tis not how well an author says,
But 'tis how much, that gathers praise.

PRIOR—*Epistle to Fleetwood Shepherd.*

22

As though I lived to write, and wrote to live.

SAM'L ROGERS—*Italy. A Character.* L. 16.

23

Ils ont les textes pour eux, mais j'en suis faché pour les textes.

They have the texts on their side, but I pity the texts.

ROYER-COLLARD, against the opinions of the Jansenists of Port-Royal on Grace. "So much the worse for the texts." Phrase attributed to VOLTAIRE.

(See also GALIANI)

24

Devise, wit; write, pen; for I am for whole volumes in folio.

Love's Labour's Lost. Act I. Sc. 2. L. 190.

25

Write till your ink be dry, and with your tears
Moist it again, and frame some feeling line
That may discover such integrity.

Two Gentlemen of Verona. Act III. Sc. 2. L. 74.

26

Of all those arts in which the wise excel,
Nature's chief masterpiece is writing well.

JOHN SHEFFIELD (Duke of Buckinghamshire) —*Essay on Poetry.*

1
Look in thy heart and write.
Sir Philip Sidney—*Wm. Gray's Life of Sir Philip Sidney.*

2
The great and good do not die even in this world. Embalmed in books, their spirits walk abroad. The book is a living voice. It is an intellect to which one still listens.
Sam'l Smiles—*Character.* Ch. X.

3
Ah, ye knights of the pen! May honour be your shield, and truth tip your lances! Be gentle to all gentle people. Be modest to women. Be tender to children. And as for the Ogre Humbug, out sword, and have at him!
Thackeray—*Roundabout Papers. Ogres.*

4
What the devil does the plot signify, except to bring in fine things?
George Villiers—*The Rehearsal.*

5
In every author let us distinguish the man from his works.
Voltaire—*A Philosophical Dictionary. Poets.*

6
But you're *our* particular author, you're our patriot and our friend,
You're the poet of the cuss-word an' the swear.
Edgar Wallace—*Tommy to his Laureate.* (R. Kipling)

7
So must the writer, whose productions should
Take with the vulgar, be of vulgar mould.
Edmund Waller—*Epistle to Mr. Killegrew.*

8
Smooth verse, inspired by no unlettered Muse.
Wordsworth—*Excursion.* V. 262 (Knight's ed.). (See also Gray)

9
This dull product of a scoffer's pen.
Wordsworth—*Excursion.* Bk. II.

10
Some write, confin'd by physic; some, by debt;
Some, for 'tis Sunday; some, because 'tis wet;
* * * * * *
Another writes because his father writ,
And proves himself a bastard by his wit.
Young—*Epistles to Mr. Pope.* Ep. I. L. 75.

11 An author! 'tis a venerable name!
How few deserve it, and what numbers claim!
Unbless'd with sense above their peers refined,
Who shall stand up dictators to mankind?
Nay, who dare shine, if not in virtue's cause?
That sole proprietor of just applause.
Young—*Epistles to Mr. Pope.* Ep. II. *From Oxford.* L. 15.

12
For who can write so fast as men run mad?
Young—*Love of Fame.* Satire I. L. 286.

13
Some future strain, in which the muse shall tell
How science dwindles, and how volumes swell.
How commentators each dark passage shun,
And hold their farthing candle to the sun.
Young—*Love of Fame.* Satire VII. L. 95.
(See also Byron)

14
And then, exulting in their taper, cry, "Behold the Sun;" and, Indian-like, adore.
Young—*Night Thoughts.* Night II.

AUTUMN

15
Now Autumn's fire burns slowly along the woods,
And day by day the dead leaves fall and melt,
And night by night the monitory blast
Wails in the key-hole, telling how it pass'd
O'er empty fields, or upland solitudes,
Or grim wide wave; and now the power is felt
Of melancholy, tenderer in its moods
Than any joy indulgent Summer dealt.
William Allingham—*Day and Night Songs. Autumnal Sonnet.*

16
O Autumn, laden with fruit, and stained
With the blood of the grape, pass not, but sit
Beneath my shady roof; there thou mayest rest
And tune thy jolly voice to my fresh pipe,
And all the daughters of the year shall dance!
Sing now the lusty song of fruits and flowers.
William Blake—*To Autumn.* St. 1.

17 Earth's crammed with heaven,
And every common bush afire with God;
And only he who sees takes off his shoes;
The rest sit round it and pluck blackberries.
E. B. Browning—*Aurora Leigh.* Bk. VII.
(See also Whittier)

18
Autumn wins you best by this, its mute
Appeal to sympathy for its decay.
Robert Browning—*Paracelsus.* Sc. 1.

19
Glorious are the woods in their latest gold and crimson,
Yet our full-leaved willows are in their freshest green.
Such a kindly autumn, so mercifully dealing
With the growths of summer, I never yet have seen.
Bryant—*Third of November.*

20
The melancholy days have come, the saddest of the year,
Of wailing winds, and naked woods, and meadows brown and sear.
Bryant—*The Death of the Flowers.*

21
All-cheering Plenty, with her flowing horn,
Led yellow Autumn, wreath'd with nodding corn.
Burns—*Brigs of Ayr.* L. 221.

22
The mellow autumn came, and with it came
The promised party, to enjoy its sweets.
The corn is cut, the manor full of game;
The pointer ranges, and the sportsman beats
In russet jacket;—lynx-like is his aim;
Full grows his bag, and wonderful his feats.
Ah, nutbrown partridges! Ah, brilliant pheasants!
And ah, ye poachers!—'Tis no sport for peasants.
Byron—*Don Juan.* Canto XIII. St. 75.

23
Yellow, mellow, ripened days,
Sheltered in a golden coating;
O'er the dreamy, listless haze,
White and dainty cloudlets floating;
Winking at the blushing trees,
And the sombre, furrowed fallow;
Smiling at the airy ease,
Of the southward flying swallow.

Sweet and smiling are thy ways,
Beauteous, golden Autumn days.
WILL CARLETON—*Autumn Days.*

1

A breath, whence no man knows,
Swaying the grating weeds, it blows;
It comes, it grieves, it goes.
Once it rocked the summer rose.
JOHN VANCE CHENEY—*Passing of Autumn.*

2

I saw old Autumn in the misty morn
Stand shadowless like silence, listening
To silence, for no lonely bird would sing
Into his hollow ear from woods forlorn,
Nor lowly hedge nor solitary thorn;—
Shaking his languid locks all dewy bright
With tangled gossamer that fell by night,
Pearling his coronet of golden corn.
HOOD—*Ode. Autumn.*

3

The Autumn is old;
The sere leaves are flying;
He hath gather'd up gold,
And now he is dying;—
Old age, begin sighing!
HOOD—*Autumn.*

4

The year's in the wane;
There is nothing adorning;
The night has no eve,
And the day has no morning;
Cold winter gives warning!
HOOD—*Autumn.*

5

Season of mists and mellow fruitfulness!
Close bosom-friend of the maturing sun;
Conspiring with him how to load and bless
With fruit the vines that round the thatch-eaves run;
To bend with apples the moss'd cottage trees,
And fill all fruit with ripeness to the core.
KEATS—*To Autumn.*

6

Third act of the eternal play!
In poster-like emblazonries
"Autumn once more begins today"—
'Tis written all across the trees
In yellow letters like Chinese.
RICHARD LE GALLIENNE—*The Eternal Play.*

7

It was Autumn, and incessant
Piped the quails from shocks and sheaves,
And, like living coals, the apples
Burned among the withering leaves.
LONGFELLOW—*Pegasus in Pound.*

8

What visionary tints the year puts on,
When falling leaves falter through motionless air
Or numbly cling and shiver to be gone!
How shimmer the low flats and pastures bare,
As with her nectar Hebe Autumn fills
The bowl between me and those distant hills,
And smiles and shakes abroad her misty, tremulous hair!
LOWELL—*An Indian Summer Reverie.*

9

Every season hath its pleasures;
Spring may boast her flowery prime,
Yet the vineyard's ruby treasures
Brighten Autumn's sob'rer time.
MOORE—*Spring and Autumn.*

10

Autumn
Into earth's lap does throw
Brown apples gay in a game of play,
As the equinoctials blow.
D. M. MULOCK—*October.*

11

Sorrow and the scarlet leaf,
Sad thoughts and sunny weather;
Ah me! this glory and this grief
Agree not well together!
T. W. PARSONS—*A Song for September.*

12

Ye flowers that drop, forsaken by the spring,
Ye birds that, left by summer, cease to sing,
Ye trees that fade, when Autumn heats remove,
Say, is not absence death to those who love?
POPE—*Pastorals. Autumn.* L. 27.

13

Thus sung the shepherds till th' approach of night,
The skies yet blushing with departing light,
When falling dews with spangles deck'd the glade,
And the low sun had lengthened every shade.
POPE—*Pastorals. Autumn.* Last lines.

14

O, it sets my heart a clickin' like the tickin' of a clock,
When the frost is on the punkin and the fodder's in the shock.
JAMES WHITCOMB RILEY—*When the Frost is on the Punkin.*

15

This sunlight shames November where he grieves
In dead red leaves, and will not let him shun
The day, though bough with bough be overrun.
But with a blessing every glade receives
High salutation.
ROSSETTI—*Autumn Idleness.*

16

The warm sun is failing, the bleak wind is wailing,
The bare boughs are sighing, the pale flowers are dying;
And the year
On the earth her deathbed, in a shroud of leaves dead,
Is lying.
Come, months, come away,
From November to May,
In your saddest array;
Follow the bier
Of the dead cold year,
And like dim shadows watch by her sepulchre.
SHELLEY—*Autumn. A Dirge.*

17

Cold autumn, wan with wrath of wind and rain,
Saw pass a soul sweet as the sovereign tune
That death smote silent when he smote again.
SWINBURNE—*Autumn and Winter.* I.

18

Autumn has come;
Storming now heaveth the deep sea with foam,
Yet would I gratefully lie there,
Willingly die there.
ESAIAS TEGNÉR—*Fridthjof's Saga. Ingeborg's Lament.*

1
How are the veins of thee, Autumn, laden?
Umbered juices,
And pulpèd oozes
Pappy out of the cherry-bruises,
Froth the veins of thee, wild, wild maiden.
With hair that musters
In globèd clusters,
In tumbling clusters, like swarthy grapes,
Round thy brow and thine ears o'ershaden;
With the burning darkness of eyes like pansies,
Like velvet pansies
Where through escapes
The splendid might of thy conflagrate fancies;
With robe gold-tawny not hiding the shapes
Of the feet whereunto it falleth down,
Thy naked feet unsandalled;
With robe gold-tawny that does not veil
Feet where the red
Is meshed in the brown,
Like a rubied sun in a Venice-sail.
FRANCIS THOMPSON—*A Corymbus for Autumn.* St. 2.

2
Crown'd with the sickle and the wheaten sheaf,
While Autumn, nodding o'er the yellow plain,
Comes jovial on.
THOMSON—*Seasons. Autumn.* L. 1.

3
We lack but open eye and ear
To find the Orient's marvels here;
The still small voice in autumn's hush,
Yon maple wood the burning bush.
WHITTIER—*Chapel of the Hermits.*
(See also E. B. BROWNING)

AVARICE

4
So for a good old-gentlemanly vice,
I think I must take up with avarice.
BYRON—*Don Juan.* Canto I. St. 216.
(See also MIDDLETON)

5
Avaritiam si tollere vultis, mater ejus est tollenda, luxuries.
If you wish to remove avarice you must remove its mother, luxury.
CICERO—*De Oratore.* II. 40.

6
Ac primam scelerum matrem, quæ semper habendo
Plus sitiens patulis rimatur faucibus aurum,
Trudis Avaritiam.
Expel avarice, the mother of all wickedness, who, always thirsty for more, opens wide her jaws for gold.
CLAUDIANUS—*De Laudibus Stilichonis.* II. 111.

7
Non propter vitam faciunt patrimonia quidam,
Sed vitio cæci propter patrimonia vivunt.
Some men make fortunes, but not to enjoy them; for, blinded by avarice, they live to make fortunes.
JUVENAL—*Satires.* XII. 50.

8
Crescit amor nummi quantum ipsa pecunia crescit.
The love of pelf increases with the pelf.
JUVENAL—*Satires.* XIV. 139.

9
That disease
Of which all old men sicken, avarice.
THOMAS MIDDLETON—*The Roaring Girl.* Act I. Sc. 1. (See also BYRON)

10
There grows,
In my most ill-compos'd affection such
A stanchless avarice, that, were I king,
I should cut off the nobles for their lands.
Macbeth. Act IV. Sc. 3. L. 76.

11
This avarice
Strikes deeper, grows with more pernicious root.
Macbeth. Act IV. Sc. 3. L. 84.

12
Desunt inopiæ multa, avaritiæ omnia.
Poverty wants much; but avarice, everything.
SYRUS—*Maxims.* 441.

AWKWARDNESS

13
Awkward, embarrassed, stiff, without the skill
Of moving gracefully or standing still,
One leg, as if suspicious of his brother,
Desirous seems to run away from t'other.
CHURCHILL—*Rosciad.* L. 438.

14
What's a fine person, or a beauteous face,
Unless deportment gives them decent grace?
Blessed with all other requisites to please,
Some want the striking elegance of ease;
The curious eye their awkward movement tires:
They seem like puppets led about by wires.
CHURCHILL—*Rosciad.* L. 741.

15
God may forgive sins, he said, but awkwardness has no forgiveness in heaven or earth.
EMERSON—*Society and Solitude.*

16
With ridiculous and awkward action,
Which, slanderer, he imitation calls.
Troilus and Cressida. Act I. Sc. 3. L. 149.

AYR (RIVER)

17
Ayr, gurgling, kissed his pebbled shore,
O'erhung with wild woods, thickening green;
The fragrant birch and hawthorn hoar
Twined amorous round the raptured scene.
BURNS—*To Mary in Heaven.*

18
Farewell, my friends! farewell, my foes!
My peace with these, my love with those.
The bursting tears my heart declare;
Farewell, the bonnie banks of Ayr.
BURNS—*The Banks of Ayr.*

AZALEA

Rhododendron

19
And in the woods a fragrance rare
Of wild azaleas fills the air,
And richly tangled overhead
We see their blossoms sweet and red.
DORA READ GOODALE—*Spring Scatters Far and Wide.*

20
The fair azalea bows
Beneath its snowy crest.
SARAH H. WHITMAN—*She Blooms no More.*

B

BABYHOOD

1
Have you not heard the poets tell
How came the dainty Baby Bell
Into this world of ours?
T. B. ALDRICH—*Baby Bell.*

2
Oh those little, those little blue shoes!
Those shoes that no little feet use.
Oh, the price were high
That those shoes would buy,
Those little blue unused shoes!
WILLIAM C. BENNETT—*Baby's Shoes.*

3
Lullaby, baby, upon the tree top;
When the wind blows the cradle will rock,
When the bough breaks the cradle will fall,
And down comes the baby, and cradle and all.
Said to be "first poem produced on American soil." Author a Pilgrim youth who came over on the Mayflower. See *Book Lover*, Feb., 1904.

4
Rock-bye-baby on the tree top,
When the wind blows the cradle will rock,
When the bough bends the cradle will fall,
Down comes the baby, cradle and all.
Old nursery rhyme, attributed in this form to CHARLES DUPEE BLAKE.

5
Sweet babe, in thy face
Soft desires I can trace,
Secret joys and secret smiles,
Little pretty infant wiles.
WILLIAM BLAKE—*A Cradle Song.*

6
How lovely he appears! his little cheeks
In their pure incarnation, vying with
The rose leaves strewn beneath them.
And his lips, too,
How beautifully parted! No; you shall not
Kiss him; at least not now; he will wake soon—
His hour of midday rest is nearly over.
BYRON—*Cain.* Act III. Sc. 1. L. 14.

7
He smiles, and sleeps!—sleep on
And smile, thou little, young inheritor
Of a world scarce less young: sleep on and smile!
Thine are the hours and days when both are cheering
And innocent!
BYRON—*Cain.* Act III. Sc. 1. L. 24.

8
Look! how he laughs and stretches out his arms,
And opens wide his blue eyes upon thine,
To hail his father; while his little form
Flutters as winged with joy. Talk not of pain!
The childless cherubs well might envy thee
The pleasures of a parent.
BYRON—*Cain.* Act III. Sc. 1. L. 171.

9
There came to port last Sunday night
The queerest little craft,
Without an inch of rigging on;
I looked and looked—and laughed.
It seemed so curious that she
Should cross the unknown water,
And moor herself within my room—
My daughter! O my daughter!
G. W. CABLE—*The New Arrival.*

10
Lo! at the couch where infant beauty sleeps;
Her silent watch the mournful mother keeps;
She, while the lovely babe unconscious lies,
Smiles on her slumbering child with pensive eyes.
CAMPBELL—*Pleasures of Hope.* Pt. I. L. 225.

11
He is so little to be so large!
Why, a train of cars, or a whale-back barge
Couldn't carry the freight
Of the monstrous weight
Of all of his qualities, good and great.
And tho' one view is as good as another,
Don't take my word for it. Ask his mother!
EDMUND VANCE COOKE—*The Intruder.*

12
"The hand that rocks the cradle"—but there is no such hand.
It is bad to rock the baby, they would have us understand;
So the cradle's but a relic of the former foolish days,
When mothers reared their children in unscientific ways;
When they jounced them and they bounced them, those poor dwarfs of long ago—
The Washingtons and Jeffersons and Adamses, you know.
Ascribed to BISHOP DOANE—*What Might Have Been.* A complaint that for hygienic reasons, he was not allowed to play with his grandchild in the old-fashioned way.
(See also WALLACE under MOTHERHOOD)

13
When you fold your hands, Baby Louise!
Your hands like a fairy's, so tiny and fair,
With a pretty, innocent, saintlike air,
Are you trying to think of some angel-taught prayer
You learned above, Baby Louise.
MARGARET EYTINGE—*Baby Louise.*

14
Baloo, baloo, my wee, wee thing.
RICHARD GALL—*Cradle Song.*

15
The morning that my baby came
They found a baby swallow dead,
And saw a something hard to name
Fly mothlike over baby's bed.
RALPH HODGSON—*The Swallow.*

16
What is the little one thinking about?
Very wonderful things, no doubt;
Unwritten history!
Unfathomed mystery!
Yet he laughs and cries, and eats and drinks,
And chuckles and crows, and nods and winks,
As if his head were as full of kinks
And curious riddles as any sphinx!
J. G. HOLLAND—*Bitter-Sweet. First Movement.* L. 6.

17
When the baby died,
On every side
Rose stranger's voices, hard and harsh and loud.

The baby was not wrapped in any shroud.
The mother made no sound. Her head was bowed
That men's eyes might not see
Her misery.
HELEN HUNT JACKSON—*When the Baby Died.*

1
Sweet is the infant's waking smile,
And sweet the old man's rest—
But middle age by no fond wile,
No soothing calm is blest.
KEBLE—*Christian Year. St. Philip and St. James.* St. 3.

2
Suck, baby! suck! mother's love grows by giving:
Drain the sweet founts that only thrive by wasting!
Black manhood comes when riotous guilty living
Hands thee the cup that shall be death in tasting.
CHARLES LAMB—*The Gypsy's Malison. Sonnet in Letter to Mrs. Procter,* Jan. 29, 1829.

3
The hair she means to have is gold,
Her eyes are blue, she's twelve weeks old,
Plump are her fists and pinky.
She fluttered down in lucky hour
From some blue deep in yon sky bower—
I call her "Little Dinky."
FRED. LOCKER-LAMPSON—*Little Dinky.*

4
A tight little bundle of wailing and flannel,
Perplex'd with the newly found fardel of life.
FRED. LOCKER-LAMPSON—*The Old Cradle.*

5
O child! O new-born denizen
Of life's great city! on thy head
The glory of the morn is shed,
Like a celestial benison!
Here at the portal thou dost stand,
And with thy little hand
Thou openest the mysterious gate
Into the future's undiscovered land.
LONGFELLOW—*To a Child.*

6
A baby was sleeping,
Its mother was weeping.
SAMUEL LOVER—*Angel's Whisper.*

7 Her beads while she numbered,
The baby still slumbered,
And smiled in her face, as she bended her knee;
Oh! bless'd be that warning,
My child, thy sleep adorning,
For I know that the angels are whispering with thee.
SAMUEL LOVER—*Angel's Whisper.*

8
He seemed a cherub who had lost his way
And wandered hither, so his stay
With us was short, and 'twas most meet,
That he should be no delver in earth's clod,
Nor need to pause and cleanse his feet
To stand before his God:
O blest word—Evermore!
LOWELL—*Threnodia.*

9
How did they all just come to be you?
God thought about me and so I grew.
GEO. MACDONALD—*Song in "At the Back of The North Wind."* Ch. XXXIII.

10
Where did you come from, baby dear?
Out of the Everywhere into here.
GEO. MACDONALD—*Song in "At The Back of The North Wind."* Ch. XXXIII.

11
Whenever a little child is born
All night a soft wind rocks the corn;
One more buttercup wakes to the morn,
Somewhere, Somewhere.
One more rosebud shy will unfold,
One more grass blade push through the mold,
One more bird-song the air will hold,
Somewhere, Somewhere.
AGNES CARTER MASON—*Somewhere.*

12
And thou hast stolen a jewel, Death!
Shall light thy dark up like a Star.
A Beacon kindling from afar
Our light of love and fainting faith.
GERALD MASSEY—*Babe Christabel.*

13
You scarce could think so small a thing
Could leave a loss so large;
Her little light such shadow fling
From dawn to sunset's marge.
In other springs our life may be
In bannered bloom unfurled,
But never, never match our wee
White Rose of all the world.
GERALD MASSEY—*Our Wee White Rose.*

14
A sweet, new blossom of Humanity,
Fresh fallen from God's own home to flower on earth.
GERALD MASSEY—*Wooed and Won.*

15
Wee Willie Winkie rins through the toun,
Up stairs and doon stairs in his nicht-goun,
Tirlin' at the window, cryin' at the lock,
"Are the weans in their bed? for it's now ten o'clock."
WILLIAM MILLER—*Willie Winkie.*

16
As living jewels dropped unstained from heaven.
POLLOCK—*Course of Time.* Bk. V. L. 158.

17
Out of the mouth of babes and sucklings hast thou ordained strength.
Psalms. VIII. 2.

18
A grievous burthen was thy birth to me;
Tetchy and wayward was thy infancy.
Richard III. Act IV. Sc. 4. L. 167.

19 God mark thee to his grace!
Thou wast the prettiest babe that e'er I nursed:
An I might live to see thee married once,
I have my wish.
Romeo and Juliet. Act I. Sc. 3. L. 59.

20
Fie, fie, how wayward is this foolish love
That, like a testy babe, will scratch the nurse
And presently all humbled kiss the rod!
Two Gentlemen of Verona. Act I. Sc. 2. L. 57.

21 A daughter and a goodly babe,
Lusty and like to live: the queen receives
Much comfort in 't.
Winter's Tale. Act II. Sc. 2. L. 27.

1
Sweetest li'l' feller, everybody knows;
Dunno what to call him, but he's mighty lak' a rose;
Lookin' at his mammy wid eyes so shiny blue
Mek' you think that Heav'n is comin' clost ter you.
FRANK L. STANTON—*Mighty Lak' a Rose.*

2
A little soul scarce fledged for earth
Takes wing with heaven again for goal,
Even while we hailed as fresh from birth
A little soul.
SWINBURNE—*A Baby's Death.*

3
But what am I?
An infant crying in the night:
An infant crying for the light:
And with no language but a cry.
TENNYSON—*In Memoriam.* Pt. LIV. St. 5.
(See also BURTON, under BIRTH; CROUCH, under DEATH; also KING LEAR, SAXE, under LIFE)

4
Beat upon mine, little heart! beat, beat!
Beat upon mine! you are mine, my sweet!
All mine from your pretty blue eyes to your feet,
My sweet!
TENNYSON—*Romney's Remorse.*

5
Baby smiled, mother wailed,
Earthward while the sweetling sailed;
Mother smiled, baby wailed,
When to earth came Viola.
FRANCIS THOMPSON—*The Making of Viola.* St. 9.

6
A babe in a house is a well-spring of pleasure.
TUPPER—*Of Education.*

7
Hush, my dear, lie still and slumber,
Holy angels guard thy bed!
Heavenly blessings without number
Gently falling on thy head.
WATTS—*A Cradle Hymn.*

BALLADS

8
I've now got the music book ready,
Do sit up and sing like a lady
A recitative from Tancredi,
And something about "Palpiti!"
Sing forte when first you begin it,
Piano the very next minute,
They'll cry "What expression there's in it!"
Don't sing English ballads to me!
THOMAS HAYNES BAYLY—*Don't Sing English Ballads to Me.*

9
The farmer's daughter hath soft brown hair
(*Butter and eggs and a pound of cheese*)
And I met with a ballad, I can't say where,
That wholly consisted of lines like these.
CHARLES S. CALVERLY—*Ballad.*

10
Thespis, the first professor of our art,
At country wakes sung ballads from a cart.
DRYDEN—*Prologue to Sophonisba.*

11
I knew a very wise man that believed that * * * if a man were permitted to make all the ballads, he need not care who should make the laws of a nation.
ANDREW FLETCHER—Quoting the EARL OF CROMARTY. *Letters to the Marquis of Montrose.* In FLETCHER'S *Works.* P. 266. (Ed. 1749)

12
Some people resemble ballads which are only sung for a certain time.
LA ROCHEFOUCAULD—*Maxims.* No. 220.

13
I have a passion for ballads. * * * They are the gypsy children of song, born under green hedgerows in the leafy lanes and by-paths of literature,—in the genial Summertime.
LONGFELLOW—*Hyperion.* Bk. II. Ch. II.

14
For a ballad's a thing you expect to find lies in.
SAMUEL LOVER—*Paddy Blake's Echo.*

15
More solid things do not show the complexion of the times so well as Ballads and Libels.
JOHN SELDON—*Libels.* (Libels-pamphlets, *libellum*, a small book.)

16
I had rather be a kitten, and cry mew!
Than one of these same metre ballad-mongers.
Henry IV. Pt. I. Act III. Sc. 1. L. 129.

17
I love a ballad but even too well; if it be doleful matter, merrily set down, or a very pleasant thing indeed, and sung lamentably.
Winter's Tale. Act IV. Sc. 4. L. 187.

18
A famous man is Robin Hood,
The English ballad-singer's joy.
WORDSWORTH—*Rob Roy's Grave.*

BANISHMENT

19
The world was all before them, where to choose
Their place of rest, and Providence their guide;
They, hand in hand, with wandering steps and slow,
Through Eden took their solitary way.
MILTON—*Paradise Lost.* Bk. XII. L. 646.

20
Had we no other quarrel else to Rome, but that
Thou art thence banish'd, we would muster all
From twelve to seventy; and pouring war
Into the bowels of ungrateful Rome,
Like a bold flood o'erbear.
Coriolanus. Act IV. Sc. 5. L. 133.

21
No, my good lord: banish Peto, banish Bardolph, banish Poins; but for sweet Jack Falstaff, kind Jack Falstaff, true Jack Falstaff, valiant Jack Falstaff, and therefore more valiant, being as he is old Jack Falstaff, banish not him thy Harry's company: banish plump Jack and banish all the world.
Henry IV. Pt. I. Act II. Sc. 4. L. 520.

22
Have stooped my neck under your injuries
And sighed my English breath in foreign clouds,
Eating the bitter bread of banishment.
Richard II. Act III. Sc. 1. L. 19.

23
Banished?
O friar, the damned use that word in hell;
Howlings attend it: How hast thou the heart,

Being a divine, a ghostly confessor,
A sin-absolver, and my friend profess'd,
To mangle me with that word—banished?
Romeo and Juliet. Act III. Sc. 3. L. 47.

BARBER (See also Hair)

1
With odorous oil thy head and hair are sleek;
And then thou kemb'st the tuzzes on thy cheek:
Of these, my barbers take a costly care.
Dryden—*Fourth Satire of Persius.* L. 89.

2
Of a thousand shavers, two do not shave so much alike as not to be distinguished.
Samuel Johnson—*Boswell's Life of Johnson.* (1777)

3
But he shaved with a shell when he chose,
'Twas the manner of primitive man.
Andrew Lang—*Double Ballad of Primitive Man.*

4
Thy boist'rous locks, no worthy match
For valour to assail, nor by the sword
* * * * * *
But by the barber's razor best subdued.
Milton—*Samson Agonistes.* L. 1,167.

5
The first (barbers) that entered Italy came out of Sicily and it was in the 454 yeare after the foundation of Rome. Brought in they were by P. Ticinius Mena as Verra doth report for before that time they never cut their hair. The first that was shaven every day was Scipio Africanus, and after him cometh Augustus the Emperor who evermore used the rasor.
Pliny—*Natural History.* Bk. VII. Ch. LIX. Holland's trans.

6
Our courteous Antony,
* * * * * *
Being barber'd ten times o'er, goes to the feast.
Antony and Cleopatra. Act II. Sc. 2. L. 227.

7
Whose beard they have sing'd off with brands of fire;
And ever, as it blaz'd, they threw on him
Great pails of puddled mire to quench the hair:
My master preaches patience to him and the while
His man with scissors nicks him like a fool.
Comedy of Errors. Act V. Sc. 1. L. 171.

8
And his chin new reap'd,
Show'd like a stubble-land at harvest-home.
Henry IV. Pt. I. Act I. Sc. 3. L. 34.

9
I must to the barber's; * * * for methinks
I am marvellous hairy about the face.
Midsummer Night's Dream. Act IV. Sc. 1. L. 23.

10
The barber's man hath been seen with him, and the old ornament of his cheek hath already stuffed tennis-balls.
Much Ado About Nothing. Act III. Sc. 2. L. 45.

11
A Fellow in a market town.
Most musical, cried Razors up and down.
John Wolcot—*Farewell Odes.* Ode 3.

BASIL

Pycnanthemum

12
The basil tuft, that waves
Its fragrant blossom over graves.
Moore—*Lalla Rookh. Light of the Harem.*

BAT

13
The sun was set; the night came on apace,
And falling dews bewet around the place;
The bat takes airy rounds on leathern wings,
And the hoarse owl his woeful dirges sings.
Gay—*Shepherd's Week. Wednesday; or, The Dumps.*

14
Far different there from all that charm'd before,
The various terrors of that horrid shore;
* * * * * *
Those matted woods where birds forget to sing.
But silent bats in drowsy clusters cling.
Goldsmith—*The Deserted Village.* L. 345.

15
Ere the bat hath flown
His cloister'd flight.
Macbeth. Act III. Sc. 2. L. 40.

16
On the bat's back I do fly
After summer merrily.
Tempest. Act V. Sc. 1. L. 91.

BEACH BIRD

17
Thou little bird, thou dweller by the sea,
Why takest thou its melancholy voice,
And with that boding cry
Along the waves dost thou fly?
Oh! rather, bird, with me
Through this fair land rejoice!
R. H. Dana—*The Little Beach Bird.*

BEAR

18
Make ye no truce with Adam-zad—the Bear that walks like a man.
Kipling—*The Truce of the Bear.*

BEAUTY

19
Beauty soon grows familiar to the lover,
Fades in his eye, and palls upon the sense.
Addison—*Cato.* Act I. Sc. 4.

20
What is lovely never dies,
But passes into other loveliness,
Star-dust, or sea-foam, flower or winged air.
T. B. Aldrich—*A Shadow of the Night.*

21
I must not say that she was true,
Yet let me say that she was fair;
And they, that lovely face who view,
They should not ask if truth be there.
Matthew Arnold—*Euphrosyne.*

22
The beautiful are never desolate;
But some one alway loves them—God or man.
If man abandons, God himself takes them.
Bailey—*Festus.* Sc. *Water and Wood Midnight.* L. 370.

1
There's nothing that allays an angry mind
So soon as a sweet beauty.
BEAUMONT AND FLETCHER—*The Elder Brother*. Act III. Sc. 5.

2
Ye Gods! but she is wondrous fair!
For me her constant flame appears;
The garland she hath culled, I wear
On brows bald since my thirty years.
Ye veils that deck my loved one rare,
Fall, for the crowning triumph's nigh.
Ye Gods! but she is wondrous fair!
And I, so plain a man am I!
BERANGER—*Qu'elle est jolie*. Translated by C. L. BETTS.

3
The beautiful seems right
By force of beauty, and the feeble wrong
Because of weakness.
E. B. BROWNING—*Aurora Leigh*. Bk. I.

4
The essence of all beauty, I call love,
The attribute, the evidence, and end,
The consummation to the inward sense
Of beauty apprehended from without,
I still call love.
E. B. BROWNING—*Sword Glare*.

5
And behold there was a very stately palace before him, the name of which was Beautiful.
BUNYAN—*Pilgrim's Progress*. Pt. I.

6
Who doth not feel, until his failing sight
Faints into dimness with its own delight,
His changing cheek, his sinking heart confess,
The might—the majesty of Loveliness?
BYRON—*Bride of Abydos*. Canto I. St. 6.

7
The light of love, the purity of grace,
The mind, the Music breathing from her face,
The heart whose softness harmonized the whole,
And, oh! the eye was in itself a Soul!
BYRON—*Bride of Abydos*. Canto I. St. 6.

8
Thou who hast
The fatal gift of beauty.
BYRON—*Childe Harold*. Canto IV. St. 42.

9
Her glossy hair was cluster'd o'er a brow
Bright with intelligence, and fair and smooth;
Her eyebrow's shape was like the aerial bow,
Her cheek all purple with the beam of youth,
Mounting, at times, to a transparent glow,
As if her veins ran lightning.
BYRON—*Don Juan*. Canto I. St. 61.

10
A lovely being, scarcely formed or moulded,
A rose with all its sweetest leaves yet folded.
BYRON—*Don Juan*. Canto XV. St. 43.

11
She walks in beauty like the night
Of cloudless climes and starry skies;
And all that's best of dark and bright
Meet in her aspect and her eyes:
Thus mellowed to that tender light
Which heaven to gaudy day denies.
BYRON—*She Walks in Beauty*.

12
No todas hermosuras enamoran, que algunas alegran la vista, y no rinden la voluntad.
All kinds of beauty do not inspire love; there is a kind which only pleases the sight, but does not captivate the affections.
CERVANTES—*Don Quixote*. II. 6.

13
Exceeding fair she was not; and yet fair
In that she never studied to be fairer
Than Nature made her; beauty cost her nothing,
Her virtues were so rare.
GEORGE CHAPMAN—*All Fools*. Act I. Sc. 1.

14
I pour into the world the eternal streams
Wan prophets tent beside, and dream their dreams.
JOHN VANCE CHENEY—*Beauty*.

15
She is not fair to outward view
As many maidens be;
Her loveliness I never knew
Until she smiled on me:
Oh! then I saw her eye was bright,
A well of love, a spring of light.
HARTLEY COLERIDGE—*Song*.

16
Her gentle limbs did she undress,
And lay down in her loveliness.
COLERIDGE—*Christabel*. Pt. I. St. 24.

17
Beauty is the lover's gift.
CONGREVE—*The Way of the World*. Act II. Sc. 2.

18
The ladies of St. James's!
They're painted to the eyes;
Their white it stays for ever,
Their red it never dies;
But Phyllida, my Phyllida!
Her colour comes and goes;
It trembles to a lily,—
It wavers to a rose.
AUSTIN DOBSON—*At the Sign of the Lyre*.

19
Old as I am, for ladies' love unfit,
The power of beauty I remember yet,
Which once inflam'd my soul, and still inspires my wit.
DRYDEN—*Cymon and Iphigenia*. L. 1.

20
When beauty fires the blood, how love exalts the mind!
DRYDEN—*Cymon and Iphigenia*. L. 41.

21
She, though in full-blown flower of glorious beauty,
Grows cold, even in the summer of her age.
DRYDEN—*Œdipus*. Act IV. Sc. 1.

22
Rhodora! if the sages ask thee why
This charm is wasted on the marsh and sky,
Tell them, dear, that if eyes were made for seeing,
Then beauty is its own excuse for being.
EMERSON—*The Rhodora*.

23
The beautiful rests on the foundations of the necessary.
EMERSON—*Essay. On the Poet*.

1
Who gave thee, O Beauty,
The keys of this breast,—
Too credulous lover
Of blest and unblest?
Say, when in lapsed ages
Thee knew I of old?
Or what was the service
For which I was sold?
EMERSON—*Ode to Beauty.* St. 1.

2
Each ornament about her seemly lies,
By curious chance, or careless art composed.
EDWARD FAIRFAX—*Godfrey of Bullogne.*

3
Any color, so long as it's red,
Is the color that suits me best,
Though I will allow there is much to be said
For yellow and green and the rest.
EUGENE FIELD—*Red.*

4
In beauty, faults conspicuous grow;
The smallest speck is seen on snow.
GAY—*Fable. The Peacock, Turkey and Goose.* L. 1.

5
Schön war ich auch, und das war mein Verderben.
I too was fair, and that was my undoing.
GOETHE—*Faust.* I. 25. 30.

6
Handsome is that handsome does.
GOLDSMITH—*The Vicar of Wakefield.* Ch. I.
FIELDING—*Tom Jones.* Bk. IV. Ch. XII.

7
'Tis impious pleasure to delight in harm.
And beauty should be kind, as well as charm.
GEO. GRANVILLE (Lord Lansdowne) — *To Myra.* L. 21.

8
The dimple that thy chin contains has beauty in its round,
That never has been fathomed yet by myriad thoughts profound.
HAFIZ—*Odes.* CXLIII.

9
There's beauty all around our paths, if but our watchful eyes
Can trace it 'midst familiar things, and through their lowly guise.
FELICIA D. HEMANS—*Our Daily Paths.*

10
Many a temptation comes to us in fine, gay colours that are but skin deep.
MATTHEW HENRY—*Commentaries. Genesis.* Ch. III.
(See also OVERBURY, RUSKIN, VENNING)

11
Beauty draws more than oxen.
HERBERT—*Jacula Prudentum.*

12
Beauty is the index of a larger fact than wisdom.
HOLMES—*Professor at the Breakfast Table.* II.

13
A heaven of charms divine Nausicaa lay.
HOMER—*Odyssey.* Bk. VI. L. 22. POPE'S trans.

14
O matre pulchra filia pulchrior.
O daughter, more beautiful than thy lovely mother.
HORACE—*Carmina.* I. 16. 1.

15
Nihil est ab omni
Parte beatum.
Nothing is beautiful from every point of view.
HORACE—*Carmina.* II. 16. 27.

16
Sith Nature thus gave her the praise,
To be the chiefest work she wrought,
In faith, methink, some better ways
On your behalf might well be sought,
Than to compare, as ye have done,
To match the candle with the sun.
HENRY HOWARD—*Sonnet to the Fair Geraldine.* "Hold their farthing candles to the sun." See YOUNG, under AUTHORSHIP.

17
Tell me, shepherds, have you seen
My Flora pass this way?
In shape and feature Beauty's queen,
In pastoral array.
The Wreath—From *The Lyre.* Vol. III. P. 27. (Ed. 1824) First lines also in a song by DR. SAMUEL HOWARD.

18
A queen, devoid of beauty is not queen;
She needs the royalty of beauty's mien.
VICTOR HUGO—*Eviradnus.* V.

19
Rara est adeo concordia formæ
Atque pudicitiæ.
Rare is the union of beauty and purity.
JUVENAL—*Satires.* X. 297.

20
A thing of beauty is a joy forever;
Its loveliness increases; it will never
Pass into nothingness; but still will keep
A bower quiet for us, and a sleep
Full of sweet dreams, and health, and quiet breathing.
KEATS—*Endymion.* Bk. I. L. 1.

21
Beauty is truth, truth beauty.
KEATS—*Ode on a Grecian Urn.*

22
L'air spirituel est dans les hommes ce que la régularité des traits est dans les femmes: c'est le genre de beauté où les plus vains puissent aspirer.
A look of intelligence in men is what regularity of features is in women: it is a style of beauty to which the most vain may aspire.
LA BRUYÈRE—*Les Caractères.* XII.

23
'Tis beauty calls, and glory shows the way.
NATHANIEL LEE—*Alexander the Great; or, The Rival Queens.* Act IV. Sc. 2. ("Leads the way" in stage ed.)

24
Beautiful in form and feature,
Lovely as the day,
Can there be so fair a creature
Formed of common clay?
LONGFELLOW—*Masque of Pandora. The Workshop of Hephæstus. Chorus of the Graces.*

1
Blue were her eyes as the fairy-flax,
  Her cheeks like the dawn of day,
And her bosom white as the hawthorn buds,
  That ope in the month of May.
  LONGFELLOW—*Wreck of the Hesperus.* St. 2.

2
Oh, could you view the melodie
Of ev'ry grace,
And musick of her face,
You'd drop a teare,
Seeing more harmonie
In her bright eye,
Then now you heare.
  LOVELACE—*Orpheus to Beasts.*

3
You are beautiful and faded
Like an old opera tune
Played upon a harpsichord.
  AMY LOWELL—*A Lady.*

4
Where none admire, 'tis useless to excel;
Where none are beaux, 'tis vain to be a belle.
  LORD LYTTLETON—*Soliloquy of a Beauty in the Country.* L. 11.

5
Beauty, like wit, to judges should be shown;
Both most are valued where they best are known.
  LORD LYTTLETON—*Soliloquy of a Beauty in the Country.* L. 13.

6
Beauty and sadness always go together.
Nature thought beauty too rich to go forth
Upon the earth without a meet alloy.
  GEORGE MACDONALD—*Within and Without.* Pt. IV. Sc. 3.

7
O, thou art fairer than the evening air
Clad in the beauty of a thousand stars.
  MARLOWE—*Faustus.*

8
'Tis evanescence that endures;
The loveliness that dies the soonest has the longest life.
The rainbow is a momentary thing,
The afterglows are ashes while we gaze.
  DON MARQUIS—*The Paradox.*

9
Too fair to worship, too divine to love.
  HENRY HART MILMAN—*Belvidere Apollo.*

10
Beauty is Nature's coin, must not be hoarded,
But must be current, and the good thereof
Consists in mutual and partaken bliss.
  MILTON—*Comus.* L. 739.

11
Beauty is nature's brag, and must be shown
In courts, at feasts, and high solemnities,
Where most may wonder at the workmanship.
  MILTON—*Comus.* L. 745.

12
Hung over her enamour'd, and beheld
Beauty, which, whether waking or asleep,
Shot forth peculiar graces.
  MILTON—*Paradise Lost.* Bk. V. L. 13.

13
She fair, divinely fair, fit love for gods.
  MILTON—*Paradise Lost.* Bk. IX. L. 489.
  (See also TENNYSON)

14
* * * for beauty stands
In the admiration only of weak minds
Led captive. Cease to admire, and all her plumes
Fall flat and shrink into a trivial toy,
At every sudden slighting quite abash'd.
  MILTON—*Paradise Regained.* Bk. II. L. 220.

15
And ladies of the Hesperides, that seemed
Fairer than feign'd of old.
  MILTON—*Paradise Regained.* Bk. II. L. 357.

16
Yet beauty, tho' injurious, hath strange power,
After offence returning, to regain
Love once possess'd.
  MILTON—*Samson Agonistes.* L. 1003.

17
The maid who modestly conceals
Her beauties, while she hides, reveals:
Gives but a glimpse, and fancy draws
Whate'er the Grecian Venus was.
  EDWARD MOORE—*Spider and the Bee.* Fable X.

18
Not more the rose, the queen of flowers,
Outblushes all the bloom of bower,
Than she unrivall'd grace discloses;
The sweetest rose, where all are roses.
  MOORE—*Odes of Anacreon.* Ode LXVI.

19
To weave a garland for the rose,
  And think thus crown'd 'twould lovelier be,
Were far less vain than to suppose
  That silks and gems add grace to thee.
  MOORE—*Songs from the Greek Anthology. To Weave a Garland.*

20
Die when you will, you need not wear
At heaven's Court a form more fair
  Than Beauty here on Earth has given:
Keep but the lovely looks we see
The voice we hear, and you will be
  An angel ready-made for heaven.
  MOORE. Versification of LORD HERBERT of Cherbury, *Life.* P. 36.
  (See also OLDHAM)

21
An' fair was her sweet bodie,
  Yet fairer was her mind:—
Menie's the queen among the flowers,
  The wale o' womankind.
  ROBERT NICOLL—*Menie.*

22
Altho' your frailer part must yield to Fate,
By every breach in that fair lodging made,
Its blest inhabitant is more displayed.
  OLDHAM—*To Madam L. E. on her Recovery.* 106.

23
And should you visit now the seats of bliss,
You need not wear another form but this.
  OLDHAM—*To Madam L. E. on her Recovery.* 115.
  (See also MOORE, WALLER)

24
Hast thou left thy blue course in heaven, golden-haired son of the sky! The west has opened its gates; the bed of thy repose is there. The waves come, to behold thy beauty. They lift their trembling heads. They see thee lovely

in thy sleep; they shrink away with fear. Rest, in thy shadowy cave, O sun! let thy return be in joy.
OSSIAN—*Carric-Thura*. St. 1.

1
And all the carnal beauty of my wife
Is but skin-deep.
SIR THOS. OVERBURY—*A Wife*. "Beauty is but skin deep" is found in *The Female Rebellion*, written about 1682.
(See also HENRY)

2
Aut formosa fores minus, aut minus improba, vellem.
Non facit ad mores tam bona forma malos.
I would that you were either less beautiful, or less corrupt. Such perfect beauty does not suit such imperfect morals.
OVID—*Amorum*. Bk. III. 11. 41.

3
Auxilium non leve vultus habet.
A pleasing countenance is no slight advantage.
OVID—*Epistolæ Ex Ponto*. II. 8. 54.

4
Raram facit misturam cum sapientia forma.
Beauty and wisdom are rarely conjoined.
PETRONIUS ARBITER—*Satyricon*. XCIV.

5
O quanta species cerebrum non habet!
O that such beauty should be so devoid of understanding!
PHÆDRUS—*Fables*. I. 7. 2.

6
Nimia est miseria nimis pulchrum esse hominem.
It is a great plague to be too handsome a man.
PLAUTUS—*Miles Gloriosus*. I. 1. 68.

7
When the candles are out all women are fair.
PLUTARCH—*Conjugal Precepts*.

8
'Tis not a lip, or eye, we beauty call,
But the joint force and full result of all.
POPE—*Essay. On Criticism*. Pt. II. L. 45.

9
Beauties in vain their pretty eyes may roll;
Charms strike the sight, but merit wins the soul.
POPE—*Rape of the Lock*. Canto V. L. 33.

10
No longer shall the bodice aptly lac'd
From thy full bosom to thy slender waist,
That air and harmony of shape express,
Fine by degrees, and beautifully less.
PRIOR—*Henry and Emma*. L. 429.

11
For, when with beauty we can virtue join,
We paint the semblance of a form divine.
PRIOR—*To the Countess of Oxford*.

12
Nimis in veritate, et similitudinis quam pulchritudinis amantior.
Too exact, and studious of similitude rather than of beauty.
QUINTILIAN—*De Institutione Oratoria*. XII. 10. 9.

13
Fair are the flowers and the children, but their subtle suggestion is fairer;
Rare is the roseburst of dawn, but the secret that clasps it is rarer;
Sweet the exultance of song, but the strain that precedes it is sweeter
And never was poem yet writ, but the meaning outmastered the meter.
RICHARD REALF—*Indirection*.

14
Is she not more than painting can express,
Or youthful poets fancy, when they love?
NICHOLAS ROWE—*The Fair Penitent*. Act III. Sc. 1.

15
Remember that the most beautiful things in the world are the most useless; peacocks and lilies, for instance.
RUSKIN.

16
The saying that beauty is but skin deep is but a skin deep saying.
RUSKIN—*Personal Beauty*.
(See also HENRY)

17
The beauty that addresses itself to the eyes is only the spell of the moment; the eye of the body is not always that of the soul.
GEORGE SAND—*Handsome Lawrence*. Ch. I.

18
All things of beauty are not theirs alone
Who hold the fee; but unto him no less
Who can enjoy, than unto them who own,
Are sweetest uses given to possess
J. G. SAXE—*The Beautiful*.

19
Damals war nichts heilig, als das Schöne.
In days of yore [in ancient Greece] nothing was sacred but the beautiful.
SCHILLER—*Die Götter Griechenlands*. St. 6.

20
Die Wahrheit ist vorhanden für den Weisen.
Die Schönheit für ein fühlend Herz.
Truth exists for the wise, beauty for the feeling heart.
SCHILLER—*Don Carlos*. IV. 21. 186.

21
Das ist das Loos des Schönen auf der Erde!
That is the lot of the beautiful on earth.
SCHILLER—*Wallenstein's Tod*. IV. 12. 26.

22
And ne'er did Grecian chisel trace
A Nymph, a Naiad, or a Grace,
Of finer form, or lovelier face!
SCOTT—*Lady of the Lake*. Canto I. St. 18.

23
There was a soft and pensive grace,
A cast of thought upon her face,
That suited well the forehead high,
The eyelash dark, and downcast eye.
SCOTT—*Rokeby*. Canto IV. St. 5.

24
Spirit of Beauty, whose sweet impulses,
Flung like the rose of dawn across the sea,
Alone can flush the exalted consciousness
With shafts of sensible divinity—
Light of the world, essential loveliness.
ALAN SEEGER—*Ode to Natural Beauty*. St. 2.

1
Why thus longing, thus forever sighing
For the far-off, unattain'd, and dim,
While the beautiful all round thee lying
Offers up its low, perpetual hymn?
HARRIET W. SEWALL—*Why Thus Longing.*

2
Beauty comes, we scarce know how, as an emanation from sources deeper than itself.
SHAIRP—*Studies in Poetry and Philosophy. Moral Motive Power.*

3
For her own person,
It beggar'd all description.
Antony and Cleopatra. Act II. Sc. 2. L. 202.

4
Beauty provoketh thieves sooner than gold.
As You Like It. Act I. Sc. 3. L. 112.

5
Heaven bless thee!
Thou hast the sweetest face I ever looked on;
Sir, as I have a soul, she is an angel.
Henry VIII. Act IV. Sc. 1. L. 43.

6
Of Nature's gifts thou may'st with lilies boast
And with the half-blown rose.
King John. Act III. Sc. 1. L. 53.

7
Beauty is bought by judgment of the eye,
Not utter'd by base sale of chapmen's tongues.
Love's Labour's Lost. Act II. Sc. 1. L. 15.

8
Beauty doth varnish age.
Love's Labour's Lost. Act IV. Sc. 3. L. 244.

9
Beauty is a witch,
Against whose charms faith melteth into blood.
Much Ado About Nothing. Act II. Sc. 1. L. 186.

10
I'll not shed her blood;
Nor scar that whiter skin of hers than snow,
And smooth as monumental alabaster.
Othello. Act V. Sc. 2. L. 3.

11
Beauty is but a vain and doubtful good;
A shining gloss that fadeth suddenly;
A flower that dies when first it 'gins to bud;
A brittle glass that's broken presently;
A doubtful good, a gloss, a glass, a flower,
Lost, faded, broken, dead within an hour.
The Passionate Pilgrim. St. 13.

12
O, she doth teach the torches to burn bright!
It seems she hangs upon the cheek of night,
Like a rich jewel in an Ethiope's ear:
Beauty too rich for use, for earth too dear!
Romeo and Juliet. Act I. Sc. 5. L. 46.
(Later editions read: "Her beauty hangs upon the cheek of night.)

13
Her beauty makes
This vault a feasting presence full of light.
Romeo and Juliet. Act V. Sc. 3. L. 85.

14
O, how much more doth beauty beauteous seem
By that sweet ornament which truth doth give!
Sonnet LIV.

15
Say that she frown; I'll say she looks as clear
As morning roses newly wash'd with dew.
Taming of the Shrew. Act II. Sc. 1. L. 173.

16
'Tis beauty truly blent, whose red and white
Nature's own sweet and cunning hand laid on.
Twelfth Night. Act I. Sc. 5. L. 257.

17
There's nothing ill can dwell in such a temple:
If the ill spirit have so fair a house,
Good things will strive to dwell with't.
Tempest. Act I. Sc. 2. L. 458.

18
A lovely lady, garmented in light
From her own beauty.
SHELLEY—*The Witch of Atlas.* St. 5.

19
She died in beauty—like a rose blown from its parent stem.
CHARLES DOYNE SILLERY—*She Died in Beauty.*

20
O beloved Pan, and all ye other gods of this place, grant me to become beautiful in the inner man.
SOCRATES. In PLATO'S *Phædrus.* End.

21
For all that faire is, is by nature good;
That is a signe to know the gentle blood.
SPENSER—*An Hymne in Honour of Beauty.* L. 139.

22
Her face so faire, as flesh it seemed not,
But heavenly pourtraict of bright angels' hew,
Cleare as the skye withouten blame or blot,
Through goodly mixture of complexion's dew.
SPENSER—*Faerie Queene.* Canto III. St. 22.

23
They seemed to whisper: "How handsome she is!
What wavy tresses! what sweet perfume!
Under her mantle she hides her wings;
Her flower of a bonnet is just in bloom."
E. C. STEDMAN—*Translation. Jean Prouvaire's Song at the Barricade.*

24
She wears a rose in her hair,
At the twilight's dreamy close:
Her face is fair,—how fair
Under the rose!
R. H. STODDARD—*Under the Rose.*

25
Fortuna facies muta commendatio est.
A pleasing countenance is a silent commendation.
SYRUS—*Maxims.*

26
A daughter of the gods, divinely tall,
And most divinely fair.
TENNYSON—*Dream of Fair Women.* St. 22.
(See also MILTON)

27
How should I gauge what beauty is her dole,
Who cannot see her countenance for her soul,
As birds see not the casement for the sky?
And as 'tis check they prove its presence by,
I know not of her body till I find
My flight debarred the heaven of her mind.
FRANCIS THOMPSON—*Her Portrait.* St. 9

1
Whose body other ladies well might bear
As soul,—yea, which it profanation were
For all but you to take as fleshy woof,
Being spirit truest proof.
FRANCIS THOMPSON—"*Manus Animam Pinxit.*" St. 3.

2
Whose form is as a grove
Hushed with the cooing of an unseen dove.
FRANCIS THOMPSON—"*Manus Animam Pinxit.*" St. 3.

3
Thoughtless of beauty, she was Beauty's self.
THOMSON—*Seasons. Autumn.* L. 209.

4
All the beauty of the world, 'tis but skin deep.
RALPH VENNING—*Orthodoxe Paradoxes.* (Third Edition, 1650) *The Triumph of Assurance.* P. 41. (See also HENRY)

5
Gratior ac pulchro veniens in corpore virtus.
Even virtue is fairer when it appears in a beautiful person.
VERGIL—*Æneid.* V. 344.

6
Nimium ne crede colori.
Trust not too much to beauty.
VERGIL—*Eclogæ.* II. 17.

7
And as pale sickness does invade
Your frailer part, the breaches made
In that fair lodging still more clear
Make the bright guest, your soul, appear.
WALLER—*A la Malade.*
(See also OLDHAM)

8
The yielding marble of her snowy breast.
WALLER—*On a Lady Passing through a Crowd of People.*

9
Beauty is its own excuse.
WHITTIER—Dedication to *Songs of Labor.* (Copied from EMERSON.)

10
Elysian beauty, melancholy grace,
Brought from a pensive, though a happy place.
WORDSWORTH—*Laodamia.*

11
Her eyes as stars of Twilight fair,
Like Twilight's, too, her dusky hair,
But all things else about her drawn
From May-time and the cheerful Dawn.
WORDSWORTH—*She was a Phantom of Delight.*

12
Alas! how little can a moment show
Of an eye where feeling plays
In ten thousand dewy rays;
A face o'er which a thousand shadows go!
WORDSWORTH—*Triad.*

13
And beauty born of murmuring sound.
WORDSWORTH—*Three Years She Grew in Sun and Shower.*

14
True beauty dwells in deep retreats,
Whose veil is unremoved
Till heart with heart in concord beats,
And the lover is beloved.
WORDSWORTH—*To——. Let Other Bards of Angels Sing.*

15
What's female beauty, but an air divine,
Through which the mind's all-gentle graces shine!
They, like the Sun, irradiate all between;
The body *charms,* because the soul is *seen.*
YOUNG—*Love of Fame.* Satire VI. L. 151.

BED

16
Matthew, Mark, Luke and John,
The bed be blest that I lye on.
THOMAS ADY—*A Cradle in the Dark.* P. 58. (London, 1656)

17
Théâtre des ris et des pleurs
Lit! où je nais, et où je meurs,
Tu nous fais voir comment voisins
Sont nos plaisirs et chagrins.
In bed we laugh, in bed we cry;
And born in bed, in bed we die;
The near approach a bed may show
Of human bliss to human woe.
ISAAC DE BENSERADE. DR. JOHNSON'S trans.

18
To rise with the lark, and go to bed with the lamb.
NICHOLAS BRETON—*Court and County.* (1618 reprint.) P. 183.

19
Like feather-bed betwixt a wall
And heavy brunt of cannon ball.
BUTLER—*Hudibras.* Pt. I. Canto II. L. 871.

20
O bed! O bed! delicious bed!
That heaven upon earth to the weary head.
HOOD—*Miss Kilmansegg. Her Dream.*

21
Rise with the lark and with the lark to bed.
JAMES HURDIS—*The Village Curate.*

22
The bed has become a place of luxury to me! I would not exchange it for all the thrones in the world.
NAPOLEON I.

BEE

23
The honey-bee that wanders all day long
The field, the woodland, and the garden o'er,
To gather in his fragrant winter store,
Humming in calm content his winter song,
Seeks not alone the rose's glowing breast,
The lily's dainty cup, the violet's lips,
But from all rank and noxious weeds he sips
The single drop of sweetness closely pressed
Within the poison chalice.
ANNE C. LYNCH BOTTA—*The Lesson of the Bee.*

24
The pedigree of honey
Does not concern the bee;
A clover, any time, to him
Is aristocracy.
EMILY DICKINSON—*Poems.* V. (Ed. 1891)

25
His labor is a chant,
His idleness a tune;
Oh, for a bee's experience
Of clovers and of noon!
EMILY DICKINSON—*Poems.* XV. *The Bee.*

1
Burly, dozing humblebee,
Where thou art is clime for me.
Let them sail for Porto Rique,
Far-off heats through seas to seek.
I will follow thee alone,
Thou animated torrid-zone!
EMERSON—*The Humble-Bee.*

2
Seeing only what is fair,
Sipping only what is sweet,
* * * * *
Leave the chaff, and take the wheat.
EMERSON—*The Humble-Bee.*

3
The careful insect 'midst his works I view,
Now from the flowers exhaust the fragrant dew,
With golden treasures load his little thighs,
And steer his distant journey through the skies.
GAY—*Rural Sports.* Canto I. L. 82.

4
Bees work for man, and yet they never bruise
Their Master's flower, but leave it having done,
As fair as ever and as fit to use;
So both the flower doth stay and honey run.
HERBERT—*The Church. Providence.*

5
For pitty, Sir, find out that Bee
Which bore my Love away
I'le seek him in your Bonnet brave,
I'le seek him in your eyes.
HERRICK—*Mad Nan's Song.*

6
"O bees, sweet bees!" I said; "that nearest field
Is shining white with fragrant immortelles.
Fly swiftly there and drain those honey wells."
HELEN HUNT JACKSON—*My Bees.*

7 Listen! O, listen!
Here ever hum the golden bees
Underneath full-blossomed trees,
At once with glowing fruit and flowers crowned.
LOWELL—*The Sirens.* L. 94.

8
As busie as a Bee.
LYLY—*Euphues and his England.* P. 252.

9
The bee is enclosed, and shines preserved, in a tear of the sisters of Phaëton, so that it seems enshrined in its own nectar. It has obtained a worthy reward for its great toils; we may suppose that the bee itself would have desired such a death.
MARTIAL—*Epigrams.* Bk. IV. Ep. 32. (For same idea see ANT, FLY, SPIDER; also POPE, under WONDERS.)

10
In the nice bee, what sense so subtly true
From pois'nous herbs extracts the healing dew?
POPE—*Essay on Man.* Ep. I. 219.

11 For so work the honey-bees,
Creatures that by a rule in nature teach
The act of order to a peopled kingdom.
They have a king and officers of sorts,
Where some, like magistrates, correct at home,
Others, like merchants, venture trade abroad,
Others like soldiers, armed in their stings,
Make boot upon the summer's velvet buds,
Which pillage they with merry march bring home.
Henry V. Act I. Sc. 2. L. 188.

12 The solitary Bee
Whose buzzing was the only sound of life,
Flew there on restless wing,
Seeking in vain one blossom where to fix.
SOUTHEY—*Thalaba.* Bk. VI. St. 13.

13
The little bee returns with evening's gloom,
To join her comrades in the braided hive,
Where, housed beside their mighty honey-comb,
They dream their polity shall long survive.
CHARLES TENNYSON TURNER—*A Summer Night in the Bee Hive.*

14
How doth the little busy bee
Improve each shining hour,
And gather honey all the day
From every opening flower.
WATTS—*Against Idleness.*

15
The wild Bee reels from bough to bough
With his furry coat and his gauzy wing,
Now in a lily cup, and now
Setting a jacinth bell a-swing,
In his wandering.
OSCAR WILDE—*Her Voice.*

BEETLE

16
O'er folded blooms
On swirls of musk,
The beetle booms adown the glooms
And bumps along the dusk.
JAMES WHITCOMB RILEY—*The Beetle.*

17
And often, to our comfort, shall we find
The sharded beetle in a safer hold
Than is the full-winged eagle.
Cymbeline. Act III. Sc. 3. L. 19.

18
And the poor beetle that we tread upon,
In corporal sufferance finds a pang as great
As when a giant dies.
Measure for Measure. Act III. Sc. 1. L. 79.

BEGGARY

19
I'd just as soon be a beggar as king,
And the reason I'll tell you for why;
A king cannot swagger, nor drink like a beggar,
Nor be half so happy as I.
* * * * *
Let the back and side go bare.
Old English Folk Song. In CECIL SHARPE'S *Folk Songs from Somerset.*

20
Beggars must be no choosers.
BEAUMONT AND FLETCHER—*Scornful Lady.* Act V. Sc. 3.

21
Homer himself must beg if he want means, and as by report sometimes he did "go from door to door and sing ballads, with a company of boys about him."
BURTON—*Anatomy of Melancholy.* Pt. I. Sec. II. Mem. 4. Subsect. 6.

1
Set a beggar on horseback, and he will ride a gallop.
BURTON—*Anatomy of Melancholy*. Pt. II. Sec. III. Memb. 2.

2
Set a beggar on horse backe, they saie, and hee will neuer alight.
ROBERT GREENE—*Card of Fancie*. HEYWOOD —*Dialogue*. CLAUDIANUS—*Eutropium*. I. 181. SHAKESPEARE—*True Tragedy of Richard, Duke of York*. Sc. 3. *Henry VI*. IV. 1. BEN JONSON—*Staple of News*. Act IV. See also collection of same in BEBEL—*Proverbia Germanica, Suringar's ed.* (1879) No. 537. (See also BURTON)

3
To get thine ends, lay bashfulnesse aside;
Who feares to aske, doth teach to be deny'd.
HERRICK—*No Bashfulnesse in Begging*. (See also SENECA)

4
Mieux vaut goujat debout qu'empereur enterré.
Better a living beggar than a buried emperor.
LA FONTAINE—*La Matrone d'Ephèse*.

5
Borgen ist nicht viel besser als betteln.
Borrowing is not much better than begging.
LESSING—*Nathan der Weise*. II. 9.

6
Der wahre Bettler ist
Doch einzig und allein der wahre König.
The real beggar is indeed the true and only king.
LESSING—*Nathan der Weise*. II. 9.

7
A beggar through the world am I,
From place to place I wander by.
Fill up my pilgrim's scrip for me,
For Christ's sweet sake and charity.
LOWELL—*The Beggar*.

8
A pampered menial drove me from the door.
THOMAS MOSS—*The Beggar*. (Altered by GOLDSMITH from "*A Liveried Servant*," *etc.*)

9
Qui timide rogat,
Docet negare.
He who begs timidly courts a refusal.
SENECA—*Hippolytus*. II. 593. (See also HERRICK)

10
Beggar that I am, I am even poor in thanks.
Hamlet. Act II. Sc. 2. L. 281.

11
Unless the old adage must be verified,
That beggars mounted, run their horse to death.
Henry VI. Pt. III. Act I. Sc. 4. L. 126. (See also GREENE)

12
Well, whiles I am a beggar I will rail
And say, there is no sin but to be rich;
And being rich, my virtue then shall be
To say, there is no vice but beggary.
King John. Act II. Sc. 1. L. 593.

13
I see, Sir, you are liberal in offers:
You taught me first to beg; and now, methinks,
You teach me how a beggar should be answer'd.
Merchant of Venice. Act IV. Sc. 1. L. 437.

BEGINNINGS

14
Incipe; dimidium facti est cœpisse. Supersit Dimidium: rursum hoc incipe, et efficies.
Begin; to begin is half the work. Let half still remain; again begin this, and thou wilt have finished.
AUSONIUS—*Epigrams*. LXXXI. 1.

15
Incipe quidquid agas: pro toto est prima operis pars.
Begin whatever you have to do: the beginning of a work stands for the whole.
AUSONIUS—*Idyllia*. XII. *Inconnexa*. 5.

16
Il n'y a que le premier obstacle qui coûte à vaincre la pudeur.
It is only the first obstacle which counts to conquer modesty.
BOSSUET—*Pensées Chrétiennes et Morales*. IX. (See also DU DEFFAND)

17
Omnium rerum principia parva sunt.
The beginnings of all things are small.
CICERO—*De Finibus Bonorum et Malorum*. V. 21.

18
In omnibus negotiis prius quam aggrediare, adhibenda est præparatio diligens.
In all matters, before beginning, a diligent preparation should be made.
CICERO—*De Officiis*. I. 21.

19
La distance n'y fait rien; il n'y a que le premier pas qui coûte.
The distance is nothing; it is only the first step that costs.
MME. DU DEFFAND—*Letter to d'Alembert*, July 7, 1763. See also GIBBON—*Decline and Fall of the Roman Empire*. Ch. XXXIX. N. 100. Phrase "C'est le premier pas qui coûte" attributed to CARDINAL POLIGNAC. (See also BOSSUET, VOLTAIRE)

20
Et redit in nihilum quod fuit ante nihil.
It began of nothing and in nothing it ends.
CORNELIUS GALLUS. Translated by BURTON in *Anat. Melan.* (1621)

21
Dimidium facti qui cœpit habet.
What's well begun, is half done.
HORACE—*Epistles*. I. 2. 40. (Traced to Hesiod.)

22
Cœpisti melius quam desinis. Ultima primis cedunt.
Thou beginnest better than thou endest. The last is inferior to the first.
OVID—*Heroides*. IX. 23.

23
Principiis obsta: sero medicina paratur,
Cum mala per longas convaluere moras.
Resist beginnings: it is too late to employ medicine when the evil has grown strong by inveterate habit.
OVID—*Remedia Amoris*. XCI.

24
Deficit omne quod nascitur.
Everything that has a beginning comes to an end.
QUINTILIAN—*De Institutione Oratoria*. V. 10.

1
Quidquid cœpit, et desinit.
Whatever begins, also ends.
SENECA—*De Consolatione ad Polybium.* I.

2
Things bad begun make strong themselves by ill.
Macbeth. Act III. Sc. 2. L. 56.

3
The true beginning of our end.
Midsummer Night's Dream. Act V. Sc. 1. L. 111.

4
C'est le commencement de la fin.
It is the beginning of the end.
Ascribed to TALLEYRAND *in the Hundred Days.* Also to GEN. AUGEREAU. (1814)

5
Le premier pas, mon fils, que l'on fait dans le monde,
Est celui dont dépend le reste de nos jours.
The first step, my son, which one makes in the world, is the one on which depends the rest of our days.
VOLTAIRE—*L'Indiscret.* I. 1.
(See also DU DEFFAND)

BELGIUM

6
Après des siècles d'esclavage,
Le Belge sortant du tombeau,
A reconquis par son courage,
Son nom, ses droits et son drapeau,
Et ta main souveraine et fière,
Peuple désormais indompté,
Grava sur ta vieille bannière
Le Roi, la loi, la liberté.
The years of slavery are past,
The Belgian rejoices once more;
Courage restores to him at last
The rights he held of yore.
Strong and firm his grasp will be—
Keeping the ancient flag unfurled
To fling its message on the watchful world:
For king, for right, for liberty.
LOUIS DECHEZ—*La Brabançonne.* Belgian National Anthem. Written during the Revolution of 1830. Music by François van Campenhout. Trans. by FLORENCE ATTENBOROUGH.

BELIEF

7
Ideo credendum quod incredibile.
It is believable because unbelievable.
BURTON—*Anatomy of Melancholy.* Quoting TERTULLIAN. (See Page 390[16].)

8
For fools are stubborn in their way,
As coins are harden'd by th' allay;
And obstinacy's ne'er so stiff
As when 'tis in a wrong belief.
BUTLER—*Hudibras.* Pt. III. Canto II. L. 481.

9
Fere libenter homines id, quod volunt, credunt.
Men willingly believe what they wish.
CÆSAR—*Bellum Gallicum.* III. 18.
(See also YOUNG)

10
No iron chain, or outward force of any kind, could ever compel the soul of man to believe or to disbelieve: it is his own indefeasible light, that judgment of his; he will reign and believe there by the grace of God alone!
CARLYLE—*Heroes and Hero Worship.* Lecture IV.

11
There is no unbelief;
Whoever plants a seed beneath the sod
And waits to see it push away the clod,
He trusts in God.
ELIZ. YORK CASE—*Unbelief.*

12
Belief consists in accepting the affirmations of the soul; unbelief, in denying them.
EMERSON—*Montaigne.*

13
Credat Judæus Apella non ego.
The Jew Apella may believe this, not I.
HORACE—*Satires.* I. 5. 100.

14
Better trust all and be deceived,
And weep that trust, and that deceiving,
Than doubt one heart that, if believed,
Had blessed one's life with true believing.
FANNY KEMBLE.

15
O thou, whose days are yet all spring,
Faith, blighted once, is past retrieving;
Experience is a dumb, dead thing;
The victory's in believing.
LOWELL—*To———.*

16
They believed—faith, I'm puzzled—I think I may call
Their belief a believing in nothing at all,
Or something of that sort; I know they all went
For a general union of total dissent.
LOWELL—*Fable for Critics.* L. 851.

17
A man may be a heretic in the truth; and if he believe things only because his pastor says so, or the assembly so determines, without knowing other reason, though his belief be true, yet the very truth he holds becomes his heresy.
MILTON—*Areopagitica.*

18
Nothing is so firmly believed as what we least know.
MONTAIGNE—*Essays. Of Divine Ordinances.* Bk. I. Ch. XXXI.

19
Tarde quæ credita lædunt credimus.
We are slow to believe what if believed would hurt our feelings.
OVID—*Heroides.* II. 9.

20
Incrédules les plus crédules. Ils croient les miracles de Vespasien, pour ne pas croire ceux de Moïse.
The incredulous are the most credulous. They believe the miracles of Vespasian that they may not believe those of Moses.
PASCAL—*Pensées.* II. XVII. 120.

21
And when religious sects ran mad,
He held, in spite of all his learning,
That if a man's belief is bad,
It will not be improved by burning.
PRAED—*Poems of Life and Manners.* Pt. II. *The Vicar.* St. 9.

1
Do not believe what I tell you here any more than if it were some tale of a tub.
RABELAIS—*Works*. Bk. IV. Ch. XXXVIII. ("*Tale of a Tub*," title of a work of SWIFT'S.)

2
Stands not within the prospect of belief.
Macbeth. Act I. Sc. 3. L. 74.

3
A thing that nobody believes cannot be proved too often.
BERNARD SHAW—*Devil's Disciple*. Act III.

4
There littleness was not; the least of things
Seemed infinite; and there his spirit shaped
Her prospects, nor did he believe,—He *saw*.
WORDSWORTH—*Excursion*. Bk. I. St. 12.

5
I have believed the best of every man,
And find that to believe it is enough
To make a bad man show him at his best,
Or even a good man swing his lantern higher.
YEATS—*Deirdre*.

6
What ardently we wish, we soon believe.
YOUNG—*Night Thoughts*. Night VII. Pt. II. L. 1311.

(See also CÆSAR)

BELLS

7
Hark! the bonny Christ-Church bells,
One, two, three, four, five, six;
They sound so woundy great,
So wound'rous sweet,
And they troul so merrily.
DEAN ALDRICH—*Hark the Merry Christ-Church Bells*.

8
That all-softening, overpowering knell,
The tocsin of the soul—the dinner bell.
BYRON—*Don Juan*. Canto V. St. 49.

9
How soft the music of those village bells,
Falling at intervals upon the ear
In cadence sweet; now dying all away,
Now pealing loud again, and louder still,
Clear and sonorous, as the gale comes on!
With easy force it opens all the cells
Where Memory slept.
COWPER—*Task*. Bk. VI. L. 6.

10
The church-going bell.
COWPER—*Verses supposed to be written by Alexander Selkirk*.

11
The vesper bell from far
That seems to mourn for the expiring day.
DANTE—*Purgatorio*. Canto 8. L. 6. CARY'S trans.

12
Your voices break and falter in the darkness,—
Break, falter, and are still.
BRET HARTE—*The Angelus*.

13
Bells call others, but themselves enter not into the Church.
HERBERT—*Jacula Prudentum*.

14
Dear bells! how sweet the sound of village bells
When on the undulating air they swim!
HOOD—*Ode to Rae Wilson*.

15
While the steeples are loud in their joy,
To the tune of the bells' ring-a-ding,
Let us chime in a peal, one and all,
For we all should be able to sing Hullah baloo.
HOOD—*Song for the Million*.

16
The old mayor climbed the belfry tower,
The ringers ran by two, by three;
"Pull, if ye never pulled before;
Good ringers, pull your best," quoth he.
"Play uppe, play uppe, O Boston bells!
Ply all your changes, all your swells,
Play uppe The Brides of Enderby."
JEAN INGELOW—*High Tide on the Coast of Lincolnshire*.

17
I call the Living—I mourn the Dead—
I break the Lightning.
Inscribed on the Great Bell of the Minster of Schaffhausen—also on that of the Church of Art, near Lucerne.

18
The cheerful Sabbath bells, wherever heard,
Strike pleasant on the sense, most like the voice
Of one, who from the far-off hills proclaims
Tidings of good to Zion.
LAMB—*The Sabbath Bells*.

19
For bells are the voice of the church;
They have tones that touch and search
The hearts of young and old.
LONGFELLOW—*Bells of San Blas*.

20
Seize the loud, vociferous bells, and
Clashing, clanging to the pavement
Hurl them from their windy tower!
LONGFELLOW—*Christus. The Golden Legend. Prologue*.

21
These bells have been anointed,
And baptized with holy water!
LONGFELLOW—*Christus. The Golden Legend. Prologue*.

22
He heard the convent bell,
Suddenly in the silence ringing
For the service of noonday.
LONGFELLOW—*Christus. The Golden Legend*. Pt. II.

23
The bells themselves are the best of preachers,
Their brazen lips are learned teachers,
From their pulpits of stone, in the upper air,
Sounding aloft, without crack or flaw,
Shriller than trumpets under the Law,
Now a sermon and now a prayer.
LONGFELLOW—*Christus. The Golden Legend*. Pt. III.

24
Bell, thou soundest merrily,
When the bridal party
To the church doth hie!
Bell, thou soundest solemnly,
When, on Sabbath morning,
Fields deserted lie!
LONGFELLOW (*quoted*)—*Hyperion*. Bk. III. Ch. III.

25
It cometh into court and pleads the cause
Of creatures dumb and unknown to the laws;

And this shall make, in every Christian clime,
The bell of Atri famous for all time.
LONGFELLOW—*Tales of a Wayside Inn. The Sicilian's Tale. The Bell of Atri.*

1
Those evening bells! those evening bells!
How many a tale their music tells!
MOORE—*Those Evening Bells.*

2
Nunquam ædepol temere tinniit tintinnabulum;
Nisi quis illud tractat aut movet, mutum est, tacet.
The Bell never rings of itself; unless some one handles or moves it it is dumb.
PLAUTUS—*Trinummus.* IV. 2. 162.

3
Hear the sledges with the bells,
Silver bells!
What a world of merriment their melody foretells!
How they tinkle, tinkle, tinkle,
In the icy air of night,
While the stars that oversprinkle
All the Heavens seem to twinkle
With a crystalline delight:
Keeping time, time, time,
In a sort of Runic rhyme
To the tintinnabulation that so musically wells
From the bells, bells, bells, bells,
Bells, bells, bells—
From the jingling and the tingling of the bells.
POE—*The Bells.* St. 1.

4
Hear the mellow wedding bells,
Golden bells!
What a world of happiness their harmony foretells
Through the balmy air of night
How they ring out their delight!
From the molten golden notes,
And all in tune
What a liquid ditty floats
To the turtle-dove that listens while she gloats
On the moon!
POE—*The Bells.* St. 2.

5
With deep affection
And recollection
I often think of
Those Shandon bells,
Whose sounds so wild would,
In the days of childhood,
Fling round my cradle
Their magic spells.
FATHER PROUT (Francis Mahony). *The Bells of Shandon.*

6
And the Sabbath bell,
That over wood and wild and mountain dell
Wanders so far, chasing all thoughts unholy
With sounds most musical, most melancholy.
SAMUEL ROGERS—*Human Life.* L. 517.

7
And this be the vocation fit,
For which the founder fashioned it:
High, high above earth's life, earth's labor
E'en to the heaven's blue vault to soar.
To hover as the thunder's neighbor,
The very firmament explore.
To be a voice as from above
Like yonder stars so bright and clear,
That praise their Maker as they move,
And usher in the circling year.
Tun'd be its metal mouth alone
To things eternal and sublime.
And as the swift wing'd hours speed on
May it record the flight of time!
SCHILLER—*Song of the Bell.* E. A. BOWRING'S trans.

8
Around, around,
Companions all, take your ground,
And name the bell with joy profound!
CONCORDIA is the word we've found
Most meet to express the harmonious sound,
That calls to those in friendship bound.
SCHILLER—*Song of the Bell.*

9
Like sweet bells jangled, out of tune and harsh.
Hamlet. Act III. Sc. 1. L. 166.

10
Then get thee gone and dig my grave thyself,
And bid the merry bells ring to thine ear
That thou art crowned, not that I am dead.
Henry IV. Pt. II. Act IV. Sc. 5. L. 111.

11
Hark, how chimes the passing bell!
There's no music to a knell;
All the other sounds we hear,
Flatter, and but cheat our ear.
This doth put us still in mind
That our flesh must be resigned,
And, a general silence made,
The world be muffled in a shade.
[Orpheus' lute, as poets tell,
Was but moral of this bell,
And the captive soul was she,
Which they called Eurydice,
Rescued by our holy groan,
A loud echo to this tone.]
SHIRLEY—*The Passing Bell.*

12
Ring in the valiant man and free,
The larger heart, the kindlier hand;
Ring out the darkness of the land;
Ring in the Christ that is to be.
TENNYSON—*In Memoriam.* Pt. CVI.

13
Ring out old shapes of foul disease;
Ring out the narrowing lust of gold;
Ring out the thousand wars of old,
Ring in the thousand years of peace.
TENNYSON—*In Memoriam.* Pt. CVI.

14
Ring out the old, ring in the new,
Ring, happy bells, across the snow.
TENNYSON—*In Memoriam.* Pt. CVI.

15
Ring out, wild bells, to the wild sky,
The flying cloud, the frosty light.
TENNYSON—*In Memoriam.* Pt. CVI.

16
Softly the loud peal dies,
In passing winds it drowns,
But breathes, like perfect joys,
Tender tones.
FREDERICK TENNYSON—*The Bridal.*

17
Curfew must not ring to-night.
ROSA H. THORPE—*Title of Poem.*

1
How like the leper, with his own sad cry
Enforcing his own solitude, it tolls!
That lonely bell set in the rushing shoals,
To warn us from the place of jeopardy!
CHARLES TENNYSON TURNER—*The Buoy Bell.*

BENEFITS (See also GIFTS, PHILANTHROPY)

2
Beneficium non in eo quod fit aut datur consistit sed in ipso dantis aut facientis animo.

A benefit consists not in what is done or given, but in the intention of the giver or doer.
SENECA—*De Beneficiis.* I. 6.

3
Eodem animo beneficium debetur, quo datur.

A benefit is estimated according to the mind of the giver.
SENECA—*De Beneficiis.* I. 1.

4
Qui dedit beneficium taceat; narret, qui accepit.

Let him that hath done the good office conceal it; let him that hath received it disclose it.
SENECA—*De Beneficiis.* II. 11.

5
Inopi beneficium bis dat, qui dat celeriter.

He gives a benefit twice who gives quickly.
SYRUS, in the collection of proverbs known as the *Proverbs of Seneca.*

6
Beneficia usque eo læta sunt dum videntur exsolvi posse; ubi multum antevenere pro gratia odium redditur.

Benefits are acceptable, while the receiver thinks he may return them; but once exceeding that, hatred is given instead of thanks.
TACITUS—*Annales.* IV. 18.

BIRCH (TREE)

Betula

7
Rippling through thy branches goes the sunshine,
Among thy leaves that palpitate forever,
And in thee, a pining nymph had prisoned
The soul, once of some tremulous inland river,
Quivering to tell her woe, but ah! dumb, dumb forever.
LOWELL—*The Birch Tree.*

BIRDS (UNCLASSIFIED)

8
Birds of a feather will gather together.
BURTON—*Anatomy of Melancholy.* Pt. III. Sec. I. Memb. 1. Subsect. 2.
(See also MINSHEU)

9
A bird in the hand is worth two in the bush.
CERVANTES—*Don Quixote.* Pt. I. Ch. IV.
(See also HERBERT, HEYWOOD, PLUTARCH)

10
You must not think, sir, to catch old birds with chaff.
CERVANTES—*Don Quixote.* Pt. I. Ch. IV.

11
Never look for birds of this year in the nests of the last.
CERVANTES—*Don Quixote.* Pt. II. Ch. LXXIV.

12
Dame Nature's minstrels.
GAVIN DOUGLAS—*Morning in May.*

13
A bird of the air shall carry the voice, and that which hath wings shall tell the matter.
Ecclesiastes. X. 20.
(See also HENRY IV)

14
To warm their little loves the birds complain.
GRAY—*Sonnet on the Death of Richard West.*
(See also SOMERVILLE)

15
A feather in hand is better than a bird in the air.
HERBERT—*Jacula Prudentum.*
(See also CERVANTES)

16
Better one byrde in hand than ten in the wood.
HEYWOOD—*Proverbs.* Pt. I. Ch. XI.
(See also CERVANTES)

17
The nightingale has a lyre of gold,
The lark's is a clarion call,
And the blackbird plays but a boxwood flute,
But I love him best of all.

For his song is all the joy of life,
And we in the mad spring weather,
We two have listened till he sang
Our hearts and lips together.
W. E. HENLEY—*Echoes.*

18
When the swallows homeward fly,
When the roses scattered lie,
When from neither hill or dale,
Chants the silvery nightingale:
In these words my bleeding heart
Would to thee its grief impart;
When I thus thy image lose
Can I, ah! can I, e'er know repose?
KARL HERRLOSSOHN—*When the Swallows Homeward Fly.*

19
I was always a lover of soft-winged things.
VICTOR HUGO—*I Was Always a Lover.*

20
Rara avis in terris, nigroque simillima cygno.

A rare bird upon the earth, and exceedingly like a black swan.
JUVENAL—*Satires.* VI. 165.

21
Do you ne'er think what wondrous beings these?
Do you ne'er think who made them, and who taught
The dialect they speak, where melodies
Alone are the interpreters of thought?
Whose household words are songs in many keys,
Sweeter than instrument of man e'er caught!
LONGFELLOW—*Tales of a Wayside Inn. The Poet's Tale. The Birds of Killingworth.*

22
That which prevents disagreeable flies from feeding on your repast, was once the proud tail of a splendid bird.
MARTIAL—*Epigrams.* Bk. XIV. Ep. 67.

23
Birdes of a feather will flocke togither.
MINSHEU. (1599)
(See also BURTON)

1
Every bird that upwards swings
Bears the Cross upon its wings.
Ascribed to JOHN MASON NEALE.

2
He is a fool who lets slip a bird in the hand for a bird in the bush.
PLUTARCH—*Of Garrulity.*
(See also CERVANTES)

3
Hear how the birds, on ev'ry blooming spray,
With joyous musick wake the dawning day!
POPE—*Pastorals. Spring.* L. 23.

4
A little bird told me.
King Henry IV. Pt. II. Last lines. See also Mahomet's pigeon, the "pious lie", *Life of Mahomet* in *Library of Useful Knowledge.* Note p. 19. ARISTOPHANES—*Aves.* See *Robinson's Antiquities.* Greek, Bk. III. Ch. XV. ad init. *Ecclesiastes.* X. 20.

5
That byrd ys nat honest
That fylythe hys owne nest.
SKELTON—*Poems against Garnesche.* III.

6
The bird
That glads the night had cheer'd the listening groves with sweet complainings.
SOMERVILLE—*The Chace.*
(See also GRAY)

BIRD OF PARADISE

7
Those golden birds that, in the spice-time, drop
About the gardens, drunk with that sweet food
Whose scent hath lur'd them o'er the summer flood;
And those that under Araby's soft sun
Build their high nests of budding cinnamon.
MOORE—*Lalla Rookh. The Veiled Prophet of Khorassan.*

BIRTH; BIRTHDAY

8
He is born naked, and falls a whining at the first.
BURTON—*Anatomy of Melancholy.* Pt. I. Sec. II. Mem. 3. Subsect. 10.
(See also PLINY, WISDOM OF SOLOMON; and TENNYSON, under BABYHOOD)

9
Esaw selleth his byrthright for a messe of potage.
Chapter heading of the Genevan version and Matthew's Bible of *Genesis* XXV. (Not in authorized version.)
(See also PENN)

10
A birthday:—and now a day that rose
With much of hope, with meaning rife—
A thoughtful day from dawn to close:
The middle day of human life.
JEAN INGELOW—*A Birthday Walk.*

11
And show me your nest with the young ones in it,
I will not steal them away;
I am old! you may trust me, linnet, linnet—
I am seven times one to-day.
JEAN INGELOW—*Songs of Seven. Seven Times One.*

12
As this auspicious day began the race
Of ev'ry virtue join'd with ev'ry grace;
May you, who own them, welcome its return,
Till excellence, like yours, again is born.
The years we wish, will half your charms impair;
The years we wish, the better half will spare;
The victims of your eyes will bleed no more,
But all the beauties of your mind adore.
JEFFREY—*Miscellanies. To a Lady on her Birthday.*

13
Believing hear, what you deserve to hear:
Your birthday as my own to me is dear.
Blest and distinguish'd days! which we should prize
The first, the kindest bounty of the skies.
But yours gives most; for mine did only lend
Me to the world; yours gave to me a friend.
MARTIAL—*Epigrams.* Bk. IX. Ep. 53.

14
My birthday!—what a different sound
That word had in my youthful ears;
And how each time the day comes round,
Less and less white its mark appears.
MOORE—*My Birthday.*

15
Lest, selling that noble inheritance for a poor mess of perishing pottage, you never enter into His eternal rest.
PENN—*No Cross no Crown.* Pt. II. Ch. XX. Sec. XXIII.
(See also *Genesis*)

16
Man alone at the very moment of his birth, cast naked upon the naked earth, does she abandon to cries and lamentations.
PLINY The Elder—*Natural History.* Bk. VII. Sec. II.
(See also BURTON)

17
Is that a birthday? 'tis, alas! too clear;
'Tis but the funeral of the former year.
POPE—*To Mrs. M. B.* L. 9.

18
The dew of thy birth is of the womb of the morning.
The Psalter. Psalms. CX. 3.

19
"Do you know who made you?" "Nobody, as I knows on," said the child, with a short laugh. The idea appeared to amuse her considerably; for her eyes twinkled, and she added—
"I 'spect I growed. Don't think nobody never made me."
HARRIET BEECHER STOWE—*Uncle Tom's Cabin.* Ch. XXI.

20
As some divinely gifted man,
Whose life in low estate began,
And on a simple village green;
Who breaks his birth's invidious bar.
TENNYSON—*In Memoriam.* Canto 64.

21
When I was born I drew in the common air, and fell upon the earth, which is of like nature, and the first voice which I uttered was crying, as all others do.
Wisdom of Solomon. VII. 3.
(See also BURTON)

BLACKBIRD

1
The birds have ceased their songs,
All save the blackbird, that from yon tall ash,
'Mid Pinkie's greenery, from his mellow throat,
In adoration of the setting sun,
Chants forth his evening hymn.
MOIR—*An Evening Sketch.*

2
Golden Bill! Golden Bill!
Lo, the peep of day;
All the air is cool and still,
From the elm-tree on the hill,
Chant away:
* * * *
Let thy loud and welcome lay
Pour alway
Few notes but strong.
MONTGOMERY—*The Blackbird.*

3
A slender young Blackbird built in a thorn-tree:
A spruce little fellow as ever could be;
His bill was so yellow, his feathers so black,
So long was his tail, and so glossy his back,
That good Mrs. B., who sat hatching her eggs,
And only just left them to stretch her poor legs,
And pick for a minute the worm she preferred,
Thought there never was seen such a beautiful bird.
D. M. MULOCK—*The Blackbird and the Rooks.*

4
O Blackbird! sing me something well:
While all the neighbors shoot thee round,
I keep smooth plats of fruitful ground,
Where thou may'st warble, eat and dwell.
TENNYSON—*The Blackbird.*

BLACKSMITH

5
Curs'd be that wretch (Death's factor sure) who brought
Dire swords into the peaceful world, and taught
Smiths (who before could only make
The spade, the plough-share, and the rake)
Arts, in most cruel wise
Man's left to epitomize!
ABRAHAM COWLEY—*In Commendation of the Time we live under, the Reign of our gracious King, Charles II.*

6
Come, see the Dolphin's anchor forged; 'tis at a white heat now:
The billows ceased, the flames decreased; though on the forge's brow
The little flames still fitfully play through the sable mound;
And fitfully you still may see the grim smiths ranking round,
All clad in leathern panoply, their broad hands only bare;
Some rest upon their sledges here, some work the windlass there.
SAMUEL FERGUSON—*The Forging of the Anchor.* St. 1.

7
The smith and his penny both are black.
HERBERT—*Jacula Prudentum.*

8
And the smith his iron measures hammered to the anvil's chime;
Thanking God, whose boundless wisdom makes the flowers of poesy bloom
In the forge's dust and cinders, in the tissues of the loom.
LONGFELLOW—*Nuremberg.* L. 34.

9
Under a spreading chestnut tree
The village smithy stands:
The smith, a mighty man is he,
With large and sinewy hands;
And the muscles of his brawny arms
Are strong as iron bands.
LONGFELLOW—*The Village Blacksmith.*

10
As great Pythagoras of yore,
Standing beside the blacksmith's door,
And hearing the hammers, as they smote
The anvils with a different note,
Stole from the varying tones, that hung
Vibrant on every iron tongue,
The secret of the sounding wire,
And formed the seven-chorded lyre.
LONGFELLOW—*To a Child.* L. 175.

11
And he sang: "Hurra for my handiwork!"
And the red sparks lit the air;
Not alone for the blade was the bright steel made;
And he fashioned the first ploughshare.
CHAS. MACKAY—*Tubal Cain.* St. 4.

12
In other part stood one who, at the forge
Labouring, two massy clods of iron and brass
Had melted.
MILTON—*Paradise Lost.* Bk. XI. L. 564.

13
I saw a smith stand with his hammer, thus,
The whilst his iron did on the anvil cool.
King John. Act IV. Sc. 2. L. 193.

14
The paynefull smith, with force of fervent heat,
The hardest yron soone doth mollify,
That with his heavy sledge he can it beat,
And fashion it to what he it list apply.
SPENSER—*Sonnet XXXII.*

BLASPHEMY (See OATHS, SWEARING)

BLESSINGS

15
'Tis not for mortals always to be blest.
ARMSTRONG—*Art of Preserving Health.* Bk. IV. L. 260.

16
Prosperity is the blessing of the Old Testament;
Adversity is the blessing of the New.
BACON—*Of Adversity.*

17
Blessings star forth forever; but a curse
Is like a cloud—it passes.
BAILEY—*Festus.* Sc. *Hades.*

18
A spring of love gushed from my heart,
And I bless'd them unaware.
COLERIDGE—*The Ancient Mariner.* Pt. IV.

19
For blessings ever wait on virtuous deeds,
And though a late, a sure reward succeeds.
CONGREVE—*Mourning Bride.* Act. V. Sc. 3.

1
Blessed shall be thy basket and thy store.
Deuteronomy. XXVIII. 5.

2
God bless us every one.
DICKENS—*Christmas Carol.* Stave 3. (Saying of Tiny Tim.)

3
O close my hand upon Beatitude!
Not on her toys.
LOUISE IMOGEN GUINEY—*Deo Optimo Maximo.*

4
To heal divisions, to relieve the oppress'd,
In virtue rich; in blessing others, bless'd.
HOMER—*Odyssey.* Bk. VII. L. 95. POPE'S trans.

5
A man's best things are nearest him,
Lie close about his feet.
MONCKTON MILNES—*The Men of Old.* St. 7.

6
The blest to-day is as completely so,
As who began a thousand years ago.
POPE—*Essay on Man.* Ep. I. L. 75.

7
God bless us every one, prayed Tiny Tim,
Crippled and dwarfed of body yet so tall
Of soul, we tiptoe earth to look on him,
High towering over all.
JAMES WHITCOMB RILEY—*God Bless Us Every One.*
(See also DICKENS)

8
The benediction of these covering heavens
Fall on their heads like dew!
Cymbeline. Act V. Sc. 5. L. 350.

9
Like birds, whose beauties languish half concealed,
Till, mounted on the wing, their glossy plumes
Expanded, shine with azure, green and gold;
How blessings brighten as they take their flight.
YOUNG—*Night Thoughts.* Night II. L. 589.

10
Amid my list of blessings infinite,
Stands this the foremost, "That my heart has bled."
YOUNG—*Night Thoughts.* Night IX. L. 497.

BLINDNESS

11
Oh, say! what is that thing call'd light,
Which I must ne'er enjoy?
What are the blessings of the sight?
Oh, tell your poor blind boy!
COLLEY CIBBER—*The Blind Boy.*

12
None so blind as those that will not see.
MATTHEW HENRY—*Commentaries.* Jeremiah XX.
(See also SWIFT)

13
Dispel this cloud, the light of heaven restore;
Give me to see, and Ajax asks no more.
HOMER—*Iliad.* Bk. XVII. L. 730. POPE'S trans.

14
If the blind lead the blind, both shall fall into the ditch.
Matthew. XV. 14.

15
O loss of sight, of thee I most complain!
Blind among enemies, O worse than chains,
Dungeon, or beggary, or decrepit age!
MILTON—*Samson Agonistes.* L. 67.

16
O dark, dark, dark, amid the blaze of noon,
Irrecoverably dark! total eclipse,
Without all hope of day.
MILTON—*Samson Agonistes.* L. 80.

17 These eyes, tho' clear
To outward view of blemish or of spot,
Bereft of light, their seeing have forgot,
Nor to their idle orbs doth sight appear
Of sun, or moon, or star, throughout the year,
Or man, or woman. Yet I argue not
Against Heaven's hand or will, nor bate a jot
Of heart or hope; but still bear up and steer
Right onward.
MILTON—*Sonnet XXII.* L. 1.

18
He that is strucken blind cannot forget
The precious treasure of his eyesight lost.
Romeo and Juliet. Act I. Sc. 1. L. 238.

19
There's none so blind as they that won't see.
SWIFT—*Polite Conversation.* Dialogue III.
(See also HENRY)

20 And when a damp
Fell round the path of Milton, in his hand
The Thing became a trumpet; whence he blew
Soul-animating strains—alas! too few.
WORDSWORTH—*Scorn Not the Sonnet; Critic, You Have Frowned.*

BLISS

21
To bliss unknown my lofty soul aspires,
My lot unequal to my vast desires.
J. ARBUTHNOT—*Gnothi Seaton.* L. 3.

22 Thin partitions do divide
The bounds where good and ill reside;
That nought is perfect here below;
But *bliss* still bordering upon woe. [P. 50 (1770).
Weekly Magazine, Edinburgh, Vol. I. XXII.
(See also DRYDEN, under WIT; POPE, under SENSE)

23
The hues of bliss more brightly glow,
Chastis'd by sabler tints of woe.
GRAY—*Ode on the Pleasure arising from Vicissitude.* L. 45.

24
Alas! by some degree of woe
We every bliss must gain;
The heart can ne'er a transport know,
That never feels a pain.
LORD LYTTLETON—*Song.*

25
And my heart rocked its babe of bliss,
And soothed its child of air,
With something 'twixt a song and kiss,
To keep it nestling there.
GERALD MASSEY—*On a Wedding Day.* St. 3.

26
But such a sacred and home-felt delight,
Such sober certainty of waking bliss,
I never heard till now.
MILTON—*Comus.* L. 262.

1
The sum of earthly bliss.
MILTON—*Paradise Lost.* Bk. VIII. L. 522.

2
Bliss in possession will not last;
Remember'd joys are never past;
At once the fountain, stream, and sea,
They were,—they are,—they yet shall be.
MONTGOMERY—*The Little Cloud.*

3
Some place the bliss in action, some in ease,
Those call it pleasure, and contentment these.
POPE—*Essay on Man.* Ep. IV. L. 21.

4
Condition, circumstance, is not the thing;
Bliss is the same in subject or in king.
POPE—*Essay on Man.* Ep. IV. L. 57.

5
The way to bliss lies not on beds of down,
And he that had no cross deserves no crown.
QUARLES—*Esther.*
(See also PAULINUS, under CHRISTIANITY)

6
I know I am—that simplest bliss
The millions of my brothers miss.
I know the fortune to be born,
Even to the meanest wretch they scorn.
BAYARD TAYLOR—*Prince Deukalion.* Act IV.

7
We thinke no greater blisse than such
To be as be we would,
When blessed none but such as be
The same as be they should.
WILLIAM WARNER—ALBION'S ENGLAND. Bk. X. Ch. LIX. St. 68.

8
The spider's most attenuated thread
Is cord, is cable, to man's tender tie
On earthly bliss; it breaks at every breeze.
YOUNG—*Night Thoughts.* Night 1. L. 178.

BLOOD

9
Le sang qui vient de se répandre, est-il donc si pur?
Was the blood which has been shed then so pure?
ANTOINE BARNAVE, on hearing a criticism of the murder of FOULON and BARTIER. (1790)

10
Blut ist ein ganz besondrer Saft.
Blood is a juice of rarest quality.
GOETHE—*Faust.* I. 4. 214.

11
Blud's thicker than water.
SCOTT—*Guy Mannering.* Ch. XXXVIII.

12
Hands across the sea
Feet on English ground,
The old blood is bold blood, the wide world round.
BYRON WEBBER—*Hands across the Sea.*

13
Blood is thicker than water.
Attributed to COMMODORE TATTNALL. See Eleventh Ed. of *Encyclopedia Britannica* in notice of Tattnall. VINCENT S. LEAN stated in *Notes and Queries.* Seventh S. XIII. 114, he had found the proverb in the British Museum copy of the 1797 Ed. of ALLAN RAMSAY'S *Collection.* (First Ed. 1737)

BLUEBELL

Campanula rotundifolia

14
Hang-head Bluebell,
Bending like Moses' sister over Moses,
Full of a secret that thou dar'st not tell!
GEORGE MACDONALD—*Wild Flowers.*

15
Oh! roses and lilies are fair to see;
But the wild bluebell is the flower for me.
LOUISA A. MEREDITH—*The Bluebell.* L. 178.

BLUEBIRD

16
"So the Bluebirds have contracted, have they, for a house?
And a nest is under way for little Mr. Wren?"
"Hush, dear, hush! Be quiet, dear! quiet as a mouse.
These are weighty secrets, and we must whisper them."
SUSAN COOLIDGE—*Secrets.*

17
In the thickets and the meadows
Piped the bluebird, the Owaissa.
On the summit of the lodges
Sang the robin, the Opechee.
LONGFELLOW—*Hiawatha.* Pt. XXI.

18
Whither away, Bluebird,
Whither away?
The blast is chill, yet in the upper sky
Thou still canst find the color of thy wing,
The hue of May.
Warbler, why speed thy southern flight? ah, why,
Thou too, whose song first told us of the Spring?
Whither away?
E. C. STEDMAN—*The Flight of the Birds.*

BLUSHES

19
An Arab, by his earnest gaze,
Has clothed a lovely maid with blushes;
A smile within his eyelids plays
And into words his longing gushes.
WM. R. ALGER—*Oriental Poetry. Love Sowing and Reaping Roses.*

20
Girls blush, sometimes, because they are alive,
Half wishing they were dead to save the shame.
The sudden blush devours them, neck and brow;
They have drawn too near the fire of life, like gnats,
And flare up bodily, wings and all.
E. B. BROWNING—*Aurora Leigh.* Bk. II. L. 732.

21
So sweet the blush of bashfulness,
E'en pity scarce can wish it less!
BYRON—*Bride of Abydos.* Canto 1. St. 8

22
Blushed like the waves of hell.
BYRON—*Devil's Drive.* St. 5.

23
'Tis not on youth's smooth cheek the blush alone, which fades so fast,
But the tender bloom of heart is gone, ere youth itself be past.
BYRON—*Stanzas for Music.*

1
Pure friendship's well-feigned blush.
BYRON—*Stanzas to Her who can Best Understand Them.* St. 12.

2
We griev'd, we sigh'd, we wept; we never blushed before.
COWLEY—*Discourse concerning the Government of* OLIVER CROMWELL. *Works.* P. 60. (Ed. 1693) Quoted in house of Commons by Sir Robert Peel repelling an attack by William Cobbett. (See also P. 707[3].)

3
I pity bashful men, who feel the pain
Of fancied scorn and undeserved disdain,
And bear the marks upon a blushing face,
Of needless shame, and self-impos'd disgrace.
COWPER—*Conversation.* L. 347.

4
Once he saw a youth blushing, and addressed him, "Courage, my boy; that is the complexion of virtue."
DIOGENES LAERTIUS—*Diogenes.* VI.

5
A blush is no language: only a dubious flag-signal which may mean either of two contradictories.
GEORGE ELIOT—*Daniel Deronda.* Bk. V. Ch. XXXV.

6
The rising blushes, which her cheek o'er-spread,
Are opening roses in the lily's bed.
GAY—*Dione.* Act II. Sc. 3.

7
Bello è il rossore, ma è incommodo qualche volta.
The blush is beautiful, but it is sometimes inconvenient.
GOLDONI—*Pamela.* I. 3.

8
Blushing is the colour of virtue.
MATTHEW HENRY—*Commentaries.* Jeremiah III.

9
Such a blush
In the midst of brown was born,
Like red poppies grown with corn.
HOOD—*Ruth.*

10
Les hommes rougissent moins de leur crimes que de leurs faiblesses et de leur vanité.
Men blush less for their crimes than for their weaknesses and vanity.
LA BRUYÈRE—*Les Caractères.* II.

11
L'innocence à rougir n'est point accoutumée.
Innocence is not accustomed to blush.
MOLIÈRE—*Don Garcie de Navarre.* II. 5.

12
While mantling on the maiden's cheek
Young roses kindled into thought.
MOORE—*Evenings in Greece.* Evening II. *Song.*

13
From every blush that kindles in thy cheeks,
Ten thousand little loves and graces spring
To revel in the roses.
NICHOLAS ROWE—*Tamerlane.* Act I. Sc. 1.

14
I will go wash;
And when my face is fair, you shall perceive
Whether I blush or no.
Coriolanus. Act I. Sc. 9. L. 68.

15
Lay by all nicety and prolixious blushes,
That banish what they sue for.
Measure for Measure. Act II. Sc. 4. L. 162.

16
By noting of the lady I have mark'd
A thousand blushing apparitions
To start into her face, a thousand innocent shames.
In angel whiteness beat away those blushes.
Much Ado About Nothing. Act IV. Sc. 1. L. 160.

17
Yet will she blush, here be it said,
To hear her secrets so bewrayed.
Passionate Pilgrim. Pt. XIX. L. 351.

18
Where now I have no one to blush with me,
To cross their arms and hang their heads with mine.
Rape of Lucrece. L. 792.

19
Two red fires in both their faces blazed;
She thought he blush'd, * * *
And, blushing with him, wistly on him gazed.
Rape of Lucrece. Line 1, 353.

20
And bid the cheek be ready with a blush
Modest as morning when she coldly eyes
The youthful Phœbus.
Troilus and Cressida. Act I. Sc. 3. L. 228.

21
Come, quench your blushes and present yourself
That which you are, mistress o' the feast.
Winter's Tale. Act IV. Sc. 4. L. 67.

22
Erubuit: salva res est.
He blushes: all is safe.
TERENCE—*Adelphi.* IV. 5. 9.

23
The man that blushes is not quite a brute.
YOUNG—*Night Thoughts.* Night VII. L. 496.

BOATING

24
Oh, swiftly glides the bonnie boat,
Just parted from the shore,
And to the fisher's chorus-note,
Soft moves the dipping oar!
JOANNA BAILLIE—*Song. Oh, Swiftly glides the Bonnie Boat.*

25
Like the watermen that row one way and look another.
BURTON—*Anatomy of Melancholy. Democritus to the Reader.*
(See also MONTAIGNE, PLUTARCH)

26
On the ear
Drops the light drip of the suspended oar.
BYRON—*Childe Harold.* Canto III. St. 86.

27
But oars alone can ne'er prevail
To reach the distant coast;
The breath of Heaven must swell the sail,
Or all the toil is lost.
COWPER—*Human Frailty.* St. 6.

28
We lie and listen to the hissing waves,
Wherein our boat seems sharpening its keel,
Which on the sea's face all unthankful graves

An arrowed scratch as with a tool of steel.
JOHN DAVIDSON—*In a Music-Hall and Other Poems. For Lovers.* L. 17.

1
The Owl and the Pussy-Cat went to sea
In a beautiful pea-green boat.
EDWARD LEAR—*The Owl and the Pussy-Cat.*

2
And all the way, to guide their chime,
With falling oars they kept the time.
ANDREW MARVELL—*Bermudas.*

3
Like the watermen who advance forward while they look backward.
MONTAIGNE—Bk. II. Ch. XXIX. *Of Profit and Honesty.*
(See also BURTON)

4
Faintly as tolls the evening chime,
Our voices keep tune and our oars keep time,
Soon as the woods on shore look dim,
We'll sing at St. Ann's our parting hymn;
Row, brothers, row, the stream runs fast,
The rapids are near and the daylight's past!
MOORE—*Canadian Boat Song.*

5
Gracefully, gracefully glides our bark
On the bosom of Father Thames,
And before her bows the wavelets dark
Break into a thousand gems.
THOS. NOEL—*A Thames Voyage.*

6
Like watermen who look astern while they row the boat ahead.
PLUTARCH—*Whether 'twas rightfully said, Live concealed.*
(See also BURTON)

7
Learn of the little nautilus to sail,
Spread the thin oar, and catch the driving gale.
POPE—*Essay on Man.* Ep. III. L. 177.

8 The oars were silver:
Which to the tune of flutes kept stroke.
Antony and Cleopatra. Act II. Sc. 2. L. 199.

BOBOLINK

9
Modest and shy as a nun is she;
One weak chirp is her only note;
Braggarts and prince of braggarts is he,
Pouring boasts from his little throat.
BRYANT—*Robert of Lincoln.*

10
Robert of Lincoln is gayly drest,
Wearing a bright black wedding-coat;
White are his shoulders and white his crest.
BRYANT—*Robert of Lincoln.*

11
One day in the bluest of summer weather,
Sketching under a whispering oak,
I heard five bobolinks laughing together,
Over some ornithological joke.
C. P. CRANCH—*Bird Language.*

12
When Nature had made all her birds,
With no more cares to think on,
She gave a rippling laugh and out
There flew a Bobolinkon.
C. P. CRANCH—*The Bobolinks.*

13
The crack-brained bobolink courts his crazy mate,
Poised on a bulrush tipsy with his weight.
O. W. HOLMES—*Spring.*

14
Out of the fragrant heart of bloom,
The bobolinks are singing;
Out of the fragrant heart of bloom
The apple-tree whispers to the room,
"Why art thou but a nest of gloom
While the bobolinks are singing?"
W. D. HOWELLS—*The Bobolinks are Singing.*

BOOKS (See also AUTHORSHIP, PRINTING, PUBLISHING, READING)

15
Books are the legacies that a great genius leaves to mankind, which are delivered down from generation to generation, as presents to the posterity of those who are yet unborn.
ADDISON—*Spectator.* No. 166.

16
That is a good book which is opened with expectation and closed with profit.
ALCOTT—*Table Talk.* Bk. I. *Learning-Books.*

17
Homo unius libri.
A man of one book.
THOMAS AQUINAS.
(See also D'ISRAELI, SOUTHEY, TAYLOR)

18
Books are delightful when prosperity happily smiles; when adversity threatens, they are inseparable comforters. They give strength to human compacts, nor are grave opinions brought forward without books. Arts and sciences, the benefits of which no mind can calculate, depend upon books.
RICHARD AUNGERVYLE (Richard De Bury)—*Philobiblon.* Ch. I.

19
You, O Books, are the golden vessels of the temple, the arms of the clerical militia with which the missiles of the most wicked are destroyed; fruitful olives, vines of Engaddi, fig-trees knowing no sterility; burning lamps to be ever held in the hand.
RICHARD AUNGERVYLE (Richard De Bury)—*Philobiblon.* Ch. XV.

20
But the images of men's wits and knowledges remain in books, exempted from the wrong of time, and capable of perpetual renovation.
BACON—*Advancement of Learning.* Bk. I. *Advantages of Learning.*

21
Some books are to be tasted, others to be swallowed, and some few to be chewed and digested
BACON—*Essay. Of Studies.*
(See also FULLER)

22
Books must follow sciences, and not sciences books.
BACON—*Proposition touching Amendment of Laws.*

23 Worthy books
Are not companions—they are solitudes:
We lose ourselves in them and all our cares.
BAILEY—*Festus.* Sc. *A Village Feast. Evening.*

1 That place that does contain
My books, the best companions, is to me
A glorious court, where hourly I converse
With the old sages and philosophers;
And sometimes, for variety, I confer
With kings and emperors, and weigh their counsels.

BEAUMONT AND FLETCHER—*The Elder Brother*. Act I. Sc. 2.

2 We get no good
By being ungenerous, even to a book,
And calculating profits—so much help
By so much reading. It is rather when
We gloriously forget ourselves, and plunge
Soul-forward, headlong, into a book's profound,
Impassioned for its beauty, and salt of truth—
'Tis then we get the right good from a book.

E. B. BROWNING—*Aurora Leigh*. Bk. I. L. 700.

3 Books, books, books!
I had found the secret of a garret room
Piled high with cases in my father's name;
Piled high, packed large,—where, creeping in and out
Among the giant fossils of my past,
Like some small nimble mouse between the ribs
Of a mastodon, I nibbled here and there
At this or that box, pulling through the gap,
In heats of terror, haste, victorious joy,
The first book first. And how I felt it beat
Under my pillow, in the morning's dark,
An hour before the sun would let me read!
My books!
At last, because the time was ripe,
I chanced upon the poets.

E. B. BROWNING—*Aurora Leigh*. Bk. I. L. 830.

4
Laws die, Books never.

BULWER-LYTTON—*Richelieu*. Act I. Sc. 2.

5 The Wise
(Minstrel or Sage,) *out* of their books are clay;
But *in* their books, as from their graves they rise.
Angels—that, side by side, upon our way,
Walk with and warn us!

BULWER-LYTTON—*The Souls of Books*. St. 3. L. 9.

6 Hark, the world so loud,
And they, the movers of the world, so still!

BULWER-LYTTON—*The Souls of Books*. St. 3. L. 14.

7
We call some books immortal! *Do they live?*
If so, believe me, TIME hath made them pure.
In Books, the veriest wicked rest in peace.

BULWER-LYTTON—*The Souls of Books*. St. 3. L. 22.

8
All books grow homilies by time; they are
Temples, at once, and Landmarks.

BULWER-LYTTON—*The Souls of Books*. St. 4. L. 1.

9
There is no Past, so long as Books shall live!

BULWER-LYTTON—*The Souls of Books*. St. 4. L. 9.

10 In you are sent
The types of Truths whose life is THE TO COME;
In you soars up the Adam from the fall;
In you the FUTURE as the PAST is given—
Ev'n in our death ye bid us hail our birth;—
Unfold these pages, and behold the Heaven,
Without one grave-stone left upon the Earth.

BULWER-LYTTON—*The Souls of Books*. St. 5. L. 11.

11
Some said, John, print it, others said, Not so;
Some said, It might do good, others said, No.

BUNYAN—*Apology for his Book*. L. 39.

12
Go now, my little book, to every place
Where my first pilgrim has but shown his face.
Call at their door: if any say "Who's there?"
Then answer thou "Christiana is here."

BUNYAN—*Pilgrim's Progress*. Pt. II.
(See also SOUTHEY)

13
Some books are lies frae end to end.

BURNS—*Death and Dr. Hornbook*.

14
'Tis pleasant, sure, to see one's name in print;
A book's a book, although there's nothing in't.

BYRON—*English Bards and Scotch Reviewers*. L. 51.

15
In the poorest cottage are Books: is one Book, wherein for several thousands of years the spirit of man has found light, and nourishment, and an interpreting response to whatever is Deepest in him.

CARLYLE—*Essays. Corn-Law Rhymes*.

16
If a book come from the heart, it will contrive to reach other hearts; all art and authorcraft are of small amount to that.

CARLYLE—*Heroes and Hero Worship*. Lecture II.

17
All that Mankind has done, thought, gained or been it is lying as in magic preservation in the pages of Books. They are the chosen possession of men.

CARLYLE—*Heroes and Hero Worship*. Lecture V.

18
In books lies the soul of the whole Past Time; the articulate audible voice of the Past, when the body and material substance of it has altogether vanished like a dream.

CARLYLE—*Heroes and Hero Worship. The Hero as a Man of Letters*.

19
The true University of these days is a collection of Books.

CARLYLE—*Heroes and Hero Worship. The Hero as a Man of Letters*.

20
"There is no book so bad," said the bachelor, "but something good may be found in it."

CERVANTES—*Don Quixote*. Pt. II. Ch. III.

21
It is chiefly through books that we enjoy intercourse with superior minds, and these invaluable means of communication are in the reach of all. In the best books, great men talk to us, give us their most precious thoughts, and pour their souls into ours.

CHANNING—*On Self-Culture*.

1
Go, litel boke! go litel myn tregedie!
CHAUCER—*Canterbury Tales. Troilus and Creseide.* Bk. V. L. 1,800.

2
O little booke, thou art so unconning,
How darst thou put thyself in prees for dred?
CHAUCER—*Flower and the Leaf.* L. 591.

3
And as for me, though than I konne but lyte,
On bokes for to rede I me delyte,
And to hem yeve I feyth and ful credence,
And in myn herte have hem in reverence
So hertely, that ther is game noon,
That fro my bokes maketh me to goon,
But yt be seldome on the holy day.
Save, certeynly, when that the monthe of May
Is comen, and that I here the foules synge,
And that the floures gynnen for to sprynge,
Farwel my boke, and my devocion.
CHAUCER—*Legende of Goode Women. Prologue.* L. 29.

4
It is saying less than the truth to affirm that an excellent book (and the remark holds almost equally good of a Raphael as of a Milton) is like a well-chosen and well-tended fruit tree. Its fruits are not of one season only. With the due and natural intervals, we may recur to it year after year, and it will supply the same nourishment and the same gratification, if only we ourselves return to it with the same healthful appetite.
COLERIDGE—*Literary Remains. Prospectus of Lectures.*

5
Books should, not Business, entertain the Light;
And Sleep, as undisturb'd as Death, the Night.
COWLEY—*Of Myself.*

6
Books cannot always please, however good;
Minds are not ever craving for their food.
CRABBE—*The Borough.* Letter XXIV. *Schools.* L. 402.

7
The monument of vanished mindes.
SIR WM. DAVENANT—*Gondibert.* Bk. II. Canto V.

8
Give me a book that does my soul embrace
And makes simplicity a grace—
Language freely flowing, thoughts as free—
Such pleasing books more taketh me
Than all the modern works of art
That please mine eyes and not my heart.
MARGARET DENBO. Suggested by
Give me a look, give me a face,
That makes simplicity a grace.
BEN JONSON—*Silent Woman.* Act I. Sc. 1.

9
Books should to one of these four ends conduce,
For wisdom, piety, delight, or use.
SIR JOHN DENHAM—*Of Prudence.*

10
He ate and drank the precious words,
His spirit grew robust;
He knew no more that he was poor,
Nor that his frame was dust.
He danced along the dingy days,
And this bequest of wings
Was but a book. What liberty
A loosened spirit brings!
EMILY DICKINSON—*A Book.*

11
There is no frigate like a book
To take us lands away,
Nor any coursers like a page
Of prancing poetry.
This traverse may the poorest take
Without oppress of toll;
How frugal is the chariot
That bears a human soul.
EMILY DICKINSON—*A Book.*

12
Golden volumes! richest treasures,
Objects of delicious pleasures!
You my eyes rejoicing please,
You my hands in rapture seize!
Brilliant wits and musing sages,
Lights who beam'd through many ages!
Left to your conscious leaves their story,
And dared to trust you with their glory;
And now their hope of fame achiev'd,
Dear volumes! you have not deceived!
ISAAC D'ISRAELI—*Curiosities of Literature. Libraries.*

13
Homo unius libri, or, cave ab homine unius libri.
Beware of the man of one book.
ISAAC D'ISRAELI, quoted in *Curiosities of Literature.*
(See also AQUINAS)

14
Not as ours the books of old—
Things that steam can stamp and fold;
Not as ours the books of yore—
Rows of type, and nothing more.
AUSTIN DOBSON—*To a Missal of the 13th Century.*

15
The spectacles of books.
DRYDEN—*Essay on Dramatic Poetry.*

16
Of making many books there is no end; and much study is a weariness of the flesh.
Ecclesiastes. XII. 12.

17
Books are the best things, well used: abused, among the worst.
EMERSON—*American Scholar.*

18
In every man's memory, with the hours when life culminated are usually associated certain books which met his views.
EMERSON—*Letters and Social Aims. Quotation and Originality.*

19
There are many virtues in books, but the essential value is the adding of knowledge to our stock by the record of new facts, and, better, by the record of intuitions which distribute facts, and are the formulas which supersede all histories.
EMERSON—*Letters and Social Aims. Persian Poetry.*

20
We prize books, and they prize them most who are themselves wise.
EMERSON—*Letters and Social Aims. Quotation and Originality.*

1
The princeps copy, clad in blue and gold.
John Ferriar—*Bibliomania.*

2
Now cheaply bought, for thrice their weight in gold.
John Ferriar—*Bibliomania.*

3
How pure the joy when first my hands unfold
The small, rare volume, black with tarnished gold.
John Ferriar—*Bibliomania.*

4
Learning hath gained most by those books by which the Printers have lost.
Fuller—*Holy and the Profane State. Of Books.*

5
Some Books are onely cursorily to be tasted of.
Fuller—*Holy and the Profane State. Of Books.* (See also Bacon)

6
Books are necessary to correct the vices of the polite; but those vices are ever changing, and the antidote should be changed accordingly—should still be new.
Goldsmith — *Citizen of the World.* Letter LXXII.

7
In proportion as society refines, new books must ever become more necessary.
Goldsmith—*Citizen of the World.* Letter LXXII.

8
I armed her against the censures of the world; showed her that books were sweet unreproaching companions to the miserable, and that if they could not bring us to enjoy life, they would at least teach us to endure it.
Goldsmith—*Vicar of Wakefield.* Ch. XXII.

9
I have ever gained the most profit, and the most pleasure also, from the books which have made me think the most: and, when the difficulties have once been overcome, these are the books which have struck the deepest root, not only in my memory and understanding, but likewise in my affections.
J. C. and A. W. Hare—*Guesses at Truth.* P. 458.

10
Thou art a plant sprung up to wither never,
But, like a laurell, to grow green forever.
Herrick—*Hesperides. To His Booke.*

11
The foolishest book is a kind of leaky boat on a sea of wisdom; some of the wisdom will get in anyhow.
Holmes—*The Poet at the Breakfast-Table.* XI.

12
Dear little child, this little book
Is less a primer than a key
To sunder gates where wonder waits
Your "Open Sesame!"
Rupert Hughes—*With a First Reader.*

13
Medicine for the soul.
Inscription over the door of the Library at Thebes. Diodorus Siculus. I. 49. 3.

14
Now go, write it before them in a table, and note it in a book.
Isaiah. XXX. 8.

15
Oh that my words were now written! oh that they were printed in a book!
Job. XIX. 23.

16
My desire is . . . that mine adversary had written a book.
Job. XXXI. 35.

17
A man will turn over half a library to make one book.
Samuel Johnson—*Boswell's Life of Johnson.* (1775)

18
Blest be the hour wherein I bought this book;
His studies happy that composed the book,
And the man fortunate that sold the book.
Ben Jonson—*Every man out of his Humour.* Act I. Sc. 1.

19
Pray thee, take care, that tak'st my book in hand,
To read it well; that is to understand.
Ben Jonson—*Epigram* 1.

20
When I would know thee * * * my thought looks
Upon thy well-made choice of friends and books;
Then do I love thee, and behold thy ends
In making thy friends books, and thy books friends.
Ben Jonson—*Epigram* 86.

21
Quicquid agunt homines, votum, timor, ira, voluptas, gaudia, discursus, nostri est farrago libelli.
The doings of men, their prayers, fear, wrath, pleasure, delights, and recreations, are the subject of this book.
Juvenal—*Satires.* I. I. 85.

22
In omnibus requiem quæsivi
Et non inveni
Nisi seorsim sedans
In angulo cum libello.
Everywhere I have sought rest and found it not except sitting apart in a nook with a little book.
Written in an autograph copy of Thomas À. Kempis's *De Imitatione*, according to Cornelius A. Lapide (Cornelius van den Steen), a Flemish Jesuit of the 17th century, who says he saw this inscription. At Zwoll is a picture of à Kempis with this inscription, the last clause being "in angello cum libello"—in a little nook with a little book. In angellis et libellis—in little nooks (cells) and little books. Given in King—*Classical Quotations* as being taken from the preface of *De Imitatione.*
(See also Wilson)

23
Every age hath its book.
Koran. Ch. XIII

1
Books which are no books.
LAMB—*Last Essay of Elia. Detached Thoughts on Books.*

2
A book is a friend whose face is constantly changing. If you read it when you are recovering from an illness, and return to it years after, it is changed surely, with the change in yourself.
ANDREW LANG—*The Library.* Ch. I.

3
A wise man will select his books, for he would not wish to class them all under the sacred name of friends. Some can be accepted only as acquaintances. The best books of all kinds are taken to the heart, and cherished as his most precious possessions. Others to be chatted with for a time, to spend a few pleasant hours with, and laid aside, but not forgotten.
LANGFORD—*The Praise of Books. Preliminary Essay.*

4
The love of books is a love which requires neither justification, apology, nor defence.
LANGFORD—*The Praise of Books. Preliminary Essay.*

5
The pleasant books, that silently among
Our household treasures take familiar places,
And are to us as if a living tongue
Spake from the printed leaves or pictured faces!
LONGFELLOW—*Seaside and Fireside. Dedication.*

6
Leaving us heirs to amplest heritages
Of all the best thoughts of the greatest sages,
And giving tongues unto the silent dead!
LONGFELLOW—*Sonnet on Mrs. Kemble's Reading from Shakespeare.*

7
Books are sepulchres of thought.
LONGFELLOW—*Wind Over the Chimney.* St. 8.

8
All books are either dreams or swords,
You can cut, or you can drug, with words.
* * * * * *
My swords are tempered for every speech,
For fencing wit, or to carve a breach
Through old abuses the world condones.
AMY LOWELL—*Sword Blades and Poppy Seed.*

9
If I were asked what book is better than a cheap book, I would answer that there is one book better than a cheap book, and that is a book honestly come by.
LOWELL—*Before the U. S. Senate Committee on Patents*, Jan. 29, 1886.

10
What a sense of security in an old book which Time has criticised for us!
LOWELL—*My Study Windows. Library of Old Authors.*

11
Gentlemen use books as Gentlewomen handle their flowers, who in the morning stick them in their heads, and at night strawe them at their heeles.
LYLY—*Euphues. To the Gentlemen Readers.*

12
That wonderful book, while it obtains admiration from the most fastidious critics, is loved by those who are too simple to admire it.
MACAULAY—*On Bunyan's Pilgrim's Progress.* (1831)

13
As you grow ready for it, somewhere or other you will find what is needful for you in a book.
GEORGE MACDONALD—*The Marquis of Lossie.* Ch. XLII.

14
You importune me, Tucca, to present you with my books. I shall not do so; for you want to sell, not to read, them.
MARTIAL—*Epigrams.* Bk. VII. Ep. 77.

15
A good book is the precious life-blood of a master-spirit imbalmed and treasured up on purpose to a life beyond life.
MILTON—*Areopagitica.*

16
As good almost kill a man as kill a good book; who kills a man kills a reasonable creature, God's image; but he who destroys a good book kills reason itself, kills the image of God, as it were, in the eye.
MILTON—*Areopagitica.*

17
Books are not absolutely dead things, but do contain a progeny of life in them to be as active as that soul was whose progeny they are; nay, they do preserve as in a vial the purest efficacy and extraction of that living intellect that bred them.
MILTON—*Areopagitica.*

18
Deep vers'd in books, and shallow in himself.
MILTON—*Paradise Regained.* Bk. IV. L. 327.

19
Un livre est un ami qui ne trompe jamais.
A book is a friend that never deceives.
Ascribed to GUILBERT DE PIXÉRÉCOURT. Claimed for DESBARREAUX BERNARD.

20
Within that awful volume lies
The mystery of mysteries!
SCOTT—*The Monastery.* Vol. I. Ch. XII.

21
Distrahit animum librorum multitudo.
A multitude of books distracts the mind.
SENECA—*Epistolæ Ad Lucilium.* II. 3.

22
That roars so loud and thunders in the index
Hamlet. Act III. Sc. 4.

23
Keep * * * thy pen from lenders' books, and defy the foul fiend.
King Lear. Act III. Sc. 4. L. 100.

24
We turn'd o'er many books together.
Merchant of Venice. Act IV. Sc. 1. L. 156.

25
I had rather than forty shillings, I had my Book of Songs and Sonnets here.
Merry Wives of Windsor. Act I. Sc. 1. L. 204.

26
That book in many's eyes doth share the glory,
That in gold clasps locks in the golden story.
Romeo and Juliet. Act I. Sc. 3. L. 91.

1
O, let my books be then the eloquence
And dumb presagers of my speaking breast;
Who plead for love and look for recompense
More than that tongue that more hath more
express'd.
Sonnet XXIII.

2
Knowing I lov'd my books, he furnished me
From mine own library with volumes that
I prize above my dukedom.
The Tempest. Act I. Sc. 2. L. 165.

3
And deeper than did ever plummet sound,
I'll drown my book.
The Tempest. Act V. Sc. 1. L. 56.

4
And in such indexes (although small pricks
To their subsequent volumes) there is seen
The baby figure of the giant mass
Of things to come at large.
Troilus and Cressida. Act I. Sc. 3.

5
Their books of stature small they take in hand,
Which with pellucid horn secured are;
To save from finger wet the letters fair.
SHENSTONE—*The Schoolmistress.* St. 18.
(See also TICKELL)

6
You shall see them on a beautiful quarto page, where a neat rivulet of text shall meander through a meadow of margin.
SHERIDAN—*School for Scandal.* Act I. Sc. 1.
(See also TICKELL)

7
Nor wyll suffer this boke
By hooke ne by crooke
Printed to be.
SKELTON—*Duke of Clout.*

8
Some books are drenched sands,
On which a great soul's wealth lies all in
heaps,
Like a wrecked argosy.
ALEXANDER SMITH—*A Life Drama.* Sc. 2.

9
When St. Thomas Aquinas was asked in what manner a man might best become learned, he answered, "By reading one book." The *homo unius libri* is indeed proverbially formidable to all conversational figurantes.
SOUTHEY—*The Doctor.* P. 164.
(See also AQUINAS)

10
Go, little Book! From this my solitude
I cast thee on the Waters,—go thy ways:
And if, as I believe, thy vein be good,
The World will find thee after many days.
Be it with thee according to thy worth:
Go, little Book; in faith I send thee forth.
SOUTHEY—*Lay of the Laureate. L'Envoy.*
(See also BUNYAN)

11
Books, the children of the brain.
SWIFT—*Tale of a Tub.* Sec. I.

12
Aquinas was once asked, with what compendium a man might become learned? He answered "By reading of one book."
JEREMY TAYLOR—*Life of Christ.* Pt. II. S. XII. 16. He also quotes ACCLUS. XI. 10. ST. GREGORY, ST. BERNARD, SENECA, QUINTILIAN, JUVENAL. See *British Critic* No. 59. P. 202.
(See also AQUINAS)

13
Books, like proverbs, receive their chief value from the stamp and esteem of ages through which they have passed.
SIR WM. TEMPLE—*Ancient and Modern Learning.*

14
But every page having an ample marge,
And every marge enclosing in the midst
A square of text that looks a little blot.
TENNYSON—*Idylls of the King. Merlin and Vivien.* L. 669.
(See also TICKELL)

15
Thee will I sing in comely wainscot bound
And golden verge enclosing thee around;
The faithful horn before, from age to age
Preserving thy invulnerable page.
Behind thy patron saint in armor shines
With sword and lance to guard the sacred lines;
Th' instructive handle's at the bottom fixed
Lest wrangling critics should pervert the text.
TICKELL—*The Hornbook.*
(See also SHENSTONE, SHERIDAN, TENNYSON)

16
They are for company the best friends, in Doubt's Counsellors, in Damps Comforters, Time's Prospective the Home Traveller's Ship or Horse, the busie Man's best Recreation, the Opiate of idle Weariness, the Mindes best Ordinary, Nature's Garden and Seed-plot of Immortality.
BULSTRODE WHITELOCK—*Zootamia.*

17
O for a Booke and a shadie nooke, eyther in-a-
doore or out;
With the grene leaves whisp'ring overhede,
or the Streete cries all about.
Where I maie Reade all at my ease,
both of the Newe and Olde;
For a jollie goode Booke whereon to looke,
is better to me than Golde.
JOHN WILSON. Motto in his second-hand book catalogues. Claimed for him by AUSTIN DOBSON. Found in SIR JOHN LUBBOCK'S *Pleasures of Life* and IRELAND'S *Enchiridion*, where it is given as an old song. (See *Notes and Queries*, Nov. 1919, P. 297, for discussion of authorship.)

18
Books, we know,
Are a substantial world, both pure and good:
Round these, with tendrils strong as flesh and
blood,
Our pastime and our happiness will grow.
WORDSWORTH—*Poetical Works. Personal Talk.*

19
Up! up! my Friend, and quit your books,
Or surely you'll grow double;
Up! up! my Friend, and clear your looks;
Why all this toil and trouble?
WORDSWORTH—*The Tables Turned.*

20
Unlearned men of books assume the care,
As eunuchs are the guardians of the fair.
YOUNG—*Love of Fame.* Satire II. L. 83.

21
A dedication is a wooden leg.
YOUNG—*Love of Fame.* Satire IV. L. 192.

BORES

1
Society is now one polished horde,
Formed of two mighty tribes, the *Bores* and *Bored.*
BYRON—*Don Juan.* Canto XIII. St. 95.

2
The bore is usually considered a harmless creature, or of that class of irrational bipeds who hurt only themselves.
MARIA EDGEWORTH—*Thoughts on Bores.*

3
Got the ill name of augurs, because they were bores.
LOWELL—*A Fable for Critics,* L. 55.

4
L'ennui naquit un jour de l'uniformité.
One day ennui was born from uniformity.
MOTTE.

5
That old hereditary bore,
The steward.
ROGERS—*Italy. A Character.* L. 13.

6
Again I hear that creaking step!—
He's rapping at the door!
Too well I know the boding sound
That ushers in a bore.
J. G. SAXE—*My Familiar.*

7
He says a thousand pleasant things,—
But never says "Adieu."
J. G. SAXE—*My Familiar.*

8
O, he's as tedious
As is a tir'd horse, a railing wife;
Worse than a smoky house; I had rather live
With cheese and garlic in a windmill, far,
Than feed on cates, and have him talk to me,
In any summer-house in Christendom.
Henry IV. Pt. I. Act III. Sc. I. L. 159.

BORROWING

9
Great collections of books are subject to certain accidents besides the damp, the worms, and the rats; one not less common is that of the *borrowers,* not to say a word of the *purloiners.*
ISAAC D'ISRAELI—*Curiosities of Literature. The Bibliomania.*

10
He who prefers to give Linus the half of what he wishes to borrow, rather than to lend him the whole, prefers to lose only the half.
MARTIAL—*Epigrams.* Bk. I. Ep. 75.

11
You give me back, Phœbus, my bond for four hundred thousand sesterces; lend me rather a hundred thousand more. Seek some one else to whom you may vaunt your empty present: what I cannot pay you, Phœbus, is my own.
MARTIAL—*Epigrams.* Bk. IX. Ep. 102.

12
I have granted you much that you asked: and yet you never cease to ask of me. He who refuses nothing, Atticilla, will soon have nothing to refuse.
MARTIAL—*Epigrams.* Bk. XII. Ep. 79.

13
The borrower is servant to the lender.
Proverbs. XXII. 7.

14
Croyez que chose divine est prester; debvoir est vertu heroïcque.
Believe me that it is a godlike thing to lend; to owe is a heroic virtue.
RABELAIS—*Pantagruel.* Bk. III. Ch. IV.

15
Neither a borrower nor a lender be:
For loan oft loses both itself and friend,
And borrowing dulls the edge of husbandry.
Hamlet. Act I. Sc. 3. L. 75.

16
What question can be here? Your own true heart
Must needs advise you of the only part:
That may be claim'd again which was but lent,
And should be yielded with no discontent,
Nor surely can we find herein a wrong,
That it was left us to enjoy it long.
RICHARD CHENEVIX TRENCH—*The Lent Jewels.*

17
Who goeth a borrowing
Goeth a sorrowing.
Few lend (but fools)
Their working tools.
TUSSER—*Five Hundred Points of Good Husbandry. September's Abstract.* First lines also in *June's Abstract.*

BOSTON

18
A Boston man is the east wind made flesh.
THOMAS APPLETON.

19
The sea returning day by day
Restores the world-wide mart.
So let each dweller on the Bay
Fold Boston in his heart
Till these echoes be choked with snows
Or over the town blue ocean flows.
EMERSON—*Boston.* St. 20.

20
One day through the primeval wood
A calf walked home as good calves should;
But made a trail all bent askew,
A crooked trail as all calves do.
* * * * *
And men two centuries and a half
Trod in the footsteps of that calf.
SAM WALTER FOSS—*The Calf-Path.*

21
A hundred thousand men were led
By one calf near three centuries dead;
They followed still his crooked way
And lost a hundred years a day;
For thus such reverence is lent
To well-established precedent.
SAM WALTER FOSS—*The Calf-Path.*

22
Boston State-house is the hub of the solar system. You couldn't pry that out of a Boston man if you had the tire of all creation straightened out for a crow-bar.
HOLMES—*Autocrat of the Breakfast Table.* VI.
(See also ZINCKLE)

23
A solid man of Boston;
A comfortable man with dividends,
And the first salmon and the first green peas.
LONGFELLOW—*New England Tragedies. John Endicott.* Act IV.

1
Solid men of Boston, banish long potations!
Solid men of Boston, make no long orations!
CHARLES MORRIS—*Pitt and Dundas's Return to London from Wimbledon.* American Song. From *Lyra Urbanica.*

2
Solid men of Boston, make no long orations;
Solid men of Boston, drink no long potations;
Solid men of Boston, go to bed at sundown;
Never lose your way like the loggerheads of London.
Billy Pitt and the Farmer. Printed in "*Asylum for Fugitive Pieces*" (1786), without author's name.

3
Massachusetts has been the wheel within New England, and Boston the wheel within Massachusetts. Boston therefore is often called the "hub of the world," since it has been the source and fountain of the ideas that have reared and made America.
REV. F. B. ZINCKLE—*Last Winter in the United States.* (1868)
(See also HOLMES)

BOYHOOD (See CHILDHOOD, YOUTH)

BRAVERY (See also COURAGE, VALOR)

4
Zwar der Tapfere nennt sich Herr der Länder
Durch sein Eisen, durch sein Blut.
The brave man, indeed, calls himself lord of the land, through his iron, through his blood.
ARNDT—*Lehre an den Menschen.* 5.

5
Hoch klingt das Lied vom braven Mann,
Wie Orgelton und Glockenklang;
Wer hohes Muths sich rühmen kann
Den lohnt nicht Gold, den lohnt Gesang.
Song of the brave, how thrills thy tone
As when the Organ's music rolls;
No gold rewards, but song alone,
The deeds of great and noble souls.
BÜRGER—*Lied von Braven Mann.*

6
Brave men were living before Agamemnon.
BYRON—*Don Juan.* Canto I. St. 5.
(See also HORACE)

7
The truly brave,
When they behold the brave oppressed with odds,
Are touched with a desire to shield and save:—
A mixture of wild beasts and demi-gods
Are they—now furious as the sweeping wave,
Now moved with pity; even as sometimes nods
The rugged tree unto the summer wind,
Compassion breathes along the savage mind.
BYRON—*Don Juan.* Canto VIII. St. 106.

8
Fortis vero, dolorem summum malum judicans; aut temperans, voluptatem summum bonum statuens, esse certe nullo modo potest.
No man can be brave who thinks pain the greatest evil; nor temperate, who considers pleasure the highest good.
CICERO—*De Officiis.* I. 2.

9
How sleep the brave, who sink to rest,
By all their country's wishes blest!
COLLINS—*Ode written in* 1746.
Authorship disputed. Found in the *Oratorio, Alfred the Great,* altered from *Alfred, a Masque,* presented Aug. 1, 1740. Written by THOMPSON and MALLET.

10
Les hommes valeureux le sont au premier coup.
Brave men are brave from the very first.
CORNEILLE—*Le Cid.* II. 3.
(See also HORACE)

11
Toll for the brave!
The brave that are no more.
COWPER—*On the Loss of the Royal George.*

12
The brave man seeks not popular applause,
Nor, overpower'd with arms, deserts his cause;
Unsham'd, though foil'd, he does the best he can,
Force is of brutes, but honor is of man.
DRYDEN—*Palamon and Arcite.* Bk. III. L. 2,015.

13
The god-like hero sate
On his imperial throne:
His valiant peers were placed around,
Their brows with roses and with myrtles bound
(So should desert in arms be crowned).
The lovely Thais. by his side,
Sate like a blooming Eastern bride
In flower of youth and beauty's pride.
Happy, happy, happy pair!
None but the brave,
None but the brave,
None but the brave deserve the fair.
DRYDEN—*Alexander's Feast.* St. 1.
(See also OVID; also BURNS and COLLIER under WOOING)

14
Then rush'd to meet the insulting foe:
They took the spear, but left the shield.
PHILIP FRENEAU—*To the Memory of the Brave Americans who fell at Eutaw Springs.*
(See also SCOTT—*Marmion.* Introd. to Canto III)

15
The brave
Love mercy, and delight to save.
GAY—*Fable. The Lion, Tiger and Traveller.* L. 33.

16
Without a sign his sword the brave man draws,
And asks no omen but his country's cause.
HOMER—*Iliad.* Bk. XII. L. 283. POPE'S trans.

17
O friends, be men; so act that none may feel
Ashamed to meet the eyes of other men.
Think each one of his children and his wife,
His home, his parents, living yet or dead.
For them, the absent ones, I supplicate,
And bid you rally here, and scorn to fly.
HOMER—*Iliad.* Bk. XV. L. 843. BRYANT'S trans.

18
Ardentem frigidus Ætnam insiluit.
In cold blood he leapt into burning Etna.
HORACE—*Ars Poetica.*

1
Vixere fortes ante Agamemnona
Multi; sed omnes illacrimabiles
Urguentur ignotique longa
Nocte, carent quia vate sacro.

Many brave men lived before Agamemnon; but, all unwept and unknown, are lost in the distant night, since they are without a divine poet (to chronicle their deeds).

HORACE—*Odes*. Bk. IV, IX. 25.
(See also BYRON)

2
True bravery is shown by performing without witness what one might be capable of doing before all the world.

LA ROCHEFOUCAULD. *Maxims*. 216.

3
There's a brave fellow! There's a man of pluck!
A man who's not afraid to say his say,
Though a whole town's against him.

LONGFELLOW—*Christus*. Pt. III. *John Endicott*. Act II. Sc. 2.

4
How well Horatius kept the bridge
In the brave days of old.

MACAULAY—*Lays of Ancient Rome. Horatius*. 70.

5
Rebus in angustis facile est contemnere vitam;
Fortiter ille facit qui miser esse potest.

In adversity it is easy to despise life; he is truly brave who can endure a wretched life.

MARTIAL—*Epigrams*. XI. 56. 15.

6
'Tis more brave
To live, than to die.

OWEN MEREDITH (*Lord Lytton*)—*Lucile*. Pt. II. Canto VI. St. 11.

7
Audentem Forsque Venusque juvant.
Fortune and love favour the brave.

OVID—*Ars Amatoria*. Bk. I. 608.
(See also DRYDEN, SCHILLER, TERENCE, VERGIL)

8
Omne solum forti patria est.
The brave find a home in every land.

OVID—*Fasti*. I. 493.

9
Audentes deus ipse juvat.
God himself favors the brave.

OVID—*Metamorphoses*. X. 586.

10
Who combats bravely is not therefore brave:
He dreads a death-bed like the meanest slave.

POPE—*Moral Essays*. Epistle I. L. 115.

11
Dem Muthigen hilft Gott.
God helps the brave.

SCHILLER—*Wilhelm Tell*. I. 2. 132.
(See also OVID)

12
Come one, come all! this rock shall fly
From its firm base as soon as I.

SCOTT—*Lady of the Lake* Canto V. St. 10.

13
He did look far
Into the service of the time, and was
Discipled of the bravest; he lasted long;
But on us both did haggish age steal on
And wore us out of act.

All's Well That Ends Well. Act I. Sc. 2. L. 26.

14
What's brave, what's noble,
Let's do it after the high Roman fashion,
And make death proud to take us.

Antony and Cleopatra. Act IV. Sc. 15. L. 86.

15
Fortes et strenuos etiam contra fortunam insistere, timidos et ignoros ad desperationem formidine properare.

The brave and bold persist even against fortune; the timid and cowardly rush to despair through fear alone.

TACITUS—*Annales*. II. 46.

16
Fortes fortuna adjuvat.
Fortune favors the brave.

TERENCE—*Phormio*. I. 4. 26. Quoted as a proverb.
(See also OVID)

17
Bravery never goes out of fashion.

THACKERAY—*Four Georges. George Second*.

18
Audentes fortuna juvat.
Fortune favours the daring.

VERGIL—*Æneid*. X. 284 and 458. Same phrase or idea found in CICERO—*De Finibus*. III. 4. and *Tusc*. II. 4. CLAUDIANUS—*Ad Probin*. XLIII. 9. ENNIUS—*Annales*. V. 262. LIVY—Bk. IV. 37; Bk. VII. 29; Bk. XXXIV. 37. MENANDER—In STOBÆUS *Flor*. VII. P. 206. Ed. 1709. OVID—*Metamorphoses*. X. 11. 27. PLINY THE YOUNGER—*Epistles*. VI. 16. TACITUS—*Annales*. IV. 17.
(See also OVID)

BRIBERY

19
And ye sall walk in silk attire,
And siller hae to spare,
Gin ye'll consent to be his bride,
Nor think o' Donald mair.

SUSANNA BLAMIRE—*The Siller Crown*.

20
'Tis pleasant purchasing our fellow-creatures;
And all are to be sold, if you consider
Their passions, and are dext'rous; some by features
Are brought up, others by a warlike leader;
Some by a place—as tend their years or natures;
The most by ready cash—but all have prices,
From crowns to kicks, according to their vices.

BYRON—*Don Juan*. Canto V. St. 27.
(See also WALPOLE)

21
Flowery oratory he [Walpole] despised. He ascribed to the interested views of themselves or their relatives the declarations of pretended patriots, of whom he said, "All those men have their price."

COXE—*Memoirs of Walpole*. Vol. IV. P. 369.
(See also BYRON, WALPOLE)

22
A hoarseness caused by swallowing gold and silver.

DEMOSTHENES, bribed not to speak against HARPALUS, he pretended to have lost his voice. PLUTARCH quotes the accusation as above. Also elsewhere refers to it as the "silver quinsey."

1
Too poor for a bribe, and too proud to importune,
He had not the method of making a fortune.
GRAY—*On His Own Character.*

2
But here more slow, where all are slaves to gold,
Where looks are merchandise, and smiles are sold.
SAMUEL JOHNSON—*London.* L. 177.

3
Our supple tribes repress their patriot throats,
And ask no questions but the price of votes.
SAMUEL JOHNSON—*Vanity of Human Wishes.* L. 95.

4
Alas! the small discredit of a bribe
Scarce hurts the lawyer, but undoes the scribe.
POPE—*Epilogue to Satire.* Dialogue II. L. 46.

5
Judges and senates have been bought for gold;
Esteem and love were never to be sold.
POPE—*Essay on Man.* Ep. IV. L. 187.

6
Auro pulsa fides, auro venalia jura,
Aurum lex sequitur, mox sine lege pudor.
By gold all good faith has been banished; by gold our rights are abused; the law itself is influenced by gold, and soon there will be an end of every modest restraint.
PROPERTIUS—*Elegiæ.* III. 13. 48.

7
No mortal thing can bear so high a price,
But that with mortal thing it may be bought.
SIR WALTER RALEIGH—*Love the Only Price of Love.*

8
'Tis gold
Which buys admittance; oft it doth; yea, and makes
Diana's rangers false themselves, yield up
Their deer to the stand o' the stealer: and 'tis gold
Which makes the true man kill'd and saves the thief;
Nay, sometimes hangs both thief and true man.
Cymbeline. Act II. Sc. 3. L. 72.

9
There is gold for you.
Sell me your good report.
Cymbeline. Act II. Sc. 3. L. 87.

10
What, shall one of us,
That struck the foremost man of all this world
But for supporting robbers, shall we now
Contaminate our fingers with base bribes?
Julius Cæsar. Act IV. Sc. 3. L. 22.

11
There is thy gold, worse poison to men's souls,
Doing more murders in this loathsome world,
Than these poor compounds that thou mayst not sell.
I sell thee poison, thou hast sold me none.
Romeo and Juliet. Act V. Sc. 1. L. 80.

12
Every man has his price.
SIR ROBERT WALPOLE—*Speech.* Nov. or Dec., 1734, according to A. F. ROBBINS, in *Gentleman's Mag.* No. IV, Pp. 589–92. 641–4. HORACE WALPOLE asserts it was attributed to Walpole by his enemies. See Letter, Aug. 26, 1785. Article in *Notes and Queries,* May 11, 1907. Pp. 367–8, asserts he said: "I know the price of every man in this house except three." See article in London *Times* March 15, 1907, Review of W. H. Craig's Life of Chesterfield. Phrase in *The Bee,* Vol. VII. P. 97, attributed to SIR W——M W——M (WILLIAM WYNDHAM)

(See also BYRON, COXE)

13
Few men have virtue to withstand the highest bidder.
GEORGE WASHINGTON—*Moral Maxims. Virtue and Vice. The Trial of Virtue.*

BRONX RIVER

14
Yet I will look upon thy face again,
My own romantic Bronx, and it will be
A face more pleasant than the face of men.
Thy waves are old companions, I shall see
A well remembered form in each old tree
And hear a voice long loved in thy wild minstrelsy.
JOSEPH RODMAN DRAKE—*Bronx.*

BROOKS

15
A noise like of a hidden brook
In the leafy month of June,
That to the sleeping woods all night
Singeth a quiet tune.
COLERIDGE—*The Ancient Mariner.* Pt. V. St. 18.

16
The streams, rejoiced that winter's work is done,
Talk of to-morrow's cowslips as they run.
EBENEZER ELLIOTT—*The Village Patriarch. Love and Other Poems. Spring.*

17
From Helicon's harmonious springs
A thousand rills their mazy progress take.
GRAY—*The Progress of Poesy.* I. 1. L. 3.

18
Sweet are the little brooks that run
O'er pebbles glancing in the sun,
Singing in soothing tones.
HOOD—*Town and Country.* St. 9.

19
Thou hastenest down between the hills to meet me at the road,
The secret scarcely lisping of thy beautiful abode
Among the pines and mosses of yonder shadowy height,
Where thou dost sparkle into song, and fill the woods with light.
LUCY LARCOM—*Friend Brook.* St. 1.

20
See, how the stream has overflowed
Its banks, and o'er the meadow road
Is spreading far and wide!
LONGFELLOW—*Christus. The Golden Legend.* Pt. III. Sc. 7. *The Nativity.*

21
The music of the brook silenced all conversation.
LONGFELLOW—*Kavanagh.* Ch. XXI.

22
I wandered by the brook-side,
I wandered by the mill;
I could not hear the brook flow.
The noisy wheel was still.
MONCKTON MILNES (Lord Houghton)—*The Brookside.*

1
Gently running made sweet music with the enameled stones and seemed to give a gentle kiss to every sedge he overtook in his watery pilgrimage.
Seven Champions. Pt. III. Ch. XII.

2
He makes sweet music with the enameled stones,
Giving a gentle kiss to every sedge,
He overtaketh in his pilgrimage.
Two Gentlemen of Verona. Act II. Sc. 7.

3
I chatter, chatter, as I flow
To join the brimming river,
For men may come and men may go,
But I go on forever.
TENNYSON—*The Brook.*

4
Brook! whose society the poet seeks,
Intent his wasted spirits to renew;
And whom the curious painter doth pursue
Through rocky passes, among flowery creeks,
And tracks thee dancing down thy water-breaks.
WORDSWORTH—*Brook! Whose Society the Poet Seeks.*

BUILDING (See ARCHITECTURE, CARPENTRY, MASONS)

BURDENS (See CARE)

BUSINESS

5
Nation of shopkeepers.
Attributed to SAMUEL ADAMS—*Oration,* said to have been delivered at Philadelphia State House, Aug. 1, 1776. Printed in Phil., reprinted for E. JOHNSON, 4 Ludgate Hill, London. (1776) According to W. V. WELLS—*Life of Adams:* "No such American edition has ever been seen, but at least four copies are known of the London issue. A German translation of this oration was printed in 1778, perhaps at Berne; the place of publication is not given."
(See also NAPOLEON under ENGLAND)

6
Talk of nothing but business, and dispatch that business quickly.
On a placard placed by ALDUS on the door of his printing office. See DIBDIN—*Introduction.* Vol. I. P. 436.

7
Business tomorrow.
Founded on the words of ARCHIAS OF THEBES.

8
Come home to men's business and bosoms.
BACON—*Essays.* Dedication of edition 9. To the Duke of Buckingham. Also in Ed. 1668.

9
The soul's Rialto hath its merchandise,
I barter curl for curl upon that mart.
E. B. BROWNING—*Sonnets from the Portuguese.* XIX.

10
Business dispatched is business well done, but business hurried is business ill done.
BULWER-LYTTON—*Caxtoniana.* Essay XXVI. *Readers and Writer.*

11
When we speak of the commerce with our colonies, fiction lags after truth, invention is unfruitful, and imagination cold and barren.
BURKE—*Speech on the Conciliation of America.*

12
In matters of commerce the fault of the Dutch
Is offering too little and asking too much.
The French are with equal advantage content—
So we clap on Dutch bottoms just 20 per cent.
GEORGE CANNING'S *dispatch to* SIR CHARLES BAGOT, Jan. 31, 1826. See *Notes and Queries,* Oct. 4, 1902. P. 270. Claimed for MARVELL in London *Morning Post,* May 25, 1904.
In making of treaties the fault of the Dutch,
Is giving too little and asking too much.
Given as a verbatim copy of the dispatch.

13
Keep thy shop, and thy shop will keep thee. Light gains make heavy purses. 'Tis good to be merry and wise.
GEORGE CHAPMAN—*Eastward Ho.* Act I. Sc. 1. (Written by CHAPMAN, JONSON and MARSTON.)

14
Despatch is the soul of business.
CHESTERFIELD—*Letters.* Feb. 5, 1750.

15
You foolish man, you don't even know your own foolish business.
CHESTERFIELD to John Anstis, the Garter King of Arms. Attributed to him in JESSE'S *Memories of the Courts of the Stuarts—Nassau and Hanover.*
(See also MAULE, WESTBURY)

16
This business will never hold water.
COLLEY CIBBER—*She Wou'd and She Wou'd Not.* Act IV.

17
They (corporations) cannot commit treason, nor be outlawed, nor excommunicated, for they have no souls.
COKE—*Reports.* Vol. V. *The Case of Sutton's Hospital.* CAMPBELL—*Lives of the Lords Chancellors.*
(See also HAZLITT, HONE, THURLOW)

18
A business with an income at its heels.
COWPER—*Retirement.* L. 614.

19
Swear, fool, or starve; for the dilemma's even;
A tradesman thou! and hope to go to heaven?
DRYDEN—*Persius.* Sat. V. L. 204.

20
The greatest meliorator of the world is selfish, huckstering trade.
EMERSON—*Work and Days.*

21
In every age and clime we see,
Two of a trade can ne'er agree.
GAY—*Fables. Rat-Catcher and Cats.* L. 43.
(See also HESIOD)

22
A manufacturing district * * * sends out, as it were, suckers into all its neighborhood.
HALLAM—*View of the State of Europe during the Middle Ages.* Ch. IX.

1
Lord Stafford mines for coal and salt,
The Duke of Norfolk deals in malt,
The Douglas in red herrings.
FITZ-GREENE HALLECK—*Alnwick Castle.*

2
They [corporations] feel neither shame, remorse, gratitude, nor goodwill.
HAZLITT—*Table Talks, Essay* XXVII.
(See also COKE)

3
Those that are above business.
MATTHEW HENRY—*Commentaries. Matthew XX.*

4
Ill ware is never cheap.
HERBERT—*Jacula Prudentum.*

5
Pleasing ware is half sold.
HERBERT—*Jacula Prudentum.*

6
The potter is at enmity with the potter.
HESIOD—*Works and Days.*
(See also GAY)

7
Mr. Howel Walsh, in a corporation case tried at the Tralee assizes, observed that a corporation cannot blush. It was a body, it was true; had certainly a head—a new one every year—an annual acquisition of intelligence in every new lord mayor. Arms he supposed it had, and very long ones too, for it could reach at anything. Legs, of course, when it made such long strides. A throat to swallow the rights of the community, and a stomach to digest them. But who ever yet discovered, in the anatomy of any corporation, either bowels or a heart?
HONE. In his *Table-Book.*
(See also COKE)

8
Quod medicorum est
Promittunt medici, tractant fabrilia fabri.
Physicians attend to the business of physicians, and workmen handle the tools of workmen.
HORACE—*Epistles.* II. 1. 115.

9
Sed tamen amoto quæramus seria ludo.
Setting raillery aside, let us attend to serious matters.
HORACE—*Satires.* I. 1. 27.

10
Aliena negotia curo,
Excussus propriis.
I attend to the business of other people, having lost my own.
HORACE—*Satires.* II. 3. 19.

11
Whose merchants are princes.
Isaiah. XXIII. 8.

12
Trade's proud empire hastes to swift decay.
SAMUEL JOHNSON—*Line added to Goldsmith's Deserted Village.*

13
The sign brings customers.
LA FONTAINE—*Fables. The Fortune Tellers.* Bk. VII. Fable 15.

14
Business today consists in persuading crowds.
GERALD STANLEY LEE—*Crowds.* Bk. II. Ch. V.

15
It is never the machines that are dead.
It is only the mechanically-minded men that are dead.
GERALD STANLEY LEE — *Crowds.* Pt. II. Ch. V.

16
Machinery is the subconscious mind of the world.
GERALD STANLEY LEE — *Crowds.* Pt. II. Ch. VIII.

17
A man's success in business today turns upon his power of getting people to believe he has something that they want.
GERALD STANLEY LEE — *Crowds.* Bk. II. Ch. IX.

18
Consilia callida et audacia prima specie læta, tractatu dura, eventu tristia sunt.
Hasty and adventurous schemes are at first view flattering, in execution difficult, and in the issue disastrous.
LIVY—*Annales.* XXXV. 32.

19
There is no better ballast for keeping the mind steady on its keel, and saving it from all risk of *crankiness*, than business.
LOWELL—*Among My Books. New England Two Centuries Ago.*

20
Everybody's business is nobody's business.
MACAULAY—*Essay on Hallam's Constit. Hist.* Quoted as an old maxim.
(See also WALTON)

21
As touching corporations, that they were invisible, immortal and that they had no soul, therefor no supœna lieth against them, because they have no conscience or soul.
SIR ROGER MANWOOD, Chief Baron of the Exchequer. (1592) See *Dictionary of National Biography.*
(See also COKE)

22
You silly old fool, you don't even know the alphabet of your own silly old business.
Attributed to JUDGE MAULE.
(See also CHESTERFIELD)

23
A blind bargain.
Merrie Tales of the Madmen of Gottam. (1630) No. 13.

24
Curse on the man who business first designed,
And by't enthralled a freeborn lover's mind!
OLDHAM—*Complaining of Absence.* 11.

25
Negotii sibi qui volet vim parare,
Navem et mulierem, hæc duo comparato.
Nam nullæ magis res duæ plus negotii
Habent, forte si occeperis exornare.
Neque unquam satis hæ duæ res ornantur,
Neque eis ulla ornandi satis satietas est.
Who wishes to give himself an abundance of business let him equip these two things, a ship and a woman. For no two things involve more business, if you have begun to fit them out. Nor are these two things ever sufficiently adorned, nor is any excess of adornment enough for them.
PLAUTUS—*Pœnulus.* I. 2. 1.

1
Non enim potest quæstus consistere, si eum sumptus superat.

There can be no profit, if the outlay exceeds it.

PLAUTUS—*Pœnulus*. I. 2. 74.

2
Nam mala emptio semper ingrata est, eo naxime, quod exprobrare stultitiam domino idetur.

For a dear bargain is always annoying, particularly on this account, that it is a reflection on the judgment of the buyer.

PLINY the Younger—*Epistles*. I. 24.

3
The merchant, to secure his treasure,
Conveys it in a borrow'd name.

PRIOR—*Ode. The Merchant, to Secure his Treasure.*

4
We demand that big business give people a square deal; in return we must insist that when any one engaged in big business honestly endeavors to do right, he shall himself be given a square deal.

ROOSEVELT. Written when Mr. Taft's administration brought suit to dissolve the Steel Trust.

5
To business that we love we rise betime,
And go to 't with delight.

Antony and Cleopatra. Act IV. Sc. 4. L. 20.

6
I'll give thrice so much land
To any well-deserving friend;
But in the way of bargain, mark ye me,
I'll cavil on the ninth part of a hair.

Henry IV. Pt. I. Act III. Sc. 1. L. 137.

7
Bad is the trade that must play fool to sorrow.

King Lear. Act IV. Sc. 1. L. 40.

8
To things of sale a seller's praise belongs.

Love's Labour's Lost. Act IV. Sc. 3. L. 240.

9
Losses,
That have of late so huddled on his back,
Enow to press a royal merchant down
And pluck commiseration of his state
From brassy bosoms and rough hearts of flint.

Merchant of Venice. Act IV. Sc. 1. L. 27.

10
It is a man's office, but not yours.

Much Ado about Nothing. Act IV. Sc. 1. L. 268.

11
A merchant of great traffic through the world.

Taming of the Shrew. Act I. Sc. 1. L. 12.

12
Traffic's thy god; and thy god confound thee!

Timon of Athens. Act I. Sc. 1. L. 246.

13
There's two words to that bargain.

SWIFT—*Polite Conversation*. Dialogue III.

14
Omnia inconsulti impetus cœpta, initiis valida, spatio languescunt.

All inconsiderate enterprises are impetuous at first, but soon languish.

TACITUS—*Annales*. III. 58.

15
Par negotiis neque supra.

Neither above nor below his business.

TACITUS—*Annales*. VI. 39.

16
Omnibus nobis ut res dant sese, ita magni atque humiles sumus.

We all, according as our business prospers or fails, are elated or cast down.

TERENCE—*Hecyra*. III. 2. 20.

17
Cujuslibet tu fidem in pecunia perspiceres,
Verere ei verba credere?

Do you fear to trust the word of a man, whose honesty you have seen in business?

TERENCE—*Phormio*. I. 2. 10.

18
Did you ever expect a corporation to have a conscience, when it has no soul to be damned, and no body to be kicked?

LORD THURLOW. See ALISON—*History of Europe*, and POYNDER—*Literary Extracts. Corporations*. WILBERFORCE—*Life of Thurlow*. Vol. II. Appendix.

(See also COKE)

19
Keep your shop, and your shop will keep you.

SIR WILLIAM TURNER.
STEELE in *Spectator* No. 509.

20
That which is everybody's business, is nobody's business.

IZAAK WALTON—*Compleat Angler*. Pt. I. Ch. II. Quoted.

21
A silly old man who did not understand even his silly old trade.

LORD WESTBURY, of a witness from the Heralds' College.

(See also CHESTERFIELD)

22
The way to stop financial "joy-riding" is to arrest the chauffeur, not the automobile.

WOODROW WILSON. See RICHARD LINTHICUM—*Wit and Wisdom of Woodrow Wilson.*

BUTCHERING

23
Whoe'er has gone thro' London street,
Has seen a butcher gazing at his meat,
And how he keeps
Gloating upon a sheep's
Or bullock's personals, as if his own;
How he admires his halves
And quarters—and his calves,
As if in truth upon his own legs grown.

HOOD—*A Butcher*.

24
Who finds the heifer dead and bleeding fresh
And sees fast by a butcher with an axe,
But will suspect 'twas he that made the slaughter?

Henry VI. Pt. II. Act III. Sc. 2. L. 188.

25
Why, that's spoken like an honest drovier; so they sell bullocks.

Much Ado About Nothing. Act II. Sc. 1. L. 201.

26
The butcher in his killing clothes.

WALT WHITMAN—*The Workingmen*. Pt. VI. St. 32.

BUTTERCUP

Ranunculus

1
The royal kingcup bold
Dares not don his coat of gold.
EDWIN ARNOLD—*Almond Blossoms.*

2
He likes the poor things of the world the best,
I would not, therefore, if I could be rich.
It pleases him to stoop for buttercups.
E. B. BROWNING—*Aurora Leigh.* Bk. IV.

3
All will be gay when noontide wakes anew
The buttercups, the little children's dower.
ROBERT BROWNING—*Home Thoughts. From Abroad.*

4
The buttercups, bright-eyed and bold,
Held up their chalices of gold
To catch the sunshine and the dew.
JULIA C. R. DORR—*Centennial Poem.* L. 165.

5
Fair is the kingcup that in meadow blows,
Fair is the daisy that beside her grows.
GAY—*Shepherd's Week. Monday.* L. 43.

6
Against her ankles as she trod
The lucky buttercups did nod.
JEAN INGELOW—*Reflections.*

7
And O the buttercups! that field
O' the cloth of gold, where pennons swam—
Where France set up his lilied shield,
His oriflamb,
And Henry's lion-standard rolled:
What was it to their matchless sheen,
Their million million drops of gold
Among the green!
JEAN INGELOW—*The Letter L Present.* St. 3.

8
The buttercups across the field
Made sunshine rifts of splendor.
D. M. MULOCK—*A Silly Song.*

9
When buttercups are blossoming,
The poets sang, 'tis best to wed:
So all for love we paired in Spring—
Blanche and I—ere youth had sped.
E. C. STEDMAN—*Bohemia.*

BUTTERFLY

10
I'd be a butterfly, born in a bower,
Where roses and lilies and violets meet.
THOMAS HAYNES BAYLY—*I'd be a Butterfly.*

11
Gray sail against the sky,
Gray butterfly!
Have you a dream for going,
Or are you only the blind wind's blowing?
DANA BURNET—*A Sail at Twilight.*

12
With the rose the butterfly's deep in love,
A thousand times hovering round;
But round himself, all tender like gold,
The sun's sweet ray is hovering found.
HEINE—*Book of Songs. New Spring.* No. 7.

13
Far out at sea,—the sun was high,
While veer'd the wind and flapped the sail,
We saw a snow-white butterfly
Dancing before the fitful gale,
Far out at sea.
RICHARD HENGIST HORNE—*Genius.*

14
The gold-barr'd butterflies to and fro
And over the waterside wander'd and wove
As heedless and idle as clouds that rove
And drift by the peaks of perpetual snow.
JOAQUIN MILLER—*Songs of the Sun-Lands. Isles of the Amazons.* Pt. III. St. 41.

15
And many an ante-natal tomb
Where butterflies dream of the life to come.
SHELLEY—*Sensitive Plant.*

16
Much converse do I find in thee,
Historian of my infancy!
Float near me; do not yet depart!
Dead times revive in thee:
Thou bring'st, gay creature as thou art!
A solemn image to my heart.
WORDSWORTH—*To a Butterfly.*

C

CALMNESS

17
O haste to shed the sovereign balm—
My shattered nerves new string:
And for my guest serenely calm,
The nymph Indifference bring.
FRANCES MCCARTNEY FULKE-GREVILLE—*Prayer for Indifference.*

18
How calm, how beautiful comes on
The stilly hour, when storms are gone!
When warring winds have died away,
And clouds, beneath the glancing ray,
Melt off, and leave the land and sea
Sleeping in bright tranquillity!
MOORE—*Lalla Rookh. Fire Worshippers.* St. 52.

19
'Tis Noon;—a calm, unbroken sleep
Is on the blue waves of the deep;
A soft haze, like a fairy dream,
Is floating over wood and stream;
And many a broad magnolia flower,
Within its shadowy woodland bower,
Is gleaming like a lovely star.
GEO. D. PRENTICE—*To an Absent Wife.* St. 2

20
The noonday quiet holds the hill.
TENNYSON—*Œnone.* L. 2.

21
Pure was the temperate Air, an even Calm
Perpetual reign'd, save what the Zephyrs bland
Breath'd o'er the blue expanse.
THOMSON—*Seasons. Spring.* L. 323.

CALUMNY

1
Calomniez, calomniez; il en reste toujours quelque chose.

Calumniate, calumniate; there will always be something which sticks.

Beaumarchais—*Barbier de Séville.* Act III. 13.

2
Nihil est autem tam volucre, quam maledictum; nihil facilius emittitur; nihil citius excipitur, latius dissipatur.

Nothing is so swift as calumny; nothing is more easily uttered; nothing more readily received; nothing more widely dispersed.

Cicero—*Oratio Pro Cnæo Plancio.* XXIII.

3
Calumny is only the noise of madmen.

Diogenes.

4
A nickname a man may chance to wear out; but a system of calumny, pursued by a faction, may descend even to posterity. This principle has taken full effect on this state favorite.

Isaac D'Israeli—*Amenities of Literature. The First Jesuits in England.*

5
Dens Theonina.

Like Theon (i.e. a calumniating disposition).

Horace—*Epistles.* Bk. I. 18. 82.

6
There are calumnies against which even innocence loses courage.

Napoleon I.

7
Virtue itself 'scapes not calumnious strokes.

Hamlet. Act I. Sc. 3. L. 38.

8
Be thou as chaste as ice, as pure as snow, thou shalt not escape calumny.

Hamlet. Act II. Sc. 1. L. 138.

9
No might nor greatness in mortality
Can censure 'scape; back-wounding calumny
The whitest virtue strikes. What king so strong,
Can tie the gall up in the slanderous tongue?

Measure for Measure. Act III. Sc. 2. L. 146.

10
Calumny will sear
Virtue itself;—these shrugs, these hums, and ha's.

Winter's Tale. Act II. Sc. 1. L. 73.

CAM (River)

11
Where stray ye, Muses! in what lawn or grove,
* * * * * *
In those fair fields where sacred Isis glides,
Or else where Cam his winding vales divides?

Pope—*Summer.* L. 23.

CAMOMILE

Anthemis nobilis

12
For though the camomile, the more it is trodden on the faster it grows.

Henry IV. Pt. I. Act II. Sc. 4. L. 441.

CANARY

13
Thou should'st be carolling thy Maker's praise,
Poor bird! now fetter'd, and here set to draw,
With graceless toil of beak and added claw,
The meagre food that scarce thy want allays!
And this—to gratify the gloating gaze
Of fools, who value Nature not a straw,
But know to prize the infraction of her law
And hard perversion of her creatures' ways!
Thee the wild woods await, in leaves attired,
Where notes of liquid utterance should engage
Thy bill, that now with pain scant forage earns.

Julian Fane—*Poems. Second Edition, with Additional Poems. To a Canary Bird.*

14
Sing away, ay, sing away,
Merry little bird
Always gayest of the gay,
Though a woodland roundelay
You ne'er sung nor heard;
Though your life from youth to age
Passes in a narrow cage.

D. M. Mulock—*The Canary in his Cage.*

15
Bird of the amber beak,
Bird of the golden wing!
Thy dower is thy carolling;
Thou hast not far to seek
Thy bread, nor needest wine
To make thy utterance divine;
Thou art canopied and clothed
And unto Song betrothed.

E. C. Stedman—*The Songster.* St. 2.

CARCASSONNE

16
How old I am! I'm eighty years!
I've worked both hard and long,
Yet patient as my life has been,
One dearest sight I have not seen—
It almost seems a wrong;
A dream I had when life was new,
Alas our dreams! they come not true;
I thought to see fair Carcassonne,
That lovely city—Carcassonne!

Gustave Nadaud—*Carcassonne.*

CARDINAL-FLOWER

Lobelia Cardinalis

17
Whence is yonder flower so strangely bright?
Would the sunset's last reflected shine
Flame so red from that dead flush of light?
Dark with passion is its lifted line,
Hot, alive, amid the falling night.

Dora Read Goodale—*Cardinal Flower.*

CARDS (See also Gambling)

18
Paciencia y barajar.

Patience and shuffle the cards.

Cervantes—*Don Quixote.* II. 23.

19
With spots quadrangular of diamond form,
Ensanguined hearts, clubs typical of strife,
And spades, the emblems of untimely graves.

Cowper—*Task.* Bk. IV. *The Winter Evening.* L. 217.

20
He's a sure card.

Dryden—*The Spanish Friar.* Act II. Sc. 2.

1
Cards were at first for benefits designed,
Sent to amuse, not to enslave the mind.
GARRICK—*Epilogue to Ed. Moore's Gamester.*

2
The pictures placed for ornament and use,
The twelve good rules, the royal game of goose.
GOLDSMITH—*Deserted Village.* L. 231.

3
A clear fire, a clean hearth, and the rigour of the game.
LAMB—*Mrs. Battle's Opinions on Whist.*

4
Vous ne jouez donc pas le whist, monsieur? Hélas! quelle triste vieilesse vous vous préparez!
You do not play then at whist, sir! Alas, what a sad old age you are preparing for yourself!
TALLEYRAND.

CARE; CAREFULNESS

5
O insensata cura dei mortali,
Quanto son defettivi sillogismi
Quei che ti fanno in basso batter l'ali!
O mortal cares insensate, what small worth,
In sooth, doth all those syllogisms fill,
Which make you stoop your pinions to the earth!
DANTE—*Paradiso.* XI. 1.

6
For want of a nail the shoe was lost; for want of a shoe the horse was lost; and for want of a horse the rider was lost; being overtaken and slain by the enemy, all for want of care about a horse-shoe nail.
FRANKLIN—*Poor Richard's Almanac.*

7
For the want of a nail the shoe was lost,
For the want of a shoe the horse was lost,
For the want of a horse the rider was lost,
For the want of a rider the battle was lost,
For the want of a battle the kingdom was lost—
And all for the want of a horseshoe nail.
Another version of FRANKLIN.

8
Every man shall bear his own burden.
Galatians. VI. 5.

9
Light burdens, long borne, grow heavy.
HERBERT—*Jacula Prudentum.*

10
Be swift to hear, slow to speak, slow to wrath.
James. I. 19.

11
Care that is entered once into the breast
Will have the whole possession ere it rest.
BEN JONSON—*Tale of a Tub.* Act I. Sc. 4.

12
Borne the burden and heat of the day.
Matthew. XX. 12.

13
And ever, against eating cares,
Lap me in soft Lydian airs.
MILTON—*L'Allegro.* L. 135.

14
Begone, old Care, and I prithee begone from me;
For i' faith, old Care, thee and I shall never agree.
PLAYFORD—*Musical Companion.* Catch 13.

15
Eat not thy heart; which forbids to afflict our souls, and waste them with vexatious cares.
PLUTARCH—*Morals. Of the Training of Children.*

16
Old Care has a mortgage on every estate,
And that's what you pay for the wealth that you get.
J. G. SAXE—*Gifts of the Gods.*

17
For some must watch, while some must sleep:
So runs the world away.
Hamlet. Act III. Sc. 2. L. 284.

18
No, no, he cannot long hold out these pangs;
The incessant care and labour of his mind
Hath wrought the mure, that should confine it in,
So thin that life looks through and will break out.
Henry IV. Pt. II. Act IV. Sc. 4. L. 117.

19
O polished perturbation! golden care!
That keep'st the ports of slumber open wide
To many a watchful night!
Henry IV. Pt. II. Act IV. Sc. 5. L. 23.

20
Care is no cure, but rather a corrosive,
For things that are not to be remedied.
Henry VI. Pt. I. Act III. Sc. 3. L. 3.

21
Things past redress are now with me past care.
Richard II. Act II. Sc. 3. L. 171.

22
Care keeps his watch in every old man's eye,
And where care lodges, sleep will never lie;
But where unbruised youth with unstuff'd brain.
Doth couch his limbs, there golden sleep doth reign.
Romeo and Juliet. Act II. Sc. 3. L. 34.

23
I am sure, care's an enemy to life.
Twelfth Night. Act I. Sc. 3. L. 2.

24
I could lie down like a tired child,
And weep away the life of care
Which I have borne, and yet must bear.
SHELLEY—*Stanzas written in Dejection, near Naples.*

25
Care to our coffin adds a nail, no doubt;
And every Grin, so merry, draws one out.
JOHN WOLCOT—*Expostulatory Odes.* Ode 15.

26
And care, whom not the gayest can outbrave,
Pursues its feeble victim to the grave.
HENRY KIRKE WHITE—*Childhood.* Pt. II. L. 17.

CARPENTRY

27
Are the tools without, which the carpenter puts forth his hands to, or are they and all the carpentry within himself; and would he not smile at the notion that chest or house is more than he?
CYRUS A. BARTOL—*The Rising Faith. Personality.*

1
Sure if they cannot cut, it may be said
His saws are toothless, and his hatchets lead.
POPE—*Epilogue to Satires.* Dialogue II. L. 151.

2
He talks of wood: it is some carpenter.
Henry VI. Pt. I. Act V. Sc. 3. L. 90.

3
Speak, what trade art thou?
Why, sir, a carpenter.
Where is thy leather apron and thy rule?
What dost thou with thy best apparel on?
Julius Cæsar. Act I. Sc. 1. L. 5.

4
A carpenter's known by his chips.
SWIFT—*Polite Conversation.* Dialogue II.

5
The carpenter dresses his plank—the tongue of his fore-plane whistles its wild ascending lisp.
WALT WHITMAN—*Leaves of Grass.* Pt. XV. St. 77.

6
The house-builder at work in cities or anywhere,
The preparatory jointing, squaring, sawing, mortising,
The hoist-up of beams, the push of them in their places, laying them regular,
Setting the studs by their tenons in the mortises, according as they were prepared,
The blows of the mallets and hammers.
WALT WHITMAN—*Song of the Broad-Axe.* Pt. III. St. 4.

CASSIA

Cassia

7
While cassias blossom in the zone of calms.
JEAN INGELOW—*Sand Martins.*

CAT

8
A cat may look at a king.
Title of a Pamphlet. (Published 1652)

9
Lauk! what a monstrous tail our cat has got!
HENRY CAREY—*The Dragon of Wantley.* Act II. Sc. 1.

10
Mrs. Crupp had indignantly assured him that there wasn't room to swing a cat there; but as Mr. Dick justly observed to me, sitting down on the foot of the bed, nursing his leg, "You know, Trotwood, I don't want to swing a cat. I never do swing a cat. Therefore what does that signify to *me!*"
DICKENS—*David Copperfield.* Vol. II. Ch. VI.

11
Confound the cats! All cats—alway—
Cats of all colours, black, white, grey;
By night a nuisance and by day—
Confound the cats!
ORLANDO THOS. DOBBIN—*A Dithyramb on Cats.*

12
The Cat in Gloves catches no Mice.
BENJ. FRANKLIN—*Poor Richard's Almanac.*

13
The cat would eat fish, and would not wet her feet.
HEYWOOD—*Proverbs.* Pt. I. Ch. XI.

14
It has been the providence of nature to give this creature nine lives instead of one.
PILPAY—*Fable III.*

CATTLE (see ANIMALS)

CAUSE

15
To all facts there are laws,
The effect has its cause, and I mount to the cause.
OWEN MEREDITH (Lord Lytton)—*Lucile.* Pt. II. Canto III. St. 8.

16
Causa latet: vis est notissima.
The cause is hidden, but the result is known.
OVID—*Metamorphoses.* IV. 287.

17
Ask you what provocation I have had?
The strong antipathy of good to bad.
POPE—*Epilogue to Satires.* Dialogue 2. L. 205.

18
Your cause doth strike my heart.
Cymbeline. Act I. Sc. 6. L. 118.

19
Find out the cause of this effect,
Or rather say, the cause of this defect,
For this effect defective comes by cause.
Hamlet. Act II. Sc. 2. L. 101.

20
God befriend us, as our cause is just!
Henry IV. Pt. I. Act V. Sc. 1. L. 120.

21
Mine's not an idle cause.
Othello. Act I. Sc. 2. L. 95.

22
Felix qui potuit rerum cognoscere causas.
Happy the man who has been able to learn the causes of things.
VERGIL—*Georgics.* II. 490.

CEDAR

Cedrus

23
O'er yon bare knoll the pointed cedar shadows
Drowse on the crisp, gray moss.
LOWELL—*An Indian-Summer Reverie.*

24
Thus yields the cedar to the axe's edge,
Whose arms gave shelter to the princely eagle.
Henry VI. Pt. III. Act V. Sc. 2. L. 11.

25
High on a hill a goodly Cedar grewe,
Of wond'rous length and streight proportion,
That farre abroad her daintie odours threwe;
'Mongst all the daughters of proud Libanon,
Her match in beautie was not anie one.
SPENSER—*Visions of the World's Vanitie.* St. 7.

CELANDINE

Chelidonium

26
Eyes of some men travel far
For the finding of a star;
Up and down the heavens they go,
Men that keep a mighty rout!
I'm as great as they, I trow,
Since the day I found thee out,
Little Flower!—I'll make a stir,
Like a sage astronomer.
WORDSWORTH—*To the Small Celandine.*

1
Long as there's a sun that sets,
  Primroses will have their glory;
Long as there are violets,
  They will have a place in story:
There's a flower that shall be mine,
'Tis the little Celandine.
  WORDSWORTH—*To the Small Celandine.*

2
Pleasures newly found are sweet
When they lie about our feet:
February last, my heart
First at sight of thee was glad;
All unheard of as thou art,
  Thou must needs, I think have had,
Celandine! and long ago,
Praise of which I nothing know.
  WORDSWORTH—*To the Same Flower.*

CEREMONY

3 What infinite heart's ease
Must kings neglect, that private men enjoy?
And what have kings that privates have not too,
Save ceremony, save general ceremony?
  Henry V. Act IV. Sc. 1. L. 253.

4
  What art thou, thou idol ceremony?
What kind of god art thou, that suffer'st more
Of mortal griefs than do thy worshippers?
  Henry V. Act IV. Sc. 1. L. 257.

5
O ceremony, show me but thy worth!
What is thy soul of adoration?
Art thou aught else but place, degree, and form,
Creating awe and fear in other men?
  Henry V. Act IV. Sc. 1. L. 261.

6
When love begins to sicken and decay,
It useth an enforced ceremony,
There are no tricks in plain and simple faith.
  Julius Cæsar. Act IV. Sc. 2. L. 20.

7 To feed were best at home;
From thence the sauce to meat is ceremony;
Meeting were bare without it.
  Macbeth. Act III. Sc. 4. L. 36.

8 Ceremony was but devised at first
To set a gloss on faint deeds, hollow welcomes,
Recanting goodness, sorry ere 'tis shown;
But where there is true friendship, there needs none.
  Timon of Athens. Act I. Sc. 2. L. 15.

CHALLENGE (See also DUELLING)

9
If not, resolve, before we go,
That you and I must pull a crow.
Y' 'ad best (quoth Ralpho), as the Ancients
Say wisely, have a care o' the main chance.
  BUTLER—*Hudibras.* Pt. II. Canto II. L. 499.

10 I never in my life
Did hear a challenge urg'd more modestly,
Unless a brother should a brother dare
To gentle exercise and proof of arms.
  Henry IV. Pt. I. Act V. Sc. 2. L. 52.

11 There I throw my gage,
To prove it on thee to the extremest point
Of mortal breathing.
  Richard II. Act IV. Sc. 1. L. 46.

12
But thou liest in thy throat; that is not the matter I challenge thee for.
  Twelfth Night. Act III. Sc. 4. L. 172.

13
An I thought he had been valiant and so cunning in fence, I'ld have seen him damned ere I'ld have challenged him.
  Twelfth Night. Act III. Sc. 4. L. 311.

CHAMPAC

Michelia Champaca

14
The maid of India, blessed again to hold
In her full lap the Champac's leaves of gold.
  MOORE—*Lalla Rookh. The Veiled Prophet of Khorassan.*

CHANCE

15
How slight a chance may raise or sink a soul!
  BAILEY—*Festus. A Country Town.*

16
Perhaps it may turn out a sang,
Perhaps turn out a sermon.
  BURNS—*Epistle to a Young Friend.*

17
Le hasard c'est peut-être le pseudonyme de Dieu, quand il ne veut pas signer.
  Chance is perhaps the pseudonym of God when He did not want to sign.
  ANATOLE FRANCE—*Le Jardin d'Epicure.* P. 132. Quoted "Le hasard, en definitive, c'est Dieu."

18
I shot an arrow into the air
It fell to earth I knew not where;
For so swiftly it flew, the sight
Could not follow it in its flight.
  LONGFELLOW—*The Arrow and the Song.*

19 Next him high arbiter
Chance governs all.
  MILTON—*Paradise Lost.* Bk. II. L. 909.

20 Or that power
Which erring men call chance.
  MILTON—*Comus.* L. 587.

21
Chance is blind and is the sole author of creation.
  J. X. B. SAINTINE—*Picciola.* Ch. III.

22
Ours is no sapling, chance-sown by the fountain,
  Blooming at Beltane, in winter to fade.
  SCOTT—*Hail to the Chief. Lady of the Lake.* Canto II. Quoted by SENATOR VEST in nominating BLAND in Chicago.

23
Chance will not do the work—Chance sends the breeze;
But if the pilot slumber at the helm,
The very wind that wafts us towards the port
May dash us on the shelves.—The steersman's part is vigilance,
Blow it or rough or smooth.
  SCOTT—*Fortunes of Nigel.* Ch. XXII.

24
I shall show the cinders of my spirits
Through the ashes of my chance.
  Antony and Cleopatra. Act V. Sc. 2. L. 173.

1
Against ill chances men are ever merry;
But heaviness foreruns the good event.
Henry IV. Pt. II. Act IV. Sc. 2. L. 82.

2
But as the unthought-on accident is guilty
To what we wildly do, so we profess
Ourselves to be the slaves of chance, and flies
Of every wind that blows.
Winter's Tale. Act IV. Sc. 4. L. 549.

3
Quam sæpe forte temere eveniunt, quæ non audeas optare!

How often things occur by mere chance, which we dared not even to hope for.

TERENCE—*Phormio*. V. 1. 31.

4
A lucky chance, that oft decides the fate
Of mighty monarchs.
THOMSON—*The Seasons*. *Summer*. L. 1,285.

5
Er spricht Unsinn; für den Vernünftigen Menschen giebt es gar keinen Zufall.

He talks nonsense; to a sensible man there is no such thing as chance.

LUDWIG TIECK—*Fortunat*.

6
Chance is a word void of sense; nothing can exist without a cause.

VOLTAIRE—*A Philosophical Dictionary*.

CHANGE (See also CONSISTENCY)

7
J'avais vu les grands, mais je n'avais pas vu les petits.

I had seen the great, but I had not seen the small.

ALFIERI—*Reason for Changing his Democratic Opinions*.

8
Nè spegner può per star nell'acqua il foco;
Nè può stato mutar per mutar loco.
Such fire was not by water to be drown'd,
Nor he his nature changed by changing ground.
ARIOSTO—*Orlando Furioso*. XXVIII. 89.

9
Joy comes and goes, hope ebbs and flows
Like the wave;
Change doth unknit the tranquil strength of men.
Love lends life a little grace,
A few sad smiles; and then,
Both are laid in one cold place,
In the grave.
MATTHEW ARNOLD—*A Question*. St. 1.

10
Il n'y a rien de changé en France; il n'y a qu'un Français de plus.

Nothing has changed in France, there is only a Frenchman the more.

Proclamation pub. in the *Moniteur*, April, 1814, as the words of COMTE D'ARTOIS (afterwards CHARLES X), on his entrance into Paris. Originated with COUNT BEUGNOT. Instigated by TALLEYRAND. See M. DE VAULABELLE—*Hist. des Deux Restaurations*. 3d Édit. II. Pp. 30, 31. Also *Contemporary Review*, Feb., 1854.

11
Earth changes, but thy soul and God stand sure.
ROBERT BROWNING—*Rabbi Ben Ezra*. St. 27.

12
Weep not that the world changes—did it keep
A stable, changeless state, it were cause indeed
to weep.
BRYANT—*Mutation*.

13
Full from the fount of Joy's delicious springs
Some bitter o'er the flowers its bubbling venom
flings.
BYRON—*Childe Harold*. Canto I. St. 82.

14
I am not now
That which I have been.
BYRON—*Childe Harold*. Canto IV. St. 185.

15
And one by one in turn, some grand mistake
Casts off its bright skin yearly like the snake.
BYRON—*Don Juan*. Canto V. St. 21.

16
A change came o'er the spirit of my dream.
BYRON—*Dream*. St. 3.

17
Shrine of the mighty! can it be,
That this is all remains of thee?
BYRON—*Giaour*. L. 106.

18
How chang'd since last her speaking eye
Glanc'd gladness round the glitt'ring room,
Where high-born men were proud to wait—
Where Beauty watched to imitate.
BYRON—*Parisina*. St. 10.

19
To-day is not yesterday: we ourselves change; how can our Works and Thoughts, if they are always to be the fittest, continue always the same? Change, indeed, is painful; yet ever needful; and if Memory have its force and worth, so also has Hope.

CARLYLE—*Essays*. *Characteristics*.

20
Tempora mutantur, nos et mutamur in illis.
Astra regunt homines, sed regit astra Deus.
Times change and we change with them.
The stars rule men but God rules the stars.
CELLARIUS—*Harmonia Macrocosmica*. (1661)

The phrase "Tempora mutantur" or "Omnia mutantur" attributed by BORBONIUS to EMPEROR LOTHARIUS I, in *Delitiæ Poetarum Germanorum*. CICERO—*De Officiis*. Bk. I. Ch. 10. OVID—*Metamor*. Bk. III. 397. LACTANTIUS. Bk. III. Fable V. WM. HARRISON—*Description of Great Britain*. (1571)

21
Sancho Panza by name is my own self, if I was not changed in my cradle.

CERVANTES—*Don Quixote*. Pt. II. Ch. XXX.

22
An id exploratum cuiquam potest esse, quomodo sese habiturum sit corpus, non dico ad annum sed ad vesperam?

Can any one find out in what condition his body will be, I do not say a year hence, but this evening?

CICERO—*De Finibus Bonorum et Malorum*. II. 228.

23
Non tam commutandarum, quam evertendarum rerum cupidi.

Longing not so much to change things as to overturn them.
CICERO—*De Officiis*. II. 1.

1
Nihil est aptius ad delectationem lectoris quam temporum varietates fortunæque vicissitudines.
There is nothing better fitted to delight the reader than change of circumstances and varieties of fortune.
CICERO—*Epistles*. V. 12.

2
Nemo doctus unquam (multa autem de hoc genere scripta sunt) mutationem consili inconstantiam dixit esse.
No sensible man (among the many things that have been written on this kind) ever imputed inconsistency to another for changing his mind.
CICERO—*Epistolæ ad Atticus*. XVI. 7. 3.

3
Asperius nihil est humili cum surgit in altum.
Nothing is more annoying than a low man raised to a high position.
CLAUDIANUS—*In Eutropium*. I. 181.

4
Still ending, and beginning still.
COWPER—*The Task*. Bk. III. L. 627.

5
On commence par être dupe,
On finit par être fripon.
We begin by being dupe, and end by being rogue.
DESCHAMPS—*Réflexion sur le Jeu*.

6
Change is inevitable in a progressive country,
Change is constant.
BENJ. DISRAELI—*Edinburgh*, Oct. 29, 1867.

7
Will change the Pebbles of our puddly thought
To *Orient* Pearls.
DU BARTAS—*Divine Weekes and Workes, Second Week, Third Day*. Pt. I.

8
Good to the heels the well-worn slipper feels
When the tired player shuffles off the buskin;
A page of Hood may do a fellow good
After a scolding from Carlyle or Ruskin.
HOLMES—*How not to Settle It*.

9
Nor can one word be chang'd but for a worse.
HOMER—*Odyssey*. Bk. VIII. L. 192. POPE'S trans.

10
Non si male nunc et olim
Sic erit.
If matters go badly now, they will not always be so.
HORACE—*Carmina*. II. 10. 17.

11
Plerumque gratæ divitibus vices.
Change generally pleases the rich.
HORACE—*Carmina*. III. 29. 13.

12
Non sum qualis eram.
I am not what I once was.
HORACE—*Carmina*. IV. 1. 3.

13
Amphora cœpit
Instituti; currente rota cur urceus exit?
A vase is begun; why, as the wheel goes round, does it turn out a pitcher?
HORACE—*Ars Poetica*. XXI.

14
Quo teneam vultus mutantem Protea nodo?
With what knot shall I hold this Proteus, who so often changes his countenance?
HORACE—*Epistles*. I. 1. 90.

15
Quod petiit spernit, repetit quod nuper omisit.
He despises what he sought; and he seeks that which he lately threw away.
HORACE—*Epistles*. I. 1. 98.

16
Diruit, ædificat, mutat quadrata rotundis.
He pulls down, he builds up, he changes squares into circles.
HORACE—*Epistles*. I. 1. 100.

17
Optat ephippia bos piger, optat arare caballus.
The lazy ox wishes for horse-trappings, and the steed wishes to plough.
HORACE—*Epistles*. I. 14. 43.

18
Deus hæc fortasse benigna
Reducet in sedem vice.
God perchance will by a happy change restore these things to a settled condition.
HORACE—*Epistles*. XIII. 7.

19
There is a certain relief in change, even though it be from bad to worse; as I have found in travelling in a stage-coach, that it is often a comfort to shift one's position and be bruised in a new place.
WASHINGTON IRVING—*Tales of a Traveller. Preface*.

20
So many great nobles, things, administrations,
So many high chieftains, so many brave nations.
So many proud princes, and power so splendid,
In a moment, a twinkling, all utterly ended.
JACOPONE—*De Contemptu Mundi*. ABRAHAM COLES—Trans. in *"Old Gems in New Settings."* P. 75.

21
As the rolling stone gathers no moss, so the roving heart gathers no affections.
MRS. JAMESON—*Studies. Detached Thoughts. Sternberg's Novels*.
(See also TUSSER)

22
Can the Ethiopian change his skin, or the leopard his spots?
Jeremiah. XIII. 23.

23
He is no wise man that will quit a certainty for an uncertainty.
SAMUEL JOHNSON—*The Idler*. No. 57.

24
The world goes up and the world goes down,
And the sunshine follows the rain;
And yesterday's sneer and yesterday's frown
Can never come over again.
CHARLES KINGSLEY—*Songs*. II.

1
Coups de fourches ni d'étrivières,
Ne lui font changer de manières.
Neither blows from pitchfork, nor from the lash, can make him change his ways.
LA FONTAINE—*Fables*. II. 18.

2
Time fleeth on,
Youth soon is gone,
Naught earthly may abide;
Life seemeth fast,
But may not last—
It runs as runs the tide.
LELAND—*Many in One*. Pt. II. St. 21.

3
I do not allow myself to suppose that either the convention or the League, have concluded to decide that I am either the greatest or the best man in America, but rather they have concluded it is not best to swap horses while crossing the river, and have further concluded that I am not so poor a horse that they might not make a botch of it in trying to swap.
LINCOLN, to a delegation of the National Union League who congratulated him on his nomination as the Republican candidate for President, June 9, 1864. As given by J. F. RHODES *Hist. of the U. S. from the Compromise of 1850*. Vol. IV. P. 370. Same in NICOLAY AND HAY *Lincoln's Complete Works*. Vol. II. P. 532. Different version in *Appleton's Cyclopedia*. RAYMOND —*Life and Public Services of Abraham Lincoln*. Ch. XVIII. P. 500. (Ed. 1865) says Lincoln quotes an old Dutch farmer, "It was best not to swap horses when crossing a stream."

4
All things must change
To something new, to something strange.
LONGFELLOW—*Kéramos*. L. 32.

5
But the nearer the dawn the darker the night,
And by going wrong all things come right;
Things have been mended that were worse,
And the worse, the nearer they are to mend.
LONGFELLOW—*Tales of a Wayside Inn. The Baron of St. Castine*. L. 265.

6
Omnia mortali mutantur lege creata,
Nec se cognoscunt terræ vertentibus annis,
Et mutant variam faciem per sæcula gentes.
Everything that is created is changed by the laws of man; the earth does not know itself in the revolution of years; even the races of man assume various forms in the course of ages.
MANILIUS—*Astronomica*. 515.

7
Do not think that years leave us and find us the same!
OWEN MEREDITH (Lord Lytton)—*Lucile*. Pt. II. Canto II. St. 3.

8
Weary the cloud falleth out of the sky,
Dreary the leaf lieth low.
All things must come to the earth by and by,
Out of which all things grow.
OWEN MEREDITH (Lord Lytton)—*The Wanderer. Earth's Havings*. Bk. III.

9
To-morrow to fresh woods, and pastures new.
MILTON—*Lycidas*. L. 193.

10
In dim eclipse, disastrous twilight sheds
On half the nations, and with fear of change
Perplexes monarchs.
MILTON—*Paradise Lost*. Bk. I. L. 597.

11
Nous avons changé tout cela.
We have changed all that.
MOLIÈRE—*Le Médecin Malgré lui*. II. 6.

12
Saturninus said, "Comrades, you have lost a good captain to make him an ill general."
MONTAIGNE—*Of Vanity*. Bk. III. Ch. IX.

13
All that's bright must fade,—
The brightest still the fleetest;
All that's sweet was made
But to be lost when sweetest.
MOORE—*National Airs. All That's Bright Must Fade*.

14
Omnia mutantur, nihil interit.
All things change, nothing perishes.
OVID—*Metamorphoses*. XV. 165.

15
My merry, merry, merry roundelay
Concludes with Cupid's curse,
They that do change old love for new,
Pray gods, they change for worse!
GEORGE PEELE—*Cupid's Curse; From the Araignment of Paris*.

16
Till Peter's keys some christen'd Jove adorn,
And Pan to Moses lends his Pagan horn.
POPE—*Dunciad*. Bk. III. L. 109.

17
See dying vegetables life sustain,
See life dissolving vegetate again;
All forms that perish other forms supply;
(By turns we catch the vital breath and die.)
POPE—*Essay on Man*. Ep. III. L. 15.

18
Alas! in truth, the man but chang'd his mind,
Perhaps was sick, in love, or had not dined.
POPE—*Moral Essays*. Ep. I. Pt. II.

19
Manners with Fortunes, Humours turn with Climes,
Tenets with Books, and Principles with Times.
POPE—*Moral Essays*. Ep. I. Pt. II.

20
Tournoit les truies au foin.
Turned the pigs into the grass. (Clover.)
RABELAIS—*Gargantua*. (Phrase meaning to change the subject.)

21
Corporis et fortunæ bonorum ut initium finis est. Omnia orta occidunt, et orta senescunt.
As the blessings of health and fortune have a beginning, so they must also find an end. Everything rises but to fall, and increases but to decay.
SALLUST—*Jugurtha*. II.

22
With every change his features play'd,
As aspens show the light and shade.
SCOTT—*Rokeby*. Canto III. St. 5.

1
As hope and fear alternate chase
Our course through life's uncertain race.
SCOTT—*Rokeby*. Canto VI. St. 2.

2
When change itself can give no more,
'Tis easy to be true.
SIR CHAS. SEDLEY—*Reasons for Constancy*.

3 Hereditary
Rather than purchased; what he cannot change,
Than what he chooses.
Antony and Cleopatra. Act I. Sc. 4. L. 14.

4
This world is not for aye, nor 'tis not strange
That even our loves should with our fortunes change.
Hamlet. Act III. Sc. 2. L. 210.

5 That we would do,
We should do when we would; for this "would" changes
And hath abatements and delays as many
As there are tongues, are hands, are accidents;
And then this "should" is like a spendthrift sigh,
That hurts by easing.
Hamlet. Act IV. Sc. 7. L. 119.

6
The love of wicked men converts to fear;
That fear to hate, and hate turns one or both
To worthy danger and deserved death.
Richard II. Act V. Sc. 1. L. 65.
(See also HENRY VIII under MAN.)

7
All things that we ordained festival,
Turn from their office to black funeral;
Our instruments to melancholy bells,
Our wedding cheer to a sad burial feast,
Our solemn hymns to sullen dirges change,
Our bridal flowers serve for a buried corse,
And all things change them to the contrary.
Romeo and Juliet. Act IV. Sc. 5. L. 84.

8 I am not so nice,
To change true rules for old inventions.
Taming of the Shrew. Act III. Sc. 1. L. 80.

9
Full fathom five thy father lies;
Of his bones are coral made;
Those are pearls that were his eyes·
Nothing of him that doth fade,
But doth suffer a sea-change
Into something rich and strange.
Tempest. Act I. Sc. 2. L. 396.

10
Life may change, but it may fly not;
Hope may vanish, but can die not;
Truth be veiled, but still it burneth;
Love repulsed,—but it returneth.
SHELLEY—*Hellas*. Semi-chorus.

11
Men must reap the things they sow,
Force from force must ever flow,
Or worse; but 'tis a bitter woe
That love or reason cannot change.
SHELLEY—*Lines Written among the Euganean Hills*. L. 232.

12
Nought may endure but Mutability.
SHELLEY—*Mutability*.

13
Neither to change, nor falter, nor repent;
This, like thy glory, Titan! is to be
Good, great, and joyous, beautiful and free;
This is alone Life, Joy, Empire and Victory.
SHELLEY—*Prometheus*. Act IV.

14
This sad vicissitude of things.
LAURENCE STERNE—*Sermons*. XVI. *The Character of Shimel*.
(See also GIFFORD under SONG; HAWTHORNE under APPLE TREE; BACON under RELIGION)

15
The life of any one can by no means be changed after death; an evil life can in no wise be converted into a good life, or an infernal into an angelic life: because every spirit, from head to foot, is of the character of his love, and therefore, of his life; and to convert this life into its opposite, would be to destroy the spirit utterly.
SWEDENBORG—*Heaven and Hell*. 527.

16
Corpora lente augescent, cito extinguuntur.
Bodies are slow of growth, but are rapid in their dissolution.
TACITUS—*Agricola*. II.

17
Not in vain the distance beacons. Forward, forward let us range.
Let the great world spin forever down the ringing grooves of change.
TENNYSON—*Locksley Hall*. St. 91.

18
The stone that is rolling can gather no moss.
Who often removeth is suer of loss.
TUSSER—*Five Hundred Points of Good Husbandry. Lessons*. St. 46.

19
So, when a raging fever burns,
We shift from side to side by turns;
And 'tis a poor relief we gain
To change the place, but keep the pain.
ISAAC WATTS—*Hymns and Spiritual Songs*. Bk. II. 146.

20
Life is arched with changing skies:
Rarely are they what they seem:
Children we of smiles and sighs—
Much we know, but more we dream.
WILLIAM WINTER—*Light and Shadow*.

21
"A jolly place," said he, "in times of old!
But something ails it now; the spot is curst."
WORDSWORTH—*Hart-leap Well*. Pt. II.

22
As high as we have mounted in delight
In our dejection do we sink as low.
WORDSWORTH—*Resolution and Independence*. St. 4.

23
I heard the old, old men say,
"Every thing alters,
And one by one we drop away."
They had hands like claws, and their knees
Were twisted like the old thorn trees
By the waters.
I heard the old, old men say,
"All that's beautiful drifts away
Like the waters."
W. B. YEATS—*The Old Men admiring themselves in the Water*.

CHAOS

1
Temple and tower went down, nor left a site:—
Chaos of ruins!
BYRON—*Childe Harold.* Canto IV. St. 80.

2 The world was void,
The populous and the powerful was a lump,
Seasonless, herbless, treeless, manless, lifeless—
A lump of death—a chaos of hard clay.
BYRON—*Darkness.* L. 69.

3
The chaos of events.
BYRON—*Prophecy of Dante.* Canto II. L. 6.

4 Chaos, that reigns here
In double night of darkness and of shades.
MILTON—*Comus.* L. 334.

5 Fate shall yield
To fickle Chance, and Chaos judge the strife.
MILTON—*Paradise Lost.* Bk. II. L. 232.

6
Then rose the seed of Chaos, and of Night,
To blot out order and extinguish light.
POPE—*Dunciad.* Bk. IV. L. 13.

7
Lo: thy dread empire, Chaos, is restored;
Light dies before thy uncreating word:
Thy hand, great Anarch! lets the curtain fall;
And universal darkness buries all.
POPE—*Dunciad.* Bk. IV. L. 649.

8 Nay, had I power, I should
Pour the sweet milk of concord into hell,
Uproar the universal peace, confound
All unity on earth.
Macbeth. Act IV. Sc. 3. L. 97.

CHARACTER

9
There is so much good in the worst of us,
And so much bad in the best of us,
That it ill behoves any of us
To find fault with the rest of us.
Sometimes quoted "To talk about the rest of us." Author not found. Attributed to R. L. STEVENSON, not found. Lloyd Osborne, his literary executor, states he did not write it. Claimed for GOVERNOR HOCH of Kansas, in *The Reader*, Sept. 7, 1907, but authorship denied by him. Accredited to ELLEN THORNEYCROFT FOWLER, who denies writing it. Claimed also for ELBERT HUBBARD.
(See also MILLER, STRINGER)

10
They love, they hate, but cannot do without him.
ARISTOPHANES. See PLUTARCH—*Life of Alcibiades.* LANGHORNE's trans.
(See also MARTIAL; also ADDISON, under LOVE)

11
In brief, I don't stick to declare, Father Dick,
So they call him for short, is a regular brick;
A metaphor taken—I have not the page aright—
From an ethical work by the Stagyrite.
BARHAM—*Brothers of Birchington.* *Nicomachean Ethics*, section I, records Aristotle's definition of a happy man, a four cornered, perfectly rectangular man, a faultless cube. ("A perfect brick.")
(See also LYCURGAS)

12
Chevalier sans peur et sans reproche.
Knight without fear and without reproach.
Applied to CHEVALIER BAYARD.

13
Zealous, yet modest; innocent, though free;
Patient of toil; serene amidst alarms;
Inflexible in faith; invincible in arms.
BEATTIE—*The Minstrel.* Bk. I. St. 11.

14
Many men are mere warehouses full of merchandise—the head, the heart, are stuffed with goods. * * * There are apartments in their souls which were once tenanted by taste, and love, and joy, and worship, but they are all deserted now, and the rooms are filled with earthy and material things.
HENRY WARD BEECHER—*Life Thoughts.*

15
Many men build as cathedrals were built, the part nearest the ground finished; but that part which soars toward heaven, the turrets and the spires, forever incomplete.
HENRY WARD BEECHER—*Life Thoughts.*

16
Most men are bad.
Attributed to BIAS of Priene.

17
Une grande incapacité inconnue.
A great unrecognized incapacity.
BISMARCK, *of Napoleon III.*, while Minister to Paris in 1862.

18
I look upon you as a gem of the old rock.
SIR THOMAS BROWNE—*Dedication to Urn Burial.*
(See also BULLEN, BURKE)

19
No, when the fight begins within himself,
A man's worth something.
ROBERT BROWNING—*Men and Women. Bishop Blougram's Apology.*

20
Your father used to come home to my mother, and why may not I be a chippe of the same block out of which you two were cutte?
BULLEN'S *Old Plays.* II. 60. *Dick of Devonshire.* (See also BROWNE)

21
Are you a bromide?
GELETT BURGESS—Title of *Essay.* First pub. in *Smart Set*, April, 1906.

22
All men that are ruined, are ruined on the side of their natural propensities.
BURKE—*Letters. Letter I. On a Regicide Peace.*

23
He was not merely a chip of the old Block, but the old Block itself.
BURKE—*About Wm. Pitt—Wraxall's Memoirs.* Vol. II. P. 342.
(See also BROWNE)

24
From their folded mates they wander far,
Their ways seem harsh and wild:
They follow the beck of a baleful star,
Their paths are dream-beguiled.
RICHARD BURTON—*Black Sheep.*

1
Hannibal, as he had mighty virtues, so had he many vices; * * * he had two distinct persons in him.
BURTON—*Anatomy of Melancholy. Democritus to the Reader.*

2
Heroic, stoic Cato, the sententious,
Who lent his lady to his friend Hortensius.
BYRON—*Don Juan.* Canto VI. St. 7.

3
So well she acted all and every part
By turns—with that vivacious versatility,
Which many people take for want of heart.
They err—'tis merely what is call'd mobility,
A thing of temperament and not of art,
Though seeming so, from its supposed facility;
And false—though true; for surely they're sincerest
Who are strongly acted on by what is nearest.
BYRON—*Don Juan.* Canto XVI.. St. 97.

4
With more capacity for love than earth
Bestows on most of mortal mould and birth,
His early dreams of good out-stripp'd the truth,
And troubled manhood follow'd baffled youth.
BYRON—*Lara.* Canto I. St. 18.

5
Genteel in personage,
Conduct, and equipage;
Noble by heritage,
Generous and free.
HENRY CAREY—*The Contrivances.* Act I. Sc. 2. L. 22.

6
Clever men are good, but they are not the best.
CARLYLE—*Goethe. Edinburgh Review.* (1828)

7
We are firm believers in the maxim that, for all right judgment of any man or thing, it is useful, nay, essential, to see his good qualities before pronouncing on his bad.
CARLYLE—*Essays. Goethe.*

8
It is in general more profitable to reckon up our defects than to boast of our attainments.
CARLYLE—*Essays. Signs of the Times.*

9
It can be said of him, When he departed he took a Man's life with him. No sounder piece of British manhood was put together in that eighteenth century of Time.
CARLYLE—*Sir Walter Scott. London and Westminster Review.* (1838)

10
Thou art a cat, and rat, and a coward to boot.
CERVANTES—*Don Quixote.* Pt. I. Bk. III. Ch. VIII.

11
Every one is the son of his own works.
CERVANTES—*Don Quixote.* Pt. I. Bk. IV. Ch. XX.

12
I can look sharp as well as another, and let me alone to keep the cobwebs out of my eyes.
CERVANTES — *Don Quixote.* Pt. II. Ch. XXXIII.

13
Cada uno es come Dios le hijo, y aun peor muchas vezes.
Every one is as God made him, and often a great deal worse.
CERVANTES—*Don Quixote.* XI. 5.

14
He was a verray perfight gentil knight.
CHAUCER—*Canterbury Tales.* Prologue. L. 72.

15
The nation looked upon him as a deserter, and he shrunk into insignificancy and an Earldom.
CHESTERFIELD—*Character of Pulteney.* (1763)

16
Importunitas autem, et inhumanitas omni ætati molesta est.
But a perverse temper and fretful disposition make any state of life unhappy.
CICERO—*De Senectute.* III.

17
Ut ignis in aquam conjectus, continuo restinguitur et refrigeratur, sic refervens falsum crimen in purissimam et castissimam vitam collatum, statim concidit et extinguitur.
As fire when thrown into water is cooled down and put out, so also a false accusation when brought against a man of the purest and holiest character, boils over and is at once dissipated, and vanishes.
CICERO—*Oratio Pro Quinto Roscio Comœdo.* VI.

18
What was said of Cinna might well be applied to him. He [Hampden] had a head to contrive, a tongue to persuade, and a hand to execute, any mischief.
ED. HYDE, LORD CLARENDON—*History of the Rebellion.* Vol. III. Bk. VII.
(See also GIBBON, JUNIUS, VOLTAIRE)

19
In numbers warmly pure, and sweetly strong.
COLLINS—*Ode to Simplicity.*

20
Not to think of men above that which is written.
I. *Corinthians.* IV. 6.

21
An honest man, close-button'd to the chin,
Broadcloth without, and a warm heart within.
COWPER—*Epistle to Joseph Hill.*

22
He cannot drink five bottles, bilk the score,
Then kill a constable, and drink five more;
But he can draw a pattern, make a tart,
And has ladies' etiquette by heart.
COWPER—*Progress of Error.* L. 191.

23
Elegant as simplicity, and warm
As ecstasy.
COWPER—*Table Talk.* L. 588.

24
Virtue and vice had boundaries in old time,
Not to be pass'd.
COWPER—*Task.* Bk. III. L. 75.

25
He's tough, ma'am,—tough is J. B.; tough and de-vilish sly.
DICKENS—*Dombey and Son.* Ch. VII.

26
O Mrs. Higden, Mrs. Higden, you was a woman and a mother, and a mangler in a million million.
DICKENS—*Mutual Friend.* Ch. IX.

1
I know their tricks and their manners.
DICKENS—*Mutual Friend.* Bk. II. Ch. I.

2
A demd damp, moist, unpleasant body.
DICKENS—*Nicholas Nickleby.* Ch. XXXIV.

3
Men of light and leading.
BENJ. DISRAELI—*Sybil.* Bk. V. Ch. I. Also in BURKE—*Reflections on the Revolution in France.* P. 419. (Ed. 1834)

4
A man so various, that he seem'd to be
Not one, but all mankind's epitome;
Stiff in opinions, always in the wrong,
Was everything by starts, and nothing long;
But in the course of one revolving moon,
Was chymist, fiddler, statesman, and buffoon.
DRYDEN—*Absalom and Achitophel.* Pt. I. L. 545.

5
So over violent, or over civil,
That every man with him was God or Devil.
DRYDEN—*Absalom and Achitophel.* Pt. I. L. 557.

6
For every inch that is not fool, is rogue.
DRYDEN—*Absalom and Achitophel.* Pt. II. L. 463.

7
Her wit was more than man, her innocence a child.
DRYDEN—*Elegy on Mrs. Killigrew.* L. 70.

8
Thus all below is strength, and all above is grace.
DRYDEN—*Epistle to Congreve.* L. 19.

9
Plain without pomp, and rich without a show.
DRYDEN—*The Flower and the Leaf.* L. 187.

10
There is a great deal of unmapped country within us which would have to be taken into account in an explanation of our gusts and storms.
GEORGE ELIOT—*Daniel Deronda.* Bk. III. Ch. XXIV.

11
She was and is (what can there more be said?)
On earth the first, in heaven the second maid.
Tribute to Queen Elizabeth. MS. 4712, in British Museum. AYSCOUGH'S Catalogue.

12
A trip-hammer, with an Æolian attachment.
EMERSON, of CARLYLE, after meeting him in 1848.

13
Character is higher than intellect. * * * A great soul will be strong to live, as well as to think.
EMERSON—*American Scholar.*

14
No change of circumstances can repair a defect of character.
EMERSON—*Essay. On Character.*

15
A great character, founded on the living rock of principle, is, in fact, not a solitary phenomenon, to be at once perceived, limited, and described. It is a dispensation of Providence, designed to have not merely an immediate, but a continuous, progressive, and never-ending agency. It survives the man who possessed it; survives his age,—perhaps his country, his language.
ED. EVERETT—*Speech. The Youth of Washington.* July 4, 1835.

16
Human improvement is from within outwards.
FROUDE—*Short Studies on Great Subjects. Divus Cæsar.*

17
Our thoughts and our conduct are our own.
FROUDE—*Short Studies on Great Subjects. Education.*

18
Every one of us, whatever our speculative opinions, knows better than he practices, and recognizes a better law than he obeys.
FROUDE—*Short Studies on Great Subjects. On Progress.* Pt. II.

19
Weak and beggarly elements.
Galatians. IV. 9.

20
In every deed of mischief, he [Andronicus Comnenus] had a heart to resolve, a head to contrive, and a hand to execute.
GIBBON—*Decline and Fall of the Roman Empire.* Vol. IX. P. 94.
(See also CLARENDON)

21
That man may last, but never lives,
Who much receives, but nothing gives;
Whom none can love, whom none can thank,—
Creation's blot, creation's blank.
THOMAS GIBBONS—*When Jesus Dwelt.*

22
A man not perfect, but of heart
So high, of such heroic rage,
That even his hopes became a part
Of earth's eternal heritage.
R. W. GILDER—*At the President's Grave. Epitaph* for President Garfield, Sept. 19, 1881.

23
To be engaged in opposing wrong affords, under the conditions of our mental constitution, but a slender guarantee for being right.
GLADSTONE—*Time and Place of Homer. Introduction.*

24
Aufrichtig zu sein kann ich versprechen; unparteiisch zu sein aber nicht.
I can promise to be upright, but not to be without bias.
GOETHE—*Sprüche in Prosa.* III.

25
Es bildet ein Talent sich in der Stille,
Sich ein Charakter in dem Strom der Welt.
Talent is nurtured in solitude; character is formed in the stormy billows of the world.
GOETHE—*Torquato Tasso.* I. 2. 66.

26
Welch' höher Geist in einer engen Brust.
What a mighty spirit in a narrow bosom.
GOETHE—*Torquato Tasso.* II. 3. 199.

27
Our Garrick's a salad; for in him we see
Oil, vinegar, sugar, and saltness agree.
GOLDSMITH—*Retaliation.* L. 11.

1
Though equal to all things, for all things unfit;
Too nice for a statesman, too proud for a wit.
GOLDSMITH—*Retaliation*. L. 37.

2
Hands, that the rod of empire might have swayed,
Or waked to ecstasy the living lyre.
GRAY—*Elegy in a Country Churchyard*. St. 12.

3
He were n't no saint—but at jedgment
I'd run my chance with Jim.
'Longside of some pious gentlemen
That wouldn't shook hands with him.
He seen his duty, a dead-sure thing—
And went for it thar and then;
And Christ ain't a-going to be too hard
On a man that died for men.
JOHN HAY—*Jim Bludso*.

4
Anyone must be mainly ignorant or thoughtless, who is surprised at everything he sees; or wonderfully conceited who expects everything to conform to his standard of propriety.
HAZLITT—*Lectures on the English Comic Writers. On Wit and Humour*.

5
Kein Talent, doch ein Charakter.
No talent, but yet a character.
HEINE—*Atta Troll*. Caput 24.

6
O Dowglas, O Dowglas!
Tendir and trewe.
SIR RICHARD HOLLAND—*The Buke of the Howlat*. St. XXXI. First printed in appendix to PINKERTON'S *Collection of Scottish Poems*. III. P. 146. (Ed. 1792)

7
We must have a weak spot or two in a character before we can love it much. People that do not laugh or cry, or take more of anything than is good for them, or use anything but dictionary-words, are admirable subjects for biographies. But we don't care most for those flat pattern flowers that press best in the herbarium.
HOLMES—*Professor at the Breakfast Table*. Ch. III. *Iris*.

8
Whatever comes from the brain carries the hue of the place it came from, and whatever comes from the heart carries the heat and color of its birthplace.
HOLMES—*Professor at the Breakfast Table*. Ch. VI.

9
In death a hero, as in life a friend!
HOMER—*Iliad*. Bk. XVII. L. 758. POPE'S trans.

10
Wise to resolve, and patient to perform.
HOMER—*Odyssey*. Bk. IV. L. 372. POPE'S trans.

11
Gentle of speech, beneficent of mind.
HOMER—*Odyssey*. Bk. IV. L. 917. POPE'S trans.

12
But he whose inborn worth his acts commend,
Of gentle soul, to human race a friend.
HOMER—*Odyssey*. Bk. XIX. L. 383. POPE'S trans.

13
Integer vitæ scelerisque purus
Non eget Mauris incidis neque arcu
Nec venenatis gravida sagittis
Fusce pharetra.
If whole in life, and free from sin,
Man needs no Moorish bow, nor dart
Nor quiver, carrying death within
By poison's art.
HORACE—*Carmina* I. 22. 1. GLADSTONE'S *trans*.

14
Paullum sepultæ distat inertiæ
Celata virtus.
Excellence when concealed, differs but little from buried worthlessness.
HORACE—*Carmina*. IV. 9. 29.

15
Argilla quidvis imitaberis uda.
Thou canst mould him into any shape like soft clay.
HORACE—*Epistles*. II. 2. 8.

16
A Soul of power, a well of lofty Thought
A chastened Hope that ever points to Heaven.
JOHN HUNTER—*Sonnet. A Replication of Rhymes*.

17
He was worse than provincial—he was parochial.
HENRY JAMES, JR.—*Of Thoreau. A Critical Life of Hawthorne*.

18
If he does really think that there is no distinction between virtue and vice, why, Sir, when he leaves our houses let us count our spoons.
SAMUEL JOHNSON—*Boswell's Life*. (1763)

19
A very unclubable man.
SAMUEL JOHNSON—*Boswell's Life*. Note. (1764)

20
Officious, innocent, sincere,
Of every friendless name the friend.
SAMUEL JOHNSON—*Verses on the Death of Mr. Robert Levet*. St. 2.

21
The heart to conceive, the understanding to direct, or the hand to execute.
JUNIUS—*City Address and the King's Answer*. Letter XXXVII. March 19, 1770.
(See also CLARENDON)

22
Nemo repente venit turpissimus.
No one ever became thoroughly bad all at once.
JUVENAL—*Satires*. II. 33.

23
He is truly great that is little in himself, and that maketh no account of any height of honors.
THOMAS À KEMPIS—*Imitation of Christ*. Bk. I. Ch. III.

24
E'en as he trod that day to God,
so walked he from his birth,
In simpleness, and gentleness and honor
and clean mirth.
KIPLING—*Barrack Room Ballads*. Dedication to Wolcott Balestier. (Adaptation of an earlier one.)

1
Oh, East is East, and West is West, and never the twain shall meet
Till earth and sky stand presently at God's great judgment seat;
But there is neither East nor West, border nor breed nor birth
When two strong men stand face to face, tho' they come from the ends of the earth!
KIPLING—*Barrack-Room Ballads. Ballad of East and West.*

2
La physionomie n'est pas une règle qui nous soit donnée pour juger des hommes; elle nous peut servir de conjecture.

Physiognomy is not a guide that has been given us by which to judge of the character of men: it may only serve us for conjecture.
LA BRUYÈRE—*Les Caractères.* XII.

3
Incivility is not a Vice of the Soul, but the effect of several Vices; of Vanity, Ignorance of Duty, Laziness, Stupidity, Distraction, Contempt of others, and Jealousy.
LA BRUYÈRE—*The Characters or Manners of the Present Age.* Vol. II. Ch. XI.

4
On n'est jamais si ridicule par les qualités que l'on a que par celles que l'on affecte d'avoir.

The qualities we have do not make us so ridiculous as those which we affect to have.
LA ROCHEFOUCAULD—*Maximes.* 134.

5
Famæ ac fidei damna majora sunt quam quæ æstimari possunt.

The injury done to character is greater than can be estimated.
LIVY—*Annales.* III. 72.

6
A tender heart; a will inflexible.
LONGFELLOW—*Christus.* Pt. III. *The New England Tragedies. John Endicott.* Act III. Sc. 2.

7
So mild, so merciful, so strong, so good,
So patient, peaceful, loyal, loving, pure.
LONGFELLOW—*Christus. The Golden Legend.* Pt. V. L. 319.

8
Sensitive, swift to resent, but as swift in atoning for error.
LONGFELLOW—*Courtship of Miles Standish.* Pt. IX. *The Wedding Day.*

9
In this world a man must either be anvil or hammer.
LONGFELLOW—*Hyperion.* Bk. IV. Ch. VI.

10
Not in the clamor of the crowded street,
Not in the shouts and plaudits of the throng,
But in ourselves, are triumph and defeat.
LONGFELLOW—*The Poets.*

11
For me Fate gave, whate'er she else denied,
A nature sloping to the southern side;
I thank her for it, though when clouds arise
Such natures double-darken gloomy skies.
LOWELL—*An Epistle to George William Curtis.* Postscript 1887. L. 53.

12
All that hath been majestical
In life or death, since time began,
Is native in the simple heart of all,
The angel heart of man.
LOWELL—*An Incident in a Railroad Car.* St.10.

13
Our Pilgrim stock wuz pethed with hardihood.
LOWELL—*Biglow Papers.* Second Series. No. 6. L. 38.

14
Soft- heartedness, in times like these,
Shows sof'ness in the upper story.
LOWELL—*Biglow Papers.* Second Series. No. 7. L. 119.

15
Endurance is the crowning quality,
And patience all the passion of great hearts.
LOWELL—*Columbus.* L. 237.

16
For she was jes' the quiet kind
Whose naturs never vary,
Like streams that keep a summer mind
Snowhid in Jenooary.
LOWELL—*The Courtin'.* St. 22.

17
His Nature's a glass of champagne with the foam on 't,
As tender as Fletcher, as witty as Beaumont;
So his best things are done in the flash of the moment.
LOWELL—*Fable for Critics.* L. 834.

18
It is by presence of mind in untried emergencies that the native metal of a man is tested.
LOWELL—*My Study Windows. Abraham Lincoln.*

19
A nature wise
With finding in itself the types of all,—
With watching from the dim verge of the time
What things to be are visible in the gleams
Thrown forward on them from the luminous past,—
Wise with the history of its own frail heart,
With reverence and sorrow, and with love,
Broad as the world, for freedom and for man.
LOWELL—*Prometheus.* L. 216.

20
Eripitur persona, manet res.

The mask is torn off, while the reality remains.
LUCRETIUS—*De Rerum Natura.* III. 58.

21
There thou beholdest the walls of Sparta, and every man a brick.
LYCURGUS, according to PLUTARCH.
(See also BARHAM)

22
We hardly know any instance of the strength and weakness of human nature so striking and so grotesque as the character of this haughty, vigilant, resolute, sagacious blue-stocking, half Mithridates and half Trissotin, bearing up against a world in arms, with an ounce of poison in one pocket and a quire of bad verses in the other.
MACAULAY—*Frederick the Great.* (1842)

23
And the chief-justice was rich, quiet, and infamous.
MACAULAY—*Warren Hastings.* (1841)

1
Men look to the East for the dawning things,
for the light of a rising sun
But they look to the West, to the crimson West,
for the things that are done, are done.
DOUGLAS MALLOCH—*East and West.*

2
Now will I show myself to have more of the serpent than the dove; that is—more knave than fool.
MARLOWE—*The Jew of Malta.* Act II. Sc. 3.

3
Au demeurant, le meilleur fils du monde.
In other respects the best fellow in the world.
CLEMENT MAROT—*Letter to Francis I.*

4
In all thy humours, whether grave or mellow,
Thou'rt such a touchy, testy, pleasant fellow;
Hast so much wit, and mirth, and spleen about thee,
That there's no living with thee, or without thee.
MARTIAL—*Epigrams.* Bk. XII. Ep. 47.
Trans. by Addison. Spectator. No. 68.
(See also ARISTOPHANES)

5
And, but herself, admits no parallel.
MASSINGER—*Duke of Milan.* Act IV. Sc. 3.
(See also SENECA, THEOBALD)

6
Hereafter he will make me know,
And I shall surely find.
He was too wise to err, and O,
Too good to be unkind.
MEDLEY—*Hymn.* Claimed for REV. THOMAS EAST, but not found.

7
Who knows nothing base,
Fears nothing known.
OWEN MEREDITH (Lord Lytton)—*A Great Man.* St. 8.

8
Sae true his heart, sae smooth his speech,
His breath like caller air,
His very foot has music in 't,
As he comes up the stair.
W. J. MICKLE—*Ballad of Cumnor Hall. Mariner's Wife.* Attributed also to JEAN ADAM, evidence in favor of Mickle. Claimed also for MCPHERSON as a MS. copy was found among his papers after his death.

9
In men whom men condemn as ill
I find so much of goodness still,
In men whom men pronounce divine
I find so much of sin and blot
I do not dare to draw a line
Between the two, where God has not.
JOAQUIN MILLER—*Byron.* St. 1. (Bear ed. 1909, changes "I hesitate" to "I do not dare.")
(See also first quotation under topic)

10
He that has light within his own clear breast
May sit i' the centre, and enjoy bright day:
But he that hides a dark soul and foul thoughts
Benighted walks under the mid-day sun;
Himself his own dungeon.
MILTON—*Comus.* L. 381.

11
Yet, where an equal poise of hope and fear
Does arbitrate the event, my nature is
That I incline to hope rather than fear,
And gladly banish squint suspicion.
MILTON—*Comus.* L. 410.

12
Quips and Cranks and wanton Wiles,
Nods and Becks and wreathèd Smiles.
MILTON—*L'Allegro.* L. 27.

13
Unrespited, unpitied, unreprieved.
MILTON—*Paradise Lost.* Bk. II. L. 185.

14
Sufficient to have stood, though free to fall.
MILTON—*Paradise Lost.* Bk. III. L. 99.

15
For contemplation he and valor formed,
For softness she and sweet attractive grace.
MILTON—*Paradise Lost.* Bk. IV. L. 297.
(See also ROYDEN under FACE)

16
Adam the goodliest man of men since born
His sons, the fairest of her daughters, Eve.
MILTON—*Paradise Lost.* Bk. IV. L. 323.

17
Her virtue and the conscience of her worth,
That would be wooed, and not unsought be won.
MILTON—*Paradise Lost.* Bk. VIII. L. 502.

18
Les hommes, fripons en détail, sont en gros de très-honnêtes gens.
Men, who are rogues individually, are in the mass very honorable people.
MONTESQUIEU—*De l'Esprit.* XXV. C. 2.

19
Good at a fight, but better at a play;
Godlike in giving, but the devil to pay.
MOORE—*On a Cast of Sheridan's Hand.*

20
To those who know thee not, no words can paint;
And those who know thee, know all words are faint!
HANNAH MORE—*Sensibility.*

21
To set the Cause above renown,
To love the game beyond the prize,
To honour, while you strike him down,
The foe that comes with fearless eyes;
To count the life of battle good,
And dear the land that gave you birth;
And dearer yet the brotherhood
That binds the brave of all the earth.
HENRY J. NEWBOLT—*The Island Race. Clifton Chapel.*

22
Video meliora proboque,
Deteriora sequor.
I see and approve better things, I follow the worse.
OVID—*Metamorphoses.* VII. 20. Same in PETRARCH—*To Laura in Life.* XXI.

23
Every man has at times in his mind the ideal of what he should be, but is not. This ideal may be high and complete, or it may be quite low and insufficient; yet in all men that really seek to improve, it is better than the actual character. * * * Man never falls so low that he can see nothing higher than himself.
THEODORE PARKER—*Critical and Miscellaneous Writings.* Essay I. *A Lesson for the Day.*

1
Il ne se déboutonna jamais.
He never unbuttons himself.
Said of SIR ROBERT PEEL, according to CROKER.

2
Udum et molle lutum es: nunc, nunc properandus et acri
Fingendus sine fine rota.
Thou art moist and soft clay; thou must instantly be shaped by the glowing wheel.
PERSIUS—*Satires*. III. 23.

3
Tecum habita, et noris quam sit tibi curta supellex.
Retire within thyself, and thou will discover how small a stock is there.
PERSIUS. *Satires*. IV. 52.

4
Grand, gloomy and peculiar, he sat upon the throne, a sceptred hermit, wrapped in the solitude of his awful originality.
CHARLES PHILLIPS—*Character of Napoleon I.*

5
Optimum et emendatissimum existimo, qui ceteris ita ignoscit, tanquam ipse quotidie peccet; ita peccatis abstinet, tanquam nemini ignoscat.
The highest of characters, in my estimation, is his, who is as ready to pardon the moral errors of mankind, as if he were every day guilty of some himself; and at the same time as cautious of committing a fault as if he never forgave one.
PLINY the Younger—*Epistles*. VIII. 22

6
Good-humor only teaches charms to last,
Still makes new conquests and maintains the past.
POPE—*Epistle to Miss Blount. With the Works of Voiture.*

7
Of Manners gentle, of Affections mild;
In Wit a man; Simplicity, a child.
POPE—*Epitaph XI.*

8
'Tis from high Life high Characters are drawn;
A Saint in Crape is twice a Saint in Lawn:
A Judge is just, a Chanc'llor juster still;
A Gownman learn'd; a Bishop what you will;
Wise if a minister; but if a King,
More wise, more learn'd, more just, more ev'ry-thing.
POPE—*Moral Essays*. Ep. I. Pt. II.

9
With too much Quickness ever to be taught;
With too much Thinking to have common Thought.
POPE—*Moral Essays*. Ep. II. L. 97.

10
From loveless youth to unrespected age,
No passion gratified, except her rage,
So much the fury still outran the wit,
That pleasure miss'd her, and the scandal hit.
POPE—*Moral Essays*. Ep. II. L. 125.

11
In men we various ruling passions find;
In women two almost divide the kind;
Those only fixed, they first or last obey,
The love of pleasure, and the love of sway.
POPE—*Moral Essays*. Ep. II. L. 207.

12
Beauty that shocks you, parts that none will trust,
Wit that can creep, and pride that licks the dust.
POPE—*Prologue to Satires*. L. 332.

13
What then remains, but well our power to use,
And keep good-humor still whate'er we lose?
And trust me, dear, good-humor can prevail,
When airs, and flights, and screams, and scolding fail.
POPE—*Rape of the Lock*. Canto V. L. 29.

14
Charms strike the sight, but merit wins the soul.
POPE—*Rape of the Lock*. Canto V. L. 34.

15
No man's defects sought they to know;
So never made themselves a foe.
No man's good deeds did they commend;
So never rais'd themselves a friend.
PRIOR—*Epitaph.*

16
So much his courage and his mercy strive,
He wounds to cure, and conquers to forgive.
PRIOR—*Ode in Imitation of Horace*. Bk. III. Ode II.

17
He that sweareth
Till no man trust him.
He that lieth
Till no man believe him;
He that borroweth
Till no man will lend him;
Let him go where
No man knoweth him.
HUGH RHODES—*Cautions.*

18
Nie zeichnet der Mensch den eignen Charakter schärfer als in seiner Manier, einen Fremden zu zeichnen.
A man never shows his own character so plainly as by his manner of portraying another's.
JEAN PAUL RICHTER—*Titan*. Zykel 110.

19
Devout yet cheerful, active yet resigned.
ROGERS—*Pleasures of Memory.*

20
Was never eie did see that face,
Was never eare did heare that tong,
Was never minde did minde his grace,
That ever thought the travell long,
But eies and eares and ev'ry thought
Were with his sweete perfections caught.
MATHEW ROYDEN—*An Elegie. On the Death of Sir Philip Sidney.*

21
It is of the utmost importance that a nation should have a correct standard by which to weigh the character of its rulers.
LORD JOHN RUSSELL—*Introduction to the 3rd Vol. of the Correspondence of the Duke of Bedford.*

22
Da krabbeln sie num, wie die Ratten auf der Keule des Hercules.
They [the present generation] are like rats crawling about the club of Hercules.
SCHILLER—*Die Räuber*. I. 2.

1 Gemeine Naturen
Zahlen mit dem, was sie thun, edle mit dem, was sie sind.

Common natures pay with what they do, noble ones with what they are.

SCHILLER—*Unterschied der Stände.*

2 Quæris Alcidæ parem?
Nemo est nisi ipse.

Do you seek Alcides' equal? None is, except himself.

SENECA—*Hercules Furens.* I. 1. 84.

(See also MASSINGER)

3 I know him a notorious liar,
Think him a great way fool, solely a coward;
Yet these fix'd evils sit so fit in him,
That they take place, when virtue's steely bones
Look bleak i' the cold wind.

All's Well That Ends Well. Act I. Sc. 1. L. 111.

4
He is deformed, crooked, old, and sere,
Ill-faced, worse-bodied, shapeless everywhere;
Vicious, ungentle, foolish, blunt, unkind,
Stigmatical in making, worse in mind.

Comedy of Errors. Act IV. Sc. 2. L. 19.

5
Though I am not splenitive and rash,
Yet have I something in me dangerous.

Hamlet. Act V. Sc. 1. L. 285.

6
There's neither honesty, manhood, nor good fellowship in thee.

Henry IV. Pt. I. Act I. Sc. 2. L. 154.

7
I am no proud Jack, like Falstaff; but a
Corinthian, glad of mettle, a good boy.

Henry IV. Pt. I. Act II. Sc. 4. L. 12.

8
What a frosty-spirited rogue is this!

Henry IV. Pt. I. Act II. Sc. 3. L. 21.

9
This bold bad man.

Henry VIII. Act II. Sc. 2.

(See also SPENSER)

10
O, he sits high in all the people's hearts:
And that which would appear offence in us.
His countenance, like richest alchemy,
Will change to virtue and to worthiness.

Julius Cæsar. Act I. Sc. 3. L. 157.

11 Thou art most rich, being poor;
Most choice, forsaken; and most lov'd, despis'd!
Thee and thy virtues here I seize upon.

King Lear. Act I. Sc. 1. L. 252.

12
I do profess to be no less than I seem; to serve him truly that will put me in trust; to love him that is honest; to converse with him that is wise, and says little; to fear judgment; to fight when I cannot choose; and to eat no fish.

King Lear. Act I. Sc. 4. L. 14.

13 What thou wouldst highly,
That wouldst thou holily; wouldst not play false,
And yet wouldst wrongly win.

Macbeth. Act I. Sc. 5. L. 21.

14 I grant him bloody,
Luxurious, avaricious, false, deceitful,
Sudden, malicious, smacking of every sin
That has a name.

Macbeth. Act IV. Sc. 3. L. 57.

15
There is a kind of character in thy life,
That to the observer doth thy history
Fully unfold.

Measure for Measure. Act I. Sc. 1. L. 28.

16
Nature hath fram'd strange fellows in her time:
Some that will evermore peep through their eyes,
And laugh, like parrots, at a bagpiper:
And other of such vinegar aspect
That they'll not show their teeth in way of smile,
Though Nestor swear the jest be laughable.

Merchant of Venice. Act I. Sc. 1. L. 51.

17
When he is best, he is a little worse than a man, and when he is worst, he is little better than a beast.

Merchant of Venice. Act I. Sc. 2. L. 94.

18
You are thought here to be the most senseless and fit man for the constable of the watch; therefore bear you the lantern.

Much Ado About Nothing. Act III. Sc. 3. L. 20.

19
Why, now I see there's mettle in thee, and even from this instant do build on thee a better opinion than ever before.

Othello. Act IV. Sc. 2. L. 205.

20
He hath a daily beauty in his life
That makes me ugly.

Othello. Act V. Sc. 1. L. 19.

21
O do not slander him, for he is kind.
Right; as snow in harvest.

Richard III. Act I. Sc. 4. L. 240.

22 Now do I play the touch,
To try if thou be current gold indeed.

Richard III. Act IV. Sc. 2. L. 9.

23 How this grace
Speaks his own standing! what a mental power
This eye shoots forth! How big imagination
Moves in this lip! to the dumbness of the gesture
One might interpret.

Timon of Athens. Act I. Sc. 1. L. 30.

24
The trick of singularity.

Twelfth Night. Act II. Sc. 5. L. 164.

25
He wants wit that wants resolved will.

Two Gentlemen of Verona. Act II. Sc. 6. L. 12.

26
His words are bonds, his oaths are oracles;
His love sincere, his thoughts immaculate;
* * * * * *
His heart as far from fraud as heaven from earth.

Two Gentlemen of Verona. Act II. Sc. 7. L. 75.

27
As headstrong as an allegory on the banks of the Nile.

SHERIDAN—*Rivals.* Act III. St. 3.

1
I'm called away by particular business. But I leave my character behind me.
SHERIDAN—*School for Scandal.* Act II. Sc. 2.

2
Messieurs, nous avons un maître, ce jeune homme fait tout, peut tout, et veut tout.
Gentlemen, we have a master; this young man does everything, can do everything and will do everything.
Attributed to SIEYÈS, who speaks of BONAPARTE.

3
It is energy—the central element of which is will—that produces the miracles of enthusiasm in all ages. Everywhere it is the main-spring of what is called force of character, and the sustaining power of all great action.
SAMUEL SMILES—*Character.* Ch. V.

4
Lax in their gaiters, laxer in their gait.
HORACE AND JAMES SMITH—*Rejected Addresses. The Theatre.*

5
Daniel Webster struck me much like a steam engine in trousers.
SYDNEY SMITH—*Lady Holland's Memoir.* Vol. I. P. 267.

6
He [Macaulay] is like a book in breeches.
SYDNEY SMITH—*Lady Holland's Memoir.* Ch. IX.

7
There is no man suddenly either excellently good or extremely evil.
SYDNEY SMITH—*Arcadia.* Bk. I.
(See also JUVENAL)

8
A bold bad man!
SPENSER—*Faerie Queene.* Bk. I. Canto I. St. 37. (See also HENRY VIII)

9
Worth, courage, honor, these indeed
Your sustenance and birthright are.
E. C. STEDMAN—*Beyond the Portals.* Pt. 10.

10
Yet though her mien carries much more invitation than command, to behold her is an immediate check to loose behaviour; and to love her is a liberal education.
STEELE—*Tatler.* No. 49. (Of Lady Elizabeth Hastings.)

11
It's the bad that's in the best of us
Leaves the saint so like the rest of us!
It's the good in the darkest-curst of us
Redeems and saves the worst of us!
It's the muddle of hope and madness;
It's the tangle of good and badness;
It's the lunacy linked with sanity
Makes up, and mocks, humanity!
ARTHUR STRINGER—*Humanity.*
(See also first quotation under topic.)

12
High characters (cries one), and he would see
Things that ne'er were, nor are, nor e'er will be.
SIR JOHN SUCKLING—*The Goblin's Epilogue.*

13
The true greatness of nations is in those qualities which constitute the greatness of the individual.
CHARLES SUMNER—*Oration on the True Grandeur of Nations.*

14
His own character is the arbiter of every one's fortune.
SYRUS—*Maxims.* 286.

15
Inerat tamen simplicitas ac liberalitas, quæ, nisi adsit modus in exitium vertuntur.
He possessed simplicity and liberality, qualities which beyond a certain limit lead to ruin.
TACITUS—*Annales.* III. 86.

16
In turbas et discordias pessimo cuique plurima vis: pax et quies bonis artibus indigent.
In seasons of tumult and discord bad men have most power; mental and moral excellence require peace and quietness.
TACITUS—*Annales.* IV. 1.

17
A man should endeavor to be as pliant as a reed, yet as hard as cedar-wood.
TALMUD—*Taanith.* 20.

18
Brama assai, poco spera e nulla chiede.
He, full of bashfulness and truth, loved much, hoped little, and desired naught.
TASSO—*Gerusalemme.* II. 16.

19
Fame is what you have taken,
Character's what you give;
When to this truth you waken,
Then you begin to live.
BAYARD TAYLOR—*Improvisations.* St. XI.

20
The hearts that dare are quick to feel;
The hands that wound are soft to heal.
BAYARD TAYLOR—*Soldiers of Peace.*

21
Such souls,
Whose sudden visitations daze the world,
Vanish like lightning, but they leave behind
A voice that in the distance far away
Wakens the slumbering ages.
HENRY TAYLOR—*Philip Van Artevelde.* Pt. I. Act I. Sc. 7.

22
He makes no friend who never made a foe.
TENNYSON—*Idylls of the King. Launcelot and Elaine.* L. 1109.
(See also YOUNG)

23
Self-reverence, self-knowledge, self-control.
TENNYSON—*Œnone.*

24
And one man is as good as another—and a great dale betther, as the Irish philosopher said.
THACKERAY—*Roundabout Papers. On Ribbons.*

25
None but himself can be his parallel.
LEWIS THEOBALD—*The Double Falsehood.* Quoted by POPE—*Dunciad.* II. 272.
Taken probably from the inscription under the portrait of COL. STRANGEWAYS, as quoted by DODD—*Epigrammatists.* P. 533. (Shee can bee immytated by none, nor paralleld by anie but by herselfe. S.R.N.I. *Votivæ Anglicæ.* (1624)
(See also MASSINGER, VERGIL)

1 Whoe'er amidst the sons
Of reason, valor, liberty and virtue,
Displays distinguished merit, is a noble
Of Nature's own creating.
THOMSON—*Coriolanus.* Act III. Sc. 3.

2
Just men, by whom impartial laws were given,
And saints, who taught and led the way to heaven!
TICKELL—*On the Death of Mr. Addison.* L. 41.

3
Nor e'er was to the bowers of bliss conveyed
A fairer spirit, or more welcome shade.
TICKELL—*On the Death of Mr. Addison.* L. 45.

4
Quantum instar in ipso est.
None but himself can be his parallel.
VERGIL—*Æneid.* VI. L. 865. He [Cæsar] was equal only to himself. SIR WILLIAM TEMPLE. As quoted by GRANGER—*Biographical History.* Found in DODD—*Epigrammatists.*
(See also THEOBALD)

5
Uni odiisque viro telisque frequentibus instant.
Ille velut rupes vastum quæ prodit in æquor,
Obvia ventorum furiis, expostaque ponto,
Vim cunctam atque minas perfert cœlique marisque,
Ipsa immota manens.

They attack this one man with their hate and their shower of weapons. But he is like some rock which stretches into the vast sea and which, exposed to the fury of the winds and beaten against by the waves, endures all the violence and threats of heaven and sea, himself standing unmoved.
VERGIL—*Æneid.* X. 692.

6
Accipe nunc Danaum insidias, et crimine ab uno
Disce omnes.

Learn now of the treachery of the Greeks, and from one example the character of the nation may be known.
VERGIL—*Æneid.* II. 65.

7
Il [le Chevalier de Belle-Isle] était capable de tout imaginer, de tout arranger, et de tout faire.

He (the Chevalier de Belle-Isle) was capable of imagining all, of arranging all, and of doing everything.
VOLTAIRE—*Siècle de Louis XV. Works.* XXI. P. 67.
(See also CLARENDON)

8
Lord of the golden tongue and smiting eyes;
Great out of season and untimely wise:
A man whose virtue, genius, grandeur, worth,
Wrought deadlier ill than ages can undo.
WM. WATSON—*The Political Luminary.*

9
I celebrate myself, and sing myself,
And what I assume you shall assume,
For every atom belonging to me as good as belongs to you.
WALT WHITMAN—*Song of Myself.* I.

10 Formed on the good old plan,
A true and brave and downright honest man!
He blew no trumpet in the market-place,
Nor in the church with hypocritic face
Supplied with cant the lack of Christian grace;
Loathing pretence, he did with cheerful will
What others talked of while their hands were still.
WHITTIER—*Daniel Neall.* II.

11
One that would peep and botanize
Upon his mother's grave.
WORDSWORTH—*A Poet's Epitaph.* St. 5.

12
But who, if he be called upon to face
Some awful moment to which Heaven has joined
Great issues, good or bad for humankind,
Is happy as a lover.
WORDSWORTH—*Character of a Happy Warrior.* L. 48.

13
Whom neither shape of danger can dismay,
Nor thought of tender happiness betray.
WORDSWORTH—*Character of a Happy Warrior.* L. 72.

14
The reason firm, the temperate will,
Endurance, foresight, strength and skill.
WORDSWORTH—*She was a Phantom of Delight.*

15
The man that makes a character, makes foes.
YOUNG—*Epistles to Mr. Pope.* Ep. I. L. 28.
(See also TENNYSON)

16 The man who consecrates his hours
By vig'rous effort and an honest aim,
At once he draws the sting of life and death;
He walks with nature and her paths are peace.
YOUNG—*Night Thoughts.* Night II. L. 187.

CHARITY (See also PHILANTHROPY)

17
In charity to all mankind, bearing no malice or ill-will to any human being, and even compassionating those who hold in bondage their fellow-men, not knowing what they do.
JOHN QUINCY ADAMS—*Letter to A. Bronson.* July 30, 1838.
(See also LINCOLN under RIGHT)

18
Charity is a virtue of the heart, and not of the hands.
ADDISON—*The Guardian.* No. 166.

19
The desire of power in excess caused the angels to fall; the desire of knowledge in excess caused man to fall; but in charity there is no excess, neither can angel or man come in danger by it.
BACON—*Essay. On Goodness.*

20
Charity and treating begin at home.
BEAUMONT AND FLETCHER—*Wit without Money.* Sc. 2.

21
Let them learn first to show pity at home.
BEAUMONT AND FLETCHER—*Wit without Money.* Sc. 2. MARSTON—*Histrio-Matrix.* 3. 165.
(See also GREFS, MONTLUC, POPE, SHERIDAN SMITH, TERENCE, TIMOTHY)

22
The voice of the world ["Charity begins at home"].
SIR THOMAS BROWNE—*Religio Medici.*

1
No sound ought to be heard in the church but the healing voice of Christian charity.
BURKE—*Reflections on the Revolution in France.* (1790)

2
Though I speak with the tongues of men and of angels, and have not charity, I am become as sounding brass, or a tinkling cymbal.
I Corinthians. XIII. 1.

3
Though I have all faith, so that I could remove mountains, and have not charity, I am nothing.
I Corinthians. XIII. 2.

4
Charity suffereth long and is kind; charity envieth not; charity vaunteth not itself, is not puffed up.
I Corinthians. XIII. 4.

5
And now abideth faith, hope, charity, these three; but the greatest of these is charity.
I Corinthians. XIII. 13.

6
True Charity, a plant divinely nurs'd.
COWPER—*Charity.* L. 573.

7
No farther seek his merits to disclose,
Or draw his frailties from their dread abode
(There they alike in trembling hope repose),
The bosom of his Father and his God.
GRAY—*Elegy in a Country Churchyard. Epitaph.*

8
When your courtyard twists, do not pour the water abroad.
GREFS.
(See also BEAUMONT)

9
Meek and lowly, pure and holy,
Chief among the "blessed three."
CHARLES JEFFERYS—*Charity.*

10
In silence, * * *
Steals on soft-handed Charity,
Tempering her gifts, that seem so free,
By time and place,
Till not a woe the bleak world see,
But finds her grace.
KEBLE—*The Christian Year. The Sunday After Ascension Day.* St. 6.

11
He is truly great who hath a great charity.
THOMAS À KEMPIS—*Imitation of Christ.* Bk. I. Ch. III. DIBDIN'S trans.

12
In necessasariis, unitas; In dubiis, libertas; in omnibus, caritas.
In things essential, unity; in doubtful, liberty; in all things, charity.
RUPERTUS MELDENIUS. So attributed by CANON FARRAR at Croyden Church Congress, 1877. Also attributed to Melancthon. Quoted as "A gude saying o' auld Mr. Guthrie" in *A Crack aboot the Kirk,* appended to *Memoirs of Norman Macleod, D.D.* Vol. I. P. 340.

13
All crush'd and stone-cast in behaviour,
She stood as a marble would stand,
Then the Saviour bent down, and the Saviour
In silence wrote on in the sand.
JOAQUIN MILLER—*Charity.*

14
Charité bien ordonné commence par soy même.
Charity well directed should begin at home.
MONTLUC—*La Comédie de Proverbes.* Act III. Sc. 7. (See also BEAUMONT)

15
Charity shall cover the multitude of sins.
I Peter. IV. 8.

16
In Faith and Hope the world will disagree,
But all mankind's concern is charity.
POPE—*Essay on Man.* Ep. III. L. 307.

17
Soft peace she brings, wherever she arrives:
She builds our quiet, as she forms our lives:
Lays the rough paths of peevish Nature even,
And opens in each heart a little Heaven.
PRIOR—*Charity.*

18
Charity itself fulfills the law,
And who can sever love from charity?
Love's Labour's Lost. Act IV. Sc. 3. L. 364.

19
Charity,
Which renders good for bad, blessings for curses.
Richard III. Act I. Sc. 2. L. 68.

20
I believe there is no sentiment he has such faith in as that "charity begins at home"
And his, I presume, is of that domestic sort which never stirs abroad at all.
SHERIDAN—*School for Scandal.* Act. V. Sc. 1.
(See also BEAUMONT)

21
Our charity begins at home,
And mostly ends where it begins.
HORACE SMITH—*Horace in London.* Bk. II. Ode 15.
(See also BEAUMONT)

22
Cold is thy hopeless heart, even as charity.
SOUTHEY—*Soldier's Wife.*

23
Proximus sum egomet mihi.
Charity begins at home. (Free trans.)
TERENCE—*Andria.* Act IV. Sc. 1. 12. Greek from MENANDER. See note to *Andria.* Act II. Sc. 5. 16. (Valpy's ed.)
(See also BEAUMONT)

24
Let them learn first to show piety at home.
I Timothy. V. 4.
(See also BEAUMONT)

CHASE, THE

25
He thought at heart like courtly Chesterfield,
Who, after a long chase o'er hills, dales, bushes,
And what not, though he rode beyond all price,
Ask'd next day, "if men ever hunted *twice?*"
BYRON—*Don Juan.* Canto XIV. St. 35.

26
They sought it with thimbles, they sought it with care;
They pursued it with forks and hope;
They threatened its life with a railway-share;
They charmed it with smiles and soap.
LEWIS CARROLL—*Hunting of the Snark.* Fit 5.

1
The dusky night rides down the sky
And ushers in the morn:
The hounds all join in glorious cry,
The huntsman winds his horn;
And a-hunting we will go.
HENRY FIELDING—*And a-Hunting We Will Go.*

2
The woods were made for the hunter of dreams,
The brooks for the fishers of song;
To the hunters who hunt for the gunless game
The streams and the woods belong.
There are thoughts that moan from the soul of pine
And thoughts in a flower bell curled;
And the thoughts that are blown with scent of the fern
Are as new and as old as the world.
SAM WALTER FOSS—*Bloodless Sportsman.*

3
Soon as Aurora drives away the night,
And edges eastern clouds with rosy light,
The healthy huntsman, with the cheerful horn,
Summons the dogs, and greets the dappled morn.
GAY—*Rural Sports.* Canto II. L. 93.

4
Love's torments made me seek the chase;
Rifle in hand, I roam'd apace.
Down from the tree, with hollow scoff,
The raven cried: "Head-off! head off!"
HEINE—*Book of Songs. Youthful Sorrows.* No. 8.

5
Of horn and morn, and hark and bark,
And echo's answering sounds,
All poets' wit hath ever writ
In dog-rel verse of hounds.
HOOD—*Epping Hunt.* St. 10.

6
D'ye ken John Peel with his coat so gay?
D'ye ken John Peel at the break of the day?
D'ye ken John Peel when he's far, far away,
With his hounds and his horn in the morning?
John Peel. Old Hunting Song. ("Coat so gray," said to be in the original)

7
It (hunting) was the labour of the savages of North America, but the amusement of the gentlemen of England.
SAMUEL JOHNSON—*Johnsoniana.*

8
With a hey, ho, chevy!
Hark forward, hark forward, tantivy!
Hark, hark, tantivy!
This day a stag must die.
JOHN O'KEEFE—Song in *Czar Peter.* Act I. Sc. 4.

9
Together let us beat this ample field,
Try what the open, what the covert yield.
POPE—*Essay on Man.* Ep. I. L. 9

10
Proud Nimrod first the bloody chase began,
A mighty hunter, and his prey was man.
POPE—*Windsor Forest.* L. 61.

11
My hoarse-sounding horn
Invites thee to the chase, the sport of kings.
WILLIAM SOMERVILLE—*The Chase.*

CHASTITY (See also PURITY)

12
There's a woman like a dew-drop,
She's so purer than the purest.
ROBERT BROWNING—*A Blot in the 'Scutcheon.* Act I. Sc. 3.

13
That chastity of honour which felt a stain like a wound.
BURKE—*Reflections on the Revolution in France.*

14
As pure as a pearl,
And as perfect: a noble and innocent girl.
OWEN MEREDITH (Lord Lytton)—*Lucile.* Pt. II. Canto VI. St. 16.

15
'Tis chastity, my brother, chastity;
She that has that is clad in complete steel,
And, like a quiver'd nymph with arrows keen,
May trace huge forests, and unharbour'd heaths,
Infamous hills, and sandy perilous wilds;
Where, through the sacred rays of chastity,
No savage fierce, bandite, or mountaineer,
Will dare to soil her virgin purity.
MILTON—*Comus.* L. 420.

16
So dear to Heaven is saintly chastity,
That, when a soul is found sincerely so,
A thousand liveried angels lacky her,
Driving far off each thing of sin and guilt.
MILTON—*Comus.* L. 453.

17
Like the stain'd web that whitens in the sun,
Grow pure by being purely shone upon.
MOORE—*Lalla Rookh. The Veiled Prophet of Khorassan.*

18
If she seem not chaste to me,
What care I how chaste she be?
SIR WALTER RALEIGH. Written the night before his death.

19
My chastity's the jewel of our house,
Bequeathed down from many ancestors.
All's Well That Ends Well. Act IV. Sc. 2. L. 46.

20
The very ice of chastity is in them.
As You Like It. Act III. Sc. 4. L. 18.

21
Chaste as the icicle
That's curded by the frost from purest snow
And hangs on Dian's temple.
Coriolanus. Act V. Sc. 3. L. 66.

22
As chaste as unsunn'd snow.
Cymbeline. Act. II. Sc. 5. L. 14.

23
A nice man is a man of nasty ideas.
SWIFT—*Preface* to one of BISHOP BURNET'S *Introductions to History of the Reformation.*

24
Neque femina amissa pudicitia alia abnuerit.
When a woman has lost her chastity, she will shrink from no crime.
TACITUS—*Annales.* IV. 3.

25
Then she rode forth, clothed on with chastity:
The deep air listen'd round her as she rode,
And all the low wind hardly breathed for fear.
TENNYSON—*Godiva.* L. 53.

1
Even from the body's purity, the mind
Receives a secret sympathetic aid.
THOMSON—*Seasons Summer.* L. 1,269.

CHATTAHOOCHEE (RIVER)

2
Out of the hills of Habersham,
Down the valleys of Hall,
I hurry amain to reach the plain;
Run the rapid and leap the fall,
Split at the rock, and together again
Accept my bed, or narrow or wide,
And flee from folly on every side
With a lover's pain to attain the plain,
Far from the hills of Habersham,
Far from the valleys of Hall.
SIDNEY LANIER—*The Song of the Chattahoochee.*

CHEERFULNESS

3
A cheerful temper joined with innocence will make beauty attractive, knowledge delightful and wit good-natured.
ADDISON—*The Tatler.* No. 192.

4
Cheered up himself with ends of verse
And sayings of philosophers.
BUTLER—*Hudibras.* Pt. I. Canto III. L. 1,011.

5
Cheerful at morn he wakes from short repose,
Breathes the keen air, and carols as he goes.
GOLDSMITH—*The Traveller.* L. 1853.

6
A cheerful look makes a dish a feast.
HERBERT—*Jacula Prudentum.*

7
Cheer up, the worst is yet to come.
PHILANDER JOHNSON. See *Everybody's Magazine*, May, 1920. P. 36. See TENNYSON—*Sea Dreams*, L. 5 from end.

8
It is good
To lengthen to the last a sunny mood.
LOWELL—*Legend of Brittany.* Pt. I. St. 35.

9
Leve fit quod bene fertur onus.
That load becomes light which is cheerfully borne.
OVID—*Amorum.* I. 2. 10.

10
Had she been light, like you,
Of such a merry, nimble, stirring spirit,
She might ha' been a grandam ere she died;
And so may you; for a light heart lives long.
Love's Labour's Lost. Act V. Sc. 2. L. 15.

11
Look cheerfully upon me.
Here, love; thou seest how dilgent I am.
Taming of the Shrew. Act IV. Sc. 3. L. 38.

12
He makes a July's day short as December,
And with his varying childness cures in me
Thoughts that would thick my blood.
Winter's Tale. Act I. Sc. 2. L. 169.

13
A cheerful life is what the Muses love,
A soaring spirit is their prime delight.
WORDSWORTH—*From the Dark Chambers.*

14
Corn shall make the young men cheerful.
Zechariah. IX. 17.

CHERRY TREE

Cerasus

15
Sweet is the air with the budding haws, and the valley stretching for miles below
Is white with blossoming cherry-trees, as if just covered with lightest snow.
LONGFELLOW—*Christus. Golden Legend.* Pt. IV.

CHESTNUT TREE

Castanea Vesca

16
When I see the chestnut letting
All her lovely blossoms falter down, I think,
"Alas the day!"
JEAN INGELOW—*The Warbling of Blackbirds.*

17
The chestnuts, lavish of their long-hid gold,
To the faint Summer, beggared now and old,
Pour back the sunshine hoarded 'neath her favoring eye.
LOWELL—*Indian-Summer Reverie.* St. 10.

CHILDHOOD (See also BABYHOOD)

18
The children in Holland take pleasure in making
What the children in England take pleasure in breaking.
Old Nursery Rhyme.

19
My lovely living Boy,
My hope, my hap, my Love, my life, my joy.
DU BARTAS—*Divine Weekes and Workes. Second Week, Fourth Day.* Bk. II.

20
'Tis not a life,
'Tis but a piece of childhood thrown away.
BEAUMONT AND FLETCHER—*Philaster.* Act V. Sc. 2. L. 15.

21
Do ye hear the children weeping, O my brothers,
Ere the sorrow comes with years?
They are leaning their young heads against their mothers,
And that cannot stop their tears.
E. B. BROWNING—*The Cry of the Children.*

22
Women know
The way to rear up children (to be just);
They know a simple, merry, tender knack
Of tying sashes, fitting baby-shoes,
And stringing pretty words that make no sense,
And kissing full sense into empty words;
Which things are corals to cut life upon,
Although such trifles.
E. B. BROWNING—*Aurora Leigh.* Bk. I. L. 48.

23
[Witches] steal young children out of their cradles, *ministerio dæmonum*, and put deformed in their rooms, which we call changelings.
BURTON—*Anatomy of Melancholy.* Pt. I. Sect. II. Memb. 1. Subsect. 3.

24
Diogenes struck the father when the son swore.
BURTON—*Anatomy of Melancholy.* Pt. III. Sect. II. Memb. 6. Subsect. 5.

25
Besides, they always smell of bread and butter.
BYRON—*Beppo.* St. 39.

1
A little curly-headed, good-for-nothing,
And mischief-making monkey from his birth.
BYRON—*Don Juan*. Canto I. St. 25.

2
Pietas fundamentum est omnium virtutum.
The dutifulness of children is the foundation of all virtues.
CICERO—*Oratio Pro Cnæo Plancio*. XII.

3
When I was a child, I spake as a child, I understood as a child, I thought as a child; but when I became a man, I put away childish things.
I Corinthians. XIII. 11.

4
Better to be driven out from among men than to be disliked of children.
R. H. DANA—*The Idle Man. Domestic Life*.

5
They are idols of hearts and of households;
They are angels of God in disguise;
His sunlight still sleeps in their tresses,
His glory still gleams in their eyes;
Those truants from home and from Heaven
They have made me more manly and mild;
And I know now how Jesus could liken
The kingdom of God to a child.
CHAS. M. DICKINSON—*The Children*.

6
When the lessons and tasks are all ended,
And the school for the day is dismissed,
The little ones gather around me,
To bid me good-night and be kissed;
Oh, the little white arms that encircle
My neck in their tender embrace
Oh, the smiles that are halos of heaven,
Shedding sunshine of love on my face.
CHAS. M. DICKINSON—*The Children*.

7
Childhood has no forebodings; but then, it is soothed by no memories of outlived sorrow.
GEORGE ELIOT—*Mill on the Floss*. Bk. I. Ch. IX.

8
Wynken, Blynken and Nod one night
Sailed off in a wooden shoe—
Sailed on a river of crystal light
Into a sea of dew.
EUGENE FIELD—*Wynken, Blynken and Nod*.

9
Teach your child to hold his tongue,
He'll learn fast enough to speak.
BENJ. FRANKLIN—*Poor Richard Maxims*. (1734)

10
By sports like these are all their cares beguil'd,
The sports of children satisfy the child.
GOLDSMITH—*The Traveller*. L. 153.

11
Alas! regardless of their doom,
The little victims play;
No sense have they of ills to come,
Nor care beyond to-day.
GRAY—*On a Distant Prospect of Eton College*. St. 6.

12
But still when the mists of doubt prevail,
And we lie becalmed by the shores of age,
We hear from the misty troubled shore
The voice of the children gone before.
Drawing the soul to its anchorage.
BRET HARTE—*A Greyport Legend*. St. 6.

13
I think that saving a little child
And bringing him to his own,
Is a derned sight better business
Than loafing around the throne.
JOHN HAY—*Little Breeches*.

14
Few sons attain the praise
Of their great sires and most their sires disgrace.
HOMER—*Odyssey*. Bk. II. L. 315. POPE'S trans.

15
Nondum enim quisquam suum parentem ipse cognosvit.
It is a wise child that knows his own father.
HOMER—*Odyssey*. Bk. I. 216. Trans. from the Greek by Clarke. Same idea in EURIPIDES. Quoted by EUSTATH—*Ad Hom.* P. 1412. ARISTOTLE—*Rhetoric*. MENANDER—*Carthaginian*. See STOBÆUS—*Anthology*. LXXVI. 7.

16
Another tumble! that's his precious nose!
HOOD—*Parental Ode to My Son*.

17
Oh, when I was a tiny boy
My days and nights were full of joy.
My mates were blithe and kind!
No wonder that I sometimes sigh
And dash the tear drop from my eye
To cast a look behind!
HOOD—*Retrospective Review*.

18
Children, ay, forsooth,
They bring their own love with them when they come,
But if they come not there is peace and rest;
The pretty lambs! and yet she cries for more:
Why, the world's full of them, and so is heaven—
They are not rare.
JEAN INGELOW—*Supper at the Mill*.

19
Nil dictu fœdum visuque hæc limina tangat
Intra quæ puer est.
Let nothing foul to either eye or ear reach those doors within which dwells a boy.
JUVENAL—*Satires*. XIV. 44.

20
Les enfants n'ont ni passé ni avenir; et, ce qui ne nous arrive guère, ils jouissent du présent.
Children have neither past nor future; and that which seldom happens to us, they rejoice in the present.
LA BRUYÈRE—*Les Caractères*. XI.

21
Mais un fripon d'enfant (cet âge est sans pitié).
But a rascal of a child (that age is without pity).
LA FONTAINE—*Fables*. IX. 2.

22
A babe is fed with milk and praise.
LAMB—*The First Tooth*. In *Poetry for Children* by CHARLES and MARY LAMB.
(See also SHELLEY)

23
Oh, would I were a boy again,
When life seemed formed of sunny years,
And all the heart then knew of pain
Was wept away in transient tears!
MARK LEMON—*Oh, Would I Were a Boy Again*.

1
There was a little girl,
And she had a little curl,
Right in the middle of her forehead;
When she was good she was very, very good,
When she was bad she was horrid.
LONGFELLOW. See BLANCHE ROOSEVELT TUCKER-MACHETTA—*Home Life of Longfellow.*

2
Ah! what would the world be to us
If the children were no more?
We should dread the desert behind us
Worse than the dark before.
LONGFELLOW—*Children.* St. 4.

3
Perhaps there lives some dreamy boy, untaught
In schools, some graduate of the field or street,
Who shall become a master of the art,
An admiral sailing the high seas of thought
Fearless and first, and steering with his fleet
For lands not yet laid down in any chart.
LONGFELLOW—*Possibilities.*

4
Who can foretell for what high cause
This darling of the gods was born?
ANDREW MARVELL—*Picture of T. C. in a Prospect of Flowers.*

5
Each one could be a Jesus mild,
Each one has been a little child,
A little child with laughing look,
A lovely white unwritten book;
A book that God will take, my friend,
As each goes out at journey's end.
MASEFIELD—*Everlasting Mercy.* St. 27.

6
And he who gives a child a treat
Makes Joy-bells ring in Heaven's street,
And he who gives a child a home
Builds palaces in Kingdom come,
And she who gives a baby birth,
Brings Saviour Christ again to Earth.
MASEFIELD—*Everlasting Mercy.* St. 50.

7
Lord, give to men who are old and rougher
The things that little children suffer,
And let keep bright and undefiled
The young years of the little child.
MASEFIELD—*Everlasting Mercy.* St. 67.

8
Rachel weeping for her children, and would not be comforted, because they are not.
Matthew. II. 18; *Jeremiah.* XXXI. 15.

9
Ay, these young things lie safe in our hearts just so long
As their wings are in growing; and when these are strong
They break it, and farewell! the bird flies!
OWEN MEREDITH (Lord Lytton)—*Lucile.* Canto VI. Pt. II. St. 29.

10
The childhood shows the man,
As morning shows the day.
MILTON—*Paradise Regained.* Bk. IV. L. 220.
(See also WORDSWORTH)

11
As children gath'ring pebbles on the shore.
MILTON—*Paradise Regained.* Bk. IV. L. 330.

12
Ah, il n'y a plus d'enfant.
Ah, there are no children nowadays.
MOLIÈRE—*Le Malade Imaginaire.* II. 2.

13
Parentes objurgatione digni sunt, qui nolunt liberos suos severa lege proficere.
Parents deserve reproof when they refuse to benefit their children by severe discipline.
PETRONIUS ARBITER—*Satyricon.* IV.

14
The wildest colts make the best horses.
PLUTARCH—*Life of Themistocles.*

15
Behold the child, by Nature's kindly law,
Pleas'd with a rattle, tickled with a straw.
POPE—*Essay on Man.* Ep. II. L. 275.

16
A wise son maketh a glad father.
Proverbs. X. 1.

17
Train up a child in the way he should go; and when he is old he will not depart from it.
Proverbs. XXII. 6.

18
Many daughters have done virtuously, but thou excellest them all.
Proverbs. XXXI. 29.

19
Happy is the man that hath his quiver full of them.
Psalms. CXXVII. 5.

20
Thy children like olive plants round about thy table.
Psalms. CXXVIII. 3.

21
There is nothing more to say,
They have all gone away
From the house on the hill.
EDWIN A. ROBINSON—*The House on the Hill.*

22
Pointing to such, well might Cornelia say,
When the rich casket shone in bright array,
"These are *my* Jewels!" Well of such as he,
When Jesus spake, well might the language be,
"Suffer these little ones to come to me!"
SAMUEL ROGERS—*Human Life.* L. 202.

23
L'enfance est le sommeil de la raison.
Childhood is the sleep of reason.
ROUSSEAU—*Émile.* Bk. II.

24
Glücklicher Säugling! dir ist ein unendlicher
Raum noch die Wiege,
Werde Mann, und dir wird eng die unendliche
Welt.
Happy child! the cradle is still to thee a vast space; but when thou art a man the boundless world will be too small for thee.
SCHILLER—*Das Kind in der Wiege.*

25
Wage du zu irren und zu träumen.
Hoher Sinn liegt oft im kind'schen Spiel.
Dare to err and to dream. Deep meaning often lies in childish plays.
SCHILLER—*Theklo.* St. 6.

26
And children know,
Instinctive taught, the friend and foe.
SCOTT—*Lady of the Lake.* Canto II. St. 14.

1
O lord! my boy, my Arthur, my fair son!
My life, my joy, my food, my all the world!
My widow-comfort, and my sorrow's cure!
King John. Act III. Sc. 4. L. 103.

2
We have no such daughter, nor shall ever see
That face of her again. Therefore begone
Without our grace, our love, our benizon.
King Lear. Act I. Sc. 1. L. 266.

3
Fathers that wear rags
Do make their children blind;
But fathers that bear bags
Shall see their children kind.
King Lear. Act II. Sc. 4. L. 48.

4
It is a wise father that knows his own child.
Merchant of Venice. Act II. Sc. 2. L. 80.

5
Oh, 'tis a parlous boy;
Bold, quick, ingenious, forward, capable;
He's all the mother's from the top to toe.
Richard III. Act III. Sc. 1. L. 154.

6
Your children were vexation to your youth,
But mine shall be a comfort to your age.
Richard III. Act IV. Sc. 4. L. 305.

7
Behold, my lords,
Although the print be little, the whole matter
And copy of the father, eye, nose, lip,
The trick of's frown, his forehead, nay, the valley,
The pretty dimples of his chin and cheek; his smiles;
The very mould and frame of hand, nail, finger.
Winter's Tale. Act II. Sc. 3. L. 98.

8
A little child born yesterday
A thing on mother's milk and kisses fed.
SHELLEY—*Homer's Hymn to Mercury.* St. 69.
(See also LAMB)

9
It is very nice to think
The world is full of meat and drink
With little children saying grace
In every Christian kind of place.
STEVENSON—*Child's Garden of Verses. A Thought.*

10
In winter I get up at night
And dress by yellow candle-light.
In summer, quite the other way,
I have to go to bed by day.
STEVENSON—*Child's Garden of Verses. Bed in Summer.*

11
When I am grown to man's estate
I shall be very proud and great
And tell the other girls and boys
Not to meddle with my toys.
STEVENSON—*Child's Garden of Verses. Looking Forward.*

12
Every night my prayers I say,
And get my dinner every day,
And every day that I've been good,
I get an orange after food.
STEVENSON—*Child's Garden of Verses. System.*

13
While here at home, in shining day,
We round the sunny garden play,
Each little Indian sleepy-head
Is being kissed and put to bed.
STEVENSON—*Child's Garden of Verses. The Sun's Travels.*

14
Children are the keys of Paradise,
They alone are good and wise,
Because their thoughts, their very lives, are prayer.
R. H. STODDARD—*The Children's Prayer.*

15
If there is anything that will endure
The eye of God, because it still is pure,
It is the spirit of a little child,
Fresh from his hand, and therefore undefiled.
R. H. STODDARD—*The Children's Prayer.*

16
"Not a child: I call myself a boy,"
Says my king, with accent stern yet mild;
Now nine years have brought him change of joy—
"Not a child."
SWINBURNE—*Not a Child.* St. 1.

17
But still I dream that somewhere there must be
The spirit of a child that waits for me.
BAYARD TAYLOR—*The Poet's Journal. Third Evening.*

18
Nam qui mentiri, aut fallere insuerit patrem, aut
Audebit: tanto magis audebit cæteros.
Pudore et liberalitate liberos
Retinere satius esse credo, quam metu.

For he who has acquired the habit of lying or deceiving his father, will do the same with less remorse to others. I believe that it is better to bind your children to you by a feeling of respect, and by gentleness, than by fear.
TERENCE—*Adelphi.* I. 1. 30.

19
Ut quisque suum vult esse, ita est.
As each one wishes his children to be, so they are.
TERENCE—*Adelphi.* III. 3. 46.

20
Birds in their little nests agree:
And 'tis a shameful sight,
When children of one family
Fall out, and chide, and fight.
ISAAC WATTS—*Divine Songs.* XVII.

21
In books, or work, or healthful play,
Let my first years be past,
That I may give for every day
Some good account at last.
ISAAC WATTS—*Against Idleness.*

22
Oh, for boyhood's time of June,
Crowding years in one brief moon,
When all things I heard or saw,
Me, their master, waited for.
WHITTIER—*The Barefoot Boy.* St. 3.

23
The sweetest roamer is a boy's young heart.
GEORGE E. WOODBERRY—*Agathon.*

24
The child is father of the man.
WORDSWORTH—*My Heart Leaps Up.*
(See also MILTON; also DRYDEN under MAN)

1
Sweet childish days, that were as long
As twenty days are now.
WORDSWORTH—*To a Butterfly.*

2 A simple child,
That lightly draws its breath,
And feels its life in every limb,
What should it know of death?
WORDSWORTH—*We Are Seven.*

3
The booby father craves a booby son,
And by heaven's blessing thinks himself undone.
YOUNG—*Love of Fame.* Satire II. L. 1.

CHOICE

4
If I were not Alexander, I should wish to be Diogenes.
ALEXANDER to DIOGENES when requested to stand a little out of his sunshine. PLUTARCH—*Life of Alexander.*

5
He that will not when he may,
When he will he shall have nay.
BURTON—*Anat. of Mel.* Pt. III. Sect. 2. Mem. 5. Subs. 5. Quoted.

6
Better to sink beneath the shock
Than moulder piecemeal on the rock!
BYRON—*The Giaour.* L. 969.

7
Of harmes two the less is for to chose.
CHAUCER—*Troilus and Criseyde.* Bk. II. L. 470.
(See also quotations under EVIL)

8
What voice did on my spirit fall,
Peschiera, when thy bridge I crost?
'Tis better to have fought and lost
Than never to have fought at all!
ARTHUR HUGH CLOUGH—*Peschiera.*
(See also TENNYSON under LOVE)

9
Life often presents us with a choice of evils, rather than of goods.
C. C. COLTON—*Lacon.* P. 362.

10
Devine, si tu peux, et choisis, si tu l'oses.
Guess, if you can, and choose, if you dare.
CORNEILLE—*Héraclius.* IV. 4.

11
The strongest principle of growth lies in human choice.
GEORGE ELIOT—*Daniel Deronda.* Bk. VI. Ch. XLII.

12
God offers to every mind its choice between truth and repose.
EMERSON—*Essay.* *Intellect.*

13
Betwixt the devil and the deep sea.
ERASMUS—*Adagia.* Ch. III. Cent. IV. 94. Quoted from the Greek. Proverb in HAZLITT—*English Proverbs.* CLARKE—*Parœmiologia.* (1639) Said by COL. MONROE—*Expedition and Observations.* Pt. III. P. 55. (Ed. 1637)

14
Inter sacrum et sazim.
Between the victim and the stone knife.
ERASMUS—*Letter to Pirkheimer.* PLAUTUS—*Captivi.* 3. 4. 84. Also said by APPULEIUS.

15
Se soumettre ou se démettre.
Submit or resign.
GAMBETTA.

16
Where passion leads or prudence points the way.
ROBERT LOWTH—*The Choice of Hercules.* 1.

17
But one thing is needful; and Mary hath chosen that good part which shall not be taken away from her.
Luke. X. 42.

18
For many are called, but few are chosen.
Matthew. XXII. 14.

19 Rather than be less
Car'd not to be at all.
MILTON—*Paradise Lost.* Bk. II. L. 47.

20
Who would not, finding way, break loose from hell,
* * * * * *
And boldly venture to whatever place
Farthest from pain?
MILTON—*Paradise Lost.* Bk. IV. L. 889.

21
The difficulty in life is the choice.
GEORGE MOORE—*Bending of the Bough.* Act IV.

22 Or fight or fly,
This choice is left ye, to resist or die.
POPE—*Homer's Odyssey.* Bk. XXII. L. 79.

23
S'asseoir entre deux selles le cul a terre.
Between two stools one sits on the ground.
RABELAIS—*Gargantua.* Bk. I. Ch. II. Entre deux arcouns chet cul a terre. In *Les Proverbes del Vilain.* MS. BODLEIAN. (About 1303)

24
Set honour in one eye and death i' the other,
And I will look on both indifferently.
Julius Cæsar. Act I. Sc. 2. L. 86.

25 Which of them shall I take?
Both? one? or neither? Neither can be enjoy'd,
If both remain alive.
King Lear. Act V. Sc. 1. L. 57.

26
I will not choose what many men desire,
Because I will not jump with common spirits,
And rank me with the barbarous multitudes.
Merchant of Venice. Act II. Sc. 9. L. 31.

27
Preferment goes by letter and affection.
Othello. Act I. Sc. 1. L. 36.

28
There's small choice in rotten apples.
Taming of the Shrew. Act I. Sc. 1. L. 138.

29
"Thy royal will be done—'tis just,"
Replied the wretch, and kissed the dust;
"Since, my last moments to assuage,
Your Majesty's humane decree
Has deigned to leave the choice to me,
I'll die, so please you, of old age."
HORACE SMITH—*The Jester Condemned to Death.*

1
Better fifty years of Europe than a cycle of Cathay.
TENNYSON—*Locksley Hall.* St. 92.

2
When to elect there is but one,
'Tis Hobson's *Choice; take that or none.*
THOS. WARD—*England's Reformation.* Canto IV. L. 896. ("Hobson's Choice" explained in *Spectator.* No. 509.)

3 Great God! I'd rather be
A Pagan, suckled in a creed outworn;
So might I, standing on this pleasant lea,
Have glimpses that would make me less forlorn;
Have sight of Proteus rising from the sea,
Or hear old Triton blow his wreathed horn.
WORDSWORTH—*Miscellaneous Sonnets.* Pt. I. Sonnet XXXIII.
(See also MOORE under CHRISTIANITY; HOLMES under MUSIC)

4
A strange alternative * * *
Must women have a doctor or a dance?
YOUNG—*Love of Fame.* Satire V. L. 189.

CHRIST

5
There is a green hill far away,
Without a city wall,
Where the dear Lord was crucified
Who died to save us all.
CECIL FRANCES ALEXANDER—*There is a Green Hill.*

6
Hail, O bleeding Head and wounded,
With a crown of thorns surrounded,
Buffeted, and bruised and battered,
Smote with reed by striking shattered,
Face with spittle vilely smeared!
Hail, whose visage sweet and comely,
Marred by fouling stains and homely,
Changed as to its blooming color,
All now turned to deathly pallor,
Making heavenly hosts affeared!
ST. BERNARD OF CLAIRVAUX—*Passion Hymn.* ABRAHAM COLES' trans.

7
In every pang that rends the heart
The Man of Sorrows had a part.
MICHAEL BRUCE—*Gospel Sonnets. Christ Ascended.* Attributed to JOHN LOGAN, who issued the poems with emendations of his own.
"Every pang that rends the heart."
See also GOLDSMITH—*The Captivity.*

8 Lovely was the death
Of Him whose life was Love! Holy with power,
He on the thought-benighted Skeptic beamed
Manifest Godhead.
COLERIDGE—*Religious Musings.* L. 29.

9
A pagan heart, a Christian soul had he.
He followed Christ, yet for dead Pan he sighed,
As if Theocritus in Sicily
Had come upon the Figure crucified,
And lost his gods in deep, Christ-given rest.
MAURICE FRANCIS EGAN—*Maurice de Guērin.*

10
Fra Lippo, we have learned from thee
A lesson of humanity:
To every mother's heart forlorn,
In every house the Christ is born.
R. W. GILDER—*A Madonna of Fra Lippo Lippi.*

11
In darkness there is no choice. It is light that enables us to see the differences between things; and it is Christ that gives us light.
J. C. AND A. W. HARE—*Guesses at Truth.*

12
Who did leave His Father's throne,
To assume thy flesh and bone?
Had He life, or had He none?
If he had not liv'd for thee,
Thou hadst died most wretchedly
And two deaths had been thy fee.
HERBERT—*The Church. Business.*

13
Vicisti, Gallilœ.
Thou hast conquered, O Galilæan.
Attributed to JULIAN the APOSTATE. MONTAIGNE — *Essays.* Bk. II. Ch. XIX. Claim dismissed by German and French scholars. EMPEROR JUSTINIAN at the dedication of the Cathedral of St. Sophia, built on the plan of the Temple of Jerusalem, said: "I have vanquished thee, O Solomon."
(See also SWINBURNE)

14
All His glory and beauty come from within, and there He delights to dwell, His visits there are frequent, His conversation sweet, His comforts refreshing; and His peace passing all understanding.
THOMAS À KEMPIS—*Imitation of Christ.* Bk. II. Ch. I. DIBDIN's trans.

15
Into the woods, my Master went,
Clean forspent, forspent.
Into the woods my Master came,
Forspent with love and shame.
But the olives they were not blind to Him,
The little gray leaves were kind to Him:
The thorn-tree had a mind to Him,
When into the woods He came.
SIDNEY LANIER—*A Ballad of Trees and the Master.*

16
God never gave man a thing to do concerning which it were irreverent to ponder how the Son of God would have done it.
GEORGE MACDONALD—*The Marquis of Lossie.* Vol. II. Ch. XVII.

17
The foxes have holes, and the birds of the air have nests; but the Son of Man hath not where to lay his head.
Matthew. VIII. 20.

18
The Pilot of the Galilean Lake.
MILTON—*Lycidas.* L. 109.

19
Near, so very near to God,
Nearer I cannot be;
For in the person of his Son
I am as near as he.
CATESBY PAGET—*Hymn.*

1 But chiefly Thou,
Whom soft-eyed Pity once led down from Heaven
To bleed for man, to teach him how to live,
And, oh! still harder lesson! how to die.
BISHOP PORTEUS—*Death*. L. 316.
(See also TICKNELL under EXAMPLE)

2 In those holy fields.
Over whose acres walk'd those blessed feet
Which, fourteen hundred years ago, were nail'd
For our advantage on the bitter cross.
Henry IV. Pt. I. Act I. Sc. 1. L. 24.

3
And on his brest a bloodie crosse he bore,
The deare remembrance of his dying Lord,
For whose sweete sake that glorious badge he wore.
SPENSER—*Faerie Queene*. Bk. I. Canto I. St. 2.

4
Thou hast conquered, O pale Galilean;
The world has grown gray from thy breath;
We have drunken from things Lethean,
And fed on the fullness of death.
SWINBURNE—*Hymn to Proserpine*.
(See also JULIAN)

5
And so the Word had breath, and wrought
With human hands the creed of creeds
In loveliness of perfect deeds,
More strong than all poetic thoughts;
Which he may read that binds the sheaf,
Or builds the house, or digs the grave,
And those wild eyes that watch the waves
In roarings round the coral reef.
TENNYSON—*In Memoriam*. XXXVI.

6
His love at once and dread instruct our thought;
As man He suffer'd and as God He taught.
EDMUND WALLER—*Of Divine Love*. Canto III. L. 41.

CHRISTIANITY

7
Almost thou persuadest me to be a Christian.
Acts. XXVI. 28.

8
Christians have burnt each other, quite persuaded.
That all the Apostles would have done as they did.
BYRON—*Don Juan*. Canto I. St. 83.

9
His Christianity was muscular.
BENJ. DISRAELI—*Endymion*. Ch. XIV.

10
A Christian is God Almighty's gentleman.
J. C. AND A. W. HARE—*Guesses at Truth*.

11
Look in, and see Christ's chosen saint
In triumph wear his Christ-like chain;
No fear lest he should swerve or faint;
"His life is Christ, his death is gain."
KEBLE—*Christian Year. St. Luke. The Evangelist*.

12
Now it is not good for the Christian's health
To hustle the Aryan brown,
For the Christian riles and the Aryan smiles, and it weareth the Christian down.
And the end of the fight is a tombstone white
With the name of the late deceased—
And the epitaph drear: "A fool lies here
Who tried to hustle the East."
KIPLING—*Naulahka*. Heading of Ch. V.

13
What was invented two thousand years ago was the spirit of Christianity.
GERALD STANLEY LEE—*Crowds*. Bk. II. Ch. XVIII.

14
Servant of God, well done, well hast thou fought
The better fight.
MILTON—*Paradise Lost*. Bk. VI. L. 29.

15
Persons of mean understandings, not so inquisitive, nor so well instructed, are made good Christians, and by reverence and obedience, implicity believe, and abide by their belief.
MONTAIGNE—*Essays. Of Vain Subleties*.

16
Yes,—rather plunge me back in pagan night,
And take my chance with Socrates for bliss,
Than be the Christian of a faith like this,
Which builds on heavenly cant its earthly sway,
And in a convert mourns to lose a prey.
MOORE—*Intolerance*. L. 68.
(See also WORDSWORTH under CHOICE)

17
Tolle crucem, qui vis auferre coronam.
Take up the cross if thou the crown would'st gain.
ST. PAULINUS, Bishop of Nola.
(See also QUARLES under BLISS)

18
Yet still a sad, good Christian at the heart.
POPE—*Moral Essay*. Ep. II. L. 68.

19
You are Christians of the best edition, all picked and culled.
RABELAIS—*Works*. Bk. IV. Ch. L.

20
Plant neighborhood and Christian-like accord
In their sweet bosoms.
Henry V. Act V. Sc. 2. L. 381.

21
O father Abram, what these Christians are,
Whose own hard dealings teaches them suspect
The thoughts of others.
Merchant of Venice. Act I. Sc. 3. L. 162.

22
The Hebrew will turn Christian: he grows kind.
Merchant of Venice. Act I. Sc. 3. L. 179.

23
My daughter! O, my ducats! O, my daughter!
Fled with a Christian! O my Christian ducats.
Merchant of Venice. Act II. Sc. 8. L. 15.

24
If thou keep promise, I shall end this strife,
Become a Christian and thy loving wife.
Merchant of Venice. Act II. Sc. 3. L. 20.

25
This making of Christians will raise the price of hogs: if we grow all to be pork-eaters, we shall not shortly have a rasher on the coals for money.
Merchant of Venice. Act III. Sc. 5. L. 24.

26
For in converting Jews to Christians, you raise the price of pork.
Merchant of Venice. Act III. Sc. 5. L. 38.

1
It is spoke as Christians ought to speak.
Merry Wives of Windsor. Act I. Sc. 1. L. 103.

2
A virtuous and a Christian-like conclusion,
To pray for them that have done scathe to us.
Richard III. Act I. Sc. 3. L. 316.

3
Methinks sometimes I have no more wit than a Christian or an ordinary man has.
Twelfth Night. Act I. Sc. 3. L. 88.

4
I thank the goodness and the grace
Which on my birth have smiled,
And made me, in these Christian days
A happy Christian child.
JANE TAYLOR—*Child's Hymn of Praise*.
(See also WATTS)

5
Vide, inquiunt ut invicem se diligant.
See how these Christians love one another.
TERTULLIAN — *Apologeticus*. Ch. XXIX.
Claimed also for JULIAN THE APOSTATE.

6
Lord, I ascribe it to Thy grace,
And not to chance, as others do,
That I was born of Christian race.
WATTS—*Divine Songs for Children*. (JANE TAYLOR'S lines are popularly ascribed to WATTS)

7
Whatever makes men good Christians, makes them good citizens.
DANIEL WEBSTER—*Speech at Plymouth*. Dec. 22, 1820. Vol. I. P. 44.

8
A Christian is the highest style of man.
YOUNG—*Night Thoughts*. Night IV. L. 788.

CHRISTMAS

9
The mistletoe hung in the castle hall,
The holly branch shone on the old oak wall.
THOS. HAYNES BAYLY—*The Mistletoe Bough*.

10
And the Baron's retainers were blithe and gay,
And keeping their Christmas holiday.
THOS. HAYNES BAYLY—*The Mistletoe Bough*.

11
No trumpet-blast profaned
The hour in which the Prince of Peace was born;
No bloody streamlet stained
Earth's silver rivers on that sacred morn.
BRYANT—*Christmas in 1875*.

12
Christians awake, salute the happy morn
Whereon the Saviour of the world was born.
JOHN BYROM—*Hymn for Christmas Day*.

13
For little children everywhere
A joyous season still we make;
We bring our precious gifts to them,
Even for the dear child Jesus' sake.
PHEBE CARY—*Christmas*.

14
It was the calm and silent night!
Seven hundred years and fifty-three
Had Rome been growing up to might
And now was queen of land and sea.
No sound was heard of clashing wars,
Peace brooded o'er the hushed domain;
Apollo, Pallas, Jove and Mars,
Held undisturbed their ancient reign,
In the solemn midnight,
Centuries ago.
ALFRED DOMETT—*Christmas Hymn*.

15
How bless'd, how envied, were our life,
Could we but scape the poulterer's knife!
But man, curs'd man, on Turkeys preys,
And Christmas shortens all our days:
Sometimes with oysters we combine,
Sometimes assist the savory chine;
From the low peasant to the lord,
The Turkey smokes on every board.
GAY—*Fables*. Pt. I. Fable 39.

16
What babe new born is this that in a manger cries?
Near on her lowly bed his happy mother lies.
Oh, see the air is shaken with white and heavenly wings—
This is the Lord of all the earth, this is the King of Kings.
R. W. GILDER—*A Christmas Hymn*. St. 4.

17
As I sat on a sunny bank
On Christmas day in the morning
I spied three ships come sailing in.
WASHINGTON IRVING—*Sketch book. The Sunny Bank*. From an old Worcestershire Song.

18
High noon behind the tamarisks, the sun is hot above us—
As at home the Christmas Day is breaking wan,
They will drink our healths at dinner, those who tell us how they love us,
And forget us till another year be gone!
KIPLING—*Christmas in India*.

19
Shepherds at the grange,
Where the Babe was born,
Sang with many a change,
Christmas carols until morn.
LONGFELLOW—*By the Fireside. A Christmas Carol*. St. 3.

20
I heard the bells on Christmas Day
Their old, familiar carols play,
And wild and sweet
The words repeat
Of peace on earth, good-will to men!
LONGFELLOW—*Christmas Bells*. St. 1.

21
Hail to the King of Bethlehem,
Who weareth in his diadem
The yellow crocus for the gem
Of his authority!
LONGFELLOW—*Christus. Golden Legend*. Pt. III.

22
"What means this glory round our feet,"
The Magi mused, "more bright than morn!"
And voices chanted clear and sweet,
"To-day the Prince of Peace is born."
LOWELL—*Christmas Carol*.

23
Let's dance and sing and make good cheer,
For Christmas comes but once a year.
G. MACFARREN—*From a Fragment*. (Before 1580) (See also TUSSER)

1
Ring out, ye crystal spheres!
Once bless our human ears,
If ye have power to touch our senses so;
And let your silver chime
Move in melodious time,
And let the bass of Heaven's deep organ blow;
And with your ninefold harmony
Make up full consort to the angelic symphony.
MILTON—*Hymn. On the Morning of Christ's Nativity.*

2
This is the month, and this the happy morn,
Wherein the Son of Heaven's eternal King,
Of wedded maid and virgin mother born,
Our great redemption from above did bring,
For so the holy sages once did sing,
That He our deadly forfeit should release,
And with His Father work us a perpetual peace.
MILTON—*Hymn. On the Morning of Christ's Nativity.*

3
'Twas the night before Christmas, when all through the house
Not a creature was stirring,—not even a mouse:
The stockings were hung by the chimney with care,
In hopes that St. Nicholas soon would be there.
CLEMENT C. MOORE—*A Visit from St. Nicholas.*

4
God rest ye, little children; let nothing you affright,
For Jesus Christ, your Saviour, was born this happy night;
Along the hills of Galilee the white flocks sleeping lay,
When Christ, the Child of Nazareth, was born on Christmas day.
D. M. MULOCK—*Christmas Carol.* St. 2.

5
As many mince pies as you taste at Christmas' so many happy months will you have.
Old English Saying.

6
England was merry England, when
Old Christmas brought his sports again.
'Twas Christmas broach'd the mightiest ale;
'Twas Christmas told the merriest tale;
A Christmas gambol oft could cheer
The poor man's heart through half the year.
SCOTT—*Marmion.* Canto VI. Introduction.

7
At Christmas I no more desire a rose,
Than wish a snow in May's new-fangled mirth.
Love's Labour's Lost. Act I. Sc. 1. L. 107.

8
The time draws near the birth of Christ:
The moon is hid; the night is still;
The Christmas bells from hill to hill
Answer each other in the mist.
TENNYSON—*In Memoriam.* XXVIII.

9
Christmas is here:
Winds whistle shrill,
Icy and chill,
Little care we:
Little we fear
Weather without,
Sheltered about
The Mahogany-Tree.
THACKERAY—*The Mahogany-Tree.*

10
At Christmas play, and make good cheer,
For Christmas comes but once a year.
TUSSER—*Five Hundred Points of Good Husbandry.* Ch. XII.

(See also MACFARREN)

11
The sun doth shake
Light from his locks, and, all the way
Breathing perfumes, doth spice the day.
HENRY VAUGHAN—*Christ's Nativity.*

12
"Hark the herald angels sing,
Glory to the new-born king."
Peace on earth, and mercy mild,
God and sinners reconciled!
CHARLES WESLEY—*Christmas Hymn.* (Altered from "Hark how all the welkin rings, Glory to the King of Kings.")

13
Blow, bugles of battle, the marches of peace;
East, west, north, and south let the long quarrel cease;
Sing the song of great joy that the angels began,
Sing the glory to God and of good-will to man!
WHITTIER—*Christmas Carmen.* St. 3.

CHRYSANTHEMUM

Chrysanthemum

14
Fair gift of Friendship! and her ever bright
And faultless image! welcome now thou art,
In thy pure loveliness—thy robes of white,
Speaking a moral to the feeling heart;
Unscattered by heats—by wintry blasts unmoved—
Thy strength thus tested—and thy charms improved.
ANNA PEYRE DINNIES—*To a White Chrysanthemum.*

15
Chrysanthemums from gilded argosy
Unload their gaudy scentless merchandise.
OSCAR WILDE—*Humanitad.* St. 11.

CHURCH

16
The nearer the church, the further from God.
BISHOP ANDREWS—*Sermon on the Nativity before James I.* (1622) Proverb quoted by FULLER—*Worthies.* II. 5. (Ed. 1811)

17
To Kerke the narre, from God more farre.
As quoted by SPENSER—*Shepherd's Calendar.* (July, 1579) DOUSE MS. 52. 15. (1450) See MURRAY, N.E.D. Used by SWIFT—*Legion Club.* Note. HEYWOOD—*Proverbs.* Given also in RAY as French. Known to Germans and Italians.

(See also BURTON)

18
Where Christ erecteth his church, the divell in the same church-yarde will have his chappell.
BANCROFT—*Anti-Puritan Sermon.* Feb. 9, 1588. MARTIN LUTHER—*Von den Conciliis und Kirchen. Werke.* 23. 378. (Ed. 1826) MELBANCKE—*Philotimus.* Sig. E. 1. CHARLES ALEYN—*Historie of that Wise and Fortunate Prince Henrie.* (1638) P. 136.

DR. JOHN DOVE—*The Conversion of Salomon.* Attributed to ERASMUS by FRANZ HORN—*Die Poesie und Beredsamkeit der Deutschen.* Bk. I. P. 35. (1822) WILLIAM ROE—*Christian Liberty.* (1662) P. 2.
(See also BURTON, DEFOE, DRUMMOND, HERBERT, NASHE, PALEOTTI)

1

Oh! St. Patrick was a gentleman
Who came of decent people;
He built a church in Dublin town,
And on it put a steeple.

HENRY BENNETT—*St. Patrick Was a Gentleman.*

2

Pour soutenir tes droits, que le ciel autorise,
Abîme tout plutôt; c'est l'esprit de l'Église.

To support those of your rights authorized by Heaven, destroy everything rather than yield; that is the spirit of the Church.

BOILEAU—*Lutrin.* Chant I. 185.

3

Where God hath a temple, the devil will have a chapel.

BURTON—*Anatomy of Melancholy.* Pt. III. Sec. IV. Memb. 1. Subsec. I.
(See also BANCROFT)

4

An instinctive taste teaches men to build their churches in flat countries with spire steeples, which, as they cannot be referred to any other object, point as with silent finger to the sky and stars.

COLERIDGE—*The Friend.*
(See also WORDSWORTH)

5

"What is a church?" Let Truth and reason speak,
They would reply, "The faithful, pure and meek,
From Christian folds, the one selected race,
Of all professions, and in every place."

CRABBE—*The Borough.* Letter II. L. 1.

6

What is a church?—Our honest sexton tells,
'Tis a tall building, with a tower and bells.

CRABBE—*The Borough.* Letter II. L. 11.

7

Whenever God erects a house of prayer
The devil always builds a chapel there;
And 'twill be found, upon examination,
The latter has the largest congregation.

DEFOE—*True Born Englishman.* Pt. I. L. 1. Note in first Edition says it is an English proverb. Omitted in later editions.
(See also BANCROFT)

8

God never had a church but there, men say,
The devil a chapel hath raised by some wiles,
I doubted of this saw, till on a day
I westward spied great Edinburgh's Saint Giles.

DRUMMOND—*Posthumous Poems. A Proverb.*
(See also BANCROFT)

9

Die Kirch' allein, meine lieben Frauen,
Kann ungerechtes Gut verdauen.
The church alone beyond all question
Has for ill-gotten goods the right digestion.

GOETHE—*Faust.* I. 9. 35.

10

It is common for those that are *farthest from God*, to boast themselves most of their *being near to the Church.*

MATTHEW HENRY—*Commentaries.* Jeremiah VII.

11

No sooner is a temple built to God but the devil builds a chapel hard by.

HERBERT—*Jacula Prudentum.*
(See also BANCROFT)

12

When once thy foot enters the church, be bare.
God is more there than thou: for thou art there
Only by his permission. Then beware,
And make thyself all reverence and fear.

HERBERT—*The Temple. The Church Porch.*

13

Well has the name of Pontifex been given
Unto the Church's head, as the chief builder
And architect of the invisible bridge
That leads from earth to heaven.

LONGFELLOW—*Golden Legend.* V.

14

In that temple of silence and reconciliation where the enmities of twenty generations lie buried, in the Great Abbey, which has during many ages afforded a quiet resting-place to those whose minds and bodies have been shattered by the contentions of the Great Hall.

MACAULAY—*Warren Hastings.*

15

A beggarly people,
A church and no steeple.

Attributed to MALONE by SWIFT. See *Prior's Life.* (1860) 381. Of St. Ann's Church, Dublin.

16

It was founded upon a rock.

Matthew. VII. 25.

17

As like a church and an ale-house, God and the devell, they manie times dwell neere to ether.

NASHE—*Works.* III. *Have with you to Saffron Walden.* Same idea in his *Christ's Teares. Works.* IV. 57. DEKKER—*Rauens Almanacke. Works.* IV. 221.
(See also BANCROFT)

18

There can be no church in which the demon will not have his chapel.

CARDINAL PALEOTTI, according to K. H. DIGBY—*Compitum.* Vol. II. P. 297.
(See also BANCROFT)

19

Non est de pastu ovium quæstio, sed de lana.

It is not about the pasture of the sheep, but about their wool.

POPE PIUS II.
(See also SUETONIUS)

20

No silver saints, by dying misers giv'n,
Here brib'd the rage of ill-requited heav'n;
But such plain roofs as Piety could raise,
And only vocal with the Maker's praise.

POPE—*Eloisa to Abelard.* L. 137.

21

Who builds a church to God, and not to Fame,
Will never mark the marble with his Name.

POPE—*Moral Essays.* Ep. III. L. 285.

1
I never weary of great churches. It is my favourite kind of mountain scenery. Mankind was never so happily inspired as when it made a cathedral.
STEVENSON—*Inland Voyage.*

2
Boni pastoris est tondere pecus non deglubere.
A good shepherd shears his flock, not flays them.
SUETONIUS. Attributed by him to TIBERIUS CÆSAR—*Life.* 32.
(See also POPE PIUS II)

3
The itch of disputation will break out
Into a scab of error.
ROWLAND WATKYNS—*The new Illiterate late Teachers.*
(See also WOTTON)

4
See the Gospel Church secure,
And founded on a Rock!
All her promises are sure;
Her bulwarks who can shock?
Count her every precious shrine;
Tell, to after-ages tell,
Fortified by power divine,
The Church can never fail.
CHARLES WESLEY—*Scriptural.* Psalm XLVIII St. 9.

5
Disputandi pruritus ecclesiarum scabies.
The itch of disputing is the scab of the churches.
SIR HENRY WOTTON—*A Panegyric to King Charles.* (*Inscribed on his tomb.*)
(See also WATKYNS; also WALTON under EPITAPHS)

CIRCLES

6
Circles and right lines limit and close all bodies, and the mortal right-lined circle must conclude and shut up all.
SIR THOMAS BROWNE—*Hydriotaphia.* Ch. V.

7
A circle may be small, yet it may be as mathematically beautiful and perfect as a large one.
ISAAC D'ISRAELI—*Miscellanies.*

8
The eye is the first circle; the horizon which it forms is the second; and throughout nature this primary figure is repeated without end. It is the highest emblem in the cipher of the world.
EMERSON—*Essays. Circles.*

9
As the small pebble stirs the peaceful lake;
The centre mov'd, a circle straight succeeds,
Another still, and still another spreads.
POPE—*Essay on Man.* Ep. IV. L. 364.

10
As on the smooth expanse of crystal lakes
The sinking stone at first a circle makes;
The trembling surface by the motion stirr'd,
Spreads in a second circle, then a third;
Wide, and more wide, the floating rings advance,
Fill all the watery plain, and to the margin dance.
POPE—*Temple of Fame.* L. 436.

11
I'm up and down and round about,
Yet all the world can't find me out;
Though hundreds have employed their leisure,
They never yet could find my measure.
SWIFT—*On a Circle.*

12
I watch'd the little circles die;
They past into the level flood.
TENNYSON—*The Miller's Daughter.* St. 10.

13
On the lecture slate
The circle rounded under female hands
With flawless demonstration.
TENNYSON—*The Princess.* II. L. 349.

14
Circles are praised, not that abound
In largeness, but the exactly round.
EDMUND WALLER—*Long and Short Life.*

CIRCUMSTANCE

15
The massive gates of circumstance
Are turned upon the smallest hinge,
And thus some seeming pettiest chance
Oft gives our life its after-tinge.

The trifles of our daily lives,
The common things, scarce worth recall,
Whereof no visible trace survives,
These are the mainsprings after all.
ANON. In *Harper's Weekly,* May 30, 1863.

16
Epicureans, that ascribed the origin and frame of the world not to the power of God, but to the fortuitous concourse of atoms.
BENTLEY—*Sermons.* II. Preached in 1692. See also Review of SIR ROBERT PEEL'S *Address.* Attributed later to SIR JOHN RUSSELL. See CROKER—*Papers.* Vol. II. P. 56.
(See also CICERO, GOLDSMITH, PALMERSTONE, SCOTT, WEBSTER)

17
And circumstance, that unspiritual god,
And miscreator, makes and helps along
Our coming evils, with a critch-like rod,
Whose touch turns hope to dust—the dust we all have trod.
BYRON—*Childe Harold.* Canto IV. St. 125.

18
Men are the sport of circumstances, when
The circumstances seem the sport of men.
BYRON—*Don Juan.* Canto V. St. 17.
(See also DISRAELI)

19
I am the very slave of circumstance
And impulse—borne away with every breath.
BYRON—*Sardanapalus.* Act IV. Sc. 1.

20
Odd instances of strange coincidence.
QUEEN CAROLINE'S Advocate in the House of Lords, referring to her association with BERGAMI.

21
The long arm of coincidence.
HADDON CHAMBERS—*Captain Swift.*

22
Nulla cogente natura, sed concursu quodam fortuito.
CICERO—*De Nat. Deorum.* Bk. I. 24. Adapted by him to:
Fortuito quodam concursu atomorum.
By some fortuitous concourse of atoms.
Same in QUINTILIAN. 7. 2. 2.
(See also BENTLEY)

1
Thus neither the praise nor the blame is our own.
COWPER—*Letter to Mr. Newton.*

2
Circumstances beyond my individual control.
DICKENS—*David Copperfield.* Ch. 20.

3
Man is not the creature of circumstances,
Circumstances are the creatures of men.
BENJ. DISRAELI—*Vivian Grey.* Vol. II. Bk. VI. Ch. 7.
(See also BYRON)

4
It is circumstances (difficulties) which show what men are.
EPICTETUS. Ch. XXIV. Quoted from OVID—*Tristia.* IV. 3. 79. Sc. 1. LONG'S trans.

5
To what fortuitous occurrence do we not owe every pleasure and convenience of our lives.
GOLDSMITH—*Vicar of Wakefield.* Ch. XXI.
(See also BENTLEY)

6
Circumstances alter cases.
HALIBURTON—*The Old Judge.* Ch. XV.

7
Man, without religion, is the creature of circumstances.
THOS. HARDY—*Guesses at Truth.* Vol. I.
(See also OWEN)

8
Thus we see, too, in the world that some persons assimilate only what is ugly and evil from the same moral circumstances which supply good and beautiful results—the fragrance of celestial flowers—to the daily life of others.
HAWTHORNE—*Mosses from an Old Manse. The Old Manse.*

9
Et mihi res, non me rebus, subjungere conor.
And I endeavour to subdue circumstances to myself, and not myself to circumstances.
HORACE—*Epistles.* I. 1. 191.

10
Quid velit et possit rerum concordia discors.
What the discordant harmony of circumstances would and could effect.
HORACE—*Epistles.* I. 12. 19.

11
For these attacks do not contribute to make us frail but rather show us to be what we are.
THOS. À KEMPIS—*Imitation of Christ.* DIBDIN'S trans. Bk. I. Ch. XVI.

12
Consilia res magis dant hominibus quam homines rebus.
Men's plans should be regulated by the circumstances, not circumstances by the plans.
LIVY—*Annales.* XXII. 39.

13
Man is the creature of circumstances.
ROBERT OWEN—*The Philanthropist.*
(See also HARDY)

14
Accidental and fortuitous concourse of atoms.
LORD PALMERSTON. Of the combination of Parties led by Disraeli and Gladstone, March 5, 1857.
(See also BENTLEY)

15
Condition, circumstance is not the thing.
POPE—*Essay on Man.* Ep. IV. L. 57.

16
The happy combination of fortuitous circumstances.
SCOTT—*Answer of the Author of Waverly to the Letter of Captain Clutterbuck. The Monastery.*
(See also BENTLEY)

17
The Lie with Circumstance.
As You Like It. Act V. Sc. 4. L. 100.

18
My circumstances
Being so near the truth as I will make them,
Must first induce you to believe.
Cymbeline. Act II. Sc. 4. L. 62.

19
Leave frivolous circumstances.
Taming of the Shrew. Act V. Sc. 1. L. 27.

20
How comes it to pass, if they be only moved by chance and accident, that such regular mutations and generations should be begotten by a fortuitous concourse of atoms.
J. SMITH—*Select Discourses.* III. P. 48. (Ed. 1660) Same phrase found in *Marcus Minucius Felix his Octavius.* Preface. (Pub. 1695)
(See also BENTLEY)

21
In all distresses of our friends
We first consult our private ends;
While Nature, kindly bent to ease us,
Points out some circumstance to please us.
SWIFT—*Paraphrase of Rochefoucauld's Maxim.*
(See also under ADVERSITY)

22
Aliena nobis, nostra plus aliis placent.
The circumstances of others seem good to us, while ours seem good to others.
SYRUS—*Maxims.*

23
Varia sors rerum.
The changeful chance of circumstances.
TACITUS—*Historiæ.* Bk. II. 70.

24
So runs the round of life from hour to hour.
TENNYSON—*Circumstance.*

25
And grasps the skirts of happy chance,
And breasts the blows of circumstance.
TENNYSON—*In Memoriam.* Pt. LXIII. St. 2.

26
This fearful concatenation of circumstances.
DANIEL WEBSTER—*Argument.* The Murder of Captain Joseph White. (1830) Vol. VI. P. 88. (See also BENTLEY)

27
F. M. the Duke of Wellington presents his compliments to Mr. —— and declines to interfere in circumstances over which he has no control.
WELLINGTON. See G. A. SALA—*Echoes of the Week* in London *Illustrated News*, Aug. 23, 1884. See CAPT. MARRYATT—*Settlers in Canada.* P. 177. GRENVILLE—*Memoirs.* Ch. II. (1823), gives early use of phrase.
(See also DICKENS)

28
Who does the best that circumstance allows,
Does well, acts nobly, angels could no more.
YOUNG—*Night Thoughts.* Night II. L. 90.
(Compare *Habakkuk.* II. 2)

CITIES

1
Smyrna, Rhodos, Colophon, Salamis, Chios, Argos, Athenæ,
Hæ septem certant de stirpe insignis Homeri.

Smyrna, Rhodes, Colophon, Salamis, Chios, Argos, Athens—these seven cities contend as to being the birthplace of the illustrious Homer. (The second line sometimes runs "Orbis de patria certat, Homere, tua.")

ANON. Tr. from Greek. Same in *Antipater of Sidon.*
(See also HEYWOOD, SEWARD)

2
A rose-red city half as old as Time.
JOHN W. BURGON—*Petra.* See LIBBEY and HOSKINS—*Jordan Valley and Petia.*
(See also ROGERS under TIME)

3
I live not in myself, but I become
Portion of that around me; and to me
High mountains are a feeling, but the hum
Of human cities torture.
BYRON—*Childe Harold.* Canto III. St. 72.
(See also MILTON)

4
This poor little one-horse town.
S. L. CLEMENS—*The Undertaker's Story.*

5
God made the country, and man made the town.
COWPER—*The Task.* Bk. I. L. 749.
(See also VARRO; also COWLEY under GARDENS)

6
The first requisite to happiness is that a man be born in a famous city.
EURIPIDES—*Encomium on Alcibiades.* (Probably quoted.) See PLUTARCH—*Life of Demosthenes.*

7
In the busy haunts of men.
FELICIA D. HEMANS—*Tale of the Secret Tribunal.* Pt. I. L. 2.

8
Seven cities warr'd for Homer being dead,
Who living had no roofe to shroud his head.
THOS. HEYWOOD—*Hierarchie of the Blessed Angells.*
(See also SEWARD)

9
The axis of the earth sticks out visibly through the centre of each and every town or city.
HOLMES—*The Autocrat of the Breakfast Table.* VI.
(See also HOLMES under BOSTON)

10
Far from gay cities, and the ways of men.
HOMER—*Odyssey.* Bk. 14. L. 410. POPE'S trans.

11
Non cuivis homini contingit adire Corinthum.
Every man cannot go to Corinth.
HORACE—*Epistles.* I. 17. 36.

12
Even cities have their graves!
LONGFELLOW—*Amalfi.* St. 6.

13
Friends and loves we have none, nor wealth, nor blest abode
But the hope, the burning hope, and the road, the lonely road.
Not for us are content, and quiet, and peace of mind,
For we go seeking cities that we shall never find.
MASEFIELD—*The Seekers.*

14
Ye are the light of the world. A city that is set on a hill cannot be hid.
Matthew. V. 14.

15
Towered cities please us then,
And the busy hum of men.
MILTON—*L'Allegro.* L. 117.

16
Nisi Dominus frustra.
Unless the Lord keep the city the watchman waketh in vain (*lit.*, unless the Lord in vain).
Motto of City of Edinburgh, adapted from *Psalms.* CVII. 1. Vulgate.

17
Fields and trees are not willing to teach me anything; but this can be effected by men residing in the city.
PLATO—*Works.* Vol. III. *The Phædrus.*

18
I dwelt in a city enchanted,
And lonely indeed was my lot;
* * * * *
Though the latitude's rather uncertain,
And the longitude also is vague,
The persons I pity who know not the City
The beautiful City of Prague.
W. J. PROWSE—*The City of Prague.* (*"Little Village on Thames."*)

19
Beautiful for situation, the joy of the whole earth, is Mount Zion, . . . the city of the great King.
Psalms. XLVIII. 2.

20
Petite ville, grand renom.
Small town, great renown.
RABELAIS—*Pantagruel.* Bk. V. Ch. XXXV.
Of Chinon, Rabelais's native town.

21
The people are the city.
Coriolanus. Act III. Sc. 1. L. 200.

22
Great Homer's birthplace seven rival cities claim,
Too mighty such monopoly of Fame.
THOMAS SEWARD—*On Shakespeare's Monument at Stratford-upon-Avon.*
(See also first quotation under topic, and HEYWOOD)

23
Urbem lateritiam accepit, mamoream relinquit.
He [Cæsar Augustus] found a city built of brick; he left it built of marble.
SUETONIUS. (Adapted.) *Cæsar Augustus.* 28.

24
The city of dreadful night.
JAMES THOMSON—*Current Literature for 1889.* P. 492.

25
Divina natura dedit agros, ars humana ædificavit urbes.
Divine Nature gave the fields, human art built the cities.
VARRO—*De Re Rustica.* III. 1.
(See also COWPER)

1
Fuimus Troes; fuit Ilium.
We have been Trojans; Troy was.
VERGIL—*Æneid*. II. 324.

CLEANLINESS

2
For cleanness of body was ever esteemed to proceed from a due reverence to God, to society, and to ourselves.
BACON—*Advancement of Learning*.

3
Todo saldrá en la colada.
All will come out in the washing.
CERVANTES. *Don Quixote*. I. 20.

4
He that toucheth pitch shall be defiled therewith.
Ecclesiasticus. XIII. 1.

5
God loveth the clean.
Koran. Ch. IX.

6
If dirt was trumps, what hands you would hold!
LAMB—*Lamb's Suppers*. Vol. II. Last Chapter.

7
I'll purge and leave sack and live cleanly.
Henry IV. Pt. I. Act V. Sc. 4. L. 168.

8
The doctrines of religion are resolved into carefulness; carefulness into vigorousness; vigorousness into guiltlessness; guiltlessness into abstemiousness; abstemiousness into cleanliness; cleanliness into godliness.
Talmud. Division of Mishna, as translated by DR. A. S. BETTELHEIM. Religious zeal leads to cleanliness, cleanliness to purity, purity to godliness, godliness to humility to the fear of sin. RABBI PINHASBEN-JAÏR —Commentary on the lines from the *Talmud*. See also *Talmudde Jerusalem*, by SCHWAB. IV. 16. Commentary on the treatise Schabbath. SCHUL—*Sentences of Proverbes du Talmud et du Midrasch*. 463.

9
Then bless thy secret growth, nor catch
At noise, but thrive unseen and dumb;
Keep clean, be as fruit, earn life, and watch,
Till the white-winged reapers come.
HENRY VAUGHAN—*The Seed Growing Secretly*.

10
Certainly this is a duty, not a sin. "Cleanliness is indeed next to godliness."
JOHN WESLEY—*Sermon XCII. On Dress*. Quoted by ROWLAND HILL as a saying of WHITEFIELD'S.
(See also TALMUD)

CLOUDS

11
Have you ever, looking up, seen a cloud like to a Centaur, a Pard, or a Wolf, or a Bull?
ARISTOPHANES—*Clouds*. GERARD'S trans.
(Compare *Hamlet*. III. 2)

12
Rocks, torrents, gulfs, and shapes of giant size
And glitt'ring cliffs on cliffs, and fiery ramparts rise.
BEATTIE—*Minstrel*. Bk. I.

13
I saw two clouds at morning
Tinged by the rising sun,
And in the dawn they floated on
And mingled into one.
JOHN G. C. BRAINARD—*I Saw Two Clouds at Morning*.

14
Were I a cloud I'd gather
My skirts up in the air,
And fly I well know whither,
And rest I well know where.
ROBERT BRIDGES—*Elegy. The Cliff Top. A Cloud*.

15
O, it is pleasant, with a heart at ease,
Just after sunset, or by moonlight skies,
To make the shifting clouds be what you please,
Or let the easily persuaded eyes
Own each quaint likeness issuing from the mould
Of a friend's fancy.
COLERIDGE—*Fancy in Nubibus*.

16
Our fathers were under the cloud.
I Corinthians. X. 1.

17
Though outwardly a gloomy shroud,
The inner half of every cloud
Is bright and shining:
I therefore turn my clouds about
And always wear them inside out
To show the lining.
ELLEN THORNEYCROFT FOWLER (Mrs. A. L. Felkin—*Wisdom of Folly*.

18
The clouds,—the only birds that never sleep.
VICTOR HUGO—*The Vanished City*.

19
There ariseth a little cloud out of the sea, like a man's hand.
I Kings. XVIII. 44.

20
See yonder little cloud, that, borne aloft
So tenderly by the wind, floats fast away
Over the snowy peaks!
LONGFELLOW—*Christus. The Golden Legend*. Pt. V. L. 145.

21
By unseen hands uplifted in the light
Of sunset, yonder solitary cloud
Floats, with its white apparel blown abroad,
And wafted up to heaven.
LONGFELLOW—*Michael Angelo*. Pt. II. 2.

22
But here by the mill the castled clouds
Mocked themselves in the dizzy water.
E. L. MASTERS—*Spoon River Anthology. Isaiah Beethoven*.

23
Was I deceiv'd, or did a sable cloud
Turn forth her silver lining on the night?
MILTON—*Comus*. L. 22.

24 There does a sable cloud
Turn forth her silver lining on the night,
And casts a gleam over this tufted grove.
MILTON—*Comus*. L. 223.

1 So when the sun in bed,
Curtain'd with cloudy red,
Pillows his chin upon an orient wave.
MILTON—*Ode on the Morning of Christ's Nativity.*

2 The low'ring element
Scowls o'er the darken'd landscape.
MILTON—*Paradise Lost.* Bk. II. L. 490.

3
If woolly fleeces spread the heavenly way
No rain, be sure, disturbs the summer's day.
Old Weather Rhyme.

4
When clouds appear like rocks and towers,
The earth's refreshed by frequent showers.
Old Weather Rhyme.

5
Clouds on clouds, in volumes driven,
Curtain round the vault of heaven.
THOMAS LOVE PEACOCK—*Rhododaphne.* Canto V. L. 257.

6
Choose a firm cloud before it fall, and in it
Catch, ere she change, the Cynthia of this minute.
POPE—*Moral Essays.* Ep. 2. L. 19.

7
Who maketh the clouds his chariot.
Psalms. CIV. 3.

8
Do you see yonder cloud, that's almost in shape of a camel?
By the mass, and 'tis like a camel, indeed.
Methinks it is like a weasel.
It is backed like a weasel.
Or, like a whale?
Very like a whale.
Hamlet. Act III. Sc. 2. L. 312.
(See also ARISTOPHANES)

9
Yon towers, whose wanton tops do buss the clouds.
Troilus and Cressida. Act IV. Sc. 5. L. 220.

10
I bring fresh showers for the thirsting flowers,
From the seas and the streams;
I bear light shade for the leaves when laid
In their noonday dreams.

From my wings are shaken the dews that waken
The sweet buds every one,
When rocked to rest on their mother's breast,
As she dances about the sun.
I wield the flail of the lashing hail,
And whiten the green plains under,
And then again I dissolve it in rain,
And laugh as I pass in thunder.
SHELLEY—*The Cloud.*

11 . . . feathery curtains,
Stretching o'er the sun's bright couch.
SHELLEY—*Queen Mab.* Bk. II.

12 Far clouds of feathery gold,
Shaded with deepest purple, gleam
Like islands on a dark blue sea.
SHELLEY—*Queen Mab.* Bk. II.

13 . . . fertile golden islands,
Floating on a silver sea.
SHELLEY—*Queen Mab.* Bk. II.

14
Bathed in the tenderest purple of distance,
Tinted and shadowed by pencils of air,
Thy battlements hang o'er the slopes and the forests,
Seats of the gods in the limitless ether,
Looming sublimely aloft and afar.
BAYARD TAYLOR—*Kilimandjaro.*

15 Yonder cloud
That rises upward always higher,
And onward drags a laboring breast,
And topples round the dreary west,
A looming bastion fringed with fire.
TENNYSON—*In Memoriam.* XV.

16
The clouds that gather round the setting sun
Do take a sober coloring from an eye
That hath kept watch o'er man's mortality.
WORDSWORTH—*Ode. Intimations of Immortality.* St. 11.

17
Once I beheld a sun, a sun which gilt
That sable cloud, and turned it all to gold.
YOUNG—*Night Thoughts.* Night VII. L. 815.

CLOVER

Trifolium

18
Where the wind-rows are spread for the butterfly's bed,
And the clover-bloom falleth around.
ELIZA COOK—*Journal.* Vol. VII. St. 2. *Song of the Haymakers.*

19
Crimson clover I discover
By the garden gate,
And the bees about her hover,
But the robins wait.
Sing, robins, sing,
Sing a roundelay,—
'Tis the latest flower of Spring
Coming with the May!
DORA READ GOODALE—*Red Clover.*

20
The clover blossoms kiss her feet,
She is so sweet, she is so sweet.
While I, who may not kiss her hand,
Bless all the wild flowers in the land.
OSCAR LEIGHTON—*Clover Blossoms. For Thee Alone.*

21
Flocks thick-nibbling through the clovered vale.
THOMSON—*The Seasons. Summer.* L. 1,235.

22
What airs outblown from ferny dells
And clover-bloom and sweet brier smells.
WHITTIER—*Last Walk in Autumn.* St. 6.

CLYDE (RIVER)

23
How sweet to move at summer's eve
By Clyde's meandering stream,
When Sol in joy is seen to leave
The earth with crimson beam;
When islands that wandered far
Above his sea couch lie,
And here and there some gem-like star
Re-opes its sparkling eye.
ANDREW PARK—*The Banks of Clyde.*

COCK

1
Good-morrow to thy sable beak,
And glossy plumage, dark and sleek,
Thy crimson moon and azure eye,
Cock of the heath, so wildly shy!
JOANNA BAILLIE—*The Black Cock.* St. 1.

2
While the cock with lively din
Scatters the rear of darkness thin,
And to the stack or the barn door
Stoutly struts his dames before.
MILTON—*L'Allegro.*

3
The cock, that is the trumpet to the morn,
Doth with his lofty and shrill-sounding throat
Awake the god of day.
Hamlet. Act I. Sc. 1. L. 150.

4
The early village cock
Hath twice done salutation to the morn.
Richard III. Act V. Sc. 3. L. 209.

5
Hark, hark! I hear
The strain of strutting chanticleer
Cry, cock-a-diddle-dow.
Tempest. Act I. Sc. 2. L. 384.

COLOGNE

6
In Köln, a town of monks and bones,
And pavement fang'd with murderous stones,
And rags and hags, and hideous wenches,
I counted two-and-seventy stenches,
All well defined, and several stinks!
Ye nymphs that reign o'er sewers and sinks,
The River Rhine, it is well known,
Doth wash your city of Cologne;
But tell me, nymphs! what power divine
Shall henceforth wash the river Rhine?
COLERIDGE—*Cologne.*

COLUMBINE

Aquilegia Canadensis

7
Or columbines, in purple dressed
Nod o'er the ground-bird's hidden nest.
BRYANT—*To the Fringed Gentian.*

8
Skirting the rocks at the forest edge
With a running flame from ledge to ledge,
Or swaying deeper in shadowy glooms,
A smoldering fire in her dusky blooms;
Bronzed and molded by wind and sun,
Maddening, gladdening every one
With a gypsy beauty full and fine,—
A health to the crimson columbine!
ELAINE GOODALE—*Columbine.*

9
O columbine, open your folded wrapper,
Where two twin turtle-doves dwell!
O cuckoopint, toll me the purple clapper
That hangs in your clear green bell!
JEAN INGELOW—*Songs of Seven. Seven Times One.*

10
There's fennel for you, and columbines: there's rue for you.
Hamlet. Act IV. Sc. 5. L. 180.

11
I am that flower,—That mint.—That columbine.
Love's Labor Lost. Act V. Sc. 2. L. 661.

COMFORT

12
It's grand, and you canna expect to be baith grand and comfortable.
BARRIE—*Little Minister.* Ch. 10.

13
They have most satisfaction in themselves, and consequently the sweetest relish of their creature comforts.
MATTHEW HENRY—*Commentaries.* Psalm XXXVII.

14
Is there no balm in Gilead?
Jeremiah. VIII. 22.
Is there no treacle in Gilead?
Version from the "Treacle Bible." (1568) Spelled also "truacle" or "tryacle" in the Great Bible (1541), Bishops' Bible. (1561)

15
Miserable comforters are ye all.
Job. XVI. 2.

16
From out the throng and stress of lies,
From out the painful noise of sighs,
One voice of comfort seems to rise:
"It is the meaner part that dies."
WM. MORRIS—*Comfort.*

17
Thy rod and thy staff they comfort me.
Psalms. XXIII. 4.

18
And He that doth the ravens feed,
Yea, providently caters for the sparrow,
Be comfort to my age!
As You Like It. Act II. Sc. 3. L. 43.

19
That comfort comes too late;
'Tis like a pardon after execution;
That gentle physic, given in time, had cur'd me;
But now I am past all comforts here, but Prayers.
Henry VIII. Act IV. Sc. 2. L. 119.

COMMERCE (See BUSINESS)

COMPANIONSHIP

20
Tell me thy company and I will tell thee what thou art.
CERVANTES—Quoted in *Don Quixote.* Vol. III. Pt. II. Ch. XXIII.

21
Pares autem vetere proverbio, cum paribus facillime congregantur.
Like, according to the old proverb, naturally goes with like.
CICERO—*Cato Major De Senectute.* III. 7.
(See also "BIRDS OF A FEATHER" under BIRDS).

22
We are in the same boat.
POPE CLEMENT I. *To the Church of Corinth.*

23
Ah, savage company; but in the church
With saints, and in the taverns with the gluttons.
DANTE—*Inferno.* XXII. 13.

24
Better your room than your company.
SIMON FORMAN—*Marriage of Wit and Wisdom.* (About 1570)

25
The right hands of fellowship.
Galatians. II. 9.

1
Solamen miseris socios habuisse doloris.
It is a comfort to the unfortunate to have companions in woe.
Quoted by DOMINICUS DE GRAVINA—*Chron. de Rebus*, in *Apul. Gest.* THOMAS À KEMPIS—*De Valle Siliorum.* Ch. 16. DIONYSIUS CATO. SPINOZA—*Ethics.* IV. 57 ("Alorum" for "doloris." THUCYDIDES—VII. 75.
(See also MARLOWE, SENECA)

2
It takes two for a kiss
Only one for a sigh,
Twain by twain we marry
One by one we die.
FREDERICK L. KNOWLES—*Grief and Joy.*

3
Joy is a partnership,
Grief weeps alone,
Many guests had Cana;
Gethsemane but one.
FREDERICK L. KNOWLES—*Grief and Joy.*

4
It is a comfort to the miserable to have comrades in misfortune, but it is a poor comfort after all.
MARLOWE—*Faustus.*
(See also GRAVINA)

5
Two i's company, three i's trumpery.
MRS. PARR—*Adam and Eve.* IX. 124.

6
Male voli solatii genus est turbu miserorum.
A crowd of fellow-sufferers is a miserable kind of comfort.
SENECA—*Consol. ad Marc.* 12. 5.
(See also MARLOWE)

7
Ante, inquit, circumspiciendum est, cum quibos edas et bibas, quam quid edas et bibas.
[Epicurus] says that you should rather have regard to the company with whom you eat and drink, than to what you eat and drink.
SENECA—*Epistles.* XIX.

8
Nullius boni sine sociis jucunda possessio est.
No possession is gratifying without a companion.
SENECA—*Epistles. Ad Lucilium.* VI.

9
How is it less or worse
That it shall hold companionship in peace
With honour, as in war?
Coriolanus. Act III. Sc. 2. L. 49.

10
No blast of air or fire of sun
Puts out the light whereby we run
With girdled loins our lamplit race,
And each from each takes heart of grace
And spirit till his turn be done.
SWINBURNE—*Songs Before Sunrise.*

11
Comes jucundus in via pro vehiculo est.
A pleasant companion on a journey is as good as a carriage.
SYRUS—*Maxims.*

12
Join the company of lions rather than assume the lead among foxes.
Talmud—Aboth. IV. 20.

COMPARISONS

13
How God ever brings like to like.
ARISTOTLE—*Ethics Mag.* 2. 11. Also *Politics.* VIII. Ch. II. 12. "One pin drives out another," as trans. by CONGREVE. ARISTOPHANES—*Pluto.* 32. EURIPIDES—*Hecuba.* 993. HOMER—*Odyssey.* 17. 218.
(See also GASCOIGNE, LYLY, WYATT)

14
Defining night by darkness, death by dust.
BAILEY—*Festus.* Sc. *Water and Wood.*

15
'Tis light translateth night; 'tis inspiration
Expounds experience; 'tis the west explains
The east; 'tis time unfolds Eternity.
BAILEY—*Festus.* Sc. *A Ruined Temple.*

16
Glass antique! 'twixt thee and Nell
Draw we here a parallel!
She, like thee, was forced to bear
All reflections, foul or fair.
Thou art deep and bright within,
Depths as bright belong'd to Gwynne;
Thou art very frail as well,
Frail as flesh is,—so was Nell.
L. BLANCHARD—*Nell Gwynne's Looking Glass.* St. 1.

17
Comparisons are odious.
ARCHBISHOP BOIARDO—*Orlando Innamorato.* Ch. VI. St. 4. BURTON—*Anatomy of Melancholy.* Pt. III. Sec. III. Memb. 1. Subsec. 2. CAREW—*Describing Mount Edgcumbe.* (About 1590) DONNE—*Elegy.* VIII. (1619) FORTESCUE—*De Laudibus Leg. Angliæ.* Ch. 19. GABRIEL HARVEY—*Archaica.* Vol. II. P. 23. (1592) HERBERT—*Jacula Prudentum.* HEYWOOD—*Woman Killed with Kindness.* Act I. Sc. 2. LODOWICH—*Lloyd Marrow of History.* P. 19. (1653)—*Much Ado About Nothing.* Act III. Sc. 5. 1. 19. has *odorous.* W. P. in *Pasquine in a Traunce.* Folio 4. (1549) WHITGIFT—*Defence of the Answer to the Administration.* (1574) Parker Society's Whitgift. Vol. II. P. 434. (See also LYDGATE)

18
Not worthy to carry the buckler unto him.
SIR THOMAS BROWNE—*Religio Medici.* Pt. I. Sec. 21.

19
It's wiser being good than bad;
It's safer being meek than fierce:
It's fitter being sane than mad.
My own hope is, a sun will pierce
The thickest cloud earth ever stretched;
That, after Last, returns the First,
Though a wide compass round be fetched;
That what began best, can't end worst,
Nor what God blessed once, prove accurst.
ROBERT BROWNING—*Apparent Failure.* VII.

20
It has all the contortions of the sibyl without the inspiration.
BURKE—*Prior's Life of Burke.*

21
To liken them to your auld-warld squad,
I must needs say comparisons are odd.
BURNS—*Brigs of Ayr.* L. 177.
(See also LYDGATE)

1
Some say, that Seignior Bononchini
Compar'd to Handel's a mere Ninny;
Others aver, to him, that Handel
Is scarcely fit to hold a candle.
Strange! that such high Disputes shou'd be
'Twixt Tweedledum and Tweedledee.

JOHN BYROM—*Epigram on the Feuds between Handel and Bononcini.* As given in the *London Journal*, June 5, 1725.

2
Some say, compared to Bononcini,
That Mynheer Handel's but a ninny;
Others aver, that he to Handel
Is scarcely fit to hold a Candle:
Strange all this difference should be,
'Twixt Tweedle-dum and Tweedle-dee!

JOHN BYROM'S *Epigram* as published later, probably changed by himself. Not fit to hold a candle to him.

From the Roman Catholic custom of holding candles before shrines, in processions.

(See also BROWNE)

3
Is it possible your pragmatical worship should not know that the comparisons made between wit and wit, courage and courage, beauty and beauty, birth and birth, are always odious and ill taken?

CERVANTES—*Don Quixote.* Pt. II. Ch. I.

(See also BOIARDO)

4
At whose sight, like the sun,
All others with diminish'd lustre shone.

CICERO—*Tusculan Disp.* Bk. III. Div. 18. YONGE'S trans.

5
Similem habent labra lactucam.

Like lips like lettuce (i. e. like has met its like).

CRASSUS. See CICERO—*De Finibus.* V. 30. 92.

6
About a donkey's taste why need we fret us?
To lips like his a thistle is a lettuce.

Free trans. by WM. EWART of the witticism that made Crassus laugh for the only time, on seeing an ass eat thistles. Quoted by FACCIOLATI (Bailey's ed.) and by MOORE in his Diary (Lord John Russell's ed.)

7
Like to like.

GASCOIGNE—*Complaynt of Philomene.*

(See also ARISTOTLE)

8
Everything *is* twice as large, measured on a three-year-old's three-foot scale as on a thirty-year-old's six-foot scale.

HOLMES—*Poet at the Breakfast Table.* I.

9
Too great refinement is false delicacy, and true delicacy is solid refinement.

LA ROCHEFOUCAULD—*Maxims.* No. 131.

10
And but two ways are offered to our will,
Toil with rare triumph, ease with safe disgrace,
The problem still for us and all of human race.

LOWELL—*Under the Old Elm.* Pt. VII. St. 3.

11
Comparisons do ofttime great grievance.

JOHN LYDGATE—*Bochas.* Bk. III. Ch. VIII.

(See also BOIARDO)

12
Who wer as lyke as one pease is to another.

LYLY—*Euphues.* P. 215.

(See also GASCOIGNE)

13
Hoc ego, tuque sumus: sed quod sum, non potes esse:
Tu quod es, e populo quilibet esse potest.

Such are thou and I: but what I am thou canst not be; what thou art any one of the multitude may be.

MARTIAL—*Epigrams.* V. 13. 9.

14
Sunt bona, sunt quædam mediocria, sunt mala plura.

Some are good, some are middling, the most are bad.

MARTIAL—*Epigrams.* I. 17. 1.

15
L'ape e la serpe spesso
Suggon l'istesso umore;

The bee and the serpent often sip from the selfsame flower.

METASTASIO—*Morte d'Abele.* I.

16
Il y a fagots et fagots.

There are fagots and fagots.

MOLIÈRE—*Le Médecin Malgré lui.* I. 6.

17
The souls of emperors and cobblers are cast in the same mould. * * * The same reason that makes us wrangle with a neighbour causes a war betwixt princes.

MONTAIGNE—*Apology for Raimond de Sebond.* Bk. II. Ch. XII.

18
A man must either imitate the vicious or hate them.

MONTAIGNE—*Essays. Of Solitude.*

19
We are nearer neighbours to ourselves than whiteness to snow, or weight to stones.

MONTAIGNE—*Essays.* Bk. II. Ch. XII.

20
No more like together than is chalke to coles.

SIR THOS. MORE—*Works.* P. 674.

21
Everye white will have its blacke,
And everye sweet its soure.

THOS. PERCY—*Reliques. Sir Curline.*

22
Another yet the same.

POPE—*Dunciad.* Bk. III. L. 90.

23
The rose and thorn, the treasure and dragon, joy and sorrow, all mingle into one.

SAADI—*The Gulistan.* Ch. VII. *Apologue* 21. Ross' trans.

24
Einem ist sie die hohe, die himmlische Göttin, dem andern
Eine tüchtige Kuh, die ihn mit Butter versorgt.

To one it is a mighty heavenly goddess, to the other an excellent cow that furnishes him with butter.

SCHILLER—*Wissenschaft.*

25
Those that are good manners at the court are as ridiculous in the country as the behaviour of the country is most mockable at the court.

As You Like It. Act III. Sc. 2. L. 46.

1
Nature hath meal and bran, contempt and grace.
Cymbeline. Act. IV Sc. 2. L. 27.

2
Hyperion to a satyr.
Hamlet. Act I. Sc. 2. L. 140.

3 No more like my father
Than I to Hercules.
Hamlet. Act I. Sc. 2. L. 152.

4 O, the more angel she,
And you the blacker devil!
Othello. Act V. Sc. 2. L. 130.

5
Crabbed age and youth cannot live together.
Passionate Pilgrim. Pt. XII.

6
What, is the jay more precious than the lark,
Because his feathers are more beautiful?
Or is the adder better than the eel,
Because his painted skin contents the eye?
Taming of the Shrew. Act IV. Sc. 3. L. 177.

7
Here and there a cotter's babe is royal—born by right divine;
Here and there my lord is lower than his oxen or his swine.
TENNYSON—*Locksley Hall. Sixty Years After.* St. 63.

8
Duo quum idem faciunt, sæpe ut possis dicere,
Hoc licet impune facere huic, illi non licet:
Non quod dissimilis res sit, sed quod is sit.

When two persons do the self-same thing, it oftentimes falls out that in the one it is criminal, in the other it is not so; not that the thing itself is different, but he who does it.
TERENCE—*Adelphi.* V. III. 37.

9
Sic canibus catulos similes, sic matribus hædos
Noram; sic parvis componere magna solebam.

Thus I knew that pups are like dogs, and kids like goats; so I used to compare great things with small.
VERGIL—*Eclogæ.* I. 23.

10
Qui n'est que juste est dur, qui n'est que sage est triste.

He who is not just is severe, he who is not wise is sad.
VOLTAIRE—*Epître au Roi de Prusse.* (1740)

11
The little may contrast with the great, in painting, but cannot be said to be contrary to it. Oppositions of colors contrast; but there are also colors contrary to each other, that is, which produce an ill effect because they shock the eye when brought very near it.
VOLTAIRE—*A Philosophical Dictionary. Essay. Contrast.*

12
For like to like, the proverb saith.
THOS. WYATT—*The Lover Complaineth.*

13
For as saith a proverb notable,
Each thing seeketh his semblable.
THOS. WYATT—*The Re-cured Lover.*
(See also ARISTOTLE)

COMPASS-PLANT

Silphium laciniatum

14
Look at this vigorous plant that lifts its head from the meadow,
See how its leaves are turned to the north, as true as the magnet;
This is the compass-flower, that the finger of God has planted
Here in the houseless wild, to direct the traveller's journey.
Over the sea-like, pathless, limitless waste of the desert,
Such in the soul of man is faith.
LONGFELLOW—*Evangeline.* Pt. II. St. 4. L. 140.

COMPENSATION

15
Each loss has its compensation
There is healing for every pain,
But the bird with a broken pinion
Never soars so high again.
HEZEKIAH BUTTERWORTH—*The Broken Pinion.*

16
Cast thy bread upon the waters; for thou shalt find it after many days.
Ecclesiastes. XI. 1.

17
As some tall cliff that lifts its awful form,
Swells from the vale, and midway leaves the storm,
Though round its breast the rolling clouds are spread,
Eternal sunshine settles on its head.
GOLDSMITH—*The Deserted Village.* L. 189.

18
Multa ferunt anni venientes commoda secum:
Multa recedentes adimunt.

The coming years bring many advantages with them: retiring they take away many.
HORACE—*Ars Poetica.* CLXXV.

19
'Tis always morning somewhere in the world.
RICHARD HENGEST HORNE—*Orion.* Bk. III. Canto II.
(See also LONGFELLOW)

20
Give unto them beauty for ashes, the oil of joy for mourning, the garment of praise for the spirit of heaviness.
Isaiah. LXI. 3.

21
O weary hearts! O slumbering eyes!
O drooping souls, whose destinies
Are fraught with fear and pain,
Ye shall be loved again.
LONGFELLOW—*Endymion.* St. 7.

22
'Tis always morning somewhere.
LONGFELLOW—*Tales of a Wayside Inn. Birds of Killingworth.* St. 16.
(See also HORNE)

23
Earth gets its price for what Earth gives us,
The beggar is taxed for a corner to die in,
The priest hath his fee who comes and shrives us,
We bargain for the graves we lie in;
At the devil's booth are all things sold,

Each ounce of dross costs its ounce of gold;
For a cap and bells our lives we pay,
Bubbles we buy with a whole soul's tasking,
'Tis heaven alone that is given away,
'Tis only God may be had for the asking,
No price is set on the lavish summer;
June may be had by the poorest comer.
LOWELL—*Vision of Sir Launfal. Prelude to Pt. I.*

1
Merciful Father, I will not complain.
I know that the sunshine shall follow the rain.
JOAQUIN MILLER—*For Princess Maud.*

2
Sæpe creat molles aspera spina rosas.
The prickly thorn often bears soft roses.
OVID—*Epistolæ Ex Ponto.* II. 2. 34.

3
Long pains are light ones,
Cruel ones are brief!
J. G. SAXE—*Compensation.*

4
The burden is equal to the horse's strength.
Talmud. Sota. 13.

5
That not a moth with vain desire
Is shrivel'd in a fruitless fire,
Or but subserves another's gain.
TENNYSON—*In Memoriam.* LIV.

6
Primo avulso non deficit alter aureus.
One plucked, another fills its room
And burgeons with like precious bloom.
VERGIL—*Æneid.* VI. 143.

7
And light is mingled with the gloom,
And joy with grief;
Divinest compensations come,
Through thorns of judgment mercies bloom
In sweet relief.
WHITTIER—*Anniversary Poem.* St. 15.

COMPLIMENTS

8
A compliment is usually accompanied with a bow, as if to beg pardon for paying it.
J. C. AND A. W. HARE—*Guesses at Truth.*

9
What honour that,
But tedious waste of time, to sit and hear
So many hollow compliments and lies.
MILTON—*Paradise Regained.* Bk. IV. L. 122.

10
'Twas never merry world
Since lowly feigning was called compliment.
Twelfth Night. Act III. Sc. 1. L. 109.

11
A woman * * * always feels herself complimented by love, though it may be from a man incapable of winning her heart, or perhaps even her esteem.
ABEL STEVENS—*Life of Madame de Staël.* Ch. III.

12
Current among men,
Like coin, the tinsel clink of compliment.
TENNYSON—*The Princess.* Pt. II. L. 40.

CONCEIT

13
I've never any pity for conceited people, because I think they carry their comfort about with them.
GEORGE ELIOT—*The Mill on the Floss.* Bk. V. Ch. IV.

14
For what are they all in their high conceit,
When man in the bush with God may meet?
EMERSON—*Good-Bye.* St. 4.

15
The world knows only two, that's Rome and I.
BEN JONSON—*Sejanus.* Act V. Sc. 1.

16
In men this blunder still you find,
All think their little set mankind.
HANNAH MORE—*Florio.* Pt. I.

17
Seest thou a man wise in his own conceit? There is more hope of a fool than of him.
Proverbs. XXVI. 12.

18
Wiser in his own conceit than seven men that can render a reason.
Proverbs. XXVI. 16.

19
Be not wise in your own conceits.
Romans. XII. 16.

20
Conceit may puff a man up, but never prop him up.
RUSKIN—*True and Beautiful. Morals and Religion. Function of the Artist.*

21
Conceit in weakest bodies strongest works.
Hamlet. Act III. Sc. 4. L. 114.

22
I am not in the roll of common men.
Henry IV. Pt. I. Act III. Sc. 1. L. 43.

23
Conceit, more rich in matter than in words,
Brags of his substance, not of ornament:
They are but beggars that can count their worth.
Romeo and Juliet. Act II. Sc. 6. L. 29.

24
Whoe'er imagines prudence all his own,
Or deems that he hath powers to speak and judge
Such as none other hath, when they are known,
They are found shallow.
SOPHOCLES—*Antigone.* 707.

25
Faith, that's as well said as if I had said it myself.
SWIFT—*Polite Conversation. Dialogue* II.

CONFESSION

26
Nor do we find him forward to be sounded
But, with a crafty madness, keeps aloof,
When we would bring him on to some confession
Of his true state.
Hamlet. Act III. Sc. 1. L. 7.

27
Confess yourself to heaven;
Repent what's past; avoid what is to come.
Hamlet. Act III. Sc. 4. L. 149.

1
Confess thee freely of thy sin;
For to deny each article with oath
Cannot remove nor choke the strong conception
That I do groan withal.
Othello. Act V. Sc. 2. L. 54.

2
I own the soft impeachment.
SHERIDAN—*The Rivals*. Act V. Sc. 3.

CONFIDENCE

3
Confidence is that feeling by which the mind embarks in great and honourable courses with a sure hope and trust in itself.
CICERO—*Rhetorical Invention*.

4
I see before me the statue of a celebrated minister, who said that confidence was a plant of slow growth. But I believe, however gradual may be the growth of confidence, that of credit requires still more time to arrive at maturity.
BENJ. DISRAELI—*Speech*. Nov. 9, 1867.
(See also PITT)

5
La confiance que l'on a en soi fait naître la plus grande partie de celle que l'on a aux autres.
The confidence which we have in ourselves gives birth to much of that which we have in others.
LA ROCHEFOUCAULD — *Premier Supplément*. 49.

6
He that wold not when he might,
He shall not when he wold-a.
THOS. PERCY—*Reliques*. *The Baffled Knight*. St. 14.

7
Confidence is a plant of slow growth in an aged bosom.
WILLIAM PITT (Earl of Chatham)—*Speech*. Jan. 14, 1766.
(See also DISRAELI)

8
Ultima talis erit quæ mea prima fides.
My last confidence will be like my first.
PROPERTIUS—*Elegiæ*. II. 20. 34.

9
Your wisdom is consum'd in confidence.
Do not go forth to-day.
Julius Cæsar. Act II. Sc. 2. L. 49.

10
I would have some confidence with you that decerns you nearly.
Much Ado About Nothing. Act III. Sc. 5. L. 3.

11
Confidence is conqueror of men; victorious both over them and in them;
The iron will of one stout heart shall make a thousand quail:
A feeble dwarf, dauntlessly resolved, will turn the tide of battle,
And rally to a nobler strife the giants that had fled.
TUPPER—*Proverbial Philosophy*. *Of Faith*. L. 11.

12
Nusquam tuta fides.
Confidence is nowhere safe.
VERGIL—*Æneid*. IV. 373.

CONGO (RIVER)

13
Then I saw the Congo, creeping through the black,
Cutting through the jungle with a golden track.
NICHOLAS VACHEL LINDSAY—*The Congo*.

CONQUEST (See also VICTORY)

14
Great things thro' greatest hazards are achiev'd,
And then they shine.
BEAUMONT AND FLETCHER—*Loyal Subject*. Act I. Sc. 5.

15
He who surpasses or subdues mankind,
Must look down on the hate of those below.
BYRON—*Childe Harold*. Canto III. St. 45.

16
Jus belli, ut qui vicissent, iis quos vicissent, quemadmodum vellent, imperarent.
It is the right of war for conquerors to treat those whom they have conquered according to their pleasure.
CÆSAR—*Bellum Gallicum*. I. 36.

17
In hoc signo vinces.
Conquer by this sign.
CONSTANTINE THE GREAT, after his defeat of Maxentius, at Saxe Rubra, Oct. 27, 312.

18
A vaincre sans péril on triomphe sans gloire.
We triumph without glory when we conquer without danger.
CORNEILLE—*Le Cid*. II. 2.

19
Like Douglas conquer, or like Douglas die.
JOHN HOME—*Douglas*. Act. V. Sc. 1. L. 100.

20
Sai, che piegar si vede
Il docile arboscello,
Che vince allor che cede
Dei turbini al furor.
Know that the slender shrub which is seen to bend, conquers when it yields to the storm.
METASTASIO—*Il Trionfo di Clelia*. I. 8.

21
Cede repugnanti; cedendo victor abibis.
Yield to him who opposes you; by yielding you conquer.
OVID—*Ars Amatoria*. II. 197.

22
Male vincetis, sed vincite.
You will hardly conquer, but conquer you must.
OVID—*Metamorphoses*. IX. 509.

23
Victi vincimus.
Conquered, we conquer.
PLAUTUS—*Casina*. Act I. 1.

24
Victor victorum cluet.
He is hailed a conqueror of conquerors.
PLAUTUS—*Trinummus*. Act II. 2.

25
Shall they hoist me up,
And show me to the shouting varletry
Of censuring Rome? Rather a ditch in Egypt
Be gentle grave unto me, rather on Nilus' mud
Lay me stark naked, and let the water-flies
Blow me into abhorring!
Antony and Cleopatra. Act V. Sc. 2. L. 55.

1
Brave conquerors! for so you are
That war against your own affections,
And the huge army of the world's desires.
Love's Labour's Lost. Act I. Sc. 1. L. 8.

2
I sing the hymn of the conquered, who fell in the battle of life,
The hymn of the wounded, the beaten who died overwhelmed in the strife;
Not the jubilant song of the victors for whom the resounding acclaim
Of nations was lifted in chorus whose brows wore the chaplet of fame,
But the hymn of the low and the humble, the weary, the broken in heart,
Who strove and who failed, acting bravely a silent and desperate part.
W. W. STORY—*Io Victis.*
(See also SCARBOROUGH under FAILURE)

3
Bis vincit qui se vincit in victoria.
He conquers twice who conquers himself in victory.
SYRUS—*Maxims.*

CONSCIENCE

4
And I know of the future judgment
How dreadful so'er it be
That to sit alone with my conscience
Would be judgment enough for me.
CHAS. WILLIAM STUBBS—*Alone with my conscience.*

5
Oh! think what anxious moments pass between
The birth of plots, and their last fatal periods,
Oh! 'tis a dreadful interval of time,
Filled up with horror all, and big with death!
ADDISON—*Cato.* Act I. Sc. 3.

6
They have cheveril consciences that will stretch.
BURTON—*Anatomy of Melancholy.* Pt III. Sec. IV. Memb. 2. Subsect. 3.

7
Why should not Conscience have vacation
As well as other Courts o' th' nation?
Have equal power to adjourn,
Appoint appearance and return?
BUTLER—*Hudibras.* Pt. II. Canto II. L. 317.

8
A quiet conscience makes one so serene!
Christians have burnt each other, quite persuaded
That all the Apostles would have done as they did.
BYRON—*Don Juan.* Canto I. St. 83.

9
But at sixteen the conscience rarely gnaws
So much, as when we call our old debts in
At sixty years, and draw the accounts of evil,
And find a deuced balance with the devil.
BYRON—*Don Juan.* Canto I. St. 167.

10
There is no future pang
Can deal that justice on the self condemn'd
He deals on his own soul.
BYRON—*Manfred.* Act III. Sc. 1.

11
Yet still there whispers the small voice within,
Heard through Gain's silence, and o'er Glory's din;
Whatever creed be taught or land be trod,
Man's conscience is the oracle of God.
BYRON—*The Island.* Canto I. St. 6.

12
The Past lives o'er again
In its effects, and to the guilty spirit
The ever-frowning Present is its image.
COLERIDGE—*Remorse.* Act I. Sc. 2.

13
The still small voice is wanted.
COWPER—*The Task.* Bk. V. L. 687.

14
Oh, Conscience! Conscience! man's most faithful friend,
Him canst thou comfort, ease, relieve, defend;
But if he will thy friendly checks forego,
Thou art, oh! woe for me, his deadliest foe!
CRABBE—*Struggles of Conscience.* Last Lines.

15
O dignitosa coscienza e netta,
Come t' è picciol fallo amaro morso.
O faithful conscience, delicately pure, how doth a little failing wound thee sore!
DANTE—*Purgatorio.* III. 8.

16
Se tosto grazia risolva le schiume
Di vostra conscienza, si che chiaro
Per essa scenda della mente il fiume.
So may heaven's grace clear away the foam from the conscience, that the river of thy thoughts may roll limpid thenceforth.
DANTE—*Purgatorio.* XIII. 88.
(For "river of thy thought," see also BYRON and LONGFELLOW under WOMAN)

17
Zwei Seelen wohnen, ach! in meiner Brust,
Die eine will sich von der andern trennen.
Two souls, alas! reside within my breast, and each withdraws from and repels its brother.
GOETHE—*Faust.* I. 2. 307.

18
Conscience is a coward, and those faults it has not strength to prevent, it seldom has justice enough to accuse.
GOLDSMITH—*Vicar of Wakefield.* Ch. XIII.

19
Hic murus aeneus esto,
Nil conscire sibi, nulla pallescere culpa.
Be this thy brazen bulwark, to keep a clear conscience, and never turn pale with guilt.
HORACE—*Epistles.* I. 1. 60.

20
A cleere conscience is a sure carde.
LYLY—*Euphues.* P. 207. Arbor's reprint. (1579)

21
He that has light within his own clear breast,
May sit i' the centre, and enjoy bright day;
But he that hides a dark soul, and foul thoughts,
Benighted walks under the mid-day sun;
Himself is his own dungeon.
MILTON—*Comus.* L. 381.

22
Now conscience wakes despair
That slumber'd, wakes the bitter memory
Of what he was, what is, and what must be
Worse; of worse deeds worse sufferings must ensue!
MILTON—*Paradise Lost.* Bk. IV. L. 23.

1
O Conscience, into what abyss of fears
And horrors hast thou driven me, out of which
I find no way, from deep to deeper plunged.
MILTON—*Paradise Lost.* Bk. X. L. 842.

2
Let his tormentor conscience find him out.
MILTON—*Paradise Regained.* Bk. IV. L. 130.

3
Whom conscience, ne'er asleep,
Wounds with incessant strokes, not loud, but deep.
MONTAIGNE—*Essays.* Bk. II. Ch. V. *Of Conscience.*

4
Conscia mens ut cuique sua est, ita concipit intra
Pectora pro facto spemque metumque suo.

According to the state of a man's conscience, so do hope and fear on account of his deeds arise in his mind.
OVID—*Fasti.* I. 485.

5
One self-approving hour whole years outweighs
Of stupid starers and of loud huzzas.
POPE—*Essay on Man.* Ep. IV. L. 255.

6
True, conscious Honour is to feel no sin,
He's arm'd without that's innocent within;
Be this thy screen, and this thy wall of Brass.
POPE—*First Book of Horace.* Ep. I. L. 93.

7
Some scruple rose, but thus he eas'd his thought,
"I'll now give sixpence where I gave a groat;
Where once I went to church, I'll now go twice—
And am so clear too of all other vice."
POPE—*Moral Essays.* Ep. III. L. 365.

8
Let Joy or Ease, let Affluence or Content,
And the gay Conscience of a life well spent,
Calm ev'ry thought, inspirit ev'ry grace,
Glow in thy heart, and smile upon thy face.
POPE—*To Mrs. M. B., on her Birthday.*

9
What Conscience dictates to be done,
Or warns me not to do;
This teach me more than Hell to shun,
That more than Heav'n pursue.
POPE—*Universal Prayer.*

10
Sic vive cum hominibus, tanquem deus videat; sic loquere cum deo, tanquam homines audiant.

Live with men as if God saw you; converse with God as if men heard you.
SENECA—*Epistolæ Ad Lucilium.* X.

11
Thus conscience does make cowards of us all;
And thus the native hue of resolution
Is sicklied o'er with the pale cast of thought.
And enterprises of great pith and moment,
With this regard, their currents turn awry,
And lose the name of action.
Hamlet. Act III. Sc. 1. L. 83.
("Away," not "awry" in folio)

12
They are our outward consciences.
Henry V. Act IV. Sc. 1. L. 8.

13
Now, if you can blush and cry, "guilty," cardinal,
You'll show a little honesty.
Henry VIII. Act III. Sc. 2. L. 306.

14
I know myself now; and I feel within me
A peace above all earthly dignities;
A still and quiet conscience.
Henry VIII. Act III. Sc. 2. L. 377.

15
Better be with the dead,
Whom we, to gain our peace, have sent to peace,
Than on the torture of the mind to lie
In restless ecstacy.
Macbeth. Act III. Sc. 2. L. 19.

16
Well, my conscience says, "Launcelot, budge not." "Budge," says the fiend: "budge not," says my conscience. "Conscience," say I, "you counsel well." "Fiend," say I, "you counsel well."
Merchant of Venice. Act II. Sc. 2.

17
I hate the murderer, love him murdered.
The guilt of conscience take thou for thy labour,
But neither my good word nor princely favour:
With Cain go wander through shades of night,
And never show thy head by day nor light.
Richard II. Act V. Sc. 6. L. 40.

18
The worm of conscience still begnaw thy soul!
Thy friends suspect for traitors while thou liv'st,
And take deep traitors for thy dearest friends!
Richard III. Act I. Sc. 3. L. 222.

19
'Tis a blushing shamefast spirit that mutinies in a man's bosom; it fills one full of obstacles.
Richard III. Act I. Sc. 4. L. 141.

20
Soft, I did but dream.
O coward conscience, how dost thou afflict me!
Richard III. Act V. Sc. 3. L. 179.

21
My conscience hath a thousand several tongues,
And every tongue brings in a several tale,
And every tale condemns me for a villain.
Richard III. Act V. Sc. 3. L. 193.

22
Conscience is but a word that cowards use,
Devised at first to keep the strong in awe.
Richard III. Act V. Sc. 3. L. 309.

23
I know thou art religious,
And hast a thing within thee called conscience,
With twenty popish tricks and ceremonies,
Which I have seen thee careful to observe.
Titus Andronicus. Act V. Sc. 1. L. 75.

24
Trust that man in nothing who has not a Conscience in everything.
STERNE—*Tristram Shandy.* Bk. II. Ch. XVII.

25
La conscience des mourants calomnie leur vie.

The conscience of the dying belies their life.
VAUVENARGUES—*Réflexions.* CXXXVI.

26
Labor to keep alive in your breast that little spark of celestial fire, called Conscience.
GEORGE WASHINGTON—*Moral Maxims. Virtue and Vice. Conscience.*

27
Men who can hear the Decalogue and feel
No self-reproach.
WORDSWORTH—*The Old Cumberland Beggar.* L. 136.

CONSIDERATION

1
Consideration, like an angel came
And whipp'd the offending Adam out of him,
Leaving his body as a paradise,
To envelope and contain celestial spirits.
Henry V. Act I. Sc. 1. L. 28.

2 What you have said
I will consider; what you have to say
I will with patience hear, and find a time
Both meet to hear and answer such high things.
Julius Cæsar. Act I. Sc. 2. L. 168.

3
A stirring dwarf we do allowance give
Before a sleeping giant.
Troilus and Cressida. Act II. Sc. 3. L. 146.

CONSISTENCY (See also CONSTANCY)

4 Of right and wrong he taught
Truths as refin'd as ever Athens heard;
And (strange to tell) he practis'd what he preach'd.
JOHN ARMSTRONG—*Art of Preserving Health*. Bk. IV. L. 302.

5
Tush! Tush! my lassie, such thoughts resigne,
Comparisons are cruele:
Fine pictures suit in frames as fine,
Consistencie's a jewell.
For thee and me coarse cloathes are best,
Rude folks in homelye raiment drest,
Wife Joan and goodman Robin.
Jolly Robyn-Roughhead. (Fake ballad. Appeared in American Newspaper, 1867.)

6
Nemo doctus unquam mutationem consilii inconstantiam dixit esse.
No well-informed person has declared a change of opinion to be inconstancy.
CICERO—*Ep. ad Atticum*. Bk. XVI. 8.
(See also EMERSON)

7
A foolish consistency is the hobgoblin of little minds, adored by little statesmen and philosophers and divines.
EMERSON—*Essays. Self-Reliance*.

8
With consistency a great soul has simply nothing to do. * * * Speak what you think to-day in words as hard as cannon balls, and to-morrow speak what to-morrow thinks in hard words again, though it contradict everything you said to-day.
EMERSON—*Essays. Self-Reliance*.
(See also HOOLE under CONSTANCY)

9
Gineral C. is a dreffle smart man:
He's been on all sides that give places or pelf;
But consistency still wuz a part of his plan;
He's been true to *one* party, and that is, himself;—
So John P.
Robinson, he
Sez he shall vote for Gineral C.
LOWELL—*The Biglow Papers*. Series I. No. 3.

10
Inconsistency is the only thing in which men are consistent.
HORATIO SMITH—*Tin Trumpet*. Vol. I. P. 273.

11
Cantilenam eandem canis.
You are harping on the same string.
TERENCE—*Phormio*. III. 2. 10.

CONSPIRACY

12
Conspiracies no sooner should be formed
Than executed.
ADDISON—*Cato*. Act I. Sc. 2.

13 O conspiracy,
Sham'st thou to show thy dang'rous brow by night,
When evils are most free?
Julius Cæsar. Act II. Sc. 1. L. 76.

14 Take no care
Who chafes, who frets; and where conspirers are:
Macbeth shall never vanquish'd be.
Macbeth. Act IV. Sc. 1. L. 89.

15
Thou dost conspire against thy friend, Iago,
If thou but think'st him wrong'd and mak'st his ear
A stranger to thy thoughts.
Othello. Act III. Sc. 3. L. 142.

16
Open-eye conspiracy
His time doth take.
Tempest. Act II. Sc. 1. *Song*. L. 301.

CONSTANCY

17
Through perils both of wind and limb,
Through thick and thin she follow'd him.
BUTLER—*Hudibras*. Pt. I. Canto II. L. 369.
(See also SPENSER; also DRYDEN under POETRY and "THROUGH THICK AND THIN" under PROVERBS)

18
'Tis often constancy to change the mind.
HOOLE—*Metastasio. Sieves*.
(See also EMERSON under CONSISTENCY, and CICERO under OPINION)

19
Changeless march the stars above,
Changeless morn succeeds to even;
And the everlasting hills,
Changeless watch the changeless heaven.
CHARLES KINGSLEY—*Saint's Tragedy*. Act II. Sc. 2.

20
Abra was ready ere I call'd her name;
And, though I call'd another, Abra came.
PRIOR—*Solomon on the Vanity of the World*. Bk. II. L. 364.

21 Now from head to foot
I am marble-constant: now the fleeting moon
No planet is of mine.
Antony and Cleopatra. Act V. Sc. 2. L. 238.

22
O constancy, be strong upon my side,
Set a huge mountain 'tween my heart and tongue!
I have a man's mind, but a woman's might.
Julius Cæsar. Act II. Sc. 4. L. 7.

23
I could be well moved if I were as you;
If I could pray to move, prayers would move me;
But I am constant as the northern star,
Of whose true fix'd and resting quality
There is no fellow in the firmament.
Julius Cæsar. Act III. Sc. 1. L. 58.

1
He that parts us shall bring a brand from heaven,
And fire us hence like foxes.
King Lear. Act V. Sc. 3. L. 22.

2
Sigh no more, ladies, sigh no more,
Men were deceivers ever,
One foot in sea and one on shore;
To one thing constant never.
Much Ado About Nothing. Act II. Sc. 3. L. 64. See also THOS. PERCY—*The Friar of Orders Gray.*

3 If ever thou shalt love,
In the sweet pangs of it remember me;
For such as I am all true lovers are;
Unstaid and skittish in all motions else,
Save in the constant image of the creature
That is belov'd.
Twelfth Night. Act II. Sc. 4. L. 15.

4
I would have men of such constancy put to sea, that their business might be everything and their intent everywhere; for that's it that always makes a good voyage of nothing.
Twelfth Night. Act II. Sc. 4. L. 77.

5 O heaven! were man
But constant, he were perfect. That one error
Fills him with faults; makes him run through all the sins:
Inconstancy falls off ere it begins.
Two Gentlemen of Verona. Act V. Sc. 4. L. 109.

6
Through thick and thin, both over banck and bush,
In hope her to attaine by hooke or crooke.
SPENSER—*Faerie Queene.* Bk. III. Canto I. St. 17.
(See also BUTLER)

7
Out upon it! I have lov'd
Three whole days together;
And am like to love three more,
If it prove fair weather.
SIR JOHN SUCKLING—*Constancy.*

CONTEMPLATION

8
The act of contemplation then creates the thing contemplated.
ISAAC D'ISRAELI—*Literary Character.* Ch. XII.

9
But first and chiefest, with thee bring
Him that yon soars on golden wing,
Guiding the fiery-wheeled throne,
The Cherub Contemplation.
MILTON—*Il Penseroso.* L. 51.

10 In discourse more sweet,
(For Eloquence the Soul, Song charms the sense,)
Others apart sat on a hill retir'd,
In thoughts more elevate, and reasoned high
Of Providence, Foreknowledge, Will and Fate,
Fixed fate, free will, foreknowledge absolute;
And found no end, in wand'ring mazes lost.
MILTON—*Paradise Lost.* Bk. II. L. 555.

11
When holy and devout religious men
Are at their beads, 'tis hard to draw them thence;
So sweet is zealous contemplation.
Richard III. Act III. Sc. 7. L. 92.

12
Contemplation makes a rare turkey-cock of him: how he jets under his advanced plumes.
Twelfth Night. Act II. Sc. 5. L. 35.

CONTEMPT (See also SCORN)

13
Go—let thy less than woman's hand
Assume the distaff—not the brand.
BYRON—*Bride of Abydos.* Canto I. St. 4.

14
When they talk'd of their Raphaels, Correggios, and stuff,
He shifted his trumpet, and only took snuff.
GOLDSMITH—*Retaliation.* L. 145.

15
Grown all to all, from no one vice exempt,
And most contemptible to shun contempt.
POPE—*Moral Essays.* Pt. III. L. 21.

16
Call me what instrument you will, though you can fret me, yet you cannot play upon me.
Hamlet. Act III. Sc. 2. L. 378.

17
I had rather chop this hand off at a blow,
And with the other fling it at thy face,
Than bear so low a sail, to strike to thee.
Henry VI. Pt. III. Act V. Sc. 1. L. 49.

CONTENT

18
Ten poor men sleep in peace on one straw heap, as Saadi sings,
But the immensest empire is too narrow for two kings.
WM. R. ALGER—*Oriental Poetry. Elbow Room.*

19
Ah, sweet Content, where doth thine harbour hold?
BARNABE BARNES—*Parthenophil and Parthenophe.*

20
Happy am I; from care I'm free!
Why aren't they all contented like me?
Opera of La Bayadère.

21
From labour health, from health contentment spring;
Contentment opes the source of every joy.
JAMES BEATTIE—*The Minstrel.* Bk. I. St. 13.

22
In Paris a queer little man you may see,
A little man all in gray;
Rosy and round as an apple is he,
Content with the present whate'er it may be,
While from care and from cash he is equally free,
And merry both night and day!
"Ma foi! I laugh at the world," says he,
"I laugh at the world, and the world laughs at me!"
What a gay little man in gray.
BERANGER—*The Little Man all in Gray.* Trans. by AMELIA B. EDWARDS.

1
There was a jolly miller once,
  Lived on the River Dee;
He worked and sang, from morn to night;
  No lark so blithe as he.
And this the burden of his song,
  Forever used to be,—
"I care for nobody, not I,
  If no one cares for me."
  BICKERSTAFF—*Love in a Village.* Act I. Sc. 5.
  (See also BURNS)

2
Some things are of that nature as to make
One's fancy chuckle, while his heart doth ache.
  BUNYAN—*The Author's Way of Sending Forth his Second Part of the Pilgrim.* L. 126.

3
Contented wi' little, and cantie wi' mair.
  BURNS—*Contented wi' Little.*

4
I'll be merry and free,
  I'll be sad for nae-body;
If nae-body cares for me,
  I'll care for nae-body.
  BURNS—*Nae-body.*
  (See also BICKERSTAFF)

5
With more of thanks and less of thought,
  I strive to make my matters meet;
To seek what ancient sages sought,
  Physic and food in sour and sweet,
To take what passes in good part,
And keep the hiccups from the heart.
  JOHN BYROM—*Careless Content.*

6
I would do what I pleased, and doing what I pleased, I should have my will, and having my will, I should be contented; and when one is contented, there is no more to be desired; and when there is no more to be desired, there is an end of it.
  CERVANTES—*Don Quixote.* Pt. I. Bk. IV. Ch. XXIII.

7
In a cottage I live, and the cot of content,
  Where a few little rooms for ambition too low,
Are furnish'd as plain as a patriarch's tent,
  With all for convenience, but nothing for show:
Like Robinson Crusoe's, both peaceful and pleasant,
  By industry stor'd, like the hive of a bee;
And the peer who looks down with contempt on a peasant,
  Can ne'er be look'd up to with envy by me.
  JOHN COLLINS—*How to be Happy.* Song in his *Scripscrapologia.*

8
We'll therefore relish with content,
Whate'er kind Providence has sent,
  Nor aim beyond our pow'r;
For, if our stock be very small,
'Tis prudent to enjoy it all,
  Nor lose the present hour.
  NATHANIEL COTTON—*The Fireside.* St. 10.

9
Enjoy the present hour, be thankful for the past,
And neither fear nor wish th' approaches of the last.
  COWLEY—*Imitations. Martial.* Bk. X. Ep. XLVII.

10
Give what thou wilt, without thee we are poor;
And with thee rich, take what thou wilt away.
  COWPER—*Task. Winter Morning Walk.* Last lines.

11
What happiness the rural maid attends,
In cheerful labour while each day she spends!
She gratefully receives what Heav'n has sent,
And, rich in poverty, enjoys content.
  GAY—*Rural Sports.* Canto II. L. 148.

12
Where wealth and freedom reign, contentment fails,
And honour sinks where commerce long prevails.
  GOLDSMITH—*The Traveller.* L. 91.

13
Their wants but few, their wishes all confin'd.
  GOLDSMITH—*The Traveller.* L. 210.

14
Happy the man, of mortals happiest he,
Whose quiet mind from vain desires is free;
Whom neither hopes deceive, nor fears torment,
But lives at peace, within himself content;
In thought, or act, accountable to none
But to himself, and to the gods alone.
  GEO. GRANVILLE (Lord Lansdowne)—*Epistle to Mrs. Higgons,* 1690. L. 79.

15
Sweet are the thoughts that savour of content;
The quiet mind is richer than a crown;
Sweet are the nights in careless slumber spent;
The poor estate scorns fortune's angry frown:
Such sweet content, such minds, such sleep, such bliss,
Beggars enjoy, when princes oft do miss.
  ROBERT GREENE—*Song. Farewell to Folly.*

16
Let's live with that small pittance which we have;
Who covets more is evermore a slave.
  HERRICK—*The Covetous Still Captive.*

17
Quanto quisque sibi plura negaverit,
A dis plura feret. Nil cupientium
Nudus castra peto.
  The more a man denies himself, the more he shall receive from heaven. Naked, I seek the camp of those who covet nothing.
  HORACE—*Carmina.* III. 16. 21.

18
  Multa petentibus
Desunt multa; bene est cui deus obtulit
Parca quod satis est manu.
  Those who want much, are always much in need; happy the man to whom God gives with a sparing hand what is sufficient for his wants.
  HORACE—*Carmina.* III. 16. 42.

19
Quod satis est cui contigit, nihil amplius optet.
  Let him who has enough ask for nothing more.
  HORACE—*Epistles.* I. 2. 46.

20
Sit mihi quod nunc est, etiam minus et mihi vivam
Quod superest ævi—si quid superesse volunt di.
  Let me possess what I now have, or even less, so that I may enjoy my remaining days, if Heaven grant any to remain.
  HORACE—*Epistles.* I. 18. 107.

1 Sit mihi mensa tripes et
Coucha salis puri et toga quæ defendere frigus
Quamvis crassa queat.

Let me have a three-legged table, a dish of salt, and a cloak which, altho' coarse, will keep off the cold.

HORACE—*Satires*. I. 3. 13.

2
Yes! in the poor man's garden grow,
Far more than herbs and flowers,
Kind thoughts, contentment, peace of mind,
And joy for weary hours.

MARY HOWITT—*The Poor Man's Garden.*

3
Contentment furnishes constant joy. Much covetousness, constant grief. To the contented even poverty is joy. To the discontented, even wealth is a vexation.

MING LUM PAOU KEËN—*In Chinese Repository.* Trans. by DR. MILNE.

4
It is good for us to be here.

Matthew. XVII. 4.

5 So well to know
Her own, that what she wills to do or say
Seems wisest, virtuousest, discreetest, best.

MILTON—*Paradise Lost.* Bk. VIII. L. 548.

6
No eye to watch, and no tongue to wound us,
All earth forgot, and all heaven around us!

MOORE—*Come O'er the Sea.*

7
Vive sine invidia, mollesque inglorius annos
Exige; amicitias et tibi junge pares.

May you live unenvied, and pass many pleasant years unknown to fame; and also have congenial friends.

OVID—*Tristium.* III. 4. 43.

8
The eagle nestles near the sun;
The dove's low nest for me!—
The eagle's on the crag; sweet one,
The dove's in our green tree!
For hearts that beat like thine and mine
Heaven blesses humble earth;—
The angels of our Heaven shall shine
The angels of our Hearth!

J. J. PIATT—*A Song of Content.*

9
Si animus est æquus tibi satis habes, qui bene vitam colas.

If you are content, you have enough to live comfortably.

PLAUTUS—*Aulularia.* II. 2. 10.

10
Habeas ut nactus: nota mala res optima est.

Keep what you have got; the known evil is best.

PLAUTUS—*Trinummus.* I. 2. 25.

11
Whate'er the passion, knowledge, fame, or pelf,
Not one will change his neighbor with himself.

POPE—*Essay on Man.* Ep. II. L. 261.

12
I earn that I eat, get that I wear, owe no man hate, envy no man's happiness; glad of other men's good, content with my harm.

As You Like It. Act III. Sc. 2. L. 77.

13
He that commends me to mine own content
Commends me to the thing I cannot get.

Comedy of Errors. Act I. Sc. 2. L. 33.

14
For mine own part, I could be well content
To entertain the lag-end of my life
With quiet hours.

Henry IV. Pt. I. Act V. Sc. 1. L. 23.

15 The shepherd's homely curds,
His cold thin drink out of his leathern bottle,
His wonted sleep under a fresh tree's shade,
All which secure and sweetly he enjoys,
Is far beyond a prince's delicates,
His viands sparkling in a golden cup,
His body couched in a curious bed,
When care, mistrust, and treason wait on him.

Henry VI. Pt. III. Act II. Sc. 5. L. 47.

16
My crown is in my heart, not on my head;
Not deck'd with diamonds and Indian stones,
Nor to be seen: my crown is called content;
A crown it is that seldom kings enjoy.

Henry VI. Pt. III. Act III. Sc. 1. L. 63.

17
Why, I can smile, and murder whiles I smile,
And cry, "Content" to that which grieves my heart;
And wet my cheeks with artificial tears,
And frame my face to all occasions.

Henry VI. Pt. III. Act III. Sc. 2. L. 182.

18
'Tis better to be lowly born,
And range with humble livers in content,
Than to be perk'd up in a glistering grief,
And wear a golden sorrow.

Henry VIII. Act II. Sc. 3. L. 19.

19 Our content
Is our best having.

Henry VIII. Act II. Sc. 3. L. 23.

20 Shut up
In measureless content.

Macbeth. Act II. Sc. 1. L. 17.

21 If it were now to die,
'Twere now to be most happy; for I fear
My soul hath her content so absolute
That not another comfort like to this
Succeeds in unknown fate.

Othello. Act II. Sc. 1. L. 191.

22
'Tis not so deep as a well, nor so wide as a church door; but 'tis enough, 'twill serve.

Romeo and Juliet. Act III. Sc. 1. L. 100

23
Not on the outer world
For inward joy depend;
Enjoy the luxury of thought,
Make thine own self friend;
Not with the restless throng,
In search of solace roam
But with an independent zeal
Be intimate at home.

LYDIA SIGOURNEY—*Know Thyself.*

24
The noblest mind the best contentment has.

SPENSER—*Faerie Queene.* Bk. I. Canto I. St. 35.

1
Dear little head, that lies in calm content
Within the gracious hollow that God made
In every human shoulder, where He meant
Some tired head for comfort should be laid.
CELIA THAXTER—*Song.*

2
An elegant Sufficiency, Content,
Retirement, rural Quiet, Friendship, Books,
Ease and alternate Labor, useful Life,
Progressive Virtue, and approving Heaven!
THOMSON—*Seasons. Spring.* L. 1,159.

3
Vivite felices, quibus est fortuna peracta
Jam sua.
Be happy ye, whose fortunes are already completed.
VERGIL—*Æneid.* III. 493.

4
This is the charm, by sages often told,
Converting all it touches into gold:
Content can soothe, where'er by fortune placed,
Can rear a garden in the desert waste.
HENRY KIRK WHITE—*Clifton Grove.* L. 130.

5
There is a jewel which no Indian mines can buy,
No chymic art can counterfeit;
It makes men rich in greatest poverty,
Makes water wine; turns wooden cups to gold;
The homely whistle to sweet music's strain,
Seldom it comes;—to few from Heaven sent,
That much in little, all in naught, *Content.*
JOHN WILBYE—*Madrigales. There Is a Jewel.*

CONTENTION (See also DISSENSION, QUARRELLING)

6
Did thrust (as now) in others' corn his sickle.
DU BARTAS—*Divine Weekes and Workes. Second Week, Second Day.* Pt. II.

7
He that wrestles with us strengthens our nerves, and sharpens our skill. Our antagonist is our helper.
BURKE—*Reflections on the Revolution in France.* Vol. III. P. 195.

8
'Tis a hydra's head contention; the more they strive the more they may: and as Praxiteles did by his glass, when he saw a scurvy face in it, brake it in pieces; but for that one he saw many more as bad in a moment.
BURTON—*Anatomy of Melancholy.* Pt. II. Sc. 3. Mem. 7.

9
Et le combat cessa, faute de combattants.
And the combat ceased, for want of combatants.
CORNEILLE—*Le Cid.* IV. 3.

10
Great contest follows, and much learned dust
Involves the combatants; each claiming truth,
And truth disclaiming both.
COWPER—*Task.* Bk. III. L. 161.

11
So when two dogs are fighting in the streets,
When a third dog one of the two dogs meets:
With angry teeth he bites him to the bone,
And this dog smarts for what that dog has done.
HENRY FIELDING—*Tom Thumb the Great.* Act I. Sc. 5. L. 55.

(See also SMART)

12
Let there be no strife, I pray thee, between thee and me.
Genesis. XIII. 8.

13
When individuals approach one another with deep purposes on both sides they seldom come at once to the matter which they have most at heart. They dread the electric shock of a too sudden contact with it.
NATH. HAWTHORNE—*The Marble Faun.* Vol. II. Ch. XXII.

14
Not hate, but glory, made these chiefs contend;
And each brave foe was in his soul a friend.
HOMER—*The Iliad.* Bk. VII. L. 364. POPE'S trans.

15
But curb thou the high spirit in thy breast,
For gentle ways are best, and keep aloof
From sharp contentions.
HOMER—*Iliad.* Bk. IX. L. 317. BRYANT'S trans.

16
A man of strife and a man of contention.
Jeremiah. XV. 10.

17
Mansit concordia discors.
Agreement exists in disagreement.
LUCAN—*Pharsalia.* I. 98.

18
Ducibus tantum de funere pugna est.
The chiefs contend only for their place of burial.
LUCAN—*Pharsalia.* VI. 811.

19
If a house be divided against itself, that house cannot stand.
Mark. III. 25.

20
Irritabis crabrones.
You will stir up the hornets.
PLAUTUS—*Amphitruo.* Act II. 2. 75.

21
A continual dropping in a very rainy day and a contentious woman are alike.
Proverbs. XXVII. 15.

22
Irriter les freslons.
Stir up the hornets.
RABELAIS—*Pantagruel.*

23
Contentions fierce,
Ardent, and dire, spring from no petty cause.
SCOTT—*Peveril of the Peak.* Ch. XL.

24
Tota hujus mundi concordia ex discordibus constat.
The whole concord of this world consists in discords.
SENECA—*Nat. Quæst.* Bk. VII. 27.

25
Thus when a barber and collier fight,
The barber beats the luckless collier—white;
The dusty collier heaves his ponderous sack,
And, big with vengeance, beats the barber—black.
In comes the brick-dust man, with grime o'erspread,
And beats the collier and the barber—red;

Black, red, and white, in various clouds are toss'd,
And in the dust they raise the combatants are lost.
CHRISTOPHER SMART—*Soliloquy of the Princess Periwinkle* in *A Trip to Cambridge.* See CAMPBELL'S *Specimens of the British Poets.* Vol. VI. P. 185.
(See also FIELDING)

1
Nimium altercando veritas amittitur.
In excessive altercation, truth is lost.
SYRUS—*Maxims.*

CONVERSATION

2
Method is not less requisite in ordinary conversation than in writing, provided a man would talk to make himself understood.
ADDISON—*The Spectator.* No. 476.

3
With good and gentle-humored hearts
I choose to chat where'er I come
Whate'er the subject be that starts.
But if I get among the glum
I hold my tongue to tell the truth
And keep my breath to cool my broth.
JOHN BYROM—*Careless Content.*

4
In conversation avoid the extremes of forwardness and reserve.
CATO.

5
But conversation, choose what theme we may,
And chiefly when religion leads the way,
Should flow, like waters after summer show'rs,
Not as if raised by mere mechanic powers.
COWPER—*Conversation.* L. 703.

6
Conversation is a game of circles.
EMERSON—*Essays. Circles.*

7
Conversation is the laboratory and workshop of the student.
EMERSON—*Society and Solitude. Clubs.*

8
I never, with important air,
In conversation overbear.
* * * *
My tongue within my lips I rein;
For who talks much must talk in vain.
GAY—*Fables.* Pt. I. Introduction. L. 53.

9
With thee conversing I forget the way.
GAY—*Trivia.* Bk. II. L. 480.

10
They would talk of nothing but high life and high-lived company, with other fashionable topics, such as pictures, taste, Shakespeare, and the musical glasses.
GOLDSMITH—*Vicar of Wakefield.* Ch. IX.

11
And when you stick on conversation's burs,
Don't strew your pathway with those dreadful *urs.*
HOLMES—*A Rhymed Lesson. Urania.*

12
Discourse, the sweeter banquet of the mind.
HOMER—*The Odyssey.* Bk. 15. L. 433. POPE'S trans.

13
His conversation does not show the *minute* hand; but he strikes the hour very correctly.
SAMUEL JOHNSON—*Johnsoniana. Kearsley.* L. 604.

14
Tom Birch is as brisk as a bee in conversation; but no sooner does he take a pen in his hand, than it becomes a torpedo to him, and benumbs all his faculties.
SAMUEL JOHNSON—*Boswell's Life.* (1743)

15
Questioning is not the mode of conversation among gentlemen.
SAMUEL JOHNSON—*Boswell's Life.* (1776)

16
A single conversation across the table with a wise man is better than ten years' study of books.
LONGFELLOW—*Hyperion.* Ch. VII. Quoted from the Chinese.

17
Men of great conversational powers almost universally practise a sort of lively sophistry and exaggeration which deceives for the moment both themselves and their auditors.
MACAULAY—*Essay. On the Athenian Orators.*

18
With thee conversing I forget all time:
All seasons and their change, all please alike.
MILTON—*Paradise Lost.* Bk. IV. L. 639.
(See also GAY)

19
Inject a few raisins of conversation into the tasteless dough of existence.
O. HENRY—*The Complete Life of John Hopkins.*

20
Form'd by thy converse, happily to steer
From grave to gay, from lively to severe.
POPE—*Essay on Man.* Ep. IV. L. 379.
(See also BOILEAU under POETS)

21
We took sweet counsel together.
Psalms. LV. 14.

22
Ita fabulantur ut qui sciant Dominum audire.
They converse as those who know that God hears.
TERTULLIAN—*Apologeticus.* P. 36. (Ed. Rigalt)

23
A dearth of words a woman need not fear;
But 'tis a task indeed to learn to *hear:*
In that the skill of conversation lies;
That *shows* or *makes* you both polite and wise.
YOUNG—*Love of Fame.* Satire V. L. 57.

CONVOLVULUS

Convolvulus

24
There is an herb named in Latine Convolvulus (*i. e.* with wind), growing among shrubs and bushes, which carrieth a flower not unlike to this Lilly, save that it yeeldeth no smell nor hath those chives within; for whitenesse they resemble one another very much, as if Nature in making this floure were a learning and trying her skill how to frame the Lilly indeed.
PLINY—*Natural History.* Bk. XXI. Ch. X. HOLLAND'S trans.

COOKERY (See also APPETITE, EATING, HUNGER)

1
Every investigation which is guided by principles of nature fixes its ultimate aim entirely on gratifying the stomach.
ATHENÆUS. Bk. VII. Ch. 2.

2
Cookery is become an art, a noble science; cooks are gentlemen.
BURTON—*Anatomy of Melancholy.* Pt. I. Sec. II. Memb. 2. Subsec. 2.

3
And nearer as they came, a genial savour
Of certain stews, and roast-meats, and pilaus,
Things which in hungry mortals' eyes find favour.
BYRON—*Don Juan.* Canto V. St. 47.

4
Yet smelt roast meat, beheld a huge fire shine,
And cooks in motion with their clean arms bared.
BYRON—*Don Juan.* Canto V. St. 50.

5
Great pity were it if this beneficence of Providence should be marr'd in the ordering, so as to justly merit the Reflection of the old proverb, that though God sends us meat, yet the D— does cooks.
Cooks' and Confectioners' Dictionary, or the Accomplished Housewife's Companions. London. (1724)
(See also GARRICK, SMITH, TAYLOR)

6
Hallo! A great deal of steam! the pudding was out of the copper. A smell like a washing-day! That was the cloth. A smell like an eating-house and a pastrycook's next door to each other, with a laundress's next door to that. That was the pudding.
DICKENS—*Christmas Carol. Stave Three.*

7
Ever a glutton, at another's cost,
But in whose kitchen dwells perpetual frost.
DRYDEN—*Fourth Satire of Persius.* L. 58.

8
Heaven sends us good meat, but the devil sends us cooks.
DAVID GARRICK—*Epigram on Goldsmith's Retaliation.*
(See also COOKS' AND CONFECTIONERS' DICT.)

9
Poure faire un civet, prenez un lièvre.
To make a ragout, first catch your hare.
Attributed erroneously to MRS. GLASSE. In *Cook Book*, pub. 1747, said to have been written by DR. HILL. See NOTES AND QUERIES, Sept. 10, 1859. P. 206. Same in LA VARENNE'S *Le Cuisinier Français.* First ed. (1651) P. 40. Quoted by METTERNICH from MARCHIONESS OF LONDONDERRY—*Narrative of a visit to the Courts of Vienna.* (1844)

10
"Very well," cried I, "that's a good girl; I find you are perfectly qualified for making converts, and so go help your mother to make the gooseberry pye."
GOLDSMITH—*Vicar of Wakefield.* Ch. VII.

11
Her that ruled the rost in the kitchen.
THOS. HEYWOOD—*History of Women.* (Ed. 1624) P. 286.
(See also PRIOR, SKELTON)

12
Digestion, much like Love and Wine, no trifling will brook:
His cook once spoiled the dinner of an Emperor of men;
The dinner spoiled the temper of his Majesty, and then
The Emperor made history—and no one blamed the cook.
F. J. MACBEATH—*Cause and Effect.* In *Smart Set.* Vol. I. No. 4.

13
I seem to you cruel and too much addicted to gluttony, when I beat my cook for sending up a bad dinner. If that appears to you too trifling a cause, say for what cause you would have a cook flogged.
MARTIAL—*Epigrams.* Bk. VIII. Ep. 23.

14
If your slave commits a fault, do not smash his teeth with your fists; give him some of the (hard) biscuit which famous Rhodes has sent you.
MARTIAL—*Epigrams.* Bk. XIV. Ep. 68.

15
A cook should double one sense have: for he
Should taster for himself and master be.
MARTIAL—*Epigrams.* Bk. XIV. Ep. 220.

16
Oh, better no doubt is a dinner of herbs,
When season'd by love, which no rancour disturbs
And sweeten'd by all that is sweetest in life
Than turbot, bisque, ortolans, eaten in strife!
But if, out of humour, and hungry, alone
A man should sit down to dinner, each one
Of the dishes of which the cook chooses to spoil
With a horrible mixture of garlic and oil,
The chances are ten against one, I must own,
He gets up as ill-tempered as when he sat down.
OWEN MEREDITH (Lord Lytton)—*Lucile.* Pt. I. Canto II. St. 27.

17
Of herbs, and other country messes,
Which the neat-handed Phillis dresses.
MILTON—*L'Allegro.* L. 85.

18
The vulgar boil, the learned roast, an egg.
POPE—*Satires. Horace. Epistle II.* Bk. II. L. 85.

19
I never strove to rule the roast,
She ne'er refus'd to pledge my toast.
PRIOR—*Turtle and Sparrow.*
(See also HEYWOOD)

20
A crier of green sauce.
RABELAIS—*Works.* Bk. II. Ch. XXXI.

21
He ruleth all the roste
With bragging and with boste.
SKELTON—*Why come ye not to Court?* Of Cardinal Wolsey.
(See also HEYWOOD)

22
The capon burns, the pig falls from the spit,
The clock hath strucken twelve.
Comedy of Errors. Act I. Sc. 2. L. 44.

1
Carve him as a dish fit for the gods.
Julius Cæsar. Act II. Sc. 1. L. 173

2
Would the cook were of my mind!
Much Ado About Nothing. Act I. Sc. 3. L. 74.

3
She would have made Hercules have turned spit.
Much Ado About Nothing. Act II. Sc. 1. L. 260.

4
Let housewives make a skillet of my helm.
Othello. Act I. Sc. 3. L. 273.

5
Hire me twenty cunning cooks.
Romeo and Juliet. Act IV. Sc. 2. L. 2.

6
Were not I a little pot and soon hot, my very lips might freeze to my teeth.
Taming of the Shrew. Act IV. Sc. 1. L. 5.

7
Where's the cook? is supper ready, the house trimmed, rushes strewed, cobwebs swept?
Taming of the Shrew. Act IV. Sc. 1. L. 47.

8
'Tis burnt; and so is all the meat.
What dogs are these! Where is the rascal cook?
How durst you, villains, bring it from the dresser,
And serve it thus to me that love it not?
Taming of the Shrew. Act IV. Sc. 1. L. 164.

9
Weke, weke! so cries a pig prepared to the spit.
Titus Andronicus. Act IV. Sc. 2. L. 146.

10
He that will have a cake out of the wheat must needs tarry the grinding.
Have I not tarried?
Ay, the grinding: but you must tarry the bolting.
Have I not tarried?
Ay, the bolting: but you must tarry the leavening.
Still have I tarried.
Ay, to the leavening: but here's yet in the word "hereafter" the kneading, the making of the cake, the heating of the oven and the baking: nay, you must stay the cooling too, or you may chance to burn your lips.
Troilus and Cressida. Act I. Sc. 1. L. 15.

11
The waste of many good materials, the vexation that frequently attends such mismanagements, and the curses not unfrequently bestowed on cooks with the usual reflection, that whereas God sends good meat, the devil sends cooks.
E. Smith—*The Compleat Housewife*. (1727)
(See also Cook and Confectioners' Dict.)

12
Let onion atoms lurk within the bowl,
And, half-suspected, animate the whole.
Sydney Smith—*Recipe for Salad Dressing*. Lady Holland's *Memoir*. Vol. I. P. 426. Ed. 3d. ("Scarce suspected" in several versions.)

13
Velocius (or citius) quam asparagi coquantur.
More quickly than asparagus is cooked.
Suetonius—*Augustus*. 87. A saying of Augustus Cæsar.

14
God sends meat, and the Devil sends cooks.
John Taylor—*Works*. Vol. II. P. 85. (1630)
(See also Cook and Confectioners' Dict.)

15
This Bouillabaisse a noble dish is—
A sort of soup or broth, or brew,
Or hotchpotch of all sorts of fishes,
That Greenwich never could outdo;
Green herbs, red peppers, mussels, saffron,
Soles, onions, garlic, roach, and dace;
All these you eat at Terre's tavern,
In that one dish of Bouillabaisse.
Thackeray—*Ballad of Bouillabaisse*.

16
Corne, which is the staffe of life.
Winslow—*Good News from New England*.

17
"Very astonishing indeed! strange thing!"
(Turning the Dumpling round, rejoined the King),
" 'Tis most extraordinary, then, all this is;
It beats Penetti's conjuring all to pieces;
Strange I should never of a Dumpling dream!
But, Goody, tell me where, where, where's the Seam?"
"Sire, there's no Seam," quoth she; "I never knew
That folks did Apple-Dumplings sew."
"No!" cried the staring Monarch with a grin;
"How, how the devil got the Apple in?"
John Wolcot (Peter Pindar)—*The Apple Dumplings and a King*.

COQUETRY (See also Flirtation)

18
Or light or dark, or short or tall,
She sets a springe to snare them all:
All's one to her—above her fan
She'd make sweet eyes at Caliban.
T. B. Aldrich—*Quatrains. Coquette.*

19
Like a lovely tree
She grew to womanhood, and between whiles
Rejected several suitors, just to learn
How to accept a better in his turn.
Byron—*Don Juan*. Canto II. St. 128.

20
Such is your cold coquette, who can't say "No,"
And won't say "Yes," and keeps you on and off-ing
On a lee-shore, till it begins to blow,
Then sees your heart wreck'd, with an inward scoffing.
Byron—*Don Juan*. Canto XII. St. 63.

21
In the School of Coquettes
Madam Rose is a scholar;—
O, they fish with all nets
In the School of Coquettes!
When her brooch she forgets
'Tis to show her new collar;
In the School of Coquettes
Madam Rose is a scholar!
Austin Dobson—*Rose-Leaves. Circe.*

22
Coquetry is the essential characteristic, and the prevalent humor of women; but they do not all practise it, because the coquetry of some it restrained by fear or by reason.
La Rochefoucauld—*Maxims*. No. 252.

1
It is a species of coquetry to make a parade of never practising it.
LA ROCHEFOUCAULD—*Maxims*. No. 110.

2
Women know not the whole of their coquetry.
LA ROCHEFOUCAULD—*Maxims*. No. 342.

3
The greatest miracle of love is the cure of coquetry.
LA ROCHEFOUCAULD—*Maxims*. No. 359.

4
Coquetry whets the appetite; flirtation depraves it. Coquetry is the thorn that guards the rose—easily trimmed off when once plucked. Flirtation is like the slime on water-plants, making them hard to handle, and when caught, only to be cherished in slimy waters.
IK MARVEL—*Reveries of a Bachelor. Sea Coal*. I.

CORPORATIONS (See BUSINESS)

CORRUPTION

5
Spiritalis enim virtus sacramenti ita est ut lux: etsi per immundos transeat, non inquinatur.
The spiritual virtue of a sacrament is like light: although it passes among the impure, it is not polluted.
ST. AUGUSTINE—*Works*. Vol. III. In *Johannis Evang*. Cap. I. Tr. V. Sect. XV.

6
Corruption is a tree, whose branches are
Of an immeasurable length: they spread
Ev'rywhere; and the dew that drops from thence
Hath infected some chairs and stools of authority.
BEAUMONT AND FLETCHER — *Honest Man's Fortune*. Act III. Sc. 3.

7
* * * thieves at home must hang; but he that puts
Into his overgorged and bloated purse
The wealth of Indian provinces, escapes.
COWPER—*Task*. Bk. I. L. 736.

8
'Tis the most certain sign, the world's accurst
That the best things corrupted, are the worst;
'Twas the corrupted Light of knowledge, hurl'd
Sin, Death, and Ignorance o'er all the world;
That Sun like this (from which our sight we have)
Gaz'd on too long, resumes the light he gave.
SIR JOHN DENHAM—*Progress of Learning*.
(See also PURCHAS)

9
I know, when they prove bad, they are a sort of the vilest creatures: yet still the same reason gives it: for, *Optima corrupta pessima:* the best things corrupted become the worst.
FELTHAM—*Resolves*. XXX. *Of Woman*. P. 70. Pickering's Reprint of Fourth Ed. (1631)
(See also PURCHAS)

10
When rogues like these (a sparrow cries)
To honours and employments rise,
I court no favor, ask no place,
For such preferment is disgrace.
GAY—*Fables*. Pt. II. Fable 2.

11
At length corruption, like a general flood
(So long by watchful ministers withstood),
Shall deluge all; and avarice, creeping on,
Spread like a low-born mist, and blot the sun.
POPE—*Moral Essays*. Ep. III. L. 135.

12
So true is that old saying, Corruptio optimi pessima.
PURCHAS—*Pilgrimage. To the Reader*. Of religion. Saying may be traced to THOMAS AQUINAS. *Prim. Soc*. Art. I. 5. ARISTOTLE. *Eth. Nic*. VIII. 10. 12. EUSEBIUS—*Demon. Evang*. I. IV. Ch. XII. ST. GREGORY—*Moralia on Job*.
(See also DENHAM, FELTON, ST. AUGUSTINE, also BACON under SUN)

13
The men with the muck-rake are often indispensable to the well-being of society, but only if they know when to stop raking the muck.
ROOSEVELT—*Address at the Corner-stone laying of the Office Building of House of Representatives*, April 14, 1906.

COST (See VALUE, WORTH)

COUNSEL (See ADVICE)

COUNTRIES (See also AMERICA, ENGLAND, FRANCE, GERMANY, etc.); COUNTRY LIFE

14
The East bow'd low before the blast,
In patient, deep disdain.
She let the legions thunder past,
And plunged in thought again.
MATTHEW ARNOLD—*Obermann Once More*. St. 28. (See also MALLOCH under CHARACTER)

15
Nor rural sights alone, but rural sounds
Exhilarate the spirit, and restore
The tone of languid Nature.
COWPER—*The Task*. Bk. I. L. 181.

16
The town is man's world, but this (country life) is of God.
COWPER—*The Task*. Bk. V. L. 16.

17
There are Batavian graces in all he says.
BENJ. DISRAELI—*Retort* to Beresford Hope (descended from an Amsterdam family), who had referred to Disraeli as an "Asian Mystery."

18
O crassum ingenium. Suspicor fuisse Batavum.
Oh, dense intelligence. I suspect that it was Batavian (i.e. from the Netherlands–Batavia.)
ERASMUS—*Naufragium*.

19
A land flowing with milk and honey.
Exodus. III. 8; *Jeremiah*. XXXII. 22.

20
I hate the countrie's dirt and manners, yet
I love the silence; I embrace the wit;
A courtship, flowing here in full tide.
But loathe the expense, the vanity and pride.
No place each way is happy.
WILLIAM HABINGTON—*To my Noblest Friend, I. C. Esquire*.

21
Far from the gay cities, and the ways of men.
HOMER—*Odyssey*. Bk. XIV. L. 410. POPE'S trans.

1
To one who has been long in city pent,
'Tis very sweet to look into the fair
And open face of heaven,—to breathe a prayer
Full in the smile of the blue firmament.
KEATS—*Sonnet XIV*. L. 1.

2
And as I read
I hear the crowing cock, I hear the note
Of lark and linnet, and from every page
Rise odors of ploughed field or flowery mead.
LONGFELLOW—*Chaucer*.

3
The country is lyric,—the town dramatic. When mingled, they make the most perfect musical drama.
LONGFELLOW—*Kavanagh*. Ch. XIII.

4
Somewhat back from the village street
Stands the old-fashion'd country seat,
Across its antique portico
Tall poplar-trees their shadows throw;
And from its station in the hall
An ancient time-piece says to all,—
"Forever! never!
Never—forever!"
LONGFELLOW—*The Old Clock on the Stairs*.

5
Rus in urbe.
Country in town.
MARTIAL—*Epigrams*. Bk. XII. 57. 21.

6
Mine be a cot beside the hill;
A beehive's hum shall soothe my ear;
A willowy brook, that turns a mill,
With many a fall, shall linger near.
SAM'L ROGERS—*A Wish*.

7
Nec sit terris ultima Thule.
Nor shall Thule be the extremity of the world.
SENECA—*Med*. Act. III. 375. VERGIL—*Georgics*. I. 30.
Thule, the most remote land known to the Greeks and Romans, perhaps Tilemark, Norway, or Iceland. One of the Shetland Islands. Thylensel, according to Camden.

COUNTRY (LOVE OF) (See also PATRIOTISM)

8
There ought to be a system of manners in every nation which a well-formed mind would be disposed to relish. To make us love our country, our country ought to be lovely.
BURKE—*Reflections on the Revolution in France*. Vol. III. P. 100.

9
My dear, my native soil!
For whom my warmest wish to Heav'n is sent,
Long may thy hardy sons of rustic toil
Be blest with health, and peace, and sweet content!
BURNS—*Cotter's Saturday Night*. St. 20.

10
I can't but say it is an awkward sight
To see one's native land receding through
The growing waters; it unmans one quite,
Especially when life is rather new.
BYRON—*Don Juan*. Canto II. St. 12.

11
Oh, Christ! it is a goodly sight to see
What Heaven hath done for this delicious land!
BYRON—*Childe Harold*. Canto I. St. 15.

12
Yon Sun that sets upon the sea
We follow in his flight;
Farewell awhile to him and thee,
My native land—Good Night!
BYRON—*Childe Harold*. Canto I. St. 13.

13
There came to the beach a poor Exile of Erin,
The dew on his thin robe was heavy and chill;
For his country he sigh'd, when at twilight repairing,
To wander alone by the wind-beaten hill.
CAMPBELL—*The Exile of Erin*.

14
From the lone shielding on the misty island
Mountains divide us, and the waste of seas—
But still the blood is strong, the heart is Highland,
And we in dreams behold the Hebrides.
Canadian Boat Song. First appeared in *Blackwood's Magazine*, Sept., 1829. Attributed to JOHN G. LOCKHART, JOHN GALT and EARL OF EGLINGTON (died 1819). Founded on EGLINGTON's lines according to PROF. MACKINNON. Also in article in *Tait's Magazine*. (1849) Wording changed by SKELTON.

15
Patria est, ubicunque est bene.
Our country is wherever we are well off.
CICERO — *Tusculan Disputations*. V. 37. Quoting PACUVIUS. Same quoted by ARISTOPHANES, PLAUTUS, EURIPIDES—*Fragmenta Incerta*.
(See also VOLTAIRE)

16
He made all countries where he came his own.
DRYDEN—*Astræa Redux*. L. 76.

17
And nobler is a limited command,
Given by the love of all your native land,
Than a successive title, long and dark,
Drawn from the mouldy rolls of Noah's Ark.
DRYDEN—*Absalom and Achitophel*. Pt. I. L. 299.

18
So the loud torrent, and the whirlwind's roar,
But bind him to his native mountains more.
GOLDSMITH—*The Traveller*. L. 207.

19
They love their land, because it is their own,
And scorn to give aught other reason why;
Would shake hands with a king upon his throne,
And think it kindness to his majesty.
FITZ-GREENE HALLECK—*Connecticut*.

20
To be really cosmopolitan a man must be at home even in his own country.
T. W. HIGGINSON—*Short Studies of American Authors. Henry James, Jr.*

21
Patriæ quis exul se quoque fugit.
What exile from his country is able to escape from himself?
HORACE—*Carmina*. II. 16. 19.

22
Our hearts, our hopes, are all with thee,
Our hearts, our hopes, our prayers, our tears,
Our faith triumphant o'er our fears,
Are all with thee,—are all with thee!
LONGFELLOW—*The Building of the Ship*.

1
Who dare to love their country, and be poor.
POPE—*On his Grotto at Twickenham.*

2
Un enfant en ouvrant ses yeux doit voir la patrie, et jusqu'à la mort ne voir qu'elle.
The infant, on first opening his eyes, ought to see his country, and to the hour of his death never lose sight of it.
ROUSSEAU.

3
Breathes there the man with soul so dead,
Who never to himself hath said,
This is my own, my native land!
Whose heart hath ne'er within him burn'd,
As home his footsteps he hath turn'd,
From wandering on a foreign strand!
SCOTT—*Lay of the Last Minstrel.* Canto VI. St. 1.

4
Land of my sires! what mortal hand
Can e'er untie the filial band
That knits me to thy rugged strand!
SCOTT—*Lay of the Last Minstrel.* Canto VI. St. 2.

5
My foot is on my native heath, and my name is MacGregor.
SCOTT—*Rob Roy.* Ch. XXXIV.

6
La patrie est aux lieux où l'âme est enchainée.
Our country is that spot to which our heart is bound.
VOLTAIRE—*Le Fanatisme.* I. 2.
(See also CICERO)

COURAGE (See also BRAVERY, DARING)

7
I think the Romans call it Stoicism.
ADDISON—*Cato.* Act 1. Sc. 4.

8
The soul, secured in her existence, smiles
At the drawn dagger, and defies its point.
ADDISON—*Cato.* Act V. Sc. 1.

9
The schoolboy, with his satchel in his hand,
Whistling aloud to bear his courage up.
BLAIR—*The Grave.* Pt. I. L. 58.
(See also DRYDEN, also DRYDEN under THOUGHT)

10
One who never turned his back but marched breast forward,
Never doubted clouds would break,
Never dreamed, though right were worsted, wrong would triumph,
Held we fall to rise, are baffled to fight better,
Sleep to wake.
ROBERT BROWNING—*Epilogue. Asolando.*

11
We are not downhearted, but we cannot understand what is happening to our neighbours.
JOSEPH CHAMBERLAIN—*Speech at Southwick,* Jan. 15, 1906.

12
A man of courage is also full of faith.
CICERO—*The Tusculan Disputations.* Bk. III. Ch. VIII. YONGE's trans.

13
Sta come torre ferma, che non crolla
Giammai la cima per soffiar de' venti.
Be steadfast as a tower that doth not bend its stately summit to the tempest's shock.
DANTE—*Purgatorio.* V. 14.

14
Whistling to keep myself from being afraid.
DRYDEN—*Amphitryon.* Act III. Sc. 1.
(See also BLAIR)

15
The charm of the best courages is that they are inventions, inspirations, flashes of genius.
EMERSON—*Society and Solitude. Courage.*

16
Courage, the highest gift, that scorns to bend
To mean devices for a sordid end.
Courage—an independent spark from Heaven's bright throne,
By which the soul stands raised, triumphant high, alone.
Great in itself, not praises of the crowd,
Above all vice, it stoops not to be proud.
Courage, the mighty attribute of powers above,
By which those great in war, are great in love.
The spring of all brave acts is seated here,
As falsehoods draw their sordid birth from fear.
FARQUHAR—*Love and a Bottle. Part of dedication to the Lord Marquis of Carmarthen.*

17
Stop shallow water still running, it will rage; tread on a worm and it will turn.
ROBERT GREENE—*Worth of Wit.*
(See also HENRY VI)

18
Few persons have courage enough to appear as good as they really are.
J. C. AND A. W. HARE—*Guesses at Truth.*

19
Tender handed stroke a nettle,
And it stings you for your pains;
Grasp it like a man of mettle,
And it soft as silks remains.
AARON HILL—*Verses Written on a Window.*

20
O friends, be men, and let your hearts be strong,
And let no warrior in the heat of fight
Do what may bring him shame in others' eyes;
For more of those who shrink from shame are safe
Than fall in battle, while with those who flee
Is neither glory nor reprieve from death.
HOMER—*Iliad.* Bk. V. L. 663. BRYANT'S trans.

21
Justum et tenacem propositi virum
Non civium ardor prava jubentium,
Non vultus instantis tyranni,
Mente quatit solida.
The man who is just and resolute will not be moved from his settled purpose, either by the misdirected rage of his fellow citizens, or by the threats of an imperious tyrant.
HORACE—*Carmina.* III. 3. 1.

22
"Be bold!" *first gate;* "Be bold, be bold, and evermore be bold," *second gate;* "Be not too bold!" *third gate.*
Inscription on the Gates of Busyrane.
(See also DANTON under AUDACITY)

1
On ne peut répondre de son courage quand on n'a jamais été dans le péril.
We can never be certain of our courage until we have faced danger.
LA ROCHEFOUCAULD—*Premier Supplément*. 42.

2
Write on your doors the saying wise and old,
"Be bold! be bold!" and everywhere—"Be bold;
Be not too bold!" Yet better the excess
Than the defect; better the more than less;
Better like Hector in the field to die,
Than like a perfumed Paris turn and fly.
LONGFELLOW—*Morituri Salutamus*.

3
What! shall one monk, scarce known beyond his cell,
Front Rome's far-reaching bolts, and scorn her frown?
Brave Luther answered, "Yes"; that thunder's swell
Rocked Europe, and discharmed the triple crown.
LOWELL—*To W. L. Garrison*. St. 5.

4
Be of good cheer: it is I; be not afraid.
Matthew. XIV. 27.

5
I argue not
Against Heaven's hand or will, nor bate a jot
Of heart or hope; but still bear up and steer
Right onward.
MILTON—*Sonnet. To Cyriack Skinner*.

6
Leve fit quod bene fertur onus.
The burden which is well borne becomes light.
OVID—*Amorum*. I. 2. 10.

7
Animus tamen omnia vincit.
Ille etiam vires corpus habere facit.
Courage conquers all things: it even gives strength to the body.
OVID—*Epistolæ Ex Ponto*. II. 7. 75.

8
Pluma haud interest, patronus an cliens probior sit
Homini, cui nulla in pectore est audacia.
It does not matter a feather whether a man be supported by patron or client, if he himself wants courage.
PLAUTUS—*Mostellaria*. II. 1. 64.

9
Bonus animus in mala re, dimidium est mali.
Courage in danger is half the battle.
PLAUTUS—*Pseudolus*. I. 5. 37.

10
Non solum taurus ferit uncis cornibus hostem,
Verum etiam instanti læsa repugnat ovis.
Not only does the bull attack its foe with its crooked horns, but the injured sheep will fight its assailant.
PROPERTIUS—*Elegiæ*. II. 5. 19.

11
Cowards may fear to die; but courage stout,
Rather than live in snuff, will be put out.
SIR WALTER RALEIGH—*The night before he died. Bayley's Life of Raleigh*. P. 157.

12
C'est dans les grands dangers qu'on voit les grands courages.
It is in great dangers that we see great courage.
REGNARD—*Le Légataire*.

13
Come one, come all! this rock shall fly
From its firm base, as soon as I.
SCOTT—*Lady of the Lake*. Canto V. St. 10.

14
Virtus in astra tendit, in mortem timor.
Courage leads to heaven; fear, to death.
SENECA—*Hercules Œtæus*. LXXI.

15
Fortuna opes auferre, non animum potest.
Fortune can take away riches, but not courage.
SENECA—*Medea*. CLXXVI.

16
You must not think
That we are made of stuff so fat and dull
That we can let our beard be shook with danger
And think it pastime.
Hamlet. Act IV. Sc. 7. L. 29.

17
O, the blood more stirs
To rouse a lion than to start a hare!
Henry IV. Pt. I. Act I. Sc. 3. L. 198.

18
The smallest worm will turn being trodden on,
And doves will peck in safeguard of their brood.
Henry VI. Pt. III. Act II. Sc. 2. L. 17.
(See also GREENE)

19
Why, courage then! what cannot be avoided
'Twere childish weakness to lament or fear.
Henry VI. Pt. III. Act V. Sc. 4. L. 37.

20
We fail!
But screw your courage to the sticking-place,
And we'll not fail.
Macbeth. Act I. Sc. 7. L. 59.

21
By how much unexpected, by so much
We must awake endeavour for defence;
For courage mounteth with occasion.
King John. Act II. Sc. 1. L. 80.

22
Muster your wits: stand in your own defence;
Or hide your heads like cowards, and fly hence.
Love's Labour's Lost. Act V. Sc. 2. L. 85.

23
He hath borne himself beyond the promise of his age, doing, in the figure of a lamb, the feats of a lion.
Much Ado About Nothing. Act I. Sc. 1. L. 13.

24
The thing of courage
As rous'd with rage doth sympathise,
And, with an accent tun'd in self-same key,
Retorts to chiding fortune.
Troilus and Cressida. Act I. Sc. 3. L. 51.

25
Ei di virilità grave e maturo,
Mostra in fresco vigor chiome canute.
Grave was the man in years, in looks, in word,
His locks were gray, yet was his courage green.
TASSO—*Gerusalemme*. I. 53.

1
Quod sors feret feremus æquo animo.
Whatever chance shall bring, we will bear with equanimity.
TERENCE—*Phormio.* I. 2. 88.

2
Who stemm'd the torrent of a downward age.
THOMSON—*The Seasons. Summer.* L. 1,516.

COURTESY

3
A moral, sensible, and well-bred man
Will not affront me, and no other can.
COWPER—*Conversation.* L. 193.

4
Life is not so short but that there is always time enough for courtesy.
EMERSON—*Social Aims.*

5
How sweet and gracious, even in common speech,
Is that fine sense which men call Courtesy!
Wholesome as air and genial as the light,
Welcome in every clime as breath of flowers,
It transmutes aliens into trusting friends,
And gives its owner passport round the globe.
JAMES T. FIELDS—*Courtesy.*

6
Their accents firm and loud in conversation,
Their eyes and gestures eager, sharp and quick
Showed them prepared on proper provocation
To give the lie, pull noses, stab and kick!
And for that very reason it is said
They were so very courteous and well-bred.
JOHN HOOKHAM FRERE—*Prospectus and Specimen of an Intended National Work.*

7
When the king was horsed thore,
Launcelot lookys he upon,
How courtesy was in him more
Than ever was in any mon.
MORTE D'ARTHUR—*Harleian Library.* (British Museum.) MS. 2,252.

8
In thy discourse, if thou desire to please;
All such is courteous, useful, new, or wittie:
Usefulness comes by labour, wit by ease;
Courtesie grows in court; news in the citie.
HERBERT—*Church. Church Porch.* St. 49.

9
Shepherd, I take thy word,
And trust thy honest offer'd courtesy,
Which oft is sooner found in lowly sheds
With smoky rafters, than in tap'stry halls,
And courts of princes.
MILTON—*Comus.* L. 322.

10
The thorny point
Of bare distress hath ta'en from me the show
Of smooth civility.
As You Like It. Act II. Sc. 7. L. 94.

11
The Retort Courteous.
As You Like It. Act V. Sc. 4. L. 76.

12
Dissembling courtesy! How fine this tyrant
Can tickle where she wounds!
Cymbeline. Act I. Sc. 1. L. 84.

13
The mirror of all courtesy.
Henry VIII. Act II. Sc. 1. L. 53.

14
I am the very pink of courtesy.
Romeo and Juliet. Act II. Sc. 4. L. 61.

15
That's too civil by half.
SHERIDAN—*The Rivals.* Act III. Sc. 4.

16
High erected thoughts seated in a heart of courtesy.
SIR PHILIP SIDNEY—*The Arcadia.* Bk. I. Par. II.

COURTIERS

17
To laugh, to lie, to flatter to face,
Foure waies in court to win men's grace.
ROGER ASCHAM—*The Schoolmaster.*

18
A mere court butterfly,
That flutters in the pageant of a monarch.
BYRON—*Sardanapalus.* Act V. Sc. 1.

19
To shake with laughter ere the jest they hear,
To pour at will the counterfeited tear;
And, as their patron hints the cold or heat,
To shake in dog-days, in December sweat.
SAMUEL JOHNSON—*London.* L. 140.

20
There is, betwixt that smile we would aspire to,
That sweet aspect of princes, and their ruin,
More pangs and fears than wars or women have.
Henry VIII. Act III. Sc. 2. L. 368.

21
At the throng'd levee bends the venal tribe:
With fair but faithless smiles each varnish'd o'er,
Each smooth as those that mutually deceive,
And for their falsehood each despising each.
THOMSON—*Liberty.* Pt. V. L. 190.

COVETOUSNESS

22
Excess of wealth is cause of covetousness.
MARLOWE—*The Jew of Malta.* Act I. Sc. 2.

23
Quicquid servatur, cupimus magis: ipsaque furem
Cura vocat. Pauci, quod sinit alter, amant.
We covet what is guarded; the very care invokes the thief. Few love what they may have.
OVID—*Amorum.* III. 4. 25.

24
Verum est aviditas dives, et pauper pudor.
True it is that covetousness is rich, modesty starves.
PHÆDRUS—*Fables.* II. 1. 12.

25
Alieni appetens sui profusus.
Covetous of the property of others and prodigal of his own.
SALLUST—*Catilina.* V.

26
I am not covetous for gold,
Nor care I who doth feed upon my cost;
It yearns me not if men my garments wear;
Such outward things dwell not in my desires:
But if it be a sin to covet honor
I am the most offending soul alive.
Henry V. Act IV. Sc. 3. L. 24.

27
When workmen strive to do better than well,
They do confound their skill in covetousness.
King John. Act IV. Sc. 2 L. 28.

COW

1
I never saw a Purple Cow,
I never hope to see one;
But I can tell you, anyhow
I'd rather see than be one.
GELETT BURGESS—*The Purple Cow.*

2
The Moo-cow-moo's got a tail like a rope
En it's ravelled down where it grows,
En it's just like feeling a piece of soap
All over the moo-cow's nose.
EDMUND VANCE COOKE—*The Moo-Cow-Moo.*

3
You may rezoloot till the cows come home.
JOHN HAY—*Little Breeches. Banty Tim.*
(See also SWIFT)

4
A curst cow hath short horns.
HERBERT—*Jacula Prudentum.*

5
A cow is a very good animal in the field; but we turn her out of a garden.
SAMUEL JOHNSON—*Boswell's Life of Johnson.* (1772)

6
The friendly cow all red and white,
I love with all my heart:
She gives me cream with all her might
To eat with apple-tart.
STEVENSON—*Child's Garden of Verses. The Cow.*

7
I warrant you lay abed till the cows came home.
SWIFT—*Polite Conversations.* Dialog. 2.
(See also HAY)

8
Thank you, pretty cow, that made
Pleasant milk to soak my bread.
ANNE TAYLOR—*The Cow.*

COWARDICE; COWARDS

9
To see what is right and not to do it is want of courage.
CONFUCIUS—*Analects.* Bk. II. Ch. XXIV.

10
Grac'd with a sword, and worthier of a fan.
COWPER—*Task.* Bk. I. L. 771.

11
That all men would be cowards if they dare,
Some men we know have courage to declare.
CRABBE—*Tale I. The Dumb Orators.* L. 11.

12
The coward never on himself relies,
But to an equal for assistance flies.
CRABBE—*Tale III. The Gentleman Farmer.* L. 84.

13
Cowards are cruel, but the brave
Love mercy, and delight to save.
GAY—*Fables.* Pt. I. Fable 1.

14
Der Feige droht nur, wo er sicher ist.
The coward only threatens when he is safe.
GOETHE—*Torquato Tasso.* II. 3. 207.

15
When desp'rate ills demand a speedy cure,
Distrust is cowardice, and prudence folly.
SAMUEL JOHNSON—*Irene.* Act IV. Sc. 1.

16
He
That kills himself to avoid misery, fears it,
And, at the best, shows but a bastard valour.
This life's a fort committed to my trust,
Which I must not yield up, till it be forced:
Nor will I. He's not valiant that dares die,
But he that boldly bears calamity.
MASSINGER—*Maid of Honour.* Act IV. Sc. 3.

17
Men lie, who lack courage to tell truth—the cowards!
JOAQUIN MILLER—*Ina.* Sc. 3.

18
Timidi est optare necem.
To wish for death is a coward's part.
OVID—*Metamorphoses.* IV. 115.

19
Virtutis expers verbis jactans gloriam
Ignotos fallit, notis est derisui.
A coward boasting of his courage may deceive strangers, but he is a laughing-stock to those who know him.
PHÆDRUS—*Fables.* I. 11. 1.

20
Vous semblez les anguilles de Melun; vous criez devant qu'on vous escorche.
You are like the eels of Melun; you cry out before you are skinned.
RABELAIS—*Gargantua.*

21
Canis timidus vehementius latrat quam mordet.
A cowardly cur barks more fiercely than it bites.
QUINTUS CURTIUS RUFUS—*De Rebus Gestis Alexandri Magni.* VII. 4. 13.

22
When all the blandishments of life are gone,
The coward sneaks to death, the brave live on.
DR. SEWELL—*The Suicide.*

23
Who knows himself a braggart,
Let him fear this, for it will come to pass
That every braggart shall be found an ass.
All's Well That Ends Well. Act IV. Sc. 3. L. 369.

24
You souls of geese,
That bear the shapes of men, how have you run
From slaves that apes would beat!
Coriolanus. Act I. Sc. 4. L. 35.

25
What a slave art thou, to hack thy sword as thou hast done, and then say it was in fight!
Henry IV. Pt. I. Act II. Sc. 4. L. 286.

26
I may speak it to my shame,
I have a truant been to chivalry.
Henry IV. Pt. I. Act V. Sc. 1. L. 93.

27
I would give all my fame for a pot of ale and safety.
Henry V. Act III. Sc. 2. L. 13.

28
So bees with smoke and doves with noisome stench
Are from their hives and houses driven away.
They call'd us for our fierceness English dogs;
Now like to whelps, we crying run away.
Henry VI. Pt. I. Act I. Sc. 5. L. 23.

1
Becomes it thee to taunt his valiant age
And twit with cowardice a man half dead?
Henry VI. Pt. I. Act III. Sc. 2. L. 55.

2
So cowards fight when they can fly no further;
As doves do peck the falcon's piercing talons;
So desperate thieves, all hopeless of their lives,
Breathe out invectives 'gainst the officers.
Henry VI. Pt. III. Act I. Sc. 4. L. 39.

3 I hold it cowardice
To rest mistrustful where a noble heart
Hath pawn'd an open hand in sign of love.
Henry VI. Pt. III. Act IV. Sc. 2. L. 6.

4
Thou slave, thou wretch, thou coward!
Thou little valiant, great in villany!
Thou ever strong upon the stronger side!
Thou Fortune's champion, that dost never fight
But when her humorous ladyship is by
To teach thee safety!
King John. Act III. Sc. 1. L. 116.

5
Dost thou now fall over to my foes?
Thou wear a lion's hide! doff it for shame,
And hang a calf's skin on those recreant limbs.
King John. Act III. Sc. 1. L. 127.

6 Milk-liver'd man!
That bear'st a cheek for blows, a head for wrongs,
Who hast not in thy brows an eye discerning
Thine honor from thy suffering.
King Lear. Act IV. Sc. 2. L. 50.

7 Wouldst thou have that
Which thou esteem'st the ornament of life,
And live a coward in thine own esteem,
Letting "I dare not" wait upon, "I would";
Like the poor cat i' the adage?
Macbeth. Act I. Sc. 7. L. 41.

8
How many cowards, whose hearts are all as false
As stairs of sand, wear yet upon their chins
The beards of Hercules and frowning Mars,
Who, inward search'd, have livers white as milk.
Merchant of Venice. Act III. Sc. 2. L. 83.

9
That which in mean men we entitle patience
Is pale cold cowardice in noble breasts.
Richard II. Act I. Sc. 2. L. 33.

10
By this good light, this is a very shallow monster!—I afear'd of him!—A very weak monster! —The man i' the moon!—A most poor, credulous monster!—Well drawn, monster, in good sooth!
Tempest. Act II. Sc. 2. L. 144.

11
A coward, a most devout coward, religious in it.
Twelfth Night. Act III. Sc. 4. L. 427.

12
Timidus se vocat cautum, parcum sordidus.
The coward calls himself cautious, the miser thrifty.
Syrus—*Maxims*.

13
Ignavissimus quisque, et ut res docuit, in periculo non ausurus, nimis verbis et lingua feroces.
Every recreant who proved his timidity in the hour of danger, was afterwards boldest in words and tongue.
Tacitus—*Annales*. IV. 62.

14
The man that lays his hand on woman,
Save in the way of kindness, is a wretch
Whom 'twere gross flattery to name a coward.
Tobin—*The Honeymoon*. Act II. Sc. 1.

15
Adieu, canaux, canards, canaille.
Voltaire, summing up his *Impressions de Voyage, on his return from the Netherlands.*

COWSLIP

Primula

16
Smiled like yon knot of cowslips on a cliff.
Blair—*The Grave*. L. 520.

17
Yet soon fair Spring shall give another scene.
And yellow cowslips gild the level green.
Anne E. Bleecker—*Return to Tomhanick*.

18
And wild-scatter'd cowslips bedeck the green dale.
Burns—*The Chevalier's Lament*.

19
Ilk cowslip cup shall kep a tear.
Burns—*Elegy on Capt. Matthew Henderson*.

20
The nesh yonge coweslip bendethe wyth the dewe.
Thomas Chatterton—*Rowley Poems. Ælla.*

21
The cowslip is a country wench.
Hood—*Flowers*.

22 The first wan cowslip, wet
With tears of the first morn.
Owen Meredith (Lord Lytton)—*Ode to a Starling*.

23
Through tall cowslips nodding near you,
Just to touch you as you pass.
Owen Meredith (Lord Lytton)—*Song*.

24
Thus I set my printless feet
O'er the cowslip's velvet head,
That bends not as I tread.
Milton—*Comus. Song.*

25
The even mead, that erst brought sweetly forth
The freckled cowslip, burnet and green clover.
Henry V. Act V. Sc. 2. L. 48.

26
The cowslips tall her pensioners be;
In their gold coats spots you see:
Those be rubies, fairy favours;
In those freckles live their savours.
Midsummer Night's Dream. Act II. Sc. I. L. 10.

27
And ye talk together still,
In the language wherewith Spring
Letters cowslips on the hill.
Tennyson—*Adeline*. St. 5.

28
And by the meadow-trenches blow the faint sweet cuckoo-flowers.
Tennyson—*The May Queen*. St. 8.

CREATION

1
Had I been present at the creation, I would have given some useful hints for the better ordering of the universe.
ALPHONSO X, THE WISE.

2
For we also are his offspring.
ARATUS—*Phænomena.* Said to be the passage quoted by St. Paul. *Acts.* XVII. 28.

3
You own a watch the invention of the mind,
Though for a single motion 'tis designed,
As well as that which is with greater thought
With various springs, for various motions wrought.
BLACKMORE—*The Creation.* Bk. III. The creation and the watch. HALLAM—*Literature of Europe.* II. 385, traces its origin to CICERO—*De Natura Deorum.* Found also in HERBERT OF CHERBURY'S treatise *De Religione Gentilium.* HALE—*Primitive Origination of Mankind.* BOLINGBROKE, in a letter to POUILLY. PALEY used the illustration, which he took from NIUWENTYT.
(See also VOLTAIRE)

4
Are we a piece of machinery that, like the Æolian harp, passive, takes the impression of the passing accident? Or do these workings argue something within us above the trodden clod?
BURNS—*Letter to Mrs. Dunlop.* New Year-Day Morning, 1789.

5
Creation is great, and cannot be understood.
CARLYLE—*Essays. Characteristics.*

6
[This saying of Alphonso about Ptolemy's astronomy, that] "it seemed a crank machine; that it was pity the Creator had not taken advice."
CARLYLE—*History of Frederick the Great.* Bk. II. Ch. VII.
(See also ALPHONSO)

7
And what if all of animated nature
Be but organic harps diversely framed,
That tremble into thought, as o'er them sweeps,
Plastic and vast, one intellectual breeze,
At once the soul of each, and God of all?
COLERIDGE—*The Eolian Harp.* (1795)

8
From harmony, from heavenly harmony,
This universal frame began:
From harmony, to harmony
Through all the compass of the notes it ran,
The diapason closing full in man.
DRYDEN—*A Song for St. Cecilia's Day.* L. 11.

9
Two urns by Jove's high throne have ever stood,
The source of evil, one, and one of good.
HOMER—*Iliad.* Bk. 24. L. 663. POPE's trans.

10
Nature they say, doth dote,
And cannot make a man
Save on some worn-out plan,
Repeating us by rote.
LOWELL—*Ode at the Harvard Commemoration,* July 21, 1865. VI.

11 Though to recount almighty works
What words of tongue or seraph can suffice,
Or heart of man suffice to comprehend?
MILTON—*Paradise Lost.* Bk. VII. L. 112.

12
Open, ye heavens, your living doors; let in
The great Creator from his work return'd
Magnificent, his six days' work, a world!
MILTON—*Paradise Lost.* Bk. VII. L. 566.

13 What cause
Moved the Creator in his holy rest
Through all eternity so late to build
In chaos, and, the work begun, how soon
Absolved.
MILTON—*Paradise Lost.* Bk. VII. L. 90.

14
I am fearfully and wonderfully made.
Psalms. CXXXIX. 14.

15
Wie aus Duft und Glanz gemischt
Du mich schufst, dir dank ich's heut.
As thou hast created me out of mingled air and glitter, I thank thee for it.
RÜCKERT—*Die Sterbende Blume.* St. 8.

16
No man saw the building of the New Jerusalem, the workmen crowded together, the unfinished walls and unpaved streets; no man heard the clink of trowel and pickaxe; it descended *out of heaven from God.*
SEELEY—*Ecce Homo.* Ch. XXIV.
(See also HEBER under ARCHITECTURE)

17
When I consider everything that grows
Holds in perfection but a little moment;
That this huge stage presenteth nought but shows,
Whereon the stars in secret influence comment;
Then the conceit of this inconstant stay
Sets you most rich in youth before my sight.
SHAKESPEARE—*Sonnets.* XV.

18
Vitality in a woman is a blind fury of creation.
BERNARD SHAW—*Man and Superman.* Act I.

19
Through knowledge we behold the world's creation,
How in his cradle first he fostered was;
And judge of Nature's cunning operation,
How things she formed of a formless mass.
SPENSER—*Tears of the Muses. Urania.* L. 499.

20 Each moss,
Each shell, each drawling insect, holds a rank
Important in the plan of Him who fram'd
This scale of beings; holds a rank which, lost
Would break the chain, and leave behind a gap
Which Nature's self would rue.
BENJAMIN STILLINGFLEET — *Miscellaneous Tracts relating to Natural History.* P. 127. (Ed. 1762)
(See also WALLER)

21
One God, one law, one element,
And one far-off divine event,
To which the whole creation moves.
TENNYSON—*In Memoriam. Conclusion.* Last Stanza.

1
As if some lesser God had made the world,
And had not force to shape it as he would.
TENNYSON—*The Passing of Arthur*. L. 14.

2
Le monde m'embarrasse, et je ne puis pas songer
Que cette horloge existe et n'a pas d'Horloger.
The world embarrasses me, and I cannot dream
That this watch exists and has no watchmaker.
VOLTAIRE.
(See also BLACKMORE)

3
The chain that's fixed to the throne of Jove,
On which the fabric of our world depends,
One link dissolved, the whole creation ends.
EDMUND WALLER—*Of the Danger His Majesty Escaped*. L. 68.
(See also STILLINGFLEET)

CREDIT

4
Private credit is wealth; public honor is security; the feather that adorns the royal bird supports its flight; strip him of his plumage, and you fix him to the earth.
JUNIUS—*Affair of the Falkland Islands*. Vol. I. Letter XLII.

5
Blest paper-credit! last and best supply!
That lends corruption lighter wings to fly.
POPE—*Moral Essays*. Ep. 3. L. 39.

6
He smote the rock of the national resources, and abundant streams of revenue gushed forth. He touched the dead corpse of Public Credit, and it sprung upon its feet.
DANIEL WEBSTER—*Speech on Hamilton*, March 10, 1831. Vol. I. P. 200.
(See also YELVERTON under LAW)

CRIME

7 Non nella pena,
Nel delitto è la infamia.
Disgrace does not consist in the punishment, but in the crime.
ALFIERI—*Antigone*. I. 3.

8 Il reo
D'un delitto è chi'l pensa: a chi l' ordisce
La pena spetta.
The guilty is he who meditates a crime; the punishment is his who lays the plot.
ALFIERI—*Antigone*. II. 2.

9 Oh! ben provvide il cielo,
Ch' uom per delitto mai lieto non sia.
Heaven takes care that no man secures happiness by crime.
ALFIERI—*Oreste*. I. 2.

10 There's not a crime
But takes its proper change out still in crime
If once rung on the counter of this world.
E. B. BROWNING—*Aurora Leigh*. Bk. III. L. 870.

11
A man who has no excuse for crime, is indeed defenceless!
BULWER-LYTTON—*The Lady of Lyons*. Act IV. Sc. 1.

12
Nor all that heralds rake from coffin'd clay,
Nor florid prose, nor honied lies of rhyme,
Can blazon evil deeds, or consecrate a crime.
BYRON—*Childe Harold*. Canto I. St. 3.

13
Le crime fait la honte et non pas l'échafaud.
The crime and not the scaffold makes the shame.
CORNEILLE—*Essex*. IV. 3. Quoted by CHARLOTTE CORDAY in a letter to her father after the murder of Marat.

14
But many a crime deemed innocent on earth
Is registered in Heaven; and these no doubt
Have each their record, with a curse annex'd.
COWPER—*The Task*. Bk. VI. L. 439.

15
C'est plus qu'un crime, c'est une faute.
It is worse than a crime, it is a blunder.
JOSEPH FOUCHÉ. As quoted by himself in his *Memoires*, original Ed., 1824. Referring to the murder of the Duc Enghien. Fouché's sons deny that it originated with their father. Quoted by others as "C'est pis qu'un crime," and "C'estoit pire qu'un crime." (See *Notes and Queries*, Aug. 14, 1915. P. 123. Aug. 28. P. 166)

16
Crime is not punished as an offense against God, but as prejudicial to society.
FROUDE—*Short Studies on Great Subjects. Reciprocal Duties of State and Subjects.*

17
Every crime destroys more Edens than our own.
HAWTHORNE—*Marble Faun*. Vol. I. Ch. XXIII.

18
Deprendi miserum est.
It is grievous to be caught.
HORACE—*Satires*. Bk. I. 2. 134.

19
A crafty knave needs no broker.
BEN JONSON. Quoted in *Every Man in his Humour;* also in TAYLOR'S *London to Hamburgh.*

20
'Tis no sin love's fruits to steal;
But the sweet thefts to reveal;
To be taken, to be seen,
These have crimes accounted been.
BEN JONSON—*Volpone*. Act III. Sc. 6.

21
Se judice, nemo nocens absolvitur.
By his own verdict no guilty man was ever acquitted.
JUVENAL—*Satires*. XIII. 2.

22
Multi committunt eadem diverso crimina fato;
Ille crucem sceleris pretium tulit, hic diadema.
Many commit the same crimes with a very different result. One bears a cross for his crime; another a crown.
JUVENAL—*Satires*. XIII. 103.

23
Nam scelus intra se tacitum qui cogitat ullum,
Facti crimen habet.
For whoever meditates a crime is guilty of the deed.
JUVENAL—*Satires*. XIII. 209.

1
Non faciat malum, ut inde veniat bonum.
You are not to do evil that good may come of it.
Law Maxim.

2
Solent occupationis spe vel impune quædam scelesta committi.
Wicked deeds are generally done, even with impunity, for the mere desire of occupation.
AMMIANUS MARCELLINUS—*Annales.* XXX. 9.

3
Pœna potest demi, culpa perennis erit.
The punishment can be remitted; the crime is everlasting.
OVID—*Epistolæ Ex Ponto.* I. 1. 64.

4
Factis ignoscite nostris
Si scelus ingenio scitis abesse meo.
Overlook our deeds, since you know that crime was absent from our inclination.
OVID—*Fausti.* Bk. III. 309.

5
Ars fit ubi a teneris crimen condiscitur annis.
Where crime is taught from early years, it becomes a part of nature.
OVID—*Heroides.* IV. 25.

6
Le crime d'une mère est un pesant fardeau.
The crime of a mother is a heavy burden.
RACINE—*Phèdre.* III. 3.

7
With his hand upon the throttle-valve of crime.
LORD SALISBURY—*Speech* in House of Lords, 1889.

8
Prosperum ac felix scelus
Virtus vocatur; sontibus parent boni;
Jus est in armis, opprimit leges timor.
Successful crime is dignified with the name of virtue; the good become the slaves of the impious; might makes right; fear silences the power of the law.
SENECA—*Hercules Furens.* CCLI.
(See also HARRINGTON under TREACHERY)

9
Nullum caruit exemplo nefas.
No crime has been without a precedent.
SENECA—*Hippolytus.* DLIV.

10
Scelere velandum est scelus.
One crime has to be concealed by another.
SENECA—*Hippolytus.* DCCXXI.

11
Cui prodest scelus,
Is fecit.
He who profits by crime is guilty of it.
SENECA—*Medea.* D.

12
Ad auctores redit
Sceleris coacti culpa.
The guilt of enforced crimes lies on those who impose them.
SENECA—*Troades.* DCCCLXX.

13
Qui non vetat peccare, cum possit, jubet.
He who does not prevent a crime when he can, encourages it.
SENECA—*Troades.* CCXCI.

14
Dumque punitur scelus,
Crescit.
While crime is punished it yet increases.
SENECA—*Thyestes.* XXXI.

15
Foul deeds will rise,
Though all the earth o'erwhelm them, to men's eyes.
Hamlet. Act I. Sc. 2. L. 257.

16
If little faults, proceeding on distemper,
Shall not be wink'd at, how shall we stretch our eye
When capital crimes, chew'd, swallow'd, and digested,
Appear before us?
Henry V. Act II. Sc. 2. L. 54.

17
Between the acting of a dreadful thing
And the first motion, all the interim is
Like a phantasma, or a hideous dream.
Julius Cæsar. Act II. Sc. 1. L. 63.

18
Beyond the infinite and boundless reach
Of mercy, if thou didst this deed of death,
Art thou damn'd, Hubert.
King John. Act IV. Sc. 3. L. 117.

19
Tremble, thou wretch,
That has within thee undivulged crimes,
Unwhipp'd of justice.
King Lear. Act III. Sc. 2. L. 51.

20
There shall be done
A deed of dreadful note.
Macbeth. Act III. Sc. 2. L. 43.

21
Amici vitium ni feras, facis tuum.
If you share the crime of your friend, you make it your own.
SYRUS—*Maxims.*

22
Du repos dans le crime! ah! qui peut s'en flatter.
To be at peace in crime! ah, who can thus flatter himself.
VOLTAIRE—*Oreste.* I. 5.

23
La crainte suit le crime, et c'est son châtiment.
Fear follows crime and is its punishment.
VOLTAIRE—*Semiramis.* V. 1.

24
Yet each man kills the thing he loves,
By each let this be heard,
Some do it with a bitter look,
Some with a flattering word,
The coward does it with a kiss,
The brave man with a sword.
OSCAR WILDE—*Ballad of Reading Gaol.*

CRITICISM (See also AUTHORSHIP, JOURNALISM)

25
When I read rules of criticism, I immediately inquire after the works of the author who has written them, and by that means discover what it is he likes in a composition.
ADDISON—*Guardian.* No. 115.

26
He was in Logic, a great critic,
Profoundly skill'd in Analytic;
He could distinguish, and divide
A hair 'twixt south and south-west side.
BUTLER—*Hudibras.* Pt. I. Canto I. L. 65.

1

A man must serve his time to every trade
Save censure—critics all are ready made.
Take hackney'd jokes from Miller, got by rote,
With just enough of learning to misquote;
A mind well skill'd to find or forge a fault;
A turn for punning, call it Attic salt;
To Jeffrey go, be silent and discreet,
His pay is just ten sterling pounds per sheet;
Fear not to lie, 'twill seem a lucky hit;
Shrink not from blasphemy, 'twill pass for wit;
Care not for feeling—pass your proper jest,
And stand a critic, hated yet caress'd.

BYRON—*English Bards and Scotch Reviewers.* L. 63.

2

As soon
Seek roses in December—ice in June,
Hope, constancy in wind, or corn in chaff;
Believe a woman or an epitaph,
Or any other thing that's false, before
You trust in critics.

BYRON—*English Bards and Scotch Reviewers.* L. 75.

3

Dijó la sarten á la caldera, quitate allá ojinegra.

Said the pot to the kettle, "Get away, blackface."

CERVANTES—*Don Quixote.* II. 67.

4

Who shall dispute what the Reviewers say?
Their word's sufficient; and to ask a reason,
In such a state as theirs, is downright treason.

CHURCHILL—*Apology.* L. 94.

5

Though by whim, envy, or resentment led,
They damn those authors whom they never read.

CHURCHILL—*The Candidate.* L. 57.

6

A servile race
Who, in mere want of fault, all merit place;
Who blind obedience pay to ancient schools,
Bigots to Greece, and slaves to musty rules.

CHURCHILL—*The Rosciad.* L. 183.

7

But spite of all the criticizing elves,
Those who would make us feel—must feel themselves.

CHURCHILL—*The Rosciad.* L. 961.

8

Reviewers are usually people who would have been poets, historians, biographers, etc., if they could: they have tried their talents at one or the other, and have failed; therefore they turn critics.

COLERIDGE—*Lectures on Shakespeare and Milton.* P. 36.

(See also DISRAELI, MACAULAY, SHELLEY; also BISMARCK under JOURNALISM)

9

Too nicely Jonson knew the critic's part,
Nature in him was almost lost in art.

COLLINS—*Epistle to Sir Thomas Hanmer on his Edition of Shakespeare.*

10

There are some Critics so with Spleen diseased,
They scarcely come inclining to be pleased:
And sure he must have more than mortal Skill,
Who pleases one against his Will.

CONGREVE—*The Way of the World. Epilogue.*

11

La critique est aisée, et l'art est difficile.

Criticism is easy, and art is difficult.

DESTOUCHES—*Glorieux.* II. 5.

12

The press, the pulpit, and the stage,
Conspire to censure and expose our age.

WENTWORTH DILLON—*Essay on Translated Verse.* L. 7.

13

You know who critics are?—the men who have failed in literature and art.

BENJ. DISRAELI—*Lothair.* Ch. XXXV.

(See also COLERIDGE)

14

It is much easier to be critical than to be correct.

BENJ. DISRAELI—*Speech in the House of Commons.* Jan 24, 1860.

15

The most noble criticism is that in which the critic is not the antagonist so much as the rival of the author.

ISAAC D'ISRAELI — *Curiosities of Literature. Literary Journals.*

16

Those who do not read criticism will rarely merit to be criticised.

ISAAC D'ISRAELI—*Literary Character of Men of Genius.* Ch. VI.

17

Ill writers are usually the sharpest censors.

DRYDEN—*Dedication of translations from Ovid.*

18

They who write ill, and they who ne'er durst write,
Turn critics out of mere revenge and spite.

DRYDEN—*Prologue to Conquest of Granada.*

19

All who (like him) have writ ill plays before,
For they, like thieves, condemned, are hangmen made,
To execute the members of their trade.

DRYDEN—*Prologue to Rival Queens.*

20

"I'm an owl: you're another. Sir Critic, good day." And the barber kept on shaving.

JAMES T. FIELDS—*The Owl-Critic.*

21

Blame where you must, be candid where you can,
And be each critic the Good-natured Man.

GOLDSMITH—*The Good-Natured Man. Epilogue.*

22

Reviewers are forever telling authors they can't understand them. The author might often reply: Is that my fault?

J. C. AND A. W. HARE—*Guesses at Truth.*

23

The readers and the hearers like my books,
And yet some writers cannot them digest;
But what care I? for when I make a feast,
I would my guests should praise it, not the cooks.

SIR JOHN HARRINGTON—*Against Writers that Carp at other Men's Books.*

24

When Poets' plots in plays are damn'd for spite,
They critics turn and damn the rest that write.

JOHN HAYNES—*Prologue.* In *Oxford and Cambridge Miscellany Poems.* Ed. by ELIJAH FENTON.

1
Unmoved though Witlings sneer and Rivals rail;
Studious to please, yet not ashamed to fail.
SAMUEL JOHNSON—*Prologue to Tragedy of Irene.*

2
'Tis not the wholesome sharp morality,
Or modest anger of a satiric spirit,
That hurts or wounds the body of a state,
But the sinister application
Of the malicious, ignorant, and base
Interpreter; who will distort and strain
The general scope and purpose of an author
To his particular and private spleen.
BEN JONSON—*Poetaster.* Act V. Sc. 1.

3
Lynx envers nos pareils, et taupes envers nous.
Lynx-eyed toward our equals, and moles to ourselves.
LA FONTAINE—*Fables.* I. 7.

4
Critics are sentinels in the grand army of letters, stationed at the corners of newspapers and reviews, to challenge every new author.
LONGFELLOW—*Kavanagh.* Ch. XIII.

5
A wise scepticism is the first attribute of a good critic.
LOWELL—*Among My Books. Shakespeare Once More.*

6
Nature fits all her children with something to do,
He who would write and can't write, can surely review;
Can set up a small booth as critic and sell us his
Petty conceit and his pettier jealousies.
LOWELL—*Fable for Critics.*

7
In truth it may be laid down as an almost universal rule that good poets are bad critics.
MACAULAY—*Criticisms on the Principal Italian Writers. Dante.*
(See also COLERIDGE)

8
The opinion of the great body of the reading public is very materially influenced even by the unsupported assertions of those who assume a right to criticise.
MACAULAY—*Mr. Robert Montgomery's Poems.*

9
To check young Genius' proud career,
The slaves who now his throne invaded,
Made Criticism his prime Vizier,
And from that hour his glories faded.
MOORE—*Genius and Criticism.* St. 4.

10
And you, my Critics! in the chequer'd shade,
Admire new light thro' holes yourselves have made.
POPE—*Dunciad.* Bk. IV. L. 125.
(See also WALLER under MIND)

11
Ten censure wrong for one who writes amiss.
POPE—*Essay on Criticism.* Pt. I. L. 6.

12
The generous Critic fann'd the Poet's fire,
And taught the world with reason to admire.
POPE—*Essay on Criticism.* Pt. I. L. 100.

13
The line too labours, and the words move slow.
POPE—*Essay on Criticism.* Pt. II. L. 171.

14
A perfect Judge will read each work of Wit
With the same spirit that its author writ:
Survey the Whole, nor seek slight faults to find
Where nature moves, and rapture warms the mind.
POPE—*Essay on Criticism.* Pt. II. L. 235.

15
In every work regard the writer's End,
Since none can compass more than they intend;
And if the means be just, the conduct true,
Applause, in spite of trivial faults, is due.
POPE—*Essay on Criticism.* Pt. II. L. 255.

16
Be not the first by whom the new are tried,
Nor yet the last to lay the old aside.
POPE—*Essay on Criticism.* Pt. II. L. 336.

17
Ah, ne'er so dire a thirst of glory boast,
Nor in the Critic let the Man be lost.
POPE—*Essay on Criticism.* Pt. II. L. 522.

18
I lose my patience, and I own it too,
When works are censur'd, not as bad but new:
While if our Elders break all reason's laws,
These fools demand not pardon but Applause.
POPE—*Second Book of Horace.* Ep. I. L. 115.

19
For some in ancient books delight,
Others prefer what moderns write;
Now I should be extremely loth
Not to be thought expert in both.
PRIOR—*Alma.*

20
Die Kritik nimmt oft dem Baume
Raupen und Blüthen mit einander.
Criticism often takes from the tree
Caterpillars and blossoms together.
JEAN PAUL RICHTER—*Titan.* Zykel 105.

21
When in the full perfection of decay,
Turn vinegar, and come again in play.
SACKVILLE (Earl of Dorset)—*Address to Ned Howard.* Quoted in DRYDEN'S *Dedication to translation of Ovid.*
(See also SHENSTONE)

22
In such a time as this it is not meet
That every nice offence should bear his comment.
Julius Cæsar. Act IV. Sc. 3. L. 7.

23
Better a little chiding than a great deal of heart-break.
Merry Wives of Windsor. Act V. Sc. 3. L. 10.

24
For 'tis a physic
That's bitter to sweet end.
Measure for Measure. Act IV. Sc. 6. L. 7.

25
For I am nothing, if not critical.
Othello. Act II. Sc. 1. L. 120.

26
Reviewers, with some rare exceptions, are a most stupid and malignant race. As a bankrupt thief turns thief-taker in despair, so an unsuccessful author turns critic.
SHELLEY—*Fragments of Adonais.*
(See also COLERIDGE)

1
A poet that fails in writing becomes often a morose critic; the weak and insipid white wine makes at length excellent vinegar.
SHENSTONE—*On Writing and Books.*
(See also SACKVILLE)

2
Of all the cants which are canted in this canting world—though the cant of hypocrites may be the worst—the cant of criticism is the most tormenting.
STERNE — *Life and Opinions of Tristram Shandy.* (Orig. ed.) Vol. III. Ch. XII. "The cant of criticism." Borrowed from SIR JOSHUA REYNOLDS, *Idler*, Sept. 29, 1759.

3
For, poems read without a name,
We justly praise, or justly blame;
And critics have no partial views,
Except they know whom they abuse.
And since you ne'er provoke their spite,
Depend upon't their judgment's right.
SWIFT—*On Poetry.* L. 129.

4
For since he would sit on a Prophet's seat,
As a lord of the Human soul,
We needs must scan him from head to feet,
Were it but for a wart or a mole.
TENNYSON—*The Dead Prophet.* St. XIV.

5
Critics are like brushers of noblemen's clothes.
Attributed to SIR HENRY WOTTON by BACON. *Apothegms.* No. 64.

CROCUS
Crocus

6
Welcome, wild harbinger of spring!
To this small nook of earth;
Feeling and fancy fondly cling
Round thoughts which owe their birth
To thee, and to the humble spot
Where chance has fixed thy lowly lot.
BERNARD BARTON—*To a Crocus.*

7
Hail to the King of Bethlehem,
Who weareth in his diadem
The yellow crocus for the gem
Of his authority!
LONGFELLOW—*Christus.* Pt. II. *The Golden Legend.* IX.

CROW

8
To shoot at crows is powder flung away.
GAY. Ep. IV. Last line.

9
Only last night he felt deadly sick, and, after a great deal of pain, two black crows flew out of his mouth and took wing from the room.
Gesta Romanorum—Tale XLV.

10
Even the blackest of them all, the crow,
Renders good service as your man-at-arms,
Crushing the beetle in his coat of mail,
And crying havoc on the slug and snail.
LONGFELLOW—*Tales of a Wayside Inn. The Poet's Tale. Birds of Killingworth.* St. 19.

11
Light thickens; and the crow
Makes wing to the rooky wood.
Macbeth. Act III. Sc. 2. L. 49.

12
The crow doth sing as sweetly as the lark
When neither is attended.
Merchant of Venice. Act V. Sc. 1. L. 102.

13
As the many-winter'd crow that leads the clanging rookery home.
TENNYSON—*Locksley Hall.* St. 34.

CRUELTY

14
Man's inhumanity to man
Makes countless thousands mourn!
BURNS—*Man Was Made to Mourn.*
(See also YOUNG)

15
Contre les rebelles c'est cruauté que d'estre humain, et humanité d'estre cruel.
It is cruelty to be humane to rebels, and humanity is cruelty.
Attributed to CHARLES IX. According to M. FOURNIER, an expression taken from a sermon of CORNEILLE MUIS, BISHOP OF BITOUTE. Used by CATHERINE DE MEDICIS.

16
Detested sport,
That owes its pleasures to another's pain.
COWPER—*The Task.* Bk. III. L. 326.

17
It is not linen you're wearing out,
But human creatures' lives.
HOOD—*Song of the Shirt.*

18
Even bear-baiting was esteemed heathenish and unchristian: the sport of it, not the inhumanity, gave offence.
HUME—*History of England.* Vol. I. Ch. LXII.
(See also MACAULAY)

19
An angel with a trumpet said,
"Forever more, forever more,
The reign of violence is o'er!"
LONGFELLOW—*The Occultation of Orion.* St. 6.

20
Je voudrais bien voir la grimace qu'il fait à cette heure sur cet échafaud.
I would love to see the grimace he [Marquis de Cinq-Mars] is now making on the scaffold.
LOUIS XIII. See *Histoire de Louis XIII.* IV. P. 416.

21
Gaudensque viam fecisse ruina.
He rejoices to have made his way by ruin.
LUCAN—*Pharsalia.* I. 150.

22
The Puritan hated bear-baiting, not because it gave pain to the bear, but because it gave pleasure to the spectators.
MACAULAY—*History of England.* Vol. I. Ch. II. (See also HUME)

23
I must be cruel, only to be kind.
Hamlet. Act III. Sc. 4. L. 178.

1 Men so noble,
However faulty, yet should find respect
For what they have been; 'tis a cruelty
To load a falling man.
Henry VIII. Act V. Sc. 3. L. 74.

2
See what a rent the envious Casca made.
Julius Cæsar. Act III. Sc. 2. L. 179.

3
You are the cruell'st she alive,
If you will lead these graces to the grave
And leave the world no copy.
Twelfth Night. Act I. Sc. 5. L. 259.

4 If ever henceforth thou
These rural latches to his entrance open,
Or hoop his body more with thy embraces,
I will devise a death as cruel for thee
As thou art tender to't.
Winter's Tale. Act IV. Sc. 4. L. 448.

5
Inhumanity is caught from man,
From smiling man.
YOUNG—*Night Thoughts*. Night V. L. 158.
(See also BURNS)

CUCKOO

6
The Attic warbler pours her throat
Responsive to the cuckoo's note.
GRAY—*Ode on the Spring*.

7
And now I hear its voice again,
And still its message is of peace,
It sings of love that will not cease,
For me it never sings in vain.
FRED'K LOCKER-LAMPSON. *The Cuckoo*.

8
Oh, could I fly, I'd fly with thee!
We'd make, with joyful wing,
Our annual visit o'er the globe,
Companions of the spring.
JOHN LOGAN—*To the Cuckoo*. Attributed also to MICHAEL BRUCE.

9
Sweet bird! thy bower is ever green,
Thy sky is ever clear;
Thou hast no sorrow in thy song,
No winter in thy year.
JOHN LOGAN—*To the Cuckoo*. Attributed also to MICHAEL BRUCE. Arguments in favor of Logan in *Notes and Queries*, April, 1902. P. 309. In favor of Bruce, June 14, 1902. P. 469.

10
The cuckoo builds not for himself.
Antony and Cleopatra. Act II. Sc. 6. L. 28.

11
And being fed by us you used us so
As that ungentle gull, the cuckoo's bird,
Useth the sparrow.
Henry IV. Pt. I. Act V. Sc. 1. L. 59.

12
The cuckoo then on every tree,
Mocks married men; for thus sings he,
Cuckoo!
Cuckoo! Cuckoo! O word of fear,
Unpleasing to a married ear.
Love's Labour's Lost. Act V. Sc. 2. L. 908.

13
The merry cuckow, messenger of Spring,
His trumpet shrill hath thrice already sounded.
SPENSER—*Sonnet*. 19.

14 While I deduce,
From the first note the hollow cuckoo sings,
The symphony of spring.
THOMSON—*The Seasons. Spring*. L. 576.

15
List—'twas the cuckoo—O, with what delight
Heard I that voice! and catch it now, though faint,
Far off and faint, and melting into air,
Yet not to be mistaken. Hark again!
Those louder cries give notice that the bird,
Although invisible as Echo's self,
Is wheeling hitherward.
WORDSWORTH—*The Cuckoo at Laverna*.

16
O blithe New-comer! I have heard,
I hear thee and rejoice;
O Cuckoo! shall I call thee Bird,
Or but a wandering Voice?
WORDSWORTH—*To the Cuckoo*.
(See also SHELLEY under LARK)

CURIOSITY

17
Each window like a pill'ry appears,
With heads thrust through nail'd by the ears.
BUTLER—*Hudibras*. Pt. II. Canto III. L. 391.

18
I loathe that low vice—curiosity.
BYRON—*Don Juan*. Canto I. St. 23.

19
The poorest of the sex have still an itch
To know their fortunes, equal to the rich.
The dairy-maid inquires, if she shall take
The trusty tailor, and the cook forsake.
DRYDEN—*Sixth Satire of Juvenal*. L. 762.

20
Ask me no questions, and I'll tell you no fibs.
GOLDSMITH—*She Stoops to Conquer*. Act III.

21
Percunctatorem fugito, nam garrulus idem est.
Shun the inquisitive person, for he is also a talker.
HORACE—*Epistles*. I. 18. 69.

22
Rise up, rise up, Xarifa! lay your golden cushion down;
Rise up! come to the window, and gaze with all the town!
JOHN G. LOCKHART—*The Bridal of Andella*.

23 I saw and heard, for we sometimes,
Who dwell this wild, constrained by want, come forth
To town or village nigh, nighest is far,
Where aught we hear, and curious are to hear,
What happens new; fame also finds us out.
MILTON—*Paradise Regained*. Bk. I. L. 330.

24
Platon estime qu'il y ait quelque vice d'impiété à trop curieusement s'enquerir de Dieu et du monde.
Plato holds that there is some vice of impiety in *enquiring too curiously* about God and the world.
MONTAIGNE—*Essays*. Bk. II. Ch. XII.
(See also HAMLET)

1
Zaccheus, he
Did climb the tree,
His Lord to see.
New England Primer. 1814.

2
Incitantur enim homines ad agnoscenda quæ differuntur.
Our inquisitive disposition is excited by having its gratification deferred.
PLINY the Younger—*Epistles*. IX. 27.

3
'Twere to consider too curiously, to consider so.
Hamlet. Act V. Sc. 1.
(See also MONTAIGNE)

4
I have perceived a most faint neglect of late, which I have rather blamed as mine own jealous curiosity than as a very pretence and purpose of unkindness.
King Lear. Act I. Sc. 4. L. 73.

5
They mocked thee for too much curiosity.
Timon of Athens. Act IV. Sc. 3. L. 302.

CUSTOM

6
Consuetudo est secunda natura.
Custom is second nature.
ST. AUGUSTINE.

7
Vetus consuetudo naturæ vim obtinet.
An ancient custom obtains force of nature.
CICERO—*De Inventione*.

8
Only that he may conform
To (Tyrant) customs.
DU BARTAS—*Divine Weekes and Workes*. *Second Week*. *Third Day*. Pt. II.

9
Such dupes are men to custom, and so prone
To rev'rence what is ancient, and can plead
A course of long observance for its use,
That even servitude, the worst of ills,
Because deliver'd down from sire to son,
Is kept and guarded as a sacred thing!
COWPER—*Task*. Bk. V. L. 298.

10
The slaves of custom and established mode,
With pack-horse constancy we keep the road
Crooked or straight, through quags or thorny dells,
True to the jingling of our leader's bells.
COWPER—*Tirocinium*. L. 251.

11
Man yields to custom, as he bows to fate,
In all things ruled—mind, body, and estate;
In pain, in sickness, we for cure apply
To them we know not, and we know not why.
CRABBE—*Tale III*. *The Gentleman Farmer*. L. 86.

12
Che l'uso dei mortali è come fronda.
In ramo, che sen va, ed altra viene.
The customs and fashions of men change like leaves on the bough, some of which go and others come.
DANTE—*Paradiso*. XXVI. 137.

13
Great things astonish us, and small dishearten us. Custom makes both familiar.
LA BRUYÈRE—*The Characters or Manners of the Present Age*. Vol. II. Ch. I. *On Judgments*.

14
Consuetudo pro lege servatur.
Custom is held to be as a law.
Law Maxim.

15
Optimus legum interpres consuetudo.
Custom is the best interpreter of laws.
Law Maxim.

16
Vetustas pro lege semper habetur.
Ancient custom is always held or regarded as law.
Law Maxim.

17
The laws of conscience, which we pretend to be derived from nature, proceed from custom.
MONTAIGNE—*Of Custom and Law*. Ch. XXII.

18
Choose always the way that seems the best, however rough it may be. Custom will render it easy and agreeable.
PYTHAGORAS—*Ethical Sentences from Stobæus*.

19
Nicht fremder Brauch gedeiht in einem Lande.
Strange customs do not thrive in foreign soil.
SCHILLER—*Demetrius*. I. 1.

20
Ein tiefer Sinn wohnt in den alten Bräuchen.
A deep meaning often lies in old customs.
SCHILLER—*Marie Stuart*. I. 7. 131.

21
Custom calls me to 't:
What custom wills, in all things should we do't,
The dust on antique time would lie unswept,
And mountainous error be too highly heap't
For truth to o'erpeer.
Coriolanus. Act II. Sc. 3. L. 124.

22
But to my mind, though I am native here,
And to the manner born, it is a custom
More honor'd in the breach than the observance.
Hamlet. Act I. Sc. 4. L. 15.

23
That monster, custom, * * * is angel yet in this,
That to the use of actions fair and good
He likewise gives a frock or livery,
That aptly is put on.
Hamlet. Act III. Sc. 4. L. 161.

24
Nice customs curtesy to great kings.
Henry V. Act V. Sc. 2. L. 291.

25
New customs,
Though they be never so ridiculous,
Nay, let 'em be unmanly, yet are followed.
Henry VIII. Act I. Sc. 3. L. 3.

26
The tyrant custom, most grave senators,
Hath made the flinty and steel couch of war
My thrice-driven bed of down.
Othello. Act I. Sc. 3. L. 230.

27
'Tis nothing when you are used to it.
SWIFT—*Polite Conversation*. Dialogue III.

1
The old order changeth, yielding place to new;
And God fulfils himself in many ways,
Lest one good custom should corrupt the world.
TENNYSON—*Passing of Arthur*. L. 408. First line also in *Coming of Arthur*. L. 508.

CYPRESS

Cupressus

2
Dark tree! still sad when other's grief is fled,
The only constant mourner o'er the dead.
BYRON—*Giaour*. L. 286.

D

DAFFODIL

Narcissus Pseudo-Narcissus

3
The daffodil is our doorside queen;
She pushes upward the sword already,
To spot with sunshine the early green.
BRYANT—*An Invitation to the Country*.

4
What ye have been ye still shall be
When we are dust the dust among,
O yellow flowers!
AUSTIN DOBSON—*To Daffodils*.

5
Fair daffadils, we weep to see
You haste away so soone;
As yet the early-rising sun
Has not attained its noone.
* * * * *
We have short time to stay as you,
We have as short a spring;
As quick a growth to meet decay
As you or anything.
HERRICK—*Daffadills*.

6
When a daffadill I see,
Hanging down his head t'wards me,
Guesse I may, what I must be:
First, I shall decline my head;
Secondly, I shall be dead:
Lastly, safely buryed.
HERRICK—*Hesperides. Divination by a Daffadill*.

7
"O fateful flower beside the rill—
The Daffodil, the daffodil!"
JEAN INGELOW—*Persephone*. St. 16.

8
It is daffodil time, so the robins all cry,
For the sun's a big daffodil up in the sky,
And when down the midnight the owl calls "to-whoo"!
Why, then the round moon is a daffodil too;
Now sheer to the bough-tops the sap starts to climb,
So, merry my masters, it's daffodil time.
CLINTON SCOLLARD—*Daffodil Time*.

9
Daffodils,
That come before the swallow dares, and take
The winds of March with beauty.
Winter's Tale. Act IV. Sc. 3. L. 118.

10
When the face of night is fair in the dewy downs
And the shining daffodil dies.
TENNYSON—*Maud*. Pt. III. St. 1.

11
O Love-star of the unbeloved March,
When cold and shrill,
Forth flows beneath a low, dim-lighted arch
The wind that beats sharp crag and barren hill,
And keeps unfilmed the lately torpid rill!
AUBREY DE VERE—*Ode to the Daffodil*.

12
Daffy-down-dilly came up in the cold,
Through the brown mould
Although the March breeze blew keen on her face,
Although the white snow lay in many a place.
ANNA WARNER—*Daffy-Down-Dilly*.

13
There is a tiny yellow daffodil,
The butterfly can see it from afar,
Although one summer evening's dew could fill
Its little cup twice over, ere the star
Had called the lazy shepherd to his fold,
And be no prodigal.
OSCAR WILDE—*The Burden of Stys*.

14
A host of golden daffodils;
Beside the lake, beneath the trees,
Fluttering and dancing in the breeze.
WORDSWORTH—*I Wandered Lonely as a Cloud*.

DAISY

Bellis

15
And a breastplate made of daisies,
Closely fitting, leaf on leaf,
Periwinkles interlaced
Drawn for belt about the waist;
While the brown bees, humming praises,
Shot their arrows round the chief.
E. B. BROWNING—*Hector in the Garden*.

16
The daisy's for simplicity and unaffected air.
BURNS—*O Luve Will Venture In*.

17
Even thou who mournst the daisy's fate,
That fate is thine—no distant date;
Stern Ruin's ploughshare drives, elate,
Full on thy bloom,
Till crushed beneath the furrow's weight
Shall be thy doom!
BURNS—*To a Mountain Daisy*.
(See also YOUNG under RUIN)

18
Over the shoulders and slopes of the dune
I saw the white daisies go down to the sea,
A host in the sunshine, an army in June,
The people God sends us to set our heart free.
BLISS CARMAN—*Daisies*.

19
You may wear your virtues as a crown,
As you walk through life serenely,
And grace your simple rustic gown
With a beauty more than queenly.

Though only one for you shall care,
  One only speak your praises;
And you never wear in your shining hair,
  A richer flower than daisies.
  PHEBE CARY—*The Fortune in the Daisy.*

1
Yun daiseyd mantels ys the mountayne dyghte.
  CHATTERTON—*Rowley Poems. Ælla.*

2
That of all the floures in the mede,
Thanne love I most these floures white and rede,
Suche as men callen daysyes in her toune.
  CHAUCER—*Canterbury Tales. The Legend of Good Women.* L. 41.

3
That men by reason will it calle may
The daisie or elles the eye of day
The emperice, and floure of floures alle.
  CHAUCER—*Canterbury Tales. The Legend of Good Women.* L. 184.

4
Daisies infinite
Uplift in praise their little glowing hands,
O'er every hill that under heaven expands.
  EBENEZER ELLIOTT—*Miscellaneous Poems. Spring.* L. 13.

5
And daisy-stars, whose firmament is green.
  HOOD—*Plea of the Midsummer Fairies.* 36.
  (See also LONGFELLOW, MOIR)

6
Stoop where thou wilt, thy careless hand
  Some random bud will meet;
Thou canst not tread, but thou wilt find
  The daisy at thy feet.
  HOOD—*Song.*

7
All summer she scattered the daisy leaves;
  They only mocked her as they fell.
She said: "The daisy but deceives;
  'He loves me not,' 'he loves me well,'
  One story no two daisies tell."
Ah foolish heart, which waits and grieves
  Under the daisy's mocking spell.
  HELEN HUNT JACKSON—*The Sign of the Daisy.*

8
Spake full well, in language quaint and olden,
  One who dwelleth by the castled Rhine,
When he call'd the flowers, so blue and golden,
  Stars that on earth's firmament do shine.
  LONGFELLOW—*Flowers.*
  (See also HOOD)

9
Not worlds on worlds, in phalanx deep,
  Need we to prove a God is here;
The daisy, fresh from nature's sleep,
  Tells of His hand in lines as clear.
  DR. JOHN MASON GOOD. Found in the *Naturalist's Poetical Companion* by REV. EDWARD WILSON.

10
Stars are the daisies that begem
The blue fields of the sky.
  D. M. MOIR—*Dublin University Magazine,* Oct., 1852.
  (See also HOOD)

11
There is a flower, a little flower
  With silver crest and golden eye,
That welcomes every changing hour,
  And weathers every sky.
  MONTGOMERY—*A Field Flower.*

12
The Rose has but a Summer reign,
The daisy never dies.
  MONTGOMERY—*The Daisy. On Finding One in Bloom on Christmas Day.*

13
Bright flowers, whose home is everywhere
Bold in maternal nature's care
And all the long year through the heir
  Of joy and sorrow,
Methinks that there abides in thee
Some concord with humanity,
Given to no other flower I see
  The forest through.
  WORDSWORTH—*To the Daisy.*

14
The poet's darling.
  WORDSWORTH—*To the Daisy.*

15
We meet thee, like a pleasant thought,
When such are wanted.
  WORDSWORTH—*To the Daisy.*

16
Thou unassuming Commonplace
Of Nature.
  WORDSWORTH—*To the Same Flower.*

DANCING

17
This dance of death which sounds so musically
Was sure intended for the corpse de ballet.
  ANON.—*On the Danse Macabre of Saint-Saëns.*

18
O give me new figures! I can't go on dancing
The same that were taught me ten seasons ago;
The schoolmaster over the land is advancing,
Then why is the master of dancing so slow?
It is such a bore to be always caught tripping
In dull uniformity year after year;
Invent something new, and you'll set me a skipping:
I want a new figure to dance with my Dear!
  THOMAS HAYNES BAYLY—*Quadrille a la Mode.*

19
My dancing days are done.
  BEAUMONT AND FLETCHER—*Scornful Lady.* Act V. Sc. 3.
  (See also ROMEO AND JULIET)

20
A thousand hearts beat happily; and when
Music arose with its voluptuous swell,
Soft eyes look'd love to eyes which spake again,
And all went merry as a marriage bell.
  BYRON—*Childe Harold.* Canto III. St. 21.

21
On with the dance! let joy be unconfin'd;
No sleep till morn, when Youth and Pleasure meet.
  BYRON—*Childe Harold.* Canto III. St. 22.

22
And then he danced;—all foreigners excel
The serious Angles in the eloquence
Of pantomime;—he danced, I say, right well,
With emphasis, and also with good sense—
A thing in footing indispensable:
He danced without theatrical pretence,
Not like a ballet-master in the van
Of his drill'd nymphs, but like a gentleman.
  BYRON—*Don Juan.* Canto XIV. St. 38.

1
Imperial Waltz! imported from the Rhine
(Famed for the growth of pedigrees and wine),
Long be thine import from all duty free,
And hock itself be less esteem'd than thee.
BYRON—*The Waltz.* L. 29.

2
Endearing Waltz—to thy more melting tune
Bow Irish jig, and ancient rigadoon.
Scotch reels, avaunt! and country-dance forego
Your future claims to each fantastic toe!
Waltz—Waltz alone—both legs and arms demands,
Liberal of feet, and lavish of her hands.
BYRON—*The Waltz.* L. 109.

3
Hot from the hands promiscuously applied,
Round the slight waist, or down the glowing side.
BYRON—*The Waltz.* L. 234.

4
What! the girl I adore by another embraced?
What! the balm of her breath shall another man taste?
What! pressed in the dance by another's man's knee?
What! panting recline on another than me?
Sir, she's yours; you have pressed from the grape its fine blue,
From the rosebud you've shaken the tremulous dew;
What you've touched you may take. Pretty waltzer—adieu!
SIR HENRY ENGLEFIELD—*The Waltz. Dancing.*

5
Such pains, such pleasures now alike are o'er,
And beaus and etiquette shall soon exist no more
At their speed behold advancing
Modern men and women dancing;
Step and dress alike express
Above, below from heel to toe,
Male and female awkwardness.
Without a hoop, without a ruffle,
One eternal jig and shuffle,
Where's the air and where's the gait?
Where's the feather in the hat?
Where the frizzed toupee? and where
Oh! where's the powder for the hair?
CATHERINE FANSHAWE—*The Abrogation of the Birth-Night Ball.*

6 To brisk notes in cadence beating
Glance their many-twinkling feet.
GRAY—*Progress of Poesy.* Pt. I. St. 3. L. 10.

7
Alike all ages: dames of ancient days
Have led their children through the mirthful maze;
And the gay grandsire, skill'd in gestic lore,
Has frisk'd beneath the burden of threescore.
GOLDSMITH—*Traveller.* L. 251.

8
And the dancing has begun now,
And the dancers whirl round gaily
In the waltz's giddy mazes,
And the ground beneath them trembles.
HEINE—*Book of Songs. Don Ramiro.* St. 23.

9
Twelve dancers are dancing, and taking no rest,
And closely their hands together are press'd;
And soon as a dance has come to a close,
Another begins, and each merrily goes.
HEINE—*Dream and Life.*

10
Merrily, merrily whirled the wheels of the dizzying dances
Under the orchard-trees and down the path to the meadows;
Old folk and young together, and children mingled among them.
LONGFELLOW—*Evangeline.* Pt. I. IV.

11 He who esteems the Virginia reel
A bait to draw saints from their spiritual weal,
And regards the quadrille as a far greater knavery
Than crushing His African children with slavery,
Since all who take part in a waltz or cotillon
Are mounted for hell on the devil's own pillion,
Who, as every true orthodox Christian well knows,
Approaches the heart through the door of the toes.
LOWELL—*Fable for Critics.* L. 492.

12
Come, knit hands, and beat the ground
In a light fantastic round.
MILTON—*Comus.* L. 143.

13
Come and trip it as ye go,
On the light fantastic toe.
MILTON—*L'Allegro.* L. 33.

14
Dancing in the chequer'd shade.
MILTON—*L'Allegro.* L. 96.

15 Dear creature!—you'd swear
When her delicate feet in the dance twinkle round,
That her steps are of light, that her home is the air,
And she only *par complaisance* touches the ground.
MOORE—*Fudge Family in Paris. Letter V.* L. 50.

16
Others import yet nobler arts from France,
Teach kings to fiddle, and make senates dance.
POPE—*Dunciad.* Bk. IV. L. 597.

17
Oh! if to dance all night, and dress all day,
Charm'd the small-pox, or chas'd old age away;
* * * * * *
To patch, nay ogle, might become a saint,
Nor could it sure be such a sin to paint.
POPE—*Rape of the Lock.* Canto V. L. 19.

18
I know the romance, since it's over,
'Twere idle, or worse, to recall;—
I know you're a terrible rover;
But, Clarence, you'll come to our ball.
PRAED—*Our Ball.*

19
I saw her at a country ball;
There when the sound of flute and fiddle
Gave signal sweet in that old hall,
Of hands across and down the middle
Hers was the subtlest spell by far
Of all that sets young hearts romancing:
She was our queen, our rose, our star;
And when she danced—oh, heaven, her dancing!
PRAED—*The Belle of the Ball.*

1
He, perfect dancer, climbs the rope,
And balances your fear and hope.
PRIOR—*Alma*. Canto II. L. 9.

2
Once on a time, the wight Stupidity
For his throne trembled,
When he discovered in the brains of men
Something like thoughts assembled,
And so he searched for a plausible plan
One of validity,—
And racked his brains, if rack his brains he can
None having, or a very few!
At last he hit upon a way
For putting to rout,
And driving out
From our dull clay
These same intruders new—
This Sense, these Thoughts, these Speculative ills—
What could he do? He introduced quadrilles.
RUSKIN—*The Invention of Quadrilles*.

3
We are dancing on a volcano.
COMTE DE SALVANDY. At a fête given to the King of Naples. (1830)

4
They have measured many a mile,
To tread a measure with you on this grass.
Love's Labour's Lost. Act V. Sc. 2. L. 186.

5
He capers nimbly in a lady's chamber
To the lascivious pleasing of a lute.
Richard III. Act I. Sc. 1. L. 12.

6
For you and I are past our dancing days.
Romeo and Juliet. Act 1. Sc. 5.
(See also BEAUMONT)

7
When you do dance, I wish you
A wave o' th' sea, that you might ever do
Nothing but that.
Winter's Tale. Act IV. Sc. 4. L. 140.

8
Inconsolable to the minuet in Ariadne!
SHERIDAN—*The Critic*. Act II. Sc. 2.

9
While his off-heel, insidiously aside,
Provokes the caper which he seems to chide.
SHERIDAN—*Pizarro*. The Prologue.

10
But O, she dances such a way!
No sun upon an Easter-day,
Is half so fine a sight.
SUCKLING—*A Ballad Upon a Wedding*. St. 8.

11
Dance light, for my heart it lies under your feet, love.
JOHN FRANCIS WALLER—*Kitty Neil. Dance Light*.

12
And beautiful maidens moved down in the dance,
With the magic of motion and sunshine of glance:
And white arms wreathed lightly, and tresses fell free
As the plumage of birds in some tropical tree.
WHITTIER—*Cities of the Plain*. St. 4.

13
Jack shall pipe, and Jill shall dance.
GEORGE WITHER—*Poem on Christmas*.

DANDELION

Taraxacum Dens-leonis

14
You cannot forget if you would those golden kisses all over the cheeks of the meadow, queerly called *dandelions*.
HENRY WARD BEECHER—*Star Papers. A Discourse of Flowers*.

15
Upon a showery night and still,
Without a sound of warning,
A trooper band surprised the hill,
And held it in the morning.
We were not waked by bugle notes,
No cheer our dreams invaded,
And yet at dawn, their yellow coats
On the green slopes paraded.
HELEN GRAY CONE—*The Dandelions*.

16
Dear common flower, that grow'st beside the way,
Fringing the dusty road with harmless gold,
First pledge of blithesome May,
Which children pluck, and, full of pride, uphold,
High-hearted buccaneers, o'erjoyed that they
An Eldorado in the grass have found,
Which not the rich earth's ample round
May match in wealth, thou art more dear to me
Than all the prouder summer-blooms may be.
LOWELL—*To the Dandelion*.

17
Young Dandelion
On a hedge-side,
Said young Dandelion,
Who'll be my bride?

Said young Dandelion
With a sweet air,
I have my eye on
Miss Daisy fair.
D. M. MULOCK—*Young Dandelion*.

DANGER

18
Anguis sub viridi herba.
There's a snake in the grass.
BACON. Quoted in *Essays. Of a King*.
(See also VERGIL)

19
The wolf was sick, he vowed a monk to be;
But when he got well, a wolf once more was he.
In WALTER BOWER'S *Scotichronicon*. (15th cent.). Found in MS. *Black Book of Paisley* in British Museum. End.
(See also RABELAIS)

20
I have not quailed to danger's brow
When high and happy—need I now?
BYRON—*Giaour*. L. 1,035.

21
In summo periculo timor misericordiam non recipit.
In extreme danger, fear turns a deaf ear to every feeling of pity.
CÆSAR—*Bellum Gallicum*. VII. 26.

22
Let him that thinketh he standeth take heed lest he fall.
I Corinthians. X. 12.

1
A daring pilot in extremity;
Pleas'd with the danger, when the waves went high
He sought the storms.
DRYDEN—*Absalom and Achitophel.* Pt. I. L. 159.

2
Or ever the silver cord be loosed, or the golden bowl be broken, or the pitcher be broken at the fountain, or the wheel broken at the cistern.
Ecclesiastes. XII. 6.

3
Quo tendis inertem
Rex periture, fugam? Nescis heu, perdite! nescis
Quem fugias; hostes incurris, dum fugis hostem.
Incidis in Scyllam cupiens vitare Charybdim.

Where, O king, destined to perish, are you directing your unavailing flight? Alas, lost one, you know not whom you flee; you are running upon enemies, whilst you flee from your foe. You fall upon the rock Scylla desiring to avoid the whirlpool Charybdis.

PHILIPPE GAULTIER DE LILLE ("De Châtillon"). *Alexandriad.* Bk. V. 298. Found in the *Menagiana.* Ed. by BERTRAND DE LA MONNOIE. (1715) Source said to be QUINTUS CURTIUS. See ANDREWS—*Antient and Modern Anecdotes.* P. 307. (Ed. 1790)
(See also HOMER—*Odyssey.* Bk. XII. L. 85. MERCHANT OF VENICE. III. 5)

4
For all on a razor's edge it stands.
HOMER—*Iliad.* Bk. X. L. 173. Same use in HERODOTUS. VI. 11. THEOCRITUS—*Idyl.* XXII. 6. THEOGENES. 557.

5
Periculosæ plenum opus aleæ
Tractas, et incedis per ignes
Suppositos cineri doloso.

You are dealing with a work full of dangerous hazard, and you are venturing upon fires overlaid with treacherous ashes.

HORACE—*Odes.* Bk. II. 1. 6.
The following line (authorship unknown) is sometimes added: "Si morbum fugiens incidis in medicos" In fleeing disease you fall into the hands of the doctors.

6
Quid quisque vitet nunquam homini satis
Cautum est in horas.

Man is never watchful enough against dangers that threaten him every hour.

HORACE—*Carmina.* II. 13. 13.

7
Multos in summa pericula misit
Venturi timor ipse mali.

The mere apprehension of a coming evil has put many into a situation of the utmost danger.

LUCAN—*Pharsalia.* VII. 104.

8
'Twas a dangerous cliff, as they freely confessed,
Though to walk near its crest was so pleasant,
But over its terrible edge there had slipped
A Duke and full many a peasant,
So the people said something would have to be done,
But their projects did not at all tally.
Some said: "Put a fence round the edge of the cliff."
Some: "An ambulance down in the valley."
JOSEPH MALINES—*Fence or Ambulance.* Appeared in the *Virginia Health Bulletin* with title *Prevention and Cure.*

9
What a sea
Of melting ice I walk on!
MASSINGER—*Maid of Honor.* Act III. Sc. 3.

10
Nor for the pestilence that walketh in darkness; nor for . . . the destruction that wasteth at noonday.
Psalms. XCI. 6.

11
Passato il pericolo (or punto) gabbato il santo.
When the danger's past the saint is cheated.
RABELAIS—*Pantagruel.* IV. 24. Quoted as a proverb.

12
Ægrotat Dæmon; monachus tunc esse volebat,
Dæmon convaluit; Dæmon ante fuit.
Mediæval Latin.
The devil was sick, the devil a monk would be;
The devil was well, the devil a monk was he.
As trans. by URQUHART AND MOTTEUX.
(See also BOWER)

13
Sur un mince chrystal l'hyver conduit leurs pas,
Telle est de nos plaisirs la legere surface,
Glissez mortels; n'appuyez pas.
O'er the ice the rapid skater flies.
With sport above and death below,
Where mischief lurks in gay disguise
Thus lightly touch and quickly go.
PIERRE CHARLES ROY. Lines under a picture of skaters, a print of a painting by LANCRET. Trans. by SAMUEL JOHNSON. See PIOZZI, *Anecdotes.*

14
Scit eum sine gloria vinci, qui sine periculo vincitur.

He knows that the man is overcome ingloriously, who is overcome without danger.

SENECA—*De Providentia.* III.

15
Contemptum periculorum assiduitas periclitandi dabit.

Constant exposure to dangers will breed contempt for them.

SENECA—*De Providentia.* IV.

16
Il n'y a personne qui ne soit dangereux pour quelqu'un.

There is no person who is not dangerous for some one.

MME. DE SÉVIGNÉ—*Lettres.*

17
For though I am not splenitive and rash,
Yet have I something in me dangerous.
Hamlet. Act V. Sc. 1. L. 285.

18
Out of this nettle, danger, we pluck this flower, safety.
Henry IV. Pt. I. Act II. Sc. 3.

19
We have scotched the snake, not killed it:
She'll close and be herself, whilst our poor malice
Remains in danger of our former tooth.
Macbeth. Act III. Sc. 2. L. 13.

1
When I shun Scylla, your father, I fall into Charybdis, your mother.
Merchant of Venice. Act III. Sc. 5. L. 18.
(See also GAULTIER)

2
Some of us will smart for it.
Much Ado About Nothing. Act V. Sc. 1. L. 109.

3 Upon this hint I spake;
She loved me for the dangers I had passed
And I loved her that she did pity them.
Othello. Act I. Sc. 3. L. 166.

4
He is not worthy of the honeycomb
That shuns the hives because the bees have stings.
The Tragedy of Locrine. (1595) III. II. 39. *Shakespeare Apocrypha.*

5
It is no jesting with edge tools.
The True Tragedy of Richard III. (1594) Same in BEAUMONT AND FLETCHER—*Little French Lawyer.* Act IV. Sc. 7.

6
Caret periculo qui etiam tutus cavet.
He is safe from danger who is on his guard even when safe.
SYRUS—*Maxims.*

7
Citius venit periculum, cum contemnitur.
Danger comes the sooner when it is despised.
SYRUS—*Maxims.*

8
Si cadere necesse est, occurendum discrimini.
If we must fall, we should boldly meet the danger.
TACITUS—*Annales.* II. 1. 33.

9
Qui legitis flores et humi nascentia fraga,
Fridigus, O pueri, fugite hinc; latet anguis in herba.
O boys, who pluck the flowers and strawberries springing from the ground, flee hence; a cold snake lies hidden in the grass.
VERGIL—*Eclogues.* III. 92.
(See also BACON)

10
Time flies, Death urges, knells call, Heaven invites,
Hell threatens.
YOUNG—*Night Thoughts.* Night II. L. 291.

DARING (See also BRAVERY, COURAGE)

11
A decent boldness ever meets with friends.
HOMER—*Odyssey.* POPE's trans. Bk. 7. L. 67.

12
And what he greatly thought, he nobly dared.
HOMER—*Odyssey.* POPE's trans. Bk. II. L. 312.

13
And what they dare to dream of, dare to do.
LOWELL—*Ode Recited at the Harvard Commemoration.* July 21, 1865. St. 3.

14
Who dares this pair of boots displace,
Must meet Bombastes face to face.
WILLIAM B. RHODES—*Bombastes Furioso.* Act I. Sc. 4.

15
Wer nichts waget der darf nichts hoffen.
Who dares nothing, need hope for nothing.
SCHILLER—*Don Carlos.* Same idea in *Theocritus.* XV. 61. PLAUTUS—*Asin.* I. 3. 65.

16 And dar'st thou then
To beard the lion in his den,
The Douglas in his hall?
SCOTT—*Marmion*—Canto VI. St. 14.

17
I dare do all that may become a man:
Who dares do more, is none.
Macbeth. Act I. Sc. 7. L. 47.

18
What man dare, I dare:
Approach thou like the rugged Russian bear,
The arm'd rhinoceros, or the Hyrcan tiger,
Take any shape but that, and my firm nerves
Shall never tremble.
Macbeth. Act III. Sc. 4. L. 99

19
Nemo timendo ad summum pervenit locum.
No one reaches a high position without daring.
SYRUS—*Maxims.*

20
Audendum est; fortes adjuvat ipsa Venus.
Dare to act! Even Venus aids the bold.
TIBULLUS—*Carmina.* I. 2. 16.

DARKNESS

21
Dark as pitch.
BUNYAN—*Pilgrim's Progress.* Pt. I.

22
The waves were dead; the tides were in their grave,
The Moon, their Mistress, had expired before;
The winds were wither'd in the stagnant air,
And the clouds perish'd; darkness had no need
Of aid from them—she was the Universe.
BYRON—*Darkness.*

23
Darkness which may be felt.
Exodus. X. 21.

24
Darkness of slumber and death, forever sinking and sinking.
LONGFELLOW—*Evangeline.* Pt. II. V. L. 108.

25
Lo! darkness bends down like a mother of grief
On the limitless plain, and the fall of her hair
It has mantled a world.
JOAQUIN MILLER—*From Sea to Sea.* St. 4.

26 Yet from those flames
No light, but rather darkness visible.
MILTON—*Paradise Lost.* Bk. I. L. 62.

27
Brief as the lightning in the collied night,
That, in a spleen, unfolds both heaven and earth,
And ere a man had power to say, Behold!
The jaws of darkness do devour it up.
Midsummer Night's Dream. Act I. Sc. 1. L. 144.

1 The charm dissolves apace,
And as the morning steals upon the night,
Melting the darkness, so their rising senses
Begin to chase the ignorant fumes that mantle
Their clearer reason.
Tempest. Act V. Sc. 1. L. 64.

2
And out of darkness came the hands
That reach thro' nature, moulding men.
TENNYSON—*In Memoriam.* CXXIV.

DAY

3
Listen to the Exhortation of the Dawn!
Look to this Day! For it is Life,
The very Life of Life.
In its brief course lie all the Varieties
And Realities of your Existence;
The Bliss of Growth,
The Glory of Action,
The Splendor of Beauty;
For Yesterday is but a Dream,
And Tomorrow is only a Vision;
But Today well lived
Makes every Yesterday a Dream of Happiness,
And every Tomorrow a Vision of Hope.
Look well therefore to this Day!
Such is the Salutation of the Dawn.
Salutation of the Dawn. From the Sanscrit.

4
Day is a snow-white Dove of heaven
That from the East glad message brings.
T. B. ALDRICH—*Day and Night.*

5
The long days are no happier than the short ones.
BAILEY—*Festus.* Sc. *A Village Feast. Evening.*

6 Virtus sui gloria.
Think that day lost whose (low) descending sun
Views from thy hand no noble action done.
JACOB BOBART—In David Krieg's Album in British Museum. Dec. 8, 1697. (See also STANIFORD—*Art of Reading.* 3d Ed. P. 27. (1803)
(See also PIBRAC, TITUS, YOUNG)

7
From fibers of pain and hope and trouble
And toil and happiness,—one by one,—
Twisted together, or single or double,
The varying thread of our life is spun.
Hope shall cheer though the chain be galling;
Light shall come though the gloom be falling;
Faith will list for the Master calling
Our hearts to his rest,—when the day is done.
A. B. BRAGDON—*When the Day is done.*

8 Yet, behind the night,
Waits for the great unborn, somewhere afar,
Some white tremendous daybreak.
RUPERT BROOKE—*Second Best.*

9
Day!
Faster and more fast,
O'er night's brim, day boils at last;
Boils, pure gold, o'er the cloud-cup's brim.
ROBERT BROWNING—*Introduction to Pippa Passes.*

10
Is not every meanest day the confluence of two eternities?
CARLYLE—*French Revolution.* Pt. I. Bk. VI. Ch. V.

11
So here hath been dawning
Another blue day;
Think, wilt thou let it
Slip useless away?

Out of eternity
This new day is born,
Into eternity
At night will return.
CARLYLE—*To-day.*

12
All comes out even at the end of the day.
Quoted by WINSTON CHURCHILL. *Speech at the Highbury Athenæum,* Nov. 23, 1910.
(See also HAWES)

13
Dies iræ, dies illa!
Solvet sæclum in favilla,
Teste David cum Sybilla.
Day of wrath that day of burning,
Seer and Sibyl speak concerning,
All the world to ashes turning.
Attributed to THOMAS CELANO. See DANIEL—*Thesaurus Hymnology.* Vol. II. P. 103. Printed in *Missale Romanum.* Pavia. (1491) Trans. by ABRAHAM COLES. NOLKER, monk of St. Gall (about 880) says he saw the lines in a book belonging to the Convent of St. Jumièges. Assigned to CARDINAL FRANGIPANI ("Malabrancia"), died, 1294. Also to ST. GREGORY, ST. BERNARD, CARDINAL ORSINI, AGNOSTINO BIELLA, HUMBERTUS. See *Dublin Review,* No. 39

14
Beware of desperate steps. The darkest day,
Live till to-morrow, will have pass'd away.
COWPER—*Needless Alarm.* L. 132.

15
Days, that need borrow
No part of their good morrow
From a fore-spent night of sorrow.
RICHARD CRASHAW—*Wishes to His Supposed Mistress.*

16
Daughters of Time, the hypocrite Days,
Muffled and dumb like barefoot dervishes,
And marching single in an endless file,
Bring diadems and fagots in their hands;
To each they offer gifts after his will,
Bread, kingdom, stars, and sky that holds them all;
I, in my pleachéd garden watched the pomp
Forgot my morning wishes, hastily
Took a few herbs and apples, and the Day
Turned and departed silent. I too late
Under her solemn fillet saw the scorn.
EMERSON—*Days.*

17
The days are ever divine as to the first Aryans. They are of the least pretension, and of the greatest capacity of anything that exists. They come and go like muffled and veiled figures sent from a distant friendly party; but they say nothing, and if we do not use the gifts they bring, they carry them as silently away.
EMERSON—*Works and Days.*

1

After the day there cometh the derke night;
For though the day be never so longe,
At last the belles ringeth to evensonge.

STEPHEN HAWES—*Pastime of Pleasure.* (1517) As given in Percy Society Ed. Ch. XLII. P. 207. Also in the MASKELL books. *British Museum.* (1578) An old hymn found among the marginal rhymes of a *Book of Prayers* of QUEEN ELIZABETH, to accompany illuminations of *The Triumph of Death.* HAWES probably used the idea found in an old Latin hymn.

Quantumvis cursum longum fessumque moratur
Sol, sacro tandem carmine Vesper adest.

English of these lines quoted at the stake by GEORGE TANKERFIELD. (1555) Same in HEYWOOD. *Dialogue Concerning English Proverbs.* See also FOXE—*Acts and Monuments.* Vol. VII. P. 346. Ed. 1828

2

The better day, the worse deed.

MATTHEW HENRY—*Commentaries.* Genesis III.

3

Sweet day, so cool, so calm, so bright,
The bridal of the earth and sky,
The dew shall weep thy fall to-night;
For thou must die.

HERBERT—*The Temple. Virtue.*

4

I think the better day, the better deed.

CHIEF JUSTICE HOLT, *Judgment, Reports,* 1028. Ascribed to WALKER in *Woods Dict. of Quotations.* THOS. MIDDLETON—*The Phœnix.* Act III. Sc. 1.

5

Truditur dies die,
Novæque pergunt interire lunæ.

Day is pushed out by day, and each new moon hastens to its death.

HORACE—*Carmina.* Bk. II. 18. 15.

6

Cressa ne careat pulchra dies nota.

Let not a day so fair be without its white chalk mark.

HORACE—*Carmina.* Bk. I. 36. 10.

7

Inter spem curamque, timores inter et iras,
Omnem crede diem tibi diluxisse supremum:
Grata superveniet, quæ non sperabitur, hora.

In the midst of hope and anxiety, in the midst of fear and anger, believe every day that has dawned to be your last; happiness which comes unexpected will be the more welcome.

HORACE—*Epistles.* Bk. I. 4. 13.

8

Creta an carbone notandi?

To be marked with white chalk or charcoal? (*i.e.* good or bad.)

HORACE—*Satires.* Bk. II. 3. 246.
(See also PLINY)

9

O sweet, delusive Noon,
Which the morning climbs to find,
O moment sped too soon,
And morning left behind.

HELEN HUNT JACKSON—*Verses. Noon.*

10

Well, this is the end of a perfect day,
Near the end of a journey, too;
But it leaves a thought that is big and strong,
With a wish that is kind and true.
For mem'ry has painted this perfect day
With colors that never fade,
And we find at the end of a perfect day,
The soul of a friend we've made.

CARRIE JACOBS-BOND—*A Perfect Day.*

11

Car il n'est si beau jour qui n'amène sa nuit.

For there is no day however beautiful that is not followed by night.

On the tombstone of JEAN D'ORBESAN at Padua.

12

My days are swifter than a weaver's shuttle.

Job. VII. 6.

13

Clearer than the noonday.

Job. XI. 17.

14

Days should speak and multitude of years should teach wisdom.

Job. XXXII. 7.

15

Out of the shadows of night,
The world rolls into light;
It is daybreak everywhere.

LONGFELLOW—*Bells of San Blas.*

16

O summer day beside the joyous sea!
O summer day so wonderful and white,
So full of gladness and so full of pain!
Forever and forever shalt thou be
To some the gravestone of a dead delight,
To some the landmark of a new domain.

LONGFELLOW—*Summer Day by the Sea.*

17

Hide me from day's garish eye.

MILTON—*Il Penseroso.* L. 141.

18

How troublesome is day!
It calls us from our sleep away;
It bids us from our pleasant dreams awake,
And sends us forth to keep or break
Our promises to pay.
How troublesome is day!

THOMAS LOVE PEACOCK—*Fly-by-Night. Paper Money Lyrics.*

19

Jusqu'au cercuil (mon fils) vueilles apprendre,
Et tien perdu le jour qui s'est passe,
Si tu n'y as quelque chose ammasse,
Pour plus scavant et plus sage te rendre.

Cease not to learn until thou cease to live;
Think that day lost wherein thou draw'st
no letter,
To make thyself learneder, wiser, better.

GUY DE FAUR PIBRAC—*Collections of Quatrains* No. 31. Trans. by JOSHUA SYLVESTER. (About 1608) Reprinted by M. A. LEMERRE. (1874)
(See also BOBART)

20

O diem lætum, notandumque mihi candidissimo calculo.

O happy day, and one to be marked for me with the whitest of chalk.

PLINY THE YOUNGER—*Epistles.* VI. 11.
(See also HORACE)

1
Longissimus dies cito conditur.
The longest day soon comes to an end.
PLINY THE YOUNGER—*Epistles*. IX. 36.
(See also HAWES)

2
Boast not thyself of to-morrow; for thou knowest not what a day may bring forth.
Proverbs. XXVII. 1.

3
Day unto day uttereth speech, and night unto night showeth knowledge.
Psalms. XIX. 2.

4
Sweet Phosphor, bring the day!
Light will repay
The wrongs of night; sweet Phosphor, bring the day!
QUARLES—*Emblems*. Bk. I. Em. 14. St. 5.

5
We met, hand to hand,
We clasped hands close and fast,
As close as oak and ivy stand;
But it is past:
Come day, come night, day comes at last.
CHRISTINA G. ROSSETTI—*Twilight. Night*. I. St. 1. (See also HAWES)

6
Die schönen Tage in Aranjuez
Sind nun zu Ende.
The lovely days in Aranjuez are now at an end.
SCHILLER—*Don Carlos*. I. 1. 1.

7
O, such a day,
So fought, so follow'd and so fairly won.
Henry IV. Pt. II. Act I. Sc. 1. L. 20.

8
What hath this day deserv'd? what hath it done,
That it in golden letters should be set
Among the high tides in the calendar?
King John. Act III. Sc. 1. L. 84.

9
The sun is in the heaven, and the proud day,
Attended with the pleasures of the world,
Is all too wanton.
King John. Act III. Sc. 3. L. 34.

10
Day is the Child of Time,
And Day must cease to be:
But Night is without a sire,
And cannot expire,
One with Eternity.
R. H. STODDARD—*Day and Night*.

11
Discipulus est priori posterior dies.
Each day is the scholar of yesterday.
SYRUS—*Maxims*.

12
But the tender grace of a day that is dead
Will never come back to me.
TENNYSON—*Break, Break, Break*.

13
A life that leads melodious days.
TENNYSON—*In Memoriam*. XXXIII. St. 2.

14
"A day for Gods to stoop," * * * ay,
And men to soar.
TENNYSON—*The Lover's Tale*. L. 304.

15
Diem perdidi.
I have lost a day.
TITUS. See SUETONIUS—*Titus*. VIII.
(See also BOBART)

16
Expectada dies aderat.
The longed for day is at hand.
VERGIL—*Æneid*. V. 104.

17
Mes jours s'en sont allez errant.
My days are gone a-wandering.
VILLON—*Grand Testament*.

18
One of those heavenly days that cannot die.
WORDSWORTH—*Nutting*.

19
On all important time, thro' ev'ry age,
Tho' much, and warm, the wise have urged; the man
Is yet unborn, who duly weighs an hour,
"I've lost a day"—the prince who nobly cried
Had been an emperor without his crown;
Of Rome? say rather, lord of human race.
YOUNG—*Night Thoughts*. Night II. L. 97.
(See also BOBART)

20
The spirit walks of every day deceased.
YOUNG—*Night Thoughts*. Night II. L. 180.

DEATH (See also IMMORTALITY, MORTALITY)

21
Death is a black camel, which kneels at the gates of all.
ABD-EL-KADER.

22
This is the last of earth! I am content.
JOHN QUINCY ADAMS. His Last Words. JOSIAH QUINCY—*Life of John Quincy Adams*.

23
Call no man happy till he is dead.
ÆSCHYLUS—*Agamemnon*. 938. Earliest reference. Also in SOPHOCLES—*Trachiniæ*, and *Œdipus Tyrannus*.

24
But when the sun in all his state,
Illumed the eastern skies,
She passed through glory's morning gate,
And walked in Paradise.
JAMES ALDRICH—*A Death Bed*.
(See also GILDER, HOOD)

25
Somewhere, in desolate, wind-swept space,
In twilight land, in no man's land,
Two hurrying shapes met face to face
And bade each other stand.
"And who are you?" cried one, a-gape,
Shuddering in the glimmering light.
"I know not," said the second shape,
"I only died last night."
T. B. ALDRICH—*Identity*

26
The white sail of his soul has rounded
The promontory—death.
WILLIAM ALEXANDER—*The Icebound Ship*.

27
Your lost friends are not dead, but gone before,
Advanced a stage or two upon that road
Which you must travel in the steps they trod.
ARISTOPHANES—*Fragment*. II. Trans. by CUMBERLAND.
(See also JONSON)

1
He who died at Azan sends
This to comfort all his friends:
Faithful friends! It lies I know
Pale and white and cold as snow;
And ye say, "Abdallah's dead!"
Weeping at the feet and head.
I can see your falling tears,
I can hear your sighs and prayers;
Yet I smile and whisper this:
I am not the thing you kiss.
Cease your tears and let it lie;
It was mine—it is not I.
EDWIN ARNOLD—*He Who Died at Azan.*

2
Her cabin'd ample spirit,
It fluttered and fail'd for breath;
Tonight it doth inherit
The vasty hall of death.
MATTHEW ARNOLD—*Requiescat.*

3
Pompa mortis magis terret quam mors ipsa.
The pomp of death alarms us more than death itself.
Quoted by BACON as from SENECA.
(See also BURTON)

4
It is as natural to die as to be born; and to a little infant, perhaps, the one is as painful as the other.
BACON—*Essays. Of Death.*

5
Men fear Death, as children fear to go in the dark; and as that natural fear in children is increased with tales, so is the other.
BACON—*Essays. Of Death.*

6
What then remains, but that we still should cry
Not to be born, or being born to die.
Ascribed to BACON. (Paraphrase of a Greek Epigram.)

7
Death is the universal salt of states;
Blood is the base of all things—law and war.
BAILEY—*Festus.* Sc. *A Country Town.*

8
The death-change comes.
Death is another life. We bow our heads
At going out, we think, and enter straight
Another golden chamber of the king's,
Larger than this we leave, and lovelier.
And then in shadowy glimpses, disconnect,
The story, flower-like, closes thus its leaves.
The will of God is all in all. He makes,
Destroys, remakes, for His own pleasure, all.
BAILEY—*Festus.* Sc. *Home.*

9
So fades a summer cloud away;
So sinks the gale when storms are o'er;
So gently shuts the eye of day;
So dies a wave along the shore.
MRS. BARBAULD—*The Death of the Virtuous.*

10
It is only the dead who do not return.
BERTRAND BARÈRE—*Speech.* (1794)

11
To die would be an awfully big adventure.
BARRIE—*Peter Pan.*
(See also BROWNING, FROHMAN, RABELAIS)

12
But whether on the scaffold high,
Or in the battle's van,
The fittest place where man can die
Is where he dies for man.
MICHAEL J. BARRY—*The Place to Die.* In *The Dublin Nation.* Sept. 28, 1844. Vol. II. P. 809.

13
Death hath so many doors to let out life.
BEAUMONT AND FLETCHER—*The Custom of the Country.* Act II. Sc. 2.

14
We must all die!
All leave ourselves, it matters not where, when,
Nor how, so we die well; and can that man that does so
Need lamentation for him?
BEAUMONT AND FLETCHER—*Valentinian.* Act IV. Sc. 4.

15
How shocking must thy summons be, O Death!
To him that is at ease in his possessions:
Who, counting on long years of pleasure here,
Is quite unfurnish'd for that world to come!
BLAIR—*The Grave.* L. 350.

16
Sure 'tis a serious thing to die! My soul!
What a strange moment must it be, when, near
Thy journey's end, thou hast the gulf in view!
That awful gulf, no mortal e'er repass'd
To tell what's doing on the other side.
BLAIR—*The Grave.* L. 369.

17
'Tis long since Death had the majority.
BLAIR—*The Grave.* L. 451. Please "The Great Majority" found in PLAUTUS. *Trinium.* II. 214.

18
Beyond the shining and the shading
I shall be soon.
Beyond the hoping and the dreading
I shall be soon.
Love, rest and home—
Lord! tarry not, but come.
HORATIO BONAR—*Beyond the Smiling and the Weeping.*

19
Earth to earth, ashes to ashes, dust to dust, in sure and certain hope of the resurrection.
Book of Common Prayer. Burial of the Dead.

20
Man that is born of a woman hath but a short time to live, and is full of misery. He cometh up, and is cut down, like a flower; he fleeth as it were a shadow, and never continueth in one stay.
Book of Common Prayer. Burial of the Dead.
Quoted from *Job.* XIV. 1.

21
In the midst of life we are in death.
Book of Common Prayer. Burial of the Dead.
Media vita in morte sumus. From a Latin antiphon. Found in the choirbook of the monks of St. Gall. Said to have been composed by NOTKER ("The Stammerer") in 911, while watching some workmen building a bridge at Martinsbrücke, in peril of their lives. LUTHER's antiphon *"De Morte." Hymn XVIII is taken from this.*

1
'Mid youth and song, feasting and carnival,
Through laughter, through the roses, as of old
Comes Death, on shadowy and relentless feet
Death, unappeasable by prayer or gold;
Death is the end, the end.
Proud, then, clear-eyed and laughing, go to greet
Death as a friend!
RUPERT BROOKE—*Second Best.*

2
Oh! death will find me, long before I tire
Of watching you; and swing me suddenly
Into the shade and loneliness and mire
Of the last land!
RUPERT BROOKE—*Sonnet.* (Collection 1908-1911)

3
Pliny hath an odd and remarkable Passage concerning the Death of Men and Animals upon the Recess or Ebb of the Sea.
SIR THOMAS BROWNE—*Letter to a Friend.* Sec. 7. (See also DICKENS)

4
A little before you made a leap in the dark.
SIR THOMAS BROWNE—*Works.* II. 26. (Ed. 1708) *Letters from the Dead.* (1701) *Works.* II. P. 502.
(See also RABELAIS)

5
The thousand doors that lead to death.
SIR THOMAS BROWNE—*Religio Medici.* Pt. I. Sec. XLIV.

6
For I say, this is death and the sole death,
When a man's loss comes to him from his gain,
Darkness from light, from knowledge ignorance,
And lack of love from love made manifest.
ROBERT BROWNING—*A Death in the Desert.*

7
The grand perhaps.
ROBERT BROWNING—*Bishop Blougram's Apology.*
(See also RABELAIS)

8
Sustained and soothed
By an unfaltering trust, approach thy grave
Like one that wraps the drapery of his couch
About him, and lies down to pleasant dreams.
BRYANT—*Thanatopsis.*

9
All that tread
The globe are but a handful to the tribes
That slumber in its bosom.
BRYANT—*Thanatopsis.*

10
So he passed over and all the trumpets sounded
For him on the other side.
BUNYAN—*Pilgrim's Progress.* Death of Valiant for Truth. Close of Pt. II.

11
Die Todten reiten schnell.
The dead ride swiftly.
BÜRGER—*Leonore.*

12
But, oh! fell Death's untimely frost,
That nipt my flower sae early.
BURNS—*Highland Mary.*

13
There is only rest and peace
In the city of Surcease
From the failings and the wailings 'neath the sun,
And the wings of the swift years
Beat but gently o'er the biers
Making music to the sleepers every one.
RICHARD BURTON—*City of the Dead.*

14
They do neither plight nor wed
In the city of the dead,
In the city where they sleep away the hours.
RICHARD BURTON—*City of the Dead.*

15
We wonder if this can be really the close,
Life's fever cooled by death's trance;
And we cry, though it seems to our dearest of foes,
"God give us another chance."
RICHARD BURTON—*Song of the Unsuccessful.*

16
Timor mortis morte pejor.
The fear of death is worse than death.
BURTON—*Anatomy of Melancholy.* (Quoted.)
(See also BACON)

17
Friend Ralph! thou hast
Outrun the constable at last!
BUTLER—*Hudibras.* Pt. I. Canto III. L. 1,367.

18
Heaven gives its favourites—early death.
BYRON—*Childe Harold.* Canto IV. St. 102. Also *Don Juan.* Canto IV. St. 12.
(See also HERBERT, MENANDER, PLAUTUS)

19
Without a grave, unknell'd, uncoffin'd, and unknown.
BYRON—*Childe Harold.* Canto IV. St. 179.

20
Ah! surely nothing dies but something mourns!
BYRON—*Don Juan.* Canto III. St. 108.

21
"Whom the gods love die young," was said of yore.
BYRON—*Don Juan.* Canto IV. St. 12.
(See also HERBERT, MENANDER, PLAUTUS)

22
Death, so called, is a thing which makes men weep,
And yet a third of life is pass'd in sleep.
BYRON—*Don Juan.* Canto XIV. St. 3.

23
Oh, God! it is a fearful thing
To see the human soul take wing
In any shape, in any mood!
BYRON—*Prisoner of Chillon.* St. 8.

24
Down to the dust!—and, as thou rott'st away,
Even worms shall perish on thy poisonous clay.
BYRON—*A Sketch.*

25
Brougham delivered a very warm panegyric upon the ex-Chancellor, and expressed a hope that he would make a good end, although to an expiring Chancellor death was now armed with a new terror.
CAMPBELL—*Lives of the Chancellors.* Vol. VII. P. 163.

26
And I still onward haste to my last night;
Time's fatal wings do ever forward fly;
So every day we live, a day we die.
THOMAS CAMPION—*Divine and Moral Songs.*

1
His religion, at best, is an anxious wish; like that of Rabelais, "a great Perhaps."
CARLYLE—*Burns*.
(See also RABELAIS)

2
Qui nunc it per iter tenebricosum
Illuc unde negant redire quemquam.
Who now travels that dark path from whose bourne they say no one returns.
CATULLUS—*Carmina*. III. 11.
(See also HAMLET, VERGIL)

3
Soles occidere et redire possunt;
Nobis cum semel occidit brevis lux,
Nox est perpetua una dormienda.
Suns may set and rise; we, when our short day has closed, must sleep on during one never-ending night.
CATULLUS—*Carmina*. V. 4.

4
When death hath poured oblivion through my veins,
And brought me home, as all are brought, to lie
In that vast house, common to serfs and thanes,—
I shall not die, I shall not utterly die,
For beauty born of beauty—*that* remains.
MADISON CAWEIN.

5
"For all that let me tell thee, brother Panza," said Don Quixote, "that there is no recollection which time does not put an end to, and no pain which death does not remove."
"And what greater misfortune can there be," replied Panza, "than the one that waits for time to put an end to it and death to remove it?"
CERVANTES—*Don Quixote*. Pt. I. Ch. XV.

6
It singeth low in every heart,
We hear it each and all,—
A song of those who answer not,
However we may call;
They throng the silence of the breast,
We see them as of yore,—
The kind, the brave, the true, the sweet,
Who walk with us no more.
JOHN W. CHADWICK—*Auld Lang Syne*.

7
At length, fatigued with life, he bravely fell,
And health with Boerhaave bade the world farewell.
BENJ. CHURCH—*The Choice*. (1754)

8
Ex vita discedo, tanquam ex hospitio, non tanquam ex domo.
I depart from life as from an inn, and not as from my home.
CICERO—*De Senectute*. 23.

9
Emori nolo: sed me esse mortuum nihil æstimo.
I do not wish to die: but I care not if I were dead.
CICERO—*Tusculanarum Disputationum*. I. 8.
Trans. of verse of EPICHARMUS.

10
Vetat dominans ille in nobis deus, injussu hinc nos suo demigrare.
The divinity who rules within us, forbids us to leave this world without his command.
CICERO—*Tusculanarum Disputationum*. I. 30.

11
Undique enim ad inferos tantundem viæ est.
There are countless roads on all sides to the grave.
CICERO—*Tusculanarum Disputationum*. I. 43.

12
Supremus ille dies non nostri extinctionem sed commutationem affert loci.
That last day does not bring extinction to us, but change of place.
CICERO—*Tusculanarum Disputationum*. I. 49.

13
Some men make a womanish complaint that it is a great misfortune to die before our time. I would ask what time? Is it that of Nature? But she, indeed, has lent us life, as we do a sum of money, only no certain day is fixed for payment. What reason then to complain if she demands it at pleasure, since it was on this condition that you received it.
CICERO.

14
Omnia mors æquat.
Death levels all things.
CLAUDIANUS—*De Raptu Proserpinæ*. II. 302.

15
Mors dominos servis et sceptra ligonibus æquat,
Dissimiles simili conditione trahens.
Death levels master and slave, the sceptre and the law and makes the unlike like.
In WALTER COLMAN'S *La Danse Machabre* or *Death's Duell*. (Circa 1633)

16
Mors sceptra ligonibus æquat.
Inscribed over a 14th Century mural painting once at Battle Church, Sussex. Included in the 12th Century *Vers sur la Mort*. Ascribed to Thibaut de Marly. Also the motto of one of Symeoni's emblematic devices.
See *Notes and Queries*, May, 1917. P. 134.
(See also SHIRLEY)

17
Death comes with a crawl or he comes with a pounce,
And whether he's slow, or spry,
It isn't the fact that you're dead that counts,
But only, how did you die?
EDMUND VANCE COOKE—*How Did You Die?*

18
Qui ne craint point la mort ne craint point les menaces.
He who does not fear death cares naught for threats.
CORNEILLE—*Le Cid*. II. 1.

19
O death, where is thy sting? O grave, where is thy victory?
I Corinthians. XV. 55.

20
Ut non ex vita, sed ex domo in domum videretur migrare.
So that he seemed to depart not from life, but from one home to another.
CORNELIUS NEPOS—*Atticus*.

21
All flesh is grass, and all its glory fades
Like the fair flower dishevell'd in the wind;
Riches have wings, and grandeur is a dream;
The man we celebrate must find a tomb,
And we that worship him, ignoble graves.
COWPER—*Task*. Bk. III. L. 261.

1
All has its date below; the fatal hour
Was register'd in Heav'n ere time began.
We turn to dust, and all our mightiest works
Die too.
COWPER—*Task.* Bk. V. *The Winter Morning Walk.* L. 540.

2
Life, that dares send
A challenge to his end,
And when it comes, say, "Welcome, friend!"
RICHARD CRASHAW—*Wishes to his (Supposed) Mistress.* St. 29.

3
We are born, then cry,
We know not for why,
And all our lives long
Still but the same song.
NATHANIEL CROUCH. (Attributed.) In *Fly Leaves*, pub. 1854, taken from *Bristol Drollery*, 1674.
(See also TENNYSON under BABYHOOD)

4
Round, round the cypress bier
Where she lies sleeping,
On every turf a tear,
Let us go weeping!
Wail!
GEORGE DARLEY—*Dirge.*

5
And though mine arm should conquer twenty worlds,
There's a lean fellow beats all conquerors.
THOMAS DEKKER—*Old Fortunatus.* Act I. Sc. 1.

6
I expressed just now my mistrust of what is called Spiritualism— . . . I owe it a trifle for a message said to come from Voltaire's Ghost. It was asked, "Are you not now convinced of another world?" and rapped out, "There *is* no other world—Death is only an incident in Life."
WILLIAM DE MORGAN—*Joseph Vance.* Ch. XI.
(See also BARRIE)

7
"People can't die, along the coast," said Mr. Peggotty, "except when the tide's pretty nigh out. They can't be born, unless it's pretty nigh in—not properly born, till flood. He's a-going out with the tide."
DICKENS—*David Copperfield.* Ch. XXX.
(See also BROWNE, HENRY V; also TUSSER under TIDES)

8
Death, be not proud, though some have called thee
Mighty and dreadful, for thou art not so:
For those, whom thou think'st thou dost overthrow,
Die not, poor Death.
DONNE—*Divine Poems. Holy Sonnets.* No. 17.

9
One short sleep past, we wake eternally,
And Death shall be no more; Death, thou shalt die.
DONNE—*Divine Poems. Holy Sonnets.* No. 17.

10
Welcome, thou kind deceiver!
Thou best of thieves! who, with an easy key,
Dost open life, and, unperceived by us,
Even steal us from ourselves.
DRYDEN—*All for Love.* Act V. Sc. 1.
(See also POPE under TIME)

11
Death in itself is nothing; but we fear
To be we know not what, we know not where.
DRYDEN—*Aurengzebe.* Act IV. Sc. 1.

12
So was she soon exhaled, and vanished hence;
As a sweet odour, of a vast expense.
She vanished, we can scarcely say she died.
DRYDEN—*Elegiacs. To the Memory of Mrs. Anne Killegrew.* L. 303.
(See also YOUNG)

13
Of no distemper, of no blast he died,
But fell like autumn fruit that mellow'd long.
DRYDEN—*Œdipus.* Act IV. Sc. 1. L. 265.

14
Heaven gave him all at once; then snatched away,
Ere mortals all his beauties could survey;
Just like the flower that buds and withers in a day.
DRYDEN—*On the Death of Amyntas.*

15
He was exhal'd; his great Creator drew
His spirit, as the sun the morning dew.
DRYDEN—*On the Death of a Very Young Gentleman.* L. 25.
(See also YOUNG)

16
Like a led victim, to my death I'll go,
And dying, bless the hand that gave the blow.
DRYDEN—*The Spanish Friar.* Act II. Sc. 1. L. 64.

17
In the jaws of death.
DU BARTAS—*Divine Weekes and Workes.* Second Week. First day.
(See also JUVENAL, TENNYSON—*Charge of the Light Brigade*)

18
She'l bargain with them; and will giue
Them GOD; teach them how to liue
In him; or if they this deny,
For him she'l teach them how to Dy.
CRASHAW—*Hymn to the Name and Honor of Saint Teresa.*
(See also TICKELL)

19
One event happeneth to them all.
Ecclesiastes. II. 14.

20
The grasshopper shall be a burden, and desire shall fail; because man goeth to his long home, and the mourners go about the streets.
Ecclesiastes. XII. 5.

21
Judge none blessed before his death.
Ecclesiasticus. XI. 28.

22
Death is the king of this world: 'tis his park
Where he breeds life to feed him. Cries of pain
Are music for his banquet.
GEORGE ELIOT—*Spanish Gypsy.* Bk. II.

23
If we could know
Which of us, darling, would be first to go,
Who would be first to breast the swelling tide

And step alone upon the other side—
If we could know!
MRS. FOSTER ELY—*If We could Know.*

1
He thought it happier to be dead,
To die for Beauty, than live for bread.
EMERSON—*Beauty.* L. 25.

2
But learn that to die is a debt we must all pay.
EURIPIDES—*Alcestis.* 418. Also *Andromache.* 1271

3
Out of the strain of the Doing,
Into the peace of the Done;
Out in the thirst of Pursuing,
Into the rapture of Won.
Out of grey mist into brightness,
Out of pale dusk into Dawn—
Out of all wrong into rightness,
We from these fields shall be gone.
"Nay," say the saints, "Not gone but come,
Into eternity's Harvest Home."
W. M. L. FAY—Poem in *Sunday at Home.* May, 1910.

4
Sit the comedy out, and that done,
When the Play's at an end, let the Curtain fall down.
THOMAS FLATMAN—*The Whim.*
(See also RABELAIS)

5
Young Never-Grow-Old, with your heart of gold
And the dear boy's face upon you;
It is hard to tell, though we know it well,
That the grass is growing upon you.
ALICE FLEMING—*Spion Kop.*

6
A dying man can do nothing easy.
FRANKLIN—*Last Words.*

7
La montagne est passée; nous irons mieux.
The mountain is passed; now we shall get on better.
FREDERICK THE GREAT. Said to be his last words.

8
Why fear death? It is the most beautiful adventure in life.
CHARLES FROHMAN. Last words before he sank in the wreck of the Lusitania, torpedoed by the Germans, May 7, 1915. So reported by RITA JOLIET.
(See also BARRIE)

9
Drawing near her death, she sent most pious thoughts as harbingers to heaven; and her soul saw a glimpse of happiness through the chinks of her sicknesse broken body.
FULLER—*The Holy and the Profane State.* Bk. I. Ch. II.

10
Had [Christ] the death of death to death
Not given death by dying:
The gates of life had never been
To mortals open lying.
On the tombstone of REV. FYGE (?) in the churchyard of Castle-Camps, Cambridgeshire.

11
To die is landing on some silent shore,
Where billows never break nor tempests roar;
Ere well we feel the friendly stroke 'tis o'er.
SIR SAMUEL GARTH—*The Dispensary.* Canto III. L. 225.

12
The prince who kept the world in awe,
The judge whose dictate fix'd the law;
The rich, the poor, the great, the small,
Are levell'd; death confounds 'em all.
GAY—*Fables.* Pt. II. Fable 16.

13
Dead as a door nail.
GAY—*New Song of New Similes.* LANGLAND—*Piers Ploughman.* II. L. 183. (1362) WILLIAM OF PALERNE—*Romance* (About 1350) II *Henry IV.* Act V. Sc. 3. Deaf as a door nail. RABELAIS—III. 34. Trans. by URQUHART.

14
Where the brass knocker, wrapt in flannel band,
Forbids the thunder of the footman's hand,
The' upholder, rueful harbinger of death,
Waits with impatience for the dying breath.
GAY—*Trivia.* Bk. II. L. 467.

15
For dust thou art, and unto dust shalt thou return.
Genesis. III. 19.

16
What if thou be saint or sinner,
Crooked gray-beard, straight beginner,—
Empty paunch, or jolly dinner,
When Death thee shall call.
All alike are rich and richer,
King with crown, and cross-legged stitcher,
When the grave hides all.
R. W. GILDER—*Drinking Song.*

17
None who e'er knew her can believe her dead;
Though, should she die, they deem it well might be
Her spirit took its everlasting flight
In summer's glory, by the sunset sea,
That onward through the Golden Gate is fled.
Ah, where that bright soul is cannot be night.
R. W. GILDER—*"H. H."*
(See also ALDRICH, HOOD)

18
Can storied urn or animated bust
Back to its mansion call the fleeting breath?
Can honour's voice provoke the silent dust,
Or flattery soothe the dull cold ear of death?
GRAY—*Elegy.* St. 11.

19
He pass'd the flaming bounds of place and time:
The living throne, the sapphire blaze,
Where angels tremble while they gaze,
He saw; but blasted with excess of light,
Closed his eyes in endless night.
GRAY—*Progress of Poesy.* III. 2. L. 99.

20
Fling but a stone, the giant dies.
MATTHEW GREEN—*The Spleen.* L. 93.

21
When life is woe,
And hope is dumb,
The World says, "Go!"
The Grave says, "Come!"
ARTHUR GUITERMAN—*Betel-Nuts.*

1
Death borders upon our birth; and our cradle stands in our grave.
BISHOP HALL—*Epistles*. Decade III. Ep. II.

2
Come to the bridal-chamber, Death!
Come to the mother's, when she feels,
For the first time, her first-born's breath!
Come when the blessed seals
That close the pestilence are broke,
And crowded cities wail its stroke!
FITZ-GREENE HALLECK—*Marco Bozzaris*.

3
Ere the dolphin dies
Its hues are brightest. Like an infant's breath
Are tropic winds before the voice of death.
FITZ-GREENE HALLECK—*Fortune*.

4
The ancients dreaded death: the Christian can only fear dying.
J. C. AND A. W. HARE—*Guesses at Truth*.

5
And I hear from the outgoing ship in the bay
The song of the sailors in glee:
So I think of the luminous footprints that bore
The comfort o'er dark Galilee,
And wait for the signal to go to the shore,
To the ship that is waiting for me.
BRET HARTE—*The Two Ships*.
(See also TENNYSON—*Crossing the Bar*, WHITMAN)

6
On a lone barren isle, where the wild roaring billows
Assail the stern rock, and the loud tempests rave,
The hero lies still, while the dew-drooping willows,
Like fond weeping mourners, lean over his grave.
The lightnings may flash and the loud thunders rattle;
He heeds not, he hears not; he's free from all pain.
He sleeps his last sleep, he has fought his last battle;
No sound can awake him to glory again!
Attributed to LYMAN HEATH—*The Grave of Bonaparte*.

7
Death rides on every passing breeze,
He lurks in every flower.
BISHOP HEBER—*At a Funeral*. St. 3.

8
Leaves have their time to fall,
And flowers to wither at the north wind's breath,
And stars to set—but all.
Thou hast all seasons for thine own, O Death.
FELICIA D. HEMANS—*Hour of Death*.

9
"Passing away" is written on the world and all the world contains.
FELICIA D. HEMANS—*Passing Away*.

10
What is Death
But Life in act? How should the Unteeming Grave
Be victor over thee,
Mother, a mother of men?
W. E. HENLEY—*Echoes*. XLVI. *Matri Dilectissimæ*.

11
So be my passing.
My task accomplished and the long day done,
My wages taken, and in my heart
Some late lark singing,
Let me be gathered to the quiet west,
The sundown splendid and serene,
Death.
W. E. HENLEY—*Margaritæ Sorori*.

12
So many are the deaths we die
Before we can be dead indeed.
W. E. HENLEY—*Rhymes and Rhythms*. XV.

13
Into the everlasting lull,
The immortal, incommunicable dream.
W. E. HENLEY—*Rhymes and Rhythms*. XVI.

14
Not lost, but gone before.
MATTHEW HENRY—*Commentaries*. Matthew II. Title of a song published in *Smith's Edinburgh Harmony*, 1829.
(See also ARISTOPHANES, JONSON, ROGERS, SENECA)

15
They are not amissi, but præmissi;
Not lost but gone before.
PHILIP HENRY, as quoted by MATTHEW HENRY in his *Life of Philip Henry*.

16
Præmissi non amissi.
Inscription on a tombstone in Stallingborough Church, Lincolnshire, England. (1612)

17
Not lost but gone before.
Epitaph of MARY ANGELL in St. Dunstan's Church, Stephney, England. (1693)

18
Those that God loves, do not live long.
HERBERT—*Jacula Prudentum*.
(See also BYRON)

19
I know thou art gone to the home of thy rest—
Then why should my soul be so sad?
I know thou art gone where the weary are blest,
And the mourner looks up, and is glad;
I know thou hast drank of the Lethe that flows
In a land where they do not forget,
That sheds over memory only repose,
And takes from it only regret.
THOMAS KIBBLE HERVEY—*I Know Thou Art Gone*.

20
And death makes equal the high and low.
JOHN HEYWOOD—*Be Merry Friends*.
(See also SHIRLEY)

21
(Mors, mortis morti mortem nisi morte dedisset [dedisses].)
Death when to death a death by death hath given
Then shall be op't the long shut gates of heaven.
THOMAS HEYWOODE—*Nine Bookes of various History concerning Women*. Bk. II. *Of the Sybells*.

22
Now I am about to take my last voyage, a great leap in the dark.
THOMAS HOBBES. His reported last words. Hence "Hobbes' voyage," expression used by VANBRUGH in *The Provoked Wife*. Act V. Sc. 6.
(See also RABELAIS)

1
The mossy marbles rest
On the lips that he has pressed
In their bloom;
And the names he loved to hear
Have been carved for many a year
On the tomb.
HOLMES—*The Last Leaf.*

2
Behold—not him we knew!
This was the prison which his soul looked through.
HOLMES—*The Last Look.*

3 And they die
An equal death,—the idler and the man
Of mighty deeds.
HOMER—*Iliad.* Bk. IX. L. 396. BRYANT'S trans.

4
He slept an iron sleep,—
Slain fighting for his country.
HOMER—*Iliad.* Bk. XI. L. 285. BRYANT'S trans.

5
One more unfortunate
Weary of breath,
Rashly importunate,
Gone to her death!
HOOD—*Bridge of Sighs.*

6
We watch'd her breathing thro' the night,
Her breathing soft and low,
As in her breast the wave of life
Kept heaving to and fro.
* * * *
Our very hopes belied our fears,
Our fears our hopes belied;
We thought her dying when she slept,
And sleeping when she died.
HOOD—*The Death-bed.*

7
Pallida mors æquo pulsat pede pauperum tabernas
Regumque turres.

Pale death, with impartial step, knocks at the hut of the poor and the towers of kings.
HORACE—*Carmina.* I. 4. 13.

8 Omnes una manet nox,
Et calcanda semel via leti.

One night is awaiting us all, and the way of death must be trodden once.
HORACE—*Carmina.* I. 28. 15.

9
Omnes eodem cogimur; omnium
Versatur urna serius, ocius
Sors exitura.

We are all compelled to take the same road; from the urn of death, shaken for all, sooner or later the lot must come forth.
HORACE—*Carmina.* II. 3. 25.

10
Omne capax movet urna nomen.

In the capacious urn of death, every name is shaken.
HORACE—*Carmina.* III. 1. 16.

11
Cita mors ruit.
Swift death rushes upon us.
HORACE. Adapted from Sat. 1. 8.

12
We all do fade as a leaf.
Isaiah. LXIV. 6.

13
The Lord gave, and the Lord hath taken away; blessed be the name of the Lord.
Job. I. 21.

14
He shall return no more to his house, neither shall his place know him any more.
Job. VII. 10.

15
The land of darkness and the shadow of death.
Job. X. 21.

16
Then with no fiery throbbing pain,
No cold gradations of decay,
Death broke at once the vital chain,
And freed his soul the nearest way.
SAMUEL JOHNSON—*Verses on the Death of Mr. Robert Levet.* St. 9. ("No fiery throbs of pain" in first ed.)

17 Thou art but gone before,
Whither the world must follow.
BEN JONSON—*Epitaph on Sir John Roe.* In DODD'S *Epigrammatists.* P. 190.
(See also HENRY)

18 Mors sola fatetur
Quantula sint hominum corpuscula.

Death alone discloses how insignificant are the puny bodies of men.
JUVENAL—*Satires.* X. 172.

19
Trust to a plank, draw precarious breath,
At most seven inches from the jaws of death.
JUVENAL—*Satires.* XII. 57. GIFFORD'S trans.
(See also DU BARTAS, LUCRETIUS, TWELFTH NIGHT)

20
Nemo impetrare potest a papa bullam nunquam moriendi.

No one can obtain from the Pope a dispensation for never dying.
THOMAS À KEMPIS.
(See also MOLIÈRE)

21 Nay, why should I fear Death,
Who gives us life, and in exchange takes breath?
FREDERIC L. KNOWLES—*Laus Mortis.*

22
When I have folded up this tent
And laid the soiled thing by,
I shall go forth 'neath different stars,
Under an unknown sky.
FREDERIC L. KNOWLES—*The Last Word.*

23 Gone before
To that unknown and silent shore.
LAMB—*Hester.* St. 1.

24
One destin'd period men in common have,
The great, the base, the coward, and the brave,
All food alike for worms, companions in the grave.
LORD LANSDOWNE—*Meditation on Death.*

25
Neither the sun nor death can be looked at with a steady eye.
LA ROCHEFOUCAULD—*Maxims.* 36.

1
The young may die, but the old must!
LONGFELLOW—*Christus. The Golden Legend.* Pt. IV. *The Cloisters.*

2
There is no confessor like unto Death!
Thou canst not see him, but he is near:
Thou needest not whisper above thy breath,
And he will hear;
He will answer the questions,
The vague surmises and suggestions,
That fill thy soul with doubt and fear.
LONGFELLOW—*Christus. The Golden Legend.* Pt. V. *The Inn at Genoa.*

3
Death never takes one alone, but two!
Whenever he enters in at a door,
Under roof of gold or roof of thatch,
He always leaves it upon the latch,
And comes again ere the year is o'er,
Never one of a household only.
LONGFELLOW—*Christus. The Golden Legend.* Pt. VI. *The Farm-House in the Odenwald.*

4
And, as she looked around, she saw how Death, the consoler,
Laying his hand upon many a heart, had healed it forever.
LONGFELLOW—*Evangeline.* Pt. II. V.

5
There is a Reaper whose name is Death,
And with his sickle keen,
He reaps the bearded grain at a breath,
And the flowers that grow between.
LONGFELLOW—*Reaper and the Flowers.* Compare ARNIM and BRENTANO—*Erntelied,* in *Des Knaben Wunderhorn.* (Ed. 1857) Vol. I. P. 59.

6
There is no Death! What seems so is transition;
This life of mortal breath
Is but a suburb of the life elysian,
Whose portal we call Death.
LONGFELLOW—*Resignation.*
(See also MCCREERY)

7
There is no flock, however watched and tended,
But one dead lamb is there!
There is no fireside howsoe'er defended,
But has one vacant chair.
LONGFELLOW—*Resignation.*

8
Oh, what hadst thou to do with cruel Death,
Who wast so full of life, or Death with thee,
That thou shouldst die before thou hadst grown old!
LONGFELLOW—*Three Friends of Mine.* Pt. II.

9
Then fell upon the house a sudden gloom,
A shadow on those features fair and thin;
And softly, from the hushed and darkened room,
Two angels issued, where but one went in.
LONGFELLOW—*Two Angels.* St. 9.

10
J'avais cru plus difficile de mourir.
I imagined it was more difficult to die.
LOUIS XIV. To Madame de Maintenon. See MARTIN—*History of France.* XIV. Bk. XCI.

11
But life is sweet, though all that makes it sweet
Lessen like sound of friends' departing feet;
And Death is beautiful as feet of friend
Coming with welcome at our journey's end.
LOWELL—*An Epistle to George William Curtis.*

12
Victorosque dei celant, ut vivere durent felix esse mori.
The gods conceal from those destined to live how sweet it is to die, that they may continue living.
LUCAN—*Pharsalia.* IV. 519.

13
Libera Fortunæ mors est; capit omnia tellus
Quæ genuit.
Death is free from the restraint of Fortune; the earth takes everything which it has brought forth.
LUCAN—*Pharsalia.* VII. 818.

14
Pavido fortique cadendum est.
The coward and the courageous alike must die.
LUCAN—*Pharsalia.* IX. 582.

15
E mediis Orci faucibus ad hunc evasi modum.
From the very jaws of death I have escaped to this condition.
LUCRETIUS—*App. Met.* VII. P. 191.
(See also JUVENAL)

16
Adde repertores doctrinarum atque leporum;
Adde Heliconiadum comites; quorum unus Homerus
Sceptra potitus, eadem aliis sopitu quiete est.
Nay, the greatest wits and poets, too, cease to live;
Homer, their prince, sleeps now in the same forgotten sleep as do the others.
LUCRETIUS—*De Rerum Natura.* III. 1,049.

17
The axe is laid unto the root of the trees.
Luke. III. 9.

18
To every man upon this earth
Death cometh soon or late,
And how can man die better
Than facing fearful odds,
For the ashes of his fathers
And the temples of his gods?
MACAULAY—*Lays of Ancient Rome. Horatius.* XXVII.

19
There is no death! the stars go down
To rise upon some other shore,
And bright in Heaven's jeweled crown,
They shine for ever more.
JOHN L. MCCREERY. In *Arthur's Home Magazine.* July, 1863. Vol. 22. P. 41. Wrongly ascribed to BULWER-LYTTON.
(See also LONGFELLOW)

20
There is no such thing as death.
In nature nothing dies.
From each sad remnant of decay
Some forms of life arise.
CHARLES MACKAY—*There is No Such Thing as Death.*

1
All our knowledge merely helps us to die a more painful death than the animals that know nothing.
MAETERLINCK—*Joyzelle.* Act I.

2
Nascentes morimur, finiaque ab origine pendet.
We begin to die as soon as we are born, and the end is linked to the beginning.
MANILIUS—*Astronomica.* IV. 16.

3
I want to meet my God awake.
MARIA-THERESA, who refused to take a drug when dying, according to CARLYLE.

4
Hic rogo non furor est ne moriare mori?
This I ask, is it not madness to kill thyself in order to escape death?
MARTIAL—*Epigrams.* II. 80. 2.

5
When the last sea is sailed and the last shallow charted,
When the last field is reaped and the last harvest stored,
When the last fire is out and the last guest departed
Grant the last prayer that I shall pray, Be good to me, O Lord.
MASEFIELD—*D'Avalos' Prayer.*

6
When Life knocks at the door no one can wait,
When Death makes his arrest we have to go.
MASEFIELD—*Widow in the Bye Street.* Pt. II.

7
She thought our good-night kiss was given,
And like a lily her life did close;
Angels uncurtain'd that repose,
And the next waking dawn'd in heaven.
GERALD MASSEY—*The Ballad of Babe Christabel.*

8
Death hath a thousand doors to let out life.
I shall find one.
MASSINGER—*A Very Woman.* Act V. Sc. 4.

9
He whom the gods love dies young.
MENANDER—*Dis Exapaton.* Same in DIONYSIUS—*Ars Rhetorica.* Vol. V. P. 364. Reiske's Ed.
(See also BYRON)

10
There's nothing certain in man's life but this:
That he must lose it.
OWEN MEREDITH (Lord Lytton)—*Clytemnestra.* Pt. XX.

11 If I should die to-night,
My friends would look upon my quiet face
Before they laid it in its resting-place,
And deem that death had left it almost fair.
ROBERT C. V. MEYERS—*If I should Die Tonight.*
See *100 Choice Selections.* No. 27. P. 172

12
Aujourd'hui si la mort n' existait pas, il faudrait l'inventer.
Today if death did not exist, it would be necessary to invent it.
MILLAUD—When voting for the death of LOUIS XVI. BISMARCK used same expression to CHEVALIER NIGRA, referring to Italy.
(See also VOLTAIRE under GOD)

13
Death is delightful. Death is dawn,
The waking from a weary night
Of fevers unto truth and light.
JOAQUIN MILLER—*Even So.* St. 35.

14
O fairest flower; no sooner blown but blasted,
Soft, silken primrose fading timelessly.
MILTON—*Ode on the Death of a Fair Infant Dying of a Cough.*

15
So spake the grisly Terror.
MILTON—*Paradise Lost.* Bk. II. L. 704.

16 I fled, and cried out Death;
Hell trembled at the hideous name, and sigh'd
From all her caves, and back resounded Death.
MILTON—*Paradise Lost.* Bk. II. L. 787.

17
Before mine eyes in opposition sits
Grim Death, my son and foe.
MILTON—*Paradise Lost.* Bk. II. L. 803.

18 Death
Grinned horrible a ghastly smile, to hear
His famine should be filled.
MILTON—*Paradise Lost.* Bk. II. L. 845.

19 Eas'd the putting off
These troublesome disguises which we wear.
MILTON—*Paradise Lost.* Bk. IV. L. 739.

20 Behind her Death
Close following pace for pace, not mounted yet
On his pale horse.
MILTON—*Paradise Lost.* Bk. X. L. 588.

21 How gladly would I meet
Mortality my sentence, and be earth
Insensible! how glad would lay me down
As in my mother's lap!
MILTON—*Paradise Lost.* Bk. X. L. 775.

22
And over them triumphant Death his dart
Shook, but delay'd to strike, though oft invoked.
MILTON—*Paradise Lost.* Bk. XI. L. 491.

23
Nous sommes tous mortels, et chacun est pour soi.
We are all mortal, and each one is for himself.
MOLIÈRE—*L'École des Femmes.* II. 6.

24
On n'a point pour la mort de dispense de Rome.
Rome can give no dispensation from death.
MOLIÈRE—*L'Etourdi.* II. 4.
(See also KEMPIS)

25
La mort (dict on) nous acquitte de toutes nos obligations.
Death, they say, acquits us of all obligations.
MONTAIGNE—*Essays.* Bk. I. Ch. 7. La mort est la recepte a touts maulx. MONTAIGNE—*Essays.* Bk. II. Ch. III.

26
There's nothing terrible in death;
'Tis but to cast our robes away,
And sleep at night, without a breath
To break repose till dawn of day.
MONTGOMERY—*In Memory of E. G.*

1
Weep not for those whom the veil of the tomb
In life's happy morning hath hid from our eyes,
Ere sin threw a blight o'er the spirit's young bloom
Or earth had profaned what was born for the skies.
MOORE—*Song. Weep not for Those.*

2
How short is human life! the very breath
Which frames my words accelerates my death.
HANNAH MORE—*King Hezekiah.*

3
Be happy while y'er leevin,
For y'er a lang time deid.
Scotch Motto for a house, in *Notes and Queries*, Dec. 7, 1901. P. 469. Expression used by BILL NYE.

4
At end of Love, at end of Life,
At end of Hope, at end of Strife,
At end of all we cling to so—
The sun is setting—must we go?

At dawn of Love, at dawn of Life,
At dawn of Peace that follows Strife,
At dawn of all we long for so—
The sun is rising—let us go.
LOUISE CHANDLER MOULTON—*At End.*

5
There is rust upon locks and hinges,
And mould and blight on the walls,
And silence faints in the chambers,
And darkness waits in the halls.
LOUISE CHANDLER MOULTON—*House of Death.*

6
Two hands upon the breast,
And labor's done;
Two pale feet cross'd in rest,
The race is won.
D. M. MULOCK—*Now and Afterwards.*

7
Xerxes the great did die;
And so must you and I.
New England Primer. (1814)

8
When you and I behind the Veil are past.
OMAR KHAYYAM—*Rubaiyat.* St. 47. (Not in first ed.) FITZGERALD's trans.

9
Strange—is it not?—that of the myriads who
Before us passed the door of Darkness through,
Not one returns to tell us of the road
Which to discover we must travel too.
OMAR KHAYYAM—*Rubaiyat.* St. 68. FITZGERALD's trans.
(See also CATULLUS, HAMLET)

10
And die with decency.
THOMAS OTWAY—*Venice Preserved.* Act V. Sc. 3.

11
Tendimus huc omnes; metam properamus ad unam. Omnia sub leges mors vocat atra suas.
We are all bound thither; we are hastening to the same common goal. Black death calls all things under the sway of its laws.
OVID—*Ad Liviam.* 359.

12
Stulte, quid est somnus, gelidæ nisi mortis imago?
Longa quiescendi tempora fata dabunt.
Thou fool, what is sleep but the image of death? Fate will give an eternal rest.
OVID—*Amorum.* II. 9. 41.
(See also quotations under SLEEP)

13
Ultima semper
Expectanda dies homini est, dicique beatus
Ante obitum nemo et suprema funera debet.
Man should ever look to his last day, and no one should be called happy before his funeral.
OVID—*Metamorphoses.* III. 135.

14
Nec mihi mors gravis est posituro morte dolores.
Death is not grievous to me, for I shall lay aside my pains by death.
OVID—*Metamorphoses.* III. 471.

15
Quocunque adspicias, nihil est nisi mortis imago.
Wherever you look there is nothing but the image of death.
OVID—*Tristium.* I. 2. 23.

16
Death's but a path that must be trod,
If man would ever pass to God.
PARNELL—*A Night-Piece on Death.* L. 67.

17
Death comes to all. His cold and sapless hand
Waves o'er the world, and beckons us away.
Who shall resist the summons?
THOMAS LOVE PEACOCK—*Time.*

18
O lady, he is dead and gone!
Lady, he's dead and gone!
And at his head a green grass turfe,
And at his heels a stone.
THOS. PERCY—*Reliques. The Friar of Orders Gray.*

19
For death betimes is comfort, not dismay,
And who can rightly die needs no delay.
PETRARCH—*To Laura in Death.* Canzone V. St. 6.

20
Nam vita morti propior est quotidie.
For life is nearer every day to death.
PHÆDRUS—*Fables.* Bk. IV. 25. 10.

21
Quem dii diligunt,
Adolescens moritur, dum valet, sentit, sapit.
He whom the gods love dies young, whilst he is full of health, perception, and judgment.
PLAUTUS—*Bacchides.* Act IV. 7. 18.
(See also BYRON)

22
Omnibus a suprema die eadem, quæ ante primum; nec magis a morte sensus ullus aut corpori aut animæ quam ante natalem.
His last day places man in the same state as he was before he was born; nor after death has the body or soul any more feeling than they had before birth.
PLINY the Elder—*Historia Naturalis.* LVI. 1.

23
De mortuis nil nisi bonum.
Concerning the dead nothing but good shall be spoken.
PLUTARCH—*Life of Solon.* Given as a saying of Solon. Attributed also to CHILO.

1
Come! let the burial rite be read—
The funeral song be sung!—
An anthem for the queenliest dead
That ever died so young—
A dirge for her, the doubly dead
In that she died so young.
POE—*Lenore.* St. 1.

2
Out—out are the lights—out all!
And, over each quivering form,
The curtain, a funeral pall,
Comes down with the rush of a storm,
And the angels, all pallid and wan,
Uprising, unveiling, affirm
That the play is the tragedy, "Man,"
And its hero the Conqueror Worm.
POE—*The Conqueror Worm.* St. 5.

3
Tell me, my soul! can this be death?
POPE—*Dying Christian to His Soul.* Pope attributes his inspiration to HADRIAN and to a Fragment of SAPPHO. See CROLY'S ed. of POPE. (1835) THOMAS FLATMAN—*Thoughts on Death,* a similar paraphrase, pub. 1674, before Pope was born.

4
The world recedes; it disappears;
Heav'n opens on my eyes; my ears
With sounds seraphic ring:
Lend, lend your wings! I mount! I fly!
O Grave! where is thy victory?
O Death! where is thy sting?
POPE—*The Dying Christian to His Soul.*

5
Vital spark of heavenly flame!
Quit, oh quit this mortal frame.
POPE—*The Dying Christian to His Soul.*

6
By foreign hands thy dying eyes were clos'd,
By foreign hands thy decent limbs compos'd,
By foreign hands thy humble grave adorn'd,
By strangers honour'd, and by strangers mourn'd.
POPE—*Elegy to the Memory of an Unfortunate Lady.* L. 51.

7
A heap of dust remains of thee;
'Tis all thou art, and all the proud shall be!
POPE—*Elegy to the Memory of an Unfortunate Lady.* L. 73.

8
See my lips tremble and my eyeballs roll,
Suck my last breath, and catch my flying soul!
POPE—*Eloisa to Abelard.* L. 323.

9
O Death, all eloquent! you only prove
What dust we dote on, when 'tis man we love.
POPE—*Eloisa to Abelard.* L. 355.

10
Till tired, he sleeps, and life's poor play is o'er.
POPE—*Essay on Man.* Ep. II. L. 282.

11
But thousands die without or this or that,
Die, and endow a college or a cat.
POPE—*Moral Essays.* Ep. III. L. 95.

12
Teach him how to live,
And, oh! still harder lesson! how to die.
BISHOP PORTEUS—*Death.* L. 316.

13
Yet a little sleep, a little slumber, a little folding of the hands to sleep.
Proverbs. VI. 10; XXIV. 33.

14
I have said ye are gods . . . But ye shall die like men.
Psalms. LXXXII. 6. 7.

15
Death aims with fouler spite
At fairer marks.
QUARLES—*Divine Poems.* (Ed. 1669)
(See also YOUNG)

16
It is the lot of man but once to die.
QUARLES—*Emblems.* Bk. V. Em. 7.

17
Je m'en vais chercher un grand peut-être; tirez le rideau, la farce est jouée.

I am going to seek a great perhaps; draw the curtain, the farce is played.

Attributed to RABELAIS by tradition. From MOTTEUX'S *Life of Rabelais.* Quoted: "I am about to leap into the dark"; also *Notice sur Rabelais* in *Œuvres de F. Rabelais.* Paris, 1837.

(See also BROWNE, BROWNING, CARLYLE, FLATMAN, HOBBES)

18
Et l'avare Achéron ne lâche pas sa proie.

And greedy Acheron does not relinquish its prey.

RACINE—*Phèdre.* Act II. Sc. 5.

19
O eloquent, just, and mighty Death! whom none could advise, thou hast persuaded; what none hath dared, thou hast done; and whom all the world hath flattered, thou only hast cast out of the world and despised: thou hast drawn together all the far stretchèd greatness, all the pride, cruelty and ambition of man, and covered it all over with these two narrow words, Hic jacet!
SIR WALTER RALEIGH—*Historie of the World.* Bk. V. Pt. I. Ch. VI.

20
Hushed in the alabaster arms of Death,
Our young Marcellus sleeps.
JAMES R. RANDALL—*John Pelham.*

21

FORT	Very
BELLE,	Fair,
ELLE	She
DORT.	Sleeps.
SORT	Frame
FRELE,	Frail,
QUELLE	What a
MORT!	Death!
ROSE	Rose
CLOSE,	Close,
LA	The
BRISE	Breeze
L'A	Her
PRISE.	Seized.

COMTE DE RESSEGUIER.

22
Der lange Schlaf des Todes schliesst unsere Narben zu, und der kutze des Lebens unsere Wunden.

The long sleep of death closes our scars, and the short sleep of life our wounds.

JEAN PAUL RICHTER—*Hesperus.* XX.

1
Those that he loved so long and sees no more,
Loved and still loves—not dead, but gone before,
He gathers round him.
SAMUEL ROGERS—*Human Life*. L. 739.
(See also HENRY)

2
Sleep that no pain shall wake,
Night that no morn shall break,
Till joy shall overtake
Her perfect peace.
CHRISTINA G. ROSSETTI—*Dream-Land*. St. 4.

3
There is no music more for him:
His lights are out, his feast is done;
His bowl that sparkled to the brim
Is drained, is broken, cannot hold.
CHRISTINA G. ROSSETTI—*Peal of Bells*.

4
When I am dead, my dearest,
Sing no sad songs for me;
Plant thou no roses at my head,
No shady cypress tree.
CHRISTINA G. ROSSETTI—*Song*.

5
Je m'em̃ vais voir le soleil pour la dernière fois.
I go to see the sun for the last time.
ROUSSEAU's last words.

6
Death is the privilege of human nature,
And life without it were not worth our taking:
Thither the poor, the pris'ner, and the mourner
Fly for relief, and lay their burthens down.
NICHOLAS ROWE—*The Fair Penitent*. Act V. Sc. 1. L. 138.

7
Oh, stanch thy bootlesse teares, thy weeping is in vain;
I am not lost, for we in heaven shall one day meet againe.
Roxburghe Ballads. The Bride's Buriall. Edited by CHAS. HINDLEY.

8
Out of the chill and the shadow,
Into the thrill and the shine;
Out of the dearth and the famine,
Into the fulness divine.
MARGARET E. SANGSTER—*Going Home*.

9
Day's lustrous eyes grow heavy in sweet death.
SCHILLER—*Assignation*. St. 4. LORD LYTTON's trans.

10
Und setzet ihr nicht das Leben ein,
Nie wird euch das Leben gewonnen sein.
If you do not dare to die you will never win life.
SCHILLER—*Wallenstein's Lager*. XI. *Chorus*.

11
Gut' Nacht, Gordon.
Ich denke einen langen Schlaf zu thun.
Good night, Gordon. I am thinking of taking a long sleep.
SCHILLER—*Wallenstein's Tod*. V. 5. 85.

12
Haste thee, haste thee, to be gone!
Earth flits fast and time draws on:
Gasp thy gasp, and groan thy groan!
Day is near the breaking.
SCOTT—*Death Chant*.

13
Soon the shroud shall lap thee fast,
And the sleep be on thee cast
That shall ne'er know waking.
SCOTT—*Guy Mannering*. Ch. XXVII.

14
Like the dew on the mountain,
Like the foam on the river,
Like the bubble on the fountain,
Thou art gone, and for ever!
SCOTT—*Lady of the Lake*. Canto III. St. 16.

15
I have a rendezvous with Death
At some disputed barricade.
ALAN SEEGER—*I Have a Rendezvous with Death*.

16
So die as though your funeral
Ushered you through the doors that led
Into a stately banquet hall
Where heroes banqueted.
ALAN SEEGER—*Maktoob*.

17
Quid est enim novi, hominem mori, cujus tota vita nihil aliud quam ad mortem iter est?
What new thing then is it for a man to die, whose whole life is nothing else but a journey to death?
SENECA—*De Consol. ad Polyb.* 30.

18
Ultimum malorum est ex vivorum numero exire antequam moriaris.
It is an extreme evil to depart from the company of the living before you die.
SENECA—*De Tranquilitate. Animi.* 2.

19
Vivere nolunt, et mori nesciunt.
They will not live, and do not know how to die.
SENECA—*Epistles*. IV.

20
Non amittuntur sed præmittuntur.
They are not lost but sent before.
SENECA—*Epistles*. LXIII. 16. Early sources in CYPRIAN—*De Mortalitate*. S. XX.
(See also HENRY)

21
Stultitia est timore mortis mori.
It is folly to die of the fear of death.
SENECA—*Epistles*. LXIX.

22
Incertum est quo te loco mors expectet: itaque tu illam omni loco expecta.
It is uncertain in what place death may await thee; therefore expect it in any place.
SENECA—*Epistolæ Ad Lucilium*. XXVI.

23
Dies iste, quem tamquam extremum reformidas, æterni natalis est.
This day, which thou fearest as thy last, is the birthday of eternity.
SENECA—*Epistolæ Ad Lucilium*. CII.

24
Interim pœna est mori,
Sed sæpe donum; pluribus veniæ fuit.
Sometimes death is a punishment; often a gift; it has been a favor to many.
SENECA—*Hercules Oetæus*. CMXXX.

25
Eripere vitam nemo non homini potest;
At nemo mortem; mille ad hanc aditus patent.
Any one may take life from man, but no one death; a thousand gates stand open to it.
SENECA—*Phœnissæ*. CLII.

1
Optanda mors est, sine metu mortis mori.
To die without fear of death is to be desired.
SENECA—*Troades*. DCCCLXIX.

2
Death's pale flag advanced in his cheeks.
Seven Champions. Pt. III. Ch. XI.
(See also ROMEO AND JULIET)

3
Golden lads and girls all must,
As chimney-sweepers, come to dust.
Cymbeline. Act IV. Sc. 2. *Song*. L. 262.

4
Thou know'st 'tis common; all that lives must die,
Passing through nature to eternity.
Hamlet. Act I. Sc. 2. L. 72.

5
I do not set my life at a pin's fee;
And, for my soul, what can it do to that,
Being a thing immortal as itself?
Hamlet. Act I. Sc. 4. 1; L. 67.

6
Cut off even in the blossoms of my sin,
Unhousel'd, disappointed, unanel'd;
No reckoning made, but sent to my account
With all my imperfections on my head.
Hamlet. Act I. Sc. 5. L. 76.

7
To die:—to sleep:
No more; and, by a sleep to say we end
The heart-ache and the thousand natural shocks
That flesh is heir to, 'tis a consummation
Devoutly to be wished.
Hamlet. Act III. Sc. 1. L. 60.

8
For in that sleep of death what dreams may come.
Hamlet. Act III. Sc. 1. L. 66.

9
Who would fardels bear,
To grunt and sweat under a weary life;
But that the dread of something after death,
The undiscover'd country from whose bourn
No traveller returns, puzzles the will
And makes us rather bear those ills we have
Than fly to others that we know not of?
Hamlet. Act III. Sc. 1. L. 76. (*"These fardels"* in folio.)

10
We should profane the service of the dead,
To sing a requiem and such rest to her
As to peace-parted souls.
Hamlet. Act V. Sc. 1. L. 259.

11
O proud death,
What feast is toward in thine eternal cell,
That thou so many princes at a shot
So bloodily hast struck?
Hamlet. Act V. Sc. 2. L. 375.

12
Come, let us take a muster speedily:
Doomsday is near; die all, die merrily.
Henry IV. Pt. I. Act IV. Sc. 1. L. 133.

13
And we shall feed like oxen at a stall,
The better cherish'd, still the nearer death.
Henry IV. Pt. I. Act V. Sc. 2. L. 14.

14
A man can die but once; we owe God a death.
Henry IV. Pt. II. Act III. Sc. 2. L. 250.

15
What, is the old king dead?
As nail in door.
Henry IV. Pt. II. Act V. Sc. 3. L. 126.

16
A' made a finer end and went away an it had been any christom child; a' parted even just between twelve and one, e'en at the turning o' th' tide: for after I saw him fumble with the sheets, and play with flowers, and smile upon his fingers' ends, I knew there was but one way: for his nose was as sharp as a pen, and a' babbled of green fields. "How now, Sir John?" quoth I: "what, man! be o' good cheer." So a' cried out—"God, God, God!" three or four times. Now I, to comfort him, bid him a' should not think of God; I hoped there was no need to trouble himself with any such thoughts yet.
Henry V. Act II. Sc. 3. L. 12.

17
Ah, what a sign it is of evil life,
Where death's approach is seen so terrible!
Henry VI. Pt. II. Act III. Sc. 3. L. 5.

18
He dies, and makes no sign.
Henry VI. Pt. II. Act III. Sc. 3. L. 28.

19
My sick heart shows
That I must yield my body to the earth,
And, by my fall, the conquest to my foe.
Thus yields the cedar to the axe's edge,
Whose arms gave shelter to the princely eagle;
Under whose shade the ramping lion slept:
Whose top-branch overpeer'd Jove's spreading tree,
And kept low shrubs from winter's powerful wind.
Henry VI. Pt. III. Act V. Sc. 2. L. 8.

20
Why, what is pomp, rule, reign, but earth and dust?
And, live we how we can, yet die we must.
Henry VI. Pt. III. Act V. Sc. 2. L. 27.

21
He gave his honours to the world again,
His blessed part to heaven, and slept in peace.
Henry VIII. Act IV. Sc. 2. L. 29.

22
When beggars die, there are no comets seen;
The heavens themselves blaze forth the death of princes.
Julius Cæsar. Act II. Sc. 2. L. 30.

23
Cowards die many times before their deaths;
The valiant never taste of death but once.
Of all the wonders that I yet have heard,
It seems to me most strange that men should fear;
Seeing that death, a necessary end,
Will come when it will come.
Julius Cæsar. Act II. Sc. 2. L. 33.

24
That we shall die we know; 'tis but the time
And drawing days out, that men stand upon.
Julius Cæsar. Act III. Sc. 1. L. 99.

25
He that cuts off twenty years of life
Cuts off so many years of fearing death.
Julius Cæsar. Act III. Sc. 1. L. 101.

1 We must die, Messala:
With meditating that she must die once,
I have the patience to endure it now.
Julius Cæsar. Act IV. Sc. 3. L. 190.

2
Death, death; oh, amiable, lovely death!
* * * * * *
Come, grin on me, and I will think thou smilest.
King John. Act III. Sc. 4. L. 34.

3
We cannot hold mortality's strong hand.
King John. Act IV. Sc. 2. L. 82.

4
Have I not hideous death within my view,
Retaining but a quantity of life
Which bleeds away, even as a form of wax
Resolveth from its figure 'gainst the fire?
King John. Act V. Sc. 4. L. 22.

5 O, our lives' sweetness!
That we the pain of death would hourly die
Rather than die at once!
King Lear. Act V. Sc. 3. L. 184.

6 Nothing in his life
Became him like the leaving it.
Macbeth. Act I. Sc. 4. L. 7

7
After life's fitful fever, he sleeps well;
Treason has done his worst: nor steel, nor poison,
Malice domestic, foreign levy, nothing,
Can touch him further.
Macbeth. Act III. Sc. 2. L. 23.

8
Be absolute for death; either death or life
Shall thereby be the sweeter.
Measure for Measure. Act III. Sc. 1. L. 4

9 What's yet in this,
That bears the name of life? Yet in this life
Lie hid more thousand deaths: yet death we fear,
That makes these odds all even.
Measure for Measure. Act III. Sc. 1. L. 38

10 Dar'st thou die?
The sense of death is most in apprehension;
And the poor beetle that we tread upon,
In corporal sufferance feels a pang as great
As when a giant dies.
Measure for Measure. Act III. Sc. 1. L. 77

11 If I must die
I will encounter darkness as a bride,
And hug it in mine arms.
Measure for Measure. Act III. Sc. 1. L. 83.

12
Ay, but to die, and go we know not where;
To lie in cold obstruction and to rot.
Measure for Measure. Act III. Sc. 1. L. 118.

13
To be imprison'd in the viewless winds,
And blown with restless violence roundabout
The pendent world; or to be worse than worst
Of those, that lawless and incertain thought
Imagine howling; 'tis too horrible!
Measure for Measure. Act III. Sc. 1. L. 124.

14
The weariest and most loathed worldly life
That age, ache, penury and imprisonment
Can lay on nature, is a paradise
To what we fear of death.
Measure for Measure. Act III. Sc. 1. L. 129.

15
I am a tainted wether of the flock,
Meetest for death; the weakest kind of fruit
Drops earliest to the ground, and so let me.
Merchant of Venice. Act IV. Sc. 1. L. 114.

16
Here is my journey's end, here is my butt,
And very sea-mark of my utmost sail.
Othello. Act V. Sc. 2. L. 267.

17
Woe, destruction, ruin, and decay;
The worst is death, and death will have his day.
Richard II. Act III. Sc. 2. L. 102.

18
Let's choose executors and talk of wills:
And yet not so, for what can we bequeath,
Save our desposed bodies to the ground?
Richard II. Act III. Sc. 2. L. 148.

19
Nothing can we call our own but death
And that small model of the barren earth
Which serves as paste and cover to our bones.
Richard II. Act III. Sc. 2. L. 152.

20 Within the hollow crown
That rounds the mortal temples of a king,
Keeps Death his court; and there the antic sits,
Scoffing his state and grinning at his pomp.
Richard II. Act III. Sc. 2. L. 161.

21 And there at Venice gave
His body to that pleasant country's earth,
And his pure soul unto his captain Christ,
Under whose colours he had fought so long.
Richard II. Act IV. Sc. 1. L. 97.

22
Go thou, and fill another room in hell.
That hand shall burn in never-quenching fire,
That staggers thus my person. Exton, thy fierce hand
Hath with thy king's blood stain'd the king's own land.
Mount, mount, my soul! thy seat is up on high;
Whilst my gross flesh sinks downward, here to die.
Richard II. Act V. Sc. 5. L. 107.

23
Who pass'd, methought, the melancholy flood
With that grim ferryman which poets write of,
Unto the kingdom of perpetual night.
Richard III. Act I. Sc. 4. L. 45.

24
'Tis a vile thing to die, my gracious lord,
When men are unprepared and look not for it.
Richard III. Act III. Sc. 2. L. 64.

25
Death lies on her, like an untimely frost
Upon the sweetest flower of all the field.
Romeo and Juliet. Act IV. Sc. 5. L. 28.

26
How oft, when men are at the point of death,
Have they been merry! which their keepers call
A lightning before death.
Romeo and Juliet. Act V. Sc. 3. L. 88.

27
Death, that hath suck'd the honey of thy breath,
Hath had no power yet upon thy beauty;
Thou art not conquer'd; beauty's ensign yet
Is crimson in thy lips, and in thy cheeks,
And death's pale flag is not advanced there.
Romeo and Juliet. Act V. Sc. 3. L. 92.

(See also Seven Champions)

1 Eyes, look your last!
Arms, take your last embrace! and lips, O you
The doors of breath, seal with a righteous kiss
A dateless bargain to engrossing death.
Romeo and Juliet. Act V. Sc. 3. L. 112.

2
The wills above be done! but I would fain die a dry death.
Tempest. Act I. Sc. 1. L. 70.

3
He that dies pays all debts.
Tempest. Act III. Sc. 2. L. 140.

4
Come away, come away, death,
And in sad cypress let me be laid;
Fly away, fly away, breath:
I am slain by a fair cruel maid.
My shroud of white, stuck all with yew,
Oh, prepare it!
My part of death no one so true
Did share it.
Twelfth Night. Act II. Sc. 4. L. 52.

5
The youth that you see here
I snatch'd one half out of the jaws of death.
Twelfth Night. Act III. Sc. 4. L. 394. Ex faucibus fati creptam videtis, as said by CICERO.
(See also JUVENAL)

6
For he being dead, with him is beauty slain,
And, beauty dead, black chaos comes again.
Venus and Adonis. L. 1,019.

7
The babe is at peace within the womb,
The corpse is at rest within the tomb.
We begin in what we end.
SHELLEY—*Fragments.* Same idea in THOMAS BROWNE—*Hydriotaphia.* P. 221. (St. John's ed.)

8
First our pleasures die—and then
Our hopes, and then our fears—and when
These are dead, the debt is due,
Dust claims dust—and we die too.
SHELLEY—*Death.* (1820)

9
All buildings are but monuments of death,
All clothes but winding-sheets for our last knell,
All dainty fattings for the worms beneath,
All curious music but our passing bell:
Thus death is nobly waited on, for why?
All that we have is but death's livery.
SHIRLEY.

10
Death calls ye to the crowd of common men.
SHIRLEY—*Cupid and Death.*

11
The glories of our blood and state
Are shadows, not substantial things;
There is no armour against fate,
Death lays his icy hand on kings.
Scepter and crown
Must tumble down,
And, in the dust, be equal made
With the poor crooked scythe and spade.
SHIRLEY—*Contention of Ajax and Ulysses.* Sc. 3. ("Birth and State" in PERCY'S RELIQUES. These lines are said to have terrified *Cromwell.*)
(See also COLMAN, HEYWOOD)

12
He that on his pillow lies,
Fear-embalmed before he dies
Carries, like a sheep, his life,
To meet the sacrificer's knife,
And for eternity is prest,
Sad bell-wether to the rest.
SHIRLEY—*The Passing Bell.*

13
La mort sans phrase.
Death without phrases.
SIEYÈS, voting for the death of LOUIS XVI. (Denied by him.) He no doubt voted "La mort"; "sans phrase" being a note on the laconic nature of his vote, i.e. without remarks. The voting usually included explanations of the decision.

14
Yet 'twill only be a sleep:
When, with songs and dewy light,
Morning blossoms out of Night,
She will open her blue eyes
'Neath the palms of Paradise,
While we foolish ones shall weep.
EDWARD ROWLAND SILL—*Sleeping.*

15
We count it death to falter, not to die.
SIMONIDES—*Jacobs I.* 63, 20.

16 To our graves we walk
In the thick footprints of departed men.
ALEX. SMITH—*Horton.* L. 570.

17
Death! to the happy thou art terrible;
But how the wretched love to think of thee,
O thou true comforter! the friend of all
Who have no friend beside!
SOUTHEY—*Joan of Arc.* Bk. I. L. 318.

18 Death is an equall doome
To good and bad, the common In of rest.
SPENSER—*Faerie Queene.* II. 59. Also III. 3. 30.

19
Ave Cæsar, morituri te salutant (or Ave Imperator, te salutamus)
Hail Cæsar, we who are about to die salute you (or Hail Emperor, we salute you.)
SUETONIUS—*Tiberius Claudius Drusus.* XXI. 13. See Note by Samuelis Pitissus, SUETONIUS—*Opera.* Vol. I. P. 678. (1714) The salutation of the gladiators on entering the arena. Morituri te salutant. Quoted by an American officer as he saluted the Statue of Liberty on leaving New York for his place in the Great War.

20
Death, if thou wilt, fain would I plead with thee:
Canst thou not spare, of all our hopes have built,
One shelter where our spirits fain would be
Death, if thou wilt?
SWINBURNE—*A Dialogue.* St. 1.

21
For thee, O now a silent soul, my brother,
Take at my hands this garland and farewell.
Thin is the leaf, and chill the wintry smell,
And chill the solemn earth, a fatal mother.
SWINBURNE—*Ave Atque Vale.* St. 18.

1
And hands that wist not though they dug a grave,
Undid the hasps of gold, and drank, and gave,
And he drank after, a deep glad kingly draught:
And all their life changed in them, for they quaffed
Death; if it be death so to drink, and fare
As men who change and are what these twain were.
SWINBURNE—*Tristram of Lyonesse. The Sailing of the Swallow.* L. 789.

2
Honesta mors turpi vita potior.
An honorable death is better than a dishonorable life.
TACITUS—*Agricola.* XXXIII.

3
Trust not your own powers till the day of your death.
Talmud—Aboth. 2.

4
Death is not rare, alas! nor burials few,
And soon the grassy coverlet of God
Spreads equal green above their ashes pale.
BAYARD TAYLOR—*The Picture of St. John.* Bk. III. St. 84.

5
He that would die well must always look for death, every day knocking at the gates of the grave; and then the gates of the grave shall never prevail upon him to do him mischief.
JEREMY TAYLOR—*Holy Dying.* Ch. II. Pt. I.

6
But O! for the touch of a vanish'd hand,
And the sound of a voice that is still!
TENNYSON—*Break, Break, Break.*

7
Sunset and evening star,
And one clear call for me!
And may there be no moaning of the bar
When I put out to sea.
TENNYSON—*Crossing the Bar.*

8
Twilight and evening bell,
And after that the dark!
And may there be no sadness of farewell
When I embark.
TENNYSON—*Crossing the Bar.*

9
For tho' from out our bourne of Time and Place
The flood may bear me far,
I hope to see my Pilot face to face
When I have crossed the bar.
TENNYSON—*Crossing the Bar.*
(See also HARTE)

10
The great world's altar-stairs
That slope thro'darkness up to God.
TENNYSON—*In Memoriam.* Pt. LV.

11
Death has made
His darkness beautiful with thee.
TENNYSON—*In Memoriam.* LXXIV.

12
God's finger touched him, and he slept.
TENNYSON—*In Memoriam.* LXXXV.

13
The night comes on that knows not morn,
When I shall cease to be all alone,
To live forgotten, and love forlorn.
TENNYSON—*Mariana in the South.* Last stanza.

14
Whatever crazy sorrow saith,
No life that breathes with human breath
Has ever truly long'd for death.
TENNYSON—*Two Voices.* St. 132.

15
Dead men bite not.
THEODOTUS, when counselling the death of POMPEY. See PLUTARCH—*Life of Pompey.*

16
Et "Bene," discedens dicet, "placideque quiescas;
Terraque securæ sit super ossa levis."
And at departure he will say, "Mayest thou rest soundly and quietly, and may the light turf lie easy on thy bones."
TIBULLUS—*Carmina.* II. 4. 49.

17
I hear a voice you cannot hear,
Which says, I must not stay;
I see a hand you cannot see,
Which beckons me away.
TICKELL—*Colin and Lucy.*

18
These taught us how to live; and (oh, too high
The price for knowledge!) taught us how to die.
TICKELL—*On the Death of Mr. Addison.* L. 81.
(See also PORTEUS)

19
I believe if I should die,
And you should kiss my eyelids where I lie
Cold, dead, and dumb to all the world contains,
The folded orbs would open at thy breath,
And from its exile in the Isles of Death
Life would come gladly back along my veins.
MARY ASHLEY TOWNSEND—*Love's Belief. (Credo.)*

20
Go thou, deceased, to this earth which is a mother, and spacious and kind. May her touch be soft like that of wool, or a young woman, and may she protect thee from the depths of destruction. Rise above him, O Earth, do not press painfully on him, give him good things, give him consolation, as a mother covers her child with her cloth, cover thou him.
Vedic Funeral Rite. Quoted in New York *Times* on the death of "Buffalo Bill."

21
Venit summa dies et ineluctabile tempus.
The supreme day has come and the inevitable hour.
VERGIL—*Æneid.* II. 324. Same in LUCAN. VII. 197.

22
Vixi, et quem dederat cursum fortuna, peregi:
Et nunc magna mei sub terras currit imago.
I have lived, and I have run the course which fortune allotted me; and now my shade shall descend illustrious to the grave.
VERGIL—*Æneid.* IV. 653.

23
Irreameabilis unda.
The wave from which there is no return [the river Styx].
VERGIL—*Æneid.* VI. 425.

24
Usque adeone mori miserum est?
Is it then so sad a thing to die?
VERGIL—*Æneid.* XII. 646.

1
Decet imperatorem stantem mori.
It becomes an emperor to die standing (i.e. "in harness").
VESPASIAN.

2
C'est demain, ma belle amie, que je fais le saut perilleux.
It is today, my dear, that I take a perilous leap.
Last words of VOLTAIRE, quoting the words of King Henry to GABRIELLE D'ESTRÉES, when about to enter the Catholic Church.
(See also HOBBES)

3
Le lâche fuit en vain; la mort vole à sa suite:
C'est en la défiant que le brave l'évite.
It is vain for the coward to flee; death follows close behind; it is only by defying it that the brave escape.
VOLTAIRE—*Le Triumvirat.* IV. 7.

4
But God, who is able to prevail, wrestled with him, as the angel did with Jacob, and marked him; marked him for his own.
IZAAK WALTON—*Life of Donne.*

5
Softly his fainting head he lay
Upon his Maker's breast;
His Maker kiss'd his soul away,
And laid his flesh to rest.
WATTS—*Death of Moses.* In *Lyrics.*
(See also WESLEY)

6
Hark! from the tombs a doleful sound.
WATTS—*Funeral Thought.*

7
The tall, the wise, the reverend head,
Must lie as low as ours.
WATTS—*Hymns and Spiritual Songs.* Bk. II. Hymn 63.

8
I know death hath ten thousand several doors
For men to take their exits.
JOHN WEBSTER—*Duchess of Malfi.* Act IV. Sc. 2.

9
I saw him now going the way of all flesh.
JOHN WEBSTER—*Westward Ho!* 2. 2.

10
Like Moses to thyself convey,
And kiss my raptur'd soul away.
WESLEY—*Collection Hymn.* 229. Folio 221.
(See also WATTS)

11
Joy, shipmate, joy
(Pleas'd to my soul at death I cry,)
Our life is closed, our life begins,
The long, long anchorage we leave,
The ship is clear at last, she leaps!
Joy, shipmate, joy!
WALT WHITMAN—*Joy, Shipmate, Joy.*
(See also BRET HARTE, TENNYSON—*Crossing the Bar*)

12
O, I see now that life cannot exhibit all to me, as day cannot,
I see that I am to wait for what will be exhibited by death.
WALT WHITMAN—*Night on the Prairies.*

13
Nothing can happen more beautiful than death.
WALT WHITMAN—*Starting from Paumanok.* No. 12.

14
It is not the fear of death
That damps my brow;
It is not for another breath
I ask thee now;
I could die with a lip unstirred.
N. P. WILLIS. Paraphrase of ANDRÉ's letter to WASHINGTON.

15
How beautiful it is for a man to die
Upon the walls of Zion! to be called
Like a watch-worn and weary sentinel,
To put his armour off, and rest in heaven!
N. P. WILLIS—*On the Death of a Missionary.*

16
For I know that Death is a guest divine,
Who shall drink my blood as I drink this wine;
And he cares for nothing! a king is he—
Come on, old fellow, and drink with me!
With you I will drink to the solemn past,
Though the cup that I drain should be my last.
WILLIAM WINTER—*Orgia. The Song of a Ruined Man.*

17
But he lay like a warrior taking his rest,
With his martial cloak around him.
CHAS. WOLFE—*The Burial of Sir John Moore.*

18
If I had thought thou couldst have died
I might not weep for thee;
But I forgot, when by thy side,
That thou couldst mortal be;
It never through my mind had passed,
That time would e'er be o'er
When I on thee should look my last,
And thou shouldst smile no more!
CHAS. WOLFE—*Song. The Death of Mary.*

19
O, sir! the good die first,
And they whose hearts are dry as summer dust
Burn to the socket.
WORDSWORTH—*The Excursion.* Bk. I.

20
"But they are dead; those two are dead!
Their spirits are in Heaven!"
'Twas throwing words away; for still
The little Maid would have her will,
And said, "Nay, we are seven!"
WORDSWORTH—*We Are Seven.*

21
He first deceased; she for a little tried
To live without him, lik'd it not, and died.
SIR HENRY WOTTON—*On the Death of Sir Albert Morton's Wife.*

22
Men drop so fast, ere life's mid stage we tread,
Few know so many friends alive, as dead.
YOUNG—*Love of Fame.* L. 97.

23
Insatiate archer! could not one suffice?
Thy shaft flew thrice; and thrice my peace was slain!
YOUNG—*Night Thoughts.* Night I. L. 212.

24
Who can take
Death's portrait? The tyrant never sat.
YOUNG—*Night Thoughts.* Night II. L. 52.

1
The chamber where the good man meets his fate
Is privileged beyond the common walk
Of virtuous life, quite in the verge of heaven.
YOUNG—*Night Thoughts*. Night II. L. 633.

2
A death-bed's a detector of the heart.
YOUNG—*Night Thoughts*. Night II. L. 641.

3
Lovely in death the beauteous ruin lay;
And if in death still lovely, lovelier there;
Far lovelier! pity swells the tide of love.
YOUNG—*Night Thoughts*. Night III. L. 104.

4
Death is the crown of life;
Were death denyed, poor man would live in vain;
Were death denyed, to live would not be life;
Were death denyed, ev'n fools would wish to die.
YOUNG—*Night Thoughts*. Night III. L. 523.

5
The knell, the shroud, the mattock and the grave,
The deep, damp vault, the darkness, and the worm.
YOUNG—*Night Thoughts*. Night IV. L. 10.

6
And feels a thousand deaths, in fearing one.
YOUNG—*Night Thoughts*. Night IV. L. 17.
(See also BACON)

7
As soon as man, expert from time, has found
The key of life, it opes the gates of death.
YOUNG—*Night Thoughts*. Night IV. L. 122.

8
Early, bright, transient, chaste, as morning dew
She sparkled, was exhal'd, and went to heaven.
YOUNG—*Night Thoughts*. Night V. L. 600.

9
Death loves a shining mark, a signal blow.
YOUNG—*Night Thoughts*. Night V. L. 1,011.
(See also QUARLES)

DEBATE (See ARGUMENT)

DEBT (See also BORROWING)

10
I hold every man a debtor to his profession.
BACON—*Maxims of the Law. Preface.*

11
I owe you one.
GEORGE COLMAN, the Younger—*The Poor Gentleman*. Act I. 2.

12
Anticipated rents, and bills unpaid,
Force many a shining youth into the shade,
Not to redeem his time, but his estate,
And play the fool, but at the cheaper rate.
COWPER—*Retirement*. L. 559.

13
Wilt thou seal up the avenues of ill?
Pay every debt as if God wrote the bill!
EMERSON—*Suum Cuique.*

14
A national debt, if it is not excessive, will be to us a national blessing.
ALEX. HAMILTON—*Letter to Robert Morris*. April 30, 1781.
(See also WILKERSON)

15
At the time we were funding our national debt, we heard much about "a public debt being a public blessing"; that the stock representing it was a creation of active capital for the aliment of commerce, manufactures and agriculture.
THOMAS JEFFERSON—*On Public Debts*. Letter to John W. Epps. Nov. 6, 1813.
(See also WILKERSON)

16
The slender debt to Nature's quickly paid,
Discharged, perchance with greater ease than made.
QUARLES—*Emblems*. Bk. II. Emblem 13.

17
Debtes et mensonges sont ordinairement ensemble rallićs.
Debts and lies are generally mixed together.
RABELAIS—*Pantagruel*. Bk. III. Ch. V.

18
Our national debt a national blessing.
SAMUEL WILKERSON. Used as a broadside issued by JAY COOKE, June, 1865. Qualified by H. C. Fahnstock, "How our national debt may be a national blessing."
(See also HAMILTON, JEFFERSON)

DECAY

19
You have the Pyrrhic dance as yet,
Where is the Pyrrhic phalanx gone?
Of two such lessons, why forget
The nobler and the manlier one?
You have the letters Cadmus gave—
Think ye he meant them for a slave?
BYRON—*Don Juan*. Canto III. St. 86. 10.

20
A gilded halo hovering round decay.
BYRON—*Giaour*. L. 100.

21
He that loves a rosy cheek,
Or a coral lip admires,
Or from star-like eyes doth seek
Fuel to maintain his fires;—
As old Time makes these decay,
So his flames must waste away.
THOMAS CAREW—*Disdain Returned.*

22
A worm is in the bud of youth,
And at the root of age.
COWPER—*Stanzas Subjoined to a Bill of Mortality.*
(See also TWO GENTLEMEN OF VERONA)

23
An age that melts with unperceiv'd decay,
And glides in modest innocence away.
SAMUEL JOHNSON—*Vanity of Human Wishes*. L. 293.

24
There seems to be a constant decay of all our ideas; even of those which are struck deepest, and in minds the most retentive, so that if they be not sometimes renewed by repeated exercises of the senses, or reflection on those kinds of objects which at first occasioned them, the print wears out, and at last there remains nothing to be seen.
LOCKE—*Human Understanding*. Bk. II. Ch. 10.

25
All that's bright must fade,—
The brightest still the fleetest;
All that's sweet was made
But to be lost when sweetest.
MOORE—*National Airs. Indian Air.*

1
The ripest fruit first falls, and so doth he;
His time is spent.
Richard II. Act II. Sc. 1. L. 153.

2
As is the bud bit with an envious worm,
Ere he can spread his sweet leaves to the air,
Or dedicate his beauty to the sun.
Romeo and Juliet. Act I. Sc. 1. L. 157. (Folio and earlier editions give "same" for "sun.")

3
In the sweetest bud
The eating canker dwells.
Two Gentlemen of Verona. Act I. Sc. 1. L. 42. (See also COWPER)

4
I shall be like that tree,—I shall die at the top.
SWIFT—*Scott's Life of Swift.*

5
Fires that shook me once, but now to silent ashes fall'n away.
Cold upon the dead volcano sleeps the gleam of dying day.
TENNYSON—*Locksley Hall. Sixty Years After.* St. 21.

DECEIT

6
God is not averse to deceit in a holy cause.
ÆSCHYLUS—*Frag. Incert.* II.

7
There is a cunning which we in England call the turning of the cat in the pan.
BACON—*Essays. Of Cunning.*

8
Think'st thou there are no serpents in the world
But those who slide along the grassy sod,
And sting the luckless foot that presses them?
There are who in the path of social life
Do bask their spotted skins in Fortune's sun,
And sting the soul.
JOANNA BAILLIE—*De Montfort.* Act I. Sc. 2.

9
What song the Syrens sang, or what name Achilles assumed when he hid himself among women.
SIR THOMAS BROWNE—*Urn-Burial.* Ch. V.

10
If the world will be gulled, let it be gulled.
BURTON—*Anatomy of Melancholy.* Pt. III. Sec. IV. Memb. 1. Subsect. 2.

11
Populus vult decipi; decipiatur.
The people wish to be deceived; let them be deceived.
CARDINAL CARAFA, Legate of PAUL IV., is said to have used this expression in reference to the devout Parisians. Origin in DE THOU. I. XVII. See JACKSON'S *Works.* Bk. III. Ch. XXXII. Note 9.
(See also LINCOLN)

12
Improbi hominis est mendacio fallere.
It is the act of a bad man to deceive by falsehood.
CICERO—*Oratio Pro Murena.* XXX.

13
A delusion, a mockery, and a snare.
LORD DENMAN—*O'Connell vs. The Queen. Clark and Finnelly Reports.*

14
But Esau's hands suit ill with Jacob's voice.
DRYDEN—*Absalom and Achitopel.* Pt. I. L. 982.

15
Man wird betrogen, man betrügt sich selbst.
We are never deceived; we deceive ourselves.
GOETHE—*Sprüche in Prosa.* III.

16
Non mancano pretesti quando si vuole.
Pretexts are not wanting when one wishes to use them.
GOLDONI—*La Villeggiatura.* I. 12.

17
Which I wish to remark—
And my language is plain,—
That for ways that are dark
And for tricks that are vain,
The heathen Chinee is peculiar.
BRET HARTE—*Plain Language from Truthful James.* (*Heathen Chinee.*)

18
The angel answer'd, "Nay, sad soul; go higher!
To be deceived in your true heart's desire
Was bitterer than a thousand years of fire!"
JOHN HAY—*A Woman's Love.*

19
Hateful to me as are the gates of hell,
Is he who, hiding one thing in his heart,
Utters another.
HOMER—*Iliad.* Bk. IX. L. 386. BRYANT'S trans.

20
Vous le croyez votre dupe: s'il feint de l'être, qui est plus dupe, de lui ou de vous?
You think him to be your dupe; if he feigns to be so who is the greater dupe, he or you?
LA BRUYÈRE—*Les Caractéres.* V.

21
On ne trompe point en bien; la fourberie ajoute la malice au mensonge.
We never deceive for a good purpose: knavery adds malice to falsehood.
LA BRUYÈRE—*Les Caractéres.* XI.

22
Car c'est double plaisir de tromper le trompeur.
It is double pleasure to deceive the deceiver.
LA FONTAINE—*Fables.* II. 15.

23
Le bruit est pour le fat, la plainte pour le sot;
L'honnête homme trompé s'éloigne et ne dit mot.
The silly when deceived exclaim loudly; the fool complains; the honest man walks away and is silent.
LA NOUE—*La Coquette Corrigée.* I. 3.

24
On peut être plus fin qu'un autre, mais non pas plus fin que tous les autres.
One may outwit another, but not all the others.
LA ROCHEFOUCAULD—*Maxim.* 394.
(See also LINCOLN)

25
You can fool some of the people all of the time, and all of the people some of the time, but you cannot fool all of the people all the time.
Attributed to LINCOLN. Credited to P. T. Barnum by Nicolay, E. S. Bragg, Spofford. Wm. P. Kellogg and Richard Price Morgan

claim to have heard Lincoln say it in a speech at Bloomington, Ill., May 29, 1856.
(See also PLINY, LA ROCHEFOUCAULD)

1
It is vain to find fault with those arts of deceiving, wherein men find pleasure to be deceived.
LOCKE—*Human Understanding.* Bk. III. Ch. X. 34.

2
Where the lion's skin falls short it must be eked out with the fox's.
LYSANDER. Remark upon being told that he resorted too much to craft. PLUTARCH—*Life of Lysander.*

3
He seemed
For dignity compos'd and high exploit:
But all was false and hollow.
MILTON—*Paradise Lost.* Bk. II. L. 110.

4
On est aisément dupé par ce qu'on aime.
One is easily fooled by that which one loves.
MOLIÈRE—*Le Tartuffe.* IV. 3.

5
Impia sub dulci melle venena latent.
Deadly poisons are concealed under sweet honey.
OVID—*Amorum.* I. 8. 104.

6
Pia fraus.
A pious fraud.
OVID—*Metamorphoses.* IX. 711.

7
Furtum ingeniosus ad omne,
Qui facere assueret, patriæ non degener artis,
Candida de nigris, et de candentibus atra.
Skilled in every trick, a worthy heir of his paternal craft, he would make black look white, and white look black.
OVID—*Metamorphoses.* XI. 313.

8
Fronte politus
Astutam vapido servas sub pectore vulpem.
Though thy face is glossed with specious art thou retainest the cunning fox beneath thy vapid breast.
PERSIUS—*Satires.* V. 116.

9
Habent insidias hominis blanditiæ mali.
The smooth speeches of the wicked are full of treachery.
PHÆDRUS—*Fables.* I. 19. 1.

10
Altera manu fert lapidem panem ostentat altera.
He carries a stone in one hand, and offers bread with the other.
PLAUTUS—*Aulularia.* II. 2. 18.

11
Singuli enim decipere et decipi possunt: nemo omnes, neminem omnes fefellunt.
Individuals indeed may deceive and be deceived; but no one has ever deceived all men, nor have all men ever deceived any one.
PLINY the Younger—*Panegyr. Traj.* 62.
(See also LINCOLN)

12
Engin mieulx vault que force.
Machination is worth more than force.
RABELAIS—*Pantagruel.* Ch. XXVII.

13
Wir betrügen und schmeicheln niemanden durch so feine Kunstgriffe als uns selbst.
We deceive and flatter no one by such delicate artifices as we do our own selves.
SCHOPENHAUER—*Die Welt als Wille.* I. 350.

14
With an auspicious and a dropping eye,
With mirth in funeral, and with dirge in marriage,
In equal scale weighing delight and dole.
Hamlet. Act I. Sc. 2. L. 12.

15
They fool me to the top of my bent. I will come by and by.
Hamlet. Act III. Sc. 2. L. 401.

16
But when the fox hath once got in his nose,
He'll soon find means to make the body follow.
Henry VI. Pt. III. Act IV. Sc. 7. L. 25.

17
A quicksand of deceit.
Henry VI. Pt. III. Act V. Sc. 4. L. 26.

18
The instruments of darkness tell us truths,
Win us with honest trifles, to betray us
In deepest consequence.
Macbeth. Act I. Sc. 3. L. 124.

19
The world is still deceiv'd with ornament,
In law, what plea so tainted and corrupt,
But, being season'd with a gracious voice,
Obscures the show of evil? In religion,
What damned error, but some sober brow
Will bless it and approve it with a text,
Hiding the grossness with fair ornament?
Merchant of Venice. Act III. Sc. 2. L. 74.

20
Make the Moor thank me, love me and reward me,
For making him egregiously an ass.
Othello. Act II. Sc. 1. L. 317.

21
Who makes the fairest show means most deceit.
Pericles. Act I. Sc. 4. L. 75.

22
Oh, that deceit should steal such gentle shapes,
And with a virtuous vizard hide foul guile.
Richard III. Act II. Sc. 2. L. 27.

23
O, that deceit should dwell
In such a gorgeous palace!
Romeo and Juliet. Act III. Sc. 2. L. 84.

24
Orlando's helmet in Augustine's cowl.
HORACE AND JAMES SMITH—*Rejected Addresses. Cui Bono. Imitation of Byron.*

25
Hinc nunc præmium est, qui recta prava faciunt.
There is a demand in these days for men who can make wrong conduct appear right.
TERENCE—*Phormio.* VIII. 2. 6.

26
Deceit and treachery skulk with hatred, but an honest spirit flieth with anger.
TUPPER—*Of Hatred and Anger.*

27
Or shipwrecked, kindles on the coast
False fires, that others may be lost.
WORDSWORTH—*To the Lady Fleming.*

DECEMBER

1
Only the sea intoning,
Only the wainscot-mouse,
Only the wild wind moaning
Over the lonely house.
T. B. ALDRICH—*December*, 1863.

2
Wild was the day; the wintry sea
Moaned sadly on New England's strand,
When first the thoughtful and the free,
Our fathers, trod the desert land.
BRYANT—*The Twenty-second of December.*

3
December drops no weak, relenting tear,
By our fond Summer sympathies ensnared,
Nor from the perfect circle of the year
Can even Winter's crystal gems be spared.
C. P. CRANCH—*December.*

4
Shout now! The months with loud acclaim,
Take up the cry and send it forth;
May breathing sweet her Spring perfumes,
November thundering from the North.
With hands upraised, as with one voice,
They join their notes in grand accord;
Hail to December! say they all,
It gave to Earth our Christ the Lord!
J. K. HOYT—*The Meeting of the Months.*

5
In a drear-nighted December,
Too happy, happy brook,
Thy bubblings ne'er remember
Apollo's summer look;
But with a sweet forgetting,
They stay their crystal fretting,
Never, never petting
About the frozen time
KEATS—*Stanzas.*

6
In cold December fragrant chaplets blow,
And heavy harvests nod beneath the snow.
POPE—*Dunciad.* Bk. I. L. 77.

7
When we shall hear
The rain and wind beat dark December, how,
In this our pinching cave, shall we discourse
The freezing hours away?
Cymbeline. Act III. Sc. 3. L. 36.

8
The sun that brief December day
Rose cheerless over hills of gray,
And, darkly circled, gave at noon
A sadder light than waning moon.
WHITTIER—*Snow-Bound.*

DECISION

9
And her *yes*, once said to you,
SHALL be Yes for evermore.
E. B. BROWNING—*The Lady's Yes.*

10
He only is a well-made man who has a good determination.
EMERSON—*Essay. Culture.*

11
Multitudes in the valley of decision.
Joel. III. 14.

12
Decide not rashly. The decision made
Can never be recalled. The gods implore not,
Plead not, solicit not; they only offer
Choice and occasion, which once being passed
Return no more. Dost thou accept the gift?
LONGFELLOW—*Masque of Pandora. Tower of Prometheus on Mount Caucasus.*

13
Once to every man and nation comes the moment to decide,
In the strife of Truth with Falsehood, for the good or evil side.
LOWELL—*The Present Crisis.*

14
Men must be decided on what they will NOT do, and then they are able to act with vigor *in what they ought to do.*
MENCIUS—*Works.* Bk. IV. Pt. II. Ch. VIII.

15
Determine on some course,
More than a wild exposure to each chance
That starts i' the way before thee.
Coriolanus. Act IV. Sc. 1. L. 35.

16
For what I will, I will, and there an end.
Two Gentlemen of Verona. Act I. Sc. 3. L. 65.

17
Pleasure and revenge
Have ears more deaf than adders to the voice
Of any true decision.
Troilus and Cressida. Act II. Sc. 2. L. 171.

18
There is no mistake; there has been no mistake; and there shall be no mistake.
DUKE OF WELLINGTON—*Letter to Mr. Huskisson.*

DEE (RIVER)

19
Flow on, lovely Dee, flow on, thou sweet river,
Thy banks' purest stream shall be dear to me ever.
JOHN TAIT—*The Banks of the Dee.*

20
"O Mary, go and call the cattle home,
And call the cattle home,
And call the cattle home,
Across the sands o' Dee;"
The western wind was wild and dank wi' foam
And all alone went she.
CHARLES KINGSLEY—*The Sands o' Dee.*

DEEDS (See also ACTION)

21
Who doth right deeds
Is twice born, and who doeth ill deeds vile.
EDWIN ARNOLD—*Light of Asia.* Bk. VI. L. 78.

22
Deeds, not words.
BEAUMONT AND FLETCHER—*Lover's Progress.* Act III. Sc. 6.
(See also BUTLER, CICERO, PLAUTUS)

23
All your better deeds
Shall be in water writ, but this in marble.
BEAUMONT AND FLETCHER—*Philaster.* Act V. Sc. 3.
(See also BERTAUT, MORE; also HENRY VIII under MANNERS, BACON under LIFE)

1
L'injure se grave en métal; et le bienfait s'escrit en l'onde.

An injury graves itself in metal, but a benefit writes itself in water.

JEAN BERTAUT. *Défense de L'Amour.*
(See also BEAUMONT)

2
Qui facit per alium facit per se.

Anything done for another is done for oneself.

BONIFACE VIII—*Maxim. Sexti. Corp. Jur.* Bk. V. 12. Derived from PAULUS—*Digest.* Bk. I. 17. (Quod jessu alterius solvitur pro eo est quasi ipsi solutum esset.)

3
We have left undone those things which we ought to have done; and we have done those things which we ought not to have done.

Book of Common Prayer. General Confession.

4
To be nameless in worthy deeds, exceeds an infamous history.

SIR THOMAS BROWNE—*Hydriotaphia.* Ch. V.

5
'Tis not what man Does which exalts him, but
what man Would do.

ROBERT BROWNING—*Saul.* XVIII.

6
For now the field is not far off
Where we must give the world a proof
Of deeds, not words.

BUTLER—*Hudibras.* Pt. I. Canto I. L. 867.
(See also BEAUMONT)

7
Little deeds of kindness, little words of love,
Make our earth an Eden like the heaven above.

JULIA A. CARNEY—*Little Things.* (Originally "make this pleasant earth below.")

8
His deedes inimitable, like the Sea
That shuts still as it opes, and leaves no tracts
Nor prints of Precedent for poore men's facts.

GEORGE CHAPMAN—*Bussy d'Ambois.* Act I. Sc. 1.

9
So our lives
In acts exemplarie, not only winne
Ourselves good Names, but doth to others give
Matter for virtuous Deedes, by which wee live.

GEORGE CHAPMAN—*Bussy d'Ambois.* Act I. Sc. 1.

10
Whatever is worth doing at all is worth doing well.

EARL OF CHESTERFIELD—*Letters.* March 10, 1746.

11
The will for the deed.

COLLEY CIBBER—*The Rival Fools.* Act III.
(See also DU BARTAS, PLAUTUS, RABELAIS, SWIFT)

12
Facta ejus cum dictis discrepant.

His deeds do not agree with his words.

CICERO—*De Finibus.* Bk. II. 30.
(See also BEAUMONT)

13
This is the Thing that I was born to do.

SAMUEL DANIEL—*Musophilus.* St. 100.

14
Deeds are males, words females are.

SIR JOHN DAVIES—*Scene of Folly.* P. 147.
(See also JOHNSON under WORDS)

15
"I worked for men," my Lord will say,
When we meet at the end of the King's highway;
"I walked with the beggar along the road,
I kissed the bondsman stung by the goad,
I bore my half of the porter's load.
And what did you do," my Lord will say,
"As you traveled along the King's highway?"

ROBERT DAVIES—*My Lord and I.*

16
Thy Will for Deed I do accept.

DU BARTAS—*Divine Weekes and Workes.* Second Week. Third Day. Pt. II.
(See also CIBBER)

17
Our deeds determine us, as much as we determine our deeds.

GEORGE ELIOT—*Adam Bede.* Ch. XXIX.

18
Our deeds still travel with us from afar,
And what we have been makes us what we are.

GEORGE ELIOT—*Motto to Middlemarch.* Ch. LXX.

19
Things of to-day?
Deeds which are harvest for Eternity!

EBENEZER ELLIOTT—*Hymn.* L. 22.

20
Go put your creed into your deed,
Nor speak with double tongue.

EMERSON—*Ode. Concord.* July 4, 1857.

21
Did nothing in particular,
And did it very well.

W. S. GILBERT—*Iolanthe.*

22
Und künftige Thaten drangen wie die Sterne
Rings um uns her unzählig aus der Nacht.

And future deeds crowded round us as the countless stars in the night.

GOETHE—*Iphigenia auf Tauris.* II. 1. 121.

23
For as one star another far exceeds,
So souls in heaven are placèd by their deeds.

ROBERT GREENE—*A Maiden's Dream.*

24
If thou do ill, the joy fades, not the pains.
If well, the pain doth fade, the joy remains.

GEORGE HERBERT—*Church Porch.* Last lines. Same idea in CATO and MUSONIUS.

25
My hour at last has come;
Yet not ingloriously or passively
I die, but first will do some valiant deed,
Of which mankind shall hear in after time.

HOMER—*Iliad.* Bk. XXII. BRYANT's trans.

26
Oh! 'tis easy
To beget great deeds; but in the rearing of them—
The threading in cold blood each mean detail,
And furze brake of half-pertinent circumstance—
There lies the self-denial.

CHARLES KINGSLEY—*Saint's Tragedy.* Act IV. Sc. 3.

27
When a man dies they who survive him ask what property he has left behind. The angel who bends over the dying man asks what good deeds he has sent before him.

The Koran.

1
But the good deed, through the ages
Living in historic pages,
Brighter grows and gleams immortal,
Unconsumed by moth or rust.
LONGFELLOW—*Norman Baron.*

2
We are our own fates. Our own deeds
Are our doomsmen. Man's life was made
Not for men's creeds,
But men's actions.
OWEN MEREDITH (Lord Lytton)—*Lucile.* Pt. II. Canto V. St. 8.

3
See golden days, fruitful of golden deeds,
With joy and love triumphing.
MILTON—*Paradise Lost.* Bk. III. L. 336.

4 Nor think thou with wind
Of æry threats to awe whom yet with deeds
Thou canst not.
MILTON—*Paradise Lost.* Bk. VI. L. 282.

5 I on the other side
Us'd no ambition to commend my deeds;
The deeds themselves, though mute, spoke loud the doer.
MILTON—*Samson Agonistes.* L. 246.

6
For men use, if they have an evil tourne, to write it in marble; and whoso doth us a good tourne we write it in duste.
SIR THOMAS MORE—*Richard III and his miserable End.*
(See also BEAUMONT)

7
Actis ævum implet, non segnibus annis.
He fills his lifetime with deeds, not with inactive years.
OVID—*Ad Liviam.* 449. Adapted probably from ALBINOVANUS PEDO, contemporary poet with Ovid.

8
Ipse decor, recti facti si præmia desint,
Non movet.
Men do not value a good deed unless it brings a reward.
OVID—*Epistolæ Ex Ponto.* II. 3. 13.

9
Di pia facta vident.
The gods see the deeds of the righteous.
OVID—*Fasti.* II. 117.

10 The deed I intend is great,
But what, as yet, I know not.
OVID—*Metamorphoses.* SANDY's trans.

11
Acta deos nunquam mortalia fallunt.
The deeds of men never escape the gods.
OVID—*Tristium.* I. 2. 97.

12
Les belles actions cachées sont les plus estimables.
Noble deeds that are concealed are most esteemed.
PASCAL—*Pensées.* I. IX. 21.

13
Dictis facta suppetant.
Let deeds correspond with words.
PLAUTUS—*Pseudolus.* Act I. 1.
(See also BEAUMONT)

14
Nequam illud verbum est, Bene vult, nisi qui benefacit.
"He wishes well" is worthless, unless the deed go with it.
PLAUTUS—*Trinummus.* II. 4. 38.
(See also CIBBER)

15
We'll take the good-will for the deed.
RABELAIS—*Works.* Bk. IV. Ch. XLIX.
(See also CIBBER)

16 Your deeds are known,
In words that kindle glory from the stone.
SCHILLER—*The Walk.*

17
Wer gar zu viel bedenkt wird wenig leisten.
He who considers too much will perform little.
SCHILLER—*Wilhelm Tell.* III. 1.

18
Nemo beneficia in calendario scribit.
Nobody makes an entry of his good deeds in his day-book.
SENECA—*De Beneficiis.* I. 2.

19
From lowest place when virtuous things proceed,
The place is dignified by the doer's deed:
Where great additions swell's and virtue none,
It is a dropsied honour. Good alone
Is good without a name.
All's Well That Ends Well. Act II. Sc. 3. L. 132.

20 He covets less
Than misery itself would give; rewards
His deeds with doing them, and is content
To spend the time to end it.
Coriolanus. Act II. Sc. 2. L. 130.

21 I never saw
Such noble fury in so poor a thing;
Such precious deeds in one that promis'd nought
But beggary and poor looks.
Cymbeline. Act V. Sc. 5. L. 7.

22 There shall be done
A deed of dreadful note.
Macbeth. Act III. Sc. 2. L. 43.

23
A deed without a name.
Macbeth. Act IV. Sc. 1. L. 49.

24
The flighty purpose never is o'ertook,
Unless the deed go with it.
Macbeth. Act IV. Sc. 1. L. 146.

25 Unnatural deeds
Do breed unnatural troubles: infected minds
To their deaf pillows will discharge their secrets.
Macbeth. Act V. Sc. 1. L. 79.

26
How far that little candle throws his beams!
So shines a good deed in a naughty world.
Merchant of Venice. Act V. Sc. 1. L. 90.

27 O, would the deed were good!
For now the devil, that told me I did well,
Says that this deed is chronicled in hell.
Richard II. Act V. Sc. 5. L. 115.

1
They look into the beauty of thy mind,
And that, in guess, they measure by thy deeds.
Sonnet LXIX.

2
I give thee thanks in part of thy deserts,
And will with deeds requite thy gentleness.
Titus Andronicus. Act I. Sc. 1. L. 236.

3
Go in, and cheer the town; we'll forth and fight;
Do deeds worth praise and tell you them at night.
Troilus and Cressida. Act V. Sc. 3. L. 92.

4 One good deed dying tongueless
Slaughters a thousand waiting upon that.
Our praises are our wages.
Winter's Tale. Act I. Sc. 2. L. 92.

5 You do the deeds,
And your ungodly deeds find me the words.
SOPHOCLES—*Electra.* L. 624. MILTON'S trans.

6
You must take the will for the deed.
SWIFT—*Polite Conversation.* Dialogue II.
(See also CIBBER)

DELAY

7
Delay always heeds danger.
CERVANTES—*Don Quixote.* Bk. IV. Ch. III.
(See also HENRY VI.)

8 Il fornito
Sempre con danno l'attender sofferse.
It is always those who are ready who suffer in delays.
DANTE—*Inferno.* XXVIII. 98.
(See also LUCAN)

9
Unus homo nobis cunctando restituit rem,
Non ponebat enim rumores ante salutem.
One man by delay restored the state, for he preferred the public safety to idle report.
ENNIUS—*Quoted by* CICERO.

10
With sweet, reluctant, amorous delay.
HOMER—*Odyssey.* Bk. I. 1. POPE'S trans.

11
Nulla unquam de morte cunctatio longa est.
When a man's life is at stake no delay is too long.
JUVENAL—*Satires.* VI. 221.

12 Do not delay,
Do not delay: the golden moments fly!
LONGFELLOW—*Masque of Pandora.* Pt. VII.

13
Ah! nothing is too late
Till the tired heart shall cease to palpitate.
LONGFELLOW—*Morituri Salutamus.* St. 24.

14
Tolle moras—semper nocuit differre paratis.
Away with delay—it always injures those who are prepared.
LUCAN—*Pharsalia.* I. 281.
(See also DANTE)

15
Longa mora est nobis omnis, quæ gaudia differt.
Every delay that postpones our joys, is long.
OVID—*Heroides.* XIX. 3.

16
Tardo amico nihil est quidquam iniquius.
Nothing is more annoying than a tardy friend.
PLAUTUS—*Pœnulus.* III. 1. 1.

17
Quod ratio nequiit, sæpe sanavit mora.
What reason could not avoid, has often been cured by delay.
SENECA—*Agamemnon.* CXXX.

18
Omnis nimium longa properanti mora est.
Every delay is too long to one who is in a hurry.
SENECA—*Agamemnon.* CCCCXXVI.

19
Maximum remedium est iræ mora.
Delay is the greatest remedy for anger.
SENECA—*De Ira.* II. 28. (Same in Bk. III, with "dilatio" for "mora.")

20
Delays have dangerous ends.
Henry VI. Pt. I. Act III. Sc. 2. L. 33.
(See also CERVANTES)

21
Delay leads impotent and snail-paced beggary.
Richard III. Act IV. Sc. 3. L. 53.

22
Pelle moras; brevis est magni fortuna favoris.
Away with delay; the chance of great fortune is short-lived.
SILIUS ITALICUS—*Punica.* IV. 734.

23
Late, late, so late! but we can enter still.
Too late, too late! ye cannot enter now.
TENNYSON—*Idylls of the King. Guinevere.* L. 169.

24
And Mecca saddens at the long delay.
THOMSON—*The Seasons. Summer.* L. 979.

25
Like St. George, always in his saddle, never on his way.
Proverb quoted in CLEMENT WALKER'S *History of Independency. The Mysterie of the Two Juntos.*

DELFT

26
What land is this? Yon pretty town
Is Delft, with all its wares displayed:
The pride, the market-place, the crown
And centre of the Potter's trade.
LONGFELLOW—*Keramos.* L. 66.

DELIGHT

27
I am convinced that we have a degree of delight, and that no small one, in the real misfortunes and pains of others.
BURKE—*The Sublime and Beautiful.* Pt. I. Sec. 14.

28
Man delights not me: no, nor woman neither, though, by your smiling, you seem to say so.
Hamlet. Act II. Sc. 2. L. 321.

29
Why, all delights are vain; and that most vain,
Which with pain purchas'd, doth inherit pain.
Love's Labour's Lost. Act I. Sc. 1. L. 72.

1
Their tables were stor'd full, to glad the sight,
And not so much to feed on as delight:
All poverty was scorn'd, and pride so great,
The name of help grew odious to repeat.
Pericles. Act I. Sc. 4. L. 28.

2
These violent delights have violent ends
And in their triumph die, like fire and powder,
Which as they kiss consume.
Romeo and Juliet. Act II. Sc. 6. L. 9.

DEMOCRACY (See also GOVERNMENT, PUBLIC, STATESMANSHIP)

3
For poets (bear the word)
Half-poets even, are still whole democrats.
E. B. BROWNING—*Aurora Leigh*. Bk. 4.

4
A perfect democracy is therefore the most shameless thing in the world.
BURKE—*Reflections on the Revolution in France*.

5
And wrinkles, the d—d democrats, won't flatter.
BYRON—*Don Juan*. Canto X. St. XXIV.

6
You can never have a revolution in order to establish a democracy. You must have a democracy in order to have a revolution.
G. K. CHESTERTON—*Tremendous Trifles. Wind and the trees*.

7
Le Césarisme, c'est la démocratie sans la liberté.
Cæsarism is democracy without liberty.
TAXILE DELORD—*L'Histoire du Second Empire*.

8
The world is weary of statesmen whom democracy has degraded into politicians.
BENJ. DISRAELI—*Lothair*. Ch. XVII.

9
Democracy is on trial in the world, on a more colossal scale than ever before.
CHARLES FLETCHER DOLE—*The Spirit of Democracy*.

10
Drawn to the dregs of a democracy.
DRYDEN—*Absalom and Achitopel*. Pt. I. L. 227.

11
Puritanism, believing itself quick with the seed of religious liberty, laid, without knowing it, the egg of democracy.
LOWELL—*Among My Books. New England Two Centuries Ago*.

12
Democ'acy gives every man
A right to be his own oppressor.
LOWELL—*Biglow Papers*. Series 2. No. 7.

13
Thus our democracy was from an early period the most aristocratic, and our aristocracy the most democratic.
MACAULAY—*History*. Vol. I. P. 20.

14
To one that advised him to set up a democracy in Sparta, "Pray," said Lycurgus, "do you first set up a democracy in your own house."
LYCURGUS in PLUTARCH'S *Apophthegms of Kings and Great Commanders*.

15
Thunder on! Stride on! Democracy. Strike with vengeful strokes.
WALT WHITMAN—*Drum-Taps. Rise O Days From Your Fathomless Deep*. No. 3.

16
But the right is more precious than peace, and we shall fight for the things which we have always carried nearest our hearts—for democracy, for the right of those who submit to authority to have a voice in their own Governments, for the rights and liberties of small nations, for a universal dominion of right by such a concert of free peoples as shall bring peace and safety to all nations and make the world itself at last free.
WOODROW WILSON—*Address to Congress*. April 2, 1917.
(See also under WAR)

17
I believe in Democracy because it releases the energies of every human being.
WOODROW WILSON—*At the Workingman's Dinner*, New York, Sept. 4, 1912.

18
The world must be made safe for democracy. Its peace must be planted upon the tested foundations of political liberty. We have no selfish ends to serve. We desire no conquest, no dominion. We seek no indemnities for ourselves, no material compensation for the sacrifices we shall freely make. We are but one of the champions of the rights of mankind. We shall be satisfied when those rights have been made as secure as the faith and the freedom of nations can make them.
WOODROW WILSON—*Address to Congress*. April 2, 1917. (State of War with Germany.)

DENTISTRY

19
My curse upon thy venom'd stang,
That shoots my tortured gums alang;
And through my lugs gies monie a twang,
Wi' gnawing vengeance,
Tearing my nerves wi' bitter pang,
Like racking engines!
BURNS—*Address to the Toothache*.

20
One said a tooth drawer was a kind of unconscionable trade, because his trade was nothing else but to take away those things whereby every man gets his living.
HAZLITT—*Shakespeare Jest Books. Conceits, Clinches, Flashes and Whimzies*. No. 84.

21
Some ask'd how pearls did grow, and where,
Then spoke I to my girle,
To part her lips, and showed them there
The quarelets of pearl.
HERRICK—*The Rock of Rubies, and the Quarrie of Pearls*.

22
Those cherries fairly do enclose
Of orient pearl a double row,
Which, when her lovely laughter shows,
They look like rosebuds fill'd with snow.
Set to music by RICHARD ALISON—*An Howre's Recreation in Musike*. See OLIPHANT'S *La Messa Madrigalesca*. P. 229.

1
I am escaped with the skin of my teeth.
Job. XIX. 20.

2
Thais has black, Læcania white teeth; what is the reason? Thais has her own, Læcania bought hers.
MARTIAL—*Epigrams.* Bk. V. Ep. 43.

3
I have the toothache.
* * * * * *
What! sigh for the toothache?
Much Ado About Nothing. Act III. Sc. 2. L. 21.

4
For there was never yet philosopher
That could endure the toothache patiently.
Much Ado About Nothing. Act V. Sc. 1. L. 35.

5
In the spyght of his tethe.
SKELTON—*Why Come Ye nat to Courte.* L. 939

DESIRE

6
Passing into higher forms of desire, that which slumbered in the plant, and fitfully stirred in the beast, awakes in the man.
HENRY GEORGE—*Progress and Poverty.* Bk. II. Ch. 3.

7
Nil cupientium
Nudus castra peti.
Naked I seek the camp of those who desire nothing.
HORACE—*Carmina.* Bk. III. 16. 22.

8
The thing we long for, that we are
For one transcendent moment.
LOWELL—*Longing.*

9
Nitimur in vetitum semper, cupimusque negata.
We are always striving for things forbidden, and coveting those denied us.
OVID—*Amorum.* III. 4. 17.

10
Velle suum cuique est, nec voto vivitur uno.
Each man has his own desires; all do not possess the same inclinations.
PERSIUS—*Satires.* V. 53.

11
As the hart panteth after the water-brooks.
Psalms. XLII. 1.

12
Oh! could I throw aside these earthly bands
That tie me down where wretched mortals sigh—
To join blest spirits in celestial lands!
PETRARCH—*To Laura in Death. Sonnet XLV.*

13
I have
Immortal longings in me.
Antony and Cleopatra. Act V. Sc. 2. L. 282.

14
I do desire we may be better strangers.
As You Like It. Act III. Sc. 2. L. 274.

15
Can one desire too much of a good thing?
As You Like It. Act IV. Sc. 1. L. 123.

16
Methinks I have a great desire to a bottle of hay: good hay, sweet hay, hath no fellow.
Midsummer Night's Dream. Act IV. Sc. 1. L. 36.

17
Had doting Priam checked his son's desire,
Troy had been bright with fame and not with fire.
Rape of Lucrece. L. 1,490.

18
There are two tragedies in life. One is not to get your heart's desire. The other is to get it.
BERNARD SHAW—*Man and Superman.* Act IV.

19
The desire of the moth for the star,
Of the night for the morrow,
The devotion to something afar
From the sphere of our sorrow.
SHELLEY—*To——. One Word is too Often Profaned.*

20
We grow like flowers, and bear desire,
The odor of the human flowers.
R. H. STODDARD—*The Squire of Low Degree. The Princess Answers.* I. L. 13.

DESOLATION

21
None are so desolate but something dear,
Dearer than self, possesses or possess'd
A thought, and claims the homage of a tear.
BYRON—*Childe Harold.* Canto II. St. 24.

22
Desolate—Life is so dreary and desolate—
Women and men in the crowd meet and mingle,
Yet with itself every soul standeth single,
Deep out of sympathy moaning its moan—
Holding and having its brief exultation—
Making its lonesome and low lamentation—
Fighting its terrible conflicts alone.
ALICE CARY—*Life.*

23
No one is so accursed by fate,
No one so utterly desolate,
But some heart, though unknown,
Responds unto his own.
LONGFELLOW—*Endymion.*

24
Abomination of desolation.
Matthew. XXIV. 15; *Mark.* XIII. 14.

25
My desolation does begin to make
A better life.
Antony and Cleopatra. Act V. Sc. 2. L. 1

DESPAIR

26
I will indulge my sorrows, and give way
To all the pangs and fury of despair.
ADDISON—*Cato.* Act IV. Sc. 3.

27
Despair of ever being saved, "except thou be born again," or of seeing God "without holiness," or of having part in Christ except thou "love him above father, mother, or thy own life." This kind of despair is one of the first steps to heaven.
BAXTER—*Saint's Rest.* Ch. VI.

28
The world goes whispering to its own,
"This anguish pierces to the bone;"
And tender friends go sighing round,
"What love can ever cure this wound?"
My days go on, my days go on.
E. B. BROWNING—*De Profundis.* St. 5.

1
The name of the Slough was Despond.
BUNYAN—*Pilgrim's Progress*. Pt. I. Ch. II.

2
The nympholepsy of some fond despair.
BYRON—*Childe Harold*. Canto IV. St. 115.

3
Darkness our guide, Despair our leader was.
JOHN DENHAM—*Essay on Vergil's Æneid*.

4
Night was our friend, our leader was Despair.
DRYDEN. Trans. of VERGIL'S *Æneid*. Bk. II. 487.

5
Nil desperandum Teucro duce et auspice Teucro.
Never despair while under the guidance and auspices of Teucer.
HORACE—*Carmina*. I. 7. 27.

6
Stood up, the strongest and the fiercest spirit
That fought in heaven, now fiercer by despair.
MILTON—*Paradise Lost*. Bk. II. L. 44.

7 Thus repuls'd, our final hope
Is flat despair.
MILTON—*Paradise Lost*. Bk. II. L. 141.

8
Desperatio magnum ad honeste moriendum incitamentum.
Despair is a great incentive to honorable death.
QUINTUS CURTIUS RUFUS—*De Rebus Gestis Alexandri Magni*. IX. 5. 6.

9
O, that this too too solid flesh would melt,
Thaw and resolve itself into a dew!
Hamlet. Act I. Sc. 2. L. 129.

10
They have tied me to a stake; I cannot fly.
But, bear-like, I must fight the course.
Macbeth. Act V. Sc. 7. L. 1.

11
For nothing canst thou to damnation add
Greater than that.
Othello. Act III. Sc. 3. L. 372.

12 Discomfort guides my tongue
And bids me speak of nothing but despair.
Richard II. Act III. Sc. 2. L. 65.

13
Oh, break, my heart! poor bankrupt, break at once!
To prison, eyes, ne'er look on liberty!
Vile earth, to earth resign; end motion here;
And thou and Romeo press one heavy bier!
Romeo and Juliet. Act III. Sc. 2. L. 57.

14 Thou tyrant!
Do not repent these things, for they are heavier
Than all thy woes can stir: therefore, betake thee
To nothing but despair.
Winter's Tale. Act III. Sc. 2. L. 208.

15
No change, no pause, no hope! Yet I endure.
SHELLEY—*Prometheus Unbound*. Act I. L. 24

16 * * * then black despair,
The shadow of a starless night, was thrown
Over the world in which I moved alone.
SHELLEY—*Revolt of Islam*. *Dedication*. St. 6.

17
Alas for him who never sees
The stars shine through his cypress-trees
Who, hopeless, lays his dead away,
Nor looks to see the breaking day
Across the mournful marbles play!
WHITTIER—*Snow-Bound*. L. 204.

DESTINY (See also FATE)

18 My death and life,
My bane and antidote, are both before me.
ADDISON—*Cato*. Act V. Sc. 1.

19
Che l'uomo il suo destin fugge di raro.
For rarely man escapes his destiny.
ARIOSTO—*Orlando Furioso*. XVIII. 58.

20
Life treads on life, and heart on heart;
We press too close in church and mart
To keep a dream or grave apart.
E. B. BROWNING—*A Vision of Poets*. Conclusion.

21
There are certain events which to each man's life are as comets to the earth, seemingly strange and erratic portents; distinct from the ordinary lights which guide our course and mark our seasons, yet true to their own laws, potent in their own influences.
BULWER-LYTTON—*What Will He do with It?* Bk. II. Ch. XIV.

22 For I am a weed,
Flung from the rock, on Ocean's foam, to sail,
Where'er the surge may sweep, the tempest's breath prevail.
BYRON—*Childe Harold*. Canto III. St. 2.

23
Art and power will go on as they have done,—will make day out of night, time out of space, and space out of time.
EMERSON—*Society and Solitude*. *Work and Days*.

24
Character is fate. (Destiny).
HERACLITUS. In MULLACH'S *Fragmenta Philosophorum Græcorum*.

25
No living man can send me to the shades
Before my time; no man of woman born,
Coward or brave, can shun his destiny.
HOMER—*Iliad*. Bk. VI. L. 623. BRYANT'S trans.

26
All, soon or late, are doom'd that path to tread.
HOMER—*Odyssey*. Bk. XII. L. 31. POPE'S trans.

27
The future works out great men's destinies:
The present is enough for common souls,
Who, never looking forward, are indeed
Mere clay wherein the footprints of their age
Are petrified forever.
LOWELL—*Act for Truth*.

28
We are but as the instrument of Heaven.
Our work is not design, but destiny.
OWEN MEREDITH (Lord Lytton)—*Clytemnestra*. Pt. XIX.

1 We are what we must
And not what we would be. I know that one hour
Assures not another. The will and the power
Are diverse.
OWEN MEREDITH (Lord Lytton)—*Lucile*. Pt. I. Canto III. St. 19.

2 Unseen hands delay
The coming of what oft seems close in ken,
And, contrary, the moment, when we say
"'Twill never come!" comes on us even then.
OWEN MEREDITH (Lord Lytton)—*Thomas Muntzer to Martin Luther*. L. 382.

3
They only fall, that strive to move,
Or lose, that care to keep.
OWEN MEREDITH (Lord Lytton)—*Wanderer*. Bk. III. Futility. St. 6.

4 The irrevocable Hand
That opes the year's fair gate, doth ope and shut
The portals of our earthly destinies;
We walk through blindfold, and the noiseless doors
Close after us, forever.
D. M. MULOCK—*April*.

5
Every man meets his Waterloo at last.
WENDELL PHILLIPS—*Speech*. Nov. 1, 1859.

6
Ich fühl 's das ich der Mann des Schicksals bin.
I feel that I am a man of destiny.
SCHILLER—*Wallenstein's Tod*. III. XV. 171.

7
Truly some men there be
That live always in great horrour,
And say it goeth by destiny
To hang or wed: both hath one hour;
And whether it be, I am well sure,
Hanging is better of the twain;
Sooner done, and shorter pain.
The School-house. Pub. about 1542.

8
What a falling-off was there!
Hamlet. Act I. Sc. 5. L. 47.

9
A man may fish with the worm that hath eat of a king, and eat of the fish that hath fed of that worm.
Hamlet. Act IV. Sc. 3. L. 28.

10
Imperious Cæsar, dead and turn'd to clay,
Might stop a hole to keep the wind away:
O, that that earth, which kept the world in awe,
Should patch a wall to expel the winter's flaw!
Hamlet. Act V. Sc. 1. L. 234.
(See also TENNYSON)

11
Let Hercules himself do what he may,
The cat will mew and dog will have his day.
Hamlet. Act V. Sc. 1. L. 315.

12
We shall be winnow'd with so rough a wind
That even our corn shall seem as light as chaff,
And good from bad find no partition.
Henry IV. Pt. II. Act IV. Sc. 1. L. 194.

13
Here burns my candle out; ay, here it dies,
Which, whiles it lasted, gave King Henry light.
Henry VI. Pt. III. Act II. Sc. 6. L. 1.

14
Think you I bear the shears of destiny?
Have I commandment on the pulse of life?
King John. Act IV. Sc. 2. L. 91.

15 For it is a knell
That summons thee to heaven or to hell.
Macbeth. Act II. Sc. 1. L. 63.

16
What, will the line stretch out to the crack of doom?
Macbeth. Act IV. Sc. 1. L. 117.

17
Things at the worst will cease or else climb upward
To what they were before.
Macbeth. Act IV. Sc. 2. L. 24.

18
If he had been as you and you as he,
You would have slipt like him.
Measure for Measure. Act II. Sc. 2. L. 64.

19
A man whom both the waters and the wind,
In that vast tennis-court, hath made the ball
For them to play upon.
Pericles. Act II. Sc. 1. L. 63.

20
They that stand high have many blasts to shake them;
And if they fall, they dash themselves to pieces.
Richard III. Act I. Sc. 3. L. 259.

21
What is done cannot be now amended.
Richard III. Act IV. Sc. 4. L. 291.

22
But He, that hath the steerage of my course,
Direct my sail!
Romeo and Juliet. Act I. Sc. 4. L. 112 ("Direct my suit" in folio and quarto of 1690.)

23
The seed ye sow, another reaps;
The wealth ye find, another keeps;
The robes ye weave, another wears;
The arms ye forge, another bears.
SHELLEY—*Song. To Men of England*.

24
And all the bustle of departure—sometimes sad, sometimes intoxicating—just as fear or hope may be inspired by the new chances of coming destiny.
MADAME DE STAËL—*Corinne*. Bk. X. Ch. VI.

25
And from his ashes may be made
The violet of his native land.
TENNYSON—*In Memoriam*. XVIII. St. 1.
(See also HAMLET)

26
Thou cam'st not to thy place by accident,
It is the very place God meant for thee;
And should'st thou there small room for action see,
Do not for this give room for discontent.
ARCHBISHOP TRENCH—*Sonnet*.

27
Quisque suos patimur manes.
We bear each one our own destiny.
VERGIL—*Æneid*. VI. 743.

1
Tes destins sont d'un homme, et tes vœux sont d'un dieu.
Your destiny is that of a man, and your vows those of a god.
VOLTAIRE—*La Liberté.*

2
Pluck one thread, and the web ye mar;
Break but one
Of a thousand keys, and the paining jar
Through all will run.
WHITTIER—*My Soul and I.* St. 38.

3
To be a Prodigal's favourite,—then worse truth,
A Miser's Pensioner,—behold our lot!
WORDSWORTH—*The Small Celandine.*

DEVIL, THE

4
Renounce the Devil and all his works.
Book of Common Prayer. Baptism of Infants.

5
Every man for himself, his own ends, the devil for all.
BURTON—*Anatomy of Melancholy.* Pt. III. Sec. I. Memb. III.

6
The Devil himself, which is the author of confusion and lies.
BURTON—*Anatomy of Melancholy.* Pt. III. Sec. IV. Memb. I. Subsect. III.

7
And bid the devil take the hin'most.
BUTLER—*Hudibras.* Pt. I. Canto II. L. 633. BURNS—*To a Haggis. The Tragedy of Bouduca.* Act IV. Sc. 2.
(See also PRIOR)

8
Nick Machiavel had ne'er a trick
(Though he gave his name to our Old Nick).
BUTLER—*Hudibras.* Pt. III. Canto I. L. 1,313.

9
Here is the devil-and-all to pay.
CERVANTES—*Don Quixote.* Bk. IV. Pt. I. Ch. X.

10
Therefore it behooveth hire a full long spoon
That shal ete with a feend.
CHAUCER—*The Squire's Tale.* L. 602. Same idea in GEORGE MERITON—*Praise of Yorkshire Ale.* DEKKER—*Batchelars' Banquet. Works.* I. 170. (Grosart's ed.) HEYWOOD—*Proverbs.* Pt. II. Ch. V. KEMP—*Nine Days Wonder.* (1600) MARLOWE—*Jew of Malta.* III. IV. *Comedy of Errors.* IV. III. 64. *Tempest.* II. 2.

11
Auch die Kultur, die alle Welt beleckt,
Hat auf den Teufel sich erstreckt.
Culture which smooth the whole world licks,
Also unto the devil sticks.
GOETHE—*Faust.* I. 6. 160.

12
Nein, nein! Der Teufel ist ein Egoist
Und thut nicht leicht um Gottes Willen,
Was einem Andern nützlich ist.
No, no! The devil is an egotist,
And is not apt, without why or wherefore,
"For God's sake," others to assist.
GOETHE—*Faust.* I. 4. 124.

13
I call'd the devil, and he came,
And with wonder his form did I closely scan;
He is not ugly, and is not lame,
But really a handsome and charming man.
A man in the prime of life is the devil,
Obliging, a man of the world, and civil;
A diplomatist too, well skill'd in debate,
He talks quite glibly of church and state.
HEINE—*Pictures of Travels. The Return Home.* No. 37.

14
When the devil drives, needs must. (Needs must when the devil drives.)
HEYWOOD—*Johan the Husband. Proverbs.* Ch. VII. CERVANTES—*Don Quixote.* Pt. I. Bk. IV. Ch. 4. GOSSON—*Ephemerides of Phialo.* MARLOWE—*Dr. Faustus.* PEELE—*Edward I. All's Well that Ends Well.* I. 3.

15
How art thou fallen from heaven, O Lucifer, son of the morning!
Isaiah. XIV. 12.

16
What is got over the devil's back is spent under his belly.
Attributed to ISOCRATES by ALAIN. RENÉ LE SAGE—*Gil Blas.* Bk. III. Ch. X.

17
Resist the Devil, and he will flee from you.
James. IV. 7.

18
The king of terrors.
Job. XVIII. 14.

19
The Devil is an ass, I do acknowledge it.
BEN JONSON—*The Devil is an Ass.* Act IV. Sc. 1.

20
It is Lucifer,
The son of mystery;
And since God suffers him to be,
He, too, is God's minister,
And labors for some good
By us not understood.
LONGFELLOW—*Christus. The Golden Legend.* Epilogue. Last stanza.

21
Tell your master that if there were as many devils at Worms as tiles on its roofs, I would enter.
MARTIN LUTHER, April 16, 1521. See BUNSEN'S *Life of Luther.* P. 61.

22
The devil, my friends, is a woman just now.
'Tis a woman that reigns in Hell.
OWEN MEREDITH (Lord Lytton)—*News.*

23
Swings the scaly horror of his folded tail.
MILTON—*Hymn on Christ's Nativity.* L. 172.

24
The infernal serpent; he it was whose guile,
Stirr'd up with envy and revenge, deceived
The mother of mankind.
MILTON—*Paradise Lost.* Bk. I. L. 34.

25
His form had yet not lost
All his original brightness, nor appear'd
Less than arch-angel ruined, and th' excess
Of glory obscured.
MILTON—*Paradise Lost.* Bk. I. L. 591.

1 From morn
To noon he fell, from noon to dewy eve,
A summer's day; and with the setting sun
Dropt from the zenith like a falling star.
MILTON—*Paradise Lost.* Bk. I. L. 742.

2
Satan exalted sat, by merit raised
To that bad eminence.
MILTON—*Paradise Lost.* Bk. II. L. 5.

3 Black it stood as night,
Fierce as ten furies, terrible as hell,
And shook a dreadful dart; what seem'd his head
The likeness of a kingly crown had on.
Satan was now at hand.
MILTON—*Paradise Lost.* Bk. II. L. 670.

4
Incens'd with indignation Satan stood
Unterrified, and like a comet burn'd,
That fires the length of Ophiucus huge
In th' arctic sky, and from his horrid hair
Shakes pestilence and war.
MILTON—*Paradise Lost.* Bk. II. L. 707.

5 Abashed the Devil stood,
And felt how awful goodness is, and saw
Virtue in her own shape how lovely; saw
And pined his loss.
MILTON—*Paradise Lost.* Bk. IV. L. 846.

6
Satan; so call him now, his former name
Is heard no more in heaven.
MILTON—*Paradise Lost.* Bk. V. L. 658.

7
Be sober, be vigilant; because your adversary, the Devil, as a roaring lion, walketh about, seeking whom he may devour.
I Peter. V. 8.

8
Bid the Devil take the slowest.
PRIOR—*On the Taking of Namur.*
(See also BUTLER)

9
Verflucht wer mit dem Teufel spielt.
Accursed be he who plays with the devil.
SCHILLER—*Wallenstein's Tod.* I. 3. 64.

10
I charge thee, Satan, hous'd within this man,
To yield possession to my holy prayers,
And to thy state of darkness hie thee straight;
I conjure thee by all the saints in heaven!
Comedy of Errors. Act IV. Sc. 4. L. 57.

11 The devil hath power
To assume a pleasing shape.
Hamlet. Act II. Sc. 2. L. 628.

12
Nay, then, let the devil wear black, for I'll have a suit of sables.
Hamlet. Act III. Sc. 2. L. 136.

13
He will give the devil his due.
Henry IV. Pt. I. Act I. Sc. 2. L. 132. DRYDEN—*Epilogue to the Duke of Guise.*

14
The prince of darkness is a gentleman.
King Lear. Act III. Sc. 4. L. 147. SIR JOHN SUCKLING—*The Goblins.* Song. Act III.

15
Let me say "amen" betimes, lest the devil cross my prayer.
Merchant of Venice. Act III. Sc. 1. L. 22.

16
The lunatic, the lover and the poet,
Are of imagination all compact:
One sees more devils than vast hell can hold.
Midsummer Night's Dream. Act V. Sc. 1. L. 7.

17
This is a devil, and no monster; I will leave him; I have no long spoon.
Tempest. Act II. Sc. 2. L. 101.
(See also CHAUCER)

18
What, man! defy the devil: consider, he's an enemy to mankind.
Twelfth Night. Act III. Sc. 4. L. 107.

19
From his brimstone bed, at break of day,
A-walking the Devil is gone,
To look at his little snug farm of the world,
And see how his stock went on.
SOUTHEY AND COLERIDGE—*The Devil's Walk.* St. 1. Title originally *Devils' Thoughts.* COLERIDGE assigns to SOUTHEY the first four stanzas. See his *Sibylline Leaves.* (1817) P. 98. Claim of PORSON a hoax.

20
The Satanic school.
SOUTHEY—*Vision of Judgment.* Original Preface. III.

21
The bane of all that dread the Devil!
WORDSWORTH—*The Idiot Boy.* St. 67.

DEW

22
The Dewdrop slips into the shining sea!
EDWIN ARNOLD—*Light of Asia.* Bk. VIII. Last Line.

23 Dewdrops, Nature's tears, which she
Sheds in her own breast for the fair which die.
The sun insists on gladness; but at night,
When he is gone, poor Nature loves to weep.
BAILEY—*Festus.* Sc. *Water and Wood. Midnight.*

24 The dew,
'Tis of the tears which stars weep, sweet with joy.
BAILEY—*Festus.* Sc. *Another and a Better World.*

25
The dews of the evening most carefully shun;
Those tears of the sky for the loss of the sun.
CHESTERFIELD—*Advice to a Lady in Autumn.*

26
Dew-drops are the gems of morning,
But the tears of mournful eve!
COLERIDGE—*Youth and Age.*

27 The dew-bead
Gem of earth and sky begotten.
GEORGE ELIOT—*The Spanish Gypsy.* Song. Bk. I.

28
Every dew-drop and rain-drop had a whole heaven within it.
LONGFELLOW—*Hyperion.* Bk. III. Ch. VII.

1
Or stars of morning, dew-drops which the sun
Impearls on every leaf and every flower.
MILTON—*Paradise Lost.* Bk. V. L. 746.

2
I must go seek some dewdrops here,
And hang a pearl in every cowslip's ear.
Midsummer Night's Dream. Act II. Sc. 1. L. 14.

3
And every dew-drop paints a bow.
TENNYSON—*In Memoriam.* Pt. CXXII.

DIFFICULTIES (See also IMPOSSIBILITY)

4
Die grössten Schwierigkeiten liegen da, wo wir sie nicht suchen.
The greatest difficulties lie where we are not looking for them.
GOETHE—*Sprüche in Prosa.* P. 236.

5
Nil agit exemplum, litem quod lite resolvit.
The illustration which solves one difficulty by raising another, settles nothing.
HORACE—*Satires.* II. 3. 103.

6
Many things difficult to design prove easy to performance.
SAMUEL JOHNSON—*Rasselas.* Ch. XIII.

7
Blind guides, which strain at a gnat, and swallow a camel.
Matthew. XXIII. 24.

8
So he with difficulty and labor hard
Mov'd on, with difficulty and labor he.
MILTON—*Paradise Lost.* Bk. II. L. 1021.

9
Ardua molimur; sed nulla nisi ardua virtus.
I attempt a difficult work; but there is no excellence without difficulty.
OVID—*Ars Amatoria.* II. 537.

10
Men might as well have hunted an hare with a tabre.
Richard the Redeles. (1399)

11
It is as hard to come as for a camel
To thread the postern of a small needle's eye.
Richard II. Act V. Sc. 5. L. 16.

12
Nil tam difficile quin quærendo investigari possiet.
Nothing is so difficult but that it may be found out by seeking.
TERENCE—*Heauton timoroumenos.* IV. 2. 8.
HERRICK—*Hesperides.* No. 1009. *Seek and Find.*

13
Nulla est tam facilis res, quin difficilis siet,
Quum invitus facias.
There is nothing so easy in itself but grows difficult when it is performed against one's will.
TERENCE—*Heauton timoroumenos.* IV. 6. 1.

14
There is such a choice of difficulties, that I own myself at a loss how to determine.
JAMES WOLFE—*Dispatch to Pitt.* Sept. 2, 1759.

DIGNITY

15
Remember this,—that there is a proper dignity and proportion to be observed in the performance of every act of life.
MARCUS AURELIUS—*Meditations.* IV. 32.

16
Otium cum dignitate.
Ease with dignity.
CICERO—*Oratio Pro Publio Sextio.* XLV.

17
The dignity of truth is lost
With much protesting.
BEN JONSON—*Catiline.* Act III. Sc. 2.

18
* * * With grave
Aspect he rose, and in his rising seem'd
A pillar of state; deep on his front engraven
Deliberation sat, and public care;
And princely counsel in his face yet shone
Majestic, though in ruin: sage he stood,
With Atlantéan shoulders, fit to bear
The weight of mightiest monarchies; his look
Drew audience and attention still as night
Or summer's noontide air.
MILTON—*Paradise Lost.* Bk. II. L. 300.

19
We have exchanged the Washingtonian dignity for the Jeffersonian simplicity, which was in truth only another name for the Jeffersonian vulgarity.
BISHOP HENRY C. POTTER—*Address at the Washington Centennial Service.* New York, April 30, 1889.

20
Facilius crescit dignitas quam incipit.
Dignity increases more easily than it begins.
SENECA—*Epistolæ Ad Lucilium.* CI.

21
But clay and clay differs in dignity,
Whose dust is both alike.
Cymbeline. Act IV. Sc. 2. L. 6.

22
Let none presume
To wear an undeserved dignity.
Merchant of Venice. Act II. Sc. 9. L. 39.

23
True dignity abides with him alone
Who, in the silent hour of inward thought,
Can still suspect, and still revere himself,
In lowliness of heart.
WORDSWORTH—*Lines left upon a seat in a Yew Tree.* Same idea in BEATTIE—*Minstrel.* II. St. 12.

24
Revere thyself, and yet thyself despise.
YOUNG—*Night Thoughts.* VI. 128.

DIMPLES

25
Then did she lift her hands unto his chin,
And praised the pretty dimpling of his skin.
BEAUMONT—*Salmacis and Hermaphroditus.* L. 661.

26
In each cheek appears a pretty dimple;
Love made those hollows; if himself were slain,
He might be buried in a tomb so simple;
Foreknowing well, if there he came to lie,
Why, there Love lived and there he could not die.
Venus and Adonis. L. 242.

DIPLOMACY (See STATESMANSHIP)

DISAPPOINTMENT

1
But evil fortune has decreed,
(The foe of mice as well as men)
The royal mouse at last should bleed,
Should fall—ne'er to arise again.
MICHAEL BRUCE—*Musiad.*

2
The best-laid schemes o' mice an' men,
Gang aft a-gley,
And leave us nought but grief and pain,
For promised joy.
BURNS—*To a Mouse.* St. 7. MRS. BARBAULD—*Rose's Petition.* DRYDEN—*Hide and Panther.* POPE—*Imitation of Horace.* Bk. II. Satire 6.
(See also BLAIR under FAME)

3
Like to the apples on the Dead Sea's shore,
All ashes to the taste.
BYRON—*Childe Harold.* III. 34.

4
As distant prospects please us, but when near
We find but desert rocks and fleeting air.
SAM'L GARTH—*The Dispensary.* Canto III. L. 27.

5
Lightly I sped when hope was high
And youth beguiled the chase,—
I follow, follow still: But I
Shall never see her face.
FRED'K LOCKER-LAMPSON.—*The Unrealized Ideal.*

6
But O! as to embrace me she inclin'd,
I wak'd, she fled, and day brought back my night.
MILTON—*On His Deceased Wife.*

7
Sed ut acerbum est, pro benefactis quom malis messem metas!

It is a bitter disappointment when you have sown benefits, to reap injuries.
PLAUTUS—*Epidicus.* V. 2. 52.

8
All is but toys; renown and grace is dead;
The wine of life is drawn, and the mere lees
Is left this vault to brag of.
Macbeth. Act II. Sc. 3. L. 99.

DISCONTENT

9
In such a strait the wisest may well be perplexed, and the boldest staggered.
BURKE—*Thoughts on the Cause of the Present Discontents.* Vol. I. P. 516.

10
Whoe'er was edified, themselves were not.
COWPER—*Task.* Bk. II. *The Time Piece.* L. 444.

11
The best things beyond their measure cloy.
HOMER—*Iliad.* Bk. XIII. L. 795. POPE'S trans.

12
Qui fit, Mæcenas, ut nemo quam sibi sortem,
Seu ratio dederit, seu fors objecerit, illa
Contentus vivat? laudet diversa sequentes.

How does it happen, Mæcenas, that no one is content with that lot in life which he has chosen, or which chance has thrown in his way, but praises those who follow a different course?
HORACE—*Satires.* I. 1. 1.

13
Æstuat infelix angusto limite mundi.

Unhappy man! He frets at the narrow limits of the world.
JUVENAL—*Satires.* X. 168.

14
To sigh, yet feel no pain,
To weep, yet scarce know why;
To sport an hour with Beauty's chain,
Then throw it idly by.
MOORE—*The Blue Stocking.*

15
Past and to come seem best; things present worst.
Henry IV. Pt. II. Act I. Sc. 3. L. 108.

16
I see your brows are full of discontent,
Your hearts of sorrow and your eyes of tears.
Richard II. Act IV. Sc. I. L. 331.

17
I know a discontented gentleman,
Whose humble means match not his haughty mind.
Richard III. Act IV. Sc. 2. L. 36.

18
We love in others what we lack ourselves, and would be everything but what we are.
R. H. STODDARD—*Arcadian Idyl.* L. 30.

19
I was *born* to other things.
TENNYSON—*In Memoriam.* CXX.

20
The thirst to know and understand,
A large and liberal discontent;
These are the goods in life's rich hand,
The things that are more excellent.
WILLIAM WATSON—*Things That Are More Excellent.* St. 8.

21
And from the discontent of man
The world's best progress springs.
ELLA WHEELER WILCOX—*Discontent.*

22
Discontent is the first step in the progress of a man or a nation.
OSCAR WILDE—*Woman of No Importance.* Act II.

23
Poor in abundance, famish'd at a feast.
YOUNG—*Night Thoughts.* Night VII. L. 44.

DISCRETION

24
It shew'd discretion, the best part of valor.
BEAUMONT AND FLETCHER—*A King and No King.* Act IV. Sc. 3.
(See also HENRY IV)

25
As a jewel of gold in a swine's snout, so is a fair woman which is without discretion.
Proverbs. XI. 22.

26
Let your own discretion be your tutor: suit the action to the word, the word to the action.
Hamlet. Act III. Sc. 2. L. 18.

1
The better part of valour is discretion; in the which better part I have saved my life.
Henry IV. Pt. I. Act V. Sc. 4. L. 121.
(See also BEAUMONT)

2
Covering discretion with a coat of folly.
Henry V. Act II. Sc. 4. L. 38.

3
I have seen the day of wrong through the little hole of discretion.
Love's Labour's Lost. Act V. Sc. 2. L. 733.

4
For 'tis not good that children should know any wickedness: old folks, you know, have discretion, as they say, and know the world.
Merry Wives of Windsor. Act II. Sc. 2. L. 131.

5
Let's teach ourselves that honourable stop,
Not to outsport discretion.
Othello. Act II. Sc. 3. L. 2.

DISEASE (See also MEDICINE, SICKNESS)

6
The remedy is worse than the disease.
BACON—*Of Seditions*. BUCKINGHAM—*Speech in House of Lords*, 1675. DRYDEN—*Juvenal*. Satire XVI. L. 31. LE SAGE—*Gil Blas*. Bk. XII. Ch. VIII. MIDDLETON—*Family of Love*. Act V. Sc. 3.
(See also SYRUS, also VERGIL under MEDICINE)

7
[Diseases] crucify the soul of man, attenuate our bodies, dry them, wither them, shrivel them up like old apples, make them as so many anatomies.
BURTON—*Anatomy of Melancholy*. Pt. I. Sc. 2. Memb. 3. Subsect. 10.

8
Apoplexie, and *Lethargie*,
As forlorn hope, assault the enemy.
DU BARTAS—*Divine Weekes and Workes*. Second Week. First Day. Pt. III. *The Furies*.

9
Disease is an experience of so-called mortal mind. It is fear made manifest on the body. Divine Science takes away this physical sense of discord, just as it removes a sense of moral or mental inharmony.
MARY B. G. EDDY—*Science and Health*, 493: 20.

10
That dire disease, whose ruthless power
Withers the beauty's transient flower.
GOLDSMITH—*Double Transformation*. L. 75.

11
A bodily disease which we look upon as whole and entire within itself, may, after all, be but a symptom of some ailment in the spiritual part.
NATH. HAWTHORNE—*Scarlet Letter*. Ch. X.
(See also PLINY)

12
Against diseases here the strongest fence,
Is the defensive vertue, abstinence.
HERRICK—*Abstinence*.

13
Extreme remedies are very appropriate for extreme diseases.
HIPPOCRATES—*Aphorisms*. 6.
(See also HAMLET)

14
D'ogni pianta palesa l'aspetto
Il difetto, che il tronco nasconde
Per le fronde, dal frutto, o dal fior.
The canker which the trunk conceals is revealed by the leaves, the fruit, or the flower.
METASTASIO—*Giuseppe Riconosciuto*. I.

15
Aëre non certo corpora languor habet.
Sickness seizes the body from bad ventilation.
OVID—*Ars Amatoria*. II. 310.

16
Vitiant artus ægræ contagia mentis.
Diseases of the mind impair the bodily powers.
OVID—*Tristium*. III. 8. 25.
(See also PLINY)

17
Utque in corporibus, sic in imperio, gravissimus est morbus qui a capite diffunditur.
And as in men's bodies, so in government, that disease is most serious which proceeds from the head.
PLINY THE YOUNGER. *Ep*. Bk. IV. 22.
SENECA—*De Clementia*. Bk. II. 2.
(See also EDDY, HAWTHORNE, OVID)

18
As man, perhaps, the moment of his breath,
Receives the lurking principle of death,
The young disease, that must subdue at length,
Grows with his growth, and strengthens with his strength.
POPE—*Essay on Man*. Ep. II. L. 133.

19
But just disease to luxury succeeds,
And ev'ry death its own avenger breeds.
POPE—*Essay on Man*. Ep. III. L. 165.

20
O, he's a limb, that has but a disease;
Mortal, to cut it off; to cure it, easy.
Coriolanus. Act III. Sc. 1. L. 296.

21
Diseases desperate grown,
By desperate appliance are reliev'd,
Or not at all.
Hamlet. Act IV. Sc. 3. L. 9.
(See also HIPPOCRATES)

22
This apoplexy is, as I take it, a kind of lethargy, an't please your lordship; a kind of sleeping in the blood, a whoreson tingling.
Henry IV. Pt. II. Act I. Sc. 2. L. 125.

23
Before the curing of a strong disease,
Even in the instant of repair and health,
The fit is strongest; evils that take leave,
On their departure most of all show evil.
King John. Act III. Sc. 4. L. 112.

24
I'll forbear;
And am fallen out with my more headier will,
To take the indispos'd and sickly fit
For the sound man.
King Lear. Act II. Sc. 4. L. 110.

25
Graviora quædam sunt remedia periculis.
Some remedies are worse than the disease.
SYRUS—*Maxims*. 301.
(See also BACON)

DISGRACE

1
Come, Death, and snatch me from disgrace.
Bulwer-Lytton—*Richelieu.* Act IV. Sc. 1.

2
The unbought grace of life, the cheap defence of nations, the nurse of manly sentiment and heroic enterprise, is gone!
Burke—*Reflections on the Revolution in France.*

3
Could he with reason murmur at his case,
Himself sole author of his own disgrace?
Cowper—*Hope.* L. 316.

4
Id demum est homini turpe, quod meruit pati.
That only is a disgrace to a man which he has deserved to suffer.
Phædrus—*Fables.* III. 11. 7.

5
Hominum immortalis est infamia;
Etiam tum vivit, cum esse credas mortuam.
Disgrace is immortal, and living even when one thinks it dead.
Plautus—*Persa.* III. 1. 27.

6
And wilt thou still be hammering treachery,
To tumble down thy husband and thyself
From top of honour to disgrace's feet?
Henry VI. Pt. II. Act I. Sc. 2. L. 47.

DISSENSION (See also Contention, Quarreling)

7
Have always been at daggers-drawing,
And one another clapper-clawing.
Butler—*Hudibras.* Pt. II. Canto II. L. 79.

8
That each pull'd different ways with many an oath,
"Arcades ambo," *id est*—blackguards both.
Byron—*Don Juan.* Canto IV. St. 93.

9
And Doubt and Discord step 'twixt thine and thee.
Byron—*The Prophecy of Dante.* Canto II. L. 140.

10
Dissensions, like small streams, are first begun,
Scarce seen they rise, but gather as they run:
So lines that from their parallel decline,
More they proceed the more they still disjoin.
Sam'l Garth—*The Dispensary.* Canto III. L. 184.

11
And bitter waxed the fray;
Brother with brother spake no word
When they met in the way.
Jean Ingelow—*Poems. Strife and Peace.*

12
An old affront will stir the heart
Through years of rankling pain.
Jean Ingelow—*Poems. Strife and Peace.*

13
Alas! how light a cause may move
Dissension between hearts that love!
Hearts that the world in vain had tried,
And sorrow but more closely tied;
That stood the storm when waves were rough,
Yet in a sunny hour fall off.
Moore—*Lalla Rookh. The Light of the Harem.* L. 183.

14
Believe me, lords, my tender years can tell
Civil dissension is a viperous worm
That gnaws the bowels of the commonwealth.
Henry VI. Pt. I. Act III. Sc. 1. L. 71.

15
If they perceive dissension in our looks
And that within ourselves we disagree,
How will their grudging stomachs be provoked
To wilful disobedience and rebel!
Henry VI. Pt. I. Act IV. Sc. 1. L. 139.

16
Discord, a sleepless hag who never dies,
With Snipe-like nose, and Ferret-glowing eyes,
Lean sallow cheeks, long chin with beard supplied,
Poor crackling joints, and wither'd parchment hide,
As if old Drums, worn out with martial din,
Had clubb'd their yellow Heads to form her Skin.
John Wolcot—*The Louisad.* Canto III. L. 121.

DISTRUST

17
Usurpator diffida
Di tutti sempre.
A usurper always distrusts the whole world.
Alfieri—*Polinice.* III. 2.

18
What loneliness is more lonely than distrust?
George Eliot—*Middlemarch.* Bk. V. Ch. XLIV.

19
When desperate ills demand a speedy cure,
Distrust is cowardice, and prudence folly.
Samuel Johnson—*Irene.* Act IV. Sc. 1. L. 87.

20
A certain amount of distrust is wholesome, but not so much of others as of ourselves; neither vanity nor conceit can exist in the same atmosphere with it.
Madame Necker.

21
Three things a wise man will not trust,
The wind, the sunshine of an April day,
And woman's plighted faith.
Southey—*Madoc in Azthan.* Pt. XXIII. L. 51.

DOCTRINE

22
For his religion, it was fit
To match his learning and his wit;
'Twas Presbyterian true blue;
For he was of that stubborn crew
Of errant saints, whom all men grant
To be the true Church Militant;
Such as do build their faith upon
The holy text of pike and gun;
Decide all controversies by
Infallible artillery;
And prove their doctrine orthodox,
By Apostolic blows and knocks.
Butler—*Hudibras.* Pt. I. Canto I. L. 189.

23
What makes all doctrines plain and clear?—
About two hundred pounds a year.
And that which was prov'd true before
Prove false again? Two hundred more.
Butler—*Hudibras.* Pt. III. Canto I. L. 1,277.

1
He was the word that spake it,
He took the bread and brake it;
And what that word did make it,
I do believe and take it.

DONNE—*Divine Poems. On the Sacrament.* FLESHER'S Ed. 1654. P. 352. Found earlier in CAMDEN'S *Remains.*

2
'Twas God the word that spake it,
He took the bread and brake it,
And what the word did make it,
That I believe and take it.

QUEEN ELIZABETH. In CLARK—*Ecclesiastical History. Life of Queen Elizabeth.* P. 94 (edition 1675), quoting the queen when asked her opinion of Christ's presence in the Sacrament. FOXE—*Acts and Monuments.* FULLER—*Holy State.* Bk. IV. P. 302. (Ed. 1648) RAPIN—*History of England.* Vol. II. P. 42. 1733. Given also "Christ was the word." Generally attributed to ANNE ASKEW. Also to LADY JANE GREY in SIR H. NICOLAS' *Life and Remains.*

3
O how far remov'd,
Predestination! is thy foot from such
As see not the First Cause entire: and ye,
O mortal men! be wary how ye judge:
For we, who see the Maker, know not yet
The number of the chosen; and esteem
Such scantiness of knowledge our delight:
For all our good is, in that primal good,
Concentrate; and God's will and ours are one.

DANTE—*Vision of Paradise.* Canto XX. L. 122.

4
The Athanasian Creed is the most splendid ecclesiastical lyric ever poured forth by the genius of man.

BENJ. DISRAELI—*Endymion.* Ch. LIV

5
You can and you can't,
You will and you won't;
You'll be damn'd if you do,
You'll be damn'd if you don't.

LORENZO DOW—*Chain* (*Definition of Calvinism*).

6
And after hearing what our Church can say,
If still our reason runs another way,
That private reason 'tis more just to curb,
Than by disputes the public peace disturb;
For points obscure are of small use to learn,
But common quiet is mankind's concern.

DRYDEN—*Religio Laici.* L. 445.

7
Carried about with every wind of doctrine.

Ephesians. IV. 14.

8
Die Theologie ist die Anthropologie.

Theology is Anthropology.

FEUERBACH—*Wesen des Christenthums.*

9
Thus this brook hath conveyed his ashes into Avon, Avon into Severn, Severn into the narrow seas, they into the main ocean. And thus the ashes of Wickliffe are the emblem of his doctrine, which now is dispersed all the world over.

FULLER—*Church History.* Sec. II. Bk. IV. Par. 53. Wickliffe's body was burned, the ashes thrown into the brook Swift, by order of the Council of Constance, 1415.

(See also WEBSTER, WORDSWORTH)

10
Shall I ask the brave soldier, who fights by my side
In the cause of mankind, if our creeds agree?
Shall I give up the friend I have valued and tried,
If he kneel not before the same altar with me?
From the heretic girl of my soul should I fly,
To seek somewhere else a more orthodox kiss?
No! perish the hearts, and the laws that try
Truth, valour, or love, by a standard like this!

MOORE—*Irish Melodies. Come Send Round the Wine.*

11
"Orthodoxy, my Lord," said Bishop Warburton, in a whisper,—"orthodoxy is my doxy,—heterodoxy is another man's doxy."

JOSEPH PRIESTLY—*Memoirs.* Vol. I. P. 572.

12
Live to explain thy doctrine by thy life.

PRIOR—*To Dr. Sherlock. On his Practical Discourse Concerning Death.*

13
The Avon to the Severn runs,
The Severn, to the sea,
And Wickliff's dust shall spread abroad
Wide as the waters be.

DANIEL WEBSTER—Quoted in an Address before the Sons of New Hampshire. (1849)

(See also FULLER)

14
As thou these ashes, little brook! will bear
Into the Avon, Avon to the tide
Of Severn, Severn to the narrow seas,
Into main ocean they, this deed accurst,
An emblem yields to friends and enemies
How the bold teacher's doctrine, sanctified
By truth, shall spread throughout the world dispersed.

WORDSWORTH—*Ecclesiastical Sketches.* Pt. II. *Wicliffe.* (See also FULLER)

DOG

15
Non stuzzicare il can che dorme.

Do not disturb the sleeping dog.

ALESSANDRO ALLEGRI—*Rime e Prose.*

16
Il fait mal éveiller le chien qi dort.

It is bad to awaken a sleeping dog.

From a MS. of 13th Cen. in LE ROUX DE LINCY'S Collection, Vol. I. P. 108; Vol. II. P. 392. *La Guerre de Genève.* Poem. (1534) FRANCK—*Sprichwörter.* (1541) An earlier version in IGNAZ VON ZINGERLE—*Sprichwörter im Mittelalter.* For Earlier idea, with cat substituted; see GABRIEL MEURIER—*Trésor des Sentences;* NUÑEZ DE GUZMAN—*Refranes, Salamanca.* Wake not a sleeping lion. COUNTRYMAN'S *New Commonwealth.* (1647) Wake not a sleeping wolf. *Henry IV.* Pt. II. Act I. Sc. 2. L. 174. *Henry VIII* Act I. Sc. I. L. 121.

(See also CHAUCER)

17
He was such a dear little cock-tailed pup.

BARHAM—*Mr. Peter's Story.*

1
Qui me amat, amet et canem meum.
Who loves me will love my dog also.
St. Bernard of Clairvaux—*Sermo Primus.* Chapman—*Widows' Tears.* Erasmus—*Adagia.* Heywood—*Proverbs.* Pt. II. Ch. IX.
(See also Le Roux de Lincy, More)

2
Mother of dead dogs.
Quoted by Carlyle in *Reminiscences.* Vol. I. P. 257; Vol. II. P. 54. Froude's ed. Also in *Life in London.* (Froude.) Vol. I. P. 196.

3
On the green banks of Shannon, when Sheelah was nigh,
No blithe Irish lad was so happy as I;
No harp like my own could so cheerily play,
And wherever I went was my poor dog Tray.
Campbell—*The Harper.*
(See also Foster)

4
His faithful dog salutes the smiling guest.
Campbell—*Pleasures of Hope.* Pt. I. L. 86.

5
It is nought good a sleeping hound to wake.
Chaucer—*Troylus and Crysede.* III. 764.
(See also Bernard)

6
A living dog is better than a dead lion.
Ecclesiastes. IX. 4.

7
Old dog Tray's ever faithful;
Grief can not drive him away;
He is gentle, he is kind—
I shall never, never find
A better friend than old dog Tray!
Stephen C. Foster—*Old Dog Tray.*
(See also Campbell)

8
And in that town a dog was found,
As many dogs there be,
Both mongrel, puppy, whelp and hound,
And curs of low degree.
Goldsmith—*Elegy on the Death of a Mad Dog.*

9
Plus on apprend a connaître l'homme, plus on apprend à estimer le chien.
The more one comes to know men, the more one comes to admire the dog.
Joussenel, quoted by Paul Franche—*La Legende Doreé des Bêtes.* P. 191. The saying is attributed generally to Mme. de Sévigné. Belloy—*Siege de Calais,* says: Ce qu'il y a de mieux dans l'homme, c'est le chien. Quoted in this form by Voltaire.
(See also Lamartine)

10
Is thy servant a dog, that he should do this great thing?
II Kings. VIII. 13.

11
There is sorrow enough in the natural way
From men and women to fill our day;
But when we are certain of sorrow in store
Why do we always arrange for more?
Brothers and sisters I bid you beware
Of giving your heart to a dog to tear.
Kipling—*The Power of the Dog.*

12
Plus je vois des représentants du peuple, plus j'aime mes chiens.
The more I see the representatives of the people, the more I love my dogs.
Lamartine. Quoted in a letter from Comte Alfred D'Orsay to John Forster. (1850) See *Notes and Queries,* Oct. 3, 1908. P. 273.
(See also Joussenel)

13
Qui m'aime il aime mon chien.
Who loves me loves my dog.
Le Roux de Lincy—*French Proverbs.* Gives date 13th Cent. In *Tresor de Jeh. de Meung.* Vers. 1,567.
(See also Bernard)

14
But in some canine Paradise
Your wraith, I know, rebukes the moon,
And quarters every plain and hill,
Seeking its master. * * * As for me
This prayer at least the gods fulfill
That when I pass the flood and see
Old Charon by Stygian coast
Take toll of all the shades who land,
Your little, faithful barking ghost
May leap to lick my phantom hand.
St. John Lucas—*To a Dog.*

15
The dogs eat of the crumbs which fall from their masters' table.
Matthew. XV. 27.

16
Whosoever loveth me loveth my hound.
Sir Thomas More—*First Sermon on the Lord's Prayer.*
(See also Bernard)

17
The dog is turned to his own vomit again.
II Peter. II. 22.

18
To be, contents his natural desire,
He asks no angel's wing, no seraph's fire;
But thinks, admitted to that equal sky,
His faithful dog shall bear him company.
Go wiser thou! and in thy scale of sense
Weigh thy opinion against Providence.
Pope—*Essay on Man.* Ep. I. L. 109.

19
I am his Highness' dog at Kew;
Pray tell me, sir, whose dog are you?
Pope—*Epigrams. On the Collar of a Dog.*

20
Histories are more full of examples of the fidelity of dogs than of friends.
Pope—*Letters to and from H. Cromwell, Esq. Letter X.* Oct. 9, 1709.

21
Canis timidus vehementius latrat quam mordet.
The cowardly dog barks more violently than it bites.
Quintus Curtius—*De Rebus Best. Alexand. Magn.* VII. 14.

22
I have a dog of Blenheim birth,
With fine long ears and full of mirth;
And sometimes, running o'er the plain,
He tumbles on his nose:
But quickly jumping up again,
Like lightning on he goes!
Ruskin—*My Dog Dash.*

1 The little dogs and all,
Tray, Blanche, and Sweetheart, see, they bark at me.
King Lear. Act III. Sc. 6. L. 65.

2
Thou hast seen a farmer's dog bark at a beggar?
King Lear. Act IV. Sc. 6. L. 159.

3
We are two travellers, Roger and I.
Roger's my dog—come here, you scamp!
Jump for the gentleman—mind your eye!
Over the table,—look out for the lamp!
The rogue is growing a little old;
Five years we've tramped through wind and weather,
And slept out-doors when nights were cold,
And ate and drank and starved together.
JOHN T. TROWBRIDGE—*The Vagabonds*.

4
Gentlemen of the Jury: The one, absolute, unselfish friend that man can have in this selfish world, the one that never deserts him, the one that never proves ungrateful or treacherous, is his dog.
Senator GEO. GRAHAM VEST—*Eulogy on the Dog*. Found in ELBERT HUBBARD'S *Pig-Pen Pete*. P. 178.

DOON (RIVER)

5
Ye banks and braes o' bonny Doon,
How can ye bloom sae fresh and fair;
How can ye chant, ye little birds,
And I sae weary fu' o' care!
BURNS—*The Banks o' Doon*.

DOUBT

6
Who never doubted, never half believed.
Where doubt there truth is—'tis her shadow.
BAILEY—*Festus*. Sc. *A Country Town*.

7
He would not, with a peremptory tone,
Assert the nose upon his face his own.
COWPER—*Conversation*. L. 121.

8
Non menno che saper, dubbiar m'aggrata.
Doubting charms me not less than knowledge.
DANTE—*Inferno*. XI. 93.

9 Uncertain ways unsafest are,
And doubt a greater mischief than despair.
SIR JOHN DENHAM—*Cooper's Hill*. L. 399.

10
Vous ne prouvez que trop que chercher à connaître
N'est souvent qu' apprendre à douter.
You prove but too clearly that seeking to know
Is too frequently learning to doubt.
MME. DESHOULIÈRES.

11
Doubt indulged soon becomes doubt realized.
F. R. HAVERGAL—*Royal Bounty. The Imagination of the Thoughts of the Heart*.

12
When in doubt, win the trick.
HOYLE—*Twenty-four rules for Learners*. Rule 12.

13
He who dallies is a dastard,
He who doubts is damned.
Attributed to GEORGE MCDUFFLE, of South Carolina, during the "Nullification" period. Used by JAMES HAMILTON, when Governor of South Carolina. Also quoted by J. C. S. BLACKBURN, of Kentucky, in Congress, Feb. 1877, during the HAYES-TILDEN dispute. Appeared in the *Louisville Courier-Journal* (COL. WATTERSON, editor), during same dispute.
(See also ROMANS. XIV. 23)

14 But the gods are dead—
Ay, Zeus is dead, and all the gods but Doubt,
And doubt is brother devil to Despair!
JOHN BOYLE O'REILLY—*Prometheus. Christ*.

15
The doubtful beam long nods from side to side.
POPE—*Rape of the Lock*. Canto V. L. 73.

16
Fain would I but dare not; I dare, and yet I may not;
I may, although I care not for pleasure when I play not.
SIR WALTER RALEIGH—*A Lover's Verses*.

17
And he that doubteth is damned if he eat.
Romans. XIV. 23.

18
But yet, madam—
I do not like, "but yet," it does allay
The good precedence; fie upon "but yet!"
"But yet" is a gaoler to bring forth
Some monstrous malefactor.
Antony and Cleopatra. Act II. Sc. 5. L. 49.

19
To be, or not to be, that is the question:
Whether 'tis nobler in the mind to suffer
The slings and arrows of outrageous fortune;
Or to take arms against a sea of troubles,
And by opposing end them?
Hamlet. Act III. Sc. 1. L. 56.

20
But now I am cabin'd, cribb'd, confin'd, bound in
To saucy doubts and fears.
Macbeth. Act III. Sc. 4. L. 24.

21
Our doubts are traitors
And make us lose the good we oft might win
By fearing to attempt.
Measure for Measure. Act I. Sc. 4. L. 77.

22 To be once in doubt
Is once to be resolv'd.
Othello. Act III. Sc. 3. L. 179.

23 No hinge nor loop,
To hang a doubt on;
Othello. Act III. Sc. 3. L. 366.

24 Modest doubt is call'd
The beacon of the wise.
Troilus and Cressida. Act II. Sc. 2. L. 15.

25
To believe with certainty we must begin with doubting.
STANISLAUS (King of Poland)—*Maxims and Moral Sentences*. No. 61.

1
There lives more faith in honest doubt,
Believe me, than in half the creeds.
TENNYSON—*In Memoriam.* Pt. XCV. St. 3.

2
I follow my law and fulfil it all duly—and look!
when your doubt runneth high—
North points to the needle!
EDITH M. THOMAS—*The Compass.*

DOVE

3
And there my little doves did sit
With feathers softly brown
And glittering eyes that showed their right
To general Nature's deep delight.
E. B. BROWNING—*My Doves.*

4
The thrustelcok made eek hir lay,
The wode dove upon the spray
She sang ful loude and cleere.
CHAUCER—*The Rime of Sir Thopas.*

5
As when the dove returning bore the mark
Of earth restored to the long labouring ark;
The relics of mankind, secure at rest,
Oped every window to receive the guest,
And the fair bearer of the message bless'd.
DRYDEN—*To Her Grace of Ormond.* L. 70.

6
Listen, sweet Dove, unto my song,
And spread thy golden wings in me;
Hatching my tender heart so long,
Till it get wing, and flie away with Thee.
HERBERT—*The Church. Whitsunday.*

7
We roar all like bears, and mourn sore like doves.
Isaiah. LIX. 11.

8
See how that pair of billing doves
With open murmurs own their loves
And, heedless of censorious eyes,
Pursue their unpolluted joys:
No fears of future want molest
The downy quiet of their nest.
LADY MARY WORTLEY MONTAGU—*Verses. Written in a Garden.* St. 1.

9
The Dove,
On silver pinions, winged her peaceful way.
MONTGOMERY—*Pelican Island.* Canto I. L. 173.

10
Ut solet accipiter trepidas agitare columbas.
As the hawk is wont to pursue the trembling doves.
OVID—*Metamorphoses.* V. 606.

11
Not half so swift the trembling doves can fly,
When the fierce eagle cleaves the liquid sky;
Not half so swiftly the fierce eagle moves,
When thro' the clouds he drives the trembling doves.
POPE—*Windsor Forest.* L. 185.

12
Oh that I had wings like a dove! for then would I fly away, and be at rest.
Psalms. LV. 6.

13
Anon, as patient as the female dove,
When that her golden couplets are disclosed,
His silence will sit drooping.
Hamlet. Act V. Sc. 1. L. 309.

14
The dove and very blessed spirit of peace.
Henry IV. Pt. II. Act IV. Sc. 1. L. 46.

15
So shows a snowy dove trooping with crows.
Romeo and Juliet. Act I. Sc. 5. L. 50.

16
And oft I heard the tender dove
In firry woodlands making moan.
TENNYSON—*Miller's Daughter.*

17
I heard a Stock-dove sing or say
His homely tale, this very day;
His voice was buried among trees,
Yet to be come at by the breeze:
He did not cease; but cooed—and cooed;
And somewhat pensively he wooed:
He sang of love, with quiet blending,
Slow to begin, and never ending;
Of serious faith, and inward glee;
That was the song,—the song for me!
WORDSWORTH—*O Nightingale! Thou Surely Art.*

DOVE (RIVER)

18
Oh, my beloved nymph, fair Dove,
Princess of rivers, how I love
Upon thy flowery banks to lie,
And view thy silver stream,
When gilded by a summer's beam!
And in it all thy wanton fry,
Playing at liberty;
And with my angle, upon them
The all of treachery
I ever learned, industriously to try!
CHARLES COTTON—*The Retirement.* L. 34.

DREAMS

19
When to soft Sleep we give ourselves away,
And in a dream as in a fairy bark
Drift on and on through the enchanted dark
To purple daybreak—little thought we pay
To that sweet bitter world we know by day.
T. B. ALDRICH—*Sonnet. Sleep.*

20
Sweet sleep be with us, one and all!
And if upon its stillness fall
The visions of a busy brain,
We'll have our pleasure o'er again,
To warm the heart, to charm the sight,
Gay dreams to all! good night, good night.
JOANNA BAILLIE—*The Phantom. Song.*

21
If there were dreams to sell,
Merry and sad to tell,
And the crier rung his bell,
What would you buy?
THOMAS LOVELL BEDDOES—*Dream-Pedlary.*

22
"Come to me, darling; I'm lonely without thee;
Daytime and nighttime I'm dreaming about thee."
JOSEPH BRENAN—*The Exile To His Wife.*

1
Oft morning dreams presage approaching fate,
For morning dreams, as poets tell, are true.
MICHAEL BRUCE—*Elegy on Spring.*
(See also OVID, RHODES)

2
I dreamt that I dwelt in marble halls,
With vassals and serfs at my side.
ALFRED BUNN—Song from *Bohemian Girl.*

3
I had a dream, which was not all a dream.
BYRON—*Darkness.*

4
And dreams in their development have breath,
And tears, and tortures, and the touch of joy;
They have a weight upon our waking thoughts,
They take a weight from off our waking toils,
They do divide our being.
BYRON—*The Dream.* St. 1.

5
A change came o'er the spirit of my dream.
BYRON—*The Dream.* St. 3.

6
The fisher droppeth his net in the stream,
And a hundred streams are the same as one;
And the maiden dreameth her love-lit dream;
And what is it all, when all is done?
The net of the fisher the burden breaks,
And always the dreaming the dreamer wakes.
ALICE CARY—*Lover's Diary.*

7
Again let us dream where the land lies sunny
And live, like the bees, on our hearts' old honey,
Away from the world that slaves for money—
Come, journey the way with me.
MADISON CAWEIN—*Song of the Road.*

8
Like the dreams,
Children of night, of indigestion bred.
CHURCHILL—*The Candidate.* L. 784.

9
My eyes make pictures, when they are shut.
COLERIDGE—*A Day Dream.*

10
And so, his senses gradually wrapt
In a half sleep, he dreams of better worlds,
And dreaming hears thee still, O singing lark;
That singest like an angel in the clouds.
COLERIDGE—*Fears in Solitude.* L. 25.

11
Dream after dream ensues;
And still they dream that they shall still succeed;
And still are disappointed.
COWPER—*Task.* Bk. III. L. 127.

12
Dreams are but interludes, which fancy makes;
When monarch reason sleeps, this mimic wakes.
DRYDEN—*Fables. The Cock and the Fox.* L. 325.

13
In blissful dream, in silent night,
There came to me, with magic might,
With magic might, my own sweet love,
Into my little room above.
HEINE—*Youthful Sorrows.* Pt. VI. St. 1.

14
Fly, dotard, fly!
With thy wise dreams and fables of the sky.
HOMER—*The Odyssey.* Bk. II. L. 207. POPE'S trans.

15
Some dreams we have are nothing else but dreams,
Unnatural and full of contradictions;
Yet others of our most romantic schemes
Are something more than fictions.
HOOD—*The Haunted House.* Pt. I.

16
And the dream that our mind had sketched in haste
Shall others continue, but never complete.
For none upon earth can achieve his scheme;
The best as the worst are futile here:
We wake at the self-same point of the dream,—
All is here begun, and finished elsewhere.
VICTOR HUGO—*Early Love Revisited.*

17
Abou Ben Adhem (may his tribe increase!)
Awoke one night from a deep dream of peace.
LEIGH HUNT—*Abou Ben Adhem.*

18
Your old men shall dream dreams, your young men shall see visions.
Joel. II. 28.

19
There's a long, long trail a-winding
Into the land of my dreams,
Where the nightingales are singing
And a white moon beams;
There's a long, long night of waiting
Until my dreams all come true,
Till the day when I'll be going down that
Long, long trail with you.
STODDARD KING—*There's a Long, Long Trail.*
(Popular in the Great War.)

20
Ever of thee I'm fondly dreaming,
Thy gentle voice my spirit can cheer.
GEORGE LINLEY—*Ever of Thee.*

21
'Twas but a dream,—let it pass,—let it vanish like so many others!
What I thought was a flower is only a weed, and is worthless.
LONGFELLOW—*Courtship of Miles Standish.* Pt. VII.

22
Is this is a dream? O, if it be a dream,
Let me sleep on, and do not wake me yet!
LONGFELLOW—*Spanish Student.* Act III. Sc. 5.

23
For dhrames always go by conthraries, my dear.
SAMUEL LOVER—*Rory O'More.* GOLDSMITH—*Citizen of the World.* No. 46.

24
Ground not upon dreams, you know they are ever contrary.
THOS. MIDDLETON—*The Family of Love.* Act IV. Sc. 3.

25
I believe it to be true that Dreams are the true Interpreters of our Inclinations; but there is Art required to sort and understand them.
MONTAIGNE—*Essays.* Bk. III. Ch. XIII.

26
One of those passing rainbow dreams,
Half light, half shade, which fancy's beams
Paint on the fleeting mists that roll,
In trance or slumber, round the soul!
MOORE—*Lalla Rookh. Fire Worshippers.* St. 54.

1
Oh! that a dream so sweet, so long enjoy'd,
Should be so sadly, cruelly destroy'd!
MOORE—*Lalla Rookh. Veiled Prophet of Khorassan.* St. 62.

2
A thousand creeds and battle cries,
A thousand warring social schemes,
A thousand new moralities
And twenty thousand, thousand dreams.
ALFRED NOYES—*Forward.*

3
I am weary of planning and toiling
In the crowded hives of men;
Heart weary of building and spoiling
And spoiling and building again;
And I long for the dear old river
Where I dreamed my youth away;
For a dreamer lives forever,
And a toiler dies in a day.
JOHN BOYLE O'REILLY—*Cry of the Dreamer.*

4
"Namque sub Aurora jam dormitante lucerna
Somnia quo cerni tempore vera solent."
Those dreams are true which we have in the morning, as the lamp begins to flicker.
OVID—*Epistles.* XIX. *Hero Leandro.* 195.
(See also BRUCE)

5
Dreams, which, beneath the hov'ring shades of night,
Sport with the ever-restless minds of men,
Descend not from the gods. Each busy brain
Creates its own.
THOMAS LOVE PEACOCK—*Dreams. From Petronius Arbiter.*

6
What was your dream?
It seemed to me that a woman in white raiment, graceful and fair to look upon, came towards me and calling me by name said:
On the third day, Socrates, thou shalt reach the coast of fertile Phthia.
PLATO—*Crito.*

7
That holy dream—that holy dream,
While all the world were chiding,
Hath cheered me as a lovely beam
A lonely spirit guiding.
POE—*A Dream.* St. 3.

8
Yet eat in dreams, the custard of the day.
POPE—*The Dunciad.* Bk. I. L. 92.

9
Till their own dreams at length deceive 'em
And oft repeating, they believe 'em.
PRIOR—*Alma.* Canto III. L. 13.

10
As a dream when one awaketh.
Psalms. LXXIII. 20.

11
This morn, as sleeping in my bed I lay,
I dreamt (and morning dreams come true they say).
W. B. RHODES—*Bombastes Furioso.* Post medium noctean bisus, quum comnia vera.
HORACE—*Satires.* Bk. I. Sat. 10. L. 33.
TIBULLUS—*Elegy.* Bk. III. 4.
(See also BRUCE)

12
O Brethren, weep to-day,
The silent God hath quenched my Torch's ray,
And the vain dream hath flown.
SCHILLER—*Resignation.* BOWRING'S trans.

13
Some must delve when the dawn is nigh;
Some must toil when the noonday beams;
But when night comes, and the soft winds sigh,
Every man is a King of Dreams.
CLINTON SCOLLARD—*King of Dreams.*

14
I'll dream no more—by manly mind
Not even in sleep is well resigned.
My midnight orisons said o'er,
I'll turn to rest and dream no more.
SCOTT—*Lady of the Lake.* Canto I. St. 35.

15
Thou hast beat me out
Twelve several times, and I have nightly since
Dreamt of encounters 'twixt thyself and me.
Coriolanus. Act IV. Sc. 5. L. 127.

16
There is some ill a-brewing towards my rest,
For I did dream of money-bags to-night.
Merchant of Venice. Act II. Sc. 5. L. 17.

17
I have had a most rare vision. I have had a dream, past the wit of man to say what dream it was.
Midsummer Night's Dream. Act IV. Sc. 1. L. 211.

18
This is the rarest dream that e'er dull sleep
Did mock sad fools withal.
Pericles. Act V. Sc. 1. L. 164.

19
Oh! I have pass'd a miserable night,
So full of ugly sights, of ghastly dreams,
That, as I am a Christian faithful man,
I would not spend another such a night,
Though 'twere to buy a world of happy days.
Richard III. Act I. Sc. 4. L. 2.

20
For never yet one hour in his bed
Have I enjoyed the golden dew of sleep,
But have been waked by his timorous dreams.
Richard III. Act IV. Sc. 1. L. 83.

21
I talk of dreams,
Which are the children of an idle brain,
Begot of nothing but vain fantasy,
Which is as thin of substance as the air
And more inconstant than the wind.
Romeo and Juliet. Act I. Sc. 4. L. 96.

22
Sometime she driveth o'er a soldier's neck,
And then dreams he of cutting foreign throats,
Of breaches, ambuscadoes, Spanish blades,
Of healths five-fathom deep.
Romeo and Juliet. Act I. Sc. 4. L. 82.

23
If I may trust the flattering truth of sleep,
My dreams presage some joyful news at hand:
My bosom's lord sits lightly in his throne;
And all this day an unaccustom'd spirit
Lifts me above the ground with cheerful thoughts.
Romeo and Juliet. Act V. Sc. 1. L. 1.

1 We are such stuff
As dreams are made on, and our little life
Is rounded with a sleep.
Tempest. Act IV. Sc. 1. L. 156.

2
Ah, the strange, sweet, lonely delight
Of the Valleys of Dream.
WILLIAM SHARP (Fiona McLeod)—*Dream Fantasy.*

3
Across the silent stream
Where the dream-shadows go,
From the dim blue Hill of Dream
I have heard the west wind blow.
WILLIAM SHARP (Fiona McLeod)—*From the Hills of Dream.*

4
In an ocean of dreams without a sound.
SHELLEY—*The Sensitive Plant.* Pt. I. St. 26.

5
Those dreams, that on the silent night intrude,
And with false flitting shades our minds delude,
Jove never sends us downward from the skies;
Nor can they from infernal mansions rise;
But are all mere productions of the brain,
And fools consult interpreters in vain.
SWIFT—*On Dreams.*

6
In the world of dreams, I have chosen my part.
To sleep for a season and hear no word
Of true love's truth or of light love's art,
Only the song of a secret bird.
SWINBURNE—*A Ballad of Dreamland. Envoi.*

7 The dream
Dreamed by a happy man, when the dark East,
Unseen, is brightening to his bridal morn.
TENNYSON—*The Gardener's Daughter.* L. 71.

8
Seeing, I saw not, hearing not, I heard.
Tho', if I saw not, yet they told me all
So often that I spake as having seen.
TENNYSON—*The Princess.* VI. L. 3.

9
Like glimpses of forgotten dreams.
TENNYSON—*The Two Voices.* St. CXXVII.

10
The chambers in the house of dreams
Are fed with so divine an air,
That Time's hoar wings grow young therein,
And they who walk there are most fair.
FRANCIS THOMPSON—*Dream Tryst.* St. 3.

11
And yet, as angels in some brighter dreams
Call to the soul when man doth sleep.
So some strange thoughts transcend our wonted dreams,
And into glory peep.
VAUGHAN—*Ascension Hymn.*

12
Hunt half a day for a forgotten dream.
WORDSWORTH—*Hart-Leap Well.* Pt. II. St. 9.

DRESDEN

13
At Dresden on the Elbe, that handsome city,
Where straw hats, verses, and cigars are made,
They've built (it well may make us feel afraid,)
A music club and music warehouse pretty.
HEINE—*Book of Songs. Sonnets. Dresden Poetry.*

DRESS (See APPAREL)

DRINKING (See also INTEMPERANCE, WINE)

14
Fill up the goblet and reach to me some!
Drinking makes wise, but dry fasting makes glum.
WM. R. ALGER—*Oriental Poetry. Wine Song of Kaitmas.*

15
Here
With my beer
I sit,
While golden moments flit:
Alas!
They pass
Unheeded by:
And as they fly,
I,
Being dry,
Sit, idly sipping here
My beer.
GEORGE ARNOLD—*Beer.*

16
Or merry swains, who quaff the nut-brown ale,
And sing enamour'd of the nut-brown maid.
BEATTIE—*The Minstrel.* Bk. I. St. 44.

17
Nose, nose, jolly red nose,
And who gave thee that jolly red nose?
Nutmegs and ginger, cinammon and cloves;
And they gave me this jolly red nose.
BEAUMONT AND FLETCHER—*Knight of the Burning Pestle.* Act I. Sc. 4.

18
"Nose, nose, nose, nose!
And who gave you that jolly red nose!
Sinamont and ginger, nutmegs and cloves,
And that gave me my jolly red nose!"
Version in RAVENCROFT'S *Deuteromela.* (1609)

19
What harm in drinking can there be,
Since punch and life so well agree?
BLACKLOCK — *Epigram on Punch.* L. 15. (1788) (See BOSWELL'S *Life of Johnson.*)

20
When the liquor's out, why clink the cannikin?
ROBERT BROWNING—*The Flight of the Duchess.* XVI.

21
There's some are fou o' love divine,
There's some are fou o' brandy.
BURNS—*The Holy Fair.* St. 30.

22
Inspiring bold John Barleycorn,
What dangers thou canst make us scorn!
Wi' tippenny, we fear nae evil;
Wi' usquebae, we'll face the devil!
BURNS—*Tam o' Shanter.* L. 105.

23
I drink when I have occasion, and sometimes when I have no occasion.
CERVANTES—*Don Quixote.* Pt. II. Ch. XXXIII.

24
And broughte of mighty ale a large quart.
CHAUCER—*Canterbury Tales. The Milleres Tale.* L. 3,497.

1
If you are invited to drink at any man's house more than you think is wholesome, you may say "you wish you could, but so little makes you both drunk and sick; that you should only be bad company by doing so."
LORD CHESTERFIELD—*Principles of Politeness and of Knowing the World. Sec. Sundry Little Accomplishments.*

2
Non est ab homine nunquam sobrio postulanda prudentia.
Prudence must not be expected from a man who is never sober.
CICERO—*Philippicæ.* II. 32.

3
Mynheer Vandunck, though he never was drunk,
Sipped brandy and water gayly.
GEORGE COLMAN ("The Younger.")—*Mynheer Vandunck.*

4
Let us eat and drink, for to-morrow we die.
I Corinthians. XV. 32. *Isaiah.* XXII. 13.
Convivæ certe tui dicunt, Bibamus moriendum est. SENECA—*Controv.* XIV.

5
Nothing in Nature's sober found,
But an eternal Health goes round.
Fill up the Bowl then, fill it high—
Fill all the Glasses there; for why
Should every Creature Drink but I?
Why, Man of Morals, tell me why?
COWLEY—*Anacreon II. Drinking.*

6
The thirsty Earth soaks up the Rain,
And drinks, and gapes for Drink again;
The Plants suck in the Earth and are
With constant Drinking fresh and fair.
COWLEY—*Anacreon II. Drinking.*

7
Let the farmer praise his grounds,
Let the huntsman praise his hounds,
The shepherd his dew scented lawn,
But I more blessed than they,
Spend each happy night and day
With my charming little cruiskeen lan, lan, lan.
Cruiskeen Lawn—Irish Song.

8
Did you ever hear of Captain Wattle?
He was all for love and a little for the bottle.
CHAS. DIBDIN—*Captain Wattle and Miss Rol.*

9
When I got up to the Peacock—where I found everybody drinking hot punch in self-preservation.
DICKENS—*The Holly Tree Inn.*

10
"Wery good power o' suction, Sammy," said Mr. Weller the elder. . . . "You'd ha' made an uncommon fine oyster, Sammy, if you'd been born in that station o' life."
DICKENS—*Pickwick Papers.* Ch. XXIII.

11
Inebriate of air am I,
And debauchee of dew,
Reeling, through endless summer days,
From inns of molten blue.
EMILY DICKINSON—*Poems.* XX.

12
How gracious those dews of solace that over my senses fall
At the clink of the ice in the pitcher the boy brings up the hall.
EUGENE FIELD—*The Clink of the Ice.*

13
Come landlord fill a flowing bowl until it does run over,
Tonight we will all merry be—tomorrow we'll get sober.
FLETCHER—*Bloody Brother.* Act II. Sc. 2.

14
Landlord fill the flowing bowl
Until it doth run over;
For to-night we'll merry be
To-morrow we'll be sober.
Version of FLETCHER'S song in *Three Jolly Postboys.* (18th century song.)

15
Drink to-day, and drown all sorrow;
You shall perhaps not do it to-morrow.
FLETCHER—*The Bloody Brother. Song.* Act II. Sc. 2.

16
Tell me I hate the bowl? Hate is a feeble word;
I loathe, abhor—my very soul and strong disgust is stirred
Whene'er I see or hear or tell of the dark beverage of hell.
Attributed to JOHN B. GOUGH; denied by him.

17
It's a long time between drinks.
The Governor of South Carolina required the return of a fugitive. The Governor of North Carolina hesitated because of powerful friends of the fugitive. He gave a banquet to his official brother. The Governor of South Carolina in a speech demanded the return of the man and ended with "What do you say?" The Governor of North Carolina replied as above. It is also attributed to JUDGE ÆDANUS BURKE.

18
Where the drink goes in, there the wit goes out.
HERBERT—*Jacula Prudentum.*

19
If you'd dip in such joys, come—the better, the quicker!—
But remember the fee—for it suits not my ends
To let you make havoc, scot free, with my liquor,
As though I were one of your heavy-pursed friends.
HORACE. Bk. IV. Ode XII. *To Vergil.* Trans. by THEO. MARTIN.

20
They who drink beer will think beer.
Quoted by WASHINGTON IRVING—*Sketch-book, Stratford-on-Avon.* They who drink water will think water.
(Travesty of the foregoing.)

21
Nor shall our cups make any guilty men;
But at our parting, we will be, as when
We innocently met.
BEN JONSON—*Epigram CI.*

22
Well, as he brews, so shall he drink.
BEN JONSON—*Every Man in His Humour.* Act II. Sc. 1.

1
Let those that merely talk and never think,
That live in the wild anarchy of drink.
BEN JONSON—*Underwoods. An Epistle, answering to One that asked to be sealed of the Tribe of Ben.*
(See also PRIOR)

2
Just a wee deoch-an-doris, just a wee yin, that's a'.
Just a wee deoch-an-doris before we gang a-wa',
There's a wee wifie waitin', in a wee but-an-ben;
If you can say "It's a braw bricht moon-licht nicht
Y're a 'richt ye ken.
HARRY LAUDER, WILL CUNLIFFE, GERALD GRAFTON—*Just a Wee Deoch-an-Doris.*

3
And I wish his soul in heaven may dwell,
Who first invented this leathern bottel!
Leathern Bottel.

4
Now to rivulets from the mountains
Point the rods of fortune-tellers;
Youth perpetual dwells in fountains,
Not in flasks, and casks, and cellars.
LONGFELLOW—*Drinking Song.* St. 8.

5
Myrtale often smells of wine, but, wise,
With eating bay-leaves thinks it to disguise:
So nott with water tempers the wine's heate,
But covers it. Henceforth if her you meete
With red face and swell'd veynes, modestly say,
"Sure Myrtale hath drunk o' th' bayes today?"
MARTIAL—*Epigrams.* Bk. V. 4. Trans. in a MS. 16th Century.

6
Attic honey thickens the nectar-like Falernian. Such drink deserves to be mixed by Ganymede.
MARTIAL—*Epigrams.* Bk. XIII. 108.

7
Let Nepos place Cæretan wine on table, and you will deem it Setine. But he does not give it to all the world; he drinks it only with a trio of friends.
MARTIAL—*Epigrams.* Bk. XIII. Ep. 124.

8
Provocarem ad Philippum, inquit, sed sobrium.
I would appeal to Philip, she said, but to Philip sober.
VALERIUS MAXIMUS. Bk. VI. II. Ext. 1.

9
One sip of this
Will bathe the drooping spirits in delight,
Beyond the bliss of dreams.
MILTON—*Comus.* L. 811.

10
Then to the spicy nut-brown ale.
MILTON—*L'Allegro.* L. 100.

11
When treading London's well-known ground
If e'er I feel my spirits tire,
I haul my sail, look up around,
In search of Whitbread's best entire.
From "The Myrtle and the Vine." A Complete Vocal Library. A Pot of Porter, Ho!

12
Drinking will make a man quaff,
Quaffing will make a man sing,
Singing will make a man laugh,
And laughing long life doth bring,
Says old Simon the King.
Old Sir Simon the King. Found in DURFEY'S *Wit and Mirth,* or *Pills to Purge Melancholy.* Referring to SIMON WADLOE, tavern-keeper at the "Devil," Fleet Street, about 1621.

13
Inter pocula.
Over their cups.
PERSIUS—*Satires.* I. 30.

14
There St. John mingles with my friendly bowl
The feast of reason and the flow of soul.
POPE—*Second Book of Horace.* Satire I. L. 128.

15
They never taste who always drink.
PRIOR—*On a Passage in the Scaligerana.*
(See also JONSON)

16
Je ne boy en plus qu'une esponge.
I do not drink more than a sponge.
RABELAIS—*Gargantua.* Bk. I. Ch. 5.

17
Il y a plus de vieux ivrongnes qu'il y a de vieux médecins.
There are more old drunkards than old physicians.
RABELAIS—*Gargantua.* Bk. I. Ch. XLII.

18
Die Limonade ist matt wie deine Seele—versuche!
This lemonade is weak like your soul—try it.
SCHILLER—*Cabale und Liebe.* V. 7.

19
Drink down all unkindness.
Merry Wives of Windsor. Act I. Sc. 1. L. 203.

20
I have very poor and unhappy brains for drinking: I could wish courtesy would invent some other custom of entertainment.
Othello. Act II. Sc. 3. L. 35.

21
This bottle's the sun of our table,
His beams are rosy wine;
We planets that are not able
Without his help to shine.
R. B. SHERIDAN—*The Duenna.* Act III. Sc. 5.

22
Si bene commemini, causæ sunt quinque bibendi;
Hospitis adventus, præsens sitis, atque futura,
Aut vini bonitas, aut quælibet altera causa.
If all be true that I do think,
There are five reasons we should drink;
Good wine—a friend—or being dry—
Or lest we should be by and by—
Or any other reason why.
Attributed to PÈRE SIRMOND by MENAGE and DE LA MONNOYE. See *Menagiana.* Vol. I. P. 172. Given in ISAAC J. REEVE'S *Wild Garland.* Vol. II. Trans by HENRY ALDRICH.

23
Let the back and sides go bare, my boys,
Let the hands and the feet gang cold;
But give to belly, boys, beer enough,
Whether it be new or old.
The Beggar. Old English Folk Song. Version in CECIL SHARPE'S *Folk-Songs from Somerset.*

1
Back and side go bare, go bare,
Both foot and hand go cold;
But belly, God send thee good ale enough,
Whether it be new or old.
BISHOP STILL—*Gammer Gurton's Needle*. Act II.

2
I cannot eat but little meat,
My stomach is not good;
But sure I think that I can drink
With him that wears a hood.
BISHOP STILL—*Gammer Gurton's Needle*. Act II. Authorship of the song claimed for WILLIAM STEVENSON of Durham. (Died 1575) In HUTCHINSON'S *Songs of the Vine*. Said to be found in old MS. See SKELTON *Works*. Vol. I. Note to pages VII–X. DYCE'S ed. *Gammer Gurton's Needle* claimed for JOHN BRIDGES.

3
Absentem lædit cum ebrio qui litigat.
He hurts the absent who quarrels with a drunken man.
SYRUS—*Maxims*.

4
While briskly to each patriot lip
Walks eager round the inspiring flip;
Delicious draught, whose pow'rs inherit
The quintessence of public spirit!
JOHN TRUMBULL—*McFingal*. Canto III. L. 21.

5
We're gaily yet, we're gaily yet,
And we're not very fow, but we're gaily yet;
Then set ye awhile, and tipple a bit,
For we's not very fow, but we're gaily yet.
VANBRUGH—*Provoked Wife*. Act III. Sc. 2. *Song—Colonel Bully*.

6
They drink with impunity, or anybody who invites them.
ARTEMUS WARD—*Moses the Sassy. Programme*.

7
Drink, pretty creature, drink!
WORDSWORTH—*The Pet Lamb*.

8
For drink, there was beer which was very strong when not mingled with water, but was agreeable to those who were used to it. They drank this with a reed, out of the vessel that held the beer, upon which they saw the barley swim.
XENOPHON—*Anabasis*. Bk. IV. Ch. V.

DUELLING (See also CHALLENGE)

9
It has a strange, quick jar upon the ear,
That cocking of a pistol, when you know
A moment more will bring the sight to bear
Upon your person, twelve yards off or so.
BYRON—*Don Juan*. Canto IV. St. 41.

10
Some fiery fop, with new commission vain,
Who sleeps on brambles till he kills his man;
Some frolic drunkard, reeling from a feast,
Provokes a broil, and stabs you for a jest.
SAMUEL JOHNSON—*London*. L. 226.

DUTY

11
Thanks to the gods! my boy has done his duty.
ADDISON—*Cato*. Act IV. Sc. 4.

12
In doing what we ought we deserve no praise, because it is our duty.
ST. AUGUSTINE.

13
He who is false to present duty breaks a thread in the loom, and will find the flaw when he may have forgotten its cause.
HENRY WARD BEECHER—*Life Thoughts*.

14
To do my duty in that state of life unto which it shall please God to call me.
Book of Common Prayer. Catechism.

15
Maintain your post: That's all the fame you need;
For 'tis impossible you should proceed.
DRYDEN—*To Mr. Congreve, on his Comedy "The Double Dealer."*

16
Not aw'd to duty by superior sway.
DRYDEN—*Eleonora*. L. 178.

17
And rank for her meant duty, various,
Yet equal in its worth, done worthily.
Command was service; humblest service done
By willing and discerning souls was glory.
GEORGE ELIOT—*Agatha*.

18
The reward of one duty is the power to fulfil another.
GEORGE ELIOT—*Daniel Deronda*. Bk. VI. Ch. XLVI.

19
So nigh is grandeur to our dust,
So near is God to man.
When Duty whispers low, *Thou must*,
The youth replies, *I can*.
EMERSON—*Voluntaries*. St. 3. L. 13.

20
When I'm not thank'd at all, I'm thank'd enough:
I've done my duty, and I've done no more.
FIELDING—*Tom Thumb*. Act I. Sc. 3.

21
In common things the law of sacrifice takes the form of positive duty.
FROUDE—*Short Studies on Great Subjects. Sea Studies*.

22
Was aber ist deine Pflicht? Die Forderung des Tages.
But what is your duty? What the day demands.
GOETHE—*Sprüche in Prosa*. III. 151.

23
Hath the spirit of all beauty
Kissed you in the path of duty?
ANNA KATHARINE GREEN—*On the Threshold*.

24
Then on! then on! where duty leads,
My course be onward still.
BISHOP HEBER—*Journal*.

25
I slept and dreamed that life was Beauty;
I woke, and found that life was Duty:—
Was thy dream then a shadowy lie?
ELLEN STURGIS HOOPER—*Duty*.

1
Take up the White Man's burden.
KIPLING—*The White Man's Burden. To the United States.* Feb. 4, 1899. In *McClure's Magazine.* Feb., 1899.

2
Thet tells the story! Thet's wut we shall git
By tryin' squirtguns on the burnin' Pit;
For the day never comes when it'll du
To kick off dooty like a worn-out shoe.
LOWELL—*The Biglow Papers.* No. 11.

3
Straight is the line of duty;
Curved is the line of beauty;
Follow the straight line, thou shalt see
The curved line ever follow thee.
WILLIAM MACCALL—*Duty.*

4
Every mission constitutes a pledge of duty. Every man is bound to consecrate his every faculty to its fulfilment. He will derive his rule of action from the profound conviction of that duty.
MAZZINI—*Life and Writings. Young Europe. General Principles.*

5
The things which must be, must be for the best,
God helps us do our duty and not shrink,
And trust His mercy humbly for the rest.
OWEN MEREDITH (Lord Lytton)—*Imperfection.*

6 Left that command
Sole daughter of his voice.
MILTON—*Paradise Lost.* Bk. IX. L. 652.
(See also WORDSWORTH)

7
Knowledge is the hill which few may wish to climb;
Duty is the path that all may tread.
LEWIS MORRIS—*Epic of Hades. Quoted by John Bright at Unveiling of Cobden Statue.*

8
Thy sum of duty let two words contain,
(O may they graven in thy heart remain!)
Be humble and be just.
PRIOR—*Solomon on the Vanity of the World.* Bk. III.

9
And I read the moral—A brave endeavour
To do thy duty, whate'er its worth,
Is better than life with love forever,
And love is the sweetest thing on earth.
JAMES J. ROCHE—*Sir Hugo's Choice.*

10
Alas! when duty grows thy law, enjoyment fades away.
SCHILLER—*The Playing Infant.*

11
I do perceive here a divided duty.
Othello. Act I. Sc. 3. L. 181.

12 I thought the remnant of mine age
Should have been cherish'd by her child-like duty.
Two Gentlemen of Verona. Act III. Sc. 1. L. 74.

13
Not once or twice in our rough island story,
The path of duty was the way to glory.
TENNYSON—*Ode on the Death of the Duke of Wellington.* St. 8.

14
Simple duty hath no place for fear.
WHITTIER—*Tent on the Beach. Abraham Davenport.* Last Line.

15
The primal duties shine aloft, like stars;
The charities that soothe, and heal, and bless
Are scattered at the feet of Man, like flowers.
WORDSWORTH—*The Excursion.* Bk. IX.

16
Give unto me, made lowly wise,
The spirit of self-sacrifice;
The confidence of reason give;
And in the light of truth thy
Bondman let me live!
WORDSWORTH—*Ode to Duty.*

17
Stern Daughter of the Voice of God.
WORDSWORTH—*Ode to Duty.*
(See also MILTON)

18
Who art a light to guide, a rod
To check the erring, and reprove.
WORDSWORTH—*Ode to Duty.*

E

EAGLE

19
So, in the Libyan fable it is told
That once an eagle, stricken with a dart,
Said, when he saw the fashion of the shaft,
"With our own feathers, not by others' hand
Are we now smitten."

ÆSCHYLUS—*Fragment.* 123. PLUMPTRE's trans. The idea of the eagle struck by a feather from her own wing is proverbial. See note by PORSON, 139, to EURIPIDES' *Medea.* DIONYSIUS OF HALICARNASSUS, REISKE's ed. 970. EUSTATHIUS—*ad Iliad.* P. 632. 489. SCHOLIAST—*On Lucian.* Vol. I. P. 794. ROGER L' ESTRANGE, *Fables of Æsop.* 48. *Eagle and the Arrow.*

(See also BYRON, MOORE, WALLER, also PHILLIPS under RELIGION)

20
So the struck eagle, stretched upon the plain,
No more through rolling clouds to soar again,
Viewed his own feather on the fatal dart,
And wing'd the shaft that quivered in his heart.
BYRON—*English Bards and Scotch Reviewers.* L. 826.

21 Tho' he inherit
Nor the pride, nor ample pinion,
That the Theban eagle bear,
Sailing with supreme dominion
Thro' the azure deep of air.
GRAY—*Progress of Poesy.*

22
King of the peak and glacier,
King of the cold, white scalps,
He lifts his head at that close tread,
The eagle of the Alps.
VICTOR HUGO—*Swiss Mercenaries.*

1
Wheresoever the carcass is, there will the eagles be gathered together.
Matthew. XXIV. 28.

2
The bird of Jove, stoop'd from his aery tour,
Two birds of gayest plume before him drove.
MILTON—*Paradise Lost*. Bk. XI. L. 184.

3
Like a young eagle, who has lent his plume,
To fledge the shaft by which he meets his doom,
See their own feathers pluck'd, to wing the dart,
Which rank corruption destines for their heart!
MOORE—*Corruption*.
(See also ÆSCHYLUS)

4
Bird of the broad and sweeping wing,
Thy home is high in heaven,
Where wide the storms their banners fling,
And the tempest clouds are driven.
PERCIVAL—*To the Eagle*.

5
And little eagles wave their wings in gold.
POPE—*Moral Essays. Ep. to Addison*. L. 30.

6
I saw Jove's bird, the Roman eagle, wing'd
From the spungy south to this part of the west,
There vanish'd in the sunbeams.
Cymbeline. Act IV. Sc. 2. L. 348.

7
But flies an eagle flight, bold and forth on,
Leaving no track behind.
Timon of Athens. Act I. Sc. 1. L. 49.

8
The eagle suffers little birds to sing,
And is not careful what they mean thereby.
Titus Andronicus. Act IV. Sc. 4. L. 83.

9
Around, around, in ceaseless circles wheeling
With clangs of wings and scream, the Eagle sailed
Incessantly.
SHELLEY—*Revolt of Islam*. Canto I. St. 10.

10
He clasps the crag with hooked hands;
Close to the sun in lonely lands,
Ring'd with the azure world, he stands.
The wrinkled sea beneath him crawls:
He watches from his mountain walls,
And like a thunderbolt he falls.
TENNYSON—*The Eagle*.

11
Shall eagles not be eagles? wrens be wrens?
If all the world were falcons, what of that?
The wonder of the eagle were the less,
But he not less the eagle.
TENNYSON—*Golden Year*. L. 37.

12
That eagle's fate and mine are one,
Which, on the shaft that made him die,
Espied a feather of his own,
Wherewith he wont to soar so high.
EDMUND WALLER—*To a Lady Singing a Song of his Composing*. Ep. XIV.
(See also ÆSCHYLUS)

EARS (See HEARING)

EASTER

13
Awake, thou wintry earth—
Fling off thy sadness!
Fair vernal flowers, laugh forth
Your ancient gladness!
Christ is risen.
THOMAS BLACKBURN—*An Easter Hymn*.

14
Tomb, thou shalt not hold Him longer;
Death is strong, but Life is stronger;
Stronger than the dark, the light;
Stronger than the wrong, the right;
Faith and Hope triumphant say
Christ will rise on Easter Day.
PHILLIPS BROOKS—*An Easter Carol*.

15
Ye Heavens, how sang they in your courts,
How sang the angelic choir that day,
When from his tomb the imprisoned God,
Like the strong sunrise, broke away?
FREDERICK WILLIAM FABER—*Jesus Risen*.

16
Hail, Day of days! in peals of praise
Throughout all ages owned,
When Christ, our God, hell's empire trod,
And high o'er heaven was throned.
FORTUNATUS (Bishop of Poictiers)—*Hail, Day of Days! in Peals of Praise*.

17
Come, ye saints, look here and wonder,
See the place where Jesus lay;
He has burst His bands asunder;
He has borne our sins away;
Joyful tidings,
Yes, the Lord has risen to-day.
THOMAS KELLY—*Come, Ye Saints, Look Here and Wonder*.

18
'Twas Easter-Sunday. The full-blossomed trees
Filled all the air with fragrance and with joy.
LONGFELLOW—*Spanish Student*. Act I. Sc. 3.

19
O chime of sweet Saint Charity,
Peal soon that Easter morn
When Christ for all shall risen be,
And in all hearts new-born!
That Pentecost when utterance clear
To all men shall be given,
When all shall say *My Brother* here,
And hear *My Son* in heaven!
LOWELL—*Godminster Chimes*. St. 7.

20
In the bonds of Death He lay
Who for our offence was slain;
But the Lord is risen to-day,
Christ hath brought us life again,
Wherefore let us all rejoice,
Singing loud, with cheerful voice,
Hallelujah!
MARTIN LUTHER—*In the Bonds of Death He Lay*.

21
Hallelujah! Hallelujah!
On the third morning He arose,
Bright with victory o'er his foes.

Sing we lauding,
And applauding,
Hallelujah!

Hallelujah! Hallelujah! From the Latin of the 12th Century. J. M. NEALE. Trans.

1
I think of the garden after the rain;
And hope to my heart comes singing,
"At morn the cherry-blooms will be white,
And the Easter bells be ringing!"

EDNA DEAN PROCTER—*Easter Bells.*

2
The fasts are done; the Aves said;
The moon has filled her horn
And in the solemn night I watch
Before the Easter morn.
So pure, so still the starry heaven,
So hushed the brooding air,
I could hear the sweep of an angel's wings
If one should earthward fare.

EDNA DEAN PROCTER—*Easter Morning.*

3
Spring bursts to-day,
For Christ is risen and all the earth's at play.

CHRISTINA G. ROSSETTI—*Easter Carol.*

4
God expects from men something more than at such times, and that it were much to be wished for the credit of their religion as well as the satisfaction of their conscience that their Easter devotions would in some measure come up to their Easter dress.

SOUTH—*Sermons.* Vol. II. Ser. 8.

5
Christ is our Passover!
And we will keep the feast
With the new leaven,
The bread of heaven:
All welcome, even the least!

A. R. THOMPSON—*We Keep the Festival.* From the Roman Breviary.

6
"Christ the Lord is risen to-day,"
Sons of men and angels say.
Raise your joys and triumphs high;
Sing, ye heavens, and earth reply.

CHARLES WESLEY—*"Christ the Lord is Risen To-day."*

7
Jesus Christ is risen to-day,
Our triumphant holy day;
Who did once upon the cross
Suffer to redeem our loss.
Hallelujah!

Jesus Christ is Risen To-day. From a Latin Hymn of the 15th Century—Translator unknown.

EATING (See also APPETITE, COOKERY, HUNGER)

8
The poor man will praise it so hath he good cause,
That all the year eats neither partridge nor quail,
But sets up his rest and makes up his feast,
With a crust of brown bread and a pot of good ale.

Old English Song. From *"An Antidote Against Melancholy."* (1661)

9
When the Sultan Shah-Zaman
Goes to the city Ispahan,
Even before he gets so far
As the place where the clustered palm-trees are,
At the last of the thirty palace-gates,
The pet of the harem, Rose-in-Bloom,
Orders a feast in his favorite room—
Glittering square of colored ice,
Sweetened with syrup, tinctured with spice,
Creams, and cordials, and sugared dates,
Syrian apples, Othmanee quinces,
Limes and citrons and apricots,
And wines that are known to Eastern princes.

T. B. ALDRICH—*When the Sultan Goes to Ispahan.*

10
Acorns were good till bread was found.

BACON—*Colours of Good and Evil.* 6. Quoted from JUVENAL—*Satires.* XIV, 181.

11
Some men are born to feast, and not to fight;
Whose sluggish minds, e'en in fair honor's field,
Still on their dinner turn—
Let such pot-boiling varlets stay at home,
And wield a flesh-hook rather than a sword.

JOANNA BAILLIE—*Basil.* Act I. Sc. 1.

12
'Tis not *her* coldness, father,
That chills my labouring breast;
It's that confounded cucumber
I've ate and can't digest.

R. H. BARHAM—*The Confession.*

13
I sing the sweets I know, the charms I feel,
My morning incense, and my evening meal,
The sweets of Hasty-Pudding.

JOEL BARLOW—*The Hasty Pudding.* Canto I.

14
Ratons and myse and soche smale dere
That was his mete that vii. yere.

Sir Bevis of Hamptoun.
(See also KING LEAR)

15
Un dîner réchauffé ne valut jamais rien.
A warmed-up dinner was never worth much.

BOILEAU—*Lutrin.* I. 104.

16
First come, first served.

HENRY BRINKLOW—*Complaint of Roderyck Mors.* Also in *Bartholomew's Fair.* Act III. 5. (1614)

17
Man is a carnivorous production,
And must have meals, at least one meal a day;
He cannot live, like woodcocks, upon suction,
But, like the shark and tiger, must have prey;
Although his anatomical construction
Bears vegetables, in a grumbling way,
Your laboring people think beyond all question,
Beef, veal, and mutton better for digestion.

BYRON—*Don Juan.* Canto II. St. 67.

18
That famish'd people must be slowly nurst,
And fed by spoonfuls, else they always burst.

BYRON—*Don Juan.* Canto II. St. 158.

19
All human history attests
That happiness for man,—the hungry sinner!—
Since Eve ate apples, much depends on dinner.

BYRON—*Don Juan.* Canto XIII. St. 99.

1
Better halfe a loafe than no bread.
CAMDEN—*Remaines. Proverbs.* P. 293.

2
A loaf of bread, the Walrus said,
Is what we chiefly need:
Pepper and vinegar besides
Are very good indeed—
Now if you're ready, Oysters, dear,
We can begin to feed!
LEWIS CARROLL—*The Walrus and the Carpenter.* From *Alice Through The Looking-Glass.*

3
Todos los duelos con pan son buenos (*or* son menos).
All sorrows are good (*or* are less) with bread.
CERVANTES—*Don Quixote.* Ch. II. 13.

4
Tripas llevan corazon, que no corazon tripas.
The stomach carries the heart, and not the heart the stomach.
CERVANTES—*Don Quixote.* Ch. II. 47.

5
The proof of the pudding is in the eating.
CERVANTES—*Don Quixote.* Ch. XXIV.

6
Nemini fidas, nisi cum quo prius multos modios salis absumpseris.
Trust no one unless you have eaten much salt with him.
CICERO—*De Amic.* 19, 67. (*Quoted.*)

7
Esse oportet ut vivas, non vivere ut edas.
Thou shouldst eat to live; not live to eat.
CICERO—*Rhetoricorum Ad C. Herennium.* IV. 7.

8
For he on honey-dew hath fed,
And drunk the milk of Paradise.
COLERIDGE—*Kubla Khan.*

9
Oh, dainty and delicious!
Food for the gods! Ambrosia for Apicius!
Worthy to thrill the soul of sea-born Venus,
Or titillate the palate of Silenus!
W. A. CROFFUT—*Clam Soup.*

10
A friendly swarry, consisting of a boiled leg of mutton with the usual trimmings.
DICKENS—*Pickwick Papers.* Ch. XXXVII.

11
The true Amphitryon.
DRYDEN—*Amphitryon.* Act IV. Sc. 1.
(See also MOLIÈRE)

12
When we sat by the fleshpots.
Exodus. XVI. 3.

13
When I demanded of my friend what viands he preferred,
He quoth: "A large cold bottle, and a small hot bird!"
EUGENE FIELD—*The Bottle and the Bird.*

14
When mighty roast beef was the Englishman's food
It ennobled our hearts and enriched our blood—
Our soldiers were brave and our courtiers were good.
Oh! the roast beef of England,
And Old England's roast beef.
HENRY FIELDING—*The Roast Beef of Old England.* In *Grub Street Opera.* Act III. Sc. 2. Claimed for R. Leveridge.

15
Fools make feasts, and wise men eat them.
BENJ. FRANKLIN—*Poor Richard.* (1733)

16
What will not luxury taste? Earth, sea, and air,
Are daily ransack'd for the bill of fare.
Blood stuffed in skins is British Christians' food,
And France robs marshes of the croaking brood.
GAY—*Trivia.* Bk. III. L. 199.

17
Blest be those feasts, with simple plenty crowned,
Where all the ruddy family around
Laugh at the jests or pranks that never fail
Or sigh with pity at some mournful tale.
GOLDSMITH—*Traveller.* L. 17.

18
"Here, dearest Eve," he exclaims, "here is food." "Well," answered she, with the germ of a housewife stirring within her, "we have been so busy to-day that a picked-up dinner must serve."
HAWTHORNE—*Mosses from an Old Manse. The New Adam and Eve.*

19
Je veux que le dimanche chaque paysan ait sa poule au pot.
I want every peasant to have a chicken in his pot on Sundays.
HENRY IV of France.

20
Such as have need of milk, and not of strong meat.
Hebrews. V. 12.

21
Strong meat belongeth to them that are of full age.
Hebrews. V. 14.

22
He rolls it under his tongue as a sweet morsel.
MATTHEW HENRY—*Commentaries.*

23
Here is *bread, which strengthens man's heart,* and therefore is called *the staff of Life.*
MATTHEW HENRY—*Commentaries.* Psalm CIV. 15. (See also SWIFT)

24
He pares his apple that will cleanly feed.
HERBERT—*Church Porch.* St. 2.

25
A cheerful look makes a dish a feast.
HERBERT—*Jacula Prudentum.*

26
Gluttony kills more than the sword
HERBERT—*Jacula Prudentum.*

27
'Tis not the food, but the content,
That makes the table's merriment.
HERRICK—*Content not Cates.*

28
Out did the meate, out did the frolick wine.
HERRICK—*Ode for Ben Jonson.*

29
God never sendeth mouth but he sendeth meat.
HEYWOOD—*Proverbs.* Pt. I. Ch. IV.

1
Born but to banquet, and to drain the bowl.
HOMER—*Odyssey*. Bk. X. L. 622. POPE'S trans.

2
"Good well-dress'd turtle beats them hollow,—
It almost makes me wish, I vow,
To have *two* stomachs, like a cow!"
And lo! as with the cud, an inward thrill
Upheaved his waistcoat and disturb'd his frill,
His mouth was oozing, and he work'd his jaw—
"I almost think that I could eat one raw."
HOOD—*The Turtles*.

3
Millia frumenti tua triverit area centum,
Non tuus hinc capiet venter plus ac meus.
Though your threshing-floor grind a hundred thousand bushels of corn, not for that reason will your stomach hold more than mine.
HORACE—*Satires*. I. 1. 45.

4
Jejunus raro stomachus vulgaria temnit.
A stomach that is seldom empty despises common food.
HORACE—*Satires*. II. 2. 38.

5
The consummate pleasure (in eating) is not in the costly flavour, but in yourself. Do you seek for sauce by sweating?
HORACE—*Satires*. II. 2.

6
Free livers on a small scale; who are prodigal within the compass of a guinea.
WASHINGTON IRVING—*The Stout Gentleman*.

7
The stay and the staff, the whole stay of bread, and the whole stay of water.
Isaiah. III. 1.

8
Let us eat and drink; for to-morrow we shall die.
Isaiah. XXII. 13.

9
A feast of fat things.
Isaiah. XXV. 6.

10
Think of the man who first tried German sausage.
JEROME K. JEROME—*Three Men in a Boat*. Ch. XIV.

11
Gather up the fragments that remain, that nothing be lost.
John. VI. 12.

12
For I look upon it, that he who does not mind his belly will hardly mind anything else.
SAMUEL JOHNSON—*Boswell's Life of Johnson*. Vol. III. Ch. 9.

13
For a man seldom thinks with more earnestness of anything than he does of his dinner.
SAMUEL JOHNSON—*Piozzi's Anecdotes of Johnson*.

14
Digestive cheese, and fruit there sure will be.
BEN JONSON—*Epigram CI*.

15
Yet shall you have to rectify your palate,
An olive, capers, or some better salad
Ushering the mutton; with a short-legged hen,
If we can get her, full of eggs, and then,
Limons, and wine for sauce: to these a coney
Is not to be despaired of for our money;
And though fowl now be scarce, yet there are clerks,
The sky not falling, think we may have larks.
BEN JONSON—*Epigram CI*.

16
The master of art or giver of wit,
Their belly.
BEN JONSON—*The Poetaster*.

17
She brought forth butter in a lordly dish.
Judges. V. 25.

18
In solo vivendi causa palato est.
In their palate alone is their reason of existence.
JUVENAL—*Satires*. II. 11.

19
Bona summa putes, aliena vivere quadra.
To eat at another's table is your ambition's height.
JUVENAL—*Satires*. V. 2.

20
And lucent syrops, tinct with cinnamon.
KEATS—*The Eve of St. Agnes*. St. 30.

21
An handful of meal in a barrel, and a little oil in a cruse.
I Kings. XVII. 12.

22
And the barrel of meal wasted not, neither did the cruse of oil fail.
I Kings. XVII. 16.

23
A woman asked a coachman, "Are you full inside?" Upon which Lamb put his head through the window and said: "I am quite full inside; that last piece of pudding at Mr. Gillman's did the business for me."
LAMB—*Autobiographical Recollections*, by CHAS. R. LESLIE.

24
He hath a fair sepulchre in the grateful stomach of the judicious epicure—and for such a tomb might be content to die.
LAMB—*Dissertation upon Roast Pig*.

25
If you wish to grow thinner, diminish your dinner,
And take to light claret instead of pale ale;
Look down with an utter contempt upon butter,
And never touch bread till its toasted—or stale.
HENRY S. LEIGH—*A Day for Wishing*.

26
Your supper is like the Hidalgo's dinner; very little meat, and a great deal of tablecloth.
LONGFELLOW—*Spanish Student*. Act I. Sc. 4.

27
I am glad that my Adonis hath a sweete tooth in his head.
LYLY—*Euphues and his England*. P. 308.

28
Ye diners out from whom we guard our spoons.
MACAULAY—*Political Georgics*.

29
Philo swears that he has never dined at home, and it is so; he does not dine at all, except when invited out.
MARTIAL—*Epigrams*. Bk. V. Ep. 47.

1
Mithriades, by frequently drinking poison, rendered it impossible for any poison to hurt him. You, Cinna, by always dining on next to nothing, have taken due precaution against ever perishing from hunger.
MARTIAL—*Epigrams*. Bk. V. Ep. 76.

2
Annius has some two hundred tables, and servants for every table. Dishes run hither and thither, and plates fly about. Such entertainments as these keep to yourselves, ye pompous; I am ill pleased with a supper that walks.
MARTIAL—*Epigrams*. Bk. VII. Ep. 48.

3
You praise, in three hundred verses, Sabellus, the baths of Ponticus, who gives such excellent dinners. You wish to dine, Sabellus, not to bathe.
MARTIAL—*Epigrams*. Bk. IX. Ep. 19.

4
As long as I have fat turtle-doves, a fig for your lettuce, my friend, and you may keep your shell-fish to yourself. I have no wish to waste my appetite.
MARTIAL—*Epigrams*. Bk. XIII. Ep. 53.

5
See, how the liver is swollen larger than a fat goose! In amazement you will exclaim: Where could this possibly grow?
MARTIAL—*Epigrams*. Bk. XIII. Ep. 58.

6
Whether woodcock or partridge, what does it signify, if the taste is the same? But the partridge is dearer, and therefore thought preferable.
MARTIAL—*Epigrams*. Bk. XIII. Ep. 76.

7
However great the dish that holds the turbot, the turbot is still greater than the dish.
MARTIAL—*Epigrams*. Bk. XIII. Ep. 81.

8
I am a shell-fish just come from being saturated with the waters of the Lucrine lake, near Baiæ; but now I luxuriously thirst for noble pickle.
MARTIAL—*Epigrams*. Bk. XIII. Ep. 82.

9
If my opinion is of any worth, the fieldfare is the greatest delicacy among birds, the hare among quadrupeds.
MARTIAL—*Epigrams*. Bk. XIII. Ep. 92.

10
Man shall not live by bread alone.
Matthew. IV. 4; *Deuteronomy*. VIII. 3.

11
Take no thought for your life, what ye shall eat, or what ye shall drink.
Matthew. VI. 25.

12
O hour, of all hours, the most bless'd upon earth,
The blessèd hour of our dinners!
OWEN MEREDITH (Lord Lytton)—*Lucile*. Pt. I. Canto II. St. 23.

13
We may live without poetry, music and art;
We may live without conscience, and live without heart;
We may live without friends; we may live without books;
But civilized man cannot live without cooks.
He may live without books,—what is knowledge but grieving?
He may live without hope,—what is hope but deceiving?
He may live without love,—what is passion but pining?
But where is the man that can live without dining?
OWEN MEREDITH (Lord Lytton)—*Lucile*. Pt. I. Canto II. St. 24.

14
They eat, they drink, and in communion sweet
Quaff immortality and joy.
MILTON—*Paradise Lost*. Bk. V. L. 637.

15
Le véritable Amphitryon
Est l'Amphitryon où l'on dine.
The genuine Amphitryon is the Amphitryon with whom we dine.
MOLIÈRE—*Amphitryon*. III. 5.
(See also DRYDEN)

16
Tenez bonne table et soignez les femmes.
Keep a good table and attend to the ladies.
NAPOLEON I.—*Instructions to* ABBÉ DE PRADT.

17
What baron or squire
Or knight of the shire
Lives half so well as a holy friar.
JOHN O'KEEFE—*I am a Friar of Orders Gray*.

18
Gula plures occidit quam gladius, estque fomes omnium malorum.
Gluttony kills more than the sword, and is the kindler of all evils.
PATRICIUS, Bishop of Gæta.

19
The way to a man's heart is through his stomach.
MRS. SARAH PAYSON ("Fanny Fern")—*Willis Parton*.

20
Magister artis ingenique largitor Venter.
The belly (*i. e.* necessity) is the teacher of art and the liberal bestower of wit.
PERSIUS—*Prologue to Satires*. 10.

21
Whose God is their belly, and whose glory is in their shame.
Philippians. III. 19.

22
Festo die si quid prodegeris,
Profesto egere liceat nisi peperceris.
Feast to-day makes fast to-morrow.
PLAUTUS—*Aulularia*.

23
Their best and most wholesome feeding is upon one dish and no more and the same plaine and simple: for surely this hudling of many meats one upon another of divers tastes is pestiferous. But sundrie sauces are more dangerous than that.
PLINY—*Natural History*. Bk. XI. Ch. LIII. HOLLAND's trans.

24
What, did you not know, then, that to-day Lucullus dines with Lucullus?
PLUTARCH—*Lives*. *Life of Lucullus*. Vol. III. P. 280.

25
And solid pudding against empty praise.
POPE—*Dunciad*. Bk. I. L. 54.

1
"Pray take them, Sir,—Enough's a Feast;
Eat some, and pocket up the rest."
POPE—*First Book of Horace.* Ep. VII. L. 24.

2
"An't it please your Honour," quoth the Peasant,
"This same Dessert is not so pleasant:
Give me again my hollow Tree,
A crust of Bread, and Liberty."
POPE—*Second Book of Horace.* Last lines.

3
One solid dish his week-day meal affords,
An added pudding solemniz'd the Lord's.
POPE—*Moral Essays.* Ep. III. L. 447.

4
"Live like yourself," was soon my lady's word,
And lo! two puddings smok'd upon the board.
POPE—*Moral Essays.* Ep. III. L. 461.

5
Better is a dinner of herbs where love is, than a stalled ox and hatred therewith.
Proverbs. XV. 17.

6
L'abstenir pour jouir, c'est l'épicurisme de la raison.
To abstain that we may enjoy is the epicurianism of reason.
ROUSSEAU.

7
Dis moi ce que tu manges, je te dirai ce que tu es.
Tell me what you eat, and I will tell you what you are.
BRILLAT SAVARIN—*Physiologie du Gout.*

8
A very man—not one of nature's clods—
With human failings, whether saint or sinner:
Endowed perhaps with genius from the gods
But apt to take his temper from his dinner.
J. G. SAXE—*About Husbands.*

9
A dinner lubricates business.
WILLIAM SCOTT. Quoted in *Boswell's Life of Johnson.*

10
But, first
Or last, your fine Egyptian cookery
Shall have the fame. I have heard that Julius Cæsar
Grew fat with feasting there.
Antony and Cleopatra. Act II. Sc. 6. L. 63.

11
Sit down and feed, and welcome to our table.
As You Like It. Act II. Sc. 7. L. 106.

12
If you do, expect spoon-meat; or bespeak a long spoon.
Comedy of Errors. Act IV. Sc. 3. L. 61.

13
Unquiet meals make ill digestions.
Comedy of Errors. Act V. Sc. 1. L. 75.

14
He hath eaten me out of house and home.
Henry IV. Pt. II. Act II. Sc. 1. L. 81.

15
He that keeps nor crust nor crum,
Weary of all, shall want some.
King Lear. Act I. Sc. 4. L. 216.

16
But mice, and rats, and such small deer,
Have been Tom's food for seven long year.
King Lear. Act III. Sc. 4.
(See also BEVIS OF HAMPTOUN)

17
Fat paunches have lean pates, and dainty bits
Make rich the ribs, but bankrupt quite the wits.
Love's Labour's Lost. Act I. Sc. 1. L. 26.

18
They are as sick that surfeit with too much, as they that starve with nothing.
Merchant of Venice. Act I. Sc. 2. L. 5.

19
A surfeit of the sweetest things
The deepest loathing to the stomach brings.
Midsummer Night's Dream. Act II. Sc. 2. L. 137.

20
I wished your venison better; it was ill kill'd.
Merry Wives of Windsor. Act I. Sc. 1. L. 83.

21
Come, we have a hot venison pasty to dinner.
Merry Wives of Windsor. Act I. Sc. 1. L. 202.

22
I will make an end of my dinner; there's pippins and cheese to come.
Merry Wives of Windsor. Act I. Sc. 2. L. 12.

23
Things sweet to taste prove in digestion sour.
Richard II. Act I. Sc. 3. L. 237.

24
I fear it is too choleric a meat.
How say you to a fat tripe finely broil'd?
Taming of the Shrew. Act IV. Sc. 3. L. 19.

25
What say you to a piece of beef and mustard?
Taming of the Shrew. Act IV. Sc. 3. L. 23.

26
My cake is dough: but I'll in among the rest,
Out of hope of all, but my share of the feast.
Taming of the Shrew. Act V. Sc. 1. L. 143.

27
I charge thee, invite them all; let in the tide
Of knaves once more: my cook and I'll provide.
Timon of Athens. Act III. Sc. 4. L. 118.

28
Each man to his stool, with that spur as he would to the lip of his mistress; your diet shall be in all places alike. Make not a city feast of it, to let the meat cool ere we can agree upon the first place.
Timon of Athens. Act III. Sc. 6. L. 73.

29
You would eat chickens i' the shell.
Troilus and Cressida. Act I. Sc. 2. L. 147.

30
Our feasts
In every mess have folly, and the feeders
Digest with it a custom, I should blush
To see you so attir'd.
Winter's Tale. Act IV. Sc. 4. L. 10.

31
Though we eat little flesh and drink no wine,
Yet let's be merry; we'll have tea and toast;
Custards for supper, and an endless host
Of syllabubs and jellies and mince-pies,
And other such ladylike luxuries.
SHELLEY—*Letter to Maria Gisborne.*

1 Oh, herbaceous treat!
'Twould tempt the dying anchorite to eat;
Back to the world he'd turn his fleeting soul,
And plunge his fingers in the salad bowl;
Serenely full the epicure would say,
"Fate cannot harm me,—I have dined to-day."
SYDNEY SMITH—*A Receipt for a Salad.*
(See also DRYDEN under TO-DAY)

2
Bad men live that they may eat and drink, whereas good men eat and drink that they may live.
Attributed to SOCRATES *by* PLUTARCH—*Morals. How a Young Man Ought to Hear Poems.*

3
Lord, Madame, I have fed like a farmer; I shall grow as fat as a porpoise.
SWIFT—*Polite Conversation.* Dialogue II.

4
They say fingers were made before forks, and hands before knives.
SWIFT—*Polite Conversation.* Dialogue II.

5
Bread is the staff of life.
SWIFT—*Tale of a Tub.*
(See also HENRY)

6
This dish of meat is too good for any but anglers, or very honest men.
IZAAK WALTON—*Compleat Angler.* Pt. I. Ch. VIII.

ECHO

7
Let echo, too, perform her part,
Prolonging every note with art;
And in a low expiring strain,
Play all the comfort o'er again.
ADDISON—*Ode for St. Cecilia's Day.*

8
Hark! to the hurried question of Despair
"Where is my child?"—An echo answers—
"Where?"
BYRON—*Bride of Abydos.* Canto II. St. 27.

9
I came to the place of my birth and cried:
"The friends of my youth, where are they?"—
and an echo answered, "Where are they?"
From an Arabic MS. quoted by ROGERS—*Pleasures of Memory.* Pt. I.

10
Even Echo speaks not on these radiant moors.
BARRY CORNWALL—*English Songs and Other Small Poems. The Sea in Calm.* Pt. III.

11
Mysterious haunts of echoes old and far,
The voice divine of human loyalty.
GEORGE ELIOT—*The Spanish Gypsy.* Bk. IV. L. 149.

12
Echo waits with art and care
And will the faults of song repair.
EMERSON—*May-day.* L. 439.

13
Multitudinous echoes awoke and died in the distance.
* * * * * *
And, when the echoes had ceased, like a sense of pain was the silence.
LONGFELLOW—*Evangeline.* Pt. II. L. 56.

14
Sweetest Echo, sweetest nymph, that liv'st unseen
Within thy airy shell,
By slow Meander's margent green,
And in the violet-embroidered vale.
MILTON—*Comus. Song.*

15
How sweet the answer Echo makes
To music at night,
When, roused by lute or horn, she wakes,
And far away, o'er lawns and lakes,
Goes answering light.
MOORE—*Echo.*

16
And more than echoes talk along the walls.
POPE—*Eloisa to Abelard.* L. 306.

17
But her voice is still living immortal,
The same you have frequently heard,
In your rambles in valleys and forests,
Repeating your ultimate word.
J. G. SAXE—*The Story of Echo.*

18
The babbling echo mocks the hounds,
Replying shrilly to the well-tun'd horns,
As if a double hunt were heard at once.
Titus Andronicus. Act II. Sc. 3. L. 17.

19
Lost Echo sits amid the voiceless mountains,
And feeds her grief.
SHELLEY—*Adonais.* St. 15.

20
Never sleeping, still awake,
Pleasing most when most I speak;
The delight of old and young,
Though I speak without a tongue.
Nought but one thing can confound me,
Many voices joining round me,
Then I fret, and rave, and gabble,
Like the labourers of Babel.
SWIFT—*An Echo.*

21 I heard * * *
* * * the great echo flap
And buffet round the hills from bluff to bluff.
TENNYSON—*Golden Year.* L. 75.

22
And a million horrible bellowing echoes broke
From the red-ribb'd hollow behind the wood,
And thunder'd up into Heaven.
TENNYSON—*Maud.* Pt. XXIII.

23
Our echoes roll from soul to soul,
And grow for ever and for ever.
Blow, bugle, blow, set the wild echoes flying,
And answer, echoes, answer, dying, dying, dying.
TENNYSON—*Princess.* IV. *Bugle Song.*

24
What would it profit thee to be the first
Of echoes, tho thy tongue should live forever,
A thing that answers, but hath not a thought
As lasting but as senseless as a stone.
FREDERICK TENNYSON—*Isles of Greece. Apollo.* L. 367.

25
Like—but oh! how different!
WORDSWORTH—*Yes, it Was the Mountain Echo.*

26
The melancholy ghosts of dead renown,
Whispering faint echoes of the world's applause.
YOUNG—*Night Thoughts.* Night IX.

ECONOMY

1
Emas non quod non opus est, sed quod necesse est. Quod non opus est, asse carum est.

Buy not what you want, but what you have need of; what you do not want is dear at a farthing.

CATO. As quoted by SENECA—*Epistles* 94.

2
Magnum vectigal est parsimonia.

Economy is a great revenue.

CICERO—*Paradoxa*. VI. 3. 49.

3
A penny saved is two pence clear,
A pin a day's a groat a year.

FRANKLIN—*Necessary Hints to those that would be Rich.*

4
Many have been ruined by buying good Pennyworths.

FRANKLIN—*Poor Richard's Almanac.*

5
Cut my cote after my cloth.

Godly Queene Hester. Interlude. (1530) Expression said to be a relic of the Sumptuary Laws.

6
Give not Saint *Peter* so much, to leave Saint *Paul* nothing.

HERBERT—*Jacula Prudentum.*
(See also RABELAIS)

7
Serviet eternum qui parvo nesciet uti.

He will always be a slave, who does not know how to live upon a little.

HORACE—*Epistles*. I. 10. 41.

8
To balance Fortune by a just expense,
Join with Economy, Magnificence.

POPE—*Moral Essays*. Ep. III. L. 223.

9
By robbing Peter he paid Paul, he kept the moon from the wolves, and was ready to catch larks if ever the heavens should fall.

RABELAIS—*Works*. Bk. I. Ch. XI. Robbing Peter to pay Paul. Westminster Abbey was called St. Peter's! St. Paul's funds were low and sufficient was taken from St. Peter's to settle the account. Expression found in COLLIER'S Reprint of THOMAS NASH—*Have with you to Saffron-Walden*. P. 9.
(See also HERBERT)

10
Sera parsimonia in fundo est.

Frugality, when all is spent, comes too late.

SENECA—*Epistolæ Ad Lucilium*. I.

11
Have more than thou showest,
Speak less than thou knowest,
Lend less than thou owest,
Ride more than thou goest,
Learn more than thou trowest,
Set less than thou throwest.

King Lear. Act I. Sc. 4. L. 131.

12
Economy, the poor man's mint.

TUPPER—*Proverbial Philosophy*. *Of Society*. L. 191.

EDUCATION (See also TEACHING)

13
Brought up in this city at the feet of Gamaliel.

Acts. XXII. 3.

14
Culture is "To know the best that has been said and thought in the world."

MATTHEW ARNOLD—*Literature and Dogma. Preface.* (1873)
(See also ARNOLD under SWEETNESS)

15
Histories make men wise; poets, witty; the mathematics, subtile; natural philosophy, deep; morals, grave; logic and rhetoric, able to contend.

BACON—*Essays*. *Of Studies*.

16
Education commences at the mother's knee, and every word spoken within the hearsay of little children tends towards the formation of character.

HOSEA BALLOU—*MS. Sermons*.

17
But to go to school in a summer morn,
Oh, it drives all joy away!
Under a cruel eye outworn,
The little ones spend the day—
In sighing and dismay.

WM. BLAKE—*The Schoolboy*. St. 2.

18
Education makes a people easy to lead, but difficult to drive; easy to govern, but impossible to enslave.

Attributed to LORD BROUGHAM.

19
Let the soldier be abroad if he will, he can do nothing in this age. There is another personage,—a personage less imposing in the eyes of some, perhaps insignificant. The schoolmaster is abroad, and I trust to him, armed with his primer, against the soldier, in full military array.

LORD BROUGHAM—*Speech*. Jan. 29, 1828.

Phrase "Look out, gentlemen, the schoolmaster is abroad" first used by BROUGHAM, in 1825, at London Mechanics' Institution, referring to the secretary, JOHN REYNOLDS, a schoolmaster.
(See also PESCHEL, VON MOLTKE)

20
Every schoolboy hath that famous testament of Grunnius Corocotta Porcellus at his fingers' ends.

BURTON—*Anatomy of Melancholy*. Pt. III. Sec. I. Mem. I. 1.
(See also SWIFT, TAYLOR, WHITEHEAD)

21
"Reeling and Writhing, of course, to begin with," the Mock Turtle replied, "and the different branches of Arithmetic—Ambition, Distraction, Uglification, and Derision."

LEWIS CARROLL—*Alice in Wonderland*. Ch. X.

22
No con quien naces, sino con quien paces.

Not with whom you are born, but with whom you are bred.

CERVANTES—*Don Quixote*. II. 10.

23
To be in the weakest camp is to be in the strongest school.

G. K. CHESTERTON—*Heretics*.

1
Quod enim munus reipublicæ afferre majus, meliusve possumus, quam si docemus atque erudimus juventutem?
What greater or better gift can we offer the republic than to teach and instruct our youth?
CICERO—*De Divinatione.* II. 2.

2
How much a dunce that has been sent to roam
Excels a dunce that has been kept at home.
COWPER—*Progress of Error.* L. 410.

3
The foundation of every state is the education of its youth.
DIOGENES. (According to STOBÆUS)

4
The Self-Educated are marked by stubborn peculiarities.
ISAAC D'ISRAELI—*Literary Character.* Ch. VI.

5
By education most have been misled.
DRYDEN—*Hind and Panther.* Pt. III. L. 389.

6
My definition of a University is Mark Hopkins at one end of a log and a student on the other.
Tradition well established that JAMES A. GARFIELD used the phrase at a New York Alumni Dinner in 1872. No such words are found, however. A letter of his, Jan., 1872, contains the same line of thought.

7
Impartially their talents scan,
Just education forms the man.
GAY—*The Owl, Swan, Cock, Spider, Ass, and the Farmer. To a Mother.* L. 9.

8
Of course everybody likes and respects self-made men. It is a great deal better to be made in that way than not to be made at all.
HOLMES—*The Autocrat of the Breakfast Table.* L. 1.

9
The true purpose of education is to cherish and unfold the seed of immortality already sown within us; to develop, to their fullest extent, the capacities of every kind with which the God who made us has endowed us.
MRS. JAMESON—*Education. Winter Studies and Summer Rambles.*

10
Much may be made of a Scotchman if he be caught young.
SAMUEL JOHNSON—*Boswell's Life of Johnson.* (1772)

11
But it was in making education not only common to all, but in some sense compulsory on all, that the destiny of the free republics of America was practically settled.
LOWELL—*Among my Books. New England Two Centuries Ago.*

12
Finally, education alone can conduct us to that enjoyment which is, at once, best in quality and infinite in quantity.
HORACE MANN—*Lectures and Reports on Education.* Lecture 1.

13
Enflamed with the study of lea[illegible] admiration of virtue; stirred up with [illegible] of living to be brave men, and worthy pat[illegible] dear to God, and famous to all ages.
MILTON—*Tract on Education.*

14
Der preussiche Schulmeister hat die Schlacht bei Sadowa gewonnen.
The Prussian schoolmaster won the battle of Sadowa.
VON MOLTKE—*In the Reichstag,* Feb. 16, 1874.
(See also BURTON, PESCHEL)

15
Tempore ruricolæ patiens fit taurus aratri.
In time the bull is brought to wear the yoke.
OVID—*Tristia.* 4. 6. 1. Trans. by THOMAS WATSON. *Hecatompathia.* No. 47.
(See also MUCH ADO ABOUT NOTHING)

16
The victory of the Prussians over the Austrians was a victory of the Prussian over the Austrian schoolmaster.
PRIVY COUNCILLOR PESCHEL, in *Ausland,* No. 19. July 17, 1866.
(See also BURTON)

17
Education is the only interest worthy the deep, controlling anxiety of the thoughtful man.
WENDELL PHILLIPS—*Speeches. Idols.*

18
Lambendo paulatim figurant.
Licking a cub into shape. (Free rendering.)
PLINY—*Nat. Hist.* VIII. 36.

19
So watchful Bruin forms with plastic care,
Each growing lump and brings it to a bear.
POPE—*Dunciad.* I. 101.

20
Then take him to develop, if you can
And hew the block off, and get out the man.
POPE—*Dunciad.* IV. 269. A notion of ARISTOTLE's that there was originally in every block of marble, a statue, which would appear on the removal of the superfluous parts. See *The Spectator.*

21
'Tis education forms the common mind;
Just as the twig is bent the tree's inclined.
POPE—*Moral Essays.* Ep. I. L. 149.

22
Twelve years ago I made a mock
Of filthy trades and traffics;
I considered what they meant by stock;
I wrote delightful sapphics;
I knew the streets of Rome and Troy,
I supped with Fates and Fairies—
Twelve years ago I was a boy,
A happy boy at Drury's.
W. M. PRAED—*School and Schoolfellows.*

23
He can write and read and cast accompt.
O monstrous!
We took him setting of boys' copies.
Here's a villain!
Henry VI. Pt. II. Act IV. Sc. 2. L. 92.

24
In time the savage bull doth bear the yoke.
Much Ado About Nothing. Act I. Sc. 1.
Quoted from KYD—*Spanish Tragedy.* Act II. Found in DODSLEY's collection.
(See also OVID)

1
God hath blessed you with a good name: to be a well-favored man is the gift of fortune, but to write and read comes by nature.
Much Ado About Nothing. Act III. Sc. 3. L. 13.

2
Only the refined and delicate pleasures that spring from research and education can build up barriers between different ranks.
MADAME DE STAËL—*Corinne*. Bk. IX. Ch. I.

3
Oh how our neighbour lifts his nose,
To tell what every schoolboy knows.
SWIFT—*Century Life*.
(See also BURTON)

4
Every school-boy knows it.
JEREMY TAYLOR—*On the Real Presence*. Sec. V. 1. Phrase attributed to MACAULAY from his frequent use of it.
(See also BURTON)

5
Of an old tale which every schoolboy knows.
WILLIAM WHITEHEAD—*The Roman Father*. *Prologue*.
(See also BURTON)

6
Still sits the school-house by the road,
A ragged beggar sunning;
Around it still the sumachs grow
And blackberry vines are running.
WHITTIER—*In School Days*.

7
Slavery is but half abolished, emancipation is but half completed, while millions of freemen with votes in their hands are left without education.
ROBERT C. WINTHROP—*Yorktown Oration*. Oct. 19, 1881.

EGOTISM (See SELF-LOVE)

EGYPT

8
Egypt! from whose all dateless tombs arose
Forgotten Pharaohs from their long repose,
And shook within their pyramids to hear
A new Cambyses thundering in their ear;
While the dark shades of forty ages stood
Like startled giants by Nile's famous flood.
BYRON—*The Age of Bronze*. V.

9
And they spoiled the Egyptians.
Exodus. XII. 36.

10
I am dying, Egypt, dying.
Antony and Cleopatra. Act IV. Sc. 15. L. 18.

ELECTRICITY

11
Stretches, for leagues and leagues, the Wire,
A hidden path for a Child of Fire—
Over its silent spaces sent,
Swifter than Ariel ever went,
From continent to continent.
WM. HENRY BURLEIGH—*The Rhyme of the Cable*.

12
And fire a mine in China, here
With sympathetic gunpowder.
BUTLER—*Hudibras*. Pt. II. Canto III. L. 295.

13
While Franklin's quiet memory climbs to heaven,
Calming the lightning which he thence hath riven.
BYRON—*Age of Bronze*. V.

14
And stoic Franklin's energetic shade
Robed in the lightnings which his hand allay'd.
BYRON—*Age of Bronze*. VIII.

15
Striking the electric chain wherewith we are darkly bound.
BYRON—*Childe Harold*. Canto IV. St. 23.
(See also CARLYLE under SYMPATHY)

16
To put a girdle round about the world.
GEO. CHAPMAN—*Bussy d'Ambois*. Act I. Sc. 1.
(See also MIDSUMMER NIGHT'S DREAM. Also CHAPMAN and WEBSTER under NAVIGATION)

17
A vast engine of wonderful delicacy and intricacy, a machine that is like the tools of the Titans put in your hands. This machinery, in its external fabric so massive and so exquisitely adjusted, and in its internal fabric making new categories of thought, new ways of thinking about life.
CHARLES FERGUSON—*Address*. *Stevens' Indicator*. Vol. XXXIV. No. 1. 1917.

18
Notwithstanding my experiments with electricity the thunderbolt continues to fall under our noses and beards; and as for the tyrant, there are a million of us still engaged at snatching away his sceptre.
FRANKLIN—*Comment on* TURGOT'S *inscription* in a letter to FELIX NOGARET, who translated the lines into French.
(See also TURGOT)

19
But matchless Franklin! What a few
Can hope to rival such as you.
Who seized from kings their sceptred pride
And turned the lightning's darts aside.
PHILIP FRENEAU—*On the Death of Benjamin Franklin*.
(See also TURGOT)

20
Is it a fact—or have I dreamt it—that by means of electricity, the world of matter has become a great nerve, vibrating thousands of miles in a breathless point of time? Rather, the round globe is a vast head, a brain, instinct with intelligence: or shall we say it is itself a thought, nothing but thought, and no longer the substance which we dreamed it.
HAWTHORNE—*The House of the Seven Gables*. *The Flight of Two Owls*.

21
A million hearts here wait our call,
All naked to our distant speech—
I wish that I could ring them all
And have some welcome news for each.
CHRISTOPHER MORLEY—*Of a Telephone Directory*. In *The Rocking Horse*.

22
An ideal's love-fraught, imperious call
That bids the spheres become articulate.
JOSEPHINE L. PEABODY—*Wireless*.

1
This is a marvel of the universe:
To fling a thought across a stretch of sky—
Some weighty message, or a yearning cry,
It matters not; the elements rehearse
Man's urgent utterance, and his words traverse
The spacious heav'ns like homing birds that fly
Unswervingly, until, upreached on high,
A quickened hand plucks off the message terse.
JOSEPHINE L. PEABODY—*Wireless.*

2
Speed the soft intercourse from soul to soul,
And waft a sigh from Indus to the Pole.
POPE—*Eloise to Abelard.* L. 57.

3
I'll put a girdle round about the earth
In forty minutes.
Midsummer Night's Dream. Act II. Sc. 1. L. 175.
(See also CHAPMAN)

4
Too like the lightning, which doth cease to be
Ere one can say "It lightens."
Romeo and Juliet. Act II. Sc. 2. L. 119.

5
Eripuit cælo fulmen, mox sceptra tyrannis.
He snatched the thunderbolt from heaven, the sceptre from tyrants.
TURGOT—*Inscription for the Houdon bust* of FRANKLIN. See CONDORCET—*Life of Turgot.* P. 200. Ed. 1786. Eripuit fulmenque Jovi, Phœboque sagittas. Modified from *Anti-Lucretius.* I. 5. 96, by CARDINAL DE POLIGNAC. Eripuit Jovi fulmen viresque tonandi. MARCUS MANLIUS—*Astronomica.* I. 104. Line claimed by FREDERICK VON DER TRENCK asserted at his trial before the Revolutionary Tribunal of Paris, July 9, 1794. See GARTENLAUBE—*Last Hours of Baron Trenck.*
(See also FRANKLIN, FRENEAU)

ELEPHANT

6
Th' unwieldy elephant,
To make them mirth, us'd all his might, and wreathed
His lithe proboscis.
MILTON—*Paradise Lost.* Bk. IV. L. 345.

7
The elephant hath joints, but none for courtesy: his legs are legs for necessity, not for flexure.
Troilus and Cressida. Act II. Sc. 3. L. 97.

ELM TREE

Ulmus

8
And the great elms o'erhead
Dark shadows wove on their aërial looms,
Shot through with golden thread.
LONGFELLOW—*Hawthorne.* St. 2.

9
In crystal vapour everywhere
Blue isles of heaven laughed between,
And far, in forest-deeps unseen,
The topmost elm-tree gather'd green
From draughts of balmy air.
TENNYSON—*Sir Launcelot and Queen Guinevere.*

ELOQUENCE

10
The most eloquent voice of our century uttered, shortly before leaving the world, a warning cry against the "Anglo-Saxon contagion."
MATTHEW ARNOLD—*Essay on Criticism,* Second Series. *Essay on Milton.* First Par. ("Most eloquent voice" said to be EMERSON'S; claimed for COLERIDGE and HUGO.)

11
He adorned whatever subject he either spoke or wrote upon, by the most splendid eloquence.
CHESTERFIELD—*Character of Bolingbroke.*
(See also FENELON, also GOLDSMITH under EPITAPHS)

12
Is enim est eloquens qui et humilia subtiliter, et magna graviter, et mediocria temperate potest dicere.
He is an eloquent man who can treat humble subjects with delicacy, lofty things impressively, and moderate things temperately.
CICERO—*De Oratore.* XXIX.

13
Discourse may want an animated "No"
To brush the surface, and to make it flow;
But still remember, if you mean to please,
To press your point with modesty and ease.
COWPER—*Conversation.* L. 101.

14
Il embellit tout qu'il touche.
He adorned whatever he touched.
FENELON—*Lettre sur les Occupations de l'Académie Française.* Sec. IV.
(See also CHESTERFIELD)

15
A good discourse is that from which nothing can be retrenched without cutting into the quick.
ST. FRANCIS DE SALES—*Letter upon Eloquence.*

16
L'éloquence est au sublime ce que le tout est à sa partie.
Eloquence is to the sublime what the whole is to its part.
LA BRUYÈRE—*Les Caractères.* Ch. I.

17
Eloquence may be found in conversations and in all kinds of writings; it is rarely found when looked for, and sometimes discovered where it is least expected.
LA BRUYÈRE—*The Characters.* Ch. I. 55.

18
Profane eloquence is transfered from the bar, where Le Maître, Pucelle, and Fourcroy formerly practised it, and where it has become obsolete, to the Pulpit, where it is out of place.
LA BRUYÈRE—*The Characters.* Ch. XVI. 2.

19
There is as much eloquence in the tone of voice, in the eyes, and in the air of a speaker as in his choice of words.
LA ROCHEFOUCAULD—*Maxims and Moral Sentences.* No. 261.

20
True eloquence consists in saying all that is necessary, and nothing but what is necessary.
LA ROCHEFOUCAULD—*Maxims and Moral Sentences.* No. 262.

1
When your crowd of attendants so loudly applaud you, Pomponius, it is not you, but your banquet, that is eloquent.
MARTIAL—*Epigrams*. Bk. VI. Ep. 48.

2
* * * as that dishonest victory
At Chæronea, fatal to liberty,
Killed with report that old man eloquent,
[Isocrates, the celebrated orator of Greece.]
MILTON—*Sonnet X*.

3
In causa facili cuivis licet esse diserto.
In an easy cause any man may be eloquent.
OVID—*Tristium*. III. 11. 21.

4
L'éloquence est une peinture de la pensée.
Eloquence is a painting of the thoughts.
PASCAL—*Pensées*. XXIV. 88.

5
It is with eloquence as with a flame; it requires fuel to feed it, motion to excite it, and it brightens as it burns.
WILLIAM PITT THE YOUNGER—*Paraphrase of Tacitus*. (See also TACITUS)

6
Pour the full tide of eloquence along,
Serenely pure, and yet divinely strong.
POPE—*Imitation of Horace*. Bk. II. Ep. II. L. 171.

7
Action is eloquence.
Coriolanus. Act III. Sc. 2. L. 76.

8
A man in all the world's new fashion planted,
That hath a mint of phrases in his brain.
Love's Labour's Lost. Act I. Sc. 1. L. 165.

9
That aged ears play truant at his tales
And younger hearings are quite ravished;
So sweet and voluble is his discourse.
Love's Labour's Lost. Act II. Sc. 1. L. 74.

10
Every tongue that speaks
But Romeo's name speaks heavenly eloquence.
Romeo and Juliet. Act III. Sc. 2. L. 32.

11
Say she be mute and will not speak a word;
Then I'll commend her volubility,
And say she uttereth piercing eloquence.
Taming of the Shrew. Act II. Sc. 1. L. 175.

12
Omnium artium domina [eloquentia].
[Eloquence] the mistress of all the arts.
TACITUS—*De Oratoribus*. XXXII.

13
Magna eloquentia, sicut flamma, materia alitur, et motibus excitatur et urendo clarescit.
It is the eloquence as of a flame; it requires matter to feed it, motion to excite it, and it brightens as it burns.
TACITUS—*De Oratoribus*. XXXVI.
(See also PITT)

14
But while listening Senates hang upon thy tongue,
Devolving through the maze of eloquence
A roll of periods, sweeter than her song.
THOMSON—*The Seasons*. *Autumn*.

15
But to a higher mark than song can reach,
Rose this pure eloquence.
WORDSWORTH—*Excursion*. Bk. VII.

EMIGRATION

16
Down where yon anch'ring vessel spreads the sail,
That, idly waiting, flaps with every gale,
Downward they move, a melancholy band,
Pass from the shore and darken all the strand.
GOLDSMITH—*Deserted Village*. L. 399.

17
Beheld the duteous son, the sire decayed,
The modest matron, and the blushing maid,
Forc'd from their homes, a melancholy train,
To traverse climes beyond the Western main.
GOLDSMITH—*Traveller*. L. 407.

18
From the vine-land, from the Rhine-land,
From the Shannon, from the Scheldt,
From the ancient homes of genius,
From the sainted home of Celt,
From Italy, from Hungary,
All as brothers join and come,
To the sinew-bracing bugle,
And the foot-propelling drum;
Too proud beneath the starry flag to die, and keep secure
The liberty they dreamed of by the Danube, Elbe, and Suir.
JOHN SAVAGE—*Muster of the North*.

19
At the gate of the West I stand,
On the isle where the nations throng.
We call them "scum o' the earth."
R. H. SCHAUFFLER—*Scum o' the Earth*.

20
Exilioque domos et dulcia limina mutant,
Atque alio patriam quærunt sub sole jacentem.
And for exile they change their homes and pleasant thresholds, and seek a country lying beneath another sun.
VERGIL—*Georgics*. Bk. II. 511.

END, THE (See also RESULTS)

21
Whatsoever thou takest in hand, remember the end, and thou shalt never do amiss.
Ecclesiasticus. VII. 36.

22
Finem respice (*or* Respice finem).
Have regard to the end.
Translation of Chilo's saying.

23
He who has put a good finish to his undertaking is said to have placed a golden crown to the whole.
EUSTATHIUS—*Commentary on the Iliad*.
(See also HOMER)

24
Si finis bonus est, totum bonum erit.
If the end be well, all will be well.
Gesta Romanorum. Tale LXVII.

25
A morning Sun, and a Wine-bred child, and a Latin-bred woman seldom end well.
HERBERT—*Jacula Prudentum*.

26
It is the end that crowns us, not the fight.
HERRICK—*Hesperides*. 340.

1
Having well polished the whole bow, he added a golden tip.
HOMER—*Iliad*. Bk. IV. III.

2
En toute chose il faut considérer la fin.
We ought to consider the end in everything.
LA FONTAINE—*Fables*. III. 5.

3
Et le chemin est long du projet à la chose.
The road is long from the project to its completion.
MOLIÈRE—*Le Tartuffe*. III. 1.

4
The end must justify the means.
PRIOR—*Hans Carvel*. L. 67.

5
Par les mêmes voies on ne va pas toujours aux mêmes fins.
By the same means we do not always arrive at the same ends.
ST. REAL.

6
All's well that ends well; still the fine's the crown;
Whate'er the course, the end is the renown.
All's Well That Ends Well. Act IV. Sc. 4. L. 35. Finis coronat opus. Proverb in LEHMANN'S *Florilegium Politicum*, etc. (1630) La Fin courronnera le tout. French saying.

7
The end crowns all;
And that old common arbitrator, Time,
Will one day end it.
Troilus and Cressida. Act IV. Sc. 5. L. 224.

8
Look to the end of a long life.
SOLON'S words to CRŒSUS.

9
It is commonly and truly also said: "Matters be ended as they be friended."
T. STARKEY—*England in the Reign of Henry VIII*. Bk. I. Ch. III. 33.

ENEMY

10
Nos amis, les ennemis.
Our friends, the enemy.
BERANGER—*L'Opinion de ces Demoiselles*.
Nos amis, nos ennemis. Our friends, our enemies.
Expression used by the French during the truce after the capture of Sebastopol, referring to the Russians. Recorded in the *London Times* of that date.
(See also MIDDLETON)

11
His father was no man's friend but his owne, and he (saith the prouerbe) is no man's foe else.
THOMAS ADAMS—*Diseases of the Soul*. (1616) P. 53.
(See BROWNE, CICERO, KING, LONGFELLOW)

12
It is better to decide a difference between enemies than friends, for one of our friends will certainly become an enemy and one of our enemies a friend.
BIAS.

13
They love him most for the enemies that he has made.
GENERAL E. S. BRAGG—*Nominating Speech for Cleveland* at the Convention of 1884.

14
Every man is his own greatest enemy, and as it were his own executioner.
SIR THOMAS BROWNE—*Religio Medici*. Same idea in CLARKE—*Parœmiologia*. (1639)
(See also ADAMS)

15
Whatever the number of a man's friends, there will be times in his life when he has one too few; but if he has only one enemy, he is lucky indeed if he has not one too many.
BULWER-LYTTON—*What Will He Do With It?* Bk. IX. Ch. III. Introduction.
(See also EMERSON)

16
A weak Invention of the Enemy.
COLLEY CIBBER—*Richard III*. (Altered) Act V. Sc. 3.
(See also RICHARD III.)

17
Nihil inimicius quam sibi ipse.
Man is his own worst enemy.
CICERO—*Epistolæ ad Atticum*. X. 12a. Sec. III.
(See also ADAMS)

18
Pereant amici, dum una inimici intercidant.
Let our friends perish, provided that our enemies fall at the same time.
CICERO—*Oratio Pro Rege Deitaro*. IX.

19
He who has a thousand friends has not a friend to spare,
And he who has one enemy will meet him everywhere.
EMERSON—*Translations. From Omar Khayyam.* Attributed to ALI BEN ABU TALEB.
(See also O'REILLY, BULWER-LYTTON)

20
Our enemies will tell the rest with pleasure.
BISHOP FLEETWOOD — *Preface to Sermons*. Ordered burned by House of Commons (May, 1712)

21
You and I were long friends; you are now my enemy, and I am yours.
BENJ. FRANKLIN—*Letter to William Strahan*. (July 5, 1775)

22
He has no enemy, you say;
My friend your boast is poor,
He who hath mingled in the fray
Of duty that the brave endure
Must have made foes. If he has none
Small is the work that he has done.
He has hit no traitor on the hip;
Has cast no cup from perjured lip;
Has never turned the wrong to right;
Has been a coward in the fight.
ANASTASIUS GRÜN. (*Free Translation*.)

23
Wee commonly say of a prodigall man that hee is no man's foe but his owne.
BISHOP JOHN KING—*Lecture on Jonas*, delivered 1594. (Ed. 1618) P. 502.
(See also ADAMS)

24
Rien n'est si dangereux qu'un ignorant ami;
Mieux vaudrait un sage ennemi.
Nothing is so dangerous as an ignorant friend. Better is it to have a wise enemy.
LA FONTAINE—*Fables*. 8, 10.

1
None but yourself who are your greatest foe.
LONGFELLOW—*Michael Angelo.* Pt. II. 3.
(See also ADAMS)

2 My nearest
And dearest enemy.
THOMAS MIDDLETON—*Anything for a Quiet Life.* Act V. Sc. 1.
(See first quotation under topic.)

3
What boots it at one gate to make defence,
And at another to let in the foe?
MILTON—*Samson Agonistes.* L. 560.

4
The world is large when its weary leagues two loving hearts divide;
But the world is small when your enemy is loose on the other side.
JOHN BOYLE O'REILLY—*Distance.*

5
His enemies shall lick the dust.
Psalms. LXXII. 9.

6
Inventé par le caloumnateur ennemy.
Invented by the calumniating enemy.
RABELAIS—*Pantagruel.* Bk. III. 11.
(See also RICHARD III.)

7
Pour tromper un rival l'artifice est permis;
On peut tout employer contre ses ennemis.
Artifice is allowable in deceiving a rival; we may employ everything against our enemies.
RICHELIEU—*Les Tuileries.*

8
If thine enemy hunger, feed him; if he thirst, give him drink: for in so doing thou shalt heap coals of fire on his head.
Romans. XII. 20.

9
In cases of defence 'tis best to weigh
The enemy more mighty than he seems;
So the proportions of defence are fill'd;
Which of a weak and niggardly projection
Doth, like a miser, spoil his coat with scanting
A little cloth.
Henry V. Act II. Sc. 4. L. 43.

10 Be advis'd;
Heat not a furnace for your foe so hot
That it do singe yourself: we may outrun,
By violent swiftness, that which we run at,
And lose by over-running.
Henry VIII. Act I. Sc. 1. L. 139

11 I do believe,
Induced by potent circumstances, that
You are mine enemy; and make my challenge
You shall not be my judge.
Henry VIII. Act II. Sc. 4. L. 76.

12
That you have many enemies, that know not
Why they are so, but, like to village-curs,
Bark when their fellows do.
Henry VIII. Act II. Sc. 4. L. 158.

13
O cunning enemy, that, to catch a saint,
With saints dost bait thy hook!
Measure for Measure. Act II. Sc. 2. L. 180.

14
I do defy him, and I spit at him;
Call him a slanderous coward and a villain:
Which to maintain I would allow him odds,
And meet him, were I tied to run afoot
Even to the frozen ridges of the Alps.
Richard II. Act I. Sc. 1. L. 60.

15
A thing devised by the enemy.
Richard III. Act V. Sc. 3. L. 306.
(See also CIBBER, RABELAIS)

16
It will let in and out the enemy
With bag and baggage.
Winter's Tale. Act I. Sc. 2. L. 205.

17
Earth could not hold us both, nor can one heaven
Contain my deadliest enemy and me.
SOUTHEY—*Roderick, the Last of the Goths.* Bk. XXI.

18
One enemy can do more hurt than ten friends can do good.
SWIFT—*Quoted in Letter.* (May 30, 1710.)

19
Le corps d'un ennemi mort sent toujours bon.
The body of a dead enemy always smells sweet.
Attributed to VESPASIAN and CHARLES IX. of France.

20
Je vais, combattre les ennemis de votre majeste, et je vous laisse au milieu des miens.
I have fought your Majesty's enemies, and I now leave you in the midst of my own.
MARECHAL DE VILLARS to LOUIS XIV, before starting for the Rhine Army. *The French Ana.* Attributed to VOLTAIRE by DUVEMET—*Vie de Voltaire.*

21
Les dons d'un ennemi leur semblainte trop à craindre.
To them it seemed that the gifts of an enemy were to be dreaded.
VOLTAIRE—*Henriade.* Ch. II.

ENGLAND

22
England! my country, great and free!
Heart of the world, I leap to thee!
BAILEY—*Festus.* Sc. *The Surface.* L. 376.

23
Let Pitt then boast of his victory to his nation of shopkeepers—(Nation Boutiquiere).
Said by BARÈRE, June 16, 1794 before the National Convention. Attributed to NAPOLEON—SCOTT'S *Life of Napoleon.* Claimed as a saying of *Francis II.* to NAPOLEON.
(See also DISRAELI, SMITH, TUCKER, also ADAMS under BUSINESS)

24
Quoique leurs chapeaux sont bien laids,
Goddam! j'aime les anglais.
In spite of their hats being very ugly, Goddam! I love the English.
BERANGER.

25
Ah! la perfide Angleterre!
Ah! the perfidious English!
BOSSUET—*Sermon on the Circumcision,* preached at Metz. Quoted by NAPOLEON on leaving England for St. Helena.

1
If I should die, think only this of me:
That there's some corner of a foreign field
That is forever England. There shall be
In that rich earth a richer dust concealed;
A dust whom England bore, shaped, made aware,
Gave, once, her flowers to love, her ways to roam,
A body of England's, breathing English air,
Washed by the rivers, blest by suns of home.

RUPERT BROOKE—*The Soldier.*
(See also INGRAM under IRELAND)

2
Oh, to be in England,
Now that April's there,
And whoever wakes in England
Sees some morning, unaware,
That the lowest boughs and the brushwood sheaf,
Round the elm-tree bole are in tiny leaf
While the chaffinch sings on the orchard bough
In England—now.

ROBERT BROWNING—*Home Thoughts from Abroad.*

3
The men of England—the men, I mean of light and leading in England.

BURKE—*Reflections on the Revolution in France.* Phrase used by DISRAELI in Speech. (Feb. 28, 1859.)

4
England is a paradise for women, and hell for horses: Italy is a paradise for horses, hell for women.

BURTON—*Anatomy of Melancholy.* Pt. III. Sec. III. Memb. 1. Subsect. 2.
(See also FULLER)

5
Men of England! who inherit
Rights that cost your sires their blood.

CAMPBELL—*Men of England.*

6
Britannia needs no bulwarks
No towers along the steep;
Her march is o'er the mountain wave,
Her home is on the deep.

CAMPBELL—*Ye Mariners of England.*

7
Il y a en Angleterre soizante sectes religieuses différentes, et une seule sauce.

In England there are sixty different religions, and only one sauce.

MARQUIS CARACCIOLI.

8
A certain man has called us, "of all peoples the wisest in action," but he added, "the stupidest in speech."

CARLYLE—*The Nigger Question.*

9
Where are the rough brave Britons to be found
With Hearts of Oak, so much of old renowned?

MRS. CENTILIVRE—*Cruel Gift. Epilogue* written by NICHOLAS ROWE. He was . . . a heart of oak, and a pillar of the land. WOOD—*Ath. Oxon.* (1691) II. 221. Yonkers that have hearts of oake at fourscore yeares. *Old Meg of Hertfordshire.* (1609)

Those pigmy tribes of Panton street,
Those hardy blades, those hearts of oak,
Obedient to a tyrant's yoke.

A Monstrous good Lounge. (1777) P. 5.
(See also GARRICK)

10
Be England what she will,
With all her faults, she is my country still.

CHURCHILL—*The Farewell.*
(See also COWPER)

11
Bind her, grind her, burn her with fire,
Cast her ashes into the sea,—
She shall escape, she shall aspire,
She shall arise to make men free;
She shall arise in a sacred scorn,
Lighting the lives that are yet unborn,
Spirit supernal, splendour eternal,
England!

HELEN GRAY CONE—*Chant of Love for England.* (1915)

12
'Tis a glorious charter, deny it who can,
That's breathed in the words, "I'm an Englishman."

ELIZA COOK—*An Englishman.*
(See also GILBERT)

13
England, with all thy faults, I love thee still—
My Country! and, while yet a nook is left
Where English minds and manners may be found,
Shall be constrained to love thee.

COWPER—*Task.* Bk. II. L. 206.
(See also CHURCHILL)

14
Without one friend, above all foes,
Britannia gives the world repose.

COWPER—*To Sir Joshua Reynolds.*

15
We are indeed a nation of shopkeepers.

BENJ. DISRAELI—*The Young Duke.* Bk. I. Ch. XI. (See also BARRÈRE)

16
Roused by the lash of his own stubborn tail,
Our lion now will foreign foes assail.

DRYDEN—*Astræa Redux.* L. 117.

17
In these troublesome days when the great Mother Empire stands splendidly isolated in Europe.

HON. GEORGE EULAS FOSTER—*Speech in the Canadian House of Commons.* (Jan. 16, 1896.)
(See also GOSCHEN, LAURIER, POINCARÉ)

18
Ils s'amusaient tristement selon la coutume de leur pays.

They [the English] amuse themselves sadly as is the custom of their country.

Attributed to FROISSART. Not found in his works. Same in DUC DE SULLY'S *Memoirs* (1630) ("l'usage" instead of "coutume.") See EMERSON—*English Traits.* Ch. VIII. HAZLITT—*Sketches and Essays. Merry England.* ("se rejouissoient" instead of "s'amusaient.")
(See also HEARNE)

19
England is a prison for men, a paradise for women, a purgatory for servants, a hell for horses.

FULLER—*Holy State.* Referred to as a proverb.
(See also BURTON)

20
Hearts of oak are our ships,
Jolly tars are our men,
We always are ready, steady, boys, steady,
We'll fight and will conquer again and again.

DAVID GARRICK—*Hearts of Oak.*
(See also CENTILIVRE)

1
Wake up England. You have been asleep too long.
KING GEORGE V., when Prince of Wales. Speech at Guildhall after a trip around the world.

2
He is an Englishman!
For he himself has said it,
And it's greatly to his credit,
That he's an Englishman!

For he might have been a Rooshian
A French or Turk or Proosian,
Or perhaps Itali-an.
But in spite of all temptations
To belong to other nations,
He remains an Englishman.
W. S. GILBERT—*H. M. S. Pinafore.*
(See also COOK)

3
The land of scholars, and the nurse of arms.
GOLDSMITH—*The Traveller.* L. 356.

4
We have stood alone in that which is called isolation—our splendid isolation, as one of our Colonial friends was good enough to call it.
LORD GOSCHEN—*Speech at Lewes.* (Feb. 26, 1896) (See also FOSTER)

5
Anglica gens est optima flens et pessima ridens.
The English race is the best at weeping and the worst at laughing.
(The English take their pleasures sadly.)
THOMAS HEARNE—*Reliquiæ Hearnianæ.* Ed. 1857. Vol. I. P. 136. (Source referred to CHAMBERLAYNE—*Anglicæ Notitia.* (1669) From old Latin saying quoted in KORNMANNUS—*De Linea Amoris.* Ch. II. P. 47. (Ed. 1610) BINDER—*Novus Thesaurus Adagiorum Latinorum.* No. 2983. NEANDER'S *Ethic Vetus et Sapiens* (1590) (With "sed" not "et," "Rustica" not "Anglica."
(See also FROISSART)

6
What have I done for you,
England, my England?
What is there I would not do,
England, my own?
W. E. HENLEY—*England, My England.*

7
His home!—the Western giant smiles,
And turns the spotty globe to find it;—
This little speck the British Isles?
'Tis but a freckle,—never mind it.
HOLMES—*A Good Time Going.*

8
Old England is our home and Englishmen are we,
Our tongue is known in every clime, our flag on every sea.
MARY HOWITT—*Old England is Our Home.*
(See also KIPLING, RICHARDS)

9
The whole [English] nation, beyond all other mortal men is most given to banquetting and feasts.
PAULUS JOVIUS—*Hist.* Bk. II. Trans. by BURTON—*Anat. of Melancholy.*
(See also CARLYLE)

10
Never was isle so little, never was sea so lone,
But over the scud and the palm-trees an English flag was flown.
KIPLING—*English Flag.*
(See also HOWITT)

11
Winds of the World give answer! They are whimpering to and fro—
And what should they know of England who only England know?—
KIPLING—*English Flag.*

12
Whether splendidly isolated or dangerously isolated, I will not now debate; but for my part, I think splendidly isolated, because this isolation of England comes from her superiority.
SIR WILFRED LAURIER—*Speech* in the Canadian House of Assembly, Feb. 5, 1896.
(See also FOSTER)

13
The New World's sons from England's breast we drew
Such milk as bids remember whence we came,
Proud of her past wherefrom our future grew,
This window we inscribe with Raleigh's fame.
LOWELL. Inscription on the Window presented to St. Margaret's Church, Westminster, London, by American citizens in honor of Sir Walter Raleigh. (1882)

14
Non seulement l'Angleterre, mais chaque Anglais est une ile.
Not only England, but every Englishman is an island.
NOVALIS—*Fragments.* (1799)

15
Let us hope that England, having saved herself by her energy, may save Europe by her example.
WILLIAM PITT. In his last Speech, made at the Lord Mayor's Banquet at Guildhall. (Nov. 9, 1805) As reported by MACAULAY—*Misc. Writings.* Vol. II. P. 368. But Europe is not to be saved by any single man. England has saved herself by her exertions, and will, as I trust, save Europe by her example. STANHOPE'S—*Life of Pitt.* Vol. IV. P. 346. Reported as told him by the DUKE OF WELLINGTON. (1838) Neither the *Morning Herald*, nor the *Times* of Nov. 11, 1805 mention these words in comment on the speech. The *London Chronicle* and *St. James's Chronicle* give different versions.

16
[King Edward] was careful not to tear England violently from the splendid isolation in which she had wrapped herself.
POINCARÉ—*Speech at Cannes.* (April 13, 1912) (See also FOSTER)

17
Oh, when shall Britain, conscious of her claim,
Stand emulous of Greek and Roman fame?
In living medals see her wars enroll'd,
And vanquished realms supply recording gold?
POPE—*Moral Essays. Epistle to Addison.* L. 53.

18
Dieu et mon droit.
God and my right.
Password of the day given by RICHARD I, to his

army at the battle of Gisors. In memory of the victory it was made the motto of the royal arms of England.

1
The martial airs of England
Encircle still the earth.
AMELIA B. RICHARDS—*The Martial Airs of England.*
(See also HOWITT)

2
O England! model to thy inward greatness,
Like little body with a mighty heart,
What might'st thou do, that honour would thee do,
Were all thy children kind and natural!
But see thy fault!
Henry V. Act II. Chorus. L. 16.

3
This royal throne of kings, this scepter'd isle,
This earth of majesty, this seat of Mars,
This other Eden, demi-paradise,
This fortress built by nature for herself
Against infection and the hand of war;
This happy breed of men, this little world,
This precious stone set in the silver sea.
Richard II. Act II. Sc. 1. L. 40.

4
There is nothing so bad or so good that you will not find Englishmen doing it; but you will never find an Englishman in the wrong. He does everything on principle. He fights you on patriotic principles; he robs you on business principles; he enslaves you on imperial principles.
G. BERNARD SHAW—*The Man of Destiny.*

5
Oh, Britannia the pride of the ocean
The home of the brave and the free,
The shrine of the sailor's devotion,
No land can compare unto thee.
DAVIS TAYLOR SHAW—*Britannia.* Probably written some time before the Crimean War, when it became popular. Changed to "Columbia the Gem of the Ocean" when sung by Shaw in America. Claimed that THOMAS À BECKET wrote words for Shaw. See *Notes and Queries.* (Aug. 26, 1899) Pp. 164, 231.

6
To found a great empire for the sole purpose of raising up a nation of shopkeepers, may at first sight appear a project fit only for a nation of shopkeepers. It is, however, a project altogether unfit for a nation of shopkeepers, but extremely fit for a nation whose government is influenced by shopkeepers.
ADAM SMITH—*Wealth of Nations.* Vol. II. Bk. IV. Ch. VII. Pt. III.
(See also BARRÈRE)

7
Saint George shalt called bee,
Saint George of mery England, the sign of victoree.
SPENSER—*Faerie Queene.* Bk. I. Canto X. St. 61.

8
There is no land like England,
Where'er the light of day be;
There are no hearts like English hearts,
Such hearts of oak as they be;
There is no land like England,
Where'er the light of day be:
There are no men like Englishmen,
So tall and bold as they be!
And these will strike for England,
And man and maid be free
To foil and spoil the tyrant
Beneath the greenwood tree.
TENNYSON—*Foresters. Song.*

9
First drink a health, this solemn night,
A health to England, every guest;
That man's the best cosmopolite,
Who loves his native country best.
May Freedom's oak forever live
With stronger life from day to day;
That man's the true Conservative
Who lops the moulder'd branch away.
Hands all round!
God the tyrant's hope confound!
To this great cause of Freedom drink, my friends,
And the great name of England round and round.
TENNYSON—*Hands all around.* In *Memoirs of* TENNYSON *by his son.* Vol. I. P. 345.

10
When Britain first at Heaven's command,
Arose from out the azure main,
This was the charter of the land,
And guardian angels sung this strain;
"Rule Britannia! rule the waves;
Britons never will be slaves."
JAMES THOMSON—*Masque of Alfred.* Written by THOMSON AND MALLET. MALLET rearranged the *Masque Alfred* for the stage, and introduced Thomson's Song. See DR. DINSDALE'S edition of MALLET. (1851) P. 292.

11
A shopkeeper will never get the more custom by beating his customers, and what is true of a shopkeeper is true of a shopkeeping nation.
JOSIAH TUCKER—*Four Tracts on Political and Commercial Subjects.*
(The words are said to have been used by Dr. Tucker, in a sermon, some years before they appeared in print.)
(See also BARRÈRE)

12
Froth at the top, dregs at bottom, but the middle excellent.
VOLTAIRE—*Description of the English Nation.*

13
Set in this stormy Northern sea,
Queen of these restless fields of tide,
England! what shall men say of thee,
Before whose feet the worlds divide?
OSCAR WILDE—*Ave Imperatrix.*

ENJOYMENT

14
For Solomon, he lived at ease, and full
Of honour, wealth, high fare, aimed not beyond
Higher design than to enjoy his state.
MILTON—*Paradise Regained.* Bk. II. L. 201.

15
Though throned in highest bliss
Equal to God, and equally enjoying
God-like fruition.
MILTON—*Paradise Lost.* Bk. III. L. 305.

16
Who can enjoy alone?
Or all enjoying what contentment find?
MILTON—*Paradise Lost.* Bk. VIII. L. 365.

1

Heaven forbids, it is true, certain gratifications, but there are ways and means of compounding such matters.

MOLIÈRE—*Tartuffe*. Act IV. Sc. 5.

2

Whether with Reason, or with Instinct blest,
Know, all enjoy that pow'r which suits them best.

POPE—*Essay on Man*. Ep. III. L. 79.

3

Sleep, riches, and health, to be truly enjoyed, must be interrupted.

RICHTER—*Flour, Fruit, and Thorn Pieces*. Ch. VIII.

4

Je l'ai toujours dit et senti, la véritable jouissance ne se décrit point.

I have always said and felt that true enjoyment can not be described.

ROUSSEAU—*Confessions*. VIII.

5

You were made for enjoyment, and the world was filled with things which you will enjoy, unless you are too proud to be pleased by them, or too grasping to care for what you cannot turn to other account than mere delight.

RUSKIN—*Stones of Venice*. Vol. I. Ch. II. 2.

6

Res severa est verum gaudium

A thing seriously pursued affords true enjoyment.

SENECA—*Epistles*. XXIII. 3. 4.

7

Quam vellem longas tecum requiescere noctes,
Et tecum longos pervigilare dies.

How could I, blest with thee, long nights employ;
And how with thee the longest day enjoy!

TIBULLUS—*Carmina*. III. 6. 53.

ENTHUSIASM

8

However, 'tis expedient to be wary:
Indifference certes don't produce distress;
And rash enthusiasm in good society
Were nothing but a moral inebriety.

BYRON—*Don Juan*. Canto XIII. St. 35.

9

No wild enthusiast ever yet could rest,
Till half mankind were like himself possess'd.

COWPER—*Progress of Error*. L. 470.

10

Enthusiasm is that secret and harmonious spirit which hovers over the production of genius, throwing the reader of a book, or the spectator of a statue, into the very ideal presence whence these works have really originated. A great work always leaves us in a state of musing.

ISAAC D'ISRAELI—*Literary Character*. Ch. XII. Last lines.

11

Nothing great was ever achieved without enthusiasm.

EMERSON—*Essay*. *On Circles*. Last Par.

12

Zwang erbittert die Schwärmer immer, aber bekehrt sie nie.

Opposition embitters the enthusiast but never converts him.

SCHILLER—*Cabale und Liebe*. III. 1.

13

Sonderbarer Schwärmer!

Enthusiast most strange.

SCHILLER—*Don Carlos*. III. 10. 277.

14

Enthusiasm is that temper of the mind in which the imagination has got the better of the judgment.

BISHOP WARBURTON—*Divine Legation*. Bk. V. App.

ENVY

15

With that malignant envy which turns pale,
And sickens, even if a friend prevail.

CHURCHILL—*The Rosciad*. L. 127.

16

Rabiem livoris acerbi
Nulla potest placare quies.

Nothing can allay the rage of biting envy.

CLAUDIANUS—*De Raptu Proserpinæ*. III. 290.

17

Envy's a sharper spur than pay:
No author ever spar'd a brother.

GAY—*Fables*. Pt. I. Fable 10.

18

Fools may our scorn, not envy, raise.
For envy is a kind of praise.

GAY—*The Hound and the Huntsman*.

19

But, oh! what mighty magician can assuage
A woman's envy?

GEO. GRANVILLE (Lord Lansdowne)—*Progress of Beauty*.

20

Envy not greatness: for thou mak'st thereby
Thyself the worse, and so the distance greater.

HERBERT—*The Church. Church Porch*. St. 44.

21

It is better to be envied than pitied.

HERODOTUS—*Thalia* (Same idea in PINDAR)

22

The artist envies what the artist gains,
The bard the rival bard's successful strains.

HESIOD—*Works and Days*. Bk. I. L. 43.

23

Invidus alterius marescit rebus opimis;
Invidia Siculi non invenere tyranni
Majus tormentum.

The envious pine at others' success; no greater punishment than envy was devised by Sicilian tyrants.

HORACE—*Epistles*. I. 2. 57.

24

Ego si risi quod ineptus
Pastillos Rufillus olet, Gargonius hircum, lividus et mordax videar?

If I smile at the strong perfumes of the silly Rufillus must I be regarded as envious and ill-natured?

HORACE—*Satires*. I. 4. 91.

25

Envy! eldest-born of hell!

CHARLES JENNENS of Gopsall. Also ascribed to NEWBURGH HAMILTON. Chorus of HANDEL's Oratorio, *Saul*.

26

Invidiam, tamquam ignem, summa petere.

Envy, like fire, soars upward.

LIVY—*Annales*. VIII. 31.

1
A proximis quisque minime anteiri vult.
No man likes to be surpassed by those of his own level.
LIVY—*Annales*. XXXVIII. 49.

2
Les envieux mourront, mais non jamais l'envie.
The envious will die, but envy never.
MOLIÈRE—*Tartuffe*. V. 3.

3
Pascitur in vivis livor; post fata quiescit.
Envy feeds on the living. It ceases when they are dead.
OVID—*Amorum*. I. 15. 39.

4
Ingenium magni detractat livor Homeri.
Envy depreciates the genius of the great Homer.
OVID—*Remedia Amoris*. CCCLXV.

5
Summa petit livor: perflant altissima venti.
Envy assails the noblest: the winds howl around the highest peaks.
OVID—*Remedia Amoris*. CCCLXIX.

6
Envy will merit as its shade pursue,
But like a shadow proves the substance true.
POPE—*Essay on Criticism*. Pt. II. L. 266.

7
Envy, to which th' ignoble mind's a slave,
Is emulation in the learn'd or brave.
POPE—*Essay on Man*. Ep. II. L. 191.

8
L'invidia, figliuol mio, se stessa macera,
E si dilegua come agnel per fascino.
Envy, my son, wears herself away, and droops like a lamb under the influence of the evil eye.
SANNAZARO—*Ecloga Sesta*.

9
It is the practice of the multitude to bark at eminent men, as little dogs do at strangers.
SENECA—*Of a Happy Life*. Ch. XIX.

10
In seeking tales and informations
Against this man, whose honesty the devil
And his disciples only envy at,
Ye blew the fire that burns ye.
Henry VIII. Act V. Sc. 3. L. 110.

11
Such men as he be never at heart's ease
Whiles they behold a greater than themselves:
And therefore are they very dangerous.
Julius Cæsar. Act I. Sc. 2. L. 208.

12
No metal can,
No, not the hangman's axe, bear half the keenness
Of thy sharp envy.
Merchant of Venice. Act IV. Sc. 1. L. 124.

13
Arise, fair sun, and kill the envious moon,
Who is already sick and pale with grief,
That thou her maid art far more fair than she:
Be not her maid, since she is envious.
Romeo and Juliet. Act II. Sc. 2. L. 4.

14
We make ourselves fools, to disport ourselves;
And spend our flatteries, to drink those men
Upon whose age we void it up again,
With poisonous spite and envy.
Timon of Athens. Act I. Sc. 2. L. 141.

15
The general's disdain'd
By him one step below; he by the next;
That next by him beneath; so every step,
Exampled by the first pace that is sick
Of his superior, grows to an envious fever
Of pale and bloodless emulation.
Troilus and Cressida. Act I. Sc. 3. L. 129.

16
Base Envy withers at another's joy,
And hates that excellence it cannot reach.
THOMSON—*The Seasons*. *Spring*. L. 28.

EPIGRAMS

17
What is an epigram? a dwarfish whole,
Its body brevity, and wit its soul.
Author unknown. See BRANDER MATTHEWS—*American Epigrams*. *Harper's Mag.*, Nov., 1903.

18
The diamond's virtues well might grace
The epigram, and both excel
In brilliancy in smallest space,
And power to cut as well.
GEORGE BIRDSEYE. See BRANDER MATTHEWS, *Harper's Mag.*, Nov., 1903.
(See also YRIARTE)

19
Lumine Acon dextre,—capta est Leonilla sinistre,
Et potis est forma vincere uterque dees:
Blande puer, lumen quod habes concede sorori,
Sic tu cæcus Amor, sic erit illa Venus.
Acon his right, Leonilla her left eye
Doth want; yet each in form, the gods out-vie.
Sweet boy, with thine, thy sister's sight improved:
So shall she Venus be, thou God of Love.
Epigram said to be the "most celebrated of modern epigrams," by WARTON, in his *Essay on Pope*. I. P. 299. (Ed. 1772) Trans. as given in a *Collection of Epigrams*. Vol. I. No. 223.

20
Unlike my subject, I will make my song.
It shall be witty, and it shan't be long.
CHESTERFIELD. See note by CROKER in BOSWELL'S *Life of Johnson*, July 19, 1763. (When SIR THOMAS ROBINSON asked for an epigram on his friend LONG.)

21
This picture, plac'd the busts between
Gives Satire all its strength;
Wisdom and Wit are little seen
While Folly glares at length.
Epigram on the portrait of BEAU NASH placed between the busts of POPE and NEWTON in the Pump Room at Bath, England. Attributed to LORD CHESTERFIELD by DR. MATTHEW MATY in his *Memoirs of Chesterfield*. Sec. IV, prefixed to second ed. of *Miscellaneous Works of the Earl of Chesterfield*. LOCKER-LAMPSON credits only four of the lines of the whole epigram to Chesterfield. JANE BRERETON given credit for them. (See poems. 1744.) A copy of the poems of HENRY NORRIS (1740) in the British Museum contains the lines. See *Notes and Queries*, Feb. 10, 1917. P. 119; also Aug., 1917. P. 379.

1
Report says that you, Fidentinus, recite my compositions in public as if they were your own. If you allow them to be called mine, I will send you my verses gratis; if you wish them to be called yours, pray buy them, that they may be mine no longer.
MARTIAL—*Epigrams*. Bk. I. Ep. 29.

2
The book which you are reading aloud is mine, Fidentinus; but, while you read it so badly, it begins to be yours.
MARTIAL—*Epigrams*. Bk. I. Ep. 38.

3
You are pretty,—we know it; and young,—it is true; and rich,—who can deny it? But when you praise yourself extravagantly, Fabulla, you appear neither rich, nor pretty, nor young.
MARTIAL—*Epigrams*. Bk. I. Ep. 64.

4
"You are too free spoken," is your constant remark to me, Chœrilus. He who speaks against you, Chœrilus, is indeed a free speaker.
MARTIAL—*Epigrams*. Bk. I. Ep. 67.

5
You complain, Velox, that the epigrams which I write are long. You yourself write nothing; your attempts are shorter.
MARTIAL—*Epigrams*. Bk. I. Ep. 110.

6
What's this that myrrh doth still smell in thy
kiss,
And that with thee no other odour is?
'Tis doubt, my Postumus, he that doth smell
So sweetly always, smells not very well.
MARTIAL—*Epigrams*. Bk. II. Ep. 12.

7
Since your legs, Phœbus, resemble the horns of the moon, you might bathe your feet in a cornucopia.
MARTIAL—*Epigrams*. Bk. II. Ep. 35.

8
In whatever place you meet me, Postumus, you cry out immediately, and your very first words are, "How do you do?" You say this, even if you meet me ten times in one single hour: you, Postumus, have nothing, I suppose, to do.
MARTIAL—*Epigrams*. Bk. II. Ep. 67.

9
If you wish, Faustinus, a bath of boiling water to be reduced in temperature,—a bath, such as scarcely Julianus could enter,—ask the rhetorician Sabinæus to bathe himself in it. He would freeze the warm baths of Nero.
MARTIAL—*Epigrams*. Bk. III. Ep. 25.

10
I could do without your face, and your neck, and your hands, and your limbs, and your bosom, and other of your charms. Indeed, not to fatigue myself with enumerating each of them, I could do without you, Chloe, altogether.
MARTIAL—*Epigrams*. Bk. III. Ep. 53.

11
Lycoris has buried all the female friends she had, Fabianus: would she were the friend of my wife!
MARTIAL—*Epigrams*. Bk. IV. Ep. 24.

12
You were constantly, Matho, a guest at my villa at Tivoli. Now you buy it—I have deceived you; I have merely sold you what was already your own.
MARTIAL—*Epigrams*. Bk. IV. Ep. 79.

13
Do you wonder for what reason, Theodorus, notwithstanding your frequent requests and importunities, I have never presented you with my works? I have an excellent reason; it is lest you should present me with yours.
MARTIAL—*Epigrams*. Bk. V. Ep. 73.

14
You put fine dishes on your table, Olus, but you always put them on covered. This is ridiculous; in the same way I could put fine dishes on my table.
MARTIAL—*Epigrams*. Bk. X. Ep. 54.

15
You ask for lively epigrams, and propose lifeless subjects. What can I do, Cæcilianus? You expect Hyblæn or Hymethian honey to be produced, and yet offer the Attic bee nothing but Corsican thyme?
MARTIAL—*Epigrams*. Bk. XI. Ep. 42.

16
And have you been able, Flaccus, to see the slender Thais? Then, Flaccus, I suspect you can see what is invisible.
MARTIAL—*Epigrams*. Bk. XI. Ep. 101.

17
When to secure your bald pate from the weather,
You lately wore a cap of black neats' leather;
He was a very wag, who to you said,
"Why do you wear your slippers on your head?"
MARTIAL—*Epigrams*. Bk. XII. Ep. 45. Trans. by HAY.

18
See how the mountain goat hangs from the summit of the cliff; you would expect it to fall; it is merely showing its contempt for the dogs.
MARTIAL—*Epigrams*. Bk. XIII. Ep. 99.

19
Never think of leaving perfumes or wine to your heir. Administer these yourself, and let him have your money.
MARTIAL—*Epigrams*. Bk. XIII. Ep. 126.

20
Sir Drake whom well the world's end knew
Which thou did'st compass round,
And whom both Poles of heaven once saw
Which North and South do bound,
The stars above would make thee known,
If men here silent were;
The sun himself cannot forget
His fellow traveller.
JOHN OWEN—Epigram on SIR FRANCIS DRAKE. Pt. II. 39 of first volume dedicated to LADY MARY NEVILLE. Trans. by COWLEY. See GROSSART's ed. of COWLEY. Vol. I. P. 156.

21
Some learned writers . . . have compared a Scorpion to an Epigram . . . because as the sting of the Scorpion lyeth in the tayl, so the force and virtue of an epigram is in the conclusion.
TOPSELL—*Serpent*. P. 756. (1653)

1
Thou art so witty, profligate and thin,
At once we think thee Satan, Death and Sin.
YOUNG—*Epigram on Voltaire,* who had criticised the characters of the same name in MILTON'S *Paradise Lost.*

2
The qualities all in a bee that we meet,
In an epigram never should fail;
The body should always be little and sweet,
And a sting should be felt in its tail.
Attributed to YRIARTE by BRANDER MATTHEWS—*American Epigrams. Harper's Monthly,* Nov., 1903.
(See also BIRDSEYE)

EPITAPH

3
Here lies the remains of James Pady, Brickmaker, in hope that his clay will be remoulded in a workmanlike manner, far superior to his former perishable materials.
Epitaph from Addiscombe Church-yard, Devonshire.

4
Stavo bene; per star meglio, sto qui.
I was well, I would be better; I am here.
ADDISON'S translation of the epitaph on the monument of an Italian Valetudinarian. *Spectator.* No. 25. *Boswell's Johnson,* April 7, 1775.
(See also DRYDEN, also WALPOLE under SCOTLAND)

5
Sufficit huic tumulus, cui non suffecerit orbis.
A tomb now suffices him for whom the whole world was not sufficient.
Epitaph on Alexander the Great.

6
If Paris that brief flight allow,
My humble tomb explore!
It bears: "Eternity, be thou
My refuge!" and no more.
MATTHEW ARNOLD—*Epitaph.*

7
Here lies who, born a man, a grocer died.
Translation of a French epitaph: Né homme—mort épicier. ALFRED AUSTIN—*Golden Age.*

8
Here lies Anne Mann; she lived an
Old maid and died an old Mann.
Bath Abbey.

9
Lie lightly on my ashes, gentle earthe.
BEAUMONT AND FLETCHER—*Tragedy of Bonduca.* Act IV. Sc. 3. ("Sit tibi terra levis," familiar inscription.)
(See also EVANS, OVID, SENECA)

10
And the voice of men shall call,
"He is fallen like us all,
Though the weapon of the Lord was in his hand:"
And thine epitaph shall be—
"He was wretched ev'n as we;"
And thy tomb may be unhonoured in the land.
ROBERT BUCHANAN—*The Modern Warrior.* St. 7.

11
And be the Spartan's epitaph on me—
"Sparta hath many a worthier son than he."
BYRON—*Childe Harold.* Canto IV. St. 10.

12
Shrine of the mighty! can it be,
That this is all remains of thee?
BYRON—*Giaour.* L. 106.

13
Kind reader! take your choice to cry or laugh;
Here HAROLD lies—but where's his Epitaph?
If such you seek, try Westminster, and view
Ten thousand, just as fit for him as you.
BYRON—*Substitute for an Epitaph.*

14
Yet at the resurrection we shall see
A fair edition, and of matchless worth,
Free from erratas, new in heaven set forth.
JOSEPH CAPEN—*Lines upon Mr. John Foster.* Borrowed from REV. B. WOODBRIDGE.
(See also FRANKLIN, GEDGE, MEADER, QUARLES, SMOLLETT)

15
Loe here the precious dust is layd;
Whose purely-temper'd clay was made
So fine that it the guest betray'd.
Else the soule grew so fast within,
It broke the outward shell of sinne
And so was hatch'd a cherubin.
THOS. CAREW—*Inscription on Tomb of Lady Maria Wentworth.* In Toddington Church, Bedfordshire, England.

16
This Mirabeau's work, then, is done. He sleeps with the primeval giants. He has gone over to the majority: "Abiit ad plures."
CARLYLE—*Essay on Mirabeau.* Close.

17
It is so soon that I am done for,
I wonder what I was begun for!
Epitaph in Cheltenham Church-yard.

18
Ere sin could blight or sorrow fade,
Death came with friendly care;
The opening bud to Heaven conveyed,
And bade it blossom there.
COLERIDGE—*Epitaph on an Infant.*

19
Peas to his Hashes.
Epitaph on a Cook (London).

20
Underneath this crust
Lies the mouldering dust
Of Eleanor Batchelor Shoven,
Well versed in the arts
Of pies, custards and tarts,
And the lucrative trade of the oven.
When she lived long enough,
She made her last puff,
A puff by her husband much praised,
And now she doth lie
And make a dirt pie,
In hopes that her crust may be raised.
Epitaph on a Cook (Yorkshire).

21
What wee gave, wee have;
What wee spent, wee had;
What wee left, wee lost.
Epitaph on EDWARD COURTENAY, EARL OF DEVON. (1419) In CLEVELAND'S *Geneal. Hist. of the Family of Courtenay.* P. 142. Said to be on a tomb in Padua. Attributed to CARLYLE; not found. Like inscriptions are found on many old tombstones. The oldest

is probably the one in the choir of St. Peter's Church at St. Albans.

(See also RAVENSHAW; also QUARLES under POSSESSION; MILLER under GIFTS)

1
Praised, wept,
And honoured, by the muse he loved.

Lines from the epitaph of JAMES CRAGGS in Westminster Abbey.
(See also POPE)

2
And when I lie in the green kirkyard,
With the mould upon my breast,
Say not that she did well—or ill,
"Only, She did her best."

MRS. CRAIK (Miss Mulock). Given in her obituary notice in the *Athenæum*, Oct. 22, 1887.

3
O man! whosoever thou art, and whensoever thou comest, for come I know thou wilt, I am Cyrus, founder of the Persian empire. Envy me not the little earth that covers my body.

PLUTARCH—*Life of Alexander. Epitaph of Cyrus.*

4
Full many a life he saved
With his undaunted crew;
He put his trust in Providence,
And Cared Not How It Blew.

Epitaph in Deal Churchyard.

5
His form was of the manliest beauty,
His heart was kind and soft,
Faithful, below, he did his duty;
But now he's gone aloft.

CHARLES DIBDIN—*Tom Bowling*. Written on the death of his brother. Inscribed on Charles Dibdin's gravestone, in the cemetery of St. Martin's-in-the-Fields, Camden Town.

6
For though his body's under hatches,
His soul has gone aloft.

CHARLES DIBDIN—*Tom Bowling*. Written on the death of his brother.

7
This comes of altering fundamental laws and overpersuading by his landlord to take physic (of which he died) for the benefit of the doctor—Stavo bene (was written on his monument) ma per star meglio, sto qui.

DRYDEN—*Dedication of the Æneïd*. XIV. 149.
(See also ADDISON)

8
Here lies Du Vall; reader, if male thou art,
Look to thy purse; if female, to thy heart.

CLAUDE DU VALL'S Epitaph in Covent Garden Church. Found in FRANCIS WATT'S *Law's Slumber Room*. 2nd Series.

9
If e'er she knew an evil thought
She spoke no evil word:
Peace to the gentle! She hath sought
The bosom of her Lord.

EBENEZER ELLIOT—*Hannah Ratcliff*.

10
"Let there be no inscription upon my tomb. Let no man write my epitaph. No man can write my epitaph. I am here ready to die. I am not allowed to vindicate my character; and when I am prevented from vindicating myself, let no man dare calumniate me. Let my character and motives repose in obscurity and peace, till other times and other men can do them justice."

ROBERT EMMET—*Speech on his Trial and Conviction for High Treason*. September, 1803.

11
Corpus requiescat a malis.
May his body rest free from evil.

ENNIUS, quoted by CICERO—*Tusc.* I. 44.

12
Under this stone, reader, survey
Dead Sir John Vanbrugh's house of clay:
Lie heavy on him, earth! for he
Laid many heavy loads on thee.

DR. ABEL EVANS—Epitaph on the architect of Blenheim Palace. (Vanbrugh is buried in St. Stephen's Church, Walbrook, England.)

13
Lie light upon him, earth! tho' he
Laid many a heavy load on thee.

As quoted by SNUFFLING—*Epitaphia; Architects*. BOX—*Elegies and Epitaphs*. VOLTAIRE—*Letters*. (1733) P. 187.
(See also BEAUMONT)

14
The body of Benjamin Franklin, Printer, (Like the cover of an old book, its contents torn out and stript of its lettering and gilding), Lies here, food for worms; But the work shall not be lost, for it will (as he believed) appear once more in a new and more elegant edition, revised and corrected by the author.

BENJAMIN FRANKLIN—*Epitaph on Himself*. Written in 1728. Revised by himself from an earlier one. JOHN DAVIS, in *Travels of Four Years and a Half in the United States of America*, gives similar epitaph in Latin, said to have been written by "An Eton scholar." (See also CAPEN)

15
Quand je serai la, je serai sans souci.
When I shall be there, I shall be without care.

FREDERICK THE GREAT. His inscription written at the foot of the statue of Flora at Sans Souci, where he wished to be buried. His body lies in the church at Potsdam.

16
Here lies Fred,
Who was alive and is dead.
Had it been his father,
I had much rather.
Had it been his brother,
Still better than another.
Had it been his sister,
No one would have missed her.
Had it been the whole generation,
Still better for the nation.
But since 'tis only Fred,
Who was alive, and is dead,
There's no more to be said.

Epitaph to FREDERICK, PRINCE OF WALES (Father of George III), as given by THACKERAY—*Four Georges*. Probably version of a French epigram "Colas est morte de maladie," found in *Les Epigrammes de Jean Ogier Gombauld*. (1658) Several early versions of same. See *Notes and Queries*. May 3, 1902. P. 345.

17
"Fuller's earth."

THOMAS FULLER—*Epitaph written by Himself*.

1
Here lies Nolly Goldsmith, for shortness called Noll,
Who wrote like an angel, and talked like poor Poll.
DAVID GARRICK.

2
Here lie together, waiting the Messiah
The little David and the great Goliath.
Note in *Thespian Dict.* appended to account of GARRICK, whose remains lie close to those of JOHNSON, in Westminster Abbey.

3
Life is a jest, and all things show it,
I thought so once, but now I know it.
GAY—*My Own Epitaph.*

4
Like a worn out type, he is returned to the Founder in the hope of being recast in a better and more perfect mould.
Epitaph on PETER GEDGE. Parish church, St. Mary, Bury St. Edmund's.
(See also CAPEN)

5
I have expended; I have given; I have kept;
I have possessed; I do possess; I have lost;
I am punished. What I formerly expended, I have; what I gave away, I have.
Gesta Romanorum. Tale XVI. Found on the golden sarcophagus of a Roman Emperor.
(See also RAVENSHAW)

6
What we say of a thing that has just come in fashion
And that which we do with the dead,
Is the name of the honestest man in the nation:
What more of a man can be said?
GOLDSMITH—Punning epitaph on JOHN NEWBERY, the publisher.

7
Qui nullum fere scribendi genus non tetigit; nullum quod tetigit non ornavit.
Who left nothing of authorship untouched, and touched nothing which he did not adorn.
GOLDSMITH'S *Epitaph in Westminster Abbey.* Written by SAMUEL JOHNSON.
(See also FENELON under ELOQUENCE)

8
And many a holy text around she strews
That teach the rustic moralist to die.
GRAY—*Elegy in a Country Churchyard.* St. 21.

9
Balnea, vina, Venus corrumpunt corpora nostra;
Sed vitam faciunt baldea, vina, Venus.
Baths, wine and Venus bring decay to our bodies; but baths, wine and Venus make up life.
Epitaph in GRUTER'S *Monumenta.*

10
Beneath these green trees rising to the skies,
The planter of them, Isaac Greentree, lies;
The time shall come when these green trees shall fall,
And Isaac Greentree rise above them all.
Epitaph at Harrow.

11
His foe was folly and his weapon wit.
ANTHONY HOPE HAWKINS—Inscribed on the bronze tablet placed in memory of Sir WILLIAM GILBERT on the Victoria Embankment, Aug. 31, 1915. Bronze is by SIR GEORGE FRAMPTON.

12
Farewell, vain world, I've had enough of thee,
And Valies't not what thou Can'st say of me;
Thy Smiles I count not, nor thy frowns I fear,
My days are past, my head lies quiet here.
What faults you saw in me take Care to shun,
Look but at home, enough is to be done.
Epitaph over WILLIAM HARVEY in Greasley Churchyard, England. (1756) A travesty of the same is over the tomb of PHILLIS ROBINSON, in that churchyard. (1866) See ALFRED STAPLETON—*The Churchyard Scribe.* P. 95.
(See also PUCCI)

13
Man's life is like unto a winter's day,
Some break their fast and so depart away,
Others stay dinner then depart full fed;
The longest age but sups and goes to bed.
Oh, reader, then behold and see,
As we are now so must you be.
BISHOP HENSHAW—*Horæ Succisivæ.*

14
But here's the sunset of a tedious day.
These two asleep are; I'll but be undrest,
And so to bed. Pray wish us all good rest.
HERRICK—*Epitaph on Sir Edward Giles.*

15
Here she lies a pretty bud,
Lately made of flesh and blood;
Who, as soone fell fast asleep,
As her little eyes did peep.
Give her strewings, but not stir
The earth that lightly covers her.
HERRICK—*Upon a Child that Dyed.*

16
Under the shadow of a leafy bough
That leaned toward a singing rivulet,
One pure white stone, whereon, like crown on brow,
The image of the vanished star was set;
And this was graven on the pure white stone
In golden letters—"WHILE SHE LIVED SHE SHONE."
JEAN INGELOW—*Star's Monument.* St. 47.

17
The hand of him here torpid lies,
That drew th' essential form of grace,
Here closed in death th' attentive eyes
That saw the manners in the face.
SAMUEL JOHNSON—*Epitaph for Hogarth.*

18
Sleep undisturbed within this peaceful shrine,
Till angels wake thee with a note like thine.
SAMUEL JOHNSON—*Epitaph on Claude Phillips.*

19
Underneath this stone doth lie
As much beauty as could die;
Which in life did harbor give
To more virtue than doth live.
If at all she had a fault,
Leave it buried in this vault.
BEN JONSON—*Epigram CXXIV. To Lady Elizabeth L. H.*

20
Underneath this sable herse
Lies the subject of all verse,—
Sydneye's sister, Pembroke's mother.
Death, ere thou hast slaine another,
Faire and learn'd and good as she,
Tyme shall throw a dart at thee.

Attributed to BEN JONSON—Epitaph on the Countess of Pembroke. Claimed for SIR THOMAS BROWNE by SIR EGERTON BRYDGES. It is in *Lansdowne MS.* No. 777, in British Museum. *Poems by* BROWNE. Vol. II. P. 342. Ed. by W. C. HAZLITT for the Roxburghe Library.

1
Here lies one whose name was writ in water.
Engraved on Keats' tombstone at his own desire. Phrase "writ in water" in HAKEWELL'S *Apologie.* (1635) P. 127. *King Henry VIII.* IV. II.

2
I conceive disgust at these impertinent and misbecoming familiarities inscribed upon your ordinary tombstone.
LAMB.

3
Satire does not look pretty upon a tombstone.
LAMB.

4
I strove with none, for none was worth my strife;
Nature I loved, and after Nature, Art;
I warmed both hands before the fire of life;
It sinks, and I am ready to depart.
WALTER SAVAGE LANDOR—*Epitaph on Himself.*

5
Emigravit, is the inscription on the tombstone where he lies;
Dead he is not, but departed,—for the artist never dies.
LONGFELLOW—*Nuremberg.*

6
Here lie I, Martin Elginbrodde:
Have mercy o' my soul, Lord God;
As I wad do, were I Lord God,
And ye were Martin Elginbrodde.
GEORGE MCDONALD—*David Elginbrod.* Ch. XIII.

7
The shameless Chloe placed on the tombs of her seven husbands the inscription, "The work of Chloe." How could she have expressed herself more plainly?
MARTIAL—*Epigrams.* Bk. IX. Ep. 15.

8
This work, newly revised and improved by its great Author, will reappear in a splendid day.
Epitaph on OSCAR MEADER in a church in Berlin. (See also CAPEN)

9
Ci gît l'enfant gâté du monde qu'il gâta.
Here lies the child spoiled by the world which he spoiled.
BARONNE de MONTOLIEU—*Epitaph on Voltaire.*

10
Requiescat in pace.
May he rest in peace.
Order of the Mass.
(See also ENNIUS)

11
Beneath this stone old Abraham lies;
Nobody laughs and nobody cries.
Where he is gone, and how he fares,
Nobody knows and nobody cares.
On the monument of ABRAHAM NEWLAND, principal cashier of the Bank of England. (Died, 1807. His own lines.)

12 Jacet ecce Tibullus;
Vix manet e toto parva quod urna capit.
Here lies Tibullus; of all that he was there scarcely remains enough to fill a small urn.
OVID—*Amorum.* Bk. III. 9, 39.

13
Molliter ossa cubent.
May his bones rest gently.
OVID—*Heroides.* VII. 162.
(See also BEAUMONT)

14
"In his last binn Sir Peter lies."
*   *   *   *
He kept at true humour's mark
The social flow of pleasure's tide:
He never made a brow look dark,
Nor caused a tear, but when he died.
THOS. LOVE PEACOCK—*To Sir Peter.*
(See also POPE, also BERANGER under ROYALTY)

15
Postquam est mortem aptus Plautus: comœdia luget
Scena deserta, dein risus ludus jocusque
Et numeri innumeri simul omnes collacrumarunt.
Plautus has prepared himself for a life beyond the grave; the comic stage deserted weeps; laughter also and jest and joke; and poetic and prosaic will bewail his loss together.
Epitaph of PLAUTUS, by himself.

16
Under this marble, or under this sill,
Or under this turf, or e'en what they will,
Whatever an heir, or a friend in his stead,
Or any good creature shall lay o'er my head,
Lies one who ne'er car'd, and still cares not a pin
What they said or may say of the mortal within;
But who, living and dying, serene, still and free,
Trusts in God that as well as he was he shall be.
POPE—*Epitaph.*

17
Kneller, by Heaven and not a master taught
Whose art was nature, and whose pictures thought,
*   *   *   *   *   *
Living great Nature fear'd he might outvie
Her works; and dying, fears herself may die.
POPE—Inscription on the monument of SIR GEOFREY KNELLER in Westminster Abbey. Imitated from the epitaph on RAPHAEL, in the Pantheon at Rome.

18
To this sad shrine, whoe'er thou art! draw near!
Here lies the friend most lov'd, the son most dear;
Who ne'er knew joy but friendship might divide,
Or gave his father grief but when he died.
POPE—*Epitaph on Harcourt.*
(See also PEACOCK)

19
Nihil unquam peccavit, nisi quod mortua est.
She never did wrong in any way, unless in the fact that she died.
On a wife's tomb at Rome.

20
Calmly he looked on either Life, and here
Saw nothing to regret, or there to fear:
From Nature's temp'rate feast rose satisfy'd,
Thank'd Heaven that he had lived, and that he died.
POPE—*Epitaph X.*

1
Statesman, yet friend to truth! of soul sincere,
In action faithful, and in honour clear;
Who broke no promise, served no private end,
Who gained no title, and who lost no friend,
Ennobled by himself, by all approved,
And praised, unenvied, by the muse he loved.

POPE—*Moral Essays*. Epistle V. L. 67. (To Addison.)
(See also CRAGGS)

2
Heralds and statesmen, by your leave,
Here lies what once was Matthew Prior;
The son of Adam and of Eve;
Can Bourbon or Nassau go higher?

PRIOR—*Epitaph. Extempore.* (As given in original edition.)

3
Johnny Carnegie lais heer
Descendit of Adam and Eve,
Gif ony cou gang hieher,
I'se willing give him leve.

Epitaph in an old Scottish Churchyard.

4
In Fortunam
Inveni portum spes et fortuna valete
Nil mihi vobiscum ludite nunc alios.
Mine haven's found; Fortune and Hope, adieu.
Mock others now, for I have done with you.

Inscription on the tomb of FRANCESCO PUCCI in the church of St. Onuphrius, (St. Onofrio), Rome. Translation by BURTON—*Anatomy of Melancholy.* Pt. II. Sec. III. Memb. 6. Quoted by him as a saying of PRUDENTIUS. Attributed to JANUS PANNONIUS. See JANI PANNONII—*Onofrio.* Pt. II. Folio 70. Found in LAURENTIUS SCHRADERN'S *Monumenta Italiæ, Folio Helmæstadii.* P. 164. Attributed to CARDINAL LA MARCK in foot-note to LE SAGE'S *Gil Blas.*

5
Jam portum inveni, Spes et Fortuna valete.
Nil mihi vobiscum est, ludite nunc alios.
Fortune and Hope farewell! I've found the port;
You've done with me: go now, with others sport.

Version of the GREEK epigram in the *Anthologia.* Trans. by MERIVALE. Latin by THOMAS MORE, in the *Progymnasmata* prefixed to first ed. of MORE'S *Epigrams.* (1520)

6
Avete multum, Spesque, Forsque; sum in vado.
Qui pone sint illudite; haud mea interest.

Version of the GREEK epigram in DR. WELLESLEY'S *Anthologia Polyglotta.* P. 464. Ed. 1849.

7
Speme e Fortuna, addio; che' in porto entrai.
Schernite gli altri; ch'io vi spregio omai.

Version of the GREEK epigram by LUIGI ALAMANNI.

8
I came at morn—'twas spring, I smiled,
The fields with green were clad;
I walked abroad at noon,—and lo!
'Twas summer,—I was glad;
I sate me down; 'twas autumn eve,
And I with sadness wept;
I laid me down at night, and then
'Twas winter,—and I slept.

MARY PYPER—*Epitaph. A Life.* Same on a tombstone in Massachusetts. See *Newhaven Mag.* Dec., 1863.

9
The world's a *book*, writ by th' *eternal Art*
Of the great Maker; printed in man's heart;
'Tis falsely *printed* though divinely penn'd,
And all the *Errata* will appear at th' *end.*

QUARLES—*Divine Fancies.*

10
The *World's* a *Printing-House*, our *words*, our *thoughts*,
Our *deeds*, are *characters* of several sizes.
Each *Soul* is a *Compos'tor*, of whose faults
The *Levites* are *Correctors; Heaven Revises.*
Death is the *common Press*, from whence being driven,
We're *gather'd*, Sheet by Sheet, and bound for *Heaven.*

QUARLES—*Divine Fancies.*
(See also CAPEN)

11
She was—but room forbids to tell thee what—
Sum all perfection up, and she was—that.

QUARLES—Epitaph on LADY LUCHYN.

12
Warm summer sun, shine friendly here;
Warm western wind, blow kindly here;
Green sod above, rest light, rest light—
Good-night, Annette!
Sweetheart, good-night.

ROBERT RICHARDSON, in his collection, *Willow and Wattle.* P. 35.

13
Warm summer sun shine kindly here;
Warm southern wind blow softly here;
Green sod above lie light, lie light—
Good night, dear heart, good night, good night.

RICHARDSON'S lines on the tombstone of SUSY CLEMENS as altered by MARK TWAIN (S. L. Clemens).

14
Quod expendi habui
Quod donavi habeo
Quod servavi perdidi.
That I spent that I had
That I gave that I have
That I left that I lost.

Epitaph under an effigy of a priest. T. F. RAVENSHAW'S *Antiente Epitaphes.* P. 5. WEEVER'S *Funeral Monuments.* Ed. 1631. P. 581. PETTIGREW'S *Chronicles of the Tombs.*
(See also GESTA ROMANORUM)

15
Ecce quod expendi habui, quod donavi habeo,
quod negavi punior, quod servavi perdidi.

On Tomb of JOHN KILLUNGWORTH. (1412) In Pitson Church, Bucks, England.

16
Lo, all that ever I spent, that sometime had I;
All that I gave in good intent, that now have I;
That I never gave, nor lent, that now aby I;
That I kept till I went, that lost I.

Trans. of the Latin on the brasses of a priest at St. Albans, and on a brass as late as 1584 at St. Olave's, Hart Street, London.

17
It that I gife, I haif,
It that I len, I craif,
It that I spend, is myue,
It that I leif, I tyne.

On very old stone in Scotland. HACKETT'S *Epitaphs.* Vol. I. P. 32. (Ed. 1737)

1

Howe: Howe: who is heare:
I, Robin of Doncaster, and Margaret my feare.
That I spent, that I had;
That I gave, that I have;
That I left, that I lost.

Epitaph of Robert Byrkes, in Doncaster Church. Richard Gough—*Sepulchral Monuments of Great Britain.*

(See also Ravenshaw)

2

The earthe goeth on the earthe
Glisteringe like gold;
The earthe goeth to the earthe
Sooner than it wold;
The earthe builds on the earthe
Castles and Towers;
The earthe says to the earthe
All shall be ours.

Epitaph in T. F. Ravenshaw's *Antiente Epitaphes.* (1878) P. 158. Also in *The Scotch Haggis.* Edinburgh, 1822. For variation of same see Montgomery—*Christian Poets.* P. 58. 3rd ed. Note states it is by William Billyng, *Five Wounds of Christ.* From an old MS. in the possession of William Bateman, of Manchester. The epitaph to Archbishop of Canterbury, time of Edward III, is the same. See Weaver's *Funeral Monuments.* (1631) Facsimile discovered in the chapel of the Guild of the Holy Cross, at Stratford. See Fisher's *Illustrations of the Paintings,* etc. (1802) Ed. by J. G. Nichols.

3

Earth walks on Earth,
Glittering in gold;
Earth goes to Earth,
Sooner than it wold;
Earth builds on Earth,
Palaces and towers;
Earth says to Earth,
Soon, all shall be ours.

Scott—*Unpublished Epigram.* In *Notes and Queries.* May 21, 1853. P. 498.

4

Traveller, let your step be light,
So that sleep these eyes may close,
For poor Scarron, till to-night,
Ne'er was able e'en to doze.

Scarron—*Epitaph written by himself.*

5

Sit tua terra levis.
May the earth rest lightly on thee.

Seneca—*Epigram* II. *Ad Corsican.*
Martial—*Epigram* V. 35; IX. 30. 11.

(See also Beaumont)

6

Good Frend for Jesvs Sake Forbeare,
To Digg the Dvst Encloased Heare.
Blese be ye Man yt Spares Thes Stones.
And Cvrst be he yt Moves my Bones.

Epitaph on Shakespeare's Tombstone at Stratford-on-Avon. (Said to be chosen by him, but not original.)

7

After your death you were better have a bad epitaph than their ill report while you live.

Hamlet. Act II. Sc. 2. L. 548.

8

Either our history shall with full mouth
Speak freely of our acts, or else our grave,
Like Turkish mute, shall have a tongueless mouth,
Not worshipp'd with a waxen epitaph.

Henry V. Act I. Sc. 2. L. 230.

9

You cannot better be employ'd, Bassanio,
Than to live still and write mine epitaph.

Merchant of Venice. Act IV. Sc. 1. L. 117.

10

On your family's old monument
Hang mournful epitaphs.

Much Ado About Nothing. Act IV. Sc. 1. L. 208.

11 And if your love
Can labour aught in sad invention,
Hang her an epitaph upon her tomb
And sing it to her bones, sing it to-night.

Much Ado About Nothing. Act V. Sc. 1. L. 291.

12 Of comfort no man speak:
Let's talk of graves, of worms and epitaphs.

Richard II. Act III. Sc. 2. L. 144.

13

These are two friends whose lives were undivided:
So let their memory be, now they have glided
Under the grave; let not their bones be parted,
For their two hearts in life were single-hearted.

Shelley—*Epitaph.*

14

He will be weighed again
At the Great Day,
His rigging refitted,
And his timbers repaired,
And with one broadside
Make his adversary
Strike in his turn.

Smollett—*Peregrine Pickle.* Vol. III. Ch. VII. *Epitaph on Commodore Trunnion.*

(See also Capen)

15

Let no man write my epitaph; let my grave
Be uninscribed, and let my memory rest
Till other times are come, and other men,
Who then may do me justice.

Southey. Written after Reading the Speech of Robert Emmet.

(See also Emmet)

16

The turf has drank a
Widow's tear;
Three of her husbands
Slumber here.

Epitaph at Staffordshire.

17

Here lies one who meant well, tried a little, failed much.

Stevenson—*Christmas Sermon.*

18

I, whom Apollo sometime visited,
Or feigned to visit, now, my day being done,
Do slumber wholly, nor shall know at all
The weariness of changes; nor perceive
Immeasurable sands of centuries
Drink up the blanching ink, or the loud sound
Of generations beat the music down.

Stevenson. Epitaph for himself.

1
Now when the number of my years
Is all fulfilled and I
From sedentary life
Shall rouse me up to die,
Bury me low and let me lie
Under the wide and starry sky.
Joying to live, I joyed to die,
Bury me low and let me lie.

STEVENSON. Poem written, 1879. Probably original of his *Requiem.*

2
Under the wide and starry sky,
Dig the grave and let me lie;
Glad did I live and gladly die,
And I laid me down with a will.
This be the verse you grave for me:
"Here he lies, where he longed to be;
Home is the sailor, home from the sea,
And the hunter home from the hill."

STEVENSON—*Requiem* written for himself. Engraved on his tombstone.

3
To the down Bow of Death
His Forte gave way,
All the Graces in sorrow were drown'd;
Hallelujah Cresendo
Shall be his glad lay
When Da'Capo the Trumpet shall sound.

Epitaph to SAMUEL TAYLOR, in Youlgreaves Churchyard, Derbyshire, England.

4
Thou third great Canning, stand among our best
And noblest, now thy long day's work hath ceased,
Here silent in our minster of the West
Who wert the voice of England in the East.

TENNYSON—*Epitaph on Lord Stratford De Redcliffe.*

5
Ne'er to these chambers where the mighty rest,
Since their foundation came a nobler guest;
Nor e'er was to the bowers of bliss conveyed
A fairer spirit or more welcome shade.

THOMAS TICKELL—*Ode on the Death of Addison.* Later placed on ADDISON's tomb in Henry the VII Chapel, Westminster.

6
Then haste, kind Death, in pity to my age,
And clap the Finis to my life's last page.
May Heaven's great *Author my foul proof revise,*
Cancel the *page* in which my *error* lies,
And *raise my form* above the etherial skies.
* * * * * * * * *
The stubborn *pressman's* form I now may scoff;
Revised, corrected, finally *worked off!*

C. H. TIMBERLEY, ed. *Songs of the Press.* (1845) (See also CAPEN)

7
Mantua me genuit; Calabri rapuere; tenet nunc Parthenope. Cecini pascua, rura, duces.

Mantua bore me; the people of Calabria carried me off; Parthenope (Naples) holds me now. I have sung of pastures, of fields, of chieftains.

VERGIL's *Epitaph.* Said to be by himself.

8
Here in this place sleeps one whom love
Caused, through great cruelty to fall.
A little scholar, poor enough,
Whom François Villon men did call.
No scrap of land or garden small
He owned. He gave his goods away,
Table and trestles, baskets—all;
For God's sake say for him this Lay.

FRANÇOIS VILLON. His own Epitaph.

9
He directed the stone over his grave to be thus inscribed:
Hic jacet hujus Sententiæ primus Author:
Disputandi pruritus ecclesiarum scabies.
Nomen alias quære.

Here lies the first author of this sentence; "The itch of disputation will prove the scab of the Church." Inquire his name elsewhere.

IZAAK WALTON—*Life of Wotton.*
(See WOTTON CHURCH, also 49[18])

10
The poet's fate is here in emblem shown,
He asked for bread, and he received a stone.

SAMUEL WESLEY—*Epigrams.* On Butler's Monument in Westminster Abbey.

11
Here lies, in a "horizontal" position
The "outside" case of
Peter Pendulum, watch-maker.
He departed this life "wound up"
In hopes of being "taken in hand" by his Maker,
And of being thoroughly "cleaned, repaired" and "set a-going"
In the world to come.

C. H. WILSON—*Polyanthea. Epitaph on a Watch-maker.* Transcribed from Aberconway Churchyard.

12
O what a monument of glorious worth,
When in a new edition he comes forth,
Without erratas, may we think he'll be
In leaves and covers of eternity!

BENJAMIN WOODBRIDGE—*Lines on John Cotton.* (1652)
(See also CAPEN)

13
He first deceas'd; she for a little tri'd
To live without him, lik'd it not, and died.

SIR HENRY WOTTON—*Upon the Death of Sir Albertus Morton's Wife.*

14
Si monumentum requiris circumspice.
If you would see his monument look around.

Inscription on the tomb of Sir Christopher Wren in St. Paul's, London. Written by his son. Trans. by ROGERS—*Italy. Florence.*

EQUALITY

15
Men are made by nature unequal. It is vain, therefore, to treat them as if they were equal.

FROUDE—*Short Studies on Great Subjects. Party Politics.*

16
Sir, your levellers wish to level *down* as far as themselves: but they cannot bear levelling *up* to themselves.

SAMUEL JOHNSON—*Boswell's Life of Johnson.* (1763)

17
For the colonel's lady an' Judy O'Grady,
Are sisters under their skins.

KIPLING—*Barrack Room Ballads. II. The Ladies.*

1
Par in parem imperium non habet.
An equal has no power over an equal.
Law Maxim.

2
Quod ad jus naturale attinet, omnes homines æquales sunt.
All men are equal before the natural law.
Law Maxim.

3
Fourscore and seven years ago, our fathers brought forth on this continent a new nation, conceived in liberty, and dedicated to the proposition that all men are created equal.
LINCOLN—*Gettysburg Address.* Nov. 19, 1863.
(See also ADAMS under RIGHTS)

4
For some must follow, and some command
Though all are made of clay!
LONGFELLOW—*Keramos.* L. 6.

5
Among unequals what society
Can sort, what harmony, or true delight?
MILTON—*Paradise Lost.* Bk. VIII. L. 383.

6
Et sceleratis sol oritur.
The sun shines even on the wicked
SENECA—*De Beneficiis.* III. 25.

7
Equality of two domestic powers
Breeds scrupulous faction.
Antony and Cleopatra. Act I. Sc. 3. L. 47.

8 Mean and mighty, rotting
Together, have one dust.
Cymbeline. Act IV. Sc. 2. L. 246.

9
Heralds, from off our towers we might behold,
From first to last, the onset and retire
Of both your armies; whose equality
By our best eyes cannot be censured:
Blood hath bought blood and blows have answer'd blows;
Strength match'd with strength, and power confronted power:
Both are alike; and both alike we like.
King John. Act II. Sc. 1. L. 325.

10 She in beauty, education, blood,
Holds hand with any princess of the world.
King John. Act II. Sc. 1. L. 493.

11
The trickling rain doth fall
Upon us one and all;
The south-wind kisses
The saucy milkmaid's cheek,
The nun's, demure and meek,
Nor any misses.
E. C. STEDMAN—*A Madrigal.* St. 3.

12
Equality is the life of conversation; and he is as much out who assumes to himself any part above another, as he who considers himself below the rest of the society.
STEELE—*Tatler.* No. 225.

13
The tall, the wise, the reverend head,
Must be as low as ours.
WATTS—*Hymns and Spiritual Songs.* Bk. II. Hymn 63.

ERROR

14
The truth is perilous never to the true,
Nor knowledge to the wise; and to the fool,
And to the false, error and truth alike,
Error is worse than ignorance.
BAILEY—*Festus.* Sc. *A Mountain Sunrise.*

15
Have too rashly charged the troops of error and remain as trophies unto the enemies of truth.
SIR THOMAS BROWNE—*Religio Medici.* Pt. I. Sec. VI.

16
Mistake, error, is the discipline through which we advance.
CHANNING—*Address on The Present Age.*

17
Errare mehercule malo cum Platone, quem tu quanti facias, scio quam cum istis vera sentire.
By Hercules! I prefer to err with Plato, whom I know how much you value, than to be right in the company of such men.
CICERO—*Tusculanarum Disputationum.* I. 17.

18
The cautious seldom err.
CONFUCIUS—*Analects.* Bk. IV. Ch. XXIII.

19
Man on the dubious waves of error toss'd.
COWPER—*Poem on Truth.* L. 1.

20
Errors, like straws, upon the surface flow;
He who would search for pearls, must dive below.
DRYDEN—*All for Love.* Prologue.

21
Brother, brother; we are both in the wrong.
GAY—*Beggar's Opera.* Act II. Sc. 2.

22
Est giebt Menschen die gar nicht irren, weil sie sich nichts Vernünftiges vorsetzen.
There are men who never err, because they never propose anything rational.
GOETHE—*Sprüche in Prosa.* III.

23
Es irrt der Mensch so lang er strebt.
While man's desires and aspirations stir,
He can not choose but err.
GOETHE—*Faust. Prolog im Himmel. Der Herr.* L. 77.

24
Ille sinistrorsum hic dextrorsum abit, unus utrique Error, sed variis illudit partibus.
One goes to the right, the other to the left; both are wrong, but in different directions.
HORACE—*Satires.* II. 3. 50.

25
Dark Error's other hidden side is truth.
VICTOR HUGO—*La Légende des Siècles.*

26
Quand tout le monde a tort, tout le monde a raison.
When every one is in the wrong, every one is in the right.
LA CHAUSSÉE—*La Gouvernante.* I. 3.

27
Knowledge being to be had only of visible and certain truth, error is not a fault of our knowledge, but a mistake of our judgment, giving assent to that which is not true.
LOCKE—*Essay Concerning Human Understanding.* Bk. IV. *Of Wrong Assent or Error.* Ch. XX.

1
Sometimes we may learn more from a man's errors than from his virtues.
LONGFELLOW—*Hyperion*. Bk. IV. Ch. III.

2
Errare humanus est.
To err is human.
MELCHIOR DE POLINAC—*Anti-Lucretius*. V. 58. GILBERTUS COGNATUS—*Adagia*. SENECA—Bk. IV. *Declam*. 3. Agam, 267. Other forms of same found in DEMOSTHENES—*De Corona*. V. IX. EURIPIDES—*Hippolytus*. 615. HOMER—*Iliad*. IX. 496. LUCAN—*Demon*. 7. MARCUS ANTONINUS. IX. 11. MENANDER—*Fragments*. 499. PLAUTUS—*Merc*. II. 2. 48. SEVERUS OF ANTIOCH—*Ep*. I. 20. SOPHOCLES—*Antigone*. 1023. THEOGNIS. V. 327. Humanum fuit errare. ST. AUGUSTINE—*Sermon* 164. 14. . . . possum falli, ut homo. CICERO—*Ad Atticum*. XIII. 21. 5. Cujusvis hominis est errare, nullius nisi insipientis in errore perseverare. CICERO—*Phillipics*. XII. 2. 5. (Same idea in his *De Invent*. II. 3. 9.) Erasse humanus est. ST. JEROME—*Epistolæ*. LVII. 12. Also in *Adv. Ruf*. III. 33. 36. Nemo nostrum non peccat. Homines sumus, non dei. PETRONIUS—*Satyricon*. Ch. 75. Ch. 130. Decipi . . . humanus est. PLUTARCH. Stephanus's ed. Ch. XXXI. Per humanes, inquit, errotes. SENECA—*Rhetoric*. *Excerpta ex Controversiis*. IV. III. Censen hominem me esse? erravi. TERENCE—*Adelphi*. IV. II. 40.

3
Les plus courtes erreurs sont toujours les meilleures.
The smallest errors are always the best.
MOLIÈRE—*L'Etourdi*. IV. 4.
(See also CHARRON under FOLLY)

4
The man who makes no mistakes does not usually make anything.
EDWARD J. PHELPS. *Speech at Mansion House*, London, Jan. 24, 1889, quoting Bishop W. C. MAGEE of Peterborough, in 1868.

5
For to err in opinion, though it be not the part of wise men, is at least human.
PLUTARCH—*Morals*. *Against Colotes the Epicurean*.

6
Some positive persisting fops we know,
Who, if once wrong, will needs be always so;
But you with pleasure own your errors past,
And make each day a critique on the last.
POPE—*Essay on Criticism*. Pt. III. L. 9.

7
When people once are in the wrong,
Each line they add is much too long;
Who fastest walks, but walks astray,
Is only furthest from his way.
PRIOR—*Alma*. Canto III. L. 194.

8
How far your eyes may pierce, I cannot tell;
Striving to better, oft we mar what's well.
King Lear. Act I. Sc. 4. L. 368.

9
Purposes mistook
Fall'n on the inventors' heads.
Hamlet. Act V. Sc. 2. L. 395.

10
The error of our eye directs our mind:
What error leads must err.
Troilus and Cressida. Act V. Sc. 2. L. 110.

11
Shall error in the round of time
Still father Truth?
TENNYSON—*Love and Duty*.

12
The progress of rivers to the ocean is not so rapid as that of man to error.
VOLTAIRE—*A Philosophical Dictionary*. *Rivers*.

ESTRIDGE

13
Prince Edward all in gold, as he great Jove had been,
The Mountfords all in plumes, like estridges were seen.
DRAYTON—*Poly-Olbion*. St. 22.

14
All furnish'd, all in arms;
All plum'd, like estridges that with the wind
Baited, like eagles having lately bath'd.
Henry IV. Pt. I. Act IV. Sc. 1. L. 97.

ETERNITY (See also FUTURITY)

15
Eternity! thou pleasing dreadful thought!
Through what variety of untried being,
Through what new scenes and changes must we pass!
ADDISON—CATO. Act V. Sc. 1.

16
Then gazing up 'mid the dim pillars high,
The foliaged marble forest where ye lie,
Hush, ye will say, it is eternity!
This is the glimmering verge of heaven, and there
The columns of the heavenly palaces.
MATTHEW ARNOLD—*The Tomb*.

17
The created world is but a small parenthesis in eternity.
SIR THOMAS BROWNE—*Works*. Bohn's ed. Vol. III. P. 143.
(See also DONNE)

18
Eternity forbids thee to forget.
BYRON—*Lara*. Canto I. St. 23.

19
Vain, weak-built isthmus, which dost proudly rise
Up between two eternities!
COWLEY—*Ode on Life and Fame*. L. 18.
(See also MILTON)

20
Nothing is there to come, and nothing past,
But an eternal Now does always last.
COWLEY—*Davideis*. Bk. I. L. 360.

21
Eternity is not an everlasting flux of time, but time is as a short parenthesis in a long period.
DONNE—*Book of Devotions Meditation* 14. (1624) (See also BROWNE)

22
Summarum summa est æternum.
The sum total of all sums total is eternal (meaning the universe).
LUCRETIUS—*De Rerum Natura*. III. 817. Also Bk. V. 362.

1 That golden key,
That opes the palace of eternity.
MILTON—*Comus.* L. 13.

2
(Eternity) a moment standing still for ever.
JAMES MONTGOMERY.

3
This speck of life in time's great wilderness
This narrow isthmus 'twixt two boundless seas,
The past, the future, two eternities!
MOORE—*Lalla Rookh. The Veiled Prophet of Khorassan.* St. 42.
(See also COWLEY)

4
Those spacious regions where our fancies roam,
Pain'd by the past, expecting ills to come,
In some dread moment, by the fates assign'd,
Shall pass away, nor leave a rack behind;
And Time's revolving wheels shall lose at last
The speed that spins the future and the past:
And, sovereign of an undisputed throne,
Awful eternity shall reign alone.
PETRARCH—*Triumph of Eternity.* L. 102.

5
The time will come when every change shall cease,
This quick revolving wheel shall rest in peace:
No summer then shall glow, nor winter freeze;
Nothing shall be to come, and nothing past,
But an eternal now shall ever last.
PETRARCH—*Triumph of Eternity.* L. 117.

6
Was man von der Minute ausgeschlagen
Gibt keine Ewigkeit zurück.
Eternity gives nothing back of what one leaves out of the minutes.
SCHILLER—*Resignation.* St. 18.

7
The Pilgrim of Eternity, whose fame
Over his living head like Heaven is bent,
An early but enduring monument,
Came, veiling all the lightnings of his song
In sorrow.
SHELLEY—*Adonais.* XXX.

8
Life, like a dome of many-coloured glass,
Stains the white radiance of eternity.
SHELLEY—*Adonais.* LII.

9
In time there is no present,
In eternity no future,
In eternity no past.
TENNYSON—*The "How" and "Why."*

10
And can eternity belong to me,
Poor pensioner on the bounties of an hour?
YOUNG—*Night Thoughts.* Night I. L. 66.

EVENING

11
At the close of the day, when the hamlet is still
And mortals the sweets of forgetfulness prove,
When nought but the torrent is heard on the hill
And nought but the nightingale's song in the grove.
JAMES BEATTIE—*Hermit.*

12
And whiter grows the foam,
The small moon lightens more;
And as I turn me home,
My shadow walks before.
ROBERT BRIDGES—*The Clouds have left the Sky.*

13
To me at least was never evening yet
But seemed far beautifuller than its day.
ROBERT BROWNING—*The Ring and the Book. Pompilia.* L. 357.

14
Hath thy heart within thee burned,
At evening's calm and holy hour?
S. G. BULFINCH—*Meditation.*

15
It is the hour when from the boughs
The nightingale's high note is heard;
It is the hour when lovers' vows
Seem sweet in every whispered word;
And gentle winds, and waters near,
Make music to the lonely ear.
Each flower the dews have lightly wet,
And in the sky the stars are met,
And on the wave is deeper blue,
And on the leaf a browner hue,
And in the heaven that clear obscure,
So softly dark, and darkly pure.
Which follows the decline of day,
As twilight melts beneath the moon away.
BYRON—*Parisina.* St. 1.

16
When day is done, and clouds are low,
And flowers are honey-dew,
And Hesper's lamp begins to glow
Along the western blue;
And homeward wing the turtle-doves,
Then comes the hour the poet loves.
GEORGE CROLY—*The Poet's Hour.*

17
The curfew tolls the knell of parting day,
The lowing herd winds slowly o'er the lea,
The ploughman homeward plods his weary way,
And leaves the world to darkness and to me.
GRAY—*Elegy in a Country Churchyard.* ("Herd wind" in 1753 ed. "Knell of parting day" taken from DANTE.)

18
Day hath put on his jacket, and around
His burning bosom buttoned it with stars.
HOLMES—*Evening.*

19
How gently rock yon poplars high
Against the reach of primrose sky
With heaven's pale candles stored.
JEAN INGELOW—*Supper at the Mill.* Song.

20
But when eve's silent footfall steals
Along the eastern sky,
And one by one to earth reveals
Those purer fires on high.
KEBLE—*The Christian Year. Fourth Sunday After Trinity.*

21
Day, like a weary pilgrim, had reached the western gate of heaven, and Evening stooped down to unloose the latchets of his sandal shoon.
LONGFELLOW—*Hyperion.* Bk. IV. Ch. V.

22
Now came still evening on; and twilight gray
Had in her sober livery all things clad:
Silence accompanied; for beast and bird,
They to their grassy couch, these to their nests,
Were slunk, all but the wakeful nightingale.
MILTON—*Paradise Lost.* Bk. IV. L. 598.

1
Just then return'd at shut of evening flowers.
MILTON—*Paradise Lost.* Bk. IX. L. 278.

2
Fly not yet, 'tis just the hour
When pleasure, like the midnight flower
That scorns the eye of vulgar light,
Begins to bloom for sons of night,
And maids who love the moon.
MOORE—*Fly Not Yet.*

3
O how grandly cometh Even,
Sitting on the mountain summit,
Purple-vestured, grave, and silent,
Watching o'er the dewy valleys,
Like a good king near his end.
D. M. MULOCK—*A Stream's Singing.*

4
One by one the flowers close,
Lily and dewy rose
Shutting their tender petals from the moon.
CHRISTINA G. ROSSETTI—*Twilight Calm.*

5
Day's lustrous eyes grow heavy in sweet death.
SCHILLER—*The Assignation.* St. 4. LORD LYTTON's trans.

6
The pale child, Eve, leading her mother, Night.
ALEXANDER SMITH—*A Life Drama.* Sc. 8.

7
The lights begin to twinkle from the rocks:
The long day wanes: the slow moon climbs: the deep
Moans round with many voices.
TENNYSON—*Ulysses.* L. 54.

8
I was heavy with the even,
When she lit her glimmering tapers
Round the day's dead sanctities.
I laughed in the morning's eyes.
FRANCIS THOMPSON—*The Hound of Heaven.* L. 84.

9
The holy time is quiet as a Nun
Breathless with adoration.
WORDSWORTH—*It is a Beauteous Evening.*

EVIL

10
Evil events from evil causes spring.
ARISTOPHANES.

11
Evil and good are God's right hand and left.
BAILEY—*Prelude to Festus.*

12
Evil beginning houres may end in good.
BEAUMONT AND FLETCHER—*The Knight of Malta.* Act II. Sc. 5.

13
Souvent la peur d'un mal nous conduit dans un pire.
Often the fear of one evil leads us into a worse.
BOILEAU—*L'Art Poétique.* I. 64.

14
From envy, hatred, and malice, and all uncharitableness.
Book of Common Prayer. Litany.

15
The world, the flesh, and the devil.
Book of Common Prayer. Litany.

16
I have wrought great use out of evil tools.
BULWER-LYTTON—*Richelieu.* Act III. Sc. 1. L. 49.

17
The authors of great evils know best how to remove them.
CATO THE YOUNGER's Advice to the Senate to put all power into POMPEY's hands. PLUTARCH—*Life of Cato the Younger.*

18
Como el hacer mal viene de natural cosecha, fácilmente se aprende el hacerle.
Inasmuch as ill-deeds spring up as a spontaneous crop, they are easy to learn.
CERVANTES—*Coloquio de los Perros.*

19
Ex malis eligere minima oportere.
Of evils one should choose the least.
CICERO—*De Officiis.* Bk. III. 1. Same idea in THOMAS À KEMPIS. *Imit Christi.* 3. 12.
(See also ERASMUS, HOOPER, PRIOR)

20
Omne malum nascens facile opprimitur; inveteratum fit pleurumque robustius.
Every evil in the bud is easily crushed: as it grows older, it becomes stronger.
CICERO—*Philippicæ.* V. 11.

21
Touch not; taste not; handle not.
Colossians. II. 21.

22
Evil communications corrupt good manners.
I Corinthians. XV. 33.
(See also MENANDER)

23
Et tous maux sont pareils alors qu'ils sont extrêmes.
All evils are equal when they are extreme.
CORNEILLE—*Horace.* III. 4.

24
Superbia, invidia ed avarizia sono
Le tre faville che hanno i cori accesi.
Three sparks—pride, envy, and avarice—have been kindled in all hearts.
DANTE—*Inferno.* VI. 74.

25
E duobus malis minimum eligendum.
Of two evils choose the least.
ERASMUS—*Adages.*
(See also CICERO)

26
Den Bösen sind sie los, die Bösen sind geblieben.
The Evil One has left, the evil ones remain.
GOETHE—*Faust.* I. 6. 174.

27
Non è male alcuno nelle cose umane che non abbia congiunto seco qualche bene.
There is no evil in human affairs that has not some good mingled with it.
GUICCIARDINI—*Storia d'Italia.*

28
He who does evil that good may come, pays a toll to the devil to let him into heaven.
J. C. AND A. W. HARE—*Guesses at Truth.* P. 444.

29
But evil is wrought by want of Thought,
As well as want of Heart!
HOOD—*The Lady's Dream.* St. 16.

1 Of two
Evils we take the less.
HOOKER—*Laws of Ecclesiastical Polity.* Bk. V. Ch. LXXXI.
(See also CICERO)

2
Quid nos dura refugimus
Ætas, quid intactum nefasti
Liquimus?
What has this unfeeling age of ours left untried, what wickedness has it shunned?
HORACE—*Carmina.* I. 35. 34.

3
Woe unto them that call evil good, and good evil.
Isaiah. V. 20.

4
Magna inter molles concordia.
There is great unanimity among the dissolute.
JUVENAL—*Satires.* II. 47.

5
Fere fit malum malo aptissimum.
Evil is fittest to consort with evil.
LIVY—*Annales.* I. 46.

6
Notissimum quodque malum maxime tolerabile.
The best known evil is the most tolerable.
LIVY—*Annales.* XXIII. 3.

7
Evil springs up, and flowers, and bears no seed,
And feeds the green earth with its swift decay,
Leaving it richer for the growth of truth.
LOWELL—*Prometheus.* L. 263.

8
Solent occupationis spe vel impune quædam scelesta committi.
Wicked acts are accustomed to be done with impunity for the mere desire of occupation.
AMMIANUS MARCELLINUS—*Historia.* XXX. 9.

9
It must be that evil communications corrupt good dispositions.
MENANDER. Found in DUBNER'S edition of his *Fragments* appended to ARISTOPHANES in DIDOT'S *Bibliotheca Græca.* P. 102. L. 101. Quoted by ST. PAUL. See *1 Corinthians.* XV. 33. Same idea in PLATO—*Republic.* 550.

10
Que honni soit celui qui mal y pense.
MÉNAGE. Ascribed to TALLEMANT in the *Historiettes of Tallemant des Reaux.* Vol. I. P. 38. Second ed. Note in Third ed., corrects this. Honi soit qui mal y pense. Evil to him who evil thinks. Motto of the Order of the Garter. Established by Edward III, April 23, 1349. See SIR WALTER SCOTT—*Essay on Chivalry.*

11
And out of good still to find means of evil.
MILTON—*Paradise Lost.* Bk. I. L. 165.

12
Genus est mortis male vivere.
An evil life is a kind of death.
OVID—*Epistolæ Ex Ponto.* III. 4. 75.

13
Mille mali species, mille salutis erunt.
There are a thousand forms of evil; there will be a thousand remedies.
OVID—*Remedia Amoris.* V. 26.

14
Omnia perversas possunt corrumpere mentes.
All things can corrupt perverse minds.
OVID—*Tristium.* II. 301.

15
Hoc sustinete, majus ne veniat malum.
Endure this evil lest a worse come upon you.
PHÆDRUS—*Fables.* Bk. I. 2. 31.

16
Ut acerbum est, pro benefactis quom mali messem metas!
How bitter it is to reap a harvest of evil for good that you have done!
PLAUTUS—*Epidicus.* V. 2. 53.

17
Pulchrum ornatum turpes mores pejus cœno collinunt.
Bad conduct soils the finest ornament more than filth.
PLAUTUS—*Mostellaria.* I. 3. 133.

18
Male partum male disperit.
Ill gotten is ill spent.
PLAUTUS—*Pœnalus.* IV. 2. 22.

19
E malis multis, malum, quod minimum est, id minimum est malum.
Out of many evils the evil which is least is the least of evils.
PLAUTUS—*Stichus.* Act I. 2.
(See also CICERO)

20
Timely advis'd, the coming evil shun.
Better not do the deed, than weep it done.
PRIOR—*Henry and Emma.* L. 308.

21
Of two evils I have chose the least.
PRIOR—*Imitation of Horace.* Bk. I. Ep. IX.
(See also CICERO)

22
Maledicus a malefico non distat nisi occasione.
An evil-speaker differs from an evil-doer only in the want of opportunity.
QUINTILIAN—*De Institutione Oratoria.* XII. 9. 9.

23
For the good that I would I do not; but the evil which I would not, that I do.
Romans. VII. 19.

24
Be not overcome of evil, but overcome evil with good.
Romans. XII. 21.

25
Multitudes think they like to do evil; yet no man ever really enjoyed doing evil since God made the world.
RUSKIN—*Stones of Venice.* Vol. I. Ch. II.

26
Al mondo mal non e senza rimedio.
There is no evil in the world without a remedy.
SANNAZARO—*Ecloga Octava.*

1
Das Leben ist der Güter höchstes nicht
Der Uebel grösstes aber ist die Schuld.

Life is not the supreme good, but the supreme evil is to realize one's guilt.
SCHILLER—*Die Braut von Messina.*

2
Das eben ist der Fluch der bösen That,
Das sie fortzeugend immer Böses muss gebären.

The very curse of an evil deed is that it must always continue to engender evil.
SCHILLER—*Piccolomini.* V. 1.

3
Per scelera semper sceleribus certum est iter.

The way to wickedness is always through wickedness.
SENECA—*Agamemnon.* CXV.

4
Si velis vitiis exui, longe a vitiorum exemplis recedendum est.

If thou wishest to get rid of thy evil propensities, thou must keep far from evil companions.
SENECA—*Epistolæ Ad Lucilium.* CIV.

5
Solent suprema facere securos mala.

Desperate evils generally make men safe.
SENECA—*Œdipus.* CCCLXXXVI.

6
Serum est cavendi tempus in mediis malis.

It is too late to be on our guard when we are in the midst of evils.
SENECA—*Thyestes.* CCCCLXXXVII.

7
Magna pars vulgi levis
Odit scelus spectatque.

Most of the giddy rabble hate the evil deed they come to see.
SENECA—*Troades.* XI. 28.

8
The evil that men do lives after them;
The good is oft interred with their bones.
Julius Cæsar. Act III. Sc. 2. L. 80.

9
But then I sigh; and, with a piece of Scripture,
Tell them that God bids us do good for evil.
Richard III. Act I. Sc. 3. L. 334.

10
We too often forget that not only is there a "soul of goodness in things evil," but very generally a soul of truth in things erroneous.
SPENCER—*First Principles.*

11
So far any one shuns evils, so far as he does good.
SWEDENBORG—*Doctrine of Life.* 21.

12
Mala mens, malus animus.

A bad heart, bad designs.
TERENCE—*Andria.* I. 1. 137.

13
Aliud ex alio malum.

One evil rises out of another.
TERENCE—*Eunuchus.* V. 7. 17.

14
But, by all thy nature's weakness,
Hidden faults and follies known,
Be thou, in rebuking evil,
Conscious of thine own.
WHITTIER—*What the Voice Said.* St. 15.

EVOLUTION (See also GROWTH, PROGRESS)

15
The stream of tendency in which all things seek to fulfil the law of their being.
MATTHEW ARNOLD. Used also by EMERSON. (See also HAZLITT, WORDSWORTH)

16
Observe constantly that all things take place by change, and accustom thyself to consider that the nature of the Universe loves nothing so much as to change the things which are, and to make new things like them.
MARCUS AURELIUS—*Meditations.* Ch. IV. 36.

17
The rise of every man he loved to trace,
Up to the very pod O!
And, in baboons, our parent race
Was found by old Monboddo.
Their A, B, C, he made them speak,
And learn their qui, quæ, quod, O!
Till Hebrew, Latin, Welsh, and Greek
They knew as well's Monboddo!
Ballad in *Blackwood's Mag.* referring to the originator of the monkey theory, JAMES BURNETT (Lord Monboddo).

18
A fire-mist and a planet,
A crystal and a cell,
A jellyfish and a saurian,
And caves where the cavemen dwell;
Then a sense of law and beauty,
And a face turned from the clod—
Some call it Evolution,
And others call it God.
W. H. CARRUTH—*Each in his Own Tongue.*

19
There was an ape in the days that were earlier,
Centuries passed and his hair became curlier;
Centuries more gave a thumb to his wrist—
Then he was a MAN and a Positivist.
MORTIMER COLLINS—*The British Birds.* St. 5.

20
I have called this principle, by which each slight variation, if useful, is preserved, by the term of Natural Selection.
CHARLES DARWIN—*The Origin of Species.* Ch. III.

21
The expression often used by Mr. Herbert Spencer of the Survival of the Fittest is more accurate, and is sometimes equally convenient.
CHARLES DARWIN—*The Origin of Species.* Ch. III. (See also SPENCER)

22
Till o'er the wreck, emerging from the storm,
Immortal NATURE lifts her changeful form:
Mounts from her funeral pyre on wings of flame,
And soars and shines, another and the same.
ERASMUS DARWIN—*Botanic Garden.* Pt. I. Canto IV. L. 389.

23
Said the little Eohippus,
"I am going to be a horse,
And on my middle fingernails
To run my earthly course!
* * *
I'm going to have a flowing tail!
I'm going to have a mane!
I'm going to stand fourteen hands high
On the Psychozoic plain!"
CHARLOTTE P. S. GILMAN—*Similar cases.*

1
A mighty stream of tendency.
HAZLITT—*Essay. Why Distant Objects Please.*
(See also ARNOLD)

2
Or ever the knightly years were gone
With the old world to the grave,
I was a king in Babylon
And you were a Christian Slave.
W. F. HENLEY—*Echoes.* XXXVII.

3
Children, behold the Chimpanzee;
He sits on the ancestral tree
From which we sprang in ages gone.
I'm glad we sprang: had we held on,
We might, for aught that I can say,
Be horrid Chimpanzees to-day.
OLIVER HERFORD—*The Chimpanzee.*

4
We seem to exist in a hazardous time,
Driftin' along here through space;
Nobody knows just when we begun,
Or how fur we've gone in the race.
BEN KING—*Evolution.*

5
Pouter, tumbler, and fantail are from the same source;
The racer and hack may be traced to one Horse;
So men were developed from monkeys of course,
Which nobody can deny.
LORD NEAVES—*The Origin of Species.*

6
I was at Euphorbus at the siege of Troy.
PYTHAGORAS.
(See also THOREAU)

7
Equidem æterna constitutione crediderim nexuque causarum latentium et multo ante destinatarum suum quemque ordinem immutabili lege percurrere.

For my own part I am persuaded that everything advances by an unchangeable law through the eternal constitution and association of latent causes, which have been long before predestinated.
QUINTUS CURTIUS RUFUS—*De Rebus Gestis Alexandri Magni.* V. 11. 10.

8
When you were a tadpole and I was a fish, in the Palæozoic time
And side by side in the sluggish tide, we sprawled in the ooze and slime.
LANGDON SMITH—*A Toast to a Lady.* (*Evolution.*) Printed in *The Scrap Book,* April, 1906.

9
Civilization is a progress from an indefinite, incoherent homogeneity toward a definite, coherent heterogeneity.
HERBERT SPENCER—*First Principles.* Ch. XVI. Par. 138; also Ch. XVII. Par. 145. He summaries the same: From a relatively diffused, uniform, and indeterminate arrangement to a relatively concentrated, multiform, and determinate arrangement.

10
This survival of the fittest, which I have here sought to express in mechanical terms, is that which Mr. Darwin has called "natural selection, or the preservation of favoured races in the struggle for life."
HERBERT SPENCER—*Principles of Biology. Indirect Equilibration.*
(See also DARWIN)

11
Out of the dusk a shadow,
Then a spark;
Out of the cloud a silence,
Then a lark;
Out of the heart a rapture,
Then a pain;
Out of the dead, cold ashes,
Life again.
JOHN BANISTER TABB—*Evolution.*

12
The Lord let the house of a brute to the soul of a man,
And the man said, "Am I your debtor?"
And the Lord—"Not yet: but make it as clean as you can,
And then I will let you a better."
TENNYSON—*By an Evolutionist.*

13
Is there evil but on earth? Or pain in every peopled sphere?
Well, be grateful for the sounding watchword "Evolution" here.
TENNYSON—*Locksley Hall Sixty Years After.* L. 198.

14
Evolution ever climbing after some ideal good
And Reversion ever dragging Evolution in the mud.
TENNYSON—*Locksley Hall Sixty Years After.* L. 200.

15
When I was a shepherd on the plains of Assyria.
THOREAU.
(See also PYTHAGORAS)

16
And hear the mighty stream of tendency
Uttering, for elevation of our thought,
A clear sonorous voice, inaudible
To the vast multitude.
WORDSWORTH—*Excursion.* IX. 87.
(See also ARNOLD)

EXAMPLE

17
Example is the school of mankind, and they will learn at no other.
BURKE—*Letter I. On a Regicide Peace.* Vol. V. P. 331.

18
Illustrious Predecessor.
BURKE—*Thoughts on the Cause of the Present Discontents.* (Edition 1775)
(See also FIELDING, VAN BUREN)

19
Why doth one man's yawning make another yawn?
BURTON—*Anatomy of Melancholy.* Pt. I. Sec. II. Memb. 3. Subsect. 2.

20
This noble ensample to his sheepe he gaf,—
That firste he wroughte and afterward he taughte.
CHAUCER—*Canterbury Tales. Prologue.* L. 496.

1
Quod exemplo fit, id etiam jure fieri putant.
Men think they may justly do that for which they have a precedent.
CICERO—*Epistles*. IV. 3.

2
Componitur orbis
Regis ad exemplum; nec sic inflectere sensus
Humanos edicta valent, quam vita regentis.
The people are fashioned according to the example of their kings; and edicts are of less power than the life of the ruler.
CLAUDIANUS—*De Quarto Consulatu Honorii Augustii Panegyris*. CCXCIX.

3
Illustrious predecessors.
FIELDING—*Covent Garden Journal*. Jan. 11, 1752. (See also BURKE)

4
Allured to brighter worlds, and led the way.
GOLDSMITH—*Deserted Village*. L. 170. (See also HOMER)

5
Since truth and constancy are vain,
Since neither love, nor sense of pain,
Nor force of reason, can persuade,
Then let example be obey'd.
GEO. GRANVILLE (Lord Lansdowne)—*To Myra*.

6
Content to follow when we lead the way.
HOMER—*The Iliad*. Bk. X. L. 141. POPE'S trans. (See also GOLDSMITH)

7
Avidos vicinum funus ut ægros
Exanimat, mortisque metu sibi parcere cogit;
Sic teneros animos aliena opprobria sæpe
Absterrent vitiis.
As a neighboring funeral terrifies sick misers, and fear obliges them to have some regard for themselves; so, the disgrace of others will often deter tender minds from vice.
HORACE—*Satires*. I. 4. 126.

8
I do not give you to posterity as a pattern to imitate, but as an example to deter.
JUNIUS—*Letter XII. To the Duke of Grafton*.

9
Unde tibi frontem libertatemque parentis,
Cum facias pejora senex?
Whence do you derive the power and privilege of a parent, when you, though an old man, do worse things (than your child)?
JUVENAL—*Satires*. XIV. 56.

10
L'exemple est un dangereux leurre;
Où la guêpe a passé, le moucheron demeure.
Example is a dangerous lure: where the wasp got through the gnat sticks fast.
LA FONTAINE—*Fables*. II. XVI.

11
Lives of great men all remind us
We can make our lives sublime,
And, departing, leave behind us
Footprints on the sands of time.
LONGFELLOW—*A Psalm of Life*.

12
He who should teach men to die, would at the same time teach them to live.
MONTAIGNE—*Essays*. Bk. I. Ch. XIX.

13
He was indeed the glass
Wherein the noble youth did dress themselves.
Henry IV. Pt. II. Act II. Sc. 3. L. 21.

14
Sheep follow sheep.
Talmud. Ketuboth 62.

15
Inspicere tamquam in speculum in vitas omnium
Jubeo atque ex aliis sumere exemplum sibi.
We should look at the lives of all as at a mirror, and take from others an example for ourselves.
TERENCE—*Adelphi*. III. 3. 62.

16
Felix quicumque dolore alterius disces posse cavere tuo.
Happy thou that learnest from another's griefs, not to subject thyself to the same.
TIBULLUS—*Carmina*. III. 6. 43.

17
I tread in the footsteps of illustrious men . . . in receiving from the people the sacred trust confided to my illustrious predecessor.
MARTIN VAN BUREN—*Inaugural Address*. March 4, 1837. (See also BURKE)

18
Sequiturque patrem non passibus æquis.
He follows his father with unequal steps.
VERGIL—*Æneid*. II. 724.

EXPECTATION

19
Serene I fold my hands and wait,
Nor care for wind or tide nor sea;
I rave no more 'gainst time or fate,
For lo! my own shall come to me.
JOHN BURROUGHS—*Waiting*.

20
"Yet doth he live!" exclaims th' impatient heir,
And sighs for sables which he must not wear.
BYRON—*Lara*. Canto I. St. 3.

21
I have known him [Micawber] come home to supper with a flood of tears, and a declaration that nothing was now left but a jail; and go to bed making a calculation of the expense of putting bow-windows to the house, "in case anything turned up," which was his favorite expression.
DICKENS—*David Copperfield*. Ch. XI.

22
I suppose, to use our national motto, *something will turn up*. [Motto of Vraibleusia.]
BENJ. DISRAELI—*Popanilla*. Ch. VII.

23
He was fash and full of faith that "something would turn up."
BENJ. DISRAELI—*Tancred*. Bk. III. Ch. VI.

24
Everything comes if a man will only wait.
BENJ. DISRAELI—*Tancred*. Bk. IV. Ch. VIII.

25
What else remains for me?
Youth, hope and love;
To build a new life on a ruined life.
LONGFELLOW—*Masque of Pandora. In the Garden*. Pt. VIII.

1
Since yesterday I have been in Alcalá.
Erelong the time will come, sweet Preciosa,
When that dull distance shall no more divide us;
And I no more shall scale thy wall by night
To steal a kiss from thee, as I do now.
LONGFELLOW—*Spanish Student.* Act I. Sc. 3.

2
Blessed is he who expects nothing for he shall never be disappointed.
POPE—*Letter to* GAY. Oct. 6, 1727. Called by POPE and GAY "The Eighth Beatitude." BISHOP HEBER refers to it as "Swift's Eighth Beatitude." Also called "The Ninth Beatitude."
(See also WALCOT)

3
Oft expectation fails and most oft there
Where most it promises, and oft it hits
Where hope is coldest and despair most fits.
All's Well That Ends Well. Act II. Sc. 1. L. 145.

4
There have sat
The live-long day, with patient expectation,
To see great Pompey pass the streets of Rome.
Julius Cæsar. Act I. Sc. 1. L. 45.

5
He hath indeed better bettered expectation than you must expect of me to tell you how.
Much Ado About Nothing. Act I. Sc. 1. L. 15.

6
Promising is the very air o' the time; it opens the eyes of expectation: performance is ever the duller for his act; and, but in the plainer and simpler kind of people, the deed of saying is quite out of use.
Timon of Athens. Act V. Sc. 1. L. 24.

7
Expectation whirls me round.
The imaginary relish is so sweet
That it enchants my sense.
Troilus and Cressida. Act III. Sc. 2. L. 19.

8
'Tis expectation makes a blessing dear;
Heaven were not Heaven, if we knew what it were.
SIR JOHN SUCKLING—*Against Fruition.*

9
Although I enter not,
Yet round about the spot
Ofttimes I hover;
And near the sacred gate,
With longing eyes I wait,
Expectant of her.
THACKERAY—*Pendennis. At the Church Gate.*

10
'Tis silence all,
And pleasing expectation.
THOMSON—*Seasons. Spring.* L. 160.

11
Blessed are those that nought expect,
For they shall not be disappointed.
JOHN WALCOT—*Ode to Pitt.*
(See also POPE)

12
It is folly to expect men to do all that they may reasonably be expected to do.
WHATELY—*Apophthegms.*

EXPERIENCE

13
Suffering brings experience.
ÆSCHYLUS—*Agamemnon.* 185.

14
Behold, we live through all things,—famine, thirst,
Bereavement, pain; all grief and misery,
All woe and sorrow; life inflicts its worst
On soul and body,—but we cannot die,
Though we be sick, and tired, and faint, and worn,—
Lo, all things can be borne!
ELIZABETH AKERS ALLEN—*Endurance.*

15
By experience we find out a shorter way by a long wandering. Learning teacheth more in one year than experience in twenty.
ROGER ASCHAM—*Schoolmaster.*

16
It is costly wisdom that is bought by experience.
ROGER ASCHAM—*Schoolmaster.*

17
Oh, who can tell, save he whose heart hath tried?
BYRON—*The Corsair.* Canto I. St. 1.

18
A sadder and a wiser man,
He rose the morrow morn.
COLERIDGE—*The Ancient Mariner.* Pt. VII. Last St.

19
To show the world what long experience gains,
Requires not courage, though it calls for pains;
But at life's outset to inform mankind
Is a bold effort of a valiant mind.
CRABBE—*Borough.* Letter VII. L. 47.

20
In her experience all her friends relied,
Heaven was her help and nature was her guide.
CRABBE—*Parish Register.* Pt. III.

21
Tu proverai si come sa di sale
Lo pane altrui, e com' è duro calle
Lo scendere e'l salir per l'altrui scale.
Thou shalt know by experience how salt the savor is of other's bread, and how sad a path it is to climb and descend another's stairs.
DANTE—*Paradiso.* XVII. 58.

22
Only so much do I know, as I have lived.
EMERSON—*Oration. The American Scholar.*

23
Experience is no more transferable in morals than in art.
FROUDE—*Short Studies on Great Subjects. Education.*

24
Experience teaches slowly, and at the cost of mistakes.
FROUDE—*Short Studies on Great Subjects. Party Politics.*

25
We read the past by the light of the present, and the forms vary as the shadows fall, or as the point of vision alters.
FROUDE—*Short Studies on Great Subjects. Society in Italy in the Last Days of the Roman Republic.*

1
Experience join'd with common sense,
To mortals is a providence.
MATTHEW GREEN—*The Spleen.* L. 312.

2
I have but one lamp by which my feet are guided, and that is the lamp of experience.
PATRICK HENRY—*Speech at Virginia Convention.* March 23, 1775.

3
Stultorum eventus magister est.
Experience is the teacher of fools.
LIVY—*Annales.* XXII. 39.

4
One thorn of experience is worth a whole wilderness of warning.
LOWELL — *Among my Books. Shakespeare Once More.*

5
Semper enim ex aliis alia proseminat usus.
Experience is always sowing the seed of one thing after another.
MANILIUS—*Astronomica.* I. 90.

6
Experience, next, to thee I owe,
Best guide; not following thee, I had remain'd
In ignorance; thou open'st wisdom's way,
And giv'st access, though secret she retire.
MILTON—*Paradise Lost.* Bk. IX. L. 807.

7
What man would be wise, let him drink of the river
That bears on his bosom the record of time;
A message to him every wave can deliver
To teach him to creep till he knows how to climb.
JOHN BOYLE O'REILLY—*Rules of the Road.*

8
Who heeds not experience, trust him not.
JOHN BOYLE O'REILLY—*Rules of the Road.*

9
Nam in omnibus fere minus valent præcepta quam experimenta.
In almost everything, experience is more valuable than precept.
QUINTILIAN—*De Institutione Oratoria.* II. 5. 5.

10
I shall the effect of this good lesson keep,
As watchman to my heart.
Hamlet. Act I. Sc. 3. L. 45.

11
I know
The past and thence I will essay to glean
A warning for the future, so that man
May profit by his errors, and derive
Experience from his folly;
For, when the power of imparting joy
Is equal to the will, the human soul
Requires no other heaven.
SHELLEY—*Queen Mab.* III. L. 6.

12
Experientia docet.
Experience teaches.
Founded on TACITUS—*Annales.* Bk. V. 6.

13
I am a part of all that I have met;
Yet all experience is an arch wherethro'
Gleams that untravl'd world whose margin fades
Forever and forever when I move.
TENNYSON — *Ulysses.* (Free rendering of DANTE'S *Inferno.* Canto XVI.)

14
And others' follies teach us not,
Nor much their wisdom teaches,
And most, of sterling worth, is what
Our own experience preaches.
TENNYSON—*Will Waterproof; Lyrical Monologue.*

15
Experto credite.
Believe one who has tried it.
VERGIL—*Æneid.* XI. 283.

16
Experto crede Roberto.
Believe Robert who has tried it.
A proverb quoted by BURTON—Introduction to *Anatomy of Melancholy.* Common in the middle ages. Experto crede Ruberto is given as a saying in a discourse of ULRICUS MELITER to SIGISMOND, Archduke of Austria. (1489) Same in CORONIS—*Apolog. pro Erasmus Coll.* First version is in an epitaph in an old chapel of Exeter College. (1627) LE ROUX DE LINCY traces it to GOMÈS de TRIER—*Jardin de Recreation.* (1611)

17
Learn the lesson of your own pain—learn to seek God, not in any single event of past history, but in your own soul—in the constant verifications of experience, in the life of Christian love.
MRS. HUMPHRY WARD—*Robert Elsmere.* Ch. XXVII.

18
Da dacht ich oft: schwatzt noch so hoch gelehrt,
Man weiss doch nichts, als was man selbst erfährt.
I have often thought that however learned you may talk about it, one knows nothing but what he learns from his own experience.
WIELAND—*Oberon.* II. 24.

EXPLANATION

19
Jolie hypothèse elle explique tant de choses.
A pretty hypothesis which explains many things.
Quoted by MR. ASQUITH, Speech in Parliament, March 29, 1917, as "a saying of a witty Frenchman."

20
Denn wenn sich Jemand versteckt erklärt, so ist Nichts unhöflicher als eine neue Frage.
For when any one explains himself guardedly, nothing is more uncivil than to put a new question.
JEAN PAUL RICHTER—*Hesperus.* II.

EXPRESSION

21
Preserving the sweetness of proportion and expressing itself beyond expression.
BEN JONSON—*The Masque of Hymen.*

22
Patience and sorrow strove
Who should express her goodliest. You have seen
Sunshine and rain at once: her smile and tears
Were like a better way.
King Lear. Act IV. Sc. 3. L. 18.

EXTREMES

1
The fierce extremes of good and ill to brook.
CAMPBELL—*Gertrude of Wyoming.*
(See also MILTON)

2
Avoid extremes.
Attributed to CLEOBULUS OF LINDOS.
(See also POPE)

3
Thus each extreme to equal danger tends,
Plenty, as well as Want, can separate friends.
COWLEY—*Davideis.* Bk. III. L. 205.

4
Extremes meet, and there is no better example than the haughtiness of humility.
EMERSON—*Letters and Social Aims. Greatness.*
(See also MERCIER)

5
Extremes are faulty and proceed from men: compensation is just, and proceeds from God.
LA BRUYÈRE—*The Characters or Manners of the Present Age.* Ch. XVII.

6
Extremes meet.
MERCIER—*Tableaux de Paris.* Vol. IV. Title of Ch. 348.
(See also EMERSON)

7
And feel by turns the bitter change
Of fierce extremes, extremes by change more fierce.
MILTON—*Paradise Lost.* II. 599.
(See also CAMPBELL)

8
He that had never seen a river imagined the first he met to be the sea; and the greatest things that have fallen within our knowledge we conclude the extremes that nature makes of the kind.
MONTAIGNE—*Essays.* Bk. I. Ch. XXVI.

9
Avoid Extremes; and shun the fault of such
Who still are pleas'd too little or too much.
POPE—*Essay on Criticism.* L. 385.
(See also CLEOBULUS)

10
Extremes in nature equal good produce;
Extremes in man concur to general use.
POPE—*Moral Essays.* Ep. III. L. 161.

11
Extrema primo nemo tentavit loco.
No one tries extreme remedies at first.
SENECA—*Agamemnon.* 153.

12
Like to the time o' the year between the extremes
Of hot and cold, he was nor sad nor merry.
Antony and Cleopatra. Act I. Sc. 5. L. 51.

13
Not fearing death, nor shrinking for distress,
But always resolute in most extremes.
Henry VI. Pt. I. Act IV. Sc. 1. L. 37.

14
Who can be patient in such extremes?
Henry VI. Pt. III. Act I. Sc. 1. L. 215.

15
And where two raging fires meet together,
They do consume the thing that feeds their fury:
Though little fire grows great with little wind,
Yet extreme gusts will blow out fire and all.
Taming of the Shrew. Act II. Sc. 1. L. 133.

16
O brother, speak with possibilities,
And do not break into these deep extremes.
Titus Andronicus. Act III. Sc. 1.

EYES

17
In her eyes a thought
Grew sweeter and sweeter, deepening like the dawn,
A mystical forewarning.
T. B. ALDRICH—*Pythagoras.*

18
A gray eye is a sly eye,
And roguish is a brown one;
Turn full upon me thy eye,—
Ah, how its wavelets drown one!
A blue eye is a true eye;
Mysterious is a dark one,
Which flashes like a spark-sun!
A black eye is the best one.
W. R. ALGER—*Oriental Poetry. Mirtsa Schaffy on Eyes.*

19
There are whole veins of diamonds in thine eyes,
Might furnish crowns for all the Queens of earth.
BAILEY—*Festus.* Sc. *A Drawing Room.*

20
Look babies in your eyes, my pretty sweet one.
BEAUMONT AND FLETCHER—*The Loyal Subject.*
(See also DONNE, HERRICK, SIDNEY)

21
The mind has a thousand eyes,
And the heart but one;
Yet the light of a whole life dies
When love is done.
F. W. BOURDILLON—*Light.*
(See also SYLVESTER, also BOURDILLON under NIGHT)

22
Eyes of gentianellas azure,
Staring, winking at the skies.
E. B. BROWNING—*Hector in the Garden.*

23
Thine eyes are springs in whose serene
And silent waters heaven is seen.
Their lashes are the herbs that look
On their young figures in the brook.
BRYANT—*Oh, Fairest of the Rural Maids.*

24
The learned compute that seven hundred and seven millions of millions of vibrations have penetrated the eye before the eye can distinguish the tints of a violet.
BULWER-LYTTON—*What Will He Do With It?* Bk. VIII. Ch. II.

25
The Chinese say that we Europeans have one eye, they themselves two, all the world else is blinde.
BURTON—*Anat. of Melancholy.* Ed. 6. P. 40.
(See also ERASMUS)

26
Her eye (I'm very fond of handsome eyes)
Was large and dark, suppressing half its fire
Until she spoke, then through its soft disguise
Flash'd an expression more of pride than ire,
And love than either; and there would arise,
A something in them which was not desire,

But would have been, perhaps, but for the soul,
Which struggled through and chasten'd down the whole.
BYRON—*Don Juan.* Canto I. St. 60.

1
With eyes that look'd into the very soul—
* * * * * *
Bright—and as black and burning as a coal.
BYRON—*Don Juan.* Canto IV. St. 94.

2
In every object there is inexhaustible meaning; the eye sees in it what the eye brings means of seeing.
CARLYLE—*Hist. of the French Revolution.* Vol. I. P. 5. People's ed. *Heroes and Hero-Worship, The Hero as Poet; Miscellaneous Essays,* Vol. VI; *Review of Vernhagen von Ense's Memoirs,* P. 241. Same idea in GOETHE'S *Zahme Xeniem.* III.

3
There are eyes half defiant,
Half meek and compliant;
Black eyes, with a wondrous, witching charm
To bring us good or to work us harm.
PHEBE CARY—*Dove's Eyes.*

4
Oculi, tanquam, speculatores, altissimum locum obtinent.
The eyes, like sentinels, hold the highest place in the body.
CICERO—*De Nat. Deorum.* Bk. II. 56.
(See also DU BARTAS)

5
The love light in her eye.
HARTLEY COLERIDGE. No. CCXVIII, in *Golden Treasury of Songs and Lyrics.*
(See also DUFFERIN)

6
My eyes make pictures, when they are shut.
COLERIDGE—*A Day-Dream.*

7
In the twinkling of an eye.
I Corinthians. XV. 52. *Merchant of Venice.* Act II. Sc. 2.

8
Eyes, that displaces
The neighbor diamond, and out-faces
That sun-shine by their own sweet graces.
RICHARD CRASHAW—*Wishes. To his (Supposed) Mistress.*

9
Not in mine eyes alone is Paradise.
DANTE—*Paradise.* XVIII. 21.

10
Parean l'occhiaje anella senza gemme.
Their eyes seem'd rings from whence the gems were gone.
DANTE—*Purgatorio.* XXIII. 31.

11
He kept him as the apple of his eye.
Deuteronomy. XXXII. 10.

12
With affection beaming in one eye and calculation shining out of the other.
DICKENS—*Martin Chuzzlewit.* Ch. VIII.

13
And pictures in our eyes to get
Was all our propagation.
DONNE—*The Ecstacy.*
(See also BEAUMONT)

14
My life lies in those eyes which have me slain.
DRUMMOND—*Sonnet XXIX.* L. 14.

15
These lovely lamps, these windows of the soul.
DU BARTAS—*Divine Weekes and Workes.* First Week. Sixth Day.
(See also CICERO)

16
The love light in your eye.
LADY DUFFERIN—*Irish Emigrant.*
(See also COLERIDGE)

17
A suppressed resolve will betray itself in the eyes.
GEORGE ELIOT—*The Mill on the Floss.* Bk. V. Ch. XIV.

18
An eye can threaten like a loaded and levelled gun, or can insult like hissing or kicking; or, in its altered mood, by beams of kindness, it can make the heart dance with joy.
EMERSON—*Conduct of Life. Behavior.*

19
Eyes are bold as lions,—roving, running, leaping, here and there, far and near. They speak all languages. They wait for no introduction; they are no Englishmen; ask no leave of age or rank; they respect neither poverty nor riches, neither learning nor power, nor virtue, nor sex, but intrude, and come again, and go through and through you in a moment of time. What inundation of life and thought is discharged from one soul into another through them!
EMERSON—*Conduct of Life. Behavior.*

20
Scitum est inter cæcos luscum regnare posse.
Among the blind the one-eyed man is king.
ERASMUS—*Adagia, Dignitas et Excellentia et Inequalitas, sub-division, Excel. et Ineq.* (about 1500). Proverbs collected by MICHAEL APOSTOLIOS, Cent. VII. 31. Latin given as: Cæcorum in patria luscus rex imperat omnis. Taken from the Greek. See CHILIADES—*Adagiorum,* quarta centuria, third Chilias No. 96. Earliest use probably in G. FULLENIUS—*Comedye of Acolastus,* trans. by JOHN PALSGRAVE from the Latin. (1540) Quoted by EDMUND CAMPION—*Rationes Decom.* (1581) CARLYLE—*Frederick the Great.* Bk. 4. Ch. II. Quoted as: Beati monoculi in regione cæcorum. Blessed are the one-eyed in the country of the blind. HERBERT—*Jacula Prudentum.* Also in *Miscellanæ.* Pt. II. Fourth Ed. P. 342. JUVENAL—*Satire X.* 227, gives it as: Ambos perdidit ille oculos et luscis invidet.
(See also BURTON, MARVEL, NÜCHTER, SKELTON)

21
To sun myself in Huncamunca's eyes.
HENRY FIELDING—*The Life and Death of Tom Thumb the Great.* Act I. Sc. 3.

22
Ils sont si transparents qu'ils laissent voir votre ame.
Eyes so transparent,
That through them one sees the soul.
THEOPHILE GAUTIER—*The Two Beautiful Eyes.* (See also MEREDITH)

1
Tell me, eyes, what 'tis ye're seeking;
For ye're saying something sweet,
Fit the ravish'd ear to greet.
Eloquently, softly speaking.
GOETHE—*April.*

2
On woman Nature did bestow two eyes,
Like Hemian's bright lamps, in matchless beauty shining,
Whose beams do soonest captivate the wise
And wary heads, made rare by art's refining.
ROBERT GREENE—*Philomela.* Sonnet.

3
Wenn ich in deine Augen seh'
So schwindet all' mein Leid und Weh.
Whene'er into thine eyes I see,
All pain and sorrow fly from me.
HEINE—*Lyrisches Intermezzo.* IV.

4
Die blauen Veilchen der Aeugelein.
Those blue violets, her eyes.
HEINE—*Lyrisches Intermezzo.* XXXI.

5
I everywhere am thinking
Of thy blue eyes' sweet smile;
A sea of blue thoughts is spreading
Over my heart the while.
HEINE—*New Spring.* Pt. XVIII. St. 2.

6
The eyes have one language everywhere.
HERBERT—*Jacula Prudentum.*

7
The ear is a less trustworthy witness than the eye.
HERODOTUS. 1. 8.

8
Her eyes the glow-worme lend thee,
The shooting starres attend thee;
And the elves also,
Whose little eyes glow
Like the sparks of fire, befriend thee.
HERRICK—*The Night Piece to Julia.*

9
We credit most our sight; one eye doth please
Our trust farre more than ten eare-witnesses.
HERRICK—*Hesperides. The Eyes Before the Ears.*

10
It is an active flame that flies
First to the babies in the eyes.
HERRICK—*The Kiss.*
(See also BEAUMONT)

11
Thine eye was on the censer,
And not the hand that bore it.
HOLMES—*Lines by a Clerk.*

12
Dark eyes—eternal soul of pride!
Deep life in all that's true!
* * * *
Away, away to other skies!
Away o'er seas and sands!
Such eyes as those were never made
To shine in other lands.
LELAND—*Callirhoe.*

13
I have neither eyes to see nor tongue to speak but as the constitution is pleased to direct me, whose servant I am.
SPEAKER LENTHAL to *Charles I.* As quoted by WENDELL PHILLIPS—*Under the Flag.* Boston, April 21, 1861.
(See also LINCOLN)

14
Der Blick des Forschers fand
Nicht selten mehr, als er zu finden wünschte.
The eye of Paul Pry often finds more than he wished to find.
LESSING—*Nathan der Weise.* II. 8.

15
As President, I have no eyes but constitutional eyes; I cannot see you.
LINCOLN to the South Carolina Commissioners. (See also LENTHAL)

16
And thy deep eyes, amid the gloom,
Shine like jewels in a shroud.
LONGFELLOW—*Christus. Golden Legend.* Pt. IV.

17
The flash of his keen, black eyes
Forerunning the thunder.
LONGFELLOW—*Christus. Golden Legend.* Pt. IV.

18
I dislike an eye that twinkles like a star. Those only are beautiful which, like the planets, have a steady, lambent light,—are luminous, but not sparkling.
LONGFELLOW—*Hyperion.* Bk. III. Ch. IV.

19
O lovely eyes of azure,
Clear as the waters of a brook that run
Limpid and laughing in the summer sun!
LONGFELLOW—*Masque of Pandora.* Pt. I.

20
Within her tender eye
The heaven of April, with its changing light.
LONGFELLOW—*Spirit of Poetry.* L. 45.

21
Since your eyes are so sharpe, that you cannot onely looke through a milstone, but cleane through the minde.
LYLY—*Euphues and his England.* P. 289.

22
The light of the body is the eye.
Matthew. VI. 22.

23
Where did you get your eyes so blue?
Out of the sky as I came through.
GEO. MACDONALD—*Song in "At the Back of the North Wind."* Ch. XXXIII.

24
Those true eyes
Too pure and too honest in aught to disguise
The sweet soul shining through them.
OWEN MEREDITH (Lord Lytton)—*Lucile.* Pt. II. Canto II. St. 3.
(See also GAUTIER)

25
Among the blind the one-eyed blinkard reigns.
ANDREW MARVEL—*Character of Holland.*
(See also ERASMUS)

26
And looks commercing with the skies,
Thy rapt soul sitting in thine eyes.
MILTON—*Il Penseroso.* L. 39.
(See also OVID under GOD)

27
Ladies, whose bright eyes
Rain influence.
MILTON—*L'Allegro.* L. 121.

1
Si vous les voulez aimer, ce sera, ma foi, pour leurs beaux yeux.

If you wish to love, it shall be, by my faith, for their beautiful eyes.

MOLIÈRE—*Les Précieuses Ridicules.* XVI.

2
And violets, transform'd to eyes,
Inshrined a soul within their blue.

MOORE—*Evenings in Greece. Second Evening.*

3
Eyes of most unholy blue!

MOORE—*Irish Melodies. By that Lake whose Gloomy Shore.*

4
Those eyes, whose light seem'd rather given
To be ador'd than to adore—
Such eyes as may have looked *from* heaven,
But ne'er were raised to it before!

MOORE—*Loves of the Angels. Third Angel's Story.* St. 7.

5
And the world's so rich in resplendent eyes,
'Twere a pity to limit one's love to a pair.

MOORE—*'Tis Sweet to Think.*

6
All German cities are blind, Nurnberg alone sees with one eye.

FREDERICH NÜCHTER—*Albrecht Dürer.* P. 8. English Trans. by LUCY D. WILLIAMS. (Given as a saying in Venice.)
(See also ERASMUS)

7
Thou my star at the stars are gazing
Would I were heaven that I might behold thee with many eyes.

PLATO. From *Greek Anthology.*

8
Pluris est oculatus testis unus, quam auriti decem.
Qui audiunt, audita dicunt; qui vident, plane sciunt.

One eye-witness is of more weight than ten hearsays. Those who hear, speak of what they have heard; those who see, know beyond mistake.

PLAUTUS—*Truculentus.* II. 6. 8.

9
Why has not man a microscopic eye?
For this plain reason, Man is not a Fly.
Say, what the use, were finer optics giv'n,
T' inspect a mite, not comprehend the heav'n?

POPE—*Essay on Man.* Ep. I. L. 193.

10
Bright as the sun her eyes the gazers strike,
And, like the sun, they shine on all alike.

POPE—*Rape of the Lock.* Canto II. L. 13.

11
The eyes of a fool are in the ends of the earth.

Proverbs. XVII. 24.

12
Dark eyes are dearer far
Than those that mock the hyacinthine bell.

J. H. REYNOLDS—*Sonnet.*

13
Thou tell'st me there is murder in mine eye;
'Tis pretty, sure, and very probable,
That eyes, that are the frail'st and softest things,
Who shut their coward gates on atomies,
Should be call'd tyrants, butchers, murderers!

As You Like It. Act III. Sc. 5. L. 10.

14
Faster than his tongue
Did make offence his eye did heal it up.

As You Like It. Act III. Sc. 5. L. 116.

15
An eye like Mars, to threaten and command.

Hamlet. Act III. Sc. 4. L. 57.

16
The image of a wicked heinous fault
Lives in his eye: that close aspect of his
Does show the mood of a much troubled breast.

King John. Act IV. Sc. 2. L. 71.

17
You have seen
Sunshine and rain at once. * * * those happy smilets,
That play'd on her ripe lip, seem'd not to know
What guests were in her eyes; which parted thence,
As pearls from diamonds dropp'd.

King Lear. Act IV. Sc. 3. L. 19.

18
For where is any author in the world
Teaches such beauty as a woman's eye?

Love's Labour's Lost. Act IV. Sc. 3. L. 312.

19
A lover's eyes will gaze an eagle blind.

Love's Labour's Lost. Act IV. Sc. 3. L. 334.

20
Sometimes from her eyes
I did receive fair speechless messages.

Merchant of Venice. Act I. Sc. 1. L. 163.

21
I see how thine eye would emulate the diamond: thou hast the right archèd beauty of the brow.

Merry Wives of Windsor. Act III. Sc. 3. L. 58.

22
I have a good eye, uncle; I can see a church by daylight.

Much Ado About Nothing. Act II. Sc. 1. L. 85.

23
Disdain and scorn ride sparkling in her eyes.

Much Ado About Nothing. Act III. Sc. 1. L. 51.

24
Her eyes, like marigolds, had sheath'd their light;
And, canopied in darkness, sweetly lay,
Till they might open to adorn the day.

Rape of Lucrece. L. 397.

25
Her eyes in heaven
Would through the airy region stream so bright,
That birds would sing and think it were not night.

Romeo and Juliet. Act II. Sc. 2. L. 20.

26
Alack, there lies more peril in thine eye
Than twenty of their swords.

Romeo and Juliet. Act II. Sc. 2. L. 71.

27
If I could write the beauty of your eyes,
And in fresh numbers number all your graces,
The age to come would say, "This poet lies;
Such heavenly touches ne'er touch'd earthly faces."

Sonnet XVII.

28
The fringed curtains of thine eye advance,
And say what thou seest yond.

Tempest. Act I. Sc. 2. L. 407.

1
Her two blue windows faintly she up-heaveth,
Like the fair sun, when in his fresh array
He cheers the morn, and all the earth relieveth;
And as the bright sun glorifies the sky,
So is her face illumin'd with her eye.
Venus and Adonis. L. 482.

2
But hers, which through the crystal tears gave light,
Shone like the moon in water seen by night.
Venus and Adonis. L. 491.

3
Black brows they say
Become some women best, so that there be not
Too much hair there, but in a semicircle
Or a half-moon made with a pen.
Winter's Tale. Act II. Sc. 1. L. 8.

4
Thine eyes are like the deep, blue, boundless heaven
Contracted to two circles underneath
Their long, fine lashes; dark, far, measureless,
Orb within orb, and line through line inwoven.
SHELLEY — *Prometheus Unbound.* Act II. Sc. 1.

5
Think ye by gazing on each other's eyes
To multiply your lovely selves?
SHELLEY — *Prometheus Unbound.* Act VI. Sc. 4.

6
So when thou saw'st in nature's cabinet
Stella thou straight'st look'st babies in her eyes.
SIR PHILIP SIDNEY—*Astrophel and Stella.*
(See also BEAUMONT)

7
But have ye not heard this,
How an one-eyed man is
Well sighted when
He is among blind men?
JOHN SKELTON—*Why come ye not to Courte?* (writing against Wolsey).
(See also ERASMUS)

8
The sight of you is good for sore eyes.
SWIFT—*Polite Conversation.* Dialog. I.

9
Were you the earth dear love, and I the skies
My love would shine on you like to the sun
And look upon you with ten thousand eyes
Till heaven waxed blind and till the world were done.
J. SYLVESTER—*Love's Omnipotence.*
(See also BOURDILLON)

10
Her eyes are homes of silent prayer.
TENNYSON—*In Memoriam.* XXXII.

11
The Father of Heaven.
Scoop, young Jesus, for her eyes,
Wood-browned pools of Paradise—
Young Jesus, for the eyes,
For the eyes of Viola.
Angels.
Tint, Prince Jesus, a
Duskèd eye for Viola!
FRANCIS THOMPSON—*The Making of Viola.* St. 2.

12
But optics sharp it needs, I ween,
To see what is not to be seen.
JOHN TRUMBULL—*McFingal.* Canto I. L. 67.

13
How blue were Ariadne's eyes
When, from the sea's horizon line,
At eve, she raised them on the skies!
My Psyche, bluer far are thine.
AUBREY DE VERE—*Psyche.*

14
Blue eyes shimmer with angel glances,
Like spring violets over the lea.
CONSTANCE F. WOOLSON—*October's Song.*

15
The harvest of a quiet eye,
That broods and sleeps on his own heart.
WORDSWORTH—*A Poet's Epitaph.* St. 13.

F

FACE

16
It is the common wonder of all men, how among so many millions of faces there should be none alike.
SIR THOMAS BROWNE—*Religio Medici.* Pt. II. Sec. II.

17
A face to lose youth for, to occupy age
With the dream of, meet death with.
ROBERT BROWNING—*A Likeness.*

18
Showing that if a good face is a letter of recommendation, a good heart is a letter of credit.
BULWER-LYTTON—*What Will He Do With It?* Bk. II. Title of Ch. XI.

19
As clear and as manifest as the nose in a man's face.
BURTON—*Anatomy of Melancholy.* Pt. III. Sec. III. Memb. 4. Subsec. I.
(See also RABELAIS, 561[4])

20
And her face so fair
Stirr'd with her dream, as rose-leaves with the air.
BYRON—*Don Juan.* Canto IV. St. 29.

21
Yet even her tyranny had such a grace,
The women pardoned all, except her face.
BYRON—*Don Juan.* Canto V. St. 113.

22
And to his eye
There was but one beloved face on earth,
And that was shining on him.
BYRON—*The Dream.* St. 2.

23
There is a garden in her face,
Where roses and white lilies blow;
A heavenly paradise is that place,
Wherein all pleasant fruits do grow.
There cherries grow that none may buy,
Till cherry ripe themselves do cry.
CAMPION claims these in note To Reader, *Fourth Book of Airs.* ARBER in *English Garner*, follows original. Attributed to

RICHARD ALLISON by W. D. ADAMS, FREDERICK LOCKER-LAMPSON, CHARLES MACKAY. To CAMPION by ERNEST RHYS, A. H. BULLEN.

1
The magic of a face.
THOMAS CAREW—*Epitaph on the Lady S——.*

2
He had a face like a benediction (blessing).
CERVANTES—*Don Quixote.* Bk. II. Pt. I. Ch. IV.

3
The face the index of a feeling mind.
CRABBE—*Tales of the Hall.*

4
Well had the boding tremblers learn'd to trace
The day's disasters in his morning face.
GOLDSMITH—*The Deserted Village.* L. 199.

5
Her face betokened all things dear and good,
The light of somewhat yet to come was there
Asleep, and waiting for the opening day,
When childish thoughts, like flowers, would drift away.
JEAN INGELOW—*Margaret in the Xebec.* St. 57.

6
How some they have died, and some they have left me,
And some are taken from me; all are departed;
All, all are gone, the old familiar faces.
LAMB—*The Old Familiar Faces.*

7
A face that had a story to tell. How different faces are in this particular! Some of them speak not. They are books in which not a line is written, save perhaps a date.
LONGFELLOW—*Hyperion.* Bk. I. Ch. IV.

8
These faces in the mirrors
Are but the shadows and phantoms of myself.
LONGFELLOW—*Masque of Pandora.* Pt. II. *The House of Epimetheus.* L. 72.

9
The light upon her face
Shines from the windows of another world.
Saints only have such faces.
LONGFELLOW—*Michael Angelo.* Pt. II. 6.

10
Oh! could you view the melody
Of every grace,
And music of her face,
You'd drop a tear,
Seeing more harmony
In her bright eye,
Than now you hear.
LOVELACE—*Orpheus to Beasts.* St. 2.

11
Was this the face that launch'd a thousand ships,
And burnt the topless towers of Ilium?
Sweet Helen, make me immortal with a kiss.—
Her lips suck forth my soul; see, where it flies!—
MARLOWE—*Faustus.*

12
Human face divine.
MILTON—*Paradise Lost.* Bk. III. L. 44.

13
In her face excuse
Came prologue, and apology too prompt.
MILTON—*Paradise Lost.* Bk. IX. L. 853.

14
Vous avez bien la face descouverte; moi je suis tout face.
You have your face bare; I am all face.
MONTAIGNE—*Essays.* Vol. I. Ch. XXXV.
Answer of a naked beggar who was asked whether he was not cold. Same in FULLER—*Worthies. Berkshire.* P. 82. 3rd Ed. (1662)

15
Cheek * * *
Flushing white and mellow'd red;
Gradual tints, as when there glows
In snowy milk the bashful rose.
MOORE—*Odes of Anacreon. Ode XV.* L. 27.

16
With faces like dead lovers who died true.
D. M. MULOCK—*Indian Summer.*

17
Sæpe tacens vocem verbaque vultus habet.
Often a silent face has voice and words.
OVID—*Ars Amatoria.* Bk. I. 574.

18
If to her share some female errors fall
Look on her face, and you'll forget 'em all.
POPE—*Rape of the Lock.* Canto II. L. 17.

19
Lift thou up the light of thy countenance upon us.
Psalms. IV. 6.

20
A sweet attractive kinde of grace,
A full assurance given by lookes,
Continuall comfort in a face
The lineaments of Gospell bookes.
MATTHEW ROYDEN. *Elegie: or a Friend's Passion for his Astrophill.* (*Sir Philip Sidney*).
(See also MILTON under CHARACTER)

21
On his bold visage middle age
Had slightly press'd its signet sage,
Yet had not quenched the open truth
And fiery vehemence of youth;
Forward and frolic glee was there,
The will to do, the soul to dare.
SCOTT—*Lady of The Lake.* Canto I. St. 21.

22
Sea of upturned faces.
SCOTT—*Rob Roy.* Vol. II. Ch. XX. DANIEL WEBSTER. *Speech.* Sept. 30, 1842.

23
All men's faces are true, whatsome'er their hands are.
Antony and Cleopatra. Act II. Sc. 6. L. 102.

24
Thou hast a grim appearance, and thy face
Bears a command in 't: though thy tackle's torn,
Thou show'st a noble vessel.
Coriolanus. Act IV. Sc. 5. L. 66.

25
A countenance more in sorrow than in anger.
Hamlet. Act I. Sc. 2. L. 232.

26
God has given you one face, and you make yourselves another.
Hamlet. Act III. Sc. 1. L. 149.

27
In thy face
I see thy fury: if I longer stay
We shall begin our ancient bickerings.
Henry VI. Pt. II. Act I. Sc. 1. L. 142.

1
There is a fellow somewhat near the door; he should be a brazier by his face.
Henry VIII. Act V. Sc. 4. L. 41.

2
I have seen better faces in my time
Than stands on any shoulder that I see.
King Lear. Act II. Sc. 2. L. 99.

3 There's no art
To find the mind's construction in the face.
Macbeth. Act I. Sc. 4. L. 11.

4
Your face, my thane, is a book where men
May read strange matters. To beguile the time,
Look like the time.
Macbeth. Act I. Sc. 5. L. 63.

5
You have such a February face,
So full of frost, of storm, of cloudiness.
Much Ado About Nothing. Act V. Sc. 4. L. 41.

6
Compare her face with some that I shall show;
And I will make thee think thy swan a crow.
Romeo and Juliet. Act I. Sc. 2. L. 91.

7
Thus is his cheek the map of days outworn.
Sonnet LXVIII.

8
An unforgiving eye, and a damned disinheriting countenance.
R. B. SHERIDAN—*School for Scandal.* Act IV. Sc. 1.

9 Her angel's face,
As the great eye of heaven, shyned bright,
And made a sunshine in the shady place.
SPENSER—*Faerie Queene.* Bk. I. Canto III. St. 4.

10
Her cheeks so rare a white was on,
No daisy makes comparison;
(Who sees them is undone);
For streaks of red were mingled there,
Such as are on a Cath'rine pear,
(The side that's next the Sun).
SIR JOHN SUCKLING—*A Ballad Upon a Wedding.* St. 10.

11
Her face is like the Milky Way i' the sky,—
A meeting of gentle lights without a name.
SIR JOHN SUCKLING—*Brennoralt.* Act III.

12
White rose in red rose-garden
Is not so white;
Snowdrops, that plead for pardon
And pine for fright
Because the hard East blows
Over their maiden vows,
Grow not as this face grows from pale to bright.
SWINBURNE—*Before the Mirror.*

13
A face with gladness overspread!
Soft smiles, by human kindness bred!
WORDSWORTH—*To a Highland Girl.*

14
My face. Is this long strip of skin
Which bears of worry many a trace,
Of sallow hue, of features thin,
This mass of seams and lines, my face?
EDMUND YATES—*Aged Forty.*

FAILURE

15
[Oxford] Home of lost causes, and forsaken beliefs and unpopular names and impossible loyalties.
MATTHEW ARNOLD—*Essays in Criticism.* Closing par. of preface.

16
In the lexicon of youth, which
Fate reserves for a bright manhood, there is no such word
As—*fail!*
BULWER-LYTTON—*Richelieu.* Act II. Sc. 2.

17 Never say
"*Fail*" again.
BULWER-LYTTON—*Richelieu.* Act II. Sc. 2.

18
He that is down needs fear no fall
He that is low, no pride.
BUNYAN—*Pilgrim's Progress.* Pt. II.
(See also BUTLER)

19
Now a' is done that men can do,
And a' is done in vain.
BURNS—*It Was a' for our Rightfu' King.*

20
He that is down can fall no lower.
BUTLER—*Hudibras.* Pt. I. Canto III. L. 878.
(See also BUNYAN)

21
Camelus desiderans cornua etiam aures perdidit.
The camel set out to get him horns and was shorn of his ears.
ERASMUS—*Adagia. Chil.* III. Cent. V. 8. heading. *Greek proverb from* APOSTOLIUS. IX. 59 b. VIII. 43. English a free translation of the same from the rendering of the Proverb applied to Baalam by the Rabbis of the Talmud. *Sanhedrin.* 106 a.

22
He ploughs in sand, and sows against the wind,
That hopes for constant love of woman kind.
FULLER—*Medicina Gymnastica.* Vol. X. P. 7.
(See also MASSINGER)

23
Failed the bright promise of your early day?
BISHOP HEBER—*Palestine.* L. 113.

24
Greatly begin! Though thou have time
But for a line, be that sublime—
Not failure, but low aim is crime.
LOWELL—*For an Autograph.*

25
You may boldly say, you did not plough
Or trust the barren and ungrateful sands
With the fruitful grain of your religious counsels.
MASSINGER—*The Renegado.* Arenas arantes. Plough the sands. Phrase used by MR. ASQUITH, Nov. 21, 1894, at Birmingham. BURTON—*Anatomy of Melancholy.* Pt. III. Sec. 2. Mem. 1. Subs. 2.
(See also FULLER, WYATT, also SANNAZARO under WOMAN)

26
"All honor to him who shall win the prize,"
The world has cried for a thousand years;
But to him who tries and fails and dies,
I give great honor and glory and tears.
JOAQUIN MILLER—*For Those Who Fail.*

1 If this fail,
The pillar'd firmament is rottenness,
And earth's base built on stubble.
MILTON—*Comus*. L. 597.

2
Nam quamvis prope to, quamvis temone sub uno
Vertentem sese, frustra sectabere cantum
Cum rota posterior curras et in axe secundo.
Why, like the hindmost chariot wheels, art curst
Still to be near but ne'er to reach the first.
PERSIUS—*Satires*. V. 71. DRYDEN's trans. English, one of the mottoes of the *Spectator*, *Tatler*, *Guardian*.

3
Quod si deficiant vires, audacia certe
Laus erit: in magnis et voluisse sat est.
Although strength should fail, the effort will deserve praise. In great enterprises the attempt is enough.
PROPERTIUS—*Elegiæ*. II. 10. 5.

4
Allow me to offer my congratulations on the truly admirable skill you have shown in keeping clear of the mark. Not to have hit once in so many trials, argues the most splendid talents for missing.
DE QUINCEY—*Works*. Vol. XIV. P. 161. Ed. 1863, quoting the EMPEROR GALERIUS to a soldier who missed the target many times in succession.

5
[Il] battoit les buissons sans prendre les ozillons.
He beat the bushes without taking the birds.
RABELAIS—*Gargantua*. Ch. II.

6
How are the mighty fallen!
II Samuel. I. 25.

7
Here's to the men who lose!
What though their work be e'er so nobly plann'd
And watched with zealous care;
No glorious halo crowns their efforts grand—
Contempt is Failure's share!
G. L. SCARBOROUGH—*To the Vanquished*.
(See also STORY under CONQUEST)

8
And each forgets, as he strips and runs
With a brilliant, fitful pace,
It's the steady, quiet, plodding ones
Who win in the lifelong race.
And each forgets that his youth has fled,
Forgets that his prime is past,
Till he stands one day, with a hope that's dead,
In the glare of the truth at last.
SERVICE—*The Men That Don't Fit In*.

9
We have scotch'd the snake, not killed it.
Macbeth. Act III. Sc. 2. L. 14.

10
Not all who seem to fail have failed indeed,
Not all who fail have therefor worked in vain.
There is no failure for the good and brave.
Attributed to ARCHBISHOP TRENCH by Prof. CONNINGTON.

11
For he that believeth, bearing in hand,
Plougheth in the water, and soweth in the sand.
SIR THOMAS WYATT.
(See also MASSINGER)

FAIRIES

12
Up the airy mountain,
Down the rushy glen,
We daren't go a-hunting
For fear of little men;
Wee folk, good folk,
Trooping all together,
Green jacket, red cap,
And white owl's feather!
WILLIAM ALLINGHAM—*The Fairies*.

13
Do you believe in fairies? If you believe clap your hands.
Don't let Tinker die.
BARRIE—*Peter Pan*. ("Tinker Bell" thought she could get well again if children believed in fairies.)

14
When the first baby laughed for the first time, the laugh broke into a million pieces, and they all went skipping about. That was the beginning of fairies.
BARRIE—*Peter Pan*.

15
Whenever a child says "I don't believe in fairies" there's a little fairy somewhere that falls right down dead.
BARRIE—*Peter Pan*.

16
Bright Eyes, Light Eyes! Daughter of a Fay!
I had not been a married wife a twelvemonth and a day,
I had not nursed my little one a month upon my knee,
When down among the blue bell banks rose elfins three times three:
They griped me by the raven hair, I could not cry for fear,
They put a hempen rope around my waist and dragged me here;
They made me sit and give thee suck as mortal mothers can,
Bright Eyes, Light Eyes! strange and weak and wan!
ROBERT BUCHANAN—*The Fairy Foster Mother*.

17
Then take me on your knee, mother;
And listen, mother of mine.
A hundred fairies danced last night,
And the harpers they were nine.
MARY HOWITT—*The Fairies of the Caldon Low*. St. 5.

18
Nothing can be truer than fairy wisdom. It is as true as sunbeams.
DOUGLAS JERROLD—*Specimens of Jerrold's Wit. Fairy Tales*.

19
Nicht die Kinder bloss speist man mit Märchen ab.
It is not children only that one feeds with fairy tales.
LESSING—*Nathan der Weise*. III. 6.

20 * * * Or fairy elves,
Whose midnight revels by a forest side
Or fountain, some belated peasant sees,
Or dreams he sees, while overhead the Moon
Sits arbitress, and nearer to the Earth

Wheels her pale course; they, on their mirth and
dance
Intent, with jocund music charm his ear;
At once with joy and fear his heart rebounds.
MILTON—*Paradise Lost.* Bk. I. L. 781.

1
The dances ended, all the fairy train
For pinks and daisies search'd the flow'ry plain.
POPE—*January and May.* L. 624.

2
This is the fairy-land; O spite of spites!
We talk with goblins, owls and sprites.
Comedy of Errors. Act II. Sc. 2. L. 191.

3
Fairies, black, grey, green, and white,
You moonshine revellers, and shades of night.
Merry Wives of Windsor. Act V. Sc. 5. L. 41.

4
They are fairies; he that speaks to them shall die:
I'll wink and couch: no man their works must eye.
Merry Wives of Windsor. Act V. Sc. 5. L. 51.

5 Set your heart at rest:
The fairyland buys not the child of me.
Midsummer Night's Dream. Act II. Sc. 1. L. 121.

6 In silence sad,
Trip we after night's shade:
We the globe can compass soon.
Swifter than the wand'ring moon.
Midsummer Night's Dream. Act IV. Sc. 1. L. 100.

7
O, then, I see Queen Mab hath been with you.
She is the fairies' midwife, and she comes
In shape no bigger than an agate-stone
On the forefinger of an alderman.
Romeo and Juliet. Act I. Sc. 4. L. 54.

8
Where the bee sucks, there suck I;
In a cowslip's bell I lie;
There I couch when owls do cry.
On the bat's back I do fly.
Tempest. Act V. Sc. 1. L. 88. Song.

9
Her berth was of the wombe of morning dew
And her conception of the joyous prime.
SPENSER—*Faerie Queene.* Bk. III. Canto VI. St. 3.

10
But light as any wind that blows
So fleetly did she stir,
The flower, she touch'd on, dipt and rose,
And turned to look at her.
TENNYSON—*The Talking Oak.* St. 33.

FAITH

11
Mahomet made the people believe that he would call a hill to him, and from the top of it offer up his prayers for the observers of his law. The people assembled; Mahomet called the hill to come to him, again and again, and when the hill stood still, he was never a whit abashed, but said, if the hill will not come to Mahomet, Mahomet will go to the hill.
BACON—*Of Boldness.*

12
Faith is a higher faculty than reason.
BAILEY—*Festus.* *Prœm.* L. 84.

13
There is one inevitable criterion of judgment touching religious faith in doctrinal matters. Can you reduce it to practice? If not, have none of it.
HOSEA BALLOU—*MS. Sermons.*

14
An outward and visible sign of an inward and spiritual grace.
Book of Common Prayer. Catechism.

15
"Take courage, soul!
Hold not thy strength in vain!
With faith o'ercome the steeps
Thy God hath set for thee.
Beyond the Alpine summits of great pain
Lieth thine Italy."
ROSE TERRY COOKE—*Beyond.*

16
We walk by faith, not by sight.
II Corinthians. V. 7.

17
His faith, perhaps, in some nice tenets might
Be wrong; his life, I'm sure, was in the right.
COWLEY—*On the Death of Crashaw.* L. 55.
(See also POPE)

18
Faith is a fine invention
For gentlemen who see;
But Microscopes are prudent
In an emergency.
EMILY DICKINSON—*Poems. Second Series.* XXX.

19
To take up half on trust, and half to try,
Name it not faith but bungling bigotry.
DRYDEN—*The Hind and the Panther.* Pt. I. L. 141.

20
We lean on Faith; and some less wise have cried,
"Behold the butterfly, the seed that's cast!"
Vain hopes that fall like flowers before the blast!
What man can look on Death unterrified?
R. W. GILDER—*Love and Death.* St. 2.

21
Die Botschaft hör' ich wohl, allein mir fehlt der
Glaube;
Das Wunder ist des Glaubens liebstes Kind.
Your messages I hear, but faith has not been
given;
The dearest child of Faith is Miracle.
GOETHE—*Faust.* I. 1. 413.

22
Faith is the substance of things hoped for, the evidence of things not seen.
Hebrews. XI. 1.

23
What sought they thus afar?
Bright jewels of the mine?
The wealth of seas, the spoils of war?—
They sought a faith's pure shrine!
MRS. HEMANS—*Landing of the Pilgrim Fathers.*

24
Mirror of constant faith, revered and mourn'd!
HOMER—*Odyssey.* Bk. IV. L. 229. POPE'S trans.

25
The German is the discipline of fear; ours is the discipline of faith—and faith will triumph.
GEN. JOFFRE, at unveiling of a statue of Lafayette in Brooklyn, 1917.

1 If he were
To be made honest by an act of parliament
I should not alter in my faith of him.
BEN JONSON—*The Devil Is an Ass.* Act IV. Sc. 1.

2
And we shall be made truly wise if we be made content; content, too, not only with what we can understand, but content with what we do not understand—the habit of mind which theologians call—and rightly—faith in God.
CHARLES KINGSLEY—*Health and Education On Bio-Geology.*

3
The only faith that wears well and holds its color in all weathers is that which is woven of conviction and set with the sharp mordant of experience.
LOWELL—*My Study Windows. Abraham Lincoln.* 1864.

4
O welcome pure-ey'd Faith, white-handed Hope,
Thou hovering angel, girt with golden wings!
MILTON—*Comus.* L. 213.

5 That in such righteousness
To them by faith imputed they may find
Justification towards God, and peace
Of conscience.
MILTON—*Paradise Lost.* Bk. XII. L. 294.

6 Yet I argue not
Again Heaven's hand or will, nor bate a jot
Of right or hope; but still bear up and steer
Right onward.
MILTON—*To Cyriac Skinner.*

7
Combien de choses nous servoient hier d'articles de foy, qui nous sont fables aujourd'hui!
How many things served us yesterday for articles of faith, which to-day are fables to us!
MONTAIGNE—*Essays.* Bk. I. Ch. XXVI.

8
But Faith, fanatic Faith, once wedded fast
To some dear falsehood, hugs it to the last.
MOORE—*Lalla Rookh. The Veiled Prophet of Khorassan.*

9
If faith produce no works, I see
That faith is not a living tree.
Thus faith and works together grow;
No separate life they e'er can know:
They're soul and body, hand and heart:
What God hath joined, let no man part.
HANNAH MORE—*Dan and Jane.*

10
For modes of faith let graceless zealots fight;
His can't be wrong whose life is in the right.
POPE—*Essay on Man.* Ep. III. L. 305.
(See also COWLEY)

11
The enormous faith of many made for one.
POPE—*Essay on Man.* Ep. III. L. 242.

12
Be thou faithful unto death.
Revelation. II. 10.

13 Set on your foot,
And with a heart new-fir'd I follow you,
To do I know not what: but it sufficeth
That Brutus leads me on.
Julius Cæsar. Act II. Sc. 1. L. 331.

14
Thou almost makest me waver in my faith
To hold opinion with Pythagoras,
That souls of animals infuse themselves
Into the trunks of men.
Merchant of Venice. Act IV. Sc. 1. L. 130.

15
The saddest thing that can befall a soul
Is when it loses faith in God and woman.
ALEXANDER SMITH—*A Life Drama.* Sc. 12.

16
Faith is the subtle chain
Which binds us to the infinite; the voice
Of a deep life within, that will remain
Until we crowd it thence.
ELIZABETH OAKES SMITH—*Atheism in Three Sonnets. Faith.*

17
It is always right that a man should be able to render a reason for the faith that is within him.
SYDNEY SMITH—*Lady Holland's Memoir.* Vol. I. P. 53.

18
Faith and unfaith can ne'er be equal powers;
Unfaith in aught is want of faith in all.
TENNYSON—*Idylls of the King. Merlin and Vivien.* L. 388.

19
Whose faith has centre everywhere,
Nor cares to fix itself to form.
TENNYSON—*In Memoriam.* XXXIII.

20
I have fought a good fight, I have finished my course, I have kept the faith.
II Timothy. IV. 7.

21
Faith, mighty faith the promise sees
And rests on that alone;
Laughs at impossibilities,
And says it shall be done.
CHARLES WESLEY—*Hymns.* No. 360.

22
Through this dark and stormy night
Faith beholds a feeble light
Up the blackness streaking;
Knowing God's own time is best,
In a patient hope I rest
For the full day-breaking!
WHITTIER—*Barclay of Ury.* St. 16.

23
A bending staff I would not break,
A feeble faith I would not shake,
Nor even rashly pluck away
The error which some truth may stay,
Whose loss might leave the soul without
A shield against the shafts of doubt.
WHITTIER—*Questions of Life.* St. 1.

24
Of one in whom persuasion and belief
Had ripened into faith, and faith become
A passionate intuition.
WORDSWORTH—*Excursion.* Bk. IV.

25
'Tis hers to pluck the amaranthine flower
Of Faith, and round the sufferer's temples bind
Wreaths that endure affliction's heaviest shower,
And do not shrink from sorrow's keenest wind.
WORDSWORTH—*Weak is the Will of Man.*

1
Faith builds a bridge across the gulf of Death,
To break the shock blind nature cannot shun,
And lands Thought smoothly on the further shore.
YOUNG—*Night Thoughts.* Night IV. L. 721.

FALCON

2
The falcon and the dove sit there together,
And th' one of them doth prune the other's feather.
DRAYTON—*Noah's Flood.*

3
Say, will the falcon, stooping from above,
Smit with her varying plumage, spare the dove?
Admires the jay the insect's gilded wings?
Or hears the hawk when Philomela sings?
POPE—*Essay on Man.* Ep. III. L. 53.

4
A falcon, tow'ring in her pride of place,
Was by a mousing owl hawk'd at and kill'd.
Macbeth. Act II. Sc. 4. L. 12.

5
My falcon now is sharp, and passing empty;
And till she stoop, she must not be full-gorg'd,
For then she never looks upon her lure.
Taming of the Shrew. Act IV. Sc. 1. L. 193.

FALSEHOOD (See LYING)

FAME

6
A niche in the temple of Fame.
Owes its origin to the establishment of the Pantheon (1791) *as a receptacle for distinguished men.*

7
Were not this desire of fame very strong, the difficulty of obtaining it, and the danger of losing it when obtained, would be sufficient to deter a man from so vain a pursuit.
ADDISON—*The Spectator.* No. 255.

8
And what after all is everlasting fame? Altogether vanity.
ANTONINUS—*Med.* 4. 33.

9
Ah! who can tell how hard it is to climb
The steep where Fame's proud temple shines afar!
BEATTIE—*The Minstrel.* St. 1.

10
Nothing can cover his high fame but Heaven:
No pyramids set off his memories
But the eternal substance of his greatness;
To which I leave him.
BEAUMONT AND FLETCHER—*The False One.* Act II. Sc. 1. L. 169.

11
The best-concerted schemes men lay for fame,
Die fast away: only themselves die faster.
The far-fam'd sculptor, and the laurell'd bard,
Those bold insurancers of deathless fame,
Supply their little feeble aids in vain.
BLAIR—*The Grave.* L. 185.
(See also BURNS under DISAPPOINTMENT)

12
Herostratus lives that burnt the temple of Diana; he is almost lost that built it.
SIR THOMAS BROWNE—*Hydriotaphia.* Ch. V.
(See also CIBBER)

13
What is the end of Fame? 'tis but to fill
A certain portion of uncertain paper:
Some liken it to climbing up a hill,
Whose summit, like all hills, is lost in vapour:
For this men write, speak, preach, and heroes kill,
And bards burn what they call their "midnight taper,"
To have, when the original is dust,
A name, a wretched picture, and worse bust.
BYRON—*Don Juan.* Canto I. St. 218.

14
I awoke one morning and found myself famous.
BYRON—From MOORE'S *Life of Bryon.*

15
Folly loves the martyrdom of fame.
BYRON—*Monody on the Death of Sheridan.* L. 68.

16
O Fame!—if I e'er took delight in thy praises,
'Twas less for the sake of thy high-sounding phrases,
Than to see the bright eyes of the dear one discover
She thought that I was not unworthy to love her.
BYRON—*Stanzas Written on the Road Between Florence and Pisa.*

17
Fame, we may understand, is no sure test of merit, but only a probability of such: it is an accident, not a property of a man.
CARLYLE—*Essay. Goethe.*

18
Scarcely two hundred years back can Fame recollect articulately at all; and there she but maunders and mumbles.
CARLYLE—*Past and Present.* Ch. XVII.

19
Men the most infamous are fond of fame,
And those who fear not guilt, yet start at shame.
CHURCHILL—*The Author.* L. 233.

20
The aspiring youth that fired the *Ephesian* dome
Outlives, in fame, the pious fool that rais'd it.
COLLEY CIBBER—*Richard III.* (Altered.) Act III. Sc. 1.
(See also BROWNE)

21
Je ne dois qu'à moi seul toute ma renommée.
To myself alone do I owe my fame.
CORNEILLE—*L'Excuse à Ariste.*

22
Non é il mondam romore altro che un fiato
Di vento, che vien quinci ed or vien quindi,
E muta nome, perchè muta lato.
The splendors that belong unto the fame of earth are but a wind, that in the same direction lasts not long.
DANTE—*Purgatoria.* XI. 100.

23
La vostra nominanza é color d'erba,
Che viene e va; e quei la discolora
Per cui ell' esce della terra acerba.
All your renown is like the summer flower that blooms and dies; because the sunny glow which brings it forth, soon slays with parching power.
DANTE—*Purgatoria.* XI. 115.

1
What shall I do to be forever known,
And make the age to come my own?
COWLEY—*The Motto.* L. 1.

2
Who fears not to do ill yet fears the name,
And free from conscience, is a slave to fame.
SIR JOHN DENHAM—*Cooper's Hill.* L. 129.

3
The Duke of Wellington brought to the post of first minister immortal fame; a quality of success which would almost seem to include all others.
BENJ DISRAELI—*Sybil.* Bk. I. Ch. III.

4
Fame then was cheap, and the first courier sped;
And they have kept it since, by being dead.
DRYDEN—*The Conquest of Granada.* Epilogue.

5
'Tis a petty kind of fame
At best, that comes of making violins;
And saves no masses, either. Thou wilt go
To purgatory none the less.
GEORGE ELIOT—*Stradivarius.* L. 85.

6
Fame is the echo of actions, resounding them to the world, save that the echo repeats only the last part, but fame relates all, and often more than all.
FULLER—*The Holy and Profane States. Of Fame.*

7
From kings to cobblers 'tis the same;
Bad servants wound their masters' fame.
GAY—*Fables. The Squire and his Cur.* Pt. II.

8
Der rasche Kampf verewigt einen Mann,
Er falle gleich, so preiset ihn das Lied.
Rash combat oft immortalizes man.
If he should fall, he is renowned in song.
GOETHE—*Iphigenia auf Tauris.* V. 6. 43.

9
The temple of fame stands upon the grave: the flame that burns upon its altars is kindled from the ashes of dead men.
HAZLITT—*Lectures on the English Poets.* Lecture VIII.

10
Thou hast a charmed cup, O Fame!
A draught that mantles high,
And seems to lift this earthly frame
Above mortality.
Away! to me—a woman—bring
Sweet water from affection's spring.
FELICIA D. HEMANS—*Woman and Fame.*

11
If that thy fame with ev'ry toy be pos'd,
'Tis a thin web, which poysonous fancies make;
But the great souldier's honour was compos'd
Of thicker stuf, which would endure a shake.
Wisdom picks friends; civility plays the rest;
A toy shunn'd cleanly passeth with the best.
HERBERT—*The Temple. The Church Porch.* St. 38.

12
Short is my date, but deathless my renown.
HOMER—*Iliad.* Bk. IX. L. 535. POPE's trans.

13
The rest were vulgar deaths unknown to fame.
HOMER—*Iliad.* Bk. XI. L. 394. POPE's trans.

14
The life, which others pay, let us bestow,
And give to fame what we to nature owe.
HOMER—*Iliad.* Bk. XII. L. 393. POPE's trans.

15
Earth sounds my wisdom, and high heaven my fame.
HOMER—*Odyssey.* Bk. IX. L. 20. POPE's trans.

16
But sure the eye of time beholds no name,
So blest as thine in all the rolls of fame.
HOMER—*Odyssey.* Bk. XI. L. 591. POPE's trans.

17
Where's Cæsar gone now, in command high and able?
Or Xerxes the splendid, complete in his table?
Or Tully, with powers of eloquence ample?
Or Aristotle, of genius the highest example?
JACOPONE—*De Contemptu Mundi.* Trans. by ABRAHAM COLES.

18
Fame has no necessary conjunction with praise: it may exist without the breath of a word: it is a *recognition of excellence* which *must be felt* but need not be *spoken.* Even the envious must feel it: feel it, and hate it in silence.
MRS. JAMESON—*Memoirs and Essays. Washington Allston.*

19
Reputation being essentially contemporaneous, is always at the mercy of the Envious and the Ignorant. But Fame, whose very birth is *posthumous,* and which is only *known to exist by the echo of its footsteps through congenial minds,* can neither be increased nor diminished by any degree of wilfulness.
MRS. JAMESON—*Memoirs and Essays. Washington Allston.*

20
Miserum est aliorum incumbere famæ.
It is a wretched thing to live on the fame of others.
JUVENAL—*Satires.* VIII. 76.

21
"Let us now praise famous men"—
Men of little showing—
For their work continueth,
And their work continueth,
Greater than their knowing.
KIPLING—*Words prefixed to Stalky & Co.* First line from *Ecclesiasticus.* XLIV. 1.

22
Fame comes only when deserved, and then is as inevitable as destiny, for it is destiny.
LONGFELLOW—*Hyperion.* Bk. I. Ch. VIII.

23
Building nests in Fame's great temple,
As in spouts the swallows build.
LONGFELLOW—*Nuremberg.* St. 16.

24
His fame was great in all the land.
LONGFELLOW—*Tales of a Wayside Inn. The Student's Tale. Emma and Eginhard.* L. 50.

25
Nolo virum facili redimit qui sanguine famam;
Hunc volo laudari qui sine morte potest.
I do not like the man who squanders life

for fame; give me the man who living makes a name.
MARTIAL—*Epigrams*. I. 9. 5.

1
Si post fata venit gloria non propero.
If fame comes after death, I am in no hurry for it.
MARTIAL—*Epigrams*. V. 10. 12.

2
Though the desire of fame be the last weakness
Wise men put off.
MASSINGER—*The Very Woman*. Act V. Sc. 4.
(See also MILTON, MONTAIGNE, TACITUS, also BARNEVELT under MIND)

3
Read but o'er the Stories
Of men most fam'd for courage or for counsaile
And you shall find that the desire of glory
Was the last frailty wise men put off;
Be they presidents.
SIR JOHN VAN OLDEN BARNEVELT. Reprinted by A. H. BULLEN.

4
Fame lulls the fever of the soul, and makes
Us feel that we have grasp'd an immortality.
JOAQUIN MILLER—*Ina*. Sc. 4. L. 273.

5
Fame is the spur that the clear spirit doth raise,
(That last infirmity of noble mind)
To scorn delights, and live laborious days;
But the fair guerdon when we hope to find,
And think to burst out into sudden blaze,
Comes the blind Fury with th' abhorred shears,
And slits the thin-spun life.
MILTON—*Lycidas*. L. 70.
(See also MASSINGER)

6
Fame is no plant that grows on mortal soil.
MILTON—*Lycidas*. L. 78.

7
Fame, if not double fac'd, is double mouth'd,
And with contrary blast proclaims most deeds;
On both his wings, one black, the other white,
Bears greatest names in his wild aery flight.
MILTON—*Samson Agonistes*. L. 971.

8
"Des humeurs desraisonnables des hommes, il semble que les philosophes mesmes se desfacent plus tard et plus envy de cette cy que de nulle autre: c'est la plus revesche et opiniastre; *quia etiam bene proficientes animos tentare non cessat*."
Of the unreasoning humours of mankind it seems that (fame) is the one of which the philosophers themselves have disengaged themselves from last and with the most reluctance: it is the most intractable and obstinate; for [as St. Augustine says] it persists in tempting even minds nobly inclined."
MONTAIGNE — *Essays*. Bk. I. Ch. XLI. Quoting the Latin from ST. AUGUSTINE—*De Civit. Dei*. 5. 14.
(See also MASSINGER)

9
I'll make thee glorious by my pen
And famous by my sword.
MARQUIS OF MONTROSE—*My Dear and Only Love*. (See also SCOTT)

10
Ingenio stimulos subdere fama solet.
The love of fame usually spurs on the mind.
OVID—*Tristium*. V. 1. 76.

11
At pulchrum est digito monstrari et dicier hic est.
It is pleasing to be pointed at with the finger and to have it said, "There goes the man."
PERSIUS—*Satires*. I. 28.

12
To the quick brow Fame grudges her best wreath
While the quick heart to enjoy it throbs beneath:
On the dead forehead's sculptured marble shown,
Lo, her choice crown—its flowers are also stone.
JOHN JAMES PIATT—*The Guerdon*.

13
Who grasp'd at earthly fame,
Grasped wind: nay, worse, a serpent grasped that through
His hand slid smoothly, and was gone; but left
A sting behind which wrought him endless pain.
POLLOK—*Course of Time*. Bk. III. L. 533.

14
All crowd, who foremost shall be damn'd to fame.
POPE—*Dunciad*. Bk. III. L. 158. *Essay on Man*. IV. 284.
(See also SAVAGE)

15
Let humble Allen, with an awkward shame,
Do good by stealth, and blush to find it Fame.
POPE—*Epilogue to Satire*. Dialogue I. L. 135.

16
Above all Greek, above all Roman fame.
POPE—*Epistles of Horace*. Ep. I. Bk. II. L. 26.
(See also DRYDEN under NAME)

17
What's fame? a fancy'd life in others' breath.
A thing beyond us, e'en before our death.
POPE—*Essay on Man*. Ep. IV. L. 237.

18
If parts allure thee, think how Bacon shin'd,
The wisest, brightest, meanest of mankind:
Or, ravish'd with the whistling of a name,
See Cromwell, damn'd to everlasting fame.
POPE—*Essay on Man*. Ep. IV. L. 281.

19
And what is Fame? the Meanest have their Day,
The Greatest can but blaze, and pass away.
POPE—*First Book of Horace*. Ep. VI. L. 46.

20
Nor fame I slight, nor for her favors call;
She comes unlooked for, if she comes at all.
POPE—*Temple of Fame*. L. 513.

21
Unblemish'd let me live or die unknown;
Oh, grant an honest fame, or grant me none!
POPE—*Temple of Fame*. L. 523.

22
Omnia post obitum fingit majora vetustas:
Majus ab exsequiis nomen in ora venit.
Time magnifies everything after death; a man's fame is increased as it passes from mouth to mouth after his burial.
PROPERTIUS—*Elegiæ*. III. 1. 23.

23
Your fame shall (spite of proverbs) make it plain
To write in water 's not to write in vain.
ANON. in preface to SIR WILLIAM SANDERSON—*Art of Painting in Water Colours*. (1658)

1
May see thee now, though late, redeem thy name,
And glorify what else is damn'd to fame.
RICHARD SAVAGE—*Character of the Rev. James Foster*. L. 43.

2
I'll make thee famous by my pen,
And glorious by my sword.
SCOTT—*Legend of Montrose*. Ch. XV.
(See also MONTROSE)

3
Better to leave undone, than by our deed
Acquire too high a fame, when him we serve's away.
Antony and Cleopatra. Act III. Sc. 1. L. 14.

4
Let fame, that all hunt after in their lives,
Live register'd upon our brazen tombs.
Love's Labour's Lost. Act I. Sc. 1. L. 1.

5
Death makes no conquest of this conqueror:
For now he lives in fame, though not in life.
Richard III. Act III. Sc. 1. L. 87.

6
He lives in fame, that died in virtue's cause.
Titus Andronicus. Act I. Sc. 1. L. 390.

7
Fame is the perfume of heroic deeds.
SOCRATES.

8
Sloth views the towers of fame with envious eyes,
Desirous still, still impotent to rise.
SHENSTONE—*Moral Pieces. The Judgment of Hercules*. L. 436.

9
No true and permanent Fame can be founded except in labors which promote the happiness of mankind.
CHARLES SUMNER—*Fame and Glory*. An Address before the Literary Societies of Amherst College. Aug. 11, 1847.

10
Censure is the tax a man pays to the public for being eminent.
SWIFT—*Thoughts on Various Subjects*.

11
Etiam sapientibus cupido gloriæ novissima exuitur.
The love of fame is the last weakness which even the wise resign.
TACITUS—*Annales*. IV.
(See also MASSINGER)

12
Modestiæ fama neque summis mortalibus spernenda est.
Modest fame is not to be despised by the highest characters.
TACITUS—*Annales*. XV. 2.

13
The whole earth is a sepulchre for famous men.
THUCYDIDES. 2. 43.

14
Fama est obscurior annis.
The fame (or report) has become obscure through age.
VERGIL—*Æneid*. 7. 205.

15
Ingrediturque solo, et caput inter nubila condit.
She (Fame) walks on the earth, and her head is concealed in the clouds.
VERGIL—*Æneid*. 4. 177.

16
In tenui labor, at tenuis non gloria.
The object of the labor was small, but not the fame.
VERGIL—*Georgics*. IV. 6.

17
Tel brille au second rang, qui s'eclipse au premier.
He shines in the second rank, who is eclipsed in the first.
VOLTAIRE—*Henriade*. I.

18
C'est un poids bien pesant qu'un nom trop tôt fameux.
What a heavy burden is a name that has become too famous.
VOLTAIRE—*Henriade*. III.

19
What rage for fame attends both great and small!
Better be d—n'd than mentioned *not at all*.
JOHN WOLCOT (Peter Pindar)—*To the Royal Academicians. Lyric Odes for the Year 1783*. Ode IX.

20
With fame, in just proportion, envy grows.
YOUNG—*Epistle to Mr. Pope*. Ep. I. L. 27.

21
Men should press forward, in fame's glorious chase;
Nobles look backward, and so lose the race.
YOUNG—*Love of Fame*. Satire I. L. 129.

22
Wouldst thou be famed? have those high acts in view,
Brave men would act though scandal would ensue.
YOUNG—*Love of Fame*. Satire VII. L. 175.

23
Fame is the shade of immortality,
And in itself a shadow. Soon as caught,
Contemn'd; it shrinks to nothing in the grasp.
YOUNG—*Night Thoughts*. Night VII. L. 363.

FAMILIARITY

24
Nimia familiaritas parit contemptum.
Familiarity breeds contempt.
THOMAS AQUINAS—*Ad Joannem fratrem Monitio*. SYRUS—*Maxims*. 640. Idea in CICERO—*Pro Murena*. Ch. IX. LIVY. Bk. XXXV. Ch. X. PLUTARCH, C. MAR. Ch. XVI. LA FONTAINE—*Fables* IV. X.

25
I find my familiarity with thee has bred contempt.
CERVANTES—*Don Quixote*. Pt. I. Bk. III. Ch. VI.

26
Quod crebro videt non miratur, etiamsi cur fiat nescit. Quod ante non vidit, id si evenerit, ostentum esse censet.
A man does not wonder at what he sees frequently, even though he be ignorant of the reason. If anything happens which he has not seen before, he calls it a prodigy.
CICERO—*De Divinatione*. II. 22.

27
I hold he loves me best that calls me Tom.
THOMAS HEYWOOD—*Hierarchie of the Blessed Angells*.

1
Be thou familiar, but by no means vulgar.
Hamlet. Act I. Sc. 3. L. 61.

2
And sweets grown common lose their dear delight.
Sonnet CII.

3
Staled by frequence, shrunk by usage into commonest commonplace!
TENNYSON—*Locksley Hall Sixty Years After*. St. 38.

FAMILY (See HOME)

FANCY (See also IMAGINATION)

4
Some things are of that nature as to make
One's fancy chuckle, while his heart doth ache.
BUNYAN—*Pilgrim's Progress. The Author's Way of Sending Forth his Second Part of the Pilgrim*. Pt. II.

5
While fancy, like the finger of a clock,
Runs the great circuit, and is still at home.
COWPER—*The Task*. Bk. IV. L. 118.

6
Ever let the Fancy roam,
Pleasure never is at home.
KEATS—*Fancy*.

7
The truant Fancy was a wanderer ever.
LAMB—*Fancy employed on Divine Subjects*. I. 1.

8
Sentiment is intellectualized emotion, emotion precipitated, as it were, in pretty crystals by the fancy.
LOWELL—*Among My Books. Rousseau and the Sentimentalists*.

9
Two meanings have our lightest fantasies,
One of the flesh, and of the spirit one.
LOWELL—*Sonnet XXXIV*. Ed. 1844.

10
She's all my fancy painted her,
She's lovely, she's divine.
WM. MEE—*Alice Gray*.

11
When at the close of each sad, sorrowing day,
Fancy restores what vengeance snatch'd away.
POPE—*Eloisa to Abelard*. L. 225.

12
The difference is as great between
The optics seeing as the objects seen.
All manners take a tincture from our own;
Or come discolor'd through our passions shown;
Or fancy's beam enlarges, multiplies,
Contracts, inverts, and gives ten thousand dyes.
POPE—*Moral Essays*. Ep. 1. L. 31.

13
Woe to the youth whom Fancy gains,
Winning from Reason's hand the reins,
Pity and woe! for such a mind
Is soft, contemplative, and kind.
SCOTT—*Rokeby*. Canto I. St. 31.

14
Pacing through the forest,
Chewing the food of sweet and bitter fancy.
As You Like It. Act IV. Sc. 3. L. 101.

15
Tell me where is fancy bred,
Or in the heart or in the head?
How begot, how nourished?
Reply, reply.
It is engender'd in the eyes,
With gazing fed; and fancy dies
In the cradle where it lies.
Merchant of Venice. Act III. Sc. 2. L. 63.

16
So full of shapes is fancy,
That it alone is high fantastical.
Twelfth Night. Act I. Sc. 1. L. 14.

17
Let fancy still my sense in Lethe steep;
If it be thus to dream, still let me sleep!
Twelfth Night. Act IV. Sc. 1. L. 66.

18
We figure to ourselves
The thing we like, and then we build it up
As chance will have it, on the rock or sand:
For Thought is tired of wandering o'er the world,
And homebound Fancy runs her bark ashore.
SIR HENRY TAYLOR—*Philip Van Artevelde*. Pt. I. Act I. Sc. 5.

19
Fancy light from Fancy caught.
TENNYSON—*In Memoriam*. Pt. XXIII.

20
Sad fancies do we then affect,
In luxury of disrespect
To our own prodigal excess
Of too familiar happiness.
WORDSWORTH—*Ode to Lycoris*.

FAREWELL (See also PARTING)

21
He turn'd him right and round about
Upon the Irish shore,
And gae his bridle reins a shake,
With Adieu for evermore,
My dear,
With Adieu for evermore.
BURNS—*It Was a' for our Rightfu' King*. Used and altered by SCOTT in *Rokeby* and *Monastery*.

22
Farewell! a word that must be, and hath been—
A sound which makes us linger;—yet—farewell!
BYRON—*Childe Harold*. Canto IV. St. 186.

23
"Farewell!"
For in that word—that fatal word—howe'er
We promise—hope—believe—there breathes despair.
BYRON—*Corsair*. Canto I. St. 15.

24
Fare thee well! and if for ever,
Still for ever, fare thee well.
BYRON—*Fare Thee Well*.

25
"Adieu," she cries, and waved her lily hand.
GAY—*Sweet William's Farewell to Black-eyed Susan*.

26
Friend, ahoy! Farewell! farewell!
Grief unto grief, joy unto joy,
Greeting and help the echoes tell
Faint, but eternal—Friend, ahoy!
HELEN HUNT JACKSON—*Verses. Friend, Ahoy!*

1
Though I often salute you, you never salute me first; I shall therefore, Pontilianus, salute you with an eternal farewell.
MARTIAL—*Epigrams.* Bk. V. Ep. 66.

2 Farewell, happy fields,
Where joy forever dwells; hail, horrors!
MILTON—*Paradise Lost.* Bk. I. L. 249.

3
Gude nicht, and joy be wi' you a'.
LADY NAIRNE—*Gude Nicht, etc.*

4
Farewell to Lochaber, and farewell, my Jean,
Where heartsome wi' thee I hae mony day been:
For Lochaber no more, Lochaber no more,
We'll maybe return to Lochaber no more.
ALLAN RAMSAY—*Farewell to Lochaber.*

5 Fare thee well;
The elements be kind to thee, and make
Thy spirits all of comfort!
Antony and Cleopatra. Act III. Sc. 2. L. 39.

6
Sweets to the sweet; farewell!
Hamlet. Act V. Sc. 1. L. 266.

7
Farewell, and stand fast.
Henry IV. Pt. I. Act II. Sc. 2. L. 75.

8
Farewell the plumed troop, and the big wars,
That make ambition virtue! O, farewell!
Farewell the neighing steed, and the shrill trump,
The spirit-stirring drum, the ear-piercing fife.
Othello. Act III. Sc. 3. L. 349.

9 Here's my hand.
And mine, with my heart in't: and now farewell,
Till half an hour hence.
Tempest. Act III. Sc. 1. L. 89.

10
Then westward ho! Grace and good disposition
Attend your ladyship!
Twelfth Night. Act III. Sc. 1. L. 146.

11
So sweetly she bade me adieu,
I thought that she bade me return.
SHENSTONE—*A Pastoral Ballad.* Pt. I. *Absence.* St. 5.

FARMING (See AGRICULTURE)

FASHION (See also APPAREL)

12 Squinting upon the lustre
Of the rich Rings which on his fingers glistre;
And, snuffing with a wrythed nose the Amber,
The Musk and Civet that perfum'd the chamber.
DU BARTAS—*Divine Weekes and Workes.* Second Week. Third Day. Pt. III.

13 Nothing is thought rare
Which is not new, and follow'd; yet we know
That what was worn some twenty years ago
Comes into grace again.
BEAUMONT AND FLETCHER—*Prologue to the Noble Gentleman.* L. 4.

14
He is only fantastical that is not in fashion.
BURTON—*Anatomy of Melancholy.* Pt. III. Sec. II. Memb. 2. Subsect. 3.

15
And as the French we conquer'd once,
Now give us laws for pantaloons,
The length of breeches and the gathers,
Port-cannons, periwigs, and feathers.
BUTLER—*Hudibras.* Pt. I. Canto III. L. 923.

16
Fashion—a word which knaves and fools may use,
Their knavery and folly to excuse.
CHURCHILL—*Rosciad.* L. 455.

17
As good be out of the World as out of the Fashion.
COLLEY CIBBER—*Love's Last Shift.* Act II.

18
The fashion of this world passeth away.
I Corinthians. VII. 31.

19
The glass of fashion and the mould of form,
The observ'd of all observers.
Hamlet. Act III. Sc. 1. L. 161.

20
Their clothes are after such a pagan cut too,
That, sure, they've worn out Christendom.
Henry VIII. Act I. Sc. 3. L. 14.

21
You, sir, I entertain for one of my hundred; only I do not like the fashion of your garments.
King Lear. Act III. Sc. 6. L. 83.

22
I see that the fashion wears out more apparel than the man.
Much Ado About Nothing. Act III. Sc. 3. L. 148.

23
I'll be at charges for a looking-glass,
And entertain some score or two of tailors,
To study fashions to adorn my body:
Since I am crept in favour with myself,
I will maintain it with some little cost.
Richard III. Act I. Sc. 2. L. 256.

FATE (See also DESTINY)

24
The dawn is overcast, the morning lowers,
And heavily in clouds brings on the day,
The great, the important day, big with the fate
Of Cato, and of Rome.
ADDISON—*Cato.* Act I. Sc. 1.
(See also OTWAY)

25
The bow is bent, the arrow flies,
The wingéd shaft of fate.
IRA ALDRIDGE—*On William Tell.* St. 12.

26
Yet who shall shut out Fate?
EDWIN ARNOLD—*Light of Asia.* Bk. III. L. 336.

27
The heart is its own Fate.
BAILEY—*Festus.* Sc. *Wood and Water. Sunset.*

28 Let those deplore their doom,
Whose hope still grovels in this dark sojourn:
But lofty souls, who look beyond the tomb,
Can smile at Fate, and wonder how they mourn.
BEATTIE—*The Minstrel.* Bk. I.

1
Many things happen between the cup and the lip.
BURTON—*Anatomy of Melancholy.* Pt. II. Sec. II. Memb. 3.
(See also GREENE)

2
Things and actions are what they are, and the consequences of them will be what they will be; why then should we desire to be deceived?
BISHOP BUTLER—*Sermon VII. On the Character of Balaam.* Last Paragraph.

3
Success, the mark no mortal wit,
Or surest hand, can always hit:
For whatsoe'er we perpetrate,
We do but row, we're steer'd by Fate,
Which in success oft disinherits,
For spurious causes, noblest merits.
BUTLER—*Hudibras.* Pt. I. Canto I. L. 879.

4
Here's a sigh to those who love me,
And a smile to those who hate;
And whatever sky's above me,
Here's a heart for every fate.
BYRON—*To Thomas Moore.* St. 2.
(See LONGFELLOW under ACTION)

5
To bear is to conquer our fate.
CAMPBELL—*On Visiting a Scene in Argyleshire.*

6
Le vin est versé, il faut le boire.
The wine is poured, you should drink it.
Attributed to M. DE CHAROST. *Spoken to Louis XIV*, at the siege of Douai, as the king attempted to retire from the firing line.

7
Tolluntur in altum
Ut lapsu graviore ruant.
They are raised on high that they may be dashed to pieces with a greater fall.
CLAUDIAN—*In Rufinum.* Bk. I. 22.

8
Fate steals along with silent tread,
Found oftenest in what least we dread;
Frowns in the storm with angry brow,
But in the sunshine strikes the blow.
COWPER—*A Fable. Moral.*

9
He has gone to the demnition bow-wows.
DICKENS—*Nicholas Nickleby.* Ch. 64.

10
All human things are subject to decay,
And when fate summons, monarchs must obey.
DRYDEN—*Mac Flecknoe.* L. 1.

11
'Tis Fate that flings the dice,
And as she flings
Of kings makes peasants,
And of peasants kings.
DRYDEN—*Works.* Vol. XV. P. 103. Ed. 1821.

12
Fate has carried me
'Mid the thick arrows: I will keep my stand—
Not shrink and let the shaft pass by my breast
To pierce another.
GEORGE ELIOT—*The Spanish Gypsy.* Bk. III.

13
Stern fate and time
Will have their victims; and the best die first,
Leaving the bad still strong, though past their prime,
To curse the hopeless world they ever curs'd,
Vaunting vile deeds, and vainest of the worst.
EBENEZER ELLIOTT—*The Village Patriarch.* Bk. IV. Pt. IV.

14
On est, quand on veut, maître de son sort.
We are, when we will it, masters of our own fate.
FERRIER—*Adraste.*
(See also HENLEY under SOUL)

15
One common fate we both must prove;
You die with envy, I with love.
GAY—*Fable. The Poet and Rose.* L. 29.

16
Du musst (herrschen und gewinnen,
Oder dienen und verlieren,
Leiden oder triumphiren),
Amboss oder Hammer sein.
Thou must (in commanding and winning, or serving and losing, suffering or triumphing) be either anvil or hammer.
GOETHE—*Grosscophta.* II.

17
Der Mensch erfährt, er sei auch wer er mag,
Ein letztes Glück und einen letzten Tag.
Man, be he who he may, experiences a last piece of good fortune and a last day.
GOETHE—*Sprüche in Reimen.* III.

18
Each curs'd his fate that thus their project cross'd;
How hard their lot who neither won nor lost.
GRAVES—*An Incident in High Life.*

19
Yet, ah! why should they know their fate,
Since sorrow never comes too late,
And happiness too swiftly flies?
Thought would destroy their paradise.
GRAY—*On a Distant Prospect of Eton College.*

20
Though men determine, the gods doo dispose: and oft times many things fall out betweene the cup and the lip.
GREENE—*Perimedes the Blacksmith.*
(See also BURTON, and Quotations under God)

21
Why doth IT so and so, and ever so,
This viewless, voiceless Turner of the Wheel?
THOMAS HARDY—*The Dynasts. Fore Scene. Spirit of the Pities.*

22
'Tis writ on Paradise's gate,
"Woe to the dupe that yields to Fate!"
HAFIZ.

23
Toil is the lot of all, and bitter woe
The fate of many.
HOMER—*Iliad.* Bk. XXI. L. 646. BRYANT'S trans.

24
Jove lifts the golden balances that show
The fates of mortal men, and things below.
HOMER—*Iliad.* Bk. XXII. L. 271. POPE'S trans.

25
And not a man appears to tell their fate.
HOMER—*Odyssey.* Bk. X. L. 308. POPE'S trans.

1
With equal pace, impartial Fate
Knocks at the palace, as the cottage gate.
HORACE—*Carmina*. I. 4. 17. FRANCIS' trans.

2
Sæpius ventis agitatur ingens
Pinus, et celsæ graviore casu
Decidunt terres feriuntque summos
Fulgura montes.

The lofty pine is oftenest shaken by the winds; high towers fall with a heavier crash; and the lightning strikes the highest mountain.
HORACE—*Carmina*. II. 10. 9. (Taken from LUCULLUS.)

3
East, to the dawn, or west or south or north!
Loose rein upon the neck of—and forth!
RICHARD HOVEY—*Faith and Fate*.

4
I do not know beneath what sky
Nor on what seas shall be thy fate;
I only know it shall be high,
I only know it shall be great.
RICHARD HOVEY—*Unmanifest Destiny*.

5
Must helpless man, in ignorance sedate,
Roll darkling down the torrent of his fate?
SAMUEL JOHNSON—*Vanity of Human Wishes*. L. 345.

6
Blue! Gentle cousin of the forest-green,
Married to green in all the sweetest flowers—
Forget-me-not,—the blue bell,—and, that queen
Of secrecy, the violet: what strange powers
Hast thou, as a mere shadow! But how great,
When in an Eye thou art alive with fate!
KEATS—*Answer to a Sonnet by J. H. Reynolds*.

7
Fate holds the strings, and Men like children move
But as they're led: Success is from above.
LORD LANSDOWNE—*Heroic Love*. Act. V. Sc. 1.

8
All are architects of Fate,
Working in these walls of Time;
Some with massive deeds and great,
Some with ornaments of rhyme.
LONGFELLOW—*Builders*. St. 1.

9
No one is so accursed by fate,
No one so utterly desolate,
But some heart, though unknown,
Responds unto his own.
LONGFELLOW—*Endymion*. St. 8.

10
A millstone and the human heart are driven ever round,
If they have nothing else to grind, they must themselves be ground.
LONGFELLOW. Trans. of FRIEDRICH VON LOGAU—*Sinnegedichte*. Same idea in LUTHER—*Table Talk*. HAZLITT's trans. (1848)

11
Kabira wept when he beheld the millstone roll,
Of that which passes 'twixt the stones, nought goes forth whole.
PROF. EASTWICK's trans. of the *Bag-o-Behar*. (*Garden and the Spring*.)

12
In se magna ruunt: lætis hunc numina rebus
Crescendi posuere modum.

Mighty things haste to destruction: this limit have the gods assigned to human prosperity.
LUCAN—*Pharsalia*. I. 81.

13
Sed quo fata trahunt, virtus secura sequetur.

Whither the fates lead virtue will follow without fear.
LUCAN—*Pharsalia*. II. 287.

14
Nulla vis humana vel virtus meruisse unquam potuit, ut, quod præscripsit fatalis ordo, non fiat.

No power or virtue of man could ever have deserved that what has been fated should not have taken place.
AMMIANUS MARCELLINUS—*Historia*. XXIII. 5.

15
It lies not in our power to love or hate,
For will in us is over-rul'd by fate.
MARLOWE—*Hero and Leander*. *First Sestiad*. L. 167.

16
Earth loves to gibber o'er her dross,
Her golden souls, to waste;
The cup she fills for her god-men
Is a bitter cup to taste.
DON MARQUIS—*Wages*.

17
For him who fain would teach the world
The world holds hate in fee—
For Socrates, the hemlock cup;
For Christ, Gethsemane.
DON MARQUIS—*Wages*.

18
He either fears his fate too much,
Or his deserts are small,
That dares not put it to the touch
To gain or lose it all.
MARQUIS OF MONTROSE—*My Dear and only Love*.

19
"That puts it not unto the touch
To win or lose it all."
Version in NAPIER's *Memorials of Montrose*.

20
Nullo fata loco possis excludere.

From no place can you exclude the fates.
MARTIAL—*Epigrams*. IV. 60. 5.

21
All the great things of life are swiftly done,
Creation, death, and love the double gate.
However much we dawdle in the sun
We have to hurry at the touch of Fate.
MASEFIELD—*Widow in the Bye Street*. Pt. II.

22
And sing to those that hold the vital shears;
And turn the adamantine spindle round,
On which the fate of gods and men is wound.
MILTON—*Arcades*.

23
Fixed, fate, free will, foreknowledge absolute.
MILTON—*Paradise Lost*. Bk. II. L. 560.

24
Necessity and chance
Approach not me, and what I will is fate.
MILTON—*Paradise Lost*. Bk. VII. L. 72.

1
The Moving Finger writes; and having writ,
Moves on; nor all your Piety nor Wit
Shall lure it back to cancel half a Line,
Nor all your Tears wash out a Word of it.
OMAR KHAYYAM—*Rubaiyat*. 71. FITZGERALD's trans. ("Thy piety" in first ed.)

2
Big with the fate of Rome.
THOS. OTWAY—*Youth Preserved*. Act. III. Sc. 1.
(See also ADDISON)

3
Geminos, horoscope, varo Producis genio.
O natal star, thou producest twins of widely different character.
PERSIUS—*Satires*. VI. 18.

4
"Thou shalt see me at Philippi," was the remark of the spectre which appeared to Brutus in his tent at Abydos [B. C. 42]. Brutus answered boldly: "I will meet thee there." At Philippi the spectre reappeared, and Brutus, after being defeated, died upon his own sword.
PLUTARCH—*Life of Cæsar. Life of Marcus Brutus.*

5
But blind to former as to future fate,
What mortal knows his pre-existent state?
POPE—*Dunciad*. Bk. III. L. 47.

6
Heaven from all creatures hides the book of fate.
POPE—*Essay on Man*. Ep. I. L. 77.

7
A brave man struggling in the storms of fate.
POPE—*Prologue to Addison's Cato.*

8
As the bird by wandering, as the swallow by flying, so the curse causeless shall not come.
Proverbs. XXVI. 2.

9
He putteth down one and setteth up another.
Psalms. LXXV. 7.

10
Fate sits on these dark battlements, and frowns;
And as the portals open to receive me,
Her voice, in sullen echoes, through the courts,
Tells of a nameless deed.
ANN RADCLIFFE—*The Motto to "The Mysteries of Udolpho."*

11
Sæpe calamitas solatium est nosse sortem suam.
It is often a comfort in misfortune to know our own fate.
QUINTUS CURTIUS RUFUS—*De Rebus Gestis Alexandri Magni*. IV. 10. 27.

12
Der Zug des Herzens ist des Schicksals Stimme.
The heart's impulse is the voice of fate.
SCHILLER—*Piccolomini*. III. 8. 82.

13
Mach deine Rechnung mit dem Himmel, Vogt!
Fort musst du, deine Uhr ist abgelaufen.
Make thine account with Heaven, governor,
Thou must away, thy sand is run.
SCHILLER—*Wilhelm Tell*. IV. 3. 7.

14
Fata volemtem ducunt, nolentem trahunt.
The fates lead the willing, and drag the unwilling.
SENECA—*Epistolæ Ad Lucilium*. CVII.

15
Multi ad fatum
Venere suum dum fata timent.
Many have reached their fate while dreading fate.
SENECA—*Œdipus*. 993.

16
Nemo fit fato nocens.
No one becomes guilty by fate.
SENECA—*Œdipus*. 1,019.

17
Eat, speak, and move, under the influence of the most received star; and though the devil lead the measure such are to be followed.
All's Well That Ends Well. Act II. Sc. 1. L. 56.

18
My fate cries out,
And makes each petty artery in this body
As hardy as the Numean lion's nerve.
Hamlet. Act. I. Sc. 4. L. 81.

19
Our wills and fates do so contrary run
That our devices still are overthrown;
Our thoughts are ours, their ends none of our own.
Hamlet. Act III. Sc. 2. L. 221.

20
O God! that one might read the book of fate,
And see the revolutions of the times
Make mountains level, and the continent
Weary of solid firmness, melt itself
Into the sea!
Henry IV. Pt. II. Act II. Sc. 1. L. 45.

21
What fates impose, that men must needs abide;
It boots not to resist both wind and tide.
Henry VI. Pt. III. Act IV. Sc. 3. L. 59.

22
If thou read this, O Cæsar, thou mayst live;
If not, the Fates with traitors do contrive.
Julius Cæsar. Act II. Sc. 3. L. 15.

23
Fates, we will know your pleasures:
That we shall die we know; 'tis but the time
And drawing days out, that men stand upon.
Julius Cæsar. Act III. Sc. 1. L. 98.

24
What should be spoken here, where our fate,
Hid within an auger-hole, may rush, and seize us?
Macbeth. Act II. Sc. 3. L. 127.

25
But yet I'll make assurance double sure,
And take a bond of fate: thou shalt not live.
Macbeth. Act IV. Sc. 1. L. 83.

26
But, O vain boast!
Who can control his fate?
Othello. Act V. Sc. 2. L. 264.

27
You fools! I and my fellows
Are ministers of Fate; the elements
Of whom your swords are temper'd, may as well
Wound the loud winds, or with bemock'd-at stabs
Kill the still-closing waters, as diminish
One dowle that's in my plume.
Tempest. Act III. Sc. 3. L. 60.

28
Fate, show thy force; ourselves we do not owe;
What is decreed must be, and be this so.
Twelfth Night. Act I. Sc. 5. L. 329.

1
As the old hermit of Prague . . . said, . . . "That that is, is."
Twelfth Night. Act IV. Sc. 2. (Referring to Jerome, called "The Hermit of Camaldoli," in Tuscany.)

2
Yet what are they, the learned and the great?
Awhile of longer wonderment the theme!
Who shall presume to prophesy their date,
Where nought is certain save the uncertainty of fate?
HORACE AND JAMES SMITH—*Rejected Addresses. By Lord Cui Bono.*

3
Two shall be born, the whole wide world apart,
And speak in different tongues, and have no thought
Each of the other's being; and have no heed;
And these, o'er unknown seas to unknown lands
Shall cross, escaping wreck, defying death;
And, all unconsciously, shape every act to this one end:
That one day out of darkness they shall meet
And read life's meanings in each other's eyes.
SUSAN M. SPALDING—*Fate.* In *Wings of Icarus.* (1802) Wrongly claimed for G. E. EDMUNDSON.

4
Jacta alea esto. (Jacta est alea.)
Let the die be cast.
SUETONIUS—*Cæsar.* 32. (Cæsar, on crossing the Rubicon.) Quoted as a proverb used by Cæsar in PLUTARCH—*Apophthegms. Opp. Mor.*

5
From too much love of living,
From hope and fear set free,
We thank with brief thanksgiving
Whatever gods may be
That no life lives forever;
That dead men rise up never;
That even the weariest river
Winds somewhere safe to sea.
SWINBURNE—*Garden of Proserpine.*

6
Sometimes an hour of Fate's serenest weather
Strikes through our changeful sky its coming beams;
Somewhere above us, in elusive ether,
Waits the fulfilment of our dearest dreams.
BAYARD TAYLOR—*Ad Amicos.*

7
Ad restim mihi quidem res rediit planissume.
Nothing indeed remains for me but that I should hang myself.
TERENCE—*Phormio.* IV. 4. 5.

8
Dare fatis vela.
To give the sails to fate.
VERGIL—*Æneid.* III. 9.

9
Quo fata trahunt retrahuntque sequamur.
Wherever the fates lead us let us follow.
VERGIL—*Æneid.* V. 709.

10
Fata viam invenient.
Fate will find a way.
VERGIL—*Æneid.* X. 113.

11
Perge; decet. Forsan miseros meliora sequentur.
Persevere: It is fitting, for a better fate awaits the afflicted.
VERGIL—*Æneid.* XII. 153.

12
Fata vocant.
The fates call.
VERGIL—*Georgics.* IV. 496.

13
I saw him even now going the way of all flesh.
JOHN WEBSTER—*Westward Ho.* Act II. Sc. 2.

14
"Ah me! what boots us all our boasted power,
Our golden treasure, and our purple state.
They cannot ward the inevitable hour,
Nor stay the fearful violence of fate."
WEST—*Monody on Queen Caroline.*

15
This day we fashion Destiny, our web of Fate we spin.
WHITTIER—*The Crisis.* St. 10.

16
Blindlings that er blos den Willen des Geschickes.
Man blindly works the will of fate.
WIELAND—*Oberon.* IV. 59.

17
Des Schiksals Zwang ist bitter.
The compulsion of fate is bitter.
WIELAND—*Oberon.* V. 60.

18
My fearful trust "en vogant la galère." (Come what may.)
SIR THOMAS WYATT—*The Lover Prayeth Venus* Vogue la galère. See MOLIÈRE—*Tartuffe* Act I. Sc. 1. MONTAIGNE—*Essays.* Bk. I. Ch. XL. RABELAIS—*Gargantua.* Bk. I. Ch. XX.

FAULTS

19
Then farewell, Horace; whom I hated so,
Not for thy faults, but mine.
BYRON—*Childe Harold.* Canto IV. St. 77.

20
The greatest of faults, I should say, is to be conscious of none.
CARLYLE—*Heroes and Hero-Worship.* Ch. II.

21
Suus quoque attributus est error:
Sed non videmus, manticæ quid in tergo est.
Every one has his faults: but we do not see the wallet on our own backs.
CATULLUS—*Carmina.* XXII. 20.
(See also PERSIUS, PHÆDRUS)

22
Ea molestissime ferre homines debent quæ ipsorum culpa ferenda sunt.
Men ought to be most annoyed by the sufferings which come from their own faults.
CICERO—*Epistolæ Ad Fratrem.* I. 1.

23
Est proprium stultitiæ aliorum vitia cernere, oblivisci suorum.
It is the peculiar quality of a fool to perceive the faults of others, and to forget his own.
CICERO—*Tusculanarum Disputationum.* III. 30.

1
Thou hast no faults, or I no faults can spy;
Thou art all beauty, or all blindness I.
Christopher Codrington—*On Garth's Dispensary.*

2
Men still had faults, and men will have them still;
He that hath none, and lives as angels do,
Must be an angel.
Wentworth Dillon—*Miscellanies. On Mr. Dryden's Religio Laici.* L. 8.

3
The defects of great men are the consolation of the dunces.
Isaac D'Israeli—*Essay on the Literary Character.* Preface. P. XXIX and Vol. I. P. 187.
(See also Irving)

4
Heureux l'homme quand il n'a pas les défauts de ses qualités.
Happy the man when he has not the defects of his qualities.
Bishop Dupanloup.

5
Who mix'd reason with pleasure, and wisdom with mirth;
If he had any faults, he has left us in doubt.
Goldsmith—*Retaliation.* L. 24.

6
Do you wish to find out a person's weak points? Note the failings he has the quickest eye for in others. They may not be the very failings he is himself conscious of; but they will be their next-door neighbors. No man keeps such a jealous lookout as a rival.
J. C. and W. A. Hare—*Guesses at Truth.*

7
His very faults smack of the raciness of his good qualities.
Washington Irving—*Sketch Book. John Bull.*
(See also D'Israeli)

8
Bad men excuse their faults, good men will leave them.
Ben Jonson—*Catiline.* Act III. Sc. 2.

9
Quis tulerit Gracchos de seditione querentes?
Who'd bear to hear the Gracchi chide sedition? (Listen to those who denounce what they do themselves.)
Juvenal—*Satires.* II. 24.

10
Her new bark is worse than ten times her old bite.
Lowell—*A Fable for Critics.* L. 28.

11
You crystal break, for fear of breaking it:
Careless and careful hands like faults commit.
Martial—*Epigrams.* Bk. XIV. Ep. 111. Trans. by Wright.

12
Qui s'excuse, s'accuse.
He who excuses himself, accuses himself.
Gabriel Meurier—*Tresor des Sentences.*
(See also King John)

13
Ut nemo in sese tentat descendere, nemo!
Sed præcedenti spectatur mantica tergo.
That no one, no one at all, should try to search into himself! But the wallet of the person in front is carefully kept in view.
Persius—*Satires.* IV. 24.
(See also Catullus)

14
Peras imposuit Jupiter nobis duas.
Propriis repletam vitiis post tergum dedit;
Alienis ante pectus suspendit gravem.
Jupiter has placed upon us two wallets. Hanging behind each person's back he has given one full of his own faults; in front he has hung a heavy one full of other people's.
Phædrus—*Fables.* Bk. IV. 9. 1.
(See also Catullus)

15
Quia, qui alterum incusat probi, eum ipsum se intueri oportet.
Because those, who twit others with their faults, should look at home.
Plautus—*Truculentus.* I. 2. 58.

16
Nihil peccat, nisi quod nihil peccat.
He has no fault except that he has no fault.
Pliny the Younger—*Epistles.* Bk. IX. 26.

17
The glorious fault of angels and of gods.
Pope—*To the Memory of an Unfortunate Lady.* L. 14.

18
I will chide no breather in the world but myself, against whom I know most faults.
As You Like It. Act III. Sc. 2. L. 298.

19
Every one fault seeming monstrous till his fellow-fault came to match it.
As You Like It. Act III. Sc. 2. L. 372.

20
Chide him for faults, and do it reverently,
When you perceive his blood inclined to mirth.
Henry IV. Pt. II. Act IV. Sc. 4. L. 37.

21
So may he rest; his faults lie gently on him!
Henry VIII. Act IV. Sc. 2. L. 31.

22
And oftentimes, excusing of a fault
Doth make the fault the worse by the excuse,
As patches set upon a little breach,
Discredit more in hiding of the fault,
Than did the fault before it was so patched.
King John. Act IV. Sc. 2. L. 30.
(See also Meurier)

23
All's not offence that indiscretion finds.
King Lear. Act II. Sc. 4. L. 198.

24
Condemn the fault, and not the actor of it?
Why, every fault's condemn'd ere it be done;
Mine were the very cipher of a function,
To fine the faults whose fine stands in record,
And let go by the actor.
Measure for Measure. Act II. Sc. 2. L. 37.

25
Go to your bosom;
Knock there, and ask your heart what it doth know
That's like my brother's fault.
Measure for Measure. Act II. Sc. 2. L. 136.

26
Roses have thorns, and silver fountains mud;
Clouds and eclipses stain both moon and sun,
And loathsome canker lives in sweetest bud.
All men make faults.
Sonnet XXXV.

1
Her only fault, and that is faults enough,
Is that she is intolerable curst
And shrewd and froward, so beyond all measure
That, were my state far worser than it is,
I would not wed her for a mine of gold.
Taming of the Shrew. Act I. Sc. 2. L. 88.

2
Faults that are rich are fair.
Timon of Athens. Act I. Sc. 2. L. 13.

3
Amici vitium ni feras, prodis tuum.
Unless you bear with the faults of a friend, you betray your own.
SYRUS—*Maxims*.

4
Invitat culpam qui delictum præterit.
He who overlooks a fault, invites the commission of another.
SYRUS—*Maxims*.

5
For tho' the faults were thick as dust
In vacant chambers, I could trust
Your kindness.
TENNYSON—*To the Queen*. St. 5.

FAVOR

6
Gratia, quæ tarda est, ingrata est: gratia namque
Cum fieri properat, gratia grata magis.
A favor tardily bestowed is no favor; for a favor quickly granted is a more agreeable favor.
AUSONIUS—*Epigrams*. LXXXII. 1.

7
Nam improbus est homo qui beneficium scit sumere et reddere nescit.
That man is worthless who knows how to receive a favor, but not how to return one.
PLAUTUS—*Persa*. V. 1. 10.

8
Nam quamlibet sæpe obligati, si quid unum neges, hoc solum meminerunt, quod negatum est.
For however often a man may receive an obligation from you, if you refuse a request, all former favors are effaced by this one denial.
PLINY THE YOUNGER—*Epistles*. III. 4.

9
Beneficium accipere, libertatem est vendere.
To accept a favor is to sell one's freedom.
SYRUS—*Maxims*.

10
Neutiquam officium liberi esse hominis puto
Cum is nihil promereat, postulare id gratiæ apponi sibi.
No free man will ask as favor, what he can not claim as reward.
TERENCE—*Andria*. II. 1. 32.

FEAR

11
No one loves the man whom he fears.
ARISTOTLE.

12
Crux est si metuas quod vincere nequeas.
It is tormenting to fear what you cannot overcome.
AUSONIUS—*Septem Sapientum Sententiæ Septenis Versibus Explicatæ*. VII. 4.

13
The brave man is not he who feels no fear,
For that were stupid and irrational;
But he, whose noble soul its fear subdues,
And bravely dares the danger nature shrinks from.
JOANNA BAILLIE—*Basil*. Act III. Sc. 1. L. 151.

14
An aching tooth is better out than in,
To lose a rotten member is a gain.
RICHARD BAXTER—*Hypocrisy*.

15
Dangers bring fears, and fears more dangers bring.
RICHARD BAXTER—*Love Breathing Thanks and Praise*.

16
The fear o' hell's the hangman's whip
To laud the wretch in order;
But where ye feel your honor grip,
Let that aye be your border.
BURNS—*Epistle to a Young Friend*.

17
Fear is an ague, that forsakes
And haunts, by fits, those whom it takes;
And they'll opine they feel the pain
And blows they felt, to-day, again.
BUTLER—*Hudibras*. Pt. I. Canto III.

18
His fear was greater than his haste:
For fear, though fleeter than the wind,
Believes 'tis always left behind.
BUTLER—*Hudibras*. Pt. III. Canto III. L. 64.

19
In summo periculo timor misericordiam non recipit.
In extreme danger fear feels no pity.
CÆSAR—*Bellum Gallicum*. VII. 26.

20
El miedo tiene muchos ojos.
Fear has many eyes.
CERVANTES—*Don Quixote*. III. 6.

21
Timor non est diuturnus magister officii.
Fear is not a lasting teacher of duty.
CICERO—*Philippicæ*. II. 36.

22
Like one, that on a lonesome road
Doth walk in fear and dread,
And having once turned round, walks on,
And turns no more his head;
Because he knows a frightful fiend
Doth close behind him tread.
COLERIDGE—*The Ancient Mariner*. Pt. VI.

23
His frown was full of terror, and his voice
Shook the delinquent with such fits of awe
As left him not, till penitence had won
Lost favor back again, and clos'd the breach
COWPER—*The Task*. Bk. II. L. 659.

24
The clouds dispell'd, the sky resum'd her light,
And Nature stood recover'd of her fright.
But fear, the last of ills, remain'd behind,
And horror heavy sat on every mind.
DRYDEN—*Theodore and Honoria*. L. 336.

25
We are not apt to fear for the fearless, when we are companions in their danger.
GEORGE ELIOT—*The Mill on the Floss*. Bk. VII. Ch. V.

1
Fear always springs from ignorance.
EMERSON—*The American Scholar.*

2
Fear is the parent of cruelty.
FROUDE—*Short Studies on Great Subjects. Party Politics.*

3
Quia me vestigia terrent
Omnia te adversum spectantia, nulla retrorsum.
I am frightened at seeing all the footprints directed towards thy den, and none returning.
HORACE—*Epistles.* I. 1. 74.

4
You are uneasy, * * * you never sailed with *me* before, I see.
ANDREW JACKSON—*Parton's Life of Jackson.* Vol. III. P. 493.

5
Shame arises from the fear of men, conscience from the fear of God.
SAMUEL JOHNSON—From MISS REYNOLDS—*Recollections of Johnson.*

6
De loin, c'est quelque chose; et de prés, ce n'est rien.
From a distance it is something; and nearby it is nothing.
LA FONTAINE—*Fables.* IV. 10.

7
Major ignotarum rerum est terror.
Apprehensions are greater in proportion as things are unknown.
LIVY—*Annales.* XXVIII. 44.

8
Oh, fear not in a world like this,
And thou shalt know ere long,—
Know how sublime a thing it is
To suffer and be strong.
LONGFELLOW—*The Light of Stars.* St. 9.

9
They are slaves who fear to speak
For the fallen and the weak.
LOWELL—*Stanzas on Freedom.* Last Stanza.

10
The direst foe of courage is the fear itself, not the object of it; and the man who can overcome his own terror is a hero and more.
GEORGE MACDONALD—*Sir Gibbie.* Ch. XX.

11
Wink and shut their apprehensions up.
MARSTON—*Antonio's Revenge. Prolog.*

12
The thing in the world I am most afraid of is fear, and with good reason; that passion alone, in the trouble of it, exceeding all other accidents.
MONTAIGNE—*Essays. Fear.*

13
Imagination frames events unknown,
In wild, fantastic shapes of hideous ruin,
And what it fears creates.
HANNAH MORE—*Belshazzar.* Pt. II.

14
Quem metuit quisque, perisse cupit.
Every one wishes that the man whom he fears would perish.
OVID—*Amorum.* II. 2. 10.

15
Membra reformidant mollem quoque saucia tactum:
Vanaque sollicitis incutit umbra metum.
The wounded limb shrinks from the slightest touch; and a slight shadow alarms the nervous.
OVID—*Epistolæ Ex Ponto.* II. 7. 13.

16
Terretur minimo pennæ stridore columba
Unguibus, accipiter, saucia facta tuis.
The dove, O hawk, that has once been wounded by thy talons, is frightened by the least movement of a wing.
OVID—*Tristium.* I. 1. 75.

17
Then flash'd the living lightning from her eyes,
And screams of horror rend th' affrighted skies,
Not louder shrieks to pitying Heaven are cast,
When husbands, or when lap dogs, breathe their last;
Or when rich China vessels fallen, from high,
In glittering dust and painted fragments lie.
POPE—*Rape of the Lock.* Canto III. L. 155.

18
A lamb appears a lion, and we fear
Each bush we see's a bear.
QUARLES—*Emblems.* Bk. I. Emblem XIII. L. 19.

19
Fain would I climb, yet fear I to fall.
SIR WALTER RALEIGH—Written on a window pane for Queen Elizabeth to see. She wrote under it "If thy heart fails thee, climb not at all." FULLER—*Worthies of England.* Vol. I. P. 419.

20
Ad deteriora credenda proni metu.
Fear makes men believe the worst.
QUINTUS CURTIUS RUFUS—*De Rebus Gestis Alexandri Magni.* IV. 3. 22.

21
Ubi explorari vera non possunt, falsa per metum augentur.
When the truth cannot be clearly made out, what is false is increased through fear.
QUINTUS CURTIUS RUFUS—*De Rebus Gestis Alexandri Magni.* IV. 10. 10.

22
Ubi intravit animos pavor, id solum metuunt, quod primum formidare cœperunt.
When fear has seized upon the mind, man fears that only which he first began to fear.
QUINTUS CURTIUS RUFUS—*De Rebus Gestis Alexandri Magni.* IV. 16. 17.

23
Quem neque gloria neque pericula excitant, nequidquam hortere; timor animi auribus officit.
The man who is roused neither by glory nor by danger it is in vain to exhort; terror closes the ears of the mind.
SALLUST—*Catilina.* LVIII.

24
Wer nichts fürchtet ist nicht weniger mächtig, als der, den Alles fürchtet.
The man who fears nothing is not less powerful than he who is feared by every one.
SCHILLER—*Die Räuber.* I. 1.

25
Wenn ich einmal zu fürchten angefangen
Hab' ich zu fürchten aufgehört.
As soon as I have begun to fear I have ceased to fear.
SCHILLER—*Don Carlos.* I. 6. 68.

1
Ich weiss, dass man vor leeren Schrecken zittert;
Doch wahres Unglück bringt der falsche Wahn.
I know that oft we tremble at an empty terror, but the false phantasm brings a real misery.
SCHILLER—*Piccolomini*. V. 1. 105.

2
Scared out of his seven senses.
SCOTT—*Rob Roy*. Ch. XXIV.

3
Necesse est multos timeat, quem multi timent.
He must necessarily fear many, whom many fear.
SENECA—*De Ira*. II. 11.

4
Si vultis nihil timere, cogitate omnia esse timenda.
If you wish to fear nothing, consider that everything is to be feared.
SENECA—*Quæstionum Naturalium*. VI. 2.

5
It is a basilisk unto mine eye,
Kills me to look on't.
Cymbeline. Act II. Sc. 4. L. 107.

6
Best safety lies in fear.
Hamlet. Act I. Sc. 3. L. 43.

7
There is not such a word
Spoke of in Scotland as this term of fear.
Henry IV. Pt. I. Act IV. Sc. 1. L. 84.

8
Thou tremblest; and the whiteness in thy cheek
Is apter than thy tongue to tell thy errand.
Henry IV. Pt. II. Act 1. Sc. 1. L. 68.

9
Things done well,
And with a care, exempt themselves from fear;
Things done without example, in their issue
Are to be feared.
Henry VIII. Act I. Sc. 2. L. 88.

10
It is the part of men to fear and tremble,
When the most mighty gods by tokens send
Such dreadful heralds to astonish us.
Julius Cæsar. Act I. Sc. 3. L. 54.

11
For I am sick and capable of fears,
Oppress'd with wrongs, and therefore full of fears,
A widow, husbandless, subject to fears,
A woman, naturally born to fears.
King John. Act III. Sc. 1. L. 12.

12
And make my seated heart knock at my ribs.
Macbeth. Act I. Sc. 3. L. 136.

13
Present fears
Are less than horrible imaginings.
Macbeth. Act I. Sc. 3. L. 137.

14
Ere we will eat our meal in fear, and sleep
In the affliction of these terrible dreams
That shake us nightly.
Macbeth. Act III. Sc. 2. L. 17.

15
Thou can'st not say I did it; never shake
Thy gory locks at me.
Macbeth. Act III. Sc. 4. L. 49.

16
You can behold such sights,
And keep the natural ruby of your cheeks,
When mine is blanch'd with fear.
Macbeth. Act III. Sc. 4. L. 114.

17
His flight was madness: when our actions do not,
Our fears do make us traitors.
Macbeth. Act IV. Sc. 2. L. 3.

18
Or in the night, imagining some fear,
How easy is a bush suppos'd a bear!
Midsummer Night's Dream. Act V. Sc. 1. L. 21.

19
To fear the foe, since fear oppresseth strength,
Gives in your weakness strength unto your foe.
Richard II. Act III. Sc. 2. L. 180.

20
Truly the souls of men are full of dread:
Ye cannot reason almost with a man
That looks not heavily and full of fear.
Richard III. Act II. Sc. 3. L. 39.

21
They spake not a word;
But, like dumb statues or breathing stones,
Gazed each on other, and look'd deadly pale.
Richard III. Act III. Sc. 7. L. 24.

22
I have a faint cold fear thrills through my veins,
That almost freezes up the heat of life.
Romeo and Juliet. Act IV. Sc. 3. L. 15.

23
Tunc plurima versat
Pessimus in dubiis augur timor.
Then fear, the very worst prophet in misfortunes, anticipates many evils.
STATIUS—*Thebais*. III. 5.

24
Primus in orbe deos fecit timor.
Fear in the world first created the gods.
STATIUS—*Thebais*. III. 661.

25
Do you think I was born in a wood to be afraid of an owl?
SWIFT—*Polite Conversation*. Dialogue I.

26
Etiam fortes viros subitis terreri.
Even the bravest men are frightened by sudden terrors.
TACITUS—*Annales*. XV. 59.

27
Bello in si bella vistà anco è l'orrore,
E di mezzo la tema esce il diletto.
Horror itself in that fair scene looks gay,
And joy springs up e'en in the midst of fear.
TASSO—*Gerusalemme*. XX. 30.

28
Fear
Stared in her eyes, and chalk'd her face.
TENNYSON—*The Princess*. IV. L. 357.

29
Desponding Fear, of feeble fancies full,
Weak and unmanly, loosens every power.
THOMSON—*The Seasons*. *Spring*. L. 286.

30
Il faut tout attendre et tout craindre du temps et des hommes.
We must expect everything and fear everything from time and from men.
VAUVENARGUES—*Réflexions*. CII.

1
Obstupui, steteruntque comæ, et vox faucibus hæsit.
I was astounded, my hair stood on end, and my voice stuck in my throat.
VERGIL—*Æneid.* II. 774, and III. 48.

2
Degeneres animos timor arguit.
Fear is the proof of a degenerate mind.
VERGIL—*Æneid.* IV. 13.

3
Pedibus timor addidit alas.
Fear gave wings to his feet.
VERGIL—*Æneid.* VIII. 224.

4
Full twenty times was Peter feared,
For once that Peter was respected.
WORDSWORTH—*Peter Bell.* Pt. I. St. 3.

5
Less base the fear of death than fear of life.
YOUNG—*Night Thoughts.* Night V. L. 441.

FEBRUARY

6
Come when the rains
Have glazed the snow and clothed the trees with ice,
While the slant sun of February pours
Into the bowers a flood of light. Approach!
The incrusted surface shall upbear thy steps
And the broad arching portals of the grove
Welcome thy entering.
BRYANT—*A Winter Piece.* L. 60.

7
The February sunshine steeps your boughs
And tints the buds and swells the leaves within.
BRYANT—*Among the Trees.* L. 53.

8
February makes a bridge, and
March breaks it.
HERBERT—*Jacula Prudentum.*

9
February, fill the dyke
With what thou dost like.
TUSSER—*Hundred Points of Good Husbandry. February's Husbandry.* (1577 Edition "With what ye like.")

FEELING

10
He thought as a sage, though he felt as a man.
BEATTIE—*The Hermit.* L. 8.

11
Era of good feeling.
Title of article in Boston *Centinel.* July 12, 1817.

12
But, spite of all the criticising elves,
Those who would make us feel, must feel themselves.
CHURCHILL—*Rosciad.* L. 961.

13
Thought is deeper than all speech,
Feeling deeper than all thought;
Souls to souls can never teach
What unto themselves was taught.
C. P. CRANCH—*Thought.*

14
The moment of finding a fellow-creature is often as full of mingled doubt and exultation, as the moment of finding an idea.
GEORGE ELIOT—*Daniel Deronda.* Bk. II. Ch. XVII.

15
Wenn ihr's nicht fühlt ihr werdet's nicht erjagen.
You'll never attain it unless you know the feeling.
GOETHE—*Faust.* I. 1. 182.

16
Feeling is deep and still; and the word that floats on the surface
Is as the tossing buoy, that betrays where the anchor is hidden.
LONGFELLOW—*Evangeline.* Pt. II. Sc. 2. L. 212.

17
For there are moments in life, when the heart is so full of emotion,
That if by chance it be shaken, or into its depths like a pebble
Drops some careless word, it overflows, and its secret,
Spilt on the ground like water, can never be gathered together.
LONGFELLOW—*Courtship of Miles Standish.* Pt. VI. *Priscilla.* L. 12.

18
The wealth of rich feelings—the deep—the pure;
With strength to meet sorrow, and faith to endure.
FRANCES S. OSGOOD—*To F. D. Maurice.*

19
The soul of music slumbers in the shell,
Till wak'd and kindled by the master's spell,
And feeling hearts touch them but lightly—pour
A thousand melodies unheard before!
SAM'L ROGERS—*Human Life.* L. 359.

20
Some feelings are to mortals given,
With less of earth in them than heaven.
SCOTT—*Lady of the Lake.* Canto II. St. 22.

21
Sensations sweet,
Felt in the blood, and felt along the heart.
WORDSWORTH—*Lines Composed a Few Miles Above Tintern Abbey.*

FESTIVITIES

22
On such an occasion as this,
All time and nonsense scorning,
Nothing shall come amiss,
And we won't go home till morning.
JOHN B. BUCKSTONE—*Billy Taylor.* Act I. Sc. 2.

23
Why should we break up
Our snug and pleasant party?
Time was made for slaves,
But never for us so hearty.
JOHN B. BUCKSTONE—*Billy Taylor.* Act I. Sc. 2.

24
As much valour is to be found in feasting as in fighting, and some of our city captains and carpet knights will make this good, and prove it.
BURTON—*Anatomy of Melancholy.* Pt. I. Sec. II. Memb. 2. Subsect. 2.

25
Let us have wine and woman, mirth and laughter,
Sermons and soda-water the day after.
BYRON—*Don Juan.* Canto II. St. 178.

1
There was a sound of revelry by night,
And Belgium's capital had gather'd then
Her Beauty and her Chivalry, and bright
The lamps shone o'er fair women and brave men.
BYRON—*Childe Harold.* Canto III. St. 21.

2
The music, and the banquet, and the wine—
The garlands, the rose odors, and the flowers,
The sparkling eyes, and flashing ornaments—
The white arms and the raven hair—the braids,
And bracelets; swan-like bosoms, and the necklace,
An India in itself, yet dazzling not.
BYRON—*Marino Faliero.* Act IV. Sc. 1. L. 51.

3
Then I commended mirth, because a man hath no better thing under the sun, than to eat, and to drink, and to be merry.
Ecclesiastes. VIII. 15. See also *Luke.* XII. 19.

4
Neque pauciores tribus, neque plures novem.
Not fewer than three nor more than nine.
Quoted by ERASMUS—*Fam. Coll.* The number for a dinner, according to a proverb.

5
The service was of great array,
That they were served with that day.
Thus they ate, and made them glad,
With such service as they had—
When they had dined, as I you say,
Lordis and ladies yede to play;
Some to tables and some to chess,
With other games more and less.
The Life of Ipomydon. Harleian Library. (British Museum.) MS. No. 2,252.

6
Non ampliter, sed munditer convivium; plus salis quam sumptus.
A feast not profuse but elegant; more of salt [refinement] than of expense.
Quoted by MONTAIGNE—*Essays.* Bk. III. Ch. IX. From an ancient poet, cited by NONNIUS MARCELLUS. XI. 19. Also from CORNELIUS NEPOS—*Life of Atticus.* Ch. XIII.

7
This night I hold an old accustom'd feast,
Whereto I have invited many a guest,
Such as I love; and you among the store,
One more, most welcome, makes my number more.
Romeo and Juliet. Act I. Sc. 2. L. 20.

8
We keep the day. With festal cheer,
With books and music, surely we
Will drink to him, whate'er he be,
And sing the songs he loved to hear.
TENNYSON—*In Memoriam.* CVII.

9
Oh, leave the gay and festive scenes,
The halls of dazzling light.
H. S. VAN DYKE—*The Light Guitar.*

10
Feast, and your halls are crowded;
Fast, and the world goes by.
ELLA WHEELER WILCOX—*Solitude.*

FIDELITY (See also FAITH)

11
No man can mortgage his injustice as a pawn for his fidelity.
BURKE—*Reflections on the Revolution in France.*

12
I never will desert Mr. Micawber.
DICKENS—*David Copperfield.* Ch. XII.

13
Thou givest life and love for Greece and Right:
I will stand by thee lest thou shouldst be weak,
Not weak of soul.—I will but hold in sight
Thy marvelous beauty.—Here is
She you seek!
W. J. LINTON—*Iphigenia at Aulis.*

14
So spake the seraph Abdiel, faithful found,
Among the faithless faithful only he.
MILTON—*Paradise Lost.* Bk. V. L. 896.

15
Be not the first by whom the new are tried,
Nor yet the last to lay the old aside.
POPE—*Essay on Criticism.* L. 336.

16
Pleas'd to the last he crops the flowery food,
And licks the hand just rais'd to shed his blood.
POPE—*Essay on Man.* Ep. I. L. 83.
(See also POMFRET under HAND)

17
Pretio parata vincitur pretio fides.
Fidelity bought with money is overcome by money.
SENECA—*Agamemnon.* 287.

18
Poscunt fidem secunda, at adversa exigunt.
Prosperity asks for fidelity; adversity exacts it.
SENECA—*Agamemnon.* 934.

19
O, where is loyalty?
If it be banish'd from the frosty head,
Where shall it find a harbour in the earth?
Henry VI. Pt. II. Act V. Sc. 1. L. 166.

20
You draw me, you hard-hearted adamant;
But yet you draw not iron, for my heart
Is true as steel.
Midsummer Night's Dream. Act II. Sc. 1. L. 195.

21
To be true to each other, let 'appen what maäy
Till the end o' the daäy
An the last loäd hoäm.
TENNYSON—*The Promise of May.* Song. Act II.

22
To God, thy countrie, and thy friend be true.
VAUGHAN—*Rules and Lessons.* St. 8.

FIG

Ficus

23
Close by a rock, of less enormous height,
Breaks the wild waves, and forms a dangerous strait;
Full on its crown, a fig's green branches rise,
And shoot a leafy forest to the skies.
HOMER—*Odyssey.* Bk. XII. L. 125. POPE'S trans.

24
So counsel'd he, and both together went
Into the thickest wood; there soon they chose
The fig-tree, not that kind for fruit renowned,

But such as at this day to Indians known
In Malabar or Decan spreads her arms,
Branching so broad and long, that in the ground
The bended twigs take root, and daughters grow
About the mother tree, a pillar'd shade
High overarch'd, and echoing walks between.
MILTON—*Paradise Lost.* Bk. IX. L. 1,099.

FIR

Abies

1
A lonely fir-tree is standing
On a northern barren height;
It sleeps, and the ice and snow-drift
Cast round it a garment of white.
HEINE—*Book of Songs. Lyrical Interlude.* No. 34.

2
I remember, I remember
The fir-trees dark and high;
I used to think their slender tops
Were close against the sky.
HOOD—*I Remember, I Remember.*

3
In a drear-nighted December,
Too happy, happy tree,
Thy branches ne'er remember
Their green felicity.
KEATS—*Stanzas.*

4
Kindles the gummy bark of fir or pine,
And sends a comfortable heat from far,
Which might supply the sun.
MILTON—*Paradise Lost.* Bk. X. L. 1,076.

FIRE

5
Yet in oure asshen olde is fyr yreke.
CHAUCER—*Canterbury Tales. The Reves Prologue.* L. 3,881.
(See also GRAY, SIDNEY)

6
Words pregnant with celestial fire.
COWPER—*Boadicea.* 33.
(See also GRAY)

7
E'en from the tomb the voice of nature cries,
E'en in our ashes live their wonted fires.
GRAY—*Elegy in a Country Churchyard.* 23.
GRAY says it was suggested by PETRARCH—*Sonnet.* 169. Same phrase in SHAKESPEARE—*Antony and Cleopatra.* Act V. Sc. 2.
(See also CHAUCER)

8
Some heart once pregnant with celestial fire.
GRAY—*Elegy.* 46.
(See also COWPER)

9
A crooked log makes a straight fire.
HERBERT—*Jacula Prudentum.*

10
Well may he smell fire, whose gown burns.
HERBERT—*Jacula Prudentum.*

11
Tua res agitur, paries cum proximus ardet.
Your own property is concerned when your neighbor's house is on fire.
HORACE—*Epistles.* I. 18. 84.

12
The burnt child dreads the fire.
BEN JONSON—*The Devil is an Ass.* Act I. Sc. 2.

13
How great a matter a little fire kindleth!
James. III. 5.

14
Be of good comfort, Master Ridley, play the man! We shall this day light such a candle, by God's grace, in England, as I trust shall never be put out.
LATIMER—*The Martyrdom.* P. 523.

15
There can no great smoke arise, but there must be some fire.
LYLY—*Euphues and his Emphœbus.* P. 153. (Arber's Reprint.)
(See also PERSIUS, PLAUTUS)

16
All the fatt's in the fire.
MARSTON—*What You Will.* 1607.

17
Whirlwinds of tempestuous fire.
MILTON—*Paradise Lost.* Bk. I. L. 77.

18
They lepe lyke a flounder out of a fryenge panne into the fyre.
THOMAS MORE—*Dial.* Bk. II. Ch. I. Folio LXIII. b.
(See also PLATO)

19
Dare pondus idonea fumo.
Fit to give weight to smoke.
PERSIUS—*Satires.* V. 20.
(See also LYLY)

20
Out of the frying pan into the fire.
Idea in PLATO—*De Repub.* VIII. P. 569. B.
THEODORET—*Therap.* III. 773.
(See also MORE)

21
Flamma fumo est proxima.
Flame is very near to smoke.
PLAUTUS—*Curculio.* Act I. 1. 53.
(See also LYLY)

22
Divert her eyes with pictures in the fire.
POPE—*Epistle to Mrs. Teresa Blount, on her leaving the Town after the Coronation.*

23
Heap coals of fire upon his head.
Proverbs. XXV. 22.

24
Parva sæpe scintilla contempta magnum excitavit incendium.
A spark neglected has often raised a conflagration.
QUINTUS CURTIUS RUFUS—*De Rebus Gestis Alexandria Magni.* VI. 3. 11.

25
A little fire is quickly trodden out;
Which, being suffer'd, rivers cannot quench.
Henry VI. Pt. III. Act IV. Sc. 8. L. 6.

26
The fire i' the flint
Shows not till it be struck.
Timon of Athens. Act I. Sc. 1. L. 22.

27
Fire that's closest kept burns most of all.
Two Gentlemen of Verona. Act I. Sc. 2. L. 30.

28
In ashes of despaire, though burnt, shall make thee live.
SIR PHILIP SIDNEY—*Arcadia.*
(See also CHAUCER)

1
O joy! that in our embers
Is something that doth live.
WORDSWORTH—*Ode.* IV. 53. (Knight's ed.)

FIREFLY

2
Before, beside us, and above
The firefly lights his lamp of love.
BISHOP HEBER—*Tour Through Ceylon.*

3
Is it where the flow'r of the orange blows,
And the fireflies dance thro' the myrtle boughs?
MRS. HEMANS—*The Better Land.*

4
And the fireflies, Wah-wah-taysee,
Waved their torches to mislead him.
LONGFELLOW—*Hiawatha.*

5
The fireflies o'er the meadow
In pulses come and go.
LOWELL—*Midnight.* St. 3.

6
Tiny Salmoneus of the air
His mimic bolts the firefly threw.
LOWELL—*The Lesson.*

7
Now, motionless and dark, eluded search
Self-shrouded: and anon, starring the sky,
Rose like a shower of fire.
SOUTHEY—*Madoc.* Pt. II. (Confounds the firefly with the lantern-fly.)

8
Many a night I saw the Pleiads rising thro' the mellow shade,
Glitter like a swarm of fireflies tangled in a silver braid.
TENNYSON—*Locksley Hall.* 9.

FISH

(See also ANGLING)

9
Wha'll buy my caller herrin'?
They're no brought here without brave darin'
Buy my caller herrin', Ye little ken their worth.
Wha'll buy my caller herrin'?
O you may ca' them vulgar farin',
Wives and mithers maist despairin'
Ca' them lives o' men.
Caller Herrin'. *Old Scotch Song.* Credited to LADY NAIRN. Claimed for NEIL GOW, who probably only wrote the music.
(See also SCOTT)

10
"Will you walk a little faster?" said a whiting to a snail,
"There's a porpoise close behind us, and he's treading on my tail!
See how eagerly the lobsters and the turtles all advance:
They are waiting on the shingle—will you come and join the dance?"
LEWIS CARROLL—*Song in Alice in Wonderland.*

11
Here when the labouring fish does at the foot arrive,
And finds that by his strength but vainly he doth strive;
His tail takes in his teeth, and bending like a bow,
That's to the compass drawn, aloft himself doth throw:
Then springing at his height, as doth a little wand,
That, bended end to end, and flerted from the hand,
Far off itself doth cast, so does the salmon vaut.
And if at first he fail, his second summersaut
He instantly assays and from his nimble ring,
Still yarking never leaves, until himself he fling
Above the streamful top of the surrounded heap.
DRAYTON—*Poly-Olbion.* Sixth Song. L. 45.

12
O scaly, slippery, wet, swift, staring wights,
What is 't ye do? what life lead? eh, dull goggles?
How do ye vary your vile days and nights?
How pass your Sundays? Are ye still but joggles
In ceaseless wash? Still nought but gapes and bites,
And drinks, and stares, diversified with boggles.
LEIGH HUNT—*Sonnets.* *The Fish, the Man, and the Spirit.*

13
Fishes that tipple in the deepe,
Know no such liberty.
LOVELACE—*To Althea from Prison.* St. 2.

14
Cut off my head, and singular I am,
Cut off my tail, and plural I appear;
Although my middle's left, there's nothing there!
What is my head cut off? A sounding sea;
What is my tail cut off? A rushing river;
And in their mingling depths I fearless play,
Parent of sweetest sounds, yet mute forever.
MACAULAY—*Enigma.* *On the Codfish.*

15
Ye monsters of the bubbling deep,
Your Maker's praises spout;
Up from the sands ye codlings peep,
And wag your tails about.
COTTON MATHER—*Hymn.*

16
Our plenteous streams a various race supply,
The bright-eyed perch with fins of Tyrian dye,
The silver eel, in shining volumes roll'd,
The yellow carp, in scales bedropp'd with gold,
Swift trouts, diversified with crimson stains,
And pikes, the tyrants of the wat'ry plains.
POPE—*Windsor Forest.* L. 141.

17
'Tis true, no turbots dignify my boards,
But gudgeons, flounders, what my Thames affords.
POPE—*Second Book of Horace.* Satire II. L. 141.

18
We have here other fish to fry.
RABELAIS—*Works.* Bk. V. Ch. 12.

19
It's no fish ye're buying—it's men's lives.
SCOTT—*The Antiquary.* Ch. XI.
(See also CALLER HERRIN')

20
Master, I marvel how the fishes live in the sea.
Why, as men do a-land: the great ones eat up the little ones.
Pericles. Act II. Sc. 1. L. 29.
(See also DE MORGAN, SWIFT under FLEA)

21
Blue, darkly, deeply, beautifully blue.
SOUTHEY—*Madoc in Wales.* Pt. V. (Referring to dolphins.) BYRON erroneously quotes this as referring to the sky.
(See also BYRON under SKY)

1
They say fish should swim thrice * * * first it should swim in the sea (do you mind me?) then it should swim in butter, and at last, sirrah, it should swim in good claret.
SWIFT—*Polite Conversation.* Dialogue II.

2
All's fish they get that cometh to net.
TUSSER—*Five Hundred Points of Good Husbandry. February Abstract.* GASCOIGNE—*Steele Glas.*

3
Now at the close of this soft summer's day,
Inclined upon the river's flowery side,
I pause to see the sportive fishes play,
And cut with finny oars the sparkling tide.
VALDARNE. In THOMAS FORSTER'S *Perennial Calendar.*

FLAG

4
Uncover when the flag goes by, boys,
'Tis freedom's starry banner that you greet,
Flag famed in song and story
Long may it wave, old glory
The flag that has never known defeat.
CHARLES L. BENJAMIN AND GEORGE D. SUTTON. *The Flag That Has Never Known Defeat.*

5
Hats off!
Along the street there comes
A blare of bugles, a ruffle of drums,
A flash of color beneath the sky:
Hats off!
The flag is passing by.
HENRY H. BENNETT—*The Flag Goes By.*

6
United States, your banner wears
Two emblems—one of fame;
Alas! the other that it bears
Reminds us of your shame.

Your banner's constellation types
White freedom with its stars,
But what's the meaning of the stripes?
They mean your negroes' scars.
CAMPBELL—*To the United States of North America.* (1838)
(See also LUNT for answer to same)

7
The meteor flag of England.
CAMPBELL—*Ye Mariners of England.*
(See also MILTON under WAR)

8
Ye mariners of England!
That guard our native seas;
Whose flag has braved a thousand years,
The battle and the breeze!
CAMPBELL—*Ye Mariners of England.*

9
Fling out, fling out, with cheer and shout,
To all the winds Our Country's Banner!
Be every bar, and every star,
Displayed in full and glorious manner!
Blow, zephyrs, blow, keep the dear ensign flying!
Blow, zephyrs, sweetly mournful, sighing, sighing, sighing!
ABRAHAM COLES—*The Microcosm and other Poems.* P. 191.

10
If any one attempts to haul down the American flag, shoot him on the spot.
JOHN A. DIX—*Speeches and Addresses.* Vol. II. P. 440. *An Official Dispatch.* Jan. 29, 1861.

11
When Freedom from her mountain height
Unfurled her standard to the air,
She tore the azure robe of night,
And set the stars of glory there.
JOSEPH RODMAN DRAKE—*The Croakers. The American Flag.* St. 1.

12
Flag of the free heart's hope and home!
By angel hands to valour given,
Thy stars have lit the welkin dome;
And all thy hues were born in heaven.
JOSEPH RODMAN DRAKE—*The Croakers. The American Flag.* St. 5.

13
A moth-eaten rag on a worm-eaten pole,
It does not look likely to stir a man's soul.
'Tis the deeds that were done 'neath the moth-eaten rag,
When the pole was a staff, and the rag was a flag.
GEN. SIR E. HAMLEY. Referring to the Colors of the 43rd Monmouth Light Infantry.

14
Ay, tear her tattered ensign down!
Long has it waved on high,
And many an eye has danced to see
That banner in the sky.
HOLMES—*A Metrical Essay.*

15
Nail to the mast her holy flag,
Set every threadbare sail,
And give her to the God of storms,
The lightning and the gale.
HOLMES—*A Metrical Essay.*

16
Oh! say can you see by the dawn's early light
What so proudly we hail'd at the twilight's last gleaming,
Whose stripes and bright stars, thro' the perilous fight,
O'er the ramparts we watch'd, were so gallantly streaming;
And the rocket's red glare, the bombs bursting in air,
Gave proof thro' the night that our flag was still there!

CHORUS

Oh! say, does that star spangled banner yet wave,
O'er the land of the free and the home of the brave!
F. S. KEY—*Star-Spangled Banner.*

To Anacreon in heaven, where he sat in full glee,
A few Sons of Harmony sent a petition,
That he their inspirer and patron would be.
RALPH TOMLINSON—*To Anacreon in Heaven.* Music by JOHN STAFFORD SMITH. Tune of *The Star-Spangled Banner* (between 1770 and 1775) to which F. S. KEY set his words.

17
Praise the Power that hath made and preserved us a nation!
Then conquer we must when our cause it is just.
And this be our motto, "In God is our trust!"

And the star-spangled banner in triumph shall wave
O'er the land of the free and the home of the brave.
F. S. Key—*Star-Spangled Banner.*
(See also Morris)

1
What is the flag of England? Ye have but my breath to dare,
Ye have but my waves to conquer. Go forth, for it is there.
Kipling—*The English Flag.*

2
England! Whence came each glowing hue
That tints your flag of meteor light,—
The streaming red, the deeper blue,
Crossed with the moonbeams' pearly white?
The blood, the bruise—the blue, the red—
Let Asia's groaning millions speak;
The white it tells of colour fled
From starving Erin's pallid cheek.
George Lunt. *Answer to Campbell.* In *Newburyport News* (Mass.)
(See also Campbell)

3
Under the sooty flag of Acheron,
Harpies and Hydras.
Milton—*Comus.* L. 604.

4
The imperial ensign; which, full high advanced,
Shone like a meteor streaming to the wind.
Milton—*Paradise Lost.* Bk. I. L. 536.
(See also Webster)

5
Under spreading ensigns moving nigh, in slow
But firm battalion.
Milton—*Paradise Lost.* Bk. VI. L. 533.

6
Bastard Freedom waves
Her fustian flag in mockery over slaves.
Moore—*To the Lord Viscount Forbes.*

7
"A song for our banner?"—The watchword recall
Which gave the Republic her station;
"United we stand—divided we fall!"
It made and preserves us a nation!
George P. Morris—*The Flag of Our Union.* Probably inspired by Dickinson. See under Unity.
(See also Key)

8
The flag of our Union forever!
George P. Morris—*The Flag of Our Union.*

9
Your flag and my flag,
And how it flies today
In your land and my land
And half a world away!
Rose-red and blood-red
The stripes forever gleam;
Snow-white and soul-white—
The good forefathers' dream;
Sky-blue and true-blue, with stars to gleam aright—
The gloried guidon of the day, a shelter through the night.
Wilbur D. Nesbit—*Your Flag and My Flag.*

10
This is the song of the wind as it came,
Tossing the flags of the Nations to flame.
Alfred Noyes—*Avenue of the Allies.*

11
Yes, we'll rally round the flag, boys, we'll rally once again,
Shouting the battle-cry of Freedom,
We will rally from the hill-side, we'll gather from the plain,
Shouting the battle-cry of Freedom.
George F. Root—*Battle-Cry of Freedom.*

12
A garish flag,
To be the aim of every dangerous shot.
Richard III. Act IV. Sc. 4. L. 89.

13
This token serveth for a flag of truce
Betwixt ourselves and our followers.
Henry VI. Pt. I. Act III. Sc. 1. L. 138.

14
She's up there—Old Glory—where lightnings are sped,
She dazzles the nations with ripples of red,
And she'll wave for us living, or droop o'er us dead—
The flag of our country forever.
Frank L. Stanton—*Our Flag Forever.*

15
Banner of England, not for a season,
O Banner of Britain, hast thou
Floated in conquering battle or flapt to the battle-cry!
Never with mightier glory than when we had rear'd thee on high,
Flying at top of the roofs in the ghastly siege of Lucknow—
Shot thro' the staff or the halyard, but ever we raised thee anew,
And ever upon the topmost roof our banner of England blew.
Tennyson—*The Defence of Lucknow.*

16
Might his last glance behold the glorious ensign of the Republic still full high advanced, its arms and trophies streaming in all their original lustre.
Webster—*Peroration of the reply to Hayne.*
(See also Milton)

17
"Shoot, if you must, this old gray head,
But spare your country's flag," she said.
Whittier—*Barbara Frietchie.*

18
A star for every State, and a State for every star.
Robert C. Winthrop—*Address on Boston Common.* (1862)

FLAG

Iris

19
The yellow flags * * * would stand
Up to their chins in water.
Jean Ingelow—*Song of the Night Watches.* Watch I.

20
And nearer to the river's trembling edge
There grew broad flag-flowers, purple, prankt with white;
And starry river buds among the sedge;
And floating water-lilies, broad and bright.
Shelley—*The Question.*

FLATTERY

1

It has been well said that "the arch-flatterer with whom all the petty flatterers have intelligence is a man's self."

Quoted by BACON—*Essays* X. *Of Love.* Variation in *Essay* XXVII. *Of Friendship;* LIII. *Of Praise.* From PLUTARCH—*De Adul. et Amico.*

2

Assentatio, vitiorum adjutrix, procul amoveatur.

Let flattery, the handmaid of the vices, be far removed (from friendship).

CICERO—*De Amicitia.* XXIV.

3

Imitation is the sincerest of flattery.

C. C. COLTON—*Lacon.* P. 127.

4

Of praise a mere glutton, he swallow'd what came,
And the puff of a dunce, he mistook it for fame;
Till his relish grown callous, almost to displease,
Who pepper'd the highest was surest to please.

GOLDSMITH—*Retaliation.* L. 109.

5

Adulandi gens prudentissima laudat
Sermonem indocti, faciem deformis amici.

The skilful class of flatterers praise the discourse of an ignorant friend and the face of a deformed one.

JUVENAL—*Satires.* III. 86.

6

Gallantry of mind consists in saying flattering things in an agreeable manner.

LA ROCHEFOUCAULD—*Maxims.* 103.

7

On croit quelquefois haïr la flatterie; mais on ne hait que la manière de flatter.

We sometimes think that we hate flattery, but we only hate the manner in which it is done.

LA ROCHEFOUCAULD—*Maximes.* 329.

8

No adulation; 'tis the death of virtue;
Who flatters, is of all mankind the lowest
Save he who courts the flattery.

HANNAH MORE—*Daniel.*

9

Qu se laudari gaudent verbis subdolis,
Sera dant pœnas turpes pœnitentia.

They who delight to be flattered, pay for their folly by a late repentance.

PHÆDRUS—*Fables.* I. 13. 1.

10

By flatterers besieged
And so obliging that he ne'er obliged.

POPE—*Prologue to Satires.* L. 207.

11

Their throat is an open sepulchre; they flatter with their tongue.

Psalms. V. 9.

12

Es ist dem Menschen leichter und geläufiger, zu schmeicheln als zu loben.

It is easier and handier for men to flatter than to praise.

JEAN PAUL RICHTER—*Titan.* Zykel 34.

13

Mine eyes
Were not in fault, for she was beautiful;
Mine ears, that heard her flattery; nor my heart,
That thought her like her seeming; it had been vicious
To have mistrusted her.

Cymbeline. Act V. Sc. 5. L. 63.

14

Why should the poor be flatter'd?
No, let the candied tongue lick absurd pomp,
And crook the pregnant hinges of the knee,
Where thrift may follow fawning.

Hamlet. Act III. Sc. 2. L. 65.

15

By God, I cannot flatter: I do defy
The tongues of soothers; but a braver place
In my heart's love, hath no man than yourself;
Nay, task me to my word; approve me, lord.

Henry IV. Pt. I. Act IV. Sc. 1. L. 6.

16

What drink'st thou oft, instead of homage sweet,
But poison'd flattery?

Henry V. Act IV. Sc. 1. L. 267.

17

But when I tell him he hates flatterers,
He says he does, being then most flattered.

Julius Cæsar. Act II. Sc. 1. L. 208.

18

They do abuse the king that flatter him:
For flattery is the bellows blows up sin.

Pericles. Act I. Sc. 2. L. 38.

19

O, that men's ears should be
To counsel deaf, but not to flattery!

Timon of Athens. Act I. Sc. 2. L. 256.

20

Take no repulse, whatever she doth say;
For, "get you gone," she doth not mean, "away."
Flatter and praise, commend, extol their graces;
Though ne'er so black, say they have angels' faces.
That man that hath a tongue, I say, is no man,
If with his tongue he cannot win a woman.

Two Gentlemen of Verona. Act III. Sc. 1. L. 100.

21

'Tis an old maxim in the schools,
That flattery's the food of fools;
Yet now and then your men of wit
Will condescend to take a bit.

SWIFT—*Cadenus and Vanessa.* L. 769.

22

Where Young must torture his invention
To flatter knaves, or lose his pension.

SWIFT—*Poetry, a Rhapsody.* L. 279.

23

Vitium fuit, nunc mos est, adsentatio.

Flattery was formerly a vice; it has now become the fashion.

SYRUS—*Maxims.*

24

Pessimum genus inimicorum laudantes.

Flatterers are the worst kind of enemies.

TACITUS—*Agricola.* XLI.

25

Of folly, vice, disease, men proud we see;
And, (stranger still,) of blockheads' flattery;
Whose praise defames; as if a fool should mean,
By spitting on your face, to make it clean.

YOUNG—*Love of Fame.* Satire I. L. 755.

26

With your own heart confer;
And dread even there to find a flatterer.

YOUNG—*Love of Fame.* Satire VI.

FLEA

1
Great fleas have little fleas upon their backs to bite 'em,
And little fleas have lesser fleas, and so *ad infinitum.*
And the great fleas themselves, in turn, have greater fleas to go on;
While these again have greater still, and greater still, and so on.
AUGUSTUS DE MORGAN—*A Budget of Paradoxes.* P. 377.
(See also SWIFT, also PERICLES under FISH)

2
"I cannot raise my worth too high;
Of what vast consequence am I!"
"Not of the importance you suppose,"
Replies a Flea upon his nose;
"Be humble, learn thyself to scan;
Know, pride was never made for man."
GAY—*The Man and the Flea.*

3
A blockhead, bit by fleas, put out the light,
And chuckling cried, "Now you can't see to bite."
In *Greek Anthology.*

4
It was many and many a year ago,
In a District styled E. C.,
That a monster dwelt whom I came to know
By the name of Cannibal Flea,
And the brute was possessed with no other thought
Than to live—and to live on me.
THOS. HOOD, JR.—*The Cannibal Flea.* Parody on POE'S *Annabel Lee.*

5
I do honour the very flea of his dog.
BEN JONSON—*Every Man in his Humour.* Act IV. Sc. 4.

6
Then mimick'd my voice with satyrical sneer,
And sent me away with a Flea in my ear.
MOCHUS—*Idyll* IX. *Eunica.* BEAUMONT AND FLETCHER—*Love's Cure.* Act III. Sc. 3.

7
Panurge auoyt la pulee en l' oreille.
Panurge had a flea in his ear.
RABELAIS—*Pantagruel.* Ch. XXXI. SIMON FORMAN—*Notes to Marriage of Wit and Wisdom.*

8
So, naturalists observe, a flea
Has smaller fleas that on him prey;
And these have smaller still to bite 'em,
And so proceed *ad infinitum.*
Thus every poet in his kind
Is bit by him that comes behind.
SWIFT—*Poetry. A Rhapsody.*
(See also DE MORGAN)

FLIRTATION (See also COQUETRY)

9
I assisted at the birth of that most significant word flirtation, which dropped from the most beautiful mouth in the world, and which has since received the sanction of our most accurate Laureate in one of his comedies.
CHESTERFIELD—*The World.* No. 101. (LADY FRANCES SHIRLEY referred to. Poet-Laureate, COLLEY CIBBER.)

10
Flirtation, attention without intention.
MAX O'RELL—*John Bull and his Island.*

11
From a grave thinking mouser, she was grown
The gayest flirt that coach'd it round the town.
PITT—*Fable. The Young Man and His Cat.*

12
Ye belles, and ye flirts, and ye pert little things,
Who trip in this frolicsome round,
Pray tell me from whence this impertinence springs,
The sexes at once to confound?
WHITEHEAD—*Song for Ranelagh.*

FLORENCE

13
Ungrateful Florence! Dante sleeps afar,
Like Scipio, buried by the upbraiding shore.
BYRON—*Childe Harold.* Canto IV. St. 57.

FLOWERS (*Unclassified*)

14
Sweet letters of the angel tongue,
I've loved ye long and well,
And never have failed in your fragrance sweet
To find some secret spell,—
A charm that has bound me with witching power,
For mine is the old belief,
That midst your sweets and midst your bloom,
There's a soul in every leaf!
M. M. BALLOU—*Flowers.*

15
Take the flower from my breast, I pray thee,
Take the flower, too, from out my tresses;
And then go hence; for, see, the night is fair,
The stars rejoice to watch thee on thy way.
Third Poem in *Bard of the Dimbovitza; Rumanian Folksongs.* Collected by HÉLÈNE VACARESCO. English by CARMEN SYLVA and ALMA STRETTELL. (Quoted by GALSWORTHY, on fly leaf of *The Dark Flower.*)

16
As for marigolds, poppies, hollyhocks, and valorous sunflowers, we shall never have a garden without them, both for their own sake, and for the sake of old-fashioned folks, who used to love them.
HENRY WARD BEECHER—*Star Papers. A Discourse of Flowers.*

17
Flowers have an expression of countenance as much as men or animals. Some seem to smile; some have a sad expression; some are pensive and diffident; others again are plain, honest and upright, like the broad-faced sunflower and the hollyhock.
HENRY WARD BEECHER—*Star Papers. A Discourse of Flowers.*

18
Flowers are Love's truest language; they betray,
Like the divining rods of Magi old,
Where precious wealth lies buried, not of gold,
But love—strong love, that never can decay!
PARK BENJAMIN—*Sonnet. Flowers, Love's Truest Language.*

19
Thick on the woodland floor
Gay company shall be,
Primrose and Hyacinth
And frail Anemone,

Perennial Strawberry-bloom,
Woodsorrel's pencilled veil,
Dishevel'd Willow-weed
And Orchis purple and pale.
ROBERT BRIDGES—*Idle Flowers.*

1
I have loved flowers that fade,
Within whose magic tents
Rich hues have marriage made
With sweet unmemoried scents.
ROBERT BRIDGES—*Shorter Poems.* Bk. II. 13.

2
Brazen helm of daffodillies,
With a glitter toward the light.
Purple violets for the mouth,
Breathing perfumes west and south;
And a sword of flashing lilies,
Holden ready for the fight.
E. B. BROWNING—*Hector in the Garden.*

3
Ah, ah, Cytherea! Adonis is dead.
She wept tear after tear, with the blood which was shed,—
And both turned into flowers for the earth's garden-close;
Her tears, to the wind-flower,—his blood, to the rose.
E. B. BROWNING—*Lament for Adonis.* St. 6.

4
The flower-girl's prayer to buy roses and pinks,
Held out in the smoke, like stars by day.
E. B. BROWNING—*The Soul's Travelling.*

5
Yet here's eglantine,
Here's ivy!—take them as I used to do
Thy flowers, and keep them where they shall not pine.
Instruct thine eyes to keep their colours true,
And tell thy soul their roots are left in mine.
E. B. BROWNING—*Trans. from the Portuguese.* XLIV.

6
The windflower and the violet, they perished long ago,
And the brier-rose and the orchis died amid the summer glow;
But on the hills the golden-rod, and the aster in the wood,
And the yellow sunflower by the brook, in autumn beauty stood,
Till fell the frost from the clear cold heaven, as falls the plague on men,
And the brightness of their smile was gone, from upland glade and glen.
BRYANT—*Death of the Flowers.*

7
Where fall the tears of love the rose appears,
And where the ground is bright with friendship's tears,
Forget-me-not, and violets, heavenly blue,
Spring glittering with the cheerful drops like dew.
BRYANT—Trans. of N. MÜLLER'S *Paradise of Tears.*

8
Who that has loved knows not the tender tale
Which flowers reveal, when lips are coy to tell?
BULWER-LYTTON—*Corn Flowers. The First Violets.* Bk. I. St. 1.

9
Mourn, little harebells, o'er the lea;
Ye stately foxgloves fair to see!
Ye woodbines, hanging bonnilie
In scented bowers!
Ye roses on your thorny tree
The first o' flow'rs.
BURNS—*Elegy on Capt. Matthew Henderson.*

10
Now blooms the lily by the bank,
The primrose down the brae;
The hawthorn's budding in the glen,
And milkwhite is the slae.
BURNS—*Lament of Mary, Queen of Scots.*

11
The snowdrop and primrose our woodlands adorn,
And violets bathe in the wet o' the morn.
BURNS—*My Nannie's Awa.*

12
Rose, what is become of thy delicate hue?
And where is the violet's beautiful blue?
Does aught of its sweetness the blossom beguile?
That meadow, those daisies, why do they not smile?
JOHN BYROM—*A Pastoral.* St. 8.

13
Ye field flowers! the gardens eclipse you 'tis true:
Yet wildings of nature, I dote upon you,
For ye waft me to summers of old,
When the earth teem'd around me with fairy delight,
And when daisies and buttercups gladden'd my sight,
Like treasures of silver and gold.
CAMPBELL—*Field Flowers.*

14
The berries of the brier rose
Have lost their rounded pride:
The bitter-sweet chrysanthemums
Are drooping heavy-eyed.
ALICE CARY—*Faded Leaves.*

15
I know not which I love the most,
Nor which the comeliest shows,
The timid, bashful violet
Or the royal-hearted rose:

The pansy in her purple dress,
The pink with cheek of red,
Or the faint, fair heliotrope, who hangs,
Like a bashful maid her head.
PHEBE CARY—*Spring Flowers.*

16
They know the time to go!
The fairy clocks strike their inaudible hour
In field and woodland, and each punctual flower
Bows at the signal an obedient head
And hastes to bed.
SUSAN COOLIDGE—*Time to Go.*

17
Not a flower
But shows some touch, in freckle, streak or stain,
Of his unrivall'd pencil.
COWPER—*The Task.* Bk. VI. L. 241.

18
Flowers are words
Which even a babe may understand.
BISHOP COXE—*The Singing of Birds.*

1
And all the meadows, wide unrolled,
Were green and silver, green and gold,
Where buttercups and daisies spun
Their shining tissues in the sun.
JULIA C. R. DORR—*Unanswered.*

2
The harebells nod as she passes by,
The violet lifts its tender eye,
The ferns bend her steps to greet,
And the mosses creep to her dancing feet.
JULIA C. R. DORR—*Over the Wall.*

3
Up from the gardens floated the perfume
Of roses and myrtle, in their perfect bloom.
JULIA C. R. DORR—*Vashti's Scroll.* L. 91.

4
The rose is fragrant, but it fades in time:
The violet sweet, but quickly past the prime:
White lilies hang their heads, and soon decay,
And white snow in minutes melts away.
DRYDEN—*Trans. from Theocritus. The Despairing Lover.* L. 57.

5
The flowers of the forest are a' wede away.
JANE ELLIOTT—*The Flowers of the Forest.*

6
Why does the rose her grateful fragrance yield,
And yellow cowslips paint the smiling field?
GAY—*Panthea.* L. 71.

7
They speak of hope to the fainting heart,
With a voice of promise they come and part,
They sleep in dust through the wintry hours,
They break forth in glory—bring flowers, bright flowers!
FELICIA D. HEMANS—*Bring Flowers.*

8
Through the laburnum's dropping gold
Rose the light shaft of orient mould,
And Europe's violets, faintly sweet,
Purpled the moss-beds at its feet.
FELICIA D. HEMANS—*Palm-Tree.*

9
Faire pledges of a fruitful tree
Why do yee fall so fast?
Your date is not so past
But you may stay yet here awhile
To blush and gently smile
And go at last.
HERRICK—*To Blossoms.*

10
The daisy is fair, the day-lily rare,
The bud o' the rose as sweet as it's bonnie.
HOGG—*Auld Joe Nicolson's Nannie.*

11
What are the flowers of Scotland,
All others that excel?
The lovely flowers of Scotland,
All others that excel!
The thistle's purple bonnet,
And bonny heather bell,
Oh, they're the flowers of Scotland.
All others that excel!
HOGG—*The Flowers of Scotland.*

12
Yellow japanned buttercups and star-disked dandelions,—just as we see them lying in the grass, like sparks that have leaped from the kindling sun of summer.
HOLMES—*The Professor at the Breakfast-Table.* X.

13
I remember, I remember
The roses, red and white,
The violets, and the lily-cups,
Those flowers made of light!
The lilacs, where the robin built,
And where my brother set
The laburnum on his birthday,—
The tree is living yet.
HOOD—*I Remember, I Remember.*

14
I may not to the world impart
The secret of its power,
But treasured in my inmost heart
I keep my faded flower.
ELLEN C. HOWARTH—*'Tis but a Little Faded Flower.*

15
'Tis but a little faded flower,
But oh, how fondly dear!
'Twill bring me back one golden hour,
Through many a weary year.
ELLEN C. HOWARTH—*'Tis but a Little Faded Flower.*

16
Growing one's own choice words and fancies
In orange tubs, and beds of pansies;
One's sighs and passionate declarations,
In odorous rhetoric of carnations.
LEIGH HUNT—*Love-Letters Made of Flowers.*

17
Roses, and pinks, and violets, to adorn
The shrine of Flora in her early May.
KEATS—*Dedication to Leigh Hunt.*

18
Above his head
Four lily stalks did their white honours wed
To make a coronal; and round him grew
All tendrils green, of every bloom and hue,
Together intertwined and trammell'd fresh;
The vine of glossy sprout; the ivy mesh,
Shading its Ethiop berries.
KEATS—*Endymion.* Bk. II. L. 413.

19
Young playmates of the rose and daffodil,
Be careful ere ye enter in, to fill
Your baskets high
With fennel green, and balm, and golden pines
Savory latter-mint, and columbines.
KEATS—*Endymion.* Bk. IV. L. 575.

20
* * * the rose
Blendeth its odor with the violet,—
Solution sweet.
KEATS—*Eve of St. Agnes.* St. 36.

21
And O and O,
The daisies blow,
And the primroses are waken'd;
And the violets white
Sit in silver plight,
And the green bud's as long as the spike end.
KEATS—*In a Letter to Haydon.*

22
Underneath large blue-bells tented
Where the daisies are rose-scented,

And the rose herself has got
Perfume which on earth is not.
KEATS—*Ode. Bards of Passion and of Mirth.*

1
The loveliest flowers the closest cling to earth,
And they first feel the sun: so violets blue;
So the soft star-like primrose—drenched in dew—
The happiest of Spring's happy, fragrant birth.
KEBLE—*Miscellaneous Poems. Spring Showers.*

2
Spake full well, in language quaint and olden,
One who dwelleth by the castled Rhine,
When he called the flowers, so blue and golden,
Stars, that in the earth's firmament do shine.
LONGFELLOW—*Flowers.* St. 1.

3
Gorgeous flowerets in the sunlight shining,
Blossoms flaunting in the eye of day,
Tremulous leaves, with soft and silver lining,
Buds that open only to decay.
LONGFELLOW—*Flowers.* St. 6.

4
The flaming rose gloomed swarthy red;
The borage gleams more blue;
And low white flowers, with starry head,
Glimmer the rich dusk through.
GEORGE MACDONALD—*Songs of the Summer Night.* Pt. III.

5
And I will make thee beds of roses,
And a thousand fragrant posies.
MARLOWE—*The Passionate Shepherd to his Love.*

6
Flowers of all hue, and without thorn the rose.
MILTON—*Paradise Lost.* Bk. IV. L. 256.

7
A wilderness of sweets.
MILTON—*Paradise Lost.* Bk. V. L. 294.

8
The bright consummate flower.
MILTON—*Paradise Lost.* Bk. V. L. 481.

9
And touched by her fair tendance, gladlier grew.
MILTON—*Paradise Lost.* Bk. VIII. L. 47.

10
* * * at shut of evening flowers.
MILTON—*Paradise Lost.* Bk. IX. L. 278.

11
The foxglove, with its stately bells
Of purple, shall adorn thy dells;
The wallflower, on each rifted rock,
From liberal blossoms shall breathe down,
(Gold blossoms frecked with iron-brown,)
Its fragrance; while the hollyhock,
The pink, and the carnation vie
With lupin and with lavender,
To decorate the fading year;
And larkspurs, many-hued, shall drive
Gloom from the groves, where red leaves lie,
And Nature seems but half alive.
D. M. MOIR—*The Birth of the Flowers.* St. 14.

12
Anemones and seas of gold,
And new-blown lilies of the river,
And those sweet flow'rets that unfold
Their buds on Camadera's quiver.
MOORE—*Lalla Rookh. Light of the Harem.*

13
Yet, no—not words, for they
But half can tell love's feeling;
Sweet flowers alone can say
What passion fears revealing:
A once bright rose's wither'd leaf,
A tow'ring lily broken,—
Oh, these may paint a grief
No words could e'er have spoken.
MOORE—*The Language of Flowers.*

14
The Wreath's of brightest myrtle wove
With brilliant tears of bliss among it,
And many a rose leaf cull'd by Love
To heal his lips when bees have stung it.
MOORE—*The Wreath and the Chain.*

15
Forget-me-not, and violets, heavenly blue,
Spring, glittering with the cheerful drops like dew.
N. MÜLLER—*The Paradise of Tears.* Trans. by BRYANT.

16
"A milkweed, and a buttercup, and cowslip," said sweet Mary,
"Are growing in my garden-plot, and this I call my dairy."
PETER NEWELL—*Her Dairy.*

17
"Of what are you afraid, my child?" inquired the kindly teacher.
"Oh, sir! the flowers, they are wild," replied the timid creature.
PETER NEWELL—*Wild Flowers.*

18
I sometimes think that never blows so red
The Rose as where some buried Cæsar bled;
That every Hyacinth the Garden wears
Dropt in her Lap from some once lovely Head.
OMAR KHAYYAM—*Rubaiyat.* St. 19. FITZGERALD'S Trans.

19
One thing is certain and the rest is lies;
The Flower that once has blown for ever dies.
OMAR KHAYYAM—*Rubaiyat.* St. 63. FITZGERALD'S Trans.

20
He bore a simple wild-flower wreath:
Narcissus, and the sweet brier rose;
Vervain, and flexile thyme, that breathe
Rich fragrance; modest heath, that glows
With purple bells; the amaranth bright,
That no decay, nor fading knows,
Like true love's holiest, rarest light;
And every purest flower, that blows
In that sweet time, which Love most blesses,
When spring on summer's confines presses.
THOMAS LOVE PEACOCK—*Rhododaphne.* Canto I. L. 107.

21
In Eastern lands they talk in flowers,
And they tell in a garland their loves and cares;
Each blossom that blooms in their garden bowers,
On its leaves a mystic language bears.
PERCIVAL—*The Language of Flowers.*

22
Here blushing Flora paints th' enamell'd ground.
POPE—*Windsor Forest.*

1
Here eglantine embalm'd the air,
Hawthorne and hazel mingled there;
The primrose pale, and violet flower,
Found in each cliff a narrow bower;
Fox-glove and nightshade, side by side,
Emblems of punishment and pride,
Group'd their dark hues with every stain
The weather-beaten crags retain.
SCOTT—*The Lady of the Lake.* Canto I. St. 12.

2 Thou shalt not lack
The flower that's like thy face, pale primrose, nor
The azur'd harebell, like thy veins.
Cymbeline. Act IV. Sc. 2. L. 220.

3
These flowers are like the pleasures of the world.
Cymbeline. Act IV. Sc. 2. L. 296.

4
When daisies pied, and violets blue,
And lady-smocks all silver-white,
And cuckoo-buds of yellow hue
Do paint the meadows with delight.
Love's Labour's Lost. Act V. Sc. 2. L. 904.

5
In emerald tufts, flowers purple, blue, and white;
Like sapphire, pearl and rich embroidery.
Merry Wives of Windsor. Act V. Sc. 5. L. 74.

6
I know a bank, where the wild thyme blows
Where ox-lips, and the nodding violet grows;
Quite over-canopied with luscious woodbine,
With sweet musk-roses, and with eglantine.
Midsummer Night's Dream. Act II. Sc. 1. L. 251. Changed by STEEVENS to "whereon the wild thyme blows," and "luscious woodbine" to "lush woodbine."

7
To strew thy green with flowers; the yellows, blues,
The purple violets, and marigolds.
Pericles. Act IV. Sc. 1. L. 15.

8 The fairest flowers o' the season
Are our carnations and streak'd gillyvors.
Winter's Tale. Act IV. Sc. 4. L. 81.

9
There grew pied wind-flowers and violets,
Daisies, those pearled Arcturi of the earth,
The constellated flower that never sets.
SHELLEY—*The Question.*

10
Day stars! that ope your frownless eyes to twinkle
From rainbow galaxies of earth's creation,
And dew-drops on her lonely altars sprinkle
As a libation.
HORACE SMITH—*Hymn to the Flowers.*

11
Ye bright Mosaics! that with storied beauty,
The floor of Nature's temple tesselate,
What numerous emblems of instructive duty
Your forms create!
HORACE SMITH—*Hymn to the Flowers.*

12
Sweet is the rose, but grows upon a brere;
Sweet is the juniper, but sharp his bough;
Sweet is the eglantine, but sticketh nere;
Sweet is the firbloome, but its braunches rough;
Sweet is the cypress, but its rynd is tough;
Sweet is the nut, but bitter is his pill;
Sweet is the broome-flowre, but yet sowre enough;
And sweet is moly, but his root is ill.
SPENSER—*Amoretti. Sonnet XXVI.*

13 Roses red and violets blew,
And all the sweetest flowres that in the forrest grew.
SPENSER—*Faerie Queene.* Bk. III. Canto VI. St. 6.

14
The violets ope their purple heads;
The roses blow, the cowslip springs.
SWIFT—*Answer to a Scandalous Poem.* L. 150.

15
Primrose-eyes each morning ope
In their cool, deep beds of grass;
Violets make the air that pass
Tell-tales of their fragrant slope.
BAYARD TAYLOR—*Home and Travel. Ariel in the Cloven Pine.* L. 57.

16
The aquilegia sprinkled on the rocks
A scarlet rain; the yellow violet
Sat in the chariot of its leaves; the phlox
Held spikes of purple flame in meadows wet,
And all the streams with vernal-scented reed
Were fringed, and streaky bells of miskodeed.
BAYARD TAYLOR—*Home and Travel. Mon-Da-Min.* St. 17.

17
With roses musky-breathed,
And drooping daffodilly,
And silver-leaved lily.
And ivy darkly-wreathed,
I wove a crown before her,
For her I love so dearly.
TENNYSON—*Anacreontics.*

18
The gold-eyed kingcups fine,
The frail bluebell peereth over
Rare broidery of the purple clover.
TENNYSON—*A Dirge.* St. 6.

19
Here are cool mosses deep,
And thro' the moss the ivies creep,
And in the stream the long-leaved flowers weep,
And from the craggy ledge the poppy hangs in sleep.
TENNYSON—*The Lotos-Eaters. Choric Song.* Pt. I.

20
The slender acacia would not shake
One long milk-bloom on the tree;
The white lake-blossom fell into the lake
As the pimpernel dozed on the lea;
But the rose was awake all night for your sake,
Knowing your promise to me;
The lilies and roses were all awake,
They sighed for the dawn and thee.
TENNYSON—*Maud.* Pt. XXII. St. 8.

21
The daisy, primrose, violet darkly blue;
And polyanthus of unnumbered dyes.
THOMSON—*The Seasons. Spring.* L. 529.

22
Along the river's summer walk,
The withered tufts of asters nod;
And trembles on its arid stalk
The hoar plume of the golden-rod.
And on a ground of sombre fir,
And azure-studded juniper,

The silver birch its buds of purple shows,
And scarlet berries tell where bloomed the sweet
wild-rose!
WHITTIER—*The Last Walk in Autumn.*

1
But when they had unloosed the linen band,
Which swathed the Egyptian's body,—lo! was
found,
Closed in the wasted hollow of her hand,
A little seed, which, sown in English ground,
Did wondrous snow of starry blossoms bear,
And spread rich odours through our springtide air.
OSCAR WILDE—*Athanasia.* St. 2.

2
The very flowers are sacred to the poor.
WORDSWORTH—*Admonition.*

3
To me the meanest flower that blows can give
Thoughts that do often lie too deep for tears.
WORDSWORTH—*Intimations of Immortality.*

4
And 'tis my faith that every flower
Enjoys the air it breathes.
WORDSWORTH—*Lines Written in Early Spring.*

5
The flower of sweetest smell is shy and lowly.
WORDSWORTH—*Sonnet. Not Love, Not War, Nor, etc.*

6
Hope smiled when your nativity was cast,
Children of Summer!
WORDSWORTH—*Staffa Sonnets. Flowers on the Top of the Pillars at the Entrance of the Cave.*

7
The mysteries that cups of flowers infold
And all the gorgeous sights which fairies do be-
hold.
WORDSWORTH—*Stanzas written in Thomson's Castle of Indolence.*

8
There bloomed the strawberry of the wilderness;
The trembling eyebright showed her sapphire
blue,
The thyme her purple, like the blush of Even;
And if the breath of some to no caress
Invited, forth they peeped so fair to view,
All kinds alike seemed favourites of Heaven.
WORDSWORTH—*The River Duddon. Flowers.* VI.

9
Pansies, lilies, kingcups, daisies,
Let them live upon their praises.
WORDSWORTH—*To the Small Celandine.*

FLOWER-DE-LUCE

IRIS

10
Born in the purple, born to joy and pleasance,
Thou dost not toil nor spin,
But makest glad and radiant with thy presence
The meadow and the lin.
LONGFELLOW—*Flower-de-Luce.* St. 3.

11
O flower-de-luce, bloom on, and let the river
Linger to kiss thy feet!
O flower of song, bloom on, and make forever
The world more fair and sweet.
LONGFELLOW—*Flower-de-Luce.* St. 8.

12
Lilies of all kinds,
The flower-de-luce being one!
Winter's Tale. Act IV. Sc. 4. L. 126.

FLY

13
We see spiders, flies, or ants entombed and preserved forever in amber, a more than royal tomb.
BACON—*Historia Vitæ et Mortis.*
(Same idea under ANT, BEE)

14
It was prettily devised of Æsop: The fly sat upon the axle-tree of the chariot-wheel, and said, What a dust do I raise!
BACON—*Of Vain-Glory,* attributed to ÆSOP but found in *Fables* of LAURENTIUS ABSTEMIUS.
(See also LA FONTAINE)

15
We see how flies, and spiders, and the like, get a sepulchre in amber, more durable than the monument and embalming of the body of any king.
BACON—*Sylvia Sylvarum.* Century I. Experiment 100.
(Same idea under ANT, BEE)

16
Haceos miel, y paparos han moscas.
Make yourself honey and the flies will devour you.
CERVANTES—*Don Quixote.* II. 43.

17
The fly that sips treacle is lost in the sweets.
GAY—*The Beggar's Opera.* Act. II. Sc. 2. L. 35.

18
To a boiling pot flies come not.
HERBERT—*Jacula Prudentum.*

19
I saw a flie within a beade
Of amber cleanly buried.
HERRICK—*The Amber Bead.*
(See also BACON)

20
The Lord shall hiss for the fly that is in the uttermost part of the rivers of Egypt.
Isaiah. VII. 18.

21
A fly sat on the chariot wheel
And said "what a dust I raise."
LA FONTAINE—*Fables.* Bk. VII. 9. PHÆDRUS. III. 6. *Musca et Mula.*
(See also BACON)

22
Busy, curious, thirsty fly,
Drink with me and drink as I!
Freely welcome to my cup,
Could'st thou sip and sip it up;
Make the most of life you may;
Life is short and wears away.
WILLIAM OLDYS—*The Fly.*

23
Oh! that the memories which survive us here
Were half so lovely as these wings of thine!
Pure relics of a blameless life, that shine
Now thou art gone.
CHARLES (TENNYSON) TURNER—*On Finding a Small Fly Crushed in a Book.*

24
Baby bye
Here's a fly,
Let us watch him, you and I,
How he crawls
Up the walls
Yet he never falls.
THEODORE TILTON—*Baby Bye.*

FOLLY

1
The folly of one man is the fortune of another.
BACON—*Of Fortune.*

2
Un sot trouve toujours un plus sot qui l'admire.
A fool always finds one still more foolish to admire him.
BOILEAU—*L'Art Poétique.* I. 232.

3
Fool me no fools.
BULWER-LYTTON—*Last Days of Pompeii.* Bk. III. Ch. 6.

4
To swallow gudgeons ere they're catch'd.
And count their chickens ere they're hatch'd.
BUTLER—*Hudibras.* Pt. II. Canto III. L. 923.

5
Fools are my theme, let satire be my song.
BYRON—*English Bards and Scotch Reviewers.* L. 6.

6
Folly loves the martyrdom of Fame.
BYRON—*Monody on the Death of the Right Hon. R. B. Sheridan.* L. 68.

7
More knave than fool.
CERVANTES—*Don Quixote.* Pt. I. Bk. IV. Ch. 2.

8
Mas acompañados y paniguados debe di tener la locura que la discrecion.
Folly is wont to have more followers and comrades than discretion.
CERVANTES—*Don Quixote.* II. 13.

9
Young men think old men are fools; but old men know young men are fools.
GEO. CHAPMAN—*All Fools.* Act V. Sc. 1. L. 292. (See also METCALF)

10
Les plus courtes folies sont les meilleures.
The shortest follies are the best.
CHARRON—*Las Sagesse.* Bk. I. Ch. 3.
(See also LA GIRONDIÈRE; also MOLIÈRE under ERROR)

11
Fool beckons fool, and dunce awakens dunce.
CHURCHILL—*Apology.* L. 42.

12
Stultorum plena sunt omnia.
All places are filled with fools.
CICERO—*Epistles.* IX. 22.

13
Culpa enim illa, bis ad eundem, vulgari reprehensa proverbio est.
To stumble twice against the same stone, is a proverbial disgrace.
CICERO—*Epistles.* X. 20.

14
Hain't we got all the fools in town on our side? And ain't that a big enough majority in any town?
S. L. CLEMENS (Mark Twain)—*Huckleberry Finn.* Ch. 26.

15
A fool must now and then be right by chance.
COWPER—*Conversation.* L. 96.

16
The solemn fop; significant and budge;
A fool with judges, amongst fools a judge.
COWPER—*Conversation.* L. 299.
(See also QUINTILIAN, also JOHNSON under WIT)

17
Defend me, therefore, common sense, say I,
From reveries so airy, from the toil
Of dropping buckets into empty wells,
And growing old in drawing nothing up.
COWPER—*Task.* Bk. III. L. 187.
(See also SMITH, YOUNG)

18
L'exactitude est le sublime des sots.
Exactness is the sublimity of fools.
Attributed to FONTENELLE, who disclaimed it.

19
A fool and a wise man are alike both in the starting-place—their birth, and at the post—their death; only they differ in the race of their lives.
FULLER—*The Holy and Profane States. Of Natural Fools.* Maxim IV.

20
A rational reaction against irrational excesses and vagaries of skepticism may * * * readily degenerate into the rival folly of credulity.
GLADSTONE—*Time and Place of Homer.* Introductory.

21
He is a fool
Who only sees the mischiefs that are past.
HOMER—*Iliad.* Bk. XVII. L. 39. BRYANT'S trans.

22
Stultorum incurata malus pudor ulcera celat.
The shame of fools conceals their open wounds.
HORACE—*Epistles.* I. 16. 24.

23
Adde cruorem
Stultitiæ, atque ignem gladio scrutare.
To your folly add bloodshed, and stir the fire with the sword.
HORACE—*Satires.* II. 3. 275.

24
A man may be as much a fool from the want of sensibility as the want of sense.
MRS. JAMESON—*Studies. Detached Thoughts.* P. 122.

25
Fears of the brave and follies of the wise.
SAMUEL JOHNSON. *Vanity of Human Wishes.*

26
Un fat celui que les sots croient un homme de mérite.
A fool is one whom simpletons believe to be a man of merit.
LA BRUYÈRE—*Les Caractères.* XII.

27
Hélas! on voit que de tout temps
Les Petits ont pâti des sottises des grands.
Alas! we see that the small have always suffered for the follies of the great.
LA FONTAINE—*Fables.* II. 4.

28
Ce livre n'est pas long, on le voit en une heure;
La plus courte folie est toujours la meilleure.
This book is not long, one may run over it in an hour; the shortest folly is always the best.
LA GIRANDIÈRE—*Le Recueil des Voyeux Epigrammes.* (See also CHARRON)

1
Qui vit sans folie n'est pas si sage qu'il croit.
He who lives without committing any folly is not so wise as he thinks.
LA ROCHEFOUCAULD—*Maximes.* 209.

2
Un sot n'a pas assez d'étoffe pour être bon.
A fool has not material enough to be good.
LA ROCHEFOUCAULD—*Maximes.* 387.

3
The right to be a cussed fool
Is safe from all devices human,
It's common (ez a gin'l rule)
To every critter born of woman.
LOWELL—*The Biglow Papers.* Second Series. No. 7. St. 16.

4
A fool! a fool! my coxcomb for a fool!
MARSTON—*Parasitaster.*

5
I have play'd the fool, the gross fool, to believe
The bosom of a friend will hold a secret
Mine own could not contain.
MASSINGER—*Unnatural Combat.* Act V. Sc. 2.

6
Young men think old men fools, and old men know young men to be so.
Quoted by CAMDEN *as a saying of* DR. METCALF.

7
Quantum est in rebus inane!
How much folly there is in human affairs.
PERSIUS—*Satires.* I. 1.

8
An old doting fool, with one foot already in the grave.
PLUTARCH—*Morals. On the Training of Children.*

9
The rest on outside merit but presume,
Or serve (like other fools) to fill a room.
POPE—*Dunciad.* Bk. I. L. 136.

10
So by false learning is good sense defac'd;
Some are bewilder'd in the maze of schools,
And some made coxcombs Nature meant but fools.
POPE—*Essay on Criticism.* Pt. I. L. 25.

11
We think our fathers fools, so wise we grow;
Our wiser sons, no doubt, will think us so.
POPE—*Essay on Criticism.* Pt. II. L. 438.

12
For fools rush in where angels fear to tread.
POPE—*Essay on Criticism.* Pt. III. L. 66.

13
The fool is happy that he knows no more.
POPE—*Essay on Man.* Ep. II. L. 264.

14
Whether the charmer sinner it, or saint it,
If folly grow romantic, I must paint it.
POPE—*Moral Essays.* Ep. II. L. 15.

15
Die and endow a college or a cat.
POPE—*Moral Essays.* Ep. III. *To Bathurst.* L. 96.

16
No creature smarts so little as a fool.
POPE—*Prologue to Satires.* L. 84.

17
Leave such to trifle with more grace and ease,
Whom Folly pleases, and whose Follies please.
POPE—*Second Book of Horace.* Ep. II. L. 326.

18
Even a fool, when he holdeth his peace, is counted wise.
Proverbs. XVII. 28.

19
Every fool will be meddling.
Proverbs. XX. 3.

20
Answer a fool according to his folly.
Proverbs. XXVI. 5.

21
Though thou shouldest bray a fool in a mortar among wheat with a pestle, yet will not his foolishness depart from him.
Proverbs. XXVII. 22.

22
The fool hath said in his heart, There is no God.
Psalms. XIV. 1; LIII. 1.

23
Qui stultis videri eruditi volunt, stulti eruditis videntur.
Those who wish to appear wise among fools, among the wise seem foolish.
QUINTILIAN. X. 7. 22.
(See also COWPER)

24
After a man has sown his wild oats in the years of his youth, he has still every year to get over a few weeks and days of folly.
RICHTER—*Flower, Fruit, and Thorn Pieces.* Bk. II. Ch. V.

25
Stultus est qui fructus magnarum arborum spectat, altitudinem non metitur.
He is a fool who looks at the fruit of lofty trees, but does not measure their height.
QUINTUS CURTIUS RUFUS—*De Rebus Gestis Alexandri Magni.* VII. 8.

26
Insipientis est dicere, Non putaram.
It is the part of a fool to say, I should not have thought.
SCIPIO AFRICANUS. See Cicero. *De Off.* XXIII. 81. VALERIUS. Bk. VII. 2. 2.

27
Where lives the man that has not tried,
How mirth can into folly glide,
And folly into sin!
SCOTT—*Bridal of Triermain.* Canto I. St. 21.

28
Inter cætera mala hoc quoque habet
Stultitia semper incipit vivere.
Among other evils folly has also this, that it is always beginning to live.
SENECA—*Epistolæ Ad Lucilium.* 13.

29
Sir, for a *quart d'écu* he will sell the fee-simple of his salvation, the inheritance of it; and cut the entail from all remainders.
All's Well That Ends Well. Act. IV. Sc. 3. L. 311.

30
A fool, a fool! I met a fool i' the forest,
A motley fool; a miserable world!
As I do live by food, I met a fool;
Who laid him down and bask'd him in the sun.
As You Like It. Act II. Sc. 7. L. 12.

1 O noble fool!
A worthy fool! Motley's the only wear.
As You Like It. Act II. Sc. 7. L. 33.

2
I had rather have a fool to make me merry than experience to make me sad: and to travel for it too!
As You Like It. Act IV. Sc. 1. L. 26.

3
The fool doth think he is wise, but the wise man knows himself to be a fool.
As You Like It. Act V. Sc. 1. L. 34.

4
Fools are not mad folks.
Cymbeline. Act II. Sc. 3. L. 105.

5
Let the doors be shut upon him, that he may play the fool nowhere but in's own house.
Hamlet. Act III. Sc. 1. L. 134.

6
Well, thus we play the fools with the time, and the spirits of the wise sit in the clouds and mock us.
Henry IV. Pt. II. Act II. Sc. 2. L. 154.

7
How ill white hairs become a fool and jester!
Henry IV. Pt. II. Act V. Sc. 5. L. 52.

8
A fool's bolt is soon shot.
Henry V. Act III. Sc. 7. L. 132.

9
The fool hath planted in his memory
An army of good words; and I do know
A many fools, that stand in better place,
Garnish'd like him, that for a tricksy word
Defy the matter.
Merchant of Venice. Act III. Sc. 5. L. 71.

10
Lord, what fools these mortals be!
Midsummer Night's Dream. Act III. Sc. 2. L. 115.

11
To wisdom he's a fool that will not yield.
Pericles. Act II. Sc. 4. L. 54.

12
This fellow is wise enough to play the fool;
And to do that well craves a kind of wit.
Twelfth Night. Act III. Sc. 1. L. 67.

13
Marry, sir, they praise me and make an ass of me; now my foes tell me plainly I am an ass; so that by my foes, sir, I profit in the knowledge of myself.
Twelfth Night. Act V. Sc. 1. L. 19.

14
I hold him but a fool that will endanger
His body for a girl that loves him not.
Two Gentlemen of Verona. Act V. Sc. 4. L. 133.

15 You may as well
Forbid the sea for to obey the moon
As or by oath remove or counsel shake
The fabric of his folly.
Winter's Tale. Act I. Sc. 2. L. 426.

16
'Tis not by guilt the onward sweep
Of truth and right, O Lord, we stay;
'Tis by our follies that so long
We hold the earth from heaven away.
E. R. Sill—*The Fool's Prayer.*

17
He has spent all his life in letting down empty buckets into empty wells, and he is frittering away his age in trying to draw them up again.
Sydney Smith—*Lady Holland's Memoir.* Vol. I. P. 259.
(See also Cowper)

18
For take thy ballaunce if thou be so wise,
And weigh the winde that under heaven doth blow;
Or weigh the light that in the east doth rise;
Or weigh the thought that from man's mind doth flow.
Spenser—*Faerie Queene.* Bk. V. Canto II. St. 43.

19
He had been eight years upon a project for extracting sunbeams out of cucumbers, which were to be put in phials hermetically sealed, and let out to warm the air in raw, inclement summers.
Swift—*Gulliver's Travels.* Pt. III. Ch. V. *Voyage to Laputa.*

20
Chi conta i colpi e la dovuta offesa,
Mentr' arde la tenzon, misura e pesa?
A fool is he that comes to preach or prate,
When men with swords their right and wrong debate.
Tasso—*Gerusalemme.* V. 57.

21
Le sot est comme le peuple, qui se croit riche de peu.
The fool is like those people who think themselves rich with little.
Vauvenargues—*Reflexions.* CCLX.

22
Qui se croit sage, ô ciel! est un grand fou.
He who thinks himself wise, O heavens! is a great fool.
Voltaire—*Le Droit du Seigneur.* IV. 1.

23
The greatest men
May ask a foolish question, now and then.
John Wolcot—*The Apple Dumpling and the King.*

24 Be wise with speed;
A fool at forty is a fool indeed.
Young—*Love of Fame.* Satire II. L. 281.

25
At thirty man suspects himself a fool;
Knows it at forty, and reforms his plan.
Young—*Night Thoughts.* Night I. L. 417.

26 To climb life's worn, heavy wheel
Which draws up nothing new.
Young—*Night Thoughts.* Night III.
(See also Cowper)

27
Men may live fools, but fools they cannot die.
Young—*Night Thoughts.* Night IV. Last line.

28
We bleed, we tremble; we forget, we smile—
The mind turns fool, before the cheek is dry.
Young—*Night Thoughts.* Night V. L. 511.

FOOT

1
My feet, they haul me Round the House,
They Hoist me up the Stairs;
I only have to steer them, and
They Ride me Everywheres.
GELETT BURGESS—*My Feet.*

2
And the prettiest foot! Oh, if a man could but fasten his eyes to her feet, as they steal in and out, and play at bo-peep under her petticoats!
CONGREVE—*Love for Love.* Act I. Sc. 1.
(See also HERRICK)

3
It is a suggestive idea to track those worn feet backward through all the paths they have trodden ever since they were the tender and rosy little feet of a baby, and (cold as they now are) were kept warm in his mother's hand.
HAWTHORNE—*The Marble Faun.* Vol. I. Ch. XXI.

4
Better a barefoot than none.
HERBERT—*Jacula Prudentum.*

5
Her pretty feet
Like snails did creep
A little out, and then,
As if they played at bo-peep
Did soon draw in agen.
HERRICK—*Upon her Feet.*
(See also CONGREVE, SUCKLING)

6
Feet that run on willing errands!
LONGFELLOW—*Hiawatha.* Pt. X. *Hiawatha's Wooing.* L. 33.

7
'Tis all one as if they should make the Standard for the measure, we call a Foot, a Chancellor's Foot; what an uncertain Measure would this be! one Chancellor has a long Foot, another a short Foot, a Third an indifferent Foot. 'Tis the same thing in the Chancellor's Conscience.
JOHN SELDEN—*Table Talk. Equity.*

8
Nay, her foot speaks.
Troilus and Cressida. Act IV. Sc. 5. L. 56.

9
O, so light a foot
Will ne'er wear out the everlasting flint.
Romeo and Juliet. Act II. Sc. 6. L. 16.

10
O happy earth,
Whereon thy innocent feet doe ever tread!
SPENSER—*Faerie Queene.* Bk. I. Canto X. St. 9.

11
Her feet beneath her petticoat,
Like little mice, stole in and out,
As if they feared the light:
But oh! she dances such a way!
No sun upon an Easter day
Is half so fine a sight.
SIR JOHN SUCKLING—*Ballad Upon a Wedding.* St. 8.
(See also HERRICK)

12
And feet like sunny gems on an English green.
TENNYSON—*Maud.* Pt. V. St. 2.

FOOTSTEPS

13
The tread
Of coming footsteps cheats the midnight watcher
Who holds her heart and waits to hear them pause,
And hears them never pause, but pass and die.
GEORGE ELIOT—*The Spanish Gypsy.* Bk. III.

14
There scatter'd oft the earliest of ye Year
By Hands unseen are showers of Vi'lets found;
The Redbreast loves to build and warble there,
And little Footsteps lightly print the ground.
GRAY—MS of *Elegy in a Country Churchyard.* Corrections made by Gray are "year" for "Spring", "showers" for "frequent", "redbreast" for "robin".

15
Vestigia terrent
Omnia te adversum spectantia, nulla retrorsum.
The footsteps are terrifying, all coming towards you and none going back again.
HORACE—*Ep.* Bk. I. 1. 74. *Quoted* Vestigia nulla retrorsum.

16
And so to tread
As if the wind, not she, did walk;
Nor prest a flower, nor bow'd a stalk.
BEN JONSON—*Masques. The Vision of Delight.*

17
Her treading would not bend a blade of grass,
Or shake the downy blow-ball from his stalk!
BEN JONSON—*The Sad Shepherd.*

18
A foot more light, a step more true,
Ne'er from the heath-flower dashed the dew.
SCOTT—*Lady of the Lake.* Canto I. St. 18.

19
The grass stoops not, she treads on it so light.
Venus and Adonis. L. 1,028.

20
Steps with a tender foot, light as on air,
The lovely, lordly creature floated on.
TENNYSON—*The Princess.* VI. L. 72.

21
Sed summa sequar fastigia rerum.
But I will trace the footsteps of the chief events.
VERGIL—*Æneid.* I. 342.

22
Methought I saw the footsteps of a throne.
WORDSWORTH—*Miscellaneous Sonnets. Methought I Saw the Footsteps of a Throne.*

FOPPERY

23
'Tis mean for empty praise of wit to write,
As fopplings grin to show their teeth are white.
BROWN—*Essay on Satire.* St. 2.

24
I marched the lobby, twirled my stick,
* * * * *
The girls all cried, "He's quite the kick."
GEO. COLMAN (The Younger)—*Broad Grins. Song.* St. 1.

25
Of all the fools that pride can boast,
A Coxcomb claims distinction most.
GAY—*Fables.* Pt. II. Fable 5.

1
A beau is one who arranges his curled locks gracefully, who ever smells of balm, and cinnamon; who hums the songs of the Nile, and Cadiz; who throws his sleek arms into various attitudes; who idles away the whole day among the chairs of the ladies, and is ever whispering into some one's ear; who reads little billets-doux from this quarter and that, and writes them in return; who avoids ruffling his dress by contact with his neighbour's sleeve, who knows with whom everybody is in love; who flutters from feast to feast, who can recount exactly the pedigree of Hirpinus. What do you tell me? is this a beau, Cotilus? Then a beau, Cotilus, is a very trifling thing.

MARTIAL—*Epigrams*. Bk. III. Ep. 6.

2
Nature made every fop to plague his brother,
Just as one beauty mortifies another.

POPE—*Satire IV*. L. 258.

3
A lofty cane, a sword with silver hilt,
A ring, two watches, and a snuff box gilt.

Recipe "*To Make a Modern Fop*." (About 1770)

4
This is the excellent foppery of the world.

King Lear. Act I. Sc. 2. L. 128.

5
A fop? In this brave, licentious age
To bring his musty morals on the stage?
Rhime us to reason? and our lives redress
In metre, as Druids did the savages.

TUKE—*The Adventures of Five Hours*. Act V.

6
Has death his fopperies?

YOUNG—*Night Thoughts*. Night II. L. 231.

FORGETFULNESS (See also OBLIVION)

7
But my thoughts ran a wool-gathering; and I did like the countryman, who looked for his ass while he was mounted on his back.

CERVANTES—*Don Quixote*. Pt. II. Ch. LVII.

8
The pyramids themselves, doting with age, have forgotten the names of their founders.

FULLER—*Holy and Profane States. Of Tombs.* Maxim VI.

9
A man must *get* a thing before he can *forget* it.

HOLMES—*Medical Essays*. 300.

10
The wind blows out, the bubble dies;
The spring entomb'd in autumn lies;
The dew dries up; the star is shot;
The flight is past—and man forgot.

Attributed to DR. HENRY KING. Credited to FRANCIS BEAUMONT (1600) in a periodical pub. about 1828.

11
God of our fathers, known of old,
  Lord of our far-flung battle-line,
Beneath whose awful Hand we hold
  Dominion over palm and pine—
Lord God of Hosts, be with us yet,
Lest we forget—lest we forget!

KIPLING—*Recessional Hymn*.

12
The tumult and the shouting dies,
  The captains and the kings depart;
Still stands thine ancient sacrifice,
  A humble and a contrite heart.
Lord God of Hosts, be with us yet
Lest we forget,—lest we forget.

KIPLING—*Recessional Hymn*.

Perhaps of Biblical inspiration. "He smelleth the battle afar off, the thunder of the captains, and the shouting."

Job. XXXIX. 25.

13
Forgotten? No, we never do forget:
We let the years go; wash them clean with tears,
Leave them to bleach out in the open day,
Or lock them careful by, like dead friends' clothes,
Till we shall dare unfold them without pain,—
But we forget not, never can forget.

D. M. MULOCK—*A Flower of a Day*.

14
Mistakes remember'd are not faults forgot.

R. H. NEWELL—*The Orpheus C. Kerr Papers. Second Series. Columbia's Agony*. St. 9.

15
Intrantis medici facies tres esse videntur
Ægrotanti; hominis, Dæmonis, atque Dei.
Cum primum accessit medicus dixitque salutem,
En Deus aut custos angelus, æger ait.

To the sick man the physician when he enters seems to have three faces, those of a man, a devil, a god. When the physician first comes and announces the safety of the patient, then the sick man says: "Behold a God or a guardian angel!

JOHN OWEN—*Works*.

16
God and the Doctor we alike adore
But only when in danger, not before;
The danger o'er, both are alike requited,
God is forgotten, and the Doctor slighted.

JOHN OWEN—*Epigram*.

17
Our God and soldier we alike adore,
When at the brink of ruin, not before;
After deliverance both alike requited,
Our God forgotten, and our soldiers slighted.

QUARLES—*Epigram*.

(See also KIPLING under SOLDIERS)

18
If I forget thee, O Jerusalem, let my right hand forget her cunning.

Psalms. CXXXVII. 5.

19
We bury love,
Forgetfulness grows over it like grass;
That is a thing to weep for, not the dead.

ALEXANDER SMITH—*City Poems. A Boy's Poem*. Pt. III.

20
One day I wrote her name upon the strand,
  But came the waves and washed it away;
Agayne I wrote it with a second hand,
  But came the tyde and made my paynes his prey.

SPENSER—*Sonnet LXXV*.

1
Etiam oblivisci quod scis interdum expedit.
It is sometimes expedient to forget what you know.
SYRUS—*Maxims.*

2
And have you been to Borderland?
Its country lies on either hand
Beyond the river I-forget.
One crosses by a single stone
So narrow one must pass alone,
And all about its waters fret—
The laughing river I-forget.
HERMAN KNICKERBOCKER VIELE—*Borderland.*

3
Go, forget me—why should sorrow
O'er that brow a shadow fling?
Go, forget me—and to-morrow
Brightly smile and sweetly sing.
Smile—though I shall not be near thee;
Sing—though I shall never hear thee.
CHARLES WOLFE—*Song. Go, Forget Me!*

FORGET-ME-NOT

Myosotis

4
The blue and bright-eyed floweret of the brook,
Hope's gentle gem, the sweet Forget-me-not.
COLERIDGE—*The Keepsake.*

5
The sweet forget-me-nots,
That grow for happy lovers.
TENNYSON—*The Brook.* L. 172.

FORGIVENESS

6
Good, to forgive;
Best to forget.
ROBERT BROWNING—*La Saisiaz. Prologue.*

7
The fairest action of our human life
Is scorning to revenge an injury;
For who forgives without a further strife,
His adversary's heart to him doth tie:
And 'tis a firmer conquest, truly said,
To win the heart than overthrow the head.
LADY ELIZABETH CAREW—*Chorus from "Maxiam."*

8
Qui pardonne aisément invite à l'offenser.
He who forgives readily only invites offense.
CORNEILLE—*Cinna.* IV. 4.

9
We read that we ought to forgive our enemies; but we do not read that we ought to forgive our friends.
Attributed to COSMUS, Duke of Florence, by BACON. *Apothegms.* No. 206.

10
Thou whom avenging pow'rs obey,
Cancel my debt (too great to pay)
Before the sad accounting day.
WENTWORTH DILLON—*On the Day of Judgment.* St. 11.

11
Forgiveness to the injured does belong,
But they ne'er pardon who have done the wrong.
DRYDEN—*Conquest of Granada.* Pt. II. Act I. Sc. 2.
(See also HERBERT, SENECA)

12
She hugged the offender, and forgave the offense,
Sex to the last.
DRYDEN—*Cymon and Iphigenia.* L. 367.

13
His heart was as great as the world, but there was no room in it to hold the memory of a wrong.
EMERSON—*Letters and Social Aims. Greatness.*

14
Bear and forbear.
EPICTETUS. See GELLIUS. Bk. XVII. 6.

15
The offender never pardons.
HERBERT—*Jacula Prudentum.* No. 563.

16
Æquum est
Peccatis veniam poscentem reddere rursus.
It is right for him who asks forgiveness for his offenses to grant it to others.
HORACE—*Satires.* I. 3. 74.

17
Ex humili magna ad fastigia rerum
Extollit, quoties voluit fortuna jocari.
Whenever fortune wishes to joke, she lifts people from what is humble to the highest extremity of affairs.
JUVENAL—*Satires.* III. 39.

18
Know all and you will pardon all.
THOMAS À KEMPIS—*Imitation of Christ.*
(See also DE STAËL)

19
For 'tis sweet to stammer one letter
Of the Eternal's language;—on earth it is called
Forgiveness!
LONGFELLOW—*The Children of the Lord's Supper.* L. 214.

20
These evils I deserve, and more
* * * * * *
Justly, yet despair not of his final pardon,
Whose ear is ever open, and his eye
Gracious to re-admit the suppliant.
MILTON—*Samson Agonistes.* L. 1,170.

21
Oh Thou, who Man of baser Earth didst make,
And ev'n with Paradise devise the snake;
For all the Sin wherewith the Face of Man
Is blackened—Man's forgiveness give and take!
OMAR KHAYYAM—*Rubaiyat.* St. 81. (later ed.) Stanza an interpolation of FITZGERALD'S own.

22
Forgiveness is better than revenge.
PITTACUS—*Quoted by Heraclitus.*

23
Humanum amare est, humanum autem ignoscere est.
To love is human, it is also human to forgive.
PLAUTUS—*Mercator.* II. 2. 46.
(See also under ERROR)

24
Good-nature and good-sense must ever join;
To err is human, to forgive, divine.
POPE—*Essay on Criticism.* L. 522.

25
What if this cursed hand
Were thicker than itself with brother's blood?
Is there not rain enough in the sweet heavens
To wash it white as snow?
Hamlet. Act III. Sc. 3. L. 43.

1
I pardon him, as God shall pardon me.
Richard II. Act V. Sc. 3. L. 131.

2
Tout comprendre rend tres-indulgent.
To understand makes one very indulgent.
MADAME DE STAËL—*Corinne.*—Bk. XVIII. Ch. V.
(See also À KEMPIS)

3
Pardon, not wrath, is God's best attribute.
BAYARD TAYLOR—*Poems of the Orient. Temptation of Hassan Ben Khaled.* St. 11. L. 31.

4
The sin
That neither God nor man can well forgive.
TENNYSON—*Sea Dreams.*

5
Ignoscito sæpe alter, nunquam tibi.
Forgive others often, yourself never.
SYRUS—*Maxims.*

6
Menschlich ist es bloss zu strafen
Aber göttlich zu verzeihn.
It is manlike to punish but godlike to forgive.
P. VON WINTER.

FORTUNE

7
To be fortunate is God, and more than God to mortals.
ÆSCHYLUS—*Choëphoræ.* 60.

8
Si fortuna juvat, caveto tolli;
Si fortuna tonat, caveto mergi.
If fortune favors you do not be elated; if she frowns do not despond.
AUSONIUS—*Septem Sapientium Sententiæ Septenis Versibus Explicatæ.* IV. 6.

9
That conceit, elegantly expressed by the Emperor Charles V., in his instructions to the King, his son, "that fortune hath somewhat the nature of a woman, that if she be too much wooed she is the farther off."
BACON—*Adv. Learning.* Bk. II.

10
Therefore if a man look sharply and attentively, he shall see Fortune: for though she be blind, yet she is not invisible.
BACON—*Essays. Of Fortune.*

11
Fortune, now see, now proudly
Pluck off thy veil, and view thy triumph; look,
Look what thou hast brought this land to!—
BEAUMONT AND FLETCHER—*The Tragedy of Bonduca.* Act V. Sc. 5.

12
Just for a handful of silver he left us,
Just for a ribbon to stick in his coat;
Found the one gift of which Fortune bereft us,
Lost all the others she lets us devote.
ROBERT BROWNING—*The Lost Leader.* Referring to WORDSWORTH when he turned Tory.
(See also GOLDSMITH under GENIUS)

13
Cæsarem vehis, Cæsarisque fortunam.
You carry Cæsar and Cæsar's fortune.
CÆSAR'S *remark to a pilot in a storm.* Sometimes given: Cæsarem portas et fortunam ejus. See BACON—*Essays. Of Fortune.*

14
Fortune, the great commandress of the world,
Hath divers ways to advance her followers:
To some she gives honor without deserving;
To other some, deserving without honor;
Some wit, some wealth,—and some, wit without wealth;
Some wealth without wit; some nor wit nor wealth.
GEO. CHAPMAN—*All Fools.* Act V. Sc. 1.

15
Vitam regit fortuna, non sapientia.
It is fortune, not wisdom, that rules man's life.
CICERO—*Tusculanarum Disputationum.* LIX.

16
Fors juvat audentes.
Fortune favors the brave.
CLAUDIANUS—*Epistles.* IV. 9. CICERO—*De Finibus.* Bk. III. Div. 4. STOBÆUS—*Floril.* Tit. XXX. P. 135. SOPHOCLES—*Deperditorum Dramatum. Fragmenta.*
(See also EURIPIDES, OVID, SOMERVILLE, STATIUS, VERGIL, also TIBULLUS under DARING)

17
Eheu! quam brevibus pereunt ingentia fatis.
Alas! by what slight means are great affairs brought to destruction.
CLAUDIANUS—*In Rufinum.* II. 49.

18
If hindrances obstruct thy way,
Thy magnanimity display.
And let thy strength be seen:
But O, if Fortune fill thy sail
With more than a propitious gale,
Take half thy canvas in.
COWPER—*Trans. of Horace.* Bk. II. Ode 10.

19
Ill fortune seldom comes alone.
DRYDEN—*Cymon and Iphigenia.* L. 592.

20
Let fortune empty her whole quiver on me.
I have a soul that, like an ample shield,
Can take in all, and verge enough for more.
DRYDEN—*Don Sebastian.* Act I. Sc. 1.
(See also GRAY under HELL)

21
Neuer thinke you fortune can beare the sway,
Where Virtue's force, can cause her to obay.
QUEEN ELIZABETH—Preserved by GEO. PUTTENHAM in his "*Art of Poesie.*" Bk. III. *Of Ornament,* "which" (he says) "our soueraigne Lady wrote in defiance of Fortune."

22
Fortune truly helps those who are of good judgment.
EURIPIDES—*Pirithous.*
(See also CLAUDIAMUS)

23
Multa intersunt calicem et labrum summum.
Many things happen between the cup and the upper lip.
AULUS GELLIUS—*Trans. of Greek Proverb.* Bk. XIII. 17. 3.

24
Vicissitudes of fortune, which spares neither man nor the proudest of his works, which buries empires and cities in a common grave.
GIBBON—*Decline and Fall of the Roman Empire.* Ch. LXXI.

1
Das Glück erhebe billig der Beglückte.
It is the fortunate who should extol fortune.
GOETHE—*Torquato Tasso.* II. 3. 115.

2
Ein Tag der Gunst ist wie ein Tag der Ernte,
Man muss geschäftig sein sobald sie reift.
The day of fortune is like a harvest day,
We must be busy when the corn is ripe.
GOETHE—*Torquato Tasso.* IV. 4. 62.

3
Too poor for a bribe, and too proud to importune;
He had not the method of making a fortune.
GRAY—*On his own Character.*

4
Fortune, men say, doth give too much to many,
But yet she never gave enough to any.
SIR JOHN HARRINGTON—*Epigram. Of Fortune.*

5
The bitter dregs of Fortune's cup to drain.
HOMER—*Iliad.* Bk. XX. L. 85. POPE's trans.

6
Laudo manentem; si celeres quatit
Pennas, resigno quæ dedit, et mea
Virtute me involvo, probamque
Pauperiem sine dote quæro.
I praise her (Fortune) while she lasts; if she shakes her quick wings, I resign what she has given, and take refuge in my own virtue, and seek honest undowered Poverty.
HORACE—*Carmina.* III. 29.

7
Curtæ nescio quid semper abest rei.
Something is always wanting to incomplete fortune.
HORACE—*Carmina.* III. 24. 64.

8
Cui non conveniet sua res, ut calceus olim,
Si pede major erit subvertet; si minor, uret.
If a man's fortune does not fit him, it is like the shoe in the story; if too large it trips him up, if too small it pinches him.
HORACE—*Epistles.* I. 10. 42.

9 Horæ
Momento cita mors venit aut victoria læta.
In a moment comes either death or joyful victory.
HORACE—*Satires.* I. 1. 7.

10
Fortune, that favours fools.
BEN JONSON—*Alchemist. Prologue. Every Man Out of His Humour.* I. 1. GOOGE—*Eglogs.* (Quoted as a saying.)
(See also CLAUDIANUS)

11
Fortune aveugle suit aveugle hardiesse.
Blind fortune pursues inconsiderate rashness.
LA FONTAINE—*Fables.* X. 14.

12
Il lit au front de ceux qu'un vain luxe environne,
Que la fortune vend ce qu'on croit qu'elle donne.
We read on the forehead of those who are surrounded by a foolish luxury, that Fortune sells what she is thought to give.
LA FONTAINE—*Philémon et Baucis.*

13
La fortune ne paraît jamais si aveugle qu' a ceux à qui elle ne fait pas de bien.
Fortune never seems so blind as to those upon whom she confers no favors.
LA ROCHEFOUCAULD—*Maxims.* 391.

14
Barbaris ex fortuna pendet fides.
The fidelity of barbarians depends on fortune.
LIVY—*Annales.* XXVIII. 17.

15
Non semper temeritas est felix.
Rashness is not always fortunate.
LIVY—*Annales.* XXVIII. 42.

16
Non temere incerta casuum reputat, quem fortuna numquam decepit.
He whom fortune has never deceived, rarely considers the uncertainty of human events.
LIVY—*Annales.* XXX. 30.

17
Raro simul hominibus bonam fortunam bonamque mentem dari.
Men are seldom blessed with good fortune and good sense at the same time.
LIVY—*Annales.* XXX. 42.

18
Fortune comes well to all that comes not late.
LONGFELLOW—*Spanish Student.* Act III. Sc. 5. L. 281.

19
Posteraque in dubio est fortunam quam vehat ætas.
It is doubtful what fortune to-morrow will bring.
LUCRETIUS—*De Rerum Natura.* III. 10. 98.

20
Quivis beatus, versa rota fortunæ, ante vesperum potest esse miserrimus.
Any one who is prosperous may by the turn of fortune's wheel become most wretched before evening.
AMMIANUS MARCELLINUS—*Historia.* XXVI. 8.

21
You are sad in the midst of every blessing. Take care that Fortune does not observe—or she will call you ungrateful.
MARTIAL—*Epigrams.* Bk. VI. Ep. 79.

22
Fortuna multis dat nimis, satis nulli.
Fortune gives too much to many, enough to none.
MARTIAL—*Epigrams.* XII. 10. 2.

23
Audentem forsque Venusque juvant.
Fortune and Love befriend the bold.
OVID—*Ars Amatoria.* I. 608.
(See also CLAUDIANUS)

24
Casus ubique valet: semper tibi pendeat hamus,
Quo minime credas gurgite, piscis erit.
Luck affects everything; let your hook always be cast; in the stream where you least expect it, there will be a fish.
OVID—*Ars Amatoria.* III. 425.

25
Fortuna miserrima tuta est:
Nam timor eventus deterioris abest.
The most wretched fortune is safe; for there is no fear of anything worse.
OVID—*Epistolæ Ex Ponto.* I. 2. 113.

1
Donec eris felix, multos numerabis amicos;
Tempora si fuerint nubila solus eris.

As long as you are fortunate you will have many friends, but if the times become cloudy you will be alone.

OVID—*Tristium.* I. 9. 5.

2
Intera fortunam quisque debet manere suam.

Every man should stay within his own fortune.

OVID—*Tristium.* III. 4. 26.

3
I wish thy lot, now bad, still worse, my friend,
For when at worst, they say, things always mend.

OWEN—*To a Friend in Distress.* COWPER'S trans.

4
C'est la fortune de France.

It is the fortune of France.

PHILIP THE FORTUNATE.

5
Fortuna humana fingit artatque ut lubet.

Fortune moulds and circumscribes human affairs as she pleases.

PLAUTUS—*Captivi.* II. 2. 54.

6
Nulli est homini perpetuum bonum.

No man has perpetual good fortune.

PLAUTUS—*Curculis.* I. 3. 32.

7
Actutum fortunæ solent mutarier; varia vita est.

Man's fortune is usually changed at once; life is changeable.

PLAUTUS—*Truculentus.* II. 1. 9.

8
Fortune had so favoured me in this war that I feared, the rather, that some tempest would follow so favourable a gale.

PLUTARCH quoting PAULUS ÆMILIUS.

9
The wheel goes round and round,
And some are up and some are on the down,
And still the wheel goes round.

JOSEPHINE POLLARD—*Wheel of Fortune.*

10
Fortune in men has some small diff'rence made,
One flaunts in rags, one flutters in brocade;
The cobbler apron'd, and the parson gown'd,
The friar hooded, and the monarch crown'd.

POPE—*Essay on Man.* Ep. IV. L. 195.

11
Who thinks that fortune cannot change her mind,
Prepares a dreadful jest for all mankind.
And who stands safest? Tell me, is it he
That spreads and swells in puff'd prosperity,
Or bless'd with little, whose preventing care
In peace provides fit arms against a war?

POPE—*Second Book of Horace.* Satire II. L. 123.

12
The lines are fallen unto me in pleasant places; yea, I have a goodly heritage.

Psalms. XVI. 6.

13
Præsente fortuna pejor est futuri metus.

Fear of the future is worse than one's present fortune.

QUINTILIAN—*De Institutione Oratoria.* XII. 5.

14
Nihil est periculosius in hominibus mutata subito fortuna.

Nothing is more dangerous to men than a sudden change of fortune.

QUINTILIAN—*De Institutione Oratoria.* CCLX.

15
Centre fortune, la diverse un chartier rompit nazardes son fouet.

Against fortune the carter cracks his whip in vain.

RABELAIS—*Pantagruel.* Bk. II. Ch. XI.

16
Chacun est artisan de sa bonne fortune.

Every one is the architect of his own fortune.

REGNIER—*Satire.* XIII. PSEUDO-SALLUST—*Ep. de Rep. Ordin.* II. 1. Quoting APPIUS CLAUDIUS CÆCUS, the Censor. Same idea in PLAUTUS—*Trinummus.* II. 2. 84. CERVANTES—*Don Quixote.* 1. 4. SCHILLER—*Wallenstein's Death.* XII. 8. 77. METASTASIO—*Morte d'Abele.* II.

17
Sed profecto Fortuna in omni re dominatur; ea res cunctas ex lubidine magis, quam ex vero, celebrat, obscuratque.

But assuredly Fortune rules in all things; she raises to eminence or buries in oblivion everything from caprice rather than from well-regulated principle.

SALLUST—*Catilina.* VIII.

18
Breves et mutabiles vices rerum sunt, et fortuna nunquam simpliciter indulget.

The fashions of human affairs are brief and changeable, and fortune never remains long indulgent.

QUINTUS CURTIUS RUFUS—*De Rebus Gestis Alexandri Magni.* IV. 14. 20.

19
Præcipites regum casus
Fortuna rotat.

Fortune turns on her wheel the fate of kings.

SENECA—*Agamemnon.* LXXI.

20
Quidquid in altum, fortuna tulit, ruitura levat.

Whatever fortune has raised to a height, she has raised only to cast it down.

SENECA—*Agamemnon.* C.

21
Quid non dedit fortuna non eripit.

Fortune cannot take away what she did not give.

SENECA—*Epistolæ Ad Lucilium.* LIX.

22
Felix, quisquis novit famulum
Rogemque pati,
Vultusque potest variare suos!
Rapuit vires pondusque malis,
Casus animo qui tulit æquo.

Happy the man who can endure the highest and the lowest fortune. He, who has endured such vicissitudes with equanimity, has deprived misfortune of its power.

SENECA—*Hercules Œtæus.* 228.

23
Aurea rumpunt tecta quietem,
Vigilesque trahit purpura noctes.
O si pateant pectora ditum,
Quantos intus sublimis agit
Fortuna metus.

Golden palaces break man's rest, and purple robes cause watchful nights.
Oh, if the breasts of the rich could be seen into, what terrors high fortune places within!
SENECA—*Hercules Œtæus*. 646.

1
Iniqua raro maximis virtutibus
Fortuna parcit. Nemo se tuto diu
Periculis offerre tam crebris potest,
Quem sæpe transit casus, aliquando invenit.
Adverse fortune seldom spares men of the noblest virtues. No one can with safety expose himself often to dangers. The man who has often escaped is at last caught.
SENECA—*Hercules Furens*. 325.

2
O Fortuna, viris invida fortibus,
Quam non æque bonis præmia dividis!
O Fortune, that enviest the brave, what unequal rewards thou bestowest on the righteous!
SENECA—*Hercules Furens*. 524.

3
Minor in parvis Fortuna furit,
Leviusque ferit leviora deus.
Fortune is gentle to the lowly, and heaven strikes the humble with a light hand.
SENECA—*Hippolytus*. Act IV. 1,124.

4
Volat ambiguis
Mobilis alis hora; nec ulli
Præstat velox Fortuna fidem.
The shifting hour flies with doubtful wings; nor does swift Fortune keep faith with anyone.
SENECA—*Hippolytus*. Act IV. 1,141.

5
Fortune knows,
We scorn her most, when most she offers blows.
Antony and Cleopatra. Act III. Sc. 11. L. 73.

6
And rail'd on Lady Fortune in good terms.
As You Like It. Act II. Sc. 7. L. 16.

7
Fortune brings in some boats, that are not steer'd.
Cymbeline. Act IV. Sc. 3. L. 46.

8
That they are not a pipe for fortune's finger
To sound what stop she please.
Hamlet. Act III. Sc. 2. L. 75.

9
The great man down, you mark his favorite flies,
The poor advanced makes friends of enemies.
Hamlet. Act III. Sc. 2. L. 214.

10
Will Fortune never come with both hands full,
But write her fair words still in foulest letters?
She either gives a stomach, and no food;
Such are the poor, in health: or else a feast,
And takes away the stomach; such are the rich,
That have abundance, and enjoy it not.
Henry IV. Pt. II. Act IV. Sc. 4. L. 103.

11
Fortune is merry,
And in this mood will give us anything.
Julius Cæsar. Act III. Sc. 2. L. 271.

12
When Fortune means to men most good,
She looks upon them with a threatening eye.
King John. Act III. Sc. 4. L. 119.

13
A good man's fortune may grow out at heels.
King Lear. Act II. Sc. 2. L. 164.

14
Fortune, that arrant whore,
Ne'er turns the key to the poor.
King Lear. Act II. Sc. 4. L. 52.

15
O fortune, fortune! all men call thee fickle.
Romeo and Juliet. Act III. Sc. 5. L. 60.

16
I find my zenith doth depend upon
A most auspicious star; whose influence
If now I court not, but omit, my fortunes
Will ever after droop.
Tempest. Act I. Sc. 2. L. 181.

17
How some men creep in skittish Fortune's hall,
While others play the idiots in her eyes!
Troilus and Cressida. Act III. Sc. 3. L. 134.

18
So is Hope
Changed for Despair—one laid upon the shelf,
We take the other. Under heaven's high cope
Fortune is god—all you endure and do
Depends on circumstance as much as you.
SHELLEY—*Epigrams. From the Greek.*

19
Fortune, my friend, I've often thought,
Is weak, if Art assist her not:
So equally all Arts are vain,
If Fortune help them not again.
SHERIDAN—*Love Epistles of Aristænetus*. Ep. XIII.

20
In losing fortune, many a lucky elf
Has found himself.
HORACE SMITH—*Moral Alchemy*. St. 12.

21
Fortune is like a widow won,
And truckles to the bold alone.
WILLIAM SOMERVILLE—*The Fortune-Hunter*. Canto II.
(See also CLAUDIANUS, also BUTLER under HONOR)

22
Fors æqua merentes
Respicit.
A just fortune awaits the deserving.
STATIUS—*Thebais*. I. 661.

23
Fortuna nimium quem favet, stultum facit.
When fortune favors a man too much, she makes him a fool.
SYRUS—*Maxims*.

24
Fortuna vitrea est, tum cum splendet frangitur.
Fortune is like glass; when she shines, she is broken.
SYRUS—*Maxims*. 283.

25
Miserrima est fortuna quæ inimico caret.
That is a very wretched fortune which has no enemy.
SYRUS—*Maxims*.

26
Felicitate corrumpimur.
We are corrupted by good fortune.
TACITUS—*Annales*. Bk. I. 15.

1
Che sovente addivien che'l saggio è'l forte.
Fabro a se stesso è di beata sorte.
They make their fortune who are stout and wise,
Wit rules the heavens, discretion guides the skies.
TASSO—*Gerusalemme*. X. 20.

2
By wondrous accident perchance one may
Grope out a needle in a load of hay;
And though a white crow be exceedingly rare,
A blind man may, by fortune, catch a hare.
J. TAYLOR—*A Kicksey Winsey*. Pt. VII.

3
The lovely young Lavinia once had friends;
And fortune smil'd, deceitful, on her birth.
THOMSON—*Seasons. Autumn.*

4
Forever, Fortune, wilt thou prove
An unrelenting foe to love,
And, when we meet a mutual heart,
Come in between, and bid us part?
THOMSON—*Song. To Fortune.*

5
For fortune's wheel is on the turn,
And some go up and some go down.
MARY F. TUCKER—*Going Up and Coming Down.*

6
Tollimur in cælum curvato gurgite, et idem
Subducta ad manes imos descendimus unda.
We are carried up to the heaven by the circling wave, and immediately the wave subsiding, we descend to the lowest depths.
VERGIL—*Æneid*. III. 564.

7
Audentes fortuna juvat.
Fortune helps the bold.
VERGIL—*Æneid*. X. 284.
(See also CLAUDIANUS)

8
Non equidem invideo: miror magis.
Indeed, I do not envy your fortune; I rather am surprised at it.
VERGIL—*Eclogæ*. I. 11.

FOX

9
Multa novit vulpes, verum echinus unum magnum.
The fox has many tricks, the hedgehog only one.
ERASMUS—*Adagia*.

10
Tar-baby ain't sayin' nuthin', en brer Fox, he lay low.
JOEL CHANDLER HARRIS—*Tar-Baby Story. Legends of the Old Plantation.* Ch. XII

11
The little foxes, that spoil the vines.
Song of Solomon. IV. 15.

12
Honteux comme un renard qu'une poule aurait pris.
As sheepish as a fox captured by a fowl.
LA FONTAINE—*Fables*. I. 18.

13
Where the lion's skin falls short it must be eked out with the fox's.
LYSANDER—PLUTARCH'S *Life of Lysander*.

FRAILTY

14
Glass antique! 'twixt thee and Nell
Draw we here a parallel.
She, like thee, was forced to bear
All reflections, foul or fair.
Thou art deep and bright within,—
Depths as bright belong'd to Gwynne;
Thou art very frail as well,
Frail as flesh is,—so was Nell.
L. BLANCHARD—*Nell Gwynne's Looking Glass.* St. 1.

15
This is the porcelain clay of human kind.
DRYDEN—*Don Sebastian*. Act I. Sc. 1.

16
Unthought-of Frailties cheat us in the Wise.
POPE—*Moral Essays*. Ep. *To Temple*. L. 69.

17
Frailty, thy name is woman!
Hamlet. Act I. Sc. 2. L. 146.

18
Sometimes we are devils to ourselves,
When we will tempt the frailty of our powers,
Presuming on their changeful potency.
Troilus and Cressida. Act. IV. Sc. 4. L. 96.

19
Alas! our frailty is the cause, not we;
For, such as we are made of, such we be.
Twelfth Night. Act II. Sc. 2. L. 32.

FRANCE

20
La France est une monarchie absolue, tempérée par des chansons.
France is an absolute monarchy, tempered by ballads.
Quoted by CHAMFORT.

21
The Frenchman, easy, debonair, and brisk,
Give him his lass, his fiddle, and his frisk,
Is always happy, reign whoever may,
And laughs the sense of mis'ry far away.
COWPER—*Table Talk*. L. 237.

22
I hate the French because they are all slaves and wear wooden shoes.
GOLDSMITH—*Essays*. 24. (Ed. 1765) Appeared in the *British Magazine*, June, 1760. Also in *Essay on the History of a Disabled Soldier*. DOVE—*English Classics*.

23
Gay, sprightly, land of mirth and social ease
Pleased with thyself, whom all the world can please.
GOLDSMITH—*The Traveller*. L. 241. (Of France.)

24
Adieu, plaisant pays de France!
O, ma patrie
La plus cherie,
Qui a nourrie ma jeune enfance!
Adieu, France—adieu, mes beaux jours.
Adieu, delightful land of France! O my country so dear, which nourished my infancy! Adieu France—adieu my beautiful days!
Lines attributed to MARY QUEEN OF SCOTS, but a forgery of DE QUERLON.

1
Yet, who can help loving the land that has taught us
Six hundred and eighty-five ways to dress eggs?
MOORE—*Fudge Family*. 8.
(See also REGNIÈRE)

2
Have the French for friends, but not for neighbors.
EMPEROR NICEPHORUS (803) while treating with ambassadors of CHARLEMAGNE.

3
On connoit en France 685 manières differentes d'accommoder les œufs.
One knows in France 685 different ways of preparing eggs.
DE LA REYNIÈRE.

4
Ye sons of France, awake to glory!
Hark! Hark! what myriads bid you rise!
Your children, wives, and grandsires hoary,
Behold their tears and hear their cries!
ROUGET DE LISLE—*The Marseilles Hymn.* (1792)

5
Une natione de singes à larynx de parroquets.
A nation of monkeys with the throat of parrots.
SIÉYES—*Note to Mirabeau.* (Of France.)

FRAUD

6
The first and worst of all frauds is to cheat one's self.
BAILEY—*Festus.* Sc. *Anywhere.*

7
Perplexed and troubled at his bad success
The Tempter stood, nor had what to reply,
Discovered in his fraud, thrown from his hope.
MILTON—*Paradise Regained.* Bk. IV. L. 1.

8
So glistered the dire Snake, and into fraud
Led Eve, our credulous mother, to the Tree
Of Prohibition, root of all our woe.
MILTON—*Paradise Lost.* Bk. IX. L. 643.

9
Some cursed fraud
Of enemy hath beguiled thee, yet unknown,
And me with thee hath ruined.
MILTON—*Paradise Lost.* Bk. IX. L. 904.

10
His heart as far from fraud as heaven from earth.
Two Gentlemen of Verona. Act II. Sc. 7. L. 78.

FREEDOM

11
Freedom all solace to man gives:
He lives at ease that freely lives.
JOHN BARBOUR—*The Bruce.* Bk. I. 225.

12
Whose service is perfect freedom.
Book of Common Prayer. Collect for Peace.

13
. . . for righteous monarchs,
Justly to judge, with their own eyes should see;
To rule o'er freemen, should themselves be free.
HENRY BROOKE—*Earl of Essex.* Act I.
(See also JOHNSON under Ox for parody of same)

14
Here the free spirit of mankind, at length,
Throws its last fetters off; and who shall place
A limit to the giant's unchained strength,
Or curb his swiftness in the forward race?
BRYANT—*The Ages.* XXXIII.

15
Hereditary bondsmen! Know ye not
Who would be free themselves must strike the blow?
BYRON—*Childe Harold.* Canto II. St. 76.

16
Yet, Freedom! yet thy banner, torn, but flying,
Streams like the thunder-storm *against* the wind.
BYRON—*Childe Harold.* Canto IV. St. 98.

17
For Freedom's battle once begun,
Bequeath'd by bleeding sire to son,
Though baffled oft is ever won.
BYRON—*Giaour.* L. 123.

18
Sound the loud timbrel o'er Egypt's dark sea!
Jehovah hath triumphed—his people are free.
BYRON—*Sacred Songs. Sound the loud Timbrel.*

19
Hope for a season bade the world farewell,
And Freedom shrieked as Kosciusko fell!
* * * * * *
O'er Prague's proud arch the fires of ruin glow.
CAMPBELL—*Pleasures of Hope.* L. 381.
(See also COLERIDGE)

20
England may as well dam up the waters of the Nile with bulrushes as to fetter the step of Freedom, more proud and firm in this youthful land than where she treads the sequestered glens of Scotland, or couches herself among the magnificent mountains of Switzerland.
LYDIA MARIA CHILD—*Supposititious Speech of James Otis. The Rebels.* Ch. IV.

21
Nulla enim minantis auctoritas apud liberos est.
To freemen, threats are impotent.
CICERO—*Epistles.* XI. 3.

22
O what a loud and fearful shriek was there!
. . .
Ah me! they view'd beneath an hireling's sword
Fallen Kosciusco.
COLERIDGE—*Sonnet*
(See also CAMPBELL)

23
No, Freedom has a thousand charms to show
That slaves, howe'er contented, never know.
COWPER—*Table Talk.* L. 260.

24
He is the freeman whom the truth makes free,
And all are slaves besides.
COWPER—*Task.* Bk. V. L. 733.

25
I want free life, and I want fresh air;
And I sigh for the canter after the cattle,
The crack of the whip like shots in battle,
The medley of horns, and hoofs, and heads
That wars, and wrangles, and scatters and spreads;
The green beneath and the blue above,
And dash, and danger, and life and love.
F. DESPREZ—*Lasca.*

26
I am as free as nature first made man,
Ere the base laws of servitude began,
When wild in woods the noble savage ran.
DRYDEN—*Conquest of Granada.* Act I. Sc. 1.

1
My angel,—his name is Freedom,—
Choose him to be your king;
He shall cut pathways east and west,
And fend you with his wing.
EMERSON—*Boston Hymn.*

2
We grant no dukedoms to the few,
We hold like rights and shall;
Equal on Sunday in the pew,
On Monday in the mall.
For what avail the plough or sail,
Or land, or life, if freedom fail?
EMERSON—*Boston.* St. 5.

3
I gave my life for freedom—This I know;
For those who bade me fight had told me so.
W. N. EWER—*Five Souls.*

4
Bred in the lap of Republican Freedom.
GODWIN—*Enquirer.* II. XII. 402.

5
Yes! to this thought I hold with firm persistence;
The last result of wisdom stamps it true;
He only earns his freedom and existence
Who daily conquers them anew.
GOETHE—*Faust.* Act V. Sc. 6.

6
Frei athmen macht das Leben nicht allein.
Merely to breathe freely does not mean to live.
GOETHE—*Iphigenia auf Tauris.* I. 2. 54.

7
Ay, call it holy ground,
The soil where first they trod,
They have left unstained, what there they found,—
Freedom to worship God.
FELICIA D. HEMANS—*Landing of the Pilgrim Fathers.*

8
Quisnam igitur liber? Sapiens, sibi qui imperiosus;
Quem neque pauperies, neque mors, neque vincula terrent
Responsare cupidinibus, contemnere honores
Fortis; et in se ipso totus, teres atque rotundus.
Who then is free? the wise man who is lord over himself;
Whom neither poverty nor death, nor chains alarm; strong to withstand his passions and despise honors, and who is completely finished and rounded off in himself.
HORACE—*Satires.* Bk. II. VII. 83.
(See also HENLEY under SOUL)

9
In the beauty of the lilies Christ was born across the sea,
With a glory in his bosom that transfigures you and me;
As he died to make men holy, let us die to make men free,
While God is marching on.
JULIA WARD HOWE—*Battle Hymn of the Republic.*

10
One should never put on one's best trousers to go out to fight for freedom.
IBSEN—*Enemy of the People.*

11
All we have of freedom—all we use or know—
This our fathers bought for us, long and long ago.
KIPLING—*The Old Issue.*

12 . . That this nation, under God shall have a new birth of freedom.
ABRAHAM LINCOLN—*Gettysburg Address.*

13
I intend no modification of my oft-expressed wish that all men everywhere could be free.
ABRAHAM LINCOLN—*Letter to Horace Greeley.* Aug. 22, 1862. See RAYMOND'S *History of Lincoln's Administration.*

14
Freedom needs all her poets; it is they
Who give her aspirations wings,
And to the wiser law of music sway
Her wild imaginings.
LOWELL—*Memorial Verses. To the Memory of Hood.* St. 4.

15
Quicquid multis peccatur, inultum est.
All go free when multitudes offend.
LUCAN—*Pharsalia.* V. 260.

16
Libertas ultima mundi
Quo steterit ferienda loco.
The remaining liberty of the world was to be destroyed in the place where it stood.
LUCAN—*Pharsalia.* VII. 580.

17
Non bene, crede mihi, servo servitur amico;
Sit liber, dominus qui volet esse meus.
Service cannot be expected from a friend in service; let him be a freeman who wishes to be my master.
MARTIAL—*Epigrams.* II. 32. 7.

18
Sufficient to have stood, though free to fall.
MILTON—*Paradise Lost.* Bk. III. L. 99.

19
They can only set free men free . . .
And there is no need of that:
Free men set themselves free.
JAMES OPPENHEIM—*The Slave.*
(See also BROOKE)

20
An quisquam est alius liber, nisi ducere vitam
Cui licet, ut voluit?
Is any man free except the one who can pass his life as he pleases?
PERSIUS—*Satires.* V. 83.

21
Oh! let me live my own, and die so too!
(To live and die is all I have to do:)
Maintain a poet's dignity and ease,
And see what friends, and read what books I please.
POPE—*Prologue to Satires.* L. 261.

22
Blandishments will not fascinate us, nor will threats of a "halter" intimidate. For, under God, we are determined that wheresoever, whensoever, or howsoever we shall be called to make our exit, we will die free men.
JOSIAH QUINCY—*Observations on the Boston Port Bill,* 1774.

23
Free soil, free men, free speech, Fremont.
Republican Rallying Cry, 1856.

1
O, nur eine freie Seele wird nicht alt.
Oh, only a free soul will never grow old!
JEAN PAUL RICHTER—*Titan*. Zykel 140.

2
Freiheit ist nur in dem Reich der Träume
Und das Schöne blüht nur im Gesang.
Freedom is only in the land of dreams, and the beautiful only blooms in song.
SCHILLER—*The Beginning of the New Century*. St. 9.

3
Der Mensch ist frei geschaffen, ist frei
Und würd' er in Ketten geboren.
Man is created free, and is free, even though born in chains.
SCHILLER—*Die Worte des Glaubens*. St. 2.

4
Nemo liber est, qui corpori servit.
No man is free who is a slave to the flesh.
SENECA—*Epistolæ Ad Lucilium*. XCII.

5
When the mind's free,
The body's delicate.
King Lear. Act III. Sc. 4. L. 11.

6
The last link is broken
That bound me to thee,
And the words thou hast spoken
Have render'd me free.
FANNY STEERS—*Song*.

7
Rara temporum felicitate, ubi sentire quæ velis, et quæ sentias dicere licet.
Such being the happiness of the times, that you may think as you wish, and speak as you think.
TACITUS—*Annales*. I. 1.

8
Of old sat Freedom on the heights
The thunders breaking at her feet:
Above her shook the starry lights;
She heard the torrents meet.
TENNYSON—*Of old sat Freedom*.

9
Red of the Dawn
Is it turning a fainter red? so be it, but when shall we lay
The ghost of the Brute that is walking and hammering us yet and be free?
TENNYSON—*The Dawn*.

10
The nations lift their right hands up and swear
Their oath of freedom.
WHITTIER—*Garibaldi*.

11
Freedom exists only where the people take care of the government.
WOODROW WILSON. At the Workingman's Dinner, N. Y., Sept. 4, 1912.

12
Our object now, as then, is to vindicate the principles of peace and justice in the life of the world as against selfish and autocratic power, and to set up among the really free and self governed peoples of the world such a concert of purpose and of action as will henceforth insure the observance of those principles.
WOODROW WILSON—*Address to Congress*. (War with Germany being declared.) April 2, 1917.

13
Only free peoples can hold their purpose and their honor steady to a common end, and prefer the interests of mankind to any narrow interest of their own.
WOODROW WILSON—*Address to Congress*. (War with Germany being declared.) April 2, 1917.

14
How does the Meadow flower its bloom unfold?
Because the lovely little flower is free
Down to its root, and in that freedom, bold.
WORDSWORTH—*A Poet! He hath put his Heart to School*.

15
We must be free or die, who speak the tongue
That Shakespeare spake; the faith and morals hold
Which Milton held.
WORDSWORTH—*Sonnets to National Independence and Liberty*. Pt. XVI.

FRIENDS (See also FRIENDSHIP)

16
No friend's a friend till [he shall] prove a friend.
BEAUMONT AND FLETCHER—*The Faithful Friends*. Act III. Sc. 3. L. 50.

17
It is better to avenge a friend than to mourn for him.
Beowulf. VII.

18
Friend, of my infinite dreams
Little enough endures;
Little howe'er it seems,
It is yours, all yours.
ARTHUR BENSON—*The Gift*.

19
I have loved my friends as I do virtue, my soul, my God.
SIR THOMAS BROWNE—*Religio Medici*. Pt. II. Sec. V.

20
Now with my friend I desire not to share or participate, but to engross his sorrows, that, by making them mine own, I may more easily discuss them; for in mine own reason, and within myself, I can command that which I cannot entreat without myself, and within the circle of another.
SIR THOMAS BROWNE—*Religio Medici*. Pt. II. Sec. V.

21
Let my hand,
This hand, lie in your own—my own true friend;
Aprile! Hand-in-hand with you, Aprile!
ROBERT BROWNING—*Paracelsus*. Sc. 5.

22
There is no man so friendless but what he can find a friend sincere enough to tell him disagreeable truths.
BULWER-LYTTON—*What Will He Do With It?* Bk. II. Ch. XIV.

23
We twa hae run about the braes,
And pu'd the gowans fine.
BURNS—*Auld Lang Syne*.

24
His ancient, trusty, drouthy crony,
Tam lo'ed him like a vera brither—
They had been fou for weeks thegither!
BURNS—*Tam o' Shanter*.

1
Ah! were I sever'd from thy side,
Where were thy friend and who my guide?
Years have not seen, Time shall not see
The hour that tears my soul from thee.
BYRON—*Bride of Abydos.* Canto I. St. 11.

2
'Twas sung, how they were lovely in their lives,
And in their deaths had not divided been.
CAMPBELL—*Gertrude of Wyoming.* Pt. III. St. 33.

3
Give me the avowed, the erect, the manly foe;
Bold I can meet—perhaps may turn his blow;
But of all plagues, good Heaven, thy wrath can send,
Save, save, oh! save me from the candid friend.
GEORGE CANNING—*New Morality.*

4
Greatly his foes he dreads, but more his friends,
He hurts me most who lavishly commends.
CHURCHILL—*The Apology.* L. 19.

5
Friends I have made, whom Envy must commend,
But not one foe whom I would wish a friend.
CHURCHILL—*Conference.* L. 297.

6
Amicus est tanquam alter idem.
A friend is, as it were, a second self.
CICERO—*De Amicitia.* XXI. 80. (Adapted.)

7
You must therefore love me, myself, and not my circumstances, if we are to be real friends.
CICERO—*De Finibus.* YONGE'S trans.

8
Our very best friends have a tincture of jealousy even in their friendship; and when they hear us praised by others, will ascribe it to sinister and interested motives if they can.
C. C. COLTON—*Lacon.* P. 80.

9
Soyons amis, Cinna, c'est moi qui t'en convie.
Let us be friends, Cinna, it is I who invite you to be so.
CORNEILLE—*Cinna.* V. 3.

10
I would not enter on my list of friends
(Though graced with polish'd manners and fine sense,
Yet wanting sensibility) the man
Who needlessly sets foot upon a worm.
COWPER—*The Task.* Bk. VI. L. 560.

11
She that asks
Her dear five hundred friends, contemns them all,
And hates their coming.
COWPER—*The Task.* Bk. II. L. 642.

12
The man that hails you Tom or Jack,
And proves by thumps upon your back
How he esteems your merit,
Is such a friend, that one had need
Be very much his friend indeed
To pardon or to bear it.
COWPER—*On Friendship.* 169.
(See also YOUNG)

13
Le sort fait les parents, le choix fait les amis.
Chance makes our parents, but choice makes our friends.
DELILLE—*Pitié.*

14
Les amis—ces parents que l'on se fait soi-même.
Friends, those relations that one makes for one's self.
DESCHAMPS—*L'Ami.*

15
"Wal'r, my boy," replied the captain; "in the Proverbs of Solomon you will find the following words: 'May we never want a friend in need, nor a bottle to give him!' When found, make a note of."
DICKENS—*Dombey and Son.* Vol. I. Ch. XV.

16
Be kind to my remains; and O defend,
Against your judgment, your departed friend.
DRYDEN—*Epistle to Congreve.* L. 72.

17
The poor make no new friends;
But oh, they love the better still
The few our Father sends.
LADY DUFFERIN—*Lament of the Irish Emigrant.*

18
Forsake not an old friend, for the new is not comparable unto him. A new friend is as new wine: when it is old thou shalt drink it with pleasure.
Ecclesiasticus. IX. 10.

19
The fallying out of faithful frends is the reunyng of love.
RICHARD EDWARDS—*The Paradise of Dainty Devices.* No. 42. St. 1.

20
Animals are such agreeable friends—they ask no questions, they pass no criticisms.
GEORGE ELIOT—*Mr. Gilfil's Love-Story.* Ch. VII.

21
Best friend, my well-spring in the wilderness!
GEORGE ELIOT—*The Spanish Gypsy.* Bk. III.

22
Friend more divine than all divinities.
GEORGE ELIOT—*The Spanish Gypsy.* Bk. IV.

23
To act the part of a true friend requires more conscientious feeling than to fill with credit and complacency any other station or capacity in social life.
MRS. ELLIS—*Pictures of Private Life.* Second Series. *The Pains of Pleasing.* Ch. IV.

24
A day for toil, an hour for sport,
But for a friend is life too short.
EMERSON—*Considerations by the Way.*

25
Our friends early appear to us as representatives of certain ideas, which they never pass or exceed. They stand on the brink of the ocean of thought and power, but they never take a single step that would bring them there.
EMERSON—*Essays. Of Experience.*

26
The only way to have a friend is to be one.
EMERSON—*Essays. Of Friendship.*

1
'Tis thus that on the choice of friends
Our good or evil name depends.
GAY—*Old Woman and Her Cats.* Pt. I.

2
An open foe may prove a curse,
But a pretended friend is worse.
GAY—*Shepherd's Dog and the Wolf.* L. 33.

3
Wer nicht die Welt in seinen Freunden sieht
Verdient nicht, dass die Welt von ihm erfahre.
He who does not see the whole world in his friends, does not deserve that the world should hear of him.
GOETHE—*Torquato Tasso.* I. 3. 68.

4
He cast off his friends, as a huntsman his pack;
For he knew, when he pleas'd, he could whistle them back.
GOLDSMITH—*Retaliation.* L. 107.

5
Dear lost companions of my tuneful art,
Dear as the light that visits these sad eyes,
Dear as the ruddy drops that warm my heart.
GRAY—*The Bard.* St. 3.
(See also JULIUS CÆSAR. II. 1)

6
A favourite has no friend.
GRAY—*On a Favourite Cat Drowned.* St. 6.

7
We never know the true value of friends. While they live, we are too sensitive of their faults; when we have lost them, we only see their virtues.
J. C. AND A. W. HARE—*Guesses at Truth.*

8
Devout, yet cheerful; pious, not austere;
To others lenient, to himself sincere.
J. M. HARVEY—*On a Friend.*
(See also ROGERS, Page 103)

9
Before you make a friend eat a bushel of salt with him.
HERBERT—*Jacula Prudentum.*

10
For my boyhood's friend hath fallen, the pillar of my trust,
The true, the wise, the beautiful, is sleeping in the dust.
HILLARD—*On Death of Motley.*

11
Two friends, two bodies with one soul inspir'd.
HOMER—*Iliad.* Bk. XVI. L. 267. POPE'S trans.
(See also BELLINGHAUSEN under LOVE)

12
Dulcis inexpertis cultura potentis amici;
Expertus metuit.
To have a great man for an intimate friend seems pleasant to those who have never tried it; those who have, fear it.
HORACE—*Epistles.* I. 18. 86.

13
True friends appear less mov'd than counterfeit.
HORACE—*Of the Art of Poetry.* L. 486. WENTWORTH DILLON'S trans.

14
The new is older than the old;
And newest friend is oldest friend in this:
That, waiting him, we longest grieved to miss
One thing we sought.
HELEN HUNT JACKSON—*My New Friend.*

15
True happiness
Consists not in the multitude of friends,
But in the worth and choice. Nor would I have
Virtue a popular regard pursue:
Let them be good that love me, though but few.
BEN JONSON—*Cynthia's Revels.* Act III. Sc. 2.

16
'Tis sweet, as year by year we lose
Friends out of sight, in faith to muse
How grows in Paradise our store.
KEBLE—*Burial of the Dead.* St. 11.

17
One faithful Friend is enough for a man's self; 'tis much to meet with such an one, yet we can't have too many for the sake of others.
LA BRUYÈRE—*The Characters or Manners of the Present Age.* Ch. V.

18
Friend of my bosom, thou more than a brother,
Why wert not thou born in my father's dwelling?
LAMB—*The Old Familiar Faces.*

19
I desire so to conduct the affairs of this administration that if at the end, when I come to lay down the reins of power, I have lost every other friend on earth, I shall at least have one friend left, and that friend shall be down inside of me.
LINCOLN—*Reply to Missouri Committee of Seventy.* (1864)

20
O friend! O best of friends! Thy absence more
Than the impending night darkens the landscape o'er!
LONGFELLOW—*Christus.* Pt. II. *The Golden Legend.* I.

21
Yes, we must ever be friends; and of all who offer you friendship
Let me be ever the first, the truest, the nearest and dearest!
LONGFELLOW—*Courtship of Miles Standish.* Pt. VI. *Priscilla.* L. 72.

22
Alas! to-day I would give everything
To see a friend's face, or hear a voice
That had the slightest tone of comfort in it.
LONGFELLOW—*Judas Maccabæus.* Act IV. Sc. 3. L. 32.

23
My designs and labors
And aspirations are my only friends.
LONGFELLOW—*Masque of Pandora. Tower of Prometheus on Mount Caucasus.* Pt. III. L. 74.

24
Ah, how good it feels!
The hand of an old friend.
LONGFELLOW—*New England Tragedies. John Endicott.* Act IV. Sc. 1.

25
Quien te conseja encobria de tus amigos.
Engañar te quiere assaz, y sin testigos.
He who advises you to be reserved to your friends wishes to betray you without witnesses.
MANUEL—*Conde Lucanor.*

26
Let the falling out of friends be a renewing of affection.
LYLY—*Euphues.*
(See also BURTON under LOVE)

1
Women, like princes, find few real friends.
LORD LYTTLETON—*Advice to a Lady*. St. 2.

2
Friends are like melons. Shall I tell you why?
To find one good, you must a hundred try.
CLAUDE MERMET—*Epigram on Friends.*

3
As we sail through life towards death,
Bound unto the same port—heaven,—
Friend, what years could us divide?
D. M. MULOCK—*Thirty Years. A Christmas Blessing.*

4
We have been friends together
In sunshine and in shade.
CAROLINE E. S. NORTON—*We Have Been Friends.*

5
Cætera fortunæ, non mea, turba fuit.
The rest of the crowd were friends of my fortune, not of me.
OVID—*Tristium.* I. 5. 34.

6
Prosperity makes friends and adversity tries them.
Idea found in PLAUTUS—*Stich.* IV. 1. 16. OVID—*Ep. ex Ponto.* II. 3. 23. OVID *Trist.* I. 9. 5. ENNIUS—*Cic. Amicit.* Ch. XVII. METASTASTIO—*Olimpiade.* III. 3. HERDER—*Denksprüche.* CALDERON—*Secret in Words.* Act III. Sc. 3. MENANDER —*Ex Incest. Comoed.* P. 272. ARISTOTLE—*Ethics* VIII. 4. EURIPIDES—*Hecuba.* L. 1226.

7
For all are friends in heaven, all faithful friends;
And many friendships in the days of time
Begun, are lasting here, and growing still.
POLLOK—*Course of Time.* Bk. V. L. 336.

8
Friends given by God in mercy and in love;
My counsellors, my comforters, and guides;
My joy in grief, my second bliss in joy;
Companions of my young desires; in doubt
My oracles; my wings in high pursuit.
Oh! I remember, and will ne'er forget
Our meeting spots, our chosen sacred hours;
Our burning words, that utter'd all the soul,
Our faces beaming with unearthly love;—
Sorrow with sorrow sighing, hope with hope
Exulting, heart embracing heart entire.
POLLOK—*Course of Time.* Bk. V. L. 315.

9
Absent or dead, still let a friend be dear,
(A sigh the absent claims, the dead a tear.)
POPE—*Epistle to Robert, Earl of Oxford.*

10
Trust not yourself; but your defects to know,
Make use of ev'ry friend—and ev'ry foe.
POPE—*Essay on Criticism.* L. 214.

11
Ah, friend! to dazzle let the vain design;
To raise the thought and touch the heart be thine.
POPE—*Moral Essays.* Ep. II. L. 248.

12
A man that hath friends must show himself friendly; and there is a friend that sticketh closer than a brother.
Proverbs. XVIII. 24.

13
Faithful are the wounds of a friend.
Proverbs. XXVII. 6.

14
Iron sharpeneth iron; so a man sharpeneth the countenance of his friend.
Proverbs. XXVII. 17.

15
Mine own familiar friend.
Psalms. XLI. 9.

16
There is no treasure the which may be compared unto a faithful friend;
Gold soone decayeth, and worldly wealth consumeth, and wasteth in the winde;
But love once planted in a perfect and pure minde indureth weale and woe;
The frownes of fortune, come they never so unkinde, cannot the same overthrowe.
Roxburghe Ballads. The Bride's Good-Morrow. Ed. by JOHN PAYNE COLLIER.

17
Dear is my friend—yet from my foe, as from my friend, comes good:
My friend shows what I can do, and my foe what I should.
SCHILLER—*Votive Tablets. Friend and Foe.*

18 Keep thy friend
Under thy own life's key.
All's Well That Ends Well. Act I. Sc. 1. L. 75.

19 We still have slept together,
Rose at an instant, learn'd, play'd, eat together;
And wheresoe'er we went, like Juno's swans,
Still we went coupled and inseparable.
As You Like It. Act I. Sc. 3. L. 75.

20
Those friends thou hast, and their adoption tried,
Grapple them to thy soul with hoops of steel;
But do not dull thy palm with entertainment
Of each new-hatch'd, unfledg'd comrade.
Hamlet. Act I. Sc. 3. L. 59.

21
For who not needs shall never lack a friend,
And who in want a hollow friend doth try,
Directly seasons him his enemy.
Hamlet. Act III. Sc. 2. L. 217.

22
Where you are liberal of your loves and counsels
Be sure you be not loose; for those you make friends
And give your hearts to, when they once perceive
The least rub in your fortunes, fall away
Like water from ye, never found again
But where they mean to sink ye.
Henry VIII. Act II. Sc. 1. L. 126.

23
As dear to me as are the ruddy drops
That visit my sad heart.
Julius Cæsar. Act II. Sc. 1. L. 290.
(See also GRAY)

24
A friend should bear his friend's infirmities,
But Brutus makes mine greater than they are.
Julius Cæsar. Act IV. Sc. 3. L. 86.

25 To wail friends lost
Is not by much so wholesome—profitable,
As to rejoice at friends but newly found.
Love's Labour's Lost. Act V. Sc. 2. L. 759.

1
I would be friends with you and have your love.
Merchant of Venice. Act I. Sc. 3. L. 139.

2
Two lovely berries moulded on one stem:
So, with two seeming bodies, but one heart.
Midsummer Night's Dream. Act III. Sc. 2. L. 211.

3
Words are easy, like the wind;
Faithful friends are hard to find.
Attributed to SHAKESPEARE—*Passionate Pilgrim*. In *Notes and Queries*, June, 1918. P. 174, it is suggested that the lines are by BARNFIELD, being a piracy from JAGGARD'S publication, (1599) a volume containing little of Shakespeare, the majority being pieces by MARLOWE, RALEIGH, BARNFIELD, and others.

4
I am not of that feather to shake off
My friend when he must need me.
Timon of Athens. Act I. Sc. 1. L. 100.

5
For by these
Shall I try friends: you shall perceive how you
Mistake my fortunes; I am wealthy in my friends.
Timon of Athens. Act II. Sc. 2. L. 191.

6
To hear him speak, and sweetly smile
You were in Paradise the while.
SIR PHILIP SIDNEY—*Friend's Passion for his Astrophel*. Attributed also to SPENSER and ROYDON.

7
For to cast away a virtuous friend, I call as bad as to cast away one's own life, which one loves best.
SOPHOCLES—*Œdipus Tyrannis*. OXFORD trans. Revised by BUCKLEY.

8
For whoever knows how to return a kindness he has received must be a friend above all price.
SOPHOCLES—*Philoctetes*. OXFORD trans. Revised by BUCKLEY.

9
'Tis something to be willing to commend;
But my best praise is, that I am your friend.
SOUTHERNE—*To* MR. CONGREVE *on the Old Bachelor*. Last lines.

10
It's an owercome sooth fo' age an' youth,
And it brooks wi' nae denial,
That the dearest friends are the auldest friends,
And the young are just on trial.
STEVENSON—*Underwoods. It's an Owercome Sooth.*

11
Amici vitium ni feras, prodis tuum.
Unless you bear with the faults of a friend you betray your own.
SYRUS—*Maxims*.

12
Amicum lædere ne joco quidem licet.
A friend must not be injured, even in jest.
SYRUS—*Maxims*.

13
Secrete amicos admone, lauda palam.
Reprove your friends in secret, praise them openly.
SYRUS—*Maxims*.

14
A good man is the best friend, and therefore soonest to be chosen, longer to be retained; and indeed, never to be parted with, unless he cease to be that for which he was chosen.
JEREMY TAYLOR—*A Discourse of the Nature, Measures, and Offices of Friendship*.

15
Choose for your friend him that is wise and good, and secret and just, ingenious and honest, and in those things which have a latitude, use your own liberty.
JEREMY TAYLOR—*Discourse of the Nature, Measures, and Offices of Friendship*.

16
When I choose my friend, I will not stay till I have received a kindness; but I will choose such a one that can do me many if I need them; but I mean such kindnesses which make me wiser, and which make me better.
JEREMY TAYLOR—*Discourse of the Nature, Measures, and Offices of Friendship*.

17
Then came your new friend: you began to change—
I saw it and grieved.
TENNYSON *Princess*. IV. L. 270.

18
Ego meorum solus sum meus.
Of my friends I am the only one I have left.
TERENCE—*Phormio*. IV. 1. 21.

19
Fidus Achates.
Faithful Achates (companion of Æneas).
VERGIL—*Æneid*. VI. 158.

20
God save me from my friends, I can protect myself from my enemies.
Attributed to MARSHAL DE VILLARS on taking leave of LOUIS XIV.

21
A slender acquaintance with the world must convince every man, that actions, not words, are the true criterion of the attachment of friends; and that the most liberal professions of good-will are very far from being the surest marks of it.
GEORGE WASHINGTON — *Social Maxims. Friendship. Actions, not Words.*

22
I have *friends* in Spirit Land,—
Not shadows in a shadowy band,
Not *others* but *themselves* are they,
And still I think of them the same
As when the Master's summons came.
WHITTIER—*Lucy Hooper*.

23
Poets, like friends to whom you are in debt, you hate.
WYCHERLEY—*The Plain Dealer*. Prologue.

24
And friend received with thumps upon the back.
YOUNG—*Love of Fame*. Satire I.
(See also COWPER)

25
A friend is worth all hazards we can run.
YOUNG—*Night Thoughts*. Night II. L. 571.

26
A foe to God was ne'er true friend to man,
Some sinister intent taints all he does.
YOUNG—*Night Thoughts*. Night VIII. L. 704.

FRIENDSHIP (See also FRIENDS)

1
Great souls by instinct to each other turn,
Demand alliance, and in friendship burn.
ADDISON—*The Campaign*. L. 102.

2
The friendships of the world are oft
Confederacies in vice, or leagues of pleasure;
Ours has severest virtue for its basis,
And such a friendship ends not but with life.
ADDISON—*Cato*. Act III. Sc. 1.

3
The friendship between me and you I will not compare to a chain; for that the rains might rust, or the falling tree might break.
BANCROFT—*History of the United States. Wm. Penn's Treaty with the Indians.*

4
Friendship! mysterious cement of the soul,
Sweet'ner of life, and solder of society.
BLAIR—*The Grave*. L. 87.

5
Hand
Grasps at hand, eye lights eye in good friendship,
And great hearts expand
And grow one in the sense of this world's life.
ROBERT BROWNING—*Saul*. St. 7.

6
Should auld acquaintance be forgot,
And never brought to mind?
Should auld acquaintance be forgot,
And days o' lang syne?
BURNS—*Auld Lang Syne*. BURNS refers to these words as an old folk song. Early version in JAMES WATSON'S *Collection of Scottish Songs*. (1711)

7
Should old acquaintance be forgot,
And never thought upon.
From an old poem by ROBERT AYTON of Kincaldie.

8
Should auld acquaintance be forgot,
Though they return with scars.
ALLAN RAMSAY'S *Version*. See his *Tea-Table Miscellany*. (1724) Transferred after to JOHNSON'S *Musical Museum*. See S. J. A. FITZGERALD'S *Stories of Famous Songs*.

9
Friendship is Love without his wings!
BYRON—*L'Amitié est l'Amour sans Ailes*. St. 1.
(See also HARE)

10
In friendship I early was taught to believe;
* * * * * *
I have found that a friend may profess, yet deceive.
BYRON—*Lines addressed to the Rev. J. T. Becher*. St. 7.

11
Oh, how you wrong our friendship, valiant youth.
With friends there is not such a word as debt:
Where amity is ty'd with band of truth,
All benefits are there in common set.
LADY CAREW—*Marian*.

12
Secundas res splendidiores facit amicitia, et adversas partiens communicansque leviores.
Friendship makes prosperity brighter, while it lightens adversity by sharing its griefs and anxieties.
CICERO—*De Amicitia*. VI.

13
Vulgo dicitur multos modios salis simul edendos esse, ut amicitia munus expletum sit.
It is a common saying that many pecks of salt must be eaten before the duties of friendship can be discharged.
CICERO—*De Amicitia*. XIX.

14
Friendship is a sheltering tree.
COLERIDGE—*Youth and Age*.

15
Then come the wild weather, come sleet or come snow,
We will stand by each other, however it blow.
SIMON DACH—*Annie of Tharaw*. LONGFELLOW'S trans. L. 7.

16
What is the odds so long as the fire of souls is kindled at the taper of conwiviality, and the wing of friendship never moults a feather?
DICKENS—*Old Curiosity Shop*. Ch. II.

17
Fan the sinking flame of hilarity with the wing of friendship; and pass the rosy wine.
DICKENS—*Old Curiosity Shop*. Ch. VII.

18
For friendship, of itself a holy tie,
Is made more sacred by adversity.
DRYDEN—*The Hind and the Panther*. Pt. III. L. 47.

19
Friendships begin with liking or gratitude—roots that can be pulled up.
GEORGE ELIOT—*Daniel Deronda*. Bk. IV. Ch. XXXII.

20
So, if I live or die to serve my friend,
'Tis for my love—'tis for my friend alone,
And not for any rate that friendship bears
In heaven or on earth.
GEORGE ELIOT—*Spanish Gypsy*.

21
Friendship should be surrounded with ceremonies and respects, and not crushed into corners. Friendship requires more time than poor, busy men can usually command.
EMERSON—*Essays. Behavior*.

22
The highest compact we can make with our fellow is,—Let there be truth between us two forevermore. * * * It is sublime to feel and say of another, I need never meet, or speak, or write to him; we need not reinforce ourselves or send tokens of remembrance; I rely on him as on myself; if he did thus or thus, I know it was right.
EMERSON—*Essays. Behavior*.

23
I hate the prostitution of the name of friendship to signify modish and worldly alliances.
EMERSON—*Essays. Of Friendship*.

24
The condition which high friendship demands is ability to do without it.
EMERSON—*Essays. Of Friendship*.

25
There can never be deep peace between two spirits, never mutual respect, until, in their dialogue, each stands for the whole world.
EMERSON—*Essays. Of Friendship*.

1

A sudden thought strikes me—Let us swear an eternal friendship.

John H. Frere—*The Rovers.* Act I.
(See also Molière, Smith, also Otway under Vows)

2

Friendship, like love, is but a name,
Unless to one you stint the flame.

Gay—*The Hare with Many Friends.*
(See also Goldsmith)

3

To friendship every burden's light.

Gay—*The Hare with Many Friends.*

4

Who friendship with a knave hath made,
Is judg'd a partner in the trade.

Gay—*Old Woman and Her Cats.*

5

And what is friendship but a name,
A charm that lulls to sleep;
A shade that follows wealth or fame,
And leaves the wretch to weep?

Goldsmith—*Edwin and Angelina, or The Hermit.* St. 19.
(See also Gay)

6

Friendship closes its eye, rather than see the moon eclipst; while malice denies that it is ever at the full.

J. C. and A. W. Hare—*Guesses at Truth.*

7

Friendship is Love, without either flowers or veil.

J. C. and A. W. Hare—*Guesses at Truth.*
(See also Byron)

8

Fast as the rolling seasons bring
The hour of fate to those we love,
Each pearl that leaves the broken string
Is set in Friendship's crown above.
As narrower grows the earthly chain,
The circle widens in the sky;
These are our treasures that remain,
But those are stars that beam on high.

Holmes—*Songs of Many Seasons. Our Classmate, F. W. C.*, 1864.

9

A generous friendship no cold medium knows,
Burns with one love, with one resentment glows;
One should our interests and our passions be,
My friend must hate the man that injures me.

Homer—*Iliad.* Bk. IX. L. 725. Pope's trans.

10

If a man does not make new acquaintances, as he advances through life, he will soon find himself left alone. A man, Sir, should keep his friendship in constant repair.

Samuel Johnson—*Boswell's Life.* (1755)

11

Friendship, peculiar boon of Heaven,
The noble mind's delight and pride,
To men and angels only given,
To all the lower world denied.

Samuel Johnson—*Friendship. An Ode.*

12

The endearing elegance of female friendship.

Samuel Johnson—*Rasselas.* Ch. XLVI.

13

In Friendship we only see those faults which may be prejudicial to our friends. In love we see no faults but those by which we suffer ourselves.

La Bruyère—*Characters or Manners of the Present Age.* Ch. V.

14

Love and friendship exclude each other.

La Bruyère—*Characters or Manners of the Present Age.* Ch. V.

15

Pure friendship is something which men of an inferior intellect can never taste.

La Bruyère—*Characters or Manners of the Present Age.* Ch. V.

16

Come back! ye friendships long departed!
That like o'erflowing streamlets started,
And now are dwindled, one by one,
To stony channels in the sun!
Come back! ye friends, whose lives are ended,
Come back, with all that light attended,
Which seemed to darken and decay
When ye arose and went away!

Longfellow—*Christus.* Pt. II. *The Golden Legend.* I.

17

"You will forgive me, I hope, for the sake of the friendship between us,
Which is too true and too sacred to be so easily broken!"

Longfellow—*The Courtship of Miles Standish. Priscilla.* Pt. VI. L. 22.

18

Nulla fides regni sociis omnisque potestas
Impatiens consortis erit.

There is no friendship between those associated in power; he who rules will always be impatient of an associate.

Lucan—*Pharsalia.* I. 92.

19

My fair one, let us swear an eternal friendship.

Molière—*Le Bourgeois Gentilhomme.* Act IV. Sc. 1. (See also Frere)

20

Oh, call it by some better name,
For Friendship sounds too cold.

Moore—*Oh, call it by some better Name.*

21

Forsooth, brethren, fellowship is heaven and lack of fellowship is hell; fellowship is life and lack of fellowship is death; and the deeds that ye do upon the earth, it is for fellowship's sake that ye do them.

William Morris—*Dream of John Ball.* Ch. IV.

22

Vulgus amicitias utilitate probat.

The vulgar herd estimate friendship by its advantages.

Ovid—*Epistolæ Ex Ponto.* II. 3. 8.

23

Scilicet ut fulvum spectatur in ignibus aurum
Tempore in duro est inspicienda fides.

As the yellow gold is tried in fire, so the faith of friendship must be seen in adversity.

Ovid—*Tristium.* I. 5. 25.

1
Quod tuum'st meum'st; omne meum est autem tuum.
What is thine is mine, and all mine is thine.
PLAUTUS—*Trinummus*. II. 2. 47.

2
What ill-starr'd rage
Divides a friendship long confirm'd by age?
POPE—*Dunciad*. Bk. III. L. 173.

3
There is nothing that is meritorious but virtue and friendship; and indeed friendship itself is only a part of virtue.
POPE—*Johnson's Lives of the Poets; Life of Pope*.

4
Idem velle et idem nolle ea demum firma amicitia est.
To desire the same things and to reject the same things, constitutes true friendship.
SALLUST—*Catilina*. XX. From Cataline's Oration to his Associates.

5
Saul and Jonathan were lovely and pleasant in their lives, and in their death they were not divided.
II Samuel. I. 23.

6
Amicitia semper prodest, amor etiam aliquando nocet.
Friendship always benefits; love sometimes injures.
SENECA—*Epistolæ Ad Lucilium*. XXXV.

7
Most friendship is feigning.
As You Like It. *Song*. Act II. Sc. 7. L. 181.

8
Out upon this half-fac'd fellowship!
Henry IV. Pt. I. Act I. Sc. 3. L. 208.

9
Call you that backing of your friends? A plague upon such backing! give me them that will face me.
Henry IV. Pt. I. Act II. Sc. 4. L. 165.

10
When did friendship take
A breed for barren metal of his friend?
Merchant of Venice. Act I. Sc. 3. L. 134.

11
Friendship is constant in all other things,
Save in the office and affairs of love:
Therefore, all hearts in love use their own tongues;
Let every eye negotiate for itself,
And trust no agent.
Much Ado About Nothing. Act II. Sc. 1. L. 182.

12
Friendship's full of dregs.
Timon of Athens. Act I. Sc. 2. L. 240.

13
The amity that wisdom knits not, folly may easily untie.
Troilus and Cressida. Act II. Sc. 3. L. 110.

14
Madam, I have been looking for a person who disliked gravy all my life; let us swear eternal friendship.
SYDNEY SMITH—*Lady Holland's Memoir*. P. 257. Let us swear an eternal friendship. Poetry of the *Anti-Jacobin*. *The Rovers*.
(See also FRERE)

15
Life is to be fortified by many friendships. To love, and to be loved, is the greatest happiness of existence.
SYDNEY SMITH—*Of Friendship. Lady Holland's Memoir*.

16
I thought you and he were hand-in-glove.
SWIFT—*Polite Conversation*. Dialogue II.

17
Friendship is like rivers, and the strand of seas, and the air, common to all the world; but tyrants, and evil customs, wars, and want of love, have made them proper and peculiar.
JEREMY TAYLOR—*A Discourse of the Nature, Measures, and Offices of Friendship*.

18
Nature and religion are the bands of friendship, excellence and usefulness are its great endearments.
JEREMY TAYLOR—*A Discourse of the Nature, Measures, and Offices of Friendship*.

19
Some friendships are made by nature, some by contract, some by interest, and some by souls.
JEREMY TAYLOR—*A Discourse of the Nature, Measures, and Offices of Friendship*.

20
O friendship, equal-poised control,
O heart, with kindliest motion warm,
O sacred essence, other form,
O solemn ghost, O crowned soul!
TENNYSON—*In Memoriam*. LXXXV.

21
True friendship is a plant of slow growth, and must undergo and withstand the shocks of adversity, before it is entitled to the appellation.
GEORGE WASHINGTON — *Social Maxims. Friendship*.

22
Friendship's the wine of life: but friendship new
* * * is neither strong nor pure.
YOUNG—*Night Thoughts*. Night II. L. 582.

FRUITS (UNCLASSIFIED)

23
The kindly fruits of the earth.
Book of Common Prayer. *Litany*.

24
Nothing great is produced suddenly, since not even the grape or the fig is. If you say to me now that you want a fig, I will answer to you that it requires time: let it flower first, then put forth fruit, and then ripen.
EPICTETUS — *Discourses*. *What Philosophy Promises*. Ch. XV. GEO. LONG's trans

25
Eve, with her basket, was
Deep in the bells and grass
Wading in bells and grass
Up to her knees,
Picking a dish of sweet
Berries and plums to eat,
Down in the bells and grass
Under the trees.
RALPH HODGSON—*Eve*.

26
Ye shall know them by their fruits.
Do men gather grapes of thorns, or figs of thistles?
Matthew. VII. 16; 20.

1 Each tree
Laden with fairest fruit, that hung to th' eye
Tempting, stirr'd in me sudden appetite
To pluck and eat.
MILTON—*Paradise Lost.* Bk. VIII. L. 30.

2
But the fruit that can fall without shaking,
Indeed is too mellow for me.
LADY MARY WORTLEY MONTAGU—*Answered for.*

3
Thus do I live, from pleasure quite debarred,
Nor taste the fruits that the sun's genial rays
Mature, john-apple, nor the downy peach.
JOHN PHILIPS—*The Splendid Shilling.* L. 115.

4
The strawberry grows underneath the nettle
And wholesome berries thrive and ripen best
Neighbour'd by fruit of baser quality.
Henry V. Act I. Sc. 1. L. 60.

5
Fruits that blossom first will first be ripe.
Othello. Act II. Sc. 3. L. 383.

6
Before thee stands this fair Hesperides,
With golden fruit, but dangerous to be touched.
Pericles. Act I. Sc. 1. L. 27.

7
The ripest fruit first falls.
Richard II. Act II. Sc. 1. L. 153.

8 Superfluous branches
We lop away, that bearing boughs may live.
Richard II. Act III. Sc. 4. L. 63.

9
The barberry and currant must escape
Though her small clusters imitate the grape.
TATE—*Cowley.*

10
Let other lands, exulting, glean
The apple from the pine,
The orange from its glossy green,
The cluster from the vine.
WHITTIER—*The Corn Song.*

FURNITURE

11
Carved with figures strange and sweet,
All made out of the carver's brain.
COLERIDGE—*Christabel.* Pt. I.

12
I love it, I love it, and who shall dare
To chide me for loving that old arm-chair?
ELIZA COOK—*Old Arm-Chair.*

13
Joint-stools were then created; on three legs
Upborne they stood. Three legs upholding firm
A massy slab, in fashion square or round.
On such a stool immortal Alfred sat.
COWPER—*Sofa.* Bk. I. L. 19.

14
Ingenious Fancy, never better pleased
Than when employ'd t' accommodate the fair,
Heard the sweet moan of pity, and devised
The soft settee; one elbow at each end,
And in the midst an elbow it received,
United yet divided, twain at once.
COWPER—*Task.* Bk. I. L. 71.

15 Necessity invented stools,
Convenience next suggested elbow-chairs,
And Luxury the accomplish'd Sofa last.
COWPER—*Task.* Bk. I. L. 86.

16
A three-legged table, O ye fates!
HORACE.

17
When on my three-foot stool I sit.
Cymbeline. Act III. Sc. 3. L. 89.

FURY (See ANGER)

FUTURE; FUTURITY

18
That what will come, and must come, shall come well.
EDWIN ARNOLD—*Light of Asia.* Bk. VI. L. 274.

19
Making all futures fruits of all the pasts.
EDWIN ARNOLD—*Light of Asia.* Bk. V. L. 432.

20
Some day Love shall claim his own
Some day Right ascend his throne,
Some day hidden Truth be known;
Some day—some sweet day.
LEWIS J. BATES—*Some Sweet Day.*

21
The year goes wrong, and tares grow strong,
Hope starves without a crumb;
But God's time is our harvest time,
And that is sure to come.
LEWIS J. BATES—*Our Better Day.*

22
Dear Land to which Desire forever flees;
Time doth no present to our grasp allow,
Say in the fixed Eternal shall we seize
At last the fleeting Now?
BULWER-LYTTON—*Corn Flowers.* Bk. I. *The First Violets.*

23
You can never plan the future by the past.
BURKE—*Letter to a Member of the National Assembly.* Vol. IV. P. 55.

24
With mortal crisis doth portend,
My days to appropinque an end.
BUTLER—*Hudibras.* Pt. I. Canto III. L. 589.

25
'Tis the sunset of life gives me mystical lore,
And coming events cast their shadows before.
CAMPBELL—*Lochiel's Warning.*

26
Certis rebus certa signa præcurrunt.
Certain signs precede certain events.
CICERO—*De Divinatione.* I. 52.

27 * * * So often do the spirits
Of great events stride on before the events,
And in to-day already walks to-morrow.
COLERIDGE—*Death of Wallenstein.* Act V. Sc. 1.

28
There shall be no more snow
No weary noontide heat,
So we lift our trusting eyes
From the hills our Fathers trod:
To the quiet of the skies:
To the Sabbath of our God.
FELICIA D. HEMANS—*Evening Song of the Tyrolese Peasants.*

1
Quid sit futurum cras, fuge quærere: et
Quem Fors dierum cunque dabit, lucro
Appone.

Cease to inquire what the future has in store, and to take as a gift whatever the day brings forth.

HORACE—*Carmina*. I. 9. 13.

2
Prudens futuri temporis exitum
Caliginosa nocte premit deus.

A wise God shrouds the future in obscure darkness.

HORACE—*Carmina*. III. 29. 29.

3
You'll see that, since our fate is ruled by chance,
Each man, unknowing, great,
Should frame life so that at some future hour
Fact and his dreamings meet.

VICTOR HUGO—*To His Orphan Grandchildren*.

4
With whom there is no place of toil, no burning heat, no piercing cold, nor any briars there . . . this place we call the Bosom of Abraham.

JOSEPHUS—*Discourse to the Greeks concerning Hades*. HOMER—*Odyssey*. VI. 42.

5
When Earth's last picture is painted, and the tubes are twisted and dried,
When the oldest colours have faded, and the youngest critic has died,
We shall rest, and faith, we shall need it—lie down for an æon or two,
Till the Master of All Good Workmen shall set us to work anew.

KIPLING—*When Earth's Last Picture Is Painted*.

6
Le présent est gros de l'avenir.

The present is big with the future.

LEIBNITZ.

7
Look not mournfully into the Past; it comes not back again. Wisely improve the Present; it is thine.

Go forth to meet the shadowy Future without fear and with a manly heart.

LONGFELLOW—*Hyperion*. Translation.

8
Trust no Future, howe'er pleasant!
Let the dead Past bury its dead!

LONGFELLOW—*A Psalm of Life*.

9
There's a good time coming, boys;
A good time coming:
We may not live to see the day,
But earth shall glisten in the ray
Of the good time coming.
Cannon-balls may aid the truth,
But thought's a weapon stronger;
We'll win our battle by its aid,
Wait a little longer.

CHAS. MACKAY—*The Good Time Coming*.

10
The future is a world limited by ourselves; in it we discover only what concerns us and, sometimes, by chance, what interests those whom we love the most.

MAETERLINCK—*Joyzelle*. Act I.

11
Take therefore no thought for the morrow; for the morrow shall take thought for the things of itself. Sufficient unto the day is the evil thereof.

Matthew. VI. 34.

12
The never-ending flight
Of future days.

MILTON—*Paradise Lost*. Bk. II. L. 221.

13
There was the Door to which I found no key;
There was the Veil through which I might not see.

OMAR KHAYYAM—*Rubaiyat*. St. 32. (Later ed.) FITZ-GERALD's trans.

14
Venator sequitur fugientia; capta relinquit;
Semper et inventis ulteriora petit.

The hunter follows things which flee from him; he leaves them when they are taken; and ever seeks for that which is beyond what he has found.

OVID—*Amorum*. Bk. II. 9. 9.

15
Ludit in humanis divina potentia rebus,
Et certam præsens vix habet hora fidem.

Heaven makes sport of human affairs, and the present hour gives no sure promise of the next.

OVID—*Epistolæ Ex Ponto*. IV. 3. 49.

16
Nos duo turba sumus.

We two [Deucalion and Pyrrha, after the deluge] form a multitude.

OVID—*Metamorphoses*. I. 355.

(See also SUETONIUS)

17
Après nous le déluge.

After us the deluge.

MME. POMPADOUR. After the battle of Rossbach. See LAROUSSE—*Fleurs Historiques*. MADAME DE HAUSSET—*Memoirs*. (Ed. 1824) P. 19. Also attributed to LOUIS XV by the French. Compare CICERO—*De Finibus*. XI. 16.

(See also SUETONIUS)

18
Oh, blindness to the future! kindly giv'n,
That each may fill the circle mark'd by heaven.

POPE—*Essay on Man*. Ep. I. L. 85.

19
In adamantine chains shall Death be bound,
And Hell's grim tyrant feel th' eternal wound.

POPE—*Messiah*. L. 47.

20
And better skilled in dark events to come.

POPE—*Odyssey*. Bk. V. 219.

21
Etwas fürchten und hoffen und sorgen,
Muss der Mensch für den kommenden Morgen.

Man must have some fears, hopes, and cares, for the coming morrow.

SCHILLER—*Die Braut von Messina*.

22
But there's a gude time coming.

SCOTT—*Rob Roy*. Ch. XXXII.

23
Calamitosus est animus futuri anxius.

The mind that is anxious about the future is miserable.

SENECA—*Epistolæ Ad Lucilium*. XCVIII.

1 How many ages hence
Shall this our lofty scene be acted over
In states unborn and accents yet unknown.
Julius Cæsar. Act III. Sc. 1. L. 111.

2 God, if Thy will be so,
Enrich the time to come with smooth-faced peace,
With smiling plenty and fair prosperous days!
Richard III. Act V. Sc. 5. L. 32.

3
Quid crastina volveret ætas,
Scire nefas homini.
Man is not allowed to know what will happen to-morrow.
STATIUS—*Thebais.* III. 562.

4 Could we but know
The land that ends our dark, uncertain travel.
E. C. STEDMAN—*Undiscovered Country.*

5
When the Rudyards cease from Kipling
And the Haggards ride no more.
J. K. STEPHEN—*Lapsus Calami.*

6
When I am dead let the earth be dissolved in fire.
SUETONIUS. Quoting Nero. *Nero.* 38. Quoted by MILTON from TIBERIUS in his *Church Government.* Bk. I. Ch. V. TIBERIUS, quoting an unknown Greek poet. See note of LEUTSCH, Appendix II. 56, to *Proverbs* LVIII. 23. EURIPIDES—*Fragment* Inc. B. XXVII.
(See also OVID, POMPADOUR)

7
Till the sun grows cold,
And the stars are old,
And the leaves of the Judgment Book unfold.
BAYARD TAYLOR—*Bedouin Song.*

8
Istuc est sapere, non quod ante pedes modo est
Videre, sed etiam illa, quæ futura sunt
Prospicere.
That is to be wise to see not merely that which lies before your feet, but to foresee even those things which are in the womb of futurity.
TERENCE—*Adelphi.* III. 3. 32.

9
I hear a voice you cannot hear,
Which says, I must not stay;
I see a hand you cannot see,
Which beckons me away.
TICKELL—*Colin and Lucy.*

10
Dabit deus his quoque finem.
God will put an end to these also.
VERGIL—*Æneid.* I. 199.

G

GAIN

11
Everywhere in life, the true question is not what we *gain*, but what we *do*.
CARLYLE—*Essays.* *Goethe's Helena.*

12
And if you mean to profit, learn to please.
CHURCHILL—*Gotham.* Bk. II. L. 88.

13 Little pains
In a due hour employ'd great profit yields.
JOHN PHILIPS—*Cider.* Bk. I. L. 126.

14
Necesse est facere sumptum, qui quærit lucrum.
He who seeks for gain, must be at some expense.
PLAUTUS—*Asinaria.* I. 3. 65.

15
Share the advice betwixt you: if both gain, all
The gift doth stretch itself as 'tis receiv'd,
And is enough for both.
All's Well That Ends Well. Act II. Sc. 1. L. 3.

16 Men that hazard all
Do it in hope of fair advantages:
A golden mind stoops not to shows of dross.
Merchant of Venice. Act II. Sc. 7. L. 18.

17
No profit grows where is no pleasure ta'en;
In brief, sir, study what you most affect.
Taming of the Shrew. Act I. Sc. 1. L. 39.

18
Lucrum malum æquale dispendio.
An evil gain equals a loss.
SYRUS—*Maxims.*

19
Hoc scitum'st periculum ex aliis facere, tibi quid ex usu sit.
From others' slips some profit from one's self to gain.
TERENCE—*Heauton timorumenos.* I. 2.

20
As to pay, Sir, I beg leave to assure the Congress that as no pecuniary consideration could have tempted me to accept this arduous employment at the expense of my domestic ease and happiness, I do not wish to make any profit from it.
GEORGE WASHINGTON—*In Congress on his Appointment as Commander-in-Chief,* June 16, 1775.

GAMBLING (See also CARDS)

21
Whose game was empires, and whose stakes were thrones;
Whose table earth, whose dice were human bones.
BYRON—*The Age of Bronze.* St. 3.

22
The gamester, if he die a martyr to his profession, is doubly ruined. He adds his soul to every other loss, and by the act of suicide, renounces earth to forfeit Heaven.
C. C. COLTON—*Lacon.* *Reflection.*

23
Our Quixote bard sets out a monster taming.
Arm'd at all points to fight that hydra, gaming.
DAVID GARRICK—*Prologue to Ed. Moore's Gamester.*

1
Shake off the shackles of this tyrant vice;
Hear other calls than those of cards and dice:
Be learn'd in nobler arts than arts of play;
And other debts than those of honour pay.
DAVID GARRICK—*Prologue to Ed. Moore's Gamester.*

2
Look round, the wrecks of play behold;
Estates dismember'd, mortgag'd, sold!
Their owners now to jails confin'd,
Show equal poverty of mind.
GAY—*Fables.* Pt. II. Fable 12.

3
Oh, this pernicious vice of gaming!
ED. MOORE—*The Gamester.* Act I. Sc. 1.

4
I'll tell thee what it says; it calls me villain, a treacherous husband, a cruel father, a false brother; one lost to nature and her charities; or to say all in one short word, it calls me—gamester.
ED MOORE—*The Gamester.* Act II. Sc. 1.

5
Ay, rail at gaming—'tis a rich topic, and affords noble declamation. Go, preach against it in the city—you'll find a congregation in every tavern.
ED. MOORE—*The Gamester.* Act IV. Sc. 1.

6
How, sir! not damn the sharper, but the dice?
POPE—*Epilogue to the Satires.* Dialogue II. L. 13.

7
It [gaming] is the child of avarice, the brother of iniquity, and the father of mischief.
GEORGE WASHINGTON—*Letter to Bushrod Washington.* Jan. 15, 1783.

GARDEN

8
God Almighty first planted a garden.
BACON—*Of Gardens.*
(See also COWPER under CITIES)

9
My garden is a lovesome thing—God wot!
Rose plot,
Fringed pool,
Fern grot—
The veriest school
Of peace; and yet the fool
Contends that God is not.—
Not God in gardens! When the sun is cool?
Nay, but I have a sign!
'Tis very sure God walks in mine.
THOS. EDWARD BROWN—*My Garden.*

10
God the first garden made, and the first city Cain.
ABRAHAM COWLEY—*The Garden.* Essay V.
(See also BACON)

11
My garden is a forest ledge
Which older forests bound;
The banks slope down to the blue lake-edge,
Then plunge to depths profound!
EMERSON—*My Garden.* St. 3.

12
One is nearer God's heart in a garden
Than anywhere else on earth.
DOROTHY FRANCES GURNEY—*God's Garden.*

13
An album is a garden, not for show
Planted, but use; where wholesome herbs should grow.
LAMB—*In an Album to a Clergyman's Lady.*

14
I walk down the garden paths,
And all the daffodils
Are blowing, and the bright blue squills.
I walk down the patterned garden-paths
In my stiff, brocaded gown.
With my powdered hair, and jewelled fan,
I too am a rare
Pattern. As I wander down
The garden paths.
AMY LOWELL—*Patterns.*

15
And add to these retired Leisure,
That in trim gardens takes his pleasure.
MILTON—*Il Pensoroso.* L. 49.

16
Grove nods at grove, each alley has a brother,
And half the platform just reflects the other.
The suff'ring eye inverted nature sees,
Trees cut in statues, statues thick as trees;
With here a fountain never to be play'd,
And there a summer-house that knows no shade.
POPE—*Moral Essays.* Ep. IV. L. 117.

17
A little garden square and wall'd;
And in it throve an ancient evergreen,
A yew-tree, and all round it ran a walk
Of shingle, and a walk divided it.
TENNYSON—*Enoch Arden.* L. 731.

18
The garden lies,
A league of grass, wash'd by a slow broad stream.
TENNYSON—*Gardener's Daughter.* L. 40.

19
Come into the garden, Maud,
For the black bat, night, has flown.
TENNYSON—*Maud.* XXII. 1.

20
The splash and stir
Of fountains spouted up and showering down
In meshes of the jasmine and the rose:
And all about us peal'd the nightingale,
Rapt in her song, and careless of the snare.
TENNYSON—*Princess.* Pt. I. L. 214.

21
A little garden Little Jowett made,
And fenced it with a little palisade;
If you would know the mind of little Jowett,
This little garden don't a little show it.
FRANCIS WRANGHAM—*Epigram on Dr. Joseph Jowett.* Familiarly known as "Jowett's little garden." Claimed for WILLIAM LORT MANSEL and MR. HORRY.

GAZELLE

22
I never nursed a dear Gazelle to glad me with its soft black eye, but when it came to know me well, and love me, it was sure to marry a market-gardener.
DICKENS—*Old Curiosity Shop.* Ch. LVI. Saying of Dick Swiveller.
(See also MOORE)

23
The gazelles so gentle and clever
Skip lightly in frolicsome mood.
HEINE—*Book of Songs, Lyrical.* Interlude No. 9.

1
I never nurs'd a dear gazelle,
To glad me with its soft black eye,
But when it came to know me well
And love me, it was sure to die.
MOORE—*The Fire Worshippers.*
(See also DICKENS, PAYN, also MIDDLETON under LOVE)

2
I never had a piece of toast particularly long and wide,
But fell upon the sanded floor,
And always on the buttered side.
Parody of MOORE. Probably by JAMES PAYN. Appeared in Chambers' Journal.

GENEROSITY (See GIFTS)

GENIUS

3
Nullum magnum ingenium sine mixtura dementia.
There is no great genius without a mixture of madness.
ARISTOTLE. Quoted by BURTON—*Anatomy of Melancholy.* Assigned to ARISTOTLE also by SENECA *Problem.* 30. Same idea in SENECA—*De Tranquillitate Animi.* XVII. 10. CICERO—*Tusculum.* I. 33. 80; also in *De Div.* I. 37.

4
Doing easily what others find it difficult is talent; doing what is impossible *for talent* is genius.
HENRI-FREDERIC AMIEL—*Journal.*

5
As diamond cuts diamond, and one hone smooths a second, all the parts of intellect are whetstones to each other; and genius, which is but the result of their mutual sharpening, is character too.
C. A. BARTOL—*Radical Problems. Individualism.*

6
Le Génie, c'est la patience.
Genius is only patience.
BUFFON, *as quoted by* MADAME DE STAËL in A. STEVENS' *Study of the Life and Times of Mme. de Staël.* Ch. III. P. 61. (Ed. 1881.) Le génie n'est qu'une plus grande aptitude à la patience. As narrated by HERAULT DE SÉCHELLES—*Voyage à Montbar.* P. 15, when speaking of a talk with BUFFON in 1785. (Not in BUFFON's works.)

7
Genius . . . means the transcendent capacity of taking trouble.
CARLYLE—*Frederick the Great.* Bk. IV. Ch. III. Genius is a capacity for taking trouble. LESLIE STEPHEN. Genius is an intuitive talent for labor. JAN WALÆUS.
(See also HOPKINS)

8
Patience is a necessary ingredient of genius.
BENJ. DISRAELI—*Contarini Fleming.* Pt. IV. Ch. 5.

9
Fortune has rarely condescended to be the companion of genius.
ISAAC D'ISRAELI—*Curiosities of Literature. Poverty of the Learned.*

10
Many men of genius must arise before a particular man of genius can appear.
ISAAC D'ISRAELI—*Literary Character of Men of Genius.*

11
To think, and to feel, constitute the two grand divisions of men of genius—the men of reasoning and the men of imaginaton.
ISAAC D'ISRAELI—*Literary Character of Men of Genius.* Ch. II.

12
Philosophy becomes poetry, and science imagination, in the enthusiasm of genius.
ISAAC D'ISRAELI—*Literary Character of Men of Genius.* Ch. XII.

13
Every work of Genius is tinctured by the feelings, and often originates in the events of times.
ISAAC D'ISRAELI—*Literary Character of Men of Genius.* Ch. XXV.

14
But genius must be born, and never can be taught.
DRYDEN—*Epistle X. To Congreve.* L. 60.

15
When Nature has work to be done, she creates a genius to do it.
EMERSON—*Method of Nature.*

16
The hearing ear is always found close to the speaking tongue; and no genius can long or often utter anything which is not invited and gladly entertained by men around him.
EMERSON—*Race.*

17
Vivitur ingenio, that damn'd motto there
Seduced me first to be a wicked player.
FARQUHAR—*Love and a Bottle. Epilogue written and spoken by* JOSEPH HAYNES. The motto "Vivitur ingenio" appears to have been displayed in Drury Lane Theatre.
(See also SPENSER)

18
Genius and its rewards are briefly told:
A liberal nature and a niggard doom,
A difficult journey to a splendid tomb.
FORSTER—*Dedication of the Life and Adventures of Oliver Goldsmith.*

19
Genius is the power of lighting one's own fire.
JOHN FOSTER.

20
Das erste und letzte, was vom Genie gefordert wird, ist Wahrheits-Liebe.
The first and last thing required of genius is the love of truth.
GOETHE—*Sprüche in Prosa.* III.

21
Here lies our good Edmund, whose genius was such
We scarcely can praise it or blame it too much;
Who, born for the universe, narrow'd his mind,
And to party gave up what was meant for mankind.
GOLDSMITH—*Retaliation.* L. 29.
(See also BROWNING under FORTUNE)

22
Perhaps, moreover, he whose genius appears deepest and truest excels his fellows in nothing save the knack of expression; he throws out

occasionally a lucky hint at truths of which every human soul is profoundly though unutterably conscious.

HAWTHORNE—*Mosses from an Old Manse. The Procession of Life.*

1

Genius, like humanity, rusts for want of use.

HAZLITT—*Table Talk. On Application to Study.*

2

Nature is the master of talents; genius is the master of nature.

J. G. HOLLAND—*Plain Talk on Familiar Subjects. Art and Life.*

3

Gift, like genius, I often think only means an infinite capacity for taking pains.

ELLICE HOPKINS—*Work amongst Working Men.* In *Notes and Queries*, Sept. 13, 1879. P. 213, a correspondent, H. P. states that he was the first to use the exact phrase, "Genius is the capacity for taking pains." (See also CARLYLE)

4

At ingenium ingens
Inculto latet sub hoc corpore.

Yet a mighty genius lies hid under this rough exterior.

HORACE—*Satires.* Bk. I. 3. 33.

5

Genius is a promontory jutting out into the infinite.

VICTOR HUGO—*Wm. Shakespeare.*

6

We declare to you that the earth has exhausted its contingent of master-spirits. Now for decadence and general closing. We must make up our minds to it. We shall have no more men of genius.

VICTOR HUGO—*Wm. Shakespeare.* Bk. V. Ch. I.

7

The true Genius is a mind of large general powers, accidentally determined to some particular direction.

SAMUEL JOHNSON—*Life of Cowley.*

8

Entre esprit et talent il y a la proportion du tout à sa partié.

Intelligence is to genius as the whole is in proportion to its part.

LA BRUYÈRE—*The Characters or Manners of the Present Age. Opinions.*

9

Many a genius has been slow of growth. Oaks that flourish for a thousand years do not spring up into beauty like a reed.

G. H. LEWES—*Spanish Drama. Life of Lope De Vega.* Ch. II.

10 All the means of action—
The shapeless masses, the materials—
Lie everywhere about us. What we need
Is the celestial fire to change the flint
Into transparent crystal, bright and clear.
That fire is genius!

LONGFELLOW—*Spanish Student.* Act I. Sc. 5.

11

There is no work of genius which has not been the delight of mankind, no word of genius to which the human heart and soul have not, sooner or later, responded.

LOWELL—*Among my Books. Rousseau and the Sentimentalists.*

12

Talent is that which is in a man's power! genius is that in whose power a man is.

LOWELL—*Among my Books. Rousseau and the Sentimentalists.*

13

Three-fifths of him genius and two-fifths sheer fudge.

LOWELL—*Fable for Critics.* L. 1,296.

14

Ubi jam valideis quassatum est viribus ævi
Corpus, et obtuseis ceciderunt viribus artus,
Claudicat ingenium delirat linguaque mensque.

When the body is assailed by the strong force of time and the limbs weaken from exhausted force, genius breaks down, and mind and speech fail.

LUCRETIUS—*De Rerum Natura.* III. 452.

15

Talk not of genius baffled. Genius is master of man;
Genius does what it must, and talent does what it can.
Blot out my name, that the spirits of Shakespeare and Milton and Burns
Look not down on the praises of fools with a pity my soul yet spurns.

OWEN MEREDITH—*Last Words.* Pub. in *Cornhill Mag.* Nov. 1860. P. 516.

16

Ingenio stat sine morte decus.

The honors of genius are eternal.

PROPERTIUS—*Elegiæ.* III. 2. 24.

17

Illud ingeniorum velut præcox genus, non temere unquam pervenit ad frugem.

It seldom happens that a premature shoot of genius ever arrives at maturity.

QUINTILIAN—*De Institutione Oratoria.* I. 3. 1.

18

Das Licht des Genie's bekam weniger
Fett, als das Licht des Lebens.

The lamp of genius burns quicker than the lamp of life.

SCHILLER—*Fiesco.* II. 17.

19

Nullum sæculum magnis ingeniis clausum est.

No age is shut against great genius.

SENECA—*Epistolæ Ad Lucilium.* CII.

20 There is none but he
Whose being I do fear; and, under him,
My Genius is rebuk'd: as, it is said,
Mark Antony's was by Cæsar.

Macbeth. Act III. Sc. 1. L. 54.

21

Marmora Mæonii vincunt monumenta libelli
Vivitur ingenio; cætera mortis erunt.

The poets' scrolls will outlive the monuments of stone. Genius survives; all else is claimed by death.

SPENSER—*Shepherd's Calendar. Colin's Emblem.* End. (1715) Quoted. PEACHAM—*Minerva Britanna I.* (1612) Said to be from *Consolatio ad Liviam*, by an anonymous author, written shortly after Mæcenas' death. Attributed to VERGIL and OVID. See

Notes and Queries, Jan., 1918, p. 12. ROBINSON ELLIS—*Appendix Vergiliana*. RIESE—*Anthologia Latina*.

(See also FARQUHAR, also HORACE under MONUMENTS)

1

Genius is essentially creative; it bears the stamp of the individual who possesses it.

MADAME DE STAËL—*Corinne*. Bk. VII. Ch. I.

2

Genius inspires this thirst for fame: there is no blessing undesired by those to whom Heaven gave the means of winning it.

MADAME DE STAËL—*Corinne*. Bk. XVI. Ch. I.

3

Genius can never despise labour.

ABEL STEVENS—*Life of Madame de Staël*. Ch. XXXVIII.

4

Genius loci.

The presiding genius of the place.

VERGIL—*Æneid*. VII. 136. Genius signifies a divinity. Monumental stones were inscribed by the ancient Romans, "Genio loci"—"To the Divinity of the locality." Altar to the Unknown God. (See ACTS XVII. 23.

GENTIAN

Gentiana

5

And the blue gentian-flower, that, in the breeze,
Nods lonely, of her beauteous race the last.

BRYANT—*November*.

6

Thou blossom! bright with autumn dew,
And colour'd with the heaven's own blue,
That openest when the quiet light
Succeeds the keen and frosty night.

BRYANT—*To the Fringed Gentian*.

7

Blue thou art, intensely blue;
Flower, whence came thy dazzling hue?

MONTGOMERY—*The Gentianella*.

8

Beside the brook and on the umbered meadow,
Where yellow fern-tufts fleck the faded ground,
With folded lids beneath their palmy shadow
The gentian nods in dewy slumbers bound.

SARAH HELEN WHITMAN—*A Still Day in Autumn*. St. 6.

GENTLEMEN

9

Oh! St. Patrick was a gentleman,
Who came of decent people.

HENRY BENNETT—*St. Patrick was a Gentleman*.

10

Of the offspring of the gentilman Jafeth come Habraham, Moyses, Aron, and the profettys; also the Kyng of the right lyne of Mary, of whom that gentilman Jhesus was borne.

JULIANA BERNERS—*Heraldic Blazonry*.

11

Tho' modest, on his unembarrass'd brow
Nature had written—"Gentleman."

BYRON—*Don Juan*. Canto IX. St. 83.

12

I was ne'er so thrummed since I was a gentleman.

THOMAS DEKKER—*The Honest Whore*. Pt. I. Act IV. Sc. 2.

13

The best of men
That e'er wore earth about him was a sufferer;
A soft, meek, patient, humble, tranquil spirit,
The first true gentleman that ever breathed.

THOMAS DEKKER—*The Honest Whore*. Pt. I. Act I. Sc. 2.

14

His tribe were God Almighty's gentlemen.

DRYDEN—*Absalom and Achitophel*. Pt. I. L. 645.

15

A gentleman I could never make him, though I could make him a lord.

JAMES I, to his old nurse, who begged him to make her son a gentleman. See SELDON—*Table Talk*.

16

My master hath been an honourable gentleman; tricks he hath had in him, which gentlemen have.

All's Well That Ends Well. Act V. Sc. 3. L. 238.

17

I freely told you, all the wealth I had
Ran in my veins, I was a gentleman.

Merchant of Venice. Act III. Sc. 2. L. 257.

18

A gentleman born, master parson; who writes himself 'Armigero;' in any bill, warrant, quittance, or obligation, 'Armigero.'

Merry Wives of Windsor. Act I. Sc. 1. L. 9.

19

We are gentlemen,
That neither in our hearts, nor outward eyes
Envy the great, nor do the low despise.

Pericles. Act II. Sc. 3. L. 25.

20

Since every Jack became a gentleman,
There's many a gentle person made a Jack.

Richard III. Act I. Sc. 3. L. 72.

21

An affable and courteous gentleman.

Taming of the Shrew. Act I. Sc. 2. L. 98.

22

"I am a gentleman." I'll be sworn thou art;
Thy tongue, thy face, thy limbs, actions and spirit,
Do give thee five-fold blazon.

Twelfth Night. Act I. Sc. 5. L. 310.

23

He is complete in feature, and in mind,
With all good grace to grace a gentleman.

Two Gentlemen of Verona. Act II. Sc. 4. L. 73.

24

You are not like Cerberus, three gentlemen at once, are you?

R. B. SHERIDAN—*The Rivals*. Act IV. Sc. 2.

25

The gentle minde by gentle deeds is knowne;
For a man by nothing is so well bewrayed
As by his manners.

SPENSER—*Faerie Queene*. Bk. VI. Canto III. St. 1.

26

And thus he bore without abuse
The grand old name of gentleman,
Defamed by every charlatan
And soiled with all ignoble use.

TENNYSON—*In Memoriam*. CX. St. 6.

GENTLENESS

1
Suaviter in modo, fortiter in re.
Gentle in manner, firm in reality.
AQUAVIVA—*Industriæ ad Curandos Animæ Morbos.*

2
He is gentil that doth gentil dedis.
CHAUCER—*Canterbury Tales. The Wyf of Bathes Tale.* L. 6,695.

3
Peragit tranquilla potestas
Quod violenta nequit; mandataque fortius urget
Imperiosa quies.
Power can do by gentleness that which violence fails to accomplish; and calmness best enforces the imperial mandate.
CLAUDIANUS—*De Consulatu Mallii Theodori Panegyris.* CCXXXIX.

4
La violence est juste où la douceur est vaine.
Severity is allowable where gentleness has no effect.
CORNEILLE—*Héraclius.* I. 1.

5
The mildest manners and the gentlest heart.
HOMER—*Iliad.* Bk. XVII. L. 756. POPE's trans.

6
Plus fait douceur que violence.
Gentleness succeeds better than violence.
LA FONTAINE—*Fables.* VI. 3.

7
At caret insidiis hominum, quia mitis, hirundo.
The swallow is not ensnared by men because of its gentle nature.
OVID—*Ars Amatoria.* II. 149.

8
Gentle to others, to himself severe.
ROGERS—*Voyage of Columbus.* Canto VI.

9
What would you have? your gentleness shall force
More than your force move us to gentleness.
As You Like It. Act II. Sc. 7. L. 102.

10
Let gentleness my strong enforcement be.
As You Like It. Act II. Sc. 7. L. 113.

11
They are as gentle
As zephyrs blowing below the violet.
Cymbeline. Act IV. Sc. 2. L. 171.

12
Those that do teach young babes
Do it with gentle means and easy tasks:
Othello. Act IV. Sc. 2. L. 111.

GERMANY

13
Setzen wir Deutschland, so zu sagen, in den Sattel! Reiten wird es schon können.
Let us put Germany, so to speak, in the saddle! you will see that she can ride.
BISMARCK. In the Parliament of the Confederation. March 11, 1867.

14
Wir Deutschen fürchten Gott, sonst aber Nichts in der Welt.
We Germans fear God, but nothing else in the world.
BISMARCK—*In the Reichstag.* (1887)
(See also RACINE under GOD)

15
Deutschland, Deutschland über alles, über alles in der Welt!
Germany, Germany over all [or, above all] in the world.
A. H. HOFFMANN VON FALLERSLEBEN. The first line of a song, "Das Lied der Deutschen," written August 26, 1841, that became very popular in Germany, especially as a marching song during the World War.
The idea may have been suggested by a song which appeared 1817, "Preussen über alles." (Prussia over all.) Or by an anonymous pamphlet, "Oestreich (Österreich?) über alles wann es nur will." (Austria over all whenever it will.) 1684.

GHOSTS (See APPARITIONS)

GIFTS (See also BENEFITS)

16
It is more blessed to give than to receive.
Acts. XX. 35

17
Like giving a pair of laced ruffles to a man that has never a shirt on his back.
TOM BROWN—*Laconics.*

18
He ne'er consider'd it as loth
To look a gift-horse in the mouth,
And very wisely would lay forth
No more upon it than 'twas worth;
But as he got it freely, so
He spent it frank and freely too:
For saints themselves will sometimes be,
Of gifts that cost them nothing, free.
BUTLER—*Hudibras.* Pt. I. Canto I. L. 489.
(See also JEROME)

19
It is not the weight of jewel or plate,
Or the fondle of silk or fur;
'Tis the spirit in which the gift is rich,
As the gifts of the Wise Ones were,
And we are not told whose gift was gold,
Or whose was the gift of myrrh.
EDMUND VANCE COOKE—*The Spirit of the Gift.*

20
The gift, to be true, must be the flowing of the giver unto me, correspondent to my flowing unto him.
EMERSON—*Essays. Of Gifts.*

21
It is said that gifts persuade even the gods.
EURIPIDES—*Medea.* 964.

22
Gleich schenken? das ist brav. Da wird er reüssieren.
Presents at once? That's good. He is sure to succeed.
GOETHE—*Faust.* I. 7. 73.

23
Denn Geben ist Sache des Reichen.
For to give is the business of the rich.
GOETHE—*Hermann und Dorothea.* I. 15.

24
Die Gaben
Kommen von oben herab, in ihren eignen Gestalten.
Gifts come from above in their own peculiar forms.
GOETHE—*Hermann und Dorothea.* Canto V. L. 69.

1
Der Mutter schenk' ich,
Die Tochter denk' ich.

I make presents to the mother, but think of the daughter.

GOETHE—*Sprüche in Reimen*. III.

2
Give an inch, he'll take an ell.

HOBBES—*Liberty and Necessity*. No. 111.
JOHN WEBSTER—*Sir Thomas Wyatt*.

3
Rare gift! but oh, what gift to fools avails!

HOMER—*Odyssey*. Bk. 10. L. 29. POPE'S trans.

4
Omne supervacuum pleno de pectore manat.

Everything that is superfluous overflows from the full bosom.

HORACE—*Ars Poetica*. 337.

5
Noli equi dentes inspicere donati.

Never look a gift horse in the mouth.

ST. JEROME—*On the Epistle to the Ephesians*. According to ARCHBISHOP TRENCH, explanation that his writings were free-will offerings, when fault was found with them. Found also in *Vulgaria Stambrigi*. (About 1510)
(See also BUTLER, RABELAIS)

6
"Presents," I often say, "endear Absents."

LAMB—*A Dissertation upon Roast Pig*.

7
Denn der Wille
Und nicht die Gabe macht den Geber.

For the will and not the gift makes the giver.

LESSING—*Nathan der Weise*. I. 5.

8
Parvis mobilis rebus animus muliebris.

A woman's mind is affected by the meanest gifts.

LIVY—*Annales*. VI. 34.

9
Not what we give, but what we share,—
For the gift without the giver is bare.

LOWELL—*Vision of Sir Launfal*. Pt. II. St. 8.

10
In giving, a man receives more than he gives, and the more is in proportion to the worth of the thing given.

GEORGE MACDONALD—*Mary Marston*. Ch. V.

11
Quisquis magna dedit, voluit sibi magna remitti.

Whoever makes great presents, expects great presents in return.

MARTIAL—*Epigrams*. V. 59. 3.

12
Or what man is there of you, whom if his son ask bread, will he give him a stone?

Matthew. VII. 9.
(See also PLAUTUS, SENECA)

13
And wisest he in this whole wide land
Of hoarding till bent and gray;
For all you can hold in your cold, dead hand
Is what you have given away.

. . . .

He gave with a zest and he gave his best;
Give him the best to come.

JOAQUIN MILLER—*Peter Cooper*.

14
All we can hold in our cold dead hands is what we have given away.

Old Sanskrit proverb.
(See also COURTENAY under EPITAPHS; QUARLES under POSSESSION)

15
Take gifts with a sigh: most men give to be paid.

JOHN BOYLE O'REILLY—*Rules of the Road*.

16
Rest est ingeniosa dare.

Giving requires good sense.

OVID—*Amorum*. I. 8. 62.

17
Majestatem res data dantis habet.

The gift derives its value from the rank of the giver.

OVID—*Epistolæ Ex Ponto*. IV. 9. 68.
(See also SENECA)

18
Acceptissima semper munera sunt auctor quæ pretiosa facit.

Those gifts are ever the most acceptable which the giver makes precious.

OVID—*Heriodes*. XVII. 71.

19
Dicta docta pro datis

Smooth words in place of gifts.

PLAUTUS—*Asinaria*. Act III.

20
Altera manu fert lapidem, panem ostentat altera.

In one hand he bears a stone, with the other offers bread.

PLAUTUS—*Aulularia*. Act II. 2. 18.
(See also MATTHEW)

21
The horseleech hath two daughters, crying Give, give.

Proverbs. XXX. 15.

22
Bis dat qui cito dat.

He gives twice who gives quickly.

Credited to PUBLIUS MIMUS by LANGIUS, in *Polyanth. Noviss*. P. 382. ERASMUS—*Adagia*. P. 265, (Ed. 1579) quoting SENECA. Compare SENECA—*De Beneficiis*. II. 1. HOMER—*Iliad*. XVIII. 98. Title of epigram in a book entitled *Joannis Owen, Oxeniensis Angli Epigrammatum*. (1632) P. 148. Also in MANIPULUS SACER—*Concionum Maralium, Collectus ex Voluminibus R. P. Hieremiæ Drexelii*. (1644) EURIPIDES—*Rhes*. 333. AUSONIUS—*Epigram*. 83. 1. (Trans.) ALCIATUS—*Emblemata*. 162.

23
He always looked a given horse in the mouth.

RABELAIS—*Works*. Bk. I. Ch. XI.
(See also JEROME)

24
Back of the sound broods the silence, back of the gift stands the giving;
Back of the hand that receives thrill the sensitive nerves of receiving.

RICHARD REALF—*Indirection*.

25
Fabius Verrucosus beneficium ab homine duro aspere datum, panem lapidosum vocabat.

Fabius Verrucosus called a favor roughly bestowed by a hard man, bread made of stone.

SENECA—*De Beneficiis*. II. 7.
(See also MATTHEW)

1
Deus quædam munera universo humano generi dedit, a quibus excluditur nemo.

God has given some gifts to the whole human race, from which no one is excluded.

SENECA—*De Beneficiis.* IV. 28.

2
Cum quod datur spectabis, et dantem adspice!

While you look at what is given, look also at the giver.

SENECA—*Thyestes.* CCCXVI.

(See also OVID)

3
Let us sit and mock the good housewife Fortune from her wheel, that her gifts may henceforth be bestowed equally.

I would we could do so, for her benefits are mightily misplaced, and the bountiful blind woman doth most mistake in her gifts to women.

As You Like It. Act I. Sc. 2. L. 34.

4
Rich gifts wax poor when givers prove unkind.

Hamlet. Act III. Sc. 1. L. 101.

5
All other gifts appertinent to man, as the malice of this age shapes them, are not worth a gooseberry.

Henry IV. Part II. Act 1. Sc. 2. L. 194.

6
Win her with gifts, if she respect not words;
Dumb jewels often in their silent kind
More than quick words do move a woman's mind.

Two Gentlemen of Verona. Act III. Sc. 1. L. 89.

7
Timeo Danaos et dona ferentes.

I fear the Greeks, even when they bring gifts.

VERGIL—*Æneid.* II. 49.

8
Parta meæ Veneri sunt munera; namque notavi
Ipse locum aëriæ quo congessere palumbes.

I have found out a gift for my fair;
I have found where the wood-pigeons breed.

VERGIL—*Eclog.* III. 68. English by SHENSTONE. *Pastoral.* II. Hope. Erroneously attributed to ROWE by THOMAS HUGHES in *Tom Brown's School Days.*

9
Denn was ein Mensch auch hat, so sind's am Ende Gaben.

For whatever a man has, is in reality only a gift.

WIELAND—*Oberon.* II. 19.

10
Behold, I do not give lectures or a little charity,
When I give I give myself.

WALT WHITMAN—*Leaves of Grass. Song of Myself.* 40.

11
Give all thou canst; high Heaven rejects the lore
Of nicely calculated less or more.

WORDSWORTH—*Ecclesiastical Sonnets.* Pt. III. No. 43.

12
She gave me eyes, she gave me ears;
And humble cares, and delicate fears;
A heart, the fountain of sweet tears;
And love, and thought, and joy.

WORDSWORTH—*The Sparrow's Nest.*

13
That every gift of noble origin
Is breathed upon by Hope's perpetual breath.

WORDSWORTH—*These Times Strike Monied Worldlings.*

GLORY

14
So may glory from defect arise.

ROBERT BROWNING—*Deaf and Dumb.*

15
The glory dies not, and the grief is past.

BRYDGES—*On the Death of Sir Walter Scott.*

16
Who track the steps of Glory to the grave.

BYRON—*Monody on the Death of the Right Hon. R. B. Sheridan.*

(See also GRAY, LOWELL, MOORE)

17
Gloria virtutem tanquam umbra sequitur.

Glory follows virtue as if it were its shadow.

CICERO—*Tusculanarum Disputationum.* I. 45.

18
Sancte pater, sic transit gloria mundi.

Holy Father, so passes away the glory of the world.

See CORNELIUS À LAPIDE—*Commentaria, 2nd. Epist. ad Cor.* Ch. XII. 7. The sentence is used in the Service of the Pope's enthronement after the burning of flax. Rite used in the triumphal processions of the Roman republic. According to ZONARÆ—*Annals.* (1553)

(See also À KEMPIS)

19
* * * glory built
On selfish principles is shame and guilt.

COWPER—*Table Talk.* L. 1.

20
The paths of glory lead but to the grave.

GRAY—*Elegy in a Country Churchyard.* St. 9.

(See also BYRON)

21
The first in glory, as the first in place.

HOMER—*Odyssey.* Bk. XI. L. 441. POPE'S trans.

22
Fulgente trahit constrictos Gloria curru
Non minus ignotos generosis.

Glory drags all men along, low as well as high, bound captive at the wheels of her glittering car.

HORACE—*Satires.* I. 6. 23.

23
O quam cito transit gloria mundi.

O how quickly passes away the glory of the earth.

THOMAS À KEMPIS—*Imitation of Christ.* Bk. I. Ch. III. 30.

(See also CORNELIUS)

24
Aucun chemin de fleurs ne conduit à la gloire.

No flowery road leads to glory.

LA FONTAINE—*Fables.* X. 14.

25
La gloire n'est jamais où la vertu n'est pas.

Glory is never where virtue is not.

LE FRANC—*Didon.*

26
The glory of Him who
Hung His masonry pendant on naught, when the world He created.

LONGFELLOW—*The Children of the Lord's Supper.* L. 177.

1
Those glories come too late
That on our ashes wait.
LOVELACE—*Inscription on Title-page of Posthumous Poems.* (1659)
(See also MARTIAL)

2
This goin' ware glory waits ye haint one agreeable feetur.
LOWELL—*The Biglow Papers.* First Series. No. II.
(See also BYRON)

3
Cineri gloria sera est.
Glory paid to our ashes comes too late
MARTIAL—*Epigrams.* I. 26. 8.
(See also LOVELACE)

4
Go where glory waits thee;
But while fame elates thee,
Oh! still remember me.
MOORE—*Go Where Glory Waits Thee.*
(See also BYRON)

5
Immensum gloria calcar habet.
The love of glory gives an immense stimulus.
OVID—*Epistolæ Ex Ponto.* IV. 2. 36.

6
Nisi utile est quod facimus, stulta est gloria.
Unless what we do is useful, our glory is vain.
PHÆDRUS—*Fables.* III. 17. 12.

7
Who pants for glory, finds but short repose;
A breath revives him, or a breath o'erthrows.
POPE—*Second Book of Horace.* Ep. I. L. 300.

8
Magnum iter adscendo; sed dat mihi gloria vires.
I am climbing a difficult road; but the glory gives me strength.
PROPERTIUS—*Elegiæ.* IV. 10. 3.

9
Sound, sound the clarion, fill the fife!
To all the sensual world proclaim,
One crowded hour of glorious life
Is worth an age without a name.
SCOTT—*Old Mortality.* Ch. XXXIV. *Introductory Stanza.* Recently discovered in *The Bee,* Edinburgh, Oct. 12, 1791. Said to have been written by MAJOR MORDAUNT. Whole poem reproduced in *Literary Digest,* Sept. 11, 1920, P. 38.

10
Glory is like a circle in the water,
Which never ceaseth to enlarge itself
Till, by broad spreading it disperse to nought.
Henry VI. Pt. I. Act I. Sc. 2. L. 133.

11
When the moon shone, we did not see the candle;
So doth the greater glory dim the less.
Merchant of Venice. Act V. Sc. 1. L. 92.

12
Some glory in their birth, some in their skill,
Some in their wealth, some in their bodies' force,
Some in their garments, though new-fangled ill;
Some in their hawks and hounds, some in their horse;
And every humor hath his adjunct pleasure,
Wherein it finds a joy above the rest.
Sonnet XCI.

13
Like madness is the glory of this life.
Timon of Athens. Act I. Sc. 2. L. 139.

14
Who would be so mock'd with glory?
Timon of Athens. Act IV. Sc. 2. L. 33.

15
Avoid shame, but do not seek glory,—nothing so expensive as glory.
SYDNEY SMITH—*Lady Holland's Memoir.* Vol. I. P. 86.

16
Heu, quam difficilis gloriæ custodia est.
Alas! how difficult it is to retain glory!
SYRUS—*Maxims.*

17
Et ipse quidem, quamquam medio in spatio integræ ætatis ereptus, quantum ad gloriam, longissimum ævum peregit.
As he, though carried off in the prime of life, had lived long enough for glory.
TACITUS—*Agricola.* XLIV.

18
Twas glory once to be a Roman;
She makes it glory, now, to be a man.
BAYARD TAYLOR—*The National Ode.*

19
I never learned how to tune a harp, or play upon a lute; but I know how to raise a small and inconsiderable city to glory and greatness.
THEMISTOCLES. On being taunted with his want of social accomplishments. PLUTARCH'S *Life.*

20
Glories, like glow-worms, afar off shine bright,
But look'd to near have neither heat nor light.
JOHN WEBSTER—*The White Devil.* Act V. Sc. 1.

21
Great is the glory, for the strife is hard!
WORDSWORTH—*To B. R. Haydon.* L. 14.

22
We rise in glory, as we sink in pride:
Where boasting ends, there dignity begins.
YOUNG—*Night Thoughts.* Night VIII. L. 508.

GLOWWORM

23
Till glowworms light owl-watchmen's flight
Through our green metropolis.
WILLIAM ALLINGHAM—*Greenwood Tree.*

24
My star, God's glowworm.
ROBERT BROWNING—*Popularity.*

25
Tasteful illumination of the night,
Bright scattered, twinkling star of spangled earth.
JOHN CLARE—*To the Glowworm.*

26
While many a glowworm in the shade
Lights up her love torch.
COLERIDGE—*The Nightingale.*

27
Glow-worms on the ground are moving,
As if in the torch-dance circling.
HEINE—*Book of Songs. Donna Clara.* St. 17.

28
Ye living lamps, by whose dear light
The nightingale does sit so late;
And studying all the summer night,
Her matchless songs does meditate.
MARVELL—*The Mower to the Glow-worm.*

1
Ye country comets, that portend
No war nor princes' funeral
Shining unto no other end
Than to presage the grass's fall.
MARVELL—*The Mower to the Glow-worm.*

2
Here's a health to the glow-worm, Death's sober lamplighter.
OWEN MEREDITH (Lord Lytton)—*Au Café.* XXXIX.

3
When evening closes Nature's eye,
The glow-worm lights her little spark
To captivate her favorite fly
And tempt the rover through the dark.
MONTGOMERY—*The Glow-worm.*

4
The glow-worm shows the matin to be near,
And 'gins to pale his uneffectual fire.
Hamlet. Act I. Sc. 5. L. 89.

5
Like a glowworm golden, in a dell of dew,
Scattering unbeholden its aërial blue
Among the flowers and grass which screen it from the view.
SHELLEY—*To a Skylark.*

6
Among the crooked lanes, on every hedge,
The glow-worm lights his gem; and through the dark,
A moving radiance twinkles.
THOMSON—*The Seasons. Summer.* L. 1,682.

GNAT

7
A work of skill, surpassing sense,
A labor of Omnipotence;
Though frail as dust it meet thine eye,
He form'd this gnat who built the sky.
MONTGOMERY—*The Gnat.*

GOD

8
Ye men of Athens, I perceive that in all things ye are too superstitious. For as I passed by, and beheld your devotions, I found an altar with this inscription, TO THE UNKNOWN GOD. Whom therefore ye ignorantly worship, him declare I unto you.
Acts. XVII. 23.
(See also VERGIL under GENIUS)

9
Nearer, my God, to Thee—
Nearer to Thee—
E'en though it be a cross
That raiseth me;
Still all my song shall be
Nearer, my God, to Thee,
Nearer to Thee!
SARAH FLOWER ADAMS—*Nearer, my God, to Thee!* An article in *Notes and Queries* states that the words were written by her sister, MRS. BYRDES FLOWER ADAMS, and the music only by SARAH FLOWER ADAMS.

10
Homo cogitat, Deus indicat.
Man thinks, God directs.
ALCUIN—*Epistles.*
(See also LANGLAND)

11
At Athens, wise men propose, and fools dispose.
ANACHARSIS.
(See also LANGLAND)

12
Ordina l'uomo, e dio dispone.
Man proposes, and God disposes.
ARIOSTO—*Orlando Furioso.* Ch. XLVI. 35.
(See also LANGLAND)

13
Man says—"So, so."
Heaven says—"No, no."
Chinese Aphorism.

14
God's Wisdom and God's Goodness!—Ah, but fools
Mis-define thee, till God knows them no more.
Wisdom and goodness they are God!—what schools
Have yet so much as heard this simpler lore.
This no Saint preaches, and this no Church rules:
'Tis in the desert, now and heretofore.
MATTHEW ARNOLD—*The Divinity.* St. 3.

15
Deus scitur melius nesciendo.
God is best known in not knowing him.
ST. AUGUSTINE—*De Ordine.* II. 16.

16
They that deny a God destroy man's nobility; for certainly man is of kin to the beasts by his body; and, if he be not of kin to God by his spirit, he is a base and ignoble creature.
BACON—*Essays. Of Atheism.*

17
From thee all human actions take their springs,
The rise of empires, and the fall of kings.
SAMUEL BOYSE—*The Deity.*

18
O Rock of Israel, Rock of Salvation, Rock struck and cleft for me, let those two streams of blood and water which once gushed out of thy side . . . bring down with them salvation and holiness into my soul.
BREVINT—*Works.* P. 17. (Ed. 1679)
(See also TOPLADY)

19
He made little, too little of sacraments and priests, because God was so intensely real to him. What should he do with lenses who stood thus full in the torrent of the sunshine.
PHILLIPS BROOKS—*Sermons. The Seriousness of Life.*

20
It never frightened a Puritan when you bade him stand still and listen to the speech of God. His closet and his church were full of the reverberations of the awful, gracious, beautiful voice for which he listened.
PHILLIPS BROOKS—*Sermons. The Seriousness of Life.*

21
That we devote ourselves to God is seen
In living just as though no God there were.
ROBERT BROWNING—*Paracelsus.* Pt. I.

22
God is the perfect poet,
Who in his person acts his own creations.
ROBERT BROWNING—*Paracelsus.* Pt. II.

23
God's in His Heaven—
All's right with the world!
ROBERT BROWNING—*Pippa Passes.* Pt. I.
(See also WHITTIER)

1
All service is the same with God,
With God, whose puppets, best and worst,
Are we: there is no last nor first.
ROBERT BROWNING—*Pippa Passes.* Pt. IV.

2 Of what I call God,
And fools call Nature.
ROBERT BROWNING—*The Ring and the Book. The Pope.* L. 1,073.

3
"There is no god but God!—to prayer—lo!
God is great!"
BYRON—*Childe Harold.* Canto II. St. 59.
(See also KORAN)

4
A picket frozen on duty—
A mother starved for her brood—
Socrates drinking the hemlock,
And Jesus on the rood;
And millions who, humble and nameless,
The straight, hard pathway trod—
Some call it Consecration,
And others call it God.
W. H. CARRUTH—*Evolution.*

5
Nihil est quod deus efficere non possit.
There is nothing which God cannot do.
CICERO—*De Divinatione.* II. 41.

6
God! sing, ye meadow-streams, with gladsome voice!
Ye pine-groves, with your soft and soul-like sounds!
And they too have a voice, yon piles of snow,
And in their perilous fall shall thunder, God!
COLERIDGE—*Hymn before Sunrise in the Vale of Chamouni.*

7
God hath chosen the foolish things of the world to confound the wise; and God hath chosen the weak things of the world to confound the things that are mighty.
I Corinthians. I. 27.

8
I have planted, Apollos watered; but God gave the increase.
I Corinthians. III. 6.

9
God moves in a mysterious way
His wonders to perform;
He plants his footsteps in the sea
And rides upon the storm.
COWPER—*Hymn. Light Shining out of Darkness.* (See also POPE)

10
God never meant that man should scale the Heavens
By strides of human wisdom. In his works,
Though wondrous, he commands us in his word
To seek him rather where his mercy shines.
COWPER—*Task.* Bk. III. L. 217.

11
But who with filial confidence inspired,
Can lift to Heaven an unpresumptuous eye,
And smiling say, My Father made them all.
COWPER—*Task.* Bk. V. *The Winter Morning Walk.* L. 745.

12
Acquaint thyself with God, if thou would'st taste
His works. Admitted once to his embrace,
Thou shalt perceive that thou wast blind before:
Thine eye shall be instructed; and thine heart
Made pure shall relish with divine delight
Till then unfelt, what hands divine have wrought.
COWPER—*Task.* Bk. V. L. 782.

13
There is a God! the sky his presence shares,
His hand upheaves the billows in their mirth,
Destroys the mighty, yet the humble spares
And with contentment crowns the thought of worth.
CHARLOTTE CUSHMAN—*There is a God.*

14
My God, my Father, and my Friend,
Do not forsake me in the end.
WENTWORTH DILLON—*Translation of Dies Iræ.*

15
'Twas much, that man was made like God before:
But, that God should be made like man, much more.
DONNE—*Holy Sonnets.* Sonnet XXII.

16
By tracing Heaven his footsteps may be found:
Behold! how awfully he walks the round!
God is abroad, and wondrous in his ways
The rise of empires, and their fall surveys.
DRYDEN—*Britannia Rediviva.* L. 75.

17
Too wise to err, too good to be unkind,—
Are all the movements of the Eternal Mind.
REV. JOHN EAST—*Songs of My Pilgrimage.*
(See also MEDLEY)

18
God is incorporeal, divine, supreme, infinite,
Mind, Spirit, Soul, Life, Truth, Love.
MARY B. G. EDDY—*Science and Health,* 465:9

19
There is no life, truth, intelligence, nor substance in matter. All is infinite Mind, and its infinite manifestation, for God is all in All. Spirit is immortal Truth; matter is mortal error.
MARY B. G. EDDY—*Science and Health,* 468: 9.
(See also KORAN)

20
When the Master of the universe has points to carry in his government he impresses his will in the structure of minds.
EMERSON—*Letters and Social Aims. Immortality.*

21
He was a wise man who originated the idea of God.
EURIPIDES—*Sisyphus.*
(See also VOLTAIRE)

22
Henceforth the Majesty of God revere;
Fear him and you have nothing else to fear.
FORDYCE—*Answer to a Gentleman who Apologized to the Author for Swearing.*
(See also RACINE)

23
Wie einer ist, so ist sein Gott,
Darum ward Gott so oft zu Spott.
As a man is, so is his God; therefore God was so often an object of mockery.
GOETHE—*Gedichte.*

1

I know

My God commands, whose power no power resists.

ROBERT GREENE—*Looking-Glass for London and England.*

2

Some men treat the God of their fathers as they treat their father's friend. They do not deny him; by no means: they only deny themselves to him, when he is good enough to call upon them.

J. C. AND A. W. HARE—*Guesses at Truth.*

3

Restore to God His due in tithe and time;
A tithe purloin'd cankers the whole estate.

HERBERT—*The Temple. The Church Porch.* St. 65.

4

I askt the seas and all the deeps below
My God to know,
I askt the reptiles, and whatever is
In the abyss;
Even from the shrimps to the leviathan
Enquiry ran;
But in those deserts that no line can sound
The God I sought for was not to be found.

THOS. HEYWOOD—*Searching after God.*

5

Forgetful youth! but know, the Power above
With ease can save each object of his love;
Wide as his will, extends his boundless grace.

HOMER—*Odyssey.* Bk. III. L. 285. POPE'S trans.

6

O thou, whose certain eye foresees
The fix'd event of fate's remote decrees.

HOMER—*Odyssey.* Bk. IV. L. 627. POPE'S trans.

7

Dangerous it were for the feeble brain of man to wade far into the doings of the Most High; whom although to know be life, and joy to make mention of his name, yet our soundest knowledge is to know that we know him not as indeed he is, neither can know him; and our safest eloquence concerning him is our silence, when we confess without confession that his glory is inexplicable, his greatness above our capacity and reach.

HOOKER—*Ecclesiastical Polity.* Bk. I. Ch. II. 3.

8

Could we with ink the ocean fill,
And were the heavens of parchment made,
Were every stalk on earth a quill,
And every man a scribe by trade;
To write the love of God above,
Would drain the ocean dry;
Nor could the scroll contain the whole,
Though stretch'd from sky to sky.

RABBI MAYIR BEN ISAAC. Trans. of *Chaldee Ode*, sung in Jewish Synagogues during the service of the first day of the Feast of the Pentecost. Given in the original Chaldee in *Notes and Queries*, Dec. 31, 1853. P. 648. In GROSE'S *Olio.* P. 292, and in *Book of Jewish Thoughts.* P. 155. Same idea in CHAUCER—*Balade Warnynge Men to Beware of Deceitful Women.* Also in *Remedie of Love.* See *Modern Universal History.* P. 430. Note. MISS C. SINCLAIR—*Hill and Valley.* P. 35. (Same idea.) SMART given as English translator by one authority. See also *Des Knaben Wunderhorn.*

9

But if the sky were paper and a scribe each star above,
And every scribe had seven hands, they could not write all my love.

Dürsli und Bäbeli. Old public house ditty of the Canton de Soleure or Solothurn. Original in Swiss dialect. Given in *Notes and Queries*, Feb. 10, 1872. P. 114.

10

From thee, great God, we spring, to thee we tend,—
Path, motive, guide, original, and end.

SAMUEL JOHNSON—*Motto to The Rambler.* No. 7.

11

The sun and every vassal star,
All space, beyond the soar of angel's wings,
Wait on His word: and yet He stays His car
For every sigh a contrite suppliant brings.

KEBLE—*The Christian Year. Ascension Day.*

12

Nam homo proponit, sed Deus disponit.
Man proposes, but God disposes.

THOS. À KEMPIS—*Imitation of Christ.* Bk. I. Ch. XIX. THOS. DIBDIN'S trans.

(See also LANGLAND)

13

O God, I am thinking Thy thoughts after Thee.

KEPLER—*When Studying Astronomy.*

14

All but God is changing day by day.

CHARLES KINGSLEY—*The Saints' Tragedy. Prometheus.*

15

God! there is no God but he, the living, the self-subsisting.

Koran Ch. II. Pt. III.

(See also EDDY)

16

There is no god but God.

Koran. Ch. III.

17

L'impossibilité où je suis de prouver que Dieu n'est pas, me decouvre son existence.

The very impossibility in which I find myself to prove that God is not, discloses to me His existence.

LA BRUYÈRE—*Les Caractères.* XVI.

(See also VOLTAIRE)

18

Homo proponit et Deus disponit.
And governeth alle goode virtues.

LANGLAND—*Vision of Piers Ploughman.* Vol. II. P. 427. L. 13,984. (Ed. 1824) JOHN GERSON is credited with same. Saying quoted in *Chronicles of Battel Abbey.* (1066 to 1177) Trans. by LOWER, 1851. P. 27. HOMER—*Iliad.* XVII. 515. PINDAR—*Olymp.* XIII. 149. DEMOSTHENES—*De Corona.* 209. PLAUTUS—*Bacchid.* I. 2. 36. AMMIANUS MARCELLINUS—*Hist.* XXV. 3. FENELON—*Sermon on the Epiphany.* 1685. MONTAIGNE—*Essay.* Bk. II. Ch. XXXVII. SENECA—*Epistles.* 107. CLEANTHUS—*Fragment.* CERVANTES—*Don Quixote.* I. 22. DANTE—*Paradise.* VIII. L. 134. SCHILLER

—*Wallenstein's Death.* I. 7. 32. ORDERICUS VITALIS—*Ecclesiastica Historia.* Bk. III. (1075)
(See also ALCUIN, ANACHARSIS, ARISTO, À KEMPIS)

1
Sire, je n'avais besoin de cet hypothèse.
Sire, I had no need for that hypothesis.
LA PLACE to NAPOLEON, who asked why God was not mentioned in *Traité de la Mécanique Céleste.*

2
Denn Gott lohnt Gutes, hier gethan, auch hier noch.
For God rewards good deeds done here below—rewards them here.
LESSING—*Nathan der Weise.* I. 2.

3
"We trust, Sir, that God is on our side." "It is more important to know that we are on God's side."
LINCOLN—Reply to deputation of Southerners during Civil War.
(See also WHATELY under TRUTH)

4
God had sifted three kingdoms to find the wheat for this planting.
LONGFELLOW—*The Courtship of Miles Standish.* IV.

5
An' you've gut to git up airly
Ef you want to take in God.
LOWELL—*The Biglow Papers.* First Series. No. 1. St. 5.

6
Estne dei sedes nisi terra et pontus et aër
Et cœlum et virtus? Superos quid quærimus ultra?
Jupiter est quodcumque vides, quodcumque moveris.
Is there any other seat of the Divinity than the earth, sea, air, the heavens, and virtuous minds? why do we seek God elsewhere? He is whatever you see; he is wherever you move.
LUCAN—*Pharsalia.* IX. 578.

7
Ein feste Burg ist unser Gott
Ein gute Wehr und Waffen,
Er hilft uns frei aus aller Not,
Die uns jetzt hat betroffen.
A mighty fortress is our God,
A bulwark never failing,
Our helper he amid the flood
Of mortal ills prevailing.
MARTIN LUTHER—*Ein feste Burg.* Trans. by F. H. HEDGE.

8
I fear no foe with Thee at hand to bless;
Ills have no weight, and tears no bitterness.
HENRY FRANCIS LYTE—*Eventide.*

9
A voice in the wind I do not know;
A meaning on the face of the high hills
Whose utterance I cannot comprehend.
A something is behind them: that is God.
GEORGE MACDONALD—*Within and Without.* Pt. I. Sc. 1.

10
Exemplumque dei quisque est in imagine parva.
Every one is in a small way the image of God.
MANILIUS—*Astronomica.* IV. 895.

11
Quis cœlum possit nisi cœli munera nosse?
Et reperire deum nisi qui pars ipse deorum est?
Who can know heaven except by its gifts? and who can find out God, unless the man who is himself an emanation from God?
MANILIUS—*Astronomica.* II. 115.

12
The Lord who gave us Earth and Heaven
Takes that as thanks for all He's given.
The book he lent is given back
All blotted red and smutted black.
MASEFIELD—*Everlasting Mercy.* St. 27.

13
One sole God;
One sole ruler,—his Law;
One sole interpreter of that law—Humanity.
MAZZINI—*Life and Writings. Young Europe. General Principles.* No. 1.

14
Too wise to be mistaken still
Too good to be unkind.
SAMUEL MEDLEY—*Hymn of God.*
(See also EAST)

15
What in me is dark,
Illumine; what is low, raise and support;
That to the height of this great argument
I may assert eternal Providence,
And justify the ways of God to men.
MILTON—*Paradise Lost.* Bk. I. L. 22.
(See also POPE)

16
These are thy glorious works, Parent of good.
MILTON—*Paradise Lost.* Bk. V. L. 153.

17
Who best
Bear his mild yoke, they serve him best: his state
Is kingly; thousands at his bidding speed,
And post o'er land and ocean without rest.
MILTON—*Sonnet. On His Blindness.*

18
Gott-trunkener Mensch.
A God-intoxicated man.
NOVALIS (*of Spinoza*).

19
Trumpeter, sound for the splendour of God!
. . . .
Trumpeter, rally us, up to the heights of it!
Sound for the City of God.
ALFRED NOYES—*Trumpet Call.* Last lines.

20
Est deus in nobis; et sunt commercia cœli.
There is a God within us and intercourse with heaven.
OVID—*Ars Amatoria.* Bk. III. 549.
(Milton's "Looks commercing with the skies" said to be inspired by this phrase.)
(See also MILTON under EYES)

21
Est deus in nobis: agitante calescimus illo.
There is a God within us, and we glow when he stirs us.
OVID—*Fasti.* Bk. VI. 5.

22
Sed tamen ut fuso taurorum sanguine centum,
Sic capitur minimo thuris honore deux.
As God is propitiated by the blood of a hundred bulls, so also is he by the smallest offering of incense.
OVID—*Tristium.* II. 75.

1
Nihil ita sublime est, supraque pericula tendit
Non sit ut inferius suppositumque deo.

Nothing is so high and above all danger that is not below and in the power of God.

OVID—*Tristium*. IV. 8. 47.

2
Fear God. Honour the King.

I Peter. II. 17.

3
One on God's side is a majority.

WENDELL PHILLIPS—*Speech*. Harper's Ferry. Nov. 1, 1859.

4
God is truth and light his shadow.

PLATO.

5
God is a geometrician.

Attributed to PLATO, but not found in his works.

6
Est profecto deus, qui, quæ nos gerimus, auditque et videt.

There is indeed a God that hears and sees whate'er we do.

PLAUTUS—*Captivi*. II. 2. 63.

7
Laugh where we must, be candid where we can,
But vindicate the ways of God to man.

POPE—*Essay on Man*. Ep. I. L. 15.
(See also MILTON)

8
Lo, the poor Indian! whose untutored mind
Sees God in clouds, or hears him in the wind.

POPE—*Essay on Man*. Ep. I. L. 99.

9
To Him no high, no low, no great, no small;
He fills, He bounds, connects and equals all!

POPE—*Essay on Man*. Ep. I. L. 277.

10
He mounts the storm, and walks upon the wind.

POPE—*Essay on Man*. Ep. II. L. 110.
(See also COWPER)

11
Slave to no sect, who takes no private road,
But looks through nature up to nature's God.

POPE—*Essay on Man*. Ep. IV. L. 330.

12
He from thick films shall purge the visual ray,
And on the sightless eyeball pour the day.

POPE—*Messiah*.

13
Thou Great First Cause, least understood.

POPE—*Universal Prayer*.

14
The heavens declare the glory of God; and the firmament showeth his handiwork.

Psalms. XIX. 1.

15
He maketh me to lie down in green pastures: he leadeth me beside the still waters.

Psalms. XXIII. 2.

16
God is our refuge and strength, a very present help in trouble.

Psalms. XLVI. 1.

17
Je crains Dieu, cher Abner, et n'ai point d'autre crainte.

I fear God, dear Abner, and I have no other fear.

RACINE—*Athalie*. Act I. Sc. 1.
(See also FORDYCE, SMYTH, also BISMARCK under GERMANY)

18
There is no respect of persons with God.

Romans. II. 11. *Acts* X. 34.

19
Fear of God before their eyes.

Romans. III. 18.

20
If God be for us, who can be against us?

Romans. VIII. 31.

21
Give us a God—a living God,
One to wake the sleeping soul,
One to cleanse the tainted blood
Whose pulses in our bosoms roll.

C. G. ROSENBERG—*The Winged Horn*. St. 7.

22
We may scavenge the dross of the nation, we may shudder past bloody sod,
But we thrill to the new revelation that we are parts of God.

ROBERT HAVEN SCHAUFFLER—*New Gods for Old*.

23
Es lebt ein Gott zu strafen und zu rächen.

There is a God to punish and avenge.

SCHILLER—*Wilhelm Tell*. IV. 3. 37.

24
Nihil ab illo [*i.e.* a Deo] vacat; opus suum ipse implet.

Nothing is void of God; He Himself fills His work.

SENECA—*De Beneficiis*. IV. 8.

25
Deum non immolationibus et sanguine multo colendum: quæ enim ex trucidatione immerentium voluptas est? sed mente pura, bono honestoque proposito. Non templa illi, congestis in altitudinem saxis, struenda sunt; in suo cuique consecrandus est pectore.

God is not to be worshipped with sacrifices and blood; for what pleasure can He have in the slaughter of the innocent? but with a pure mind, a good and honest purpose. Temples are not to be built for Him with stones piled on high; God is to be consecrated in the breast of each.

SENECA—*Fragment*. V. 204.

26
God is our fortress, in whose conquering name
Let us resolve to scale their flinty bulwarks.

Henry VI. Pt. II. Act II. Sc. 1. L. 26.
(See also LUTHER)

27
God shall be my hope,
My stay, my guide and lantern to my feet.

Henry VI. Pt. II. Act II. Sc. 3. L. 24.

28
And to add greater honours to his age
Than man could give him, he died fearing God.

Henry VIII. Act IV. Sc. 2. L. 67.

29
God helps those who help themselves.

ALGERNON SIDNEY—*Discourse Concerning Government*. Ch. II. OVID—*Metamorphoses*. X. 586. PLINY THE ELDER, *viewing the Eruption of Vesuvius*, Aug., 79. SCHILLER—

William Tell. I. 2. SIMONIDES is quoted as author by CLAUDIAN. SOPHOCLES—*Fragments.* TERENCE—*Phormio.* I. 4. VERGIL—*Æneid.* X. 284. Quoted as a proverb by old and modern writers.

1
From Piety, whose soul sincere
Fears God, and knows no other fear.
W. SMYTH—*Ode for the Installation of the Duke of Gloucester as Chancellor of Cambridge.*
(See also RACINE)

2
Ad majorem Dei gloriam.
For the greater glory of God.
Motto of the Society of Jesus.

3
The divine essence itself is love and wisdom.
SWEDENBORG—*Divine Love and Wisdom.* Par. 28.

4
God, the Great Giver, can open the whole universe to our gaze in the narrow space of a single lane.
RABINDRANATH TAGORE—*Jivan-smitri.*

5
Ha sotto i piedi il Fato e la Natura.
Ministri umili; e'l moto e chi'l misura.
Under whose feet (subjected to His grace),
Sit nature, fortune, motion, time, and place.
TASSO—*Gerusalemme.* IX. 56.

6
At last I heard a voice upon the slope
Cry to the summit, "Is there any hope?"
To which an answer pealed from that high land,
But in a tongue no man could understand;
And on the glimmering limit far withdrawn,
God made himself an awful rose of dawn.
TENNYSON—*Vision of Sin.* V.

7
I fled Him, down the nights and down the days;
I fled Him, down the arches of the years;
I fled Him, down the labyrinthine ways
Of my own mind; and in the midst of tears
I hid from Him, and under running laughter.
FRANCIS THOMPSON—*The Hound of Heaven.*

8
But I lose
Myself in Him, in Light ineffable!
Come then, expressive Silence, muse His praise.
These, as they change, Almighty Father, these
Are but the varied God. The rolling Year
Is full of Thee.
THOMSON—*Hymn.* L. 116.

9
What, but God?
Inspiring God! who boundless Spirit all,
And unremitting Energy, pervades,
Adjusts, sustains, and agitates the whole.
THOMSON—*The Seasons. Spring.* L. 849.

10
The being of God is so comfortable, so convenient, so necessary to the felicity of Mankind, that, (as Tully admirably says) Dii immortales ad usum hominum fabricati pene videantur, if God were not a necessary being of himself, he might almost seem to be made on purpose for the use and benefit of men.
ARCHBISHOP TILLOTSON—*Works. Sermon* 93. Vol. I. P. 696. (Ed. 1712) Probable origin of Voltaire's phrase.
(See also VOLTAIRE, also MILLAUD under DEATH and OVID under GODS.)

11
Rock of Ages, cleft for me,
Let me hide myself in thee.
AUGUSTUS TOPLADY—*Living and Dying Prayer.* "Rock of Ages" is trans. from the Hebrew of "everlasting strength." *Isaiah.* XXVI. 4.
(See also BREVINT)

12
None but God can satisfy the longings of an immortal soul; that as the heart was made for Him, so He only can fill it.
RICHARD CHENEVIX TRENCH—*Notes on the Parables. Prodigal Son.*

13
God, from a beautiful necessity, is Love.
TUPPER—*Of Immortality.*

14
I believe that there is no God, but that matter is God and God is matter; and that it is no matter whether there is any God or no.
The Unbeliever's Creed. Connoisseur No. IX, March 28, 1754.
(See also BYRON under MIND)

15
Si genus humanum et mortalia temnitis arma,
At sperate deos memores fandi atque nefandi.
If ye despise the human race, and mortal arms, yet remember that there is a God who is mindful of right and wrong.
VERGIL—*Æneid.* I. 542.

16
Si Dieu n'existait pas, il faudrait l'inventer.
If there were no God, it would be necessary to invent him.
VOLTAIRE—*Epitre à l'Auteur du Livre des Trois Imposteurs.* CXI. See *Œuvres Complètes de Voltaire.* Vol. I. P. 1076. Ed. Didot, 1827. Also in letter to FREDERICK, Prince Royal of Prussia.
(See also EURIPIDES, TILLOTSON)

17
Je voudrais que vous écrasassiez l'infâme.
I wish that you would crush this infamy.
VOLTAIRE to D'ALEMBERT June 23, 1760. Attributed to VOLTAIRE by ABBÉ BARRUCH—*Memoirs Illustrating the History of Jacobinism.* Generally quoted "Écrasez l'infâme." A. DE MORGAN contends that the popular idea that it refers to God is incorrect. It refers probably to the Roman Catholic Church, or the traditions in the church.

18
God on His throne is eldest of poets:
Unto His measures moveth the Whole.
WILLIAM WATSON—*England my Mother.* Pt. II.

19
The God I know of, I shall ne'er
Know, though he dwells exceeding nigh.
Raise thou the stone and find me there,
Cleave thou the wood and there am I.
Yea, in my flesh his spirit doth flow,
Too near, too far, for me to know.
WILLIAM WATSON—*The Unknown God.* Third and fourth lines are from "newly discovered sayings of Jesus." Probably an ancient Oriental proverb.

20
The Somewhat which we name but cannot know.
Ev'n as we name a star and only see

Its quenchless flashings forth, which ever show
And ever hide him, and which are not he.
WILLIAM WATSON—*Wordsworth's Grave*. I. St. 6.

1
God is and all is well.
WHITTIER—*My Birthday*.
(See also BROWNING)

2
I know not where His islands lift
Their fronded palms in air;
I only know I cannot drift
Beyond His love and care.
WHITTIER—*The Eternal Goodness*. St. 20.

3
A God all mercy is a God unjust.
YOUNG—*Night Thoughts*. Night IV. L. 234.

4
By night an atheist half believes a God.
YOUNG—*Night Thoughts*. Night V. L. 177.

5
A Deity believed, is joy begun;
A Deity adored, is joy advanced;
A Deity beloved, is joy matured.
Each branch of piety delight inspires.
YOUNG—*Night Thoughts*. Night VIII. L. 720.

6
A God alone can comprehend a God.
YOUNG—*Night Thoughts*. Night IX. L. 835.

7
Thou, my all!
My theme! my inspiration! and my crown!
My strength in age— my rise in low estate!
My soul's ambition, pleasure, wealth!—my world!
My light in darkness! and my life in death!
My boast through time! bliss through eternity!
Eternity, too short to speak thy praise!
Or fathom thy profound of love to man!
YOUNG—*Night Thoughts*. Night IV. L. 586.

8
Though man sits still, and takes his ease,
God is at work on man;
No means, no moment unemploy'd,
To bless him, if he can.
YOUNG—*Resignation*. Pt. I. St. 119.

GODS (THE)

9
Great is Diana of the Ephesians.
Acts. XIX. 28.

10
The Ethiop gods have Ethiop lips,
Bronze cheeks, and woolly hair;
The Grecian gods are like the Greeks,
As keen-eyed, cold and fair.
WALTER BAGEHOT—*Literary Studies*. II. 410. *Ignorance of Man*.

11
Speak of the gods as they are.
BIAS.

12
And that dismal cry rose slowly
And sank slowly through the air,
Full of spirit's melancholy
And eternity's despair!
And they heard the words it said—
Pan is dead! great Pan is dead!
Pan, Pan is dead!
E. B. BROWNING—*The Dead Pan*.

13
The Graces, three erewhile, are three no more;
A fourth is come with perfume sprinkled o'er.
'Tis Berenice blest and fair; were she
Away the Graces would no Graces be.
CALLIMACHUS—*Epigram*. V. GOLDWIN SMITH'S *rendering*.

14
Two goddesses now must Cyprus adore;
The Muses are ten, and the Graces are four;
Stella's wit is so charming, so sweet her fair face,
She shines a new Venus, a Muse, and a Grace.
CALLIMACHUS—*Epigram*. V. SWIFT'S *rendering*. See MELEAGER OF GADARA, in *Anthologia Græca*. IX. 16. Vol. II. P. 62. (Ed. 1672)
(See also GREEK ANTHOLOGY)

15
Omnia fanda, nefanda, malo permista furore,
Justificam nobis mentem avertere deorum.
The confounding of all right and wrong, in wild fury, has averted from us the gracious favor of the gods.
CATULLUS—*Carmina*. LXIV. 406.

16
O dii immortales! ubinam gentium sumus?
Ye immortal gods! where in the world are we?
CICERO—*In Catilinam*. I. 4.

17
Never, believe me,
Appear the Immortals,
Never alone.
COLERIDGE—*The Visits of the Gods*. Imitated from Schiller.

18
Nature's self's thy Ganymede.
COWLEY—*Anacreontics. The Grasshopper*. L. 8.

19
With ravish'd ears
The monarch hears,
Assumes the god,
Affects to nod,
And seems to shake the spheres.
DRYDEN—*Alexander's Feast*. L. 37.

20
Creator Venus, genial power of love,
The bliss of men below, and gods above!
Beneath the sliding sun thou runn'st thy race,
Dost fairest shine, and best become thy place;
For thee the winds their eastern blasts forbear,
Thy mouth reveals the spring, and opens all the year;
Thee, goddess, thee, the storms of winter fly,
Earth smiles with flowers renewing, laughs the sky.
DRYDEN—*Palamon and Arcite*. Bk. III. L. 1405.

21
Cupid is a casuist, a mystic, and a cabalist,—
Can your lurking thought surprise,
And interpret your device,
* * * * *
All things wait for and divine him,—
How shall I dare to malign him?
EMERSON—*Initial Dæmonic and Celestial Love*. Pt. I.

22
Either Zeus came to earth to shew his form to thee,
Phidias, or thou to heaven hast gone the god to see.
In *Greek Anthology*.

1
I, Phœbus, sang those songs that gained so much renown
I, Phœbus, sang them; Homer only wrote them down.
In *Greek Anthology*.

2
Say, Bacchus, why so placid? What can there be
In commune held by Pallas and by thee?
Her pleasure is in darts and battles; thine
In joyous feasts and draughts of rosy wine.
In *Greek Anthology*.

3
Some thoughtlessly proclaim the Muses nine:
A tenth is Sappho, maid divine.
In *Greek Anthology*.
(See also CALLIMACHUS)

4
Though men determine, the gods do dispose.
GREENE—*Perimedes*. (1588)
(See also LANGLAND under GOD)

5
There's a one-eyed yellow idol to the north of Khatmandu,
There's a little marble cross below the town,
There's a broken-hearted woman tends the grave of Mad Carew,
And the yellow god forever gazes down.
J. MILTON HAYES—*The Green Eye of the Yellow God*.

6
The heathen in his blindness
Bows down to wood and stone.
REGINALD HEBER—*Missionary Hymn*.

7
Who hearkens to the gods, the gods give ear.
HOMER—*Iliad*. Bk. I. L. 280. BRYANT'S trans.

8
The son of Saturn gave
The nod with his dark brows. The ambrosial curls
Upon the Sovereign One's immortal head
Were shaken, and with them the mighty mount,
Olympus trembled.
HOMER—*Iliad*. Bk. I. L. 666. BRYANT'S trans.

9
Shakes his ambrosial curls, and gives the nod,
The stamp of fate, and sanction of the god.
HOMER—*Iliad*. Bk. I. L. 684. POPE'S trans.

10
The ox-eyed awful Juno.
HOMER—*Iliad*. Bk. III. L. 144, also Bk. VII. L. 10; Bk. XVIII. L. 40.

11
Yet verily these issues lie on the lap of the gods.
HOMER—*Iliad*. Bk. XVII. 514. *Odyssey*. I. 267. BUTCHER and LANG'S trans. That lies in the laps of the gods. (Nearest to the original, which is "in" not "on.") Other translations are:
But these things in the God's Knees are repos'd.
And yet the period of these designes, lye in the Knees of Gods.
It lies in the lap of the Norns. [Fates.] From the Scandinavian.

12
Where'er he moves, the goddess shone before.
HOMER—*Iliad*. Bk. XX. L. 127. POPE'S trans.

13
The matchless Ganymede, divinely fair.
HOMER—*Iliad*. Bk. XX. L. 278. POPE'S trans.

14
Jove weighs affairs of earth in dubious scales,
And the good suffers while the bad prevails.
HOMER—*Odyssey*. Bk. VI. L. 229. POPE'S trans.

15
Nec deus intersit nisi dignus vindice nodus.
Nor let a god come in, unless the difficulty be worthy of such an intervention.
HORACE—*Ars Poetica*. CXCI.

16
Junctæque Nymphis Gratiæ decentes.
And joined with the Nymphs the lovely Graces.
HORACE—*Carmina*. I. 4. 6.

17
Di me tuentur.
The gods my protectors.
HORACE—*Carmina*. I. 17. 13.

18
Neque semper arcum
Tendit Apollo.
Nor does Apollo keep his bow continually drawn.
HORACE—*Carmina*. II. 10.

19
Quanto quisque sibi plura negaverit,
A dis plura feret.
The more we deny ourselves, the more the gods supply our wants.
HORACE—*Carmina*. III. 16. 21.

20
Scire, deos quoniam propius contingis, oportet.
Thou oughtest to know, since thou livest near the gods.
HORACE—*Satires*. XXI. 6. 52.

21
Of Pan we sing, the best of leaders Pan,
That leads the Naiads and the Dryads forth;
And to their dances more than Hermes can,
Hear, O you groves, and hills resound his worth.
BEN JONSON—*Pan's Anniversary Hymn*. I.

22
Nam pro jucundis aptissima quæque dabunt di,
Carior est illis homo quam sibi.
For the gods, instead of what is most pleasing, will give what is most proper. Man is dearer to them than he is to himself.
JUVENAL—*Satires*. X. 349.

23
To that large utterance of the early gods!
KEATS—*Hyperion*. Bk. I.

24
High in the home of the summers, the seats of the happy immortals,
Shrouded in knee-deep blaze, unapproachable; there ever youthful
Hebé, Harmonié, and the daughter of Jove, Aphrodité,
Whirled in the white-linked dance, with the gold-crowned Hours and Graces.
CHARLES KINGSLEY—*Andromeda*.

25
Le trident de Neptune est le sceptre du monde.
The trident of Neptune is the sceptre of the world.
LEMIERRE.

1
Hoeder, the blind old god
Whose feet are shod with silence.
LONGFELLOW—*Tegner's Drapa.* St. 6.

2
Janus am I; oldest of potentates!
Forward I look and backward and below
I count—as god of avenues and gates—
The years that through my portals come and go.
I block the roads and drift the fields with snow,
I chase the wild-fowl from the frozen fen;
My frosts congeal the rivers in their flow,
My fires light up the hearths and hearts of men.
LONGFELLOW—*Written for the Children's Almanac.*

3
Estne Dei sedes nisi terra, et pontus, et aer,
Et cœlum, et virtus? Superos quid quærimus ultra?
Jupiter est, quodcunque vides, quodcunque moveris.

Has God any habitation except earth, and sea, and air, and heaven, and virtue? Why do we seek the highest beyond these? Jupiter is wheresoever you look, wheresoever you move.
LUCANUS—*Pharsalia.* Bk. IX. 578.

4
A boy of five years old serene and gay,
Unpitying Hades hurried me away.
Yet weep not for Callimachus: if few
The days I lived, few were my sorrows too.
LUCIAN—In *Greek Anthology.*

5
Apparet divom numen, sedesque quietæ;
Quas neque concutiunt ventei, nec nubila nimbeis.
Aspergunt, neque nix acri concreta pruina
Cana cadens violat; semper sine nubibus æther
Integer, et large diffuso lumine ridet.

The gods and their tranquil abodes appear, which no winds disturb, nor clouds bedew with showers, nor does the white snow, hardened by frost, annoy them; the heaven, always pure, is without clouds, and smiles with pleasant light diffused.
LUCRETIUS—*De Rerum Natura.* III. 18.

6
No wonder Cupid is a murderous boy;
A fiery archer making pain his joy.
His dam, while fond of Mars, is Vulcan's wife,
And thus 'twixt fire and sword divides her life.
MELEAGER—In *Greek Anthology.*

7
Deus ex machina.

A god from a machine (artificial or mechanical contrivance).
MENANDER. (From the Greek.) *Theop.* 5. LUCAN—*Hermo.* PLATO—*Bratylus.* 425. Quoted by SOCRATES.

8
Who knows not Circe,
The daughter of the Sun, whose charmed cup
Whoever tasted, lost his upright shape,
And downward fell into a groveling swine?
MILTON—*Comus.* L. 50.

9
That moly
That Hermes once to wise Ulysses gave.
MILTON—*Comus.* L. 637.

10
Le seigneur Jupiter sait dorer la pilule.

My lord Jupiter knows how to gild the pill.
MOLIÈRE—*Amphitryon.* III. 11.

11
Man is certainly stark mad; he cannot make a flea, and yet he will be making gods by dozens.
MONTAIGNE—*Apology for Raimond Sebond.* Bk. II. Ch. XII.

12
To be a god
First I must be a god-maker.
We are what we create.
JAMES OPPENHEIM—*Jottings. To Be a God. In War and Laughter.*

13
Expedit esse deos: et, ut expedit, esse putemus.

It is expedient there should be gods, and as it is expedient, let us believe them to exist.
OVID—*Ars Amatoria.* Bk. I. L. 637. According to TERTULLIAN—*Ad Nationes.* Bk. II. Ch. 2, DIOGENES said, "I do not know, only there ought to be gods."
(See also TILLOTSON under GOD)

14
Vilia miretur vulgus; mihi flavus Apollo
Pocula Castalia plena ministret aqua.

Let the crowd delight in things of no value; to me let the golden-haired Apollo minister full cups from the Castalian spring (the fountain of Parnassus).
OVID—*Amorum.* Bk. I. 15. 35.
Motto on title-page of Shakespeare's "Venus and Adonis." Another reading: "Castaliæ aquæ," of the Castalian spring.

15
The god we now behold with opened eyes,
A herd of spotted panthers round him lies
In glaring forms; the grapy clusters spread
On his fair brows, and dangle on his head.
OVID—*Metamorphoses.* Bk. III. L. 789. ADDISON'S trans.

16
Jocos et Dii amant.

Even the gods love jokes.
PLATO—*Cratylus.* (Trans. from Greek.)

17
The Graces sought some holy ground,
Whose sight should ever please;
And in their search the soul they found
Of Aristophanes.
PLATO—In *Greek Anthology.*

18
Di nos quasi pilas homines habent.

The gods play games with men as balls.
PLAUTUS—*Captivi Prologue.* XXII.
(See also KING LEAR)

19
Cui homini dii propitii sunt aliquid objiciunt lucri.

The gods give that man some profit to whom they are propitious.
PLAUTUS—*Persa.* IV. 3. 1.

20
Miris modis Di ludos faciunt hominibus.

In wondrous ways do the gods make sport with men.
PLAUTUS—*Rudens.* Act III. 1. 1; *Mercator.* Act II. (See also KING LEAR)

1
Keep what goods the Gods provide you.
PLAUTUS—*Rudens*. Act IV. Sc. 8. RILEY'S trans.

2
Dum homo est infirmus, tunc deos, tunc hominem esse se meminit: invidet nemini, neminem miratur, neminem despicit, ac ne sermonibus quidem malignis aut attendit, aut alitur.

When a man is laboring under the pain of any distemper, it is then that he recollects there are gods, and that he himself is but a man; no mortal is then the object of his envy, his admiration, or his contempt, and having no malice to gratify, the tales of slander excite not his attention.
PLINY THE YOUNGER—*Epistles*. VII. 26.

3
Themistocles told the Adrians that he brought two gods with him, Persuasion and Force. They replied: "We also, have two gods on our side, Poverty and Despair."
PLUTARCH—*Herodotus*.

4
Thamus . . . uttered with a loud voice his message, "The great Pan is dead."
PLUTARCH—*Why the Oracles cease to give Answers*.

5
Or ask of yonder argent fields above
Why Jove's satellites are less than Jove.
POPE—*Essay on Man*. I. 42.

6
Mundus est ingens deorum omnium templum.
The world is the mighty temple of the gods.
SENECA—*Epistolæ Ad Lucilium*. X.

7
The basest horn of his hoof is more musical than the pipe of Hermes.
Henry V. Act III. Sc. 7. L. 17.

8
As flies to wanton boys, are we to the gods;
They kill us for their sport.
King Lear. Act IV. Sc. 1. L. 38.
(See also PLAUTUS)

9
The gods are just, and of our pleasant vices
Make instruments to plague us.
King Lear. Act V. Sc. 3. L. 170.

10
This senior-junior, giant-dwarf, Dan Cupid:
Regent of love-rhymes, lord of folded arms,
The anointed sovereign of sighs and groans,
Liege of all loiterers and malcontents.
Love's Labour's Lost. Act III. Sc. 1. L. 182.

11
Cupid is a knavish lad,
Thus to make poor females mad.
Midsummer Night's Dream. Act III. Sc. 2. L. 440.

12
Wilt thou draw near the nature of the gods?
Draw near them in being merciful;
Sweet mercy is nobility's true badge.
Titus Andronicus. Act I. Sc. 1. L. 117.

13
Me goatfoot Pan of Arcady—the Median fear,
The Athenian's friend, Miltiades placed here.
SIMONIDES—In *Greek Anthology*.

14
A glimpse of Breidablick, whose walls are light
As e'en the silver on the cliff it shone;
Of dark blue steel its columns azure height
And the big altar was one agate stone.
It seemed as if the air upheld alone
Its dome, unless supporting spirits bore it,
Studded with stars Odin's spangled throne,
A light inscrutable burned fiercely o'er it;
In sky-blue mantles,
Sat the gold-crowned gods before it.
TEGNER—*Fridthjof's Saga*. Canto XXIII. St. 13.

15
Speak to Him, thou, for He hears, and Spirit with Spirit can meet;
Closer is He than breathing, and nearer than hands and feet.
TENNYSON—*Higher Pantheism*.

16
But a bevy of Eroses apple-cheeked
In a shallop of crystal ivory-beaked.
TENNYSON—*The Islet*.

17
Here comes to-day
Pallas and Aphrodite, claiming each
This meed of fairest.
TENNYSON—*Œnone*. St. 9.

18
Or sweet Europa's mantle blew unclasped
From off her shoulder backward borne;
From one hand drooped a crocus: one hand grasped
The mild bull's golden horn.
TENNYSON—*Palace of Art*. St. 30.

19
Or else flushed Ganymede, his rosy thigh
Half buried in the Eagle's down,
Sole as a flying star, shot thro' the sky,
Above the pillared town.
TENNYSON—*Palace of Art*. St. 31.

20
Atlas, we read in ancient song,
Was so exceeding tall and strong,
He bore the skies upon his back,
Just as the pedler does his pack;
But, as the pedler overpress'd
Unloads upon a stall to rest,
Or, when he can no longer stand,
Desires a friend to lend a hand,
So Atlas, lest the ponderous spheres
Should sink, and fall about his ears,
Got Hercules to bear the pile,
That he might sit and rest awhile.
SWIFT—*Atlas; or, the Minister of State*.

21
Volente Deo.
The god so willing.
VERGIL—*Æneid*. I. 303.

22
Incessu patuit Dea.
By her gait the goddess was known.
VERGIL—*Æneid*. I. 405.

23
Heu nihil invitis fas quemquam fidere divis.
Alas! it is not well for anyone to be confident when the gods are adverse.
VERGIL—*Æneid*. II. 402.

1
Jamque dies, ni fallor adest quem semper acerbum
Semper honoratum (sic dii voluistis) habeo.
That day I shall always recollect with grief; with reverence also, for the gods so willed it.
VERGIL—*Æneid*. V. 49.

2
Vocat in certamina Divos.
He calls the gods to arms.
VERGIL—*Æneid*. VI. 172.

3
Habitarunt Di quoque sylvas.
The gods also dwelt in the woods.
VERGIL—*Eclogues*. II. 60.

4
Oh, meet is the reverence unto Bacchus paid!
We will praise him still in the songs of our fatherland,
We will pour the sacred wine, the chargers lade,
And the victim kid shall unresisting stand,
Led by his horns to the altar, where we turn
The hazel spits while the dripping entrails burn.
VERGIL—*Georgics*. Bk. II. St. 17. L. 31. H. W. PRESTON's trans.

GOLD (See also BRIBERY, MONEY)

5
You shall not press down upon the brow of labor this crown of thorns—you shall not crucify mankind upon a cross of gold!
W. J. BRYAN. Democratic Convention. July 9, 1896.

6
A thirst for gold,
The beggar's vice, which can but overwhelm
The meanest hearts.
BYRON—*The Vision of Judgment*. St. 43.

7
And yet he hadde "a thombe of gold" *pardee*.
CHAUCER—*Canterbury Tales*. Prologue. L. 563.

8
Every honest miller has a golden thumb.
CHAUCER—*Canterbury Tales*. Old saying, referred to No. 7.

9
For gold in phisik is a cordial;
Therefore he lovede gold in special.
CHAUCER—*Canterbury Tales*. Prologue. L. 443.

10
Gold begets in brethren hate;
Gold in families debate;
Gold does friendship separate;
Gold does civil wars create.
COWLEY—*Anacreontics*. *Gold*. L. 17.

11
What female heart can gold despise?
What cat's averse to fish?
GRAY—*On the Death of a Favorite Cat.*

12
That is gold which is worth gold.
HERBERT—*Jacula Prudentum.*

13
Gold! Gold! Gold! Gold!
Bright and yellow, hard and cold.
HOOD—*Miss Kilmansegg. Her Moral.*

14
Aurum per medios ire satellites
Et perrumpere amat saxa potentius
Ictu fulmineo.
Stronger than thunder's winged force
All-powerful gold can speed its course;
Through watchful guards its passage make,
And loves through solid walls to break.
HORACE—*Ode XVI*. Bk. III. L. 12. FRANCIS' trans.

15
The lust of gold succeeds the rage of conquest;
The lust of gold, unfeeling and remorseless!
The last corruption of degenerate man.
SAMUEL JOHNSON—*Irene*. Act I. Sc. 1.

16
L'or donne aux plus laids certain charme pour plaire,
Et que sans lui le reste est une triste affaire.
Gold gives to the ugliest thing a certain charming air,
For that without it were else a miserable affair.
MOLIÈRE—*Sganarelle*. I.

17
Aurea nunc vere sunt sæcula; plurimus auro
Venit honos; auro conciliatur amor.
Truly now is the golden age; the highest honour comes by means of gold; by gold love is procured.
OVID—*Ars Amatoria*. Bk. II. 277.

18
Not Philip, but Philip's gold, took the cities of Greece.
PLUTARCH—*Life of Paulus Æmilius*. Quoted as a common saying. It refers to PHILIP II. of Macedon.

19
What nature wants, commodious gold bestows;
'Tis thus we cut the bread another sows.
POPE—*Moral Essay*. Ep. III. L. 21.

20
L'or est une chimère.
Gold is a vain and foolish fancy.
SCRIBE AND DELAVIGNE—*Robert le Diable*. Ch. I. Sc. 7.

21
How quickly nature falls into revolt
When gold becomes her object!
For this the foolish over-careful fathers
Have broke their sleep with thoughts, their brains with care,
Their bones with industry:
For this they have engrossed and pil'd up
The canker'd heaps of strange-achieved gold;
For this they have been thoughtful to invest
Their sons with arts and martial exercises.
Henry IV. Pt. II. Act IV. Sc. 5. L. 66.

22
Thou that so stoutly hast resisted me,
Give me thy gold, if thou hast any gold;
For I have bought it with an hundred blows.
Henry VI. Pt. III. Act II. Sc. 5. L. 79.

23
Commerce has set the mark of selfishness,
The signet of its all-enslaving power
Upon a shining ore, and called it gold;
Before whose image bow the vulgar great,
The vainly rich, the miserable proud,
The mob of peasants, nobles, priests, and kings,
And with blind feelings reverence the power
That grinds them to the dust of misery.
But in the temple of their hireling hearts
Gold is a living god, and rules in scorn
All earthly things but virtue.
SHELLEY—*Queen Mab*. Pt. V. St. 4.

1
Quid non mortalia pectora cogis,
Auri sacra fames?
Accursed thirst for gold! what dost thou not compel mortals to do?
VERGIL—*Æneid*. III. 56.

GOLDENROD

Solidago

2
Still the Goldenrod of the roadside clod
Is of all, the best!
SIMEON TUCKER CLARK—*Goldenrod*.

3
I lie amid the Goldenrod,
I love to see it lean and nod;
I love to feel the grassy sod
Whose kindly breast will hold me last,
Whose patient arms will fold me fast!—
Fold me from sunshine and from song,
Fold me from sorrow and from wrong:
Through gleaming gates of Goldenrod
I'll pass into the rest of God.
MARY CLEMMER—*Goldenrod*. Last stanza.

4
Nature lies disheveled, pale,
With her feverish lips apart,—
Day by day the pulses fail,
Nearer to her bounding heart;
Yet that slackened grasp doth hold
Store of pure and genuine gold;
Quick thou comest, strong and free,
Type of all the wealth to be,—
Goldenrod!
ELAINE GOODALE—*Goldenrod*.

5
I know the lands are lit
With all the autumn blaze of Goldenrod.
HELEN HUNT JACKSON—*Asters and Goldenrod*.

6
Because its myriad glimmering plumes
Like a great army's stir and wave;
Because its golden billows blooms,
The poor man's barren walks to lave:
Because its sun-shaped blossoms show
How souls receive the light of God,
And unto earth give back that glow—
I thank him for the Goldenrod.
LUCY LARCOM—*Goldenrod*.

7
Welcome, dear Goldenrod, once more,
Thou mimic, flowering elm!
I always think that Summer's store
Hangs from thy laden stem.
HORACE H. SCUDDER—*To the Goldenrod at Midsummer*.

8
And in the evening, everywhere
Along the roadside, up and down,
I see the golden torches flare
Like lighted street-lamps in the town.
FRANK DEMSTER SHERMAN—*Golden-Rod*.

9
The hollows are heavy and dank
With the steam of the Goldenrods.
BAYARD TAYLOR—*The Guests of Night*.

10
Graceful, tossing plume of glowing gold,
Waving lonely on the rocky ledge;
Leaning seaward, lovely to behold,
Clinging to the high cliff's ragged edge.
CELIA THAXTER—*Seaside Goldenrod*.

GOODNESS

11
Whatever any one does or says, I must be good.
AURELIUS ANTONINUS—*Meditations*. Ch. VII.

12
What good I see humbly I seek to do,
And live obedient to the law, in trust
That what will come, and must come, shall come well.
EDWIN ARNOLD—*The Light of Asia*. Bk. VI. L. 273.

13
Because indeed there was never law, or sect, or opinion, did so much magnify goodness, as the Christian religion doth.
BACON—*Essays*. *Of Goodness and Goodness of Nature*.

14
For the cause that lacks assistance,
The wrong that needs resistance,
For the future in the distance,
And the good that I can do.
GEO. LINNÆUS BANKS—*What I Live For*.

15
The good he scorned
Stalked off reluctant, like an ill-used ghost,
Not to return; or if it did, in visits
Like those of angels, short and far between.
BLAIR—*The Grave*. Pt. II. L. 586.
(See also CAMPBELL under ANGELS; NORRIS under JOY)

16
One may not doubt that, somehow Good
Shall come of Water and of Mud;
And sure, the reverent eye must see
A purpose in Liquidity.
RUPERT BROOKE—*Heaven*.
(See also TENNYSON)

17
There shall never be one lost good! What was shall live as before;
The evil is null, is nought, is silence implying sound;
What was good shall be good, with, for evil, so much good more;
On the earth the broken arcs; in the heaven a perfect round.
ROBERT BROWNING—*Abt Vogler*. IX.

18
No good Book, or good thing of any sort, shows its best face at first.
CARLYLE—*Essays*. *Novalis*.

19
Can one desire too much of a good thing?
CERVANTES—*Don Quixote*. Pt. I. Bk. I. Ch. VI. *As You Like It*. Act IV. Sc. 1. L. 123.

20
Ergo hoc proprium est animi bene constituti, et lætari bonis rebus, et dolere contrariis.
This is a proof of a well-trained mind, to rejoice in what is good and to grieve at the opposite.
CICERO—*De Amicitia*. XIII.

21
Homines ad deos nulla re propius accedunt, quam salutem hominibus dando.
Men in no way approach so nearly to the gods as in doing good to men.
CICERO—*Oratio Pro Quinto Ligario*. XII.

1
Cui bono?
What's the good of it? for whose advantage?
CICERO—*Oratio Pro Sextio Roscio Amerino.* XXX. Quoted from LUCIUS CASSIUS—*Second Philippic.* ("Qui bono fueret.") See *Life of Cicero.* II. 292. Note.

2
That good diffused may more abundant grow.
COWPER—*Conversation.* L. 441.

3 Doing good,
Disinterested good, is not our trade.
COWPER—*Task.* Bk. I. *The Sofa.* L. 673.

4
Now, at a certain time, in pleasant mood,
He tried the luxury of doing good.
CRABBE—*Tales of the Hall.* Bk. III.
(See also GOLDSMITH, GARTH)

5
Who soweth good seed shall surely reap;
The year grows rich as it groweth old,
And life's latest sands are its sands of gold!
JULIA C. R. DORR—*To the "Bouquet Club."*

6
Look around the habitable world, how few
Know their own good, or knowing it, pursue.
DRYDEN—*Juvenal.* Satire X.

7
If you wish to be good, first believe that you are bad.
EPICTETUS—*Fragments.* LONG'S trans.

8
For all their luxury was doing good.
SAMUEL GARTH—*Claremont.* L. 149.
(See also CRABBE)

9
Ein guter Mensch, in seinem dunkeln Drange,
Ist sich des rechten Weges wohl bewusst.
A good man, through obscurest aspirations
Has still an instinct of the one true way.
GOETHE—*Faust. Prolog im Himmel.*

10
And learn the luxury of doing good.
GOLDSMITH—*The Traveller.* L. 22.
(See also CRABBE)

11
Impell'd with steps unceasing to pursue
Some fleeting good, that mocks me with the view,
That, like the circle bounding earth and skies,
Allures from far, yet, as I follow, flies.
GOLDSMITH—*The Traveller.* L. 25.

12
If goodness leade him not, yet wearinesse
May tosse him to my breast.
HERBERT—*The Pulley.* St. 4.

13 Vir bonus est quis?
Qui consulta patrum, qui leges juraque servat.
Who is a good man? He who keeps the decrees of the fathers, and both human and divine laws.
HORACE—*Epistles.* I. 16. 40.

14
God whose gifts in gracious flood
Unto all who seek are sent,
Only asks you to be good
And is content.
VICTOR HUGO—*God whose Gifts in Gracious Flood.*

15
He was so good he would pour rose-water on a toad.
DOUGLAS JERROLD—*Jerrold's Wit. A Charitable Man.*

16
Can there any good thing come out of Nazareth?
John. I. 46.

17
How near to good is what is fair!
BEN JONSON—*Love Freed from Ignorance and Folly.*

18
Rari quippe boni: numero vix sunt totidem quot
Thebarum portæ, vel divitis ostia Nili.
The good, alas! are few: they are scarcely as many as the gates of Thebes or the mouths of the Nile.
JUVENAL—*Satires.* XIII. 26.

19
Be good, sweet maid, and let who will be clever;
Do noble things, not dream them all day long;
And so make life, death, and that vast forever
One grand, sweet song.
CHARLES KINGSLEY—*Farewell. To* C. E. G.

20
Be good, sweet maid, and let who can be clever;
Do lovely things, not dream them, all day long;
And so make Life, and Death, and that For Ever,
One grand sweet song.
CHARLES KINGSLEY—*Farewell.* Version in ed. of 1889. Also in *Life.* Ed. by his wife. Vol. I. P. 487, with line: "And so make Life, Death, and that vast For Ever."

21 Weiss
Dass alle Länder gute Menschen tragen.
Know this, that every country can produce good men.
LESSING—*Nathan der Weise.* II. 5.

22
Segnius homines bona quam mala sentiunt.
Men have less lively perception of good than of evil.
LIVY—*Annales.* XXX. 21.

23
The soil out of which such men as he are made is good to be born on, good to live on, good to die for and to be buried in.
LOWELL—*Among my Books. Second Series. Garfield.*

24 Si veris magna paratur
Fama bonis, et si successu nuda remoto
Inspicitur virtus, quicquid laudamus in ullo
Majorum, fortuna fuit.
If honest fame awaits the truly good; if setting aside the ultimate success of excellence alone is to be considered, then was his fortune as proud as any to be found in the records of our ancestry.
LUCAN—*Pharsalia.* IX. 593.

25
The crest and crowning of all good,
Life's final star, is Brotherhood.
EDWIN MARKHAM—*Brotherhood.*

26 None
But such as are good men can give good things,
And that which is not good, is not delicious
To a well-governed and wise appetite.
MILTON—*Comus.* L. 702.

1
* * * his providence
Out of our evil seek to bring forth good.
MILTON—*Paradise Lost.* Bk. I. L. 162.
(See also TENNYSON)

2
Since good, the more
Communicated, more abundant grows.
MILTON—*Paradise Lost.* Bk. V. L. 71.

3
A glass is good, and a lass is good,
And a pipe to smoke in cold weather;
The world is good, and the people are good,
And we're all good fellows together.
JOHN O'KEEFE—*Sprigs of Laurel.* Act II. Sc. 1.

4
I know and love the good, yet ah! the worst pursue.
PETRARCH—*To Laura in Life.* Canzone XXI.

5
Itidemque ut sæpe jam in multis locis,
Plus insciens quis fecit quam prodens boni.

And so it happens oft in many instances; more good is done without our knowledge than by us intended.
PLAUTUS—*Captivi Prologue.* XLIV.

6
Bono ingenio me esse ornatam, quam auro multo mavolo.
Aurum fortuna invenitur, natura ingenium donum.
Bonam ego, quam beatam me esse nimio dici mavolo.

A good disposition I far prefer to gold; for gold is the gift of fortune; goodness of disposition is the gift of nature. I prefer much rather to be called good than fortunate.
PLAUTUS—*Phœnulus.* I. 2. 90.

7
Gute Menschen können sich leichter in schlimme hineindenken als diese injene.

Good men can more easily see through bad men than the latter can the former.
JEAN PAUL RICHTER—*Hesperus.* IV.

8
You're good for Madge or good for Cis
Or good for Kate, maybe:
But what's to me the good of this
While you're not good for me?
CHRISTINA ROSSETTI—*Jessie Cameron.* St. 3.

9
Esse quam videri bonus malebat.

He preferred to be good, rather than to seem so.
SALLUST—*Catlina.* LIV.

10
What is beautiful is good, and who is good will soon also be beautiful.
SAPPHO—*Fragment.* 101.

11
Bonitas non est pessimis esse meliorem.

It is not goodness to be better than the very worst.
SENECA—*Epistolæ Ad Lucilium.*

12
There lives within the very flame of love
A kind of wick or snuff that will abate it;
And nothing is at a like goodness still;
For goodness, growing to a pleurisy,
Dies in his own too much.
Hamlet. Act IV. Sc. 7. L. 115.

13
There is some soul of goodness in things evil,
Would men observingly distil it out.
Henry V. Act IV. Sc. 1. L. 4.

14
Your great goodness, out of holy pity,
Absolv'd him with an axe.
Henry VIII. Act III. Sc. 2. L. 263.

15
I am in this earthly world; where to do harm,
Is often laudable, to do good sometime
Accounted dangerous folly.
Macbeth. Act IV. Sc. 2. L. 75.

16
My meaning in saying he is a good man is to have you understand me that he is sufficient.
Merchant of Venice. Act I. Sc. 3. L. 14.

17
For the Lord Jesus Christ's sake,
Do all the good you can,
To all the people you can,
In all the ways you can,
As long as ever you can.
Tombstone Inscription in Shrewsbury, England. Favorite of Mr. MOODY.

18
For who is there but you? who not only claim to be a good man and a gentleman, for many are this, and yet have not the power of making others good. Whereas you are not only good yourself, but also the cause of goodness in others.
SOCRATES to PROTAGORAS. See PLATO. JOWETT'S trans.
(See also HENRY IV under WIT)

19
How pleasant is Saturday night,
When I've tried all the week to be good,
Not spoken a word that is bad,
And obliged every one that I could.
NANCY DENNIS SPROAT—*How Pleasant is Saturday Night.*

20
One person I have to make good: myself. But my duty to my neighbor is much more nearly expressed by saying that I have to make him happy —if I may.
STEVENSON—*Christmas Sermon.*

21
She has more goodness in her little finger than he has in his whole body.
SWIFT—*Polite Conversation.* Dialogue II.

22
O, yet we trust that somehow good
Will be the final goal of ill,
To pangs of nature, sins of will
Defects of doubt and taints of blood.
TENNYSON—*In Memoriam.* LIV. 1.
(See also BROOKE, MILTON, THOMSON)

23
'Tis only noble to be good.
TENNYSON—*Lady Clara Vere de Vere.* Same in JUVENAL—*Satires.* VIII. 24.

24
From seeming evil still educing good.
THOMSON—*Hymn.* L. 114.
(See also TENNYSON)

1
Man should be ever better than he seems.
Sir Aubrey de Vere—*A Song of Faith.*

2
Roaming in thought over the Universe, I saw the little that is
Good steadily hastening towards immortality,
And the vast all that is called Evil I saw hastening to merge itself and become lost and dead.
Walt Whitman—*Roaming in Thought.* (After reading Hegel.)

3
Bene facere et male audire regium est.
To do good and be evil spoken of, is kingly.
On the Town Hall of Zittau, Saxony. Noted in Carlyle—*Frederick the Great.* XV. 13.

GOOSE

4
I dare not hope to please a Cinna's ear.
Or sing what Varus might vouchsafe to hear;
Harsh are the sweetest lays that I can bring,
So screams a goose where swans melodious sing.
Beattie—Trans. of *Vergil.* Pastoral 9.

5
Shall I, like Curtius, desperate in my zeal,
O'er head and ears plunge for the common weal?
Or rob Rome's ancient geese of all their glories,
And cackling save the monarchies of Tories?
Pope—*Dunciad.* Bk. I. L. 209.

6
As wild geese that the creeping fowler eye,
Or russet-pated choughs, many in sort,
Rising and cawing at the gun's report,
Sever themselves, and madly sweep the sky.
Midsummer Night's Dream. Act III. Sc. 2. L. 20.

7
Idem Accio quod Titio jus esto.
What is sauce for the goose is sauce for the gander.
Varro, quoting Gellius. III. XVI. 13. Same used by Swift. Jan. 24, 1710.

GORSE

Ulex

8
Mountain gorses, do ye teach us
* * * * *
That the wisest word man reaches
Is the humblest he can speak?
E. B. Browning—*Lessons from the Gorse.*

9
Mountain gorses, ever-golden.
Cankered not the whole year long!
Do ye teach us to be strong,
Howsoever pricked and holden
Like your thorny blooms and so
Trodden on by rain and snow,
Up the hillside of this life, as bleak as where ye grow?
E. B. Browning—*Lessons from the Gorse.*

10
Love you not, then, to list and hear
The crackling of the gorse-flower near,
Pouring an orange-scented tide
Of fragrance o'er the desert wide?
Wm. Howitt—*A June Day.*

GOSSIP (See also Scandal)

11
Whoever keeps an open ear
For tattlers will be sure to hear
The trumpet of contention.
Cowper—*Friendship.* St. 17.

12
Gossip is a sort of smoke that comes from the dirty tobacco-pipes of those who diffuse it; it proves nothing but the bad taste of the smoker.
George Eliot—*Daniel Deronda.* Bk. II. Ch. XIII.

13
Tell tales out of school.
Heywood—*Proverbs.* Pt. I. Ch. X.

14
He's gone, and who knows how may he report
Thy words by adding fuel to the flame?
Milton—*Samson Agonistes.* L. 1,350.

15
Fabula (nec sentis) tota jactaris in urba.
You do not know it but you are the talk of all the town.
Ovid—*Art of Love.* III. 1. 21.

16
He that repeateth a matter separateth very friends.
Proverbs. XVII. 9.

17
This act is as an ancient tale new told;
And, in the last repeating, troublesome,
Being urged at a time unseasonable.
King John. Act IV. Sc. 2. L. 18.

18
Foul whisperings are abroad.
Macbeth. Act V. Sc. 1. L. 79.

19
If my gossip Report be an honest woman of her word.
Merchant of Venice. Act III. Sc. 1. L. 7.

20
I heard the little bird say so.
Swift—*Letter to Stella.* May 23, 1711.

21
Tattlers also and busybodies, speaking things which they ought not.
I Timothy. V. 13.

22
Fama, malum quo non aliud velocius ullum,
Mobilitate viget, viresque acquirit eundo.
Report, that which no evil thing of any kind is more swift, increases with travel and gains strength by its progress.
Vergil—*Æneid.* IV. 174.

GOVERNMENT (See also Democracy, Politics, Statesmanship, Trust [Public])

23
The declaration that our People are hostile to a government made by themselves, for themselves, and conducted by themselves, is an insult.
John Adams—*Address to the citizens of Westmoreland Co., Virginia.* Answered July 11, 1798. See also Thomas Cooper—*Some information respecting America.* p. 52. (1794) In Report of a Meeting of the Mass. Historical Society by Samuel A. Green, May 9, 1901. (See also Lincoln)

24
* * * The manners of women are the surest criterion by which to determine whether a

republican government is practicable in a nation or not.

JOHN ADAMS—*Diary*. June 2, 1778. CHARLES FRANCIS ADAMS' *Life of Adams*. Vol. III. P. 171.

1

Yesterday the greatest question was decided which was ever debated in America; and a greater perhaps never was, nor will be, decided among men. A resolution was passed without one dissenting colony, that those United Colonies are, and of right ought to be, free and independent States.

JOHN ADAMS—*Letter to Mrs. Adams*. July 3, 1776.

2

Not stones, nor wood, nor the art of artisans make a state; but where men are who know how to take care of themselves, these are cities and walls.

Attributed to ALCÆUS by ARISTIDES—*Orations*. Vol. II. (Jebb's edition. AUSTIN'S trans.)

3

States are great engines moving slowly.

BACON—*Advancement of Learning*. Bk. II.

4

Adeo ut omnes imperii virga sive bacillum vere superius inflexum sit.

So that every wand or staff of empire is forsooth curved at top.

BACON—*De Sapientia Veterum*. (1609) 6. *Pan, sive Natura*. Sometimes translated, "All sceptres are crooked atop." Referring to the shepherd's crook of Pan, and implying that government needs to be roundabout in method.

5

It [Calvinism] established a religion without a prelate, a government without a king.

GEORGE BANCROFT—*History of the United States*. Vol. III. Ch. VI.

6

Oh, we are weary pilgrims; to this wilderness we bring
A Church without a bishop, a State without a King.

ANON.—*Puritan's Mistake*. (1844)
(See also CHOATE, JUNIUS)

7

Yet if thou didst but know how little wit governs this mighty universe.

MRS. A. BEHN—*Comedy of The Round Heads*. Act I. Sc. 2.
(See also OXENSTIERNA)

8

"Whatever is, is not," is the maxim of the anarchist, as often as anything comes across him in the shape of a law which he happens not to like.

RICHARD BENTLEY—*Declaration of Rights*.

9

England is the mother of parliaments.

JOHN BRIGHT—*Speech at Birmingham*, Jan. 18, 1865. See THOROLD ROGERS' ed. of BRIGHT'S *Speeches*. Vol. II. P. 112. Appeared in *London Times*, Jan. 19, 1865.

10

I am for Peace, for Retrenchment, and for Reform,—thirty years ago the great watchwords of the great Liberal Party.

JOHN BRIGHT. *Speech at Birmingham Town Hall*, April 28, 1859. Attributed to JOSEPH HUME by SIR CHARLES DILKE in the *Morning Herald*, Aug. 2, 1899. Probably said by WILLIAM IV to EARL GRAY, in an interview, Nov. 17, 1830. Found in *H. B.'s Cartoons*, No. 93, pub. Nov. 26, 1830. Also in a letter of PRINCESS LIEVEN, Nov., 1830. See WARREN'S *Ten Thousand a Year*. (Inscribed on the banner of Tittlebat Titmouse.) Referred to in MOLESWORTH'S *Hist. of the Reform Bill of 1832*. P. 98.
(See also IRVING)

11

Well, will anybody deny now that the Government at Washington, as regards its own people, is the strongest government in the world at this hour? And for this simple reason, that it is based on the will, and the good will, of an instructed people.

JOHN BRIGHT—*Speech at Rochdale*. Nov. 24, 1863.

12

So then because some towns in England are not represented, America is to have no representative at all. They are "our children"; but when children ask for bread we are not to give a stone.

BURKE—*Speech on American Taxation*. Vol. II. P. 74.

13

And having looked to Government for bread, on the very first scarcity they will turn and bite the hand that fed them.

BURKE—*Thoughts and Details on Scarcity*. Vol. V. P. 156.

14

When bad men combine, the good must associate.

BURKE—*Thoughts on the Cause of the Present Discontent*.

15

Support a compatriot against a native, however the former may blunder or plunder.

R. F. BURTON—*Explorations of the Highroads of Brazil*. I. P. 11. (About 1869)
(See also DISRAELI)

16

Nothing's more dull and negligent
Than an old, lazy government,
That knows no interest of state,
But such as serves a present strait.

BUTLER—*Miscellaneous Thoughts*. L. 159.

17

A thousand years scarce serve to form a state;
An hour may lay it in the dust.

BYRON—*Childe Harold*. Canto II. St. 84.

18

A power has arisen up in the Government greater than the people themselves, consisting of many and various and powerful interests, combined into one mass, and held together by the cohesive power of the vast surplus in the banks.

JOHN C. CALHOUN—*In the U. S. Senate*. May 28, 1836. "Cohesive power of public plunder." As quoted by GROVER CLEVELAND.

19

Consider in fact, a body of six hundred and fifty-eight miscellaneous persons, set to consult about "business," with twenty-seven millions, mostly fools, assiduously listening to them, and checking and criticising them. Was there ever, since the world began, will there ever be till the world end, any "business" accomplished in these circumstances?

CARLYLE—*Latter Day Pamphlets. Parliaments.* (Referring to the relation of the Parliament to the British people. June 1, 1850.)

(See also CARLYLE under JOURNALISM)

1

There are but two ways of paying debt—increase of industry in raising income, increase of thrift in laying out.

CARLYLE—*Past and Present. Government.* Ch. X.

2

And the first thing I would do in my government, I would have nobody to control me, I would be absolute; and who but I: now, he that is absolute, can do what he likes; he that can do what he likes, can take his pleasure; he that can take his pleasure, can be content; and he that can be content, has no more to desire; so the matter's over.

CERVANTES—*Don Quixote.* Pt. I. Bk. IV. Ch. XXIII.

3

There was a State without kings or nobles; there was a church without a bishop; there was a people governed by grave magistrates which it had elected, and equal laws which it had framed.

RUFUS CHOATE—*Speech before the New England Society.* December 22, 1843.

(See also BANCROFT)

4

Who's in or out, who moves this grand machine,
Nor stirs my curiosity nor spleen:
Secrets of state no more I wish to know
Than secret movements of a puppet show:
Let but the puppets move, I've my desire,
Unseen the hand which guides the master wire.

CHURCHILL—*Night.* L. 257.

5

They have proved themselves offensive partisans and unscrupulous manipulators of local party management.

GROVER CLEVELAND—*Letter to* GEORGE WILLIAM CURTIS. Dec. 25, 1884.

6

Though the people support the government the government should not support the people.

GROVER CLEVELAND—*Veto of Texas Seedbill.* Feb. 16, 1887.

7

I have considered the pension list of the republic a roll of honor.

GROVER CLEVELAND—*Veto of Mary Ann Dougherty's Pension.* July 5, 1888.

8

The communism of combined wealth and capital, the outgrowth of overweening cupidity and selfishness which assiduously undermines the justice and integrity of free institutions, is not less dangerous than the communism of oppressed poverty and toil which, exasperated by injustice and discontent, attacks with wild disorder the citadel of misrule.

GROVER CLEVELAND—*Annual Message.* (1888)

9

Whatever was required to be done, the Circumlocution Office was beforehand with all the public departments in the art of perceiving how not to do it.

DICKENS—*Little Dorrit.* Bk. III. Ch. X.

10

The country has, I think, made up its mind to close this career of plundering and blundering.

BENJ. DISRAELI—*Letter to* LORD GREY DE WELTON. Oct., 1873.

(See also BURTON)

11

The divine right of kings may have been a plea for feeble tyrants, but the divine right of government is the keystone of human progress, and without it governments sink into police, and a nation is degraded into a mob.

BENJ. DISRAELI—*Lothair. General Preface.* (1870)

12

A Conservative Government is an organized hypocrisy.

BENJ. DISRAELI—*Speech.* March 17, 1845.

13

Individualities may form communities, but it is institutions alone that can create a nation.

BENJ. DISRAELI—*Speech at Manchester.* (1866)

14

Resolv'd to ruin or to rule the state.

DRYDEN—*Absalom and Achitophel.* Pt. I. L. 174.

15

For where's the State beneath the Firmament,
That doth excell the Bees for Government?

DU BARTAS—*Divine Weekes and Workes.* First Week. Fifth Day. Pt. I.

16

Shall we judge a country by the majority, or by the minority? By the minority, surely.

EMERSON—*Conduct of Life. Considerations by the Way.*

(See also LINCOLN)

17

Fellow-citizens: Clouds and darkness are around Him; His pavilion is dark waters and thick clouds; justice and judgment are the establishment of His throne; mercy and truth shall go before His face! Fellow citizens! God reigns and the Government at Washington lives.

JAMES A. GARFIELD—*Address.* April, 1865. From the balcony of the New York Custom House to a crowd, excited by the news of President Lincoln's assassination.

18

When constabulary duty's to be done
A policeman's lot is not a happy one.

W. S. GILBERT—*Pirates of Penzance.*

19

Welche Regierung die beste sei? Diejenige die uns lehrt uns selbst zu regieren.

What government is the best? That which teaches us to govern ourselves.

GOETHE—*Sprüche in Prosa.* III.

20

For just experience tells, in every soil,
That those who think must govern those that toil.

GOLDSMITH—*The Traveller.* L. 372.

(See also BYRON under LABOR)

1

Perish commerce. Let the constitution live!

GEORGE HARDINGE. *Debate on the Traitorous Correspondence Bill.* March 22, 1793. Quoted by WILLIAM WINDHAM.

2

Unnecessary taxation is unjust taxation.

ABRAM S. HEWITT—*Democratic Platform.* 1884.

3

No sooner does he hear any of his brothers mention reform or retrenchment, than up he jumps.

WASHINGTON IRVING—*The Sketch Book. John Bull.* (1820)

(See also BRIGHT)

4

There was one species of despotism under which he had long groaned, and that was petticoat government.

WASHINGTON IRVING—*Rip Van Winkle.*

5

Of the various executive abilities, no one excited more anxious concern than that of placing the interests of our fellow-citizens in the hands of honest men, with understanding sufficient for their stations. No duty is at the same time more difficult to fulfill. The knowledge of character possessed by a single individual is of necessity limited. To seek out the best through the whole Union, we must resort to the information which from the best of men, acting disinterestedly and with the purest motives, is sometimes incorrect.

THOMAS JEFFERSON—*Letter to Elias Shipman and others of New Haven.* July 12, 1801. Paraphrased by JOHN B. MCMASTER in his *History of the People of the United States.* II. 586. One sentence will undoubtedly be remembered till our republic ceases to exist. 'No duty the Executive had to perform was so trying,' he observed, 'as to put the right man in the right place.'

6

The trappings of a monarchy would set up an ordinary commonwealth.

SAMUEL JOHNSON—*Life of Milton.*

7

Excise, a hateful tax levied upon commodities.

SAMUEL JOHNSON—*Definition of Excise in his Dictionary.*

8

What constitutes a state?

. . . .

Men who their duties know,
But know their rights, and knowing, dare maintain.

. . . .

And sovereign law, that state's collected will,
O'er thrones and globes elate,
Sits empress, crowning good, repressing ill.

SIR WILLIAM JONES—*Ode in Imitation of Alcæus.*

9

The Americans equally detest the pageantry of a king and the supercilious hypocrisy of a bishop.

JUNIUS—*Letter XXXV.* Dec. 19, 1769.

10

Salus populi suprema lex.

The safety of the State is the highest law.

JUSTINIAN—*Twelve Tables.*

11

This end (Robespierre's theories) was the representative sovereignty of all the citizens concentrated in an election as extensive as the people themselves, and acting by the people, and for the people in an elective council, which should be all the government.

LAMARTINE—*History of the Girondists.* Vol. III. P. 104. Bohn's ed. 1850.

(See also LINCOLN)

12

Misera contribuens plebs.

The poor taxpaying people.

Law of the HUNGARIAN DIET of 1751. Article 37.

13

The Congress of Vienna does not walk, but it dances.

PRINCE DE LIGNE.

14

I go for all sharing the privileges of the government who assist in bearing its burdens. Consequently I go for admitting all whites to the right of suffrage who pay taxes or bear arms, by no means excluding females.

ABRAHAM LINCOLN. Written in 1836.

15

A house divided against itself cannot stand. I believe this government cannot endure permanently half-slave and half-free.

ABRAHAM LINCOLN—*Speech.* June 17, 1858. See W. O. STODDARD'S *Life of Lincoln.*

16

If by the mere force of numbers a majority should deprive a minority of any clearly written constitutional right, it might in a moral point of view, justify revolution—certainly would if such a right were a vital one.

ABRAHAM LINCOLN—*First Inaugural Address.* March 4, 1861. (See also EMERSON)

17

That this nation, under God, shall have a new birth of freedom, and that government of the people, by the people, for the people, shall not perish from the earth.

ABRAHAM LINCOLN—*Speech at Gettysburg.* 1863. The phrase "of the people, for the people and by the people" is not original with Lincoln. There is a tradition that the phrase, "The Bible shall be for the government of the people, for the people and by the people," appears in the preface of the Wyclif Bible of 1384, or in the Hereford Bible, or in a pamphlet of the period treating of that version. See *Notes and Queries,* Feb. 12, 1916. P. 127. Albert Mathews, of Boston, examined the reprint of 1850 of the Wyclif Bible, and finds no reference to it. There is a preface to the Old and the New Testament, and a prologue to each book, probably written by John Purvey. Phrase used by CLEON, Athenian demagogue, 430 B.C.: PATRICK HENRY, see WIRT'S *Life of Patrick Henry,* Ed. 1818: MATTHEW F. MAURY, U. S. Navy in a report, 1851: President MONROE, to Congress, 1820: SCHINZ, a Swiss, in 1830, HENRY WILSON of Mass. 1860.

(See also ADAMS. LAMARTINE, MARSHALL,

PARKER, THOMPSON, WEBSTER; also DICKENS under LITERATURE; DISRAELI under TRUST [PUBLIC]; O. H. CARMICHAEL, in *Dial*, Oct. 25, 1917: J. W. WEIK, in *Outlook*, July 12, 1913.

1
All your strength is in your union,
All your danger is in discord.
LONGFELLOW—*The Song of Hiawatha.* I. L. 112.

2
L'état!—c'est moi! The state!—it is I!
Attributed to LOUIS XIV *of France.* DULAURE —*History of Paris.* P. 387. See CHÉRUEL—*Histoire de l'Administration Monarchique en France.* II. 32.

3
That is the best government which desires to make the people happy, and knows how to make them happy.
MACAULAY—*On Mitford's History of Greece,* 1824.

4
The Commons, faithful to their system, remained in a wise and masterly inactivity.
SIR JAMES MACKINTOSH—*Vindiciæ Gallicæ.* Sec. I.

5
The government of the Union, then, is emphatically and truly a government of the people. In form and in substance it emanates from them. Its powers are granted by them, and are to be exercised directly on them and for their benefit.
CHIEF JUSTICE MARSHALL. *Case of McCulloch vs. Maryland.* 1819. 4. Wheaton. 316.

6
The all-men power; government over all, by all, and for the sake of all.
THEODORE PARKER. *Pamphlet. The Relation of Slavery to a Republican Form of Government. Speech* delivered at the New England Anti-Slavery Convention, May 26, 1858. Pamphlet used by Lincoln when preparing speeches. This phrase was underlined by him. (See also LINCOLN)

7
To make a bank, was a great plot of state;
Invent a shovel, and be a magistrate.
ANDREW MARVELL—*The Character of Holland.*

8
States are not made, nor patched; they grow:
Grow slow through centuries of pain,
And grow correctly in the main;
But only grow by certain laws,
Of certain bits in certain jaws.
MASEFIELD—*Everlasting Mercy.* St. 60.

9
Hope nothing from foreign governments. They will never be really willing to aid you until you have shown that you are strong enough to conquer without them.
MAZZINI—*Life and Writings. Young Italy.*

10
If the prince of a State love benevolence, he will have no opponent in all the empire.
MENCIUS—*Works.* Bk. IV. Pt. I. Ch. 7.

11
Unearned increment.
JOHN STUART MILL—*Political Economy.* Bk. V. Ch. II. Sec. 5. Phrase used in the land agitation of 1870–71. Undoubtedly original with Mill.

12
La corruption de chaque gouvernement commence presque toujours par celle des principes.
The deterioration of a government begins almost always by the decay of its principles.
MONTESQUIEU—*De l'Esprit.* VIII. Ch. I.

13
Les républiques finissent par le luxe; les monarchies, par la pauvreté.
Republics end through luxury; monarchies through poverty.
MONTESQUIEU—*De l'Esprit.* VII. Ch. IV.

14
Nescis, mi fili, quantilla sapientia regitur mundus.
Learn, my son, with how little wisdom the world is governed.
Attributed to AXEL VON OXENSTIERNA. BÜCHMANN—*Geflügelte Wörte,* attributes it as likely to POPE JULIUS III, also to ORSELAER, tutor to the sons of a Markgraf of Baden. LORD CHATHAM claims it for POPE ALEXANDER VI, JULES or LEO, in Letter to LORD SHELBURNE, Jan. 25, 1775. CONRAD VON BENNINGTON, Dutch Statesman, also given credit. Quoted by DR. ARBUTHNOT—*Letter to Swift,* 1732–3.
(See also BEHN, SELDEN)

15
There is what I call the American idea. * * * This idea demands, as the proximate organization thereof, a democracy,—that is, a government of all the people, by all the people, for all the people; of course, a government of the principles of eternal justice, the unchanging law of God; for shortness' sake I will call it the idea of Freedom.
THEODORE PARKER—*Speech at the N. E. Anti-Slavery Convention.* Boston, May 29, 1850.

16
First there is the democratic idea: that all men are endowed by their creator with certain natural rights; that these rights are alienable only by the possessor thereof; that they are equal in men; that government is to organize these natural, unalienable and equal rights into institutions designed for the good of the governed, and therefore government is to be of all the people, by all the people, and for all the people. Here government is development, not exploitation.
THEODORE PARKER—*Speech in Boston.* May 31, 1854.

17
Democracy is direct self-government, over all the people, for all the people, by all the people.
THEODORE PARKER. *Sermon.* Delivered at Music Hall, Boston, July 4, 1858. *On the Effect of Slavery on the American People.* P. 5. (Read and underlined by Lincoln.)

18
Slavery is in flagrant violation of the institutions of America—direct government—over all the people, by all the people, for all the people.
THEODORE PARKER. *Sermon.* Delivered at Music Hall, Boston. July 4, 1858. P. 14. (Read and underlined by Lincoln.)
(See also LINCOLN)

1
In principatu commutando civium
Nil præter domini nomen mutant pauperes.
In a change of government the poor change nothing but the name of their masters.
PHÆDRUS—*Fables*. I. 15. 1.

2
Three millions of people, so dead to all the feelings of liberty as voluntarily to submit to be slaves, would have been fit instruments to make slaves of the rest.
PITT (THE ELDER)—*Speech on America.*

3
Themistocles said, "The Athenians govern the Greeks; I govern the Athenians; you, my wife, govern me; your son governs you."
PLUTARCH—*Life of Cato the Censor.*

4
The government will take the fairest of names, but the worst of realities—mob rule.
POLYBIUS. VI. 57.

5
The right divine of kings to govern wrong.
POPE—*Dunciad*. Bk. IV. L. 188. (In quotation marks, but probably his own.)

6
For forms of government let fools contest;
Whate'er is best administer'd is best.
POPE—*Essay on Man*. Ep. III. L. 303.

7
He shall rule them with a rod of iron.
Revelations. II. 27.

8
The labor unions shall have a square deal, and the corporations shall have a square deal, and in addition, all private citizens shall have a square deal.
ROOSEVELT—*Address.*

9
Le despotisme tempéré par l'assassinat, c'est notre *magna charta.*
Despotism tempered by assassination, that is our Magna Charta.
A RUSSIAN NOBLE to COUNT MÜNSTER on the assassination of PAUL I., Emperor of Russia. (1800)

10
Say to the seceded States—*Wayward sisters, depart in peace!*
WINFIELD SCOTT—*Letter to W. H. Seward.* March 3, 1861.

11
The Pope sends for him . . . and (says he) "We will be merry as we were before, for thou little thinkest what a little foolery governs the whole world."
JOHN SELDEN—*Table Talk. Pope.*
(See also OXENSTIERNA)

12
Invisa numquam imperia retinentur diu.
A hated government does not last long.
SENECA—*Phœnissæ*. VI. 60.

13
For government, through high and low and lower,
Put into parts, doth keep in one consent,
Congreeing in a full and natural close,
Like music.
Henry V. Act I. Sc. 2. L. 190.

14
How, in one house,
Should many people, under two commands,
Hold amity? 'Tis hard; almost impossible.
King Lear. Act II. Sc. 4. L. 243.

15
Why, this it is, when men are rul'd by women.
Richard III. Act I. Sc. 1. L. 62.

16
What a man that would be had he a particle of gall or the least knowledge of the value of red tape. As Curran said of Grattan, "he would have governed the world."
SYDNEY SMITH. *Of Sir John Mackintosh.* LADY HOLLAND'S *Memoir*. P. 245. (Ed. 4.)

17
Men who prefer any load of infamy, however great, to any pressure of taxation, however light.
SYDNEY SMITH—*On American Debts.*

18
The schoolboy whips his taxed top, the beardless youth manages his taxed horse, with a taxed bridle, on a taxed road; and the dying Englishman, pouring his medicine, which has paid seven per cent., flings himself back on his chintz bed, which has paid twenty-two per cent., and expires in the arms of an apothecary who has paid a license of a hundred pounds for the privilege of putting him to death.
SYDNEY SMITH—*Review of Seybert's Annals. United States.*

19
Ill can he rule the great that cannot reach the small.
SPENSER—*Faerie Queene*. Bk. V. Canto II. St. 51.

20
Omnium consensu capax imperii, nisi imperasset.
In the opinion of all men he would have been regarded as capable of governing, if he had never governed.
TACITUS—*Annales*. I. 49.

21
In the parliament of man, the Federation of the world.
TENNYSON—*Locksley Hall*. L. 129.

22
Et errat longe mea quidem sententia
Qui imperium credit gravius esse aut stabilius,
Vi quod fit, quam illud quod amicitia adjungitur.
It is a great error, in my opinion, to believe that a government is more firm or assured when it is supported by force, than when founded on affection.
TERENCE—*Adelphi*. I. 1. 40.

23
We preach Democracy in vain while Tory and Conservative can point to the opposite side of the Atlantic and say: "There are Nineteen millions of the human race free absolutely, every man heir to the throne, governing themselves—the government of all, by all, for all; but instead of being a consistent republic it is one widespread confederacy of free men for the enslavement of a nation of another complexion."
GEORGE THOMPSON, M.P. *Speech*, 1851.
(See also LINCOLN)

1
Hæ tibi erunt artes, pacisque imponere morem
Parcere subjectis et debellare superbos.
This shall be thy work: to impose conditions of peace, to spare the lowly, and to overthrow the proud.
VERGIL—*Æneid.* VI. 852.

2
Let us raise a standard to which the wise and honest can repair; the rest is in the hands of God.
WASHINGTON—*Speech to the Constitutional Convention.* (1787)

3
A National debt is a National blessing.
Attributed to DANIEL WEBSTER. Repudiated by him. See *Speech.* Jan. 26, 1830.

4
The people's government made for the people, made by the people, and answerable to the people.
DANIEL WEBSTER—*Second Speech on Foot's Resolution.* Jan. 26, 1830.
(See also LINCOLN)

5
When my eyes shall be turned to behold, for the last time, the sun in heaven, may I not see him shining on the broken and dishonored fragments of a once glorious Union; on States dissevered, discordant, belligerent; on a land rent with civil feuds, or drenched, it may be, in fraternal blood!
DANIEL WEBSTER—*Second Speech on Foot's Resolution.* Jan. 26, 1830.

6
He touched the dead corpse of Public Credit, and it sprung upon its feet.
DANIEL WEBSTER—*Speech on Hamilton.* March 10, 1831.

7
We have been taught to regard a representative of the people as a sentinel on the watch-tower of liberty.
DANIEL WEBSTER. *To the Senate.* May 7, 1834.

8
[He would do his duty as he saw it] without regard to scraps of paper called constitutions.
KING WILLIAM to the Prussian Diet disregarding the refusal of the Representatives to grant appropriations. *Harper's Weekly,* March 26, 1887. *Article* on EMPEROR WILLIAM I, of Germany.
(See also pages 847[15], 850[10])

9
No man ever saw the people of whom he forms a part. No man ever saw a government. I live in the midst of the Government of the United States, but I never saw the Government of the United States. Its personnel extends through all the nations, and across the seas, and into every corner of the world in the persons of the representatives of the United States in foreign capitals and in foreign centres of commerce.
WOODROW WILSON—*Speech at Pittsburgh.* Jan. 29, 1916.

10
Wherever magistrates were appointed from among those who complied with the injunctions of the laws, he (Socrates) considered the government to be an aristocracy.
XENOPHON—*Memorabilia of Socrates.* Bk. IV. Ch. VI.

GRACE

11
There, but for the grace of God, goes John Bradford.
JOHN BRADFORD (seeing a criminal pass by), in his *Writings.* Vol. II. Pub. by PARKER SOCIETY, Cambridge, 1853. Biog. notice. P. 13. *Credited to him also by* DEAN FARRAR —*Eternal Hope. Fourth Sermon.* S. O. VII. 269. 351. Credited also to BAXTER, BUNYAN, JOHN WESLEY.

12
An outward and visible sign of an inward and spiritual grace.
Book of Common Prayer. Catechism.

13
Whatever he did, was done with so much ease,
In him alone 'twas natural to please.
DRYDEN—*Absalom and Achitophel.* Pt. I. L. 27.

14
Ye are fallen from grace.
Galatians. V. 4.

15
Stately and tall he moves in the hall,
The chief of a thousand for grace.
KATE FRANKLIN—*Life at Olympus. Godey's Lady's Book.* Vol. XXIII. P. 33.

16
And grace that won who saw to wish her stay.
MILTON—*Paradise Lost.* Bk. VIII. L. 43.

17
From vulgar bounds with brave disorder part,
And snatch a grace beyond the reach of art.
POPE—*Essay on Criticism.* L. 152.

18
God give him grace to groan!
Love's Labour's Lost. Act. IV. Sc. 3. L. 21.

19
O, then, what graces in my love do dwell,
That he hath turn'd a heaven unto a hell!
Midsummer Night's Dream. Act I. Sc. 1. L. 206.

20
Hail to thee, lady! and the grace of heaven,
Before, behind thee and on every hand,
Enwheel thee round!
Othello. Act II. Sc. 1. L. 85.

21
For several virtues
Have I lik'd several women; never any
With so full soul, but some defect in her
Did quarrel with the noblest grace she ow'd,
And put it to the foil.
Tempest. Act III. Sc. 1. L. 42.

22
He does it with a better grace, but I do it more natural.
Twelfth Night. Act II. Sc. 3. L. 88.

23
The three black graces, Law, Physic, and Divinity.
HORACE and JAMES SMITH—*Punch's Holiday.*

24
Narcissus is the glory of his race:
For who does nothing with a better grace?
YOUNG—*Love of Fame.* Satire IV. L. 85.

GRAFT (See Bribery, Corruption, Politics)

GRAPES

1
Nay, in death's hand, the grape-stone proves
As strong as thunder is in Jove's.
Cowley—*Elegy upon Anacreon.* L. 106.

2
The fathers have eaten sour grapes, and the children's teeth are set on edge.
Ezekiel. XVIII. 2; *Jeremiah.* XXXI. 29.

3
Is not the gleaning of the grapes of Ephraim better than the vintage of Abi-ezer?
Judges. VIII. 2.

4
Uvaque conspecta livorem ducit ab uva.
The grape gains its purple tinge by looking at another grape.
Juvenal—*Satires.* II. 81.

GRASS

5
The scented wild-weeds and enamell'd moss.
Campbell—*Theodric.*
(See also Milton)

6
Grass grows at last above all graves.
Julia C. R. Dorr—*Grass-Grown.*

7
We say of the oak, "How grand of girth!"
Of the willow we say, "How slender!"
And yet to the soft grass clothing the earth
How slight is the praise we render.
Edgar Fawcett—*The Grass.*

8
All flesh is grass.
Isaiah. XL. 6.

9
A blade of grass is always a blade of grass, whether in one country or another.
Samuel Johnson—*Mrs. Piozzi's Anecdotes of Johnson.* P. 100.

10
The green grass floweth like a stream
Into the ocean's blue.
Lowell—*The Sirens.* L. 87.

11
O'er the smooth enamell'd green
Where no print of step hath been.
Milton—*Arcades.*
(See also Campbell)

12
And pile them high at Gettysburg
And pile them high at Ypres and Verdun.
Shovel them under and let me work.
* * * * *
I am the grass.
Let me work.
Carl Sandburg—*Grass.*

13 While the grass grows—
The proverb is something musty.
Hamlet. Act III. Sc. 2. L. 358.

14
How lush and lusty the grass looks! how green!
Tempest. Act II. Sc. 1. L. 52.

15
Whylst grass doth grow, oft sterves the seely steede.
Whetstone—*Promos and Cassandra.* (1578)

GRASSHOPPER

16
Happy insect! what can be
In happiness compared to thee?
Fed with nourishment divine,
The dewy morning's gentle wine!
Nature waits upon thee still,
And thy verdant cup does fill;
'Tis fill'd wherever thou dost tread,
Nature's self's thy Ganymede.
Cowley—*Anacreontiques.* No. 10. *Grasshopper.*

17
Green little vaulter, in the sunny grass,
Catching your heart up at the feel of June,
Sole noise that's heard amidst the lazy noon,
When ev'n the bees lag at the summoning brass.
Leigh Hunt—*To the Grasshopper and the Cricket.*

18
When all the birds are faint with the hot sun,
And hide in cooling trees, a voice will run
From hedge to hedge about the new-mown mead;
That is the grasshopper's—he takes the lead
In summer luxury—he has never done
With his delights, for when tired out with fun,
He rests at ease beneath some pleasant weed.
Keats—*On the Grasshopper and Cricket.*

GRATITUDE

19
If hush'd the loud whirlwind that ruffled the deep,
The sky if no longer dark tempests deform;
When our perils are past shall our gratitude sleep?
No! Here's to the pilot that weather'd the storm!
George Canning—*Song* (on "Billy Pitt"). Sung at a public dinner, May 28, 1802.

20
Gratus animus est una virtus non solum maxima, sed etiam mater virtutum omnium reliquarum.
A thankful heart is not only the greatest virtue, but the parent of all the other virtues.
Cicero—*Oratio Pro Cnæo Plancio.* XXXIII.

21
Praise the bridge that carried you over.
Geo. Colman (the Younger)—*Heir-at-Law.* Act I. Sc. 1.

22
Gratitude is expensive.
Gibbon—*Decline and Fall of the Roman Empire.*

23
The still small voice of gratitude.
Gray—*For Music.* St. 5.

24
The gratitude of most men is but a secret desire of receiving greater benefits.
La Rochefoucauld—*Maxim.* 298.

25
La reconnaissance est la mémoire du cœur.
Gratitude is the memory of the heart.
Massieu to the Abbé Sicard.

26 A grateful mind
By owing owes not, but still pays, at once
Indebted and discharg'd.
Milton—*Paradise Lost.* Bk. IV. L. 55.

1
Gratia pro rebus merito debetur inemtis.
Thanks are justly due for things got without purchase.
OVID—*Amorum*. I. 10. 43.

2
Conveniens homini est hominem servare voluptas.
Et melius nulla quæritur arte favor.
It is a pleasure appropriate to man, for him to save a fellow-man, and gratitude is acquired in no better way.
OVID—*Epistolæ Ex Ponto*. II. 9. 39.

3
Th' unwilling gratitude of base mankind!
POPE—*Second Book of Horace*. Ep. I. L. 14.

4
Non est diuturna possessio in quam gladio ducimus; beneficiorum gratia sempiterna est.
That possession which we gain by the sword is not lasting; gratitude for benefits is eternal.
QUINTUS CURTIUS RUFUS—*De Rebus Gestis Alexandri Magni*. VIII. 8. 11.

5
Qui gratus futurus est statim dum accipit de reddendo cogitet.
Let the man, who would be grateful, think of repaying a kindness, even while receiving it.
SENECA—*De Beneficiis*. II. 25.

6
L'ingratitude attire les reproches comme la reconnaissance attire de nouveaux bienfaits.
Ingratitude calls forth reproaches as gratitude brings renewed kindnesses.
MME. DE SÉVIGNÉ—*Lettres*.

7
Now the good gods forbid
That our renowned Rome, whose gratitude
Towards her deserved children is enroll'd
In Jove's own book, like an unnatural dam
Should now eat up her own!
Coriolanus. Act III. Sc. 1. L. 290.

8
Let but the commons hear this testament—
Which, pardon me, I do not mean to read—
And they would go and kiss dead Cæsar's wounds
And dip their napkins in his sacred blood,
Yea, beg a hair of him for memory,
And, dying, mention it within their wills,
Bequeathing it as a rich legacy
Unto their issue.
Julius Cæsar. Act III. Sc. 2. L. 135.

9
I've heard of hearts unkind, kind deeds
With coldness still returning;
Alas! the gratitude of men
Hath often left me mourning.
WORDSWORTH—*Simon Lee*.

GRAVE (THE)

10
And he buried him in a valley in the land of Moab, over against Beth-peor; but no man knoweth of his sepulcher unto this day.
Deut. XXXIV. 6.

By Nebo's lonely mountain,
On this side Jordan's wave,
In a vale in the land of Moab,
There lies a lonely grave;
But no man built that sepulcher,
And no man saw it e'er,
For the angels of God upturned the sod
And laid the dead man there.
CECIL FRANCES ALEXANDER—*Burial of Moses*.

11
Inn of a traveller on his way to Jerusalem.
Translation of the Latin on the monument of DEAN ALFORD. St. Martin's Churchyard, Canterbury.
(See also SCOTT)

12
Mine be the breezy hill that skirts the down;
Where a green grassy turf is all I crave,
With here and there a violet bestrown,
Fast by a brook or fountain's murmuring wave;
And many an evening sun shine sweetly on my grave!
BEATTIE—*The Minstrel*. Bk. II. St. 17.

13
Here's an acre sown indeed,
With the richest royalest seed.
FRANCIS BEAUMONT. On the Tombs in Westminster Abbey.
(See also LONGFELLOW, TAYLOR)

14
One foot in the grave.
BEAUMONT AND FLETCHER—*The Little French Lawyer*. Act I. Sc. 1.
(See also ERASMUS)

15
See yonder maker of the dead man's bed,
The sexton, hoary-headed chronicle,
Of hard, unmeaning face, down which ne'er stole
A gentle tear.
BLAIR—*The Grave*. L. 451.

16
The grave, dread thing!
Men shiver when thou'rt named: Nature appalled,
Shakes off her wonted firmness.
BLAIR—*The Grave*.

17
Nigh to a grave that was newly made,
Leaned a sexton old on his earth-worn spade.
PARK BENJAMIN—*The Old Sexton*.

18
The grave is Heaven's golden gate,
And rich and poor around it wait;
O Shepherdess of England's fold,
Behold this gate of pearl and gold!
WM. BLAKE — *Dedication of the Designs to Blair's "Grave." To Queen Charlotte*.

19
Build me a shrine, and I could kneel
To rural Gods, or prostrate fall;
Did I not see, did I not feel.
That one GREAT SPIRIT governs all.
O Heaven, permit that I may lie
Where o'er my corse green branches wave;
And those who from life's tumults fly
With kindred feelings press my grave.
BLOOMFIELD—*Love of the Country*. St. 4.

20
Gravestones tell truth scarce forty years.
SIR THOMAS BROWNE—*Hydriotaphia*. Ch. V.

21
He that unburied lies wants not his hearse,
For unto him a tomb's the Universe.
SIR THOMAS BROWNE—*Religio Medici*. Pt. I. Sec. XLI.
(See also LUCANUS under MONUMENTS)

1
I gazed upon the glorious sky
And the green mountains round,
And thought that when I came to lie
At rest within the ground,
'Twere pleasant that in flowery June
When brooks send up a cheerful tune,
And groves a joyous sound,
The sexton's hand, my grave to make,
The rich, green mountain turf should break.
BRYANT—*June.*

2
I would rather sleep in the southern corner of a little country churchyard, than in the tombs of the Capulets.
BURKE—*Letter to Matthew Smith.*

3
Perhaps the early grave
Which men weep over may be meant to save.
BYRON—*Don Juan.* Canto IV. St. 12.

4
Of all
The fools who flock'd to swell or see the show
Who car'd about the corpse? The funeral
Made the attraction, and the black the woe;
There throbb'd not there a thought which
pierc'd the pall.
BYRON—*Vision of Judgment.* St. 10.

5
What's hallow'd ground? Has earth a clod
Its Maker mean'd not should be trod
By man, the image of his God,
Erect and free,
Unscourged by Superstition's rod
To bow the knee.
CAMPBELL—*Hallowed Ground.*

6
But an untimely grave.
CAREW—*On the Duke of Buckingham.*

7
The grave's the market place.
Death and the Lady. Ballad in DIXON'S *Ballads.* The Percy Society.

8
The solitary, silent, solemn scene,
Where Cæsars, heroes, peasants, hermits lie,
Blended in dust together; where the slave
Rests from his labors; where th' insulting proud
Resigns his powers; the miser drops his hoard:
Where human folly sleeps.
DYER—*Ruins of Rome.* L. 540.

9
Etsi alterum pedem in sepulchro haberem.
(Julian would learn something) even if he had one foot in the grave.
ERASMUS. Quoting POMPONIUS, of JULIAN. Original phrase one foot in the ferry boat, meaning Charon's boat.
(See also BEAUMONT, WORDSWORTH)

10
Alas, poor Tom! how oft, with merry heart,
Have we beheld thee play the Sexton's part;
Each comic heart must now be grieved to see
The Sexton's dreary part performed on thee.
ROBERT FERGUSSON—*Epigram on the Death of Mr. Thomas Lancashire, Comedian.*

11
Some village Hampden, that, with dauntless
breast,
The little tyrant of his fields withstood,
Some mute inglorious Milton here may rest,
Some Cromwell guiltless of his country's blood.
GRAY—*Elegy in a Country Churchyard.*

12
The boast of heraldry, the pomp of power,
And all that beauty, all that wealth e'er gave,
Await alike th' inevitable hour,
The paths of glory lead but to the grave.
GRAY—*Elegy in a Country Churchyard.*

13
Fond fool! six feet shall serve for all thy store,
And he that cares for most shall find no more.
JOSEPH HALL — *Satires.* No. III. Second Series.
(See also HERBERT, LUCANUS)

14
Such graves as his are pilgrim shrines,
Shrines to no code or creed confined,—
The Delphian vales, the Palestines,
The Meccas of the mind.
FITZ-GREENE HALLECK—*Burns.* St. 32.

15
Green be the turf above thee,
Friend of my better days;
None knew thee but to love thee
Nor named thee but to praise.
FITZ-GREENE HALLECK—*On the death of J. R. Drake.*
(See also POPE, also BURNS under LOVE)

16
Graves they say are warm'd by glory;
Foolish words and empty story.
HEINE—*Latest Poems.* Epilogue. L. 1.

17
Where shall we make her grave?
Oh! where the wild flowers wave
In the free air!
When shower and singing-bird
'Midst the young leaves are heard,
There—lay her there!
FELICIA D. HEMANS—*Dirge. Where Shall we Make her Grave?*

18
A piece of a Churchyard fits everybody.
HERBERT—*Jacula Prudentum.*
(See also HALL)

19
The house appointed for all living.
Job. XXX. 23.

20
Teach me to live that I may dread
The grave as little as my bed.
BISHOP KEN—*Evening Hymn.* The same is found in THOMAS BROWNE—*Religio Medici.* Both are taken from the old *Hymni Eclesesiæ.*

21
Then to the grave I turned me to see what therein lay;
'Twas the garment of the Christian, worn out and thrown away.
KRUMMACHER—*Death and the Christian.*

22
I like that ancient Saxon phrase, which calls
The burial-ground *God's Acre.* It is just.
LONGFELLOW—*God's Acre.*
(See also BEAUMONT)

23
This is the field and Acre of our God,
This is the place where human harvests grow!
LONGFELLOW—*God's Acre.*

1
I see their scattered gravestones gleaming white
Through the pale dusk of the impending night.
O'er all alike the imperial sunset throws
Its golden lilies mingled with the rose;
We give to each a tender thought and pass
Out of the graveyards with their tangled grass.
LONGFELLOW—*Morituri Salutamus.* L. 120.

2
Take them, O Grave! and let them lie
Folded upon thy narrow shelves,
As garments by the soul laid by,
And precious only to ourselves!
LONGFELLOW—*Suspiria.*
(See also MACDONALD, PEARSON)

3
There are slave-drivers quietly whipped under-ground,
There bookbinders, done up in boards, are fast bound,
There card-players wait till the last trump be played,
There all the choice spirits get finally laid,
There the babe that's unborn is supplied with a berth,
There men without legs get their six feet of earth,
There lawyers repose, each wrapped up in his case,
There seekers of office are sure of a place,
There defendant and plaintiff get equally cast,
There shoemakers quietly stick to the last.
LOWELL—*Fables for Critics.* L. 1,656.

4
As life runs on, the road grows strange
With faces new,—and near the end
The milestones into headstones change:—
'Neath every one a friend.
LOWELL. Written on his 68th birthday.

5
We should teach our children to think no more of their bodies when dead than they do of their hair when cut off, or of their old clothes when they have done with them.
GEORGE MACDONALD—*Annals of a Quiet Neighborhood.* P. 181.
(See also LONGFELLOW)

6
Your seventh wife, Phileros, is now being buried in your field. No man's field brings him greater profit than yours, Phileros.
MARTIAL—*Epigrams.* Bk. X. Ep. 43.

7
And so sepulchred in such pomp dost lie;
That kings for such a tomb would wish to die.
MILTON—*Epitaph on Shakespeare.*

8
There is a calm for those who weep,
A rest for weary pilgrims found,
They softly lie and sweetly sleep
Low in the ground.
MONTGOMERY—*The Grave.*

9
(Bodies) carefully to be laid up in the wardrobe of the grave.
BISHOP PEARSON—*Exposition of the Creed.* Article IV.
(See also LONGFELLOW)

10
Pabulum Acheruntis.
Food of Acheron. (Grave.)
PLAUTUS—*Casina.* Act II. Sc. 1. L. 11.

11
Yet shall thy grave with rising flow'rs be dressed,
And the green turf lie lightly on thy breast;
There shall the morn her earliest tears bestow,
There the first roses of the year shall blow.
POPE—*Elegy on an Unfortunate Lady.* L. 65.
(See also HALLECK)

12
The grave unites; where e'en the great find rest,
And blended lie th' oppressor and th' oppressed!
POPE—*Windsor Forest.* L. 317.

13
Ruhe eines Kirchhofs!
The churchyard's peace.
SCHILLER—*Don Carlos.* III. 10. 220.

14
Never the grave gives back what it has won!
SCHILLER—*Funeral Fantasy.* Last line.

15
To that dark inn, the Grave!
SCOTT—*The Lord of the Isles.* VI. L. 26.
(See also ALFORD)

16
Bear from hence his body;
And mourn you for him: let him be regarded
As the most noble corse that ever herald
Did follow to his urn.
Coriolanus. Act V. Sc. 6. L. 143.

17
The sepulchre,
Wherein we saw thee quietly inurn'd,
Hath op'd his ponderous and marble jaws.
Hamlet. Act I. Sc. 4. L. 48.

18
They bore him barefac'd on the bier;
* * * * *
And in his grave rain'd many a tear.
Hamlet. Act IV. Sc. 5. L. 164.

19
Lay her i' the earth;
And from her fair and unpolluted flesh
May violets spring!
Hamlet. Act V. Sc. 1. L. 261.

20
Has this fellow no feeling of his business that he sings at grave-making?
Custom hath made it in him a property of easiness.
Hamlet. Act V. Sc. 1. L. 73.

21
Gilded tombs do worms infold.
Merchant of Venice. Act II. Sc. 7. L. 69.

22
Let's choose executors and talk of wills:
And yet not so, for what can we bequeath
Save our deposed bodies to the ground?
Richard II. Act III. Sc. 2. L. 148.

23
Taking the measure of an unmade grave.
Romeo and Juliet. Act III. Sc. 3. L. 70.

24
The lone couch of his everlasting sleep.
SHELLEY—*Alastor.* L. 57.

25
O heart, and mind, and thoughts! what thing do you
Hope to inherit in the grave below?
SHELLEY—*Sonnet. Ye Hasten to the Dead!*

1 The grave
Is but the threshold of eternity.
SOUTHEY—*Vision of the Maid of Orleans*. Bk. II. (Originally the 9th book of *Joan of Arc;* later published as separate poem.)

2
There is an acre sown with royal seed.
JEREMY TAYLOR — *Holy Living and Dying*. Ch. I. (See also BEAUMONT)

3
Kings have no such couch as thine,
As the green that folds thy grave.
TENNYSON—*A Dirge*. St. 6.

4
Our father's dust is left alone
And silent under other snows.
TENNYSON—*In Memoriam*. Pt. CV.

5
Hark! from the tombs a doleful sound.
WATTS—*Hymns and Spiritual Songs. Funeral Thoughts*. Bk. II. Vol. IX. Hymn 63.

6 . . . The low green tent
Whose curtain never outward swings.
WHITTIER—*Snow-bound*.

7
But the grandsire's chair is empty,
The cottage is dark and still;
There's a nameless grave on the battle-field,
And a new one under the hill.
WM. WINTER—*After All*.

8 . . . In shepherd's phrase
With one foot in the grave.
WORDSWORTH—*Michael*.
(See also ERASMUS)

GREATNESS

9 Burn to be great,
Pay not thy praise to lofty things alone.
The plains are everlasting as the hills,
The bard cannot have two pursuits; aught else
Comes on the mind with the like shock as though
Two worlds had gone to war, and met in air.
BAILEY—*Festus*. Sc. *Home*.

10
Nothing can cover his high fame but heaven;
No pyramids set off his memories,
But the eternal substance of his greatness,—
To which I leave him.
BEAUMONT AND FLETCHER—*The False One*. Act II. Sc. 1.

11
Man's Unhappiness, as I construe, comes of his Greatness; it is because there is an Infinite in him, which with all his cunning he cannot quite bury under the Finite.
CARLYLE—*Sartor Resartus. The Everlasting Yea*. Bk. II. Ch. IX.

12
We have not the love of greatness, but the love of the love of greatness.
CARLYLE—*Essays. Characteristics*. Vol. III.

13
Nemo vir magnus aliquo afflatu divino unquam fuit.
No man was ever great without divine inspiration.
CICERO—*De Natura Deorum*. II. 66.

14
The great man who thinks greatly of himself, is not diminishing that greatness in heaping fuel on his fire.
ISAAC D'ISRAELI—*Literary Character of Men of Genius*. Ch. XV.

15
So let his name through Europe ring!
A man of mean estate,
Who died as firm as Sparta's king,
Because his soul was great.
SIR FRANCIS HASTINGS DOYLE—*The Private of the Buffs*.

16 No great deed is done
By falterers who ask for certainty.
GEORGE ELIOT—*The Spanish Gypsy*. Bk. I. 56th line from end.

17
He is great who is what he is from Nature, and who never reminds us of others.
EMERSON—*Essays. Second Series. Uses of Great Men*.

18
Nature never sends a great man into the planet, without confiding the secret to another soul.
EMERSON—*Uses of Great Men*.

19
He who comes up to his own idea of greatness, must always have had a very low standard of it in his mind.
HAZLITT—*Table Talk. Whether Genius is Conscious of its own Power*.

20
No really great man ever thought himself so.
HAZLITT—*Table Talk. Whether Genius is Conscious of its own Power*.

21
Ajax the great * * *
Himself a host.
HOMER—*Iliad*. Bk. III. L. 293. POPE'S trans.

22
For he that once is good, is ever great.
BEN JONSON—*The Forest. To Lady Aubigny*.

23
Urit enim fulgore suo qui prægravat artes
Intra se positas; extinctus amabitur idem.
That man scorches with his brightness, who overpowers inferior capacities, yet he shall be revered when dead.
HORACE—*Epistles*. II. 1. 13.

24
Greatnesse on goodnesse loves to slide, not stand,
And leaves, for fortune's ice, vertue's firme land.
RICHARD KNOLLES—*Turkish History*. Under a portrait of Mustapha I. L. 13.
(See also DRYDEN under AMBITION)

25
Great is advertisement! 'tis almost fate;
But, little mushroom-men, of puff-ball fame.
Ah, do you dream to be mistaken great
And to be really great are just the same?
RICHARD LE GALLIENNE—*Alfred Tennyson*.

26
Il n'appartient qu'aux grands hommes d'avoir de grands défauts.
It is the prerogative of great men only to have great defects.
LA ROCHEFOUCAULD—*Maximes*.

1
The great man is the man who can get himself made and who will get himself made out of anything he finds at hand.
GERALD STANLEY LEE—*Crowds*. Bk. II. Ch. XV.

2
Great men stand like solitary towers in the city of God.
LONGFELLOW—*Kavanagh*. Ch. I.

3
A great man is made up of qualities that meet or make great occasions.
LOWELL—*My Study Windows. Garfield.*

4
The great man is he who does not lose his child's heart.
MENCIUS—*Works*. Bk. IV. Pt. II. Ch. XII

5
That man is great, and he alone,
Who serves a greatness not his own,
For neither praise nor pelf:
Content to know and be unknown:
Whole in himself.
OWEN MEREDITH (Lord Lytton)—*A Great Man.*

6 Are not great
Men the models of nations?
OWEN MEREDITH (Lord Lytton)—*Lucile*. Pt. II. Canto VI. St. 29.

7
Les grands ne sont grands que parceque nous, les portons sur nos épaules; nous n'avons qu' à les secouer pour en joncher la terre.
The great are only great because we carry them on our shoulders; when we throw them off they sprawl on the ground.
MONTANDRÉ—*Point de l'Ovale.*

8
Lives obscurely great.
HENRY J. NEWBOLDT—*Minora Sidera.*

9
Les grands ne sont grands que parceque nous sommes à genoux: relevons nous.
The great are only great because we are on our knees. Let us rise up.
PRUD'HOMME—*Révolutions de Paris. Motto.*

10
As if Misfortune made the throne her seat,
And none could be unhappy but the great.
NICHOLAS ROWE—*Fair Penitent. Prolog.*
(See also YOUNG)

11
Es ist der Fluch der Hohen, dass die Niedern
Sich ihres offnen Ohrs bemächtigen.
The curse of greatness:
Ears ever open to the babbler's tale.
SCHILLER—*Die Braut von Messina.* I.

12
Si vir es, suspice, etiam si decidunt, magna conantes.
If thou art a man, admire those who attempt great things, even though they fail.
SENECA—*De Brevitate.* XX.

13
Greatness knows itself.
Henry IV. Pt. I. Act IV. Sc. 3. L. 74.

14
I have touched the highest point of all my greatness:
And, from that full meridian of my glory,
I haste now to my setting.
Henry VIII. Act III. Sc. 2. L. 223.

15
Farewell! a long farewell, to all my greatness!
This is the state of man: to-day he puts forth
The tender leaves of hope; to-morrow blossoms,
And bears his blushing honours thick upon him:
The third day comes a frost, a killing frost,
And, when he thinks, good easy man, full surely
His greatness is a-ripening, nips his root,
And then he falls, as I do.
Henry VIII. Act III. Sc. 2. L. 351.

16
Why, man, he doth bestride the narrow world
Like a Colossus, and we petty men
Walk under his huge legs and peep about
To find ourselves dishonorable graves.
Julius Cæsar. Act I. Sc. 2. L. 135.

17
Are yet two Romans living such as these?
The last of all the Romans, fare thee well!
Julius Cæsar. Act V. Sc. 3. L. 98.

18
But thou art fair, and at thy birth, dear boy,
Nature and Fortune join'd to make thee great.
King John. Act III. Sc. 1. L. 51.

19 Your name is great
In mouths of wisest censure.
Othello. Act II. Sc. 3. L. 192.

20
They that stand high have many blasts to shake them;
And if they fall, they dash themselves to pieces.
Richard III. Act I. Sc. 3. L. 259.

21
Some are born great, some achieve greatness, and some have greatness thrust upon 'em.
Twelfth Night. Act II. Sc. 5. L. 157.

22
Not that the heavens the little can make great,
But many a man has lived an age too late.
R. H. STODDARD—*To Edmund Clarence Stedman.*

23
Censure is the tax a man pays to the public for being eminent.
SWIFT—*Thoughts on Various Subjects.*

24
The world knows nothing of its greatest men.
HENRY TAYLOR—*Philip Van Artevelde*. Act I. Sc. 5.

25
He fought a thousand glorious wars,
And more than half the world was his,
And somewhere, now, in yonder stars,
Can tell, mayhap, what greatness is.
THACKERAY—*The Chronicle of the Drum*. Last verse.

26
O, happy they that never saw the court,
Nor ever knew great men but by report!
JOHN WEBSTER—*The White Devil; or, Vittoria Corombona*. Act V. Sc. VI.

27
Great let me call him, for he conquered me.
YOUNG—*The Revenge*. Act I. Sc. 1.

1
High stations, tumult, but not bliss, create;
None think the great unhappy, but the great.
YOUNG—*Love of Fame.* Satire I. L. 237.

GREECE

2
Know ye the land where the cypress and myrtle
Are emblems of deeds that are done in their clime,
Where the rage of the vulture, the love of the turtle,
Now melt into sorrow, now madden to crime?
BYRON—*Bride of Abydos.* Canto I.

3
Fair Greece! sad relic of departed worth!
Immortal, though no more; though fallen great!
BYRON—*Childe Harold.* Canto II. St. 73.

4
The isles of Greece, the isles of Greece!
Where burning Sappho loved and sung.
Where grew the arts of war and peace,—
Where Delos rose, and Phœbus sprung!
Eternal summer gilds them yet,
But all, except their sun, is set.
BYRON—*Don Juan.* Canto III. St. 86.

5
Such is the aspect of this shore;
'Tis Greece, but living Greece no more!
So coldly sweet, so deadly fair,
We start, for soul is wanting there.
BYRON—*The Giaour.* L. 90.

6
To Greece we give our shining blades.
MOORE—*Evenings in Greece. First Evening.*

GREETING (See FAREWELL, MEETING, PARTING)

GRIEF

7
Why wilt thou add to all the griefs I suffer
Imaginary ills, and fancy'd tortures?
ADDISON—*Cato.* Act IV. Sc. 1.

8
O, brothers! let us leave the shame and sin
Of taking vainly in a plaintive mood,
The holy name of *Grief*—holy herein,
That, by the grief of One, came all our good.
E. B. BROWNING—*Sonnets. Exaggeration.*

9
Thank God, bless God, all ye who suffer not
More grief than ye can weep for. That is well—
That is light grieving!
E. B. BROWNING—*Tears.*

10
Nullus dolor est quem non longinquitas temporis minuat ac molliat.
There is no grief which time does not lessen and soften.
CICERO—*Epistles.* IV. 5. Said by SERVIUS SUPLICIUS to CICERO.

11
Were floods of tears to be unloosed
In tribute to my grief,
The doves of Noah ne'er had roost
Nor found an olive-leaf.
IBN EZRA.
(See also MONTROSE)

12
In all the silent manliness of grief.
GOLDSMITH—*Deserted Village.* L. 384.

13
Grief tears his heart, and drives him to and fro,
In all the raging impotence of woe.
HOMER—*Iliad.* Bk. XXII. L. 526. POPE'S trans.

14
Quis desiderio sit pudor aut modus
Tam cari capitis?
What impropriety or limit can there be in our grief for a man so beloved?
HORACE—*Carmina.* I. 24. 1.

15
On me, on me
Time and change can heap no more!
The painful past with blighting grief
Hath left my heart a withered leaf.
Time and change can do no more.
RICHARD HENGIST HORNE—*Dirge.*

16
Ponamus nimios gemitus: flagrantior æquo
Non debet dolor esse viri, nec vulnere major.
Let us moderate our sorrows. The grief of a man should not exceed proper bounds, but be in proportion to the blow he has received.
JUVENAL—*Satires.* XIII. 11.

17
The only cure for grief is action.
G. H. LEWES—*The Spanish Drama. Life of Lope De Vega.* Ch. II.

18
Oh, well has it been said, that there is no grief like the grief which does not speak!
LONGFELLOW—*Hyperion.* Bk. II. Ch. II.
(See also SPENSER)

19
Illa dolet vere qui sine teste dolet.
She grieves sincerely who grieves unseen.
MARTIAL—*Epigrams.* I. 34. 4.

20
There is a solemn luxury in grief.
WM. MASON—*The English Garden.* L. 596.

21
Se a ciascun l'interno affanno
Si leggesse in fronte scritto,
Quanti mai, che invidia fanno,
Ci farebbero pietà!
If our inward griefs were seen written on our brow, how many would be pitied who are now envied!
METASTASIO—*Giuseppe Riconosciuto.* I.

22
What need a man forestall his date of grief,
And run to meet what he would most avoid?
MILTON—*Comus.* L. 362.

23
Great, good, and just, could I but rate
My grief with thy too rigid fate,
I'd weep the world in such a strain
As it should deluge once again;
But since thy loud-tongued blood demands supplies
More from Briareus' hands than Argus' eyes,
I'll sing thy obsequies with trumpet sounds
And write thy epitaph in blood and wounds.
MONTROSE. On Charles I.
(See also IBN EZRA)

24
Strangulat inclusus dolor, atque exæstuat intus,
Cogitur et vires multiplicare suas.
Suppressed grief suffocates, it rages within the breast, and is forced to multiply its strength
OVID—*Tristium.* V. 1. 63.

1
Curæ leves loquuntur, ingentes stupent.
Light griefs are communicative, great ones stupefy.
SENECA—*Hippolytus*. 607.

2
Levis est dolor qui capere consilium potest.
That grief is light which can take counsel.
SENECA—*Medea*. I. 55.

3
Magnus sibi ipse non facit finem dolor.
Great grief does not of itself put an end to itself.
SENECA—*Troades*. 786.

4
If thou engrossest all the griefs are thine,
Thou robb'st me of a moiety.
All's Well That Ends Well. Act III. Sc. 2. L. 68.

5
For grief is crowned with consolation.
Antony and Cleopatra. Act I. Sc. 2. L. 173.

6
O, grief hath chang'd me since you saw me last,
And careful hours with time's deform'd hand
Have written strange defeatures in my face.
Comedy of Errors. Act V. Sc. 1. L. 297.

7
That we two are asunder; let that grieve him;
Some griefs are medicinable.
Cymbeline. Act III. Sc. 2. L. 32.

8
Great griefs, I see, medicine the less.
Cymbeline. Act IV. Sc. 2. L. 243.

9
Oft have I heard that grief softens the mind
And makes it fearful and degenerate.
Henry VI. Pt. II. Act IV. Sc. 4. L. 1.

10
What private griefs they have, alas, I know not,
That made them do it.
Julius Cæsar. Act III. Sc. 2. L. 216.

11
For grief is proud and makes his owner stoop.
King John. Act III. Sc. 1. L. 69.

12
I am not mad; I would to heaven I were!
For then, 'tis like I should forget myself:
O, if I could, what grief should I forget!
King John. Act III. Sc. 4. L. 48.

13
Grief fills the room up of my absent child,
Lies in his bed, walks up and down with me,
Puts on his pretty looks, repeats his words,
Remembers me of all his gracious parts,
Stuffs out his vacant garments with his form;
Then, have I reason to be fond of grief?
King John. Act III. Sc. 4. L. 93.

14
But then the mind much sufferance doth o'erskip,
When grief hath mates.
King Lear. Act III. Sc. 6. L. 113.

15
Every one can master a grief but he that has it.
Much Ado About Nothing. Act III. Sc. 2. L. 29.

16
Men
Can counsel and speak comfort to that grief
Which they themselves not feel; but, tasting it,
Their counsel turns to passion, which before
Would give preceptial medicine to rage,
Fetter strong madness in a silken thread,
Charm ache, with air and agony with words.
Much Ado About Nothing. Act V. Sc. 1. L. 20.

17
Nor doth the general care
Take hold on me, for my particular grief
Is of so flood-gate and o'erbearing nature
That it engluts and swallows other sorrows
And it is still itself.
Othello. Act I. Sc. 3. L. 54.

18
When remedies are past, the griefs are ended
By seeing the worst, which late on hopes depended.
Othello. Act I. Sc. 3. L. 202.

19
Each substance of a grief hath twenty shadows,
Which shows like grief itself, but is not so;
For sorrow's eye, glazed with blinding tears,
Divides one thing entire to many objects.
Richard II. Act II. Sc. 2. L. 14.

20
You may my glories and my state depose,
But not my griefs; still am I king of those.
Richard II. Act IV. Sc. 1. L. 192.

21
My grief lies all within;
And these external manners of laments
Are merely shadows to the unseen grief
That swells with silence in the tortur'd soul.
Richard II. Act IV. Sc. 1. L. 295.

22
Griefs of mine own lie heavy in my breast,
Which thou wilt propagate, to have it prest
With more of thine.
Romeo and Juliet. Act I. Sc. 1. L. 193.

23
Some griefs show much of love;
But much of grief shows still some want of wit.
Romeo and Juliet. Act III. Sc. 5. L. 73.

24
My grief lies onward and my joy behind.
Sonnet L.

25
Alas, poor man! grief has so wrought on him,
He takes false shadows for true substances.
Titus Andronicus. Act III. Sc. 2. L. 79.

26
But I have
That honourable grief lodg'd here which burns
Worse than tears drown.
Winter's Tale. Act II. Sc. 1. L. 110.

27
What's gone and what's past help
Should be past grief.
Winter's Tale. Act III. Sc. 2. L. 223.

28
Winter is come and gone,
But grief returns with the revolving year.
SHELLEY—*Adonais*. St. 18.

29
Dark is the realm of grief: but human things
Those may not know of who cannot weep for them.
SHELLEY—*Otho*. (A projected poem.)

30
"Oh, but," quoth she, "great griefe will not be tould,
And can more easily be thought than said."
SPENSER—*Faerie Queene*. Bk. I. Canto VII. St. 41. (See also LONGFELLOW)

1
He gave a deep sigh; I saw the iron enter into his soul.
STERNE—*Sentimental Journey. The Captive.*

2
Nulli jactantius mœrent quam qui maxime lætantur.
None grieve so ostentatiously as those who rejoice most in heart.
TACITUS—*Annales.* II. 77.

3
Men are we, and must grieve when even the Shade
Of that which once was great is passed away.
WORDSWORTH—*On the Extinction of the Venetian Republic.*

GROWTH (See also EVOLUTION, PROGRESS, SUCCESS)

4
What? Was man made a wheel-work to wind up,
And be discharged, and straight wound up anew?
No! grown, his growth lasts; taught, he ne'er forgets;
May learn a thousand things, not twice the same.
ROBERT BROWNING—*A Death in the Desert.* L. 447.

5
Treading beneath their feet all visible things,
As steps that upwards to their Father's throne
Lead gradual.
COLERIDGE—*Religious Musings.*
(See also TENNYSON)

6
Jeshurun waxed fat, and kicked.
Deuteronomy. XXXII. 15.

7
The lofty oak from a small acorn grows.
LEWIS DUNCOMBE—*Translation of De Minimis Maxima.*
(See also EVERETT under ORATORY)

8
Man seems the only growth that dwindles here.
GOLDSMITH—*The Traveller.* L. 126.

9
It is not growing like a tree
In bulk, doth make man better be;
Or standing long an oak, three hundred year,
To fall a log at last, dry, bald, and sere:
A lily of a day
Is fairer far in May,
Although it falls and die that night—
It was the plant and flower of Light.
BEN JONSON—*Pindaric Ode on the Death of Sir H. Morison.*

10
Nor deem the irrevocable Past,
As wholly wasted, wholly vain,
If, rising on its wrecks, at last
To something nobler we attain.
LONGFELLOW—*Ladder of St. Augustine.*
(See also TENNYSON)

11
Our pleasures and our discontents,
Are rounds by which we may ascend.
LONGFELLOW—*Ladder of St. Augustine.* St. 2.
(See also LONGFELLOW under VICE)

12
And so all growth that is not towards God
Is growing to decay.
GEORGE MACDONALD—*Within and Without.* Pt. I. Sc. 3.

13
Arts and sciences are not cast in a mould, but are found and perfected by degrees, by often handling and polishing, as bears leisurely lick their cubs into shape.
MONTAIGNE—*Apology for Raimond Sebond.* Bk. II. Ch. XII.
(See also VERGIL)

14
"Oh! what a vile and abject thing is man unless he can erect himself above humanity." Here is a *bon mot* and a useful desire, but equally absurd. For to make the handful bigger than the hand, the armful bigger than the arm, and to hope to stride further than the stretch of our legs, is impossible and monstrous. . . . He may lift himself if God lend him His hand of special grace; he may lift himself . . . by means wholly celestial. It is for our Christian religion, and not for his Stoic virtue, to pretend to this divine and miraculous metamorphosis.
MONTAIGNE—*Essays.* Bk. II. Ch. XII.
(See also WORDSWORTH)

15
Heu quotidie pejus! haec colonia retroversus crescit tanquam coda vituli.
Alas! worse every day! this colony grows backward like the tail of a calf.
PETRONIUS—*Cena.* 44.

16
Fungino genere est; capite se totum tegit.
He is of the race of the mushroom; he covers himself altogether with his head.
PLAUTUS—*Trinummus.* IV. 2. 9.

17
Post id, frumenti quum alibi messis maxima'st
Tribus tantis illi minus reddit, quam obseveris.
Heu! istic oportet obseri mores malos,
Si in obserendo possint interfieri.
Besides that, when elsewhere the harvest of wheat is most abundant, there it comes up less by one-fourth than what you have sowed. There, methinks, it were a proper place for men to sow their wild oats, where they would not spring up.
PLAUTUS—*Trinummus.* IV. 4. 128.

18
Grows with his growth, and strengthens with his strength.
POPE—*Essay on Man.* Ep. II. L. 136.

19
'Tis thus the mercury of man is fix'd,
Strong grows the virtue with his nature mix'd.
POPE—*Essay on Man.* Ep. II. L. 178.

20
Im engen Kreis verengert sich der Sinn.
Es wächst der Mensch mit seinen grössern Zwecken.
In a narrow circle the mind contracts.
Man grows with his expanded needs.
SCHILLER—*Prolog.* I. 59.

21
Jock, when ye hae naething else to do, ye may be aye sticking in a tree; it will be growing, Jock, when ye're sleeping.
SCOTT—*The Heart of Midlothian.* Ch. VIII.

22
Gardener, for telling me these news of woe,
Pray God the plants thou graft'st may never grow.
Richard II. Act III. Sc. 4. L. 100.

1
"Ay," quoth my uncle Gloucester,
"Small herbs have grace, great weeds do grow apace:"
And since, methinks, I would not grow so fast,
Because sweet flowers are slow and weeds make haste.
Richard III. Act II. Sc. 4. L. 12.

2 O, my lord,
You said that idle weeds are fast in growth:
The prince my brother hath outgrown me far.
Richard III. Act III. Sc. 1. L. 102.

3
I held it truth, with him who sings
To one clear harp in divers tones,
That men may rise on stepping-stones
Of their dead selves to higher things.
TENNYSON—*In Memoriam.* Pt. I.
(See also COLERIDGE, LONGFELLOW, MONTAIGNE, WORDSWORTH, YOUNG, also LONGFELLOW under VICE)

4
The great world's altar stairs
That slope through darkness up to God.
TENNYSON—*In Memoriam.* LV.

5
Then bless thy secret growth, nor catch
At noise, but thrive unseen and dumb;
Keep clean, be as fruit, earn life, and watch
Till the white-wing'd reapers come.
HENRY VAUGHAN—*The Seed Growing Secretly.*

6
Lambendo effingere.
Lick into shape.
VERGIL. See SUETONIUS—*Life of Vergil.* Lambendo paulatim figurant. Licking a cub into shape. PLINY—*Nat. Hist.* VIII. 36.
(See also MONTAIGNE)

7
And that unless above himself he can
Erect himself, how poor a thing is man.
WORDSWORTH—*Excursion.* V. 158. (Knight's ed.) From DANIEL'S *Essay* XIV, in COLERIDGE—*Friend. Introductory.* Quam contempta res est homo, nisi super humana se erexerit. As said by SENECA.
Amator Jesu et veritatis . . . potest se . . . elevare supra seipsum in spiritu.
A lover of Jesus and of the truth . . . can lift himself above himself in spirit.
THOMAS À KEMPIS—*Imitatio.* II. 1.
(See also MONTAIGNE, TENNYSON)

8
Teach me, by this stupendous scaffolding,
Creation's golden steps, to climb to Thee.
YOUNG—*Night Thoughts.* Night IX.
(See also TENNYSON)

GUESTS (See also HOSPITALITY, WELCOME)

9
Hail, guest, we ask not what thou art;
If friend, we greet thee, hand and heart;
If stranger, such no longer be;
If foe, our love shall conquer thee.
PAUL ELMER MORE says this is an Old Welsh door Verse.

10
For whom he means to make an often guest,
One dish shall serve; and welcome make the rest.
JOSEPH HALL—*Come Dine with Me.*

11
Quo me cumque rapit tempestas deferor hospes.
Wherever the storm carries me, I go a willing guest.
HORACE—*Epistles.* I. 1. 15.

12
Sometimes, when guests have gone, the host remembers
Sweet courteous things unsaid.
We two have talked our hearts out to the embers,
And now go hand in hand down to the dead.
MASEFIELD—*The Faithful.*

13 Unbidden guests
Are often welcomest when they are gone.
Henry VI. Pt. I. Act II. Sc. 2. L. 55.

14
Here's our chief guest.
If he had been forgotten,
It had been as a gap in our great feast.
Macbeth. Act III. Sc. 1. L. 11.

15
Be bright and jovial among your guests to-night.
Macbeth. Act III. Sc. 2. L. 28.

16 See, your guests approach:
Address yourself to entertain them sprightly,
And let's be red with mirth.
Winter's Tale. Act IV. Sc. 4. L. 52.

17
Methinks a father
Is at the nuptial of his son a guest
That best becomes the table.
Winter's Tale. Act IV. Sc. 4. L. 405.

18
You must come home with me and be my guest;
You will give joy to me, and I will do
All that is in my power to honour you.
SHELLEY—*Hymn to Mercury.* St. 5.

19
To the guests that must go, bid God's speed and brush away all traces of their steps.
RABINDRANATH TAGORE—*Gardener.* 45.

GUILT

20
In ipsa dubitatione facinus inest, etiamsi ad id non pervenerint.
Guilt is present in the very hesitation, even though the deed be not committed.
CICERO—*De Officiis.* III. 8.

21
Let no guilty man escape, if it can be avoided. No personal consideration should stand in the way of performing a public duty.
ULYSSES S. GRANT—*Indorsement of a Letter relating to the Whiskey Ring,* July 29, 1875.

22
What we call real estate—the solid ground to build a house on—is the broad foundation on which nearly all the guilt of this world rests.
HAWTHORNE—*The House of the Seven Gables. The Flight of Two Owls.*

23
How guilt once harbour'd in the conscious breast,
Intimidates the brave, degrades the great.
SAMUEL JOHNSON—*Irene.* Act IV. Sc. 8.

24 The gods
Grow angry with your patience. 'Tis their care,
And must be yours, that guilty men escape not:
As crimes do grow, justice should rouse itself.
BEN JONSON—*Catiline.* Act III. Sc. 5.

1
Exemplo quodcumque malo committitur, ipsi Displicet auctori. Prima est hæc ultio, quod se Judice nemo nocens absolvitur.

Whatever guilt is perpetrated by some evil prompting, is grievous to the author of the crime. This is the first punishment of guilt that no one who is guilty is acquitted at the judgment seat of his own conscience.

JUVENAL—*Satires*. XIII. 1.

2
Ingenia humana sunt ad suam cuique levandam culpam nimio plus facunda.

Men's minds are too ingenious in palliating guilt in themselves.

LIVY—*Annales*. XXVIII. 25.

3
Facinus quos inquinat æquat.

Those whom guilt stains it equals.

LUCAN—*Pharsalia*. V. 290.

4
Nulla manus belli, mutato judice, pura est.

Neither side is guiltless if its adversary is appointed judge.

LUCAN—*Pharsalia*. VII. 263.

5
These false pretexts and varnished colours failing,
Bare in thy guilt how foul must thou appear.

MILTON—*Samson Agonistes*. L. 901.

6
Heu! quam difficile est crimen non prodere vultu.

Alas! how difficult it is to prevent the countenance from betraying guilt.

OVID—*Metamorphoses*. II. 447.

7
Dum ne ob male facta peream, parvi æstimo.

I esteem death a trifle, if not caused by guilt.

PLAUTUS—*Captivi*. III. 5. 24.

8
Nihil est miserius quam animus hominis conscius.

Nothing is more wretched than the mind of a man conscious of guilt.

PLAUTUS—*Mostellaria*. Act III. 1. 13.

9
How glowing guilt exalts the keen delight!

POPE—*Eloisa to Abelard*. L. 230.

10
Haste, holy Friar,
Haste, ere the sinner shall expire!
Of all his guilt let him be shriven,
And smooth his path from earth to heaven!

SCOTT—*Lay of the Last Minstrel*. Canto V. St. 22.

11
Haud est nocens, quicumque non sponte est nocens.

He is not guilty who is not guilty of his own free will.

SENECA—*Hercules Œtæus*. 886.

12
Multa trepidus solet
Detegere vultus.

The fearful face usually betrays great guilt.

SENECA—*Thyestes*. CCCXXX.

13
And then it started like a guilty thing
Upon a fearful summons.

Hamlet. Act I. Sc. 1. L. 148.

14
O, she is fallen
Into a pit of ink, that the wide sea
Hath drops too few to wash her clean again.

Much Ado About Nothing. Act IV. Sc. 1. L. 141.

15
Fatetur facinus is qui judicium fugit.

He who flees from trial confesses his guilt.

SYRUS—*Maxims*.

16
Let guilty men remember, their black deeds
Do lean on crutches made of slender reeds.

JOHN WEBSTER—*The White Devil; or, Vittoria Corombona*. Act V. Sc. 6.

17
A land of levity is a land of guilt.

YOUNG—*Night Thoughts*. Night VII. Preface.

H

HABIT

18
A civil habit
Oft covers a good man.

BEAUMONT AND FLETCHER—*Beggar's Bush*. Act II. Sc. 3. L. 210.

19
Consuetudo quasi altera natura effici.

Habit is, as it were, a second nature.

CICERO—*De Finibus Bonorum et Malorum*. V. 25. *Tusculanarum Disputationum*. II. 17.

20
Habit with him was all the test of truth;
"It must be right: I've done it from my youth."

CRABBE—*The Borough*. Letter III.

21
We sow our thoughts, and we reap our actions; we sow our actions, and we reap our habits; we sow our habits, and we reap our characters; we sow our characters, and we reap our destiny.

C. A. HALL.

(See also KAINES, MURRAY, READE, also BORDMAN under THOUGHT)

22
Clavus clavo pellitur, consuetudo consuetudine vincitur.

A nail is driven out by another nail, habit is overcome by habit.

ERASMUS—*Diluculum*.

(See also À KEMPIS)

23
A man used to vicissitudes is not easily dejected.

SAMUEL JOHNSON—*Rasselas*. Ch. XII.

24
Habits form character and character is destiny.

JOSEPH KAINES—*Address*. Oct. 21, 1883. *Our Daily Faults and Failings*.

(See also HALL)

1
Consuetudo consuetudine vincitur.
Habit is overcome by habit.
THOMAS À KEMPIS. Bk. I. 21.
(See also ERASMUS)

2
Small habits, well pursued betimes,
May reach the dignity of crimes.
HANNAH MORE—*Florio*. Pt. I.

3
Sow an action, reap a habit.
DAVID CHRISTY MURRAY.
(See also HALL)

4
Nil consuetudine majus.
Nothing is stronger than habit.
OVID—*Ars Amatoria*. II. 345.

5
Abeunt studia in mores.
Pursuits become habits.
OVID—*Heroides*. XV. 83.

6
Morem fecerat usus.
Habit had made the custom.
OVID—*Metamorphoses*. II. 345.

7
Ill habits gather by unseen degrees,
As brooks make rivers, rivers run to seas.
OVID—*Metamorphoses*. Bk. XV. L. 155. DRYDEN'S trans.

8
Frangas enim citius quam corrigas quæ in pravum induerunt.

Where evil habits are once settled, they are more easily broken than mended.

QUINTILIAN—*De Institutione Oratoria*. I. 3. 3.

9
Sow an act and you reap a habit. Sow a habit and you reap a character. Sow a character and you reap a destiny.

CHAS. READE.
(See also HALL)

10
Consuetudo natura potentior est.
Habit is stronger than nature.
QUINTUS CURTIUS RUFUS—*De Rebus. Gestis Alexandri Magni*. V. 5. 21.

11
How use doth breed a habit in a man!
This shadowy desert, unfrequented woods,
I better brook than flourishing peopled towns.
Two Gentlemen of Verona. Act V. Sc. 4. L. 1.

12
Vulpem pilum mutare, non mores.
The fox changes his skin but not his habits.
SUETONIUS—*Vespasianus*. 16.

13
Inepta hæc esse, nos quæ facimus sentio;
Verum quid facias? ut homo est, ita morem geras.

I perceive that the things that we do are silly; but what can one do? According to men's habits and dispositions, so one must yield to them.

TERENCE—*Adelphi*. III. 3. 76.

14
Quam multa injusta ac prava fiunt moribus!

How many unjust and wicked things are done from mere habit.

TERENCE—*Heauton timoroumenos*. IV. 7. 11.

15
In ways and thoughts of weakness and of wrong,
Threads turn to cords, and cords to cables strong.
ISAAC WILLIAMS—*The Baptistry*. Image 18.

HAIR (See also BARBER)

16
And from that luckless hour my tyrant fair
Has led and turned me by a single hair.
BLAND—*Anthology*. P. 20. (Ed. 1813)
(See also DRYDEN)

17
His hair stood upright like porcupine quills.
BOCCACCIO—*Decameron*. Fifth Day. Nov. 8.
(See also HAMLET)

18
Dear, dead women, with such hair, too—what's become of all the gold
Used to hang and brush their bosoms?
ROBERT BROWNING—*Men and Women. A Toccata of Galuppi's*. St. 15.

19
And though it be a two-foot trout,
'Tis with a single hair pulled out.
BUTLER—*Hudibras*.

20
Those curious locks so aptly twin'd,
Whose every hair a soul doth bind.
CAREW—*To A. L. Persuasions to Love*. L. 37.

21
Stultum est in luctu capillum sibi evellere, quasi calvitio mæror levaretur.

It is foolish to pluck out one's hair for sorrow, as if grief could be assuaged by baldness.

CICERO—*Tusculanarum Disputationum*. III. 26.

22
Within the midnight of her hair,
Half-hidden in its deepest deeps.
BARRY CORNWALL—*Pearl Wearers*.
(See also HOOD, TENNYSON)

23
An harmless flaming meteor shone for hair,
And fell adown his shoulders with loose care.
ABRAHAM COWLEY—*Davideis*. Bk. II. L. 803.
(See also GRAY, SHAKESPEARE, also MILTON under WAR)

24
His head,
Not yet by time completely silver'd o'er,
Bespoke him past the bounds of freakish youth,
But strong for service still, and unimpair'd.
COWPER—*The Task*. Bk. II. *The Timepiece*. L. 702.

25
Tresses, that wear
Jewels, but to declare
How much themselves more precious are.
RICHARD CRASHAW—*Wishes to his (supposed) Mistress*.

26
She knows her man, and when you rant and swear,
Can draw you to her with a single hair.
DRYDEN—*Persius*. Satire V. L. 246.
(See also BLAND, HOWELL, POPE)

27 When you see fair hair
Be pitiful.
GEORGE ELIOT—*The Spanish Gypsy*. Bk. IV.

1
Bring down my gray hairs with sorrow to the grave.
Genesis. XLII. 38.

2
Beware of her fair hair, for she excels
All women in the magic of her locks;
And when she winds them round a young man's neck,
She will not ever set him free again.
GOETHE—*Scenes from Faust*. Sc. *The Hartz Mountain*. L. 335. SHELLEY's trans.

3
Loose his beard, and hoary hair
Stream'd, like a meteor, to the troubled air.
GRAY—*The Bard*. I. 2. L. 5.
(See also COWLEY)

4
It was brown with a golden gloss, Janette,
It was finer than silk of the floss, my pet;
'Twas a beautiful mist falling down to your wrist,
'Twas a thing to be braided, and jewelled, and kissed—
'Twas the loveliest hair in the world, my pet.
CHAS. G. HALPINE (MILES O'REILLY)—*Janette's Hair*.

5
And yonder sits a maiden,
The fairest of the fair,
With gold in her garment glittering,
And she combs her golden hair.
HEINE—*The Lorelei*. St. 3.

6
I pray thee let me and my fellow have
A hair of the dog that bit us last night.
JOHN HEYWOOD—*Proverbs*. Pt. I. Ch. XI. L. 424.

7
But she is vanish'd to her shady home
Under the deep, inscrutable; and there
Weeps in a midnight made of her own hair.
HOOD—*Hero and Leander*. 116.
(See also CORNWALL)

8
Cui flavam religas comam
Simplex munditiis?
For whom do you bind your hair, plain in your neatness?
HORACE—*Carmina*. I. 5. 4. MILTON's trans.

9
One hair of a woman can draw more than a hundred pair of oxen.
JAMES HOWELL—*Familiar Letters*. Bk. 2. Sect. 4. *To T. D., Esq.*
(See also DRYDEN)

10
The little wind that hardly shook
The silver of the sleeping brook
Blew the gold hair about her eyes,—
A mystery of mysteries.
So he must often pause, and stoop,
And all the wanton ringlets loop
Behind her dainty ear—emprise
Of slow event and many sighs.
W. D. HOWELLS—*Through the Meadow*.

11
My mother bids me bind my hair
With bands of rosy hue,
Tie up my sleeves with ribbands rare,
And lace my bodice blue;
For why, she cries, sit still and weep,
While others dance and play?
Alas, I scarce can go or creep,
While Rubin is away.
ANNE HUNTER—*My Mother Bids Me Bind My Hair*.

12
Though time has touched it in his flight,
And changed the auburn hair to white.
LONGFELLOW—*Christus. The Golden Legend*. Pt. IV. L. 388.

13
Her cap of velvet could not hold
The tresses of her hair of gold,
That flowed and floated like the stream.
And fell in masses down her neck.
LONGFELLOW—*Christus. The Golden Legend*. Pt. VI. L. 375.

14
You manufacture, with the aid of unguents, a false head of hair, and your bald and dirty skull is covered with dyed locks. There is no need to have a hairdresser for your head. A sponge, Phœbus, would do the business better.
MARTIAL—*Epigrams*. Bk. VI. Ep. 57.

15
You collect your straggling hairs on each side, Marinus, endeavoring to conceal the vast expanse of your shining bald pate by the locks which still grow on your temples. But the hairs disperse, and return to their own place with every gust of wind; flanking your bare poll on either side with crude tufts. We might imagine we saw Hermeros of Cydas standing between Speudophorus and Telesphorus. Why not confess yourself an old man? Be content to seem what you really are, and let the barber shave off the rest of your hair. There is nothing more contemptible than a bald man who pretends to have hair.
MARTIAL—*Epigrams*. Bk. X. Ep. 83.

16
The very hairs of your head are all numbered.
Matthew. X. 30.

17
Munditiis capimur: non sine lege capillis.
We are charmed by neatness of person; let not thy hair be out of order.
OVID—*Ars Amatoria*. III. 133.

18
Her head was bare;
But for her native ornament of hair;
Which in a simple knot was tied above,
Sweet negligence, unheeded bait of love!
OVID—*Metamorphoses*. *Meleager and Atalanta*. L. 68. DRYDEN's trans.

19
Fair tresses man's imperial race insnare,
And beauty draws us with a single hair.
POPE—*Rape of the Lock*. Canto II. L. 27.
(See also DRYDEN)

20
Hoary whiskers and a forky beard.
POPE—*Rape of the Lock*. Canto III. L. 37.

21
Then cease, bright nymph! to mourn thy ravish'd hair
Which adds new glory to the shining sphere;
Not all the tresses that fair head can boast
Shall draw such envy as the lock you lost,
For after all the murders of your eye,
When, after millions slain, yourself shall die;

When those fair suns shall set, as set they must,
And all those tresses shall be laid in dust,
This Lock the Muse shall consecrate to fame,
And 'midst the stars inscribe Belinda's name.
POPE—*Rape of the Lock.* Canto V. Last lines.

1
Ere on thy chin the springing beard began
To spread a doubtful down, and promise man.
PRIOR—*An Ode to the Memory of the Honourable Colonel George Villiers.* L. 5.

2
The hoary beard is a crown of glory if it be found in the way of righteousness.
Proverbs. XVI. 31.

3
Tarry at Jericho until your beards be grown.
II Samuel. X. 5.

4
Golden hair, like sunlight streaming
On the marble of her shoulder.
J. G. SAXE—*The Lover's Vision.* St. 3.

5
His hair is of a good colour.
An excellent colour; your chestnut was ever the only colour.
As You Like It. Act III. Sc. 4. L. 11.

6
Thy knotted and combined locks to part,
And each particular hair to stand an-end,
Like quills upon the fretful porpentine.
Hamlet. Act. I. Sc. 5. L. 18.
(See also BOCCACCIO)

7
And his chin new reap'd,
Show'd like a stubble-land at harvest-home.
Henry IV. Pt. I. Act I. Sc. 3. L. 34.

8
How ill white hairs become a fool and jester!
Henry IV. Pt. II. Act V. Sc. 5. L. 52.

9
Comb down his hair; look, look! it stands upright.
Henry VI. Pt. II. Act III. Sc. 3. L. 15.

10
Bind up those tresses. O, what love I note
In the fair multitude of those her hairs!
Where but by chance a silver drop hath fallen,
Even to that drop ten thousand wiry friends
Do glue themselves in sociable grief,
Like true, inseparable, faithful loves,
Sticking together in calamity.
King John. Act III. Sc. 4. L. 61.

11
And her sunny locks
Hang on her temples like a golden fleece.
Merchant of Venice. Act I. Sc. 1. L. 169.

12
What a beard hast thougot! thou hast got more hair on thy chin than Dobbin my fill-horse has on his tail.
Merchant of Venice. Act II. Sc. 2. L. 99.

13
Alas, poor chin! many a wart is richer.
Troilus and Cressida. Act I. Sc. 2. L. 154.

14
Her hair is auburn, mine is perfect yellow:
If that be all the difference in his love,
I'll get me such a colour'd periwig.
Two Gentlemen of Verona. Act IV. Sc. 4. L. 194.

15
Thy fair hair my heart enchained.
SIR PHILIP SIDNEY—*Neapolitan Villanell.*

16
Her long loose yellow locks lyke golden wyre,
Sprinckled with perle, and perling flowres atweene,
Doe lyke a golden mantle her attyre.
SPENSER—*Epithalamion.* St. 9.

17
Ah, thy beautiful hair! so was it once braided for me, for me;
Now for death is it crowned, only for death, lover and lord of thee.
SWINBURNE—*Choriambics.* St. 5.

18
But, rising up,
Robed in the long night of her deep hair, so
To the open window moved.
TENNYSON—PRINCESS.
(See also CORNWALL)

19
The Father of Heaven.
Spin, daughter Mary, spin,
Twirl your wheel with silver din;
Spin, daughter Mary, spin,
Spin a tress for Viola.
FRANCIS THOMPSON—*The Making of Viola.* St. 1.

20
Come let me pluck that silver hair
Which 'mid thy clustering curls I see;
The withering type of time or care
Has nothing, sure, to do with thee.
ALARIC ALEX WATTS—*The Grey Hair.*

21
Her hair is bound with myrtle leaves,
(Green leaves upon her golden hair!)
Green grasses through the yellow sheaves
Of Autumn corn are not more fair.
OSCAR WILDE—*La Bella Donna della mia Mente.*

HAND

22
Even to the delicacy of their hand
There was resemblance such as true blood wears.
BYRON—*Don Juan.* Canto IV. St. 45.

23
For through the South the custom still commands
The gentleman to kiss the lady's hands.
BYRON—*Don Juan.* Canto V. St. 105.

24
Bless the hand that gave the blow.
DRYDEN—*The Spanish Friar.* Act II. Sc. 1.
(See also POMFRET)

25
Una mano lava l'altra, ed ambedue lavano il volto.
One hand washeth another, both the face.
JOHN FLORIO—*Vocabolario Italiano & Inglese.*

26
His hand will be against every man, and every man's hand against him.
Genesis. XVI. 12.

27
The voice is Jacob's voice, but the hands are the hands of Esau.
Genesis. XXVII. 22.

28
Rubente dextra.
Red right hand.
HORACE—*Carmina.* I. 2. 2.
(See also MILTON)

1 'Twas a hand
White, delicate, dimpled, warm, languid, and bland.
The hand of a woman is often, in youth,
Somewhat rough, somewhat red, somewhat graceless in truth;
Does its beauty refine, as its pulses grow calm,
Or as sorrow has crossed the life line in the palm?
OWEN MEREDITH (Lord Lytton)—*Lucile.* Pt. I. Canto III. St. 18.

2
His red right hand.
MILTON—*Paradise Lost.* Bk. II. L. 174.
(See also HORACE)

3
We bear it calmly, though a ponderous woe,
And still adore the hand that gives the blow.
JOHN POMFRET—*Verses to his Friend under Affliction.*
(See also DRYDEN, also POPE under FIDELITY)

4
Without the bed her other fair hand was,
On the green coverlet; whose perfect white
Show'd like an April daisy on the grass,
With pearly sweat, resembling dew of night.
Lucrece. L. 393.

5
All the perfumes of Arabia will not sweeten this little hand.
Macbeth. Act V. Sc. 1. L. 57.

6 They may seize
On the white wonder of dear Juliet's hand.
Romeo and Juliet. Act III. Sc. 3. L. 35.

7 O, that her hand,
In whose comparison all whites are ink,
Writing their own reproach, to whose soft seizure
The cygnet's down is harsh and spirit of sense
Hard as the palm of ploughman.
Troilus and Cressida. Act I. Sc. 1. L. 55.

8
Puras deus non plenas adspicit manus.
God looks at pure, not full, hands.
SYRUS—*Maxims.*

9
Dextra mihi Deus.
My right hand is to me as a god.
VERGIL—*Æneid.* X. 773.

HAPPINESS

10
Hold him alone truly fortunate who has ended his life in happy well-being.
ÆSCHYLUS—*Agamemnon.* 928.

11
'Twas a jolly old pedagogue, long ago,
Tall and slender, and sallow and dry;
His form was bent, and his gait was slow,
His long thin hair was white as snow,
But a wonderful twinkle shone in his eye.
And he sang every night as he went to bed,
"Let us be happy down here below;
The living should live, though the dead be dead,"
Said the jolly old pedagogue long ago.
GEORGE ARNOLD—*The Jolly Old Pedagogue.*

12
Real happiness is cheap enough, yet how dearly we pay for its counterfeit.
HOSEA BALLOU—*MS. Sermons.*

13
To have been happy, madame, adds to calamity.
BEAUMONT AND FLETCHER—*The Fair Maid of the Inn.* Act I. Sc. 1. L. 250.

14
La massima felicita divisa nel maggior numero.
The greatest happiness of the greatest number.
BECCARIA—*Trattato dei Delitti e delle Pene* (Treatise of Crimes and of Punishment). Introd. (1764) (See also HUTCHESON)

15
Priestly was the first (unless it was Beccaria) who taught my lips to pronounce this sacred truth—that the greatest happiness of the greatest number is the foundation of morals and legislation.
BENTHAM—Vol. X. P. 142.

16
Quid enim est melius quam memoria recte factorum, et libertate contentum negligere humana?
What can be happier than for a man, conscious of virtuous acts, and content with liberty, to despise all human affairs?
BRUTUS—*to Cicero. Cicero's Letters.* I. 16. 9.

17
Oh, Mirth and Innocence! Oh, Milk and Water!
Ye happy mixtures of more happy days!
BYRON—*Beppo.* St. 80.

18
* * * all who joy would win
Must share it,—Happiness was born a twin.
BYRON—*Don Juan.* Canto II. St. 172.

19 There comes
For ever something between us and what
We deem our happiness.
BYRON—*Sardanapalus.* Act I. Sc. 2.

20
Quid datur a divis felici optatius hora?
What is there given by the gods more desirable than a happy hour?
CATULLUS—*Carmina.* LXII. 30.

21
The message from the hedge-leaves,
Heed it, whoso thou art;
Under lowly eaves
Lives the happy heart.
JOHN VANCE CHENEY—*The Hedge-bird's Message.*

22
In animi securitate vitam beatam ponimus.
We think a happy life consists in tranquillity of mind.
CICERO—*De Natura Deorum.* I. 20.

23
Le bonheur semble fait pour être partagé.
Happiness seems made to be shared.
CORNEILLE—*Notes par Rochefoucauld.*

24
If solid happiness we prize,
Within our breast this jewel lies,
And they are fools who roam;
The world has nothing to bestow,
From our own selves our bliss must flow,
And that dear hut,—our home.
NATHANIEL COTTON—*The Fireside.*

1
Thus happiness depends, as Nature shows,
Less on exterior things than most suppose.
COWPER—*Table Talk.* L. 246.

2
Domestic Happiness, thou only bliss
Of Paradise that hast survived the Fall!
COWPER—*Task.* Bk. III. L. 41.

3
Who is the happiest of men? He who values the merits of others,
And in their pleasure takes joy, even as though t'were his own.
GOETHE—*Distichs.*

4
Das beste Glück, des Lebens schönste Kraft
Ermattet endlich.
The highest happiness, the purest joys of life, wear out at last.
GOETHE—*Iphigenia auf Tauris.* IV. 5. 9.

5
Still to ourselves in every place consign'd,
Our own felicity to make or find.
GOLDSMITH—*The Traveller.* L. 431.
(Lines added by JOHNSON)

6
Now happiness consists in activity: such is the constitution of our nature: it is a running stream, and not a stagnant pool.
GOOD—*The Book of Nature.* Series III. Lecture VII.

7
The loss of wealth is loss of dirt,
As sages in all times assert;
The happy man's without a shirt.
JOHN HEYWOOD—*Be Merry Friends.*

8
And there is ev'n a happiness
That makes the heart afraid.
HOOD—*Ode to Melancholy.*

9
Fuge magna, licet sub paupere tecto
Reges et regum vita procurrere amicos.
Avoid greatness; in a cottage there may be more real happiness than kings or their favorites enjoy.
HORACE—*Epistles.* I. 10. 32.

10
Non possidentem multa vocaveris
Recte beatum; rectius occupat
Nomen beati, qui Deorum
Muneribus sapienter uti,
Duramque callet pauperiem pati,
Pejusque leto flagitium timet.
You will not rightly call him a happy man who possesses much; he more rightly earns the name of happy who is skilled in wisely using the gifts of the gods, and in suffering hard poverty, and who fears disgrace as worse than death.
HORACE—*Carmina.* IX. Bk. 4. 9. 45.

11
That Action is best which procures the greatest Happiness for the greatest Numbers; and that worst, which, in like manner, occasions misery.
FRANCIS HUTCHESON—*Inquiry into the Original of our Ideas of Beauty and Virtue.* (1725) Treatise II. Sec. 3. *An Inquiry concerning Moral Good and Evil.*
(See also BECCARIA)

12
Upon the road to Romany
It's stay, friend, stay!
There's lots o' love and lots o' time
To linger on the way;
Poppies for the twilight,
Roses for the noon,
It's happy goes as lucky goes,
To Romany in June.
WALLACE IRWIN—*From Romany to Rome.*

13
Happiness consists in the multiplicity of agreeable consciousness.
SAMUEL JOHNSON—*Boswell's Life.* (1766)

14
Ducimus autem
Hos quoque felices, qui ferre incommoda vitæ,
Nec jactare jugum vita didicere magistra.
We deem those happy who, from the experience of life, have learned to bear its ills, without being overcome by them.
JUVENAL—*Satires.* XII. 20.

15
On n'est jamais si heureux, ni si malheureux, qu'on se l'imagine.
We are never so happy, nor so unhappy, as we suppose ourselves to be.
LA ROCHEFOUCAULD—*Maximes.*

16
A sound Mind in a sound Body, is a short but full description of a happy State in this World.
LOCKE—*Thoughts Concerning Education.*

17
To be strong
Is to be happy!
LONGFELLOW—*Christus. The Golden Legend.* Pt. II. L. 731.

18
The rays of happiness, like those of light, are colorless when unbroken.
LONGFELLOW—*Kavanagh.* Ch. XIII.

19
Happiness, to some elation;
Is to others, mere stagnation.
AMY LOWELL—*Happiness.*

20
Now the heart is so full that a drop overfills it,
We are happy now because God wills it.
LOWELL—*The Vision of Sir Launfal.* Prelude to Pt. I. L. 61.

21
Sive ad felices vadam post funera campos,
Seu ferar ardentem rapidi Phlegethontis ad undam,
Nec sine te felix ero, nec tecum miser unquam.
Heaven would not be Heaven were thy soul not with mine, nor would Hell be Hell were our souls together.
BAPTISTA MANTUANUS—*Eclogue.* III. 108.
(See also SCOTT, HENRY V)

22
Neminem, dum adhuc viveret, beatum dici debere arbitrabatur.
He (Solon) considered that no one ought to be called happy as long as he was alive.
VALERIUS MAXIMUS. Bk. VII. 2. Ext. 2.
Same in SOPHOCLES—*Œdipus Rex.* End.
HERODOTUS—*Clio.* 32. SOLON to CRŒSUS.
Repeated by CRŒSUS to CYRUS when on his funeral pyre, thus obtaining his pardon.
(See also OVID, also ÆSCHYLUS under DEATH)

1
And feel that I am happier than I know.
MILTON—*Paradise Lost.* Bk. VIII. L. 282.

2
No eye to watch and no tongue to wound us,
All earth forgot, and all heaven around us.
MOORE—*Come o'er the Sea.*

3
The foolish man seeks happiness in the distance;
The wise grows it under his feet.
JAMES OPPENHEIM—*The Wise.*

4
Dicique beatus
Ante obitum nemo supremaque funera debet.

Before he is dead and buried no one ought to be called happy.

OVID—*Metamorphoses.* Bk. III. 136.
(See also MAXIMUS)

5
Thus we never live, but we hope to live; and always disposing ourselves to be happy, it is inevitable that we never become so.
BLAISE PASCAL—*Thoughts.* Ch. V. Sec. I.

6
Said Scopas of Thessaly, "But we rich men count our felicity and happiness to lie in these superfluities, and not in those necessary things."
PLUTARCH—*Morals.* Vol. II. *Of the Love of Wealth.*
(See also HOLMES under PARADOX)

7
Oh happiness! our being's end and aim!
Good, Pleasure, Ease, Content! whate'er thy name;
That something still which prompts th' eternal sigh,
For which we bear to live, or dare to die.
POPE—*Essay on Man.* Ep. IV. L. 1.

8
Fix'd to no spot is Happiness sincere;
'Tis nowhere to be found, or ev'rywhere;
'Tis never to be bought, but always free.
POPE—*Essay on Man.* Ep. IV. L. 15.
(See also WYNNE)

9
Heaven to mankind impartial we confess,
If all are equal in their happiness;
But mutual wants this happiness increase,
All nature's difference keeps all nature's peace.
POPE—*Essay on Man.* Ep. IV. L. 53.

10
Le bonheur des méchants comme un torrent s'écoule.

The happiness of the wicked flows away as a torrent.

RACINE—*Athalie.* II. 7.

11
Happiness lies in the consciousness we have of it, and by no means in the way the future keeps its promises.
GEORGE SAND—*Handsome Lawrence.* Ch. III.

12
Des Menschen Wille, das ist sein Glück.
The will of a man is his happiness.
SCHILLER—*Wallenstein's Lager.* VII. 25.

13
O mother, mother, what is bliss?
O mother, what is bale?
Without my William what were heaven,
Or with him what were hell?
SCOTT. Trans. of a ballad of BÜRGER'S.
(See also MANTUANUS)

14
Non potest quisquam beate degere, qui se tantum intuetur, qui omnia ad utilitates suas convertit; alteri vivas oportet, si vis tibi vivere.

No man can live happily who regards himself alone, who turns everything to his own advantage. Thou must live for another, if thou wishest to live for thyself.

SENECA—*Epistolæ Ad Lucilium.* XLVIII.

15
But, O, how bitter a thing it is to look into happiness through another man's eyes!
As You Like It. Act V. Sc. 2. L. 47.

16
Would I were with him, wheresome'er he is, either in heaven or in hell.
Henry V. Act II. Sc. 3. L. 6.
(See also MANTUANUS)

17
Ye seek for happiness—alas, the day!
Ye find it not in luxury nor in gold,
Nor in the fame, nor in the envied sway
For which, O willing slaves to Custom old,
Severe taskmistress! ye your hearts have sold.
SHELLEY—*Revolt of Islam.* Canto XI. St. 17.

18
Magnificent spectacle of human happiness.
SYDNEY SMITH—*America.* *Edinburgh Review*, July, 1824.

19
Mankind are always happier for having been happy; so that if you make them happy now, you make them happy twenty years hence by the memory of it.
SYDNEY SMITH—*Lecture on Benevolent Affections.*

20
Be happy, but be happy through piety.
MADAME DE STAËL—*Corinne.* Bk. XX. Ch. III.

21
Wealth I ask not, hope nor love,
Nor a friend to know me;
All I ask, the heavens above,
And the road below me.
STEVENSON—*The Vagabond.*

22
O terque quaterque beati.
O thrice, four times happy they!
VERGIL—*Æneid.* I. 94.

23
For it stirs the blood in an old man's heart;
And makes his pulses fly,
To catch the thrill of a happy voice,
And the light of a pleasant eye.
N. P. WILLIS—*Saturday Afternoon.* St. 1.

24
True happiness is to no spot confined.
If you preserve a firm and constant mind,
'Tis here, 'tis everywhere.
JOHN HUDDLESTONE WYNNE—*History of Ireland.* (See also POPE)

25
We're charm'd with distant views of happiness,
But near approaches make the prospect less.
THOS. YALDEN—*Against Enjoyment.* L. 23.

26
True happiness ne'er entered at an eye;
True happiness resides in things unseen.
YOUNG—*Night Thoughts.* Night VIII. L. 1,021.

HAREBELL

Campanula Rotundifolia

1
I love the fair lilies and roses so gay,
They are rich in their pride and their splendor;
But still more do I love to wander away
To the meadow so sweet,
Where down at my feet,
The harebell blooms modest and tender.
DORA READ GOODALE—*Queen Harebell.*

2
With drooping bells of clearest blue
Thou didst attract my childish view,
Almost resembling
The azure butterflies that flew
Where on the heath thy blossoms grew
So lightly trembling.
BISHOP HEBER—*The Harebell.*

3
Simplest of blossoms! To mine eye
Thou bring'st the summer's painted sky;
The May-thorn greening in the nook;
The minnows sporting in the brook;
The bleat of flocks; the breath of flowers;
The song of birds amid the bowers;
The crystal of the azure seas;
The music of the southern breeze;
And, over all, the blessed sun,
Telling of halcyon days begun.
MOIR—*The Harebell.*

4
High in the clefts of the rock 'mid the cedars
Hangeth the harebell the waterfall nigh;
Blue are its petals, deep-blue tinged with purple,
Mystical tintings that mirror the sky.
L. D. PYCHOWSKA—*Harebells.*

HARVEST (See also AGRICULTURE)

5
For now, the corn house filled, the harvest home,
Th' invited neighbors to the husking come;
A frolic scene, where work and mirth and play
Unite their charms to cheer the hours away.
JOEL BARLOW—*The Hasty Pudding.*

6
He that observeth the wind shall not sow; and he that regardeth the clouds shall not reap.
Ecclesiastes. XI. 4.

7
In the morning sow thy seed, and in the evening withhold not thine hand.
Ecclesiastes. XI. 6.

8
Whatsoever a man soweth, that shall he also reap.
Galatians. VI. 7.

9
The harvest truly is plenteous, but the labourers are few.
Matthew. IX. 37.

10
Who eat their corn while yet 'tis green,
At the true harvest can but glean.
SAADI—*Gulistan.* (*Garden of Roses.*)

11
To glean the broken ears after the man
That the main harvest reaps.
As You Like It. Act III. Sc. 5. L. 102.

12
And thus of all my harvest-hope I have
Nought reaped but a weedye crop of care.
SPENSER—*The Shepherd's Calendar. December.* L. 121.

13
Think, oh, grateful think!
How good the God of Harvest is to you;
Who pours abundance o'er your flowing fields,
While those unhappy partners of your kind
Wide-hover round you, like the fowls of heaven,
And ask their humble dole.
THOMSON—*Autumn.* L. 169.

14
Fancy with prophetic glance
Sees the teeming months advance;
The field, the forest, green and gay;
The dappled slope, the tedded hay;
Sees the reddening orchard blow,
The Harvest wave, the vintage flow.
WARTON—*Ode. The First of April.* L. 97.

HASTE

15
Festination may prove Precipitation;
Deliberating delay may be wise cunctation.
SIR THOMAS BROWNE—*Christian Morals.* Pt. I. Sec. XXIII. (Paraphrasing CÆSAR.)

16
Then horn for horn they stretch and strive;
Deil tak the hindmost, on they drive.
BURNS—*To a Haggis.*

17
Festina lente.
Hasten deliberately.
AUGUSTUS CÆSAR. Quoting a Greek Proverb, according to AULLUS GELLIUS. X. 11. 5. (See also RUFUS, ROMEO AND JULIET)

18
The more haste, ever the worst speed.
CHURCHILL—*The Ghost.* Bk. IV. L. 1,162.

19
I'll be with you in the squeezing of a lemon.
GOLDSMITH—*She Stoops to Conquer.* Act I. Sc. 2

20
Sat cito, si sat bene.
Quick enough, if good enough.
ST. JEROME—*Epistle.* LXVI. Par. 9. (Valler's ed.) Quoted from CATO. Phrase used by LORD ELDON. In TWISS's *Life of Lord C. Eldon.* Vol. I. P. 46.

21
Haste is of the Devil.
The Koran.

22
Le trop de promptitude à l'erreur nous expose.
Too great haste leads us to error.
MOLIÈRE—*Sganarelle.* I. 12.

23
Stay awhile that we may make an end the sooner.
Attributed to SIR AMICE PAWLET by BACON. *Apothegms.* No. 76.

24
On wings of winds came flying all abroad.
POPE—*Prologue to the Satires.* L. 208.

25
Festinatio tarda est.
Haste is slow.
QUINTUS CURTIUS RUFUS. IX. 9. 12.
(See also CÆSAR)

1
Celerity is never more admired
Than by the negligent.
Antony and Cleopatra. Act III. Sc. 7. L. 25.

2
Nay, but make haste; the better foot before.
King John. Act IV. Sc. 2. L. 170.

3
Stand not upon the order of your going,
But go at once.
Macbeth. Act III. Sc. 4. L. 119.

4
Swifter than arrow from the Tartar's bow.
Midsummer Night's Dream. Act III. Sc. 2. L. 101.

5
He tires betimes that spurs too fast betimes;
With eager feeding food doth choke the feeder.
Richard II. Act II. Sc. 1. L. 36.

6
It is too rash, too unadvised, too sudden;
Too like the lightning, which doth cease to be
Ere one can say "It lightens."
Romeo and Juliet. Act II. Sc. 2. L. 118.

7
Wisely, and slow; they stumble that run fast.
Romeo and Juliet. Act II. Sc. 3. L. 94.
(See also Cæsar)

HATRED

8
Hatred is self-punishment.
Hosea Ballou—*MS. Sermons.*

9
Now hatred is by far the longest pleasure;
Men love in haste, but they detest at leisure.
Byron—*Don Juan.* Canto XII. St. 6.

10
These two hated with a hate
Found only on the stage.
Byron—*Don Juan.* Canto IV. St. 93.

11
I pray that every passing hour
Your hearts may bruise and beat,
I pray that every step you take
May bruise and burn your feet.
Emile Cammaerts—*Vœux du Nouvel An,* 1915, *A L'Armée Allemand.* Trans. by Lord Curzon. *England's Response.* In *Observer,* Jan. 10, 17, 1915.
(See also Lissauer)

12
Odi et amo. Quare id faciam, fortasse requiris.
Nescio, sed fieri sentio et excrucior.
I hate and I love. Perchance you ask why I do that. I know not, but I feel that I do and I am tortured.
Catullus—*Carmina.* LXXXV. 1.

13
Qui vit haï de tous ne saurait longtemps vivre.
He who is hated by all can not expect to live long.
Corneille—*Cinna.* I. 2.

14
There are glances of hatred that stab and raise no cry of murder.
George Eliot—*Felix Holt. Introduction.*

15
Quem metuunt oderunt, quem quisque odit periisse expetit.
Whom men fear they hate, and whom they hate, they wish dead.
Quintus Ennius—*Thyestes.* (Atreus log.)

16
High above hate I dwell,
O storms! farewell.
Louise Imogen Guiney—*The Sanctuary.*

17
Wir haben lang genug geliebt,
Und wollen endlich hassen.
We've practiced loving long enough,
Let's come at last to hate.
Georg Herwegh—*Lied vom Hasse.* Trans. by Thackeray in *Foreign Quarterly Review,* April, 1843.
(See also Lissauer)

18
Then let him know that hatred without end
Or intermission is between us two.
Homer—*Iliad.* Bk. XV. L. 270. Bryant's trans.

19
"He was a very good *hater.*"
Samuel Johnson—*Mrs. Piozzi's Anecdotes of Johnson.* P. 38.

20
I like a good hater.
Samuel Johnson—*Mrs. Piozzi's Anecdotes of Johnson.* P. 89.

21
But I do hate him as I hate the devil.
Ben Jonson—*Every Man Out of his Humour.* Act I. Sc. 1.

22
Wir haben nur einen einzigen Hass,
Wir lieben vereint, wir hassen vereint,
Wir haben nur einen einzigen Feind.
We have but one, and only hate,
We love as one, we hate as one,
We have one foe and one alone.
Ernst Lissauer—*Hassgesang gegen England.* Trans. by Barbara Henderson. In the *Nation,* March 11, 1915.
(See also Cammaerts, Herweg)

23
There's no hate lost between us.
Thos. Middleton—*The Witch.* Act IV. Sc. 3.

24
For never can true reconcilement grow,
Where wounds of deadly hate have pierced so deep.
Milton—*Paradise Lost.* Bk. IV. L. 98.

25
Hatreds are the cinders of affection.
Sir Walter Raleigh—*Letter to* Sir Robert Cecil. May 10, 1593.

26
Der grösste Hass ist, wie die grösste Tugend und die schlimmsten Hunde, still.
The greatest hatred, like the greatest virtue and the worst dogs, is silent.
Jean Paul Richter—*Hesperus.* XII.

27
Quos læserunt et oderunt.
Whom they have injured they also hate.
Seneca—*De Ira.* Bk. II. Ch. 33.
(See also Tacitus)

1
In time we hate that which we often fear.
Antony and Cleopatra. Act I. Sc. 3. L. 12.

2
Yet 'tis greater skill
In a true hate, to pray they have their will.
Cymbeline. Act II Sc. 5. L. 33.

3
How like a fawning publican he looks!
I hate him for he is a Christian,
But more for that in low simplicity
He lends out money gratis and brings down
The rate of usance here with us in Venice.
Merchant of Venice. Act I. Sc. 3. L. 42.

4
Though I do hate him as I do hell-pains.
Othello. Act I. Sc. 1. L. 155.

5
Id agas tuo te merito ne quis oderit.
Take care that no one hates you justly.
SYRUS—*Maxims.*

6
Proprium humani ingenii, est odisse quem læseris.
It is human nature to hate those whom we have injured.
TACITUS—*Agricola.* XLII. 4.
(See also SENECA)

7
Accerima proximorum odia.
The hatred of relatives is the most violent.
TACITUS—*Annales.* IV. 70.

8
Procul O procul este profani.
Hence, far hence, ye vulgar herd!
VERGIL—*Æneid.* VI. 258.

HATTERS

9
"Sye," he seyd, "be the same hatte
I can knowe yf my wyfe be badde
To me by eny other man;
If my floures ouver fade or falle,
Then doth my wyfe me wrong wyth alle
As many a woman can."
ADAM of Cobsham—*The Wright's Chaste Wife.*

10
So Britain's monarch once uncovered sat,
While Bradshaw bullied in a broad-brimmed hat.
JAMES BRAMSTON—*Man of Taste.*

11
And her hat was a beaver, and made like a man's.
RICHARD HARRIS BARHAM—*Ingoldsby Legends, Patty Morgan the Milkmaid's Story.*

12
A hat not much the worse for wear.
COWPER—*History of John Gilpin.*

13
My new straw hat that's trimly lin'd with green,
Let Peggy wear.
GAY—*Shepherd's Week. Friday.* L. 125.

14
I know it is a sin
For me to sit and grin
At him here;
But the old three-cornered hat
And the breeches and all that
Are so queer.
HOLMES—*The Last Leaf.*

15
The hat is the *ultimatum moriens* of respectability.
HOLMES—*The Autocrat of the Breakfast Table.* VIII.

16
The Quaker loves an ample brim,
A hat that bows to no Salaam;
And dear the beaver is to him
As if it never made a dam.
Hood—*All Round my Hat.*

17
A sermon on a hat: "'The hat, my boy, the hat, whatever it may be, is in itself nothing—makes nothing, goes for nothing; but, be sure of it, everything in life depends upon the cock of the hat.' For how many men—we put it to your own experience, reader—have made their way through the thronging crowds that beset fortune, not by the innate worth and excellence of their hats, but simply, as Sampson Piebald has it, by 'the cock of their hats'? The cock's all."
DOUGLAS JERROLD—*The Romance of a Keyhole.* Ch. III.

18
He wears his faith but as the fashion of his hat; it ever changes with the next block.
Much Ado About Nothing. Act I. Sc. 1. L. 75.

19
I never saw so many shocking bad hats in my life.
Attributed to DUKE OF WELLINGTON, upon seeing the first Reformed Parliament. SIR WILLIAM FRASER, in *Words on Wellington* (1889), P. 12, claims it for the Duke. CAPTAIN GRONOW, in his *Recollections,* accredits it to the Duke of York, second son of George III., about 1817.

HAWK

20
I am but mad north-north-west: when the wind is southerly, I know a hawk from a handsaw.
Hamlet. Act II. Sc. 2. L. 395. ("Handsaw" is given by MALONE, COLLIER, DYCE, CLARK and WRIGHT. Others give "hernshaw." The corruption was proverbial in Shakespeare's time.)

21
When I bestride him I soar, I am a hawk.
Henry V. Act III. Sc. 7. L. 14.

22
No marvel, an it like your majesty,
My lord protector's hawks do tower so well;
They know their master loves to be aloft
And bears his thoughts above his falcon's pitch.
Henry VI. Pt. II. Act II. Sc. 1. L. 9.

23
Between two hawks, which flies the higher pitch.
Henry VI. Pt. I. Act II. Sc. 4. L. 11.

24
Dost thou love hawking? thou hast hawks will soar
Above the morning lark.
Taming of the Shrew. Induction. Sc. 2. L. 45.

25
The wild hawk stood with the down on his beak
And stared with his foot on the prey.
TENNYSON—*The Poet's Song.*

1
Non rete accipitri tenditur, neque miluo,
Qui male faciunt nobis: illis qui nihil faciunt tenditur.
The nets not stretched to catch the hawk,
Or kite, who do us wrong; but laid for those
Who do us none at all.
TERENCE—*Phormio.* Act II. Sc. 2. L. 16. COLMAN's trans.

2
She rears her young on yonder tree;
She leaves her faithful mate to mind 'em;
Like us, for fish she sails to sea,
And, plunging, shows us where to find 'em.
Yo, ho, my hearts! let's seek the deep,
Ply every oar, and cheerly wish her,
While slow the bending net we sweep,
God bless the fish-hawk and the fisher.
ALEXANDER WILSON—*The Fisherman's Hymn.*

HAWTHORN

Cratægus Oxyacanthus

3
The hawthorn-trees blow in the dew of the morning.
BURNS—*Chevalier's Lament.*

4
The hawthorn I will pu' wi' its lock o' siller gray,
Where, like an aged man, it stands at break o' day.
BURNS—*O Luve Will Venture In.*

5
Yet, all beneath the unrivall'd rose,
The lowly daisy sweetly blows;
Tho' large the forest's monarch throws
His army shade,
Yet green the juicy hawthorn grows,
Adown the glade.
BURNS—*Vision.* Duan II. St. 21.

6
Yet walk with me where hawthorns hide
The wonders of the lane.
EBENEZER ELLIOTT—*The Wonders of the Lane.* L. 3.

7
The hawthorn-bush, with seats beneath the shade
For talking age and whispering lovers made!
GOLDSMITH—*The Deserted Village.* L. 13.

8
And every shepherd tells his tale
Under the hawthorn in the dale.
MILTON—*L'Allegro.* L. 67.

9
Then sing by turns, by turns the Muses sing;
Now hawthorns blossom.
POPE—*Spring.* L. 41.

10
Gives not the hawthorn-bush a sweeter shade
To shepherds looking on their silly sheep
Than doth a rich embroider'd canopy
To kings that fear their subjects' treachery?
Henry VI. Pt. III. Act II. Sc. 5. L. 42.

11
In hawthorn-time the heart grows light.
SWINBURNE—*Tale of Balen.* I.

12
The Hawthorn whitens; and the juicy Groves
Put forth their buds, unfolding by degrees,
Till the whole leafy Forest stands displayed,
In full luxuriance, to the sighing gales.
THOMSON—*Seasons. Spring.* L. 90.

HEALTH

13
Health and cheerfulness mutually beget each other.
ADDISON—*The Spectator.* No. 387.

14
When health, affrighted, spreads her rosy wing,
And flies with every changing gale of spring.
BYRON—*Childish Recollections.* L. 3.

15
Homines ad deos nulla re propius accedunt quam salutem hominibus dando.
In nothing do men more nearly approach the gods than in giving health to men.
CICERO—*Pro Ligario.* XII.

16
Of all the garden herbes none is of greater vertue than sage.
THOMAS COGAN—*Heaven of Health.* (1596) Quoting from *Schola Salerni.* P. 32.

17
Cur moriatur homo, cui salvia crescit in horto?
Why should (need) a man die who has sage in his garden?
Regimen Sanitatis Salernitanum. L. 177. Original and trans. pub. by SIR ALEX. CROPE. (1830)

18
Nor love, nor honour, wealth nor pow'r,
Can give the heart a cheerful hour
When health is lost. Be timely wise;
With health all taste of pleasure flies.
GAY—*Fables.* Pt. I. Fable 31.

19
Health that snuffs the morning air.
JAMES GRAINGER—*Solitude.* An Ode. L. 35.

20
A cool mouth, and warm feet, live long.
HERBERT—*Jacula Prudentum.*

21
He that goes to bed thirsty rises healthy.
HERBERT—*Jacula Prudentum.*

22
There are three wicks you know to the lamp of a man's life: brain, blood, and breath. Press the brain a little, its light goes out, followed by both the others. Stop the heart a minute, and out go all three of the wicks. Choke the air out of the lungs, and presently the fluid ceases to supply the other centres of flame, and all is soon stagnation, cold, and darkness.
HOLMES—*Professor at the Breakfast Table.* XI.

23
Orandum est ut sit mens sana in corpore sano.
Our prayers should be for a sound mind in a healthy body.
JUVENAL—*Satires.* X. 356.

24
Preserving the health by too strict a regimen is a wearisome malady.
LA ROCHEFOUCAULD—*Maxims.* No. 285.

25
Health consists with Temperance alone.
POPE—*Essay on Man.* Ep. IV. L. 81.

26
Pars sanitatis velle sanari fuit.
It is part of the cure to wish to be cured.
SENECA—*Hippolytus.* CCXLIX.

1 May be he is not well:
Infirmity doth still neglect all office
Whereto our health is bound.
King Lear. Act II. Sc. 4. L. 107.

2
Ah! what avail the largest gifts of Heaven,
When drooping health and spirits go amiss?
How tasteless then whatever can be given!
Health is the vital principle of bliss,
And exercise of health.
Thomson—*Castle of Indolence*. Canto II. St. 55.

3
Qui salubrem locum negligit, mente est captus atque ad agnatos et gentiles deducendus.
He who overlooks a healthy spot for the site of his house is mad and ought to be handed over to the care of his relations and friends.
Varro—*De Re Rustica*. I. 2.

4
Health is the second blessing that we mortals are capable of: a blessing that money cannot buy.
Izaak Walton—*The Compleat Angler*. Pt. I. Ch. XXI.

5
Gold that buys health can never be ill spent,
Nor hours laid out in harmless merriment.
John Webster—*Westward Ho*. Act V. Sc. 3. L. 345.

HEARING

6
He ne'er presumed to make an error clearer;—
In short, there never was a better hearer.
Byron—*Don Juan*. Canto XIV. St. 37

7
One eare it heard, at the other out it went.
Chaucer—*Canterbury Tales*. Bk. IV. L. 435.
(See also Heywood)

8
Within a bony labyrinthean cave,
Reached by the pulse of the aërial wave,
This sibyl, sweet, and Mystic Sense is found,
Muse, that presides o'er all the Powers of Sound.
Abraham Coles—*Man, the Microcosm; and the Cosmos*. P. 51.

9
None so deaf as those that will not hear.
Matthew Henry—*Commentaries*. Psalm LVIII. (See also Herbert)

10
Little pitchers have wide ears.
Herbert—*Jacula Prudentum*.

11
Who is so deaf as he that will not hear?
Herbert—*Jacula Prudentum*.
(See also Henry)

12
Went in at the one eare and out at the other.
Heywood—*Proverbs*. Pt. II. Ch. IX.
(See also Chaucer)

13 Hear ye not the hum
Of mighty workings?
Keats—*Addressed to Haydon*. Sonnet X.

14
Where did you get that pearly ear?
God spoke and it came out to hear.
George MacDonald—*Song. At the Back of the North Wind*. Ch. XXXIII.

15
He that hath ears to hear, let him hear.
Mark. IV. 9.

16 I was all ear,
And took in strains that might create a soul
Under the ribs of death.
Milton—*Comus*. L. 560.

17
Where more is meant than meets the ear.
Milton—*Il Penseroso*. L. 120.

18
Such an exploit have I in hand, Ligarius,
Had you a healthful ear to hear of it.
Julius Cæsar. Act II. Sc. 1. L. 318.

19
Hear me for my cause, and be silent, that you may hear.
Julius Cæsar. Act III. Sc. 2. L. 13.

20
Friends, Romans, countrymen, lend me your ears.
Julius Cæsar. Act III. Sc. 2. L. 78.

21
They never would hear,
But turn the deaf ear,
As a matter they had no concern in.
Swift—*Dingley and Brent*.

22
He that has ears to hear, let him stuff them with cotton.
Thackeray—*Virginians*. Ch. XXXII.
(See also Mark)

23
Strike, but hear me.
Themistocles—*Rollin's Ancient History*. Bk. VI. Ch. II. Sec. VIII.

HEART

24
A man's first care should be to avoid the reproaches of his own heart.
Addison—*Sir Roger on the Bench*.

25
I have a heart with room for every joy.
Bailey—*Festus*. Sc. *A Mountain*.

26
My favoured temple is an humble heart.
Bailey—*Festus*. Sc. *Colonnade and Lawn*.

27
My heart's in the Highlands, my heart is not here;
My heart's in the Highlands a-chasing the deer.
Burns—*My Heart's in the Highlands*. (From an old song, *The Strong Walls of Derry*.)

28
His heart was one of those which most enamour us,
Wax to receive, and marble to retain.
Byron—*Beppo*. St. 34.

29
Maid of Athens, ere we part,
Give, oh, give me back my heart!
Byron—*Maid of Athens*. St. 1.

30
Alma de esparto y corazon de encina.
Soul of fibre and heart of oak.
Cervantes—*Don Quixote*. II. 70.
(See also Old Meg, also Garrick under Navy)

31
My heart is wax to be moulded as she pleases, but enduring as marble to retain.
Cervantes—*The Little Gypsy*.

1
No command of art,
No toil, can help you hear;
Earth's minstrelsy falls clear
But on the listening heart.
JOHN VANCE CHENEY—*The Listening Heart.*

2
Some hearts are hidden, some have not a heart.
CRABBE—*The Borough.* Letter XVII.

3
"There are strings," said Mr. Tappertit, ". . . in the human heart that had better not be wibrated."
DICKENS—*Barnaby Rudge.* Ch. XXII.
(See also DICKENS under SYMPATHY)

4
The heart asks pleasure first,
And then, excuse from pain;
And then, those little anodynes
That deaden suffering;

And then, to go to sleep;
And then, if it should be
The will of its Inquisitor,
The liberty to die.
EMILY DICKINSON—*Poems.* IX. (Ed. 1891)

5
Meine Ruh ist hin,
Mein Herz ist schwer.
My peace is gone, my heart is heavy.
GOETHE—*Faust.* I. 15.

6
Ganz unbefleckt geniesst sich nur das Herz.
Only the heart without a stain knows perfect ease.
GOETHE—*Iphigenia auf Tauris.* IV. 4. 123.

7
Doch ein gekränktes Herz erholt sich schwer.
A wounded heart can with difficulty be cured.
GOETHE—*Torquato Tasso.* IV. 4. 24.

8
There is an evening twilight of the heart,
When its wild passion-waves are lulled to rest.
FITZ-GREENE HALLECK—*Twilight.*

9
I caused the widow's heart to sing for joy.
Job. XXIX. 13.

10
Let not your heart be troubled.
John. XIV. 1.

11
The head is always the dupe of the heart.
LA ROCHEFOUCAULD—*Maxims.* No. 105.

12
Wo das Herz reden darf braucht es keiner Vorbereitung.
When the heart dares to speak, it needs no preparation.
LESSING—*Mina von Barnhelm.* V. 4.

13
For his heart was in his work, and the heart
Giveth grace unto every Art.
LONGFELLOW—*The Building of the Ship.* L. 7.

14
Something the heart must have to cherish,
Must love, and joy, and sorrow learn;
Something with passion clasp, or perish,
And in itself to ashes burn.
LONGFELLOW—*Hyperion.* Bk. II. Introduction.

15
Better to have the poet's heart than brain,
Feeling than song.
GEORGE MACDONALD—*Within and Without.* Pt. III. Sc. 9. L. 30.

16
The heart is like an instrument whose strings
Steal nobler music from Life's many frets:
The golden threads are spun thro' Suffering's fire,
Wherewith the marriage-robes for heaven are woven:
And all the rarest hues of human life
Take radiance, and are rainbow'd out in tears.
GERALD MASSEY—*Wedded Love.*

17
Where your treasure is, there will your heart be also.
Matthew. VI. 21.

18
But the beating of my own heart
Was all the sound I heard.
RICHARD MONCKTON MILNES (Lord Houghton)—*The Brookside.*

19
And when once the young heart of a maiden is stolen,
The maiden herself will steal after it soon.
MOORE—*Ill Omens.*

20
Zwei Kammern hat das Herz.
Drin wohnen,
Die Freude und der Schmerz.
Two chambers hath the heart.
There dwelling,
Live Joy and Pain apart.
HERMANN NEUMANN—*Das Herz.* Trans. by T. W. H. ROBINSON. Found in *Echoes from Kottabos.* Another trans. by ERNEST RADFORD—*Chambers Twain.*

21
Yonkers that have hearts of oak at fourscore yeares.
Old Meg of Herefordshire. (1609)
(See also CERVANTES)

22
Oh, the heart is a free and a fetterless thing,—
A wave of the ocean, a bird on the wing.
JULIA PARDOE—*The Captive Greek Girl.*

23
The incense of the heart may rise.
PIERPONT—*Every Place a Temple.*
(See also COTTON under RESIGNATION)

24
The heart knoweth his own bitterness.
Proverbs. XIV. 10.

25
A merry heart maketh a cheerful countenance.
Proverbs. XV. 13.

26
He that is of a merry heart hath a continual feast.
Proverbs. XV. 15.

27
A man's heart deviseth his way; but the Lord directeth his steps.
Proverbs. XVI. 9.

28
He fashioneth their hearts alike.
Psalms. XXXIII. 15.

1
The heart is a small thing, but desireth great matters. It is not sufficient for a kite's dinner, yet the whole world is not sufficient for it.
QUARLES—*Emblems*. Bk. I. *Hugo de Anima*.

2
This house is to be let for life or years,
Her rent is sorrow, and her income tears;
Cupid, 't has long stood void; her bills make known,
She must be dearly let, or let alone.
QUARLES—*Emblems*. Bk. II. Epigram X.

3
My heart is like a singing bird
Whose nest is in a water'd shoot;
My heart is like an apple-tree
Whose boughs are bent with thick-set fruit;
My heart is like a rainbow shell
That paddles in a halcyon sea;
My heart is gladder than all these,
Because my love is come to me.
CHRISTINA G. ROSSETTI—*A Birthday*.

4
Malebranche dirait qu'il n'y a plus une âme:
Nous pensons humblement qu'il reste encor des cœurs.
Malebranche would have it that not a soul is left; we humbly think that there still are hearts.
EDMOND ROSTAND—*Chantecler*. *Prélude*.

5
C'est toujours un mauvais moyen de lire dans le cœur des autres que d'affecter de cacher le sien.
It is always a poor way of reading the hearts of others to try to conceal our own.
ROUSSEAU—*Confessions*. II.

6
Nicht Fleisch und Blut; das Herz macht uns zu Vätern und Söhnen.
It is not flesh and blood but the heart which makes us fathers and sons.
SCHILLER—*Die Räuber*. I. 1.

7
Even at this sight
My heart is turn'd to stone: and while 'tis mine,
It shall be stony.
Henry VI. Pt. II. Act V. Sc. 2. L. 49.

8
The very firstlings of my heart shall be
The firstlings of my hand.
Macbeth. Act IV. Sc. 1. L. 147.

9
He hath a heart as sound as a bell and his tongue is the clapper, for what his heart thinks his tongue speaks.
Much Ado About Nothing. Act III. Sc. 2. L. 12.

10
But I will wear my heart upon my sleeve
For daws to peck at; I am not what I am.
Othello. Act I. Sc. 1. L. 64.

11
Worse than a bloody hand is a hard heart.
SHELLEY—*The Cenci*. Act V. Sc. 2.

12
My heart, the bird of the wilderness, has found its sky in your eyes.
RABINDRANATH TAGORE—*Gardener*. 31.

13
Never morning wore
To evening, but some heart did break.
TENNYSON—*In Memoriam*. Pt. VI. Same idea in LUCRETIUS. II. 579.

14
L'oreille est le chemin du cœur.
The ear is the avenue to the heart.
VOLTAIRE—*Réponse au Roi de Prusse*.

15
La bouche obéit mal lorsque le cœur murmure.
The mouth obeys poorly when the heart murmurs.
VOLTAIRE—*Tancrède*. I. 4.

16
Who, for the poor renown of being smart,
Would leave a sting within a brother's heart?
YOUNG—*Love of Fame*. Satire II. L. 113.

17
Heaven's Sovereign saves all beings but himself,
That hideous sight, a naked human heart.
YOUNG—*Night Thoughts*. Night III. L. 226.

HEAVEN

18
Love lent me wings; my path was like a stair;
A lamp unto my feet, that sun was given;
And death was safety and great joy to find;
But dying now, I shall not climb to Heaven.
MICHAEL ANGELO—*Sonnet LXIII*. *After Sunset*.

19
Nunc ille vivit in sinu Abraham.
Now he [Nebridius] lives in Abraham's bosom.
St. AUGUSTINE—*Confessions*. Bk. IX. 3. *De Anima*. Bk. IV. 16. 24. He explains that Abraham's bosom is the remote and secret abode of quiet. Founded on *Luke*. XVI. 23.
(See also HENRY V)

20
Spend in pure converse our eternal day;
Think each in each, immediately wise;
Learn all we lacked before; hear, know, and say
What this tumultuous body now denies;
And feel, who have laid our groping hands away;
And see, no longer blinded by our eyes.
RUPERT BROOKE—*New Numbers*.

21
God keeps a niche
In Heaven, to hold our idols; and albeit
He brake them to our faces, and denied
That our close kisses should impair their white,—
I know we shall behold them raised, complete,
The dust swept from their beauty, glorified,
New Memnons singing in the great God-light.
E. B. BROWNING—*Sonnet. Futurity with the Departed*.

22
All places are distant from heaven alike.
BURTON—*Anatomy of Melancholy*. Pt. II. Sec. III. Memb. 4.
(See also COLLIER)

23
In hope to merit Heaven by making earth a Hell.
BYRON—*Childe Harold*. Canto I. St. 20.

24
To appreciate heaven well
'Tis good for a man to have some fifteen minutes of hell.
WILL CARLETON—*Farm Ballads*. *Gone with a Handsomer Man*.

1
The road to heaven lies as near by water as by land.
JEREMY COLLIER—*Eccl. Hist.* Ed. 1852. IV. 241. FRIAR ELSTON'S words, when threatened with drowning by HENRY VIII, according to STOW, quoted by GASQUET. Same idea ascribed to SIR HUMPHRY GILBERT when his ship was wrecked off Newfoundland. (1583) Idea taken from an Epigram of LEONIDAS *of* TARENTUM. See STOBÆUS—*Greek Anthology*. JACOB'S appendix. No. 48.
(See also BURTON, MORE)

2
Heaven means to be one with God.
CONFUCIUS, quoted by CANON FARRAR. *Sermons. Eternal Hopes. What Heaven Is.* Last line.

3
Where tempests never beat nor billows roar.
COWPER—*On the Receipt of My Mother's Picture.*
(See also GARTH)

4
And so upon this wise I prayed,—
Great Spirit, give to me
A heaven not so large as yours
But large enough for me.
EMILY DICKINSON—*A Prayer.*

5
Nor can his blessed soul look down from heaven,
Or break the eternal sabbath of his rest.
DRYDEN—*The Spanish Friar.* Act V. Sc. 2.

6
Since heaven's eternal year is thine.
DRYDEN—*Elegy on Mrs. Killegrew.* L. 15.

7
'Twas whispered in Heaven, 'twas muttered in hell
And echo caught faintly the sound as it fell.
On the confines of earth 'twas permitted to rest,
And the depths of the ocean its presence confessed.
CATHERINE M. FANSHAWE—*Enigma.* (*The letter H.*) (" 'Twas in Heaven pronounced, it was muttered in hell." In the original MS.)

8
Where billows never break, nor tempests roar.
GARTH—*Dispensary.* Canto III. L. 226.
(See also COWPER)

9
While resignation gently slopes the way;
And, all his prospects brightening to the last,
His heaven commences ere the world be past.
GOLDSMITH—*The Deserted Village.* L. 110.

10
They had finished her own crown in glory, and she couldn't stay away from the coronation.
GRAY—*Enigmas of Life.*

11
Eye hath not seen it, my gentle boy!
Ear hath not heard its deep songs of joy;
Dreams cannot picture a world so fair—
Sorrow and death may not enter there;
Time doth not breathe on its fadeless bloom,
For beyond the clouds, and beyond the tomb,
It is there, it is there, my child!
FELICIA D. HEMANS—*The Better Land.*

12
All this, and Heaven too!
PHILIP HENRY—*Matthew Henry's Life of Philip Henry.* P. 70.

13
Just are the ways of heaven; from Heaven proceed
The woes of man; Heaven doom'd the Greeks to bleed.
HOMER—*Odyssey.* Bk. VIII. L. 128. POPE'S trans.

14
Nil mortalibus arduum est;
Cœlum ipsum petimus stultitia.
Nothing is difficult to mortals; we strive to reach heaven itself in our folly.
HORACE—*Carmina.* Bk. I. 3. 37.

15
There the wicked cease from troubling, and there the weary be at rest.
Job. III. 17.

16
In my father's house are many mansions.
John. XIV. 2.

17
Sperre dich, so viel du willst!
Des Himmels Wege sind des Himmels Wege.
Struggle against it as thou wilt, yet Heaven's ways are Heaven's ways.
LESSING—*Nathan der Weise.* III. 1.

18
Booth led boldly with his big bass drum
(Are you washed in the blood of the Lamb?)
The Saints smiled gravely, and they said "He's come."
(Are you washed in the blood of the Lamb?)
NICHOLAS VACHEL LINDSAY—*General Booth Enters Heaven.*

19
The heaven of poetry and romance still lies around us and within us.
LONGFELLOW—*Drift-Wood. Twice-Told Tales.*

20
When Christ ascended
Triumphantly from star to star
He left the gates of Heaven ajar.
LONGFELLOW—*Golden Legend.* Pt. II.

21
We see but dimly through the mists and vapors;
Amid these earthly damps
What seem to us but sad, funereal tapers
May be heaven's distant lamps.
LONGFELLOW—*Resignation.* St. 4.

22
Cedit item retro, de terra quod fuit ante,
In terras; et, quod missum est ex ætheris oreis,
Id rursum cæli relatum templa receptant.
What came from the earth returns back to the earth, and the spirit that was sent from heaven, again carried back, is received into the temple of heaven.
LUCRETIUS—*De Rerum Natura.* II. 999.

23
Heaven to me's a fair blue stretch of sky,
Earth's jest a dusty road.
MASEFIELD—*Vagabond.*

24
Lay up for yourselves treasures in heaven.
Matthew. VI. 20.

25
It were a journey like the path to heaven,
To help you find them.
MILTON—*Comus.* L. 302.

1 The hasty multitude
Admiring enter'd, and the work some praise,
And some the architect: his hand was known
In heaven by many a tower'd structure high,
Where scepter'd angels held their residence,
And sat as princes.
MILTON—*Paradise Lost.* Bk. I. L. 730.

2
A heaven on earth.
MILTON—*Paradise Lost.* Bk. IV. L. 208.

3 The starry cope
Of heaven.
MILTON—*Paradise Lost.* Bk. IV. L. 992.

4 Though in heav'n the trees
Of life ambrosial fruitage bear, and vines
Yield nectar.
MILTON—*Paradise Lost.* Bk. V. L. 426.

5 Heaven open'd wide
Her ever-during gates, harmonious sound
On golden hinges moving.
MILTON—*Paradise Lost.* Bk. VII. L. 205.

6
There is a world above,
Where parting is unknown;
A whole eternity of love,
Form'd for the good alone;
And faith beholds the dying here
Translated to that happier sphere.
MONTGOMERY—*Friends.*

7
A Persian's Heaven is eas'ly made,
'Tis but black eyes and lemonade.
MOORE—*Intercepted Letters.* Letter VI.

8
The way to heaven out of all places is of like length and distance.
SIR THOMAS MORE—*Utopia.*
(See also COLLIER)

9
There's nae sorrow there, John,
There's neither cauld nor care, John,
The day is aye fair,
In the land o' the leal.
LADY NAIRNE—*The Land o' the Leal.*

10 A sea before
The Throne is spread;—its pure still glass
Pictures all earth-scenes as they pass.
We, on its shore,
Share, in the bosom of our rest,
God's knowledge, and are blest.
CARDINAL NEWMAN—*A Voice from Afar.*

11
Heav'n but the Vision of fulfill'd Desire.
And Hell the Shadow from a Soul on fire.
OMAR KHAYYAM—*Rubaiyat.* St. 67. FITZ-GERALD's trans.

12
A day in thy courts is better than a thousand. I had rather be a door-keeper in the house of my God than to dwell in the tents of wickedness.
Psalms. LXXXIV. 10.

13
The blessed Damozel lean'd out
From the gold bar of Heaven:
Her eyes knew more of rest and shade
Of waters still'd at even;
She had three lilies in her hand,
And the stars in her hair were seven.
ROSSETTI—*The Blessed Damozel.* (Version in Oxford Ed. of *Golden Treasury.*)

14
It was the rampart of God's house
That she was standing on;
By God built over the sheer depth,
The which is Space begun;
So high, that looking downward thence,
She scarce could see the sun.
ROSSETTI—*The Blessed Damozel.*

15
Non est ad astra mollis e terris via.
The ascent from earth to heaven is not easy.
SENECA—*Hercules Furens.* CCCCXXXVII.

16
Heaven's face doth glow.
Hamlet. Act III. Sc. 4. L. 48.

17
Sure he's not in hell; he's in Arthur's bosom, if ever man went to Arthur's bosom.
Henry V. Act II. Sc. 3. L. 8. *Richard II.* Act IV. Sc. 1. L. 104.
(See also ST. AUGUSTINE)

18
Were it not good your grace could fly to heaven?
The treasury of everlasting joy.
Henry VI. Pt. II. Act II. Sc. 1. L. 17.

19
And, father cardinal, I have heard you say
That we shall see and know our friends in heaven:
If that be true, I shall see my boy again;
For since the birth of Cain, the first male child,
To him that did but yesterday suspire,
There was not such a gracious creature born.
King John. Act III. Sc. 4. L. 76.

20 There's husbandry in heaven;
Their candles are all out.
Macbeth. Act II. Sc. 1. L. 5.

21
Well, God's above all; and there be souls must be saved, and there be souls must not be saved.
Othello. Act II. Sc. 3. L. 105.

22
All places that the eye of heaven visits,
Are to a wise man ports and happy havens.
Richard II. Act I. Sc. 3. L. 275.

23 For the selfsame heaven
That frowns on me looks sadly upon him.
Richard III. Act V. Sc. 3. L. 285.

24
Straight is the way to Acheron,
Whether the spirit's race is run
From Athens or from Meröe:
Weep not, far from home to die;
The wind doth blow in every sky
That wafts us to that doleful sea.
J. A. SYMONDS. Trans. P. 37 in TOMSON's *Selections from the Greek Anthology,* in the *Canterbury Poets.* (Greek is found in *Palantine Anthology.* No. 3.)

25
Who seeks for Heaven alone to save his soul
May keep the path, but will not reach the goal;
While he who walks in love may wander far,
Yet God will bring him where the blessed are.
HENRY VAN DYKE—*Story of the Other Wise Man.* V.

26
So all we know of what they do above
Is that they happy are, and that they love.
EDMUND WALLER—*On the Death of Lady Rich.*

1
For all we know
Of what the blessed do above
Is, that they sing, and that they love.
EDMUND WALLER—*Song. While I Listen to Thy Voice.* St. 2.

2
I have been there, and still would go;
'Tis like a little heaven below.
ISAAC WATTS—*Divine Songs.* 28.

3
There is a land of pure delight,
Where saints immortal reign;
Infinite day excludes the night,
And pleasures banish pain.
ISAAC WATTS—*Hymns and Spiritual Songs.* Bk. II. 66.

4
One eye on death, and one full fix'd on heaven.
YOUNG—*Night Thoughts.* Night V. L. 838.

HELIOTROPE

Heliotropium

5
I drink deep draughts of its nectar
E. C. STEDMAN—*Heliotrope.*

6
O sweetest of all the flowrets
That bloom where angels tread!
But never such marvelous odor,
From heliotrope was shed.
E. C. STEDMAN—*Heliotrope.*

HELL

7
Curiosis fabricavit inferos.
He fashioned hell for the inquisitive.
ST. AUGUSTINE—*Confessions.* Bk. XI. Ch. XII. Quoting an unnamed author.
Adapted from
"Alta, scrutantibus gehennas parabat."
God prepared hell, for those who are inquisitive about high things.
(See also SOUTHEY)

8
Hell is more bearable than nothingness.
BAILEY—*Festus.* Sc. *Heaven.*

9
Hell is the wrath of God—His hate of sin.
BAILEY—*Festus.* Sc. *Hell.* L. 194.

10
Hell is paved with good intentions.
Quoted as BAXTER'S saying by COLERIDGE. *Notes Theol., Polit. and Miscel.* P. 259. Ed. 1853.
(See also BERNARD, CHRYSOSTOM, DE SALES)

11
Hell is paved with infants' skulls.
BAXTER. In HAZLITT—*Table Talk.* He was stoned by the women of Kidderminster for quoting this in the pulpit.
(See also GUEVARA)

12
L'enfer est plein de bonnes volontés ou désirs.
Hell is full of good wishes or desires.
ST. BERNARD of Clairvaux. Archbishop Trench calls it "queen of all proverbs."
(See also BAXTER, DE SALES)

13
The heart of man is the place the devil dwells in; I feel sometimes a hell dwells within myself.
SIR THOMAS BROWNE—*Religio Medici.* Pt. I. Sec. LI.
(See also MILTON under MIND)

14
But quiet to quick bosoms is a hell,
And there hath been thy bane.
BYRON—*Childe Harold.* Canto III. St. 42.

15
Nor ear can hear nor tongue can tell
The tortures of that inward hell!
BYRON—*The Giaour.* L. 748.

16
Quien ha infierene nula es retencio.
In hell there is no retention.
CERVANTES—*Don Quixote.* I. 25. Sancho Panza, misquoting the saying.
(See also BERNARD)

17
Hell is paved with priests' skulls.
ST. CHRYSOSTOM.
(See also BAXTER, FIRMIN, WANDER)

18
Undique ad inferos tantundem viæ est.
From all sides there is equally a way to the lower world.
CICERO—*Tusc. Quæst.* Bk. I. 43. 104. Quoted as a saying of ANAXAGORAS.
(See also MORE under HEAVEN)

19
There is in hell a place stone-built throughout,
Called Malebolge, of an iron hue,
Like to the wall that circles it about.
DANTE—*Inferno.* Canto XVIII. L. 1.

20
We spirits have just such natures
We had for all the world, when human creatures;
And, therefore, I, that was an actress here,
Play all my tricks in hell, a goblin there.
DRYDEN—*Tyrannick Love.* Epilogue.

21
The way of sinners is made plain with stones, but at the end thereof is the pit of hell.
Ecclesiasticus. XXI. 10.

22
Hell is paved with the skulls of great scholars, and paled in with the bones of great men.
GILES FIRMIN—*The Real Christian.* (1670) Quoted as a proverb.
(See also CHRYSOSTOM)

23
Weave the warp, and weave the woof,
The winding sheet of Edward's race;
Give ample room and verge enough
The characters of Hell to trace.
GRAY—*Bard.* Canto II.
(See also DRYDEN under FORTUNE)

24
El infierno es lleno de buenas intenciones.
Hell is full of good intentions.
Adapted probably from a saying of ANTONIO GUEVARA, quoted by the Portuguese as "Hell is paved with good intentions, and roofed with lost opportunities."
(See also BAXTER, BERNARD, DE SALES)

25
Hell is full of good meanings and wishings.
HERBERT—*Jacula Prudentum.* No. 176.
(See also BERNARD)

1
Hell is no other but a soundlesse pit,
Where no one beame of comfort peeps in it.
HERRICK—*Noble Numbers. Hell.*

2
Hell from beneath is moved for thee to meet thee at thy coming.
Isaiah. XIV. 9.

3
And, bid him go to hell, to hell he goes.
SAMUEL JOHNSON—*London.* L. 116.

4
Hell is paved with good intentions.
SAMUEL JOHNSON—(*Quoted*) *Boswell's Life of Johnson.* (1775)
(See also BERNARD)

5
Et metus ille foras præceps Acheruntis agundus,
Funditus humanam qui vitam turbat ab imo,
Omnia suffuscans mortis nigrore, neque ullam
Esse voluptatem liquidam puramque relinquit.
The dreadful fear of hell is to be driven out, which disturbs the life of man and renders it miserable, overcasting all things with the blackness of darkness, and leaving no pure, unalloyed pleasure.
LUCRETIUS—*De Rerum Natura.* III. 37.

6
Look where he goes! but see he comes again
Because I stay! Techelles, let us march
And weary death with bearing souls to hell.
MARLOWE—*Tamburlane the Great.* Act V. Sc. III. L. 75.

7
A dungeon horrible, on all sides round,
As one great furnace, flamed; yet from those flames
No light, but rather darkness visible
Serv'd only to discover sights of woe,
Regions of sorrow, doleful shades, where peace
And rest can never dwell, hope never comes
That comes to all; but torture without end.
MILTON—*Paradise Lost.* Bk. I. L. 61.

8
Hail, horrors, hail,
Infernal world! and thou profoundest hell,
Receive thy new possessor.
MILTON—*Paradise Lost.* Bk. I. L. 251.

9
Long is the way
And hard, that out of hell leads up to light.
MILTON—*Paradise Lost.* Bk. II. L. 432.

10
Hell
Grew darker at their frown.
MILTON—*Paradise Lost.* Bk. II. L. 719.

11
On a sudden open fly
With impetuous recoil and jarring sound
Th' infernal doors, and on their hinges grate
Harsh thunder.
MILTON—*Paradise Lost.* Bk. II. L. 879.

12
Nor from hell
One step no more than from himself can fly
By change of place.
MILTON—*Paradise Lost.* Bk. IV. L. 21.

13
Myself am Hell;
And, in the lowest deep, a lower deep,
Still threat'ning to devour me, opens wide;
To which the hell I suffer seems a heaven.
MILTON—*Paradise Lost.* Bk. IV. L. 75.

14
All hell broke loose.
MILTON—*Paradise Lost.* Bk. IV. L. 918.

15
The gates that now
Stood open wide, belching outrageous flame
Far into Chaos, since the fiend pass'd through.
MILTON—*Paradise Lost.* Bk. X. L. 232.

16
In inferno nulla est redemptio.
There is no redemption from hell.
POPE PAUL III, when Michael Angelo refused to alter a portrait introduced among the condemned in his "Last Judgment."

17
To rest, the cushion and soft dean invite,
Who never mentions hell to ears polite.
POPE—*Moral Essays.* Ep. IV. L. 149.

18
He knoweth not that the dead are there; and that her guests are in the depths of hell.
Proverbs. IX. 18.

19
Do not be troubled by St. Bernard's saying that "Hell is full of good intentions and wills."
FRANCIS DE SALES—*Letter to* MADAME DE CHANTAL. (1605) *Letter* XII. P. 70. Selections from the *Spiritual Letters* of S. FRANCIS DE SALES. Trans. by the author of "A Dominican Artist." *Letter* LXXIV in BLAISE ed. Quoted also in *Letter* XXII, Bk. II. of LEONARD's ed. (1726) COLLET'S *La Vraie et Solide Piété.* Pt. I. Ch. LXXV.
(See also BAXTER)

20
Black is the badge of hell,
The hue of dungeons and the suit of night.
Love's Labour's Lost. Act IV. Sc. 3. L. 254.

21
I think the devil will not have me damned, lest the oil that's in me should set hell on fire.
Merry Wives of Windsor. Act V. Sc. 5. L. 38.

22
Hell is empty,
And all the devils are here.
Tempest. Act I. Sc. 2. L. 214.

23
It has been more wittily than charitably said that hell is paved with good intentions; they have their place in heaven also.
SOUTHEY—*Colloquies on Society.*
(See also BERNARD)

24
St. Austin might have returned another answer to him that asked him, "What God employed himself about before the world was made?" "He was making hell."
SOUTHEY—*Commonplace Book,* Fourth Series. P. 591. (See also AUGUSTINE)

25
Self-love and the love of the world constitute hell.
SWEDENBORG—*Apocalypse Explained.* Par. 1,144.

26
Nay, then, what flames are these that leap and swell
As 'twere to show, where earth's foundations crack,
The secrets of the sepulchres of hell
On Dante's track?
SWINBURNE—*In Guernsey.* Pt. IV. St. 3.

1 Facilis descensus Averno est;
Noctes atque dies patet atri janua Ditis;
Sed revocare gradum, superasque evadere ad auras,
Hoc opus, hic labor est.

Easy is the descent to Lake Avernus (mouth of Hades); night and day the gate of gloomy Dis (god of Hades) is open; but to retrace one's steps, and escape to the upper air, this indeed is a task; this indeed is a toil.

VERGIL—*Æneid.* VI. 26. ("Averni" in some editions.)

2 In the throat
Of Hell, before the very vestibule
Of opening Orcus, sit Remorse and Grief,
And pale Disease, and sad Old Age and Fear,
And Hunger that persuades to crime, and Want:
Forms terrible to see. Suffering and Death
Inhabit here, and Death's own brother Sleep;
And the mind's evil lusts and deadly War,
Lie at the threshold, and the iron beds
Of the Eumenides; and Discord wild
Her viper-locks with bloody fillets bound.

VERGIL—*Ænid.* Bk. VI. L. 336. C. P. CRANCH's trans.

3
In the deepest pits of 'Ell,
Where the worst defaulters dwell
(Charcoal devils used as fuel as you require 'em),
There's some lovely coloured rays,
Pyrotechnical displays,
But you can't expect the burning to admire 'em!

EDGAR WALLACE—*Nature Fails. L'Envoi.*

4
Die Helle ist mit Mönchskappen, Pfaffenfalten, und Pickelhauben gepflastert.

Hell is paved with monks' cowls, priests' drapery, and spike-helmets.

WANDER traces the saying to 1605.

(See also CHRYSOSTOM)

5
That's the greatest torture souls feel in hell,
In hell, that they must live, and cannot die.

JOHN WEBSTER—*Duchess of Malfi.* Act IV. Sc. 1. L. 84.

HELP

6
To the man who himself strives earnestly, God also lends a helping hand.

ÆSCHYLUS—*Persæ.* 742.

(See also CERVANTES)

7
The foolish ofttimes teach the wise:
I strain too much this string of life, belike,
Meaning to make such music as shall save.
Mine eyes are dim now that they see the truth,
My strength is waned now that my need is most;
Would that I had such help as man must have,
For I shall die, whose life was all men's hope.

EDWIN ARNOLD—*Light of Asia.* Bk. VI. L. 109.

8
He that wrestles with us strengthens our nerves, and sharpens our skill. Our antagonist is our helper.

BURKE—*Reflections on the Revolution in France.*

9
The careful pilot of my proper woe.

BYRON—*Epistle to Augusta.* No. 3. St. 3.

10
Ayude Dios con lo suyo á cada uno.

God helps everyone with what is his own.

CERVANTES—*Don Quixote.* Pt. II. 26.

(See also ÆSCHYLUS, EURIPIDES, SIDNEY)

11
Heaven's help is better than early rising.

CERVANTES—*Don Quixote.* Vol. III. Pt. II. Ch. XXXIV.

12
If I can stop one heart from breaking,
I shall not live in vain;
If I can ease one life the aching,
Or cool one pain,
Or help one fainting robin
Into his nest again,
I shall not live in vain.

EMILY DICKINSON—*Life.*

13
Homo qui erranti comiter monstrat viam,
Quasi lumen de suo lumine accendit, facit:
Nihilominus ipsi luceat, cum illi accenderit.

He who civilly shows the way to one who has missed it, is as one who has lighted another's lamp from his own lamp; it none the less gives light to himself when it burns for the other.

ENNIUS. Quoted by CICERO. *De Officiis.* 1. 16.

14
God helps him who strives hard.

EURIPIDES—*Eumenidæ.*

(See also CERVANTES)

15
Turn, gentle Hermit of the Dale,
And guide my lonely way
To where yon taper cheers the vale
With hospitable ray.

GOLDSMITH—*Vicar of Wakefield. The Hermit.* Ch. VIII.

16
Light is the task when many share the toil.

HOMER—*Iliad.* Bk. XII. L. 493. BRYANT's trans.

17
Nabis sine cortice.

You will swim without cork (without help).

HORACE—*Satires.* Bk. I. 4. 120.

18
Make two grins grow where there was only a grouch before.

ELBERT HUBBARD—*Pig-Pen Pete. Why I Ride Horseback.*

19
Is not a patron, my lord, one who looks with unconcern on a man struggling for life in the water, and when he has reached ground encumbers him with help?

SAMUEL JOHNSON—*Boswell's Life of Johnson.* (1754)

20
I want to help you to grow as beautiful as God meant you to be when he thought of you first.

GEORGE MACDONALD—*The Marquis of Lossie.* Ch. XXII.

21
Aid the dawning, tongue and pen:
Aid it, hopes of honest men!

CHARLES MACKAY—*Clear the Way.*

22
Truths would you teach, or save a sinking land?
All fear, none aid you, and few understand.

POPE—*Essay on Man.* Ep. IV. L. 264.

1
In man's most dark extremity
Oft succor dawns from Heaven.
SCOTT—*Lord of the Isles.* Canto I. St. 20.

2
Now, ye familiar spirits, that are cull'd
Out of the powerful regions under earth,
Help me this once.
Henry VI. Pt. I. Act V. Sc. 3. L. 10.

3
Help me, Cassius, or I sink!
Julius Cæsar. Act I. Sc. 2. L. 111.

4
And he that stands upon a slippery place
Makes nice of no vile hold to stay him up.
King John. Act III. Sc. 4. L. 138.

5
God helps those who help themselves.
ALGERNON SIDNEY—*Discourse Concerning Government.* Ch. II. Pt. XXIII.
(See also CERVANTES)

HEMLOCK

Tsuga Canadensis

6
O Tannenbaum, O Tannenbaum,
Wie treu sind deine Blätter.
Du grünst nicht nur zur Sommerzeit,
Nein, auch im Winter wenn es schneet,
O Tannenbaum, O Tannenbaum,
Wie treu sind deine Blätter.
O hemlock-tree! O hemlock-tree! how faithful are thy branches!
Green not alone in summer time,
But in the winter's frost and rime!
O hemlock-tree! O hemlock-tree! how faithful are thy branches!
AUGUST ZARNACK's version of Old German Folk Song. Trans. by LONGFELLOW—*The Hemlock-Tree.*

HEN

7
Alas! my child, where is the Pen
That can do justice to the Hen?
Like Royalty, she goes her way,
Laying foundations every day,
Though not for Public Buildings, yet
For Custard, Cake and Omelette.
Or if too old for such a use
They have their fling at some abuse,
As when to censure Plays Unfit
Upon the stage they make a Hit
Or at elections seal the Fate
Of an Obnoxious Candidate.
No wonder, Child, we prize the Hen,
Whose Egg is Mightier than the Pen.
OLIVER HERFORD—*The Hen.*

HEPATICA

Hepatica

8
All the woodland path is broken
By warm tints along the way,
And the low and sunny slope
Is alive with sudden hope
When there comes the silent token
Of an April day,—
Blue hepatica!
DORA READ GOODALE—*Hepatica.*

HEROES

9
My valet-de-chambre sings me no such song.
ANTIGONUS I. See PLUTARCH—*Apothegms.* Also *Concerning Isis and Osiris.* Ch. XXIV.
(See also CORNUEL)

10
The hero is the world-man, in whose heart
One passion stands for all, the most indulged.
BAILEY—*Festus. Proem.* L. 114.

11
Tel maître, tel valet.
As the master so the valet.
Like master, like man.
Attributed to CHEVALIER BAYARD by M. CIMBER.
(See also CORNUEL)

12
Ferryman ho! In the night so black
Hark to the clank of iron;
'Tis heroes of the Yser,
'Tis sweethearts of glory,
'Tis lads who are unafraid!
Ferryman, ho!
LUCIEN BOYER—*La Maison du Passeur.*

13
I want a hero: an uncommon want,
When every year and month sends forth a new one.
BYRON—*Don Juan.* Canto I. St. 1.

14
Worship of a hero is transcendent admiration of a great man.
CARLYLE—*Heroes and Hero-Worship.* Lecture 1.

15
If Hero mean *sincere man*, why may not every one of us be a Hero?
CARLYLE—*Heroes and Hero-Worship.* Lecture IV.

16
Hero-worship exists, has existed, and will forever exist, universally among Mankind.
CARLYLE—*Sartor Resartus. Organic Filaments.*

17
Il faut être bien héros pour l'être aux yeux de son valet-de-chambre.
A man must indeed be a hero to appear such in the eyes of his valet.
MARSHAL CATINAT.
(See also CORNUEL)

18 He's of stature somewhat low—
Your hero always should be tall, you know.
CHURCHILL—*The Rosciad.* L. 1,029.

19
Il n'y a pas de grand homme pour son valet-de-chambre.
No man is a hero to his valet.
MME. DE CORNUEL. See MLLE. AISSÉ—*Letters.* 161. (Paris, 1853.)
(See also ANTIGONUS, BAYARD, GOETHE, LA BRUYÈRE, MONTAIGNE, PLUTARCH)

20
The hero is not fed on sweets,
Daily his own heart he eats;
Chambers of the great are jails,
And head-winds right for royal sails.
EMERSON—*Essays. Heroism. Introduction.*

1
Self-trust is the essence of heroism.
EMERSON—*Essay. Heroism.*

2
Each man is a hero and an oracle to somebody, and to that person whatever he says has an enhanced value.
EMERSON—*Letters and Social Aims. Quotation and Originality.*

3
Es gibt für den Kammerdiener keinen Helden.
To a valet no man is a hero.
GOETHE—*Wahlverwandtschaften.* II. 5. *Aus Ottilien's Tagebüche.*
(See also CORNUEL)

4
But to the hero, when his sword
Has won the battle for the free,
Thy voice sounds like a prophet's word,
And in its hollow tones are heard
The thanks of millions yet to be.
FITZ-GREENE HALLECK—*Marco Bozzaris.*

5
It hath been an antient custom among them [Hungarians] that none should wear a fether but he who had killed a Turk, to whom onlie yt was lawful to shew the number of his slaine enemys by the number of fethers in his cappe.
RICHARD HANSARD—*Description of Hungary, Anno 1599.* Lansdowne MS. 775. Vol. 149. British Museum.

6
The boy stood on the burning deck
Whence all but he had fled;
The flame that lit the battle's wreck,
Shone round him o'er the dead.
* * * * *
The flames roll'd on—he would not go
Without his Father's word;
That Father, faint in death below,
His voice no longer heard.
FELICIA D. HEMANS—*Casabianca.*

7
Heroes as great have died, and yet shall fall.
HOMER—*Iliad.* Bk. XV. L. 157. POPE'S trans.

8
Hail, Columbia! happy land!
Hail, ye heroes! heaven-born band!
Who fought and bled in Freedom's cause.
JOSEPH HOPKINSON—*Hail, Columbia!*

9
Vixere fortes ante Agamemnona
Multi: sed omnes illacrimabiles
Urgentur, ignotique longa
Nocte, carent quia vate sacro.
Many heroes lived before Agamemnon, but they are all unmourned, and consigned to oblivion, because they had no bard to sing their praises.
HORACE—*Carmina.* IV. 9. 25.

10
The idol of to-day pushes the hero of yesterday out of our recollection; and will, in turn, be supplanted by his successor of to-morrow.
WASHINGTON IRVING—*The Sketch Book. Westminster Abbey.*

11
Still the race of hero spirits pass the lamp from hand to hand.
CHARLES KINGSLEY—*The World's Age.*

12
Rarement ils sont grands vis-à-vis de leur valets-de-chambre.
Rarely do they appear great before their valets.
LA BRUYÈRE—*Caractères.*
(See also CORNUEL)

13
There are heroes in evil as well as in good.
LA ROCHEFOUCAULD—*Maxims.* No. 194.

14
Crowds speak in heroes.
GERALD STANLEY LEE—*Crowds.* Bk. IV. Ch. III.

15
There is never any real danger in allowing a pedestal for a hero. He never has time to sit on it. One sees him always over and over again kicking his pedestal out from under him, and using it to batter a world with.
GERALD STANLEY LEE—*Crowds.* Bk. V. Pt. III. Ch. XVI.

16
Dost thou know what a hero is? Why, a hero is as much as one should say,—a hero.
LONGFELLOW—*Hyperion.* Bk. I. Ch. I.

17
'Tis as easy to be heroes as to sit the idle slaves
Of a legendary virtue carved upon our father's graves.
LOWELL—*The Present Crisis.* St. 15.

18
Tel a esté miraculeux au monde, auquel sa femme et son valet n'ont rien veu seulement de remarquable; peu d'hommes ont esté admirez par leur domestiques.
Such an one has been, as it were, miraculous in the world, in whom his wife and valet have seen nothing even remarkable; few men have been admired by their servants.
MONTAIGNE—*Essays.* Bk. III. Ch. II.
(See also CORNUEL)

19
See the conquering hero comes!
Sound the trumpets, beat the drums!
DR. THOS. MORELL—Words used by HANDEL in *Joshua,* and *Judas Maccabæus.* (Introduced in stage version of LEE'S *Rival Queens.* Act II. Sc. 1.)

20
My personal attendant does not think so much of these things as I do.
PLUTARCH—*De Iside.* Ch. XXIV. Also in *Regnum et Imperatorum. Apothegmata.* II. 28. (Tauchnitz Ed.)
(See also CORNUEL)

21
Do we weep for the heroes who died for us,
Who living were true and tried for us,
And dying sleep side by side for us;
The martyr band
That hallowed our land
With the blood they shed in a tide for us?
ABRAM J. RYAN—*C. S. A.*

22
The last flash . . . and the hideous attack
Dies like a wisp of storm—discouraged flame;
And soon these battered heroes will come back,
The same but yet not the same.
LOUIS UNTERMEYER—*Return of the Soldiers.*

HILLS (See MOUNTAINS)

HISTORY

1
Happy is the nation without a history.
BECCARIA—*Trattato dei Delitti e delle Pene* (Treatise of Crimes and of Punishment). Introduction. Adapted from French text.

2
History is a pageant, not a philosophy.
AUGUSTINE BIRRELL—*Obiter Dicta. The Muse of History.*

3
I have read somewhere or other, in Dionysius of Halicarnassus, I think, that history is philosophy teaching by examples.
LORD BOLINGBROKE (Henry St. John)—*On the Study and Use of History.* Letter 2. Also quoted by CARLYLE—*Essays. History.*
(See also DIONYSIUS)

4
The dignity of history.
LORD BOLINGBROKE (Henry St. John)—*On the Study and Use of History.* Letter V. FIELDING—*Tom Jones.* Bk. XI. Ch. II.
(See also MACAULAY)

5
What want these outlaws conquerors should have
But History's purchased page to call them great?
BYRON—*Childe Harold.* Canto III. St. 48.

6
And history with all her volumes vast,
Hath but *one* page.
BYRON—*Childe Harold.* Canto IV. St. 108.

7
Histories are as perfect as the Historian is wise, and is gifted with an eye and a soul.
CARLYLE—*Cromwell's Letters and Speeches. Introduction.* Ch. I.

8
History, a distillation of rumor.
CARLYLE—*French Revolution.* Pt. I. Bk. VII. Ch. V.

9
History is the essence of innumerable Biographies.
CARLYLE—*Essays. On History.*
(See also EMERSON)

10
In a certain sense all men are historians.
CARLYLE—*Essays. On History.*

11
History, as it lies at the root of all science, is also the first distinct product of man's spiritual nature; his earliest expression of what can be called Thought.
CARLYLE—*Essays. On History.*

12
All history . . . is an inarticulate Bible.
CARLYLE—*Latter Day Pamphlets.* 405.

13
All history is a Bible—a thing stated in words by me more than once.
CARLYLE—Quoted in FROUDE'S *Early Life of Carlyle.*

14
Happy the People whose Annals are blank in History-Books.
CARLYLE—*Life of Frederick the Great.* Bk. XVI. Ch. I.

15
Que voulez-vous de plus? Il a inventé l'histoire.
What more would you have? He has invented history.
MADAME DU DEFFAND of Voltaire, who was accused by critics of lack of invention. See FOURIER—*L'Esprit dans Histoire.* P. 141.

16
The contact with manners then is education; and this Thucydides appears to assert when he says history is philosophy learned from examples.
DIONYSIUS of HALICARNASSUS—*Ars Rhetorica.* XI. 2. P. 212. (Tauchnitz Ed.) See THUCYDIDES—*Works.* I. 22.
(See also BOLINGBROKE)

17
Assassination has never changed the history of the world.
BENJ. DISRAELI—*Speech.* May, 1865.

18
There is properly no history, only biography.
EMERSON—*Essays. History.*
(See also CARLYLE)

19
The reign of Antoninus is marked by the rare advantage of furnishing very few materials for history, which is indeed little more than the register of the crimes, follies, and misfortunes of mankind.
GIBBON—*Decline and Fall of the Roman Empire.* (1776) Ch. III.
(See also VOLTAIRE)

20
And read their history in a nation's eyes.
GRAY—*Elegy in a Country Churchyard.* St. 16.

21
The long historian of my country's woes.
HOMER—*Odyssey.* Bk. III. L. 142. POPE'S trans.

22
History casts its shadow far into the land of song.
LONGFELLOW—*Outre-Mer. Ancient Spanish Ballads.*

23
They who live in history only seemed to walk the earth again.
LONGFELLOW—*The Belfry of Bruges.* St. 9.

24
I shall cheerfully bear the reproach of having descended below the dignity of history.
MACAULAY—*History of England.* Vol. I. Ch. I. (See also BOLINGBROKE)

25
Happy the people whose annals are tiresome.
MONTESQUIEU.

26
[History] hath triumphed over Time, which besides it, nothing but Eternity hath triumphed over.
SIR WALTER RALEIGH—*The History of the World. Preface.*

27
In a word, we may gather out of history a policy no less wise than eternal; by the comparison and application of other men's forepassed miseries with our own like errors and ill deservings.
SIR WALTER RALEIGH—*History of the World. Preface.* Par. IX.
(See also TACITUS)

1
Die Weltgeschichte ist das Weltgericht.
The world's history is the world's judgment.
SCHILLER—*Resignation.* 17.

2
Der Historiker ist ein rückwärts gekehrter Prophet.
The historian is a prophet looking backwards.
SCHLEGEL—*Athenæum. Berlin.* I. 2. 20.
(See also CARLYLE)

3
Præcipium munus annalium reor, ne virtutes sileantur, utque pravis dictis, factisque ex posteritate et infamia metus sit.
The principal office of history I take to be this: to prevent virtuous actions from being forgotten, and that evil words and deeds should fear an infamous reputation with posterity.
TACITUS—*Annales.* III. 65.
(See also RALEIGH)

4
L'histoire n'est que le tableau des crimes et des malheurs.
History is only the register of crimes and misfortunes.
VOLTAIRE—*L'Ingénu.* X.
(See also GIBBON)

5
Oh do not read history, for that I know must be false.
ROBERT WALPOLE. I. *Walpoliana.* No. CXLI. Also in *Advertisement* to *Letters to Horace Mann.*

6
Those old credulities, to nature dear,
Shall they no longer bloom upon the stock
Of History.
WORDSWORTH—*Memorials of a Tour in Italy.* IV. *At Rome.*

HOLIDAYS

7
The second day of July, 1776, will be the most memorable epoch in the history of America. I am apt to believe that it will be celebrated by succeeding generations as the great anniversary festival. It ought to be commemorated as the day of deliverance, by solemn acts of devotion to God Almighty. It ought to be solemnized with pomp and parade, with shows, games, sports, guns, bells, bonfires, and illuminations, from one end of this continent to the other, from this time forward forevermore.
JOHN ADAMS—*Letter to Mrs. Adams.* July 3, 1776.

8
There were his young barbarians all at play
There was their Dacian mother—he, their sire,
Butcher'd to make a Roman holiday.
BYRON—*Childe Harold.* Canto IV. St. 141.

9
And that was the way
The deuce was to pay
As it always is, at the close of the day
That gave us—
Hurray! Hurray! Hurray!
(With some restrictions, the fault-finders say)
That which, please God, we will keep for aye
Our National Independence!
WILL CARLETON—*How We Kept the Day.*

10
The holiest of all holidays are those
Kept by ourselves in silence and apart;
The secret anniversaries of the heart,
When the full river of feeling overflows;—
The happy days unclouded to their close;
The sudden joys that out of darkness start
As flames from ashes; swift desires that dart
Like swallows singing down each wind that blows!
LONGFELLOW—*Holidays.* L. 1.

11
For now I am in a holiday humour.
As You Like It. Act IV. Sc. 1. L. 69.

12
If all the year were playing holidays,
To sport would be as tedious as to work.
Henry IV. Pt. I. Act I. Sc. 2. L. 228.

13
Being holiday, the beggar's shop is shut.
Romeo and Juliet. Act V. Sc. 1. L. 56.

14
You sunburnt sicklemen, of August weary,
Come hither from the furrow and be merry:
Make holiday; your rye-straw hats put on
And these fresh nymphs encounter every one
In country footing.
Tempest. Act IV. Sc. 1. L. 134.

15
Time for work,—yet take
Much holiday for art's and friendship's sake.
GEORGE JAMES DE WILDE—*Sonnet. On the Arrival of Spring.*

HOLINESS

16
Might make a saintship of an anchorite.
BYRON—*Childe Harold.* Canto I. St. 11.

17
Where'er we tread 'tis haunted, holy ground.
BYRON—*Childe Harold.* Canto II. St. 88.

18
God attributes to place
No sanctity, if none be thither brought
By men who there frequent.
MILTON—*Paradise Lost.* Bk. XI. L. 836.

19
Whoso lives the holiest life
Is fittest far to die.
MARGARET J. PRESTON—*Ready.*

20
But all his mind is bent to holiness,
To number Ave-Maries on his beads;
His champions are the prophets and apostles,
His weapons holy saw of sacred writ,
His study is his tilt-yard, and his loves
Are brazen images of canonized saints.
Henry VI. Pt. II. Act I. Sc. 3. L. 58.

21
He who the sword of heaven will bear
Should be as holy as severe;
Pattern in himself to know,
Grace to stand, and virtue go;
More or less to others paying
Than by self-offences weighing.
Shame to him whose cruel striking
Kills for faults of his own liking!
Measure for Measure. Act III. Sc. 2. L. 275.

1
Our holy lives must win a new world's crown.
Richard II. Act V. Sc. 1. L. 24.

2
Holiness is the architectural plan upon which God buildeth up His living temple.
SPURGEON—*Gleanings Among the Sheaves. Holiness.*

HOLLY

(*Ilex*)

3
Green, slender, leaf-clad holly-boughs
Were twisted gracefu' round her brows,
I took her for some Scottish Muse,
By that same token,
An' come to stop those reckless vows,
Would soon be broken.
BURNS—*The Vision.* Duan I. St. 9.

4
Those hollies of themselves a shape
As of an arbor took.
COLERIDGE—*The Three Graves.* Pt. IV. St. 24.

5
All green was vanished save of pine and yew,
That still displayed their melancholy hue;
Save the green holly with its berries red,
And the green moss that o'er the gravel spread.
CRABBE—*Tales of the Hall.*

6
And as, when all the summer trees are seen
So bright and green,
The Holly leaves a sober hue display
Less bright than they,
But when the bare and wintry woods we see,
What then so cheerful as the Holly-tree?
SOUTHEY—*The Holly-Tree.*

7
O Reader! hast thou ever stood to see
The Holly-tree?
The eye that contemplates it well perceives
Its glossy leaves
Ordered by an Intelligence so wise
As might confound the Atheist's sophistries.
SOUTHEY—*The Holly-Tree.* St. 1.

HOME

8
No outward doors of a man's house can in general be broken open to execute any civil process; though in criminal cases the public safety supersedes the private.
BLACKSTONE (STEPHEN'S) Vol. IV. P. 108. (Ed. 1880)
(See also COKE, EMERSON, INGALLS, LAMBARD, MASSINGER, PITT, STAUNFORDE)

9
At length his lonely cot appears in view,
Beneath the shelter of an aged tree;
Th' expectant *wee-things*, toddlin, stacher thro'
To meet their Dad, wi' flichterin noise an' glee.
BURNS—*The Cotter's Saturday Night.* St. 3.

10
To make a happy fireside clime
To weans and wife,
That's the true pathos and sublime
Of human life.
BURNS—*Epistle to Dr. Blacklock.*

11
I've read in many a novel, that unless they've souls that grovel—
Folks *prefer* in fact a hovel to your dreary marble halls.
CALVERLEY—*In the Gloaming.*

12
My whinstone house my castle is,
I have my own four walls.
CARLYLE—*My Own Four Walls.*

13
When the hornet hangs in the holly hock,
And the brown bee drones i' the rose,
And the west is a red-streaked four-o'clock,
And summer is near its close—
It's—Oh, for the gate, and the locust lane;
And dusk, and dew, and home again!
MADISON CAWEIN—*In the Lane.*

14
Old homes! old hearts! Upon my soul forever
Their peace and gladness lie like tears and laughter.
MADISON CAWEIN—*Old Homes.*

15
Nullus est locus domestica sede jucundior.
There is no place more delightful than one's own fireside.
CICERO—*Epistles.* IV. 8.

16
Home is home, though it be never so homely.
JOHN CLARKE—*Paroemiologia.* P. 101.

17
For a man's house is his castle.
SIR EDWARD COKE—*Institutes.* Pt. III. *Against Going, or Riding Armed.* P. 162.

18
The house of every one is to him as his castle and fortress, as well for his defence against injury and violence, as for his repose.
SIR EDWARD COKE—*Reports, Semaynes' Case.* Vol. III. Pt. V. P. 185.
(See also BLACKSTONE)

19
For the whole world, without a native home,
Is nothing but a prison of larger room.
COWLEY—*To the Bishop of Lincoln.* L. 27.

20
I am far frae my hame, an' I'm weary aften whiles,
For the longed-for hame-bringing an' my Father's welcome smiles.
ERASTUS ELLSWORTH—*My Ain Countrie.* See MOODY and SANKEY'S *Hymns*, No. 5.

21
The house is a castle which the King cannot enter.
EMERSON—*English Traits. Wealth.*
(See also BLACKSTONE)

22
There's nobody at home
But Jumping Joan,
And father and mother and I.
GEORGE GASCOIGNE—*Tale of Ieronimi.* (1577)

23
The whitewash'd wall, the nicely sanded floor,
The varnish'd clock that click'd behind the door;
The chest contriv'd a double debt to pay,
A bed by night, a chest of drawers by day.
GOLDSMITH—*The Deserted Village.* L. 227.
(See also GREENE)

1
At night returning, every labour sped,
He sits him down, the monarch of a shed;
Smiles by his cheerful fire, and round surveys
His children's looks, that brighten at the blaze;
While his lov'd partner, boastful of her hoard,
Displays her cleanly platter on the board.
GOLDSMITH—*The Traveller*. L. 191.

2
How small of all that human hearts endure,
That part which laws or kings can cause or cure!
Still to ourselves in every place consigned,
Our own felicity we make or find.
With secret course, which no loud storms annoy,
Glides the smooth current of domestic joy.
GOLDSMITH—*The Traveller*. L. 429.

3
What if in Scotland's wilds we veil'd our head,
Where tempests whistle round the sordid bed;
Where the rug's two-fold use we might display,
By night a blanket, and a plaid by day.
E. B. G.—*Attributed in the British Museum Cat.* to EDWARD BURNABY GREENE. (1764) *The Satires of Juvenal Paraphrastically Imitated, and adapted to the Times.*

4
The stately Homes of England,
How beautiful they stand!
Amidst their tall ancestral trees,
O'er all the pleasant land.
FELICIA D. HEMANS—*Homes of England*.

5
My house, my house, though thou art small,
Thou art to me the Escurial.
HERBERT—*Jacula Prudentum*. No. 416.

6
His native home deep imag'd in his soul.
HOMER—*Odyssey*. Bk. XIII. L. 38. POPE'S trans.

7
Peace and rest at length have come,
All the day's long toil is past;
And each heart is whispering, "Home,
Home at last!"
HOOD—*Home At Last*.

8
Who hath not met with home-made bread,
A heavy compound of putty and lead—
And home-made wines that rack the head,
And home-made liquors and waters?
Home-made pop that will not foam,
And home-made dishes that drive one from home—
* * * * * *
Home-made by the homely daughters.
HOOD—*Miss Kilmansegg*.

9
The beauty of the house is order,
The blessing of the house is contentment,
The glory of the house is hospitality.
House Motto.

10
Appeles us'd to paint a good housewife upon a snayl; which intimated that she should be as slow from gadding abroad, and when she went she should carry her house upon her back; that is, she should make all sure at home.
HOWELL—*Parly of Beasts*. (1660) P. 58.
(See also BRITAINE under WOMAN)

11
I think some orator commenting upon that fate said that though the winds of heaven might whistle around an Englishman's cottage, the King of England could not.
JOHN J. INGALLS. *In the U. S. Senate*. May 10, 1880.
(See also EMERSON)

12
As a lodge in a garden of cucumbers.
Isaiah. I. 8.

13
Our law calleth a man's house, his castle, meaning that he may defend himselfe therein.
LAMBARD—*Eiren*. II. VII. 257. (1588)
(See also BLACKSTONE)

14
Cling to thy home! If there the meanest shed
Yield thee a hearth and shelter for thy head,
And some poor plot, with vegetables stored,
Be all that Heaven allots thee for thy board,
Unsavory bread, and herbs that scatter'd grow
Wild on the river-brink or mountain-brow;
Yet e'en this cheerless mansion shall provide
More heart's repose than all the world beside.
LEONIDAS—*Home*.

15
Stay, stay at home, my heart, and rest;
Home-keeping hearts are happiest,
For those that wander they know not where
Are full of trouble and full of care;
To stay at home is best.
LONGFELLOW—*Song*. St. 1.

16
A house of dreams untold,
It looks out over the whispering treetops,
And faces the setting sun.
EDWARD MACDOWELL. Heading to *From a Log Cabin*. Inscribed on memorial tablet near his grave.

17
I in my own house am an emperor,
And will defend what's mine.
MASSINGER—*Roman Actor*. Act I. Sc. 2.
(See also BLACKSTONE)

18
It is for homely features to keep home.
They had their name thence.
MILTON—*Comus*. L. 748.

19
Far from all resort of mirth,
Save the cricket on the hearth.
MILTON—*Il Penseroso*. L. 81.

20
His home, the spot of earth supremely blest,
A dearer, sweeter spot than all the rest.
MONTGOMERY—*West Indies*. Pt. III. L. 67.

21
Who has not felt how sadly sweet
The dream of home, the dream of home,
Steals o'er the heart, too soon to fleet,
When far o'er sea or land we roam?
MOORE—*The Dream of Home*. St. 1.

22
Subduing and subdued, the petty strife,
Which clouds the colour of domestic life;
The sober comfort, all the peace which springs
From the large aggregate of little things;
On these small cares of daughter, wife or friend,
The almost sacred joys of home depend.
HANNAH MORE—*Sensibility*.

1
'Mid pleasures and palaces though we may roam,
Be it ever so humble, there's no place like Home.
J. HOWARD PAYNE—*Home Sweet Home.* Song in *Clari, The Maid of Milan.*

2
The poorest man may in his cottage bid defiance to all the force of the Crown. It may be frail, its roof may shake; the wind may blow through it; the storms may enter,—the rain may enter,—but the King of England cannot enter; all his forces dare not cross the threshold of the ruined tenement!
WILLIAM PITT (Earl of Chatham)—*Speech on the Excise Bill.*
(See also BLACKSTONE)

3
Home is where the heart is.
PLINY.

4
My lodging is in Leather-Lane,
A parlor that's next to the sky;
'Tis exposed to the wind and the rain,
But the wind and the rain I defy.
W. B. RHODES—*Bombastes Furioso.* Sc. 4.

5
Just the wee cot—the cricket's chirr—
Love and the smiling face of her.
JAMES WHITCOMB RILEY—*Ike Walton's Prayer.*

6
To fireside happiness, to hours of ease
Blest with that charm, the certainty to please.
SAM'L ROGERS—*Human Life.* L. 347.

7
Gallus in sterquilinio suo plurimum potest.
The cock is at his best on his own dunghill
SENECA—*De Morte Claudii.*

8
And I'll still stay, to have thee still forget,
Forgetting any other home but this.
Romeo and Juliet. Act II. Sc. 2. L. 175.

9
That is my home of love.
Sonnet CIX.

10
Home-keeping youth have ever homely wits.
Two Gentlemen of Verona. Act I. Sc. 1. L. 2.

11
Ma meason est a moy come mon castel, hors de quel le ley ne moy arta a fuer.
My house is to me as my castle, since the law has not the art to destroy it.
STAUNFORDE—*Plees del Coron.* 14 B. (1567)

12
Home is the resort
Of love, of joy, of peace, and plenty; where
Supporting and supported, polished friends
And dear relations mingle into bliss.
THOMSON—*The Seasons. Autumn.* L. 65.

13
Though home be but homely, yet huswife is taught
That home hath no fellow to such as have aught.
TUSSER—*Points of Huswifery. Instructions to Huswifery.* VIII. P. 243. (1561)

14
I read within a poet's book
A word that starred the page,
"Stone walls do not a prison make,
Nor iron bars a cage."
Yes, that is true, and something more:
You'll find, where'er you roam,
That marble floors and gilded walls
Can never make a home.
But every house where Love abides
And Friendship is a guest,
Is surely home, and home, sweet home;
For there the heart can rest.
HENRY VAN DYKE—*Home Song.*
(See also LOVELACE under PRISON)

15
They dreamt not of a perishable home.
WORDSWORTH—*Inside of King's College Chapel, Cambridge.*

16
The man who builds, and wants wherewith to pay,
Provides a home from which to run away.
YOUNG—*Love of Fame.* Satire I. L. 171.

HONESTY

17
Honesty is the best policy.
CERVANTES—*Don Quixote.* Pt. II. Ch. XXXIII.
(See also WHATELY)

18
A honest man's word is as good as his bond.
CERVANTES—*Don Quixote.* Vol. III. Pt. II. Ch. XXXIV.
(See also GAY)

19
Omnia quæ vindicaris in altero, tibi ipsi vehementer fugienda sunt.
Everything that thou reprovest in another, thou must most carefully avoid in thyself.
CICERO—*In Verrem.* II. 3. 2.

20
Barring that natural expression of villainy which we all have, the man looked honest enough.
S. L. CLEMENS (Mark Twain)—*A Mysterious Visit.*

21
He is one that will not plead that cause wherein his tongue must be confuted by his conscience.
FULLER—*Holy and Profane States. The Good Advocate.* Bk. II. Ch. I.

22
When rogues fall out, honest men get into their own.
SIR MATTHEW HALE.

23
He that departs with his own honesty
For vulgar praise, doth it too dearly buy.
BEN JONSON—*Epigram II.*

24
The measure of life is not length, but honestie.
LYLY—*Euphues. The Anatomy of Wit. Letters of Euphues. Euphues and Eubulus.*

25
Friends, if we be honest with ourselves, we shall be honest with each other.
GEORGE MACDONALD—*The Marquis of Lossie.* Ch. LXXI.

26
Semper bonus homo tiro est.
An honest man is always a child.
MARTIAL—*Epigrams.* XII. 51. 2.

27
An honest man's the noblest work of God.
POPE—*Essay on Man.* Ep. IV. L. 247.

1
Yet Heav'n, that made me honest, made me more
Than ever king did, when he made a lord.
NICHOLAS ROWE—*Jane Shore*. Act II. Sc. 1. L. 261.

2
Mens regnum bona possidet.
An honest heart possesses a kingdom.
SENECA—*Thyestes*. CCCLXXX

3
No legacy is so rich as honesty.
All's Well That Ends Well. Act III. Sc. 5. L. 13.

4
Ay, sir; to be honest, as this world goes, is to be one man picked out of ten thousand.
Hamlet. Act II. Sc. 2. L. 178. ("Two Thousand" in Folio "ten" in quartos.)

5
What's the news?
None, my lord, but that the world's grown honest.
Then is doomsday near.
Hamlet. Act II. Sc. 2. L. 240.

6
There is no terror, Cassius, in your threats,
For I am arm'd so strong in honesty
That they pass by me as the idle wind,
Which I respect not.
Julius Cæsar. Act IV. Sc. 3. L. 66.

7
Take note, take note, O world,
To be direct and honest is not safe.
Othello. Act III. Sc. 3. L. 378.

8
An honest tale speeds best being plainly told.
Richard III. Act IV. Sc. 4. L. 358.

9
At many times I brought in my accounts,
Laid them before you; you would throw them off,
And say, you found them in mine honesty.
Timon of Athens. Act II. Sc. 2. L. 142.

10
I hope I shall always possess firmness and virtue enough to maintain what I consider the most enviable of all titles, the character of an "Honest Man."
GEORGE WASHINGTON—*Moral Maxims*.

11
Let us raise a standard to which the wise and honest can repair; the rest is in the hands of God.
WASHINGTON—*Speech to the Constitutional Convention*. (1787)

12
Were there no heaven nor hell
I should be honest.
JOHN WEBSTER—*Duchess of Malfi*. Act I. Sc. I.

13
"Honesty is the best policy," but he who acts on that principle is not an honest man.
ARCHBISHOP WHATELY—*Thoughts and Apothegms*. Pt. II. Ch. XVIII. *Pious Frauds*.
(See also CERVANTES)

14
How happy is he born and taught
That serveth not another's will;
Whose armour is his honest thought,
And simple truth his utmost skill.
SIR HENRY WOTTON—*The Character of a Happy Life*.

HONEYSUCKLE

Lonicera

15
Around in silent grandeur stood
The stately children of the wood;
Maple and elm and towering pine
Mantled in folds of dark woodbine.
JULIA C. R. DORR—*At the Gate*.

16
I sat me down to watch upon a bank
With ivy canopied and interwove
With flaunting honeysuckle.
MILTON—*Comus*. L. 543.

17
I plucked a honeysuckle where
The hedge on high is quick with thorn,
And climbing for the prize, was torn,
And fouled my feet in quag-water;
And by the thorns and by the wind
The blossom that I took was thinn'd,
And yet I found it sweet and fair.
D. G. ROSSETTI—*The Honeysuckle*.

18
And honeysuckle loved to crawl
Up the low crag and ruin'd wall.
SCOTT—*Marmion*. Canto III. *Introduction*.

19
And bid her steal into the pleached bower,
Where honeysuckles, ripen'd by the sun,
Forbid the sun to enter, like favorites,
Made proud by princes, that advance their pride
Against that power that bred it.
Much Ado About Nothing. Act III. Sc. 1. L. 7.

HONOR

20
Better to die ten thousand deaths,
Than wound my honour.
ADDISON—*Cato*. Act I. Sc. 4.

21
Content thyself to be obscurely good.
When vice prevails and impious men bear sway,
The post of honor is a private station.
ADDISON—*Cato*. Act IV. Sc. 4.

22
The sense of honour is of so fine and delicate a nature, that it is only to be met with in minds which are naturally noble, or in such as have been cultivated by good examples, or a refined education.
ADDISON—*The Guardian*. No. 161.

23
Turpe quid ausurus, te sine teste time.
When about to commit a base deed, respect thyself, though there is no witness.
AUSONIUS—*Septem Sapientum Sententiæ Septenis Veribus Explicatæ*. III. 7.

24
The best memorial for a mighty man is to gain honor ere death.
Beowulf. VII.

25
L'honneur est comme une île escarpée et sans bords;
On n'y peut plus rentrer dès qu'on en est dehors.
Honor is like an island, rugged and without shores; we can never re-enter it once we are on the outside.
BOILEAU—*Satires*. X. 167.

1
Honour is like a widow, won
With brisk attempt and putting on.
BUTLER—*Hudibras.* Pt. II. Canto I.
(See also SOMERVILLE under FORTUNE)

2
Now, while the honour thou hast got
Is spick and span new.
BUTLER—*Hudibras.* Pt. I. Canto III. L. 397.

3
If he that in the field is slain
Be in the bed of honour lain,
He that is beaten may be said
To lie in Honour's truckle-bed.
BUTLER—*Hudibras.* Pt. I. Canto III. L. 1,047.

4
As quick as lightning, in the breach
Just in the place where honour's lodged,
As wise philosophers have judged,
Because a kick in that place more
Hurts honour than deep wounds before.
BUTLER—*Hudibras.* Pt. II. Canto III. L. 1,066.

5
Semper in fide quid senseris, non quid dixeris, cogitandum.

In honorable dealing you should consider what you intended, not what you said or thought.
CICERO—*De Officiis.* I. 13.

6
Nulla est laus ibi esse integrum, ubi nemo est, qui aut possit aut conetur rumpere.

There is no praise in being upright, where no one can, or tries to corrupt you.
CICERO—*In Verrem.* II. 1. 16.

7
Nec tibi quid liceat, sed quid fecisse decebit
Occurrat, mentemque domet respectus honesti.

Do not consider what you may do, but what it will become you to have done, and let the sense of honor subdue your mind.
CLAUDIANUS—*De Quarto Consulatu Honorii Augusti Panegyris.* CCLXVII.

8
Honor lies in honest toil.
GROVER CLEVELAND—*Letter Accepting Nomination for President.* Aug. 18, 1884. WM. Q. STODDARD. *Life of Grover Cleveland.* Ch. XV.

9
Ici l'honneur m'oblige, et j'y veux satisfaire.

Here honor binds me, and I wish to satisfy it.
CORNEILLE—*Polyeucte.* IV. 3.

10
And all at Worcester but the honour lost.
DRYDEN—*Astraea Redux.*
(See also FRANCIS I)

11
These were honoured in their generations, and were the glory of the times.
Ecclesiasticus. XLIV. 7.

12
Titles of honour add not to his worth,
Who is himself an honour to his titles.
JOHN FORD—*The Lady's Trial.* Act I. Sc. 3. L. 30.

13
Madame, pour vous faire savoir comme se porte le resté de mon infortune, de toutes choses m'est demeuré que l'honneur et la vie qui est sauvé.

Madame, that you may know the state of the rest of my misfortune, there is nothing left to me but honor, and my life, which is saved.
FRANCIS I—*to his mother.* Written in the Letter of safe conduct given to the Viceroy of Naples for the Commander Penalosa the morning after Pavia. See AIMÉ CHAMPOLLION—*Captivité de François I.* Figeac P. 129 (Ed. 1847) In MARTIN—*Histoire de France.* Vol. VIII. SISMONDI. Vol. XVI. P. 241.
(See also DRYDEN)

14
Give me, kind Heaven, a private station,
A mind serene for contemplation:
Title and profit I resign;
The post of honor shall be mine.
GAY—*Fables.* Pt. II. *The Vulture, the Sparrow and other Birds.*
(See also ADDISON)

15
Your word is as good as the Bank, sir.
HOLCROFT—*The Road to Ruin.* Act I. Sc. 3. L. 235.
(See also CERVANTES)

16
Honour is but an itch in youthful blood
Of doing acts extravagantly good.
HOWARD—*Indian Queen.*

17
Great honours are great burdens, but on whom
They are cast with envy, he doth bear two loads.
His cares must still be double to his joys,
In any dignity.
BEN JONSON—*Catiline. His Conspiracy.* Act III. Sc. 1. L. 1.

18
Summum crede nefas, animum præferre pudori,
Et propter vitam vivendi perdere causas.

Believe it to be the greatest of all infamies, to prefer your existence to your honor, and for the sake of life to lose every inducement to live.
JUVENAL—*Satires.* VIII. 83.

19
Dead on the field of honour.
Answer given in the roll-call of LA TOUR D'AUVERGNE'S *regiment after his death.*

20
Quod pulcherrimum idem tutissimum est.
What is honorable is also safest.
LIVY—*Annales.* XXXIV. 14.

21
Perchè non i titoli illustrano gli uomini, ma gli uomini i titoli.

For titles do not reflect honor on men, but rather men on their titles.
MACHIAVELLI—*Dei Discorsi.* III. 38.

22
Honour is purchas'd by the deeds we do;
* * * honour is not won,
Until some honourable deed be done.
MARLOWE—*Hero and Leander. First Sistiad.* L. 276.

23
To set the cause above renown,
To love the game beyond the prize,
To honor while you strike him down,

The foe that comes with fearless eyes;
To count the life of battle good
And dear the land that gave you birth,
And dearer yet the brotherhood
That binds the brave of all the earth.
HENRY NEWBOLDT—*Clifton Chapel.*

1
When honor comes to you be ready to take it;
But reach not to seize it before it is near.
JOHN BOYLE O'REILLY—*Rules of the Road.*

2
Honour, the spur that pricks the princely mind,
To follow rule and climb the stately chair.
GEORGE PEELE—*The Battle of Alcazar.* Act I.

3
We'll shine in more substantial honours,
And to be noble, we'll be good.
THOS. PERCY—*Reliques. Winifreda.*

4
Et ille quidem plenus annis abiit, plenus honoribus, illis etiam quos recusavit.

He died full of years and of honors, equally illustrious by those he refused as by those he accepted.
PLINY the Younger—*Epistles.* II. 1.

5
A Quixotic sense of the honorable—of the chivalrous.
POE—*Letter to Mrs. Whitman.* Oct. 18, 1848.

6
Honour and shame from no condition rise;
Act well your part, there all the honour lies.
POPE—*Essay on Man.* Ep. IV. L. 193.

7
A bon entendeur ne faut qu'un parole.
A good intention does not mean honor.
RABELAIS—*Pantagruel.* Bk. V. Ch. VII.

8
Faisons ce que l'honneur exige.
Let us do what honor demands.
RACINE—*Bérénice.* IV. 4.

9
Mais sans argent l'honneur n'est qu'une maladie.

But without money honor is nothing but a malady.
RACINE—*Plaideurs.* I. 1.

10
Nichtswürdig ist die Nation, die nicht
Ihr alles freudig setzt an ihre Ehre.

That nation is worthless which does not joyfully stake everything on her honor.
SCHILLER—*Die Jungfrau von Orleans.* I. 5. 81.

11
Das Herz und nicht die Meinung ehrt den Mann.

What he feels and not what he does honors a man.
SCHILLER—*Wallenstein's Tod.* IV. 8. 70.

12 See that you come
Not to woo honour, but to wed it.
All's Well That Ends Well. Act II. Sc. 1. L. 14.

13 Honours thrive,
When rather from our acts we them derive
Than our foregoers.
All's Well That Ends Well. Act II. Sc. 3. L. 142.

14
A scar nobly got, or a noble scar, is a good livery of honour.
All's Well That Ends Well. Act IV. Sc. 5. L. 105.

15 If I lose mine honour,
I lose myself; better I were not yours
Than yours so branchless.
Antony and Cleopatra. Act III. Sc. 4. L. 22.

16 For he's honourable
And doubling that, most holy.
Cymbeline. Act III. Sc. 4. L. 179.

17 Methinks it were an easy leap,
To pluck bright honour from the pale-fac'd moon.
Henry IV. Pt. I. Act I. Sc. 3. L. 201.

18
And pluck up drowned honour by the locks.
Henry IV. Pt. I. Act I. Sc. 3. L. 205.

19
Well, 'tis no matter; honour pricks me on. Yea, but how if honour prick me off, when I come on? how then? Can honour set to a leg? no: or an arm? no: or take away the grief of a wound? no: Honour hath no skill in surgery, then? no. What is honour? a word. What is that word honour? air. A trim reckoning! Who hath it? he that died o' Wednesday. Doth he feel it? no. Doth he hear it? no. Is it insensible, then? Yea, to the dead. But will it not live with the living? no. Why? detraction will not suffer it. Therefore, I'll none of it: honour is a mere scutcheon; and so ends my catechism.
Henry IV. Pt. I. Act V. Sc. 1. L. 129.

20
For Brutus is an honourable man;
So are they all, all honourable men.
Julius Cæsar. Act III. Sc. 2. L. 87.

21
Thou art a fellow of a good respect;
Thy life hath had some smatch of honour in it.
Julius Cæsar. Act V. Sc. 5. L. 45.

22 Let none presume
To wear an undeserv'd dignity.
O, that estates, degrees and offices
Were not deriv'd corruptly, and that clear honour
Were purchas'd by the merit of the wearer!
Merchant of Venice. Act II. Sc. 9. L. 39.

23 Mine honour let me try:
In that I live, and for that will I die.
Richard II. Act I. Sc. I. L. 184.

24
And as the sun breaks through the darkest clouds,
So honour peereth in the meanest habit.
Taming of the Shrew. Act IV. Sc. 3. L. 175.

25
I had rather crack my sinews, break my back,
Than you should such dishonour undergo.
Tempest. Act III. Sc. 1. L. 26.

26
For honour travels in a strait so narrow,
Where one but goes abreast.
Troilus and Cressida. Act III. Sc. 3. L. 154.

27
Honour sits smiling at the sale of truth.
SHELLEY—*Queen Mab.* Canto IV. L. 218.

1
His honor rooted in dishonor stood,
And faith unfaithful kept him falsely true.
TENNYSON—*Idyls of the King. Lancelot and Elaine.* L. 886.

2
The nation's honor is dearer than the nation's comfort; yes, than the nation's life itself.
WOODROW WILSON—*Speech.* Jan. 29, 1916.

HOPE

3
Know then, whatever cheerful and serene
Supports the mind, supports the body too:
Hence, the most vital movement mortals feel
Is hope, the balm and lifeblood of the soul.
JOHN ARMSTRONG—*Art of Preserving Health.* Bk. IV. L. 310.

4
Our greatest good, and what we least can spare,
Is hope: the last of all our evils, fear.
JOHN ARMSTRONG—*Art of Preserving Health.* Bk. IV. L. 318.

5
It is to hope, though hope were lost.
MRS. BARBAULD—*Come here, Fond Youth.*

6
For the hopes of men have been justly called waking dreams.
BASIL, BISHOP OF CÆSAREA. (About 370) *Letter to Gregory of Nazianzus.* Found in A. VON HUMBOLDT'S *Cosmos.*
(See also DIOGENES, QUINTILIAN)

7
Hope! thou nurse of young desire.
BICKERSTAFF—*Love in a Village.* Act I. Sc. 1. L. 1.

8
The heart bowed down by weight of woe
To weakest hope will cling.
ALFRED BUNN—*Bohemian Girl.*

9
Hope springs exulting on triumphant wing.
BURNS—*Cotter's Saturday Night.* St. 16.

10
Hope, withering, fled—and Mercy sighed farewell.
BYRON—*Corsair.* Canto I. St. 9.

11
Farewell!
For in that word that fatal word,—howe'er
We promise, hope, believe,—there breathes despair.
BYRON—*Corsair.* St. 15.

12
Auspicious Hope! in thy sweet garden grow
Wreaths for each toil, a charm for every woe.
CAMPBELL—*Pleasures of Hope.* Pt. I. L. 45.

13
Cease, every joy, to glimmer in my mind,
But leave,—oh! leave the light of Hope behind!
CAMPBELL—*Pleasures of Hope.* Pt. II. L. 375.

14
Con la vida muchas cosas se remedian.
With life many things are remedied.
(While there's life there's hope.)
CERVANTES—*Don Quixote.*

15
Hasta la muerte todo es vida.
Until death all is life.
(While there's life there's hope.)
CERVANTES—*Don Quixote.*
(See also CICERO)

16
I laugh, for hope hath happy place with me,
If my bark sinks, 'tis to another sea.
WM. ELLERY CHANNING—*A Poet's Hope.* St. 13.

17
Ægroto dum anima est, spes est.
To the sick, while there is life there is hope.
CICERO—*Epistolæ Ad Atticum.* IX. 10.
(See also CERVANTES, GAY, MÆCENAS, MONTAIGNE)

18
Maxima illecebra est peccandi impunitatis spes.
The hope of impunity is the greatest inducement to do wrong.
CICERO—*Oratio Pro Animo Milone.* XVI.

19
Work without hope draws nectar in a sieve,
And hope without an object cannot live.
COLERIDGE—*Work Without Hope.* St. 2.

20
And Hope enchanted smiled, and waved her golden hair.
COLLINS—*Ode on the Passions.* L. 3.

21
But thou, O Hope, with eyes so fair,
What was thy delighted measure?
Still it whisper'd promised pleasure,
And bade the lovely scenes at distance hail!
COLLINS—*Ode on the Passions.* L. 29.

22
Hope! of all ills that men endure,
The only cheap and universal cure.
ABRAHAM COWLEY—*The Mistress. For Hope.*

23
Lasciate ogni speranza voi ch'entrate.
Abandon hope, all ye who enter here
DANTE—*Inferno.* III. 1. 9.

24
Senza speme vivemo in desio.
Still desiring, we live without hope.
DANTE—*Inferno.* IV. 42.

25
You ask what hope is. He (Aristotle) says it is a waking dream.
DIOGENES LAERTIUS. Bk. V. 18. Ascribed to PINDAR by STOBÆUS—*Sermon* CIX; to PLATO by ÆLIAN—*Var. Hist.* XIII. 29.
(See also BASIL)

26
Hopes have precarious life.
They are oft blighted, withered, snapped sheer off
In vigorous growth and turned to rottenness.
GEORGE ELIOT—*The Spanish Gypsy.* Bk. III.

27
While there is life there's hope (he cried,)
Then why such haste?—so groan'd and died
GAY—*The Sick Man and The Angel.*
(See also CICERO)

28
Bei so grosser Gefahr kommt die leichteste Hoffnung in Anschlag.
In so great a danger the faintest hope should be considered.
GOETHE—*Egmont.* II.

1
Wir hoffen immer, und in allen Dingen
Ist besser hoffen als verzweifeln.
We always hope, and in all things it is better to hope than to despair.
GOETHE—*Torquato Tasso.* III. 4. 197.

2
Hope, like the gleaming taper's light,
Adorns and cheers our way;
And still, as darker grows the night,
Emits a brighter ray.
GOLDSMITH—*The Captivity.* Act II. Sc. 1.

3
In all my wanderings round this world of care,
In all my griefs—and God has given my share—
I still had hopes my latest hours to crown,
Amidst these humble bowers to lay me down.
GOLDSMITH—*The Deserted Village.* L. 81.

4
The wretch condemn'd with life to part,
Still, still on hope relies;
And every pang that rends the heart
Bids expectation rise.
GOLDSMITH—*Captivity. Song.*

5
Gay hope is theirs by fancy fed,
Less pleasing when possest;
The tear forgot as soon as shed,
The sunshine of the breast.
GRAY—*On a Distant Prospect of Eton College.* St. 5.

6
Youth fades; love droops, the leaves of friendship fall;
A mother's secret hope outlives them all.
HOLMES—*A Mother's Secret.*

7
In all the wedding cake, hope is the sweetest of the plums.
DOUGLAS JERROLD—*Jerrold's Wit. The Catspaw.*

8
When there is no hope, there can be no endeavor.
SAMUEL JOHNSON—*The Rambler.* No. 110.

9
So, when dark thoughts my boding spirit shroud,
Sweet Hope! celestial influence round me shed
Waving thy silver pinions o'er my head.
KEATS—*Hope.* St. 8.

10
L' espérance, toute trompeuse qu'elle est, sert au moins à nous mener à la fin de la vie par un chemin agréable.
Hope, deceitful as it is, serves at least to lead us to the end of life along an agreeable road.
LA ROCHEFOUCAULD—*Maximes.* 168.

11
One only hope my heart can cheer,—
The hope to meet again.
GEO. LINLEY—*Song.*

12
Races, better than we, have leaned on her wavering promise,
Having naught else but Hope.
LONGFELLOW—*The Children of the Lord's Supper.* L. 230.

13
The setting of a great hope is like the setting of the sun. The brightness of our life is gone.
LONGFELLOW—*Hyperion.* Bk. I. Ch. I.

14
Who bids me Hope, and in that charming word
Has peace and transport to my soul restor'd.
LORD LYTTLETON—*The Progress of Love. Hope.* Eclogue II. L. 41.

15
Vita dum superest, bene est.
While life remains it is well.
MÆCENAS, *quoted by* SENECA, *Epist.*, 101.
(See also CICERO)

16
Our dearest hopes in pangs are born,
The kingliest Kings are crown'd with thorn.
GERALD MASSEY—*The Kingliest Kings.*

17
Where peace
And rest can never dwell, hope never comes,
That comes to all.
MILTON—*Paradise Lost.* Bk. I. L. 65.

18
What reinforcement we may gain from hope;
If not, what resolution from despair.
MILTON—*Paradise Lost.* Bk. I. L. 190.

19
So farewell hope, and with hope farewell fear,
Farewell remorse: all good to me is lost;
Evil, be thou my good.
MILTON—*Paradise Lost.* Bk. IV. L. 108.
(See also HENRY VI)

20
Hope elevates, and joy
Brightens his crest.
MILTON—*Paradise Lost.* Bk. IX. L. 633.

21
Toutes choses, disoit un mot ancien, sont esperables à un homme, pendant qu'il vit.
All things, said an ancient saw, may be hoped for by a man as long as he lives.
MONTAIGNE—*Essays.* Bk. II. Ch. III.
(See also CICERO)

22
Hope against hope, and ask till ye receive.
MONTGOMERY—*The World before the Flood.* Canto V.

23
Oh! ever thus, from childhood's hour,
I've seen my fondest hopes decay;
I never loved a tree or flower,
But 'twas the first to fade away.
MOORE—*Lalla Rookh. Fire Worshippers.*
(See also MOORE under GAZELLE)

24
The Worldly Hope men set their Hearts upon
Turns Ashes—or it prospers; and anon,
Like Snow upon the Desert's dusty Face,
Lighting a little hour or two—is gone.
OMAR KHAYYAM—*Rubaiyat.* St. 16. FITZGERALD's trans.

25
Et res non semper, spes mihi semper adest.
My hopes are not always realized, but I always hope.
OVID—*Heroides.* XVIII. 178.

1
Nam multa præter spem scio multis bona evenisse,
At ego etiam qui speraverint, spem decepisse multos.

For I know that many good things have happened to many, when least expected; and that many hopes have been disappointed.

PLAUTUS—*Rudens*. II. 3. 69; *Mostellaria*. Act I. Sc. 3. L. 71.

2
Hope springs eternal in the human breast;
Man never *is*, but always *to be* blest.

POPE—*Essay on Man*. Ep. I. L. 95.
(See also BROWNING under PROGRESS)

3
Hope travels through, nor quits us when we die.

POPE—*Essay on Man*. Ep. II. L. 273.

4
For hope is but the dream of those that wake!

PRIOR—*Solomon on the Vanity of the World*. Bk. III. L. 102.
(See also QUINTILIAN)

5
Our hopes, like tow'ring falcons, aim
At objects in an airy height;
The little pleasure of the game
Is from afar to view the flight.

PRIOR—*To Hon. Chas. Montague*.

6
Hope deferred maketh the heart sick.

Proverbs. XIII. 12.

7
Et spes inanes, et velut somnia quædam, vigilantium.

Vain hopes are like certain dreams of those who wake.

QUINTILIAN. VI. 2. 27.
(See also BASIL, PRIOR)

8
Who against hope believed in hope.

Romans. IV. 18.

9
Hope dead lives nevermore,
No, not in heaven.

CHRISTINA G. ROSSETTI—*Dead Hope*.

10
Who in Life's battle firm doth stand
Shall bear Hope's tender blossoms
Into the Silent Land.

J. G. VAN SALIS—*Song of the Silent Land*.

11
Verzweifle keiner je, dem in der trübsten Nacht
Der Hoffnung letzte Sterne schwinden.

Let no one despair, even though in the darkest night the last star of hope may disappear.

SCHILLER—*Oberon*. I. 27.

12
The sickening pang of hope deferr'd.

SCOTT—*Lady of the Lake*. Canto III. St. 22.

13
Hope is brightest when it dawns from fears.

SCOTT—*Lady of the Lake*. Canto IV. St. 1.

14
Omnia homini, dum vivit, speranda sunt.

All things are to be hoped by a man as long as he is alive. ("A very effeminate saying.")

SENECA—*Epistles*. 70.
(See also CICERO)

15
Our hap is loss, our hope but sad despair.

Henry VI. Pt. III. Act II. Sc. 3. L. 9.
(See also MILTON)

16
Farewell
The hopes of court! my hopes in heaven do dwell.

Henry VIII. Act III. Sc. 2. L. 458.

17
The miserable have no other medicine
But only hope:
I've hope to live, and am prepar'd to die.

Measure for Measure. Act III. Sc. 1. L. 2.

18
True hope is swift, and flies with swallow's wings:
Kings it makes gods, and meaner creatures kings.

Richard III. Act V. Sc. 2. L. 23.

19
Hope is a lover's staff; walk hence with that
And manage it against despairing thoughts.

Two Gentlemen of Verona. Act III. Sc. 1. L. 246.

20
Worse than despair,
Worse than the bitterness of death, is hope.

SHELLEY—*The Cenci*. Act V. Sc. 4.

21
Through the sunset of hope,
Like the shapes of a dream,
What paradise islands of glory gleam!

SHELLEY—*Hellas*. Semi-chorus I.

22
To hope till hope creates
From its own wreck the thing it contemplates.

SHELLEY—*Prometheus*. Act IV. Last stanza.

23
But hope will make thee young, for Hope and Youth
Are children of one mother, even Love.

SHELLEY—*Revolt of Islam*. Canto VIII. St. 27.

24
It is never right to consider that a man has been made happy by fate, until his life is absolutely finished, and he has ended his existence.

SOPHOCLES—*Frag. Tyndarus*.

25
We do not stray out of all words into the ever silent;
We do not raise our hands to the void for things beyond hope.

RABINDRANATH TAGORE—*Gardener*. 16.

26
Behold, we know not anything;
I can but trust that good shall fall
At last—far off—at last, to all,
And every winter change to spring.

TENNYSON—*In Memoriam*. LIV

27
The mighty hopes that make us men.

TENNYSON—*In Memoriam*. LXXXV.

28
Ego spem pretio non emo.

I do not buy hope with money.

TERENCE—*Adelphi*. II. 2. 12.

29
Væ misero mihi! quanta de spe decidi.

Woe to my wretched self! from what a height of hope have I fallen!

TERENCE—*Heauton timorumenos*. II. 3. 9.

1
For the living there is hope, for the dead there is none.
THEOCRITUS—*Idyl.* IV. 42.

2
Spes fovet, et fore cras semper ait melius.
Hope ever urges on, and tells us to-morrow will be better.
TIBULLUS—*Carmina.* II. 6. 20.

3
Vestras spes uritis.
You burn your hopes.
VERGIL—*Æneid.* V. 68.

4
Speravimus ista
Dum fortuna fuit.
Such hopes I had while fortune was kind.
VERGIL—*Æneid.* X. 42.

5
Behind the cloud the starlight lurks,
Through showers the sunbeams fall;
For God, who loveth all his works,
Has left his Hope with all.
WHITTIER—*Dream of Summer.*

6
Hope told a flattering tale
That joy would soon return;
Ah, naught my sighs avail
For love is doomed to mourn.
JOHN WOLCOT. Song introduced into the Opera, *Artaxerxes.*
(See also WROTHER)

7
Is Man
A child of hope? Do generations press
On generations, without progress made?
Halts the individual, ere his hairs be gray,
Perforce?
WORDSWORTH—*The Excursion.* Bk. V.

8
Hopes, what are they?—Beads of morning
Strung on slender blades of grass;
Or a spider's web adorning
In a straight and treacherous pass.
WORDSWORTH—*Hopes, What are They?*

9
Hope tells a flattering tale,
Delusive, vain and hollow.
Ah! let not hope prevail,
Lest disappointment follow.
MISS WROTHER—*In the Universal Songster.* Vol. II. P. 86.
(See also WOLCOT)

10
Hope of all passions, most befriends us here.
YOUNG—*Night Thoughts.* Night VII. L. 1,470.

11
Hope, like a cordial, innocent, though strong,
Man's heart, at once, inspirits, and serenes;
Nor makes him pay his wisdom for his joys.
YOUNG—*Night Thoughts.* Night VII. L. 1,514

12
Confiding, though confounded; hoping on,
Untaught by trial, unconvinced by proof,
And ever looking for the never-seen.
YOUNG—*Night Thoughts.* Night VIII. L. 116.

13
Prisoners of hope.
Zechariah. IX. 12.

HORSE

14
Then I cast loose my buff coat, each halter let fall,
Shook off both my jack-boots, let go belt and all,
Stood up in the stirrup, leaned, patted his ear,
Called my Roland his pet name, my horse without peer;
Clapped my hands, laughed and sang, any noise bad or good,
'Til at length into Aix Roland galloped and stood.
ROBERT BROWNING—*How They Brought the News from Ghent.*

15
Gamaun is a dainty steed,
Strong, black, and of a noble breed,
Full of fire, and full of bone,
With all his line of fathers known;
Fine his nose, his nostrils thin,
But blown abroad by the pride within;
His mane is like a river flowing,
And his eyes like embers glowing
In the darkness of the night,
And his pace as swift as light.
BARRY CORNWALL—*The Blood Horse.*

16
Morgan!—She ain't nothing else, and I've got the papers to prove it.
Sired by Chippewa Chief, and twelve hundred dollars won't buy her.
Briggs of Turlumne owned her. Did you know Briggs of Turlumne?—
Busted hisself in White Pine and blew out his brains down in Frisco?
BRET HARTE—*Chiquita.*

17
Like the driving of Jehu, the son of Nimshi; for he driveth furiously.
II Kings. IX. 20.

18
Villain, a horse—Villain, I say, give me a horse to fly,
To swim the river, villain, and to fly.
GEORGE PEELE—*Battle of Alcazar.* Act V. L. 104. (1588-9)

19
Steed threatens steed, in high and boastful neighs,
Piercing the night's dull ear.
Henry V. Chorus to Act IV. L. 10.

20
An two men ride of a horse, one must ride behind.
Much Ado About Nothing. III. 5.

21
For young hot colts being rag'd, do rage the more.
Richard II. Act II. Sc. I. L. 70.

22
Give me another horse: bind up my wounds.
Richard III. Act V. Sc. 3. L. 177.

23
A horse! a horse! my kingdom for a horse!
Richard III. Act V. Sc. 4. L. 7. Taken from an old play, *The True Tragedy of Richard the Third.* (1594) In *Shakespeare Society Reprint.* P. 64.

24
Round-hoof'd, short-jointed, fetlocks shag and long,
Broad breast, full eye, small head and nostril wide,

High crest, short ears, straight legs and passing strong,
Thin mane, thick tail, broad buttock, tender hide:
Look, what a horse should have he did not lack,
Save a proud rider on so proud a back.
Venus and Adonis. L. 295.

1
I saw them go; one horse was blind,
The tails of both hung down behind,
Their shoes were on their feet.
HORACE AND JAMES SMITH—*Rejected Addresses. The Baby's Début.* (Parody of WORDSWORTH.)

2
Quadrupedumque putrem cursu quatit ungula campum.
And the hoof of the horses shakes the crumbling field as they run.
VERGIL—*Æneid.* XI. 875. Cited as an example of onomatopœia.

3
Ardua cervix,
Argumtumque caput, brevis alvos, obesaque terga,
Luxuriatque toris animosum pectus.
His neck is high and erect, his head replete with intelligence, his belly short, his back full, and his proud chest swells with hard muscle.
VERGIL—*Georgics.* III. 79.

HOSPITALITY (See also GUESTS, WELCOME)

4
When friends are at your hearthside met,
Sweet courtesy has done its most
If you have made each guest forget
That he himself is not the host.
ALDRICH—*Hospitality.*

5
If my best wines mislike thy taste,
And my best service win thy frown,
Then tarry not, I bid thee haste;
There's many another Inn in town.
ALDRICH—*Quits.*

6
There are hermit souls that live withdrawn
In the peace of their self-content;
There are souls like stars that dwell apart,
In a fellowless firmament;
There are pioneer souls that blaze their paths
Where highways never ran,—
But let me live by the side of the road,
And be a friend to man.
SAM WALTER FOSS—*House by the Side of the Road.*
(See also HOMER, JEREMIAH, TAGORE)

7
Let me live in my house by the side of the road,
Where the race of men go by;
They are good, they are bad; they are weak, they are strong,
Wise, foolish,—so am I;
Then why should I sit in the scorner's seat,
Or hurl the cynic's ban?
Let me live in my house by the side of the road,
And be a friend to man.
SAM WALTER FOSS—*House by the Side of the Road.*

8
He kept no Christmas-house for once a yeere,
Each day his boards were fild with Lordly fare:
He fed a rout of yeomen with his cheer,
Nor was his bread and beefe kept in with care;
His wine and beere to strangers were not spare,
And yet beside to all that hunger greved,
His gates were ope, and they were there relived.
ROBERT GREENE—*A Maiden's Dream.* L. 232.

9
Axylos, Teuthranos's son that dwelt in stablished Arisbe; a man of substance dear to his fellows; for his dwelling was by the road-side and he entertained all men.
HOMER—*Iliad.* Bk. VI. L. 12. LANG'S Trans.
(See also FOSS)

10
True friendship's laws are by this rule express'd,
Welcome the coming, speed the parting guest.
HOMER—*Odyssey.* Bk. XV. L. 83. POPE'S trans. (See also POPE)

11
For 't is always fair weather
When good fellows get together
With a stein on the table and a good song ringing clear.
RICHARD HOVEY—*Spring.*

12
Oh that I had in the wilderness a lodging-place of wayfaring men!
Jeremiah. IX. 2.
(See also FOSS)

13
Hospitality sitting with gladness.
LONGFELLOW — *Translation from Frithiof's Saga.*

14
So saying, with despatchful looks in haste
She turns, on hospitable thoughts intent.
MILTON—*Paradise Lost.* Bk. V. L. 331.

15
Hospes nullus tam in amici hospitium diverti potest,
Quin ubi triduum continuum fuerit jam odiosus siet.
No one can be so welcome a guest that he will not become an annoyance when he has stayed three continuous days in a friend's house.
PLAUTUS—*Miles Gloriosus.* III. 3. 12.

16
For I, who hold sage Homer's rule the best,
Welcome the coming, speed the going guest.
POPE—*Satire II.* Bk. II. L. 159.
(See also HOMER)

17
Given to hospitality.
Romans. XII. 13.

18
My master is of churlish disposition
And little recks to find the way to heaven
By doing deeds of hospitality.
As You Like It. Act II. Sc. 4. L. 80.

19
I am your host;
With robbers' hands my hospitable favours
You should not ruffle thus.
King Lear. Act III. Sc. 7. L. 39.

20
I charge thee, invite them all: let in the tide
Of knaves once more; my cook and I'll provide.
Timon of Athens. Act III. Sc. 4. L. 118.

1
Ah me, why did they build my house by the road
to the market town?
RABINDRANATH TAGORE—*Gardener*. 4.
(See also Foss)

2
The lintel low enough to keep out pomp and
pride;
The threshold high enough to turn deceit aside;
The doorband strong enough from robbers to defend;
This door will open at a touch to welcome every
friend.
HENRY VAN DYKE—*Inscription for a Friend's House.*

3
A host in himself.
WELLINGTON. Of LORD JOHN RUSSELL. Related by SAMUEL ROGERS. (1839) *Paraphrase of* HOMER's *epithet of* AJAX. See POPE's trans. of *Iliad*. III. 293.

HOUSE (See HOME, HOSPITALITY)

HUMANITY (See also PHILANTHROPY)

4
Love, hope, fear, faith—these make humanity;
These are its sign and note and character.
ROBERT BROWNING—*Paracelsus*. Sc. 3.

5
An inadvertent step may crush the snail
That crawls at evening in the public path.
But he that has humanity, forewarned,
Will turn aside and let the reptile live.
COWPER—*Task*. Bk. VI.

6
W'en you see a man in woe,
Walk right up and say "hullo."
Say "hullo" and "how d'ye do,"
"How's the world a-usin' you?"

. . . . .

W'en you travel through the strange
Country t'other side the range,
Then the souls you've cheered will know
Who you be, an' say "hullo."
SAM WALTER FOSS—*Hullo*.

7
He held his seat; a friend to human race.
HOMER—*Iliad*. Bk. VI. L. 18. POPE's trans.

8
Respect us, human, and relieve us, poor.
HOMER—*Odyssey*. Bk. IX. L. 338. POPE's trans.

9
Over the brink of it
Picture it—think of it,
Dissolute man.
Lave in it—drink of it
Then, if you can.
HOOD—*Bridge of Sighs*.

10
Oh, God! that bread should be so dear,
And flesh and blood so cheap!
HOOD—*Song of a Shirt*.

11
For He, who gave this vast machine to roll,
Breathed *Life* in them, in us a *Reasoning Soul;*
That kindred feelings might our state improve,
And mutual wants conduct to mutual love.
JUVENAL—*Satire XV*. L. 203.

12
Every human heart is human.
LONGFELLOW—*Hiawatha. Introduction*. L. 91.

13
Laborin' man an' laborin' woman
Hev one glory an' one shame;
Ev'ythin' thet's done inhuman
Injers all on 'em the same.
LOWELL—*The Biglow Papers*. First Series. No. 1. St. 10.

14
It is good to be often reminded of the inconsistency of human nature, and to learn to look without wonder or disgust on the weaknesses which are found in the strongest minds.
MACAULAY—*Warren Hastings*.

15
For nothing human foreign was to him.
THOMSON—*To the Memory of Lord Talbot.* Translation of "Humani nihil a me alienum puto."

16
For the interesting and inspiring thing about America, gentlemen, is that she asks nothing for herself except what she has a right to ask for humanity itself.
WOODROW WILSON—*Speech*, at the luncheon of the Mayor of New York, May 17, 1915.

17
Never to blend our pleasure or our pride
With sorrow of the meanest thing that feels.
WORDSWORTH—*Hart-leap Well*. Pt. II.

18 But hearing oftentimes
The still, sad music of humanity.
WORDSWORTH—*Tintern Abbey*.

HUMILITY

19 Lowliness is the base of every virtue,
And he who goes the lowest builds the safest.
BAILEY—*Festus*. Sc. *Home*.

20
He saw a cottage with a double coach-house,
A cottage of gentility!
And the Devil did grin, for his darling sin
Is pride that apes humility.
COLERIDGE—*Devil's Walk*. Original title, *Devil's Thoughts*. Written jointly by COLERIDGE and SOUTHEY.
(See also SOUTHEY under DEVIL)

21
I am well aware that I am the 'umblest person going * * * let the other be where he may.
DICKENS—*David Copperfield*. Vol. I. Ch. XVI.

22
'Umble we are, 'umble we have been, 'umble we shall ever be.
DICKENS—*David Copperfield*. Vol. I. Ch. XVII.

23
Parvum parva decent.
Humble things become the humble.
HORACE—*Epistles*. I. 7. 44.

24
God hath sworn to lift on high
Who sinks himself by true humility.
KEBLE—*Miscellaneous Poems. At Hooker's Tomb.*

1 O be very sure
That no man will learn anything at all,
Unless he first will learn humility.
OWEN MEREDITH (Lord Lytton)—*Vanini.* L. 327.

2
One may be humble out of pride.
MONTAIGNE—*Of Presumption.* Bk. II. Ch. XVII.

3
Fairest and best adorned is she
Whose clothing is humility.
MONTGOMERY—*Humility.*

4
Nearest the throne itself must be
The footstool of humility.
MONTGOMERY—*Humility.*

5
Humility, that low, sweet root,
From which all heavenly virtues shoot.
MOORE—*Loves of the Angels. Third Angel's Story.* St. 11.

6
I was not born for Courts or great affairs;
I pay my debts, believe, and say my pray'rs.
POPE—*Prologue to Satires.* L. 268.

7
Humility is to make a right estimate of one's self. It is no humility for a man to think less of himself than he ought, though it might rather puzzle him to do that.
SPURGEON—*Gleanings Among the Sheaves. Humility.*

8
The higher a man is in grace, the lower he will be in his own esteem.
SPURGEON—*Gleanings Among the Sheaves. The Right Estimate.*

9
Da locum melioribus.
Give place to your betters.
TERENCE—*Phormio.* III. 2. 37.

HUMMING-BIRD

10 Jewelled coryphée
With quivering wings like shielding gauze outspread.
EDNAH PROCTOR CLARKE—*Humming-Bird.*

11
Quick as a humming bird is my love,
Dipping into the hearts of flowers—
She darts so eagerly, swiftly, sweetly
Dipping into the flowers of my heart.
JAMES OPPENHEIM—*Quick as a Humming Bird.*

12
And the humming-bird that hung
Like a jewel up among
The tilted honeysuckle horns
They mesmerized and swung
In the palpitating air,
Drowsed with odors strange and rare,
And, with whispered laughter, slipped away
And left him hanging there.
JAMES WHITCOMB RILEY—*The South Wind and the Sun.*

13
A flash of harmless lightning,
A mist of rainbow dyes,
The burnished sunbeams brightening
From flower to flower he flies.
JOHN BANISTER TABB—*Humming Bird.*

HUMOR (See also JESTING, RIDICULE)

14
Unconscious humor.
SAMUEL BUTLER—*Life and Habit.* (Pub. 1877) BUTLER claims to have been the first user of the phrase as a synonym for dullness.

15
Humor has justly been regarded as the finest perfection of poetic genius.
CARLYLE—*Essays. Schiller.*

16 I never dare to write
As funny as I can.
HOLMES—*The Height of the Ridiculous.*

17
Now I perceive the devil understands Welsh;
And 'tis no marvel he is so humorous.
Henry IV. Pt. I. Act III. Sc. 1. L. 233.

18
There's the humour of it.
Merry Wives of Windsor. Act I. Sc. 1. (Inserted by THEOBALD from the quarto.)

HUNGER (See also APPETITE, COOKERY, EATING)

19
Hunger is sharper than the sword.
BEAUMONT AND FLETCHER—*The Honest Man's Fortune.* Act II. Sc. 2. L. 1.

20
Bone and Skin, two millers thin,
Would starve us all, or near it;
But be it known to Skin and Bone
That Flesh and Blood can't bear it.
JOHN BYROM—*Epigram on Two Monopolists.*

21
It is difficult to speak to the belly, because it has no ears.
CATO THE CENSOR, when the Romans demanded corn. See PLUTARCH'S *Life of Cato the Censor.* (See also RABELAIS)

22
La mejor salsa del mundo es la hambre.
Hunger is the best sauce in the world.
CERVANTES—*Don Quixote.*
(See also CICERO, CYMBELINE)

23
Enough is as good as a feast.
GEORGE CHAPMAN—*Eastward Ho!* Act III. Sc. 2. Written by CHAPMAN, JONSON, MARSTON.

24
Socratem audio dicentem, cibi condimentum esse famem, potionis sitim.
I hear Socrates saying that the best seasoning for food is hunger; for drink, thirst.
CICERO—*De Finibus Bonorum et Malorum.* II. 28. (See also CERVANTES)

25
Oliver Twist has asked for more.
DICKENS—*Oliver Twist.* Ch. II.

26
A fishmonger's wife may feed of a conger; but a serving-man's wife may starve for hunger.
Health to the Gentlemanly Profession of Serving-men. (1598)

27
They that die by famine die by inches.
MATTHEW HENRY—*Commentaries.* Psalm LIX.

1
Græculus esuriens in cœlum, jusseris, ibit.
Bid the hungry Greek go to heaven, he will go.
JUVENAL—*Satires.* III. 78.

2
Magister artis ingeniique largitor venter.
The belly is the teacher of art and the bestower of genius.
PERSIUS—*Satires. Prologue.* X.

3
Famem fuisse suspicor matrem mihi.
I suspect that hunger was my mother.
PLAUTUS—*Stichus.* Act II. 1. 1.
(See also FRANCK under NECESSITY)

4
Obliged by hunger and request of friends.
POPE—*Epistle to Dr. Arbuthnot. Prologue to the Satires.* L. 44.

5
La ventre affamé n'point d'oreilles.
Hungry bellies have no ears.
RABELAIS—*Pantagruel.* Bk. III. Ch. XV.
(See also CATO)

6
Nec rationem patitur, nec æquitate mitigatur nec ulla prece flectitur, populus esuriens.
A hungry people listens not to reason, nor cares for justice, nor is bent by any prayers.
SENECA—*De Brevitate Vitæ.* XVIII.

7
They said they were an-hungry; sigh'd forth proverbs,
That hunger broke stone walls, that dogs must eat,
That meat was made for mouths, that the gods sent not
Corn for the rich men only: with these shreds
They vented their complainings.
Coriolanus. Act I. Sc. 1. L. 209.

8
Our stomachs
Will make what's homely savoury.
Cymbeline. Act III. Sc. 6. L. 32.
(See also CERVANTES)

9
Yond Cassius has a lean and hungry look.
Julius Cæsar. Act I. Sc. 2. L. 194.

10
My more-having would be as a sauce
To make me hunger more.
Macbeth. Act IV. Sc. 3. L. 81.

11
Cruel as death, and hungry as the grave.
THOMSON—*The Seasons. Winter.* L. 393.

12
Malesuada fames.
Hunger that persuades to evil.
VERGIL—*Æneid.* VI. 276.

HUSBAND (See also MATRIMONY)

13
But O ye lords of ladies intellectual,
Inform us truly, have they not henpecked you all?
BYRON—*Don Juan.* Canto I. St. 22.

14
And truant husband should return, and say,
"My dear, I was the first who came away."
BYRON—*Don Juan.* Canto I. St. 141.

15
The lover in the husband may be lost.
LORD LYTTLETON—*Advice to a Lady.* L. 112.

16
God is thy law, thou mine.
MILTON—*Paradise Lost.* Bk. IV. L. 637.

17
The wife, where danger or dishonour lurks,
Safest and seemliest by her husband stays,
Who guards her, or with her the worst endures.
MILTON—*Paradise Lost.* Bk. IX. L. 267.

18
And to thy husband's will
Thine shall submit; he over thee shall rule.
MILTON—*Paradise Lost.* Bk. X. L. 195.

19
With thee goes
Thy husband, him to follow thou art bound;
Where he abides, think there thy native soil.
MILTON—*Paradise Lost.* Bk. XI. L. 290.

20
The stoic husband was the glorious thing.
The man had courage, was a sage, 'tis true,
And lov'd his country.
POPE—*Epilogue to Rowe's Jane Shore.*

21
Well, if our author in the wife offends
He has a husband that will make amends;
He draws him gentle, tender, and forgiving,
And sure such kind good creatures may be living.
POPE—*Epilogue to Rowe's Jane Shore.*

22
No worse a husband than the best of men.
Antony and Cleopatra. Act II. Sc. 2. L. 131.

23
I will attend my husband, be his nurse,
Diet his sickness, for it is my office.
Comedy of Errors. Act V. Sc. 1. L. 98.

24
That lord whose hand must take my plight shall carry
Half my love with him, half my care and duty.
King Lear. Act I. Sc. 1. L. 103.

25
If I should marry him, I should marry twenty husbands.
Merchant of Venice. Act I. Sc. 2. L. 67.

26
Thy husband is thy lord, thy life, thy keeper,
Thy head, thy sovereign; one that cares for thee,
And for thy maintenance.
Taming of the Shrew. Act V. Sc. 2. L. 146.

27
Such duty as the subject owes the prince,
Even such a woman oweth to her husband.
Taming of the Shrew. Act V. Sc. 2. L. 155.

HYACINTH

Hyacinthus

28
The hyacinth for constancy wi' its unchanging blue.
BURNS—*O Luve Will Venture In.*

29
Art thou a hyacinth blossom
The shepherds upon the hills
Have trodden into the ground?
Shall I not lift thee?
BLISS CARMAN. Trans. of SAPPHO.

30
Come, evening gale! the crimsonne rose
Is drooping for thy sighe of dewe;
The hyacinthe wooes thy kisse to close
In slumberre sweete its eye of blue.
GEORGE CROLY—*Inscription for a Grotto.*

1
By field and by fell, and by mountain gorge,
Shone Hyacinths blue and clear.
LUCY HOOPER—*Legends of Flowers*. St. 3.

2
Here hyacinths of heavenly blue
Shook their rich tresses to the morn.
MONTGOMERY—*The Adventure of a Star*.

3
If of thy mortal goods thou art bereft,
And from thy slender store two loaves alone to thee are left,
Sell one, and with the dole
Buy hyacinths to feed thy soul.
MOSLEH EDDIN SAADI—*Gulistan*. (*Garden of Roses*.)
(See also CRAWFURD under NARCISSUS)

4
And the hyacinth purple, and white, and blue,
Which flung from its bells a sweet peal anew
Of music so delicate, soft, and intense,
It was felt like an odour within the sense.
SHELLEY—*The Sensitive Plant*. Pt. I.

HYPOCRISY (See also DECEIT)

5
And the veil
Spun from the cobweb fashion of the times,
To hide the feeling heart?
AKENSIDE—*Pleasures of Imagination*. Bk. II. L. 147.

6
Saint abroad, and a devil at home.
BUNYAN—*Pilgrim's Progress*. Pt. I.

7
Oh, for a *forty-parson power* to chant
Thy praise, Hypocrisy! Oh, for a hymn
Loud as the virtues thou dost loudly vaunt,
Not practise!
BYRON—*Don Juan*. Canto X. St. 34.

8
Be hypocritical, be cautious, be
Not what you *seem* but always what you *see*.
BYRON—*Don Juan*. Canto XI. St. 86.

9
And prate and preach about what others prove,
As if the world and they were hand and glove.
COWPER—*Table Talk*. L. 173.

10
A hypocrite is in himself both the archer and the mark, in all actions shooting at his own praise or profit.
FULLER—*The Holy and Profane States. The Hypocrite*. Maxim 1. Bk. V. Ch. VIII.

11
Thus 'tis with all; their chief and constant care
Is to seem everything but what they are.
GOLDSMITH—*Epilogue to The Sisters*. L. 25.

12
When a man puts on a Character he is a stranger to, there's as much difference between what he appears, and what he is really in himself, as there is between a Vizor and a Face.
LA BRUYÈRE—*The Characters or Manners of the Present Age. Of Men*. Ch. XI.

13
Some hypocrites and seeming mortified men, that held down their heads, were like the little images that they place in the very bowing of the vaults of churches, that look as if they held up the church, but are but puppets.
Attributed to DR. LAUD by BACON—*Apothegms*. No. 273.

14
L'hypocrisie est un hommage que le vice rend à la vertu.
Hypocrisy is the homage which vice renders to virtue.
LA ROCHEFOUCAULD—*Maximes*. 218.

15
For neither man nor angel can discern
Hypocrisy, the only evil that walks
Invisible, except to God alone,
By his permissive will, through heav'n and earth.
MILTON—*Paradise Lost*. Bk. III. L. 682.

16
He was a man
Who stole the livery of the court of Heaven
To serve the Devil in.
POLLOK—*Course of Time*. Bk. VIII. L. 616.

17
Constant at Church and 'Change; his gains were sure;
His givings rare, save farthings to the poor.
POPE—*Moral Essays*. Ep. III. L. 347.

18
Thou hast prevaricated with thy friend,
By underhand contrivances undone me:
And while my open nature trusted in thee,
Thou hast stept in between me and my hopes,
And ravish'd from me all my soul held dear.
Thou hast betray'd me.
NICHOLAS ROWE—*Lady Jane Grey*. Act II. Sc. 1. L. 235.

19
Not he who scorns the Saviour's yoke
Should wear his cross upon the heart.
SCHILLER—*The Fight with the Dragon*. St. 24.

20
'Tis too much proved—that with devotion's visage
And pious action we do sugar o'er
The devil himself.
Hamlet. Act III. Sc. 1. L. 47.

21
I will speak daggers to her, but use none;
My tongue and soul in this be hypocrites.
Hamlet. Act III. Sc. 2. L. 414.

22
Away, and mock the time with fairest show;
False face must hide what the false heart doth know.
Macbeth. Act I. Sc. 7. L. 81.

23
O, what may man within him hide,
Though angel on the outward side!
Measure for Measure. Act III. Sc. 2. L. 285.

24
So smooth he daub'd his vice with show of virtue,
* * * * * *
He liv'd from all attainder of suspect.
Richard III. Act III. Sc. 5. L. 29.

25
O serpent heart, hid with a flowering face!
Did ever a dragon keep so fair a cave?
Romeo and Juliet. Act III. Sc. 2. L. 73.

1
How inexpressible is the meanness of being a hypocrite! how horrible is it to be a mischievous and malignant hypocrite.
VOLTAIRE—*A Philosophical Dictionary. Philosopher.* Sec. I.

2
I hope you have not been leading a double life, pretending to be wicked and being really good all the time. That would be hypocrisy.
OSCAR WILDE—*Importance of Being Earnest.* Act II.

3
A man I knew who lived upon a smile,
And well it fed him; he look'd plump and fair,
While rankest venom foam'd through every vein.
YOUNG—*Night Thoughts.* Night VIII. L. 336.

I

IDEAS (See THOUGHT)

IDLENESS

4
Idleness is emptiness; the tree in which the sap is stagnant, remains fruitless.
HOSEA BALLOU—*MS. Sermons.*

5
Diligenter per vacuitatem suam.
In the diligence of his idleness.
Book of Wisdom. XIII. 13. (*Vulgate* LXX.)
(See also WORDSWORTH)

6
For idleness is an appendix to nobility.
BURTON—*Anatomy of Melancholy.* Pt. I. Sec. II. Memb. 2. Subsect. 6.

7
An idler is a watch that wants both hands;
As useless if it goes as when it stands.
COWPER—*Retirement.*

8
How various his employments whom the world
Calls idle; and who justly in return
Esteems that busy world an idler too!
COWPER—*Task.* Bk. III. *The Garden.* L. 342.

9
Thus idly busy rolls their world away.
GOLDSMITH—*The Traveller.* L. 256.

10
What heart can think, or tongue express,
The harm that groweth of idleness?
JOHN HEYWOOD—*Idleness.*

11
I live an idle burden to the ground.
HOMER—*Iliad.* Bk. XVIII. L. 134. POPE'S trans.

12
Strenua nos exercet inertia.
Busy idleness urges us on.
HORACE—*Epistles.* Bk. I. XI. 28. Same idea in PHÆDRUS—*Fables.* II. V. 3; SENECA—*De Brevitate Vitæ.* Ch. XIII and XV.
(See also WORDSWORTH)

13
Vitanda est improba syren—desidia.
That destructive siren, sloth, is ever to be avoided.
HORACE—*Satires.* II. 3. 14.

14
Gloomy calm of idle vacancy.
SAMUEL JOHNSON—*Boswell's Life of Johnson.* Dec. 8, 1763.

15
Variam semper dant otia mentem.
An idle life always produces varied inclinations.
LUCAN—*Pharsalia.* IV. 704.

16
The frivolous work of polished idleness.
SIR JAMES MACKINTOSH—*Dissertation on Ethical Philosophy. Remarks on Thomas Brown.*

17
Cernis ut ignavum corrumpant otia corpus
Ut capiant vitium ni moveantur aquæ.
Thou seest how sloth wastes the sluggish body, as water is corrupted unless it moves.
OVID—*Epistolæ Ex Ponto.* I. 5. 5.

18
Thee too, my Paridel! she mark'd thee there,
Stretch'd on the rack of a too easy chair,
And heard thy everlasting yawn confess
The Pains and Penalties of Idleness.
POPE—*Dunciad.* Bk. IV. L. 341.

19
Difficultas patrocinia prætextimus segnitiæ.
We excuse our sloth under the pretext of difficulty.
QUINTILIAN—*De Institutione Oratoria.* I. 12.

20
I rather would entreat thy company,
To see the wonders of the world abroad
Than living, dully sluggardized at home,
Wear out thy youth with shapeless idleness.
Two Gentlemen of Verona. Act I. Sc. 1. L. 5.

21
Blandoque veneno
Desidiæ virtus paullatim evicta senescit.
Valor, gradually overpowered by the delicious poison of sloth, grows torpid.
SILIUS ITALICUS—*Punica.* III. 580.

22
Utque alios industria, ita hunc ignavia ad famam protulerat.
Other men have acquired fame by industry, but this man by indolence.
TACITUS—*Annales.* XVI. 18.

23
Their only labour was to kill the time;
And labour dire it is, and weary woe,
They sit, they loll, turn o'er some idle rhyme,
Then, rising sudden, to the glass they go,
Or saunter forth, with tottering steps and slow.
THOMSON—*Castle of Indolence.* Canto I. 72.

24
L'indolence est le sommeil des esprits.
Indolence is the sleep of the mind.
VAUVENARGUES—*Reflexions.* 390.

25
There is no remedy for time misspent;
No healing for the waste of idleness,
Whose very languor is a punishment

Heavier than active souls can feel or guess.
SIR AUBREY DE VERE—*A Song of Faith, Devout Exercises, and Sonnets.*

1
For Satan finds some mischief still
For idle hands to do.
WATTS—*Against Idleness.*

2
'Tis the voice of the sluggard, I heard him complain:
"You have waked me too soon, I must slumber again";
As the door on its hinges, so he on his bed,
Turns his sides, and his shoulders and his heavy head.
WATTS—*The Sluggard.*

3
But how can he expect that others should
Build for him, sow for him, and at his call
Love him, who for himself will take no heed at all?
WORDSWORTH—*Resolution and Independence.* St. 6.

4
Worldlings revelling in the fields
Of strenuous idleness.
WORDSWORTH—*This Lawn, a Carpet all alive.*
(See also BOOK OF WISDOM, HORACE)

IGNORANCE

5
Be ignorance thy choice, where knowledge leads to woe.
BEATTIE—*The Minstrel.* Bk. II. St. 30.

6
For "ignorance is the mother of devotion," as all the world knows.
BURTON—*Anatomy of Melancholy.* Pt. III. Sec. IV. Memb. 1. Subsect. 2. Phrase used by DR. COLE—*Disputation with the Papists at Westminster,* March 31, 1559. Quoted from COLE by BISHOP JEWEL—*Works.* Vol. III. Pt. II. P. 1202. Quoted as a "Popish maxim" by THOS. VINCENT—*Explicatory Catechism. Epistle to the Reader* about 1622. Said by JEREMY TAYLOR—*To a person newly converted to the Church of England.* (1657) Same found in *New Custome.* I. I. A Morality printed 1573. (True devotion.)
(See also DRYDEN)

7
The truest characters of ignorance
Are vanity, and pride, and annoyance.
BUTLER—*Hudibras.*

8
Causarum ignoratio in re nova mirationem facit.
In extraordinary events ignorance of their causes produces astonishment.
CICERO—*De Divinatione.* II. 22.

9
Ignoratione rerum bonarum et malarum maxime hominum vita vexatur.
Through ignorance of what is good and what is bad, the life of men is greatly perplexed.
CICERO—*De Finibus Bonorum et Malorum.* I. 13.

10
Non me pudet fateri nescire quod nesciam.
I am not ashamed to confess that I am ignorant of what I do not know.
CICERO—*Tusc. Quæst.* I. 25. 60.

11
Ignorance seldom vaults into knowledge, but passes into it through an intermediate state of obscurity, even as night into day through twilight.
COLERIDGE—*Essay XVI.*

12
Ignorance never settles a question.
BENJ. DISRAELI—*Speech in House of Commons,* May 14, 1866.

13
Mr. Kremlin himself was distinguished for ignorance, for he had only one idea, and that was wrong.
BENJ. DISRAELI—*Sybil.* Bk. IV. Ch. V.

14
For your ignorance is the mother of your devotion to me.
DRYDEN—*The Maiden Queen.* Act I. Sc. 2.
(See also BURTON)

15
Ignorance gives one a large range of probabilities.
GEORGE ELIOT—*Daniel Deronda.* Bk. II. Ch. XIII.

16
Ignorance is the dominion of absurdity.
FROUDE—*Short Studies on Great Subjects. Party Politics.*

17
Often the cock-loft is empty, in those whom nature hath built many stories high.
FULLER—*Andronicus.* Sec. VI. Par. 18. 1.

18
Es ist nichts schrecklicher als eine thätige Unwissenheit.
There is nothing more frightful than an active ignorance.
GOETHE—*Sprüche in Prosa.* III.

19
And his best riches, ignorance of wealth.
GOLDSMITH—*Deserted Village.* L. 61.

20
Where ignorance is bliss,
'Tis folly to be wise.
GRAY—*On a Distant Prospect of Eton College.* St. 10. Same idea in EURIPIDES—*Fragment. Antip.* XIII.
(See also PRIOR)

21
Who ne'er knew salt, or heard the billows roar.
HOMER—*Odyssey.* Bk. XI. L. 153. POPE'S trans.

22
It was a childish ignorance,
But now 'tis little joy
To know I'm further off from heaven
Than when I was a boy.
HOOD—*I Remember, I Remember.*

23
Ignorance, madam, pure ignorance.
SAMUEL JOHNSON, in reply to the lady who asked why "pastern" was defined in the dictionary as "the knee of the horse." BOSWELL'S—*Life.* (1755)

24
Rien n'est si dangereux qu'un ignorant ami:
Mieux vaudrait un sage ennemi.
Nothing is so dangerous as an ignorant friend; a wise enemy is worth more.
LA FONTAINE—*Fables.* VIII. 10.

1
A man may live long, and die at last in ignorance of many truths, which his mind was capable of knowing, and that with certainty.
LOCKE—*Human Understanding.* Bk. I. Ch. II.

2
But let a man know that there are things to be known, of which he is ignorant, and it is so much carved out of his domain of universal knowledge.
HORACE MANN—*Lectures on Education.* Lecture VI.

3
Not to know me argues yourselves unknown,
The lowest of your throng.
MILTON—*Paradise Lost.* Bk. IV. L. 830.

4
The living man who does not learn, is dark, dark, like one walking in the night.
MING LUM PAOU KEËN. Trans. for *Chinese Repository* by DR. WM. MILNE.

5
Quod latet ignotum est; ignoti nulla cupido.
What is hid is unknown: for what is unknown there is no desire.
OVID—*Ars Amatoria.* III. 397.

6
It is better to be unborn than untaught: for ignorance is the root of misfortune.
PLATO.

7
Etiam illud quod scies nesciveris;
Ne videris quod videris.
Know not what you know, and see not what you see.
PLAUTUS—*Miles Gloriosus.* II. 6. 89.

8
From ignorance our comfort flows,
The only wretched are the wise.
PRIOR—*To the Hon. Chas. Montague.* (1692)
(See also GRAY)

9
Illi mors gravis incubat qui notus nimis omnibus ignotus moritur sibi.
Death presses heavily on that man, who, being but too well known to others, dies in ignorance of himself.
SENECA—*Thyestes.* CCCCI.

10
O thou monster, Ignorance, how deformed dost thou look!
Love's Labour's Lost. Act IV. Sc. 2. L. 21.

11
Madam, thou errest: I say, there is no darkness, but ignorance; in which thou art more puzzled, than the Egyptians in their fog.
Twelfth Night. Act IV. Sc. 2. L. 44.

12
The more we study, we the more discover our ignorance.
SHELLEY—*Scenes from the Magico Prodigioso of Calderon.* Sc. 1.

13
Omne ignotum pro magnifico est.
Everything unknown is magnified.
TACITUS—*Agricola.* XXX. Quoting GALGACUS, the British leader, to his subjects before the battle of the Grampian Hills. RITTER says the sentence may be a "marginal gloss" and brackets it. Anticipated by THUCYDIDES—*Speech of Nicias.* VI. 11. 4.

14
* * * Where blind and naked Ignorance
Delivers brawling judgments, unashamed,
On all things all day long.
TENNYSON—*Idylls of the King. Vivien.* L. 515.

15
Homine imperito nunquam quidquid injustius,
Qui nisi quod ipse facit nihil rectum putat.
Nothing can be more unjust than the ignorant man, who thinks that nothing is well done by himself.
TERENCE—*Adelphi.* I. 2. 18.

16
Ita me dii ament, ast ubi sim nescio.
As God loves me, I know not where I am.
TERENCE—*Heauton timoroumenos.* II. 3. 67.

17
Namque inscitia est,
Adversum stimulum calces.
It is consummate ignorance to kick against the pricks.
TERENCE—*Phormio.* I. 2. 27.

IMAGINATION

18
Imagination is the air of mind.
BAILEY—*Festus.* Sc. *Another and a Better World.*

19
Build castles in the air.
BURTON—*Anatomy of Melancholy.* Pt. I. Sec. II. Memb. 1. Subsect. 3. Also in *Romaunt of the Rose.*
Come nous dicimus in nubibus.
(As we said in the clouds.)
JOHN RASTELL—*Les Termes de la Ley.* (1527)
* * * his master was in a manner always in a wrong Boxe and building castels in the ayre or catching Hares with Tabers.
Letter by F. A. to L. B. 1575-76. Repr. in *Miscell. Antiq. Anglic.*
(See also GASCOIGNE, HERBERT, STORER, VILLARS, WATSON)

20
Thou hast the keys of Paradise, O just, subtle, and mighty opium!
DE QUINCEY—*Confessions of an Opium Eater.* Pt. II.

21
And castels buylt above in lofty skies,
Which never yet had good foundation.
GASCOIGNE—*Steel Glass.* ARBER's reprint. P. 55. (See also BURTON)

22
Es ist nichts fürchterlicher als Einbildungskraft ohne Geschmack.
There is nothing more fearful than imagination without taste.
GOETHE—*Sprüche in Prosa.* III.

23
Build castles in Spain.
HERBERT—*Jacula Prudentum.* Lors feras chastiaus en Espaigne. GUILLAUME DE LORRIS—*Roman de la Rose.* 2452. Et fais chasteaulx en Espaigne et en France. CHARLES D'ORLEANS—*Rondeau.* Et le songer fait chasteaux en Asie. PIERRE GRANGOIRE—*Menus Propos.* Tout fin seullet les chasteaux d'Albanye. *Le Verger d'Honneur.* (See also BURTON)

1
Seem'd washing his hands with invisible soap
In imperceptible water.
HOOD—*Miss Kilmansegg. Her Christening.*

2
Delphinum appingit sylvis, in fluctibus aprum.
He paints a dolphin in the woods, and a boar in the waves.
HORACE—*Ars Poetica.* XXX.

3
Celui qui a de l'imagination sans érudition a des ailes, et n'a pas de pieds.
He who has imagination without learning has wings but no feet.
JOUBERT.

4
These are the gloomy comparisons of a disturbed imagination; the melancholy madness of poetry, without the inspiration.
JUNIUS—*Letter VIII. To Sir W. Draper.*

5
When I could not sleep for cold
I had fire enough in my brain,
And builded with roofs of gold
My beautiful castles in Spain!
LOWELL—*Aladdin.* St. 1.
(See also HERBERT)

6
His imagination resembled the wings of an ostrich. It enabled him to run, though not to soar.
MACAULAY—*On John Dryden.* (1828)

7
C'est l'imagination qui gouverne le genre humain.
The human race is governed by its imagination.
NAPOLEON I.

8
In my mind's eye, Horatio.
Hamlet. Act I. Sc. 2. L. 186.

9
This is the very coinage of your brain:
This bodiless creation ecstasy.
Hamlet. Act III. Sc. 4. L. 137.

10
This is a gift that I have, simple, simple; a foolish extravagant spirit, full of forms, figures, shapes, objects, ideas, apprehensions, motions, revolutions; these are begot in the ventricle of memory, nourished in the womb of *pia mater*, and delivered upon the mellowing of occasion.
Love's Labour's Lost. Act IV. Sc. 2. L. 67.

11
The lunatic, the lover and the poet
Are of imagination all compact.
Midsummer Night's Dream. Act V. Sc. 1. L. 7.

12
And as imagination bodies forth
The forms of things unknown, the poet's pen
Turns them to shapes and gives to airy nothing
A local habitation and a name.
Midsummer Night's Dream. Act V. Sc. 1. L. 14.

13
The best in this kind are but shadows; and the worst are no worse, if imagination amend them.
Midsummer Night's Dream. Act V. Sc. 1. L. 213.

14
Look, what thy soul holds dear, imagine it
To lie that way thou go'st, not whence thou com'st:
Suppose the singing birds musicians;
The grass whereon thou tread'st the presence strew'd;
The flowers fair ladies, and thy steps no more
Than a delightful measure or a dance.
Richard II. Act I. Sc. 3. L. 286.

15
Castles in Spain.
STORER—*Peter the Cruel.* P. 280, ascribes the origin of this phrase to the time of DON ENRIQUE of SPAIN, on account of his favors being lavishly bestowed before they were earned. *Mercure Français.* (1616) Given as source by LITTRÉ.
(See also HERBERT)

16
It is only in France that one builds castles in Spain.
MME. DE VILLARS, when made dame d'honneur to the wife of PHILIP V, of Spain, grandson of LOUIS XIV. of France.
(See also HERBERT)

17
I build nought els but castles in the ayre.
THOS. WATSON—*Poems.* ARBER'S reprint. P. 82. See also LYLY—*Mother Bombie.* Act V. Sc. 3.
(See also BURTON)

18
But thou, that did'st appear so fair
To fond imagination,
Dost rival in the light of day
Her delicate creation.
WORDSWORTH—*Yarrow Visited.*

IMITATION (See also FLATTERY)

19
L'imitazione del male supera sempre l'esempio; comme per il contrario, l'imitazione del bene è sempre inferiore.
He who imitates what is evil always goes beyond the example that is set; on the contrary, he who imitates what is good always falls short.
GUICCIARDINI—*Storia d' Italia.*

20
Respicere exemplar vitæ morumque jubebo
Doctum imitatorem, et veras hinc ducere voces.
I would advise him who wishes to imitate well, to look closely into life and manners, and thereby to learn to express them with truth.
HORACE—*Ars Poetica.* CCCXVII.

21
Pindarum quisquis studet æmulari,
Iule ceratis ope Dædalea
Nititur pennis, vitreo daturus
Nomina ponto.
He who studies to imitate the poet Pindar, O Julius, relies on artificial wings fastened on with wax, and is sure to give his name to a glassy sea.
HORACE—*Carmina.* IV. 2. 1.

22
Dociles imitandis
Turpibus ac pravis omnes sumus.
We are all easily taught to imitate what is base and depraved.
JUVENAL—*Satires.* XIV. 40.

1
C'est un bétail servile et sot à mon avis
Que les imitateurs.

Imitators are a slavish herd and fools in my opinion.

La Fontaine—*Clymène*. V. 54.

2
Der Mensch ist ein nachahmendes Geschöpf.
Und wer der Vorderste ist, führt die Heerde.

An imitative creature is man; whoever is foremost, leads the herd.

Schiller—*Wallenstein's Tod*. III. 4. 9.

IMMORTALITY (See also Death)

3
It must be so—Plato, thou reasonest well!—
Else whence this pleasing hope, this fond desire,
This longing after immortality?
Or whence this secret dread, and inward horror,
Of falling into nought? Why shrinks the soul
Back on herself, and startles at destruction?
'Tis the divinity that stirs within us;
'Tis heaven itself, that points out an hereafter,
And intimates eternity to man.

Addison—*Cato*. Act V. Sc. 1.

4
The stars shall fade away, the sun himself
Grow dim with age, and nature sink in years,
But thou shalt flourish in immortal youth,
Unhurt amidst the wars of elements,
The wrecks of matter, and the crush of worlds.

Addison—*Cato*. Act V. Sc. 1.

5
No, no! The energy of life may be
Kept on after the grave, but not begun;
And he who flagg'd not in the earthly strife,
From strength to strength advancing—only he
His soul well-knit, and all his battles won,
Mounts, and that hardly, to eternal life.

Matthew Arnold—*Sonnet. Immortality.*

6
On the cold cheek of Death smiles and roses are
blending,
And beauty immortal awakes from the tomb.

James Beattie—*The Hermit*. St. 6. Last lines.

7
Fish say, they have their Stream and Pond;
But is there anything Beyond?

Rupert Brooke—*Heaven.*

8
There is nothing strictly immortal, but immortality. Whatever hath no beginning may be confident of no end.

Sir Thomas Browne—*Hydriotaphia*. Ch. V.

9
If I stoop
Into a dark tremendous sea of cloud,
It is but for a time; I press God's lamp
Close to my breast; its splendor soon or late
Will pierce the gloom; I shall emerge one day.

Robert Browning—*Paracelsus*. Last lines.

10
I have been dying for twenty years, now I am going to live.

Jas. Drummond Burns—*His Last Words.*

11
A good man never dies.

Callimachus—*Epigrams*. X.

12
Immortality is the glorious discovery of Christianity.

Wm. Ellery Channing—*Immortality.*

13
'Tis immortality to die aspiring,
As if a man were taken quick to heaven.

Geo. Chapman—*Byron's Conspiracy*. Act I. Sc. 1. L. 254.

14
Nemo unquam sine magna spe immortalitatis se pro patria offerret ad mortem.

No one could ever meet death for his country without the hope of immortality.

Cicero—*Tusculanarum Disputationum*. I. 15.

15
For I never have seen, and never shall see, that the cessation of the evidence of existence is necessarily evidence of the cessation of existence.

William De Morgan—*Joseph Vance*. Ch. XL.

16
Then shall the dust return to the earth as it was; and the spirit shall return unto God who gave it.

Ecclesiastes. XII. 7.

17
Thus God's children are immortall whiles their
Father hath anything for them to do on earth.

Fuller—*Church History*. Bk. II. Century VIII. 18. *On Bede's Death.*
(See also Livingston, Williams)

18
Yet spirit immortal, the tomb cannot bind thee,
But like thine own eagle that soars to the sun
Thou springest from bondage and leavest behind
thee
A name which before thee no mortal hath won.

Attributed to Lyman Heath—*The Grave of Bonaparte.*

19
'Tis true; 'tis certain; man though dead retains
Part of himself; the immortal mind remains.

Homer—*Iliad*. Bk. XXIII. L. 122. Pope's trans.

20
Dignum laude virum Musa vetat mori;
Cœlo Musa beat.

The muse does not allow the praise-deserving hero to die: she enthrones him in the heavens.

Horace—*Carmina*. IV. 8. 28.

21
But all lost things are in the angels' keeping,
Love;
No past is dead for us, but only sleeping, Love;
The years of Heaven with all earth's little pain
Make good,
Together there we can begin again
In babyhood.

Helen Hunt Jackson—*At Last*. St. 6.

22
No, no, I'm sure,
My restless spirit never could endure
To brood so long upon one luxury,
Unless it did, though fearfully, espy
A hope beyond the shadow of a dream.

Keats—*Endymion*. Bk. I.

1
He ne'er is crowned with immortality
Who fears to follow where airy voices lead.
KEATS—*Endymion.* Bk. II.

2
I long to believe in immortality. * * * If I am destined to be happy with you here—how short is the longest life. I wish to believe in immortality—I wish to live with you forever.
KEATS—*Letters to Fanny Brawne.* XXXVI.

3
Men are immortal till their work is done.
DAVID LIVINGSTONE—*Letter.* Describing the death of BISHOP MACKENZIE in Africa. March, 1862.
(See also FULLER)

4
And in the wreck of noble lives
Something immortal still survives.
LONGFELLOW—*The Building of the Ship.* L. 375.

5
Safe from temptation, safe from sin's pollution,
She lives, whom we call dead.
LONGFELLOW—*Resignation.* St. 7.

6
I came from God, and I'm going back to God, and I won't have any gaps of death in the middle of my life.
GEORGE MACDONALD—*Mary Marston.* Ch. LVII.

7
Of such as he was, there be few on earth;
Of such as he is, there are few in Heaven:
And life is all the sweeter that he lived,
And all he loved more sacred for his sake:
And Death is all the brighter that he died,
And Heaven is all the happier that he's there.
GERALD MASSEY—*In Memoriam for Earl Brownlow.*

8
For who would lose,
Though full of pain, this intellectual being,
Those thoughts that wander through eternity,
To perish rather, swallow'd up and lost
In the wide womb of uncreated night,
Devoid of sense and motion?
MILTON—*Paradise Lost.* Bk. II. L. 146.

9
They eat, they drink, and in communion sweet
Quaff immortality and joy.
MILTON—*Paradise Lost.* Bk. V. L. 637.

10
For spirits that live throughout
Vital in every part, not as frail man,
In entrails, heart or head, liver or reins,
Cannot but by annihilating die.
MILTON—*Paradise Lost.* Bk. VI. L. 345.

11
When the good man yields his breath
(For the good man never dies).
MONTGOMERY—*The Wanderer of Switzerland.* Pt. V.

12
Immortality
Alone could teach this mortal how to die.
D. M. MULOCK—*Looking Death in the Face.* L. 77.

13
Tamque opus exegi quod nec Jovis ira necignes
Nec poterit ferrum, nec edax abolere vetustas.
Cum volet illa dies quæ nil nisi corporis hujus
Jus habet, incerti spatium mihi siniat ævi;
Parte tamen meliore mei super alta perennis
Astra ferar, nomenque erit indelebile nostrum.

And now have I finished a work which neither the wrath of Jove, nor fire, nor steel, nor all-consuming time can destroy. Welcome the day which can destroy only my physical man in ending my uncertain life. In my better part I shall be raised to immortality above the lofty stars, and my name shall never die.
OVID—*Metamorphoses.* XV. 871.

14
Sunt aliquid Manes; letum non omnia finit.
Luridaque evictos effugit umbra rogos.

There is something beyond the grave; death does not put an end to everything, the dark shade escapes from the consumed pile.
PROPERTIUS—*Elegiæ.* IV. 7. 1.

15
Look, here's the warrant, Claudio, for thy death:
'Tis now dead midnight, and by eight tomorrow
Thou must be made immortal.
Measure for Measure. Act IV. Sc. 2. L. 66.

16
I hold it ever,
Virtue and cunning were endowments greater
Than nobleness and riches: careless heirs
May the two latter darken and expend;
But immortality attends the former,
Making a man a god.
Pericles. Act III. Sc. 2. L. 26.

17
And her immortal part with angels lives.
Romeo and Juliet. Act V. Sc. 1. L. 19.

18
What a world were this,
How unendurable its weight, if they
Whom Death hath sundered did not meet again!
SOUTHEY—*Inscription XVII. Epitaph.*

19
Thy lord shall never die, the whiles this verse
Shall live, and surely it shall live for ever:
For ever it shall live, and shall rehearse
His worthy praise, and vertues dying never,
Though death his soule do from his bodie sever:
And thou thyselfe herein shalt also live;
Such grace the heavens doe to my verses give.
SPENSER—*The Ruines of Time.* L. 253.

20
I am restless. I am athirst for faraway things.
My soul goes out in a longing to touch the skirt of the dim distance.
O Great Beyond, O the keen call of thy flute!
I forget, I ever forget, that I have no wings to fly, that I am bound in this spot evermore.
RABINDRANATH TAGORE—*Gardener.* 5.

21
Ah, Christ, that it were possible,
For one short hour to see
The souls we loved, that they might tell us
What and where they be.
TENNYSON—*Maud.* Pt. XXVI.

22
It may be we shall touch the Happy Isles,
And see the great Achilles, whom we knew.
TENNYSON—*Ulysses.* L. 65.

23
But felt through all this fleshly dresse
Bright shootes of everlastingnesse.
HENRY VAUGHAN—*The Retreate.*

1
Facte nova virtute, puer; sic itur ad astra.
Go on and increase in valor, O boy! this is the path to immortality.
VERGIL—*Æneid.* IX. 641.

2
Happy he whose inward ear
Angel comfortings can hear,
O'er the rabble's laughter;
And, while Hatred's fagots burn,
Glimpses through the smoke discern
Of the good hereafter.
WHITTIER—*Barclay of Ury.*

3
Man is immortal till his work is done.
JAMES WILLIAMS—*Sonnet Ethandune.* Claimed for WILLIAMS in the *Guardian,* Nov. 17, 1911; also Nov. 24.
(See also FULLER)

4
Though inland far we be,
Our souls have sight of that immortal sea
Which brought us hither.
WORDSWORTH—*Ode. Intimations of Immortality.* St. 9.

5
'Tis immortality, 'tis that alone,
Amid life's pains, abasements, emptiness,
The soul can comfort, elevate, and fill.
That only, and that amply this performs.
YOUNG—*Night Thoughts.* Night VI. L. 573.

IMPATIENCE

6
Impatient straight to flesh his virgin sword.
HOMER—*Odyssey.* Bk. 20. L. 381. POPE'S trans.

7
I wish, and I wish that the spring would go faster,
Nor long summer bide so late;
And I could grow on like the foxglove and aster,
For some things are ill to wait.
JEAN INGELOW—*Song of Seven. Seven Times Two.*

8
I am on fire
To hear this rich reprisal is so nigh
And yet not ours.
Henry IV. Pt. I. Act IV. Sc. 1. L. 117.

IMPOSSIBILITY (See also DIFFICULTIES)

9
You cannot make a crab walk straight.
ARISTOPHANES—*Pax.* 1083.

10
It is not a lucky word, this same *impossible;* no good comes of those that have it so often in their mouth.
CARLYLE—*French Revolution.* Pt. III. Bk. III. Ch. X.

11
And what's impossible, can't be,
And never, never comes to pass.
GEO. COLMAN (The Younger)—*Broad Grins. The Maid of the Moor.*

12
Hope not for impossibilities.
FULLER—*The Holy and Profane States. Of Expecting Preferment.* Maxim I.

13
Few things are impossible to diligence and skill.
SAMUEL JOHNSON—*Rasselas.* Ch. XII.

14
Simul flare sorbereque haud facile
Est: ego hic esse et illic simul, haud potui.
To blow and to swallow at the same time is not easy; I cannot at the same time be here and also there.
PLAUTUS—*Mostellaria.* Act III. 2. 105.

15
Certainly nothing is unnatural that is not physically impossible.
R. B. SHERIDAN—*The Critic.* Act II. Sc. 1.

16
Certum est quia impossibile est.
The fact is certain because it is impossible.
TERTULLIAN—*De Carne Christi.* Ch. V. Pt. II. Called "Tertullian's rule of faith." Also given "Credo quia impossibile." I believe because it is impossible. Same idea in ST. AUGUSTINE—*Confessions.* VI. 5. (7) Credo quia absurdum est. An anonymous rendering of the same.

17
You cannot make, my Lord, I fear,
A velvet purse of a sow's ear.
JOHN WALCOT—*Lord B. and his Notions.*

INCONSTANCY

18
I hate inconstancy—I loathe, detest,
Abhor, condemn, abjure the mortal made
Of such quicksilver clay that in his breast
No permanent foundation can be laid.
BYRON—*Don Juan.* Canto II. St. 209.

19
They are not constant but are changing still.
Cymbeline. Act II. Sc. 5. L. 30.

20
O, swear not by the moon, the inconstant moon,
That monthly changes in her circled orb,
Lest that thy love prove likewise variable.
Romeo and Juliet. Act II. Sc. 2. L. 109.

21
Love is not love
Which alters when it alteration finds,
Or bends with the remover to remove;
O, no! it is an ever-fixed mark
That looks on tempests and is never shaken;
It is the star to every wandering bark,
Whose worth's unknown, although his height be taken.
Sonnet CXVI.

22
Or as one nail by strength drives out another,
So the remembrance of my former love
Is by a newer object quite forgotten.
Two Gentlemen of Verona. Act II. Sc. 4. L. 193.

23
I loved a lass, a fair one,
As fair as e'er was seen;
She was indeed a rare one,
Another Sheba queen:
But, fool as then I was,
I thought she loved me too:
But now, alas! she's left me,
Falero, lero, loo!
GEORGE WITHER—*I Loved a Lass.*

INDEPENDENCE

1
I never thrust my nose into other men's porridge. It is no bread and butter of mine: Every man for himself and God for us all.
CERVANTES—*Don Quixote*. Pt. I. Bk. III. Ch. XI.

2
All we ask is to be let alone.
JEFFERSON DAVIS—*First Message to the Confederate Congress*. April 29, 1861.

3
When in the course of human events, it becomes necessary for one people to dissolve the political bonds which have connected them with another, and to assume among the powers of the earth the separate and equal station to which the laws of nature and of nature's God entitle them, a decent respect to the opinions of mankind requires that they should declare the causes which impel them to the separation.
THOMAS JEFFERSON—*Declaration of Independence*.

4
The whole trouble is that we won't let God help us.
GEORGE MACDONALD—*The Marquis of Lossie*. Ch. XXVII.

5
Voyager upon life's sea:—
To yourself be true,
And whate'er your lot may be,
Paddle your own canoe.
DR. EDWARD P. PHILPOTS—*Paddle your own Canoe*. Written for HARRY CLIFTON. Appeared in *Harper's Monthly*, May 1854. See *Notes and Queries*, May 25, 1901. P. 414. Another song written by MRS. S. K. BOLTON has same refrain. Pub. in *Family Herald*, 1853. Also in SONG by MRS. SARAH TITTLE. (BARRITT.)

6
I'll never
Be such a gosling to obey instinct, but stand,
As if a man were author of himself
And knew no other kin.
Coriolanus. Act. V. Sc. 3. L. 34.

7
Speak then to me, who neither beg nor fear
Your favours nor your hate.
Macbeth. Act I. Sc. 3. L. 60.

8
Thy spirit, Independence, let me share!
Lord of the lion-heart and eagle-eye,
Thy steps I follow with my bosom bare,
Nor heed the storm that howls along the sky.
SMOLLETT—*Ode to Independence*. L. 1.

9
* * * but while
I breathe Heaven's air, and Heaven looks down on me,
And smiles at my best meanings, I remain
Mistress of mine own self and mine own soul.
TENNYSON—*The Foresters*. Act IV. Sc. 1.

10
Hail! Independence, hail! Heaven's next best gift,
To that of life and an immortal soul!
THOMSON—*Liberty*. Pt. V. L. 124.

11
L'injustice à la fin produit l'indépendance.
Injustice in the end produces independence.
VOLTAIRE—*Tancrède*. III. 2.

12
Independence *now:* and INDEPENDENCE FOREVER.
DANIEL WEBSTER—*Eulogy on Adams and Jefferson*, Aug. 2, 1826.

INDIAN PIPE

Monotropa Uniflora

13
Pale, mournful flower, that hidest in shade
Mid dewy damps and murky glade,
With moss and mould,
Why dost thou hang thy ghastly head,
So sad and cold?
CATHERINE E. BEECHER—*To the Monotropa, or Ghost Flower*.

14
Where the long, slant rays are beaming,
Where the shadows cool lie dreaming,
Pale the Indian pipes are gleaming—
Laugh, O murmuring Spring!
SARAH F. DAVIS—*Summer Song*.

15
I hear, I hear
The twang of harps, the leap
Of fairy feet and know the revel's ripe,
While like a coral stripe
The lizard cool doth creep,
Monster, but monarch there, up the pale Indian Pipe.
CHARLES DE KAY—*Arcana Sylvarum*.

16
Death in the wood,—
In the death-pale lips apart;
Death in a whiteness that curdled the blood,
Now black to the very heart:
The wonder by her was formed
Who stands supreme in power;
To show that life by the spirit comes
She gave us a soulless flower!
ELAINE GOODALE—*Indian Pipe*. St. 4.

INDOLENCE (See IDLENESS)

INFLUENCE

17
God in making man intended by him to reduce all His Works back again to Himself.
MATTHEW BARKER—*Natural Theology*. P. 85. (See also HOMER)

18
My heart is feminine, nor can forget—
To all, except one image, madly blind;
So shakes the needle, and so stands the pole,
As vibrates my fond heart to my fix'd soul.
BYRON—*Don Juan*. Canto I. St. 196. (See also NORRIS)

19
The work an unknown good man has done is like a vein of water flowing hidden underground, secretly making the ground green.
CARLYLE—*Essays*. *Varnhagen von Ense's Memoirs*.

20
Be a pattern to others, and then all will go well; for as a whole city is affected by the licentious passions and vices of great men, so it is likewise reformed by their moderation.
CICERO.

1
He raised a mortal to the skies;
She drew an angel down.
DRYDEN—*Alexander's Feast*. L. 169.
(See also WEBSTER)

2
Blessed influence of one true loving human soul on another.
GEORGE ELIOT—*Janet's Repentance*. Ch. XIX.

3
O may I join the choir invisible
Of those immortal dead who live again
In minds made better by their presence; live
In pulses stirred to generosity,
In deeds of daring rectitude, in scorn
For miserable aims that end with self.
In thoughts sublime that pierce the night like stars,
And with their mild persistence urge man's search
To vaster issues.
GEORGE ELIOT—*O May I Join the Choir Invisible*.

4
Nor knowest thou what argument
Thy life to thy neighbor's creed has lent,
All are needed by each one;
Nothing is fair or good alone
EMERSON—*Each and All*.

5
Ah, qui jamais auroit pu dire
Que ce petit nez retroussé
Changerait les lois d'un empire.
Ah, who could have ever foretold that that little retroussé nose would change the laws of an empire.
CHARLES SIMON FAVART—*Les Trois Sultanes*. (1710) FAVART used the story of *Soleiman*, by MARMONTEL.
(See also PASCAL)

6
A little leaven leaveneth the whole lump.
Galatians. V. 9.

7
Nor ease nor peace that heart can know,
That like the needle true,
Turns at the touch of joy or woe;
But turning, trembles too.
MRS. GREVILLE—*Prayer for Indifference*. Same idea in BISHOP LEIGHTON'S *Works*.
(See also NORRIS)

8
Lay ye down the golden chain
From Heaven, and pull at its inferior links
Both Goddesses and Gods.
HOMER—*Iliad*. Bk. 8. COWLEY's trans. See also in MILTON—*Paradise Lost*. Bk. II. 1. 1004; 1. 1050. COTTON MATHER. Treatise entitled *Schola et Scala Naturæ*. Idea found in LUCAN. "Aurea Catena Homeri," sometimes called "The Hermetic or Mercurial chain." Idea used by JOHN ARNDT—*True Christianity*. Bk. I. Ch. 4. SOUTHEY, quoting WESLEY in *Life of Wesley*. PROFESSOR SEDGWICK—*Review of a Free Inquiry into the Nature and Origin of Evil*.
(See also PLATO, TENNYSON, also BUTLER under LOVE)

9
Spontaneously to God should turn the soul,
Like the magnetic needle to the pole;
But what were that intrinsic virtue worth,
Suppose some fellow, with more zeal than knowledge,
Fresh from St. Andrew's College,
Should nail the conscious needle to the north?
HOOD—*Poem addressed to Rae Wilson*.
(See also NORRIS)

10
Our life's a flying shadow, God the pole,
The needle pointing to Him is our soul.
On a slab in BISHOP JOCELINE'S crypt in Glasgow Cathedral.

11
So when a great man dies,
For years beyond our ken,
The light he leaves behind him lies
Upon the paths of men.
LONGFELLOW—*Charles Sumner*. St. 9.

12
The very room, coz she was in,
Seemed warm f'om floor to ceilin'.
LOWELL—*The Biglow Papers*. Second Series. *The Courtin'*. St. 6.

13
You've got to save your own soul first, and then the souls of your neighbors if they will let you; and for that reason you must cultivate, not a spirit of criticism, but the talents that attract people to the hearing of the Word.
GEO. MACDONALD—*The Marquis of Lossie*. Ch. XXVII.

14
No life
Can be pure in its purpose or strong in its strife
And all life not be purer and stronger thereby.
OWEN MEREDITH (Lord Lytton)—*Lucile*. Pt. II. Canto VI. St. 40.

15
No star ever rose or set without influence somewhere.
OWEN MEREDITH—*Lucile*. Pt. II. Canto VI.

16
Even here Thy strong magnetic charms I feel,
And pant and tremble like the amorous steel.
To lower good, and beauties less divine,
Sometimes my erroneous needle does incline;
But yet (so strong the sympathy)
It turns, and points again to Thee.
NORRIS OF BEMERTON—*Aspiration*. Same idea in his *Contemplation and Love*, and *The Prayer*. Simile of the magnetic needle and the soul found in: ROBERT CAWDRAY'S—*Treasure or Store-house of Similes*, printed in London, 1609. Vol. VI and VII. GREGORY—*Works*. Ch. XXXVII; also Ch. XII. (Ed. 1684) RAIMOND LULL of Majorica—*Memorials of Christian Life*. (Before 1315) SOUTHEY—*The Partidas*. In his *Omniana*. Vol. I. P. 210.
(See also GREVILLE, HOOD, POPE, QUARLES)

17
Si possem sanior essem.
Sed trahit invitam nova vis; aliudque Cupido,
Mens aliud.
If it were in my power, I would be wiser; but a newly felt power carries me off in spite of myself; love leads me one way, my understanding another.
OVID—*Metamorphoses*. VII. 18.

1
If the nose of Cleopatra had been shorter, the whole face of the earth would have been changed.
PASCAL—*Thoughts.* Ch. VIII. 29. (1623)
(See also FAVART)

2
Thus does the Muse herself move men divinely inspired, and through them thus inspired a Chain hangs together of others inspired divinely likewise.
PLATO—*Ion.* Par. V. Simile called "Plato's Rings." (See also HOMER)

3
By the golden chain Homer meant nothing else than the sun.
PLATO in KIRCHER'S *Magnes Sive de Arte Magnetica.* See also HARE'S *Guesses at Truth.* 2nd Series. Ed. 3. P. 377.
(See also HOMER)

4
Thou wert my guide, philosopher, and friend.
POPE—*Essay on Man.* Ep. IV. L. 390.

5
And the touch'd needle trembles to the pole.
POPE—*Temple of Fame.* L. 431.
(See also NORRIS)

6
They are like the deaf adder that stoppeth her ear; which will not hearken to the voice of charmers, charming never so wisely.
Psalms. LVIII. 4. 5.

7
Even as the needle that directs the hour,
(Touched with the loadstone) by the secret power
Of hidden Nature, points upon the pole;
Even so the wavering powers of my soul,
Touch'd by the virtue of Thy spirit, flee
From what is earth, and point alone to Thee.
QUARLES—*Job Mil. Med.* IV. Also in *Emblems.* Bk. I. Emblem 13.
(See also NORRIS)

8
Such souls,
Whose sudden visitations daze the world,
Vanish like lightning, but they leave behind
A voice that in the distance far away
Wakens the slumbering ages.
SIR HENRY TAYLOR—*Philip Van Artevelde.* Pt. I. Act I. Sc. 7.

9
For so the whole round Earth is every way
Bound by Gold Chains about the Feet of God.
TENNYSON—*Morte D'Arthur.*
(See also HOMER)

10
I am a part of all that I have met.
TENNYSON—*Ulysses.* L. 18.

11
I thank God that if I am gifted with little of the spirit which is said to be able to raise mortals to the skies, I have yet none, as I trust, of that other spirit, which would drag angels down.
DANIEL WEBSTER—*Second Speech on Foot's Resolution,* Jan. 26, 1830.
(See also DRYDEN)

12
It is very true that I have said that I considered Napoleon's presence in the field equal to forty thousand men in the balance. This is a very loose way of talking; but the idea is a very different one from that of his presence at a battle being equal to a reinforcement of forty thousand men.
DUKE OF WELLINGTON—*Memorandum.* Sept. 18, 1836.

13
Controls them and subdues, transmutes, bereaves
Of their bad influence, and their good receives.
WORDSWORTH—*Character of the Happy Warrior.*

14
Whose powers shed round him in the common strife,
Or mild concerns of ordinary life,
A constant influence, a peculiar grace.
WORDSWORTH—*Character of the Happy Warrior.*

INGRATITUDE

15
Nil homine terra pejus ingrato creat.
Earth produces nothing worse than an ungrateful man.
AUSONIUS—*Epigrams.* CXL. 1.

16
Deserted, at his utmost need,
By those his former bounty fed;
On the bare earth exposed he lies,
With not a friend to close his eyes.
DRYDEN—*Alexander's Feast.* St. 4.

17
Ingratitude's a weed of every clime,
It thrives too fast at first, but fades in time.
SAM'L GARTH—*Epistle to the Earl of Godolphin.* L. 27.

18
That man may last, but never lives,
Who much receives, but nothing gives;
Whom none can love, whom none can thank,
Creation's blot, creation's blank.
THOMAS GIBBONS—*When Jesus Dwelt.*

19
A man is very apt to complain of the ingratitude of those who have risen far above him.
SAMUEL JOHNSON—*Boswell's Life of Johnson.* 1776.

20
Nihil amas, cum ingratum amas.
You love a nothing when you love an ingrate.
PLAUTUS—*Persa.* II. 2. 46.

21
Ingratus est, qui beneficium accepisse se negat, quod accepit: ingratus est, qui dissimulat; ingratus, qui non reddit; ingratissimus omnium, qui oblitus est.
He is ungrateful who denies that he has received a kindness which has been bestowed upon him; he is ungrateful who conceals it; he is ungrateful who makes no return for it; most ungrateful of all is he who forgets it.
SENECA—*De Beneficiis.* III. 1.

22
Blow, blow, thou winter wind,
Thou art not so unkind
As man's ingratitude:
Thy tooth is not so keen,
Because thou art not seen,
Although thy breath be rude.
As You Like It. Act II. Sc. 7. L. 174.

1
Ingratitude is monstrous; and for the multitude to be ingrateful, were to make a monster of the multitude.
Coriolanus. Act II. Sc. 3. L. 8.

2
This was the most unkindest cut of all;
For when the noble Cæsar saw him stab,
Ingratitude, more strong than traitor's arms,
Quite vanquish'd him; then burst his mighty heart;
And, in his mantle muffling, up his face,
Even at the base of Pompey's statue,
Which all the while ran blood, great Cæsar fell.
Julius Cæsar. Act III. Sc. 2. L. 187.

3
Ingratitude! thou marble-hearted fiend,
More hideous, when thou show'st thee in a child,
Than the sea-monster!
King Lear. Act I. Sc. 4. L. 28.

4
All the stor'd vengeances of heaven fall
On her ungrateful top.
King Lear. Act II. Sc. 4. L. 164.

5
What, would'st thou have a serpent sting thee twice?
Merchant of Venice. Act IV. Sc. 1. L. 69.

6
I hate ingratitude more in a man,
Than lying, vainness, babbling, drunkenness,
Or any taint of vice.
Twelfth Night. Act III. Sc. 4. L. 388.

7
Ingratus unus miseris omnibus nocet.
One ungrateful man does an injury to all who are in suffering.
SYRUS—*Maxims*.

8
He that's ungrateful, has no guilt but one;
All other crimes may pass for virtues in him.
YOUNG—*Busiris*.

INHERITANCE

9
And all to leave what with his toil he won,
To that unfeather'd two-legged thing, a son.
DRYDEN—*Absalom and Achitophel*. Pt. I. L. 169.

10
What we have inherited from our fathers and mothers is not all that 'walks in us.' There are all sorts of dead ideas and lifeless old beliefs. They have no tangibility, but they haunt us all the same and we can not get rid of them. Whenever I take up a newspaper I seem to see Ghosts gliding between the lines. Ghosts must be all over the country, as thick as the sands of the sea.
IBSEN—*Ghosts*.

11
He lives to build, not boast, a generous race;
No tenth transmitter of a foolish face.
RICHARD SAVAGE—*The Bastard*. L. 7.

12
De male quæsitis vix gaudet tertius pæres,
Nec habet eventus sordida præda bonos.
What's ill-got scarce to a third heir descends,
Nor wrongful booty meets with prosperous ends.
Quoted by WALSINGHAM—*History*. P. 260.

INJURY

13
'Twas he
Gave heat unto the injury, which returned
Like a petard ill lighted, unto the bosom
Of him gave fire to it.
BEAUMONT—*Fair Maid of the Inn*. Act II.
(See also HAMLET, HERBERT)

14
Accipere quam facere injuriam præstat.
It is better to receive than to do an injury.
CICERO—*Tusculanarum Disputationum*. V. 19.

15
Wit's an unruly engine, wildly striking
Sometimes a friend, sometimes the engineer.
HERBERT—*Church Porch*.
(See also BEAUMONT)

16
Plerumque dolor etiam venustos facit.
A strong sense of injury often gives point to the expression of our feelings.
PLINY the Younger—*Epistles*. III. 9.

17
Aut potentior te, aut imbecillior læsit: si imbecillior, parce illi; si potentior, tibi.
He who has injured thee was either stronger or weaker. If weaker, spare him; if stronger, spare thyself.
SENECA—*De Ira*. III. 5.

18
For 'tis the sport to have the engineer
Hoist with his own petar.
Hamlet. Act III. Sc. 4.
(See also BEAUMONT)

INJUSTICE (See JUSTICE, LAW)

INN, TAVERN

19
You may go to Carlisle's and to Almack's too;
And I'll give you my Head if you find such a Host,
For Coffee, Tea, Chocolate, Butter, or Toast;
How he welcomes at once all the World and his Wife,
And how civil to Folks he ne'er saw in his Life.
ANSTEY—*New Bath Guide*. Fourth Ed. (1767) P. 130. Phrase "the world and his wife" also found in SWIFT—*Polite Conversation*. Third Dialogue. Another version "All the world and Little Billing." A parish in Northamptonshire.

20
He who has not been at a tavern knows not what a paradise it is. O holy tavern! O miraculous tavern!—holy, because no carking cares are there, nor weariness, nor pain; and miraculous, because of the spits, which themselves turn round and round!
ARETINO—Quoted by Longfellow in *Hyperion*. Bk. III. Ch. II.

21
He had scarcely gone a short league, when Fortune, that was conducting his affairs from good to better, discovered to him the road, where he also espied an Inn. Sancho positively maintained it was an Inn, and his master that it was a castle; and the dispute lasted so long that they arrived there before it was determined.
CERVANTES—*Don Quixote*. Pt. I. Ch. XV.

1
Now musing o'er the changing scene
Farmers behind the tavern screen
Collect; with elbows idly press'd
On hob, reclines the corner's guest,
Reading the news to mark again
The bankrupt lists or price of grain.
Puffing the while his red-tipt pipe
He dreams o'er troubles nearly ripe,
Yet, winter's leisure to regale,
Hopes better times, and sips his ale.
CLARE—*Shepherd's Calendar.*

2
Along the varying road of life,
In calm content, in toil or strife,
At morn or noon, by night or day,
As time conducts him on his way,
How oft doth man, by care oppressed,
Find in an Inn a place of rest.
WM. COMBE—*Dr. Syntax in Search of the Picturesque.* Canto IX. L. 1.
(See also SHENSTONE)

3
Where'er his fancy bids him roam,
In ev'ry Inn he finds a home—
* * * * *
Will not an Inn his cares beguile,
Where on each face he sees a smile?
WM. COMBE—*Dr. Syntax in Search of the Picturesque.* Canto IX. L. 13.

4
Where you have friends you should not go to inns.
GEORGE ELIOT—*Agatha.*

5
There is nothing which has yet been contrived by man, by which so much happiness is produced as by a good tavern or inn.
SAMUEL JOHNSON—*Boswell's Life of Johnson.* (1776)

6
Souls of poets dead and gone,
What Elysium have ye known,
Happy field or mossy cavern,
Choicer than the Mermaid Tavern?
KEATS—*Mermaid Tavern.*

7
The atmosphere
Breathes rest and comfort and the many chambers
Seem full of welcomes.
LONGFELLOW—*Masque of Pandora.* Pt. V. L. 33.

8
A region of repose it seems,
A place of slumber and of dreams.
LONGFELLOW—*Tales of a Wayside Inn.* Pt. I. *Prelude.* L. 18.

9
In the worst inn's worst room, with mat half hung.
POPE—*Moral Essays.* Ep. 3. L. 299.

10
Shall I not take mine ease in mine inn?
Henry IV. Pt. I. Act III. Sc. 3. L. 92.

11
The west yet glimmers with some streaks of day:
Now spurs the lated traveler apace
To gain the timely inn.
Macbeth. Act III. Sc. 3. L. 7.

12
Whoe'er has travel'd life's dull round,
Where'er his stages may have been,
May sigh to think he still has found
The warmest welcome, at an inn.
SHENSTONE—*Written at an Inn at Henley.*
Different version in DODSLEY'S *Collection.*
(See also COMBE)

13
What care if the day
Be turned to gray,
What care if the night come soon!
We may choose the pace
Who bow for grace,
At the Inn of the Silver Moon.
HERMAN KNICKERBOCKER VIELÉ—*The Good Inn.*

INNOCENCE

14
To see a world in a grain of sand,
And a heaven in a wild flower:
Hold infinity in the palm of your hand,
And eternity in an hour.
WILLIAM BLAKE—*Auguries of Innocence.*

15
E'en drunken Andrew felt the blow
That innocence can give,
When its resistless accents flow
To bid affection live.
BLOOMFIELD—*The Drunken Father.* St. 18.

16
O mon Dieu, conserve-moi innocente, donne la grandeur aux autres!
O God, keep me innocent; make others great!
CAROLINE MATILDA—*Scratched on a window of the Castle Fredericksburg, Denmark.*

17
As innocent as a new-laid egg.
W. S. GILBERT—*Engaged.* Act I.

18
An age that melts with unperceiv'd decay,
And glides in modest innocence away.
SAMUEL JOHNSON—*Vanity of Human Wishes.* L. 293.

19
On devient innocent quand on est malheureux.
We become innocent when we are unfortunate.
LA FONTAINE—*Nymphes de Vaux.*

20
What can innocence hope for,
When such as sit her judges are corrupted!
MASSINGER—*Maid of Honor.* Act V. Sc. 2.

21
He's armed without that's innocent within.
POPE—*Epistles of Horace.* Ep. I. Bk. I. L. 93.

22
Mais l'innocence enfin n'a rien à redouter.
But innocence has nothing to dread.
RACINE—*Phèdre.* III. 6.

23
Quam angusta innocentia est, ad legem bonum esse.
What narrow innocence it is for one to be good only according to the law.
SENECA—*De Ira.* II. 27.

24
O, take the sense, sweet, of my innocence,
Love takes the meaning in love's conference.
Midsummer Night's Dream. Act II. Sc. 2. L. 45.

1
Hence, bashful cunning!
And prompt me, plain and holy innocence!
Tempest. Act III. Sc. 1. L. 81.

2
We were as twinn'd lambs that did frisk i' the sun,
And bleat the one at the other; what we chang'd
Was innocence for innocence; we knew not
The doctrine of ill-doing, nor dream'd
That any did.
Winter's Tale. Act I. Sc. 2. L. 67.

3
I doubt not then but innocence shall make
False accusation blush, and tyranny
Tremble at patience.
Winter's Tale. Act III. Sc. 2. L. 31.

4
O, white innocence,
That thou shouldst wear the mask of guilt to hide
Thine awful and serenest countenance
From those who know thee not!
SHELLEY—*The Cenci.* Act V. Sc. 3. L. 24.

INSANITY

5
Like men condemned to thunderbolts,
Who, ere the blow, become mere dolts.
BUTLER—*Hudibras.* Pt. III. Canto II. L. 565. (See also EURIPIDES)

6
Much madness is divinest sense
To a discerning eye;
Much sense the starkest madness.
'Tis the majority
In this, as all, prevails
Assent, and you are sane;
Demur,—you're straightway dangerous,
And handled with a chain.
EMILY DICKINSON—*Poems.* XI. (Ed. 1891)

7
For those whom God to ruin has designed
He fits for fate, and first destroys their mind.
DRYDEN—*Fables. The Hind and the Panther.* Pt. III. L. 2,387.
(See also EURIPIDES)

8
There is a pleasure, sure,
In being mad, which none but madmen know!
DRYDEN—*Spanish Friar.* Act II. St. 1.
(See also COWPER under POETS)

9
The alleged power to charm down insanity, or ferocity in beasts, is a power behind the eye.
EMERSON—*Essays. Conduct of Life. Of Behaviour.*

10
At dæmon, homini quum struit aliquid malum,
Pervertit illi primitus mentem suam.
But the devil when he purports any evil against man, first perverts his mind.
EURIPIDES. *Fragment* 25. BARNES Ed. Attributed to ATHENAGORUS. Also ed. pub. at Padua, 1743-53. Vol. X. P. 268. The Translator, P. CARMELI, gives the Italian as: Quondo vogliono gli Dei far perire alcuno, gli tiglie la mente.
(See also DRYDEN, FRASER, SOPHOCLES)

11
But when Fate destines one to ruin it begins by blinding the eyes of his understanding.
JAMES FRASER—*Short Hist. of the Hindostan Emperors of the Moghol Race.* (1742) P. 57. See also story of the *Christian Broker. Arabian Nights.* LANE's trans. Ed. 1859. Vol. I. P. 307.
(See also EURIPIDES)

12
Mad as a March hare.
HALLIWELL—*Archaic Dict.* Vol. II. *Art. "March Hare."* HEYWOOD—*Proverbs.* Pt. II. Ch. V. SKELTON—*Replycacion Agaynst Certayne Yong Scolers, etc.* L. 35.
(See also THACKERAY)

13
Doceo insanire omnes.
I teach that all men are mad.
HORACE—*Satires.* II. 3. 81.
(See also MANTUANUS)

14
Nimirum insanus paucis videatur, eo quod
Maxima pars hominum morbo jactatur eodem.
He appears mad indeed but to a few, because the majority is infected with the same disease.
HORACE—*Satires.* II. 3. 120.

15
Quisnam igitur sanus? Qui non stultus.
Who then is sane? He who is not a fool.
HORACE—*Satires.* II. 3. 158.

16
O major tandem parcas, insane, minori.
Oh! thou who art greatly mad, deign to spare me who am less mad.
HORACE—*Satires.* II. 3. 326.

17
I demens! et sævas curre per Alpes,
Ut pueris placeas et declamatio fias.
Go, madman! rush over the wildest Alps, that you may please children and be made the subject of declamation.
JUVENAL—*Satires.* X. 166.

18
O, hark! what mean those yells and cries?
His chain some furious madman breaks;
He comes—I see his glaring eyes;
Now, now, my dungeon grate he shakes.
Help! Help! He's gone!—O fearful woe,
Such screams to hear, such sights to see!
My brain, my brain,—I know, I know
I am *not* mad but soon *shall be.*
MATTHEW GREGORY LEWIS ("Monk Lewis")—*The Maniac.*

19
Id commune malum; semel insanivimus omnes.
It is a common calamity; at some one time we have all been mad.
JOH. BAPTISTA MANTUANUS—*Ecl.* I.

20
My dear Sir, take any road, you can't go amiss.
The whole state is one vast insane asylum.
JAMES L. PETIGRU—*On being asked the way to the Charleston, S. C., Insane Asylum.* (1860)

21
Hei mihi, insanire me ajunt, ultro cum ipsi insaniunt.
They call me mad, while they are all mad themselves.
PLAUTUS—*Menæchmi.* V. 2. 90.
(See also HORACE)

1
Nullum magnum ingenium sine mixtura dementiæ fuit.
There has never been any great genius without a spice of madness.
SENECA—*De Animi Tranquillitate.* XV. 10.

2
Quid est dementius quam bilem in homines collectam in res effundere.
What is more insane than to vent on senseless things the anger that is felt towards men?
SENECA—*De Ira.* II. 26.

3
Madam, I swear I use no art at all.
That he is mad, 'tis true, 'tis true 'tis pity;
And pity 'tis 'tis true.
Hamlet. Act II. Sc. 2. L. 96.

4
Though this be madness, yet there is method in 't.
Hamlet. Act II. Sc. 2. L. 208.

5
It shall be so:
Madness in great ones must not unwatch'd go.
Hamlet. Act III. Sc. 1. L. 196.

6
I am not mad; I would to heaven I were!
For then, 'tis like I should forget myself.
King John. Act III. Sc. 4. L. 48.

7
We are not ourselves
When nature, being oppress'd, commands the mind
To suffer with the body.
King Lear. Act II. Sc. 4. L. 109.

8
Were such things here as we do speak about?
Or have we eaten on the insane root
That takes the reason prisoner?
Macbeth. Act I. Sc. 3. L. 83.

9
You will never run mad, niece;
No, not till a hot January.
Much Ado About Nothing. Act I. Sc. 1. L. 93.

10
Fetter strong madness in a silken thread.
Much Ado About Nothing. Act V. Sc. 1. L. 25.

11
Quem Jupiter vult perdere, dementat primus.
Whom Jupiter would destroy he first drives mad.
SOPHOCLES—*Antigone.* JOHNSON'S ed. (1758) L. 632. Sophocles quotes it as a saying. The passage in *Antigone* is explained by Tricinius as "The gods lead to error him whom they intend to make miserable." Quoted by ATHENAGORAS in *Legat.* P. 106. Oxon Ed. Found in a fragment of ÆSCHYLUS preserved by PLUTARCH—*De Audiend. Poet.* P. 63. Oxon ed. See also CONSTANTINUS MANASSES. *Fragments.* Bk. VIII. L. 40. Ed. by BOISSONADE. (1819) DUPORT'S *Gnomologia Homerica.* P. 282. (1660) *Oracula Sibylliana.* Bk. VIII. L. 14. LEUTSCH AND SCHNEIDEWIN —*Corpus Parœmiographorum Græcorum* Vol. I. P. 444. SEXTUS EMPIRICUS is given as the first writer to present the whole of the adage as cited by PLUTARCH. ("Concerning such whom God is slow to punish.") HESIOD—*Scutum Herculis.* V. 89. Note by ROBINSON gives it to PLATO. See also STOBŒUS—*Germ.* II. *de Malitia.*
(See also EURIPIDES)

12
Insanus omnis furere credit ceteros.
Every madman thinks all other men mad.
SYRUS—*Maxims.*

13
Mad as a hatter.
THACKERAY—*Pendennis.* Ch. X.
(See also HALLIWELL)

INSTINCT

14
Instinct is untaught ability.
BAIN—*Senses and Intellect.* (1855) P. 256.

15
Ein guter Mensch in seinem dunkeln Drange
Ist sich des rechten Weges wohl bewusst.
A good man, through obscurest aspirations,
Has still an instinct of the one true way.
GOETHE—*Faust. Prolog im Himmel. Der Herr.* L. 88.

16
Nous n'écoutons d'instincts que ceux qui sont les nôtres.
Et ne croyons le mal que quand il est venu.
'Tis thus we heed no instincts but our own,
Believe no evil, till the evil's done.
LA FONTAINE—*Fables.* I. 8.

17
A fierce unrest seethes at the core
Of all existing things:
It was the eager wish to soar
That gave the gods their wings.
* * * * *
There throbs through all the worlds that are
This heart-beat hot and strong,
And shaken systems, star by star,
Awake and glow in song.
DON MARQUIS—*Unrest.*

18
Great thoughts, great feelings, came to them,
Like instincts, unawares.
RICH. MONCKTON MILNES—*The Men of Old.*

19
But honest instinct comes a volunteer;
Sure never to o'er-shoot, but just to hit,
While still too wide or short in human wit.
POPE—*Essay on Man.* Ep. III. L. 85.

20
How instinct varies in the grov'lling swine,
Compar'd, half-reasoning elephant, with thine!
'Twixt that and reason what a nice barrier!
Forever sep'rate, yet forever near!
POPE—*Essay on Man.* Ep. I. L. 221.

21
Instinct and reason how can we divide?
'Tis the fool's ignorance, and the pedant's pride.
PRIOR—*Solomon on the Vices of the World.* Bk. I. L. 231.

22
Instinct is a great matter; I was a coward on instinct.
Henry IV. Pt. I. Act II. Sc. 4. L. 299.

23
A few strong instincts and a few plain rules.
WORDSWORTH—*Alas! What Boots the Long Laborious Quest?*

INSTRUCTION (See Education, Teaching)

INSULT

1
Qui se laisse outrager, mérite qu'on l'outrage
Et l'audace impunie enfle trop un courage.

He who allows himself to be insulted deserves to be so; and insolence, if unpunished, increases!

Corneille—*Heraclius*. I. 2.

2
Kein Heiligthum heisst uns den Schimpf ertragen.

No sacred fane requires us to submit to insult.

Goethe—*Torquato Tasso*. III. 3. 191.

3
Quid facies tibi,
Injuriæ qui addideris contumeliam?

What wilt thou do to thyself, who hast added insult to injury?

Phædrus—*Fables*. V. 3. 4.

4
Contumeliam si dices, audies.

If you speak insults you will hear them also.

Plautus—*Pseudolus*. Act IV. 7. 77.

5
Sæpe satius fuit dissimulare quam ulcisci.

It is often better not to see an insult than to avenge it.

Seneca—*De Ira*. II. 32.

INTELLECT

6
The hand that follows intellect can achieve.

Michael Angelo—*The Artist*. Longfellow's trans.

7
In short, intelligence, considered in what seems to be its original feature, is the faculty of manufacturing artificial objects, especially tools to make tools, and of indefinitely urging the manufacture.

Henri Bergson—*Creative Evolution*. Ch. II.

8
Instinct perfected is a faculty of using and even constructing organized instruments; intelligence perfected is the faculty of making and using unorganized instruments.

Henri Bergson—*Creative Evolution*. Ch. II.

9
For the eye of the intellect "sees in all objects what it brought with it the means of seeing."

Carlyle—*Varnhagen Von Ense's Memoirs. London and Westminster Review*. 1838.

(See also Carlyle under Eyes)

10
The growth of the intellect is spontaneous in every expansion. The mind that grows could not predict the times, the means, the mode of that spontaneity. God enters by a private door into every individual.

Emerson—*Essays. Intellect*.

11
'Tis good-will makes intelligence.

Emerson—*The Titmouse*. L. 65.

12
Works of the intellect are great only by comparison with each other.

Emerson—*Literary Ethics*.

13
Thou living ray of intellectual fire.

Falconer—*The Shipwreck*. Canto I. L. 104.

14
Glorious indeed is the world of God around us, but more glorious the world of God within us. There lies the Land of Song; there lies the poet's native land.

Longfellow—*Hyperion*. Bk. I. Ch. VIII.

15
A man is not a wall, whose stones are crushed upon the road; or a pipe, whose fragments are thrown away at a street corner. The fragments of an intellect are always good.

George Sand—*Handsome Lawrence*. Ch. II.

16
The march of intellect.

Southey—*Sir Thos. More; or, Colloquies on the Progress and Prospects of Society*. Vol. II. P. 361.

17
The intellectual power, through words and things,
Went sounding on, a dim and perilous way!

Wordsworth—*Excursion*. Bk. III.

18
Three sleepless nights I passed in sounding on,
Through words and things, a dim and perilous way.

Wordsworth—*Borderers*. Written eighteen years before Excursion.

INTEMPERANCE (See also Drinking, Wine)

19
Beware the deadly fumes of that insane elation
Which rises from the cup of mad impiety,
And go, get drunk with that divine intoxication
Which is more sober far than all sobriety.

Wm. R. Alger—*Oriental Poetry. The Sober Drunkenness*.

20
Man, being reasonable, must get drunk;
The best of life is but intoxication:
Glory, the grape, love, gold, in these are sunk
The hopes of all men and of every nation;
Without their sap, how branchless were the trunk
Of life's strange tree, so fruitful on occasion:
But to return,—Get very drunk; and when
You wake with headache, you shall see what then.

Byron—*Don Juan*. Canto II. St. 179.

21
Libidinosa etenim et intemperans adolescentia effœtum corpus tradit senectuti.

A sensual and intemperate youth hands over a worn-out body to old age.

Cicero—*De Senectute*. IX.

22
Ha! see where the wild-blazing Grog-Shop appears,
As the red waves of wretchedness swell,
How it burns on the edge of tempestuous years
The horrible Light-House of Hell!

M'Donald Clarke—*The Rum Hole*.

23
All learned, and all drunk!

Cowper—*The Task*. Bk. IV. L. 478.

24
Gloriously drunk, obey the important call.

Cowper—*The Task*. Bk. IV. L. 510.

1
He calls drunkenness an expression identical with ruin.
DIOGENES LAERTIUS—*Lives of the Philosophers. Pythagoras.* VI.

2
Then hasten to be drunk, the business of the day.
DRYDEN—*Cymon and Iphigenia.* L. 407.

3
Petition me no petitions, Sir, to-day;
Let other hours be set apart for business,
To-day it is our pleasure to be drunk;
And this our queen shall be as drunk as we.
HENRY FIELDING—*Tom Thumb the Great.* Act I. Sc. 2.

4 He that is drunken * * *
Is outlawed by himself; all kind of ill
Did with his liquor slide into his veins.
HERBERT—*The Temple. The Church Porch.* St. 6.

5
Shall I, to please another wine-sprung minde,
Lose all mine own? God hath giv'n me a measure
Short of His can and body; must I find
A pain in that, wherein he finds a pleasure?
HERBERT—*The Temple. The Church Porch.* St. 7.

6
Quid non ebrietas designat? Operta recludit;
Spes jubet esse ratas; in prælia trudit inermem.
What does drunkenness not accomplish? It discloses secrets, it ratifies hopes, and urges even the unarmed to battle.
HORACE—*Epistles.* I. 5. 16.

7
Touch the goblet no more!
It will make thy heart sore
To its very core!
LONGFELLOW—*Christus. The Golden Legend.* Pt. I.

8
Soon as the potion works, their human count'-nance,
Th' express resemblance of the gods, is chang'd
Into some bruitish form of wolf or bear,
Or ounce or tiger, hog, or bearded goat,
All other parts remaining as they were;
And they, so perfect in their misery,
Not once perceive their foul disfigurement.
MILTON—*Comus.* L. 64.

9 And when night
Darkens the streets, then wander forth the sons
Of Belial, flown with insolence and wine.
MILTON—*Paradise Lost.* Bk. I. L. 500.

10
In vain I trusted that the flowing bowl
Would banish sorrow, and enlarge the soul.
To the late revel, and protracted feast,
Wild dreams succeeded, and disorder'd rest.
PRIOR—*Solomon.* Bk. II. L. 106.

11
Nihil aliud est ebrietas quam voluntaria insania.
Drunkenness is nothing but voluntary madness.
SENECA—*Epistolæ Ad Lucilium.* LXXXIII.

12
O monstrous! but one half-penny-worth of bread to this intolerable deal of sack!
Henry IV. Pt. I. Act II. Sc. 4. L. 591.

13 Sweet fellowship in shame!
One drunkard loves another of the name.
Love's Labour's Lost. Act IV. Sc. 3. L. 48.

14 Boundless intemperance
In nature is a tyranny, it hath been
Th' untimely emptying of the happy throne,
And fall of many kings.
Macbeth. Act IV. Sc. 3. L. 66.

15 And now, in madness,
Being full of supper and distempering draughts,
Upon malicious bravery, dost thou come
To start my quiet.
Othello. Act I. Sc. I. L. 98.

16
O God, that men should put an enemy in their mouths to steal away their brains! that we should, with joy, pleasance, revel, and applause, transform ourselves into beasts!
Othello. Act II. Sc. 3. L. 293.

17
I will ask him for my place again; he shall tell me, I am a drunkard! Had I as many mouths as Hydra, such an answer would stop them all. To be now a sensible man, by and by a fool, and presently a beast!
Othello. Act II. Sc. 3. L. 305.

18
Every inordinate cup is unblessed and the ingredient is a devil.
Othello. Act II. Sc. 3. L. 309.

19
I told you, sir, they were red-hot with drinking;
So full of valour that they smote the air
For breathing in their faces; beat the ground
For kissing of their feet.
Tempest. Act IV. Sc. 1. L. 171.

20
What's a drunken man like, fool?
Like a drowned man, a fool and a madman: one draught above heat makes him a fool; the second mads him; and a third drowns him.
Twelfth Night. Act I. Sc. 5. L. 136.

21
Drunkenness is an immoderate affection and use of drink. That I call immoderation that is besides or beyond that order of good things for which God hath given us the use of drink.
JEREMY TAYLOR—*Holy Living. Of Drunkenness.* Ch. II. Pt. 2.

22
The wine of Love is music,
And the feast of Love is song:
And when Love sits down to the banquet,
Love sits long:
* * * * *
Sits long and rises drunken,
But not with the feast and the wine;
He reeleth with his own heart,
That great, rich Vine.
JAMES THOMSON—*The Vine.*

23
A drunkard clasp his teeth and not undo 'em,
To suffer wet damnation to run through 'em.
CYRIL TOURNEUR—*The Revenger's Tragedy.* Act III. Sc. 1.

INTENTION (See Motive)

INVENTION

1
A tool is but the extension of a man's hand, and a machine is but a complex tool. And he that invents a machine augments the power of a man and the well-being of mankind.
HENRY WARD BEECHER—*Proverbs from Plymouth Pulpit. Business.*

2
Se non è vere è ben trovato.
It is not true, it is a happy invention.
GIORDANO BRUNO—*Gli Froici Furori.* Attributed erroneously to CARDINAL D'ESTE. Quoted in PASQUIER *Recherces* (1600) *as* "Si cela n'est vray, il est bien trouve."

3
Want, the mistress of invention.
MRS. CENTLIVRE—*The Busy Body.* Act I. Sc. 1.

4
The golden hour of invention must terminate like other hours, and when the man of genius returns to the cares, the duties, the vexations, and the amusements of life, his companions behold him as one of themselves—the creature of habits and infirmities.
ISAAC D'ISRAELI—*Literary Character of Men of Genius.* Ch. XVI.

5
God hath made man upright; but they have sought out many inventions.
Ecclesiastes. VII. 29.

6
Only an inventor knows how to borrow, and every man is or should be an inventor.
EMERSON—*Letters and Social Aims. Quotation and Originality.*

7
Take the advice of a faithful friend, and submit thy inventions to his censure.
FULLER—*The Holy and Profane States.* Bk. III. *Of Fancy.*

8
Electric telegraphs, printing, gas,
Tobacco, balloons, and steam,
Are little events that have come to pass
Since the days of the old *régime.*
And, spite of Lemprière's dazzling page,
I'd give—though it might seem bold—
A hundred years of the Golden Age
For a year of the Age of Gold.
HENRY S. LEIGH—*The Two Ages.*

9
This is a man's invention and his hand.
As You Like It. Act IV. Sc. 3. L. 29.

10
He had been eight years upon a project for extracting sunbeams out of cucumbers, which were to be put in phials hermetically sealed, and let out to warm the air in raw, inclement summers.
SWIFT—*Gulliver's Travels.* Pt. III. Ch. V. *Voyage to Laputa.*

11
We issued gorged with knowledge, and I spoke:
"Why, Sirs, they do all this as well as we."
"They hunt old trails" said Cyril, "very well;
But when did woman ever yet invent?"
TENNYSON—*Princess.* II. L. 366.

INVESTIGATION

12
Nothing has such power to broaden the mind as the ability to investigate systematically and truly all that comes under thy observation in life.
MARCUS AURELIUS—*Meditations.* Ch. II.

13
Attempt the end and never stand to doubt;
Nothing's so hard but search will find it out.
HERRICK—*Hesperides. Seeke and Finde.*

14
Hail, fellow, well met,
All dirty and wet:
Find out, if you can,
Who's master, who's man.
SWIFT—*My Lady's Lamentation.*

IRELAND

15
There came to the beach a poor exile of Erin,

* * * * * *

But the day star attracted his eyes' sad devotion,
For it rose o'er his own native isle of the ocean,
Where once in the fire of his youthful emotion
He sang the bold anthem of Erin-go-bragh.
CAMPBELL—*The Exile of Erin.*

16
There's a dear little plant that grows in our isle,
'Twas St. Patrick himself sure that set it;
And the sun on his labor with pleasure did smile,
And with dew from his eye often wet it.
It thrives through the bog, through the brake, and the mireland;
And he called it the dear little shamrock of Ireland—
The sweet little shamrock, the dear little shamrock,
The sweet little, green little, shamrock of Ireland!
ANDREW CHERRY—*Green little Shamrock of Ireland.*

17
Dear Erin, how sweetly thy green bosom rises!
An emerald set in the ring of the sea.
Each blade of thy meadows my faithful heart prizes,
Thou queen of the west, the world's cushla ma chree.
JOHN PHILPOT CURRAN—*Cushla ma Chree.*

18
When Erin first rose from the dark-swelling flood,
God blessed the green island, he saw it was good.
The Emerald of Europe, it sparkled and shone
In the ring of this world, the most precious stone.
WILLIAM DRENNAN—*Erin.* Supposed to be origin of term "Emerald Isle." Phrase taken from an old song, *"Erin to her own Tune."* (1795)

19
Arm of Erin, prove strong, but be gentle as brave,
And, uplifted to strike, still be ready to save;
Nor one feeling of vengeance presume to defile
The cause or the men of the Emerald Isle.
WILLIAM DRENNAN—*Erin.*

20
Every Irishman has a potatoe in his head.
J. C. AND A. W. HARE—*Guesses at Truth.*

1
The dust of some is Irish earth,
Among their own they rest.
JOHN KELLS INGRAM—*Who dares to speak of ninety-eight.*
(See also BROOKE under ENGLAND)

2
Old Dublin City there is no doubtin'
Bates every city upon the say.
'Tis there you'd hear O'Connell spoutin'
And Lady Morgan making tay.
For 'tis the capital of the finest nation,
With charmin' pisintry upon a fruitful sod,
Fightin' like devils for conciliation,
And hatin' each other for the Love of God.
CHARLES J. LEVER. Attributed to him in article in *Notes and Queries*, Jan. 2, 1897. P. 14. Claimed to be an old Irish song by LADY MORGAN in her *Diary*, Oct. 10, 1826.

3
Th' an'am an Dhia, but there it is—
The dawn on the hills of Ireland.
God's angels lifting the night's black veil
From the fair sweet face of my sireland!
O Ireland, isn't it grand, you look
Like a bride in her rich adornin',
And with all the pent up love of my heart
I bid you the top of the morning.
JOHN LOCKE—*The Exile's Return.*

4
The groves of Blarney
They look so charming
Down by the purling
Of sweet, silent brooks.
RICHARD ALFRED MILLIKEN—*Groves of Blarney.*

5
There is a stone there,
That whoever kisses,
Oh! he never misses
To grow eloquent.
'Tis he may clamber
To a lady's chamber
Or become a member
Of Parliament.
FATHER PROUT's addition to *Groves of Blarney.* In *Reliques of Father Prout.*

6
When law can stop the blades of grass from growing as they grow;
And when the leaves in Summer-time their colour dare not show;
Then will I change the colour too, I wear in my caubeen;
But till that day, plaze God, I'll stick to wearin' o' the Green.
Wearin' o' the Green. (*Shan-Van-Voght.*) Old Irish Song found in W. STEUART TRENCH's *Realities of Irish Life.* DION BOUCICAULT used first four lines, and added the rest himself, in *Arrah-na-Pogue.* See article in *The Citizen*, Dublin, 1841. Vol. III. P. 65.

7
For dear is the Emerald Isle of the ocean,
Whose daughters are fair as the foam of the wave,
Whose sons unaccustom'd to rebel commotion,
Tho' joyous, are sober—tho' peaceful, are brave.
HORACE AND JAMES SMITH—*Rejected Addresses. Imitation of* MOORE.

8
O, love is the soul of a true Irishman;
He loves all that's lovely, loves all that he can,
With his sprig of shillelagh and shamrock so green.
Sprig of Shillelagh. Claimed for LYSAGHT.

9
Whether on the scaffold high
Or on the battle-field we die,
Oh, what matter, when for Erin dear we fall.
T. D. SULLIVAN—*God Save Ireland.*

ISAR (RIVER)

10
On Linden, when the sun was low,
All bloodless lay the untrodden snow,
And dark as winter was the flow
Of Isar, rolling rapidly.
CAMPBELL—*Hohenlinden.*

ISLANDS

11
From the sprinkled isles,
Lily on lily, that o'erlace the sea.
ROBERT BROWNING—*Cleon.*

12
Beautiful isle of the sea,
Smile on the brow of the waters.
GEO. COOPER—*Song.*

13
Fast-anchor'd isle.
COWPER—*The Task.* Bk. II. *The Timepiece.* L. 151.

14
O, it's a snug little island!
A right little, tight little island!
THOS. DIBDIN—*The Snug Little Island.*

15
Sprinkled along the waste of years
Full many a soft green isle appears:
Pause where we may upon the desert road,
Some shelter is in sight, some sacred safe abode.
KEBLE—*The Christian Year. The First Sunday in Advent.* St. 8.

16
Your isle, which stands
As Neptune's park, ribbed and paled in
With rocks unscalable, and roaring waters.
Cymbeline. Act III. Sc. 1. L. 18.

17
Ay, many flowering islands lie
In the waters of wide Agony.
SHELLEY—*Lines written among the Euganean Hills.* L. 66.

18
Sark, fairer than aught in the world that the lit skies cover,
Laughs inly behind her cliffs, and the seafarers mark
As a shrine where the sunlight serves, though the blown clouds hover, Sark.
SWINBURNE—*Insularum Ocelle.*

19
Summer isles of Eden, lying in dark purple spheres of sea.
TENNYSON—*Locksley Hall.* 164.

20
Island of bliss! amid the subject Seas,
That thunder round thy rocky coasts, set up,
At once the wonder, terror, and delight
Of distant nations; whose remotest shore

Can soon be shaken by thy naval arm;
Not to be shook thyself, but all assaults
Baffling, like thy hoar cliffs the loud sea-wave.
THOMSON—*Seasons. Summer.* L. 1,597.

ITALY

1
For whereso'er I turn my ravished eyes,
Gay gilded scenes and shining prospects rise;
Poetic fields encompass me around,
And still I seem to tread on classic ground.
ADDISON—*Letter from Italy.*

2
Italy, my Italy!
Queen Mary's saying serves for me—
(When fortune's malice
Lost her Calais)—
Open my heart and you will see
Graved inside of it, "Italy."
ROBERT BROWNING—*Men and Women. "De Gustibus."*

3
Italia, Italia, O tu cui feo la sorte,
Dono infelice di bellezza, ond' hai
Funesta dote d'infiniti guai
Che in fronte scritti per gran doglia porte.
Italia! O Italia! thou who hast
The fatal gift of beauty, which became
A funeral dower of present woes and past,
On thy sweet brow is sorrow plough'd by shame,
And annals graved in characters of flame.
VICENZO FILICAJA—*Italia.* English rendering by BYRON—*Childe Harold.* Canto IV. St. 42.

4
Beyond the Alps lies Italy.
J. W. FOLEY—*Graduation Time.* Expression found in LIVY—*Ab Urbe.* Bk. 21. 30.

5
L'Italie est un nom geographique.
Italy is only a geographical expression.
PRINCE METTERNICH to LORD PALMERSTON, 1847. See his Letter to COUNT PROKESCH-OSTEN, Nov. 19, 1849. *Correspondence of Prokesch.* II. 343. First used by METTERNICH in his *Memorandum to the Great Powers,* Aug. 2, 1814.

6
Gli Italiani tutti ladroni.
All Italians are plunderers.
NAPOLEON BONAPARTE *when in Italy.*
Non tutti, ma buona parte.
Not all but a good part.
Response by a lady who overheard him. See COLERIDGE—*Biographia Literaria. Satyrane's Letters.* No. 2. (Ed. 1870)
I Francesci son tutti ladri—Non tutti—ma buona parte.
PASQUIN when the French were in possession of Rome. *See* CATHERINE TAYLOR'S *Letters from Italy.* Vol. I. P. 239. (Ed. 1840) *Quoted also by* CHARLOTTE EATON—*Rome in the Nineteenth Cent.* Vol. II. P. 120. (Ed. 1852)

7
On desperate seas long wont to roam,
Thy hyacinth hair, thy classic face,
Thy naiad airs have brought me home
To the glory that was Greece
And the grandeur that was Rome.
POE—*Helen.*

8
My soul to-day
Is far away
Sailing the Vesuvian Bay.
T. B. READ—*Drifting.*

IVY

Hedera Helix

9
For ivy climbs the crumbling hall
To decorate decay.
BAILEY—*Festus.* Sc. *A Large Party and Entertainment.*

10
That headlong ivy! not a leaf will grow
But thinking of a wreath, * * *
I like such ivy; bold to leap a height
'Twas strong to climb! as good to grow on graves
As twist about a thyrsus; pretty too
(And that's not ill) when twisted round a comb.
E. B. BROWNING—*Aurora Leigh.* Bk. II.

11
Walls must get the weather stain
Before they grow the ivy.
E. B. BROWNING—*Aurora Leigh.* Bk. VIII.

12
The rugged trees are mingling
Their flowery sprays in love;
The ivy climbs the laurel
To clasp the boughs above.
BRYANT—*The Serenade.*

13
As creeping ivy clings to wood or stone,
And hides the ruin that it feeds upon.
COWPER—*The Progress of Error.* L. 285.

14
Oh, a dainty plant is the ivy green,
That creepeth o'er ruins old!
Of right choice food are his meals I ween,
In his cell so lone and cold.
* * * *
Creeping where no life is seen,
A rare old plant is the ivy green.
DICKENS—*Pickwick.* Ch. VI.

15
Direct
The clasping ivy where to climb.
MILTON—*Paradise Lost.* Bk. IX. L. 216.

16
On my velvet couch reclining,
Ivy leaves my brow entwining,
While my soul expands with glee,
What are kings and crowns to me?
MOORE—*Odes of Anacreon. Ode* XLVIII.

17
Bring, bring the madding Bay, the drunken vine;
The creeping, dirty, courtly Ivy join.
POPE—*The Dunciad.* Bk. I. L. 303.

18
Round broken columns clasping ivy twin'd.
POPE—*Windsor Forest.* L. 69.

19
Where round some mould'ring tow'r pale ivy creeps,
And low-brow'd rocks hang nodding o'er the deeps.
POPE—*Eloisa to Abelard.* L. 243.

J

JACKDAW

1
The Jackdaw sat in the Cardinal's chair!
Bishop and Abbot and Prior were there,
Many a monk and many a friar,
Many a knight and many a squire,
With a great many more of lesser degree,—
In sooth a goodly company;
And they served the Lord Primate on bended knee.
Never, I ween,
Was a prouder seen,
Read of in books or dreamt of in dreams,
Than the Cardinal Lord Archbishop of Rheims.
R. H. BARHAM—*Ingoldsby Legends. The Jackdaw of Rheims.*

2
An old miser kept a tame jackdaw, that used to steal pieces of money, and hide them in a hole, which a cat observing, asked, "Why he would hoard up those round shining things that he could make no use of?" "Why," said the jackdaw, "my master has a whole chestfull, and makes no more use of them than I do."
SWIFT—*Thoughts on Various Subjects.*

JANUARY

3
Janus was invoked at the commencement of most actions; even in the worship of the other gods the votary began by offering wine and incense to Janus. The first month in the year was named from him; and under the title of Matutinus he was regarded as the opener of the day. Hence he had charge of the gates of Heaven, and hence, too, all gates, *Januæ*, were called after him, and supposed to be under his care. Hence, perhaps, it was, that he was represented with a staff and key, and that he was named the Opener (*Patulcius*), and the Shutter (*Clusius*).
M. A. DWIGHT—*Grecian and Roman Mythology. Janus.*

4
That blasts of January
Would blow you through and through.
Winter's Tale. Act IV. Sc. 4. L. 111.

JASMINE

Jasminum

5
And at my silent window-sill
The jessamine peeps in.
BRYANT—*The Hunter's Serenade.*

6
Jasmine is sweet, and has many loves.
HOOD—*Flowers.*

7
Jas in the Arab language is despair,
And *Min* the darkest meaning of a lie.
Thus cried the Jessamine among the flowers,
How justly doth a lie
Draw on its head despair!
Among the fragrant spirits of the bowers
The boldest and the strongest still was I.
Although so fair,
Therefore from Heaven
A stronger perfume unto me was given
Than any blossom of the summer hours.
LELAND—*Jessamine.*

8
Among the flowers no perfume is like mine;
That which is best in me comes from within.
So those in this world who would rise and shine
Should seek internal excellence to win.
And though 'tis true that falsehood and despair
Meet in my name, yet bear it still in mind
That where they meet they perish. All is fair
When they are gone and nought remains behind.
LELAND—*Jessamine.*

9
And the jasmine flower in her fair young breast,
(O the faint, sweet smell of that jasmine flower!)
And the one bird singing alone to his nest.
And the one star over the tower.
OWEN MEREDITH (Lord Lytton)—*Aux Italiens.* St. 13.

10
It smelt so faint, and it smelt so sweet,
It made me creep and it made me cold.
Like the scent that steals from the crumbling sheet
Where a mummy is half unroll'd.
OWEN MEREDITH (Lord Lytton)—*Aux Italiens.*
(See also HARTE under PERFUME)

11
Out in the lonely woods the jasmine burns
Its fragrant lamps, and turns
Into a royal court with green festoons
The banks of dark lagoons.
HENRY TIMROD—*Spring.*

JAY

12
What, is the jay more precious than the lark,
Because his feathers are more beautiful?
Taming of the Shrew. Act IV. Sc. 3. L. 177.

JEALOUSY

13
The damning tho't stuck in my throat and cut me like a knife,
That she, whom all my life I'd loved, should be another's wife.
H. G. BELL—*The Uncle.* Written for and recited by HENRY IRVING.

14
Yet he was jealous, though he did not show it,
For jealousy dislikes the world to know it.
BYRON—*Don Juan.* Canto I. St. 65.

15
Anger and jealousy can no more bear to lose sight of their objects than love.
GEORGE ELIOT—*The Mill on the Floss.* Bk. I. Ch. X.

16
Jealousy is never satisfied with anything short of an omniscience that would detect the subtlest fold of the heart.
GEORGE ELIOT—*The Mill on the Floss.* Bk. VI. Ch. X.

17
Then grew a wrinkle on fair Venus' brow,
The amber sweet of love is turn'd to gall!
Gloomy was Heaven; bright Phœbus did avow
He would be coy, and would not love at all:

Swearing no greater mischief could be wrought,
Than love united to a jealous thought.
ROBERT GREENE—*Jealousy.*

1
Jealousy is said to be the offspring of Love. Yet, unless the parent makes haste to strangle the child, the child will not rest till it has poisoned the parent.
J. C. AND A. W. HARE—*Guesses at Truth.*

2
Les hommes sont la cause que les femmes ne s'aiment point.
Men are the cause of women not loving one another.
LA BRUYÈRE.

3
In jealousy there is more self-love than love.
LA ROCHEFOUCAULD—*Maxims.* No. 334.

4
No true love there can be without
Its dread penalty—jealousy.
OWEN MEREDITH (Lord Lytton)—*Lucile.* Pt. II. Canto I. St. 24. L. 8.

5
Nor jealousy
Was understood, the injur'd lover's hell.
MILTON—*Paradise Lost.* Bk. V. L. 449.

6
Can't I another's face commend,
Or to her virtues be a friend,
But instantly your forehead louers,
As if her merit lessen'd yours?
EDWARD MOORE—*The Farmer, the Spaniel, and the Cat.* Fable 9. L. 5.

7
O jealousy,
Thou ugliest fiend of hell! thy deadly venom
Preys on my vitals, turns the healthful hue
Of my fresh cheek to haggard sallowness,
And drinks my spirit up!
HANNAH MORE—*David and Goliath.* Pt. V.

8
Bear, like the Turk, no brother near the throne.
POPE—*Prologue to the Satires.* L. 197.

9
O, der alles vergrössernden Eifersucht.
O jealousy! thou magnifier of trifles.
SCHILLER—*Fiesco.* I. 1.

10
So full of artless jealousy is guilt,
It spills itself in fearing to be spilt!
Hamlet. Act IV. Sc. 5. L. 19.

11
Though I perchance am vicious in my guess,
As, I confess, it is my nature's plague
To spy into abuses, and oft my jealousy
Shapes faults that are not.
Othello. Act III. Sc. 3. L. 146.

12
O, beware, my lord of jealousy;
It is the green-eyed monster which doth mock
The meat it feeds on; that cuckold lives in bliss,
Who, certain of his fate, loves not his wronger;
But, O, what damned minutes tells he o'er,
Who dotes, yet doubts, suspects, yet strongly loves!
Othello. Act III. Sc. 3. L. 166. ("Fondly loves" in some editions.)

13
Trifles light as air
Are to the jealous confirmations strong
As proofs of holy writ.
Othello. Act III. Sc. 3. L. 322.

14
But jealous souls will not be answer'd so;
They are not ever jealous for the cause,
But jealous for they are jealous.
Othello. Act III. Sc. 4. L. 158.

15
If I shall be condemn'd
Upon surmises, all proofs sleeping else
But what your jealousies awake, I tell you,
'Tis rigour, and not law.
Winter's Tale. Act III. Sc. 2. L. 112.

16
Entire affection hateth nicer hands.
SPENSER—*Faerie Queene.* Bk. I. Canto VIII. St. 40.

17
But through the heart
Should Jealousy its venom once diffuse,
'Tis then delightful misery no more,
But agony unmix'd, incessant gall,
Corroding every thought, and blasting all
Love's paradise.
THOMSON—*The Seasons. Spring.* L. 1,073.

JESTING

18
A joke's a very serious thing.
CHURCHILL—*Ghost.* Bk. 4.

19
A man who could make so vile a pun would not scruple to pick a pocket.
JOHN DENNIS—In *The Gentleman's Magazine.* Vol. LI. P. 324. Claimed for DANIEL PURCELL but given to DENNIS by HOOD, also by VICTOR in an Epistle to STEELE.
(See also HOOD)

20
Jest not with the two-edged sword of God's word.
FULLER—*The Holy and Profane States. Of Jesting.* Maxim II.

21
He that will lose his friend for a jest, deserves to die a beggar by the bargain.
FULLER—*The Holy and Profane States. Of Jesting.* Maxim VII.

22
No time to break jests when the heartstrings are about to be broken.
FULLER—*The Holy and Profane States. Of Jesting.* Maxim VIII.

23
Less at thine own things laugh; lest in the jest
Thy person share, and the conceit advance,
Make not thy sport abuses: for the fly
That feeds on dung is colored thereby.
HERBERT—*Temple. Church Porch.* St. 39.

24
People that make puns are like wanton boys that put coppers on the railroad tracks.
HOLMES—*The Autocrat of the Breakfast Table.* I

25
And however our Dennises take offence,
A double meaning shows double sense;
And if proverbs tell truth,
A double tooth
Is wisdom's adopted dwelling.
HOOD—*Miss Kilmansegg.*
(See also DENNIS)

1
Of all the griefs that harass the distress'd,
Sure the most bitter is a scornful jest;
Fate never wounds more deep the generous heart,
Than when a blockhead's insult points the dart.
SAMUEL JOHNSON—*London*. L. 165. *Imitation of Juvenal*. *Satire*. III. V. 152.

2
La moquerie est souvent une indigence d'esprit.
Jesting, often, only proves a want of intellect.
LA BRUYÈRE.

3
Joking decides great things,
Stronger and better oft than earnest can.
MILTON—*Horace*.

4
That's a good joke but we do it much better in England.
GENERAL OGLETHORPE to a Prince of Würtemberg who at dinner flicked some wine in Oglethorpe's face. *Assuming the insult to be a joke* Oglethorpe threw a whole wine glass in the Prince's face in return. BOSWELL'S—*Life of Johnson*. (1772)

5
Diseur de bon mots, mauvais caractère.
A jester, a bad character.
PASCAL—*Pensées*. Art. VI. 22.

6
Si quid dictum est per jocum,
Non æquum est id te serio prævortier.
If anything is spoken in jest, it is not fair to turn it to earnest.
PLAUTUS—*Amphitruo*. III. 2. 39.

7
Omissis jocis.
Joking set aside.
PLINY THE YOUNGER—*Epistles*. I. 21.

8
Der Spass verliert Alles, wenn der Spassmacher selber lacht.
A jest loses its point when the jester laughs himself.
SCHILLER—*Fiesco*. I. 7.

9
Alas, poor Yorick! I knew him, Horatio: a fellow of infinite jest, of most excellent fancy.
Hamlet—Act V. Sc. 1. L. 203.

10
Jesters do often prove prophets.
King Lear. Act V. Sc. 3. L. 71.

11
A jest's prosperity lies in the ear
Of him that hears it, never in the tongue
Of him that makes it.
Love's Labour's Lost. Act V. Sc. 2. L. 871.

12
A dry jest, sir. . . . I have them at my fingers' end.
Twelfth Night. Act I. Sc. 3. L. 80.

13
A college joke to cure the dumps.
SWIFT—*Cassinus and Peter*.

14
Asperæ facetiæ, ubi nimis ex vero traxere,
Acram sui memoriam relinquunt.
A bitter jest, when it comes too near the truth, leaves a sharp sting behind it.
TACITUS—*Annales*. XV. 68.

JEWELS; JEWELRY

15
January
By her who in this month is born,
No gems save *Garnets* should be worn;
They will insure her constancy,
True friendship and fidelity.
February
The February born will find
Sincerity and peace of mind;
Freedom from passion and from care,
If they the *Pearl* (*also green amethyst*) will wear.
March
Who in this world of ours their eyes
In March first open shall be wise;
In days of peril firm and brave,
And wear a *Bloodstone* to their grave.
April
She who from April dates her years,
Diamonds should wear, lest bitter tears
For vain repentance flow; this stone,
Emblem of innocence is known.
May
Who first beholds the light of day
In Spring's sweet flowery month of May
And wears an *Emerald* all her life,
Shall be a loved and happy wife.
June
Who comes with Summer to this earth
And owes to June her day of birth,
With ring of *Agate* on her hand,
Can health, wealth, and long life command.
July
The glowing *Ruby* should adorn
Those who in warm July are born,
Then will they be exempt and free
From love's doubt and anxiety.
August
Wear a *Sardonyx* or for thee
No conjugal felicity.
The August-born without this stone
'Tis said must live unloved and lone.
September
A maiden born when Autumn leaves
Are rustling in September's breeze,
A *Sapphire* on her brow should bind,
'Twill cure diseases of the mind.
October
October's child is born for woe,
And life's vicissitudes must know;
But lay an *Opal* on her breast,
And hope will lull those woes to rest.
November
Who first comes to this world below
With drear November's fog and snow
Should prize the *Topaz'* amber hue—
Emblem of friends and lovers true.
December
If cold December gave you birth,
The month of snow and ice and mirth,
Place on your hand a *Turquoise* blue,
Success will bless whate'er you do.
In *Notes and Queries*, May 11, 1889. P. 371.

16
If that a pearl may in a toad's head dwell,
And may be found too in an oyster shell.
BUNYAN—*Apology for his Book*. L. 89.

17
Black is a pearl in a woman's eye.
GEORGE CHAPMAN—*An Humorous Day's Mirth*.

1
Stones of small worth may lie unseen by day,
But night itself does the rich gem betray.
ABRAHAM COWLEY—*Davideis*. Bk. III. L. 37.

2
These gems have life in them: their colors speak,
Say what words fail of.
GEORGE ELIOT—*The Spanish Gypsy*. Bk. I.

3
And I had lent my watch last night to one
That dines to-day at the sheriff's.
BEN JONSON—*Alchemist*. Act I. Sc. 1.

4
It strikes! one, two,
Three, four, five, six. Enough, enough, dear watch,
Thy pulse hath beat enough. Now sleep and rest;
Would thou could'st make the time to do so too;
I'll wind thee up no more.
BEN JONSON—*Staple of News*. Act I. Sc. 1.

5
Après l'esprit de discernement, ce qu'il y a au monde de plus rare, ce sont les diamants et les perles.

The rarest things in the world, next to a spirit of discernment, are diamonds and pearls.
LA BRUYÈRE—*Les Caractères*. XII.

6
Pearl of great price.
Matthew. XIII. 46.

7
Rich and rare were the gems she wore,
And a bright gold ring on her wand she bore.
MOORE—*Irish Melodies. Rich and Rare were the Gems She Wore.*

8
On her white breast a sparkling cross she wore,
Which Jews might kiss and Infidels adore.
POPE—*Rape of the Lock*. Canto II. L. 7.

9
Nay, tarry a moment, my charming girl;
Here is a jewel of gold and pearl;
A beautiful cross it is I ween
As ever on beauty's breast was seen;
There's nothing at all but love to pay;
Take it and wear it, but only stay!
Ah! Sir Hunter, what excellent taste!
I'm not—in such—particular—haste.
J. G. SAXE—*The Hunter and the Milkmaid*. Trans.

10 I see the jewel best enameled
Will lose his beauty; and the gold 'bides still,
That others touch, and often touching will
Wear gold.
Comedy of Errors. Act II. Sc. 1. L. 109.

11
'Tis plate of rare device, and jewels
Of rich and exquisite form; their value's great;
And I am something curious, being strange,
To have them in safe stowage.
Cymbeline. Act I. Sc. 6. L. 189.

12 Your ring first;
And here the bracelet of the truest princess
That ever swore her faith.
Cymbeline. Act V. Sc. 5. L. 416.

13 Ever out of frame,
And never going right, being a watch,
But being watch'd that it may still go right!
Love's Labour's Lost. Act III. Sc. 1. L. 193.

14
And jewels, two stones, two rich and precious stones,
Stol'n by my daughter!
Merchant of Venice. Act II. Sc. 8. L. 20.

15 A quarrel * * *
About a hoop of gold, a paltry ring.
Merchant of Venice. Act V. Sc. 1. L. 146.

16
I'll give my jewels for a set of beads.
Richard II. Act III. Sc. 3. L. 147.

17
The clock upbraids me with the waste of time.
Twelfth Night. Act III. Sc. 1. L. 141.

18
The tip no jewel needs to wear:
The tip is jewel of the ear.
SIR PHILIP SIDNEY—*Sonnet. What Tongue can Her Perfection Tell?*

19
The lively Diamond drinks thy purest rays,
Collected light, compact.
THOMSON—*The Seasons. Summer*. L. 142.

JEWS

20
The Jews are among the aristocracy of every land; if a literature is called rich in the possession of a few classic tragedies, what shall we say to a national tragedy lasting for fifteen hundred years, in which the poets and the actors were also the heroes.
GEORGE ELIOT—*Daniel Deronda*. Bk. VI. Ch. XLII.

21
The Jews spend at Easter.
HERBERT—*Jacula Prudentum*. No. 244.

22
A Hebrew knelt in the dying light,
His eye was dim and cold;
The hairs on his brow were silver white,
And his blood was thin and old.
THOMAS K. HERVEY—*The Devil's Progress*.

23
Who hateth me but for my happiness?
Or who is honored now but for his wealth?
Rather had I, a Jew, be hated thus,
Than pitied in a Christian poverty.
MARLOWE—*The Jew of Malta*. Act I. Sc. 1.

24
To undo a Jew is charity, and not sin.
MARLOWE—*The Jew of Malta*. Act IV. Sc. 6.

25
This is the Jew that Shakespeare drew.
Attributed to POPE when MACKLIN was performing Shylock. Feb. 14, 1741. See *Biographia Dramatica*. Vol. I. Pt. II. P. 469.

26
Still have I borne it with a patient shrug,
(For sufferance is the badge of all our tribe.)
You call me misbeliever, cut-throat dog.
Merchant of Venice. Act. I. Sc. 3. L. 110.

27
I am a Jew: Hath not a Jew eyes? hath not a Jew hands, organs, dimensions, senses, affections, passions? fed with the same food, hurt with the same weapons, subject to the same diseases, healed by the same means, warmed and cooled by the same winter and summer, as a Christian is?
Merchant of Venice. Act III. Sc. 1. L. 60.

JOURNALISM (See also AUTHORSHIP, CRITICS, NEWS)

1
I would * * * earnestly advise them for their good to order this paper to be punctually served up, and to be looked upon as a part of the tea equipage.
ADDISON—*Spectator*. No. 10.

2
They consume a considerable quantity of our paper manufacture, employ our artisans in printing, and find business for great numbers of indigent persons.
ADDISON—*Spectator*. No. 367.

3
Advertisements are of great use to the vulgar. First of all, as they are instruments of ambition. A man that is by no means big enough for the Gazette, may easily creep into the advertisements; by which means we often see an apothecary in the same paper of news with a plenipotentiary, or a running footman with an ambassador.
ADDISON—*Tatler*. No. 224.

4
The great art in writing advertisements is the finding out a proper method to catch the reader's eye; without which a good thing may pass over unobserved, or be lost among commissions of bankrupt.
ADDISON—*Tatler*. No. 224.

5
Ask how to live? Write, write, write, anything;
The world's a fine believing world, write news.
BEAUMONT AND FLETCHER—*Wit without Money*. Act II.

6
[The opposition Press] which is in the hands of malecontents who have failed in their career.
BISMARCK. To a deputation from Rügen to the King. Nov. 10, 1862.

7
Hear, land o' cakes, and brither Scots,
Frae Maidenkirk to Johnny Groat's;
If there's a hole in a' your coats,
I rede you tent it:
A chiel's amang you taking notes,
And, faith, he'll prent it.
BURNS—*On Capt. Grose's Peregrinations Through Scotland.*

8
A would-be satirist, a hired buffoon,
A monthly scribbler of some low lampoon,
Condemn'd to drudge, the meanest of the mean,
And furbish falsehoods for a magazine.
BYRON—*English Bards and Scotch Reviewers.* L. 975.

9
The editor sat in his sanctum, his countenance furrowed with care,
His mind at the bottom of business, his feet at the top of a chair,
His chair-arm an elbow supporting, his right hand upholding his head,
His eyes on his dusty old table, with different documents spread.
WILL CARLETON—*Farm Ballads. The Editor's Guests.*

10
A Fourth Estate, of Able Editors, springs up.
CARLYLE—*French Revolution.* Pt. I. Bk. VI. Ch. 5.

11
Great is journalism. Is not every able editor a ruler of the world, being the persuader of it?
CARLYLE—*French Revolution.* Pt. II. Bk. 1. Ch. 4.

12
Burke said there were Three Estates in Parliament; but, in the Reporter's gallery yonder, there sat a fourth estate more important far than they all.
CARLYLE—*Heroes and Hero-Worship.* Lecture V. Not in Burke's published works. See Macaulay's essay on Hallam's "Constitutional History," paragraph 8 from end. The "three estates of the realm" are the Lords Spiritual, The Lords Temporal, and the Commons. DAVID LINDSLAY—*Satyre of the Three Estatis.* (1535) RABELAIS—in *Pantagruel*, 4–48 describes a monk, a falconer, a lawyer, and a husbandman called the "four estates of the island."

13
A parliament speaking through reporters to Buncombe and the Twenty-seven millions, mostly fools.
CARLYLE—*Latter Day Pamphlets.* No. VI. *Parliaments.*
(See also CARLYLE under GOVERNMENT)

14
Get your facts first, and then you can distort 'em as much as you please.
S. L. CLEMENS (Mark Twain)—*Interview with* KIPLING. In *From Sea to Sea.* Epistle 37.

15
Only a newspaper! Quick read, quick lost,
Who sums the treasure that it carries hence?
Torn, trampled under feet, who counts thy cost,
Star-eyed intelligence?
MARY CLEMMER—*The Journalist.* St. 9.

16
To serve thy generation, this thy fate:
"Written in water," swiftly fades thy name;
But he who loves his kind does, first and late,
A work too great for fame.
MARY CLEMMER—*The Journalist.* Last Stanza.

17
I believe it has been said that one copy of the *Times* contains more useful information than the whole of the historical works of Thucydides.
RICHARD COBDEN—*Speech* at the Manchester Athenæum, Dec. 27, 1850. See The *Times*, Dec. 30, 1830. P. 7. Quoted in MORLEY'S *Life of Cobden.* Note. Vol. II. P. 429. Also reference to same. P. 428.

18
Did Charity prevail, the press would prove
A vehicle of virtue, truth, and love.
COWPER—*Charity.* L. 624.

19
How shall I speak thee, or thy power address,
Thou God of our idolatry, the Press.
* * * * *
Like Eden's dead probationary tree,
Knowledge of good and evil is from thee.
COWPER—*Progress of Error.* L. 452.

1

He comes, the herald of a noisy world,
With spatter'd boots, strapp'd waist, and frozen locks;
News from all nations lumbering at his back.

COWPER—*The Task.* Bk. IV. L. 5.

2

When found, make a note of.

DICKENS—*Dombey and Son.* Ch. 15.

3

Miscellanists are the most popular writers among every people; for it is they who form a communication between the learned and the unlearned, and, as it were, throw a bridge between those two great divisions of the public.

ISAAC D'ISRAELI—*Literary Character of Men of Genius. Miscellanists.*

4

None of our political writers . . take notice of any more than three estates, namely, Kings, Lords and Commons . : . passing by in silence that very large and powerful body which form the fourth estate in the community . . . the Mob.

FIELDING—*Covent Garden Journal.* June 13, 1752.

(See also CARLYLE)

5

Caused by a dearth of scandal should the vapors
Distress our fair ones—let them read the papers.

GARRICK—Prologue to SHERIDAN'S *School for Scandal.*

6

The liberty of the press is the *palladium* of all the civil, political, and religious rights of an Englishman.

JUNIUS—*Dedication to Letters.*

7

The highest reach of a news-writer is an empty Reasoning on Policy, and vain Conjectures on the public Management.

LA BRUYÈRE—*The Characters or Manners of the Present Age.* Ch. I.

8

The News-writer lies down at Night in great Tranquillity, upon a piece of News which corrupts before Morning, and which he is obliged to throw away as soon as he awakes.

LA BRUYÈRE—*The Characters or Manners of the Present Age.* Ch. I.

9

Tout faiseur de journaux doit tribut au Malin.

Every newspaper editor owes tribute to the devil.

LA FONTAINE—*Lettre à Simon de Troyes.* 1686.

10

Newspapers always excite curiosity. No one ever lays one down without a feeling of disappointment.

CHARLES LAMB—*Essays of Elia. Detached Thoughts on Books and Reading.*

11

Behold the whole huge earth sent to me hebdomadally in a brown paper wrapper.

LOWELL—*Biglow Papers.* Series I. No. 6.

12

I fear three newspapers more than a hundred thousand bayonets.

NAPOLEON I.

13

The penny-papers of New York do more to govern this country than the White House at Washington.

WENDELL PHILLIPS.

14

We live under a government of men and morning newspapers.

WENDELL PHILLIPS.

15

The press is like the air, a chartered libertine.

PITT—*To Lord Grenville.* (About 1757)

(See also HENRY V under SPEECH)

16

The mob of gentlemen who wrote with ease.

POPE—*Epistles of Horace.* Ep. I. Bk. II. L. 108.

17

Cela est escrit. Il est vray.

The thing is written. It is true.

RABELAIS—*Pantagruel.*

18

Can it be maintained that a person of any education can learn anything worth knowing from a penny paper? It may be said that people may learn what is said in Parliament. Well, will that contribute to their education?

SALISBURY (Lord Robert Cecil)—*Speeches.* House of Commons, 1861. On the Repeal of the Paper Duties.

19

But I'll report it
Where senators shall mingle tears with smiles.

Coriolanus. Act I. Sc. 9. L. 2.

20

Report me and my cause aright
To the unsatisfied.

Hamlet. Act V. Sc. 2. L. 350.

21

Bring me no more reports.

Macbeth. Act V. Sc. 3. L. 1.

22

The newspapers! Sir, they are the most villanous—licentious—abominable—infernal—not that I ever read them—no—I make it a rule never to look into a newspaper.

R. B. SHERIDAN—*The Critic.* Act I. Sc. 1.

23

Trade hardly deems the busy day begun
Till his keen eye along the sheet has run;
The blooming daughter throws her needle by,
And reads her schoolmate's marriage with a sigh;
While the grave mother puts her glasses on,
And gives a tear to some old crony gone.
The preacher, too, his Sunday theme lays down
To know what last new folly fills the town;
Lively or sad, life's meanest, mightiest things,
The fate of fighting cocks, or fighting kings.

SPRAGUE—*Curiosity.*

24

Here shall the Press the People's right maintain,
Unawed by influence and unbribed by gain;
Here Patriot Truth her glorious precepts draw,
Pledged to Religion, Liberty, and Law.

JOSEPH STORY—*Motto of the Salem Register.* Adopted 1802. WM. W. STORY'S *Life of Joseph Story.* Vol. I. Ch. VI.

25

The thorn in the cushion of the editorial chair.

THACKERAY—*Roundabout Papers. The Thorn in the Cushion.*

JOY

1
And these are joys, like beauty, but skin deep.
BAILEY—*Festus*. Sc. *A Village Feast*. L. 26.

2 Joys
Are bubble-like—what makes them bursts them too.
BAILEY—*Festus*. Sc. *A Library and Balcony. A Summer Night*. L. 62.

3
The joy late coming late departs.
LEWIS J. BATES—*Some Sweet Day*.

4
Capacity for joy
Admits temptation.
E. B. BROWNING—*Aurora Leigh*. Bk. I. L. 703.

5
An infant when it gazes on a light,
A child the moment when it drains the breast,
A devotee when soars the Host in sight,
An Arab with a stranger for a guest,
A sailor when the prize has struck in fight,
A miser filling his most hoarded chest,
Feel rapture; but not such true joy are reaping
As they who watch o'er what they love while sleeping.
BYRON—*Don Juan*. Canto II. St. 196.

6
There's not a joy the world can give like that it takes away.
BYRON—*Stanzas for Music. There's not a joy*, etc.

7
Oh, frabjous day! Callooh. Callay!
He chortled in his joy.
LEWIS CARROLL—*Jabberwocky. Alice Through the Looking Glass*.

8
Sing out my soul, thy songs of joy;
Such as a happy bird will sing,
Beneath a Rainbow's lovely arch,
In early spring.
W. H. DAVIES—*Songs of Joy*.

9
Joy rul'd the day, and Love the night.
DRYDEN—*The Secular Masque*. L. 82.

10
Our joy is dead, and only smiles on us.
GEORGE ELIOT—*Spanish Gypsy*. Bk. III.

11
All human joys are swift of wing,
For heaven doth so allot it;
That when you get an easy thing,
You find you haven't got it.
EUGENE FIELD—*Ways of Life*.

12
There's a hope for every woe,
And a balm for every pain,
But the first joys of our heart
Come never back again!
ROBERT GILFILLAN—*The Exile's Song*.

13
And, e'en while fashion's brightest arts decoy,
The heart, distrusting, asks if this be joy.
GOLDSMITH—*The Deserted Village*. L. 263.

14
They hear a voice in every wind,
And snatch a fearful joy.
GRAY—*On a Distant Prospect of Eton College*. St. 4.

15
But were there ever any
Writhed not at passed joy?
KEATS—*Stanzas. In Drear Nighted December*.

16
Die Freude macht drehend, wirblicht.
Joy makes us giddy, dizzy.
LESSING—*Minna von Barnhelm*. II. 3.

17
Medio de fonte leporum
Surgit amari aliquid, quod in ipsis floribus angat.
Full from the fount of joy's delicious springs
Some bitter o'er the flowers its bubbling venom flings.
LUCRETIUS—*De Rerum Natura*. IV. 1,129.
BYRON's trans. in *Childe Harold*. I. 82.

18
Gaudia non remanent, sed fugitiva volant.
Joys do not stay, but take wing and fly away.
MARTIAL.—*Epigrams*. Bk. I. 16. 8.

19
Joys too exquisite to last,
And yet more exquisite when past.
MONTGOMERY—*The Little Cloud*.

20
How fading are the joys we dote upon!
Like apparitions seen and gone;
But those which soonest take their flight
Are the most exquisite and strong;
Like angel's visits short and bright,
Mortality's too weak to bear them long.
JOHN NORRIS—*The Parting*. St. 4.

(See also BLAIR under GOODNESS, CAMPBELL under ANGELS)

21
Joy, in Nature's wide dominion,
Mightiest cause of all is found;
And 'tis joy that moves the pinion
When the wheel of time goes round.
SCHILLER—*Hymn to Joy*. BOWRING's trans.

22
At Earth's great market where Joy is trafficked in,
Buy while thy purse yet swells with golden Youth.
ALAN SEEGER—*Ode to Antares*. Last lines.

23
For bonny sweet Robin is all my joy.
Hamlet. Act IV. Sc. 5. L. 186.

24 My plenteous joys,
Wanton in fulness, seek to hide themselves
In drops of sorrow.
Macbeth. Act I. Sc. 4. L. 35.

25
'Tis safer to be that which we destroy
Than by destruction dwell in doubtful joy.
Macbeth. Act III. Sc. 2. L. 9.

26
I wish you all the joy that you can wish.
Merchant of Venice. Act III. Sc. 2. L. 192.

27
Sweets with sweets war not, joy delights in joy.
Sonnet VIII.

28 I have drunken deep of joy,
And I will taste no other wine to-night.
SHELLEY—*The Cenci*. Act I. Sc. 3. L. 92.

1
There is a sweet joy which comes to us through sorrow.
SPURGEON—*Gleanings Among the Sheaves. Sweetness in Sorrow.*

2
Beauty for Ashes, and oil of joy!
WHITTIER—*The Preacher.* St. 26. Quoting *Isaiah LXI.* 3.

3
And often, glad no more,
We wear a face of joy, because
We have been glad of yore.
WORDSWORTH—*The Fountain.*

4
Joys season'd high, and tasting strong of guilt.
YOUNG—*Night Thoughts.* Night VIII. L. 835.

JUDGES (See also JUDGMENT)

5
Judges ought to be more learned than witty, more reverend than plausible, and more advised than confident. Above all things, integrity is their portion and proper virtue.
BACON—*Essays. Of Judicature.*

6
The cold neutrality of an impartial judge.
BURKE—*Preface to Brissot's Address.* Vol. V. P. 67.

7
A justice with grave justices shall sit;
He praise their wisdom, they admire his wit.
GAY—*The Birth of the Squire.* L. 77.

8
Art thou a magistrate? then be severe:
If studious, copy fair what time hath blurr'd,
Redeem truth from his jaws: if soldier,
Chase brave employments with a naked sword
Throughout the world. Fool not, for all may have
If they dare try, a glorious life, or grave.
HERBERT—*The Church Porch.* St. 15.

9
Male verum examinat omnis
Corruptus judex.
A corrupt judge does not carefully search for the truth.
HORACE—*Satires.* II. 2. 8.

10
So wise, so grave, of so perplex'd a tongue,
And loud withal, that would not wag, nor scarce
Lie still without a fee.
BEN JONSON—*Volpone.* Act I. Sc. 1.

11
Le devoir des juges est de rendre justice, leur métier est de la différer; quelques uns savent leur devoir, et font leur métier.
A judge's duty is to grant justice, but his practice is to delay it: even those judges who know their duty adhere to the general practice.
LA BRUYÈRE—*Les Caractères.*

12
Half as sober as a judge.
CHARLES LAMB.—*Letter to Mr. and Mrs. Moxon.* August, 1833.

13
Bisogna che i giudici siano assai, perchè pochi sempre fanno a modo de' pochi.
There should be many judges, for few will always do the will of few.
MACHIAVELLI—*Dei Discorsi.* I. 7.

14
My suit has nothing to do with the assault, or battery, or poisoning, but is about three goats, which, I complain, have been stolen by my neighbor. This the judge desires to have proved to him; but you, with swelling words and extravagant gestures, dilate on the Battle of Cannæ, the Mithridatic war, and the perjuries of the insensate Carthaginians, the Syllæ, the Marii, and the Mucii. It is time, Postumus, to say something about my three goats.
MARTIAL—*Epigrams.* Bk. VI. Ep. 19.

15
I pleaded your cause, Sextus, having agreed to do so for two thousand sesterces. How is it that you have sent me only a thousand? "You said nothing," you tell me; "and this cause was lost through you." You ought to give me so much the more, Sextus, as I had to blush for you.
MARTIAL—*Epigrams.* Bk. VIII. Ep. 18.

16
Judicis officium est ut res ita tempora rerum
Quærere.
The judge's duty is to inquire about the time, as well as the facts.
OVID—*Tristium.* I. 1. 37.

17
The hungry judges soon the sentence sign,
And wretches hang that jurymen may dine.
POPE—*Rape of the Lock.* Canto III. L. 21.

18
Since twelve honest men have decided the cause,
And were judges of fact, tho' not judges of laws.
PULTENEY—*The Honest Jury.* In the *Craftsman.* Vol. 5. 337. Refers to SIR PHILIP YORKE's unsuccessful prosecution of *The Craftsman.* (1792) Quoted by LORD MANSFIELD.

19
Si judicas, cognosce: si regnas, jude.
If you judge, investigate; if you reign, command.
SENECA—*Medea.* CXCIV.

20
Therefore I say again,
I utterly abhor, yea from my soul
Refuse you for my judge; whom, yet once more,
I hold my most malicious foe, and think not
At all a friend to truth.
Henry VIII. Act II. Sc. 4. L. 80.

21
Heaven is above all yet; there sits a judge,
That no king can corrupt.
Henry VIII. Act III. Sc. 1. L. 100.

22
Thieves for their robbery have authority
When judges steal themselves.
Measure for Measure. Act II. Sc. 2. L. 176.

23
He who the sword of heaven will bear
Should be as holy as severe;
Pattern in himself to know,
Grace to stand, and virtue go;
More nor less to others paying
Than by self-offenses weighing.
Shame to him, whose cruel striking
Kills for faults of his own liking!
Measure for Measure. Act III. Sc. 2. L. 275.

1
To offend, and judge, are distinct offices
And of opposed natures.
Merchant of Venice. Act II. Sc. 9. L. 61.

2
It doth appear you are a worthy judge;
You know the law; your exposition
Hath been most sound.
Merchant of Venice. Act IV. Sc. 1. L. 236.

3
What is my offence?
Where are the evidence that do accuse me?
What lawful quest have given their verdict up
Unto the frowning judge?
Richard III. Act I. Sc. 4. L. 187.

4
Four things belong to a judge: to hear courteously, to answer wisely, to consider soberly, and to decide impartially.
SOCRATES.

5
Judex damnatur cum nocens absolvitur.
The judge is condemned when the guilty is acquitted.
SYRUS—*Maxims.*

6
Initia magistratuum nostrorum meliora, ferme finis inclinat.
Our magistrates discharge their duties best at the beginning; and fall off toward the end.
TACITUS—*Annales.* XV. 31.

JUDGMENT (See also JUDGES)

7
On you, my lord, with anxious fear I wait,
And from your judgment must expect my fate.
ADDISON—*A Poem to His Majesty.* L. 21.

8
Cruel and cold is the judgment of man,
Cruel as winter, and cold as the snow;
But by-and-by will the deed and the plan
Be judged by the motive that lieth below.
LEWIS J. BATES—*By-and-By.*

9
Meanwhile "Black sheep, black sheep!" we cry,
Safe in the inner fold;
And maybe they hear, and wonder why,
And marvel, out in the cold.
RICHARD BURTON—*Black Sheep.*

10
My friend, judge not me,
Thou seest I judge not thee;
Betwixt the stirrop and the ground,
Mercy I askt, mercy I found.
CAMDEN—*Remaines Concerning Britaine.* 1637. P. 392. Quoted by DR. HILL on epitaph to a man killed by a fall from his horse.

11
Woe to him, * * * who has no court of appeal against the world's judgment.
CARLYLE—*Essays. Mirabeau.*

12
Thou art weighed in the balances, and art found wanting.
Daniel. V. 27.

13
We judge others according to results; how else?—not knowing the process by which results are arrived at.
GEORGE ELIOT—*The Mill on the Floss.* Bk. VII. Ch. II.

14
In other men we faults can spy,
And blame the mote that dims their eye;
Each little speck and blemish find,
To our own stronger errors blind.
GAY—*The Turkey and the Ant.* Pt. I. L. 1.

15
So comes a reck'ning when the banquet's o'er,
The dreadful reck'ning, and men smile no more.
GAY—*The What D'ye Call It.* Act II. Sc. 9.

16
I know of no way of judging the future but by the past.
PATRICK HENRY—*Speech in the Virginia Convention.* (1775)

17
Demens
Judicio vulgi, sanus fortasse tuo.
Mad in the judgment of the mob, sane, perhaps, in yours.
HORACE—*Satires.* Bk. I. 6. 97.

18
Verso pollice.
With thumb turned.
JUVENAL—*Satires.* III. 36.
"Vertero" or "convertere pollicem" was the sign of condemnation; "premere" or "comprimere pollicem" (to press or press down the thumb) signified popular favour. To press down both thumbs (utroque pollice compresso) signified a desire to caress one who had fought well. See HORACE. Ep. I. 18. 66. PRUDENTIUS—*Ado. Sym.* 1098, gives it "Converso pollice."

19
Quid tam dextro pede concipis ut te conatus non pœniteat votique peracti?
What is there that you enter upon so favorably as not to repent of the undertaking and the accomplishment of your wish?
JUVENAL—*Satires.* X. 5.

20
On est quelquefois un sot avec de l'esprit; mais on ne l'est jamais avec du jugement.
We sometimes see a fool possessed of talent, but never of judgment.
LA ROCHEFOUCAULD—*Maximes.* 456.

21
He that judges without informing himself to the utmost that he is capable, cannot acquit himself of judging amiss.
LOCKE—*Human Understanding.* Bk. II. Ch. XXI.

22
We judge ourselves by what we feel capable of doing, while others judge us by what we have already done.
LONGFELLOW—*Kavanagh.* Ch. I.

23
Give your decisions, never your reasons; your decisions may be right, your reasons are sure to be wrong.
LORD MANSFIELD'S *Advice.*

24
When thou attended gloriously from heaven,
Shalt in the sky appear, and from thee send
Thy summoning archangels to proclaim
Thy dread tribunal.
MILTON—*Paradise Lost.* Bk. III. L. 323.

1 *There* written all
Black as the damning drops that fall
From the denouncing Angel's pen,
Ere Mercy weeps them out again.
MOORE—*Lalla Rookh. Paradise and the Peri.* St. 28.

2
'Tis with our judgments as our watches, none
Go just alike, yet each believes his own.
POPE—*Essay on Criticism.* L. 9.
(See also SUCKLING)

3
Denn aller Ausgang ist ein Gottesurtheil.
For every event is a judgment of God.
SCHILLER—*Wallenstein's Tod.* I. 7. 32.

4
Commonly we say a Judgment falls upon a Man for something in him we cannot abide.
JOHN SELDEN—*Table Talk. Judgments.*

5
For I do not distinguish by the eye, but by the mind, which is the proper judge of the man.
SENECA—*On a Happy Life.* Ch. I.

6
We shall be judged, not by what we might have been, but what we have been.
SEWELL—*Passing Thoughts on Religion. Sympathy in Gladness.*

7
He that of greatest works is finisher
Oft does them by the weakest minister:
So holy writ in babes hath judgment shown,
When judges have been babes.
All's Well That Ends Well. Act II. Sc. 1. L. 139.

8 I see men's judgments are
A parcel of their fortunes; and things outward
Do draw the inward quality after them,
To suffer all alike.
Antony and Cleopatra. Act III. Sc. 13. L. 31.

9
Give every man thy ear, but few thy voice;
Take each man's censure, but reserve thy judgment.
Hamlet. Act I. Sc. 3. L. 68.

10
Forbear to judge, for we are sinners all.
Henry VI. Pt. II. Act III. Sc. 3. L. 31.

11 What we oft do best,
By sick interpreters, once weak ones, is
Not ours, or not allow'd; what worst, as oft,
Hitting a grosser quality, is cried up
For our best act.
Henry VIII. Act I. Sc. 2. L. 81.

12
O judgment! thou art fled to brutish beasts,
And men have lost their reason!
Julius Cæsar. Act III. Sc. 2. L. 109.

13
The jury, passing on the prisoner's life,
May in the sworn twelve have a thief or two
Guiltier than him they try.
Measure for Measure. Act II. Sc. 1. L. 19.

14 How would you be,
If He, which is the top of judgment, should
But judge you as you are?
Measure for Measure. Act II. Sc. 2. L. 76.

15
I stand for judgment: answer: shall I have it?
Merchant of Venice. Act IV. Sc. 1. L. 103.

16
A Daniel come to judgment! yea, a Daniel.
Merchant of Venice. Act IV. Sc. 1. L. 223.

17 I charge you by the law,
Whereof you are a well deserving pillar,
Proceed to judgment.
Merchant of Venice. Act IV. Sc. 1. L. 238.

18
The urging of that word, judgment, hath bred a kind of remorse in me.
Richard III. Act I. Sc. 4. L. 109.

19
But as when an authentic watch is shown,
Each man winds up and rectifies his own,
So in our very judgments.
SIR JOHN SUCKLING—*Aglaura.* Epilogue.
(See also POPE)

20 Though our works
Find righteous or unrighteous judgment, this
At least is ours, to make them righteous.
SWINBURNE—*Marino Faliero.* Act III. Sc. 1.

21 Where blind and naked Ignorance
Delivers brawling judgments, unashamed,
On all things all day long.
TENNYSON—*Idyls of the King. Merlin and Vivien.* L. 662.

22
Ita comparatam esse naturam omnium, aliena ut melius videant et dijudicent, quam sua.
The nature of all men is so formed that they see and discriminate in the affairs of others, much better than in their own.
TERENCE—*Heauton timoroumenos.* III. 1. 94.

23
One cool judgment is worth a thousand hasty councils. The thing to do is to supply light and not heat. At any rate, if it is heat it ought to be white heat and not sputter, because sputtering heat is apt to spread the fire. There ought, if there is any heat at all, to be that warmth of the heart which makes every man thrust aside his own personal feeling, his own personal interest, and take thought of the welfare and benefit of others.
WOODROW WILSON—*Speech at Pittsburgh,* Jan. 29, 1916.

JULY

24 The linden, in the fervors of July,
Hums with a louder concert. When the wind
Sweeps the broad forest in its summer prime,
As when some master-hand exulting sweeps
The keys of some great organ, ye give forth
The music of the woodland depths, a hymn
Of gladness and of thanks.
BRYANT—*Among the Trees.* L. 62.

25
Loud is the summer's busy song
The smallest breeze can find a tongue,
While insects of each tiny size
Grow teasing with their melodies,
Till noon burns with its blistering breath
Around, and day lies still as death.
CLARE—*July.*

26
The Summer looks out from her brazen tower,
Through the flashing bars of July.
FRANCIS THOMPSON—*A Corymbus for Autumn.* St. 3.

JUNE

1
Do you recall that night in June
Upon the Danube River;
We listened to the ländler-tune,
We watched the moonbeams quiver.
CHARLES H. AIDÉ—*Danube River.*

2
I gazed upon the glorious sky
And the green mountains round,
And thought that when I came to lie
At rest within the ground,
'Twere pleasant, that in flowery June,
When brooks send up a cheerful tune,
And groves a joyous sound,
The sexton's hand, my grave to make,
The rich, green mountain-turf should break.
BRYANT—*June.*

3
What joy have I in June's return?
My feet are parched—my eyeballs burn,
I scent no flowery gust;
But faint the flagging Zephyr springs,
With dry Macadam on its wings,
And turns me "dust to dust."
HOOD—*Town and Country. Ode Imitated from Horace.*

4
June falls asleep upon her bier of flowers;
In vain are dewdrops sprinkled o'er her,
In vain would fond winds fan her back to life,
Her hours are numbered on the floral dial.
LUCY LARCOM—*Death of June.* L. 1.

5
And what is so rare as a day in June?
Then, if ever, come perfect days;
Then Heaven tries earth if it be in tune,
And over it softly her warm ear lays.
LOWELL—*The Vision of Sir Launfal.*

6
So sweet, so sweet the roses in their blowing,
So sweet the daffodils, so fair to see;
So blithe and gay the humming-bird a-going
From flower to flower, a-hunting with the bee.
NORA PERRY—*In June.*

7
It is the month of June,
The month of leaves and roses,
When pleasant sights salute the eyes
And pleasant scents the noses.
N. P. WILLIS—*The Month of June.*

JUSTICE

8
Justice discards party, friendship, kindred, and is therefore always represented as blind
ADDISON—*The Guardian.* No. 99.

9
There is no virtue so truly great and godlike as justice.
ADDISON—*The Guardian.* No. 99.

10
Justice is that virtue of the soul which is distributive according to desert.
ARISTOTLE—*Metaphysics. On the Virtues and Vices. Justice.*

11
God's justice, tardy though it prove perchance,
Rests never on the track until it reach
Delinquency.
ROBERT BROWNING—*Ceuciaja.*

12
Justice is itself the great standing policy of civil society; and any eminent departure from it, under any circumstances, lies under the suspicion of being no policy at all.
BURKE—*Reflections on the Revolution in France.*

13
It looks to me to be narrow and pedantic to apply the ordinary ideas of criminal justice to this great public contest. I do not know the method of drawing up an indictment against a whole people.
BURKE—*Speech on Conciliation with America.* Works. Vol. II. P. 136.

14
So justice while she winks at crimes,
Stumbles on innocence sometimes.
BUTLER—*Hudibras.* Canto II. Pt. I. L. 1177.

15
Amongst the sons of men how few are known
Who dare be just to merit not their own.
CHURCHILL—*Epistle to Hogarth.* L. 1.

16
Justitia suum cuique distribuit.
Justice renders to every one his due.
CICERO—*De Legibus.* I. 15.

17
Justitia nihil exprimit præmii, nihil pretii: per se igitur expetitur.
Justice extorts no reward, no kind of price: she is sought, therefore, for her own sake.
CICERO—*De Legibus.* I. 18.

18
Meminerimus etiam adversus infimos justitiam esse servandam.
Let us remember that justice must be observed even to the lowest.
CICERO—*De Natura Deorum.* III. 15.

19
Summum jus, summa injuria.
Extreme justice is extreme injustice.
CICERO—*De Officiis.* I. 10. Also in *De Republica.* V. Ch. III. Same idea in ARISTOTLE—*Ethics* V. 14. TERENCE—*Heauton timorumenos.* Act IV. Sc. 5. 48. COLUMELLA—*De Re Rustica.* Bk. I. Ch. VII. (Ed. Bipont, 1787.) RACINE—*La Thébaide.* Act IV. Sc. 3. *Les Frères Ennemis.* IV. 3. (See also SOPHOCLES)

20
Fundamenta justitiæ sunt, ut ne cui noceatur, deinde ut communi utilitati serviatur.
The foundations of justice are that no one shall suffer wrong; then, that the public good be promoted.
CICERO—*De Officiis.* I. 10.

21
Observantior æqui
Fit populus, nec ferre negat, cum viderit ipsum
Auctorem parere sibi.
The people become more observant of justice, and do not refuse to submit to the laws when they see them obeyed by their enactor.
CLAUDIANUS—*De Quarto Consulatu Honorii Augusti Panegyris.* CCXCVII.

22
Cima di giudizio non s'avvalla.
Justice does not descend from its pinnacle.
DANTE—*Purgatorio.* VI. 37.

1
Justice is truth in action.
BENJ. DISRAELI—*Speech*, Feb. 11, 1851.

2
Whoever fights, whoever falls,
Justice conquers evermore.
EMERSON—*Voluntaries*.

3
Justice without wisdom is impossible.
FROUDE—*Short Studies on Great Subjects. Party Politics.*

4
That which is unjust can really profit no one; that which is just can really harm no one.
HENRY GEORGE—*The Land Question.* Ch. XIV.

5
Dilexi justitiam et odi iniquitatem, propterea morior in exilio.
I have loved justice and hated iniquity; and therefore I die in exile.
POPE GREGORY VII. (HILDEBRAND.) *Bowden's Life of Gregory VII.* Vol. II. Bk. III. Ch. XX.

6
The spirits of just men made perfect.
Hebrews. XII. 23.

7
Raro antecedentem scelestum
Deseruit pede pœna claudo.
Justice, though moving with tardy pace, has seldom failed to overtake the wicked in their flight.
HORACE—*Carmina.* III. 2. 31.

8
L'amour de la justice n'est, en la plupart des hommes, que la crainte de souffrir l'injustice.
The love of justice is, in most men, nothing more than the fear of suffering injustice.
LA ROCHEFOUCAULD—*Maximes.*

9
Man is unjust, but God is just; and finally justice
Triumphs.
LONGFELLOW—*Evangeline.* Pt. I. 3. L. 34.

10 Arma tenenti
Omnia dat qui justa negat.
He who refuses what is just, gives up everything to him who is armed.
LUCAN—*Pharsalia.* I. 348.

11
But the sunshine aye shall light the sky,
As round and round we run;
And the Truth shall ever come uppermost,
And Justice shall be done.
CHARLES MACKAY—*Eternal Justice.* St. 4.

12
I'm armed with more than complete steel,—
The justice of my quarrel.
MARLOWE—*Lust's Dominion.* Act III. Sc. 4.
(See also HENRY VI., SHAW)

13 Yet I shall temper so
Justice with mercy, as may illustrate most
Them fully satisfied, and thee appease.
MILTON—*Paradise Lost.* Bk. X. L. 77.

14
Just are the ways of God,
And justifiable to men.
MILTON—*Samson Agonistes.* L. 293.

15
Prompt sense of equity! to thee belongs
The swift redress of unexamined wrongs!
Eager to serve, the cause perhaps untried,
But always apt to choose the suffering side!
HANNAH MORE—*Sensibility.* L. 243.

16
A just man is not one who does no ill,
But he, who with the power, has not the will.
PHILEMON—*Sententiæ.* II.

17
The path of the just is as the shining light, that shineth more and more unto the perfect day.
Proverbs. IV. 18.

18
Render therefore to all their dues.
Romans. XIII. 7.

19
Qui statuit aliquid, parte inaudita altera,
Aequum licet statuerit, haud æquus fuerit.
He who decides a case without hearing the other side, though he decide justly, cannot be considered just.
SENECA—*Medea.* CXCIX.

20
There is more owing her than is paid; and more shall be paid her than she'll demand.
All's Well That Ends Well. Act I. Sc. 3. L. 107.

21
Use every man after his desert, and who should 'Scape whipping!
Hamlet. Act II. Sc. 2. L. 554.

22
Thrice is he arm'd that hath his quarrel just,
And he but naked, though lock'd up in steel,
Whose conscience with injustice is corrupted.
Henry VI. Pt. II. Act III. Sc. 2. L. 232.
(See also MARLOWE)

23
This shows you are above
Your justicers; that these our nether crimes
So speedily can venge!
King Lear. Act IV. Sc. 2. L. 78.

24 This even-handed justice
Commends the ingredients of our poison'd chalice
To our own lips.
Macbeth. Act I. Sc. 7. L. 9.

25
I show it most of all when I show justice;
For then I pity those I do not know,
Which a dismiss'd offence would after gall;
And do him right that, answering one foul wrong,
Lives not to act another.
Measure for Measure. Act II. Sc. 2. L. 99

26 This bond is forfeit;
And lawfully by this the Jew may claim
A pound of flesh.
Merchant of Venice. Act IV. Sc. 1. L. 230.

27 Thyself shalt see the act:
For, as thou urgest justice, be assur'd
Thou shalt have justice more than thou desir'st.
Merchant of Venice. Act IV. Sc. 1. L. 315.

28
He shall have merely justice and his bond.
Merchant of Venice. Act IV. Sc. 1. L. 339.

1
O, I were damn'd beneath all depth in hell,
But that I did proceed upon just grounds
To this extremity.
Othello. Act V. Sc. 2. L. 137.

2
I have done the state some service, and they know't;
No more of that, I pray you, in your letters,
When you shall these unlucky deeds relate,
Speak of me as I am; nothing extenuate,
Nor set down aught in malice.
Othello. Act V. Sc. 2. L. 339.

3
Thrice is he armed that hath his quarrel just;
And four times he who gets his fist in fust.
Accredited to HENRY WHEELER SHAW. (Josh Billings.)
(See also MARLOWE)

4
Truth is its [justice's] handmaid, freedom is its child, peace is its companion, safety walks in its steps, victory follows in its train; it is the brightest emanation from the gospel; it is the attribute of God.
SYDNEY SMITH—*Lady Holland's Memoir.* Vol. I. P. 29.

5
There is a point at which even justice does injury.
SOPHOCLES—*Electra.*
(See also CICERO)

6
A sense of justice is a noble fancy.
TEGNER—*Frithjof's Saga.* Canto VIII.

7
Suo sibi gladio hunc jugulo.
With his own sword do I stab this man
TERENCE—*Adelphi.* V. 8. 35.

8
On ne peut être juste si on n'est pas humain.
One can not be just if one is not humane.
VAUVENARGUES—*Réflexions.* XXVIII.

9
Discite justitiam moniti et non temnere divos.
Being admonished, learn justice and despise not the gods.
VERGIL—*Æneid.* VI. 620.

10
Fiat justitia, ruat cœlum.
Let justice be done, though the heavens fall.
WILLIAM WATSON—*Decacordon of Ten Quodlibeticall Questions.* (1602) PRYNNE—*Fresh Discovery of Prodigious New Wandering-Blazing Stars.* Sec. ed. London, 1646. WARD—*Simple Cobbler of Aggawam in America.* (1647) Motto of the EMPEROR FERDINAND. DUKE OF RICHMOND—*Speech before the House of Lords.* Jan. 31, 1642. See *Parliamentary History.* Vo. X. P. 28. Idea in THEOGNIS V. 869. In *Anthologia Lyrica.* 1868 ed. P. 72. TERENCE—*Heut.* IV, III, 41. VARRO—Ap. Nonn. Ch. IX, 7. HORACE—*Carmina.* III, III, 8.
Fiat Justitia et ruat Mundus.—*Egerton Papers* (1552) P. 25. *Camden Society.* (1840) AIKIN—*Court and Times of James I.* Vol. II. P. 500. (1625)

11
Justice, sir, is the great interest of man on earth.
DANIEL WEBSTER—*On Mr. Justice Story* (1845)

K

KATYDID

12
Thou art a female, Katydid!
I know it by the trill
That quivers through thy piercing notes
So petulant and shrill.
I think there is a knot of you
Beneath the hollow tree,
A knot of spinster Katydids,—
Do Katydids drink tea?
HOLMES—*To an Insect.*

13
Where the katydid works her chromatic reed on the walnut-tree over the well.
WALT WHITMAN—*Leaves of Grass. Song of Myself.* Pt. 33. L. 61.

KEEDRON (RIVER)

14
Thou soft-flowing Keedron by thy silver stream
Our Saviour at midnight when Cynthia's pale beam
Shone bright on the waters, would oftentimes stray
And lose in thy murmurs the toils of the day.
MARIA DE FLEURY—*Thou soft-flowing Keedron.*

KINDNESS

15
Kindness is wisdom. There is none in life
But needs it and may learn.
BAILEY—*Festus.* Sc. *Home.*

16
Both man and womankind belie their nature
When they are not kind.
BAILEY—*Festus.* Sc. *Home*

17
Have you had a kindness shown?
Pass it on;
'Twas not given for thee alone,
Pass it on;
Let it travel down the years,
Let it wipe another's tears,
'Till in Heaven the deed appears—
Pass it on.
REV. HENRY BURTON—*Pass It On.*

18
I would help others out of a fellow-feeling.
BURTON—*Anatomy of Melancholy. Democritus to the Reader.*
(See also GARRICK)

19
Sed tamen difficile dictu est, quantopere conciliat animos hominum comitas affabilitasque sermonis.
It is difficult to tell how much men's minds are conciliated by a kind manner and gentle speech.
CICERO—*De Officiis.* II. 14.

1
Their cause I plead—plead it in heart and mind;
A fellow-feeling makes one wondrous kind.
DAVID GARRICK—*Epilogue on Quitting the Stage.* June, 1776.
(See also BURTON)

2
And Heaven, that every virtue bears in mind,
E'en to the ashes of the just is kind.
HOMER—*Iliad.* Bk. XXIV. L. 523. POPE'S trans.

3
Though he was rough, he was kindly.
LONGFELLOW—*Courtship of Miles Standish.* Pt. III.

4
The greater the kindred is, the lesse the kindnesse must bee.
LYLY—*Mother Bombie.* Act III. Sc. 1.
(See also HAMLET)

5
There's no dearth of kindness
In this world of ours;
Only in our blindness
We gather thorns for flowers.
GERALD MASSEY—*There's no Dearth of Kindness.*

6
Colubram sustulit
Sinuque fovet, contra se ipse misericors.
He carried and nourished in his breast a snake, tender-hearted against his own interest.
PHÆDRUS—*Fables.* Bk. IV. 18.

7
Sociis atque amicis auxilia portabant Romani, magisque dandis quam accipiundis beneficiis amicitias parabant.
The Romans assisted their allies and friends, and acquired friendships by giving rather than receiving kindness.
SALLUST—*Catilina.* VI.

8
Ubicumque homo est, ibi beneficio locus est.
Wherever there is a human being there is an opportunity for a kindness.
SENECA—*Thyestes.* CCXIV.

9
A little more than kin, and less than kind.
Hamlet. Act I. Sc. 2. L. 65.
(See also LYLY)

10 When your head did but ache,
I knit my handkerchief about your brows,
The best I had, a princess wrought it me,
And I did never ask it you again;
And with my hand at midnight held your head,
And, like the watchful minutes to the hour,
Still and anon cheer'd up the heavy time,
Saying, "What lack you?" and, "Where lies your grief?"
King John. Act IV. Sc. 1. L. 41.

11 Yet do I fear thy nature;
It is too full o' the milk of human kindness.
Macbeth. Act I. Sc. 5. L. 14.

12
Bis gratum est, quod dato opus est, ultro si offeras.
If what must be given is given willingly the kindness is doubled.
SYRUS—*Maxims.*

13
Pars beneficii est, quod petitur, si cito neges.
It is kindness immediately to refuse what you intend to deny.
SYRUS—*Maxims.*

14
On that best portion of a good man's life,
His little, nameless, unremembered acts
Of kindness and of love.
WORDSWORTH—*Lines Composed Above Tintern Abbey.*

KISSES

15
Blush, happy maiden, when you feel
The lips which press love's glowing seal;
But as the slow years darklier roll,
Grown wiser, the experienced soul
Will own as dearer far than they
The lips which kiss the tears away.
ELIZABETH AKERS ALLEN—*Kisses.*

16 But is there nothing else,
That we may do but only walk? Methinks,
Brothers and sisters lawfully may kiss.
BEAUMONT AND FLETCHER—*A King and No King.* Act IV. Sc. 4.

17
Kiss till the cows come home.
BEAUMONT AND FLETCHER—*Scornful Lady* Act II. Sc. 2.

18
Remember the Viper:—'twas close at your feet,
How you started and threw yourself into my arms;
Not a strawberry there was so ripe nor so sweet
As the lips which I kiss'd to subdue your alarms.
BLOOMFIELD—*Nancy.* St. 4.

19
* * * And when my lips meet thine
Thy very soul is wedded unto mine.
H. H. BOYESEN—*Thy Gracious Face I Greet with Glad Surprise.*

20
Thy lips which spake wrong counsel, I kiss close.
E. B. BROWNING—*Drama of Exile.* Sc. *Farther on, etc.* L. 992.

21 I was betrothed that day;
I wore a troth kiss on my lips I could not give away.
E. B. BROWNING—*Lay of the Brown Rosary.* Pt. II.

22
First time he kiss'd me, he but only kiss'd
The fingers of this hand wherewith I write;
And ever since it grew more clean and white.
E. B. BROWNING—*Sonnets from the Portuguese.* Sonnet XXXVIII.

23
Something made of nothing, tasting very sweet,
A most delicious compound, with ingredients complete;
But if as on occasion the heart and mind are sour,
It has no great significance, it loses half its power.
MARY E. BUELL—*The Kiss.*

1
Comin' through the rye, poor body,
  Comin' through the rye,
She draigl't a' her petticoatie,
  Comin' through the rye
  * * * *
Gin a body meet a body
  Comin' through the rye,
Gin a body kiss a body
  Need a body cry?

BURNS. Taken from an old song, *The Bobtailed Lass.* Found in *Ane Pleasant Garden of Sweet-scented Flowers.* Also in JOHNSON'S *Scots Musical Museum,* in the British Museum. Vol. V. P. 430. Ed. 1787. While it seems evident that the river Rye is referred to, the Editor of the *Scottish American* decides it is a field of grain that is meant, not the river.
(See also BLAMIRE, CROSS)

2
Jenny, she's aw weet, peer body,
  Jenny's like to cry;
For she hes weet her petticoats
  In gangin' thro' the rye,
    Peer body.

Said to be the joint production of MISS BLAMIRE AND MISS GILPIN, before 1794.
(See also BURNS)

3
Come, lay thy head upon my breast,
And I will kiss thee into rest.

BYRON—*The Bride of Abydos.* Canto I. St. 11.

4
A long, long kiss, a kiss of youth, and love.

BYRON—*Don Juan.* Canto II. St. 186.

5
When age chills the blood, when our pleasures are past—
  For years fleet away with the wings of the dove—
The dearest remembrance will still be the last,
  Our sweetest memorial the first kiss of love.

BYRON—*The First Kiss of Love.* St. 7.

6
Kisses kept are wasted;
Love is to be tasted.
There are some you love, I know;
Be not loath to tell them so.
Lips go dry and eyes grow wet
Waiting to be warmly met,
Keep them not in waiting yet;
Kisses kept are wasted.

EDMUND VANCE COOKE—*Kisses Kept Are Wasted.*

7
If a body meet a body going to the Fair,
If a body kiss a body need a body care?

JAMES C. CROSS. Written for the pantomime, *Harlequin Mariner.* (1796)
(See also BURNS)

8
Since there's no help, come let us kiss and part.

DRAYTON—*Sonnet.*

9
Kisses honeyed by oblivion.

GEORGE ELIOT—*The Spanish Gypsy.* Bk. III. L. 251 from end of Bk.

10
It was thy kiss, Love, that made me immortal.

MARGARET W. FULLER—*Dryad Song.*
(See also WEST)

11
The kiss you take is paid by that you give:
The joy is mutual, and I'm still in debt.

GEO. GRANVILLE (Lord Lansdowne)—*Heroic Love.* Act V. Sc. 1.

12
Tell me who first did kisses suggest?
It was a mouth all glowing and blest;
It kissed and it thought of nothing beside.
The fair month of May was then in its pride,
The flowers were all from the earth fast springing,
The sun was laughing, the birds were singing.

HEINE—*Book of Songs. New Spring. Prologue.* No. 25. St. 2.

13
Give me a kisse, and to that kisse a score;
Then to that twenty, adde a hundred more;
A thousand to that hundred; so kiss on,
To make that thousand up a million;
Treble that million, and when that is done,
Let's kisse afresh, as when we first begun.

HERRICK—*Hesperides. To Anthea.*

14
What is a kisse? Why this, as some approve:
The sure sweet cement, glue, and lime of love.

HERRICK—*Hesperides. A Kiss.*

15
Then press my lips, where plays a flame of bliss,—
  A pure and holy love-light,—and forsake
The angel for the woman in a kiss,
    At once I wis,
      My soul will wake!

VICTOR HUGO—*Come When I Sleep.*

16
Jenny kissed me when we met,
  Jumping from the chair she sat in;
Time, you thief, who love to get
  Sweets into your list, put that in.
Say I'm weary, say I'm sad,
  Say that health and wealth have missed me:
Say I'm growing old, but add
  Jenny kissed me.

LEIGH HUNT—*Jenny Kissed Me.* ("Jenny" was Mrs. Carlyle.)

17
Drink to me only with thine eyes
And I will pledge with mine.
Or leave a kiss but in the cup,
And I'll not look for wine.

BEN JONSON—*The Forest. To Celia.*
(See also PHILOSTRATUS)

18
    A soft lip,
Would tempt you to eternity of kissing!

BEN JONSON—*Volpone; or, the Fox.* Act I. Sc. 1.

19
Favouritism governed kissage,
Even as it does in this age.

KIPLING—*Departmental Ditties. General Summary.*

20
My lips the sextons are
Of thy slain kisses.

GEORGE ERIC LANCASTER—In *Pygmalion in Cyprus.* P. 18. (Ed. 1880)

1
When she kissed me once in play,
Rubies were less bright than they;
And less bright were those which shone
In the palace of the Sun.
Will they be as bright again?
Not if kiss'd by other men.
WALTER SAVAGE LANDOR—*Rubies.*

2
What is a kiss? Alacke! at worst,
A single Dropp to quenche a Thirst,
Tho' oft it prooves, in happie Hour,
The first swete Dropp of our long Showre.
LELAND—*In the Old Time.*

3
Says he—"I'd better call agin;"
Says she—"Think likely, Mister!"
Thet last word pricked him like a pin,
An'—Wal, he up an' kist her.
LOWELL—*The Courtin'.*

4
The kiss, in which he half forgets even such a yoke as yours.
MACAULAY—*Lays of Ancient Rome. Virginia.* L. 138.

5
Why do I not kiss you, Philænis? you are bald. Why do I not kiss you, Philænis? you are carrotty. Why do I not kiss you, Philænis? you are one-eyed. He who kisses you, Philænis, sins against nature.
MARTIAL—*Epigrams.* Bk. II. Ep. 33.

6
I throw a kiss across the sea,
I drink the winds as drinking wine,
And dream they all are blown from thee,
I catch the whisper'd kiss of thine.
JOAQUIN MILLER—*England.* 1871. *Introduction.*

7
I rest content; I kiss your eyes,
I kiss your hair in my delight:
I kiss my hand and say "Good-night."
JOAQUIN MILLER—*Songs of the Sun-Lands. Isles of the Amazons.* Pt. V. Introd. St.

8
One kiss the maiden gives, one last,
Long kiss, which she expires in giving.
MOORE—*Lalla Rookh. Paradise and the Peri.* L. 200.

9
Kiss—kiss—thou hast won me,
Bright, beautiful sin.
MOTHERWELL—*The Demon Lady.*

10
How should great Jove himself do else than miss
To win the woman he forgets to kiss.
COVENTRY PATMORE—*De Natura Deorum.*

11
Drink to me with thine eyes alone; or if thou wilt, having put it to thy lips, fill the cup with kisses, and so give it me.
PHILOSTRATUS—*Epistles.* 24.
(See also JONSON)

12
A kiss, when all is said, what is it?
. . . a rosy dot
Placed on the "i" in loving; 'tis a secret
Told to the mouth instead of to the ear.
ROSTAND—*Cyrano de Bergerac.*

13
Young gentlemen, pray recollect, if you please,
Not to make appointments near mulberry trees.
Should your mistress be missing, it shows a weak head
To be stabbing yourself, till you know she is dead.
Young ladies, you should not go strolling about
When your ancient mammas don't know you are out;
And remember that accidents often befall
From kissing young fellows through holes in the wall!
J. G. SAXE—*Pyramus and Thisbe.*

14
Give me kisses! Nay, 'tis true
I am just as rich as you;
And for every kiss I owe,
I can pay you back, you know.
Kiss me, then,
Every moment—and again.
J. G. SAXE—*To Lesbia.*

15
Thou knowest the maiden who ventures to kiss a sleeping man, wins of him a pair of gloves.
SCOTT—*Fair Maid of Perth.* Ch. V.

16
Yet whoop, Jack! kiss Gillian the quicker,
Till she bloom like a rose, and a fig for the vicar!
SCOTT—*Lady of the Lake.* VI. 5.

17
Strangers and foes do sunder, and not kiss.
All's Well That Ends Well. Act II. Sc. 5. L. 91.

18
We have kiss'd away
Kingdoms and provinces.
Antony and Cleopatra. Act III. Sc. 10. L. 5.

19
And his kissing is as full of sanctity as the touch of holy bread.
As You Like It. Act III. Sc. 4. L. 17.

20
O, a kiss,
Long as my exile, sweet as my revenge!
Now, by the jealous queen of heaven, that kiss
I carried from thee, dear.
Coriolanus. Act V. Sc. 3. L. 44.

21
Or ere I could
Give him that parting kiss, which I had set
Betwixt two charming words, comes in my father
And like the tyrannous breathing of the north
Shakes all our buds from growing.
Cymbeline. Act I. Sc. 3. L. 33.

22
I understand thy kisses, and thou mine,
And that's a feeling disputation.
Henry IV. Pt. I. Act III. Sc. 1. L. 205.

23
It is not a fashion for the maids in France to kiss before they are married.
Henry V. Act V. Sc. 2. L. 286.

24
Upon thy cheek lay I this zealous kiss,
As seal to this indenture of my love.
King John. Act II. Sc. 1. L. 19.

25
Take, O take those lips away,
That so sweetly were foreswom;
And those eyes, the break of day,
Lights that do mislead the morn;

But my kisses bring again,
Seals of love, but sealed in vain.
Measure for Measure. Act IV. Sc. 1. L. 1. This stanza, with an additional one, is found in BEAUMONT AND FLETCHER'S *Rollo.* Act V. 2. Possibly a ballad current in Shakespeare's time. Malone and other editors claim it is by Shakespeare.

1
But, thou know'st this,
'Tis time to fear when tyrants seem to kiss.
Pericles. Act I. Sc. 2. L. 78.

2
Teach not thy lips such scorn; for they were made
For kissing, lady, not for such contempt.
Richard III. Act I. Sc. 2. L. 172.

3
Their lips were four red roses on a stalk,
Which in their summer beauty kiss'd each other.
Richard III. Act IV. Sc. 3. L. 12.

4
And steal immortal blessing from her lips;
Who, even in pure and vestal modesty,
Still blush, as thinking their own kisses sin.
Romeo and Juliet. Act III. Sc. 3. L. 36.

5
This done, he took the bride about the neck
And kiss'd her lips with such a clamorous smack
That at the parting, all the church did echo.
Taming of the Shrew. Act III. Sc. 2. L. 179.

6
I'll take that winter from your lips.
Troilus and Cressida. Act IV. Sc. 5. L. 23.

7
Why, then we'll make exchange; here, take you this,
And seal the bargain with a holy kiss.
Two Gentlemen of Verona. Act II. Sc. 2. L. 6.

8
Kissing with inside lip? stopping the career
Of laughter with a sigh?
Winter's Tale. Act I. Sc. 2. L. 287.

9
Kiss me, so long but as a kiss may live;
And in my heartless breast and burning brain
That word, that kiss shall all thoughts else survive,
With food of saddest memory kept alive.
SHELLEY—*Adonais.* St. 26.

10
As in the soft and sweet eclipse,
When soul meets soul on lover's lips.
SHELLEY—*Prometheus Unbound.*

11
My lips till then had only known
The kiss of mother and of sister,
But somehow, full upon her own
Sweet, rosy, darling mouth,—I kissed her.
E. C. STEDMAN—*The Door-Step.*

12
My love and I for kisses played;
She would keep stakes: I was content;
But when I won she would be paid;
This made me ask her what she meant.
Pray, since I see (quoth she) "your wrangling vain,
Take your own kisses; give me mine again."
DR. WILLIAM STRODE. Verses in *Gentleman's Magazine,* July, 1823. "Wrangling vayne," or "wrangle in vane." Also found in DRYDEN—*Miscellany.* Poems pub. 1716. with three lines added by DRYDEN.

13
Lord! I wonder what fool it was that first invented kissing.
SWIFT—*Polite Conversation.* Dialogue II.

14
Once he drew
With one long kiss my whole soul thro'
My lips, as sunlight drinketh dew.
TENNYSON—*Fatima.* St. 3.

15
And our spirits rushed together at the touching of the lips.
TENNYSON—*Locksley Hall.* St. 19.

16
Girl, when he gives you kisses twain,
Use one, and let the other stay;
And hoard it, for moons may die, red fades,
And you may need a kiss—some day.
RIDGELY TORRENCE—*House of a Hundred Lights.*

17
A kiss from my mother made me a painter.
BENJAMIN WEST.
(See also FULLER)

KNAVERY

18
Now I will show myself
To have more of the serpent than the dove;
That is—more knave than fool.
MARLOWE—*The Jew of Malta.* Act II. Sc. 3.

19
Zeno first started that doctrine, that knavery is the best defence against a knave.
PLUTARCH—*Morals.* Vol. I. *Of Bashfulness.*

20
There's ne'er a villain dwelling in all Denmark
But he's an arrant knave.
Hamlet. Act I. Sc. 5. L. 124.

21
A knave; a rascal; an eater of broken meats.
King Lear. Act II. Sc. 2. L. 14.

22
Whip me such honest knaves.
Othello. Act I. Sc. 1. L. 49.

23
His nunc præmium est qui recta prava faciunt.
Knavery's now its own reward.
TERENCE—*Phormio.* V. 1. 6.

KNOWLEDGE

24
Knowledge is, indeed, that which, next to virtue, truly and essentially raises one man above another.
ADDISON—*The Guardian. Letter of Alexander to Aristotle.* No. 111.

25
There are four kinds of people, three of which are to be avoided and the fourth cultivated: those who don't know that they don't know; those who know that they don't know; those who don't know that they know; and those who know that they know.
ANON. Rendering of the Arab Proverb.
(See also SIDGEWICK)

1
For all knowledge and wonder (which is the seed of knowledge) is an impression of pleasure in itself.
BACON—*Advancement of Learning.* Bk. I.

2
Knowledge and human power are synonymous, since the ignorance of the cause frustrates the effect.
BACON—*Novum Organum.* Aphorism III.

3
Knowledge bloweth up, but charity buildeth up.
BACON—*Rendering of I Cor. VIII.* I.

4
Nam et ipsa scientia potestas est.
For knowledge, too, is itself a power.
BACON—*Treatise. De Hæresiis.* HOBBES—*Leviathan.* Ch. IX; Ch. X. Used phrase "Knowledge is power."
(See also EMERSON, JOHNSON)

5
Pursuit of knowledge under difficulties.
Title given by LORD BROUGHAM to a book published under the superintendence of the Society for the Diffusion of Useful Knowledge. (1830) DUKE OF SUSSEX—*Address to the Royal Society.* (1839) PROF. CRAIK—Volume bearing this title. (1828)

6
Men are four:
He who knows not and knows not he knows not, he is a fool—shun him;
He who knows not and knows he knows not, he is simple—teach him;
He who knows and knows not he knows, he is asleep—wake him;
He who knows and knows he knows, he is wise—follow him!
LADY BURTON—*Life of Sir Richard Burton.* Given as an Arabian Proverb. Another rendering in the *Spectator*, Aug. 11, 1894. P. 176. In HESIOD—*Works and Days.* 293. 7. Quoted by ARISTOTLE—*Nic. Eth.* I. 4. CICERO—*Pro Cluent.* 31. LIVY—*Works.* XXII. 29.

7
He knew what's what, and that's as high
As metaphysic wit can fly.
BUTLER—*Hudibras.* Pt. I. Canto I. L. 149.

8
Deep sighted in intelligences,
Ideas, atoms, influences.
BUTLER—*Hudibras.* Pt. I. Canto I. L. 533.

9
Nor do I know what is become
Of him, more than the Pope of Rome.
BUTLER—*Hudibras.* Pt. I. Canto III. L. 263.

10
He knew whats'ever 's to be known,
But much more than he knew would own.
BUTLER—*Hudibras.* Pt. II. Canto III. L. 297.
(See also SKELTON)

11
The tree of knowledge is not that of life.
BYRON—*Manfred.* Act I. Sc. 1.

12
Knowledge is not happiness, and science
But an exchange of ignorance for that
Which is another kind of ignorance.
BYRON—*Manfred.* Act II. Sc. 4.

13
There's lots of people—this town wouldn't hold them;
Who don't know much excepting what's told them.
WILL CARLETON—*City Ballads.* P. 143.

14
For love is ever the beginning of Knowledge, as fire is of light.
CARLYLE—*Essays. Death of Goethe.*

15
What is all Knowledge too but recorded Experience, and a product of History; of which, therefore, Reasoning and Belief, no less than Action and Passion, are essential materials?
CARLYLE—*Essays.* On History.

16
Ne quis nimis. (*From the Greek.*)
Know thyself.
Inscription attributed to CHILO OF THALES, PYTHAGORAS, SOLON, on the Temple of Apollo at Delphi.
(See also CICERO, COLERIDGE, DIOGENES, JUVENAL, LA FONTAINE, TERENCE)

17
Nam non solum scire aliquid, artis est, sed quædam ars etiam docendi.
Not only is there an art in knowing a thing, but also a certain art in teaching it.
CICERO—*De Legibus.* II. 19.

18
Minime sibi quisque notus est, et difficillime de se quisque sentit.
Every one is least known to himself, and it is very difficult for a man to know himself.
CICERO—*De Oratore.* III. 9.
(See also CHILO)

19
Nescire autem quid ante quam natus sis acciderit, id est semper esse puerum.
Not to know what happened before one was born is always to be a child.
CICERO—*De Oratore.* XXXIV.

20
And is this the prime
And heaven-sprung message of the olden time?
COLERIDGE. Referring to "Know thyself."
(See also CHILO)

21
When you know a thing, to hold that you know it; and when you do not know a thing, to allow that you do not know it; this is knowledge.
CONFUCIUS—*Analects.* Bk. II. Ch. XVII.
(See also SOCRATES)

22
Knowledge and Wisdom, far from being one,
Have oft-times no connexion. Knowledge dwells
In heads replete with thoughts of other men,
Wisdom in minds attentive to their own.
COWPER—*The Task.* Bk. VI. L. 88. "Knowledge dwells," etc., found in: MILTON—*Paradise Lost.* VII. SELDON—*Table Talk.* YOUNG—*Satires.* VI. Night Thoughts. V.

23
Many shall run to and fro, and knowledge shall be increased.
Daniel. XII. 4.

24
Knowledge comes
Of learning well retain'd, unfruitful else.
DANTE—*Vision of Paradise.* Canto V. L. 41.

1
But ask not bodies (doomed to die),
To what abode they go;
Since knowledge is but sorrow's spy,
It is not safe to know.
DAVENANT—*The Just Italian.* Act V. Sc. 1.

2
Thales was asked what was very difficult; he said: "To know one's self."
DIOGENES LAERTIUS—*Thales.* IX.
(See also CHILO)

3
To be conscious that you are ignorant is a great step to knowledge.
BENJ. DISRAELI—*Sybil.* Bk. I. Ch. V.

4
He that increaseth knowledge increaseth sorrow.
Ecclesiastes. I. 18.

5
Our knowledge is the amassed thought and experience of innumerable minds.
EMERSON—*Letters and Social Aims. Quotation and Originality.*

6
Knowledge is the antidote to fear,—
Knowledge, Use and Reason, with its higher aids.
EMERSON—*Society and Solitude. Courage.*

7
There is no knowledge that is not power.
EMERSON—*Society and Solitude. Old Age.*
(See also BACON)

8
Was man nicht versteht, besitzt man nicht.
What we do not understand we do not possess.
GOETHE—*Sprüche in Prosa.*

9
Eigentlich weiss man nur wenn man wenig weiss; mit dem Wissen wächst der Zweifel.
We know accurately only when we know little; with knowledge doubt increases.
GOETHE—*Sprüche in Prosa.*

10
Who can direct, when all pretend to know?
GOLDSMITH—*The Traveller.* L. 64.

11
The first step to self-knowledge is self-distrust. Nor can we attain to any kind of knowledge, except by a like process.
J. C. AND A. W. HARE—*Guesses at Truth.* P. 454.

12
Nec scire fas est omnia.
One cannot know everything.
HORACE—*Carmina.* IV. 4. 22.

13
Si quid novisti rectius istis.
Candidus imperti, si non, his utere mecum.
If you know anything better than this candidly impart it; if not, use this with me.
HORACE—*Epistles.* I. 6. 67.

14
A desire of knowledge is the natural feeling of mankind; and every human being whose mind is not debauched, will be willing to give all that he has to get knowledge.
SAMUEL JOHNSON—*Boswell's Life of Johnson.* Conversation on Saturday, July 30, 1763.

15
Knowledge is of two kinds. We know a subject ourselves, or we know where we can find information upon it.
SAMUEL JOHNSON—*Boswell's Life of Johnson.* (1775)

16
Knowledge is more than equivalent to force.
SAMUEL JOHNSON—*Rasselas.* Ch. XIII.
(See also BACON)

17
E cœlo descendit nosce te ipsum.
This precept descended from Heaven: know thyself.
JUVENAL—*Satires.* XI. 27.
(See also CHILO)

18
There are gems of wondrous brightness
Ofttimes lying at our feet,
And we pass them, walking thoughtless,
Down the busy, crowded street.
If we knew, our pace would slacken,
We would step more oft with care,
Lest our careless feet be treading
To the earth some jewel rare.
If We Only Understood. Erroneously attributed to KIPLING in *Masonic Standard,* May 16, 1908. Claimed for BESSIE SMITH.

19
Laissez dire les sots: le savoir a son prix.
Let fools the studious despise,
There's nothing lost by being wise.
LA FONTAINE—*Fables.* VIII. 19.

20
Il connoît l'univers, et ne se connoît pas.
He knoweth the universe, and himself he knoweth not.
LA FONTAINE—*Fables.* VIII. 26.
(See also CHILO)

21
Not if I know myself at all.
CHARLES LAMB—*Essays of Elia. The Old and the New Schoolmaster.*

22
Wer viel weiss
Hat viel zu sorgen.
He who knows much has many cares.
LESSING—*Nathan der Weise.* IV. 2.

23
The improvement of the understanding is for two ends: first, for our own increase of knowledge; secondly, to enable us to deliver and make out that knowledge to others.
LOCKE—*Some Thoughts Concerning Reading and Study. Appendix B.*

24
'Tain't a knowin' kind of cattle
Thet is ketched with mouldy corn.
LOWELL—*Biglow Papers.* No. 1. L. 3.

25
Scire est nescire, nisi id me scire alius scierit.
To know is not to know, unless someone else has known that I know.
LUCILIUS—*Fragment.*
(See also PERSIUS)

26
Quid nobis certius ipsis
Sensibus esse potest? qui vera ac falso notemus.
What can give us more sure knowledge than our senses? How else can we distinguish between the true and the false?
LUCRETIUS—*De Rerum Natura.* I. 700.

1
A kind of semi-Solomon, half-knowing everything, from the cedar to the hyssop.
MACAULAY—(*About Brougham*). *Life and Letters.* Vol. I. P. 175.

2
Diffused knowledge immortalizes itself.
SIR JAMES MACKINTOSH—*Vindiciæ Gallicæ.*

3
Every addition to true knowledge is an addition to human power.
HORACE MANN—*Lectures and Reports on Education.* Lecture I.

4
Et teneo melius ista quam meum nomen.
I know all that better than my own name.
MARTIAL—*Epigrams.* IV. 37. 7.

5
Only by knowledge of that which is not Thyself, shall thyself be learned.
OWEN MEREDITH (Lord Lytton)—*Know Thyself.* (See also CHILO)

6
I went into the temple, there to hear
The teachers of our law, and to propose
What might improve my knowledge or their own.
MILTON—*Paradise Regained.* Bk. I. L. 211.

7
Vous parlez devant un homme à qui tout Naples est connu.
You speak before a man to whom all Naples is known.
MOLIÈRE—*L'Avare.* V. 5.

8
Faites comme si je ne le savais pas.
Act as though I knew nothing.
MOLIÈRE—*Le Bourgeois Gentilhomme.* II. 6.

9
All things I thought I knew; but now confess
The more I know I know, I know the less.
OWEN—*Works.* Bk. VI. 39.
(See also SOCRATES)

10
Scire tuum nihil est, nisi te scire hoc sciat alter?
Is then thy knowledge of no value, unless another know that thou possessest that knowledge?
PERSIUS—*Satires.* I. 27.
(See also LUCILIUS)

11
Ego te intus et in cute novi.
I know you even under the skin.
PERSIUS—*Satires.* III. 30. Same in ERASMUS—*Adagia.*

12
Plus scire satius est, quam loqui.
It is well for one to know more than he says.
PLAUTUS—*Epidecus.* I. 1. 60.

13
That virtue only makes our bliss below,
And all our knowledge is ourselves to know.
POPE—*Essay on Man.* Ep. IV. L. 397.
(See also CHILO)

14
In vain sedate reflections we would make
When half our knowledge we must snatch, not take.
POPE—*Moral Essays.* Ep. I. L. 39.

15
He that hath knowledge spareth his words.
Proverbs. XVII. 27.

16
I may tell all my bones.
Psalms. XXII. 17.

17
Que nuist savoir tousjours et tousjours apprendre, fust ce
D'un sot, d'une pot, d'une que—doufle
D'un mouffe, d'un pantoufle.
What harm in learning and getting knowledge even from a sot, a pot, a fool, a mitten, or a slipper.
RABELAIS—*Pantagruel.* III. 16.

18
Then I began to think, that it is very true which is commonly said, that the one-half of the world knoweth not how the other half liveth.
RABELAIS—*Works.* Bk. II. Ch. XXXII.

19
For the more a man knows, the more worthy he is.
ROBERT OF GLOUCESTER—*Rhyming Chronicle.*

20
Far must thy researches go
Wouldst thou learn the world to know;
Thou must tempt the dark abyss
Wouldst thou prove what *Being* is;
Naught but firmness gains the prize,
Naught but fullness makes us wise,
Buried deep truth e'er lies.
SCHILLER—*Proverbs of Confucius.* BOWRING'S trans.

21
Willst du dich selber erkennen, so sieh' wie die andern es treiben;
Willst du die andern versteh'n, blick in dein eigenes Herz.
If you wish to know yourself observe how others act.
If you wish to understand others look into your own heart.
SCHILLER—*Votire Tablets. Xenien.*

22
Natura semina scientiæ nobis dedit, scientiam non dedit.
Nature has given us the seeds of knowledge, not knowledge itself.
SENECA—*Epistolæ Ad Lucilium.* CXX.

23
Crowns have their compass—length of days their date—
Triumphs their tomb—felicity, her fate—
Of nought but earth can earth make us partaker,
But knowledge makes a king most like his Maker.
SHAKESPEARE ON KING JAMES I. See PAYNE COLLIER—*Life of Shakespeare.*

24
We know what we are, but know not what we may be.
Hamlet. Act IV. Sc. 5. L. 42.

25
And seeing ignorance is the curse of God,
Knowledge the wing wherewith we fly to heaven.
Henry VI. Pt. II. Act IV. Sc. 7. L. 78.

26
Too much to know is to know naught but fame.
Love's Labour's Lost. Act I. Sc. 1. L. 92.

1
If you can look into the seeds of time,
And say which grain will grow and which will not;
Speak then to me.
Macbeth. Act I. Sc. 3. L. 58.

2
But the full sum of me * *
Is an unlesson'd girl, unschool'd, unpractis'd;
Happy in this, she is not yet so old
But she may learn.
Merchant of Venice. Act III. Sc. 2. L. 159.

3
We think so because other people all think so;
Or because—or because—after all, we do think so;
Or because we were told so, and think we must think so;
Or because we once thought so, and think we still think so;
Or because, having thought so, we think we will think so.
HENRY SIDGEWICK. Lines which came to him in his sleep. Referred to by DR. WILLIAM OSLER—*Harveian Oration*, given in the *South Place Magazine*, Feb., 1907.
(See also BURTON)

4
And thou my minde aspire to higher things;
Grow rich in that which never taketh rust.
SIR PHILIP SIDNEY—*Sonnet. Leave me, O Love.*

5
Sweet food of sweetly uttered knowledge.
SIR PHILIP SIDNEY—*Defence of Poesy.*

6
He knew what is what.
SKELTON—*Why Come Ye nat to Courte*. L. 1,106.
(See also BUTLER)

7
A life of knowledge is not often a life of injury and crime.
SYDNEY SMITH—*Pleasures of Knowledge.*

8
As for me, all I know is that I know nothing.
SOCRATES—*Plato. Phædrus*. Sec. CCXXXV
(See also CONFUCIUS, OWEN, STIRLING)

9
Yet all that I have learn'd (hugh toyles now past)
By long experience, and in famous schooles,
Is but to know my ignorance at last,
Who think themselves most wise are greatest fools.
WILLIAM, EARL OF STIRLING—*Recreation with the Muses*. London. Fol. 1637. P. 7.
(See also SOCRATES)

10
Knowledge alone is the being of Nature,
Giving a soul to her manifold features,
Lighting through paths of the primitive darkness,
The footsteps of Truth and the vision of Song.
BAYARD TAYLOR—*Kilimandjaro*. St. 2.

11
Knowledge comes, but wisdom lingers.
TENNYSON—*Locksley Hall*. St. 71.

12
Who loves not Knowledge? Who shall rail
Against her beauty? May she mix
With men and prosper! Who shall fix
Her pillars? Let her work prevail.
TENNYSON—*In Memoriam*. CXIV.

13
Faciunt næ intelligendo, ut nihil intelligant.
By too much knowledge they bring it about that they know nothing.
TERENCE—*Andria. Prologue*. XVII.

14
Namque inscitia est,
Adversum stimulum calces.
For it shows want of knowledge to kick against the goad.
TERENCE—*Phormio*. I. 24. 27.

15
Knowledge, in truth, is the great sun in the firmament. Life and power are scattered with all its beams.
DANIEL WEBSTER—*Address*. Delivered at the Laying of the Corner-Stone of Bunker Hill Monument, 1825.

16
Knowledge is the only fountain, both of the love and the principles of human liberty.
DANIEL WEBSTER—*Address Delivered on Bunker Hill, June* 17, 1843.

17
He who binds
His soul to knowledge, steals the key of heaven.
N. P. WILLIS—*The Scholar of Thibèt Ben Khorat*. II.

18
Oh, be wise, Thou!
Instructed that true knowledge leads to love.
WORDSWORTH—*Lines left upon a Seat in a Yew-tree.*

L

19
LABOR (See also WORK)

Labour in vain; or coals to Newcastle.
ANON. In a sermon to the people of Queen-Hith. Advertised in the *Daily Courant*, Oct. 6, 1709. Published in Paternoster Row, London. "Coals to Newcastle," or "from Newcastle," found in HEYWOOD—*If you Know Not Me*. Pt. II. (1606) GAUNT—*Bills of Mortality* (1661) MIDDLETON—*Phœnix*. Act I. Sc. 5. R. THORESBY—*Correspondence. Letter* June 29, 1682. Owls to Athens. (Athenian coins were stamped with the owl.) ARISTOPHANES—*Aves*. 301. DIOGENES LAERTIUS—*Lives of Eminent Philosophers. Plato*. XXXII. You are importing pepper into Hindostan. From the *Bustan* of SADI.
(See also FULLER, HORACE)

20
Qui laborat, orat.
He who labours, prays.
Attr. to ST. AUGUSTINE.
(See also BERNARD, MULOCK, also TENNYSON under PRAYER)

1
Qui orat et laborat, cor levat ad Deum cum manibus.

He who prays and labours lifts his heart to God with his hands.

St. Bernard—*Ad sororem.* A similar expression is found in the works of Gregory the Great—*Moral in Libr. Job.* Bk. XVIII. Also in *Pseudo-Hieron,* in *Jerem.,* Thren. III. 41. See also "What worship, for example, is there not in mere washing!" Carlyle—*Past and Present.* Ch. XV., referring to "Work is prayer."

2
Such hath it been—shall be—beneath the sun
The many still must labour for the one.

Byron—*The Corsair.* Canto I. St. 8.

(See also Shelley, Thompson, Tupper, Watson, also Goldsmith under Government)

3
Not all the labor of the earth
Is done by hardened hands.

Will Carleton—*A Working Woman.*

4
And yet without labour there were no ease, no rest, so much as conceivable.

Carlyle—*Essays. Characteristics.*

5
They can expect nothing but their labor for their pains.

Cervantes—*Don Quixote. Author's Preface.*
Edward Moore—*Boy and the Rainbow.*
(See also Troilus and Cressida)

6
Labor is discovered to be the grand conqueror, enriching and building up nations more surely than the proudest battles.

Wm. Ellery Channing—*War.*

7
Vulgo enim dicitur, *Jucundi acti labores:* nec male Euripides: concludam, si potero, Latine: Græcum enim hunc versum nostis omnes: *Suavis laborum est præteritorum memoria.*

It is generally said, "Past labors are pleasant," Euripides says, for you all know the Greek verse, "The recollection of past labors is pleasant."

Cicero—*De Finibus Bonorum et Malorum.* II. 32.

8
A truly American sentiment recognises the dignity of labor and the fact that honor lies in honest toil.

Cleveland—*Letter accepting the nomination for President.* Aug. 18, 1884.

9
American labor, which is the capital of our workingmen.

Cleveland—*Annual Message.* Dec., 1885.

10
When admirals extoll'd for standing still,
Of doing nothing with a deal of skill.

Cowper—*Table Talk.* L. 192.
(See also Woodward)

11
Honest labour bears a lovely face.

Thos. Dekker—*Patient Grissell.* Act I. Sc. 1.

12
Labour itself is but a sorrowful song,
The protest of the weak against the strong.

F. W. Faber—*The Sorrowful World.*

13
It is so far from being needless pains, that it may bring considerable profit, to carry Charcoals to Newcastle.

Fuller—*Pisgah. Sight of Palestine.* Ed. 1650. P. 128. *Worthies.* P. 302. (Ed. 1661) (See also first Quotation.)

14
For as labor cannot produce without the use of land, the denial of the equal right to the use of land is necessarily the denial of the right of labor to its own produce.

Henry George—*Progress and Poverty.* Bk. VII. Ch. I.

15
How blest is he who crowns in shades like these,
A youth of labour with an age of ease.

Goldsmith—*The Deserted Village.* L. 99.

16
Vitam perdidi laboricose agendo.

I have spent my life laboriously doing nothing.

Quoted by Grotius on his death bed.
(See also Woodward)

17
If little labour, little are our gaines:
Man's fortunes are according to his paines.

Herrick—*Hesperides. No Paines, No Gaines.*

18
To labour is the lot of man below;
And when Jove gave us life, he gave us woe.

Homer—*Iliad.* Bk. X. L. 78. Pope's trans.

19
Our fruitless labours mourn,
And only rich in barren fame return.

Homer—*Odyssey.* Bk. X. L. 46. Pope's trans.

20
With fingers weary and worn,
With eyelids heavy and red,
A woman sat in unwomanly rags,
Plying her needle and thread.

Hood—*Song of the Shirt.*

21
Qui studet optatam cursu contingere metam
Multa tulit fecitque puer, sudavit et alsit.

He who would reach the desired goal must, while a boy, suffer and labor much and bear both heat and cold.

Horace—*Ars Poetica.* CCCCXII.

22
O laborum
Dulce lenimen.

O sweet solace of labors.

Horace—*Carmina.* I. 32. 14.

23
In silvam ligna ferre.

To carry timber into the wood.

Horace—*Satires.* I. 10. 24.
(See also Aristophanes)

24
Cur quæris quietem, quam natus sis ad laborem?

Why seekest thou rest, since thou art born to labor?

Thomas à Kempis—*De Imitatione Christi.* II. 10. 1.

1
The heights by great men reached and kept
Were not attained by sudden flight,
But they, while their companions slept,
Were toiling upward in the night.
LONGFELLOW—*Birds of Passage. The Ladder of St. Augustine.* St. 10.

2
Taste the joy
That springs from labor.
LONGFELLOW—*Masque of Pandora.* Pt. VI. *In the Garden.*

3
From labor there shall come forth rest.
LONGFELLOW—*To a Child.* L. 162.

4
Labor est etiam ipsa voluptas.
Labor is itself a pleasure.
MANILIUS—*Astronomica.* IV. 155.

5
Bowed by the weight of centuries he leans
Upon his hoe and gazes on the ground,
The emptiness of ages in his face,
And on his back the burden of the world.
EDWIN MARKHAM—*The Man with the Hoe.* Written after seeing Millet's picture "Man with the Hoe."

6
But now my task is smoothly done,
I can fly, or I can run.
MILTON—*Comus.* L. 1,012.

7
Lo! all life this truth declares,
Laborare est orare;
And the whole earth rings with prayers.
MISS MULOCK—*Labour is Prayer.* St. 4.
(See also AUGUSTINE)

8
Labor is life! 'Tis the still water faileth;
Idleness ever despaireth, bewaileth;
Keep the watch wound, for the dark rust assaileth.
FRANCES S. OSGOOD—*To Labor is to Pray.*

9
Labor is rest—from the sorrows that greet us;
Rest from all petty vexations that meet us,
Rest from sin-promptings that ever entreat us,
Rest from the world-sirens that hire us to ill.
Work—and pure slumbers shall wait on thy pillow;
Work—thou shalt ride over Care's coming billow;
Lie not down wearied 'neath Woe's weeping willow!
Work with a stout heart and resolute will!
FRANCES S. OSGOOD—*To Labor is to Pray.*

10
Dum vires annique sinunt, tolerate labores.
Jam veniet tacito curva senecta pede.
While strength and years permit, endure labor; soon bent old age will come with silent foot.
OVID—*Ars Amatoria.* II. 669.

11
And all labor without any play, boys,
Makes Jack a dull boy in the end.
H. A. PAGE—*Vers de Société.*

12
Grex venalium.
The herd of hirelings. (A venal pack.)
PLAUTUS—*Cistellaria.* IV. 2. 67.

13
Oleum et operam perdidi.
I have lost my oil and my labor. (Labored in vain.)
PLAUTUS—*Pœnulus.* I. 2. 119.

14
The man who by his labour gets
His bread, in independent state,
Who never begs, and seldom eats,
Himself can fix or change his fate
PRIOR—*The Old Gentry.*

15
Why, Hal, 'tis my vocation. Hal: 'tis no sin for a man to labour in his vocation.
Henry IV. Pt. I. Act I. Sc. 2. L. 116.

16
The labour we delight in physics pain.
Macbeth. Act II. Sc. 3. L. 55.

17
I have had my labour for my travail.
Troilus and Cressida. Act I. Sc. 1. L. 72.
(See also CERVANTES)

18
Many faint with toil,
That few may know the cares and woe of sloth.
SHELLEY—*Queen Mab.* Canto III.
(See also BYRON)

19
Labour of love.
I Thessalonians. I. 3.

20
With starving labor pampering idle waste;
To tear at pleasure the defected land.
THOMSON—*Liberty.* Pt. IV. L. 1160.
(See also BYRON)

21
The labourer is worthy of his reward.
I Timothy. V. 18; *Luke.* X. 7. (hire)

22
Clamorous pauperism feasteth
While honest Labor, pining, hideth his sharp ribs.
MARTIN TUPPER—*Of Discretion.*
(See also BYRON)

23
Labor omnia vincit improbus.
Stubborn labor conquers everything.
VERGIL—*Georgics.* I. 145.

24
Too long, that some may rest,
Tired millions toil unblest.
WILLIAM WATSON—*New National Anthem.*
(See also BYRON)

25
Labor in this country is independent and proud. It has not to ask the patronage of capital, but capital solicits the aid of labor.
DANIEL WEBSTER—*Speech.* April, 1824.

26
Ah, little recks the laborer,
How near his work is holding him to God,
The loving Laborer through space and time.
WALT WHITMAN—*Song of the Exposition.* I.

27
Ah vitam perdidi operse nihil agendo.
Ah, my life is lost in laboriously doing nothing.
JOSIAH WOODWARD—*Fair Warnings to a Careless World.* P. 97. Ed. 1736, quoting Méric Casaubon.
(See also COWPER, GROTIUS; also HORACE under IDLENESS)

LAMB

1
Mary had a little lamb
Its fleece was white as snow,
And everywhere that Mary went
The lamb was sure to go.

Mrs. Sarah J. Hale—*Mary's Little Lamb.* First pub. in her Poems for our Children, 1830. Claimed for John Roulston by Mary Sawyer Tyler. Disproved by Mrs. Hale's son, in Letter to *Boston Transcript,* April 10, 1889. Mrs. Hale definitely asserted her claim to authorship before her death.

LANGUAGE (See also Linguist, Speech, Words)

2
Well languag'd Danyel.

William Browne—*Britannia's Pastorals.* Bk. II. Song 2. L. 303.

3
Pedantry consists in the use of words unsuitable to the time, place, and company.

Coleridge—*Biographia Literaria.* Ch. X.

4
And who in time knows whither we may vent
The treasure of our tongue? To what strange shores
This gain of our best glory shall be sent,
T' enrich unknowing nations with our stores?
What worlds in th' yet unformed Occident
May come refin'd with th' accents that are ours?

Sam. Daniel—*Musophilus.* Last lines.

5
Who climbs the grammar-tree, distinctly knows
Where noun, and verb, and participle grows.

Dryden—*Sixth Satire of Juvenal.* L. 583.

6
Language is fossil poetry.

Emerson—*Essays. The Poet.*

7
Language is a city to the building of which every human being brought a stone.

Emerson—*Letters and Social Aims. Quotation and Originality.*

8
And don't confound the language of the nation
With long-tailed words in *osity* and *ation.*

J. Hookham Frere—*King Arthur and his Round Table. Introduction.* St. 6.

9
Language is the only instrument of science, and words are but the signs of ideas.

Samuel Johnson—*Preface to his English Dictionary.*

10
L'accent du pays où l'on est né demeure dans l'esprit et dans le cœur comme dans le langage.

The accent of one's country dwells in the mind and in the heart as much as in the language.

La Rochefoucauld—*Maximes.* 342.

11
Writ in the climate of heaven, in the language spoken by angels.

Longfellow—*The Children of the Lord's Supper.* L. 262.

12
La grammaire, qui sait régenter jusqu'aux rois,
Et les fait, la main haute, obéir à ses lois.

Grammar, which knows how to lord it over kings, and with high hands makes them obey its laws.

Molière—*Les Femmes Savantes.* II. 6.

13
Une louange en grec est d'une merveilleuse efficace à la tête d'un livre.

A laudation in Greek is of marvellous efficacy on the title-page of a book.

Molière—*Preface. Les Précieuses Ridicules.*

14
L'accent est l'âme du discours, il lui donne le sentiment et la vérité.

Accent is the soul of a language; it gives the feeling and truth to it.

Rousseau—*Emile.* I.

15
Syllables govern the world.

John Selden—*Table Talk. Power.*

16
He has strangled
His language in his tears.

Henry VIII. Act V. Sc. 1. L. 158.

17
Thou whoreson Zed! thou unnecessary letter!

King Lear. Act II. Sc. 2. L. 66.

18
You taught me language; and my profit on't
Is, I know how to curse. The red plague rid you
For learning me your language!

Tempest. Act I. Sc. 2. L. 363.

19
Fie, fie upon her!
There's language in her eye, her cheek, her lip,
Nay, her foot speaks; her wanton spirits look out
At every joint and motive of her body.

Troilus and Cressida. Act IV. Sc. 5. L. 55.

20
There was speech in their dumbness, language in their very gesture.

Winter's Tale. Act V. Sc. 2. L. 12.

21
Ego sum rex Romanus, et supra grammaticam.

I am the King of Rome, and above grammar.

Sigismund. At the Council of Constance. (1414) To a prelate who objected to his grammar.

(See also Molière)

22
Don Chaucer, well of English undefyled
On Fame's eternall beadroll worthie to be fyled.

Spenser—*Faerie Queene.* IV. 2. 32.

(See also Whittier)

23
Language is the expression of ideas, and if the people of one country cannot preserve an identity of ideas they cannot retain an identity of language.

Noah Webster—*Preface to Dictionary.* Ed. of 1828.

24
From purest wells of English undefiled
None deeper drank than he, the New World's Child,
Who in the language of their farm field spoke
The wit and wisdom of New England folk.

Whittier—*James Russell Lowell.*

(See also Spenser)

25
Oft on the dappled turf at ease
I sit, and play with similes,
Loose type of things through all degrees.

Wordsworth—*To the Daisy.*

LAPWING

1
Changed to a lapwing by th' avenging god,
He made the barren waste his lone abode,
And oft on soaring pinions hover'd o'er
The lofty palace then his own no more.
BEATTIE—*Vergil*. Pastoral 6.

2
The false lapwynge, full of trecherye.
CHAUCER—*The Parlement of Fowles*. L. 47.

3
Amid thy desert-walks the lapwing flies,
And tires their echoes with unvaried cries.
GOLDSMITH—*Deserted Village*. L. 44.

4
For look where Beatrice, like a lapwing, runs
Close by the ground, to hear our conference.
Much Ado About Nothing. Act III. Sc. 1. L. 25.

LARK

5
The music soars within the little lark,
And the lark soars.
E. B. BROWNING—*Aurora Leigh*. Bk. III. L. 155.

6
Oh, stay, sweet warbling woodlark, stay,
Nor quit for me the trembling spray,
A hapless lover courts thy lay,
Thy soothing, fond complaining.
BURNS—*Address to the Woodlark*.

7
The merry lark he soars on high,
No worldly thought o'ertakes him.
He sings aloud to the clear blue sky,
And the daylight that awakes him.
HARTLEY COLERIDGE—*Song*.

8
The lark now leaves his watery nest,
And climbing, shakes his dewy wings.
He takes your window for the East
And to implore your light he sings.
SIR WILLIAM DAVENANT — *The Lark now Leaves his Watery Nest*.

9
The pretty Lark, climbing the Welkin cleer,
Chaunts with a cheer, Heer peer—I neer my Deer;
Then stooping thence (seeming her fall to rew)
Adieu (she saith) adieu, deer Deer, adieu.
DU BARTAS—*Weekes and Workes*. Fifth Day.

10
Musical cherub, soar, singing, away!
Then, when the gloaming comes,
Low in the heather blooms
Sweet will thy welcome and bed of love be!
Emblem of happiness,
Blest is thy dwelling-place—
O, to abide in the desert with thee!
HOGG—*The Skylark*.

11
Rise with the lark, and with the lark to bed.
HURDIS—*The Village Curate*. L. 276.

12
None but the lark so shrill and clear;
Now at heaven's gate she claps her wings,
The morn not waking till she sings.
LYLY—*Alexander and Campaspe*. Act V. Sc. 1. (See also CYMBELINE)

13
To hear the lark begin his flight,
And singing startle the dull Night,
From his watch-tower in the skies,
Till the dappled dawn doth rise.
MILTON—*L'Allegro*. L. 41.

14
And now the herald lark
Left his ground-nest, high tow'ring to descry
The morn's approach, and greet her with his song.
MILTON—*Paradise Regained*. Bk. II. L. 279.

15
The bird that soars on highest wing,
Builds on the ground her lowly nest;
And she that doth most sweetly sing,
Sings in the shade when all things rest:
In lark and nightingale we see
What honor hath humility.
MONTGOMERY—*Humility*.

16
I said to the sky-poised Lark:
"Hark—hark!
Thy note is more loud and free
Because there lies safe for thee
A little nest on the ground."
D. M. MULOCK—*A Rhyme About Birds*.

17
No more the mounting larks, while Daphne sings,
Shall, list'ning, in mid-air suspend their wings.
POPE—*Pastorals. Winter*. L. 53.

18
The sunrise wakes the lark to sing.
CHRISTINA G. ROSSETTI—*Bird Raptures*.

19
O happy skylark springing
Up to the broad, blue sky,
Too fearless in thy winging,
Too gladsome in thy singing,
Thou also soon shalt lie
Where no sweet notes are ringing.
CHRISTINA G. ROSSETTI—*Gone Forever*. St. 2.

20
Then my dial goes not true; I took this lark for a bunting.
All's Well That Ends Well—Act II. Sc. 5. L. 5.

21
Hark! hark! the lark at heaven's gate sings,
And Phœbus 'gins arise,
His steeds to water at those springs
On chalic'd flowers that lies.
And winking Mary-buds begin
To ope their golden eyes;
With everything that pretty is,
My lady sweet, arise!
Cymbeline. Act II. Sc. 3. *Song*. L. 21.
(See also LYLY)

22
Some say, that ever 'gainst that season comes
Wherein our Saviour's birth is celebrated,
The bird of dawning singeth all night long:
And then, they say, no spirit dare stir abroad;
The nights are wholesome; then no planets strike,
No fairy takes, nor witch hath power to charm,
So hallow'd and so gracious is the time.
Hamlet. Act I. Sc. 1. L. 158.

23
It was the lark, the herald of the morn.
Romeo and Juliet. Act III. Sc. 5. L. 6.

1
It is the lark that sings so out of tune,
Straining harsh discords and unpleasing sharps.
Romeo and Juliet. Act III. Sc. 5. L. 27

2
Lo! here the gentle lark, weary of rest,
From his moist cabinet mounts up on high,
And wakes the morning, from whose silver breast
The sun ariseth in his majesty.
Venus and Adonis. L. 853.

3
Hail to thee blithe Spirit!
Bird thou never wert,
That from Heaven, or near it,
Pourest thy full heart
In profuse strains of unpremeditated art.
SHELLEY—*To a Skylark.* St. 1.
(See also WORDSWORTH under CUCKOO)

4
Better than all measures
Of delightful sound,
Better than all treasures
That in books are found,
Thy skill to poet were, thou scorner of the ground!
SHELLEY—*To a Skylark.* St. 20.

5
Up springs the lark,
Shrill-voiced, and loud, the messenger of morn;
Ere yet the shadows fly, he mounted sings
Amid the dawning clouds, and from their haunts
Calls up the tuneful nations.
THOMSON—*The Seasons. Spring.* L. 587.

6
The lark that shuns on lofty boughs to build
Her humble nest, lies silent in the field.
EDMUND WALLER—*Of the Queen.*

7
Ethereal minstrel! pilgrim of the sky!
Dost thou despise the earth where cares abound?
Or, while the wings aspire, are heart and eye
Both with thy nest upon the dewy ground?
Thy nest which thou canst drop into at will,
Those quivering wings composed, that music still!
WORDSWORTH—*Poems of the Imagination. To a Skylark.*

8
Leave to the nightingale her shady wood;
A privacy of glorious light is thine:
Whence thou dost pour upon the world a flood
Of harmony, with instinct more divine:
Type of the wise who soar, but never roam:
True to the kindred points of Heaven and Home!
WORDSWORTH—*Poems of the Imagination. To a Skylark.*

LAUGHTER

9
He laughs best who laughs last.
Old English Proverb.
Better the last smile than the first laughter.
RAY—*Collection of Old English Proverbs.*
Il rit bien qui rit le dernier. (French)
Rira bien que rira le dernier. (French)
Ride bene chi ride l'ultimo. (Italian)
Wer zuletzt lacht, lacht am besten. (German)
Den leer bedst som leer sidst. (Danish)
(See also OTHELLO)

10
Je me hâte de me moquer de tous, de peur d'être obligé d'en pleurer.
I hasten to laugh at everything, for fear of being obliged to weep.
BEAUMARCHAIS—*Barbier de Séville.* Act I. Sc. 2. (See also BYRON)

11
When the green woods laugh with the voice of joy,
And the dimpling stream runs laughing by;
When the air does laugh with our merry wit,
And the green hill laughs with the noise of it.
WILLIAM BLAKE—*Laughing Song.*

12
Truth's sacred fort th' exploded laugh shall win,
And coxcombs vanquish Berkeley with a grin.
JOHN BROWN—*Essay on Satire.* Pt. II. V. 224. *On the death of Pope.* Prefixed to POPE'S *Essay on Man,* in WARBURTON'S Ed. of Pope's Works.

13
The landlord's laugh was ready chorus.
BURNS—*Tam o' Shanter.*

14
And if I laugh at any mortal thing,
'Tis that I may not weep.
BYRON—*Don Juan.* Canto IV. St. 4.
(See also BEAUMARCHAIS)

15
How much lies in Laughter: the cipher-key, wherewith we decipher the whole man.
CARLYLE—*Sartor Resartus.* Bk. I. Ch. IV.

16
Nam risu inepto res ineptior nulla est.
Nothing is more silly than silly laughter.
CATULLUS—*Carmina.* XXXIX. 16.

17
La plus perdue de toutes les journées est celle où l'on n'a pas rit.
The most completely lost of all days is that on which one has not laughed.
CHAMFORT.

18
The vulgar only laugh, but never smile; whereas well-bred people often smile, but seldom laugh.
CHESTERFIELD—*Letter to his Son.* Feb. 17, 1754.
(See also HERBERT, MEYNELL)

19
Loud laughter is the mirth of the mob, who are only pleased with silly things; for true wit or good sense never excited a laugh since the creation of the world.
CHESTERFIELD—*Letters.* Vol. I. P. 211. Ed. by MAHON.

20
A gentleman is often seen, but very seldom heard to laugh.
CHESTERFIELD—*Letters.* Vol. II. P. 164; also 404. Ed. by MAHÓN.

21
Cio ch'io vedeva mi sembrava un riso
Dell' universo.
What I saw was equal ecstasy:
One universal smile it seemed of all things.
DANTE—*Paradiso.* XXVII. 5.

22
As the crackling of thorns under a pot, so is the laughter of a fool.
Ecclesiastes. VII. 6.

1
Ce n'est pas être bien aisé que de rire.
He is not always at ease who laughs.
St. Evremond.

2
I have known sorrow—therefore I
May laugh with you, O friend, more merrily
Than those who never sorrowed upon earth
And know not laughter's worth.

I have known laughter—therefore I
May sorrow with you far more tenderly
Than those who never guess how sad a thing
Seems merriment to one heart's suffering.
Theodosia Garrison—*Knowledge.*

3
I am the laughter of the new-born child
On whose soft-breathing sleep an angel smiled.
R. W. Gilder—*Ode.*

4
Your laugh is of the sardonic kind.
Caius Gracchus. When his adversaries laughed at his defeat.

5
Low gurgling laughter, as sweet
As the swallow's song i' the South,
And a ripple of dimples that, dancing, meet
By the curves of a perfect mouth.
Paul Hamilton Hayne—*Ariel.*

6
Laugh not too much; the witty man laughs least:
For wit is news only to ignorance.
Lesse at thine own things laugh; lest in the jest
Thy person share, and the conceit advance.
Herbert—*The Temple. Church Porch.* St. 39. (See also Chesterfield)

7
And unextinguish'd laughter shakes the skies.
Homer—*Iliad.* Bk. I. L. 771. *Odyssey.* Bk. VIII. L. 116. Pope's trans.

8
Discit enim citius, meminitque libentius ilud
Quod quis deridet, quam quod probat et veneratur.

For a man learns more quickly and remembers more easily that which he laughs at, than that which he approves and reveres.
Horace—*Epistles.* Bk. II. 1. 262.

9
Laugh, and be fat, sir, your penance is known.
They that love mirth, let them heartily drink,
'Tis the only receipt to make sorrow sink.
Ben Jonson—*Entertainments. The Penates.*

10
We must laugh before we are happy, for fear we die before we laugh at all.
La Bruyère—*The Characters or Manners of the Present Age.* Ch. IV.

11
The sense of humor has other things to do than to make itself conspicuous in the act of laughter.
Alice Meynell—*Laughter.*
(See also Chesterfield)

12
Haste thee, Nymph, and bring with thee
Jest, and youthful Jollity,
Quips, and Cranks, and wanton Wiles,
Nods, and Becks, and wreathed Smiles,
Such as hang on Hebe's cheek,
And love to live in dimple sleek;
Sport that wrinkled Care derides,
And Laughter holding both his sides.
Milton—*L'Allegro.* L. 25.

13
To laugh, if but for an instant only, has never been granted to man before the fortieth day from his birth, and then it is looked upon as a miracle of precocity.
Pliny the Elder—*Natural History.* Bk. VII. Ch. I. Holland's trans.

14
Laugh at your friends, and if your friends are sore;
So much the better, you may laugh the more.
Pope—*Epilogue to Satire.* Dialogue I. L. 55.

15
The man that loves and laughs must sure do well.
Pope—*Imitations of Horace.* Ep. VI. Bk. I. L. 129.

16
To laugh were want of goodness and of grace;
And to be grave, exceeds all pow'r of face.
Pope—*Prologue to Satires.* L. 35.

17
Nimium risus pretium est, si probitatis impendio constat.

A laugh costs too much when bought at the expense of virtue.
Quintilian—*De Institutione Oratoria.* VI. 3. 5.

18
One inch of joy surmounts of grief a span,
Because to laugh is proper to the man.
Rabelais—*To the Readers.*

19
Tel qui rit vendredi, dimanche pleurera.

He who laughs on Friday will weep on Sunday.
Racine—*Plaideurs.* I. 1.

20
Is he gone to a land of no laughter,
The man who made mirth for us all?
James Rhoades—*Death of Artemus Ward.*

21
Niemand wird tiefer traurig als wer zu viel lächelt.

No one will be more profoundly sad than he who laughs too much.
Jean Paul Richter—*Hesperus.* XIX.

22
Castigat ridendo mores.
He chastizes manners with a laugh.
Santeul—*Motto of the Comédie Italienne, and Opéra Comique.* Paris.

23
With his eyes in flood with laughter.
Cymbeline. Act I. Sc. 6. L. 74.

24
O, you shall see him laugh till his face be like a wet cloak ill laid up.
Henry IV. Pt. II. Act V. Sc. 1. L. 88.

25
The brain of this foolish-compounded clay, man, is not able to invent anything that tends to laughter, more than I invent or is invented on me.
Henry IV. Pt. II. Act I. Sc. 2. L. 6.

26
O, I am stabb'd with laughter.
Love's Labour's Lost. Act V. Sc. 2. L. 79.

1
They laugh that win.
Othello. Act IV. Sc. 1. L. 124.
(See also first quotation)

2
Laughter almost ever cometh of things most disproportioned to ourselves and nature: delight hath a joy in it either permanent or present; laughter hath only a scornful tickling.
SIR PHILIP SIDNEY—*The Defence of Poesy.*

3
Laugh and be fat.
JOHN TAYLOR—*Title of a Tract.* (1615)

4
For still the World prevail'd, and its dread
laugh,
Which scarce the firm Philosopher can scorn.
THOMSON—*The Seasons. Autumn.* L. 233.

5
Fight Virtue's cause, stand up in Wit's defence,
Win us from vice and laugh us into sense.
TICKELL—*On the Prospect of Peace.* St. 38.

6
Laugh and the world laughs with you,
Weep and you weep alone;
For the sad old earth must borrow its mirth,
But has trouble enough of its own.
ELLA WHEELER WILCOX—*Solitude.* Claimed by COL. JOHN A. JOYCE, who had it engraved on his tombstone.

7
Care to our coffin adds a nail, no doubt;
And every Grin, so merry, draws one out.
JOHN WOLCOT (Peter Pindar)—*Expostulatory Odes. Ode* 15.

8
The house of laughter makes a house of woe.
YOUNG—*Night Thoughts.* Night VIII. L. 757.

LAUREL

9
Laurus Nobilis
The laurel-tree grew large and strong,
Its roots went searching deeply down;
It split the marble walls of Wrong,
And blossomed o'er the Despot's crown.
RICHARD HENGIST HORNE—*The Laurel Seed.*

10
This flower that smells of honey and the sea,
White laurustine, seems in my hand to be
A white star made of memory long ago
Lit in the heaven of dear times dead to me.
SWINBURNE—*Relics.*

LAW

11
Ove son leggi,
Tremar non dee chi leggi non infranse.
Where there are laws, he who has not broken them need not tremble.
ALFIERI—*Virginia.* II. 1.

12
Law is king of all.
HENRY ALFORD—*School of the Heart.* Lesson 6.

13
Written laws are like spiders' webs, and will like them only entangle and hold the poor and weak, while the rich and powerful will easily break through them.
ANACHARSIS to SOLON when writing his laws.
(See also SOLON for answer; and BACON, SHENSTONE, SWIFT)

14
Law is a bottomless pit.
J. ARBUTHNOT—*Title of a Pamphlet.* (About 1700)

15
One of the Seven was wont to say: "That laws were like cobwebs; where the small flies were caught, and the great brake through."
BACON—*Apothegms.* No. 181.
(See also ANACHARSIS)

16
All this is but a web of the wit; it can work nothing.
BACON—*Essays on Empire.*

17
There was an ancient Roman lawyer, of great fame in the history of Roman jurisprudence, whom they called Cui Bono, from his having first introduced into judicial proceedings the argument, "What end or object could the party have had in the act with which he is accused."
BURKE—*Impeachment of Warren Hastings.*

18
I do not know the method of drawing up an indictment against an whole people.
BURKE—*Speech on the Conciliation of America.*

19
A good parson once said that where mystery begins religion ends. Cannot I say, as truly at least, of human laws, that where mystery begins, justice ends?
BURKE—*Vindication of Natural Society.*

20
The law of England is the greatest grievance of the nation, very expensive and dilatory.
BISHOP BURNET—*History of His Own Times.*

21
Our wrangling lawyers * * * are so litigious and busy here on earth, that I think they will plead their clients' causes hereafter, some of them in hell.
BURTON—*Anatomy of Melancholy. Democritus to the Reader.*

22
Your pettifoggers damn their souls,
To share with knaves in cheating fools.
BUTLER—*Hudibras.* Pt. II. Canto I. L. 515.

23
Is not the winding up witnesses,
And nicking, more than half the bus'ness?
For witnesses, like watches, go
Just as they're set, too fast or slow;
And where in Conscience they're strait-lac'd,
'Tis ten to one that side is cast.
BUTLER—*Hudibras.* Pt. II. Canto II. L. 359.

24
The law of heaven and earth is life for life.
BYRON—*The Curse of Minerva.* St. 15.

25
Arms and laws do not flourish together.
JULIUS CÆSAR. PLUTARCH—*Life of Cæsar.*
(See also CICERO, MARIUS, MONTAIGNE)

26
Who to himself is law, no law doth need,
Offends no law, and is a king indeed.
GEORGE CHAPMAN—*Bussy d'Ambois.* Act II. Sc. 1.

27
Jus gentium.
The law of nations.
CICERO—*De Officiis.* III. 17.

1
For as the law is set over the magistrate, even so are the magistrates set over the people. And therefore, it may be truly said, "that the magistrate is a speaking law, and the law is a silent magistrate."

CICERO—*On the Laws.* Bk. III. I.

2
Silent enim leges inter arma.

For the laws are dumb in the midst of arms.

CICERO—*Pro Milone.* IV.

(See also CÆSAR)

3
After an existence of nearly twenty years of almost innocuous desuetude these laws are brought forth.

GROVER CLEVELAND—*Message.* March 1, 1886.

4
Magna Charta is such a fellow that he will have no sovereign.

SIR EDWARD COKE—*Debate in the Commons.* May 17, 1628.

5
Reason is the life of the law; nay, the common law itself is nothing else but reason. * * * The law which is perfection of reason.

SIR EDWARD COKE—*First Institute.*

(See also POWELL)

6
The gladsome light of jurisprudence.

SIR EDWARD COKE—*First Institute.*

7
According to the law of the Medes and Persians, which altereth not.

Daniel. VI. 8.

8
Trial by jury itself, instead of being a security to persons who are accused, shall be a delusion, a mockery, and a snare.

LORD DENMAN—In his *Judgment* in *O'Connell vs. the Queen.* II. C. and F., 351. Sept. 4, 1894.

9
Whatever was required to be done, the Circumlocution Office was beforehand with all the public departments in the art of perceiving—HOW NOT TO DO IT.

DICKENS—*Little Dorrit.* Pt. I. Ch. X.

10
"If the law supposes that," said Mr. Bumble, "the law is a ass, a idiot."

DICKENS—*Oliver Twist.* Ch. LI.

11
If it's near dinner time, the foreman takes out his watch when the jury have retired and says: "Dear me, gentlemen, ten minutes to five, I declare! I dine at five, gentlemen." "So do I," says everybody else except two men who ought to have dined at three, and seem more than half disposed to stand out in consequence. The foreman smiles, and puts up his watch: "Well, gentlemen, what do we say? Plaintiff, defendant, gentlemen? I rather think so far as I am concerned, gentlemen—I say I rather think—but don't let that influence you—I rather think the plaintiff's the man." Upon this two or three other men are sure to say they think so too—as of course they do; and then they get on very unanimously and comfortably.

DICKENS—*Pickwick Papers.* Vol. II. Ch. VI.

12
I know'd what 'ud come o' this here mode o' doin' business. Oh, Sammy, Sammy, vy worn't there a alleybi!

DICKENS—*Pickwick Papers.* Vol. II. Ch. VI.

13
When the judges shall be obliged to go armed, it will be time for the courts to be closed.

S. J. FIELD—*When advised to arm himself. California.* (1889)

14
Our human laws are but the copies, more or less imperfect, of the eternal laws, so far as we can read them.

FROUDE—*Short Studies on Great Subjects. Calvinism.*

15
Just laws are no restraint upon the freedom of the good, for the good man desires nothing which a just law will interfere with.

FROUDE—*Short Studies on Great Subjects. Reciprocal Duties of State and Subject.*

16
Whenever the offence inspires less horror than the punishment, the rigour of penal law is obliged to give way to the common feelings of mankind.

GIBBON—*The Decline and Fall of the Roman Empire.* Ch. XIV. Vol. I.

17
Es erben sich Gesetz und Rechte
Wie eine ew'ge Krankheit fort.

All rights and laws are still transmitted,
Like an eternal sickness to the race.

GOETHE—*Faust.* I. 4. 449.

18
Laws grind the poor, and rich men rule the law.

GOLDSMITH—*The Traveller.* L. 386. Same in *Vicar of Wakefield.*

19
I know no method to secure the repeal of bad or obnoxious laws so effective as their stringent execution.

U. S. GRANT—*Inaugural Address.* March 4, 1869.

20
A cloud of witnesses.

Hebrews. XII. 1.

21
Quid leges sine moribus
Vanæ proficiunt?

Of what use are laws, inoperative through public immorality?

HORACE—*Carmina.* III. 24. 35.

22
To the law and to the testimony.

Isaiah. VIII. 20.

23
The law is the last result of human wisdom acting upon human experience for the benefit of the public.

SAMUEL JOHNSON. *Johnsoniana.* Piozzi's Anecdotes, 58.

24
Dat veniam corvis, vexat censura columbas.

The verdict acquits the raven, but condemns the dove.

JUVENAL—*Satires.* II. 63.

1
Ad quæstionem juris respondeant judices ad quæstionem facti respondeant juratores.
Let the judges answer to the question of law, and the jurors to the matter of the fact.
Law Maxim.

2
We must never assume that which is incapable of proof.
G. H. LEWES—*The Physiology of Common Life.* Ch. XIII.

3
Hominem improbum non accusari tutius est quam absolvi.
It is safer that a bad man should not be accused, than that he should be acquitted.
LIVY—*Annales.* XXXIV. 4.

4
La charte sera désormais une vérité.
The charter will henceforth be a reality.
LOUIS PHILIPPE.

5
And folks are beginning to think it looks odd,
To choke a poor scamp for the glory of God.
LOWELL—*A Fable for Critics.* L. 492.

6
Perchè, cosi come i buoni costumi, per mantenersi, hanno bisogno delli leggi; cosi le leggi per ossevarsi, hanno bisogno de' buoni costumi.
For as laws are necessary that good manners may be preserved, so there is need of good manners that laws may be maintained.
MACHIAVELLI—*Dei Discorsi.* I. 18.

7
The law is a sort of hocus-pocus science, that smiles in yeer face while it picks yeer pocket: and the glorious uncertainty of it is of mair use to the professors than the justice of it.
MACKLIN—*Love à la Mode.* Act II. Sc. 1.

8
Nisi per legale judicium parum suorum.
Unless by the lawful judgment of their peers.
Magna Charta. Privilege of Barons of Parliament.

9
Certis * * * legibus omnia parent.
All things obey fixed laws.
MANILIUS—*Astronomica.* I. 479.

10
The law speaks too softly to be heard amidst the din of arms.
CAIUS MARIUS. When complaint was made of his granting the freedom of Rome to a thousand Camerians. In PLUTARCH'S *Life of Caius Marius.*
(See also CÆSAR)

11
Render therefore unto Cæsar the things which are Cæsar's.
Matthew. XXII. 21.

12
As the case stands.
MIDDLETON—*Old Law.* Act II. Sc. 1.

13
Litigious terms, fat contentions, and flowing fees.
MILTON—*Prose Works.* Vol. I. *Of Education.*

14
Le bruit des armes l'empeschoit d'entendre la voix des lois.
The clatter of arms drowns the voice of the law.
MONTAIGNE—*Essays.* III. I.
(See also CÆSAR)

15
There is no man so good, who, were he to submit all his thoughts and actions to the laws would not deserve hanging ten times in his life.
MONTAIGNE—*Essays. Of Vanity.*

16
Neque enim lex est æquior ulla,
Quam necis artifices arte perire sua.
Nor is there any law more just, than that he who has plotted death shall perish by his own plot.
OVID—*Ars Amatoria.* I. 665.
(See also BYRON)

17
Sunt superis sua jura.
The gods have their own laws.
OVID—*Metamorphoses.* IX. 499.

18
Where law ends, there tyranny begins.
WILLIAM PITT (Earl of Chatham)—*Case of Wilkes. Speech.* Jan. 9, 1770. Last line.

19
Nescis tu quam meticulosa res sit ire ad judicem.
You little know what a ticklish thing it is to go to law.
PLAUTUS—*Mostellaria.* V. 1. 52.

20
Non est princeps super leges, sed leges supra principem.
The prince is not above the laws, but the laws above the prince.
PLINY THE YOUNGER—*Paneg. Traj.* 65.

21
Curse on all laws but those which love has made.
POPE—*Eloisa to Abelard.* L. 74.

22
All, look up with reverential awe,
At crimes that 'scape, or triumph o'er the law.
POPE—*Epilogue to Satire.* Dialogue I. L. 167.

23
Mark what unvary'd laws preserve each state,
Laws wise as Nature, and as fixed as Fate.
POPE—*Essay on Man.* Ep. III. L. 189.

24
Piecemeal they win this acre first then, that,
Glean on, and gather up the whole estate.
POPE—*Satires of Dr. Donne.* Satire II. L. 91.

25
Once (says an Author; where, I need not say)
Two Trav'lers found an Oyster in their way;
Both fierce, both hungry; the dispute grew strong,
While Scale in hand Dame Justice pass'd along.
Before her each with clamour pleads the Laws.
Explain'd the matter, and would win the cause,
Dame Justice weighing long the doubtful Right,
Takes, open, swallows it, before their sight.
The cause of strife remov'd so rarely well,
"There take" (says Justice), "take ye each a shell.
We thrive at Westminster on Fools like you:
'Twas a fat oyster—live in peace—Adieu."
POPE—*Verbatim from Boileau.*

26
Let us consider the reasons of the case. For nothing is law that is not reason.
SIR JOHN POWELL—*Coggs vs. Bernard. 2 Ld. Raym. 911.*
(See also COKE)

1
He that is surety for a stranger shall smart for it.
Proverbs. XI. 15.

2
That very law which moulds a tear,
And bids it trickle from its source,
That law preserves the earth a sphere,
And guides the planets in their course.
SAM'L ROGERS—*On a Tear.* St. 6.

3
La loi permet souvent ce que défend l'honneur.
The law often allows what honor forbids.
SAURIN—*Spartacus.* III. 3.

4
Si judicas, cognosce; si regnas, jube.
If you judge, investigate; if you reign, command.
SENECA—*Medea.* CXCIV.

5
Qui statuit aliquid, parte inaudita altera,
Æquum licet statuerit, haud æquus fuerit.
He who decides a case without hearing the other side, though he decide justly, cannot be considered just.
SENECA—*Medea.* CXCIX.

6
Inertis est nescire, quid liceat sibi.
Id facere, laus est, quod decet; non, quod licet.
It is the act of the indolent not to know what he may lawfully do. It is praiseworthy to do what is becoming, and not merely what is lawful.
SENECA—*Octavia.* CCCCLIII.

7
There is a higher law than the Constitution.
W. H. SEWARD—*Speech.* March 11, 1850.

8
You who wear out a good wholesome forenoon in hearing a cause between an orange-wife and a fosset-seller; and then rejourn the controversy of three pence to a second day of audience.
Coriolanus. Act II. Sc. 1. L. 77.

9
He hath resisted law,
And therefore law shall scorn him further trial
Than the severity of the public power.
Coriolanus. Act III. Sc. 1. L. 267.

10
In the corrupted currents of this world,
Offence's gilded hand may shove by justice;
And oft 'tis seen the wicked prize itself
Buys out the law: but 'tis not so above;
There is no shuffling, there the action lies
In his true nature; and we ourselves compell'd,
Even to the teeth and forehead of our faults,
To give in evidence.
Hamlet. Act III. Sc. 3. L. 57.

11
But is this law?
Ay, marry is 't; crowner's quest law.
Hamlet. Act V. Sc. 1. L. 23.

12
But, I prithee, sweet wag, shall there be gallows standing in England when thou art king? and resolution thus fobbed as it is with the rusty curb of old father antic the law?
Henry IV. Pt. I. Act I. Sc. 2. L. 65.

13
Faith, I have been a truant in the law,
And never yet could frame my will to it;
And therefore frame the law unto my will.
Henry VI. Pt. I. Act II. Sc. 4. L. 7.

14
But in these nice sharp quillets of the law,
Good faith, I am no wiser than a daw.
Henry VI. Pt. I. Act II. Sc. 4. L. 11.

15
The first thing we do, let's kill all the lawyers.
Henry VI. Pt. II. Act IV. Sc. 2. L. 84.

16
Press not a falling man too far! 'tis virtue:
His faults lie open to the laws; let them,
Not you, correct him.
Henry VIII. Act III. Sc. 2. L. 333.

17
When law can do no right,
Let it be lawful that law bar no wrong.
King John. Act III. Sc. 1. L. 185.

18
'Tis like the breath of an unfee'd lawyer; you gave me nothing for 't.
King Lear. Act I. Sc. 4. L. 142.

19
Bold of your worthiness, we single you
As our best-moving fair solicitor.
Love's Labour's Lost. Act II. Sc. 1. L. 28.

20
We have strict statutes and most biting laws.
Measure for Measure. Act I. Sc. 3. L. 19.

21
We must not make a scarecrow of the law,
Setting it up to fear the birds of prey,
And let it keep one shape, till custom make it
Their perch and not their terror.
Measure for Measure. Act II. Sc. 1. L. 1.

22
To offend, and judge, are distinct offices
And of opposed natures.
Merchant of Venice. Act II. Sc. 9. L. 61.

23
In law, what plea so tainted and corrupt
But, being season'd with a gracious voice,
Obscures the show of evil?
Merchant of Venice. Act III. Sc. 2. L. 75.

24
It must not be; there is no power in Venice
Can alter a decree established:
'Twill be recorded for a precedent;
And many an error by the same example
Will rush into the state.
Merchant of Venice. Act IV. Sc. 1. L. 218.

25
The bloody book of law
You shall yourself read in the bitter letter
After your own sense.
Othello. Act I. Sc. 3. L. 67.

26
I am a subject,
And I challenge law: attorneys are denied me;
And therefore personally I lay my claim
To my inheritance of free descent.
Richard II. Act II. Sc. 3. L. 133.

27
Before I be convict by course of law,
To threaten me with death is most unlawful.
Richard III. Act I. Sc. 4. L. 192.

1
Do as adversaries do in law,
Strive mightily, but eat and drink as friends.
Taming of the Shrew. Act I. Sc. 2. L. 278.

2
We are for law; he dies.
Timon of Athens. Act III. Sc. 5. L. 86.

3
They have been grand-jurymen since before Noah was a sailor.
Twelfth Night. Act III. Sc. 2. L. 16.

4
Still you keep o' the windy side of the law.
Twelfth Night. Act III. Sc. 4. L. 181.

5
Laws are generally found to be nets of such a texture, as the little creep through, the great break through, and the middle-sized alone are entangled in.
SHENSTONE—*On Politics.*
(See also ANACHARSIS)

6
When to raise the wind some lawyer tries,
Mysterious skins of parchment meet our eyes;
On speeds the smiling suit—

. . . . . .

Till stript—nonsuited—he is doomed to toss
In legal shipwreck, and redeemless loss,
Lucky, if like Ulysses, he can keep
His head above the waters of the deep.
HORACE AND JAMES SMITH—*Rejected Addresses. Architectural Atoms.* Trans. by Dr. B. T.

7
Men keep their engagements when it is an advantage to both parties not to break them.
SOLON—*Answer to Anacharsis.* In PLUTARCH—*Life of Solon.*
(See also ANACHARSIS)

8
Laws are like cobwebs, which may catch small flies, but let wasps and hornets break through.
SWIFT—*Essay on the Faculties of the Mind.*
(See also ANACHARSIS)

9
Bonis nocet quisquis pepercerit malis.
He hurts the good who spares the bad.
SYRUS—*Maxims.*

10
Judex damnatur cum nocens absolvitur.
The judge is condemned when the guilty is acquitted.
SYRUS—*Maxims.*

11
Corruptissima republica, plurimæ leges.
The more corrupt the state, the more laws.
TACITUS—*Annales.* III. 27.

12
Rebus cunctis inest quidam velut orbis.
In all things there is a kind of law of cycles
TACITUS—*Annales.* III. 55.

13
Initia magistratum nostrorum meliora, ferme finis inclinat.
Our magistrates discharge their duties best at the beginning; and fall off toward the end.
TACITUS—*Annales.* XV. 31.

14
A man must not go to law because the musician keeps false time with his foot.
JEREMY TAYLOR—Vol. VIII. P. 145. *The Worthy Communicant.* Chap. IV. Sect. IV. Quoted from SCHOTT—*Adagia.* P. 351. Prov. E, Suida. Cent. II. 17.

15
Quod vos jus cogit, id voluntate impetret.
What the law insists upon, let it have of your own free will.
TERENCE—*Adelphi.* III. 4. 44.

16
Jus summum sæpe summa est malitia.
The strictest law sometimes becomes the severest injustice.
TERENCE—*Heauton timoroumenos.* IV. 5. 48.

17
The law is good, if a man use it lawfully.
I Timothy. I. 8.

18
No man e'er felt the halter draw,
With good opinion of the law.
JOHN TRUMBULL—*McFingal.* Canto III. L. 489.

19
The Law: It has honored us, may we honor it.
DANIEL WEBSTER—*Toast at the Charleston Bar Dinner.* May 10, 1847.

20
The glorious uncertainty of law.
Toast of WILBRAHAM at a dinner of judges and counsel at Serjeants' Inn Hall, 1756. Quoted by MR. SHERIDAN in 1802.

21
And he that gives us in these days
New Lords may give us new laws.
GEORGE WITHER—*Contented Man's Morrice.*

22
And through the heat of conflict keeps the law
In calmness made, and sees what he foresaw.
WORDSWORTH—*Character of a Happy Warrior.* L. 53.

23
He it was that first gave to the law the air of a science. He found it a skeleton, and clothed it with life, colour, and complexion; he embraced the cold statue, and by his touch it grew into youth, health, and beauty.
BARRY YELVERTON (Lord Avonmore)—*On Blackstone.*
(See also WEBSTER under CREDIT)

LEARNING

24
Much learning doth make thee mad.
Acts. XXVI. 24.
(See also BURTON)

25
It is always in season for old men to learn.
ÆSCHYLUS—*Agamemnon.*

26
The green retreats
Of Academus.
AKENSIDE—*Pleasures of the Imagination.* Canto I. L. 591.

27
Learning hath his infancy, when it is but beginning and almost childish; then his youth, when it is luxuriant and juvenile; then his strength of years, when it is solid and reduced; and lastly his old age, when it waxeth dry and exhaust.
BACON—*Essays Civil and Moral. Of Vicissitude of Things.*

1
Reading maketh a full man; conference a ready man; and writing an exact man.
BACON—*Essays. Of Studies.*

2
The king to Oxford sent a troop of horse,
For Tories own no argument but force;
With equal care, to Cambridge books he sent,
For Whigs allow no force but argument.
SIR WILLIAM BROWNE—*Epigram. In reply to Dr. Trapp.*
(See also TRAPP)

3
Learning will be cast into the mire and trodden down under the hoofs of a swinish multitude.
BURKE—*Reflections on the Revolution in France.*

4
Out of too much learning become mad.
BURTON—*Anatomy of Melancholy.* Pt. III. Sec. 4. Memb. 1. Subsec. 2.
(See also ACTS)

5
In mathematics he was greater
Than Tycho Brahe, or Erra Pater;
For he, by geometric scale,
Could take the size of pots of ale.
BUTLER—*Hudibras.* Pt. I. Canto I. L. 119.

6
And wisely tell what hour o' th' day
The clock does strike by Algebra.
BUTLER—*Hudibras.* Pt. I. Canto I. L. 125.

7
The languages, especially the dead,
The sciences, and most of all the abstruse,
The arts, at least all such as could be said
To be the most remote from common use,
In all these he was much and deeply read.
BYRON—*Don Juan.* Canto I. St. 40.

8
And gladly wolde he lerne and gladly teche.
CHAUCER—*Canterbury Tales. Prologue.* L. 308.

9
Doctrina est ingenii naturale quoddam pabulum.
Learning is a kind of natural food for the mind.
CICERO—Adapted from *Acad. Quaest.* 4. 41, and *De Sen.* 14.
(See also CICERO under MIND)

10
When Honor's sun declines, and Wealth takes wings,
Then Learning shines, the best of precious things.
COCKER—*Urania.* (1670)

11
Learning without thought is labor lost; thought without learning is perilous.
CONFUCIUS—*Analects.* Bk. II. Ch. XV.

12
There is the love of knowing without the love of learning; the beclouding here leads to dissipation of mind.
CONFUCIUS—*Analects.* Bk. XVII. Ch. VIII.

13
Here the heart
May give a useful lesson to the head,
And learning wiser grow without his books.
COWPER—*The Task.* Bk. VI. *Winter Walk at Noon.* L. 85.

14
Next these learn'd Jonson in this list I bring
Who had drunk deep of the Pierian Spring.
DRAYTON—*Of Poets and Poesie.*
(See also POPE)

15
Consider that I laboured not for myself only, but for all them that seek learning.
Ecclesiasticus. XXXIII. 17.

16
Extremæ est dementiæ discere dediscenda.
It is the worst of madness to learn what has to be unlearnt.
ERASMUS—*De Ratione Studii.*

17
There is no other Royal path which leads to geometry.
EUCLID to PTOLEMY I. See Proclus' *Commentaries on Euclid's Elements.* Bk. II. Ch. IV.

18
Learning by study must be won;
'Twas ne'er entail'd from son to son.
GAY—*The Pack Horse and Carrier.* L. 41.

19
Whence is thy learning? Hath thy toil
O'er books consum'd the midnight oil?
GAY—*Shepherd and Philosopher.* L. 15.

20
Walkers at leisure learning's flowers may spoil
Nor watch the wasting of the midnight oil.
GAY—*Trivia.* Bk. II. L. 558.
(See also SHENSTONE)

21
I've studied now Philosophy
And Jurisprudence, Medicine
And even, alas, Theology
From end to end with labor keen;
And here, poor fool; with all my lore
I stand no wiser than before.
GOETHE—*Faust.* I. *Night.* BAYARD TAYLOR'S trans.

22
Yet, he was kind, or, if severe in aught,
The love he bore to learning was in fault;
The village all declar'd how much he knew,
'Twas certain he could write and cipher too.
GOLDSMITH—*The Deserted Village.* L. 205.

23
While words of learned length and thundering sound
Amaz'd the gazing rustics rang'd around.
GOLDSMITH—*The Deserted Village.* L. 211.

24
And still they gazed, and still the wonder grew,
That one small head should carry all it knew.
GOLDSMITH—*The Deserted Village.* L. 215. Ed. 1822, printed for John Sharp. Other editions give "could" for "should," "brain" for "head."

25
Men of polite learning and a liberal education.
MATTHEW HENRY—*Commentaries.* The Acts. Ch. X.

26
Deign on the passing world to turn thine eyes
And pause awhile from Learning to be wise;
Yet think what ills the scholar's life assail,
Toil, envy, want, the patron, and the goal.
See nations, slowly wise and meanly just,

To buried merit raise the tardy bust.
SAMUEL JOHNSON—*Vanity of Human Wishes.* L. 157. *Imitation of Juvenal. Satire X.* "Garret" instead of "patron" in 4th Ed. See BOSWELL'S—*Life.* (1754)

1
Nosse velint omnes, mercedem solvere nemo.
All wish to be learned, but no one is willing to pay the price.
JUVENAL—*Satires.* VII. 157.

2
The Lord of Learning who upraised mankind
From being silent brutes to singing men.
LELAND—*The Music-lesson of Confucius.*

3
Thou art an heyre to fayre lyving, that is nothing, if thou be disherited of learning, for better were it to thee to inherite righteousnesse then riches, and far more seemly were it for thee to haue thy Studie full of bookes, then thy pursse full of mony.
LYLY—*Euphues. Letters to a Young Gentleman in Naples named Alcius.*

4
He [Steele] was a rake among scholars, and a scholar among rakes.
MACAULAY—*Review of Aikin's Life of Addison.* (See also SANNAZARIUS)

5
He [Temple] was a man of the world among men of letters, a man of letters among men of the world.
MACAULAY—*Review of Life and Writings of Sir William Temple.*

6
Il ne l'en fault pas arrouser, il l'en fault teindre.
Not merely giving the mind a slight tincture but a thorough and perfect dye.
MONTAIGNE.
(See also POPE)

7
Ils n'ont rien appris, ni rien oublie.
They have learned nothing, and forgotten nothing.
CHEVALIER DE PANET to MALLET DU PAN. Jan., 1796. (Of the Bourbons.) Attributed also to TALLEYRAND.

8
A little learning is a dangerous thing;
Drink deep, or taste not the Pierian spring;
Their shallow draughts intoxicate the brain,
And drinking largely sobers us again.
POPE—*Essays on Criticism.* L. 215.
(See also DRAYTON, MONTAIGNE)

9
Learn from the birds what food the thickets yield;
Learn from the beasts the physic of the field;
The arts of building from the bee receive;
Learn of the mole to plough, the worm to weave.
POPE—*Essay on Man.* Ep. III. L. 173.

10
Ask of the Learn'd the way? The Learn'd are blind;
This bids to serve, and that to shun mankind;
Some place the bliss in action, some in ease,
Those call it Pleasure, and Contentment these.
POPE—*Essay on Man.* Ep. IV. L. 19.

11
Ein Gelehrter hat keine Langweile.
A scholar knows no ennui.
JEAN PAUL RICHTER—*Hesperus.* 8.

12
Delle belle eruditissima, delle erudite bellissima.
Most learned of the fair, most fair of the learned.
SANNAZARIUS — Inscription to CASSANDRA MARCHESIA in an edition of the latter's poems. See GRESWELL—*Memoirs of Politian.* (See also MACAULAY)

13
Few men make themselves Masters of the things they write or speak.
JOHN SELDEN—*Table Talk. Learning.*

14
No man is the wiser for his Learning * * *
Wit and Wisdom are born with a man.
JOHN SELDEN—*Table Talk. Learning.*

15
Homines, dum docent, discunt.
Men learn while they teach.
SENECA—*Epistolæ Ad Lucilium.* VII.

16
Learning is but an adjunct to ourself
And where we are our learning likewise is.
Love's Labour's Lost. Act IV. Sc. 3. L. 314.

17
Well, for your favour, sir, why, give God thanks, and make no boast of it; and for your writing and reading, let that appear when there is no need of such vanity.
Much Ado About Nothing. Act III. Sc. 3. L. 17.

18
O this learning, what a thing it is!
Taming of the Shrew. Act I. Sc. 2. L. 160.

19
I trimmed my lamp, consumed the midnight oil.
SHENSTONE—*Elegies.* XI. St. 7.
(See also GAY; also PLUTARCH under ARGUMENT)

20
I would by no means wish a daughter of mine to be a progeny of learning.
R. B. SHERIDAN—*The Rivals.* Act I. Sc. 2.

21
Learn to live, and live to learn,
Ignorance like a fire doth burn,
Little tasks make large return.
BAYARD TAYLOR—*To My Daughter.*

22
Wearing his wisdom lightly.
TENNYSON—*A Dedication.*

23
Wearing all that weight
Of learning lightly like a flower.
TENNYSON—*In Memoriam. Conclusion.* St. 10.

24
The King, observing with judicious eyes,
The state of both his universities,
To one he sent a regiment, for why?
That learned body wanted loyalty;
To the other he sent books, as well discerning,
How much that loyal body wanted learning.
JOSEPH TRAPP—*Epigram.* On George I.'s Donation of Bishop Ely's Library to Cambridge University.
(See also BROWNE)

25
Our gracious monarch viewed with equal eye
The wants of either university;
Troops he to Oxford sent, well knowing why,
That learned body wanted loyalty;

But books to Cambridge sent, as well discerning
That that right loyal body wanted learning.
Another version of TRAPP.

1
Our royal master saw with heedful eyes
The state of his two universities;
To one he sends a regiment, for why?
That learned body wanted loyalty.
To the other books he gave, as well discerning,
How much that loyal body wanted learning.
Version attributed to THOS. WARTON.
(See also BROWNE for answer.)

2
Ab uno disce omnes.
From one learn all.
VERGIL—*Æneid*. II. 65.

3
Disce, puer, virtutem ex me, verumque laborem;
Fortunam ex aliis.
Learn, O youth, virtue from me and true labor; fortune from others.
VERGIL—*Æneid*. XII. 435.

4
Aut disce, aut discede; manet sors tertia, cædi.
Either learn, or depart; a third course is open to you, and that is, submit to be flogged.
Winchester College. Motto of the Schoolroom.

5
Much learning shows how little mortals know,
Much wealth, how little worldlings can enjoy.
YOUNG—*Night Thoughts*. Night VI. L. 519.

6
Were man to live coeval with the sun,
The patriarch-pupil would be learning still.
YOUNG—*Night Thoughts*. Night VII. L. 86.

LEE (RIVER)

7
On this I ponder
Where'er I wander,
And thus grow fonder,
Sweet Cork, of thee,—
With thy bells of Shandon,
That sounds so grand on
The pleasant waters
Of the river Lee.
FATHER PROUT (Francis Mahoney)—*The Bells of Shandon.*

LEISURE

8
And leave us leisure to be good.
GRAY—*Hymn. Adversity.* Sc. 3.

9
No blessed leisure for Love or Hope,
But only time for Grief.
HOOD—*The Song of the Shirt.*

10
Retired Leisure,
That in trim gardens takes his pleasure.
MILTON—*Il Penseroso*. L. 49.

11
Mend when thou canst, be better at thy leisure.
King Lear. Act II. Sc. 4. L. 232.

12
Leisure is pain; take off our chariot wheels,
How heavily we drag the load of life!
Blest leisure is our curse; like that of Cain,
It makes us wander, wander earth around
To fly that tyrant, thought.
YOUNG—*Night Thoughts*. Night II. L. 125.

LEMON

13
My living in Yorkshire was so far out of the way, that it was actually twelve miles from a lemon.
SYDNEY SMITH—*Lady Holland's Memoir*. Vol. I. P. 262.

LETTERS (See POST, WRITING)

LEVEN (RIVER)

14
On Leven's banks, while free to rove,
And tune the rural pipe to love,
I envied not the happiest swain
That ever trod the Arcadian plain.
Pure stream! in whose transparent wave
My youthful limbs I wont to lave;
No torrents stain thy limpid source,
No rocks impede thy dimpling course,
That sweetly warbles o'er its bed,
With white, round, polish'd pebbles spread.
SMOLLETT—*Ode to Leven Water.*

LIBERALITY (See also GENEROSITY, GIFTS)

15
He that's liberal
To all alike, may do a good by chance,
But never out of judgment.
BEAUMONT AND FLETCHER—*The Spanish Curate*. Act I. Sc. 1.

16
Then gently scan your brother man,
Still gentler sister woman;
Tho' they may gang a kennin' wrang,
To step aside is human.
BURNS—*Address to the Unco Guid.*

17
It is better to believe that a man does possess good qualities than to assert that he does not.
Chinese Moral Maxims. Compiled by JOHN FRANCIS DAVIS, F. R. S. China, 1823.

18
The liberal soul shall be made fat.
Proverbs. XI. 25.

19
Shall I say to Cæsar
What you require of him? for he partly begs
To be desir'd to give. It much would please him,
That of his fortunes you should make a staff
To lean upon.
Antony and Cleopatra. Act III. Sc. 13. L. 67.

LIBERTY

20
A day, an hour, of virtuous liberty
Is worth a whole eternity in bondage.
ADDISON—*Cato*. Act II. Sc. 1.

21
L'arbre de la liberté ne croit qu'arrosé par le sang des tyrans.
The tree of liberty grows only when watered by the blood of tyrants.
BARÈRE—*Speech in the Convention Nationale.* (1792)

22
But what is liberty without wisdom, and without virtue? It is the greatest of all possible evils; for it is folly, vice, and madness, without tuition or restraint.
BURKE—*Reflections on the Revolution in France.*

1
My vigour relents. I pardon something to the spirit of liberty.
BURKE—*Speech on the Conciliation of America.* Vol. II. P. 118.

2
The people never give up their liberties but under some delusion.
BURKE—*Speech at a County Meeting at Bucks.* (1784)

3
Liberty's in every blow!
Let us do or die.
BURNS—*Bruce to His Men at Bannockburn.*

4
Eternal Spirit of the chainless Mind!
Brightest in dungeons, Liberty! thou art,
For there thy habitation is the heart—
The heart which love of thee alone can bind;
And when thy sons to fetters are consign'd—
To fetters and damp vault's dayless gloom,
Their country conquers with their martyrdom.
BYRON—*Sonnet. Introductory to Prisoner of Chillon.*

5
When Liberty from Greece withdrew,
And o'er the Adriatic flew,
To where the Tiber pours his urn,
She struck the rude Tarpeian rock;
Sparks were kindled by the shock—
Again thy fires began to burn.
HENRY F. CARY—*Power of Eloquence.*

6
Yes, while I stood and gazed, my temples bare,
And shot my being through earth, sea, and air,
Possessing all things with intensest love,
O Liberty! my spirit felt thee there.
COLERIDGE—*France. An Ode.* V.

7
Where the spirit of the Lord is, there is Liberty.
II Corinthians. III. 17.

8
'Tis liberty alone that gives the flower
Of fleeting life its lustre and perfume;
And we are weeds without it.
COWPER—*The Task.* Bk. V. L. 446.

9
Then liberty, like day,
Breaks on the soul, and by a flash from Heaven
Fires all the faculties with glorious joy.
COWPER—*The Task.* Bk. V. L. 882.

10
The condition upon which God hath given liberty to man is eternal vigilance.
JOHN PHILPOT CURRAN—*Speech.* July 10, 1790.

11
Eternal vigilance is the price of liberty.
JOHN PHILPOT CURRAN—*Speech.* Dublin. (1808)

12
Rendre l'homme infâme, et le laisser libre, est une absurdité qui peuple nos forêts d'assassins.
To brand man with infamy, and let him free, is an absurdity that peoples our forests with assassins.
DIDEROT.

13
The love of liberty with life is given,
And life itself the inferior gift of Heaven.
DRYDEN—*Palamon and Arcite.* Bk. II. L. 291.

14
The sun of liberty is set; you must light up the candle of industry and economy.
BENJ. FRANKLIN. In Correspondence.

15
Those who would give up essential liberty to purchase a little temporary safety deserve neither liberty nor safety.
BENJ. FRANKLIN—*Motto to Historical Review of Pennsylvania.*

16
Where liberty dwells, there is my country.
BENJ. FRANKLIN.

17
Give me liberty, or give me death.
PATRICK HENRY—*Speech.* March, 1775.

18
The God who gave us life, gave us liberty at the same time.
THOMAS JEFFERSON—*Summary View of the Rights of British America.*

19
As so often before, liberty has been wounded in the house of its friends. Liberty in the wild and freakish hands of fanatics has once more, as frequently in the past, proved the effective helpmate of autocracy and the twin-brother of tyranny.
OTTO KAHN—*Speech at University of Wisconsin.* Jan. 14, 1918.

20
The deadliest foe of democracy is not autocracy but liberty frenzied. Liberty is not foolproof. For its beneficent working it demands self-restraint, a sane and clear recognition of the practical and attainable, and of the fact that there are laws of nature which are beyond our power to change.
OTTO KAHN—*Speech at University of Wisconsin.* Jan. 14, 1918.

21
Libertas, inquit, populi quem regna coercent,
Libertate perit.
The liberty of the people, he says, whom power restrains unduly, perishes through liberty.
LUCANUS—*Pharsalia.* Bk. III. 146.

22
License they mean when they cry, Liberty!
For who loves that, must first be wise and good.
MILTON—*On the Detraction which followed upon my Writing Certain Treatises.*

23
Justly thou abhorr'st
That son, who on the quiet state of men
Such trouble brought, affecting to subdue
Rational liberty; yet know withal,
Since thy original lapse, true liberty
Is lost.
MILTON—*Paradise Lost.* Bk. XII. L. 79.

24
Oh! if there be, on this earthly sphere,
A boon, an offering Heaven holds dear,
'Tis the last libation Liberty draws
From the heart that bleeds and breaks in her cause!
MOORE—*Lalla Rookh. Paradise and the Peri.* St. 11.

1
Give me again my hollow tree
A crust of bread, and liberty!
POPE—*Imitations of Horace.* Bk. II. Satire VI. L. 220.

2
O liberté! que de crimes on commêt dans ton nom!
O liberty! how many crimes are committed in thy name!
MADAME ROLAND—*Memoirs. Appendix.* The actual expression used is said to have been "O liberté, comme on t'a jouée!"—"O Liberty, how thou hast been played with!" Spoken as she stood before a statue of Liberty.

3
That treacherous phantom which men call Liberty.
RUSKIN—*Seven Lamps of Architecture.* Ch. VIII. Sect. XXI.

4
I must have liberty
Withal, as large a charter as the wind,
To blow on whom I please.
As You Like It. Act II. Sc. 7. L. 47.

5
Why, headstrong liberty is lash'd with woe;
There's nothing, situate under heaven's eye
But hath his bound, in earth, in sea, in sky.
Comedy of Errors. Act II. Sc. 1. L. 15.

6
So every bondman in his own hand bears
The power to cancel his captivity.
Julius Cæsar. Act I. Sc. 3. L. 101.

7
Deep in the frozen regions of the north,
A goddess violated brought thee forth,
Immortal Liberty!
SMOLLETT—*Ode to Independence.* L. 5.

8
Behold! in Liberty's unclouded blaze
We lift our heads, a race of other days.
CHARLES SPRAGUE—*Centennial Ode.* St. 22.

9
Libertatem natura etiam mutis animalibus datam.
Liberty is given by nature even to mute animals.
TACITUS—*Annales.* IV. 17.

10
Eloquentia, alumna licentiæ, quam stulti libertatem vocabant.
[That form of] eloquence, the foster-child of license, which fools call liberty.
TACITUS—*Dialogus de Oratoribus.* 46.

11
If the true spark of religious and civil liberty be kindled, it will burn.
DANIEL WEBSTER—*Address.* Charlestown, Mass. June 17, 1825. Bunker Hill Monument.

12
On the light of Liberty you saw arise the light of Peace, like
"another morn,
Risen on mid-noon;"
and the sky on which you closed your eye was cloudless.
DANIEL WEBSTER—*Speeches.* The Bunker Hill Monument. (1825)

13
God grants liberty only to those who love it, and are always ready to guard and defend it.
DANIEL WEBSTER—*Speech.* June 3, 1834.

14
Liberty exists in proportion to wholesome restraint.
DANIEL WEBSTER—*Speech at the Charleston Bar Dinner.* May 10, 1847.

15
I shall defer my visit to Faneuil Hall, the cradle of American liberty, until its doors shall fly open, on golden hinges, to lovers of Union as well as of Liberty.
DANIEL WEBSTER—*Letter.* April, 1851. When refused the use of the Hall after his speech on the Compromise Measures. (March 7, 1850) The Aldermen reversed their decision. MR. WEBSTER began his speech: "This is Faneuil Hall—Open!"

LIBRARIES (See also BOOKS)

16
The medicine chest of the soul.
Inscription on a Library. From the Greek.

17
Nutrimentum spiritus.
Food for the soul.
Inscription on Berlin Royal Library.
(See also CICERO under LEARNING, MIND)

18
The richest minds need not large libraries.
AMOS BRONSON ALCOTT—*Table Talk.* Bk. I. *Learning-Books.*

19
Libraries are as the shrines where all the relics of the ancient saints, full of true virtue, and that without delusion or imposture, are preserved and reposed.
BACON—*Libraries.*

20
That place that does contain
My books, the best companions, is to me
A glorious court, where hourly I converse
With the old sages and philosophers;
And sometimes, for variety, I confer
With kings and emperors, and weigh their counsels;
Calling their victories, if unjustly got,
Unto a strict account, and, in my fancy,
Deface their ill-placed statues.
BEAUMONT AND FLETCHER—*The Elder Brother.* Act I. Sc. 2. L. 177.

21
A library is but the soul's burial-ground. It is the land of shadows.
HENRY WARD BEECHER—*Star Papers. Oxford. Bodleian Library.*

22
All round the room my silent servants wait,
My friends in every season, bright and dim.
BARRY CORNWALL—*My Books.*

23
A great library contains the diary of the human race.
DAWSON—*Address on Opening the Birmingham Free Library.*

24
It is a vanity to persuade the world one hath much learning, by getting a great library.
FULLER—*The Holy and Profane States. Of Books.* Maxim 1.

1
Every library should try to be complete on something, if it were only the history of pinheads.
HOLMES—*Poet at the Breakfast Table.* VIII.

2
The first thing naturally when one enters a scholar's study or library, is to look at his books. One gets a notion very speedily of his tastes and the range of his pursuits by a glance round his book-shelves.
HOLMES—*Poet at the Breakfast Table.* VIII.

3
What a place to be in is an old library! It seems as though all the souls of all the writers that have bequeathed their labours to these Bodleians were reposing here as in some dormitory, or middle state. I do not want to handle, to profane the leaves, their winding-sheets. I could as soon dislodge a shade. I seem to inhale learning, walking amid their foliage; and the odor of their old moth-scented coverings is fragrant as the first bloom of those sciential apples which grew amid the happy orchard.
LAMB—*Essays of Elia. Oxford in the Vacation.*

4
I love vast libraries; yet there is a doubt,
If one be better with them or without,—
Unless he use them wisely, and, indeed,
Knows the high art of what and how to read.
J. G. SAXE—*The Library.*

5
'Tis well to borrow from the good and great;
'Tis wise to learn; 'tis God-like to create!
J. G. SAXE—*The Library.*

6
Come, and take choice of all my library,
And so beguile thy sorrow.
Titus Andronicus. Act IV. Sc. 1. L. 34.

7
A circulating library in a town is as an evergreen tree of diabolical knowledge.
R. B. SHERIDAN—*The Rivals.* Act I. Sc. 2.

8 Shelved around us lie
The mummied authors.
BAYARD TAYLOR—*The Poet's Journal. Third Evening.*

9
Thou can'st not die. Here thou art more than safe
Where every book is thy epitaph.
HENRY VAUGHAN. On SIR THOMAS BODLEY'S Library.

LIES (See LYING)

LIFE

10
I expect to pass through this world but once. Any good therefore that I can do, or any kindness that I can show to any fellow creature, let me do it now. Let me not defer or neglect it, for I shall not pass this way again.
Author unknown. General proof lies with STEPHEN GRELLET as author. Not found in his writings. Same idea found in *The Spectator*. (Addison.) No. I. Vol. I. March 1. 1710. CANON JEPSON positively claimed it for EMERSON. Attributed to EDWARD COURTENAY, due to the resemblance of the Earl's epitaph. See *Literary World*, March 15, 1905. Also to CARLYLE, MISS A. B. HAGEMAN, ROWLAND HILL, MARCUS AURELIUS.
(See also CHESTERFIELD)

11
If you will do some deed before you die,
Remember not this caravan of death,
But have belief that every little breath
Will stay with you for an eternity.
ABU'L ALA.
(See also BACCHYLIDES, VAUVENARGUES)

12 Spesso è da forte,
Più che il morire, il vivere.
Ofttimes the test of courage becomes rather to live than to die.
ALFIERI—*Oreste.* IV. 2.

13
I know not if the dark or bright
Shall be my lot;
If that wherein my hopes delight
Be best or not.
HENRY M. ALFORD—*Life's Answer.*

14
Every man's life is a fairy-tale written by God's fingers.
HANS CHRISTIAN ANDERSEN—*Preface to Works.*

15
And by a prudent flight and cunning save
A life which valour could not, from the grave.
A better buckler I can soon regain,
But who can get another life again?
ARCHILOCHUS—See PLUTARCH'S *Morals.* Vol. I. *Essay on the Laws, etc., of the Lacedemonians.*

16
There is a cropping-time in the races of men, as in the fruits of the field; and sometimes, if the stock be good, there springs up for a time a succession of splendid men; and then comes a period of barrenness.
ARISTOTLE—*Rhetoric.* II. 15. Par. III. Quoted by BISHOP FRASER. *Sermon.* Feb. 9, 1879.

17
We are the voices of the wandering wind,
Which moan for rest and rest can never find;
Lo! as the wind is so is mortal life,
A moan, a sigh, a sob, a storm, a strife.
EDWIN ARNOLD—*Light of Asia.*

18
Life, which all creatures love and strive to keep
Wonderful, dear and pleasant unto each,
Even to the meanest; yea, a boon to all
Where pity is, for pity makes the world
Soft to the weak and noble for the strong.
EDWIN ARNOLD—*Light of Asia.*

19
With aching hands and bleeding feet
We dig and heap, lay stone on stone;
We bear the burden and the heat
Of the long day, and wish 'twere done.
Not till the hours of light return
All we have built do we discern.
MATTHEW ARNOLD—*Morality.* St. 2.

20
Saw life steadily and saw it whole.
MATTHEW ARNOLD—*Sonnet to a Friend.* (Said of SOPHOCLES.)

1
This strange disease of modern life,
With its sick hurry, its divided aims.
MATTHEW ARNOLD—*Scholar-Gypsy*. St. 21.

2
They live that they may eat, but he himself [Socrates] eats that he may live.
ATHENÆUS. IV. 15. See AULUS GELLIUS. XVIII. 2. 8.

3
As a mortal, thou must nourish each of two forebodings—that tomorrow's sunlight will be the last that thou shalt see; and that for fifty years thou wilt live out thy life in ample wealth.
BACCHYLIDES.
(See also ABU)

4
I would live to study, and not study to live.
BACON—*Memorial of Access*. From a Letter to KING JAMES I. See Birch's ed. of BACON—*Letters, Speeches, etc.* P. 321. (Ed. 1763) (See also JOHNSON)

5
The World's a bubble, and the Life of Man less than a span:
In his conception wretched, from the womb so to the tomb;
Curst from his cradle, and brought up to years with cares and fears.
Who then to frail mortality shall trust,
But limns the water, or but writes in dust.
BACON—*Life. Preface to the Translation of Certain Psalms.* For "Man's a Bubble," see PETRONIUS under MAN. For "Writ in Water," see BEAUMONT under DEEDS.
(See also BROWNE, COOKE, GORDON, OMAR, POPE, YOUNG, also BACON. P. 912[1])

6
We live in deeds, not years: in thoughts, not breaths;
In feelings, not in figures on a dial.
We should count time by heart-throbs. He most lives
Who thinks most, feels the noblest, acts the best.
BAILEY—*Festus*. Sc. *A Country Town*.

7
It matters not how long we live, but how.
BAILEY—*Festus*. Sc. *Wood and Water*.

8
Life hath more awe than death.
BAILEY—*Festus*. Sc. *Wood and Water*.

9
I live for those who love me,
For those who know me true;
For the heaven so blue above me,
And the good that I can do.
GEORGE LINNÆUS BANKS—*My Aim*. In *Daisies of the Grass*. P. 21. (Ed. 1865)

10
Life! we've been long together
Through pleasant and through cloudy weather:
'Tis hard to part when friends are dear:
Perhaps 'twill cost a sigh, a tear;
Then steal away, give little warning,
Choose thine own time,
Say not Good-night,—but in some brighter clime
Bid me Good-morning.
ANNA LETITIA BARBAULD—*Life*.

11
Life is a long lesson in humility.
BARRIE—*Little Minister*. Ch. III.

12
Loin des sépultures célebres
Vers un cimitière isolé
Mon cœur, comme un tambour voilé
Va battant des marches funèbres.
To the solemn graves, near a lonely cemetery, my heart like a muffled drum is beating funeral marches.
BAUDELAIRE—*Les Fleurs du Mal. Le Guignon.*
(See also LONGFELLOW)

13
Our lives are but our marches to the grave.
BEAUMONT AND FLETCHER—*The Humorous Lieutenant*. Act III. Sc. 5. L. 76.

14
We sleep, but the loom of life never stops and the pattern which was weaving when the sun went down is weaving when it comes up to-morrow.
HENRY WARD BEECHER—*Life Thoughts*. P. 12.

15
The day is short, the work is much.
Saying of BEN SYRA. (From the Hebrew.)

16
We are all but Fellow-Travelers,
Along Life's weary way;
If any man can play the pipes,
In God's name, let him play.
JOHN BENNETT—Poem in *The Century*.

17
Life does not proceed by the association and addition of elements, but by dissociation and division.
HENRI BERGSON—*Creative Evolution*. Ch. I.

18
For life is tendency, and the essence of a tendency is to develop in the form of a sheaf, creating, by its very growth, divergent directions among which its impetus is divided.
HENRI BERGSON—*Creative Revolution*. Ch. II.

19
Nasci miserum, vivere pœna, angustia mori.
It is a misery to be born, a pain to live, a trouble to die.
ST. BERNARD—Ch. III.

20
Alas, how scant the sheaves for all the trouble,
The toil, the pain and the resolve sublime—
A few full ears; the rest but weeds and stubble,
And withered wild-flowers plucked before their time.
A. B. BRAGDON—*The Old Campus*.

21
For life is the mirror of king and slave,
'Tis just what we are and do;
Then give to the world the best you have,
And the best will come back to you.
MADELEINE BRIDGES—*Life's Mirror*.

22
There are loyal hearts, there are spirits brave,
There are souls that are pure and true;
Then give to the world the best you have,
And the best will come back to you.
MADELEINE BRIDGES—*Life's Mirror*.

23
Life, believe, is not a dream,
So dark as sages say;
Oft a little morning rain
Foretells a pleasant day!
CHARLOTTE BRONTË—*Life*.

1
A little sun, a little rain,
A soft wind blowing from the west,
And woods and fields are sweet again,
And warmth within the mountain's breast

A little love, a little trust,
A soft impulse, a sudden dream,
And life as dry as desert dust,
Is fresher than a mountain stream.
STOPFORD A. BROOKE—*Earth and Man.*

2
I would not live over my hours past . . . not unto Cicero's ground because I have lived them well, but for fear I should live them worse.
SIR THOMAS BROWNE.
(See also FRANKLIN, GORDON, MONTAIGNE)

3
Life is a pure flame, and we live by an invisible sun within us.
SIR THOMAS BROWNE—*Hydriotaphia.* Ch. V.

4
The long habit of living indisposeth us for dying.
SIR THOMAS BROWNE—*Hydriotaphia.*
(See also DICKENS)

5
Whose life is a bubble, and in length a span.
WM. BROWNE—*Britannia Pastorals.* Bk. I. Song II. (See also BACON)

6
I know—is all the mourner saith,
Knowledge by suffering entereth;
And Life is perfected by Death.
E. B. BROWNING—*Vision of Poets.* St. 321.

7
Have you found your life distasteful?
My life did, and does, smack sweet.
Was your youth of pleasure wasteful?
Mine I saved and hold complete.
Do your joys with age diminish?
When mine fail me, I'll complain.
Must in death your daylight finish?
My sun sets to rise again.
ROBERT BROWNING—*At the "Mermaid."* St. 10.

8
I count life just a stuff
To try the soul's strength on.
ROBERT BROWNING—*In a Balcony.*

9
No! let me taste the whole of it, fare like my peers,
The heroes of old,
Bear the brunt, in a minute pay glad life's arrears
Of pain, darkness and cold.
ROBERT BROWNING—*Prospice.*

10
O Life! thou art a galling load,
Along a rough, a weary road,
To wretches such as I!
BURNS—*Despondency.*

11
O, Life! how pleasant is thy morning,
Young Fancy's rays the hills adorning!
Cold pausing Caution's lesson scorning,
We frisk away,
Like schoolboys, at the expected warning,
To joy and play.
BURNS—*Epistle to James Smith.*

12
Life is but a day at most.
BURNS—*Friars' Carse Hermitage.*

13
Did man compute
Existence by enjoyment, and count o'er
Such hours 'gainst years of life, say, would he name threescore?
BYRON—*Childe Harold.* Canto III. St. 34.

14
All is concentred in a life intense,
Where not a beam, nor air, nor leaf is lost,
But hath a part of being.
BYRON—*Childe Harold.* Canto, III. St. 89.

15
Through life's road, so dim and dirty,
I have dragged to three and thirty;
What have these years left to me?
Nothing, except thirty-three.
BYRON—*Diary.* Jan. 22, 1821. In MOORE'S *Life of Byron.* Vol. II. P. 414. First Ed.

16
Our life is two-fold; sleep hath its own world,
A boundary between the things misnamed
Death and existence.
BYRON—*Dream.* St. 1. L. 1.

17
The dust we tread upon was once alive.
BYRON—*Sardanapalus.* Act IV. Sc. 1. L. 66.

18
Life is with such all beer and skittles.
They are not difficult to please
About their victuals.
C. S. CALVERLEY—*Contentment.*
(See also DICKENS, HUGHES)

19
Heaven gives our years of fading strength
Indemnifying fleetness;
And those of Youth a seeming length,
Proportioned to their sweetness.
CAMPBELL—*A Thought Suggested by the New Year.*

20
A well-written life is almost as rare as a well-spent one.
CARLYLE—*Essays. Jean Paul Friedrich Richter.*

21
There is no life of a man, faithfully recorded, but is a heroic poem of its sort, rhymed or unrhymed.
CARLYLE—*Essays. Memoirs on the Life of Scott.*

22
One life;—a little gleam of Time between two Eternities.
CARLYLE—*Heroes and Hero Worship. The Hero as a Man of Letters.*
(See also LILLO)

23
How many lives we live in one,
And how much less than one, in all.
ALICE CARY—*Life's Mysteries.*

24
Bien predica quien bien vive.
He who lives well is the best preacher.
CERVANTES—*Don Quixote.* VI. 19.

1
On entre, on crie,
Et c'est la vie!
On bâille, on sort,
Et c'est la mort!

We come and we cry, and that is life; we yawn and we depart, and that is death!

AUSONE DE CHANCEL—*Lines in an Album.* (1836) (See also DE PIIS, SAXE)

2
However, while I crawl upon this planet I think myself obliged to do what good I can in my narrow domestic sphere, to all my fellow-creatures, and to wish them all the good I cannot do.

CHESTERFIELD—In a letter to the Bishop of Waterford, Jan. 22, 1780. (See First Quotation)

3
Brevis a natura nobis vita data est; at memoria bene reditæ vitæ sempiterna.

The life given us by nature is short; but the memory of a well-spent life is eternal.

CICERO—*Philippicæ.* XIV. 12.

4
Natura dedit usuram vitæ tanquam pecuniæ nulla præstitua die.

Nature has lent us life at interest, like money, and has fixed no day for its payment.

CICERO—*Tusculanarum Disputationum.* I. 39.

5
Nemo parum diu vixit, qui virtuis perfectæ perfecto functus est munere.

No one has lived a short life who has performed its duties with unblemished character.

CICERO—*Tusculanarum Disputationum.* I. 45.

6
To know, to esteem, to love,—and then to part,
Makes up life's tale to many a feeling heart.

COLERIDGE—*On Taking Leave of——.*

7
Life is but thought.

COLERIDGE—*Youth and Age.*

8
This life's a hollow bubble,
Don't you know?
Just a painted piece of twoubble,
Don't you know?
We come to earth to cwy,
We gwow oldeh and we sigh,
Oldeh still, and then we die!
Don't you know?

EDMUND VANCE COOKE—*Fin de Siècle.* (See also BACON)

9
Life for delays and doubts no time does give,
None ever yet made haste enough to live.

ABRAHAM COWLEY—*Martial.* Lib. II. XC.

10
His faith, perhaps, in some nice tenets might
Be wrong; his life, I'm sure, was in the right.

ABRAHAM COWLEY—*On the Death of Mr. Crashaw.* L. 56.

11
Life is an incurable disease.

ABRAHAM COWLEY—*To Dr. Scarborough.*

12
Men deal with life as children with their play,
Who first misuse, then cast their toys away.

COWPER—*Hope.* L. 127.

13
Still ending, and beginning still.

COWPER—*Task.* Bk. III. L. 627.

14
What is it but a map of busy life,
Its fluctuations, and its vast concerns?

COWPER—*Task.* Bk. IV. L. 55.

15
Let's learn to live, for we must die alone.

CRABBE—*Borough.* Letter X.

16
Shall he who soars, inspired by loftier views,
Life's little cares and little pains refuse?
Shall he not rather feel a double share
Of mortal woe, when doubly arm'd to bear?

CRABBE—*Library.*

17
Life's bloomy flush was lost.

CRABBE—*Parish Register.* Pt. II. 453. (See also GOLDSMITH)

18
Life is not measured by the time we live.

CRABBE—*Village.* Bk. II.

19
Chaque instant de la vie est un pas vers la mort.

Every moment of life is a step toward the grave.

CRÉBILLON—*Tite et Bérénice.* I. 5.

20
Non è necessario
Vivere, si scolpire olte quel termine
Nostro nome: quæsto è necessario.
It is not necessary to live,
But to carve our names beyond that point,
This is necessary.

GABRIELE d'ANNUNZIO—*Canzone di Umberto Cagni.*

21
Nel mezzo del cammin di nostra vita
Mi ritrovai per una selva oscura,
Che la diritta via era smarrita.
In the midway of this our mortal life,
I found me in a gloomy wood, astray,
Gone from the path direct.

DANTE—*Inferno.* I.

22
Questo misero modo
Tengon l'anime triste di coloro
Che visser senza infamia e senza lodo.

This sorrow weighs upon the melancholy souls of those who lived without infamy or praise.

DANTE—*Inferno.* III. 36.

23
. . . There are two distinct classes of people in the world; those that feel that they themselves are *in* a body; and those that feel that they themselves *are* a body, with something working it. *I* feel like the contents of a bottle, and am curious to know what will happen when the bottle is uncorked. Perhaps I shall be *mousseux*—who knows? Now I *know* that many people feel like a strong moving engine, self-stoking, and often so anxious to keep the fire going that they put too much fuel on, and it has to be raked out and have the bars cleared.

WILLIAM DE MORGAN—*Joseph Vance.* Ch. XL.

24
Learn to live well, that thou may'st die so too;
To live and die is all we have to do.

SIR JOHN DENHAM—*Of Prudence.* L. 93.

1
Cette longue et cruelle maladie qu'on appele la vie.

That long and cruel malady which one calls life.

DESCHAMPS.

2
Mr. Wopsle's great-aunt conquered a confirmed habit of living into which she had fallen.

DICKENS—*Great Expectations*. Ch. 16.
(See also BROWNE, OLDHAM, THACKERAY)

3
My life is one demd horrid grind.

DICKENS—*Nicholas Nickleby*. Vol. II. Ch. XXXII.

4
They don't mind it: its a reg'lar holiday to them—all porter and skittles.

DICKENS—*Pickwick Papers*. Ch. XL, of original Ed.
(See also CALVERLY)

5
"Live, while you live," the epicure would say,
"And seize the pleasures of the present day;"
"Live, while you live," the sacred *preacher* cries,
"And give to God each moment as it flies."
"Lord, in my views let both united be;
I live in *pleasure*, when I live to *Thee*."

PHILIP DODDRIDGE—"*Dum vivimus vivamus.*" Lines written under Motto of his Family Arms.

6
So that my life be brave, what though not long?

DRUMMOND—*Sonnet*.

7
Bankrupt of life, yet prodigal of ease.

DRYDEN—*Absalom and Achitophel*. L. 168.

8
'Tis not for nothing that we life pursue;
It pays our hopes with something still that's new.

DRYDEN—*Aureng-Zebe*. Act IV. Sc. 1.

9
When I consider life, 'tis all a cheat;
Yet, fooled with hope, men favour the deceit.

DRYDEN—*Aureng-Zebe*. Act IV. Sc. 1.

10
Like pilgrims to th' appointed place we tend;
The World's an Inn, and Death the journey's end.

DRYDEN—*Palamon and Arcite*. III. 887.
(See also ELLIS, JENKYNS, QUARLES, SENECA; also COMBE and SHENSTONE under INN)

11
Take not away the life you cannot give:
For all things have an equal right to live.

DRYDEN—*Pythagorean Phil*. L. 705.

12
The wheels of weary life at last stood still.

DRYDEN and LEE—*Œdipus*. Act IV. Sc. 1.

13
Living from hand to mouth.

DU BARTAS—*Divine Weekes and Workes*. Second Week. First Day. Pt. IV.

14
A little rule, a little sway,
A sunbeam in a winter's day,
Is all the proud and mighty have
Between the cradle and the grave.

JOHN DYER—*Grongar Hill*. L. 89.
(See also MONTENAEKIN)

15
A man's ingress into the world is naked and bare,
His progress through the world is trouble and care;
And lastly, his egress out of the world, is nobody knows where.
If we do well here, we shall do well there;
I can tell you no more if I preach a whole year.

JOHN EDWIN—*The Eccentricities of John Edwin* (second edition). Vol. I. P. 74. Quoted in LONGFELLOW'S *Tales of a Wayside Inn*. Pt. II. *Student's Tale*.

16
Life's a vast sea
That does its mighty errand without fail,
Painting in unchanged strength though waves are changing.

GEORGE ELIOT—*Spanish Gypsy*. Bk. III.

17
Life is short, and time is swift;
Roses fade, and shadows shift.

EBENEZER ELLIOT—*Epigram*.

18
Sooner or later that which is now life shall be poetry, and every fair and manly trait shall add a richer strain to the song.

EMERSON—*Letters and Social Aims. Poetry and Imagination*.

19
When life is true to the poles of nature, the streams of truth will roll through us in song.

EMERSON—*Letters and Social Aims. Poetry and Imagination*.

20
Life's like an inn where travelers stay,
Some only breakfast and away;
Others to dinner stop, and are full fed;
The oldest only sup and go to bed.

Epitaph on tomb in Silkstone, England, to the memory of JOHN ELLIS. (1766)
(See also DRYDEN)

21
Life's an Inn, my house will shew it;—
I thought so once, but now I know it.

Epitaphs printed by MR. FAIRLEY. *Epitaphiana*. (Ed. 1875) On an Innkeeper at Eton. The lines that follow are like those of Quarles.
(See also GAY under EPITAPHS)

22
This world's a city full of crooked streets,
Death's the market-place where all men meet;
If life were merchandise that men should buy,
The rich would always live, the poor might die.

Epitaph to JOHN GADSDEN, died 1739, in Stoke Goldington, England. See E. R. SUFFLING —*Epitaphia*. P. 401. On P. 405 is a Scotch version of 1689. Same idea in GAY. *The Messenger of Mortality*, in *Ancient Poems, Ballads, and Songs of the Peasantry*. A suggestion from CHAUCER'S *Knight's Tale*. L. 2487. SHAKESPEARE and FLETCHER. *Two Noble Kinsmen*. Act I. Sc. 5. L. 15. WALLER—*Divine Poems*.

23
Nulli desperandum, quam diu spirat.

No one is to be despaired of as long as he breathes. (While there is life there is hope.)

ERASMUS—*Colloq. Epicureus*.
(See also CICERO under HOPE)

1
So likewise all this life of martall men,
What is it but a certaine kynde of stage plaie?
Where men come forthe disguised one in one arraie,
An other in an other eche plaiying his part.
ERASMUS — *Praise of Folie.* CHALLONER'S Trans. (1549) P. 43.
(See also ACTING)

2
Life is short, yet sweet.
EURIPIDES.

3
For like a child, sent with a fluttering light
To feel his way along a gusty night,
Man walks the world. Again, and yet again,
The lamp shall be by fits of passion slain;
But shall not He who sent him from the door
Relight the lamp once more, and yet once more?
EDWARD FITZGERALD—Translation of ATTAR'S *Mantik-ut-Tair.* (Bird Parliament.) In *Letters and Literary Remains of FitzGerald.* Vol. II. P. 457.

4
The King in a carriage may ride,
And the Beggar may crawl at his side;
But in the general race,
They are traveling all the same pace.
EDWARD FITZGERALD—*Chrononoros.*

5
Were the offer made true, I would engage to run again, from beginning to end, the same career of life. All I would ask should be the privilege of an author, to correct, in a second edition, certain errors of the first.
BENJ. FRANKLIN. In his *Life.*
(See also BROWNE)

6
Dost thou love life? Then do not squander time, for that is the stuff life is made of.
BENJ. FRANKLIN—*Poor Richard.*

7
We live merely on the crust or rind of things.
FROUDE—*Short Studies on Great Subjects. Lucian.*

8
The old Quaker was right: "I expect to pass through life but once. If there is any kindness, or any good thing I can do to my fellow beings, let me do it now. I shall pass this way but once."
W. C. GANNETT—*Blessed be Drudgery.*
(See First Quotation.)

9
How short is life! how frail is human trust!
GAY—*Trivia.* Bk. III. L. 235.

10
Lebe, wie Du, wenn du stirbst,
Wünschen wirst, gelebt zu haben.
Live in such a way as, when you come to die, you will wish to have lived.
C. F. GELLERT—*Geistliche Oden und Lieder. Vom Tode.*

11
We are in this life as it were in another man's house. . . . In heaven is our home, in the world is our Inn: do not so entertain thyself in the Inn of this world for a day as to have thy mind withdrawn from longing after thy heavenly home.
GERHARDT—*Meditations.* XXXVIII. (About 1630)
(See also DRYDEN, QUARLES)

12
Die uns das Leben gaben, herrliche Gefühle,
Erstarren in dem irdischen Gewühle.
The fine emotions whence our lives we mold
Lie in the earthly tumult dumb and cold.
GOETHE—*Faust.* I. 1. 286.

13
Grau, theurer Freund, ist alle Theorie
Und grün des Lebens goldner Baum.
My worthy friend, gray are all theories
And green alone Life's golden tree.
GOETHE—*Faust.* I. 4. 515.

14
Ein unnütz Leben ist ein früher Tod.
A useless life is an early death.
GOETHE—*Iphigenia auf Tauris.* I. 2. 63.

15
Singet nicht in Trauertönen.
Sing it not in mournful numbers.
GOETHE—*Wilhelm Meister. Philine.*
(See also LONGFELLOW)

16
All the bloomy flush of life is fled.
GOLDSMITH—*Deserted Village.* 128.
(See also CRABBE)

17
The pregnant quarry teem'd with human form.
GOLDSMITH—*Traveller.* L. 138.

18
I would live the same life over if I had to live again,
And the chances are I go where most men go.
ADAM LINDSAY GORDON.
(See also BROWNE)

19
Life is mostly froth and bubble;
Two things stand like stone:
Kindness in another's trouble
Courage in our own.
ADAM LINDSAY GORDON—*Ye Weary Wayfarer. Finis Exoptatus.*
(See also BACON)

20
Along the cool sequestered vale of life,
They kept the noiseless tenour of their way.
GRAY—*Elegy in a Country Churchyard.* St. 19.
(See also PORTEUS)

21
Qui n'a pas vécu dans les années voisines de 1789 ne sait pas ce que c'est le palisir de vivre.
Whoever did not live in the years neighboring 1789 does not know what the pleasure of living means.
TALLEYRAND to GUIZOT. GUIZOT—*Memoirs pour Servir a l'histoire de nous Temps.* Vol. I. P. 6.

22
Life's little ironies.
THOS. HARDY. Title of a collection of stories.

23
[George Herbert] a conspicuous example of plain living and high thinking.
HAWEIS—*Sermon on George Herbert.* In *Evenings for the People.*
(See also WORDSWORTH)

24
Who but knows
How it goes!
Life's a last year's Nightingale,
Love's a last year's rose.
HENLEY—*Echoes.* XLV.

1
Life is a smoke that curls—
Curls in a flickering skein,
That winds and whisks and whirls,
A figment thin and vain,
Into the vast inane.
One end for hut and hall.
HENLEY—*Of the Nothingness of Things.*

2
One doth but break-fast here, another dine; he that lives longest does but suppe; we must all goe to bed in another World.
BISHOP HENSHAW—*Horæ Subcessivæ.* (1631) P. 80.
(See also DRYDEN, QUARLES)

3
Let all live as they would die.
HERBERT—*Jacula Prudentum.*

4
I made a posy, while the day ran by:
Here will I smell my remnant out, and tie
My life within this band.
But time did beckon to the flowers, and they
By noon most cunningly did steal away,
And wither'd in my hand.
HERBERT—*Life.*

5
No arts; no letters; no society; and which is worst of all, continual fear, and danger of violent death; and the life of man, solitary, poor, nasty, brutish, and short.
THOMAS HOBBES—*Leviathan.* Pt. I. *Of Man.* Ch. XVIII.

6
Life is not to be bought with heaps of gold;
Not all Apollo's Pythian treasures hold,
Or Troy once held, in peace and pride of sway,
Can bribe the poor possession of the day.
HOMER—*Iliad.* Bk. IX. L. 524. POPE'S trans.

7
For Fate has wove the thread of life with pain,
And twins ev'n from the birth are Misery and Man!
HOMER—*Odyssey.* Bk. VII. L. 263. POPE'S trans.

8
Vitæ summa brevis spem nos vetat inchoare longam.
Jam te premet nox, fabulæque Manes,
Et domus exilis Plutonia.
The short span of life forbids us to spin out hope to any length. Soon will night be upon you, and the fabled Shades, and the shadowy Plutonian home.
HORACE—*Carmina.* I. 4. 15.

9
Ille potens sui
Lætusque deget, cui licet in diem
Dixisse Vixi; cras vel atra
Nube polum pater occupato,
Vel sole puro, non tamen irritum
Quodcunque retro est efficiet.
That man lives happy and in command of himself, who from day to day can say I have lived. Whether clouds obscure, or the sun illumines the following day, that which is past is beyond recall.
HORACE—*Carmina.* III. 29. 41.

10
Vivendi recte qui prorogat horam
Rusticus expectat dum defluat amnis; at ille
Labitur et labetur in omne volubilis ævum.
He who postpones the hour of living as he ought, is like the rustic who waits for the river to pass along (before he crosses); but it glides on and will glide on forever.
HORACE—*Epistles.* I. 2. 41.

11
Nec vixit male qui natus moriensque fefellit.
Nor has he spent his life badly who has passed it in privacy.
HORACE—*Epistles.* I. 17. 10.

12
Exacto contentus tempore vita cedat uti conviva satur.
Content with his past life, let him take leave of life like a satiated guest.
HORACE—*Satires.* I. 1. 118.

13
Life isn't all beer and skittles; but beer and skittles or something better of the same sort, must form a good part of every Englishman's education.
THOMAS HUGHES—*Tom Brown's Schooldays.* Ch. II.
(See also CALVERLY)

14
The chess-board is the world, the pieces are the phenomena of the universe, the rules of the game are what we call the laws of Nature. The player on the other side is hidden from us.
HUXLEY—*Liberal Education.* In *Science and Education.*
(See also OMAR, TERENCE, WARE)

15
There is but halting for the wearied foot;
The better way is hidden. Faith hath failed;
One stronger far than reason mastered her.
It is not reason makes faith hard, but life.
JEAN INGELOW—*A Pastor's Letter to a Young Poet.* Pt. II. L. 231.

16
Study as if you were to live forever. Live as if you were to die tomorrow.
ISIDORE OF SEVILLE.

17
A fair, where thousands meet, but none can stay;
An inn, where travellers bait, then post away.
SOAME JENKYNS—*Immortality of the Soul.* Translated from the Latin of ISAAC HAWKINS BROWNE.
(See also DRYDEN)

18
All that a man hath will he give for his life.
Job. II. 4.

19
I would not live alway.
Job. VII. 16.

20
The land of the living.
Job. XXVIII. 13.

21
Learn that the present hour alone is man's.
SAMUEL JOHNSON—*Irene.* Act III. Sc. 2. L. 33.

22
Reflect that life, like every other blessing,
Derives its value from its use alone.
SAMUEL JOHNSON—*Irene.* Act III. Sc. 8. L. 28.

1
The drama's laws the drama's patrons give.
For we that live to please must please to live.
SAMUEL JOHNSON. Prologue to opening of Drury Lane Theatre. (1747)
(See also BACON)

2
"Enlarge my life with multitude of days!"
In health, in sickness, thus the suppliant prays:
Hides from himself its state, and shuns to know,
That life protracted is protracted woe.
SAMUEL JOHNSON—*Vanity of Human Wishes.* L. 255.

3
In life's last scene what prodigies surprise,
Fears of the brave, and follies of the wise!
From Marlborough's eyes the streams of dotage flow,
And Swift expires a driveller and a show.
SAMUEL JOHNSON—*Vanity of Human Wishes.* L. 315.

4
Catch, then, oh! catch the transient hour,
Improve each moment as it flies;
Life's a short summer—man a flower;
He dies—alas! how soon he dies!
SAMUEL JOHNSON—*Winter. An Ode.* L. 33.

5
Our whole life is like a play.
BEN JONSON—*Discoveries de Vita Humana.*

6
Festinat enim decurrere velox
Flosculus angustæ miseræque brevissima vitæ
Portio; dum bibimus dum serta unguenta puellas
Poscimus obrepit non intellecta senectus.

The short bloom of our brief and narrow life flies fast away. While we are calling for flowers and wine and women, old age is upon us.
JUVENAL—*Satires.* IX. 127.

7
A sacred burden is this life ye bear,
Look on it, lift it, bear it solemnly,
Stand up and walk beneath it steadfastly;
Fail not for sorrow, falter not for sin,
But onward, upward, till the goal ye win.
FRANCES ANNE KEMBLE—*Lines to the Young Gentlemen leaving the Lennox Academy, Mass.*

8
I have fought my fight, I have lived my life,
I have drunk my share of wine;
From Trier to Coln there was never a knight
Led a merrier life than mine.
CHARLES KINGSLEY — *The Knight's Leap.* Similar lines appear under the picture of FRANZ HALS, The Laughing Cavalier.

9
La plupart des hommes emploient la première partie de leur vie à rendre l'autre misérable.

Most men employ the first part of life to make the other part miserable.
LA BRUYÈRE—*Les Caractères.* XI.

10
Life will be lengthened while growing, for
Thought is the measure of life.
LELAND—*The Return of the Gods.* L. 85.

11
What shall we call this undetermin'd state,
This narrow isthmus 'twixt two boundless oceans,
That whence we came, and that to which we tend?
LILLO—*Arden of Feversham.* Act III. Sc. 2.
(See also CARLYLE, MOORE, POPE, PRIOR, WESLEY, YOUNG)

12
This life of ours is a wild æolian harp of many a joyous strain,
But under them all there runs a loud perpetual wail, as of souls in pain.
LONGFELLOW—*Christus. The Golden Legend.* Pt. IV. St. 2.

13
Love is sunshine, hate is shadow,
Life is checkered shade and sunshine.
LONGFELLOW—*Hiawatha.* Pt. X. *Hiawatha's Wooing.* L. 265.

14
Life hath quicksands, Life hath snares!
LONGFELLOW—*Maidenhood.* St. 9.

15
Tell me not, in mournful numbers,
Life is but an empty dream!
LONGFELLOW—*A Psalm of Life.* St. 1.
(See also GOETHE)

16
Art is long, and Time is fleeting,
And our hearts, though stout and brave,
Still, like muffled drums, are beating
Funeral marches to the grave.
LONGFELLOW—*A Psalm of Life.* St. 4.
(See also BAUDELAIRE)

17
Thus at the flaming forge of life
Our fortunes must be wrought;
Thus on its sounding anvil shaped
Each burning deed and thought!
LONGFELLOW—*The Village Blacksmith.* St. 8.

18
Live and think.
SAMUEL LOVER—*Father Roach.*

19
Truly there is a tide in the affairs of men; but there is no gulf-stream setting forever in one direction.
LOWELL—*Among my Books. First Series. New England Two Centuries Ago.*

20
Our life must once have end; in vain we fly
From following Fate; e'en now, e'en now, we die.
LUCRETIUS—*De Rerum Natura*, 3, 1093 (*Creech tr.*).

21
Vita dum superest, bene est.
Whilst life remains it is well.
MÆCENAS. Quoted by SENECA. Ep. 101.
(See also Quotations under HOPE.)

22
An ardent throng, we have wandered long,
We have searched the centuries through,
In flaming pride, we have fought and died,
To keep its memory true.
We fight and die, but our hopes beat high,
In spite of the toil and tears,
For we catch the gleam of our vanished dream
Down the path of the Untrod Years.
WILMA KATE MCFARLAND—*The Untrod Years.* Pub. in *Methodist Journal.* July, 1912.

23
Victuros agimus semper, nec vivimus unquam.
We are always beginning to live, but are never living.
MANILIUS—*Astronomica.* IV. 899.

1
Non est, crede mihi sapientis dicere "vivam."
Sera nimis vita est crastina, vive hodie.

It is not, believe me, the act of a wise man to say, "I will live." To-morrow's life is too late; live to-day.

MARTIAL—*Epigrams*. I. 16. 11.

2
Cras vives; hodie jam vivere, Postume, serum est.
Ille sapit, quisquis, Postume, vixit heri.

To-morrow I will live, the fool does say;
To-day itself's too late, the wise lived yesterday.

MARTIAL—*Epigrams*. V. 58. COWLEY'S Trans. *Danger of Procrastination*. Quoted by VOLTAIRE in *Letter to Thieriot*.

3
He who thinks that the lives of Priam and of Nestor were long is much deceived and mistaken. Life consists not in living, but in enjoying health.

MARTIAL—*Epigrams*. Bk. VI.

4
Ampliat ætatis spatium sibi vir bonus: hoc est vivere bis, vita posse priore frui.

A good man doubles the length of his existence; to have lived so as to look back with pleasure on our past existence is to live twice.

MARTIAL—*Epigrams*. X. 23. 7.

5
On the long dusty ribbon of the long city street,
The pageant of life is passing me on multitudinous feet,
With a word here of the hills, and a song there of the sea
And—the great movement changes—the pageant passes me.

MASEFIELD—*All ye that pass by!*

6
While we least think it he prepares his Mate.
Mate, and the King's pawn played, it never ceases,
Though all the earth is dust of taken pieces.

MASEFIELD—*Widow in the Bye Street*. Pt. I. Last lines.

7
Man cannot call the brimming instant back;
Time's an affair of instants spun to days;
If man must make an instant gold, or black,
Let him, he may; but Time must go his ways.
Life may be duller for an instant's blaze.
Life's an affair of instants spun to years,
Instants are only cause of all these tears.

MASEFIELD—*Widow in the Bye Street*. Pt. V.

8
Wide is the gate and broad is the way that leadeth to destruction.

Matthew. VII. 13.

9
Strait is the gate and narrow is the way which leadeth unto life.

Matthew. VII. 14.

10
Life is a mission. Every other definition of life is false, and leads all who accept it astray. Religion, science, philosophy, though still at variance upon many points, all agree in this, that every existence is an aim.

MAZZINI—*Life and Writings*. Ch. V.

11
Life hath set
No landmarks before us.

OWEN MEREDITH (Lord Lytton)—*Lucile*. Pt. II. Canto V. St. 14.

12
When life leaps in the veins, when it beats in the heart,
When it thrills as it fills every animate part,
Where lurks it? how works it? * * * we scarcely detect it.

OWEN MEREDITH (Lord Lytton)—*Lucile*. Pt. II. Canto I. St. 5.

13
Il torre altrui la vita
È facoltà commune
Al più vil della terra; il darla è solo
De' Numi, e de' Regnanti.

To take away life is a power which the vilest of the earth have in common; to give it belongs to gods and kings alone.

METASTASIO—*La Clemenza di Tito*. III. 7.

14
A man's best things are nearest him,
Lie close about his feet.

RICHARD MONCKTON MILNES (Lord Houghton)—The Men of Old. St. 7.
(See also WORDSWORTH under WISDOM)

15
For men to tell how human life began
Is hard; for who himself beginning knew?

MILTON—*Paradise Lost*. Bk. VIII. L. 250.

16
Nor love thy life, nor hate; but what thou liv'st
Live well; how long or short permit to heav'n.

MILTON—*Paradise Lost*. Bk. XI. L. 553.

17
Were I to live my life over again, I should live it just as I have done. I neither complain of the past, nor do I fear the future.

MONTAIGNE—*Essays On Repentance*. Bk. III. Ch. II.
(See also BROWNE, MOORE)

18
La vie est vaine:
Un peu d'amour,
Un peu de haine—
Et puis-bonjour!

La vie est brève:
Un peu d'espoir,
Un peu de rêve—
Et puis—bon soir!

Life is but jest:
A dream, a doom;
A gleam, a gloom—
And then—good rest!

Life is but play;
A throb, a tear:
A sob, a sneer;
And then—good day.

LEON DE MONTENAEKEN—*Peu de Chose et Presque Trop*. (Nought and too Much.) English Trans. by Author. Quoted by DU MAURIER in *Trilby*
(See also CHANCEL, DE PIIS)

19
'Tis not the whole of life to live;
Nor all of death to die.

MONTGOMERY—*The Issues of Life and Death*.

1
Vain were the man, and false as vain,
Who said, were he ordained to run
His long career of life again
He would do all that he had done.
MOORE—*My Birthday*. In a footnote Moore refers to FONTENELLE, "Si je recommençais ma carrière, je ferai tout ce que j'ai fait."
(See also MONTAIGNE)

2
The longer one lives the more he learns.
MOORE—*Dream of Hindoostan*.

3
A narrow isthmus 'twixt two boundless seas,
The past, the future, two eternities.
MOORE—*Lalla Rookh. Veiled Prophet*. Idea given as a quotation in the *Spectator*. No. 590, Sept. 6, 1714.
(See also LILLO)

4
Life is a waste of wearisome hours,
Which seldom the rose of enjoyment adorns,
And the heart that is soonest awake to the flowers,
Is always the first to be touch'd by the thorns.
MOORE—*Oh! Think not My Spirits are always as Light*.

5
Nor on one string are all life's jewels strung.
WILLIAM MORRIS—*Life and Death of Jason*. Bk. 17. L. 1170.

6
I would not live alway; I ask not to stay
Where storm after storm rises dark o'er the way.
WILLIAM A. MUHLENBERG—*I would not Live Alway*.

7
Our days begin with trouble here, our life is but a span,
And cruel death is always near, so frail a thing is man.
New England Primer. (1777)

8
While some no other cause for life can give
But a dull habitude to live.
OLDHAM—*To the Memory of Norwent*. Par. 5.
(See also DICKENS)

9
You know how little while we have to stay,
And, once departed, may return no more.
OMAR KHAYYAM—*Rubaiyat*. St. III. FITZGERALD'S Trans.

10
Ah Love! could you and I with him conspire
To grasp this sorry Scheme of Things entire
Would we not shatter it to bits—and then
Re-mould it nearer to the Heart's Desire?
OMAR KHAYYAM—*Rubaiyat*. St. IX. FITZGERALD'S Trans.

11
Think, in this batter'd Caravanserai
Whose portals are alternate Night and Day,
How Sultan after Sultan with his Pomp
Abode his destin'd Hour and went his way.
OMAR KHAYYAM—*Rubaiyat*. St. XVII. FITZGERALD'S Trans.

12
I came like Water, and like Wind I go.
OMAR KHAYYAM—*Rubaiyat*. St. XXVIII.

13
A Moment's Halt—a momentary taste
Of BEING from the Well amid the Waste—
And, Lo! the phantom Caravan has reach'd
The NOTHING it set out from. Oh, make haste!
OMAR KHAYYAM—*Rubaiyat*. St. XLVIII. FITZGERALD'S Trans.

14
But helpless Pieces of the Game He plays
Upon this Checker-board of Nights and Days;
Hither and thither moves, and checks, and slays,
And one by one back in the Closet lays.
OMAR KHAYYAM—*Rubaiyat*. LXIX. FITZGERALD'S trans.
(See also HUXLEY)

15
And fear not lest Existence closing your
Account should lose or know the type no more:
The Eternal Sáki from that Bowl has poured
Millions of Bubbles like us and will pour.
OMAR KHAYYAM—*Rubaiyat*. FITZGERALD'S Trans. (In the edition of 1889 the second line reads: Account and mine, should know the like no more.)
(See also BACON)

16
My life is like the summer rose
That opens to the morning sky,
But ere the shade of evening close
Is scatter'd on the ground to die.
Claimed by PATRICK O'KELLY. *The Simile*. Pub. 1824. Authorship doubted. The lines appeared in a Philadelphia paper about 1815–16, attributed to RICHARD HENRY WILDE.

17
Id quoque, quod vivam, munus habere dei.
This also, that I live, I consider a gift of God.
OVID—*Tristium*. I. 1. 20.

18
This life a theatre we well may call,
Where very actor must perform with art,
Or laugh it through, and make a farce of all,
Or learn to bear with grace his tragic part.
PALLADAS. Epitaph in *Palatine Anthology*. X. 72. As translated by ROBERT BLAND. (From the Greek.) Part of this SIR THOMAS SHADWELL wished to have inscribed on the monument in Westminster Abbey to his father, THOMAS SHADWELL.
(See Quotations under ACTING, WORLD)

19
Condition de l'homme, inconstance, ennui, inquietude.
The state of man is inconstancy, ennui, anxiety.
PASCAL—*Pensées*. Art. VI. 46.

20
On s'eveille, on se léve, on s'habille, et l'on sort;
On rentre, on dine, on soupe, on se couche, et l'on dort.
One awakens, one rises, one dresses, and one goes forth;
One returns, one dines, one sups, one retires and one sleeps.
DE PIIS.
(See also MONTENAEKEN)

21
Natura vero nihil hominibus brevitate vitæ præstitit melius.
Nature has given man no better thing than shortness of life.
PLINY the Elder—*Historia Naturalis*. VII. 51. 3.

1
She went from opera, park, assembly, play,
To morning walks, and prayers three hours a day.
To part her time 'twixt reading and bohea,
To muse, and spill her solitary tea,
Or o'er cold coffee trifle with the spoon,
Count the slow clock, and dine exact at noon.

Pope—*Ep. to Miss Blount on Leaving Town.* L. 13.

2
Let us (since life can little more supply
Than just to look about us and to die)
Expatiate free o'er all this scene of man;
A mighty maze! but not without a plan.

Pope—*Essay on Man.* Ep. I. L. 1.

3
Placed on this isthmus of a middle state.

Pope—*Essay on Man.* Ep. II. L. 3.
(See also Lillo)

4
Fix'd like a plant on his peculiar spot,
To draw nutrition, propagate and rot.

Pope—*Essay on Man.* Ep. II. L. 63.
(See also As You Like It)

5
On life's vast ocean diversely we sail,
Reason the card, but passion is the gale.

Pope—*Essay on Man.* Ep. II. L. 107.

6
Like bubbles on the sea of matter borne,
They rise, they break, and to that sea return.

Pope—*Essay on Man.* Ep. III. L. 19.
(See also Omar)

7
Like following life through creatures you dissect,
You lose it in the moment you detect.

Pope—*Moral Essays.* Ep. I. L. 29.

8
See how the World its Veterans rewards!
A Youth of Frolics, an old Age of Cards;
Fair to no purpose, artful to no end,
Young without Lovers, old without a Friend;
A Fop their Passion, but their Prize a Sot;
Alive ridiculous, and dead forgot.

Pope—*Moral Essays.* Ep. II. L. 243.

9
Learn to live well, or fairly make your will;
You've play'd, and lov'd, and ate, and drank your fill:
Walk sober off, before a sprightlier age
Comes titt'ring on, and shoves you from the stage.

Pope—*Second Book of Horace.* Ep. II. L. 322.

10
Through the sequester'd vale of rural life
The venerable patriarch guileless held
The tenor of his way.

Porteus—*Death.* L. 109.
(See also Gay)

11
Amid two seas, on one small point of land,
Wearied, uncertain, and amazed we stand.

Prior—*Solomon on the Vanity of Human Wishes.* Pt. III. L. 616.
(See also Lillo)

12
Who breathes must suffer; and who thinks, must mourn;
And he alone is bless'd who ne'er was born.

Prior—*Solomon on the Vanity of the World.* Bk. III. L. 240.

13
So vanishes our state; so pass our days;
So life but opens now, and now decays;
The cradle and the tomb, alas! so nigh,
To live is scarce distinguish'd from to die.

Prior—*Solomon on the Vanity of the World.* Bk. III. L. 527.

14
Half my life is full of sorrow,
Half of joy, still fresh and new;
One of these lives is a fancy,
But the other one is true.

Adelaide A. Procter—*Dream-Life.*

15
Lord, make me to know mine end, and the measure of my days, what it is; that I may know how frail I am.

Psalms. XXXIX. 4.

16
As for man his days are as grass; as a flower of the field so he flourisheth.

Psalms. CIII. 15.

17
The wind passeth over it, and it is gone; and the place thereof shall know it no more.

Psalms. CIII. 16.

18
Our Life is nothing but a Winter's day;
Some only break their Fast, and so away:
Others stay to Dinner, and depart full fed:
The deepest Age but Sups, and goes to Bed:
He's most in debt that lingers out the Day:
Who dies betime, has less, and less to pay.

Quarles—*Divine Fancies. On The Life of Man.* (1633) Quoted in different forms for epitaphs.
(See also Dryden, Gerhard, Henslaw, Jenkyns, Seneca)

19
Man's life is like a Winter's day:
Some only breakfast and away;
Others to dinner stay and are full fed,
The oldest man but sups and goes to bed.
Long is his life who lingers out the day,
Who goes the soonest has the least to pay;
Death is the Waiter, some few run on tick,
And some alas! must pay the bill to Nick!
Tho' I owed much, I hope long trust is given,
And truly mean to pay all bills in Heaven.

Epitaph in *Barnwell Churchyard*, near Cambridge, England.

20
Et là commençay à penser qu'il est bien vray ce que l'on dit, que la moitié du monde ne sçait comment l'aultre vit.

And there I began to think that it is very true, which is said, that half the world does not know how the other half lives.

Rabelais—*Pantagruel.* Ch. XXXII.

21
Vivat, fifat, pipat, bibat.

May he live, fife, pipe, drink.

Rabelais—*Pantagruel.* Bk. IV. Ch. 53.

Called by Epistemon, "O secret apocalyptique." It suggests "Old King Cole."

22
The romance of life begins and ends with two blank pages. Age and extreme old age.

Jean Paul Richter.

1
Der Mensch hat hier dritthalb Minuten, eine zu lächeln—eine zu seufzen—und eine halbe zu lieben: denn mitten in dieser Minute stirbt er.

Man has here two and a half minutes—one to smile, one to sigh, and a half to love: for in the midst of this minute he dies.

JEAN PAUL RICHTER—*Hesperus*. IV.

2
Jeder Mensch hat eine Regen-Ecke seines Lebens aus der ihm das schlimme Wetter nachzieht.

Every man has a rainy corner of his life out of which foul weather proceeds and follows after him.

JEAN PAUL RICHTER—*Titan*. Zykel 123.

3
Die Parzen und Furien ziehen auch mit verbundnen Händen um das Leben, wie die Grazien und die Sirenen.

The Fates and Furies, as well as the Graces and Sirens, glide with linked hands over life.

JEAN PAUL RICHTER—*Titan*. Zykel 140.

4
Nur Thaten geben dem Leben Stärke, nur Maas ihm Reiz.

Only deeds give strength to life, only moderation gives it charm.

JEAN PAUL RICHTER—*Titan*. Zykel 145.

5
I bargained with Life for a penny,
And Life would pay no more,
However I begged at evening
When I counted my scanty store.

JESSIE B. RITTENHOUSE—*My Wage*.

6
I worked for a menial's hire,
Only to learn, dismayed,
That any wage I had asked of Life,
Life would have paid.

JESSIE B. RITTENHOUSE—*My Wage*.

7
In speaking to you men of the greatest city of the West, men of the state which gave to the country Lincoln and Grant, men who preeminently and distinctly embody all that is most American in the American character, I wish to preach not the doctrine of ignoble ease, but the doctrine of the strenuous life.

ROOSEVELT. At Appomattox Day celebration of the Hamilton Club of Chicago. April 10, 1899.

8
This life is but the passage of a day,
This life is but a pang and all is over;
But in the life to come which fades not away
Every love shall abide and every lover.

CHRISTINA G. ROSSETTI—*Saints and Angels*.

9
Life's but a span, or a tale, or a word,
That in a trice, or suddaine, is rehearsèd.

The Roxburghe Ballads. A Friend's Advice. Pt. II. Edited by Wm. Chappell.

(See also KING LEAR, NEW ENGLAND PRIMER)

10
Vita ipsa qua fruimur brevis est.

The very life which we enjoy is short.

SALLUST—*Catilina*. I.

11
Ignavia nemo immortalis factus: neque quisquam parens liberis, uti æterni forent, optavit; magis, uti boni honestique vitam exigerent.

No one has become immortal by sloth; nor has any parent prayed that his children should live forever; but rather that they should lead an honorable and upright life.

SALLUST—*Jugurtha*. LXXXV.

12
Say, what is life? 'Tis to be born,
A helpless Babe, to greet the light
With a sharp wail, as if the morn
Foretold a cloudy noon and night;
To weep, to sleep, and weep again,
With sunny smiles between; and then?

J. G. SAXE—*The Story of Life*.

(See also DYER, KING LEAR, also TENNYSON under BABYHOOD)

13
Wir, wir leben! Unser sind die Stunden
Und der Lebende hat Recht.

We, we live! ours are the hours, and the living have their claims.

SCHILLER—*An die Freude*. St. 1.

14
Nicht der Tummelplatz des Lebens—sein Gehalt bestimmt seinen Werth.

'Tis not the mere stage of life but the part we play thereon that gives the value.

SCHILLER—*Fiesco*. III. 2.

15
Nicht seine Freudenseite kehrte dir
Das Leben zu.

Life did not present its sunny side to thee.

SCHILLER—*Marie Stuart*. II. 3. 136.

16
Wouldst thou wisely, and with pleasure,
Pass the days of life's short measure,
From the slow one counsel take,
But a tool of him ne'er make;
Ne'er as friend the swift one know,
Nor the constant one as foe.

SCHILLER—*Proverbs of Confucius*. E. A. BOWRING's trans.

17
Des Lebens Mai blüht einmal und nicht wieder.

The May of life blooms once and never again.

SCHILLER—*Resignation*. St. 2.

18
O'er Ocean, with a thousand masts, sails forth the stripling bold—
One boat, hard rescued from the deep, draws into port the old!

SCHILLER—*Votive Tablets. Expectation and Fulfilment*.

19
I've lived and loved.

SCHILLER—*Wallenstein*. Pt. I. Piccolomini. Song in Act II. Sc. 6. COLERIDGE's trans.

20
Das Spiel des Lebens sieht sich heiter an,
Wenn man den sichern Schatz im Herzen trägt.

The game of life looks cheerful when one carries a treasure safe in his heart.

SCHILLER—*Wallenstein*. Pt. I. Piccolomini. Act III. 4.

1
Sein Spruch war: leben und leben lassen.
His saying was: live and let live.
SCHILLER—*Wallenstein's Lager.* VI. 106. 110.

2
From a boy
I gloated on existence. Earth to me
Seemed all-sufficient and my sojourn there
One trembling opportunity for joy.
ALAN SEEGER—*Sonnet. I Loved.*

3
Tota vita nihil aliud quam ad mortem iter est.
The whole of life is nothing but a journey to death.
SENECA—*Consol. ad Polybium.* 29.

4
Vita, si scias uti, longa est.
Life, if thou knowest how to use it, is long enough.
SENECA—*De Brevitate Vitæ.* II.

5
Exigua pars est vitæ quam nos vivimus.
The part of life which we really live is short.
SENECA—*De Brevitate Vitæ.* II.

6
Si ad naturam vivas, nunquam eris pauper; si ad opinionem, numquam dives.
If you live according to nature, you never will be poor; if according to the world's caprice, you will never be rich.
SENECA—*Epistolæ Ad Lucilium.* XVI.

7
Molestum est, semper vitam inchoare; male vivunt qui semper vivere incipiunt.
It is a tedious thing to be always beginning life; they live badly who always begin to live.
SENECA—*Epistolæ Ad Lucilium.* XXIII.

8
Ante senectutem curavi ut bene viverem, in senectute (curo) ut bene moriar; bene autem mori est libenter mori.
Before old age I took care to live well; in old age I take care to die well; but to die well is to die willingly.
SENECA—*Epistolæ Ad Lucilium.* LXI.

9
Non vivere bonum est, sed bene vivere.
To live is not a blessing, but to live well.
SENECA—*Epistolæ Ad Lucilium.* LXX.

10
Atqui vivere, militare est.
But life is a warfare.
SENECA—*Epistolæ Ad Lucilium.* XCVI.

11
Propra vivere et singulos dies singulas vitas puta.
Make haste to live, and consider each day a life.
SENECA—*Epistolæ Ad Lucilium.* CI.

12
Non domus hoc corpus sed hospitium et quidem breve.
This body is not a home, but an inn; and that only for a short time.
SENECA—*Epistolæ Ad Lucilium.* CXX.
(See also DRYDEN)

13
Quomodo fabula, sic vita: non quam diu, sed quam bene acta sit, refert.
As is a tale, so is life: not how long it is, but how good it is, is what matters.
SENECA—*Epistles.* LXXXVII.
(See also AS YOU LIKE IT)

14
Prima quæ vitam dedit hora, carpit.
The hour which gives us life begins to take it away.
SENECA—*Hercules Furens.* VIII. 74.

15
The web of our life is of a mingled yarn, good and ill together.
All's Well That Ends Well. Act IV. Sc. 3. L. 80.

16
O excellent! I love long life better than figs.
Antony and Cleopatra. Act I. Sc. 2. L. 32.

17
And this our life, exempt from public haunt,
Finds tongues in trees, books in the running brooks,
Sermons in stones, and good in everything.
As You Like It. Act II. Sc. 1. L. 15.

18
And so, from hour to hour, we ripe and ripe.
And then, from hour to hour, we rot and rot;
And thereby hangs a tale.
As You Like It. Act II. Sc. 7. L. 26.
Last phrase in *The Taming of the Shrew.* Act IV. Sc. 1; *Othello.* Act III. Sc. 1. *The Merry Wives of Windsor.* Act I. Sc. 4. *As You Like It.* Act II. Sc. 7. RABELAIS. Bk. V. Ch. IV.
(See also POPE, SENECA)

19
Why, what should be the fear?
I do not set my life at a pin's fee.
Hamlet. Act I. Sc. 4. L. 66.

20
And a man's life's no more than to say "One."
Hamlet. Act V. Sc. 2. L. 74.

21
O gentlemen, the time of life is short!
To spend that shortness basely were too long,
If life did ride upon a dial's point,
Still ending at the arrival of an hour.
Henry IV. Pt. I. Act V. Sc. 2. L. 82.

22
Let life be short; else shame will be too long.
Henry V. Act IV. Sc. 5. L. 23.

23
The sands are number'd that make up my life;
Here must I stay, and here my life must end.
Henry VI. Pt. III. Act I. Sc. 4. L. 25

24
I cannot tell what you and other men
Think of this life; but, for my single self,
I had as lief not be as live to be
In awe of such a thing as I myself.
Julius Cæsar. Act I. Sc. 2. L. 93.

25
This day I breathed first: time is come round,
And where I did begin there shall I end;
My life is run his compass.
Julius Cæsar. Act V. Sc. 3. L. 23.

1
Life is as tedious as a twice-told tale,
Vexing the dull ear of a drowsy man.
King John. Act III. Sc. 4. L. 108.
(See also HOMER under STORY TELLING)

2
Thy life's a miracle.
King Lear. Act IV. Sc. 6. L. 55.

3
When we are born, we cry, that we are come
To this great stage of fools.
King Lear. Act IV. Sc. 6. L. 186.
(See also SAXE)

4
Nor stony tower, nor walls of beaten brass,
Nor airless dungeon, nor strong links of iron,
Can be retentive to the strength of spirit;
But life, being weary of these worldly bars,
Never lacks power to dismiss itself.
Julius Cæsar. Act I. Sc. 3. L. 93.

5
That but this blow
Might be the be-all and the end-all here,
But here, upon this bank and shoal of time,
We'ld jump the life to come.
Macbeth. Act I. Sc. 7. L. 4.

6
Had I but died an hour before this chance,
I had liv'd a blessed time; for, from this instant,
There's nothing serious in mortality:
All is but toys; renown, and grace is dead;
The wine of life is drawn, and the mere lees
Is left this vault to brag of.
Macbeth. Act II. Sc. 3. L. 96.

7
So weary with disasters, tugg'd with fortune,
That I would set my life on any chance,
To mend, or be rid on't.
Macbeth. Act III. Sc. I. L. 113.

8
Out, out, brief candle!
Life's but a walking shadow.
Macbeth. Act V. Sc. 5. L. 23.

9
I bear a charmed life.
Macbeth. Act V. Sc. 8. L. 12.

10
Reason thus with life:
If I do lose thee, I do lose a thing
That none but fools would keep.
Measure for Measure. Act III. Sc. 1. L. 6.

11
Life is a shuttle.
Merry Wives of Windsor. Act V. Sc. 1. L. 20.

12
Her father lov'd me; oft invited me;
Still question'd me the story of my life,
From year to year, the battles, sieges, fortunes,
That I have pass'd.
Othello. Act I. Sc. 3. L. 128.

13
It is silliness to live when to live is torment; and then have we a prescription to die when death is our physician.
Othello. Act I. Sc. 3. L. 309.

14
Life was driving at brains—at its darling object: an organ by which it can attain not only self-consciousness but self-understanding.
BERNARD SHAW—*Man and Superman.* Act III.

15
J'ai vécu.
I have survived.
SIÈYES. After the Reign of Terror, when asked what he had done.

16
We have two lives;
The soul of man is like the rolling world,
One half in day, the other dipt in night;
The one has music and the flying cloud,
The other, silence and the wakeful stars.
ALEX. SMITH—*Horton.* L. 76.

17
Yes, this is life; and everywhere we meet,
Not victor crowns, but wailings of defeat.
ELIZABETH OAKES SMITH—*Sonnet. The Unattained.*

18
"Life is not lost," said she, "for which is bought
Endlesse renowne."
SPENSER—*Faerie Queene.* Bk. III. Canto XI. St. 19.

19
Away with funeral music—set
The pipe to powerful lips—
The cup of life's for him that drinks
And not for him that sips.
STEVENSON. At Boulogne. (1872)

20
To be honest, to be kind—to earn a little and to spend a little less, to make upon the whole a family happier for his presence, to renounce when that shall be necessary and not be embittered, to keep a few friends but these without capitulation—above all, on the same grim condition to keep friends with himself—here is a task for all that a man has of fortitude and delicacy.
STEVENSON—*Christmas Sermon.*

21
Man is an organ of life, and God alone is life.
SWEDENBORG—*True Christian Religion.* Par. 504.

22
Gaudeamus igitur,
Juvenes dum sumus
Post jucundam juventutem.
Post molestam senectutem.
Nos habebit humus.
Let us live then, and be glad
While young life's before us
After youthful pastime had,
After old age hard and sad,
Earth will slumber over us.
Author Unknown. JOHN ADDINGTON SYMONDS' Trans.

23
O vita, misero longa! felici brevis!
O life! long to the wretched, short to the happy.
SYRUS—*Maxims.*

24
Let your life lightly dance on the edges of Time like dew on the tip of a leaf.
RABINDRANATH TAGORE—*Gardener.* 45.

25
. . . The wise man warns me that life is but a dewdrop on the lotus leaf.
RABINDRANATH TAGORE—*Gardener.* 46.

1
So his life has flowed
From its mysterious urn a sacred stream,
In whose calm depth the beautiful and pure
Alone are mirrored; which, though shapes of ill
May hover round its surface, glides in light,
And takes no shadow from them.

THOMAS NOON TALFOURD—*Ion.* Act I. Sc. 1. L. 138.

2
For life lives only in success.

BAYARD TAYLOR—*Amran's Wooing.* St. 5.

3
Our life is scarce the twinkle of a star
In God's eternal day.

BAYARD TAYLOR—*Autumnal Vespers.*

4
The white flower of a blameless life.

TENNYSON—*Dedication to Idylls of the King.*

5
Life is not as idle ore,
But iron dug from central gloom,
And heated hot with burning fears,
And dipt in baths of hissing tears,
And batter'd with the shocks of doom,
To shape and use.

TENNYSON—*In Memoriam.* Pt. CXVIII. St. 5.

6
I cannot rest from travel: I will drink
Life to the lees.

TENNYSON—*Ulysses.* L. 6.

7
Life is like a game of tables, the chances are not in our power, but the playing is.

TERENCE—*Adelphi;* also PLATO—*Commonwealth.* Quoted by JEREMY TAYLOR—*Holy Living.* Sec. VI. *Of Contentedness.*
(See also HUXLEY)

8
No particular motive for living, except the custom and habit of it.

THACKERAY. Article on Thackeray and his Novels in *Blackwood's Mag.* Jan. 1854.
(See also DICKENS)

9
My life is like a stroll upon the beach.

THOREAU—*A Week on the Concord and Merrimack Rivers.*

10
The tree of deepest root is found
Least willing still to quit the ground;
'Twas therefore said by ancient sages,
That love of life increased with years
So much, that in our latter stages,
When pain grows sharp, and sickness rages,
The greatest love of life appears.

HESTER L. THRALE—*Three Warnings.*

11
We live not in our moments or our years:
The present we fling from us like the rind
Of some sweet future, which we after find
Bitter to taste.

RICHARD CHENEVIX TRENCH—*To——.*

12
Life let us cherish, while yet the taper glows,
And the fresh flow'ret pluck ere it close;
Why are we fond of toil and care?
Why choose the rankling thorn to wear?

J. M. USTERI—*Life let us Cherish.*

13
Pour exécuter de grandes choses, il faut vivre comme si on ne devait jamais mourir.

To execute great things, one should live as though one would never die.

VAUVENARGUES.

14
Qu'est-ce qu'une grande vie? C'est un rêve de jeunesse réalisé dans l'âge mûr.

What is a great life? It is the dreams of youth realised in old age.

ALFRED DE VIGNY, quoted by LOUIS RATISBONNE in an article in the *Journal des Débats,* Oct. 4, 1863.

15
Ma vie est un combat.
My life is a struggle.

VOLTAIRE—*Le Fanatisme.* II. 4.

16
Life is a comedy.

WALPOLE—Letter to SIR HORACE MANN, Dec. 31, 1769. In a letter to same, March 5, 1772. "This world is a comedy, not Life."
(See also WALPOLE under WORLD)

17
Life is a game of whist. From unseen sources
The cards are shuffled, and the hands are dealt.
Blind are our efforts to control the forces
That, though unseen, are no less strongly felt.

I do not like the way the cards are shuffled,
But yet I like the game and want to play;
And through the long, long night will I, unruffled,
Play what I get, until the break of day.

EUGENE F. WARE—*Whist.*
(See also HUXLEY)

18
Since the bounty of Providence is new every day,
As we journey through life let us live by the way.

WALTER WATSON—*Drinking Song.*

19
Yet I know that I dwell in the midst of the roar
of the Cosmic Wheel
In the hot collision of Forces, and the clangor
of boundless Strife,
Mid the sound of the speed of worlds, the rushing
worlds, and the peal
Of the thunder of Life.

WILLIAM WATSON—*Dawn on the Headland.*

20
Our life contains a thousand springs,
And dies if one be gone.
Strange! that a harp of thousand strings
Should keep in tune so long.

WATTS—*Hymns and Spiritual Songs.* Bk. II. Hymn XIX.

21
Lo! on a narrow neck of land,
'Twixt two unbounded seas, I stand.
Secure, insensible.

CHARLES WESLEY—*Hymn.* (1749)
(See also LILLO)

22
I desire to have both heaven and hell ever in my eye, while I stand on this isthmus of life, between two boundless oceans.

JOHN WESLEY—*Letter to Charles Wesley.* (1747) (See also LILLO)

1
Long and long has the grass been growing,
Long and long has the rain been falling,
Long has the globe been rolling round.
WALT WHITMAN—*Exposition.* I.

2
I swear the earth shall surely be complete to him or her who shall be complete,
The earth remains jagged and broken only to him or her who remains jagged and broken.
WALT WHITMAN—*Song of the Rolling Earth.* 3.

3
Our lives are albums written through
With good or ill, with false or true;
And as the blessed angels turn
The pages of our years,
God grant they read the good with smiles,
And blot the ill with tears!
WHITTIER—*Written in a Lady's Album.*

4
The days grow shorter, the nights grow longer,
The headstones thicken along the way;
And life grows sadder, but love grows stronger
For those who walk with us day by day.
ELLA WHEELER WILCOX—*Interlude.*

5
Our lives are songs; God writes the words
And we set them to music at pleasure;
And the song grows glad, or sweet or sad,
As we choose to fashion the measure.
ELLA WHEELER WILCOX—*Our Lives.* St. 102.
Claimed for REV. THOMAS GIBBONS. Appears in his 18th Century Book. See *Notes and Queries*, April 1, 1905. P. 249.

6
Ah! somehow life is bigger after all
Than any painted angel could we see
The God that is within us!
OSCAR WILDE—*Humanitad.* St. 60.

7
The Book of Life begins with a man and a woman in a garden.
It ends with Revelations.
OSCAR WILDE—*Woman of No Importance.* Act I.

8
We live by Admiration, Hope, and Love;
And, even as these are well and wisely fixed,
In dignity of being we ascend.
WORDSWORTH—*Excursion.* Bk. IV.

9
Plain living and high thinking are no more.
WORDSWORTH—*Sonnet dedicated to National Independence and Liberty.* No. XIII. Written in London, Sept. 1802.
(See also HAWEIS)

10
For what are men who grasp at praise sublime,
But bubbles on the rapid stream of time,
That rise, and fall, that swell, and are no more,
Born, and forgot, ten thousand in an hour?
YOUNG—*Love of Fame.* Satire II. L. 285.
(See also OMAR)

11
While man is growing, life is in decrease.
And cradles rock us nearer to the tomb:
Our birth is nothing but our death begun.
YOUNG—*Night Thoughts.* Night V. L. 718.

12
That life is long, which answers life's great end.
YOUNG—*Night Thoughts.* Night V. L. 773.

13
Still seems it strange, that thou shouldst live forever?
Is it less strange, that thou shouldst live at all?
This is a miracle; and that no more.
YOUNG—*Night Thoughts.* Night VII. L. 1,396.

14
A narrow isthmus betwixt time and eternity.
YOUNG—*On Pleasure. Letter.* III.
(See also LILLO)

LIGHT

15
Now that the sun is gleaming bright,
Implore we, bending low,
That He, the Uncreated Light,
May guide us as we go.
Attributed to ADAM DE SAINT VICTOR. Old Latin Hymn said to have been sung at the death-bed of WILLIAM THE CONQUEROR.

16
Corruption springs from light: 'tis one same power
Creates, preserves, destroys; matter whereon
It works, on e'er self-transmutative form,
Common to now the living, now the dead.
BAILEY—*Festus.* Sc. *Water and Wood.*

17
Misled by Fancy's meteor-ray,
By passion driven;
But yet the light that led astray,
Was light from Heaven.
BURNS—*The Vision.*
(See also WORDSWORTH)

18
For I light my candle from their torches.
BURTON—*Anatomy of Melancholy.* Pt. III. Sect. II. Memb. 5. Subsec. 1.

19
Hinc lucem et pocula sacra.
Hence light and the sacred vessels.
Motto of Cambridge University.

20
Light is the first of painters. There is no object so foul that intense light will not make it beautiful.
EMERSON—*Nature.* Ch. III.

21
I shall light a candle of understanding in thine heart, which shall not be put out.
II Esdras. XIV. 25.

22
Light (God's eldest daughter!).
FULLER—*The Holy and Profane States.* Bk. III. *Of Building.*

23
And God said, Let there be light: and there was light.
Genesis. I. 3.
(See also POPE)

24
Against the darkness outer
God's light his likeness takes,
And he from the mighty doubter
The great believer makes.
R. W. GILDER—*The New Day.* Pt. IV. *Song XV.*

1
Mehr Licht!
More light!
Said to be the last words of Goethe.
(See also Longfellow)

2
Wo viel Licht is, ist starker Schatten.
Where there is much light, the shadows are deepest.
Goethe—*Götz von Berlichingen.* I. 24.

3
Blasted with excess of light.
Gray—*Progress of Poesy.*
(See also Milton)

4
Like our dawn, merely a sob of light.
Victor Hugo—*La Legende des Siècles.*

5
The true light, which lighteth every man that cometh into the world.
John. I. 9.

6
He was a burning and a shining light.
John. V. 35.

7
Walk while ye have the light, lest darkness come upon you.
John. XII. 35.

8
The Light that Failed.
Kipling—*Title of Story*

9
The prayer of Ajax was for light;
Through all that dark and desperate fight,
The blackness of that noonday night.
Longfellow—*The Goblet of Life.* St. 8.
(See also Goethe, Tennyson)

10
Fra l' ombre un lampo solo
Basta al nocchier fugace
Che già ritrova il polo,
Già riconosce il mar.
In the dark a glimmering light is often sufficient for the pilot to find the polar star and to fix his course.
Metastasio—*Achille.* I. 6.

11
With thy long levell'd rule of streaming light.
Milton—*Comus.* L. 340.

12
He that has light within his own clear breast
May sit i' th' centre and enjoy bright day;
But he that hides a dark soul and foul thoughts
Benighted walks under the mid-day sun.
Milton—*Comus.* L. 381.

13
Where glowing embers through the room
Teach light to counterfeit a gloom.
Milton—*Il Penseroso.* L. 79.

14
But let my due feet never fail
To walk the studious cloisters pale,
And love the high embowed roof,
With antique pillars massy proof,
And storied windows richly dight;
Casting a dim religious light.
Milton—*Il Penseroso.* L. 155.
Compare Euripides—*Bacchæ.* 486.

15
Hail, holy light! offspring of heaven firstborn!
Or of th' eternal co-eternal beam,
May I express thee unblam'd? since God is light
And never but in unapproached light
Dwelt from eternity, dwelt then in thee,
Bright effluence of bright essence increate!
Milton—*Paradise Lost.* Bk III. L. 1.

16
Dark with excessive bright.
Milton—*Paradise Lost.* Bk. III. L. 380.
(See also Gray)

17
And from her native east,
To journey through the aery gloom began,
Spher'd in a radiant cloud, for yet the sun
Was not.
Milton—*Paradise Lost.* Bk. VII. L. 245.

18
There swift return
Diurnal, merely to officiate light
Round this opacous earth, this punctual spot.
Milton—*Paradise Lost.* Bk. VIII. L. 21.

19
And this I know; whether the one True Light
Kindle to Love, or Wrath consume me quite,
One flash of it within the Tavern caught
Better than in the temple lost outright.
Omar Khayyam—*Rubaiyat.* St. 77. Fitz-Gerald's trans.

20
Where art thou, beam of light? Hunters from the mossy rock, saw ye the blue-eyed fair?
Ossian—*Temora.* Bk. VI.

21
Ex luce lucellum.
Out of light a little profit.
Pitt's description of the Window Tax. Also suggested by Robert Lowe, Chancellor, as a motto for matchboxes, when the British Government introduced a match tax, 1871.

22
Those having lamps will pass them on to others.
Plato—*Republic.* 328.

23
Nature and Nature's laws lay hid in night:
God said, "Let Newton be!" and all was light.
Pope—*Epitaph Intended for Sir Isaac Newton.*
(See also *Genesis*)

24
Nur der Gewissenswurm schwärmt mit der Eule. Sünder und böse Geister scheun das Licht.
Only the worm of conscience consorts with the owl. Sinners and evil spirits shun the light.
Schiller—*Liebe und Cabale.* V. I.

25
Light seeking light doth light of light beguile:
So, ere you find where light in darkness lies,
Your light grows dark by losing of your eyes.
Love's Labour's Lost. Act I. Sc. 1. L. 77.

26
But it is not necessary to light a candle to the sun.
Algernon Sidney—*Discourses on Government.* Ch. II. Sec. XXIII.

27
'Twas a light that made
Darkness itself appear
A thing of comfort.
Southey—*The Curse of Kehama. Padalon.* St. 2.

1
An unreflected light did never yet
Dazzle the vision feminine.
SIR HENRY TAYLOR—*Philip Van Artevelde.* Pt. I. Act I. Sc. 5. L. 88.

2
Thy prayer was "Light—more Light"—while Time shall last
Thou sawest a glory growing on the night,
But not the shadows which that light would cast,
Till shadows vanish in the Light of Light.
TENNYSON—*Inscription on the Window in memory of* CAXTON, in St. Margaret's Church, Westminster, London.
(See also LONGFELLOW)

3
Where God and Nature met in light.
TENNYSON—*In Memoriam.* Pt. CXI. St. 5.

4
A remnant of uneasy light.
WORDSWORTH—*The Matron of Jedborough, and Her Husband.*

5
The light that never was on sea or land,
The consecration, and the poet's dream.
WORDSWORTH—*Elegiac Stanzas.* Suggested by a picture of Peele Castle in a storm.

6
But ne'er to a seductive lay let faith be given;
Nor deem that "light that leads astray" is light from Heaven.
WORDSWORTH—*To the Sons of Burns.*
(See also BURNS)

LILAC

Syringa Vulgaris

7
The lilac spread
Odorous essence.
JEAN INGELOW—*Laurance.* Pt. III.

8
Go down to Kew in lilac-time, in lilac-time, in lilac-time;
Go down to Kew in lilac-time (it isn't far from London).
And you shall wander hand in hand with love in summer's wonderland;
Go down to Kew in lilac-time (it isn't far from London).
ALFRED NOYES—*The Barrel Organ.*

9
I am thinking of the lilac-trees,
That shook their purple plumes,
And when the sash was open,
Shed fragrance through the room.
MRS. ANNA S. STEPHENS—*The Old Apple-Tree.*

10
The purple clusters load the lilac-bushes.
AMELIA B. WELBY—*Hopeless Love.*

11
When lilacs last in the door-yard bloom'd,
And the great star early droop'd in the western sky in the night,
I mourn'd—and yet shall mourn with ever-returning spring.
WALT WHITMAN—*When Lilacs Last in the Door-Yard Bloom'd.* I. *Leaves of Grass.*

12
With every leaf a miracle . . . and from this bush in the door-yard,
With delicate-colour'd blossoms, and heart-shaped leaves of rich green
A sprig, with its flower, I break.
WALT WHITMAN—*When Lilacs Last in the Door-Yard Bloom'd.* III. *Leaves of Grass.*

LILY

Lilium

13
I like not lady-slippers,
Nor yet the sweet-pea blossoms,
Nor yet the flaky roses,
Red or white as snow;
I like the chaliced lilies,
The heavy Eastern lilies,
The gorgeous tiger-lilies,
That in our garden grow.
T. B. ALDRICH—*Tiger Lilies.* St. 1.

14
And lilies are still lilies, pulled
By smutty hands, though spotted from their white.
E. B. BROWNING—*Aurora Leigh.* Bk. III.

15
* * * Purple lilies Dante blew
To a larger bubble with his prophet breath.
E. B. BROWNING—*Aurora Leigh.* Bk. VII.

16
And lilies white, prepared to touch
The whitest thought, nor soil it much,
Of dreamer turned to lover.
E. B. BROWNING—*A Flower in a Letter.*

17
Very whitely still
The lilies of our lives may reassure
Their blossoms from their roots, accessible
Alone to heavenly dews that drop not fewer;
Growing straight out of man's reach, on the hill.
God only, who made us rich, can make us poor.
E. B. BROWNING—*Sonnets from the Portuguese.* XXIV.

18
I wish I were the lily's leaf
To fade upon that bosom warm,
Content to wither, pale and brief,
The trophy of thy paler form.
DIONYSIUS.

19
And the stately lilies stand
Fair in the silvery light,
Like saintly vestals, pale in prayer;
Their pure breath sanctifies the air,
As its fragrance fills the night.
JULIA C. R. DORR—*A Red Rose.*

20
Yet, the great ocean hath no tone of power
Mightier to reach the soul, in thought's hushed hour,
Than yours, ye Lilies! chosen thus and graced!
MRS. HEMANS—*Sonnet. The Lilies of the Field.*

21
The lily is all in white, like a saint,
And so is no mate for me.
HOOD—*Flowers.*

22
We are Lilies fair,
The flower of virgin light;
Nature held us forth, and said,
"Lo! my thoughts of white."
LEIGH HUNT—*Songs and Chorus of the Flowers. Lilies.*

1
O lovely lily clean,
O lily springing green,
O lily bursting white,
Dear lily of delight,
Spring in my heart agen
That I may flower to men.
MASEFIELD—*Everlasting Mercy.* Last St.

2
Consider the lilies of the field, how they grow; they toil not, neither do they spin.
Matthew. VI. 28.

3
"Look to the lilies how they grow!"
'Twas thus the Saviour said, that we,
Even in the simplest flowers that blow,
God's ever-watchful care might see.
MOIR—*Lilies.*

4
For her, the lilies hang their heads and die.
POPE—*Pastorals. Autumn.* L. 26.

5
Gracious as sunshine, sweet as dew
Shut in a lily's golden core.
MARGARET J. PRESTON—*Agnes.*

6
Is not this lily pure?
What fuller can procure
A white so perfect, spotless clear
As in this flower doth appear?
QUARLES—*The School of the Heart. Ode XXX.* St. 4.

7
How bravely thou becomest thy bed, fresh lily.
Cymbeline. Act II. Sc. 2. L. 15

8
Like the lily,
That once was mistress of the field and flourish'd,
I'll hang my head and perish.
Henry VIII. Act III. Sc. 1. L. 151.

9
And the wand-like lily which lifted up,
As a Mænad, its moonlight-coloured cup,
Till the fiery star, which is its eye,
Gazed through clear dew on the tender sky.
SHELLEY—*The Sensitive Plant.* Pt. I.

10
"Thou wert not, Solomon! in all thy glory
Array'd," the lilies cry, "in robes like ours;
How vain your grandeur! Ah, how transitory
Are human flowers!"
HORACE SMITH—*Hymn to the Flowers.* St. 10.

11
But who will watch my lilies,
When their blossoms open white?
By day the sun shall be sentry,
And the moon and the stars by night!
BAYARD TAYLOR—*The Poets' Journal. The Garden of Roses.* St. 14.

12
But lilies, stolen from grassy mold,
No more curlèd state unfold,
Translated to a vase of gold;
In burning throne though they keep still
Serenities unthawed and chill.
FRANCIS THOMPSON—*Gilded Gold.* St. 1.

13
Yet in that bulb, those sapless scales,
The lily wraps her silver vest,
Till vernal suns and vernal gales
Shall kiss once more her fragrant breast.
MARY TIGHE—*The Lily.*

LILY-OF-THE-VALLEY

Convallaria Majalis

14
The lily of the vale, of flowers the queen,
Puts on the robe she neither sew'd nor spun.
MICHAEL BRUCE—*Elegy.*

15
White bud! that in meek beauty dost lean
Thy cloistered cheek as pale as moonlight snow,
Thou seem'st, beneath thy huge, high leaf of green,
An Eremite beneath his mountain's brow.
GEORGE CROLY—*The Lily of the Valley.*

16 And in his left he held a basket full
Of all sweet herbs that searching eye could cull
Wild thyme, and valley-lilies whiter still
Than Leda's love, and cresses from the rill.
KEATS—*Endymion.* Bk. I. L. 155.

17
And the Naiad-like lily of the vale,
Whom youth makes so fair and passion so pale,
That the light of its tremulous bells is seen,
Through their pavilions of tender green.
SHELLEY—*The Sensitive Plant.* Pt. I.

18
Where scattered wild the Lily of the Vale
Its balmy essence breathes.
THOMSON—*The Seasons. Spring.* L. 445.

19 And leaves of that shy plant,
(Her flowers were shed) the lily of the vale.
That loves the ground, and from the sun withholds
Her pensive beauty, from the breeze her sweets.
WORDSWORTH—*The Excursion.* Bk. IX. L. 540.

LINCOLN

20
"Railsplitter."
Lincoln and John Hanks in 1830 split 3,000 rails. Incident related in the House of Representatives by WASHBURN, and quoted in the Republican State Convention at Decatur, Macon County.

21
Some opulent force of genius, soul, and race,
Some deep life-current from far centuries
Flowed to his mind and lighted his sad eyes,
And gave his name, among great names, high place.
JOEL BENTON—*Another Washington.* (Lincoln.)

22
To set the stones back in the wall
Lest the divided house should fall.
The beams of peace he laid,
While kings looked on, afraid.
JOHN VANCE CHENEY—*Lincoln.*

23
Unheralded, God's captain came
As one that answers to his name;
Nor dreamed how high his charge,
His privilege how large.
JOHN VANCE CHENEY—*Lincoln.*

1

If so men's memories not a monument be,
None shalt thou have. Warm hearts, and not cold stone,
Must mark thy grave, or thou shalt lie, unknown.
Marbles keep not themselves; how then, keep thee?

JOHN VANCE CHENEY—*Thy Monument.*

2

O, Uncommon Commoner! may your name
Forever lead like a living flame!
Unschooled scholar! how did you learn
The wisdom a lifetime may not earn?
Unsainted martyr! higher than saint!
You were a *man* with a man's constraint.
In the world, *of* the world was your lot;
With it and for it the fight you fought,
And never till Time is itself forgot
And the heart of man is a pulseless clot
Shall the blood flow slow, when we think the thought Of Lincoln!

EDMUND VANCE COOKE—*The Uncommon Commoner.*

3

A martyr to the cause of man,
His blood is freedom's eucharist,
And in the world's great hero list
His name shall lead the van.

CHARLES G. HALPIN—*Death of Lincoln.*

4

When Lincoln died, hate died—
* * * * * *
And anger, came to North and South
When Lincoln died.

W. J. LAMPTON—*Lincoln.*

5

That nation has not lived in vain which has given the world Washington and Lincoln, the best great men and the greatest good men whom history can show. * * * You cry out in the words of Bunyan, "So Valiant-for-Truth passed over, and all the trumpets sounded for him on the other side."

HENRY CABOT LODGE—*Lincoln.* Address before the Mass. Legislature, Feb. 12, 1909.

6

Nature, they say, doth dote,
And cannot make a man
Save on some worn-out plan
Repeating us by rote:
For him her Old World moulds aside she threw
And, choosing sweet clay from the breast
Of the unexhausted West,
With stuff untainted shaped a hero new.

LOWELL—*A Hero New.*

7

When the Norn-mother saw the Whirlwind Hour,
Greatening and darkening as it hurried on,
She bent the strenuous Heavens and came down
To make a man to meet the mortal need.
She took the tried clay of the common road—
Clay warm yet with the genial heat of Earth,
Dashed through it all a strain of prophecy;
Then mixed a laughter with the serious stuff.
It was a stuff to wear for centuries,
A man that matched the mountains, and compelled
The stars to look our way and honor us.

EDWIN MARKHAM—*Lincoln, The Man of the People.*

8

Look on this cast, and know the hand
That bore a nation in its hold;
From this mute witness understand
What Lincoln was—how large of mould.

E. C. STEDMAN—*Hand of Lincoln.*

9

Lo, as I gaze, the statured man,
Built up from yon large hand appears:
A type that nature wills to plan
But once in all a people's years.

E. C. STEDMAN—*Hand of Lincoln.*

10

No Cæsar he whom we lament,
A Man without a precedent,
Sent, it would seem, to do
His work, and perish, too.

R. H. STODDARD—*The Man We Mourn Today.*

11

You lay a wreath on murdered Lincoln's bier,
You, who with mocking pencil wont to trace,
Broad for the self-complacent British sneer,
His length of shambling limb, his furrowed face.

TOM TAYLOR—*Britannia Sympathises with Columbia.* In *Punch*, May 6, 1865. Assigned to Taylor by SHIRLEY BROOKS in his *Diary*, May 10, 1865. See G. S. LAYARD's *Life, Letters, and Diaries of Shirley Brooks of Punch.*

12

He [Lincoln] has doctrines, not hatreds, and is without ambition except to do good and serve his country.

E. B. WASHBURN in the House of Representatives on the nomination of Lincoln, May 29, 1860.

13

This dust was once the man,
Gentle, plain, just and resolute, under whose cautious hand,
Against the foulest crime in history known in any land or age,
Was saved the Union of these States.

WALT WHITMAN—*Memories of President Lincoln. This Dust Was Once the Man.*

14

O captain! my captain! our fearful trip is done;
The ship has weather'd every rack; the prize we sought is won;
The port is near, the bells I hear, the people all exulting,
While follow eyes the steady keel, the vessel grim and daring?
But O heart! heart! heart! O the bleeding drops of red,
Where on the deck my captain lies, fallen cold and dead.

WALT WHITMAN—*Captain! My Captain!*

15

The ship is anchor'd safe and sound, its voyage is closed and done.
From fearful trip the victor ship comes in with object won.
Exult, O shores, and ring, O bells; but I with mournful tread
Walk the deck my captain lies, fallen cold and dead.

WALT WHITMAN—*Captain! My Captain!*

LINDEN

Tilia

1
The linden in the fervors of July
Hums with a louder concert.
BRYANT—*Among the Trees.*

2
If thou lookest on the lime-leaf,
Thou a heart's form will discover;
Therefore are the lindens ever
Chosen seats of each fond lover.
HEINE—*Book of Songs. New Spring.* No. 31. St. 3.

LINGUISTS

3
Besides 'tis known he could speak Greek
As naturally as pigs squeak;
That Latin was no more difficile
Than to a blackbird 'tis to whistle.
BUTLER—*Hudibras.* Pt. I. Canto I. L. 51.

4
A Babylonish dialect
Which learned pedants much affect.
BUTLER—*Hudibras.* Pt. I. Canto I. L. 93.

5
For though to smatter ends of Greek
Or Latin be the rhetoric
Of pedants counted, and vain-glorious,
To smatter French is meritorious.
BUTLER—*Remains in Verse and Prose. Satire. Upon Our Ridiculous Imitation of the French.* Line 127. A Greek proverb condemns the man of two tongues.

6
I love the language, that soft bastard Latin,
Which melts like kisses from a female mouth.
BYRON—*Beppo.* St. 44.

7
* * * Philologists, who chase
A panting syllable through time and space
Start it at home, and hunt it in the dark,
To Gaul, to Greece, and into Noah's Ark.
COWPER—*Retirement.* L. 691.

8
He Greek and Latin speaks with greater ease
Than hogs eat acorns, and tame pigeons peas.
CRANFIELD—*Panegyric on Tom Coriate.*

9
Lash'd into Latin by the tingling rod.
GAY—*The Birth of the Squire.* L. 46.

10
Wer fremde Sprachen nicht kennt, weiss nichts von seiner eigenen.
He who is ignorant of foreign languages, knows not his own.
GOETHE—*Kunst und Alterthum.*

11
Small Latin, and less Greek.
BEN JONSON—*To the Memory of Shakespeare.*

12
Omnia Græce!
Cum sit turpe magis nostris nescire Latine.
Everything is Greek, when it is more shameful to be ignorant of Latin.
JUVENAL—*Satires.* VI. 187. (Second line said to be spurious.)

13
Languages are no more than the keys of Sciences. He who despises one, slights the other.
LA BRUYÈRE—*The Characters or Manners of the Present Age.* Ch. XII.

14
C'est de l'hebreu pour moi.
It is Hebrew to me.
MOLIÈRE—*L'Etourdi.* Act III. Sc. 3.

15
Negatas artifex sequi voces.
He attempts to use language which he does not know.
PERSIUS—*Satires. Prologue.* XI.

16
This is your devoted friend, sir, the manifold linguist.
All's Well That Ends Well. Act IV. Sc. 3. L. 262.

17
Away with him, away with him! he speaks Latin.
Henry VI. Pt. II. Act IV. Sc. 7. L. 62.

18
O! good my lord, no Latin;
I'm not such a truant since my coming,
As not to know the language I have liv'd in.
Henry VIII. Act III. Sc. 1. L. 42.

19
But, for my own part, it was Greek to me.
Julius Cæsar. Act I. Sc. 2. L. 287.

20
Speaks three or four languages word for word without a book.
Twelfth Night. Act I. Sc. 3. L. 28.

21
By your own report
A linguist.
Two Gentlemen of Verona. Act IV. Sc. 1. L. 56.

22
Egad, I think the interpreter is the hardest to be understood of the two!
R. B. SHERIDAN—*The Critic.* Act I. Sc. 2.

LINNET

23
Is it for thee the linnet pours his throat?
Loves of his own, and raptures swell the note.
POPE—*Essay on Man.* Ep. III. L. 33

24
Perch'd on the cedar's topmost bough,
And gay with gilded wings,
Perchance the patron of his vow,
Some artless linnet sings.
SHENSTONE—*Valentine's Day.*

25
I do sing because I must,
And pipe but as the linnets sing.
TENNYSON—*In Memoriam.* Pt. XXI. St. 6.

26
Linnets * * * sit
On the dead tree, a dull despondent flock.
THOMSON—*The Seasons. Autumn.* L. 974.

27
Hail to thee, far above the rest
In joy of voice and pinion!
Thou, linnet! in thy green array,
Presiding spirit here to-day,
Dost lead the revels of the May;
And this is thy dominion.
WORDSWORTH—*The Green Linnet.*

LION

1
The lion is not so fierce as they paint him.
HERBERT—*Jacula Prudentum.*

2 Noli
Barbam vellere mortuo leoni.
Do not pluck the beard of a dead lion.
MARTIAL—*Epigrams.* Bk. X. 90.

3 They rejoice
Each with their kind, lion with lioness,
So fitly them in pairs thou hast combined.
MILTON—*Paradise Lost.* Bk. VII. L. 392.

4
Rouse the lion from his lair.
SCOTT—*The Talisman.* Heading of Ch. VI.

5
The man that once did sell the lion's skin
While the beast lived, was killed with hunting him.
Henry V. Act IV. Sc. 3. L. 93.

LIPS (See MOUTH)

LISTENING (See also HEARING)

6
But yet she listen'd—'tis enough—
Who listens once will listen twice;
Her heart, be sure, is not of ice,
And one refusal no rebuff.
BYRON—*Mazeppa.* St. 6.

7
He holds him with his glittering eye—
* * * * * *
And listens like a three years' child.
COLERIDGE—*The Ancient Mariner.* Pt. I. St. 4. Last line claimed by Wordsworth. See note to his *We are Seven.*

8 Listen, every one
That listen may, unto a tale
That's merrier than the nightingale.
LONGFELLOW—*Tales of a Wayside Inn.* Pt. III. *The Sicilian's Tale. Interlude Before the Monk of Casal-Maggiore.*

9
In listening mood she seemed to stand,
The guardian Naiad of the strand.
SCOTT—*The Lady of the Lake.* Canto I. St. 17.

10
And this cuff was but to knock at your ear, and beseech listening.
Taming of the Shrew. Act IV. Sc. 1. L. 66.

LITERATURE (See also AUTHORSHIP, BOOKS)

11
Literature is the thought of thinking Souls.
CARLYLE—*Essays. Memoirs of the Life of Scott.*

12
Literary Men are * * * a perpetual priesthood.
CARLYLE—*Essays. State of German Literature.*

13
I made a compact with myself that in my person literature should stand by itself, of itself, and for itself.
DICKENS. Speech at Liverpool Banquet, 1869.
(See also LINCOLN under GOVERNMENT)

14
But, indeed, we prefer books to pounds; and we love manuscripts better than florins; and we prefer small *pamphlets* to war horses.
ISAAC D'ISRAELI—*Curiosities of Literature. Pamphlets.*

15
Time the great destroyer of other men's happiness, only enlarges the patrimony of literature to its possessor.
ISAAC D'ISRAELI—*Literary Character of Men of Genius.* Ch. XXII.

16
Literature is an avenue to glory, ever open for those ingenious men who are deprived of honours or of wealth.
ISAAC D'ISRAELI—*Literary Character of Men of Genius.* Ch. XXIV.

17
Republic of letters.
HENRY FIELDING—*Tom Jones.* Bk. XIV. Ch. I. (See also MOLIÈRE)

18
Our poetry in the eighteenth century was prose; our prose in the seventeenth, poetry.
J. C. AND A. W. HARE—*Guesses at Truth.*

19
The death of Dr. Hudson is a loss to the republick of letters.
WILLIAM KING—*Letter.* Jan. 7, 1719. Same phrase occurs in the *Spectator.* Commonwealth of letters is used by ADDISON—*Spectator.* No. 529. Nov. 6, 1712.
(See also MOLIÈRE)

20
* * * A man of the world amongst men of letters, a man of letters amongst men of the world.
MACAULAY—*On Sir William Temple.*

21
La république des lettres.
The republic of letters.
MOLIÈRE—*Le Mariage forcé.* Sc. 6. (1664)
(See also FIELDING)

22
There is first the literature of *knowledge,* and secondly, the literature of *power.* The function of the first is—to *teach;* the function of the second is—to *move,* the first is a rudder, the second an oar or a sail. The first speaks to the *mere* discursive understanding; the second speaks ultimately, it may happen, to the higher understanding or reason, but always *through* affections of pleasure and sympathy.
THOMAS DE QUINCEY—*Essays on the Poets. Alexander Pope.*

23
La mode d'aimer Racine passera comme la mode du café.
The fashion of liking Racine will pass away like that of coffee.
MME. DE SÉVIGNÉ—According to VOLTAIRE, *Letters,* Jan. 29, 1690, who connected two remarks of hers to make the phrase; one from a letter March 16, 1679, the other, March 10, 1672. LA HARPE reduced the *mot* to "Racine passera comme le café."

24
We cultivate literature on a little oat-meal.
SYDNEY SMITH—*Lady Holland's Memoir.* Vol. I. P. 23.

25
The great Cham of literature. [Samuel Johnson.]
SMOLLETT—*Letter to Wilkes,* March 16, 1759.

LIVERY

1
Ne sait on pas où viennent ces gondoles Parisiennes?
Does anyone know where these gondolas of Paris came from?
BALZAC—*Physiologie du Mariage.* (1827) N. Q. S. 5. IV. 499. V. 195.

2
Go, call a coach, and let a coach be called;
And let the man who calleth be the caller;
And in the calling, let him nothing call,
But coach! coach! coach! O for a coach, ye gods!
HENRY CAREY—*Chrononhotonthologos.* Act II. Sc. 4. L. 46.

3
The gondola of London [a hansom].
DISRAELI—*Lothair.* Ch. XXVII. H. SCHUTZ WILSON in *Three Paths,* claims to have originated the phrase. (1759)

4
Our chariots and our horsemen be in readiness.
Cymbeline. Act III. Sc. 5. L. 23.

5
Come, my coach! Good-night, ladies.
Hamlet. Act IV. Sc. 5. L. 72.

6
Many carriages he hath dispatched.
King John. Act V. Sc. 7. L. 90.

7
When I am in my coach, which stays for us
At the park gate.
Merchant of Venice. Act III. Sc. 4. L. 82.

8
"There beauty half her glory veils,
In cabs, those gondolas on wheels."
Said to be taken from *May Fair,* a satire pub. 1827.

LONDON

9
As I came down the Highgate Hill,
The Highgate Hill, the Highgate Hill,
As I came down the Highgate Hill
I met the sun's bravado,
And saw below me, fold on fold,
Grey to pearl and pearl to gold,
This London like a land of old,
The land of Eldorado.
HENRY BASHFORD—*Romances.*

10
Veni Gotham, ubi multos,
Si non omnes, vidi stultos.
I came to Gotham, where I saw many who were fools, if not all.
RICHARD BRATHWAIT—*Drunken Barnaby's Journal.*

11
A mighty mass of brick, and smoke, and shipping,
Dirty and dusty, but as wide as eye
Could reach, with here and there a sail just skipping
In sight, then lost amidst the forestry
Of masts; a wilderness of steeples peeping
On tiptoe through their sea-coal canopy;
A huge, dun cupola, like a foolscap crown
On a fool's head—and there is London Town.
BYRON—*Don Juan.* Canto X. St. 82.

12
London is the clearing-house of the world.
JOS. CHAMBERLAIN—*Speech,* Guildhall, London. Jan. 19, 1904.

13
If the parks be "the lungs of London" we wonder what Greenwich Fair is—a periodical breaking out, we suppose—a sort of spring rash.
DICKENS—*Greenwich Fair.*
(See also WINDHAM)

14
London is a roost for every bird.
BENJ. DISRAELI—*Lothair.* Ch. XI.

15
London is the epitome of our times, and the Rome of to-day.
EMERSON—*English Traits. Result.*

16
He was born within the sound of Bow-bell.
FULLER—*Gnomologia.*

17
London! the needy villain's general home,
The common sewer of Paris and of Rome!
With eager thirst, by folly or by fate,
Sucks in the dregs of each corrupted state.
SAMUEL JOHNSON—*London.* L. 93.

18
In town let me live then, in town let me die
For in truth I can't relish the country, not I.
If one *must* have a villa in summer to dwell,
Oh give me the sweet shady side of Pall Mall.
CAPTAIN CHARLES MORRIS—*The Contrast.*

19
The way was long and weary,
But gallantly they strode,
A country lad and lassie,
Along the heavy road.
The night was dark and stormy,
But blithe of heart were they,
For shining in the distance
The lights of London lay.
O gleaming lights of London, that gem of the city's crown;
What fortunes be within you, O Lights of London Town!
GEORGE R. SIMS. Song in *Lights of London.*

20
The lungs of London. (Parks)
WINDHAM. Debate in House of Commons. June 30, 1808, attributes it to LORD CHATHAM. (See also DICKENS)

LOSS

21
Losers must have leave to speak.
COLLEY CIBBER—*The Rival Fools.* Act I. L. 17.

22
Our wasted oil unprofitably burns,
Like hidden lamps in old sepulchral urns.
COWPER—*Conversation.* L. 357. Referring to the story told by PANCIROLLUS and others, of the lamp which burned for fifteen hundred years in the tomb of TULLIA, daughter of CICERO.
(See also BUTLER under LOVE)

23
For 'tis a truth well known to most,
That whatsoever thing is lost,
We seek it, ere it comes to light,
In every cranny but the right.
COWPER—*The Retired Cat.* L. 95.

1
Gli huomini dimenticano più teste la morte del padre, che la perdita del patrimonie.

A son could bear with great complacency, the death of his father, while the loss of his inheritance might drive him to despair.

MACHIAVELLI—*Del. Prin.* Ch. XVII. Same idea in TAYLOR—*Philip Van Artevelde.* (See also BYRON under THIEVING)

2
Things that are not at all, are never lost.

MARLOWE—*Hero and Leander. First Sestiad.* L. 276. (See also WALTON)

3
What's saved affords
No indication of what's lost.

OWEN MEREDITH (Lord Lytton)—*The Scroll.*

4
A wise man loses nothing, if he but save himself.

MONTAIGNE—*Essays. Of Solitude.*

5
When wealth is lost, nothing is lost;
When health is lost, something is lost;
When character is lost, all is lost!

Motto Over the Walls of a School in Germany.

6
That puts it not unto the touch
To win or lose it all.

NAPIER—*Montrose and the Covenanters. Montrose's Poems.* No. 1. Vol. II. P. 566.

7
Si quis mutuum quid dederit, sit pro proprio perditum;
Cum repetas, inimicum amicum beneficio invenis tuo.
Si mage exigere cupias, duarum rerum exoritur optio;
Vel illud, quod credideris perdas, vel illum amicum, amiseris.

What you lend is lost; when you ask for it back, you may find a friend made an enemy by your kindness. If you begin to press him further, you have the choice of two things—either to lose your loan or lose your friend.

PLAUTUS—*Trinummus.* IV. 3. 43.

8
Periere mores, jus, decus, pietas, fides,
Et qui redire nescit, cum perit, pudor.

We have lost morals, justice, honor, piety and faith, and that sense of shame which, once lost, can never be restored.

SENECA—*Agamemnon.* CXII.

9
Like the dew on the mountain,
Like the foam on the river,
Like the bubble on the fountain,
Thou art gone, and forever!

SCOTT—*Lady of the Lake.* Canto III. St. 16.

10
Wise men ne'er sit and wail their loss,
But cheerly seek how to redress their harms.

Henry VI. Pt. III. Act V. Sc. 4. L. 1.

11
That loss is common would not make
My own less bitter, rather more:
Too common! Never morning wore
To evening, but some heart did break.

TENNYSON—*In Memoriam.* Pt. VI. St. 2.

12
But over all things brooding slept
The quiet sense of something lost.

TENNYSON—*In Memoriam.* Pt. LXXVIII. St. 2.

13
No man can lose what he never had.

IZAAK WALTON—*The Compleat Angler.* Pt. I. Ch. V. (See also MARLOWE)

LOTUS

Zizyphus Lotus

14
Where drooping lotos-flowers, distilling balm,
Dream by the drowsy streamlets sleep hath crown'd,
While Care forgets to sigh, and Peace hath balsamed Pain.

PAUL H. HAYNE—*Sonnet. Pent in this Common Sphere.*

15
The lotus flower is troubled
At the sun's resplendent light;
With sunken head and sadly
She dreamily waits for the night.

HEINE—*Book of Songs. Lyrical Interlude.* No. 10.

16
Lotos, the name; divine, nectareous juice!

HOMER—*Odyssey.* Bk. IX. L. 106. POPE'S trans.

17
Stone lotus cups, with petals dipped in sand.

JEAN INGELOW—*Gladys and her Island.* L. 460.

18
Oh! what are the brightest that e'er have blown
To the lote-tree, springing by Alla's throne,
Whose flowers have a soul in every leaf.

MOORE—*Lalla Rookh. Paradise and the Peri.*

19
They wove the lotus band to deck
And fan with pensile wreath their neck.

MOORE—*Odes of Anacreon.* Ode LXX.

20
A spring there is, whose silver waters show
Clear as a glass the shining sands below:
A flowering lotos spreads its arms above,
Shades all the banks, and seems itself a grove.

POPE—*Sappho to Phaon.* L. 177.

21
The lotos bowed above the tide and dreamed.

MARGARET J. PRESTON—*Rhodope's Sandal.*

22
The Lotos blooms below the barren peak:
The Lotos blooms by every winding creek:
All day the wind breathes low with mellower tone:
Thro' every hollow cave and alley lone,
Round and round the spicy downs the yellow Lotos-dust is blown.

TENNYSON—*The Lotos-Eaters. Choric Song.* St. 8.

23
In that dusk land of mystic dream
Where dark Osiris sprung,
It bloomed beside his sacred stream
While yet the world was young;
And every secret Nature told,
Of golden wisdom's power,
Is nestled still in every fold,
Within the Lotos flower.

WM. WINTER—*A Lotos Flower.*

LOUSE

1
Ha! Whare ye gaun, ye crawlin' ferlie?
Your impudence protects you sairly;
I canna say but ye strunt rarely
Owre gauze an' lace;
Though faith! I fear ye dine but sparely
On sic a place.
BURNS—*To a Louse.*

LOVE

2
When love's well-timed 'tis not a fault to love;
The strong, the brave, the virtuous, and the wise,
Sink in the soft captivity together.
ADDISON—*Cato.* Act III. Sc. 1.

3
When love once pleads admission to our hearts,
(In spite of all the virtue we can boast),
The woman that deliberates is lost.
ADDISON—*Cato.* Act IV. Sc. 1.

4
Mysterious love, uncertain treasure,
Hast thou more of pain or pleasure!
* * * *
Endless torments dwell about thee:
Yet who would live, and live without thee!
ADDISON—*Rosamond.* Act III. Sc. 2.

5
Che amar chi t'odia, ell'è impossibil cosa.
For 'tis impossible
Hate to return with love.
ALFIERI—*Polinice.* II. 4.

6
Somewhere there waiteth in this world of ours
For one lone soul another lonely soul,
Each choosing each through all the weary hours,
And meeting strangely at one sudden goal,
Then blend they, like green leaves with golden flowers,
Into one beautiful and perfect whole;
And life's long night is ended, and the way
Lies open onward to eternal day.
EDWIN ARNOLD—*Somewhere There Waiteth.*

7
Ma vie a son secret, mon âme a son mystére:
Un amour éternel en un moment concu.
La mal est sans remède, aussi j'ai dû le taire,
Et elle qui l'a fait n'en a jamais rien su.
One sweet, sad secret holds my heart in thrall;
A mighty love within my breast has grown,
Unseen, unspoken, and of no one known;
And of my sweet, who gave it, least of all.
FELIX ARVERS—*Sonnet.* Trans. by JOSEPH KNIGHT. In *The Athenæum*, Jan. 13, 1906. Arvers in *Mes Heures Perdues,* says that the sonnet was "mite de l'italien."

8
Ask not of me, love, what is love?
Ask what is good of God above;
Ask of the great sun what is light;
Ask what is darkness of the night;
Ask sin of what may be forgiven;
Ask what is happiness of heaven;
Ask what is folly of the crowd;
Ask what is fashion of the shroud;
Ask what is sweetness of thy kiss;
Ask of thyself what beauty is.
BAILEY—*Festus.* Sc. *A Party and Entertainment.*

9
Could I love less, I should be happier now.
BAILEY—*Festus.* Sc. *Garden and Bower by the Sea.*

10
I cannot love as I have loved,
And yet I know not why;
It is the one great woe of life
To feel all feeling die.
BAILEY—*Festus.* Sc. *A Party and Entertainment.*

11
Love spends his all, and still hath store.
BAILEY—*Festus.* Sc. *A Party and Entertainment.*

12
The sweetest joy, the wildest woe is love.
BAILEY—*Festus.* Sc. *Alcove and Garden.*

13
How many times do I love, again?
Tell me how many beads there are
In a silver chain
Of evening rain
Unravelled from the trembling main
And threading the eye of a yellow star:—
So many times do I love again.
THOS. LOVELL BEDDOES—*How Many Times.*

14
Mein Herz ich will dich fragen,
Was ist denn Liebe, sag?
"Zwei Seelen und ein Gedanke,
Zwei Herzen und ein Schlag."
My heart I fain would ask thee
What then is Love? say on.
"Two souls and one thought only
Two hearts that throb as one."
VON MÜNCH BELLINGHAUSEN (Friedrich Halm)—*Der Sohn der Wildniss.* Act II. Trans. by W. H. CHARLTON. (Commended by author.) Popular trans. of the play is by MARIE LOVELL—*Ingomar the Barbarian.*
Two souls with but a single thought,
Two hearts that beat as one.
(See also DU BARTAS)

15
To Chloe's breast young Cupid slily stole,
But he crept in at Myra's pocket-hole.
WILLIAM BLAKE—*Couplets and Fragments.* IV.

16
Love in a shower safe shelter took,
In a rosy bower beside a brook,
And winked and nodded with conscious pride
To his votaries drenched on the other side.
Come hither, sweet maids, there's a bridge below,
The toll-keeper, Hymen, will let you through.
Come over the stream to me.
BLOOMFIELD—*Glee.* St. 1.

17
Love is like fire. * * * Wounds of fire are hard to bear; harder still are those of love.
HJALMAR HJORTH BOYESEN—*Gunnar.* Ch. IV.

18
Le premier soupir de l'amour
Est le dernier de la sagesse.
The first sigh of love is the last of wisdom.
ANTOINE BRET—*Ecole amoureuse* Sc. 7.

19
Much ado there was, God wot;
He woold love, and she woold not,

She sayd, "Never man was trewe;"
He sayes, "None was false to you."
NICHOLAS BRETON—*Phillida and Corydon.*

1
In your arms was still delight,
Quiet as a street at night;
And thoughts of you, I do remember,
Were green leaves in a darkened chamber,
Were dark clouds in a moonless sky.
RUPERT BROOKE—*Retrospect.*

2
There is musick, even in the beauty and the silent note which Cupid strikes, far sweeter than the sound of an instrument.
SIR THOMAS BROWNE—*Religio Medici.* Pt. II. Sec. IX.

3
Whoever lives true life, will love true love.
E. B. BROWNING—*Aurora Leigh.* Bk. I. L. 1096.

4
I would not be a rose upon the wall
A queen might stop at, near the palace-door,
To say to a courtier, "Pluck that rose for me,
It's prettier than the rest." O Romney Leigh!
I'd rather far be trodden by his foot,
Than lie in a great queen's bosom.
E. B. BROWNING—*Aurora Leigh.* Bk. IV.

5
But I love you, sir:
And when a woman says she loves a man,
The man must hear her, though he love her not.
E. B. BROWNING—*Aurora Leigh.* Bk. IX.

6
For none can express thee, though all should approve thee.
I love thee so, Dear, that I only can love thee.
E. B. BROWNING—*Insufficiency.*

7
Behold me! I am worthy
Of thy loving, for I love thee!
E. B. BROWNING—*Lady Geraldine's Courtship.* St. 79.

8
How do I love thee? Let me count the ways.
E. B. BROWNING—*Sonnets from the Portuguese.*

9
Who can fear
Too many stars, though each in heaven shall roll—
Too many flowers, though each shall crown the year?
Say thou dost love me, love me, love me—toll
The silver iterance!—only minding, Dear,
To love me also in silence, with thy soul.
E. B. BROWNING—*Sonnets from the Portuguese.* Sonnet XXI.

10
Unless you can feel when the song is done
No other is sweet in its rhythm;
Unless you can feel when left by one
That all men else go with him.
E. B. BROWNING—*Unless.*

11
I think, am sure, a brother's love exceeds
All the world's loves in its unworldliness.
ROBERT BROWNING—*Blot on the 'Scutcheon.* Act II. Sc. 1.

12
Never the time and the place
And the loved one all together.
ROBERT BROWNING—*Never the Time and the Place.*

13
God be thanked, the meanest of his creatures
Boasts two soul-sides, one to face the world with,
One to show a woman when he loves her.
ROBERT BROWNING—*One Word More.* St. XVII.

14
Love has no thought of self!
Love buys not with the ruthless usurer's gold
The loathsome prostitution of a hand
Without a heart! Love sacrifices all things
To bless the thing it loves!
BULWER-LYTTON—*The Lady of Lyons.* Act V. Sc. 2. L. 23.

15
Love thou, and if thy love be deep as mine,
Thou wilt not laugh at poets.
BULWER-LYTTON—*Richelieu.* Act I. Sc. 1. L. 177.

16
No matter what you do, if your heart is ever true,
And his heart *was* true to Poll.
F. C. BURNAND—*His Heart was true to Poll.*

17
To see her is to love her,
And love but her forever;
For nature made her what she is,
And never made anither!
BURNS—*Bonny Lesley.*
(See also ROGERS; also HALLECK under GRAVE)

18
The wisest man the warl' e'er saw,
He dearly loved the lasses, O.
BURNS—*Green Grow the Rashes.*

19
The golden hours on angel wings
Flew o'er me and my dearie,
For dear to me as light and life
Was my sweet Highland Mary.
BURNS—*Highland Mary.*

20
Oh my luve's like a red, red rose,
That's newly sprung in June;
Oh my luve's like the melodie
That's sweetly played in tune.
BURNS—*Red, Red Rose.*

21
What is life, when wanting love?
Night without a morning;
Love's the cloudless summer sun,
Nature gay adorning.
BURNS—*Thine am I, my Faithful Fair.*
(See also CAMPBELL)

22
And this is that Homer's golden chain, which reacheth down from heaven to earth, by which every creature is annexed, and depends on his Creator.
BURTON—*Anatomy of Melancholy.* Pt. III. Sec. 1. Memb. 1. Subsec. 7.
(See also SPENSER; also HOMER under INFLUENCE)

23
No cord nor cable can so forcibly draw, or hold so fast, as love can do with a twined thread.
BURTON—*Anatomy of Melancholy.* Pt. III. Sec. 2. Memb. 1. Subsec. 2.

1
The falling out of lovers is the renewing of love.
BURTON—*Anatomy of Melancholy.* Pt. III. Sec. 2. TERENCE—*Andria.* III. 23.
(See also LYLY under FRIENDS)

2
Love in your hearts as idly burns
As fire in antique Roman urns.
BUTLER—*Hudibras.* Pt. II. Canto I.
(See also COWPER under LOSS)

3
Love is a boy by poets styl'd:
Then spare the rod and spoil the child.
BUTLER—*Hudibras.* Pt. II. Canto I. L. 843.

4
What mad lover ever dy'd,
To gain a soft and gentle bride?
Or for a lady tender-hearted,
In purling streams or hemp departed?
BUTLER—*Hudibras.* Pt. III. Canto I.

5
When things were as fine as could possibly be
I thought 'twas the spring; but alas it was she.
JOHN BYROM—*A Pastoral.*

6
Oh Love! young Love! bound in thy rosy band,
Let sage or cynic prattle as he will,
These hours, and only these, redeem Life's years of ill.
BYRON—*Childe Harold.* Canto II. St. 81.

7
Who loves, raves—'tis youth's frenzy—but the cure
Is bitterer still.
BYRON—*Childe Harold.* Canto IV. St. 123.

8
O! that the Desert were my dwelling place,
With one fair Spirit for my minister,
That I might all forget the human race,
And, hating no one, love but only her!
BYRON—*Childe Harold.* Canto IV. St. 177.

9
Man's love is of man's life a thing apart,
'Tis woman's whole existence: man may range
The court, camp, church, the vessel, and the mart,
Sword, gown, gain, glory, offer in exchange
Pride, fame, ambition, to fill up his heart,
And few there are whom these cannot estrange;
Men have all these resources, we but one,
To love again, and be again undone.
BYRON—*Don Juan.* Canto I. St. 194.
(See also CROWE, DE STAËL)

10
Alas! the love of women! it is known
To be a lovely and a fearful thing.
BYRON—*Don Juan.* Canto II. St. 199.

11
In her first passion woman loves her lover;
In all the others, all she loves is love.
BYRON—*Don Juan.* Canto III. St. 3. LA ROCHEFOUCAULD. Maxims, No. 497.

12
And to his eye
There was but one beloved face on earth,
And that was shining on him.
BYRON—*The Dream.* St. 2.

13
She knew she was by him beloved,—she knew
For quickly comes such knowledge, that his heart
Was darken'd with her shadow.
BYRON—*The Dream.* St. 3.

14
The cold in clime are cold in blood,
Their love can scarce deserve the name.
BYRON—*The Giaour.* L. 1,099.

15
Yes, Love indeed is light from heaven;
A spark of that immortal fire
With angels shared, by Allah given
To lift from earth our low desire.
BYRON—*The Giaour.* L. 1,131.

16
Why did she love him? Curious fool!—be still—
Is human love the growth of human will?
BYRON—*Lara.* Canto II. St. 22.

17
I'll bid the hyacinth to blow,
I'll teach my grotto green to be;
And sing my true love, all below
The holly bower and myrtle tree.
CAMPBELL—*Caroline.* Pt. I.

18
My love lies bleeding.
CAMPBELL—*O'Connor's Child.* St. 5.

19
He that loves a rosy cheek,
Or a coral lip admires,
Or from star-like eyes doth seek
Fuel to maintain his fires,
As Old Time makes these decay,
So his flames must waste away.
THOS. CAREW—*Disdain Returned.*

20
Then fly betimes, for only they
Conquer love, that run away.
THOS. CAREW—*Song. Conquest by Flight.*
(See also BUTLER under WAR)

21
Of all the girls that are so smart
There's none like pretty Sally;
She is the darling of my heart,
And lives in our alley.
HENRY CAREY—*Sally in our Alley.*

22
Let Time and Chance combine, combine!
Let Time and Chance combine!
The fairest love from heaven above,
That love of yours was mine,
My Dear!
That love of yours was mine.
CARLYLE—*Adieu.*

23
Vivamus, mea Lesbia atque amemus.
My Lesbia, let us live and love.
CATULLUS—*Carmina.* V. 1.

24
Mulier cupido quod dicit amanti,
In vento et rapida scribere oportet aqua.
What woman says to fond lover should be written on air or the swift water.
CATULLUS—*Carmina.* LXX. 3.

25
Difficile est longum subito deponere amorem.
It is difficult at once to relinquish a long-cherished love.
CATULLUS—*Carmina.* LXXVI. 13.

1
Odi et amo. Quare id faciam, fortasse requiris.
Nescio: sed fieri sentio, et excrucior.

I hate and I love. Why do I do so you perhaps ask.
I cannot say; but I feel it to be so, and I am tormented accordingly.

CATULLUS—*Carmina*. LXXXV.
(See also MARTIAL)

2
There's no love lost between us.

CERVANTES—*Don Quixote*. Bk. IV. Ch. 13. FIELDING—*Grub Street*. Act I. Sc. 4. GARRICK—*Correspondence*. (1759) GOLDSMITH—*She Stoops to Conquer*. Act IV. BEN JONSON—*Every Man Out of His Humour*. Act II. Sc. 1. LE SAGE—*Gil Blas*. Bk. IX. Ch. VII. As trans. by SMOLLETT.

3
It's love, it's love that makes the world go round.

Popular French song in *Chansons Nationales et Populaires de France*. Vol. II. P. 180. (About 1821)

4
I tell thee Love is Nature's second sun,
Causing a spring of virtues where he shines.

GEORGE CHAPMAN—*All Fools*. Act I. Sc. 1. L. 98.

5
None ever loved, but at first sight they loved.

GEORGE CHAPMAN—*The Blind Beggar of Alexandria*.
(See also MARLOWE)

6
Banish that fear; my flame can never waste,
For love sincere refines upon the taste.

COLLEY CIBBER—*The Double Gallant*. Act V. Sc. 1.

7
So mourn'd the dame of Ephesus her love.

COLLEY CIBBER—*Richard III*. Act II. Altered from SHAKESPEARE.

8
What have I done? What horrid crime committed?
To me the worst of crimes—outliv'd my liking.

COLLEY CIBBER—*Richard III*. Act III. Sc. 2. Altered from SHAKESPEARE.
(See also CRASHAW)

9
Vivunt in venerem frondes omnisque vicissim
Felix arbor amat; mutant ad mutua palmæ
Fœdera.

The leaves live but to love, and in all the lofty grove the happy trees love each his neighbor.

CLAUDIANUS—*De Nuptiis Honorii et Mariæ*. LXV.

10
Her very frowns are fairer far
Than smiles of other maidens are.

HARTLEY COLERIDGE—*Song. She is not Fair.*

11
Alas! they had been friends in youth;
But whispering tongues can poison truth,
And constancy lives in realms above;
And life is thorny, and youth is vain;
And to be wroth with one we love
Doth work like madness in the brain.

COLERIDGE—*Christabel*. Pt. II.

12
All thoughts, all passions, all delights,
Whatever stirs this mortal frame,
All are but ministers of Love,
And feed his sacred flame.

COLERIDGE—*Love*. St. 1.

13
I have heard of reasons manifold
Why love must needs be blind,
But this is the best of all I hold—
His eyes are in his mind.

COLERIDGE—*To a Lady*. St. 2.

14
He that can't live upon love deserves to die in a ditch.

CONGREVE.

15
Say what you will, 'tis better to be left
Than never to have loved.

CONGREVE—*Way of the World*. Act II. Sc. 1.
(See also CRABBE, GUARINI, TENNYSON)

16
If there's delight in love, 'tis when I see
The heart, which others bleed for, bleed for me.

CONGREVE—*Way of the World*. Act III. Sc. 3.

17
I know not when the day shall be,
I know not when our eyes may meet;
What welcome you may give to me,
Or will your words be sad or sweet,
It may not be 'till years have passed,
'Till eyes are dim and tresses gray;
The world is wide, but, love, at last,
Our hands, our hearts, must meet some day.

HUGH CONWAY—*Some Day*.

18
How wise are they that are but fools in love!

How a man may choose a Good Wife. Act I. 1. Attributed to JOSHUA COOKE in Dict. of Nat. Biog.

19
A mighty pain to love it is,
And 'tis a pain that pain to miss;
But, of all pains, the greatest pain
Is to love, but love in vain.

ABRAHAM COWLEY—Trans. of *Anacreontic Odes. VII. Gold.* (Anacreon's authorship doubted.)
(See also MOORE)

20
Our love is principle, and has its root
In reason, is judicious, manly, free.

COWPER—*The Task*. Bk. V. L. 353.

21
Better to love amiss than nothing to have loved.

CRABBE—*The Struggles of Conscience*. *Tale* 14.
(See also CONGREVE)

22
Heaven's great artillery.

CRASHAW—*Flaming Heart*. L. 56.

23
Love's great artillery.

CRASHAW—*Prayer*. L. 18.

24
Mighty Love's artillery.

CRASHAW—*Wounds of the Lord Jesus*. L. 2.

25
And I, what is my crime I cannot tell,
Vnless it be a crime to haue lou'd too well.

CRASHAW—*Alexias*.
(See also CIBBER, POPE)

1
Poor love is lost in men's capacious minds,
In ours, it fills up all the room it finds.
JOHN CROWNE—*Thyestes.*
(See also BYRON)

2
Amor, ch'al cor gentil ratto s'apprende.
Love, that all gentle hearts so quickly know.
DANTE—*Inferno.* V. 100.

3
Amor ch' a nullo amato amar perdona.
Love, which insists that love shall mutual be.
DANTE—*Inferno.* V. 103.

4
We are all born for love. * * * It is the principle of existence and its only end.
BENJ. DISRAELI—*Sybil.* Bk. V. Ch. IV.

5
He who, being bold
For life to come, is false to the past sweet
Of mortal life, hath killed the world above.
For why to live again if not to meet?
And why to meet if not to meet in love?
And why in love if not in that dear love of old?
SYDNEY DOBELL—*Sonnet. To a Friend in Bereavement.*

6
Give, you gods,
Give to your boy, your Cæsar,
The rattle of a globe to play withal,
This gewgaw world, and put him cheaply off;
I'll not be pleased with less than Cleopatra.
DRYDEN—*All for Love.* Act II. Sc. 1.

7
Love taught him shame, and shame with love at strife
Soon taught the sweet civilities of life.
DRYDEN—*Cymon and Iphigenia.* L. 134.

8
How happy the lover,
How easy his chain,
How pleasing his pain,
How sweet to discover
He sighs not in vain.
DRYDEN—*King Arthur.* IV. 1. *Song.*

9
Fool, not to know that love endures no tie,
And Jove but laughs at lovers' perjury.
DRYDEN—*Palamon and Arcite.* Bk. II. L. 75. *Amphitron.* Act I. Sc. 2.
(See also MASSINGER, OVID, ROMEO and JULIET, TIBULLUS)

10
Pains of love be sweeter far
Than all other pleasures are.
DRYDEN—*Tyrannic Love.* Act IV. Sc. 1.

11
Two souls in one, two hearts into one heart.
DU BARTAS—*Divine Weekes and Workes.* First Week. Pt. I. Sixth day. L. 1,057.
(See also BELLINGHAUSEN)

12
I'm sitting on the stile, Mary,
Where we sat side by side.
LADY DUFFERIN—*Lament of the Irish Emigrant.*

13
Oh, tell me whence Love cometh!
Love comes uncall'd, unsent.
Oh, tell me where Love goeth!
That was not Love that went.
Burden of a Woman. Found in J. W. EBSWORTH'S *Roxburghe Ballads.*

14
The solid, solid universe
Is pervious to Love;
With bandaged eyes he never errs,
Around, below, above.
His blinding light
He flingeth white
On God's and Satan's brood,
And reconciles
By mystic wiles
The evil and the good.
EMERSON—*Cupido.*

15
But is it what we love, or how we love,
That makes true good?
GEORGE ELIOT—*The Spanish Gypsy.* Bk. I.

16
'Tis what I love determines how I love.
GEORGE ELIOT—*The Spanish Gypsy.* Bk. I.

17
Women know no perfect love:
Loving the strong, they can forsake the strong;
Man clings because the being whom he loves
Is weak and needs him.
GEORGE ELIOT—*The Spanish Gypsy.* Bk. III.

18
A ruddy drop of manly blood
The surging sea outweighs;
The world uncertain comes and goes,
The lover rooted stays.
EMERSON—*Essays. First Series. Epigraph to Friendship.*

19
Love, which is the essence of God, is not for levity, but for the total worth of man.
EMERSON—*Essays. Of Friendship.*

20
All mankind love a lover.
EMERSON—*Essays. Of Love.*

21
Venus, when her son was lost,
Cried him up and down the coast,
In hamlets, palaces, and parks,
And told the truant by his marks,—
Golden curls, and quiver, and bow.
EMERSON—*Initial, Demoniac and Celestial Love.* St. 1.

22
Mais on revient toujours
A ses premières amours.
But one always returns to one's first loves.
Quoted by ÉTIENNE in *Joconde.* Act III. 1.
Same idea in PLINY—*Natural History.* X. 63.

23
Venus, thy eternal sway
All the race of men obey.
EURIPIDES—*Iphigenia in Aulis.*

24
He is not a lover who does not love for ever.
EURIPIDES—*Troades.* 1,051.

25
Wedded love is founded on esteem.
ELIJAH FENTON—*Mariamne.*
(See also VILLIERS)

26
Love is the tyrant of the heart; it darkens
Reason, confounds discretion; deaf to Counsel
It runs a headlong course to desperate madness.
JOHN FORD—*The Lover's Melancholy.* Act III. Sc. 3. L. 105.

1
If you would be loved, love and be lovable.
BENJ. FRANKLIN—*Poor Richard.* (1755)
(See also SENECA)

2
Love, then, hath every bliss in store;
'Tis friendship, and 'tis something more.
Each other every wish they give;
Not to know love is not to live.
GAY—*Plutus, Cupid and Time.* L. 135.

3
I saw and loved.
GIBBON—*Autobiographic Memoirs.* P. 48.

4
I love her doubting and anguish;
I love the love she withholds,
I love my love that loveth her,
And anew her being moulds.
R. W. GILDER.—*The New Day.* Pt. III. *Song XV.*

5
Love, Love, my Love.
The best things are the truest!
When the earth lies shadowy dark below
Oh, then the heavens are bluest!
R. W. GILDER—*The New Day.* Pt. IV. *Song I.*

6
Not from the whole wide world I chose thee,
Sweetheart, light of the land and the sea!
The wide, wide world could not inclose thee,
For thou art the whole wide world to me.
R. W. GILDER—*Song.*

7
I seek for one as fair and gay,
But find none to remind me,
How blest the hours pass'd away
With the girl I left behind me.
The Girl I Left Behind Me. (1759)

8
Es ist eine der grössten Himmelsgaben,
So ein lieb' Ding im Arm zu haben.
It is one of Heaven's best gifts to hold such a dear creature in one's arms.
GOETHE—*Faust.*

9
Und Lust und Liebe sind die Fittige zu grossen Thaten.
Love and desire are the spirit's wings to great deeds.
GOETHE—*Iphigenia auf Tauris.* II. 1. 107.

10
In einem Augenblick gewährt die Liebe
Was Mühe kaum in langer Zeit erreicht.
Love grants in a moment
What toil can hardly achieve in an age.
GOETHE—*Torquato Tasso.* II. 3. 76.

11
Man liebt an dem Mädchen was es ist,
Und an dem Jüngling was er ankündigt.
Girls we love for what they are;
Young men for what they promise to be.
GOETHE — *Die Wahrheit und Dichtung.* III. 14.

12
Wenn ich dich lieb habe, was geht's dich an?
If I love you, what business is that of yours?
GOETHE—*Wilhelm Meister.* IV. 9.

13
The bashful virgin's sidelong looks of love.
GOLDSMITH—*The Deserted Village.* L. 29.

14
Thus let me hold thee to my heart,
And every care resign:
And we shall never, never part,
My life—my all that's mine!
GOLDSMITH—*The Hermit.* St. 39.

15
As for murmurs, mother, we grumble a little now and then, to be sure; but there's no love lost between us.
GOLDSMITH—*She Stoops to Conquer.* Act IV. L. 255.

16
Whoe'er thou art, thy Lord and master see,
Thou wast my Slave, thou art, or thou shalt be.
GEORGE GRANVILLE (Lord Lansdowne)—*Inscription for a Figure representing the God of Love.* See *Genuine Works.* (1732) I. 129. Version of a Greek couplet from the Greek Anthology.
(See also VOLTAIRE)

17
Dear as the light that visits these sad eyes,
Dear as the ruddy drops that warm my heart.
GRAY—*The Bard.* I. 3. L. 12.

18
O'er her warm cheek, and rising bosom, move
The bloom of young Desire and purple light of love.
GRAY—*The Progress of Poesy.* I. 3. L. 16.

19
Love is a lock that linketh noble minds,
Faith is the key that shuts the spring of love.
ROBERT GREENE—*Alcida. Verses Written under a Carving of Cupid Blowing Bladders in the Air.*

20
Greensleeves was all my joy,
Greensleeves was my delight,
Greensleeves was my heart of gold,
And who but Lady Greensleeves?
A new Courtly Sonnet of the Lady Greensleeves, to the new tune of "Greensleeves." From "A Handful of Pleasant Delites." (1584)

21
Che mai
Non v'avere ò provate, ò possedute.
Far worse it is
To lose than never to have tasted bliss.
GUARINI—*Pastor Fido.*
(See also TENNYSON)

22
The chemist of love
Will this perishing mould,
Were it made out of mire,
Transmute into gold.
HAFIZ—*Divan.*

23
Love understands love; it needs no talk.
F. R. HAVERGAL—*Royal Commandments. Loving Allegiance.*

24
What a sweet reverence is that when a young man deems his mistress a little more than mortal and almost chides himself for longing to bring her close to his heart.
HAWTHORNE—*The Marble Faun.* Vol. II. Ch. XV.

25
Whom the Lord loveth he chasteneth.
Hebrews. XII. 6.

1
Du bist wie eine Blume, so hold, so schön und rein;
Ich shau' dich an und Wehmut schleicht mir ins Herz hinein.
Oh fair, oh sweet and holy as dew at morning tide,
I gaze on thee, and yearnings, sad in my bosom hide.
HEINE—*Du bist wie eine Blume.*

2
Es ist eine alte Geschichte,
Doch bleibt sie immer neu.
It is an ancient story
Yet is it ever new.
HEINE—*Lyrisches Intermezzo.* 39.

3
And once again we plighted our troth,
And titter'd, caress'd, kiss'd so dearly.
HEINE—*Youthful Sorrows.* No. 57. St. 2.

4
Alas! for love, if thou art all,
And nought beyond, O earth.
FELICIA D. HEMANS—*The Graves of a Household.*

5
Open your heart and take us in,
Love—love and me.
W. E. HENLEY—*Rhymes and Rhythms.* V.

6
Love your neighbor, yet pull not down your hedge.
HERBERT—*Jacula Prudentum.*

7
No, not Jove
Himselfe, at one time, can be wise and love.
HERRICK—*Hesperides. To Silvia.*
(See also SPENSER)

8
You say to me-wards your affection's strong;
Pray love me little, so you love me long.
HERRICK—*Love me Little, Love me Long.*
(See also MARLOWE)

9
There is a lady sweet and kind,
Was never face so pleased my mind;
I did but see her passing by,
And yet I love her till I die.
Ascribed to HERRICK in the *Scottish Student's Song-Book.* Found on back of leaf 53 of *Popish Kingdome or reigne of Antichrist,* in Latin verse by THOMAS NAOGEORGUS, and Englished by BARNABE GOOGE. Printed 1570. See *Notes and Queries.* S. IX. X. 427. Lines from *Elizabethan Song-books.* BULLEN. P. 31. Reprinted from THOMAS FORD's *Music of Sundry Kinds.* (1607)
(See also ARVERS)

10
Bid me to live, and I will live
Thy Protestant to be:
Or bid me love, and I will give
A loving heart to thee,
A heart as soft, a heart as kind,
A heart as sound and free
As in the whole world thou canst find,
That heart I'll give to thee.
HERRICK—*To Anthea, who may command him anything.* No. 268.

11
They do not love that do not show their love.
HEYWOOD—*Proverbs.* Pt. II. Ch. IX.

12
Let never man be bold enough to say,
Thus, and no farther shall my passion stray:
The first crime, past, compels us into more,
And guilt grows *fate,* that was but *choice,* before.
AARON HILL—*Athelwold.* Act V. Sc. *The Garden.*

13
To love is to know the sacrifices which eternity exacts from life.
JOHN OLIVER HOBBES—*School for Saints.* Ch. XXV.

14
O, love, love, love!
Love is like a dizziness;
It winna let a poor body
Gang about his biziness!
HOGG—*Love is like a Dizziness.* L. 9.

15
Cupid "the little greatest enemy."
HOLMES—*Professor at the Breakfast Table.*
(See also SOUTHEY)

16
Soft is the breath of a maiden's Yes:
Not the light gossamer stirs with less;
But never a cable that holds so fast
Through all the battles of wave and blast.
HOLMES—*Songs of Many Seasons. Dorothy.* II. St. 7.

17
Who love too much, hate in the like extreme.
HOMER—*Odyssey.* Bk. XV. L. 79. POPE's trans.

18
For love deceives the best of woman kind.
HOMER—*Odyssey.* Bk. XV. L. 463. POPE's trans.

19
Si sine amore, jocisque
Nil est jucundum, vivas in amore jocisque.
If nothing is delightful without love and jokes, then live in love and jokes.
HORACE—*Epistles.* I. 6. 65.

20
What's our baggage? Only vows,
Happiness, and all our care,
And the flower that sweetly shows
Nestling lightly in your hair.
VICTOR HUGO—*Eviradnus.* XI.

21
If you become a Nun, dear,
The bishop Love will be;
The Cupids every one, dear!
Will chant—'We trust in thee!'
LEIGH HUNT—*The Nun.*

22
From henceforth thou shalt learn that there is love
To long for, pureness to desire, a mount
Of consecration it were good to scale.
JEAN INGELOW—*A Parson's Letter to a Young Poet.* Pt. II. L. 55.

23
That divine swoon.
INGERSOLL—*Orthodoxy. Works.* Vol. II. P. 420.

24
But great loves, to the last, have pulses red;
All great loves that have ever died dropped dead.
HELEN HUNT JACKSON—*Dropped Dead.*

1
Love has a tide!
HELEN HUNT JACKSON—*Tides.*

2
When love is at its best, one loves
So much that he cannot forget.
HELEN HUNT JACKSON—*Two Truths.*

3
Love's like the flies, and, drawing-room or garret, goes all over a house.
DOUGLAS JERROLD—*Jerrold's Wit. Love.*

4
Greater love hath no man than this, that a man lay down his life for his friends.
John. XV. 13.

5
There is no fear in love; but perfect love casteth out fear.
I John. IV. 18.

6
Love in a hut, with water and a crust,
Is—Love, forgive us!—cinders, ashes, dust.
KEATS—*Lamia.* Pt. II.

7
I wish you could invent some means to make me at all happy without you. Every hour I am more and more concentrated in you; everything else tastes like chaff in my mouth.
KEATS—*Letters.* No. XXXVII.

8
When late I attempted your pity to move,
Why seemed you so deaf to my prayers?
Perhaps it was right to dissemb'e your love
But—why did you kick me downstairs?
J. P. KEMBLE—*Panel.* Act I. Sc. 1. Quoted from *Asylum for Fugitive Pieces.* Vol. I. P. 15. (1785) where it appeared anonymously. Kemble is credited with its authorship. *The Panel* is adapted from BICKERSTAFF'S *'Tis Well 'Tis No Worse,* but these lines are not therein. It may also be found in *Annual Register.* Appendix. (1783) P. 201.

9
What's this dull town to me?
Robin's not near—
He whom I wished to see,
Wished for to hear;
Where's all the joy and mirth
Made life a heaven on earth?
O! they're all fled with thee,
Robin Adair.
CAROLINE KEPPEL—*Robin Adair.*

10
The heart of a man to the heart of a maid—
Light of my tents, be fleet—
Morning awaits at the end of the world,
And the world is all at our feet.
KIPLING—*Gypsy Trail.*

11
The white moth to the closing vine,
The bee to the open clover,
And the Gypsy blood to the Gypsy blood
Ever the wide world over.
KIPLING—*Gypsy Trail.*

12
The wild hawk to the wind-swept sky,
The deer to the wholesome wold;
And the heart of a man to the heart of a maid,
As it was in the days of old.
KIPLING—*Gypsy Trail.*

13
The hawk unto the open sky,
The red deer to the wold;
The Romany lass for the Romany lad,
As in the days of old.
Given in the *N. Y. Times* Review of Books as a previously written poem by F. C. WEATHERBY. Not found.
(See also THEOCRITUS under SONG)

14
Sing, for faith and hope are high—
None so true as you and I—
Sing the Lovers' Litany:
"Love like ours can never die!"
KIPLING—*Lovers Litany.*

15
By the old Moulmein Pagoda, lookin' eastward to the sea,
There's a Burma girl a-settin', and I know she thinks o' me;
For the wind is in the palm-trees, and the temple-bells they say:
"Come you back, you British soldier; come you back to Mandalay!"
KIPLING—*Mandalay.*
(See also HAYES under GODS)

16
If Love were jester at the court of Death,
And Death the king of all, still would I pray,
"For me the motley and the bauble, yea,
Though all be vanity, as the Preacher saith,
The mirth of love be mine for one brief breath!"
FREDERIC L. KNOWLES—*If Love were Jester at the Court of Death.*

17
Love begins with love.
LA BRUYÈRE—*The Characters and Manners of the Present Age.* Ch. IV.

18
Le commencement et le déclin de l'amour se font sentir par l'embarras où l'on est de se trouver seuls.
The beginning and the end of love are both marked by embarrassment when the two find themselves alone.
LA BRUYÈRE—*Les Caractères.* IV.

19
Amour! Amour! quand tu nous tiens
On peut bien dire, Adieu, prudence.
O tyrant love, when held by you,
We may to prudence bid adieu.
LA FONTAINE—*Fables.* IV. 1.

20
The pleasure of love is in loving. We are happier in the passion we feel than in what we excite.
LA ROCHEFOUCAULD—*Maxims.* 78.

21
The more we love a mistress, the nearer we are to hating her.
LA ROCHEFOUCAULD—*Maxims.* 114.

22
Ce qui fait que amants et les maitresses ne s'ennuient point d'être ensemble; c'est qu'ils parlent toujours d'eux mêmes.
The reason why lovers and their mistresses never tire of being together is that they are always talking of themselves.
LA ROCHEFOUCAULD—*Maximes.* 312.

1
Do you know you have asked for the costliest thing
Ever made by the Hand above—
A woman's heart, and a woman's life,
And a woman's wonderful love?

MARY T. LATHROP. *A Woman's Answer to a Man's Question.* Erroneously credited to MRS. BROWNING.

2
I love a lassie, a bonnie, bonnie lassie,
She's as pure as the lily in the dell.
She's as sweet as the heather,
The bonnie, bloomin' heather,
Mary, ma Scotch Blue-bell.

HARRY LAUDER and GERALD GRAFTON. *I Love a Lassie.*

3
Et c'est dans la première flamme
Qu'est tout le nectar du baiser.
And in that first flame
Is all the nectar of the kiss.

LEBRUN—*Mes Souvenirs, ou les Deux Rives de la Seine.*

4
Love leads to present rapture,—then to pain;
But all through Love in time is healed again.

LELAND—*Sweet Marjoram.*

5
A warrior so bold, and a virgin so bright,
Conversed as they sat on the green.
They gazed on each other with tender delight,
Alonzo the Brave was the name of the knight—
The maiden's the Fair Imogene.

M. G. LEWIS—*Alonzo the Brave and the Fair Imogene.* First appeared in his novel *Ambrosio the Monk.* Found in his *Tales of Wonder.* Vol. III. P. 63. Lewis's copy of his poem is in the British Museum.

6
Ah, how skillful grows the hand
That obeyeth Love's command!
It is the heart and not the brain
That to the highest doth attain,
And he who followeth Love's behest
Far excelleth all the rest.

LONGFELLOW—*Building of the Ship.*

7
Love contending with friendship, and self with each generous impulse.
To and fro in his breast his thoughts were heaving and dashing,
As in a foundering ship.

LONGFELLOW—*Courtship of Miles Standish.* Pt. III. L. 7.

8
Like Dian's kiss, unask'd, unsought,
Love gives itself, but is not bought.

LONGFELLOW—*Endymion.* St. 4.

9
Does not all the blood within me
Leap to meet thee, leap to meet thee,
As the springs to meet the sunshine.

LONGFELLOW—*Hiawatha. Wedding Feast.* L. 153.

10
O, there is nothing holier, in this life of ours, than the first consciousness of love,—the first fluttering of its silken wings.

LONGFELLOW—*Hyperion.* Bk. III. Ch. VI.

11
It is difficult to know at what moment love begins; it is less difficult to know that it has begun.

LONGFELLOW—*Kavanagh.* Ch. XXI.

12
I do not love thee less for what is done,
And cannot be undone. Thy very weakness
Hath brought thee nearer to me, and henceforth
My love will have a sense of pity in it,
Making it less a worship than before.

LONGFELLOW—*Masque of Pandora.* Pt. VIII. *In the Garden.* L. 39.

13
That was the first sound in the song of love!
Scarce more than silence is, and yet a sound.
Hands of invisible spirits touch the strings
Of that mysterious instrument, the soul,
And play the prelude of our fate. We hear
The voice prophetic, and are not alone.

LONGFELLOW—*Spanish Student.* Act I. Sc. 3. L. 109.

14
I love thee, as the good love heaven.

LONGFELLOW—*Spanish Student.* Act I. Sc. 3. L. 146.

15
Love keeps the cold out better than a cloak.
It serves for food and raiment.

LONGFELLOW—*Spanish Student.* Act I. Sc. 5. L. 52.

16
How can I tell the signals and the signs
By which one heart another heart divines?
How can I tell the many thousand ways
By which it keeps the secret it betrays?

LONGFELLOW—*Tales of a Wayside Inn.* Pt. III. *Student's Tale. Emma and Eginhard.* L. 75.

17
So they grew, and they grew, to the church steeple tops
And they couldn't grow up any higher;
So they twin'd themselves into a true lover's knot,
For all lovers true to admire.

Lord Lovel. Old Ballad.
History found in Professor Child's *English and Scottish Popular Ballads.* II. 204. Also in *The New Comic Minstrel.* Pub. by JOHN CAMERON, Glasgow. The original version seems to be as given there.

18
Under floods that are deepest,
Which Neptune obey,
Over rocks that are steepest,
Love will find out the way.

Love will find out the way. Ballad in PERCY'S *Reliques.*

19
Tell me not, sweet, I am unkind,
That from the nunnery
Of thy chaste breast and quiet mind
To war and arms I fly.

. . . .

Yet this inconstancy is such
As you too shall adore:—
I could not love thee, dear, so much,
Loved I not honour more.

L[illegible]ACE—*To Lucasta, on going to the Wars.* [illegible] erroneously to MONTROSE by SCOTT.

1
True love is but a humble, low born thing,
And hath its food served up in earthenware;
It is a thing to walk with, hand in hand,
Through the every-dayness of this workday world.

LOWELL—*Love*. L. 1.

2
Not as all other women are
Is she that to my soul is dear;
Her glorious fancies come from far,
Beneath the silver evening star,
And yet her heart is ever near.

LOWELL—*My Love*. St. 1.

3
Wer nicht liebt Wein, Weib, und Gesang,
Der bleibt ein Narr sein Leben lang.
He who loves not wine, woman, and song,
Remains a fool his whole life long.

Attributed to LUTHER by UHLAND in *Die Geisterkelter*. Found in LUTHER'S *Tischreden, Proverbs* at end. Credited to J. H. Voss by REDLICH, *Die poetischen Beiträge zum Waudsbecker Bothen*, Hamburg, 1871. P. 67.
(See BURTON under TEMPTATION)

4
As love knoweth no lawes, so it regardeth no conditions.

LYLY—*Euphues*. P. 84.

5
Cupid and my Campaspe play'd
At cards for kisses; Cupid paid;
He stakes his quiver, bow and arrows,
His mother's doves, and team of sparrows;
Loses them too; then down he throws
The coral of his lip,—the rose
Growing on 's cheek (but none knows how)
With these, the crystal on his brow,
And then the dimple of his chin;
All these did my Campaspe win.
At last he set her both his eyes,
She won, and Cupid blind did rise.
O Love! hath she done this to thee?
What shall, alas! become of me?

LYLY—*Alexander and Campaspe*. Act III. Sc. V. *Song*.

6
It is better to poyson hir with the sweet bait of love.

LYLY—*Euphues*.
(See also ROMEO AND JULIET)

7
Nothing is more hateful than love.

LYLY—*Euphues*.
(See also TROILUS AND CRESSIDA)

8
The lover in the husband may be lost.

LORD LYTTLETON—*Advice to a Lady*. St. 13.

9
None without hope e'er lov'd the brightest fair:
But Love can hope where Reason would despair.

LORD LYTTLETON—*Epigram*.

10
But thou, through good and evil, praise and blame,
Wilt not thou love me for myself alone?
Yes, thou wilt love me with exceeding love,
And I will tenfold all that love repay;
Still smiling, though the tender may reprove,
Still faithful, though the trusted may betray.

MACAULAY—*Lines Written July 30*, 1847.

11
This lass so neat, with smile so sweet,
Has won my right good will,
I'd crowns resign to call her mine,
Sweet lass of Richmond Hill.

Ascribed to LEONARD MCNALLY, who married MISS I'ANSON, one of the claimants for the "Lass," by SIR JOSEPH BARRINGTON in *Sketches of His Own Times*. Vol. II. P. 47. Also credited to WILLIAM UPTON. It appeared in *Public Advertiser*, Aug. 3, 1789. "Sweet Lass of Richmond Hill" erroneously said to have been a sweetheart of King George III.

12
When Madelon comes out to serve us drinks,
We always know she's coming by her song.
And every man he tells his little tale,
And Madelon, she listens all day long.
Our Madelon is never too severe—
A kiss or two is nothing much to her—
She laughs us up to love and life and God—
Madelon, Madelon, Madelon.

Madelon—Song of the French Soldiers in the Great War.

13
Who ever lov'd, that lov'd not at first sight?

MARLOWE—*Hero and Leander. First Sestiad*. L. 176. Quoted as a "dead shepherd's saw." Found in *As You Like It*.
(See also CHAPMAN)

14
Love me little, love me long.

MARLOWE—*The Jew of Malta*. Act IV. Sc. 6.
(See also HERRICK)

15
Come live with me, and be my love,
And we will all the pleasures prove,
That valleys, groves, or hills, or fields,
Or woods and steepy mountains, yield.

MARLOWE—*The Passionate Shepherd to his Love*. St. 1.

16
Quand on n'a pas ce que l'on aime, il faut aimer ce que l'on a.

If one does not possess what one loves, one should love what one has.

MARMONTEL. Quoted by MOORE in *Irish Melodies. The Irish Peasant to His Mistress*. Note. (See also 615[3])

17
Non amo te, Sabidi, nec possum dicere quare;
Hoc tantum possum dicere: non amo te.

I do not love thee, Sabidius, nor can I say why; I can only say this, "I do not love thee."

MARTIAL—*Epigrams*. I. 32. (Name sometimes given "Savidi.")
(See also CATULLUS)

18
I do not love thee, Dr. Fell.
But why I cannot tell;
But this I know full well,
I do not love thee, Dr. Fell.

Paraphrase of MARTIAL by TOM BROWN, as given in his *Works*, ed. by DRAKE. (1760) Answer to DEAN JOHN FELL, of Oxford. IV. 100.

19
Je ne vous aime point, Hylas;
Je n'en saurois dire la cause;
Je sais seulement une chose.

C'est que je ne vous aime pas.
Paraphrase of MARTIAL by ROBERT RABUTIN (De Bussy)—Epigram 32. Bk. I.

1
I love thee not, Nel
But why I can't tell.
Paraphrase of MARTIAL in THOS. FORDE'S *Virtus Rediviva.*

2
I love him not, but show no reason wherefore,
but this, I do not love the man.
Paraphrase of MARTIAL by ROWLAND WATKYNS—*Antipathy.*

3
Love is a flame to burn out human wills,
Love is a flame to set the will on fire,
Love is a flame to cheat men into mire.
MASEFIELD—*Widow in the Bye Street.* Pt. II.

4
Great men,
Till they have gained their ends, are giants in
Their promises, but, those obtained, weak pigmies
In their performance. And it is a maxim
Allowed among them, so they may deceive,
They may swear anything; for the queen of love,
As they hold constantly, does never punish,
But smile, at lovers' perjuries.
MASSINGER—*Great Duke of Florence.* Act II. Sc. 3. (See also OVID)

5
'Tis well to be merry and wise,
'Tis well to be honest and true;
'Tis well to be off with the old love,
Before you are on with the new.
As used by MATURIN, for the motto to *"Bertram,"* produced at Drury Lane, 1816.

6
It is good to be merry and wise,
It is good to be honest and true,
It is best to be off with the old love,
Before you are on with the new.
Published in *"Songs of England and Scotland."* London, 1835. Vol. II. P. 73.

7
I loved you ere I knew you; know you now,
And having known you, love you better still.
OWEN MEREDITH (Lord Lytton)—*Vanini.*

8
Love is all in fire, and yet is ever freezing;
Love is much in winning, yet is more in leesing:
Love is ever sick, and yet is never dying;
Love is ever true, and yet is ever lying;
Love does doat in liking, and is mad in loathing;
Love indeed is anything, yet indeed is nothing.
THOS. MIDDLETON—*Blurt, Master Constable.* Act II. Sc. 2.

9
I never heard
Of any true affection but 'twas nipped.
THOS. MIDDLETON—*Blurt, Master Constable.* Act III. Sc. 2.
(See also MOORE under GAZELLE)

10
He who for love hath undergone
The worst that can befall,
Is happier thousandfold than one
Who never loved at all.
MONCKTON MILNES—*To Myrzha. On Returning.* (See also TENNYSON)

11
Such sober certainty of waking bliss.
MILTON—*Comus.* 263.
(See also WORDSWORTH)

12
Imparadis'd in one another's arms.
MILTON—*Paradise Lost.* Bk. IV. L. 50.

13
So dear I love him, that with him all deaths
I could endure, without him live no life.
MILTON—*Paradise Lost.* Bk. IX. L. 832.

14
It is not virtue, wisdom, valour, wit,
Strength, comeliness of shape, or amplest merit,
That woman's love can win, or long inherit;
But what it is, hard is to say,
Harder to hit.
MILTON—*Samson Agonistes.* L. 1,010.

15
La fleur nommée héliotrope tourne sans cesse vers cet astre du jour, aussi mon cœur dorénavant tournera-t-il toujours vers les astres resplendissants de vos yeux adorables, ainsi que son pôle unique.

The flower called heliotrope turns without ceasing to that star of the day, so also my heart henceforth will turn itself always towards the resplendent stars of your adorable eyes, as towards its only pole.
MOLIÈRE—*Le Malade Imaginaire.* Act II. Sc. 6. (See also MOORE)

16
L'amour est souvent un fruit de mariage.
Love is often a fruit of marriage.
MOLIÈRE—*Sganarelle.* I. 1.

17
If a man should importune me to give a reason why I loved him, I find it could no otherwise be expressed than by making answer, Because it was he; because it was I. There is beyond all that I am able to say, I know not what inexplicable and fated power that brought on this union.
MONTAIGNE—*Essays.* Bk. I. Ch. XXVII.

18
Celuy ayme peu qui ayme à la mesure.
He loves little who loves by rule.
MONTAIGNE. Bk. I. Ch. XXVIII.

19
Yes, loving is a painful thrill,
And not to love more painful still;
But oh, it is the worst of pain,
To love and not be lov'd again.
MOORE—*Anacreontic.* Ode 29.
(See also COWLEY)

20
No, the heart that has truly loved never forgets,
But as truly loves on to the close,
As the sunflower turns on her god, when he sets,
The same look which she turn'd when he rose.
MOORE—*Believe Me, If All Those Endearing Young Charms.* St. 2.
(See also MOLIÈRE)

21
I know not, I ask not, if guilt's in that heart,
I but know that I love thee, whatever thou art.
MOORE—*Come, Rest in This Bosom.* St. 2.

22
Love on through all ills, and love on till they die!
MOORE—*Lalla Rookh. The Light of the Harem.* L. 653.

1
A boat at midnight sent alone
  To drift upon the moonless sea,
A lute, whose leading chord is gone,
  A wounded bird, that hath but one
Imperfect wing to soar upon,
  Are like what I am, without thee.
  MOORE—*Loves of the Angels. Second Angel's Story.*

2
But there's nothing half so sweet in life
As love's young dream.
  MOORE—*Love's Young Dream.* St. 1.

3
"Tell me, what's Love;" said Youth, one day,
To drooping Age, who crost his way.—
"It is a sunny hour of play;
For which repentance dear doth pay;
  Repentance! Repentance!
And this is Love, as wise men say."
  MOORE—*Youth and Age.*

4
I've wandered east, I've wandered west,
  I've bourne a weary lot;
But in my wanderings far or near
  Ye never were forgot.
The fount that first burst frae this heart
  Still travels on its way
And channels deeper as it rins
  The luve o' life's young day.
  WM. MOTHERWELL—*Jeanie Morrison.*

5
  Duty's a slave that keeps the keys,
But Love, the master goes in and out
Of his goodly chambers with song and shout,
  Just as he please—just as he please.
  D. M. MULOCK—*Plighted.*

6
Ah, dearer than my soul . . .
Dearer than light, or life, or fame.
  OLDHAM—*Lament for Saul and Jonathan.*
  (See also WORDSWORTH)

7
Militat omnis amans.
  Every lover is a soldier. (Love is a warfare.)
  OVID—*Amorum.* I. 9. 1.

8
Qui non vult fieri desidiosus, amet.
  Let the man who does not wish to be idle, fall in love.
  OVID—*Amorum.* I. 9. 46.

9
Sic ego nec sine te nec tecum vivere possum
Et videor voti nescius esse mei.
  Thus I am not able to exist either with you or without you; and I seem not to know my own wishes.
  OVID—*Amorum.* Bk. III. 10. 39.

10
Jupiter ex alto perjuria ridet amantum.
  Jupiter from on high laughs at the perjuries of lovers.
  OVID—*Ars Amatoria.* Bk. I. 633.
  (See also DRYDEN)

11
Res est soliciti plena timoris amor.
  Love is a thing full of anxious fears.
  OVID—*Heroides.* I. 12.

12
Quicquid Amor jussit non est contemnere tutum.
Regnat, et in dominos jus habet ille deos.
  It is not safe to despise what Love commands. He reigns supreme, and rules the mighty gods.
  OVID—*Heroides.* IV. 11.

13
Hei mihi! quod nullis amor est medicabilis herbis.
  Ah me! love can not be cured by herbs.
  OVID—*Metamorphoses.* I. 523.

14
Non bene conveniunt, nec in una sede morantur,
Majestas et amor.
  Majesty and love do not well agree, nor do they live together.
  OVID—*Metamorphoses.* II. 846.

15
Credula res amor est.
  Love is a credulous thing.
  OVID—*Metamorphoses.* VII. 826. *Heroides.* VI. 21.

16
Otia si tollas, periere cupidinis arcus.
  If you give up your quiet life, the bow of Cupid will lose its power.
  OVID—*Remedia Amoris.* CXXXIX.

17
Qui finem quæris amoris,
(Cedit amor rebus) res age; tutus eris.
  If thou wishest to put an end to love, attend to business (love yields to employment); then thou wilt be safe.
  OVID—*Remedia Amoris.* CXLIII.

18
Let those love now who never lov'd before,
Let those who always loved now love the more.
  THOS. PARNELL—*Trans. of the Pervigilium Veneris.* Ancient poem. Author unknown. Ascribed to CATULLUS. See also BURTON —*Anatomy of Melancholy.* Pt. III. Sec. II. Memb. 5. 5.

19
The moods of love are like the wind,
And none knows whence or why they rise.
  COVENTRY PATMORE—*The Angel in the House. Sarum Plain.*

20
My merry, merry, merry roundelay
  Concludes with Cupid's curse,
They that do change old love for new,
  Pray gods, they change for worse!
  GEORGE PEELE—*Cupid's Curse; From the Arraignment of Paris.*

21
What thing is love?—for (well I wot) love is a thing.
It is a prick, it is a sting.
It is a pretty, pretty thing;
It is a fire, it is a coal,
Whose flame creeps in at every hole!
  GEORGE PEELE—*Miscellaneous Poems. The Hunting of Cupid.*

22
  Love will make men dare to die for their beloved—love alone; and women as well as men.
  PLATO—*The Symposium.*

23
Qui amat, tamen hercle si esurit, nullum esurit.
  He that is in love, faith, if he be hungry, is not hungry at all.
  PLAUTUS—*Casina.* IV. 2. 16.

1
Amor et melle et felle est fœcundissimus:
Gustu dat dulce, amarum ad satietatem usque aggerit.

Love has both its gall and honey in abundance: it has sweetness to the taste, but it presents bitterness also to satiety.

PLAUTUS—*Cistellaria*. I. 1. 71.

2
Auro contra cedo modestum amatorem.

Find me a reasonable lover against his weight in gold.

PLAUTUS—*Curculio*. I. 3. 45.

3
Qui in amore præcipitavit pejus perit, quam si saxo saliat.

He who falls in love meets a worse fate than he who leaps from a rock.

PLAUTUS—*Trinummus*. II. 1. 30.

4
A lover's soul lives in the body of his mistress.

PLUTARCH.

5
Ah! what avails it me the flocks to keep,
Who lost my heart while I preserv'd my sheep.

POPE—*Autumn*. L. 79.

6
Is it, in Heav'n, a crime to love too well?
To bear too tender or too firm a heart,
To act a lover's or a Roman's part?
Is there no bright reversion in the sky
For those who greatly think, or bravely die?

POPE—*Elegy on an Unfortunate Lady*.
(See also CRASHAW)

7
Of all affliction taught a lover yet,
'Tis true the hardest science to forget.

POPE—*Eloisa to Abelard*. L. 189.

8
One thought of thee puts all the pomp to flight;
Priests, tapers, temples, swim before my sight.

POPE—*Eloisa to Abelard*. L. 273.
(See also SMITH)

9
Love, free as air, at sight of human ties,
Spreads his light wings, and in a moment flies.

POPE—*Epistle to Eloisa*. Last Line.

10
Ye gods, annihilate but space and time,
And make two lovers happy.

POPE—*Martinus Scriblerus on the Art of Sinking in Poetry*. Ch. XI.

11
O Love! for Sylvia let me gain the prize,
And make my tongue victorious as her eyes.

POPE—*Spring*. L. 49.

12
Scilicent insano nemo in amore videt.

Everybody in love is blind.

PROPERTIUS—*Elegiæ*. II. 14. 18.
(See also MIDSUMMER NIGHT'S DREAM, MERCHANT OF VENICE)

13
Divine is Love and scorneth worldly pelf,
And can be bought with nothing but with self.

SIR WALTER RALEIGH—*Love the Only Price of Love*.

14
If all the world and love were young,
And truth in every shepherd's tongue,
These pretty pleasures might me move
To live with thee, and be thy love.

SIR WALTER RALEIGH—*The Nymph's Reply to the Passionate Shepherd*.

15
Ach die Zeiten der Liebe rollen nicht zurück, sondern ewig weiter hinab.

Ah! The seasons of love roll not backward but onward, downward forever.

JEAN PAUL RICHTER—*Hesperus*. IX.

16
Die Liebe vermindert die weibliche
Feinheit und verstärkt die männliche.

Love lessens woman's delicacy and increases man's.

JEAN PAUL RICHTER—*Titan*. Zykel 34.

17
Ein liebendes Mädchen wird unbewust kühner.

A loving maiden grows unconsciously more bold.

JEAN PAUL RICHTER—*Titan*. Zykel 71.

18
As one who cons at evening o'er an album all alone,
And muses on the faces of the friends that he has known,
So I turn the leaves of Fancy, till in shadowy design
I find the smiling features of an old sweetheart of mine.

JAMES WHITCOMB RILEY—*An Old Sweetheart of Mine*.

19
The hours I spent with thee, dear heart,
Are as a string of pearls to me;
I count them over, every one apart,
My rosary, my rosary.

ROBERT CAMERON ROGERS—*My Rosary*.

20
Oh! she was good as she was fair.
None—none on earth above her!
As pure in thought as angels are,
To know her was to love her.

SAMUEL ROGERS—*Jacqueline*. Pt. I. L. 68.
(See also BURNS, also HALLECK under GRAVE)

21
Love is the fulfilling of the law.

Romans. XIII. 10.

22
Trust thou thy Love: if she be proud, is she not sweet?
Trust thou thy love: if she be mute, is she not pure?
Lay thou thy soul full in her hands, low at her feet —
Fail, Sun and Breath!—yet, for thy peace, she shall endure.

RUSKIN—*Trust Thou Thy Love*.

23
Whither thou goest, I will go; and where thou lodgest, I will lodge: thy people shall be my people, and thy God my God.

Ruth. I. 16.

24
Et l'on revient toujours à ses premiers amours.

One always returns to his first love.

ST. JUST.

25
L'amour est un égoïsme à deux.

Love is an egotism of two.

ANTOINE DE SALLE.

1
Thy love to me was wonderful, passing the love of women.
II Samuel. I. 26.

2
Raum ist in der kleinsten Hütte
Für ein glücklich liebend Paar.
In the smallest cot there is room enough for a loving pair.
SCHILLER—*Der Jüngling am Bache.* St. 4.

3
Arm in Arm mit dir,
So fordr' ich mein Jahrhundert in die Schranken.
Thus Arm in Arm with thee I dare defy my century into the lists.
SCHILLER—*Don Carlos.* I. 9. 97.

4
Ah, to that far distant strand
Bridge there was not to convey,
Not a bark was near at hand,
Yet true love soon found the way.
SCHILLER—*Hero and Leander.* BOWRING'S trans.

5
O dass sie ewig grünen bliebe,
Die schöne Zeit der jungen Liebe.
O that it might remain eternally green,
The beautiful time of youthful love.
SCHILLER—*Lied von der Glocke.*

6
Ich habe genossen das irdische Glück,
Ich habe gelebt und geliebt.
I have enjoyed earthly happiness,
I have lived and loved.
SCHILLER—*Piccolomini.* III. 7. 9.

7
Mortals, while through the world you go,
Hope may succor and faith befriend,
Yet happy your hearts if you can but know,
Love awaits at the journey's end!
CLINTON SCOLLARD—*The Journey's End—Envoy.*

8
And love is loveliest when embalm'd in tears.
SCOTT—*Lady of the Lake.* Canto IV. St. 1.

9
In peace, Love tunes the shepherd's reed;
In war, he mounts the warrior's steed;
In halls, in gay attire is seen;
In hamlets, dances on the green.
Love rules the court, the camp, the grove,
And men below, and saints above;
For love is heaven, and heaven is love.
SCOTT—*Lay of the Last Minstrel.* Canto III. St. 2.

10
Her blue eyes sought the west afar,
For lovers love the western star.
SCOTT—*Lay of the Last Minstrel.* Canto III. St. 24.

11
True love's the gift which God has given
To man alone beneath the heaven.
* * * * *
It is the secret sympathy,
The silver link, the silken tie,
Which heart to heart, and mind to mind,
In body and in soul can bind.
SCOTT—*Lay of the Last Minstrel.* Canto V. St. 13. (See also SPENSER)

12
Where shall the lover rest,
Whom the fates sever
From his true maiden's breast,
Parted for ever?
Where, through groves deep and high,
Sounds the far billow,
Where early violets die,
Under the willow.
SCOTT—*Marmion.* Canto III. St. 10.

13
Magis gauderes quod habueras, quam moereres quod amiseras.
Better to have loved and lost, than not to have loved at all. (Free trans.)
SENECA—*Epistles.* 99.
(See also TENNYSON)

14
Odit verus amor nec patitur moras.
True love hates and will not bear delay.
SENECA—*Hercules Furens.* 588.

15
Qui blandiendo dulce nutrivit malum,
Sero recusat ferre, quod subiit, jugum.
He who has fostered the sweet poison of love by fondling it, finds it too late to refuse the yoke which he has of his own accord assumed.
SENECA—*Hippolytus.* CXXXIV.

16
Si vis amari, ama.
If you wish to be loved, love.
SENECA—*Epistolæ Ad Lucilium.* IX. AUSONIUS—*Epigrams.* XCI. 6. MARTIAL—*Epigrams.* VI. 11. OVID—*Ars Amatoria.* II. 107. Attributed to PLATO by BURTON.
(See also FRANKLIN)

17
But love that comes too late,
Like a remorseful pardon slowly carried,
To the great sender turns a sour offence.
All's Well That Ends Well. Act V. Sc. 3. L. 5.

18
There's beggary in the love that can be reckoned.
Antony and Cleopatra. Act I. Sc. 1. L. 15.

19
If thou remember'st not the slightest folly
That ever love did make thee run into,
Thou hast not lov'd.
As You Like It. Act II. Sc. 4. L. 34.

20
It is as easy to count atomies as to resolve the propositions of a lover.
As You Like It. Act III. Sc. 2. L. 245

21
But are you so much in love as your rhymes speak?
Neither rhyme nor reason can express how much.
As You Like It. Act III. Sc. 2. L. 418.

22
O coz, coz, coz, my pretty little coz, that thou didst know how many fathom deep I am in love! But it cannot be sounded; my affection hath an unknown bottom, like the bay of Portugal.
As You Like It. Act IV. Sc 1. L. 208.

1
No sooner met but they looked, no sooner looked but they loved, no sooner loved but they sighed, no sooner sighed but they asked one another the reason.
As You Like It. Act V. Sc. 2. L. 36.

2
Good shepherd, tell this youth what 'tis to love.
It is to be all made of sighs and tears;—
* * * * *
It is to be all made of faith and service;—
* * * * *
It is to be all made of fantasy.
As You Like It. Act V. Sc. 2. L. 89.

3
I know not why
I love this youth; and I have heard you say,
Love's reason's without reason.
Cymbeline. Act IV. Sc. 2. L. 20.

4
This is the very ecstasy of love,
Whose violent property foredoes itself,
And leads the will to desperate undertakings.
Hamlet. Act II. Sc. 1. L. 102.

5
He is far gone, far gone: and truly in my youth I suffered much extremity for love; very near this.
Hamlet. Act II. Sc. 2. L. 188.

6
Where love is great, the littlest doubts are fear;
When little fears grow great, great love grows there.
Hamlet. Act III. Sc. 2. L. 181.

7
Forty thousand brothers
Could not, with all their quantity of love,
Make up my sum.
Hamlet. Act V. Sc. 1. L. 292.

8
Love thyself last: cherish those hearts that hate thee.
Henry VIII. Act III. Sc. 2. L. 444.

9
Though last, not least in love!
Julius Cæsar. Act III. Sc. 1. L. 189.

10
Which of you shall we say doth love us most?
That we our largest bounty may extend
Where nature doth with merit challenge.
King Lear. Act I. Sc. 1. L. 52.

11
Love, whose month is ever May,
Spied a blossom passing fair,
Playing in the wanton air:
Through the velvet leaves the wind,
All unseen can passage find;
That the lover, sick to death,
Wish'd himself the heaven's breath.
Love's Labour's Lost. Act IV. Sc. 3. *Song.*

12
By heaven, I do love: and it hath taught me to rhyme, and to be melancholy.
Love's Labour's Lost. Act IV. Sc. 3. L. 10.

13
You would for paradise break faith and troth,
And Jove, for your love, would infringe an oath.
Love's Labour's Lost. Act IV. Sc. 3. L. 143.

14
A lover's eyes will gaze an eagle blind.
A lover's ear will hear the lowest sound.
Love's Labour's Lost. Act IV. Sc. 3. L. 334.

15
Love's tongue proves dainty Bacchus gross in taste:
For valour, is not Love a Hercules,
Still climbing trees in the Hesperides?
Love's Labour's Lost. Act IV. Sc. 3. L. 339.

16
And when Love speaks, the voice of all the gods
Makes heaven drowsy with the harmony.
Love's Labour's Lost. Act IV. Sc. 3. L. 344.

17
But love is blind, and lovers cannot see
The pretty follies that themselves commit.
Merchant of Venice. Act II. Sc. 6. L. 36.
(See also PROPERTIUS)

18
Yet I have not seen
So likely an ambassador of love;
A day in April never came so sweet,
To show how costly summer was at hand,
As this fore-spurrer comes before his lord.
Merchant of Venice. Act II. Sc. 9. L. 91.

19
And swearing till my very roof was dry
With oaths of love.
Merchant of Venice. Act III. Sc. 2. L. 206.

20
Love like a shadow flies when substance love pursues;
Pursuing that that flies, and flying what pursues.
Merry Wives of Windsor. Act II. Sc. 2. L. 217.

21
Ay me! for aught that I ever could read,
Could ever hear by tale or history,
The course of true love never did run smooth.
Midsummer Night's Dream. Act I. Sc. 1. L. 132.

22
Love looks not with the eyes, but with the mind;
And therefore is winged Cupid painted blind.
Midsummer Night's Dream. Act I. Sc. 1. L. 234. (See also PROPERTIUS)

23
Love, therefore, and tongue-tied simplicity
In least speak most, to my capacity.
Midsummer Night's Dream. Act V. Sc. 1. L. 104.

24
Speak low, if you speak love.
Much Ado About Nothing. Act II. Sc. 1. L. 102.

25
Friendship is constant in all other things
Save in the office and affairs of love:
Therefore, all hearts in love use their own tongues;
Let every eye negotiate for itself
And trust no agent.
Much Ado About Nothing. Act II. Sc. 1. L. 182.

26
Some Cupid kills with arrows, some with traps.
Much Ado About Nothing. Act III. Sc. 1. L. 106.

27
Upon this hint I spake;
She lov'd me for the dangers I had pass'd,
And I lov'd her, that she did pity them.
This only is the witchcraft I have us'd:
Here comes the lady; let her witness it.
Othello. Act I. Sc. 3. L. 166.

1 Perdition catch my soul,
But I do love thee! and when I love thee not,
Chaos is come again.
Othello. Act III. Sc. 3. L. 89.

2
What! keep a week away? seven days and nights?
Eight score eight hours? and lovers' absent hours,
More tedious than the dial eight score times?
O, weary reckoning!
Othello. Act III. Sc. 4. L. 173.

3
If heaven would make me such another world
Of one entire and perfect chrysolite,
I'ld not have sold her for it.
Othello. Act V. Sc. 2. L. 144.

4
Speak of me as I am; nothing extenuate
Nor set down aught in malice: then must you speak
Of one that loved not wisely, but too well;
Of one not easily jealous, but, being wrought,
Perplexed in the extreme: of one, whose hand
Like the base Indian, threw a pearl away,
Richer than all his tribe: of one, whose subdued eyes,
Albeit unused to the melting mood,
Drop tears as fast as the Arabian trees
Their medicinal gum.
Othello. Act V. Sc. 2. L. 383. ("Base Indian" is "base Judean" in first folio.)

5
There is no creature loves me,
And if I die, no soul shall pity me.
Richard III. Act V. Sc. 3. L. 200.

6
From love's weak childish bow she lives unharmed.
Romeo and Juliet. Act I. Sc. 1. ("Uncharmed" instead of "unharmed" in Folio and early ed.)

7
Love is a smoke rais'd with the fume of sighs;
Being purg'd, a fire sparkling in a lover's eyes;
Being vex'd, a sea nourish'd with lovers' tears:
What is it else? a madness most discreet,
A choking gall and a preserving sweet.
Romeo and Juliet. Act I. Sc. 1. L. 196.

8
Steal love's sweet bait from fearful hooks.
Romeo and Juliet. Act I. Sc. 5. *Chorus at end*. (Not in Folio.)
(See also Lyly)

9
Speak but one rhyme, and I am satisfied;
Cry but—"Ay me!" pronounce but "love" and "dove."
Romeo and Juliet. Act II. Sc. 1. L. 9.

10
See, how she leans her cheek upon her hand!
O, that I were a glove upon that hand,
That I might touch that cheek!
Romeo and Juliet. Act II. Sc. 2. L. 23.

11
O, Romeo, Romeo! wherefore art thou, Romeo?
Romeo and Juliet. Act II. Sc. 2. L. 33.

12
For stony limits cannot hold love out,
And what love can do that dares love attempt.
Romeo and Juliet. Act II. Sc. 2. L. 67.

13 At lovers' perjuries,
They say, Jove laughs.
Romeo and Juliet. Act II. Sc. 2. L. 92.
(See also Dryden)

14
My bounty is as boundless as the sea,
My love as deep; the more I give to thee
The more I have, for both are infinite.
Romeo and Juliet. Act II. Sc. 2. L. 133.

15
Love goes toward love as school-boys from their books,
But love from love, toward school with heavy looks.
Romeo and Juliet. Act II. Sc. 2. L. 157.

16
It is my soul that calls upon my name;
How silver-sweet sound lovers' tongues by night,
Like soft music to attending ears.
Romeo and Juliet. Act II. Sc. 2. L. 165.

17
'Tis almost morning; I would have thee gone:
And yet no further than a wanton's bird;
Who lets it hop a little from her hand,
Like a poor prisoner in his twisted gyves,
And with a silk thread plucks it back again,
So loving-jealous of his liberty.
Romeo and Juliet. Act II. Sc. 2. L. 177.

18 Love's heralds should be thoughts,
Which ten times faster glide than the sun's beams,
Driving back shadows over louring hills;
Therefore do nimble-pinion'd doves draw love,
And therefore hath the wind-swift Cupid wings.
Romeo and Juliet. Act II. Sc. 5. L. 4.

19
Therefore love moderately; long love doth so;
Too swift arrives as tardy as too slow.
Romeo and Juliet. Act II. Sc. 6. L. 14.

20
Give me my Romeo; and, when he shall die,
Take him, and cut him out in little stars,
And he will make the face of heaven so fine,
And all the world will be in love with night,
And pay no worship to the garish sun.
Romeo and Juliet. Act III. Sc. 2. L. 21.

21
Love's not Time's fool, though rosy lips and cheeks
Within his bending sickle's compass come;
Love alters not with his brief hours and weeks,
But bears it out even to the edge of doom.
Sonnet CXVI.

22
They say all lovers swear more performance than they are able, and yet reserve an ability that they never perform.
Troilus and Cressida. Act III. Sc. 2. L. 91.

23 For to be wise, and love
Exceeds man's might; that dwells with gods above.
Troilus and Cressida. Act III. Sc. 2. L. 163.

24
The noblest hateful love that e'er I heard of.
Troilus and Cressida. Act IV. Sc. 1. L. 33.
(See also Lyly)

25
O spirit of love! how quick and fresh art thou,
That notwithstanding thy capacity
Receiveth as the sea, nought enters there,

Of what validity and pitch soe'er,
But falls into abatement and low price,
Even in a minute!
Twelfth Night. Act I. Sc. 1. L. 9.

1
Then let thy love be younger than thyself,
Or thy affection cannot hold the bent.
Twelfth Night. Act II. Sc. 4. L. 37.

2
She never told her love,
But let concealment, like a worm i' the bud,
Feed on her damask cheek; she pin'd in thought,
And with a green and yellow melancholy
She sat like patience on a monument,
Smiling at grief.
Twelfth Night. Act II. Sc. 4. L. 114.

3
Love sought is good, but given unsought is better.
Twelfth Night. Act III. Sc. 1. L. 167.

4
For he was more than over shoes in love.
Two Gentlemen of Verona. Act I. Sc. 1. L. 23.

5
Love is your master, for he masters you;
And he that is so yoked by a fool,
Methinks, should not be chronicled for wise.
Two Gentlemen of Verona. Act I. Sc. 1. L. 39.

6
And writers say, as the most forward bud
Is eaten by the canker ere it blow,
Even so by love the young and tender wit
Is turn'd to folly, blasting in the bud,
Losing his verdure even in the prime.
Two Gentlemen of Verona. Act I. Sc. 1. L. 45.

7
How wayward is this foolish love,
That, like a testy babe, will scratch the nurse
And presently, all humbled, kiss the rod.
Two Gentlemen of Verona. Act I. Sc. 2. L. 57.

8
O, how this spring of love resembleth
Th' uncertain glory of an April day,
Which now shows all the beauty of the sun,
And by and by a cloud takes all away!
Two Gentlemen of Verona. Act I. Sc. 3. L. 84.

9
Didst thou but know the inly touch of love,
Thou wouldst as soon go kindle fire with snow,
As seek to quench the fire of love with words.
Two Gentlemen of Verona. Act II. Sc. 7. L. 18.

10
I do not seek to quench your love's hot fire,
But qualify the fire's extreme rage,
Lest it should burn above the bounds of reason.
Two Gentlemen of Verona. Act II. Sc. 7. L. 21.

11
Except I be by Sylvia in the night,
There is no music in the nightingale.
Two Gentlemen of Verona. Act III. Sc. 1. L. 178.

12
Love keeps his revels where there are but twain.
Venus and Adonis. L. 123.

13
What 'tis to love? how want of love tormenteth?
Venus and Adonis. L. 202.

14
When you loved me I gave you the whole sun and stars to play with. I gave you eternity in a single moment, strength of the mountains in one clasp of your arms, the volume of all the seas in one impulse of your soul. A moment only; but was it not enough? Were you not paid then for all the rest of your struggle on earth? . . . When I opened the gates of paradise, were you blind? Was it nothing to you? When all the stars sang in your ears and all the winds swept you the heart of heaven, were you deaf? were you dull? was I no more to you than a bone to a dog? Was it not enough? We spent eternity together; and you ask me for a little lifetime more. We possessed all the universe together; and you ask me to give you my scanty wages as well. I have given you the greatest of all things; and you ask me to give you little things. I gave you your own soul: you ask me for my body as a plaything. Was it not enough? Was it not enough?
BERNARD SHAW—*Getting Married.*

15
The fickleness of the woman I love is only equalled by the infernal constancy of the women who love me.
BERNARD SHAW—*The Philanderer.* Act II.

16
Love's Pestilence, and her slow dogs of war.
SHELLEY—*Hellas.* L. 321.

17
Yet all love is sweet
Given or returned. Common as light is love,
And its familiar voice wearies not ever
* * * * *
They who inspire it most are fortunate,
As I am now: but those who feel it most
Are happier still after long sufferings
As I shall soon become.
SHELLEY—*Prometheus Unbound.* Act II. Sc. 5.

18
My true-love hath my heart, and I have his,
By just exchange, one for the other given;
I hold his dear, and mine he cannot miss,
There never was a better bargain driven.
SIR PHILIP SIDNEY—*My True Love Hath my Heart.*

19
They love indeed who quake to say they love.
SIR PHILIP SIDNEY—*Astrophel and Stella.* LIV.

20
Priests, altars, victims, swam before my sight.
EDMUND SMITH—*Phædra and Hippolytus.* Act I. Sc. 1. (See also POPE)

21
Thy fatal shafts unerring move;
I bow before thine altar, Love!
SMOLLETT—*Roderick Random.* Ch. XL. St. 1.

22
Love is strong as death; jealousy is cruel as the grave.
Song of Solomon. VIII. 6.

23
Many waters cannot quench love, neither can the floods drown it.
Song of Solomon. VIII. 7.

1
And when my own Mark Antony
Against young Cæsar strove,
And Rome's whole world was set in arms,
The cause was,—all for love.
SOUTHEY—*All for Love.* Pt. II. St. 26.

2
Cupid "the little greatest god."
SOUTHEY—*Commonplace Book.* 4th Series. P. 462. (See also HOLMES)

3
They sin who tell us Love can die:
With life all other passions fly,
All others are but vanity.
In Heaven Ambition cannot dwell,
Nor Avarice in the vaults of Hell.
SOUTHEY—*Curse of Kehama. Mount Meru.* St. 10.

4
Together linkt with adamantine chains.
SPENSER—*Hymn in Honour of Love.* Phrase used by DRUMMOND—*Flowers of Sion.* BELVOIR, in HARLEIAN *Miscellany.* IV. 559. PHINEAS FLETCHER—*Purple Island.* Ch. XII. 64. (1633) MANILIUS. Bk. I. 921. MARINI—*Sospetto d'Herode.* Sts. 14 and 18, CRASHAW's trans. SHELLEY—*Revolt of Islam.* III. 19.
(See also BURTON, SCOTT, also HOMER under INFLUENCE)

5
To be wise and eke to love,
Is granted scarce to gods above.
SPENSER—*Shepheard's Calendar. March.* (See also HERRICK)

6
Love is the emblem of eternity: it confounds all notion of time: effaces all memory of a beginning, all fear of an end.
MADAME DE STAËL—*Corinne.* Bk. VIII. Ch. II.

7
Where we really love, we often dread more than we desire the solemn moment that exchanges hope for certainty.
MADAME DE STAËL—*Corinne.* Bk. VIII. Ch. IV.

8
L'amour est l'histoire de la vie des femmes; c'est un épisode dans celle des hommes.
Love is the history of a woman's life; it is an episode in man's.
MADAME DE STAËL—*De l'influence des passions. Works.* III. P. 135. (Ed. 1820) (See also BYRON)

9
Sweetheart, when you walk my way,
Be it dark or be it day;
Dreary winter, fairy May,
I shall know and greet you.
For each day of grief or grace
Brings you nearer my embrace;
Love hath fashioned your dear face,
I shall know you when I meet you.
FRANK L. STANTON—*Greeting.*

10
To love her was a liberal education.
STEELE—*Of Lady Elizabeth Hastings.* In *The Tatler.* No. 49. AUGUSTINE BIRRELL in *Obiter Dicta* calls this "the most magnificent compliment ever paid by man to a woman."

11
I who all the Winter through,
Cherished other loves than you
And kept hands with hoary policy in marriage-bed and pew;
Now I know the false and true,
For the earnest sun looks through,
And my old love comes to meet me in the dawning and the dew.
STEVENSON. Poem written 1876.

12
And my heart springs up anew,
Bright and confident and true,
And the old love comes to meet me, in the dawning and the dew.
STEVENSON. Poem written 1876

13
Just like Love is yonder rose,
Heavenly fragrance round it throws,
Yet tears its dewy leaves disclose,
And in the midst of briars it blows
Just like Love.
VISCOUNT STRANGFORD—*Just like Love.* Trans. of *Poems* of CAMOENS.

14
Why so pale and wan, fond lover,
Prithee, why so pale?
Will, when looking well can't move her,
Looking ill prevail?
Prithee, why so pale?
SIR JOHN SUCKLING—*Song.* St. 1.

15
Love in its essence is spiritual fire.
SWEDENBORG—*True Christian Religion.* Par. 31.

16
In all I wish, how happy should I be,
Thou grand Deluder, were it not for thee?
So weak thou art that fools thy power despise;
And yet so strong, thou triumph'st o'er the wise.
SWIFT—*To Love.*

17
Love, as is told by the seers of old,
Comes as a butterfly tipped with gold,
Flutters and flies in sunlit skies,
Weaving round hearts that were one time cold.
SWINBURNE—*Song.*

18
If love were what the rose is,
And I were like the leaf,
Our lives would grow together
In sad or singing weather.
SWINBURNE—*A Match.*

19
O Love, O great god Love, what have I done,
That thou shouldst hunger so after my death?
My heart is harmless as my life's first day:
Seek out some false fair woman, and plague he.
Till her tears even as my tears fill her bed.
SWINBURNE—*The Complaint of Lisa.*

20
Love laid his sleepless head
On a thorny rose bed:
And his eyes with tears were red,
And pale his lips as the dead.
SWINBURNE—*Love Laid his Sleepless Head.*

21
I that have love and no more
Give you but love of you, sweet;
He that hath more, let him give;
He that hath wings, let him soar;

Mine is the heart at your feet
Here, that must love you to live.
SWINBURNE—*The Oblation.*

1
Cogas amantem irasci, amare si velis.
You must make a lover angry if you wish him to love.
SYRUS—*Maxims.*

2
Tum, ut adsolet in amore et ira, jurgia, preces, exprobratio, satisfactio.
Then there is the usual scene when lovers are excited with each other, quarrels, entreaties, reproaches, and then fondling reconcilement.
TACITUS—*Annales.* XIII. 44.

3
When gloaming treads the heels of day
And birds sit cowering on the spray,
Along the flowery hedge I stray,
To meet mine ain dear somebody.
ROBERT TANNAHILL—*Love's Fear.*

4
I love thee, I love but thee,
With a love that shall not die
Till the sun grows cold,
And the stars are old,
And the leaves of the Judgment Book unfold!
BAYARD TAYLOR—*Bedouin Song.*

5
Love better is than Fame.
BAYARD TAYLOR—*Christmas Sonnets. Lyrics. To J. L. G.*

6
Love's history, as Life's, is ended not
By marriage.
BAYARD TAYLOR—*Lars.* Bk. III.

7
For love's humility is Love's true pride.
BAYARD TAYLOR—*Poet's Journal. Third Evening. The Mother.*

8
And on her lover's arm she leant,
And round her waist she felt it fold,
And far across the hills they went
In that new world which is the old.
TENNYSON—*Day Dream. The Departure.* I.

9
Love lieth deep; Love dwells not in lip-depths.
TENNYSON—*Lover's Tale.* L. 466.

10
Where love could walk with banish'd Hope no more.
TENNYSON—*Lover's Tale.* L. 813.

11
Love's arms were wreathed about the neck of Hope,
And Hope kiss'd Love, and Love drew in her breath
In that close kiss and drank her whisper'd tales.
They said that Love would die when Hope was gone.
And Love mourn'd long, and sorrow'd after Hope;
At last she sought out Memory, and they trod
The same old paths where Love had walked with Hope,
And Memory fed the soul of Love with tears.
TENNYSON—*Lover's Tale.* L. 815.

12
'Tis better to have loved and lost,
Than never to have loved at all.
TENNYSON—*In Memoriam.* Pt. XXVII. St. 4.
(See also CONGREVE, GUARINI, MILNE, SENECA, THACKERAY, also CONGREVE under WOOING)

13
For love reflects the thing beloved.
TENNYSON—*In Memoriam.* Pt. LII.

14
Love's too precious to be lost,
A little grain shall not be spilt.
TENNYSON—*In Memoriam.* Pt. LXV.

15
I loved you, and my love had no return,
And therefore my true love has been my death.
TENNYSON—*Lancelot and Elaine.* L. 1,298.

16
Shall it not be scorn to me to harp on such a moulder'd string?
I am shamed through all my nature to have lov'd so slight a thing.
TENNYSON—*Locksley Hall.* St. 74.

17
There has fallen a splendid tear
From the passion-flower at the gate.
She is coming, my dove, my dear;
She is coming, my life, my fate;
The red rose cries, "She is near, she is near;"
And the white rose weeps, "She is late;"
The larkspur listens, "I hear; I hear;"
And the lily whispers, "I wait."
TENNYSON—*Maud.* Pt. XXII. St. 10.

18
She is coming, my own, my sweet;
Were it ever so airy a tread,
My heart would hear her and beat,
Were it earth in an earthly bed;
My dust would hear her and beat,
Had I lain for a century dead;
Would start and tremble under her feet,
And blossom in purple and red.
TENNYSON—*Maud.* Pt. XXII. St. 11.

19
Love is hurt with jar and fret;
Love is made a vague regret.
TENNYSON—*The Miller's Daughter.* St. 28.

20
It is best to love wisely, no doubt; but to love foolishly is better than not to be able to love at all.
THACKERAY—*Pendennis.* Ch. VI.
(See also TENNYSON)

21
Werther had a love for Charlotte,
Such as words could never utter;
Would you know how first he met her?
She was cutting bread and butter.
THACKERAY—*The Sorrows of Werther.*

22
Like to a wind-blown sapling grow I from
The cliff, Sweet, of your skyward-jetting soul,—
Shook by all gusts that sweep it, overcome
By all its clouds incumbent; O be true
To your soul, dearest, as my life to you!
For if that soil grow sterile, then the whole
Of me must shrivel, from the topmost shoot
Of climbing poesy, and my life, killed through,
Dry down and perish to the foodless root.
FRANCIS THOMPSON—*Manus Animam Pinxit*

1
Why should we kill the best of passions, love?
It aids the hero, bids ambition rise
To nobler heights, inspires immortal deeds,
Even softens brutes, and adds a grace to virtue.
THOMSON—*Sophonisba*. Act V. Sc. 2.

2
O, what are you waiting for here? young man!
What are you looking for over the bridge?—
A little straw hat with the streaming blue ribbons
Is soon to come dancing over the bridge.
THOMSON—*Waiting*.

3
Nec jurare time; Veneris perjuria venti
Irrita per terras et freta summa ferunt,
Gratia magna Jovi; vetuit pater ipse valere,
Jurasset cupide quicquid ineptus amor.

Fear not to swear; the winds carry the perjuries of lovers without effect over land and sea, thanks to Jupiter. The father of the gods himself has denied effect to what foolish lovers in their eagerness have sworn.
TIBULLUS—*Carmina*. I. 4. 21.
(See also DRYDEN)

4
Perjuria ridet amantium Jupiter et ventos irrita ferre jubet.

At lovers' perjuries Jove laughs and throws them idly to the winds.
TIBULLUS—*Carmina*. III. 6. 49.
(See also DRYDEN)

5
Die Liebe wintert nicht;
Nein, nein! Ist und bleibt Frühlings-Schein.

Love knows no winter; no, no! It is, and remains the sign of spring.
LUDWIG TIECK—*Herbstlied*.

6
At first, she loved nought else but flowers,
And then—she only loved the rose;
And then—herself alone; and then—
She knew not what, but now—she knows.
RIDGELY TORRENCE—*House of a Hundred Lights*.

7
For Truth makes holy Love's illusive dreams,
And their best promise constantly redeems.
TUCKERMAN—*Sonnets*. XXII.

8
The warrior for the True, the Right,
Fights in Love's name;
The love that lures thee from that fight
Lures thee to shame:
That love which lifts the heart, yet leaves
The spirit free,—
That love, or none, is fit for one
Man-shaped like thee.
AUBREY THOS. DE VERE—*Miscellaneous Poems. Song*.

9
Quis fallere possit amantem?
Who can deceive a lover?
VERGIL—*Æneid*. IV. 296.

10
Omnia vincit amor, et nos cedamus amori.
Love conquers all things; let us yield to love.
VERGIL—*Eclogæ*. X. 69.

11
For all true love is grounded on esteem.
VILLIERS (Duke of Buckingham).
(See also FENTON)

12
Qui que tu sois, voici ton maître;
Il l'est—le fut—ou le doit être.
Whoe'er thou art, thy master see;
He was—or is—or is to be.
VOLTAIRE—*Works*. II. P. 765. (Ed. 1837)
Used as an inscription for a statue of Cupid.
(See also LANSDOWNE)

13
To love is to believe, to hope, to know;
'Tis an essay, a taste of Heaven below!
EDMUND WALLER—*Divine Poems. Divine Love*. Canto III. L. 17.

14
Could we forbear dispute, and practise love,
We should agree as angels do above.
EDMUND WALLER—*Divine Poems. Divine Love*. Canto III. L. 25.

15
And the King with his golden sceptre,
The Pope with Saint Peter's key,
Can never unlock the one little heart
That is opened only to me.
For I am the Lord of a Realm,
And I am Pope of a See;
Indeed I'm supreme in the kingdom
That is sitting, just now, on my knee.
C. H. WEBB—*The King and the Pope*.

16
O, rank is good, and gold is fair,
And high and low mate ill;
But love has never known a law
Beyond its own sweet will!
WHITTIER—*Amy Wentworth*. St. 18.

17
"I'm sorry that I spell'd the word;
I hate to go above you,
Because"—the brown eyes lower fell,—
"Because, you see, I love you!"
WHITTIER—*In School-Days*. St. 4.

18
Your love in a cottage is hungry,
Your vine is a nest for flies—
Your milkmaid shocks the Graces,
And simplicity talks of pies!
You lie down to your shady slumber
And wake with a bug in your ear,
And your damsel that walks in the morning
Is shod like a mountaineer.
N. P. WILLIS—*Love in a Cottage*. St. 3.

19
He loves not well whose love is bold!
I would not have thee come too nigh.
The sun's gold would not seem pure gold
Unless the sun were in the sky:
To take him thence and chain him near
Would make his beauty disappear.
WILLIAM WINTER—*Love's Queen*.

20
The unconquerable pang of despised love.
WORDSWORTH—*Excursion*. Bk. VI. *Hamlet*. Act III. Sc. 1.

21
For mightier far
Than strength of nerve or sinew, or the sway
Of magic potent over sun and star,
Is love, though oft to agony distrest,
And though his favourite be feeble woman's breast.
WORDSWORTH—*Laodamia*. St. 15

1
O dearer far than light and life are dear.
WORDSWORTH—*Poems Founded on the Affections.* No. XIX. To ——. VII. 114. (Knight's ed.)

2
While all the future, for thy purer soul,
With "sober certainties" of love is blest.
WORDSWORTH—*Poems Founded on the Affections.* VII. 115. (Knight's ed.)
(See also MILTON)

3
Farewell, Love, and all thy laws for ever.
SIR THOMAS WYATT—*Songs and Sonnets. A Renouncing of Love.*

LOVE LIES BLEEDING

Amarantus Caudatus

4
Love lies bleeding in the bed whereover
Roses lean with smiling mouths or pleading:
Earth lies laughing where the sun's dart clove her:
Love lies bleeding.
SWINBURNE—*Love Lies Bleeding.*

5
This flower that first appeared as summer's guest
Preserves her beauty 'mid autumnal leaves
And to her mournful habits fondly cleaves.
WORDSWORTH—*Love Lies Bleeding.* (Companion Poem.)

LOYALTY (See FIDELITY, PATRIOTISM, ROYALTY)

LUCK

6
O, once in each man's life, at least,
Good luck knocks at his door;
And wit to seize the flitting guest
Need never hunger more.
But while the loitering idler waits
Good luck beside his fire,
The bold heart storms at fortune's gates,
And conquers its desire.
LEWIS J. BATES—*Good Luck.*

7
As ill-luck would have it.
CERVANTES—*Don Quixote.* Pt. I. Bk. I. Ch. II.

8
As they who make
Good luck a god count all unlucky men.
GEORGE ELIOT—*The Spanish Gypsy.* Bk. I.

9
A farmer travelling with his load
Picked up a horseshoe on the road,
And nailed it fast to his barn door,
That luck might down upon him pour;
That every blessing known in life
Might crown his homestead and his wife,
And never any kind of harm
Descend upon his growing farm.
JAMES T. FIELDS—*The Lucky Horseshoe.*

10
Now for good lucke, cast an old shooe after mee.
HEYWOOD—*Proverbs.* Pt. I. Ch. IX.
(See also TENNYSON)

11
Some people are so fond of ill-luck that they run half-way to meet it.
DOUGLAS JERROLD—*Jerrold's Wit. Meeting Trouble Half-Way.*

12
Felix ille tamen corvo quoque rarior albo.
A lucky man is rarer than a white crow.
JUVENAL—*Satires.* VII. 202.

13
Happy art thou, as if every day thou hadst picked up a horseshoe.
LONGFELLOW—*Evangeline.* Pt. I. St. 2.

14
"Then here goes another," says he, "to make sure,
For there's luck in odd numbers," says Rory O'More.
SAMUEL LOVER—*Rory O'More.*
(See also MERRY WIVES OF WINDSOR)

15
Good luck befriend thee, Son; for at thy birth
The fairy ladies danced upon the hearth.
MILTON—*At a Vacation Exercise in the College.*

16
By the luckiest stars.
All's Well That Ends Well. Act I. Sc. 3. L. 252.

17
When mine hours were nice and lucky.
Antony and Cleopatra. Act III. Sc. 13. L. 179.

18
And good luck go with thee.
Henry V. Act IV. Sc. 3. L. 11.

19
As good luck would have it.
Merry Wives of Windsor. Act III. Sc. 5. L. 83.

20
Good luck lies in odd numbers * * * They say there is divinity in odd numbers, either in nativity, chance, or death.
Merry Wives of Windsor. Act V. Sc. 1. L. 2.
(See also LOVER)

21
And wheresoe'er thou move, good luck
Shall fling her old shoe after.
TENNYSON—*Will Waterproof's Lyrical Monologue.* St. 27.
(See also HEYWOOD)

LUXURY

22
Blesses his stars, and thinks it luxury.
ADDISON—*Cato.* Act I. Sc. 4.

23
To treat a poor wretch with a bottle of Burgundy, and fill his snuff-box, is like giving a pair of laced ruffles to a man that has never a shirt on his back.
TOM BROWN—*Laconics.*
(See also SORBIENNE)

24
Sofas 'twas half a sin to sit upon,
So costly were they; carpets, every stitch
Of workmanship so rare, they make you wish
You could glide o'er them like a golden fish.
BYRON—*Don Juan.* Canto V. St. 65.

25
Blest hour! It was a luxury—to be!
COLERIDGE—*Reflections on having left a Place of Retirement.* L. 43.

26
O Luxury! thou curst by Heaven's decree.
GOLDSMITH—*Deserted Village.* L. 385.

1
Such dainties to them, their health it might hurt:
It's like sending them ruffles, when wanting a shirt.
GOLDSMITH—*Haunch of Venison.*
(See also SORBIENNE)

2
Then there is that glorious Epicurean paradox, uttered by my friend, the Historian in one of his flashing moments: "Give us the luxuries of life, and we will dispense with its necessaries."
HOLMES—*Autocrat of the Breakfast Table.* VI.

3
Fell luxury! more perilous to youth
Than storms or quicksands, poverty or chains.
HANNAH MORE—*Belshazzar.*

4
Luxury and dissipation, soft and gentle as their approaches are, and silently as they throw their silken chains about the heart, enslave it more than the most active and turbulent vices.
HANNAH MORE—*Essays. Dissipation.*

5
On his weary couch
Fat Luxury, sick of the night's debauch,
Lay groaning, fretful at the obtrusive beam
That through his lattice peeped derisively.
POLLOK—*Course of Time.* Bk. VII. L. 69.

6
Luxury is an enticing pleasure, a bastard mirth, which hath honey in her mouth, gall in her heart, and a sting in her tail.
QUARLES—*Emblems.* Bk. I. *Hugo.*

7
Rings put upon his fingers,
A most delicious banquet by his bed,
And brave attendants near him when he wakes,
Would not the beggar then forget himself?
Taming of the Shrew. Induction. Sc. 1. L. 38.

8
Like sending them ruffles, when wanting a shirt.
SORBIENNE.
(See also BROWN, GOLDSMITH)

9
Falsely luxurious, will not man awake?
THOMSON—*The Seasons. Summer.* L. 67.

LYING

10
A giurar presti i mentitor son sempre.
Liars are always most disposed to swear.
ALFIERI—*Virginia.* II. 3.

11
Se non volea pulir sua scusa tanto,
Che la facesse di menzogna rea.
But that he wrought so high the specious tale,
As manifested plainly 'twas a lie.
ARIOSTO—*Orlando Furioso.* XVIII. 84.

12
And none speaks false, when there is none to hear.
BEATTIE—*The Minstrel.* Bk. II. St. 24.

13
And, after all, what is a lie? 'Tis but
The truth in masquerade.
BYRON—*Don Juan.* Canto XI. St. 37.

14
I tell him, if a clergyman, he lies!
If captains the remark, or critics, make,
Why they lie also—*under a mistake.*
BYRON—*Don Juan.*
(See also CALDERON, SWIFT)

15
Resolved to die in the last dyke of prevarication.
BURKE—*Impeachment of Warren Hastings.* (May 7, 1789.)

16
Quoth Hudibras, I smell a rat;
Ralpho, thou dost prevaricate.
BUTLER—*Hudibras.* Pt. I. Canto I. L. 821.

17
You lie—under a mistake—
For this is the most civil sort of lie
That can be given to a man's face, I now
Say what I think.
CALDERON—*El Magico Prodigioso.* Sc. 1. Trans. by SHELLEY.
(See also BYRON)

18
Ita enim finitima sunt falsa veris ut in præcipitem locum non debeat se sapiens committere.
So near is falsehood to truth that a wise man would do well not to trust himself on the narrow edge.
CICERO—*Academici.* IV. 21.

19
Mendaci homini ne verum quidem dicenti credere solemus.
A liar is not believed even though he tell the truth.
CICERO—*De Divinatione.* II. 71. Same idea in PHÆDRUS—*Fables.* I. 10. 1.

20
The silent colossal National Lie that is the support and confederate of all the tyrannies and shams and inequalities and unfairnesses that afflict the peoples—that is the one to throw bricks and sermons at.
S. L. CLEMENS (Mark Twain)—*My First Lie.*

21
An experienced, industrious, ambitious, and often quite picturesque liar.
S. L. CLEMENS (Mark Twain)—*My Military Campaign.*

22
Un menteur est toujours prodigue de serments.
A liar is always lavish of oaths.
CORNEILLE—*Le Menteur.* III. 5.

23
Il faut bonne mémoire après qu'on a menti.
A good memory is needed once we have lied.
CORNEILLE—*Le Menteur.* IV. 5.
(See also MONTAIGNE, QUINTILIAN, SIDNEY)

24
Some truth there was, but dash'd and brew'd with lies,
To please the fools, and puzzle all the wise.
DRYDEN—*Absalom and Achitophel.*

25
Wenn ich irre kann es jeder bemerken; wenn ich lüge, nicht.
When I err every one can see it, but not when I lie.
GOETHE—*Sprüche in Prosa.* III.

26
As ten millions of circles can never make a square, so the united voice of myriads cannot lend the smallest foundation to falsehood.
GOLDSMITH—*Vicar of Wakefield.* Vol. II. Ch. VIII.

27
Half the world knows not how the other half lies.
HERBERT—*Jacula Prudentum.*

1
Show me a liar, and I will show thee a thief.
HERBERT—*Jacula Prudentum.*

2
Dare to be true: nothing can need a lie;
A fault which needs it most, grows two thereby.
HERBERT—*Church Porch.*
(See also WATTS)

3
Sin has many tools, but a lie is the handle which fits them all.
HOLMES—*Autocrat of the Breakfast Table.* VI.

4
Who dares think one thing, and another tell,
My heart detests him as the gates of hell.
HOMER—*Iliad.* Bk. IX. L. 412. POPE'S trans.

5
Urge him with truth to frame his fair replies;
And sure he will; for wisdom never lies.
HOMER—*Odyssey.* Bk. III. L. 25. POPE'S trans.

6
For my part getting up seems not so easy
By half as lying.
HOOD—*Morning Meditations.*

7
Splendide mendax.
Splendidly mendacious.
HORACE—*Carmina.* III. 11. 35.

8
Round numbers are always false.
SAMUEL JOHNSON—*Johnsoniana. Apothegms, Sentiment, etc.* From HAWKINS' Collective Edition.

9
Falsus in uno, falsus in omnibus.
False in one thing, false in everything.
Law Maxim.

10 For no falsehood can endure
Touch of celestial temper.
MILTON—*Paradise Lost.* Bk. IV. L. 811.

11
Qui ne sent point assez ferme de memoire, ne se doit pas mêler d'être menteur.
Who is not sure of his memory should not attempt lying.
MONTAIGNE—*Of Liars.* Bk. I. Ch. IX.
(See also CORNEILLE)

12
Hercle audivi esse optimum mendacium.
Quicquid dei dicunt, id rectum est dicere.
By Hercules! I have often heard that your piping-hot lie is the best of lies: what the gods dictate, that is right.
PLAUTUS—*Mostellaria.* III. 1. 134.

13
Playing the Cretan with the Cretans (*i.e.* lying to liars).
PLUTARCH, quoting Greek prov. used by Paulus Æmilius.

14
Some lie beneath the churchyard stone,
And some before the Speaker.
PRAED—*School and School Fellows.*

15
I said in my haste, All men are liars.
Psalms. CXVI. 11.

16
Mendacem memorem esse oportet.
It is fitting that a liar should be a man of good memory.
QUINTILIAN. IV. 2. 91.
(See also CORNEILLE)

17
Ce mensonge immortel.
That immortal lie.
REV. PÈRE DE RAVIGNAN. Found in POUJOULAT'S *Sa Vie, ses Œuvres.*

18
He will lie, sir, with such volubility, that you would think truth were a fool.
All's Well That Ends Well. Act IV. Sc. 3. L. 283.

19 To lapse in fulness
Is sorer than to lie for need, and falsehood
Is worse in kings than beggars.
Cymbeline. Act III. Sc. 6. L. 12.

20
Your bait of falsehood takes this carp of truth.
Hamlet. Act II. Sc. 1. L. 63.

21
'Tis as easy as lying.
Hamlet. Act III. Sc. 2. L. 372.

22
These lies are like the father that begets them; gross as a mountain, open, palpable.
Henry IV. Pt. I. Act II. Sc. 4. L. 249.

23
Lord, Lord, how this world is given to lying! I grant you I was down and out of breath; and so was he: but we rose both at an instant and fought a long hour by Shrewsbury clock.
Henry IV. Pt. I. Act V. Sc. 4. L. 149.

24
For my part, if a lie may do thee grace,
I'll gild it with the happiest terms I have.
Henry IV. Pt. I. Act V. Sc. 4. L. 161.

25
Lord, Lord, how subject we old men are to the vice of lying!
Henry IV. Pt. II. Act III. Sc. 2. L. 325.

26 Whose tongue soe'er speaks false,
Not truly speaks; who speaks not truly, lies.
King John. Act IV. Sc. 3. L. 91.

27
An evil soul producing holy witness
Is like a villain with a smiling cheek;
A goodly apple rotten at the heart:
O, what a goodly outside falsehood hath!
Merchant of Venice. Act I. Sc. 3. L. 100.

28
Had I a heart for falsehood framed.
I ne'er could injure you.
R. B. SHERIDAN—*The Duenna.* Act I. Sc. 5.

29
This shows that liars ought to have good memories.
ALGERNON SIDNEY—*Discourses on Government.* Ch. II. Sec. XV.
(See also CORNEILLE)

30
A lie never lives to be old.
SOPHOCLES—*Acrisius.* Frag. 59.

1
I mean you lie—under a mistake.
SWIFT—*Polite Conversation*. Dialogue 1.
Same phrase used by DE QUINCEY, SOUTHEY, LANDOR. (See also BYRON)

2
That a lie which is half a truth is ever the blackest of lies;
That a lie which is all a lie may be met and fought with outright—
But a lie which is part a truth is a harder matter to fight.
TENNYSON—*The Grandmother*. St. 8.

3
And he that does one fault at first,
And lies to hide it, makes it two.
WATTS—*Song XV*.
(See also HERBERT)

4
I give him joy that's awkward at a lie.
YOUNG—*Night Thoughts*. Night VIII. L. 361.

M

MAGNOLIA

Magnolia

5
Fragrant o'er all the western groves
The tall magnolia towers unshaded.
MARIA BROOKS—*Written on Seeing Pharamond.*

6
Majestic flower! How purely beautiful
Thou art, as rising from thy bower of green,
Those dark and glossy leaves so thick and full,
Thou standest like a high-born forest queen
Among thy maidens clustering round so fair,—
I love to watch thy sculptured form unfolding,
And look into thy depths, to image there
A fairy cavern, and while thus beholding,
And while thy breeze floats o'er thee, matchless flower,
I breathe the perfume, delicate and strong,
That comes like incense from thy petal-bower;
My fancy roams those southern woods along,
Beneath that glorious tree, where deep among
The unsunned leaves thy large white flower-cups hung!
C. P. CRANCH—*Poem to the Magnolia Grandiflora.*

MAMMON (See also MONEY, WEALTH)

7
I rose up at the dawn of day,—
"Get thee away! get thee away!
Pray'st thou for riches? Away, away!
This is the throne of Mammon grey."
WILLIAM BLAKE—*Mammon.*

8
Maidens, like moths, are ever caught by glare,
And Mammon wins his way where seraphs might despair.
BYRON—*Childe Harold*. Canto I. St. 9.

9
Cursed Mammon be, when he with treasures
To restless action spurs our fate!
Cursed when for soft, indulgent leisures,
He lays for us the pillows straight.
GOETHE—*Faust.*

10
We cannot serve God and Mammon.
Matthew. VI. 24.

11
Mammon led them on—
Mammon, the least erected Spirit that fell
From Heaven: for even in Heaven his looks and thoughts
Were always downward bent, admiring more
The riches of Heaven's pavement, trodden gold,
Than aught divine or holy else enjoyed
In vision beatific.
MILTON—*Paradise Lost*. Bk. I. L. 678.

12
Who sees pale Mammon pine amidst his store,
Sees but a backward steward for the poor.
POPE—*Moral Essays*. Ep. III. L. 171.

13
What treasures here do Mammon's sons behold!
Yet know that all that which glitters is not gold.
QUARLES—*Emblems*. Bk. II. Emblem V.
(See also QUOTATIONS under APPEARANCES)

MAN

14
The man forget not, though in rags he lies,
And know the mortal through a crown's disguise.
AKENSIDE—*Epistle to Curio.*

15
Man only,—rash, refined, presumptuous Man—
Starts from his rank, and mars Creation's plan!
Born the free heir of nature's wide domain,
To art's strict limits bounds his narrow'd reign;
Resigns his native rights for meaner things,
For Faith and Fetters, Laws and Priests and Kings.
Poetry of the Anti-Jacobin. The Progress of Man. L. 55.

16
Non è un si bello in tante altre persone,
Natura il fece, e poi roppa la stampa.
There never was such beauty in another man.
Nature made him, and then broke the mould.
ARIOSTO—*Orlando Furioso*. Canto X. St. 84.
L'on peut dire sans hyperbole, que la nature, que la après l'avoir fait en cassa la moule.
ANGELO CONSTANTINI—*La Vie de Scaramouche*. L. 107. (Ed. 1690)
(See also BYRON, MONTGOMERY)

17
Ye children of man! whose life is a span
Protracted with sorrow from day to day,
Naked and featherless, feeble and querulous,
Sickly, calamitous creatures of clay.
ARISTOPHANES—*Birds*. Trans. by JOHN HOOKHAM FRERE.

18
Let each man think himself an act of God.
His mind a thought, his life a breath of God.
BAILEY—*Festus. Proem*. L. 162.

19
Man is the nobler growth our realms supply
And souls are ripened in our northern sky.
ANNA LETITIA BARBAULD—*The Invitation.*

1
Thou wilt scarce be a man before thy mother.
BEAUMONT AND FLETCHER—*Love's Cure.* Act II. Sc. 2.
(See also COWPER)

2
All sorts and conditions of men.
Book of Common Prayer. Prayer for all Conditions of Men.

3
Man is a noble animal, splendid in ashes and pompous in the grave.
SIR THOMAS BROWNE—*Urn Burial.* Ch. V.

4
A man's a man for a' that!
BURNS—*For A' That and A' That.*

5
A prince can mak a belted knight,
A marquis, duke, and a' that;
But an honest man's aboon his might:
Guid faith, he maunna fa' that.
BURNS—*For A' That and A' That.*
(See also GOWER, WYCHERLY; also WATTS under SOUL)

6
The rank is but the guinea's stamp,
The man's the gowd for a' that.
BURNS—*For A' That and A' That.*
(See also CAREW)

7
Man,—whose heaven-erected face
The smiles of love adorn,—
Man's inhumanity to man
Makes countless thousands mourn!
BURNS—*Man Was Made to Mourn.*

8
Where the virgins are soft as the roses they twine,
And all, save the spirit of man, is divine?
BYRON—*Bride of Abydos.* Canto I. St. 1.
(See also HEBER)

9
Man!
Thou pendulum betwixt a smile and tear.
BYRON—*Childe Harold.* Canto IV. St. 109.

10
The precious porcelain of human clay.
BYRON—*Don Juan.* Canto IV. St. 11.
(See also DRYDEN)

11
Lord of himself;—that heritage of woe!
BYRON—*Lara.* Canto I. St. 2.

12
But we, who name ourselves its sovereigns, we,
Half dust, half deity, alike unfit
To sink or soar.
BYRON—*Manfred.* Act I. Sc. 2. L. 39.

13
Sighing that Nature formed but one such man,
And broke the die—in moulding Sheridan.
BYRON—*Monody on the Death of the Rt. Hon. R. B. Sheridan.* L. 117.
(See also ARIOSTO)

14
And say without our hopes, without our fears,
Without the home that plighted love endears,
Without the smile from partial beauty won,
Oh! what were man?—a world without a sun.
CAMPBELL—*Pleasures of Hope.* Pt. II. L. 21.

15
To lead, or brass, or some such bad
Metal, a prince's stamp may add
That value, which it never had.
But to the pure refined ore,
The stamp of kings imparts no more
Worth, than the metal held before.
THOMAS CAREW—*To T. H. A Lady Resembling My Mistress.*
(See also BURNS)

16
No sadder proof can be given by a man of his own littleness than disbelief in great men.
CARLYLE—*Heroes and Hero Worship.* Lecture 1.

17
Charms and a man I sing, to wit—a most superior person,
Myself, who bear the fitting name of George Nathaniel Curzon.
Charma Virumque Cano. Pub. in *Poetry of the Crabbet Club,* 1892. P. 36.
(See also VERGIL under WAR)

18
La vraie science et le vrai étude de l'homme c'est l'homme.
The proper Science and Subject for Man's Contemplation is *Man* himself.
CHARRON—*Of Wisdom.* Bk. I. Ch. I. STANHOPE's trans.
(See also POPE)

19
Men the most infamous are fond of fame:
And those who fear not guilt, yet start at shame.
CHURCHILL—*The Author.* L. 233.

20
A self-made man? Yes—and worships his creator.
HENRY CLAPP. Said also by JOHN BRIGHT of DISRAELI.

21
I am made all things to all men.
I Corinthians. IX. 22.

22
The first man is of the earth, earthy.
I Corinthians. XV. 47.

23
An honest man, close-buttoned to the chin,
Broadcloth without, and a warm heart within.
COWPER—*Epistle to Joseph Hill.*

24
But strive still to be a man before your mother.
COWPER—*Motto of No. III. Connoisseur.*
(See also BEAUMONT)

25
So man, the moth, is not afraid, it seems,
To span Omnipotence, and measure might
That knows no measure, by the scanty rule
And standard of his own, that is to-day,
And is not ere to-morrow's sun go down.
COWPER—*The Task.* Bk. VI. L. 211.

26
A sacred spark created by his breath,
The immortal mind of man his image bears;
A spirit living 'midst the forms of death,
Oppressed, but not subdued, by mortal cares.
SIR H. DAVY—*Written After Recovery from a Dangerous Illness.*

27
His tribe were God Almighty's gentlemen.
DRYDEN—*Absalom and Achitophel.* Pt. I. L. 645.

28
Men are but children of a larger growth,
Our appetites as apt to change as theirs,
And full of cravings too, and full as vain.
DRYDEN—*All for Love.* Act IV. Sc. 1.
(See also WORDSWORTH under CHILDHOOD)

1
This is the porcelain clay of humankind.
DRYDEN—*Don Sebastian.* Act I. Sc. 1.
(See also BYRON)

2
How dull, and how insensible a beast
Is man, who yet would lord it o'er the rest.
DRYDEN—*Essay on Satire.* I. 1. Written by DRYDEN and the EARL OF MULGRAVE.

3
There is no Theam more plentiful to scan,
Then is the glorious goodly Frame of Man.
DU BARTAS—*Divine Weekes and Workes. First Week, Sixth Day.* L. 421.
(See also POPE)

4
Men's men: gentle or simple, they're much of a muchness.
GEORGE ELIOT—*Daniel Deronda.* Bk. IV. Ch. XXXI.

5
A man is the whole encyclopedia of facts. The creation of a thousand forests is in one acorn, and Egypt, Greece, Rome, Gaul, Britain, America, lie folded already in the first man.
EMERSON—*Essays. History.*

6
Man is his own star, and the soul that can
Render an honest and a perfect man,
Commands all light.
JOHN FLETCHER—*Upon an Honest Man's Fortune.* L. 33.

7
Man is a tool making animal.
FRANKLIN.

8
Aye, think! since time and life began,
Your mind has only feared and slept;
Of all the beasts they called you man
Only because you toiled and wept.
ARTURO GIOVANNITTI—*The Thinker.* (On Rodin's Statue.)

9
Stood I, O Nature! man alone in thee,
Then were it worth one's while a man to be.
GOETHE—*Faust.*

10
Die Menschen fürchtet nur, wer sie nicht kennt
Und wer sie meidet, wird sie bald verkennen.
He only fears men who does not know them, and he who avoids them will soon misjudge them.
GOETHE—*Torquato Tasso.* I. 2. 72.

11
Lass uns, geliebter Bruder, nicht vergessen,
Dass von sich selbst der Mensch nicht scheiden kann.
Beloved brother, let us not forget that man can never get away from himself.
GOETHE—*Torquato Tasso.* I. 2. 85.

12
Lords of humankind.
GOLDSMITH—*The Traveller.* L. 327.

13
A king may spille, a king may save;
A king may make of lorde a knave;
And of a knave a lorde also.
GOWER—*Confessio Amantis.* Bk. VII. I. 1,895.
(See also WYCHERLEY)

14
We are coming we, the young men,
Strong of heart and millions strong;
We shall work where you have trifled,
Cleanse the temple, right the wrong,
Till the land our fathers visioned
Shall be spread before our ken,
We are through with politicians;
Give us Men! Give us Men!
ARTHUR GUITERMAN—*Challenge of the Young Men.* In *Life*, Nov. 2, 1911.
(See also HOLLAND)

15
What though the spicy breezes
Blow soft o'er Ceylon's isle;
Though every prospect pleases,
And only man is vile.
REGINALD HEBER—*Missionary Hymn.* ("Java" in one version.)
(See also BYRON)

16
Man is all symmetrie,
Full of proportions, one limbe to another,
And all to all the world besides:
Each part may call the farthest, brother:
For head with foot hath privite amitie,
And both with moons and tides.
HERBERT—*Temple. The Church Man.*

17
Man is one world, and hath
Another to attend him.
HERBERT—*Temple. The Church Man.*

18
God give us men. A time like this demands
Strong minds, great hearts, true faith and ready hands!
Men whom the lust of office does not kill,
Men whom the spoils of office cannot buy,
Men who possess opinions and a will,
Men who love honor, men who cannot lie.
J. G. HOLLAND—*Wanted.*
(See also GUITERMAN, MARSTON, PHÆDRUS, STEDMAN, TENNYSON, also FOSS under AMERICA)

19
Like leaves on trees the race of man is found,—
Now green in youth, now withering on the ground;
Another race the following spring supplies;
They fall successive; and successive rise.
HOMER—*Iliad.* Bk. VI. L. 181. POPE's trans.

20
Forget the brother and resume the man.
HOMER—*Odyssey.* Bk. IV. L. 732. POPE'S trans.

21
The fool of fate, thy manufacture, man.
HOMER—*Odyssey.* Bk. XX. L. 254. POPE'S trans.

22
Pulvis et umbra sumus.
We are dust and shadow.
HORACE—*Carmina.* Bk. IV. 7. L. 16.

23
Metiri se quemque suo modulo ac pede verum est.
Every man should measure himself by his own standard.
HORACE—*Epistles.* I. 7. 98.
(See also JAMESON)

1
Ad unguem factus homo.
A man polished to the nail.
HORACE—*Satires.* I. 5. 32.

2
Man dwells apart, though not alone,
He walks among his peers unread;
The best of thoughts which he hath known
For lack of listeners are not said.
JEAN INGELOW—*Afternoon at a Parsonage. Afterthought.*

3
Man passes away; his name perishes from record and recollection; his history is as a tale that is told, and his very monument becomes a ruin.
WASHINGTON IRVING—*The Sketch Book. Westminster Abbey.*

4
Cease ye from man, whose breath is in his nostrils.
Isaiah. II. 22.

5
The only competition worthy a wise man is with himself.
MRS. JAMESON—*Memoirs and Essays. Washington Allston.*
(See also HORACE)

6
Man that is born of a woman is of few days, and full of trouble.
Job. XIV. 1.

7
Where soil is, men grow,
Whether to weeds or flowers.
KEATS—*Endymion.* Bk. II.

8
Though I've belted you and flayed you,
By the livin' Gawd that made you,
You're a better man than I am, Gunga Din.
KIPLING—*Gunga Din.*

9
If you can keep your head when all about you
Are losing theirs and blaming it on you,
If you can trust yourself when all men doubt you,
But make allowance for their doubting too;
* * * * * *
Yours is the Earth and every thing that's in it,
And—which is more—you'll be a man, my son!
KIPLING—*If.* First and Last Lines.

10
Limited in his nature, infinite in his desires, man is a fallen god who remembers the heavens.
LAMARTINE—*Second Meditations.*

11
Il est plus aisé de connaître l'homme en général que de connaître un homme en particulier.
It is easier to know mankind in general than man individually.
LA ROCHEFOUCAULD—*Maximes.* 436.

12
As man; false man, smiling destructive man.
NATHANIEL LEE—*Theodosius.* Act III. Sc. 2. L. 50.

13
A man of mark.
LONGFELLOW—*Tales of a Wayside Inn.* Pt. I. *The Musician's Tale. Saga of King Olaf.* Pt. IX. St. 2.

14
Before man made us citizens, great Nature made us men.
LOWELL—*The Capture of Fugitive Slaves Near Washington.*

15
The hearts of men are their books; events are their tutors; great actions are their eloquence.
MACAULAY—*Essays. Conversation Touching the Great Civil War.*

16
A man! A man! My kingdom for a man!
MARSTON—*Scourge of Villainy.*
(See also HOLLAND)

17
Hominem pagina nostra sapit.
Our page (*i.e.* our book) has reference to man.
MARTIAL—*Epigrams.* Bk. X. 4. 10.

18
But in our Sanazarro 'tis not so,
He being pure and tried gold; and any stamp
Of grace, to make him current to the world,
The duke is pleased to give him, will add honour
To the great bestower; for he, though allow'd
Companion to his master, still preserves
His majesty in full lustre.
MASSINGER—*Great Duke of Florence.* Act I. Sc. 1. (See also WYCHERLY)

19
Ah! pour être devot, je n'en suis pas moins homme.
Ah! to be devout, I am none the less human.
MOLIÈRE—*Tartuffe.* III. 3.

20
The mould is lost wherein was made
This a *per se* of all.
ALEXANDER MONTGOMERY.
(See also ARIOSTO)

21
I teach you beyond Man [Uebermensch; over-man-superman]. Man is something that shall be surpassed. What have you done to surpass him?
NIETZSCHE—*Thus Spake Zarathustra.*
(See also SHAW)

22
T'is but a Tent where takes his one day's rest
A Sultan to the realm of Death addrest.
A Sultan rises, and the dark Ferrash
Strikes, and prepares it for another Guest.
OMAR KHAYYAM—*Rubaiyat.* St. 45. FITZGERALD's Trans.

23
Man's the bad child of the universe.
JAMES OPPENHEIM—*Laughter.*

24
Os homini sublime dedit cœlumque tueri
Jussit; et erectos ad sidera tollere vultus.
God gave man an upright countenance to survey the heavens, and to look upward to the stars.
OVID—*Metamorphoses.* I. 85.

25
What a chimera, then, is man! what a novelty, what a monster, what a chaos, what a subject of contradiction, what a prodigy! A judge of all things, feeble worm of the earth, depositary of the truth, *cloaca* of uncertainty and error, the glory and the shame of the universe!
PASCAL—*Thoughts.* Ch. X.

1
Nos non pluris sumus quam bullæ.
We are not more than a bubble.
PETRONIUS. 42.
(See also VARRO, also BACON under LIFE)

2
Piper, non homo.
He is pepper, not a man.
PETRONIUS.

3
Hominem quæro.
I am in search of a man.
PHÆDRUS—*Fables*. Bk. III. 19. 9.
(See also HOLLAND)

4
Man is the plumeless genus of bipeds, birds are the plumed.
PLATO—*Politicus*. 266. Diogenes produced a plucked cock, saying, "Here is Plato's man." DIOGENES LAERTIUS. Bk. VI. 2.

5
Homo homini lupus.
Man is a wolf to man.
PLAUTUS—*Asinaria*. II. 4. 88.

6
A minister, but still a man.
POPE—*Epistle to James Craggs*.

7
So man, who here seems principal alone,
Perhaps acts second to some sphere unknown
Touches some wheel, or verges to some goal;
'Tis but a part we see, and not a whole.
POPE—*Essay on Man*. Ep. I. L. 57.

8
Know then thyself, presume not God to scan;
The proper study of mankind is man.
POPE—*Essay on Man*. Ep. II. L. 1. In POPE's first ed. of *Moral Essays* it read "The only science of mankind is man." For the last phrase see GROTE—*History of Greece*. Vol. IX. P. 573. Ascribed to SOCRATES; also to XENOPHON—*Memor*. I. 1.
(See also CHARRON, QUARLES, also DIOGENES under KNOWLEDGE)

9
Chaos of thought and passion, all confused;
Still by himself abused and disabused;
Created half to rise, and half to fall;
Great lord of all things, yet a prey to all;
Sole judge of truth, in endless error hurled;
The glory, jest and riddle of the world!
POPE—*Essay on Man*. Ep. II. L. 13.

10
Virtuous and vicious every man must be,
Few in the extreme, but all in the degree.
POPE—*Essay on Man*. Ep. II. L. 231.

11
An honest man's the noblest work of God.
POPE—*Essay on Man*. Ep. IV. L. 248.

12
No more was seen the human form divine.
POPE—*Homer's Odyssey*. Bk. X. L. 278.

13
So, if unprejudiced you scan
The going of this clock-work, man,
You find a hundred movements made
By fine devices in his head;
But 'tis the stomach's solid stroke
That tells his being what's o'clock.
PRIOR—*Alma*. Pt. III. L. 272.

14
Man is the measure of all things.
PROTAGORAS. Quoted as his philosophical principle.

15
Thou hast made him a little lower than the angels.
Psalms. VIII. 5.

16
Mark the perfect man, and behold the upright.
Psalms. XXXVII. 37.

17
Man is man's A, B, C. There's none that can
Read God aright, unless he first spell man.
QUARLES—*Hieroglyphics of the Life of Man*.
(See also POPE)

18
Quit yourselves like men.
I Samuel. IV. 9.

19
A man after his own heart.
I Samuel. XIII. 14.

20
Thou art the man.
II Samuel. XII. 7.

21
Der Mensch ist, der lebendig fühlende,
Der leichte Raub des mächt'gen Augenblicks.
Man, living, feeling man is the easy prey of the powerful present.
SCHILLER—*Die Jungfrau von Orleans*. III. 4. 54.

22
"How poor a thing is man!" alas 'tis true,
I'd half forgot it when I chanced on you.
SCHILLER—*The Moral Poet*.
(See also DANIEL)

23
Men have died from time to time and worms have eaten them, but not for love.
As You Like It. Act IV. Sc. 1. L. 105.

24
He was a man, take him for all in all,
I shall not look upon his like again.
Hamlet. Act I. Sc. 2. L. 187.

25
What a piece of work is a man! how noble in reason! how infinite in faculty! in form and moving how express and admirable! in action how like an angel! in apprehension how like a god! the beauty of the world! the paragon of animals! And, yet, to me, what is this quintessence of dust? man delights not me: no, nor woman neither, though by your smiling, you seem to say so.
Hamlet. Act II. Sc. 2. L. 313.

26
I have thought some of Nature's journeymen had made men and not made them well, they imitated humanity so abominably.
Hamlet. Act III. Sc. 2. L. 37.

27
Give me that man
That is not passion's slave, and I will wear him
In my heart's core, ay, in my heart of heart
As I do thee.
Hamlet. Act III. Sc. 2. L. 76.

28
What is a man,
If his chief good and market of his time
Be but to sleep and feed?
Hamlet. Act IV. Sc. 4. L. 33.

1
This is the state of man: to-day he puts forth
The tender leaves of hope; to-morrow blossoms,
And bears his blushing honours thick upon him:
The third day comes a frost, a killing frost,
And, when he thinks, good easy man, full surely
His greatness is a-ripening, nips his root,
And then he falls, as I do.
Henry VIII. Act III. Sc. 2. L. 352.

2
Men that make
Envy and crooked malice nourishment,
Dare bite the best.
Henry VIII. Act V. Sc. 3. L. 43.

3
Men at some time are masters of their fates:
The fault, dear Brutus, is not in our stars,
But in ourselves, that we are underlings.
Julius Cæsar. Act I. Sc. 2. L. 139.

4
The foremost man of all this world.
Julius Cæsar. Act IV. Sc. 3. L. 22.

5
His life was gentle, and the elements
So mix'd in him that Nature might stand up,
And say to all the world, This was a man!
Julius Cæsar. Act V. Sc. 5. L. 73.

6
God made him, and therefore let him pass for a man.
Merchant of Venice. Act I. Sc. 2. L. 60.

7
A proper man as one shall see in a summer's day.
Midsummer Night's Dream. Act I. Sc. 2. L. 89.

8
Are you good men and true?
Much Ado About Nothing. Act III. Sc. 3. L. 1.

9
Why, he's a man of wax.
Romeo and Juliet. Act I. Sc. 3. L. 76.

10
I wonder men dare trust themselves with men.
Timon of Athens. Act I. Sc. 2. L. 42.

11
For men, like butterflies,
Show not their mealy wings but to the summer.
Troilus and Cressida. Act III. Sc. 3. L. 78.

12
Every man is odd.
Troilus and Cressida. Act IV. Sc. 5. L. 42.

13
Nietzsche . . . he was a confirmed Life Force worshipper. It was he who raked up the Superman, who is as old as Prometheus; and the 20th century will run after this newest of the old crazes when it gets tired of the world, the flesh, and your humble servant.
BERNARD SHAW—*Man and Superman.* Act. III. (See also NIETZSCHE)

14
Man is of soul and body, formed for deeds
Of high resolve; on fancy's boldest wing.
SHELLEY—*Queen Mab.* Canto IV. L. 160.

15
Of the king's creation you may be; but he who makes a count, ne'er made a man.
THOMAS SOUTHERNE—*Sir Anthony Love.* Act II. Sc. 1.
(See also BURNS)

16
Man's wretched state,
That floures so fresh at morne, and fades at evening late.
SPENSER—*Faerie Queene.* Bk. III. Canto IX. St. 39.

17
Give us a man of God's own mould
Born to marshall his fellow-men;
One whose fame is not bought and sold
At the stroke of a politician's pen.
Give us the man of thousands ten,
Fit to do as well as to plan;
Give us a rallying-cry, and then
Abraham Lincoln, give us a *Man.*
E. C. STEDMAN—*Give us a Man.*
(See also HOLLAND)

18
Titles of honour are like the impressions on coin—which add no value to gold and silver, but only render brass current.
STERNE—*Koran.* Pt. II.
(See also BURNS)

19
A man's body and his mind, with the utmost reverence to both I speak it, are exactly like a jerkin and a jerkin's lining;—rumple the one,—you rumple the other.
STERNE—*Tristram Shandy.* Bk. III. Ch. IV.

20
When I beheld this I sighed, and said within myself, Surely man is a Broomstick!
SWIFT—*A Meditation upon a Broomstick.*

21
Homo vitæ commodatus, non donatus est.
Man has been lent, not given, to life.
SYRUS—*Maxims.*

22
Man is man, and master of his fate.
TENNYSON—*Enid. Song of Fortune and Her Wheel.*
(See also HENLEY under SOUL)

23
Ah God, for a man with heart, head, hand,
Like some of the simple great gone
Forever and ever by,
One still strong man in a blatant land,
Whatever they call him, what care I,
Aristocrat, democrat, autocrat—one
Who can rule and dare not lie.
TENNYSON—*Maud.* X. 5.
(See also HOLLAND)

24
I am a part of all that I have met.
TENNYSON—*Ulysses.* L. 18.
(See also BYRON under CITIES)

25
Homo sum, humani nihil a me alienum puto.
I am a man, nothing that is human do I think unbecoming in me.
TERENCE—*Heauton timoroumenos.* Act I. Sc. 1. F. W. RICORD's trans.
(See also POPE)

26
Der edle Mensch ist nur ein Bild von Gott.
The noble man is only God's image.
LUDWIG TIECK—*Genoveva.*

27
Quod, ut dictur, si est homo bulla, eo magis senex.
What, if as said, man is a bubble.
VARRO—*Preface* to *De Re Rustica.* Found also in SENECA—*Apocolocyntosis.* LUCAN—*Cha-*

ron. 19. CARDINAL ARMELLINI'S *Epitaph* in *Revue des Deux Mondes*, April 15, 1892.
ERASMUS—*Adagia*.
(See also PETRONIUS)

1
Silver is the king's stamp; man God's stamp, and a woman is man's stamp; we are not current till we pass from one man to another.
WEBSTER—*Northward Hoe.* I. 186. HAZLITT's ed.
(See also WYCHERLY)

2
I am an acme of things accomplished, and I am encloser of things to be.
WALT WHITMAN—*Song of Myself.* 44.

3
When faith is lost, when honor dies,
The man is dead!
WHITTIER—*Ichabod.* St. 8.

4
I weigh the man, not his title: 'tis not the king's inscription can make the metal better or heavier.
WYCHERLY—*Plain Dealer.* Act I. Sc. 1. (Altered by Bickerstaff.)
(See also BURNS, CAREW, GOWER, MASSINGER, STERNE, WEBSTER)

5
How poor, how rich, how abject, how august,
How complicate, how wonderful, is man!
How passing wonder He, who made him such!
YOUNG—*Night Thoughts.* Night I. L. 68.

6
Ah! how unjust to nature, and himself,
Is thoughtless, thankless, inconsistent man.
YOUNG—*Night Thoughts.* Night II. L. 112.

MANNERS

7
He was the mildest manner'd man
That ever scuttled ship or cut a throat.
BYRON—*Don Juan.* Canto III. St. 41.

8
Now as to politeness . . . I would venture to call it benevolence in trifles.
LORD CHATHAM—*Correspondence.* I. 79.

9
Manners must adorn knowledge, and smooth its way through the world. Like a great rough diamond, it may do very well in a closet by way of curiosity, and also for its intrinsic value; but it will never be worn, nor shine, if it is not polished.
CHESTERFIELD—*Letters.* July 1, 1748.

10
A moral, sensible, and well-bred man
Will not affront me, and no other can.
COWPER—*Conversation.* L. 193.

11
Nobody ought to have been able to resist her coaxing manner; and nobody had any business to try. Yet she never seemed to know it was her manner at all. That was the best of it.
DICKENS—*Martin Chuzzlewit.* Vol. II. Ch. XIV.

12
Fine manners need the support of fine manners in others.
EMERSON—*The Conduct of Life. Behavior.*

13
Good manners are made up of petty sacrifices.
EMERSON—*Letters and Social Aims.*

14
Das Betragen ist ein Spiegel in welchem jeder sein Bild zeigt.
Behavior is a mirror in which every one shows his image.
GOETHE—*Die Wahlverwandtschaften.* II. 5. *Aus Ottiliens Tagebuche.*

15
The mildest manners with the bravest mind.
HOMER—*Iliad.* Bk. XXIV. L. 963. POPE'S trans.

16
He was so generally civil, that nobody thanked him for it.
SAMUEL JOHNSON—*Boswell's Life of Johnson.* (1777)

17
Ah, ah Sir Thomas, Honores mutant *Mores.*
MANNERS (Lord Rutland). To SIR THOS. MORE.
Not so, in faith, but have a care lest we translate the proverb and say, 'Honours change *Manners.*'
Answer of SIR THOS. MORE to MANNERS.
MARGARET MORE—*Diary.* October, 1524.

18
My lords, we are vertebrate animals, we are mammalia! My learned friend's manner would be intolerable in Almighty God to a black beetle.
MAULE. *To the Court.* On the Authority of LORD COLERIDGE.

19
We call it only pretty Fanny's way.
THOMAS PARNELL—*An Elegy to an Old Beauty.* Compare LEIGH HUNT Trans. of *Dulces Amaryllidis Iræ.*

20
Eye nature's walks, shoot folly as it flies,
And catch the manners, living as they rise;
Laugh where we must, be candid where we can,
But vindicate the ways of God to man.
POPE—*Essay on Man.* Ep. I. L. 13.

21
"What sort of a doctor is he?" "Well, I don't know much about his ability; but he's got a very good bedside manner."
Punch, March 15, 1884, accompanying a drawing by G. DU MAURIER.

22
Quæ fuerant vitia mores sunt.
What once were vices, are now the manners of the day.
SENECA—*Epistolæ Ad Lucilium.* XXXIX.

23
Men's evil manners live in brass; their virtues
We write in water.
Henry VIII. Act IV. Sc. 2. L. 46.
(See also BEAUMONT under DEEDS, BACON under LIFE)

24
Ecrivez les injures sur le sable,
Mais les bienfaits sur le marbre.
Write injuries in dust,
But kindnesses in marble.
French saying.

25
Fit for the mountains and the barb'rous caves,
Where manners ne'er were preach'd.
Twelfth Night. Act IV. Sc. 1. L. 52.

1
Her manners had not that repose
Which stamps the caste of Vere de Vere.
TENNYSON—*Lady Clara Vere de Vere*. St. 5.

2
Ut homo est, ita morem geras.
Suit your manner to the man.
TERENCE—*Adelphi*. III. 3. 78.

3
Obsequium amicos, veritas odium parit.
Obsequiousness begets friends; truth, hatred.
TERENCE—*Andria*. I. 1. 41.

MAPLE

4
The scarlet of the maples can shake me like a cry,
Of bugles going by.
BLISS CARMAN—*Vagabond Song*.

5
That was a day of delight and wonder.
While lying the shade of the maple trees under—
He felt the soft breeze at its frolicksome play;
He smelled the sweet odor of newly mown hay.
THOS. DUNN ENGLISH—*Under the Trees*.

6
I mark me how today the maples wear
A look of inward burgeoning, and I feel
Colours I see not in the naked air,
Lance-keen, and with the little blue of steel.
EDWARD O'BRIEN—*In Late Spring*.

MARCH

7
March. Its tree, Juniper. Its stone, Bloodstone. Its motto, "Courage and strength in times of danger."
Old Saying.

8
Ah, March! we know thou art
Kind-hearted, spite of ugly looks and threats,
And, out of sight, art nursing April's violets!
HELEN HUNT JACKSON—*Verses. March*.

9
Slayer of the winter, art thou here again?
O welcome, thou that bring'st the summer nigh!
The bitter wind makes not the victory vain,
Nor will we mock thee for thy faint blue sky.
WILLIAM MORRIS—*March*. St. 1.

10
The ides of March are come.
Julius Cæsar. Act III. Sc. 1. L. 1.

11
In fierce March weather
White waves break tether,
And whirled together
At either hand,
Like weeds uplifted,
The tree-trunks rifted
In spars are drifted,
Like foam or sand.
SWINBURNE—*Four Songs of Four Seasons*. St. 11.

12
With rushing winds and gloomy skies
The dark and stubborn Winter dies:
Far-off, unseen, Spring faintly cries,
Bidding her earliest child arise;
March!
BAYARD TAYLOR—*March*.

13
All in the wild March-morning I heard the angels call;
It was when the moon was setting, and the dark was over all;
The trees began to whisper, and the wind began to roll,
And in the wild March-morning I heard them call my soul.
TENNYSON—*The May Queen*. Conclusion.

14
Up from the sea, the wild north wind is blowing
Under the sky's gray arch;
Smiling I watch the shaken elm boughs, knowing
It is the wind of March.
WHITTIER—*March*.

15
Like an army defeated
The snow hath retreated,
And now doth fare ill
On the top of the bare hill;
The Ploughboy is whooping—anon—anon!
There's joy in the mountains:
There's life in the fountains;
Small clouds are sailing,
Blue sky prevailing;
The rain is over and gone.
WORDSWORTH—*Written in March*.

MARIGOLD

Tagetes

16
The marigold, whose courtier's face
Echoes the sun, and doth unlace
Her at his rise, at his full stop
Packs and shuts up her gaudy shop.
JOHN CLEVELAND—*On Phillis Walking Before Sunrise*.

17
The marigold abroad her leaves doth spread,
Because the sun's and her power is the same.
HENRY CONSTABLE—*Diana*.

18
No marigolds yet closed are,
No shadows great appeare.
HERRICK—*Hesperides. To Daisies. Not to Shut so Soone*.

19
Open afresh your round of starry folds,
Ye ardent marigolds!
Dry up the moisture from your golden lips.
KEATS—*I Stood Tiptoe Upon a Little Hill*.

20
The sun-observing marigold.
QUARLES—*The School of the Heart. Ode XXX*. St. 5.

21
Nor shall the marigold unmentioned die,
Which Acis once found out in Sicily;
She Phœbus loves, and from him draws his hue,
And ever keeps his golden beams in view.
RAPIN—*In His Latin Poem on Gardens*. Trans. by GARDINER in 1706.

22
And winking Mary-buds begin
To ope their golden eyes.
Cymbeline. Act II. Sc. 3. *Song*. L. 25.

1
Here's flowers for you:
Hot lavender, mints, savory, marjoram:
The marigold, that goes to bed wi' the sun,
And with him rises weeping.
Winter's Tale. Act IV. Sc. 4. L. 103.

2
When with a serious musing I behold
The graceful and obsequious marigold,
How duly every morning she displays
Her open breast, when Titan spreads his rays.
GEORGE WITHER—*The Marigold.*

MARSH MARIGOLD

Caltha Palustris

3
The seal and guerdon of wealth untold
We clasp in the wild marsh marigold.
ELAINE GOODALE—*Nature's Coinage.*

4
Fair is the marigold, for pottage meet.
GAY—*Shepherd's Week. Monday.* L. 46.

5
A little marsh-plant, yellow green,
And prick'd at lip with tender red.
Tread close, and either way you tread,
Some faint black water jets between
Lest you should bruise the curious head.
SWINBURNE—*The Sundew.*

MARTLET

6
The martlet
Builds in the weather on the outward wall,
Even in the force and road of casualty.
Merchant of Venice. Act II. Sc. 9. L. 28.

7
This guest of summer,
The temple-haunting martlet, does approve,
By his lov'd mansionry, that the heaven's breath
Smells wooingly here; no jutty, frieze,
Buttress, nor coign of vantage, but this bird
Hath made its pendent bed, and procreant cradle:
Where they most breed and haunt, I have observ'd,
The air is delicate.
Macbeth. Act I. Sc. 6. L. 3.

MARTYRDOM

8
For a tear is an intellectual thing;
And a sigh is the sword of an angel-king;
And the bitter groan of a martyr's woe
Is an arrow from the Almighty's bow.
WILLIAM BLAKE—*The Grey Monk.*

9
The noble army of martyrs.
Book of Common Prayer. Te Deum Laudamus.

10
Strangulatus pro republica.
Tortured for the Republic.
JAMES A. GARFIELD—*Last Words.* Written as he was dying, July 17, 1882.

11
Who falls for love of God, shall rise a star.
BEN JONSON—*Underwoods. An Epistle to a Friend.*

12
He strove among God's suffering poor
One gleam of brotherhood to send;
The dungeon oped its hungry door
To give the truth one martyr more,
Then shut,—and here behold the end!
LOWELL—*On the Death of C. T. Torrey.*

13
Martyrs! who left for our reaping
Truths you had sown in your blood—
Sinners! whom long years of weeping
Chasten'd from evil to good.
MOORE—*Where is Your Dwelling, Ye Sainted?*

14
It is the cause, and not the death, that makes the martyr.
NAPOLEON I.

15
His wife and children, being eleven in number, ten able to walk, and one sucking on her breast, met him by the way as he went towards Smithfield: this sorrowful sight of his own flesh and blood, dear as they were to him, could yet nothing move him, but that he constantly and cheerfully took his death with wonderful patience, in the defence and support of Christ's Gospel.
Martyrdom of JOHN ROGERS. See RICHMOND'S *Selection from the Writings of the Reformers and Early Protestant Divines of the Church of England.*

16
Like a pale martyr in his shirt of fire.
ALEX. SMITH—*A Life Drama.* Sc. 2. L. 225.

MASONS

17
The elder of them, being put to nurse,
Was by a beggar-woman stolen away;
And, ignorant of his birth and parentage,
Became a bricklayer when he came to age.
Henry VI. Pt. II. Act IV. Sc. 2. L. 150.

18
Sir, he made a chimney in my father's house, and the bricks are alive at this day to testify it.
Henry VI. Pt. II. Act IV. Sc. 2. L. 156.

19
The crowded line of masons with trowels in their right hands, rapidly laying the long side-wall,
The flexible rise and fall of backs, the continual click of the trowels striking the bricks,
The bricks, one after another, each laid so workmanlike in its place, and set with a knock of the trowel-handle.
WALT WHITMAN—*Song of the Broad-Axe.* Pt. III. St. 4.

MATRIMONY

20
He that hath a wife and children hath given hostages to fortune; for they are impediments to great enterprises, either of virtue or mischief.
BACON—*Essays. Of Marriage and Single Life.*

21
No jealousy their dawn of love o'ercast,
Nor blasted were their wedded days with strife;
Each season looked delightful as it past,
To the fond husband and the faithful wife.
JAMES BEATTIE—*The Minstrel.* Bk. I. St. 14.

22
To have and to hold from this day forward, for better, for worse, for richer, for poorer, in sickness, and in health, to love and to cherish, till death us do part.
Book of Common Prayer. Solemnization of Matrimony.

1

To love, cherish, and to obey.

Book of Common Prayer. Solemnization of Matrimony.

2

With this ring I thee wed, with my body I thee worship, and with all my wordly goods I thee endow.

Book of Common Prayer. Solemnization of Matrimony.

3

He that said it was not good for man to be alone, placed the celibate amongst the inferior states of perfection.

BOYLE—*Works.* Vol. VI. P. 292. *Letter from Mr. Evelyn.*

4

I'd rather die Maid, and lead apes in Hell
Than wed an inmate of Silenus' Cell.

RICHARD BRATHWAIT—*English Gentelman and Gentelwoman* (1640), in a supplemental tract, *The Turtle's Triumph.* Phrase "lead apes in hell" found in his *Drunken Barnaby's Journal. Bessy Bell.* MASSINGER—*City Madam.* Act II. Sc. 2. SHIRLEY—*School of Compliments.* (1637)
(See also TAMING OF THE SHREW)

5

Cursed be the man, the poorest wretch in life,
The crouching vassal, to the tyrant wife,
Who has no will but by her high permission;
Who has not sixpence but in her possession;
Who must to her his dear friend's secret tell;
Who dreads a curtain lecture worse than hell.
Were such the wife had fallen to my part,
I'd break her spirit or I'd break her heart.

BURNS—*The Henpecked Husband.*

6

Marriage and hanging go by destiny; matches are made in heaven.

BURTON—*Anatomy of Melancholy.* Pt. III. Sec. II. Mem. 5. Subs. 5.
(See also LYLY, MERCHANT OF VENICE)

7

'Cause grace and virtue are within
Prohibited degrees of kin;
And therfore no true Saint allows,
They shall be suffer'd to espouse.

BUTLER—*Hudibras.* Pt. III. Canto I. L. 1,293.

8

For talk six times with the same single lady,
And you may get the wedding dresses ready.

BYRON—*Don Juan.* Canto XII. St. 59.

9

There was no great disparity of years,
Though much in temper; but they never clash'd,
They moved like stars united in their spheres,
Or like the Rhône by Leman's waters wash'd,
Where mingled and yet separate appears
The river from the lake, all bluely dash'd
Through the serene and placid glassy deep,
Which fain would lull its river-child to sleep.

BYRON—*Don Juan.* Canto XIV. St. 87.

10

Una muger no tiene.
Valor para el consejo, y la conviene Casarse.

A woman needs a stronger head than her own for counsel—she should marry.

CALDERON—*El Purgatorio de Sans Patricio.* III. 4.

11

To sit, happy married lovers; Phillis trifling with a plover's
Egg, while Corydon uncovers with a grace the Sally Lunn,
Or dissects the lucky pheasant—that, I think, were passing pleasant
As I sit alone at present, dreaming darkly of a dun.

CALVERLEY—*In the Gloaming.* (*Parody on Mrs. Browning.*)

12

We've been together now for forty years,
An' it don't seem a day too much;
There ain't a lady livin' in the land
As I'd swop for my dear old Dutch.

ALBERT CHEVALIER—*My Old Dutch.*

13

Man and wife,
Coupled together for the sake of strife.

CHURCHILL—*Rosciad.* L. 1,005.

14

Oh! how many torments lie in the small circle of a wedding ring.

COLLEY CIBBER.

15

Prima societas in ipso conjugio est: proxima in liberis; deinde una domus, communia omnia.

The first bond of society is marriage; the next, our children; then the whole family and all things in common.

CICERO—*De Officiis.* I. 17.

16

Thus grief still treads upon the heels of pleasure,
Marry'd in haste, we may repent at leisure.

CONGREVE—*The Old Bachelor.* Act V. Sc. 1.
(See also MOLIÈRE, TAMING OF THE SHREW)

17

Misses! the tale that I relate
This lesson seems to carry—
Choose not alone a proper mate,
But proper time to marry.

COWPER—*Pairing Time Anticipated.* (*Moral.*)

18

Wedlock, indeed, hath oft compared been
To public feasts, where meet a public rout,
Where they that are without would fain go in,
And they that are within would fain go out.

SIR JOHN DAVIES—*Contention Betwixt a Wife, etc.*
(See also EMERSON, MONTAIGNE, QUITARD, WEBSTER)

19

At length cried she, I'll marry:
What should I tarry for?
I may lead apes in hell forever.

DIBDIN—*Tack and Tack.*
(See also BRATHWAIT)

20

The wictim o' connubiality

DICKENS—*Pickwick Papers.* Ch. XX.

21

Every woman should marry—and no man.

BENJ. DISRAELI—*Lothair.* Ch. XXX.

22

Is not marriage an open question, when it is alleged, from the beginning of the world, that such as are in the institution wish to get out, and such as are out wish to get in.

EMERSON—*Representative Men. Montaigne.*
(See also DAVIES)

1
Magis erit animorum quam corporum conjugium.
The wedlock of minds will be greater than that of bodies.
ERASMUS—*Procus et Puella.*

2
The joys of marriage are the heaven on earth,
Life's paradise, great princess, the soul's quiet,
Sinews of concord, earthly immortality,
Eternity of pleasures.
JOHN FORD—*The Broken Heart.* Act II. Sc. 2. L. 102.

3
A bachelor
May thrive by observation on a little,
A single life's no burthen: but to draw
In yokes is chargeable, and will require
A double maintenance.
JOHN FORD—*The Fancies Chaste and Noble.* Act I. Sc. 3. L. 82.

4
Where there's marriage without love, there will be love without marriage.
BENJ. FRANKLIN—*Poor Richard.* (1734)

5
My son is my son till he have got him a wife,
But my daughter's my daughter all the days of her life.
Proverb from FULLER'S *Gnomologia.* (1732)

6
They that marry ancient people, merely in expectation to bury them, hang themselves, in hope that one will come and cut the halter.
FULLER—*Holy and Profane States.* Bk. III. *Of Marriage.*

7
You are of the society of the wits and railers; . . the surest sign is, you are an enemy to marriage, the common butt of every railer.
GARRICK—*The Country Girl.* Act II. 1. Play taken from WYCHERLY'S *Country Wife.*
(See also WYCHERLY)

8
The husband's sullen, dogged, shy,
The wife grows flippant in reply;
He loves command and due restriction,
And she as well likes contradiction.
She never slavishly submits;
She'll have her way, or have her fits.
He his way tugs, she t'other draws;
The man grows jealous and with cause.
GAY—*Cupid, Hymen, and Plutus.*

9
It is not good that the man should be alone.
Genesis. II. 18.

10
Bone of my bones, and flesh of my flesh.
Genesis. II. 23.

11
Denn ein wackerer Mann verdient ein begütertes Mädchen.
For a brave man deserves a well-endowed girl.
GOETHE—*Hermann und Dorothea.* III. 19.

12
So, with decorum all things carry'd;
Miss frown'd, and blush'd, and then was—married.
GOLDSMITH—*The Double Transformation.* St. 3.

13
Le divorce est le sacrement de l'adultere.
Divorce is the sacrament of adultery.
G. F. GUICHARD.

14
An unhappy gentleman, resolving to wed nothing short of perfection, keeps his heart and hand till both get so old and withered that no tolerable woman will accept them.
HAWTHORNE—*Mosses from an Old Manse.*

15
I should like to see any kind of a man, distinguishable from a gorilla, that some good and even pretty woman could not shape a husband out of.
HOLMES—*The Professor at the Breakfast Table.*
(See also POPE, THACKERAY)

16
Yet while my Hector still survives, I see
My father, mother, brethren, all in thee.
HOMER—*Iliad.* Bk. VI. L. 544. POPE'S trans.

17
Andromache! my soul's far better part.
HOMER—*Iliad.* Bk. VI. L. 624. POPE'S trans.

18
Felices ter et amplius
Quos irrupta tenet copula, nec malis
Divulsus querimoniis
Suprema citius solvet amor die.
Happy and thrice happy are they who enjoy an uninterrupted union, and whose love, unbroken by any complaints, shall not dissolve until the last day.
HORACE—*Carmina.* I. 13. 17.

19
Marriages would in general be as happy, if not more so, if they were all made by the Lord Chancellor.
SAMUEL JOHNSON—*Boswell's Life.* (1776)

20
I have met with women whom I really think would like to be married to a Poem, and to be given away by a Novel.
KEATS—*Letters to Fanny Brawne.* Letter II.

21
Ay, marriage is the life-long miracle,
The self-begetting wonder, daily fresh.
CHARLES KINGSLEY—*Saint's Tragedy.* Act II. Sc. 9.

22
You should indeed have longer tarried
By the roadside before you married.
WALTER SAVAGE LANDOR—*To One Ill-mated.*

23
As unto the bow the cord is,
So unto the man is woman;
Though she bends him she obeys him,
Though she draws him, yet she follows,
Useless each without the other!
LONGFELLOW—*Hiawatha.* Pt. X. L. 1.

24
Sure the shovel and tongs
To each other belongs.
SAMUEL LOVER—*Widow Machree.*

25
Take heede, Camilla, that seeking al the Woode for a streight sticke, you chuse not at the last a crooked staffe.
LYLY—*Euphues.*

1
Marriage is destinie, made in heaven.
LYLY'S *Mother Bombie*. Same in CLARKE—*Parœmologia*. P. 230. (Ed. 1639)
(See also BURTON, TENNYSON)

2
Cling closer, closer, life to life,
Cling closer, heart to heart;
The time will come, my own wed Wife,
When you and I must part!
Let nothing break our band but Death,
For in the world above
'Tis the breaker Death that soldereth
Our ring of Wedded Love.
GERALD MASSEY—*On a Wedding Day*. St. 11.

3
And, to all married men, be this a caution,
Which they should duly tender as their life,
Neither to doat too much, nor doubt a wife.
MASSINGER—*Picture*. Act V. Sc. 3.

4
The sum of all that makes a just man happy
Consists in the well choosing of his wife:
And there, well to discharge it, does require
Equality of years, of birth, of fortune;
For beauty being poor, and not cried up
By birth or wealth, can truly mix with neither.
And wealth, when there's such difference in years,
And fair descent, must make the yoke uneasy.
MASSINGER—*New Way to Pay Old Debts*. Act IV. Sc. 1.

5
What therefore God hath joined together let not man put asunder.
Matthew. XIX. 6.

6
Hail, wedded love, mysterious law; true source
Of human offspring.
MILTON—*Paradise Lost*. Bk. IV. L. 750.

7
To the nuptial bower
I led her, blushing like the morn; all Heaven,
And happy constellations on that hour
Shed their selectest influence; the earth
Gave sign of gratulation, and each hill;
Joyous the birds; fresh gales and gentle airs
Whisper'd it to the woods, and from their wings
Flung rose, flung odours from the spicy shrub.
MILTON—*Paradise Lost*. Bk. VIII. L. 510.

8
Therefore God's universal law
Gave to the man despotic power
Over his female in due awe,
Not from that right to part an hour,
Smile she or lour.
MILTON—*Samson Agonistes*. L. 1,053.

9
Par un prompt désespoir souvent on se marie.
Qu'on s'en repent après tout le temps de sa vie.
Men often marry in hasty recklessness and repent afterward all their lives.
MOLIÈRE—*Les Femmes Savantes*. V. 5.
(See also CONGREVE)

10
Women when they marry buy a cat in the bag.
MONTAIGNE—*Essays*. Bk. III. Ch. V.

11
Il en advient ce qui se veoid aux cages; les oyseaux qui en sont dehors, desesperent d'y entrer; et d'un pareil soing en sortir, ceulx qui sont au dedans.
It happens as one sees in cages: the birds which are outside despair of ever getting in, and those within are equally desirous of getting out.
MONTAIGNE—*Essays*. Bk. III. Ch. V.
(See also DAVIES)

12
There's a bliss beyond all that the minstrel has told,
When two, that are link'd in one heavenly tie,
With heart never changing, and brow never cold,
Love on thro' all ills, and love on till they die.
MOORE—*Lalla Rookh*. *Light of the Harem*. St. 42.

13
Drink, my jolly lads, drink with discerning,
Wedlock's a lane where there is no turning;
Never was owl more blind than a lover,
Drink and be merry, lads, half seas over.
D. M. MULOCK—*Magnus and Morna*. Sc. 3.

14
Hac quoque de causa, si te proverbia tangunt,
Mense malos Maio nubere vulgus ait.
For this reason, if you believe proverbs, let me tell you the common one: "It is unlucky to marry in May."
OVID—*Fasti*. V. 489.

15
Si qua voles apte nubere, nube pari.
If thou wouldst marry wisely, marry thine equal.
OVID—*Heroides*. IX. 32.

16
Some dish more sharply spiced than this
Milk-soup men call domestic bliss.
COVENTRY PATMORE—*Olympus*.

17
The garlands fade, the vows are worn away;
So dies her love, and so my hopes decay.
POPE—*Autumn*. L. 70.

18
Grave authors say, and witty poets sing,
That honest wedlock is a glorious thing.
POPE—*January and May*. L. 21.

19
There swims no goose so gray, but soon or late
She finds some honest gander for her mate.
POPE—*Wife of Bath*. *Her Prologue*. From CHAUCER. L. 98.
(See also HOLMES)

20
Before I trust my Fate to thee,
Or place my hand in thine,
Before I let thy Future give
Color and form to mine,
Before I peril all for thee,
Question thy soul to-night for me.
ADELAIDE ANN PROCTER—*A Woman's Question*.

21
A prudent wife is from the Lord.
Proverbs. XIX. 14.

22
Advice to persons about to marry —Don't.
"Punch's Almanack." (1845) Attributed to HENRY MAYHEW.

23
Le mariage est comme une forteresse assiégée; ceux qui sont dehors veulent y entrer et ceux qui sont dedans en sortir.
Marriage is like a beleaguered fortress; those

who are without want to get in, and those within want to get out.

QUITARD—*Études sur les Proverbes Français.* P. 102. (See also DAVIES)

1

Widowed wife and wedded maid.

SCOTT—*The Betrothed.* Ch. XV.

2

Marriage is a desperate thing.

JOHN SELDEN—*Table Talk. Marriage.*

3

If you shall marry,
You give away this hand, and that is mine;
You give away heaven's vows, and those are mine;
You give away myself, which is known mine.

All's Well That Ends Well. Act V. Sc. 3. L. 169.

4

Men are April when they woo, December when they wed; maids are May when they are maids, but the sky changes when they are wives.

As You Like It. Act IV. Sc. 1. L. 147.

5

I will fasten on this sleeve of thine:
Thou art an elm, my husband, I, a vine.

Comedy of Errors. Act II. Sc. 2. L. 175.

6

Men's vows are women's traitors! All good seeming,
By thy revolt, O husband, shall be thought
Put on for villany; not born where 't grows,
But worn a bait for ladies.

Cymbeline. Act III. Sc. 4. L. 55.

7

Ere yet the salt of most unrighteous tears
Had left the flushing in her galled eyes,
She married.

Hamlet. Act I. Sc. 2. L. 154.

8

The instances that second marriage move
Are base respects of thrift, but none of love.

Hamlet. Act III. Sc. 2. L. 192.

9

God, the best maker of all marriages,
Combine your hearts in one.

Henry V. Act I. Sc. 2. L. 387.

10

He is the half part of a blessed man,
Left to be finished by such as she;
And she a fair divided excellence,
Whose fulness of perfection lies in him.

King John. Act II. Sc. 1. L. 437.

11

A world-without-end bargain.

Love's Labour's Lost. Act V. Sc. 2. L. 799.

12

Hanging and wiving goes by destiny.

Merchant of Venice. Act II. Sc. 9. L. 83.
Same in *Schole House for Women.* (1541)
(See also BURTON)

13

As are those dulcet sounds in break of day
That creep into the dreaming bridegroom's ear
And summon him to marriage.

Merchant of Venice. Act III. Sc. 2. L. 51.

14

Happiest of all, is, that her gentle spirit
Commits itself to yours to be directed,
As from her lord, her governor, her king.

Merchant of Venice. Act III. Sc. 2. L. 162.

15

I will marry her, sir, at your request; but if there be no great love in the beginning, yet heaven may decrease it upon better acquaintance * * * I hope, upon familiarity will grow more contempt: I will marry her; that I am freely dissolved, and dissolutely.

Merry Wives of Windsor. Act I. Sc. 1. L. 253.

16

But earthlier happy is the rose distill'd,
Than that which with'ring on the virgin thorn
Grows, lives and dies in single blessedness.

Midsummer Night's Dream. Act I. Sc. 1. L. 76.

17

I would not marry her, though she were endowed with all that Adam had left him before he transgressed: she would have made Hercules have turned spit, yea, and have cleft his club to make the fire too. * * * I would to God some scholar would conjure her; for certainly, while she is here, a man may live as quiet in hell as in a sanctuary.

Much Ado About Nothing. Act II. Sc. 1. L. 258.

18

No, the world must be peopled. When I said, I would die a bachelor, I did not think I should live till I were married.

Much Ado About Nothing. Act II. Sc. 1. L. 353.

19

Let husbands know,
Their wives have sense like them: they see, and smell,
And have their palates both for sweet and sour,
As husbands have.

Othello. Act IV. Sc. 3. L. 94.

20

She is not well married that lives married long:
But she's best married that dies married young.

Romeo and Juliet. Act IV. Sc. 5. L. 77.

21

She is your treasure, she must have a husband;
I must dance barefoot on her wedding day
And for your love to her lead apes in hell.

Taming of the Shrew. Act II. Sc. 1. L. 32.
(See also BRATHWAIT)

22

If she deny to wed, I'll crave the day
When I shall ask the banns and when be married.

Taming of the Shrew. Act II. Sc. 1. L. 180.

23

Who wooed in haste, and means to wed at leisure.

Taming of the Shrew. Act III. Sc. 2. L. 11.
(See also CONGREVE)

24

She shall watch all night:
And if she chance to nod I'll rail and brawl
And with the clamour keep her still awake.
This is the way to kill a wife with kindness.

Taming of the Shrew. Act IV. Sc. 1. L. 218.

25

Thy husband * * * commits his body
To painful labour, both by sea and land,

* * * * * *

And craves no other tribute at thy hands,
But love, fair looks, and true obedience;
Too little payment for so great a debt.

Taming of the Shrew. Act V. Sc. 2. L. 152.

1 Let still the woman take
An elder than herself: so wears she to him,
So sways she level in her husband's heart:
For, boy, however we do praise ourselves,
Our fancies are more giddy and unfirm,
More longing, wavering, sooner lost and worn
Than women's are.
Twelfth Night. Act II. Sc. 4. L. 29.

2
Then let thy love be younger than thyself,
Or thy affection cannot hold the bent:
For women are as roses, whose fair flower
Being once display'd, doth fall that very hour.
Twelfth Night. Act II. Sc. 4. L. 37.

3
Now go with me and with this holy man
Into the chantry by: there, before him,
And underneath that consecrated roof,
Plight me the full assurance of your faith.
Twelfth Night. Act IV. Sc. 3. L. 23.

4
To disbelieve in marriage is easy: to love a married woman is easy; but to betray a comrade, to be disloyal to a host, to break the covenant of bread and salt, is impossible.
BERNARD SHAW—*Getting Married.*

5
What God hath joined together no man shall ever put asunder: God will take care of that.
BERNARD SHAW—*Getting Married.*

6
The whole world is strewn with snares, traps, gins and pitfalls for the capture of men by women.
BERNARD SHAW—*Epistle Dedicatory to Man and Superman.*

7
Lastly no woman should marry a teetotaller, or a man who does not smoke. It is not for nothing that this "ignoble tobagie" as Michelet calls it, spreads all over the world.
STEVENSON—*Virginibus Puerisque.* Pt. I.

8
Under this window in stormy weather
I marry this man and woman together;
Let none but Him who rules the thunder
Put this man and woman asunder.
SWIFT—*Marriage Service from His Chamber Window.*

9
The reason why so few marriages are happy is because young ladies spend their time in making nets, not in making cages.
SWIFT—*Thoughts on Various Subjects.*

10
Celibate, like the fly in the heart of an apple, dwells in a perpetual sweetness, but sits alone, and is confined and dies in singularity.
JEREMY TAYLOR—*Sermon.* XVII. *The Marriage Ring.* Pt. I.

11
Marriages are made in Heaven.
TENNYSON—*Aylmer's Field.* L. 188.
(See also LYLY)

12
As the husband is the wife is; thou art mated with a clown,
And the grossness of his nature will have weight to drag thee down.
TENNYSON—*Locksley Hall.* St. 24.

13
Remember, it is as easy to marry a rich woman as a poor woman.
THACKERAY—*Pendennis.* Bk. I. Ch. XXVIII.

14
This I set down as a positive truth. A woman with fair opportunities and without a positive hump, may marry whom she likes.
THACKERAY—*Vanity Fair.* Ch. IV.
(See also HOLMES)

15
What woman, however old, has not the bridal-favours and raiment stowed away, and packed in lavender, in the inmost cupboards of her heart?
THACKERAY—*Virginians.* Bk. I. Ch. XXVIII.

16
But happy they, the happiest of their kind!
Whom gentler stars unite, and in one fate
Their Hearts, their Fortunes, and their Beings blend.
THOMSON—*Seasons. Spring.* L. 1,111.

17
Thrice happy is that humble pair,
Beneath the level of all care!
Over whose heads those arrows fly
Of sad distrust and jealousy.
EDMUND WALLER—*Of the Marriage of the Dwarfs.* L. 7.

18
The happy married man dies in good stile at home, surrounded by his weeping wife and children. The old bachelor don't die at all—he sort of rots away, like a pollywog's tail.
ARTEMUS WARD—*Draft in Baldinsville.*

19
'Tis just like a summer bird cage in a garden; the birds that are without despair to get in, and the birds that are within despair, and are in a consumption, for fear they shall never get out.
JOHN WEBSTER—*White Devil.* Act I. Sc. 2.
(See also DAVIES)

20
Why do not words, and kiss, and solemn pledge,
And nature that is kind in woman's breast,
And reason that in man is wise and good,
And fear of Him who is a righteous Judge,—
Why do not these prevail for human life,
To keep two hearts together, that began
Their spring-time with one love.
WORDSWORTH—*Excursion.* Bk. VI.

21
'Tis my maxim, he's a fool that marries; but he's a greater that does not marry a fool.
WYCHERLY—*Country Wife.* Act I. Sc. 1. L. 502.

22
You are of the society of the wits and railleurs . . . the surest sign is, since you are an enemy to marriage,—for that, I hear, you hate as much as business or bad wine.
WYCHERLY—*Country Wife.*
(See also GARRICK)

23
Body and soul, like peevish man and wife,
United jar, and yet are loth to part.
YOUNG—*Night Thoughts.* Night II. L. 175.

MAY

1
Hebe's here, May is here!
The air is fresh and sunny;
And the miser-bees are busy
Hoarding golden honey.
T. B. ALDRICH—*May.*

2
As it fell upon a day
In the merry month of May,
Sitting in a pleasant shade
Which a grove of myrtles made.
RICHARD BARNFIELD—*Address to the Nightingale.*

3
Spring's last-born darling, clear-eyed, sweet,
Pauses a moment, with white twinkling feet,
And golden locks in breezy play,
Half teasing and half tender, to repeat
Her song of "May."
SUSAN COOLIDGE—*May.*

4
But winter lingering chills the lap of May.
GOLDSMITH—*The Traveller.* L. 172.

5
Sweet May hath come to love us,
Flowers, trees, their blossoms don;
And through the blue heavens above us
The very clouds move on.
HEINE—*Book of Songs. New Spring.* No. 5.

6
O month when they who love must love and wed.
HELEN HUNT JACKSON—*Verses. May.*

7
O May, sweet-voiced one, going thus before,
Forever June may pour her warm red wine
Of life and passion,—sweeter days are thine!
HELEN HUNT JACKSON—*Verses. May.*

8
Oh! that we two were Maying
Down the stream of the soft spring breeze;
Like children with violets playing,
In the shade of the whispering trees.
CHARLES KINGSLEY—*Saint's Tragedy.* Act II. Sc. 9.

9
Ah! my heart is weary waiting,
Waiting for the May:
Waiting for the pleasant rambles
Where the fragrant hawthorn brambles,
With the woodbine alternating,
Scent the dewy way;
Ah! my heart is weary, waiting,
Waiting for the May.
DENIS FLORENCE MCCARTHY—*Summer Longings.*

10
Now the bright morning star, day's harbinger,
Comes dancing from the east, and leads with her
The flowery May, who from her green lap throws
The yellow cowslip, and the pale primrose.
Hail, bounteous May, that doth inspire
Mirth, and youth, and warm desire;
Woods and groves are of thy dressing,
Hill and dale doth boast thy blessing,
Thus we salute thee with our early song,
And welcome thee, and wish thee long.
MILTON—*Song. On May Morning.*

11
In the under-wood and the over-wood
There is murmur and trill this day,
For every bird is in lyric mood,
And the wind will have its way.
CLINTON SCOLLARD—*May Magic.*

12
As full of spirit as the month of May.
King Henry IV. Pt. I. Act IV. Sc. 1. L. 101.

13
No doubt they rose up early to observe
The rite of May.
Midsummer Night's Dream. Act IV. Sc. 1. L. 137.

14
In beauty as the first of May.
Much Ado About Nothing. Act I. Sc. 1. L. 194.

15
Rough winds do shake the darling buds of May.
Sonnet XVIII.

16
More matter for a May morning.
Twelfth Night. Act III. Sc. 4. L. 145.

17
Another May new buds and flowers shall bring:
Ah! why has happiness no second Spring?
CHARLOTTE SMITH—*Elegiac Sonnets and Other Poems.* Sonnet II.

18
When May, with cowslip-braided locks,
Walks through the land in green attire.
And burns in meadow-grass the phlox
His torch of purple fire:
* * * * * *
And when the punctual May arrives,
With cowslip-garland on her brow,
We know what once she gave our lives,
And cannot give us now!
BAYARD TAYLOR—*The Lost May.*

19
For I'm to be Queen o' the May, mother, I'm to be Queen o' the May.
TENNYSON—*The May Queen.* St. 1.

20
Among the changing months, May stands confest
The sweetest, and in fairest colors dressed.
THOMSON—*On May.*

21
May, queen of blossoms,
And fulfilling flowers,
With what pretty music
Shall we charm the hours?
Wilt thou have pipe and reed,
Blown in the open mead?
Or to the lute give heed
In the green bowers?
LORD THURLOW—*To May.*

22
For every marriage then is best in tune,
When that the wife is May, the husband June.
ROWLAND WATKINS—*To the most Courteous and Fair Gentlewoman, Mrs. Elinor Williams.*

23
What is so sweet and dear
As a prosperous morn in May,
The confident prime of the day,
And the dauntless youth of the year,
When nothing that asks for bliss,
Asking aright, is denied,
And half of the world a bridegroom is
And half of the world a bride?
WILLIAM WATSON—*Ode in May.*

(See also LOWELL under JUNE)

MEDICINE

(See also Disease, Health, Sickness)

1

Medicus curat, Natura sanat morbus.
The physician heals, Nature makes well.
Idea in Aristotle—*Nicomachean Ethics.* Bk. VII. 15. 7. Oxford text.

2

A man's own observation, what he finds good of, and what he finds hurt of, is the best physic to preserve health.
Bacon—*Essays. Of Regimen of Health.*

3

I find the medicine worse than the malady.
Beaumont and Fletcher—*Love's Cure.* Act III. Sc. 2.
(See also Vergil, also Bacon under Disease)

4

Dat Galenus opes, dat Justinianus honores,
Sed genus species cogitur ire pedes;
The rich Physician, honor'd Lawyers ride,
Whil'st the poor Scholar foots it by their side.
Burton—*Anatomy of Melancholy.* I. 2. 3. 15. Quoted by Dr. Robert F. Arnold. A like saying may be found in Franciscus Floridus Sabinus—*Lectiones Subcisive.* Bk. I. Ch. I. Also John Owen—*Medicus et I. C.* Ovid—*Fasti.* I. 217; *Amores.* III. VIII. 55.

5

'Tis not amiss, ere ye're giv'n o'er,
To try one desp'rate med'cine more;
For where your case can be no worse,
The desp'rat'st is the wisest course.
Butler—*Epistle of Hudibras to Sidrophel.* L. 5.

6

Learn'd he was in medic'nal lore,
For by his side a pouch he wore,
Replete with strange hermetic powder
That wounds nine miles point-blank would solder.
Butler—*Hudibras.* Pt. I. Canto II. L. 223.

7

This is the way that physicians mend or end us,
Secundum artem: but although we sneer
In health—when ill, we call them to attend us,
Without the least propensity to jeer.
Byron—*Don Juan.* Canto X. St. 42.

8

Dios que dá la llaga, dá la medicina.
God who sends the wound sends the medicine.
Cervantes—*Don Quixote.* II. 19.

9

Ægri quia non omnes convalescunt, idcirco ars nulla medicina est.
Because all the sick do not recover, therefore medicine is not an art.
Cicero—*De Natura Deorum.* II. 4.

10

When taken
To be well shaken.
George Colman (the Younger)—*Broad Grins. The Newcastle Apothecary.* St. 12.

11

Take a little rum
The less you take the better,
Pour it in the lakes
Of Wener or of Wetter.

Dip a spoonful out
And mind you don't get groggy,
Pour it in the lake
Of Winnipissiogie.

Stir the mixture well
Lest it prove inferior,
Then put half a drop
Into Lake Superior.

Every other day
Take a drop in water,
You'll be better soon
Or at least you oughter.
Bishop G. W. Doane—*Lines on Homeopathy.*

12

Better to hunt in fields for health unbought,
Than fee the doctor for a nauseous draught.
The wise for cure on exercise depend;
God never made his work for man to mend.
Dryden—*Epistle to John Dryden of Chesterton.* L. 92.

13

So liv'd our sires, ere doctors learn'd to kill,
And multiplied with theirs the weekly bill.
Dryden—*To John Dryden, Esq.* L. 71.

14

Even as a Surgeon, minding off to cut
Some cureless limb, before in use he put
His violent Engins on the vicious member,
Bringeth his Patient in a senseless slumber,
And grief-less then (guided by use and art),
To save the whole, sawes off th' infected part.
Du Bartas—*Divine Weekes and Workers. First Week. Sixth Day.* L. 1,018.

15

For of the most High cometh healing.
Ecclesiasticus. XXXVIII. 2.

16

One doctor, singly like the sculler plies,
The patient struggles, and by inches dies;
But two physicians, like a pair of oars,
Waft him right swiftly to the Stygian shores.
Quoted by Garth—*The Dispensary.*

17

A single doctor like a sculler plies,
And all his art and all his physic tries;
But two physicians, like a pair of oars,
Conduct you soonest to the Stygian shores.
Epigrams Ancient and Modern. Edited by Rev. John Booth, London, 1863. P. 144. Another version signed D, (probably John Dunscombe) in note to Nichols' *Select Collection of Poems.*

18

"Is there no hope?" the sick man said,
The silent doctor shook his head,
And took his leave with signs of sorrow,
Despairing of his fee to-morrow.
Gay—*The Sick Man and the Angel.*

19

Oh, powerful bacillus,
With wonder how you fill us,
Every day!
While medical detectives,
With powerful objectives,
Watch your play.
Wm. Tod Helmuth—*Ode to the Bacillus.*

1
I firmly believe that if the whole *materia medica* could be sunk to the bottom of the sea, it would be all the better for mankind and all the worse for the fishes.
HOLMES—*Lecture before the Harvard Medical School.*

2
A pill that the present moment is daily bread to thousands.
DOUGLAS JERROLD—*The Catspaw.* Act I. Sc. 1.

3
Orandum est, ut sit mens sana in corpore sano.
A sound mind in a sound body is a thing to be prayed for.
JUVENAL—*Satires.* X. 356.
(See also QUOTATIONS under DISEASE)

4
You behold in me
Only a travelling Physician;
One of the few who have a mission
To cure incurable diseases,
Or those that are called so.
LONGFELLOW—*Christus. The Golden Legend.* Pt. I.

5
Physician, heal thyself.
Luke. IV. 23. Quoted as a proverb

6
And in requital ope his leathern scrip,
And show me simples of a thousand names,
Telling their strange and vigorous faculties.
MILTON—*Comus.* L. 626.

7
Adrian, the Emperor, exclaimed incessantly, when dying, "That the crowd of physicians had killed him."
MONTAIGNE—*Essays.* Bk. II. Ch. XXXVII.

8
How the Doctor's brow should smile,
Crown'd with wreaths of camomile.
MOORE—*Wreaths for Ministers.*

9
Dulcia non ferimus; succo renovamus amaro.
We do not bear sweets; we are recruited by a bitter potion.
OVID—*Ars Amatoria.* III. 583.

10
Medicus nihil aliud est quam animi consolatio.
A physician is nothing but a consoler of the mind.
PETRONIUS ARBITER—*Satyricon.*

11
I have heard that Tiberius used to say that that man was ridiculous, who after *sixty* years, appealed to a physician.
PLUTARCH—*De Sanitate tuenda.* Vol. II.
(See also TACITUS)

12
So modern 'pothecaries, taught the art
By doctor's bills to play the doctor's part,
Bold in the practice of mistaken rules,
Prescribe, apply, and call their masters fools.
POPE—*Essay on Criticism.* L. 108.

13
Learn from the beasts the physic of the field.
POPE—*Essay on Man.* Ep. III. L. 174.

14
Who shall decide when doctors disagree,
And soundest casuists doubt, like you and me?
POPE—*Moral Essays.* Ep. III.

15
Banished the doctor, and expell'd the friend.
POPE—*Moral Essays.* Ep. III. L. 330.

16
You tell your doctor, that y' are ill
And what does he, but write a bill,
Of which you need not read one letter,
The worse the scrawl, the dose the better.
For if you knew but what you take,
Though you recover, he must break.
PRIOR—*Alma.* Canto III. L. 97.

17
But, when the wit began to wheeze,
And wine had warm'd the politician,
Cur'd yesterday of my disease,
I died last night of my physician.
PRIOR—*The Remedy Worse than the Disease.*

18
Physicians, of all men, are most happy: whatever good success soever they have, the world proclaimeth and what faults they commit, the earth covereth.
QUARLES—*Hieroglyphics of the Life of Man.*

19
Use three Physicians,
Still-first Dr. Quiet,
Next Dr. Merry-man
And Dr. Dyet.
From *Regimen Sanitatis Salernitanum.* Edition 1607.

20
By medicine life may be prolonged, yet death
Will seize the doctor too.
Cymbeline. Act V. Sc. 5. L. 29.

21
No cataplasm so rare,
Collected from all simples that have virtue
Under the moon, can save the thing from death.
Hamlet. Act IV. Sc. 7. L. 144.

22
In poison there is physic; and these news,
Having been well, that would have made me sick;
Being sick, have in some measure made me well.
Henry IV. Pt. II. Act I. Sc. 1. L. 137

23
'Tis time to give 'em physic, their diseases
Are grown so catching.
Henry VIII. Act I. Sc. 3. L. 36.

24
In this point
All his tricks founder, and he brings his physic
After his patient's death.
Henry VIII. Act III. Sc. 2. L. 39.

25
Take physic, pomp;
Expose thyself to feel what wretches feel.
King Lear. Act III. Sc. 4. L. 33.

26
How does your patient, doctor?
Not so sick, my lord,
As she is troubled with thick-coming fancies.
Macbeth. Act V. Sc. 3. L. 37.

27
Canst thou not minister to a mind diseas'd,
Pluck from the memory a rooted sorrow,
Raze out the written troubles of the brain,
And with some sweet oblivious antidote
Cleanse the stuff'd bosom of that perilous stuff
Which weighs upon the heart?
Therein the patient

Must minister to himself.
Throw physic to the dogs; I'll none of it.
Macbeth. Act V. Sc. 3. L. 40.

1 If thou couldst, doctor, cast
The water of my land, find her disease,
And purge it to a sound and pristine health,
I would applaud thee to the very echo,
That should applaud again.
Macbeth. Act V. Sc. 3. L. 50.

2 In such a night
Medea gather'd the enchanted herbs
That did renew old Æson.
Merchant of Venice. Act V. Sc. 1. L. 12.

3
I do remember an apothecary,—
And hereabouts he dwells,—whom late I noted
In tatter'd weeds, with overwhelming brows,
Culling of simples; meagre were his looks,
Sharp misery had worn him to the bones:
And in his needy shop a tortoise hung,
An alligator stuff'd, and other skins
Of ill-shaped fishes; and about his shelves
A beggarly account of empty boxes,
Green earthen pots, bladders and musty seeds,
Remnants of packthread and old cakes of roses,
Were thinly scatter'd to make up a show.
Romeo and Juliet. Act V. Sc. 1. L. 37.

4 You rub the sore,
When you should bring the plaster.
Tempest. Act II. Sc. 1. L. 138.

5 Trust not the physician;
His antidotes are poison, and he slays
More than you rob.
Timon of Athens. Act IV. Sc. 3. L. 434

6
When I was sick, you gave me bitter pills.
Two Gentlemen of Verona. Act II. Sc. 4. L. 149.

7
Crudelem medicum intemperans æger facit.
A disorderly patient makes the physician cruel.
Syrus—*Maxims.*

8
He (Tiberius) was wont to mock at the arts of physicians, and at those who, after thirty years of age, needed counsel as to what was good or bad for their bodies.
Tacitus—*Annals.* Bk. VI. Ch. XLVI. Same told by Suetonius—*Life of Tiberius.* Ch. LXVIII.
(See also Plutarch)

9
Ægrescitque medendo.
The medicine increases the disease.
Vergil—*Æneid.* XII. 46.

10
But nothing is more estimable than a physician who, having studied nature from his youth, knows the properties of the human body, the diseases which assail it, the remedies which will benefit it, exercises his art with caution, and pays equal attention to the rich and the poor.
Voltaire—*A Philosophical Dictionary. Physicians.*

MEDITATION

11
Thy thoughts to nobler meditations give,
And study how to die, not how to live.
Geo. Granville (Lord Lansdowne)—*Meditations on Death.* St. 1.

12
Happy the heart that keeps its twilight hour,
And, in the depths of heavenly peace reclined,
Loves to commune with thoughts of tender power,—
Thoughts that ascend, like angels beautiful,
A shining Jacob's-ladder of the mind!
Paul H. Hayne—*Sonnet IX.*

13
In maiden meditation, fancy-free.
Midsummer Night's Dream. Act II. Sc. 1. L. 164.

14
Divinely bent to meditation;
And in no worldly suits would he be mov'd,
To draw him from his holy exercise.
Richard III. Act III. Sc. 7. L. 61.

MEETING

15
As two floating planks meet and part on the sea,
O friend! so I met and then drifted from thee.
Wm. R. Alger—*Oriental Poetry. The Brief Chance Encounter.*
(See also Arnold, Bulwer, Longfellow, Moore, Smith, Stedman)

16
Like a plank of driftwood
Tossed on the watery main,
Another plank encountered,
Meets, touches, parts again;
So tossed, and drifting ever,
On life's unresting sea,
Men meet, and greet, and sever,
Parting eternally.
Edwin Arnold—*Book of Good Counsel.* Trans. from the Sanscrit of the *Hitopadéesa.* A literal trans. by Max Müller appeared in *The Fortnightly,* July, 1898. He also translated the same idea from the *Mahavastu.*

17
Like driftwood spars which meet and pass
Upon the boundless ocean-plain,
So on the sea of life, alas!
Man nears man, meets, and leaves again.
Matthew Arnold—*Terrace at Berne.*
(See also Alger)

18
As drifting logs of wood may haply meet
On ocean's waters surging to and fro,
And having met, drift once again apart,
So, fleeting is the intercourse of men.

E'en as a traveler meeting with the shade
Of some o'erhung tree, awhile reposes,
Then leaves its shelter to pursue his ways,
So men meet friends, then part with them for ever.
Trans. of the *Code of Manu.* In *Words of Wisdom.*

19
We met—'twas in a crowd.
Thomas Haynes Bayly—*We Met.*

1
Two lives that once part, are as ships that divide
When, moment on moment, there rushes between
The one and the other, a sea;—
Ah, never can fall from the days that have been
A gleam on the years that shall be!
BULWER-LYTTON—*A Lament.* L. 10.
(See also ALGER)

2
As vessels starting from ports thousands of miles apart pass close to each other in the naked breadths of the ocean, nay, sometimes even touch in the dark.
HOLMES—*Professor at the Breakfast Table.*
(See also ALGER)

3
The joy of meeting not unmixed with pain.
LONGFELLOW—*Morituri Salutamus.* L. 113.

4
Ships that pass in the night, and speak each other in passing,
Only a signal shown and a distant voice in the darkness:
So on the ocean of life, we pass and speak one another,
Only a look and a voice, then darkness again and a silence.
LONGFELLOW—*Tales of a Wayside Inn. The Theologian's Tale. Elizabeth.* Pt. IV.
(See also ALGER)

5
In life there are meetings which seem
Like a fate.
OWEN MEREDITH (Lord Lytton)—*Lucile.* Pt. II. Canto III. St. 8.

6
And soon, too soon, we part with pain,
To sail o'er silent seas again.
THOMAS MOORE—*Meeting of the Ships.*
(See also ALGER)

7
Some day, some day of days, threading the street
With idle, heedless pace,
Unlooking for such grace,
I shall behold your face!
Some day, some day of days, thus may we meet.
NORA PERRY—*Some Day of Days.*

8
And so he'll die; and, rising so again,
When I shall meet him in the court of heaven
I shall not know him.
King John. Act III. Sc. 4. L. 86.

9
When shall we three meet again
In thunder, lightning, or in rain?
Macbeth. Act I. Sc. 1. L. 1.

10
We twain have met like the ships upon the sea,
Who behold an hour's converse, so short, so sweet;
One little hour! and then, away they speed
On lonely paths, through mist, and cloud, and foam,
To meet no more.
ALEXANDER SMITH—*Life Drama.* Sc. IV.
(See also ALGER)

11
Alas, by what rude fate
Our lives, like ships at sea, an instant meet,
Then part forever on their courses fleet.
E. C. STEDMAN—*Blameless Prince.* St. 51.
(See also ALGER)

12
We shall meet but we shall miss her.
H. S. WASHBURN—*Song.*

MELANCHOLY

13
All my griefs to this are jolly,
Naught so damn'd as melancholy.
BURTON—*Abstract to Anatomy of Melancholy.*

14
All my joys to this are folly,
Naught so sweet as melancholy.
BURTON—*Abstract to Anatomy of Melancholy.*
(See also STRODE)

15
As melancholy as an unbraced drum.
CENTLIVRE—*Wonder.* Act II. Sc. 1.

16
With eyes upraised, as one inspired,
Pale Melancholy sate retired;
And, from her wild, sequester'd seat,
In notes by distance made more sweet,
Pour'd through the mellow horn her pensive soul.
COLLINS—*The Passions.* L. 57.

17
Tell us, pray, what devil
This melancholy is, which can transform
Men into monsters.
JOHN FORD—*The Lover's Melancholy.* Act III. Sc. 1. L. 107.

18
Melancholy
Is not, as you conceive, indisposition
Of body, but the mind's disease.
JOHN FORD—*The Lover's Melancholy.* Act III. Sc. 1. L. 111.

19
Here rests his head upon the lap of earth,
A youth, to fortune and to fame unknown;
Fair Science frowned not on his humble birth,
And Melancholy marked him for her own.
GRAY—*Elegy in a Country Churchyard. The Epitaph.*

20
There's not a string attuned to mirth
But has its chord in melancholy.
HOOD—*Ode to Melancholy.*
(See also BURTON)

21
Employment, sir, and hardships, prevent melancholy.
SAMUEL JOHNSON—*Boswell's Life of Johnson.* (1777)

22
Moping melancholy,
And moon-struck madness.
MILTON—*Paradise Lost.* Bk. XI. L. 485.

23
Go—you may call it madness, folly,
You shall not chase my gloom away.
There's such a charm in melancholy,
I would not, if I could, be gay!
SAMUEL ROGERS—*To——.* St. 1.

24
I can suck melancholy out of a song.
As You Like It. Act II. Sc. 5. L. 12.

25
O melancholy!
Who ever yet could sound thy bottom? find
The ooze, to show what coast thy sluggish crare
Might easiliest harbour in?
Cymbeline. Act IV. Sc. 2. L. 205.

1
The greatest note of it is his melancholy.
Much Ado About Nothing. Act III. Sc. 2. L. 53.

2
And melancholy is the nurse of frenzy.
Taming of the Shrew. Induction. Sc. 2. L. 135.

3
Hence, all you vain delights,
As short as are the nights
Wherein you spend your folly!
There's nought in this life sweet,
If man were wise to see 't,
But only melancholy,
Oh, sweetest melancholy!
DR. STRODE—*Song in Praise of Melancholy.* As given in MALONE'S MSS. in the Bodleian Library. MS. No. 21. It appears in DR. STRODE'S play, *The Floating Island.* Attributed to FLETCHER, who inserted it in *The Nice Valour.* Act III. Sc. 3.
(See also BURTON)

MEMORY

4
Far from our eyes th' Enchanting Objects set,
Advantage by the friendly Distance get.
ALEXIS. *A poem against Fruition.* From *Poems by Several Hands.* Pub. 1685.

5
I do perceive that the old proverb be not alwaies trew, for I do finde that the absence of my Nath. doth breede in me the more continuall remembrance of him.
ANNE, LADY BACON—*To Jane Lady Cornwallis.* (1613)
(See also BROOKE, HENDYNG, KEMPIS, LINLEY)

6
Out of sighte, out of mynde.
Quoted as a saying by NATHANIEL BACON. In *Private Correspondence of Lady Cornwallis.* P. 19. GOOGE. *Title of Eclog.*
(See also LADY BACON)

7
Tell me the tales that to me were so dear,
Long, long ago, long, long ago.
THOMAS HAYNES BAYLY—*Long, Long Ago.*

8
Oh, I have roamed o'er many lands,
And many friends I've met;
Not one fair scene or kindly smile
Can this fond heart forget.
THOMAS HAYNES BAYLY—*O, Steer my Bark to Erin's Isle.*

9
Friends depart, and memory takes them
To her caverns, pure and deep.
THOMAS HAYNES BAYLY—*Teach Me to Forget.*

10
Out of mind as soon as out of sight.
LORD BROOKE—*Sonnet.* LVI.
(See also BACON)

11
The mother may forget the child
That smiles sae sweetly on her knee;
But I'll remember thee, Glencairn,
And all that thou hast done for me!
BURNS—*Lament for Glencairn.*

12
Yet how much less it were to gain,
Though thou hast left me free,
The loveliest things that still remain,
Than thus remember thee.
BYRON—*And Thou art Dead as Young and Fair.*

13
To live in hearts we leave behind,
Is not to die.
CAMPBELL—*Hallowed Ground.* St. 6.

14
When promise and patience are wearing thin,
When endurance is almost driven in,
When our angels stand in a waiting hush,
Remember the Marne and Ferdinand Foch.
BLISS CARMAN—*The Man of the Marne.*

15
Though sands be black and bitter black the sea,
Night lie before me and behind me night,
And God within far Heaven refuse to light
The consolation of the dawn for me,—
Between the shadowy burns of Heaven and Hell,
It is enough love leaves my soul to dwell
With memory.
MADISON CAWEIN—*The End of All.*

16
Les souvenirs embellissent la vie, l'oubli seul la rend possible.
Remembrances embellish life but forgetfulness alone makes it possible.
GEN'L CIALDINI—*Written in an album.*

17
Memoria est thesaurus omnium rerum e custos.
Memory is the treasury and guardian of all things.
CICERO—*De Oratore.* I. 5.

18
Vita enim mortuorum in memoria vivorum est posita.
The life of the dead is placed in the memory of the living.
CICERO—*Philippicæ.* IX. 5.

19
Oh, how cruelly sweet are the echoes that start
When Memory plays an old tune on the heart!
ELIZA COOK—*Journal.* Vol. IV. *Old Dobbin.* St. 16.

20
What peaceful hours I once enjoy'd!
How sweet their memory still!
But they have left an aching void
The world can never fill.
COWPER—*Walking with God.*

21
Don't you remember, sweet Alice, Ben Bolt?
Sweet Alice, whose hair was so brown;
Who wept with delight when you gave her a smile,
And trembl'd with fear at your frown!
THOMAS DUNN ENGLISH—*Ben Bolt.*

22
But woe to him, who left to moan,
Reviews the hours of brightness gone.
EURIPIDES—*Iphigenia in Taurus.* L. 1121. Trans. by ANSTICE.

23
Memory [is] like a purse,—if it be over-full that it cannot shut, all will drop out of it. Take heed of a gluttonous curiosity to feed on many things, lest the greediness of the appetite of thy memory spoil the digestion thereof.
FULLER—*Holy and Profane States.* Bk. III. *Of Memory.*

1
By every remove I only drag a greater length of chain.
GOLDSMITH—*Citizen of the World*. No. 3. See also his *Traveller*.

2
Remembrance wakes with all her busy train,
Swells at my breast, and turns the past to pain.
GOLDSMITH—*Deserted Village*. L. 81.

3
Where'er I roam, whatever realms to see,
My heart untravell'd fondly turns to thee;
Still to my brother turns, with ceaseless pain,
And drags at each remove a lengthening chain.
GOLDSMITH—*Traveller*. L. 7. See also his *Citizen of the World*.

4
A place in thy memory, Dearest!
Is all that I claim:
To pause and look back when thou hearest
The sound of my name.
GERALD GRIFFIN—*A Place in Thy Memory, Dearest*.

5
Fer from eze, fer from herte,
Quoth Hendyng.
HENDYNG—*Proverbs, MSS*. (Circa 1320)
(See also BACON)

6
So may it be: that so dead Yesterday,
No sad-eyed ghost but generous and gay,
May serve you memories like almighty wine,
When you are old.
HENLEY—*When You Are Old*.

7
I remember, I remember,
The house where I was born,
The little window where the sun
Came peeping in at morn;
He never came a wink too soon,
Nor brought too long a day,
But now, I often wish the night
Had borne my breath away!
HOOD—*I Remember, I Remember*.
(See also PRAED)

8
Where is the heart that doth not keep,
Within its inmost core,
Some fond remembrance hidden deep,
Of days that are no more?
ELLEN C. HOWARTH—*'Tis but a Little Faded Flower*.

9
And when he is out of sight, quickly also is he out of mind.
THOS. À KEMPIS—*Imitation of Christ*. Bk. I. Ch. XXIII.
(See also BACON)

10
Badness of memory every one complains of, but nobody of the want of judgment.
LA ROCHEFOUCAULD—*Reflections and Moral Maxims*. No. 463.

11
Tho' lost to sight to mem'ry dear
Thou ever wilt remain.
GEO. LINLEY—*Though Lost to Sight*. First line found as an axiom in *Monthly Magazine*, Jan., 1827. HORACE F. CUTLER published a poem with same refrain, calling himself "Ruthven Jenkyns," crediting its publication in a fictitious magazine, *Greenwich Mag. for Marines*, 1707. (Hoax.) It appeared in MRS. MARY SHERWOOD's novel, *The Nun*. Same idea in POPE—*Epistle to Robert, Earl of Oxford, and Earl Mortimer*.
Though lost to sight to memory dear
The absent claim a sigh, the dead a tear.
SIR DAVID DUNDAS offered 5 shillings during his life (1799–1877) to any one who could produce the origin of this first line. See *Notes and Queries*, Oct. 21, 1916. P. 336.
Dem Augen fern dem Herzen ewig nah'.
On a tomb in Dresden, near that of VON WEBER's. See *Notes and Queries*, March 27, 1909. P. 249.
(See also BACON, RIDER)

12
I recollect a nurse called Ann,
Who carried me about the grass,
And one fine day a fine young man
Came up and kissed the pretty lass.
She did not make the least objection.
Thinks I, "*Aha,*
When I can talk I'll tell Mama,"
And that's my earliest recollection.
FRED. LOCKER-LAMPSON—*A Terrible Infant*.

13
The leaves of memory seemed to make
A mournful rustling in the dark.
LONGFELLOW—*The Fire of Drift-Wood*.

14
The heart hath its own memory, like the mind,
And in it are enshrined
The precious keepsakes, into which is wrought
The giver's loving thought.
LONGFELLOW—*From My Arm-Chair*. St. 12.

15
This memory brightens o'er the past,
As when the sun concealed
Behind some cloud that near us hangs,
Shines on a distant field.
LONGFELLOW—*A Gleam of Sunshine*.

16
There comes to me out of the Past
A voice, whose tones are sweet and wild,
Singing a song almost divine,
And with a tear in every line.
LONGFELLOW—*Tales of a Wayside Inn*. Pt. III. *Interlude before "The Mother's Ghost."*

17
Nothing now is left
But a majestic memory.
LONGFELLOW—*Three Friends of Mine*. L. 10.

18
Wakes the bitter memory
Of what he was, what is, and what must be
Worse.
MILTON—*Paradise Lost*. Bk. IV. L. 24.

19
Il se veoid par expérience, que les mémoires excellentes se joignent volontiers aux jugements débiles.
Experience teaches that a good memory is generally joined to a weak judgment.
MONTAIGNE—*Essays*. I. 9.

20
To live with them is far less sweet
Than to remember thee!
MOORE—*I Saw Thy Form in Youthful Prime*.

1
Oft in the stilly night
E'er slumber's chain has bound me,
Fond memory brings the light
Of other days around me.
MOORE—*Oft in the Stilly Night.*

2
When I remember all
The friends so link'd together,
I've seen around me fall,
Like leaves in wintry weather
I feel like one who treads alone
Some banquet hall deserted,
Whose lights are fled, whose garlands dead,
And all but he departed.
MOORE—*Oft in the Stilly Night.*

3
And the tear that we shed, though in secret it rolls,
Shall long keep his memory green in our souls.
MOORE—*Oh, Breathe not his Name.*
(See also HAMLET)

4
When time who steals our years away
Shall steal our pleasures too,
The mem'ry of the past will stay
And half our joys renew.
MOORE—*Song. From Juvenile Poems.*

5
All to myself I think of you,
Think of the things we used to do,
Think of the things we used to say,
Think of each happy bygone day.
Sometimes I sigh, and sometimes I smile,
But I keep each olden, golden while
All to myself.
WILBUR D. NESBIT—*All to Myself.*

6
Many a man fails to become a thinker for the sole reason that his memory is too good.
NIETZSCHE—*Maxims.*

7
At cum longa dies sedavit vulnera mentis,
Intempestive qui fovet illa novat.
When time has assuaged the wounds of the mind, he who unseasonably reminds us of them, opens them afresh.
OVID—*Epistolæ Ex Ponto.* IV. 11. 19.

8
Impensa monumenti supervacua est: memoria nostra durabit, si vita meruimus.
The erection of a monument is superfluous; the memory of us will last, if we have deserved it in our lives.
PLINY the Younger—*Epistles.* IX. 19.

9
I remember, I remember
How my childhood fleeted by,—
The mirth of its December,
And the warmth of its July.
PRAED—*I Remember, I Remember.*

10
If I do not remember thee, let my tongue cleave to the roof of my mouth.
Psalms. CXXXVII. 6.

11
Tho' lost to sight, within this filial breast
Hendrick still lives in all his might confest.
W. RIDER, in the *London Magazine*, 1755. P. 589. (See also LINLEY)

12
Hail, memory, hail! in thy exhaustless mine
From age to age unnumbered treasures shine!
Thought and her shadowy brood thy call obey,
And Place and Time are subject to thy sway!
SAM'L ROGERS—*Pleasures of Memory.* Pt. II. L. 428.

13
I have a room whereinto no one enters
Save I myself alone:
There sits a blessed memory on a throne,
There my life centres.
CHRISTINA G. ROSSETTI—*Memory.* Pt. II.

14
I wept for memory.
CHRISTINA G. ROSSETTI—*Song. She Sat and Sang Always.*

15
Though varying wishes, hopes, and fears,
Fever'd the progress of these years,
Yet now, days, weeks, and months but seem
The recollection of a dream.
SCOTT—*Marmion. Introduction to* Canto IV.

16
Still so gently o'er me stealing,
Mem'ry will bring back the feeling,
Spite of all my grief revealing
That I love thee,—that I dearly love thee still.
SCRIBE—*Opera of La Sonnambula.*

17
Though yet of Hamlet, our dear brother's death,
The memory be green.
Hamlet. Act I. Sc. 2. L. 1.
(See also MOORE)

18
Remember thee!
Yea, from the table of my memory
I'll wipe away all trivial fond records.
Hamlet. Act I. Sc. 5. L. 97.

19
Die two months ago, and not forgotten yet?
Then there's hope a great man's memory may outlive his life half a year.
Hamlet. Act III. Sc. 2. L. 137.

20
Briefly thyself remember.
King Lear. Act IV. Sc. 6. L. 233.

21
That memory, the warder of the brain,
Shall be a fume.
Macbeth. Act I. Sc. 7. L. 65.

22
I cannot but remember such things were,
That were most precious to me.
Macbeth. Act IV. Sc. 3. L. 222.

23
If a man do not erect in this age his own tomb ere he dies, he shall live no longer in monument than the bell rings, and the widow weeps. * * * An hour in clamour and a quarter in rheum.
Much Ado About Nothing. Act V. Sc. 2. L. 76?

24
I count myself in nothing else so happy
As in a soul rememb'ring my good friends;
And, as my fortune ripens with thy love,
It shall be still thy true love's recompense.
Richard II. Act II. Sc. 3. L. 46.

25
How sharp the point of this remembrance is!
Tempest. Act V. Sc. 1. L. 137.

1 Looking on the lines
Of my boy's face, my thoughts I did recoil
Twenty-three years; and saw myself unbreech'd,
In my green velvet coat, my dagger muzzled,
Lest it should bite its master, and so prove,
As ornaments oft do, too dangerous.
Winter's Tale. Act I. Sc. 2. L. 153.

2
Thou comest as the memory of a dream,
Which now is sad because it hath been sweet.
SHELLEY—*Prometheus Unbound*. Act II. Sc. 1.

3
Heu quanto minus est cum reliquis versari quam tui meminisse.
Ah, how much less all living loves to me,
Than that one rapture of remembering thee.
The Latin is SHENSTONE'S *Epitaph* to the memory of his cousin MARY DOLMAN, on an ornamental Urn. The trans. is by ARTHUR J. MUNBY.

4
The Right Honorable gentleman is indebted to his memory for his jests and to his imagination for his facts.
R. B. SHERIDAN—Attributed to him in report of a *Speech in Reply to Mr. Dundas*. Not found in his works but the idea exists in loose sketches for a comedy.

5
Nobis meminisse relictum.
Left behind as a memory for us.
STATIUS—*Silvæ*. Bk. II. 1. 55.

6 In vain does Memory renew
The hours once tinged in transport's dye:
The sad reverse soon starts to view
And turns the past to agony.
MRS. DUGALD STEWART—*The Tear I Shed*.

7
I shall remember while the light lives yet
And in the night time I shall not forget.
SWINBURNE—*Erotion*.

8
Facetiarum apud præpotentes in longum memoria est.
The powerful hold in deep remembrance an ill-timed pleasantry.
TACITUS—*Annales*. V. 2.

9
The sweet remembrance of the just
Shall flourish when he sleeps in dust.
TATE AND BRADY—*Paraphrase of Psalm CXII*. St. 6.

10
A land of promise, a land of memory,
A land of promise flowing with the milk
And honey of delicious memories!
TENNYSON—*The Lover's Tale*. L. 333.

11
Faciam, hujus loci, dieique, meique semper memineris.
I will make you always remember this place, this day, and me.
TERENCE—*Eunuchus*. V. 7. 31.

12
Memory, in widow's weeds, with naked feet stands on a tombstone.
AUBREY DE VERE—*Widowhood*.

13
Forsan et hæc olim meminisse juvabit.
Perhaps the remembrance of these things will prove a source of future pleasure.
VERGIL—*Æneid*. I. 203.

14
Quique sui memores alios fecere merendo.
These who have ensured their remembrance by their deserts.
VERGIL—*Æneid*. VI. 664.

15
As the dew to the blossom, the bud to the bee,
As the scent to the rose, are those memories to me.
AMELIA B. WELBY—*Pulpit Eloquence*.

16
Out of the cradle endlessly rocking,
Out of the mocking bird's throat, the musical shuttle,
* * * * * *
A reminiscence sing.
WALT WHITMAN—*Sea-Drift*.

17
Ah! memories of sweet summer eves,
Of moonlit wave and willowy way,
Of stars and flowers, and dewy leaves,
And smiles and tones more dear than they!
WHITTIER—*Memories*. St. 4.

18 And when the stream
Which overflowed the soul was passed away,
A consciousness remained that it had left,
Deposited upon the silent shore
Of memory, images and precious thoughts,
That shall not die, and cannot be destroyed.
WORDSWORTH—*Excursion*. Bk. VII.

19
The vapours linger round the Heights,
They melt, and soon must vanish;
One hour is theirs, nor more is mine,—
Sad thought, which I would banish,
But that I know, where'er I go,
Thy genuine image, Yarrow!
Will dwell with me,—to heighten joy,
And cheer my mind in sorrow.
WORDSWORTH—*Yarrow Visited*.

MERCANTILE (See BUSINESS)

MERCY

20
When all thy mercies, O my God,
My rising soul surveys,
Transported with the view I'm lost,
In wonder, love and praise.
ADDISON—*Hymn*.

21
Have mercy upon us miserable sinners.
Book of Common Prayer. *Litany*.

22
Mercy to him that shows it, is the rule.
COWPER—*Task*. Bk. VI. L. 595.

23
And shut the gates of mercy on mankind.
GRAY—*Elegy in a Country Churchyard*. St. 17.

24
A sentinel angel sitting high in glory
Heard this shrill wail ring out from Purgatory:
"Have mercy, mighty angel, hear my story!"
JOHN HAY—*A Woman's Love*.

1
Being all fashioned of the self-same dust,
Let us be merciful as well as just.
LONGFELLOW—*Tales of a Wayside Inn.* Pt. III. *The Student's Tale. Emma and Eginhard.* L. 177.

2
The corn that makes the holy bread
By which the soul of man is fed,
The holy bread, the food unpriced,
Thy everlasting mercy, Christ.
MASEFIELD—*Everlasting Mercy.* St. 88.

3
Mercy stood in the cloud, with eye that wept
Essential love.
POLLOK—*The Course of Time.* Bk. III. L. 658.

4
To hide the fault I see:
That mercy I to others show,
That mercy show to me.
POPE—*Universal Prayer.*

5
'Tis vain to flee; till gentle Mercy show
Her better eye, the farther off we go,
The swing of Justice deals the mightier blow.
QUARLES—*Emblems.* Bk. III. Emblem XVI.

6
Think not the good,
The gentle deeds of mercy thou hast done,
Shall die forgotten all; the poor, the prisoner,
The fatherless, the friendless, and the widow,
Who daily owe the bounty of thy hand,
Shall cry to Heaven, and pull a blessing on thee.
NICHOLAS ROWE—*Jane Shore.* Act I. Sc. 2. L. 173.

7
Mortem misericors sæpe pro vita dabit.
Mercy often inflicts death.
SENECA—*Troades.* 329.

8
Whereto serves mercy,
But to confront the visage of offence?
Hamlet. Act III. Sc. 3. L. 46.

9
You must not dare, for shame, to talk of mercy;
For your own reasons turn into your bosoms,
As dogs upon their masters, worrying you.
Henry V. Act II. Sc. 2. L. 81.

10
Open thy gate of mercy, gracious God!
My soul flies through these wounds to seek out thee.
Henry VI. Pt. III. Act I. Sc. 4. L. 177.

11
Mercy is not itself, that oft looks so;
Pardon is still the nurse of second woe.
Measure for Measure. Act II. Sc. 1. L. 297.

12
The quality of mercy is not strain'd
It droppeth as the gentle rain from heaven
Upon the place beneath: it is twice blest;
It blesseth him that gives and him that takes;
'Tis mightiest in the mightiest; it becomes
The throned monarch better than his crown;
His sceptre shows the force of temporal power,
The attribute to awe and majesty,
Wherein doth sit the dread and fear of kings;
But mercy is above this sceptred sway;
It is enthroned in the hearts of kings,
It is an attribute to God himself;
And earthly power doth then show likest God's
When mercy seasons justice.
Merchant of Venice. Act IV. Sc. 1. L. 184.

13
We do pray for mercy;
And that same prayer doth teach us all to render
The deeds of mercy.
Merchant of Venice. Act IV. Sc. 1. L. 198.

14
Mercy but murders, pardoning those that kill.
Romeo and Juliet. Act III. Sc. 1. L. 202.

15
Who will not mercie unto others show,
How can he mercie ever hope to have?
SPENSER—*Faerie Queene.* Bk. VI. Canto I. St. 42.

16
Pulchrum est vitam donare minori.
It is noble to grant life to the vanquished.
STATIUS—*Thebais.* VI. 816.

17
Sweet Mercy! to the gates of Heaven
This Minstrel lead, his sins forgiven;
The rueful conflict, the heart riven
With vain endeavour,
And memory of earth's bitter leaven
Effaced forever.
WORDSWORTH—*Thoughts Suggested on the Banks of the Nith.*

MERIT (See also WORTH)

18
Thy father's merit sets thee up to view,
And shows thee in the fairest point of light,
To make thy virtues, or thy faults, conspicuous.
ADDISON—*Cato.* Act I. Sc. 2.

19
View the whole scene, with critic judgment scan,
And then deny him merit if you can.
Where he falls short, 'tis Nature's fault alone
Where he succeeds, the merit's all his own.
CHURCHILL—*Rosciad.* L. 1,023.

20
It sounds like stories from the land of spirits,
If any man obtain that which he merits,
Or any merit that which he obtains.
COLERIDGE—*Complaint.*

21
On their own merits modest men are dumb.
GEORGE COLMAN (The Younger)—*Epilogue to The Heir-at-Law.*

22
La faveur des princes n'exclut pas le mérite, et ne le suppose pas aussi.
The favor of princes does not preclude the existence of merit, and yet does not prove that it exists.
LA BRUYÈRE—*Les Caractères.* XII.

23
Du même fonds dont on néglige un homme de mérite l'on sait encore admirer un sot.
The same principle leads us to neglect a man of merit that induces us to admire a fool.
LA BRUYÈRE—*Les Caractères.* XII.

24
Le monde récompense plus souvent les apparences de mérite que le mérite même.
The world rewards the appearance of merit oftener than merit itself.
LA ROCHEFOUCAULD—*Maximes.* 166.

1
Le mérite des hommes a sa saison aussi bien que les fruits.

There is a season for man's merit as well as for fruit.

LA ROCHEFOUCAULD—*Maximes*. 291.

2
Il y a du mérite sans élévation mais il n'y a point d'élévation sans quelque mérite.

There is merit without elevation, but there is no elevation without some merit.

LA ROCHEFOUCAULD—*Maximes*. 401.

3
By merit raised
To that bad eminence.

MILTON—*Paradise Lost*. Bk. II. L. 5.

4
Virtute ambire oportet, non favitoribus.
Sat habet favitorum semper, qui recte facit.

We should try to succeed by merit, not by favor. He who does well will always have patrons enough.

PLAUTUS—*Amphitruo*. *Prologue*. LXXVIII.

5
The sufficiency of merit is to know that my merit is not sufficient.

QUARLES—*Emblems*. Bk. II. Em. I.

6
The spurns
That patient merit of the unworthy takes.

Hamlet. Act III. Sc. 1. L. 73.

7
The force of his own merit makes his way.

Henry VIII. Act I. Sc. 1. L 64.

MERMAIDS

8
O, train me not, sweet mermaid, with thy note,
To drown me in thy sister's flood of tears.

Comedy of Errors. Act III. Sc. 2. L. 45.

9
Since once I sat upon a promontory,
And heard a mermaid on a dolphin's back
Uttering such dulcet and harmonious breath,
That the rude sea grew civil at her song:
And certain stars shot madly from their spheres,
To hear the sea-maid's music.

Midsummer Night's Dream. Act II. Sc. 1. L. 149.

10
Who would be
A mermaid fair,
Singing alone,
Combing her hair
Under the sea,
In a golden curl
With a comb of pearl,
On a throne?
I would be a mermaid fair;
I would sing to myself the whole of the day;
With a comb of pearl I would comb my hair;
And still as I comb I would sing and say,
"Who is it loves me? who loves not me?"

TENNYSON—*The Mermaid*.

11
Slow sail'd the weary mariners and saw,
Betwixt the green brink and the running foam,
Sweet faces, rounded arms, and bosoms prest
To little harps of gold; and while they mused
Whispering to each other half in fear,
Shrill music reach'd them on the middle sea.

TENNYSON—*The Sea Fairies*.

MERRIMENT

12
An ounce of mirth is worth a pound of sorrow.

BAXTER—*Self Denial*.

13
As Tammie glow'red, amazed and curious,
The mirth and fun grew fast and furious.

BURNS—*Tam o' Shanter*.

14
Go then merrily to Heaven.

BURTON—*Anatomy of Melancholy* Pt. II. Sec. 3. Memb. 1.

15
Plus on est de fous, plus on rit.

The more fools the more one laughs.

DANCOURT—*Maison de Campagne*. Sc. 11.
(See also GASCOIGNE)

16
Some credit in being jolly.

DICKENS—*Martin Chuzzlewit*. Ch. V.

17
A very merry, dancing, drinking,
Laughing, quaffing, and unthinking time.

DRYDEN—*The Secular Masque*. L. 40.

18
And mo the merier is a Prouerbe eke.

GASCOIGNE—*Works*. Ed. by Hazlitt. I. 64.
(The more the merrier.)
HEYWOOD—*Proverbes*. Pt. II. Ch. VII.
BEAUMONT AND FLETCHER—*Scornful Lady*. I. 1. HENRY PARROTT—*The Sea Voyage*. I. 2. Given credit in BRYDGES—*Censura Literaria*. Vol. III. P. 337. KING JAMES I., according to the *Westminster Gazette*.
(See also DANCOURT)

19
Ride si sapis.

Be merry if you are wise.

MARTIAL—*Epigrams*. II. 41. 1.

20
Mirth, admit me of thy crew,
To live with her, and live with thee,
In unreprov'd pleasures free.

MILTON—*L'Allegro*. L. 38.

21
A merry heart doeth good like a medicine.

Proverbs. XVII. 22.

22
Forward and frolic glee was there,
The will to do, the soul to dare.

SCOTT—*Lady of the Lake*. Canto I. St. 21.

23
What should a man do but be merry?

Hamlet. Act III. Sc. 2. L. 131.

24
Hostess, clap to the doors; watch to-night, pray to-morrow. Gallants, lads, boys, hearts of gold, all the titles of good fellowship come to you! What, shall we be merry? Shall we have a play extempore?

Henry IV. Pt. I. Act II. Sc. 4. L. 305.

25
As 'tis ever common
That men are merriest when they are from home.

Henry V. Act I. Sc. 2. L. 271.

26
And, if you can be merry then, I'll say
A man may weep upon his wedding day.

Henry VIII. *Prologue*. L. 31.

27
But a merrier man,
Within the limit of becoming mirth,
I never spent an hour's talk withal.

Love's Labour's Lost. Act II. Sc. 1. L. 66.

1
Mirth cannot move a soul in agony.
Love's Labour's Lost. Act V. Sc. 2. L. 867.

2
Be large in mirth; anon we'll drink a measure
The table round.
Macbeth. Act III. Sc. 4. L. 11.

3
With mirth and laughter let old wrinkles come,
And let my liver rather heat with wine
Than my heart cool with mortifying groans.
Merchant of Venice. Act I. Sc. 1. L. 80.

4
As merry as the day is long.
Much Ado About Nothing. Act II. Sc. 1. L. 45.

5
You have a merry heart.
Yea, my lord; I thank it, poor fool, it keeps on the windy side of care.
Much Ado About Nothing. Act II. Sc. 1. L. 323.

6
Your silence most offends me, and to be merry best becomes you; for out of question, you were born in a merry hour.
No, sure, my lord, my mother cried; but then there was a star danced, and under that I was born.
Much Ado About Nothing. Act II. Sc. 1. L. 345.

7
I am not merry; but I do beguile
The thing I am by seeming otherwise.
Othello. Act II. Sc. 1. L. 123.

8
And frame your mind to mirth and merriment,
Which bars a thousand harms and lengthens life.
Taming of the Shrew. Induction. Sc. 2. L. 137.

9
Merrily, merrily, shall I live now
Under the blossom that hangs on the bough.
Tempest. Act V. Sc. 1. L. 93.

10
When every room
Hath blaz'd with lights and brayed with minstrelsy.
Timon of Athens. Act II. Sc. 2. L. 169.

11
Jog on, jog on, the foot-path way,
And merrily hent the stile-a:
A merry heart goes all the day,
Your sad tires in a mile-a.
Winter's Tale. Act IV. Sc. 3. L. 132.

12
And let's be red with mirth.
Winter's Tale. Act IV. Sc. 4. L. 54.

13
The glad circle round them yield their souls
To festive mirth, and wit that knows no gall.
THOMSON—*The Seasons. Summer.* L. 403.

14
'Tis merry in hall
Where beards wag all.
TUSSER—*Five Hundred Points of Good Husbandry. August's Abstract.* ADAM DAVIE—*Life of Alexander.* (About 1312) In WARTON'S—*History of English Poetry.* Vol. II. P. 10. Quoted by BEN JONSON—*Masque of Christmas.*

MIDGE

15
Meanwhile, there is dancing in yonder green bower,
A swarm of young midges, they dance high and low;
'Tis a sweet little species that lives but one hour,
And the eldest was born half an hour ago.
OWEN MEREDITH (Lord Lytton)—*Midges.*

16
The midge's wing beats to and fro
A thousand times ere one can utter "O."
COVENTRY PATMORE—*The Cry at Midnight.*

MIDNIGHT

17
Is there not
A tongue in every star that talks with man,
And wooes him to be wise? nor wooes in vain;
This dead of midnight is the noon of thought,
And wisdom mounts her zenith with the stars.
ANNA LETITIA BARBAULD—*A Summer Evening's Meditation.* L. 48.

18
That hour o' night's black arch the keystane.
BURNS—*Tam o' Shanter.*

19
It was evening here,
But upon earth the very noon of night.
DANTE—*Purgatorio.* Canto XV. L. 5.

20
I stood on the bridge at midnight,
As the clocks were striking the hour,
And the moon rose over the city,
Behind the dark church tower.
LONGFELLOW—*Bridge.*

21
Midnight! the outpost of advancing day!
The frontier town and citadel of night!
LONGFELLOW—*Two Rivers.* Pt. I.

22
O wild and wondrous midnight,
There is a might in thee
To make the charmed body
Almost like spirit be,
And give it some faint glimpses
Of immortality!
LOWELL—*Midnight.*

23
'Tis midnight now. The bent and broken moon,
Batter'd and black, as from a thousand battles,
Hangs silent on the purple walls of Heaven.
JOAQUIN MILLER—*Ina.* Sc. 2.

24
Soon as midnight brought on the dusky hour
Friendliest to sleep and silence.
MILTON—*Paradise Lost.* Bk. V. L. 667.

25
The iron tongue of midnight hath told twelve;
Lovers, to bed; 'tis almost fairy time.
Midsummer Night's Dream. Act V. Sc. 1. L. 370.

26
Midnight, yet not a nose
From Tower Hill to Piccadilly snored!
HORACE AND JAMES SMITH—*Rejected Addresses. The Rebuilding.* (*Imitation of Southey.*)

27
Midnight, and yet no eye
Through all the Imperial City closed in sleep.
SOUTHEY—*Curse of Kehama.* Pt. I. 1.

MILITARY (See NAVY, SOLDIERS, WAR)

MIND

1
I had rather believe all the fables in the Legends and the Talmud and the Alcoran, than that this universal frame is without a mind.
BACON—*Essays. Of Atheism.*

2
That last infirmity of noble mind.
The Tragedy of SIR JOHN VAN OLDEN BARNEVELT. (1622)
(See also MILTON under FAME)

3
All the choir of heaven and furniture of earth—in a word, all those bodies which compose the mighty frame of the world—have not any subsistence without a mind.
GEORGE BERKELEY (Bishop of Cloyne)—*Principles of Human Knowledge.*
(See also EDDY)

4
Measure your mind's height by the shade it casts.
ROBERT BROWNING—*Paracelsus.* II.

5
The march of the human mind is slow.
BURKE—*Speech on the Conciliation of America.*

6
Such as take lodgings in a head
That's to be let unfurnished.
BUTLER—*Hudibras.* Pt. I. Canto I. L. 161.

7
I love my neighbor as myself,
Myself like him too, by his leave,
Nor to his pleasure, power or pelf
Came I to crouch, as I conceive.
Dame Nature doubtless has designed
A man the monarch of his mind.
JOHN BYROM—*Careless Content.*
(See also HENLEY under SOUL)

8
When Bishop Berkeley said "there was no matter,"
And proved it,—'Twas no matter what he said.
BYRON—*Don Juan.* Canto IX. St. 1. Allusion to a dissertation by BERKELEY on Mind and Matter, found in a note by DR. HAWKESWORTH to SWIFT's *Letters*, pub. 1769.
(See also KEY; also UNBELIEVER'S CREED under GOD)

9
'Tis strange the mind, that very fiery particle,
Should let itself be snuff'd out by an article.
BYRON—*Don Juan.* Canto XI. St. 60.

10
Constant attention wears the active mind,
Blots out our pow'rs, and leaves a blank behind.
CHURCHILL—*Epistle to Hogarth.* L. 647.

11
Animi cultus quasi quidam humanitatis cibus.
The cultivation of the mind is a kind of food supplied for the soul of man.
CICERO—*De Finibus Bonorum et Malorum.* V. 19.

12
Frons est animi janua.
The forehead is the gate of the mind.
CICERO—*Oratio De Provinciis Consularibus.* XI.

13
Morbi perniciores pluresque animi quam corporis.
The diseases of the mind are more and more destructive than those of the body.
CICERO—*Tusculanarum Disputationum.* III. 3.

14
In animo perturbato, sicut in corpore, sanitas esse non potest.
In a disturbed mind, as in a body in the same state, health can not exist.
CICERO—*Tusculanarum Disputationum.* III. 4. (See also EDDY)

15
Absence of occupation is not rest,
A mind quite vacant is a mind distress'd.
COWPER—*Retirement.*

16
His mind his kingdom, and his will his law.
COWPER—*Truth.* Line 405.
(See also DYER)

17
How fleet is a glance of the mind!
Compared with the speed of its flight,
The tempest itself lags behind,
And the swift-winged arrows of light.
COWPER—*Verses supposed to be written by Alexander Selkirk.*

18
Nature's first great title—mind.
GEORGE CROLY—*Pericles and Aspasia.*

19
As that the walls worn thin, permit the mind
To look out through, and his Frailty find.
SAMUEL DANIEL—*History of the Civil War.* Bk. IV. St. 84.
(See also HENRY IV., WALLER)

20
Babylon in all its desolation is a sight not so awful as that of the human mind in ruins.
SCROPE DAVIES—*Letter to Thomas Raikes.* May 25, 1835.

21
My mynde to me a kingdome is
Such preasent joyes therein I fynde
That it excells all other blisse
That earth afforde or growes by kynde
Though muche I wante which moste would have
Yet still my mynde forbiddes to crave.
EDWARD DYER—*Rawlinson MSS.* 85. P. 17. (In the Bodleian Library at Oxford.) Words changed by Byrd when he set it to music. Quoted by BEN JONSON—*Every Man out of his Humour.* I. 1. Found in PERCY's *Reliques.* Series I. Bk. III. No. V. And in J. SYLVESTER's *Works.* P. 651.

22
My minde to me a kingdome is,
Such perfect joy therein I finde
As farre exceeds all earthly blisse
That God or Nature hath assignde
Though much I want that most would have
Yet still my minde forbids to crave.
WM. BYRD's rendering of DYER's verse, when he set it to music. See his *Psalmen, Sonets and Songs made into Musicke.* Printed by THOMAS EAST. (No date. Later edition, 1588)

23
God is Mind, and God is All; hence all is Mind.
MARY B. G. EDDY—*Science and Health*, 492: 25. (See also SENNAZARO)

1
A great mind is a good sailor, as a great heart is.
EMERSON—*English Traits. Voyage to England.* Ch. II.

2
Each mind has its own method.
EMERSON—*Essays. Intellect.*

3
Wer fertig ist, dem ist nichts recht zu machen,
Ein Werdender wird immer dankbar sein.
A mind, once formed, is never suited after,
One yet in growth will ever grateful be.
GOETHE—*Faust. Vorspiel auf dem Theater.* L. 150.

4
Vain, very vain, my weary search to find
That bliss which only centers in the mind.
GOLDSMITH—*Traveler.* L. 423.

5
A noble mind disdains to hide his head,
And let his foes triumph in his overthrow.
ROBERT GREENE—*Alphonso, King of Arragon.* Act I.

6
The mind is like a sheet of white paper in this, that the impressions it receives the oftenest, and retains the longest, are black ones.
J. C. AND A. W. HARE—*Guesses at Truth.*

7
Lumen siccum optima anima.
The most perfect mind is a dry light.
The "obscure saying" of HERACLITUS, quoted by BACON, who explains it as a mind not "steeped and infused in the humors of the affections."

8
Whose little body lodged a mighty mind.
HOMER—*Iliad.* Bk. V. L. 999. POPE'S trans.

9
A faultless body and a blameless mind.
HOMER—*Odyssey.* Bk. III. L. 138. POPE'S trans.

10
The glory of a firm capacious mind.
HOMER—*Odyssey.* Bk. IV. L. 262. POPE'S trans.

11
And bear unmov'd the wrongs of base mankind,
The last, and hardest, conquest of the mind.
HOMER—*Odyssey.* Bk. XIII. L. 353. POPE'S trans.

12
Sperat infestis, metuit secundis
Alteram sortem, bene preparatum
Pectus.
A well-prepared mind hopes in adversity and fears in prosperity.
HORACE—*Carmina.* II. 10. 13.

13
Quæ lædunt oculum festinas demere; si quid
Est animum, differs curandi tempus in annum.
If anything affects your eye, you hasten to have it removed; if anything affects your mind, you postpone the cure for a year.
HORACE—*Epistles.* I. 238.

14
Acclinis falsis animus meliora recusat.
A mind that is charmed by false appearances refuses better things.
HORACE—*Satires.* II. 2. 6.

15
Quin corpus onustum
Hesternis vitiis, animum quoque prægravat una
Atque affigit humo divinæ particulam auræ.
The body loaded by the excess of yesterday, depresses the mind also, and fixes to the ground this particle of divine breath.
HORACE—*Satires.* II. 2. 77.

16
The true, strong, and sound mind is the mind that can embrace equally great things and small.
SAMUEL JOHNSON—*Boswell's Life of Johnson.* (1778)

17
What is mind? No matter. What is matter? Never mind.
T. H. KEY, once Head Master of University School—On the authority of F. J. FURNIVALL. (See also BYRON)

18
Seven Watchmen sitting in a tower,
Watching what had come upon Mankind,
Showed the Man the Glory and the Power
And bade him shape the Kingdom to his mind.
. . . . . .
That a man's mind is wont to tell him more
Than Seven Watchmen sitting in a tower
KIPLING—*Dedication to Seven Watchmen.*

19
La gravité est un mystère du corps inventé pour cacher les défauts de l'esprit.
Gravity is a mystery of the body invented to conceal the defects of the mind.
LA ROCHEFOUCAULD—*Maximes.* 257.

20
Nobody, I believe, will deny, that we are to form our judgment of the true nature of the human mind, not from sloth and stupidity of the most degenerate and vilest of men, but from the sentiments and fervent desires of the best and wisest of the species.
ARCHBISHOP LEIGHTON—*Theological Lectures.* No. 5. *Of the Immortality of the Soul.*

21
Stern men with empires in their brains.
LOWELL—*The Biglow Papers. Second Series.* No. 2.

22
O miseras hominum menteis! oh, pectora cæca!
How wretched are the minds of men, and how blind their understandings.
LUCRETIUS—*De Rerum Natura.* II. 14.

23
Cum corpore ut una
Crescere sentimus pariterque senescere mentem.
We plainly perceive that the mind strengthens and decays with the body.
LUCRETIUS—*De Rerum Natura.* III. 446.

24
The conformation of his mind was such, that whatever was little seemed to him great, and whatever was great seemed to him little.
MACAULAY—*On Horace Walpole.*

25
Rationi nulla resistunt.
Claustra nec immensæ moles, ceduntque recessus:
Omnia succumbunt, ipsum est penetrabile cœlum.
No barriers, no masses of matter, however enormous, can withstand the powers of the

mind the remotest corners yield to them; all things succumb, the very heaven itself is laid open.
MANILIUS—*Astronomica*. I. 541.

1
Clothed, and in his right mind.
Mark. V. 15; *Luke*. VIII. 35.

2
The social states of human kinds
Are made by multitudes of minds,
And after multitudes of years
A little human growth appears
Worth having, even to the soul
Who sees most plain it's not the whole.
MASEFIELD—*Everlasting Mercy*. St. 60.

3
The mind is its own place, and in itself
Can make a heaven of hell, a hell of heaven.
MILTON—*Paradise Lost*. Bk. I. L. 254.

4
Mensque pati durum sustinet ægra nihil.
The sick mind can not bear anything harsh.
OVID—*Epistolæ Ex Ponto*. I. 5. 18.

5
Mens sola loco non exulat.
The mind alone can not be exiled.
OVID—*Epistolæ Ex Ponto*. IV. 9. 41.

6
Conscia mens recti famæ mendacia risit.
A mind conscious of right laughs at the falsehoods of rumour.
OVID—*Fasti*. Bk. IV. 311.

7
Pro superi! quantum mortalia pectora cæcæ,
Noctis habent.
Heavens! what thick darkness pervades the minds of men.
OVID—*Metamorphoses*. VI. 472.

8
It is the mind that makes the man, and our vigour is in our immortal soul.
OVID—*Metamorphoses*. XIII.
(See also EDDY, SENECA)

9
Corpore sed mens est ægro magis ægra; malique
In circumspectu stat sine fine sui.
The mind is sicker than the sick body; in contemplation of its sufferings it becomes hopeless.
OVID—*Tristium*. IV. 6. 43.

10
Be ye all of one mind.
I Peter. III. 8.

11
Animus quod perdidit optat,
Atque in præterita se totus imagine versat.
The mind wishes for what it has missed, and occupies itself with retrospective contemplation.
PETRONIUS ARBITER—*Satyricon*.

12
Habet cerebrum sensus arcem; hic mentis est regimen.
The brain is the citadel of the senses: this guides the principle of thought.
PLINY the Elder—*Historia Naturalis*. XI. 49. 2.

13
Strength of mind is exercise, not rest.
POPE—*Essay on Man*. Ep. II. L. 104.

14
Love, Hope, and Joy, fair pleasure's smiling train,
Hate, Fear, and Grief, the family of pain,
These mix'd with art, and to due bounds confin'd
Make and maintain the balance of the mind.
POPE—*Essay on Man*. Ep. II. L. 117.

15
My mind's my kingdom.
QUARLES—*School of the Heart*. Ode IV. St. 3.
(See also DYER)

16
Mens mutatione recreabitur; sicut in cibis, quorum diversitate reficitur stomachus, et pluribus minore fastidio alitur.
Our minds are like our stomachs; they are whetted by the change of their food, and variety supplies both with fresh appetite.
QUINTILIAN—*De Institutione Oratoria*. I. 11. 1.

17
Whose cockloft is unfurnished.
RABELAIS—*The Author's Prologue to the Fifth Book*.

18
Let every man be fully persuaded in his own mind.
Romans. XIV. 5.

19
Un corps débile affoiblit l'âme.
A feeble body weakens the mind.
ROUSSEAU—*Émile*. I.

20
Tanto è miser l'uom quant' ei si riputa.
Man is only miserable so far as he thinks himself so.
SANNAZARO—*Ecloga Octava*.
(See also EDDY)

21
Magnam fortunam magnus animus decet.
A great mind becomes a great fortune.
SENECA—*De Clementia*. I. 5.

22
Valentior omni fortuna animus est: in utramque partem ipse res suas ducit, beatæque miseræ vitæ sibi causa est.
The mind is the master over every kind of fortune: itself acts in both ways, being the cause of its own happiness and misery.
SENECA—*Epistolæ Ad Lucilium*. XCVIII.

23
For I do not distinguish them by the eye, but by the mind, which is the proper judge of the man.
SENECA—*Of a Happy Life*. Ch. I. (*L'Estrange's Abstract.*)
(See also OVID)

24
Mens bona regnum possidet.
A good mind possesses a kingdom.
SENECA—*Thyestes*. Act II. 380.

25
O, what a noble mind is here o'erthrown!
The courtier's, soldier's, scholar's, eye, tongue, sword!
Hamlet. Act III. Sc. 1. L. 158.

26
The incessant care and labour of his mind
Hath wrought the mure that should confine it in
So thin that life looks through and will break out.
Henry IV. Pt. II. Act IV. Sc. 4. L. 118.

1
And when the mind is quicken'd, out of doubt,
The organs, though defunct and dead before,
Break up their drowsy grave and newly move
With casted slough and fresh legerity.
Henry V. Act IV. Sc. 1. L. 20.

2
'Tis but a base, ignoble mind
That mounts no higher than a bird can soar.
Henry VI. Pt. II. Act II. Sc. 1. L. 13.

3
For 'tis the mind that makes the body rich.
Taming of the Shrew. Act IV. Sc. 3. L. 174.

4
'Tis pity bounty had not eyes behind,
That man might ne'er be wretched for his mind.
Timon of Athens. Act I. Sc. 2. L. 170.

5
Now, the melancholy god protect thee; and the tailor make thy doublet of changeable taffeta, for thy mind is a very opal.
Twelfth Night. Act II. Sc. 4. L. 74.

6
Not body enough to cover his mind decently with; his intellect is improperly exposed.
SYDNEY SMITH—*Lady Holland's Memoir*. Vol. I. P. 258.

7
I feel no care of coin;
Well-doing is my wealth;
My mind to me an empire is,
While grace affordeth health.
ROBT. SOUTHWELL—*Content and Rich*. (*Look Home*) (See also DYER)

8
Man's mind a mirror is of heavenly sights,
A brief wherein all marvels summèd lie,
Of fairest forms and sweetest shapes the store,
Most graceful all, yet thought may grace them more.
ROBT. SOUTHWELL—*Content and Rich*. (*Look Home*.)

9
A flower more sacred than far-seen success
Perfumes my solitary path; I find
Sweet compensation in my humbleness,
And reap the harvest of a quiet mind.
TROWBRIDGE—*Twoscore and Ten*. St. 28.

10
Mens sibi conscia recti.
A mind conscious of its own rectitude.
VERGIL—*Æneid*. I. 604.

11
Mens agitat molem.
Mind moves matter.
VERGIL—*Æneid*. VI. 727.

12
Nescia mens hominum fati sortisque futuræ,
Et servare modum, rebus sublata secundis.
The mind of man is ignorant of fate and future destiny, and can not keep within due bounds when elated by prosperity.
VERGIL—*Æneid*. X. 501.

13
The soul's dark cottage, batter'd and decay'd,
Lets in new light through chinks that Time has made.
WALLER—*Verses upon his Divine Poesy*.
Compare LONGINUS—*De Sub*. Sect. XXII.
(See also DANIELS, also POPE under CRITICISM)

14
Mind is the great lever of all things; human thought is the process by which human ends are alternately answered.
DANIEL WEBSTER—*Address at the Laying of the Corner Stone of the Bunker Hill Monument*.

15
You will turn it over once more in what you are pleased to call your mind.
LORD WESTBURY, to a solicitor. See NASH—*Life of Lord Westbury*. Vol. II. P. 292.

16
A man of hope and forward-looking mind.
WORDSWORTH—*Excursion*. Bk. VII. 278.

17
In years that bring the philosophic mind.
WORDSWORTH—*Ode. Intimations of Immortality*. St. 10.

18
Minds that have nothing to confer
Find little to perceive.
WORDSWORTH—*Yes! Thou Art Fair*.

MIRACLE

19
Every believer is God's miracle.
BAILEY—*Festus*. Sc. *Home*.
(See also INGELOW)

20
Thou water turn'st to wine, fair friend of life;
Thy foe, to cross the sweet arts of Thy reign,
Distils from thence the tears of wrath and strife,
And so turns wine to water back again.
CRASHAW—*Steps to the Temple. To Our Lord upon the Water Made Wine*.

21
When Christ at Cana's feast by pow'r divine,
Inspir'd cold water, with the warmth of wine,
See! cry'd they while, in red'ning tide, it gush'd,
The bashful stream hath seen its God and blush'd.
AARON HILL—*Translation of Crashaw's Latin lines. Works*. Vol. III. O. 241. (Ed. 1754)
See also VIDA—*Christiad*. Bk. III. 9984, and Bk. II. 431. Also *Hymn* of ANDREW—*Vel Hydriis plenis Æqua*.
(See also SEDULIUS)

22
Man is the miracle in nature. God
Is the One Miracle to man. Behold,
"There is a God," thou sayest. Thou sayest well:
In that thou sayest all. To Be is more
Of wonderful, than being, to have wrought,
Or reigned, or rested.
JEAN INGELOW—*Story of Doom*. Bk. VII. L. 271. (See also BAILEY)

23
Accept a miracle; instead of wit,—
See two dull lines by Stanhope's pencil writ.
POPE to LORD CHESTERFIELD on using his pencil, according to JOHN TAYLOR—*Records of My Life*. I. 161, and GOLDSMITH—In NEWBERY'S *Art of Poetry on a New Plan*. Vol. I. 57. (1762)

24
The water owns a power Divine,
And conscious blushes into wine;
Its very nature changed displays
The power Divine that it obeys.
SEDULIUS ("SCOTUS HYBERNICUS"). Hymn

written in Fifth century. *A solis ortus cardine.* Found in *Lyra Hibernica Sacra.* English trans. by CANON MACILWAINE, editor of the *Lyra.*

(See also HILL)

1 Great floods have flown
From simple sources, and great seas have dried
When miracles have by the greatest been denied.

All's Well That Ends Well. Act II. Sc. 1. L. 142.

2
It must be so; for miracles are ceased
And therefore we must needs admit the means
How things are perfected.

Henry V. Act I. Sc. 1. L. 67.

3
What is a miracle?—'Tis a reproach,
'Tis an implicit satire on mankind;
And while it satisfies, it censures too.

YOUNG—*Night Thoughts.* Night IX. L. 1,245

MISCHIEF

4
In life it is difficult to say who do you the most mischief, enemies with the worst intentions, or friends with the best.

BULWER-LYTTON—*What Will He Do With It?* Bk. III. Heading to Ch. XVII.

5
What plaguy mischief and mishaps
Do dog him still with after claps!

BUTLER—*Hudibras.* Pt. I. Canto III. L. 3.

6 Let them call it mischief:
When it is past and prospered 'twill be virtue.

BEN JONSON—*Catiline.* Act III. Sc. 3.

7
When to mischief mortals bend their will,
How soon they find it instruments of ill.

POPE—*Rape of the Lock.* Canto III. St. 125.

8
Now let it work: Mischief, thou art afoot,
Take thou what course thou wilt.

Julius Cæsar. Act III. Sc. 2. L. 265.

9
To mourn a mischief that is past and gone
Is the next way to draw new mischief on.

Othello. Act I. Sc. 3. L. 204.

10 O mischief, thou art swift
To enter in the thoughts of desperate men!

Romeo and Juliet. Act V. Sc. 1. L. 35.

MISERS (See also AVARICE)

11
And were it not that they are loath to lay out money on a rope, they would be hanged forthwith, and sometimes die to save charges.

BURTON—*Anatomy of Melancholy.* Pt. I. Sec. II. Memb. 3. Subsec. 12.

12
A mere madness, to live like a wretch, and die rich.

BURTON—*Anatomy of Melancholy.* Pt. I. Sec. II. Memb. 3. Subsec. 13.

13
If I knew a miser, who gave up every kind of comfortable living, all the pleasure of doing good to others, all the esteem of his fellow-citizens, and the joys of benevolent friendship, for the sake of accumulating wealth, Poor man, said I, you pay too much for your whistle.

BENJ. FRANKLIN—*The Whistle.*

14
Hoards after hoards his rising raptures fill;
Yet still he sighs, for hoards are wanting still.

GOLDSMITH—*The Traveller.*

15
Quærit, et inventis miser abstinet, ac timet uti.

The miser acquires, yet fears to use his gains.

HORACE—*Ars Poetica.* 170.

16
The unsunn'd heaps
Of miser's treasures.

MILTON—*Comus.* L. 398.

17
Abiturus illuc priores abierunt,
Quid mente cæca torques spiritum?
Tibi dico, avare.

Since you go where all have gone before, why do you torment your disgraceful life with such mean ambitions, O miser?

PHÆDRUS—*Fables.* IV. 19. 16.

18
He sat among his bags, and, with a look
Which hell might be ashamed of, drove the poor
Away unalmsed; and midst abundance died—
Sorest of evils!—died of utter want.

POLLOK—*Course of Time.* Bk. III. L. 276.

19
'Tis strange the miser should his cares employ
To gain those riches he can ne'er enjoy;
Is it less strange the prodigal should waste
His wealth to purchase what he ne'er can taste?

POPE—*Moral Essays.* Ep. IV. L. 1.

20
Decrepit miser; base, ignoble wretch;
I am descended of a gentler blood.

Henry VI. Pt. I. Act V. Sc. 4. L. 7.

21
Tam deest avaro quod habet, quam quod non habet.

The miser is as much in want of what he has, as of what he has not.

SYRUS—*Maxims.*

MISERY (See also SORROW, WOE)

22
Levis est consolatio ex miseria aliorum.

The comfort derived from the misery of others is slight.

CICERO—*Epistles.* VI. 3.

23
Horatio looked handsomely miserable, like Hamlet slipping on a piece of orange-peel.

DICKENS—*Sketches by Boz. Horatio Sparkins.* (Omitted in some editions)

24 The worst of misery
Is when a nature framed for noblest things
Condemns itself in youth to petty joys,
And, sore athirst for air, breathes scanty life
Gasping from out the shallows.

GEORGE ELIOT—*The Spanish Gypsy.* Bk. III.

25
Grim-visaged, comfortless despair.

GRAY—*Ode on Eton College.*

(See also COMEDY OF ERRORS)

1
There are a good many real miseries in life that we cannot help smiling at, but they are the smiles that make wrinkles and not dimples.
HOLMES—*The Poet at the Breakfast Table.* III.

2
This, this is misery! the last, the worst,
That man can feel.
HOMER—*Iliad.* Bk. XXII. L. 106. POPE'S trans.

3
That to live by one man's will became the cause of all men's misery.
RICHARD HOOKER—*Ecclesiastical Polity.* Bk. I. Ch. X. 5.

4
Il ne se faut jamais moquer des misérables,
Car qui peut s'assurer d'être toujours heureux?
We ought never to scoff at the wretched, for who can be sure of continued happiness?
LA FONTAINE—*Fables.* V. 17.

5
The child of misery, baptized in tears!
J. LANGHORNE—*The Country Justice.* Pt. I. L. 166.

6 But O yet more miserable!
Myself my sepulchre, a moving grave.
MILTON—*Samson Agonistes.* L. 101.

7
And bear about the mockery of woe
To midnight dances and the public show.
POPE—*To the Memory of an Unfortunate Lady.* L. 57.

8
Frei geht das Unglück durch die ganze Erde!
Misery travels free through the whole world!
SCHILLER—*Wallenstein's Tod.* IV. 11. 31.

9
Ignis aurum probat, misera fortes viros.
Fire tries gold, misery tries brave men.
SENECA—*De Providentia.* V.

10 Miserias properant suas
Audire miseri.
The wretched hasten to hear of their own miseries.
SENECA—*Hercules Œtæus.* 754.

11
Grim and comfortless despair.
Comedy of Errors. V. I. 80.
(See also GRAY)

12
Misery makes sport to mock itself.
Richard II. Act II. Sc. 1. L. 85.

13 Meagre were his looks,
Sharp misery had worn him to the bones.
Romeo and Juliet. Act V. Sc. 1. L. 40.

14
Misery acquaints a man with strange bedfellows.
Tempest. Act II. Sc. 2. L. 40.

15
Quæque ipse misserrima vidi, et quorum pars magna fui.
All of which misery I saw, part of which I was.
VERGIL—*Æneid.* L. 5.

MISFORTUNE

16
It is the nature of mortals to kick a fallen man.
ÆSCHYLUS—*Agamemnon.* 884. (Adapted.)

17
Calamity is man's true touch-stone.
BEAUMONT AND FLETCHER—*Four Plays in One. The Triumph of Honour.* Sc. 1. L. 67.

18
Conscientia rectæ voluntatis maxima consolatio est rerum incommodarum.
The consciousness of good intention is the greatest solace of misfortunes.
CICERO—*Epistles.* V. 4.

19
He went like one that hath been stunn'd,
And is of sense forlorn:
A sadder and a wiser man,
He rose the morrow morn.
COLERIDGE — *Ancient Mariner.* Pt. VII. Last Stanza.

20
Most of our misfortunes are more supportable than the comments of our friends upon them.
C. C. COLTON—*Lacon.* P. 238.

21
A raconter ses maux souvent on les soulage.
By speaking of our misfortunes we often relieve them.
CORNEILLE—*Polyeucte.* I. 3.

22
I was a stricken deer that left the herd
Long since.
COWPER—*The Task.* Bk. III. L. 108.

23
Fallen, fallen, fallen, fallen,
Fallen from his high estate,
And welt'ring in his blood;
Deserted at his utmost need,
By those his former bounty fed;
On the bare earth expos'd he lies,
With not a friend to close his eyes.
DRYDEN—*Alexander's Feast.* L. 77.

24
Quando la mala ventura se duerme, nadie la despierte.
When Misfortune is asleep, let no one wake her.
Quoted by FULLER—*Gnomologia.* (French proverb has "sorrow" for "Misfortune.")

25 But strong of limb
And swift of foot misfortune is, and, far
Outstripping all, comes first to every land,
And there wreaks evil on mankind, which prayers
Do afterwards redress.
HOMER—*Iliad.* Bk. IX. L. 625. BRYANT'S trans.

26 Take her up tenderly,
Lift her with care;
Fashioned so slenderly,
Young and so fair!
HOOD—*Bridge of Sighs.*

27 One more unfortunate
Weary of breath,
Rashly importunate,
Gone to her death.
HOOD—*Bridge of Sighs.*

1
Let us be of good cheer, however, remembering that the misfortunes hardest to bear are those which never come.
LOWELL—*Democracy and Addresses. Democracy.*

2
Suave mari magno, turbantibus æquora ventis
E terra magnum alterius spectare laborum.
It is pleasant, when the sea runs high, to view from land the great distress of another.
LUCRETIUS—*De Rerum Natura.* II. 1.
(See also TERENCE)

3
Rocks whereon greatest men have oftest wreck'd.
MILTON—*Paradise Regained.* Bk. II. L. 228.

4
Quicumque amisit dignitatem pristinam
Ignavis etiam jocus est in casu gravi.
Whoever has fallen from his former high estate is in his calamity the scorn even of the base.
PHÆDRUS—*Fables.* I. 21. 1.

5
Paucis temeritas est bono, multis malo.
Rashness brings success to few, misfortune to many.
PHÆDRUS—*Fables.* V. 4. 12.

6
I never knew any man in my life, who could not bear another's misfortunes perfectly like a Christian.
POPE. See SWIFT'S *Thoughts on Various Subjects.*

7
As if Misfortune made the Throne her Seat,
And none could be unhappy but the Great.
NICHOLAS ROWE—*The Fair Penitent. Prologue.* L. 3.
(See also YOUNG)

8
Nihil infelicius eo, cui nihil unquam evenit adversi, non licuit enim illi se experiri.
There is no one more unfortunate than the man who has never been unfortunate, for it has never been in his power to try himself.
SENECA—*De Providentia.* III.

9
Calamitas virtutis occasio est.
Calamity is virtue's opportunity.
SENECA—*De Providentia.* IV.

10
Nil est nec miserius nec stultius quam prætimere. Quæ ista dementia est, malum suum antecedere!
There is nothing so wretched or foolish as to anticipate misfortunes. What madness it is in your expecting evil before it arrives!
SENECA—*Epistolæ Ad Lucilium.* XCVIII.

11
Quemcumque miserum videris, hominem scias.
When you see a man in distress, recognize him as a fellow man.
SENECA—*Hercules Furens.* 463.

12
The worst is not
So long as we can say "This is the worst."
King Lear. Act IV. Sc. 1. L. 29.

13
O, give me thy hand,
One writ with me in sour misfortune's book.
Romeo and Juliet. Act V. Sc. 3. L. 81.

14
Such a house broke!
So noble a master fallen! All gone! and not
One friend to take his fortune by the arm,
And go along with him.
Timon of Athens. Act IV. Sc. 2. L. 5.

15
We have seen better days.
Timon of Athens. Act IV. Sc. 2. L. 27.

16
From good to bad, and from bad to worse,
From worse unto that is worst of all,
And then return to his former fall.
SPENSER—*The Shepherd's Calendar.* Feb. L. 12.

17
Misfortune had conquered her, how true it is, that sooner or later the most rebellious must bow beneath the same yoke.
MADAME DE STAËL—*Corinne.* Bk. XVII. Ch. II.

18
Bonum est fugienda adspicere in alieno malo.
It is good to see in the misfortunes of others what we should avoid.
SYRUS—*Maxims.*

19
I shall not let a sorrow die
Until I find the heart of it,
Nor let a wordless joy go by
Until it talks to me a bit;
And the ache my body knows
Shall teach me more than to another,
I shall look deep at mire and rose
Until each one becomes my brother.
SARA TEASDALE—*Servitors.*

20
Hoccin est credibile, aut memorabile,
Tanta vecordia innata cuiquam ut siet,
Ut malis gaudeant alienis, atque ex incommodis
Alterius, sua ut comparent commoda?
It is to be believed or told that there is such malice in men as to rejoice in misfortunes, and from another's woes to draw delight.
TERENCE—*Andria.* IV. 1. 1.
(See also LUCRETIUS)

21
Tu ne cede malis, sed contra audentior ito.
Yield not to misfortunes, but advance all the more boldly against them.
VERGIL—*Æneid.* VI. 95.

22
So fallen! so lost! the light withdrawn
Which once he wore;
The glory from his gray hairs gone
For evermore!
WHITTIER—*Ichabod.*

23
None think the great unhappy, but the great.
YOUNG—*Love of Fame. Satire.*
(See also ROWE)

MOCCASIN FLOWER

Cypripedium

24
With careless joy we thread the woodland ways
And reach her broad domain.
Thro' sense of strength and beauty, free as air.
We feel our savage kin,—
And thus alone with conscious meaning wear
The Indian's moccasin!
ELAINE GOODALE—*Moccasin Flower.*

MOCKING-BIRD

1
Then from the neighboring thicket the mocking-bird, wildest of singers,
Swinging aloft on a willow spray that hung o'er the water,
Shook from his little throat such floods of delirious music,
That the whole air and the woods and the waves seemed silent to listen.
LONGFELLOW—*Evangeline.* Pt. II. St. 2.

2
Winged mimic of the woods! thou motley fool!
Who shall thy gay buffoonery describe?
Thine ever-ready notes of ridicule
Pursue thy fellows still with jest and jibe:
Wit, sophist, songster, Yorick of thy tribe;
Thou sportive satirist of Nature's school;
To thee the palm of scoffing we ascribe,
Arch-mocker and mad abbot of misrule!
ROBERT WILDE, D.D.—*Sonnet. To the Mocking-Bird.*

MODERATION

3
This only grant me, that my means may lie
Too low for envy, for contempt too high.
COWLEY—*Essays in Prose and Verse. Of Myself.* (Trans. of HORACE.)

4
Moderation is the silken string running through the pearl-chain of all virtues.
FULLER—*Holy and Profane States.* Bk. III. *Of Moderation.* See also BISHOP HALL—*Christian Moderation.* Introduction.

5
Aus Mässigkeit entspringt ein reines Glück.
True happiness springs from moderation.
GOETHE—*Die Naturliche Tochter.* II. 5. 79

6
Auream quisquis mediocritatem deligit tutus caret obsoleti sordibus tecti, caret invidenda sobrius aula.
Who loves the golden mean is safe from the poverty of a tenement, is free from the envy of a palace.
HORACE—*Carmina.* II. 10. 5.

7
Est modus in rebus, sunt certi denique fines
Quos ultra citraque nequit consistere rectum.
There is a mean in all things; and, moreover, certain limits on either side of which right cannot be found.
HORACE—*Satires.* I. 1. 106.

8
The moderation of fortunate people comes from the calm which good fortune gives to their tempers.
LA ROCHEFOUCAULD—*Maxims.* No. 18.

9
Le juste milieu.
The proper mean.
Phrase used by LOUIS PHILIPPE in an address to the deputies of Gaillac. First occurs in a letter of VOLTAIRE's to COUNT D'ARGENTAL, Nov. 29, 1765. Also in PASCAL—*Pensées.*

10
Medio tutissimus ibis.
Safety lies in the middle course.
OVID—*Metamorphoses.* Bk. II. L. 136.

11
Take this at least, this last advice, my son:
Keep a stiff rein, and move but gently on:
The coursers of themselves will run too fast,
Your art must be to moderate their haste.
OVID—*Metamorphoses. Story of Phaeton.* Bk. II. L. 147. ADDISON's trans.

12
Modus omnibus in rebus, soror, optimum est habitu;
Nimia omnia nimium exhibent negotium hominibus ex se.
In everything the middle course is best: all things in excess bring trouble to men.
PLAUTUS—*Pœnulus.* I. 2. 29.

13
He knows to live who keeps the middle state,
And neither leans on this side nor on that.
POPE—Bk. II. Satire II. L. 61.

14
Give me neither poverty nor riches.
Proverbs. XXX. 8.

15
Souhaitez donc mediocrité.
Wish then for mediocrity.
RABELAIS—*Pantagruel.* Bk. IV. *Prologue.*

16
Modica voluptas laxat animos et temperat.
Moderate pleasure relaxes the spirit, and moderates it.
SENECA—*De Ira.* II. 20.

17
Be moderate, be moderate.
Why tell you me of moderation?
The grief is fine, full, perfect, that I taste,
And violenteth in a sense as strong
As that which causeth it: how can I moderate it?
Troilus and Cressida. Act IV. Sc. 4. L. 1.

18
Bonarum rerum consuetudo pessima est.
The too constant use even of good things is hurtful.
SYRUS—*Maxims.*

19
Id arbitror
Adprime in vita esse utile, Ut ne quid nimis.
Excess in nothing,—this I regard as a principle of the highest value in life.
TERENCE—*Andria.* I. 1. 33.

20
There is a limit to enjoyment, though the sources of wealth be boundless,
And the choicest pleasures of life lie within the ring of moderation.
TUPPER—*Proverbial Philosophy. Of Compensation.* L. 15.

21
Give us enough but with a sparing hand.
WALLER—*Reflections.*

MODESTY

22
Maximum ornamentum amicitiæ tollit, qui ex ea tollit verecundiam.
He takes the greatest ornament from friendship, who takes modesty from it.
CICERO—*De Amicitia.* XX.

23
Modesty is that feeling by which honorable shame acquires a valuable and lasting authority.
CICERO—*Rhetorical Invention.* Bk. II. Sec. LVI.

1
Modesty antedates clothes and will be resumed when clothes are no more.
Modesty died when clothes were born.
Modesty died when false modesty was born.
S. L. CLEMENS (Mark Twain)—*Memoranda.* PAINE'S *Biography of Mark Twain.* Vol. III. P. 1513

2
Immodest words admit of no defence;
For want of decency is want of sense.
WENTWORTH DILLON—*Essay on Translated Verse.* L. 113.

3
Thy modesty's a candle to thy merit.
HENRY FIELDING—*Tom Thumb the Great.* Act I. Sc. 3. L. 8.

4
Her modest looks the cottage might adorn,
Sweet as the primrose peeps beneath the thorn.
GOLDSMITH—*The Deserted Village.* L. 329.

5
Like the violet, which alone
Prospers in some happy shade,
My Castara lives unknown
To no looser eye betrayed.
HABINGTON—*Castara.* (1634) In ELTON'S ed. P. 166.

6
Why, to hear Betsy Bobbet talk about wimmin's throwin' their modesty away, you would think if they ever went to the political pole, they would have to take their dignity and modesty and throw 'em against the pole, and go without any all the rest of their lives.
MARIETTA HOLLEY—*My Opinions and Betsy Bobbet's.*

7
Cui pudor et justitiæ soror incorrupta fides nudaque veritas quando ullum inveniet parem?
What can be found equal to modesty, uncorrupt faith, the sister of justice, and undisguised truth?
HORACE—*Carmina.* I. 24. 6.

8
Modesty is to merit, what shade is to figures in a picture; it gives it strength and makes it stand out.
LA BRUYÈRE—*The Characters or Manners of the Present Age.* Ch. II. Sec. 17.

9
Adolescentem verecundum esse decet.
Modesty becomes a young man.
PLAUTUS—*Asinaria.* V. 1. 8.

10
Wenn jemand bescheiden bleibt, nicht beim Lobe, sondern beim Tadel, dann ist er's.
When one remains modest, not after praise but after blame, then is he really so.
JEAN PAUL RICHTER—*Hesperus.* 12.

11
Can it be
That modesty may more betray our sense
Than woman's lightness? Having waste ground enough,
Shall we desire to raze the sanctuary
And pitch our evils there?
Measure for Measure. Act II. Sc. 2. L. 167.

12
Not stepping o'er the bounds of modesty.
Romeo and Juliet. Act IV. Sc. 2. L. 27.

13
Da locum melioribus.
Give place to your betters.
TERENCE—*Phormio.* III. 2. 37.

14
He saw her charming, but he saw not half
The charms her downcast modesty conceal'd.
THOMSON—*The Seasons. Autumn.* L. 229.

MONEY (See also GOLD, MAMMON)

15
Up and down the City Road,
In and out the Eagle,
That's the way the money goes—
Pop goes the weasel!
Popular street song in England in the late Fifties, sung at the Grecian Theatre. Attributed to W. R. MANDALE.

16
Money makes the man.
ARISTODEMUS. See ALCÆUS—*Fragment. Miscel. Songs.*

17
L'argent est un bon serviteur, mais un méchant maître.
Money is a good servant but a bad master.
Quoted by BACON. (French Proverb.) In *Menegiana.* II. 296. 1695.

18
Money is like muck, not good except it be spread.
BACON—*Of Sedition.*

19
The sinews of business (or state).
BION. In *Life of Bion* by DIOGENES LAERTIUS Bk. IV. Ch. VII. Sec. 3.
(See also DEMOSTHENES)

20
Penny wise, pound foolish.
BURTON—*Anatomy of Melancholy. Democritus to the Reader.* P. 35. (Ed. 1887)

21
Still amorous, and fond, and billing,
Like Philip and Mary on a shilling.
BUTLER—*Hudibras.* Pt. III. Canto I. L. 687.

22
How beauteous are rouleaus! how charming chests
Containing ingots, bags of dollars, coins
(Not of old victors, all whose heads and crests
Weigh not the thin ore where their visage shines,
But) of fine unclipt gold, where dully rests
Some likeness, which the glittering cirque confines,
Of modern, reigning, sterling, stupid stamp;—
Yes! ready money is Aladdin's lamp.
BYRON—*Don Juan.* Canto XII. St. 12.

23
Money, which is of very uncertain value, and sometimes has no value at all and even less.
CARLYLE—*Frederick the Great.* Bk. IV. Ch. III.

24
Make ducks and drakes with shillings.
GEORGE CHAPMAN—*Eastward Ho.* Sc. 1. Act I. (Written by CHAPMAN, JONSON, MARSTON.)

1
The way to resumption is to resume.
SALMON P. CHASE—*Letter to Horace Greeley.* May 17, 1866.

2
I knew once a very covetous, sordid fellow who used to say, "Take care of the pence, for the pounds will take care of themselves."
CHESTERFIELD—*Letters.* Nov. 6, 1747; also Feb. 5, 1750. Quoting LOWNDES.
(See also LOWNDES; also CHESTERFIELD under TIME)

3
As I sat at the Café I said to myself,
They may talk as they please about what they call pelf,
They may sneer as they like about eating and drinking,
But help it I cannot, I cannot help thinking
How pleasant it is to have money, heigh-ho!
How pleasant it is to have money!
ARTHUR HUGH CLOUGH—*Spectator Ab Extra.*

4
Money was made, not to command our will,
But all our lawful pleasures to fulfil.
Shame and woe to us, if we our wealth obey;
The horse doth with the horseman run away.
ABRAHAM COWLEY—*Imitations. Tenth Epistle of Horace.* Bk. I. L. 75.

5
Stamps God's own name upon a lie just made,
To turn a penny in the way of trade.
COWPER—*Table Talk.* L. 421.

6
The sinews of affairs are cut.
Attributed to DEMOSTHENES by ÆSCHINES. Adv. *Ctesiphon.*
(See also BION; also CICERO under WAR)

7
The sweet simplicity of the three per cents.
BENJ. DISRAELI. In the House of Commons, Feb. 19, 1850. *Endymion.* Ch. XCVI.
(See also ELDON)

8
"The American nation in the Sixth Ward is a fine People," he says. "They love th' eagle," he says. "On the back iv a dollar."
F. P. DUNNE—*Mr. Dooley in Peace and War. Oratory on Politics.*

9
Wine maketh merry: but money answereth all things.
Ecclesiastes. X. 19.

10
The elegant simplicity of the three per cents.
LORD ELDON. See CAMPBELL—*Lives of the Lord Chancellors.* Vol. X. Ch. CCXII.
(See also DISRAELI)

11
Almighty gold.
FARQUHAR—*Recruiting Officer.* III. 2.

12
If you would know the value of money, go and try to borrow some.
FRANKLIN—*Poor Richard's Almanac.* Same idea in HERBERT—*Jacula Prudentum.*

13
This bank-note world.
FITZ-GREENE HALLECK—*Alnwick Castle.*

14
Get to live;
Then live, and use it; else, it is not true
That thou hast gotten. Surely use alone
Makes money not a contemptible stone.
HERBERT—*The Temple. The Church Porch.* St. 26.

15
Fight thou with shafts of silver, and o'ercome
When no force else can get the masterdome.
HERRICK—*Money Gets the Mastery.*

16
How widely its agencies vary,—
To save, to ruin, to curse, to bless,—
As even its minted coins express,
Now stamp'd with the image of good Queen Bess,
And now of a Bloody Mary.
HOOD—*Miss Kilmansegg. Her Moral.*

17
Quærenda pecunia primum est; virtus post nummos.
Money is to be sought for first of all; virtue after wealth.
HORACE—*Epistles.* I. 1. 53.

18
Rem facias rem,
Recte si possis, si non, quocumque modo rem.
Money, make money; by honest means if you can; if not, by any means make money.
HORACE—*Epistles.* I. 1. 65.
(See also JONSON)

19
Quo mihi fortunam, si non conceditur uti?
Of what use is a fortune to me, if I can not use it?
HORACE—*Epistles.* I. 5. 12.

20
Et genus et formam regina pecunia donat.
All powerful money gives birth and beauty.
HORACE—*Epistles.* I. 6. 37.

21
Licet superbus ambules pecuniæ,
Fortuna non mutat genus.
Though you strut proud of your money, yet fortune has not changed your birth.
HORACE—*Epodi.* IV. 5.

22
Populus me sibilat, at mihi plaudo
Ipse domi, simul ac nummos contemplor in arca.
The people hiss me, but I applaud myself at home, when I contemplate the money in my chest.
HORACE—*Satires.* I. 1. 66.

23
The almighty dollar, that great object of universal devotion throughout our land, seems to have no genuine devotees in these peculiar villages.
WASHINGTON IRVING—*Creole Village. In Wolfert's Roost.* Appeared in *Knickerbocker Mag.* Nov., 1836.
(See also WOLCOT)

24
Whilst that for which all virtue now is sold,
And almost every vice, almighty gold.
BEN JONSON—*Epistle to Elizabeth, Countess of Rutland.*

25
Get money; still get money, boy;
No matter by what means.
BEN JONSON—*Every Man in His Humour.* Act II. Sc. 3.
(See also HORACE, POPE)

1
Quantum quisque sua nummorum condit in arca,
Tantum habet et fidei.

Every man's credit is proportioned to the money which he has in his chest.

JUVENAL—*Satires*. III. 143.

2
Ploratur lacrimis amissa pecunia veris.

Money lost is bewailed with unfeigned tears.

JUVENAL—*Satires*. XIII. 134.

3
Crescit amor nummi quantum ipsa pecunia crescit.

The love of money grows as the money itself grows.

JUVENAL—*Satires*. XIV. 139.

4
Dollar Diplomacy.

Term applied to Secretary Knox's activities in securing opportunities for the investment of American capital abroad, particularly in Latin America and China; also in Honduras and Liberia. Defended by President Taft, Message to Congress, Dec. 3, 1912. Huntington Wilson aided Knox in framing the Policy. See *Harper's Weekly*, April 23, 1910. P. 8.

5
Luat in corpore, qui non habet in ære.

Who can not pay with money, must pay with his body.

Law Maxim.

6
Nec quicquam acrius quam pecuniæ damnum stimulat.

Nothing stings more deeply than the loss of money.

LIVY—*Annales*. XXX. 44.

7
Take care of the pence, and the pounds will take care of themselves.

WILLIAM LOWNDES, Sec. of Treasury under William III, George I.

(See also CHESTERFIELD, also CARROLL under SENSE)

8
Money brings honor, friends, conquest, and realms.

MILTON—*Paradise Regained*. Bk. II. L. 422

9
Les beaux yeux de ma cassette!
Il parle d'elle comme un amant d'une maitresse.

The beautiful eyes of my money-box!
He speaks of it as a lover of his mistress.

MOLIÈRE—*L'Avare*. V. 3.

10
Ah, take the Cash, and let the Credit go,
Nor heed the rumble of a distant Drum!

OMAR KHAYYAM—*Rubaiyat*. St. 13. FITZGERALD's trans. ("Promise" for "credit"; "Music" for "rumble" in 2nd ed.)

11
In pretio pretium nunc est; dat census honores,
Census amicitias; pauper ubique jacet.

Money nowadays is money; money brings office; money gains friends; everywhere the poor man is down.

OVID—*Fasti*. I. 217.

12
"Get Money, money still!
And then let virtue follow, if she will."
This, this the saving doctrine preach'd to all,
From low St. James' up to high St. Paul.

POPE—*First Book of Horace*. Ep. I. L. 79.

(See also JONSON)

13
Trade it may help, society extend,
But lures the Pirate, and corrupts the friend:
It raises armies in a nation's aid,
But bribes a senate, and the land's betray'd.

POPE—*Moral Essays*. Ep. III. L. 29.

14
Subject to a kind of disease, which at that time they called lack of money.

RABELAIS—*Works*. Bk. II. Ch. XVI.

15
Point d'argent, point de Suisse.

No money, no Swiss.

RACINE—*Plaideurs*. I. 1.

16
When I was stamp'd, some coiner with his tools
Made me a counterfeit.

Cymbeline. Act II. Sc. 5. L. 5.

17
For they say, if money go before, all ways do lie open.

Merry Wives of Windsor. Act II. Sc. 2. L. 173.

18
Money is a good soldier, sir, and will on.

Merry Wives of Windsor. Act II. Sc. 2. L. 175.

19
Why, give him gold enough and marry him to a puppet or an aglet-baby or an old trot with ne'er a tooth in her head, though she have as many diseases as two-and-fifty horses; why, nothing comes amiss, so money comes withal.

Taming of the Shrew. Act I. Sc. 2. L. 78.

20
But the jingling of the guinea helps the hurt that
Honor feels.

TENNYSON—*Locksley Hall*. St. 53.

21
Pecuniam in loco negligere maximum est lucrum.

To despise money on some occasions is a very great gain.

TERENCE—*Adelphi*. II. 2. 8.

22
Not greedy of filthy lucre.

I Timothy. III. 3.

23
The love of money is the root of all evil.

I Timothy. VI. 10.

24
A fool and his money be soon at debate.

TUSSER—*Good Husbandry*.

A fool and his money are soon parted.

GEORGE BUCHANAN, tutor to James VI. of Scotland, to a courtier after winning a bet as to which could make the coarser verse. See WALSH—*Handy Book of Literary Curiosities*.

25
It is money makes the mare to trot.

WOLCOT—*Ode to Pitt*.

26
No, let the monarch's bags and coffers hold
The flattering, mighty, nay, *all*-mighty gold.

WOLCOT—*To Kieu Long*. Ode IV.

(See also IRVING)

1
I think this piece will help to boil thy pot.
WOLCOT—*The bard complimenteth Mr. West on his Lord Nelson* (c. 1790) (Probably first use of "pot-boiler.")

MONTHS (UNCLASSIFIED)

2
Fourth, eleventh, ninth, and sixth,
Thirty days to each affix;
Every other thirty-one,
Except the second month alone.
Common in Chester Co., Pa., among the Friends.

3
Thirty days hath September,
April, June, and November;
All the rest have thirty-one
Excepting February alone:
Which hath but twenty-eight, in fine,
Till leap year gives it twenty-nine.
Common in New England States.

4
Thirty days hath November,
April, June, and September,
February hath xxviii alone,
And all the rest have xxxi.
RICHARD GRAFTON—*Abridgement of the Chronicles of Englande.* (1570) 8vo. "A rule to knowe how many dayes every moneth in the yeare hath."

5
Thirty days hath September,
April, June, and November;
February eight-and-twenty all alone,
And all the rest have thirty-one:
Unless that leap-year doth combine,
And give to February twenty-nine.
Return from Parnassus. (London. 1606)

MONTREAL

6
Oh God! Oh Montreal!
SAMUEL BUTLER—*Psalm of Montreal.* See *Spectator.* May 18, 1878. Writer in the *Dial* Jan. 6, 1916, attributes it to W. H. HURLBERT.

MONUMENTS

7
The tap'ring pyramid, the Egyptian's pride,
And wonder of the world, whose spiky top
Has wounded the thick cloud.
BLAIR—*The Grave.* L. 190.

8
Gold once out of the earth is no more due unto it; what was unreasonably committed to the ground, is reasonably resumed from it; let monuments and rich fabricks, not riches, adorn men's ashes.
SIR THOMAS BROWNE—*Hydriotaphia.* Ch. III.

9
To extend our memories by monuments, whose death we daily pray for, and whose duration we cannot hope, without injury to our expectations in the advent of the last day, were a contradiction to our belief.
SIR THOMAS BROWNE—*Hydriotaphia.* Ch. V.

10
But monuments themselves memorials need.
CRABBE—*The Borough.* Letter II.

11
You shall not pile, with servile toil,
Your monuments upon my breast,
Nor yet within the common soil
Lay down the wreck of power to rest,
Where man can boast that he has trod
On him that was "the scourge of God."
EDWARD EVERETT—*Alaric the Visigoth.*

12
He made him a hut, wherein he did put
The carcass of Robinson Crusoe.
O poor Robinson Crusoe!
SAMUEL FOOTE—*Mayor of Garratt.* Act I. Sc. 1.

13
Tombs are the clothes of the dead. A grave is but a plain suit, and a rich monument is one embroidered.
FULLER—*The Holy and Profane States.* Bk. III. *Of Tombs.*

14
Exegi monumentum ære perennius
Regalique situ pyramidum altius,
Quod non imber edax, non Aquilo impotens
Possit diruere aut innumerabilis
Annorum series et fuga temporum.
Non omnis moriar, multaque pars mei
Vitabit Libitinam.

I have reared a memorial more enduring than brass, and loftier than the regal structure of the pyramids, which neither the corroding shower nor the powerless north wind can destroy; no, not even unending years nor the flight of time itself. I shall not entirely die. The greater part of me shall escape oblivion.
HORACE—*Carmina.* III. 30. 1.
(See also MOORE, WEBSTER, also SPENSER under GENIUS)

15
Incisa notis marmora publicis,
Per quæ spiritus et vita redit bonis
Post mortem ducibus.

Marble statues, engraved with public inscriptions, by which the life and soul return after death to noble leaders.
HORACE—*Carmina.* IV. 8.

16
Cœlo tegitur qui non habet urnam.
He is covered by the heavens who has no sepulchral urn.
LUCANUS—*Pharsalia.* Bk. VII. 831.
(See also BROWNE under GRAVE)

17
Thou, in our wonder and astonishment
Hast built thyself a life-long monument.
MILTON—*Epitaph. On Shakespeare.*

18
For men use, if they have an evil tourne, to write it in marble; and whoso doth us a good tourne we will write it in duste.
THOS. MORE—*Richard III.*
(See also HORACE)

19
Towers of silence.
ROBERT X. MURPHY, according to SIR GEORGE BIRDWOOD, in a letter to the London *Times,* Aug. 8, 1905.

20
Soldats, du haut ces Pyramides quarante siècles vous contemplent.

Soldiers, forty centuries are looking down upon you from these pyramids.

NAPOLEON. To his army before the Battle of the Pyramids, July 2, 1797. Also quoted "twenty centuries."

1

Factum abiit; monumenta manent.

The need has gone; the memorial thereof remains.

OVID—*Fasti*. Bk. IV. 709.

2

Where London's column, pointing at the skies,
Like a tall bully, lifts the head and lies.

POPE—*Moral Essays*. Ep. III. L. 339.

3

Jove, thou regent of the skies.

Hamlet. Act V. Sc. 1. L. 320.

4

Let it rise! let it rise, till it meet the sun in his coming; let the earliest light of the morning gild it, and the parting day linger and play on its summit.

DANIEL WEBSTER—*Address on Laying the Corner Stone of the Bunker Hill Monument*. Works. Vol. I. P. 62.

5

If we work upon marble it will perish. If we work upon brass time will efface it. If we rear temples they will crumble to dust. But if we work upon men's immortal minds, if we imbue them with high principles, with the just fear of God and love of their fellow men, we engrave on those tablets something which no time can efface, and which will brighten and brighten to all eternity.

DANIEL WEBSTER—*Speech in Faneuil Hall*. (1852)

MOON (THE)

6

Soon as the evening shades prevail,
The moon takes up the wondrous tale,
And nightly to the listening earth
Repeats the story of her birth.

ADDISON—*Spectator*. No. 465. *Ode*.

7

The moon is a silver pin-head vast,
That holds the heaven's tent-hangings fast.

WM. R. ALGER—*Oriental Poetry*. *The Use of the Moon*.

8

The moon is at her full, and riding high,
Floods the calm fields with light.
The airs that hover in the summer sky
Are all asleep to-night.

BRYANT—*The Tides*.

9

Doth the moon care for the barking of a dog?

BURTON—*Anatomy of Melancholy*. Pt. II. Sec. III. Mem. 7.

10

The moon pull'd off her veil of light,
That hides her face by day from sight
(Mysterious veil, of brightness made,
That's both her lustre and her shade),
And in the lantern of the night,
With shining horns hung out her light.

BUTLER—*Hudibras*. Pt. II. Canto I. L. 905.

11

He made an instrument to know
If the moon shine at full or no;
That would, as soon as e'er she shone straight,
Whether 'twere day or night demonstrate;
Tell what her d'ameter to an inch is,
And prove that she's not made of green cheese.

BUTLER—*Hudibrus*. Pt. II. Canto III. L. 261.

12

The devil's in the moon for mischief; they
Who call'd her chaste, methinks, began too soon
Their nomenclature; there is not a day,
The longest, not the twenty-first of June,
Sees half the business in a wicked way,
On which three single hours of moonshine smile—
And then she looks so modest all the while!

BYRON—*Don Juan*. Canto I. St. 113.

13

Into the sunset's turquoise marge
The moon dips, like a pearly barge;
Enchantment sails through magic seas,
To fairyland Hesperides,
Over the hills and away.

MADISON CAWEIN—*At Sunset*. St. 1

14

The sun had sunk and the summer skies
Were dotted with specks of light
That melted soon in the deep moon-rise
That flowed over Groton Height.

M'DONALD CLARKE—*The Graveyard*.

15

The moving moon went up the sky,
And nowhere did abide;
Softly she was going up,
And a star or two beside.

COLERIDGE—*The Ancient Mariner*. Pt. IV.

16

When the hollow drum has beat to bed
And the little fifer hangs his head,
When all is mute the Moorish flute,
And nodding guards watch wearily,
Oh, then let me,
From prison free,
March out by moonlight cheerily.

GEORGE COLMAN the Younger—*Mountaineers*. Act I. Sc. 2.

17

How like a queen comes forth the lonely Moon
From the slow opening curtains of the clouds
Walking in beauty to her midnight throne!

GEORGE CROLY—*Diana*.

18

And hail their queen, fair regent of the night.

ERASMUS DARWIN—*Botanic Garden*. Pt. I. Canto II. L. 90.

19

Now Cynthia, named fair regent of the night.

GAY—*Trivia*. Bk. III.

(See also MICKLE, MORE, POPE)

20

On the road, the lonely road,
Under the cold, white moon;
Under the rugged trees he strode,
Whistled and shifted his heavy load—
Whistled a foolish tune.

W. W. HARNEY—*The Stab*.

21

He who would see old Hoghton right
Must view it by the pale moonlight.

HAZLITT—*English Proverbs and Provincial Phrases*. (1869) P. 196. (Hoghton Tower is not far from Blackburn.)

(See also SCOTT)

1
As the moon's fair image quaketh
In the raging waves of ocean,
Whilst she, in the vault of heaven,
Moves with silent peaceful motion.
HEINE—*Book of Songs. New Spring. Prologue.* No. 23.

2
Mother of light! how fairly dost thou go
Over those hoary crests, divinely led!
Art thou that huntress of the silver bow
Fabled of old? Or rather dost thou tread
Those cloudy summits thence to gaze below,
Like the wild chamois from her Alpine snow,
Where hunters never climbed—secure from dread?
HOOD—*Ode to the Moon.*

3
The moon, the moon, so silver and cold,
Her fickle temper has oft been told,
Now shady—now bright and sunny—
But of all the lunar things that change,
The one that shows most fickle and strange,
And takes the most eccentric range,
Is the moon—so called—of honey!
HOOD—*Miss Kilmansegg. Her Honeymoon.*

4
The stars were glittering in the heaven's dusk meadows,
Far west, among those flowers of the shadows,
The thin, clear crescent lustrous over her,
Made Ruth raise question, looking through the bars
Of heaven, with eyes half-oped, what God, what comer
Unto the harvest of the eternal summer,
Had flung his golden hook down on the field of stars.
VICTOR HUGO—*Boaz Asleep.*

5
Such a slender moon, going up and up,
Waxing so fast from night to night,
And swelling like an orange flower-bud, bright,
Fated, methought, to round as to a golden cup,
And hold to my two lips life's best of wine.
JEAN INGELOW—*Songs of the Night Watches. The First Watch.* Pt. II.

6
The moon looks upon many night flowers; the night flowers see but one moon.
SIR WILLIAM JONES.
(See also MOORE)

7
Queen and huntress, chaste and fair,
Now the sun is laid to sleep,
Seated in thy silver car,
State in wonted manner keep.
Hesperus entreats thy light,
Goddess, excellently bright!
BEN JONSON—*Hymn. To Cynthia.*

8
The moon put forth a little diamond peak
No bigger than an unobserved star,
Or tiny point of fairy cimetar.
KEATS—*Endymion.* Bk. IV. L. 499.

9
See yonder fire! It is the moon
Slow rising o'er the eastern hill.
It glimmers on the forest tips,
And through the dewy foliage drips
In little rivulets of light,
And makes the heart in love with night.
LONGFELLOW—*Christus. The Golden Legend.* Pt. VI. L. 462.

10
It is the Harvest Moon! On gilded vanes
And roofs of villages, on woodland crests
And their aerial neighborhoods of nests
Deserted, on the curtained window-panes
Of rooms where children sleep, on country lanes
And harvest-fields, its mystic splendor rests.
LONGFELLOW—*Harvest Moon.*

11
The dews of summer night did fall;
The moon (sweet regent of the sky)
Silver'd the walls of Cumnor Hall,
And many an oak that grew thereby.
WM. J. MICKLE—*Cumnor Hall.* (Authorship of *Cumnor Hall* claimed for JEAN ADAM. Conceded generally to MICKLE.)
(See also DARWIN)

12
Let the air strike our tune,
Whilst we show reverence to yond peeping moon.
THOMAS MIDDLETON—*The Witch.* Act V. Sc. 2.

13
Unmuffle, ye faint stars; and thou fair Moon,
That wont'st to love the traveller's benison,
Stoop thy pale visage through an amber cloud,
And disinherit Chaos.
MILTON—*Comus.* L. 331.

14
* * * now glow'd the firmament
With living sapphires; Hesperus, that led
The starry host rode brightest, till the Moon,
Rising in clouded majesty, at length,
Apparent queen, unveil'd her peerless light,
And o'er the dark her silver mantle threw.
MILTON—*Paradise Lost.* Bk. IV. L. 604.

15
The moon looks
On many brooks,
The brook can see no moon but this.
MOORE—*Irish Melodies. While Gazing on the Moon's Light.*
(See also JONES)

16
He should, as he list, be able to prove the moon made of grene cheese.
SIR THOMAS MORE—*English Works.* P. 256. Same phrase in BLACKLOCH—*Hatchet of Heresies.* (1565) RABELAIS. Bk. I. Ch. XI. *Jack Jugler* in DODSLEY'S *Old Plays.* Ed. by HAZLITT. Vol. II.
(See also BURTON)

17
Hail, pallid crescent, hail!
Let me look on thee where thou sitt'st for aye
Like memory—ghastly in the glare of day,
But in the evening, light.
D. M. MULOCK—*The Moon in the Morning.*

18
No rest—no dark.
Hour after hour that passionless bright face
Climbs up the desolate blue.
D. M. MULOCK—*Moon-Struck.*

1 Au clair de la lune
Mon ami Pierrot,
Prête moi ta plume
Pour écrire un mot;
Ma chandelle est morte,
Je n'ai plus de feu,
Ouvre moi ta porte,
Pour l'amour de Dieu.
Lend me thy pen
To write a word
In the moonlight,
Pierrot, my friend!
My candle's out,
I've no more fire;—
For love of God
Open thy door!
French Folk Song.

2
Late, late yestreen I saw the new moone,
Wi' the auld moon in hir arme.
THOMAS PERCY—*Reliques. Sir Patrick Spens.* See also SCOTT—*Minstrelsy of the Scottish Border.*

3
Jove, thou regent of the skies.
POPE—*Odyssey.* Bk. II. L. 42.
(See also DARWIN)

4
Day glimmer'd in the east, and the white Moon
Hung like a vapor in the cloudless sky.
SAMUEL ROGERS—*Italy. The Lake of Geneva.*

5
Again thou reignest in thy golden hall,
Rejoicing in thy sway, fair queen of night!
The ruddy reapers hail thee with delight:
Theirs is the harvest, theirs the joyous call
For tasks well ended ere the season's fall.
ROSCOE—*Sonnet. To the Harvest Moon.*

6
The sun was gone now; the curled moon was like a little feather
Fluttering far down the gulf.
D. G. ROSSETTI—*The Blessed Damozel.* St. 10.

7
That I could clamber to the frozen moon
And draw the ladder after me.
Quoted by SCHOPENHAUER in *Parerga and Paralipomena.*

8
Good even, good fair moon, good even to thee;
I prithee, dear moon, now show to me
The form and the features, the speech and degree,
Of the man that true lover of mine shall be.
SCOTT—*Heart of Mid-Lothian.* Ch. XVII.

9
If thou would'st view fair Melrose aright,
Go visit it by the pale moonlight;
For the gay beams of lightsome day
Gild, but to flout, the ruins gray.
SCOTT—*Lay of the Last Minstrel.* Canto II. St. 1.
(See also HAZLITT)

10
The moon of Rome, chaste as the icicle
That's curded by the frost from purest snow.
Coriolanus. Act V. Sc. 3. L. 65.

11 How slow
This old moon wanes! she lingers my desires,
Like to a step-dame or a dowager
Long withering out a young man's revenue.
Midsummer Night's Dream. Act I. Sc. 1. L. 3.

12
Therefore the moon, the governess of floods,
Pale in her anger, washes all the air,
That rheumatic diseases do abound:
And through this distemperature we see
The seasons alter.
Midsummer Night's Dream. Act II. Sc. 1. L. 103.

13
It is the very error of the moon:
She comes more nearer earth than she was wont,
And makes men mad.
Othello. Act V. Sc. 2. L. 109.

14
The wat'ry star.
Winter's Tale. Act I. Sc. 2.

15
That orbed maiden, with white fire laden,
Whom mortals call the moon.
SHELLEY—*The Cloud.* IV.

16
The young moon has fed
Her exhausted horn
With the sunset's fire.
SHELLEY—*Hellas. Semi-Chorus II.*

17
Art thou pale for weariness
Of climbing heaven, and gazing on the earth,
Wandering companionless
Among the stars that have a different birth,—
And ever changing, like a joyous eye
That finds no object worth its constancy?
SHELLEY—*To the Moon.*

18
With how sad steps, O moon, thou climb'st the skies!
How silently, and with how wan a face!
SIR PHILIP SIDNEY—*Astrophel and Stella. Sonnet XXXI.*

19
The Moon arose: she shone upon the lake,
Which lay one smooth expanse of silver light;
She shone upon the hills and rocks, and cast
Upon their hollows and their hidden glens
A blacker depth of shade.
SOUTHEY—*Madoc.* Pt. II. *The Close of the Century.*

20
Transcendental moonshine.
Found in *Life of John Sterling.* P. 84. (People's Ed.) Applied to the teaching of COLERIDGE. Said to have been applied by CARLYLE to EMERSON.

21
I with borrow'd silver shine,
What you see is none of mine.
First I show you but a quarter,
Like the bow that guards the Tartar:
Then the half, and then the whole,
Ever dancing round the pole.
SWIFT.—*On the Moon.*

22
As like the sacred queen of night,
Who pours a lovely, gentle light
Wide o'er the dark, by wanderers blest,
Conducting them to peace and rest.
THOMSON—*Ode to Seraphina.*

1
The crimson Moon, uprising from the sea,
With large delight, foretells the harvest near.
LORD THURLOW—*Select Poems. The Harvest Moon.*

2
Meet me by moonlight alone,
And then I will tell you a tale
Must be told by the moonlight alone,
In the grove at the end of the vale!
You must promise to come, for I said
I would show the night-flowers their queen.
Nay, turn not away that sweet head,
'T is the loveliest ever was seen.
J. AUGUSTUS WADE—*Meet Me by Moonlight.*

3
And suddenly the moon withdraws
Her sickle from the lightening skies,
And to her sombre cavern flies,
Wrapped in a veil of yellow gauze.
OSCAR WILDE—*La Faite de la Lune.*

MORALITY

4
Kant, as we all know, compared moral law to the starry heavens, and found them both sublime. On the naturalistic hypothesis we should rather compare it to the protective blotches on a beetle's back, and find them both ingenious.
ARTHUR J. BALFOUR—*Foundations of Belief.*

5
No mere man since the Fall, is able in this life perfectly to keep the Commandments.
Book of Common Prayer. Shorter Catechism.

6
Rough Johnson, the great moralist.
BYRON—*Don Juan.* Canto XIII. St. 7.
(See also HAWTHORNE)

7
"Tut, tut, child," said the Duchess. "Everything's got a moral if only you can find it."
LEWIS CARROLL—*Alice in Wonderland.* Ch. VIII.

8
The Bearings of this observation lays in the application on it.
DICKENS—*Dombey and Son.* Ch. XXIII.

9
The moral system of the universe is like a document written in alternate ciphers, which change from line to line.
FROUDE—*Short Studies on Great Subjects. Calvinism.*

10
Morality, when vigorously alive, sees farther than intellect, and provides unconsciously for intellectual difficulties.
FROUDE—*Short Studies on Great Subjects. Divus Cæsar.*

11
Dr. Johnson's morality was as English an article as a beefsteak.
HAWTHORNE—*Our Old Home. Lichfield and Uttoxeter.* (See also BYRON)

12
Turning the other cheek is a kind of moral jiu-jitsu.
GERALD STANLEY LEE—*Crowds.* Bk. IV. Ch. X.

13
Morality without religion is only a kind of dead reckoning,—an endeavor to find our place on a cloudy sea by measuring the distance we have run, but without any observation of the heavenly bodies.
LONGFELLOW—*Kavanagh.* Ch. XIII.

14
We know no spectacle so ridiculous as the British public in one of its periodical fits of morality.
MACAULAY—*On Moore's Life of Lord Byron.* (1830)

15
I find the doctors and the sages
Have differ'd in all climes and ages,
And two in fifty scarce agree
On what is pure morality.
MOORE—*Morality.*

MORNING

16
Sacrament of morning.
E. B. BROWNING—*Sabbath at Sea.* St. 6. Last Line.

17
The summer morn is bright and fresh, the birds are darting by
As if they loved to breast the breeze that sweeps the cool clear sky.
BRYANT—*Strange Lady.*

18
The morn is up again, the dewy morn,
With breath all incense, and with cheek all bloom,
Laughing the clouds away with playful scorn,
And living as if earth contained no tomb,—
And glowing into day.
BYRON—*Childe Harold.* Canto III. St. 98.

19
Slow buds the pink dawn like a rose
From out night's gray and cloudy sheath;
Softly and still it grows and grows,
Petal by petal, leaf by leaf.
SUSAN COOLIDGE—*The Morning Comes Before the Sun.*

20
Awake thee, my Lady-Love!
Wake thee, and rise!
The sun through the bower peeps
Into thine eyes.
GEORGE DARLEY—*Sylvia; or, The May Queen.* Act IV. Sc. 1.

21
I saw myself the lambent easy light
Gild the brown horror, and dispel the night.
DRYDEN—*Hind and Panther.* Pt. II. L. 1,230.

22
The breezy call of incense-breathing morn.
GRAY—*Elegy in a Country Churchyard.* St. 5.

23
Now from the smooth deep ocean-stream the sun
Began to climb the heavens, and with new rays
Smote the surrounding fields.
HOMER—*Iliad.* Bk. VII. L. 525. BRYANT'S trans.

24
In saffron-colored mantle from the tides
Of Ocean rose the Morning to bright light
To gods and men.
HOMER—*Iliad.* Bk. XIX. L. 1. BRYANT'S trans.

1
The Morn! she is the source of sighs,
The very face to make us sad;
If but to think in other times
The same calm quiet look she had.
HOOD—*Ode to Melancholy.*

2
The blessed morn has come again;
The early gray
Taps at the slumberer's window pane,
And seems to say,
Break, break from the enchanter's chain,
Away, away!
RALPH HOYT—*Snow. A Winter Sketch.*

3
I have heard the mavis singing
Its love-song to the morn;
I've seen the dew-drop clinging
To the rose just newly born.
CHARLES JEFFREYS—*Mary of Argyle.*

4
Hues of the rich unfolding morn,
That, ere the glorious sun be born,
By some soft touch invisible
Around his path are taught to swell.
KEBLE—*The Christian Year. Morning.*

5
A fine morning,
Nothing's the matter with it that I know of.
I have seen better and I have seen worse.
LONGFELLOW—*Christus.* Pt. III. *John Endicott.* Act V. Sc. 2.

6
Far off I hear the crowing of the cocks,
And through the opening door that time unlocks
Feel the fresh breathing of To-morrow creep.
LONGFELLOW—*To-morrow.*

7
Like pearl
Dropt from the opening eyelids of the morn
Upon the bashful rose.
MIDDLETON—*Game of Chess.*

8
Under the opening eyelids of the morn.
MILTON—*Lycidas.* L. 26.

9
Flames in the forehead of the morning sky.
MILTON—*Lycidas.* L. 171.

10
Sweet is the breath of morn, her rising sweet,
With charm of earliest birds.
MILTON—*Paradise Lost.* Bk. IV. L. 641.

11
Now morn, her rosy steps in th' eastern clime
Advancing, sow'd the earth with Orient pearl.
MILTON—*Paradise Lost.* Bk. V. L. 1.

12
Morn,
Wak'd by the circling hours, with rosy hand
Unbarr'd the gates of light.
MILTON—*Paradise Lost.* Bk. VI. L. 2.

13
Till morning fair
Came forth with pilgrim steps in amice gray.
MILTON—*Paradise Regained.* Bk. IV. L. 426.

14
When did morning ever break,
And find such beaming eyes awake?
MOORE—*Fly not Yet.*

15
Morgen Stunde hat Gold im Munde.
The morning hour has gold in the mouth.
For history of the saying see MAX MÜLLER—*Lectures on the Science of Language.* Sec. Series. P. 378. (Ed. 1864)

16
Hadn't he been blowing kisses to Earth millions of years before I was born?
JAMES OPPENHEIM—*Morning and I.*

17
Bright chanticleer proclaims the dawn
And spangles deck the thorn.
JOHN O'KEEFE—*Tzar Peter.* Act I. Sc. 4.
(Originally "bold" for "bright.")

18
If I take the wings of the morning, and dwell in the uttermost parts of the sea.
Psalms. CXXXIX. 9.

19
At length the morn and cold indifference came.
ROWE—*Fair Penitent.* Act I. 1.
(See also SCOTT)

20
Clothing the palpable and familiar
With golden exhalations of the dawn.
SCHILLER—*The Death of Wallenstein.* Act V. Sc. 1. COLERIDGE's trans.

21
But with the morning cool reflection came.
SCOTT—*Highland Widow. Introductory.* Ch. IV.

22
But with the morning cool repentance came.
SCOTT—*Rob Roy.* Ch. XII.
(See also ROWE)

23
But, look, the morn, in russet mantle clad,
Walks o'er the dew of yon high eastern hill.
Hamlet. Act I. Sc. 1. L. 166.

24
The day begins to break, and night is fled,
Whose pitchy mantle over-veil'd the earth.
Henry VI. Pt. I. Act II. Sc. 2. L. 1.

25
See how the morning opes her golden gates,
And takes her farewell of the glorious sun!
How well resembles it the prime of youth,
Trimm'd like a younker prancing to his love.
Henry VI. Pt. III. Act II. Sc. 1. L. 21.

26
An hour before the worshipp'd sun
Peer'd from the golden window of the east.
Romeo and Juliet. Act I. Sc. 1. L. 125.

27
The grey-ey'd morn smiles on the frowning night,
Chequering the eastern clouds with streaks of light.
Romeo and Juliet. Act II. Sc. 3. L. 1.

28
Night's candles are burnt out, and jocund day
Stands tiptoe on the misty mountain tops.
Romeo and Juliet. Act III. Sc. 5. L. 9.

29
As when the golden sun salutes the morn,
And, having gilt the ocean with his beams,
Gallops the zodiac in his glistening coach.
Titus Andronicus. Act II. Sc. 1. L. 5.

1 The busy day,
Wak'd by the lark, hath rous'd the ribald crows.
And dreaming night will hide our joys no longer.
Troilus and Cressida. Act IV. Sc. 2. L. 8.

2
Hail, gentle Dawn! mild blushing goddess, hail!
Rejoic'd I see thy purple mantle spread
O'er half the skies, gems pave thy radiant way,
And orient pearls from ev'ry shrub depend.
WM. SOMERVILLE—*The Chase*. Bk. II. L. 79.

3
Now the frosty stars are gone:
I have watched them one by one,
Fading on the shores of Dawn.
Round and full the glorious sun
Walks with level step the spray,
Through his vestibule of Day.
BAYARD TAYLOR—*Ariel in the Cloven Pine.*

4
And yonder fly his scattered golden arrows,
And smite the hills with day.
BAYARD TAYLOR—*The Poet's Journal. Third Evening. Morning.*

5
There in the windy flood of morning
Longing lifted its weight from me,
Lost as a sob in the midst of cheering,
Swept as a sea-bird out to sea.
SARA TEASDALE—*Leaves.*

6
Rise, happy morn, rise, holy morn,
Draw forth the cheerful day from night;
O Father, touch the east, and light
The light that shone when Hope was born.
TENNYSON—*In Memoriam.* Pt. XXX.

7
Morn in the white wake of the morning star
Came furrowing all the orient into gold.
TENNYSON—*The Princess*. Pt. III. L. 1.

8
The meek-eyed Morn appears, mother of Dews.
THOMSON—*Seasons. Summer.* L. 47.

9
The yellow fog came creeping down
The bridges, till the houses' walls
Seemed changed to shadows, and St. Paul's
Loomed like a bubble o'er the town.
OSCAR WILDE—*Impression du Matin.*

10
And the fresh air of incense-breathing morn
Shall wooingly embrace it.
WORDSWORTH—*Ecclesiastical Sonnets.* XL.

(See also GRAY)

MORNING-GLORY

Ipomœa

11 Wondrous interlacement!
Holding fast to threads by green and silky rings,
With the dawn it spreads its white and purple wings;
Generous in its bloom, and sheltering while it clings,
Sturdy morning-glory.
HELEN HUNT JACKSON—*Morning-Glory.*

12
The morning-glory's blossoming
Will soon be coming round
We see their rows of heart-shaped leaves
Upspringing from the ground.
MARIA WHITE LOWELL—*Morning-Glory.*

MORTALITY (See also DEATH)

13
"O Charidas, what of the underworld?"
"Great darkness."
"And what of the resurrection?"
"A lie."
"And Pluto?"
"A fable; we perish utterly."
CALLIMACHUS. Trans. by MACNAIL in *Select Epigrams from the Greek Anthology.* See also CALLIMACHUS—*Epigrams.* XIV. L. 3. *Anthologia Palatina.* VII. 524.

14
To smell to a turf of fresh earth is wholesome for the body; no less are thoughts of mortality cordial to the soul.
FULLER—*Holy and Profane States.* Bk. IV. *The Court Lady.*

15
That flesh is but the glasse, which holds the dust
That measures all our time; which also shall
Be crumbled into dust.
HERBERT—*The Temple. Church Monuments.*

16 Consider
The lilies of the field whose bloom is brief:—
We are as they;
Like them we fade away
As doth a leaf.
CHRISTINA G. ROSSETTI—*Consider.*

17
Hier ist die Stelle wo ich sterblich bin.
This is the spot where I am mortal.
SCHILLER—*Don Carlos.* I. 6. 67.

18
The immortal could we cease to contemplate,
The mortal part suggests its every trait.
God laid His fingers on the ivories
Of her pure members as on smoothèd keys,
And there out-breathed her spirit's harmonies.
FRANCIS THOMPSON—*Her Portrait.* St. 7.

19
At thirty, man suspects himself a fool,
Knows it at forty, and reforms his plan;
At fifty, chides his infamous delay,
Pushes his prudent purpose to resolve,
In all the magnanimity of thought;
Resolves, and re-resolves, then dies the same.
And why? because he thinks himself immortal,
All men think all men mortal but themselves.
YOUNG—*Night Thoughts.* Night I. L. 417.

MOSQUITO

20
Fair insect! that, with threadlike legs spread out,
And blood-extracting bill and filmy wing,
Dost murmur, as thou slowly sail'st about,
In pitiless ears full many a plaintive thing,
And tell how little our large veins would bleed,
Would we but yield them to thy bitter need.
BRYANT—*To a Mosquito.*

MOTH

21
What gained we, little moth? Thy ashes,
Thy one brief parting pang may show:
And withering thoughts for soul that dashes,
From deep to deep, are but a death more slow.
CARLYLE—*Tragedy of the Night Moth.* St. 14.

MOTHERHOOD

1

Stabat mater, dolorosa
Juxta crucem lacrymosa
Que pendebat Filius.
At the cross, her station keeping,
Stood the mournful mother, weeping,
Where He hung, the dying Lord.

ANON. Trans. by DR. IRONS.

2

Alma mater.
Fostering mother.

Applied by students to the university where they have graduated.

3

[Milton] calls the university "A stony-hearted step-mother."

AUGUSTINE BIRRELL—*Obiter Dicta.* Phrase used also by DE QUINCEY—*Confessions of an Opium Eater.* Pt. I. Referring to Oxford Street, London.

4

A mother is a mother still,
The holiest thing alive.

COLERIDGE—*The Three Graves.* St. 10.

5

The mother of all living.

Genesis. III. 20.

6

There is none,
In all this cold and hollow world, no fount
Of deep, strong, deathless love, save that within
A mother's heart.

MRS. HEMANS—*Siege of Valencia.* Sc. *Room in a Palace of Valencia.*

7

The mother said to her daughter, "Daughter, bid thy daughter tell her daughter that her daughter's daughter hath a daughter."

GEORGE HAKEWILL—*Apologie.* Bk. III. Ch. V. Sec. 9.

Mater ait natæ die natæ filia natum
Ut moneat natæ plangere filiolam.

The mother says to her daughter: Daughter bid thy daughter, to tell her daughter, that her daughter's daughter is crying.

See GRESWELL—*Account of Runcorn.* P. 34.

Another trans.: Rise up daughter, and go to thy daughter, For her daughter's daughter hath a daughter. Another old form in WILLETS' *Hexapla, in Leviticum.* Ch. XXVI. 9.

8

I arose a mother in Israel.

Judges. V. 7.

9

If I were hanged on the highest hill,
Mother o' mine, O mother o' mine!
I know whose love would follow me still,
Mother o' mine, O mother o' mine!

KIPLING—*Mother O' Mine.*

10

There was a place in childhood that I remember well,
And there a voice of sweetest tone bright fairy tales did tell.

SAMUEL LOVER—*My Mother Dear.*

11

A woman's love
Is mighty, but a mother's heart is weak,
And by its weakness overcomes.

LOWELL—*Legend of Brittany.* Pt. II. St. 43.

12

The bravest battle that ever was fought;
Shall I tell you where and when?
On the maps of the world you will find it not;
It was fought by the mothers of men.

JOAQUIN MILLER—*The Bravest Battle. Mothers of Men.*

13

Her children arise up and call her blessed.

Proverbs. XXXI. 28.

14

They say man rules the universe,
That subject shore and main
Kneel down and bless the empery
Of his majestic reign;
But a sovereign, gentler, mightier,
Man from his throne has hurled,
For the hand that rocks the cradle
Is the hand that rules the world.

WILLIAM STEWART ROSS ("Saladin"). Poem in *Woman: Her Glory, her Shame, and her God.* Vol. II. P. 420. 1894.

(See also WALLACE)

15

So loving to my mother
That he might not esteem the winds of heaven
Visit her face too roughly.

Hamlet. Act. I. Sc. 2. L. 140.

16

And all my mother came into mine eyes
And gave me up to tears.

Henry V. Act. IV. Sc. 6. L. 32.

17

And say to mothers what a holy charge
Is theirs—with what a kingly power their love
Might rule the fountains of the new-born mind.

MRS. SIGOURNEY—*The Mother of Washington.* L. 33.

18

Who ran to help me when I fell,
And would some pretty story tell,
Or kiss the place to make it well?
My mother.

ANNE TAYLOR—*My Mother.* St. 6.

19

The bearing and the training of a child
Is woman's wisdom.

TENNYSON—*Princess.* Canto V. L. 456.

20

Happy he
With such a mother! faith in womankind
Beats with his blood, and trust in all things high
Comes easy to him, and though he trip and fall,
He shall not blind his soul with clay.

TENNYSON—*Princess.* Canto VII. L. 308.

21

Mother is the name for God in the lips and hearts of children.

THACKERAY—*Vanity Fair.* Vol. II. Ch. XII.

22

They say that man is mighty,
He governs land and sea,
He wields a mighty scepter
O'er lesser powers that be;
But a mightier power and stronger
Man from his throne has hurled,
For the hand that rocks the cradle
Is the hand that rules the world.

WM. ROSS WALLACE—*What Rules the World.* Written about 1865-6.

(See also ROSS, also J. A. WALLACE under PRAYER)

1
All women become like their mothers. That is their tragedy. No man does. That is his.
OSCAR WILDE—*Importance of Being Earnest.* Act I.

2
Sure I love the dear silver that shines in your hair,
And the brow that's all furrowed, and wrinkled with care.
I kiss the dear fingers, so toil-worn for me,
Oh, God bless you and keep you, Mother Machree.
RIDA JOHNSON YOUNG—*Mother Machree.*

MOTIVE

3
Iago's soliloquy—the motive-hunting of a motiveless malignity—how awful it is!
COLERIDGE—*Shakespeare. Notes on Othello.*

4
What makes life dreary is the want of motive.
GEORGE ELIOT—*Daniel Deronda.* Bk. VIII. Ch. LXV.

5
A good intention clothes itself with sudden power.
EMERSON—*Essays. Fate.*

6
For there's nothing we read of in torture's inventions,
Like a well-meaning dunce, with the best of intentions.
LOWELL—*A Fable for Critics.* L. 250.

7
Men's minds are as variant as their faces. Where the motives of their actions are pure, the operation of the former is no more to be imputed to them as a crime, than the appearance of the latter; for both, being the work of nature, are alike unavoidable.
GEORGE WASHINGTON—*Social Maxims. Difference of Opinion no Crime.*

MOUNTAINS

8
Mont Blanc is the monarch of mountains;
They crown'd him long ago
On a throne of rocks, in a robe of clouds,
With a diadem of snow.
BYRON—*Manfred.* Act I. Sc. 1. L. 62.

9
'Tis distance lends enchantment to the view,
And robes the mountain in its azure hue.
CAMPBELL—*Pleasures of Hope.* Pt. I. L. 7.

10
Whose sunbright summit mingles with the sky.
CAMPBELL—*Pleasures of Hope.* Pt. I. L. 4.

11
Mountains interposed
Make enemies of nations, who had else
Like kindred drops been mingled into one.
COWPER—*The Task.* Bk. II. L. 17.

12
To make a mountain of a mole-hill.
HENRY ELLIS—*Original Letters. Second Series.* P. 312.
(See also HORACE)

13
Over the hills, and over the main,
To Flanders, Portugal, or Spain;
The Queen commands, and we'll obey,
Over the hills and far away.
GEORGE FARQUHAR—*The Recruiting Officer.* Act II. Sc. 2.

14
Over the hills and far away.
GAY—*The Beggar's Opera.* Act I. Sc. 1.
(See also HENLEY, MERRY COMPANION, TENNYSON, also FARQUHAR under MUSIC)

15
Round its breast the rolling clouds are spread,
Eternal sunshine settles on its head.
GOLDSMITH—*The Deserted Village.* L. 192.

16
What is the voice of strange command
Calling you still, as friend calls friend,
With love that cannot brook delay,
To rise and follow the ways that wend
Over the hills and far away.
HENLEY—*Rhymes and Rhythms.* 1.
(See also GAY)

17
Heav'd on Olympus tottering Ossa stood;
On Ossa, Pelion nods with all his wood.
HOMER—*Odyssey.* Bk. XI. L. 387. POPE'S trans.
(See also HORACE, OVID, RABELAIS, VERGIL)

18
Quid dignum tanto feret hic promissor hiatu?
Parturiunt montes; nascetur ridiculus mus.
What will this boaster produce worthy of this mouthing? The mountains are in labor; a ridiculous mouse will be born.
HORACE—*Ars Poetica.* 138. ATHENÆUS—*Deipnosophists.* 14. 7. (A preserved fragment.) PHÆDRUS. IV. 22.
(See also ELLIS, TACHOS)

19
Pelion imposuisse Olympo.
To pile Pelion upon Olympus.
HORACE—*Odes.* Bk. III. 4. 52.
(See also HOMER)

20
Daily with souls that cringe and plot,
We Sinais climb and know it not.
LOWELL—*The Vision of Sir Launfal. Prelude* to Pt. I.

21
Then the Omnipotent Father with his thunder made Olympus tremble, and from Ossa hurled Pelion.
OVID—*Metamorphoses.* I.
(See also HOMER)

22
Over the hills and o'er the main,
To Flanders, Portugal and Spain,
Queen Anne commands and we'll obey,
Over the hills and far away.
The Merry Companion. Song 173. P. 149.
(See also GAY)

23
Hills peep o'er hills, and Alps on Alps arise.
POPE—*Essay on Criticism.* Pt. II. L. 32.

24
I would have you call to mind the strength of the ancient giants, that undertook to lay the high mountain Pelion on the top of Ossa, and set among those the shady Olympus.
RABELAIS—*Works.* Bk. IV. Ch. XXXVIII.
(See also HOMER)

25
Mountains are the beginning and the end of all natural scenery.
RUSKIN—*True and Beautiful. Nature. Mountains.* P. 91.

1
Who digs hills because they do aspire,
Throws down one mountain to cast up a higher.
Pericles. Act I. Sc. 4. L. 6.

2
The mountain was in labour, and Jove was afraid, but it brought forth a mouse.
TACHOS, King of Egypt.
(See also HORACE)

3
And o'er the hills and far away,
Beyond their utmost purple rim,
Beyond the night, across the day,
Thro' all the world she followed him.
TENNYSON—*Daydream. The Departure.* IV.
(See also GAY)

4
Imponere Pelio Ossam.
To pile Ossa upon Pelion.
VERGIL—*Georgics.* I. 281.
(See also HOMER)

MOURNING

5
He had kept
The whiteness of his soul, and thus men o'er him wept.
BYRON—*Childe Harold.* Canto III. St. 57.

6
O! sing unto my roundelay,
O! drop thy briny tear with me.
Dance no more at holiday,
Like a running river be;
My love is dead,
Gone to his death bed
All under the willow tree.
THOS. CHATTERTON—*Ælla. Minstrel's Songs.*

7
Each lonely scene shall thee restore;
For thee the tear be duly shed;
Belov'd till life can charm no more,
And mourn'd till Pity's self be dead.
COLLINS—*Dirge in Cymbeline.*

8
It is better to go to the house of mourning than to go to the house of feasting.
Ecclesiastes. VII. 2.

9
When I am dead, no pageant train
Shall waste their sorrows at my bier,
Nor worthless pomp of homage vain
Stain it with hypocritic tear.
EDWARD EVERETT—*Alaric the Visigoth.*

10
Forever honour'd, and forever mourn'd.
HOMER—*Iliad.* Bk. XXII. L. 422. POPE'S trans.

11
Si vis me flere, dolendum est
Primum ipsi tibi.
If you wish me to weep, you must mourn first yourself.
HORACE—*Ars Poetica.* CII.

12
Seems, madam! Nay, it is; I know not "seems."
'Tis not alone my inky cloak, good mother,
Nor customary suits of solemn black,
Nor windy suspiration of forced breath.
No, nor the fruitful river in the eye,
Nor the dejected 'haviour of the visage,
Together with all forms, modes, shapes of grief,
That can denote me truly; these indeed seem,
For they are actions that a man might play,
But I have that within which passeth show;
These but the trappings and the suits of woe.
Hamlet. Act I. Sc. 2. ("Moods" for "modes" in folio and quarto.)

13
He that lacks time to mourn, lacks time to mend.
Eternity mourns that. 'Tis an ill cure
For life's worst ills to have no time to feel them.
SIR HENRY TAYLOR—*Philip Van Artevelde.* Pt. I. Act I. Sc. 5.

14
Let us weep in our darkness—but weep not for him!
Not for him—who, departing, leaves millions in tears!
Not for him—who has died full of honor and years!
Not for him—who ascended Fame's ladder so high.
From the round at the top he has stepped to the sky.
N. P. WILLIS—*The Death of Harrison.* St. 6.

15
He mourns the dead who lives as they desire.
YOUNG—*Night Thoughts.* Night II. L. 24.

MOUSE

16
I holde a mouses herte nat worth a leek.
That hath but oon hole for to sterte to.
CHAUCER—*Paraphrase of the Prologue of The Wyves Tale of Bath.* L. 572.
(See also POPE)

17
The mouse that hath but one hole is quickly taken.
HERBERT—*Jacula Prudentum.* PLAUTUS—*Truncülentus.* IV.

18
It had need to bee
A wylie mouse that should breed in the cat's eare.
HEYWOOD—*Proverbs.* Pt. II. Ch. V.

19
"Once on a time there was a mouse," quoth she,
"Who sick of worldly tears and laughter, grew
Enamoured of a sainted privacy;
To all terrestrial things he bade adieu,
And entered, far from mouse, or cat, or man,
A thick-walled cheese, the best of Parmesan."
LORENZO PIGNOTTI—*The Mouse Turned Hermit.*

20
When a building is about to fall down all the mice desert it.
PLINY the Elder—*Natural History.* Bk. VIII. Sec. CIII.

21
The mouse that always trusts to one poor hole,
Can never be a mouse of any soul.
POPE—*The Wife of Bath. Her Prologue.* L. 298.
(See also CHAUCER)

22
The mouse ne'er shunn'd the cat as they did budge
From rascals worse than they.
Coriolanus. Act I. Sc. 6. L. 44.

MOUTH

1
Some asked me where the rubies grew,
And nothing I did say,
But with my finger pointed to
The lips of Julia.
HERRICK—*The Rock of Rubies, and the Quarrie of Pearls.*

2
Lips are no part of the head, only made for a double-leaf door for the mouth.
LYLY—*Midas.*

3
Divers philosophers hold that the lips is parcel of the mouth.
Merry Wives of Windsor. Act I. Sc. 1. Theobald's reading is "mind." Pope changed "mouth" to "mind."

4
Her lips were red, and one was thin,
Compared to that was next her chin,
(Some bee had stung it newly).
SUCKLING—*A Ballad Upon a Wedding.* St. 11.

5
With that she dasht her on the lippes,
So dyed double red;
Hard was the heart that gave the blow,
Soft were those lippes that bled.
WILLIAM WARNER—*Albion's England.* Bk. VIII. Ch. XLI. St. 53.

6
As a pomegranate, cut in twain,
White-seeded is her crimson mouth.
OSCAR WILDE—*La Bella Donna della Mia Mente.*

MULBERRY TREE

Morus

7
O, the mulberry-tree is of trees the queen!
Bare long after the rest are green;
But as time steals onwards, while none perceives
Slowly she clothes herself with leaves—
Hides her fruit under them, hard to find.
* * * * *
But by and by, when the flowers grow few
And the fruits are dwindling and small to view—
Out she comes in her matron grace
With the purple myriads of her race;
Full of plenty from root to crown,
Showering plenty her feet adown.
While far over head hang gorgeously
Large luscious berries of sanguine dye,
For the best grows highest, always highest,
Upon the mulberry-tree.
D. M. MULOCK—*The Mulberry-Tree.*

MURDER

8
Carcasses bleed at the sight of the murderer.
BURTON—*Anatomy of Melancholy.* Pt. I. Sec. I. Memb. II. Subsec. V.

9
Et tu, Brute fili.
You also, O son Brutus.
CÆSAR. Words on being stabbed by Brutus, according to SUETONIUS. Quoted as "Et tu Brutus" and "Tu quoque Brute." *True Tragedy of Richarde, Duke of York.* (1600) Also found in S. NICHOLSON'S *Acolastus his Afterwitte.* (1600) *Cæsar's Legend,* in *Mirror for Magistrates.* (1587) MALONE suggests that the Latin words appeared in the old Latin play by RICHARD EEDES—*Epilogus Cæsaris Interfecti,* given at Christ Church Oxford. (1582)

10
Blood, though it sleep a time, yet never dies.
The gods on murtherers fix revengeful eyes.
GEO. CHAPMAN—*The Widow's Tears.* Act V. Sc. IV.

11
Mordre wol out, that see we day by day.
CHAUCER—*Canterbury Tales. The Nonnes Preestes Tale.* L. 15,058.

12
Murder may pass unpunish'd for a time,
But tardy justice will o'ertake the crime.
DRYDEN—*The Cock and the Fox.* L. 285.

13
Murder, like talent, seems occasionally to run in families.
GEORGE HENRY LEWES—*Physiology of Common Life.* Ch. XII.

14
Absolutism tempered by assassination.
COUNT MÜNSTER, Hanoverian envoy at St. Petersburg, writing of the Russian Constitution.

15
Neque enim lex est æquior ulla,
Quam necis artifices arte perire sua.
Nor is there any law more just, than that he who has plotted death shall perish by his own plot.
OVID—*Ars Amatoria.* I. 655.

16
One murder made a villain,
Millions a hero.—Princes were privileg'd
To kill, and numbers sanctified the crime.
Ah! why will kings forget that they are men,
And men that they are brethren?
BISHOP PORTEUS—*Death.* L. 154.
(See also YOUNG)

17
Murder most foul, as in the best it is;
But this most foul, strange and unnatural.
Hamlet. Act I. Sc. 5. L. 27.

18
For murder, though it have no tongue, will speak
With most miraculous organ.
Hamlet. Act II. Sc. 2. L. 622.

19
He took my father grossly, full of bread;
With all his crimes broad blown, as flush as May;
And how his audit stands who knows save heaven?
Hamlet. Act III. Sc. 3. L. 80.

20
No place, indeed, should murder sanctuarize.
Hamlet. Act IV. Sc. 7. L. 128.

21
O, pardon me, thou bleeding piece of earth,
That I am meek and gentle with these butchers!
Thou art the ruins of the noblest man
That ever lived in the tide of times.
Woe to the hand that shed this costly blood
Over thy wounds now do I prophesy.
Julius Cæsar. Act III. Sc. 1. L. 254.

1
Will all great Neptune's ocean wash this blood
Clean from my hand? No, this my hand will rather
The multitudinous seas incardine,
Making the green one red.
Macbeth. Act II. Sc. 2. L. 60.

2
Blood hath been shed ere now i' the olden time,
Ere humane statute purg'd the gentle weal;
Ay, and since too, murders have been perform'd
Too terrible for the ear: the time has been,
That, when the brains were out, the man would die,
And there an end; but now they rise again,
With twenty mortal murders on their crowns,
And push us from our stools: this is more strange
Than such a murder is.
Macbeth. Act III. Sc. 4. L. 76.

3
The great King of kings
Hath in the table of his law commanded
That thou shalt do no murder: and wilt thou, then,
Spurn at his edict and fulfill a man's?
Richard III. Act I. Sc. 4. L. 200.

4
E un incidente del mestiere.
It is one of the incidents of the profession.
UMBERTO I, of Italy, *after escaping death.* Assassination is the perquisite of kings. Ascribed to him by other authorities. (Quoted "métier" erroneously.)

5
Cast not the clouded gem away,
Quench not the dim but living ray,—
My brother man, Beware!
With that deep voice which from the skies
Forbade the Patriarch's sacrifice.
God's angel, cries, Forbear!
WHITTIER—*Human Sacrifice.* Pt. VII.

6
One to destroy is murder by the law,
And gibbets keep the lifted hand in awe;
To murder thousands takes a specious name,
War's glorious art, and gives immortal fame.
YOUNG—*Love of Fame.* Satire VII. L. 55.
(See also PORTEUS)

7
Killing no murder.
Title of a tract in *Harleian Miscellany*, ascribed to COL. SILAS TITUS, recommending the murder of CROMWELL.

MUSIC

8
Music religious heat inspires,
It wakes the soul, and lifts it high,
And wings it with sublime desires,
And fits it to bespeak the Deity.
ADDISON—*A Song for St. Cecilia's Day.* St. 4.

9
Music exalts each joy, allays each grief,
Expels diseases, softens every pain,
Subdues the rage of poison, and the plague.
JOHN ARMSTRONG—*Art of Preserving Health.* Bk. IV. L. 512.

10
That rich celestial music thrilled the air
From hosts on hosts of shining ones, who thronged
Eastward and westward, making bright the night.
EDWIN ARNOLD—*Light of Asia.* Bk. IV. L. 418.

11
Music tells no truths.
BAILEY—*Festus.* Sc. *A Village Feast.*

12
Rugged the breast that music cannot tame.
J. C. BAMPFYLDE—*Sonnet.*
(See also BRAMSTON)

13
If music and sweet poetry agree.
BARNFIELD—*Sonnet.*

14
Gayly the troubadour
Touched his guitar.
THOMAS HAYNES BAYLY—*Welcome Me Home.*

15
I'm saddest when I sing.
THOMAS HAYNES BAYLY—*You think I have a merry heart.*
(See also ARTEMUS WARD)

16
God is its author, and not man; he laid
The key-note of all harmonies; he planned
All perfect combinations, and he made
Us so that we could hear and understand.
J. G. BRAINARD—*Music.*

17
The rustle of the leaves in summer's hush
When wandering breezes touch them, and the sigh
That filters through the forest, or the gush
That swells and sinks amid the branches high,—
'Tis all the music of the wind, and we
Let fancy float on this æolian breath.
J. G. BRAINARD—*Music.*

18
"Music hath charms to soothe the savage beast,"
And therefore proper at a sheriff's feast.
JAMES BRAMSTON—*Man of Taste.* First line quoted from PRIOR.
(See also BAMPFYLDE, CONGREVE, PRIOR)

19
And sure there is music even in the beauty, and the silent note which Cupid strikes, far sweeter than the sound of an instrument; for there is music wherever there is harmony, order, or proportion; and thus far we may maintain the music of the spheres.
SIR THOMAS BROWNE—*Religio Medici.* Pt. II. Sec. IX. Use of the phrase "Music of the Spheres" given by BISHOP MARTIN FOTHERBY—*Athconastrix.* P. 315. (Ed. 1622) Said by BISHOP JOHN WILKINS—*Discovery of a New World.* I. 42. (Ed. 1694)
(See also BUTLER, BYRON, COWLEY, JOB, MILTON, MONTAIGNE, MOORE)

20
Yet half the beast is the great god Pan,
To laugh, as he sits by the river,
Making a poet out of a man.
The true gods sigh for the cost and the pain—
For the reed that grows never more again
As a reed with the reeds of the river.
E. B. BROWNING—*A Musical Instrument.*

21
Her voice, the music of the spheres,
So loud, it deafens mortals' ears;
As wise philosophers have thought,
And that's the cause we hear it not.
BUTLER—*Hudibras.* Pt. II. Canto I. L. 617.
(See also BROWNE)

1
For discords make the sweetest airs.
BUTLER—*Hudibras.* Pt. III. Canto I. L. 919.
(See also SPENSER)

2
Soprano, basso, even the contra-alto
Wished him five fathom under the Rialto.
BYRON—*Beppo.* St. 32.

3
Music arose with its voluptuous swell,
Soft eyes look'd love to eyes which spake again,
And all went merry as a marriage bell.
BYRON—*Childe Harold.* Canto III. St. 21.

4
There's music in the sighing of a reed;
There's music in the gushing of a rill;
There's music in all things, if men had ears:
Their earth is but an echo of the spheres.
BYRON—*Don Juan.* Canto XV. St. 5.

5
And hears thy stormy music in the drum!
CAMPBELL—*Pleasures of Hope.* Pt. I.

6
Merrily sang the monks in Ely
When Cnut, King, rowed thereby;
Row, my knights, near the land,
And hear we these monkes' song.
Attributed to KING CANUTE—*Song of the Monks of Ely*, in SPENS—*History of the English People. Historia Eliensis.* (1066) *Chambers' Ency. of English Literature.*

7
Music is well said to be the speech of angels.
CARLYLE—*Essays. The Opera.*

8
When music, heavenly maid, was young,
While yet in early Greece she sung,
The Passions oft, to hear her shell,
Throng'd around her magic cell.
COLLINS—*Passions.* L. 1.

9
In notes by distance made more sweet.
COLLINS—*Passions.* L. 60.
(See also WORDSWORTH)

10
In hollow murmurs died away.
COLLINS—*Passions.* L. 68.

11
Music has charms to soothe a savage breast,
To soften rocks, or bend a knotted oak.
I've read that things inanimate have moved,
And, as with living souls, have been inform'd,
By magic numbers and persuasive sound.
CONGREVE—*The Mourning Bride.* Act I. Sc. 1.
(See also BRAMSTON)

12
And when the music goes te-toot,
The monkey acts so funny
That we all hurry up and scoot
To get some monkey-money.
M-double-unk for the monkey,
M-double-an for the man;
M-double unky, hunky monkey,
Hunkey monkey-man.
Ever since the world began
Children danced and children ran
When they heard the monkey-man,
The m-double-unky man.
EDMUND VANCE COOKE—*The Monkey-Man. I rule the House.*

13
Water and air He for the Tenor chose,
Earth made the Base, the Treble Flame arose,
To th' active Moon a quick brisk stroke he gave,
To Saturn's string a touch more soft and grave.
The motions strait, and round, and swift, and slow,
And short and long, were mixt and woven so,
Did in such artful Figures smoothly fall,
As made this decent measur'd Dance of all.
And this is Musick.
COWLEY—*Davideis.* Bk. I. P. 13. (1668)
(See also BROWNE)

14
With melting airs, or martial, brisk, or grave;
Some chord in unison with what we hear
Is touch'd within us, and the heart replies.
COWPER—*The Task.* Bk. VI. *Winter Walk at Noon.* L. 3.

15
The soft complaining flute
In dying notes discovers
The woes of hopeless lovers,
Whose dirge is whisper'd by the warbling lute.
DRYDEN—*A Song for St. Cecilia's Day.*

16
Music sweeps by me as a messenger
Carrying a message that is not for me.
GEORGE ELIOT—*Spanish Gypsy.* Bk. III.

17
'Tis God gives skill,
But not without men's hands: He could not make
Antonio Stradivari's violins
Without Antonio.
GEORGE ELIOT—*Stradivarius.* L. 151.

18
The silent organ loudest chants
The master's requiem.
EMERSON—*Dirge.*

19
Our 'prentice, Tom, may now refuse
To wipe his scoundrel master's shoes;
For now he's free to sing and play
Over the hills and far away.
FARQUHAR—*Over the Hills and Far Away.* Act II. Sc. 3.
(See also STEVENSON, also GAY under MOUNTAINS, FARQUHAR under PATRIOTISM)

20
But Bellenden we needs must praise,
Who as down the stairs she jumps
Sings o'er the hill and far away,
Despising doleful dumps.
Distracted Jockey's Lamentation. Pills to Purge Melancholy.

21
Tom he was a piper's son,
He learned to play when he was young;
But all the tune that he could play
Was "Over the hills and far away."
Distracted Jockey's Lamentation. Pills to Purge Melancholy found in *The Nursery Rhymes of England* by HALLIWELL PHILLIPS.

22
When I was young and had no sense
I bought a fiddle for eighteen pence,
And all the tunes that I could play
Was, "Over the Hills and Far Away."
Old Ballad, in the *Pedlar's Pack of Ballads and Songs.*

1
Blasen ist nicht flöten, ihr müsst die Finger bewegen.
To blow is not to play on the flute; you must move the fingers.
GOETHE—*Sprüche in Prosa*. III.

2
Jack Whaley had a cow,
And he had nought to feed her;
He took his pipe and played a tune,
And bid the cow consider.
Old Scotch and North of Ireland ballad.
LADY GRANVILLE uses it in a letter. (1836)

3
Where through the long-drawn aisle and fretted vault
The pealing anthem swells the note of praise.
GRAY—*Elegy in a Country Church Yard*. St. 10.

4
He stood beside a cottage lone,
And listened to a lute,
One summer's eve, when the breeze was gone,
And the nightingale was mute.
THOS. HERVEY—*The Devil's Progress*.

5
Why should the devil have all the good tunes?
ROWLAND HILL—*Sermons*. In his biography by E. W. BROOME. P. 93.

6
Music was a thing of the soul—a rose-lipped shell that murmured of the eternal sea — a strange bird singing the songs of another shore.
J. G. HOLLAND—*Plain Talks on Familiar Subjects. Art and Life.*
(See also ROGERS; also HAMILTON under OCEAN)

7
From thy dead lips a clearer note is born
Than ever Triton blew from wreathèd horn.
HOLMES—*Chambered Nautilus*.
(See also WORDSWORTH under CHOICE)

8 Citharœdus
Ridetur chorda qui semper oberrat eadem.
The musician who always plays on the same string, is laughed at.
HORACE—*Ars Poetica*. 355.

9
Play uppe, play uppe, O Boston bells!
Ply all your changes, all your swells,
Play uppe "The Brides of Enderby."
JEAN INGELOW—*High Tide on the Coast of Lincolnshire*.

10
When the morning stars sang together, and all the sons of God shouted for joy.
Job. XXXVIII. 7.
(See also BROWNE)

11 Ere music's golden tongue
Flattered to tears this aged man and poor.
KEATS—*The Eve of St. Agnes*. St. 3.

12
The silver, snarling trumpets 'gan to chide.
KEATS—*The Eve of St. Agnes*. St. 4.

13
Heard melodies are sweet, but those unheard
Are sweeter; therefore, ye soft pipes, play on;
Not to the sensual ear, but, more endear'd,
Pipe to the spirit ditties of no tone.
KEATS—*Ode on a Grecian Urn*.

14
I even think that, sentimentally, I am disposed to harmony. But organically I am incapable of a tune.
LAMB—*A Chapter on Ears*.

15
A velvet flute-note fell down pleasantly,
Upon the bosom of that harmony,
And sailed and sailed incessantly,
As if a petal from a wild-rose blown
Had fluttered down upon that pool of tone,
And boatwise dropped o' the convex side
And floated down the glassy tide
And clarified and glorified
The solemn spaces where the shadows bide.
From the warm concave of that fluted note
Somewhat, half song, half odour forth did float
As if a rose might somehow be a throat.
SIDNEY LANIER—*The Symphony*.
(See also SHERMAN)

16
Music is in all growing things;
And underneath the silky wings
Of smallest insects there is stirred
A pulse of air that must be heard;
Earth's silence lives, and throbs, and sings.
LATHROP—*Music of Growth*.

17
Writ in the climate of heaven, in the language spoken by angels.
LONGFELLOW—*The Children of the Lord's Supper*. L. 262.

18
Yea, music is the Prophet's art
Among the gifts that God hath sent,
One of the most magnificent!
LONGFELLOW—*Christus*. Pt. III. Second Interlude. St. 5.

19
When she had passed, it seemed like the ceasing of exquisite music.
LONGFELLOW—*Evangeline*. Pt. I. 1.

20
He is dead, the sweet musician!
* * * *
He has moved a little nearer
To the Master of all music.
LONGFELLOW—*Hiawatha*. Pt. XV. L. 56.

21
Music is the universal language of mankind.
LONGFELLOW—*Outre-Mer. Ancient Spanish Ballads*.

22
Who, through long days of labor,
And nights devoid of ease,
Still heard in his soul the music
Of wonderful melodies.
LONGFELLOW—*The Day is Done*. St. 8.

23
Such sweet compulsion doth in music lie.
MILTON—*Arcades*. L. 68.

24
Who shall silence all the airs and madrigals that whisper softness in chambers?
MILTON—*Areopagitica*.

25
Can any mortal mixture of earth's mould
Breathe such divine enchanting ravishment?
MILTON—*Comus*. L. 244.

1

Ring out ye crystal spheres!
Once bless our human ears,
If ye have power to touch our senses so;
And let your silver chime
Move in melodious time;
And let the base of Heaven's deep organ blow,
And with your ninefold harmony,
Make up full consort to the angelic symphony.
MILTON—*Hymn on the Nativity*. St. 13.

2

There let the pealing organ blow,
To the full voiced quire below,
In service high, and anthems clear,
As may with sweetness, through mine ear,
Dissolve me into ecstasies,
And bring all heaven before mine eyes.
MILTON—*Il Penseroso*. L. 161.

3

Untwisting all the chains that tie the hidden soul of harmony.
MILTON—*L'Allegro*. L. 143.

4

As in an organ from one blast of wind
To many a row of pipes the soundboard breathes.
MILTON—*Paradise Lost*. Bk. I. L. 708.

5

And in their motions harmony divine
So smoothes her charming tones, that God's own ear
Listens delighted.
MILTON—*Paradise Lost*. Bk. V. 620.
(See also BROWNE)

6

Mettez, pour me jouer, vos flûtes mieux d'accord.
If you want to play a trick on me, put your flutes more in accord.
MOLIÈRE—*L'Etourdi*. Act I. 4.

7

La musique celeste.
The music of the spheres.
MONTAIGNE. Bk. I. Ch. XXII.
(See also BROWNE)

8

If the pulse of the patriot, soldier, or lover,
Have throbb'd at our lay, 'tis thy glory alone;
I was but as the wind, passing heedlessly over,
And all the wild sweetness I wak'd was thy own.
MOORE—*Dear Harp of My Country*. St. 2.

9

"This *must* be music," said he, "of the *spears*,
For I am cursed if each note of it doesn't run through one!"
MOORE—*Fudge Family in Paris*. Letter V. L. 28. (See also BROWNE)

10

The harp that once through Tara's halls
The soul of music shed,
Now hangs as mute on Tara's walls,
As if that soul were fled.
MOORE—*Harp That Once*.

11

If thou would'st have me sing and play
As once I play'd and sung,
First take this time-worn lute away,
And bring one freshly strung.
MOORE—*If Thou Would'st Have Me Sing and Play*.

12

And music too—dear music! that can touch
Beyond all else the soul that loves it much—
Now heard far off, so far as but to seem
Like the faint, exquisite music of a dream.
MOORE—*Lalla Rookh. The Veiled Prophet of Khorassan*.

13

'Tis believ'd that this harp which I wake now for thee
Was a siren of old who sung under the sea.
MOORE—*Origin of the Harp*.

14

She played upon her music-box a fancy air by chance,
And straightway all her polka-dots began a lively dance.
PETER NEWELL—*Her Polka Dots*.

15

Apes and ivory, skulls and roses, in junks of old Hong-Kong,
Gliding over a sea of dreams to a haunted shore of song.
ALFRED NOYES—*Apes and Ivory*.

16

There's a barrel-organ carolling across a golden street
In the city as the sun sinks low;
And the music's not immortal; but the world has made it sweet
And fulfilled it with the sunset glow.
ALFRED NOYES—*Barrel Organ*.

17

Wagner's music is better than it sounds.
BILL NYE.

18

We are the music-makers,
And we are the dreamers of dreams,
Wandering by lone sea-breakers,
And sitting by desolate streams;
World-losers and world-forsakers,
Of whom the pale moon gleams:
Yet we are the movers and shakers
Of the world for ever, it seems.
A. W. E. O'SHAUGHNESSY—*Music Makers*.

19

One man with a dream, at pleasure,
Shall go forth and conquer a crown
And three with a new song's measure
Can trample a kingdom down.
A. W. E. O'SHAUGHNESSY—*Music Makers*.

20

How light the touches are that kiss
The music from the chords of life!
COVENTRY PATMORE—*By the Sea*.

21

He touched his harp, and nations heard, entranced,
As some vast river of unfailing source,
Rapid, exhaustless, deep, his numbers flowed,
And opened new fountains in the human heart.
POLLOK—*Course of Time*. Bk. IV. L. 674.

22

Music resembles poetry: in each
Are nameless graces which no methods teach
And which a master-hand alone can reach.
POPE—*Essay on Criticism*. L. 143.

23 As some to Church repair,
Not for the doctrine, but the music there.
POPE—*Essay on Criticism*. L. 343.

1
What woful stuff this madrigal would be
In some starv'd hackney sonneteer, or me!
But let a Lord once own the happy lines,
How the wit brightens! how the style refines!
POPE—*Essay on Criticism*. L. 418.

2
Light quirks of music, broken and uneven,
Make the soul dance upon a jig to Heav'n.
POPE—*Moral Essays*. Ep. IV. L. 143.

3
By music minds an equal temper know,
Nor swell too high, nor sink too low.
* * * * *
Warriors she fires with animated sounds.
Pours balm into the bleeding lover's wounds.
POPE—*Ode on St. Cecilia's Day*.

4
Hark! the numbers soft and clear,
Gently steal upon the ear;
Now louder, and yet louder rise
And fill with spreading sounds the skies.
POPE—*Ode on St. Cecilia's Day*.

5
In a sadly pleasing strain
Let the warbling lute complain.
POPE—*Ode on St. Cecilia's Day*.

6
Music's force can tame the furious beast.
PRIOR. (See also BRAMSTON)

7
Seated one day at the organ,
I was weary and ill at ease,
And my fingers wandered idly
Over the noisy keys.
I do not know what I was playing,
Or what I was dreaming then,
But I struck one chord of music
Like the sound of a great Amen.
ADELAIDE A. PROCTER—*Lost Chord*. (As set to music, 5th line reads, "I know not what I was playing.")

8
We hanged our harps upon the willows in the midst thereof.
Psalms. CXXXVII. 2.

9
Above the pitch, out of tune, and off the hinges.
RABELAIS—*Works*. Bk. IV. Ch. XIX.

10
Musik ist Poesie der Luft.
Music is the poetry of the air.
JEAN PAUL RICHTER.

11
Sie zog tief in sein Herz, wie die Melodie eines Liedes, die aus der Kindheit heraufklingt.
It sank deep into his heart, like the melody of a song sounding from out of childhood's days.
JEAN PAUL RICHTER—*Hesperus*. XII.

12
The soul of music slumbers in the shell,
Till waked and kindled by the Master's spell;
And feeling hearts—touch them but lightly—pour
A thousand melodies unheard before!
SAM'L ROGERS—*Human Life*. L. 363.
(See also HOLLAND)

13
Give me some music; music, moody food
Of us that trade in love.
Antony and Cleopatra. Act II. Sc. 5. L. 1.

14
I am advised to give her music o' mornings; they say it will penetrate.
Cymbeline. Act II. Sc. 3. L. 12.

15
And it will discourse most eloquent music.
Hamlet. Act III. Sc. 2. L. 374. ("Excellent music" in Knight's ed.)

16
You would play upon me; you would seem to know my stops; you would pluck out the heart of my mystery; you would sound me from my lowest note to the top of my compass.
Hamlet. Act III. Sc. 2. L. 379.

17
How irksome is this music to my heart!
When such strings jar, what hope of harmony?
Henry VI. Pt. II. Sc. 1. L. 56.

18
Orpheus with his lute made trees,
And the mountain-tops that freeze,
Bow themselves, when he did sing:
To his music, plants and flowers
Ever sprung; as sun and showers,
There had made a lasting spring.
Henry VIII. Act III. Sc. 1. L. 3.

19
Everything that heard him play,
Even the billows of the sea,
Hung their heads, and then lay by;
In sweet music is such art:
Killing care and grief of heart
Fall asleep, or, hearing, die.
Henry VIII. Act III. Sc. 1. L. 9.

20
The choir,
With all the choicest music of the kingdom,
Together sung *Te Deum*.
Henry VIII. Act IV. Sc. 1. L. 90.

21
One whom the music of his own vain tongue
Doth ravish like enchanting harmony.
Love's Labour's Lost. Act I. Sc. 1. L. 167.

22
Though music oft hath such a charm
To make bad good, and good provoke to harm.
Measure for Measure. Act IV. Sc. 1. L. 14.

23
Let music sound while he doth make his choice;
Then, if he lose, he makes a swan-like end,
Fading in music.
Merchant of Venice. Act III. Sc. 2. L. 43.

24
How sweet the moonlight sleeps upon this bank!
Here will we sit and let the sounds of music
Creep in our ears: soft stillness, and the night
Becomes the touches of sweet harmony.
Merchant of Venice. Act V. Sc. 1. L. 54.

25
There's not the smallest orb which thou behold'st
But in his motion like an angel sings,
Still quiring to the young-eyed cherubins;
Such harmony is in immortal souls;
But, whilst this muddy vesture of decay
Doth grossly close it in, we cannot hear it.
Merchant of Venice. Act V. Sc. 1. L. 57.

1 Therefore the poet
Did feign that Orpheus drew trees, stones and floods;
Since nought so stockish, hard and full of rage,
But music for the time doth change his nature.
Merchant of Venice. Act V. Sc. 1. L. 79.

2
The man that hath no music in himself,
Nor is not moved with concord of sweet sounds,
Is fit for treasons, stratagems and spoils.
Merchant of Venice. Act V. Sc. 1. L. 83.

3 Music do I hear?
Ha! ha! keep time: how sour sweet music is,
When time is broke and no proportion kept!
Richard II. Act V. Sc. 5. L. 41.

4
Wilt thou have music? hark! Apollo plays
And twenty caged nightingales do sing.
Taming of the Shrew. Induction. Sc. 2. L. 37.

5
Preposterous ass, that never read so far
To know the cause why music was ordain'd!
Was it not to refresh the mind of man,
After his studies or his usual pain?
Taming of the Shrew. Act III. Sc. 1. L. 9.

6
This music crept by me upon the waters,
Allaying both their fury and my passion
With its sweet air.
Tempest. Act I. Sc. 2. L. 391.

7
Take but degree away, untune that string,
And, hark, what discord follows!
Troilus and Cressida. Act I. Sc. 3. L. 109.

8
If music be the food of love, play on;
Give me excess of it, that, surfeiting,
The appetite may sicken, and so die.
That strain again! it had a dying fall:
O, it came o'er my ear like the sweet sound
That breathes upon a bank of violets,
Stealing and giving odour.
Twelfth Night. Act I. Sc. 1. L. 1.

9
Song like a rose should be;
Each rhyme a petal sweet;
For fragrance, melody,
That when her lips repeat
The words, her heart may know
What secret makes them so.
Love, only Love.
FRANK DEMPSTER SHERMAN—*Song, in Lyrics for a Lute.*
(See also LANIER)

10
Musick! soft charm of heav'n and earth,
Whence didst thou borrow thy auspicious birth?
Or art thou of eternal date,
Sire to thyself, thyself as old as Fate.
EDMUND SMITH—*Ode in Praise of Musick*

11
See to their desks Apollo's sons repair,
Swift rides the rosin o'er the horse's hair!
In unison their various tones to tune,
Murmurs the hautboy, growls the hoarse bassoon;
In soft vibration sighs the whispering lute,
Tang goes the harpsichord, too-too the flute,
Brays the loud trumpet, squeaks the fiddle sharp,
Winds the French-horn, and twangs the tingling harp;
Till, like great Jove, the leader, figuring in,
Attunes to order the chaotic din.
HORACE AND JAMES SMITH—*Rejected Addresses. The Theatre.* L. 20.

12
So dischord ofte in musick makes the sweeter lay.
SPENSER—*Faerie Queene.* Bk. III. Canto II. St. 15. (See also BUTLER)

13
Music revives the recollections it would appease.
MADAME DE STAËL—*Corinne.* Bk. IX. Ch. II.

14
The gauger walked with willing foot,
And aye the gauger played the flute;
And what should Master Gauger play
But *Over the Hills and Far Away.*
ROBT. LOUIS STEVENSON—*Underwoods. A Song of the Road.*
(See also FARQUHAR)

15
How her fingers went when they moved by note
Through measures fine, as she marched them o'er
The yielding plank of the ivory floor.
BENJ. F. TAYLOR—*Songs of Yesterday. How the Brook Went to Mill.* St. 3.

16
It is the little rift within the lute
That by and by will make the music mute,
And ever widening slowly silence all.
TENNYSON—*Idylls of the King. Merlin and Vivien.* L. 393.

17
Music that brings sweet sleep down from the blissful skies.
TENNYSON—*The Lotos Eaters. Choric Song.* St. 1.

18
Music that gentlier on the spirit lies
Than tir'd eyelids upon tir'd eyes.
TENNYSON—*The Lotos Eaters. Choric Song.* St. 1.

19
I can't sing. As a singist I am not a success. I am saddest when I sing. So are those who hear me. They are sadder even than I am.
ARTEMUS WARD—*Lecture.*
(See also BAYLEY)

20
Strange! that a harp of thousand strings
Should keep in tune so long.
WATTS—*Hymns and Spiritual Songs.* Bk. II. 19.

21 And with a secret pain,
And smiles that seem akin to tears,
We hear the wild refrain.
WHITTIER—*At Port Royal.*

22
I'm the sweetest sound in orchestra heard
Yet in orchestra never have been.
DR. WILBERFORCE—*Riddle.* First lines.

23
Her ivory hands on the ivory keys
Strayed in a fitful fantasy,
Like the silver gleam when the poplar trees
Rustle their pale leaves listlessly
Or the drifting foam of a restless sea

When the waves show their teeth in the flying breeze.
OSCAR WILDE—*In the Gold Room. A Harmony.*

1
What fairy-like music steals over the sea,
Entrancing our senses with charmed melody?
MRS. M. C. WILSON—*What Fairy-like Music.*

2
Where music dwells
Lingering, and wandering on as loth to die;
Like thoughts whose very sweetness yieldeth proof
That they were born for immortality.
WORDSWORTH—*Ecclesiastical Sonnets.* Pt. III. 63. *Inside of King's Chapel, Cambridge.*

3
Bright gem instinct with music, vocal spark.
WORDSWORTH—*A Morning Exercise.*

4
Soft is the music that would charm forever:
The flower of sweetest smell is shy and lowly.
WORDSWORTH—*Not Love, Not War.*

5
Sweetest melodies
Are those that are by distance made more sweet.
WORDSWORTH—*Personal Talk.* St. 2.

6
The music in my heart I bore,
Long after it was heard no more.
WORDSWORTH—*The Solitary Reaper.*

MYRTLE

Myrtus Communis

7
Nor myrtle—which means chiefly love: and love
Is something awful which one dare not touch
So early o' mornings.
E. B. BROWNING—*Aurora Leigh.* Bk. II.

8
The myrtle (ensign of supreme command,
Consigned by Venus to Melissa's hand)
Not less capricious than a reigning fair,
Oft favors, oft rejects a lover's prayer;
In myrtle shades oft sings the happy swain,
In myrtle shades despairing ghosts complain.
SAMUEL JOHNSON—*Written at the Request of a Gentleman.* L. 3.

9
Dark-green and gemm'd with flowers of snow,
With close uncrowded branches spread
Not proudly high, nor meanly low,
A graceful myrtle rear'd its head.
MONTGOMERY—*The Myrtle.*

10
While the myrtle, now idly entwin'd with his crown.
Like the wreath of Harmodius, shall cover his sword.
MOORE—*O, Blame Not The Bard.*

N

NAME

11
Oh! no! we never mention her,
Her name is never heard;
My lips are now forbid to speak
That once familiar word.
THOMAS HAYNES BAYLY—*Melodies of Various Nations. Oh! No! We Never Mention Her.*

12
Je ne puis rien nommer si ce n'est par son nom;
J'appelle un chat un chat, et Rollet un fripon.
I can call nothing by name if that is not his name. I call a cat a cat, and Rollet a rogue.
BOILEAU—*Satires.* I. 51.

13
Call a spade a spade.
BURTON—*Anatomy of Melancholy. Democritus Junior to the Reader.* P. 11. SCALIGER—*Note on the Priapeia Sive Diversorum Poetarum.* BAXTER—*Narrative of the Most Memorable Passages of Life and Times.* (1696) DR. ARBUTHNOT—*Dissertations on the Art of Selling Bargains.* PHILIP OF MACEDON. See PLUTARCH'S *Life of Philip.*
(See also BOILEAU, ERASMUS, GIFFORD, JONSON, SWIFT)

14
He left a Corsair's name to other times,
Linked with one virtue, and a thousand crimes.
BYRON—*The Corsair.* Canto III. St. 24.

15
I have a passion for the name of "Mary,"
For once it was a magic sound to me,
And still it half calls up the realms of fairy,
Where I beheld what never was to be.
BYRON—*Don Juan.* Canto V. St. 4.

16
Oh, Amos Cottle!—Phœbus! what a name!
BYRON—*English Bards and Scotch Reviewers.* L. 399.

17
Who hath not own'd, with rapture-smitten frame,
The power of grace, the magic of a name.
CAMPBELL—*Pleasures of Hope.* Pt. II. L. 5.

18
Ah! replied my gentle fair,
Beloved, what are names but air?
Choose thou whatever suits the line:
Call me Sappho, call me Chloris,
Call me Lalage, or Doris,
Only, only, call me thine.
COLERIDGE—*What's in a Name.*

19
Some to the fascination of a name,
Surrender judgment hoodwinked.
COWPER—*Task.* Bk. VI. L. 101.

20
"Brooks of Sheffield": "'Somebody's sharp.' 'Who is?'" asked the gentleman, laughing. I looked up quickly, being curious to know. "Only Brooks of Sheffield," said Mr. Murdstone. I was glad to find it was only Brooks of Sheffield; for at first I really thought that it was I.
DICKENS—*David Copperfield.* Ch. 2.
I know that man; he comes from Sheffield.
SIDNEY GRUNDY—*A Pair of Spectacles.*

1
Known by the *sobriquet* of "The Artful Dodger."
DICKENS—*Oliver Twist*. Ch. 8.

2
The dodgerest of all the dodgers.
DICKENS—*Our Mutual Friend*. Ch. XIII.

3
Called me wessel, Sammy—a wessel of wrath.
DICKENS—*Pickwick Papers*. Ch. 22.

4
He lives who dies to win a lasting name.
DRUMMOND—*Sonnet*. XII.

5
Above any Greek or Roman name.
DRYDEN—*Upon the Death of Lord Hastings*. L. 76.
(See also POPE under FAME)

6
A good name is better than precious ointment.
Ecclesiastes. VII. 1.

7
There be of them that have left a name behind them.
Ecclesiasticus. XLIV. 8.

8
Ficum vocamus ficum, et scapham scapham.
We call a fig a fig, and a skiff a skiff.
ERASMUS—*Colloquy*. *Philetymus et Pseudocheus*. Also in *Dilucalum Philyphnus*. In his *Adagia* he refers to ARISTOPHANES as user of a like phrase. Quoted by LUCIAN—*Quom, Hist. sit. conscribend*. 41. Also in his *Jov. Trag*. 32. Found also in PLUTARCH—*Apopthegms*. P. 178. (Ed. 1624) Old use of same idea in TAVERNER—*Garden of Wysdom*. Pt. I. Ch. VI. (Ed. 1539)
(See also BURTON)

9
The blackest ink of fate was sure my lot,
And when fate writ my name it made a blot.
FIELDING—*Amelia*. II. 9.

10
I cannot say the crow is white,
But needs must call a spade a spade.
HUMPHREY GIFFORD—*A Woman's Face is Full of Wiles*.
(See also BURTON)

11
"Whose name was writ in water!" What large laughter
Among the immortals when that word was brought!
Then when his fiery spirit rose flaming after,
High toward the topmost heaven of heavens up-caught!
"All hail! our younger brother!" Shakespeare said,
And Dante nodded his imperial head.
R. W. GILDER—*Keats*.

12
My name may have buoyancy enough to float upon the sea of time.
Quoted by GLADSTONE. *Eton Miscellany*. Nov. 1827.

13
One of the few, the immortal names,
That were not born to die.
FITZ-GREENE HALLECK—*Marco Bozzaris*.

14
A nickname is the hardest stone that the devil can throw at a man.
Quoted by HAZLITT—*Essays*. *On Nicknames*.

15
Fate tried to conceal him by naming him Smith.
HOLMES—*The Boys*. (Of S. F. Smith)

16
My name is Norval; on the Grampian hills
My father feeds his flocks; a frugal swain,
Whose constant cares were to increase his store,
And keep his only son, myself, at home.
JOHN HOME—*Douglas*. Act II. Sc. 1. L. 42.

17
And, lo! Ben Adhem's name led all the rest.
LEIGH HUNT—*Abou Ben Adhem*.

18
He left the name, at which the world grew pale,
To point a moral, or adorn a tale.
SAMUEL JOHNSON—*Vanity of Human Wishes*. L. 221.

19
Ramp up my genius, be not retrograde,
But boldly nominate a spade a spade.
JONSON—*Poetaster*. Act V. 3.
(See also BURTON)

20
Have heard her sigh and soften out the name.
WALTER SAVAGE LANDOR—*Gebir*. Bk. V. L. 145.

21
Stat magni nominis umbra.
He stands the shadow of a mighty name.
LUCAN—*Pharsalia*. I. 135. JUNIUS adapted this as motto affixed to his *Letters*. (Stat nominis umbra) CLAUDIANUS—*Epigrams*. 42. gives "Nominis umbra manet veteris."

22
Clarum et venerabile nomen.
An illustrious and ancient name.
LUCAN—*Pharsalia*. IX. 203.

23
Out of his surname they have coined an epithet for a knave, and out of his Christian name a synonym for the Devil.
MACAULAY—*On Machiavelli*. 1825.

24
But unto you that fear my name shall the Sun of righteousness arise with healing in his wings.
Malachi. IV. 2.

25
The name that dwells on every tongue,
No minstrel needs.
DON JORGE MANRIQUE—*Coplas de Manrique*. St. 54. LONGFELLOW'S trans.

26
My name is Legion.
Mark. V. 9.

27
I, a parrot, am taught by you the names of others; I have learned of myself to say, "Hail! Cæsar!"
MARTIAL—*Epigrams*. Bk. XIV. Ep. 73.

28
"What is thy name, faire maid?" quoth he.
"Penelophon, O King," quoth she.
THOS. PERCY—*Reliques*. *King Cophetua and the Beggar-Maid*.

1
O name forever sad! forever dear!
Still breath'd in sighs, still usher'd with a tear.
POPE—*Eloisa to Abelard*. L. 31.

2
A good name is rather to be chosen than great riches.
Proverbs. XXII. 1.

3
Byzantine Logothete.
Term applied by ROOSEVELT to PRESIDENT WILSON. Taken from HODGKIN'S *Italy and Her Invaders*, or BURY'S *Hist. of the Later Roman Empire*. The officials of Byzantium were called Logothetes, "men of learning," "academic"; their foes were "barbarians." These men wrote notes to their foes, who read the notes and conquered the empire. Term defined by PROF. BASIL GILDERSLEEVE as "a scrivener," a subordinate who draws up papers." See N. Y. *Tribune*, Dec. 13, 1915.

4
Your name hangs in my heart like a bell's tongue.
ROSTAND—*Cyrano de Bergerac*.

5
Ich bin der Letzte meines Stamms; mein Name
Endet mit mir.
I am the last of my race. My name ends with me.
SCHILLER—*Wilhelm Tell*. II. 1. 100.

6
My foot is on my native heath, and my name is MacGregor!
SCOTT—*Rob Roy*. Ch. XXXIV.

7
Who, noteless as the race from which he sprung,
Saved others' names, but left his own unsung.
SCOTT—*Waverley*. Ch. XIII.

8
The one so like the other
As could not be distinguish'd but by names.
Comedy of Errors. Act I. Sc. 1. L. 52.

9
I would to God thou and I knew where a commodity of good names were to be bought.
Henry IV. Pt. I. Act I. Sc. 2. L. 92.

10
Then shall our names,
Familiar in his mouth as household words—
* * * * * *
Be in their flowing cups freshly remembered.
Henry V. Act IV. Sc. 3. L. 51.

11
And if his name be George, I'll call him Peter;
For new-made honour doth forget men's names.
King John. Act I. Sc. 1. L. 186.

12
When we were happy we had other names.
King John. Act V. Sc. 4. L. 7.

13
I cannot tell what the dickens his name is.
Merry Wives of Windsor. Act III. Sc. 2. L. 17.

14
Good name in man and woman, dear my lord,
Is the immediate jewel of their souls:
Who steals my purse steals trash; 'tis something, nothing;
'Twas mine, 'tis his, and has been slave to thousands;
But he that filches from me my good name
Robs me of that which not enriches him,
And makes me poor indeed.
Othello. Act III. Sc. 3. L. 157.

15
What's in a name? that which we call a rose
By any other name would smell as sweet.
Romeo and Juliet. Act II. Sc. 2. L. 43.
("Name" is "word" in Folio, and quarto of 1609.) (See also TALMUD)

16
I do beseech you—
Chiefly, that I might set it in my prayers—
What is your name?
Tempest. Act III. Sc. 1. L. 32.

17
I am thankful that my name is obnoxious to no pun.
SHENSTONE—*Egotisms*.

18
Ye say they all have passed away,
That noble race and brave;
That their light canoes have vanished
From off the crested wave;
That mid the forests where they roamed
There rings no hunter's shout;
But their name is on your waters;
Ye may not wash it out.
LYDIA SIGOURNEY—*Indian Names*.

19
And last of all an Admiral came,
A terrible man with a terrible name,—
A name which you all know by sight very well;
But which no one can speak, and no one can spell.
SOUTHEY—*The March to Moscow*. St. 8.

20
I'll give you leave to call me anything, if you don't call me spade.
SWIFT—*Polite Conversation*. Dialogue II.
(See also BURTON)

21
And the best and the worst of this is
That neither is most to blame,
If you have forgotten my kisses
And I have forgotten your name.
SWINBURNE—*An Interlude*.

22
The myrtle that grows among thorns is a myrtle still.
Talmud. Sanhedrin. 44.
(See also ROMEO AND JULIET)

23
No sound is breathed so potent to coerce
And to conciliate, as their names who dare
For that sweet mother-land which gave them birth
Nobly to do, nobly to die.
TENNYSON—*Tiresias*.

24
O, Sophonisba, Sophonisba, O!
THOMSON—*Sophonisba*.

25
Charmed with the foolish whistling of a name.
VERGIL—*Georgics*. Bk. II. L. 72. COWLEY'S trans.

26
Neither holy, nor Roman, nor Empire.
VOLTAIRE—*Essay on the Morals of the Holy Empire of the Hapsburgs*.

NAPLES

1
Naples sitteth by the sea, keystone of an arch
of azure.
TUPPER—*Proverbial Philosophy. Of Death.* L. 53.

NARCISSUS

2
If thou hast a loaf of bread, sell half and buy the flowers of the narcissus; for bread nourisheth the body, but the flowers of the narcissus the soul.
OSWALD CRAWFURD—*Round the Calendar in Portugal.* P. 114. Quoting it from MOHAMMED.
(See also SAADI under HYACINTH)

NATURE

3
If there's a power above us, (and that there is
all nature cries aloud
Through all her works) he must delight in virtue.
ADDISON—*Cato.* Act V. Sc. 1.

4
No one finds fault with defects which are the result of nature.
ARISTOTLE—*Ethics.* III. 5.

5
Nature's great law, and law of all men's minds?—
To its own impulse every creature stirs;
Live by thy light, and earth will live by hers!
MATTHEW ARNOLD—*Religious Isolation.* St. 4.

6
Nature means Necessity.
BAILEY—*Festus. Dedication.*

7
The course of Nature seems a course of Death,
And nothingness the whole substantial thing.
BAILEY—*Festus.* Sc. *Water and Wood.*

8
At the close of the day, when the hamlet is still,
And mortals the sweets of forgetfulness prove,
When nought but the torrent is heard on the hill,
And nought but the nightingale's song in the
grove.
BEATTIE—*The Hermit.*

9
Nature too unkind;
That made no medicine for a troubled mind!
BEAUMONT AND FLETCHER—*Philaster.* Act III. Sc. 1.

10
Rich with the spoils of nature.
SIR THOMAS BROWNE—*Religio Medici.* Pt. XIII.
(See also Gray under TIME)

11
There are no grotesques in nature; not anything framed to fill up empty cantons, and unnecessary spaces.
SIR THOMAS BROWNE—*Religio Medici.* Pt. XV.

12
Now nature is not at variance with art, nor art with nature, they being both servants of his providence: art is the perfection of nature; were the world now as it was the sixth day, there were yet a chaos; nature hath made one world, and art another. In brief, all things are artificial; for nature is the art of God.
SIR THOMAS BROWNE—*Religio Medici.* Pt. XVI. (See also YOUNG)

13
I trust in Nature for the stable laws
Of beauty and utility. Spring shall plant
And Autumn garner to the end of time.
I trust in God—the right shall be the right
And other than the wrong, while he endures;
I trust in my own soul, that can perceive
The outward and the inward, Nature's good
And God's.
ROBERT BROWNING—*A Soul's Tragedy.* Act I.

14
Go forth under the open sky, and list
To Nature's teachings.
BRYANT—*Thanatopsis.*

15
To him who in the love of Nature holds
Communion with her visible forms, she speaks
A various language.
BRYANT—*Thanatopsis.*

16
See one promontory (said Socrates of old) one mountain, one sea, one river, and see all.
BURTON—*Anatomy of Melancholy.* Pt. I. Sec. 2. Memb. 4. Subsec. 7.

17
I am a part of all you see
In Nature: part of all you feel:
I am the impact of the bee
Upon the blossom; in the tree
I am the sap—that shall reveal
The leaf, the bloom—that flows and flutes
Up from the darkness through its roots.
MADISON CAWEIN—*Penetralia.*

18
Nature vicarye of the Almighty Lord.
CHAUCER—*Parlement of Foules.* L. 379.

19
Not without art, but yet to Nature true.
CHURCHILL—*The Rosciad.* L. 699.

20
Ab interitu naturam abhorrere.
Nature abhors annihilation.
CICERO—*De Finibus.* V. 11. 3.
(See also RABELAIS)

21
Meliora sunt ea quæ natura quam illa quæ arte perfecta sunt.
Things perfected by nature are better than those finished by art.
CICERO—*De Natura Deorum.* II. 34.

22
All argument will vanish before one touch of nature.
GEORGE COLMAN the Younger—*Poor Gentleman.* Act V. 1.

23
Nature, exerting an unwearied power,
Forms, opens, and gives scent to every flower;
Spreads the fresh verdure of the field, and leads
The dancing Naiads through the dewy meads.
COWPER—*Table Talk.* L. 690.

24
Nor rural sights alone, but rural sounds,
Exhilarate the spirit, and restore
The tone of languid Nature.
COWPER—*The Task.* Bk. I. *The Sofa.* L. 187.

1
What is bred in the bone will not come out of the flesh.
Quoted by DEFOE—*Further Adventures of Robinson Crusoe.*

2
Chassez le naturel, il revient au galop.
Drive the natural away, it returns at a gallop.
DESTOUCHES—*Glorieux.* IV. 3. Idea in LA FONTAINE—*Fables.* Bk. II. 18.
Chassez les prejugés par la porte, ils rentreront par la fenêtre.
As used by FREDERICK THE GREAT. *Letter to* VOLTAIRE. March 19, 1771.
(See also HORACE)

3
Whate'er he did, was done with so much ease,
In him alone 't was natural to please.
DRYDEN—*Absalom and Achitophel.* Pt. I. L. 27.

4
By viewing nature, nature's handmaid, art,
Makes mighty things from small beginnings grow;
Thus fishes first to shipping did impart,
Their tail the rudder, and their head the prow.
DRYDEN—*Annus Mirabilis.* St. 155.

5
For Art may err, but Nature cannot miss.
DRYDEN—*Fables. The Cock and the Fox.* L. 452.

6
Out of the book of Nature's learned breast.
DU BARTAS—*Divine Weekes and Workes.* Second Week. Fourth Day. Bk. II. L. 566.
(See also LONGFELLOW)

7
Ever charming, ever new,
When will the landscape tire the view?
JOHN DYER—*Grongar Hill.* L. 102.

8
Nature is a mutable cloud which is always and never the same.
EMERSON—*Essays. First Series. History.*

9
By fate, not option, frugal Nature gave
One scent to hyson and to wall-flower,
One sound to pine-groves and to water-falls,
One aspect to the desert and the lake.
It was her stern necessity: all things
Are of one pattern made; bird, beast, and flower,
Song, picture, form, space, thought, and character
Deceive us, seeming to be many things,
And are but one.
EMERSON—*Xenophones.*

10
Nature seems to wear one universal grin.
HENRY FIELDING—*Tom Thumb the Great.* Act I. Sc. 1.

11
As distant prospects please us, but when near
We find but desert rocks and fleeting air.
GARTH—*The Dispensary.* Canto III. L. 27.

12
To me more dear, congenial to my heart,
One native charm, than all the gloss of art.
GOLDSMITH—*Deserted Village.* L. 253.

13
E'en from the tomb the voice of nature cries,
E'en in our ashes live their wonted fires.
GRAY—*Elegy in a Country Churchyard.* St. 23.
(See also CHAUCER under FIRE)

14
What Nature has writ with her lusty wit
Is worded so wisely and kindly
That whoever has dipped in her manuscript
Must up and follow her blindly.
Now the summer prime is her blithest rhyme
In the being and the seeming,
And they that have heard the overword
Know life's a dream worth dreaming.
HENLEY—*Echoes.* XXXIII.
(See also LONGFELLOW)

15
That undefined and mingled hum,
Voice of the desert never dumb!
HOGG—*Verses to Lady Anne Scott.*

16
Naturam expellas furca, tamen usque recurrit.
You may turn nature out of doors with violence, but she will still return.
HORACE—*Epistles.* I. 10. 24. ("Expelles" in some versions.)
(See also DESTOUCHES)

17
Nunquam aliud Natura aliud Sapientia dicit.
Nature never says one thing, Wisdom another.
JUVENAL—*Satires.* XIV. 321.

18
No stir of air was there,
Not so much life as on a summer's day
Robs not one light seed from the feather'd grass,
But where the dead leaf fell, there did it rest.
KEATS—*Hyperion.* Bk. I. L. 7.

19
Ye marshes, how candid and simple and nothing-with-holding and free
Ye publish yourselves to the sky and offer yourselves to the sea!
SIDNEY LANIER—*Marshes of Glynn.*

20
O what a glory doth this world put on
For him who, with a fervent heart, goes forth
Under the bright and glorious sky, and looks
On duties well performed, and days well spent!
For him the wind, ay, and the yellow leaves,
Shall have a voice, and give him eloquent teachings.
LONGFELLOW—*Autumn.* L. 30.

21
And Nature, the old nurse, took
The child upon her knee,
Saying: "Here is a story-book
Thy Father has written for thee."

"Come, wander with me," she said,
"Into regions yet untrod;
And read what is still unread
In the manuscripts of God."
LONGFELLOW—*Fiftieth Birthday of Agassiz.*
(See also DU BARTAS, ANTONY AND CLEOPATRA)

22
The natural alone is permanent.
LONGFELLOW—*Kavanagh.* Ch. XIII.

23
So Nature deals with us, and takes away
Our playthings one by one, and by the hand
Leads us to rest so gently, that we go,

Scarce knowing if we wish to go or stay,
Being too full of sleep to understand
How far the unknown transcends the what we know.
LONGFELLOW—*Nature*. L. 9.

1
No tears
Dim the sweet look that Nature wears.
LONGFELLOW—*Sunrise on the Hills*. L. 35.

2
Nature with folded hands seemed there,
Kneeling at her evening prayer!
LONGFELLOW—*Voices of the Night. Prelude*. St. 11.

3
I'm what I seem; not any dyer gave,
But nature dyed this colour that I have.
MARTIAL—*Epigrams*. Bk. XIV. Ep. 133. Trans. by WRIGHT.

4
O maternal earth which rocks the fallen leaf to sleep!
E. L. MASTERS—*Spoon River Anthology. Washington McNeely*.

5
But on and up, where Nature's heart
Beats strong amid the hills.
RICHARD MONCKTON MILNES (Lord Houghton)—*Tragedy of the Lac de Gaube*. St. 2.

6
Beldam Nature.
MILTON—*At a Vacation Exercise in the College*. l. 48.

7
Wherefore did Nature pour her bounties forth
With such a full and unwithdrawing hand,
Covering the earth with odours, fruits, and flocks,
Thronging the seas with spawn innumerable,
But all to please and sate the curious taste?
MILTON—*Comus*. L. 710.

8
And live like Nature's bastards, not her sons.
MILTON—*Comus*. L. 727.

9
Into this wild abyss,
The womb of Nature and perhaps her grave.
MILTON—*Paradise Lost*. Bk. II. L. 910.

10
Thus with the year
Seasons return, but not to me returns
Day, or the sweet approach of even or morn,
Or sight of vernal bloom, or summer's rose,
Or flocks, or herds, or human face divine;
But cloud instead, and ever-during dark
Surrounds me, from the cheerful ways of men
Cut off, and for the book of knowledge fair
Presented with a universal blank
Of Nature's works to me expunged and rased,
And wisdom at one entrance quite shut out.
MILTON—*Paradise Lost*. Bk. III. L. 40.

11
And liquid lapse of murmuring streams.
MILTON—*Paradise Lost*. Bk. VIII. L. 263.

12
Accuse not Nature, she hath done her part;
Do thou but thine!
MILTON—*Paradise Lost*. Bk. VIII. L. 561.

13
Let us a little permit Nature to take her own way; she better understands her own affairs than we.
MONTAIGNE—*Essays. Experience*.

14
And not from Nature up to Nature's God,
But down from Nature's God look Nature through.
ROBERT MONTGOMERY—*Luther. A Landscape of Domestic Life*.
(See also POPE)

15
There is not in the wide world a valley so sweet
As that vale in whose bosom the bright waters meet.
MOORE—*The Meeting of the Waters*.

16
And we, with Nature's heart in tune,
Concerted harmonies.
WM. MOTHERWELL—*Jeannie Morrison*.

17
Eye Nature's walks, shoot folly as it flies,
And catch the manners living as they rise.
POPE—*Essay on Man*. Ep. I. L. 13.

18
Seas roll to waft me, suns to light me rise;
My footstool Earth, my canopy the skies.
POPE—*Essay on Man*. Ep. I. L. 139.

19
All are but parts of one stupendous whole,
Whose body Nature is, and God the soul;
That chang'd thro' all, and yet in all the same,
Great in the earth as in th' ethereal frame;
Warms in the sun, refreshes in the breeze,
Glows in the stars, and blossoms in the trees;
Lives thro' all life, extends thro' all extent,
Spreads undivided, operates unspent;
Breathes in our soul, informs our mortal part,
As full, as perfect, in a hair as heart.
POPE—*Essay on Man*. Ep. I. L. 267.

20
See plastic Nature working to this end,
The single atoms each to other tend,
Attract, attracted to, the next in place
Form'd and impell'd its neighbor to embrace.
POPE—*Essay on Man*. Ep. III. L. 9.

21
Slave to no sect, who takes no private road,
But looks through Nature up to Nature's God.
POPE—*Essay on Man*. Ep. IV. L. 331. (Verbatim from BOLINGBROKE—*Letters to Pope*, according to WARTON.)
(See also MONTGOMERY)

22
Ut natura dedit, sic omnis recta figura.
Every form as nature made it is correct.
PROPERTIUS—*Elegiæ*. II. 18. 25.

23
Naturæ sequitur semina quisque suæ.
Every one follows the inclinations of his own nature.
PROPERTIUS—*Elegiæ*. III. 9. 20.

24
Natura abhorret vacuum.
Nature abhors a vacuum.
RABELAIS—*Gargantua*. Ch. V.
(See also CICERO)

25
Der Schein soll nie die Wirklichkeit erreichen
Und siegt Natur, so muss die Kunst entweichen.
The ideal should never touch the real;
When nature conquers, Art must then give way.
SCHILLER. To GOETHE when he put VOLTAIRE'S *Mahomet* on the Stage. St. 6.

1
Some touch of Nature's genial glow.
SCOTT—*Lord of the Isles*. Canto III. St. 14.

2
Oh, Brignall banks are wild and fair,
And Greta woods are green,
And you may gather garlands there
Would grace a summer queen.
SCOTT—*Rokeby*. Canto III. St. 16.

3
In Nature's infinite book of secrecy
A little I can read.
Antony and Cleopatra. Act I. Sc. 2. L. 9.
(See also LONGFELLOW)

4
How hard it is to hide the sparks of Nature!
Cymbeline. Act III. Sc. 3. L. 79.

5
To hold, as 'twere, the mirror up to Nature; to shew virtue her own feature, scorn her own image, and the very age and body of the time his form and pressure.
Hamlet. Act III. Sc. 2. L. 24.

6
Diseased Nature oftentimes breaks forth
In strange eruptions.
Henry IV. Pt. I. Act III. Sc. 1. L. 27.

7
And Nature does require
Her times of preservation, which perforce
I, her frail son, amongst my brethren mortal,
Must give my tendance to.
Henry VIII. Act III. Sc. 2. L. 147.

8
One touch of nature makes the whole world kin.
Troilus and Cressida. Act III. Sc. 3. L. 175.

9
How sometimes Nature will betray its folly,
Its tenderness, and make itself a pastime
To harder bosoms!
Winter's Tale. Act I. Sc. 2. L. 151.

10
Yet nature is made better by no mean
But nature makes that mean: so, over that art
Which, you say, adds to nature, is an art
That nature makes.
Winter's Tale. Act IV. Sc. 4. L. 89.

11
My banks they are furnish'd with bees,
Whose murmur invites one to sleep;
My grottoes are shaded with trees,
And my hills are white over with sheep.
SHENSTONE—*A Pastoral Ballad*. Pt. II. *Hope*.

12
Certainly nothing is unnatural that is not physically impossible.
R. B. SHERIDAN—*The Critic*. Act II. Sc. 1.

13
Yet neither spinnes, nor cards, ne cares nor fretts,
But to her mother Nature all her care she letts.
SPENSER—*Faerie Queene*. Bk. II. Canto VI.

14
For all that Nature by her mother-wit
Could frame in earth.
SPENSER—*Faerie Queene*. Bk. IV. Canto X. St. 21.

15
What more felicitie can fall to creature
Than to enjoy delight with libertie,
And to be lord of all the workes of Nature,
To raine in th' aire from earth to highest skie,
To feed on flowres and weeds of glorious feature.
SPENSER—*The Fate of the Butterfly*. L. 209.

16
Once, when the days were ages,
And the old Earth was young,
The high gods and the sages
From Nature's golden pages
Her open secrets wrung.
R. H. STODDARD—*Brahma's Answer*.

17
A voice of greeting from the wind was sent;
The mists enfolded me with soft white arms;
The birds did sing to lap me in content,
The rivers wove their charms,—
And every little daisy in the grass
Did look up in my face, and smile to see me pass!
R. H. STODDARD—*Hymn to the Beautiful*. St. 4.

18
In the world's audience hall, the simple blade of grass sits on the same carpet with the sunbeams, and the stars of midnight.
RABINDRANATH TAGORE—*Gardener*. 74.

19
Nothing in Nature is unbeautiful.
TENNYSON—*Lover's Tale*. L. 348.

20
Myriads of rivulets hurrying through the lawn,
The moan of doves in immemorial elms,
And murmuring of innumerable bees.
TENNYSON—*Princess*. Canto VII. L. 205.

21
I care not, Fortune, what you me deny;
You cannot rob me of free Nature's grace,
You cannot shut the windows of the sky,
Through which Aurora shows her brightening face;
You cannot bar my constant feet to trace
The woods and lawns, by living stream, at eve.
THOMSON—*Castle of Indolence*. Canto II. St. 3.

22
O nature! * * *
Enrich me with the knowledge of thy works;
Snatch me to Heaven.
THOMSON—*Seasons*. *Autumn*. L. 1,352.

23
Rocks rich in gems, and Mountains big with mines,
That on the high Equator, ridgy, rise,
Whence many a bursting Stream auriferous plays.
THOMSON—*Seasons*. *Summer*. L. 646.

24
Nature is always wise in every part.
LORD THURLOW—*Select Poems*. *The Harvest Moon*.

25
Talk not of temples, there is one
Built without hands, to mankind given;
Its lamps are the meridian sun
And all the stars of heaven,
Its walls are the cerulean sky,
Its floor the earth so green and fair,
The dome its vast immensity
All Nature worships there!
DAVID VEDDER—*Temple of Nature*.

1
La Nature a toujours été en eux plus forte que l'education.
Nature has always had more force than education.
VOLTAIRE—*Life of Molière.*

2
And recognizes ever and anon
The breeze of Nature stirring in his soul.
WORDSWORTH—*The Excursion.* Bk. IV.

3
Ah, what a warning for a thoughtless man,
Could field or grove, could any spot of earth,
Show to his eye an image of the pangs
Which it hath witnessed; render back an echo
Of the sad steps by which it hath been trod!
WORDSWORTH—*The Excursion.* Bk. VI.

4
The streams with softest sound are flowing,
The grass you almost hear it growing,
You hear it now, if e'er you can.
WORDSWORTH—*The Idiot Boy.* St. 57.

5
Nature never did betray
The heart that loved her.
WORDSWORTH—*Lines Composed Above Tintern Abbey.*

6
As in the eye of Nature he has lived,
So in the eye of Nature let him die!
WORDSWORTH—*The Old Cumberland Beggar.* Last Lines.

7
The stars of midnight shall be dear
To her; and she shall lean her ear
In many a secret place
Where rivulets dance their wayward round,
And beauty born of murmuring sound
Shall pass into her face.
WORDSWORTH—*Three Years She Grew in Sun and Shower.*

8
Nature's old felicities.
WORDSWORTH—*The Trosachs.*

9
To the solid ground
Of Nature trusts the Mind that builds for aye.
WORDSWORTH—*A Volant Tribe of Bards on Earth.*

10
Such blessings Nature pours,
O'erstock'd mankind enjoy but half her stores.
In distant wilds, by human eyes unseen,
She rears her flowers, and spreads her velvet green;
Pure gurgling rills the lonely desert trace
And waste their music on the savage race.
YOUNG—*Love of Fame.* Satire V. L. 232.
(See also CHAMBERLAYNE under OBSCURITY)

11
Nothing in Nature, much less conscious being,
Was e'er created solely for itself.
YOUNG—*Night Thoughts.* Night IX. L. 711.

12
The course of nature governs all!
The course of nature is the heart of God.
The miracles thou call'st for, this attest;
For say, could nature nature's course control?
But, miracles apart, who sees Him not?
YOUNG—*Night Thoughts.* Night IX. L. 1,280.
(See also BROWNE)

NAVIGATION (See also NAVY, OCEAN, SHIPS)

13
O pilot! 'tis a fearful night,
There's danger on the deep.
THOMAS HAYNES BAYLY—*The Pilot.*

14
How Bishop Aidan foretold to certain seamen a storm that would happen, and gave them some holy oil to lay it.
BEDE—Heading of Chapter in his *Ecclesiastical History.* III. 15.
(See also PLINY, PLUTARCH)

15
O'er the glad waters of the dark blue sea,
Our thoughts as boundless, and our souls as free,
Far as the breeze can bear, the billows foam,
Survey our empire, and behold our home!
BYRON—*The Corsair.* Canto I. St. 1.

16
Here's to the pilot that weathered the storm.
CANNING—*The Pilot that Weathered the Storm.*

17
And as great seamen, using all their wealth
And skills in Neptune's deep invisible paths,
In tall ships richly built and ribbed with brass,
To put a girdle round about the world.
GEO. CHAPMAN—*Bussy d'Ambois.* Act I. Sc. 1. L. 20.
(See also WEBSTER, also CHAPMAN, MIDSUMMER NIGHT'S DREAM under ELECTRICITY)

18
A wet sheet and a flowing sea,
A wind that follows fast
And fills the white and rustling sails,
And bends the gallant mast!
And bends the gallant mast, my boys,
While, like the eagle free,
Away the good ship flies, and leaves
Old England in the lee.
ALLAN CUNNINGHAM—*Songs of Scotland. A Wet Sheet and a Flowing Sea.*

19
Soon shall thy arm, unconquered steam, afar
Drag the slow barge, or drive the rapid car;
Or on wide waving wings expanded bear
The flying chariot through the fields of air.
ERASMUS DARWIN—*The Botanic Garden.* Pt. I. 1. 289.

20
For they say there's a Providence sits up aloft
To keep watch for the life of poor Jack.
CHARLES DIBDEN—*Poor Jack.*

21
There's a sweet little cherub that sits up aloft,
To keep watch for the life of poor Jack.
CHARLES DIBDEN—*Poor Jack.*

22
Skill'd in the globe and sphere, he gravely stands,
And, with his compass, measures seas and lands.
DRYDEN—*Sixth Satire of Juvenal.* L. 760.

23
The winds and waves are always on the side of the ablest navigators.
GIBBON—*Decline and Fall of the Roman Empire.* Ch. LXVIII.

24
Oh, I am a cook and a captain bold
And the mate of the *Nancy* brig,
And a bo'sun tight and a midshipmite
And the crew of the captain's gig.
W. S. GILBERT—*Yarn of the "Nancy Bell."*

1
Thus, I steer my bark, and sail
On even keel, with gentle gale.
MATTHEW GREEN—*Spleen.* L. 814.

2
Though pleas'd to see the dolphins play,
I mind my compass and my way.
MATTHEW GREEN—*Spleen.* L. 826.

3
What though the sea be calm? trust to the shore,
Ships have been drown'd, where late they danc'd before.
HERRICK—*Safety on the Shore.*

4
Yet the best pilots have need of mariners, besides sails, anchor and other tackle.
BEN JONSON—*Discoveries. Illiteratus Princeps.*

5
—They write here one Cornelius—Son
Hath made the Hollanders an invisible eel
To swim the haven at Dunkirk, and sink all
The shipping there.
—But how is't done?
—I'll show you, sir.
It is automa, runs under water
With a snug nose, and has a nimble tail
Made like an auger, with which tail she wriggles
Betwixt the costs of a ship and sinks it straight.
BEN JONSON—*Staple of News.* Act III. Sc. 1.

6
Some love to roam o'er the dark sea's foam,
Where the shrill winds whistle free.
CHARLES MACKAY—*Some Love to Roam.*

7
Thus far we run before the wind.
ARTHUR MURPHY—*The Apprentice.* Act I. Sc. 1. L. 344.

8
Nos fragili vastum ligno sulcavimus æquor.
We have ploughed the vast ocean in a fragile bark.
OVID—*Epistolæ ex Pont.* I. 14. 35.

9
Ye gentlemen of England
That live at home at ease,
Ah! little do you think upon
The dangers of the seas.
MARTIN PARKER—*Ye Gentlemen of England.*
(See also SOUTHEY)

10
A strong nor'wester's blowing, Bill!
Hark! don't ye hear it roar now?
Lord help 'em, how I pities them
Unhappy folks on shore now!
The Sailor's Consolation. Attributed to BILLY PITT, COLMAN.

11
And that all seas are made calme and still with oile; and therefore the Divers under the water doe spirt and sprinkle it aboard with their mouthes because it dulceth and allaieth the unpleasant nature thereof, and carrieth a light with it.
PLINY—*Natural History.* Bk. II. Ch. CIII. HOLLAND's trans.
(See also BEDE)

12
Why does pouring Oil on the Sea make it Clear and Calm? Is it for that the winds, slipping the smooth oil, have no force, nor cause any waves?
PLUTARCH—*Morals. Natural Questions.* XII.
(See also BEDE)

13
Well, then—our course is chosen—spread the sail—
Heave oft the lead, and mark the soundings well—
Look to the helm, good master—many a shoal
Marks this stern coast, and rocks, where sits the Siren
Who, like ambition, lures men to their ruin.
SCOTT—*Kenilworth.* Ch. XVII. Verses at head of Chapter.

14
Merrily, merrily goes the bark
On a breeze from the northward free,
So shoots through the morning sky the lark,
Or the swan through the summer sea.
SCOTT—*Lord of the Isles.* Canto IV. St. 10.

15
Upon the gale she stoop'd her side,
And bounded o'er the swelling tide,
As she were dancing home;
The merry seamen laugh'd to see
Their gallant ship so lustily
Furrow the green sea-foam.
SCOTT—*Marmion.* Canto II. St. 1.

16
Behold the threaden sails,
Borne with the invisible and creeping wind,
Draw the huge bottomes through the furrow'd sea,
Breasting the lofty surge.
Henry V. Act III. Chorus. L. 10.

17
Ye who dwell at home,
Ye do not know the terrors of the main.
SOUTHEY—*Madoc in Wales.* Pt. IV.
(See also PARKER)

18
Cease, rude Boreas, blustering railer!
List, ye landsmen all, to me:
Messmates, hear a brother sailor
Sing the dangers of the sea.
GEORGE A. STEVENS—*The Storm.*

19
Thou bringest the sailor to his wife,
And travell'd men from foreign lands,
And letters unto trembling hands;
And, thy dark freight, a vanish'd life.
TENNYSON—*In Memoriam.* Pt. X.

20
There were three sailors of Bristol City
Who took a boat and went to sea.
But first with beef and captain's biscuits
And pickled pork they loaded she.
There was gorging Jack and guzzling Jimmy,
And the youngest he was little Billee.
Now when they got as far as the Equator
They'd nothing left but one split pea.
THACKERAY—*Little Billee.*

21
On deck beneath the awning,
I dozing lay and yawning;
It was the gray of dawning,
Ere yet the Sun arose;
And above the funnel's roaring,
And the fitful wind's deploring,
I heard the cabin snoring
With universal noise.
THACKERAY—*The White Squall.*

1
He hath put a girdle 'bout the world
And sounded all her quicksands.
WEBSTER—*Duchess of Malfi.* Act II. Sc. 1.
(See also CHAPMAN)

NAVY (See also SOLDIERS, WAR)

2
Britain's best bulwarks are her wooden walls.
T. AUGUSTINE ARNE—*Britain's Best Bulwarks.*
(See also BLACKSTONE, COVENTRY, LINSCHOTEN)

3
Our ships were British oak,
And hearts of oak our men.
S. J. ARNOLD—*Death of Nelson.*
(See also GARRICK, also RABELAIS under HEART)

4
The royal navy of England has ever been its greatest defence and ornament; it is its ancient and natural strength; the floating bulwark of the island.
SIR WM. BLACKSTONE—*Commentaries.* Vol. I. Bk. I. Ch. XIII.

5
Cooped in their winged sea-girt citadel.
BYRON—*Childe Harold.* Canto II. St. 28.

6
Right—that will do for the marines.
BYRON—*The Island.* II. XXI.
(See also SCOTT)

7
The wooden walls are the best walls of this kingdom.
LORD KEEPER COVENTRY—*Speech to the Judges,* June 17, 1635, given in GARDINER—*History of England.* Vol. III. P. 79.
(See also ARNE)

8
Hearts of oak are our ships,
Gallant tars are our men.
GARRICK—*Hearts of Oak.*

9
Hearts of oak are our ships,
Hearts of oak are our men.
GARRICK—*Other version of Hearts of Oak.*
(See also ARNOLD)

10
All in the Downs the fleet was moor'd.
GAY—*Sweet William's Farewell to Black-Eyed Susan.*

11
Now landsmen all, whoever you may be,
If you want to rise to the top of the tree,
If your soul isn't fettered to an office stool,
Be careful to be guided by this golden rule—
Stick close to your desks and *never go to sea,*
And you all may be Rulers of the Queen's Navee.
W. S. GILBERT—*H. M. S. Pinafore.*

12
Scarce one tall frigate walks the sea
Or skirts the safer shores
Of all that bore to victory
Our stout old Commodores.
HOLMES—At a dinner given to ADMIRAL FARRAGUT, July 6, 1865.

13
The credite of the Realme, by defending the same with Wodden Walles, as Themistocles called the Ship of Athens.
LINSCHOTEN—*London.* Preface to English Trans. (See also ARNE)

14
Lysander when handing over the command of the fleet to Callicratidas, the Spartan, said to him, "I deliver you a fleet that is mistress of the seas."
LYSANDER. See PLUTARCH—*Life of Lysander.*

15
There were gentlemen and there were seamen in the navy of Charles the Second. But the seamen were not gentlemen; and the gentlemen were not seamen.
MACAULAY—*History of England.* Vol. I. Ch. III. Pt. XXXII.

16
Now the sunset breezes shiver,
And she's fading down the river,
But in England's song forever
She's the Fighting Téméraire.
HENRY NEWBOLDT—*The Fighting Téméraire.*

17
Tell that to the Marines—the sailors won't believe it.
Old saying quoted by SCOTT—*Redgauntlet.* Ch. XIII. TROLLOPE—*Small House at Allington.*
(See also BYRON)

NECESSITY

18
Necessity is stronger far than art.
ÆSCHYLUS—*Prometheus Chained.* L. 513.

19
Thanne is it wysdom, as thynketh me,
To maken vertu of necessité,
And take it weel, that we may not eschu,
And namely that that to us alle is due.
CHAUCER—*Canterbury Tales. The Knighte's Tale.* L. 2,182.
(See also HADRIANUS)

20
Necessity hath no law. Feigned necessities, imaginary necessities, are the greatest cozenage men can put upon the Providence of God, and make pretences to break known rules by.
CROMWELL—*Speeches. To Parliament,* Sept. 12, 1654.
(See also SKELTON)

21
Necessità c'induce, e non diletto.
It is necessity and not pleasure that compels us.
DANTE—*Inferno.* XII. 87.

22
Art imitates nature, and necessity is the mother of invention.
RICHARD FRANCK—*Northern Memoirs.* Written in 1658. P. 52.
(See also SCOTT, WYCHERLY, also PERSIUS under HUNGER)

23
Necessitatem in virtutem commutarum.
To make necessity a virtue (a virtue of necessity).
HADRIANUS JULIUS—*Addition to Adages of Erasmus.* F. GERONIMO BERMUDES—*Nise Lastimosa.* Act IV. Sc. 2. (1577) BURTON—*Anatomy of Melancholy.* Pt. III. Sec. 3. Memb. 4. Subsec. 1. DRYDEN—*Palamon and Arcite.* Bk. III. L. 1,084. MATTHEW HENRY—*Paraphrase of Psalm 37.* HIERONYMUS—*In Ruf. 3.* Also in *Epistles*

54. PETTIE—*Civile Conversation.* I. 5. QUINTILIAN—*Inst. Orat.* I. 8. 14. RABELAIS —*Gargantua.* I. II. *Pantagruel.* Sec. 5. Ch. XXII.

(See also CHAUCER, RICHARD II)

1
Æqua lege necessitas
Sortitur insignes et imos.

Necessity takes impartially the highest and the lowest.

HORACE—*Carmina.* III. 1. 14.

2
Necessitas ultimum et maximum telum est.

Necessity is the last and strongest weapon.

LIVY—*Annales.* IV. 28.

3
Discite quam parvo liceat producere vitam,
Et quantum natura petat.

Learn on how little man may live, and how small a portion nature requires.

LUCAN—*Pharsalia.* IV. 377.

4
So spake the Fiend, and with necessity,
The tyrant's plea, excused his devilish deed.

MILTON—*Paradise Lost.* Bk. IV. L. 393.

(See also PITT)

5
C'est une violente maistresse d'eschole que la necessité.

Necessity is a violent school-mistress.

MONTAIGNE—*Essays.* Bk. I. 47.

6
My steps have pressed the flowers,
That to the Muses' bowers
The eternal dews of Helicon have given:
And trod the mountain height,
Where Science, young and bright,
Scans with poetic gaze the midnight-heaven.
Yet have I found no power to vie
With thine, severe necessity!

THOMAS LOVE PEACOCK—*Necessity.*

7
Necessity is the plea for every infringement of human freedom. It is the argument of tyrants; it is the creed of slaves.

WILLIAM PITT the Elder—*Speeches. The India Bill,* November 18, 1783.

(See also MILTON)

8
Qui e nuce nucleum esse vult, frangat nucem.

He who would eat the kernel, must crack the shell.

PLAUTUS—*Curculio.* I. 1. 55.

9
Efficacior omni arte imminens necessitas.

Necessity when threatening is more powerful than device of man.

QUINTUS CURTIUS RUFUS—*De Rebus Gestis Alexandri Magni.* IV. 3. 23.

10
Necessitas etiam timidos fortes facit.

Necessity makes even the timid brave.

SALLUST—*Catilina.* 58.

11
Ernst ist der Anblick der Nothwendigkeit.

Stern is the visage of necessity.

SCHILLER—*Wallenstein's Tod.* I. 4. 45.

12
It is in these useless and superfluous things that I am rich and happy.

SCOPAS. In PLUTARCH'S *Life of Cato.*

(See also VOLTAIRE)

13
Necessity—thou best of peacemakers,
As well as surest prompter of invention.

SCOTT—*Peveril of the Peak.* Heading of Ch. XXVI.

(See also FRANCK)

14
Malum est necessitati vivere; sed in necessitate vivere necessitas nulla est.

It is bad to live for necessity; but there is no necessity to live in necessity.

SENECA—*Epistles.* 58.

15
Now sit we close about this taper here,
And call in question our necessities.

Julius Cæsar. Act IV. Sc. 3. L. 165.

16
Necessity's sharp pinch!

King Lear. Act II. Sc. 4. L. 214.

17
Teach thy necessity to reason thus:
There is no virtue like necessity.

Richard II. Act I. Sc. 3. L. 277.

(See also HADRIANUS)

18
Omission to do what is necessary
Seals a commission to a blank of danger.

Troilus and Cressida. Act III. Sc. 3. L. 230.

19
Spirit of Nature! all-sufficing Power!
Necessity, thou mother of the world!

SHELLEY—*Queen Mab.* Pt. VI.

20
Sheer necessity—the proper parent of an art so nearly allied to invention.

SHERIDAN—*The Critic.* Act I. Sc. 2.

(See also FRANCK)

21
The gods do not fight against necessity.

SIMONIDES. 3. 20.

22
Nede hath no lawe.

SKELTON—*Colyn Cloute.* L. 865. LANGLAND —*Piers Ploughman.* Passus. 23. L. 10.

(See also CROMWELL, SYRUS)

23
I hold that to need nothing is divine, and the less a man needs the nearer does he approach divinity.

SOCRATES. Quoted by XENOPHON—*Mem.* Bk. I. 6. 10.

24
A wise man never refuses anything to necessity.

SYRUS—*Maxims.* 540.

25
Necessity knows no law except to conquer.

SYRUS—*Maxims.* 553.

(See also SKELTON)

26
Le superflu, chose très nécessaire.

The superfluous, a very necessary thing.

VOLTAIRE—*Le Mondain.*

(See also SCOPAS)

27
Who, doomed to go in company with Pain
And Fear and Bloodshed,—miserable train!—
Turns his necessity to glorious gain.

WORDSWORTH—*Character of a Happy Warrior.*

28
Necessity, the mother of invention.

WYCHERLY—*Love in a Wood.* Act III. Sc. 3.

(See also FRANCK)

NEGLECT

1
A wise and salutary neglect.

BURKE—*Speech on the Conciliation of America.* Vol. II. P. 117.

2
Give me a look, give me a face,
That makes simplicity a grace:
Robes loosely flowing, hair as free;
Such sweet neglect more taketh me
Than all the adulteries of art;
They strike mine eyes, but not my heart.

BEN JONSON—*The Silent Woman.* Act I. Sc. 1.

(See also DENBO under BOOKS)

3
His noble negligences teach
What others' toils despair to reach.

PRIOR—*Alma.* Canto II. L. 7.

NEW YORK CITY

4
Stream of the living world
Where dash the billows of strife!—
One plunge in the mighty torrent
Is a year of tamer life!
City of glorious days,
Of hope, and labour and mirth,
With room and to spare, on thy splendid bays
For the ships of all the earth!

R. W. GILDER—*The City.*

5
Silent, grim, colossal, the Big City has ever stood against its revilers. They call it hard as iron; they say that nothing of pity beats in its bosom; they compare its streets with lonely forests and deserts of lava. But beneath the hard crust of the lobster is found a delectable and luscious food. Perhaps a different simile would have been wiser. Still nobody should take offence. We would call nobody a lobster with good and sufficient claws.

O. HENRY—*Between Rounds.* In *Four Million.*

6
New York is the Caoutchouc City. * * * They have the furor rubberendi.

O. HENRY—*Comedy in Rubber.* In *The Voice of the City.*

7
In dress, habits, manners, provincialism, routine and narrowness, he acquired that charming insolence, that irritating completeness, that sophisticated crassness, that overbalanced poise that makes the Manhattan gentleman so delightfully small in his greatness.

O. HENRY—*Defeat of the City.* In *The Voice of the City.*

8
Far below and around lay the city like a ragged purple dream. The irregular houses were like the broken exteriors of cliffs lining deep gulches and winding streams. Some were mountainous; some lay in long, monotonous rows like the basalt precipices hanging over desert cañons. Such was the background of the wonderful, cruel, enchanting, bewildering, fatal, great city. But into this background were cut myriads of brilliant parallelograms and circles and squares through which glowed many colored lights. And out of the violet and purple depths ascended like the city's soul, sounds and odors and thrills that make up the civic body. There arose the breath of gaiety unrestrained, of love, of hate, of all the passions that man can know. There below him lay all things, good or bad, that can be brought from the four corners of the earth to instructt please, thrill, enrich, elevate, cast down, nurture or kill. Thus the flavor of it came up to him and went into his blood.

O. HENRY—*The Duel.* In *Strictly Business.*

9
Well, little old Noisyville-on-the-Subway is good enough for me * * * Me for it from the rathskellers up. Sixth Avenue is the West now to me.

O. HENRY—*The Duel.* In *Strictly Business.*

10
"If you don't mind me asking," came the bell-like tones of the Golden Diana, "I'd like to know where you got that City Hall brogue. I did not know that Liberty was necessarily Irish." "If ye'd studied the history of art in its foreign complications, ye'd not need to ask," replied Mrs. Liberty, "If ye wasn't so light and giddy ye'd know that I was made by a Dago and presented to the American people on behalf of the French Government for the purpose of welcomin' Irish immigrants into the Dutch city of New York. 'Tis that I've been doing night and day since I was erected."

O. HENRY—*The Lady Higher Up.* In *Sixes and Sevens.*

11
GEORGE WASHINGTON, with his right arm upraised, sits his iron horse at the lower corner of Union Square * * * Should the General raise his left hand as he has raised his right, it would point to a quarter of the city that forms a haven for the oppressed and suppressed of foreign lands. In the cause of national or personal freedom they have found refuge here, and the patriot who made it for them sits his steed, overlooking their district, while he listens through his left ear to vaudeville that caricatures the posterity of his protégés.

O. HENRY—*A Philistine in Bohemia.* In *Voice of the City.*

12
If there ever was an aviary overstocked with jays it is that Yaptown-on-the-Hudson, called New York. Cosmopolitan they call it, you bet. So's a piece of fly-paper. You listen close when they're buzzing and trying to pull their feet out of the sticky stuff. "Little old New York's good enough for us"—that's what they sing.

O. HENRY—*A Tempered Wind.* In *The Gentle Grafter.*

13
You'd think New York people was all wise; but no, they can't get a chance to learn. Every thing's too compressed. Even the hay-seeds are bailed hayseeds. But what else can you expect from a town that's shut off from the world by the ocean on one side and New Jersey on the other?

O. HENRY—*A Tempered Wind.* In *The Gentle Grafter.*

14
Not like the brazen giant of Greek fame,
With conquering limbs astride from land to land;
Here at our sea-washed, sunset gates shall stand

A mighty woman with a torch, whose flame
Is the imprisoned lightning, and her name
Mother of exiles.
EMMA LAZARUS—*The New Colossus.*

1
Some day this old Broadway shall climb to the skies,
As a ribbon of cloud on a soul-wind shall rise,
And we shall be lifted, rejoicing by night,
Till we join with the planets who choir their delight.
The signs in the streets and the signs in the skies
Shall make a new Zodiac, guiding the wise,
And Broadway make one with that marvelous stair
That is climbed by the rainbow-clad spirits of prayer.
VACHEL LINDSAY—*Rhyme about an Electrical Advertising Sign.*

2
Up in the heights of the evening skies I see my City of Cities float
In sunset's golden and crimson dyes: I look and a great joy clutches my throat!
Plateau of roofs by canyons crossed: windows by thousands fire-furled—
O gazing, how the heart is lost in the Deepest City in the World.
JAMES OPPENHEIM—*New York from a Skyscraper.*

3
Just where the Treasury's marble front
Looks over Wall Street's mingled nations,—
Where Jews and Gentiles most are wont
To throng for trade and last quotations;
Where, hour, by hour, the rates of gold
Outrival, in the ears of people,
The quarter-chimes, serenely tolled
From Trinity's undaunted steeple.
E. C. STEDMAN—*Pan in Wall Street.*

4
Lo! body and soul!—this land!
Mighty Manhattan, with spires, and
The sparkling and hurrying tides, and the ships;
The varied and ample land,—the South
And the North in the light—Ohio's shores, and flashing Missouri,
And ever the far-spreading prairies, covered with grass and corn.
WALT WHITMAN—*Sequel to Drum-Taps. When Lilacs Last in the Door-Yard Bloom'd.* St. 12.

NEWS (See also JOURNALISM, NOVELTY)

5
By evil report and good report
II Corinthians. VI. 8.

6
Ill news is wing'd with fate, and flies apace.
DRYDEN—*Threnodia Augustalis.* L. 49.
(See also MASSINGER)

7
Where village statesmen talk'd with looks profound.
And news much older than their ale went round.
GOLDSMITH—*The Deserted Village.* L. 223.

8
It is good news, *worthy of all acceptation*, and yet not too good to be true.
MATTHEW HENRY—*Commentaries.* I Timothy. I. 15.

9
Stay a little, and news will find you.
HERBERT—*Jacula Prudentum.*

10
What, what, what,
What's the news from Swat?
Sad news,
Bad news,
Comes by the cable; led
Through the Indian Ocean's bed,
Through the Persian Gulf, the Red
Sea, and the Med-
Iterranean—he's dead;
The Akhoond is dead.
GEORGE THOMAS LANIGAN—*The Akhoond of Swat.* Written after seeing the item in the London papers, Jan. 22, 1878, "The Akhoond of Swat is dead."

11
Who, or why, or which, or what,
Is the Akhond of Swat?
EDWARD LEAR—*The Akhond of Swat.*

12 Ill news, madam,
Are swallow-winged, but what's good
Walks on crutches.
MASSINGER—*Picture.* Act II. 1.
(See also DRYDEN)

13
News, news, news, my gossiping friends,
I have wonderful news to tell,
A lady by me her compliments sends;
And this is the news from Hell!
OWEN MEREDITH (Lord Lytton)—*News.*

14
He's gone, and who knows how he may report
Thy words by adding fuel to the flame?
MILTON—*Samson Agonistes.* L. 1,350.

15
For evil news rides post, while good news baits.
MILTON—*Samson Agonistes.* L. 1,538.

16
As cold waters to a thirsty soul, so is good news from a far country.
Proverbs. XXV. 25.

17
Ram thou thy fruitful tidings in mine ears,
That long time have been barren.
Antony and Cleopatra. Act II. Sc. 5. L. 24.

18 Prithee, friend,
Pour out the pack of matter to mine ear,
The good and bad together.
Antony and Cleopatra. Act II. Sc. 5. L. 53.

19
Though it be honest, it is never good
To bring bad news; give to a gracious message
An host of tongues; but let ill tidings tell
Themselves when they be felt.
Antony and Cleopatra. Act II. Sc. 5. L. 85.

20
Here comes Monsieur le Beau
With his mouth full of news,
Which he will put on us, as pigeons feed their young.
Then shall we be news-crammed.
As You Like It. Act I. Sc. 2. L. 96.

21 If it be summer news,
Smile to 't before: if winterly, thou need'st
But keep that countenance still.
Cymbeline. Act III. Sc. 4. L. 12.

1
There's villainous news abroad.
Henry IV. Pt. I. Act II. Sc. 4. L. 365.

2
Yet the first bringer of unwelcome news
Hath but a losing office; and his tongue
Sounds ever after as a sullen bell,
Remember'd tolling a departed friend.
Henry IV. Pt. II. Act I. Sc. 1. L. 100.

3
And tidings do I bring, and lucky joys,
And golden times, and happy news of price
I pr'ythee now, deliver them like a man of the world.
Henry IV. Pt. II. Act V. Sc. 3. L. 101.

4
I drown'd these news in tears.
Henry VI. Pt. III. Act II. Sc. 1. L. 104.

5
News fitting to the night,
Black, fearful, comfortless and horrible.
King John. Act V. Sc. 6. L. 19.

6
My heart hath one poor string to stay it by,
Which holds but till thy news be uttered.
King John. Act V. Sc. 7. L. 55.

7
Master, master! news, old news, and such news as you never heard of!
Taming of the Shrew. Act III. Sc. 2. L. 30.

8
How goes it now, sir? this news which is called true is so like an old tale, that the verity of it is in strong suspicion.
Winter's Tale. Act V. Sc. 2. L. 25.

9
Ce n'est pas un événement, c'est une nouvelle.
It is not an event, it is a piece of news.
TALLEYRAND. On hearing of Napoleon's death.

NEWSPAPERS (See JOURNALISM, NEWS)

NIAGARA

10
"Niagara! wonder of this western world,
And half the world beside! hail, beauteous queen
Of cataracts!" An angel who had been
O'er heaven and earth, spoke thus, his bright wings furled,
And knelt to Nature first, on this wild cliff unseen.
MARIA BROOKS—*To Niagara.*

11
Fools-to-free-the-world, they go,
Primeval hearts from Buffalo.
Red cataracts of France to-day
Awake, three thousand miles away,
An echo of Niagara
The cataract Niagara.
VACHEL LINDSAY—*Niagara.*

12
Flow on, forever, in thy glorious robe
Of terror and of beauty. Yea, flow on
Unfathomed and resistless. God hath set
His rainbow on thy forehead: and the cloud
Mantled around thy feet. And He doth give
Thy voice of thunder power to speak of Him
Eternally—bidding the lip of man
Keep silence—and upon thine altar pour
Incense of awe-struck praise.
LYDIA H. SIGOURNEY—*Niagara.*

NIGHT

13
Night is a stealthy, evil Raven,
Wrapt to the eyes in his black wings.
T. B. ALDRICH—*Day and Night.*

14
Night comes, world-jewelled, * * *
The stars rush forth in myriads as to wage
War with the lines of Darkness; and the moon,
Pale ghost of Night, comes haunting the cold earth
After the sun's red sea-death—quietless.
BAILEY—*Festus*. Sc. *Garden and Bower by the Sea.*

15
I love night more than day—she is so lovely;
But I love night the most because she brings
My love to me in dreams which scarcely lie.
BAILEY—*Festus*. Sc. *Water and Wood. Midnight.*

16
Wan night, the shadow goer, came stepping in.
Beowulf. III.

17
When it draws near to witching time of night.
BLAIR—*The Grave*. L. 55.
(See also HAMLET, KEATS)

18
The Night has a thousand eyes,
The Day but one;
Yet the light of the bright world dies
With the dying sun.
F. W. BOURDILLON—*Light.*
(See also LYLY, also BOURDILLON, PLATO and SYLVESTER under EYES)

19
Most glorious night!
Thou wert not sent for slumber!
BYRON—*Childe Harold*. Canto III. St. 93.

20
For the night
Shows stars and women in a better light.
BYRON—*Don Juan*. Canto II. St. 152.

21
The stars are forth, the moon above the tops
Of the snow-shining mountains—Beautiful!
I linger yet with Nature, for the night
Hath been to me a more familiar face
Than that of man; and in her starry shade
Of dim and solitary loveliness
I learn'd the language of another world.
BYRON—*Manfred*. Act III. Sc. 4.

22
Night's black Mantle covers all alike.
DU BARTAS—*Divine Weekes and Workes. First Week. First Day.* L. 562.

23
Dark the Night, with breath all flowers,
And tender broken voice that fills
With ravishment the listening hours,—
Whisperings, wooings,
Liquid ripples, and soft ring-dove cooings
In low-toned rhythm that love's aching stills!
Dark the night
Yet is she bright,
For in her dark she brings the mystic star,
Trembling yet strong, as is the voice of love,
From some unknown afar.
GEORGE ELIOT—*Spanish Gypsy. Song.* Bk. I.

1
O radiant Dark! O darkly fostered ray!
Thou hast a joy too deep for shallow Day.
GEORGE ELIOT—*Spanish Gypsy.* Bk. I.

2
The watch-dog's voice that bay'd the whispering wind,
And the loud laugh that spoke the vacant mind:
These all in sweet confusion sought the shade,
And fill'd each pause the nightingale had made.
GOLDSMITH—*Deserted Village.* L. 121.

3
A late lark twitters from the quiet skies:
And from the west,
Where the sun, his day's work ended,
Lingers as in content,
There falls on the old, gray city
An influence luminous and serene,
A shining peace.
HENLEY—*Margaritæ Sorori.*

4
The smoke ascends
In a rosy-and-golden haze. The spires
Shine and are changed. In the valley
Shadows rise. The lark sings on. The sun
Closing his benediction,
Sinks, and the darkening air
Thrills with the sense of the triumphing night,—
Night with train of stars
And her great gift of sleep.
HENLEY—*Margaritæ Sorori.*

5
Now deep in ocean sunk the lamp of light,
And drew behind the cloudy vale of night.
HOMER—*Iliad.* Bk. VIII. L. 605. POPE'S trans.

6
At night, to his own dark fancies a prey,
He lies like a hedgehog rolled up the wrong way,
Tormenting himself with his prickles.
HOOD—*Miss Kilmansegg and her precious Leg.*

7
Watchman, what of the night?
Isaiah. XXI. 11.

8
Night, when deep sleep falleth on men.
Job. IV. 13; XXXIII. 15.

9
The night cometh when no man can work.
John. IX. 4.

10
'Tis the witching hour of night,
Orbed is the moon and bright,
And the stars they glisten, glisten,
Seeming with bright eyes to listen-
For what listen they?
KEATS—*A Prophecy.* L. 1.

11
I heard the trailing garments of the Night
Sweep through her marble halls.
LONGFELLOW—*Hymn to the Night.*
(See also WHITMAN)

12
O holy Night! from thee I learn to bear
What man has borne before!
Thou layest thy fingers on the lips of Care,
And they complain no more.
LONGFELLOW—*Hymn to the Night.*

13
Then stars arise, and the night is holy.
LONGFELLOW—*Hyperion.* Bk. I. Ch. I.

14
And the night shall be filled with music
And the cares, that infest the day,
Shall fold their tents, like the Arabs,
And as silently steal away.
LONGFELLOW—*The Day is Done.*

15
God makes sech nights, all white an' still
Fur'z you can look or listen,
Moonshine an' snow on field an' hill,
All silence an' all glisten.
LOWELL—*The Courtin'.*

16
Night hath a thousand eyes.
LYLY—*Maydes Metamorphose.* Act III. Sc. 1.
(See also BOURDILLON)

17
Quiet night, that brings
Rest to the labourer, is the outlaw's day,
In which he rises early to do wrong,
And when his work is ended dares not sleep.
MASSINGER—*The Guardian.* Act II. Sc. 4.

18
A night of tears! for the gusty rain
Had ceased, but the eaves were dripping yet;
And the moon look'd forth, as tho' in pain,
With her face all white and wet.
OWEN MEREDITH (Lord Lytton)—*The Wanderer.* Bk. II. *The Portrait.*

19
O thievish Night,
Why shouldst thou, but for some felonious end,
In thy dark lantern thus close up the stars,
That nature hung in heaven, and filled their lamps
With everlasting oil, to give due light
To the misled and lonely traveller?
MILTON—*Comus.* L. 195.

20
* * * And when night
Darkens the streets, then wander forth the sons
Of Belial, flown with insolence and wine.
MILTON—*Paradise Lost.* Bk. I. L. 500.

21
Where eldest Night
And Chaos, ancestors of nature, hold
Eternal anarchy, amidst the noise
Of endless wars, and by confusion stand.
MILTON—*Paradise Lost.* Bk II. L. 894.

22
Sable-vested Night, eldest of things.
MILTON—*Paradise Lost.* Bk. II. L. 962.

23
* * * For now began
Night with her sullen wings to double-shade
The desert; fowls in their clay nests were couch'd,
And now wild beasts came forth, the woods to roam.
MILTON—*Paradise Regained.* Bk. I. L. 499,

24
Darkness now rose,
As daylight sunk, and brought in low'ring Night
Her shadowy offspring.
MILTON—*Paradise Regained.* Bk. IV. L. 397.

25
Night is the time for rest;
How sweet, when labours close,
To gather round an aching breast
The curtain of repose,
Stretch the tired limbs, and lay the head
Down on our own delightful bed!
MONTGOMERY—*Night.* St. 1.

1
Then awake! the heavens look bright, my dear;
'Tis never too late for delight, my dear;
And the best of all ways
To lengthen our days
Is to steal a few hours from the night, my dear.
MOORE—*The Young May Moon.*
(See also MACBETH, ROTRON)

2
But we that have but span-long life,
The thicker must lay on the pleasure;
And since time will not stay,
We'll add night to the day,
Thus, thus we'll fill the measure.
Duet printed 1795. Probably of earlier date.

3
There never was night that had no morn.
D. M. MULOCK—*The Golden Gate.*
(See also MACBETH)

4
The wind was a torrent of darkness among the gusty trees,
The moon was a ghostly galleon tossed upon cloudy seas,
The road was a ribbon of moonlight over the purple moor,
And the highwayman came riding.
ALFRED NOYES—*The Highwayman.*

5
Day is ended, Darkness shrouds
The shoreless seas and lowering clouds.
THOMAS LOVE PEACOCK—*Rhododaphne.* Canto V. L. 264.

6
Silence, ye wolves! while Ralph to Cynthia howls,
And makes night hideous;—Answer him, ye owls!
POPE—*Dunciad.* Bk. III. L. 165.
(See also HAMLET)

7
O Night, most beautiful and rare!
Thou giv'st the heavens their holiest hue,
And through the azure fields of air
Bring'st down the gentle dew.
THOMAS BUCHANAN READ—*Night.*

8
Ce que j'ôte à mes nuits, je l'ajoute à mes jours.
What I take from my nights, I add to my days.
Ascribed to ROTROU in *Venceslas.* (1647)
See also (MOORE)

9
Qu'une nuit paraît longue à la douleur qui veille!
How long the night seems to one kept awake by pain.
SAURIN—*Blanche et Guiscard.* V. 5.

10
On dreary night let lusty sunshine fall.
SCHILLER—*Pompeii and Herculaneum.*

11
To all, to each, a fair good night,
And pleasing dreams; and slumbers light.
SCOTT—*Marmion.* Canto VI. Last lines.

12
In the dead vast and middle of the night.
Hamlet. Act I. Sc. 2. L. 198. ("Waist" in many editions; afterwards printed "waste." "Vast" in the quarto of 1603.)

13
Making night hideous.
Hamlet. Act I. Sc. 4. L. 54.
(See also POPE)

14
'Tis now the very witching time of night,
When churchyards yawn and hell itself breathes out
Contagion to this world.
Hamlet. Act III. Sc. 2. L. 404.

15
And night is fled,
Whose pitchy mantle overveil'd the earth.
Henry VI. Pt. I. Act II. Sc. 2. L. 1.

16
I must become a borrower of the night
For a dark hour or twain.
Macbeth. Act III. Sc. 1. L. 27.
(See also MOORE)

17
Come, seeling night,
Skarf up the tender eye of pitiful day;
And with thy bloody and invisible hand,
Cancel and tear to pieces that great bond
Which keeps me pale!
Macbeth. Act III. Sc. 2. L. 46.

18
Light thickens; and the crow
Makes wing to the rooky wood:
Good things of the day begin to droop and drowse;
Whiles night's black agents to their preys do rouse.
Macbeth. Act III. Sc. 2. L. 50.

19
The night is long that never finds the day.
Macbeth. Act IV. Sc. 3. L. 240.
(See also MULOCK)

20
Now the hungry lion roars,
And the wolf behowls the moon;
Whilst the heavy ploughman snores,
All with weary task foredone.
Midsummer Night's Dream. Act V. Sc. 1. L. 378.

21
This is the night
That either makes me or fordoes me quite.
Othello. Act V. Sc. 1. L. 128.

22
Come, gentle night, come, loving, blackbrow'd night.
Romeo and Juliet. Act III. Sc. 2. L. 20.

23
How beautiful this night! the balmiest sigh
Which Vernal Zephyrs breathe in evening's ear
Were discord to the speaking quietude
That wraps this moveless scene. Heaven's ebon vault,
Studded with stars, unutterably bright,
Through which the moon's unclouded grandeur rolls,
Seems like a canopy which love has spread
To curtain her sleeping world.
SHELLEY—*Queen Mab.* Pt. IV.

24
Swiftly walk over the western wave,
Spirit of Night!
SHELLEY—*To Night.*

25
How beautiful is night!
A dewy freshness fills the silent air;
No mist obscures, nor cloud nor speck nor stain
Breaks the serene of heaven.
SOUTHEY—*Thalaba.* Bk. I.

26
Dead sounds at night come from the inmost hills,
Like footsteps upon wool.
TENNYSON—*Œnone.* St. 20.

1
I was heavy with the even,
When she lit her glimmering tapers
Round the day's dead sanctities.
FRANCIS THOMPSON—*Hound of Heaven*. L. 84.

2
Now black and deep the Night begins to fall,
A shade immense! Sunk in the quenching Gloom,
Magnificent and vast, are heaven and earth.
Order confounded lies; all beauty void,
Distinction lost, and gay variety
One universal blot: such the fair power
Of light, to kindle and create the whole.
THOMSON—*The Seasons. Autumn*. L. 113.

3
Come, drink the mystic wine of Night,
Brimming with silence and the stars;
While earth, bathed in this holy light,
Is seen without its scars.
LOUIS UNTERMEYER—*The Wine of Night*.

4
When, upon orchard and lane, breaks the white foam of the Spring
When, in extravagant revel, the Dawn, a Bacchante upleaping,
Spills, on the tresses of Night, vintages golden and red
When, as a token at parting, munificent Day for remembrance,
Gives, unto men that forget, Ophirs of fabulous ore.
WILLIAM WATSON—*Hymn to the Sea*. Pt. III. 12.

5
Mysterious night! when our first parent knew
Thee from report divine, and heard thy name,
Did he not tremble for this lovely frame,
This glorious canopy of light and blue?
JOSEPH BLANCO WHITE—*Night and Death*.

6
The summer skies are darkly blue,
The days are still and bright,
And Evening trails her robes of gold
Through the dim halls of Night.
SARAH H. P. WHITMAN—*Summer's Call*.
(See also LONGFELLOW)

7
Night begins to muffle up the day.
WITHERS—*Mistresse of Philarete*.

8
Night, sable goddess! from her ebon throne,
In rayless majesty, now stretches forth
Her leaden sceptre o'er a slumbering world.
Silence, how dead! and darkness, how profound!
Nor eye, nor list'ning ear, an object finds;
Creation sleeps. 'Tis as the general pulse
Of life stood still, and nature made a pause;
An awful pause! prophetic of her end.
YOUNG—*Night Thoughts*. Night I. L. 18.

9
How is night's sable mantle labor'd o'er,
How richly wrought with attributes divine!
What wisdom shines! what love! this midnight pomp,
This gorgeous arch, with golden worlds inlaid
Built with divine ambition!
YOUNG—*Night Thoughts*. Night IV. L. 385.

10
Mine is the night, with all her stars.
YOUNG—*Paraphrase on Job*. L. 147.

NIGHTINGALE

11
I have heard the nightingale herself.
KING AGESILAUS when asked to listen to a man imitate the nightingale. PLUTARCH—*Life of Agesilaus*.

12
Hark! ah, the nightingale—
The tawny-throated!
Hark from that moonlit cedar what a burst!
What triumph! hark!—what pain!

* * * * * *

Listen, Eugenia—
How thick the bursts come crowding through the leaves!
Again—thou hearest?
Eternal passion!
Eternal pain!
MATTHEW ARNOLD—*Philomela*. L. 32.

13
For as nightingales do upon glow-worms feed,
So poets live upon the living light.
BAILEY—*Festus*. Sc. *Home*.

14
As it fell upon a day
In the merry month of May,
Sitting in a pleasant shade
Which a grove of myrtles made.
RICHARD BARNFIELD—*Address to the Nightingale*.

15
It is the hour when from the boughs
The nightingale's high note is heard;
It is the hour when lovers' vows
Seem sweet in every whisper'd word.
BYRON—*Parisina*. St. 1.

16
"Most musical, most melancholy" bird!
A melancholy bird! Oh! idle thought!
In nature there is nothing melancholy.
COLERIDGE—*The Nightingale*. L. 13.

17
'Tis the merry nightingale
That crowds, and hurries, and precipitates
With fast thick warble his delicious notes,
As he were fearful that an April night
Would be too short for him to utter forth
His love-chant, and disburthen his full soul
Of all its music!
COLERIDGE—*The Nightingale*. L. 43.

18
Sweet bird, that sing'st away the early hours,
Of winter's past or coming void of care,
Well pleaséd with delights which present are,
Fair seasons, budding sprays, sweet-smelling flowers.
DRUMMOND—*Sonnet. To a Nightingale*.

19
Like a wedding-song all-melting
Sings the nightingale, the dear one.
HEINE—*Book of Songs. Donna Clara*.

20
The nightingale appear'd the first,
And as her melody she sang,
The apple into blossom burst,
To life the grass and violets sprang.
HEINE—*Book of Songs. New Spring*. No. 9.

1
Where the nightingale doth sing
Not a senseless, tranced thing,
But divine melodious truth.
KEATS—*Ode. Bards of Passion and of Mirth.*

2
Adieu! adieu! thy plaintive anthem fades
Past the near meadows, over the still stream,
Up the hill-side; and now 'tis buried deep
In the next valley-glades:
Was it a vision, or a waking dream?
Fled is that music:—do I wake or sleep?
KEATS—*To a Nightingale.*

3
Thou wast not born for death, immortal bird!
No hungry generations tread thee down;
The voice I hear this passing night was heard
In ancient days by emperor and clown.
KEATS—*To a Nightingale.*

4
Soft as Memnon's harp at morning,
To the inward ear devout,
Touched by light, with heavenly warning
Your transporting chords ring out.
Every leaf in every nook,
Every wave in every brook,
Chanting with a solemn voice
Minds us of our better choice.
JOHN KEBLE—*The Nightingale.*

5
To the red rising moon, and loud and deep
The nightingale is singing from the steep.
LONGFELLOW—*Keats.*

6
What bird so sings, yet does so wail?
O, 'tis the ravish'd nightingale
Jug, jug, jug, jug—tereu—she cries,
And still her woes at midnight rise.
LYLY—*The Songs of Birds.*

7
Sweet bird that shunn'st the noise of folly,
Most musical, most melancholy!
Thee, chauntress, oft, the woods among,
I woo, to hear thy even-song.
MILTON—*Il Penseroso.* L. 61.

8
O nightingale, that on yon bloomy spray
Warblest at eve, when all the woods are still;
Thou with fresh hope the lover's heart dost fill
While the jolly hours lead on propitious May.
MILTON—*Sonnet. To the Nightingale.*

9
Thy liquid notes that close the eye of day
First heard before the shallow cuckoo's bill,
Portend success in love.
MILTON—*Sonnet. To the Nightingale.*

10
I said to the Nightingale:
"Hail, all hail!
Pierce with thy trill the dark,
Like a glittering music-spark,
When the earth grows pale and dumb."
D. M. MULOCK—*A Rhyme About Birds.*

11
Yon nightingale, whose strain so sweetly flows,
Mourning her ravish'd young or much-loved mate,
A soothing charm o'er all the valleys throws
And skies, with notes well tuned to her sad state.
PETRARCH—*To Laura in Death.* Sonnet XLIII.

12
The sunrise wakes the lark to sing,
The moonrise wakes the nightingale.
Come, darkness, moonrise, everything
That is so silent, sweet, and pale:
Come, so ye wake the nightingale.
CHRISTINA G. ROSSETTI—*Bird Raptures.*

13
Hark! that's the nightingale,
Telling the self-same tale
Her song told when this ancient earth was young:
So echoes answered when her song was sung
In the first wooded vale.
CHRISTINA G. ROSSETTI—*Twilight Calm.* St. 7.

14
The angel of spring, the mellow-throated nightingale.
SAPPHO. Fragm. 39.

15
The nightingale, if she should sing by day,
When every goose is cackling, would be thought
No better a musician than the wren.
How many things by season season'd are
To their right praise, and true perfection!
Merchant of Venice. Act V. Sc. 1. L. 104.

16
Wilt thou be gone? it is not yet near day:
It was the nightingale, and not the lark,
That pierc'd the fearful hollow of thine ear;
Nightly she sings on yon pomegranate tree:
Believe me, love, it was the nightingale.
Romeo and Juliet. Act III. Sc. 5. L. 1.

17 O Nightingale,
Cease from thy enamoured tale.
SHELLEY—*Scenes from "Magico Prodigioso."* Sc. 3.

18
One nightingale in an interfluous wood
Satiate the hungry dark with melody.
SHELLEY—*Woodman and the Nightingale.*

19
The nightingale as soon as April bringeth
Unto her rested sense a perfect waking,
While late bare earth, proud of new clothing, springeth,
Sings out her woes, a thorn her song-book making.
And mournfully bewailing,
Her throat in tunes expresseth
What grief her breast oppresseth.
SIR PHILIP SIDNEY—*O Philomela Fair.*

20
Where beneath the ivy shade,
In the dew-besprinkled glade,
Many a love-lorn nightingale,
Warbles sweet her plaintive tale.
SOPHOCLES—*Œdipus Coloneus.* Trans. by THOMAS FRANCKLIN.

21
Lend me your song, ye Nightingales! O, pour
The mazy-running soul of melody
Into my varied verse.
THOMSON—*The Seasons. Spring.* L. 574.

1
The rose looks out in the valley,
And thither will I go,
To the rosy vale, where the nightingale
Sings his song of woe.
GIL VICENTE—*The Nightingale.* BOWRING'S trans.

2
—Under the linden,
On the meadow,
Where our bed arranged was,
There now you may find e'en
In the shadow
Broken flowers and crushed grass.
—Near the woods, down in the vale,
Tandaradi!
Sweetly sang the nightingale.
WALTER VON DER VOGELWEIDE—Trans. in *The Minnesinger of Germany. Under the Linden.*

3
Last night the nightingale woke me,
Last night, when all was still.
It sang in the golden moonlight,
From out the woodland hill.
CHRISTIAN WINTHER—*Sehnsucht.* Trans. used by MARZIALS in his song. *Last Night.*

NILE

4
It flows through old hushed Egypt and its sands,
Like some grave mighty thought threading a dream.
LEIGH HUNT—*Sonnet. The Nile.*

5
Son of the old moon-mountains African!
Stream of the Pyramid and Crocodile!
We call thee fruitful, and that very while
A desert fills our seeing's inward span.
KEATS—*Sonnet. To the Nile.*
(See also SHELLEY)

6
The Nile, forever new and old,
Among the living and the dead,
Its mighty, mystic stream has rolled.
LONGFELLOW—*Christus. The Golden Legend.* Pt. I.

7
The higher Nilus swells,
The more it promises; as it ebbs, the seedsman
Upon the slime and ooze scatters his grain,
And shortly comes the harvest.
Antony and Cleopatra. Act II. Sc. 7. L. 23.

8
Whose tongue
Outvenoms all the worms of Nile.
Cymbeline. Act III. Sc. 4. L. 33.

9
O'er Egypt's land of memory floods are level,
And they are thine, O Nile! and well thou knowest
The soul-sustaining airs and blasts of evil,
And fruits, and poisons spring where'er thou flowest.
SHELLEY—*Sonnet. To the Nile.*
(See also KEATS)

10
Mysterious Flood,—that through the silent sands
Hast wandered, century on century,
Watering the length of great Egyptian lands,
Which were not, but for thee.
BAYARD TAYLOR—*To the Nile.*

NOBILITY

11
If there is anything good about nobility it is that it enforces the necessity of avoiding degeneracy.
From the Latin of BÖETHIUS.

12
Inquinat egregios adjuncta superbia mores.
The noblest character is stained by the addition of pride.
CLAUDIANUS—*De Quarto Consulatu Honorii Augustii Panegyris.* 305.

13
Ay, these look like the workmanship of heaven;
This is the porcelain clay of human kind,
And therefore cast into these noble moulds.
DRYDEN—*Don Sebastian.* Act I. Sc. 1.

14
O lady, nobility is thine, and thy form is the reflection of thy nature!
EURIPIDES—*Ion.* 238.

15
There are epidemics of nobleness as well as epidemics of disease.
FROUDE—*Short Studies on Great Subjects. Calvinism.*

16
Ein edler Mensch zieht edle Menschen an,
Und weiss sie fest zu halten, wie ihr thut.
A noble soul alone can noble souls attract;
And knows alone, as ye, to hold them.
GOETHE—*Torquato Tasso.* I. 1. 59.

17
Il sangue nobile è un accidente della fortuna; le azioni nobili caratterizzano il grande.
Noble blood is an accident of fortune; noble actions characterize the great.
GOLDONI—*Pamela.* I. 6.

18
Par nobile fratrum.
A noble pair of brothers.
HORACE—*Satires.* II. 3. 243.

19
Fond man! though all the heroes of your line
Bedeck your halls, and round your galleries shine
In proud display; yet take this truth from me—
Virtue alone is true nobility!
JUVENAL—*Satire VIII.* L. 29. GIFFORD'S trans. "Virtus sola nobilitat," is the Latin of last line.

20
Noblesse oblige.
There are obligations to nobility.
COMTE DE LABORDE, in a notice to the French Historical Society in 1865, attributes the phrase to DUC DE LEVIS, who used it in 1808, apropos of the establishment of the nobility.

21
Be noble in every thought
And in every deed!
LONGFELLOW—*Christus. The Golden Legend.* Pt. II.

22
Noble by birth, yet nobler by great deeds.
LONGFELLOW—*Tales of a Wayside Inn.* Pt. III. *The Student's Tale. Emma and Eginhard.* L. 82.

1
Be noble! and the nobleness that lies
In other men, sleeping, but never dead,
Will rise in majesty to meet thine own.
LOWELL—*Sonnet IV.*

2
Let wealth and commerce, laws and learning die,
But leave us still our old nobility.
LORD JOHN MANNERS—*England's Trust.* Pt. III. L. 227.

3
Be aristocracy the only joy:
Let commerce perish—let the world expire.
Modern Gulliver's Travels. P. 192. (Ed. 1796)

4 His nature is too noble for the world:
He would not flatter Neptune for his trident,
Or Jove for's power to thunder.
Coriolanus. Act III. Sc. 1. L. 255.

5
This was the noblest Roman of them all:
All the conspirators save only he
Did that they did in envy of great Cæsar;
He only, in a general honest thought
And common good to all, made one of them.
Julius Cæsar. Act V. Sc. 5. L. 68.

6
Better not to be at all
Than not be noble.
TENNYSON—*The Princess.* Pt. II. L. 79.

7 Whoe'er amidst the sons
Of reason, valor, liberty, and virtue
Displays distinguished merit, is a noble
Of Nature's own creating.
THOMSON—*Coriolanus.* Act III. Sc. 3.

8
Titles are marks of *honest* men, and *wise:*
The fool or knave that wears a title *lies.*
YOUNG—*Love of Fame.* Satire I. L. 145.

NONSENSE

9
A little nonsense now and then
Is relished by the wisest men.
ANONYMOUS.
(See also WALPOLE)

10
He killed the noble Mudjokivis.
Of the skin he made him mittens,
Made them with the fur side inside,
Made them with the skin side outside.
He, to get the warm side inside,
Put the inside skin side outside;
He, to get the cold side outside,
Put the warm side fur side inside.
That's why he put the fur side inside,
Why he put the skin side outside,
Why he turned them inside outside.
Given as Anon. in CAROLYN WELLS—*Parody Anthology.* P. 120.
(See also STRONG)

11
When Bryan O'Lynn had no shirt to put on,
He took him a sheep skin to make him a' one.
"With the skinny side out, and the wooly side in,
'Twill be warm and convanient," said Bryan O'Lynn.
Old Irish Song.

12
For blocks are better cleft with wedges,
Than tools of sharp or subtle edges,
And dullest nonsense has been found
By some to be the most profound.
BUTLER—*Pindaric Ode.* IV. L. 82.

13
'T was brillig, and the slithy toves
Did gyre and gimble in the wabe;
All mimsy were the borogoves,
And the mome raths outgrabe.
LEWIS CARROLL—*Through the Looking-glass.* Ch. I.

14
To varnish nonsense with the charms of sound.
CHURCHILL—*The Apology.* L. 219.

15
Conductor, when you receive a fare,
Punch in the presence of the passenjare.
A blue trip slip for an eight-cent fare,
A buff trip slip for a six-cent fare,
A pink trip slip for a three-cent fare,
Punch in the presence of the passenjare!
Chorus
Punch, brothers! punch with care!
Punch in the presence of the passenjare!
S. L. CLEMENS (Mark Twain)—*Punch, Brothers, Punch.* Used in *Literary Nightmare.* Notice posted in a car and discovered by Mark Twain. Changed into the above jingle, which became popular, by Isaac Bromley and others. See ALBERT BIGELOW PAINE—*Biography of Mark Twain.*

16
Misce stultitiam consiliis brevem:
Dulce est desipere in loco.
Mingle a little folly with your wisdom; a little nonsense now and then is pleasant.
HORACE—*Carmina.* IV. 12. 27.

17
How pleasant to know Mr. Lear!
Who has written such volumes of stuff!
Some think him ill-tempered and queer,
But a few think him pleasant enough.
EDWARD LEAR—*Lines to a Young Lady.*

18
No one is exempt from talking nonsense; the misfortune is to do it solemnly.
MONTAIGNE—*Essays.* Bk. III. Ch. I.

19
There's a skin without and a skin within,
A covering skin and a lining skin,
But the skin within is the skin without
Doubled and carried complete throughout.
POWER of Atherstone.
(See also STRONG)

20
From the Squirrel skin Marcosset
Made some mittens for our hero.
Mittens with the fur-side inside,
With the fur-side next his fingers
So's to keep the hand warm inside.
G. STRONG ("Marc Antony Henderson")—*Song of the Milgenwater.* Parody of Hiawatha.
(See also ANON QUOTATION, POWER)

21
A careless song, with a little nonsense in it now and then, does not misbecome a monarch.
HORACE WALPOLE—*Letter to Sir Horace Mann.* (1770)

NOSE

1
Jolly nose! there are fools who say drink hurts the sight,
Such dullards know nothing about it;
'Tis better with wine to extinguish the light
Than live always in darkness without it.
Paraphrase of OLIVIER BASSELIN'S *Vaux-de-vire*. Quoted by AINSWORTH in *Jack Sheppard*. Vol. I. P. 213.

2
As clear and as manifest as the nose in a man's face.
BURTON—*Anatomy of Melancholy*. Pt. III. Sec. III. Memb. 4. Subsec. I.

3
Give me a man with a good allowance of nose, . . . when I want any good head-work done I choose a man—provided his education has been suitable—with a long nose.
NAPOLEON. Related in *Notes on Noses*. P. 43. (Ed. 1847)

4
Plain as a nose in a man's face.
RABELAIS—*Works. The Author's Prologue to the Fifth Book.*

NOTHINGNESS

5
Nothing proceeds from nothingness, as also nothing passes away into non-existence.
MARCUS AURELIUS—*Meditations*. IV. 4.

6
Why and Wherefore set out one day,
To hunt for a wild Negation.
They agreed to meet at a cool retreat
On the Point of Interrogation.
OLIVER HERFORD—*Metaphysics*.

7
Nothing to do but work,
Nothing to eat but food,
Nothing to wear but clothes,
To keep one from going nude.
BEN KING—*The Pessimist*.

8
Nil actum credens, dum quid superesset agendum.
Believing nothing done whilst there remained anything else to be done.
LUCANUS—*Pharsalia*. Bk. II. 657.

9
Nil igitur fieri de nilo posse putandum es
Semine quando opus est rebus.
We cannot conceive of matter being formed of nothing, since things require a seed to start from.
LUCRETIUS—*De Rerum Natura*. Bk. I. L. 206.

10
Haud igitur redit ad Nihilum res ulla, sed omnes
Discidio redeunt in corpora materiai.
Therefore there is not anything which returns to nothing, but all things return dissolved into their elements.
LUCRETIUS—*De Rerum Natura*. Bk. I. 250.

11
Nothing's new, and nothing's true, and nothing matters.
Attributed to LADY MORGAN.

12
Gigni
De nihilo nihil, in nihilum nil posse reverti.
Nothing can be born of nothing, nothing can be resolved into nothing.
PERSIUS.—*Satires*. I, 111. 83.

13
Gratis anhelans, multa agendo nihil agens.
Sibi molesta, et aliis odiosissima.
Out of breath to no purpose, in doing much doing nothing. A race (of busybodies) hurtful to itself and most hateful to all others.
PHÆDRUS—*Fables*. Bk. II. 5. 3.

14
It is, no doubt, an immense advantage to have done nothing, but one should not abuse it.
RIVAROL—Preface to *Petit Almanach de nos Grands Hommes*.

15
Nothing, thou elder brother e'en to shade.
ROCHESTER—*Poem on Nothing*.

16
Operose nihil agunt.
They laboriously do nothing.
SENECA—*De Brev. Vitæ*. Bk. I. 13.

17
Where every something, being blent together
Turns to a wild of nothing.
Merchant of Venice. Act III. Sc. 2.

18
A life of nothing's nothing worth,
From that first nothing ere his birth,
To that last nothing under earth.
TENNYSON—*Two Voices*.

NOVELTY (See also NEWS)

19
There is nothing new except what is forgotten.
MADEMOISELLE BERTIN (Milliner to Marie Antoinette.)

20
Spick and span new.
CERVANTES—*Don Quixote*. Pt. II. Ch. LVIII.
THOS. MIDDLETON—*The Family of Love*. Act IV. Sc. 3.

21
There is no new thing under the sun.
Ecclesiastes. I. 9.

22
Is there anything whereof it may be said, See, this is new? It hath been already of old time, which was before us.
Ecclesiastes. I. 10.

23
Wie machen wir's, dass alles frisch und neu
Und mit Bedeutung auch gefällig sei?
How shall we plan, that all be fresh and new—
Important matter yet attractive too?
GOETHE—*Faust. Vorspiel auf dem Theater*. L. 15.

24
Dulcique animos novitate tenebo.
And I will capture your minds with sweet novelty.
OVID—*Metamorphoses*. Bk. IV. 284.

25
Est natura hominum novitatis avida.
Human nature is fond of novelty.
PLINY the Elder—*Historia Naturalis*. XII. 5. 3.

1
Ex Africa semper aliquid novi.
Always something new out of Africa.
PLINY the Elder—*Historia Naturalis*. 8. 6.

2
Afrique est coustumiere toujours choses produire nouvelles et monstrueuses.
It is the custom of Africa always to produce new and monstrous things.
RABELAIS—*Pantagruel*. Bk. V. Ch. III.

3
Sehen Sie, die beste Neuigkeit verliert, sobald sie Stadtmärchen wird.
Observe, the best of novelties palls when it becomes town talk.
SCHILLER—*Fiesco*. III. 10.

4
What is valuable is not new, and what is new is not valuable.
DANIEL WEBSTER. At Marshfield. Sept. 1, 1848. Criticism of the platform of the Free Soil party. Phrase used in *Edinburgh Review* by LORD BROUGHAM in an article on the work of DR. THOMAS YOUNG.

NOVEMBER

5
On my cornice linger the ripe black grapes ungathered;
Children fill the groves with the echoes of their glee,
Gathering tawny chestnuts, and shouting when beside them
Drops the heavy fruit of the tall black-walnut tree.
BRYANT—*The Third of November*. (1861)

6
When shrieked
The bleak November winds, and smote the woods,
And the brown fields were herbless, and the shades
That met above the merry rivulet
Were spoiled, I sought, I loved them still; they seemed
Like old companions in adversity.
BRYANT—*A Winter Piece*. L. 22.

7
The dusky waters shudder as they shine,
The russet leaves obstruct the straggling way
Of oozy brooks, which no deep banks define,
And the gaunt woods, in ragged scant array,
Wrap their old limbs with sombre ivy twine.
HARTLEY COLERIDGE—*November*.

8
Dry leaves upon the wall,
Which flap like rustling wings and seek escape,
A single frosted cluster on the grape
Still hangs—and that is all.
SUSAN COOLIDGE—*November*.

9
Fie upon thee, November! thou dost ape
The airs of thy young sisters, * * * thou hast stolen
The witching smile of May to grace thy lip,
And April's rare capricious loveliness
Thou'rt trying to put on!
JULIA C. R. DORR—*November*.

10
My sorrow when she's here with me,
Thinks these dark days of autumn rain
Are beautiful as days can be;
She loves the bare, the withered tree;
She walks the sodden pasture lane.
ROBERT FROST—*My November Guest*.

11
No park—no ring—no afternoon gentility—
No company—no nobility—
No warmth, no cheerfulness, no healthful ease.
No comfortable feel in any member—
No shade, no shine, no butterflies, no bees,
No fruits, no flowers, no leaves, no birds,
November!
HOOD—*November*.

12
The dead leaves their rich mosaics
Of olive and gold and brown
Had laid on the rain-wet pavements,
Through all the embowered town.
SAMUEL LONGFELLOW—*November*.

13
Now Neptune's sullen month appears,
The angry night cloud swells with tears,
And savage storms infuriate driven,
Fly howling in the face of heaven!
Now, now, my friends, the gathering gloom
With roseate rays of wine illume:
And while our wreaths of parsley spread
Their fadeless foliage round our head,
We'll hymn th' almighty power of wine,
And shed libations on his shrine!
MOORE—*Odes of Anacreon. Ode LXVIII*.

14
The wild November come at last
Beneath a veil of rain;
The night wind blows its folds aside,
Her face is full of pain.

The latest of her race, she takes
The Autumn's vacant throne:
She has but one short moon to live,
And she must live alone.
R. H. STODDARD—*November*.

15
Wrapped in his sad-colored cloak, the Day, like a Puritan, standeth
Stern in the joyless fields, rebuking the lingering color,—
Dying hectic of leaves and the chilly blue of the asters,—
Hearing, perchance, the croak of a crow on the desolate tree-top.
BAYARD TAYLOR—*Home Pastorals. November*. I.

NUREMBURG

16
In the valley of the Pegnitz, where,
Across broad meadow-lands,
Rise the blue Franconian mountains,
Nuremburg, the ancient, stands.

Quaint old town of toil and traffic,
Quaint old town of art and song,
Memories haunt thy pointed gables,
Like the rooks that round thee throng.
LONGFELLOW—*Nuremburg*.

O

OAK

Quercus

1
A song to the oak, the brave old oak,
Who hath ruled in the greenwood long;
Here's health and renown to his broad green crown,
And his fifty arms so strong.
There's fear in his frown when the Sun goes down,
And the fire in the West fades out;
And he showeth his might on a wild midnight,
When the storms through his branches shout.
H. F. CHORLEY—*The Brave Old Oak.*

2
The oak, when living, monarch of the wood;
The English oak, which, dead, commands the flood.
CHURCHILL—*Gotham.* I. 303.

3
Old noted oak! I saw thee in a mood
Of vague indifference; and yet with me
Thy memory, like thy fate, hath lingering stood
For years, thou hermit, in the lonely sea
Of grass that waves around thee!
JOHN CLARE—*The Rural Muse. Burthorp Oak.*

4
The monarch oak, the patriarch of the trees,
Shoots rising up, and spreads by slow degrees.
Three centuries he grows, and three he stays
Supreme in state; and in three more decays.
DRYDEN—*Palamon and Arcite.* Bk. III. L. 1,058.

5
Tall oaks from little acorns grow.
DAVID EVERETT—*Lines for a School Declamation.*

6
The oaks with solemnity shook their heads;
The twigs of the birch-trees, in token
Of warning, nodded,—and I exclaim'd:
"Dear Monarch, forgive what I've spoken!"
HEINE—*Songs. Germany.* Caput XVII.

7
Those green-robed senators of mighty woods,
Tall oaks, branch-charmed by the earnest stars,
Dream, and so dream all night without a stir.
KEATS—*Hyperion.* Bk. I. L. 73.

8
The tall Oak, towering to the skies,
The fury of the wind defies,
From age to age, in virtue strong.
Inured to stand, and suffer wrong.
MONTGOMERY—*The Oak.*

9
There grewe an aged tree on the greene;
A goodly Oake sometime had it bene,
With armes full strong and largely displayed,
But of their leaves they were disarayde·
The bodie bigge, and mightely pight,
Thoroughly rooted, and of wond'rous hight;
Whilome had bene the king of the field,
And mochell mast to the husband did yielde,
And with his nuts larded many swine:
But now the gray mosse marred his rine;
His bared boughes were beaten with stormes,
His toppe was bald, and wasted with wormes,
His honour decayed, his braunches sere.
SPENSER—*Shepheard's Callender. Februarie.*

OATHS (See also SWEARING, VOWS)

10
Oaths were not purpos'd, more than law,
To keep the Good and Just in awe,
But to confine the Bad and Sinful,
Like mortal cattle in a penfold.
BUTLER—*Hudibras.* Pt. II. Canto II. L. 197.

11
He that imposes an Oath makes it,
Not he that for Convenience takes it.
Then how can any man be said
To break an oath he never made?
BUTLER—*Hudibras.* Pt. II. Canto II. L. 377.

12
I will take my corporal oath on it.
CERVANTES—*Don Quixote.* Pt. I. Bk. IV. Ch. X.

13
Juravi lingua, mentem injuratam gero.
I have sworn with my tongue, but my mind is unsworn.
CICERO—*De Officiis.* III. 29.

14
They fix attention, heedless of your pain,
With oaths like rivets forced into the brain;
And e'en when sober truth prevails throughout,
They swear it, till affirmance breeds a doubt.
COWPER—*Conversation.* L. 63.

15
And hast thou sworn on every slight pretence,
Till perjuries are common as bad pence,
While thousands, careless of the damning sin,
Kiss the book's outside, who ne'er look'd within?
COWPER—*Expostulation.* L. 384.

16
In lapidary inscriptions a man is not upon oath.
SAMUEL JOHNSON—*Boswell's Life of Johnson.* (1775)

17
I take the official oath to-day with no mental reservations and with no purpose to construe the Constitution by any hypercritical rules.
LINCOLN—*First Inaugural Address.* March 4, 1861.

18
You can have no oath registered in heaven to destroy the Government; while I shall have the most solemn one to "preserve, protect, and defend" it.
LINCOLN—*First Inaugural Address.* March 4, 1861.

19
He that sweareth to his own hurt and changeth not.
Psalms. XV. 4.

20
'Tis not the many oaths that makes the truth,
But the plain single vow that is vow'd true.
All's Well That Ends Well. Act IV. Sc. 2. L. 21

21
Trust none;
For oaths are straws, men's faiths are wafer-cakes,
And hold-fast is the only dog.
Henry V. Act II. Sc. 3. L. 52.

1
It is a great sin to swear unto a sin,
But greater sin to keep a sinful oath.
Henry VI. Pt. II. Act V. Sc. 1. L. 182.

2
Or, having sworn too hard a keeping oath,
Study to break it and not break my troth.
Love's Labour's Lost. Act I. Sc. 1. L. 65.

3 What fool is not so wise
To lose an oath to win a paradise?
Love's Labour's Lost. Act IV. Sc. 3. L. 72.

4
An oath, an oath, I have an oath in heaven:
Shall I lay perjury upon my soul?
No, not for Venice.
Merchant of Venice. Act IV. Sc. 1. L. 228

5
I'll take thy word for faith, not ask thine oath;
Who shuns not to break one will sure crack both.
Pericles. Act I. Sc. 2. L. 120.

6
I write a woman's oaths in water.
SOPHOCLES—*Fragment*. 694.

OBEDIENCE

7
Obedience is the mother of success, the wife of safety.
ÆSCHYLUS—*Septem. Duces*. 224.

8
The fear of some divine and supreme powers keeps men in obedience.
BURTON—*Anatomy of Melancholy*. Pt. III. Sec. 4. Memb. 1. Subsec. 2.

9
Qui modeste paret, videtur qui aliquando imperet dignus esse.
He who obeys with modesty appears worthy of being some day a commander.
CICERO—*De Legibus*. III. 2.

10
Tis the *same*, with *common* natures,
Use 'em *kindly*, they *rebel*,
But, be *rough* as *nutmeg graters*,
And the rogues *obey* you well.
AARON HILL—*Verses written on a Window in a Journey to Scotland*.

11
All arts his own, the hungry Greekling counts;
And bid him mount the skies, the skies he mounts.
JUVENAL—*Third Satire*. Trans. by GIFFORD.

12
All sciences a fasting Monsieur knows;
And bid him go to hell—to hell he goes.
JUVENAL — *Third Satire*. Paraphrased by JOHNSON—*London*.

13
No nice extreme a true Italian knows;
But bid him go to hell, to hell he goes.
JUVENAL—*Third Satire*. Paraphrased by PHILLIPS, in a letter to the king in reference to the Italian witnesses at the trial of QUEEN CAROLINE.

14
Obedience is the key to every door.
GEORGE MACDONALD—*The Marquis of Lossie*. Ch. LIII.

15
I find the doing of the will of God, leaves me no time for disputing about His plans.
GEORGE MACDONALD—*The Marquis of Lossie*. Ch. LXXII.

16 Son of Heav'n and Earth,
Attend! That thou art happy, owe to God;
That thou continuest such, owe to thyself,
That is, to thy obedience; therein stand.
MILTON—*Paradise Lost*. Bk. V. L. 519.

17
Ascend, I follow thee, safe guide, the path
Thou lead'st me, and to the hand of heav'n submit.
MILTON—*Paradise Lost*. Bk. XI. L. 371.

18
Though a god I have learned to obey the times.
PALLADAS—*Epigram*. In *Palatine Anthology*. IX. 441.

19
Through obedience learn to command.
Founded on a passage in PLATO—*Leges*. 762 E. Same idea in PLINY—*Letters*. VIII. 14. 5.

20
The eye that mocketh at his father, and despiseth to obey his mother, the ravens of the valley shall pick it out, and the young eagles shall eat it.
Proverbs. XXX. 17.

21
Obedience decks the Christian most.
SCHILLER—*Fight with the Dragon*. BOWRING'S trans.

22
Let them obey that know not how to rule.
Henry VI. Pt. II. Act V. Sc. 1. L. 6.

23
It fits thee not to ask the reason why,
Because we bid it.
Pericles. Act I. Sc. 1. L. 157.

24 One so small
Who knowing nothing knows but to obey.
TENNYSON—*Idylls of the King. Guinevere*. L. 183.

OBLIVION (See also FORGETFULNESS)

25
Oblivion is not to be hired.
SIR THOMAS BROWNE—*Hydriotaphia*. Ch. V.

26 For those sacred powers
Tread on oblivion: no desert of ours
Can be entombed in their celestial breasts.
WM. BROWNE—*Britannia's Pastorals*. Bk. III. Song II. St. 23.

27
It is not in the storm nor in the strife
We feel benumb'd, and wish to be no more,
But in the after-silence on the shore,
When all is lost, except a little life.
BYRON—*Lines on Hearing that Lady Byron was Ill*. L. 9.

28
Without oblivion, there is no remembrance possible. When both oblivion and memory are wise, when the general soul of man is clear,

melodious, true, there may come a modern Iliad as memorial of the Past.
CARLYLE—*Cromwell's Letters and Speeches. Introduction.* Ch. I.

1
And o'er the past oblivion stretch her wing.
HOMER — *Odyssey.* Bk. XXIV. L. 557. POPE'S trans.

2
He shall return no more to his house, neither shall his place know him any more.
Job. VII. 10.

3
Injuriarum remedium est oblivio.
Oblivion is the remedy for injuries.
SENECA—*Epistles.* 94. Quoting from an old poet, also found in SYRUS.

4
What's past and what's to come is strew'd with husks
And formless ruin of oblivion.
Troilus and Cressida. Act IV. Sc. 5. L. 166.

5
Eo magis præfulgebant quod non videbantur.
They shone forth the more that they were not seen.
TACITUS. Adapted from *Annals.* Bk. III. 76.

6
But from your mind's chilled sky
It needs must drop, and lie with stiffened wings
Among your soul's forlornest things;
A speck upon your memory, alack!
A dead fly in a dusty window-crack.
FRANCIS THOMPSON—"*Manus Animam Pinxit.*" St. 2.

OBSCURITY

7
Content thyself to be obscurely good.
ADDISON—*Cato.* Act IV. Sc. 4.

8
I give the fight up; let there be an end,
A privacy, an obscure nook for me,
I want to be forgotten even by God.
ROBERT BROWNING—*Paracelsus.* Pt. V.

9
Like beauteous flowers which vainly waste their scent
Of odours in unhaunted deserts.
CHAMBERLAYNE—*Pharonida.* Part II. Bk. IV.
(See also GRAY, also YOUNG under NATURE, POPE under ROSE, CHURCHILL under SWEETNESS)

10
As night the life-inclining stars best shows,
So lives obscure the starriest souls disclose.
GEORGE CHAPMAN—*Hymns and Epigrams of Homer. The Translator's Epilogue.* L. 74.

11
Full many a flower is born to blush unseen,
And waste its sweetness on the desert air.
GRAY—*Elegy in a Country Churchyard.* St. 14.
(See also CHAMBERLAYNE)

12
Yet still he fills affection's eye,
Obscurely wise, and coarsely kind.
SAMUEL JOHNSON—*On the Death of Robert Levet.*

13
Some write their wrongs in marble: he more just,
Stoop'd down serene and wrote them on the dust,
Trod under foot, the sport of every wind,
Swept from the earth and blotted from his mind,
There, secret in the grave, he bade them lie,
And grieved they could not 'scape the Almighty eye.
SAMUEL MADDEN—*Boulter's Monument.*

14
The palpable obscure.
MILTON—*Paradise Lost.* Bk. II. L. 406.

15
Bene qui latuit, bene vixit.
He who has lived obscurely and quietly has lived well.
OVID—*Tristium.* III. 4. 25.

16
Ut sæpe summa ingenia in occulto latent!
How often the highest talent lurks in obscurity!
PLAUTUS—*Captivi.* I. 2. 62.

17
How happy is the blameless vestal's lot!
The world forgetting, by the world forgot.
POPE—*Eloisa to Abelard.* L. 207.

18
Thus let me live, unseen, unknown,
Thus unlamented let me die;
Steal from the world, and not a stone
Tell where I lie.
POPE—*Ode on Solitude.*

19
Yet was he but a squire of low degree.
SPENSER—*Faerie Queene.* Bk. IV. Canto VII. St. 15.

20
Eo magis præfulgebat quod non videbatur.
He shone with the greater splendor, because he was not seen.
TACITUS—*Annales.* III. 76.

21
She dwelt among the untrodden ways
Beside the springs of Dove,
A maid whom there were none to praise
And very few to love.
WORDSWORTH—*She Dwelt Among the Untrodden Ways.*

OCCUPATION (See also LABOR, WORK, and Different OCCUPATIONS)

22
I hold every man a debtor to his profession; from the which as men of course do seek to receive countenance and profit, so ought they of duty to endeavor themselves, by way of amends, to be a help and ornament thereunto.
BACON—*Maxims of the Law.* Preface.

23
Quam quisque novit artem, in hac se exerceat.
Let a man practise the profession which he best knows.
CICERO — *Tusculanarum Disputationum.* I. 18.

24
The ugliest of trades have their moments of pleasure. Now, if I were a grave-digger, or even a hangman, there are some people I could work for with a great deal of enjoyment.
DOUGLAS JERROLD — *Jerrold's Wit. Ugly Trades.*

25
And sure the Eternal Master found
The single talent well employ'd.
SAMUEL JOHNSON—*On the Death of Robert Levet.* St. 7.

1
The hand of little employment hath the daintier sense.
Hamlet. Act V. Sc. 1. L. 77.

2
Thus Nero went up and down Greece and challenged the fiddlers at their trade. Æropus, a Macedonian king, made lanterns; Harcatius, the king of Parthia, was a mole-catcher; and Biantes, the Lydian, filed needles.
JEREMY TAYLOR—*Holy Living.* Ch. I. Sec. I. *Rules for Employing Our Time.*

OCEAN

3
Ye waves
That o'er th' interminable ocean wreathe
Your crisped smiles.
ÆSCHYLUS—*Prometheus Chained.* L. 95.
"The multitudinous laughter of the sea."
As trans. by DE QUINCEY. "The many-twinkling smile of ocean," is used by KEBLE—*Christian Year. 2nd Sunday After Trinity.*

4
The sea heaves up, hangs loaded o'er the land,
Breaks there, and buries its tumultuous strength.
ROBERT BROWNING—*Luria.* Act I.

5
That make the meadows green; and, poured round all,
Old Ocean's gray and melancholy waste,—
Are but the solemn decorations all
Of the great tomb of man.
BRYANT—*Thanatopsis.* L. 43.

6
Once more upon the waters! yet once more!
And the waves bound beneath me as a steed
That knows his rider.
BYRON—*Childe Harold.* Canto III. St. 2.

7
Roll on, thou deep and dark blue Ocean—roll!
Ten thousand fleets sweep over thee in vain;
Man marks the earth with ruin—his control
Stops with the shore.
BYRON—*Childe Harold.* Canto IV. St. 179.

8
Time writes no wrinkle on thine azure brow,
Such as Creation's dawn beheld, thou rollest now.
BYRON—*Childe Harold.* Canto IV. St. 182.
Same idea found in MME. DE STAËL—*Corinne.* Bk. I. Ch. IV. (Pub. before Byron.)
(See also MONTGOMERY)

9
The image of Eternity—the throne
Of the Invisible; even from out thy slime
The monsters of the deep are made; each zone
Obeys thee; thou goest forth, dread, fathomless, alone.
BYRON—*Childe Harold.* Canto IV. St. 183.

10
And I have loved thee, Ocean! and my joy
Of youthful sports was on thy breast to be
Borne, like thy bubbles, onward; from a boy
I wanton'd with thy breakers.

* * * * * *

And laid my hand upon thy mane—as I do here.
BYRON—*Childe Harold.* Canto IV. St. 184.
(See also POLLOK)

11
There's not a sea the passenger e'er pukes in,
Turns up more dangerous breakers than the Euxine.
BYRON—*Don Juan.* Canto V. St. 5.

12
What are the wild waves saying,
Sister, the whole day long,
That ever amid our playing
I hear but their low, lone song?
JOSEPH E. CARPENTER—*What are the Wild Waves Saying?*

13
I never was on the dull, tame shore,
But I loved the great sea more and more.
BARRY CORNWALL—*The Sea.*

14
The sea! the sea! the open sea!
The blue, the fresh, the ever free!
Without a mark, without a bound,
It runneth the earth's wide regions round;
It plays with the clouds; it mocks the skies;
Or like a cradled creature lies.
BARRY CORNWALL—*The Sea.*

15
Behold the Sea,
The opaline, the plentiful and strong,
Yet beautiful as is the rose in June,
Fresh as the trickling rainbow of July;
Sea full of food, the nourisher of kinds,
Purger of earth, and medicine of men;
Creating a sweet climate by my breath,
Washing out harms and griefs from memory,
And, in my mathematic ebb and flow,
Giving a hint of that which changes not.
EMERSON—*Sea Shore.*

16
The sea is flowing ever,
The land retains it never.
GOETHE—*Hikmet Nameh. Book of Proverbs.*

17
Alone I walked on the ocean strand,
A pearly shell was in my hand;
I stooped, and wrote upon the sand
My name, the year, the day.
As onward from the spot I passed,
One lingering look behind I cast,
A wave came rolling high and fast,
And washed my lines away.
HANNAH FLAGG GOULD—*A Name in the Sand.*

18
Full many a gem of purest ray serene,
The dark unfathomed caves of ocean bear.
GRAY—*Elegy in a Country Churchyard.* St. 14.
Original found in a poem by CARDINAL BARBERINI.
(See also HALL, MILTON, RICHARD II., YOUNG)

19
There is many a rich stone laid up in the bowells of the earth, many a fair pearle in the bosome of the sea, that never was seene nor never shall bee.
BISHOP HALL—*Contemplations. Veil of Moses.* I. VI. P. 872. See *Quarterly Review,* No. XXII. P. 314.
(See also GRAY)

20
The hollow sea-shell, which for years hath stood
On dusty shelves, when held against the ear
Proclaims its stormy parent, and we hear
The faint, far murmur of the breaking flood.

We hear the sea. The Sea? It is the blood
In our own veins, impetuous and near.
EUGENE LEE-HAMILTON—*Sonnet. Sea-shell Murmurs.*
(See also LANDOR, WEBB, WORDSWORTH, also HOLLAND under MUSIC)

1
The sea appears all golden
Beneath the sun-lit sky.
HEINE—*Book of Songs. New Poems. Seraphina.* No. 15.

2
The breaking waves dashed high
On a stern and rock-bound coast,
And the woods against a stormy sky,
Their giant branches toss'd.
FELICIA D. HEMANS—*The Landing of the Pilgrim Fathers in New England.*

3
Praise the sea, but keep on land.
HERBERT—*Jacula Prudentum.*

4
Of the loud resounding sea.
HOMER—*Iliad.* Bk. IX. 182.

5
Whilst breezy waves toss up their silvery spray.
HOOD—*Ode to the Moon.*

6
Quoth the Ocean, "Dawn! O fairest, clearest,
Touch me with thy golden fingers bland;
For I have no smile till thou appearest
For the lovely land."
JEAN INGELOW—*Winstanley. The Apology.*

7
The burden of the desert of the sea.
Isaiah. XXI. 1.

8
Come o'er the moonlit sea,
The waves are brightly glowing.
CHARLES JEFFERYS—*The Moonlit Sea.*

9
Tut! the best thing I know between France and England is the sea.
DOUGLAS JERROLD—*Jerrold's Wit. The Anglo-French Alliance.*

10
Love the sea? I dote upon it—from the beach.
DOUGLAS JERROLD—*Specimen of Jerrold's Wit. Love of the Sea.*

11
Hitherto thou shalt come, but no further; and here shall thy proud waves be stayed.
Job. XXXVIII. 11.

12
He maketh the deep to boil like a pot.
Job. XLI. 31.

13
Past are three summers since she first beheld
The ocean; all around the child await
Some exclamation of amazement here:
She coldly said, her long-lasht eyes abased,
Is this the mighty ocean? is this all?
WALTER SAVAGE LANDOR—*Gebir.* Bk. V

14
But I have sinuous shells of pearly hue;
* * * * *
Shake one, and it awakens; then apply
Its polished lips to your attentive ear,
And it remembers its august abodes,
And murmurs as the ocean murmurs there.
WALTER SAVAGE LANDOR—*Gebir.* Bk. V.
(See also HAMILTON)

15
The land is dearer for the sea,
The ocean for the shore.
LUCY LARCOM—*On the Beach.* St. 11.

16
"Would'st thou,"—so the helmsman answered,
"Learn the secret of the sea?
Only those who brave its dangers
Comprehend its mystery!"
LONGFELLOW—*The Secret of the Sea.* St. 8.

17
It is a pleasure for to sit at ease
Upon the land, and safely for to see
How other folks are tossed on the seas
That with the blustering winds turmoiled be.
LUCRETIUS. Translated from AMYOT'S *Introduction to Plutarch,* by SIR THOMAS NORTH. (1579)

18
Rich and various gems inlay
The unadorned bosom of the deep.
MILTON—*Comus.* 22.
(See also GRAY)

19
Distinct as the billows, yet one as the sea.
JAMES MONTGOMERY—*The Ocean.* St. 6.

20
And Thou, vast Ocean! on whose awful face
Time's iron feet can print no ruin trace.
ROBERT MONTGOMERY—*The Omnipresence of the Deity.* Pt. I. St. 20.
(See also BYRON)

21
He laid his hand upon "the Ocean's mane,"
And played familiar with his hoary locks.
POLLOK—*Course of Time.* Bk. IV. L. 689.
(See also BYRON)

22
Deep calleth unto deep.
Psalms. XLII. 7.

23
If I take the wings of the morning, and dwell in the uttermost parts of the sea.
Psalms. CXXXIX. 9.

24
Why does the sea moan evermore?
Shut out from heaven it makes its moan,
It frets against the boundary shore;
All earth's full rivers cannot fill
The sea, that drinking thirsteth still.
CHRISTINA G. ROSSETTI—*By the Sea.* St. 1.

25
Streak of silver sea.
LORD SALISBURY. Quoted from COL. CHESNEY, who also quoted it. Used by GLADSTONE, writing of the English Channel, in *Edinburgh Review,* Oct. 18, 1870.

26
The Channel is that silver strip of sea which severs merry England from the tardy realms of Europe.
In the *Church and State Review,* April 1, 1863.

27
A life on the ocean wave!
A home on the rolling deep;
Where the scattered waters rave,
And the winds their revels keep!
EPES SARGENT—*Life on the Ocean Wave.*

1
The always wind-obeying deep.
Comedy of Errors. Act I. Sc. 1. L. 64.

2
The precious stone set in the silver sea.
Richard II. Act II. Sc. I. L. 46.

3 There the sea I found
Calm as a cradled child in dreamless slumber bound.
SHELLEY—*The Revolt of Islam*. Canto I. St. 15.

4 *I loved the Sea.*
Whether in calm it glassed the gracious day
With all its light, the night with all its fires;
Whether in storm it lashed its sullen spray,
Wild as the heart when passionate youth expires;
Or lay, as now, a torture to my mind,
In yonder land-locked bay, unwrinkled by the wind.
R. H. STODDARD—*Carmen Naturæ Triumphale*. L. 192.

5
Thou wert before the Continents, before
The hollow heavens, which like another sea
Encircles them and thee, but whence thou wert,
And when thou wast created, is not known,
Antiquity was young when thou wast old.
R. H. STODDARD—*Hymn to the Sea*. L. 104.

6 We follow and race
In shifting chase,
Over the boundless ocean-space!
Who hath beheld when the race begun?
Who shall behold it run?
BAYARD TAYLOR—*The Waves*.

7
Break, break, break,
On thy cold gray stones, oh sea!
And I would that my tongue could utter
The thoughts that arise in me.
TENNYSON—*Break, Break, Break*.

8
Rari nantes in gurgite vasto.
A few swimming in the vast deep.
VERGIL—*Æneid*. I. 118.

9
Litus ama; altum alii teneant.
Love the shore; let others keep to the deep sea.
VERGIL—*Æneid*. V. 163-4. (Adapted)

10
I send thee a shell from the ocean-beach;
But listen thou well, for my shell hath speech.
Hold to thine ear
And plain thou'lt hear
Tales of ships.
CHAS. H. WEBB—*With a Nantucket Shell*.
(See also HAMILTON)

11
Rocked in the cradle of the deep,
I lay me down in peace to sleep.
EMMA WILLARD—*The Cradle of the Deep*.

12 I have seen
A curious child, who dwelt upon a tract
Of inland ground, applying to his ear
The convolutions of a smooth-lipped shell;
To which, in silence hushed, his very soul
Listened intensely; and his countenance soon
Brightened with joy; for from within were heard
Murmurings, whereby the monitor expressed
Mysterious union with its native sea.
WORDSWORTH—*The Excursion*. Bk. IV.
(See also HAMILTON)

13 Ocean into tempest wrought,
To waft a feather, or to drown a fly.
YOUNG—*Night Thoughts*. Night I. L. 153.

14
In chambers deep,
Where waters sleep,
What unknown treasures pave the floor.
YOUNG—*Ocean*. St. 24.
(See also GRAY)

OCTOBER

15
October turned my maple's leaves to gold;
The most are gone now; here and there one lingers;
Soon these will slip from out the twig's weak hold,
Like coins between a dying miser's fingers.
T. B. ALDRICH—*Maple Leaves*.

16
And suns grow meek, and the meek suns grow brief,
And the year smiles as it draws near its death.
BRYANT—*October*.

17
The sweet calm sunshine of October, now
Warms the low spot; upon its grassy mould
The purple oak-leaf falls; the birchen bough
Drops its bright spoil like arrow-heads of gold.
BRYANT—*October*. (1866)

18
There is something in October sets the gypsy blood astir:
We must rise and follow her,
When from every hill of flame
She calls, and calls each vagabond by name.
BLISS CARMAN—*Vagabond Song*.

19
Is it the shrewd October wind
Brings the tears into her eyes?
Does it blow so strong that she must fetch
Her breath in sudden sighs?
W. D. HOWELLS—*Gone*.

20
October's foliage yellows with his cold.
RUSKIN—*The Months*.

21
No clouds are in the morning sky,
The vapors hug the stream,
Who says that life and love can die
In all this northern gleam?
At every turn the maples burn,
The quail is whistling free,
The partridge whirs, and the frosted burs
Are dropping for you and me.
Ho! hillyho! heigh O!
Hillyho!
In the clear October morning.
E. C. STEDMAN—*Autumn Song*.

22
And close at hand, the basket stood
With nuts from brown October's wood.
WHITTIER—*Snow-bound*.

OLIVE

Olea Europæa

1
See there the olive grove of Academe,
Plato's retirement, where the Attic bird
Trills her thick-warbled notes the summer long.
MILTON—*Paradise Regained.* Bk. IV. L. 244.

OPINION

2
Where an opinion is general, it is usually correct.
JANE AUSTEN—*Mansfield Park.* Ch. XI.
(See also CICERO)

3
Facts are cheels that winna ding,
An' downa be disputed.
BURNS—*A Dream.*
(See also SMOLLETT, TINDAL)

4
Sure 'tis an orthodox opinion,
That grace is founded in dominion.
BUTLER—*Hudibras.* Pt. I. Canto III. L. 1,173.

5
With books and money placed, for show
Like nest eggs, to make clients lay,
And for his false opinion pay.
BUTLER—*Hudibras.* Pt. III. Canto III. L. 624.

6
For most men (till by losing rendered sager)
Will back their own opinions by a wager.
BYRON—*Beppo.* St. 27.

7
Nor prints of Precedent for poore men's facts.
GEORGE CHAPMAN—*Bussy d'Ambois.* Act I. Sc. 1.

8
Omni autem in re consensio omnium gentium lex naturæ putanda est.

But in every matter the consensus of opinion among all nations is to be regarded as the law of nature.
CICERO—*Tusc. Quæst.* I. 13. 30.
(See also AUSTEN)

9
Stiff in opinion, always in the wrong.
DRYDEN—*Absalom and Achitophel.* I. 545.

10
As the saying is, So many heades, so many wittes.
QUEEN ELIZABETH—*Godly Meditacyon of the Christian Sowle.* (1548)
(See also TERENCE)

11
Intolerant only of intolerance.
I. S. S. G. in *Fraser's Mag.* Aug., 1863. Article on *Mr. Buckle in the East.*

12
It is not often that an opinion is worth expressing, which cannot take care of itself.
HOLMES—*Medical Essays.* 211.

13
Denique non omnes eadem mirantur amantque.

All men do not, in fine, admire or love the same thing.
HORACE—*Epistles.* II. 2. 58.

14
Monuments of the safety with which errors of opinion may be tolerated where reason is left free to combat it.
THOMAS JEFFERSON—*First Inaugural Address.* March 4, 1801.

15
Dogmatism is puppyism come to its full growth.
JERROLD—*Man Made of Money.* In the *Wit and Opinions of Jerrold.* P. 28. Attributed to DEAN MANSEL by BURGON in *Lives of Twelve Good Men.*

16
How long halt ye between two opinions?
I Kings. XVIII. 21.

17
We hardly find any persons of good sense save those who agree with us.
LA ROCHEFOUCAULD—*Maxims.* 347.
(See also SWIFT)

18
The deep slumber of a decided opinion.
Thoughts for the Cloister and Crowd. London, 1835. P. 21. Quoted by MILL—*Liberty.*

19
Even opinion is of force enough to make itself to be espoused at the expense of life.
MONTAIGNE—*Of Good and Evil.* Ch. XL.

20
There never was in the world two opinions alike, no more than two hairs, or two grains; the most universal quality is diversity.
MONTAIGNE—*Essays.* *Of the Resemblance of Children to their Fathers.*

21
Il opine du bonnet comme un moine en Sorbonne.

He adopts the opinion of others like a monk in the Sorbonne.
PASCAL—*Lettres Provinciales.* II.

22
La force est la reine du monde, et non pas l'opinion; mais l'opinion est celle qui use de la force.

Force and not opinion is the queen of the world; but it is opinion that uses the force.
PASCAL—*Pensées.* Art. XXIV. 92.

23
Della opinione regina del mondo.
Opinion is the queen of the world.
PASCAL quotes this as the title of an Italian work.

24
He (Cato) never gave his opinion in the Senate upon any other point whatever, without adding these words, "And, in my opinion Carthage should be destroyed." ["Delenda est Carthago."]
PLUTARCH—*Life of Cato the Censor.*

25
Some praise at morning what they blame at night,
But always think the last opinion right.
POPE—*Essay on Criticism.* Pt. II. L. 230.

26
I have bought
Golden opinions from all sorts of people,
Which would be worn now in their newest gloss,
Not cast aside so soon.
Macbeth. Act I. Sc. 7. L. 32.

1
Opinion's but a fool, that makes us scan
The outward habit by the inward man.
Pericles. Act II. Sc. 2. L. 56.

2
Facts are stubborn things.
SMOLLETT. Trans. of *Gil Blas*. Bk. X. Ch. I.
ELLIOT—*Essay on Field Husbandry*. P. 35.
(See also BURNS)

3
"That was excellently observed," say I when I read a passage in another where his opinion agrees with mine. When we differ, then I pronounce him to be mistaken.
SWIFT—*Thoughts on Various Subjects*.
(See also LA ROCHEFOUCAULD)

4
Je connais quelqu'un qui a plus d'esprit que Napoléon, que Voltaire, que tous les ministres présents et futurs: c'est l'opinion.
I know where there is more wisdom than is found in Napoleon, Voltaire, or all the ministers present and to come—in public opinion.
TALLEYRAND—*In the Chamber of Peers*. (1821)

5
Quot homines, tot sententiæ; suus cuique mos.
So many men, so many opinions; everyone has his own fancy.
TERENCE—*Phormio*. II. 3, 14. Same idea in GASCOIGNE—*Glass of Government*.
(See also QUEEN ELIZABETH)

6
Matters of fact, as Mr. Budgell somewhere observes, are very stubborn things.
In copy of the Will of MATTHEW TINDAL. P. 23. (1733)
(See also BURNS)

OPPORTUNITY

7
A thousand years a poor man watched
Before the gate of Paradise:
But while one little nap he snatched,
It oped and shut. Ah! was he wise?
WM. R. ALGER—*Oriental Poetry. Swift Opportunity.*

8
There is an hour in each man's life appointed
To make his happiness, if then he seize it.
BEAUMONT AND FLETCHER—*Custom of the Country*. Act II. Sc. 3. L. 85.

9
This could but have happened once,
And we missed it, lost it forever.
ROBERT BROWNING—*Youth and Art*. XVII.

10
He that will not when he may,
When he will he shall have nay.
BURTON—*Quoted in Anatomy of Melancholy*. Pt. III. Sec. 2. Memb. 5. Subsec. 5.

11
There is a nick in Fortune's restless wheel
For each man's good.
CHAPMAN—*Bussy d'Ambois*.
(See also JULIUS CÆSAR)

12
Holding occasion by the hand,
Not over nice 'twixt weed and flower,
Waiving what none can understand,
I take mine hour.
JOHN VANCE CHENEY—*This My Life*.

13
Who lets slip fortune, her shall never find:
Occasion once past by, is bald behind.
COWLEY—*Pyramus and Thisbe*. XV.
(See also PHÆDRUS)

14
Rem tibi quam nosces aptam dimittere noli;
Fronte capillata, post est occasio calva.
Let nothing pass which will advantage you;
Hairy in front, Occasion's bald behind.
DIONYSIUS CATO—*Disticha de Moribus*. II. 26. (See also PHÆDRUS)

15
Observe the opportunity.
Ecclesiasticus. IV. 20.

16
Seek not for fresher founts afar,
Just drop your bucket where you are;
And while the ship right onward leaps,
Uplift it from exhaustless deeps.
Parch not your life with dry despair;
The stream of hope flows everywhere—
So under every sky and star,
Just drop your bucket where you are!
SAM WALTER FOSS—*Opportunity*.

17
"Oh, ship ahoy!" rang out the cry;
"Oh, give us water or we die!"
A voice came o'er the waters far,
"Just drop your bucket where you are."
And then they dipped and drank their fill
Of water fresh from mead and hill;
And then they knew they sailed upon
The broad mouth of the Amazon.
SAM WALTER FOSS—*Opportunity*. "Let down your buckets where you are," quoted by Booker T. Washington. *Address at Atlanta Exposition*. See his Life, *Up From Slavery*.

18
Der den Augenblick ergreift,
Das ist der rechte Mann.
Yet he who grasps the moment's gift,
He is the proper man.
GOETHE—*Faust*. I. 4. 494.

19
Man's extremity is God's opportunity.
JOHN HAMILTON (Lord Belhaven). *In the Scottish Parliament, Nov. 2, 1706, protesting against the Union of England and Scotland.* Also found in JOHN FLAVEL'S *Faithful and Ancient Account of Some Late and Wonderful Sea Deliverances*. Pub. before 1691.

20
I beseech you not to blame me if I be desirous to strike while the iron is hot.
SIR EDWARD HOBY—*To Cecil*. Oct. 14, 1587.

21
Rapiamus, amici,
Occasionem de die.
Let us seize, friends, our opportunity from the day as it passes.
HORACE—*Epodon*. XIII. 3.

22
The actual fact is that in this day Opportunity not only knocks at your door but is playing an anvil chorus on every man's door, and then lays for the owner around the corner with a club. The world is in sore need of men who can do things. Indeed, cases can easily be recalled by every one where Opportunity actually smashed in the door and collared her candidate and

dragged him forth to success. These cases are exceptional, usually you have to meet Opportunity half-way. But the only place where you can get away from Opportunity is to lie down and die. Opportunity does not trouble dead men, or dead ones who flatter themselves that they are alive.
ELBERT HUBBARD. In *The Philistine*.

1
I knock unbidden once at every gate—
If sleeping, wake—if feasting, rise before
I turn away—it is the hour of fate,
And they who follow me reach every state
Mortals desire, and conquer every foe
Save death, but those who doubt or hesitate,
Condemned to failure, penury and woe,
Seek me in vain and uselessly implore,
I answer not, and I return no more.
JOHN J. INGALLS—*Opportunity*.
(See also HUBBARD, MALONE)

2
They do me wrong who say I come no more,
When once I knock and fail to find you in;
For every day I stand outside your door
And bid you wait, and rise to fight and win.
JUDGE WALTER MALONE—*Opportunity*.
(See also INGALLS)

3
Not by appointment do we meet delight
Or joy; they heed not our expectancy;
But round some corner of the streets of life
They of a sudden greet us with a smile.
GERALD MASSEY—*Bridegroom of Beauty*.

4
Danger will wink on opportunity.
MILTON—*Comus*. L. 401.

5 Zeal and duty are not slow
But on occasion's forelock watchful wait.
MILTON—*Paradise Regained*. Bk. III. L. 172.
(See also PHÆDRUS)

6
Nostra sine auxilio fugiunt bona. Carpite florem.
Our advantages fly away without aid. Pluck the flower.
OVID—*Ars Amatoria*. III. 79.

7
Casus ubique valet; semper tibi pendeat hamus.
Quo minime credas gurgite, piscis erit.
Opportunity is ever worth expecting; let your hook be ever hanging ready. The fish will be in the pool where you least imagine it to be.
OVID—*Ars Amatoria*. Bk. III. 425.

8
Oh! Who art thou so fast proceeding,
Ne'er glancing back thine eyes of flame?
Mark'd but by few, through earth I'm speeding,
And Opportunity's my name.
What form is that which scowls beside thee?
Repentance is the form you see:
Learn then, the fate may yet betide thee.
She seizes them who seize not me.
THOMAS LOVE PEACOCK—*Love and Opportunity*, in *Headlong Hall*. Imitated from MACHIAVELLI'S *Capitolo dell' Occasione*.

9
He that would not when he might,
He shall not when he wolda.
THOS. PERCY—*Reliques*. *The Baffled Knight*.

10
Occasio prima sui parte comosa, posteriore calva
Quam si occupasis, teneas elapsum
Non isse possit Jupiter reprehendre.
Opportunity has hair on her forehead, but is bald behind. If you meet her seize her, for once let slip, Jove himself cannot catch her again.
PHÆDRUS. Bk. V. Fable 8. Same idea in LUCAN—*Pharsalia*. Bk. I. L. 513. Also in RABELAIS—*Gargantua*. Bk. I. Ch. 37.
(See also COWLEY, DIONYSIUS, MILTON, POSIDIPPUS, TASSO)

11
Why hast thou hair upon thy brow?
To seize me by, when met.
Why is thy head then bald behind?
Because men wish in vain,
When I have run past on wingèd feet
To catch me e'er again.
POSIDIPPUS—*Epigram* 13. In BRUNCK'S ed. of *Anthologia*. Vol. II. P. 49. Imitated by AUSONIUS—*Epigram* 12.
(See also PHÆDRUS)

12
There's place and means for every man alive.
All's Well That Ends Well. Act IV. Sc. 3. L. 375.

13
Who seeks, and will not take when once 'tis offer'd,
Shall never find it more.
Antony and Cleopatra. Act II. Sc. 7. L. 89.

14
A staff is quickly found to beat a dog.
Henry VI. Pt. II. Act III. Sc. 1. L. 471.

15
There is a tide in the affairs of men,
Which, taken at the flood, leads on to fortune;
Omitted, all the voyage of their life
Is bound in shallows and in miseries.
Julius Cæsar. Act IV. Sc. 3. L. 218.
(See also CHAPMAN)

16 Urge them while their souls
Are capable of this ambition,
Lest zeal, now melted by the windy breath
Of soft petitions, pity and remorse,
Cool and congeal again to what it was.
King John. Act II. Sc. 2. L. 475.

17
O opportunity, thy guilt is great!
'Tis thou that executest the traitor's treason;
Thou set'st the wolf where he the lamb may get;
Whoever plots the sin, thou 'point'st the season;
'Tis thou that spurn'st at right, at law, at reason.
The Rape of Lucrece. L. 876.

18
Occasio ægre offertur, facile amittitur.
A good opportunity is seldom presented, and is easily lost.
SYRUS—*Maxims*.

19
Deliberando sæpe perit occasio.
The opportunity is often lost by deliberating.
SYRUS—*Maxims*.

20
Crespe hà le chiome e d'oro,
E in quella guisa appunto,
Che Fortuna si pinge

Ha lunghi e folti in sulla fronte i crini;
Ma nuda hà poi la testa
Agli opposti confini.
TASSO—*Amore Fuggitivo.*
(See also PHÆDRUS for translation)

1
An opportunity well taken is the only weapon of advantage.
JOHN UDALE—*To the Earl of Essex.* May 15, 1598.

2
L'occasion de faire du mal se trouve cent fois par jour, et celle de faire du bien une fois dans l'année.
The opportunity for doing mischief is found a hundred times a day, and of doing good once in a year.
VOLTAIRE—*Zadig.*

3
Turning for them who pass, the common dust
Of servile opportunity to gold.
WORDSWORTH—*Desultory Stanzas.*

ORACLE

4
Ibis redibis non morieris in bello.
Thou shalt go thou shalt return never in battle shalt thou perish.
Utterance of the Oracle which through absence of punctuation and position of word "non" may be interpreted favorably or the reverse.

5
A Delphic sword.
ARISTOTLE—*Politica.* I. 2. (Referring to the ambiguous Delphic Oracles.)

6
The oracles are dumb,
No voice or hideous hum
Runs thro' the arched roof in words deceiving.
MILTON—*Hymn on Christ's Nativity.* L. 173.

7
I am Sir Oracle,
And when I ope my lips let no dog bark!
Merchant of Venice. Act I. Sc. 1. L. 93.

ORANGE

8
The happy bells shall ring Marguerite;
The summer birds shall sing Marguerite;
You smile but you shall wear
Orange blossoms in your hair, Marguerite.
T. B. ALDRICH—*Wedded.*

9
Kennst du das Land wo die Citronen blühen,
Im dunkeln Laub die Gold-Orangen glühn,
Ein sanfter Wind vom blauen Himmel weht
Die Myrthe still und hoch der Lorbeer steht?
Kennst du es wohl?
Dahin! Dahin,
Möcht' ich mit dir, O mein Geliebter, ziehn.
Knowest thou the land where the lemon-trees flourish, where amid the shadowed leaves the golden oranges glisten,—a gentle zephyr breathes from the blue heavens, the myrtle is motionless, and the laurel rises high? Dost thou know it well? Thither, thither, fain would I fly with thee, O my beloved!
GOETHE—*Wilhelm Meister. Mignon's Lied.*

10
Yes, sing the song of the orange-tree,
With its leaves of velvet green:
With its luscious fruit of sunset hue,
The fairest that ever were seen;
The grape may have its bacchanal verse,
To praise the fig we are free;
But homage I pay to the queen of all,
The glorious orange-tree.
J. K. HOYT—*The Orange-Tree.*

11
If I were yonder orange-tree
And thou the blossom blooming there,
I would not yield a breath of thee
To scent the most imploring air!
MOORE—*If I Were Yonder Wave, My Dear.*

12
'Twas noon; and every orange bud
Hung languid o'er the crystal flood,
Faint as the lids of maiden eyes
Beneath a lover's burning sighs!
MOORE—*I Stole Along the Flowery Bank.*

13
Beneath some orange-trees,
Whose fruit and blossoms in the breeze
Were wantoning together free,
Like age at play with infancy.
MOORE—*Lalla Rookh. Paradise and the Peri.*

ORATORY (See also ELOQUENCE)

14
Solon wished everybody to be ready to take everybody else's part; but surely Chilo was wiser in holding that public affairs go best when the laws have much attention and the orators none.
REV. J. BEACON—*Letter to Earl Grey on Reform.* (1831) See PLUTARCH—*Symposium. Septem Sapientintium Convivium.* Ch. XI. I. (Chilo.)

15
Ce que l'on conçoit bien s'énonce clairement,
Et les mots pour le dire arrivent aisément.
Whatever we conceive well we express clearly, and words flow with ease.
BOILEAU—*L'Art Poètique.* I. 153.

16
For rhetoric, he could not ope
His mouth, but out there flew a trope.
BUTLER—*Hudibras.* Pt. I. Canto I. L. 81.

17
The Orator persuades and carries all with him, he knows not how; the Rhetorician can prove that he ought to have persuaded and carried all with him.
CARLYLE—*Essays. Characteristics.*

18
Its Constitution—the glittering and sounding generalities of natural right which make up the Declaration of Independence.
RUFUS CHOATE—*Letter to the Maine Whig Committee.* (1856)
(See also DICKMAN, EMERSON)

19
He mouths a sentence as curs mouth a bone.
CHURCHILL—*The Rosciad.* L. 322.

20
I asked of my dear friend Orator Prig:
"What's the first part of oratory?" He said, "A great wig."
"And what is the second?" Then, dancing a jig
And bowing profoundly, he said, "A great wig."

"And what is the third?" Then he snored like a pig,
And puffing his cheeks out, he replied, "A great wig."
GEO. COLMAN the Younger—*Orator Prig.*
(See also PLUTARCH)

1
We fear that the glittering generalities of the speaker have left an impression more delightful than permanent.
F. J. DICKMAN—*Review of Lecture by Rufus Choate. Providence Journal,* Dec. 14, 1849.
(See also CHOATE)

2
There is no true orator who is not a hero.
EMERSON—*Letters and Social Aims. Eloquence.*

3
Glittering generalities! They are blazing ubiquities.
EMERSON—*Remark on Choate's words.*
(See also CHOATE)

4
You'd scarce expect one of my age
To speak in public on the stage;
And if I chance to fall below
Demosthenes or Cicero,
Don't view me with a critic's eye,
But pass my imperfections by.
Large streams from little fountains flow,
Tall oaks from little acorns grow.
DAVID EVERETT—*Lines Written for a School Declamation.*
(See also DUNCOMBE under GROWTH)

5
Allein der Vortrag macht des Redners Glück,
Ich fühl es wohl noch bin ich weit zurück.
Yet through delivery orators succeed,
I feel that I am far behind indeed.
GOETHE—*Faust.* I. 1. 194.

6
Es trägt Verstand und rechter Sinn,
Mit wenig Kunst sich selber vor.
With little art, clear wit and sense
Suggest their own delivery.
GOETHE—*Faust.* I. 1. 198.

7
Intererit multum Davusne loquatur an heros.
It makes a great difference whether Davus or a hero speaks.
HORACE—*Ars Poetica.* CXIV.

8
The passions are the only orators that always persuade: they are, as it were, a natural art, the rules of which are infallible; and the simplest man with passion is more persuasive than the most eloquent without it.
LA ROCHEFOUCAULD—*Maxims.* No. 9.

9
The object of oratory alone is not truth, but persuasion.
MACAULAY—*Essay on Athenian Orators.*

10
Thence to the famous orators repair,
Those ancient, whose resistless eloquence
Wielded at will that fierce democratie,
Shook the Arsenal, and fulmined over Greece,
To Macedon, and Artaxerxes' throne.
MILTON—*Paradise Regained.* Bk. IV. L. 267.

11
The capital of the orator is in the bank of the highest sentimentalities and the purest enthusiasms.
EDW. G. PARKER—*The Golden Age of American Oratory.* Ch. I.

12
Præterea multo magis, ut vulgo dicitur viva vox afficit: nam licet acriora sint, quæ legas, ultius tamen in ammo sedent, quæ pronuntiatio, vultus, habitus, gestus dicentis adfigit.
Besides, as is usually the case, we are much more affected by the words which we hear, for though what you read in books may be more pointed, yet there is something in the voice, the look, the carriage, and even the gesture of the speaker, that makes a deeper impression upon the mind.
PLINY the Younger—*Epistles.* II. 3.

13
When Demosthenes was asked what was the first part of Oratory, he answered, "Action," and which was the second, he replied, "Action," and which was the third, he still answered "Action."
PLUTARCH—*Morals. Lives of the Ten Orators.* Referred to by CICERO—*De Oratore.* III. 214. *Oration* 55, and *Brutus.* 234.
(See also COLMAN)

14
It is a thing of no great difficulty to raise objections against another man's oration,—nay, it is a very easy matter; but to produce a better in its place is a work extremely troublesome.
PLUTARCH—*Of Hearing.* VI.

15
Fire in each eye, and papers in each hand,
They rave, recite, and madden round the land.
POPE—*Prologue to Satires.* L. 5.

16
Very good orators, when they are out, they will spit.
As You Like It. Act IV. Sc. 1. L. 75.

17
Be not thy tongue thy own shame's orator.
Comedy of Errors. Act III. Sc. 2. L. 10.

18
List his discourse of war, and you shall hear
A fearful battle render'd you in music.
Henry V. Act I. Sc. 1. L. 43.

19
What means this passionate discourse,
This peroration with such circumstance?
Henry VI. Pt. II. Act I. Sc. 1. L. 104.

20
I come not, friends, to steal away your hearts:
I am no orator, as Brutus is;
* * * I only speak right on.
Julius Cæsar. Act III. Sc. 2. L. 220.

21
Fear not, my lord, I'll play the orator
As if the golden fee for which I plead
Were for myself.
Richard III. Act III. Sc. 5. L. 95.

22
Bid me discourse, I will enchant thine ear,
Or, like a fairy, trip upon the green.
Venus and Adonis. L. 145.

23
Charm us, orator, till the lion look no larger than the cat.
TENNYSON—*Locksley Hall Sixty Years After.* L. 112.

ORCHID

Orchis

1
In the marsh pink orchid's faces,
With their coy and dainty graces,
Lure us to their hiding places—
Laugh, O murmuring Spring!
SARAH F. DAVIS—*Summer Song.*

2
Around the pillars of the palm-tree bower
The orchids cling, in rose and purple spheres;
Shield-broad the lily floats; the aloe flower
Foredates its hundred years.
BAYARD TAYLOR—*Canopus.*

ORDER

3
Let all things be done decently and in order.
I Corinthians. XIV. 40.

4
For the world was built in order
And the atoms march in tune;
Rhyme the pipe, and Time the warder,
The sun obeys them, and the moon.
EMERSON—*Monadnock.* St. 12.

5
Can any man have a higher notion of the rule of right and the eternal fitness of things?
HENRY FIELDING—*Tom Jones.* Bk. IV. Ch. IV. SAMUEL CLARKE—*Being and Attributes of God.* JOHN LELAND—*Review of Morgan's Moral Philosopher.* I. 154. (Ed. 1807) Also his *Inquiry into Lord Bolingbroke's Writings.* Letter XXII. I. 451.

6
Set thine house in order.
Isaiah. XXXVIII. 1.

7
To make the plough go before the horse.
JAMES I—*Letter to the Lord Keeper.* July, 1617.
(See also RABELAIS)

8
Confusion heard his voice, and wild uproar
Stood ruled, stood vast infinitude confined;
Till at his second bidding darkness fled,
Light shone, and order from disorder sprung.
MILTON—*Paradise Lost.* Bk. III. L. 710.

9
Order is Heaven's first law; and this confess,
Some are and must be greater than the rest.
POPE—*Essay on Man.* Ep. IV. L. 49.
(See also TUSSER)

10
Not chaos-like together crush'd and bruis'd,
But, as the world, harmoniously confused:
Where order in variety we see,
And where tho' all things differ, all agree.
POPE—*Windsor Forest.* L. 13.

11
Folie est mettre la charrue devant les bœufs.
It is folly to put the plough in front of the oxen.
RABELAIS—*Gargantua.* Ch. XI.
(See also JAMES I)

12
Not a mouse
Shall disturb this hallow'd house:
I am sent with broom before,
To sweep the dust behind the door.
Midsummer Night's Dream. Act V. Sc. 1. L. 394.

13
The heavens themselves, the planets and this centre
Observe degree, priority and place,
Insisture, course, proportion, season, form,
Office and custom, in all line of order.
Troilus and Cressida. Act I. Sc. 3. L. 85.

14
As order is heavenly, where quiet is had,
So error is hell, or a mischief as bad.
TUSSER—*Points of Huswifery, Huswifery Admonitions.* XII. P. 251. (1561)
(See also POPE)

OWL

15
The large white owl that with eye is blind,
That hath sate for years in the old tree hollow.
Is carried away in a gust of wind.
E. B. BROWNING—*Isobel's Child.* St. 19.

16
The Roman senate, when within
The city walls an owl was seen,
Did cause their clergy, with lustrations
* * * *
The round-fac'd prodigy t' avert,
From doing town or country hurt.
BUTLER—*Hudibras.* Pt. II. Canto III. L. 709.

17
In the hollow tree, in the old gray tower,
The spectral Owl doth dwell;
Dull, hated, despised, in the sunshine hour,
But at dusk—he's abroad and well!
Not a bird of the forest e'er mates with him—
All mock him outright, by day:
But at night, when the woods grow still and dim,
The boldest will shrink away!
O, when the night falls, and roosts the fowl,
Then, then, is the reign of the Horned Owl!
BARRY CORNWALL—*The Owl.*

18
St. Agnes' Eve—Ah, bitter chill it was!
The owl, for all his feathers, was a-cold.
KEATS—*The Eve of St. Agnes.*

19
The wailing owl
Screams solitary to the mournful moon.
MALLET—*Excursion.*

20
The screech-owl, with ill-boding cry,
Portends strange things, old women say;
Stops every fool that passes by,
And frights the school-boy from his play.
LADY MONTAGU—*The Politicians.* St. 4.

21
Then nightly sings the staring owl,
Tu-whit;
Tu-who, a merry note.
Love's Labour's Lost. Act V. Sc. 2. L. 928.

22
It was the owl that shriek'd, the fatal bellman,
Which gives the stern'st good night.
Macbeth. Act II. Sc. 2. L. 3.

23
The clamorous owl, that nightly hoots and wonders
At our quaint spirits.
Midsummer Night's Dream. Act II. Sc. 2. L. 6.

24
O you virtuous owle,
The wise Minerva's only fowle.
SIR PHILIP SIDNEY—*A Remedy for Love.* L. 77.

1
When cats run home and light is come,
And dew is cold upon the ground,
And the far-off stream is dumb,
And the whirring sail goes round,
And the whirring sail goes round;
Alone and warming his five wits,
The white owl in the belfry sits.
TENNYSON—*Song. The Owl.*

2
Then lady Cynthia, mistress of the shade,
Goes, with the fashionable owls, to bed.
YOUNG—*Love of Fame.* Satire V. L. 209.

OX

3
The ox knoweth his owner, and the ass his master's crib.
Isaiah. I. 3.

4
Who drives fat oxen should himself be fat.
SAMUEL JOHNSON. Parody on "Who rules o'er freemen should himself be free," from HENRY BROOKE'S *Earl of Essex.* In BOSWELL'S *Life of Johnson.* (1784)

5
As an ox goeth to the slaughter.
Proverbs. VII. 22. *Jeremiah.* XI. 19.

6 And the plain ox,
That harmless, honest, guileless animal,
In what has he offended? he whose toil,
Patient and ever ready, clothes the land
With all the pomp of harvest.
THOMSON—*The Seasons.*

OYSTER

7
It is unseasonable and unwholesome in all months that have not an R in their names to eat an oyster.
BUTLER—*Dyet's Dry Dinner.* (1599)

8
'Twere better to be born a stone
Of ruder shape, and feeling none,
Than with a tenderness like mine
And sensibilities so fine!
Ah, hapless wretch! condemn'd to dwell
Forever in my native shell,
Ordained to move when others please,
Not for my own content or ease;
But toss'd and buffeted about,
Now *in* the water and now *out.*
COWPER—*The Poet, the Oyster and Sensitive Plant.*

9
Secret, and self-contained, and solitary as an oyster.
DICKENS—*Christmas Carol.* Stave I.

10
"It's a wery remarkable circumstance, sir," said Sam, "that poverty and oysters always seem to go together."
DICKENS—*Pickwick Papers.* Ch. XXII.

11
I will not be sworn but love may transform me to an oyster; but I'll take my oath on it, till he have made an oyster of me, he shall never make me such a fool.
Much Ado About Nothing. Act II. Sc. 3. L. 20.

12
An oyster may be crossed in love! Who says
A whale's a bird?—Ha! did you call my love?—
He's here! he's there! he's everywhere!
Ah me! he's nowhere!
R. B. SHERIDAN—*The Critic. A Tragedy Rehearsed.* Act III. Sc. 1.

13
He was a bold man that first eat an oyster.
SWIFT—*Polite Conversation.* Dialogue II.

P

PAIN

14
World's use is cold, world's love is vain,
World's cruelty is bitter bane;
But pain is not the fruit of pain.
E. B. BROWNING—*A Vision of Poets.* St. 146.

15
Nature knows best, and she says, *roar!*
MARIA EDGEWORTH—*Ormond.* Ch. V. *King Corny in a Paroxysm of the Gout.*

16
So great was the extremity of his pain and anguish, that he did not only sigh but roar.
MATTHEW HENRY—*Commentaries.* Job III. V. 24.

17
There is purpose in pain,
Otherwise it were devilish.
OWEN MEREDITH (Lord Lytton)—*Lucile.* Pt. II. Canto V. St. 8.

18
You purchase pain with all that joy can give,
And die of nothing but a rage to live.
POPE—*Moral Essays.* Ep. II. L. 99.

19
Pain is no longer pain when it is past.
MARGARET J. PRESTON—*Old Songs and New. Nature's Lesson.*

20
Ah, to think how thin the veil that lies
Between the pain of hell and Paradise.
G. W. RUSSELL—*Janus.*

21
Why, all delights are vain; but that most vain,
Which, with pain purchas'd, doth inherit pain.
Love's Labour's Lost. Act I. Sc. 1. L. 72.

22 One fire burns out another's burning,
One pain is lessen'd by another's anguish.
Romeo and Juliet. Act I. Sc. 2. L. 46.

23
The scourge of life, and death's extreme disgrace,
The smoke of hell,—that monster callèd Paine.
SIR PHILIP SIDNEY—*Sidera. Paine.*

24
There's a pang in all rejoicing,
And a joy in the heart of pain;

And the wind that saddens, the sea that gladdens,
Are singing the selfsame strain.
BAYARD TAYLOR—*Wind and the Sea.*

1
Nothing begins, and nothing ends,
That is not paid with moan;
For we are born in others' pain,
And perish in our own.
FRANCIS THOMPSON—*Daisy.* St. 15.

2
The mark of rank in nature is capacity for pain,
And the anguish of the singer marks the sweetness of the strain.
SARAH WILLIAMS—*Twilight Hours. Is it so, O Christ, in Heaven.*

3
A man of pleasure is a man of pains.
YOUNG—*Night Thoughts.* Night VIII. L. 793.

4
When pain can't bless, heaven quits us in despair.
YOUNG—*Night Thoughts.* Night IX. L. 500.

PAINTING

5
And those who paint 'em truest praise 'em most.
ADDISON—*The Campaign.* Last line.

6
As certain as the Correggiosity of Correggio.
AUGUSTINE BIRRELL—*Obiter Dicta. Emerson.* Phrase found also in STERNE—*Tristram Shandy.* Ch. XII.
(See also CARLYLE)

7
From the mingled strength of shade and light
A new creation rises to my sight,
Such heav'nly figures from his pencil flow,
So warm with light his blended colors glow.
* * * * * *
The glowing portraits, fresh from life, that bring
Home to our hearts the truth from which they spring.
BYRON—*Monody on the death of the Rt. Hon. R. B. Sheridan.* St. 3.

8
If they could forget for a moment the correggiosity of Correggio and the learned babble of the sale-room and varnishing Auctioneer.
CARLYLE—*Frederick the Great.* Bk. IV. Ch. III.
(See also BIRRELL)

9
A picture is a poem without words.
CORNIFICUS—*Anet. ad Her.* 4. 28.

10
Paint me as I am. If you leave out the scars and wrinkles, I will not pay you a shilling.
CROMWELL—*Remark to the Painter, Lely.*
(See also FIELDS, GOLDSMITH, LA ROCHEFOUCAULD)

11
Hard features every bungler can command:
To draw true beauty shows a master's hand.
DRYDEN—*To Mr. Lee, on his Alexander.* L. 53.

12
Pictures must not be too picturesque.
EMERSON—*Essays. Of Art.*

13
"Paint me as I am," said Cromwell,
"Rough with age and gashed with wars;
Show my visage as you find it,
Less than truth my soul abhors."
JAMES T. FIELDS—*On a Portrait of Cromwell.*
(See also CROMWELL)

14
A flattering painter, who made it his care
To draw men as they ought to be, not as they are.
GOLDSMITH—*Retaliation.* L. 63.
(See also CROMWELL)

15
The fellow mixes blood with his colors.
Said by GUIDO RENI of RUBENS.
(See also OPIE)

16
One picture in ten thousand, perhaps, ought to live in the applause of mankind, from generation to generation until the colors fade and blacken out of sight or the canvas rot entirely away.
HAWTHORNE—*Marble Faun.* Bk. II. Ch. XII.

17
Well, something must be done for May,
The time is drawing nigh—
To figure in the Catalogue,
And woo the public eye.

Something I must invent and paint;
But oh my wit is not
Like one of those kind substantives
That answer Who and What?
HOOD—*The Painter Puzzled.*

18
Delphinum sylvis appingit, fluctibus aprum.
He paints a dolphin in the woods, a boar in the waves.
HORACE—*Ars Poetica.* XXX.

19
He that seeks popularity in art closes the door on his own genius: as he must needs paint for other minds, and not for his own.
MRS. JAMESON—*Memoirs and Essays. Washington Allston.*

20
Nequeo monstrare et sentio tantum.
I only feel, but want the power to paint.
JUVENAL—*Satires.* VII. 56.

21
The only good copies are those which exhibit the defects of bad originals.
LA ROCHEFOUCAULD—*Maxims.* No. 136.

22
The picture that approaches sculpture nearest
Is the best picture.
LONGFELLOW—*Michael Angelo.* Pt. II. 4.

23
Vain is the hope by colouring to display
The bright effulgence of the noontide ray
Or paint the full-orb'd ruler of the skies
With pencils dipt in dull terrestrial dyes.
MASON—*Fresnoy's Art of Painting.*

24
I mix them with my brains, sir.
JOHN OPIE. Answer when asked with what he mixed his colors. See SAMUEL SMILES—*Self Help.* Chap. V.
(See also GUIDO RENI)

25
He best can paint them who shall feel them most.
POPE—*Eloisa and Abelard.* Last line.

26
Lely on animated canvas stole
The sleepy eye, that spoke the melting soul.
POPE—*Second Book of Horace.* Ep. I. L. 149.

1
Painting with all its technicalities, difficulties, and peculiar ends, is nothing but a noble and expressive language, invaluable as the vehicle of thought, but by itself nothing.
RUSKIN—*True and Beautiful. Painting. Introduction.*

2
If it is the love of that which your work represents—if, being a landscape painter, it is love of hills and trees that moves you—if, being a figure painter, it is love of human beauty, and human soul that moves you—if, being a flower or animal painter, it is love, and wonder, and delight in petal and in limb that move you, then the Spirit is upon you, and the earth is yours, and the fullness thereof.
RUSKIN—*The Two Paths.* Lect. I.

3
Look here, upon this picture, and on this.
Hamlet. Act III. Sc. 4. L. 53.

4
What demi-god
Hath come so near creation?
Merchant of Venice. Act III. Sc. 2. L. 116.

5
I will say of it,
It tutors nature: artificial strife
Lives in these touches, livelier than life.
Timon of Athens. Act I. Sc. 1. L. 36.

6
The painting is almost the natural man:
For since dishonour traffics with man's nature,
He is but outside; pencill'd figures are
Ev'n such as they give out.
Timon of Athens. Act I. Sc. 1. L. 157.

7
Wrought he not well that painted it?
He wrought better that made the painter; and yet he's but a filthy piece of work.
Timon of Athens. Act I. Sc. 1. L. 200.

8
With hue like that when some great painter dips
His pencil in the gloom of earthquake and eclipse.
SHELLEY—*The Revolt of Islam.* Canto V. St. 23.

9
There is no such thing as a dumb poet or a handless painter. The essence of an artist is that he should be articulate.
SWINBURNE—*Essays and Studies. Matthew Arnold's New Poems.*

10
But who can paint
Like nature? Can Imagination boast,
Amid its gay creation, hues like hers?
THOMSON—*Seasons. Spring.* L. 465.

11
They dropped into the yolk of an egg the milk that flows from the leaf of a young fig-tree, with which, instead of water, gum or gumdragant, they mixed their last layer of colours.
WALPOLE—*Anecdotes of Painting.* Vol. I. Ch. II.

12
I would I were a painter, for the sake
Of a sweet picture, and of her who led,
A fitting guide, with reverential tread,
Into that mountain mystery.
WHITTIER—*Mountain Pictures.* No. 2.

PALM

Palmaceæ

13
As the palm-tree standeth so straight and so tall,
The more the hail beats, and the more the rains fall.
LONGFELLOW—*Annie of Tharaw.* Trans. from the German of SIMON DACH. L. 11.

14
First the high palme-trees, with braunches faire,
Out of the lowly vallies did arise,
And high shoote up their heads into the skyes.
SPENSER—*Virgil's Gnat.* L. 191.

15
Next to thee, O fair gazelle,
O Beddowee girl, beloved so well;

Next to the fearless Nedjidee,
Whose fleetness shall bear me again to thee;

Next to ye both I love the Palm,
With his leaves of beauty, his fruit of balm;

Next to ye both I love the Tree
Whose fluttering shadow wraps us three
With love, and silence, and mystery!
BAYARD TAYLOR—*The Arab to the Palm.*

16
Of threads of palm was the carpet spun
Whereon he kneels when the day is done,
And the foreheads of Islam are bowed as one!

To him the palm is a gift divine,
Wherein all uses of man combine,—
House and raiment and food and wine!

And, in the hour of his great release,
His need of the palms shall only cease
With the shroud wherein he lieth in peace.

"Allah il Allah!" he sings his psalm,
On the Indian Sea, by the isles of balm;
"Thanks to Allah, who gives the palm!"
WHITTIER—*The Palm-Tree.*

17
What does the good ship bear so well?
The cocoa-nut with its stony shell,
And the milky sap of its inner cell.
WHITTIER—*The Palm-Tree.*

PANSY

Viola Tricolor

18
Pansies for ladies all—(I wis
That none who wear such brooches miss
A jewel in the mirror).
E. B. BROWNING—*A Flower in a Letter.*

19
Pansies? You praise the ones that grow today
Here in the garden; had you seen the place
When Sutherland was living!
Here they grew,
From blue to deeper blue, in midst of each
A golden dazzle like a glimmering star,
Each broader, bigger than a silver crown;
While here the weaver sat, his labor done,
Watching his azure pets and rearing them,
Until they seem'd to know his step and touch,
And stir beneath his smile like living things:
The very sunshine loved them, and would lie
Here happy, coming early, lingering late,
Because they were so fair.
ROBERT BUCHANAN—*Hugh Sutherland's Pansies.*

1
I pray, what flowers are these?
The pansy this,
O, that's for lover's thoughts.
GEO. CHAPMAN—*All Fools.* Act II. Sc. 1. L. 248. (See also HAMLET)

2
I send thee pansies while the year is young,
Yellow as sunshine, purple as the night;
Flowers of remembrance, ever fondly sung
By all the chiefest of the Sons of Light;
And if in recollection lives regret
For wasted days and dreams that were not true,
I tell thee that the "pansy freak'd with jet"
Is still the heart's ease that the poets knew
Take all the sweetness of a gift unsought,
And for the pansies send me back a thought.
SARAH DOWDNEY—*Pansies.*
(See also MILTON)

3
The delicate thought, that cannot find expression,
For ruder speech too fair,
That, like thy petals, trembles in possession,
And scatters on the air.
BRET HARTE—*The Mountain Heart's Ease.*

4
Heart's ease! one could look for half a day
Upon this flower, and shape in fancy out
Full twenty different tales of love and sorrow,
That gave this gentle name.
MARY HOWITT—*Heart's Ease.*

5
They are all in the lily-bed, cuddled close together—
Purple, Yellow-cap, and little Baby-blue;
How they ever got there you must ask the April weather,
The morning and the evening winds, the sunshine and the dew.
NELLIE M. HUTCHINSON—*Vagrant Pansies.*

6
The pansy freaked with jet.
MILTON—*Lycidas.* L. 144.

7
The beauteous pansies rise
In purple, gold, and blue,
With tints of rainbow hue
Mocking the sunset skies.
THOMAS J. OUSELEY—*The Angel of the Flowers.*

8
Pray, love, remember: and there is pansies, that's for thoughts.
Hamlet. Act IV. Sc. 5. L. 176.
(See also CHAPMAN)

9
The bolt of Cupid fell:
* * * upon a little western flower,
Before milk-white, now purple with love's wound,
And maidens call it love-in-idleness.
Midsummer Night's Dream. Act II. Sc. 1. L. 165.

10
Heart's ease or pansy, pleasure or thought,
Which would the picture give us of these?
Surely the heart that conceived it sought
Heart's ease.
SWINBURNE—*A Flower Piece by Fanten.*

11
Pansies in soft April rains
Fill their stalks with honeyed sap
Drawn from Earth's prolific lap.
BAYARD TAYLOR—*Home and Travel. Ariel in the Cloven Pine.* L. 37.

12
Darker than darkest pansies.
TENNYSON—*Gardener's Daughter.*

PARADISE

13
In the nine heavens are eight Paradises;
Where is the ninth one? In the human breast.
Only the blessed dwell in th' Paradises,
But blessedness dwells in the human breast.
WM. R. ALGER—*Oriental Poetry. The Ninth Paradise.*

14
Or were I in the wildest waste,
Sae bleak and bare, sae bleak and bare,
The desert were a paradise
If thou wert there, if thou wert there.
BURNS—*Oh! Wert Thou in the Cold Blast.*
(See also OMAR, also MANTUANUS under HAPPINESS)

15
In this fool's paradise, he drank delight.
CRABBE—*The Borough Players.* Letter XII.

16
Nor count compartments of the floors,
But mount to paradise
By the stairway of surprise.
EMERSON—*Merlin.*

17
Unto you is paradise opened.
II Esdras. VIII. 52.

18
The meanest floweret of the vale,
The simplest note that swells the gale,
The common sun, the air, the skies,
To him are open paradise.
GRAY—*Ode on the Pleasure Arising from Vicissitudes.* L. 53.

19
Dry your eyes—O dry your eyes,
For I was taught in Paradise
To ease my breast of melodies.
KEATS—*Fairy Song.*

20
Mahomet was taking his afternoon nap in his Paradise. An houri had rolled a cloud under his head, and he was snoring serenely near the fountain of Salsabil.
ERNEST L'EPINE—*Croquemitaine.* Bk. II Ch. IX. HOOD'S trans.

21
A limbo large and broad, since call'd
The Paradise of Fools to few unknown.
MILTON—*Paradise Lost.* Bk. III. L. 495.

22
So on he fares, and to the border comes,
Of Eden, where delicious Paradise,
Now nearer, crowns with her enclosure green,
As with a rural mound, the champain head
Of a steep wilderness.
MILTON—*Paradise Lost.* Bk. IV. L. 131.

23
One morn a Peri at the gate
Of Eden stood disconsolate.
MOORE—*Lalla Rookh. Paradise and the Peri.*

1
A Book of Verses underneath the Bough,
A Jug of Wine, a Loaf of Bread—and Thou
Beside me singing in the Wilderness—
Oh, Wilderness were Paradise enow!
OMAR KHAYYAM—*Rubaiyat*. St. 12. FITZ-GERALD's trans.

2
The loves that meet in Paradise shall cast out fear,
And Paradise hath room for you and me and all.
CHRISTINA G. ROSSETTI—*Saints and Angels*. St. 10.

3
There is no expeditious road
To pack and label men for God,
And save them by the barrel-load.
Some may perchance, with strange surprise,
Have blundered into Paradise.
FRANCIS THOMPSON—*Epilogue*. St. 2.

PARADOX

4 For thence,—a paradox
Which comforts while it mocks,—
Shall life succeed in that it seems to fail:
What I aspired to be,
And was not, comforts me:
A brute I might have been, but would not sink i' the scale.
ROBERT BROWNING—*Rabbi-Ben-Ezra*. St. 7.

5
Then there is that glorious Epicurean paradox, uttered by my friend, the Historian, in one of his flashing moments: "Give us the luxuries of life, and we will dispense with its necessaries."
HOLMES—*The Autocrat of the Breakfast Table*. VI.
(See also PLUTARCH under HAPPINESS)

6
These are old fond paradoxes to make fools laugh i' the alehouse.
Othello. Act II. Sc. 1. L. 139.

7
You undergo too strict a paradox,
Striving to make an ugly deed look fair.
Timon of Athens. Act III. Sc. 5. L. 24.

8
The mind begins to boggle at unnatural substances as things paradoxical and incomprehensible.
BISHOP SOUTH—*Sermons*.

PARDON (See FORGIVENESS, UNDERSTANDING)

PARIS

9
Good Americans when they die go to Paris.
Attributed to THOS. APPLETON by O. W. HOLMES—*Autocrat of the Breakfast Table*. VI.

10
When you've walked up the Rue la Paix at Paris,
Been to the Louvre and the Tuileries,
And to Versailles, although to go so far is
A thing not quite consistent with your ease,
And—but the mass of objects quite a bar is
To my describing what the traveller sees.
You who have ever been to Paris, know;
And you who have not been to Paris—go!
RUSKIN—*A Tour Through France*. St. 12.

11
Prince, give praise to our French ladies
For the sweet sound their speaking carries;
'Twixt Rome and Cadiz many a maid is,
But no good girl's lip out of Paris.
SWINBURNE—*Translation from Villon. Ballad of the Women of Paris*.

PARTING

12 Till then, good-night!
You wish the time were now? And I.
You do not blush to wish it so?
You would have blush'd yourself to death
To own so much a year ago.
What! both these snowy hands? ah, then
I'll have to say, Good-night again.
T. B. ALDRICH—*Palabras Carinosas*.

13
Good night! I have to say good night,
To such a host of peerless things!
T. B. ALDRICH—*Palabras Carinosas*.

14
Adieu! 'tis love's last greeting,
The parting hour is come!
And fast thy soul is fleeting
To seek its starry home.
BERANGER—*L'Adieu*. Free translation.

15
Such partings break the heart they fondly hope to heal.
BYRON—*Childe Harold*. Canto I. St. 10.

16
Fare thee well! and if for ever,
Still for ever, fare thee well.
BYRON—*Fare Thee Well*.

17
Let's not unman each other—part at once;
All farewells should be sudden, when forever,
Else they make an eternity of moments,
And clog the last sad sands of life with tears.
BYRON—*Sardanapalus*. Act V. Sc. 1.

18
We two parted
In silence and tears,
Half broken-hearted
To sever for years.
BYRON—*When We Two Parted*.

19
Kathleen Mavourneen, the gray dawn is breaking,
The horn of the hunter is heard on the hill,
The lark from her light wing the bright dew is shaking—
Kathleen Mavourneen, what, slumbering still?
Oh hast thou forgotten how soon we must sever?
Oh hast thou forgotten this day we must part?
It may be for years and it may be forever;
Oh why art thou silent, thou voice of my heart?
Ascribed to MRS. JULIA CRAWFORD—*Kathleen Mavourneen*. First pub. in *Metropolitan Magazine*. London, between 1830 and 1840.

20
One kind kiss before we part,
Drop a tear, and bid adieu;
Though we sever, my fond heart
Till we meet shall pant for you.
DODSLEY—*Colin's Kisses. The Parting Kiss*.

21
In every parting there is an image of death.
GEORGE ELIOT—*Amos Barton*. Ch. X.

1
The king of Babylon stood at the parting of the way.
Ezekiel. XXI. 21. See also XENOPHON—*Memorabilia.* II. 1. *"Choice of Hercules."* Referred to by CARLYLE—*Sartor Resartus.* Bk. II.

2
We only part to meet again.
GAY—*Black-eyed Susan.* St. 4.

3
Excuse me, then! you know my heart;
But dearest friends, alas! must part.
GAY—*The Hare and Many Friends.* L. 61.

4
Good-night! good-night! as we so oft have said
Beneath this roof at midnight, in the days
That are no more, and shall no more return.
Thou hast but taken up thy lamp and gone to bed;
I stay a little longer, as one stays
To cover up the embers that still burn.
LONGFELLOW—*Three Friends of Mine.* Pt. IV.

5
My Book and *Heart*
Shall never part.
New England Primer. (1814)

6
If we must part forever,
Give me but one kind word to think upon,
And please myself with, while my heart's breaking.
THOS. OTWAY—*The Orphan.* Act III. Sc. 1.

7
Shall I bid her goe? what and if I doe?
Shall I bid her goe and spare not?
Oh no, no, no, I dare not.
THOMAS PERCY—*Reliques. Corydon's Farewell to Phillis.*

8
Now fitted the halter, now travers'd the cart,
And often took leave; but was loth to part.
PRIOR—*The Thief and the Cordelier.*

9
But in vain she did conjure him,
To depart her presence so,
Having a thousand tongues t' allure him
And but one to bid him go.
When lips invite,
And eyes delight,
And cheeks as fresh as rose in June,
Persuade delay,—
What boots to say
Forego me now, come to me soon.
SIR WALTER RALEIGH—*Dulcina.* See CAYLEY'S *Life of Raleigh.* Vol. I. Ch. III.

10
Say good-bye er howdy-do—
What's the odds betwixt the two?
Comin'—goin'—every day—
Best friends first to go away—
Grasp of hands you'd ruther hold
Than their weight in solid gold,
Slips their grip while greetin' you,—
Say good-bye er howdy-do?
JAMES WHITCOMB RILEY—*Good-Bye er Howdy-Do.*

11
If we do meet again, we'll smile indeed;
If not, 'tis true this parting was well made.
Julius Cæsar. Act V. Sc. 1. L. 121.

12
They say he parted well, and paid his score;
And so, God be with him!
Macbeth. Act V. Sc. 8. L. 52.

13
Good-night, good-night! parting is such sweet sorrow,
That I shall say good-night till it be morrow.
Romeo and Juliet. Act II. Sc. 2. L. 185.

14
Gone—flitted away,
Taken the stars from the night and the sun
From the day!
Gone, and a cloud in my heart.
TENNYSON—*The Window. Gone.*

15
She went her unremembering way,
She went and left in me
The pang of all the partings gone,
And partings yet to be.
FRANCIS THOMPSON—*Daisy.* St. 12.

16
But fate ordains that dearest friends must part.
YOUNG—*Love of Fame.* Satire II. L. 232.

PARTRIDGE

17
Ah, nut-brown partridges! Ah, brilliant pheasants!
And ah, ye poachers!—'Tis no sport for peasants.
BYRON—*Don Juan.* Canto XIII. St. 75.

18
Or have you mark'd a partridge quake,
Viewing the towering falcon nigh?
She cuddles low behind the brake:
Nor would she stay; nor dares she fly.
PRIOR—*The Dove.* St. 14.

19
Who finds the partridge in the puttock's nest,
But may imagine how the bird was dead,
Although the kite soar with unbloodied beak?
Henry VI. Pt. II. Act III. Sc. 2. L. 191.

20
Like as a feareful partridge, that is fledd
From the sharpe hauke which her attacked neare,
And falls to ground to seeke for succor theare,
Whereas the hungry spaniells she does spye,
With greedy jawes her ready for to teare.
SPENSER—*Faerie Queene.* Bk. III. Canto VIII. St. 33.

PASSION

21
Fountain-heads and pathless groves,
Places which pale passion loves!
BEAUMONT AND FLETCHER—*The Nice Valour. Song.* Act III. Sc. 3.

22
Only I discern
Infinite passion, and the pain
Of finite hearts that yearn.
ROBERT BROWNING—*Two in the Campagna.* St. 12.

23
For one heat, all know, doth drive out another,
One passion doth expel another still.
GEORGE CHAPMAN—*Monsieur D'Olive.* Act V. Sc. 1. L. 8.

24
Filled with fury, rapt, inspir'd.
COLLINS—*The Passions.* L. 10.

1
We are ne'er like angels till our passion dies.
THOMAS DEKKER—*The Honest Whore.* Pt. II. Act I. Sc. 2.

2
Bee to the blossom, moth to the flame;
Each to his passion; what's in a name?
HELEN HUNT JACKSON—*Vanity of Vanities.*

3
If we resist our passions it is more from their weakness than from our strength.
LA ROCHEFOUCAULD—*Maxims.* No. 125.

4
Toutes les passions ne sont autre chose que les divers degrés de la chaleur et de la froideur du sang.
All the passions are nothing else than different degrees of heat and cold of the blood.
LA ROCHEFOUCAULD—*Premier Supplement.* VIII.

5
Where passion leads or prudence points the way.
ROBERT LOWTH—*Choice of Hercules.*

6 Take heed lest passion sway
Thy judgment to do aught, which else free will
Would not admit.
MILTON—*Paradise Lost.* Bk. VIII. L. 634.

7
Search then the ruling passion; there alone,
The wild are constant, and the cunning known;
The fool consistent, and the false sincere;
Priests, princes, women, no dissemblers here.
POPE—*Moral Essays.* Ep. I. L. 174.

8
And you, brave Cobham! to the latest breath
Shall feel your ruling passion strong in death.
POPE—*Moral Essays.* Ep. I. L. 262.

9
In men, we various ruling passions find;
In women two almost divide the kind;
Those only fix'd, they first or last obey.
The love of pleasure, and the love of sway.
POPE—*Moral Essays.* Ep. II. L. 207.

10
The ruling passion, be it what it will,
The ruling passion conquers reason still.
POPE—*Moral Essays.* Ep. III. L. 153.

11
May I govern my passions with absolute sway,
And grow wiser and better as my strength wears away.
WALTER POPE—*The Old Man's Wish.*

12
Passions are likened best to floods and streams,
The shallow murmur, but the deep are dumb.
SIR WALTER RALEIGH—*The Silent Lover.* See CAYLEY'S *Life of Raleigh.* Vol. I. Ch. III.

13 Give me that man
That is not passion's slave.
Hamlet. Act III. Sc. 2. L. 75.

14
What to ourselves in passion we propose,
The passion ending, doth the purpose lose.
Hamlet. Act III. Sc. 2. L. 204.

15
O, that my tongue were in the thunder's mouth!
Then with a passion would I shake the world.
King John. Act III. Sc. 4. L. 38.

16
Alas, why gnaw you so your nether lip?
Some bloody passion shakes your very frame;
These are portents; but yet I hope, I hope,
They do not point on me.
Othello. Act V. Sc. 2. L. 43.

17
He will hold thee, when his passion shall have spent its novel force,
Something better than his dog, a little dearer than his horse.
TENNYSON—*Locksley Hall.* St. 25.

18
The seas are quiet when the winds give o'er;
So calm are we when passions are no more!
EDMUND WALLER—*On Divine Poems.* L. 7.

19
But, children, you should never let
Such angry passions rise;
Your little hands were never made
To tear each other's eyes.
ISAAC WATTS—*Divine Songs. Song XVI.*

20
And beauty, for confiding youth,
Those shocks of passion can prepare
That kill the bloom before its time,
And blanch, without the owner's crime,
The most resplendent hair.
WORDSWORTH—*Lament of Mary, Queen of Scots.*

PASSION FLOWER

Passiflora

21
Art thou a type of beauty, or of power,
Of sweet enjoyment, or disastrous sin?
For each thy name denoteth, Passion flower!
O no! thy pure corolla's depth within
We trace a holier symbol; yea, a sign
'Twixt God and man; a record of that hour
When the expiatory act divine
Cancelled that curse which was our mortal dower.
It is the Cross!
SIR AUBREY DE VERE—*A Song of Faith. Devout Exercises and Sonnets. The Passion Flower.*

PAST (See also Time, To-Day)

22
Therefore Agathon rightly says: "Of this alone even God is deprived, the power of making things that are past never to have been."
ARISTOTLE—*Ethics.* Bk. VI. Ch. II. R. W. BROWNE'S trans. Same idea in MILTON—*Paradise Lost.* 9. 926. PINDAR—*Olympia.* 2. 17. PLINY the Elder—*Historia Naturalis.* 2. 5. 10.

23
The present contains nothing more than the past, and what is found in the effect was already in the cause.
HENRI BERGSON—*Creative Evolution.* Ch. I. (See also CARLYLE)

24
No traces left of all the busy scene,
But that remembrances says: The things have been.
SAMUEL BOYSE—*The Deity.*

25
But how carve way i' the life that lies before,
If bent on groaning ever for the past?
ROBERT BROWNING—*Balaustion's Adventure.*

1
Thou unrelenting past.
BRYANT—*To the Past.*

2
The light of other days is faded,
And all their glories past.
ALFRED BUNN—*The Maid of Artois.*

3
The age of chivalry is gone.
BURKE—*Reflections on the Revolution in France.*
(See also KINGSLEY)

4
John Anderson, my jo, John,
When we were first acquent,
Your locks were like the raven,
Your bonny brow was brent.
BURNS—*John Anderson.*

5
Gone—glimmering through the dream of things that were.
BYRON—*Childe Harold.* Canto II. St. 2.

6
The best of prophets of the future is the past.
BYRON—*Letter.* Jan. 28, 1821.

7
The Present is the living sum-total of the whole Past.
CARLYLE—*Essays. Characteristics.*
(See also BERGSON)

8
O, to bring back the great Homeric time,
The simple manners and the deeds sublime:
When the wise Wanderer, often foiled by Fate,
Through the long furrow drave the ploughshare straight.
MORTIMER COLLINS—*Letter to the Rt. Hon. B. Disraeli, M.P.* Pub. anon. 1869. "Ploughing his lonely furrow." Used by LORD ROSEBERY. July, 1901.

9
Listen to the Water-Mill:
Through the live-long day
How the clicking of its wheel
Wears the hours away!
Languidly the Autumn wind
Stirs the forest leaves,
From the field the reapers sing
Binding up their sheaves:
And a proverb haunts my mind
As a spell is cast,
"The mill cannot grind
With the water that is past."
SARAH DOUDNEY—*Lesson of the Water-Mill.*
(See also TRENCH)

10
Not heaven itself upon the past has power;
But what has been, has been, and I have had my hour.
DRYDEN—*Imitation of Horace.* Bk. III. *Ode XXIX.* L. 71.

11
Ils sont passés ces jours de fête.
The days of rejoicing are gone forever.
DU LORENS—*Le Tableau Parlant.*

12
Oh le bon temps où étions si malheureux.
Oh! the good times when we were so unhappy.
DUMAS—*Le Chevalier d'Harmental.* II. 318.

13
Un jeune homme d'un bien beau passé.
A young man with a very good past.
HEINE of ALFRED DE MUSSET. Quoted by SWINBURNE—*Miscellanies.* P. 233.

14
O Death! O Change! O Time!
Without you, O! the insufferable eyes
Of these poor Might-Have-Beens,
These fatuous, ineffectual yesterdays.
HENLEY—*Rhymes and Rhythms.* XIII.

15
Praise they that will times past, I joy to see
My selfe now live: this age best pleaseth mee.
HERRICK—*The Present Time Best Pleaseth.*

16
O God! Put back Thy universe and give me yesterday.
HENRY ARTHUR JONES—*Silver King.*

17
Some say that the age of chivalry is past, that the spirit of romance is dead. The age of chivalry is never past so long as there is a wrong left unredressed on earth.
CHARLES KINGSLEY—*Life.* Vol. II. Ch. XXVIII.
(See also BURKE)

18
Enjoy the spring of love and youth,
To some good angel leave the rest;
For time will teach thee soon the truth,
There are no birds in last year's nest.
LONGFELLOW—*It is not always May.*

19
We remain
Safe in the hallowed quiets of the past.
LOWELL—*The Cathedral.* L. 234.

20
Prisca juvent alios; ego me nunc denique natum
Gratulor.
The good of other times let people state;
I think it lucky I was born so late.
OVID—*Ars Amatoria.* III. 121. Trans. by SYDNEY SMITH.

21
Weep no more, lady, weep no more,
Thy sorrowe is in vaine,
For violets pluckt, the sweetest showers
Will ne'er make grow againe.
THOS. PERCY—*Reliques. The Friar of Orders Gray.* See FLETCHER—*The Queen of Corinth.* Act III. Sc. 2.

22
O there are Voices of the Past,
Links of a broken chain,
Wings that can bear me back to Times
Which cannot come again;
Yet God forbid that I should lose
The echoes that remain!
ADELAIDE A. PROCTER—*Voices of the Past.*

23
In tanta inconstantia turbaque rerum nihil nisi quod preteriit certum est.
In the great inconstancy and crowd of events, nothing is certain except the past.
SENECA—*De Consolatione ad Marciam.* XXII.

24
What's past is prologue.
Tempest. Act II. Sc. 1. L. 253.

1
The past Hours weak and gray
With the spoil which their toil
Raked together
From the conquest but One could foil.
SHELLEY—*Prometheus Unbound.* Act IV. Sc. 1.

2
I need not ask thee if that hand, now calmed,
Has any Roman soldier mauled and knuckled,
For thou wert dead, and buried and embalmed,
Ere Romulus and Remus had been suckled:
Antiquity appears to have begun
Long after that primeval race was run.
HORACE SMITH—*Address to the Mummy in Belzoni's Exhibition.*

3
Oh, had I but Aladdin's lamp
Tho' only for a day,
I'd try to find a link to bind
The joys that pass away.
CHARLES SWAIN—*Oh, Had I but Aladdin's Lamp.*

4
The eternal landscape of the past.
TENNYSON—*In Memoriam.* Pt. XLVI.

5
Oh seize the instant time; you never will
With waters once passed by impel the mill.
TRENCH—*Poems.* (Ed. 1865) P. 303. *Proverbs, Turkish* and *Persian.*
(See also DOUDNEY)

6
Many a woman has a past; but I am told she has at least a dozen, and that they all fit.
OSCAR WILDE—*Lady Windermere's Fan.* Act I. A Woman with a Past. Title of a Novel by MRS. BERENS. Pub. 1886.

7
Though nothing can bring back the hour
Of splendour in the grass, of glory in the flower.
WORDSWORTH—*Ode. Intimations of Immortality.* St. 10.

8
For old, unhappy, far-off things,
And battles long ago.
WORDSWORTH—*The Solitary Reaper.*

9
That awful independent on to-morrow!
Whose work is done; who triumphs in the past;
Whose yesterdays look backward with a smile
Nor, like the Parthian, wound him as they fly.
YOUNG—*Night Thoughts.* Night II. L. 322.

PATIENCE

10
With strength and patience all his grievous loads are borne,
And from the world's rose-bed he only asks a thorn.
WM. R. ALGER—*Oriental Poetry, Mussud's Praise of the Camel.*

11
I worked with patience which means almost power.
E. B. BROWNING—*Aurora Leigh.* Bk. III. L. 205.

12
And I must bear
What is ordained with patience, being aware
Necessity doth front the universe
With an invincible gesture.
E. B. BROWNING—*Prometheus Bound.*

13
But there are times when patience proves at fault.
ROBERT BROWNING—*Paracelsus.* Sc. 3.

14
There is however a limit at which forbearance ceases to be a virtue.
BURKE—*Observations on a Late Publication on the Present State of the Nation.*

15
Patience and shuffle the cards.
CERVANTES—*Don Quixote.* Pt. II. Bk. I. Ch. VI.

16
Thus with hir fader for a certeyn space
Dwelleth this flour of wyfly pacience,
That neither by hir wordes ne hir face
Biforn the folk, ne eek in her absence,
Ne shewed she that hir was doon offence.
CHAUCER—*The Clerkes Tale.* V. L. 13,254.

17
Patience is sorrow's salve.
CHURCHILL—*Prophecy of Famine.* L. 363.

18
His patient soul endures what Heav'n ordains,
But neither feels nor fears ideal pains.
CRABBE—*The Borough.* Letter XVII.

19
Patience is a necessary ingredient of genius.
BENJ. DISRAELI—*Contarini Fleming.* Pt. IV. Ch. V.

20
But the waiting time, my brothers,
Is the hardest time of all.
SARAH DOUDNEY—*Psalms of Life. The Hardest Time of All.*

21
The worst speak something good; if all want sense,
God takes a text, and preacheth patience.
HERBERT—*The Church Porch.* St. 72.

22
Durum! sed levius fit patientia
Quicquid corrigere est nefas.
It is hard! But what can not be removed, becomes lighter through patience.
HORACE—*Carmina.* I. 24. 19.

23
For patience, sov'reign o'er transmuted ill.
SAMUEL JOHNSON—*The Vanity of Human Wishes.* L. 352.

24
Patience et longueur de temps.
Font plus que force ni que rage.
By time and toil we sever
What strength and rage could never.
LA FONTAINE—*Fables.* II. 11.

25
Rule by patience, Laughing Water!
LONGFELLOW—*Hiawatha.* Pt. X. *Hiawatha's Wooing.*

26
Still achieving, still pursuing,
Learn to labor and to wait.
LONGFELLOW—*A Psalm of Life.* St. 9.

27
All things come round to him who will but wait.
LONGFELLOW—*Tales of a Wayside Inn. The Student's Tale.* Pt. I.
(See also MILTON under SERVICE)

1
Endurance is the crowning quality,
And patience all the passion of great hearts.
LOWELL—*Columbus*. L. 241.

2 Or arm th' obdured breast
With stubborn patience as with triple steel.
MILTON—*Paradise Lost*. Bk. II. L. 568.

3
Perfer et obdura; dolor hic tibi proderit olim.
Have patience and endure; this unhappiness will one day be beneficial.
OVID—*Amorum*. III. 11. 7.

4
Sua quisque exempla debet æquo animo pati.
Every one ought to bear patiently the results of his own conduct.
PHÆDRUS—*Fables*. I. 26. 12.

5
La patience est amère, mais son fruit est doux.
Patience is bitter, but its fruit is sweet.
ROUSSEAU.

6
Nihil tam acerbum est in quo non æquus animus solatium inveniat.
There is nothing so disagreeable, that a patient mind can not find some solace for it.
SENECA—*De Animi Tranquilitate*. X.

7
And makes us rather bear those ills we have
Than fly to others that we know not of?
Hamlet. Act III. Sc. 1. L. 81.

8
I will with patience hear, and find a time
Both meet to hear and answer such high things.
Till then, my noble friend, chew upon this.
Julius Cæsar. Act I. Sc. 2. L. 169.

9
A high hope for a low heaven: God grant us patience!
Love's Labour's Lost. Act I. Sc. 1. L. 195.

10
Sufferance is the badge of all our tribe.
Merchant of Venice. Act I. Sc. 3. L. 111.

11 I do oppose
My patience to his fury, and am arm'd
To suffer, with a quietness of spirit,
The very tyranny and rage of his.
Merchant of Venice. Act IV. Sc. 1. L. 10.

12 'Tis all men's office to speak patience
To those that wring under the load of sorrow,
But no man's virtue nor sufficiency
To be so moral when he shall endure
The like himself.
Much Ado About Nothing. Act V. Sc. 1. L. 27.

13
How poor are they that have not patience!
What wound did ever heal but by degrees?
Othello. Act II. Sc. 3. L. 376.

14 Had it pleas'd heaven
To try me with affliction * * *
I should have found in some place of my soul
A drop of patience.
Othello. Act IV. Sc. 2. L. 47.

15
Like Patience gazing on kings' graves, and smiling
Extremity out of act.
Pericles. Act V. Sc. 1. L. 139.

16
She sat like patience on a monument
Smiling at grief.
Twelfth Night. Act II. Sc. 4. L. 117.

17
Furor fit læsa sæpius patientia.
Patience, when too often outraged, is converted into madness.
SYRUS—*Maxims*. 289.

18
La patience est l'art d'espérer.
Patience is the art of hoping.
VAUVENARGUES—*Réflexions*. CCLI.

19
Durate, et vosmet rebus servate secundis.
Persevere and preserve yourselves for better circumstances.
VERGIL—*Æneid*. I. 207.

20
Superanda omnis fortuna ferendo est.
Every misfortune is to be subdued by patience.
VERGIL—*Æneid*. V. 710.

PATRIOTISM

21
The die was now cast; I had passed the Rubicon. Swim or sink, live or die, survive or perish with my country was my unalterable determination.
JOHN ADAMS—*Works*. Vol. IV. P. 8. In a conversation with Jonathan Sewell. (1774) (PEELE in *Edward I* [1584?] used the phrase "Live or die, sink or swim.")

22
Who would not be that youth? What pity is it
That we can die but once to save our country!
ADDISON—*Cato*. Act IV. Sc. 4.

23
Our ships were British oak,
And hearts of oak our men.
S. J. ARNOLD—*Death of Nelson*.

24
From distant climes, o'er wide-spread seas we come,
Though not with much éclat or beat of drum;
True patriots all; for be it understood
We left our country for our country's good.
No private views disgraced our generous zeal,
What urged our travels was our country's weal.
GEORGE BARRINGTON—*Prologue for the Opening of the Playhouse at Sydney, New South Wales*, Jan. 16, 1796. DR. YOUNG'S *Revenge* was played by convicts.
(See also FARQUHAR, FITZGEFFREY)

25
The unbought grace of life, the cheap defence of nations, the nurse of manly sentiment and heroic enterprise, is gone!
BURKE—*Reflections on the Revolution in France*. Vol. III. P. 331.

26
Be Briton still to Britain true,
Among oursel's united;
For never but by British hands
Maun British wrangs be righted.
BURNS—*Dumfries Volunteers*.

27
Again to the battle, Achaians!
Our hearts bid the tyrants defiance!

Our land, the first garden of liberty's tree—
It has been, and shall yet be, the land of the free.
CAMPBELL—*Song of the Greeks.*

1
God save our gracious king,
Long live our noble king,
God save the king.
HENRY CAREY—*God Save the King.*

2
I realize that patriotism is not enough. I must have no hatred toward any one.
EDITH CAVELL. Quoted by the Newspapers as her last words before she was shot to death by the Germans in Brussels, Oct. 12, 1915.

3
"My country, right or wrong," is a thing that no patriot would think of saying except in a desperate case. It is like saying, "My mother, drunk or sober."
G. K. CHESTERTON—*The Defendant.*
(See also DECATUR)

4
We join ourselves to no party that does not carry the flag and I keep step to the music of the Union.
RUFUS CHOATE—*Letter to a Worcester Whig Convention.* Oct. 1, 1855.

5
Patria est communis omnium parens.
Our country is the common parent of all.
CICERO—*Orationes in Catilinam.* I. 7.

6
I have heard something said about allegiance to the South: I know no South, no North, no East, no West, to which I owe any allegiance.
HENRY CLAY—*In the U. S. Senate.* (1848)

7
I hope to find my country in the right: however I will stand by her, right or wrong.
JOHN J. CRITTENDEN. In Congress, when President Polk sent a message after the defeat of the Mexican General Arista by General Taylor. May, 1846.
(See also CHESTERTON, DECATUR)

8
Our country! In her intercourse with foreign nations, may she always be in the right; but our country, right or wrong.
STEPHEN DECATUR—*Toast given at Norfolk, April,* 1816. See MACKENZIE'S *Life of Stephen Decatur.* Ch. XIV.
(See also CRITTENDEN, SCHURZ, WINTHROP)

9
I wish I was in de land ob cotton,
Ole times dar am not forgotten,
Look-a-way! Look-a-way! Look-a-way, Dixie Land!
* * * * *
Den I wish I was in Dixie, Hooray! Hooray!
In Dixie Land I'll take my stand
To lib and die in Dixie.
DANIEL D. EMMETT—*Dixie Land.* See account in *Century,* Aug., 1887. A Southern version was written by ALBERT PIKE.

10
'Twas for the good of my country that I should be abroad. Anything for the good of one's country—I'm a Roman for that.
GEO. FARQUHAR—*The Beaux' Stratagem.* Act III. Sc. 2. L. 89.
(See also BARRINGTON)

11
Liberté, égalité, fraternité.
Liberty, equality, fraternity.
Watchword of French Revolution.

12
And bold and hard adventures t' undertake,
Leaving his country for his country's sake.
CHARLES FITZGEFFREY—*Life and Death of Sir Francis Drake.* St. 213. (1600)
(See also BARRINGTON)

13
Our country is the world—our countrymen are all mankind.
WILLIAM LLOYD GARRISON—*Motto of the Liberator.,* 1837–1839. "My country" originally—later changed to "Our country."
(See also PLUTARCH)

14
Such is the patriot's boast, where'er we roam,
His first best country ever is at home.
GOLDSMITH—*The Traveler.* L. 73.

15
I only regret that I have but one life to lose for my country.
NATHAN HALE—His Last Words, Sept. 22, 1776. STEWART'S *Life of Capt. Nathan Hale.* Ch. VII.

16
Strike—for your altars and your fires;
Strike—for the green graves of your sires;
God—and your native land!
FITZ-GREENE HALLECK—*Marco Bozzaris.*

17
And have they fixed the where, and when?
And shall Trelawny die?
Here's thirty thousand Cornish men
Will know the reason why!
ROBERT STEPHEN HAWKER — *Song of the Western Men.* Mr. Hawker asserts that he wrote the ballad in 1825, all save the chorus and the last two lines, which since the imprisonment by James II, 1688, of the seven Bishops, have been popular throughout Cornwall. (Trelawny was Bishop of Bristol.) First appearance in the *Royal Devonport Telegram* and *Plymouth Chronicle,* Sept. 2, 1826. Story of the ballad in MACAULAY'S *History of England.* Footnote for HAWKER.

18
He serves his party best who serves the country best.
RUTHERFORD B. HAYES. *Inaugural Address,* March 5, 1877.
(See also HOMER)

19
I am not a Virginian but an American.
PATRICK HENRY—*In the Continental Congress,* Sept. 5, 1774.

20
One flag, one land, one heart, one hand,
One Nation evermore!
HOLMES—*Voyage of the Good Ship Union. Poems of the Class of '29.*

21
He serves me most who serves his country best.
HOMER—*Iliad.* Bk. X. L. 206. POPE'S trans.
(See also HAYES)

22
And for our country 'tis a bliss to die.
HOMER—*Iliad.* Bk. XV. L. 583. POPE'S trans.

1
Who fears to speak of Ninety-eight?
Who blushes at the name?
When cowards mock the patriot's fate,
Who hangs his head for shame?

JOHN K. INGRAM—In *The Dublin Nation.* April 1, 1843. Vol. II. P. 339.

2
Our federal Union: it must be preserved.

ANDREW JACKSON—*Toast given at the Jefferson Birthday Celebration in* 1830. See W. J. SUMNER'S *Life of Jackson.*

3
Patriotism is the last refuge of a scoundrel.

SAMUEL JOHNSON—*Boswell's Life of Johnson.* (1775)

4
That man is little to be envied, whose patriotism would not gain force upon the plain of *Marathon*, or whose piety would not grow warmer among the ruins of *Iona.*

SAMUEL JOHNSON—*A Journey to the Western Islands. Inch Kenneth.*

5
Pater patriæ.

Father of his country.

JUVENAL—*Sat.* VIII. 244. Title bestowed on Cicero (B.C. 64) after his consulship, "a mark of distinction which none ever gained before." PLUTARCH—*Life of Cicero.* PLINY. Bk. VII, calls CICERO "Parens patriæ." Title conferred on Peter the Great by the Russian Senate. (1721) See *Post-Boy,* Dec. 28–30, 1721. Also applied to AUGUSTUS CÆSAR and MARIUS.

(See also MARTIAL, MASSINGER, SENECA, also KNOX under WASHINGTON)

6
Je meurs content, je meurs pour la liberté de mon pays.

I die content, I die for the liberty of my country.

Attributed to LE PELLETIER, also to MARSHAL LANNES.

7
The mystic chords of memory, stretching from every battlefield and patriot grave to every living heart and hearthstone all over this broad land, will yet swell the chorus of the Union, when again touched, as surely they will be, by the better angels of our nature.

LINCOLN—*Inaugural Address.* March 4, 1861.

8
Is it an offence, is it a mistake, is it a crime to take a hopeful view of the prospects of your own country? Why should it be? Why should patriotism and pessimism be identical? Hope is the mainspring of patriotism.

D. LLOYD GEORGE—*House of Commons, Oct.* 30, 1919.

9
And how can man die better
Than facing fearful odds,
For the ashes of his fathers
And the temples of his gods?

MACAULAY—*Horatius keeps the Bridge.*

10
'Twere sweet to sink in death for Truth and Freedom!
Yes, who would hesitate, for who could bear
The living degradation we may know
If we do dread death for a sacred cause?

TERENCE MCSWINEY—Lines written when a boy. In the *Nation,* Nov. 3, 1920.

11
Our spirit is . . . to show ourselves eager to work for, and if need be, to die for the Irish Republic. Facing our enemy we must declare an attitude simply. . . . We ask for no mercy and we will make no compromise.

TERENCE MCSWINEY, Lord Mayor of Cork. From a document in his possession when he was sentenced, in August, 1920.

12
Vox diversa sonat: populorum est vox tamen una,
Cum verus PATRIÆ diceris esse PATER.

There are many different voices and languages; but there is but one voice of the peoples when you are declared to be the true "Father of your country."

MARTIAL—*De Spectaculis.* III. 11.

(See also JUVENAL)

13
We, that would be known
The father of our people, in our study
And vigilance for their safety, must not change
Their ploughshares into swords, and force them from
The secure shade of their own vines, to be
Scorched with the flames of war.

MASSINGER—*The Maid of Honour.* Act I. 1.

(See also JUVENAL)

14
Nescio qua natale solum dulcedine captos
Ducit, et immemores non sinit esse sui.

Our native land charms us with inexpressible sweetness, and never allows us to forget that we belong to it.

OVID—*Epistolæ Ex Ponto.* I. 3. 35.

15
Omne solum forti patria est.

The whole earth is the brave man's country.

OVID—*Fasti.* I. 501.

(See also PAINE, PLUTARCH)

16
Patria est, ubicunque est bene.

Our country is wherever we are well off.

PACUVIUS, quoted by CICERO—*Tusculan. Disputations.* V. 37. ARISTOPHANES. PLAUTUS. EURIPIDES—*Fragmenta Incerta.* PHIPISKUS—*Dion Cassius.* I. 171.

(See also QUINTUS)

17
My country is the world, and my religion is to do good.

THOS. PAINE—*Rights of Man.* Ch. V.

(See also OVID)

18
They know no country, own no lord,
Their home the camp, their law the sword.

Free rendering of passage in SILVIO PELLICO'S *Enfernio de Messina.* Act V. Sc. 2.

19
Millions for defence, but not one cent for tribute.

Attributed to CHAS. C. PINCKNEY when Ambassador to the French Republic. (1796) Denied by him. Said to have been "Not a penny—not a sixpence." Attributed also to ROBERT GOODLOE HARPER, of South Carolina.

I have ten thousand for defense, but none to surrender; if you want our weapons, come and get them.

The response of an ancient General.

1
If I were an American, as I am an Englishman, while a foreign troop was landed in my country I never would lay down my arms, never! never! never!

WILLIAM PITT (Earl of Chatham)—*Speech.* Nov. 18, 1777.

2
Socrates said he was not an Athenian or a Greek, but a citizen of the world.

PLUTARCH—*On Banishment.*

(See also GARRISON, OVID)

3
Patria est ubicumque vir fortis sedem elegerit.

A brave man's country is wherever he chooses his abode.

QUINTUS CURTIUS RUFUS—*De Rebus Gestis Alexandri Magni.* VI. 4. 13.

4
Our country, right or wrong! When right, to be kept right; when wrong, to be put right!

CARL SCHURZ—*Speech in U. S. Senate.* (1872).

(See also DECATUR)

5
Where's the coward that would not dare
To fight for such a land?

SCOTT—*Marmion.* Canto IV. St. 30.

6
Servare cives, major est virtus patriæ patri.

To preserve the life of citizens, is the greatest virtue in the father of his country.

SENECA—*Octavia* 444.

7
Had I a dozen sons,—each in my love alike, * * * I had rather have eleven die nobly for their country, than one voluptuously surfeit out of action.

Coriolanus. Act I. Sc. 3. L. 24.

8
I do love
My country's good with a respect more tender,
More holy and profound, than mine own life.

Coriolanus. Act III. Sc. 3. L. 111.

9
Where liberty is, there is my country.

ALGERNON SIDNEY'S *motto.*

10
He held it safer to be of the religion of the King or Queen that were in being, for he knew that he came raw into the world, and accounted it no point of wisdom to be broiled out of it.

JOHN TAYLOR—*The Old, Old, Very Old Man.* (Parr.)

11
A saviour of the silver-coasted isle.

TENNYSON—*Ode on Death of Duke of Wellington.* Pt. VI.

12
Put none but Americans on guard tonight.

Attributed to WASHINGTON. The only basis for this order seems to be found in Washington's circular letter to regimental commanders, dated April 30, 1777, regarding recruits for his body guard. "You will therefore send me none but natives." A few months before, Thomas Hickey, a deserter from the British army, had tried to poison Washington, had been convicted and hanged.

13
Hands across the sea,
Feet on English ground,
The old blood is bold blood, the wide world round.

BYRON WEBBER—*Hands Across the Sea.*

14
Let our object be, our country, our whole country, and nothing but our country.

DANIEL WEBSTER—*Address at the Laying of the Corner-Stone of the Bunker Hill Monument.* June 17, 1825.

15
Thank God, I—I also—am an American!

DANIEL WEBSTER—*Completion of Bunker Hill Monument.* June 17, 1843.

16
Sink or swim, live or die, survive or perish, I give my hand and heart to this vote.

DANIEL WEBSTER—*Eulogy on Adams and Jefferson.*

17
I was born an American; I live an American; I shall die an American!

DANIEL WEBSTER—*Speech.* July 17, 1850.

18
Patriotism has become a mere national self assertion, a sentimentality of flag-cheering with no constructive duties.

H. G. WELLS—*Future in America.*

19
The lines of red are lines of blood, nobly and unselfishly shed by men who loved the liberty of their fellowmen more than they loved their own lives and fortunes. God forbid that we should have to use the blood of America to freshen the color of the flag. But if it should ever be necessary, that flag will be colored once more, and in being colored will be glorified and purified.

WOODROW WILSON—*Flag Day Speech.* May 7, 1915.

20
Our country—whether bounded by the St. John's and the Sabine, or however otherwise bounded or described, and be the measurements more or less;—still our country, to be cherished in all our hearts, and to be defended by all our hands.

ROBT. C. WINTHROP—*Toast at Faneuil Hall.* July 4, 1845.

Our country, however bounded.

Toast founded on the speech of WINTHROP.

(See also DECATUR)

21
There are no points of the compass on the chart of true patriotism.

ROBT. C. WINTHROP—*Letter to Boston Commercial Club.* June 12, 1879.

22
Our land is the dearer for our sacrifices. The blood of our martyrs sanctifies and enriches it. Their spirit passes into thousands of hearts. How costly is the progress of the race. It is only by the giving of life that we can have life.

REV. E. J. YOUNG—*Lesson of the Hour.* In *Mag. of History.* Extra. No. 43. Originally pub. in *Monthly Religious Mag.*, Boston, May, 1865.

(See also LINCOLN under SOLDIERS)

23
America is the crucible of God. It is the melting pot where all the races are fusing and reforming . . . these are the fires of God you've come to. . . . Into the crucible with you all. God is making the American.

ZANGWILL—*The Melting Pot.*

PEACE

1
This hand, to tyrants ever sworn the foe,
For freedom only deals the deadly blow;
Then sheathes in calm repose the vengeful blade,
For gentle peace in freedom's hallowed shade.
JOHN QUINCY ADAMS—*Written in an Album.*

2
The fiercest agonies have shortest reign;
And after dreams of horror, comes again
The welcome morning with its rays of peace.
BRYANT—*Mutation.* L. 4.

3
The trenchant blade Toledo trusty,
For want of fighting was grown rusty,
And ate into itself for lack
Of somebody to hew and hack.
BUTLER—*Hudibras.* Pt. I. Canto I. L. 359.

4
Mark! where his carnage and his conquests cease,
He makes a solitude and calls it—peace!
BYRON—*Bride of Abydos.* Canto II. St. 20.
(See also COWPER, TACITUS)

5
Oh that the desert were my dwelling-place!
BYRON—*Childe Harold.* Canto IV. L. 177.
(See also COWPER)

6
Cedant arma togæ.
War leads to peace.
CICERO—*De Officiis.* I. 22.

7
Mihi enim omnis pax cum civibus bello civili utilior videbatur.
For to me every sort of peace with the citizens seemed to be of more service than civil war.
CICERO—*Philippics.* 2. 15. 37.

8
Iniquissimam pacem justissimo bello antefero.
I prefer the most unfair peace to the most righteous war.
Adapted from CICERO. Same idea used by BUTLER in the Rump Parliament. See also CICERO—*Epistola ad Atticum.* 7. 14. Also said by FRANKLIN—*Letter to Quincey.* Sept. 11, 1783. BISHOP COLET, St. Paul's, London, 1512. See GREEN'S *History of the English People. The New Learning.*

9
Mars gravior sub pace latet.
A severe war lurks under the show of peace.
CLAUDIANUS—*De Sexto Consulatu Honorii Augusti Panegyris.* 307.

10
Nec sidera pacem
Semper habent.
Nor is heaven always at peace.
CLAUDIANUS—*De Bello Getico.* LXII.

11
The gentleman [Josiah Quincy] cannot have forgotten his own sentiment, uttered even on the floor of this House, "Peaceably if we can, forcibly if we must."
HENRY CLAY—*Speech. On the New Army Bill* (1813)

12
Peace rules the day, where reason rules the mind.
COLLINS—*Eclogue II. Hassan.* L. 68.

13
O for a lodge in some vast wilderness,
Some boundless contiguity of shade;
Where rumor of oppression and deceit,
Of unsuccessful or successful war,
Might never reach me more.
COWPER—*The Task.* Bk. II. L. 1.
(See also BYRON, also JOHNSON under SUMMER)

14
Though peace be made, yet it's interest that keeps peace.
Quoted by OLIVER CROMWELL, in Parliament, Sept. 4, 1654, as "a maxim not to be despised."

15
Such subtle covenants shall be made,
Till peace itself is war in masquerade.
DRYDEN—*Absalom and Achitopel.* Pt. I. L. 752; Pt. II. L. 268.

16
At home the hateful names of parties cease,
And factious souls are wearied into peace.
DRYDEN—*Astræa Redux.* L. 312.

17
Nothing can bring you peace but yourself. Nothing can bring you peace but the triumph of principles.
EMERSON—*Essays. Of Self-Reliance.*

18
Breathe soft, ye winds! ye waves, in silence sleep!
GAY—*To a Lady.* Ep. I. L. 17.

19
Pax vobiscum.
Peace be with you.
Vulgate. Genesis. XLIII. 23.

20
Let us have peace.
U. S. GRANT. Accepting the Presidential nomination. May 20, 1868.

21
I accept your nomination in the confident trust that the masses of our countrymen, North and South, are eager to clasp hands across the bloody chasm which has so long divided them.
HORACE GREELEY. Accepting the Liberal Republican nomination for President. May 20, 1872.

22
But—a stirring thrills the air
Like to sounds of joyance there,
That the rages
Of the ages
Shall be cancelled, and deliverance offered from the darts that were,
Consciousness the Will informing, till it fashion all things fair.
THOMAS HARDY—*Dynasts. Semichorus I of the Years.*

23
So peaceful shalt thou end thy blissful days,
And steal thyself from life by slow decays.
HOMER—*Odyssey.* Bk. XI. L. 164. POPE'S trans.

24
In pace ut sapiens aptarit idonea bello.
Like as a wise man in time of peace prepares for war.
HORACE—*Satires.* II. 2. 111.
(See also VEGETIUS)

1
They shall beat their swords into ploughshares, and their spears into pruning-hooks; nation shall not lift up sword against nation neither shall they learn war any more.
Isaiah. II. 4. *Joel.* III. 10. *Micah.* IV. 3.

2
The wolf also shall dwell with the lamb, and the leopard shall lie down with the kid.
Isaiah. XI. 6.

3
We love peace as we abhor pusillanimity; but not peace at any price. There is a peace more destructive of the manhood of living man than war is destructive of his material body. Chains are worse than bayonets.
DOUGLAS JERROLD—*Jerrold's Wit. Peace.*

4
It is thus that mutual cowardice keeps us in peace. Were one-half of mankind brave and one-half cowards, the brave would be always beating the cowards. Were all brave, they would lead a very uneasy life; all would be continually fighting; but being all cowards, we go on very well.
SAMUEL JOHNSON—*Boswell's Life.* (1778)

5
Sævis inter se convenit ursis.
Savage bears keep at peace with one another.
JUVENAL—*Satires.* XV. 164.

6
The days of peace and slumberous calm are fled.
KEATS—*Hyperion.* Bk. II.

7
Paix à tout prix.
Peace at any price.
LAMARTINE, as quoted by A. H. CLOUGH in *Letters and Remains.* (Ed. 1865) P. 105. Le Ministère de la Paix à tout prix. ARMAND CARREL in the *National,* March 13, 1831. (Of the Perier ministry.)

8
Peace will come soon and come to stay, and so come as to be worth keeping in all future time. It will then have been proved that among free men there can be no successful appeal from the ballot to the bullet, and that they who take such appeal are sure to lose their cases and pay the cost.
LINCOLN. Quoted by E. J. YOUNG—*The Lesson of the Hour.* In *Magazine of History.* No. 43. (Extra number.)

9
Peace! and no longer from its brazen portals
The blast of War's great organ shakes the skies!
But beautiful as songs of the immortals,
The holy melodies of love arise.
LONGFELLOW—*Arsenal at Springfield.*

10
Buried was the bloody hatchet;
Buried was the dreadful war-club;
Buried were all warlike weapons,
And the war-cry was forgotten.
Then was peace among the nations.
LONGFELLOW—*Hiawatha.* Pt. XIII. L. 7.

11
Ef you want peace, the thing you've gut to du
Is jes' to show you're up to fightin', tu.
LOWELL—*Biglow Papers.* 2nd Series. 2.

12
Glory to God in the highest, and on earth peace, good will toward men.
Luke. II. 14.

13
Pax huic domui.
Peace be to this house.
Luke. X. 5; *Matthew.* X. 12. (*Vulgate.*)

14
In the inglorious arts of peace.
ANDREW MARVELL—*Upon Cromwell's Return from Ireland.*

15
Peace hath her victories,
No less renowned than war.
MILTON—*Sonnet. To the Lord General Cromwell.*

16
I knew by the smoke that so gracefully curled
Above the green elms, that a cottage was near,
And I said, "If there's peace to be found in the world,
A heart that was humble might hope for it here."
MOORE—*Ballad Stanzas.*

17
How calm, how beautiful comes on
The stilly hour, when storms are gone.
MOORE—*Lalla Rookh. The Fire Worshippers.* Pt. III. St. 7.

18
L'empire, c'est la paix.
The Empire means peace.
LOUIS NAPOLEON—*Speech to the Chamber of Commerce in Toulouse,* Oct. 9, 1852. See B. JERROLD'S *Life of Louis Napoleon.* "L'empire, c'est l'epée." Parody of same in *Kladderdatsch,* Nov. 8, 1862.

19
Would you end war?
Create great Peace.
JAMES OPPENHEIM—*War and Laughter, 1914, And After.* IV.

20
For peace do not hope; to be just you must break it.
Still work for the minute and not for the year.
JOHN BOYLE O'REILLY—*Rules of the Road.*

21
Candida pax homines, trux decet ira feras.
Fair peace becomes men; ferocious anger belongs to beasts.
OVID—*Ars Amatoria.* III. 502.

22
His helmet now shall make a hive for bees,
And lover's sonnets turn'd to holy psalms;
A man at arms must now serve on his knees,
And feed on prayers, which are his age's alms.
GEO. PEELE—*Sonnet ad fin. Polyhymnia.*

23
An equal doom clipp'd Time's blest wings of peace.
PETRARCH—*To Laura in Death. Sonnet XLVIII.* L. 18.

24
Allay the ferment prevailing in America by removing the obnoxious hostile cause—obnoxious and unserviceable—for their merit can only be in action. "Non dimicare et vincare."
WILLIAM PITT the Elder—*Speech.* Jan. 20, 1775. Referring to the American Colonies.
(See also WILSON)

1
Concession comes with better grace and more salutary effect from superior power.
WILLIAM PITT the Elder—*Speech to Recall Troops from Boston.*
(See also WILSON)

2
The peace of God, which passeth all understanding.
Philippians. IV. 7.

3
Her ways are ways of pleasantness, and all her paths are peace.
Proverbs. III. 17.

4
Mercy and truth are met together: righteousness and peace have kissed each other.
Psalms. LXXXV. 10.

5
Peace be within thy walls, and prosperity within thy palaces.
Psalms. CXXII. 7.

6
People are always expecting to get peace in heaven: but you know whatever peace they get there will be ready-made. Whatever making of peace *they* can be blest for, must be on the earth here.
RUSKIN—*The Eagle's Nest.* Lecture IX.

7
If peace cannot be maintained with honor, it is no longer peace.
LORD JOHN RUSSELL—*Speech at Greenoch.* Sept., 1853.

8
Es kann der Frömmste nicht im Frieden bleiben,
Wenn es dem bösen Nachbar nicht gefällt.
The most pious may not live in peace, if it does not please his wicked neighbor.
SCHILLER—*Wilhelm Tell.* IV. 3. 124.

9
All these you may avoid but the Lie Direct; and you may avoid that too, with an If. I knew when seven justices could not take up a quarrel, but when the parties were met themselves, one of them thought but of an If, as, "If you said so then I said so"; and they shook hands and swore brothers. Your If is the only peace-maker; much virtue in If.
As You Like It. Act V. Sc. 4. L. 100.

10
That it should hold companionship in peace
With honour, as in war; since that to both
It stands in like request.
Coriolanus. Act III. Sc. 2. L. 49.

11
A peace is of the nature of a conquest;
For then both parties nobly are subdued,
And neither party loser.
Henry IV. Pt. II. Act IV. Sc. 2. L. 89.

12
In peace there's nothing so becomes a man
As modest stillness and humility.
Henry V. Act III. Sc. 1. L. 3.

13 Peace,
Dear nurse of arts, plenties and joyful births.
Henry V. Act V. Sc. 2. L. 34.

14
Still in thy right hand carry gentle peace,
To silence envious tongues.
Henry VIII. Act III. Sc. 2. L. 445.

15
To reap the harvest of perpetual peace,
By this one bloody trial of sharp war.
Richard III. Act V. Sc. 2. L. 15.

16
And for the peace of you I hold such strife
As 'twixt a miser and his wealth is found.
Sonnet LXXV.

17
When it is peace, then we may view again
With new-won eyes each other's truer form
And wonder. Grown more loving-kind and warm
We'll grasp firm hands and laugh at the old pain
When it is peace. But until peace, the storm
The darkness and the thunder and the rain.
CHARLES SORLEY—*To Germany.*

18
Let the bugles sound the *Truce of God* to the whole world forever.
CHARLES SUMNER—*Oration on the True Grandeur of Nations.*

19
In this surrender—if such it may be called—the National Government does not even stoop to conquer. It simply lifts itself to the height of its original principle. The early efforts of its best negotiators, the patriotic trial of its soldiers . . . may at last prevail.
CHARLES SUMNER. *Sustaining President Lincoln in the U. S. Senate, in the Trent Affair.* Jan. 7, 1862.
(See also WILSON)

20
Auferre, trucidare, rapere, falsis nominibus imperium, atque, ubi solitudinem faciunt, pacem appellant.
To rob, to ravage, to murder, in their imposing language, are the arts of civil policy. When they have made the world a solitude, they call it peace.
TACITUS—*Agricola.* XXX. Ascribing the speech to Galgacus, Britain's leader against the Romans.
(See also BYRON)

21
Miseram pacem vel bello bene mutari.
A peace may be so wretched as not to be ill exchanged for war.
TACITUS—*Annales.* III. 44.

22
Bellum magis desierat, quam pax cœperat.
It was rather a cessation of war than a beginning of peace.
TACITUS—*Annales.* IV. 1.

23
Peace the offspring is of Power.
BAYARD TAYLOR—*A Thousand Years.*

24 No more shall * * * Peace
Pipe on her pastoral hillock a languid note,
And watch her harvest ripen.
TENNYSON—*Maud.* St. 28.

25
Peace with honor.
THEOBALD, COUNT OF CHAMPAGNE—*Letter to King Louis the Great.* (1108–1137) See WALTER MAP—*De Nugis Curialium.* (Ed. Camden Society. P. 220.) SIR KENELM DIGBY—*Letter to* LORD BRISTOL, May 27, 1625. See his Life, pub. by Longmans. Same in *Coriolanus.* III. II.

1
Si vis pacem, para bellum.
In time of peace prepare for war.
Original not found, but probably suggested by "qui desiderat pacem, præparet bellum." He who desires peace will prepare for war. VEGETIUS—*Epitoma Rei Militaris.* Lib. III. *End of Prolog.* A similar thought also in DION CHRYSOSTOM. LIVY. VI. 18. 7. CORNELIUS NEPOS—*Epaminondas.* V. STATIUS—*Thebais.* VII. 554. SYRUS—*Maxims.* 465.
(See also HORACE)

2
He had rather spend £100,000 on Embassies to keep or procure peace with dishonour, than £100,000 on an army that would have forced peace with honour.
SIR ANTHONY WELDON—*The Court and Character of King James.* P. 185. (1650) Used by DISRAELI on his return from the Berlin Congress on the Eastern Question, July, 1878.

3
But dream not helm and harness
The sign of valor true;
Peace hath higher tests of manhood
Than battle ever knew.
WHITTIER—*Poems. The Hero.* St. 19.

4
As on the Sea of Galilee,
The Christ is whispering "Peace."
WHITTIER—*Tent on the Beach. Kallundborg Church.*

5
When earth as if on evil dreams
Looks back upon her wars,
And the white light of Christ outstreams
From the red disc of Mars,
His fame, who led the stormy van
Of battle, well may cease;
But never that which crowns the man
Whose victory was peace.
WHITTIER—*William Francis Bartlett.*

6
The example of America must be the example not merely of peace because it will not fight, but of peace because peace is the healing and elevating influence of the world, and strife is not. There is such a thing as a man being too proud to fight. There is such a thing as a nation being so right that it does not need to convince others by force that it is right.
WOODROW WILSON—*Address in Convention Hall.* Philadelphia, May 10, 1915.
(See also PITT, SUMNER)

7
Ne'er to meet, or ne'er to part, is peace.
YOUNG—*Night Thoughts.* Night V. L. 1,058.

PEA, SWEET

Lathyrus Odoratus

8
The pea is but a wanton witch
In too much haste to wed,
And clasps her rings on every hand.
HOOD—*Flowers.*

9
Here are sweet peas, on tiptoe for a flight;
With wings of gentle flush o'er delicate white,
And taper fingers catching at all things,
To bind them all about with tiny rings.
KEATS—*I Stood Tiptoe Upon a Little Hill.*

PEACOCK

10
For everything seemed resting on his nod,
As they could read in all eyes. Now to them,
Who were accustomed, as a sort of god,
To see the sultan, rich in many a gem,
Like an imperial peacock stalk abroad
(That royal bird, whose tail's a diadem,)
With all the pomp of power, it was a doubt
How power could condescend to do without.
BYRON—*Don Juan.* Canto VII. St. 74.

11
To frame the little animal, provide
All the gay hues that wait on female pride:
Let Nature guide thee; sometimes golden wire
The shining bellies of the fly require;
The peacock's plumes thy tackle must not fail,
Nor the dear purchase of the sable's tail.
GAY—*Rural Sports.* Canto I. L. 177.

12
To Paradise, the Arabs say,
Satan could never find the way
Until the peacock led him in.
LELAND—*The Peacock.*

13
"Fly pride," says the peacock.
Comedy of Errors. Act IV. Sc. 3. L. 81.

14
Let frantic Talbot triumph for a while
And like a peacock sweep along his tail.
Henry VI. Pt. I. Act III. Sc. 3. L. 5.

15
Why, he stalks up and down like a peacock,—a stride and a stand.
Troilus and Cressida. Act III. Sc. 3. L. 251.

16
And there they placed a peacock in his pride,
Before the damsel.
TENNYSON—*Gareth and Lynette.*

PEACH

17
A little peach in an orchard grew,—
A little peach of emerald hue;
Warmed by the sun and wet by the dew
It grew.
EUGENE FIELD—*The Little Peach.*

18
As touching peaches in general, the very name in Latine whereby they are called Persica, doth evidently show that they were brought out of Persia first.
PLINY—*Natural History.* Bk. XV. Ch. 13. HOLLAND's trans.

19
The ripest peach is highest on the tree.
JAMES WHITCOMB RILEY—*The Ripest Peach.*
(See CARMAN under APPLES)

PEAR

20
"Now, Sire," quod she, "for aught that may bityde,
I moste haue of the peres that I see,
Or I moote dye, so soore longeth me
To eten of the smalle peres grene."
CHAUCER—*Canterbury Tales. The Merchantes Tale.* L. 14,669.

21
The great white pear-tree dropped with dew from leaves
And blossom, under heavens of happy blue.
JEAN INGELOW—*Songs with Preludes. Wedlock.*

1 A pear-tree planted nigh:
'Twas charg'd with fruit that made a goodly show,
And hung with dangling pears was every bough.
POPE—*January and May.* L. 602.

PELICAN

2
What, wouldst thou have me turn pelican, and feed thee out of my own vitals?
CONGREVE—*Love for Love.* Act II. Sc. 1.

3
By them there sat the loving pelican,
Whose young ones, poison'd by the serpent's sting,
With her own blood to life again doth bring.
DRAYTON—*Noah's Flood.*

4
Nature's prime favourites were the Pelicans;
High-fed, long-lived, and sociable and free.
MONTGOMERY—*Pelican Island.* Canto V. L. 144.

5
Nimbly they seized and secreted their prey,
Alive and wriggling in the elastic net,
Which Nature hung beneath their grasping beaks;
Till, swoln with captures, the unwieldy burden
Clogg'd their slow flight, as heavily to land,
These mighty hunters of the deep return'd.
There on the cragged cliffs they perch'd at ease,
Gorging their hapless victims one by one;
Then full and weary, side by side, they slept,
Till evening roused them to the chase again.
MONTGOMERY—*Pelican Island.* Canto IV. L. 141.

6
The nursery of brooding Pelicans,
The dormitory of their dead, had vanish'd,
And all the minor spots of rock and verdure,
The abodes of happy millions, were no more.
MONTGOMERY—*Pelican Island.* Canto VI. L. 74.

PEN (See also AUTHORSHIP, JOURNALISM)

7
Art thou a pen, whose task shall be
To drown in ink
What writers think?
Oh, wisely write,
That pages white
Be not the worse for ink and thee.
ETHEL LYNN BEERS—*The Gold Nugget.*

8 Whose noble praise
Deserves a quill pluckt from an angel's wing.
DOROTHY BERRY—*Sonnet.* Prefixed to DIANA PRIMROSE'S *Chain of Pearls.* (1699)
(See also BYRON, CONSTABLE, DAVIES, NETHERSOLE, WORDSWORTH)

9
Beneath the rule of men entirely great
The pen is mightier than the sword.
BULWER-LYTTON—*Richelieu.* Act II. Sc. 2.
(See also BURTON)

10
Hinc quam sit calamus sævior euse, patet.
From this it appears how much more cruel the pen may be than the sword.
BURTON—*Anatomy of Melancholy.* Pt. I. Sec. XXI. Mem. 4. Subsec. 4.
(See also BULWER, MARVIN, ST. SIMON)

11
Oh! nature's noblest gift—my gray-goose quill!
Slave of my thoughts, obedient to my will,
Torn from thy parent-bird to form a pen,
That mighty instrument of little men!
BYRON—*English Bards and Scotch Reviewers.* L. 7.
(See also BERRY, also BYRON under EAGLE)

12
The pen wherewith thou dost so heavenly sing
Made of a quill from an angel's wing.
HENRY CONSTABLE—*Sonnet.* Found in Notes to TODD'S *Milton.* Vol. V. P. 454. (Ed. 1826.) (See also BERRY)

13
For what made that in glory shine so long
But poets' Pens, pluckt from Archangels' wings?
JOHN DAVIES—*Bien Venu.*
(See also BERRY)

14
The pen is mightier than the sword.
FRANKLIN—*Oration.* (1783)
(See also BULWER)

15
Anser, apie, vitellus, populus et regna gubernant.
Goose [pen] bee [wax] and calf [parchment] govern the world.
Quoted by JAMES HOWELL. *Letters.* Bk. II. Letter 2.

16
The pen became a clarion.
LONGFELLOW—*Monte Cassino.* St. 13.

17
The swifter hand doth the swift words outrun:
Before the tongue hath spoke the hand hath done.
MARTIAL—*Epigrams.* Bk. XIV. Ep. 208. Trans. by WRIGHT. (On a shorthand writer.)

18
The sacred Dove a quill did lend
From her high-soaring wing.
F. NETHERSOLE. Prefixed to GILES FLETCHER'S *Christ's Victorie.*
(See also BERRY)

19
Non sest aliena res, quæ fere ab honestis negligi solet, cura bene ac velociter scribendi.
Men of quality are in the wrong to undervalue, as they often do, the practise of a fair and quick hand in writing; for it is no immaterial accomplishment.
QUINTILIAN—*De Institutione Oratoria.* I. 5.

20
Qu'on me donne six lignes écrites de la main du plus honnête homme, j'y trouverai de quoi le faire pendre.
If you give me six lines written by the hand of the most honest of men, I will find something in them which will hang him.
Attributed to RICHELIEU, denied by FOURNIER—*L'Esprit dans l'Histoire.* Ch. 39. P. 159. (1857)

21
Tant la plume a eu sous le roi d'avantage sur l'épée.
So far had the pen, under the king, the superiority over the sword.
SAINT SIMON—*Mémoires.* Vol. III. P. 517. (1702) (Ed. 1856)
(See also BURTON)

1
Let there be gall enough in thy ink, though thou write with a goose-pen, no matter.
Twelfth Night. Act III. Sc. 2. L. 52.

2
You write with ease, to show your breeding,
But easy writing's curst hard reading.
R. B. SHERIDAN—*Clio's Protest.* See MOORE'S *Life of Sheridan.* Vol. I. P. 55.

3
The feather, whence the pen
Was shaped that traced the lives of these good men,
Dropped from an Angel's wing.
WORDSWORTH—*Ecclesiastical Sonnets.* Pt. III. V. *Walton's Book of Lives.*
(See also BERRY)

PEOPLE (See PUBLIC, The)

PERCEPTION (See also MIND, SIGHT)

4
As men of inward light are wont
To turn their optics in upon't.
BUTLER—*Hudibras.* Pt. III. Canto I. L. 481.

5
He gives us the very quintessence of perception.
LOWELL—*My Study Window. Coleridge.*

PERFECTION

6
Trifles make perfection, and perfection is no trifle.
MICHAEL ANGELO. See C. C. COLTON—*Lacon.*

7
What's come to perfection perishes,
Things learned on earth we shall practise in heaven;
Works done least rapidly Art most cherishes.
ROBERT BROWNING—*Old Pictures in Florence.* St. 17.

8
The very pink of perfection.
GOLDSMITH—*She Stoops to Conquer.* Act I. Sc. 1.

9
Whoever thinks a faultless piece to see,
Thinks what ne'er was, nor is, nor e'er shall be.
POPE—*Essay on Criticism.* Pt. II. L. 53.

10
Whose dear perfection hearts that scorn'd to serve
Humbly call'd mistress.
All's Well That Ends Well. Act V. Sc. 3. L. 16.

11
How many things by season season'd are
To their right praise and true perfection!
Merchant of Venice. Act V. Sc. 1. L. 107.

12
It is the witness still of excellency
To put a strange face on his own perfection.
Much Ado About Nothing. Act II. Sc. 3. L. 48.

13
A man cannot have an idea of perfection in another, which he was never sensible of in himself.
STEELE—*The Tatler.* No. 227.

14
In this broad earth of ours,
Amid the measureless grossness and the slag,
Enclosed and safe within its central heart,
Nestles the seed perfection.
WALT WHITMAN—*Song of the Universal.*

PERFUME

15
In virtue, nothing earthly could surpass her,
Save thine "incomparable oil," Macassar!
BYRON—*Don Juan.* Canto I. St. 17.

16
And the ripe harvest of the new-mown hay
Gives it a sweet and wholesome odour.
COLLEY CIBBER—*Richard III.* (*Altered.*) Act V. Sc. 3. L. 44.

17
I cannot talk with civet in the room,
A fine puss gentleman that's all perfume.
COWPER—*Conversation.* L. 283.

18
Soft carpet-knights all scenting musk and amber.
DU BARTAS—*Divine Weekes and Workes. Third Day.* Pt. I.

19
And ever since then, when the clock strikes two,
She walks unbidden from room to room,
And the air is filled that she passes through
With a subtle, sad perfume.
The delicate odor of mignonette,
The ghost of a dead and gone bouquet,
Is all that tells of her story—yet
Could she think of a sweeter way?
BRET HARTE—*Newport Legend.* Quoted by AUGUSTUS THOMAS in *The Witching Hour.*
(See also MEREDITH under JASMINE)

20
Look not for musk in a dog's kennel.
HERBERT—*Jacula Prudentum.*

21
A stream of rich distill'd perfumes.
MILTON—*Comus.* 556.

22
Sabean odours from the spicy shore
Of Arabie the blest.
MILTON—*Paradise Lost.* Bk. IV. L. 162.

23
An amber scent of odorous perfume
Her harbinger.
MILTON—*Samson Agonistes.* L. 720.

24
And all your courtly civet cats can vent
Perfume to you, to me is excrement.
POPE—*Epilogue to the Satires.* Dialogue II. L. 188.

25
And all Arabia breathes from yonder box.
POPE—*The Rape of the Lock.* Canto I. L. 134.

26
So perfumed that
The winds were love-sick.
Antony and Cleopatra. Act II. Sc. 2. L. 198.

27
From the barge
A strange invisible perfume hits the sense
Of the adjacent wharfs.
Antony and Cleopatra. Act II. Sc. 2. L. 216.

1 Hast thou not learn'd me how
To make perfumes? distil? preserve? yea, so
That our great king himself doth woo me oft
For my confections?
Cymbeline. Act I. Sc. 5. L. 12.

2
The perfumed tincture of the roses.
Sonnet LIV.

3 Take your paper, too,
And let me have them very well perfumed,
For she is sweeter than perfume itself
To whom they go to.
Taming of the Shrew. Act I. Sc. 2. L. 151.

4
Perfume for a lady's chamber.
Winter's Tale. Act IV. Sc. 4. L. 225.

PERILS

5
Ay me! what perils do environ
The man that meddles with cold iron!
BUTLER—*Hudibras.* Pt. I. Canto III. L. 1.

6
Ay me, how many perils doe enfold
The righteous man to make him daily fall!
SPENSER—*Faerie Queene.* Bk. I. Canto VIII. St. 1.

PERSEVERANCE

7
Attempt the end and never stand to doubt;
Nothing's so hard, but search will find it out.
HERRICK—*Seeke and Finde.*

8
The waters wear the stones.
Job. XIV. 19.
(See also LYLY)

9
God is with those who persevere.
Koran. Ch. VIII.

10
For thine own purpose, thou hast sent
The strife and the discouragement!
LONGFELLOW—*Christus. The Golden Legend.* Pt. II.

11
The soft droppes of rain perce the hard marble; many strokes overthrow the tallest oaks.
LYLY—*Euphues.* P. 81. ARBER'S Reprint. (1579)
(See also JOB, MENAGIANA, PLUTARCH, HENRY VI)

12
Gutta cavat lapidem non vi, sed sæpe cadendo.
The drop hollows out the stone not by strength, but by constant falling.
Quoted in the *Menagiana*, 1713. Probably first to use it was RICHARD, MONK OF S. VICTOR; Paris. (Died about 1172. Scotchman by birth.) In his *Adnotationes mysticæ in Psalmos* he says: "Quid lapide durius, quid aqua mollius? Verumtamen gutta cavat lapidem non vi sed sæpe cadendo." See MIGNE'S *Patrologia Latina.* Vol. CXCVI. P. 389. Said to be by CHŒRILUS OF SAMOS, by SIMPLICIUS—*Ad Aristot. Physic. Auscult.* VIII. 2. P. 429. (Brand's ed.) Same idea in LUCRETIUS I. 314; also in IV. 1282. Trans. of a proverb quoted by GALEN. Vol. VIII. P. 27. Ed. by KÜHN, 1821, Given there: "Gutta cavat lapidem sæpe cadentis aquæ." Quoted by BION. Also in OVID—*Ex Ponte.* IV. X. L. 5. Note by Burman states CLAUDIAN was earliest user found in MS.
(See also LYLY)

13
So Satan, whom repulse upon repulse
Met ever, and to shameful silence brought,
Yet gives not o'er, though desperate of success.
MILTON—*Paradise Regained.* Bk. IV. L. 21.

14
Water continually dropping will wear hard rocks hollow.
PLUTARCH—*Of the Training of Children.*
(See also LYLY)

15
We shall escape the uphill by never turning back.
CHRISTINA G. ROSSETTI—*Amor Mundi.*

16
Many strokes, though with a little axe,
Hew down and fell the hardest-timber'd oak.
Henry VI. Pt. III. Act II. Sc. 1. L. 54.

17 Perseverance, dear my lord,
Keeps honour bright: to have done is to hang
Quite out of fashion, like a rusty mail
In monumental mockery.
Troilus and Cressida. Act III. Sc. 3. L. 150.

PHEASANT

18
Fesaunt excedeth all fowles in sweetnesse and holsomnesse, and is equall to capon in nourishynge.
SIR T. ELYOT—*The Castle of Helth.* Ch. VIII.

19
The fesant hens of Colchis, which have two ears as it were consisting of feathers, which they will set up and lay down as they list.
PLINY—*Natural History.* Bk. X. Ch. XLVIII. HOLLAND'S trans.

20
See! from the brake the whirring pheasant springs,
And mounts exulting on triumphant wings:
Short is his joy; he feels the fiery wound,
Flutters in blood, and panting beats the ground.
POPE—*Windsor Forest.* L. 111.

PHILADELPHIA

21
They say that the lady from Philadelphia who is staying in town is very wise. Suppose I go ask her what is best to be done.
LUCRETIA P. HALE—*Peterkin Papers.* Ch. I.

22
Hail! Philadelphia, tho' Quaker thou be,
The birth-day of medical honors to thee
In this country belongs; 'twas thou caught the flame,
That crossing the ocean from Englishmen came
And kindled the fires of Wisdom and Knowledge,
Inspired the student, erected a college,
First held a commencement with suitable state,
In the year of our Lord, seventeen sixty-eight.
WM. TODD HELMUTH—*The Story of a City Doctor.*

PHILANTHROPY (See also BENEFITS, CHARITY)

1
Now there was at Joppa a certain disciple named Tabitha, which by interpretation is called Dorcas: this woman was full of good works and almsdeeds which she did.
Acts. IX. 36.

2
Gifts and alms are the expressions, not the essence, of this virtue.
ADDISON—*The Guardian*. No. 166.

3
He scorn'd his own, who felt another's woe.
CAMPBELL—*Gertrude of Wyoming*. Pt. I. St. 24.

4
Our sympathy is cold to the relation of distant misery.
GIBBON—*Decline and Fall of the Roman Empire*. Ch. XLIX.

5
His house was known to all the vagrant train,
He chid their wanderings but reliev'd their pain;
The long remembered beggar was his guest,
Whose beard descending swept his aged breast.
GOLDSMITH—*Deserted Village*. L. 149.

6
Careless their merits or their faults to scan,
His pity gave ere charity began.
GOLDSMITH—*Deserted Village*. L. 161.

7
A kind and gentle heart he had,
To comfort friends and foes;
The naked every day he clad
When he put on his clothes.
GOLDSMITH—*Elegy on the Death of a Mad Dog*.

8
Large was his bounty, and his soul sincere,
Heaven did a recompense as largely send;
He gave to misery (all he had) a tear,
He gain'd from Heaven ('twas all he wish'd) a friend.
GRAY—*Elegy. The Epitaph*.

9
Scatter plenty o'er a smiling land.
GRAY—*Elegy in a Country Churchyard*. St. 16.

10
Steal the hog, and give the feet for alms.
HERBERT—*Jacula Prudentum*.

11
By Jove the stranger and the poor are sent,
And what to those we give, to Jove is lent.
HOMER—*Odyssey*. Bk. VI. L. 247. POPE'S trans.

12
It never was our guise
To slight the poor, or aught humane despise.
HOMER—*Odyssey*. Bk. XIV. L. 65. POPE'S trans.

13
In every sorrowing soul I pour'd delight,
And poverty stood smiling in my sight.
HOMER—*Odyssey*. Bk. XVII. L. 505. POPE'S trans.

14
Alas! for the rarity
Of Christian charity
Under the sun.
Oh! it was pitiful!
Near a whole city full,
Home had she none.
HOOD—*The Bridge of Sighs*.

15
He is one of those wise philanthropists who, in a time of famine, would vote for nothing but a supply of toothpicks.
DOUGLAS JERROLD—*Douglas Jerrold's Wit*.

16
I was eyes to the blind, and feet was I to the lame.
Job. XXIX. 15.

17
In Misery's darkest caverns known,
His useful care was ever nigh,
Where hopeless Anguish pour'd his groan,
And lonely want retir'd to die.
SAMUEL JOHNSON—*On the Death of Mr. Robert Levet*. St. 5. In BOSWELL'S *Life of Johnson*. (1782) ("Useful care" reads "ready help" in first ed.)

18
Shut not thy purse-strings always against painted distress.
LAMB—*Complaint of the Decay of Beggars in the Metropolis*.

19
Help thi kynne, Crist bit (biddeth), for ther bygynneth charitie.
LANGLAND—*Piers Plowman. Passus*. 18. L. 61.

20
Who gives himself with his alms feeds three,
Himself, his hungering neighbor, and me.
LOWELL—*The Vision of Sir Launfal*. Pt. II. VIII.

21
Nec sibi sed toti genitum se credere mundo.
He believed that he was born, not for himself, but for the whole world.
LUCAN—*Pharsalia*. II. 383.

22
To pity distress is but human; to relieve it is Godlike.
HORACE MANN—*Lectures on Education*. Lecture VI.

23
Take heed that ye do not your alms before men, to be seen of them.
Matthew. VI. 1.

24
When thou doest alms, let not thy left hand know what thy right hand doeth.
Matthew. VI. 3.

25
Pity the sorrows of a poor old man,
Whose trembling limbs have brought him to your door.
THOS. MOSS—*The Beggar's Petition*.

26
The organized charity, scrimped and iced,
In the name of a cautious, statistical Christ.
JOHN BOYLE O'REILLY—*In Bohemia*.

27
Misero datur quodcunque, fortunæ datur.
Whatever we give to the wretched, we lend to fortune.
SENECA—*Troades*. 697.

1
For his bounty
There was no winter in't; an autumn 'twas
That grew the more by reaping: his delights
Were dolphin-like.
Antony and Cleopatra. Act V. Sc. 2. L. 87.

2
For this relief, much thanks: 'tis bitter cold,
And I am sick at heart.
Hamlet. Act I. Sc. 1. L. 8.

3
A tear for pity and a hand
Open as day for melting charity.
Henry IV. Pt. II. Act IV. Sc. 4. L. 31.

4
Speak with me, pity me, open the door:
A beggar begs that never begg'd before.
Richard II. Act V. Sc. 3. L. 77.

5
'Tis not enough to help the feeble up,
But to support him after.
Timon of Athens. Act I. Sc. 1. L. 107.

6
You find people ready enough to do the Samaritan, without the oil and twopence.
SYDNEY SMITH—*Lady Holland's Memoir.* Vol. I. P. 261. 1st Ed. London.

7
'Tis a little thing
To give a cup of water; yet its draught
Of cool refreshment, drain'd by fever'd lips,
May give a shock of pleasure to the frame
More exquisite than when nectarean juice
Renews the life of joy in happiest hours.
THOS. NOON TALFOURD—*Ion.* Act I. Sc. 2.

8
Non ignara mali miseris succurrere disco.

Being myself no stranger to suffering, I have learned to relieve the sufferings of others.
VERGIL—*Æneid.* I. 630.

9
The poor must be wisely visited and liberally cared for, so that mendicity shall not be tempted into mendacity, nor want exasperated into crime.
ROBERT C. WINTHROP—*Yorktown Oration in 1881.*

PHILOSOPHY

10
A little philosophy inclineth man's mind to atheism; but depth in philosophy bringeth men's minds about to religion.
BACON—*Essays. Atheism.*

11
Sublime Philosophy!
Thou art the patriarch's ladder, reaching heaven;
And bright with beckoning angels —but alas!
We see thee, like the patriarch, but in dreams,
By the first step,—dull slumbering on the earth.
BULWER-LYTTON—*Richelieu.* Act III. Sc. 1. L. 4.

12
Beside, he was a shrewd philosopher,
And had read ev'ry text and gloss over
Whate'er the crabbed'st author hath,
He understood b' implicit faith.
BUTLER—*Hudibras.* Pt. I. Canto I. L. 127.

13
Before Philosophy can teach by Experience, the Philosophy has to be in readiness, the Experience must be gathered and intelligibly recorded.
CARLYLE—*Essays. On History.*
(See also CARLYLE under HISTORY)

14
O vitæ philosophia dux! O virtutis indagatrix, expultrixque vitiorum! Quid non modo nos, sed omnino vita hominum sine et esse potuisset? Tu urbes peperisti; tu dissipatos homines in societatum vitæ convocasti.

O philosophy, life's guide! O searcher-out of virtue and expeller of vices! What could we and every age of men have been without thee? Thou hast produced cities; thou hast called men scattered about into the social enjoyment of life.
CICERO—*Tusc. Quæst.* Bk. V. 2. 5.

15
The first step towards philosophy is incredulity.
DENIS DIDEROT—*Last Conversation.*

16
The Beginning of Philosophy * * * is a Consciousness of your own Weakness and inability in necessary things.
EPICTETUS—*Discourses.* Bk. II. Ch. XI. St. 1.

17
Philosophy goes no further than probabilities, and in every assertion keeps a doubt in reserve.
FROUDE—*Short Studies on Great Subjects. Calvinism.*

18
This same philosophy is a good horse in the stable, but an arrant jade on a journey.
GOLDSMITH—*The Good-Natured Man.* Act I.

19
How charming is divine philosophy!
Not harsh, and crabbed, as dull fools suppose,
But musical as is Apollo's lute,
And a perpetual feast of nectar'd sweets,
Where no crude surfeit reigns.
MILTON—*Mask of Comus.* L. 476.

20
That stone, * * *
Philosophers in vain so long have sought.
MILTON—*Paradise Lost.* Bk. III. L. 600.

21
Se moquer de la philosophie c'est vraiment philosophe.

To ridicule philosophy is truly philosophical.
PASCAL—*Pensées.* Art. VII. 35.

22
Philosophy is nothing but Discretion.
JOHN SELDEN—*Table Talk. Philosophy.*

23
There are more things in heaven and earth, Horatio,
Than are dreamt of in your philosophy.
Hamlet. Act I. Sc. 5. L. 166. ("Our philosophy" in some readings.)

24
Adversity's sweet milk, philosophy.
Romeo and Juliet. Act III. Sc. 3. L. 55.

25
The philosopher is Nature's pilot. And there you have our difference: to be in hell is to drift: to be in heaven is to steer.
BERNARD SHAW—*Man and Superman.* Act III.

26
La clarté est la bonne foi des philosophes.

Clearness marks the sincerity of philosophers.
VAUVENARGUES—*Pensées Diverses.* No. 372. GILBERT's ed. 1857. Vol. I. P. 475.

1
The bosom-weight, your stubborn gift,
That no philosophy can lift.
WORDSWORTH—*Presentiments.*

2
Why should not grave Philosophy be styled.
Herself, a dreamer of a kindred stock,
A dreamer, yet more spiritless and dull?
WORDSWORTH—*The Excursion.* Bk. III.

PHRENOLOGY

3
'Tis strange how like a very dunce,
Man, with his bumps upon his sconce,
Has lived so long, and yet no knowledge he
Has had, till lately, of Phrenology—
A science that by simple dint of
Head-combing he should find a hint of,
When scratching o'er those little pole-hills
The faculties throw up like mole hills.
HOOD—*Craniology.*

PIGEON

4
Wood-pigeons cooed there, stock-doves nestled there;
My trees were full of songs and flowers and fruit,
Their branches spread a city to the air.
CHRISTINA G. ROSSETTI—*From House to Home.* St. 7.

5
With his mouth full of news
Which he will put on us, as pigeons feed their young.
As You Like It. Act I. Sc. 2. L. 98.

6
Thou pigeon-egg of discretion.
Love's Labour's Lost. Act V. Sc. 1. L. 75.

7
This fellow pecks up wit as pigeons pease.
Love's Labour's Lost. Act V. Sc. 2. L. 315.

8
'Tis a bird I love, with its brooding note,
And the trembling throb in its mottled throat;
There's a human look in its swelling breast,
And the gentle curve of its lowly crest;
And I often stop with the fear I feel—
He runs so close to the rapid wheel.
WILLIS—*The Belfry Pigeon.*

PINE

Pinus

9
Shaggy shade
Of desert-loving pine, whose emerald scalp
Nods to the storm.
BYRON—*The Prophecy of Dante.* Canto II. L. 63.

10
Risest from forth thy silent sea of pines.
COLERIDGE—*Hymn Before Sunrise in the Vale of Chamouni.*

11
'Twas on the inner bark, stripped from the pine,
Our father pencilled this epistle rare;
Two blazing pine knots did his torches shine,
Two braided pallets formed his desk and chair.
DURFEE—*What-Cheer.* Canto II.

12
As sunbeams stream through liberal space
And nothing jostle or displace,
So waved the pine-tree through my thought
And fanned the dreams it never brought.
EMERSON—*Woodnotes.* II.

13
Like two cathedral towers these stately pines
Uplift their fretted summits tipped with cones;
The arch beneath them is not built with stones,
Not Art but Nature traced these lovely lines,
And carved this graceful arabesque of vines;
No organ but the wind here sighs and moans,
No sepulchre conceals a martyr's bones,
No marble bishop on his tomb reclines.
Enter! the pavement, carpeted with leaves,
Gives back a softened echo to thy tread!
Listen! the choir is singing; all the birds,
In leafy galleries beneath the eaves,
Are singing! listen, ere the sound be fled,
And learn there may be worship without words.
LONGFELLOW—*Sonnets. My Cathedral.*

14
Under the yaller pines I house,
When sunshine makes 'em all sweet-scented,
An' hear among their furry boughs
The baskin' west-wind purr contented.
LOWELL—*The Biglow Papers.* Second Series. No. 10.

15
The pine is the mother of legends.
LOWELL—*The Growth of a Legend.*

16
To archèd walks of twilight groves,
And shadows brown that Sylvan loves,
Of pine.
MILTON—*Il Penseroso.* L. 133.

17
Here also grew the rougher rinded pine,
The great Argoan ship's brave ornament.
SPENSER—*Virgil's Gnat.* L. 209.

18
Ancient Pines,
Ye bear no record of the years of man.
Spring is your sole historian.
BAYARD TAYLOR—*The Pine Forest of Monterey.*

19
Stately Pines,
But few more years around the promontory
Your chant will meet the thunders of the sea.
BAYARD TAYLOR—*The Pine Forest of Monterey.*

PINK

Dianthus

20
You take a pink,
You dig about its roots and water it,
And so improve it to a garden-pink,
But will not change it to a heliotrope.
E. B. BROWNING—*Aurora Leigh.* Bk. VI.

21
And I will pu' the pink, the emblem o' my dear,
For she's the pink o' womankind, and blooms without a peer.
BURNS—*O Luve Will Venture In.*

22
The beauteous pink I would not slight,
Pride of the gardener's leisure.
GOETHE—*The Floweret Wondrous Fair.* St. 8.
JOHN S. DWIGHT's trans.

PITY

1
Of all the paths that lead to a woman's love
Pity's the straightest.
BEAUMONT AND FLETCHER—*Knight of Malta.* Act I. Sc. 1. L. 73.
(See also DRYDEN, SHERIDAN, SOUTHERNE)

2
Pity, some say, is the parent of future love.
BEAUMONT AND FLETCHER—*Spanish Curate.* Act V. Sc. 1.

3
Pity speaks to grief
More sweetly than a band of instruments.
BARRY CORNWALL—*Florentine Party.*

4
For pity melts the mind to love.
Softly sweet, in Lydian measures,
Soon he sooth'd his soul to pleasures.
War, he sung, is toil and trouble;
Honour but an empty bubble.
DRYDEN—*Alexander's Feast.* L. 96.
(See also BEAUMONT)

5
More helpful than all wisdom is one draught of simple human pity that will not forsake us.
GEORGE ELIOT—*Mill on the Floss.* Bk. VII. Ch. I.

6
Taught by that Power that pities me,
I learn to pity them.
GOLDSMITH—*Hermit.* St. 6.

7
La plaincte et la commiseration sont meslees à quelque estimation de la chose qu'on plaind.
Pity and commiseration are mixed with some regard for the thing which one pities.
MONTAIGNE—*Essays.* Bk. I. Ch. L.

8
At length some pity warm'd the master's breast
('Twas then, his threshold first receiv'd a guest),
Slow creaking turns the door with jealous care,
And half he welcomes in the shivering pair.
PARNELL—*The Hermit.* L. 97.

9
O God, show compassion on the wicked.
The virtuous have already been blessed by Thee in being virtuous.
Prayer of a Persian Dervish.

10
My pity hath been balm to heal their wounds,
My mildness hath allay'd their swelling griefs.
Henry VI. Pt. III. Act IV. Sc. 8. L. 41.

11
My friend, I spy some pity in thy looks;
O, if thine eye be not a flatterer,
Come thou on my side, and entreat for me,
As you would beg, were you in my distress:
A begging prince what beggar pities not?
Richard III. Act I. Sc. 4. L. 270.

12
Tear-falling pity dwells not in his eye.
Richard III. Act IV. Sc. 2. L. 66.

13
I shall despair. There is no creature loves me;
And if I die, no soul shall pity me:
Nay, wherefore should they, since that I myself
Find in myself no pity to myself?
Richard III. Act V. Sc. 3. L. 200.

14
Is there no pity sitting in the clouds,
That sees into the bottom of my grief?
Romeo and Juliet. Act III. Sc. 5. L. 198.

15
But, I perceive,
Men must learn now with pity to dispense;
For policy sits above conscience.
Timon of Athens. Act III. Sc. 2. L. 92.

16
Pity is the virtue of the law,
And none but tyrants use it cruelly.
Timon of Athens. Act III. Sc. 5. L. 8.

17
Soft pity never leaves the gentle breast
Where love has been received a welcome guest.
R. B. SHERIDAN—*The Duenna.* Act II.
(See also BEAUMONT)

18
Pity's akin to love; and every thought
Of that soft kind is welcome to my soul.
THOS. SOUTHERNE—*Oroonoko.* Act II. Sc. 2. L. 64.
(See also BEAUMONT)

PLAGIARISM

19
They lard their lean books with the fat of others' works.
BURTON—*Anatomy of Melancholy. Democritus to the Reader.*

20
We can say nothing but what hath been said,
* * * Our poets steal from Homer * * *
Our storydressers do as much; he that comes last is commonly best.
BURTON—*Anatomy of Melancholy. Democritus to the Reader.*
(See also KIPLING)

21
Who, to patch up his fame—or fill his purse—
Still pilfers wretched plans, and makes them worse;
Like gypsies, lest the stolen brat be known,
Defacing first, then claiming for his own.
CHURCHILL—*The Apology.* L. 232.
(See also DAVENANT, D'ISRAELI, MONTAIGNE, SHERIDAN, YOUNG)

22
Because they commonly make use of treasure found in books, as of other treasure belonging to the dead and hidden underground; for they dispose of both with great secrecy, defacing the shape and image of the one as much as of the other.
DAVENANT—*Gondibert. Preface.*
(See also CHURCHILL)

23
The Plagiarism of orators is the art, or an ingenious and easy mode, which some adroitly employ to change, or disguise, all sorts of speeches of their own composition, or that of other authors, for their pleasure, or their utility; in such a manner that it becomes impossible even for the author himself to recognise his own work, his own genius, and his own style, so skilfully shall the whole be disguised.
ISAAC D'ISRAELI—*Curiosities of Literature. Professors of Plagiarism and Obscurity.*

1
Pereant qui ante nos nostra dixerent.

Perish those who said our good things before we did.

ÆLIUS DONATUS, according to ST. JEROME—*Commentary on Ecclesiastes*. Ch. I. Referring to the words of TERENCE.

2
When Shakespeare is charged with debts to his authors, Landor replies, "Yet he was more original than his originals. He breathed upon dead bodies and brought them into life."

EMERSON—*Letters and Social Aims*. *Quotation and Originality*.

3
It has come to be practically a sort of rule in literature, that a man, having once shown himself capable of original writing, is entitled thenceforth to steal from the writings of others at discretion.

EMERSON—*Shakespeare*.

4
He that readeth good writers and pickes out their flowres for his own nose, is lyke a foole.

STEPHEN GOSSON—*In the School of Abuse. Loyterers.*

5
When 'Omer smote 'is bloomin' lyre,
He'd 'eard men sing by land an' sea;
An' what he thought 'e might require,
'E went an' took—the same as me.

KIPLING—*Barrack-Room Ballads*. *Introduction.*

(See also BURTON)

6
My books need no one to accuse or judge you: the page which is yours stands up against you and says, "You are a thief."

MARTIAL—*Epigrams*. Bk. I. Ep. 53.

7
Why, simpleton, do you mix your verses with mine? What have you to do, foolish man, with writings that convict you of theft? Why do you attempt to associate foxes with lions, and make owls pass for eagles? Though you had one of Ladas's legs, you would not be able, blockhead, to run with the other leg of wood.

MARTIAL—*Epigrams*. Bk. X. Ep. 100.

8
For such kind of borrowing as this, if it be not bettered by the borrower, among good authors is accounted plagiary.

MILTON—*Iconoclastes*. XXIII.

9
Je reprends mon bien où je le trouve.

I recover my property wherever I find it.

MOLIÈRE. CYRANO DE BERGERAC incorporated a scene confidentially communicated to him by MOLIÈRE, in his *Pédant Joué*. II. 4. MOLIÈRE taking possession, used it in his *Les Fourberies de Scapin*. EMERSON—*Letters and Social Aims,* attributes the mot to MARMONTEL.

10
Les abeilles pillotent deçà delà les fleurs; mais elles en font aprez le miel, qui est tout leur; ce n'est plus thym, ny marjolaine: ainsi les pièces empruntées d'aultruy, il les transformera et confondra pour en faire un ouvrage tout sien.

The bees pillage the flowers here and there but they make honey of them which is all their own; it is no longer thyme or marjolaine: so the pieces borrowed from others he will transform and mix up into a work all his own.

MONTAIGNE—*Essays*. Bk. I. Ch. XXV.

11
Amongst so many borrowed things, am glad if I can steal one, disguising and altering it for some new service.

MONTAIGNE—*Essays. Of Physiognomy.*

(See also CHURCHILL)

12
He liked those literary cooks
Who skim the cream of others' books;
And ruin half an author's graces
By plucking *bon-mots* from their places.

HANNAH MORE—*Florio, the Bas Blue.*

13
Take the whole range of imaginative literature, and we are all wholesale borrowers. In every matter that relates to invention, to use, or beauty or form, we are borrowers.

WENDELL PHILLIPS—*Lecture*. *The Lost Arts.*

14
Leurs écrits sont des vois qu'ils nous ont faits d'avance.

Their writings are thoughts stolen from us by anticipation.

PIRON—*La Métromanie*. III. 6.

15
Next o'er his books his eyes began to roll,
In pleasing memory of all he stole;
How here he sipp'd, how there he plunder'd snug,
And suck'd all o'er like an industrious bug.

POPE—*Dunciad*. Bk. I. L. 127.

16
With him most authors steal their works, or buy;
Garth did not write his own Dispensary.

POPE—*Essay on Criticism*. L. 618.

17
The seed ye sow, another reaps;
The wealth ye find, another keeps:
The robes ye weave, another wears:
The arms ye forge another bears.

SHELLEY—*To the Men of England.*

(See also VERGIL)

18
Steal!—to be sure they may; and egad, serve your best thoughts as gypsies do stolen children, disfigure them to make 'em pass for their own.

R. B. SHERIDAN—*The Critic*. Act I. Sc. 1.

(See also CHURCHILL)

19
Libertas et natale solum.

Fine words! I wonder where you stole 'em.

SWIFT. Upon CHIEF JUSTICE WHITSHED'S *Motto* for his coach. (1724)

20
Nullum est jam dictum quod non dictum sit primus.

Nothing is said nowadays that has not been said before.

TERENCE—*Eunuchus*. *Prologue*. XLI. As quoted by Donatus. See WARTON—*Essay on Pope*. Note I. P. 88. Ed. 1806.

(See also DONATUS)

21
Hos ego versiculos feci, tulit alter honores
Sic vos non vobis nidificatis aves:
Sic vos non vobis vellera fertis oves:
Sic vos non vobis mellificatis apes:
Sic vos non vobis fertis aratra boves.

I wrote these lines; another wears the bays:
Thus you for others build your nests, O birds:
Thus you for others bear your fleece, O sheep:
Thus you for others honey make, O bees:
Thus you for others drag the plough, O kine.
VERGIL—*Claudius Donatus.* Delphin ed. of *Life of Vergil.* 1830. P. 17.
(See also SHELLEY)

1
Call them if you please bookmakers, not authors; range them rather among second-hand dealers than plagiarists.
VOLTAIRE—*A Philosophical Dictionary. Plagiarism.*

2
Who borrow much, then fairly make it known,
And damn it with improvements of their own.
YOUNG—*Love of Fame.* Satire III. L. 23.

PLANTS (See TREES)

PLEASURE

3
O Athenians, what toil do I undergo to please you!
ALEXANDER THE GREAT. Quoted by CARLYLE—*Essay on Voltaire.*

4
It is happy for you that you possess the talent of pleasing with delicacy. May I ask whether these pleasing attentions proceed from the impulse of the moment, or are the result of previous study?
JANE AUSTEN—*Pride and Prejudice.* Ch. XIV.
(See also LYTTLETON)

5
Pleasures lie thickest where no pleasures seem;
There's not a leaf that falls upon the ground
But holds some joy of silence or of sound,
Some sprite begotten of a summer dream.
BLANCHARD—*Sonnet VII. Hidden Joys.*

6
Every age has its pleasures, its style of wit, and its own ways.
NICHOLAS BOILEAU-DESPREAUX—*The Art of Poetry.* Canto III. L. 374.

7
But pleasures are like poppies spread;
You seize the flower, its bloom is shed.
Or like the snow falls in the river,
A moment white—then melts forever.
BURNS—*Tam o' Shanter.* L. 59.
(See also TAGORE)

8
The rule of my life is to make business a pleasure, and pleasure my business.
AARON BURR—*Letter to Pichon.*

9
Doubtless the pleasure is as great
Of being cheated as to cheat.
BUTLER—*Hudibras.* Pt. II. Canto III. L. 1.

10
There is a pleasure in the pathless woods,
There is a rapture on the lonely shore,
There is society where none intrudes
By the deep Sea, and music in its roar.
BYRON—*Childe Harold.* Canto IV. St. 178.

11
Ludendi etiam est quidam modus retinendus, ut ne nimis omnia profundamus, elatique voluptate in aliquam turpitudinem delabamur.
In our amusements a certain limit is to be placed that we may not devote ourselves to a life of pleasure and thence fall into immorality.
CICERO—*De Officiis.* I. 29.

12
Omnibus in rebus voluptatibus maximis fastidium finitimum est.
In everything satiety closely follows the greatest pleasures.
CICERO—*De Oratore.* III. 25.

13
Voluptas mentis (ut ita dicam) præstringit oculos, nec habet ullum cum virtute commercium.
Pleasure blinds (so to speak) the eyes of the mind, and has no fellowship with virtue.
CICERO—*De Senectute.* XII.

14
Divine Plato escam malorum appeliat voluptatem, quod ea videlicet homines capiantur, ut pisces hamo.
Plato divinely calls pleasure the bait of evil, inasmuch as men are caught by it as fish by a hook.
CICERO—*De Senectute.* XIII. 44.

15
Who pleases one against his will.
CONGREVE—*The Way of the World. Epilogue.*

16
That, though on pleasure she was bent,
She had a frugal mind.
COWPER—*History of John Gilpin.* St. 8.

17
Pleasure admitted in undue degree
Enslaves the will, nor leaves the judgment free.
COWPER—*Progress of Error.* L. 267.

18
Rich the treasure,
Sweet the pleasure,
Sweet is pleasure after pain.
DRYDEN—*Alexander's Feast.* L. 58.
(See also HORACE, MEREDITH, SPENSER)

19
Men may scoff, and men may pray,
But they pay
Every pleasure with a pain.
HENLEY—*Ballade of Truisms.*

20
Follow pleasure, and then will pleasure flee,
Flee pleasure, and pleasure will follow thee.
HEYWOOD—*Proverbs.* Pt. I. Ch. X.

21
Ficta voluptatis causa sint proxima veris.
Let the fictitious sources of pleasure be as near as possible to the true.
HORACE—*Ars Poetica.* 338.

22
Sperne voluptates; nocet empta dolore voluptas.
Despise pleasure; pleasure bought by pain is injurious.
HORACE—*Epistles.* I. 2. 55.

23
Vivo et regno, simul ista reliqui
Quæ vos ad cœlum effertis rumore secundo.
I live and reign since I have abandoned those pleasures which you by your praises extol to the skies.
HORACE—*Epistles.* I. 10. 8.

24
I fly from pleasure, because pleasure has ceased to please: I am lonely because I am miserable.
SAMUEL JOHNSON—*Rasselas.* Ch. III.

1
Pleasure the servant, Virtue looking on.
Ben Jonson—*Pleasure Reconciled to Virtue.*

2
Voluptates commendat rarior usus.
Rare indulgence produces greater pleasure.
Juvenal—*Satires.* XI. 208.

3
Medio de fonte leporum
Surgit amari aliquid, quod in ipsis floribus angat.
From the midst of the fountains of pleasures there rises something of bitterness which torments us amid the very flowers.
Lucretius—*De Rerum Nat.* Bk. IV. 11. 26.

4
Ah, no! the conquest was obtained with ease;
He pleased you by not studying to please.
George Lyttleton—*Progress of Love.* 3.

5
There is a pleasure which is born of pain.
Owen Meredith (Lord Lytton)—*The Wanderer.* Bk. I. *Prologue.* Pt. I.
(See also Dryden)

6
Take all the pleasures of all the spheres,
And multiply each through endless years,
One minute of Heaven is worth them all.
Moore—*Lalla Rookh. Paradise and the Peri.*

7
The roses of pleasure seldom last long enough to adorn the brow of him who plucks them; for they are the only roses which do not retain their sweetness after they have lost their beauty.
Hannah More—*Essays on Various Subjects. On Dissipation.*

8
God made all pleasures innocent.
Mrs. Norton—*Lady of La Garaye.* Pt. I.

9
Quod licet est ingratum quod non licet acrius urit.
What is lawful is undesirable; what is unlawful is very attractive.
Ovid—*Amorum.* II. 19. 3.
(See also Quintilian, Tacitus)

10
Blanda truces animos fertur mollisse voluptas.
Alluring pleasure is said to have softened the savage dispositions (of early mankind).
Ovid—*Ars Amatoria.* Bk. II. 477.

11
Usque adeo nulli sincera voluptas,
Solicitique aliquid lætis intervenit.
No one possesses unalloyed pleasure; there is some anxiety mingled with the joy.
Ovid—*Metamorphoses.* VII. 453.

12
Pleasures are ever in our hands or eyes;
And when in act they cease, in prospect rise.
Pope—*Essay on Man.* Ep. II. L. 123.

13
Reason's whole pleasure, all the joys of sense,
Lie in three words,—health, peace, and competence.
Pope—*Essay on Man.* Ep. IV. L. 79.

14
The little pleasure of the game
Is from afar to view the flight.
Prior—*To the Hon. C. Montague.*
But all the pleasure of the game,
Is afar off to view the flight. (In ed. of 1692.)

15
Dum licet inter nos igitur lætemur amantes;
Non satis est ullo tempore longus amor.
Let us enjoy pleasure while we can; pleasure is never long enough.
Propertius—*Elegiæ.* I. 19. 25.

16
Diliguntur immodice sola quæ non licent; * * * non nutrit ardorem concupiscendi, ubi frui licet.
Forbidden pleasures alone are loved immoderately; when lawful, they do not excite desire.
Quintilian—*Declamationes.* XIV. 18.
(See also Ovid)

17
Continuis voluptatibus vicina satietas.
Satiety is a neighbor to continued pleasures.
Quintilian—*Declamationes.* XXX. 6.

18
Spangling the wave with lights as vain
As pleasures in this vale of pain,
That dazzle as they fade.
Scott—*Lord of the Isles.* Canto I. St. 23.

19
Boys who, being mature in knowledge,
Pawn their experience to their present pleasure.
Antony and Cleopatra. Act I. Sc. 4. L. 31.

20
And painefull pleasure turnes to pleasing paine.
Spenser—*Faerie Queene.* Bk. III. Canto X. St. 60.
(See also Dryden)

21
Non quam multis placeas, sed qualibus stude.
Do not care how many, but whom, you please.
Syrus—*Maxims.*

22
Prævalent illicita.
Things forbidden have a secret charm.
Tacitus—*Annales.* XIII. 1.
(See also Ovid)

23
Pleasure is frail like a dewdrop, while it laughs it dies. But sorrow is strong and abiding. Let sorrowful love wake in your eyes.
Rabindrath Tagore—*Gardener.* 27.
(See also Burns)

24
I built my soul a lordly pleasure-house,
Wherein at ease for aye to dwell.
Tennyson—*The Palace of Art.* St. 1.

25
Nam id arbitror
Adprime in vita esse utile ut ne quid nimis.
I hold this to be the rule of life, "Too much of anything is bad."
Terence—*Andria.* I. 1. 33.

26
They who are pleased themselves must always please.
Thomson—*The Castle of Indolence.* Canto I. St. 15.

27
Trahit sua quemque voluptas.
His own especial pleasure attracts each one.
Vergil—*Eclogæ.* II. 65.

28
Zu oft ist kurze Lust die Quelle langer Schmerzen!
Too oft is transient pleasure the source of long woes.
Wieland—*Oberon.* II. 52.

1 Sure as night follows day,
Death treads in Pleasure's footsteps round the world,
When Pleasure treads the paths which Reason shuns.
YOUNG—*Night Thoughts.* Night V. L. 863.

2
To frown at pleasure, and to smile in pain.
YOUNG—*Night Thoughts.* Night VIII. L. 1,045.

POETRY (See also POETS)

3
Poetry is itself a thing of God;
He made his prophets poets; and the more
We feel of poesie do we become
Like God in love and power,—under-makers.
BAILEY—*Festus.* Proem. L. 5.

4 You speak
As one who fed on poetry.
BULWER-LYTTON—*Richelieu.* Act I. Sc. 1.

5
For rhyme the rudder is of verses,
With which, like ships, they steer their courses.
BUTLER—*Hudibras.* Pt. I. Canto I. L. 463.

6
Some force whole regions, in despite
O' geography, to change their site;
Make former times shake hands with latter,
And that which was before come after;
But those that write in rhyme still make
The one verse for the other's sake;
For one for sense, and one for rhyme,
I think's sufficient at one time.
BUTLER—*Hudibras.* Pt. II. Canto I. L. 23.

7
Nor florid prose, nor honied lies of rhyme,
Can blazon evil deeds, or consecrate a crime.
BYRON—*Childe Harold.* Canto I. St. 3.

8
The fatal facility of the octosyllabic verse.
BYRON—*Corsair. Preface.*

9
Poetry, therefore, we will call *Musical Thought.*
CARLYLE—*Heroes and Hero Worship.* 3.

10
For there is no heroic poem in the world but is at bottom a biography, the life of a man; also, it may be said, there is no life of a man, faithfully recorded, but is a heroic poem of its sort, rhymed or unrhymed.
CARLYLE—*Sir Walter Scott. London and Westminster Review.* (1838)
(See also EMERSON)

11
In the hexameter rises the fountain's silvery column:
In the pentameter aye falling in melody back.
COLERIDGE—*The Ovidian Elegiac Metre.*

12
Prose—words in their best order;—poetry—the best words in their best order.
COLERIDGE—*Table Talk.* July 12, 1827.

13
Made poetry a mere mechanic art.
COWPER—*Table Talk.* L. 654.

14
Feel you the barren flattery of a rhyme?
Can poets soothe you, when you pine for bread,
By winding myrtle round your ruin'd shed?
CRABBE—*The Village.* Bk. I.

15
Why then we should drop into poetry.
DICKENS—*Our Mutual Friend.* Bk. I. Ch. V.

16
When the brain gets as dry as an empty nut,
When the reason stands on its squarest toes,
When the mind (like a beard) has a "formal cut,"—
There is a place and enough for the pains of prose;
But whenever the May-blood stirs and glows,
And the young year draws to the "golden prime,"
And Sir Romeo sticks in his ear a rose,—
Then hey! for the ripple of laughing rhyme!
AUSTIN DOBSON—*The Ballad of Prose and Rhyme.*

17
Doeg, though without knowing how or why,
Made still a blundering kind of melody;
Spurr'd boldly on, and dash'd through thick and thin,
Through sense and nonsense, never out nor in;
Free from all meaning whether good or bad,
And in one word, heroically mad.
DRYDEN—*Absalom and Achitophel.* Pt. II. L. 412. "Thick and thin."
(See also BUTLER, SPENSER under CONSTANCY)

18
'Twas he that ranged the words at random flung,
Pierced the fair pearls and them together strung.
EASTWICK—*Anvari Suhaili.* Rendering of BIDPAI.
(See also LOWELL, TENNYSON)

19
The true poem is the poet's mind.
EMERSON—*Essays. Of History.*

20
For it is not metres, but a metre-making argument that makes a poem.
EMERSON—*Essays. The Poet.*

21
It does not need that a poem should be long. Every word was once a poem.
EMERSON—*Essays. The Poet.*

22
The finest poetry was first experience.
EMERSON—*Shakespeare.*
(See also CARLYLE)

23
Oh love will make a dog howl in rhyme.
JOHN FLETCHER—*Queen of Corinth.* Act IV. Sc. 1.

24
What is a Sonnet? 'Tis the pearly shell
That murmurs of the far-off, murmuring sea;
A precious jewel carved most curiously;
It is a little picture painted well.
What is a Sonnet? 'Tis the tear that fell
From a great poet's hidden ecstasy;
A two-edged sword, a star, a song—ah me!
Sometimes a heavy tolling funeral bell.
R. W. GILDER—*The Sonnet.*

25
To write a verse or two, is all the praise
That I can raise.
HERBERT—*The Church. Praise.*

26
A verse may finde him who a sermon flies,
And turn delight into a sacrifice.
HERBERT—*The Temple. The Church Porch.*

1
For dear to gods and men is sacred song.
Self-taught I sing; by Heaven and Heaven alone,
The genuine seeds of poesy are sown.
HOMER—*Odyssey*. Bk. XXII. L. 382. POPE'S trans.

2
Versibus exponi tragicis res comica non vult.
A comic matter cannot be expressed in tragic verse.
HORACE—*Ars Poetica*. 89.

3
Non satis est pulchra esse poemata, dulcia sunto.
It is not enough that poetry is agreeable, it should also be interesting.
HORACE—*Ars Poetica*. 99.

4
Versus inopes rerum, nugæque canoræ.
Verses devoid of substance, melodious trifles.
HORACE—*Ars Poetica*. 322.

5
Ubi plura nitent in carmine, non ego paucis
Offendar maculis, quas aut incuria fudit,
Aut humana parum cavit natura.
Where there are many beauties in a poem I shall not cavil at a few faults proceeding either from negligence or from the imperfection of our nature.
HORACE—*Ars Poetica*. 351.

6
Nonumque prematur in annum.
Let your poem be kept nine years.
HORACE—*Ars Poetica*. 388.

7
Wheresoe'er I turn my view,
All is strange, yet nothing new:
Endless labor all along,
Endless labor to be wrong:
Phrase that Time has flung away;
Uncouth words in disarray,
Trick'd in antique ruff and bonnet,
Ode, and elegy, and sonnet.
SAMUEL JOHNSON—*Parody of the style of* THOMAS WARTON. See CROKER'S note to BOSWELL'S *Johnson*. Sept. 18, 1777. Also in MRS. PIOZZI'S *Anecdotes*.

8
The essence of poetry is invention; such invention as, by producing something unexpected, surprises and delights.
SAMUEL JOHNSON—*The Lives of the English Poets. Life of Waller.*

9
Still may syllables jar with time,
Still may reason war with rhyme,
Resting never!
BEN JONSON—*Underwoods. Fit of Rhyme Against Rhyme.*

10
These are the gloomy companions of a disturbed imagination; the melancholy madness of poetry, without the inspiration.
JUNIUS—*Letter No. VII. To Sir W. Draper.*

11
Facit indignatio versum.
Indignation leads to the making of poetry. Quoted "Facit indignatio versus"—*i.e.*, verses.
JUVENAL—*Satires*. I. 79.

12
The poetry of earth is never dead;
* * * * *
The poetry of earth is ceasing never.
KEATS—*On the Grasshopper and Cricket.*

13
A drainless shower
Of light is poesy: 'tis the supreme of power;
'Tis might half slumbering on its own right arm.
KEATS—*Sleep and Poetry*. L. 237.

14
There are nine and sixty ways of constructing tribal lays,
And—every—single—one—of—them—is—right.
KIPLING—*In the Neolithic Age.*

15
The time for Pen and Sword was when
"My ladye fayre," for pity,
Could tend her wounded knight, and then
Grow tender at his ditty.
Some ladies now make pretty songs,
And some make pretty nurses:
Some men are good for righting wrongs,
And some for writing verses.
FREDERICK LOCKER-LAMPSON—*The Jester's Plea.*

16
It ["The Ancient Mariner"] is marvellous in its mastery over that delightfully fortuitous inconsequence that is the adamantine logic of dreamland.
LOWELL—*Among My Books. Coleridge.*

17
For, of all compositions, he thought that the sonnet
Best repaid all the toil you expended upon it.
LOWELL—*Fable for Critics*. L. 368.

18
Never did Poesy appear
So full of heaven to me, as when
I saw how it would pierce through pride and fear
To the lives of coarsest men.
LOWELL—*Incident in a Railroad Car*. St. 18.

19
These pearls of thought in Persian gulfs were bred,
Each softly lucent as a rounded moon;
The diver Omar plucked them from their bed,
FitzGerald strung them on an English thread.
LOWELL—*In a Copy of Omar Khayyam.*
(See also EASTWICK)

20
Musæo contigens cuncta lepore.
Gently touching with the charm of poetry.
LUCRETIUS—*De Rerum Natura*. IV. 9.

21
The merit of poetry, in its wildest forms, still consists in its truth—truth conveyed to the understanding, not directly by the words, but circuitously by means of imaginative associations, which serve as its conductors.
MACAULAY—*Essays. On the Athenian Orators.*

22
We hold that the most wonderful and splendid proof of genius is a great poem produced in a civilized age.
MACAULAY—*On Milton*. (1825)

1
Lap me in soft Lydian airs,
Married to immortal verse,
Such as the meeting soul may pierce,
In notes, with many a winding bout
Of linkèd sweetness long drawn out.
MILTON—*L'Allegro*. L. 136.
(See also WORDSWORTH)

2
My unpremeditated verse.
MILTON—*Paradise Lost*. Bk. IX. L. 24.

3
Yea, marry, now it is somewhat, for now it is rhyme; before it was neither rhyme nor reason.
SIR THOS. MORE. Advising an author to put his MS. into rhyme.

Rhyme nor reason.
Said by PEELE—*Edward I*. In *As You Like It*. Act III. Sc. 2. *Comedy of Errors*. Act II. Sc. 2. *Merry Wives of Windsor*. Act V. Sc. 5. *Farce du Vendeur des Lieures*. (16th Cen.) *L'avocat Patelin* (Quoted by TYNDALE, 1530.) *The Mouse Trap*. (1606) See BELOE *Anecdotes of Literature*. II. 127. Also in MS. in Cambridge University Library, England. 2. 5. Folio 9b. (Before 1500)
(See also SPENSER)

4
An erit, qui velle recuset
Os populi meruisse? et cedro digna locutus
Linquere, nec scombros metuentia carmina nec thus.

Lives there the man with soul so dead as to disown the wish to merit the people's applause, and having uttered words worthy to be kept in cedar oil to latest times, to leave behind him rhymes that dread neither herrings nor frankincense.
PERSIUS—*Satires*. I. 41.

5
Verba togæ sequeris, junctura callidus acri,
Ore teres modico, pallentes radere mores
Doctus, et ingenuo culpam defigere ludo.
Confined to common life thy numbers flow,
And neither soar too high nor sink too low;
There strength and ease in graceful union meet,
Though polished, subtle, and though poignant, sweet;
Yet powerful to abash the front of crime
And crimson error's cheek with sportive rhyme.
PERSIUS—*Satires*. V. 14. GIFFORD'S trans.

6
A needless Alexandrine ends the song,
That, like a wounded snake, drags its slow length along.
POPE—*Essay on Criticism*. Pt. II. L. 156.

7
What woful stuff this madrigal would be,
In some starv'd hackney sonneteer or me!
But let a lord once own the happy lines,
How the wit brightens! how the style refines.
POPE—*Essay on Criticism*. Pt. II. L. 418.

8
The varying verse, the full resounding line,
The long majestic march, and energy divine.
POPE—*Horace*. Bk. II. Ep. I. L. 267.

9
Curst be the verse, how well soe'er it flow,
That tends to make one worthy man my foe,
Give virtue scandal, innocence a fear,
Or from the soft-eyed virgin steal a tear!
POPE—*Prologue to Satires*. L. 283.

10
O for a Muse of fire, that would ascend
The brightest heaven of invention.
Henry V. *Chorus*. L. 1.

11
The elegancy, facility, and golden cadence of poesy.
Love's Labour's Lost. Act IV. Sc. 2. L. 126.

12
I consider poetry very subordinate to moral and political science.
SHELLEY — *Letter to Thomas L. Peacock*. Naples. Jan. 26, 1819.

13
A poem round and perfect as a star.
ALEX. SMITH—*A Life Drama*. Sc. 2.

14
I was promised on a time,
To have reason for my rhyme;
From that time unto this season,
I received nor rhyme nor reason.
SPENSER—*Lines on His Promised Pension*. See *Fuller's Worthies*, by NUTTALL. Vol. II. P. 379.
(See also MORE)

15
Jewels five-words-long,
That on the stretch'd forefinger of all Time
Sparkle for ever.
TENNYSON—*Princess*. Pt. II. L. 355.
(See also EASTWICK)

16
Tale tuum carmen nobis, divine poeta,
Quale sopor fessis in gramine.
Thy verses are as pleasing to me, O divine poet, as sleep is to the wearied on the soft turf.
VERGIL—*Eclogæ*. V. 45.

17
One merit of poetry few persons will deny: it says more and in fewer words than prose.
VOLTAIRE—*A Philosophical Dictionary*. *Poets*.

18
Old-fashioned poetry, but choicely good.
IZAAK WALTON—*The Compleat Angler*. Pt. I. Ch. IV.

19
And so no force, however great,
Can strain a cord, however fine,
Into a horizontal line
That shall be absolutely straight.
WILLIAM WHEWELL. Given as an accidental instance of metre and poetry.

20
Give lettered pomp to teeth of Time,
So "Bonnie Doon" but tarry:
Blot out the epic's stately rhyme,
But spare his Highland Mary!
WHITTIER—*Burns*. Last stanza.

21
The vision and the faculty divine;
Yet wanting the accomplishment of verse.
WORDSWORTH—*The Excursion*. Bk. I.

1
Wisdom married to immortal verse.
WORDSWORTH—*The Excursion*. Bk. VII.
(See also MILTON)

2 There is in Poesy a decent pride,
Which well becomes her when she speaks to Prose,
Her younger sister.
YOUNG—*Night Thoughts*. Night V. L. 64.

POETS (See also POETRY)

3
Poets are all who love,—who feel great truths,
And tell them.
BAILEY—*Festus*. Sc. *Another and a Better World*.

4
A poet not in love is out at sea;
He must have a lay-figure.
BAILEY—*Festus*. Sc. *Home*.

5
Heureux qui, dans ses vers, sait d'une voix légère
Passer du grave au doux, du plaisant au sévère
Happy the poet who with ease can steer
From grave to gay, from lively to severe.
BOILEAU—*L'Art Poetique*. I. 75.
(See also DRYDEN, also POPE under CONVERSATION)

6
Ah, poet-dreamer, within those walls
What triumphs shall be yours!
For all are happy and rich and great
In that City of By-and-by.
A. B. BRAGDON—*Two Landscapes*.

7 "There's nothing great
Nor small," has said a poet of our day,
Whose voice will ring beyond the curfew of eve
And not be thrown out by the matin's bell.
E. B. BROWNING—*Aurora Leigh*. Bk. VII.
Probably EMERSON—*Epigram to History*.
"There is no great and no small."

8
O brave poets, keep back nothing;
Nor mix falsehood with the whole!
Look up Godward! speak the truth in
Worthy song from earnest soul!
Hold, in high poetic duty,
Truest Truth the fairest Beauty.
E. B. BROWNING—*Dead Pan*. St. 39.

9
God's prophets of the Beautiful,
These Poets were.
E. B. BROWNING—*Vision of Poets*. St. 98.

10 One fine day,
Says Mister Mucklewraith to me, says he,
"So! you've a poet in your house," and smiled.
"A poet? God forbid," I cried; and then
It all came out: how Andrew slyly sent
Verse to the paper; how they printed it
In Poet's Corner.
ROBERT BUCHANAN—*Poet Andrew*. L. 161.

11
Poets alone are sure of immortality; they are the truest diviners of nature.
BULWER-LYTTON—*Caxtoniana*. Essay XXVII.

12
And poets by their sufferings grow,—
As if there were no more to do,
To make a poet excellent,
But only want and discontent.
BUTLER—*Miscellaneous Thoughts*.

13
Ovid's a rake, as half his verses show him,
Anacreon's morals are a still worse sample,
Catullus scarcely has a decent poem,
I don't think Sappho's Ode a good example,
Although Longinus tells us there is no hymn
Where the sublime soars forth on wings more ample;
But Virgil's songs are pure, except that horrid one
Beginning with "Formosum Pastor Corydon."
BYRON—*Don Juan*. Canto I. St. 42.

14
A Poet without Love were a physical and metaphysical impossibility.
CARLYLE—*Essays*. *Burns*.

15
Most joyful let the Poet be;
It is through him that all men see.
WILLIAM E. CHANNING—*The Poet of the Old and New Times*.

16
He koude songes make and wel endite.
CHAUCER—*Canterbury Tales*. *Prologue*. L. 95.

17
Who all in raptures their own works rehearse,
And drawl out measur'd prose, which they call verse.
CHURCHILL—*Independence*. L. 295.

18
Adhuc neminem cognovi poetam, qui sibi non optimus videretur.
I have never yet known a poet who did not think himself super-excellent.
CICERO—*Tusculanarum Disputationum*. V. 22.

19
Poets by Death are conquer'd but the wit
Of poets triumphs over it.
ABRAHAM COWLEY—*On the Praise of Poetry*. Ode I. L. 13.

20
And spare the poet for his subject's sake.
COWPER—*Charity*. Last line.

21
Ages elapsed ere Homer's lamp appeared,
And ages ere the Mantuan Swan was heard;
To carry nature lengths unknown before,
To give a Milton birth, asked ages more.
COWPER—*Table Talk*.
(See also DRYDEN)

22
Greece, sound thy Homer's, Rome thy Virgil's name,
But England's Milton equals both in fame.
COWPER—*To John Milton*.
(See also DRYDEN)

23
There is a pleasure in poetic pains,
Which only poets know.
COWPER—*The Task*. Bk. II. L. 285. Same in WORDSWORTH—*Miscellaneous Sonnets*. Knight's ed. VII. 160.

1
They best can judge a poet's worth,
  Who oft themselves have known
The pangs of a poetic birth
  By labours of their own.
  COWPER—*To Dr. Darwin.* St. 2.

2
Sure there are poets which did never dream
Upon Parnassus, nor did taste the stream
Of Helicon; we therefore may suppose
Those made not poets, but the poets those.
  SIR JOHN DENHAM—*Cooper's Hill.*

3
I can no more believe old Homer blind,
Than those who say the sun hath never shined;
The age wherein he lived was dark, but he
Could not want sight who taught the world to see.
  SIR JOHN DENHAM—*Progress of Learning.* L. 61.

4
The poet must be alike polished by an intercourse with the world as with the studies of taste; one to whom labour is negligence, refinement a science, and art a nature.
  ISAAC D'ISRAELI—*Literary Character of Men of Genius. Vers de Société.*

5
For that fine madness still he did retain,
Which rightly should possess a poet's brain.
  DRAYTON—*To Henry Reynolds. Of Poets and Poesy.* L. 109.
  (See also DRYDEN under INSANITY)

6
Happy who in his verse can gently steer
From grave to light, from pleasant to severe.
  DRYDEN—*The Art of Poetry.* Canto I. L. 75.
  (See also BOILEAU)

7
Three poets in three distant ages born,
Greece, Italy, and England did adorn.
The first in loftiness of thought surpass'd;
The next, in majesty; in both, the last.
The force of nature could no further go;
To make a third, she join'd the former two.
  DRYDEN—*Under Mr. Milton's Picture.* Homer, Virgil, Milton.
  (See also COWPER, SALVAGGI)

8
Poets should be law-givers; that is, the boldest lyric inspiration should not chide and insult, but should announce and lead the civil code, and the day's work.
  EMERSON—*Essays. Of Prudence.*

9
All men are poets at heart.
  EMERSON—*Literary Ethics.*

10
"Give me a theme," the little poet cried,
  "And I will do my part,"
"'Tis not a theme you need," the world replied;
  "You need a heart."
  R. W. GILDER—*Wanted, a Theme.*

11
Wer den Dichter will verstehen
Muss in Dichters Lande gehen.
  Whoever would understand the poet
  Must go into the poet's country.
  GOETHE—*Noten auf West-O. Divans.*

12
Neuere Poeten thun viel Wasser in die Tinte.
  Modern poets mix too much water with their ink.
  GOETHE—*Sprüche in Prosa.* III. Quoting STERNE—*Koran.* 2. 142.

13
Thou best-humour'd man with the worst-humour'd muse.
  GOLDSMITH—*Retaliation.* Postscript.
  (See also ROCHESTER)

14
Singing and rejoicing,
As aye since time began,
The dying earth's last poet
Shall be the earth's last man.
  ANASTASIUS GRÜN—*The Last Poet.*

15
His virtues formed the magic of his song.
  Inscription on the Tomb of Cowper. L. 10. See HAYLEY'S *Life of Cowper.* Vol. IV. P. 189.

16
Lo! there he lies, our Patriarch Poet, dead!
  The solemn angel of eternal peace
Has waved a wand of mystery o'er his head,
  Touched his strong heart, and bade his pulses cease.
  PAUL H. HAYNE—*To Bryant, Dead.*

17
We call those poets who are first to mark
Through earth's dull mist the coming of the dawn,—
Who see in twilight's gloom the first pale spark,
While others only note that day is gone.
  HOLMES—*Memorial Verses. Shakespeare.*

18
Where go the poet's lines?—
Answer, ye evening tapers!
Ye auburn locks, ye golden curls,
Speak from your folded papers!
  HOLMES—*The Poet's Lot.* St. 3.

19
In his own verse the poet still we find,
In his own page his memory lives enshrined,
As in their amber sweets the smothered bees,—
As the fair cedar, fallen before the breeze,
Lies self-embalmed amidst the mouldering trees.
  HOLMES—*Songs of Many Seasons. Bryant's Seventieth Birthday.* St. 17 and 18. For same idea see ANT, FLY, SPIDER.

20
Mediocribus esse poetis
Non homines, non di, non concessere columnæ.
  Neither men, nor gods, nor booksellers' shelves permit ordinary poets to exist.
  HORACE—*Ars Poetica.* 372.

21
Poets, the first instructors of mankind,
Brought all things to their proper native use.
  HORACE—*Of the Art of Poetry.* L. 449. WENTWORTH DILLON'S trans.

22
Quod si me lyricis vatibus inseris,
Sublimi feriam sidera vertice.
  If you rank me with the lyric poets, my exalted head shall strike the stars.
  HORACE—*Carmina.* I. 1. 35.

23
Genus irritabile vatum.
  The irritable tribe of poets.
  HORACE—*Epistles.* II. 2. 102.

1
Disjecti membra poetæ.
The scattered remnants of the poet.
HORACE—*Satires.* I. 4. 62.

2
Aut insanit homo, aut versus facit.
The man is either mad or he is making verses.
HORACE—*Satires.* II. 7. 117.

3
Was ever poet so trusted before!
SAMUEL JOHNSON—*Boswell's Life of Johnson.* (1774)

4
For a good poet's made, as well as born.
BEN JONSON—*To the Memory of Shakespeare.*
Trans. of Solus aut rex aut poeta non quotannis nascitur. FLORUS—*De Qualitate Vitæ. Fragment.* VIII. Poeta nascitur non fit. The poet is born not made. Earliest use in CÆLIUS RHODIGINUS—*Lectiones Antiquæ.* I. VII. Ch. IV. P. 225. (Ed. 1525)

5
O 'tis a very sin
For one so weak to venture his poor verse
In such a place as this.
KEATS—*Endymion.* Bk. III. L. 965.

6
Much have I travell'd in the realms of gold,
And many goodly states and kingdoms seen;
Round many western islands have I been
Which bards in fealty to Apollo hold.
Oft of one wide expanse had I been told
That deep-brow'd Homer ruled as his demesne,
Yet did I never breathe its pure serene
Till I heard Chapman speak out loud and bold:
Then felt I like some watcher of the skies
When a new planet swims into his ken;
Or like stout Cortez when with eagle eyes
He stared at the Pacific,—and all his men
Look'd at each other with a wild surmise,—
Silent, upon a peak in Darien.
KEATS. On first looking into CHAPMAN'S HOMER. Cortez confused with Balboa.

7
Je chantais comme l'oiseau gémit.
I was singing as a bird mourns.
LAMARTINE—*Le Poète Mourant.*
(See also TENNYSON)

8
For next to being a great poet is the power of understanding one.
LONGFELLOW—*Hyperion.* Bk. II. Ch. III.

9
All that is best in the great poets of all countries is not what is national in them, but what is universal.
LONGFELLOW—*Kavanagh.* Ch. XX.

10
For voices pursue him by day,
And haunt him by night,—
And he listens, and needs must obey,
When the Angel says: "Write!"
LONGFELLOW—*L'Envoi. The Poet and His Songs.* St. 7.

11
Like the river, swift and clear,
Flows his song through many a heart.
LONGFELLOW—*Oliver Basselin.* St. 11.

12
O ye dead Poets, who are living still
Immortal in your verse, though life be fled,
And ye, O living Poets, who are dead
Though ye are living, if neglect can kill,
Tell me if in the darkest hours of ill,
With drops of anguish falling fast and red
From the sharp crown of thorns upon your head,
Ye were not glad your errand to fulfill?
LONGFELLOW—*The Poets.*

13
The clear, sweet singer with the crown of snow
Not whiter than the thoughts that housed below!
LOWELL—*Epistle to George William Curtis.* L. 43. Postscript.

14
A terrible thing to be pestered with poets!
But, alas, she is dumb, and the proverb holds good,
She never will cry till she's out of the wood!
LOWELL—*Fable for Critics.* L. 73.

15
Sithe of our language he was the lodesterre.
LYDGATE—*The Falls of Princes.* Referring to CHAUCER.
(See also SPENSER)

16
For his chaste Muse employed her heaven-taught lyre
None but the noblest passions to inspire,
Not one immoral, one corrupted thought,
One line, which dying he could wish to blot.
LORD LYTTLETON—*Prologue to Thomson's Coriolanus.*
(See also SWIFT)

17
Non scribit, cujus carmina nemo legit.
He does not write whose verses no one reads.
MARTIAL—*Epigrams.* III. 9. 2.

18
You admire, Vacerra, only the poets of old and praise only those who are dead. Pardon me, I beseech you, Vacerra, if I think death too high a price to pay for your praise.
MARTIAL—*Epigrams.* Bk. VIII. Ep. 49.

19
Poets are sultans, if they had their will:
For every author would his brother kill.
ORRERY—*Prologues.* (According to JOHNSON.)

20
Valeant mendacia vatum.
Good-bye to the lies of the poets.
OVID—*Fasti.* VI. 253.

21
Poets utter great and wise things which they do not themselves understand.
PLATO—*The Republic.* Bk. II. Sec. V.

22
Tamen poetis mentiri licet.
Nevertheless it is allowed to poets to lie. (Poetical license.)
PLINY the Younger—*Epistles.* Bk. VI. 21.

23
While pensive poets painful vigils keep,
Sleepless themselves to give their readers sleep.
POPE—*Dunciad.* Bk. I. L. 93.

24
Dulness! whose good old cause I yet defend,
With whom my muse began, with whom shall end.
POPE—*Dunciad.* Bk. I. L. 165.

1
Poets like painters, thus unskill'd to trace
The naked nature and the living grace,
With gold and jewels cover every part,
And hide with ornaments their want of art.
POPE—*Essay on Criticism.* L. 293.

2
Vain was the chief's, the sage's pride!
They had no poet, and they died.
POPE—*Odes of Horace.* Bk. IV. Ode 9.

3
Then from the Mint walks forth the man of rhyme,
Happy to catch me, just at dinner-time.
POPE—*Prologue to Satires.* L. 13.

4
The bard whom pilfer'd pastorals renown,
Who turns a Persian tale for half a crown,
Just writes to make his barrenness appear,
And strains from hard-bound brains eight lines a year.
POPE—*Prologue to Satires.* L. 179.

5
And he whose fustian's so sublimely bad,
It is not poetry, but prose run mad.
POPE—*Prologue to Satires.* L. 185.

6
For pointed satire I would Buckhurst choose,
The best good man with the worst-natured muse.
EARL OF ROCHESTER. An allusion to HORACE—*Satire X.* Bk. I.
(See also GOLDSMITH)

7
Græcia Mæonidam, jactet sibi Roma Maronem
Anglia Miltonum jactat utrique parem.
Greece boasts her Homer, Rome can Virgil claim;
England can either match in Milton's fame.
SALVAGGI—*Ad Joannem Miltonum.*
(See also DRYDEN)

8
* * * For ne'er
Was flattery lost on Poet's ear;
A simple race! they waste their toil
For the vain tribute of a smile.
SCOTT—*Lay of the Last Minstrel.* Canto IV. Last stanza.

9
Call it not vain:—they do not err,
Who say that, when the Poet dies,
Mute Nature mourns her worshipper,
And celebrates his obsequies.
SCOTT—*Lay of the Last Minstrel.* Canto V. St. 1.

10
I would the gods had made thee poetical.
As You Like It. Act III. Sc. 3. L. 15.

11
Never durst poet touch a pen to write
Until his ink were temper'd with Love's sighs.
Love's Labour's Lost. Act IV. Sc. 3. L. 346.

12
The poet's eye, in a fine frenzy rolling,
Doth glance from heaven to earth, from earth to heaven;
And as imagination bodies forth
The forms of things unknown, the poet's pen
Turns them to shapes and gives to airy nothing
A local habitation and a name.
Midsummer Night's Dream. Act V. Sc. 1. L. 12.

13
Most wretched men
Are cradled into poetry by wrong;
They learn in suffering what they teach in song.
SHELLEY—*Julian and Maddalo.* L. 556.

14
Dan Chaucer, well of English undefyled,
On Fame's eternall beadroll worthie to be fyled.
SPENSER—*Faerie Queene.* Bk. IV. Canto II. St. 32.
(See also LYDGATE)

15
I learnt life from the poets.
MADAME DE STAËL—*Corinne.* Bk. XVIII. Ch. V.

16
With no companion but the constant Muse,
Who sought me when I needed her—ah, when
Did I not need her, solitary else?
R. H. STODDARD—*Proem.* L. 87.

17
The Poet in his Art
Must intimate the whole, and say the smallest part.
W. W. STORY—*The Unexpressed.*

18
Then, rising with Aurora's light,
The Muse invoked, sit down to write;
Blot out, correct, insert, refine,
Enlarge, diminish, interline.
SWIFT—*On Poetry.*
(See also LYTTLETON, WALLER)

19
Unjustly poets we asperse:
Truth shines the brighter clad in verse,
And all the fictions they pursue
Do but insinuate what is true.
SWIFT—*To Stella.*

20
Villon, our sad bad glad mad brother's name.
SWINBURNE—*Ballad of François Villon.*

21
To have read the greatest works of any great poet, to have beheld or heard the greatest works of any great painter or musician, is a possession added to the best things of life.
SWINBURNE—*Essays and Studies. Victor Hugo. L'Année Terrible.*

22
The Poet's leaves are gathered one by one,
In the slow process of the doubtful years.
BAYARD TAYLOR—*Poet's Journal. Third Evening.*

23
I do but sing because I must,
And pipe but as the linnets sing.
TENNYSON—*In Memoriam.* XXI. 6.
(See also LAMARTINE)

24
The poet in a golden clime was born,
With golden stars above;
Dower'd with the hate of hate, the scorn of scorn,
The love of love.
TENNYSON—*The Poet.*

25
For now the Poet cannot die,
Nor leave his music as of old,
But round him ere he scarce be cold
Begins the scandal and the cry.
TENNYSON—*To ——, after Reading a Life and Letters.* St. 4.

1
A bard here dwelt, more fat than bard becomes
Who void of envy, guile and lust of gain,
On virtue still and nature's pleasing themes
Poured forth his unpremeditated strain.
THOMSON—*Castle of Indolence.* Canto I. St. 68. (*Last line said to be* "writ by a friend of the author.")

2
Poets lose half the praise they should have got,
Could it be known what they discreetly blot.
EDMUND WALLER—*Miscellanies.* Upon the EARL OF ROSCOMMON'S Translation of HORACE—*Ars Poetica.* L. 41.
(See also SWIFT)

3
God, eldest of Poets.
WILLIAM WATSON—*England, my England.*

4
He saw wan Woman toil with famished eyes;
He saw her bound, and strove to sing her free.
He saw her fall'n; and wrote "The Bridge of Sighs";
And on it crossed to immortality.
WILLIAM WATSON—*Hood.*

5
Threadbare his songs seem now, to lettered ken:
They were worn threadbare next the hearts of men.
WILLIAM WATSON—*Longfellow.*

6
A dreamer of the common dreams,
A fisher in familiar streams,
He chased the transitory gleams
That all pursue;
But on his lips the eternal themes
Again were new.
WILLIAM WATSON—*The Tomb of Burns.*

7
It was Homer who inspired the poet.
WAYLAND—*The Iliad and the Bible.*

8
In Spring the Poet is glad,
And in Summer the Poet is gay;
But in Autumn the Poet is sad,
And has something sad to say.
BYRON FORCEYTHE WILLSON—*Autumn Song.*

9 That mighty orb of song,
The divine Milton.
WORDSWORTH—*Excursion.* Bk. I. L. 252.

10 And, when a damp
Fell round the path of Milton, in his hand
The Thing became a trumpet; whence he blew
Soul-animating strains,—alas! too few.
WORDSWORTH—*Miscellaneous Sonnets.* Pt. II. *Scorn not the Sonnet.*

11
Blessings be with them, and eternal praise,
Who gave us nobler loves, and nobler cares,—
The Poets, who on earth have made us heirs
Of truth and pure delight by heavenly lays!
WORDSWORTH—*Personal Talk.*

12
I thought of Chatterton, the marvellous Boy,
The sleepless Soul that perished in his pride;
Of him who walked in glory and in joy,
Following his plough, along the mountain side.
WORDSWORTH—*Resolution and Independence.* St. 7.

POISON

13
What's one man's poison, signior,
Is another's meat or drink.
BEAUMONT AND FLETCHER—*Love's Cure.* Act III. Sc. 2. Same in LUCRETIUS. IV. 627.

14
Vipera Cappadocem nocitura mormordit; at illa Gustato perit sanguine Cappadocis.
A deadly echidna once bit a Cappadocian; she herself died, having tasted the Poison-flinging blood.
DEMODOCUS. Trans. of his Greek Epigram.
(See also GOLDSMITH, WOLCOT)

15
Un gros serpent mordit Aurèle.
Que croyez-vous qu'il arriva?
Qu' Aurèle en mourut? Bagatelle!
Ce fut le serpent qui creva.
In a MS. commonplace book, written probably at end of 18th Cen. See *Notes and Queries.* March 30, 1907. P. 246. Same attributed to MARTINIERE—*Nat. ad Loc.* II. 421.

16
Hier auprès de Charenton
Un serpent morait Jean Fréron,
Que croyez-vous qu'il arriva?
Ce fut le serpent qui creva.
Imitation from the Greek. Found also in *Œuvres Complèts de* VOLTAIRE. III. P. 1002. (1817) Printed as VOLTAIRE'S; attributed to PIRON; claimed for FRÉRON.

17
The man recover'd of the bite,
The dog it was that died.
GOLDSMITH—*Elegy on the Death of a Mad Dog.* Same idea in MANASSES—*Fragmenta.* Ed. BOISSONADE. I. 323. (1819)
(See also DEMODOCUS)

18
While Fell was reposing himself in the hay,
A reptile concealed bit his leg as he lay;
But, all venom himself, of the wound he made light,
And got well, while the scorpion died of the bite.
LESSING—*Paraphrase of Demodocus.*
(See also DEMODOCUS)

19
All men carry about them that which is poyson to serpents: for if it be true that is reported, they will no better abide the touching with man's spittle than scalding water cast upon them: but if it happen to light within their chawes or mouth, especially if it come from a man that is fasting, it is present death.
PLINY—*Natural History.* Bk. VII. Ch. II. HOLLAND'S trans.

20
In gährend Drachengift hast du
Die Milch der frommen Denkart mir verwandelt.
To rankling poison hast thou turned in me the milk of human kindness.
SCHILLER—*Wilhelm Tell.* IV. 3. 3.

21
Venenum in auro bibitur.
Poison is drunk out of gold.
SENECA—*Thyestes.* Act III. 453.

1 Let me have
A dram of poison, such soon-speeding gear
As will disperse itself through all the veins
That the life-weary taker may fall dead
And that the trunk may be discharg'd of breath
As violently as hasty powder fir'd
Doth hurry from the fatal cannon's womb.
Romeo and Juliet. Act V. Sc. 1. L. 59.

2
Talk no more of the lucky escape of the head
From a flint so unhappily thrown;
I think very different from thousands; indeed
'Twas a lucky escape for the stone.
WOLCOT (Peter Pindar). On a Stone thrown at GEORGE III.
(See also GOLDSMITH)

POLICY

3
Mahomet made the people believe that he would call a hill to him, and from the top of it offer up his prayers for the observers of his law. The people assembled; Mahomet called the hill to come to him, again and again; and when the hill stood still, he was never a whit abashed, but said, "If the hill will not come to Mahomet, Mahomet will go to the hill."
BACON—*Essays. Of Boldness.*

4
Kings will be tyrants from policy, when subjects are rebels from principle.
BURKE—*Reflections on the Revolution in France.*

5
Like Æsop's fox, when he had lost his tail, would have all his fellow foxes cut off theirs.
BURTON—*Anatomy of Melancholy. Democritus to the Reader.*

6
They had best not stir the rice, though it sticks to the pot.
CERVANTES—*Don Quixote.* Pt. II. Ch. XXXVII.

7
It is better to walk than to run; it is better to stand than to walk; it is better to sit than to stand; it is better to lie than to sit.
Hindu Proverb.

8
Don't throw a monkey-wrench into the machinery.
PHILANDER JOHNSON. See *Everybody's Magazine.* May, 1920. P. 36.

9
Masterly inactivity.
SIR JAMES MACKINTOSH—*Vindiciæ Gallicæ.* Probably from "Strenua inertia." HORACE—*Epistles.* XI. 28.

10
When I see a merchant over-polite to his customers, begging them to taste a little brandy and throwing half his goods on the counter,—thinks I, that man has an axe to grind.
CHARLES MINER—*Who'll turn Grindstones? Essays from the Desk of Poor Robert the Scribe.* In *Wilkesbarre Gleaner.* (1811)

11
The publick weal requires that a man should betray, and lye, and massacre.
MONTAIGNE—*Essays. Of Profit and Honesty.*

12
Turn him to any cause of policy,
The Gordian knot of it he will unloose,
Familiar as his garter: that, when he speaks,
The air, a charter'd libertine, is still.
Henry V. Act I. Sc. 1. L. 45.

13 To beguile the time,
Look like the time; bear welcome in your eye,
Your hand, your tongue: look like the innocent flower,
But be the serpent under 't.
Macbeth. Act I. Sc. 5. L. 65.

14
We shall not, I believe, be obliged to alter our policy of watchful waiting.
WOODROW WILSON—*Annual Message.* Dec. 2, 1913. Alluding to Mexico.

15
We have stood apart, studiously neutral.
WOODROW WILSON—*Message to Congress.* Dec. 7, 1915.

POLITICS (See also GOVERNMENT, STATESMANSHIP)

16
I consider biennial elections as a security that the sober, second thought of the people shall be law.
FISHER AMES—*Speech.* Jan., 1788.

17
Man is by nature a civic animal.
ARISTOTLE—*Polit.* I. 2.

18
All political parties die at last of swallowing their own lies.
Attributed to JOHN ARBUTHNOT, M.D. In *"Life of Emerson."* P. 165.

19
Listen! John A. Logan is the Head Centre, the Hub, the King Pin, the Main Spring, Mogul, and Mugwump of the final plot by which partisanship was installed in the Commission.
ISAAC H. BROMLEY—*Editorial in the New York Tribune.* Feb. 16, 1877.
(See also PORTER)

20
It is necessary that I should qualify the doctrine of its being not men, but measures, that I am determined to support. In a monarchy it is the duty of parliament to look at the men as well as at the measures.
LORD BROUGHAM—*In the House of Commons.* Nov., 1830.
(See also BURKE, CANNING, GOLDSMITH)

21
We are Republicans, and don't propose to leave our party and identify ourselves with the party whose antecedents have been Rum, Romanism, and Rebellion.
SAMUEL D. BURCHARD—*One of the Deputation visiting Mr. Blaine.* Oct. 29, 1884.

22
You had that action and counteraction which, in the natural and in the political world, from the reciprocal struggle of discordant powers draws out the harmony of the universe.
BURKE—*Reflexions on the Revolution in France.* Vol. III. P. 277.

1
Of this stamp is the cant of, not men, but measures.
BURKE—*Thoughts on the Cause of the Present Discontent.* EARL OF SHELBURNE quotes the phrase in a letter, July 11, 1765, before Burke's use of it.
(See also BROUGHAM)

2
Protection and patriotism are reciprocal.
CALHOUN—*Speech delivered in the House of Representatives.* (1812)

3
Away with the cant of "Measures, not men!"—the idle supposition that it is the harness and not the horses that draw the chariot along. No Sir, if the comparison must be made, if the distinction must be taken, men are everything, measures comparatively nothing.
CANNING—*Speech against the Addington Ministry.* (1801)
(See also BROUGHAM)

4
The Duty of an Opposition is to oppose.
Quoted by RANDOLPH CHURCHILL.
(See also STANLEY)

5
One of the greatest of Romans, when asked what were his politics, replied, "Imperium et libertas." That would not make a bad programme for a British Ministry.
RANDOLPH CHURCHILL—*Speech.* Mansion House, London. Nov. 10, 1879.

3
Here the two great interests IMPERIUM ET LIBERTAS, res olim insociabiles (saith Tacitus), began to incounter each other.
SIR WINSTON CHURCHILL—*Divi Britannici.* P. 849. (1675)

7
Nam ego in ista sum sententia, qua te fuisse semper scio, nihil ut feurit in suffragiis voce melius.
I am of the opinion which you have always held, that "viva voce" voting at elections is the best method.
CICERO—*De Legibus.* III. 15. *Philippics.* IV. 4. TACITUS—*Agricola.* Ch. III.

8
It is a *condition* which confronts us—not a theory.
GROVER CLEVELAND — *Annual Message.* (1887)
(See also DISRAELI)

9
Party honesty is party expediency.
GROVER CLEVELAND—*Interview in New York Commercial Advertiser.* Sept. 19, 1889.

10
Laissez faire, laissez passer.
Let it alone. Let it pass by.
COLBERT, according to LORD JOHN RUSSELL. See report of his speech in the London *Times,* April 2, 1840. Attributed to GOURNAY, Minister of Commerce, at Paris, 1751. Also to QUESNAY. Quoted by ADAM SMITH—*Wealth of Nations.*

11
Free trade is not a principle, it is an expedient.
BENJ. DISRAELI—*On Import Duties.* April 25, 1843.
(See also CLEVELAND)

12
The Right Honorable gentleman [Sir Robert Peel] caught the Whigs bathing and walked away with their clothes.
BENJ. DISRAELI—*Speech.* House of Commons, Feb. 28, 1845.

13
Party is organized opinion.
BENJ. DISRAELI—*Speech.* Oxford, Nov. 25, 1864.

14
Principle is ever my motto, no expediency.
BENJ. DISRAELI—*Sybil.* Bk. II. Ch. II.
(See also CLEVELAND)

15
Information upon points of practical politics.
BENJ. DISRAELI—*Vivian Gray.* Ch. XIV. Given by WALSH as first appearance of the phrase "practical politics."

16
All the ten-to-oners were in the rear, and a *dark* horse, which had never been thought of, and which the careless St. James had never even observed in the list, rushed past the grand stand in sweeping triumph.
BENJ. DISRAELI—*The Young Duke.* Bk. II. Ch. V.
(See also THACKERAY)

17
Damned Neuters, in their Middle way of Steering,
Are neither Fish, nor Flesh, nor good Red Herring.
DRYDEN—*Duke of Guise. Epilogue.* Phrase used by DR. SMITH. *Ballet.* Ch. IX. In *Musarum Deliciæ.*

18
What is a Communist? One who has yearnings
For equal division of unequal earnings.
EBENEZER ELLIOT—*Corn Law Rhymes.*

19
All political power is a trust.
CHARLES JAMES FOX. (1788)

20
Oh! we'll give 'em Jessie
When we rally round the polls.
Popular song of FREMONT'S Supporters in the Presidential Campaign of 1856.

21
I always voted at my party's call,
And I never thought of thinking for myself at all.
W. S. GILBERT—*H. M. S. Pinafore.*

22
Measures, not men, have always been my mark.
GOLDSMITH—*Good-Natured Man.* Act II.
(See also BURKE)

23
Who, born for the universe, narrow'd his mind,
And to party gave up what was meant for mankind.
GOLDSMITH—*Retaliation.* L. 31.

24
Who will burden himself with your liturgical parterre when the burning questions [brennende Fragen] of the day invite to very different toils?
HAGENBACH—*Grundlinien der Liturgik und Homiletik.* (1803) "Burning question" used by EDWARD MIALL, M.P., also by DISRAELI in the House of Commons, March, 1873.

1
He serves his party best who serves the country best.
RUTHERFORD B. HAYES—*Inaugural Address.* March 5, 1877.

2
The freeman casting, with unpurchased hand,
The vote that shakes the turrets of the land.
HOLMES—*Poetry. A Metrical Essay.* L. 83.

3
Non ego ventosæ plebis suffragia venor.
I court not the votes of the fickle mob.
HORACE—*Epistles.* I. 19. 37.

4
Like an armed warrior, like a plumed knight, James G. Blaine marched down the halls of the American Congress and threw his shining lance full and fair against the brazen foreheads of the defamers of his country, and the maligners of his honor.
ROBERT G. INGERSOLL—*The Plumed Knight.* Speech in nomination of BLAINE for President in the Republican Convention. Cincinnati, June 15, 1876.
(See also PHILLIPS)

5
Whenever a man has cast a longing eye on offices, a rottenness begins in his conduct.
THOS. JEFFERSON—*Letter to Coxe.* (1799)

6
If a due participation of office is a matter of right, how are vacancies to be obtained? Those by death are few; by resignation, none.
Usually quoted, "Few die and none resign."
THOS. JEFFERSON—*Letter to Elias Shipman and Merchants of New Haven.* July 12, 1801.

7
Of the various executive abilities, no one excited more anxious concern than that of placing the interests of our fellow-citizens in the hands of honest men, with understanding sufficient for their stations. No duty is at the same time more difficult to fulfil. The knowledge of character possessed by a single individual is of necessity limited. To seek out the best through the whole Union, we must resort to the information which from the best of men, acting disinterestedly and with the purest motives, is sometimes incorrect.
THOS. JEFFERSON—*Letter to Elias Shipman and Merchants of New Haven.* July 12, 1801. Paraphrased, "Put the right man in the right place" by MCMASTER—*History of the People of the U. S.* Vol. II. P. 586.

8
We are swinging round the circle.
ANDREW JOHNSON—*Of the Presidential "Reconstruction."* August, 1866.

9
I have always said the first Whig was the Devil.
SAMUEL JOHNSON—*Boswell's Johnson.* (1778)

10
Skilled to pull wires he baffles nature's hope, who sure intended him to stretch a rope.
LOWELL—*The Boss.* (Tweed.)

11
Free trade, one of the greatest blessings which a government can confer on a people, is in almost every country unpopular.
MACAULAY—*On Mitford's History of Greece.*

12
Factions among yourselves; preferring such
To offices and honors, as ne'er read
The elements of saving policy;
But deeply skilled in all the principles
That usher to destruction.
MASSINGER—*The Bondman.* Act I. Sc. 3. L. 210.

13
Agitate, agitate, agitate.
LORD MELBOURNE. In TORRENS—*Life of Lord Melbourne.* Vol. I. P. 320, and in WALPOLE'S *History of England from Conclusion of the Great War.* Vol. III. P. 143.

14
Every time I fill a vacant office I make ten malcontents and one ingrate.
MOLIÈRE. Quoting LOUIS XIV, in *Siècle de Louis Quatorze.*

15
Those who would treat politics and morality apart will never understand the one or the other.
JOHN MORLEY—*Rousseau.* P. 380.

16
Car c'est en famille, ce n'est pas en public, qu'un lave son linge sale.
But it is at home and not in public that one should wash ones dirty linen.
NAPOLEON—*On his return from Elba.* Speech to the Legislative Assembly.
(See also VOLTAIRE)

17
Better a hundred times an honest and capable administration of an erroneous policy than a corrupt and incapable administration of a good one.
E. J. PHELPS—*At Dinner of the N. Y. Chamber of Commerce.* Nov. 19, 1889.

18
The White Plume of Navarre.
Name given to N. Y. *Tribune* during the Civil War. See WENDELL PHILLIPS—*Under the Flag.* Boston, April 21, 1861.
(See also INGERSOLL)

19
A weapon that comes down as still
As snowflakes fall upon the sod;
But executes a freeman's will,
As lightning does the will of God;
And from its force, nor doors nor locks
Can shield you; 'tis the ballot-box.
PIERPONT—*A Word from a Petitioner.*

20
Party-spirit, which at best is but the madness of many, for the gain of a few.
POPE—*Letter to Blount.* Aug. 27, 1714.

21
Old politicians chew on wisdom past,
And totter on in business to the last.
POPE—*Moral Essays.* Ep. I. L. 228.

22
Party is the madness of many for the gain of a few.
POPE in *Thoughts on Various Subjects,* written by SWIFT and POPE. Evidence in favor of Pope.

23
A mugwump is a person educated beyond his intellect.
HORACE PORTER—*A Bon-Mot in Cleveland-Blaine Campaign.* (1884)
(See also BROMLEY)

1
Abstain from beans.
PYTHAGORAS. Advice against political voting, which was done by means of beans. See LUCIAN GALLUS. IV. 5. *Vitarum Auctio.* Sect. 6. The superstition against beans was prevalent in Egypt however. See HERODOTUS. II. 37, also SEXTUS EMPIRICUS. Explanations to abstain from beans from lost treatise of ARISTOTLE in DIOG. LAERTES. VIII. 34. Beans had an oligarchical character on account of their use in voting. PLUTARCH gives a similar explanation in *De Educat.* Ch. XVII. Caution against entering public life, for the votes by which magistrates were elected were originally given by beans. PYTHAGORAS referred to by JEREMY TAYLOR—*Holy Living.* Sect. IV. P. 80.

2
I will drive a coach and six through the Act of Settlement.
STEPHEN RICE—Quoted by MACAULAY—*History of England.* Ch. XII. Familiarly known as "Drive a coach and six through an Act of Parliament."

3
There is a homely old adage which runs: "Speak softly and carry a big stick; you will go far." If the American nation will speak softly and yet build and keep at a pitch of the highest training a thoroughly efficient navy, the Monroe Doctrine will go far.
ROOSEVELT. *Address at Minnesota State Fair,* Sept. 2, 1901.

4
The first advice I have to give the party is that it should clean its slate.
LORD ROSEBERY (Fifth Earl)—*Speech.* Chesterfield. Dec. 16, 1901.

5
Something is rotten in the state of Denmark.
Hamlet. Act I. Sc. 4. L. 90.

6
Get thee glass eyes;
And, like a scurvy politician, seem
To see the things thou dost not.
King Lear. Act IV. Sc. 6. L. 174.

7
O, that estates, degrees, and offices
Were not deriv'd corruptly, and that clear honour
Were purchased by the merit of the wearer!
Merchant of Venice. Act II. Sc. 9. L. 41.

8
Persuade me not; I will make a Star-chamber matter of it.
Merry Wives of Windsor. Act I. Sc. 1. L. 1.

9
When I first came into Parliament, Mr. Tierney, a great Whig authority, used always to say that the duty of an Opposition was very simple—it was to oppose everything and propose nothing.
LORD STANLEY—*Debate,* June 4, 1841. See *Hansard's Parliamentary Debates.*
(See also CHURCHILL)

10
Who is the dark horse he has in his stable?
THACKERAY—*Adventures of Philip*
(See also DISRAELI)

11
As long as I count the votes what are you going to do about it? Say.
WM. M. TWEED—*The Ballot in* 1871.

12
Defence, not defiance.
Motto adopted by the "VOLUNTEERS," when there was fear of an invasion of England by Napoleon. (1859)

13
The king [Frederick] has sent me some of his dirty linen to wash; I will wash yours another time.
VOLTAIRE—*Reply to General Manstein.* CXI.
(See also NAPOLEON)

14
The gratitude of place expectants is a lively sense of future favours.
Ascribed to WALPOLE by HAZLITT—*Wit and Humour.* Same in LA ROCHFOUCAULD—*Maxims.*

15
I am not a politician, and my other habits air good.
ARTEMUS WARD—*Fourth of July Oration.*

16
Politics I conceive to be nothing more than the science of the ordered progress of society along the lines of greatest usefulness and convenience to itself.
WOODROW WILSON. *To the Pan-American Scientific Congress.* Washington, Jan. 6, 1916.

17
Tippecanoe and Tyler too.
Political slogan, attributed to ORSON E. WOODBURY. (1840)

POLLUTION (See CORRUPTION)

POPPY

Papaver

18
I sing the Poppy! The frail snowy weed!
The flower of Mercy! that within its heart
Doth keep "a drop serene" for human need,
A drowsy balm for every bitter smart.
For happy hours the Rose will idly blow—
The Poppy hath a charm for pain and woe.
MARY A. BARR—*White Poppies.*

19
Central depth of purple,
Leaves more bright than rose,
Who shall tell what brightest thought
Out of darkness grows?
Who, through what funereal pain,
Souls to love and peace attain?
LEIGH HUNT—*Songs and Chorus of the Flowers. Poppies.*

20
We are slumberous poppies,
Lords of Lethe downs,
Some awake and some asleep,
Sleeping in our crowns.
What perchance our dreams may know,
Let our serious beauty show.
LEIGH HUNT—*Songs and Chorus of the Flowers. Poppies.*

1
The poppy opes her scarlet purse of dreams.
SCHARMEL IRIS—*Early Nightfall.*

2
Through the dancing poppies stole
A breeze most softly lulling to my soul.
KEATS—*Endymion.* Bk. I. L. 565.

3 The poppies hung
Dew-dabbled on their stalks.
KEATS—*Endymion.* Bk. I. L. 681.

4
Every castle of the air
Sleeps in the fine black grains, and there
Are seeds for every romance, or light
Whiff of a dream for a summer night.
AMY LOWELL—*Sword Blades and Poppy Seed.*

5
Visions for those too tired to sleep,
These seeds cast a film over eyes which weep.
AMY LOWELL—*Sword Blades and Poppy Seed.*

6
In Flanders' fields the poppies blow
Between the crosses, row on row,
That mark our place, and in the sky,
The larks, still bravely singing, fly
Scarce heard among the guns below.
COL. JOHN MCCRAE—*In Flander's Fields.* (*We shall not Sleep.*)
(See also MCCRAE under WAR)

7
Find me next a Poppy posy,
Type of his harangues so dozy.
MOORE—*Wreaths for the Ministers.*

8
And would it not be proud romance
Falling in some obscure advance,
To rise, a poppy field of France?
WILLIAM A. PERCY—*Poppy Fields.*

9
Let but my scarlet head appear
And I am held in scorn;
Yet juice of subtile virtue lies
Within my cup of curious dyes.
CHRISTINA G. ROSSETTI—*"Consider the Lilies of the Field."*

10 Gentle sleep!
Scatter thy drowsiest poppies from above;
And in new dreams not soon to vanish, bless
My senses with the sight of her I love.
HORACE SMITH—*Poppies and Sleep.*

11
And far and wide, in a scarlet tide,
The poppy's bonfire spread.
BAYARD TAYLOR—*Poems of the Orient. The Poet in the East.* St. 4.

12
Summer set lip to earth's bosom bare,
And left the flushed print in a poppy there:
Like a yawn of fire from the grass it came,
And the fanning wind puffed it to flapping flame.
With burnt mouth red like a lion's it drank
The blood of the sun as he slaughtered sank,
And dipped its cup in the purpurate shine
When the eastern conduits ran with wine.
FRANCIS THOMPSON—*The Poppy.*

13
Bring poppies for a weary mind
That saddens in a senseless din.
WM. WINTER—*The White Flag.*

POPLAR

Populus Fastigiata

14
Trees that, like the poplar, lift upward all their boughs, give no shade and no shelter, whatever their height. Trees the most lovingly shelter and shade us, when, like the willow, the higher soar their summits, the lowlier droop their boughs.
BULWER-LYTTON—*What Will He Do With It?* Bk. XI. Ch. X. Introductory lines.

POPULARITY

15
Their poet, a sad trimmer, but no less
In company a very pleasant fellow,
Had been the favorite of full many a mess
Of men, and made them speeches when half mellow;
And though his meaning they could rarely guess,
Yet still they deign'd to hiccup or to bellow
The glorious meed of popular applause,
Of which the first ne'er knows the second cause.
BYRON—*Don Juan.* Canto III. St. 82.

16
Some shout him, and some hang upon his car,
To gaze in his eyes, and bless him. Maidens wave
Their 'kerchiefs, and old women weep for joy;
While others, not so satisfied, unhorse
The gilded equipage, and turning loose
His steeds, usurp a place they well deserve.
COWPER—*The Task.* Bk. VI. L. 708.

17
And to some men popularity is always suspicious. Enjoying none themselves, they are prone to suspect the validity of those attainments which command it.
GEO. HENRY LEWES—*The Spanish Drama.* Ch. III.

18
There was ease in Casey's manner as he stept into his place,
There was pride in Casey's bearing and a smile on Casey's face,
And when responding to the cheers he lightly doft his hat,
No stranger in the crowd could doubt, 't was Casey at the bat.
ERNEST L. THAYER—*Casey at the Bat.*

19
All tongues speak of him, and the bleared sights
Are spectacled to see him.
Coriolanus. Act II. Sc. 1. L. 221.

20
I have seen the dumb men throng to see him, and
The blind to hear him speak: matrons flung gloves,
Ladies and maids their scarfs and handkerchers
Upon him as he passed; the nobles bended,
As to Jove's statue, and the commons made
A shower and thunder with their caps and shouts.
Coriolanus. Act II. Sc. 1. L. 278.

21 The ladies call him sweet;
The stairs, as he treads on them, kiss his feet.
Love's Labour's Lost. Act V. Sc. 2. L. 329.

POSSESSION

1
When I behold what pleasure is Pursuit,
What life, what glorious eagerness it is,
Then mark how full Possession falls from this,
How fairer seems the blossom than the fruit,—
I am perplext, and often stricken mute.
Wondering which attained the higher bliss,
The wing'd insect, or the chrysalis
It thrust aside with unreluctant foot.

T. B. ALDRICH—*Sonnet. Pursuit and Possession.*

2
La propriété exclusive est un vol dans la nature.
Exclusive property is a theft against nature.

BRISSOT. (See also PRUD'HON)

3
Quand on n'a pas ce que l'on aime,
Il faut aimer ce que l'on a.
When we have not what we love, we must love what we have.

BUSSY-RABUTIN—*Lettre à Mme. de Sevigné.* (1667)

4
I die,—but first I have possess'd,
And come what may, I *have been* bless'd.

BYRON—*The Giaour.* L. 1,114.

5
Britannia needs no bulwarks, no towers along the steep:
Her march is o'er the mountain waves; her home is on the deep.

CAMPBELL—*Ye Mariners of England.*
(See also CARLYLE)

6
Providence has given to the French the empire of the land, to the English that of the sea, to the Germans that of—the air!

CARLYLE—*Essays. Richter.*
(See also CAMPBELL, LOUIS XVIII, WALLER, WEBSTER)

7
This is the truth as I see it, my dear,
Out in the wind and the rain:
They who have nothing have little to fear,
Nothing to lose or to gain.

MADISON CAWEIN—*The Bellman.*

8
Male parta, male dilabuntur.
What is dishonorably got, is dishonorably squandered.

CICERO—*Philippicæ.* II. 27.

9
As having nothing, and yet possessing all things.

II Corinthians. VI. 10.

10
Ah, yet, e'er I descend to th' grave,
May I a *small House* and a *large Garden* have.
And a *few Friends*, and *many Books* both true,
Both wise, and both delightful too.
And since *Love* ne'er will from me flee,
A *Mistress* moderately fair,
And good as *Guardian angels* are,
Only belov'd and loving me.

ABRAHAM COWLEY—*The Wish.* St. 2.

11
Of a rich man who was mean and niggardly, he said, "That man does not possess his estate, but his estate possesses him."

DIOGENES LAERTIUS—*Lives of Eminent Philosophers.* Bion. III.

12
Property has its duties as well as its rights.

THOMAS DRUMMOND—*Letter to the Tipperary Magistrates.* May 22, 1838. Letter composed jointly by DRUMMOND, WOLFE and PIGOT. Phrase quoted by GLADSTONE, also by DISRAELI—*Sybil.* Bk. I. Ch. 11.

13
My apple trees will never get across
And eat the cones under his pines, I tell him.
He only says, "Good fences make good neighbors."

ROBERT FROST—*Mending Wall.*

14
It maybe said of them [the Hollanders], as of the Spaniards, that the sun never sets upon their Dominions.

THOS. GAGE—*New Survey of the West Indies. Epistle Dedicatory.* London, 1648. ALEXANDER THE GREAT claimed the same for his dominions. See WILLIAMS—*Life*—Ch. XIII. HOWELL—*Familiar Letters* claimed for PHILIP II. Also in FULLER—*Life of Drake;* in *The Holy State*, and in CAMDEN—*Summary of Career of Philip.* II. *Annals.* Ed. HEARNE. P. 778. Claimed for Portugal by CAMOENS—*Luciad.* I. 8. Claimed for Rome by CLAUDIAN. XXIV. 138. MINUTIUS FELIX—*Octavius.* VI. 3. OVID—*Fasti.* II. 136. RUTILIUS. I. 53. TIBULLUS—*Elegiæ.* Bk. II. V. VERGIL—*Æneid.* VI. 795.
(See also GUARINI, PASCAL, SCHILLER, SCHUPPIUS, SCOTT, SMITH, WEBSTER, WILHELM II)

15
Denn was man schwarz auf weiss besitzt
Kann man getrost nach Hause tragen.
For what one has in black and white,
One can carry home in comfort.

GOETHE—*Faust.* I. 4. 42.

16
Altera figlia
Di quel monarca a cui
Nè anco, quando annotta, il Sol tramonta.
The proud daughter of that monarch to whom when it grows dark [elsewhere] the sun never sets.

GUARINI—*Pastor Fido.* (1590) On the marriage of the Duke of Savoy with Catherine of Austria.
(See also GAGE)

17
Wouldst thou both eat thy cake and have it?

HERBERT—*The Church. The Size.*
(See also PLAUTUS)

18
Possession means to sit astride the world
Instead of having it astride of you.

CHARLES KINGSLEY—*Saint's Tragedy.* I. 4.

19
Un tiens vaut, ce dit-on, mieux que deux tu l'auras.
L'un est sûr, l'autre ne l'est pas.
It is said, that the thing you possess is worth more than two you may have in the future. The one is sure and the other is not.

LA FONTAINE—*Fables.* V. 3.

20
Les Anglais, nation trop fière,
S'arrogent l'empire des mers;

Les Français, nation légère,
S'emparent de celui des airs.

The English, a spirited nation, claim the empire of the sea; the French, a calmer nation, claim that of the air.

LOUIS XVIII, when Comte de Provence, 1783. *Impromter sur nos decouverte ærostatiques.* Year of the aeronautical experiments of the brothers MONTGOLFIER, PILATRE DE ROZIER, and MARQUIS D'ARLANDES.

(See also CARLYLE)

1

Aspiration sees only one side of every question; possession, many.

LOWELL—*Among my Books. New England Two Centuries Ago.*

2

Cleon hath ten thousand acres,—
Ne'er a one have I;
Cleon dwelleth in a palace,—
In a cottage I.

CHARLES MACKAY—*Cleon and I.*

3

Property in land is capital; property in the funds is income without capital; property in mortgage is both capital and income.

LORD MANSFIELD.

4

Extra fortunam est, quidquid donatur amicis;
Quas dederis, selas semper habebis opes.

Who gives to friends so much from Fate secures,
That is the only wealth for ever yours.

MARTIAL—*Epigrams.* V. 42.

(See also QUARLES)

5

Is it not lawful for me to do what I will with mine own?

Matthew. XX. 15.

6

Unto every one that hath shall be given, and he shall have abundance; but from him that hath not shall be taken away even that which he hath.

Matthew. XXV. 29.

7

Ce chien est à moi, disaient ces pauvres enfants; c'est là ma place au soleil. Voilà le commencement et l'image de l'usurpation de toute la terre.

That dog is mine said those poor children; that place in the sun is mine; such is the beginning and type of usurpation throughout the earth.

PASCAL—*La Pensées.* Ch. VII. 1.

(See also GAGE)

8

Male partum, male disperit.

Badly gotten, badly spent.

PLAUTUS—*Pœn.* IV. 2. 22.

9

What is yours is mine, and all mine is yours.

PLAUTUS—*Trinummus.* Act II. Sc. 2. RILEY's trans.

10

Non tibi illud apparere si sumas potest.

If you spend a thing you can not have it.

PLAUTUS—*Trinummus.* II. 4. 12.

(See also HERBERT)

11

Nihil enim æque gratum est adeptis, quam concupiscentibus.

An object in possession seldom retains the same charms which it had when it was longed for.

PLINY the Younger—*Epistles.* II. 15.

12

La propriété, c'est le vol.

Property, it is theft.

PRUD'HON—*Principle of Right.* Ch. I. Attributed to FOURNIER by LOUIS BLANC—*Organization du Travail.*

(See also BRISSOT)

13

The goods we spend we keep; and what we save
We lose; and only what we lose we have.

QUARLES—*Divine Fancies.* Bk. IV. Art. 70. Early instances of same in SENECA—*De Beneficiis.* LVI. Ch. III. *Gesta Romanorum.* Ch. XVI. Ed. 1872. P. 300. JEREMY TAYLOR. Note to *Holy Dying.* Ch. II. Sec. XIII. Vol. III. of Works. C. P. Eden's ed.

(See also MARTIAL, also COURTENAY under EPITAPHS, MILLER under GIFTS)

14

Ich heisse
Der reichste Mann in der getauften Welt;
Die Sonne geht in meinem Staat nicht unter.

I am called the richest man in Christendom.
The sun never sets on my dominions.

SCHILLER—*Don Carlos.* I. 6. 60.

(See also GAGE)

15

The king of Spain is a great potentate, who stands with one foot in the east and the other in the west; and the sun never sets that it does not shine on some of his dominions.

BALTHASAR SCHUPPIUS—*Abgenötigte Ehrenrettung.* (1660)

(See also GAGE)

16

The sun never sets on the immense empire of Charles V.

SCOTT—*Life of Napoleon.* Ch. LIX.

(See also GAGE)

17

That what we have we prize not to the worth
Whiles we enjoy it, but being lack'd and lost,
Why, then we rack the value, then we find
The virtue that possession would not show us
While it was ours.

Much Ado About Nothing. Act IV. Sc. 1. L. 220.

18

I ne'er could any lustre see
In eyes that would not look on me;
I ne'er saw nectar on a lip
But where my own did hope to sip.

R. B. SHERIDAN—*Duenna. Air.* Act I. Sc. 2.

19

Why should the brave Spanish soldiers brag? The sunne never sets in the Spanish dominions, but ever shineth on one part or other we have conquered for our king.

CAPTAIN JOHN SMITH—*Advertisements for the Unexperienced, etc.* Mass. Hist. Soc. Coll. Third Series. Vol. III. P. 49.

(See also GAGE)

1
Possession, they say, is eleven points of the law.
SWIFT—*Works*. Vol. XVII. P. 270. COLLEY CIBBER—*Woman's Wit*. Act I.

2
Others may use the ocean as their road;
Only the English make it their abode.
WALLER—*On a War with Spain*.
(See also CAMPBELL)

3
A power which has dotted over the surface of the whole globe with her possessions and military posts, whose morning drum-beat, following the sun, and keeping company with the hours, circles the earth with one continuous and unbroken strain of the martial airs of England.
DANIEL WEBSTER—*Speech. The Presidential Protest*. May 7, 1834.

4
Germany must have her place in the sun.
Attributed to WILHELM II., German Kaiser, July, 1908.
(See also GAGE)

5
People may have *too much* of a good *thing:*
Full as an egg of wisdom thus I sing.
JOHN WOLCOT (Peter Pindar)—*Subjects for Painters. The Gentleman and his Wife*.

6
For why? because the good old rule
Sufficeth them, the simple plan
That they should take, who have the power,
And they should keep, who can.
WORDSWORTH—*Rob Roy's Grave*. Motto of SCOTT'S *Rob Roy*.

7
Lord of himselfe, though not of lands,
And having nothing, yet hath all.
SIR HENRY WOTTON—*The Character of a Happy Life*. St. 6.

POST (LETTERS)

8
(He) put that which was most material in the postscript.
BACON—*Essays*. Arber's Ed. 93.
(See also STEELE)

9
He whistles as he goes, light-hearted wretch,
Cold and yet cheerful; messenger of grief
Perhaps to thousands, and of joy to some.
COWPER—*Winter Evening*. Bk. IV. L. 12. (Of the Postman.)

10
Belshazzar had a letter,—
He never had but one;
Belshazzar's correspondence
Concluded and begun
In that immortal copy
The conscience of us all
Can read without its glasses
On revelation's wall.
EMILY DICKINSON—*Poems*. XXV. (Ed. 1891) *Belshazzar had a Letter*.

11
The welcome news is in the letter found;
The carrier's not commission'd to expound;
It speaks itself, and what it does contain,
In all things needful to be known, is plain.
DRYDEN—*Religio Laici*. L. 366.

12
Carrier of news and knowledge,
Instrument of trade and industry,
Promoter of mutual acquaintance,
Of peace and good-will
Among men and nations.
CHARLES W. ELIOT—*Inscription on Southeast corner of Post-office*, Washington, D. C.

13
Messenger of sympathy and love,
Servant of parted friends,
Consoler of the lonely,
Bond of the scattered family,
Enlarger of the common life.
CHARLES W. ELIOT—*Inscription on Southwest corner of Post-office*, Washington, D. C.

14
Every day brings a ship,
Every ship brings a word;
Well for those who have no fear,
Looking seaward well assured
That the word the vessel brings
Is the word they wish to hear.
EMERSON—*Letters*.

15
Sent letters by posts . . . being hastened and pressed on.
Esther. VIII. 10. 14.

16
Thy letter sent to prove me,
Inflicts no sense of wrong;
No longer wilt thou love me,—
Thy letter, though, is long.
HEINE—*Book of Songs. New Spring*. No. 34.

17
Neither snow, nor rain, nor heat, nor night stays these couriers from the swift completion of their appointed rounds.
HERODOTUS—*Inscription on the front of the Post office*, New York City.

18
Letters, from *absent* friends, extinguish *fear*,
Unite *division*, and draw distance *near;*
Their *magic* force each *silent* wish conveys,
And wafts *embodied* thought, a thousand ways:
Could *souls* to *bodies* write, *death's* pow'r were *mean*,
For minds could then *meet* minds with heav'n between.
AARON HILL—*Verses Written on a Window in a Journey to Scotland*.

19
An exquisite invention this,
Worthy of Love's most honeyed kiss,—
This art of writing billet-doux—
In buds, and odors, and bright hues!
In saying all one feels and thinks
In clever daffodils and pinks;
In puns of tulips; and in phrases,
Charming for their truth, of daisies.
LEIGH HUNT—*Love-Letters Made of Flowers*.

20
A piece of simple goodness—a letter gushing from the heart; a beautiful unstudied vindication of the worth and untiring sweetness of human nature—a record of the invulnerability of man, armed with high purpose, sanctified by truth.
DOUGLAS JERROLD—*Specimens of Jerrold's Wit. The Postman's Budget*.

1
A strange volume of real life in the daily packet of the postman. Eternal love and instant payment!
DOUGLAS JERROLD—*Specimens of Jerrold's Wit. The Postman's Budget.*

2
My days are swifter than a post.
Job. IX. 25.

3
Kind messages, that pass from land to land;
Kind letters, that betray the heart's deep history,
In which we feel the pressure of a hand,—
One touch of fire,—and all the rest is mystery!
LONGFELLOW—*The Seaside and Fireside. Dedication.* St. 5.

4
Good-bye—my paper's out so nearly,
I've only room for, Yours sincerely.
MOORE—*The Fudge Family in Paris.* Letter VI.

5
Je n'ai fait celle-ci plus longue que parceque je n'ai pas eu le loisir de la faire plus courte.
I have only made this letter rather long because I have not had time to make it shorter.
PASCAL—*Lettres provinciales.* 16. Dec. 14, 1656.

6
Soon as thy letters trembling I unclose,
That well-known name awakens all my woes.
POPE—*Eloisa to Abelard.* L. 29.

7
Line after line my gushing eyes o'erflow,
Led thro' a sad variety of woe:
Now warm in love, now with'ring in my bloom,
Lost in a convent's solitary gloom!
POPE—*Eloisa to Abelard.* L. 35.

8
Heav'n first taught letters for some wretch's aid,
Some banish'd lover, or some captive maid.
POPE—*Eloisa to Abelard.* L. 51.

9
Ev'n so, with all submission, I
* * * * *
Send you each year a homely letter,
Who may return me much a better.
PRIOR—*Epistle to Fleetwood Shepherd.* L. 23.

10
And oft the pangs of absence to remove
By letters, soft interpreters of love.
PRIOR—*Henry and Emma.* L. 147.

11
I will touch
My mouth unto the leaves, caressingly;
And so wilt thou. Thus, from these lips of mine
My message will go kissingly to thine,
With more than Fancy's load of luxury,
And prove a true love-letter.
J. G. SAXE—*Sonnet.* (*With a Letter.*)

12
The letter is too long by half a mile.
Love's Labour's Lost. Act V. Sc. 2. L. 54.

13
Here are a few of the unpleasant'st words
That ever blotted paper!
Merchant of Venice. Act III. Sc. 2. L. 254.

14
Tell him there's a post come from my master, with his horn full of good news.
Merchant of Venice. Act V. Sc. 1. L. 46.

15
What! have I 'scaped love-letters in the holiday-time of my beauty, and am I now a subject for them?
Merry Wives of Windsor. Act II. Sc. 1. L. 1.

16
I have a letter from her
Of such contents as you will wonder at:
The mirth whereof so larded with my matter,
That neither singly can be manifested,
Without the show of both.
Merry Wives of Windsor. Act IV. Sc. 6. L. 12.

17
Jove and my stars be praised! Here is yet a postcript.
Twelfth Night. Act II. Sc. 5. L. 187.

18
If this letter move him not, his legs cannot. I'll give 't him.
Twelfth Night. Act III. Sc. 4. L. 188.

19
Let me hear from thee by letters.
Two Gentlemen from Verona. Act I. Sc. 1. L. 57.

20
A woman seldom writes her Mind, but in her Postscript.
STEELE—*Spectator.* No. 79.
(See also BACON)

21
Go, little letter, apace, apace,
Fly;
Fly to the light in the valley below—
Tell my wish to her dewy blue eye.
TENNYSON—*The Letter.* St. 2.

22
I read
Of that glad year that once had been,
In those fall'n leaves which kept their green,
The noble letters of the dead:
And strangely on the silence broke
The silent-speaking words.
TENNYSON—*In Memoriam.* Pt. XCV.

23
Thou bringest * * *
* * * letters unto trembling hands.
TENNYSON—*In Memoriam.* Pt. X.

POSTERITY (See also ANCESTRY)

24
Think of your forefathers! Think of your posterity!
JOHN Q. ADAMS—*Speech at Plymouth.* Dec. 22, 1802.

25
Herself the solitary scion left
Of a time-honour'd race.
BYRON—*The Dream.* St. 2.

26
He thinks posterity is a pack-horse, always ready to be loaded.
BENJ. DISRAELI—*Speech.* June 3, 1862.

27
Posterity is a most limited assembly. Those gentlemen who reach posterity are not much more numerous than the planets.
BENJ. DISRAELI—*Speech.* June 3, 1862.

1
Was glänzt ist für den Augenblick geboren;
Das Aechte bleibt der Nachwelt unverloren.
What dazzles, for the moment spends its spirit;
What's genuine, shall posterity inherit.
GOETHE—*Faust. Vorspiel auf dem Theater.* L. 41.

2
Muore per metà chi lascia un' immagine di se stesso nei figli.
He only half dies who leaves an image of himself in his sons.
GOLDONI—*Pamela.* II. 2.

3
As to posterity, I may ask (with somebody whom I have forgot) what has it ever done to oblige me?
GRAY—*Letter to Dr. Wharton.* March 8, 1758.
(See also ROCHE)

4
Audiet pugnas, vitio parentum
Rara juventus.
Posterity, thinned by the crime of its ancestors, shall hear of those battles.
HORACE—*Odes.* Bk. I. 2. 23.

5
Ich verachte die Menschheit in allen ihren Schichten; ich sehe es voraus, dass unsere Nachkommen noch weit unglücklicher sein werden, als wir. Sollte ich nicht ein Sünder sein, wenn ich trotz dieser Ansicht für Nachkommen, d. h. für Unglückliche sorgte?
I despise mankind in all its strata; I foresee that our descendants will be still far unhappier than we are. Would I not be a criminal if, notwithstanding this view, I should provide for progeny, i. e. for unfortunates?
ALEXANDER VON HUMBOLDT, during a conversation with ARAGO in 1812.

6
The man was laughed at as a blunderer who said in a public business: "We do much for posterity; I would fain see them do something for us."
MRS. ELIZABETH MONTAGU—*Letters.* Jan. 1, 1742.
(See also ROCHE)

7
Why should we put ourselves out of our way to do anything for posterity; for what has posterity done for us?
SIR BOYLE ROCHE. During *Grattan's Parliament.* See C. LITTON FLAKINER'S *Studies in Irish History and Biography.*
(See also GRAY, MONTAGUE, STEELE, TRUMBULL)

8
Culpam majorum posteri luunt.
Posterity pays for the sins of their fathers.
QUINTUS CURTIUS RUFUS—*De Rebus Gestis Alexandri Magni.* VII. 5.

9
Quid quæris, quamdiu vixit? Vixit ad posteros.
Why do you ask, how long has he lived? He has lived to posterity.
SENECA—*Epistles.* XCIII.

10
Les étrangers sont la postérité contemporaine.
Strangers are contemporary posterity.
MADAME DE STAËL. See the *Journal* of CAMILLE DESMOULINS.
(See also WALLACE)

11
The survivorship of a worthy man in his son is a pleasure scarce inferior to the hopes of the continuance of his own life.
STEELE—*Spectator.* Oct. 10, 1711.

12
We are always doing, says he, something for Posterity, but I would fain see Posterity do something for us.
STEELE—*Spectator.* Vol. VIII. No. 583.
(See also ROCHE)

13
Suum cuique decus posteritas rependet.
Posterity gives to every man his true honor.
TACITUS—*Annales.* IV. 35.

14
What has poster'ty done for us,
That we, lest they their rights should lose,
Should trust our necks to gripe of noose?
JOHN TRUMBULL—*McFingal.* Canto II. L. 121. (See also ROCHE)

15
A foreign nation is a kind of contemporaneous posterity.
H. B. WALLACE—*Stanley.* Vol. II. P. 89.
(See also DE STAËL. Same idea in FRANKLIN'S Letter to WM. STRAHAN, 1745).

POTOMAC (RIVER)

16
And Potomac flowed calmly, scarce heaving her breast,
With her low-lying billows all bright in the west,
For a charm as from God lulled the waters to rest
Of the fair rolling river.
PAUL HAMILTON HAYNE—*Beyond the Potomac.*

POTTERY

17
I am content to be a *bric-a-bracker* and a Ceramiker.
S. L. CLEMENS (Mark Twain)—*Tramp Abroad.* Ch. XX.

18
For a male person *bric-a-brac* hunting is about as robust a business as making doll-clothes.
S. L. CLEMENS (Mark Twain)—*Tramp Abroad.* Ch. XX.

19
The very "marks" on the bottom of a piece of rare crockery are able to throw me into a gibbering ecstasy.
S. L. CLEMENS (Mark Twain)—*Tramp Abroad.* Ch. XX.

20
Thou spring'st a leak already in thy crown,
A flaw is in thy ill-bak'd vessel found;
'Tis hollow, and returns a jarring sound,
Yet thy moist clay is pliant to command,
Unwrought, and easy to the potter's hand:
Now take the mould; now bend thy mind to feel
The first sharp motions of the forming wheel.
DRYDEN—*Third Satire of Persius.* L. 35.

21
There's a joy without canker or cark,
There's a pleasure eternally new,
Tis to gloat on the glaze and the mark
Of china that's ancient and blue;
Unchipp'd, all the centuries through
It has pass'd, since the chime of it rang,
And they fashion'd it, figures and hue,
In the reign of the Emperor Hwang.

Here's a pot with a cot in a park,
In a park where the peach-blossoms blew,
Where the lovers eloped in the dark,
Lived, died, and were changed into two
Bright birds that eternally flew
Through the boughs of the May, as they sang;
'Tis a tale was undoubtedly true
In the reign of the Emperor Hwang.
ANDREW LANG—*Ballade of Blue China.*

1
Turn, turn, my wheel! Turn round and round
Without a pause, without a sound:
So spins the flying world away!
This clay, well mixed with marl and sand,
Follows the motion of my hand;
For some must follow, and some command,
Though all are made of clay!
LONGFELLOW—*Keramos.* L. 1.

2
Figures that almost move and speak.
LONGFELLOW—*Keramos.* L. 236.

3
And yonder by Nankin, behold!
The Tower of Porcelain, strange and old,
Uplifting to the astonished skies
Its ninefold painted balconies,
With balustrades of twining leaves,
And roofs of tile, beneath whose eaves
Hang porcelain bells that all the time
Ring with a soft, melodious chime;
While the whole fabric is ablaze
With varied tints, all fused in one
Great mass of color, like a maze
Of flowers illumined by the sun.
LONGFELLOW—*Keramos.* L. 336.

4
Said one among them: "Surely not in vain
My substance of the common Earth was ta'en
And to this Figure moulded, to be broke,
Or trampled back to shapeless Earth again."
OMAR KHAYYAM—*Rubaiyat.* St. 84. FITZ-GERALD's trans.

5
All this of Pot and Potter—Tell me then,
Who is the Potter, pray, and who the Pot?
OMAR KHAYYAM—*Rubaiyat.* St. 87. FITZ-GERALD's trans.

6
Hath not the potter power over the clay, of the same lump to make one vessel unto honour, and another unto dishonour?
Romans. IX. 21.

POVERTY

7
Paupertas omnium artium repertrix.
Poverty is the discoverer of all the arts.
APOLLONIUS—*De Magia.* P. 285. 35.

8
Leave the poor
Some time for self-improvement. Let them not
Be forced to grind the bones out of their arms
For bread, but have some space to think and feel
Like moral and immortal creatures.
BAILEY—*Festus.* Sc. *A Country Town.*

9
L'or même à la laideur donne un teint de beauté:
Mais tout devient affreux avec la pauvreté.
Gold gives an appearance of beauty even to ugliness: but with poverty everything becomes frightful.
BOILEAU—*Satires.* VIII. 209.

10
Oh, the little more, and how much it is!
And the little less, and what worlds away.
ROBERT BROWNING—*By the Fireside.* St. 39.

11
Needy knife-grinder! whither are ye going?
Rough is the road, your wheel is out of order;
Bleak blows the blast—your hat has got a hole in it.
So have your breeches.
CANNING—*The Friend of Humanity and the Knife-Grinder.*

12
Thank God for poverty
That makes and keeps us free,
And lets us go our unobtrusive way,
Glad of the sun and rain,
Upright, serene, humane,
Contented with the fortune of a day.
BLISS CARMAN—*The Word at Saint Kavin's.*

13
Paupertatis onus patienter ferre memento.
Patiently bear the burden of poverty.
DIONYSIUS CATO—*Disticha.* Lib. I. 21.

14
He is now fast rising from affluence to poverty.
S. L. CLEMENS (Mark Twain)—*Henry Ward Beecher's Farm.*

15
The beggarly last doit.
COWPER—*The Task.* Bk. V. *The Winter Morning Walk.* L. 316.

16
And plenty makes us poor.
DRYDEN—*The Medal.* L. 126.

17
Content with poverty, my soul I arm;
And virtue, though in rags, will keep me warm.
DRYDEN—*Third Book of Horace. Ode* 29.

18
Living from hand to mouth.
DU BARTAS—*Divine Weekes and Workes.* Second Week. First Day. Pt. IV.

19
The greatest man in history was the poorest.
EMERSON—*Domestic Life.*

20
Thou source of all my bliss and all my woe,
That found'st me poor at first, and keep'st me so.
GOLDSMITH—*Deserted Village.* L. 413.

21
The nakedness of the indigent world may be clothed from the trimmings of the vain.
GOLDSMITH—*Vicar of Wakefield.* Ch. IV.
(See also SHELLEY under LABOR)

22
Chill penury repress'd their noble rage,
And froze the genial current of the soul.
GRAY—*Elegy in a Country Churchyard.* St. 13.

23
Poverty is no sin.
HERBERT—*Jacula Prudentum.*

24
Yes, child of suffering, thou may'st well be sure
He who ordained the Sabbath loves the poor!
O. W. HOLMES—*Urania; or, A Rhymed Lesson.* L. 325.

25
O God! that bread should be so dear,
And flesh and blood so cheap!
HOOD—*The Song of the Shirt.*

1 Stitch! stitch! stitch!
In poverty, hunger, and dirt,
And still with a voice of dolorous pitch,
Would that its tone could reach the Rich,
She sang this "Song of the Shirt!"
HOOD—*Song of the Shirt.* St. 11.

2
Magnas inter opes inops.
Penniless amid great plenty.
HORACE—*Carmina.* Bk. III. 16. 28.

3
Pauper enim non est cui rerum suppetet usus.
He is not poor who has the use of necessary things.
HORACE—*Epistles.* I. 12. 4.

4
Ibit eo quo vis qui zonam perdidit.
The man who has lost his purse will go wherever you wish.
HORACE—*Epistles.* II. 2. 40.

5
Grind the faces of the poor.
Isaiah. III. 15.

6
The poor always ye have with you.
John. XII. 8.

7
All this [wealth] excludes but one evil,—poverty.
SAMUEL JOHNSON—*Boswell's Life of Johnson.* (1777)

8
Nil habet infelix paupertas durius in se
Quam quod ridiculos homines facit.
Cheerless poverty has no harder trial than this, that it makes men the subject of ridicule.
JUVENAL—*Satires.* III. V. 152.

9
Haud facile emergunt quorum virtutibus obstat
Res angusta domi.
They do not easily rise whose abilities are repressed by poverty at home.
JUVENAL—*Satires.* III. 164.

10
Hic vivimus ambitiosa
Paupertate omnes.
Here we all live in ambitious poverty.
JUVENAL—*Satires.* III. 182.

11
O Poverty, thy thousand ills combined
Sink not so deep into the generous mind,
As the contempt and laughter of mankind.
JUVENAL—*Satires.* III. L. 226. GIFFORD'S trans.

12
Cantabit vacuus coram latrone viator.
The traveler without money will sing before the robber.
JUVENAL—*Satires.* X. 22.

13
Paupertas fugitur, totoque arcessitur orbe.
Poverty is shunned and persecuted all over the globe.
LUCAN—*Pharsalia.* I. 166.

14
If you are poor now, Æmilianus, you will always be poor. Riches are now given to none but the rich.
MARTIAL—*Epigrams.* Bk. V. Ep. 8.

15
Non est paupertas, Nestor, habere nihil.
To have nothing is not poverty.
MARTIAL—*Epigrams.* XI. 32. 8.

16
La pauvreté des biens est aysee à guerir; la pauvreté de l'âme, impossible.
The lack of wealth is easily repaired; but the poverty of the soul is irreparable.
MONTAIGNE—*Essays.* III. 10.

17
Rattle his bones over the stones!
He's only a pauper whom nobody owns!
THOMAS NOEL—*The Pauper's Drive.*

18
Horrea formicæ tendunt ad inania nunquam
Nullus ad amissas ibit amicus opes.
Ants do not bend their ways to empty barns, so no friend will visit the place of departed wealth.
OVID—*Tristium.* I. 9. 9.

19
Inops, potentem dum vult imitari. perit.
The poor, trying to imitate the powerful, perish.
PHÆDRUS—*Fables.* I. 24. 1.

20
Paupertas . . . omnes artes perdocet.
Poverty is a thorough instructress in all the arts.
PLAUTUS—*Stichus.* Act II. 1.

21
But to the world no bugbear is so great,
As want of figure and a small estate.
POPE—*First Book of Horace.* Ep. I. L. 67.

22
Where are those troops of poor, that throng'd of yore
The good old landlord's hospitable door?
POPE—*Satires of Dr. Donne.* Satire II. L. 113.

23
So shall thy poverty come as one that travelleth, and thy want as an armed man.
Proverbs. VI. 11.

24
The destruction of the poor is their poverty.
Proverbs. X. 15.

25
He that hath pity upon the poor lendeth unto the Lord.
Proverbs. XIX. 17.

26
Blessed is he that considereth the poor.
Psalms. XLI. 1.

27
Whene'er I walk the public ways,
How many poor that lack ablution
Do probe my heart with pensive gaze,
And beg a trivial contribution.
OWEN SEAMAN—*Bitter Cry of the Great Unpaid.*
(See also WATTS)

28
Non qui parum habet, sed qui plus cupit, pauper est.
Not he who has little, but he who wishes for more, is poor.
SENECA—*Epistolæ Ad Lucilium.* II.

29
Nemo tam pauper vivit quam natus est.
No one lives so poor as he is born.
SENECA—*Quare bonis viris.*

1
No, madam, 'tis not so well that I am poor, though many of the rich are damned.
All's Well That Ends Well. Act I. Sc. 3. L. 17.

2
I am as poor as Job, my lord, but not so patient.
Henry IV. Pt. II. Act I. Sc. 2. L. 144.

3
It is still her use
To let the wretched man outlive his wealth,
To view with hollow eye and wrinkled brow
An age of poverty.
Merchant of Venice. Act IV. Sc. 1. L. 268.

4
Poor and content is rich and rich enough,
But riches fineless is as poor as winter
To him that ever fears he shall be poor.
Othello. Act III. Sc. 3. L. 172.

5
Steep'd me in poverty to the very lips.
Othello. Act IV. Sc. 2. L. 50.

6
The world affords no law to make thee rich;
Then be not poor, but break it, and take this.
My poverty, but not my will, consents.
I pay thy poverty, and not thy will.
Romeo and Juliet. Act V. Sc. 1. L. 73.

7
Whose plenty made him pore.
SPENSER—*Faerie Queene.* Bk. I. Canto IV. St. 29.

8
His rawbone cheekes, through penurie and pine,
Were shronke into his jawes, as he did never dyne.
SPENSER—*Faerie Queene.* Bk. I. Canto IX. St. 35.

9
Paupertas sanitatis mater.
Poverty is the mother of health.
VINCENT OF BEAUVAIS—*Speculum Historiale.* Bk. X. Ch. LXXI. HERBERT—*Jacula Prudentum.*

10
Whene'er I take my walks abroad,
How many poor I see!
WATTS—*Praise for Mercies.*
(See also SEAMAN)

POWER

11
Give me a lever long enough
And a prop strong enough,
I can single handed move the world.
ARCHIMEDES.

12
Odin, thou whirlwind, what a threat is this
Thou threatenest what transcends thy might, even thine,
For of all powers the mightiest far art thou,
Lord over men on earth, and Gods in Heaven;
Yet even from thee thyself hath been withheld
One thing—to undo what thou thyself hast ruled.
MATTHEW ARNOLD—*Balder Dead. The Funeral.*

13
He hath no power that hath not power to use.
BAILEY—*Festus.* Sc. *A Visit.*

14
Then, everlasting Love, restrain thy will;
'Tis god-like to have power, but not to kill.
BEAUMONT AND FLETCHER—*The Chances.* Act II. Sc. 2. *Song.*

15
The balance of power.
BURKE—*Speech.* (1741) SIR ROBT. WALPOLE—*Speech.* (1741) JOHN WESLEY—*Journal*, Sept. 20, 1790, ascribes it to "the King of Sweden." A German Diet, or the Ballance of Europe. Title of a Folio of 1653.
(See also WELLINGTON)

16
Dim with the mist of years, gray flits the shade of power.
BYRON—*Childe Harold.* Canto II. St. 2.

17
Men are never very wise and select in the exercise of a new power.
WM. ELLERY CHANNING—*The Present Age. An Address.* (1841)

18
Iron hand in a velvet glove.
Attributed to CHARLES V. Used also by NAPOLEON. See CARLYLE—*Latter Day Pamphlets, No.* II.

19
To know the pains of power, we must go to those who have it; to know its pleasures, we must go to those who are seeking it: the pains of power are real, its pleasures imaginary.
C. C. COLTON—*Lacon.* P. 255.

20
Qui peut ce qui lui plaît, commande alors qu'il prie.
Whoever can do as he pleases, commands when he entreats.
CORNEILLE—*Sertorius.* IV. 2.

21
So mightiest powers by deepest calms are fed,
And sleep, how oft, in things that gentlest be!
BARRY CORNWALL—*Songs. The Sea in Calm.* L. 13.

22
For what can power give more than food and drink,
To live at ease, and not be bound to think?
DRYDEN—*Medal.* L. 235.

23
Du bist noch nicht der Mann den Teufel festzuhalten.
Neither art thou the man to catch the fiend and hold him!
GOETHE—*Faust.* I. 3. 336.

24
Patience and Gentleness is Power.
LEIGH HUNT—*Sonnet. On a Lock of Milton's Hair.*

25
O what is it proud slime will not believe
Of his own worth, to hear it equal praised
Thus with the gods?
BEN JONSON—*Sejanus.* Act I.

26
Nihil est quod credere de se
Non possit, quum laudatur dis æqua potestas.
There is nothing which power cannot believe of itself, when it is praised as equal to the gods
JUVENAL—*Satires.* IV. 70.

1
Et qui nolunt occidere quemquam
Posse volunt.
Those who do not wish to kill any one, wish they had the power.
JUVENAL—*Satires*. X. 96.

2 Without his rod revers'd,
And backward mutters of dissevering power.
MILTON—*Comus*. L. 816.

3
Ut desint vires tamen est laudanda voluntas.
Though the power be wanting, yet the wish is praiseworthy.
OVID—*Epistolæ Ex Ponto*. III. 4. 79.

4
A cane non magno sæpe tenetur aper.
The wild boar is often held by a small dog.
OVID—*Remedia Amoris*. 422.

5
Nunquam est fidelis cum potente societas.
A partnership with men in power is never safe.
PHÆDRUS—*Fables*. I. 5. 1.

6
Unlimited power corrupts the possessor.
PITT—*Speaking of the case of John Wilkes*. (1770)

7
And deal damnation round the land.
POPE—*The Universal Prayer*. St. 7.

8
The powers that be are ordained of God.
Romans. XIII. 1.

9
Kann ich Armeen aus der Erde stampfen?
Wächst mir ein Kornfeld in der flachen Hand?
Can I summon armies from the earth?
Or grow a cornfield on my open palm?
SCHILLER—*Die Jungfrau von Orleans*. I. 3.

10
Ich fühle eine Armee in meiner Faust.
I feel an army in my fist.
SCHILLER—*Die Rauber*. II. 3.

11
Quod non potest vult posse, qui nimium potest.
He who is too powerful, is still aiming at that degree of power which is unattainable.
SENECA—*Hippolytus*. 215.

12
Minimum decet libere cui multum licet.
He who has great power should use it lightly.
SENECA—*Troades*. 336.

13
No pent-up Utica contracts your powers,
But the whole boundless continent is yours.
JONATHAN SEWALL—*Epilogue to* ADDISON'S *Cato*. Written for the performance at the Bow Street Theatre, Portsmouth, N. H.

14
The awful shadow of some unseen Power
Floats, tho' unseen, amongst us.
SHELLEY—*Hymn to Intellectual Beauty*.

15
Power, like a desolating pestilence,
Pollutes whate'er it touches; and obedience,
Bane of all genius, virtue, freedom, truth,
Makes slaves of men, and of the human frame
A mechanized automaton.
SHELLEY—*Queen Mab*. Pt. III.

16
Male imperando summum imperium amittitur.
The highest power may be lost by misrule.
SYRUS—*Maxims*.

17
Suspectum semper invisumque dominantibus qui proximus destinaretur.
Rulers always hate and suspect the next in succession.
TACITUS—*Annales*. I. 21.

18
Imperium flagitio acquisitum nemo unquam bonis artibus exercuit.
Power acquired by guilt was never used for a good purpose.
TACITUS—*Annales*. I. 30.

19
Imperium cupientibus nihil medium inter summa et præcipitia.
In the struggle between those seeking power there is no middle course.
TACITUS—*Annales*. II. 74.

20
Potentiam cautis quam acribus consiliis tutius haberi.
Power is more safely retained by cautious than by severe councils.
TACITUS—*Annales*. XI. 29.

21
Cupido dominandi cunctis affectibus flagrantior est.
Lust of power is the most flagrant of all the passions.
TACITUS—*Annales*. XV. 53.

22
I thought that my invincible power would hold the world captive, leaving me in a freedom undisturbed. Thus night and day I worked at the chain with huge fires and cruel hard strokes. When at last the work was done and the links were complete and unbreakable, I found that it held me in its grip.
RABINDRANATH TAGORE—*Gitanjali*. 31.

23
He never sold the truth to serve the hour,
Nor paltered with Eternal God for power.
TENNYSON—*Ode on the Death of the Duke of Wellington*.

24
Et errat longe, mea quidem sententia,
Qui imperium credat esse gravius, aut stabilius,
Vi quod fit, quam illud quod amicitia adjungitur.
And he makes a great mistake, in my opinion at least, who supposes that authority is firmer or better established when it is founded by force than that which is welded by affection.
TERENCE—*Adelph*. Act I. 1. L. 40.

25
Flectere si nequeo superos, Acheronta movebo.
If I can not influence the gods, I shall move all hell.
VERGIL—*Æneid*. VII. 312.

26
An untoward event. (Threatening to disturb the balance of power.)
WELLINGTON. On the destruction of the Turkish Navy at the battle of Navarino, Oct. 20, 1827. (See also BURKE)

1
A power is passing from the earth.
WORDSWORTH. *Lines on the Expected Dissolution of Mr. Fox.*

PRAISE

2
Praise undeserved is satire in disguise.
BROADHURST—*British Beauties.* *Epigram* in the *Garland* signed B. (1721) Attributed also to DR. KENDRICK. Appears also in TONSON'S *Miscellanies.* Anon. *The Celebrated Beauties of the British Court.*
(See also POPE)

3
Trahimur omnes laudis studio, et optimus quisque maxime gloria ducitur.
We are all excited by the love of praise, and the noblest are most influenced by glory.
CICERO—*Oratio Pro Licinio Archia.* XI.

4 Lætus sum
Laudari me abs te, pater, laudato viro.
I am pleased to be praised by a man so praised as you, father. [Words used by Hector.]
Quoted by CICERO—*Tusc. Quæst.* IV. 31, 67; *Epist.* Bk. XV. 6.

5
Earth, with her thousand voices, praises God.
COLERIDGE—*Hymn Before Sunrise in the Vale of Chamouni.* Last line.

6
Praise the bridge that carried you over.
GEO. COLMAN (the Younger)—*Heir-at-Law.* Act I. Sc. 1.

7 Praise enough
To fill the ambition of a private man,
That Chatham's language was his mother-tongue.
COWPER—*The Task.* Bk. II. L. 235.

8
When needs he must, yet faintly then he praises;
Somewhat the deed, much more the means he raises:
So marreth what he makes, and praising most, dispraises.
PHINEAS FLETCHER — *The Purple Island.* Canto VII. St. 67.

9
Long open panegyric drags at best,
And praise is only praise when well address'd.
GAY. Ep. I. L. 29.

10
Good people all, with one accord,
Lament for Madame Blaize,
Who never wanted a good word—
From those who spoke her praise.
GOLDSMITH—*Elegy on Mrs. Mary Blaize.*

11 Praise me not too much,
Nor blame me, for thou speakest to the Greeks
Who know me.
HOMER—*Iliad.* Bk. X. L. 289. BRYANT'S trans.

12
Praise from a friend, or censure from a foe,
Are lost on hearers that our merits know.
HOMER—*Iliad.* Bk. X. L. 293. POPE'S trans.

13
Laudator temporis acti.
A eulogist of past times.
HORACE—*Ars Poetica.* 173.

14
Principibus placuisse viris non ultima laus est.
To please great men is not the last degree of praise.
HORACE—*Epistles.* I. 17. 35.

15
A refusal of praise is a desire to be praised twice.
LA ROCHEFOUCAULD—*Maxims.* No. 152.

16
Cela est beau, et je vous louerais davantage si vous m'aviez loué moins.
That is fine, and I would have praised you more had you praised me less.
Attributed to LOUIS XIV.

17
The sweeter sound of woman's praise.
MACAULAY—*Lines Written on the Night of 30th of July, 1847.*

18
Join voices, all ye living souls: ye birds,
That singing up to heaven-gate ascend,
Bear on your wings and in your notes his praise.
MILTON—*Paradise Lost.* Bk. V. L. 197.

19
And touch'd their golden harps, and hymning praised
God and his works.
MILTON—*Paradise Lost.* Bk. VII. L. 258.

20
Of whom to be disprais'd were no small praise.
MILTON—*Paradise Regained.* Bk. III. L. 56.

21
Approbation from Sir Hubert Stanley is praise indeed.
THOS. MORTON—*Cure for the Heartache.* Act V. Sc. 2.

22
Solid pudding against empty praise.
POPE—*Dunciad.* Bk. I. L. 54.

23
To what base ends, and by what abject ways,
Are mortals urg'd through sacred lust of praise!
POPE—*Essay on Criticism.* L. 520.

24
Praise undeserved is scandal in disguise.
POPE—*First Epistle of Second Book of Horace.*
(See also BROADHURST)

25
Delightful praise!—like summer rose,
That brighter in the dew-drop glows,
The bashful maiden's cheek appear'd,
For Douglas spoke, and Malcolm heard.
SCOTT—*Lady of the Lake.* Canto II. St. 24.

26
Id facere laus est quod decet, non quod licet.
He deserves praise who does not what he may, but what he ought.
SENECA—*Octavia.* 454.

27 Praising what is lost
Makes the remembrance dear.
All's Well That Ends Well. Act V. Sc. 3. L. 19.

28
Thou wilt say anon he is some kin to thee,
Thou spend'st such high-day wit in praising him.
Merchant of Venice. Act II. Sc. 9. L. 97.

29
Our praises are our wages.
Winter's Tale. Act I. Sc. 2. L. 94.

1
We bow our heads before Thee, and we laud
And magnify Thy name, Almighty God!
But Man is Thy most awful instrument,
In working out a pure intent.
WORDSWORTH—*Ode. Imagination ne'er before Content.*

2
With faint praises one another damn.
WYCHERLEY—*Plain Dealer. Prologue.*
(See also POPE under SATIRE)

3
The love of praise, howe'er conceal'd by art,
Reigns more or less, and glows, in ev'ry heart.
YOUNG—*The Love of Fame.* Satire I. L. 51.

4
I grant the man is vain who writes for praise.
Praise no man e'er deserved who sought no more.
YOUNG—*Night Thoughts.* Night V. L. 3.

5
The most pleasing of all sounds that of your own praise.
XENOPHON—*Hiero.* I. 14. WATSON's trans.

PRAYER

6
Yet then from all my grief, O Lord,
Thy mercy set me free,
Whilst in the confidence of pray'r
My soul took hold on thee.
ADDISON—*Miscellaneous Poems. Divine Ode, made by a Gentleman on the Conclusion of his Travels.* Verse 6.

7
Prayer is the spirit speaking truth to Truth.
BAILEY—*Festus.* Sc. *Elsewhere.*

8
And from the prayer of Want, and plaint of Woe,
O never, never turn away thine ear!
Forlorn, in this bleak wilderness below,
Ah! what were man, should Heaven refuse to hear!
BEATTIE—*Minstrel.* Bk. I. St. 29.

9
God answers sharp and sudden on some prayers,
And thrusts the thing we have prayed for in our face,
A gauntlet with a gift in 't.
E. B. BROWNING—*Aurora Leigh.* Bk. II.

10
Every wish
Is like a prayer—with God.
E. B. BROWNING—*Aurora Leigh.* Bk. II.

11
Hope, he called, belief
In God,—work, worship * * * therefore let us pray!
E. B. BROWNING—*Aurora Leigh.* Bk. III.

12
She knows omnipotence has heard her prayer
And cries, "It shall be done — sometime, somewhere."
OPHELIA G. BROWNING—*Unanswered.*

13
Just my vengeance complete,
The man sprang to his feet,
Stood erect, caught at God's skirts, and prayed!
So, I was afraid!
ROBERT BROWNING—*Instans Tyrannus.* VII.

14
They never sought in vain that sought the Lord aright!
BURNS—*The Cotter's Saturday Night.* St. 6.

15
Father! no prophet's laws I seek,—
Thy laws in Nature's works appear;—
I own myself corrupt and weak,
Yet will I pray, for thou wilt hear.
BYRON—*Prayer of Nature.*

16
Father of Light! great God of Heaven!
Hear'st thou the accents of despair?
Can guilt like man's be e'er forgiven?
Can vice atone for crimes by prayer?
BYRON—*Prayer of Nature.*

17
Pray to be perfect, though material leaven
Forbid the spirit so on earth to be;
But if for any wish thou darest not pray,
Then pray to God to cast that wish away.
HARTLEY COLERIDGE—*Poems.* (*Posthumous.*) *Prayer.*

18
He prayeth best who loveth best
All things, both great and small.
COLERIDGE—*Ancient Mariner.* Pt. VII.

19
He prayeth well who loveth well
Both man and bird and beast.
COLERIDGE—*Ancient Mariner.* Pt. VII.

20
The saints will aid if men will call:
For the blue sky bends over all.
COLERIDGE—*Christabel. Conclusion to* Pt. 1.

21
But maybe prayer is a road to rise,
A mountain path leading toward the skies
To assist the spirit who truly tries.
But it isn't a shibboleth, creed, nor code,
It isn't a pack-horse to carry your load,
It isn't a wagon, it's *only* a road.
And perhaps the reward of the spirit who tries
Is not the goal, but the exercise!
EDMUND VANCE COOKE—*Prayer. The Uncommon Commoner.*

22
Not as we wanted it,
But as God granted it.
QUILLER COUCH—*To Bearers.*

23
And Satan trembles when he sees
The weakest saint upon his knees.
COWPER—*Hymns. Exhortation to Prayer.*

24
I ask not a life for the dear ones,
All radiant, as others have done,
But that life may have just enough shadow
To temper the glare of the sun;
I would pray God to guard them from evil,
But my prayer would bound back to myself:
Ah! a seraph may pray for a sinner,
But a sinner must pray for himself.
CHARLES M. DICKINSON—*The Children.*

25
Our vows are heard betimes! and Heaven takes care
To grant, before we can conclude the prayer:
Preventing angels met it half the way,
And sent us back to praise, who came to pray.
DRYDEN—*Britannia Rediviva.* First lines.
(See also GOLDSMITH)

1
Grant folly's prayers that hinder folly's wish,
And serve the ends of wisdom.
GEORGE ELIOT—*The Spanish Gypsy*. Bk. IV.

2
Almighty Father! let thy lowly child,
Strong in his love of truth, be wisely bold,—
A patriot bard, by sycophants reviled,
Let him live usefully, and not die old!
EBENEZER ELLIOTT—*Corn Law Rhymes. A Poet's Prayer*.

3
Though I am weak, yet God, when prayed,
Cannot withhold his conquering aid.
EMERSON—*The Nun's Aspiration*.

4
To pray, * * * is to desire; but it is to desire what God would have us desire.
He who desires not from the bottom of his heart, offers a deceitful prayer.
FÉNELON—*Pious Thoughts. Advice Concerning Prayer*. MRS. MANT'S trans.

5
Ejaculations are short prayers darted up to God on emergent occasions.
FULLER—*Good Thoughts in Bad Times. Meditations on all Kinds of Prayers. Ejaculations, their Use*. V.

6
So a good prayer, though often used, is still fresh and fair in the ears and eyes of Heaven.
FULLER—*Good Thoughts in Bad Times. Meditations on all Kinds of Prayers*. XII.

7
O Lord of Courage grave,
O Master of this night of Spring!
Make firm in me a heart too brave
To ask Thee anything.
JOHN GALSWORTHY—*The Prayer*.

8
At church, with meek and unaffected grace,
His looks adorn'd the venerable place;
Truth from his lips prevailed with double sway,
And fools, who came to scoff, remain'd to pray.
GOLDSMITH—*The Deserted Village*. L. 177.
(See also DRYDEN)

9
He that will learn to pray, let him go to Sea.
HERBERT—*Jacula Prudentum*. No. 89.

10
Who goes to bed, and doth not pray,
Maketh two nights to every day!
HERBERT — *Temple. The Church. Charms and Knots*. St. 4.

11
Resort to sermons, but to prayers most:
Praying's the end of preaching.
HERBERT—*Temple. The Church Porch*. St. 69.

12
In prayer the lips ne'er act the winning part
Without the sweet concurrence of the heart.
HERRICK—*Hesperides. The Heart*.

13
The prayer of Noah,
He cried out in the darkness, Hear, O God,
Hear HIM: hear this one; through the gates of death,
If life be all past praying for, O give
To Thy great multitude a way to peace;
Give them to HIM.
JEAN INGELOW—*A Story of Doom*. Bk. IX. St. 6.

14
Is there never a chink in the world above
Where they listen for words from below?
JEAN INGELOW—*Supper at the Mill*.

15
O God, if in the day of battle I forget Thee, do not Thou forget me.
WILLIAM KING attributes the prayer to a soldier, in his *Anecdotes of his own time*. P 7. (Ed. 1818)

16
My brother kneels, so saith Kabir,
To stone and brass in heathen-wise,
But in my brother's voice I hear
My own unanswered agonies.
His God is as his fates assign
His prayer is all the world's—and mine.
KIPLING—*Song of Kabir*.
(See also DON MARQUIS under WORSHIP)

17
I ask and wish not to appear
More beauteous, rich or gay:
Lord, make me wiser every year,
And better every day.
LAMB—*A Birthday Thought*.

18
You know I say
Just what I think, and nothing more nor less,
And, when I pray, my heart is in my prayer.
I cannot say one thing and mean another:
If I can't pray, I will not make believe!
LONGFELLOW—*Christus*. Pt. III. *Giles Corey*. Act II. Sc. 3.

19
Let one unceasing, earnest prayer
Be, too, for light,—for strength to bear
Our portion of the weight of care,
That crushes into dumb despair
One half the human race.
LONGFELLOW—*Goblet of Life*. St. 10.

20
Like one in prayer I stood.
LONGFELLOW—*Voices of the Night. Prelude*. St. 11.

21
Vigilate et orate.
Watch and pray.
Mark. XIII. 33. (From the Vulgate.)

22
O Domine Deus! speravi in te;
O care mi Jesu! nunc libera me.
In dura catena, in misera poena,
Disidero te.
Languendo, jemendo, et genuflectendo,
Adoro, imploro, ut liberes me!
O Lord, my God,
I have trusted in Thee;
O Jesu, my dearest One,
Now set me free.
In prison's oppression,
In sorrow's obsession,
I weary for Thee.
With sighing and crying,
Bowed down in dying,
I adore Thee, I implore Thee, set me free.
MARY, QUEEN OF SCOTS. Written in her Book of Devotion before her execution. Trans. by SWINBURNE, in *Mary Stuart*.

1
God warms his hands at man's heart when he prays.
MASEFIELD—*Widow in the Bye Street.* Pt. VI.

2
Ask, and it shall be given you; seek, and ye shall find; knock, and it shall be opened unto you.
Matthew. VII. 7.

3
Every one that asketh receiveth; and he that seeketh findeth.
Matthew. VII. 8.

4
Not what we wish, but what we want,
Oh! let thy grace supply,
The good unask'd, in mercy grant;
The ill, though ask'd, deny.
MERRICK—*Hymn.*

5
Hear his sighs though mute;
Unskillful with what words to pray, let me
Interpret for him.
MILTON—*Paradise Lost.* Bk. XI. L. 31.

6
But that from us aught should ascend to Heav'n
So prevalent as to concern the mind
Of God, high-bless'd, or to incline His will,
Hard to belief may seem; yet this will prayer.
MILTON—*Paradise Lost.* Bk. XI. L. 143.

7
And if by prayer
Incessant I could hope to change the will
Of Him who all things can, I would not cease
To weary Him with my assiduous cries.
MILTON—*Paradise Lost.* Bk. XI. L. 307.

8
Prayer is the soul's sincere desire,
Uttered or unexpressed,
The motion of a hidden fire
That trembles in the breast.
JAMES MONTGOMERY—*Original Hymns. What is Prayer?*

9
Prayer moves the arm
Which moves the world,
And brings salvation down.
JAMES MONTGOMERY—*Prayer.*

10
As down in the sunless retreats of the ocean
Sweet flowers are springing no mortal can see,
So deep in my soul the still prayer of devotion
Unheard by the world, rises silent to Thee.
MOORE—*As Down in the Sunless Retreats.*

11
O sad estate
Of human wretchedness; so weak is man,
So ignorant and blind, that did not God
Sometimes withhold in mercy what we ask,
We should be ruined at our own request.
HANNAH MORE—*Moses in the Bulrushes.* Pt. I.

12
Now I lay me down to take my sleep,
I pray thee, Lord, my soul to keep;
If I should die before I wake,
I pray thee, Lord, my soul to take.
New England Primer. (1814)

13
He pray'd by quantity,
And with his repetitions, long and loud,
All knees were weary.
POLLOK—*Course of Time.* Pt. VIII. L. 628.

14
Father of All! in every age,
In every clime ador'd,
By saint, by savage, and by sage,
Jehovah, Jove, or Lord!
POPE—*Universal Prayer.*

15
If I am right, Thy grace impart,
Still in the right to stay;
If I am wrong, O teach my heart
To find that better way!
POPE—*Universal Prayer.*

16
In all thou dost first let thy Prayers ascend,
And to the Gods thy Labours first commend,
From them implore Success, and hope a prosperous End.
PYTHAGORAS—*Golden Verses.* L. 49. See M. DACIER'S *Life of Pythagoras.*

17
They were ordinary soldiers, just the common Jean and Hans,
One from the valley of the Rhine and one from fair Provence.
They were simple-hearted fellows—every night each said his prayer:
The one prayed Vater Unser and the other Notre Père.
C. A. RICHMOND—*Lord's Prayer.*

18
At the muezzin's call for prayer,
The kneeling faithful thronged the square,
And on Pushkara's lofty height
The dark priest chanted Brahma's might.
Amid a monastery's weeds
An old Franciscan told his beads;
While to the synagogue there came
A Jew to praise Jehovah's name.
The one great God looked down and smiled
And counted each His loving child;
For Turk and Brahmin, monk and Jew
Had reached Him through the gods they knew.
HARRY ROMAINE—*Ad Cœlum.* In *Munsey's Mag.* Jan. 1895.

19
I pray the prayer the Easterners do,
May the peace of Allah abide with you;
Wherever you stay, wherever you go,
May the beautiful palms of Allah grow;
Through days of labor, and nights of rest,
The love of Good Allah make you blest;
So I touch my heart—as the Easterners do,
May the peace of Allah abide with you.
Salaam Alaikum. (Peace be with you).
Author unknown.

20
In vota miseros ultimus cogit timor.
Fear of death drives the wretched to prayer.
SENECA—*Agamemnon.* 560.

21
Nulla res carius constat quam quæ precibus empta est.
Nothing costs so much as what is bought by prayers.
SENECA—*De Beneficiis.* II. 1.

1
The first petition that we are to make to Almighty God is for a good *conscience*, the next for *health of mind*, and then of *body*.
SENECA—*Epistles*. XIV.

2
Bow, stubborn knees; and, heart, with strings of steel,
Be soft as sinews of the new-born babe.
Hamlet. Act III. Sc. 3. L. 70.

3
All his mind is bent to holiness,
To number Ave-Maries on his beads.
Henry VI. Pt. II. Act I. Sc. 3. L. 58.

4 Rather let my head
Stoop to the block than these knees bow to any
Save to the God of heaven and to my king.
Henry VI. Pt. II. Act IV. Sc. 1. L. 124.

5
Go with me, like good angels, to my end;
And, as the long divorce of steel falls on me,
Make of your prayers one sweet sacrifice,
And lift my soul to heaven.
Henry VIII. Act II. Sc. 1. L. 75.

6 My prayers
Are not words duly hallow'd nor my wishes
More worth than empty vanities; yet prayers and wishes
Are all I can return.
Henry VIII. Act II. Sc. 3. L. 67.

7 "Amen"
Stuck in my throat.
Macbeth. Act II. Sc. 2. L. 32.

8
When I would pray and think, I think and pray
To several subjects; Heaven hath my empty words.
Measure for Measure. Act II. Sc. 4. L. 1.

9
His worst fault is, that he is given to prayer; he is something peevish that way; but nobody but has his fault; but let that pass.
Merry Wives of Windsor. Act I. Sc. 4. L. 13.

10
Well, if my wind were but long enough to say my prayers, I would repent.
Merry Wives of Windsor. Act IV. Sc. 5. L. 104.

11
If you bethink yourself of any crime
Unreconcil'd as yet to heaven and grace,
Solicit for it straight.
Othello. Act V. Sc. 2. L. 26.

12
Earth bears no balsams for mistakes;
Men crown the knave, and scourge the tool
That did his will: but thou, O Lord,
Be merciful to me, a fool.
EDWARD ROWLAND SILL—*The Fool's Prayer*.

13
Four things which are not in thy treasury,
I lay before thee, Lord, with this petition:—
My nothingness, my wants,
My sins, and my contrition.
SOUTHEY—*Occasional Pieces*. XIX. Imitated from the Persian.

14
Prayers are heard in heaven very much in proportion to our faith. Little faith will get very great mercies, but great faith still greater.
SPURGEON—*Gleanings Among the Sheaves. Believing Prayer*.

15
To pray together, in whatever tongue or ritual, is the most tender brotherhood of hope and sympathy that men can contract in this life.
MADAME DE STAËL—*Corinne*. Bk. X. Ch. V.

16
Holy Father, in thy mercy,
Hear our anxious prayer.
Keep our loved ones, now far absent,
'Neath Thy care.
ISABELLA S. STEPHENSON—*Hymn*. Sung universally among the British troops in the Great War.

17
Lord, thy most pointed pleasure take,
And stab my spirit broad awake;
Or, Lord, if too obdurate I,
Choose Thou, before that spirit die,
A piercing pain, a killing sin,
And to my dead heart turn them in.
STEVENSON—*Celestial Surgeon*.

18
My debts are large, my failures great, my shame secret and heavy; yet when I come to ask for my good, I quake in fear lest my prayer be granted.
RABINDRANATH TAGORE—*Gitanjali*. 28.

19
Speak to Him thou for He hears, and spirit with spirit can meet—
Closer is He than breathing, and nearer than hands and feet.
TENNYSON—*Higher Pantheism*.

20 More things are wrought by prayer
Than this world dreams of. Wherefore, let thy voice
Rise like a fountain for me night and day.
For what are men better than sheep or goats
That nourish a blind life within the brain,
If, knowing God, they lift not hands of prayer
Both for themselves and those who call them friend?
TENNYSON—*Morte d'Arthur*. L. 247.

21
Battering the gates of heaven with storms of prayer.
TENNYSON—*St. Simeon Stylites*. L. 7.

22
"'Twas then belike," Honorious cried,
"When you the public fast defied,
Refused to heav'n to raise a prayer,
Because you'd no connections there."
JOHN TRUMBULL—*McFingal*. Canto I. L. 541.

23
From compromise and things half done,
Keep me with stern and stubborn pride;
And when at last the fight is won,
God, keep me still unsatisfied.
LOUIS UNTERMEYER—*Prayer*.

24
God, though this life is but a wraith,
Although we know not what we use,

Although we grope with little faith,
Give me the heart to fight—and lose.
LOUIS UNTERMEYER—*Prayer.*

1 Prayer is
The world in tune,
A spirit-voyce,
And vocall joyes,
Whose Eccho is heaven's blisse.
HENRY VAUGHAN—*The Morning Watch.*

2
Desine fata deum flecti sperare precando.
Cease to think that the decrees of the gods can be changed by prayers.
VERGIL—*Æneid.* VI. 376.

3
Audiit, et voti Phœbus succedere partem
Mente didit, partem volucres dispersit in auras.
Ae half the prayer wi' Phœbus grace did find
The t'other half he whistled down the wind.
VERGIL—*Æneid.* XI. 794. Trans. by SCOTT—*Waverley.* Ch. XLIII. Same idea in HOMER—*Iliad.* XVI. 250.

4
Prayer moves the Hand which moves the world
JOHN AIKMAN WALLACE—*There is an Eye that Never Sleeps.* L. 19.
(See also W. R. WALLACE under MOTHERHOOD)

5
Who is this before whose presence idols tumble to the sod?
While he cries out—"Allah Akbar! and there is no god but God!"
WM. ROSS WALLACE—*El Amin. The Faithful.*

6
Making their lives a prayer.
WHITTIER—*To A. K. on Receiving a Basket of Sea Mosses.*

7
Though smooth be the heartless prayer, no ear in heaven will mind it;
And the finest phrase falls dead, if there is no feeling behind it.
ELLA WHEELER WILCOX—*Art and Heart.* St. 2.

8
The imperfect offices of prayer and praise.
WORDSWORTH—*Excursion.* Bk. I.

9
"What is good for a bootless bene?"
With these dark words begins my Tale;
And their meaning is, whence can comfort spring
When Prayer is of no avail?
WORDSWORTH—*Force of Prayer.*

10
The bells of Ryleston seemed to say,
While she sat listening in the shade,
With vocal music, "God us ayde!"
And all the hills were glad to bear
Their part in this effectual prayer.
WORDSWORTH—*White Doe of Rylstone.* Canto VII. St. 11.

11
Prayer ardent opens heaven.
YOUNG—*Night Thoughts.* Night VIII. L. 721.

12
Doubt not but God who sits on high,
Thy secret prayers can hear;
When a dead wall thus cunningly
Conveys soft whispers to the ear.
Verse inscribed in the Whispering Gallery of Gloucester Cathedral.

PREACHING

13 Of right and wrong he taught
Truths as refined as ever Athens heard;
And (strange to tell) he practis'd what he preach'd.
JOHN ARMSTRONG—*The Art of Preserving Health.* Bk. IV. L. 301.

14
I met a preacher there I knew, and said,
Ill and overworked, how fare you in this scene?
Bravely! said he; for I of late have been
Much cheered with thoughts of Christ, the living bread.
MATTHEW ARNOLD—*East London.*

15
I preached as never sure to preach again,
And as a dying man to dying men.
RICHARD BAXTER—*Love Breathing Thanks and Praise.* Pt. 2. St. 29.

16
Faites ce que nous disons, et ne faites pas ce que nous faisons.
Do as we say, and not as we do.
BOCCACCIO—*Decameron.* From the French of SABATIER DE CASTRES—*Troisième Journée.* Novelle VII.
(See also VILLIERS)

17
For the preacher's merit or demerit,
It were to be wished that the flaws were fewer
In the earthen vessel, holding treasure,
But the main thing is, does it hold good measure?
Heaven soon sets right all other matters!
ROBERT BROWNING—*Christmas Eve.* Canto XXII.
(See also HERBERT)

18
Hear how he clears the points o' Faith
Wi' rattlin' an' thumpin'!
Now meekly calm, now wild in wrath,
He's stampin', an' he's jumpin'!
BURNS—*Holy Fair.* St. 13.

19
And pulpit, drum ecclesiastic,
Was beat with fist instead of a stick.
BUTLER—*Hudibras.* Pt. I. Canto I. L. 11.
(See also STANLEY)

20
Take time enough: all other graces
Will soon fill up their proper places.
JOHN BYROM—*Advice to Preach Slow.*
(See also WALKER under READING)

21
Oh, for a *forty-parson power* to chant
Thy praise, Hypocrisy!
BYRON—*Don Juan.* Canto X. St. 34. SYDNEY SMITH quotes this as "a twelve-parson power of conversation."

22
But Cristes loore, and his Apostles twelve,
He taughte, but first he folowed it hymselfe.
CHAUCER—*Canterbury Tales. Prologue.* L. 527.

1
There goes the parson, oh illustrious spark!
And there, scarce less illustrious, goes the clerk.
COWPER—*On Observing Some Names of Little Note.*

2
I venerate the man whose heart is warm,
Whose hands are pure, whose doctrine and whose life,
Coincident, exhibit lucid proof
That he is honest in the sacred cause.
COWPER—*Task.* Bk. II. L. 372.

3
Would I describe a preacher,
* * * *
I would express him simple, grave, sincere;
In doctrine uncorrupt; in language plain,
And plain in manner; decent, solemn, chaste,
And natural in gesture; much impress'd
Himself, as conscious of his awful charge,
And anxious mainly that the flock he feeds
May feel it too; affectionate in look,
And tender in address, as well becomes
A messenger of grace to guilty men.
COWPER—*Task.* Bk. II. L. 394.

4
The things that mount the rostrum with a skip,
And then skip down again, pronounce a text,
Cry hem; and reading what they never wrote
Just fifteen minutes, huddle up their work,
And with a well-bred whisper close the scene!
COWPER—*Task.* Bk. II. L. 408.

5
He that negotiates between God and man,
As God's ambassador, the grand concerns
Of judgment and of mercy, should beware
Of lightness in his speech.
COWPER—*Task.* Bk. II. L. 463.

6
The priest he merry is, and blithe
Three-quarters of a year,
But oh! it cuts him like a scythe
When tithing time draws near.
COWPER—*Yearly Distress.* St. 2.

7
A kick that scarce would move a horse,
May kill a sound divine.
COWPER—*Yearly Distress.* St. 16.

8
Go forth and preach impostures to the world,
But give them truth to build on.
DANTE—*Vision of Paradise.* Canto XXIX. L. 116.

9
God preaches, a noted clergyman,
And the sermon is never long;
So instead of getting to heaven at last,
I'm going all along.
EMILY DICKINSON—*Poems.* VI. *A Service of Song.*

10
The proud he tam'd, the penitent he cheer'd:
Nor to rebuke the rich offender fear'd.
His preaching much, but more his practice wrought;
(A living sermon of the truths he taught;)
For this by rules severe his life he squar'd:
That all might see the doctrines which they heard.
DRYDEN—*Character of a Good Parson.* L. 75.

11
Alas for the unhappy man that is called to stand in the pulpit, and *not* give the bread of life.
EMERSON—*An Address to the Senior Class in Divinity College, Cambridge.* July 15, 1838.

12
But in his duty prompt at every call,
He watch'd and wept, he pray'd and felt for all.
GOLDSMITH—*Deserted Village.* L. 165.

13
They shall knaw a file, and flee unto the mountains of Hepsidam whar the lion roareth and the Wang Doodle mourneth for its first born—ah!
Burlesque Sermon in *Cole's Fun Doctor.* Attributed to ANDREW HARPER as a travesty on sermons preached by itinerant preachers on the Mississippi. Found in *Speaker's Garland.* Vol. VIII. Also claimed for Dow—*Patent Sermons.*

14
Judge not the preacher; for he is thy judge:
If thou mislike him, thou conceiv'st him not.
God calleth preaching folly. Do not grudge
To pick out treasures from an earthen pot.
The worst speak something good. If all want sense,
God takes a text, and preaches patience.
HERBERT—*The Temple. The Church Porch.* St. 72. Quoting, "But we have this treasure in earthen vessels." *II Corinthians.* IV. 7.
(See also BROWNING)

15
Even ministers of good things are like torches, a light to others, waste and destruction to themselves.
HOOKER. Quoted by GLADSTONE, 1880. See MORLEY'S *"Life of Gladstone."* Bk. VIII. Ch. I.

16
Sir, a woman preaching is like a dog's walking on his hind legs. It is not done well: but you are surprised to find it done at all.
SAMUEL JOHNSON—*Boswell's Life of Johnson.* (1763)

17
And he played on a harp of a thousand strings,
Spirits of just men made perfect.
Burlesque Sermon, ascribed to REV. HENRY TALIAFERRO LEWIS, in the Brandon (Miss.) *Republic* (1854) Claimed for ST. GEORGE LEE and WILLIAM P. BRANNAN. Found in Dow's *Patent Sermons.* T. L. MASSON'S *Masterpieces of Humor.*

18
As pleasant songs, at morning sung,
The words that dropped from his sweet tongue
Strengthened our hearts; or, heard at night,
Made all our slumbers soft and light.
LONGFELLOW—*Christus. The Golden Legend.* Pt. I.

19
Skilful alike with tongue and pen,
He preached to all men everywhere
The Gospel of the Golden Rule,
The New Commandment given to men,
Thinking the deed, and not the creed,
Would help us in our utmost need.
LONGFELLOW—*Prelude to Tales of a Wayside Inn.* L. 217.

1
It is by the Vicar's skirts that the
Devil climbs into the Belfry.
LONGFELLOW—*The Spanish Student.* Act I. Sc. 2.

2
So clomb the first grand thief into God's fold;
So since into his church lewd hirelings climb.
MILTON—*Paradise Lost.* Bk. IV. L. 192.

3
He of their wicked ways
Shall them admonish, and before them set
The paths of righteousness.
MILTON—*Paradise Lost.* Bk. XI. L. 812.

4
And truths divine came mended from that tongue.
POPE—*Eloisa to Abelard.* L. 66.

5
The gracious Dew of Pulpit Eloquence,
And all the well-whip'd Cream of Courtly Sense.
POPE—*Epilogue to the Satires. Dialogue I.* L. 70.

6
He was a shrewd and sound divine
Of loud Dissent the mortal terror;
And when, by dint of page and line,
He 'stablished Truth, or startled Error,
The Baptist found him far too deep,
The Deist sighed with saving sorrow,
And the lean Levite went to sleep,
And dreamt of eating pork to-morrow.
PRAED—*The Vicar.*

7
His sermon never said or showed
That Earth is foul, that Heaven is gracious,
Without refreshment on the road
From Jerome, or from Athanasius.
And sure a righteous zeal inspired,
The hand and head that penned and planned them,
For all who understood, admired—
And some who did not understand them.
PRAED—*The Vicar.*

8
The lilies say: Behold how we
Preach without words of purity.
CHRISTINA G. ROSSETTI—*Consider the Lilies of the Field.*

9
I have taught you, my dear flock, for above thirty years how to live; and I will show you in a very short time how to die.
SANDYS—*Anglorum Speculum.* P. 903.

10
Sermons in stones and good in every thing.
As You Like It. Act II. Sc. 1. L. 17.

11
Show me the steep and thorny way to heaven,
Whiles, like a puff'd and reckless libertine,
Himself the primrose path of dalliance treads,
And recks not his own rede.
Hamlet. Act I. Sc. 3. L. 47.

12
He who the sword of heaven will bear
Should be as holy as severe;
Pattern in himself to know,
Grace to stand, and virtue go.
Measure for Measure. Act III. Sc. 2. L. 275.

13
It is a good divine that follows his own instructions; I can easier teach twenty what were good to be done, than be one of the twenty to follow mine own teaching.
Merchant of Venice. Act I. Sc. 2. L. 15.

14
Perhaps thou wert a priest,—if so, my struggles
Are vain, for priestcraft never owns its juggles.
HORACE SMITH—*Address to a Mummy.* St. 4.

15
He taught them how to live and how to die.
WM. SOMERVILLE—*In Memory of the Rev. Mr. Moore.* L. 21.

16
By thy language cabalistic,
By thy cymbal, drum, and his stick.
THOMAS STANLEY—*The Debauchée.* (1651)
(See also BUTLER)

17
With a little hoard of maxims preaching down a daughter's heart.
TENNYSON—*Locksley Hall.* L. 94.

18
A little, round, fat, oily man of God.
THOMSON—*Castle of Indolence.* Canto I. St. 69.

19
"Dear sinners all," the fool began, "man's life is but a jest,
A dream, a shadow, bubble, air, a vapour at the best.
In a thousand pounds of law I find not a single ounce of love,
A blind man killed the parson's cow in shooting at the dove;
The fool that eats till he is sick must fast till he is well,
The wooer who can flatter most will bear away the belle."
* * * * * *
And then again the women screamed, and every staghound bayed;
And why? because the motley fool so wise a sermon made.
GEORGE W. THORNBURY—*The Jester's Sermon.*

20
Le sermon edifie, et l'example detruit.
The sermon edifies, the example destroys.
(Practice what you preach)
ABBÉ DE VILLIERS. From a story in *L'Art de Prêcher.*
(See also BOCCACCIO)

PREJUDICE

21
He hears but half who hears one party only.
ÆSCHYLUS—*Eum.* 428.

22
Prejudice renders a man's virtue his habit, and not a series of unconnected acts. Through just prejudice, his duty becomes a part of his nature.
BURKE—*Reflections on the Revolution in France.*

23
Chi non esce dal suo paese, vive pieno di pregiudizi.
He who never leaves his country is full of prejudices.
GOLDONI—*Pamela.* I. 14.

1
Remember, when the judgment's weak,
The prejudice is strong.
KANE O'HARA—*Midas. Air.* Act I. Sc. 3.

PRESENT (See TODAY)

PRESENTS (See GENEROSITY, GIFTS)

PRESUMPTION

2
Presume to lay their hand upon the ark
Of her magnificent and awful cause.
COWPER—*The Task.* Bk. II. *The Timepiece.* L. 231.

3
It is not so with Him that all things knows
As 'tis with us that square our guess by shows:
But most it is presumption in us when
The help of heaven we count the act of men.
All's Well That Ends Well. Act II. Sc. 1. L. 152.

4
He will steal himself into a man's favour and for a week escape a great deal of discoveries; but when you find him out, you have him ever after.
All's Well That Ends Well. Act III. Sc. 6. L. 97.

5
How dare the plants look up to heaven, from whence
They have their nourishment?
Pericles. Act I. Sc. 2. L. 55.

PRIDE

6
As proud as Lucifer.
BAILEY—*Festus.* Sc. *A Country Town.*

7
Ay, do despise me, I'm the prouder for it;
I like to be despised.
BICKERSTAFF—*The Hypocrite.* Act V. Sc. 1.

8
They are proud in humility, proud in that they are not proud.
BURTON—*Anatomy of Melancholy.* Pt. I. Sec. II. Memb. 3. Subsect. 14.

9
Let pride go afore, shame will follow after.
GEORGE CHAPMAN—*Eastward Ho.* Act III. Sc. 1. (Written by CHAPMAN, JONSON, and MARSTON.)

10
Pride (of all others the most dang'rous fault)
Proceeds from want of sense, or want of thought.
WENTWORTH DILLON—*Essay on Translated Verse.* L. 161.

11
Lord of human kind.
DRYDEN—*Spanish Friar.* Act II. Sc. 1.
(See also GOLDSMITH, SHULDHAM)

12
Zu strenge Ford'rung ist verborgner Stolz.
Too rigid scruples are concealed pride.
GOETHE—*Iphigenia auf Tauris.* IV. 4. 120.

13
Pride in their port, defiance in their eye,
I see the lords of humankind pass by.
GOLDSMITH—*The Traveller.* L. 327.
(See also DRYDEN)

14
Oh! Why should the spirit of mortal be proud?
Like a swift-fleeting meteor, a fast flying cloud,
A flash of the lightning, a break of the wave,
Man passes from life to his rest in the grave.
WM. KNOX—*Mortality.* (Lincoln's favorite hymn.)

15
What the weak head with strongest bias rules,
Is pride, the never-failing vice of fools.
POPE—*Essay on Criticism.* L. 203.

16
In pride, in reas'ning pride, our error lies;
All quit their sphere and rush into the skies.
Pride still is aiming at the bless'd abodes,
Men would be angels, angels would be gods.
POPE—*Essay on Man.* Ep. I. L. 124.

17
Thus unlamented pass the proud away,
The gaze of fools and pageant of a day;
So perish all, whose breast ne'er learn'd to glow
For others' good, or melt at others' woe.
POPE—*Memory of an Unfortunate Lady.* L. 4.

18
Pride goeth before destruction, and an haughty spirit before a fall.
Proverbs. XVI. 18.

19
Is this that haughty, gallant, gay Lothario?
NICHOLAS ROWE—*The Fair Penitent.* Act V. Sc. 1. L. 37. Taken from MASSINGER'S *Fatal Dowry.*

20
In general, pride is at the bottom of all great mistakes.
RUSKIN—*True and Beautiful. Morals and Religion. Conception of God.* P. 426.

21
Why, who cries out on pride,
That can therein tax any private party?
Doth it not flow as hugely as the sea.
As You Like It. Act II. Sc. 7. L. 70.

22
Prouder than rustling in unpaid-for silk.
Cymbeline. Act III. Sc. 3. L. 24.

23
She bears a duke's revenues on her back,
And in her heart she scorns our poverty.
Henry VI. Pt. II. Act I. Sc. 3. L. 83.

24
I have ventur'd,
Like little wanton boys that swim on bladders,
This many summers in a sea of glory,
But far beyond my depth: my high-blown pride
At length broke under me.
Henry VIII. Act III. Sc. 2. L. 358.

25
He that is proud eats up himself: pride is his own glass, his own trumpet, his own chronicle; and whatever praises itself but in the deed, devours the deed in the praise.
Troilus and Cressida. Act II. Sc. 3. L. 164.

26
I do hate a proud man, as I hate the engendering of toads.
Troilus and Cressida. Act II. Sc. 3. L. 169.

27
He is so plaguy proud that the death tokens of it
Cry "No recovery."
Troilus and Cressida. Act II. Sc. 3. L. 187.

1 Pride hath no other glass
To show itself but pride, for supple knees
Feed arrogance and are the proud man's fees.
Troilus and Cressida. Act III. Sc. 3. L. 47.

2
O world, how apt the poor are to be proud!
Twelfth Night. Act III. Sc. 1. L. 138.

3
The Lords of creation men we call.
EMILY ANNE SHULDHAM—*Lords of Creation.*
(See also DRYDEN)

4
Pride, like hooded hawks, in darkness soars
From blindness bold, and towering to the skies.
YOUNG—*Night Thoughts.* Night VI. L. 324.

PRIMROSE

Primula

5
Ring-ting! I wish I were a primrose,
A bright yellow primrose blowing in the spring!
The stooping boughs above me,
The wandering bee to love me,
The fern and moss to creep across,
And the elm-tree for our king!
WM. ALLINGHAM—*Wishing. A Child's Song.*

6
The primrose banks how fair!
BURNS—*My Chloris, Mark How Green the Groves.*

7
"I could have brought you some primroses, but I do not like to mix violets with anything."
"They say primroses make a capital salad," said Lord St. Jerome.
BENJ. DISRAELI—*Lothair.* Ch. XIII.

8
Her modest looks the cottage might adorn,
Sweet as the primrose peeps beneath the thorn.
GOLDSMITH—*The Deserted Village.* L. 329.

9
Why doe ye weep, sweet babes? Can tears
Speak griefe in you,
Who were but borne
Just as the modest morne
Teemed her refreshing dew?
HERRICK—*To Primroses.*

10 A tuft of evening primroses,
O'er which the mind may hover till it dozes;
O'er which it well might take a pleasant sleep,
But that 'tis ever startled by the leap
Of buds into ripe flowers.
KEATS—*I Stood Tiptoe Upon a Little Hill.*

11
Bountiful Primroses,
With outspread heart that needs the rough leaves' care.
GEORGE MACDONALD—*Wild Flowers.*

12
Mild offspring of a dark and sullen sire!
Whose modest form, so delicately fine,
Was nursed in whirling storms,
And cradled in the winds.
Thee when young spring first question'd winter's sway,
And dared the sturdy blusterer to the fight,
Thee on his bank he threw
To mark his victory.
HENRY KIRKE WHITE—*To an Early Primrose.*

13
A primrose by a river's brim,
A yellow primrose was to him,
And it was nothing more.
WORDSWORTH—*Peter Bell.* Pt. I. St. 12.

14
Primroses, the Spring may love them;
Summer knows but little of them.
WORDSWORTH—*Foresight.*

15
The Primrose for a veil had spread
The largest of her upright leaves;
And thus for purposes benign,
A simple flower deceives.
WORDSWORTH—*A Wren's Nest.*

PRINCIPLE

16
A precedent embalms a principle.
BENJ. DISRAELI—*Speech on the Expenditures of the Country.* Feb. 22, 1848.

17
I *don't* believe in princerple,
But, oh, I *du* in interest.
LOWELL—*The Biglow Papers.* First Series. No. VI. St. 9.

18
Ez to my princerples, I glory
In hevin' nothin' o' the sort.
LOWELL—*The Biglow Papers.* First Series. No. VII. St. 10.

PRINTING

19
Memoriæ sacrum
Typographia
Ars artium omnium
Conservatrix
Hic primum inventa
Circa annum mccccxl.

Sacred to the memory of printing, the art preservative of all arts. This was first invented about the year 1440.
Inscription on the façade of the house once occupied by LAURENT KOSTER at Harlem. "The art preservative of all arts," probably taken from this.

20
He who first shortened the labor of Copyists by device of *Movable Types* was disbanding hired Armies and cashiering most Kings and Senates, and creating a whole new Democratic world: he had invented the Art of printing.
CARLYLE—*Sartor Resartus.* Bk. I. Ch. V.

21 Transforms old print
To zigzag manuscript, and cheats the eyes
Of gallery critics by a thousand arts.
COWPER—*The Task.* Bk. II. *The Time Piece.* L. 363.

22
Every school boy and school girl who has arrived at the age of reflection ought to know something about the history of the art of printing.
HORACE MANN—*The Common School Journal.* February, 1843. *Printing and Paper Making.*

23
Though an angel should write, still 'tis *devils* must print.
MOORE—*The Fudge Family in England.* Letter III.

1 I'll print it,
And shame the fools.
POPE—*Prologue to Satires*. L. 61.

2
Thou hast most traitorously corrupted the youth of the realm in erecting a grammar school: and whereas, before, our forefathers had no other books but the score and the tally, thou hast caused printing to be used, and, contrary to the king, his crown and dignity, thou hast built a paper-mill.
Henry VI. Pt. II. Act IV. Sc. 7. L. 35.

3
The jour printer with gray head and gaunt jaws works at his case,
He turns his quid of tobacco, while his eyes blur with the manuscript.
WALT WHITMAN—*Leaves of Grass. Walt Whitman*. Pt. XV. St. 77.

PRISON

4
In durance vile here must I wake and weep,
And all my frowsy couch in sorrow steep.
BURNS—*Epistle from Esopus to Maria* in CHAMBERS' *Burns' Life and Work*. Vol. IV. P. 54.
(See also KENDRICK)

5
Whene'er with haggard eyes I view
This dungeon that I'm rotting in,
I think of those companions true
Who studied with me at the U-
Niversity of Göttingen.
GEORGE CANNING—*Song. Of One Eleven Years in Prison*. Found in *The Poetry of the Anti-Jacobin*. Also in *Burlesque Plays and Poems*, edited by HENRY MORLEY.

6
Prison'd in a parlour snug and small,
Like bottled wasps upon a southern wall.
COWPER—*Retirement*. L. 493.

7
"And a bird-cage, sir," said Sam. "Veels vithin veels, a prison in a prison."
DICKENS—*Pickwick Papers*. Ch. XL.

8
As if a wheel had been in the midst of a wheel.
Ezekiel. X. 10.

9
In durance vile.
WILLIAM KENDRICK—*Falstaff's Wedding*. Act I. Sc. 2. BURKE—*Thoughts on the Present Discontent*.
(See also BURNS)

10
That which the world miscalls a jail,
A private closet is to me.
* * * * *
Locks, bars, and solitude together met,
Make me no prisoner, but an anchoret.
Attributed to SIR ROGER L'ESTRANGE. Also to LORD CAPEL. Found in the *New Foundling Hospital for Wit*. (Ed. 1786) IV. 40, as a supplementary stanza. See *Notes and Queries*, April 10, 1909. P. 288.

11
Stone walls do not a prison make,
Nor iron bars a cage,
Minds innocent and quiet take
That for an hermitage.
LOVELACE—*To Althea, from Prison*. IV.

12
Doubles grilles à gros cloux,
Triples portes, forts verroux,
Aux âmes vraiment méchantes
Vous représentez l'enfer;
Mais aux âmes innocentes
Vous n'etes que du bois, des pierres, du fer.
Fast closed with double grills
And triple gates—the cell
To wicked souls is hell;
But to a mind that's innocent
'Tis only iron, wood and stone.
PELISSON—*Written on the walls of his cell in the Bastile*. (About 1661)

13
Nor stony tower, nor walls of beaten brass,
Nor airless dungeon, nor strong links of iron,
Can be retentive to the strength of spirit;
But life, being weary of these worldly bars,
Never lacks power to dismiss itself.
Julius Cæsar. Act I. Sc. 3. L. 93.

14
I have been studying how I may compare
This prison where I live unto the world:
And for because the world is populous
And here is not a creature but myself,
I cannot do it; yet I'll hammer it out.
Richard II. Act V. Sc. 5. L. 1.

PROBABILITY

15
Probability is the very guide of life.
CICERO—*De Natura*. 5. 12. Quoted by BISHOP BUTLER. Also used by HOOKER—*Ecclesiastical Polity*. Bk. I. Ch. VIII., and Bk. II. Ch. VII. Found in LOCKE—*Essays*. Bk. IV. Ch. XV. Also in HOBBES *Leviathan*.

PROCRASTINATION (See TIME, TO-MORROW)

PROGRESS (See also EVOLUTION, GROWTH)

16
Westward the star of empire takes its way.
JOHN QUINCY ADAMS—*Oration at Plymouth*. (1802) Misquoted from BERKELEY on inside cover of an early edition of BANCROFT'S *History of United States*.
(See also BERKELEY)

17
Laws and institutions are constantly tending to gravitate. Like clocks, they must be occasionally cleansed, and wound up, and set to true time.
HENRY WARD BEECHER—*Life Thoughts*.

18
Westward the course of empire takes its way;
The four first Acts already past,
A fifth shall close the Drama with the day;
Time's noblest offspring is the last.
BISHOP BERKELEY—*Verses. on the Prospect of Planting Arts and Learning in America*.
(See also ADAMS)

19 What is art
But life upon the larger scale, the higher,
When, graduating up in a spiral line
Of still expanding and ascending gyres,
It pushed toward the intense significance
Of all things, hungry for the Infinite?

Art's life—and where we live, we suffer and toil.
E. B. BROWNING—*Aurora Leigh*. Bk. IV. L. 1150.
(See also EMERSON, GOETHE, MEREDITH, DE STAËL)

1
Finds progress, man's distinctive mark alone,
Not God's, and not the beast's;
God is, they are,
Man partly is, and wholly hopes to be.
ROBERT BROWNING—*A Death in the Desert*.
(See also POPE under HOPE)

2
Progress is
The law of life, man is not
Man as yet.
ROBERT BROWNING—*Paracelsus*. Pt. V.

3
Like plants in mines, which never saw the sun,
But dream of him, and guess where he may be,
And do their best to climb, and get to him.
ROBERT BROWNING—*Paracelsus*. Last page.

4
Hombre apercebido medio combatido.
A man prepared has half fought the battle.
CERVANTES—*Don Quixote*. 2. 17.

5
All things journey: sun and moon,
Morning, noon, and afternoon,
Night and all her stars;
'Twixt the east and western bars
Round they journey,
Come and go!
We go with them!
GEORGE ELIOT—*Spanish Gypsy*. Bk. III. *Song*.

6
And striving to be Man, the worm
Mounts through all the spires of form.
EMERSON—*Mayday*.
(See also BROWNING)

7
So long as all the increased wealth which modern progress brings, goes but to build up great fortunes, to increase luxury, and make sharper the contest between the House of Have and the House of Want, progress is not real and cannot be permanent.
HENRY GEORGE—*Progress and Poverty. Introductory. The Problem.*

8
Progress has not followed a straight ascending line, but a spiral with rhythms of progress and retrogression, of evolution and dissolution.
GOETHE.
(See also BROWNING)

9
He who moves not forward goes backward!
A capital saying!
GOETHE—*Herman and Dorothea*. Canto III. L. 66.

10
To look up and not down,
To look forward and not back,
To look out and not in—and
To lend a hand.
EDWARD EVERETT HALE—*Rule of the "Harry Wadsworth Club."* From *Ten Times One is Ten*. (1870) Ch. IV.

11
I have seen that Man moves over with each new generation into a bigger body, more awful, more reverent and more free than he has had before.
GERALD STANLEY LEE—*Crowds*. Pt. II. Ch. III.

12
From lower to the higher next,
Not to the top, is Nature's text;
And embryo good, to reach full stature,
Absorbs the evil in its nature.
LOWELL—*Festina Lente. Moral.*

13
New occasions teach new duties, time makes ancient good uncouth;
They must upward still and onward, who would keep abreast of truth.
LOWELL—*Present Crisis*.

14
"Spiral" the memorable Lady terms
Our mind's ascent.
GEORGE MEREDITH—*The World's Advance*. G. M. TREVELYAN in notes to MEREDITH'S *Poetical Works* says the "memorable Lady" is MRS. BROWNING.
(See also E. B. BROWNING)

15
That in our proper motion we ascend
Up to our native seat; descent and fall
To us is adverse.
MILTON—*Paradise Lost*. Bk. II. L. 75.

16
Quod sequitur, fugio; quod fugit, usque sequor.
What follows I flee; what flees I ever pursue.
OVID—*Amorum*. II. 19, 36.

17
Vogue la galère.
Row on [whatever happens].
RABELAIS—*Gargantua*. I. 3.

18
Il est un terme de la vie au-delà duquel en rétrograde en avançant.
There is a period of life when we go back as we advance.
ROUSSEAU—*Émile*. II.

19
The march of intellect.
ROBERT SOUTHEY—*Sir T. More, or Colloquies on the Progress and Prospects of Society*. Vol. II. P. 361. Quoted by CARLYLE—*Miscel. Essays*. Vol. I. P. 162. (Ed. 1888)

20
L'esprit humain fait progrès toujours, mais c'est progrès en spirale.
The human mind always makes progress, but it is a progress in spirals.
MADAME DE STAËL.
(See also BROWNING)

21
If you strike a thorn or rose,
Keep a-goin'!
If it hails or if it snows,
Keep a-goin'!
'Tain't no use to sit and whine
'Cause the fish ain't on your line;
Bait you hook an' keep on tryin',
Keep a-goin'!
FRANK L. STANTON—*Keep a-goin.'*

1
When old words die out on the tongue, new melodies break forth from the heart; and where the old tracks are lost, new country is revealed with its wonders.
RABINDRANATH TAGORE—*Gitanjali*. 37.

2
The stone that is rolling, can gather no moss.
TUSSER—*Five Hundred Points of Good Husbandry. Huswifely Admonitions*. GOSSON—*Ephemendes of Phialo*. MARSTON—*The Faun*. SYRUS—*Maxims*. 524. Pierre volage ne queult mousse. *De l'hermite qui se désepéra pour le larron que ala en paradis avant que lui*. 13th Cent.

3
Qui n'a pas l'esprit de son âge,
De son âge a tout le malheur.
He who has not the spirit of his age, has all the misery of it.
VOLTAIRE—*Lettre à Cideville*.

4
Press on!—"for in the grave there is no work
And no device"—Press on! while yet ye may!
N. P. WILLIS—*From a Poem Delivered at Yale College*, 1827. L. 45.

PROMISES

5
Promise is most given when the least is said.
GEORGE CHAPMAN—Trans. of MUSŒUS—*Hero and Leander*. L. 234.

6
Promettre c'est donner, espérer c'est jouir.
To promise is to give, to hope is to enjoy.
DELILLE—*Jardins*. I.

7
You never bade me hope, 'tis true;
I asked you not to swear:
But I looked in those eyes of blue,
And read a promise there.
GERALD GRIFFIN—*You Never Bade Me Hope*.

8
We promise according to our hopes, and perform according to our fears.
LA ROCHEFOUCAULD—*Maxims*. No. 39.
(See also MACBETH)

9
Giants in
Their promises, but those obtained, weak pigmies
In their performance.
MASSINGER—*Great Duke*. Act II. Sc. 3.

10
Thy promises are like Adonis' gardens
That one day bloomed and fruitful were the next.
Henry VI. Pt.. Act I. Sc. 6. L. 6.

11
His promises were, as he then was, mighty;
But his performance, as he is now, nothing.
Henry VIII. Act IV. Sc. 2. L. 41.

12
And be these juggling fiends no more believ'd,
That palter with us in a double sense:
That keep the word of promise to our ear,
And break it to our hope.
Macbeth. Act V. Sc. 8. L. 19.
(See also LA ROCHEFOUCAULD)

13
There buds the promise of celestial worth.
YOUNG—*The Last Day*. Bk. III. L. 317.

PROOF

14
You may prove anything by figures.
Quoted by CARLYLE—*Chartism*. No. 2.

15
You cannot demonstrate an emotion or prove an aspiration.
JOHN MORLEY—*Rousseau*. P. 402.

16
For when one's proofs are aptly chosen,
Four are as valid as four dozen.
PRIOR—*Alma*. Canto I. End.

17
Prove all things; hold fast that which is good.
I Thessalonians. V. 21.

PROPERTY (See POSSESSION)

PROPHECY

18
Be thou the rainbow to the storms of life!
The evening beam that smiles the clouds away,
And tints to-morrow with prophetic ray!
BYRON—*Bride of Abydos*. Canto II. St. 20.

19
Of all the horrid, hideous notes of woe,
Sadder than owl-songs or the midnight blast;
Is that portentous phrase, "I told you so."
BYRON—*Don Juan*. Canto XIV. St. 50.

20
The prophet's mantle, ere his flight began,
Dropt on the world—a sacred gift to man.
CAMPBELL—*Pleasures of Hope*. Pt. I. L. 43.

21
Bene qui conjiciet, vatem hunc perhibebo optimum.
I shall always consider the best guesser the best prophet.
CICERO—*De Divinatione*. II. 5. (Greek adage.)
(See also LOWELL, WALPOLE)

22
Ancestral voices prophesying war.
COLERIDGE—*Kubla Khan*.

23
We know in part, and we prophesy in part.
I Corinthians. XIII. 9.

24
From hence, no question, has sprung an observation . . . confirmed now into a settled opinion, that some long experienced souls in the world, before their dislodging, arrive to the height of prophetic spirits.
ERASMUS—*Praise of Folly*. (Old translation.)
(See also MILTON)

25
Thy voice sounds like a prophet's word;
And in its hollow tones are heard
The thanks of millions yet to be.
FITZ-GREENE HALLECK—*Marco Bozzaris*.

26
Prophet of evil! never hadst thou yet
A cheerful word for me. To mark the signs
Of coming mischief is thy great delight,
Good dost thou ne'er foretell nor bring to pass.
HOMER—*Iliad*. Bk. I. L. 138. BRYANT'S trans.

1
A tunnel underneath the sea from Calais straight
to Dover, Sir,
The squeamish folks may cross by land from
shore to shore,
With sluices made to drown the French, if e'er
they would come over, Sir,
Has long been talk'd of, till at length 'tis
thought a *monstrous bore.*
THEODORE HOOK—*Bubbles of 1825.* In *John Bull*, 1825.

2
This solemn moment of triumph, one of the greatest moments in the history of the world . . . this great hour which rings in a new era . . . and which is going to lift up humanity to a higher plane of existence for all the ages of the future.
DAVID LLOYD GEORGE. *Speech* at Guildhall after the signing of the Armistice, Nov. 11, 1918.

3
My gran'ther's rule was safer 'n 't is to crow:
Don't never prophesy—onless ye know.
LOWELL—*Biglow Papers.* No. 2. *Mason and Slidell.*
(See also CICERO)

4
It takes a mind like Dannel's, fact, ez big ez all
ou'doors
To find out thet it looks like rain arter it fairly
pours.
LOWELL—*Biglow Papers.* No. 9. L. 97.

5
A prophet is not without honour, save in his own country and in his own house.
Matthew. XIII. 57.

6
No mighty trance, or breathed spell
Inspires the pale-eyed priest from the prophetic
cell.
MILTON—*Hymn on Christ's Nativity.* L. 173.

7
Till old experience do attain
To something like prophetic strain.
MILTON—*Il Penseroso.* L. 173.
(See also ERASMUS)

8
Is Saul also among the prophets?
I Samuel. X. 11.

9
O my prophetic soul!
My uncle!
Hamlet. Act I. Sc. 5. L. 40.

10
There is a history in all men's lives,
Figuring the nature of the times deceas'd,
The which observed, a man may prophesy
With a near aim, of the main chance of things
As yet not come to life, which in their seeds
And weak beginnings lie intreasured.
Henry IV. Pt. II. Act III. Sc. 1. L. 80.

11
Prognostics do not always prove prophecies, at least the wisest prophets make sure of the event first.
HORACE WALPOLE—*Letter to Thos. Walpole.* Feb. 9, 1785.
(See also CICERO)

12
Your fathers, where are they? And the prophets, do they live forever?
Zechariah. I. 5.

PROPRIETY (See MANNERS)

PROSPERITY (See also SUCCESS)

13
In rebus prosperis, superbiam, fastidium arrogantiamque magno opere fugiamus.
In prosperity let us most carefully avoid pride, disdain, and arrogance.
CICERO—*De Officiis.* I. 26.

14
Ut adversas res, secundas immoderate ferre, levitatis est.
It shows a weak mind not to bear prosperity as well as adversity with moderation.
CICERO—*De Officiis.* I. 26.

15
C'est un faible roseau que la prospérité.
Prosperity is a feeble reed.
DANIEL D'ANCHÈRES—*Tyr et Sidon.*

16
Alles in der Welt lässt sich ertragen,
Nur nicht eine Reihe von schönen Tagen.
Everything in the world may be endured, except only a succession of prosperous days.
GOETHE—*Sprüche in Reimen.* III.

17
Prosperity lets go the bridle.
HERBERT—*Jacula Prudentum.*

18
The desert shall rejoice, and blossom as the rose.
Isaiah. XXXV. 1.

19
I wish you every kind of prosperity, with a little more taste.
ALAIN RENÉ LE SAGE—*Gil Blas.* Bk. VII. Ch. IV. HENRI VAN LAUN'S trans.

20
Felix se nescit amari.
The prosperous man does not know whether he is loved.
LUCAN—*Pharsalia.* VII. 727.

21
They shall sit every man under his vine and under his fig-tree.
Micah. IV. 4.

22
Surer to prosper than prosperity could have assur'd us.
MILTON—*Paradise Lost.* Bk. II. L. 39.

23
Length of days is in her right hand; and in her left hand riches and honour.
Proverbs. III. 16.

24
Est felicibus difficilis miserarium vera æstimatio.
The prosperous can not easily form a right idea of misery.
QUINTILIAN—*De Institutione Oratoria.* IX. 6.

25
Res secundæ valent commutare naturam, et raro quisquam erga bona sua satis cautus est.
Prosperity can change man's nature; and seldom is any one cautious enough to resist the effects of good fortune.
QUINTUS CURTIUS RUFUS—*De Rebus Gestis Alexandri Magni.* X. 1. 40.

1
Quantum caliginis mentibus nostris objicit magna felicitas!
How much does great prosperity overspread the mind with darkness.
SENECA—*De Brevitate Vitæ.* XIII.

2
Semel profecto premere felices deus
Cum cœpit, urget; hos habent magna exitus.
When God has once begun to throw down the prosperous, He overthrows them altogether: such is the end of the mighty.
SENECA—*Hercules Œtæus.* 713.

3
There shall be in England seven halfpenny loaves sold for a penny: the three-hooped pot shall have ten hoops; and I will make it felony to drink small beer.
Henry VI. Pt. II. Act IV. Sc. 2. L. 70.

4
Prosperity's the very bond of love.
Winter's Tale. Act IV. Sc. 4. L. 584.

5
La prospérité fait peu d'amis.
Prosperity makes few friends.
VAUVENARGUES—*Réflexions.* XVII.

6
Prosperity doth bewitch men, seeming clear;
As seas do laugh, show white, when rocks are near.
JOHN WEBSTER—*White Devil.* Act V. Sc. 6.

7
Oh, how portentous is prosperity!
How comet-like, it threatens while it shines.
YOUNG—*Night Thoughts.* Night V. L. 915.

PROVERBS (Introduction)

8
I'll tell the names and sayings and the places of their birth,
Of the seven great ancient sages so renowned on Grecian earth,
The Lindian Cleobulus said, "The mean was still the best";
The Spartan Chilo, "Know thyself," a heaven-born phrase confessed.
Corinthian Periander taught "Our anger to command,"
"Too much of nothing," Pittacus, from Mitylene's strand;
Athenian Solon this advised, "Look to the end of life,"
And Bias from Priene showed, "Bad men are the most rife";
Milesian Thales urged that "None should e'er a surety be";
Few were their words, but if you look, you'll much in little see.
From the Greek. Author unknown.

9
Know thyself.—SOLON.
Consider the end.—CHILO.
Know thy opportunity.—PITTACUS.
Most men are bad.—BIAS.
Nothing is impossible to industry.—PERIANDER.
Avoid excess.—CLEOBULUS.
Suretyship is the precursor of ruin.—THALES.
Mottoes of the Seven Wise Men of Greece. Inscribed in later days in the Delphian Temple.

10
The genius, wit, and spirit of a nation are discovered in its proverbs.
BACON.

11
Proverbs are short sentences drawn from long and wise experience.
CERVANTES—*Don Quixote.*

12
No hay refran que no sea verdadero.
There is no proverb which is not true.
CERVANTES—*Don Quixote.*

13
As Love and I late harbour'd in one inn,
With proverbs thus each other entertain:
"In love there is no lack," thus I begin;
"Fair words make fools," replieth he again;
"Who spares to speak doth spare to speed," quoth I;
"As well," saith he, "too forward as too slow";
"Fortune assists the boldest," I reply;
"A hasty man," quoth he, "ne'er wanted woe";
"Labour is light where love," quoth I," doth pay";
Saith he, "Light burden's heavy, if far borne";
Quoth I, "The main lost, cast the by away";
"Y'have spun a fair thread," he replies in scorn.
And having thus awhile each other thwarted
Fools as we met, so fools again we parted.
MICHAEL DRAYTON—*Proverbs.*

14
Proverbs like the sacred books of each nation, are the sanctuary of the intuitions.
EMERSON—*Compensation.*

15
Much matter decocted into few words.
FULLER—*Definition of a proverb. Worthies.* Ch. II.

16
A proverb and a byword among all people.
I Kings. IX. 7.

17
Maxims are the condensed good sense of nations.
SIR J. MACKINTOSH. Quoted on the title page of BROOM'S *Legal Maxims.* (1911)

18
This formal fool, your man, speaks naught but proverbs,
And speak men what they can to him he'll answer
With some rhyme, rotten sentence, or old saying,
Such spokes as ye ancient of ye parish use.
HENRY PORTER—*The Proverb Monger.* From *Two Angry Women of Abindon.*

19
A proverb is one man's wit and all men's wisdom.
LORD JOHN RUSSELL. In Notes to ROGER'S *Italy.* (1848) Claimed by him as his original definition of a proverb.

20
Wickedness proceedeth from the wicked.
I Samuel. XXIV. 13. Said to be the oldest proverb on record.

21
I can tell thee where that saying was born.
Twelfth Night. Act I. Sc. 5. L. 9.

22
Scoundrel maxim.
THOMSON—*The Castle of Indolence.* Canto I. St. 50.

Les maximes des hommes décèlent leur cœur.
The maxims of men reveal their characters.
VAUVENARGUES—*Réflexions*. CVII.

PROVERBS AND POPULAR PHRASES

(Alphabetically arranged)

2
A baker's dozen.
RABELAIS—*Works*. Bk. V. Ch. XXII.

3
Add to golden numbers golden numbers.
THOS. DEKKER—*Patient Grissell*. Act I. Sc. 1.

4
A flea in his ear.
R. ARMIN—*Nest of Ninnies*. (1608) T. NASH—*Pierce Penniless*. (1592) R. GREENE—*Quip for an upstart Courier*. (1592) TEUTON—*Tragicall Discourses*. (1579) FRANCIS DE L'ISLE—*Legendarie Life and Behavior of Charles, Cardinal of Lorraine*. (1577)
(See also RABELAIS under FLEA)

5
After supper walk a mile.
BEAUMONT and FLETCHER—*Philaster*. II. 4.

6
A new broome sweepeth cleane.
LYLY—*Euphues*. Arber's Reprint. P. 89.

7
An inch in a miss is as good as an ell.
CAMDEN'S *Remains*. (1614)

8
An inch in missing is as bad as an ell.
FULLER—*Gnomologia*. (1732)

9
As clear as a whistle.
JOHN BYROM—*Epistle to Lloyd*. I.

10
As cold as cucumbers.
BEAUMONT AND FLETCHER—*Cupid's Revenge*. Act I. Sc. 1.

11
As high as Heaven, as deep as Hell.
BEAUMONT AND FLETCHER—*Honest Man's Fortune*. Act IV. Sc. 1.

12
A thorn in the flesh.
II Corinthians. XII. 7.

13
Bag and baggage.
RICHARD HULOET—*Abecedarium Anglico-Latinum pro Tyrunculas*. (1552) *As You Like It*. III. 2. How erst wee did them thence, sans bag and baggage, tosse. BURDET—*Mirror for Magistrates*. St. 75.
With bag and baggage, selye wretch,
I yelded into Beautie's hand.
TOTTEL'S *Miscellany*. Arber's Reprint. P. 173. Appears in trans. of POLYDORE VERGIL'S *English History*, edited by SIR HENRY ELLIS, Camden Society (1844) MS., in the handwriting of the reign of HENRY VIII. (About 1540–50) Also in Camden Society Reprint, No. 53. P. 47. (1500) In Life of LORD GREY, Camden Society MS. P. 37. (About 1570) Credited to FROISSART, in LORD BERNER'S trans. Vol. I. Ch. CCCXX. P. 497. (Ed. 1523)
(See also GLADSTONE under TURKEY)

14
Barkis is willin'.
DICKENS—*David Copperfield*. Ch. I.

15
Beat all your feathers as flat as pancakes.
MIDDLETON—*Roaring Girl*. Act II. Sc. 1.

16
Better a bad excuse, than none at all.
CAMDEN—*Remaines*. *Proverbs*. P. 293.

17
Big-endians and small-endians.
SWIFT—*Gulliver's Travels*. Pt. I. Ch. IV. *Voyage to Lilliput*.

18
But me no buts.
HENRY FIELDING—*Rape upon Rape*. Act II. Sc. 2. AARON HILL—*Snake in the Grass*. Sc. 1.

19
By all that's good and glorious.
BYRON—*Sardanapalus*. Act I. Sc. 2.

20
By hooke or crooke.
HEYWOOD—*Proverbs*. Pt. I. Ch. XI. In a letter of SIR RICHARD MORYSIN to the Privy Council in LODGE'S *Illustrations &c.* I. 154. HOLLAND'S *Suetonius*. P. 169. JOHN WYCLIF—*Works*. Ed. by ARNOLD. III. 331. RABELAIS—Bk. V. Ch. XIII. DU BARTAS—*The Map of Man*. SPENSER—*Faerie Queene*. Bk. III. Canto I. St. 17. BEAUMONT AND FLETCHER—*Women Pleased*. Act I. Sc. 3. SKELTON—*Duke of Clout*. See also "Which he by hook or crook."

21
Curses are like young chickens,
And still come home to roost!
Arabian Proverb quoted by BULWER-LYTTON—*The Lady of Lyons*. Act V. Sc. 2. CHAUCER—*Persones Tale*. Sec. 41.
(See also HESIOD under WISH)

22
Cut and come again.
CRABBE—*Tales VII*. L. 26.

23
Se couper le nez pour faire dépit à son visage.
Cut off your nose to spite your face.
TALLEMENT DES RÉAUX—*Historiettes*. Vol. I. Ch. I. (About 1657–1659)

24
Diamonds cut diamonds.
JOHN FORD—*The Lover's Melancholy*. Act I. Sc. 3.

25
Every fat (vat) must stand upon his bottom.
BUNYAN—*Pilgrim's Progress*. Pt. I

26
Every one stretcheth his legs according to his coverlet.
HERBERT—*Jacula Prudentum*.

27
Every why hath a wherefore.
Comedy of Errors. Act II. Sc. 2. L. 44.

28
Facts are stubborn things.
LE SAGE—*Gil Blas*. Bk. X. Ch. I. SMOLLET'S trans.

29
Every tub must stand upon its bottom.
MACKLIN—*Man of the World*. Act I. Sc. 2.

1 Fast bind, fast find;
A proverb never stale in thrifty mind.
Merchant of Venice. Act II. Sc. 5. L. 54.

2
First come, first served.
BEAUMONT AND FLETCHER—*Little French Lawyer.* II. 1.

3
Fitted him to a T.
SAMUEL JOHNSON—*Boswell's Life of Johnson.* (1784) (See also "performed, etc.")

4
From the crown of our head to the sole of our foot.
BEAUMONT AND FLETCHER—*The Honest Man's Fortune.* Act II. Sc. 2. THOS. MIDDLETON—*A Mad World, My Masters.* Act I. Sc. 3. PLINY—*Natural History.* Bk. VII. Ch. XVII *Much Ado About Nothing.* Act III. Sc. 2.

5
Glass, China, and Reputation, are easily crack'd and never well mended.
BENJ. FRANKLIN—*Poor Richard.* (1750)

6
God save the mark!
Henry IV. Pt. I. Act I. Sc. 3. L. 57.

7
Going as if he trod upon eggs.
BURTON—*Anatomy of Melancholy.* Pt. III. Sect. II. Memb. 3.

8
Go to Jericho.
Let them all go to Jericho,
And ne'er be seen againe.
MERCURIUS AULICUS. (1648) Quoted in the *Athenæum,* Nov. 14, 1874.

9
Go West, young man! Go West.
JOHN L. B. SOULE—*In the Terre Haute Express.* (1851)

10
Go West, young man, and grow up with the country.
HORACE GREELEY—*Hints toward Reform.* In an editorial in the *Tribune.*
(See also "WESTWARD HO")

11
Hail, fellow, well met.
SWIFT—*My Lady's Lamentation.*

12
Harp not on that string.
Richard III. Act IV. Sc. 4. L. 366.

13
He can give little to his servant that licks his knife.
HERBERT—*Jacula Prudentum.*

14
He comes not in my books.
BEAUMONT AND FLETCHER—*The Widow.*

15
He did not care a button for it.
RABELAIS—*Works.* Bk. II. Ch. XVI.

16
Here's metal more attractive.
Hamlet. Act III. Sc. 2. L. 115.

17
Hide their diminished heads.
MILTON—*Paradise Lost.* Bk. IV. L. 35.

18
Hier lies that should fetch a perfect woman over the coles.
SIR GYLES GOOSECAPPE. (1606)

19
His bark is worse than his bite.
HERBERT—*Country Parson.* Ch. XXIX.

20
Hit the nail on the head.
BEAUMONT AND FLETCHER—*Love's Cure.* Act II. Sc. 1.

21
Hold one another's noses to the grindstone hard.
BURTON—*Anatomy of Melancholy.* Pt. III. Sec. I. Memb. 3.

22
Hold their noses to the grindstone.
THOS. MIDDLETON—*Blurt, Master Constable.* Act III. Sc. 3.

23
Honey of Hybla.
Henry IV. Pt. I. Act I. Sc. 2. L. 47.

24
How well I feathered my nest.
RABELAIS—*Works.* Bk. II. Ch. XVII.

25
I have other fish to fry.
CERVANTES — *Don Quixote.* Pt. II. Ch. XXXV.

26
I have you on the hip.
Merchant of Venice. Act IV. Sc. 1. L. 334.

27
I'll have a fling.
BEAUMONT AND FLETCHER—*Rule a Wife and Have a Wife.* III. 5.

28 I'll make the fur
Fly 'bout the ears of the old cur.
BUTLER—*Hudibras.* Pt. I. Canto III. L. 278.

29
I'll put a spoke among your wheels.
BEAUMONT AND FLETCHER—*Mad Lover.* III. 5.

30
In the name of the Prophet—figs.
HORACE AND JAMES SMITH—*Rejected Addresses. Johnson's Ghost.*

31
Leap out of the frying pan into the fire.
CERVANTES—*Don Quixote.* Pt. I. Bk. III. Ch. IV.

32
Let the worst come to the worst.
CERVANTES—*Don Quixote.* Bk. III. Ch. V. MARSTON—*Dutch Courtezan.* Act III. Sc. 1.

33
Love all, trust a few,
Do wrong to none.
All's Well That Ends Well. Act I. Sc. 1. L. 73.

34
Love, and a Cough, cannot be hid.
HERBERT—*Jacula Prudentum.*

35
Made no more bones.
DU BARTAS—*The Maiden Blush.*

36
Make ducks and drakes with shillings.
GEORGE CHAPMAN—*Eastward Ho.* Act I. Sc. I.

1
Make three bites of a cherry.
RABELAIS—*Works*. Bk. V. Ch. XXVIII.

2
Many a smale maketh a grate.
CHAUCER—*Persones Tale*.

3
Many go out for wool, and come home shorn themselves.
CERVANTES — *Don Quixote*. Pt. II. Ch. XXXVII.

4
Mariana in the moated grange.
TENNYSON. Motto for *Mariana*. Taken from "There, at the moated grange, resides this dejected Mariana." *Comedy of Errors*. Act II. Sc. 1.

5
Mind your P's and Q's.
Said to be due to the old custom of hanging up a slate in the tavern with P. and Q. (for pints and quarts), under which were written the names of customers and ticks for the number of "P's and Q's." Another explanation is that the expression referred to "toupées" (artificial locks of hair) and "queues" (tails).

6
Moche Crye and no Wull.
FORTESCUE—*De Laudibus Leg. Angliæ*. Ch. X.

7
Much of a muchness.
VANBRUGH—*The Provoked Husband*. Act I. Sc. 1.

8
Needle in a bottle of hay.
FIELD—*A Woman's a Weathercock*. Reprint 1612. P. 20.

9
Neither fish, flesh nor good red herring.
TOM BROWNE — *Æneus Sylvius*. *Letter*. DRYDEN—*Epilogue to Duke of Guise*. MARSDEN—*History of Christian Churches*. Vol. I. P. 267. In SIR JOHN MENNES' (Mennis) *Musarum Deliciæ*. (1651) THOS. NASH—*Lenten Stuff*. (1599) Reprinted in *Harleian Miscellany*. SIR H. SHERES—*Satyr on the sea officers*. *Rede me and be nott wrothe*. I. III. (1528)

10
No better than you should be.
BEAUMONT AND FLETCHER—*The Coxcomb*. Act IV. Sc. 3.

11
No rule is so general, which admits not some exception.
BURTON—*Anatomy of Melancholy*. Pt. I. Sec. II. Memb. 2. Subsect. 3.

12
Nought venter nought have.
HEYWOOD—*Proverbs*. Pt. I. Ch. XI. THOS. TUSSER—*Five Hundred Points of Good Husbandry*. *October's Extract*.

13
Old Lady of Threadneedle Street.
WILLIAM COBBETT. Also Gilray *Caricature*. May 22, 1797, after the bank stopped cash payments, Feb. 26, 1797. SHERIDAN—*Life* by WALTER SICHEL. P. 16. Refers to the bank as an elderly lady in the city, of great credit and long standing, who had recently made a *faux pas* which was not altogether inexcusable.

14
On his last legs.
THOS. MIDDLETON—*The Old Law*. Act V. Sc. 1.

15
One good turn deserves another.
BEAUMONT AND FLETCHER—*Little French Lawyer*. III. 2.

16
Originality provokes originality.
GOETHE.

17
Passing the Rubicon.
When he arrived at the banks of the Rubicon, which divides Cisalpine Gaul from the rest of Italy . . . he stopped to deliberate. . . . At last he cried out: "The die is cast" and immediately passed the river.
PLUTARCH—*Life of Julius Cæsar*.

18
Performed to a T.
RABELAIS—*Works*. Bk. IV. Ch. LI. See also "Fitted, etc."

19
Pons Asinorum.
The asses' bridge.
Applied to Proposition 5 of the first book of Euclid.

20
Present company excepted.
O'KEEFE—*London Hermit*. (1793)

21
Push on—keep moving.
THOS. MORTON—*A Cure for the Heartache*. Act III. Sc. 1.

22
Put himself upon his good behaviour.
BYRON—*Don Juan*. Canto V. St. 47.

23
Put your toong in your purse.
HEYWOOD—*Dialogue of Wit and Folly*. Pt. II. L. 263.

24
Quo vadis?
Whither goest thou?
From The *Vulgate*. *John*. XIII. 36. Domine, quo vadis? [St. Peter's question.] ST. THOMAS asks a similar question in *John*. XIV. 5. The traditional story is told by ST. AMBROSE — *Contra Auxentium*. (Ed. Paris, 1690) II. 867.

25
Safe bind, safe find.
TUSSER—*Five Hundred Points of Good Husbandry*. *Washing*.

26
Scared out of his seven senses.
SCOTT—*Rob Roy*. Ch. XXIV.

27
Set all at sixe and seven.
HEYWOOD—*Proverbs*. Pt. I. Ch. XI. CHAUCER—*Troilus and Cresseide*. L. 623. Also *Towneley Mysteries*. 143. *Morte Arture*. MS. at Lincoln. DEGREVANT. (1279) *Richard II*. Act II. Sc. 2. L. 122.

1
Smell a rat.
BUTLER—*Hudibras*. Pt. I. Canto I. L. 821. CERVANTES—*Don Quixote*. Pt. I. Bk. IV. Ch. X. BEN JONSON—*Tale of a Tub*. Act IV. Sc. 3. THOS. MIDDLETON—*Blurt, Master Constable*. Act III. Sc. 3.

2
Snug as a bug in a rug.
The Stratford Jubilee. II. 1. 1779. *Letter to Miss Georgiana Shipley*. September, 1772.

3
Something given that way.
BEAUMONT AND FLETCHER—*The Lovers' Progress*. Act I. Sc. 1.

4
So obliging that he ne'er oblig'd.
POPE—*Prologue to Satires*. L. 207.

5
Sop to Cerebus.
If I can find that Cerebus a sop, I shall be at rest for one day.
CONGREVE—*Love for Love*. Act I. Sc. 1.

6
So was hir jolly whistel wel y-wette.
CHAUCER—*Canterbury Tales*. *The Reeve's Tale*. L. 4,155.

7
Spare your breath to cool your porridge.
CERVANTES—*Don Quixote*. Pt. II. Ch. V. RABELAIS—*Works*. Bk. V. Ch. XXVIII.

8
Strike the iron whilst it is hot.
RABELAIS—*Works*. Bk. II. Ch. XXXI.

9
Strike while the iron is hot.
FARQUHAR—*The Beaux' Stratagem*. Act IV. Sc. 2. SCOTT—*The Fair Maid of Perth*. Ch. V. WEBSTER—*Westward Ho*. III. 2. CHAUCER—*Troylus and Cresseyde*. Bk. II. St. 178.

10
That was laid on with a trowel.
As You Like It. Act I. Sc. 2. L. 112.

11
The coast was clear.
MICHAEL DRAYTON—*Nymphidia*.

12
The fat's all in the fire.
COBBE—*Prophecies*. BULLEN'S reprint. (1614) MARSTON—*What You Will*. (1607) *The Balancing Captain*. Whole poem quoted by WALPOLE in a letter to MANN, Nov. 2, 1741.

13
The finest edge is made with the blunt whetstone.
LYLY—*Euphues*. Arber's Reprint. (1579) P. 47.

14
The foule Toade hath a faire stone in his head.
LYLY—*Euphues*. Arber's Reprint. (1679) P. 53.

15
The man that heweth over high,
Some chip falleth in his eye.
Story of Sir Eglamour of Artoys. MSS. in *Garrick Collection*.

16
The more thou stir it the worse it will be.
CERVANTES—*Don Quixote*. Bk. III. Ch. VIII.

17
The next way home's the farthest way about.
QUARLES—*Emblems*. Bk. IV. Em. 2. Ep. 2.

18
The point is plain as a pike staff.
JOHN BYROM—*Epistle to a Friend*.

19
The short and the long of it.
Merry Wives of Windsor. Act II. Sc. 2. L. 60.

20
The total depravity of inanimate things.
KATHERINE K. C. WALKER—*Title of an Essay in the Atlantic Monthly*. Sept., 1864. MARY ABIGAIL DODGE—*Epigram*.

21
This is a pretty flimflam.
BEAUMONT AND FLETCHER—*Little French Lawyer*. III. 3.

22
Though this may be play to you,
'Tis death to us.
ROGER L'ESTRANGE—*Fables*. 398.

23
Thou will scarce be a man before thy mother.
BEAUMONT AND FLETCHER—*Love's Cure*. Act II. Sc. 2.

24
Three things are men most likely to be cheated in, a horse, a wig, and a wife.
BENJ. FRANKLIN—*Poor Richard*. 1736.

25
Through thick and thin, both over bank and bush.
SPENSER—*Faerie Queene*. Bk. III. Canto I. St. 17.

26
Through thick and thin, both over Hill and Plain.
DU BARTAS—*Divine Weekes and Workes*. Second Week. Fourth Day. Bk. IV.

27
Through thick and thin.
BUTLER—*Hudibras*. Pt. I. Canto II. L. 370. COWPER—*John Gilpin*. DRAYTON—*Nymphidia*. DRYDEN—*Absalom and Achitophel*. Pt. II. L. 414. KEMP—*Nine Days' Wonder*. MIDDLETON—*The Roaring Girl*. Act IV. Sc. 2. POPE—*Dunciad*. Bk. II.
(See also BUTLER under CONSTANCY)

28
Though last, not least in love.
Julius Cæsar. Act III. Sc. 1. L. 189.
Although the last, not least.
King Lear. Act I. Sc. 1. L. 85. SPENSER—*Colin Clout*. L. 444.

29
Thursday come, and the week is gone.
HERBERT—*Jacula Prudentum*.

30
'Tis as cheap sitting as standing.
SWIFT—*Polite Conversation*. Dialogue I.

31
'Tis a stinger.
THOS. MIDDLETON—*More Dissemblers Besides Women*. Act III. Sc. 2.

32
'Tis in grain, sir, 'twill endure wind and weather.
Twelfth Night. Act I. Sc. 5. L. 253.

33
'Tis neither here nor there.
Othello. Act IV. Sc. 3. L. 58.

1
To rise with the lark, and go to bed with the lamb.
BRETON—*Court and Country*. (1618)

2
To take the nuts from the fire with the dog's foot.
HERBERT—*Jacula Prudentum*.

Tirer les marrons de la patte du chat.
To pull the chestnuts from the fire with the cat's paw.
MOLIÈRE—*L'Étourdi*. Act III. 6.

3
Turn over a new leaf.
BURKE—*Letter to Miss Haviland*. THOS. DEKKER—*The Honest Whore*. Pt. II. Act II. Sc. 1. Also *A Health to the Gentlemanly Profession of Serving-Men*. (1598) MIDDLETON—*Anything for a Quiet Life*. Act III. Sc. 3.

4
Two heads are better than one.
HEYWOOD—*Proverbs*. Pt. I. Ch. IX.

5
Walls have tongues, and hedges ears.
SWIFT—*Pastoral Dialogue*. L. 7. HAZLITT—*English Proverbs, etc.* (Ed. 1869) P. 446.

Wode has erys, felde has sigt.
King Edward and the Shepherd, MS. (Circa 1300)

Felde hath eyen, and wode hath eres.
CHAUCER—*Canterbury Tales. The Knight's Tale*. L. 1,522.

Fieldes have eies and woodes have eares.
HEYWOOD—*Proverbes*. Pt. II. Ch. V.

6
Westward-ho!
Twelfth Night. Act III. Sc. 1. L. 146.

7
What is bred in the bone will never come out of the flesh.
PILPAY—*The Two Fishermen*. Fable XIV.

It will never come out of the flesh that's bred in the bone.
JONSON—*Every Man in his Humour*. Act I. Sc. 1.

8
What is not in a man cannot come out of him surely.
GOETHE—*Herman and Dorothea*. Canto III. L. 3.

9
What is sauce for the goose is sauce for a gander.
TOM BROWN—*New Maxims*. P. 123.
(See also VARRO under GOOSE)

10
What is the matter with Kansas?
W. A. WHITE. Title of an editorial in the *Emporia Gazette*, August 15, 1896.

11
What mare's nest hast thou found?
BEAUMONT AND FLETCHER—*Bonduca*. IV. 2.

12
What you would not have done to yourselves, never do unto others.
ALEXANDER SEVERUS. See also "Golden Rule." *Matthew*. VII. 12.

13
When a dog is drowning, every one offers him drink.
HERBERT—*Jacula Prudentum*.

14
Where McGregor sits, there is the head of the table.
Quoted in *American Scholar* by EMERSON. Attributed to The McGregor, a Highland Chief.

15
Whether the pitcher hits the stone or the stone hits the pitcher, it goes ill with the pitcher.
CERVANTES—*Don Quixote*. Vol. II. Ch. XLIII.

16
Which he by hook or crook has gather'd
And by his own inventions father'd.
BUTLER—*Hudibras*. Pt. III. Canto I. L. 109. See also "By hooke or crooke."

17
Whistle, and I'll come to you, my lad.
BURNS—*Whistle, and I'll Come to You*.

18
Whistle, and she'll come to you.
BEAUMONT AND FLETCHER—*Wit Without Money*. Act IV. Sc. 4.

19
Wind puffs up empty bladders; opinion, fools.
SOCRATES.

20
With tooth and nail.
DU BARTAS—*Divine Weekes and Workes*. First Week. Second Day.

21
Within a stone's throw of it.
CERVANTES—*Don Quixote*. Pt. I. Bk. III. Ch. IX.

22
Whose house is of glass, must not throw stones at another.
HERBERT—*Jacula Prudentum*.

23
Why, then, do you walk as if you had swallowed a ramrod?
EPICTETUS—*Discourses*. Ch. XXI.

24
You shall never want rope enough.
RABELAIS—*Works. Prologue to the Fifth Book*.

25
You whirled them to the back of beyont.
SCOTT—*Antiquary*.

PROVIDENCE

26
And pleas'd th' Almighty's orders to perform,
Rides in the whirlwind and directs the storm.
ADDISON—*The Campaign*.

27
Fear not, but trust in Providence,
Wherever thou may'st be.
THOMAS HAYNES BAYLY—*The Pilot*.

28
But they that are above
Have ends in everything.
BEAUMONT AND FLETCHER—*The Maid's Tragedy*. Act V. Sc. 4.

29
If heaven send no supplies,
The fairest blossom of the garden dies.
WILLIAM BROWNE—*Visions*. Ch. V.

30
In some time, his good time, I shall arrive;
He guides me and the bird
In his good time.
ROBERT BROWNING—*Paracelsus*. Pt. I.

1
Le hasard est un sobriquet de la Providence.
Chance is a nickname for Providence.
CHAMFORT.

2
'Tis Providence alone secures
In every change both mine and yours.
COWPER—*A Fable. Moral.*

3
Behind a frowning Providence
He hides a smiling face.
COWPER—*Light Shining Out of Darkness.*

4
God made bees, and bees made honey,
God made man, and man made money,
Pride made the devil, and the devil made sin;
So God made a cole-pit to put the devil in.
Transcribed by JAMES HENRY DIXON, from the fly-sheet of a Bible, belonging to a pitman who resided near Hutton-Henry, in County of Denham.

5
Whatever is, is in its causes just.
DRYDEN—*Œdipus.* Act III. Sc. 1.

6
Dieu mesure le froid à la brebis tondue.
God tempers the cold to the shorn sheep.
HENRI ÉTIENNE—*Le Livre de Proverbs Epigrammatique.* Quoted from an older collection, possibly LEBON'S. (1557. Reprint of 1610)
(See also HERBERT, STERNE, also GIBBON under NAVIGATION)

7
We sometimes had those little rubs which Providence sends to enhance the value of its favours.
GOLDSMITH—*Vicar of Wakefield.* Ch. I.

8
To a close shorn sheep, God gives wind by measure.
HERBERT—*Jacula Prudentum.*
(See alfo ÉTIENNE)

9
God sends cold according to clothes.
HERBERT—*Jacula Prudentum.*
God sendeth cold after clothes.
As given in CAMDEN'S *Remains.*
(See also ÉTIENNE)

10
Deus haec fortasse benigna
Reducet in sedem vice.
Perhaps Providence by some happy change will restore these things to their proper places.
HORACE—*Epodi.* XIII. 7.

11
Behind the dim unknown,
Standeth God within the shadow, keeping watch above his own.
LOWELL—*The Present Crisis.* St. 8.

12
Eye me, blest Providence, and square my trial
To my proportion'd strength.
MILTON—*Comus.* L. 329.

13
Who sees with equal eye, as God of all,
A hero perish, or a sparrow fall,
Atoms or systems into ruin hurl'd,
And now a bubble burst, and now a world.
POPE—*Essay on Man.* Ep. I. L. 87.

14
Destroy all creatures for thy sport or gust,
Yet cry, if man's unhappy, God's unjust.
POPE—*Essay on Man.* Ep. I. L. 117.

15
Who finds not Providence all good and wise,
Alike in what it gives, and what denies.
POPE—*Essay on Man.* Ep. I. L. 205.

16
Warms in the sun, refreshes in the breeze.
Glows in the stars, and blossoms in the trees.
POPE—*Essay on Man.* Ep. I. L. 271.

17
Lap of providence.
PRIDEAUX—*Directions to Churchwardens.* P. 105. (Ed. 1712)
(See also HOMER under GODS)

18
The sun shall not smite thee by day, nor the moon by night.
Psalm. CXXI. 6.

19
Mutos enim nasci, et egere omni ratione satius fuisset, quam providentiæ munera in mutuam perniciem convertere.
For it would have been better that man should have been born dumb, nay, void of all reason, rather than that he should employ the gifts of Providence to the destruction of his neighbor.
QUINTILIAN—*De Institutione Oratoria.* XII. 1. 1.

20
Dieu modère tout à son plaisir.
God moderates all at His pleasure.
RABELAIS—*Pantagruel.* (1533)

21
He that doth the ravens feed,
Yea, providently caters for the sparrow,
Be comfort to my age!
As You Like It. Act II. Sc. 3. L. 43.

22
There is a divinity that shapes our ends,
Rough-hew them how we will.
Hamlet. Act V. Sc. 2. L. 10.

23
We defy augury: there's a special providence in the fall of a sparrow. If it be now, 'tis not to come; if it be not to come, it will be now; if it be not now, yet it will come; the readiness is all.
Hamlet. Act V. Sc. 2. L. 230.

24
O God, thy arm was here;
And not to us, but to thy arm alone,
Ascribe we all!
Henry V. Act IV. Sc. 8. L. 111.

25
For nought so vile that on the earth doth live
But to the earth some special good doth give.
Romeo and Juliet. Act II. Sc. 3. L. 17.

26
He maketh kings to sit in soverainty;
He maketh subjects to their powre obey;
He pulleth downe, he setteth up on hy:
He gives to this, from that he takes away;
For all we have is his: what he list doe he may.
SPENSER—*Faerie Queene.* Bk. V. Canto II. St. 41.

1
God tempers the wind to the shorn lamb.
STERNE—*Sentimental Journey*. (Given in Italics as a quotation.)
(See also ÉTIENNE)

2
And I will trust that He who heeds
The life that hides in mead and wold,
Who hangs yon alder's crimson beads,
And stains these mosses green and gold,
Will still, as He hath done, incline
His gracious care to me and mine.
WHITTIER—*Last Walk in Autumn*. St. 26.

PRUDENCE

3
Multis terribilis, caveto multos.
If thou art terrible to many, then beware of many.
AUSONIUS—*Septem Sapientum Sententiæ Septenis Versibus Explicatæ*. IV. 5.

4
It is always good
When a man has two irons in the fire.
BEAUMONT AND FLETCHER—*The Faithful Friends*. Act I. Sc. 2.
(See also BUTLER)

5
Et vulgariter dicitur, quod primum oportet cervum capere, et postea, cum captus fuerit, illum excoriare.
And it is a common saying that it is best first to catch the stag, and afterwards, when he has been caught, to skin him.
BRACTON—*Works*. Bk. IV. Tit. I. C. 2. Sec. IV.
(See also GLASSE under COOKERY)

6
Look before you ere you leap.
BUTLER—*Hudibras*. Pt. II. Canto II. HEYWOOD—*Proverbs*. Pt. I. Ch. II. TOTTEL—*Miscellany*. (1557)
(See also TRAPP)

7
'Tis true no lover has that pow'r
T' enforce a desperate amour,
As he that has two strings t' his bow,
And burns for love and money too.
BUTLER—*Hudibras*. Pt. III. Canto I. L. 1.
CHURCHILL—*The Ghost*. Bk. IV.
(See also BEAUMONT, CHAPMAN, ELIZABETH, FIELDING, HEYWOOD, HOOKER, PARKER, TERENCE)

8
No arrojemos la soga tras el caldero.
Let us not throw the rope after the bucket.
CERVANTES—*Don Quixote*. II. 9.

9
Archers ever
Have two strings to a bow; and shall great Cupid
(Archer of archers both in men and women),
Be worse provided than a common archer?
CHAPMAN—*Bussy d'Ambois*. Act II. Sc. 1.
(See also BUTLER)

10
Prudentia est rerum expectandarum fugiendarumque scientia.
Prudence is the knowledge of things to be sought, and those to be shunned.
CICERO—*De Officiis*. I. 43.

11
Malo indisertam prudentiam, quam loquacem stultitiam.
I prefer silent prudence to loquacious folly.
CICERO—*De Oratore*. III. 35.

12
Præstat cautela quam medela.
Precaution is better than cure.
COKE.
(See also RALEIGH)

13
According to her cloth she cut her coat.
DRYDEN—*Fables*. *Cock and the Fox*. L. 20.
(See also GODLY QUEEN HESTER under ECONOMY)

14
* * * Therefore I am wel pleased to take any coulor to defend your honour and hope you wyl remember that who seaketh two strings to one bowe, he may shute strong but neuer strait.
QUEEN ELIZABETH TO JAMES VI.—*Letter X*. Edited by JOHN BRUCE.
(See also BUTLER)

15
For chance fights ever on the side of the prudent.
EURIPIDES—*Pirithous*. (Adapted.)

16
Yes, I had two strings to my bow; both golden ones, egad! and both cracked.
FIELDING—*Love in Several Masques*. Act V. Sc. 13.
(See also BUTLER)

17
Great Estates may venture more. Little Boats must keep near Shore.
BENJ. FRANKLIN—*Poor Richard*. (1751)
(See also VERGIL)

18
Wer sich nicht nach der Decke streckt,
Dem bleiben die Füsse unbedeckt.
He who does not stretch himself according to the coverlet finds his feet uncovered.
GOETHE—*Sprüche in Reimen*. III.

19
Better is to bow than breake.
HEYWOOD—*Proverbs*. Pt. I. Ch. IX. CHRISTYNE—*Morale Proverbs*.
(See also LA FONTAINE)

20
It is good to have a hatch before the durre.
HEYWOOD—*Proverbs*. Pt. I. Ch. XI.

21
Yee have many strings to your bowe.
HEYWOOD—*Proverbs*. Pt. I. Ch. XI.
(See also BUTLER)

22
So that every man lawfully ordained must bring a bow which hath two strings, a title of present right and another to provide for future possibility or chance.
RICHARD HOOKER—*Laws of Ecclesiastical Polity*. Bk. V. Ch. LXXX. No. 9.
(See also BUTLER)

23
Fænum habet in cornu, longe fuge.
He is a dangerous fellow, keep clear of him. (That is: he has hay on his horns, showing he is dangerous.)
HORACE—*Satires*. I. IV. 34.

1
Fasten him as a nail in a sure place.
Isaiah. XXII. 23.

2
The first years of man must make provision for the last.
SAMUEL JOHNSON—*Rasselas*. Ch. XVII.

3
Nullum numen habes si sit prudentia.
One has no protecting power save prudence.
JUVENAL—*Satires*. X. 365. Also *Satires*. XIV. 315.

4
Je plie et ne romps pas.
I bend and do not break.
LA FONTAINE—*Fables*. I. 22.
(See also HEYWOOD)

5
Le trop d'expédients peut gâter une affaire.
Too many expedients may spoil an affair.
LA FONTAINE—*Fables*. IX. 14.

6
Don't cross the bridge till you come to it,
Is a proverb old, and of excellent wit.
LONGFELLOW—*Christus. The Golden Legend*. Pt. VI.

7
Let your loins be girded about, and your lights burning.
Luke. XII. 35.

8
Entre l'arbre et l'écorce il n'y faut pas mettre le doigt.
Between the tree and the bark it is better not to put your finger.
MOLIÈRE—*Médecin Malgre Lui*. Act I. Sc. 2.

9
Il faut reculer pour mieux sauter.
One must draw back in order to leap better.
MONTAIGNE—*Essays*. Bk. I. Ch. XXXVIII.

10
Crede mihi; miseros prudentia prima relinquit.
Believe me; it is prudence that first forsakes the wretched.
OVID—*Epistolæ Ex Ponto*. IV. 12. 47.

11
In ancient times all things were cheape,
'Tis good to looke before thou leape,
When corne is ripe 'tis time to reape.
MARTIN PARKER—*The Roxburghe Ballads. An Excellent New Medley*.
(See also BUTLER)

12
Cito rumpes arcum, semper si tensum habueris.
You will soon break the bow if you keep it always stretched.
PHÆDRUS—*Fab*. Bk. III. 14. 10. SYRUS—*Maxims*. 388.

13
Cum grano salis.
With a grain of salt.
PLINY—*Natural History*. XXIII. 8. 77. Giving the story of POMPEY, who when he took the palace of MITHRIDATES, found hidden the antidote against poison, "to be taken fasting, addite salis grano."

14
Ne clochez pas devant les boyteux. (Old French.)
Do not limp before the lame.
RABELAIS—*Gargantua*.

15
Prevention is the daughter of intelligence.
SIR WALTER RALEIGH—*Letter to Sir Robert Cecil*. May 10, 1593.
(See also COKE)

16
Be prudent, and if you hear, * * * some insult or some threat, * * * have the appearance of not hearing it.
GEORGE SAND—*Handsome Lawrence*. Ch. II.

17
Love all, trust a few,
Do wrong to none: be able for thine enemy
Rather in power than use, and keep thy friend
Under thy own life's key: be check'd for silence,
But never tax'd for speech.
All's Well That Ends Well. Act I. Sc. 1. L. 73.

18
Think him as a serpent's egg
Which, hatch'd, would, as his kind, grow mischievous,
And kill him in the shell.
Julius Cæsar. Act II. Sc. 1. L. 32.

19
In my school days. when I had lost one shaft,
I shot his fellow of the self-same flight
The self-same way with more advised watch,
To find the other forth, and by adventuring both
I oft found both.
Merchant of Venice. Act I. Sc. 1. L. 139.

20
I won't quarrel with my bread and butter.
SWIFT—*Polite Conversation. Dialogue* I.

21
Consilio melius vinces quam iracundia.
You will conquer more surely by prudence than by passion.
SYRUS—*Maxims*.

22
Deliberandum est diu, quod statuendum semel.
That should be considered long which can be decided but once.
SYRUS—*Maxims*.

23
It is well to moor your bark with two anchors.
SYRUS—*Maxims*. 119.

24
Plura consilio quam vi perficimus.
We accomplish more by prudence than by force.
TACITUS—*Annales*. II. 26.

25
Ratio et consilium, propriæ ducis artes.
Forethought and prudence are the proper qualities of a leader.
TACITUS—*Annales*. XIII. 20.

26
Ut quimus, aiunt, quando ut volumus, non licet.
As we can, according to the old saying, when we can not, as we would.
TERENCE—*Andria*. IV. 5. 10.

27
Commodius esse opinor duplici spe utier.
I think it better to have two strings to my bow.
TERENCE—*Phormio*. IV. 2. 13.
(See also BUTLER)

28
Try therefor before ye trust; look before ye leap.
JOHN TRAPP—*Commentary on I Peter*. III. 17. Tracing the saying to ST. BERNARD.
(See also BUTLER, PARKER)

1
Litus ama: * * * altum alii teneant.
Keep close to the shore: let others venture on the deep.
VERGIL—*Æneid.* V. 163.
(See also FRANKLIN)

PUBLIC (The)

2
Report uttered by the people is everywhere of great power.
ÆSCHYLUS—*Agamemnon.* 938.
(See also HESIOD)

3
Nec audiendi sunt qui solent dicere vox populi, vox dei; cum tumultus vulgi semper insaniæ proxima sit.
We would not listen to those who were wont to say the voice of the people is the voice of God, for the voice of the mob is near akin to madness.
ALCUIN—*Epistle to Charlemagne.* FROBEN'S Ed. Vol. I. P. 191. (Ed. 1771) Also credited to EADMER.
(See also REYNOLDS)

4
Vox populi habet aliquid divinum: nam quomo do aliter tot capita in unum conspirare possint?
The voice of the people has about it something divine: for how otherwise can so many heads agree together as one?
BACON—*9. Laus, Existimatio.*
(See also ALCUIN)

5
The great unwashed.
Attributed to LORD BROUGHAM.

6
The individual is foolish; the multitude, for the moment is foolish, when they act without deliberation; but the species is wise, and, when time is given to it, as a species it always acts right.
BURKE—*Speech.* Reform of Representation in the House of Commons. May 7, 1782.

7
The tyranny of a multitude is a multiplied tyranny.
BURKE—*To Thomas Mercer.* Feb. 26, 1790.

8
The public! why, the public's nothing better than a great baby.
THOS. CHALMERS—*Letter.* Quoted by RUSKIN—*Sesame and Lilies.* Sec. I. 40.

9
Le public! le public! combien faut-il de sots pour faire un public?
The public! the public! how many fools does it require to make the public?
CHAMFORT.

10
Qui ex errore imperitæ multitudinis pendet, hic in magnis viris non est habendus.
He who hangs on the errors of the ignorant multitude, must not be counted among great men.
CICERO—*De Officiis.* I. 19.

11
Vulgus ex veritate pauca, ex opinione multa æstimat.
The rabble estimate few things according to their real value, most things according to their prejudices.
CICERO—*Oratio Pro Quinto Roscio Comœdo.* X. 29.

12
Mobile mutatur semper cum principe vulgus.
The fickle populace always change with the prince.
CLAUDIANUS—*De Quarto Consulatu Honorii Augusti Panegyris.* CCCII.

13
Hence ye profane; I hate you all;
Both the great vulgar, and the small.
COWLEY—*Of Greatness.* Translation of HORACE, Ode I. Bk. III.
(See also HORACE, JUVENAL)

14
This many-headed monster, Multitude.
DANIEL—*History of the Civil War.* Bk. II. St. 13.
(See also PSEUDO-PHOCYL, SCOTT, SIDNEY)

15
La clef des champs.
The key of the fields (street).
Used by DICKENS in *Pickwick Papers.* Ch. XLVII. Also by GEORGE AUGUSTUS SALA in *Household Words,* Sept. 6, 1851.

16
The multitude is always in the wrong.
WENTWORTH DILLON—*Essay on Translated Verse.* L. 184.

17
For who can be secure of private right,
If sovereign sway may be dissolved by might?
Nor is the people's judgment always true:
The most may err as grossly as the few.
DRYDEN—*Absalom and Achitophel.* Pt. I. L. 779.

18
The man in the street does not know a star in the sky.
EMERSON—*Conduct of Life. Worship.*
(See also GREVILLE)

19
Bona prudentiæ pars est nosse stultas vulgi cupiditates, et absurdas opiniones.
It is a good part of sagacity to have known the foolish desires of the crowd and their unreasonable notions.
ERASMUS—*De Utilitate Colloquiorum. Preface.*

20
A stiff-necked people.
Exodus. XXXIII. 3.

21
Classes and masses.
Used by GLADSTONE. See MOORE—*Fudges in England. Letter* 4.

22
Ich wünschte sehr, der Menge zu behagen,
Besonders weil sie lebt und leben lässt.
I wish the crowd to feel itself well treated,
Especially since it lives and lets me live.
GOETHE—*Faust Vorspiel auf dem Theater.* L. 5.

23
Wer dem Publicum dient, ist ein armes Thier;
Er quält sich ab, niemand bedankt sich dafür.
He who serves the public is a poor animal; he worries himself to death and no one thanks him for it.
GOETHE—*Sprüche in Reimen.* III.

1
Knowing as "the man in the street" (as we call him at Newmarket) always does, the greatest secrets of kings, and being the confidant of their most hidden thoughts.
GREVILLE—*Memoirs*. March 22, 1830.
(See also EMERSON)

2
No whispered rumours which the many spread can wholly perish.
HESIOD—*Works and Days*. I. 763.
(See also ÆSCHYLUS)

3
The leader, mingling with the vulgar host,
Is with the common mass of matter lost!
HOMER—*Odyssey*. Bk. IV. L. 397. POPE'S trans.

4
Mobilium turba Quiritium.
The crowd of changeable citizens.
HORACE—*Odes*. Bk. I. 1. 7.

5
Malignum
Spernere vulgus.
To scorn the ill-conditioned rabble.
HORACE—*Odes*. Bk. II. 16, 39.

6
Odi profanum vulgus et arceo.
Favete linguis.
I hate the uncultivated crowd and keep them at a distance. Favour me by your tongues (keep silence).
HORACE—*Odes*. Bk. III. 1. ("Favete linguis" also found in CICERO, OVID.)
(See also COWLEY)

7
Reason stands aghast at the sight of an "unprincipled, immoral, incorrigible" publick; And the word of God abounds in such threats and denunciations, as must strike terror into the heart of every believer.
RICHARD HURD—*Works*. Vol. IV. Sermon 1.

8
Venale pecus.
The venal herd.
JUVENAL—*Satires*. VIII. 62.
(See also COWLEY, SUETONIUS)

9
Paucite paucarum diffundere crimen in omnes.
Do not lay on the multitude the blame that is due to a few.
OVID—*Ars Amatoria*. III. 9.

10
The people's voice is odd,
It is, and it is not, the voice of God.
POPE—*To Augustus*. Bk. II. Ep. I. L. 89.

11
Trust not the populace; the crowd is many-minded.
PSEUDO-PHOCYL. 89.
(See also DANIEL)

12
The proverbial wisdom of the populace in the streets, on the roads, and in the markets, instructs the ear of him who studies man more fully than a thousand rules ostentatiously arranged.
Proverbs, or the Manual of Wisdom. On the Title Page. Printed for Tabart & Co., London. (1804)

13
The public is a bad guesser.
DE QUINCEY—*Essays*. *Protestantism*.

14
Vox Populi, vox Dei.
The voice of the people, the voice of God.
WALTER REYNOLDS, Archbishop of Canterbury. *Text of Sermon when* EDWARD III *ascended the throne*, Feb. 1, 1327. (*Called also* DE REYNEL and REGINALD.) *See* JOHN TOLAND—*Angelia Libera*. Attributed also to WALTER MEPHAN. See G. C. LEWIS —*Essay on Influence of Authority*. P. 172. See *Aphorismi Politici*, (Simon given erroneously for Walter.) Collected by LAMBERTUM DANÆUM. Alluded to as an old proverb by WILLIAM OF MALMESBURY—*De Gestis Pont*. Folio 114. (About 920)
HESIOD—*Works and Days*. 763.
(See also ALCUIN)

15
Who o'er the herd would wish to reign,
Fantastic, fickle, fierce, and vain?
Vain as the leaf upon the stream,
And fickle as a changeful dream;
Fantastic as a woman's mood,
And fierce as Frenzy's fever'd blood—
Thou many-headed monster thing,
Oh, who would wish to be thy king?
SCOTT—*Lady of the Lake*. Canto V. St. 30.
(See also DANIEL)

16
Faith, there have been many great men that have flattered the people, who ne'er loved them; and there be many that they have loved, they know not wherefore; so that, if they love they know not why, they hate upon no better a ground.
Coriolanus. Act II. Sc. 2. L. 7.

17
He himself stuck not to call us the many-headed multitude.
Coriolanus. Act II. Sc. 3. L. 14.
(See also DANIEL, also SCOTT under ACTING)

18
The play, I remember, pleased not the million; 'twas caviare to the general.
Hamlet. Act II. Sc. 2. L. 456.

19
Was ever feather so lightly blown to and fro as this multitude?
Henry VI. Pt. II. Act IV. Sc. 8. L. 57.

20
Look, as I blow this feather from my face,
And as the air blows it to me again,
Obeying with my wind when I do blow,
And yielding to another when it blows,
Commanded always by the greater gust;
Such is the lightness of you common men.
Henry VI. Pt. III. Act III. Sc. 1. L. 85.

21
Many-headed multitude.
SIR PHILIP SIDNEY—*Arcadia*. Bk. II.
(See also CORIOLANUS, DANIEL)

22
Laymen say, indeed,
How they take no heed
Their sely sheep to feed,
But pluck away and pull
The fleeces of their wool.
SKELTON—*Colin Clout*. Partly from WALTER MAPES—*Apocalypse of Golias*.

1
Grex venalium.
A flock of hirelings (venal pack).
SUETONIUS—*De Clar. Rhet.* I.
(See also JUVENAL)

2
Vulgus ignavum et nihil ultra verba ausurum.
A cowardly populace which will dare nothing beyond talk.
TACITUS—*Annales.* Bk. III. 58.

3
Neque mala, vel bona, quæ vulgus putet.
The views of the multitude are neither bad nor good.
TACITUS—*Annales.* Bk. VI. 22.

4
It is to the middle class we must look for the safety of England.
THACKERAY—*Four Georges. George the Third.*

5
The public be damned.
W. H. VANDERBILT'S amused retort when asked whether the public should be consulted about luxury trains. As reported by CLARENCE DRESSER in Chicago *Tribune,* about 1883. See Letter by ASHLEY W. COLE in N. Y. *Times,* Aug. 25, 1918. Also Letter in *Herald,* Oct. 1, 1918, which was answered in same, Oct. 28, 1918.

6 Sævitque animis ignobile vulgus,
Jamque faces et saxa volant.
The rude rabble are enraged; now firebrands and stones fly.
VERGIL—*Æneid.* I. 149.

7
Scinditur incertum studia in contraria vulgus.
The uncertain multitude is divided by opposite opinions.
VERGIL—*Æneid.* II. 39.

8
Vox omnibus una.
One cry was common to them all.
VERGIL—*Æneid.* V. 616.

9
Les préjugés, ami, sont les rois du vulgaire.
Prejudices, friend, govern the vulgar crowd.
VOLTAIRE—*Le Fanatisme.* II. 4.

10
Our supreme governors, the mob.
HORACE WALPOLE—*Letter to Horace Mann.* Sept. 7, 1743.

11 [The] public path of life
Is dirty.
YOUNG—*Night Thoughts.* VIII. 373.

PUBLISHING (See also BOOKS, PRINTING)

12
But I account the use that a man should seek of the publishing of his own writings before his death, to be but an untimely anticipation of that which is proper to follow a man, and not to go along with him.
BACON—*An Advertisement Touching a Holy War. Epistle Dedicatory.*

13
Yon second-hand bookseller is second to none in the worth of the treasures which he dispenses.
LEIGH HUNT—*On the Beneficence of Bookstalls.*

14
If I publish this poem for you, speaking as a trader, I shall be a considerable loser. Did I publish all I admire, out of sympathy with the author, I should be a ruined man.
BULWER-LYTTON—*My Novel.* Bk. VI. Ch. XIV.

15
If the bookseller happens to desire a privilege for his merchandize, whether he is selling Rabelais or the Fathers of the Church, the magistrate grants the privilege without answering for the contents of the book.
VOLTAIRE—*A Philosophical Dictionary. Books.* Sec. 1.

PUMPKIN

16
I don't know how to tell it—but ef such a thing could be
As the angels wantin' boardin', and they'd call around on *me*—
I'd want to 'commodate 'em—all the whole-indurin' flock—
When the frost is on the punkin and the fodder's in the shock.
JAMES WHITCOMB RILEY—*When the Frost is on the Punkin.*

17
And the Creole of Cuba laughs out to behold,
Through orange leaves shining the broad spheres of gold.
WHITTIER—*The Pumpkin.*

18
O,—fruit loved of boyhood!—the old days recalling,
When wood grapes were purpling and brown nuts were falling!
When wild, ugly faces we carved in its skin,
Glaring out through the dark with a candle within!
When we laughed round the corn-heap, with hearts all in tune,
Our chair a broad pumpkin,—our lantern the moon,
Telling tales of the fairy who travelled like steam
In a pumpkin-shell coach, with two rats for her team!
WHITTIER—*The Pumpkin.*

PUN (See HUMOR, JESTING, WIT)

PUNISHMENT

19 See they suffer death,
But in their deaths remember they are men,
Strain not the laws to make their tortures grievous.
ADDISON—*Cato.* Act III. Sc 5.

20
Let them stew in their own grease (or juice).
BISMARCK, at the time of the Franco-German war, to Mr. Malet at Meaux. See LABOUCHERE—*Diary of a Besieged Resident.* Stewing in our own gravy. NED WARD—*London Spy.* Pt. IX. P. 219. (1709) (Describing a Turkish bath.) Idea in PLAUTUS—*Captives.* Act I. Ver. 80-84. TEUBNER'S ed.
(See also CHAUCER)

1
Some have been beaten till they know
What wood a cudgel's of by th' blow:
Some kick'd until they can feel whether
A shoe be Spanish or neat's leather.
BUTLER—*Hudibras*. Pt. II. Canto I. L. 221.

2
Frieth in his own grease.
CHAUCER—*Wife of Bathes Tale*. V. 6069. *Prologue*. L. 487. MORRIS' ed. HEYWOOD—*Proverbs*. Pt. I. Ch. XI. ("her" for "his.")
(See also BISMARCK, COTTON)

3
Noxiæ pœna par esto.
Let the punishment be equal with the offence.
CICERO—*De Legibus*. Bk. III. 20.
(See also GILBERT)

4
Cavendum est ne major pœna quam culpa sit; et ne iisdem de causis alii plectantur, alii ne appellentur quidem.
Care should be taken that the punishment does not exceed the guilt; and also that some men do not suffer for offenses for which others are not even indicted.
CICERO—*De Officiis*. I. 23.

5
Diis proximus ille est
Quem ratio non ira movet: qui factor rependens
Consilio punire potest.
He is next to the gods whom reason, and not passion, impels; and who, after weighing the facts, can measure the punishment with discretion.
CLAUDINAUS—*De Consulatu Malii Theodori Panegyris*. CCXXVII.

6
I stew all night in my own grease.
COTTON—*Virgil Travestie*. P. 35. (Ed. 1807) Fat enough to be stewed in their own liquor. FULLER—*Holy State and the Profane State*. P. 396. (Ed. 1840)
(See also CHAUCER)

7
Eye for eye, tooth for tooth, hand for hand, foot for foot.
Deuteronomy. XIX. 21.

8
'Tis I that call, remember Milo's end,
Wedged in that timber which he strove to rend.
WENTWORTH DILLON—*Essay on Translated Verse. Ovid*.

9
That is the bitterest of all,—to wear the yoke of our own wrong-doing.
GEORGE ELIOT—*Daniel Deronda*. Bk. V. Ch. XXXVI.

10
Send them into everlasting Coventry.
EMERSON—*Essays. Manners*. During the Civil War in England officers were sent for punishment to the garrison at Coventry.

11
Vengeance comes not slowly either upon you or any other wicked man, but steals silently and imperceptibly, placing its foot on the bad.
EURIPIDES—*Fragment*.

12
My punishment is greater than I can bear.
Genesis. IV. 13.

13
Whoso sheddeth man's blood, by man shall his blood be shed.
Genesis. IX. 6.

14
Something lingering with boiling oil in it . . . . something humorous but lingering—with either boiling oil or melted lead.
W. S. GILBERT—*Mikado*.

15
My object all sublime
I shall achieve in time—
To let the punishment fit the crime.
W. S. GILBERT—*Mikado*.
(See also CICERO)

16
The wolf must die in his own skin.
HERBERT—*Jacula Prudentum*.

17
Culpam pœna premit comes.
Punishment follows close on crime.
HORACE—*Carmina*. IV. 5. 24.

18
Ne scutica dignum horribili sectere flagello.
Do not pursue with the terrible scourge him who deserves a slight whip.
HORACE—*Satires*. I. 3. 119.

19
For whoso spareth the spring [switch] spilleth his children.
LANGLAND—*Piers Ploughman*.
(See also PROVERBS)

20
Breach for breach, eye for eye, tooth for tooth.
Leviticus. XXIV. 20.

21
Quidquid multis peccatur inultum est.
The sins committed by many pass unpunished.
LUCAN—*Pharsalia*. V. 260.

22
It were better for him that a millstone were hanged about his neck, and he cast into the sea.
Luke. XVII. 2.

23
The object of punishment is, prevention from evil; it never can be made impulsive to good.
HORACE MANN—*Lectures and Reports on Education*. Lecture VII.

24
Where their worm dieth not, and the fire is not quenched.
Mark. IX. 44.

25
Unrespited, unpitied, unrepriev'd.
MILTON—*Paradise Lost*. Bk. II. L. 185.

26
Our torments also may in length of time
Become our elements.
MILTON—*Paradise Lost*. Bk. II. L. 274.

27
Back to thy punishment,
False fugitive, and to thy speed add wings.
MILTON—*Paradise Lost*. Bk. II. L. 699.

28
Just prophet, let the damn'd one dwell
Full in the sight of Paradise,
Beholding heaven and feeling hell.
MOORE—*Lalla Rookh. Fire Worshippers*. L. 1,028.

1
Ay—down to the dust with them, slaves as they are,
From this hour, let the blood in their dastardly veins,
That shrunk at the first touch of Liberty's war,
Be wasted for tyrants, or stagnant in chains.
MOORE—*Lines on the Entry of the Austrians into Naples.* (1821)

2
Die and be damned.
THOMAS MORTIMER—*Against the Calvinistic doctrine of eternal punishment.*

3
Æquo animo pœnam, qui meruere, ferant.
Let those who have deserved their punishment, bear it patiently.
OVID—*Amorum.* II. 7. 12.

4
Paucite paucarum diffundere crimen in omnes.
Do not lay on the multitude the blame that is due to a few.
OVID—*Ars Amatoria.* III. 9.

5
Estque pati pœnas quam meruisse minus.
It is less to suffer punishment than to deserve it.
OVID—*Epistolæ Ex Ponto.* I. 1. 62.

6
Deos agere curam rerum humanarum credi, ex usu vitæ est: pœnasque maleficiis, aliquando seras, nunquam autem irritas esse.
It is advantageous that the gods should be believed to attend to the affairs of man; and the punishment for evil deeds, though sometimes late, is never fruitless.
PLINY the Elder—*Historia Naturalis.* II. 5. 10.

7
Heaven is not always angry when he strikes,
But most chastises those whon most he likes.
JOHN POMFRET—*To a Friend Under Affliction.* L. 89.

8
But if the first Eve
Hard doom did receive
When only one apple had she,
What a punishment new
Must be found out for you,
Who eating hath robb'd the whole tree.
POPE—*To Lady Montague.*

9
He that spareth his rod hateth his son.
Proverbs. XIII. 24.
(See also LANGLAND, SKELTON, VENNING)

10
To kiss the rod.
History of Reynard the Fox. WILLIAM CAXTON's trans., printed by him. (1481) ARBER's *English Scholar's Library.* Ch. XII.
(See also TWO GENTLEMEN OF VERONA)

11
Quod antecedit tempus, maxima venturi supplicii pars est.
The time that precedes punishment is the severest part of it.
SENECA—*De Beneficiis.* II. 5.

12
Corrigendus est, qui peccet, et admonitione et vi, et molliter et aspere, meliorque tam sibi quam alii faciendus, non sine castigatione, sed sine ira.
He, who has committed a fault, is to be corrected both by advice and by force, kindly and harshly, and to be made better for himself as well as for another, not without chastisement, but without passion.
SENECA—*De Ira.* I. 14.

13
Maxima est factæ injuriæ pæna, fecisse: nec quisquam gravius adficitur, quam qui ad supplicium pœnitentiæ traditur.
The severest punishment a man can receive who has injured another, is to have committed the injury; and no man is more severely punished than he who is subject to the whip of his own repentance.
SENECA—*De Ira.* III. 26.

14
Nec ulla major pœna nequitiæ est, quam quod sibi et suis displicet.
There is no greater punishment of wickedness than that it is dissatisfied with itself and its deeds.
SENECA—*Epistolæ Ad Lucilium.* XLII.

15
Sequitur superbos ultor a tergo deus.
An avenging God closely follows the haughty.
SENECA—*Hercules Furens.* 385.

16
Minor in parvis fortuna furit,
Leviusque ferit leviora Deus.
Fortune is less severe against those of lesser degree, and God strikes what is weak with less power.
SENECA—*Hippolytus.* Act IV. 1124.

17
Thou shalt be whipp'd with wire, and stew'd in brine,
Smarting in ling'ring pickle.
Antony and Cleopatra. Act II. Sc. 5. L. 65.

18
Vex not his ghost: Oh; let him pass! he hates him,
That would upon the rack of this tough world
Stretch him out longer.
King Lear. Act V. Sc. 2. "Tough world" altered by Pope to "rough world."

19
Some of us will smart for it.
Much Ado About Nothing. Act V. Sc. 1. L. 109.

20
Off with his head! so much for Buckingham!
Richard III. Act IV. Sc. 3. As altered by COLLEY CIBBER.

21
A testy babe will scratch the nurse,
And presently all humbled kiss the rod.
Two Gentlemen of Verona. Act I. Sc. 2. 59.
(See also REYNARD THE FOX)

22
There is nothynge that more dyspleaseth God
Than from theyr children to spare the rod.
SKELTON—*Magnyfycence.* L. 1,954.
(See also PROVERBS)

23
Punitis ingeniis, gliscit auctoritas.
When men of talents are punished, authority is strengthened.
TACITUS—*Annales.* IV. 35.

1
Habet aliquid ex iniquo omne magnum exemplum, quod contra singulos, utilitate publica rependitus.

Every great example of punishment has in it some injustice, but the suffering individual is compensated by the public good.

TACITUS—*Annales.* XIV. 44.

2
The woman, Spaniel, the walnut tree,
The more you beat them the better they be.

JOHN TAYLOR. From an early song. Same idea in GILBERTUS COGNATUS—*Adagia.* Included in GRYNÆUS—*Adagia.* P. 484. (Ed. 1629)

3
Verbera sed audi.

Strike, but hear.

THEMISTOCLES. When EURYBIADES, commander of the Spartan fleet, raised his staff to strike him. In PLUTARCH'S *Life of Themistocles.* Ch. XI.

4
Ah, miser! et si quis primo perjuria celat,
Sera tamen tacitis Pœna venit pedibus.

Ah, wretch! even though one may be able at first to conceal his perjuries, yet punishment creeps on, though late, with noiseless step.

TIBULLUS—*Carmina.* I. 9. 3.

5
They spare the rod, and spoyle the child.

RALPH VENNING—*Mysteries and Revelations.* P. 5. (1649)

(See also PROVERBS)

6
What heavy guilt upon him lies!
How cursed is his name!
The ravens shall pick out his eyes,
And eagles eat the same.

ISAAC WATTS—*Obedience.*

7
Du spottest noch? Erzittre! Immer schlafen
Des Rächers Blitze nicht.

Thou mockest? Tremble! the avenger's lightning bolts do not forever dormant lie.

WIELAND—*Oberon.* I. 50.

8
Hanging was the worst use a man could be put to.

SIR HENRY WOTTON—*The Disparity between Buckingham and Essex.*

9
Jupiter is late in looking into his note-book.

ZENOBIUS—*Cent.* IV. 11. Same idea in HORACE—*Odes.* III. 2. 30. PERSIUS—*Satires.* II. 24.

PURITY (See also CHASTITY)

10
Quell' onda, che ruina
Dalla pendice alpina,
Balza, si frange, e mormora
Ma limpida si fa.

That water which falls from some Alpine height is dashed, broken, and will murmur loudly, but grows limpid by its fall.

METASTASIO—*Alcide al Bivio.*

11
Qual diverrà quel fiume,
Nel lungo suo cammino,
Se al fonte ancor vicino
È torbido così?

What will the stream become in its lengthened course, if it be so turbid at its source?

METASTASIO—*Morte d' Abele.* I.

12
Les choses valent toujours mieux dans leur source.

The stream is always purer at its source.

PASCAL—*Lettres Provinciales.* IV.

13
Whiter than new snow on a raven's back.

Romeo and Juliet. Act III. Sc. 2. L. 19.

14
Unto the pure all things are pure.

Titus. I. 15.

Q

QUACKERY (See also MEDICINE)

15
Void of all honor, avaricious, rash,
The daring tribe compound their boasted trash—
Tincture of syrup, lotion, drop, or pill;
All tempt the sick to trust the lying bill.

CRABBE—*Borough.* Letter VII. L. 75.

16
From powerful causes spring the empiric's gains,
Man's love of life, his weakness, and his pains;
These first induce him the vile trash to try,
Then lend his name, that other men may buy.

CRABBE—*Borough.* Letter VII. L. 124.

17
Out, you impostors!
Quack salving, cheating mountebanks! your skill
Is to make sound men sick, and sick men kill.

MASSINGER—*Virgin-Martyr.* Act IV. Sc. 1.

18
I bought an unction of a mountebank,
So mortal that, but dip a knife in it,
Where it draws blood no cataplasm so rare,
Collected from all simples that have virtue
Under the moon, can save the thing from death
That is but scratch'd withal.

Hamlet. Act IV. Sc. 7. L. 142.

QUAIL

19
In jalousie I rede eek thou hym bynde
And thou shalt make him couche as doeth a quaille.

CHAUCER—*The Clerke's Tale.* L. 13,541.

20
The song-birds leave us at the summer's close,
Only the empty nests are left behind,
And pipings of the quail among the sheaves.

LONGFELLOW—*The Harvest Moon.*

21
An honest fellow enough, and one that loves quails.

Troilus and Cressida. Act V. Sc. 1. L. 58.

QUALITY

1
Things that have a common quality ever quickly seek their kind.
MARCUS AURELIUS—*Meditations*. Ch. IX. 9.

2
A demd, damp, moist, unpleasant body!
DICKENS—*Nicholas Nickelby*. Ch. XXXIV.

3
Hard as a piece of the nether millstone.
Job. XLI. 24.

4
Ye are the salt of the earth: but if the salt have lost his savour, wherewith shall it be salted?
Matthew. V. 13.

5
Fine by defect, and delicately weak.
POPE—*Moral Essays*. Ep. II. L. 43.

6
That air and harmony of shape express,
Fine by degrees, and beautifully less.
PRIOR—*Henry and Emma*. L. 432.

7
Come, give us a taste of your quality.
Hamlet. Act II. Sc. 2. L. 451.

8
Innocence in genius, and candor in power, are both noble qualities.
MADAME DE STAËL—*Germany*. Pt. II. Ch. VIII.

9
Nothing endures but personal qualities.
WALT WHITMAN—*Leaves of Grass*. *Song of the Broad-Axe*. St. 4.

QUARRELING (See also CONTENTION, DISSENSION)

10
Those who in quarrels interpose,
Must often wipe a bloody nose.
GAY—*Fables*. *The Mastiffs*. L. 1.

11
L'aimable siècle où l'homme dit à l'homme,
Soyons frères, ou je t'assomme.
Those glorious days, when man said to man,
Let us be brothers, or I will knock you down.
LE BRUN.

12
Cadit statim simultas, ab altera parte deserta; nisi pariter, non pugnant.
A quarrel is quickly settled when deserted by one party: there is no battle unless there be two.
SENECA—*De Ira*. II. 34.

13
But greatly to find quarrel in a straw
When honour's at the stake.
Hamlet. Act IV. Sc. 4. L. 55.

14
In a false quarrel there is no true valour.
Much Ado About Nothing. Act V. Sc. 1. L. 120.

15
Thou! why, thou wilt quarrel with a man that hath a hair more, or a hair less, in his beard than thou hast: thou wilt quarrel with a man for cracking nuts, having no other reason but because thou hast hazel eyes.
Romeo and Juliet. Act III. Sc. 1. L. 18.

16
Thy head is as full of quarrels as an egg is full of meat.
Romeo and Juliet. Act III. Sc. 1. L. 23.

17
The quarrel is a very pretty quarrel as it stands; we should only spoil it by trying to explain it.
R. B. SHERIDAN—*The Rivals*. Act IV. Sc. 3.

18
I won't quarrel with my bread and butter.
SWIFT—*Polite Conversation*. *Dialogue* I.

19
O we fell out, I know not why,
And kiss'd again with tears.
TENNYSON—*The Princess*. Canto II. *Song*.

20
Weakness on both sides is, as we know, the motto of all quarrels.
VOLTAIRE—*A Philosophical Dictionary*. *Weakness on Both Sides*.

21
Let dogs delight to bark and bite,
For God hath made them so;
Let bears and lions growl and fight,
For 'tis their nature too.
ISAAC WATTS—*Against Quarrelling*.

22
But children you should never let
Such angry passions rise,
Your little hands were never made
To tear each other's eyes.
ISAAC WATTS—*Against Quarrelling*.

QUOTATION

23
There is not less wit nor invention in applying rightly a thought one finds in a book, than in being the first author of that thought. Cardinal du Perron has been heard to say that the happy application of a verse of Virgil has deserved a talent.
BAYLE—*Dictionnaire*. Vol. II. P. 1077. Ed. 1720. (See also EMERSON)

24
One whom it is easier to hate, but still easier to quote—Alexander Pope.
AUGUSTINE BIRRELL—*Alexander Pope*.

25
All which he understood by rote,
And, as occasion serv'd, would quote.
BUTLER—*Hudibras*. Pt. I. Canto I. L. 135.

26
With just enough of learning to misquote.
BYRON—*English Bards and Scotch Reviewers*. L. 66.

27
Perverts the Prophets, and purloins the Psalms.
BYRON—*English Bards and Scotch Reviewers*. L. 326.

28
To copy beauties, forfeits all pretence
To fame—to copy faults, is want of sense.
CHURCHILL—*The Rosciad*. L. 457.

29
The greater part of our writers, * * * have become so original, that no one cares to imitate them: and those who never quote in return are seldom quoted.
ISAAC D'ISRAELI—*Curiosities of Literature*. *Quotation*.

1
The art of quotation requires more delicacy in the practice than those conceive who can see nothing more in a quotation than an extract.
ISAAC D'ISRAELI—*Curiosities of Literature. Quotation.*

2
One may quote till one compiles.
ISAAC D'ISRAELI—*Curiosities of Literature. Quotation.*

3
The wisdom of the wise and the experience of ages may be preserved by QUOTATION.
ISAAC D'ISRAELI—*Curiosities of Literature. Quotation.*

4
A book which hath been culled from the flowers of all books.
GEORGE ELIOT—*The Spanish Gypsy.* Bk. II.
(See also MONTAIGNE)

5
A great man quotes bravely, and will not draw on his invention when his memory serves him with a word as good.
EMERSON—*Letters and Social Aims. Quotation and Originality.*

6
By necessity, by proclivity, and by delight, we quote. We quote not only books and proverbs, but arts, sciences, religion, customs, and laws; nay, we quote temples and houses, tables and chairs by imitation.
EMERSON—*Letters and Social Aims. Quotation and Originality.*

7
Next to the originator of a good sentence is the first quoter of it.
EMERSON—*Letters and Social Aims. Quotation and Originality.*
(See also BAYLE, LOWELL)

8
We are as much informed of a writer's genius by what he selects as by what he originates.
EMERSON—*Letters and Social Aims. Quotation and Originality.*

9
Every quotation contributes something to the stability or enlargement of the language.
SAMUEL JOHNSON—*Preface to Dictionary.*

10
Classical quotation is the parole of literary men all over the world.
SAMUEL JOHNSON—*Remark to Wilkes.* (1781)

11
C'est souvent hasarder un bon mot et vouloir le perdre que de le donner pour sien.
A good saying often runs the risk of being thrown away when quoted as the speaker's own.
LA BRUYÈRE—*Les Caractères.* II.

12
'Twas not an Age ago since most of our Books were nothing but Collections of Latin Quotations; there was not above a line or two of French in a Page.
LA BRUYÈRE—*The Character or Manners of the Present Age.* Ch. XV. *Of the Pulpit.*

13
Though old the thought and oft exprest,
'Tis his at last who says it best.
LOWELL—*For an Autograph.* St. 1.
(See also EMERSON)

14
Comme quelqu'un pourroit dire de moy, que j'ay seulement faict icy un amas des fleurs estrangieres, n'y ayant fourny du mien que le filet à les lier.
As one might say of me that I have only made here a collection of other people's flowers, having provided nothing of my own but the cord to bind them together.
MONTAIGNE—*Essays.* Bk. III. Ch. XII.
(See also ELIOT)

15
. . . I have seen books made of things neither studied nor ever understood . . . the author contenting himself for his own part, to have cast the plot and projected the design of it, and by his industry to have bound up the fagot of unknown provisions; at least the ink and paper his own. This may be said to be a buying or borrowing, and not a making or compiling of a book.
MONTAIGNE—*Essays.* Bk. III. Ch. XII.

16
Nor suffers Horace more in wrong translations
By wits, than critics in as wrong quotations.
POPE—*Essay on Criticism.* Pt. III. L. 104.

17
He ranged his tropes, and preached up patience,
Backed his opinion with quotations.
PRIOR—*Paulo Purganti and his Wife.* L. 143.

18
Always to verify your references.
REV. DR. ROUTH—*to Dean Burgon.* Nov. 29, 1847. See VERY REV. JOHN BURGON—*Lives of Twenty Good Men.* "Reference" in ed. of 1891; "quotation" in earlier ed.

19
The little honesty existing among authors is to be seen in the outrageous way in which they misquote from the writings of others.
SCHOPENHAUER—*On Authorship.*

20
They had been at a great feast of languages, and stolen the scraps.
Love's Labour's Lost. Act V. Sc. 1. L. 39.

21
The devil can cite Scripture for his purpose.
Merchant of Venice. Act I. Sc. 3. L. 99.

22
A forward critic often dupes us
With sham quotations *peri hupsos*,
And if we have not read Longinus,
Will magisterially outshine us.
Then, lest with Greek he over-run ye,
Procure the book for love or money,
Translated from Boileau's translation,
And quote quotation on quotation.
SWIFT—*On Poetry.*

23
I am but a gatherer and disposer of other men's stuff.
SIR HENRY WOTTON—*Preface to the Elements of Architecture.*

24
To patchwork learn'd quotations are allied,
Both strive to make our poverty our pride.
YOUNG—*Love of Fame.* Satire I.

25
Some, for *renown*, on scraps of learning dote,
And think they grow immortal as they *quote.*
YOUNG—*Love of Fame.* Satire I. L. 89.

R

RAIN

1
We knew it would rain, for the poplars showed
The white of their leaves, the amber grain
Shrunk in the wind,—and the lightning now
Is tangled in tremulous skeins of rain.
T. B. Aldrich—*Before the Rain.*

2
A little rain will fill
The lily's cup which hardly moists the field.
Edwin Arnold—*The Light of Asia.* Bk. VI. L. 215.

3
She waits for me, my lady Earth,
Smiles and waits and sighs;
I'll say her nay, and hide away,
Then take her by surprise.
Mary Mapes Dodge—*How the Rain Comes. April.*

4
How it pours, pours, pours,
In a never-ending sheet!
How it drives beneath the doors!
How it soaks the passer's feet!
How it rattles on the shutter!
How it rumples up the lawn!
How 'twill sigh, and moan, and mutter,
From darkness until dawn.
Rossiter Johnson—*Rhyme of the Rain.*

5
Be still, sad heart, and cease repining;
Behind the clouds the sun is shining;
Thy fate is the common fate of all,
Into each life some rain must fall,
Some days must be dark and dreary.
Longfellow—*An April Day.*

6
And the hooded clouds, like friars,
Tell their beads in drops of rain.
Longfellow—*Midnight Mass for the Dying Year.* St. 4.

7
The day is cold, and dark, and dreary;
It rains, and the wind is never weary;
The vine still clings to the mouldering wall,
But at every gust the dead leaves fall,
And the day is dark and dreary.
Longfellow—*The Rainy Day.*

8
The ceaseless rain is falling fast,
And yonder gilded vane,
Immovable for three days past,
Points to the misty main.
Longfellow—*Travels by the Fireside.* St. 1.

9
It is not raining rain to me,
It's raining daffodils;
In every dimpled drop I see
Wild flowers on distant hills.
Robert Loveman—*April Rain.* Appeared in *Harper's Mag.* May, 1901. Erroneously attributed to Swama Rama, who copied it in the *Thundering Dawn.* Lahore.
(See also Eliot under Rose)

10
He shall come down like rain upon the mown grass.
Psalms. LXXII. 6.

11
For the rain it raineth every day.
Twelfth Night. Act V. Sc. 1. *Song.* L. 401.

12
I bring fresh showers for the thirsting flowers,
From the seas and the streams;
I bear light shade for the leaves when laid
In their noonday dreams.
Shelley—*The Cloud.*

13
I know Sir John will go, though he was sure it would rain cats and dogs.
Swift—*Polite Conversation. Dialogue* II.

14
The Clouds consign their treasures to the fields,
And, softly shaking on the dimpled pool
Prelusive drops; let all their moisture flow,
In large effusion, o'er the freshen'd world.
Thomson—*The Seasons. Spring.* L. 172.

RAINBOW

15
God's glowing covenant.
Hosea Ballou—*MS. Sermons.*

16
And, lo! in the dark east, expanded high,
The rainbow brightens to the setting Sun.
Beattie—*The Minstrel.* Bk. I. St. 30.

17
'Tis sweet to listen as the night winds creep
From leaf to leaf; 'tis sweet to view on high
The rainbow, based on ocean, span the sky.
Byron—*Don Juan.* Canto I. St. 122.

18
Triumphal arch, that fill'st the sky
When storms prepare to part,
I ask not proud Philosophy
To teach me what thou art.
Campbell—*To the Rainbow.*

19
Over her hung a canopy of state,
Not of rich tissue, nor of spangled gold,
But of a substance, though not animate,
Yet of a heavenly and spiritual mould,
That only eyes of spirits might behold.
Giles Fletcher—*The Rainbow.* L. 33.

20
O beautiful rainbow;—all woven of light!
There's not in thy tissue one shadow of night;
Heaven surely is open when thou dost appear,
And, bending above thee, the angels draw near,
And sing,—"The rainbow! the rainbow!
The smile of God is here."
Mrs. Sarah J. Hale—*Poems.*

21
God loves an idle rainbow,
No less than laboring seas.
Ralph Hodgson—*Three Poems.* II.

22
There was an awful rainbow once in heaven;
We know her woof, her texture; she is given
In the dull catalogue of common things.
Philosophy will clip an Angel's wings.
Keats—*Lamia.* Pt. II. L. 231.

23
Pride of the dewy morning,
The swain's experienced eye
From thee takes timely warning,

Nor trusts the gorgeous sky.
KEBLE—*Christian Year.* (25th Sunday after Trinity.) *On the Rainbow.*

1
A rainbow in the morning
Is the Shepherd's warning;
But a rainbow at night
Is the Shepherd's delight.
Old Weather Rhyme.

2
What skilful limner e'er would choose
To paint the rainbow's varying hues,
Unless to mortal it were given
To dip his brush in dyes of heaven?
SCOTT—*Marmion.* Canto VI. St. 5.

3
Mild arch of promise! on the evening sky
Thou shinest fair with many a lovely ray,
Each in the other melting.
SOUTHEY—*Sonnets. The Evening Rainbow.*

4
Rain, rain, and sun! a rainbow in the sky!
TENNYSON—*Idylls of the King. The Coming of Arthur.* L. 401.

5
Hung on the shower that fronts the golden West,
The rainbow bursts like magic on mine eyes!
In hues of ancient promise there impress;
Frail in its date, eternal in its guise.
CHARLES TENNYSON TURNER—*Sonnets and Fugitive Pieces. The Rainbow.*

6
Bright pledge of peace and sunshine! the sure tie
Of thy Lord's hand, the object of His eye!
When I behold thee, though my light be dim,
Distinct, and low, I can in thine see Him
Who looks upon thee from His glorious throne,
And minds the covenant between all and One.
VAUGHAN—*The Rainbow.*

RAVEN

7
That Raven on yon left-hand oak
(Curse on his ill-betiding croak)
Bodes me no good.
GAY—*Fables. The Farmer's Wife and the Raven.*

8
The Raven's house is built with reeds,—
Sing woe, and alas is me!
And the Raven's couch is spread with weeds,
High on the hollow tree;
And the Raven himself, telling his beads
In penance for his past misdeeds,
Upon the top I see.
THOS. D'ARCY MCGEE—*The Penitent Raven.*

9
The raven once in snowy plumes was drest,
White as the whitest dove's unsullied breast,
Fair as the guardian of the Capitol,
Soft as the swan; a large and lovely fowl
His tongue, his prating tongue had changed him quite
To sooty blackness from the purest white.
OVID—*Metamorphoses. Story of Coronis.* ADDISON'S trans.

10
Ghastly, grim, and ancient Raven, wandering from the Nightly shore,—
Tell me what thy lordly name is on the Night's Plutonian shore!
Quoth the Raven "Nevermore!"
POE—*The Raven.* St. 8.

11
And the Raven, never flitting,
Still is sitting, still is sitting
On the pallid bust of Pallas
Just above my chamber door;
And his eyes have all the seeming
Of a demon's that is dreaming,
And the lamplight o'er him streaming
Throws his shadow on the floor,
And my soul from out that shadow,
That lies floating on the floor,
Shall be lifted—nevermore.
POE—*The Raven.* St. 18.

12
The croaking raven doth bellow for revenge.
Hamlet. Act III. Sc. 2. L. 264.

13
The raven himself is hoarse
That croaks the fatal entrance of Duncan
Under my battlements.
Macbeth. Act I. Sc. 5. L. 40.

14
O, it comes o'er my memory,
As doth the raven o'er the infected house,
Boding to all.
Othello. Act IV. Sc. 1. L. 20.

15
Did ever raven sing so like a lark,
That gives sweet tidings of the sun's uprise?
Titus Andronicus. Act III. Sc. 1. L. 158.

READING

16
Reading is to the mind, what exercise is to the body. As by the one, health is preserved, strengthened, and invigorated: by the other, virtue (which is the health of the mind) is kept alive, cherished, and confirmed.
ADDISON—*The Tatler.* No. 147.

17
Reading maketh a full man.
BACON—*Of Studies.*

18
Read, mark, learn, and inwardly digest.
Book of Common Prayer. Collect for the Second Sunday in Advent.

19
In science, read, by preference, the newest works; in literature, the oldest. The classic literature is always modern.
BULWER-LYTTON—*Caxtoniana. Hints on Mental Culture.*

20
If time is precious, no book that will not improve by repeated readings deserves to be read at all.
CARLYLE—*Essays. Goethe's Helena.*

21
We have not *read* an author till we have seen his object, whatever it may be, as *he* saw it.
CARLYLE—*Essays. Goethe's Helena.*

22
The mind, relaxing into needful sport,
Should turn to writers of an abler sort,
Whose wit well managed, and whose classic style,
Give truth a lustre, and make wisdom smile.
COWPER—*Retirement.* L. 715.

1
But truths on which depends our main concern,
That 'tis our shame and misery not to learn,
Shine by the side of every path we tread
With such a lustre he that runs may read.
COWPER—*Tirocinium*. L. 77.
(See also HABAKKUK)

2
The delight of opening a new pursuit, or a new course of reading, imparts the vivacity and novelty of youth even to old age.
ISAAC D'ISRAELI—*Literary Character of Men of Genius*. Ch. XXII.

3
I like to be beholden to the great metropolitan English speech, the sea which receives tributaries from every region under heaven. I should as soon think of swimming across the Charles river when I wish to go to Boston, as of reading all my books in originals, when I have them rendered for me in my mother tongue.
EMERSON—*Essays. Books.*

4
If we encountered a man of rare intellect, we should ask him what books he read.
EMERSON—*Letters and Social Aims. Quotation and Originality.*

5
Our high respect for a well-read man is praise enough of literature.
EMERSON—*Letters and Social Aims. Quotation and Originality.*

6
My early and invincible love of reading, * * * I would not exchange for the treasures of India.
GIBBON—*Memoirs.*

7
The sagacious reader who is capable of reading between these lines what does not stand written in them, but is nevertheless implied, will be able to form some conception.
GOETHE—*Autobiography*. Bk. XVIII. *Truth and Beauty.*

8
Zwar sind sie an das Beste nicht gewöhnt,
Allein sie haben schrecklich viel gelesen.
What they're accustomed to is no great matter,
But then, alas! they've read an awful deal.
GOETHE—*Faust. Vorspiel auf dem Theater*. L. 13. BAYARD TAYLOR'S trans.

9
In a polite age almost every person becomes a reader, and receives more instruction from the Press than the Pulpit.
GOLDSMITH—*The Citizen of the World*. Letter LXXV.

10
The first time I read an excellent book, it is to me just as if I had gained a new friend. When I read over a book I have perused before, it resembles the meeting with an old one.
GOLDSMITH—*The Citizen of the World*. Letter LXXXIII.

11
Write the vision, and make it plain upon tables, that he may run that readeth it.
Habakkuk. II. 2.
Ut percurrat qui legerit eum.
That he that readeth it may run over it.
Rendering in the Vulgate.
(See also COWPER, TENNYSON)

12
Books have always a secret influence on the understanding; we cannot at pleasure obliterate ideas: he that reads books of science, though without any desire fixed of improvement, will grow more knowing; he that entertains himself with moral or religious treatises, will imperceptibly advance in goodness; the ideas which are often offered to the mind, will at last find a lucky moment when it is disposed to receive them.
SAMUEL JOHNSON—*The Adventurer*. No. 137.

13
A man ought to read just as inclination leads him; for what he reads as a task will do him little good.
SAMUEL JOHNSON—*Boswell's Life of Johnson*. (1763)

14
What is twice read is commonly better remembered than what is transcribed.
SAMUEL JOHNSON—*The Idler*. No. 74.

15
It may be well to wait a century for a reader, as God has waited six thousand years for an observer.
JOHN KEPLER—In *Martyrs of Science*. P. 197.

16
I love to lose myself in other men's minds.
When I am not walking, I am reading;
I cannot sit and think. Books think for me.
CHARLES LAMB—*Last Essays of Elia. Detached Thoughts on Books and Reading.*

17
Night after night,
He sat and bleared his eyes with books.
LONGFELLOW—*Christus. The Golden Legend.* Pt. I.

18
Many readers judge of the power of a book by the shock it gives their feelings.
LONGFELLOW—*Kavanagh*. Ch. XIII.

19
Seria cum possim, quod delectantia malim
Scribere, tu causa es lector.
Thou art the cause, O reader, of my dwelling on lighter topics, when I would rather handle serious ones.
MARTIAL—*Epigrams*. V. 16. 1.

20
His classical reading is great: he can quote
Horace, Juvenal, Ovid, and Martial by rote.
He has read Metaphysics * * * Spinoza and Kant
And Theology too: I have heard him descant
Upon Basil and Jerome. Antiquities, art,
He is fond of. He knows the old masters by heart,
And his taste is refined.
OWEN MEREDITH (Lord Lytton) — *Lucile*. Canto II. Pt. IV.

21
Who reads
Incessantly, and to his reading brings not
A spirit and judgment equal or superior,
(And what he brings what need he elsewhere seek?)
Uncertain and unsettled still remains,
Deep versed in books and shallow in himself,

Crude or intoxicate, collecting toys
And trifles for choice matters, worth a sponge,
As children gathering pebbles on the shore.
MILTON—*Paradise Regained*. Bk. IV. L. 322.

1
He that I am reading seems always to have the most force.
MONTAIGNE—*Apology for Raimond Sebond*

2
And better had they ne'er been born,
Who read to doubt, or read to scorn.
SCOTT—*The Monastery*. Ch. XII.

3
He hath never fed of the dainties that are bred in a book; he hath not eat paper, as it were; he hath not drunk ink: his intellect is not replenished; he is only an animal, only sensible in the duller parts.
Love's Labour's Lost. Act IV. Sc. 2. L. 26.

4
Read Homer once, and you can read no more,
For all books else appear so mean, so poor,
Verse will seem prose; but still persist to read,
And Homer will be all the books you need.
JOHN SHEFFIELD (Duke of Buckinghamshire) —*An Essay on Poetry*. L. 323.

5
He that runs may read.
TENNYSON—*The Flower*. St. 5.
(See also HABAKKUK)

6
Studious let me sit,
And hold high converse with the mighty Dead.
THOMSON—*Seasons. Winter*. L. 431.

7
Learn to read slow; all other graces
Will follow in their proper places.
WM. WALKER—*Art of Reading*.

REASON

8
Il n'est pas nécessaire de tenir les choses pour en raisonner.
It is not necessary to retain facts that we may reason concerning them.
BEAUMARCHAIS—*Barbier de Séville*. V. 4.

9
Domina omnium et regina ratio.
Reason is the mistress and queen of all things.
CICERO—*Tusculanarum Disputationum*. II. 21.

10
Aristophanes turns Socrates into ridicule . . . as making the worse appear the better reason.
DIOGENES LAERTIUS—*Socrates*. V.
(See also MILTON, QUINTILIAN)

11
He who will not reason, is a bigot; he who cannot is a fool; and he who dares not, is a slave.
WILLIAM DRUMMOND—*Academical Question*. End of preface.

12
Two angels guide
The path of man, both aged and yet young,
As angels are, ripening through endless years,
On one he leans: some call her Memory,
And some Tradition; and her voice is sweet,
With deep mysterious accords: the other,
Floating above, holds down a lamp which streams
A light divine and searching on the earth,
Compelling eyes and footsteps. Memory yields,
Yet clings with loving check, and shines anew,
Reflecting all the rays of that bright lamp
Our angel Reason holds. We had not walked
But for Tradition; we walk evermore
To higher paths by brightening Reason's lamp.
GEORGE ELIOT—*Spanish Gypsy*. Bk. II.

13
Reasons are not like garments, the worse for wearing.
EARL OF ESSEX to *Lord Willoughby*. Jan. 4, 1598–9.

14
Setting themselves against reason, as often as reason is against them.
HOBBES—*Works*. III. P. 91. Ed. 1839. Also in *Epistle Dedicatory to Tripos*. IV. XIII.

15
Hoc volo, sic jubeo, sit pro ratione voluntas.
I will it, I so order, let my will stand for a reason.
JUVENAL—*Satires*. VI. 223.

16
You have ravished me away by a Power I cannot resist; and yet I could resist till I saw you; and even since I have seen you I have endeavored often "to reason against the reasons of my Love."
KEATS—*Letters to Fanny Braune*. VIII.

17
La raison du plus fort est toujours la meilleure.
The reasoning of the strongest is always the best.
LA FONTAINE—*Fables*. I. 10.

18
To be rational is so glorious a thing, that two-legged creatures generally content themselves with the title.
LOCKE—*Letter to Antony Collins, Esq.*

19
But all was false and hollow; though his tongue
Dropt manna, and could make the worse appear
The better reason, to perplex and dash
Maturest counsels.
MILTON—*Paradise Lost*. Bk. II. L. 112.
(See also QUINTILIAN)

20
Subdue
By force, who reason for their law refuse,
Right reason for their law.
MILTON—*Paradise Lost*. Bk. VI. L. 40

21
Indu'd
With sanctity of reason.
MILTON—*Paradise Lost*. Bk. VII. L. 507.

22
Mais la raison n'est pas ce qui règle l'amour.
But it is not reason that governs love.
MOLIÈRE—*Le Misanthrope*. I. 1.

23
La parfaite raison fuit toute extremité,
Et veut que l'on soit sage avec sobriété.
All extremes does perfect reason flee,
And wishes to be wise quite soberly.
MOLIÈRE—*Le Misanthrope*. I. 1.

24
Say first, of God above or man below,
What can we reason but from what we know?
POPE—*Essay on Man*. Ep. I. L. 17.

1
Reason, however able, cool at best,
Cares not for service, or but serves when prest,
Stays till we call, and then not often near.
POPE—*Essay on Man*. Ep. III. L. 85.

2
Who reasons wisely is not therefore wise;
His pride in reasoning, not in acting lies.
POPE—*Moral Essays*. Ep. I. L. 117.

3
Omnia sunt risus, sunt pulvis, et omnia nil sunt:
Res hominum cunctæ, nam ratione carent.
All is but a jest, all dust, all not worth two peason:
For why in man's matters is neither rime nor reason.
PUTTENHAM—*Arte of English Poesie*. P. 125. Attributed by him to DEMOCRITUS.
(See also MORE under POETRY)

4
Nam et Socrati objiciunt comici, docere eum quomodo pejorem causam meliorem faciat.
For comic writers charge Socrates with making the worse appear the better reason.
QUINTILIAN—*De Institutione Oratoria*. II. 17. 1.
(See also DIOGENES, MILTON)

5
On aime sans raison, et sans raison l'on hait.
We love without reason, and without reason we hate.
REGNARD—*Les Folies Amoureuses*.

6
Nihil potest esse diuturnum cui non subest ratio.
Nothing can be lasting when reason does not rule.
QUINTUS CURTIUS RUFUS—*De Rebus Gestis Alexandri Magni*. IV. 14. 19.

7
Id nobis maxime nocet, quod non ad rationis lumen sed ad similitudinem aliorum vivimus.
This is our chief bane, that we live not according to the light of reason, but after the fashion of others.
SENECA—*Octavia*. Act II. 454.

8
Every why hath a wherefore.
Comedy of Errors. Act II. Sc. 2. L. 44.

9
Sure, he that made us with such large discourse,
Looking before and after, gave us not
That capability and god-like reason
To fust in us unus'd.
Hamlet. Act IV. Sc. 4. L. 36.

10
Give you a reason on compulsion! if reasons were as plentiful as blackberries, I would give no man a reason upon compulsion, I.
Henry IV. Pt. I. Act II. Sc. 4. L. 263.

11
Good reasons must, of force, give place to better.
Julius Cæsar. Act IV. Sc. 3. L. 203.

12
But since the affairs of men rest still incertain,
Let's reason with the worst that may befall.
Julius Cæsar. Act V. Sc. 1. L. 96.

13
Strong reasons make strong actions.
King John. Act III. Sc. 4. L. 182.

14
His reasons are as two grains of wheat hid in two bushels of chaff; you shall seek all day ere you find them; and when you have them, they are not worth the search.
Merchant of Venice. Act I. Sc. 1. L. 116.

15
I have no other but a woman's reason
I think him so because I think him so.
Two Gentlemen of Verona. Act I. Sc. 2. L. 23

16
While Reason drew the plan, the Heart inform'd
The moral page and Fancy lent it grace.
THOMSON—*Liberty*. Pt. IV. L. 262.

17
Reason progressive, Instinct is complete;
Swift Instinct leaps; slow reason feebly climbs.
Brutes soon their zenith reach. * * * In ages they no more
Could know, do, covet or enjoy.
YOUNG—*Night Thoughts*. Night VII. L. 81.

18
And what is reason? Be she thus defined:
Reason is upright stature in the soul.
YOUNG—*Night Thoughts*. Night VII. L. 1,526.

REBELLION (See also REVOLUTION)

19
The worst of rebels never arm
To do their king or country harm,
But draw their swords to do them good,
As doctors cure by letting blood.
BUTLER—*Miscellaneous Thoughts*. L. 181.

20
Men seldom, or rather never for a length of time and deliberately, rebel against anything that does not deserve rebelling against.
CARLYLE—*Essays*. *Goethe's Works*.

21
Rebellion to tyrants is obedience to God.
Inscription on a Cannon near which the ashes of President John Bradshaw were lodged, on the top of hill near Martha Bay in Jamaica. See STILES—*History of the Three Judges of Charles I*. Attributed also to FRANKLIN in RANDALL'S *Life of Jefferson*. Vol. III. P. 585. Motto on Jefferson's seal.

22
Rebellion in this land shall lose his sway,
Meeting the check of such another day.
Henry IV. Pt. I. Act V. Sc. 5. L. 41.

23
Unthread the rude eye of rebellion.
King John. Act V. Sc. 4. L. 11.

RECKLESSNESS

24
I tell thee, be not rash; a golden bridge
Is for a flying enemy.
BYRON—*The Deformed Transformed*. Act II. Sc. 2.

25
Who falls from all he knows of bliss,
Cares little into what abyss.
BYRON—*The Giaour*. L. 1,091.

26
I am one, my liege,
Whom the vile blows and buffets of the world
Have so incens'd that I am reckless what
I do to spite the world.
Macbeth. Act III. Sc. 1. L. 108.

REDEMPTION

1
In cruce salus.
Salvation by the cross.
THOMAS À KEMPIS—*De Imitatio Christi*. Bk. II. 2. Adapted from "A cruce salus."

2
Say, heavenly pow'rs, where shall we find such love?
Which of ye will be mortal to redeem
Man's mortal crime, and just th' unjust to save.
MILTON—*Paradise Lost*. Bk. III. L. 213.

3
And now without redemption all mankind
Must have been lost, adjudged to death and hell
By doom severe.
MILTON—*Paradise Lost*. Bk. III. L. 222.

4
Why, all the souls that are were forfeit once;
And He that might the vantage best have took
Found out the remedy.
Measure for Measure. Act II. Sc. 2. L. 73.

5
Condemned into everlasting redemption for this.
Much Ado About Nothing. Act IV. Sc. 2. L. 58.

REED

Phragmites

6
Those tall flowering-reeds which stand,
In Arno like a sheaf of sceptres, left
By some remote dynasty of dead gods.
E. B. BROWNING—*Aurora Leigh*. Bk. VII.

REFLECTION

7
The next time you go out to a smoking party, young feller, fill your pipe with that 'ere reflection.
DICKENS—*Pickwick Papers*. Ch. XVI.
(See also RICHMOND ENQUIRER)

8
The solitary side of our nature demands leisure for reflection upon subjects on which the dash and whirl of daily business, so long as its clouds rise thick about us, forbid the intellect to fasten itself.
FROUDE—*Short Studies on Great Subjects. Sea Studies.*

9
The learn'd reflect on what before they knew.
POPE—*Essay on Criticism*. Pt. III. L. 180.

10
Let the *Tribune* put all this in its pipe and smoke it.
Richmond, Va., *Enquirer*. Feb. 7. 1860.
(See also DICKENS)

11
For take thy ballaunce if thou be so wise,
And weigh the winde that under heaven doth blow;
Or weigh the light that in the east doth rise;
Or weigh the thought that from man's mind doth flow.
SPENSER—*Faerie Queene*. Bk. V. Canto II. St. 43.

12
A soul without reflection, like a pile
Without inhabitant, to ruin runs.
YOUNG—*Night Thoughts*. Night V. L. 596.

REFORM; REFORMATION

13
Grant that the old Adam in these persons may be so buried, that the new man may be raised up in them.
Book of Common Prayer. Baptism of those of Riper Years.

14
The oyster-women lock'd their fish up,
And trudged away to cry, No Bishop.
BUTLER—*Hudibras*. Pt. I. Canto II. L. 537.

15
All zeal for a reform, that gives offence
To peace and charity, is mere pretence.
COWPER—*Charity*. L. 533.

16
But 'tis the talent of our English nation,
Still to be plotting some new reformation.
DRYDEN—*Prologue to Sophonisba*. L. 9.

17
He bought a Bible of the new translation,
And in his life he show'd great reformation;
He walkèd mannerly and talkèd meekly;
He heard three lectures and two sermons weekly;
He vow'd to shun all companions unruly,
And in his speech he used no oath but "truly;"
And zealously to keep the Sabbath's rest.
SIR JOHN HARRINGTON—*Of a Precise Tailor*.

18
The Bolshevists would blow up the fabric with high explosive, with horror. Others would pull down with the crowbars and with cranks—especially with cranks. . . . Sweating, slums, the sense of semi-slavery in labour, must go. We must cultivate a sense of manhood by treating men as men.
LLOYD GEORGE—*Speech*, Dec. 6, 1919.

19
My desolation does begin to make
A better life.
Antony and Cleopatra. Act V. Sc. 2. L. 1.

20
And like bright metal on a sullen ground,
My reformation, glittering o'er my fault,
Shall show more goodly and attract more eyes
Than that which hath no foil to set it off.
Henry IV. Pt. I. Act I. Sc. 2. L. 236.

21
Never came reformation in a flood.
Henry V. Act I. Sc. 1. L. 33.

22
I do not mean to be disrespectful, but the attempt of the Lords to stop the progress of reform, reminds me very forcibly of the great storm of Sidmouth, and of the conduct of the excellent Mrs. Partington on that occasion. In the winter of 1824, there set in a great flood upon that town—the tide rose to an incredible height: the waves rushed in upon the houses, and everything was threatened with destruction. In the midst of this sublime and terrible storm, Dame Partington, who lived upon the beach, was seen at the door of her house with mop and pattens, trundling her mop, squeezing out the sea water, and vigorously pushing away the Atlantic Ocean. The Atlantic was roused. Mrs. Partington's spirit was up; but I need not tell you that the contest was unequal. The Atlantic Ocean beat Mrs. Partington. She was excellent at a slop or a puddle, but she should not have meddled with a tempest.
SYDNEY SMITH—*Speech at Taunton*. Oct., 1831.

REGRET

1
Keen were his pangs, but keener far to feel,
He nursed the pinion, which impell'd the steel.
BYRON—*English Bards and Scotch Reviewers.* L. 823.

2
Thou wilt lament
Hereafter, when the evil shall be done
And shall admit no cure.
HOMER—*Iliad.* Bk. IX. L. 308. BRYANT'S trans.

3
No simple word
That shall be uttered at our mirthful board,
Shall make us sad next morning; or affright
The liberty that we'll enjoy to-night.
BEN JONSON—*Epigram CI.*

4
O lost days of delight, that are wasted in doubting and waiting!
O lost hours and days in which we might have been happy!
LONGFELLOW—*Tales of a Wayside Inn.* Pt. III. *The Theologian's Tale. Elizabeth.*

5
For who, alas! has lived,
Nor in the watches of the night recalled
Words he has wished unsaid and deeds undone.
SAM'L ROGERS—*Reflections.* L. 52.

6
I could have better spar'd a better man.
Henry IV. Pt. I. Act V. Sc. 4. L. 104.

RELIGION

7
Children of men! the unseen Power, whose eye
Forever doth accompany mankind,
Hath look'd on no religion scornfully
That men did ever find.
MATTHEW ARNOLD—*Progress.* St. 10.

8
There was never law, or sect, or opinion did so much magnify goodness, as the Christain religion doth.
BACON—*Essays. Of Goodness, and Goodness of Nature.*

9
The greatest vicissitude of things amongst men, is the vicissitude of sects and religions.
BACON—*Of Vicissitude of Things.*
(See also GIFFORD under SONG)

10
Religio peperit divitias et filia devoravit matrem.
Religion brought forth riches, and the daughter devoured the mother.
Saying of ST. BERNARD. Religio censum peperit, sed filia matri caussa suæ leti perniti osa fuit. See REUSNER'S *Ænigmatographia.* Ed. 2. 1602. Pt. I. Page 361. *Heading of an epigram ascribed to* HENRICUS MEIBOMIUS.

11
Tant de fiel entre-t-il dans l'âme des dévots?
Can such bitterness enter into the heart of the devout?
BOILEAU—*Lutrin.* I. 12.

12
No mere man since the Fall, is able in this life perfectly to keep the commandments.
Book of Common Prayer. Shorter Catechism.

13
Curva trahit mites, pars pungit acuta rebelles.
The crooked end obedient spirits draws,
The pointed, those rebels who spurn at Christian laws.
BROUGHTON—*Dictionary of all Religions.* (1756) The croisier is pointed at one end and crooked at the other. "Curva trahit, quos virga regit, pars ultima pungit"; is the Motto on the Episcopal staff said to be preserved at Toulouse.
(See also BACON under GOVERNMENT)

14
Persecution is a bad and indirect way to plant religion.
SIR THOMAS BROWNE—*Religio Medici.* XXV.

15
Speak low to me, my Saviour, low and sweet
From out the hallelujahs, sweet and low,
Lest I should fear and fall, and miss Thee so
Who art not missed by any that entreat.
E. B. BROWNING—*Comfort.*

16
The body of all true religion consists, to be sure, in obedience to the will of the Sovereign of the world, in a confidence in His declarations, and in imitation of His perfections.
BURKE—*Reflections on the Revolution in France.*

17
But the religion most prevalent in our northern colonies is a refinement on the principle of resistance, it is the dissidence of dissent, and the protestantism of the Protestant religion.
BURKE—*Speech on Conciliation with America.*

18
The writers against religion, whilst they oppose every system, are wisely careful never to set up any of their own.
BURKE—*A Vindication of Natural Society. Preface.* Vol. I. P. 7.

19
People differ in their discourse and profession about these matters, but men of sense are really but of one religion. * * * "What religion?" * * * the Earl said, "Men of sense never tell it."
BISHOP BURNET—*History of his Own Times.* Vol. I. Bk. I. Sec. 96. Footnote by ONSLOW, referring to Earl of Shaftesbury.
(See also DISRAELI, EMERSON, JOHNSON, SHAFTESBURY)

20
An Atheist's laugh's a poor exchange
For Deity offended!
BURNS—*Epistle to a Young Friend.*

21
G— knows I'm no the thing I should be,
Nor am I even the thing I could be,
But twenty times I rather would be
An atheist clean,
Than under gospel colours hid be,
Just for a screen.
BURNS—*Epistle to Rev. John M'Math.* St. 8.

22
One religion is as true as another.
BURTON—*Anatomy of Melancholy.* Bk. III. Sec. IV. Memb. 2. Subsec. 1.

23
As if Religion were intended
For nothing else but to be mended.
BUTLER—*Hudibras.* Pt. I. Canto I. L. 205.

1

Synods are mystical Bear-gardens,
Where Elders, Deputies, Church-wardens,
And other Members of the Court,
Manage the Babylonish sport.

BUTLER—*Hudibras*. Pt. I. Canto III. L. 1,095.

2

So 'ere the storm of war broke out,
Religion spawn'd a various rout
Of petulant capricious sects,
The maggots of corrupted texts,
That first run all religion down,
And after every swarm its own.

BUTLER—*Hudibras*. Pt. III. Canto II. L. 7.

3

There's naught, no doubt, so much the spirit calms as rum and true religion.

BYRON—*Don Juan*. Canto II. St. 34.

4

His religion at best is an anxious wish,—like that of Rabelais, a great Perhaps.

CARLYLE—*Essays*. *Burns*.

(See also RABELAIS under DEATH)

5

On the whole we must repeat the often repeated saying, that it is unworthy a religious man to view an irreligious one either with alarm or aversion; or with any other feeling than regret, and hope, and brotherly commiseration.

CARLYLE—*Essays*. *Voltaire*.

6

I realized that ritual will always mean throwing away something; *Destroying* our corn or wine upon the altar of our gods.

G. K. CHESTERTON—*Tremendous Trifles. Secret of a Train.*

7

The rigid saint, by whom no mercy's shown
To saints whose lives are better than his own.

CHURCHILL—*Epistle to Hogarth*. L. 25.

8

Deos placatos pietas efficiet et sanctitas.

Piety and holiness of life will propitiate the gods.

CICERO—*De Officiis*. II. 3.

9

Res sacros non modo manibus attingi, sed ne cogitatione quidem violari fas fuit.

Things sacred should not only be untouched with the hands, but unviolated in thought.

CICERO—*Orationes in Verrem*. II. 4. 45

10

Forth from his dark and lonely hiding place,
(Portentous sight!) the owlet atheism,
Sailing on obscene wings athwart the noon,
Drops his blue-fring'd lids, and holds them close,
And hooting at the glorious sun in Heaven,
Cries out, "Where is it?"

COLERIDGE—*Fears in Solitude*.

11

Life and the Universe show spontaneity;
Down with ridiculous notions of Deity!
Churches and creeds are lost in the mists;
Truth must be sought with the Positivists.

MORTIMER COLLINS—*The Positivists*.

12

Men will wrangle for religion; write for it; fight for it; die for it; anything but—live for it.

C. C. COLTON—*Lacon*. Vol. I. XXV.

13

Religion, if in heavenly truths attired,
Needs only to be seen to be admired.

COWPER—*Expostulation*. L. 492.

14

The Cross!
There, and there only (though the deist rave,
And atheist, if Earth bears so base a slave);
There and there only, is the power to save.

COWPER—*The Progress of Error*. L. 613.

15

Religion does not censure or exclude
Unnumbered pleasures, harmlessly pursued.

COWPER—*Retirement*. L. 782.

16

Pity! Religion has so seldom found
A skilful guide into poetic ground!
The flowers would spring where'er she deign'd to stray
And every muse attend her in her way.

COWPER—*Table Talk*. L. 688.

17

Sacred religion! Mother of Form and Fear!

SAMUEL DANIEL—*Musophilus*. St. 47.

18

"As for that," said Waldenshare, "sensible men are all of the same religion." "Pray, what is that?" inquired the Prince. "Sensible men never tell."

BENJ. DISRAELI—*Endymion*. Ch. LXXXI. Borrowed from SIR ANTHONY ASHLEY COOPER (Lord Shaftesbury.)

(See also BURNET)

19

You can and you can't,—You shall and you shan't—You will and you won't—And you will be damned if you do—And you will be damned if you don't.

DOW ("Crazy Dow") defining Calvinism, in *Reflections on the Love of God*, by L. D.

20

Gardez-vous bien de lui les jours qu'il communie.

Beware of him the days that he takes Communion.

DU LORENS—*Satires*. I.

21

L'institut des Jesuites est une épée dont la poignée est à Rome et la pointe partout.

The Order of Jesuits is a sword whose handle is at Rome and whose point is every where.

ANDRÉ M. J. DUPIN—*Procès de tendance*. (1825) Quoted by him as found in a letter to MLLE. VOLAND from ABBÉ RAYNAL. ROUSSEAU quotes it from D'AUBIGNÉ—*Anti-Coton*, who ascribes it to the saying of the Society of Jesus which is "a sword, the blade of which is in France, and the handle in Rome."

22

I do not find that the age or country makes the least difference; no, nor the language the actors spoke, nor the religion which they professed, whether Arab in the desert or Frenchman in the Academy, I see that sensible men and conscientious men all over the world were of one religion.

EMERSON—*Lectures and Biographical Sketches. The Preacher*. P. 215.

(See also BURNET)

1
I like the church, I like a cowl,
I love a prophet of the soul;
And on my heart monastic aisles
Fall like sweet strains or pensive smiles;
Yet not for all his faith can see,
Would I that cowlèd churchman be.
EMERSON—*The Problem.*

2
Die Theologie ist die Anthropologie.
Theology is Anthropology.
FEUERBACH—*Wesen des Christenthums.*

3
There are at bottom but two possible religions—that which rises in the moral nature of man, and which takes shape in moral commandments, and that which grows out of the observation of the material energies which operate in the external universe.
FROUDE—*Short Studies on Great Subjects. Calvinism.* P. 20.

4
Sacrifice is the first element of religion, and resolves itself in theological language into the love of God.
FROUDE—*Short Studies on Great Subjects. Sea Studies.*

5
But our captain counts the image of God, nevertheless, his image—cut in ebony as if done in ivory; and in the blackest Moors he sees the representation of the King of heaven.
FULLER—*Holy and Profane States. The Good Sea-Captain.* Maxim 5.

6
Indeed, a *little skill* in antiquity inclines a man to Popery; but *depth in that study* brings him about again to our religion.
FULLER—*Holy and Profane States. The True Church Antiquary.* Maxim 1.

7
Am I my brother's keeper?
Genesis. IV. 9.

8
We do ourselves wrong, and too meanly estimate the holiness above us, when we deem that any act or enjoyment good in itself, is not good to do religiously.
HAWTHORNE—*Marble Faun.* Bk. II. Ch. VII.

9
From Greenland's icy mountains,
From India's coral strand,
Where Afric's sunny fountains
Roll down their golden sand;
From many an ancient river,
From many a palmy plain,
They call us to deliver
Their land from error's chain.
REGINALD HEBER—*Missionary Hymn.*

10
La couronne vaut bien une messe (Paris vaut bien une messe.)
The crown, (or Paris), is well worth a mass.
Attributed to HENRY IV.

11
Religion stands on tiptoe in our land,
Ready to pass to the American strand.
HERBERT—*The Church Militant.* L. 235.

12
Dresse and undresse thy soul: mark the decay
And growth of it: if, with thy watch, that too
Be down, then winde up both: since we shall be
Most surely judged, make thy accounts agree.
HERBERT—*Temple. Church Porch.* St. 76.

13
My Fathers and Brethren, this is never to be forgotten that New England is originally a plantation of religion, not a plantation of trade.
JOHN HIGGINSON—*Election Sermon. The Cause of God and His People in New England.* May 27, 1663.

14
No solemn, sanctimonious face I pull,
Nor think I'm pious when I'm only bilious—
Nor study in my sanctum supercilious
To frame a Sabbath Bill or forge a Bull.
HOOD—*Ode to Rae Wilson.*

15
Should all the banks of Europe crash,
The bank of England smash,
Bring all your notes to Zion's bank,
You're sure to get your cash.
HENRY HOYT—*Zion's Bank, or Bible Promises Secured to all Believers.* Pub. in Boston, 1857. Probably a reprint of English origin.

16
My creed is this:
Happiness is the only good.
The place to be happy is here.
The time to be happy is now.
The way to be happy is to help make others so.
ROBERT G. INGERSOLL—On the Title Page of Vol. XII. FARRELL's Ed. of his Works.

17
I belong to the Great Church which holds the world within its starlit aisles; that claims the great and good of every race and clime; that finds with joy the grain of gold in every creed, and floods with light and love the germs of good in every soul.
ROBERT G. INGERSOLL—Declaration in Discussion with REV. HENRY M. FIELD on *Faith and Agnosticism.* FARRELL'S *Life.* Vol. VI.

18
I envy them, those monks of old
Their books they read, and their beads they told.
G. P. R. JAMES—*The Monks of Old.*

19
Sir, I think all Christians, whether Papists or Protestants, agree in the essential articles, and that their religious differences are trivial, and rather political than religious.
SAMUEL JOHNSON—*Boswell's Life.* Ch.V. 1763.

20
To be of no Church is dangerous.
SAMUEL JOHNSON—*Life of Milton.*

21
Other hope had she none, nor wish in life, but to follow
Meekly, with reverent steps, the sacred feet of her Saviour.
LONGFELLOW—*Evangeline.* Pt. II. V. L. 35.

22
Puritanism, believing itself quick with the seed of religious liberty, laid, without knowing it, the egg of democracy.
LOWELL—*Among My Books. New England Two Centuries Ago.*

1
God is not dumb, that he should speak no more;
If thou hast wanderings in the wilderness
And find'st not Sinai, 'tis thy soul is poor.
LOWELL—*Bibliolatres.*

2
But he turned up his nose at their murmuring and shamming,
And cared (shall I say?) not a d—n for their damning;
So they first read him out of their church and next minute
Turned round and declared he had never been in it.
LOWELL—*A Fable for Critics.* L. 876.

3
Tantum religio potuit suadere malorum!
How many evils has religion caused!
LUCRETIUS—*De Rerum Natura.* I. 102.

4
Blessed is the man that hath not walked in the way of the Sacramentarians, nor sat in the seat of the Zwinglians, nor followed the Council of the Zurichers.
MARTIN LUTHER—*Parody of First Psalm.*

5
The Puritan hated bear-baiting, not because it gave pain to the bear, but because it gave pleasure to the spectators.
MACAULAY—*History of England.* Vol. I. Ch. II.

6
No pain, no palm; no thorns, no throne; no gall, no glory; no cross, no crown.
WILLIAM PENN—*No Cross, No Crown.*
(See also QUARLES)

7
It was a friar of orders grey
Walked forth to tell his beads.
THOS. PERCY—*The Friar of Orders Grey.*

8
Religion, which true policy befriends,
Designed by God to serve man's noblest ends,
Is by that old deceiver's subtle play
Made the chief party in its own decay,
And meets the eagle's destiny, whose breast
Felt the same shaft which his own feathers drest.
K. PHILLIPS. *On Controversies in Religion.*
(See also ÆSCHYLUS under EAGLE)

9
The Puritan did not stop to think; he recognized God in his soul, and acted.
WENDELL PHILLIPS—*Speech.* Dec. 18, 1859.

10
We have a Calvinistic creed, a Popish liturgy, and an Arminian clergy.
WILLIAM PITT (Earl of Chatham)—See *Prior's Life of Burke.* Ch. X. (1790)

11
So upright Quakers please both man and God.
POPE—*The Dunciad.* Bk. IV. L. 208.

12
To happy convents, bosom'd deep in vines,
Where slumber abbots purple as their wines.
POPE—*The Dunciad.* Bk. IV. L. 301.

13
Religion, blushing, veils her sacred fires,
And unawares Morality expires.
POPE—*The Dunciad.* Bk. IV. L. 649.

14
For virtue's self may too much zeal be had;
The worst of madmen is a saint run mad.
POPE—*To Murray.* Ep. VI. of *Horace.* L. 26.

15
I think while zealots fast and frown,
And fight for two or seven,
That there are fifty roads to town,
And rather more to Heaven.
PRAED—*Chant of Brazen Head.* St. 8.

16
He that hath no cross deserves no crown.
QUARLES—*Esther.*
(See also PENN)

17
Ils ont les textes pour eux; disait-il, j'en suis faché pour les textes.
They have the texts in their favor; said he, so much the worse for the texts.
ROYER-COLLARD—*Words of disapproval of the Fathers of Port Royal on their doctrine of grace.*

18
Humanity and Immortality consist neither in reason, nor in love; not in the body, nor in the animation of the heart of it, nor in the thoughts and stirrings of the brain of it;—but in the dedication of them all to Him who will raise them up at the last day.
RUSKIN—*Stones of Venice.* Vol I. Ch. II.

19
Religion is like the fashion, one man wears his doublet slashed, another laced, another plain; but every man has a doublet; so every man has a religion. We differ about the trimming.
JOHN SELDEN—*Table Talk.* P. 157. (Ed. 1696)

20
[Lord Shaftesbury said] "All wise men are of the same religion." Whereupon a lady in the room . . . demanded what that religion was. To whom Lord Shaftesbury straight replied, "Madam, wise men never tell."
LORD SHAFTESBURY (Said by first and third Earl). JOHN TOLAND—CLIDOPHORUS. Ch. XIII. Attributed to SAMUEL ROGERS by FROUDE—*Short Studies on Great Subjects. Plea for the Free Discussion of Theological Difficulties.* Attributed also to FRANKLIN.
(See also BURNET)

21
I always thought
It was both impious and unnatural
That such immanity and bloody strife
Should reign among professors of one faith.
Henry VI. Pt. I. Act V. Sc. 1. L. 11.

22
In religion,
What damned error, but some sober brow
Will bless it and approve it with a text.
Merchant of Venice. Act III. Sc. 2. L. 77.

23
The moon of Mahomet
Arose, and it shall set:
While, blazoned as on heaven's immortal noon,
The cross leads generations on.
SHELLEY—*Hellas.* L. 237.

24
A religious life is a struggle and not a hymn.
MADAME DE STAËL—*Corinne.* Bk. X. Ch. V.

1
Religion has nothing more to fear than not being sufficiently understood.
STANISLAUS (King of Poland)—*Maxims*. No. 36.

2
What religion is he of?
Why, he is an Anythingarian.
SWIFT—*Polite Conversation. Dialogue* I.

3
He made it a part of his religion, never to say grace to his meat.
SWIFT—*Tale of a Tub*. Sec. XI.

4
We have enough religion to make us hate, but not enough to make us love one another.
SWIFT—*Thoughts on Various Subjects*. Collected by POPE and SWIFT. Found in *Spectator* No. 459.

5
Honour your parents; worship the gods; hurt not animals.
TRIPTOLEMUS, *according to* PLUTARCH. *From his traditional laws or precepts.*

6
Once I journeyd far from home
To the gate of holy Rome;
There the Pope, for my offence,
Bade me straight, in penance, thence
Wandering onward, to attain
The wondrous land that height Cokaigne.
ROBERT WACE—*The Land of Cokaigne.*

7
When I can read my title clear
To mansions in the skies,
I'll bid farewell to every fear,
And wipe my weeping eyes.
WATTS—*Songs and Hymns*. Bk. II. No. 65.

8
The world has a thousand creeds, and never a one have I;
Nor church of my own, though a million spires are pointing the way on high.
But I float on the bosom of faith, that bears me along like a river;
And the lamp of my soul is alight with love, for life, and the world, and the Giver.
ELLA WHEELER WILCOX—*Heresy.*

9
So many gods, so many creeds—
So many paths that wind and wind
While just the art of being kind
Is all the sad world needs.
ELLA WHEELER WILCOX—*The World's Need.*

10
Who God doth late and early pray
More of his Grace than Gifts to lend;
And entertains the harmless day
With a Religious Book or Friend.
SIR HENRY WOTTON—*The Character of a Happy Life*. St. 5.

11
Religion's all. Descending from the skies
To wretched man, the goddess in her left
Holds out this world, and, in her right, the next.
YOUNG—*Night Thoughts*. Night IV. L. 550.

12
But if man loses all, when life is lost,
He lives a coward, or a fool expires.
A daring infidel (and such there are,
From pride, example, lucre, rage, revenge,
Or pure heroical defect of thought),
Of all earth's madmen, most deserves a chain.
YOUNG—*Night Thoughts*. Night VII. L. 199.

REMORSE

13
Cruel Remorse! where Youth and Pleasure sport,
And thoughtless Folly keeps her court,—
Crouching 'midst rosy bowers thou lurk'st unseen
Slumbering the festal hours away,
While Youth disports in that enchanting scene;
Till on some fated day
Thou with a tiger-spring dost leap upon thy prey,
And tear his helpless breast, o'erwhelmed with wild dismay.
ANNA LETITIA BARBAULD—*Ode to Remorse*. St. 6.

14
Remorse is as the heart in which it grows;
If that be gentle, it drops balmy dews
Of true repentance; but if proud and gloomy,
It is the poison tree, that pierced to the inmost,
Weeps only tears of poison.
COLERIDGE—*Remorse*. Act I. Sc. 1.

15
Man, wretched man, whene'er he stoops to sin,
Feels, with the act, a strong remorse within.
JUVENAL—*Satires. Satire XIII*. L. 1. WM. GIFFORD's trans.

16
Farewell, remorse: all good to me is lost;
Evil, be thou my good.
MILTON—*Paradise Lost*. Bk. IV. L. 108.

17
Le remords s'endort durant un destin prospère et s'aigrit dans l'adversité.
Remorse goes to sleep during a prosperous period and wakes up in adversity.
ROUSSEAU—*Confessions*. I. II.

18
High minds, of native pride and force,
Most deeply feel thy pangs, Remorse;
Fear, for their scourge, mean villains have,
Thou art the torturer of the brave!
SCOTT—*Marmion*. Canto III. St. 13.

19
Abandon all remorse;
On horror's head horrors accumulate.
Othello. Act III. Sc. 3. L. 369.

REPENTANCE

20
O ye powers that search
The heart of man, and weigh his inmost thoughts,
If I have done amiss, impute it not!
The best may err, but you are good.
ADDISON—*Cato*. Act V. Sc. 4.

21
D'uomo è il fallir, ma dal malvagio il buono
Scerne il dolor del fallo.
To err is human; but contrition felt for the crime distinguishes the virtuous from the wicked.
ALFIERI—*Rosmunda*. III. 1.

22
To sigh, yet not recede; to grieve, yet not repent!
CRABBE—*Tales of the Hall*. Bk. III. *Boys at School*. Last line.

1
When prodigals return great things are done.
A. A. Dowty—*The Siliad.* In Beeton's *Christmas Annual.* 1873.

2
I do not buy repentance at so heavy a cost as a thousand drachmæ.
Aulus Gellius. Bk. I. Ch. VI. 6. Quoting Demosthenes to Lais.

3
When iron scourge, and tort'ring hour
The bad affright, afflict the best.
Gray—*Ode to Adversity.* Same phrase "the torturing hour" in Campbell—*Pleasures of Hope.* Pt. I. *Midsummer Night's Dream.* Act V. Sc. 1.
(See also Milton)

4
Restore to God his due in tithe and time:
A tithe purloin'd cankers the whole estate.
Herbert—*The Temple. The Church Porch.*

5
Who after his transgression doth repent,
Is halfe, or altogether, innocent.
Herrick—*Hesperides. Penitence.*
(See also Seneca)

6
He comes never late who comes repentant.
Juan de Horozco—*Manasses, Rey de India.* Jorn. III.

7
Woman, amends may never come too late.
Thos. Lodge and Robt. Greene—*A Looking Glass for London and England.*

8
God dropped a spark down into everyone,
And if we find and fan it to a blaze,
It'll spring up and glow, like—like the sun,
And light the wandering out of stony ways.
Masefield—*Widow in the Bye Street.* Pt. VI.

9
When the scourge
Inexorable, and the torturing hour
Calls us to penance.
Milton—*Paradise Lost.* Bk. II. L. 90.
(See also Gray)

10
He [Cato] used to say that in all his life he never repented but of three things. The first was that he had trusted a woman with a secret; the second that he had gone by sea when he might have gone by land; and the third, that he had passed one day without having a will by him.
Plutarch—*Life of Cato.* Vol. II. P. 495. Langhorne's trans. Same in Simplicius—*Commentary on the Enchiridion* of Epictetus. Ch. IX. P. 52. (Ed. 1670)

11
Der Wahn ist kurtz, die Reu ist lang.
The dream is short, repentance long.
Schiller—*Lied von der Glocke.*

12
But with the morning cool repentance came.
Scott—*Rob Roy.* Ch. XII. *The Monastery.* Ch. III. Note 11. "But with the morning cool reflection came." In *Chronicles of Canongate.* Ch. IV. "Calm" substituted for "cool" in *The Antiquary.* Ch. V.

13
Nam sera nunquam est ad bonos mores via.
Quem pœnitet peccasse, pæne est innocens.
It is never too late to turn from the errors of our ways:
He who repents of his sins is almost innocent.
Seneca—*Agamemnon.* 242.
(See also Herbert)

14
Nec unquam primi consilii deos pœnitet.
God never repents of what He has first resolved upon.
Seneca—*De Beneficiis.* VI. 23.

15
What then? what rests?
Try what repentance can: what can it not?
Yet what can it when one cannot repent?
O wretched state! O bosom black as death!
O limed soul, that struggling to be free
Art more engag'd!
Hamlet. Act III. Sc. 3. L. 64.

16
Well, I'll repent, and that suddenly, while I am in some liking; I shall be out of heart shortly, and then I shall have no strength to repent.
Henry IV. Pt. I. Act III. Sc. 3. L. 5.

17
Under your good correction, I have seen,
When, after execution, judgment hath
Repented o'er his doom.
Measure for Measure. Act II. Sc. 2. L. 10.

18
And wet his grave with my repentant tears.
Richard III. Act I. Sc. 2. L. 216.

19
Cave ne quidquam incipias, quod post pœniteat.
Take care not to begin anything of which you may repent.
Syrus—*Maxims.*

20
Velox consilium sequitur pœnitentia.
Repentance follows hasty counsels.
Syrus—*Maxims.*

21
Amid the roses, fierce Repentance rears
Her snaky crest; a quick-returning pang
Shoots through the conscious heart.
Thomson—*Seasons. Spring.* L. 995.

22
And while the lamp holds out to burn,
The vilest sinner may return.
Isaac Watts—*Hymns and Spiritual Songs.* Bk. I. Hymn 88.

REPOSE (See also Rest)

23
But quiet to quick bosoms is a hell.
Byron—*Childe Harold.* Canto III. St. 42.

24
What sweet delight a quiet life affords.
Drummond—*Sonnet.* P. 38.

25
To husband out life's taper at the close,
And keep the flames from wasting by repose.
Goldsmith—*Deserted Village.* L. 87.

26
The toils of honour dignify repose.
Hoole—*Metastasia. Achilles in Lucias.* Act III. Last Scene.

27
The wind breath'd soft as lover's sigh,
And, oft renew'd, seem'd oft to die,
With breathless pause between,

O who, with speech of war and woes,
Would wish to break the soft repose
Of such enchanting scene!
SCOTT—*Lord of the Isles.* Canto IV. St. 13.

1
These should be hours for necessities,
Not for delights; times to repair our nature
With comforting repose, and not for us
To waste these times.
Henry VIII. Act V. Sc. 1. L. 3.

2
Our foster-nurse of nature is repose,
The which he lacks; that to provoke in him,
Are many simples operative, whose power
Will close the eye of anguish.
King Lear. Act IV. Sc. 4. L. 12.

3
Study to be quiet.
Thessalonians. IV. 11.

4
The best of men have ever loved repose:
They hate to mingle in the filthy fray;
Where the soul sours, and gradual rancour grows,
Imbitter'd more from peevish day to day.
THOMSON—*The Castle of Indolence.* Canto I. St. 17.

5
Dulcis et alta quies, placidæque simillima morti.
Sweet and deep repose, very much resembling quiet death.
VERGIL—*Æneid.* VI. 522.

6
Deus nobis hæc otia fecit.
God has given us this repose.
VERGIL—*Eclogæ.* I. 6.

7
Chacun s'égare, et le moins imprudent,
Est celui-là qui plus tôt se repent.
Every one goes astray, but the least imprudent are they who repent the soonest.
VOLTAIRE—*Nanine.* II. 10.

REPUTATION (See also NAME)

8
It is a maxim with me that no man was ever written out of reputation but by himself.
RICHARD BENTLEY—MONK'S *Life of Bentley.* Vol. I. Ch. VI.
(See also EMERSON)

9
And reputation bleeds in ev'ry word.
CHURCHILL—*Apology.*

10
Negligere quid de se quisque sentiat, non solum arrogantis est, sed etiam omnino dissoluti.
To disregard what the world thinks of us is not only arrogant but utterly shameless.
CICERO—*De Officiis.* 1. 28.

11
No book was ever written down by any but itself.
EMERSON—*Spiritual Laws.*
(See also BENTLEY)

12
Nemo me lacrymis decoret, nec funera fletu.
Faxit cur? Volito vivu' per ora virum.
Let no one honour me with tears, or bury me with lamentation. Why? Because I fly hither and thither, living in the mouths of men.
Attributed to ENNIUS. Quoted by CICERO—*Tusc. Quæst.* I. 15. 34. Latter part said to be ENNIUS' *Epitaph.*

13
A lost good name is ne'er retriev'd.
GAY—*Fables. The Fox at the Point of Death.* L. 46.

14
Denn ein wanderndes Mädchen ist immer von schwankendem Rufe.
For a strolling damsel a doubtful reputation bears.
GOETHE—*Hermann und Dorothea.* VII. 93.

15
Ich halte nichts von dem, der von sich denkt
Wie ihn das Volk vielleicht erheben möchte.
I consider him of no account who esteems himself just as the popular breath may chance to raise him.
GOETHE—*Iphigenia auf Tauris.* II. 1. 140.

16
That man is thought a dangerous knave,
Or zealot plotting crime,
Who for advancement of his kind
Is wiser than his time.
Attributed to LORD HOUGHTON (MONCKTON MILNES)—*Men of Old.*

17
Reputation is but a synonyme of popularity: dependent on suffrage, to be increased or diminished at the will of the voters.
MRS. JAMESON—*Memoirs and Essays. Washington Allston.*

18
Reputations, like beavers and cloaks, shall last some people twice the time of others.
DOUGLAS JERROLD—*Specimens of Jerrold's Wit. Reputations.*

19
How many worthy men have we seen survive their own reputation!
MONTAIGNE—*Essays. Of Glory.*

20
To be pointed out with the finger.
PERSIUS—*Satires.* I. L. 28.

21
In various talk th' instructive hours they past,
Who gave the ball, or paid the visit last;
One speaks the glory of the British queen,
And one describes a charming Indian screen;
A third interprets motions, looks, and eyes;
At every word a reputation dies.
POPE—*Rape of the Lock.* Pt. III. L. 11. (This stanza not found in his printed works.)

22
Das Aergste weiss die Welt von mir, und ich
Kann sagen, ich bin besser als mein Ruf.
The worst of me is known, and I can say that I am better than the reputation I bear.
SCHILLER—*Marie Stuart.* III. 4. 208.

23
I have offended reputation,
A most unnoble swerving.
Antony and Cleopatra. Act III. Sc. 11. L. 49.

24
O, I have lost my reputation! I have lost the immortal part of myself, and what remains is bestial.
Othello. Act II. Sc. 3. L. 262.

1
Reputation is an idle and most false imposition; oft got without merit, and lost without deserving.
Othello. Act II. Sc. 3. L. 268.

2
The purest treasure mortal times afford
Is spotless reputation; that away,
Men are but gilded loam or painted clay.
Richard II. Act I. Sc. 1. L. 177.

3
Thy death-bed is no lesser than thy land
Wherein thou liest in reputation sick.
Richard II. Act II. Sc. 1. L. 95.

4
I see my reputation is at stake:
My fame is shewdly gor'd.
Troilus and Cressida. Act III. Sc. 3. L. 227.

5
Convey a libel in a frown.
And wink a reputation down!
Swift—*Journal of a Modern Lady*. L. 185.

RESIGNATION

6
To be resign'd when ills betide,
Patient when favours are denied,
And pleased with favours given;—
Dear Chloe, this is wisdom's part,
This is that incense of the heart
Whose fragrance smells to heaven.
Nathaniel Cotton—*The Fireside*. St. 11.
(See also Pierpont under Heart)

7
Give what thou canst, without thee we are poor;
And with thee rich, take what thou wilt away.
Cowper—*The Task*. Bk. V. Last lines.

8
Dare to look up to God and say, Deal with me in the future as Thou wilt; I am of the same mind as Thou art; I am Thine; I refuse nothing that pleases Thee; lead me where Thou wilt; clothe me in any dress Thou choosest.
Epictetus—*Discourses*. Bk. II. Ch. XVI.

9
Bends to the grave with unperceived decay,
While resignation gently slopes the way
And, all his prospects brightening to the last,
His heaven commences ere the world be past.
Goldsmith—*Deserted Village*. L. 110.

10
To will what God doth will, that is the only science
That gives us any rest.
Malherbe—*Consolation*. St. 7. Longfellow's trans.

11
That's best
Which God sends. 'Twas His will: it is mine.
Owen Meredith (Lord Lytton)—*Lucile*. Pt. II. Canto VI. St. 29.

12
The pious farmer, who ne'er misses pray'rs,
With patience suffers unexpected rain;
He blesses Heav'n for what its bounty spares,
And sees, resign'd, a crop of blighted grain.
But, spite of sermons, farmers would blaspheme,
If a star fell to set their thatch on flame.
Lady Mary Wortley Montagu—*Poem*. Written Oct., 1736.

13
Placato possum non miser esse deo.
If God be appeased, I can not be wretched.
Ovid—*Tristium*. III. 40.

14
Unum est levamentum malorum pati et necessitatibus suis obsequi.
One alleviation in misfortune is to endure and submit to necessity.
Seneca—*De Ira*. III. 16.

15
Placeat homini quidquid deo placuit.
Let that please man which has pleased God.
Seneca—*Epistolæ Ad Lucilium*. LXXIV.

16
Thus ready for the way of life or death,
I wait the sharpest blow.
Pericles. Act I. Sc. 1. L. 54.

17
It seem'd so hard at first, mother, to leave the blessed sun,
And now it seems as hard to stay—and yet His will be done!
But still I think it can't be long before I find release;
And that good man, the clergyman, has told me words of peace.
Tennyson—*The May-Queen*. *Conclusion*. St. 3.

RESOLUTION

18
Videlicit,
That each man swore to do his best
To damn and perjure all the rest.
Butler—*Hudibras*. Pt. I. Canto II. L. 630.

19
I am in earnest—I will not equivocate—I will not excuse—I will not retreat a single inch AND I WILL BE HEARD.
William Lloyd Garrison—*Salutatory of the Liberator*. Vol. I. No. 1. Jan. 1, 1831.

20
I will be as harsh as truth and as uncompromising as justice.
William Lloyd Garrison—*Salutatory of the Liberator*. Vol. I. No. 1. Jan. 1, 1831.

21
Nor cast one longing, ling'ring look behind.
Gray—*Elegy in a Country Churchyard*. St. 22.

22
In truth there is no such thing in man's nature as a settled and full resolve either for good or evil, except at the very moment of execution.
Hawthorne — *Twice-Told Tales*. *Fancy's Show Box*.

23
Hast thou attempted greatnesse?
Then go on;
Back-turning slackens resolution.
Herrick—*Regression Spoils Resolution*.

24
For when two
Join in the same adventure, one perceives
Before the other how they ought to act;
While one alone, however prompt, resolves
More tardily and with a weaker will.
Homer—*Iliad*. Bk. X. L. 257. Bryant's trans.

25
Resolve, and thou art free.
Longfellow—*Masque of Pandora*. Pt. VI. *In the Garden*.

1
In life's small things be resolute and great
To keep thy muscle trained: know'st thou when
Fate
Thy measure takes, or when she'll say to thee,
"I find thee worthy; do this deed for me?"
LOWELL—*Epigram.*

2
Never tell your resolution beforehand.
JOHN SELDEN—*Table Talk. Wisdom.*

3
Be stirring as the time; be fire with fire;
Threaten the threat'ner and outface the brow
Of bragging horror: so shall inferior eyes,
That borrow their behaviours from the great,
Grow great by your example and put on
The dauntless spirit of resolution.
King John. Act V. Sc. 1. L. 48.

4
And hearts resolved and hands prepared
The blessings they enjoy to guard.
SMOLLETT—*Humphry Clinker. Ode to Leven Water.*

REST (See also REPOSE)

5
In the rest of Nirvana all sorrows surcease:
Only Buddha can guide to that city of Peace
Whose inhabitants have the eternal release.
WM. R. ALGER—*Oriental Poetry. A Leader to Repose.*

6 Silken rest
Tie all thy cares up!
BEAUMONT AND FLETCHER—*Four Plays in One.* Sc. 4. *Triumph of Love.*

7
O! quid solutis est beatius curis!
Cum mens onus reponit, ac peregrino
Labore fessi venimus larem ad nostrum
Desideratoque acquiescimus lecto.
Hoc est, quod unum est pro laboribus tantis.

O, what is more sweet than when the mind, set free from care, lays its burden down; and, when spent with distant travel, we come back to our home, and rest our limbs on the wished-for bed? This, this alone, repays such toils as these!
CATULLUS—*Carmina.* 31. 7.

8
Absence of occupation is not rest;
A mind quite vacant is a mind distress'd.
COWPER—*Retirement.* L. 623.

9
Rest is not quitting the busy career;
Rest is the fitting of self to its sphere.
JOHN S. DWIGHT—*True Rest.* (From his translation of GOETHE. Main part original.)

10
Sweet is the pleasure itself cannot spoil.
Is not true leisure one with true toil?
JOHN S. DWIGHT—*True Rest.*

11
Amidst these restless thoughts this rest I find,
For those that rest not here, there's rest behind.
THOMAS GATAKER—*B. D.* Nat. 4. Sept., 1574.

12
On every mountain height
Is rest.
GOETHE—*Ein Gleiches.*

13
Calm on the bosom of thy God,
Fair spirit! rest thee now!
MRS. HEMANS—*Siege of Valencia. Dirge.* Sc. 9.

14
For too much rest itself becomes a pain.
HOMER—*Odyssey.* Bk. XV. L. 429. POPE'S trans.

15
Rest is sweet after strife.
OWEN MEREDITH (Lord Lytton)—*Lucile.* Pt. I. Canto VI. St. 25.

16
Anything for a quiet life.
THOMAS MIDDLETON. *Title of a Play*

17
Da requiem; requietus ager bene credita reddit.

Take rest; a field that has rested gives a bountiful crop.
OVID—*Ars Amatoria.* II. 351.

18
Life's race well run,
Life's work well done,
Life's victory won,
Now cometh rest.
DR. EDWARD HAZEN PARKER—*Funeral Ode on President Garfield.* Claimed for him by his brother in *Notes and Queries*, May 25, 1901. P. 406. Claimed by MRS. JOHN MILLS, for JOHN MILLS of Manchester, 1878. Appears in the Life of John Mills with account of origin. See *Notes and Queries.* Ser. 9. Vol. IV. P. 167. Also Vol. VII. P. 406.

19
Master, I've filled my contract, wrought in Thy many lands;
Not by my sins wilt Thou judge me, but by the work of my hands.
Master, I've done Thy bidding, and the light is low in the west,
And the long, long shift is over . . . Master, I've earned it—Rest.
ROBERT SERVICE—*Song of the Wage Slave.*

20 Weariness
Can snore upon the flint, when resty sloth
Finds the down pillow hard.
Cymbeline. Act III. Sc. 6. L. 33.

21
Who, with a body filled and vacant mind,
Gets him to rest, cramm'd with distressful bread.
Henry V. Act IV. Sc. 1. L. 286.

22
Sleepe after toyle, port after stormie seas,
Ease after warre, death after life, does greatly please.
SPENSER—*Faerie Queene.* Bk. I. Canto IX. St. 40.

23
Arcum intensio frangit, animum remissio.

Straining breaks the bow, and relaxation the mind.
SYRUS—*Maxims.*

24
And rest, that strengthens unto virtuous deeds,
Is one with Prayer.
BAYARD TAYLOR—*Temptation of Hassan Ben Khaled.* St. 4.

1
The camel at the close of day
Kneels down upon the sandy plain
To have his burden lifted off
And rest again.
ANNA TEMPLE—*Kneeling Camel.*

2
Now is done thy long day's work
Fold thy palms across thy breast,
Fold thine arms, turn to thy rest.
Let them rave.
TENNYSON—*A Dirge.*

3
Thou hadst, for weary feet, the gift of rest.
WILLIAM WATSON—*Wordsworth's Grave.* II. St. 3.

4
Father Abbot, I am come to lay my weary bones among you.
WOLSEY. At Leicester Abbey, Nov. 26, 1529.

RESULTS

5
From hence, let fierce contending nations know,
What dire effects from civil discord flow.
ADDISON—*Cato.* Act V. Sc. 4.
(See also POPE)

6
As you sow y' are like to reap.
BUTLER—*Hudibras.* Pt. II. Canto II. L. 504.
(See also CICERO)

7
The thorns which I have reap'd are of the tree
I planted—they have torn me—and I bleed!
I should have known what fruit would spring from such a seed.
BYRON—*Childe Harold.* Canto IV. St. 10.

8
Tantas veces va el cantarillo á la fuente.
The pitcher goes so often to the fountain (that it gets broken).
CERVANTES—*Don Quixote.* I. 30.
Tant va li poz au puis qu'il brise.
Quoted by GAUTIER DE COINCI. Early 13th century.

9
Al freir de los huevos lo vera.
It will be seen in the frying of the eggs.
CERVANTES—*Don Quixote.* 1. 37.

10
Ut sementem feceris, ita metes.
As thou sowest, so shalt thou reap
CICERO—*De Oratore.* II. 65.
(See also BUTLER)

11
O! lady, we receive but what we give,
And in our life alone doth nature live;
Ours is her wedding-garment, ours her shroud!
COLERIDGE—*Dejection. An Ode.* IV.

12
From little spark may burst a mighty flame.
DANTE—*Paradise.* Canto I. L. 34.
(See also HERBERT, POPE, SCOTT)

13
Consequences are unpitying. Our deeds carry their terrible consequences, quite apart from any fluctuations that went before—consequences that are hardly ever confined to ourselves.
GEORGE ELIOT—*Adam Bede.* Ch. XVI.

14
A bad ending follows a bad beginning.
EURIPIDES—*Frag. Melanip.* (*Stobæus.*)

15
So comes a reck'ning when the banquet's o'er,
The dreadful reck'ning, and men smile no more.
GAY—*What D'ye Call't?* Act II. Sc. 4.

16
That from small fires comes oft no small mishap.
HERBERT—*The Temple. Artillerie.*
(See also DANTE)

17
They have sown the wind, and they shall reap the whirlwind.
Hosea. VIII. 7.

18
By their fruits ye shall know them.
Matthew. VII. 20.

19
What dire offence from am'rous causes springs,
What mighty contests rise from trivial things.
POPE—*Rape of the Lock.* Canto I. "Contests" is "quarrels" in first ed. Same idea in ERASMUS—*Adagia.* CLAUDIANUS—*In Refinum.* II. 49.
(See also ADDISON, DANTE, SCOTT, also ARISTOTLE under REVOLUTION)

20
Whoso diggeth a pit shall fall therein.
Proverbs. XXVI. 27.

21
Contentions fierce,
Ardent, and dire, spring from no petty cause.
SCOTT—*Peveril of the Peak.* Ch. XL.

22
Great floods have flown
From simple sources.
All's Well That Ends Well. Act II. Sc. 1. L. 142.

23
Is not this a lamentable thing, that of the skin of an innocent lamb should be made parchment? that parchment, being scribbled o'er, should undo a man?
Henry VI. Pt. II. Act IV. Sc. 2. L. 85.

24
Striving to better, oft we mar what's well.
King Lear. Act I. Sc. 4. L. 369.

25
Things bad begun make strong themselves by ill.
Macbeth. Act III. Sc. 2. L. 55.

26
O most lame and impotent conclusion!
Othello. Act II. Sc. 1. L. 162.

27
Every unpunished delinquency has a family of delinquencies.
HERBERT SPENCER—*Sociology.*

28
The evening shows the day, and death crowns life.
JOHN WEBSTER—*A Monumental Column.* Last line.

29
The Fates are just: they give us but our own;
Nemesis ripens what our hands have sown.
WHITTIER—*To a Southern Statesman.* (1864)

30
The blood will follow where the knife is driven,
The flesh will quiver where the pincers tear.
YOUNG—*The Revenge.* Act V.

RESURRECTION

1
The last loud trumpet's wondrous sound,
Shall thro' the rending tombs rebound,
And wake the nations under ground.

WENTWORTH DILLON—*On the Day of Judgment.* St. 3.

2
The trumpet! the trumpet! the dead have all heard:
Lo, the depths of the stone-cover'd charnels are stirr'd:
From the sea, from the land, from the south and the north,
The vast generations of man are come forth.

MILMAN—*Hymns for Church Service. Second Sunday in Advent.* St. 3.

3
Shall man alone, for whom all else revives,
No resurrection know? Shall man alone,
Imperial man! be sown in barren ground,
Less privileged than grain, on which he feeds?

YOUNG—*Night Thoughts.* Night VI. L. 704.

4
I see the Judge enthroned; the flaming guard:
The volume open'd!—open'd every heart!

YOUNG—*Night Thoughts.* Night IX. L. 262.

RETALIATION

5
Ich bin gewohnt in der Münze wiederzuzahlen in der man mich bezahlt.

I am accustomed to pay men back in their own coin.

BISMARCK—*To the Ultramontanes.* (1870)
(See also SWIFT)

6
Repudiate the repudiators.

WM. P. FESSENDEN. Presidential Canvass of 1868.

7
And would'st thou evil for his good repay?

HOMER—*Odyssey.* Bk. XVI. L. 448. POPE'S trans.

8
She pays him in his own coin.

SWIFT—*Polite Conversation. Dialogue* III.
(See also BISMARCK)

RETRIBUTION (See also PUNISHMENT)

9
God's mills grind slow,
But they grind woe.

WM. R. ALGER—*Poetry of the East. Delayed Retribution.*
(See also EURIPIDES, JUVENAL, LOGAU, MAXIMUS)

10
The divine power moves with difficulty, but at the same time surely.

EURIPIDES—*Bacchæ.* 382.

11
The ways of the gods are long, but in the end they are not without strength.

EURIPIDES—*Ion.* I. 1615.
(See also ALGER)

12
Ut sit magna tamen certe lenta ira deorum est.

But grant the wrath of Heaven be great, 'tis slow.

JUVENAL—*Satires.* XIII. 100. GIFFORD'S trans. (See also ALGER)

13
Though the mills of God grind slowly, yet they grind exceeding small;
Though with patience He stands waiting, with exactness grinds He all.

FRIEDRICH VON LOGAU—*Retribution.* From the *Sinngedichte.* See LONGFELLOW'S trans. *Poetic Aphorisms.* First line from the Greek *Oracula Sibyllina.* VIII. 14. Same idea in PLUTARCH—*Sera Humanis Vindicta. Ch. VIII,* quoting SEXTUS EMPIRICUS—*Adversus Grammaticos.* I. 13. Sect. 287. Found also in *Proverbia e cad. Coisl.* in GAISFORD. —*Parœm. Græc.* Oxon. 1836. P. 164. HORACE—*Carmina.* III. 2. 31. TIBULLUS—*Elegies.* I. 9.
(See also ALGER)

14
To be left alone
And face to face with my own crime, had been
Just retribution.

LONGFELLOW—*Masque of Pandora.* Pt. VIII. *In the Garden.*

15
Lento quidem gradu ad vindictam divina procedit ira, sed tarditatem supplicii gravitate compensat.

The divine wrath is slow indeed in vengeance, but it makes up for its tardiness by the severity of the punishment.

VALERIUS MAXIMUS. I. 1. 3.
(See also ALGER)

16
Be ready, gods, with all your thunderbolts;
Dash him to pieces!

Julius Cæsar. Act IV. Sc. 3. L. 81.

17
But as some muskets so contrive it
As oft to miss the mark they drive at,
And though well aimed at duck or plover
Bear wide, and kick their owners over.

JOHN TRUMBULL—*McFingal.* Canto I. L. 95.

REVELATION

18
Lochiel, Lochiel! beware of the day;
For, dark and despairing, my sight I may seal
But man cannot cover what God would reveal.

CAMPBELL—*Lochiel's Warning.*

19
'Tis Revelation satisfies all doubts,
Explains all mysteries except her own,
And so illuminates the path of life,
That fools discover it, and stray no more.

COWPER—*The Task.* Bk. II. *The Time-Piece.* L. 526.

20
Nature is a revelation of God;
Art a revelation of man.

LONGFELLOW—*Hyperion.* Bk. III. Ch. V.

REVENGE

21
Revenge is a kind of wild justice; which the more man's nature runs to, the more ought law to weed it out.

BACON—*Of Revenge.*

22
Women do most delight in revenge.

SIR THOS. BROWNE—*Christian Morals.* Part III. Sec. XII.
(See also BYRON, JUVENAL)

1
Sweet is revenge—especially to women.
BYRON—*Don Juan.* Canto I. St. 124.
(See also BROWNE)

2
'Tis more noble to forgive, and more manly to despise, than to revenge an Injury.
BENJ. FRANKLIN—*Poor Richard.* (1752)

3
Revenge is profitable.
GIBBON—*Decline and Fall of the Roman Empire.* Ch. XI.

4
It [revenge] is sweeter far than flowing honey.
HOMER—*Iliad.* XVIII. 109.

5
Behold, on wrong
Swift vengeance waits; and art subdues the strong.
HOMER—*Odyssey.* Bk. VIII. L. 367. POPE'S trans.

6
At vindicta bonum vita jucundius ipsa nempe hoc indocti.
Revenge is sweeter than life itself. So think fools.
JUVENAL—*Satires.* XIII. 180.

7
Minuti
Semper et infirmi est animi exiguique voluptas
Ultio.
Revenge is always the weak pleasure of a little and narrow mind.
JUVENAL—*Satires.* XIII. 189.

8
Vindicta
Nemo magis gaudet quam fœmina.
No one rejoices more in revenge than woman.
JUVENAL—*Satires.* XIII. 191.
(See also BROWNE)

9
Which, if not victory, is yet revenge.
MILTON—*Paradise Lost.* Bk. II. L. 105.

10
Revenge, at first though sweet,
Bitter ere long back on itself recoils.
MILTON—*Paradise Lost.* Bk. IX. L. 171.

11
Je ne te quitterai point que je ne t'aie vu pendu.
I will not leave you until I have seen you hanged.
MOLIÈRE—*Le Medecin Malgré Lui.* III. 9.

12
One sole desire, one passion now remains
To keep life's fever still within his veins,
Vengeance! dire vengeance on the wretch who cast
O'er him and all he lov'd that ruinous blast.
MOORE—*Lalla Rookh. The Veiled Prophet of Khorassan.*

13
Sæpe intereunt aliis meditantes necem.
Those who plot the destruction of others often fall themselves.
PHÆDRUS—*Fables. Appendix.* VI. 11.

14
'Tis an old tale, and often told;
But did my fate and wish agree,
Ne'er had been read, in story old,
Of maiden true betray'd for gold,
That loved, or was avenged, like me!
SCOTT—*Marmion.* Canto II. St. 27.

15
Vengeance to God alone belongs;
But, when I think of all my wrongs.
My blood is liquid flame!
SCOTT—*Marmion.* Canto VI. St. 7.

16
Inhumanum verbum est ultio.
Revenge is an inhuman word.
SENECA—*De Ira.* II. 31.

17
If I can catch him once upon the hip,
I will feed fat the ancient grudge I bear him.
Merchant of Venice. Act I. Sc. 3. L. 47.

18
If it will feed nothing else, it will feed my revenge.
Merchant of Venice. Act III. Sc. 1. L. 55.

19
Now, infidel, I have you on the hip.
Merchant of Venice. Act IV. Sc. 1. L. 334.

20
Vengeance is in my heart, death in my hand,
Blood and revenge are hammering in my head.
Titus Andronicus. Act II. Sc. 3. L. 38.

21
Malevolus animus abditos dentes habet.
The malevolent have hidden teeth.
SYRUS—*Maxims.*

22
Odia in longum jaciens, quæ reconderet, auctaque promeret.
Laying aside his resentment, he stores it up to bring it forward with increased bitterness.
TACITUS—*Annales.* I. 69.

23
Souls made of fire and children of the sun,
With whom Revenge is virtue.
YOUNG—*The Revenge.* Act V.

REVOLUTION (See also REBELLION, WAR)

24
Revolutions are not about trifles, but spring from trifles.
ARISTOTLE—*Politics.* Bk. VII. Ch. IV.
(See also POPE under RESULTS)

25
A reform is a correction of abuses; a revolution is a transfer of power.
BULWER-LYTTON—*Speech.* In the House of Commons, on the Reform Bill. (1866)

26
Voulez-vous donc qu'on vous fasse des révolutions à l'eau-rose?
Do you think then that revolutions are made with rose water?
SEBASTIAN CHAMFORT to MARMOTEL, who regretted the excesses of the Revolution.

27
Ce n'est pas une révolte, c'est une révolution.
It is not a revolt, it is a revolution.
DUC DE LIANCOURT to LOUIS XVI, July 14, 1789. Found in CARLYLE'S *French Revolution.* Pt. I. Bk. V. Ch. VII.

28
Je suis le signet qui marque la page où la révolution s'est arrêtée; mais quand je serai mort, elle tournera le feuillet et reprendra sa marche.
I am the signet which marks the page where the revolution has been stopped; but when I die it will turn the page and resume its course.
NAPOLEON I. to COUNT MOLÉ.

1
Revolutions are not made; they come.
WENDELL PHILLIPS—*Speech. Public Opinion.* Jan. 28, 1852.

2
Revolutions never go backward.
WENDELL PHILLIPS—*Speech. Progress.* Feb. 17, 1861.

3
I know and all the world knows, that revolutions never go backwards.
SEWARD—*Speech on the Irrepressible Conflict.* Oct., 1858.

4
O God! that one might read the book of fate,
And see the revolutions of the times
Make mountains level, and the continent
Weary of solid firmness, melt itself
Into the sea!
Henry IV. Pt. II. Act III. Sc. 1. L. 45.

5
Seditiosissimus quisque ignavus.
The most seditious is the most cowardly.
TACITUS—*Annales.* IV. 34.

RHINE

6
Sie sollen ihn nicht haben
Den freien, deutschen Rhein.
You shall never have it,
The free German Rhine.
BECKER—*Der Rhein.* Popular in 1840. Answered by ALFRED DE MUSSET—*Nous l'avons eu, votre Rhin Allemand.* Appeared in the *Athenæum*, Aug. 13, 1870.

7
The castled crag of Drachenfels,
Frowns o'er the wide and winding Rhine,
Whose breast of waters broadly swells
Between the banks which bear the vine,
And hills all rich with blossom'd trees,
And fields which promise corn and wine,
And scatter'd cities crowning these,
Whose far white walls along them shine.
BYRON—*Childe Harold.* Cants III. St. 55.

8
Am Rhein, am Rhein, da wachsen uns're Reben.
On the Rhine, on the Rhine, there grow our vines.
CLAUDIUS—*Rheinweinlied.*

9
The air grows cool and darkles,
The Rhine flows calmly on;
The mountain summit sparkles
In the light of the setting sun.
HEINE—*The Lorelei.*

10
The Rhine! the Rhine! a blessing on the Rhine!
LONGFELLOW—*Hyperion.* Bk. I. Ch. II.

11
Beneath me flows the Rhine, and, like the stream of Time, it flows amid the ruins of the Past.
LONGFELLOW—*Hyperion.* Bk. I. Ch. III.

12
I've seen the Rhine with younger wave,
O'er every obstacle to rave.
I see the Rhine in his native wild
Is still a mighty mountain child.
RUSKIN—*A Tour on the Continent. Via Mala.*

13
Lieb Vaterland magst ruhig sein,
Fest steht und treu die Wacht am Rhein!
Dear Fatherland no danger thine,
Firm stand thy sons to watch the Rhine!
MAX SCHNECKENBURGER—*Die Wacht am Rhein.*

14
Oh, sweet thy current by town and by tower,
The green sunny vale and the dark linden bower;
Thy waves as they dimple smile back on the plain,
And Rhine, ancient river, thou'rt German again!
HORACE WALLACE—*Ode on the Rhine's Returning into Germany from France.*

RHONE

15
Is it not better, then, to be alone,
And love Earth only for its earthly sake?
By the blue rushing of the arrowy Rhone
Or the pure bosom of its nursing lake.
BYRON—*Childe Harold.* Canto III. St. 71.

16
Thou Royal River, born of sun and shower
In chambers purple with the Alpine glow,
Wrapped in the spotless ermine of the snow
And rocked by tempests!
LONGFELLOW—*To the River Rhone.*

RICHES (See MONEY, POSSESSION, WEALTH)

RIDICULE

17
It frequently happens that where the second line is sublime, the third, in which he meant to rise still higher, is perfectly bombast.
BLAIR. Commenting on Lucan's style. Borrowed from LONGINUS—*Treatise on the Sublime.* Sect. III.
(See also COLERIDGE, DESLAUDES, FONTENELLE, MARMONTEL, NAPOLEON, PAINE)

18
We have oftener than once endeavoured to attach some meaning to that aphorism, vulgarly imputed to Shaftesbury, which however we can find nowhere in his works, that "ridicule is the test of truth."
CARLYLE—*Essays. Voltaire.*

19
That passage is what I call the sublime dashed to pieces by cutting too close with the fiery four-in-hand round the corner of nonsense.
COLERIDGE—*Table Talk.* Jan. 20, 1834.
WIELAND—*Abdereiten.* III. Ch. XII.
(See also BLAIR)

20
Jane borrow'd maxims from a doubting school,
And took for truth the test of ridicule;
Lucy saw no such virtue in a jest,
Truth was with her of ridicule the test.
CRABBE—*Tales of the Hall.* Bk. VIII. L. 126.

21
I distrust those sentiments that are too far removed from nature, and whose sublimity is blended with ridicule; which two are as near one another as extreme wisdom and folly.
DESLAUDES—*Reflexions sur les Grands Hommes qui sont morts en Plaisantant.*
(See also BLAIR)

1
L'on ne saurait mieux faire voir que le magnifique et le ridicule sont si voisins qu'ils se touchent.

There is nothing one sees oftener than the ridiculous and magnificent, such close neighbors that they touch.

DE FONTENELLE—*Œuvres. Dialogues des Morts.* (1683) IV. 32. Ed. 1825. Used by EDWARD, LORD OXFORD—*Ms. Common Place Book.*

(See also BLAIR)

2
Ridiculum acri
Fortius ac melius magnas plerumque secat res.

Ridicule more often settles things more thoroughly and better than acrimony.

HORACE—*Satires.* Bk. I. 10. 14.

(See also SHAFTESBURY)

3
En général, le ridicule touche au sublime.

Generally the ridiculous touches the sublime.

MARMONTEL—*Œuvres Complettes.* (1787) V. 188.

(See also BLAIR)

4
Du sublime au ridicule il n'y a qu'un pas.

There is only one step from the sublime to the ridiculous.

NAPOLEON I to *Abbé du Pradt, at Warsaw.* See *Histoire de l'Ambassade dans la Grande Duché de Vasovie.* Ed. 2. P. 219. Attributed also to TALLEYRAND. (Traced from Napoleon to Paine, Paine to Blair.)

5
The sublime and the ridiculous are often so nearly related that it is difficult to class them separately. One step above the sublime makes the ridiculous, and one step above the ridiculous makes the sublime again.

THOMAS PAINE—*The Age of Reason.* Pt. II.

(See also BLAIR)

6
How comes it to pass, then, that we appear such cowards in reasoning, and are so afraid to stand the test of ridicule?

SHAFTESBURY—*Characteristics. Letter Concerning Enthusiasm.* Pt. I. Sec. II.

7
'Twas the saying of an ancient sage that humour was the only test of gravity, and gravity of humour. For a subject which would not bear raillery was suspicious; and a jest which would not bear a serious examination was certainly false wit.

SHAFTESBURY—*Characteristics. Letter Concerning Enthusiasm.* Pt. I. Sect. V. Referring to Leontinus.

(See also LEONTINUS under ARGUMENT)

(See also HORACE)

8
Truth, 'tis supposed, may bear all lights; and one of those principal lights or natural mediums by which things are to be viewed in order to a thorough recognition is ridicule itself.

SHAFTESBURY—*Essay on the Freedom of Wit and Humour.* Pt. I. Sec. I.

9
I have always made one prayer to God, a very short one. Here it is: "My God, make our enemies very ridiculous!" God has granted it to me.

VOLTAIRE—*Letter to M. Damilaville,* May 16, 1767.

RIGHT; RIGHTS

10
Among the natural rights of the colonists are these: First a right to life, secondly to liberty, thirdly to property; together with the right to defend them in the best manner they can.

SAMUEL ADAMS—*Statement of the Rights of the Colonists, etc.* (1772)

(See also JEFFERSON, also LINCOLN under EQUALITY)

11
Right as a trivet.

R. H. BARHAM—*The Ingoldsby Legends. Auto-da-fé.*

12
They made and recorded a sort of institute and digest of anarchy, called the rights of man.

BURKE—*On the Army Estimates.* Vol. III. P. 221.

13
Sir, I would rather be right than be President.

HENRY CLAY—*Speech.* (1850) *Referring to the Compromise Measure.*

14
He will hew to the line of right, let the chips fly where they may.

ROSCOE CONKLING—*Speech at the National Convention,* Chicago, 1880, when GENERAL GRANT was nominated for a third term.

15
But 'twas a maxim he had often tried,
That right was right, and there he would abide.

CRABBE—*Tales.* Tale XV. *The Squire and the Priest.*

16
Be sure you are right, then go ahead.

DAVID CROCKETT—*Motto.* In War of 1812.

17
The rule of the road is a paradox quite,
If you drive with a whip or a thong;
If you go to the left you are sure to be right,
If you go to the right you are wrong.

HENRY ERSKINE—*Rule of the Road.*

18
For right is right, since God is God,
And right the day must win;
To doubt would be disloyalty,
To falter would be sin.

F. W. FABER—*The Right Must Win.* St. 18.

19
Wherever there is a human being, I see God-given rights inherent in that being, whatever may be the sex or complexion.

WILLIAM LLOYD GARRISON. In his *Life.* Vol. III. P. 390.

20
The equal right of all men to the use of land is as clear as their equal right to breathe the air—it is a right proclaimed by the fact of their existence. For we cannot suppose that some men have a right to be in this world, and others no right.

HENRY GEORGE—*Progress and Poverty.* Bk. VII. Ch. I.

(See also MORE)

21
And wanting the right rule they take chalke for cheese, as the saying is.

NICHOLAS GRIMALD—*Preface* to his Trans. of MARCUS TULLIUS CICERO. *Three Bookes of Duties to Marcus his Sonne.* Same expression in GOWER—*Confessio Amantis.*

1
For the ultimate notion of right is that which tends to the universal good; and when one's acting in a certain manner has this tendency he has a right thus to act.
FRANCIS HUTCHESON—*A System of Moral Philosophy. The General Notions of Rights and Laws Explained.* Bk. II. Ch. III.

2
Equal rights for all, special privileges for none.
THOMAS JEFFERSON.

3
We hold these truths to be self-evident,—that all men are created equal; that they are endowed by their Creator with certain inalienable rights; that among these are Life, Liberty, and the pursuit of happiness.
THOMAS JEFFERSON—*Declaration of Independence of the U. S. of America.*

4
Let us have faith that Right makes Might, and in that faith let us to the end dare to do our duty as we understand it.
ABRAHAM LINCOLN—*Address.* New York City. Feb. 21, 1859. See HENRY J. RAYMOND'S *Life and Public Services of Lincoln.* Ch. III.

5
With malice toward none, with charity for all, with firmness in the right, as God gives us to see the right.
ABRAHAM LINCOLN—*Second Inaugural Address.* March 4, 1865.

6
Mensuraque juris
Vis erat.
Might was the measure of right.
LUCAN—*Pharsalia.* I. 175. Found in THUCYDIDES. IV. 86. PLAUTUS—*Truncul.* IV. 3. 30. LUCAN. I. 175. SENECA—*Hercules Furens.* 291. SCHILLER—*Wallenstein's Camp.* VI. 144.

7
All men are born free and equal, and have certain natural, essential, and unalienable rights.
Constitution of Massachusetts.

8
Every man has by the law of nature a right to such a waste portion of the earth as is necessary for his subsistence.
MORE—*Utopia.* Bk. II.
(See also GEORGE)

9
Reparation for our rights *at home*, and security against the like future violations.
WILLIAM PITT (Earl of Chatham)—*Letter to the Earl of Shelburne.* Sept. 29, 1770.

10
All Nature is but art unknown to thee;
All chance direction, which thou canst not see;
All discord, harmony not understood;
All partial evil, universal good;
And spite of pride, in erring reason's spite,
One truth is clear, Whatever is is right.
POPE—*Essay on Man.* Ep. I. L. 289.

11
No question is ever settled
Until it is settled right.
ELLA WHEELER WILCOX.

RIGHTEOUSNESS

12
Be not righteous overmuch.
Ecclesiastes. VII. 16.

13
Every one that useth milk is unskilful in the word of righteousness: for he is a babe.
Hebrews. V. 13.

14
A righteous man regardeth the life of his beast; but the tender mercies of the wicked are cruel.
Proverbs. XII. 10.

15
Righteousness exalteth a nation.
Proverbs. XIV. 34.

16
I have been young, and now am old; yet have I not seen the righteous forsaken, nor his seed begging bread.
Psalms. XXXVII. 25.

17
The righteous shall flourish like the palm-tree: he shall grow like a cedar in Lebanon.
Psalms. XCII. 12.

RIVERS (GENERAL TOPIC)

18
And see the rivers how they run
Through woods and meads, in shade and sun,
Sometimes swift, sometimes slow,—
Wave succeeding wave, they go
A various journey to the deep,
Like human life to endless sleep!
JOHN DYER—*Grongar Hill.* L. 93.

19
The fountains of sacred rivers flow upwards, (*i.e.* everything is turned topsy turvy).
EURIPIDES—*Medea.* 409.

20
Two ways the rivers
Leap down to different seas, and as they roll
Grow deep and still, and their majestic presence
Becomes a benefaction to the towns
They visit, wandering silently among them,
Like patriarchs old among their shining tents.
LONGFELLOW—*Christus. The Golden Legend.* Pt. V.

21
By shallow rivers, to whose falls
Melodious birds sing madrigals.
MARLOWE—*The Passionate Shepherd to His Love.* Same idea in *Merry Wives of Windsor.* Act III. Sc. 1. *Passionate Shepherd* said to be written by SHAKESPEARE and MARLOWE.

22
Les rivières sont des chemins qui marchant et qui portent où l'on veut aller.
Rivers are roads that move and carry us whither we wish to go.
PASCAL—*Pensées.* VII. 38.

23
Viam qui nescit qua deveniat ad mare
Eum oportet amnem quærere comitem sibi.
He who does not know his way to the sea should take a river for his guide.
PLAUTUS—*Pœnulus.* III. 3. 14.

24
Now scantier limits the proud arch confine,
And scarce are seen the prostrate Nile or Rhine;
A small Euphrates thro' the piece is roll'd,

And little eagles wave their wings in gold.
POPE—*Moral Essays. Epistle to Addison.* L. 27.

1
From Stirling Castle we had seen
The mazy Forth unravelled;
Had trod the banks of Clyde and Tay,
And with the Tweed had travelled;
And when we came to Clovenford,
Then said "my winsome marrow,"
"Whate'er betide, we'll turn aside,
And see the braes of Yarrow."
WORDSWORTH—*Yarrow Unvisited.*

ROBIN

2
The redbreast oft, at evening hours,
Shall kindly lend his little aid,
With hoary moss, and gathered flowers,
To deck the ground where thou art laid.
WILLIAM COLLINS—*Odes. Dirge in Cymbeline.*

3
Bearing His cross, while Christ passed forth forlorn,
His God-like forehead by the mock crown torn,
A little bird took from that crown one thorn.
To soothe the dear Redeemer's throbbing head,
That bird did what she could; His blood, 'tis said,
Down dropping, dyed her tender bosom red.
Since then no wanton boy disturbs her nest;
Weasel nor wild cat will her young molest;
All sacred deem the bird of ruddy breast.
HOSKYNS-ABRAHALL—*The Redbreast. A Brèton Legend.* In *English Lyrics.*

4
On fair Britannia's isle, bright bird,
A legend strange is told of thee,—
'Tis said thy blithesome song was hushed
While Christ toiled up Mount Calvary,
Bowed 'neath the sins of all mankind;
And humbled to the very dust
By the vile cross, while viler men
Mocked with a crown of thorns the Just.
Pierced by our sorrows, and weighed down
By our transgressions,—faint and weak,
Crushed by an angry Judge's frown,
And agonies no word can speak,—
'Twas then, dear bird, the legend says
That thou, from out His crown, didst tear
The thorns, to lighten the distress,
And ease the pain that he must bear,
While pendant from thy tiny beak
The gory points thy bosom pressed,
And crimsoned with thy Saviour's blood
The sober brownness of thy breast!
Since which proud hour for thee and thine,
As an especial sign of grace
God pours like sacramental wine
Red signs of favor o'er thy race!
DELLE W. NORTON—*To the Robin Redbreast.*

5
You have learned, like Sir Proteus, to wreathe your arms, like a malcontent; to relish a love-song, like a robin redbreast.
Two Gentlemen of Verona. Act II. Sc. 1. L. 16.

6
The Redbreast, sacred to the household gods,
Wisely regardful of the embroiling sky,
In joyless fields and thorny thickets leaves
His shivering mates, and pays to trusted Man
His annual visit.
THOMSON—*The Seasons. Winter.* L. 246.

7
Call for the robin-red-breast, and the wren,
Since o'er shady groves they hover,
And with leaves and flowers do cover
The friendless bodies of unburied men.
JOHN WEBSTER—*The White Devil, or Vittoria Corombona. A Dirge.*

8
Now when the primrose makes a splendid show,
And lilies face the March-winds in full blow,
And humbler growths as moved with one desire
Put on, to welcome spring, their best attire,
Poor Robin is yet flowerless; but how gay
With his red stalks upon this sunny day!
WORDSWORTH—*Poor Robin.*

9
Art thou the bird whom Man loves best,
The pious bird with the scarlet breast,
Our little English Robin;
The bird that comes about our doors
When autumn winds are sobbing?
WORDSWORTH—*The Redbreast Chasing the Butterfly.*

10
Stay, little cheerful Robin! stay,
And at my casement sing,
Though it should prove a farewell lay
And this our parting spring.
* * * * *
Then, little Bird, this boon confer,
Come, and my requiem sing,
Nor fail to be the harbinger
Of everlasting spring.
WORDSWORTH—*To a Redbreast. In Sickness.*

ROMANCE

11
Parent of golden dreams, Romance!
Auspicious queen of childish joys,
Who lead'st along, in airy dance,
Thy votive train of girls and boys.
BYRON—*To Romance.*

12
Romances paint at full length people's wooings,
But only give a bust of marriages:
For no one cares for matrimonial cooings.
There's nothing wrong in a connubial kiss.
Think you, if Laura had been Petrarch's wife,
He would have written sonnets all his life?
BYRON—*Don Juan.* Canto III. St. 8.

13
He loved the twilight that surrounds
The border-land of old romance;
Where glitter hauberk, helm, and lance,
And banner waves, and trumpet sounds,
And ladies ride with hawk on wrist,
And mighty warriors sweep along,
Magnified by the purple mist,
The dusk of centuries and of song.
LONGFELLOW—*Prelude to Tales of a Wayside Inn.* Pt. V. L. 130.

14
Romance is the poetry of literature.
MADAME NECKER.

15
Lady of the Mere,
Sole-sitting by the shores of old romance.
WORDSWORTH—*A Narrow Girdle of Rough Stones and Crags.*

ROOK

1
Those Rooks, dear, from morning till night,
They seem to do nothing but quarrel and fight,
And wrangle and jangle, and plunder.
D. M. MULOCK—*Thirty Years. The Blackbird and the Rooks.*

2
Invite the rook who high amid the boughs.
In early spring, his airy city builds,
And ceaseless caws amusive.
THOMSON—*The Seasons. Spring.* L. 756.

3
Where in venerable rows
Widely waving oaks enclose
The moat of yonder antique hall,
Swarm the rooks with clamorous call;
And, to the toils of nature true,
Wreath their capacious nests anew.
WARTON—*Ode X.*

ROME

4
Si fueris Romæ, Romano vivito more;
Si fueris alibi, vivito sicut ibi.
If you are at Rome live in the Roman style; if you are elsewhere live as they live elsewhere.
ST. AMBROSE to ST. AUGUSTINE. Quoted by JEREMY TAYLOR. *Ductor Dubitantium.* I. 1. 5.

5
When I am at Rome I fast as the Romans do; when I am at Milan I do not fast. So likewise you, whatever church you come to, observe the custom of the place, if you would neither give offence to others, nor take offence from them.
Another version of ST. AMBROSE's advice.

6
When I am at Rome, I fast on a Saturday: when I am at Milan I do not. Do the same. Follow the custom of the church where you are.
ST. AUGUSTINE gives this as the advice of ST. AMBROSE to him. See *Epistle to Januarius.* II. 18. Also *Epistle* 36.
(See also BURTON, CERVANTES)

7
Now conquering Rome doth conquered Rome inter,
And she the vanquished is, and vanquisher.
To show us where she stood there rests alone
Tiber; and that too hastens to be gone.
Learn, hence what fortune can. Towns glide away;
And rivers, which are still in motion, stay.
JOACHIM DU BELLAY—*Antiquitez de Rome.* (Third stanza of this poem taken from JANUS VITALIS.) Trans. by WILLIAM BROWNE, from a Latin version of the same by JANUS VITALIS—*In Urbem Romam Qualis est hodie.* See GORDON GOODWIN's ed. of Poems of WILLIAM BROWNE. Trans. also by SPENSER, in *Complaints.*

8
Every one soon or late comes round by Rome.
ROBERT BROWNING—*Ring and the Book.* V. 296.
(See also LA FONTAINE)

9
When they are at Rome, they do there as they see done.
BURTON—*Anatomy of Melancholy.* III. 4. 2.
(See also AUGUSTINE)

10
O Rome! my country! city of the soul!
BYRON—*Childe Harold.* Canto IV. St. 78.

11
When falls the Coliseum, Rome shall fall;
And when Rome falls—the World.
BYRON—*Childe Harold.* Canto IV St. 145.

12
You cheer my heart, who build as if Rome would be eternal.
AUGUSTUS CÆSAR to PISO. See PLUTARCH—*Apothegms.* "Eternal Rome" said by TIBULLUS. II. 5. 23. Repeated by AMMIANUS MARCELLINUS—*Rerum Gestarum.* XVI. Ch. X. 14.

13
Cuando á Roma fueres, haz como vieres.
When you are at Rome, do as you see.
CERVANTES—*Don Quixote.*
(See also AUGUSTINE)

14
Y á Roma por todo.
To Rome for everything.
CERVANTES—*Don Quixote.* 2. 13. 55.

15
Quod tantis Romana manus contexuit annis
Proditor unus iners angusto tempore vertit.
What Roman power slowly built, an unarmed traitor instantly overthrew.
CLAUDIANUS—*In Rufinum.* II. 52.

16
Veuve d'un peuple-roi, mais reine encore du monde.
[Rome] Widow of a King-people, but still queen of the world.
GABRIEL GILBERT—*Papal Rome.*

17
Rome, Rome, thou art no more
As thou hast been!
On thy seven hills of yore
Thou sat'st a queen.
MRS. HEMANS—*Roman Girl's Song.*

18
Omitte mirari beatæ
Fumum et opes strepitumque Romæ.
Cease to admire the smoke, wealth, and noise of prosperous Rome.
HORACE—*Carmina.* III. 29. 11.

19
In tears I tossed my coin from Trevi's edge.
A coin unsordid as a bond of love—
And, with the instinct of the homing dove,
I gave to Rome my rendezvous and pledge.
And when imperious Death
Has quenched my flame of breath,
Oh, let me join the faithful shades that throng that fount above.
ROBERT UNDERWOOD JOHNSON—*Italian Rhapsody.*

20
Tous chemins vont à Rome; ainsi nos concurrents
Crurent pouvoir choisir des sentiers différents.
All roads lead to Rome, but our antagonists think we should choose different paths.
LA FONTAINE—*Le Juge Arbitre. Fable XII.* 28. 4.
(See also BROWNING)

1
Rome was not built in a day.
Latin in PALINGENIUS. (1537) BEAUMONT AND FLETCHER—*Little French Lawyer*. Act I. Sc. 3. Same idea "No se ganó Zamora en una hora.—Zamora was not conquered in an hour." CERVANTES—*Don Quixote*. II. 23.

2
See the wild Waste of all-devouring years!
How Rome her own sad Sepulchre appears,
With nodding arches, broken temples spread!
The very Tombs now vanish'd like their dead!
POPE—*Moral Essays. Epistle to Addison.*

3
I am in Rome! Oft as the morning ray
Visits these eyes, waking at once I cry,
Whence this excess of joy? What has befallen me?
And from within a thrilling voice replies,
Thou art in Rome! A thousand busy thoughts
Rush on my mind, a thousand images;
And I spring up as girt to run a race!
SAM'L ROGERS—*Rome.*

4
I had rather be a dog, and bay the moon,
Than such a Roman.
Julius Cæsar. Act IV. Sc. 3. L. 27.

5
Utinam populus Romanus unam cervicem haberet!
Would that the Roman people had but one neck!
SUETONIUS. In *Life of Caligula* ascribes it to Caligula. SENECA and DION CASSIUS credit it to the same. Ascribed to NERO by others.

ROSE

Rosa

6
She wore a wreath of roses,
The night that first we met.
THOS. HAYNES BAYLY—*She Wore a Wreath of Roses.*

7
The rose that all are praising
Is not the rose for me.
THOS. HAYNES BAYLY—*The Rose That all are Praising.*

8
Go pretty rose, go to my fair,
Go tell her all I fain would dare,
Tell her of hope; tell her of spring,
Tell her of all I fain would sing,
Oh! were I like thee, so fair a thing.
MIKE BEVERLY—*Go Pretty Rose.*

9
Thus to the Rose, the Thistle:
Why art thou not of thistle-breed?
Of use thou'dst, then, be truly,
For asses might upon thee feed.
F. M. BODENSTEDT—*The Rose and Thistle.* Trans. from the German by FREDERICK RICORD.

10
The full-blown rose, mid dewy sweets
Most perfect dies.
MARIA BROOKS—*Written on Seeing Pharamond.*

11
This guelder rose, at far too slight a beck
Of the wind, will toss about her flower-apples.
E. B. BROWNING—*Aurora Leigh.* Bk. II.

12
O rose, who dares to name thee?
No longer roseate now, nor soft, nor sweet,
But pale, and hard, and dry, as stubblewheat,—
Kept seven years in a drawer, thy titles shame thee.
E. B. BROWNING—*A Dead Rose.*

13
'Twas a yellow rose,
By that south window of the little house,
My cousin Romney gathered with his hand
On all my birthdays, for me, save the last;
And then I shook the tree too rough, too rough,
For roses to stay after.
E. B. BROWNING—*Aurora Leigh.* Bk. VI.

14
And thus, what can we do,
Poor rose and poet too,
Who both antedate our mission
In an unprepared season?
E. B. BROWNING—*A Lay of the Early Rose.*

15
"For if I wait," said she,
"Till time for roses be,—
For the moss-rose and the musk-rose,
Maiden-blush and royal-dusk rose,—

"What glory then for me
In such a company?—
Roses plenty, roses plenty
And one nightingale for twenty?"
E. B. BROWNING—*A Lay of the Early Rose.*

16
Red as a rose of Harpocrate.
E. B. BROWNING—*Isobel's Child.*
(See also BURMANN under SECRECY)

17
You smell a rose through a fence:
If two should smell it, what matter?
E. B. BROWNING—*Lord Walter's Wife.*

18
A white rosebud for a guerdon.
E. B. BROWNING—*Romance of the Swan's Nest.*

19
All June I bound the rose in sheaves,
Now, rose by rose, I strip the leaves.
ROBERT BROWNING—*One Way of Love.*

20
Loveliest of lovely things are they
On earth that soonest pass away.
The rose that lives its little hour
Is prized beyond the sculptured flower.
BRYANT—*A Scene on the Banks of the Hudson.*

21
I'll pu' the budding rose, when Phœbus peeps in view,
For its like a baumy kiss o'er her sweet bonnie mou'!
BURNS—*The Posie.*

22
Yon rose-buds in the morning dew,
How pure amang the leaves sae green!
BURNS—*To Chloris.*

23
When love came first to earth, the Spring
Spread rose-beds to receive him.
CAMPBELL—*Song. When Love Came First to Earth.*

24
Roses were sette of swete savour,
With many roses that thei bere.
CHAUCER—*The Romaunt of the Rose.*

1
Je ne suis pas la rose, mais j'ai vécu pres d'elle.
I am not the rose, but I have lived near the rose.
Attributed to H. B. CONSTANT by A. HAYWARD in *Introduction to Letters of Mrs. Piozzi.* SAADI, the Persian poet, represents a lump of clay with perfume still clinging to it from the petals fallen from the rose-trees. In his *Gulistan.* (Rose Garden.)

2
Till the rose's lips grow pale
With her sighs.
ROSE TERRY COOKE—*Rêve Du Midi.*

3
I wish I might a rose-bud grow
And thou wouldst cull me from the bower,
To place me on that breast of snow
Where I should bloom a wintry flower.
DIONYSIUS.

4
O beautiful, royal Rose,
O Rose, so fair and sweet!
Queen of the garden art thou,
And I—the Clay at thy feet!
* * * *
Yet, O thou beautiful Rose!
Queen rose, so fair and sweet,
What were lover or crown to thee
Without the Clay at thy feet?
JULIA C. R. DORR—*The Clay to the Rose.*

5
It never will rain roses: when we want
To have more roses we must plant more trees.
GEORGE ELIOT—*Spanish Gypsy.* Bk. III.
(See also LOVEMAN under RAIN)

6
Oh, raise your deep-fringed lids that close
To wrap you in some sweet dream's thrall;
I am the spectre of the rose
You wore but last night at the ball.
GAUTIER—*Spectre of the Rose.* (From the French.) See WERNER's *Readings* No. 8.

7
In Heaven's happy bowers
There blossom two flowers,
One with fiery glow
And one as white as snow;
While lo! before them stands,
With pale and trembling hands,
A spirit who must choose
One, and one refuse.
R. W. GILDER—*The White and Red Rose.*

8
Pflücke Rosen, weil sie blühn,
Morgen ist nicht heut!
Keine Stunde lass entfliehn.
Morgen ist nicht heut.
Gather roses while they bloom,
To-morrow is yet far away.
Moments lost have no room
In to-morrow or to-day.
GLEIM—*Benutzung der Zeit.*
(See also HERRICK under TIME)

9
It is written on the rose
In its glory's full array:
Read what those buds disclose—
"Passing away."
FELICIA D. HEMANS—*Passing Away.*

10
Sweet rose, whose hue, angry and brave,
Bids the rash gazer wipe his eye,
Thy root is even in the grave,
And thou must die.
HERBERT—*Vertue.* St. 2.

11
Roses at first were white,
'Till they co'd not agree,
Whether my Sappho's breast
Or they more white sho'd be.
HERRICK—*Hesperides.* Found in DODD's *Epigrammatists.*

12
But ne'er the rose without the thorn.
HERRICK—*The Rose.*

13
He came and took me by the hand,
Up to a red rose tree,
He kept His meaning to Himself,
But gave a rose to me.

I did not pray Him to lay bare
The mystery to me,
Enough the rose was Heaven to smell,
And His own face to see.
RALPH HODGSON—*The Mystery.*

14
It was not in the winter
Our loving lot was cast:
It was the time of roses
We pluck'd them as we pass'd.
HOOD—*Ballad. It was not in the Winter.*

15
Poor Peggy hawks nosegays from street to street
Till—think of that who find life so sweet!—
She hates the smell of roses.
HOOD—*Miss Kilmansegg.*

16 And the guelder rose
In a great stillness dropped, and ever dropped,
Her wealth about her feet.
JEAN INGELOW—*Laurance.* Pt. III.

17
The roses that in yonder hedge appear
Outdo our garden-buds which bloom within;
But since the hand may pluck them every day,
Unmarked they bud, bloom, drop, and drift away.
JEAN INGELOW—*The Four Bridges.* St. 61.

18 The vermeil rose had blown
In frightful scarlet, and its thorns outgrown
Like spiked aloe.
KEATS—*Endymion.* Bk. I. L. 694.

19
But the rose leaves herself upon the brier,
For winds to kiss and grateful bees to feed.
KEATS—*On Fame.*

20
Woo on, with odour wooing me,
Faint rose with fading core;
For God's rose-thought, that blooms in thee,
Will bloom forevermore.
GEORGE MACDONALD—*Songs of the Summer Night.* Pt. III.

21
Mais elle était du mond, où les plus belles choses
Ont le pire destin;
Et Rose, elle a vécu ce que vivent les roses,
L'espace d'un matin.

But she bloomed on earth, where the most beautiful things have the saddest destiny;
And Rose, she lived as live the roses, for the space of a morning.
FRANÇOIS DE MALHERBE. In a letter of condolence to M. DU PERRIER on the loss of his daughter.

1
And I will make thee beds of roses,
And a thousand fragrant posies.
MARLOWE—*The Passionate Shepherd to his Love.* St. 3. Said to be written by SHAKESPEARE and MARLOWE.
(See also MERRY WIVES OF WINDSOR)

2
Flowers of all hue, and without thorn the rose.
MILTON—*Paradise Lost.* Bk. IV. L. 256.

3
Rose of the desert! thou art to me
An emblem of stainless purity,—
Of those who, keeping their garments white,
Walk on through life with steps aright.
D. M. MOIR—*The White Rose.*

4
While rose-buds scarcely show'd their hue,
But coyly linger'd on the thorn.
MONTGOMERY—*The Adventures of a Star.*

5
Two roses on one slender spray
In sweet communion grew,
Together hailed the morning ray
And drank the evening dew.
MONTGOMERY—*The Roses.*

6
Sometimes, when on the Alpine rose
The golden sunset leaves its ray,
So like a gem the flow'ret glows,
We thither bend our headlong way;
And though we find no treasure there,
We bless the rose that shines so fair.
MOORE—*The Crystal-Hunters.*

7
Long, long be my heart with such memories fill'd!
Like the vase, in which roses have once been distill'd—
You may break, you may shatter the vase if you will,
But the scent of the roses will hang round it still.
MOORE—*Farewell! but Whenever you Welcome the Hour.*
(See also CONSTANT)

8
There's a bower of roses by Bendemeer's stream,
And the nightingale sings round it all the day long,
In the time of my childhood 'twas like a sweet dream,
To sit in the roses and hear the bird's song.
MOORE—*Lalla Rookh. The Veiled Prophet of Khorassan.*

9
No flower of her kindred,
No rosebud is nigh,
To reflect back her blushes,
Or give sigh for sigh.
MOORE—*Last Rose of Summer.*

10
'Tis the last rose of summer,
Left blooming alone.
MOORE—*Last Rose of Summer.*

11
What would the rose with all her pride be worth,
Were there no sun to call her brightness forth?
MOORE—*Love Alone.*

12
Why do we shed the rose's bloom
Upon the cold, insensate tomb?
Can flowery breeze, or odor's breath,
Affect the slumbering chill of death?
MOORE—*Odes of Anacreon. Ode XXXII.*

13
Rose! thou art the sweetest flower,
That ever drank the amber shower;
Rose! thou art the fondest child
Of dimpled Spring, the wood-nymph wild.
MOORE—*Odes of Anacreon. Ode XLIV.*

14
Oh! there is naught in nature bright
Whose roses do not shed their light;
When morning paints the Orient skies,
Her fingers burn with roseate dyes.
MOORE—*Odes of Anacreon. Ode LV.*

15
The rose distils a healing balm
The beating pulse of pain to calm.
MOORE—*Odes of Anacreon. Ode LV.*

16
Rose of the Desert! thus should woman be
Shining uncourted, lone and safe, like thee.
MOORE—*Rose of the Desert.*

17
Rose of the Garden! such is woman's lot—
Worshipp'd while blooming—when she fades, forgot.
MOORE—*Rose of the Desert.*

18
Each Morn a thousand Roses brings, you say;
Yes, but where leaves the Rose of Yesterday?
OMAR KHAYYAM—*Rubaiyat.* FITZGERALD'S trans.
(See also VILLON under SNOW)

19
O rose! the sweetest blossom,
Of spring the fairest flower,
O rose! the joy of heaven.
The god of love, with roses
His yellow locks adorning,
Dances with the hours and graces.
J. G. PERCIVAL—*Anacreontic.* St. 2.

20
The sweetest flower that blows,
I give you as we part
For you it is a rose
For me it is my heart.
FREDERICK PETERSON—*At Parting.*

21
There was never a daughter of Eve but once, ere the tale of her years be done,
Shall know the scent of the Eden Rose, but once beneath the sun;
Though the years may bring her joy or pain, fame, sorrow or sacrifice,
The hour that brought her the scent of the Rose, she lived it in Paradise.
SUSAN K. PHILLIPS—*The Eden Rose.* Quoted by KIPLING in *Mrs. Hauksbee Sits it Out.* Published anonymously in *St. Louis Globe Democrat,* July 13, 1878.

1
There is no gathering the rose without being pricked by the thorns.
PILPAY—*The Two Travellers*. Ch. II. Fable VI.

2
Let opening roses knotted oaks adorn,
And liquid amber drop from every thorn.
POPE—*Autumn*. L. 36.

3
Die of a rose in aromatic pain.
POPE—*Essay on Man*. Ep. I. L. 200.

4
Like roses, that in deserts bloom and die.
POPE—*Rape of the Lock*. Canto IV. L. 158.
(See also CHAMBERLAYNE under OBSCURITY)

5
And when the parent-rose decays and dies,
With a resembling face the daughter-buds arise.
PRIOR—*Celia to Damon*.

6
We bring roses, beautiful fresh roses,
Dewy as the morning and coloured like the dawn;
Little tents of odour, where the bee reposes,
Swooning in sweetness of the bed he dreams upon.
THOS. BUCHANAN READ—*The New Pastoral*. Bk. VII. L. 51.

7
Die Rose blüht nicht ohne Dornen. Ja: wenn nur aber nicht die Dornen die Rose überlebten.
The rose does not bloom without thorns.
True: but would that the thorns did not outlive the rose.
JEAN PAUL RICHTER—*Titan*. *Zykel* 105.

8
The rose saith in the dewy morn,
I am most fair;
Yet all my loveliness is born
Upon a thorn.
CHRISTINA G. ROSSETTI—*Consider the Lilies of the Field*.

9
I watched a rose-bud very long
Brought on by dew and sun and shower,
Waiting to see the perfect flower:
Then when I thought it should be strong
It opened at the matin hour
And fell at even-song.
CHRISTINA G. ROSSETTI—*Symbols*.

10
The rose is fairest when 'tis budding new,
And hope is brightest when it dawns from fears;
The rose is sweetest wash'd with morning dew,
And love is loveliest when embalm'd in tears.
SCOTT—*Lady of the Lake*. Canto IV.

11
From off this brier pluck a white rose with me.
Henry VI. Pt. I. Act II. Sc. 4. L. 30.

12
Then will I raise aloft the milk-white rose,
With whose sweet smell the air shall be perfumed.
Henry VI. Pt. II. Act I. Sc. 1. L. 254.

13
There will we make our peds of roses,
And a thousand fragrant posies.
Merry Wives of Windsor. Act III. Sc. 1. L. 19. *Song*.
(See also MARLOWE)

14
Hoary-headed frosts
Fall in the fresh lap of the crimson rose.
Midsummer Night's Dream. Act II. Sc. 1. L. 107.

15
The red rose on triumphant brier.
Midsummer Night's Dream. Act III. Sc. 1. L. 96.

16
And the rose like a nymph to the bath addrest,
Which unveiled the depth of her glowing breast,
Till, fold after fold, to the fainting air,
The soul of her beauty and love lay bare.
SHELLEY—*The Sensitive Plant*. Pt. I.

17
Should this fair rose offend thy sight,
Placed in thy bosom bare,
'Twill blush to find itself less white,
And turn Lancastrian there.
JAMES SOMERVILLE—*The White Rose*. Other versions of traditional origin.

18
I am the one rich thing that morn
Leaves for the ardent noon to win;
Grasp me not, I have a thorn,
But bend and take my being in.
HARRIET PRESCOTT SPOFFORD—*Flower Songs. The Rose*.

19
It was nothing but a rose I gave her,—
Nothing but a rose
Any wind might rob of half its savor,
Any wind that blows.
* * * * *
Withered, faded, pressed between these pages,
Crumpled, fold on fold,—
Once it lay upon her breast, and ages
Cannot make it old!
HARRIET PRESCOTT SPOFFORD—*A Sigh*.

20
The year of the rose is brief;
From the first blade blown to the sheaf,
From the thin green leaf to the gold,
It has time to be sweet and grow old,
To triumph and leave not a leaf.
SWINBURNE—*The Year of the Rose*.

21
And half in shade and half in sun;
The Rose sat in her bower,
With a passionate thrill in her crimson heart.
BAYARD TAYLOR—*Poems of the Orient. The Poet in the East*. St. 5.

22
And is there any moral shut
Within the bosom of the rose?
TENNYSON—*The Day-Dream. Moral*.

23
The fairest things have fleetest end:
Their scent survives their close,
But the rose's scent is bitterness
To him that loved the rose!
FRANCIS THOMPSON—*Daisy*. St. 10.

24
I saw the rose-grove blushing in pride,
I gathered the blushing rose—and sigh'd—
I come from the rose-grove, mother,
I come from the grove of roses.
GIL VICENTE—*I Come from the Rose-grove, Mother*. Trans. by JOHN BOWRING.

1
Go, lovely Rose!
Tell her that wastes her time and me
That now she knows.
When I resemble her to thee,
How sweet and fair she seems to be.
EDMUND WALLER—*The Rose.*

2
How fair is the Rose! what a beautiful flower.
The glory of April and May!
But the leaves are beginning to fade in an hour,
And they wither and die in a day.
Yet the Rose has one powerful virtue to boast,
Above all the flowers of the field;
When its leaves are all dead, and fine colours are lost,
Still how sweet a perfume it will yield!
ISAAC WATTS—*The Rose.*

3
The rosebuds lay their crimson lips together.
AMELIA B. WELBY—*Hopeless Love.* St. 5.

4
Let us crown ourselves with rosebuds before they be withered.
Wisdom of Solomon. II. 8.

5
The budding rose above the rose full blown.
WORDSWORTH—*The Prelude.* Bk. XI.

6
Far off, most secret, and inviolate Rose,
Enfold me in my hour of hours; where those
Who sought thee in the Holy Sepulchre
Or in the wine vat, dwell beyond the stir
And tumult of defeated dreams.
W. B. YEATS—*The Secret Rose.*

ROSE, MUSK

Rosa Moschata

7
I saw the sweetest flower wild nature yields,
A fresh-blown musk-rose; 'twas the first that threw
Its sweets upon the summer.
KEATS—*To a Friend who Sent some Roses.*

8 And mid-May's eldest child,
The coming musk-rose, full of dewy wine,
The murmurous haunt of flies on summer eyes.
KEATS—*Ode to a Nightingale.*

ROSE, SWEETBRIER

(*Eglantine*), *Rosa Rubiginosa*

9
The fresh eglantine exhaled a breath,
Whose odours were of power to raise from death.
DRYDEN—*The Flower and the Leaf.* L. 96.

10
Wild-rose, Sweetbriar, Eglantine,
All these pretty names are mine,
And scent in every leaf is mine,
And a leaf for all is mine,
And the scent—Oh, that's divine!
Happy-sweet and pungent fine,
Pure as dew, and pick'd as wine.
LEIGH HUNT—*Songs and Chorus of the Flowers. Sweetbriar.*

11 Rain-scented eglantine
Gave temperate sweets to that well-wooing sun.
KEATS—*Endymion.* Bk. I. L. 100.

12
Its sides I'll plant with dew-sweet eglantine.
KEATS—*Endymion.* Bk. IV. L. 700.

13 As through the verdant maze
Of sweetbriar hedges I pursue my walk;
Or taste the smell of dairy.
THOMSON—*The Seasons. Spring.* L. 105.

14
The garden rose may richly bloom
In cultured soil and genial air,
To cloud the light of Fashion's room
Or droop in Beauty's midnight hair,
In lonelier grace, to sun and dew
The sweetbrier on the hillside shows
Its single leaf and fainter hue,
Untrained and wildly free, yet still a sister rose!
WHITTIER—*The Bride of Pennacook.* Pt. III. *The Daughter.*

ROSE, WILD

Rosa Lucida

15
A wild rose roofs the ruined shed,
And that and summer well agree.
COLERIDGE—*A Day Dream.*

16 A brier rose, whose buds
Yield fragrant harvest for the honey bee.
L. E. LANDON—*The Oak.* L. 17.

17
A waft from the roadside bank
Tells where the wild rose nods.
BAYARD TAYLOR—*The Guests of Night.*

ROSEMARY

Rosmarinus

18 Dreary rosmarye
That always mourns the dead.
HOOD—*Flowers.*

19 The humble rosemary
Whose sweets so thanklessly are shed
To scent the desert and the dead.
MOORE—*Lalla Rookh. Light of the Harem.*

20
There's rosemary, that's for remembrance.
Hamlet. Act IV. Sc. 5. L. 175.

ROYALTY

21
Ten poor men sleep in peace on one straw heap, as Saadi sings.
But the immensest empire is too narrow for two kings.
WM. R. ALGER—*Oriental Poetry. Elbow Room.*

22
Princes are like to heavenly bodies, which cause good or evil times; and which have much veneration, but no rest.
BACON—*Essays. Of Empire.*

23
Malheureuse France! Malheureux roi!
Unhappy France! Unhappy king!
ÉTIENNE BÉQUET. Heading in the *Journal des Débats*, when CHARLES X. was driven from the throne.

1
Ce n'est que lorsqu'il expira
Que le peuple, qui l'enterra, pleura.
And in the years he reigned; through all the country wide,
There was no cause for weeping, save when the good man died.
BERANGER—*Le Roi Yvetot.* Rendering of THACKERAY—*King of Brentford.*
(See also PEACOCK under EPITAPH)

2
Der König herrscht aber regiert nicht.
The king reigns but does not govern.
BISMARCK—*In a debate in the Reichstag.* Jan. 24, 1882. He denied the application of this maxim to Germany.
(See also HÉNAULT, THIERS)

3
The Prussian Sovereigns are in possession of a crown not by the grace of the people, but by God's grace.
BISMARCK—*Speech in the Prussian Parliament.* (1847)

4
St. George he was for England; St. Dennis was for France.
Sing, "Honi soit qui mal y pense."
Black-letter Ballad. London. (1512)

5
That the king can do no wrong is a necessary and fundamental principle of the English constitution.
BLACKSTONE. Bk. III. Ch. XVII.

6
The king never dies.
BLACKSTONE—*Commentaries.* IV. 249.

7 Many a crown
Covers bald foreheads.
E. B. BROWNING—*Aurora Leigh.* Bk. I. L. 754.

8
I loved no King since Forty One
When Prelacy went down,
A Cloak and Band I then put on,
And preached against the Crown.
SAMUEL BUTLER—*The Turn-Coat.* In Posthumous Works.

9
Whatever I can say or do,
I'm sure not much avails;
I shall still Vicar be of Bray,
Whichever side prevails.
SAMUEL BUTLER—*Tale of the Cobbler and the Vicar of Bray.* In Posthumous Works.

10
I dare be bold, you're one of those
Have took the covenant,
With cavaliers are cavaliers
And with the saints, a saint.
SAMUEL BUTLER—*Tale of the Cobbler and the Vicar of Bray.*

11
In good King Charles's golden days
When royalty no harm meant,
A zealous high-churchman was I,
And so I got preferment.
Vicar of Bray. English song. Written before 1710. Also said to have been written by an officer in George the First's army, Col. Fuller's regiment. The Vicar of Bray was said to be REV. SYMON SYMONDS; also DR. FRANCIS CASWELL. A Vicar of Bray, in Berkshire, Eng., was alternately Catholic and Protestant under Henry VIII., Edward VI., Mary, and Elizabeth. See FULLER—*Worthies of Berkshire.* SIMON ALEYN (ALLEN) named in BROM's *Letters from the Bodleian.* Vol. II. Pt. I. P. 100.

12
God bless the King—I mean the faith's defender;
God bless (no harm in blessing) the pretender;
But who the pretender is, or who is King—
God bless us all—that's quite another thing.
JOHN BYROM—*Miscellaneous Pieces.*

13
Every noble crown is, and on Earth will forever be, a crown of thorns.
CARLYLE—*Past and Present.* Bk. III. Ch. VIII.

14
Fallitur egregio quisquis sub principe credet
Servitutem. Nunquam libertas gratior extat
Quam sub rege pio.
That man is deceived who thinks it slavery to live under an excellent prince. Never does liberty appear in a more gracious form than under a pious king.
CLAUDIANUS—*De Laudibus Stilichonis.* III. 113.

15
'Tis a very fine thing to be father-in-law
To a very magnificent three-tailed bashaw.
GEORGE COLMAN (The Younger)—*Blue Beard.* Act III. Sc. 4.

16
La clémence est la plus belle marque
Qui fasse à l'univers connaître un vrai monarque.
Clemency is the surest proof of a true monarch.
CORNEILLE—*Cinna.* IV. 4.

17
I am monarch of all I survey,
My right there is none to dispute,
From the centre all round to the sea,
I am lord of the fowl and the brute.
COWPER—*Verses supposed to be written by Alexander Selkirk.*

18
Now let us sing, long live the king.
COWPER—*History of John Gilpin.*

19
And kind as kings upon their coronation day.
DRYDEN—*Fables. The Hind and the Panther.* Pt. I. L. 271.

20 A man's a man,
But when you see a king, you see the work
Of many thousand men.
GEORGE ELIOT—*Spanish Gypsy.* Bk. I.

21
Who made thee a prince and a judge over us?
Exodus. II. 14.

22
Tout citoyen est roi sous un roi citoyen.
Every citizen is king under a citizen king.
FAVART—*Les Trois Sultanes.* II. 3.

23
Es war ein König in Tule
Gar treu bis an das Grab,
Dem sterbend seine Buhle

Einen gold'nen Becher gab.
There was a king of Thule,
Was faithful till the grave,
To whom his mistress dying,
A golden goblet gave.
GOETHE—*Faust. The King of Thule.* BAYARD TAYLOR's trans.

1
Der Kaiser of dis Faderland,
Und Gott on high all dings commands,
We two—ach! Don't you understand?
Myself—und Gott.
A. M. R. GORDON (McGregor Rose)—*Kaiser & Co.* Later called *Hoch der Kaiser.* Pub. in Montreal *Herald,* Oct., 1897, after the Kaiser's Speech on the Divine Right of Kings. Recited by CAPTAIN COGHLAN at a banquet.

2
As yourselves your empires fall,
And every kingdom hath a grave.
WILLIAM HABINGTON—*Night.*

3
Elle gouvernait, mais elle ne régnait pas.
She governs but she does not reign.
HÉNAULT—*Memoirs.* 161. Said of Mme. des Ursins, favorite of PHILIP V. of Spain.
(See also BISMARCK)

4
The Royal Crown cures not the headache.
HERBERT—*Jacula Prudentum.*

5
The rule
Of the many is not well. One must be chief
In war and one the king.
HOMER—*Iliad.* Bk. II. L. 253. BRYANT'S trans.

6
Quidquid delirant reges, plectuntur Achivi.
Whenever monarchs err, the people are punished.
HORACE—*Epistles.* I. 2. 14.

7
On the king's gate the moss grew gray;
The king came not. They call'd him dead;
And made his eldest son, one day,
Slave in his father's stead.
HELEN HUNT JACKSON—*Coronation.*

8
God gives not kings the stile of Gods in vaine,
For on his throne his sceptre do they sway;
And as their subjects ought them to obey,
So kings should feare and serve their God againe.
KING JAMES—*Sonnet Addressed to his son, Prince Henry.*

9
Si la bonne foi était bannie du reste du monde, il faudrait qu'on la trouvât dans la bouche des rois.

Though good faith should be banished from the rest of the world, it should be found in the mouths of kings.
JEAN II. See *Biographie Universelle.*

10
The trappings of a monarchy would set up an ordinary commonwealth.
SAMUEL JOHNSON—*Life of Milton.*

11
Princes that would their people should do well
Must at themselves begin, as at the head;
For men, by their example, pattern out
Their imitations, and regard of laws:
A virtuous court a world to virtue draws.
BEN JONSON—*Cynthia's Revels.* Act V. Sc. 3.

12
A prince without letters is a Pilot without eyes. All his government is groping.
BEN JONSON—*Discoveries. Illiteratus. Princeps.*

13
They say Princes learn no art truly, but the art of horsemanship. The reason is, the brave beast is no flatterer. He will throw a Prince as soon as his groom.
BEN JONSON—*Discoveries. Illiteratus Princeps.*

14
Over all things certain, this is sure indeed,
Suffer not the old King, for we know the breed.
KIPLING—*The Old Issue.* In the *Five Nations.*

15
'Ave you 'eard o' the Widow at Windsor
With a hairy old crown on 'er 'ead?
She 'as ships on the foam—she 'as millions at 'ome,
An' she pays us poor beggars in red.
KIPLING—*The Widow at Windsor.*

16
La cour est comme un édifice bâti de marbre; je veux dire qu'elle est composée d'hommes fort durs mais fort polis.

The court is like a palace built of marble; I mean that it is made up of very hard but very polished people.
LA BRUYÈRE—*Les Caractères.* VIII.

17
Ah! vainest of all things
Is the gratitude of kings.
LONGFELLOW—*Belisarius.* St. 8.

18
Qui ne sait dissimuler, ne sait régner.
He who knows not how to dissimulate, can not reign.
LOUIS XI. See ROCHE ET CHASLES—*Hist. de France.* Vol. II. P. 30.

19
L'état c'est moi.
I am the State.
Attributed to LOUIS XIV of France. Probably taken from a phrase of BOSSUET's referring to the King: "tout l'état est en lui"; which may be freely translated: "he embodies the State."

20
Qui nescit dissimulare, nescit regnare.
He who knows how to dissimulate knows how to reign.
VICENTIUS LUPANUS—*De Magistrat. Franc.* Lib. I. See LIPSIUS—*Politica sive Civilis Doctrina.* Lib. IV. Cap. 14. CONRAD LYCOSTHENES—*Apopothegmata. De Simulatione & Dissimulatione.* BURTON—*Anatomy of Melancholy.* Pt. I. Sect. II. Mem. III. Subsec. 15. PALINGENIUS—*Zodiacus Vitæ.* Lib. IV. 684. Also given as a saying of EMPEROR FREDERICK I., (Barbarossa), LOUIS XI, and PHILIP II, of Spain. TACITUS—*Annales.* IV. 71.

21
A crown
Golden in show, is but a wreath of thorns,
Brings dangers, troubles, cares, and sleepless nights
To him who wears the regal diadem.
MILTON—*Paradise Regained.* Bk. II. L. 458.

1
His fair large front and eye sublime declared
Absolute rule; and hyacinthine locks
Round from his parted forelock manly hung
Clustering, but not beneath his shoulders broad.
MILTON—*Paradise Lost.* Bk. IV. L. 300.

2
'Tis so much to be a king, that he only is so by being so.
MONTAIGNE—*Essays. Of the Inconveniences of Greatness.*

3
A crown! what is it?
It is to bear the miseries of a people!
To hear their murmurs, feel their discontents,
And sink beneath a load of splendid care!
HANNAH MORE—*Daniel.* Pt. VI.

4
An nescis longos regibus esse manus?
Knowest thou not that kings have long hands?
OVID—*Heroides.* XVII. 166.

5
Est aliquid valida sceptra tenere manu.
It is something to hold the scepter with a firm hand.
OVID—*Remedia Amoris.* 480.

6
The King is dead! Long live the King!
PARDOE—*Life of Louis XIV.* Vol. III. P. 457.

7
But all's to no end, for the times will not mend
Till the King enjoys his own again.
MARTIN PARKER. *Upon Defacing of White-Hall.* (1645)

8
What is a king? a man condemn'd to bear
The public burthen of the nation's care.
PRIOR—*Solomon.* Bk. III. L. 275.

9
Put not your trust in princes.
Psalms. CXLVI. 3.

10
Savoir dissimuler est le savoir des rois.
To know how to dissemble is the knowledge of kings.
RICHELIEU—*Miranne.*

11
A merry monarch, scandalous and poor.
EARL OF ROCHESTER—*On the King.*

12
Here lies our sovereign lord, the king,
Whose word no man relies on,
Who never said a foolish thing,
And never did a wise one.
ROCHESTER. To CHARLES II. "That is very true, for my words are my own. My actions are my minister's." Answer of CHARLES II, according to the account in HUME's *History of England.* VIII. P. 312.

13
Here lies our mutton-looking king,
Whose word no man relied on,
Who never said a foolish thing,
Nor ever did a wise one.
Another version of ROCHESTER's Epitaph on CHARLES II, included in works of QUARLES.
(See also OVERBURY under WISDOM)

14
Wenn die Könige bau'n, haben die Kärrner zu thun.
When kings are building, draymen have something to do.
SCHILLER—*Kant und Seine Ausleger.*

15
For monarchs seldom sigh in vain.
SCOTT—*Marmion.* Canto V. St. 9.

16
O Richard! O my king!
The universe forsakes thee!
MICHEL JEAN SEDAINE—*Richard Cœur de Lion. Blondel's Song.*

17
Alieno in loco
Haud stabile regnum est.
The throne of another is not stable for thee.
SENECA—*Hercules Furens.* CCCXLIV.

18
Ars prima regni posse te invidiam pati.
The first art to be learned by a ruler is to endure envy.
SENECA—*Hercules Furens.* CCCLIII.

19
Omnes sub regno graviore regnum est.
Every monarch is subject to a mightier one.
SENECA—*Hercules Furens.* DCXIV.

20
His legs bestrid the ocean; his rear'd arm
Crested the world: his voice was propertied
As all the tuned spheres, and that to friends;
But when he meant to quail and shake the orb,
He was as rattling thunder.
Antony and Cleopatra. Act V. Sc. 2. L. 28.

21
The gates of monarchs
Are arch'd so high that giants may jet through
And keep their impious turbans on.
Cymbeline. Act III. Sc. 3. L. 4.

22
There's such divinity doth hedge a king,
That treason can but peep to what it would.
Hamlet. Act IV. Sc. 5. L. 123.

23
Uneasy lies the head that wears a crown.
Henry IV. Pt. II. Act III. Sc. 1. L. 31.

24
Every subject's duty is the king's; but every subject's soul is his own.
Henry V. Act IV. Sc. 1. L. 186.

25
And fearless minds climb soonest unto crowns.
Henry VI. Pt. III. Act IV. Sc. 7. L. 63.

26
O, how wretched
Is that poor man that hangs on princes' favors!
There is, betwixt that smile we would aspire to,
That sweet aspect of princes, and their ruin,
More pangs and fears than wars and women have;
And when he falls, he falls like Lucifer,
Never to hope again.
Henry VIII. Act III. Sc. 2. L. 366.

27
She had all the royal makings of a queen;
As holy oil, Edward Confessor's crown,
The rod, and bird of peace, and all such emblems
Laid nobly on her.
Henry VIII. Act IV. Sc. 1. L. 87.

1
Ay, every inch a king.
King Lear. Act IV. Sc. 6. L. 109.

2 The king-becoming graces,
As justice, verity, temperance, stableness,
Bounty, perseverance, mercy, lowliness,
Devotion, patience, courage, fortitude,
I have no relish of them.
Macbeth. Act IV. Sc. 3. L. 91.

3
A substitute shines brightly as a king
Until a king be by, and then his state
Empties itself, as doth an inland brook
Into the main waters.
Merchant of Venice. Act V. Sc. 1. L. 94.

4
We are enforc'd to farm our royal realm;
The revenue whereof shall furnish us
For our affairs in hand.
Richard II. Act I. Sc. 4. L. 45.

5 Let us sit upon the ground
And tell sad stories of the death of kings:
How some have been depos'd, some slain in war,
Some haunted by the ghosts they have depos'd.
Some poison'd by their wives, some sleeping kill'd,
All murder'd.
Richard II. Act III. Sc. 2. L. 155.

6
Yet looks he like a king; behold, his eye,
As bright as is the eagle's, lightens forth
Controlling majesty.
Richard II. Act III. Sc. 3. L. 68.

7
I give this heavy weight from off my head,
And this unwieldy sceptre from my hand,
The pride of kingly sway from out my heart;
With mine own tears I wash away my value,
With mine own hands I give away my crown,
With mine own tongue deny my sacred state,
With mine own breath release all duteous oaths.
Richard II. Act IV. Sc. 1. L. 204.

8
The king's name is a tower of strength,
Which they upon the adverse party want.
Richard III. Act V. Sc. 3. L. 12.

9
Kings are like stars—they rise and set, they have
The worship of the world, but no repose.
SHELLEY—*Hellas. Mahmud to Hassan.* L. 195.

10
Hail, glorious edifice, stupendous work!
God bless the Regent, and the Duke of York!
HORACE AND JAMES SMITH—*Rejected Addresses. Loyal Effusion.* L. 1.

11
A prince, the moment he is crown'd,
Inherits every virtue sound,
As emblems of the sovereign power,
Like other baubles in the Tower:
Is generous, valiant, just, and wise,
And so continues till he dies.
SWIFT—*On Poetry.* L. 191.

12
Hener was the hero-king,
Heaven-born, dear to us,
Showing his shield
A shelter for peace.
ESAIAS TEGNÉR—*Fridthjof's Saga.* Canto XXI. St. 7.

13
Broad-based upon her people's will,
And compassed by the inviolate sea.
TENNYSON—*To the Queen.* St. 9.
(See also WORDSWORTH)

14
In that fierce light which beats upon a throne.
TENNYSON—*Idylls of the King. Dedication.* L. 26.

15
Titles are abolished; and the American Republic swarms with men claiming and bearing them.
THACKERAY—*Round Head Papers. On Ribbons.*

16
Le roi règne, il ne gouverne pas.
The king reigns but does not govern.
THIERS. In an early number of the *National*, a newspaper under the direction of himself and his political friends six months before the dissolution of the monarchy. July 1, 1830. JAN ZAMOYSKI, in the Polish and Hungarian Diets.
(See also BISMARCK)

17
Le premier qui fut roi, fut un soldat heureux;
Qui sert bien son pays, n'a pas besoin d'aïeux.
The first king was a successful soldier;
He who serves well his country has no need of ancestors.
VOLTAIRE—*Mérope.* I. 3.

18
Hail to the crown by Freedom shaped—to gird
An English sovereign's brow! and to the throne
Whereon he sits! whose deep foundations lie
In veneration and the people's love.
WORDSWORTH—*Excursion.* Bk. IV.
(See also TENNYSON)

19
A partial world will listen to my lays,
While Anna reigns, and sets a female name
Unrival'd in the glorious lists of fame.
YOUNG—*Force of Religion.* Bk. I. L. 6.

RUIN

20
Should the whole frame of nature round him break
In ruin and confusion hurled,
He, unconcerned, would hear the mighty crack,
And stand secure amidst a falling world.
ADDISON—*Horace. Ode III.* Bk. III.

21
And when 'midst fallen London they survey
The stone where Alexander's ashes lay,
Shall own with humble pride the lesson just
By Time's slow finger written in the dust.
MRS. BARBAULD—*Eighteen Hundred and Eleven.*
(See also GOLDSMITH, LONDON MAGAZINE, MACAULAY, SHELLEY, VOLNEY, WALPOLE, WHITE)

22
There is a temple in ruin stands,
Fashion'd by long forgotten hands:
Two or three columns, and many a stone,
Marble and granite, with grass o'ergrown!
BYRON—*Siege of Corinth.* St. 18.

23
While in the progress of their long decay,
Thrones sink to dust, and nations pass away.
EARL OF CARLISLE—*On the Ruins of Pæstum.*
Same idea in POPE'S *Messiah.*

1
What cities, as great as this, have . . . promised themselves immortality! Posterity can hardly trace the situation of some. The sorrowful traveller wanders over the awful ruins of others. . . . Here stood their citadel, but now grown over with weeds; there their senate-house, but now the haunt of every noxious reptile; temples and theatres stood here, now only an undistinguished heap of ruins.

GOLDSMITH—*The Bee.* No. IV. *A City Night-Piece.* (1759)

(See also BARBAULD)

2
The ruins of himself! now worn away
With age, yet still majestic in decay.

HOMER—*Odyssey.* Bk. XXIV. L. 271. POPE'S trans.

3
For, to make deserts, God, who rules mankind,
Begins with kings, and ends the work by wind.

VICTOR HUGO—*The Vanished City.*

4
History fades into fable; fact becomes clouded with doubt and controversy; the inscription moulders from the tablet: the statue falls from the pedestal. Columns, arches, pyramids, what are they but heaps of sand; and their epitaphs, but characters written in the dust?

IRVING—*The Sketch Book. Westminster Abbey.*

5
Babylon is fallen, is fallen.

Isaiah. XXI. 9.

6
When I have been indulging this thought I have, in imagination, seen the Britons of some future century, walking by the banks of the Thames, then overgrown with weeds and almost impassable with rubbish. The father points to his son where stood St. Paul's, the Monument, the Bank, the Mansion House, and other places of the first distinction.

London Magazine, 1745. Article, *Humorous Thoughts on the Removal of the Seat of Empire and Commerce.*

(See also BARBAULD)

7
Gaudensque viam fecisse ruina.
And rejoicing that he has made his way by ruin.

LUCANUS—*Pharsalia.* Bk. I. 150. (Referring to Julius Cæsar.)

8
She [the Roman Catholic Church] may still exist in undiminished vigour, when some traveller from New Zealand shall, in the midst of a vast solitude, take his stand on a broken arch of London Bridge to sketch the ruins of St. Paul's.

MACAULAY—*Ranke's History of the Popes.* Same idea in his Review of MITFORD'S *Greece.* Last Par. (1824) Also in his Review of MILL'S *Essay on Government.* (1829) Same thought also in *Poems of a Young Nobleman lately deceased*—supposed to be written by THOMAS, second LORD LYTTLETON, describing particularly the State of England, and the once flourishing City of London. In a letter from an American Traveller, dated from the Ruinous Portico of St. Paul's, in the year 2199, to a friend settled in Boston, the Metropolis of the Western Empire. (1771) The original said to be taken from LOUIS S. MERCIER—*L'An Deux Mille Quatre Cent-Quarante.* Written 1768, pub. 1770. Disowned in part by his executors.

(See also BARBAULD)

9
For such a numerous host
Fled not in silence through the frighted deep
With ruin upon ruin, rout on rout,
Confusion worse confounded.

MILTON—*Paradise Lost.* Bk. II. L. 993.

10
Prostrate the beauteous ruin lies; and all
That shared its shelter, perish in its fall.

WM. PITT—In *Poetry of the Anti-Jacobin.*

11
In the firm expectation that when London shall be a habitation of bitterns, when St. Paul and Westminster Abbey shall stand shapeless and nameless ruins in the midst of an unpeopled marsh, when the piers of Waterloo Bridge shall become the nuclei of islets of reeds and osiers, and cast the jagged shadows of their broken arches on the solitary stream, some Transatlantic commentator will be weighing in the scales of some new and now unimagined system of criticism the respective merits of the Bells and the Fudges and their historians.

SHELLEY—*Dedication to Peter Bell the Third.*

(See also BARBAULD)

12
Red ruin and the breaking-up of all.

TENNYSON—*Idylls of the King. Guinevere.* Fifth line.

13
Behold this ruin! 'Twas a skull
Once of ethereal spirit full!
This narrow cell was Life's retreat;
This place was Thought's mysterious seat!
What beauteous pictures fill'd that spot,
What dreams of pleasure, long forgot!
Nor Love, nor Joy, nor Hope, nor Fear,
Has left one trace, one record here.

ANNA JANE VARDILL (Mrs. James Niven.) Appeared in *European Magazine,* Nov., 1816, with signature V. Since said to have been found near a skeleton in the Royal College of Surgeons, Lincoln's Inn, London. Falsely claimed for J. D. GORDMAN. ROBERT PHILIP claims it in a newspaper pub. 1826.

14
Etiam quæ sibi quisque timebat
Unius in miseri exitium conversa tulere.

What each man feared would happen to himself, did not trouble him when he saw that it would ruin another.

VERGIL—*Æneid.* II. 130.

15
Who knows but that hereafter some traveller like myself will sit down upon the banks of the Seine, the Thames, or the Zuyder Zee, where now, in the tumult of enjoyment, the heart and the eyes are too slow to take in the multitude of sensations? Who knows but he will sit down solitary amid silent ruins, and weep a people inurned and their greatness changed into an empty name?

VOLNEY—*Ruins.* Ch. II.

(See also BARBAULD)

1
The next Augustan age will dawn on the other side of the Atlantic. There will, perhaps, be a Thucydides at Boston, a Xenophon at New York, in time a Vergil at Mexico, and a Newton at Peru. At last some curious traveller from Lima will visit England, and give a description of the ruins of St. Paul's, like the editions of Balbec and Palmyra.
HORACE WALPOLE—*Letter to* HORACE MANN. Nov. 24, 1774.
(See also BARBAULD)

2 I do love these ancient ruins.
We never tread upon them but we set
Our foot upon some reverend history.
JOHN WEBSTER—*The Duchess of Malfi.* Act V. Sc. 3.

3
Where now is Britain?
* * * *
Even as the savage sits upon the stone
That marks where stood her capitols, and hears
The bittern booming in the weeds, he shrinks
From the dismaying solitude.
HENRY KIRKE WHITE—*Time.*
(See also BARBAULD)

4 Final Ruin fiercely drives
Her ploughshare o'er creation.
YOUNG—*Night Thoughts.* Night IX. L. 167.
(See also BURNS under DAISY)

RUMOR

5
Vana quoque ad veros accessit fama timores.
Idle rumors were also added to well-founded apprehensions.
LUCAN—*Pharsalia.* I. 469.

6
Hi narrata ferunt alio; mensuraque ficti
Crescit et auditus aliquid novus adjicit auctor.
Some report elsewhere whatever is told them; the measure of fiction always increases, and each fresh narrator adds something to what he has heard.
OVID—*Metamorphoses.* XII. 57.

7
Nam inimici famam non ita ut nata est ferunt.
Enemies carry a report in form different from the original.
PLAUTUS—*Persa.* III. 1. 23.

8
The flying rumours gather'd as they roll'd,
Scarce any tale was sooner heard than told;
And all who told it added something new.
And all who heard it made enlargements too.
POPE—*Temple of Fame.* L. 468.

9
I cannot tell how the truth may be;
I say the tale as 'twas said to me.
SCOTT—*Lay of the Last Minstrel.* Canto II. St 22.

10 I will be gone:
That pitiful rumour may report my flight,
To consolate thine ear.
All's Well That Ends Well. Act III. Sc. 2. L. 129.

11 Rumour is a pipe
Blown by surmises, jealousies, conjectures,
And of so easy and so plain a stop
That the blunt monster with uncounted heads,
The still-discordant wavering multitude,
Can play upon it.
Henry IV. Pt. II. Act I. Induction. L. 15.

12
Rumour doth double, like the voice and echo,
The numbers of the fear'd.
Henry IV. Pt. II. Act III. Sc. 1. L. 97.

13
The rolling fictions grow in strength and size,
Each author adding to the former lies.
SWIFT—*Tr. of Ovid. Examiner,* No. 15.

14
What some invent the rest enlarge.
SWIFT—*Journal of a Modern Lady.*

15
Ad calamitatem quilibet rumor valet.
Every rumor is believed against the unfortunate.
SYRUS—*Maxims.*

16
Haud semper erret fama; aliquando et elegit.
Rumor does not always err; it sometimes even elects a man.
TACITUS—*Agricola.* IX.

17
There is nothing which cannot be perverted by being told badly.
TERENCE—*Phormio.* Act IV.

18
Tattlers also and busybodies, speaking things which they ought not.
I Timothy. V. 13.

19
Extemplo Libyæ magnas it Fama per urbes:
Fama malum quo non velocius ullum;
Mobilitate viget, viresque acquirit eundo;
Parva metu primo; mox sese attollit in auras,
Ingrediturque solo, et caput inter nubilia condit.
* * * * * *
Monstrum, horrendum ingens; cui quot sunt corpore plumæ
Tot vigiles oculi subter, mirabile dictu,
Tot linguæ, totidem ora sonant, tot subrigit aures.
Straightway throughout the Libyan cities flies rumor;—the report of evil things than which nothing is swifter; it flourishes by its very activity and gains new strength by its movements; small at first through fear, it soon raises itself aloft and sweeps onward along the earth. Yet its head reaches the clouds. * * * A huge and horrid monster covered with many feathers: and for every plume a sharp eye, for every pinion a biting tongue. Everywhere its voices sound, to everything its ears are open.
VERGIL—*Æneid.* IV. 173.

20
Fama volat parvam subito vulgata per urbem.
The rumor forthwith flies abroad, dispersed throughout the small town.
VERGIL—*Æneid.* VIII. 554.

21
Linguæ centum sunt, oraque centum
Ferrea vox.
It (rumour) has a hundred tongues, a hundred mouths, a voice of iron.
VERGIL—*Georgics.* II. 44. (Adapted.)

S

SABBATH

1
On Sundays, at the matin-chime,
The Alpine peasants, two and three,
Climb up here to pray;
Burghers and dames, at summer's prime,
Ride out to church from Chamberry,
Dight with mantles gay,
But else it is a lonely time
Round the Church of Brou.
MATTHEW ARNOLD—*The Church of Brou.* II. St. 3.

2
Thou art my single day, God lends to leaven
What were all earth else, with a feel of heaven.
ROBERT BROWNING—*Pippa Passes.* Sc. 1.

3
Of all the days that's in the week,
I dearly love but one day,
And that's the day that comes betwixt
A Saturday and Monday.
HENRY CAREY—*Sally in Our Alley.*

4
How still the morning of the hallow'd day!
Mute is the voice of rural labour, hush'd
The ploughboy's whistle, and the milkmaid's song.
JAMES GRAHAME—*The Sabbath. Song.*

5
Gently on tiptoe Sunday creeps,
Cheerfully from the stars he peeps,
Mortals are all asleep below,
None in the village hears him go;
E'en chanticleer keeps very still,
For Sunday whispered, 'twas his will.
JOHN PETER HEBEL—*Sunday Morning.*

6
Sundaies observe: think when the bells do chime,
'Tis angel's musick; therefore come not late.
HERBERT—*Temple. The Church Porch.* St. 65.

7
The Sundaies of man's life,
Thredded together on time's string,
Make bracelets to adorn the wife
Of the eternal, glorious King.
On Sunday heaven's gates stand ope;
Blessings are plentiful and rife.
More plentiful than hope.
HERBERT—*Temple. The Church. Sunday.*

8
Now, really, this appears the common case
Of putting too much Sabbath into Sunday—
But what is your opinion, Mrs. Grundy?
HOOD—*An Open Question.* St. 1.

9
Day of the Lord, as all our days should be!
LONGFELLOW—*Christus.* Pt. III. *John Endicott.* Act I. Sc. 2.

10
The Sabbath was made for man, and not man for the Sabbath.
Mark. II. 27.

11
So sang they, and the empyrean rung
With Hallelujahs. Thus was Sabbath kept.
MILTON—*Paradise Lost.* Bk. VII. L. 632.

12
For, bless the gude mon, gin he had his ain way,
He'd na let a cat on the Sabbath say "mew;"
Nae birdie maun whistle, nae lambie maun play,
An' Phœbus himsel' could na travel that day,
As he'd find a new Joshua in Andie Agnew.
MOORE—*Sunday Ethics.* St. 3.

13
See Christians, Jews, one heavy sabbath keep,
And all the western world believe and sleep.
POPE—*Dunciad.* Bk. III. L. 99.

14
E'en Sunday shines no Sabbath day to me.
POPE—*Epistle to Dr. Arbuthnot. Prologue to the Satires.* L. 12.

15
The sabbaths of Eternity,
One sabbath deep and wide.
TENNYSON—*St. Agnes' Eve.* St. 3.

SACRIFICE

16
What millions died—that Cæsar might be great!
CAMPBELL—*Pleasures of Hope.* Pt. II.

17
Sacrifice to the Graces.
DIOGENES LAERTIUS. Bk. IV. 6. LORD CHESTERFIELD—*Letter.* March 9, 1748.
(See also PLUTARCH, VOLTAIRE)

18
He is brought as a lamb to the slaughter.
Isaiah. LIII. 7.

19
Sacrifice to the Muses.
PLUTARCH—*Banquet of the Seven Wise Men.*

20
Plato used to say to Xenocrates the philosopher, who was rough and morose, "Good Xenocrates, sacrifice to the Graces."
PLUTARCH—*Life of Marius.*

21
The ancients recommended us to sacrifice to the Graces, but Milton sacrificed to the Devil.
VOLTAIRE. Of Milton's Genius.

SADNESS

22
Child of mortality, whence comest thou? Why is thy countenance sad, and why are thine eyes red with weeping?
ANNA LETITIA BARBAULD—*Hymns in Prose.* XIII.

23
Of all tales 'tis the saddest—and more sad,
Because it makes us smile.
BYRON—*Don Juan.* Canto XIII. St. 9.

24
A feeling of sadness and longing,
That is not akin to pain,
And resembles sorrow only
As the mist resembles the rain.
LONGFELLOW—*The Day is Done.* St. 3.

25
Yet be sad, good brothers,
* * * * *
Sorrow so royally in you appears,
That I will deeply put the fashion on.
Henry IV. Pt. II. Act V. Sc. 2. L. 49.

1
We look before and after,
And pine for what is not,
Our sincerest laughter
With some pain is fraught:
Our sweetest songs are those that tell of saddest thought.
SHELLEY—*To a Skylark*. St. 18.

2
'Tis impious in a good man to be sad.
YOUNG—*Night Thoughts*. Night IV. L. 676.

SAFFLOWER

Carthamus

3
And the saffron flower
Clear as a flame of sacrifice breaks out.
JEAN INGELOW—*The Doom*. Bk. II.

SAILORS (See NAVY)

SAND-PIPER

4
Across the narrow beach we flit,
One little sand-piper and I;
And fast I gather, bit by bit,
The scattered drift-wood, bleached and dry,
The wild waves reach their hands for it,
The wild wind raves, the tide runs high,
As up and down the beach we flit,
One little sand-piper and I.
CELIA THAXTER—*The Sand-Piper*.

SATIRE

5
Why should we fear; and what? The laws?
They all are armed in virtue's cause;
And aiming at the self-same end,
Satire is always virtue's friend.
CHURCHILL—*Ghost*. Bk. III. L. 943.

6
Unless a love of virtue light the flame,
Satire is, more than those he brands, to blame;
He hides behind a magisterial air
His own offences, and strips others' bare.
COWPER—*Charity*. L. 490.

7
Difficile est satiram non scribere.
It is difficult not to write satire.
JUVENAL—*Satires*. I. 29.

8
Men are more satirical from vanity than from malice.
LA ROCHEFOUCAULD—*Maxims*. No. 508.

9
Satire should, like a polished razor keen,
Wound with a touch that's scarcely felt or seen.
Thine is an oyster knife, that hacks and hews;
The rage but not the talent to abuse.
LADY MARY WORTLEY MONTAGU—*To the Imitator of the First Satire of Horace*. (Pope.)

10
I wear my Pen as others do their Sword.
To each affronting sot I meet, the word
Is *Satisfaction:* straight to thrusts I go,
And pointed satire runs him through and through.
JOHN OLDHAM—*Satire upon a Printer*. L. 35.

11
Damn with faint praise, assent with civil leer,
And without sneering, teach the rest to sneer;
Willing to wound, and yet afraid to strike,
Just hint a fault, and hesitate dislike;
Alike reserv'd to blame, or to commend,
A tim'rous foe, and a suspicious friend.
POPE—*Prologue to Satires*. L. 201.
(See also WYCHERLEY under PRAISE)

12
Satire or sense, alas! Can Sporus feel?
Who breaks a butterfly upon a wheel?
POPE—*Prologue to Satires*. L. 307. ("Sporus," LORD JOHN HERVEY.)

13
There are, to whom my satire seems too bold;
Scarce to wise Peter complaisant enough,
And something said of Chartres much too rough.
POPE—*Second Book of Horace*. Satire I. L. 2.

14
Satire's my weapon, but I'm too discreet
To run amuck and tilt at all I meet.
POPE—*Second Book of Horace*. Satire I. L. 71.

15
It is a pretty mocking of the life.
Timon of Athens. Act I. Sc. 1. L. 35.

16
La satire ment sur les gens de lettres pendant leur vie, et l'éloge ment après leur mort.
Satire lies about literary men while they live and eulogy lies about them when they die.
VOLTAIRE—*Lettre à Bordes*. Jan. 10, 1769.

SATISFACTION

17
Il plaît à tout le monde et ne saurait se plaire.
He [Molière] pleases every one but can not please himself.
BOILEAU—*Satires*. II.

18
Nul n'est content de sa fortune;
Ni mécontent de son esprit.
No one is satisfied with his fortune, nor dissatisfied with his intellect.
DESHOULIÈRES.

19
Multa petentibus
Desunt multa.
Bene est, cui Deus obtulit
Parca, quod satis est manu.
Those who seek for much are left in want of much. Happy is he to whom God has given, with sparing hand, as much as is enough.
HORACE—*Carmina*. Bk. III. 16. 42.

20
Ohe! jam satis est.
Now, that's enough.
HORACE—*Epistles*. I. 5. 12. MARTIAL—*Epigrams*. IV. 91. 1.

21
Sed tacitus pasci si posset corvus, haberet
Plus dapis, et rixæ multo minus invidiæque.
If the crow had been satisfied to eat his prey in silence, he would have had more meat and less quarreling and envy.
HORACE—*Epistles*. I. 17. 50.

22
Les délicats sont malheureux,
Rien ne saurait les satisfaire.
The fastidious are unfortunate: nothing can satisfy them.
LA FONTAINE—*Fables*. II. 1.

1
Est bien fou du cerveau
Qui prétend contenter tout le monde et son père.

He is very foolish who aims at satisfying all the world and his father.

LA FONTAINE—*Fables*. III. 1.

2
My cup runneth over.

Psalms. XXIII. 5.

3
Mach' es Wenigen recht; vielen gefallen ist schlimm.

Satisfy a few to please many is bad.

SCHILLER—*Votivtafeln*.

4
Nullius boni sine sociis jucunda possessio est.

There is no satisfaction in any good without a companion.

SENECA—*Epistolæ Ad Lucilium*. VI.

5
He is well paid that is well satisfied.

Merchant of Venice. Act IV. Sc. 1. L. 415.

6
Enough is as good as a feast.

JOSHUA SYLVESTER—*Works*. (1611)

7
Give me, indulgent gods! with mind serene,
And guiltless heart, to range the sylvan scene;
No splendid poverty, no smiling care,
No well-bred hate, or servile grandeur, there.

YOUNG—*Love of Fame*. Satire I. L. 235.

SCANDAL (See also GOSSIP)

8
Dead scandals form good subjects for dissection.

BYRON—*Don Juan*. Canto I. St. 31.

9
To converse with Scandal is to play at Losing Loadum, you must lose a good name to him, before you can win it for yourself.

CONGREVE—*Love for Love*. Act I. Sc. 2. ("Losing Loadum" an old game which one plays to lose tricks.)

10
Assail'd by scandal and the tongue of strife,
His only answer was a blameless life;
And he that forged, and he that threw the dart,
Had each a brother's interest in his heart.

COWPER—*Hope*. L. 570.

11
And though you duck them ne'er so long,
Not one salt drop e'er wets their tongue;
'Tis hence they scandal have at will,
And that this member ne'er lies still.

GAY—*The Mad Dog*.

12
And there's a lust in man no charm can tame
Of loudly publishing our neighbour's shame;
On eagles' wings immortal scandals fly,
While virtuous actions are but borne to die.

JUVENAL—*Satires*. IX. HARVEY'S trans.

13
Conscia mens recti famæ mendacia risit:
Sed nos in vitium credula turba sumus.

The mind conscious of innocence despises false reports: but we are a set always ready to believe a scandal.

OVID—*Fasti*. IV. 311.

14
The mightier man, the mightier is the thing
What makes him honour'd, or begets him hate;
For greatest scandal waits on greatest state.

Rape of Lucrece. L. 1,004.

15
He rams his quill with scandal and with scoff,
But 'tis so very foul, it won't go off.

YOUNG—*Epistles to Pope*. Ep. I. L. 199.

SCHELD (RIVER)

16
Remote, unfriended, melancholy, slow,
Or by the lazy Scheld or wandering Po!

GOLDSMITH—*The Traveller*. L. 1.

SCHOOL (See EDUCATION, TEACHING)

SCHUYLKILL (RIVER)

17
Alone by the Schuylkill a wanderer rov'd,
And bright were its flowery banks to his eye;
But far, very far, were the friends that he lov'd.
And he gaz'd on its flowery banks with a sigh.

MOORE—*Lines Written on Leaving Philadelphia*.

SCIENCE

18
'Twas thus by the glare of false science betray'd,
That leads to bewilder, and dazzles to blind.

BEATTIE—*The Hermit*.

19
O star-eyed Science, hast thou wander'd there,
To waft us home the message of despair?

CAMPBELL—*Pleasures of Hope*. Pt. II. L. 325.

20
Respectable Professors of the Dismal Science.

CARLYLE — *Latter Day Pamphlets*. No. 1. (1850)

21
What we might call, by way of Eminence, the Dismal Science.

CARLYLE—*The Nigger Question*.

22
Philosophia vero omnium mater artium.

Philosophy is true mother of the arts. (Science)

CICERO—*Tusculum Disp*. Bk. I.

23
There are very few persons who pursue science with true dignity.

SIR HUMPHREY DAVY—*Consolations in Travel. Dialogue* V. *The Chemical Philosopher*.

24
Wissenschaft und Kunst gehören der Welt an, und vor ihnen verschwinden die Schranken der Nationalität.

Science and art belong to the whole world, and before them vanish the barriers of nationality.

GOETHE—*In a conversation with a German historian*. (1813)

25
While bright-eyed Science watches round.

GRAY—*Ode for Music. Chorus*. L. 11.

26
Science is the topography of ignorance.

HOLMES—*Medical Essays*. 211.

27
For science is * * * like virtue, its own exceeding great reward.

CHAS. KINGSLEY—*Health and Education. Science*.

1
The science of fools with long memories.
PLANCHÉ—*Preliminary Observations. Pursuivant of Arms.* Speaking of Heraldry.

2
How index-learning turns no student pale,
Yet holds the eel of science by the tail.
POPE—*Dunciad.* Bk. I. L. 279.
(See also SMOLLETT)

3
One science only will one genius fit,
So vast is art, so narrow human wit.
POPE—*Essay on Criticism.* Pt. I. L. 60.

4
To the natural philosopher, to whom the whole extent of nature belongs, all the individual branches of science constitute the links of an endless chain, from which not one can be detached without destroying the harmony of the whole.
FRIEDRICH SCHOEDLER—*Treasury of Science. Astronomy.*

5
A mere index hunter, who held the eel of science by the tail.
SMOLLETT—*Peregrine Pickle.* Ch. XLIII.
(See also POPE)

6
Science is organised knowledge.
SPENCER—*Education.* Ch. II.

7
Science when well digested is nothing but good sense and reason.
STANISLAUS (King of Poland)—*Maxims.* No. 43.

8
Science falsely so called.
I Timothy. VI. 20.

9
But beyond the bright searchlights of science,
Out of sight of the windows of sense,
Old riddles still bid us defiance,
Old questions of Why and of Whence.
W. C. D. WHETHAM—*Recent Development of Physical Science.* P. 10.

SCORN

10
So let him stand, through ages yet unborn,
Fix'd statue on the pedestal of Scorn.
BYRON—*Curse of Minerva.* L. 206.

11
He will laugh thee to scorn.
Ecclesiasticus. XIII. 7.

12
He hears
On all sides, from innumerable tongues
A dismal universal hiss, the sound
Of public scorn.
MILTON—*Paradise Lost.* Bk. X. L. 506.

13
A drop of patience: but, alas, to make me
A fixed figure, for the time of scorn
To point his slow unmoving finger at!
Othello. Act IV. Sc. 2. L. 53. In the folio:
"The fixed figure for the time of scorn
To point his slow and moving finger at."

14
O, what a deal of scorn looks beautiful
In the contempt and anger of his lip!
Twelfth Night. Act III. Sc. 1. L. 156.

SCOTLAND

15
Give me but one hour of Scotland,
Let me see it ere I die.
WM. E. AYTOUN—*Lays of the Scottish Cavaliers—Charles Edward at Versailles.* L. 111.

16
Hear, Land o' Cakes and brither Scots
Frae Maiden Kirk to Johnny Groat's.
BURNS—*On Capt. Grose's Peregrinations Thro' Scotland.*

17
O Scotia! my dear, my native soil!
For whom my warmest wish to heaven is sent;
Long may thy hardy sons of rustic toil
Be blest with health, and peace, and sweet content.
BURNS—*Cotter's Saturday Night.* St. 20.

18
It's guid to be merry and wise,
It's guid to be honest and true,
It's guid to support Caledonia's cause,
And bide by the buff and the blue!
BURNS—*Here's a Health to Them that's Awa'.*

19
Only a few industrious Scots perhaps, who indeed are dispersed over the face of the whole earth. But as for them, there are no greater friends to Englishmen and England, when they are out on't, in the world, than they are. And for my own part, I would a hundred thousand of them were there [Virginia] for we are all one countrymen now, ye know, and we should find ten times more comfort of them there than we do here.
CHAPMAN—*Eastward Ho.* Act III. Sc. 2. Written by CHAPMAN, JONSON, MARSTON. JAMES I was offended at the reflexion on Scotchmen and the authors were threatened with imprisonment. Extract now found only in a few editions.

20
The Scots are poor, cries surly English pride;
True is the charge, nor by themselves denied.
Are they not then in strictest reason clear,
Who wisely come to mend their fortunes here?
CHURCHILL—*Prophecy of Famine.* L. 195.

21
The noblest prospect which a Scotchman ever sees is the high-road that leads him to England.
SAMUEL JOHNSON—*Boswell's Life of Johnson.* Vol. II. Ch. V. 1763.

22
In all my travels I never met with any one Scotchman but what was a man of sense. I believe everybody of that country that has any, leaves it as fast as they can.
FRANCIS LOCKIER—*Scotchmen.*

23
O Caledonia! stern and wild,
Meet nurse for a poetic child!
Land of brown heath and shaggy wood,
Land of the mountain and the flood,
Land of my sires! what mortal hand
Can e'er untie the filial band,
That knits me to thy rugged strand!
SCOTT—*Lay of the Last Minstrel.* Canto VI. St. 2.

1
It requires a surgical operation to get a joke well into a Scotch understanding.
SYDNEY SMITH—*Lady Holland's Memoir*. Vol. I. P. 15.

2
That knuckle-end of England—that land of Calvin, oat-cakes, and sulphur.
SYDNEY SMITH—*Lady Holland's Memoir*. Vol. II. P. 17.

3
Now the summer's in prime
Wi' the flowers richly blooming,
And the wild mountain thyme
A' the moorlands perfuming.
To own dear native scenes
Let us journey together,
Where glad innocence reigns
'Mang the braes o' Balquhither.
ROBERT TANNAHILL—*The Braes o' Balquhither*.

4
In short, he and the Scotch have no way of redeeming the credit of their understandings, but by avowing that they have been consummate villains. Stavano bene; per star meglio, stanno qui.
HORACE WALPOLE — *To the Rev. William Mason*. Aug. 2, or 6, 1778.
(See also ADDISON under EPITAPHS)

SCRIPTURE

5
His studie was but litel on the Bible.
CHAUCER—*Canterbury Tales*. *Prologue*. L. 4.

6
A glory gilds the sacred page,
Majestic like the sun,
It gives a light to every age,
It gives, but borrows none.
COWPER—*Olney Hymns*. No. 30.

7
One day at least in every week,
The sects of every kind
Their doctrines here are sure to seek,
And just as sure to find.
AUGUSTUS DE MORGAN. In preface to *From Matter to Spirit, by C. D.*

8
And that the Scriptures, though not everywhere
Free from corruption, or entire, or clear,
Are uncorrupt, sufficient, clear, entire
In all things which our needful faith require.
DRYDEN—*Religio Laici*. L. 297.

9
Out from the heart of nature rolled
The burdens of the Bible old.
EMERSON—*The Problem*.

10
The word unto the prophet spoken
Was writ on tablets yet unbroken:
The word by seers or sibyls told,
In groves of oak or fanes of gold,
Still floats upon the morning wind,
Still whispers to the willing mind.
EMERSON—*The Problem*.

11
It was a common saying among the Puritans, "Brown bread and the Gospel is good fare."
MATTHEW HENRY — *Commentaries*. Isaiah XXX.

12
Shallows where a lamb could wade and depths where an elephant would drown.
MATTHEW HENRY—*Of Solomon's Song*.

13
Bibles laid open, millions of surprises.
HERBERT—*The Church*. *Sin*.

14
Starres are poore books, and oftentimes do misse;
This book of starres lights to eternal blisse.
HERBERT—*The Church*. *The Holy Scriptures*. Pt. II.

15
So *we*'re all right, an' I, for one,
Don't think our cause'll lose in vally
By rammin' Scriptur' in our gun,
An' gittin' Natur' for an ally.
LOWELL—*The Biglow Papers*. Second Series. No. 7. St. 17.

16
The history of every individual man should be a Bible.
NOVALIS—*Christianity or Europe*. CARLYLE'S trans.

17
Most wondrous book! bright candle of the Lord!
Star of Eternity! The only star
By which the bark of man could navigate
The sea of life, and gain the coast of bliss
Securely.
POLLOK—*Course of Time*. Bk. II. L. 270.

18
I have more understanding than all my teachers: for thy testimonies are my meditations.
Psalms. CXIX. 99.

19
Thy word is a lamp unto my feet and a light unto my path.
Psalms. CXIX. 105.

20
The sweet psalmist of Israel.
II Samuel. XXIII. 1.

21
Within that awful volume lies
The mystery of mysteries!
Happiest they of human race,
To whom God has granted grace
To read, to fear, to hope, to pray,
To lift the latch, and force the way:
And better had they ne'er been born,
Who read to doubt, or read to scorn.
SCOTT—*Monastery*. Ch. XII.

22
But Thy good word informs my soul
How I may climb to heaven.
WATTS—*Excellency of the Bible*.

23
How glad the heathens would have been,
That worship idols, wood and stone,
If they the book of God had seen.
WATTS—*Praise for the Gospel*.

24
The Bible is a book of faith, and a book of doctrine, and a book of morals, and a book of religion, of especial revelation from God.
DANIEL WEBSTER—*Completion of Bunker Hill Monument*. June 17, 1843.

25
We search the world for truth; we cull
The good, the pure, the beautiful,
From all old flower fields of the soul;

And, weary seekers of the best,
We come back laden from our quest,
To find that all the sages said
Is in the Book our mothers read.
WHITTIER—*Miriam.*

SCULPTURE

1
The stone unhewn and cold
Becomes a living mould,
The more the marble wastes
The more the statue grows.
MICHAEL ANGELO—*Sonnet.* MRS. HENRY ROSCOE'S trans.

2
Ex quovis ligno non fit Mercurius.
A Mercury is not made out of any block of wood.
Quoted by APPULEIUS as a saying of PYTHAGORAS.

3
A sculptor wields
The chisel, and the stricken marble grows
To beauty.
BRYANT—*The Flood of Years.*

4
Not from a vain or shallow thought
His awful Jove young Phidias brought.
EMERSON—*The Problem.*

5
In sculpture did ever anybody call the Apollo a fancy piece? Or say of the Laocoön how it might be made different? A masterpiece of art has in the mind a fixed place in the chain of being, as much as a plant or a crystal.
EMERSON—*Society and Solitude. Art.*

6
Ex pede Herculem.
From the feet, Hercules.
HERODOTUS. Bk. IV. Sec. LXXXII. PLUTARCH. As quoted by AULUS GELLIUS. I. 1. DIOGENES. V. 15.

7
Sculpture is more divine, and more like Nature,
That fashions all her works in high relief,
And that is Sculpture. This vast ball, the Earth,
Was moulded out of clay, and baked in fire;
Men, women, and all animals that breathe
Are statues, and not paintings.
LONGFELLOW—*Michael Angelo.* Pt. III. 5.

8
Sculpture is more than painting. It is greater
To raise the dead to life than to create
Phantoms that seem to live.
LONGFELLOW—*Michael Angelo.* Pt. III. 5.

9
And the cold marble leapt to life a God.
H. H. MILMAN—*The Belvedere Apollo.*

10
The Paphian Queen to Cnidos made repair
Across the tide to see her image there:
Then looking up and round the prospect wide,
When did Praxiteles see me thus? she cried.
PLATO. In *Greek Anthology.*

11
Then marble, soften'd into life, grew warm.
POPE—*Second Book of Horace.* Ep. I. L. 146.

12
The sculptor does not work for the anatomist, but for the common observer of life and nature.
RUSKIN—*True and Beautiful. Sculpture.*

13
So stands the statue that enchants the world,
So bending tries to veil the matchless boast,
The mingled beauties of exulting Greece.
THOMSON—*The Seasons. Summer.* L. 1,346.

14
The marble index of a mind forever
Voyaging through strange seas of thought, alone.
WORDSWORTH—*The Prelude.* Bk. III.

SEA BIRD

15
How joyously the young sea-mew
Lay dreaming on the waters blue,
Whereon our little bark had thrown
A little shade, the only one;
But shadows ever man pursue.
E. B. BROWNING—*The Sea-Mew.*

16
Vainly the fowler's eye
Might mark thy distant flight to do thee wrong,
As, darkly painted on the crimson sky,
Thy figure floats along.
BRYANT—*To a Water Fowl.*

17
Up and down! Up and down!
From the base of the wave to the billow's crown;
And amidst the flashing and feathery foam
The Stormy Petrel finds a home,—
A home, if such a place may be,
For her who lives on the wide, wide sea,
On the craggy ice, in the frozen air,
And only seeketh her rocky lair
To warm her young and to teach them spring
At once o'er the waves on their stormy wing!
BARRY CORNWALL—*The Stormy Petrel.*

18
Between two seas the sea-bird's wing makes halt,
Wind-weary; while with lifting head he waits
For breath to reinspire him from the gates
That open still toward sunrise on the vault
High-domed of morning.
SWINBURNE—*Songs of the Spring Tides. Introductory lines to Birthday Ode to Victor Hugo.*

SEASONS (UNCLASSIFIED)

19
Therefore all seasons shall be sweet to thee,
Whether the summer clothe the general earth
With greenness, or the redbreast sit and sing
Betwixt the tufts of snow on the bare branch
Of mossy apple-tree, while the nigh thatch
Smokes in the sunthaw; whether the eve-drops fall,
Heard only in the trances of the blast,
Or if the secret ministry of frost
Shall hang them up in silent icicles,
Quietly shining to the quiet moon.
COLERIDGE—*Frost at Midnight.*

20
Our seasons have no fixed returns,
Without our will they come and go;
At noon our sudden summer burns,
Ere sunset all is snow.
LOWELL—*To ——.*

21
Autumn to winter, winter into spring,
Spring into summer, summer into fall,—
So rolls the changing year, and so we change;
Motion so swift, we know not that we move.
D. M. MULOCK—*Immutable.*

1
January grey is here,
Like a sexton by her grave;
February bears the bier,
March with grief doth howl and rave,
And April weeps—but, O ye hours!
Follow with May's fairest flowers.
SHELLEY—*Dirge for the Year*. St. 4.

2 Ah! well away!
Seasons flower and fade.
TENNYSON—*Every Day hath its Night*.

SECRECY

3
For this thing was not done in a corner.
Acts. XXVI. 26.

4
A man can hide all things, excepting twain—
That he is drunk, and that he is in love.
ANTIPHANES — *Fragmenta*. See MEINEKE'S *Fragmenta Comicorum Græcorum*. Vol. III. P. 3. *Seq*. Also in DIDOT'S *Poet. Com. Græ*. P. 407.

5
When we desire to confine our words, we commonly say they are spoken under the rose.
SIR THOMAS BROWNE—*Vulgar Errors. Of Speaking Under the Rose.—Pseudodoxia*. 5. 23.

6
Est rosa flos Veneris cujus quo furta laterent.
As given in BURMANN'S *Anthologia*. Bk. V. 217. (1778)

Sub rosa. Under the rose (*i.e.*, secretly). The rose was emblematic of secrecy with the ancients. Cupid bribed Harpocrates, god of silence, with a rose, not to divulge the amours of Venus. Hence a host hung a rose over his tables that his guests might know that under it words spoken were to remain secret. Harpocrates is Horus, god of the rising sun.
Found in GREGORY NAZIANZEN—*Carmen*. Vol. II. P. 27. (Ed. 1611)
(See also SWIFT)

7
For thre may kepe a counsel, if twain be awaie.
CHAUCER—*The Ten Commandments of Love*. 41. HERBERT—*Jacula Prudentum*. HEYWOOD—*Proverbs*. Pt. II. Ch. V.
(See also FRANKLIN, SHAKESPEARE)

8
The secret things belong unto the Lord our God.
Deuteronomy. XXIX. 29.

9
Three may keep a secret if two of them are dead.
BENJ. FRANKLIN—*Poor Richard*. (1735)
(See also CHAUCER)

10
As witnesses that the things were not done in a corner.
GEN. THOMAS HARRISON—*Defence at his trial. Account of the Trial of Twenty Regicides*. (1660) P. 39.
(See also ACTS)

11
Arcanum neque tu scrutaveris ullius unquam, commissumve teges et vino tortus et ira.
Never inquire into another man's secret; but conceal that which is intrusted to you, though pressed both by wine and anger to reveal it.
HORACE—*Epistles*. I. 18. 37.

12
There is a skeleton on every house.
Saying from story in *Italian Tales of Humour, Gallantry and Romance*.

13
L'on confie son secret dans l'amitié, mais il échappe dans l'amour.
We trust our secrets to our friends, but they escape from us in love.
LA BRUYÈRE—*Les Caractères*. IV.

14
Toute révélation d'un secret est la faute de celui qui l'a confié.
When a secret is revealed, it is the fault of the man who confided it.
LA BRUYÈRE—*Les Caractères*. V.

15
Rien ne pèse tant qu'un secret:
Le porter loin est difficile aux dames;
Et je sais même sur ce fait
Bon nombre d'hommes que sont femmes.
Nothing is so oppressive as a secret: women find it difficult to keep one long; and I know a goodly number of men who are women in this regard.
LA FONTAINE—*Fables*. VIII. 6.

16
How can we expect another to keep our secret if we cannot keep it ourselves.
LA ROCHEFOUCAULD—*Maxims*. No. 90.

17
Vitæ poscœnia celant.
Men conceal the past scenes of their lives.
LUCRETIUS—*Re Rerum Natura*. IV. 1,182.

18
Nothing is secret which shall not be made manifest.
Luke. VIII. 17.

19
I have play'd the fool, the gross fool, to believe
The bosom of a friend will hold a secret
Mine own could not contain.
MASSINGER—*Unnatural Combat*. Act V. Sc. 2.

20
A secret at home is like rocks under tide.
D. M. MULOCK—*Magnus and Morna*. Sc. 2.

21
Wer den kleinsten Theil eines Geheimnisses hingibt, hat den andern nicht mehr in der Gewalt.
He who gives up the smallest part of a secret has the rest no longer in his power.
JEAN PAUL RICHTER—*Titon*. Zykel 123.

22
Tell it not in Gath; publish it not in the streets of Askelon.
II Samuel. I. 20.

23
Alium silere quod voles, primus sile.
If you wish another to keep your secret, first keep it yourself.
SENECA—*Hippolytus*. 876. Also ST. MARTIN of Braga.

24
Latere semper patere, quod latuit diu.
Leave in concealment what has long been concealed.
SENECA—*Œdipus*. 826.

1
If you have hitherto conceal'd this sight,
Let it be tenable in your silence still.
And whatsoever else shall hap to-night,
Give it an understanding, but no tongue.
Hamlet. Act I. Sc. 2. L. 249.

2
But that I am forbid,
To tell the secrets of my prison-house,
I could a tale unfold whose lightest word
Would harrow up thy soul.
Hamlet. Act I. Sc. 5. L. 13.

3
Two may keep counsel, putting one away.
Romeo and Juliet. Act II. Sc. 4. L. 209.
(See also CHAUCER)

4
Two may keep counsel when the third's away.
Titus Andronicus. Act IV. Sc. 2. L. 144.
(See also CHAUCER)

5
Under the rose, since here are none but friends,
(To own the truth) we have some private ends.
SWIFT—*Epilogue to a Benefit Play for the Distressed Weavers.*
(See also BROWNE)

6
Miserum est tacere cogi, quod cupias loqui.
You are in a pitiable condition when you have to conceal what you wish to tell.
SYRUS—*Maxims.*

7
Let your left hand turn away what your right hand attracts.
Talmud. Sota. 47.

8
Tacitum vivit sub pectore vulnus.
The secret wound still lives within the breast.
VERGIL—*Æneid.* IV. 67.

SELF-EXAMINATION

9
As I walk'd by myself, I talk'd to myself
And myself replied to me;
And the questions myself then put to myself,
With their answers I give to thee.
BARNARD BARTON—*Colloquy with Myself.* Appeared in *Youth's Instructor*, Dec., 1826.

10
Summe up at night what thou hast done by day;
And in the morning what thou hast to do.
Dresse and undresse thy soul; mark the decay
And growth of it; if, with thy watch, that too
Be down then winde up both; since we shall be
Most surely judg'd, make thy accounts agree.
HERBERT—*The Temple. The Church Porch.* Next to last stanza.

11
One self-approving hour whole years out-weighs
Of stupid starers and of loud huzzas.
POPE—*Essay on Man.* Ep. IV. L. 249.

12
Speak no more:
Thou turn'st mine eyes into my very soul;
And there I see such black and grained spots
As will not leave their tinct.
Hamlet. Act III. Sc. 4. L. 88.

13
Go to your bosom;
Knock there, and ask your heart what it doth know.
Measure for Measure. Act II. Sc. 2. L. 136.

14
Let not soft slumber close your eyes,
Before you've collected thrice
The train of action through the day!
Where have my feet chose out their way?
What have I learnt, where'er I've been,
From all I've heard, from all I've seen?
What have I more that's worth the knowing?
What have I done that's worth the doing?
What have I sought that I should shun?
What duty have I left undone,
Or into what new follies run?
These self-inquiries are the road
That lead to virtue and to God.
ISAAC WATTS—*Self Examination.*

15
There is a luxury in self-dispraise;
And inward self-disparagement affords
To meditative spleen a grateful feast.
WORDSWORTH—*The Excursion.* Bk. IV.

16
'Tis greatly wise to talk with our past hours;
And ask them what report they bore to heaven:
And how they might have borne more welcome news.
YOUNG—*Night Thoughts.* Night II. L. 376.

SELFISHNESS

17
Chacun chez soi, chacun pour soi.
Every one for his home, every one for himself.
M. DUPIN.

18
Where all are selfish, the sage is no better than the fool, and only rather more dangerous.
FROUDE—*Short Studies on Great Subjects. Party Politics.*

19
Esto, ut nunc multi, dives tibi pauper amicis.
Be, as many now are, luxurious to yourself, parsimonious to your friends.
JUVENAL—*Satires.* V. 113.

20
As for the largest-hearted of us, what is the word we write most often in our cheque-books?—"Self."
EDEN PHILLPOTTS—*A Shadow Passes.*

21
Despite those titles, power, and pelf,
The wretch, concentred all in self,
Living, shall forfeit fair renown,
And, doubly dying, shall go down
To the vile dust from whence he sprung,
Unwept, unhonour'd and unsung.
SCOTT—*Lay of the Last Minstrel.* Canto VI. St. 1.

22
What need we any spur but our own cause,
To prick us to redress?
Julius Cæsar. Act II. Sc. 1. L. 123.

23
Love took up the harp of Life, and smote on all the chords with might;
Smote the chord of Self, that, trembling, pass'd in music out of sight.
TENNYSON—*Locksley Hall.* L. 33.

24
Selfishness is the only real atheism; aspiration, unselfishness, the only real religion.
ZANGWILL—*Children of the Ghetto.* Bk. II. Ch. 16.

SELF-LOVE

1

Self-love is a principle of action; but among no class of human beings has nature so profusely distributed this principle of life and action as through the whole sensitive family of genius.

ISAAC D'ISRAELI—*Literary Character of Men of Genius.* Ch. XV.

2

He was like a cock who thought the sun had risen to hear him crow.

GEORGE ELIOT—*Adam Bede.* Ch. XXXIII.
(See also ROSTAND)

3

Wer sich nicht zu viel dünkt ist viel mehr als er glaubt.

He who does not think too much of himself is much more esteemed than he imagines.

GOETHE—*Sprüche in Prosa.* III.

4

A gentleman is one who understands and shows every mark of deference to the claims of self-love in others, and exacts it in return from them.

HAZLITT—*Table Talk. On the Look of a Gentleman.*

5

Self-love is the greatest of all flatterers.

LA ROCHEFOUCAULD—*Maxims.* No. 3.

6

Voyez le beau rendez-vous qu'il me donne; cet homme là n'a jamais aimé que lui-même.

Behold the fine appointment he makes with me; that man never did love any one but himself.

MME. DE MAINTENON, when LOUIS XIV. in dying said, "Nous nous renverrons bientôt." (We shall meet again).

7

Ofttimes nothing profits more
Than self-esteem, grounded on just and right
Well manag'd.

MILTON—*Paradise Lost.* Bk. VIII. L. 571.

8

Le moi est haïssable.

Egoism is hateful.

PASCAL—*Pensées Diverses.*

9

To observations which ourselves we make,
We grow more partial for th' observer's sake.

POPE—*Moral Essays.* Ep. I. L. 11.

10

But respect yourself most of all.

Golden Verses of the Pythagoreans.

11

Sans doute
Je peux apprendre à coqueriquer: je glougloute.

Without doubt
I can teach crowing: for I gobble.

ROSTAND—*Chanticleer.* Act I. Sc. 2.

12

Et sonnant d'avance sa victoire,
Mon chant jaillit si net, si fier, si peremptoire,
Que l'horizon, saisi d'un rose tremblement,
M'obéit.

And sounding in advance its victory,
My song jets forth so clear, so proud, so peremptory,
That the horizon, seized with a rosy trembling,
Obeys me.

ROSTAND—*Chanticleer.* Act II. Sc. 3.

13

Je recule
Ébloui de me voir moi même tout vermeil
Et d'avoir, moi, le coq, fait élever le soleil.

I fall back dazzled at beholding myself all rosy red,
At having, I myself, caused the sun to rise.

ROSTAND—*Chanticleer.* Act II. Sc. 3.
(See also ELIOT)

14

Self-love, my liege, is not so vile a sin
As self-neglecting.

Henry V. Act II. Sc. 4. L. 74.

15

O villainous! I have looked upon the world for four times seven years; and since I could distinguish betwixt a benefit and an injury, I never found man that knew how to love himself.

Othello. Act I. Sc. 3. L. 312.

16

I to myself am dearer than a friend.

Two Gentlemen of Verona. Act II. Sc. 6. L. 23.

17

I am the most concerned in my own interests.

TERENCE—*Andria.* IV. 1.

18

L'amour-propre offensé ne pardonne jamais.

Offended self-love never forgives.

VIGÉE—*Les Aveux Difficiles.* VII.

19

This self-love is the instrument of our preservation; it resembles the provision for the perpetuity of mankind:—it is necessary, it is dear to us, it gives us pleasure, and we must conceal it.

VOLTAIRE—*Philosophical Dictionary. Self-Love.*

SENSE; SENSES

20

I am almost frightened out of my seven senses.

CERVANTES—*Don Quixote.* Pt. I. Bk. III. Ch. IX.
(See also ECCLESIASTICUS)

21

Take care of the sense and the sounds will take care of themselves.

LEWIS CARROLL—*Alice in Wonderland.* Ch. IX.
(See also LOWNDES under MONEY, CHESTERFIELD under TIME)

22

He had used the word in its Pickwickian sense . . . he had merely considered him a humbug in a Pickwickian point of view.

DICKENS—*Pickwick Papers.* Ch. I. The quarrel in the Pickwick Club is a literal paraphrase of a scene in the House of Commons during a debate, April 17, 1823, when Brougham and Canning quarreled over an accusation which was decided should be taken as political, not personal.

23

Him of the western dome, whose weighty sense
Flows in fit words and heavenly eloquence.

DRYDEN—*Absalom and Achitophel.* Pt. I. L. 868.

24

They received the use of the five operations of the Lord and in the sixth place he imparted them understanding, and in the seventh speech, an interpreter of the cogitations thereof.

Ecclesiasticus. XVII. 5.
(See also CERVANTES, SPECTATOR)

1
Be sober, and to doubt prepense,
These are the sinews of good sense.
SIR WILLIAM HAMILTON—*Notes on Reid.* From the *Fragments of Epicharmus.* 255.

2
Rarus enim ferme sensus communis in illa Fortuna.
Generally common sense is rare in that (higher) rank.
JUVENAL—*Satires.* VIII. 73.

3
If Poverty is the Mother of Crimes, want of Sense is the Father.
LA BRUYÈRE—*The Characters or Manners of the Present Age.* Vol. II. Ch. II.

4
Entre le bon sens et le bon goût il y a la différence de la cause à son effet.
Between good sense and good taste there is the difference between cause and effect.
LA BRUYÈRE—*Les Caractères.* XII.

5
Il n'est rien d'inutile aux personnes de sens.
Sensible people find nothing useless.
LA FONTAINE—*Fables.* V. 19.

6
Whate'er in her Horizon doth appear,
She is one Orb of Sense, all Eye, all aiery Ear.
HENRY MORE—*Antidote against Atheism.*

7
What thin partitions sense from thought divide.
POPE—*Essay on Man.* Ep. I. L. 226. And thin partitions do their bounds divide. DRYDEN—*Absalom and Achitophel.*
(See also BURNS under BLISS)

8
Good sense which only is the gift of Heaven,
And though no science, fairly worth the seven.
POPE—*Moral Essays.* Ep. IV. L. 43.

9
'Tis use alone that sanctifies expense
And splendor borrows all her rays from sense.
POPE—*Moral Essyas.* Ep. IV. L. 179.

10
Fool, 'tis in vain from wit to wit to roam:
Know, sense, like charity, begins at home.
POPE—*Umbra.*

11
Oft has good nature been the fool's defence,
And honest meaning gilded want of sense.
SHENSTONE—*Ode to a Lady.*

12
Huzzaed out of my seven senses.
Spectator. No. 616. Nov. 5, 1774.
(See also ECCLESIASTICUS)

13
Le sens commun n'est pas si commun.
Common sense is not so common.
VOLTAIRE—*Philosophical Dict. Self Love.*

14
Sense is our helmet, wit is but the plume;
The plume exposes, 'tis our helmet saves.
Sense is the diamond, weighty, solid, sound;
When cut by wit, it casts a brighter beam;
Yet, wit apart, it is a diamond still.
YOUNG—*Night Thoughts.* Night VIII. L. 1,254.

SENSIBILITY; SENTIMENT (See also INFLUENCE)

15
Chords that vibrate sweetest pleasure
Thrill the deepest notes of wo.
BURNS—*Sweet Sensibility.*

16
Susceptible persons are more affected by a change of tone than by unexpected words.
GEORGE ELIOT—*Adam Bede.* Ch. XXVII.

17
Noli me tangere.
Do not wish to touch me. Touch me not.
John. XX. 17. From the *Vulgate.*

18
And the heart that is soonest awake to the flowers
Is always the first to be touch'd by the thorns.
MOORE—*O Think Not My Spirits.*

19
It seem'd as if each thought and look
And motion were that minute chain'd
Fast to the spot such root she took,
And—like a sunflower by a brook,
With face upturn'd—so still remain'd!
MOORE—*Loves of the Angels. First Angel's Story.* L. 33.

20
To touch the quick.
SOPHOCLES—*Ajax.* 786.

21
Too quick a sense of constant infelicity.
JEREMY TAYLOR—*Sermon.*

22
I sit with my toes in a brook,
And if any one axes forwhy?
I hits them a rap with my crook,
For 'tis sentiment does it, says I.
HORACE WALPOLE. See CUNNINGHAM'S *Walpole.*

SENSITIVE PLANT

Mimosa Pudica

23
A Sensitive Plant in a garden grew,
And the young winds fed it with silver dew,
And it opened its fan-like leaves to the light,
And clothed them beneath the kisses of night.
SHELLEY—*The Sensitive Plant.* Pt. I.

24
For the Sensitive Plant has no bright flower;
Radiance and odour are not its dower;
It loves, even like Love, its deep heart is full,
It desires what it has not, the beautiful.
SHELLEY—*The Sensitive Plant.* Pt. I.

SEPTEMBER

25
O sweet September, thy first breezes bring
The dry leaf's rustle and the squirrel's laughter,
The cool fresh air whence health and vigor spring
And promise of exceeding joy hereafter.
GEORGE ARNOLD—*September Days.*

26
Come out 'tis now September,
The hunter's moon's begun,
And through the wheaten stubble
Is heard the frequent gun.
All Among the Barley. Made popular by the part-song of MRS. ELIZABETH STIRLING BRIDGE. Pub. in *The Musical Times,* No. 187. Supplement.

1
The morrow was a bright September morn;
The earth was beautiful as if new-born;
There was that nameless splendor everywhere,
That wild exhilaration in the air,
Which makes the passers in the city street
Congratulate each other as they meet.

LONGFELLOW—*Tales of a Wayside Inn.* Pt. I. *The Student's Tale. The Falcon of Sir Federigo.* L. 135.

SERVICE

2
If I had always served God as I have served you, Madam, I should not have a great account to render at my death.

BACON—*Life and Times of Francis the First.* Vol. I. P. 46, of ed. 2.

(See also BOURDEILLE, OAKLEY, HENRY VIII)

3
And Master Kingston, this I will say—had I but served God as diligently as I have served the king, he would not have given me over in my grey hairs.

PIERRE DE BOURDEILLE (Brantome), quoting THOMAS CROMWELL to his keeper.

(See also BACON, FIRDUSI)

4
We are his,
To serve him nobly in the common cause,
True to the death, but not to be his slaves.

COWPER—*Task.* Bk. V. L. 340.

5
When I have attempted to join myself to others by services, it proved an intellectual trick,—no more. They eat your service like apples, and leave you out. But love them, and they feel you, and delight in you all the time.

EMERSON—*Essays. Of Gifts.*

6
Had I but written as many odes in praise of Muhammad and Ali as I have composed for King Mahmud, they would have showered a hundred blessings on me.

FIRDUSI. (See also BACON)

7
Is thy servant a dog, that he should do this great thing?

II Kings. VIII. 13.

8
"Sidney Godolphin," said Charles (II), "is never in the way and never out of the way."

MACAULAY—*History of England.* Vol. I. P. 265. Cabinet Ed. Phrase used later to describe a good valet.

9
Who seeks for aid
Must show how service sought can be repaid.

OWEN MEREDITH (Lord Lytton)—*Siege of Constantinople.*

10
Servant of God, well done.

MILTON—*Paradise Lost.* Bk. VI. L. 29.

11
They also serve who only stand and wait.

MILTON—*Sonnet. On his Blindness.*

(See also MILTON under God, LONGFELLOW under PATIENCE)

12
They serve God well,
Who serve his creatures.

MRS. NORTON—*The Lady of La Garaye. Conclusion.* L. 9.

13
God curse Moawiyah. If I had served God so well as I have served him, he would never have damned me to all eternity.

Found in OCKLEY'S *History of the Saracens.* An. Hegira 54, A. D. 673.

(See also BACON)

14
Domini pudet non servitutis.

I am ashamed of my master and not of my servitude.

SENECA—*Troades.* 989.

15
Master, go on, and I will follow thee,
To the last gasp, with truth and loyalty.

As You Like It. Act II. Sc. 3. L. 69.

16
I am an ass, indeed, you may prove it by my long ears. I have served him from the hour of my nativity to this instant, and have nothing at his hands for my service but blows. When I am cold, he heats me with beating.

Comedy of Errors. Act IV. Sc. 4. L. 29.

17
Had I but serv'd my God with half the zeal
I serv'd my king, he would not in mine age
Have left me naked to mine enemies.

Henry VIII. Act III. Sc. 2. L. 455.

(See also BACON, also IBNU under ZEAL)

18
We cannot all be masters, nor all masters cannot be truly followed.

Othello. Act I. Sc. 1. L. 43.

19
My heart is ever at your service.

Timon of Athens. Act I. Sc. 2. L. 76.

20
The swallow follows not summer more willing than we your lordship.

Timon of Athens. Act III. Sc. 6. L. 31.

21
You know that love
Will creep in service where it cannot go.

Two Gentlemen of Verona. Act IV. Sc. 2. L. 19.

22
Small service is true service while it lasts:
Of humblest friends, bright Creature! scorn not one;
The Daisy, by the shadow that it casts,
Protects the lingering dew drop from the Sun.

WORDSWORTH—*To a Child: Written in Her Album.*

SHADOWS

23
The worthy gentleman [Mr. Coombe], who has been snatched from us at the moment of the election, and in the middle of the contest, while his desires were as warm, and his hopes as eager as ours, has feelingly told us, what shadows we are, and what shadows we pursue.

BURKE—*Speech at Bristol on Declining the Poll.*

(See also HOMER, JONSON)

24
Thus shadow owes its birth to light.

GAY—*The Persian, Sun, and Cloud.* L. 10.

1
(Orion) A hunter of shadows, himself a shade.
HOMER—*Odyssey*. II. 572.
(See also BURKE)

2
Follow a shadow, it still flies you;
Seem to fly it, it will pursue.
BEN JONSON—*Song. That Women are but Men's Shadows.*
(See also BURKE)

3
The picture of a shadow is a positive thing.
LOCKE—*Essay concerning Human Understanding*. Bk. II. Ch. VIII. Par. 5.

4 Alas! must it ever be so?
Do we stand in our own light, wherever we go,
And fight our own shadows forever?
OWEN MEREDITH (Lord Lytton)—*Lucile*. Pt. II. Canto II. St. 5.

5
Shadows are in reality, when the sun is shining, the most conspicuous thing in a landscape, next to the highest lights.
RUSKIN—*Painting*.

6
Come like shadows, so depart!
Macbeth. Act IV. Sc. 1. L. 111.

7
Some there be that shadows kiss;
Such have but a shadow's bliss.
Merchant of Venice. Act II. Sc. 9. L. 66.

8 Shadows to-night
Have struck more terror to the soul of Richard
Than can the substance of ten thousand soldiers
Armed in proof, and led by shallow Richmond.
Richard III. Act V. Sc. 3. L. 216.

9
Chequer'd shadow.
Titus Andronicus. Act II. Sc. 3. L. 15.

10
Like Hezekiah's, backward runs
The shadow of my days.
TENNYSON—*Will Waterproof's Lyrical Monologue*. (Ed. 1842) Changed in 1853 ed. to
"Against its fountain upward runs
The current of my days."

11
Majoresque cadunt altis de montibus umbræ.
And the greater shadows fall from the lofty mountains.
VERGIL—*Eclogue*. I. 84.

SHAKESPEARE

12 This Booke
When Brasse and Marble fade, shall make thee looke
Fresh to all Ages.
Commendatory Verses prefixed to the folio of SHAKESPEARE. (1623)

13 This was Shakespeare's form;
Who walked in every path of human life,
Felt every passion; and to all mankind
Doth now, will ever, that experience yield
Which his own genius only could acquire.
AKENSIDE—*Inscription*. IV.

14
Others abide our question. Thou art free.
We ask and ask—Thou smilest and art still,
Out-topping knowledge.
MATTHEW ARNOLD—*Shakespeare*.

15
Renowned Spenser, lie a thought more nigh
To learned Chaucer, and rare Beaumont lie
A little nearer Spenser, to make room
For Shakespeare in your threefold, fourfold tomb.
WILLIAM BASSE—*On Shakespeare*.
(See also JONSON)

16
There, Shakespeare, on whose forehead climb
The crowns o' the world. Oh, eyes sublime
With tears and laughter for all time.
E. B. BROWNING—*A Vision of Poets*.

17 "With this same key
Shakespeare unlocked his heart," once more!
Did Shakespeare? If so, the less Shakespeare he!
ROBERT BROWNING—*House*. X.
(See also WORDSWORTH)

18
If I say that Shakespeare is the greatest of intellects, I have said all concerning him. But there is more in Shakespeare's intellect than we have yet seen. It is what I call an unconscious intellect; there is more virtue in it than he himself is aware of.
CARLYLE—*Essays. Characteristics of Shakespeare*.

19
Voltaire and Shakespeare! *He* was all
The other feigned to be.
The flippant Frenchman speaks: I weep;
And Shakespeare weeps with me.
MATTHIAS CLAUDIUS—*A Comparison*.

20
Our myriad-minded Shakespeare.
COLERIDGE—*Biographia Literaria*. Ch. XV. Borrowed from a Greek monk who applied it to a Patriarch of Constantinople.

21 When great poets sing,
Into the night new constellations spring,
With music in the air that dulls the craft
Of rhetoric. So when Shakespeare sang or laughed
The world with long, sweet Alpine echoes thrilled
Voiceless to scholars' tongues no muse had filled
With melody divine.
C. P. CRANCH—*Shakespeare*.

22
But Shakespeare's magic could not copied be;
Within that circle none durst walk but he.
DRYDEN—*The Tempest. Prologue*.

23
The passages of Shakespeare that we most prize were never quoted until within this century.
EMERSON—*Letters and Social Aims. Quotation and Originality*.

24
Nor sequent centuries could hit
Orbit and sum of Shakespeare's wit.
EMERSON—*May Day and Other Pieces. Solution*. L. 39.

1
What point of morals, of manners, of economy, of philosophy, of religion, of taste, of the conduct of life, has he not settled? What mystery has he not signified his knowledge of? What office, or function, or district of man's work, has he not remembered? What king has he not taught state, as Talma taught Napoleon? What maiden has not found him finer than her delicacy? What lover has he not outloved? What sage has he not outseen? What gentleman has he not instructed in the rudeness of his behavior?

EMERSON—*Representative Men. Shakespeare.*

2
Now you who rhyme, and I who rhyme,
Have not we sworn it, many a time,
That we no more our verse would scrawl,
For Shakespeare he had said it all!

R. W. GILDER—*The Modern Rhymer.*

3
If we wish to know the force of human genius we should read Shakespeare. If we wish to see the insignificance of human learning we may study his commentators.

HAZLITT—*Table Talk. On the Ignorance of the Learned.*

4
Mellifluous *Shakespeare,* whose enchanting Quill
Commandeth Mirth or Passion, was but *Will.*

THOMAS HEYWOOD—*Hierarchie of the Blessed Angels.*

5
The stream of Time, which is continually washing the dissoluble fabrics of other poets, passes without injury by the adamant of Shakspere.

SAMUEL JOHNSON—*Preface to Works of Shakspere.*

6
I remember, the players have often mentioned it as an honour to Shakespeare, that in his writing (whatsoever he penned) he never blotted out a line. My answer hath been, would he had blotted a thousand.

BEN JONSON—*Discoveries. De Shakespeare nostrat.*

7
This figure that thou here seest put,
It was for gentle Shakespeare cut,
Wherein the graver had a strife
With Nature, to outdo the life:
Oh, could he but have drawn his wit
As well in brass, as he has hit
His face, the print would then surpass
All that was ever writ in brass;
But since he cannot, reader, look
Not on his picture, but his book.

BEN JONSON—*Lines on a Picture of Shakespeare.*

8
He was not of an age, but for all time!
And all the Muses still were in their prime,
When, like Apollo, he came forth to warm
Our ears, or like a Mercury to charm!

BEN JONSON—*Lines to the Memory of Shakespeare.*

9
Nature herself was proud of his designs,
And joyed to wear the dressing of his lines!
Which were so richly spun, and woven so fit,
As since, she will vouchsafe no other wit.

BEN JONSON—*Lines to the Memory of Shakespeare*

10
Soul of the Age!
The applause! delight! the wonder of our stage!
My Shakespeare rise! I will not lodge thee by
Chaucer, or Spenser, or bid Beaumont lie
A little further off, to make thee room:
Thou art a monument without a tomb,
And art alive still, while thy book doth live
And we have wits to read, and praise to give.

BEN JONSON—*Lines to the Memory of Shakespeare.* (See also BASSE)

11
Sweet Swan of Avon! What a sight it were
To see thee in our water yet appear.

BEN JONSON—*Lines to the Memory of Shakespeare.*

12
For a good poet's made, as well as born,
And such wast thou! Look how the father's face
Lives in his issue; even so the race
Of Shakespeare's mind and manners brightly shine
In his well-turned and true-filèd lines;
In each of which he seems to shake a lance,
As brandished at the eyes of ignorance.

BEN JONSON—*Lines to the Memory of Shakespeare.*

13
Thou hadst small Latin and less Greek.

BEN JONSON—*Lines to the Memory of Shakespeare.*

14
Shakespeare is not our poet, but the world's,
Therefore on him no speech!

WALTER SAVAGE LANDOR—*To Robert Browning.* L. 5.

15
Then to the well-trod stage anon
If Jonson's learned sock be on,
Or sweetest Shakespeare, Fancy's child,
Warble his native wood-notes wild.

MILTON—*L'Allegro.* L. 131.

16
What needs my Shakespeare for his honored bones
The labors of an age in piled stones?
Or that his hallowed reliques should be hid
Under a starre-y-pointing pyramid?
Dear son of Memory, great heir of fame,
What need'st thou such weak witness of thy name?
Thou in our wonder and astonishment
Hath built thyself a livelong monument.

MILTON—*An Epitaph.* Similar phrases in the entire epitaph are found in the epitaph on SIR THOMAS STANLEY, supposed to have been written by SHAKESPEARE. Also, same ideas found in CRASHAW.

17
Shakspeare (whom you and every playhouse bill
Style the divine! the matchless! what you will),
For gain, not glory, wing'd his roving flight,
And grew immortal in his own despite.

POPE—*Imitations of Horace.* Ep. I. Bk. II. L. 69.

1
Few of the university pen plaies well, they smell too much of that writer *Ovid* and that writer *Metamorphosis* and talk too much of Proserpina and Jupiter. Why, here's our fellow Shakespeare puts them all down. Aye, and Ben Jonson too. O that B. J. is a pestilent fellow, he brought up Horace giving the poets a pill, but our fellow, Shakespeare, hath given him a purge that made him beray his credit.
The Return from Parnassus; or, the Scourge of Simony. Act IV. Sc. 3.

2
Shikspur, Shikspur! Who wrote it?
No, I never read Shikspur.
Then you have an immense pleasure to come.
JAMES TOWNLEY—*High Life Below Stairs*. Act II. Sc. 1. (Ed. 1759)

3
Scorn not the Sonnet. Critic, you have frowned,
Mindless of its just honours; with this key
Shakespeare unlocked his heart.
WORDSWORTH—*Scorn not the Sonnet*.
(See also BROWNING)

SHAME

4
Shame is an ornament to the young; a disgrace to the old.
ARISTOTLE.

5
A nightingale dies for shame if another bird sings better.
BURTON—*Anatomy of Melancholy*. Pt. I. Sec. II. Memb. 3. Subsec. 6.

6
Maggior difetto men vergogna lava.
Less shame a greater fault would palliate.
DANTE—*Inferno*. XXX. 142.

7
Love taught him shame, and shame, with love at strife,
Soon taught the sweet civilities of life.
DRYDEN—*Cymon and Iphigenia*. L. 133.

8
The only art her guilt to cover,
To hide her shame from every eye,
To give repentance to her lover,
And wring his bosom, is—to die.
GOLDSMITH—*Vicar of Wakefield*. Ch. XXIV.

9
If yet not lost to all the sense of shame.
HOMER—*Iliad*. Bk. VI. L. 350. POPE'S trans.

10
Næ simul pudere quod non oportet cœperit; quod oportet non pudebit.
As soon as she (woman) begins to be ashamed of what she ought not, she will not be ashamed of what she ought.
LIVY—*Annales*. XXXIV. 4.

11
Pessimus quidem pudor vel est parsimoniæ vel frugalitatis.
The worst kind of shame is being ashamed of frugality or poverty.
LIVY—*Annales*. XXXIV. 4.

12
Pudet hæc opprobria nobis
Et dici potuisse et non potuisse repelli.
I am not ashamed that these reproaches can be cast upon us, and that they can not be repelled.
OVID—*Metamorphoses*. Bk. I. 758.

13
Here shame dissuades him, there his fear prevails,
And each by turns his aching heart assails.
OVID—*Metamorphoses*. Bk. III. *Transformation of Actæon*. L. 73. ADDISON'S trans.

14
Nam ego illum periisse duco, cui quidem periit pudor.
I count him lost, who is lost to shame.
PLAUTUS—*Bacchides*. III. 3. 80.

15
O shame! Where is thy blush?
Hamlet. Act III. Sc. 4. L. 82.

16
All is confounded, all!
Reproach and everlasting shame
Sits mocking in our plumes.
Henry V. Act IV. Sc. 5. L. 3.

17
He was not born to shame:
Upon his brow shame was asham'd to sit;
For 'tis a throne where honour may be crown'd
Sole monarch of the universal earth.
Romeo and Juliet. Act III. Sc. 2. L. 91.

18
We live in an atmosphere of shame. We are ashamed of everything that is real about us; ashamed of ourselves, of our relatives, of our incomes, of our accents, of our opinion, of our experience, just as we are ashamed of our naked skins.
BERNARD SHAW—*Man and Superman*. Act I.

19
The most curious offspring of shame is shyness.
SYDNEY SMITH—*Lecture on the Evil Affections*.

SHAMROCK

Trifolium Repens

20
I'll seek a four-leaved shamrock in all the fairy dells,
And if I find the charmèd leaves, oh, how I'll weave my spells!
SAMUEL LOVER—*The Four-Leaved Shamrock*.

21
O, the Shamrock, the green, immortal Shamrock!
Chosen leaf
Of Bard and Chief,
Old Erin's native Shamrock.
MOORE—*Oh, the Shamrock*.

SHEEP

22
A black sheep is a biting beast.
BASTARD'S CHRESTOLEROS. P. 90. (1598)

23
She walks—the lady of my delight—
A sheperdess of sheep.
Her flocks are thoughts. She keeps them white;
She guards them from the steep.
She feeds them on the fragrant height,
And folds them in for sleep.
ALICE MEYNELL—*The Lady of the Lambs*.

1
A leap year
Is never a good sheep year.
Old English Saying.

2
The mountain sheep are sweeter,
But the valley sheep are fatter.
We therefore deemed it meeter
To carry off the latter.
THOS. L. PEACOCK—*The Misfortunes of Elphin. The War-Song of Dinas Vawr.*

SHIPS (See also NAVIGATION, NAVY, SHIPWRECK)

3
She walks the waters like a thing of life,
And seems to dare the elements to strife.
BYRON—*The Corsair.* Canto I. St. 3.

4
She bears her down majestically near,
Speed on her prow, and terror in her tier.
BYRON—*The Corsair.* Canto III. St. 15.

5
For why drives on that ship so fast,
Without or wave or wind?
The air is cut away before,
And closes from behind.
COLERIDGE—*Ancient Mariner.*

6
A strong nor'wester's blowing, Bill;
Hark! don't ye hear it roar now?
Lord help 'em, how I pities them
Unhappy folks on shore, now.
CHARLES DIBDEN—*Sailor's Consolation.* Attributed to PITT (song writer) and HOOD.

7
The true ship is the ship builder.
EMERSON—*Essays. Of History.*

8
For she *is* such a smart little craft,
Such a neat little, sweet little craft—
Such a bright little,
Tight little,
Slight little,
Light little,
Trim little, slim little craft!
W. S. GILBERT—*Ruddigore.*

9
A great ship asks deep waters.
HERBERT—*Jacula Prudentum.*

10
The wooden wall alone should remain unconquered.
HERODOTUS. VII. 141. Relating the second reply of the *Pythian Oracle to the Athenians.* B. C. 480. THEMISTOCLES interpreted this to mean the ships. See GROTE—*History of Greece,* quoted in TIMBS—*Curiosities of History.* NEPOS—*Themistocles.*

11
Ships that sailed for sunny isles,
But never came to shore.
THOS. KIBBLE HERVEY—*The Devil's Progress.*

12
Morn on the waters, and purple and bright
Bursts on the billows the flushing of light.
O'er the glad waves, like a child of the sun,
See the tall vessel goes gallantly on.
THOMAS KIBBLE HERVEY—*The Convict Ship.*

13
Being in a ship is being in a jail, with the chance of being drowned.
SAMUEL JOHNSON—*Boswell's Life of Johnson.* (1759)

14
Lord, Thou hast made this world below the shadow of a dream,
An', taught by time, I tak' it so—exceptin' always steam.
From coupler-flange to spindle-guide I see thy Hand, O God—
Predestination in the stride o' yon connectin'-rod.
KIPLING—*McAndrew's Hymn.*

15
The Liner she's a lady, an' she never looks nor 'eeds—
The Man-o'-War's 'er 'usband an' 'e gives 'er all she needs;
But, oh, the little cargo-boats, that sail the wet seas roun',
They're just the same as you an' me, a'-plyin' up an' down.
KIPLING—*The Liner She's a Lady.*

16
Her plates are scarred by the sun, dear lass,
And her ropes are taut with the dew,
For we're booming down on the old trail, our own trail, the out trail,
We're sagging south on the Long Trail, the trail that is always new.
KIPLING—*L'Envoi. There's a Whisper down the Field.*

17
Build me straight, O worthy Master!
Staunch and strong, a goodly vessel
That shall laugh at all disaster,
And with wave and whirlwind wrestle!
LONGFELLOW—*Building of the Ship.* L. 1.

18
There's not a ship that sails the ocean,
But every climate, every soil,
Must bring its tribute, great or small,
And help to build the wooden wall!
LONGFELLOW—*Building of the Ship.* L. 66.

19
And the wind plays on those great sonorous harps, the shrouds and masts of ships.
LONGFELLOW—*Hyperion.* Bk. I. Ch. VII.

20
Like ships that have gone down at sea,
When heaven was all tranquillity.
MOORE—*Lalla Rookh. The Light of the Harem.*

21
They that go down to the sea in ships, that do business in great waters.
Psalms. CVII. 23.

22
And let our barks across the pathless flood
Hold different courses.
SCOTT—*Kenilworth.* Ch. XXIX. Introductory verses.

23
She comes majestic with her swelling sails,
The gallant Ship: along her watery way,
Homeward she drives before the favouring gales;
Now flirting at their length the streamers play,
And now they ripple with the ruffling breeze.
SOUTHEY—*Sonnet XIX.*

1
The barge she sat in, like a burnish'd throne,
Burn'd on the water: the poop was beaten gold;
Purple the sails, and so perfumed that
The winds were love-sick with them: the oars were silver,
Which to the tune of flutes kept stroke, and made
The water which they beat to follow faster,
As amorous of their strokes.

Antony and Cleopatra. Act II. Sc. 2. L. 196.

2
It would have been as though he [Pres. Johnson] were in a boat of stone with masts of steel, sails of lead, ropes of iron, the devil at the helm, the wrath of God for a breeze, and hell for his destination.

EMORY A. STORRS—*Speech* in Chicago, about 1865–6, when PRESIDENT JOHNSON threatened to imitate CROMWELL and force Congress with troops to adjourn. As reported in the Chicago *Tribune.*

3
And the stately ships go on
To their haven under the hill.

TENNYSON—*Break, Break, Break.* St. 3.

4
Ships, dim discover'd, dropping from the clouds.

THOMSON—*The Seasons. Summer.* L. 946.

5
Whoever you are, motion and reflection are especially for you,
The divine ship sails the divine sea for you.

WALT WHITMAN—*Song of the Rolling Earth.* 2.

6
Speed on the ship;—But let her bear
No merchandise of sin,
No groaning cargo of despair
Her roomy hold within;
No Lethean drug for Eastern lands,
Nor poison-draught for ours;
But honest fruits of toiling hands
And Nature's sun and showers.

WHITTIER—*The Ship-Builders.*

7
If all the ships I have at sea
Should come a-sailing home to me,
Ah, well! the harbor would not hold
So many ships as there would be
If all my ships came home from sea.

ELLA WHEELER WILCOX—*My Ships.* From *Poems of Passion.*

8
One ship drives east and another drives west
With the self-same winds that blow,
'Tis the set of the sails and not the gales
Which tells us the way to go.

ELLA WHEELER WILCOX—*Winds of Fate.*

SHIPWRECK (See also SHIPS)

9
Some hoisted out the boats, and there was one
That begged Pedrillo for an absolution,
Who told him to be damn'd,—in his confusion.

BYRON—*Don Juan.* Canto II. St. 44.

10
Then rose from sea to sky the wild farewell—
Then shriek'd the timid, and stood still the brave,—
Then some leap'd overboard with fearful yell,
As eager to anticipate their grave.

BYRON—*Don Juan.* Canto II. St. 52.

11
Again she plunges! hark! a second shock
Bilges the splitting vessel on the rock;
Down on the vale of death, with dismal cries,
The fated victims shuddering cast their eyes
In wild despair; while yet another stroke
With strong convulsion rends the solid oak:
Ah Heaven!—behold her crashing ribs divide!
She loosens, parts, and spreads in ruin o'er the tide.

FALCONER—*Shipwreck.* Canto III. L. 642.

12
And fast through the midnight dark and drear,
Through the whistling sleet and snow,
Like a sheeted ghost, the vessel swept
Towards the reef of Norman's Woe.

LONGFELLOW—*The Wreck of the Hesperus.* St. 15.

13
Naufragium sibi quisque facit.
Each man makes his own shipwreck.

LUCANUS—*Pharsalia.* I. 499.

14
Through the black night and driving rain
A ship is struggling, all in vain,
To live upon the stormy main;—
Miserere Domine!

ADELAIDE A. PROCTER—*The Storm.*

15
But hark! what shriek of death comes in the gale,
And in the distant ray what glimmering sail
Bends to the storm?—Now sinks the note of fear!
Ah! wretched mariners!—no more shall day
Unclose his cheering eye to light ye on your way!

MRS. RADCLIFFE — *Mysteries of Udolpho. Shipwreck.*

16
O, I have suffer'd
With those that I saw suffer: a brave vessel,
Who had, no doubt, some noble creature in her,
Dash'd all to pieces. O, the cry did knock
Against my very heart! Poor souls, they perished.

Tempest. Act I. Sc. 2. L. 5.

17
A rotten carcass of a boat, not rigged,
Nor tackle, sail, nor mast; the very rats
Instinctively have quit it.

Tempest. Act I. Sc. 2. L. 146.

18
Every drunken skipper trusts to Providence. But one of the ways of Providence with drunken skippers is to run them on the rocks.

BERNARD SHAW—*Heartbreak House.* Act III.

19
Improbe Neptunum accusat, qui iterum naufragium facit.

He wrongly accuses Neptune, who makes shipwreck a second time.

SYRUS. GELLIUS. 17. 14; MACROBIUS—*Satires.* II. 7.

20
Apparent rari nantes in gurgite vasto.

Here and there they are seen swimming in the vast flood.

VERGIL—*Æneid.* I. 118.

21
Or shipwrecked, kindles on the coast
False fires, that others may be lost.

WORDSWORTH—*To the Lady Fleming.*

SHOEMAKING

1
A cobbler, * * * produced several new grins of his own invention, having been used to cut faces for many years together over his last.
ADDISON—*Spectator*. No. 173.

2
To one commending an orator for his skill in amplifying petty matters, Agesilaus said: "I do not think that shoemaker a good workman that makes a great shoe for a little foot."
AGESILAUS THE GREAT—*Laconic Apophthegmns.*

3
Him that makes shoes go barefoot himself.
BURTON—*Anatomy of Melancholy. Democritus to the Reader*. P. 34. (Ed. 1887)
(See also MONTAIGNE)

4
Ye tuneful cobblers! still your notes prolong,
Compose at once a slipper and a song;
So shall the fair your handiwork peruse,
Your sonnets sure shall please—perhaps your shoes.
BYRON—*English Bards and Scotch Reviewers*. L. 751.

5
I can tell where my own shoe pinches me.
CERVANTES—*Don Quixote*. Pt. I. Ch. IV.
(See also ERASMUS, HERBERT, PLUTARCH)

6
The shoemaker makes a good shoe because he makes nothing else.
EMERSON—*Letters and Social Aims. Greatness.*

7
Si calceum induisses, tum demum sentires qua parte te urgeret.
If you had taken off the shoe then, at length you would feel in what part it pinched you.
Quoted by ERASMUS as founded on the remarks of PAULUS ÆMILIUS when he divorced his wife.
(See also CERVANTES)

8
Let firm, well hammer'd soles protect thy feet
Through freezing snows, and rains, and soaking sleet;
Should the big last extend the shoe too wide,
Each stone will wrench the unwary step aside;
The sudden turn may stretch the swelling vein,
The cracking joint unhinge, or ankle sprain;
And when too short the modish shoes are worn,
You'll judge the seasons by your shooting corn.
GAY—*Trivia*. Bk. I. L. 33.

9
I was not made of common calf,
Nor ever meant for country loon;
If with an axe I seem cut out,
The workman was no cobbling clown;
A good jack boot with double sole he made,
To roam the woods, or through the rivers wade.
GIUSEPPE GIUSTI—*The Chronicle of the Boot.*

10
Marry because you have drank with the king,
And the king hath so gracicusly pledged you,
You shall no more be called shoemakers.
But you and yours to the world's end
Shall be called the trade of the gentle craft.
Probably a play of GEORGE A. GREENE. *Time of Edward IV.*

11
As he cobbled and hammered from morning till dark,
With the footgear to mend on his knees,
Stitching patches, or pegging on soles as he sang,
Out of tune, ancient catches and glees.
OSCAR H. HARPEL—*The Haunted Cobbler.*

12
One said he wondered that leather was not dearer than any other thing. Being demanded a reason: because, saith he, it is more stood upon than any other thing in the world.
HAZLITT—*Shakespeare Jest Books. Conceits, Clinches, Flashes and Whimzies*. No. 86.

13
The title of Ultracrepidarian critics has been given to those persons who find fault with small and insignificant details.
HAZLITT—*Table-talk. Essay.* 22.

14
The wearer knows where the shoe wrings.
HERBERT—*Jacula Prudentum.*
(See also CERVANTES)

15
A careless shoe string, in whose tie
I see a wilde civility.
HERRICK—*Delight in Disorder.*

16
Cinderella's *lefts and rights*
To Geraldine's were frights,
And I trow
The damsel, deftly shod,
Has dutifully trod
Until now.
FREDERICK LOCKER-LAMPSON—*To My Mistress's Boots.*

17
Oh, where did hunter win
So delicate a skin
For her feet?
You lucky little kid,
You perished, so you did,
For my sweet.
FREDERICK LOCKER-LAMPSON—*To My Mistress's Boots.*

18
The fairy stitching gleams
On the sides and in the seams,
And it shows
That Pixies were the wags
Who tipped these funny tags
And these toes.
FREDERICK LOCKER-LAMPSON—*To My Mistress's Boots.*

19
Memento, in pellicula, cerdo, tenere tuo.
Remember, cobbler, to keep to your leather.
MARTIAL. 3. 16. 6.
(See also PLINY)

20
Quand nous veoyons un homme mal chaussé, nous disons que ce n'est pas merveille, s'il est chaussetier.
When we see a man with bad shoes, we say it is no wonder, if he is a shoemaker.
MONTAIGNE—*Essays*. Bk. I. Ch. XXIV.
(See also BURTON)

21
A chaque pied son soulier.
To each foot its own shoe.
MONTAIGNE—*Essays*. Bk. III. Ch. XIII.

1
But from the hoop's bewitching round,
Her very shoe has power to wound.
EDWARD MOORE—*The Spider and the Bee. Fable X.* L. 29.

2
Ne supra crepidam judicaret.
Shoemaker, stick to your last.
Proverb quoted by PLINY the Elder—*Historia Naturalis.* XXXV. 10. 36. According to CARDINAL WISEMAN, it should read "a shoemaker should not go above his latchet." See his *Points of Contact between Science and Art.* Note under *Sculpture.*
Ne sutor supra crepidam.
Given by BÜCHMANN—*Geflügelte Worte*, as correct phrase. Ne sutor ultra crepidam, as quoted by ERASMUS. Same idea in Non sentis, inquit, te ultra malleum loqui?
Do you not perceive that you are speaking beyond your hammer? To a blacksmith criticising music.
ATHENÆUS.
(See also MARTIAL)

3
* * * And holding out his shoe, asked them whether it was not new and well made. "Yet," added he, "none of you can tell where it pinches me."
PLUTARCH—*Lives.* Vol. II. *Life of Æmilius Paulus.*
(See also CERVANTES)

4
Hans Grovendraad, an honest clown,
By cobbling in his native town,
Had earned a living ever.
His work was strong and clean and fine,
And none who served at Crispin's shrine
Was at his trade more clever.
JAN VAN RYSWICK—*Hans Grovendraad.* Translated from the French by F. W. RICORD.

5
What trade are you?
Truly, sir, in respect of a fine workman, I am but, as you would say, a cobbler.
Julius Cæsar. Act I. Sc. 1. L. 9.

6
What trade art thou? answer me directly.
A trade, sir, that, I hope, I may use with a safe conscience; which is, indeed sir, a mender of bad soles.
Julius Cæsar. Act I. Sc. 1. L. 12.

7
Thou art a cobbler, art thou?
Truly, sir, all that I live by is with the awl: * * * I am indeed, sir, a surgeon to old shoes.
Julius Cæsar. Act I. Sc. 1. L. 23.

8
Wherefore art not in thy shop to-day?
Why dost thou lead these men about the streets?
Truly, sir, to wear out their shoes, to get myself into more work.
Julius Cæsar. Act I. Sc. 1. L. 31.

9
You cannot put the same shoe on every foot.
SYRUS—*Maxims.* 596.

10
When bootes and shoes are torne up to the lefts,
Coblers must thrust their awles up to the hefts.
NATHANIEL WARD—*The Simple Cobler of Aggawam in America.* Title Page.

11
Rap, rap! upon the well-worn stone,
How falls the polished hammer!
Rap, rap! the measured sound has grown
A quick and merry clamor.
Now shape the sole! now deftly curl
The glassy vamp around it,
And bless the while the bright-eyed girl
Whose gentle fingers bound it!
WHITTIER—*The Shoemakers.*

SICKNESS (See also DISEASE, MEDICINE)

12
The best of remedies is a beefsteak
Against sea-sickness; try it, sir, before
You sneer, and I assure you this is true,
For I have found it answer—so may you.
BYRON—*Don Juan.* Canto II. St. 13.

13
But when ill indeed,
E'en dismissing the doctor don't *always* succeed.
GEORGE COLMAN (the Younger)—*Broad Grins. Lodgings for Single Gentlemen.* St. 7.

14
Sickness is a belief, which must be annihilated by the divine Mind.
MARY B. G. EDDY—*Science and Health*, 493: 18.

15
Prevention is better than cure.
ERASMUS—*Adagia.* Same idea in OVID—*De Remedia Amoris.* 91. PERSIUS—*Satires.* III. 63. LIVY—*Works.* III. 61 and V. 36.

16
I've that within for which there are no plasters.
GARRICK—*Prologue* to GOLDSMITH'S *She Stoops to Conquer.*

17
Some maladies are rich and precious and only to be acquired by the right of inheritance or purchased with gold.
HAWTHORNE—*Mosses from an Old Manse. The Old Manse. The Procession of Life.*

18
The whole head is sick, and the whole heart faint.
Isaiah. I. 5.

19
A malady
Preys on my heart that med'cine cannot reach.
MATURIN—*Bertram.* Act IV. Sc. 2.

20
This sickness doth infect
The very life-blood of our enterprise.
Henry IV. Pt. I. Act IV. Sc. 1. L. 28.

21
He had a fever when he was in Spain,
And when the fit was on him, I did mark
How he did shake; 'tis true, this god did shake:
His coward lips did from their colour fly,
And that same eye whose bend doth awe the world
Did lose his lustre.
Julius Cæsar. Act I. Sc. 2. L. 119.

22
What, is Brutus sick,
And will he steal out of his wholesome bed,
To dare the vile contagion of the night?
Julius Cæsar. Act II. Sc. 1. L. 263.

23
My long sickness
Of health and living now begins to mend,
And nothing brings me all things.
Timon of Athens. Act V. Sc. 1. L. 189.

1
An' I thowt 'twur the will o' the Lord, but Miss
Annie she said it wur draäins,
For she hedn't naw coomfut in 'er, an' arn'd
naw thanks fur 'er paäins.
TENNYSON—*Village Wife.*

2
I've known my lady (for she loves a tune)
For *fevers* take an opera in June:
And, though perhaps you'll think the practice
bold,
A midnight park is sov'reign for a *cold.*
YOUNG—*Love of Fame.* Satire V. L. 185.

SIGHS

3
Sighed and wept and said no more.
Isle of Ladies. Erroneously attributed to CHAUCER as *Dream.* L. 931.

4
Sigh'd and look'd, and sigh'd again.
DRYDEN—*Alexander's Feast.* L. 120.

5
Implores the passing tribute of a sigh.
GRAY—*Elegy in a Country Churchyard.* St. 20.

6
To sigh, yet feel no pain.
MOORE—*Songs from M. P.; or, The Blue Stocking.*

7
My soul has rest, sweet sigh! alone in thee.
PETRARCH—*To Laura in Death. Sonnet LIV.* L. 14.

8
Oh, if you knew the pensive pleasure
That fills my bosom when I sigh,
You would not rob me of a treasure
Monarchs are too poor to buy.
SAMUEL ROGERS—*To ——.* St. 2.

9
Yet sighes, deare sighes, indeede true friends
you are
That do not leave your left friend at the wurst,
But, as you with my breast, I oft have nurst
So, gratefull now, you waite upon my care.
SIR PHILIP SIDNEY—*Sighes.*

10
Sighs
Which perfect Joy, perplexed for utterance,
Stole from her sister Sorrow.
TENNYSON—*The Gardener's Daughter.* L. 249.

SIGHT

11
And finds with keen, discriminating sight,
Black's not so black— nor white so very white.
CANNING—*New Morality.*

12
And for to se, and eek for to be seye.
CHAUCER—*Canterbury Tales. The Wife of Bath. Preamble.* L. 6134.

13
The age, wherein he lived was dark; but he
Could not want sight, who taught the world to
see.
DENHAM. In TODD'S *Johnson.*

14
The rarer sene, the lesse in mynde,
The lesse in mynde, the lesser payne.
BARNABY GOOGE—*Sonnettes. Out of Syght, Out of Mynde.*

15
See and to be seen.
BEN JONSON—*Epithalamion.* St. 3. L. 4.
GOLDSMITH—*Citizen of the World.* Letter 71.

16
And every eye
Gaz'd as before some brother of the sky.
HOMER—*Odyssey.* Bk. VIII. L. 17. POPE'S trans.

17
For sight is woman-like and shuns the old.
(Ah! he can see enough, when years are told,
Who backwards looks.)
VICTOR HUGO—*Eviradnus.* IX.

18
Two men look out through the same bars:
One sees the mud, and one the stars.
FREDERICK LANGBRIDGE—In *A Cluster of Quiet Thoughts.* Pub. by the Religious Tract Society.

19
Then purg'd with euphrasy and rue
The visual nerve, for he had much to see.
MILTON—*Paradise Lost.* Bk. XI. L. 414.

20
He that had neither beene kithe nor kin,
Might have seene a full fayre sight.
THOMAS PERCY—*Reliques of Ancient Poetry. Robin Hood and Guy of Gisborne.*

21
For any man with half an eye,
What stands before him may espy;
But optics sharp it needs I ween,
To see what is not to be seen.
JOHN TRUMBULL—*McFingal.* Canto I. L. 67.

22
Monstrum horrendum, informe, ingens, cui lumen ademptum.
A monster frightful, formless, immense, with sight removed.
VERGIL—*Æneid.* III. 658.

SILENCE

23
But silence never shows itself to so great an advantage, as when it is made the reply to calumny and defamation, provided that we give no just occasion for them.
ADDISON—*The Tatler.* No. 133.

24
Alta vendetta
D'alto silenzio è figlia.
Deep vengeance is the daughter of deep silence.
ALFIERI—*La Congiura de' Pazzi.* I. 1.

25
Qui tacet, consentire videtur.
Silence gives consent.
POPE BONIFACE VIII. Taken from the Canon Law. *Decretals.* Bk. V. 12. 43. FULLER—*Wise Sentences.* GOLDSMITH—*The Good-Natured Man.* Act II.

26
Le silence est l'esprit des sots,
Et l'une des vertus du sage.
Silence is the genius of fools and one of the virtues of the wise.
BONNARD.

27
Three things are ever silent—Thought, Destiny, and the Grave.
BULWER-LYTTON—*Harold.* Bk. X. Ch. II.

1
All Heaven and Earth are still, though not in sleep,
But breathless, as we grow when feeling most.
BYRON—*Childe Harold.* Canto III. St. 89.

2
There was silence deep as death;
And the boldest held his breath,
For a time.
CAMPBELL—*Battle of the Baltic.*

3
Speech is great; but silence is greater.
CARLYLE—*Essays. Characteristics of Shakespeare.*

4
Under all speech that is good for anything there lies a silence that is better. Silence is deep as Eternity; speech is shallow as Time.
CARLYLE—*Essays. Memoir of the Life of Scott.*

5
Silence is more eloquent than words.
CARLYLE—*Heroes and Hero Worship.* Lecture II.

6
Silence is the element in which great things fashion themselves together; that at length they may emerge, full-formed and majestic, into the daylight of Life, which they are thenceforth to rule.
CARLYLE—*Sartor Resartus.* Bk. III. Ch. III.

7
There are haunters of the silence, ghosts that hold the heart and brain.
MADISON CAWEIN—*Haunters of the Silence.*

8
Cum tacent clamant.
When they hold their tongues they cry out.
CICERO—*In Catilinam.* 1. 8.

9
And they three passed over the white sands, between the rocks, silent as the shadows.
COLERIDGE—*The Wanderings of Cain.*

10
Striving to tell his woes, words would not come;
For light cares speak, when mighty griefs are dumb.
SAMUEL DANIEL—*Complaint of Rosamond.* St. 114.

11
Il ne voit que la nuit, n'entend que le silence.
He sees only night, and hears only silence.
DELILLE—*Imagination.* IV.

12
Silence is the mother of Truth.
BENJ. DISRAELI—*Tancred.* Bk. IV. Ch. IV.

13
A horrid stillness first invades the ear,
And in that silence we the tempest fear.
DRYDEN—*Astræa Redux.* L. 7.

14
Stillborn silence! thou that art
Flood-gate of the deeper heart!
RICHARD FLECKNO—*Silence.*

15
Take heed of still waters, they quick pass away.
HERBERT—*Jacula Prudentum.*
(See also LYLY)

16
Small griefs find tongues: full casques are ever found
To give, if any, yet but little sound.
Deep waters noyselesse are; and this we know,
That chiding streams betray small depth below.
HERRICK—*Hesperides. To His Mistresse Objecting to Him Neither Toying or Talking.*
(See also JEWELL)

17
And silence, like a poultice, comes
To heal the blows of sound.
HOLMES—*The Music Grinder.*

18
There is a silence where hath been no sound,
There is a silence where no sound may be,
In the cold grave—under the deep, deep sea,
Or in wide desert where no life is found,
Which hath been mute, and still must sleep profound.
HOOD—*Sonnets. Silence.*

19
Est et fideli tuta silentio merces.
There is likewise a reward for faithful silence.
HORACE—*Carmina.* III. 2. 25.

20
Not much talk—a great, sweet silence.
HENRY JAMES, JR.—*A Bundle of Letters.* Letter IV.

21
Vessels never give so great a sound as when they are empty.
BISHOP JOHN JEWELL—*Defense of the Apology for the Church of England.*

22
Rarus sermo illis et magna libido tacendi.
Their conversation was brief, and their desire was to be silent.
JUVENAL—*Satires.* II. 14.

23
Thou foster-child of Silence and slow Time.
KEATS—*Ode on a Grecian Urn.*

24
Les gens sans bruit sont dangereux;
Il n'en est pas ainsi des autres.
Silent people are dangerous; others are not so.
LA FONTAINE—*Fables.* VIII. 23.

25
Some sipping punch, some sipping tea,
But as you by their faces see
All silent and all damned.
LAMB—*Lines made up from a stanza in* WORDSWORTH's *Peter Bell.*

26
All was silent as before—
All silent save the dripping rain.
LONGFELLOW—*A Rainy Day.*

27
What shall I say to you? What can I say
Better than silence is?
LONGFELLOW—*Morituri Salutamus.* L. 128.

28
Three Silences there are: the first of speech,
The second of desire, the third of thought.
LONGFELLOW—*The Three Silences of Molinos.*

29
Where the streame runneth smoothest, the water is deepest.
LYLY—*Euphues and His England.* P. 287.
(See also HERBERT, RUFUS, HENRY IV, SIDNEY)

1
I have known the silence of the stars and of the sea,
And the silence of the city when it pauses,
And the silence of a man and a maid,
And the silence for which music alone finds the word.
EDGAR LEE MASTERS—*Silence.*

2
Dixisse me, inquit, aliquando pœnituit, tacuisse nunquam.
He [Xenocrates] said that he had often repented speaking, but never of holding his tongue.
VALERIUS MAXIMUS. Bk. VII. 2, Ext. 7.

3
Nothing is more useful than silence.
MENANDER—*Ex Incert. Comœd.* P. 216.

4
You know
There are moments when silence, prolong'd and unbroken,
More expressive may be than all words ever spoken,
It is when the heart has an instinct of what
In the heart of another is passing.
OWEN MEREDITH (Lord Lytton)—*Lucile.* Pt. II. Canto I. St. 20.

5
That silence is one of the great arts of conversation is allowed by Cicero himself, who says, there is not only an art, but even an eloquence in it.
HANNAH MORE—*Essays on Various Subjects. Thoughts on Conversation.*

6
Silence sweeter is than speech.
D. M. MULOCK—*Magnus and Morna.* Sc. 3.

7
Be silent and safe—silence never betrays you.
JOHN BOYLE O'REILLY—*Rules of the Road.* St. 2.

8
Sed taciti fecere tamen convicia vultus.
But still her silent looks loudly reproached me.
OVID—*Amorum.* I. 7. 21.

9
Sæpe tacens vocem verbaque vultus habet.
The silent countenance often speaks.
OVID—*Ars Amatoria.* I. 574.

10
Exigua est virtus præstare silentia rebus;
At contra, gravis est culpa tacenda loqui.
Slight is the merit of keeping silence on a matter, on the other hand serious is the guilt of talking on things whereon we should be silent.
OVID—*Ars Amatoria.* Bk. II. 603.

11
Silence sleeping on a waste of ocean.
PERCY SOMERS PAYNE—*Rest.*

12
Remember what Simonides said,—that he never repented that he had held his tongue, but often that he had spoken.
PLUTARCH—*Morals.* Vol. I. *Rules for the Preservation of Health.*

13
Said Periander, "Hesiod might as well have kept his breath to cool his pottage."
PLUTARCH—*Morals.* Vol. II. *The Banquet of the Seven Wise Men.*

14
La douleur qui se tait n'en est que plus funeste.
Silent anguish is the more dangerous.
RACINE—*Andromaque.* III. 3.

15
Silence in love bewrays more woe
Than words, though ne'er so witty;
A beggar that is dumb, you know,
May challenge double pity.
SIR WALTER RALEIGH—*The Silent Lover.* St. 9.

16
The silente man still suffers wrong.
The Rock of Regard. J. P. COLLIER'S *Reprint.* (1576)

17
Silence more musical than any song.
CHRISTINA G. ROSSETTI—*Sonnet. Rest.*

18
Altissima quæque flumina minimo sono labuntur.
The deepest rivers flow with the least sound.
QUINTUS CURTIUS RUFUS—*De Rebus Gestis Alexandri Magni.* VII. 4. 13.
(See also LYLY)

19
Doch grosse Seelen dulden still.
Great souls suffer in silence.
SCHILLER—*Don Carlos.* I. 4. 52.

20
Bekker schweigt in sieben Sprachen.
Bekker is silent in seven languages.
SCHLEIERMACHER. See *Letter of Zelter to Goethe.* March 15, 1830.

21
Wise Men say nothing in dangerous times.
JOHN SELDEN—*Table Talk. Wisdom.*

22
Tacere multis discitur vitæ malis.
Silence is learned by the many misfortunes of life.
SENECA—*Thyestes.* 319.

23
Be check'd for silence,
But never tax'd for speech.
All's Well That Ends Well. Act I. Sc. 1. L. 76.

24
I'll speak to thee in silence.
Cymbeline. Act V. Sc. 4. L. 29.

25
The rest is silence.
Hamlet. Act V. Sc. 2. L. 368.

26
The saying is true "The empty vessel makes the greatest sound."
Henry V. Act IV. Sc. 4. L. 72.

27
Smooth runs the water where the brook is deep.
Henry VI. Pt. II. Act III. Sc. 1. L. 58.
(See also LYLY)

28
Silence is only commendable
In a neat's tongue dried and a maid not vendible.
Merchant of Venice. Act I. Sc. 1. L. 111.

29
'Tis old, but true, still swine eat all the draff.
Merry Wives of Windsor. Act IV. Sc. 2. L. 96.

30
Silence is the perfectest herald of joy:
I were but little happy, if I could say how much.
Much Ado About Nothing. Act II. Sc. 1. L. 317.

1 What; gone without a word?
Ay, so true love should do: it cannot speak;
For truth hath better deeds than words to grace it.
Two Gentlemen of Verona. Act II. Sc. 2. L. 16.

2
Silence! Oh, well are Death and Sleep and Thou
Three brethren named, the guardians gloomy-winged,
Of one abyss, where life and truth and joy
Are swallowed up.
SHELLEY—*Fragments. Silence.*

3
Shallow brookes murmur moste, deepe silent slide away.
SIR PHILIP SIDNEY—*The Arcadia. Thirsis and Dorus.*
(See also LYLY)

4
Macaulay is like a book in breeches * * *
He has occasional flashes of silence, that make his conversation perfectly delightful.
SYDNEY SMITH—*Lady Holland's Memoir*. Vol. I. P. 363.

5
Le silence du peuple est la leçon des rois.
The silence of the people is a lesson for kings.
SOANEN, Bishop of Senax; also ABBÉ DE BEAUVAIS—*Funeral oration over Louis XV.*

6
Woman, to women silence is the best ornament.
SOPHOCLES—*Ajax*. 293.

7
To me so deep a silence portends some dread event; a clamorous sorrow wastes itself in sound.
SOPHOCLES—*Antigone*. 1251.

8
The deepest rivers make least din,
The silent soule doth most abound in care.
EARL OF STIRLING—*Aurora*. (1604) *Song.*

9 But let me silent be:
For silence is the speech of love,
The music of the spheres above.
R. H. STODDARD—*Speech of Love*. St. 4.

10
Of every noble work the silent part is best,
Of all expression, that which cannot be expressed.
W. W. STORY—*The Unexpressed.*

11
Silence, beautiful voice.
TENNYSON—*Maud*. Pt. V. St. 3.

12
And *I* too talk, and lose the touch
I talk of. Surely, after all,
The noblest answer unto such
Is kindly silence when they brawl.
TENNYSON—*The After Thought*. In *Punch*, March 7, 1846. (Altered in the published poems to: "Is perfect stillness when they brawl.")

13
Our noisy years seem moments in the being
Of the eternal Silence.
WORDSWORTH—*Intimations of Immortality*. IX.

14
No sound is uttered,—but a deep
And solemn harmony pervades
The hollow vale from steep to steep,
And penetrates the glades.
WORDSWORTH—*Composed upon an Evening of Extraordinary Splendour and Beauty.*

15
The silence that is in the starry sky.
WORDSWORTH—*Song at the Feast of Brougham Castle.*

SIMPLICITY

16
Nothing is more simple than greatness; indeed, to be simple is to be great.
EMERSON—*Literary Ethics.*

17
Generally nature hangs out a sign of simplicity in the face of a fool.
FULLER—*The Holy and Profane States. Of Natural Fools. Maxim* I.

18
To me more dear, congenial to my heart,
One native charm, than all the gloss of art.
GOLDSMITH—*Deserted Village*. L. 253.

19
The greatest truths are the simplest: and so are the greatest men.
J. C. AND A. W. HARE—*Guesses at Truth.*

20
Simplicity is a state of mind.
CHARLES WAGNER—*Simple Life*. Ch. II.

21
A man is simple when his chief care is the wish to be what he ought to be, that is honestly and naturally human.
CHARLES WAGNER—*Simple Life*. Ch. II.

22
Humanity lives and always has lived on certain elemental provisions.
CHARLES WAGNER—*Simple Life*. Ch. III.

SIN

23
I waive the quantum o' the sin,
The hazard of concealing:
But, och! it hardens a' within,
And petrifies the feeling!
BURNS—*Epistle to a Young Friend.*

24
Compound for sins they are inclin'd to,
By damning those they have no mind to.
BUTLER—*Hudibras*. Pt. I. Canto I. L. 215.

25
But, sad as angels for the good man's sin,
Weep to record, and blush to give it in.
CAMPBELL—*Pleasures of Hope*. Pt. II. L. 357.

26
Sin let loose speaks punishment at hand.
COWPER—*Expostulation*. L. 160.

27
Come, now again, thy woes impart,
Tell all thy sorrows, all thy sin;
We cannot heal the throbbing heart
Till we discern the wounds within.
CRABBE—*Hell of Justice*. Pt. II.

28
I couldn't live in peace if I put the shadow of a wilful sin between myself and God.
GEORGE ELIOT—*The Mill on the Floss*. Bk. VI. Ch. XIV.

1
He that falls into sin is a man; that grieves at it, is a saint; that boasteth of it, is a devil.
FULLER—*Holy State. Of Self-Praising.* (1642) (See also LOGAU)

2
Das Uebel macht eine Geschichte und das Gute keine.
Sin writes histories, goodness is silent.
GOETHE. See RIEMER—*Mittheilungen über Goethe.* II. 9. 1810.

3
Man-like is it to fall into sin,
Fiend-like is it to dwell therein,
Christ-like is it for sin to grieve,
God-like is it all sin to leave.
FRIEDRICH VON LOGAU—*Sinngedichte. Sin.* See LONGFELLOW's trans. *Poetic Aphorisms.*

4
Deus propitius esto mihi peccatori.
God be merciful to me a sinner.
Luke. XVIII. 13. *Vulgate.*

5
Nor custom, nor example, nor vast numbers
Of such as do offend, make less the sin.
MASSINGER—*The Picture.* Act IV. Sc. 2.

6
Her rash hand in evil hour
Forth reaching to the fruit, she pluck'd, she eat;
Earth felt the wound, and Nature from her seat
Sighing through all her works gave signs of woe
That all was lost.
MILTON—*Paradise Lost.* Bk. IX. L. 780.

7
Law can discover sin, but not remove,
Save by those shadowy expiations weak.
MILTON—*Paradise Lost.* Bk. XII. L. 290.

8
So many laws argues so many sins.
MILTON—*Paradise Lost.* Bk. XII. L. 283.

9
But the trail of the serpent is over them all.
MOORE—*Lalla Rookh. Paradise and the Peri.* L. 206.

10
In *Adam's* fall—
We sinned all.
New England Primer. (1814)

11
Young Timothy
Learnt sin to fly.
New England Primer. (1777)

12
Di faciles, peccasse semel concedite tuto:
Id satis est. Pœnam culpa secunda ferat.
Indulgent gods, grant me to sin once with impunity. That is sufficient. Let a second offence bear its punishment.
OVID—*Amorum.* Bk. II. 14. 43.

13
Cui peccare licet peccat minus. Ipsa potestas
Semina nequitiæ languidiora facit.
He who has it in his power to commit sin, is less inclined to do so. The very idea of being able, weakens the desire.
OVID—*Amorum.* III. 4. 9.

14
Si quoties homines peccant sua fulmina mittat
Jupiter, exiguo tempore inermis erit.
If Jupiter hurled his thunderbolt as often as men sinned, he would soon be out of thunderbolts.
OVID—*Tristium.* II. 33.

15
Palam mutire plebeio piaculum est.
It is a sin for a plebeian to grumble in public.
PHÆDRUS—*Fables.* III. *Epilogue.* 34.

16
How shall I lose the sin yet keep the sense,
And love th' offender, yet detest the offence?
POPE—*Eloise to Abelard.* L. 191.

17
See sin in state, majestically drunk;
Proud as a peeress, prouder as a punk.
POPE—*Moral Essays.* Ep. II. L. 69.

18
My son, if sinners entice thee, consent thou not.
Proverbs. I. 10.

19
The way of transgressors is hard.
Proverbs. XIII. 15.

20
The wages of sin is death.
Romans. VI. 23.

21
Aliena vitia in oculis habemus; a tergo nostra sunt.
Other men's sins are before our eyes; our own behind our backs.
SENECA—*De Ira.* II. 28.

22
Magna pars hominum est, quæ non peccatis irascitur sed peccantibus.
The greater part of mankind are angry with the sinner and not with the sin.
SENECA—*De Ira.* II. 28.

23
Omnes mali sumus. Quidquid itaque in alio reprehenditur, id unusquisque in suo sinu inveniet.
We are all sinful. Therefore whatever we blame in another we shall find in our own bosoms.
SENECA—*De Ira.* III. 26.

24
Sin is a state of mind, not an outward act.
SEWELL—*Passing Thoughts on Religion. Wilful Sin.*

25
Commit
The oldest sins the newest kind of ways?
Henry IV. Pt. II. Act IV. Sc. 5. L. 126.

26
It is great sin to swear unto a sin,
But greater sin to keep a sinful oath.
Henry VI. Pt. II. Act V. Sc. 1. L. 182.

27
Some sins do bear their privilege on earth.
King John. Act I. Sc. 1. L. 261.

28
I am a man
More sinn'd against than sinning.
King Lear. Act III. Sc. 2. L. 58.

29
Robes and furr'd gowns hide all. Plate sin with gold,
And the strong lance of justice hurtless breaks;
Arm it in rags, a pigmy's straw doth pierce it.
King Lear. Act IV. Sc. 6. L. 169.

1
Some rise by sin, and some by virtue fall;
Some run from breaks of ice, and answer none:
And some condemned for a fault alone.
Measure for Measure. Act II. Sc. 1. L. 38.

2 O, fie, fie, fie!
Thy sin's not accidental, but a trade.
Measure for Measure. Act III. Sc. 1. L. 148.

3
O, what authority and show of truth
Can cunning sin cover itself withal!
Much Ado About Nothing. Act IV. Sc. 1. L. 36.

4
Few love to hear the sins they love to act.
Pericles. Act I. Sc. 1. L. 92.

5
Though some of you with Pilate wash your hands
Showing an outward pity; yet you Pilates
Have here deliver'd me to my sour cross,
And water cannot wash away your sin.
Richard II. Act IV. Sc. 1. L. 239.

6
They say sin touches not a man so near
As shame a woman; yet he too should be
Part of the penance, being more deep than she
Set in the sin.
SWINBURNE—*Tristram of Lyonesse. Sailing of the Swallow.* L. 360.

7
To abstain from sin when a man cannot sin is to be forsaken by sin, not to forsake it.
JEREMY TAYLOR—*Works.* Vol. VII. P. 206. Eden's Ed. Rendering of ST. AUGUSTINE—*Sermon* CCXCIII *De Pœnitentibus.*

8
Nec tibi celandi spes sit peccare paranti;
Est deus, occultos spes qui vetat esse dolos.
When thou art preparing to commit a sin, think not that thou wilt conceal it; there is a God that forbids crimes to be hidden.
TIBULLUS—*Carmina.* I. 9. 23.

9
But he who never sins can little boast
Compared to him who goes and sins no more!
N. P. WILLIS—*The Lady Jane.* Canto II. St. 44.

SINCERITY

10
Loss of sincerity is loss of vital power.
BOVEE—*Summaries of Thought. Sincerity.*

11
Of all the evil spirits abroad at this hour in the world, insincerity is the most dangerous.
FROUDE—*Short Studies on Great Subjects. Education.*

12
Sincerity is impossible, unless it pervade the whole being, and the pretence of it saps the very foundation of character.
LOWELL—*Essay on Pope.*

13
There is no greater delight than to be conscious of sincerity on self-examination.
MENCIUS—*Works.* Bk. VII. Ch. IV.

14
Bashful sincerity and comely love.
Much Ado About Nothing. Act IV. Sc. 1. L. 55.

15
Men should be what they seem;
Or those that be not, would they might seem none!
Othello. Act III. Sc. 3. L. 126.

16
A little sincerity is a dangerous thing, and a great deal of it is absolutely fatal.
OSCAR WILDE—*The Critic as Artist.* Pt. I.

SINGING (See also SONG)

17
Ce qui ne vaut pas la peine d'être dit, on le chante.
That which is not worth speaking they sing.
BEAUMARCHAIS—*Barbier de Séville.* I. 1.

18
Three merry boys, and three merry boys,
And three merry boys are we,
As ever did sing in a hempen string
Under the gallow-tree.
BEAUMONT AND FLETCHER—*Bloody Brother.* Act III. Sc. 2. *Song.*

19
Come, sing now, sing; for I know you sing well;
I see you have a singing face.
BEAUMONT AND FLETCHER—*Wild Goose Chase.* Act II. 2.
(See also FARQUHAR, RHODES)

20
The tenor's voice is spoilt by affectation,
And for the bass, the beast can only bellow;
In fact, he had no singing education,
An ignorant, noteless, timeless, tuneless fellow.
BYRON—*Don Juan.* Canto IV. St. 87.

21
Quien canta, sus males espanta.
He who sings frightens away his ills.
CERVANTES—*Don Quixote.* I. 22.

22
At every close she made, th' attending throng
Replied, and bore the burden of the song:
So just, so small, yet in so sweet a note,
It seemed the music melted in the throat.
DRYDEN—*Flower and the Leaf.* L. 197.

23
Y'ought to hyeah dat gal a-warblin'
Robins, la'ks an' all dem things
Heish de mouffs an' hides dey faces
When Malindy sings.
PAUL LAURENCE DUNBAR—*When Malindy Sings.*

24
Olympian bards who sung
Divine ideas below,
Which always find us young
And always keep us so.
EMERSON—*Ode to Beauty.*

25
I see you have a singing face—a heavy, dull, sonata face.
FARQUHAR—*The Inconstant.* Act II. 1.
(See also BEAUMONT)

26
When I but hear her sing, I fare
Like one that raised, holds his ear
To some bright star in the supremest Round;
Through which, besides the light that's seen
There may be heard, from Heaven within,
The rests of Anthems, that the Angels sound.
OWEN FELLTHAM—*Lusoria.* XXXIV. Ap-

peared as a poem of SUCKLING's—beginning "When dearest I but think of thee." Claimed by FELLTHAM in note to ed. 1690, 1696 of his *Resolves, Divine, Moral, Biblical.*

1
Then they began to sing
That extremely lovely thing,
"*Scherzando! ma non troppo, ppp.*"
W. S. GILBERT—*Bab Ballads. Story of Prince Agib.*

2
So she poured out the liquid music of her voice to quench the thirst of his spirit.
HAWTHORNE—*Mosses from an Old Manse. The Birthmark.*

3
He the sweetest of all singers.
LONGFELLOW—*Hiawatha.* Pt. VI. L. 21.

4
Sang in tones of deep emotion,
Songs of love and songs of longing.
LONGFELLOW—*Hiawatha.* Pt. XI. L. 136.

5
God sent his Singers upon earth
With songs of sadness and of mirth,
That they might touch the hearts of men,
And bring them back to heaven again.
LONGFELLOW—*The Singers.*

6
Ils chantent, ils payeront.
They sing, they will pay.
CARDINAL MAZARIN. Originally "S'ils cantent la cansonette ils pageront." A patois.

7
Who, as they sung, would take the prison'd soul
And lap it in Elysium.
MILTON—*Comus.* L. 256.

8
Or bid the soul of Orpheus sing
Such notes as, warbled to the string,
Drew iron tears down Pluto's cheek.
MILTON—*Il Penseroso.* L. 105.

9
O Carril, raise again thy voice! let me hear the song of Selma, which was sung in my halls of joy, when Fingal, king of shields, was there, and glowed at the deeds of his fathers.
OSSIAN—*Fingal.* Bk. III. St. 1.

10
Sweetest the strain when in the song
The singer has been lost.
ELIZABETH STUART PHELPS—*The Poet and the Poem.*

11
But would you sing, and rival Orpheus' strain.
The wond'ring forests soon should dance again;
The moving mountains hear the powerful call.
And headlong streams hang listening in their fall!
POPE—*Summer.* L. 81.

12
You know you haven't got a singing face.
RHODES—*Bombastes Furioso.*
(See also BEAUMONT)

13
Every night he comes
With musics of all sorts and songs compos'd
To her unworthiness: it nothing steads us
To chide him from our eaves; for he persists
As if his life lay on't.
All's Well That Ends Well. Act III. Sc. 7. L. 39.

14
Thou hast by moonlight at her window sung
With feigning voice verses of feigning love.
Midsummer Night's Dream. Act I. Sc. 1. L. 30.

15
O! she will sing the savageness out of a bear.
Othello. Act IV. Sc. 1. L. 200.

16
His tongue is now a stringless instrument.
Richard II. Act II. Sc. 1. L. 149.

17
Nay, now you are too flat
And mar the concord with too harsh a descant.
Two Gentlemen of Verona. Act I. Sc. 2. L. 94.

18
But one puritan amongst them, and he sings psalms to hornpipes.
Winter's Tale. Act IV. Sc. 3. L. 46.

19
Sing again, with your dear voice revealing
A tone
Of some world far from ours,
Where music and moonlight and feeling
Are one.
SHELLEY—*To Jane. The Keen Stars were Twinkling.*

SKY (THE)

20
And they were canopied by the blue sky,
So cloudless, clear, and purely beautiful,
That God alone was to be seen in Heaven.
BYRON—*The Dream.* St. 4.

21
"Darkly, deeply, beautifully blue,"
As some one somewhere sings about the sky.
BYRON—*Don Juan.* Canto IV. St. 110.
(See also SOUTHEY under FISH)

22
Arrestment, sudden really as a bolt out of the blue has hit strange victims.
CARLYLE—*French Revolution.* Vol. III. P. 347. (See also HOMER, VERGIL)

23
The mountain at a given distance
In amber lies;
Approached, the amber flits a little,—
And that's the skies!
EMILY DICKINSON—*Poems.* XIX. Second Series. (Ed. 1891)

24
How bravely Autumn paints upon the sky
The gorgeous fame of Summer which is fled!
HOOD—*Written in a Volume of Shakspeare.*

25
Bolt from the blue.
HORACE—*Ode.* I. 34.
(See also CARLYLE)

26
The sky
is that beautiful old parchment
in which the sun
and the moon
keep their diary.
ALFRED KREYMBORG—*Old Manuscript.*

27
When it is evening, ye say it will be fair weather: for the sky is red.
Matthew. XVI. 2.

1
The planets in their station list'ning stood.
MILTON—*Paradise Lost.* Bk. VII. L. 563.

2
And that inverted Bowl they call the Sky,
Whereunder crawling coop'd we live and die,
Lift not your hands to it for help—for it
As impotently moves as you or I.
OMAR KHAYYAM—*Rubaiyat.* FITZGERALD'S trans. St. 72.

3 From hyperborean skies,
Embodied dark, what clouds of vandals rise.
POPE—*Dunciad.* III. L. 85.

4
A sky full of silent suns.
RICHTER—*Flower, Fruit, and Thorn Pieces.* Ch. II.

5
Sometimes gentle, sometimes capricious, sometimes awful, never the same for two moments together; almost human in its passions, almost spiritual in its tenderness, almost Divine in its infinity.
RUSKIN—*The True and Beautiful. The Sky.*

6
The moon has set
In a bank of jet
That fringes the Western sky,
The pleiads seven
Have sunk from heaven
And the midnight hurries by;
My hopes are flown
And, alas! alone
On my weary couch I lie.
SAPPHO—*Fragment.* J. S. EASBY-SMITH'S trans.

7
This majestical roof fretted with golden fire.
Hamlet. Act II. Sc. 2. L. 312.

8 Heaven's ebon vault,
Studded with stars unutterably bright,
Through which the moon's unclouded grandeur rolls,
Seems like a canopy which love has spread
To curtain her sleeping world.
SHELLEY—*Queen Mab.* Pt. IV.

9
Redeo ad illes qui aiunt: quid si cœlum ruat?
I go back to those who say: what if the heavens fall?
TERENCE—*Heauton timoroumenos.* IV. 3. 41.

10 Of evening tinct,
The purple-streaming Amethyst is thine.
THOMSON—*Seasons. Summer.* L. 150.

11
Non alias cælo ceciderunt plura sereno.
Never till then so many thunderbolts from cloudless skies. (Bolt from the blue.)
VERGIL—*Georgics.* I. 487.
(See also CARLYLE)

12
Green calm below, blue quietness above.
WHITTIER—*The Pennsylvania Pilgrim.* St. 113.

13
The soft blue sky did never melt
Into his heart; he never felt
The witching of the soft blue sky!
WORDSWORTH—*Peter Bell.* Pt. I. St. 15.

SLANDER (See also GOSSIP, SCANDAL)

14
There are * * * robberies that leave man or woman forever beggared of peace and joy, yet kept secret by the sufferer.
GEORGE ELIOT—*Felix Holt. Introduction.*

15
I hate the man who builds his name
On ruins of another's fame.
GAY—*The Poet and the Rose.*

16
A generous heart repairs a slanderous tongue.
HOMER—*Odyssey.* Bk. VIII. L. 43. POPE'S trans.

17
If slander be a snake, it is a winged one—it flies as well as creeps.
DOUGLAS JERROLD—*Specimens of Jerrold's Wit. Slander.*

18 Where it concerns himself,
Who's angry at a slander, makes it true.
BEN JONSON—*Catiline.* Act III. Sc. 1.

19 Cut
Men's throats with whisperings.
BEN JONSON—*Sejanus.* Act I. Sc. 1.

20
For enemies carry about slander not in the form in which it took its rise. * * * The scandal of men is everlasting; even then does it survive when you would suppose it to be dead.
PLAUTUS—*Persa.* Act III. Sc. 1. RILEY'S trans.

21
Homines qui gestant, quique auscultant crimina,
Si meo arbitratu liceat, omnes pendeant,
Gestores linguis, auditores auribus.
Your tittle-tattlers, and those who listen to slander, by my good will should all be hanged —the former by their tongues, the latter by the ears.
PLAUTUS—*Pseudolus.* I. 5. 12.

22
'Twas slander filled her mouth with lying words;
Slander, the foulest whelp of Sin.
POLLOK—*Course of Time.* Bk. VIII. L. 725.

23
For slander lives upon succession,
Forever housed where it gets possession.
Comedy of Errors. Act III. Sc. 1. L. 105.

24 'Tis slander,
Whose edge is sharper than the sword, whose tongue
Outvenoms all the worms of Nile, whose breath
Rides on the posting winds and doth belie
All corners of the world; kings, queens and states,
Maids, matrons, nay, the secrets of the grave
This viperous slander enters.
Cymbeline. Act III. Sc. 4. L. 35.

25 One doth not know
How much an ill word may empoison liking.
Much Ado About Nothing. Act III. Sc. 1. L. 85.

26 Slander'd to death by villains,
That dare as well answer a man indeed
As I dare take a serpent by the tongue:
Boys, apes, braggarts, Jacks, milksops!
Much Ado About Nothing. Act V. Sc. 1. L. 88.

1
Done to death by slanderous tongues
Was the Hero that here lies.
Much Ado About Nothing. Act V. Sc. 3. L. 3.

2
I will be hang'd, if some eternal villain,
Some busy and insinuating rogue,
Some cogging, cozening slave, to get some office,
Have not devis'd this slander.
Othello. Act IV. Sc. 2. L. 130.

3
I am disgrac'd, impeach'd and baffled here,—
Pierc'd to the soul with slander's venom'd spear.
Richard II. Act I. Sc. 1. L. 170.

4
That thou art blamed shall not be thy defect,
For slander's mark was ever yet the fair;
* * * *
So thou be good, slander doth but approve
Thy worth the greater.
Sonnet LXX.

5
If I can do it
By aught that I can speak in his dispraise,
She shall not long continue love to him.
Two Gentlemen of Verona. Act III. Sc. 2. L. 46.

6
Soft-buzzing Slander; silly moths that eat
An honest name.
THOMSON—*Liberty*. Pt. IV. L. 609.

SLAVERY (See also FREEDOM)

7
Servi peregrini, ut primum Galliæ fines penetraverint eodem momento liberi sunt.

Foreign slaves, as soon as they come within the limits of Gaul, that moment they are free.
BODINUS. Bk. I. Ch. V.
(See also CAMPBELL)

8
Lord Mansfield first established the grand doctrine that the air of England is too pure to be breathed by a slave.
LORD CAMPBELL—*Lives of the Chief Justices*. Vol. II. P. 418.
(See also BODINUS, COWPER, LOFFT, MANSFIELD)

9
No more slave States and no more slave territory.
SALMON P. CHASE—*Resolutions Adopted at the Free-Soil National Convention*. Aug. 9, 1848.

10
Cotton is king; or slavery in the Light of Political Economy.
DAVID CHRISTY—*Title of Book*, pub. 1855.
(See also HAMMOND)

11
It [Chinese Labour in South Africa] could not, in the opinion of His Majesty's Government, be classified as slavery in the extreme acceptance of the word without some risk of terminological inexactitude.
WINSTON CHURCHILL in the British House of Commons. Feb. 22, 1906.

12
Nimia libertas et populis et privatis in nimiam servitutem cadit.

Excessive liberty leads both nations and individuals into excessive slavery.
CICERO—*De Republica*. I. 44.

13
Fit in dominatu servitus, in servitute dominatus.

He is sometimes slave who should be master; and sometimes master who should be slave.
CICERO—*Oratio Pro Rege Deiotaro*. XI.

14
I would not have a slave to till my ground,
To carry me, to fan me while I sleep,
And tremble when I wake, for all the wealth
That sinews bought and sold have ever earn'd.
COWPER—*Task*. Bk. II. L. 29.

15
Slaves cannot breathe in England; if their lungs
Receive our air, that moment they are free;
They touch our country, and their shackles fall.
COWPER—*Task*. Bk. II. L. 40.
(See also CAMPBELL)

16
I do not see how a barbarous community and a civilized community can constitute a state. I think we must get rid of slavery or we must get rid of freedom.
EMERSON—*The Assault upon Mr. Sumner's Speech*. May 26, 1856.

17
Corrupted freemen are the worst of slaves.
DAVID GARRICK—*Prologue to* ED. MOORE'S *Gamesters*.

18
Resolved, That the compact which exists between the North and the South is a covenant with death and an agreement with hell; involving both parties in atrocious criminality, and should be immediately annulled.
WM. LLOYD GARRISON—*Adopted by the Mass. Anti-Slavery Society. Fanueil Hall*. Jan. 27, 1843.

19
The man who gives me employment, which I must have or suffer, that man is my master, let me call him what I will.
HENRY GEORGE—*Social Problems*. Ch. V.

20
The very mudsills of society. * * * We call them slaves. * * * But I will not characterize that class at the North with that term; but you have it. It is there, it is everywhere, it is eternal.
JAMES H. HAMMOND—*Speech in the U. S. Senate*. March, 1858.

21
Cotton is King.
JAMES H. HAMMOND. Phrase used in the Senate, March, 1858. GOV. MANNING *of South Carolina, Speech at Columbia, S. C.* (1858)
(See also CHRISTY)

22
Whatever day
Makes man a slave, takes half his worth away.
HOMER—*Odyssey*. Bk. XVII. L. 392. POPE'S trans.

23
I believe this government cannot endure permanently half slave and half free.
ABRAHAM LINCOLN—*Speech*. June 17, 1858.

24
In giving freedom to the slave we assure freedom to the free,—honorable alike in what we give and what we preserve.
ABRAHAM LINCOLN—*Annual Message to Congress*. Dec. 1, 1862.

1
[England] a soil whose air is deemed too pure for slaves to breathe in.
LOFFT—*Reports.* P. 2. *Margrave's Argument.* May 14, 1772.
(See also CAMPBELL)

2
They are slaves who fear to speak
For the fallen and the weak;
* * * *
They are slaves who dare not be
In the right with two or three.
LOWELL—*Stanzas on Freedom.*

3
The air of England has long been too pure for a slave, and every man is free who breathes it.
LORD MANSFIELD. Said in the case of a negro, James Somersett, carried from Africa to Jamaica and sold.
(See also CAMPBELL)

4
Execrable son! so to aspire
Above his brethren, to himself assuming
Authority usurp'd, from God not given.
He gave us only over beast, fish, fowl,
Dominion absolute; that right we hold
By his donation; but man over men
He made not lord; such title to himself
Reserving, human left from human free.
MILTON—*Paradise Lost.* Bk. XII. L. 64.

5 Where bastard Freedom waves
Her fustian flag in mockery over slaves.
MOORE—*To the Lord Viscount Forbes.* Written from the City of Washington.

6
And ne'er shall the sons of Columbia be slaves,
While the earth bears a plant, or the sea rolls its waves.
ROBERT PAINE—*Ode. Adams and Liberty.* (1798)

7
Base is the slave that pays.
Henry V. Act II. Sc. 1. L. 100.

8
You have among you many a purchas'd slave,
Which, like your asses and your dogs and mules,
You use in abject and in slavish parts,
Because you bought them.
Merchant of Venice. Act IV. Sc. 1. L. 90.

9
Englishmen never will be slaves; they are free to do whatever the Government and public opinion allow them to do.
BERNARD SHAW—*Man and Superman.*

10
Disguise thyself as thou wilt, still,
Slavery! said I—still thou art a bitter draught.
STERNE—*Sentimental Journey. The Passport. The Hotel at Paris.*

11
By the Law of Slavery, man, created in the image of God, is divested of the human character, and declared to be a mere chattel.
CHAS. SUMNER—*The Anti-Slavery Enterprise.* Address at New York. May 9, 1859.

12
Where Slavery is there Liberty cannot be; and where Liberty is there Slavery cannot be.
CHAS. SUMNER—*Slavery and the Rebellion.* Speech before the New York Young Men's Republican Union. Nov. 5, 1864.

13
They [the blacks] had no rights which the white man was bound to respect.
ROGER B. TANEY—*The Dred Scot Case.* See HOWARD'S *Rep.* Vol. XIX. P. 407.

14
Slavery is also as ancient as war, and war as human nature.
VOLTAIRE—*Philosophical Dictionary. Slaves.*

15
I never mean, unless some particular circumstances should compel me to do it, to possess another slave by purchase, it being among my first wishes to see some plan adopted by which slavery in this country may be abolished by law.
GEORGE WASHINGTON—*Farewell Address.*

16
That execrable sum of all villanies commonly called the Slave-trade.
JOHN WESLEY—*Journal.* Feb. 12, 1792.

17 A Christian! going, gone!
Who bids for God's own image?—for his grace,
Which that poor victim of the market-place
Hath in her suffering won?
WHITTIER—*Voices of Freedom. The Christian Slave.*

18
Our fellow-countrymen in chains!
Slaves—in a land of light and law!
Slaves—crouching on the very plains
Where rolled the storm of Freedom's war!
WHITTIER—*Voices of Freedom. Stanzas.*

19
What! mothers from their children riven!
What! God's own image bought and sold!
AMERICANS to market driven,
And bartered as the brute for gold!
WHITTIER—*Voices of Freedom. Stanzas.*

SLEEP

20
What means this heaviness that hangs upon me?
This lethargy that creeps through all my senses?
Nature, oppress'd and harrass'd out with care,
Sinks down to rest.
ADDISON—*Cato.* Act V. Sc. 1.

21 What probing deep
Has ever solved the mystery of sleep?
T. B. ALDRICH—*Human Ignorance.*

22
But I, in the chilling twilight stand and wait
At the portcullis, at thy castle gate,
Longing to see the charmèd door of dreams
Turn on its noiseless hinges, delicate sleep!
T. B. ALDRICH—*Invocation to Sleep.*

23
Come to me now! O, come! benignest sleep!
And fold me up, as evening doth a flower,
From my vain self, and vain things which have power
Upon my soul to make me smile or weep.
And when thou comest, oh, like Death be deep.
PATRICK PROCTOR ALEXANDER—*Sleep.* Appeared in the *Spectator.*

24 How happy he whose toil
Has o'er his languid pow'rless limbs diffus'd
A pleasing lassitude; he not in vain
Invokes the gentle Deity of dreams.

His pow'rs the most voluptuously dissolve
In soft repose; on him the balmy dews
Of Sleep with double nutriment descend.
ARMSTRONG—*The Art of Preserving Health.* Bk. III. L. 385.

1
When the sheep are in the fauld, and a' the kye at hame,
And all the weary world to sleep are gane.
LADY ANN BARNARD—*Auld Robin Gray.*

2
Still believe that ever round you
Spirits float who watch and wait;
Nor forget the twain who found you
Sleeping nigh the Golden Gate.
BESANT AND RICE—*Case of Mr. Lucraft and other Tales.* P. 92. (Ed. 1877)
(See also MORRIS)

3
Since the Brother of Death daily haunts us with dying mementoes.
SIR THOMAS BROWNE—*Hydriotaphia.* Same idea in BUTLER—*Anatomy of Melancholy.* P. 107. (Ed. 1849) Also in an old French poet RACAN.

4
Sleep is a death, O make me try,
By sleeping, what it is to die:
And as gently lay my head
On my grave, as now my bed.
SIR THOMAS BROWNE—*Religio Medici.* Pt. II. Sec. XII.
(See also DANIEL, FLETCHER, HOMER, OVID, SACKVILLE, CYMBELINE, MACBETH, SHELLEY, SPENSER, VERGIL)

5
How he sleepeth! having drunken
Weary childhood's mandragore,
From his pretty eyes have sunken
Pleasures to make room for more—
Sleeping near the withered nosegay which he pulled the day before.
E. B. BROWNING—*A Child Asleep.*

6
Of all the thoughts of God that are
Borne inward unto souls afar,
Along the Psalmist's music deep,
Now tell me if that any is.
For gift or grace, surpassing this—
"He giveth His beloved sleep."
E. B. BROWNING—*The Sleep.*

7
Sleep on, Baby, on the floor,
Tired of all the playing,
Sleep with smile the sweeter for
That you dropped away in!
On your curls' full roundness stand
Golden lights serenely—
One cheek, pushed out by the hand,
Folds the dimple inly.
E. B. BROWNING—*Sleeping and Watching*

8
Sleep hath its own world,
A boundary between the things misnamed
Death and existence: Sleep hath its own world,
And a wide realm of wild reality,
And dreams in their development have breath,
And tears, and tortures, and the touch of joy.
BYRON—*The Dream.* St. 1.

9
Now, blessings light on him that first invented this same sleep! it covers a man all over, thoughts and all, like a cloak; it is meat for the hungry, drink for the thirsty, heat for the cold, and cold for the hot. It is the current coin that purchases all the pleasures of the world cheap; and the balance that sets the king and the shepherd, the fool and the wise man, even. There is only one thing, which somebody once put into my head, that I dislike in sleep; it is, that it resembles death; there is very little difference between a man in his first sleep, and a man in his last sleep.
CERVANTES—*Don Quixote.* Pt. II. Ch. LXVIII.
(See also SAXE)

10
It is not good a sleping hound to wake.
CHAUCER—*Troilus.* I. 640. Wake not a sleeping lion. *The Countryman's New Commonwealth.* (1647) Esveiller le chat qui dort. RABELAIS—*Pantagruel.* Wake not a sleeping wolf. *Henry IV.* Pt. II.

11
O sleep! it is a gentle thing,
Beloved from pole to pole!
To Mary Queen the praise be given!
She sent the gentle sleep from Heaven
That slid into my soul.
COLERIDGE—*Ancient Mariner.* Pt. V. St. 1.

12
Visit her, gentle Sleep! with wings of healing,
And may this storm be but a mountain-birth,
May all the stars hang bright above her dwelling,
Silent as though they watched the sleeping Earth!
COLERIDGE—*Dejection. An Ode.* St. 8.

13
Care-charmer Sleep, son of the sable Night,
Brother to Death, in silent darkness born;
Relieve my languish, and restore the light.
SAMUEL DANIEL—*Sonnet.* 46. *To Delia.*

14
Awake thee, my Lady-Love!
Wake thee, and rise!
The sun through the bower peeps
Into thine eyes.
GEORGE DARLEY—*Waking Song.*

15
Golden slumbers kiss your eyes,
Smiles awake you when you rise.
THOS. DEKKER—*The Comedy of Patient Grissil.* (Play written by DEKKER, HENRY CHETTLE, WM. HOUGHTON.)

16
Sister Simplicitie!
Sing, sing a song to me,—
Sing me to sleep!
Some legend low and long,
Slow as the summer song
Of the dull Deep.
SIDNEY DOBELL—*A Sleep Song.*

17
Two gates the silent house of Sleep adorn:
Of polished ivory this, that of transparent horn:
True visions through transparent horn arise;
Through polished ivory pass deluding lies.
DRYDEN—*Æneid.* Bk. VI. 894. Same in POPE'S trans. of *Odyssey.* Bk. XIX. 562.
(See also MORRIS)

1
The sleep of a labouring man is sweet.
Ecclesiastes. V. 12.

2
She took the cup of life to sip,
Too bitter 'twas to drain;
She meekly put it from her lip,
And went to sleep again.
Epitaph in Meole Churchyard. Found in *Sabrinæ Corolla*. P. 246 of third ed.

3
If thou wilt close thy drowsy eyes,
My mulberry one, my golden son,
The rose shall sing thee lullabies,
My pretty cosset lambkin!
EUGENE FIELD—*Armenian Lullaby*.

4
The mill goes toiling slowly round
With steady and solemn creak,
And my little one hears in the kindly sound
The voice of the old mill speak;
While round and round those big white wings
Grimly and ghostlike creep,
My little one hears that the old mill sings,
Sleep, little tulip, sleep.
EUGENE FIELD—*Nightfall in Dordrecht*.

5
Care-charming Sleep, thou easer of all woes,
Brother to Death . . . thou son of Night.
JOHN FLETCHER—*The Tragedy of Valentinian*. Act V. 2.

(See also BROWNE)

6
O sleep! in pity thou art made
A double boon to such as we;
Beneath closed lids and folds of deepest shade
We think we see.
FROTHINGHAM *The Sight of the Blind*.

7
Sleep sweet within this quiet room,
O thou! whoe'er thou art;
And let no mournful Yesterday,
Disturb thy peaceful heart.
ELLEN M. H. GATES—*Sleep Sweet*.

8
Oh! lightly, lightly tread!
A holy thing is sleep,
On the worn spirit shed,
And eyes that wake to weep.
FELICIA D. HEMANS—*The Sleeper*.

9
One hour's sleep before midnight is worth three after.
HERBERT—*Jacula Prudentum*.

10
Then Sleep and Death, two twins of winged race,
Of matchless swiftness, but of silent pace.
HOMER—*Iliad*. Bk. XVI. L. 831. POPE'S trans.

(See also BROWNE)

11
Et idem
Indignor quandoque bonus dormitat Homerus;
Verum opere longo fas est obrepere somnum.
I, too, am indignant when the worthy Homer nods; yet in a long work it is allowable for sleep to creep over the writer.
HORACE—*Ars Poetica*. 358.

12
I lay me down to sleep,
With little thought or care
Whether my waking find
Me here, or there.
MRS. R. S. HOWLAND (Miss Woolsey)—*Rest*. Found under the pillow of a soldier who, in the War of the Rebellion, died in the hospital at Port Royal. For a time attributed to this unknown soldier.

13
O sleep, we are beholden to thee, sleep;
Thou bearest angels to us in the night,
Saints out of heaven with palms.
Seen by thy light
Sorrow is some old tale that goeth not deep;
Love is a pouting child.
JEAN INGELOW—*Sleep*.

14
I never take a nap after dinner but when I have had a bad night, and then the nap takes me.
SAMUEL JOHNSON—*Boswell's Life of Johnson*. (1775)

15
O magic sleep! O comfortable bird,
That broodest o'er the troubled sea of the mind
Till it is hush'd and smooth! O unconfined
Restraint! imprisoned liberty! great key
To golden palaces.
KEATS—*Endymion*. Bk. I. L. 452.

16
Over the edge of the purple down,
Where the single lamplight gleams,
Know ye the road to the Merciful Town
That is hard by the Sea of Dreams—
Where the poor may lay their wrongs away,
And the sick may forget to weep?
But we—pity us! Oh pity us!
We wakeful; Ah, pity us!—
KIPLING—*City of Sleep*.

17
But who will reveal to our waiting ken
The forms that swim and the shapes that creep
under the waters of sleep?
And I would I could know what swimmeth below
when the tide comes in
On the length and the breadth of the marvelous
Marches of Glynn.
SIDNEY LANIER—*Marches of Glynn*. Last lines.

18
Breathe thy balm upon the lonely,
Gentle Sleep!
As the twilight breezes bless
With sweet scents the wilderness,
Ah, let warm white dove-wings only
Round them sweep!
LUCY LARCOM—*Sleep Song*.

19
For I am weary, and am overwrought
With too much toil, with too much care distraught,
And with the iron crown of anguish crowned.
Lay thy soft hand upon my brow and cheek,
O peaceful Sleep!
LONGFELLOW—*Sleep*.

20
Dreams of the summer night!
Tell her, her lover keeps
Watch! while in slumbers light
She sleeps!
My lady sleeps!
Sleeps!
LONGFELLOW—*Spanish Student*. Act I. Sc. 3. *Serenade*. St. 4.

1
Thou driftest gently down the tides of sleep.
LONGFELLOW—*To a Child.* L. 115.

2
While the bee with honied thigh,
That at her flowery work doth sing,
And the waters murmuring
With such a consort as they keep,
Entice the dewy-feather'd sleep.
MILTON—*Il Penseroso.* L. 142.

3 The timely dew of sleep
Now falling with soft slumb'rous weight inclines
Our eyelids.
MILTON—*Paradise Lost.* Bk. IV. L. 615.

4 For his sleep
Was aery light, from pure digestion bred.
MILTON—*Paradise Lost.* Bk. V. L. 3.

5
Dreamer of dreams, born out of my due time,
Why should I strive to set the crooked straight?
Let it suffice me that my murmuring rhyme
Beat with light wing against the ivory gate,
Telling a tale not too importunate
To those who in the sleepy region stay,
Lulled by the singer of an empty day.
WILLIAM MORRIS—Apology to *The Earthly Paradise.*
(See also BESANT, DRYDEN)

6
O, we're a' noddin', nid, nid, noddin';
O we're a' noddin' at our house at hame.
LADY NAIRNE—*We're a' Noddin'.*

7
Stulte, quid est somnus, gelidæ nisi mortis imago?
Longa quiescendi tempora fata dabunt.
Fool, what is sleep but the likeness of icy death? The fates shall give us a long period of rest.
OVID—*Amorum.* Bk. II. 10. 40.
(See also BROWNE)

8
Alliciunt somnos tempus motusque merumque.
Time, motion and wine cause sleep.
OVID—*Fasti.* VI. 681.

9
Somne, quies rerum, placidissime, somne, Deorum,
Pax animi, quem cura fugit, qui corda diurnis
Fessa ministeriis mulces, reparasque labori!
Sleep, rest of nature, O sleep, most gentle of the divinities, peace of the soul, thou at whose presence care disappears, who soothest hearts wearied with daily employments, and makest them strong again for labour!
OVID—*Metamorphoses.* XI. 624.

10
Balow, my babe, lye still and sleipe,
It grieves me sair to see thee weipe.
PERCY—*Reliques. Lady Anne Bothwell's Lament.*

11 Sleep, baby, sleep
Thy father's watching the sheep,
Thy mother's shaking the dreamland tree,
And down drops a little dream for thee.
ELIZABETH PRENTISS—*Sleep, Baby, Sleep.*

12
Drowsiness shall clothe a man with rags.
Proverbs. XXIII. 21.

13
I will both lay me down in peace, and sleep: for thou, LORD, only makest me dwell in safety.
Psalms. IV. 8.

14
He giveth his beloved sleep.
Psalms. CXXVII. 2.

15
I will not give sleep to mine eyes, or slumber to mine eyelids.
Psalms. CXXXII. 4.; *Proverbs.* VI. 4.

16
Je ne dors jamais bien à mon aise sinon quand je suis au sermon, ou quand je prie Dieu.
I never sleep comfortably except when I am at sermon or when I pray to God.
RABELAIS—*Gargantua.* Bk. I. Ch. XLI.

17
Elle s'endormit du sommeil des justes.
She slept the sleep of the just.
RACINE—*Abrégé de l'histoire de Port Royal.* Vol. IV. 517. Mesnard's ed.

18
When the Sleepy Man comes with the dust on his eyes
(Oh, weary, my Dearie, so weary!)
He shuts up the earth, and he opens the skies.
(So hush-a-by, weary my Dearie!)
C. G. D. ROBERTS—*Sleepy Man.*

19
Heavy Sleep, the Cousin of Death.
SACKVILLE—*Sleep.*
(See also BROWNE)

20
Yes; bless the man who first invented sleep
(I really can't avoid the iteration):
But blast the man with curses loud and deep,
Whate'er the rascal's name or age or station,
Who first invented, and went round advertising,
That artificial cut-off—Early Rising.
J. G. SAXE—*Early Rising.*

21
"God bless the man who first invented sleep!"
So Sancho Panza said and so say I;
And bless him, also, that he didn't keep
His great discovery to himself, nor try
To make it,—as the lucky fellow might—
A close monopoly by patent-right.
J. G. SAXE—*Early Rising.*
(See also CERVANTES)

22
Sleep the sleep that knows not breaking,
Morn of toil, nor night of waking.
SCOTT—*Lady of the Lake.* Canto I. St. 31.

23
To all, to each, a fair good-night,
And pleasing dreams, and slumbers light.
SCOTT—*Marmion. L'Envoy. To the Reader.*

24
O sleep, thou ape of death, lie dull upon her
And be her sense but as a monument.
Cymbeline. Act II. Sc. 2. L. 31.
(See also BROWNE)

25
He that sleeps feels not the tooth-ache.
Cymbeline. Act V. Sc. 4. L. 177.

26
To sleep! perchance to dream; ay, there's the rub;
For in that sleep of death what dreams may come,
When we have shuffled off this mortal coil,
Must give us pause.
Hamlet. Act III. Sc. 1. L. 65.

1
On your eyelids crown the god of sleep,
Charming your blood with pleasing heaviness:
Making such difference 'twixt wake and sleep,
As is the difference betwixt day and night,
The hour before the heavenly-harness'd team
Begins his golden progress in the east.
Henry IV. Pt. I. Act III. Sc. 1. L. 217.

2 O sleep, O gentle sleep,
Nature's soft nurse, how have I frighted thee,
That thou no more wilt weigh my eyelids down
And steep my senses in forgetfulness?
Henry IV. Pt. II. Act III. Sc. 1. L. 4.

3
Why rather, sleep, liest thou in smoky cribs,
Upon uneasy pallets stretching thee
And hushed with buzzing night-flies to thy slumber,
Than in the perfum'd chambers of the great,
Under the canopies of costly state,
And lull'd with sound of sweetest melody?
Henry IV. Pt. II. Act III. Sc. 1. L. 9.

4
O polish'd perturbation! golden care!
That keep'st the ports of slumber open wide
To many a watchful night! sleep with it now!
Yet not so sound and half so deeply sweet
As he whose brow with homely biggen bound
Snores out the watch of night.
Henry IV. Pt. II. Act IV. Sc. 5. L. 23.

5
This sleep is sound indeed, this is a sleep
That from this golden rigol hath divorc'd
So many English kings.
Henry IV. Pt. II. Act IV. Sc. 5. L. 35.

6
Winding up days with toil and nights with sleep.
Henry V. Act IV. Sc. 1. L. 296.

7 Fast asleep? It is no matter;
Enjoy the honey-heavy dew of slumber;
Thou hast no figures nor no fantasies,
Which busy care draws in the brains of men;
Therefore thou sleep'st so sound.
Julius Cæsar. Act II. Sc. 1. L. 229.

8 Bid them come forth and hear me,
Or at their chamber-door I'll beat the drum
Till it cry sleep to death.
King Lear. Act II. Sc. 4. L. 118.

9
Sleep shall neither night nor day
Hang upon his pent-house lid.
Macbeth. Act I. Sc. 3. L. 19.

10
Methought I heard a voice cry, "Sleep no more!
Macbeth does murder sleep," the innocent sleep.
Macbeth. Act II. Sc. 2. L. 35.

11
Sleep that knits up the ravell'd sleave of care,
The death of each day's life, sore labour's bath,
Balm of hurt minds, great nature's second course,
Chief nourisher in life's feast.
Macbeth. Act II. Sc. 2. L. 36.

12
Shake off this downy sleep, death's counterfeit,
And look on death itself!
Macbeth. Act II. Sc. 3. L. 81.
(See also BROWNE)

13 He sleeps by day
More than the wild-cat.
Merchant of Venice. Act II. Sc. 5. L. 47.

14 Thou lead them thus,
Till o'er their brows death-counterfeiting sleep
With leaden legs and batty wings doth creep.
Midsummer Night's Dream. Act III. Sc. 2. L. 363.

15
Sleep, that sometimes shuts up sorrow's eye,
Steal me awhile from mine own company.
Midsummer Night's Dream. Act III. Sc. 2. L. 435.

16
But I pray you, let none of your people stir me: I have an exposition of sleep come upon me.
Midsummer Night's Dream. Act IV. Sc. 1. L. 42.

17 Not poppy, nor mandragora,
Nor all the drowsy syrups of the world
Shall ever medicine thee to that sweet sleep
Which thou ow'dst yesterday.
Othello. Act III. Sc. 3. L. 330.

18
I let fall the windows of mine eyes.
Richard III. Act V. Sc. 3. L. 116.

19 Thy eyes' windows fall,
Like death, when he shuts up the day of life;
Each part, depriv'd of supple government,
Shall, stiff and stark and cold, appear like death.
Romeo and Juliet. Act IV. Sc. 1. L. 100.

20
Sleep, the fresh dew of languid love, the rain
Whose drops quench kisses till they burn again.
SHELLEY—*Epipsychidion*. L. 571.

21
How wonderful is Death, Death and his brother Sleep!
SHELLEY—*Queen Mab*. L. 1.
(See also BROWNE)

22
And on their lids * * *
The baby Sleep is pillowed.
SHELLEY—*Queen Mab*. Pt. I.

23
Come, Sleep: O Sleep! the certain knot of peace,
The baiting place of wit, the balm of woe,
The poor man's wealth, the prisoner's release,
Th' indifferent judge between the high and low.
SIR PHILIP SIDNEY—*Astrophel and Stella*. St. 39.

24
Take thou of me, sweet pillowes, sweetest bed;
A chamber deafe of noise, and blind of light,
A rosie garland and a weary hed.
SIR PHILIP SIDNEY—*Astrophel and Stella*. St. 39.

25
Thou hast been called, O Sleep, the friend of Woe,
But 'tis the happy who have called thee so.
SOUTHEY—*The Curse of Kehama*. Canto XV. St. 12.

26
For next to Death is Sleepe to be compared;
Therefore his house is unto his annext:
Here Sleepe, ther Richesse, and hel-gate them both betwext.
SPENSER—*Faerie Queene*. Bk. II. Canto VII. St. 25.
(See also BROWNE)

1
All gifts but one the jealous God may keep
From our soul's longing, one he cannot—sleep.
This, though he grudge all other grace to prayer,
This grace his closed hand cannot choose but spare.
SWINBURNE—*Tristram of Lyonesse. Prelude to Tristram and Iseult.* L. 205.

2
She sleeps: her breathings are not heard
In palace chambers far apart,
The fragrant tresses are not stirr'd
That lie upon her charmed heart.
She sleeps: on either hand upswells
The gold fringed pillow lightly prest:
She sleeps, nor dreams, but ever dwells
A perfect form in perfect rest.
TENNYSON—*Day Dream. The Sleeping Beauty.* St. 3.

3
The mystery
Of folded sleep.
TENNYSON—*Dream of Fair Women.* St. 66.

4
When in the down I sink my head,
Sleep, Death's twin-brother, times my breath.
TENNYSON—*In Memoriam.* Pt. LXVIII.

5
For is there aught in Sleep can charm the wise?
To lie in dead oblivion, loosing half
The fleeting moments of too short a life—
* * * * * *
Who would in such a gloomy state remain
Longer than Nature craves?
THOMSON—*Seasons. Summer.* L. 71.

6
Who can wrestle against Sleep?—Yet is that giant very gentleness.
MARTIN TUPPER—*Of Beauty.*

7
Yet never sleep the sun up. Prayer shou'd
Dawn with the day. There are set, awful hours
'Twixt heaven and us. The manna was not good
After sun-rising; far day sullies flowres.
Rise to prevent the sun; sleep doth sin glut,
And heaven's gate opens when the world's is shut.
HENRY VAUGHAN—*Rules and Lessons.* St. 2.

8
Softly, O midnight hours!
Move softly o'er the bowers
Where lies in happy sleep a girl so fair:
For ye have power, men say,
Our hearts in sleep to sway
And cage cold fancies in a moonlight snare.
AUBREY THOS. DE VERE—*Song. Softly, O Midnight Hours.*

9
Deep rest and sweet, most like indeed to death's own quietness.
VERGIL—*Æneid.* Bk. VI. L. 522. WM. MORRIS' trans.
(See also BROWNE)

10
Tu dors, Brutus, et Rome est dans les fers.
Thou sleepest, Brutus, and yet Rome is in chains.
VOLTAIRE—*La Mort de César.* II. 2.

11
Hush, my dear, lie still and slumber!
Holy angels guard thy bed!
Heavenly blessings without number
Gently falling on thy head.
WATTS—*Cradle Hymn.*

12
'Tis the voice of the sluggard I hear him complain;
"You've waked me too soon, I must slumber again.
* * * * * *
A little more sleep and a little more slumber."
WATTS—*Moral Songs. The Sluggard.*

13
Come, gentle sleep! attend thy votary's prayer,
And, though death's image, to my couch repair;
How sweet, though lifeless, yet with life to lie,
And, without dying, O how sweet to die!
JOHN WOLCOT (Peter Pindar). Trans. of THOS. WARTON'S Latin Epigram on Sleep for a statue of Somnus in the garden of Mr. Harris.

14
And to tired limbs and over-busy thoughts,
Inviting sleep and soft forgetfulness.
WORDSWORTH—*The Excursion.* Bk. IV.

15
Tired Nature's sweet restorer, balmy sleep!
He, like the world, his ready visit pays
Where fortune smiles; the wretched he forsakes.
YOUNG—*Night Thoughts.* Night I. L. 1.

16
Creation sleeps. 'Tis as the general pulse
Of life stood still, and nature made a pause.
YOUNG—*Night Thoughts.* Night I. L. 23.

SLOE

Prunus Spinosa

17
From the white-blossomed sloe, my dear Chloe requested,
A sprig her fair breast to adorn.
No! by Heav'n, I exclaim'd, may I perish,
If ever I plant in that bosom a thorn.
JOHN O'KEEFE—*The Thorn.*

SMILES

18
What's the use of worrying?
It never was worth while, so
Pack up your troubles in your old kit-bag,
And smile, smile, smile.
GEORGE ASAF—*Smile, Smile, Smile.*

19
Smiles form the channels of a future tear.
BYRON—*Childe Harold.* Canto II. St. 97.

20
Cervantes smiled Spain's chivalry away;
A single laugh demolished the right arm
Of his own country;—seldom since that day
Has Spain had heroes.
BYRON—*Don Juan.* Canto XIII. St. 11.

21
But owned that smile, if oft observed and near,
Waned in its mirth, and wither'd to a sneer.
BYRON—*Lara.* Canto I. St. 17. L. 11.

22
From thy own smile I snatched the snake.
BYRON—*Manfred.*
(See also SHELLEY)

1
Her very frowns are fairer far
Than smiles of other maidens are.
HARTLEY COLERIDGE—*She is not Fair.*

2
In came Mrs. Fezziwig, one vast substantial smile.
DICKENS—*Christmas Carol.* Stave 2.

3
The smile of her I love is like the dawn
Whose touch makes Memnon sing:
O see where wide the golden sunlight flows—
The barren desert blossoms as the rose!
R. W. GILDER—*The Smile of Her I Love.*

4
With the smile that was childlike and bland.
BRET HARTE—*Language of Truthful James.* (*Heathen Chinee.*)

5
Reproof on her lip, but a smile in her eye.
SAMUEL LOVER—*Rory O'More.*
(See also SCOTT)

6
Whence that three-cornered smile of bliss?
Three angels gave me at once a kiss.
GEORGE MACDONALD—*Baby.* St. 7.

7 ——— A smile that glow'd
Celestial rosy red, love's proper hue.
MILTON—*Paradise Lost.* Bk. VIII. L. 618.

8 For smiles from reason flow
To brute deny'd, and are of love the food.
MILTON—*Paradise Lost.* Bk. IX. L. 239.

9
The thing that goes the farthest towards making life worth while,
That costs the least, and does the most, is just a pleasant smile.
* * * * * *
It's full of worth and goodness too, with manly kindness blent,
It's worth a million dollars and it doesn't cost a cent.
W. D. NESBIT—*Let us Smile.*

10
Eternal smiles his emptiness betray,
As shallow streams run dimpling all the way.
POPE—*Prologue to Satires.* L. 315.

11
With a smile on her lips, and a tear in her eye.
SCOTT—*Marmion.* Canto V. St. 12.
(See also LOVER)

12 Nobly he yokes
A smiling with a sigh, as if the sigh
Was that it was, for not being such a smile:
The smile mocking the sigh, that it would fly
From so divine a temple, to commix
With winds that sailors rail at.
Cymbeline. Act IV. Sc. 2. L. 51.

13
My tables,—meet it is I set it down,
That one may smile, and smile, and be a villain;
At least I'm sure it may be so in Denmark.
Hamlet. Act I. Sc. 5. L. 107.

14
Seldom he smiles, and smiles in such a sort
As if he mock'd himself, and scorn'd his spirit
That could be mov'd to smile at anything.
Julius Cæsar. Act I. Sc. 2. L. 205.

15 Those happy smilets,
That play'd on her ripe lip, seem'd not to know
What guests were in her eyes; which parted thence,
As pearls from diamonds dropp'd.
King Lear. Act IV. Sc. 3. L. 21.

16
There is a snake in thy smile, my dear,
And bitter poison within thy tear.
SHELLEY—*Beatrice Cenci.*
(See also BYRON)

17
The smile that flickers on baby's lips when he sleeps—does anybody know where it was born? Yes, there is a rumor that a young pale beam of a crescent moon touched the edge of a vanishing autumn cloud, and there the smile was first born in the dream of a dew-washed morning.
RABINDRANATH TAGORE—*Gitanjali.* 61.

18
'Tis easy enough to be pleasant,
When life flows along like a song;
But the man worth while is the one who will smile
When everything goes dead wrong;
For the test of the heart is trouble,
And it always comes with the years,
But the smile that is worth the praise of earth
Is the smile that comes through tears.
* * * * *
But the virtue that conquers passion,
And the sorrow that hides in a smile—
It is these that are worth the homage of earth,
For we find them but once in a while.
ELLA WHEELER WILCOX—*Worth While.*

19
I feel in every smile a chain.
JOHN WOLCOT (Peter Pindar)—*Pindariana.*

20
And she hath smiles to earth unknown—
Smiles that with motion of their own
Do spread, and sink, and rise.
WORDSWORTH—*I met Louisa in the Shade.* St. 2. (Afterwards cancelled by him, not found in complete ed. of poems.)

21
A tender smile, our sorrows' only balm.
YOUNG—*Love of Fame.* Satire V. L. 108.

22
A man I knew who lived upon a smile,
And well it fed him; he look'd plump and fair,
While rankest venom foam'd through every vein.
YOUNG—*Night Thoughts.* Night VIII. L. 336.

SMOKING (See TOBACCO)

SNEER (See also CONTEMPT, SCORN)

23
Sapping a solemn creed with a solemn sneer.
BYRON—*Childe Harold.* Canto III. St. 107.

24
There was a laughing Devil in his sneer,
That raised emotions both of rage and fear.
BYRON—*Corsair.* Canto I. St. 9.

25
Who can refute a sneer?
PALEY—*Moral Philosophy. Of Reverencing the Deity.* Vol. II. Bk. V. Ch. IX.

SNOW

1
Lo, sifted through the winds that blow,
Down comes the soft and silent snow,
White petals from the flowers that grow
In the cold atmosphere.
GEORGE W. BUNGAY—*The Artists of the Air.*

2
Through the sharp air a flaky torrent flies,
Mocks the slow sight, and hides the gloomy skies;
The fleecy clouds their chilly bosoms bare,
And shed their substance on the floating air.
CRABBE—*Inebriety.*

3
Announced by all the trumpets of the sky,
Arrives the snow, and, driving o'er the fields,
Seems nowhere to alight: the whited air
Hides hills and woods, the river, and the heaven,
And veils the farmhouse at the garden's end.
The sled and traveller stopped, the courier's feet
Delayed, all friends shut out, the housemates sit
Around the radiant fireplace, enclosed
In a tumultuous privacy of storm.
EMERSON—*The Snow-Storm.*

4
Come, see the north-wind's masonry.
Out of an unseen quarry evermore
Furnished with tile, the fierce artificer
Curves his white bastions with projected roof
Round every windward stake, or tree, or door.
Speeding, the myriad-handed, his wild work
So fanciful, so savage, naught cares he
For number or proportion.
EMERSON—*The Snow-Storm.*

5
Out of the bosom of the Air,
Out of the cloud-folds of her garments shaken,
Over the woodlands brown and bare,
Over the harvest-fields forsaken,
Silent, and soft, and slow
Descends the snow.
LONGFELLOW—*Snow-Flakes.*

6
Where's the snow
That fell the year that's fled—where's the snow?
LOVER—*The Snow.*
(See also VILLON)

7
Notre Dame des Neiges.
Our Lady of the Snows.
EMILE NELLIGAN. Title of a poem.

8
Sancta Maria ad Nives.
Name of the basilica dedicated to Our Lady, now known as Santa Maria Maggiora. Many Catholic churches so called after the famous legend.

9
As I saw fair Chloris walk alone,
The feather'd snow came softly down,
As Jove, descending from his tow'r
To court her in a silver show'r.
The wanton snow flew to her breast,
As little birds into their nest;
But o'ercome with whiteness there,
For grief dissolv'd into a tear.
Thence falling on her garment hem,
To deck her, froze into a gem.
On Chloris walking in the Snow. In *Wit's Recreations.* J. C. HOTTEN's reprint. P. 308. (1640)

10
Mais où sont les neiges d'antan? C'estoit le plus grand soucy qu'eust Villon, le poëte parisien.
But where are the snows of last year? That was the greatest concern of Villon, the Parisian poet.
RABELAIS—*Pantagruel.* Ch. XIV.
(See also VILLON)

11
A little snow, tumbled about, anon becomes a mountain.
King John. Act III. Sc. 4. L. 176.

12
O that I were a mockery king of snow,
Standing before the sun of Bolingbroke,
To melt myself away in water drops!
Richard II. Act IV. Sc. 1. L. 260.

13
For thou wilt lie upon the wings of night
Whiter than new snow on a raven's back.
Romeo and Juliet. Act III. Sc. 2. L. 18.

14
Lawn as white as driven snow.
Winter's Tale. Act IV. Sc. 4. L. 220.

15
Mais où sont les neiges d'antan?
But where are the snows of yester year?
VILLON—*Ballade des Dames du Temps Jadis.*
(See also LOVER, RABELAIS, also OMAR under ROSE)

16
O the snow, the beautiful snow,
Filling the sky and earth below;
Over the house-tops, over the street,
Over the heads of the people you meet,
Dancing, flirting, skimming along.
JAMES W. WATSON—*Beautiful Snow*

SNOW-DROP

Galanthus Nivalis

17
At the head of Flora's dance;
Simple Snow-drop, then in thee
All thy sister-train I see;
Every brilliant bud that blows,
From the blue-bell to the rose;
All the beauties that appear,
On the bosom of the Year,
All that wreathe the locks of Spring,
Summer's ardent breath perfume,
Or on the lap of Autumn bloom,
All to thee their tribute bring.
MONTGOMERY—*Snow-Drop.*

18
The morning star of flowers.
MONTGOMERY—*Snow-Drop.*

19
Nor will I then thy modest grace forget,
Chaste Snow-drop, venturous harbinger of Spring,
And pensive monitor of fleeting years!
WORDSWORTH—*To a Snow-Drop.*

20
Lone Flower, hemmed in with snows and white as they
But hardier far, once more I see thee bend
Thy forehead, as if fearful to offend,
Like an unbidden guest. Though day by day,
Storms, sallying from the mountain tops, waylay
The rising sun, and on the plains descend;
Yet art thou welcome, welcome as a friend
Whose zeal outruns his promise!
WORDSWORTH—*To a Snow-Drop.*

SOCIETY

1
For it is most true that a natural and secret hatred and aversation towards society in any man, hath somewhat of the savage beast.
BACON—*Essays. Civil and Moral. Of Friendship.*

2
A people is but the attempt of many
To rise to the completer life of one—
And those who live as models for the mass
Are singly of more value than they all.
ROBERT BROWNING—*Luria.* Act V. L. 334.

3
But now being lifted into high society,
And having pick'd up several odds and ends
Of free thoughts in his travels for variety,
He deem'd, being in a lone isle, among friends,
That without any danger of a riot, he
Might for long lying make himself amends;
And singing as he sung in his warm youth,
Agree to a short armistice with truth.
BYRON—*Don Juan.* Canto III. St. 83.

4
Those families, you know, are our upper crust, not upper ten thousand.
COOPER—*The Ways of the Hour.* Ch. VI.
(See also WILLIS)

5
The rout is Folly's circle, which she draws
With magic wand. So potent is the spell,
That none decoy'd into that fatal ring,
Unless by Heaven's peculiar grace, escape.
There we grow early gray, but never wise.
COWPER—*Task.* Bk. II. L. 627.

6
Every man is like the company he is wont to keep.
EURIPIDES—*Phœnissæ.* Frag. 809.

7
For every social wrong there must be a remedy. But the remedy can be nothing less than the abolition of the wrong.
HENRY GEORGE—*Social Problems.* Ch. IX.

8
The noisy and extensive scene of crowds without company, and dissipation without pleasure.
GIBBON—*Memoirs.* Vol. I. P. 116.

9
I live in the crowds of jollity, not so much to enjoy company as to shun myself.
SAMUEL JOHNSON—*Rasselas.* Ch. XVI.

10
Le sage quelquefois évite le monde de peur d'être ennuyé.
The wise man sometimes flees from society from fear of being bored.
LA BRUYÈRE—*Les Caractères.* V.

11
He might have proved a useful adjunct, if not an ornament to society.
LAMB—*Captain Starkey.*

12
Society is like a large piece of frozen water; and skating well is the great art of social life.
L. E. LANDON.

13
The Don Quixote of one generation may live to hear himself called the savior of society by the next.
LOWELL—*Don Quixote.*

14
A system in which the two great commandments were, to hate your neighbour and to love your neighbour's wife.
MACAULAY—*Essays. Moore's Life of Lord Byron.*

15
Old Lady T-sh-nd [Townshend] formerly observed that the human race might be divided into three separate classes—men, women and H-v-eys [Herveys].
Attributed to LADY MARY WORTLEY MONTAGU in LORD WHARNCLIFFE'S Ed. of her *Letters and Works.* LADY LOUISA STUART, in introductory anecdotes to the same, also credits the saying to Lady Montague. Vol. I. P. 67. Attributed to CHARLES PIGOTT in *The Jockey Club.* Pt. II. P. 4. (Ed. 1792)
(See also SMITH)

16
La Société est l'union des hommes, et non pas les hommes.
Society is the union of men and not the men themselves.
MONTESQUIEU—*De l'Esprit.* X. 3.

17
This new rage for rhyming badly,
Which late hath seized all ranks and classes,
Down to that new estate 'the masses.'
MOORE—*The Fudges in England.* Letter 4.
The classes and the masses.
A phrase used by GLADSTONE.

18
What will Mrs. Grundy say?
THOS. MORTON—*Speed the Plough.* Act I. Sc. 1. (Ed. 1808)

19
Heav'n forming each on other to depend,
A master, or a servant, or a friend,
Bids each on other for assistance call,
Till one man's weakness grows the strength of all.
POPE—*Essay on Man.* Ep. II. L. 249.

20
Sociale animal est.
[Man] is a social animal.
SENECA—*De Beneficiis.* Bk. VII. 1.

21
Society is no comfort
To one not sociable.
Cymbeline. Act IV. Sc. 2. L. 12.

22
Whilst I was big in clamour came there in a man,
Who, having seen me in my worst estate,
Shunn'd my abhorr'd society.
King Lear. Act V. Sc. 3. L. 208.

23
To make society
The sweeter welcome, we will keep ourself
Till supper-time alone.
Macbeth. Act III. Sc. 1. L. 42.

24
Men lived like fishes; the great ones devoured the small.
ALGERNON SIDNEY—*Discourses on Government.* Ch. II. Sec. XVIII.

25
As the French say, there are three sexes,—men women, and clergymen.
SYDNEY SMITH—*Lady Holland's Memoir.* Vol. I. P. 262.
(See also MONTAGU)

1
Ah, you flavour everything; you are the vanille of society.
SYDNEY SMITH—*Lady Holland's Memoir*. Vol. I. P. 262.

2
It is impossible, in our condition of Society, not to be sometimes a Snob.
THACKERAY—*Book of Snobs*. Ch. III.

3
Society therefore is as ancient as the world.
VOLTAIRE—*Philosophical Dictionary. Policy.*

4
Other people are quite dreadful. The only possible society is oneself.
OSCAR WILDE—*An Ideal Husband*. Act III.

5
I suppose Society is wonderfully delightful.
To be in it is merely a bore. But to be out of it is simply a tragedy.
OSCAR WILDE—*Woman of No Importance*. Act III.

6
At present there is no distinction among the upper ten thousand of the city.
N. P. WILLIS—*Necessity for a Promenade Drive.*
(See also COOPER)

7
Society became my glittering bride,
And airy hopes my children.
WORDSWORTH—*The Excursion*. Bk. III.

8
Nor greetings where no kindness is, nor all
The dreary intercourse of daily life.
WORDSWORTH—*Lines composed a few miles above Tintern Abbey.*

9
There is
One great society alone on earth:
The noble Living and the noble Dead.
WORDSWORTH—*The Prelude*. Bk. XI.

SOLDIERS (See also NAVY, WAR)

10
O Dormer, how can I behold thy fate,
And not the wonders of thy youth relate;
How can I see the gay, the brave, the young,
Fall in the cloud of war, and lie unsung!
In joys of conquest he resigns his breath,
And, filled with England's glory, smiles in death.
ADDISON—*Campaign. To Philip Dormer.*

11
God and a soldier all people adore
In time of war, but not before;
And when war is over and all things are righted,
God is neglected and an old soldier slighted.
ANON. Lines chalked on a sentry-box on Europa Guard. Compare KIPLING—*Tommy*. OTWAY'S *Soldier's Fortune*, SHAKESPEARE'S *Sonnet XXV*.
(See also OWEN under FORGETFULNESS)

12
O little Force that in your agony
Stood fast while England girt her armour on,
Held high our honour in your wounded hands,
Carried our honour safe with bleeding feet—
We have no glory great enough for you,
The very soul of Britain keeps your day.
ANON—*Published in a London Newspaper*, 1917.

13
An Austrian army awfully arrayed.
Siege of Belgrade.
Poem arranged with "Apt alliteration's artful aid." First appeared in *The Trifler*, May 7, 1817, printed at Winchester, Eng. Found in *Bentley's Miscellany*, March, 1838. P. 313. Quoted in *Wheeler's Mag.* Winchester, Eng. Vol. I. P. 344. (1828) Attributed to REV. B. POULTER, of Winchester. In the *Wild Garland* to ISAAC J. REEVE. Claimed for ALARIC A. WATTS by his son in a biography of Watts. Vol. I. P. 118.

14
See! There is Jackson standing like a stone wall.
BERNARD E. BEE—*Battle of Manassas (Bull Run)*. July 21, 1861.

15
Each year his mighty armies marched forth in gallant show,
Their enemies were targets, their bullets they were tow.
BERENGER—*Le Roi d'Yvetot*. Trans. by THACKERAY—*The King of Brentford.*

16
The king of France with twenty thousand men
Went up the hill, and then came down again:
The king of Spain with twenty thousand more
Climbed the same hill the French had climbed before.
From *Sloane MS*. 1489. Written time of CHARLES I. Later version in *Old Tarleton's Song* in *Pigge's Corantol or News from the North*. HALLIWELL gives several versions in his *Nursery Rhymes.*

17
L'infanterie anglaise est la plus redoubtable de l'Europe; heureusement, il n'y en a pas beaucoup.
The English Infantry is the most formidable in Europe, but fortunately there is not much of it.
MARSHAL BUGEAUD—*Œuvres Militaires*. Collected by WEIL.

18
You led our sons across the haunted flood,
Into the Canaan of their high desire—
No milk and honey there, but tears and blood
Flowed where the hosts of evil trod in fire,
And left a worse than desert where they passed.
AMELIA J. BURR—*To General Pershing.*

19
Ay me! what perils do environ
The man that meddles with cold iron!
BUTLER—*Hudibras*. Pt. I. Canto III. L. 1.
(See also ENGLISH under WOMAN)

20
Earth! render back from out thy breast
A remnant of our Spartan dead!
Of the three hundred grant but three,
To make a new Thermopylæ!
BYRON—*Don Juan*. Canto III. St. 86.

21
His breast with wounds unnumber'd riven,
His back to earth, his face to heaven.
BYRON—*Giaour*. L. 675.

22
For the army is a school in which the miser becomes generous, and the generous prodigal; miserly soldiers are like monsters, but very rarely seen.
CERVANTES—*Don Quixote*. Ch. XXXIX.

1
The knight's bones are dust,
And his good sword rust;
His soul is with the saints, I trust.
COLERIDGE—*The Knight's Tomb.*

2
How sleep the brave, who sink to rest,
By all their country's wishes blest!
* * * * *
By fairy hands their knell is rung,
By forms unseen their dirge is sung.
COLLINS—*Ode Written in* 1746.

3
Who passes down this road so late?
Compagnon de la Majaloine?
Who passes down this road so late,
Always gay!

Of all the King's Knights 'tis the flower,
Compagnon de la Majaloine,
Of all the King's Knights 'tis the flower,
Always gay!
Compagnon de la Majaloine. Old French Song.

4
Back of the boy is Wilson,
Pledge of his high degree,
Back of the boy is Lincoln,
Lincoln and Grant and Lee;
Back of the boy is Jackson,
Jackson and Tippecanoe,
Back of each son is Washington,
And the old red, white and blue!
EDMUND VANCE COOKE—*Back of the Boy.*

5
I have seen men march to the wars, and then
I have watched their homeward tread,
And they brought back bodies of living men,
But their eyes were cold and dead.
So, Buddy, no matter what else the fame,
No matter what else the prize,
I want you to come back thru The Flame
With the boy-look still in your eyes!
EDMUND VANCE COOKE—*The Boy-Look.*

6
He stands erect; his slouch becomes a walk;
He steps right onward, martial in his air,
His form and movement.
COWPER—*The Task.* Bk. IV. L. 638.

7
Far in foreign fields from Dunkirk to Belgrade
Lie the soldiers and chiefs of the Irish Brigade.
THOMAS DAVIS—*Battle Eve of the Brigade.*
(See also BROOKE under ENGLAND, INGRAHAM under IRELAND)

8
Terrible he rode alone,
With his yemen sword for aid;
Ornament it carried none
But the notches on the blade.
The Death Feud. An Arab War Song. St. 14. *Tait's Edinburgh Magazine.* July, 1850. Trans. signed J. S. M.

9
His helmet now shall make
A hive for bees.
ROBERT DEVEREUX—*Sonnet.*

10
So let his name through Europe ring!
A man of mean estate,
Who died as firm as Sparta's king,
Because his soul was great.
SIR FRANCIS HASTINGS DOYLE—*The Private of the Buffs.*

11
Mouths without hands; maintained at vast expense,
In peace a charge, in war a weak defense:
Stout once a month they march, a blustering band,
And ever, but in times of need, at hand.
DRYDEN—*Cymon and Iphigenia.* L. 401.

12
Under the sod and the dew,
Waiting the Judgment Day;
Love and tears for the Blue,
Tears and love for the Gray.
FRANCIS M. FINCH—*The Blue and the Gray.*

13
Hunde, wollt ihr ewig leben?
Dogs, would you live forever?
Traditional saying of FREDERICK THE GREAT to his troops at Kolin, June 18. 1757 (or at Kunersdorf, Aug. 12, 1759). Doubted by CARLYLE.

14
We are coming, Father Abraham, three hundred thousand more.
J. S. GIBBONS. Pub. anon. in New York *Evening Post,* July 16, 1862.

15
The broken soldier, kindly bade to stay;
Sat by his fire, and talked the night away,
Wept o'er his wounds, or tales of sorrow done,
Shoulder'd his crutch, and show'd how fields were won.
GOLDSMITH—*Deserted Village.* L. 155.

16
Wake, soldier wake, thy war-horse waits
To bear thee to the battle back;—
Thou slumberest at a foeman's gates,—
Thy dog would break thy bivouac;
Thy plume is trailing in the dust,
And thy red falchion gathering rust.
T. K. HERVEY—*Dead Trumpeter.*

17
He slept an iron sleep,—
Slain fighting for his country.
HOMER—*Iliad.* Bk. XI. L. 285. BRYANT'S trans.

18
The sex is ever to a soldier kind.
HOMER—*Odyssey.* Bk. XIV. L. 246. POPE'S trans.

19
Ben Battle was a soldier bold,
And used to war's alarms;
But a cannon-ball took off his legs,
So he laid down his arms.
HOOD—*Faithless Nellie Gray.*

20
But for you, it shall be forever Spring,
And only you shall be forever fearless,
And only you shall have white, straight, tireless limbs,
And only you, where the water lily swims,
Shall walk along pathways, thro' the willows
Of your West.
You who went West,

And only you on silvery twilight pillows
Shall take your rest
In the soft, sweet glooms
Of twilight rooms.
FORD MADOX HUEFFER—*One Day's List.*

1
The Seconds that tick as the clock moves along
Are Privates who march with a spirit so strong.
The Minutes are Captains. The Hours of the day
Are Officers brave, who lead on to the fray.
So, remember, when tempted to loiter and dream
You've an army at hand; your command is supreme;
And question yourself, as it goes on review—
Has it helped in the fight with the best it could do?
PHILANDER JOHNSON. Lines selected by PAYMASTER GEN. MCGOWAN to distribute to those under his command during the Great War. See *Everybody's Magazine*, May, 1920. P. 36.

2
He smote them hip and thigh.
Judges. XV. 8.

3
In a wood they call the Rouge Bouquet,
There is a new-made grave today,
Built by never a spade nor pick,
Yet covered with earth ten meters thick.
There lie many fighting men,
Dead in their youthful prime.
JOYCE KILMER—*Rouge Bouquet.*

4
Let not him that girdeth on his harness boast himself as he that putteth it off.
I Kings. XX. 11.

5
As we pledge the health of our general, who fares as rough as we,
What can daunt us, what can turn us, led to death by such as he?
CHARLES KINGSLEY—*A March.*

6
"What are the bugles blowin' for?" said Files-on-Parade.
"To turn you out, to turn you out," the Colour Sergeant said.
KIPLING—*Danny Deever.*

7
"For they're hangin' Danny Deever, you can 'ear the Dead March play,
The regiment's in 'ollow square—They're hangin' him to-day;
They're taken of his buttons off an' cut his stripes away,
An' they're hangin' Danny Deever in the morning."
KIPLING—*Danny Deever.*

8
The 'eathen in 'is blindness bows down to wood an' stone;
'E don't obey no orders unless they is 'is own;
'E keeps 'is side-arms awful: 'e leaves 'em all about,
An' then comes up the Regiment an' pokes the 'eathen out.
KIPLING—*The 'Eathen.*

9
So 'ere's to you, Fuzzy-Wuzzy, at your 'ome in the Soudan;
You're a pore benighted 'eathen but a first-class fightin' man;
And 'ere's to you, Fuzzy-Wuzzy, with your 'ayrick 'ead of 'air;
You big black boundin' beggar—for you broke a British square!
KIPLING—*Fuzzy-Wuzzy.*

10
For it's Tommy this an' Tommy that, an' "Chuck 'im out, the brute!"
But it's "Savior of 'is country," when the guns begin to shoot.
KIPLING—*Tommy.*

11
It is not the guns or armament
Or the money they can pay,
It's the close co-operation
That makes them win the day.
It is not the individual
Or the army as a whole,
But the everlastin' teamwork
Of every bloomin' soul.
J. MASON KNOX. Claimed for him by his wife in a communication in New York *Times.*

12
But in a large sense we cannot dedicate, we cannot hallow this ground. The brave men, living and dead, who struggled here, have consecrated it far above our poor power to add or detract.
LINCOLN—*Gettysburg Address.* Nov. 19, 1863.

13
Nulla fides pietasque viris qui castra sequuntur.
Good faith and probity are rarely found among the followers of the camp.
LUCAN—*Pharsalia.* X. 407.

14
Ned has gone, he's gone away, he's gone away for good.
He's called, he's killed.
Him and his drum lies in the rain, lies where they was stood.
Where they was stilled.
A. NEIL LYONS ("Edwin Smallweed")—*Drums.* Appeared in the London *Weekly Dispatch.*

15
Nicanor lay dead in his harness.
II Maccabees. XV. 28.

16
Here's to the Blue of the wind-swept North
When we meet on the fields of France,
May the spirit of Grant be with you all
As the sons of the North advance!

* * * * *

Here's to the Gray of the sun-kissed South
When we meet on the fields of France,
May the spirit of Lee be with you all
As the sons of the South advance!

* * * * *

And here's to the Blue and the Gray as One!
When we meet on the fields of France,
May the spirit of God be with us all
As the sons of the Flag advance!
GEORGE MORROW MAYO—*A Toast.*

1
"Companions," said he [Saturninus], "you have lost a good captain, to make of him a bad general."
MONTAIGNE—*Essays. Of Vanity.*

2
Napoleon's troops fought in bright fields where every helmet caught some beams of glory; but the British soldier conquered under the cold shade of aristocracy.
SIR W. F. P. NAPIER—*Hist. of the Peninsular War.* II. 401. (Ed. 1851)

3
The greatest general is he who makes the fewest mistakes.
Saying attributed to NAPOLEON.

4
Judge not that ye be not judged; we carried the torch to the goal.
The goal is won: guard the fire: it is yours: but remember our soul
Breathes through the life that we saved, when our lives went out in the night:
Your body is woven of ours: see that the torch is alight.
EDWARD J. O'BRIEN—*On the Day of Achievement.*

5
The muffled drum's sad roll has beat
The soldier's last tattoo;
No more on Life's parade shall meet
The brave and fallen few.
On Fame's eternal camping-ground
Their silent tents are spread,
And Glory guards, with solemn round
The bivouac of the dead.
THEODORE O'HARA—*The Bivouac of the Dead.*

6
Miles gloriosus.
The bragging soldier.
PLAUTUS. Title of a comedy.

7
But off with your hat and three times three for
Columbia's true-blue sons;
The men below who batter the foe—the men
behind the guns!
JOHN JEROME ROONEY—*The Men Behind the Guns.*

8
I want to see you shoot the way you shout.
ROOSEVELT. At the meeting of the Mayor's Committee on National Defense. Madison Square, Oct., 1917. Speech to the audience after their enthusiastic demonstration over the patriotic addresses.

9
A thousand leagues of ocean, a company of kings,
You came across the watching world to show how heroes die.
When the splendour of your story
Builds the halo of its glory,
'Twill belt the earth like Saturn's rings
And diadem the sky.
"M.R.C.S." In *Anzac.* On Colonial Soldiers. (1919)

10
'Tis a far, far cry from the "Minute-Men,"
And the times of the buff and blue
To the days of the withering Jorgensen
And the hand that holds it true.
'Tis a far, far cry from Lexington
To the isles of the China Sea,
But ever the same the man and the gun—
Ever the same are we.
EDWIN L. SABIN—*The American Soldier.* In *Munsey's Mag.* July, 1899.

11
Abner . . . smote him under the fifth rib.
II Samuel. II. 23.

12
Soldier, rest! thy warfare o'er,
Dream of fighting fields no more:
Sleep the sleep that knows not breaking,
Morn of toil, nor night of waking.
SCOTT—*Lady of the Lake.* Canto I. St. 31.

13
Although too much of a soldier among sovereigns, no one could claim with better right to be a sovereign among soldiers.
SCOTT—*Life of Napoleon.*

14
Warriors!—and where are warriors found,
If not on martial Britain's ground?
And who, when waked with note of fire,
Love more than they the British lyre?
SCOTT—*Lord of the Isles.* Canto IV. St. 20.

15
Yet what can they see in the longest kingly line in Europe, save that it runs back to a successful soldier?
SCOTT—*Woodstock.* Ch. XXXVII.

16
Then a soldier,
Full of strange oaths and bearded like the pard,
Jealous in honour, sudden and quick in quarrel,
Seeking the bubble reputation
Even in the cannon's mouth.
As You Like It. Act II. Sc. 7. L. 149.

17
Arm'd at point exactly, cap-à-pie.
Hamlet. Act I. Sc. 2. L. 200.

18
I thought upon one pair of English legs
Did march three Frenchmen.
Henry V. Act III. Sc. 6. L. 158.

19
Give them great meals of beef and iron and steel, they will eat like wolves and fight like devils.
Henry V. Act III. Sc. 7. L. 161.

20
I am a soldier and unapt to weep
Or to exclaim on fortune's fickleness.
Henry VI. Pt. I. Act V. Sc. 3. L. 134.

21
I said an elder soldier, not a better.
Did I say, better?
Julius Cæsar. Act IV. Sc. 3. L. 56.

22
Fie, my Lord, fie! a soldier, and afear'd?
Macbeth. Act V. Sc. 1. L. 41.

23
Blow, wind! come, wrack!
At least we'll die with harness on our back.
Macbeth. Act V. Sc. 5. L. 51.

24
God's soldier be he!
Had I as many sons as I have hairs,
I would not wish them to a fairer death:
And so his knell is knoll'd.
Macbeth. Act V. Sc. 8. L. 47.

1
He is a soldier fit to stand by Cæsar
And give direction.
Othello. Act II. Sc. 3. L. 127.

2
The painful warrior famoused for fight,
After a thousand victories once foiled,
Is from the book of honour razed quite,
And all the rest forgot for which he toiled,
Sonnet XXV. "Fight" is "worth" in original.
(See also KIPLING)

3
A soldier is an anachronism of which we must get rid.
BERNARD SHAW—*Devil's Disciple.* Act III.

4
When the military man approaches, the world locks up its spoons and packs off its womankind.
BERNARD SHAW—*Man and Superman.*

5
Prostrate on earth the bleeding warrior lies,
And Isr'el's beauty on the mountains dies.
How are the mighty fallen!
Hush'd be my sorrow, gently fall my tears,
Lest my sad tale should reach the alien's ears:
Bid Fame be dumb, and tremble to proclaim
In heathen Gath, or Ascalon, our shame
Lest proud Philistia, lest our haughty foe,
With impious scorn insult our solemn woe.
W. C. SOMERVILLE—*The Lamentation of David over Saul and Jonathan.*

6
Sleep, soldiers! still in honored rest
Your truth and valor wearing:
The bravest are the tenderest,—
The loving are the daring.
BAYARD TAYLOR—*The Song of the Camp.*

7
Foremost captain of his time,
Rich in saving common sense.
TENNYSON—*Ode on the Death of the Duke of Wellington.*

8
For this is England's greatest son,
He that gain'd a hundred fights,
And never lost an English gun.
TENNYSON—*Ode on the Death of the Duke of Wellington.*

9
Home they brought her warrior dead.
TENNYSON—*The Princess.* Song at end of Canto V.

10
Home they brought him slain with spears,
They brought him home at even-fall.
TENNYSON. Version of the song in *The Princess.* Canto V, as published in the *Selections.* (1865) T. J. WISE—*Bibliography of Tennyson.* Only reprinted in the *Miniature Edition.* (1870) Vol. III. P. 147.

11
Dans ce pays-ci il est bon de tuer de temps en temps un admiral pour encourager les autres.
In this country it is found necessary now and then to put an admiral to death in order to encourage the others.
VOLTAIRE—*Candide.* Ch. XXIII.

12
Old soldiers never die;
They fade away!
War Song, popular in England. (1919)

13
Under the tricolor, long khaki files of them
Through the Étoile, down the Champs Elysées
Marched, while grisettes blew their kisses to miles of them,
And only the old brushed the tear stains away—
Out where the crows spread their ominous pinions
Shadowing France from Nancy to Fay,
Singing they marched 'gainst the Kaiser's gray minions,
Singing the song of boyhood at play.
CHARLES LAW WATKINS—*The Boys who never grew up.* To the Foreign Legion. Written on the Somme, Dec., 1916.

14
The more we work, the more we may,
It makes no difference to our pay.
We are the Royal Sappers. War Song, popular in England. (1915)

15
Our youth has stormed the hosts of hell and won;
Yet we who pay the price of their oblation
Know that the greater war is just begun
Which makes humanity the nations' Nation.
WILLARD WATTLES—*The War at Home.*

16
Where are the boys of the old Brigade,
Who fought with us side by side?
F. E. WEATHERLEY—*The Old Brigade.*

17
Oh, a strange hand writes for our dear son—O, stricken mother's soul!
All swims before her eyes—flashes with black—she catches the main words only;
Sentences broken—*gun-shot wound in the breast, cavalry skirmish, taken to hospital;*
At present low, but will soon be better.
WALT WHITMAN—*Drum-Taps. Come up from the Fields, Father.*

18
Not a drum was heard, not a funeral note,
As his corse to the rampart we hurried.
CHAS. WOLFE—*The Burial of Sir John Moore at Carunna.* St. 1.

19
No useless coffin enclosed his breast,
Not in sheet nor in shroud we wound him;
But he lay like a warrior taking his rest
With his martial cloak around him.
CHAS. WOLFE—*The Burial of Sir John Moore at Carunna.* St. 3.

20
Of boasting more than of a bomb afraid,
A soldier should be modest as a maid.
YOUNG—*Love of Fame.* Satire IV.

21
Some for hard masters, broken under arms,
In battle lopt away, with half their limbs,
Beg bitter bread thro' realms their valour saved.
YOUNG—*Night Thoughts.* Night I. L. 250.
(See also KIPLING)

SOLITUDE

22
Converse with men makes sharp the glittering wit,
But God to man doth speak in solitude.
JOHN STUART BLACKIE—*Sonnet. Highland Solitude.*

1
I am as one who is left alone at a banquet, the lights dead and the flowers faded.
BULWER-LYTTON—*Last Days of Pompeii*. Ch. V. (See also MOORE)

2 *Alone!*—that worn-out word,
So idly spoken, and so coldly heard;
Yet all that poets sing, and grief hath known,
Of hope laid waste, knells in that word—ALONE!
BULWER-LYTTON—*New Timon*. Pt. II.

3
But 'midst the crowd, the hum, the shock of men,
To hear, to see, to feel, and to possess,
And roam along, the world's tired denizen,
With none who bless us, none whom we can bless.
BYRON—*Childe Harold*. Canto II. St. 26.

4
This is to be alone; this, this is solitude!
BYRON—*Childe Harold*. Canto II. St. 26.

5
In solitude, when we are *least* alone.
BYRON—*Childe Harold*. Canto III. St. 90. (See also CICERO)

6
Among them, but not of them.
BYRON—*Childe Harold*. Canto III. St. 113.

7
'Tis solitude should teach us how to die;
It hath no flatterers; vanity can give
No hollow aid; alone—man with his God must strive.
BYRON—*Childe Harold*. Canto IV. St. 33.

8
Nunquam se minus otiosum esse quam cum otiosus; nec minus solum quam cum solus esset.
That he was never less at leisure than when at leisure; nor that he was ever less alone than when alone.
CICERO—*De Officiis*. Bk. III. Ch. I. Also in Rep. I. 17. 27. A saying of SCIPIO AFRICANUS, as quoted by CATO. Also attributed to ST. BERNARD OF CLAIRVAUX. (See also BYRON, DRUMMOND, GIBBON)

9
Alone, alone, all, all alone,
Alone on a wide, wide sea.
COLERIDGE—*Ancient Mariner*. Pt. IV.

10
So lonely 'twas that God himself
Scarce seemed there to be.
COLERIDGE—*Ancient Mariner*. Pt. VII.

11
I praise the Frenchman; his remark was shrewd,—
"How sweet, how passing sweet is solitude."
But grant me still a friend in my retreat,
Whom I may whisper—Solitude is sweet.
COWPER—*Retirement*. L. 739. The quotation is attributed to LA BRUYÈRE and to JEAN GUEZ DE BALZAC.

12
Oh, for a lodge in some vast wilderness,
Some boundless contiguity of shade,
Where rumour of oppression and deceit,
Of unsuccessful or successful war,
Might never reach me more!
COWPER—*Task*. Bk. II. L. 1. (See also JOHNSON under SUMMER)

13
O solitude, where are the charms
That sages have seen in thy face?
Better dwell in the midst of alarms,
Than reign in this horrible place.
COWPER—*Verses supposed to be written by Alexander Selkirk*.

14
Solitude is the nurse of enthusiasm, and enthusiasm is the true parent of genius. In all ages solitude has been called for—has been flown to.
ISAAC D'ISRAELI—*Literary Character of Men of Genius*. Ch. X.

15
There is a society in the deepest solitude.
ISAAC D'ISRAELI—*Literary Character of Men of Genius*. Ch. X.

16
So vain is the belief
That the sequestered path has fewest flowers.
THOMAS DOUBLEDAY—*Sonnet. The Poet's Solitude*.

17
Thrice happy he, who by some shady grove,
Far from the clamorous world; doth live his own;
Though solitary, who is not alone,
But doth converse with that eternal love.
DRUMMOND—*Urania; or, Spiritual Poems*. (See also CICERO)

18
We enter the world alone, we leave it alone.
FROUDE—*Short Studies on Great Subjects. Sea Studies*.

19
I was never less alone than when by myself.
GIBBON—*Memoirs*. Vol. I. P. 117. (See also CICERO)

20
Wer sich der Einsamkeit ergiebt,
Ach! der ist bald allein.
Whoever gives himself up to solitude,
Ah! he is soon alone.
GOETHE—*Wilhelm Meister*. II. 13.

21
Nobody with me at sea but myself.
GOLDSMITH—*The Haunch of Venison*.

22
Far from the madding crowd's ignoble strife.
GRAY—*Elegy in a Country Churchyard*. St. 19.

23
O Solitude! if I must with thee dwell,
Let it not be among the jumbled heap
Of murky buildings: climb with me the steep,—
Nature's observatory—whence the dell,
In flowery slopes, its river's crystal swell,
May seem a span; let me thy vigils keep
'Mongst boughs pavilion'd, where the deer's swift leap
Startles the wild bee from the foxglove bell.
KEATS—*Sonnet. O Solitude! If I Must With Thee Dwell*.

24
Why should we faint and fear to live alone,
Since all alone, so Heaven has willed, we die,
Nor even the tenderest heart and next our own
Knows half the reasons why we smile and sigh.
KEBLE—*Christian Year. Twenty-Fourth Sunday after Trinity*.

1
Solitude is as needful to the imagination as society is wholesome for the character.
LOWELL—*Among my Books. Dryden.*

2
And Wisdom's self
Oft seeks to sweet retired solitude,
Where, with her best nurse, Contemplation,
She plumes her feathers, and lets grow her wings,
That in the various bustle of resort
Were all too ruffled, and sometimes impaired.
MILTON—*Comus.* L. 375.

3
For solitude sometimes is best society,
And short retirement urges sweet return.
MILTON—*Paradise Lost.* Bk. IX. L. 249.

4
I feel like one who treads alone
Some banquet hall deserted,
Whose lights are fled, whose garlands dead,
And all but he departed.
MOORE—*Oft in the Stilly Night.*
(See also BULWER-LYTTON)

5
Until I truly loved, I was alone.
MRS. NORTON—*The Lady of La Garaye.* Pt. II. L. 381.

6
Now the New Year reviving old Desires,
The thoughtful Soul to Solitude retires.
OMAR KHAYYAM — *Rubaiyat.* FITZGERALD'S trans. St. 4.

7
You must show him . . . by leaving him severely alone.
CHAS. STEWART PARNELL—*Speech at Ennis.* Sept. 19, 1880.

8
Far in a wild, unknown to public view,
From youth to age a reverend hermit grew;
The moss his bed, the cave his humble cell,
His food the fruits, his drink the crystal well,
Remote from man, with God he pass'd the days;
Prayer all his business, all his pleasure praise.
THOMAS PARNELL—*The Hermit.*

9
Whosoever is delighted in solitude, is either a wild beast or a god.
PLATO—*Protag.* I. 337.

10
Shall I, like an hermit, dwell
On a rock or in a cell?
SIR WALTER RALEIGH—*Poem.* See CAYLEY'S *Life of Raleigh.* Vol. I.

11
Then never less alone than when alone.
SAMUEL ROGERS—*Human Life.* L. 759.
(See also BROWNE)

12
When, musing on companions gone,
We doubly feel ourselves alone.
SCOTT—*Marmion.* Canto II. *Introduction.*

13
Atque ubi omnia nobis mala solitudo persuadet.
And when Solitude leads us into all manner of evil.
SENECA—*Epistle* 25. Quoting GALGACUS, leader of the Britains.

14
I love tranquil solitude
And such society
As is quiet, wise, and good.
SHELLEY—*Rarely, Rarely, Comest Thou.*

15
Solitude is the best nurse of wisdom.
STERNE—*Letters.* No. 82.

16
A wise man is never less alone than when he is alone.
SWIFT—*Essay on the Faculties of the Mind.*
(See also CICERO)

17
Alone each heart must cover up its dead;
Alone, through bitter toil, achieve its rest.
BAYARD TAYLOR—*The Poet's Journal. First Evening. Conclusion.*

18
'Tis not for golden eloquence I pray,
A godlike tongue to move a stony heart—
Methinks it were full well to be apart
In solitary uplands far away,
Betwixt the blossoms of a rosy spray,
Dreaming upon the wonderful sweet face
Of Nature, in a wild and pathless place.
FREDERICK TENNYSON — *Sonnet.* From *A Treasury Of English Sonnets.* Edited by DAVID M. MAIN.

19
I never found the companion that was so companionable as solitude.
THOREAU—*Solitude.*

20
I could live in the woods with thee in sight,
Where never should human foot intrude:
Or with thee find light in the darkest night,
And a social crowd in solitude.
TIBULLUS—*Elegies.* Elegy I.

21
Impulses of deeper birth
Have come to him in solitude.
WORDSWORTH—*A Poet's Epitaph.*

22
They flash upon that inward eye
Which is the bliss of solitude.
WORDSWORTH—*I Wandered Lonely.* Lines in the poem written by MRS. WORDSWORTH.

23
Often have I sighed to measure
By myself a lonely pleasure,—
Sighed to think I read a book,
Only read, perhaps, by me.
WORDSWORTH—*To the Small Celandine.*

24
O sacred solitude! divine retreat!
Choice of the prudent! envy of the great,
By thy pure stream, or in thy waving shade,
We court fair wisdom, that celestial maid.
YOUNG—*Love of Fame.* Satire V. L. 254.

25
O! lost to virtue, lost to manly thought,
Lost to the noble sallies of the soul!
Who think it solitude to be alone.
YOUNG—*Night Thoughts.* Night III. L. 6.

26
This sacred shade and solitude, what is it?
'Tis the felt presence of the Deity,
Few are the faults we flatter when alone.
YOUNG—*Night Thoughts.* Night V. L. 172.

SONG (See also MUSIC, SINGING)

1
Tout finit par des chansons.
Everything ends with songs.
BEAUMARCHAIS—*Mariage de Figaro. End.*

2
Sing a song of sixpence.
BEAUMONT AND FLETCHER—*Bonduca.* Act V. Sc. 2.

3
I cannot sing the old songs
Though well I know the tune,
Familiar as a cradle-song
With sleep-compelling croon;
Yet though I'm filled with music,
As choirs of summer birds,
"I cannot sing the old songs"—
I do not know the words.
ROBERT J. BURDETTE—*Songs Without Words.*
(See also CALVERLEY)

4
All this for a song.
BURLEIGH—*To Queen Elizabeth* (when ordered to give £100 to Spenser).

5
I can not sing the old songs now!
It is not that I deem them low,
'Tis that I can't remember how
They go.
CHAS. S. CALVERLEY—*Changed.*
(See also BURDETTE)

6
Unlike my subject now * * * shall be my song,
It shall be witty and it sha'n't be long!
CHESTERFIELD—*Preface to Letters.* Vol. I.

7
A song of hate is a song of Hell;
Some there be who sing it well.
Let them sing it loud and long,
We lift our hearts in a loftier song:
We lift our hearts to Heaven above,
Singing the glory of her we love,
England.
HELEN GRAY CONE—*Chant of Love for England.*
(See also LISSAUER under HATRED)

8
And heaven had wanted one immortal song.
DRYDEN—*Absalom and Achitophel.* Pt. I. L. 197.

9
Verse sweetens toil, however rude the sound;
She feels no biting pang the while she sings,
Nor as she turns the giddy wheel around,
Revolves the sad vicissitudes of things.
GIFFORD—*Contemplation.* SAMUEL JOHNSON altered the second line to: "All at her work the village maiden sings"; and in the third line substituted "while" for "as." For "sad vicissitude of things" see STERNE under CHANGE, HAWTHORNE under APPLE, BACON under RELIGION.
(See also OVERBURY, QUINTILIAN, SIDNEY)

10
He play'd an ancient ditty long since mute,
In Provence call'd, "La belle dame sans merci."
KEATS—*The Eve of St. Agnes.* St. 33. "La Belle Dame, sans Merci" is a poem by ALAIN CHARTIER. Attributed to JEAN MAROT by M. PAULIN—*Manuscript Français.* VII. 252. In Harleian MS. 373, a translation is attributed to SIR RICHARD ROS.

11
We are tenting tonight on the old camp ground,
Give us a song to cheer.
WALTER KITTRIDGE—*Tenting on the Old Camp Ground.*

12
In the ink of our sweat we will find it yet,
The song that is fit for men!
FREDERIC L. KNOWLES.

13
The song on its mighty pinions
Took every living soul, and lifted it gently to heaven.
LONGFELLOW—*Children of the Lord's Supper.* L. 44.

14
Listen to that song, and learn it!
Half my kingdom would I give,
As I live,
If by such songs you would earn it!
LONGFELLOW—*Tales of a Wayside Inn.* Pt. I. *The Musician's Tale. The Saga of King Olaf.* Pt. V.

15
Such songs have power to quiet
The restless pulse of care,
And come like the benediction
That follows after prayer.
LONGFELLOW—*The Day is Done.* St. 9.

16
And grant that when I face the grisly Thing,
My song may trumpet down the gray Perhaps
Let me be as a tune-swept fiddlestring
That feels the Master Melody—and snaps.
JOHN G. NEIHARDT—*Let me live out my Years.*

17
She makes her hand hard with labour, and her heart soft with pity: and when winter evenings fall early (sitting at her merry wheel), she sings a defiance to the giddy wheel of fortune . . . and fears no manner of ill because she means none.
THOS. OVERBURY—*A Fair and Happy Milkmaid.*
(See also GIFFORD)

18
I think, whatever mortals crave,
With impotent endeavor,
A wreath—a rank—a throne—a grave—
The world goes round forever;
I think that life is not too long,
And therefore I determine,
That many people read a song,
Who will not read a sermon.
W. M. PRAED—*Chant of the Brazen Head.*

19
Odds life! must one swear to the truth of a song?
PRIOR—*A Better Answer.*

20
Etiam singulorum fatigatio quamlibet se rudi modulatione solatur.
Men, even when alone, lighten their labors by song, however rude it may be.
QUINTILIAN—*De Institutione Oratoria.* I. 81.
(See also GIFFORD)

1
Builders, raise the ceiling high,
Raise the dome into the sky,
Hear the wedding song!
For the happy groom is near,
Tall as Mars, and statelier,
Hear the wedding song!
SAPPHO—*Fragments*. J. S. EASBY SMITH'S trans.

2
Song forbids victorious deeds to die.
SCHILLER—*The Artists*.

3
The lively Shadow-World of Song.
SCHILLER—*The Artists*.

4
Now, good Cesario, but that piece of song,
That old and antique song we heard last night;
Methought it did relieve my passion much,
More than light airs and recollected terms
Of these most brisk and giddy-paced times:
Come, but one verse.
Twelfth Night. Act II. Sc. 4. L. 2.

5
Songs consecrate to truth and liberty.
SHELLEY—*To Wordsworth*. L. 12.

6
Knitting and withal singing, and it seemed that her voice comforted her hands to work.
SIR PHILIP SIDNEY—*Arcadia*. Bk. I.
(See also GIFFORD)

7
Because the gift of Song was chiefly lent,
To give consoling music for the joys
We lack, and not for those which we possess.
BAYARD TAYLOR—*The Poet's Journal. Third Evening*.

8
They sang of love and not of fame;
Forgot was Britain's glory;
Each heart recalled a different name,
But all sang "Annie Laurie."
BAYARD TAYLOR—*A Song of the Camp*.

9
Short swallow-flights of song, that dip
Their wings in tears, and skim away.
TENNYSON—*In Memoriam*. Pt. XLVIII. St. 4.

10
Cantilenam eandem canis.
You sing the same old song.
TERENCE—*Phormio*. III. 2. 10.

11
Cicala to cicala is dear, and ant to ant, and hawks to hawks, but to me the muse and song.
THEOCRITUS—*Idyl*. IX. Trans. by ANDREW LANG. St. 2.

12
Grasshopper to grasshopper, ant to ant is dear,
Hawks love hawks, but I the muse and song.
THEOCRITUS—*Idyl*. IX. Trans. by MAURICE THOMPSON.

13
Swift, swift, and bring with you
Song's Indian summer!
FRANCIS THOMPSON—*A Carrier Song*. St. 2.

14
Martem accendere cantu.
To kindle war by song.
VERGIL—*Æneid*. VI. 165.

15
Soft words, with nothing in them, make a song.
EDMUND WALLER—*To Mr. Creech*. L. 10.

16
A careless song, with a little nonsense in it now and then, does not mis-become a monarch.
HORACE WALPOLE—*Letter to Sir Horace Mann*. (1770)

17
Bring the good old bugle, boys! we'll sing another song—
Sing it with a spirit that will start the world along—
Sing it as we used to sing it, fifty thousand strong,
While we were marching through Georgia.
HENRY CLAY WORK—*Marching Through Georgia*.

SORROW

18
Oh c'etait le bon temps, j'etais bien malheureuse.
Oh, that was a good time, when I was unhappy.
SOPHIE ARNOULD, the actress, accredited with the phrase. Quoted as hers by RULHIÈRE—*Êpître à Monsieur de Cha—*.

19
Ah, nothing comes to us too soon but sorrow.
BAILEY—*Festus*. Sc. *Home*.

20
Night brings out stars as sorrow shows us truths.
BAILEY—*Festus*. Sc. *Water and Wood. Midnight*.

21
In omni adversitate fortunæ, infelicissimum genus est infortunii fuisse felicem.
In every adversity of fortune, to have been happy is the most unhappy kind of misfortune.
BOETHIUS—*De Consolatione Philosophiæ*. Bk. II. Pt. IV.
(See also CHAUCER, DANTE, MUSSET, PETRARCH, TENNYSON, WORDSWORTH)

22
Sorrow preys upon
Its solitude, and nothing more diverts it
From its sad visions of the other world
Than calling it at moments back to this.
The busy have no time for tears.
BYRON—*The Two Foscari*. Act IV. Sc. 1.

23
Ah, don't be sorrowful, darling,
And don't be sorrowful, pray;
Taking the year together, my dear,
There isn't more night than day.
ALICE CARY—*Don't be Sorrowful, Darling*.

24
For of Fortune's sharpe adversite,
The worste kynde of infortune is this,
A man to hav bent in prosperite,
And it remembren whan it passed is.
CHAUCER—*Canterbury Tales. Troylus and Crysseyde*. Bk. III. L. 1,625.
(See also BOETHIUS)

25
Men die, but sorrow never dies;
The crowding years divide in vain,
And the wide world is knit with ties
Of common brotherhood in pain.
SUSAN COOLIDGE—*The Cradle Tomb in Westminster Abbey*.

1
The path of sorrow, and that path alone,
Leads to the lands where sorrow is unknown
COWPER—*To an Afflicted Protestant Lady.*

2 Nessun maggior dolore
Che ricordarsi del tempo felice
Nella miseria.
There is no greater sorrow
Than to be mindful of the happy time
In misery.
DANTE—*Inferno.* V. 121. LONGFELLOW'S Trans. Same in FORTINGUERRA—*Ricciardetto.* Ch. XI. St. 83. MARINO—*Adone.* Ch. XIV. St. 100.
(See also BOETHIUS)

3
Mes malheurs sont comblés, mais ma vertu me reste.
My sorrows are overwhelming, but my virtue is left to me.
DUCIS—*Hamlet.* Last lines.

4
In the bitter waves of woe,
Beaten and tossed about
By the sullen winds which blow
From the desolate shores of doubt.
WASHINGTON GLADDEN—*Ultima Veritas.*

5
Ach! aus dem Glück entwickelt oft sich Schmerz.
Alas! sorrow from happiness is oft evolved.
GOETHE—*Die Natürliche Tochter.* II. 3. 17.

6
Wer nie sein Brod mit Thränen ass,
Wer nicht die kummervollen Nächte
Auf seinem Bette weinend sass,
Der kennt euch nicht, ihr himmlischen Mächte.
Who never ate his bread in sorrow,
Who never spent the darksome hours
Weeping, and watching for the morrow,—
He knows ye not, ye gloomy Powers.
GOETHE—*Wilhelm Meister.* Bk. II. Ch. XIII

7
Since sorrow never comes too late,
And happiness too swiftly flies.
GRAY—*Ode on a Distant Prospect of Eton College.*

8
I walked a mile with Sorrow
And ne'er a word said she;
But, oh, the things I learned from her
When Sorrow walked with me.
ROBERT BROWNING HAMILTON—*Along the Road.*

9 A happier lot were mine,
If I must lose thee, to go down to earth,
For I shall have no hope when thou art gone,—
Nothing but sorrow. Father have I none,
And no dear mother.
HOMER—*Iliad.* Bk. VI. L. 530. BRYANT'S trans.

10
Sinks my sad soul with sorrow to the grave.
HOMER—*Iliad.* Bk. XXII. L. 543. POPE'S trans.

11
Oderunt hilarem tristes tristemque jocosi.
The sorrowful dislike the gay, and the gay the sorrowful.
HORACE—*Epistles.* I. 18. 89.

12
When sparrows build and the leaves break forth
My old sorrow wakes and cries.
JEAN INGELOW—*Song of Old Love.*

13
Hang sorrow, care 'll kill a cat.
BEN JONSON—*Every Man in his Humour.* Act I. Sc. 3.
(See also WITHER)

14 O, sorrow!
Why dost borrow
Heart's lightness from the merriment of May?
KEATS—*Endymion.* Bk. IV.

15 To Sorrow
I bade good-morrow,
And thought to leave her far away behind;
But cheerly, cheerly,
She loves me dearly:
She is so constant to me, and so kind.
KEATS—*Endymion.* Bk. IV.

16
How beautiful, if sorrow had not made
Sorrow more beautiful than Beauty's self.
KEATS—*Hyperion.* Bk. I. L. 36.

17 Our days and nights
Have sorrows woven with delights.
MALHERBE—*To Cardinal Richelieu.* LONGFELLOW'S Trans.

18
Day-thoughts feed nightly dreams;
And sorrow tracketh wrong,
As echo follows song.
HARRIET MARTINEAU—*Hymn.*

19
A grace within his soul hath reigned
Which nothing else can bring;
Thank God for all that I have gained
By that high sorrowing.
MONCKTON MILNES (Lord Houghton).

20
Weep on; and, as thy sorrows flow,
I'll taste the luxury of woe.
MOORE—*Anacreontic.*

21
Ecoute, moribonde! Il n'est pire douleur
Qu'un souvenir heureux dans le jour de malheur.
Listen, dying one! There is no worse sorrow than remembering happiness in the day of sorrow.
ALFRED DE MUSSET—*Le Saule.* (The opposite opinion in his *Un Souvenir.*)
(See also DANTE)

22
Con dolor rimembrando il tempo lieto.
With sorrow remembering happy times.
PETRARCH—*Canzone.* 46.
(See also DANTE)

23
Sorrows remembered sweeten present joy.
POLLOK—*Course of Time.* Bk. I. L. 464.

1
Do not cheat thy Heart and tell her,
"Grief will pass away,
Hope for fairer times in future,
And forget to-day."
Tell her, if you will, that sorrow
Need not come in vain;
Tell her that the lesson taught her
Far outweighs the pain.
ADELAIDE A. PROCTER—*Friend Sorrow.*

2
Die Leiden sind wie die Gewitterwolken; in der Ferne sehen sie schwartz aus, über uns kaum grau.
Sorrows are like thunderclouds—in the distance they look black, over our heads scarcely gray.
JEAN PAUL RICHTER—*Hesperus.* XIV.

3
Kurz ist der Schmerz, und ewig ist die Freude!
Brief is sorrow, and endless is joy.
SCHILLER—*Die Jungfrau von Orleans.* V. 14. 44.

4 Quæ fuit durum pati,
Miminisse dulce est.
Those things which were hard to bear, are sweet to remember.
SENECA—*Hercules Furens.* 656.
(See also DANTE)

5
Curæ leves loquuntur, ingentes stupent.
Light sorrows speak, but deeper ones are dumb.
SENECA—*Hippolytus.* 607. THUCYDIDES. Bk. VII. Ch. LXXV. Given as from ÆSCHYLUS. Compare ÆSCHYLUS—*Agamemnon.* 860. OVID—*Metamorphoses.* VI. 301–312. HERODOTUS. VII. 147; also III. 14.
(See also MACBETH)

6
Nulla dies mærore caret.
There is no day without sorrow.
SENECA—*Troades.* 77.

7
Wherever sorrow is, relief would be:
If you do sorrow at my grief in love,
By giving love, your sorrow and my grief were both extermin'd.
As You Like It. Act III. Sc. 5. L. 86.

8
When sorrows come, they come not single spies,
But in battalions.
Hamlet. Act IV. Sc. 5. L. 78.

9 'Tis better to be lowly born,
And range with humble livers in content,
Than to be perk'd up in a glistering grief,
And wear a golden sorrow.
Henry VIII. Act II. Sc. 3. L. 19.

10
I will instruct my sorrows to be proud.
King John. Act III. Sc. 1. L. 68.

11 Here I and sorrows sit:
Here is my throne, bid kings come bow to it.
King John. Act III. Sc. 1. L. 73.

12
Down, thou climbing sorrow.
King Lear. Act II. Sc. 4. L. 57.

13 Each new morn,
New widows howl, new orphans cry, new sorrows
Strike heaven on the face, that it resounds
As if it felt with Scotland and yell'd out
Like syllable of dolour.
Macbeth. Act IV. Sc. 3. L. 4.

14
Give sorrow words; the grief that does not speak
Whispers the o'er-fraught heart and bids it break.
Macbeth. Act IV. Sc. 3. L. 209.
(See also SENECA)

15 Your cause of sorrow
Must not be measur'd by his worth, for then
It hath no end.
Macbeth. Act V. Sc. 8. L. 44.

16 This sorrow's heavenly;
It strikes where it doth love.
Othello. Act V. Sc. 2. L. 21.

17
One sorrow never comes but brings an heir,
That may succeed as his inheritor.
Pericles. Act I. Sc. 4. L. 63.
(See also YOUNG under WOE)

18
Sorrow ends not when it seemeth done.
Richard II. Act I. Sc. 2. L. 61.

19 Joy, being altogether wanting,
It doth remember me the more of sorrow.
Richard II. Act III. Sc. 4. L. 13.

20
Sorrow breaks seasons and reposing hours,
Makes the night morning, and the noon-tide night.
Richard III. Act I. Sc. 4. L. 76.

21
Eighty odd years of sorrow have I seen,
And each hour's joy wrecked with a week of teen.
Richard III. Act IV. Sc. 1. L. 96.

22
If sorrow can admit society,
Tell o'er your woes again by viewing mine.
Richard III. Act IV. Sc. 4. L. 38.

23
To weep with them that weep doth ease some deal;
But sorrow flouted at is double death.
Titus Andronicus. Act III. Sc. 1. L. 245.

24
I have, as when the sun doth light a storm,
Buried this sigh in wrinkle of a smile:
But sorrow, that is couch'd in seeming gladness,
Is like that mirth fate turns to sudden sadness.
Troilus and Cressida. Act I. Sc. 1. L. 37.

25
Forgive me, Valentine: if hearty sorrow
Be a sufficient ransom for offence,
I tender 't here: I do as truly suffer,
As e'er I did commit.
Two Gentlemen of Verona. Act V. Sc. 4. L. 74.

26 Each time we love,
We turn a nearer and a broader mark
To that keen archer, Sorrow, and he strikes.
ALEXANDER SMITH—*City Poems. A Boy's Dream.*

27
When sorrow sleepeth, wake it not,
But let it slumber on.
MISS M. A. STODART—*Song.*

1
Time, thy name is sorrow, says the stricken
Heart of life, laid waste with wasting flame
Ere the change of things and thoughts requicken,
Time, thy name.
SWINBURNE—*Time and Life*. St. 1.

2
What shall be done for sorrow
With love whose race is run?
Where help is none to borrow,
What shall be done?
SWINBURNE—*Wasted Love*.

3
Joy was a flame in me
Too steady to destroy.
Lithe as a bending reed,
Loving the storm that sways her—
I found more joy in sorrow
Than you could find in joy.
SARA TEASDALE—*The Answer*.

4
O sorrow, wilt thou rule my blood,
Be sometimes lovely, like a bride,
And put thy harsher moods aside,
If thou wilt have me wise and good.
TENNYSON—*In Memoriam*. Pt. LVIII.

5
Smit with exceeding sorrow unto Death.
TENNYSON—*The Lover's Tale*. L. 597.

6
That a sorrow's crown of sorrow is remembering happier things.
TENNYSON—*Locksley Hall*. St. 38. CHURTON COLLINS, in *Illustrations of Tennyson*. P. 62, refers to PINDAR—*Pythian* 4. 510, and THUCYDIDES II. 44, as inspiring these lines.
(See also DANTE)

7
When I was young, I said to Sorrow,
"Come and I will play with thee!"
He is near me now all day,
And at night returns to say,
"I will come again to-morrow—
I will come and stay with thee."
AUBREY THOS. DE VERE—*Song. When I was Young I said to Sorrow*.

8
Past sorrows, let us moderately lament them;
For those to come, seek wisely to prevent them.
JOHN WEBSTER—*Duchess of Malfi*. Act III. Sc. 2.

9
Sorrow is held the eldest child of sin.
JOHN WEBSTER—*Duchess of Malfi*. Act V. Sc. 5.

10
Where there is sorrow, there is holy ground.
OSCAR WILDE—*De Profundis*.

11
Hang sorrow, care will kill a cat,
And therefore let's be merry.
WITHER—*Christmas*.
(See also JONSON)

12
Some natural sorrow, loss, or pain,
That has been and may be again.
WORDSWORTH—*The Solitary Reaper*.

13
So joys remembered without wish or will
Sharpen the keenest edge of present ill.
WORDSWORTH—*Sonnet on Captivity*. VI. 172.
(See also DANTE)

SOUL (THE)

14
Today the journey is ended,
I have worked out the mandates of fate;
Naked, alone, undefended,
I knock at the Uttermost Gate.
Behind is life and its longing,
Its trial, its trouble, its sorrow,
Beyond is the Infinite Morning
Of a day without a tomorrow.
WENONAH STEVENS ABBOTT—*A Soul's Soliloquy*.

15
But thou shall flourish in immortal youth,
Unhurt amidst the wars of elements,
The wrecks of matter, and the crush of worlds.
ADDISON—*Cato*. Act V. Sc. 1.

16
What sculpture is to a block of marble, education is to the soul.
ADDISON—*Spectator*. No. 215.

17
And see all sights from pole to pole,
And glance, and nod, and bustle by,
And never once possess our soul
Before we die.
MATTHEW ARNOLD—*A Southern Night*. St. 18.
(See also *Luke*)

18
But each day brings its petty dust
Our soon choked souls to fill.
MATTHEW ARNOLD—*Switzerland*. Pt. VI.

19
Anima certe, quia spiritus, in sicco habitare non potest; ideo in sanguine fertur habitare.
The soul, which is spirit, can not dwell in dust; it is carried along to dwell in the blood.
ST. AUGUSTINE—*Decretum*. IX. 32. 2.

20
A soul as white as Heaven.
BEAUMONT AND FLETCHER—*The Maid's Tragedy*. Act IV. Sc. 1.

21
John Brown's body lies a mould'ring in the grave,
His soul goes marching on.
THOS. BRIGHAM BISHOP—*John Brown's Body*.

22
And I have written three books on the soul,
Proving absurd all written hitherto,
And putting us to ignorance again.
ROBERT BROWNING—*Cleon*.

23
And he that makes his soul his surety,
I think, does give the best security.
BUTLER—*Hudibras*. Pt. III. Canto I. L. 203.

24
The dome of Thought, the palace of the Soul.
BYRON—*Childe Harold*. Canto II. St. 6.

25
Everywhere the human soul stands between a hemisphere of light and another of darkness; on the confines of two everlasting hostile empires, Necessity and Freewill.
CARLYLE—*Essays*. *Goethe's Works*.

26
Imago animi vultus est, indices oculi.
The countenance is the portrait of the soul, and the eyes mark its intentions.
CICERO—*De Oratore*. III. 59.

1
From the looks—not the lips, is the soul reflected.
M'Donald Clarke—*The Rejected Lover.*

2
The soul of man is larger than the sky,
Deeper than ocean, or the abysmal dark
Of the unfathomed centre.
Hartley Coleridge—*Poems. To Shakespeare.*

3
My father was an eminent button-maker at Birmingham, . . . but I had a soul above buttons.
George Colman the Younger—*Sylvester Daggerwood.* Act I. 1. Also in Marryat's *Peter Simple.*

4
A happy soul, that all the way
To heaven hath a summer's day.
Richard Crashaw—*In Praise of Lessius' Rule of Health.* L. 33.

5
A fiery soul, which, working out its way,
Fretted the pygmy-body to decay,
And o'er-inform'd the tenement of clay.
Dryden—*Absalom and Achitophel.* Pt. I. L. 156. (See also Fuller)

6
Lord of oneself, uncumbered with a name.
Dryden—*Epistle to John Dryden.*
(See also Henley)

7
I have a soul that, like an ample shield,
Can take in all, and verge enough for more.
Dryden—*Sebastian.* Act I. Sc. 1.

8
The one thing in the world, of value, is the active soul.
Emerson—*American Scholar.*

9
Gravity is the ballast of the soul, which keeps the mind steady.
Fuller—*Holy and Profane States. Gravity.*

10
He was one of a lean body and visage, as if his eager soul, biting for anger at the clog of his body, desired to fret a passage through it.
Fuller—*Life of the Duke of Alva.*
(See also Dryden)

11
Animula, vagula, blandula
Hospes comesque corporis!
Quæ nunc abibis in loca,
Pallidula, frigida nudula
Nec ut soles dabis joca?
O fleeting soul of mine, my body's friend and guest, whither goest thou, pale, fearful, and pensive one? Why laugh not as of old?
Hadrian—*Ad Animam,* according to Ælius Spartianus. See Pope's paraphrase, *A Dying Christian to His Soul.*

12
It matters not how strait the gate,
How charged with punishments the scroll,
I am the master of my fate:
I am the captain of my soul.
Henley—*Echoes.* IV. To R. J. H. B.
(See also Dryden, Kenyon, Oldham, Shelley, Tennyson, Watts, Wotton, also Horace under Freedom)

13
Salute thyself; see what thy soul doth wear.
Herbert—*Church Porch.*

14
Build thee more stately mansions, O my soul,
As the swift seasons roll!
Leave thy low-vaulted past!
Let each new temple, nobler than the last,
Shut thee from heaven with a dome more vast,
Till thou at length art free,
Leaving thine outgrown shell by life's unresting sea!
Holmes—*The Chambered Nautilus.* St. 5.

15
And rest at last where souls unbodied dwell,
In ever-flowing meads of Asphodel.
Homer—*Odyssey.* Bk. XXIV. L. 19. Pope's trans.

16
The production of souls is the secret of unfathomable depth.
Victor Hugo—*Shakespeare.* Bk. V. Ch. I.

17
The limbs will quiver and move after the soul is gone.
Samuel Johnson—See Northcote's *Johnsoniana.* 487.

18
Awake, my soul, and with the sun
Thy daily course of duty run.
Bishop Ken—*Evening Hymn.* Taken from *Salvator Mundi, Domine.* In *Hymni Ecclesiæ.*

19
Arise, O Soul, and gird thee up anew,
Though the black camel Death kneel at thy gate;
No beggar thou that thou for alms shouldst sue:
Be the proud captain still of thine own fate.
James Benjamin Kenyon.
(See also Henley, also Abd-el-Kader under Death)

20
Ah, the souls of those that die
Are but sunbeams lifted higher.
Longfellow—*Christus. The Golden Legend.* Pt. IV. *The Cloisters.*

21
Ignoratur enim, quæ sit natura animai;
Nata sit, an contra nascentibus insinuetur;
Et simul intereat nobiscum, morte diremta,
An tenebras Orci visat, vastasque lacunas:
An pecudes alias divinitus insinuet se.
For it is unknown what is the real nature of the soul, whether it be born with the bodily frame or be infused at the moment of birth, whether it perishes along with us, when death separates the soul and body, or whether it visits the shades of Pluto and bottomless pits, or enters by divine appointment into other animals.
Lucretius—*De Rerum Natura.* I. 113.

22
Soul, thou hast much goods laid up for many years; take thine ease, eat, drink, and be merry.
Luke. XII. 19. *Ecclesiastes.* VIII. 15.

23
In your patience possess ye your souls.
Luke. XXI. 19.
(See also Arnold)

1
This ae nighte, this ae nighte
Every nighte and all;
Fire and sleete, and candle lighte
And Christe receive thye saule.
Lyke-Wake Dirge. In SCOTT's *Minstrelsy of the Border.* Vol. III. P. 163. T. F. HENDERSON's ed. (1902) "Fire and fleet" in version given in JOHN AUBREY's—*Remaines of Gentilisme and Judaisme.* (1686–7) Lansdowne MSS. in British Museum. ("Fleet" given as meaning water; "Sleete" meaning salt.) Compare with chant to the departing spirit in *Guy Mannering.*

2
The soul of the river had entered my soul,
And the gathered power of my soul was moving
So swiftly, it seemed to be at rest
Under cities of cloud and under
Spheres of silver and changing worlds—
Until I saw a flash of trumpets
Above the battlements over Time!
EDGAR LEE MASTERS—*Spoon River Anthology. Isaiah. Beethoven.*

3
The dust's for crawling, heaven's for flying,
Wherefore, O Soul, whose wings are grown,
Soar upward to the sun!
EDGAR LEE MASTERS—*Spoon River Anthology. Julian Scott.*

4
What is a man profited, if he shall gain the whole world, and lose his own soul?
Matthew. XVI. 26.

5
The soul, aspiring, pants its source to mount,
As streams meander level with their fount.
ROBERT MONTGOMERY—*Omnipresence of the Deity.* Pt. I. Ridiculed by MACAULAY as "the worst similitude in the world." Omitted in later editions.

6
There was a little man, and he had a little soul;
And he said, "Little Soul, let us try, try, try!"
MOORE—*Little Man and Little Soul.*

7
I reflected how soon in the cup of desire
The pearl of the soul may be melted away;
How quickly, alas, the pure sparkle of fire
We inherit from heaven, may be quenched in the clay.
MOORE—*Stanzas. A Beam of Tranquillity.*

8
Above the vulgar flight of common souls.
ARTHUR MURPHY—*Zenobia.* Act V. Sc. 1. L. 154.

9
Lord of myself, accountable to none.
But to my conscience, and my God alone.
JOHN OLDHAM—*Satire addressed to a Friend.*
(See also HENLEY)

10
I sent my Soul through the Invisible,
Some letter of that After-life to spell,
And by and by my Soul returned to me,
And answered "I Myself am Heav'n and Hell."
OMAR KHAYYAM—*Rubaiyat.* FITZGERALD's Trans.

11
Est deus in nobis, et sunt commercia cœli.
Sedibus ætheriis spiritus ille venit.
There is a god within us, and we have intercourse with heaven. That spirit comes from abodes on high.
OVID—*Ars Amatoria.* III. 549.

12
Deus est in pectore nostro.
There is a divinity within our breast.
OVID—*Epistolæ Ex Ponto.* III. 4. 93.

13
Egomet sum mihi imperator.
I am myself my own commander.
PLAUTUS—*Mercator.* Act V.
(See also HENLEY)

14
No craving void left aching in the soul.
POPE—*Eloisa.*
(See also WESLEY)

15
The soul, uneasy and confin'd from home,
Rests and expatiates in a life to come.
POPE—*Essay on Man.* Ep. I. L. 97.

16
Stript to the naked soul.
POPE—*Lines to Mrs. Grace Butler.* Found in *Sussex Garland.* Nos. 9 and 10. Under Warminghurst. Attributed also to CHARLES YORKE.

17
Vital spark of heav'nly flame!
POPE—*Paraphrase of Emperor Hadrian's "Ode of the Dying Christian to His Soul."* Also inspired by SAPPHO—*Fragment.* In *Spectator,* Nov. 15, 1711.
(See also HADRIAN)

18
Or looks on heav'n with more than mortal eyes,
Bids his free soul expatiate in the skies,
Amid her kindred stars familiar roam,
Survey the region, and confess her home.
POPE—*Windsor Forest.* L. 264.

19
The iron entered into his soul.
Psalms. CV. 18. In the *Psalter.*

20
Anima mea in manibus meis semper.
My soul is continually in my hand.
Psalms. CXIX. 109. (Latin in *Vulgate.*)

21
My soul, the seas are rough, and thou a stranger
In these false coasts; O keep aloof; there's danger;
Cast forth thy plummet; see, a rock appears;
Thy ships want sea-room; make it with thy tears.
QUARLES—*Emblems.* Bk. III. Ep. XI.

22
Goe sowle, the bodies gueste
vpon a thankeles errant;
feare not to touche the beste,
the trueth shalbe thie warrant,
goe, since I nedes muste die
and tell them all they lie.
Generally believed to be by RALEIGH—*The Lie. (Souls Errand.) Harleian MS.* 2296. Folio 135. Also in MS. 6910. Folio 141. Assigned to him in *Chetham MS.* 8012. P. 103. *Collier MS.* Bibl. Cat. Vol. II. P. 244. Printed as DAVIDSON's in his *Poetical Rhapsody* (Second Ed.) Pub. 1608. Claim for JOHN SYLVESTER discredited by author-

ities, although it appears in the folio of his posthumous works. (1641) Printed in LORD PEMBROKE's *Poems*. Attributed also to RICHARD EDWARDS by CAMPBELL. Not proven that Raleigh wrote it 1618 or 1603. May have been written by him 1592–3(?) during his imprisonment.

1
Yet stab at thee who will,
No stab the soul can kill!
SIR WALTER RALEIGH—*The Farewell.*

2
—'Tis my soul
That I thus hold erect as if with stays,
And decked with daring deeds instead of ribbons,
Twirling my wit as it were my moustache,
The while I pass among the crowd, I make
Bold truths ring out like spurs.
ROSTAND—*Cyrano de Bergerac.*

3
Animus hoc habet argumentum divinitatis suæ, quod illum divina delectant.

The soul has this proof of its divinity: that divine things delight it.
SENECA—*Quæstionum Naturalium.* Præfet ad 1 lib.

4 Man who man would be
Must rule the empire of himself.
SHELLEY—*Sonnet on Political Greatness.*
(See also HENLEY)

5 Within this wall of flesh
There is a soul counts thee her creditor.
King John. Act III. Sc. 3. L. 20.

6 Thy soul's flight,
If it find heaven, must find it out to-night.
Macbeth. Act III. Sc. 1. L. 141.

7
Think'st thou I'll endanger my soul gratis?
Merry Wives of Windsor. Act II. Sc. 2. L. 14.

8
Whate'er of earth is form'd, to earth returns,
* * * The soul
Of man alone, that particle divine,
Escapes the wreck of worlds, when all things fail.
W. C. SOMERVILLE—*The Chase.* Bk. IV. L. 1.

9
For of the soule the bodie forme doth take;
For soule is forme and doth the bodie make.
SPENSER—*An Hymn in Honour of Beauty.* L. 132.

10
The soul is a fire that darts its rays through all the senses; it is in this fire that existence consists; all the observations and all the efforts of philosophers ought to turn towards this ME, the centre and moving power of our sentiments and our ideas.
MADAME DE STAËL—*Germany.* Pt. III. Ch. II.

11
My soul is a dark ploughed field
In the cold rain;
My soul is a broken field
Ploughed by pain.
SARA TEASDALE—*The Broken Field.*

12
But this main-miracle that thou art thou,
With power on thine own act and on the world.
TENNYSON—*De Profundis.* Last lines.
(See also HENLEY)

13 But while
I breathe Heaven's air, and Heaven looks down on me,
And smiles at my best meanings, I remain
Mistress of mine own self and mine own soul.
TENNYSON—*The Foresters.* Act IV. Sc. 1.
(See also HENLEY)

14
What profits now to understand
The merits of a spotless shirt—
A dapper boot—a little hand—
If half the little soul is dirt.
TENNYSON—*The New Timon and the Poets.* Appeared in *Punch*, Feb. 28, 1846. Signed ALCIBIADES. Answer to attack made by BULWER-LYTTON in *The New Timon* when TENNYSON received a pension.

15
Her soul from earth to Heaven lies,
Like the ladder of the vision,
Wheron go
To and fro,
In ascension and demission,
Star-flecked feet of Paradise.
FRANCIS THOMPSON—*Scala Jacobi Portaque Eburnea.* St. 1.

16
What then do you call your soul? What idea have you of it? You cannot of yourselves, without revelation, admit the existence within you of anything but a power unknown to you of feeling and thinking.
VOLTAIRE—*A Philosophical Dictionary. Soul.*

17
And keeps that palace of the soul serene.
EDMUND WALLER—*Of Tea.* L. 9.

18
Were I so tall to reach the pole,
Or grasp the ocean with my span,
I must be measur'd by my soul:
The mind's the standard of the man.
WATTS—*False Greatness. Horæ Lyricæ.* Bk. II.
(See also HENLEY, also OVID, SENECA under MIND, BURNS under MAN)

19
My soul is all an aching void.
CHARLES WESLEY—*Hymn.*
(See also COWPER)

20
A charge to keep I have,
A God to glorify:
A never-dying soul to save,
And fit it for the sky.
CHARLES WESLEY—*Hymns.* 318.

21
I loafe and invite my soul,
I lean and loafe at my ease, observing a spear of summer grass.
WALT WHITMAN—*Song of Myself.*

22
But who would force the Soul, tilts with a straw
Against a Champion cased in adamant.
WORDSWORTH—*Ecclesiastical Sonnets.* Pt. III. VII. *Persecution of the Scottish Covenanters.*

23 For the Gods approve
The depth, and not the tumult, of the soul.
WORDSWORTH—*Laodamia.*

1
Lord of himself, though not of lands;
And having nothing, yet hath all.
Sir Henry Wotton—*The Character of a Happy Life.*
(See also Henley)

SOUND

2
A thousand trills and quivering sounds
In airy circles o'er us fly,
Till, wafted by a gentle breeze,
They faint and languish by degrees,
And at a distance die.
Addison—*An Ode for St. Cecilia's Day.* VI.

3
A noise like of a hidden brook
In the leafy month of June,
That to the sleeping woods all night
Singeth a quiet tune.
Coleridge—*Ancient Mariner.* Pt. V. St. 18.

4
By magic numbers and persuasive sound.
Congreve—*Mourning Bride.* Act I. Sc. 1.

5
I hear a sound so fine there's nothing lives
'Twixt it and silence.
James Sheridan Knowles—*Virginius.* Act V. Sc. 2.

6
Parent of sweetest sounds, yet mute forever.
Macaulay—*Enigma.* "Cut off my head, etc." Last line.

7
And filled the air with barbarous dissonance.
Milton—*Comus.* L. 550.

8
Sonorous metal blowing martial sounds,
At which the universal host up sent
A shout that tore hell's concave, and beyond
Frighted the reign of Chaos and old Night.
Milton—*Paradise Lost.* Bk. I. L. 540.

9
Their rising all at once was as the sound
Of thunder heard remote.
Milton—*Paradise Lost.* Bk. II. L. 476.

10
To all proportioned terms he must dispense
And make the sound a picture of the sense.
Christopher Pitt—*Translation of Vida's Art of Poetry.*
(See also Pope)

11
The murmur that springs
From the growing of grass.
Poe—*Al Aaraaf.* Pt. II. L. 124.

12
The sound must seem an echo to the sense.
Pope—*Essay on Criticism.* L. 365.
(See also Pitt)

13
The empty vessel makes the greatest sound.
Henry V. Act IV. Sc. 4. L. 73.

14
What's the business,
That such a hideous trumpet calls to parley
The sleepers of the house? Speak, speak!
Macbeth. Act II. Sc. 3. L. 86.

15
Hark! from the tombs a doleful sound.
Isaac Watts—*Hymns and Spiritual Songs.* Bk. II. Hymn 63.

16
My eyes are dim with childish tears,
My heart is idly stirred,
For the same sound is in my ears
Which in those days I heard.
Wordsworth—*The Fountain.*

SPAIN

17
Fair land! of chivalry the old domain,
Land of the vine and olive, lovely Spain!
Though not for thee with classic shores to vie
In charms that fix th' enthusiast's pensive eye;
Yet hast thou scenes of beauty richly fraught
With all that wakes the glow of lofty thought.
Felicia D. Hemans—*Abencerrage.* Canto II. L. 1.

SPARROW

18
Tell me not of joy: there's none
Now my little sparrow's gone;
He, just as you,
Would toy and woo,
He would chirp and flatter me,
He would hang the wing awhile,
Till at length he saw me smile,
Lord! how sullen he would be!
Wm. Cartwright—*Lesbia and the Sparrow.*

19
The sparrows chirped as if they still were proud
Their race in Holy Writ should mentioned be.
Longfellow—*Tales of a Wayside Inn. The Poet's Tale. The Birds of Killingworth.* St. 2.

20
The hedge-sparrow fed the cuckoo so long,
That it had it head bit off by it young.
King Lear. Act I. Sc. 4. L. 235.

21
Behold, within the leafy shade,
Those bright blue eggs together laid!
On me the chance-discovered sight
Gleamed like a vision of delight.
Wordsworth—*The Sparrow's Nest.*

SPEECH

22
I have but nine-pence in ready money, but I can draw for a thousand pounds.
Addison, to a lady who complained of his having talked little in company. See *Boswell's Life of* Johnson. (1773)

23
And let him be sure to leave other men their turns to speak.
Bacon—*Essays. Civil and Moral. Of Discourse.* No. 32.

24
Discretion of speech is more than eloquence; and to speak agreeably to him with whom we deal is more than to speak in good words or in good order.
Bacon—*Essays. Of Discourse.*

25
Though I say't that should not say't.
Beaumont and Fletcher—*Wit at Several Weapons.* Act II. Sc. 2.

26
Speak boldly, and speak truly, shame the devil.
Beaumont and Fletcher—*Wit Without Money.* Act IV. Sc. 4.

1
Revenons à nos moutons.

To return to the subject. (Lit. "to our mutton.")

PIERRE BLANCHET—*Pierre Pathelin*. III. 2. Same used by BRUEYS in his *L'Avocat Patelin* (*Maître Patelin*) which he says in the preface he took from BLANCHET's play. JACOB's ed. in *Recueil de Farces Soties*. P. 96 gives text as "Revenons a ces mouton." PASQUIER—*Recherches de la France* gives "nos mouton." RABELAIS—*Pantagruel*. Bk. III. 34. ("Retournous" for "Revenons.")

2
Tout ce qu'on dit de trop est fade et rebutant.

That which is repeated too often becomes insipid and tedious.

BOILEAU—*L'Art Poétique*. I. 61.

3
Let him now speak, or else hereafter for ever hold his peace.

Book of Common Prayer. Solemnization of Matrimony.

4
For brevity is very good,
Where we are, or are not understood.

BUTLER—*Hudibras*. Pt. I. Canto I. L. 669.

(See also PLINY)

5
He who does not make his words rather serve to conceal than discover the sense of his heart deserves to have it pulled out like a traitor's and shown publicly to the rabble.

BUTLER—*The Modern Politician*.

(See also VOLTAIRE)

6
His speech was a fine sample, on the whole,
Of rhetoric, which the learn'd call "*rigmarole*."

BYRON—*Don Juan*. Canto I. St. 174.

7
Le cœur sent rarement ce que la bouche exprime.

The heart seldom feels what the mouth expresses.

CAMPISTRON—*Pompeia*. XI. 5.

8
Speech is silvern, silence is golden.

CARLYLE—*A Swiss Inscription*. Quoted in *Sartor Resartus*. Bk. III. Ch. III.

9
Speak not at all, in any wise, till you have somewhat to speak; care not for the reward of your speaking, but simply and with undivided mind for the truth of your speaking.

CARLYLE—*Essays. Biography.*

10
Sermo hominum mores et celat et indicat idem.

The same words conceal and declare the thoughts of men.

DIONYSIUS CATO—*Disticha de Moribus ad Filium*. Bk. IV. 26.

(See also VOLTAIRE)

11
He mouths a sentence as curs mouth a bone.

CHURCHILL—*The Rosiad*. L. 322.

12
Ipse dixit.

He himself has said it.

Quoted by CICERO—*De Nat. Deorum*. I. 5, 10 as the unreasoning answer given by Pythagoras.

13
Nullum simile quatuor pedibus currit.

It is not easy to make a simile go on all-fours.

SIR EDWARD COKE. *Institutes*.

14
Let your speech be alway with grace, seasoned with salt.

Colossians. IV. 6.

15
But though I be rude in speech, yet not in knowledge.

II Corinthians. XI. 6.

(See also OTHELLO)

16
Seeing then that we have such hope, we use great plainness of speech.

II Corinthians. III. 12.

17
Lo tuo ver dir m'incuora
Buona umilta e gran tumor m'appiani.

The truth thy speech doth show, within my heart reproves the swelling pride.

DANTE—*Purgatorio*. XI. 118.

18
Think all you speak; but speak not all you think:
Thoughts are your own; your words are so no more.
Where Wisdom steers, wind cannot make you sink:
Lips never err, when she does keep the door.

DELAUNE—*Epigram*.

19
As a vessel is known by the sound, whether it be cracked or not; so men are proved, by their speeches, whether they be wise or foolish.

DEMOSTHENES.

20
That's a Blazing strange answer.

DICKENS—*A Tale of Two Cities*. Bk. I. Ch. II.

21
Abstruse and mystic thoughts you must express
With painful care, but seeming easiness;
For truth shines brightest thro' the plainest dress.

WENTWORTH DILLON—*Essay on Translated Verse*. L. 216.

22
I will sit down now, but the time will come when you will hear me.

BENJ. DISRAELI—*Maiden Speech in the House of Commons*. (1837)

23
A sophistical rhetorician, inebriated with the exuberance of his own verbosity.

BENJ. DISRAELI—*Speech at the Riding School*. London, July 27, 1878. (Of Gladstone.)

24
A series of congratulatory regrets.

BENJ. DISRAELI—July 30, 1878. In reference to Lord Harrington's resolution on the Berlin Treaty.

25
The hare-brained chatter of irresponsible frivolity.

BENJ. DISRAELI—*Speech at Guildhall*. London, November 9, 1878.

26
Miss not the discourse of the elders.

Ecclesiasticus. VIII. 9.

1

Blessed is the man who having nothing to say, abstains from giving us wordy evidence of the fact.

George Eliot—*Impressions of Theophrastus Such*. Ch. IV. P. 97.

2

Speech is but broken light upon the depth
Of the unspoken.

George Eliot—*The Spanish Gypsy*. Bk. I.

3

O that grave speech would cumber our quick souls,
Like bells that waste the moments with their loudness.

George Eliot—*The Spanish Gypsy*. Bk. III.

4

Speech is better than silence; silence is better than speech.

Emerson—*Essay on Nominalist and Realist*.

5

When Harel wished to put a joke or witticism into circulation, he was in the habit of connecting it with some celebrated name, on the chance of reclaiming it if it took. Thus he assigned to Talleyrand, in the "Nain Jaune," the phrase, "Speech was given to man to disguise his thoughts."

Fournier—*L'Esprit dans l'Histoire*.

(See also Voltaire)

6

Mir wird von alledem so dumm,
Als ging 'mir ein Mühlrad im Kopf herum.
I feel as stupid, from all you've said
As if a mill-wheel whirled in my head.

Goethe—*Faust*. Act I. *Schulerszene*.

7

Du sprichst ein grosses Wort gelassen aus.
Thou speakest a word of great moment calmly.

Goethe—*Iphigenia auf Tauris*. I. 3. 88. 1.

8

The true use of speech is not so much to express our wants as to conceal them.

Goldsmith—*The Bee*. No. 3.

(See also Voltaire)

9

All the heart was full of feeling: love had ripened into speech,
Like the sap that turns to nectar, in the velvet of the peach.

Wm. Wallace Harney—*Adonais*.

10

Know when to speake; for many times it brings
Danger to give the best advice to kings.

Herrick—*Hesperides. Caution in Councell*.

11

In man speaks God.

Hesiod—*Works and Days*.

12

These authors do not avail themselves of the invention of letters for the purpose of conveying, but of concealing their ideas.

Lord Holland—*Life of Lope de Vega*.

(See also Voltaire)

13

I love to hear thine earnest voice,
Wherever thou art hid. * *
Thou say'st an undisputed thing
In such a solemn way.

Holmes—*To an Insect*.

14

The flowering moments of the mind
Drop half their petals in our speech.

Holmes—*To My Readers*. St. 11.

15

His speech flowed from his tongue sweeter than honey.

Homer—*Iliad*. Bk. I. 124.

16

He spake, and into every heart his words
Carried new strength and courage.

Homer—*Iliad*. Bk. V. L. 586. Bryant's trans.

17

He, from whose lips divine persuasion flows.

Homer—*Iliad*. Bk. VII. L. 143. Pope's trans.

18

For that man is detested by me as the gates of hell, whose outward words conceal his inmost thoughts.

Homer—*Iliad*. IX. 312.

(See also Voltaire)

19

Persuasive speech, and more persuasive sighs,
Silence that spoke, and eloquence of eyes.

Homer—*Iliad*. Bk. XIV. L. 251. Pope's trans.

20

And endless are the modes of speech, and far
Extends from side to side the field of words.

Homer—*Iliad*. Bk. XX. L. 315. Bryant's trans.

21

Brevis esse laboro, obscurus fio.
In laboring to be concise, I become obscure.

Horace—*Ars Poetica*. XXV.

22

I am a man of unclean lips.

Isaiah. VI. 5.

23

That fellow would vulgarize the day of judgment.

Douglas Jerrold—*A Comic Author*.

24

Speak gently! 'tis a little thing
Dropp'd in the heart's deep well:
The good, the joy, that it may bring
Eternity shall tell.

G. W. Langford—*Speak Gently*.

25

It is never so difficult to speak as when we are ashamed of our silence.

La Rochefoucauld—*Maxims*. No. 178.

26

L'allégorie habite un palais diaphane.
Allegory dwells in a transparent palace.

Lemierre—*Peinture*. III.

27

Speech was made to open man to man, and not to hide him; to promote commerce, and not betray it.

David Lloyd—*State Worthies*. Vol. I. P. 503. Whitworth's Ed. (1665)

(See also Voltaire)

28

In general those who nothing have to say
Contrive to spend the longest time in doing it.

Lowell—*To Charles Eliot Norton*.

1
Woe unto you, when all men shall speak well of you!
Luke. VI. 26.

2
They think that they shall be heard for their much speaking.
Matthew. VI. 7.

3
Out of the abundance of the heart the mouth speaketh.
Matthew. XII. 34.

4
Though his tongue
Dropp'd manna, and could make the worse
appear
The better reason, to perplex and dash
Maturest counsels.
MILTON—*Paradise Lost*. Bk. II. L. 112.

5
When Adam first of men,
To first of women Eve, thus moving speech,
Turn'd him all ear to hear new utterance flow.
MILTON—*Paradise Lost*. Bk. IV. L. 408.

6
Faire de la prose sans le savoir.
To speak prose without knowing it.
MOLIÈRE—*Bourgeois Gentilhomme*. II. 6.

7
Quand on se fait entendre, on parle toujours bien,
Et tous vos beaux dictons ne servent de rien.
When we are understood, we always speak well, and then all your fine diction serves no purpose.
MOLIÈRE—*Les Femmes Savantes*. II. 6.

8
Je vous ferai un impromptu à loisir.
I shall make you an impromptu at my leisure.
MOLIÈRE—*Les Précieuses Ridicules*. I. 12.

9
If you your lips would keep from slips,
Five things observe with care;
To whom you speak, of whom you speak,
And how, and when, and where.
W. E. NORRIS—*Thirlby Hall*. Vol. I. P. 315.

10
Barbarus hic ego sum, quia non intelligor ulli.
I am a barbarian here, because I am not understood by anyone.
OVID—*Tristia*. Bk. V. 10. 37.

11
Voulez-vous qu'on croie du bien de vous? N'en dites point.
Do you wish people to speak well of you? Then do not speak at all yourself.
PASCAL—*Pensées*. VI. 59.

12
Verba togæ sequeris.
You follow words of the toga (language of the cultivated class).
PERSIUS—*Satires*. 5. 14.

13
Rhetoric is the art of ruling the minds of men.
PLATO. See PLUTARCH—*Life of Pericles*.

14
Odiosa est oratio, cum rem agas, longinquum loqui.
It is a tiresome way of speaking, when you should despatch the business, to beat about the bush.
PLAUTUS—*Mercator*. III. 4. 23.

15
Verba facit mortuo.
He speaks to a dead man (*i.e.* wastes words).
PLAUTUS—*Pœnulus*. Act IV. 2. 18.

16
In the pleading of cases nothing pleases so much as brevity.
PLINY the Younger—*Epistles*. Bk. I. 20.
(See also BUTLER)

17
Abstruse questions must have abstruse answers.
Saying in PLUTARCH—*Life of Alexander*.

18
Speech is like cloth of Arras opened and put abroad, whereby the imagery doth appear in figure; whereas in thoughts they lie but as in packs.
PLUTARCH—*Life of Themistocles*.

19
In their declamations and speeches they made use of words to veil and muffle their design.
PLUTARCH—*On Hearing*. V. (Of the Sophists.)
(See also VOLTAIRE)

20
And empty heads console with empty sound.
POPE—*Dunciad*. Bk. IV. L. 542.

21
A soft answer turneth away wrath.
Proverbs. XV. 1.

22
Deus ille princeps, parens rerum fabricatorque mundi, nullo magis hominem separavit a ceteris, quæ quidem mortalia sunt, animalibus, quam dicendi facultate.
God, that all-powerful Creator of nature and Architect of the world, has impressed man with no character so proper to distinguish him from other animals, as by the faculty of speech.
QUINTILIAN—*De Institutione Oratoria*. II. 17. 2.

23
Il ne rend que monosyllables. Je croy qu'il feroit d'une cerise trois morceaux.
He replies nothing but monosyllables. I believe he would make three bites of a cherry.
RABELAIS—*Pantagruel*. Bk. V. Ch. XXVIII.

24
Man lernt Verschwiegenheit am meisten unter Menschen, die Keine haben—und Plauderhaftigheit unter Verschwiegenen.
One learns taciturnity best among people who have none, and loquacity among the taciturn.
JEAN PAUL RICHTER—*Hesperus*. XII.

25
Speak after the manner of men.
Romans. VI. 19.

26
Was ist der langen Rede kurzer Sinn?
What is the short meaning of this long harangue?
SCHILLER—*Piccolomini*. I. 2. 160.

27
Just at the age 'twixt boy and youth,
When thought is speech, and speech is truth.
SCOTT—*Marmion*. Canto II. *Introduction*.

28
Talis hominibus est oratio qualis vita.
Men's conversation is like their life.
SENECA—*Epistolæ Ad Lucilium*. 114.

1 I had a thing to say,
But I will fit it with some better time.
King John. Act III. Sc. 3. L. 25.

2
The tongues of mocking wenches are as keen
As is the razor's edge invisible,
Cutting a smaller hair than may be seen
Above the sense of sense; so sensible
Seemeth their conference; their conceits have wings
Fleeter than arrows, bullets, wind, thought, swifter things.
Love's Labour's Lost. Act V. Sc. 2. L. 256.

3
A heavy heart bears not a humble tongue.
Love's Labour's Lost. Act V. Sc. 2. L. 747.

4
It may be right; but you are i' the wrong
To speak before your time.
Measure for Measure. Act V. Sc. 1. L. 86.

5
Here will be an old abusing of God's patience
and the king's English.
Merry Wives of Windsor. Act I. Sc. 4. L. 4.

6
She speaks poniards, and every word stabs.
Much Ado About Nothing. Act II. Sc. 1. L. 255.

7 Rude am I in my speech,
And little blessed with the soft phrase of peace;
For since these arms of mine had seven years' pith,
Till now some nine moons wasted, they have us'd
Their dearest action in the tented field,
And little of this great world can I speak,
More than pertains to feats of broil and battle,
And therefore little shall I grace my cause
In speaking for myself.
Othello. Act I. Sc. 3. L. 81.
(See also CORINTHIANS)

8
Your fair discourse hath been as sugar,
Making the hard way sweet and delectable.
Richard II. Act II. Sc. 3. L. 6.

9
I would be loath to cast away my speech, for besides that it is excellently well penn'd, I have taken great pains to con it.
Twelfth Night. Act I. Sc. 5. L. 183.

10
No one minds what Jeffrey says—it is not more than a week ago that I heard him speak disrespectfully of the equator.
SYDNEY SMITH. LADY HOLLAND'S *Memoir.* Vol. I.

11
God giveth speech to all, song to the few.
WALTER C. SMITH—*Editorial.* L. 15. *Olrig Grange.* Bk. I.

12
Speech was given to the ordinary sort of men, whereby to communicate their mind; but to wise men, whereby to conceal it.
BISHOP SOUTH—*Sermon.* April 30, 1676.
(See also VOLTAIRE)

13
Sæpius locutum, nunquam me tacuisse pœnitet.
I have often regretted having spoken, never having kept silent.
SYRUS—*Maxims.*

14
Sermo animi est imago; qualis vir, talis et oratio est.
Conversation is the image of the mind; as the man, so is his speech.
SYRUS—*Maxims.*

15
La parole a été donnée à l'homme pour déguiser sa pensée.
Speech was given to man to disguise his thoughts.
Attributed to TALLEYRAND by BARRÈRE in *Memoirs.*
(See also FOURNIER, VOLTAIRE)

16
Doubtless there are men of great parts that are guilty of downright bashfulness, that by a strange hesitation and reluctance to speak murder the finest and most elegant thoughts and render the most lively conceptions flat and heavy.
The Tatler. No. 252.

17
Nullum est jam dictum quod non dictum sit prius.
Nothing is said nowadays that has not been said before.
TERENCE—*Eunuchus. Prologue.* XLI.

18
On the day of the dinner of the Oyster-mongers' Company, what a noble speech I thought of in the cab!
THACKERAY—*Roundabout Papers. On Two Papers I intended to write.*

19
Oh, but the heavenly grammar did I hold
Of that high speech which angels' tongues turn gold!
So should her deathless beauty take no wrong,
Praised in her own great kindred's fit and cognate tongue.
Or if that language yet with us abode
Which Adam in the garden talked with God!
But our untempered speech descends—poor heirs!
Grimy and rough-cast still from Babel's brick layers:
Curse on the brutish jargon we inherit,
Strong but to damn, not memorise, a spirit!
A cheek, a lip, a limb, a bosom, they
Move with light ease in speech of working-day;
And women we do use to praise even so.
FRANCIS THOMPSON—*Her Portrait.*

20
Quand celui à qui l'on parle ne comprend pas et celui qui parle ne se comprend pas, c'est de la métaphysique.
When he to whom one speaks does not understand, and he who speaks himself does not understand, this is Metaphysics.
VOLTAIRE.

21
Ils ne se servent de la pensée que pour autoriser leurs injustices, et emploient les paroles que pour déguiser leurs pensées.
Men use thought only to justify their wrong doings, and employ speech only to conceal their thoughts.
VOLTAIRE—*Dialogue* XIV. *Le Chapon et la Poularde.* (1766)
(See also BUTLER, CATO, FOURNIER, GOLDSMITH, HOLLAND LLOYD, PLUTARCH, SOUTH, TALLEYRAND, YOUNG)

1
Il faut distinguer entre parler pour tromper et se taire pour être impénétrable.
We must distinguish between speaking to deceive and being silent to be reserved.
VOLTAIRE—*Essai sur les Mœurs.* Ch. CLXIII.

2
Choice word and measured phrase, above the
reach
Of ordinary men.
WORDSWORTH—*Resolution and Independence.* St. 14.

3
Where nature's end of language is declined,
And men talk only to conceal the mind.
YOUNG—*Love of Fame.* Satire II. L. 207.
Same idea in ST. AUGUSTINE—*Enchiridion ad Laurentium.* HOMER—*Iliad.* IX. 313. Traced from GOLDSMITH to BUTLER; YOUNG to SOUTH.
(See also VOLTAIRE)

SPICE

Umbellularia Californica

4
The Spice-Tree lives in the garden green,
Beside it the fountain flows;
And a fair Bird sits the boughs between,
And sings his melodious woes.
* * * * * *
That out-bound stem has branches three;
On each a thousand blossoms grow;
And old as aught of time can be,
The root stands fast in the rocks below.
JOHN STERLING—*The Spice-Tree.* Sts. 1 and 3.

SPIDER

5
I've lately had two spiders
Crawling upon my startled hopes—
Now though thy friendly hand has brushed 'em
from me,
Yet still they crawl offensive to mine eyes:
I would have some kind friend to tread upon 'em.
COLLEY CIBBER—*Richard III* (Altered). Act IV. Sc. 2. L. 15.

6
Much like a subtle spider, which doth sit
In middle of her web, which spreadeth wide:
If aught do touch the utmost thread of it,
She feels it instantly on every side.
SIR JOHN DAVIES—*The Immortality of the Soul.* Sec. XVIII. *Feeling.*

7
Or (almost) like a Spider, who, confin'd
In her Web's centre, shakt with every winde,
Moves in an instant, if the buzzing Flie
Stir but a string of her Lawn Canopie.
DU BARTAS—*Divine Weekes and Workes. First Week. Sixth Day.* L. 998.

8
"Will you walk into my parlour?"
Said a spider to a fly;
"'Tis the prettiest little parlour
That ever you did spy."
MARY HOWITT—*The Spider and the Fly.*

9
The spider's touch, how exquisitely fine!
Feels at each thread, and lives along the line.
POPE—*Essay on Man.* Ep. I. L. 217.

SPIRIT; SPIRITS (See also APPARITIONS)

10
Why, a spirit is such a little, little thing, that I have heard a man, who was a great scholar, say that he'll dance ye a hornpipe upon the point of a needle.
ADDISON—*The Drummer.* Act I. Sc. 1.
(See also CUDWORTH)

11
Not of the letter, but of the spirit; for the letter killeth, but the spirit giveth life.
II Corinthians. III. 6.

12
Some who are far from atheists, may make themselves merry with that conceit of thousands of spirits dancing at once upon a needle's point.
CUDWORTH—*True Intellectual System of the Universe.* Vol. III. P. 497. Ed. 1829. ISAAC D'ISRAELI in *Curiosities of Literature. Quodlibets,* quotes from AQUINAS, "How many angels can dance on the point of a very fine needle without jostling each other." The idea, not the words, are in AQUINAS—*Summa* and *Sentences.* Credited also to BERNARDO DE CARPINO and ALAGONA.
(See also ADDISON)

13
A Corpse or a Ghost— . . . I'd sooner be one or t'other, square and fair, than a Ghost in a Corpse, which is my feelins at present.
WILLIAM DE MORGAN—*Joseph Vance.* Ch. XXXIX.

14
I am the spirit of the morning sea,
I am the awakening and the glad surprise.
R. W. GILDER—*Ode.*

15
Ich bin der Geist stets verneint.
I am the Spirit that denies.
GOETHE—*Faust.* I. 3. 163.

16
Aërial spirits, by great Jove design'd
To be on earth the guardians of mankind:
Invisible to mortal eyes they go,
And mark our actions, good or bad, below:
The immortal spies with watchful care preside,
And thrice ten thousand round their charges
glide:
They can reward with glory or with gold,
A power they by Divine permission hold.
HESIOD—*Works and Days.* L. 164.
(See also MILTON, POPE)

17
The spirit indeed is willing, but the flesh is weak.
Matthew. XXVI. 41.

18
Millions of spiritual creatures walk the earth
Unseen, both when we wake, and when we sleep.
MILTON—*Paradise Lost.* Bk. IV. L. 678.
(See also HESIOD)

19
Teloque animus præstantior omni.
A spirit superior to every weapon.
OVID—*Metamorphoses.* III. 54.

20
Ornament of a meek and quiet spirit.
I Peter. III. 4.

1
Know then, unnumber'd Spirits round thee fly,
The light Militia of the lower sky.
POPE—*Rape of the Lock*. I. 41.
(See also HESIOD)

2
He that is slow to anger is better than the mighty; and he that ruleth his spirit than he that taketh a city.
Proverbs. XVI. 32. *Mishna*. *Ethics of the Fathers*. IV. 2.

3
A wounded spirit who can bear?
Proverbs. XVIII. 14.

4
After the spiritual powers, there is no thing in the world more unconquerable than the spirit of nationality. . . The spirit of nationality in Ireland will persist even though the mightiest of material powers be its neighbor.
GEORGE W. RUSSELL—*The Economics of Ireland*. P. 23.

5
Black spirits and white,
Red spirits and grey,
Mingle, mingle, mingle,
You that mingle may.
Macbeth. Act IV. Sc. 1. MIDDLETON—*The Witch*. Act V. Sc. 2.

6 Spirits are not finely touched
But to fine issues.
Measure for Measure. Act I. Sc. 1. L. 36.

7
The spirit, Sir, is one of mockery.
STEVENSON—*Suicide Club*. In *New Arabian Nights*.

8
Of my own spirit let me be
In sole though feeble mastery.
SARA TEASDALE—*Mastery*.
(See also HENLEY under SOUL)

9
Boatman, come, thy fare receive;
Thrice thy fare I gladly give,
For unknown, unseen by thee,
Spirits twain have crossed with me.
UHLAND—*The Ferry Boat*. SKEAT'S trans.

SPORT (See also AMUSEMENT)

10
By sports like these are all their cares beguil'd,
The sports of children satisfy the child.
GOLDSMITH—*The Traveller*. L. 153.

11
It is a poor sport that is not worth the candle.
HERBERT—*Jacula Prudentum*.

12
Nec luisse pudet, sed non incidere ludum.
The shame is not in having sported, but in not having broken off the sport.
HORACE—*Epistles*. I. 14. 36.

13
When I play with my cat, who knows whether I do not make her more sport, than she makes me?
MONTAIGNE—*Apology for Raimond de Sebonde*.

SPRING

14
As quickly as the ice vanishes when the Father unlooses the frost fetters and unwounds the icy ropes of the torrent.
Beowulf. VII.

15
Now Spring returns; but not to me returns
The vernal joy my better years have known;
Dim in my breast life's dying taper burns,
And all the joys of life with health have flown.
MICHAEL BRUCE—*Elegy, written in Spring*.

16
Now Nature hangs her mantle green
On every blooming tree,
And spreads her sheets o' daisies white
Out o'er the grassy lea.
BURNS—*Lament of Mary Queen of Scots*.

17
And the spring comes slowly up this way.
COLERIDGE—*Christabel*. Pt. I.

18
Spring hangs her infant blossoms on the trees,
Rock'd in the cradle of the western breeze.
COWPER—*Tirocinium*. L. 43.

19
If there comes a little thaw,
Still the air is chill and raw,
Here and there a patch of snow,
Dirtier than the ground below,
Dribbles down a marshy flood;
Ankle-deep you stick in mud
In the meadows while you sing,
"This is Spring."
C. P. CRANCH—*A Spring Growl*.

20
Starred forget-me-nots smile sweetly,
Ring, blue-bells, ring!
Winning eye and heart completely,
Sing, robin, sing!
All among the reeds and rushes,
Where the brook its music hushes,
Bright the caloposon blushes,—
Laugh, O murmuring Spring!
SARAH F. DAVIS—*Summer Song*.

21
Daughter of heaven and earth, coy Spring,
With sudden passion languishing,
Teaching barren moors to smile,
Painting pictures mile on mile,
Holds a cup of cowslip wreaths
Whence a smokeless incense breathes.
EMERSON—*May Day*. St. 1.

22
Eternal Spring, with smiling Verdure here
Warms the mild Air, and crowns the youthful Year.
* * * * * *
The Rose still blushes, and the vi'lets blow.
SIR SAM'L GARTH—*The Dispensary*. Canto IV. L. 298.

23
Lo! where the rosy bosom'd Hours
Fair Venus' train appear,
Disclose the long-expecting flowers,
And wake the purple year.
GRAY—*Ode on Spring*. Compare *Homeric Hymn to Aphrodite*. (Hymn E.)

1
When Spring unlocks the flowers to paint the laughing soil.
BISHOP HEBER—*Hymn for Seventh Sunday after Trinity.*

2
The spring's already at the gate
With looks my care beguiling;
The country round appeareth straight
A flower-garden smiling.
HEINE—*Book of Songs. Catherine.* No. 6.

3
The beauteous eyes of the spring's fair night
With comfort are downward gazing.
HEINE—*Book of Songs. New Spring.* No. 3.

4
I come, I come! ye have called me long,
I come o'er the mountain with light and song:
Ye may trace my step o'er the wakening earth,
By the winds which tell of the violet's birth,
By the primrose-stars in the shadowy grass,
By the green leaves, opening as I pass.
FELICIA D. HEMANS—*Voice of Spring.*

5
Sweet Spring, full of sweet dayes and roses,
A box where sweets compacted lie,
My musick shows ye have your closes,
And all must die.
HERBERT—*The Church. Vertue.* St. 3.

6
For surely in the blind deep-buried roots
Of all men's souls to-day
A secret quiver shoots.
RICHARD HOVEY—*Spring.*

7
They know who keep a broken tryst,
Till something from the Spring be missed
We have not truly known the Spring.
ROBERT UNDERWOOD JOHNSON—*The Wistful Days.*

8
All flowers of Spring are not May's own;
The crocus cannot often kiss her;
The snow-drop, ere she comes, has flown:—
The earliest violets always miss her.
LUCY LARCOM—*The Sister Months.*

9
And softly came the fair young queen
O'er mountain, dale, and dell;
And where her golden light was seen
An emerald shadow fell.
The good-wife oped the window wide,
The good-man spanned his plough;
'Tis time to run, 'tis time to ride,
For Spring is with us now.
LELAND—*Spring.*

10
The lovely town was white with apple-blooms,
And the great elms o'erhead
Dark shadows wove on their aerial looms,
Shot through with golden thread.
LONGFELLOW—*Hawthorne.* St. 2.

11
Came the Spring with all its splendor,
All its birds and all its blossoms,
All its flowers, and leaves, and grasses.
LONGFELLOW—*Hiawatha.* Pt. XXI. L. 109.

12
Thus came the lovely spring with a rush of blossoms and music,
Flooding the earth with flowers, and the air with melodies vernal.
LONGFELLOW—*Tales of a Wayside Inn.* Pt. III. *The Theologian's Tale. Elizabeth.*

13
The holy spirit of the Spring
Is working silently.
GEORGE MACDONALD—*Songs of the Spring Days.* Pt. II.

14
Awake! the morning shines, and the fresh field
Calls us; we lose the prime, to mark how spring
Our tended plants, how blows the citron grove,
What drops the myrrh, and what the balmy reed.
How nature paints her colours, how the bee
Sits on the bloom, extracting liquid sweet.
MILTON—*Paradise Lost.* Bk. V. L. 20.

15
On many a green branch swinging,
Little birdlets singing
Warble sweet notes in the air.
Flowers fair
There I found.
Green spread the meadow all around.
NITHART—Spring-Song. Trans. in *The Minnesinger of Germany.*

16
Yet Ah, that Spring should vanish with the Rose.
That Youth's sweet-scented manuscript should close!
The Nightingale that in the branches sang
Ah whence and whither flown again, who knows?
OMAR KHAYYAM—*Rubaiyat.* FITZGERALD'S Trans. St. 96.

17
Gentle Spring!—in sunshine clad,
Well dost thou thy power display!
For Winter maketh the light heart sad,
And thou,—thou makest the sad heart gay.
CHARLES D'ORLÉANS—*Spring.* LONGFELLOW'S trans.

18
Hark! the hours are softly calling
Bidding Spring arise,
To listen to the rain-drops falling
From the cloudy skies,
To listen to Earth's weary voices,
Louder every day,
Bidding her no longer linger
On her charm'd way;
But hasten to her task of beauty
Scarcely yet begun.
ADELAIDE A. PROCTER—*Spring.*

19
I wonder if the sap is stirring yet,
If wintry birds are dreaming of a mate,
If frozen snowdrops feel as yet the sun,
And crocus fires are kindling one by one.
CHRISTINA G. ROSSETTI—*The First Spring Day.* St. 1.

20
There is no time like Spring,
When life's alive in everything,
Before new nestlings sing,
Before cleft swallows speed their journey back
Along the trackless track.
CHRISTINA G. ROSSETTI—*Spring.* St. 3.

1
Spring flies, and with it all the train it leads:
And flowers, in fading, leave us but their seeds.
SCHILLER—*Farewell to the Reader.*

2
I sing the first green leaf upon the bough,
The tiny kindling flame of emerald fire,
The stir amid the roots of reeds, and how
The sap will flush the briar.
CLINTON SCOLLARD—*Song in March.*

3
For, lo! the winter is past, the rain is over and gone; the flowers appear on the earth; the time of the singing of birds is come, and the voice of the turtle is heard in our land.
The Song of Solomon. II. 11, 12.

4
So forth issew'd the Seasons of the yeare:
First, lusty Spring, all dight in leaves of flowres
That freshly budded and new bloomes did beare,
In which a thousand birds had built their bowres
That sweetly sung to call forth paramours;
And in his hand a javelin he did beare,
And on his head (as fit for warlike stoures)
A guilt, engraven morion he did weare:
That, as some did him love, so others did him feare.
SPENSER—*Faerie Queene.* Bk. VII. Canto VII. *Legend of Constancie.* St. 28.

5
Now the hedged meads renew
Rustic odor, smiling hue,
And the clean air shines and twinkles as the world goes wheeling through;
And my heart springs up anew,
Bright and confident and true,
And my old love comes to meet me in the dawning and the dew.
STEVENSON—*Poem written in 1876.*

6
It is the season now to go
About the country high and low,
Among the lilacs hand in hand,
And two by two in fairyland.
STEVENSON—*Underwoods. It is the Season Now to Go.*

7
O tender time that love thinks long to see,
Sweet foot of Spring that with her footfall sows
Late snow-like flowery leavings of the snows,
Be not too long irresolute to be;
O mother-month, where have they hidden thee?
SWINBURNE—*A Vision of Spring in Winter.*

8
Once more the Heavenly Power
Makes all things new,
And domes the red-plough'd hills
With loving blue;
The blackbirds have their wills,
The throstles too.
TENNYSON—*Early Spring.*

9
The bee buzz'd up in the heat,
"I am faint for your honey, my sweet."
The flower said, "Take it, my dear,
For now is the Spring of the year.
So come, come!"
"Hum!"
And the bee buzz'd down from the heat.
TENNYSON—*The Forester.* Act IV. Sc. 1.

10
Dip down upon the northern shore,
O sweet new year, delaying long;
Thou doest expectant nature wrong,
Delaying long; delay no more.
TENNYSON—*In Memoriam,* 82.

11
In the Spring a livelier iris changes on the burnish'd dove;
In the Spring a young man's fancy lightly turns to thoughts of love.
TENNYSON—*Locksley Hall.* St. 9.

12
The boyhood of the year.
TENNYSON—*Sir Launcelot and Queen Guinevere.* St. 3.

13
Come, gentle Spring; ethereal Mildness, come!
THOMSON—*Seasons. Spring.* L. 1.

14
The Clouds consign their treasures to the fields,
And, softly shaking on the dimpled pool,
Prelusive drops, let all their moisture flow
In large effusion, o'er the freshen'd world.
THOMSON—*Seasons. Spring.* L. 173.

15
Fair-handed Spring unbosoms every grace:
Throws out the snowdrop and the crocus first.
THOMSON—*Seasons. Spring.* L. 527.

16
'Tis spring-time on the eastern hills!
Like torrents gush the summer rills;
Through winter's moss and dry dead leaves
The bladed grass revives and lives,
Pushes the mouldering waste away,
And glimpses to the April day.
WHITTIER—*Mogg Megone.* Pt. III.

17
And all the woods are alive with the murmur and sound of spring,
And the rosebud breaks into pink on the climbing briar,
And the crocus bed is a quivering moon of fire
Girdled round with the belt of an amethyst ring.
OSCAR WILDE—*Magdalen Walks.*

18
The Spring is here—the delicate footed May,
With its slight fingers full of leaves and flowers,
And with it comes a thirst to be away,
In lovelier scenes to pass these sweeter hours.
N. P. WILLIS—*Spring.*

STAGE, THE (See ACTING)

STARS

19
The spacious firmament on high,
With all the blue ethereal sky,
And spangled heavens, a shining frame,
Their great Original proclaim.
Forever singing, as they shine,
The hand that made us is divine.
ADDISON—*Ode. The Spacious Firmament on High.*

20
Surely the stars are images of love.
BAILEY—*Festus.* Sc. *Garden and Bower by the Sea.*

1
What are ye orbs?
The words of God? the Scriptures of the skies?
BAILEY—*Festus*. Sc. *Everywhere*.

2
The stars,
Which stand as thick as dewdrops on the fields
Of heaven.
BAILEY—*Festus*. Sc. *Heaven*.

3
The sad and solemn night
Hath yet her multitude of cheerful fires;
The glorious host of light
Walk the dark hemisphere till she retires;
All through her silent watches, gliding slow,
Her constellations come, and climb the heavens, and go.
BRYANT—*Hymn to the North Star*.

4
When stars are in the quiet skies,
Then most I pine for thee;
Bend on me then thy tender eyes,
As stars look on the sea.
BULWER-LYTTON—*When Stars are in the Quiet Skies*.

5
The number is certainly the cause. The apparent disorder augments the grandeur, for the appearance of care is highly contrary to our ideas of magnificence. Besides, the stars lie in such apparent confusion, as makes it impossible on ordinary occasions to reckon them. This gives them the advantage of a sort of infinity.
BURKE—*On the Sublime and the Beautiful. Magnificence*.

6
A grisly meteor on his face.
BUTLER—*Cobbler and Vicar of Bray*.

7
This hairy meteor did announce
The fall of sceptres and of crowns.
BUTLER—*Hudibras*. Pt. I. Canto I. 247.
(See also CAMPBELL, TASSO, TAYLOR)

8
Cry out upon the stars for doing
Ill offices, to cross their wooing.
BUTLER—*Hudibras*. Pt. III. Canto I. L. 17.

9
Like the lost pleiad seen no more below.
BYRON—*Beppo*. St. 14.

10
And the sentinel stars set their watch in the sky.
CAMPBELL—*The Soldier's Dream*.
(See also LEE)

11
Where Andes, giant of the western star,
With meteor standard to the winds unfurl'd.
CAMPBELL—*Pleasures of Hope*. Pt. I.
(See also BUTLER)

12
In yonder pensile orb, and every sphere
That gems the starry girdle of the year.
CAMPBELL—*Pleasures of Hope*. Pt. II. L. 194.

13
Now twilight lets her curtain down
And pins it with a star.
LYDIA MARIA CHILD. Adapted from M'DONALD CLARK. Appeared thus in his obituary notice.
(See also CLARK)

14
Quod est ante pedes nemo spectat: cœli scrutantur plagas.
No one sees what is before his feet: we all gaze at the stars.
CICERO—*De Divinatione*. II. 13.

15
While twilight's curtain gathering far,
Is pinned with a single diamond star.
M'DONALD CLARK—*Death in Disguise*. L. 227.

16
Whilst twilight's curtain spreading far,
Was pinned with a single star.
M'DONALD CLARK—*Death in Disguise*. L. 227. As it appeared in Boston Ed. 1833.
(See also CHILD)

17
Hast thou a charm to stay the morning-star
In his steep course?
COLERIDGE—*Hymn in the Vale of Chamouni*.

18
Or soar aloft to be the spangled skies
And gaze upon her with a thousand eyes.
COLERIDGE—*Lines on an Autumnal Evening*.
(See also PLATO, SHELLEY)

19
All for Love, or the Lost Pleiad.
STIRLING COYNE. Title of play. Produced in London, Jan. 16, 1838.

20
The stars that have most glory have no rest.
SAMUEL DANIEL—*History of the Civil War*. Bk. VI. St. 104.

21
The stars are golden fruit upon a tree
All out of reach.
GEORGE ELIOT—*The Spanish Gypsy*. Bk. II.

22
Hitch your wagon to a star.
EMERSON—*Society and Solitude. Civilization*.

23
The starres, bright sentinels of the skies.
WM. HABINGTON—*Dialogue between Night and Araphil*. L. 3.
(See also LEE)

24
Why, who shall talk of shrines, of sceptres riven?
It is too sad to think on what *we* are,
When from its height afar
A world sinks thus; and yon majestic Heaven
Shines not the less for that one vanish'd star!
FELICIA D. HEMANS—*The Lost Pleiad*.
(See also LEE)

25
The starres of the night
Will lend thee their light,
Like tapers cleare without number.
HERRICK—*The Night Piece*.

26
Micat inter omnes
Iulium sidus, velut inter ignes
Luna minores.
And yet more bright
Shines out the Julian star,
As moon outglows each lesser light.
HORACE—*Carmina*. I. 12. 47.
(See also WOTTON)

1
The dawn is lonely for the sun,
And chill and drear;
The one lone star is pale and wan,
As one in fear.
RICHARD HOVEY—*Chanson de Rosemonde.*

2
When, like an Emir of tyrannic power,
Sirius appears, and on the horizon black
Bids countless stars pursue their mighty track.
VICTOR HUGO—*The Vanished City.*

3
The morning stars sang together, and all the sons of God shouted for joy.
Job. XXXVIII. 7.

4
Canst thou bind the sweet influences of Pleiades, or loose the bands of Orion?
Job. XXXVIII. 31.

5
Canst thou guide Arcturus with his sons?
Job. XXXVIII. 32.

6
When sunset flows into golden glows,
And the breath of the night is new,
Love finds afar eve's eager star—
That is my thought of you.
ROBERT UNDERWOOD JOHNSON—*Star Song.*

7
Who falls for love of God shall rise a star.
JONSON—*Underwoods.* 32. *To a friend.*

8
The stars in their courses fought against Sisera.
Judges. V. 20.

9
God be thanked for the Milky Way that runs across the sky.
That's the path that my feet would tread whenever I have to die.

Some folks call it a Silver Sword, and some a Pearly Crown.
But the only thing I think it is, is Main Street, Heaventown.
JOYCE KILMER—*Main Street.*

10
The stars, heav'n sentry, wink and seem to die.
LEE—*Theodosius.* Probably inspired CAMPBELL's lines.
(See also CAMPBELL, HABINGTON, HEMANS, MONTGOMERY, NORRIS)

11
Just above yon sandy bar,
As the day grows fainter and dimmer,
Lonely and lovely, a single star
Lights the air with a dusky glimmer.
LONGFELLOW—*Chrysaor.* St. 1.

12
Silently, one by one, in the infinite meadows of heaven,
Blossomed the lovely stars, the forget-me-nots of the angels.
LONGFELLOW—*Evangeline.* Pt. I. St. 3.
(See also DE LA MARE, MOIR)

13
The night is calm and cloudless,
And still as still can be,
And the stars come forth to listen
To the music of the sea.
They gather, and gather, and gather,
Until they crowd the sky,
And listen, in breathless silence,
To the solemn litany.
LONGFELLOW—*Christus. The Golden Legend.* Pt. V.

14
There is no light in earth or heaven
But the cold light of stars;
And the first watch of night is given
To the red planet Mars.
LONGFELLOW—*Light of Stars.* St. 2.

15
Stars of the summer night!
Far in yon azure deeps
Hide, hide your golden light!
She sleeps!
My lady sleeps!
Sleeps.
LONGFELLOW—*Spanish Student. Serenade.*

16
A wise man,
Watching the stars pass across the sky,
Remarked:
In the upper air the fireflies move more slowly.
AMY LOWELL—*Meditation.*

17
Wide are the meadows of night
And daisies are shining there,
Tossing their lovely dews,
Lustrous and fair;
And through these sweet fields go,
Wanderers amid the stars—
Venus, Mercury, Uranus, Neptune,
Saturn, Jupiter, Mars.
WALTER DE LA MARE—*The Wanderers.*
(See also LONGFELLOW)

18
The star that bids the shepherd fold,
Now the top of heaven doth hold.
MILTON—*Comus.* L. 93.

19
So sinks the day-star in the ocean-bed,
And yet anon repairs his drooping head,
And tricks his beams, and with new-spangled ore
Flames in the forehead of the morning sky.
MILTON—*Lycidas.* L. 168.

20
Brightest seraph, tell
In which of all these shining orbs hath man
His fixed seat, or fixed seat hath none,
But all these shining orbs his choice to dwell.
MILTON—*Paradise Lost.* Bk. III. L. 667.

21
At whose sight all the stars
Hide their diminish'd heads.
MILTON—*Paradise Lost.* Bk. IV. L. 34.
(See also POPE)

22
Now glowed the firmament
With living sapphires; Hesperus, that led
The starry host, rode brightest, till the Moon,
Rising in clouded majesty, at length
Apparent queen, unveiled her peerless light,
And o'er the dark her silver mantle threw.
MILTON—*Paradise Lost.* Bk. IV. L. 604.

23
The starry cope
Of heaven.
MILTON—*Paradise Lost.* Bk. IV. L. 992.

24
And made the stars,
And set them in the firmament of heav'n,
T' illuminate the earth, and rule the day
In their vicissitude, and rule the night.
MILTON—*Paradise Lost.* Bk. VII. L. 348.

1
Hither, as to their fountain, other stars
Repairing in their golden urns draw light,
And hence the morning planet gilds her horns.
MILTON—*Paradise Lost.* Bk. VII. L. 364.

2
A broad and ample road, whose dust is gold,
And pavement stars.
MILTON—*Paradise Lost.* Bk. VII. L. 577.

3
Now the bright morning-star, day's harbinger,
Comes dancing from the east.
MILTON—*Song on May Morning.*

4
Stars are the Daisies that begem
The blue fields of the sky,
Beheld by all, and everywhere,
Bright prototypes on high.
MOIR—*The Daisy.* St. 5.
(See also LONGFELLOW)

5
The quenchless stars, so eloquently bright,
Untroubled sentries of the shadow'y night.
MONTGOMERY—*Omnipresence of the Deity.*
(See also LEE)

6
But soon, the prospect clearing,
By cloudless starlight on he treads
And thinks no lamp so cheering
As that light which Heaven sheds.
MOORE—*I'd Mourn the Hopes.*

7
The stars stand sentinel by night.
JOHN NORRIS.
(See also LEE)

8
And the day star arise in your hearts.
II. *Peter* I. 19.

9
Would that I were the heaven, that I might be
All full of love-lit eyes to gaze on thee.
PLATO—*To Stella.* In *Anthologia Palat.* Vol. V. P. 317.
(See also COLERIDGE)

10
Led by the light of the Mæonian star.
POPE—*Essay on Criticism.* Pt. III. L. 89.

11
Ye little stars, hide your diminish'd rays.
POPE—*Moral Essays.* Ep. III. L. 282.
(See also MILTON)

12
Starry Crowns of Heaven
Set in azure night!
Linger yet a little
Ere you hide your light:—
Nay; let Starlight fade away,
Heralding the day!
ADELAIDE A. PROCTER—*Give Place.*

13
No star is ever lost we once have seen,
We always may be what we might have been.
ADELAIDE A. PROCTER—*Legend of Provence.*

14
One naked star has waded through
The purple shallows of the night,
And faltering as falls the dew
It drips its misty light.
JAMES WHITCOMB RILEY—*The Beetle.*

15
Thus some who have the Stars survey'd
Are ignorantly led
To think those glorious Lamps were made
To light *Tom Fool* to bed.
NICHOLAS ROWE—*Song on a Fine Woman Who Had a Dull Husband.*

16
Hesperus bringing together
All that the morning star scattered.—
SAPPHO. XIV. Trans. by BLISS CARMAN.

17
Her blue eyes sought the west afar,
For lovers love the western star.
SCOTT—*Lay of the Last Minstrel.* Canto III. St. 24.

18
Non est ad astra mollis e terris via.—
There is no easy way to the stars from the earth.
SENECA — *Hercules Furens.* Act II. 437.
Same idea in USENER—*Scholia.* LUCAN. I. 300. PRUDENTIUS—*Cathem.* 10. 92.

19
Our Jovial star reign'd at his birth.
Cymbeline. Act V. Sc. 4. L. 105.

20
Two stars keep not their motion in one sphere.
Henry IV. Pt. I. Act V. Sc. 4. L. 65.

21
The skies are painted with unnumber'd sparks,
They are all fire and every one doth shine,
But there's but one in all doth hold his place.
Julius Cæsar. Act III. Sc. 1. L. 63.

22
The stars above us govern our conditions.
King Lear. Act IV. Sc. 3. L. 35.

23
The unfolding star calls up the shepherd.
Measure for Measure. Act IV. Sc. 2. L. 218.

24 Look how the floor of heaven
Is thick inlaid with patines of bright gold:
There's not the smallest orb which thou behold'st
But in his motion like an angel sings,
Still quiring to the young-ey'd cherubins:
Such harmony is in immortal souls;
But whilst this muddy vesture of decay
Doth grossly close it in, we cannot hear it.
Merchant of Venice. Act V. Sc. 1. L. 58.
("Pattens" in Folio.)

25
These blessed candles of the night.
Merchant of Venice. Act V. Sc. 1. L. 220.

26
O that my spirit were yon heaven of night,
Which gazes on thee with its thousand eyes.
SHELLEY—*Revolt of Islam.* IV. 36.
(See also COLERIDGE)

27
He that strives to touch a star,
Oft stumbles at a straw.
SPENSER—*Shepherd's Calendar.* *July.*

28
Clamorem ad sidera mittunt.
They send their shout to the stars.
STATIUS—*Thebais.* XII. 521.

1
As shaking terrors from his blazing hair,
A sanguine comet gleams through dusky air.
Tasso—*Jerusalem Delivered.* Hoole's trans. L. 581.
(See also Butler)

2
Twinkle, twinkle, little star!
How I wonder what you are,
Up above the world so high,
Like a diamond in the sky!
Anne Taylor—*Rhymes for the Nursery. The Star.*

3
Each separate star
Seems nothing, but a myriad scattered stars
Break up the Night, and make it beautiful.
Bayard Taylor—*Lars.* Bk. III. Last lines.

4
The stars shall be rent into threds of light,
And scatter'd like the beards of comets.
Jeremy Taylor—*Sermon* I. *Christ's Advent to Judgment.*
(See also Butler)

5
Many a night I saw the Pleiads, rising thro' the mellow shade,
Glitter like a swarm of fire-flies tangled in a silver braid.
Tennyson—*Locksley Hall.* St. 5.

6
She saw the snowy poles and moons of Mars,
That marvellous field of drifted light
In mid Orion, and the married stars—
Tennyson—*Palace of Art.* Unfinished lines withdrawn from later editions. Appears in foot-note to Ed. of 1833.

7
But who can count the stars of Heaven?
Who sing their influence on this lower world?
Thomson—*Seasons. Winter.* L. 528.

8
The twilight hours, like birds flew by,
As lightly and as free;
Ten thousand stars were in the sky,
Ten thousand on the sea.

For every wave with dimpled face
That leap'd upon the air,
Had caught a star in its embrace
And held it trembling there.
Amelia B. Welby—*Musings. Twilight at Sea.* St. 4.

9
But He is risen, a later star of dawn.
Wordsworth—*A Morning Exercise.*

10
You meaner beauties of the night,
That poorly satisfy our eyes
More by your number than your light;
You common people of the skies,—
What are you when the moon shall rise?
Sir Henry Wotton—*On His Mistress, the Queen of Bohemia.* ("Sun" in some editions.)
(See also Horace)

11
Hence Heaven looks down on earth with all her eyes.
Young—*Night Thoughts.* Night VII. L. 1,103.

12
One sun by day, by night ten thousand shine;
And light us deep into the Deity;
How boundless in magnificence and might.
Young—*Night Thoughts.* Night IX. L. 728.

13
Who rounded in his palm these spacious orbs
* * * * * *
Numerous as glittering gems of morning dew,
Or sparks from populous cities in a blaze,
And set the bosom of old night on fire.
Young—*Night Thoughts.* Night IX. L. 1,260.

STATESMANSHIP

14
It is strange so great a statesman should
Be so sublime a poet.
Bulwer-Lytton—*Richelieu.* Act I. Sc. 2.

15
A disposition to preserve, and an ability to improve, taken together, would be my standard of a statesman.
Burke—*Reflections on the Revolution in France.*

16
Learn to think imperially.
Joseph Chamberlain—*Speech at Guildhall.* Jan. 19, 1904.
(See also Hamilton, Lowell, Roosevelt)

17
No statesman e'er will find it worth his pains
To tax our labours and excise our brains.
Churchill—*Night.* L. 271.

18
The people of the two nations [French and English] must be brought into mutual dependence by the supply of each other's wants. There is no other way of counteracting the antagonism of language and race. It is God's own method of producing an *entente cordiale*, and no other plan is worth a farthing.
Richard Cobden—*Letter to M. Michel Chevalier.* Sept., 1859. "Entente cordiale," used by Queen Victoria to Lord John Russell, Sept. 7, 1848. Littré (Dict.) dates its use to speech in The Chamber of Deputies, 1840-41. Phrase in a letter written by the Dutch Governor-General at Batavia to the Bewinikebbers (directors) at Amsterdam, Dec. 15, 1657. See *Notes and Queries*, Sept. 11, 1909. P. 216. Early examples given in Stanford Dict. Cobden probably first user to make the phrase popular. Quoted also by Lord Aberdeen. Phrase appeared in the *Foreign Quarterly Review.* Oct., 1844. Used by Louis Philippe in a speech from the throne, Jan., 1843, to express friendly relations between France and England.

19
La cordiale entente qui existe entre le gouvernement français et celui de la Grande-Bretagne.
The cordial agreement which exists between the governments of France and Great Britain.
Le Charivari. Jan. 6, 1844. Review of a Speech by Guizot, about 1840.

20
Si l'on n'a pas de meilleurs moyen de sèduction a lui offrir, l'entente cordiale nous paraît fort compromise.

If one has no better method of enticement to offer, the cordial agreement seems to us to be the best compromise.
Le Charivari. Vol. XV. No. 3. P. 4. (1846), referring to the ambassador of Morocco, then in Paris.

1
I have the courage of my opinions, but I have not the temerity to give a political blank cheque to Lord Salisbury.
GOSCHEN. In Parliament, Feb. 19, 1884.

2
Spheres of influence.
Version of EARL GRANVILLE'S phrase. "Spheres of action," found in his letter to COUNT MÜNSTER, April 29, 1885. HERTSLET'S *Map of Africa by Treaty*. P. 596. Trans. May 7, 1885. See also phrase used in Convention between Great Britain and France, Aug. 10, 1889, in same. P. 562.

3
Gli ambasciadori sono l'occhio e l'orecchio degli stati.
Ambassadors are the eye and ear of states.
GUICCIARDINI—*Storia d'Italia*.

4
Learn to think continentally.
ALEXANDER HAMILTON. Paraphrase of his words in a Speech to his American fellow countrymen.
(See also CHAMBERLAIN)

5
Peace, commerce, and honest friendship with all nations—entangling alliances with none.
THOS. JEFFERSON—*First Inaugural Address*. March 4, 1801.
(See also WASHINGTON)

6
Nursed by stern men with empires in their brains.
LOWELL—*Biglow Papers. Mason and Slidell*.
(See also CHAMBERLAIN)

7
Statesman, yet friend to truth; of soul sincere,
In action faithful, and in honour clear;
Who broke no promise, serv'd no private end,
Who gain'd no title, and who lost no friend;
Ennobled by himself, by all approv'd,
And prais'd, unenvy'd, by the Muse he lov'd.
POPE—*Epistle to Addison*. L. 67.

8
Who would not praise Patricio's high desert,
His hand unstain'd, his uncorrupted heart,
His comprehensive head? all interests weigh'd,
All Europe sav'd, yet Britain not betray'd.
POPE—*Moral Essays*. Ep. I. L. 82.

9
It is well indeed for our land that we of this generation have learned to think nationally.
ROOSEVELT—*Builders of the State*.
(See also CHAMBERLAIN)

10
If you wish to preserve your secret wrap it up in frankness.
ALEXANDER SMITH—*Dreamthorp. On the Writing of Essays*.
(See also WOTTON)

11
And lives to clutch the golden keys,
To mould a mighty state's decrees,
And shape the whisper of the throne.
TENNYSON—*In Memoriam*. Pt. LXIII.

12
And statesmen at her council met
Who knew the seasons when to take
Occasion by the hand, and make
The bounds of freedom wider yet.
TENNYSON—*To the Queen*. St. 8.

13
Why don't you show us a statesman who can rise up to the emergency, and cave in the emergency's head.
ARTEMUS WARD—*Things in New York*.

14
Why forego the advantages of so peculiar a situation?—Why quit our own to stand upon foreign ground?—Why by interweaving our destiny with that of any part of Europe, entangle our peace and prosperity in the toils of European ambition, rivalship, interest, humour or caprice?
WASHINGTON—*Farewell Address*. Sept. 17, 1796.

15
'Tis our true policy to steer clear of permanent alliances, with any portion of the foreign world—so far, I mean, as we are now at liberty to do it.
WASHINGTON—*Farewell Address*. Sept. 17, 1796.
(See also JEFFERSON)

16
Tell the truth, and so puzzle and confound your adversaries.
WOTTON—Advice to a young diplomat.
(See also SMITH)

17
Legatus est vir bonus peregre missus ad mentiendem rei publicæ causæ.
An ambassador is an honest man sent to lie abroad for the commonwealth.
WOTTON. In the autograph album of CHRISTOPHER FLECKAMORE. (1604) Eight years later JASPER SCIOPPIUS published it with malicious intent. WOTTON apologized, but insisted on the double meaning of *lie* as a jest. A leiger is an ambassador. So used by BUTLER—*Hudibras*. Pt. II. III. 139. Also by FULLER—*Holy State*. P. 306.

STORM

18
Rides in the whirlwind, and directs the storm.
ADDISON—*The Campaign*.
(See also MILTON)

19
I have heard a greater storm in a boiling pot.
ATHENÆUS—*Deipnosophistæ*. VIII. 19. Dorian, a flutist, ridiculing Timotheos, a zither player, who imitated a storm at sea.
(See also CICERO)

20
The earth is rocking, the skies are riven—
Jove in a passion, in god-like fashion,
Is breaking the crystal urns of heaven.
ROBERT BUCHANAN—*Horatius Cogitandibus*. St. 16.

21
A storm in a cream bowl.
JAMES BUTLER, First Duke of Ormond, to the EARL OF ARLINGTON, Dec. 28, 1678. *Ormond MSS. Commission New Series*. Vol. IV. P. 292.
(See also CICERO)

1
Excitabat enim fluctus in simpulo.
He used to raise a storm in a teapot.
CICERO—*De Legibus*. III. 16. ERASMUS—*Adagia Occulta*. P. 548. (Ed. 1670) BERNARD BAYLE—*Storm in a Teacup*. Comedietta performed March 20, 1854, Princess Theatre, London.
(See also ATHENÆUS, BUTLER, PAUL)

2
Bursts as a wave that from the clouds impends,
And swell'd with tempests on the ship descends;
White are the decks with foam; the winds aloud
Howl o'er the masts, and sing through every shroud:
Pale, trembling, tir'd, the sailors freeze with fears;
And instant death on every wave appears.
HOMER—*Iliad*. Bk. XV. L. 752. POPE'S trans.

3
Roads are wet where'er one wendeth,
And with rain the thistle bendeth,
And the brook cries like a child!
Not a rainbow shines to cheer us;
Ah! the sun comes never near us,
And the heavens look dark and wild.
MARY HOWITT—*The Wet Summer*. From the German.

4
Ride the air
In whirlwind.
MILTON—*Paradise Lost*. Bk. II. L. 545.
(See also ADDISON)

5
C'est une tempête dans un verre d'eau.
It is a tempest in a tumbler of water.
PAUL, GRAND-DUC DE RUSSIE—*Of the insurrection in Geneva*.
(See also ATHENÆUS)

6
The winds grow high;
Impending tempests charge the sky;
The lightning flies, the thunder roars;
And big waves lash the frightened shores.
PRIOR—*The Lady's Looking-Glass*.

7
Lightnings, that show the vast and foamy deep,
The rending thunders, as they onward roll,
The loud, loud winds, that o'er the billows sweep—
Shake the firm nerve, appal the bravest soul!
MRS. RADCLIFFE—*Mysteries of Udolpho. The Mariner*. St. 9.

8
Der Sturm ist Meister; Wind und Welle spielen
Ball mit dem Menschen.
The storm is master. Man, as a ball, is tossed twixt winds and billows.
SCHILLER—*Wilhelm Tell*. IV. 1. 59.

9
Loud o'er my head though awful thunders roll,
And vivid lightnings flash from pole to pole,
Yet 'tis Thy voice, my God, that bids them fly,
Thy arm directs those lightnings through the sky.
Then let the good Thy mighty name revere,
And hardened sinners Thy just vengeance fear.
SCOTT—*On a Thunderstorm*. Written at the age of twelve. Found in LOCKHART'S *Life of Scott*. Vol. I. Ch. III.

10
As far as I could ken thy chalky cliffs,
When from thy shore the tempest beat us back,
I stood upon the hatches in the storm.
Henry VI. Pt. II. Act III. Sc. 2. L. 101.

11
A little gale will soon disperse that cloud
. . . for every cloud engenders not a storm.
Henry VI. Pt. III. Act V. Sc. 3. L. 9.

12
I have seen tempests, when the scolding winds
Have riv'd the knotty oaks, and I have seen
The ambitious ocean swell and rage and foam,
To be exalted with the threat'ning clouds
But never till to-night, never till now,
Did I go through a tempest dropping fire.
Julius Cæsar. Act I. Sc. 3. L. 5.

13
Blow wind, swell billow, and swim bark!
The storm is up, and all is on the hazard.
Julius Cæsar. Act V. Sc. 1. L. 67.

14
Blow, winds, and crack your cheeks! rage! blow!
You cataracts and hurricanoes, spout
Till you have drench'd our steeples.
King Lear. Act III. Sc. 2. L. 1.

15
Merciful Heaven,
Thou rather with thy sharp and sulphurous bolt
Split'st the unwedgeable and gnarled oak
Than the soft myrtle.
Measure for Measure. Act II. Sc. 2. L. 114.

16
Swift as a shadow, short as any dream;
Brief as the lightning in the collied night,
That in a spleen, unfolds both heaven and earth,
And ere a man hath power to say "Behold"
The jaws of darkness do devour it up.
Midsummer Night's Dream. Act I. Sc. 1. L. 144.

17
His rash fierce blaze of riot cannot last,
For violent fires soon burn out themselves;
Small showers last long, but sudden storms are short.
Richard II. Act II. Sc. 1. L. 33.

18
When clouds appear, wise men put on their cloaks;
When great leaves fall, then winter is at hand;
When the sun sets, who doth not look for night?
Untimely storms make men expect a dearth.
Richard III. Act II. Sc. 3. L. 32.

19
At first, heard solemn o'er the verge of Heaven,
The Tempest growls; but as it nearer comes,
And rolls its awful burden on the wind,
The Lightnings flash a larger curve, and more
The Noise astounds; till overhead a sheet
Of livid flame discloses wide, then shuts,
And opens wider; shuts and opens still
Expansive, wrapping ether in a blaze.
Follows the loosen'd aggravated Roar,
Enlarging, deepening, mingling, peal on peal,
Crush'd, horrible, convulsing Heaven and Earth.
THOMSON—*Seasons. Summer*. L. 1,133.

20
For many years I was self-appointed inspector of snow-storms and rain-storms and did my duty faithfully.
THOREAU—*Walden*.

STORY-TELLING

1
A schoolboy's tale, the wonder of an hour!
BYRON—*Childe Harold.* Canto II. St. 2.

2
A story, in which native humour reigns,
Is often useful, always entertains;
A graver fact, enlisted on your side,
May furnish illustration, well applied;
But sedentary weavers of long tales
Give me the fidgets, and my patience fails.
COWPER—*Conversation.* L. 203.

3
In this spacious isle I think there is not one
But he hath heard some talk of Hood and Little John,
Of Tuck, the merry friar, which many a sermon made
In praise of Robin Hood, his outlaws, and their trade.
DRAYTON—*Polyolbion.*

4
This story will never go down.
HENRY FIELDING—*Tumble-Down Dick.* Air I.

5
Ich weiss nicht was soll es bedeuten,
Dass ich so traurig bin:
Ein Märchen aus alten Zeiten
Das kommt mir nicht aus dem Sinn.
In vain would I seek to discover
Why sad and mournful am I,
My thoughts without ceasing brood over
A tale of the times gone by.
HEINE—*Die Lorelei.* E. A. BOWRING'S trans.

6
When thou dost tell another's jest, therein
Omit the oaths, which true wit cannot need;
Pick out of tales the mirth, but not the sin.
HERBERT—*Temple. Church Porch.* St. 11.

7
Soft as some song divine, thy story flows.
HOMER—*Odyssey.* Bk. XI. L. 458. POPE'S trans.

8
I hate
To tell again a tale once fully told.
HOMER—*Odyssey.* Bk. XII. L. 566. BRYANT'S trans.

9
And what so tedious as a twice-told tale.
HOMER—*Odyssey.* Bk. XII. Last line. POPE'S trans.
(See also KING JOHN under LIFE)

10
Quid rides?
Mutato nomine de te fabula narratur.
Why do you laugh? Change but the name, and the story is told of yourself.
HORACE—*Satires.* I. 1. 69.

11
But that's another story.
KIPLING—*Mulvaney. Soldiers Three.* FARQUHAR—*Recruiting Officer.* Last scene. STERNE—*Tristram Shandy.* Ch. XVII.

12
It is a foolish thing to make a long prologue, and to be short in the story itself.
II Maccabees. II. 32.

13
An' all us other children, when the supper things is done,
We set around the kitchen fire an' has the mostest fun
A-list'nin' to the witch tales 'at Annie tells about
An' the gobble-uns 'at gits you
Ef you
Don't
Watch
Out!
JAMES WHITCOMB RILEY—*Little Orphant Annie.*

14
I cannot tell how the truth may be;
I say the tale as 'twas said to me.
SCOTT—*Lay of the Last Minstrel.* Canto II. St. 22.

15
I could a tale unfold whose lightest word
Would harrow up thy soul, freeze thy young blood,
Make thy two eyes, like stars, start from their spheres,
Thy knotted and combined locks to part
And each particular hair to stand on end,
Like quills upon the fretful porcupine.
Hamlet. Act I. Sc. 5. L. 15.

16
Which his fair tongue—conceit's expositor—
Delivers in such apt and gracious words,
That aged ears play truant at his tales,
And younger hearings are quite ravished.
Love's Labour's Lost. Act II. Sc. 1. L. 72.
(See also SIDNEY)

17
And thereby hangs a tale.
Taming of the Shrew. Act IV. Sc. 1. L. 60. Also found in *Othello.* Act III. 1; *Merry Wives of Windsor.* Act I. 4; *As you Like it.* Act II. 7.

18
For seldom shall she hear a tale
So sad, so tender, yet so true.
SHENSTONE—*Jemmy Dawson.* St. 20.

19
With a tale forsooth he cometh unto you, with a tale which holdeth children from play, and old men from the chimney corner.
SIR PHILIP SIDNEY—*The Defense of Poesy.*

20
In after-dinner talk,
Across the walnuts and the wine.
TENNYSON—*The Miller's Daughter.*

21
A tale in everything.
WORDSWORTH—*Simon Lee.*

STRATEGY (See also DECEIT)

22
There webs were spread of more than common size,
And half-starved spiders prey'd on half-starved flies.
CHURCHILL—*The Prophecy of Famine.* L. 327

23
Those oft are stratagems which errors seem,
Nor is it Homer nods, but we that dream.
POPE—*Essay on Criticism.* Pt. I. L. 177.

1
For her own breakfast she'll project a scheme,
Nor take her tea without a stratagem.
YOUNG—*Love of Fame.* Satire VI. L. 187.

STRAWBERRY

Fragaria

2
Like strawberry wives, that laid two or three great strawberries at the mouth of their pot, and all the rest were little ones.
BACON—*Apothegms.* No. 54.

3
The strawberry grows underneath the nettle
And wholesome berries thrive and ripen best
Neighbour'd by fruit of baser quality.
Henry V. Act I. Sc. 1. L. 60.

STRENGTH

4
My strength is made perfect in weakness.
II Corinthians. XII. 9.

5
As thy days, so shall thy strength be.
Deuteronomy. XXXIII. 25.

6
A threefold cord is not quickly broken.
Ecclesiastes. IV. 12.

7
Like strength is felt from hope, and from despair.
HOMER—*Iliad.* Bk. XV. L. 853. POPE'S trans.

8
A mass enormous! which, in modern days
No two of earth's degenerate sons could raise.
HOMER—*The Iliad.* Bk. XX. L. 338. Also in Bk. V. 371. POPE'S trans.

9
Strong are her sons, though rocky are her shores.
HOMER—*Odyssey.* Bk. IX. L. 28. POPE'S trans.

10
Their strength is to sit still.
Isaiah. XXX. 7.

11
And, weaponless himself,
Made arms ridiculous.
MILTON—*Samson Agonistes.* L. 130.

12
Minimæ vires frangere quassa valent.
The least strength suffices to break what is bruised.
OVID—*Tristia.* Bk. III. 11, 22.

13
Plus potest qui plus valet.
The stronger always succeeds.
PLAUTUS—*Truculentus.* IV. 3. 30.

14
They go from strength to strength.
Psalms. LXXXIV. 7.

15
I feel like a Bull Moose.
ROOSEVELT. On landing from Cuba with his Rough Riders, after the Spanish War.

16
Profan'd the God-given strength, and marr'd the lofty line.
SCOTT—*Marmion. Introduction.* Canto I.

17
In that day's feats,
* * * * * *
He prov'd best man i' the field, and for his meed
Was brow-bound with the oak.
Coriolanus. Act II. Sc. 2. L. 99.

18
O, it is excellent
To have a giant's strength, but it is tyrannous
To use it like a giant.
Measure for Measure. Act II. Sc. 2. L. 107.

19
So let it be in God's own might
We gird us for the coming fight,
And, strong in Him whose cause is ours
In conflict with unholy powers,
We grasp the weapons he has given,—
The Light, and Truth, and Love of Heaven.
WHITTIER—*The Moral Warfare.*

STUDENTS

20
Rocking on a lazy billow
With roaming eyes,
Cushioned on a dreamy pillow,
Thou art now wise.
Wake the power within thee slumbering,
Trim the plot that's in thy keeping,
Thou wilt bless the task when reaping
Sweet labour's prize.
JOHN STUART BLACKIE—*Address to the Edinburgh Students.* Quoted by LORD IDDLESLEIGH—*Desultory Reading.*

21
Strange to the world, he wore a bashful look,
The fields his study, nature was his book.
BLOOMFIELD—*Farmer's Boy. Spring.* L. 31.

22
Experience is the best of schoolmasters, only the school-fees are heavy.
CARLYLE—*Miscellaneous Essays.* I. 137. (Ed. 1888) Same idea in FRANKLIN—*Preliminary Address to the Pennsylvania Almanac for* 1758.
(See also quotations under EXPERIENCE)

23
The scholar who cherishes the love of comfort, is not fit to be deemed a scholar.
CONFUCIUS—*Analects.* Bk. XIV. Ch. III.

24
The studious class are their own victims; they are thin and pale, their feet are cold, their heads are hot, the night is without sleep, the day a fear of interruption,—pallor, squalor, hunger, and egotism. If you come near them and see what conceits they entertain—they are abstractionists, and spend their days and nights in dreaming some dream; in expecting the homage of society to some precious scheme built on a truth, but destitute of proportion in its presentment, of justness in its application, and of all energy of will in the schemer to embody and vitalize it.
EMERSON—*Representative Men. Montaigne.*

25
The world's great men have not commonly been great scholars, nor its great scholars great men.
HOLMES—*Autocrat of the Breakfast-Table.* VI.

1
Ah, pensive scholar, what is fame?
A fitful tongue of leaping flame;
A giddy whirlwind's fickle gust,
That lifts a pinch of mortal dust;
A few swift years, and who can show
Which dust was Bill, and which was Joe?
HOLMES—*Poems of the Class of '29. Bill and Joe.* St. 7.

2
Where should the scholar live? In solitude, or in society? in the green stillness of the country, where he can hear the heart of Nature beat, or in the dark, gray town where he can hear and feel the throbbing heart of man?
LONGFELLOW—*Hyperion.* Bk. I. Ch. VIII.

3
And then the whining schoolboy, with his satchel
And shining morning face, creeping like snail
Unwillingly to school.
As You Like It. Act II. Sc. 7. L. 145.

4
He was a scholar, and a ripe and good one;
Exceeding wise, fair-spoken, and persuading;
Lofty and sour to them that lov'd him not;
But to those men that sought him sweet as summer.
Henry VIII. Act IV. Sc. 2. L. 51.

5
And with unwearied fingers drawing out
The lines of life, from living knowledge hid.
SPENSER—*Faerie Queene.* Bk. IV. Canto II. St. 48.

STUDY

6
O Granta! sweet Granta! where studious of ease,
I slumbered seven years, and then lost my degrees.
CHRISTOPHER ANSTEY—*New Bath Guide. Epilogue.*
(See also PHILIPS)

7
Histories make men wise; poets, witty; the mathematics, subtile; natural philosophy, deep; morals, grave; logic and rhetoric, able to contend.
BACON—*Of Studies.*

8
When night hath set her silver lamp on high,
Then is the time for study.
BAILEY—*Festus.* Sc. *A Village Feast.*

9
Exhausting thought,
And hiving wisdom with each studious year.
BYRON—*Childe Harold.* Canto III. St. 107.

10
Hæc studia adolescentiam alunt, senectutem oblectant, secundas res ornant, adversis solatium et perfugium præbent, delectant domi, non impediunt foris, pernoctant nobiscum, peregrinantur, rusticantur.

These (literary) studies are the food of youth, and consolation of age; they adorn prosperity, and are the comfort and refuge of adversity; they are pleasant at home, and are no incumbrance abroad; they accompany us at night, in our travels, and in our rural retreats.
CICERO—*Oratio Pro Licinio Archia.* VII.

11
Me therefore studious of laborious ease.
COWPER—*Task.* Bk. III. *The Garden.*
(See also PHILIPS)

12
Studious of elegance and ease.
GAY—*Fables.* Pt. II. No. 8.

13
For he was studious—of his ease.
GAY—*Poems on Several Occasions.* (Ed. 1752) II. 49.
(See also PHILIPS)

14
As turning the logs will make a dull fire burn, so changes of studies a dull brain.
LONGFELLOW—*Drift-Wood. Table Talk.*

15
You are in some brown study.
LYLY—*Euphues.* Arber's Reprint. P. 80. (1579) The phrase is used by GREENE—*Menaphon.* Arber's Reprint. P. 24. (1589) Also in HALLIWELL's Reprint for the PERCY SOCIETY of *Manifest Detection . . . of the use of Dice at Play.* (1532)

16
Beholding the bright countenance of truth in the quiet and still air of delightful studies.
MILTON *Reason of Church Government. Introduction.* Bk. II.

17
Studious of ease, and fond of humble things.
AMBROSE PHILIPS—*Epistles from Holland, to a Friend in England.* L. 21.
(See also ANSTEY, COWPER, GAY, VERGIL)

18
I'll talk a word with this same learned Theban.
What is your study?
King Lear. Act III. Sc. 4. L. 162.

19
What is the end of study? Let me know?
Why, that to know, which else we should not know.
Things hid and barr'd, you mean, from common sense?
Ay, that is study's god-like recompense.
Love's Labour's Lost. Act I. Sc. 1. L. 55.

20
Study is like the heaven's glorious sun
That will not be deep-searched with saucy looks;
Small have continual plodders ever won,
Save base authority from others' books.
Love's Labour's Lost. Act I. Sc. 1. L. 84.

21
So study evermore is overshot;
While it doth study to have what it would
It doth forget to do the thing it should,
And when it hath the thing it hunteth most,
'Tis won as towns with fire, so won, so lost.
Love's Labour's Lost. Act I. Sc. 1. L. 143.

22
One of the best methods of rendering study agreeable is to live with able men, and to suffer all those pangs of inferiority which the want of knowledge always inflicts.
SYDNEY SMITH—*Second Lecture on the Conduct of the Understanding.*

23
Studiis florentem ignobilis oti.
Priding himself in the pursuits of an inglorious ease.
VERGIL—*Georgics.* 4. 564.
(See also PHILIPS)

STUPIDITY

1
We are growing serious, and, let me tell you, that's the very next step to being dull.
ADDISON—*The Drummer.* Act IV. 6. (1715)

2
With various readings stored his empty skull,
Learn'd without sense, and venerably dull.
CHURCHILL—*The Rosciad.* L. 591.

3
I find we are growing serious, and then we are in great danger of being dull.
CONGREVE—*Old Bachelor.* Act II. 2. (1693)
(See also ADDISON)

4
The fool of nature stood with stupid eyes
And gaping mouth, that testified surprise.
DRYDEN—*Cymon and Iphigenia.* L. 107.

5
La faute en est aux dieux, qui la firent si bête.
The fault rests with the gods, who have made her so stupid.
GRESSET—*Méchant.* II. 7.

6
Why, Sir, Sherry is dull, naturally dull; but it must have taken him a great deal of pains to become what we now see him. Such an excess of stupidity, Sir, is not in Nature.
SAMUEL JOHNSON. Of SHERIDAN. *Boswell's Life of Johnson.* (1763)

7
He is not only dull himself, but the cause of dulness in others.
SAMUEL JOHNSON—*Boswell's Life of Johnson.* (1783)

8
The impenetrable stupidity of Prince George (son-in-law of James II.) served his turn. It was his habit, when any news was told him, to exclaim, "Est il possible?"—"Is it possible?"
MACAULAY—*History of England.* Vol. I. Ch. IX.

9
The bookful blockhead, ignorantly read,
With loads of learned lumber in his head.
POPE—*Essay on Criticism.* L. 612.

10
Mit der Dummheit kämpfen Götter selbst vergebens.
Against stupidity the very gods
Themselves contend in vain.
SCHILLER—*Maid of Orleans.* Act III. Sc. 6.

11
Schad'um die Leut'! Sind sonst wackre Brüder.
Aber das denkt, wie ein Seifensieder.
A pity about the people! they are brave enough comrades, but they have heads like a soapboiler's.
SCHILLER—*Wallenstein's Lager.* XI. 347.

12
Peter was dull; he was at first
Dull,—Oh, so dull—so very dull!
Whether he talked, wrote, or rehearsed—
Still with his dulness was he cursed—
Dull—beyond all conception—dull.
SHELLEY—*Peter Bell the Third.* Pt. VII. XI.

13
Personally, I have a great admiration for stupidity.
OSCAR WILDE—*An Ideal Husband.* Act II.

STYLE

14
A chaste and lucid style is indicative of the same personal traits in the author.
HOSEA BALLOU—*MS. Sermons.*

15
Le style c'est l'homme.
The style is the man.
BUFFON—*Discourse on taking his seat in the French Academie.* Aug. 25, 1753. Le style c'est l'homme même. *Œuvres Completes.* (1778) *Histoire Naturelle.* (1769) Le style est de l'homme. *Discours sur Style.*

16
Style is the dress of thoughts.
CHESTERFIELD—*Letter to his Son. On Education.* Nov. 24, 1749.

17
And, after all, it is style alone by which posterity will judge of a great work, for an author can have nothing truly his own but his style.
ISAAC D'ISRAELI—*Literary Miscellanies. Style.*

18
Style! style! why, all writers will tell you that it is the very thing which can least of all be changed. A man's style is nearly as much a part of him as his physiognomy, his figure, the throbbing of his pulse,—in short, as any part of his being is at least subjected to the action of the will.
FÉNELON.
(See also BUFFON)

19
The gloomy companions of a disturbed imagination, the melancholy madness of poetry without the inspiration.
JUNIUS—*To Sir W. Draper.* Letter No. VII.
(See also PRIOR)

20
Neat, not gaudy.
LAMB—*Letter to Wordsworth.* June, 1806.

21
Che stilo oltra l'ingegno non si stende.
For style beyond the genius never dares.
PETRARCH—*Morte di Laura. Sonnet* 68.

22
Such labour'd nothings, in so strange a style,
Amaze th' learn'd, and make the learned smile.
POPE—*Essay on Criticism.* Pt. II. L. 126.

23
Expression is the dress of thought, and still
Appears more decent as more suitable;
A vile conceit in pompous words express'd,
Is like a clown in regal purple dress'd.
POPE—*Essay on Criticism.* L. 318.

24
When Croft's "Life of Dr. Young" was spoken of as a good imitation of Dr. Johnson's style, "No, no," said he, "it is not a good imitation of Johnson; it has all his pomp without his force; it has all the nodosities of the oak, without its strength; it has all the contortions of the sibyl, without the inspiration."
PRIOR—*Life of Burke.*
(See also JUNIUS)

25
La clarté orne les pensées profondes.
Clearness ornaments profound thoughts.
VAUVENARGUES—*Reflexions et Maximes.* 4.

1
L'obscurité est le royaume de l'erreur.
Obscurity is the realm of error.
VAUVENARGUES—*Reflexions et Maxims.* 5.

2
Tous les genres sont bons, hors le genre ennuyeux.
All styles are good except the tiresome kind.
VOLTAIRE—*L'Enfant Prodigue. Preface.*

3
The flowery style is not unsuitable to public speeches or addresses, which amount only to compliment. The lighter beauties are in their place when there is nothing more solid to say; but the flowery style ought to be banished from a pleading, a sermon, or a didactic work.
VOLTAIRE—*Philosophical Dictionary. Style.*

SUBMARINE (See NAVIGATION)

SUCCESS

4
'Tis not in mortals to command success,
But we'll do more, Sempronius,—
We'll deserve it.
ADDISON—*Cato.* Act I. Sc. 2.

5
Médiocre et rampant, et l'on arrive à tout.
Be commonplace and creeping, and you attain all things.
BEAUMARCHAIS—*Barbier de Seville.* III. 7.

6
That low man seeks a little thing to do,
Sees it and does it:
This high man with a great thing to pursue,
Dies ere he knows it.
That low man goes on adding one to one,
His hundred's soon hit:
This high man, aiming at a million,
Misses an unit.
ROBERT BROWNING—*Grammarian's Funeral.*

7
Better have failed in the high aim, as I,
Than vulgarly in the low aim succeed
As, God be thanked! I do not.
ROBERT BROWNING—*The Inn Album.* IV.

8
We are the doubles of those whose way
Was festal with fruits and flowers;
Body and brain we were sound as they,
But the prizes were not ours.
RICHARD BURTON—*Song of the Unsuccessful.*

9
They never fail who die
In a great cause.
BYRON—*Marino Faliero.* Act II. Sc. 2.

10
Be it jewel or toy,
Not the prize gives the joy,
But the striving to win the prize.
PISISTRATUS CAXTON (First Earl Lytton)—*The Boatman.*

11
These poor mistaken people think they shine, and they do indeed, but it is as putrefaction shines,—in the dark.
CHESTERFIELD—*Letters.* Compare COWPER—*Conversation.* 675.

12
Now, by St. Paul, the work goes bravely on.
COLLEY CIBBER—*Richard III.* Act III. Sc. 1.

13
Hast thou not learn'd what thou art often told,
A truth still sacred, and believed of old,
That no success attends on spears and swords
Unblest, and that the battle is the Lord's?
COWPER—*Expostulation.* L. 350.

14
One never rises so high as when one does not know where one is going.
CROMWELL to M. BELLIÈVRE. Found in *Memoirs* of CARDINAL DE RETZ.

15
Th' aspirer, once attain'd unto the top,
Cuts off those means by which himself got up.
SAMUEL DANIEL—*Civil War.* Bk. II.

16
Three men, together riding,
Can win new worlds at their will;
Resolute, ne'er dividing,
Lead, and be victors still.
Three can laugh and doom a king,
Three can make the planets sing.
MARY CAROLINE DAVIES—*Three.* Pub. in *American Mag.* July, 1914.

17
Success is counted sweetest
By those who ne'er succeed.
EMILY DICKINSON—*Success.* (Ed. 1891)

18
Rien ne réussit comme le succès.
Nothing succeeds like success.
DUMAS—*Ange Pitou.* Vol. I. P. 72.

19
The race is not to the swift, nor the battle to the strong.
Ecclesiastes. IX. 11.

20
If the single man plant himself indomitably on his instincts, and there abide, the huge world will come round to him.
EMERSON—*Of the American Scholar.* In *Nature Addresses and Lectures.*

21
If a man has good corn, or wood, or boards, or pigs to sell, or can make better chairs or knives, crucibles, or church organs, than anybody else, you will find a broad, hard-beaten road to his house, tho it be in the woods. And if a man knows the law, people will find it out, tho he live in a pine shanty, and resort to him. And if a man can pipe or sing, so as to wrap the prisoned soul in an elysium; or can paint landscape, and convey into oils and ochers all the enchantments of spring or autumn; or can liberate or intoxicate all people who hear him with delicious songs and verses, 'tis certain that the secret can not be kept: the first witness tells it to a second, and men go by fives and tens and fifties to his door.
EMERSON—*Works.* Vol. VIII. In his *Journal.* (1855) P. 528. (Ed. 1912)

22
If a man write a better book, preach a better sermon, or make a better mouse-trap than his neighbor, tho he build his house in the woods, the world will make a beaten path to his door.
MRS. SARAH S. B. YULE credits the quotation to EMERSON in her *Borrowings* (1889), asserting that she copied this in her handbook from a lecture delivered by EMERSON. The "mouse-trap" quotation was the occa-

sion of a long controversy, owing to ELBERT HUBBARD's claim to its authorship. This was asserted by him in a conversation with S. Wilbur Corman, of N. W. Ayer & Son, Philadelphia, and in a letter to Dr. Frank H. Vizetelly, Managing Editor of the Standard Dictionary. In *The Literary Digest* for May 15, 1915, "The Lexicographer" reaffirmed his earlier finding, "Mr. Hubbard is the author."

(See also PAXTON)

1

One thing is forever good;
That one thing is Success.
EMERSON—*Fate.*

2

Born for success, he seemed
With grace to win, with heart to hold,
With shining gifts that took all eyes.
EMERSON—*In Memoriam.* L. 60.

3

If you wish in this world to advance,
Your merits you're bound to enhance;
You must stir it and stump it,
And blow your own trumpet,
Or trust me, you haven't a chance.
W. S. GILBERT—*Ruddigore.*

4

Successfully to accomplish any task it is necessary not only that you should give it the best there is in you, but that you should obtain for it the best there is in those under your guidance.
GEORGE W. GOETHALS. In the *Nat. Ass. of Corporation Schools Bulletin.* Feb., 1918.

5

Die That ist alles, nichts der Ruhm.
The deed is everything, the glory naught.
GOETHE—*Faust.* Pt. II. Act IV. Sc. 1.
BAYARD TAYLOR's trans.
(See also MILNES)

6

Ja, meine Liebe, wer lebt, verliert * * * aber er gewinnt auch.

Yes, my love, who soever lives, loses, * * * but he also wins.
GOETHE—*Stella.* I.

7

Somebody said that it couldn't be done,
But he with a chuckle replied
That "maybe it couldn't," but he would be one
Who wouldn't say so till he'd tried.
So he buckled right in with the trace of a grin
On his face. If he worried he hid it.
He started to sing as he tackled the thing
That couldn't be done, and he did it.
EDGAR A. GUEST—*It Couldn't be Done.*
(See also WESLEY)

8

Ha sempre dimostrato l'esperienza, e lo dimostra la ragione, che mai succedono bene le cose che dipendono da molti.

Experience has always shown, and reason also, that affairs which depend on many seldom succeed.
GUICCIARDINI—*Storia d'Italia.*

9

Like the British Constitution, she owes her success in practice to her inconsistencies in principle.
THOS. HARDY—*Hand of Ethelberta.* Ch. IX.

10

Sink not in spirit; who aimeth at the sky
Shoots higher much than he that means a tree.
HERBERT—*The Church Porch.*
(See also SIDNEY)

11

Omne tulit punctum qui miscuit utile dulci.

He has carried every point, who has mingled the useful with the agreeable.
HORACE—*Ars Poetica.* 343.

12

Quid te exempta juvat spinis e pluribus una.

What does it avail you, if of many thorns only one be removed?
HORACE—*Epistles.* II. 2. 212.

13

Peace courts his hand, but spreads her charms in vain;
"Think nothing gain'd," he cries, "till naught remain."
SAMUEL JOHNSON—*The Vanity of Human Wishes.* L. 201.

14

When the shore is won at last,
Who will count the billows past?
KEBLE—*Christian Year. St. John the Evangelist's Day.* St. 5.

15

Il n'y a au monde que deux manières de s'élever, ou par sa propre industrie, ou par l'imbécilité des autres.

There are but two ways of rising in the world: either by one's own industry or profiting by the foolishness of others.
LA BRUYÈRE—*Les Caractères.* VI.

16

Rien ne sert de courir: il faut partir à point.
To win a race, the swiftness of a dart
Availeth not without a timely start.
LA FONTAINE—*Fables.* VI. 10.

17

Facile est ventis dare vela secundis,
Fecundumque solum varias agitare per artes,
Auroque atque ebori decus addere, cum rudis ipsa
Materies niteat.

It is easy to spread the sails to propitious winds, and to cultivate in different ways a rich soil, and to give lustre to gold and ivory, when the very raw material itself shines.
MANILIUS—*Astronomica.* 3.

18

Tametsi prosperitas simul utilitasque consultorum non obique concordent, quoniam captorum eventus superæ sibi vindicant potestates.

Yet the success of plans and the advantage to be derived from them do not at all times agree, seeing the gods claim to themselves the right to decide as to the final result.
AMMIANUS MARCELLINUS—*Annales.* XXV. 3.

19

In tauros Libyci ruunt leones;
Non sunt papilionibus molesti.

The African lions rush to attack bulls; they do not attack butterflies.
MARTIAL—*Epigrams.* Bk. XII. 62. 5.

20 The virtue lies
In the struggle, not the prize.
RICHARD MONCKTON MILNES (Lord Houghton)
—*The World to the Soul.* 9. 1.
(See also GOETHE)

1
J'ai toujours vu que, pour réussir dans le monde, il fallait avoir l'air fou et être sage.

I have always observed that to succeed in the world one should appear like a fool but be wise.

MONTESQUIEU—*Pensées Diverses.*

2
Le succès de la plupart des choses dépend de savoir combien il faut de temps pour réussir.

The success of most things depends upon knowing how long it will take to succeed.

MONTESQUIEU—*Pensées Diverses.*

3
How far high failure overleaps the bound
Of low successes.

LEWIS MORRIS—*Epic of Hades. Story of Marsyasy.*

4
Aut non tentaris, aut perfice.

Either do not attempt at all, or go through with it.

OVID—*Ars Amatoria.* Bk. I. 389.

5
Acer et ad palmæ per se cursurus honores,
Si tamen horteris fortius ibit equus.

The spirited horse, which will of itself strive to beat in the race, will run still more swiftly if encouraged.

OVID—*Epistolæ Ex Ponto.* II. 11. 21.

6
A man can't be hid. He may be a pedler in the mountains, but the world will find him out to make him a king of finance. He may be carrying cabbages from Long Island, when the world will demand that he shall run the railways of a continent. He may be a groceryman on the canal, when the country shall come to him and put him in his career of usefulness. So that there comes a time finally when all the green barrels of petroleum in the land suggest but two names and one great company.

DR. JOHN PAXTON—*Sermon. He Could not be Hid.* Aug. 25, 1889. Extract from The *Sun.* Aug. 26, 1889.
(See also EMERSON)

7
He that will not stoop for a pin will never be worth a pound.

PEPYS—*Diary.* Jan. 3, 1668. Quoted as a proverb by SIR W. COVENTRY to CHARLES II.

8
Successus improborum plures allicit.

The success of the wicked entices many more.

PHÆDRUS—*Fables.* II. 3. 7.

9
Sperat quidem animus: quo eveniat, diis in manu est.

The mind is hopeful; success is in God's hands.

PLAUTUS—*Bacchides.* I. 2. 36.

10
It may well be doubted whether human ingenuity can construct an enigma of the kind which human ingenuity may not, by proper application resolve.

POE—*The Gold Bug.*

11
The race by vigour, not by vaunts, is won.

POPE—*Dunciad.* Bk. II. L. 59.

12
Say, shall my little bark attendant sail,
Pursue the triumph, and partake the gale?

POPE—*Essay on Man.* Ep. 4. L. 385.

13
In medio spatio mediocria firma locantur.

It is best for man not to seek to climb too high, lest he fall.

Free rendering of the Latin by LORD CHIEF JUSTICE POPHAM in sentencing RALEIGH to death, quoting NICHOLAS BACON.
(See also RALEIGH under FEAR)

14
Promotion cometh neither from the east, nor from the west, nor from the south.

Psalms. LXXV. 6.

15
Qui bien chante et bien danse fait un métier qui peu avance.

Singing and dancing alone will not advance one in the world.

ROUSSEAU—*Confessions.* V.

16
He that climbs the tall tree has won right to the fruit,
He that leaps the wide gulf should prevail in his suit.

SCOTT—*The Talisman.* Ch. XXVI.

17
Honesta quædam scelera successus facit.

Success makes some crimes honorable.

SENECA—*Hippolytus.* 598.

18
Such a nature,
Tickled with good success, disdains the shadow
Which he treads on at noon.

Coriolanus. Act I. Sc. 1. L. 263.

19
Didst thou never hear
That things ill-got had ever bad success?

Henry VI. Pt. III. Act II. Sc. 2. L. 45.

20
To climb steep hills
Requires slow pace at first.

Henry VIII. Act I. Sc. 1. L. 131.

21
Ye gods, it doth amaze me,
A man of such a feeble temper should
So get the start of the majestic world,
And bear the palm alone.

Julius Cæsar. Act I. Sc. 2. L. 128.

22
A great devotee of the Gospel of Getting On.

BERNARD SHAW—*Mrs. Warren's Profession.* Act IV.

23
Have I caught my heav'nly jewel.

SIR PHILIP SIDNEY—*Astrophel and Stella.* Song II. *Merry Wives of Windsor.* Act III. Sc. 3. L.45.

24
Who shootes at the midday Sunne, though he be sure, he shall never hit the marke; yet as sure he is, he shall shoot higher than who ayms but at a bush.

SIR PHILIP SIDNEY—*Countess of Pembroke's Arcadia.* P. 118. (Ed. 1638)
(See also HERBERT)

1
And he gave it for his opinion, that whoever could make two ears of corn, or two blades of grass, to grow upon a spot of ground where only one grew before, would deserve better of mankind and do more essential service to his country, than the whole race of politicians put together.
SWIFT—*Gulliver's Travels. Voyage to Brobdingnag.* Pt. II. Ch. VII.
(See also EMERSON)

2
There may come a day
Which crowns Desire with gift, and Art with truth,
And Love with bliss, and Life with wiser youth!
BAYARD TAYLOR—*The Picture of St. John.* Bk. IV. St. 86.

3
Attain the unattainable.
TENNYSON—*Timbuctoo.*
(See also GUEST)

4
You might have painted that picture,
I might have written that song;
Not ours, but another's the triumph,
'Tis done and well done—so 'long!
EDITH M. THOMAS—*Rank-and-File.*

5
Not to the swift, the race:
Not to the strong, the fight:
Not to the righteous, perfect grace:
Not to the wise, the light.
HENRY VAN DYKE—*Reliance.*

6
(He) set his heart upon the goal,
Not on the prize.
WILLIAM WATSON—*Tribute to Matthew Arnold. Spectator.* Aug. 30, 1890.

7
Faith, mighty faith, the promise sees,
And looks to that alone;
Laughs at impossibilities,
And cries it shall be done.
CHARLES WESLEY—*Hymns.*
(See also GUEST)

8
Others may sing the song,
Others may right the wrong.
WHITTIER—*My Triumph.*

SUFFERING

9
It is hard for thee to kick against the pricks.
Acts. IX. 5. Same idea in ÆSCHYLUS—*Agamemnon.* L. 1635.

10
Knowledge by suffering entereth,
And Life is perfected by Death.
E. B. BROWNING—*A Vision of Poets. Conclusion.*

11
To each his suff'rings; all are men,
Condemn'd alike to groan;
The tender for another's pain,
Th' unfeeling for his own.
Yet ah! why should they know their fate,
Since sorrow never comes too late,
And happiness too swiftly flies?
Thought would destroy their paradise.
GRAY—*On a Distant Prospect of Eton College.* St. 10.

12
Ho! why dost thou shiver and shake, Gaffer Grey?
And why does thy nose look so blue?
THOMAS HOLCROFT—*Gaffer Grey.*

13
And taste
The melancholy joys of evils pass'd,
For he who much has suffer'd, much will know.
HOMER—*Odyssey.* Bk. XV. L. 434. POPE's trans.

14
I have trodden the wine-press alone.
Isaiah. LXIII. 3.

15
Graviora quæ patiantur videntur jam hominibus quam quæ metuant.
Present sufferings seem far greater to men than those they merely dread.
LIVY—*Annales.* III. 39.

16
They, the holy ones and weakly,
Who the cross of suffering bore,
Folded their pale hands so meekly,
Spake with us on earth no more!
LONGFELLOW—*Footsteps of Angels.* St. 5.

17
Perfer et obdura; dolor hic tibi proderit olim.
Have patience and endure; this unhappiness will one day be beneficial.
OVID—*Amorum.* III. 11. 7.

18
Leniter ex merito quidquid patiare ferendum est,
Quæ venit indigne pœna dolenda venit.
What is deservedly suffered must be borne with calmness, but when the pain is unmerited, the grief is resistless.
OVID—*Heriodes.* V. 7.

19
Si stimulos pugnis cædis manibus plus dolet.
If you strike the goads with your fists, your hands suffer most.
PLAUTUS—*Truculentus.* IV. 2. 54.

20
Levia perpessi sumus
Si flenda patimur.
We have suffered lightly, if we have suffered what we should weep for.
SENECA—*Agamemnon.* 665.

21
Oh, I have suffered
With those that I saw suffer.
Tempest. Act I. Sc. 2. L. 5.
(See also WORDSWORTH)

22
For there are deeds
Which have no form, sufferings which have no tongue.
SHELLEY—*The Cenci.* Act III. Sc. 1.

23
Those who inflict must suffer, for they see
The work of their own hearts, and that must be
Our chastisement or recompense.
SHELLEY—*Julian and Maddalo.* L. 494.

24
Is it so, O Christ in heaven, that the highest suffer most,
That the strongest wander furthest, and more hopelessly are lost?
SARAH WILLIAMS—*Is it so, O Christ in Heaven?* St. 3. In *Twilight Hours.*

1 He could *afford* to suffer
With those whom he saw suffer.
WORDSWORTH—*Excursion.* I. 370. (V. 40 in Knight's ed.)
(See also TEMPEST)

SUICIDE

2
Who doubting tyranny, and fainting under
Fortune's false lottery, desperately run
To death, for dread of death; that soul's most stout,
That, bearing all mischance, dares last it out.
BEAUMONT AND FLETCHER—*The Honest Man's Fortune.* Act IV. Sc. 1.

3 But if there be an hereafter,
And that there is, conscience, uninfluenc'd
And suffer'd to speak out, tells every man,
Then must it be an awful thing to die;
More horrid yet to die by one's *own* hand.
BLAIR—*The Grave.* L. 398.

4
Our time is fixed, and all our days are number d;
How long, how short, we know not:—this we know,
Duty requires we calmly wait the summons,
Nor dare to stir till Heaven shall give permission.
BLAIR—*The Grave.* L. 417.

5
The common damn'd shun their society.
BLAIR—*The Grave.* Referring to suicides in Hell. Attributed to LAMB, but not found in his works.
(See also LEE)

6
The beasts (Conservatives) had committed suicide to save themselves from slaughter.
JOHN BRIGHT—*Speech at Birmingham.* (1867)
(See also MARTIAL)

7 Fool! I mean not
That poor-souled piece of heroism, self-slaughter;
Oh no! the miserablest day we live
There's many a better thing to do than die!
DARLEY—*Ethelstan.*

8
If suicide be supposed a crime, it is only cowardice can impel us to it. If it be no crime, both prudence and courage should engage us to rid ourselves at once of existence when it becomes a burden. It is the only way that we can then be useful to society, by setting an example which, if imitated, would preserve every one his chance for happiness in life, and would effectually free him from all danger or misery.
DAVID HUME—*Essay on Suicide.*

9
While foulest fiends shun thy society.
LEE—*Rival Queens.* V. I. 86.
(See also BLAIR)

10
Ah, yes, the sea is still and deep,
All things within its bosom sleep!
A single step, and all is o'er,
A plunge, a bubble, and no more.
LONGFELLOW—*Christus. The Golden Legend.* Pt. V.

11
When Fannius from his foe did fly
Himself with his own hands he slew;
Who e'er a greater madness knew?
Life to destroy for fear to die.
MARTIAL—*Epigrams.* Bk. II. 80. Same idea in ANTIPHANES—*Fragment. Comicorum Græcorum.* P. 567. Meineke's ed.
(See also BRIGHT)

12 He
That kills himself to avoid misery, fears it,
And, at the best, shows but a bastard valour.
This life's a fort committed to my trust,
Which I must not yield up till it be forced:
Nor will I. He's not valiant that dares die,
But he that boldly bears calamity.
MASSINGER—*The Maid of Honour.* Act IV. Sc. 3.

13
If you like not hanging, drown yourself;
Take some course for your reputation.
MASSINGER—*New Way to pay Old Debts.* Act II. Sc. 1.

14 Bravest at the last,
She levell'd at our purposes, and, being royal,
Took her own way.
Antony and Cleopatra. Act V. Sc. 2. L. 338.

15 Against self-slaughter
There is a prohibition so divine
That cravens my weak hand.
Cymbeline. Act III. Sc. 4. L. 78.

16
For who would bear the whips and scorns of time,
The oppressor's wrong, the proud man's contumely,
The pangs of despised love, the law's delay,
The insolence of office, and the spurns
That patient merit of the unworthy takes,
When he himself might his quietus make
With a bare bodkin?
Hamlet. Act III. Sc. 1. L. 76. ("Poor" for "proud"; "despriz'd" for "despised" in folio.)

17
The more pity that great folk should have countenance in this world to drown or hang themselves, more than their even Christian.
Hamlet. Act V. Sc. 1. L. 29.

18
He that cuts off twenty years of life
Cuts off so many years of fearing death.
Julius Cæsar. Act III. Sc. 1. L. 101.

19
You ever-gentle gods, take my breath from me;
Let not my worser spirit tempt me again
To die before you please!
King Lear. Act IV. Sc. 6. L. 221.

20
There is no refuge from confession but suicide; and suicide is confession.
DANIEL WEBSTER—*Argument on the Murder of Captain White.* April 6, 1830.

21
Britannia's shame! There took her gloomy flight,
On wing impetuous, a black sullen soul . . .
Less base the fear of death than fear of life.
O Britain! infamous for suicide.
YOUNG—*Night Thoughts.* Night V. L. 436.
(See also SEWELL under COWARDICE, HAMLET under DOUBT, HOOD under MISFORTUNE)

SUMMER

1

In lang, lang days o' simmer,
When the clear and cloudless sky
Refuses ae wee drap o' rain
To Nature parched and dry,
The genial night, wi' balmy breath,
Gars verdure spring anew,
An' ilka blade o' grass
Keps its ain drap o' dew.

BALLANTINE—*Its Ain Drap o' Dew.*

2

O thou who passest through our valleys in
Thy strength, curb thy fierce steeds, allay the heat
That flames from their large nostrils! Thou, O Summer,
Oft pitchest here thy golden tent, and oft
Beneath our oaks hast slept, while we beheld
With joy thy ruddy limbs and flourishing hair.

WM. BLAKE—*To Summer.*

3

Now simmer blinks on flowery braes,
And o'er the crystal streamlet plays.

BURNS—*The Birks of Aberfeldy.*

4

I question not if thrushes sing,
If roses load the air;
Beyond my heart I need not reach
When all is summer there.

JOHN VANCE CHENEY—*Love's World.*

5

The Indian Summer, the dead Summer's soul.

MARY CLEMMER—*Presence.* L. 62.

6

Oh, father's gone to market-town, he was up before the day,
And Jamie's after robins, and the man is making hay,
And whistling down the hollow goes the boy that minds the mill,
While mother from the kitchen door is calling with a will,
"Polly!—Polly!—The cows are in the corn!
Oh, where's Polly?"

R. W. GILDER—*A Midsummer Song.*

7

Here is the ghost
Of a summer that lived for us,
Here is a promise
Of summer to be.

WM. ERNEST HENLEY—*Rhymes and Rhythms.*

8

All labourers draw hame at even,
And can to others say,
"Thanks to the gracious God of heaven,
Whilk sent this summer day."

ALEXANDER HUME—*Evening.* St. 2.

9

Sumer is y cumen in.

Famous old Round. The music is the oldest piece of polyphonic and canonical composition in existence. This portion was written probably in 1226 by a monk, JOHN OF FORNSETE, at the Abbey of Reading. Original is in *Harleian MS.* 978.

10

As a lodge in a garden of cucumbers.

Isaiah. I. 8.

11

O for a lodge in a garden of cucumbers!
O for an iceberg or two at control!
O for a vale that at midday the dew cumbers!
O for a pleasure trip up to the pole!

ROSSITER JOHNSON—*Ninety-Nine in the Shade.*

(See also COWPER under PEACE)

12

Summer, as my friend Coleridge waggishly writes, has set in with its usual severity.

LAMB—*To V. Novello.* May 9, 1826.

13

That beautiful season
* * * the Summer of All-Saints!
Filled was the air with a dreamy and magical light; and the landscape
Lay as if new created in all the freshness of childhood.

LONGFELLOW—*Evangeline.* Pt. I. St. 2.

14

Very hot and still the air was,
Very smooth the gliding river,
Motionless the sleeping shadows.

LONGFELLOW—*Hiwatha.* Pt. XVIII. L. 54.

15

O summer day beside the joyous sea!
O summer day so wonderful and white,
So full of gladness and so full of pain!
Forever and forever shalt thou be
To some the gravestone of a dead delight,
To some the landmark of a new domain.

LONGFELLOW—*A Summer Day by the Sea.*

16

Where'er you walk cool gales shall fan the glade,
Trees where you sit shall crowd into a shade.
Where'er you tread the blushing flowers shall rise,
And all things flourish where you turn your eyes.

POPE—*Pastorals. Summer.*

17

But see, the shepherds shun the noonday heat,
The lowing herds to murmuring brooks retreat,
To closer shades the panting flocks remove;
Ye gods! and is there no relief for love?

POPE—*Pastorals. Summer.*

18

Oh, the summer night
Has a smile of light
And she sits on a sapphire throne.

B. W. PROCTER (Barry Cornwall)—*The Nights.*

19

Before green apples blush,
Before green nuts embrown,
Why, one day in the country
Is worth a month in town.

CHRISTINA G. ROSSETTI—*Summer.*

20

The summer dawn's reflected hue
To purple changed Loch Katrine blue,
Mildly and soft the western breeze
Just kiss'd the lake, just stirr'd the trees,
And the pleased lake, like maiden coy,
Trembled but dimpled not for joy.

SCOTT—*Lady of the Lake.* Canto III. St. 2.

21

Summer's parching heat.

Henry VI. Pt. II. Act I. Sc. 1. L. 81.

22

The middle summer's spring.

Midsummer Night's Dream. Act II. Sc. 1. L. 82.

1
Now is the winter of our discontent
Made glorious summer by this sun of York;
And all the clouds that lour'd upon our house
In the deep bosom of the ocean buried.
Richard III. Act I. Sc. 1. L. 1.

2
Thy eternal summer shall not fade.
Sonnet XVIII.

3
Heat, ma'am! it was so dreadful here, that I found there was nothing left for it but to take off my flesh and sit in my bones.
SYDNEY SMITH—*Lady Holland's Memoir.* Vol. I. P. 267.

4
Then came the jolly sommer, being dight
In a thin silken cassock, coloured greene,
That was unlyned all, to be more light.
SPENSER—*Faerie Queene.* Bk. VII. Canto VII. St. 29.

5
From brightening fields of ether fair-disclosed,
Child of the Sun, refulgent Summer comes,
In pride of youth, and felt through Nature's depth;
He comes, attended by the sultry Hours,
And ever-fanning breezes, on his way.
THOMSON—*Seasons. Summer.* L. 1.

6
All-conquering Heat, O, intermit thy wrath!
And on my throbbing temples, potent thus,
Beam not so fierce! incessant still you flow,
And still another fervent flood succeeds,
Pour'd on the head profuse. In vain I sigh,
And restless turn, and look around for night;
Night is far off; and hotter Hours approach.
THOMSON—*Seasons. Summer.* L. 451.

7
Patient of thirst and toil,
Son of the desert, e'en the Camel feels,
Shot through his wither'd heart, the fiery blast.
THOMSON—*Seasons. Summer.* L. 965.

SUN (THE)

8
When the Sun
Clearest shineth
Serenest in the heaven,
Quickly are obscured
All over the earth
Other stars.
KING ALFRED. Trans. of BOETHIUS—*Consolation.*

9
The sun, which passeth through pollutions and itself remains as pure as before.
BACON—*Advancement of Learning.* Bk. II.
(See also DIOGENES, LYLY, TAYLOR, also AUGUSTINE under CORRUPTION)

10
The sun, centre and sire of light,
The keystone of the world-built arch of heaven.
BAILEY—*Festus.* Sc. *Heaven.*

11
See the sun!
God's crest upon His azure shield, the Heavens.
BAILEY—*Festus.* Sc. *A Mountain.*

12
See the gold sunshine patching,
And streaming and streaking across
The gray-green oaks; and catching,
By its soft brown beard, the moss.
BAILEY—*Festus.* Sc. *The Surface.* L. 409.

13
Pleasantly, between the pelting showers, the sunshine gushes down.
BRYANT—*The Cloud on the Way.* L. 18.

14
Make hay while the sun shines.
CERVANTES—*Don Quixote.* Pt. I. Bk. III. Ch. 11.

15
The sun, too, shines into cesspools, and is not polluted.
DIOGENES LAERTIUS—Bk. VI. Sec. 63.
(See also BACON)

16
Behold him setting in his western skies,
The shadows lengthening as the vapours rise.
DRYDEN—*Absalom and Achitophel.* St. 1. L. 268.

17
The glorious lamp of heaven, the radiant sun,
Is Nature's eye.
DRYDEN—*The Story of Acis, Polyphemus, and Galatea from the Thirteenth Book of Ovid's Metamorphoses.* L. 165.

18
Out of the solar walk and Heaven's highway.
DRYDEN—*Threnodia Augustalis.*
(See also GRAY)

19
High in his chariot glow'd the lamp of day.
FALCONER—*The Shipwreck.* Canto I. III. L. 3.

20
Such words fall too often on our cold and careless ears with the triteness of long familiarity; but to Octavia . . . they seemed to be written in sunbeams.
DEAN FARRAR—*Darkness and Dawn.* Chap. XLVI.
(See also JORTIN, TERTULLIAN)

21
Let others hail the rising sun:
I bow to that whose course is run.
GARRICK—*On the Death of Henry Pelham.*
(See also PLUTARCH)

22
In climes beyond the solar road.
GRAY—*Progress of Poesy.*
(See also DRYDEN)

23
Failing yet gracious,
Slow pacing, soon homing,
A patriarch that strolls
Through the tents of his children,
The sun as he journeys
His round on the lower
Ascents of the blue,
Washes the roofs
And the hillsides with clarity.
W. E. HENLEY—*Rhymes and Rhythms.*

24
Father of rosy day,
No more thy clouds of incense rise;
But waking flow'rs,
At morning hours,
Give out their sweets to meet thee in the skies.
HOOD—*Hymn to the Sun.* St. 4.

1
She stood breast-high amid the corn,
Clasp'd by the golden light of morn,
Like the sweetheart of the sun,
Who many a glowing kiss had won.
HOOD—*Ruth.*

2
The great duties of life are written with a sunbeam.
JORTIN—*Sermon.* (1751)
(See also FARRAR)

3
When the sun sets, shadows, that showed at noon
But small, appear most long and terrible.
NATHANIEL LEE—*Œdipus.* Said to be written by LEE and DRYDEN.
(See also VERGIL)

4
Thou shalt come out of a warme Sunne into God's blessing.
LYLY—*Euphues.* HOWELL—*Instructions for Ferreine Travell.* (1642), ARBER's reprint, 1869.

5
The sun shineth upon the dunghill and is not corrupted.
LYLY—*Euphues.* P. 43.
(See also BACON)

6
Thou shalt sleep in thy clouds, careless of the voice of the morning.
MACPHERSON—*Ossian. Carthon. Ossian's Address to the Sun.*

7
Whence are thy beams, O sun! thy everlasting light? Thou comest forth, in thy awful beauty; the stars hide themselves in the sky; the moon, cold and pale, sinks in the western wave. But thou, thyself, movest alone.
MACPHERSON—*Ossian. Carthon. Ossian's Address to the Sun.*

8
The gay motes that people the sunbeams.
MILTON—*Il Penseroso.* L. 8.

9
The great luminary
Aloof the vulgar constellations thick,
That from his lordly eye keep distance due,
Dispenses light from far.
MILTON—*Paradise Lost.* Bk. III. L. 576.

10
Thou sun, of this great world both eye and soul.
MILTON—*Paradise Lost.* Bk. V. L. 171.

11
And see—the Sun himself!—on wings
Of glory up the East he springs.
Angel of Light! who from the time
Those heavens began their march sublime,
Hath first of all the starry choir
Trod in his Maker's steps of fire!
MOORE—*Lalla Rookh. The Fire Worshippers.*

12
As sunshine, broken in the rill,
Though turn'd astray, is sunshine still!
MOORE—*Lalla Rookh. The Fire Worshippers.*

13
Blest power of sunshine!—genial day,
What balm, what life is in thy ray!
To feel there is such real bliss,
That had the world no joy but this,
To sit in sunshine calm and sweet,—
It were a world too exquisite
For man to leave it for the gloom,
The deep, cold shadow, of the tomb.
MOORE—*Lalla Rookh. The Fire Worshippers.*

14
Finge datos currus, quid agas?
Suppose the chariot of the sun were given you, what would you do? (Apollo's question to Phaeton.)
OVID—*Metamorphoses.* Bk. II. 74.

15
Si numeres anno soles et nubila toto,
Invenies nitidum sæpius isse diem.
If you count the sunny and the cloudy days of the whole year, you will find that the sunshine predominates.
OVID—*Tristium.* V. 8. 31.

16
Pompey bade Sylla recollect that more worshipped the rising than the setting sun.
PLUTARCH—*Life of Pompey.*
(See also GARRICK, TIMON OF ATHENS, TIBERIUS)

17
And the sun had on a crown
Wrought of gilded thistledown,
And a scarf of velvet vapor
And a raveled rainbow gown;
And his tinsel-tangled hair
Tossed and lost upon the air
Was glossier and flossier
Than any anywhere.
JAMES WHITCOMB RILEY—*The South Wind and the Sun.*

18
It's hame, and it's hame, and it's hame we fain would be,
Though the cloud is in the lift and the wind is on the lea;
For the sun through the mirk blinks blithe on mine e'e,
Says, "I'll shine on ye yet in your ain countrie."
SCOTT—*Fortunes of Nigel.* Ch. XXXI. Probably quoted.

19
When the sun shines let foolish gnats make sport,
But creep in crannies when he hides his beams.
Comedy of Errors. Act II. Sc. 2. L. 30.

20
I 'gin to be aweary of the sun,
And wish the estate o' the world were now undone.
Macbeth. Act V. Sc. 5. L. 49.

21
Shine out, fair sun, till I have bought a glass,
That I may see my shadow as I pass.
Richard III. Act I. Sc. 2. L. 263.

22
Gilding pale streams with heavenly alchemy.
Sonnet XXXIII.

23
It shall be what o'clock I say it is.
Why, so this gallant will command the sun.
Taming of the Shrew. Act IV. Sc. 3. L. 196.

24
Men shut their doors against a setting sun.
Timon of Athens. Act 1. Sc. 2. L. 129.
(See also PLUTARCH)

25
That orbed continent the fire
That severs day from night.
Twelfth Night. Act V. Sc. 1. L. 278.

1
The selfsame sun that shines upon his court
Hides not his visage from our cottage, but
Looks on alike.
Winter's Tale. Act IV. Sc. 4. L. 455.

2
In the warm shadow of her loveliness;—
He kissed her with his beams.
SHELLEY—*The Witch of Atlas.* St. 2.

3
"But," quoth his neighbor, "when the sun
From East to West his course has run,
How comes it that he shows his face
Next morning in his former place?"
"Ho! there's a pretty question, truly!"
Replied our wight, with an unruly
Burst of laughter and delight,
So much his triumph seemed to please him.
"Why, blockhead! he goes back at night,
And that's the reason no one sees him!"
HORACE SMITH—*The Astronomical Alderman.* St. 5.

4
* * * Because as the sun reflecting upon the wind of strands and shores is unpolluted in its beams, so is God not dishonored when we suppose him in every of his creatures, and in every part of every one of them.
JEREMY TAYLOR—*Holy Living.* Ch. II. Sec. III.
(See also BACON)

5
There sinks the nebulous star we call the sun.
TENNYSON—*The Princess.* Pt. IV.

6
Written as with a sunbeam.
TERTULLIAN—*De Resurrectione Carnis.* Ch. XLVII.
(See also FARRAR)

7
The sopped sun—toper as ever drank hard—
Stares foolish, hazed,
Rubicund, dazed,
Totty with thine October tankard.
FRANCIS THOMPSON—*A Corymbus for Autumn.* St. 1.

8
You leave the setting to court the rising sun.
TIBERIUS. To the Romans who welcomed his successor, CALIGULA. Also POMPEY to SULLA.
(See also PLUTARCH)

9
Sol crescentes decedens duplicat umbras.
The sun when setting makes the increasing shadows twice as large.
VERGIL—*Eclogues.* II. 67.
(See also LEE)

10
Fairest of all the lights above,
Thou sun, whose beams adorn the spheres,
And with unwearied swiftness move,
To form the circles of our years.
ISAAC WATTS—*Sun, Moon and Stars, Praise Ye the Lord.*

11
Whose dwelling is the light of setting suns.
WORDSWORTH—*On Revisiting the Banks of Wye.*

SUN DIAL MOTTOES

12
I go away and come again each day,
But thou shalt go away and ne'er return.
ANON. Found on Sun Dial in England.

13
Vivite, ait, fugie.
Live ye, he says, I flee.
BISHOP ATTERBURY'S Sun Dial.

14
True as the needle to the pole,
Or as the dial to the sun.
BARTON BOOTH—*Song.*

15
True as the dial to the sun,
Although it be not shin'd upon.
BUTLER—*Hudibras.* Pt. III. Canto II. L. 175.

16
Amende to-day and slack not,
Deythe cometh and warneth not,
Tyme passeth and speketh not.
Sun Dial at Moccas Hall near Hereford, belonging to SIR GEORGE CORNEWALL. (1630)

17
"Horas non numero nisi serenas."
There stands in the garden of old St. Mark
A sun dial quaint and gray.
It takes no heed of the hours which in dark
Pass o'er it day by day.
It has stood for ages amid the flowers
In that land of sky and song.
"I number none but the cloudless hours,"
Its motto the live day long.
WM. C. DOANE. Of a Sun Dial in Venice.

18
Let not the sun go down upon your wrath.
Ephesians. IV. 26.

19
Give God thy heart, thy service, and thy gold;
The day wears on, and time is waxing old.
Sun Dial in the Cloister-garden of Gloucester Cathedral.

20
Our life's a flying shadow, God's the pole,
The index pointing at Him is our soul;
Death the horizon, when our sun is set,
Which will through Christ a resurrection get.
Sun Dial inscription once on the South wall of Glasgow Cathedral.

21
The night cometh when no man can work.
John. IX. 9.

22
Thou breathing dial! since thy day began
The present hour was ever mark'd with shade.
LANDOR—*Miscellaneous Poems.* Vol. VIII. P. 92. (1846)

23
A lumine motus.
I am moved by the light.
MAETERLINCK—*Measure of the Hours. Motto.*

24
Horas non numero nisi serenas.
I count only the hours that are serene.
MAETERLINCK—*Measure of the Hours.* Mentioned as found by HAZLITT on a Sun Dial near Venice.

25
L'heure de la justice ne sonne pas
Aux cadrans de ce monde:

The hour of justice does not strike
On the dials of this world.

MAETERLINCK—*Measure of the Hours.* Motto on a Sun Dial on a church at Tourette-sur-Loup.

1
Let others tell of storms and showers,
I'll only mark your sunny hours.

On a Sun Dial at Pittsfield, Mass.

2
Once at a potent leader's voice I stayed;
Once I went back when a good monarch prayed;
Mortals, howe'er we grieve, howe'er deplore,
The flying shadow will return no more.

In CYRUS REDDING—*Fifty Years Recollections.* Vol. III. P. 86. Attributed to WILLIAM HAMILTON in CHALMER'S *Poets.* Vol. XV. P. 620.

3
The Natural Clock-work by the mighty ONE
Wound up at first, and ever since have gone.

Part of Sun Dial motto on the South Porch of Seaham Church, Durham, England.

4
As the long hours do pass away,
So doth the life of man decay.

Inscription on a Sun Dial in the garden of the Royal hotel at Sevenoaks, Kent, England.

5
Carve out dials, quaintly, point by point
Thereby to set the minutes, how they run,
How many make the Hour full, complete,
How many hours bring about the Day.

King Henry VI. Pt. III. Act II. Sc. 5.

6
If o'er the dial glides a shade, redeem
The time for lo! it passes like a dream;
But if 'tis all a blank, then mark the loss
Of hours unblest by shadows from the cross.

On a Sun Dial in a churchyard at Shenstone, England.

7
I mark my hours by shadow;
Mayest thou mark thine
By sunshine.

HILTON TURVEY. In his novel—*The Van Haavens.*

8
Begone about your business.

On a Sun Dial once in The Temple, London.

9
Hours fly,
Flowers die.
New days,
New ways,
Pass by.
Love stays.

HENRY VAN DYKE—*Motto for Katrina's Sun Dial.*

10
Time is
Too Slow for those who Wait,
Too Swift for those who Fear,
Too Long for those who Grieve,
Too Short for those who Rejoice,
But for those who Love
Time is not.

HENRY VAN DYKE—*Motto for Katrina's Sun Dial.* In Mrs. Spencer Trask's Garden of Yaddo, Saratoga Springs.

11
In the day, do the day's work.

Sun Dial against the residence of Spencer Wells, Hamstead, England.

12
With warning hand I mark Time's rapid flight,
From Life's glad morning to its solemn night;
Yet, through the dear Lord's love, I also show
There's light above me by the shade I throw.

WHITTIER—*Inscription on a Sun Dial* for the Rev. Henry T. Bowditch.

13
He knows but from its shade the present hour.

WORDSWORTH—*An Evening Walk.*

SUNFLOWER

Helianthus

14
Ah, Sunflower, weary of time,
Who countest the steps of the sun;
Seeking after that sweet golden clime,
Where the traveller's journey is done;

Where the youth pined away with desire,
And the pale virgin shrouded in snow,
Arise from their graves, and aspire
Where my Sunflower wishes to go!

WILLIAM BLAKE—*The Sunflower.*

15
Light-enchanted sunflower, thou
Who gazest ever true and tender
On the sun's revolving splendour.

CALDERON—*Magico Prodigioso.* Sc. 3. SHELLEY's trans.

16
Restless sunflower; cease to move.

CALDERON—*Magico Prodigioso.* Sc. 3. SHELLEY's trans.

17
The Sunflow'r, thinking 'twas for him foul shame
To nap by daylight, strove t' excuse the blame;
It was not sleep that made him nod, he said,
But too great weight and largeness of his head.

COWLEY—*Of Plants.* Bk. IV. *Of Flowers. The Poppy.* L. 102.

18
With zealous step he climbs the upland lawn,
And bows in homage to the rising dawn;
Imbibes with eagle eye the golden ray,
And watches, as it moves, the orb of day.

ERASMUS DARWIN—*Loves of the Plants.* Canto I. L. 225.

19
Space for the sunflower, bright with yellow glow,
To court the sky.

CAROLINE GILMAN—*To the Ursulines.*

20
Eagle of flowers! I see thee stand,
And on the sun's noon-glory gaze;
With eye like his, thy lids expand,
And fringe their disk with golden rays:
Though fix'd on earth, in darkness rooted there,
Light is thy element, thy dwelling air,
Thy prospect heaven.

MONTGOMERY—*The Sunflower.*

21
As the sunflower turns on her god when he sets,
The same look which she turn'd when he rose.

MOORE—*Believe Me, if all Those Endearing Young Charms.*

1
But one, the lofty follower of the Sun,
Sad when he sets, shuts up her yellow leaves
Drooping all night; and, when he warm returns,
Points her enamoured bosom to his ray.
THOMSON—*The Seasons. Summer.* L. 216.

SUNRISE

2
The sun had long since in the lap
Of Thetis taken out his nap,
And, like a lobster boil'd, the morn
From black to red began to turn.
BUTLER—*Hudibras.* Pt. II. Canto II. L. 29.

3
Oh the road to Mandalay
Where the flyin'-fishes play
An' the dawn comes up like thunder outer
China 'crost the Bay!
KIPLING—*Mandalay.*
(See also THOMPSON)

4
The east is blossoming! Yea, a rose,
Vast as the heavens, soft as a kiss,
Sweet as the presence of woman is,
Rises and reaches, and widens and grows
Large and luminous up from the sea,
And out of the sea, as a blossoming tree,
Richer and richer, so higher and higher,
Deeper and deeper it takes its hue;
Brighter and brighter it reaches through
The space of heaven and the place of stars,
Till all is as rich as a rose can be,
And my rose-leaves fall into billows of fire.
JOAQUIN MILLER—*Sunrise in Venice.*

5
Night is the time for rest;
How sweet, when labours close,
To gather round an aching breast
The curtain of repose,
Stretch the tired limbs, and lay the head
Down on our own delightful bed!
MONTGOMERY—*Night.* St. 1.

6
The whole east was flecked
With flashing streaks and shafts of amethyst,
While a light crimson mist
Went up before the mounting luminary,
And all the strips of cloud began to vary
Their hues, and all the zenith seemed to ope
As if to show a cope beyond the cope!
EPES SARGENT—*Sunrise at Sea.*

7
The heavenly-harness'd team
Begins his golden progress in the east.
Henry IV. Pt. I. Act III. Sc. 1. L. 221.

8
He fires the proud tops of the eastern pines
And darts his light through every guilty hole.
Richard II. Act III. Sc. 2. L. 42.

9
As when the golden sun salutes the morn,
And, having gilt the ocean with his beams,
Gallops the zodiac in his glistering coach,
And overlooks the highest-peering hills.
Titus Andronicus. Act II. Sc. 1. L. 5.

10
Hail, gentle Dawn! mild blushing goddess, hail!
Rejoic'd I see thy purple mantle spread
O'er half the skies, gems pave thy radiant way,
And orient pearls from ev'ry shrub depend.
WM. SOMERVILLE—*The Chase.* Bk. II. L. 79.

11
And yonder fly his scattered golden arrows,
And smite the hills with day.
BAYARD TAYLOR—*The Poet's Journal. Third Evening. Morning.*

12
See! led by Morn, with dewy feet,
Apollo mounts his golden seat,
Replete with seven-fold fire;
While, dazzled by his conquering light,
Heaven's glittering host and awful night
Submissively retire.
THOMAS TAYLOR—*Ode to the Rising Sun.*

13
See how there
The cowlèd night
Kneels on the Eastern sanctuary-stair.
FRANCIS THOMPSON—*A Corymbus for Autumn* St. 5.

14
East, oh, east of Himalay
Dwell the nations underground,
Hiding from the shock of day,
For the sun's uprising sound . . .
So fearfully the sun doth sound,
Clanging up beyond Cathay;
For the great earthquaking sunrise
Rolling up beyond Cathay.
FRANCIS THOMPSON—*The Mistress of Vision.*
(See also KIPLING)

15
But yonder comes the powerful King of Day,
Rejoicing in the East.
THOMSON—*Seasons. Summer.* L. 81.

16
The rising sun complies with our weak sight,
First gilds the clouds, then shows his globe of light
At such a distance from our eyes, as though
He knew what harm his hasty beams would do.
EDMUND WALLER — *To the King upon His Majesty's Happy Return.* L. 1.

SUNSET

17
Come watch with me the shaft of fire that glows
In yonder West: the fair, frail palaces,
The fading Alps and archipelagoes,
And great cloud-continents of sunset-seas.
T. B. ALDRICH—*Sonnet. Miracles.*

18
The death-bed of a day, how beautiful!
BAILEY—*Festus.* Sc. *A Library and Balcony.*

19
It was the cooling hour, just when the rounded
Red sun sinks down behind the azure hill,
Which then seems as if the whole earth is bounded,
Circling all nature, hush'd, and dim, and still,
With the far mountain-crescent half surrounded
On one side, and the deep sea calm and chill
Upon the other, and the rosy sky
With one star sparkling through it like an eye.
BYRON—*Don Juan.* Canto II. St. 183.

20
See! he sinks
Without a word; and his ensanguined bier
Is vacant in the west, while far and near
Behold! each coward shadow eastward shrinks,
Thou dost not strive, O sun, nor dost thou cry
Amid thy cloud-built streets.
FABER—*The Rosary and Other Poems. On the Ramparts at Angoulême.*

1 The sacred lamp of day
Now dipt in western clouds his parting ray.
FALCONER—*The Shipwreck.* Canto II. L. 27.

2
Oft did I wonder why the setting sun
Should look upon us with a blushing face:
Is't not for shame of what he hath seen done,
Whilst in our hemisphere he ran his race?
HEATH—*First Century. On the Setting Sun.*

3
Forming and breaking in the sky,
I fancy all shapes are there;
Temple, mountain, monument, spire;
Ships rigged out with sails of fire,
And blown by the evening air.
J. K. HOYT—*A Summer Sunset.*

4
Down sank the great red sun, and in golden, glimmering vapors
Veiled the light of his face, like the Prophet descending from Sinai.
LONGFELLOW—*Evangeline.* Pt. I. Sec. IV.

5
Softly the evening came. The sun from the western horizon
Like a magician extended his golden wand o'er the landscape;
Twinkling vapors arose; and sky and water and forest
Seemed all on fire at the touch, and melted and mingled together.
LONGFELLOW—*Evangeline.* Pt. II. Sec. II.

6
After a day of cloud and wind and rain
Sometimes the setting sun breaks out again,
And, touching all the darksome woods with light,
Smiles on the fields until they laugh and sing,
Then like a ruby from the horizon's ring,
Drops down into the night.
LONGFELLOW—*Hanging of the Crane.* Pt. VII.

7
And the gilded car of day,
His glowing axle doth allay
In the steep Atlantic stream.
MILTON—*Comus.* L. 95.

8
Now in his Palace of the West,
Sinking to slumber, the bright Day,
Like a tired monarch fann'd to rest,
'Mid the cool airs of Evening lay;
While round his couch's golden rim
The gaudy clouds, like courtiers, crept—
Struggling each other's light to dim,
And catch his last smile e'er he slept.
MOORE—*The Summer Fête.* St. 22.

9
Long on the wave reflected lustres play.
SAMUEL ROGERS—*The Pleasures of Memory.* Pt. I. L. 94.

10
Methought little space 'tween those hills intervened,
But nearer,—more lofty,—more shaggy they seemed.
The clouds o'er their summits they calmly did rest,
And hung on the ether's invisible breast;
Than the vapours of earth they seemed purer, more bright,—
Oh! could they be clouds? 'Twas the necklace of night.
RUSKIN—*The Iteriad. Sunset at Low-Wood.*

11
The lonely sunsets flare forlorn
Down valleys dreadly desolate;
The lonely mountains soar in scorn
As still as death, as stern as fate.
ROBERT SERVICE—*The Land God Forgot.*

12
The setting sun, and music at the close,
At the last taste of sweets, is sweetest last.
Richard II. Act II. Sc. 1. L. 12.

13
When the sun sets, who doth not look for night?
Richard III. Act II. Sc. 3. L. 34.

14 The sun was down,
And all the west was paved with sullen fire.
I cried, "Behold! the barren beach of hell
At ebb of tide."
ALEXANDER SMITH—*A Life Drama.* Sc. 4.

15
How fine has the day been! how bright was the sun,
How lovely and joyful the course that he run!
Though he rose in a mist when his race he begun,
And there followed some droppings of rain:
But now the fair traveller's come to the west,
His rays are all gold, and his beauties are best;
He paints the skies gay as he sinks to his rest,
And foretells a bright rising again.
WATTS—*Moral Songs. A Summer Evening.*

SUPERSTITION

16
Foul Superstition! howsoe'er disguised,
Idol, saint, virgin, prophet, crescent, cross,
For whatsoever symbol thou art prized,
Thou sacerdotal gain, but general loss!
Who from true worship's gold can separate thy dross?
BYRON—*Childe Harold.* Canto II. St. 44.

17
Superstitione tollenda religio non tollitur.
Religion is not removed by removing superstition.
CICERO—*De Divinatione.* II. 72.

18
Accedit etiam mors, quæ quasi saxum Tantalo semper impendit: tum superstitio, qua qui est imbutus quietus esse numquam potest.
Death approaches, which is always impending like the stone over Tantalus: then comes superstition with which he who is imbued can never have peace of mind.
CICERO—*De Finibus Bonorum et Malorum.* I. 8.

19
Superstitio, in qua inest inanis timor
Dei; religio, quæ dei pio cultu continetur.
There is in superstition a senseless fear of God; religion consists in the pious worship of Him.
CICERO—*De Natura Deorum.* I. 42.

20
My right eye itches, some good luck is near.
DRYDEN—*Paraphrase of Amaryllis. Third Idyllium of Theocritus.* L. 86.

1
Alas! you know the cause too well;
The salt is spilt, to me it fell.
Then to contribute to my loss,
My knife and fork were laid across;
On Friday, too! the day I dread;
Would I were safe at home, in bed!
Last night (I vow to Heaven 'tis true)
Bounce from the fire a coffin flew.
Next post some fatal news shall tell:
God send my Cornish friends be well!
GAY—*Fables*. Pt. I. Fable 37.

2
Dish yer rabbit foot'll gin you good luck. De man w'at tote it mighty ap'fer ter come out right en' up wen deys any racket gwine on in de neighborhoods, let 'er be whar she will en w'en she may; mo' espeshually ef de man w'at got it know 'zactly w'at he got ter do.
JOEL CHANDLER HARRIS—*Brother Rabbit and his famous Foot*.

3
Minimis etiam rebus prava religio inserit deos.
A foolish superstition introduces the influences of the gods even in the smallest matters.
LIVY—*Annales*. XXVII. 23.

4
Why is it that we entertain the belief that for every purpose odd numbers are the most effectual?
PLINY—*Natural History*. Bk. XXVIII. Ch. V.
(See also LOVER under LUCK)

5
Midnight hags,
By force of potent spells, of bloody characters,
And conjurations horrible to hear,
Call fiends and spectres from the yawning deep,
And set the ministers of hell at work.
NICHOLAS ROWE—*Jane Shore*. Act IV. Sc. 1. L. 240.

6
Some devils ask but the parings of one's nail,
A rush, a hair, a drop of blood, a pin, a nut, a cherry stone;
But she, more coveteous, would have a chain.
Master, be wise: an if you give it her,
The devil will shake her chain and fright us with it.
Comedy of Errors. Act IV. Sc. 3. L. 72.

7
I pull in resolution, and begin
To doubt the equivocation of the fiend
That lies like truth: "Fear not, till Birnam wood
Do come to Dunsinane."
Macbeth. Act V. Sc. 5. L. 42.

8
Number three is always fortunate.
SMOLLETT—*Peregrine Pickle*. Quoted as a well-known proverb.
(See also PLINY)

9
Superstition is related to this life, religion to the next; superstition is allied to fatality, religion to virtue; it is by the vivacity of earthly desires that we become superstitious; it is, on the contrary, by the sacrifice of these desires that we become religious.
MADAME DE STAËL. See ABEL STEVENS' *Life of Madame de Staël*. Ch. XXXIV.

SUSPICION

10
Quoth Sidrophel, If you suppose,
Sir Knight, that I am one of those,
I might suspect, and take th' alarm,
Your bus'ness is but to inform;
But if it be, 'tis ne'er the near,
You have a wrong sow by the ear.
BUTLER—*Hudibras*. Pt. II. Canto III. L. 575.

11
Multorum te etiam oculi et aures non sentientem, sicuti adhuc fecerunt, speculabuntur atque custodient.
Without your knowledge, the eyes and ears of many will see and watch you, as they have done already.
CICERO—*Orationes In Catilinam*. I. 2.

12
Cautus enim metuit foveam lupus, accipiterque
Suspectos laqueos, et opertum milvius hamum.
The wolf dreads the pitfall, the hawk suspects the snare, and the kite the covered hook.
HORACE—*Epistles*. I. 16. 50.

13
Argwohnen folgt auf Misstrauen.
Suspicion follows close on mistrust.
LESSING—*Nathan der Weise*. V. 8.

14
Que diable alloit-il faire dans cette galère?
What the devil was he doing in this galley?
MOLIÈRE—*Fourberies de Scapin*. Act II. 11.
CYRANO DE BERGERAC—*Pédant Joué*. Act II. Sc. 4.

15
Julius Cæsar divorced his wife Pompeia, but declared at the trial that he knew nothing of what was alleged against her and Clodius. When asked why, in that case, he had divorced her, he replied: "Because I would have the chastity of my wife clear even of suspicion."
PLUTARCH—*Life of Julius Cæsar*. Same in SUETONIUS—*Life of Cæsar*.

16
As to Cæsar, when he was called upon, he gave no testimony against Clodius, nor did he affirm that he was certain of any injury done to his bed. He only said, "He had divorced Pompeia because the wife of Cæsar ought not only to be clear of such a crime, but of the very suspicion of it."
PLUTARCH—*Life of Cicero*.

17
All seems infected that the infected spy,
As all looks yellow to the jaundiced eye.
POPE—*Essay on Criticism*. L. 568.

18
Les soupçons importuns
Sont d'un second hymen les fruits les plus communs.
Disagreeable suspicions are usually the fruits of a second marriage.
RACINE—*Phèdre*. II. 5.

19
All is not well;
I doubt some foul play.
Hamlet. Act I. Sc. 2. L. 255.

20
Suspicion always haunts the guilty mind;
The thief doth fear each bush an officer.
Henry VI. Pt. III. Act V. Sc. 6. L. 11.

1
Would he were fatter! But I fear him not:
Yet if my name were liable to fear,
I do not know the man I should avoid
So soon as that spare Cassius.
Julius Cæsar. Act I. Sc. 2. L. 198.

2
Ad tristem partem strenua est suspicio.
The losing side is full of suspicion.
SYRUS—*Maxims*.

3
Omnes quibus res sunt minus secundæ magis sunt, nescio quomodo,
Suspiciosi; ad contumeliam omnia accipiunt magis;
Propter suam impotentiam se credunt negligi.
All persons as they become less prosperous, are the more suspicious. They take everything as an affront; and from their conscious weakness, presume that they are neglected.
TERENCE—*Adelphi*. IV. 3. 14.

SWALLOW

4
One swallow does not make spring.
ARISTOTLE—*Ethic. Nicom*. Bk. I.
(See also CERVANTES, NORTHBROOKE)

5
Una golondrina sola no hace verano.
One swallow alone does not make the summer.
CERVANTES—*Don Quixote*. Pt. I. Ch. XIII.

6
Down comes rain drop, bubble follows;
On the house-top one by one
Flock the synagogue of swallows,
Met to vote that autumn's gone.
THEOPHILE GAUTIER—*Life, a Bubble. A Bird's-Eye View Thereof*.

7
But, as old Swedish legends say,
Of all the birds upon that day,
The swallow felt the deepest grief,
And longed to give her Lord relief,
And chirped when any near would come.
"*Hugswala swala swal honom!*"
Meaning, as they who tell it deem,
Oh, cool, oh, cool and comfort Him!
LELAND—*The Swallow*.

8
The swallow is come!
The swallow is come!
O, fair are the seasons, and light
Are the days that she brings,
With her dusky wings,
And her bosom snowy white!
LONGFELLOW—*Hyperion*. Bk. II. Ch. I.

9
One swallowe proveth not that summer is neare.
NORTHBROOKE—*Treatise against Dancing*. (1577)
(See also ARISTOTLE)

10
It's surely summer, for there's a swallow:
Come one swallow, his mate will follow,
The bird race quicken and wheel and thicken.
CHRISTINA G. ROSSETTI—*A Bird Song*. St. 2.

11
There goes the swallow,—
Could we but follow!
Hasty swallow, stay,
Point us out the way;
Look back swallow, turn back swallow, stop swallow.
CHRISTINA G. ROSSETTI—*Songs in a Cornfield*. St. 7.

12
The swallow follows not summer more willing than we your lordship.
Timon of Athens. Act III. Sc. 6. L. 31.

13
Now to the Goths as swift as swallow flies.
Titus Andronicus. Act IV. Sc. 2. L. 172.

14
The swallow sweeps
The slimy pool, to build his hanging house.
THOMSON—*The Seasons. Spring*. L. 651.

15
When autumn scatters his departing gleams,
Warn'd of approaching winter, gather'd, play
The swallow-people; and toss'd wide around,
O'er the calm sky, in convolution swift,
The feather'd eddy floats; rejoicing once,
Ere to their wintry slumbers they retire.
THOMSON—*Seasons. Autumn*. L. 836.

SWAN

16
All our geese are swans.
BURTON—*Anatomy of Melancholy*. Pt. I. Sec. II. Memb. 3. Subsect. 14.

17
Place me on Sunium's marbled steep,
Where nothing save the waves and I
May hear our mutual murmurs sweep;
There, swan-like, let me sing and die.
BYRON—*Don Juan*. Canto III. St. 86. 16.
(See also DOANE, FLETCHER, MARTIAL, OVID, SHAKESPEARE, SOCRATES, TENNYSON)

18
The jelous swan, agens hire deth that syngith.
CHAUCER—*Parlement of Fowles*. L. 342.

19
Cignoni non sine causa Apoloni dicati sint, quod ab eo divinationem habere videantur, qua providentes quid in morte boni sit, cum cantu et voluptate moriantur.
The swan is not without cause dedicated to Apollo because, foreseeing his happiness in death, he dies with singing and pleasure.
CICERO—*Tusculanarum Disputationum*. I. 30.
(See also BYRON, SOCRATES)

20
Death darkens his eyes, and unplumes his wings,
Yet the sweetest song is the last he sings:
Live so, my Love, that when death shall come,
Swan-like and sweet it may waft thee home.
G. W. DOANE.
(See also BYRON)

21
The immortal swan that did her life deplore.
GILES FLETCHER—*Temptation and Victory of Christ*.

22
The dying swan, when years her temples pierce,
In music-strains breathes out her life and verse,
And, chanting her own dirge, tides on her wat'ry hearse.
PHINEAS FLETCHER—*Purple Island*. Canto I.
(See also BYRON)

1
The swan in the pool is singing,
And up and down doth he steer,
And, singing gently ever,
Dips under the water clear.
HEINE—*Book of Songs. Lyrical Interlude.* No. 64.

2
And over the pond are sailing
Two swans all white as snow;
Sweet voices mysteriously wailing
Pierce through me as onward they go.
They sail along, and a ringing
Sweet melody rises on high;
And when the swans begin singing,
They presently must die.
HEINE—*Early Poems. Evening Songs.* No. 2.

3
The swan, like the soul of the poet,
By the dull world is ill understood.
HEINE—*Early Poems. Evening Songs.* No. 3.

4
There's a double beauty whenever a swan
Swims on a lake with her double thereon.
HOOD—*Her Honeymoon.*
(See also WORDSWORTH)

5
The swan murmurs sweet strains with a faltering tongue, itself the singer of its own dirge.
MARTIAL — *Epigrams.* Bk. XIII. Ep. LXXVII.
(See also BYRON)

6
The swan, with arched neck
Between her white wings mantling proudly, rows
Her state with oary feet.
MILTON—*Paradise Lost.* Bk. VII. L. 438.

7
Thus does the white swan, as he lies on the wet grass, when the
Fates summon him, sing at the fords of Mæander.
OVID—Ep. VII. RILEY's trans.
(See also BYRON)

8
The swan's down-feather,
That stands upon the swell at full of tide,
And neither way inclines.
Antony and Cleopatra. Act III. Sc. 2. L. 48.

9
As I have seen a swan
With bootless labour swim against the tide
And spend her strength with over-matching waves.
Henry VI. Pt. III. Act I. Sc. 4. L. 19.

10
I am the cygnet to this pale faint swan,
Who chants a doleful hymn to his own death;
And, from the organ-pipe of frailty, sings
His soul and body to their lasting rest.
King John. Act V. Sc. 7. L. 21.
(See also BYRON)

11
(Let music sound while he doth make his choice)
Then if he lose he makes a swan-like end.
Merchant of Venice. Act III. Sc. 2.
(See also BYRON)

12
I will play the swan
And die in music.
Othello. Act V. Sc. 2.
(See also BYRON)

13
For all the water in the ocean,
Can never turn the swan's black legs to white,
Although she lave them hourly in the flood.
Titus Andronicus. Act IV. Sc. 2. L. 101.

14
You think that upon the score of fore-knowledge and divining I am infinitely inferior to the swans. When they perceive approaching death they sing more merrily than before, because of the joy they have in going to the God they serve.
SOCRATES. See PLATO—*Phaedo.* 77.
(See also BYRON, CICERO)

15
The wild swan's death-hymn took the soul
Of that waste place with joy
Hidden in sorrow: at first to the ear
The warble was low, and full and clear.
TENNYSON—*The Dying Swan.*
(See also BYRON)

16
Some full-breasted swan
That, fluting a wild carol ere her death,
Ruffles her pure cold plume, and takes the flood
With swarthy webs.
TENNYSON—*Passing of Arthur.*

17
The stately-sailing swan
Gives out his snowy plumage to the gale;
And, arching proud his neck, with oary feet
Bears forward fierce, and guards his osier isle,
Protective of his young.
THOMSON—*The Seasons. Spring.* L. 775.

18
The swan on still St. Mary's lake
Float double, swan and shadow!
WORDSWORTH—*Yarrow Unvisited.*
(See also HOOD)

SWANEE RIVER

19
Way down upon de Swanee Ribber,
Far, far away,
Dere's whar ma heart am turning ebber,
Dere's whar de old folks stay.
All up and down de whole creation,
Sadly I roam,
Still longing for de old plantation,
And for de old folks at home.
STEPHEN COLLINS FOSTER—*Old Folks at Home.* (*Swanee Ribber.*)

SWEARING (See also OATHS, VOWS)

20
A demon holds a book, in which are written the sins of a particular man; an Angel drops on it from a phial, a tear which the sinner had shed in doing a good action, and his sins are washed out.
MS. of ALBERIC, Monk of Monte-Cassino. Found in an article on DANTE. Selections from *Edinburgh Review.* Vol. I. P. 67.
(See also MOORE, STERNE)

21
Jack was embarrassed—never hero more,
And as he knew not what to say, he swore.
BYRON—*The Island.* Canto III. St. 5.

22
Bad language or abuse
I never, never use,
Whatever the emergency;

Though "Bother it" I may
Occasionally say,
I never never use a big, big D.
W. S. Gilbert—*H. M. S. Pinafore.*

1
Take not His name, who made thy mouth, in vain;
It gets thee nothing, and hath no excuse.
Herbert—*Temple. Church Porch.* St. 10.

2 There written all
Black as the damning drops that fall
From the denouncing Angel's pen
Ere Mercy weeps them out again.
Moore—*Lalla Rookh. Paradise and the Peri.*
(See also Alberic)

3
And each blasphemer quite escape the rod,
Because the insult's not on man, but God?
Pope—*Epilogue to Satires.* Dialogue II. L. 199.

4
In totum jurare, nisi ubi necesse est, gravi viro parum convenit.

To swear, except when necessary, is unbecoming to an honorable man.
Quintilian—*De Institutione Oratoria.* IX. 2.

5
And then a whoreson jackanapes must take me up for swearing; as if I borrowed mine oaths of him and might not spend them at my pleasure.
Cymbeline. Act II. Sc. 1. L. 3.

6
When a gentleman is disposed to swear, it is not for any standers-by to curtail his oaths.
Cymbeline. Act II. Sc. 1. L. 11.

7
I'll be damned for never a king's son in Christendom.
Henry IV. Part I. Act. I. Sc. 2. L. 109.

8
That in the captain's but a choleric word,
Which in the soldier is flat blasphemy.
Measure for Measure. Act II. Sc. 2. L. 130.

9 Do not swear at all;
Or, if thou wilt, swear by thy gracious self,
Which is the god of my idolatry,
And I'll believe thee.
Romeo and Juliet. Act II. Sc. 2. L. 112.

10
For it comes to pass oft that a terrible oath, with a swaggering accent sharply twanged off, gives manhood more approbation than ever proof itself would have earned him.
Twelfth Night. Act III. Sc. 4. L. 196.

11
"He shall not die, by God," cried my uncle Toby. The Accusing Spirit which flew up to heaven's chancery with the oath, blushed as he gave it in: and the Recording Angel as he wrote it down, dropped a tear upon the word and blotted it out forever.
Sterne—*Tristram Shandy.* Bk. VI. Ch. VIII.
(See also Alberic)

12
Our armies swore terribly in Flanders.
Sterne—*Tristram Shandy.* Bk. III. Ch. XI.

SWEET BASIL

13 *Ocymum Basilicum*
I pray your Highness mark this curious herb:
Touch it but lightly, stroke it softly, Sir,
And it gives forth an odor sweet and rare;
But crush it harshly and you'll make a scent
Most disagreeable.
Leland—*Sweet Basil.*

SWEETNESS

14
The Greek word *euphuia*, a finely tempered nature, gives exactly the notion of perfection as culture brings us to perceive it; a harmonious perfection, a perfection in which the characters of beauty and intelligence are both present, which unites "the two noblest of things"—as Swift . . . most happily calls them in his Battle of the Books, "the two noblest of things, sweetness and light."
Matthew Arnold—*Culture and Anarchy.*
(See also Swift)

15
The pursuit of the perfect, then, is the pursuit of sweetness and light.
Matthew Arnold—*Culture and Anarchy.*

16
Culture is the passion for sweetness and light, and (what is more) the passion for making them prevail.
Matthew Arnold—*Literature and Dogma. Preface.*

17
Everye white will have its blacke
And everye sweete its soure.
Sir Carline. 15th century ballad.
(See also Emerson, Jonson)

18
Nor waste their sweetness in the desert air.
Churchill—*Gotham.* Bk. II. L. 20.
(See also Gray under Obscurity)

19
Every sweet hath its sour, every evil its good.
Emerson—*Compensation.*

20
Sweet meat must have sour sauce.
Jonson—*Poetaster.* Act III. 3.
(See also Carline)

21
To pile up honey upon sugar, and sugar upon honey, to an interminable tedious sweetness.
Lamb—*On Ears.*

22
Sweeter also than honey and the honeycomb.
Psalms. XIX. 10.

23
Sweets to the sweet: farewell.
Hamlet. Act V. Sc. 1. L. 268.

24
Instead of dirt and poison, we have rather chosen to fill our hives with honey and wax, thus furnishing mankind with the two noblest of things, which are *sweetness* and *light*.
Swift—*Battle of the Books.* Fable on the merits of the bee (the ancients) and the spider (the moderns).
(See also Arnold)

25
The sweetest thing that ever grew
Beside a human door.
Wordsworth—*Lucy Gray.* St. 2.

SWINE

1

Shear swine, all cry and no wool.

BUTLER—*Hudibras*. Pt. I. Canto I. L. 852.

2

You have a wrong sow by the ear.

BUTLER—*Hudibras*. Pt. II. Canto III. L. 580. JONSON—*Every Man in his Humour*. Act II. Sc. 1.

3

Me pinguem et nitidum bene curata cute vises,
. . . Epicuri de grege porcum.

You may see me, fat and shining, with well-cared for hide, . . . a hog from Epicurus' herd.

HORACE—*Epistles*. Bk. I. IV. 15. 16.

4

The fattest hog in Epicurus' sty.

WILLIAM MASON—*Heroic Epistle*.

5

Neither cast ye your pearls before swine.

Matthew. VII. 6.

6

Then on the grounde
Togyder rounde
With manye a sadde stroke,
They roll and rumble,
They turne and tumble,
As pigges do in a poke.

SIR THOMAS MORE—*How a Sergeant would learn to Playe the Frere*.

7

How Instinct varies in the grov'ling swine.

POPE—*Essay on Man*. Ep. I. L. 221.

8

The hog that ploughs not, nor obeys thy call,
Lives on the labours of this lord of all.

POPE—*Essay on Man*. Ep. III. L. 41.

SYMBOLS

9

With crosses, relics, crucifixes,
Beads, pictures, rosaries, and pixes;
The tools of working out salvation
By mere mechanic operation.

BUTLER—*Hudibras*. Pt. III. Canto I. L. 1,495.

10

Science sees signs; Poetry the thing signified.

J. C. AND A. W. HARE—*Guesses at Truth*.

11

It [Catholicism] supplies a multitude of external forms in which the spiritual may be clothed and manifested.

HAWTHORNE—*Marble Faun*. Vol. II. Ch. XIII.

12

All things are symbols: the external shows
Of Nature have their image in the mind,
As flowers and fruits and falling of the leaves.

LONGFELLOW—*The Harvest Moon*.

13

Sometime we see a cloud that's dragonish;
A vapour sometime like a bear or lion,
A tower'd citadel, a pendant rock,
A forked mountain, or blue promontory
With trees upon 't, that nod unto the world,
And mock our eyes with air: thou hast seen
these signs;
They are black vesper's pageants.

Antony and Cleopatra. Act IV. St. 14. L. 2.

14

If he be not in love with some woman, there is no believing old signs: a' brushes his hat o' mornings; what should that bode?

Much Ado About Nothing. Act III. Sc. 2. L. 40.

SYMPATHY

15

Strengthen me by sympathizing with my strength not my weakness.

AMOS BRONSON ALCOTT—*Table-Talk*. *Sympathy*.

16

Pity and need
Make all flesh kin. There is no caste in blood.

EDWIN ARNOLD—*Light of Asia*. Bk. VI. L. 73.

(See also CARLYLE, also TROILUS AND CRESIDA under NATURE)

17

But there is one thing which we are responsible for, and that is for our sympathies, for the manner in which we regard it, and for the tone in which we discuss it. What shall we say, then, with regard to it? On which side shall we stand?

JOHN BRIGHT—*Speech on Slavery and Secession*. Feb. 3, 1863.

18

In the desert a fountain is springing,
In the wide waste there still is a tree,
And a bird in the solitude singing,
Which speaks to my spirit of *thee*.

BYRON—*Stanzas to Augusta*.

19

Of a truth, men are mystically united: a mystic bond of brotherhood makes all men one.

CARLYLE—*Essays*. *Goethe's Works*.

(See also ARNOLD and BYRON under ELECTRICITY)

20

There is in souls a sympathy with sounds.

COWPER—*The Task*. Bk. VI. L. 1.

21

Jobling, there *are* chords in the human mind.

DICKENS—*Bleak House*. Ch. XX.

(See also DICKENS under HEART)

22

Our souls sit close and silently within,
And their own web from their own entrails spin;
And when eyes meet far off, our sense is such,
That, spider like, we feel the tenderest touch.

DRYDEN—*Mariage à la Mode*. Act II. Sc. 1.

23

The secrets of life are not shown except to sympathy and likeness.

EMERSON—*Representative Men*. *Montaigne*.

24

The man who melts
With social sympathy, though not allied,
Is of more worth than a thousand kinsmen.

EURIPIDES—*Orestes*. L. 846.

25

He watch'd and wept, he pray'd and felt for all.

GOLDSMITH—*The Deserted Village*. L. 166.

26

The craving for sympathy is the common boundary-line between joy and sorrow.

J. C. AND A. W. HARE—*Guesses at Truth*.

1
We pine for kindred natures
To mingle with our own.
Felicia D. Hemans—*Psyche borne by Zephyrs to the Island of Pleasure.*

2
Yet, taught by time, my heart has learned to glow
For other's good, and melt at other's woe.
Homer — *Odyssey.* Bk. XVIII. L. 269. Pope's trans.

3
Bowels of compassion.
I John. III. 17.

4
World-wide apart, and yet akin,
As showing that the human heart
Beats on forever as of old.
Longfellow—*Tales of a Wayside Inn.* Pt. III. *The Theologian's Tale. Interlude.*

5
For I no sooner in my heart divin'd,
My heart, which by a secret harmony
Still moves with thine, joined in connection sweet.
Milton—*Paradise Lost.* Bk. X. L. 357.

6
Never elated while one man's oppress'd;
Never dejected while another's blessed.
Pope—*Essay on Man.* Ep. IV. L. 323.

7
Somewhere or other there must surely be
The face not seen, the voice not heard,
The heart that not yet—never yet—ah me!
Made answer to my word.
Christina G. Rossetti—*Somewhere or Other.*

8
If thou art something bring thy soul and interchange with mine.
Schiller—*Votive Tablets. Value and Worth.*

9
It [true love] is the secret sympathy,
The silver link, the silken tie,
Which heart to heart, and mind to mind
In body and in soul can bind.
Scott—*Lay of the Last Minstrel.* Canto V. St. 13.

10
For thou hast given me in this beauteous face,
A world of earthly blessings to my soul,
If sympathy of love unite our thoughts.
Henry VI. Pt. II. Act I. Sc. 1. L. 21.

11
A sympathy in choice.
Midsummer Night's Dream. Act I. Sc. 1. L. 141.

12
A heart at leisure from itself,
To soothe and sympathise.
Anna L. Waring—*Father I know that all my Life.*

T

TAILORS (See also Apparel)

13
'Twas when young Eustace wore his heart in's breeches.
Beaumont and Fletcher—*Elder Brother.* Act V.

14
Thy clothes are all the soul thou hast.
Beaumont and Fletcher—*Honest Man's Fortune.* Act V. Sc. 3. L. 170.

15
May Moorland weavers boast Pindaric skill,
And tailors' lays be longer than their bill!
While punctual beaux reward the grateful notes,
And pay for poems—when they pay for coats.
Byron—*English Bards and Scotch Reviewers.* L. 781.

16
Great is the Tailor, but not the greatest.
Carlyle—*Essays. Goethe's Works.*

17
Sister, look ye,
How, by a new creation of my tailor's
I've shook off old mortality.
John Ford—*The Fancies Chaste and Noble.* Act I. Sc. 3.

18
A tailor, though a man of upright dealing,—
True but for lying,—honest but for stealing,—
Did fall one day extremely sick by chance
And on the sudden was in wondrous trance.
Sir John Harrington—*Of a Precise Tailor.*

19
One commending a Tayler for his dexteritie in his profession, another standing by ratified his opinion, saying tailors had their business at their fingers' ends.
Hazlitt—*Shakespeare Jest Books. Conceits, Clinches, Flashes and Whimzies.* No. 93.

20
'Tis not the robe or garment I affect;
For who would marry with a suit of clothes?
Heywood—*Royal King and Loyal Subject.* Act II. Sc. 2.

21
Yes, if they would thank their maker,
And seek no further; but they have new creators,
God tailor and god mercer.
Massinger—*A Very Woman.* Act III. Sc. 1. L. 161.

22
What a fine man
Hath your tailor made you!
Massinger—*City Madam.* Act I. Sc. 2.

23
As if thou e'er wert angry
But with thy tailor! and yet that poor shred
Can bring more to the making up of a man,
Than can be hoped from thee; thou art his creature;
And did he not, each morning, new create thee,
Thou'dst stink and be forgotten.
Massinger—*Fatal Dowry.* Act III. Sc. 1.

24
Get me some French tailor
To new-create you.
Massinger—*Renegade.* Act III. Sc. 1.

1
King Stephen was a worthy peere,
His breeches cost him but a crowne;
He held them sixpence all too deere,
Therefore he call'd the taylor lowne.
THOMAS PERCY—*Reliques. Take Thy Old Cloak About Thee.* St. 7. Quoted in *Othello.* Act II. Sc. 2.

2
Th' embroider'd suit at least he deem'd his prey;
That suit an unpaid tailor snatch'd away.
POPE—*The Dunciad.* Bk. II. L. 117.

3 Thou villain base,
Know'st me not by my clothes?
No, nor thy tailor, rascal,
Who is thy grandfather: he made those clothes,
Which, as it seems, make thee.
Cymbeline. Act IV. Sc. 2. L. 80.

4
Thou art a strange fellow: a tailor make a man?
Ay, a tailor, sir; a stone-cutter or a painter could not have made him so ill, though he had been but two hours at the trade.
King Lear. Act II. Sc. 2. L. 61.

5
Thy gown? why, ay;—come, tailor, let us see't.
O mercy, God! what masquing stuff is here?
What's this? a sleeve? 'tis like a demi-cannon:
What, up and down, carv'd like an apple-tart?
Here's snip and nip and cut and slish and slash,
Like to a censer in a barber's shop:
Why, what i' devil's name, tailor, call'st thou this!
Taming of the Shrew. Act IV. Sc. 3. L. 86.

6
Il faut neuf tailleurs pour faire un homme.
It takes nine tailors to make a man.
Quoted by COMTE DE LA VILLEMARQUE as a Breton proverb.

7 All his reverend wit
Lies in his wardrobe.
WEBSTER—*White Devil.* Act II. Sc. 1.

TALENT

8
Magni est ingenii revocare mentem a sensibus, et cogitationem a consuetudine abducere.
It is a proof of great talents to recall the mind from the senses, and to separate thought from habit.
CICERO — *Tusculanarum Disputationum.* I. 16.

9
Occultæ musices nullus respectus.
Concealed talent brings no reputation.
ERASMUS—*Adagia.* SUETONIUS—*Nero.* 20.

10
Ne forçons point notre talent;
Nous ne ferions rien avec grâce:
Jamais un lourdaud, quoi qu'il fasse,
Ne saurait passer pour galant.
Let us not overstrain our talents, lest we do nothing gracefully: a clown, whatever he may do, will never pass for a gentleman.
LA FONTAINE—*Fables.* IV. 5.

11
Talent is that which is in a man's power!
Genius is that in whose power a man is.
LOWELL—*Among my Books. Rousseau and the Sentimentalists.*

TALK (See also CONVERSATION, SPEECH)

12
It would talk;
Lord, how it talked!
BEAUMONT AND FLETCHER—*The Scornful Lady.* Act IV. Sc. 1.
(See also LEE)

13
But still his tongue ran on, the less
Of weight it bore, with greater ease.
BUTLER—*Hudibras.* Pt. III. Canto II. L. 443.

14
With vollies of eternal babble.
BUTLER—*Hudibras.* Pt. III. Canto II. L. 453.

15
"The time has come," the Walrus said,
"To talk of many things:
Of shoes—and ships—and sealing-wax—
Of cabbages—and kings—
And why the sea is boiling hot—
And whether pigs have wings.
LEWIS CARROLL—*Through the Looking Glass.* Ch. III.

16
Persuasion tips his tongue whene'er he talks.
COLLEY CIBBER—*Parody on Pope's lines.*

17
Words learn'd by rote a parrot may rehearse,
But talking is not always to converse,
Not more distinct from harmony divine
The constant creaking of a country sign.
COWPER—*Conversation.* L. 7.

18
But far more numerous was the herd of such,
Who think too little, and who talk too much.
DRYDEN—*Absalom and Achitophel.* Pt. I. L. 533.

19
Whose talk is of bullocks.
Ecclesiasticus. XXXVIII. 25.

20
My tongue within my lips I rein;
For who talks much must talk in vain.
GAY—*Introduction to the Fables.* Pt. I. L. 57.

21
Chi parla troppo non può parlar sempre bene.
He who talks much cannot always talk well.
GOLDONI—*Pamela.* I. 6.

22
Stop not, unthinking, every friend you meet
To spin your wordy fabric in the street;
While you are emptying your colloquial pack,
The fiend *Lumbago* jumps upon his back.
HOLMES—*Urania. A Rhymed Lesson.* L. 439.

23
No season now for calm, familiar talk.
HOMER—*Iliad.* Bk. XXII. L. 169. POPE'S trans.

24
Talk to him of Jacob's ladder, and he would ask the number of the steps.
DOUGLAS JERROLD—*A Matter-of-Fact Man.*

1
And the talk slid north, and the talk slid south
With the sliding puffs from the hookah-mouth;
Four things greater than all things are—
Women and Horses and Power and War.
Kipling—*Ballad of the King's Jest.*

2
Then he will talk—good gods, how he will talk!
Nathaniel Lee—*Alexander the Great.* Act I. Sc. 1.
(See also Beaumont)

3
In general those who nothing have to say
Contrive to spend the longest time in doing it.
Lowell—*An Oriental Apologue.* St. 15.

4
Oft has it been my lot to mark
A proud, conceited, talking spark.
James Merrick—*The Chameleon.*

5
His talk was like a stream which runs
With rapid change from rock to roses;
It slipped from politics to puns;
It passed from Mahomet to Moses;
Beginning with the laws that keep
The planets in their radiant courses,
And ending with some precept deep
For dressing eels or shoeing horses.
Praed—*The Vicar.*

6
They never taste who always drink;
They always talk who never think.
Prior—*Upon a Passage in the Scaligerana.*

7
I prythee, take the cork out of thy mouth that I may drink thy tidings.
As You Like It. Act III. Sc. 2. L. 12.

8
If I chance to talk a little wild, forgive me;
I had it from my father.
Henry VIII. Act I. Sc. 4. L. 26.

9
The red wine first must rise
In their fair cheeks, my lord; then we shall have 'em
Talk us to silence.
Henry VIII. Act I. Sc. 4. L. 43.

10
What cracker is this same that deafs our ears
With this abundance of superfluous breath?
King John. Act II. Sc. 1. L. 147.

11 No, pray thee, let it serve for table-talk;
Then, howsoe'er thou speak'st, 'mong other things
I shall digest it.
Merchant of Venice. Act III. Sc. 5. L. 93.

12
Talk with a man out at a window—a proper saying.
Much Ado About Nothing. Act IV. Sc. 1 L. 190.

13
My lord shall never rest:
I'll watch him, tame and talk him out of patience:
His bed shall seem a school, his board a shrift.
Othello. Act III. Sc. 3. L. 22.

14
Talkers are no good doers; be assur'd
We come to use our hands and not our tongues.
Richard III. Act I. Sc. 3. L. 352.

15
A gentleman, nurse, that loves to hear himself talk, and will speak more in a minute than he will stand to in a month.
Romeo and Juliet. Act II. Sc. 4. L. 155.

16
She sits tormenting every guest,
Nor gives her tongue one moment's rest,
In phrases batter'd, stale, and trite,
Which modern ladies call polite.
Swift—*The Journal of a Modern Lady.*

17
Good talkers are only found in Paris.
François Villon—*Des Femmes de Paris.* II.

18
Le secret d'ennuyer est celui de tout dire.
The secret of being tiresome is in telling everything.
Voltaire—*Discours Preliminaire.*

19
Little said is soonest mended.
George Wither—*The Shepherd's Hunting.*

TASTE

20
De gustibus non disputandum.
There is no disputing about taste.
Quoted by Sterne—*Tristram Shandy.* Also by Jeremy Taylor—*Reflections upon Ridicule.* P. 122. (1707)

TAXATION (See Government, Politics)

TEA

21
Matrons, who toss the cup, and see
The grounds of *fate* in *grounds of tea.*
Churchill—*The Ghost.* Bk. I. L. 117.

22
Tea! thou soft, thou sober, sage, and venerable liquid, * * * thou female tongue-running, smile-smoothing, heart-opening, wink-tippling cordial, to whose glorious insipidity I owe the happiest moment of my life, let me fall prostrate.
Colley Cibber—*Lady's Last Stake.* Act I. Sc. 1.

23
Now stir the fire, and close the shutters fast,
Let fall the curtains, wheel the sofa round,
And while the bubbling and loud-hissing urn
Throws up a steamy column, and the cups,
That cheer but not inebriate, wait on each,
So let us welcome peaceful evening in.
Cowper—*Task.* Bk. IV. L. 36.
(See also Berkeley under Temperance)

24
Here, thou, great Anna! whom three realms obey,
Dost sometimes counsel take—and sometimes tea.
Pope—*Rape of the Lock.* Canto III. L. 7.

25
Thank God for tea! What would the world do without tea? how did it exist? I am glad I was not born before tea.
Sydney Smith—*Lady Holland's Memoir.* Vol. I. P. 383.

26
Tea does our fancy aid,
Repress those vapours which the head invade
And keeps that palace of the soul serene.
Edmund Waller—*Of Tea.*

TEACHING (See also EDUCATION)

1
We must not contradict, but instruct him that contradicts us; for a madman is not cured by another running mad also.
ANTISTHENES.

2
What's a' your jargon o' your schools,
Your Latin names for horns and stools;
If honest nature made you fools.
BURNS—*Epistle to J. L.——k.*
(See also COWPER, POMFRET, PRIOR)

3
O ye! who teach the ingenious youth of nations,
Holland, France, England, Germany or Spain,
I pray ye flog them upon all occasions,
It mends their morals, never mind the pain.
BYRON—*Don Juan.* Canto II. St. 1.

4
'Tis pleasing to be school'd in a strange tongue
By female lips and eyes—that is, I mean,
When both the teacher and the taught are young,
As was the case, at least, where I have been;
They smile so when one's right; and when one's wrong
They smile still more.
BYRON—*Don Juan.* Canto II. St. 164.

5
He is wise who can instruct us and assist us in the business of daily virtuous living.
CARLYLE—*Essays. Schiller.*

6
You cannot teach old dogs new tricks.
Quoted by JOS. CHAMBERLAIN, at Greenock, Oct., 1903.

7
Seek to delight, that they may mend mankind.
And, while they captivate, inform the mind.
COWPER—*Hope.* L. 770.

8
The sounding jargon of the schools.
COWPER—*Truth.* L. 367.
(See also BURNS)

9
The twig is so easily bended
I have banished the rule and the rod:
I have taught them the goodness of knowledge,
They have taught me the goodness of God;
My heart is the dungeon of darkness,
Where I shut them for breaking a rule;
My frown is sufficient correction;
My love is the law of the school.
CHARLES M. DICKINSON—*The Children.*

10
There is no teaching until the pupil is brought into the same state or principle in which you are; a transfusion takes place; he is you, and you are he; there is a teaching; and by no unfriendly chance or bad company can he ever quite lose the benefit.
EMERSON—*Essays. Of Spiritual Laws.*

11
Instruction does not prevent waste of time or mistakes; and mistakes themselves are often the best teachers of all.
FROUDE—*Short Studies on Great Subjects. Education.*

12
A boy is better unborn than untaught.
GASCOIGNE.

13
Full well they laughed, wit
At all his jokes, for many a
Full well the busy whisper, cir
Convey'd the dismal tidings when h
GOLDSMITH—*Deserted Village.* L. 20

14
Grave is the Master's look; his forehead wears
Thick rows of wrinkles, prints of worrying cares:
Uneasy lies the heads of all that rule,
His worst of all whose kingdom is a school.
Supreme he sits; before the awful frown
That binds his brows the boldest eye goes down;
Not more submissive Israel heard and saw
At Sinai's foot the Giver of the Law.
HOLMES—*The School Boy.*

15
Doctrina sed vim promovet insitam.
Instruction enlarges the natural powers of the mind.
HORACE—*Carmina.* IV. 4. 33.

16
Fingit equum tenera docilem cervice magister
Ire viam qua monstret eques.
The trainer trains the docile horse to turn, with his sensitive neck, whichever way the rider indicates.
HORACE—*Epistles.* Bk. I. 2. 64. ("Quam" for "qua" in some texts.)

17
If you be a lover of instruction, you will be well instructed.
ISOCRATES—*Ad Dœmonicum.* Inscribed in golden letters over his school, according to ROGER ASCHAM, in his *Schoolmaster.*

18
Speak to the earth, and it shall teach thee.
Job. XII. 8.

19
Whilst that the childe is young, let him be instructed in vertue and lytterature.
LYLY—*Euphues. The Anatomy of Wit. Of the Education of Youth.*

20
Adde, quod ingenuas didicisse fideliter artes
Emollit mores, nec sinit esse fervos.
To be instructed in the arts, softens the manners and makes men gentle.
OVID—*Epistolæ Ex Ponto.* II. 9. 47.

21
Fas est ab hoste doceri.
It is lawful to be taught by an enemy.
OVID—*Metamorphoses.* IV. 428.

22
What's all the noisy jargon of the schools?
POMFRET—*Reason.* L. 57. (1700)
(See also BURNS)

23
Men must be taught as if you taught them not,
And things unknown propos'd as things forgot.
POPE—*Essay on Criticism.* Pt. III. L. 15.

24
To dazzle let the vain design,
To raise the thought and touch the heart, be thine!
POPE—*Moral Essays.* Ep. II. L. 249.

25
All jargon of the schools.
PRIOR—*An Ode on Exodus III. 14. "I am that I am."*
(See also BURNS)

1
When I am forgotten, as I shall be,
And sleep in dull cold marble,
* * * *
Say, I taught thee.
Henry VIII. Act III. Sc. 2. L. 433.

2
We'll set thee to school to an ant, to teach thee there's no labouring i' the winter.
King Lear. Act II. Sc. 4. L. 67.

3
Schoolmasters will I keep within my house,
Fit to instruct her youth. * * *
* * * To cunning men
I will be very kind, and liberal
To mine own children in good bringing up.
Taming of the Shrew. Act I. Sc. 1. L. 94.

4
I do present you with a man of mine,
Cunning in music and the mathematics,
To instruct her fully in those sciences.
Taming of the Shrew. Act II. Sc. 1. L. 55.

5
I am not a teacher: only a fellow-traveller of whom you asked the way. I pointed ahead—ahead of myself as well as of you.
Shaw—*Getting Married*.

6
A little bench of heedless bishops here,
And there a chancellor in embryo.
Shenstone—*The School Mistress*. St. 28.

7
Whoe'er excels in what we prize,
Appears a hero in our eyes;
Each girl, when pleased with what is taught,
Will have the teacher in her thought.
* * * * *
A blockhead with melodious voice,
In boarding-schools may have his choice.
Swift—*Cadenus and Vanessa*. L. 733.

8
Better fed than taught.
John Taylor—*Jack a Lent*.

9
Domi habuit unde disceret.
He need not go away from home for instruction.
Terence—*Adelphi*. III. 3. 60.

10
Delightful task! to rear the tender Thought,
To teach the young Idea how to shoot,
To pour the fresh Instruction o'er the Mind,
To breathe the enlivening Spirit, and to fix
The generous Purpose in the glowing breast.
Thomson—*The Seasons. Spring*. L. 1,150.

TEARS

11
Fons lacrymarum.
Fountains of tears.
Æschylus—*Agamemnon*. 861. *Jeremiah*. IX. 1. Sophocles—*Antigones*. 803.

12
We weep when we are born,
Not when we die!
T. B. Aldrich — *Metempsychosis*. Phrase found in *Les Paroles Remarquables, les Bon Mots et les Maximes Orientaux*. Ed. by Galland. (1694)
(See also King Lear)

13
Dear Lord, though I be changed to senseless clay,
And serve the Potter as he turn his wheel,
I thank Thee for the gracious gift of tears!
T. B. Aldrich—*Two Moods*.

14
Filius istarum lacrymarum.
A child of those tears.
St. Augustine—*Confessions*. Bk. III. 12.
It cannot be, that a child of those tears (of mine) shall perish.
Words of his mother when St. Augustine was influenced by the Manichean Heresy.

15
And friends, dear friends,—when it shall be
That this low breath is gone from me,
And round my bier ye come to weep,
Let One, most loving of you all,
Say, "Not a tear must o'er her fall;
He giveth His beloved sleep."
E. B. Browning—*The Sleep*. St. 9.

16
Thank God for grace,
Ye who weep only! If, as some have done,
Ye grope tear-blinded in a desert place
And touch but tombs,—look up! Those tears will run
Soon in long rivers down the lifted face,
And leave the vision clear for stars and sun.
E. B. Browning—*Tears*.

17
So bright the tear in Beauty's eye,
Love half regrets to kiss it dry.
Byron—*Bride of Abydos*. Canto I. St. 8.

18
Oh! too convincing—dangerously dear—
In woman's eye the unanswerable tear!
That weapon of her weakness she can wield,
To save, subdue—at once her spear and shield.
Byron—*Corsair*. Canto II. St. 15.

19
What gem hath dropp'd, and sparkles o'er his chain?
The tear most sacred, shed for other's pain,
That starts at once—bright pure—from Pity's mine,
Already polish'd by the hand divine!
Byron—*Corsair*. Canto II. St. 15.

20
She was a good deal shock'd; not shock'd at tears,
For women shed and use them at their liking;
But there is something when man's eye appears
Wet, still more disagreeable and striking.
Byron—*Don Juan*. Canto V. St. 118.

21
There is a tear for all who die,
A mourner o'er the humblest grave.
Byron—*Elegiac Stanzas. On the Death of Sir Peter Parker, Bart.*

22
A stoic of the woods,—a man without a tear.
Campbell—*Gertrude of Wyoming*. Pt. I. St. 23.

23
For Beauty's tears are lovelier than her smile.
Campbell—*Pleasures of Hope*. Pt. I. L. 180.

1
We look through gloom and storm-drift
Beyond the years:
The soul would have no rainbow
Had the eyes no tears.
JOHN VANCE CHENEY—*Tears*.

2
Nihil enim lacryma citius arescit.
Nothing dries sooner than a tear.
CICERO—*Ad Herrenium*. II. 31. 50. *De Inventione*. I. 56. (Quoting APOLLONIUS.)

3
Words that weep and tears that speak.
ABRAHAM COWLEY—*The Prophet*. St. 2.

4
And the tear that is wiped with a little address,
May be follow'd perhaps by a smile.
COWPER—*The Rose*.

5
No radiant pearl, which crested Fortune wears,
No gem that twinkling hangs from Beauty's ears,
Not the bright stars which Night's blue arch adorn,
Nor rising suns that gild the vernal morn,
Shine with such lustre as the tear that flows
Down Virtue's manly cheek for others' woes.
ERASMUS DARWIN—*The Botanic Garden*. Pt. II. Canto III. L. 459.

6
What precious drops are those,
Which silently each other's track pursue,
Bright as young diamonds in their infant dew?
DRYDEN—*The Conquest of Grenada*. Pt. II. Act III. Sc. 1.

7
Weep no more, nor sigh, nor groan,
Sorrow calls no time that's gone:
Violets plucked the sweetest rain
Makes not fresh nor grow again.
JOHN FLETCHER—*Queen of Corinth*. Act IV. Sc. 1. Not in original folio. Said to be spurious.

8
The tear forgot as soon as shed,
The sunshine of the breast.
GRAY—*Eton College*. St. 5.

9
Ope the sacred source of sympathetic tears.
GRAY—*Progress of Poesy*. III. 1. L. 12.

10
And weep the more, because I weep in vain.
GRAY—*Sonnet. On the Death of Mr. West*.

11
Never a tear bedims the eye
That time and patience will not dry.
BRET HARTE—*Lost Galleon*.

12
Accept these grateful tears! for thee they flow,
For thee, that ever felt another's woe!
HOMER—*Iliad*. Bk. XIX. L. 319. POPE's trans.

13
My tears must stop, for every drop
Hinders needle and thread.
HOOD—*Song of the Shirt*.

14
Oh! would I were dead now,
Or up in my bed now,
To cover my head now
And have a good cry!
HOOD—*A Table of Errata*.

15
Si vis me flere, dolendum est
Primum ipsi tibi.
If you wish me to weep, you yourself must first feel grief.
HORACE—*Ars Poetica*. V. 102.

16
Hinc illæ lacrymæ.
Hence these tears.
HORACE—*Epistles*. I. 19. 41. TERENCE—*Andria*. I. 1. 99.

17
If the man who turnips cries,
Cry not when his father dies,
'Tis a proof that he had rather
Have a turnip than his father.
SAMUEL JOHNSON. Ridiculing LOPE DE VEGA's lines, "Se acquien los leones vence," etc.

18
On parent knees, a naked new-born child
Weeping thou sat'st while all around thee smiled;
So live, that sinking in thy last long sleep
Calm thou may'st smile, while all around thee weep.
SIR WILLIAM JONES. Taken from *Enchanted Fruit*. *Six Hymns to Hindu Deities*. See sketch prefixed to his *Poetical Works*. (1847) Also in his *Life*. P. 110.
(See also WESLEY)

19
E'en like the passage of an angel's tear
That falls through the clear ether silently.
KEATS—*To One Who Has Been Long in City Pent*.

20
All kin' o' smily round the lips
An' teary roun' the lashes.
LOWELL—*Biglow Papers*. Second Series. *The Courtin'*. St. 21.

21
Tell me, ye wingèd winds
That round my pathway roar,
Know ye not some spot
Where mortals weep no more?
CHARLES MACKAY—*Tell Me Ye Winged Winds*. *The Inquiry*.

22
Without the meed of some melodious tear.
MILTON—*Lycidas*. L. 14.

23
Thrice he assay'd, and, thrice in spite of scorn,
Tears, such as angels weep, burst forth.
MILTON—*Paradise Lost*. Bk. I. L. 619.

24
The glorious Angel, who was keeping
The gates of Light, beheld her weeping;
And, as he nearer drew and listen'd
To her sad song, a tear-drop glisten'd
Within his eyelids, like the spray
From Eden's fountain, where it lies
On the blue flow'r, which—Bramins say—
Blooms nowhere but in Paradise.
MOORE—*Lalla Rookh*. *Paradise and the Peri*.

25
O dear, dear Jeanie Morrison,
The thochts o' bygane years
Still fling their shadows ower my path,
And blind my een wi' tears.
WM. MOTHERWELL—*Jeanie Morrison*.

1
Peter deny'd
His Lord and cry'd.
New England Primer. (1777)

2
If you go over desert and mountain,
Far into the country of Sorrow,
To-day and to-night and to-morrow,
And maybe for months and for years;
You shall come with a heart that is bursting
For trouble and toiling and thirsting,
You shall certainly come to the fountain
At length,—to the Fountain of Tears.
A. W. E. O'Shaughnessy—*The Fountain of Tears.*

3
Interdum lacrymæ pondera vocis habent.
Tears are sometimes as weighty as words.
Ovid—*Epistolæ Ex Ponto.* III. 1. 158.

4
Flere licet certe: flendo diffundimus iram:
Perque sinum lacrimæ, fluminis instar enim.
Truly it is allowed us to weep: by weeping we disperse our wrath; and tears go through the heart, even like a stream.
Ovid—*Heroides.* 8. 61.

5 Est quædam flere voluptas;
Expletur lacrymis egeriturque dolor.
It is some relief to weep; grief is satisfied and carried off by tears.
Ovid—*Tristium.* IV. 3. 37.

6
Behold who ever wept, and in his tears
Was happier far than others in their smiles.
Petrarch—*The Triumph of Eternity!* L. 95. (*Charlemont.*)

7
Sweet tears! the awful language, eloquent
Of infinite affection; far too big
For words.
Pollok—*Course of Time.* Bk. V. L. 633.

8
Sweet drop of pure and pearly light;
In thee the rays of Virtue shine;
More calmly clear, more mildly bright,
Than any gem that gilds the mine.
Samuel Rogers—*On a Tear.*

9
But woe awaits a country, when
She sees the tears of bearded men.
Scott—*Marmion.* Canto V. St. 16.

10
The tear, down childhood's cheek that flows,
Is like the dewdrop on the rose;
When next the summer breeze comes by
And waves the bush, the flower is dry.
Scott—*Rokeby.* Canto IV. St. 11.

11
'Tis the best brine a maiden can season her praise in.
All's Well That Ends Well. Act I. Sc. 1. L. 55.

12
The tears live in an onion that should water this sorrow.
Antony and Cleopatra. Act I. Sc. 2. L. 176.

13 The big round tears
Coursed one another down his innocent nose
In piteous chase.
As You Like It. Act II. Sc. 1. L. 38.

14
I had not so much of man in me,
And all my mother came into my eyes,
And gave me up to tears.
Henry V. Act IV. Sc. 6. L. 30.

15
With sad unhelpful tears; and with dimm'd eyes
Look after him, and cannot do him good.
Henry VI. Pt. II. Act III. Sc. 1. L. 218.

16
I cannot weep; for all my body's moisture
Scarce serves to quench my furnace-burning heart.
Henry VI. Pt. III. Act II. Sc. 1. L. 79.

17 See, see what showers arise,
Blown with the windy tempest of my heart.
Henry VI. Pt. III. Act II. Sc. 5. L. 85.

18 What I should say
My tears gainsay; for every word I speak,
Ye see, I drink the water of mine eyes.
Henry VI. Pt. III. Act V. Sc. 4. L. 73.

19
I am about to weep; but, thinking that
We are a queen, or long have dream'd so, certain
The daughter of a king, my drops of tears
I'll turn to sparks of fire.
Henry VIII. Act II. Sc. 4. L. 70.

20 I did not think to shed a tear
In all my miseries; but thou hast forc'd me,
Out of thy honest truth, to play the woman.
Henry VIII. Act III. Sc. 2. L. 428.

21 He has strangled
His language in his tears.
Henry VIII. Act V. Sc. 1. L. 157.

22
If you have tears, prepare to shed them now.
Julius Cæsar. Act III. Sc. 2. L. 173.

23
When that the poor have cried, Cæsar hath wept:
Ambition should be made of sterner stuff:
Yet Brutus says he was ambitious;
And Brutus is an honourable man.
Julius Cæsar. Act III. Sc. 2. L. 96.

24 There she shook
The holy water from her heavenly eyes,
And clamour moisten'd.
King Lear. Act IV. Sc. 3. L. 31.

25
When we are born we cry that we are come
To this great stage of fools.
King Lear. Act IV. Sc. 6. L. 186. Marston, in his observations on King Lear, quotes this from Dryden's trans. of Lucretius. See Drake—*Memorials of Shakespeare.* 336.
(See also Aldrich)

26 That instant shut
My woeful self up in a mourning house,
Raining the tears of lamentation.
Love's Labour's Lost. Act V. Sc. 2. L. 817

27 My plenteous joys,
Wanton in fullness, seek to hide themselves
In drops of sorrow.
Macbeth. Act I. Sc. 4. L. 33.

1

And he, a marble to her tears, is washed with them, but relents not.

Measure for Measure. Act III. Sc. 1. L. 238.

2

Did he break into tears?
In great measure.
A kind overflow of kindness: there are no faces truer than those that are so washed.

Much Ado About Nothing. Act I. Sc. 1. L. 24.

3

If that the earth could teem with woman's tears,
Each drop she falls would prove a crocodile.

Othello. Act IV. Sc. 1. L. 256.

4 One, whose subdu'd eyes,
Albeit unused to the melting mood,
Drop tears as fast as the Arabian trees
Their medicinal gum.

Othello. Act V. Sc. 2. L. 348.

5

Those eyes of thine from mine have drawn salt tears,
Sham'd their aspect with store of childish drops.

Richard III. Act I. Sc. 2. L. 154.

6

The liquid drops of tears that you have shed
Shall come again, transform'd to orient pearl,
Advantaging their loan with interest
Of ten times double gain of happiness.

Richard III. Act IV. Sc. 4. L. 321.

7

If the boy have not a woman's gift
To rain a shower of commanded tears,
An onion will do well for such a shift.

Taming of the Shrew. *Induction.* Sc. 1. L. 124.

8 Then fresh tears
Stood on her cheeks, as doth the honey-dew
Upon a gather'd lily almost wither'd.

Titus Andronicus. Act III. Sc. 1. L. 111.

9

Eye-offending brine.

Twelfth Night. Act I. Sc. 1. L. 30.

10

Why, man, if the river were dry, I am able to fill it with my tears: if the wind were down, I could drive the boat with my sighs.

Two Gentlemen of Verona. Act II. Sc. 3. L. 57.

11 I so lively acted with my tears
That my poor mistress, moved therewithal,
Wept bitterly.

Two Gentlemen of Verona. Act IV. Sc. 4. L. 174.

12

The silver key of the fountain of tears.

SHELLEY—*Two Fragments to Music.*

13

Heaven is not gone, but we are blind with tears,
Groping our way along the downward slope of Years!

R. H. STODDARD—*Hymn to the Beautiful.* L. 33.

14

Tears, idle tears, I know not what they mean,
Tears from the depths of some divine despair.

TENNYSON—*The Princess.* Canto IV. L. 21.

15

Why wilt thou ever scare me with thy tears,
And make me tremble lest a saying learnt,
In days far-off, on that dark earth, be true?
The gods themselves cannot recall their gifts.

TENNYSON—*Tithonus.* St. 5.

16

Two aged men, that had been foes for life,
Met by a grave, and wept—and in those tears
They washed away the memory of their strife;
Then wept again the loss of all those years.

FREDERICK TENNYSON—*The Golden City.* Pt. I.

17

The big round tears run down his dappled face;
He groans in anguish.

THOMSON—*Seasons.* *Autumn.* L. 454.

18

The tears of the young who go their way, last a day;
But the grief is long of the old who stay.

TROWBRIDGE—*A Home Idyll.* 15.

19

Sunt lacrymæ rerum et mentem mortalia tangunt.

Tears are due to human misery, and human sufferings touch the mind.

VERGIL—*Æneid.* I. 462.

20

Tears are the silent language of grief.

VOLTAIRE—*A Philosophical Dictionary.* *Tears.*

21

When summoned hence to thine eternal sleep,
Oh, may'st thou smile while all around thee weep.

CHARLES WESLEY—*On an Infant.*

(See also JONES)

22

Yet tears to human suffering are due;
And mortal hopes defeated and o'erthrown
Are mourned by man, and not by man alone.

WORDSWORTH—*Laodamia.*

23

Lorenzo! hast thou ever weigh'd a sigh?
Or studied the philosophy of tears?—
* * * * *
Hast thou descended deep into the breast,
And seen their source? If not, descend with me,
And trace these briny riv'lets to their springs.

YOUNG—*Night Thoughts.* Night V. L. 516.

TEMPERANCE (See also DRINKING, INTEMPERANCE)

24

And he that will to bed go sober,
Falls with the leaf still in October.

BEAUMONT AND FLETCHER—*Bloody Brother.* *Song.* Act II. Sc. 2. (From an old "Catch.")

25

Of a nature so mild and benign and proportioned to the human constitution as to warm without heating, to cheer but not inebriate. [Tar Water.]

BISHOP BERKELEY—*Siris.* Par. 217.

(See also COWPER under TEA)

26

Call'd to the temple of impure delight
He that abstains, and he alone, does right.
If a wish wander that way, call it home;
He cannot long be safe whose wishes roam.

COWPER—*Progress of Error.* L. 557.

1
Temp'rate in every place—abroad, at home,
Thence will applause, and hence will profit come;
And health from either—he in time prepares
For sickness, age, and their attendant cares.
CRABBE—*Borough.* Letter XVII. L. 198.

2
Abstinence is whereby a man refraineth from any thyng which he may lawfully take.
ELYOT—*Governour.* Bk. III. Ch. XVI.

3
Drink not the third glass, which thou canst not tame,
When once it is within thee; but before
Mayst rule it, as thou list: and pour the shame,
Which it would pour on thee, upon the floor.
It is most just to throw that on the ground,
Which would throw me there, if I keep the round.
HERBERT—*Temple. The Church Porch. Perirrhanterium.* St. 5.

4
Abstinence is as easy to me as temperance would be difficult.
SAMUEL JOHNSON—HANNAH MORE'S *Johnsoniana.* 467.

5
Of my merit
On that pint you yourself may jedge:
All is, I never drink no sperit,
Nor I haint never signed no pledge.
LOWELL—*Biglow Papers.* First Series. No. VII. St. 9.

6
If all the world
Should in a pet of temp'rance, feed on pulse,
Drink the clear stream, and nothing wear but frieze,
Th' All-giver would be unthank'd, would be unprais'd.
MILTON—*Comus.* L. 720.

7
Impostor; do not charge most innocent Nature,
As if she would her children should be riotous
With her abundance; she, good cateress,
Means her provision only to the good,
That live according to her sober laws,
And holy dictate of spare temperance.
MILTON—*Comus.* L. 762.

8
Well observe
The rule of Not too much, by temperance taught
In what thou eat'st and drink'st.
MILTON—*Paradise Lost.* Bk. XI. L. 531.

9
O madness to think use of strongest wines
And strongest drinks our chief support of health,
When God with these forbidden made choice to rear
His mighty champion, strong above compare,
Whose drink was only from the liquid brook.
MILTON—*Samson Agonistes.* L. 553.

10
Make less thy body hence, and more thy grace;
Leave gormandizing.
Henry IV. Pt. II. Act V. Sc. 5. L. 56.

11
Ask God for temperance; that's the appliance only
Which your disease requires.
Henry VIII. Act I. Sc. 1. L. 124.

TEMPTATION

12
Why comes temptation but for man to meet
And master and make crouch beneath his foot,
And so be pedestaled in triumph?
ROBERT BROWNING—*The Ring and the Book. The Pope.* L. 1,185.

13
What's done we partly may compute,
But know not what's resisted.
BURNS—*Address to Unco Guid.* St. 8.

14
I may not here omit those two main plagues, and common dotages of human kind, wine and women, which have infatuated and besotted myriads of people: they go commonly together.
BURTON—*Anatomy of Melancholy.* Pt. I. Sec. II. Memb. 3. Subsect. XIII.

15
So you tell yourself you are pretty fine clay
To have tricked temptation and turned it away,
But wait, my friend, for a different day;
Wait till you want to want to!
EDMUND VANCE COOKE—*Desire.*

16
The devil tempts us not—'tis we tempt him,
Reckoning his skill with opportunity.
GEORGE ELIOT—*Felix Holt.* Ch. XLVII.

17
Entbehren sollst du! sollst entbehren.
Thou shalt abstain,
Renounce, refrain.
GOETHE—*Faust.* I. 4.

18
Many a dangerous temptation comes to us in fine gay colours, that are but skin-deep.
MATTHEW HENRY—*Commentaries.* Genesis. III.

19
Temptations hurt not, though they have accesse;
Satan o'ercomes none but by willingnesse.
HERRICK—*Hesperides. Temptations.*

20
Blessed is the man that endureth temptation; for when he is tried, he shall receive the crown of life.
James. I. 12.

21
Honest bread is very well—it's the butter that makes the temptation.
DOUGLAS JERROLD—*The Catspaw.*

22
Get thee behind me, Satan.
Matthew. XVI. 23.

23
But Satan now is wiser than of yore,
And tempts by making rich, not making poor.
POPE—*Moral Essays.* Ep. III. L. 351.

24
Bell, book and candle shall not drive me back,
When gold and silver becks me to come on.
King John. Act III. Sc. 3. L. 12.

25
How oft the sight of means to do ill deeds
Makes ill deeds done!
King John. Act IV. Sc. 2. L. 219.

26
Devils soonest tempt, resembling spirits of light.
Love's Labour's Lost. Act IV. Sc. 3. L. 257.

1
I am that way going to temptation,
Where prayers cross.
Measure for Measure. Act II. Sc. 2. L. 158.

2 Most dangerous
Is that temptation that doth goad us on
To sin in loving virtue.
Measure for Measure. Act II. Sc. 2. L. 181.

3
To beguile many and be beguil'd by one.
Othello. Act IV. Sc. 1. L. 98.

4
Know'st thou not any whom corrupting gold
Would tempt unto a close exploit of death?
Richard III. Act IV. Sc. 2. L. 34.

5 Sometimes we are devils to ourselves,
When we will tempt the frailty of our powers,
Presuming on their changeful potency.
Troilus and Cressida. Act IV. Sc. 4. L. 97.

6
Let a man be but in earnest in praying against a temptation as the tempter is in pressing it, and he needs not proceed by a surer measure.
BISHOP SOUTH. Vol. VI. Sermon 10.

7
Could'st thou boast, O child of weakness!
O'er the sons of wrong and strife,
Were their strong temptations planted
In thy path of life?
WHITTIER—*What the Voice Said.*

TEVIOT (RIVER)

8
Sweet Teviot! on thy silver tide
The glaring bale-fires blaze no more;
No longer steel-clad warriors ride
Along thy wild and willow'd shore.
SCOTT—*Lay of the Last Minstrel.* Canto IV. St. 1.

THAMES

9
O, could I flow like thee! and make thy stream
My great example, as it is my theme;
Though deep yet clear, though gentle yet not dull;
Strong without rage, without o'erflowing full.
SIR JOHN DENHAM—*Cooper's Hill.* L. 189. Latin prose with same idea found in a letter of ROGER ASCHAM'S to SIR WILLIAM PETRE. *Epistles.* P. 254. (Ed. 1590)

10
Serene yet strong, majestic yet sedate,
Swift without violence, without terror great.
PRIOR—*Carmen Seculare.* L. 200. Imitation of DENHAM.

11
Slow let us trace the matchless vale of Thames;
Fair winding up to where the Muses haunt
In Twit'nham bowers, and for their Pope implore.
THOMSON—*Seasons. Summer.* L. 1,425.

12
Never did sun more beautifully steep
In his first splendor, valley, rock, or hill;
Ne'er saw I, never felt, a calm so deep!
The river glideth at his own sweet will.
Dear God! the very houses seem asleep;
And all that mighty heart is lying still!
WORDSWORTH—*Sonnet. Composed upon Westminster Bridge.*

THANKFULNESS

13
Thank you for nothing.
CERVANTES—*Don Quixote.* Pt. I. Bk. III. Ch. VIII.

14
When I'm not thank'd at all, I'm thank'd enough,
I've done my duty, and I've done no more.
HENRY FIELDING—*The Life and Death of Tom Thumb the Great.* Act I. Sc. 3.

15
I am glad that he thanks God for anything.
SAMUEL JOHNSON—*Boswell's Life of Johnson.* (1775)

16
To receive honestly is the best thanks for a good thing.
GEORGE MACDONALD—*Mary Marston.* Ch. V.

17
Your bounty is beyond my speaking;
But though my mouth be dumb, my heart shall thank you.
NICHOLAS ROWE—*Jane Shore.* Act II. Sc. 1.

18
Thou thought'st to help me; and such thanks I give
As one near death to those that wish him live.
All's Well That Ends Well. Act II. Sc. 1. L. 133.

19
Let never day nor night unhallow'd pass,
But still remember what the Lord hath done.
Henry VI. Pt. II. Act II. Sc. 1. L. 85.

20
How sharper than a serpent's tooth it is
To have a thankless child.
King Lear. Act I. Sc. 4. L. 310.

21
From too much love of living,
From hope and fear set free,
We thank with brief thanksgiving
Whatever gods may be,
That no life lives forever,
That dead men rise up never;
That even the weariest river
Winds somewhere safe to sea.
SWINBURNE—*The Garden of Proserpine.* St. 11.

THANKSGIVING DAY

22
Thanksgiving-day, I fear,
If one the solemn truth must touch,
Is celebrated, not so much
To thank the Lord for blessings o'er,
As for the sake of getting more!
WILL CARLETON—*Captain Young's Thanksgiving.*

23
And taught by thee the Church prolongs
Her hymns of high thanksgiving still.
KEBLE—*The Christian Year. St. Luke the Evangelist.* St. 18.

24
Great as the preparations were for the dinner, everything was so contrived that not a soul in the house should be kept from the morning service of Thanksgiving in the church.
H. B. STOWE—*Oldtown Folks.* P. 345.

1
Ah! on Thanksgiving day, when from East and from West,
From North and South, come the pilgrim and guest,
When the gray-haired New Englander sees round his board
The old broken links of affection restored,
When the care-wearied man seeks his mother once more,
And the worn matron smiles where the girl smiled before.
What moistens the lips and what brightens the eye?
What calls back the past, like the rich pumpkin pie?
WHITTIER—*The Pumpkin.*

2
And let these altars, wreathed with flowers
And piled with fruits, awake again
Thanksgivings for the golden hours,
The early and the latter rain!
WHITTIER—*For an Autumn Festival.*

THEOLOGY (See CHURCH, DOCTRINE, RELIGION)

THIEVING

3
Who steals a bugle-horn, a ring, a steed,
Or such like worthless thing, has some discretion;
'Tis petty larceny: not such his deed
Who robs us of our fame, our best possession.
BERNI—*Orlando Innamorata.* Canto LV.
(See also OTHELLO under NAME)

4
To keep my hands from picking and stealing.
Book of Common Prayer—Catechism.

5
—To live
On means not yours—be brave in silks and laces,
Gallant in steeds; splendid in banquets; all
Not yours. Given, uninherited, unpaid for;
This is to be a trickster; and to filch
Men's art and labour, which to them is wealth,
Life, daily bread;—quitting all scores with "friend,
You're troublesome!" Why this, forgive me,
Is what, when done with a less dainty grace,
Plain folks call "Theft."
BULWER-LYTTON—*Richelieu.* Act I. Sc. 2.

6
No Indian prince has to his palace
More followers than a thief to the gallows.
BUTLER—*Hudibras.* Pt. II. Canto I. L. 273.

7
Kill a man's family, and he may brook it,
But keep your hands out of his breeches' pocket.
BYRON—*Don Juan.* Canto X. St. 79.
(See also MACHIAVELLI under LOSS)

8
'Tis bad enough in man or woman
To steal a goose from off a common;
But surely he's without excuse
Who steals a common from the goose.
Epigram in CAREY'S *Commonplace Book of Epigrams.* (1872) Different versions of the same were prompted by the Enclosure Acts. One version given in *Sabrinæ Corolla* was written when CHARLES PRATT, first Earl of Camden, took a common strip of land in front of Camden House. Oct. 7, 1764.

9
Stolen sweets are best.
COLLEY CIBBER—*Rival Fools.* Act I.
(See also PROVERBS, RANDOLPH)

10
The Friar preached against stealing, and had a goose in his sleeve.
HERBERT—*Jacula Prudentum.*

11
In vain we call old notions fudge
And bend our conscience to our dealing.
The Ten Commandments will not budge
And stealing will continue stealing.
Motto of American Copyright League. Written Nov. 20, 1885.

12
Stolen waters are sweet, and bread eaten in secret is pleasant.
Proverbs. IX. 17.
(See also CIBBER)

13
Stolen sweets are always sweeter:
Stolen kisses much completer;
Stolen looks are nice in chapels:
Stolen, stolen be your apples.
THOMAS RANDOLPH—*Song of Fairies.*
(See also CIBBER)

14
Thou hast stolen both mine office and my name;
The one ne'er got me credit, the other mickle blame.
Comedy of Errors. Act III. Sc. 1. L. 44.

15
A cutpurse of the empire and the rule,
That from a shelf the precious diadem stole,
And put it in his pocket!
Hamlet. Act III. Sc. 4. L. 99.

16
A plague upon it when thieves cannot be true one to another!
Henry IV. Pt. I. Act II. Sc. 2. L. 29.

17
Let me tell you, Cassius, you yourself
Are much condemn'd to have an itching palm.
Julius Cæsar. Act IV. Sc. 3. L. 9.

18
The robb'd that smiles steals something from the thief:
He robs himself that spends a bootless grief.
Othello. Act I. Sc. 3. L. 208.

19
He that is robb'd, not wanting what is stol'n,
Let him not know't, and he's not robb'd at all.
Othello. Act III. Sc. 3. L. 342.

20
In limited professions there's boundless theft.
Timon of Athens. Act IV. Sc. 3. L. 430.

21
The sun's a thief, and with his great attraction
Robs the vast sea; the moon's an arrant thief,
And her pale fire she snatches from the sun:
The sea's a thief, whose liquid surge resolves
The moon into salt tears: the earth's a thief,
That feeds and breeds by a composture stolen
From general excrement: each thing's a thief;
The laws, your curb and whip, in their rough power
Have uncheck'd theft.
Timon of Athens. Act IV. Sc. 3. L. 439.

1
Well, well, be it so, thou strongest thief of all,
For thou hast stolen my will, and made it thine.
TENNYSON—*The Foresters*. Act III. Sc. 1.

THISTLE

Cnicus

2
Up wi' the flowers o' Scotland,
The emblems o' the free,
Their guardians for a thousand years,
Their guardians still we'll be.
A foe had better brave the de'il
Within his reeky cell,
Than our thistle's purple bonnet,
Or bonny heather bell.
HOGG—*The Flowers of Scotland*.

3
When on the breath of Autumn's breeze,
From pastures dry and brown,
Goes floating, like an idle thought,
The fair, white thistle-down;
O, then what joy to walk at will,
Upon the golden harvest-hill!
MARY HOWITT—*Corn-Fields*.

THORN

Cratægus

4
Beneath the milk-white thorn that scents the evening gale.
BURNS—*The Cotter's Saturday Night*. St. 9.

5
There is a Thorn,—it looks so old,
In truth, you'd find it hard to say
How it could ever have been young,
It looks so old and gray.
Not higher than a two years child
It stands erect, this aged Thorn;
No leaves it has, no prickly points;
It is a mass of knotted joints,
A wretched thing forlorn.
It stands erect, and like a stone
With lichens is it overgrown.
WORDSWORTH—*The Thorn*.

THOUGHT

6
Upon the cunning loom of thought
We weave our fancies, so and so.
T. B. ALDRICH—*Cloth of Gold. Prelude*.

7
Sempre il miglior non è il parer primiero.
First thoughts are not always the best.
ALFIERI—*Don Garzia*. III. 1.
(See also DRYDEN)

8
The kings of modern thought are dumb.
MATTHEW ARNOLD—*Stanzas from the Grande Chartreuse*.

9
Great thoughts, like great deeds, need
No trumpet.
BAILEY—*Festus*. Sc. *Home*.

10
I'll put that in my considering cap.
BEAUMONT AND FLETCHER—*Loyal Subject*. Act II. Sc. 1.

11
Qui sait si l'on ne verra pas que le phosphore et l'esprit vont ensemble?
Who knows whether it is not true that phosphorus and mind are not the same thing?
HENRI BEYLE (STENDHAL)—*Histoire de la Peinture en Italie*. Ch. XCI. P. 209. (Ed. 1854)
(See also MOLESCHOTT)

12
Sow a thought and reap an act.
Quoted by G. D. BOARDMAN.
(See also HALL under HABIT)

13
Thought is valuable in proportion as it is generative.
BULWER-LYTTON—*Caxtoniana*. Essay XIV.

14
The first thought is often the best.
BISHOP BUTLER—*Sermon on the Character of Balaam. Seventh Sermon*.
(See also DRYDEN)

15
What exile from himself can flee?
To zones, though more and more remote,
Still, still pursues, where'er I be,
The blight of life—the demon Thought.
BYRON—*Childe Harold. To Inez*. Canto I. St. 84. L. 6.

16
I stood
Among them, but not of them: in a shroud
Of thoughts which were not their thoughts.
BYRON—*Childe Harold*. Canto III. St. 113.

17
Whatsoe'er thy birth,
Thou wert a beautiful thought and softly bodied forth.
BYRON—*Childe Harold*. Canto IV. St. 115.

18
The power of Thought,—the magic of the Mind!
BYRON—*Corsair*. Canto I. St. 8.

19
Nay, in every epoch of the world, the great event, parent of all others, is it not the arrival of a Thinker in the world?
CARLYLE—*Heroes and Hero Worship*. Lecture I.

20
Thought once awakened does not again slumber.
CARLYLE—*Heroes and Hero Worship*. Lecture I.

21
My thoughts ran a wool-gathering.
CERVANTES—*Don Quixote*. Pt. II. Ch. LVII.

22
With curious art the brain, too finely wrought,
Preys on herself, and is destroyed by thought.
CHURCHILL—*Epistle to Wm. Hogarth*. L. 645.

23
Cujusvis hominis est errare; nullius, nisi insipientis, in errore perseverare. Posteriores enim cogitationes (ut aiunt) sapientiores solent esse.
Any man may make a mistake; none but a fool will stick to it. Second thoughts are best as the proverb says.
CICERO—*Philippicæ*. XII. 2.
(See also DRYDEN)

24
Old things need not be therefore true,
O brother men, nor yet the new;

Ah! still awhile the old thought retain,
And yet consider it again!
ARTHUR HUGH CLOUGH—*Ah, yet Consider it Again.*

1
Perhaps 'tis pretty to force together
Thoughts so all unlike each other;
To mutter and mock a broken charm,
To dally with wrong that does no harm.
COLERIDGE—*Christabel.* Conclusion to Part II.

2
In indolent vacuity of thought.
COWPER—*Task.* Bk. IV. *The Winter Evening.* L. 297.

3
Je pense, donc je suis.
I think, therefore I am.
DESCARTES—*Principes de la Philosophie.* I. Sec. VII. Cogito, ergo sum. (Latin of same.) Vivere est cogitare. CICERO.

4
He trudg'd along, unknowing what he sought,
And whistled as he went, for want of thought.
DRYDEN—*Cymon and Iphigenia.* L. 84.
(See also BLAIR under COURAGE)

5
Second thoughts, they say, are best.
DRYDEN—*The Spanish Friar.* Act II. Sc. 2.
EURIPIDES—*Hippolytus.* 438.
(See also ALFIERI, BUTLER, CICERO, HENRY, SHENSTONE, also AMES under POLITICS)

6
For thoughts are so great—aren't they, sir?
They seem to lie upon us like a deep flood.
GEORGE ELIOT—*Adam Bede.* Ch. VIII.

7
Our growing thought
Makes growing revelation.
GEORGE ELIOT—*Spanish Gypsy.* Bk. II.

8
The revelation of thought takes men out of servitude into freedom.
EMERSON—*Conduct of Life. Fate.*

9
Every thought which genius and piety throw into the world, alters the world.
EMERSON—*Essays. Of Politics.*

10
Great men are they who see that spiritual is stronger than any material force, that thoughts rule the world.
EMERSON—*Letters and Social Aims. Progress of Culture.*

11
Wer kann was Dummes, wer was Kluges denken,
Das nicht die Vorwelt schon gedacht.
Who can think wise or stupid things at all that were not thought already in the past.
GOETHE—*Faust.* II. 2. 1.

12
Those who think must govern those that toil.
GOLDSMITH—*The Traveller.* L. 372.

13
Thoughts that breathe and words that burn.
GRAY—*Progress of Poesy.* III. 3. L. 4.
(See also COWPER under WORDS)

14
Their own second and sober thoughts.
MATTHEW HENRY—*Exposition.* Job VI. 29.
(See also DRYDEN)

15
A thought is often original, though you have uttered it a hundred times.
HOLMES—*The Autocrat of the Breakfast Table.* I.

16
Why can't somebody give us a list of things that everybody thinks and nobody says, and another list of things that everybody says and nobody thinks?
HOLMES—*Professor at the Breakfast Table.*

17
Every man who speaks out loud and clear is tinting the "Zeitgeist." Every man who expresses what he honestly thinks is true is changing the Spirit of the Times. Thinkers help other people to think, for they formulate what others are thinking. No person writes or thinks alone —thought is in the air, but its expresson is necessary to create a tangible Spirit of the Times.
ELBERT HUBBARD—*Pig-Pen Pete. The Bee.*

18
That fellow seems to me to possess but one idea, and that is a wrong one.
SAMUEL JOHNSON. BOSWELL'S *Life of Johnson.* (1770)

19
My thoughts and I were of another world.
BEN JONSON—*Every Man Out of His Humour.* Act III. Sc. 3.

20
Sudden a thought came like a full-blown rose,
Flushing his brow.
KEATS—*The Eve of St. Agnes.* St. 16.

21
The thoughts that come often unsought, and, as it were, drop into the mind, are commonly the most valuable of any we have, and therefore should be secured, because they seldom return again.
LOCKE—*Letter to Mr. Sam'l Bold,* May 16, 1699.

22
A thought often makes us hotter than a fire.
LONGFELLOW—*Drift-Wood. Table-Talk.*

23
The surest pledge of a deathless name
Is the silent homage of thoughts unspoken.
LONGFELLOW—*Herons of Elmwood.* St. 9.

24
My own thoughts
Are my companions.
LONGFELLOW—*Masque of Pandora.* Pt. III. *Tower of Prometheus on Mount Caucasus.*

25
Thoughts so sudden, that they seem
The revelations of a dream.
LONGFELLOW—*Prelude to Tales of a Wayside Inn.* Pt. I. L. 233.

26
All thoughts that mould the age begin
Deep down within the primitive soul.
LOWELL—*An Incident in a Railroad Car.*

27
A penny for your thought.
LYLY—*Euphues.* SWIFT—*Polite Conversation. Introduction.*

28
Annihilating all that's made
To a green thought in a green shade.
ANDREW MARVELL—*The Garden.* Translated.

1
Grand Thoughts that never can be wearied out,
Showing the unreality of Time.
RICHARD MONCKTON MILNES (Lord Houghton)—*Sonnet To Charles Lamb.*

2 Thoughts that voluntary move
Harmonious numbers.
MILTON—*Paradise Lost.* Bk. III. L. 37.

3
Ohne Phosphor kein Gedanke.
No thought without phosphorus.
JACOB MOLESCHOTT—*Lehre der Nahrungsmittel.* II. 1. 4.
(See also BEYLE)

4
His thoughts have a high aim, though their dwelling be in the vale of a humble heart.
MONTAIGNE.
(See also WEBSTER)

5
It is often said that second thoughts are best. So they are in matters of judgment, but not in matters of conscience. In matters of duty, first thoughts are commonly best. They have more in them of the voice of God.
CARDINAL NEWMAN.
(See also TAYLOR)

6
Man is but a reed, the weakest in nature, but he is a thinking reed.
BLAISE PASCAL—*Thoughts.* Ch. II. 10.

7 Thought can wing its way
Swifter than lightning-flashes or the beam
That hastens on the pinions of the morn.
PERCIVAL—*Sonnet.*

8
As he thinketh in his heart, so is he.
Proverbs. XXIII. 7.

9
Gaily I lived as ease and nature taught,
And spent my little life without a thought,
And am amazed that Death, that tyrant grim,
Should think of me, who never thought of him.
ABBÉ REGNIER.

10
Sweetest mother, I can weave no more to-day,
For thoughts of him come thronging,
Him for whom my heart is longing—
For I know not where my weary fingers stray.
SAPPHO — *Fragment.* J. S. EASBY-SMITH'S trans.

11
At Learning's fountain it is sweet to drink,
But 'tis a nobler privilege to think.
J. G. SAXE—*The Library.*

12
Es lebt ein anders denkendes Geschlecht!
There lives a race which otherwise does think.
SCHILLER—*Wilhelm Tell.* II. 1. 206.

13
Still are the thoughts to memory dear.
SCOTT—*Rokeby.* Canto I. St. 33.

14
Ah! comme vous dites, il faut glisser sur bien des pensées, et ne faire pas semblant de les voir.
Ah! as you say, we should slip over many thoughts and act as though we did not perceive them.
MME. DE SÉVIGNÉ—*Lettres.* 70.

15 But now behold,
In the quick forge and working-house of thought,
How London doth pour out her citizens!
Henry V. Act V. *Prologue.* L. 22.

16
My thoughts are whirled like a potter's wheel.
Henry VI. Pt. I. Act I. Sc. 5. L. 19.

17
A maiden hath no tongue but thought.
Merchant of Venice. Act III. Sc. 2. L. 8.

18
Men's first thoughts in this matter are generally better than their second; their natural notions better than those refin'd by study, or consultation with casuists.
EARL OF SHAFTESBURY—*Characteristics. Essay on The Freedom of Wit and Humour.* Sect. I.
(See also DRYDEN, SHENSTONE)

19
Strange thoughts beget strange deeds.
SHELLEY—*The Cenci.* Act IV. Sc. 4.

20
A thought by thought is piled, till some great truth
Is loosened, and the nations echo round,
Shaken to their roots, as do the mountains now.
SHELLEY—*Prometheus Unbound.* Act II. Sc. 3.

21 Come near me! I do weave
A chain I cannot break—I am possest
With thoughts too swift and strong for one lone human breast.
SHELLEY—*Revolt of Islam.* Canto IX. St. 33.

22
Second thoughts oftentimes are the very worst of all thoughts.
SHENSTONE—*Detached Thoughts on Men and Manners.*
(See also DRYDEN)

23
They are never alone that are accompanied with noble thoughts.
SIR PHILIP SIDNEY—*The Arcadia.* Bk. I.

24
If I could think how these my thoughts to leave,
Or thinking still, my thoughts might have good end:
If rebel sense would reason's law receive;
Or reason foil'd would not in vain contend:
Then might I think what thoughts were best to think:
Then might I wisely swim, or gladly sink.
SIR PHILIP SIDNEY—*Sonnet.*

25
Oh, the fetterless mind! how it wandereth free
Through the wildering maze of Eternity!
HENRY SMITH—*Thought.*

26
Thinking is but an idle waste of thought,
And naught is everything, and everything is naught.
HORACE AND JAMES SMITH—*Rejected Addresses. Cui Bono?* (Imitation of BYRON.)

27
Thought can never be compared with action, but when it awakens in us the image of truth.
MADAME DE STAËL—*Germany.* Pt. I. Ch. VIII.

1
Time to me this truth has taught,
('Tis a treasure worth revealing)
More offend from want of thought
Than from any want of feeling.
CHARLES SWAIN—*Want of Thought.*

2
What a man *thinks* in his spirit in the world, that he *does* after his departure from the world when he becomes a spirit.
SWEDENBORG—*Divine Providence.* 101.

3
Though man a thinking being is defined,
Few use the grand prerogative of mind.
How few think justly of the thinking few!
How many never think, who think they do.
JANE TAYLOR—*Essays in Rhyme. On Morals and Manners. Prejudice.* Essay I. St. 45.

4
In matters of conscience that is the best sense which every wise man takes in before he hath sullied his understanding with the designs of sophisters and interested persons.
JEREMY TAYLOR—*Ductor Dubitantium* (*Rule of Conscience*) Bk. I. Ch. I. Rule VI. (1660)
(See also SHAFTESBURY)

5
And Thought leapt out to wed with Thought,
Ere Thought could wed itself with Speech.
TENNYSON—*In Memoriam.* Pt. XXIII. St. 4.

6
Large elements in order brought,
And tracts of calm from tempest made,
And world-wide fluctuation sway'd,
In vassal tides that follow'd thought.
TENNYSON—*In Memoriam.* CXII. St. 4.

7
Yet I doubt not thro' the ages one increasing purpose runs,
And the thoughts of men are widened with the process of the suns.
TENNYSON—*Locksley Hall.* St. 69.

8
And yet, as angels in some brighter dreams
Call to the soul when man doth sleep,
So some strange thoughts transcend our wonted themes,
And into glory peep.
HENRY VAUGHAN—*They are all gone into the World of Light.* St. 7.

9
Lorsqu'une pensée est trop faible pour porter une expression simple, c'est la marque pour la rejeter.
When a thought is too weak to be expressed simply, it is a proof that it should be rejected.
VAUVENARGUES—*Reflexions.* III.

10
Les grandés pensées viennent du cœur.
Great thoughts come from the heart.
VAUVENARGUES—*Reflexions.* CXXVII.

11
His high-erected thoughts look'd down upon
The smiling valley of his fruitful heart.
DANIEL WEBSTER—*A Monumental Column.*
(See also MONTAIGNE)

12
But hushed be every thought that springs
From out the bitterness of things.
WORDSWORTH—*Elegiac Stanzas. Addressed to Sir G. H. B.*

13
Yet, sometimes, when the secret cup
Of still and serious thought went round,
It seemed as if he drank it up,
He felt with spirit so profound.
WORDSWORTH—*Matthew.*

14
Like thoughts whose very sweetness yieldeth proof
That they were born for immortality.
WORDSWORTH—*Sonnet. On King's College Chapel, Cambridge.*

15
Knocks at our hearts, and finds our thoughts at home.
YOUNG—*Love of Fame.* Satire I. L. 99.

THRUSH

16
Across the noisy street
I hear him careless throw
One warning utterance sweet;
Then faint at first, and low,
The full notes closer grow;
Hark, what a torrent gush!
They pour, they overflow—
Sing on, sing on, O thrush!
AUSTIN DOBSON—*Ballad of the Thrush.*

17
O thrush, your song is passing sweet,
But never a song that you have sung
Is half so sweet as thrushes sang
When my dear love and I were young.
WM. MORRIS—*Other Days.*

18
In the gloamin' o' the wood
The throssil whusslit sweet.
WM. MOTHERWELL—*Jeanie Morrison.*

19
I said to the brown, brown thrush:
"Hush—hush!
Through the wood's full strains I hear
Thy monotone deep and clear,
Like a sound amid sounds most fine."
D. M. MULOCK—*A Rhyme About Birds.*

20
The throstle with his note so true,
The wren with little quill.
Midsummer Night's Dream. Act III. Sc. 1. L. 130.

21
Sing, sweet thrushes, forth and sing!
Meet the moon upon the lea;
Are the emeralds of the spring
On the angler's trysting-tree?
Tell, sweet thrushes, tell to me,
Are there buds on our willow-tree?
Buds and birds on our trysting-tree?
THOMAS TOD STODDART—*The Angler's Trysting-Tree.*

22
Hush!
With sudden gush
As from a fountain sings in yonder bush
The Hermit Thrush.
JOHN BANNISTER TABB—*Overflow.*

23
When rosy plumelets tuft the larch,
And rarely pipes the mounted thrush.
TENNYSON—*In Memoriam.* Pt. XCI.

1
At the corner of Wood Street, when daylight appears,
Hangs a thrush that sings loud, it has sung for three years.
WORDSWORTH—*Reverie of Poor Susan.*

2
And hark! how blithe the throstle sings!
He, too, is no mean preacher:
Come forth into the light of things,
Let Nature be your teacher.
WORDSWORTH—*The Tables Turned.*

THUNDER (See also STORM)

3
The sky is changed!—and such a change! O night,
And storm, and darkness, ye are wondrous strong,
Yet lovely in your strength, as is the light
Of a dark eye in woman! Far along,
From peak to peak the rattling crags among
Leaps the live thunder!
BYRON—*Childe Harold.* Canto III. St. 92

4
Hark, hark! Deep sounds, and deeper still,
Are howling from the mountain's bosom:
There's not a breath of wind upon the hill,
Yet quivers every leaf, and drops each blossom:
Earth groans as if beneath a heavy load.
BYRON—*Heaven and Earth.* Pt. I. Sc. 3.

5
Loud roared the dreadful thunder,
The rain a deluge showers.
ANDREW CHERRY—*Bay of Biscay.*

6
Thy thunder, conscious of the new command,
Rumbles reluctant o'er our fallen house.
KEATS—*Hyperion.* L. 60.

7
As a storm-cloud lurid with lightning
And a cry of lamentation,
Repeated and again repeated,
Deep and loud
As the reverberation
Of cloud answering unto cloud,
Swells and rose away in the distance,
As if the sheeted
Lightning retreated,
Baffled and thwarted by the wind's resistance.
LONGFELLOW—*Christus. The Golden Legend. Epilogue.* L. 62.

8
The thunder,
Wing'd with red lightning and impetuous rage,
Perhaps hath spent his shafts, and ceases now
To bellow through the vast and boundless deep.
MILTON—*Paradise Lost.* Bk. I. L. 174.

9
To stand against the deep, dread-bolted thunder?
In the most terrible and nimble stroke
Of quick, cross lightning?
King Lear. Act IV. Sc. 7. L. 33.

10
Are there no stones in heaven
But what serve for the thunder?
Othello. Act V. Sc. 2. L. 234.

11
The thunder,
That deep and dreadful organ-pipe, pronounc'd
The name of Prosper; it did bass my trespass.
Tempest. Act III. Sc. 3. L. 97.

12
C'est l'éclair qui paraît, la foudre va partir.
It is the flash which appears, the thunderbolt will follow.
VOLTAIRE—*Oreste.* II. 7.

THYME

Thymus

13
I know a bank where the wild thyme blows.
Midsummer Night's Dream. Act II. Sc. 1. L. 249.

TIBER (See also ROME)

14
Thou hast fair forms that move
With queenly tread;
Thou hast proud fanes above
Thy mighty dead.
Yet wears thy Tiber's shore
A mournful mien:—
Rome, Rome, thou art no more
As thou hast been.
FELICIA D. HEMANS—*Roman Girl's Song.*

15
Those graceful groves that shade the plain,
Where Tiber rolls majestic to the main,
And flattens, as he runs, the fair campagne.
OVID—*Metamorphoses.* Bk. XIV. *Æneas Arrives in Italy.* L. 8. SIR SAM'L GARTH'S trans.

16
Draw them to Tiber banks, and weep your tears
Into the channel, till the lowest stream
Do kiss the most exalted shores of all.
Julius Cæsar. Act I. Sc. 1. L. 63.

TIDES

17
All night the thirsty beach has listening lain
With patience dumb,
Counting the slow, sad moments of her pain;
Now morn has come,
And with the morn the punctual tide again.
SUSAN COOLIDGE—*Flood-Tide.*

18
The punctual tide draws up the bay,
With ripple of wave and hiss of spray.
SUSAN COOLIDGE—*On the Shore.*

19
The western tide crept up along the sand,
And o'er and o'er the sand,
And round and round the sand,
As far as eye could see
The rolling mist came down and hid the land:
And never home came she.
CHARLES KINGSLEY—*The Sands o' Dee.* St. 2.

20
I saw the long line of the vacant shore,
The sea-weed and the shells upon the sand,
And the brown rocks left bare on every hand,
As if the ebbing tide would flow no more.
LONGFELLOW—*The Tides.*

21
The tide rises, the tide falls,
The twilight darkens, the curlew calls;
* * * * * *
The little waves, with their soft, white hands,
Efface the footprints in the sands,
And the tide rises, the tide falls.
LONGFELLOW—*The Tide Rises, the Tide Falls.*

1
Tide flowing is feared, for many a thing,
Great danger to such as be sick, it doth bring;
Sea ebb, by long ebbing, some respite doth give,
And sendeth good comfort, to such as shall live.
TUSSER—*Five Hundred Points of Good Husbandrie*. Ch. XIV. St. 5.
(See also DICKENS under DEATH)

TIGER

2
Tiger, tiger, burning bright
In the forests of the night,
What immortal hand or eye,
Could frame thy fearful symmetry?
WILLIAM BLAKE—*The Tiger*.

TIME

3
Six years—six little years—six drops of time.
MATTHEW ARNOLD—*Mycerinus*. St. 11.

4
Modo, et modo, non habebent modum.
By-and-by has no end.
ST. AUGUSTINE—*Confessions*. Bk. VIII. 5. 12.

5
Backward, flow backward, O full tide of years!
I am so weary of toil and of tears,
Toil without recompense—tears all in vain,
Take them and give me my childhood again.
I have grown weary of dust and decay,
Weary of flinging my heart's wealth away—
Weary of sowing for others to reap;
Rock me to sleep, mother, rock me to sleep.
ELIZABETH AKERS ALLEN—*Rock me to Sleep, Mother*. Claimed for A. M. W. BALL. See *Northern Monthly*. Vol. II. 1860. Pub. by ALLEN L. BASSETT, Newark, N.J. Appendix to March, Vol. II. 1868. Ball shows proof that he wrote it in 1856–7. Produces witness who saw it before 1860. Mrs. Allen says she wrote it in Italy, 1860. It was published in *The Knickerbocker Mag.*, May, 1861.

6
Backward, turn backward, O Time in your flight;
Make me a child again just for tonight.
Mother, come back from the echoeless shore,
Take me again to your heart as of yore.
ELIZABETH AKERS ALLEN—*Rock me to Sleep, Mother*.

7
Why slander we the times?
What crimes
Have days and years, that we
Thus charge them with iniquity?
If we would rightly scan,
It's not the times are bad, but man.
DR. J. BEAUMONT—*Original Poems*.

8
Wherever anything lives, there is, open somewhere, a register in which time is being inscribed.
HENRI BERGSON—*Creative Evolution*. Ch. I.

9
Le temps fuit, et nous traîne avec soi:
Le moment où je parle est déjà loin de moi.
Time flies and draws us with it. The moment in which I am speaking is already far from me.
BOILEAU—*Épîtres*. III. 47.

10
What's not destroyed by Time's devouring hand?
BRAMSTON—*Art of Politicks*.

11
Think not thy time short in this world, since the world itself is not long. The created world is but a small parenthesis in eternity, and a short interposition, for a time, between such a state of duration as was before it and may be after it.
SIR THOMAS BROWNE—*Christian Morals*. Pt. III. XXIX.

12
Time was made for slaves.
JOHN B. BUCKSTONE—*Billy Taylor*.
(See also EMERSON)

13
Time is money.
BULWER-LYTTON—*Money*. Act III. Sc. 3.

14
Behind, he hears Time's iron gates close faintly,
He is now far from them;
For he has reached the city of the saintly,
The New Jerusalem.
REV. JAMES D. BURNS—*Poem of a Death Believer*. In the *Vision of Prophecy*.

15
Some wee short hour ayont the twal.
BURNS—*Death and Dr. Hornbook*.

16
Nae man can tether time or tide.
BURNS—*Tam o' Shanter*.

17
How slowly time creeps till my Phœbe returns!
While amidst the soft zephyr's cool breezes I burn.
Methinks if I knew whereabouts he would tread,
I could breathe on his wings and 'twould melt down the lead.
Fly swifter, ye minutes, bring hither my dear,
And rest so much longer for 't when she is here.
JOHN BYROM—*A Pastoral*.

18
The good old times—all times when old are good—
Are gone.
BYRON—*Age of Bronze*.
(See also ECCLESIASTES)

19
Yet Time, who changes all, had altered him
In soul and aspect as in age; years steal
Fire from the mind as vigour from the limb;
And life's enchanted cup but sparkles near the brim.
BYRON—*Childe Harold*. Canto III. St. 8.

20
When Youth and Pleasure meet
To chase the glowing Hours with flying feet.
BYRON—*Childe Harold*. Canto III. St. 22.

21
O Time! the beautifier of the dead,
Adorner of the ruin, comforter
And only healer when the heart hath bled—
Time! the corrector where our judgments err,
The test of truth, love, sole philosopher,
For all besides are sophists, from thy thrift
Which never loses though it doth defer—
Time, the avenger! unto thee I lift
My hands, and eyes, and heart, and crave of thee a gift.
BYRON—*Childe Harold*. Canto IV. St. 130.

1 Spared and blessed by Time,
Looking tranquility.
BYRON—*Childe Harold.* Canto IV. 146.
Same expression used by CONGREVE—*Mourning Bride.* Act II. Sc. 1, and by LAMB—*A Quaker's Meeting.*

2
Thinkst thou existence doth depend on time?
It doth; but actions are our epochs; mine
Have made my days and nights imperishable,
Endless, and all alike.
BYRON—*Manfred.* Act II. Sc. 1.

3
Out upon Time! it will leave no more
Of the things to come than the things before!
Out upon Time! who forever will leave
But enough of the past for the future to grieve.
BYRON—*Siege of Corinth.* St. 18.

4
The more we live, more brief appear
Our life's succeeding stages;
A day to childhood seems a year,
And years like passing ages.
CAMPBELL—*A Thought Suggested by the New Year.*

5
Time's fatal wings do ever forward fly;
To every day we live, a day we die.
THOMAS CAMPION—*Come, Cheerful Day.*

6
That great mystery of TIME, were there no other; the illimitable, silent, never-resting thing called Time, rolling, rushing on, swift, silent, like an all-embracing ocean tide, on which we and all the Universe swim like exhalations, like apparitions which *are*, and then *are not:* this is forever very literally a miracle; a thing to strike us dumb,—for we have no word to speak about it.
CARLYLE—*Heroes and Hero Worship.* Lecture I.

7
No ay memoria à quien el tiempo no acabe, ni dolor que nuerte no le consuma.
There is no remembrance which time does not obliterate, nor pain which death does not put an end to.
CERVANTES—*Don Quixote.* III. 1.

8
I recommend you to take care of the minutes, for the hours will take care of themselves.
CHESTERFIELD—*Letter.* Oct. 4 1746.
(See also LOWDES under MONEY, CARROLL under SENSE)

9
Know the true value of time; snatch, seize, and enjoy every moment of it. No idleness, no laziness, no procrastination: never put off till to-morrow what you can do to-day.
CHESTERFIELD—*Letters to his Son.* Dec. 26, 1749.

10
Opinionum enim commenta delet dies; naturæ judicia confirmat.
Time destroys the groundless conceits of men; it confirms decisions founded on reality.
CICERO—*De Natura Deorum.* II. 2.

11
O tempora! O mores!
O what times (are these)! what morals!
CICERO—*Orationes in Catilinam.* I. 2.

12
No! no arresting the vast wheel of time,
That round and round still turns with onward might,
Stern, dragging thousands to the dreaded night
Of an unknown hereafter.
CHARLES COWDEN CLARKE—*Sonnet. The Course of Time.*

13
Hours are Time's shafts, and one comes winged with death.
On the clock at Keir House, near Denblane, the Seat of Sir William Stirling Maxwell.

14
Sex horas somno, totidem des legibus æquis
Quatuor orabis, des epulisque duas;
Quod superest ultro sacris largire Camœnis.
Six hours in sleep, in law's grave study six,
Four spend in prayer, the rest on nature fix.
COKE introduced this as "ancient verses" in *Institutes of the Laws of England.* Bk. II. Ch. I. Section 85. See also GILBERT's *Law of Evidence.* (1784)

Sex horis dormire sat est juvenique senique:
Septem vix pigro; nulli concedimus octo.
Six hours in sleep is enough for youth and age. Perhaps seven for the lazy, but we allow eight to no one.
Version from *Collectio Salernitans.* Ed. De Renzi. Vol. II. L. 130.
(See also FROUDE, HESIOD, JONES)

15
Now is the accepted time.
II Corinthians. VI. 2.

16
Touch us gently, Time!
Let us glide adown thy stream
Gently,—as we sometimes glide
Through a quiet dream!
BARRY CORNWALL—*A Petition to Time.*

17
Begin, be bold, and venture to be wise,
He who defers this work from day to day,
Does on a river's bank expecting stay,
Till the whole stream, which stopped him, should be gone,
That runs, and as it runs, for ever will run on.
COWLEY—*The Danger of Procrastination.* Translation of HORACE. 1. Ep. II. 4.

18
Nothing is there to come, and nothing past,
But an eternal Now does always last.
COWLEY—*Davideis.* Bk. I. L. 361.

19
His time's forever, everywhere his place.
COWLEY—*Friendship in Absence.* St. 3.

20
Time, as he passes us, has a dove's wing,
Unsoil'd, and swift, and of a silken sound.
COWPER—*The Task.* Bk. IV. L. 211.

21
See Time has touched me gently in his race,
And left no odious furrows in my face.
CRABBE—*Tales of the Hall.* Bk. XVII. *The Widow.* St. 3.

22
Swift speedy Time, feathered with flying hours,
Dissolves the beauty of the fairest brow.
SAMUEL DANIEL—*Delia.*

1
Che'l perder tempo a chi più sa più spiace.
The wisest are the most annoyed at the loss of time.
DANTE—*Purgatorio*. III. 78.

2
Old Time, that greatest and longest established spinner of all! . . . his factory is a secret place, his work is noiseless, and his Hands are mutes.
DICKENS—*Hard Times*. I. 14.

3
But what minutes! Count them by sensation, and not by calendars, and each moment is a day and the race a life.
BENJ. DISRAELI—*Sybil*. Bk. I. Ch. II.

4
Time, to the nation as to the individual, is nothing absolute; its duration depends on the rate of thought and feeling.
DRAPER—*History of the Intellectual Development of Europe*. Vol. I. Ch. I.

5
When Time shall turne those Amber Lockes to
Gray.
DRAYTON—*England's Heroical Epistles*.
(See also PEELE)

6
(Time) with his silent sickle.
DRYDEN—*Astræa Redux*. L. 110.

7
And write whatever Time shall bring to pass
With pens of adamant on plates of brass.
DRYDEN—*Palamon and Arcite*.
(See also YOUNG)

8
Who well lives, long lives: for this age of ours
Should not be numbered by years, daies and
hours.
DU BARTAS—*Divine Weekes and Workes. Second Week. Fourth Day*. Bk. II.

9
To everything there is a season, and a time to every purpose under the heaven.
Ecclesiastes. III. 1.

10
Say not thou, What is the cause that the former days were better than these? for thou dost not inquire wisely concerning this.
Ecclesiastes. VII. 10.
(See also BYRON)

11
Let us leave hurry to slaves.
EMERSON—*Essay on Manners*.
(See also BUCKSTONE)

12
Write it on your heart that every day is the best day in the year. No man has learned anything rightly, until he knows that every day is Doomsday.
EMERSON—*Society and Solitude. Work and Days*.

13
Dilatio damnum habet, mora periculum.
Procrastination brings loss, delay danger.
ERASMUS—*Adolescens*.
(See also YOUNG)

14
The four eights, that ideal of operative felicity, are here (New Zealand) a realized fact.
J. A. FROUDE—*Oceana*. Ch. XIV. The four eights are explained in a footnote to be "Eight to work, eight to play, eight to sleep, and eight shillings a day."
(See also COKE)

15
I count my time by times that I meet thee;
These are my yesterdays, my morrows, noons,
And nights, these are my old moons and my
new moons.
Slow fly the hours, fast the hours flee,
If thou art far from or art near to me:
If thou art far, the bird's tunes are no tunes;
If thou art near, the wintry days are Junes.
R. W. GILDER—*The New Day*. Pt. IV. *Sonnet VI*.

16
So schaff' ich am sausenden Webstuhl der Zeit.
Thus at Time's humming loom I ply.
GOETHE—*Faust*. I. 1. 156.

17
Ein stiller Geist ist Jahre lang geschäftig;
Die Zeit nur macht die feine Gährung kräftig.
Long is the calm brain active in creation;
Time only strengthens the fine fermentation.
GOETHE—*Faust*. I. 6. 36.

18
Mein Vermächtniss, wie herrlich weit und breit;
Die Zeit ist mein Vermächtniss, mein Acker ist
die Zeit.
My inheritance, how wide and fair
Time is my estate; to Time I'm heir.
GOETHE—*Wilhelm Meister's Travels*. Trans. by CARLYLE in *Sartor Resartus*.
My inheritance how lordly wide and fair;
Time is my fair seed-field, to Time I'm heir.
CARLYLE's version in *Chartism*. Ch. X.
Mein Erbteil wie herrlich, weit und breit;
Die Zeit ist mein Besitz, mein Acker ist die Zeit.
GOETHE—*Westöstliche Divan*. VI. *Buch der Sprüche*. (Original version.)

19
Die Zeit ist selbst ein Element.
Time is itself an element.
GOETHE—*Sprüche in Prosa*. III.

20
Rich with the spoils of time.
GRAY—*Elegy in a Country Churchyard*. St. 13.
(See also BROWNE under NATURE)

21
I made a posy while the day ran by;
Here will I smell my remnant out, and tie
My life within this band.
But time did beckon to the flowers, and they
By noon most cunningly did steal away,
And wither'd in my hand.
HERBERT—*The Temple. Life*.

22
Thus times do shift; each thing his turne does
hold;
New things succeed, as former things grow old.
HERRICK—*Ceremonies for Candlemas Eve*.

23
Gather ye rose-buds while ye may,
Old Time is still a flying,
And this same flower that smiles to-day,
To-morrow will be dying.
HERRICK—*Hesperides*. 208. Same found in AUSONIUS—*Idyllia*. 14.
(See also SPENSER, WYATT, also GLEIM under ROSE)

1
But what says the Greek? "In the morning of life, work; in the midday, give counsel; in the evening, pray."

HESIOD—*Fragments*.

(See also COKE)

2
Old Time, in whose banks we deposit our notes,
Is a miser who always wants guineas for groats;
He keeps all his customers still in arrears
By lending them minutes and charging them years.

HOLMES—*Poems of the Class of '29. Our Banker*. (1874)

3
Dum loquimur, fugerit invida
Ætas: carpe diem.

While we are speaking envious time will have fled. Seize the present day.

HORACE—*Carmina*. Bk. I. 11. 7.

4
Carpe diem, quam minime credula postero.

Enjoy the present day, trusting very little to the morrow.

HORACE—*Carmina*. Bk. I. 11. 8.

5
Eheu fugaces Postume, Postume,
Labuntur anni, nec pietas moram
Rugis et instanti senectæ
Afferet, indomitæ que morti.

Postumus, Postumus, the years glide by us:
Alas! no piety delays the wrinkles,
Nor the indomitable hand of Death.

HORACE—*Carmina*. Bk. II. 14. 1.

6
Damnosa quid non imminuit dies?

What does not destructive time destroy?

HORACE—*Carmina*. Bk. III. 6. 45.

7
Quidquid sub terra est, in apricum proferet ætas;
Defodiet condetque nitentia.

Time will bring to light whatever is hidden; it will cover up and conceal what is now shining in splendor.

HORACE—*Epistles*. I. 6. 24.

8
Singula de nobis anni prædantur euntes.

Each passing year robs us of some possession.

HORACE—*Epistles*. II. 2. 55.

(See also POPE)

9
Horæ
Memento cita mors venit, aut victoria læta.

In the hour's short space comes swift death, or joyful victory.

HORACE—*Satires*. Bk. I. 1. 7.

10
How short our happy days appear!
How long the sorrowful!

JEAN INGELOW—*The Mariner's Cave*. St. 38.

11
To the true teacher, time's hour-glass should still run gold-dust.

DOUGLAS JERROLD—*Specimens of Jerrold's Wit. Time*.

12
My days are swifter than a weaver's shuttle.

Job. VII. 6.

13
And panting Time toil'd after him in vain.

SAMUEL JOHNSON—*Prologue on Opening the Drury Lane Theatre*. L. 6.

14
Seven hours to law, to soothing slumber seven,
Ten to the world allot, and all to heaven.

SIR WM. JONES—*Ode in Imitation of Alcæus*. See LORD TEIGNMOUTH—*Memoirs of the Life and Writings of Sir William Jones. Letter to Charles Chapman*. Aug. 30, 1784. Also Errata. P. 251. "The muses claim the rest," or "the muse claims all beside" are the changes made by JONES, according to ANDREW AMOS—*Four Lectures on the Advantages of a Classical Education*. London, 1846. P. 78.

(See also COKE)

15
That old bald cheater, Time.

BEN JONSON—*The Poetaster*. Act I. Sc. 5.

16
The noiseless foot of Time steals swiftly by
And ere we dream of manhood, age is nigh.

JUVENAL—*Satires*. IX. 129. GIFFORD'S trans.

17
Time, that aged nurse
Rocked me to patience.

KEATS—*Endymion*. Bk. I.

18
Time's waters will not ebb nor stay.

KEBLE—*Christian Year. First Sunday after Christmas*.

19
Memento semper finis, et quia perditum non redit tempus.

Remember always your end, and that lost time does not return.

THOMAS À KEMPIS. Bk. I. Ch. XXV. 11.

20
Time, which strengthens Friendship, weakens Love.

LA BRUYÈRE—*The Characters or Manners of the Present Age*. Ch. IV.

21
Vingt siècles descendus dans l'éternelle nuit.
Y sont sans mouvement, sans lumière et sans bruit.

Twenty ages sunk in eternal night. They are without movement, without light, and without noise.

LEMOINE—*Œuvres Poétiques. Saint Louis*.

22
Potius sero quam nunquam.

Better late than never.

LIVY. IV. II. 11. BUNYAN—*Pilgrim's Progress*. Pt. I. DIONYSIUS of Halicarnassus. IX. 9. MATTHEW HENRY—*Commentaries Matthew* XXI. MURPHY—*School for Guardians*. Act I. TUSSER—*Five Hundred Points of Good Husbandry. An Habitation enforced*.

23
Time has laid his hand
Upon my heart, gently, not smiting it,
But as a harper lays his open palm
Upon his harp, to deaden its vibrations.

LONGFELLOW—*The Golden Legend*.

24
Time is the Life of the Soul.

LONGFELLOW—*Hyperion*. Bk. II. Ch. VI.

1
Alas! it is not till Time, with reckless hand, has torn out half the leaves from the Book of Human Life to light the fires of human passion with, from day to day, that man begins to see that the leaves which remain are few in number.
LONGFELLOW—*Hyperion.* Bk. IV. Ch. VIII.

2
A handful of red sand from the hot clime
Of Arab deserts brought,
Within this glass becomes the spy of Time,
The minister of Thought.
LONGFELLOW—*Sand of the Desert in an Hour-Glass.*

3
What we want, we have for our pains
The promise that if we but wait
Till the want has burned out of our brains,
Every means shall be present to state;
While we send for the napkin the soup gets cold,
While the bonnet is trimming the face grows old,
When we've matched our buttons the pattern is sold,
And everything comes too late—too late.
FITZHUGH LUDLOW—*Too Late.*

4
Volat hora per orbem.
The hours fly around in a circle.
MANILIUS—*Astronomica.* I. 641.

5
Æquo stat fœdare tempus.
Time stands with impartial law.
MANILIUS—*Astronomica.* III. 360.

6
But at my back I always hear
Time's wingèd chariot hurrying near.
MARVELL—*To his coy Mistress.*

7
Such phantom blossoms palely shining
Over the lifeless boughs of Time.
E. L. MASTERS—*Spoon River Anthology. Russell Kincaid.*

8
The signs of the times.
Matthew. XVI. 3.

9
Time is a feathered thing,
And, whilst I praise
The sparkling of thy looks, and call them rays,
Takes wing,
Leaving behind him as he flies
An unperceivèd dimness in thine eyes.
JASPER MAYNE—*Time.*

10
However we pass Time, he passes still,
Passing away whatever the pastime,
And, whether we use him well or ill,
Some day he gives us the slip for the last time.
OWEN MEREDITH (Lord Lytton)—*The Dead Pope.*

11
Who can undo
What time hath done? Who can win back the wind?
Beckon lost music from a broken lute?
Renew the redness of a last year's rose?
Or dig the sunken sunset from the deep?
OWEN MEREDITH—*Orval, or the Fool of Time.* Second Epoch. Sc. 1. Said to be a translation of a French translation of *The Inferno.* See *Saturday Review.* London. Feb. 27, 1869.

12
When time is flown, how it fled
It is better neither to ask nor tell,
Leave the dead moments to bury their dead.
OWEN MEREDITH (Lord Lytton)—*Wanderer.* Bk. IV. *Two out of the Crowd.* St. 17.

13
Time, eftsoon will tumble
All of us together like leaves in a gust,
Humbled indeed down into the dust.
JOAQUIN MILLER—*Fallen Leaves Down into the Dust.* St. 5.

14
Time will run back and fetch the age of gold.
MILTON—*Hymn on the Nativity.* L. 135.

15
Day and night,
Seed-time and harvest, heat and hoary frost
Shall hold their course, till fire purge all things new.
MILTON—*Paradise Lost.* Bk. XI. L. 898.

16
Le temps . . . souverain médecin de nos passions.
Time is the sovereign physician of our passions.
MONTAIGNE—*Essays.* Bk. III. Ch. IV. Same idea in EURIPIDES—*Alcestis.*
(See also OVID)

17
Time softly there
Laughs through the abyss of radiance with the gods.
W. V. MOODY—*The Fire-Bringer.* Act I.

18
How long, old builder Time, wilt bide
Till at thy thrilling word
Life's crimson pride shall have to bride
The spirit's white accord,
Within that gate of good estate
Which thou must build us soon or late,
Hoar workman of the Lord.
W. V. MOODY—*At Assisi.* II.

19
Time, still as he flies, adds increase to her truth,
And gives to her mind what he steals from her youth.
EDWARD MOORE—*The Happy Marriage.*

20
Surely in a matter of this kind we should endeavor to do something, that we may say that we have not lived in vain, that we may leave some impress of ourselves on the sands of time.
From an alleged Letter of NAPOLEON to his Minister of the Interior on the Poor Laws. Pub. in *The Press*, Feb. 1, 1868.

21
For each age is a dream that is dying,
Or one that is coming to birth.
ARTHUR O'SHAUGHNESSY—*Ode. We are the Music Makers.*

22
Labitur occulte, fallitque volubilis ætas,
Ut celer admissis labitur amnis aquis.
Time steals on and escapes us, like the swift river that glides on with rapid stream.
OVID—*Amorum.* I. 8. 49.

1
Dum loquor hora fugit.
While I am speaking the hour flies.
OVID—*Amorum.* Bk. I. 11. 15.

2
Tempore difficiles veniunt ad aratra juvenci;
Tempore lenta pati frena docentur equi.
In time the unmanageable young oxen come to the plough; in time the horses are taught to endure the restraining bit.
OVID—*Ars Amatoria.* Bk. I. 471.

3
Nec, quæ præteriit, iterum revocabitur unda:
Nec, quæ præteriit, hora redire potest.
Neither will the wave which has passed be called back; nor can the hour which has gone by return.
OVID—*Ars Amatoria.* Bk. III. 63.

4
Ludit in humanis divina potentia rebus,
Et certam præsens vix habet hora fidem.
Heaven makes sport of human affairs, and the present hour gives no sure promise of the next.
OVID—*Epistolæ Ex Ponto.* IV. 3. 49.

5
Tempora labuntur, tacitisque senescimus annis;
Et fugiunt fræno non remorante dies.
Time glides by, and we grow old with the silent years; and the days flee away with no restraining curb.
OVID—*Fasti.* VI. 771.

6
Assiduo labuntur tempora motu,
Non secus ad flumen. Neque enim consistere flumen.
Nec levis hora potest.
Time glides by with constant movement, not unlike a stream. For neither can a stream stay its course, nor can the fleeting hour.
OVID—*Metamorphoses.* XV. 180.

7
Tempus edax rerum.
Time that devours all things.
OVID—*Metamorphoses.* XV. 234.

8
Temporis ars medicina fere est.
Time is generally the best medicine.
OVID—*Remedia Amoris.* 131.

9
These are the times that try men's souls.
THOMAS PAINE—*The American Crisis.* No. 1.

10
Let time that makes you homely, make you sage.
PARNELL—*An Elegy to an Old Beauty.* L. 35.

11
Time, the foe of man's dominion,
Wheels around in ceaseless flight,
Scattering from his hoary pinion
Shades of everlasting night.
THOMAS LOVE PEACOCK—*The Genius of the Thames.* Pt. II. St. 42.

12
The present is our own; but while we speak,
We cease from its possession, and resign
The stage we tread on, to another race,
As vain, and gay, and mortal as ourselves.
THOMAS LOVE PEACOCK—*Time.* L. 9.

13
Man yields to death; and man's sublimest works
Must yield at length to Time.
THOMAS LOVE PEACOCK—*Time.* L. 65.

14
Time is lord of thee:
Thy wealth, thy glory, and thy name are his.
THOMAS LOVE PEACOCK—*Time.* L. 71.

15
His golden locks Time hath to silver turned,
O time too swift! O swiftness never ceasing!
His youth 'gainst Time and Age hath ever spurned,
But spurned in vain! Youth waneth by increasing.
GEORGE PEELE—*Sonnet. Polyhymnia.* Another version published in SEGER'S *Honor Military and Civil.* (1602)
(See also DRAYTON)

16
Seize time by the forelock.
PITTACUS of Mitylene. THALES of Miletus.
(See also PHÆDRUS under OPPORTUNITY)

17
Tanto brevius omne, quanto felicius tempus.
The happier the time, the quicker it passes.
PLINY the Younger—*Epistles.* VII. 14.

18
From a wild weird clime that lieth, sublime
Out of Space—out of Time.
POE—*Dreamland.* L. 7.

19
Years following years steal something ev'ry day.
At last they steal us from ourselves away.
POPE—*Imitations of Horace.* Bk. II. Ep. 2. L. 72.
(See also HORACE, also DRYDEN under DEATH)

20
Time conquers all, and we must time obey.
POPE—*Winter.* L. 88.

21
Gone! gone forever!—like a rushing wave
Another year has burst upon the shore
Of earthly being—and its last low tones,
Wandering in broken accents in the air,
Are dying to an echo.
GEORGE D. PRENTICE—*Flight of Years.*

22
A thousand years in thy sight are but as yesterday when it is past, and as a watch in the night.
Psalms. XC. 4.

23
We spend our years as a tale that is told.
Psalms. XC. 9.

24
Expect, but fear not, Death: Death cannot kill,
Till Time (that first must seal his patent) will.
Would'st thou live long? keep Time in high esteem:
Whom gone, if thou canst not recall, redeem.
QUARLES—*Hieroglyphics of the Life of Man.* Ep. 6.

25
Dum deliberamus quando incipiendum sit, incipiere jam serum est.
Whilst we deliberate how to begin a thing, it grows too late to begin it.
QUINTILIAN. XII. 6. 3.

1
He briskly and cheerfully asked him how a man should kill time.
RABELAIS—*Works*. Bk. IV. Ch. LXIII.

2
E'en such is time! which takes in trust
Our youth, our joys, and all we have;
And pays us naught but age and dust,
Which, in the dark and silent grave,
When we have wandered all our ways,
Shuts up the story of our days.
And from which grave, and earth, and dust,
The Lord will raise me up, I trust.
SIR WALTER RALEIGH. Written in his Bible.
CAYLEY'S *Life of Raleigh*. Vol. II. Ch. IX.

3
Hour after hour departs,
Recklessly flying;
The golden time of our hearts
Is fast a-dying:
O, how soon it will have faded!
Joy droops, with forehead shaded;
And Memory starts.
JOHN HAMILTON REYNOLDS—*Hour After Hour*.

4
Time, like a flurry of wild rain,
Shall drift across the darkened pane!
C. G. D. ROBERTS—*The Unsleeping*.

5
By many a temple half as old as Time.
SAMUEL ROGERS—*Italy*.
(See also BURGON under CITIES)

6
To vanish in the chinks that Time has made.
SAMUEL ROGERS—*Italy*. *Pæstum*. L. 59.
(See also WALLER)

7
Que pour les malheureux l'heure lentement fuit!
How slowly the hours pass to the unhappy.
SAURIN—*Blanche et Guiscard*. V. 5.

8
Tag wird es auf die dickste Nacht, und, kommt
Die Zeit, so reifen auch die spät'sten Früchte.
Day follows on the murkiest night, and, when the time comes, the latest fruits will ripen.
SCHILLER—*Die Jungfrau von Orleans*. III. 2. 60.

9
O, wer weiss
Was in der Zeiten Hintergrunde schlummert.
Who knows what may be slumbering in the background of time!
SCHILLER—*Don Carlos*. I. 1. 44.

10
Time flies on restless pinions—constant never.
Be constant—and thou chainest time forever.
SCHILLER—*Epigram*.

11
Spät kommt ihr—doch ihr kommt!
You come late, yet you come!
SCHILLER—*Piccolomini*. I. 1. 1.

12
Dreifach ist der Schritt der Zeit:
Zögernd kommt die Zukunft hergezogen,
Pfeilschnell ist das Jetzt entflogen,
Ewig still steht die Vergangenheit.
Threefold the stride of Time, from first to last:
Loitering slow, the Future creepeth—
Arrow-swift, the Present sweepeth—
And motionless forever stands the Past.
SCHILLER—*Sprüche des Confucius*.

13
Doch zittre vor der langsamen,
Der stillen Macht der Zeit.
Yet tremble at the slow, silent power of time.
SCHILLER—*Wallenstein's Tod*. I. 3. 32.

14
Upon my lips the breath of song,
Within my heart a rhyme,
Howe'er time trips or lags along,
I keep abreast with time!
CLINTON SCOLLARD—*The Vagrant*.

15
Time rolls his ceaseless course.
SCOTT—*The Lady of the Lake*. Canto III. St. 1.

16
Infinita est velocitas temporis quæ magis apparet respicientibus.
The swiftness of time is infinite, which is still more evident to those who look back upon the past.
SENECA—*Epistolæ Ad Lucilium*. XLIX.

17
Volat ambiguis
Mobilis alis hora.
The swift hour flies on double wings.
SENECA—*Hippolytus*. 1141.

18
Nullum ad nocendum tempus angustum est malis.
No time is too short for the wicked to injure their neighbors.
SENECA—*Medea*. 292.

19
Urbes constituit ætas: hora dissolvit: momento fit cinis: diu sylva.
An age builds up cities: an hour destroys them. In a moment the ashes are made, but a forest is a long time growing.
SENECA—*Quæstionum Naturalium*. Bk. III. 27.

20
Nemo tam divos habuit faventes,
Crastinum ut possit sibi polliceri.
Nobody has ever found the gods so much his friends that he can promise himself another day.
SENECA—*Thyestes*. 619.

21
Let's take the instant by the forward top;
For we are old, and on our quick'st decrees
The inaudible and noiseless foot of Time
Steals ere we can effect them.
All's Well That Ends Well. Act V. Sc. 3. L. 39.
(See also PITTACUS)

22
And, looking on it with lack-lustre eye,
Says very wisely, "It is ten o'clock:
Thus we may see," quoth he, "how the world wags."
As You Like It. Act II. Sc. 7. L. 21.

23
Time travels in divers paces with divers persons. I'll tell you who Time ambles withal, who Time trots withal, who Time gallops withal, and who he stands still withal.
As You Like It. Act III. Sc. 2. L. 326.

24
Time is the old justice that examines all such offenders, and let Time try.
As You Like It. Act IV. Sc. 1. L. 203.

1
There's a time for all things.
Comedy of Errors. Act II. Sc. 2. L. 66.

2
The time is out of joint.
Hamlet. Act I. Sc. 5. L. 189.

3
Time, that takes survey of all the world,
Must have a stop.
Henry IV. Pt. I. Act V. Sc. 4. L. 82.

4 See the minutes, how they run,
How many make the hour full complete;
How many hours bring about the day;
How many days will finish up the year;
How many years a mortal man may live.
Henry VI. Pt. III. Act II. Sc. 5. L. 25.

5
So many hours must I take my rest;
So many hours must I contemplate.
Henry VI. Pt. III. Act II. Sc. 5. L. 32.
(See also COKE)

6
Minutes, hours, days, months, and years,
Pass'd over to the end they were created,
Would bring white hairs unto a quiet grave.
Ah, what a life were this!
Henry VI. Pt. III. Act II. Sc. 5. L. 35.

7
Time shall unfold what plighted cunning hides;
Who cover faults, at last shame them derides.
King Lear. Act I. Sc. 1. L. 283.

8 Come what come may,
Time and the hour runs through the roughest day.
Macbeth. Act I. Sc. 3. L. 146.

9 'Gainst the tooth of time
And razure of oblivion.
Measure for Measure. Act V. Sc. 1. L. 12.

10
We should hold day with the Antipodes,
If you would walk in absence of the sun.
Merchant of Venice. Act V. Sc. 1. L. 127.

11
Time goes on crutches till love have all his rites.
Much Ado About Nothing. Act II. Sc. 1. L. 372.

12
Pleasure and action make the hours seem short.
Othello. Act II. Sc. 3. L. 385.

13 Time's the king of men,
He's both their parent, and he is their grave,
And gives them what he will, not what they crave.
Pericles. Act II. Sc. 3. L. 45.

14
O, call back yesterday, bid time return.
Richard II. Act III. Sc. 2. L. 69.

15
Yet, do thy worst, old Time; despite thy wrong,
My love shall in my verse ever live young.
Sonnet XIX.

16
Time doth transfix the flourish set on youth
And delves the parallels in beauty's brow.
Sonnet LX.

17
O, how shall summer's honey breath hold out
Against the wreckful siege of battering days,
When rocks impregnable are not so stout,
Nor gates of steel so strong, but Time decays?
O fearful meditation! where, alack,
Shall Time's best jewel from Time's chest lie hid?
Or what strong hand can hold his swift foot back?
Or who his spoil of beauty can forbid?
Sonnet LXV.

18
Time hath, my lord, a wallet at his back,
Wherein he puts alms for oblivion,
A great-sized monster of ingratitudes;
Those scraps are good deeds past; which are devour'd
As fast as they are made, forgot as soon
As done.
Troilus and Cressida. Act III. Sc. 3. L. 145.

19 Time is like a fashionable host
That slightly shakes his parting guest by the hand,
And with his arms outstretch'd, as he would fly
Grasps in the comer: welcome ever smiles.
Troilus and Cressida. Act III. Sc. 3. L. 165.

20 Beauty, wit,
High birth, vigour of bone, desert in service,
Love, friendship, charity, are subjects all
To envious and calumniating time.
Troilus and Cressida. Act III. St. 3. L. 171.

21 The end crowns all,
And that old common arbitrator, Time,
Will one day end it.
Troilus and Cressida. Act IV. Sc. 5. L. 224.

22
The whirligig of time brings in his revenges.
Twelfth Night. Act V. Sc. 1. L. 384.

23
Time is the nurse and breeder of all good.
Two Gentlemen of Verona. Act III. Sc. 1. L. 243.

24
Make use of time, let not advantage slip;
Beauty within itself should not be wasted:
Fair flowers that are not gather'd in their prime
Rot and consume themselves in little time.
Venus and Adonis. L. 129.

25
The flood of time is rolling on;
We stand upon its brink, whilst *they* are gone
To glide in peace down death's mysterious stream.
Have ye done well?
SHELLEY—*Revolt of Islam.* Canto XII. St. 27.

26
Unfathomable Sea! whose waves are years,
Ocean of Time, whose waters of deep woe
Are brackish with the salt of human tears!
Thou shoreless flood, which in thy ebb and flow
Claspest the limits of mortality!
And sick of prey, yet howling on for more,
Vomitest thy wrecks on its inhospitable shore,
Treacherous in calm, and terrible in storm,
Who shall put forth on thee,
Unfathomable sea?
SHELLEY—*Time.*

1
Per varios præceps casus rota volvitur ævi.
The wheel of time rolls downward through various changes.
SILIUS ITALICUS—*Punica.* VI. 121.

2
For time would, with us, 'stead of sand,
Put filings of steel in his glass,
To dry up the blots of his hand,
And spangle life's page as they pass.
Since all flesh is grass ere 'tis hay,
O may I in clover lie snug,
And when old Time mow me away,
Be stacked with defunct Lady Mugg!
HORACE AND JAMES SMITH—*Rejected Addresses. The Beautiful Incendiary, by the Hon. W. S.* 10.

3
For the next inn he spurs amain,
In haste alights, and skuds away,
But time and tide for no man stay.
W. C. SOMERVILLE—*The Sweet-Scented Miser.* L. 98.

4
Time wears all his locks before,
Take thou hold upon his forehead;
When he flies he turns no more,
And behind his scalp is naked.
Works adjourn'd have many stays,
Long demurs breed new delays.
ROB'T SOUTHWELL—*Loss in Delay.*
(See also PHÆDRUS under OPPORTUNITY)

5
Goe to my Love where she is carelesse layd
Yet in her winter's bowere not well awake;
Tell her the joyous time will not be staid
Unlesse she doe him by the forelock take
SPENSER—*Amoretti.* LXX.

6
Gather the rose of love whilst yet is time.
SPENSER—*The Faerie Queene.* Bk. III. Canto XII. St. 75.

7
Too late I staid, forgive the crime,
Unheeded flew the hours;
How noiseless falls the foot of Time
That only treads on flow'rs!
What eye with clear account remarks
The ebbing of his glass,
When all its sands are diamond sparks
That dazzle as they pass?
Ah! who to sober measurement
Time's happy swiftness brings,
When birds of Paradise have lent
Their plumage for his wings?
W. R. SPENCER—*To the Lady Anne Hamilton.*

8
Long ailments wear out pain, and long hopes joy.
STANISLAUS (King of Poland)—*Maxims.*

9
I see that time divided is never long, and that regularity abridges all things.
ABEL STEVENS—*Life of Madame de Staël.* Ch. XXXVIII. Quoting Mme. de Staël.

10
In time take time while time doth last, for time
Is no time when time is past.
Written on the title page of MS. account book of NICHOLAS STONE, mason to JAMES I. In the SOANE MUSEUM.

11
Nick of Time!
SIR JOHN SUCKLING—*The Goblins.* Act V.

12
Ever eating, never cloying,
All-devouring, all-destroying,
Never finding full repast,
Till I eat the world at last.
SWIFT—*On Time.*

13
Lauriger Horatius
Quam dixisti verum;
Fugit euro citius
Tempus edax rerum.
Laurel crowned Horatius
True, how true thy saying,
Swift as wind flies over us
Time devouring, slaying.
Anon. Trans. by JOHN ADDINGTON SYMONDS.

14
A wonderful stream is the River Time,
As it runs through the realms of Tears,
With a faultless rhythm, and a musical rhyme,
And a broader sweep, and a surge sublime
As it blends with the ocean of Years.
BENJAMIN F. TAYLOR—*The Long Ago.*

15
He that lacks time to mourn, lacks time to mend:
Eternity mourns that. 'Tis an ill cure
For life's worst ills to have no time to feel them.
SIR HENRY TAYLOR—*Philip Van Artevelde.* Act I. Sc. 5.

16
Come, Time, and teach me many years,
I do not suffer in dream;
For now so strange do these things seem,
Mine eyes have leisure for their tears.
TENNYSON—*In Memoriam.* Pt. XIII.

17
Every moment dies a man,
Every moment one is born.
TENNYSON—*Vision of Sin.* St. 9. ("Minute" for "moment" in early Ed.)
Every minute dies a man,
And one and one-sixteenth is born.
Parody on TENNYSON by a Statistician.

18
Heu! universum triduum!
Alas! three whole days to wait!
TERENCE—*Works.* II. 1. 17. (Sometimes "totum" given for "universum.")

19
I dimly guess what Time in mists confounds;
Yet ever and anon a trumpet sounds
From the hid battlements of Eternity;
Those shaken mists a space unsettle, then
Round the half-glimpsed turrets slowly wash again.
FRANCIS THOMPSON—*Hound of Heaven.* L. 143.

20
Once in Persia reigned a king
Who upon his signet ring
Graved a maxim true and wise,
Which if held before the eyes
Gave him counsel at a glance
Fit for every change and chance.
Solemn words, and these are they:
"Even this shall pass away."
THEODORE TILTON—*The King's Ring.* (*All Things Shall Pass Away.*)
(See also WILCOX)

1
Time tries the troth in everything.
TUSSER—*Five Hundred Points of Good Husbandrie. The Author's Epistle.* Ch. I.

2
Sed fugit interea, fugit irreparabile tempus.
But meanwhile time flies; it flies never to be regained.
VERGIL—*Georgics.* III. 284.

3
The soul's dark cottage, batter'd and decay'd,
Lets in new light through chinks that Time has made.
WALLER—*On the Divine Poems. Epilogue.*
(See also ROGERS)

4
To wind the mighty secrets of the past,
And turn the key of time.
HENRY KIRK WHITE—*Time.* L. 249.

5
And let its meaning permeate
Whatever comes, This too shall pass away.
ELLA WHEELER WILCOX—*This too shall pass away.*
(See also TILTON)

6
He was always late on principle, his principle being that punctuality is the thief of time.
OSCAR WILDE—*Picture of Dorian Gray.* Ch. III.

7
Our time is a very shadow that passeth away.
Wisdom of Solomon. II. 5.

8
Delivered from the galling yoke of time.
WORDSWORTH—*Laodamia.*

9
Therefore fear not to assay
To gather, ye that may,
The flower that this day
Is fresher than the next.
THOS. WYATT—*That the Season of Enjoyment is Short.*
(See also HERRICK)

10
Nought treads so silent as the foot of Time;
Hence we mistake our autumn for our prime.
YOUNG—*Love of Fame.* Satire V. L. 497.

11
The bell strikes one. We take no note of time
But from its loss: to give it then a tongue
Is wise in man.
YOUNG—*Night Thoughts.* Night I. L. 55.

12
Procrastination is the thief of time:
Year after year it steals, till all are fled,
And to the mercies of a moment leaves
The vast concerns of an eternal scene.
YOUNG—*Night Thoughts.* Night I. L. 390.
(See also ERASMUS)

13
Time is eternity;
Pregnant with all eternity can give;
Pregnant with all that makes archangels smile.
Who murders Time, he crushes in the birth
A power ethereal, only not adorn'd.
YOUNG—*Night Thoughts.* Night II. L. 107.

14
Time wasted is existence, used is life.
YOUNG—*Night Thoughts.* Night II. L. 149.

15
We push time from us, and we wish him back;
* * * * * *
Life we think long and short; death seek and shun.
YOUNG—*Night Thoughts.* Night II. L. 174.

16
In leaves, more durable than leaves of brass,
Writes our whole history.
YOUNG—*Night Thoughts.* Night II. L. 275.
(See also DRYDEN)

17
We see time's furrows on another's brow,
* * * * *
How few themselves in that just mirror see!
YOUNG—*Night Thoughts.* Night V. L. 627.

18
In records that defy the tooth of time.
YOUNG—*The Statesman's Creed.*

TOASTS

19
Then here's to the City of Boston
The town of the cries and the groans
Where the Cabots can't see the Kabotschniks
And the Cabots won't speak to the Cohns.
FRANKLIN P. ADAMS. *Revised.* In "So Much Velvet." (See also BOSSIDY)

20
Waes-hael! for Lord and Dame!
O! merry be their Dole;
Drink-hael! in Jesu's name,
And fill the tawny bowl.
KING ARTHUR'S *Waes-Hael.*

21
The wind that blows, the ship that goes
And the lass that loves a sailor.
Popular Toast in England about 1820.

22
Here's a health to poverty; it sticks by us when all friends forsake us.
Toast given in the *Boston Bee.*

23
Some hae meat, and canna eat,
And some wad eat that want it;
But we hae meat, and we can eat,
And sae the Lord be thankit.
BURNS—*The Selkirk Grace.* As attributed to him.

24
Some have meat but cannot eat;
Some could eat but have no meat;
We have meat and can all eat;
Blest, therefore, be God for our meat.
The Selkirk Grace, in the MSS. of Dr. Plume, of Maldon, Essex, in a handwriting of about 1650.

25
Here's to old Massachusetts,
The home of the sacred cod,
Where the Adamses vote for Douglas
And the Cabots walk with God.
Anonymous. *Toast at 25th anniversary dinner of Harvard Class of 1880.*

26
And this is good old Boston,
The home of the bean and the cod,
Where the Lowells talk to the Cabots
And the Cabots talk only to God.
DR. JOHN C. BOSSIDY—*Toast at Annual dinner of the Alumni of the Holy Cross College.* (See also JONES)

1
My boat is on the shore,
  And my bark is on the sea:
But, before I go, Tom Moore,
  Here's a double health to thee!
  BYRON—*To Thomas Moore.*

2
Were't the last drop in the well,
  As I gasp'd upon the brink,
Ere my fainting spirit fell,
  'Tis to thee that I would drink.
  BYRON—*To Thomas Moore.*

3
Drink to her that each loves best,
  And if you nurse a flame
That's told but to her mutual breast,
  We will not ask her name.
  THOS. CAMPBELL—*A Toast.*

4
Here's to the red of it,
There's not a thread of it,
No, not a shred of it,
In all the spread of it,
    From foot to head,
But heroes bled for it,
Faced steel and lead for it,
Precious blood shed for it,
    Bathing in red.
  JOHN DALY—*A Toast to the Flag.*

5
But the standing toast that pleased me most
Was, "The wind that blows, the ship that goes,
And the lass that loves a sailor!"
  DIBDIN—*The Standing Toast.* From the Comic Opera, *The Round Robin*, produced June 21, 1811.

6
Ho! stand to your glasses steady!
  'Tis all we have left to prize.
A cup to the dead already,—
  Hurrah for the next that dies.
  BARTHOLOMEW DOWLING—*Revelry in India.* Different version of same given in DORAN'S *Table Traits.* Said to have been written during first Burmese War.

7
And he that will this health deny,
Down among the dead men let him lie.
  DYER—*From a Toast published during the reign of Queen Anne.*

8
Here's to Great Britain, the sun that gives light to all nations of the earth.
  An Englishman's Toast at a banquet in England.

Here's to France, the moon whose magic rays move the tides of the world.
  A Frenchman's Toast at the same.

Here's to our beloved George Washington, the Joshua of America, who commanded the sun and the moon to stand still—and they obeyed.
  FRANKLIN'S *Toast.* At the Close.

9
L'Abbé de Ville proposed a toast,
  His master, as the rising Sun:
Reisbach then gave the Empress Queen,
  As the bright Moon and much praise won.

The Earl of Stair, whose turn next came,
  Gave for his toast his own King Will,
As Joshua the son of Nun,
  Who made both Sun and Moon stand still.
  A metrical version of the Toast of LORD STAIR. From the *Anecdote Library*, 1822. The Empress Maria Theresa was the "Empress Queen." Also given as a toast at a banquet during the war between England, France, and Holland. LOUIS XIV was alluded to as the rising sun, England as the moon, Holland which had broken its dikes and forced the other army to retreat, was compared to Joshua.

10
Here's to old Adam's crystal ale,
  Clear sparkling and divine,
Fair H_2O, long may you flow,
  We drink your health (in wine).
  OLIVER HERFORD — *Toast. Adam's Crystal Ale.*

11
The bubble winked at me, and said,
"You'll miss me brother, when you're dead."
  OLIVER HERFORD—*Toast. The Bubble Winked.*

12
You to the left and I to the right,
  For the ways of men must sever—
And it may be for a day and a night,
  And it well may be forever.
But whether we meet or whether we part,
  (For our ways are past our knowing)
A pledge from the heart to its fellow heart,
  On the ways we all are going!
Here's luck!
  For we know not where we are going.
  RICHARD HOVEY—*At the Crossroads.*

13
Here's to your good health, and your family's good health, and may you all live long and prosper.
  IRVING—*Rip Van Winkle.* As used by JOSEPH JEFFERSON.

14
Here's to the town of New Haven,
  The home of the truth and the light,
    Where God speaks to Jones,
    In the very same tones,
  That he uses with Hadley and Dwight.
  DEAN JONES—*Reply to Dr. Bushnell's Toast.* (See also BOSSIDY)

15
Drink to me only with thine eyes,
  And I will pledge with mine;
Or leave a kiss but in the cup,
  And I'll not look for wine.
  BEN JONSON—*The Forest. To Celia.* See also PHILOSTRATUS, from whom it was taken.

16
The thirst that from the soul doth rise,
  Doth ask a drink divine;
But might I of Jove's nectar sup,
  I would not change for thine.
  BEN JONSON—*The Forest. To Celia.*

17
To the old, long life and treasure;
To the young, all health and pleasure.
  BEN JONSON—*Metamorphosed Gipsies. Third Song.*

18
May all your labors be in vein.
  Mining Toast in Yorkshire.

1
A glass is good, and a lass is good,
And a pipe to smoke in cold weather;
The world is good and the people are good,
And we're all good fellows together.
JOHN O'KEEFE—*Sprigs of Laurel.* II. 1.

2
Here's a health to all those that we love,
Here's a health to all those that love us,
Here's a health to all those that love them that love those
That love them that love those that love us.
Old Toast.

3
Here's a health to you and yours who have done such things for us and ours.
And when we and ours have it in our powers to do for you and yours what you and yours have done for us and ours,
Then we and ours *will* do for you and yours what you and yours have done for us and ours.
Old Toast.

4
Here's to you, as good as you are,
And here's to me, as bad as I am;
But as good as you are, and as bad as I am,
I am as good as you are, as bad as I am.
Old Scotch Toast.

5
Drink to me with your eyes alone. . . . And if you will, take the cup to your lips and fill it with kisses, and give it so to me.
PHILOSTRATUS—*Letters.* XXIV.
(See also JONSON)

6
I, whenever I see thee, thirst, and holding the cup, apply it to my lips more for thy sake than for drinking.
PHILOSTRATUS—*Letters.* XXV.

7
I fill this cup to one made up
Of loveliness alone,
A woman, of her gentle sex
The seeming paragon;
To whom the better elements
And kindly stars have given
A form so fair that, like the air,
'Tis less of earth than heaven.
EDWARD C. PINKNEY—*A Health.* To Georgiana McCausland, Pinkney's wife, according to Wm. Leggett. Also said to be written for Peggy O'Neil, a famous beauty.

8
May the hinges of friendship never rust, or the wings of luve lose a feather.
Toast from DEAN RAMSEY'S *Reminiscences of Scottish Life.*
(See also DICKENS under FRIENDSHIP)

9
I'll drink a cup to Scotland yet,
Wi' a' the honours three.
REV. HENRY SCOTT RIDDELL—*Toast to Scotland.*

10
St. Leon raised his kindling eye,
And lifts the sparkling cup on high;
"I drink to one," he said,
"Whose image never may depart,
Deep graven on this grateful heart,
Till memory be dead."
* * *
St. Leon paused, as if he would
Not breathe her name in careless mood
Thus lightly to another;
Then bent his noble head, as though
To give the word the reverence due,
And gently said, "My mother!"
SCOTT—*The Knight's Toast.*

11
The cannons to the heavens, the heavens to earth,
"Now the king drinks to Hamlet."
Hamlet. Act V. Sc. 2. L. 288.

12
Here's to the maiden of bashful fifteen;
Here's to the widow of fifty;
Here's to the flaunting, extravagant quean;
And here's to the housewife that's thrifty.
Chorus: Let the toast pass,—
Drink to the lass,
I'll warrant she'll prove an excuse for the glass.
R. B. SHERIDAN—*School for Scandal.* Act III. Sc. 3. *Song.*

13
A health to the nut-brown lass,
With the hazel eyes: let it pass.
* * * *
As much to the lively grey
'Tis as good i' th' night as day:
* * * *
She's a savour to the glass,
An excuse to make it pass.
SUCKLING—*Goblins.* Act III.

14
May you live all the days of your life.
SWIFT—*Polite Conversation. Dialogue* II.

15
First pledge our Queen this solemn night,
Then drink to England, every guest;
That man's the best Cosmopolite
Who loves his native country best.
TENNYSON—*Hands All Round.*

16
Here's a health to the lass with the merry black eyes!
Here's a health to the lad with the blue ones!
WM. WINTER—*Blue and Black.*

TOBACCO

17
It's all one thing—both tend into one scope—
To live upon Tobacco and on Hope,
The one's but smoke, the other is but wind.
SIR ROBERT AYTOUN—*Sonnet on Tobacco.*

18
The Elizabethan age might be better named the beginning of the smoking era.
BARRIE—*My Lady Nicotine.* Ch. XIV.

19
Little tube of mighty pow'r,
Charmer of an idle hour,
Object of my warm desire.
ISAAC HAWKINS BROWNE—*A Pipe of Tobacco.* Parody in imitation of A. PHILLIPS.

20
The man who smokes, thinks like a sage and acts like a *Samaritan!*
BULWER-LYTTON—*Night and Morning.* Bk. I. Ch. VI.

1
He who doth not smoke hath either known no great griefs, or refuseth himself the softest consolation, next to that which comes from heaven.
BULWER-LYTTON—*What Will He Do With It?* Bk. I. Ch. VI.

2
Woman in this scale, the weed in that, Jupiter, hang out thy balance, and weigh them both; and if thou give the preference to woman, all I can say is, the next time Juno ruffles thee—O Jupiter, try the weed.
BULWER-LYTTON—*What Will He Do With It?* Bk. I. Ch. VI.

3
Tobacco, divine, rare superexcellent tobacco, which goes far beyond all panaceas, potable gold and philosopher's stones, a sovereign remedy to all diseases.
BURTON—*Anatomy of Melancholy.*

4
After he had administer'd a dose
Of snuff mundungus to his nose;
And powder'd th' inside of his skull,
Instead of th' outward jobbernol,
He shook it with a scornful look
On th' adversary, and thus he spoke.
BUTLER—*Hudibras.* Pt. III. Canto II. L. 1,005.

5
Sublime tobacco! which from east to west,
Cheers the tar's labour or the Turkman's rest;
Which on the Moslem's ottoman divides
His hours, and rivals opium and his brides;
Magnificent in Stamboul, but less grand,
Though not less loved, in Wapping or the Strand:
Divine in hookas, glorious in a pipe,
When tipp'd with amber, mellow, rich, and ripe;
Like other charmers wooing the caress,
More dazzlingly when daring in full dress;
Yet thy true lovers more admire by far
Thy naked beauties—Give me a cigar!
BYRON—*The Island.* Canto II. St. 19.

6
Contented I sit with my pint and my pipe,
Puffing sorrow and care far away,
And surely the brow of grief nothing can wipe,
Like smoking and moist'ning our clay;
* * * * *
For tho' at my simile many may joke,
Man is but a pipe—and his life but smoke.
Content and a Pipe. Old ballad.

7
The pipe, with solemn interposing puff,
Makes half a sentence at a time enough;
The dozing sages drop the drowsy strain,
Then pause, and puff—and speak, and pause again.
COWPER—*Conversation.* L. 245.

8
Pernicious weed! whose scent the fair annoys
Unfriendly to society's chief joys,
Thy worst effect is banishing for hours
The sex whose presence civilizes ours.
COWPER—*Conversation.* L. 251.

9
The Indian weed, withered quite,
Green at noon, cut down at night,
Shows thy decay.
All flesh is hay.
Thus think, then drink tobacco.
* * * *
And when the smoke ascends on high,
Then thou behold'st vanity
Of worldly stuff,
Gone at a puff.
Thus think, then drink tobacco.
Attributed to ERSKINE—*Gospel Sonnets. Meditations on Tobacco.* Pt. I. Printed in a Collection *Two Broadsides against Tobacco.* (1672) ERSKINE claimed only Pt. II. Pt. I. is from an old poem.
(See also SCOTT, G. W.)

10
Tobacco, an outlandish weed,
Doth in the land strange wonders breed;
It taints the breath, the blood it dries,
It burns the head, it blinds the eyes;
It dries the lungs, scourgeth the lights,
It 'numbs the soul, it dulls the sprites;
It brings a man into a maze,
And makes him sit for others' gaze;
It mars a man, it mars a purse,
A lean one fat, a fat one worse;
A white man black, a black man white,
A night a day, a day a night;
It turns the brain like cat in pan,
And makes a Jack a gentleman.
FAIRHOLT—*J. Payne Collier's MS.*

11
With pipe and book at close of day,
Oh, what is sweeter? mortal say.
It matters not what book on knee,
Old Isaak or the Odyssey,
It matters not meerschaum or clay.
RICHARD LE GALLIENNE. In *Volumes in Folio.* See COPE's *Smoker's Garland.*

12
Tobacco is a traveler,
Come from the Indies hither;
It passed sea and land
Ere it came to my hand,
And 'scaped the wind and weather.

Tobacco's a musician,
And in a pipe delighteth;
It descends in a close,
Through the organ of the nose,
With a relish that inviteth.
BARTEN HOLIDAY—*Texnotamia.* (1630)

13
Some sigh for this and that;
My wishes don't go far;
The world may wag at will,
So I have my cigar.
HOOD—*The Cigar.*

14
Neither do thou lust after that tawney weed tobacco.
BEN JONSON—*Bartholomew Fair.* Act II. Sc. 6.

15
Ods me I marle what pleasure or felicity they have in taking their roguish tobacco. It is good for nothing but to choke a man, and fill him full of smoke and embers.
BEN JONSON—*Every Man in His Humour.* Act III. Sc. 2.

16
And a woman is only a woman, but a good cigar is a smoke.
KIPLING—*The Betrothed.*

1
For Maggie has written a letter to give me my choice between
The wee little whimpering Love and the great god Nick O'Teen.

And I have been servant of Love for barely a twelvemonth clear,
But I have been priest of Partagas a matter of seven year.

And the gloom of my bachelor days is flecked with the cherry light
Of stumps that I burned to friendship, and pleasure and work and fight.
KIPLING—*The Betrothed.*

2
For I hate, yet love thee, so,
That, whichever thing I show,
The plain truth will seem to be
A constrained hyperbole,
And the passion to proceed
More from a mistress than a weed.
LAMB—*A Farewell to Tobacco.*

3
For thy sake, tobacco, I
Would do anything but die.
LAMB—*A Farewell to Tobacco.*

4
Nay, rather,
Plant divine, of rarest virtue;
Blisters on the tongue would hurt you.
LAMB—*A Farewell to Tobacco.*

5
Thou in such a cloud dost bind us,
That our worst foes cannot find us,
And ill fortune, that would thwart us,
Shoots at rovers, shooting at us;
While each man, through thy height'ning steam,
Does like a smoking Etna seem.
LAMB—*A Farewell to Tobacco.*

6
Thou through such a mist dost show us,
That our best friends do not know us.
LAMB—*A Farewell to Tobacco.*

7
Tobac! dont mon âme est ravie,
Lorsque je te vois te perdre en l'air,
Aussi promptement q'un éclair,
Je vois l'image de ma vie.
Tobacco, charmer of my mind,
When like the meteor's transient gleam,
Thy substance gone to air I find,
I think, alas! my life's the same.
MISSON—*Memoirs of his travels over England.* (1697) Trans. by OZELL.

8
I would I were a cigarette
Between my Lady's lithe sad lips,
Where Death like Love, divinely set.
With exquisite sighs and sips,
Feeds and is fed.
* * * *
For life is Love and Love is death,
It was my hap, a well-a-day!
To burn my little hour away.
H. A. PAGE—*Vers de Société. Madonna Mia.*

9
Old man, God bless you, does your pipe taste sweetly?
A beauty, by my soul!
A ruddy flower-pot, rimmed with gold so neatly,
What ask you for the bowl?
O sir, that bowl for worlds I would not part with;
A brave man gave it me,
Who won it—now what think you—of a bashaw?
At Belgrade's victory.
GOTTFRIED KONRAD PFEFFEL—*The Tobacco Pipe.*

10
Sir Plume, of amber snuff-box justly vain,
And the nice conduct of a clouded cane.
POPE—*Rape of the Lock.* Canto IV. L. 122.

11
Just where the breath of life his nostrils drew,
A charge of snuff the wily virgin threw;
The gnomes direct, to every atom just,
The pungent grains of titillating dust,
Sudden, with starting tears each eye o'erflows,
And the high dome re-echoes to his nose.
POPE—*Rape of the Lock.* Canto V. L. 81.

12
Tobacco's but an Indian weed,
Grows green at morn, cut down at eve;
It shows our decay, we are but clay.
Think on this when you smoak Tobacco.
As quoted by SCOTT—*Rob Roy.* First printed in *Wit and Mirth,* or *Pills to Purge Melancholy.* Vol. I. P. 315. (Ed. 1707)
(See also ERSKINE)

13
And 'twixt his finger and his thumb he held
A pouncet-box, which ever and anon
He gave his nose and took 't away again;
Who therefor angry, when it next came there,
Took it in snuff.
Henry IV. Pt. I. Act I. Sc. 3. L. 37.

14
Divine Tobacco.
SPENSER—*Faerie Queene.* Bk. III. Canto V. St. 32.

15
Yes, social friend, I love thee well,
In learned doctors' spite;
Thy clouds all other clouds dispel
And lap me in delight.
CHARLES SPRAGUE—*To My Cigar.*

16
It is not for nothing that this "ignoble tabagie," as Michelet calls it, spreads over all the world. Michelet rails against it because it renders you happily apart from thought or work; . . . Whatever keeps a man in the front garden, whatever checks wandering fancy and all inordinate ambition, whatever makes for lounging and contentment, makes just so surely for domestic happiness.
STEVENSON—*Virginibus Puerisque.* I.
(See also STEVENSON under MATRIMONY)

17
Am I not—a smoker and a brother?
A VETERAN OF SMOKEDOM—*The Smoker's Guide.* Ch. IV. Last line.

18
Look at me—follow me—smell me! The "stunning" cigar I am smoking is one of a sample intended for the Captain General of Cuba, and the King of Spain, and positively cost a shilling! Oh! * * * I have some dearer at home. Yes, the expense is frightful, but——it!

who can smoke the monstrous rubbish of the shops?
A VETERAN OF SMOKEDOM—*The Smoker's Guide.* Ch. IV.

1
To smoke a cigar through a mouthpiece is equivalent to kissing a lady through a respirator.
A VETERAN OF SMOKEDOM—*The Smoker's Guide.* Ch. V.

2
Dick Stoype
Was a dear friend and lover of the pipe.
He used to say one pipe of Wishart's best
Gave life a zest.
To him 'twas meat and drink and physic,
To see the friendly vapor
Curl round his midnight taper,
And the black fume
Clothe all the room,
In clouds as dark as sciences metaphysic.
CHARLES WESTMACOTT—*Points of Misery.*

3
A cigarette is the perfect type of a perfect pleasure. It is exquisite, and it leaves one unsatisfied. What more can you want?
OSCAR WILDE—*Picture of Dorian Gray.* Ch. IV.

4
Lastly, the ashes left behind,
May daily show to move the mind,
That to ashes and dust return we must:
Then think, and drink tobacco.
G. W. Probably GEORGE WITHERS, in MS. of 17th. Cent. owned by J. PAYNE COLLIER. Printed in *My Little Book of Songs and Ballads from Ancient Musick Books* MS. (1851) "Drink tobacco" means drinking in, or smoking.
(See also ERSKINE)

TO-DAY (See also TO-MORROW)

5
Out of Eternity
The new Day is born;
Into Eternity
At night will return.
CARLYLE—*To-day.*

6
To-day is ours; what do we fear?
To-day is ours; we have it here.
Let's treat it kindly, that it may
Wish, at least, with us to stay.
Let's banish business, banish sorrow;
To the gods belongs to-morrow.
ABRAHAM COWLEY—*Anacreontique. The Epicure.* L. 7.

7
To-morrow let my sun his beams display,
Or in clouds hide them: I have lived to-day.
ABRAHAM COWLEY—*A Vote.* Last lines.
(See also DRYDEN)

8
Days that need borrow
No part of their good morrow,
From a fore-spent night of sorrow.
RICHARD CRASHAW—*Wishes to his (Supposed) Mistress.* St. 27.

9
What dost thou bring to me, O fair To-day,
That comest o'er the mountains with swift feet?
JULIA C. R. DORR—*To-Day.*

10
Happy the man, and happy he alone,
He, who can call to-day his own:
He who, secure within, can say,
To-morrow, do thy worst, for I have liv'd to-day.
DRYDEN—*Imitation of Horace.* Bk. III. Ode XXIX. L. 65.
(See also COWLEY, also SMITH under EATING)

11
Die Gegenwart ist eine mächtige Göttin.
The present is a powerful deity.
GOETHE—*Torquato Tasso.* IV. 4. 67.

12
The acts of to-day become the precedents of to-morrow.
F. HERSCHELL—*Speech* in support of LORD HARRINGTON'S resolution, May 23, 1878.

13
What yesterday was fact to-day is doctrine.
JUNIUS. Dedication of his *Letters.*

14
Nothing that is can pause or stay;
The moon will wax, the moon will wane,
The mist and cloud will turn to rain,
The rain to mist and cloud again,
To-morrow be to-day.
LONGFELLOW—*Kéramos.* L. 34.

15
Oh, the nursery is lonely and the garden's full of rain,
And there's nobody at all who wants to play,
But I think if I should only run with all my might and main,
I could leave this dreary country of To-day.
CAROLINE MCCORMICK—*Road to Yesterday.*

16
To-day what is there in the air
That makes December seem sweet May?
There are no swallows anywhere,
Nor crocuses to crown your hair
And hail you down my garden way.
Last night the full moon's frozen stare
Struck me, perhaps; or did you say
Really—you'd come, sweet Friend and fair!
To-day?
THEOPHILE MARZIALS—*Rondel.*

17
Rise! for the day is passing,
And you lie dreaming on;
The others have buckled their armour,
And forth to the fight have gone:
A place in the ranks awaits you,
Each man has some part to play;
The Past and the Future are nothing,
In the face of the stern To-day.
ADELAIDE PROCTER—*Legends and Lyrics.*

TO-MORROW

18
Dreaming of a to-morrow, which to-morrow
Will be as distant then as 'tis to-day.
TOME BURGUILLOS—*To-morrow, and To-morrow.* JOHN BOWRING'S trans.

19
How oft my guardian angel gently cried,
"Soul, from thy casement look, and thou shalt see
How he persists to knock and wait for thee!"
And, O! how often to that voice of sorrow,
"To-morrow we will open," I replied,

1 You play the spaniel,
And think with wagging of your tongue to win me.
Henry VIII. Act V. Sc. 3. L. 126.

2
So on the tip of his subduing tongue
All kinds of arguments and question deep,
All replication prompt, and reason strong,
For his advantage still did wake and sleep;
To make the weeper laugh, the laugher weep,
He had the dialect and different skill,
Catching all passions in his craft of will.
Lover's Complaint. L. 120.

3
My tongue's use is to me no more
Than an unstringed viol or a harp.
Richard II. Act I. Sc. 3. L. 161.

4 The heart hath treble wrong
When it is barr'd the aidance of the tongue.
Venus and Adonis. L. 329.

5
Is there a tongue like Delia's o'er her cup,
That runs for ages without winding up?
YOUNG—*Love of Fame*. Satire I. L. 281.

TONSORIAL (See BARBER, HAIR)

TRAVELING

6
The traveled mind is the catholic mind educated from exclusiveness and egotism.
AMOS BRONSON ALCOTT—*Table-Talk. Traveling*.

7
Traveling is no fool's errand to him who carries his eyes and itinerary along with him.
AMOS BRONSON ALCOTT—*Table-Talk. Traveling*.

8
Travel, in the younger sort, is a part of education; in the elder, a part of experience. He that travelleth into a country before he hath some entrance into the language, goeth to school, and not to travel.
BACON—*Of Travel*.

9
Go far—too far you cannot, still the farther
The more experience finds you: And go sparing;—
One meal a week will serve you, and one suit,
Through all your travels; for you'll find it certain,
The poorer and the baser you appear,
The more you look through still.
BEAUMONT AND FLETCHER—*The Woman's Prize*. Act IV. Sc. 5. L. 199.

10 I depart,
Whither I know not; but the hour's gone by
When Albion's lessening shores could grieve or glad mine eye.
BYRON—*Childe Harold*. Canto III. St. 1.

11
He travels safest in the dark night who travels lightest.
FERNANDO CORTEZ. See PRESCOTT—*Conquest of Mexico*. Bk. V. Ch. III.

12 In travelling
I shape myself betimes to idleness
And take fools' pleasure.
GEORGE ELIOT—*The Spanish Gypsy*. Bk. I.

13
I have been a stranger in a strange land.
Exodus. II. 22.

14
Know most of the rooms of thy native country before thou goest over the threshold thereof.
FULLER—*The Holy and Profane States. Of Travelling*. Maxim IV.

15
Un viaggiatore prudente non disprezza mai il suo paese.
A wise traveler never despises his own country.
GOLDONI—*Pamela*. I. 16.

16 One who journeying
Along a way he knows not, having crossed
A place of drear extent, before him sees
A river rushing swiftly toward the deep,
And all its tossing current white with foam,
And stops and turns, and measures back his way.
HOMER—*Iliad*. Bk. V. L. 749. BRYANT'S trans.

17
Cœlum, non animum mutant, qui trans mare currunt.
Strenua nos exercet inertia, navibus atque
Quadrigis petimus bene vivere; quod petis hic est.
They change their sky, not their mind, who cross the sea. A busy idleness possesses us: we seek a happy life, with ships and carriages: the object of our search is present with us.
HORACE—*Epistles*. I. 11. 27.

18
I am fevered with the sunset,
I am fretful with the bay,
For the wander-thirst is on me
And my soul is in Cathay.
RICHARD HOVEY—*A Sea Gypsy*.

19
The wonders of each region view,
From frozen Lapland to Peru.
SOAME JENKYNS—*Epistle to Lord Lovelace*. Suggested JOHNSON'S lines.
(See also JOHNSON, STEELE, TENNYSON)

20
Let him go abroad to a distant country; let him go to some place where he is not known. Don't let him go to the devil where he is known.
SAMUEL JOHNSON—*Boswell's Life of Johnson*. (1773)

21
As the Spanish proverb says, "He who would bring home the wealth of the Indies must carry the wealth of the Indies with him." So it is in travelling: a man must carry knowledge with him, if he would bring home knowledge.
SAMUEL JOHNSON—*Boswell's Life of Johnson*. (1778)

22
The use of travelling is to regulate imagination by reality, and, instead of thinking how things may be, to see them as they are.
SAMUEL JOHNSON—PIOZZI'S *Johnsoniana*. 154.

23
Let observation with extensive view,
Survey mankind from China to Peru;
Remark each anxious toil, each eager strife,
And watch the busy scenes of crowded life.
SAMUEL JOHNSON—*Vanity of Human Wishes*.
(See also JENKYNS, WARTON)

1
Follow the Romany Patteran
Sheer to the Austral light,
Where the bosom of God is the wild west wind,
Sweeping the sea floors white.
KIPLING—*The Gypsy Trail.*

2
Down to Gehenna or up to the throne,
He travels the fastest who travels alone.
KIPLING—*The Winners.*

3
The marquise has a disagreeable day for her journey.
LOUIS XV.—*While Looking at Mme. de Pompadour's Funeral.*

4
Better sit still where born, I say,
Wed one sweet woman and love her well,
Love and be loved in the old East way,
Drink sweet waters, and dream in a spell,
Than to wander in search of the Blessed Isles,
And to sail the thousands of watery miles
In search of love, and find you at last
On the edge of the world, and a curs'd outcast.
JOAQUIN MILLER—*Pace Implora.*

5
We sack, we ransack to the utmost sands
Of native kingdoms, and of foreign lands:
We travel sea and soil; we pry, and prowl,
We progress, and we prog from pole to pole.
QUARLES—*Divine Emblems.* Bk. II. II.

6
Qui veut voyager loin ménage sa monture.
He who will travel far spares his steed.
RACINE—*Plaideurs.* I. 1.

7
Does the road wind up-hill all the way?
Yes, to the very end.
Will the day's journey take the whole long day?
From morn to night, my friend.
CHRISTINA ROSSETTI—*Up-Hill.*

8
Zählt der Pilger Meilen,
Wenn er zum fernen Gnadenbilde wallt?
Does the pilgrim count the miles
When he travels to some distant shrine?
SCHILLER—*Wallenstein's Tod.* IV. 11.

9
Nusquam est, qui ubique est.
He who is everywhere is nowhere.
SENECA—*Epistolæ Ad Lucilium.* II.

10
When I was at home, I was in a better place; but travellers must be content.
As You Like It. Act II. Sc. 4. L. 17.

11
And in his brain,
Which is as dry as the remainder biscuit
After a voyage, he hath strange places cramm'd
With observation, the which he vents
In mangled forms.
As You Like It. Act II. Sc. 7. L. 38.

12
* * * The sundry contemplation of my travels, in which my often rumination wraps me in a most humorous sadness.
As You Like It. Act IV. Sc. 1. L. 17.

13
Farewell, Monsieur Traveller: look you lisp and wear strange suits, disable all the benefits of your own country.
As You Like It. Act IV. Sc. 1. L. 33.

14
Travell'd gallants,
That fill the court with quarrels, talk, and tailors.
Henry VIII. Act I. Sc. 3. L. 19.

15
I spake of most disastr'us chances,
* * * *
Of being taken by the insolent foe
And sold to slavery; of my redemption thence
And portance in my travellers' history;
Wherein of antres vast, and deserts idle,
Rough quarries, rocks and hills whose heads touch heaven,
It was my hint to speak—such was the process;—
And of the cannibals that each other eat.
Othello. Act I. Sc. 3. L. 134.

16
I think it was Jekyll who used to say that the further he went west, the more convinced he felt that the wise men came from the east.
SYDNEY SMITH—*Lady Holland's Memoir.* Vol. I.

17
'Tis nothing when a fancied scene's in view
To skip from Covent Garden to Peru.
STEELE—*Prologue* to AMBROSE PHILLIP'S *Distressed Mother.*
(See also JENKYNS)

18
I pity the man who can travel from Dan to Beersheba and cry, " 'Tis all barren!"
STERNE—*Sentimental Journey. In the Street. Calais.*

19
When we have discovered a continent, or crossed a chain of mountains, it is only to find another ocean or another plain upon the further side . . . O toiling hands of mortals! O wearied feet, travelling ye know not whither! Soon, soon, it seems to you, you must come forth on some conspicuous hilltop, and but a little way further, against the setting sun, descry the spires of El Dorado. Little do ye know your own blessedness; for to travel hopefully is a better thing than to arrive, and the true success is to labour.
STEVENSON—*El Dorado.*

20
I always love to begin a journey on Sundays, because I shall have the prayers of the church to preserve all that travel by land or by water.
SWIFT—*Polite Conversation. Dialogue* II.

21
'Tis a mad world (my masters) and in sadnes
I travail'd madly in these dayes of madnes.
JOHN TAYLOR—*Wandering to see the Wonders of the West.*

22
Let observation with extended observation observe extensively.
TENNYSON, paraphrasing JOHNSON. See LOCKER-LAMPSON'S *Recollections of a tour with Tennyson,* in *Memoirs of Tennyson* by his son. II. 73. See also Criticism by BYRON in his *Diary,* Jan. 9, 1821.
Let observation with observant view,
Observe mankind from China to Peru.

GOLDSMITH's paraphrase. CAROLINE SPURGEON—*Works of Dr. Johnson.* (1898) DE QUINCEY quotes it from some writer, according to DR. BIRKBECK HILL—*Boswell.* I. 194. COLERIDGE quotes it, *Lecture* VI, on *Shakespeare and Milton.*

(See also JENKYNS)

1
For always roaming with a hungry heart,
Much have I seen and known.

TENNYSON—*Ulysses.*

2
Good company in a journey makes the way to seem the shorter.

IZAAK WALTON—*The Compleat Angler.* Pt. I. Ch. I.

3
All human race from China to Peru,
Pleasure, howe'er disguis'd by art, pursue.

THOMAS WARTON—*The Universal Love of Pleasure.*

(See also JOHNSON)

4
The dust is old upon my "sandal shoon,"
And still I am a pilgrim; I have roved
From wild America to Bosphor's waters,
And worshipp'd at innumerable shrines
Of beauty; and the painter's art, to me,
And sculpture, speak as with a living tongue,
And of dead kingdoms, I recall the soul,
Sitting amid their ruins.

N. P. WILLIS—*Florence Gray.* L. 46.

TREACHERY; TREASON

5
Is there not some chosen curse,
Some hidden thunder in the stores of heaven,
Red with uncommon wrath, to blast the man
Who owes his greatness to his country's ruin?

ADDISON—*Cato.* Act I. Sc. 1.

6
Nemo unquam sapiens proditori credendum putavit.

No wise man ever thought that a traitor should be trusted.

CICERO—*Orationes In Verrem.* II. 1. 15.

7
This principle is old, but true as fate,
Kings may love treason, but the traitor hate.

THOMAS DEKKER—*The Honest Whore.* Pt. I. Act IV. Sc. 4.

(See also PLUTARCH)

8
Treason is not own'd when 'tis descried;
Successful crimes alone are justified.

DRYDEN—*Medals.* L. 207.

(See also HARRINGTON)

9
O that a soldier so glorious, ever victorious in fight,
Passed from a daylight of honor into the terrible night;
Fell as the mighty archangel, ere the earth glowed in space, fell—
Fell from the patriot's heaven down to the loyalist's hell!

THOS. DUNN ENGLISH—*Arnold at Stillwater.*

10
With evil omens from the harbour sails
The ill-fated ship that worthless Arnold bears;
God of the southern winds, call up thy gales,
And whistle in rude fury round his ears.

PHILIP FRENEAU—*Arnold's Departure.*

11
Rebellion must be managed with many swords; treason to his prince's person may be with one knife.

FULLER—*The Holy and Profane States. The Traitor.*

12
Treason doth never prosper: what's the reason?
Why if it prosper, none dare call it treason.

SIR JOHN HARRINGTON—*Epigrams.* Bk. IV. Ep. V.

(See also DEKKER, also SENECA under CRIME)

13
Judas had given them the slip.

MATTHEW HENRY—*Commentaries.* Matthew. XXII.

14
Tarquin and Cæsar had each his Brutus—Charles the First, his Cromwell—and George the Third—("Treason!" shouted the Speaker) may profit by their example. If this be treason, make the most of it.

PATRICK HENRY—*Speech* (1765)

15
The man who pauses on the paths of treason,
Halts on a quicksand, the first step engulfs him.

AARON HILL—*Henry V.* Act I. Sc. 1.

16
For while the treason I detest,
The traitor still I love.

HOOLE—*Metastatio. Romulus and Hersilia.* Act I. Sc. 5.

(See also PLUTARCH)

17
Ipsa se fraus, etiamsi initio cautior fuerit, detegit.

Treachery, though at first very cautious, in the end betrays itself.

LIVY—*Annales.* XLIV. 15.

18
The traitor to Humanity is the traitor most accursed;
Man is more than Constitutions; better rot beneath the sod,
Than be true to Church and State while we are doubly false to God.

LOWELL—*On the Capture of Certain Fugitive Slaves near Washington.*

19
Hast thou betrayed my credulous innocence
With vizor'd falsehood and base forgery?

MILTON—*Comus.* L. 697.

20
Oh, colder than the wind that freezes
Founts, that but now in sunshine play'd,
Is that congealing pang which seizes
The trusting bosom, when betray'd.

MOORE—*Lalla Rookh. The Fire Worshippers.*

21
Oh, for a tongue to curse the slave
Whose treason, like a deadly blight,
Comes o'er the councils of the brave,
And blasts them in their hour of might!

MOORE—*Lalla Rookh. The Fire-Worshippers.*

22
He [Cæsar] loved the treason, but hated the traitor.

PLUTARCH—*Life of Romulus.*

(See also DEKKER, HOOLE)

1 The man was noble,
But with his last attempt he wiped it out:
Destroy'd his country, and his name remains
To the ensuing age abhorr'd.
Coriolanus. Act V. Sc. 3. L. 145.

2 Though those that are betray'd
Do feel the treason sharply, yet the traitor
Stands in worse case of woe.
Cymbeline. Act III. Sc. 4. L. 87.

3
I did pluck allegiance from men's hearts,
Loud shouts and salutations from their mouths,
Even in the presence of the crowned king.
Henry IV. Pt. I. Act III. Sc. 2. L. 52.

4
Treason is but trusted like the fox
Who, ne'er so tame, so cherish'd and locked up,
Will have a wild trick of his ancestors.
Henry IV. Pt. I. Act V. Sc. 2. L. 9.

5
Some guard these traitors to the block of death;
Treason's true bed and yielder up of breath.
Henry IV. Pt. II. Act IV. Sc. 2. L. 122.

6
Treason and murder ever kept together,
As two yoke-devils sworn to either's purpose,
Working so grossly in a natural cause,
That admiration did not hoop at them.
Henry V. Act II. Sc. 2. L. 105.

7
Smooth runs the water where the brook is deep;
And in his simple show he harbours treason.
Henry VI. Pt. II. Act III. Sc. 1. L. 53.

8
To say the truth, so Judas kiss'd his master,
And cried "all hail!" whereas he meant all harm.
Henry VI. Pt. III. Act V. Sc. 7. L. 33.

9
Et tu Brute! Then fall, Cæsar!
Julius Cæsar. Act III. Sc. 1. L. 77.

10 Know, my name is lost;
By treason's tooth bare-gnawn and canker-bit.
King Lear. Act V. Sc. 3. L. 121.

11
Tellest thou me of "ifs"? Thou art a traitor:
Off with his head!
Richard III. Act III. Sc. 4. L. 77.
Off with his head! so much for Buckingham!
As altered by COLLEY CIBBER.

TREES AND PLANTS

Unclassified

12
The place is all awave with trees,
Limes, myrtles, purple-beaded,
Acacias having drunk the lees
Of the night-dew, faint headed,
And wan, grey olive-woods, which seem
The fittest foliage for a dream.
E. B. BROWNING—*An Island.*

13
Stranger, if thou hast learned a truth which needs
No school of long experience, that the world
Is full of guilt and misery, and hast seen
Enough of all its sorrows, crimes and cares,
To tire thee of it, enter this wild wood
And view the haunts of Nature. The calm shade
Shall bring a kindred calm, and the sweet breeze
That makes the green leaves dance, shall waft a balm
To thy sick heart.
BRYANT—*Inscription for the Entrance to a Wood.*

14
The groves were God's first temples. Ere man learned
To hew the shaft, and lay the architrave,
And spread the roof above them,—ere he framed
The lofty vault, to gather and roll back
The sound of anthems; in the darkling wood,
Amidst the cool and silence, he knelt down
And offered to the Mightiest solemn thanks
And supplication.
BRYANT—*A Forest Hymn.*

15 The shad-bush, white with flowers,
Brightened the glens; the new leaved butternut
And quivering poplar to the roving breeze
Gave a balsamic fragrance.
BRYANT—*The Old Man's Counsel.* L. 28.

16
Oh, leave this barren spot to me!
Spare, woodman, spare the beechen tree!
CAMPBELL—*The Beech-Tree's Petition.*
(See also MORRIS)

17
As by the way of innuendo
Lucus is made *a non lucendo.*
CHURCHILL—*The Ghost.* Bk. II. V. 257.
Lucus a non lucendo.—Lucus (a grove), from non lucendo (not admitting light).
A derivation given by QUINTILIAN I. 16, and by others.

18
No tree in all the grove but has its charms,
Though each its hue peculiar.
COWPER—*The Task.* Bk. I. L. 307.

19
Some boundless contiguity of shade.
COWPER—*The Task.* Bk. II.
(See also THOMSON)

20
In the place where the tree falleth, there it shall be.
Ecclesiastes. XI. 3.

21
Es ist dafür gesorgt, dass die Bäume nicht in den Himmel wachsen.
Care is taken that trees do not grow into the sky.
GOETHE—*Wahrheit und Dichtung.* Motto to Pt. III.

22
Where is the pride of Summer,—the green prime,—
The many, many leaves all twinkling?—three
On the mossed elm; three on the naked lime
Trembling,—and one upon the old oak tree!
Where is the Dryad's immortality?
HOOD—*Ode. Autumn.*

23
Nullam vare, sacra vite prius arborem.
Plant no other tree before the vine.
HORACE—*Carmina.* I. 18. Imitation, in sense and meter from ALCÆUS.

1
I think that I shall never scan
A tree as lovely as a man.
* * * *
A tree depicts divinest plan,
But God himself lives in a man.
JOYCE KILMER—*Trees.*

2
I think that I shall never see
A poem lovely as a tree.
* * * *
Poems are made by fools like me,
But only God can make a tree.
JOYCE KILMER—*Trees.*

3
It was the noise
Of ancient trees falling while all was still
Before the storm, in the long interval
Between the gathering clouds and that light breeze
Which Germans call the Wind's bride.
LELAND—*The Fall of the Trees.*

4
This is the forest primeval.
LONGFELLOW—*Evangeline. Introduction.*

5
The tree is known by his fruit.
Matthew. XII. 33.

6
The gadding vine.
MILTON—*Lycidas.* L. 40.

7
Cedar, and pine, and fir, and branching palm,
A sylvan scene, and as the ranks ascend
Shade above shade, a woody theatre
Of stateliest view.
MILTON—*Paradise Lost.* Bk. IV. L. 139.

8
And all amid them stood the Tree of Life,
High eminent, blooming ambrosial fruit
Of vegetable gold.
MILTON—*Paradise Lost.* Bk. IV. L. 218.

9
A pillar'd shade
High over-arch'd, and echoing walks between.
MILTON—*Paradise Lost.* Bk. IX. L. 1,106.

10
Woodman, spare that tree!
Touch not a single bough!
In youth it sheltered me,
And I'll protect it now.
GEORGE P. MORRIS—*Woodman, Spare That Tree.*
(See also CAMPBELL)

11
When the sappy boughs
Attire themselves with blooms, sweet rudiments
Of future harvest.
JOHN PHILLIPS—*Cider.* Bk. II. L. 437.

12
Grove nods at grove.
POPE—*Moral Essays.* Ep. IV. L. 117.

13
Spreading himself like a green bay-tree.
Psalms. XXXVII. 35.

14
The highest and most lofty trees have the most reason to dread the thunder.
ROLLIN—*Ancient History.* Bk. VI. Ch. II. Sec. I.

15
Stultus est qui fructus magnarum arborum spectat, altitudinem non metitur.
He is a fool who looks at the fruit of lofty trees, but does not measure their height.
QUINTUS CURTIUS RUFUS—*De Rebus Gestis Alexandri Magni.* VII. 8.

16
So bright in death I used to say,
So beautiful through frost and cold!
A lovelier thing I know to-day,
The leaf is growing old,
And wears in grace of duty done,
The gold and scarlet of the sun.
MARGARET E. SANGSTER—*A Maple Leaf.*

17
Hath not old custom made this life more sweet
Than that of painted pomp? Are not these woods
More free from peril than the envious court?
As You Like It. Act II. Sc. 1. L. 2.

18
But, poor old man, thou prunest a rotten tree,
That cannot so much as a blossom yield
In lieu of all thy pains and husbandry.
As You Like It. Act II. Sc. 3. L. 63.

19
Under the greenwood tree
Who loves to lie with me,
And tune his merry note
Unto the sweet bird's throat,
Come hither, come hither, come hither:
No enemy here shall he see,
But winter and rough weather.
As You Like It. Act II. Sc. 5. L. 1.

20
If aught possess thee from me, it is dross,
Usurping ivy, brier, or idle moss;
Who, all for want of pruning, with intrusion
Infect thy sap and live on thy confusion.
Comedy of Errors. Act II. Sc. 2. L. 179.

21
Who am no more but as the tops of trees,
Which fence the roots they grow by and defend them.
Pericles. Act I. Sc. 2. L. 29.

22
A barren detested vale, you see it is;
The trees, though summer, yet forlorn and lean,
O'ercome with moss and baleful mistletoe.
Titus Andronicus. Act II. Sc. 3. L. 93.

23
Now all the tree-tops lay asleep,
Like green waves on the sea,
As still as in the silent deep
The ocean-woods may be.
SHELLEY—*The Recollection.* II.

24
Pun-provoking thyme.
SHENSTONE—*The Schoolmistress.* St. 11.

25
The trees were gazing up into the sky,
Their bare arms stretched in prayer for the snows.
ALEX. SMITH—*A Life-Drama.* Sc. 2.

26
The laurell, meed of mightie conquerours
And poets sage; the firre that weepeth still;
The willow, worne of forlorne paramours;
The eugh, obedient to the bender's will;
The birch, for shafts; the sallow for the mill;
The mirrhe sweete-bleeding in the bitter wound;
The warlike beech; the ash for nothing ill;

The fruitfull olive; and the platane round;
The carver holme; the maple seldom inward sound.
SPENSER—*Faerie Queene.* Bk. I. Canto I. St. 8.

1
A temple whose transepts are measured by miles,
Whose chancel has morning for priest,
Whose floor-work the foot of no spoiler defiles,
Whose musical silence no music beguiles,
No festivals limit its feast.
SWINBURNE—*Palace of Pan.* St. 8.

2 The woods appear
With crimson blotches deeply dashed and crossed,—
Sign of the fatal pestilence of Frost.
BAYARD TAYLOR—*Mon-Da-Min.* St. 38.

3
The linden broke her ranks and rent
The woodbine wreaths that bind her,
And down the middle buzz! she went
With all her bees behind her!
The poplars, in long order due,
With cypress promenaded,
The shock-head willows two and two
By rivers gallopaded.
TENNYSON—*Amphion.* St. 5.

4
O Love, what hours were thine and mine,
In lands of palm and southern pine;
In lands of palm, of orange-blossom,
Of olive, aloe, and maize, and vine.
TENNYSON—*The Daisy.* St. 1.

5
The woods are hush'd, their music is no more;
The leaf is dead, the yearning past away;
New leaf, new life—the days of frost are o'er;
New life, new love, to suit the newer day:
New loves are sweet as those that went before:
Free love—free field—we love but while we may.
TENNYSON—*Idylls of the King. The Last Tournament.* L. 276.

6
Now rings the woodland loud and long,
The distance takes a lovelier hue,
And drowned in yonder living blue
The lark becomes a sightless song.
TENNYSON—*In Memoriam.* Pt. CXV.

7
But see the fading many-coloured Woods,
Shade deep'ning over shade, the country round
Imbrown; crowded umbrage, dusk and dun,
Of every hue from wan declining green
To sooty dark.
THOMSON—*Seasons. Autumn.* L. 950.

8 Some to the holly hedge
Nestling repair; and to the thicket some;
Some to the rude protection of the thorn.
THOMSON—*Seasons. Spring.* L. 634.

9
Welcome, ye shades! ye bowery Thickets hail!
Ye lofty Pines! ye venerable Oaks!
Ye Ashes wild, resounding o'er the steep!
Delicious is your shelter to the soul.
THOMSON—*Seasons. Summer.* L. 469.

10
Or ruminate in the contiguous shade.
THOMSON—*Seasons. Winter.*
(See also COWPER)

11
Sure thou did'st flourish once! and many springs,
Many bright mornings, much dew, many showers,
Passed o'er thy head; many light hearts and wings,
Which now are dead, lodg'd in thy living bowers.

And still a new succession sings and flies;
Fresh groves grow up, and their green branches shoot
Towards the old and still-enduring skies;
While the low violet thrives at their root.
VAUGHAN—*The Timber.*

12
In such green palaces the first kings reign'd,
Slept in their shades, and angels entertain'd;
With such old counsellors they did advise,
And by frequenting sacred groves grew wise.
EDMUND WALLER—*On St. James' Park.* L. 71.

13
A brotherhood of venerable Trees.
WORDSWORTH—*Sonnet composed at Castle——.*

14
One impulse from a vernal wood
May teach you more of man,
Of moral evil and of good,
Than all the sages can.
WORDSWORTH—*The Tables Turned.*

TRIALS

15
Pray, pray, thou who also weepest,—
And the drops will slacken so;
Weep, weep—and the watch thou keepest,
With a quicker count will go.
Think,—the shadow on the dial
For the nature most undone,
Marks the passing of the trial,
Proves the presence of the sun.
E. B. BROWNING—*Fourfold Aspect.*

16
The child of trial, to mortality
And all its changeful influences given;
On the green earth decreed to move and die,
And yet by such a fate prepared for heaven.
SIR HUMPHREY DAVY—*Written after Recovery from a Dangerous Illness.*

17
'Tis a lesson you should heed,
Try, try, try again.
If at first you don't succeed,
Try, try, try again.
W. E. HICKSON—*Try and try again.*

18
But noble souls, through dust and heat,
Rise from disaster and defeat
The stronger.
LONGFELLOW—*The Sifting of Peter.* St. 7.

19
Rocks whereon greatest men have oftest wreck'd.
MILTON—*Paradise Regained.* Bk. 2. L. 228.

20
There are no crown-wearers in heaven who were not cross-bearers here below.
SPURGEON—*Gleanings among the Sheaves. Cross-Bearers.*

1
As sure as ever God puts His children in the furnace, He will be in the furnace with them.
SPURGEON—*Gleanings among the Sheaves. Privileges of Trial.*

2
Trials teach us what we are; they dig up the soil, and let us see what we are made of; they just turn up some of the ill weeds on to the surface.
SPURGEON—*Gleanings among the Sheaves. The Use of Trial.*

TRIFLES

3
Seeks painted trifles and fantastic toys,
And eagerly pursues imaginary joys.
AKENSIDE—*The Virtuoso.* St. 10.

4
This is a gimcrack
That can get nothing but new fashions on you.
BEAUMONT AND FLETCHER—*Older Brother.* Act III. Sc. 3.

5
Little drops of water, little grains of sand
Make the mighty ocean, and the pleasant land
JULIA FLETCHER CARNEY—*Little Things.*
(See also YOUNG)

6
Little deeds of kindness, little words of love,
Help to make earth happy, like the heaven above.
Changed by later compilers to "make this earth an Eden."
JULIA FLETCHER CARNEY—*Little Things.*

7
He that contemneth small things shall fall by little and little.
Ecclesiasticus. XIX. 1.

8
He that despiseth small things will perish by little and little.
EMERSON—*Prudence.*

9
Small things are best:
Grief and unrest
To rank and wealth are given;
But little things
On little wings
Bear little souls to Heaven.
REV. F. W. FABER—*Written in a Little Lady's Little Album.*

10
Das kleinste Haar wirft seinen Schatten.
The smallest hair throws its shadow.
GOETHE—*Sprüche in Prosa.* III.

11
These little things are great to little man.
GOLDSMITH—*The Traveller.* L. 42.

12
Coups d'épingle.
Policy of pin pricks.
L. M. DE LA HAYE—*Vicomte de Cormenin.*
Des coups d'épée. . . Mais pas de coups d'épingle.
A stroke of the sword . . . but not a pin prick.
DAUDET—*Tartarin de Tarascon.* Part of title of Ch. XI. Phrase at end of chapter.
J'aime à rêver, mais ne veux pas
Qu'à coups d'épingle on me réveille.
I love to dream, but do not wish
To have a pin prick rouse me.
As used by JACQUES DELILLE—*La Conversation*, earlier than DAUDET.
Ce ne sont jamais les coups d'épingle qui décident de la fortune des États.
It is never the pin pricks which decide the fortune of states.
DE VERGENNES—*Letter to D'Angiviller.* Aug. 11, 1777.
(See also NAPOLEON)

13
Hæ nugæ seria ducent
In mala.
These trifles will lead to serious mischief.
HORACE—*Ars Poetica.* 451.

14
For precept must be upon precept, precept upon precept; line upon line, line upon line; here a little, and there a little.
Isaiah. XXVIII. 10.

15
A little one shall become a thousand, and a small one a strong nation.
Isaiah. LX. 22.

16
Atque utinam his potius nugis tota illa dedisset
Tempora sævitiæ.
Would to heaven he had given up to trifles like these all the time which he devoted to cruelty.
JUVENAL—*Satires.* IV. 150.

17
Ex parvis sæpe magnarum momenta rerum pendent.
Events of great consequence often spring from trifling circumstances.
LIVY—*Annales.* XXVII. 9.

18
The soft droppes of raine perce the hard
Marble, many strokes overthrow the tallest Oke.
LYLY—*Euphues.* ARBER'S reprint. P. 81. (1579)

19
They made light of it.
Matthew. XXII. 5.

20
It was possible to live under the regulations established by Sir George [Cockburn], but now we are tortured to death by pin-point wounds.
NAPOLEON according to LADY MALCOLM—*Diary of St. Helena.*

21
For the maintenance of peace, nations should avoid the pin-pricks which forerun cannon-shots.
NAPOLEON to the CZAR ALEXANDER. At Tilsit, June 22, 1807.
(See also HAYE)

22
De multis grandis acervus erit.
Out of many things a great heap will be formed.
OVID—*Remedia Amoris.* 424.

23
Peu de chose nous console, parceque peu de chose nous afflige.
A little thing comforts us because a little thing afflicts us.
PASCAL—*Pensées.* VI. 25.

24
At every trifle scorn to take offence;
That always shows great pride or little sense.
POPE—*Essay on Criticism.* L. 386.

1
What dire offence from amorous causes springs,
What mighty contests rise from trivial things.
POPE—*Rape of the Lock.* Canto I. L. 1.

2
And many strokes, though with a little axe,
Hew down and fell the hardest-timber'd oak.
Henry VI. Pt. III. Act II. Sc. 1. L. 54.

3
Trifles, light as air.
Othello. Act III. Sc. 3. L. 322.

4
Come, gentlemen, we sit too long on trifles,
And waste the time, which looks for other revels.
Pericles. Act II. Sc. 3. L. 92.

5
A snapper-up of unconsidered trifles.
A Winter's Tale. Act IV. Sc. 3. L. 26.

6
A trifle makes a dream, a trifle breaks.
TENNYSON—*Sea Dreams.* L. 140.

7
Magno iam conatu magnas nugas.
By great efforts obtain great trifles.
TERENCE—*Heauton timorumenos.* IV. 1. 8.

8
Think nought a trifle, though it small appear;
Small sands the mountain, moments make the year.
YOUNG—*Love of Fame.* Satire VI. L. 205.
(See also CARNEY)

9
For who hath despised the day of small things?
Zechariah. IV. 10.

TROUBLE

10
Le chagrin monte en croupe et galope avec lui.
Trouble rides behind and gallops with him.
BOILEAU—*Épître.* V. 44

11
This peck of troubles.
CERVANTES—*Don Quixote.* Pt. II. Ch. LIII.

12
Jucunda memoria est præteritorum malorum.
The memory of past troubles is pleasant.
CICERO—*De Finibus.* Bk. II. 32.

13
You may batter your way through the thick of the fray,
You may sweat, you may swear, you may grunt;
You may be a jack-fool, if you must, but this rule
Should ever be kept at the front;—
Don't fight with your pillow, but lay down your head
And kick every worriment out of the bed.
EDMUND VANCE COOKE—*Don't take your Troubles to Bed.*

14
I survived that trouble so likewise may I survive this one.
Complaint of Deor. II. 7. STOPFORD BROOKE's rendering in modern English.

15
Sweet is the remembrance of troubles when you are in safety.
EURIPIDES—*Andromeda.* 10. 2. (Fragm.)

16
Die Müh'ist klein, der Spass ist gross.
The trouble is small, the fun is great.
GOETHE—*Faust.* I. 21. 218.

17
Man is born unto trouble, as the sparks fly upward.
Job V. 7.

18
Curæ leves loquuntur, ingentes stupent.
Light troubles speak; immense troubles are silent.
SENECA—*Hippolytus.* Act II. Sc. 3. L. 607.

19
Dubiam salutem qui dat adflictis negat.
He who tenders doubtful safety to those in trouble refuses it.
SENECA—*Œdipus.* CCXIII.

20
To take arms against a sea of troubles.
Hamlet. Act III. Sc. 1. L. 59. Sea of troubles found in EURIPIDES—*Hippolytus.*

TRUST

21
The greatest trust between man and man is the trust of giving counsel.
BACON—*Essays.* *Of Counsel.*

22
Build a little fence of trust
Around to-day;
Fill the space with loving work,
And therein stay;
Look not through the sheltering bars
Upon to-morrow;
God will help thee bear what comes
Of joy or sorrow.
MARY FRANCES BUTTS—*Trust.*

23
Who would not rather trust and be deceived?
ELIZA COOK—*Love On.*

24
Trust in God, and keep your powder dry.
CROMWELL. In COL. BLACKER—*Oliver's Advice.* See *Ballads of Ireland.* I. 191.

25
A little trust that when we die
We reap our sowing, and so—Good-bye.
GEORGE B. DUMAURIER—*Trilby.* Inscribed on his Memorial Tablet, Hampstead Churchyard.

26
Dear, I trusted you
As holy men trust God. You could do naught
That was not pure and loving—though the deed
Might pierce me unto death.
GEORGE ELIOT—*The Spanish Gypsy.* Bk. III.

27
Trust men, and they will be true to you; treat them greatly, and they will show themselves great.
EMERSON—*Essays.* *On Prudence.*

28
I too
Will cast the spear and leave the rest to Jove.
HOMER—*Iliad.* Bk. XVII. L. 622. BRYANT'S trans.

29
Thou trustest in the staff of this broken reed.
Isaiah. XXXVI. 6.

1
O holy trust! O endless sense of rest!
Like the beloved John
To lay his head upon the Saviour's breast,
And thus to journey on!
LONGFELLOW—*Hymn.* St. 5.

2
To be trusted is a greater compliment than to be loved.
GEORGE MACDONALD—*The Marquis of Lossie.* Ch. IV.

3
That, in tracing the shade, I shall find out the sun,
Trust to me!
OWEN MEREDITH (Lord Lytton)—*Lucile.* Pt. II. Canto VI. St. 15.

4
"Eyes to the blind"
Thou art, O God! Earth I no longer see,
Yet trustfully my spirit looks to thee.
ALICE BRADLEY NEAL—*Blind.* Pt. II.

5
You may trust him in the dark.
Roman proverb cited by CICERO.

6
I well believe
Thou wilt not utter what thou dost not know;
And so far will I trust thee.
Henry IV. Pt. I. Act II. Sc. 3. L. 114.

7
Let every eye negotiate for itself,
And trust no agent.
Much Ado About Nothing. Act II. Sc. 1. L. 185.

8
My life upon her faith!
Othello. Act I. Sc. 3. L. 295.

9
I am sorry I must never trust thee more,
But count the world a stranger for thy sake:
The private wound is deepest.
Two Gentlemen of Verona. Act V. Sc. 4. L. 69.

TRUST (PUBLIC) (See also GOVERNMENT)

10
All government is a trust. Every branch of government is a trust, and immemorially acknowledged to be so.
JEREMY BENTHAM.

11
All persons possessing any portion of power ought to be strongly and awfully impressed with an idea that they act in trust, and that they are to account for their conduct in that trust to the one great Master, Author, and Founder of society.
BURKE—*Reflections on the Revolution in France.*

12
To execute laws is a royal office; to execute orders is not to be a king. However, a political executive magistracy, though merely such, is a great trust.
BURKE—*Reflections on the Revolution in France.*

13
The very essence of a free government consists in considering offices as public trusts, bestowed for the good of the country, and not for the benefit of an individual or a party.
JOHN C. CALHOUN—*Speech.* July 13, 1835.

14
Government is a trust, and the officers of the government are trustees; and both the trust and the trustees are created for the benefit of the people.
HENRY CLAY—*Speech at Lexington.* May 16, 1829.

15
Public officers are the servants and agents of the people, to execute laws which the people have made and within the limits of a constitution which they have established.
GROVER CLEVELAND—*Letter of Acceptance as Candidate for Governor.* Oct. 7, 1882. See W. O. STODDARD'S *Life of Cleveland.* Ch. IX.

16
Your every voter, as surely as your chief magistrate, under the same high sanction, though in a different sphere, exercises a public trust.
GROVER CLEVELAND — *Inaugural Address.* March 4, 1885. See also speech in accepting the nomination to the Mayoralty of Buffalo. First Message as Mayor. Reply to the committee appointed by the Nat. Democratic Convention to inform him of his nomination to the Presidency, July 28, 1884.

17
The appointing power of the Pope is treated as a public trust, and not as a personal perquisite.
W. W. CRAPO.

18
All power is a trust; that we are accountable for its exercise; that from the people and for the people all springs, and all must exist.
BENJ. DISRAELI—*Vivian Grey.* Bk. VI. Ch. VII.
(See also LINCOLN under GOVERNMENT)

19
Public office is a public trust, the authority and opportunities of which must be used as absolutely as the public moneys for the public benefit, and not for the purposes of any individual or party.
DORMAN B. EATON—*The "Spoils" System and Civil-Service Reform.* Ch. III. *The Merit System.*

20
If you use your office as you would a private trust, and the moneys as trust funds, if you faithfully perform your duty, we, the people, may put you in the Presidential chair.
HON. R. P. FLOWER. On the night of Mr. Cleveland's election as Governor of New York.

21
It is not fit the public trusts should be lodged in the hands of any till they are first proved and found fit for the business they are to be entrusted with.
MATTHEW HENRY—*Commentaries.* Timothy. III.

22
When a man assumes a public trust, he should consider himself as public property.
THOS. JEFFERSON. To BARON HUMBOLDT. See RAYNER'S *Life of Jefferson.* P. 356.

23
The English doctrine that all power is a trust for the public good.
MACAULAY—*Essay on Horace Walpole.* (1833)

1
The phrase "public office is a public trust," has of late become common property.

CHAS. SUMNER—*Speech in the United States Senate.* May 31, 1872. According to COL. JOHN S. WOLF, of Champaign, it originated in a decision of JUSTICE SAMUEL D. LOCKWOOD, of the Illinois Supreme Court, prior to 1840. He served from 1825 to 1848. *Washington Star*, May 5, 1891, assigns it to THOMAS M. COOLEY. See *Constitutional Law.* (Pub. 1880.) P. 303. CHARLES JAMES FOX. (1788) SYDNEY SMITH in *Edinburgh Review.* (1825) WEBSTER—*Bunker Hill Address.* (1825) PRESIDENT ANDREW JOHNSON'S *Message.* (1867) ABRAM S. HEWITT—*Speech.* (1883) DANIEL S. LAMONT. *Motto of Pamphlet.* (1884)

TRUTH

2
Yet the deepest truths are best read between the lines, and, for the most part, refuse to be written.

AMOS BRONSON ALCOTT — *Concord Days. June. Goethe.*

3
But no pleasure is comparable to the standing upon the vantage ground of Truth.

BACON—*Essays. Of Truth.*

4
How sweet the words of Truth, breath'd from
the lips of Love.

BEATTIE—*The Minstrel.* Bk. II. St. 53.

5
To say the truth, though I say 't that should not say 't.

BEAUMONT AND FLETCHER—*Wit at Several Weapons.* Act II.

6
La vérité n'a point cet air impétueux.
Truth has not such an urgent air.

BOILEAU—*L'Art Poétique.* I. 198.

7
Le vrai peut quelquefois n'être pas vraisemblable.
At times truth may not seem probable.

BOILEAU—*L'Art Poétique.* III. 48.

8
Think truly, and thy thoughts
Shall the world's famine feed.
Speak truly, and each word of thine
Shall be a fruitful seed.
Live truly, and thy life shall be
A great and noble creed.

HORATIUS BONAR—*Hymns of Faith and Hope.* P. 113. (Ed. 1867)

9
Magna est veritas et prævalebit.
Truth is mighty and will prevail.

THOMAS BROOKS is said to have been the first to use the expression. (1662) Found in SCOTT — *Talisman.* Ch. XIX. Bishop JEWEL. PURCHAS—*Microcosmus.* THACKERAY—*Roundabout Papers.*

O magna vis veritas. Found in CICERO—*Oratio Pro Cœlio Rufo.* XXVI.

10
Se non è vero, è molto ben trovato.
If it is not true it is very well invented.

GIORDANO BRUNO—*Degli Eroici Furori.* CARDINAL D'ESTE. Of ARIOSTO'S *Orlando Furioso.*

11
Truth crushed to earth shall rise again:
Th' eternal years of God are hers;
But Error, wounded, writhes in pain,
And dies among his worshippers.

BRYANT—*The Battle Field.* St. 9.

12
Truth makes on the ocean of nature no one track of light—every eye looking on finds its own.

BULWER-LYTTON—*Caxtoniana.* Essay XIV.

13
Arm thyself for the truth!

BULWER-LYTTON—*Lady of Lyons.* Act V. Sc. 1.

14
Better be cheated to the last,
Than lose the blessed hope of truth.

MRS. BUTLER (Fanny Kemble).

15
For truth is precious and divine;
Too rich a pearl for carnal swine.

BUTLER—*Hudibras.* Pt. II. Canto II. L. 257.

16
'Tis not antiquity, nor author,
That makes truth truth, altho' time's daughter.

BUTLER—*Hudibras.* Pt. II. Canto III.
(See also GELLIUS)

17
More proselytes and converts use t' accrue
To false persuasions than the right and true;
For error and mistake are infinite,
But truth has but one way to be i' th' right.

BUTLER—*Miscellaneous Thoughts.* L. 113.

18
No words suffice the secret soul to show,
For Truth denies all eloquence to Woe.

BYRON—*Corsair.* Canto III. St. 22.

19
'Tis strange—but true; for truth is always
strange,
Stranger than fiction.

BYRON—*Don Juan.* Canto XIV. St. 101.

20
A man protesting against error is on the way towards uniting himself with all men that believe in truth.

CARLYLE—*Heroes and Hero Worship.* IV.

21
Truths turn into dogmas the moment they are disputed.

G. K. CHESTERTON—*Heretics.*

22
When fiction rises pleasing to the eye,
Men will believe, because they love the lie;
But truth herself, if clouded with a frown,
Must have some solemn proof to pass her down.

CHURCHILL—*Epistle to Hogarth.* L. 291.

23
Qui semel a veritate deflexit, hic non majore religione ad perjurium quam ad mendacium perduci consuevit.

He who has once deviated from the truth, usually commits perjury with as little scruple as he would tell a lie.

CICERO—*Oratio Pro Quinto Roscio Comœdo.* XX.

1
Natura inest mentibus nostris insatiabilis quædam cupiditas veri videndi.

Our minds possess by nature an insatiable desire to know the truth.

CICERO—*Tusculanarum Disputationum.* I. 18.

2
Tell the truth or trump—but get the trick.

S. L. CLEMENS (Mark Twain)—*Pudd'nhead Wilson.*

3
For truth is unwelcome, however divine.

COWPER—*The Flatting Mill.* St. 6.

4
But what is truth? 'Twas Pilate's question put
To Truth itself, that deign'd him no reply.

COWPER—*The Task.* Bk. III. L. 270.

5
Nature * * * has buried truth deep in the bottom of the sea.

DEMOCRITUS. Quoted by CICERO—*Academic Questions.* Bk. II. Ch. X. C. D. YONGE'S trans. Credited to DEMOCRITUS by LACTANTIUS—*Institutiones.* Bk. III. Ch. XXVIII.
(See also RABELAIS)

6
"It was as true," said Mr. Barkis, . . . "as taxes is. And nothing's truer than them."

DICKENS—*David Copperfield.* Ch. XXI.

7
The first great work (a task performed by few)
Is that yourself may to yourself be true.

WENTWORTH DILLON—*An Essay on Translated Verse.* L. 71.
(See also HAMLET)

8
For truth has such a face and such a mien,
As to be lov'd needs only to be seen.

DRYDEN—*The Hind and the Panther.* Pt. I. L. 33.
(See also POPE under VICE)

9
Truth is immortal; error is mortal.

MARY B. G. EDDY—*Science and Health,* 466: 13.

10
Truth has rough flavours if we bite it through.

GEORGE ELIOT—*Armgart.* Sc. 2.

11
The greater the truth the greater the libel.

Attributed to LORD ELLENBOROUGH. (About 1789) BURNS credits it to LORD MANSFIELD.
(See also MOORE)

12
The nobler the truth or sentiment, the less imports the question of authorship.

EMERSON—*Letters and Social Aims. Quotation and Originality.*

13
Though love repine and reason chafe,
There came a voice without reply,
"'Tis man's perdition to be safe,
When for the truth he ought to die."

EMERSON—*Quatrains. Sacrifice.*

14
Vincer veris.

I am conquered by truth.

ERASMUS—*Diluculum.*

15
But above all things truth beareth away the victory.

I Esdras. III. 12. Inscription on the New York Public Library.

16
Great is truth, and mighty above all things.

I Esdras. IV. 41.

17
Si je tenais toutes les vérités dans ma main, je me donnerais bien de garde de l'ouvrir aux hommes.

If I held all of truth in my hand I would beware of opening it to men.

FONTENELLE.

18
Truth only smells sweet forever, and illusions, however innocent, are deadly as the canker worm.

FROUDE—*Short Studies on Great Subjects. Calvinism.*

19
Lest men suspect your tale untrue,
Keep probability in view.

GAY—*The Painter who Pleased Nobody and Everybody.*

20
Alius quidam veterum pœtarum cuius nomen mihi nunc memoriæ non est veritatem temporis filiam esse dixit.

There is another old poet whose name I do not now remember who said Truth is the daughter of Time.

AULUS GELLIUS—*Noctes Atticæ.* XII. 11. Par. 2. Veritas temporis filia. Found on the reverse of several coins of QUEEN MARY I.
(See also BUTLER)

21
Her terrible tale
You can't assail,
With truth it quite agrees;
Her taste exact
For faultless fact
Amounts to a disease.

W. S. GILBERT—*Mikado.* Act II.

22
Truth like a torch, the more 'tis shook, it shines.

SIR WILLIAM HAMILTON—*Discussions on Philosophy.* Title Page.
(See also LOGAU)

23
One truth discovered is immortal, and entitles its author to be so: for, like a new substance in nature, it cannot be destroyed.

HAZLITT—*The Spirit of the Age. Jeremy Bentham.*

24
All truths are not to be told.

HERBERT—*Jacula Prudentum.*

25
Dare to be true, nothing can need a lie;
A fault which needs it most, grows two thereby.

HERBERT—*The Temple. The Church Porch.*

26
Truth is tough. It will not break, like a bubble, at a touch; nay, you may kick it about all day, like a foot-ball, and it will be round and full at evening.

HOLMES—*Professor at the Breakfast Table.* V.

1
Nuda veritas. (Nudaque veritas.)
The naked truth.
HORACE—*Carmina*. I. 24. 7.
(See also PENN)

2
Quid verum atque decens curo et rogo, et omnis in hoc sum.
My cares and my inquiries are for decency and truth, and in this I am wholly occupied.
HORACE—*Epistles*. I. 1. 11.

3
Ridentem dicere verum,
Quid vetat.
What forbids a man to speak the truth in a laughing way?
HORACE—*Satires*. I. 24.

4
The truth shall make you free.
John. VIII. 32.

5
There is no truth in him.
John. VIII. 44.

6
Le contraire des bruits qui courent des affaires ou des personnes est souvent la vérité.
The opposite of what is noised about concerning men and things is often the truth.
LA BRUYÈRE—*Les Caractères*. XII.

7
La vérité ne fait pas tant de bien dans le monde, que ses apparences y font de mal.
Truth does not do so much good in the world, as the appearance of it does evil.
LA ROCHEFOUCAULD—*Maximes*. 59.

8
Veritatem laborare nimis sæpe, aiunt, extingui nunquam.
It is said that truth is often eclipsed but never extinguished.
LIVY—*Annales*. XXII. 39.

9
The best way to come to truth being to examine things as really they are, and not to conclude they are, as we fancy of ourselves, or have been taught by others to imagine.
LOCKE—*Human Understanding*. Bk. II. Ch. XII.

10
To love truth for truth's sake is the principal part of human perfection in this world, and the seed-plot of all other virtues.
LOCKE—*Letter to Anthony Collins, Esq.* Oct. 29, 1703.

11
When by night the frogs are croaking, kindle but a torch's fire;
Ha! how soon they all are silent! Thus Truth silences the liar.
FRIEDRICH VON LOGAU. See LONGFELLOW'S trans. *Poetic Aphorisms. Truth.*
(See also HAMILTON)

12
Who dares
To say that he alone has found the truth?
LONGFELLOW—*Christus*. Pt. III. *John Endicott.* Act II. Sc. 3.

13
Get but the truth once uttered, and 'tis like
A star new-born that drops into its place
And which, once circling in its placid round,
Not all the tumult of the earth can shake.
LOWELL—*A Glance Behind the Curtain*. L. 173.

14
Put golden padlocks on Truth's lips, be callous as ye will,
From soul to soul, o'er all the world, leaps one electric thrill.
LOWELL—*On the Capture of Certain Fugitive Slaves near Washington.*

15
Then to side with Truth is noble when we share her wretched crust,
Ere her cause bring fame and profit, and 'tis prosperous to be just;
Then it is the brave man chooses, while the coward stands aside,
Doubting in his abject spirit, till his Lord is crucified.
LOWELL—*The Present Crisis.*

16
Truth forever on the scaffold. Wrong forever on the throne.
LOWELL—*The Present Crisis.*

17
Children and fooles speake true.
LYLY—*Endymion.*

18
But there is no veil like light—no adamantine armor against hurt like the truth.
GEORGE MACDONALD—*The Marquis of Lossie*. Ch. LXXI.

19
Veritatis absolutus sermo ac semper est simplex.
The language of truth is unadorned and always simple.
AMMIANUS MARCELLINUS—*Annales*. XIV. 10.

20
Pericula veritati sæpe contigua.
Truth is often attended with danger.
AMMIANUS MARCELLINUS—*Annales*. XXVI. 1.

21
Truth, when not sought after, sometimes comes to light.
MENANDER—*Ex Verberata*. P. 160.

22
Not a truth has to art or to science been given,
But brows have ached for it, and souls toil'd and striven;
And many have striven, and many have fail'd,
And many died, slain by the truth they assail'd.
OWEN MEREDITH (Lord Lytton)—*Lucile*. Pt. II. Canto VI. St. 1.

23
Who ever knew truth put to the worse in a free and open encounter?
MILTON—*Areopagitica.*

24
Truth is as impossible to be soiled by any outward touch as the sunbeam.
MILTON—*Doctrine and Discipline of Divorce.*

25
Ev'n them who kept thy truth so pure of old,
When all our fathers worshipp'd stocks and stones,
Forget not.
MILTON—*Sonnet. Massacre in Piedmont.*

1
I speak truth, not so much as I would, but as much as I dare; and I dare a little the more as I grow older.
MONTAIGNE—*Essays. Of Repentance.*

2
For oh, 'twas nuts to the Father of Lies,
(As this wily fiend is named in the Bible)
To find it settled by Laws so wise
That the greater the truth, the worse the libel.
MOORE—*A Case of Libel. Odes on Cash, Corn, etc.*
(See also ELLENBOROUGH)

3
I seem to have been only like a boy playing on the seashore and diverting myself in now and then finding a smoother pebble or a prettier shell than ordinary, whilst the great ocean of truth lay all undiscovered before me.
ISAAC NEWTON—*Statement.* In BREWSTER—*Memoirs.* Vol. II. Ch. XXVII.
As children gathering pebbles on the shore.
MILTON—*Paradise Regained.* Bk. IV. L. 330.

4
In the mountains of truth, you never climb in vain.
NIETZSCHE—*Thus spake Zarathustra.*

5
We know the truth, not only by the reason, but also by the heart.
PASCAL—*Thoughts.* Ch. X. 1.

6
Naked Truth needs no shift.
WILLIAM PENN—*Title of a Broadside.* (1674)
(See also HORACE)

7
Ego verum amo, verum volo mihi dici; mendacem odi.
I love truth and wish to have it always spoken to me: I hate a liar.
PLAUTUS—*Mostellaria.* I. 3. 26.

8
When truth or virtue an affront endures,
Th' affront is mine, my friend, and should be yours.
POPE—*Epilogue to Satires.* Dialogue I. L. 207.

9
'Tis not enough your counsel still be true;
Blunt truths more mischief than nice falsehoods do.
POPE—*Essay on Criticism.* Pt. III. L. 13.

10
Farewell then, verse, and love, and ev'ry toy,
The rhymes and rattles of the man or boy;
What right, what true, what fit we justly call,
Let this be all my care—for this is all.
POPE—*First Book of Horace.* Ep. I. L. 17.

11
Dum omnia quærimus, aliquando ad verum, ubi minime expectavimus, pervenimus.
While we are examining into everything we sometimes find truth where we least expected it.
QUINTILIAN—*De Institutione Oratoria.* XII. 8. 3.

12
Let us seek the solution of these doubts at the bottom of the inexhaustible well, where Heraclitus says that truth is hidden.
RABELAIS—*Pantagruel.* Ch. XVIII.
(See also DEMOCRITUS, SENECA, WOLCOT)

13
Die Treue warnt vor drohenden Verbrechen,
Die Rachgier spricht von den begangenen.
Truth warns of threatening crimes,
Malice speaks of those which were committed.
SCHILLER—*Don Carlos.* III. 4. 124.

14
Involuta veritas in alto latet.
Truth lies wrapped up and hidden in the depths.
SENECA—*De Beneficiis.* VII. 1.
(See also RABELAIS)

15
Veritatem dies aperit.
Time discovers truth.
SENECA—*De Ira.* II. 22.

16
Veritatis simplex oratio est.
The language of truth is simple.
SENECA—*Epistolæ Ad Lucilium.* XLIX.

17
Veritas odit moras.
Truth hates delays.
SENECA—*Œdipus.* 850.

18
That truth should be silent I had almost forgot.
Antony and Cleopatra. Act II. Sc. 2. L. 110.

19
To thine own self be true,
And it must follow, as the night the day,
Thou canst not then be false to any man.
Hamlet. Act I. Sc. 3. L. 78.
(See also DILLON)

20
If circumstances lead me, I will find
Where truth is hid, though it were hid indeed
Within the centre.
Hamlet. Act II. Sc. 2. L. 157.

21
Mark now, how a plain tale shall put you down.
Henry IV. Pt. I. Act II. Sc. 4. L. 281.

22
Tell truth and shame the devil.
If thou have power to raise him, bring him hither,
And I'll be sworn I have power to shame him hence.
Henry IV. Pt. I. Act III. Sc. 1. L. 59.
(See also SWIFT)

23
What, can the devil speak true?
Macbeth. Act I. Sc. 3. L. 107.

24
But 'tis strange:
And oftentimes, to win us to our harm,
The instruments of darkness tell us truths,
Win us with honest trifles, to betray's
In deepest consequence.
Macbeth. Act I. Sc. 3. L. 122.

25
Truth is truth
To the end of reckoning.
Measure for Measure. Act V. Sc. 1. L. 45.

26
But wonder on, till truth make all things plain.
Midsummer Night's Dream. Act V. Sc. 1. L. 129.

27
They breathe truth that breathe their words in pain.
Richard II. Act II. Sc. 1. L. 8.

1
Methinks the truth should live from age to age,
As 'twere retail'd to all posterity,
Even to the general all-ending day.
Richard III. Act III. Sc. 1. L. 76.

2
My man's as true as steel.
Romeo and Juliet. Act II. Sc. 4. L. 209.
Troilus and Cressida. Act III. Sc. 2. L. 166.

3
And simple truth miscall'd simplicity,
And captive good attending captain ill.
Sonnet LXVI.

4
Truth needs no colour, with his colour fix'd;
Beauty no pencil, beauty's truth to lay;
But best is best, if never intermix'd.
Sonnet CI.

5
When my love swears that she is made of truth,
I do believe her, though I know she lies.
Sonnet. CXXXVIII.

6
All great truths begin as blasphemies.
BERNARD SHAW—*Annajanska*.

7
My way of joking is to tell the truth. It's the funniest joke in the world.
BERNARD SHAW—*John Bull's Other Island*. Act II.

8
Truth and, by consequence, liberty, will always be the chief power of honest men.
MADAME DE STAËL—*Coppet et Weimar. Letter to Gen. Moreau.*

9
Tell truth, and shame the devil.
SWIFT—*Mary, the Cookmaid's Letter*. RABELAIS—*Works*. Author's *Prologue* to Bk. V. BEAUMONT AND FLETCHER—*Wit Without Money*. Act IV. Sc. 1. *Henry IV*. Pt. I. Sc. 1. L. 59.

10
Veritas visu et mora, falsa festinatione et incertis valescunt.
Truth is confirmed by inspection and delay: falsehood by haste and uncertainty.
TACITUS—*Annales*. II. 39.

11
Truth-teller was our England's Alfred named?
TENNYSON—*Ode on the Death of the Duke of Wellington.*

12
And friendly free discussion calling forth
From the fair jewel Truth its latent ray.
THOMSON—*Liberty*. Pt. II. L. 220.

13
It takes two to speak the truth—one to speak, and another to hear.
THOREAU—*A Week on the Concord and Merrimack Rivers*. P. 283.

14
There are truths which are not for all men, nor for all times.
VOLTAIRE—*Letter to Cardinal de Bernis*. April 23, 1761.

15
There is nothing so powerful as truth; and often nothing so strange.
DANIEL WEBSTER—*Arguments on the Murder of Captain White*. Vol. VI. P. 68.

16
I have ever thought,
Nature doth nothing so great for great men,
As when she's pleas'd to make them lords of truth.
Integrity of life is fame's best friend,
Which nobly, beyond death, shall crown the end.
JOHN WEBSTER—*The Duchess of Malfi*. Act V. Sc. 5.

17
It is one thing to wish to have truth on our side, and another to wish sincerely to be on the side of truth.
ARCHBISHOP WHATELEY—*Essay on some of the Difficulties in the Writings of the Apostle Paul.*—No. 1. *On the Love of Truth.*
(See also LINCOLN under GOD)

18
The sages say, Dame Truth delights to dwell
(Strange Mansion!) in the bottom of a well:
Questions are then the Windlass and the rope
That pull the grave old Gentlewoman up.
JOHN WOLCOT (Peter Pindar)—*Birthday Ode.*
(See also RABELAIS)

19
Truths that wake
To perish never.
WORDSWORTH—*Ode. Intimations of Immortality*. St. 9.

20
Truth never was indebted to a lie.
YOUNG—*Night Thoughts*. Night VIII. L. 587.

TUBEROSE

Polianthes Tuberosa

21
The tuberose, with her silvery light,
That in the gardens of Malay
Is call'd the Mistress of the Night,
So like a bride, scented and bright;
She comes out when the sun's away.
MOORE—*Lalla Rookh. Light of the Harem.*

TULIP

Tulipa

22
You believe
In God, for your part?—ay? that He who makes,
Can make good things from ill things, best from worst,
As men plant tulips upon dunghills when
They wish them finest.
E. B. BROWNING—*Aurora Leigh*. Bk. II.

23
And tulips, children love to stretch
Their fingers down, to feel in each
Its beauty's secret nearer.
E. B. BROWNING—*A Flower in a Letter*.

24
'Mid the sharp, short emerald wheat, scarce risen three fingers well,
The wild tulip at end of its tube, blows out its great red bell,
Like a thin clear bubble of blood, for the children to pick and sell.
ROBERT BROWNING—*Up at a Villa. Down in the City*. St. 6.

25
The tulip is a courtly quean,
Whom, therefore, I will shun.
HOOD—*Flowers*.

1
Guarded within the old red wall's embrace,
Marshalled like soldiers in gay company,
The tulips stand arrayed. Here infantry
Wheels out into the sunlight.
AMY LOWELL—*A Tulip Garden.*

2
Dutch tulips from their beds
Flaunted their stately heads.
MONTGOMERY—*The Adventure of a Star.*

3
Not one of Flora's brilliant race
A form more perfect can display;
Art could not feign more simple grace
Nor Nature take a line away.
MONTGOMERY—*On Planting a Tulip-Root.*

4
The tulip's petals shine in dew,
All beautiful, but none alike.
MONTGOMERY—*On Planting a Tulip-Root.*

5
Like tulip-beds of different shape and dyes,
Bending beneath the invisible west-wind's sighs.
MOORE—*Lalla Rookh. The Veiled Prophet of Khorassan.*

TULIP-TREE

Liriodendron Tulipifera

6
Heed not the night; a summer lodge amid the wild is mine—
'Tis shadowed by the tulip-tree, 'tis mantled by the vine.
BRYANT—*A Strange Lady.* St. 6.

7
The tulip-tree, high up,
Opened, in airs of June, her multitude
Of golden chalices to humming birds
And silken-winged insects of the sky.
BRYANT—*The Fountain.* St. 3.

TURKEY; THE TURKS

8
The unspeakable Turk should be immediately struck out of the question, and the country be left to honest European guidance.
CARLYLE—*Letter.* To a meeting at St. James Hall, London, 1876. See also his article on *Das Niebelungen Lied* in *Westminster Review.* 1831. No. 29. Also his Letter to GEORGE HOWARD, Nov. 24, 1876.

9
[Turks] one and all, bag and baggage, shall I hope clear out from the province they have desolated and profaned.
GLADSTONE—*Speech.* May 7, 1877.
For "Bag and baggage," see under PROVERBS.

10
The Lofty Gate of the Royal Tent.
MAHOMET II. It was translated "La Porte Sublima" by the Italians. See E. S. CREASY—*History of the Ottoman Turks.* P. 96, ed. 1877.

11
[The Ottoman Empire] whose sick body was not supported by a mild and regular diet, but by a powerful treatment, which continually exhausted it.
MONTESQUIEU—*Persian Letters.* I. 19.

12
We have on our hands a sick man,—a very sick man. [The sick man of Europe, the Turk.]
NICHOLAS I, of Russia. Conversation with SIR GEORGE HAMILTON SEYMOUR. (1853) See *Blue Book.* (1854)

13
[The Ottoman Empire] has the body of a sick old man, who tried to appear healthy, although his end was near.
SIR THOMAS ROE, Ambassador to Constantinople. See BUCHANAN—*Letter.* 375.

14
Your Majesty may think me an impatient sick man, and that the Turks are even sicker.
VOLTAIRE to CATHERINE II. In the *Rundschau.* April, 1878.

TWILIGHT

15
The sunbeams dropped
Their gold, and, passing in porch and niche,
Softened to shadows, silvery, pale, and dim,
As if the very Day paused and grew Eve.
EDWIN ARNOLD—*Light of Asia.* Bk. II. L. 466.

16
Fair Venus shines
Even in the eye of day; with sweetest beam
Propitious shines, and shakes a trembling flood
Of softened radiance from her dewy locks.
ANNA LETITIA BARBAULD—*A Summer Evening's Meditation.* L. 10.

17
The summer day is closed, the sun is set:
Well they have done their office, those bright hours,
The latest of whose train goes softly out
In the red west.
BRYANT—*An Evening Reverie.*

18
Parting day
Dies like the dolphin, whom each pang imbues
With a new colour as it gasps away,
The last still loveliest, till—'tis gone—and all is gray.
BYRON—*Childe Harold.* Canto IV. St. 29.

19
'Twas twilight, and the sunless day went down
Over the waste of waters; like a veil,
Which, if withdrawn, would but disclose the frown
Of one whose hate is mask'd but to assail.
BYRON—*Don Juan.* Canto II. St. 49.

20
How lovely are the portals of the night,
When stars come out to watch the daylight die.
THOMAS COLE—*Twilight.* See LOUIS L. NOBLE'S *Life and Works of Cole.* Ch. XXXV.

21
Beauteous Night lay dead
Under the pall of twilight, and the love-star sickened and shrank.
GEORGE ELIOT—*Spanish Gypsy.* Bk. II.

22
In the twilight of morning to climb to the top of the mountain,—
Thee to salute, kindly star, earliest herald of day,—
And to await, with impatience, the gaze of the ruler of heaven.—

Youthful delight, oh, how oft lur'st thou me out in the night.
GOETHE—*Venetian Epigrams.*

1
Sweet shadows of twilight! how calm their repose,
While the dewdrops fall soft in the breast of the rose!
How blest to the toiler his hour of release
When the vesper is heard with its whisper of peace!
HOLMES—*Poems of the Class of '29. Our Banker.* St. 12.

2 The lengthening shadows wait
The first pale stars of twilight.
HOLMES—*Poems of the Class of '29. Even Song.* St. 6.

3
The gloaming comes, the day is spent,
The sun goes out of sight,
And painted is the occident
With purple sanguine bright.
ALEXANDER HUME—*Story of a Summer Day.*

4
The sun is set; and in his latest beams
Yon little cloud of ashen gray and gold,
Slowly upon the amber air unrolled,
The falling mantle of the Prophet seems.
LONGFELLOW—*A Summer Day by the Sea.*

5
The twilight is sad and cloudy,
The wind blows wild and free,
And like the wings of sea-birds
Flash the white caps of the sea.
LONGFELLOW—*Twilight.*

6
The west is broken into bars
Of orange, gold, and gray;
Gone is the sun, come are the stars,
And night infolds the day.
GEORGE MACDONALD—*Songs of the Summer Nights.*

7
Dim eclipse, disastrous twilight.
MILTON—*Paradise Lost.* Bk. I. L. 597.

8
From that high mount of God whence light and shade
Spring both, the face of brightest heaven had changed
To grateful twilight.
MILTON—*Paradise Lost.* Bk. V. L. 643.

9
Our lady of the twilight,
She hath such gentle hands,
So lovely are the gifts she brings
From out the sunset-lands,
So bountiful, so merciful,
So sweet of soul is she;
And over all the world she draws
Her cloak of charity.
ALFRED NOYES—*Our Lady of the Twilight.*

10
* * * th' approach of night
The skies yet blushing with departing light,
When falling dews with spangles deck'd the glade,
And the low sun had lengthen'd ev'ry shade.
POPE—*Pastorals. Autumn.* L. 98.

11
Night was drawing and closing her curtain up above the world, and down beneath it.
RICHTER—*Flower, Fruit, and Thorn Pieces.* Ch. II.

12
Twilight's soft dews steal o'er the village-green,
With magic tints to harmonize the scene.
Stilled is the hum that through the hamlet broke
When round the ruins of their ancient oak
The peasants flocked to hear the minstrel play,
And games and carols closed the busy day.
SAM'L ROGERS—*Pleasures of Memory.* Pt. I. L. 1.

13
Twilight, a timid fawn, went glimmering by,
And Night, the dark-blue hunter, followed fast.
G. W. RUSSELL—*Refuge.*

14
Her feet along the dewy hills
Are lighter than blown thistledown;
She bears the glamour of one star
Upon her violet crown.
CLINTON SCOLLARD—*Dusk.*

15
Then the nun-like twilight came, violet-vestured and still,
And the night's first star outshone afar on the eve of Bunker Hill.
CLINTON SCOLLARD—*On the Eve of Bunker Hill.*

16
Ah, County Guy, the hour is nigh,
The sun has left the lea,
The orange flower perfumes the bower,
The breeze is on the sea.
SCOTT—*Quentin Durward.* Ch. IV.

17
The hour before the heavenly-harness'd team
Begins his golden progress in the east.
Henry IV. Pt. I. Act III. Sc. 1. L. 221.

18 Look, the gentle day
Before the wheels of Phœbus, round about
Dapples the drowsy east with spots of grey.
Much Ado About Nothing. Act V. Sc. 3. L. 25.

19
The weary sun hath made a golden set,
And, by the bright track of his fiery car,
Gives signal of a goodly day to-morrow.
Richard III. Act V. Sc. 3. L. 19.

20
Twilight, ascending slowly from the east,
Entwined in duskier wreaths her braided locks
O'er the fair front and radiant eyes of day;
Night followed, clad with stars.
SHELLEY—*Alastor.*

21 Now the soft hour
Of walking comes; for him who lonely loves
To seek the distant hills, and there converse
With Nature, there to harmonize his heart,
And in pathetic Song to breathe around
The harmony to others.
THOMSON—*Seasons. Summer.* L. 1,378.

22
Her eyes as stars of twilight fair,
Like twilight's too her dusky hair.
WORDSWORTH—*She was a Phantom of Delight.*

23
As pensive evening deepens into night.
WORDSWORTH—*To ———.*

TYRANNY

1
A king ruleth as he ought, a tyrant as he lists, a king to the profit of all, a tyrant only to please a few.
ARISTOTLE.

2
The tyrant now
Trusts not to men: nightly within his chamber
The watch-dog guards his couch, the only friend
He now dare trust.
JOANNA BAILLIE—*Ethwald.* Pt. II. Act V. Sc. 3.

3
Th' oppressive, sturdy, man-destroying villains,
Who ravag'd kingdoms, and laid empires waste,
And in a cruel wantonness of power,
Thinn'd states of half their people, and gave up
To want the rest.
BLAIR—*The Grave.* L. 9.

4
Tyranny
Absolves all faith; and who invades our rights,
Howe'er his own commence, can never be
But an usurper.
HENRY BROOKE—*Gustavus Vasa.* Act IV. Sc. 1.

5
Think'st thou there is no tyranny but that
Of blood and chains? The despotism of vice—
The weakness and the wickedness of luxury—
The negligence—the apathy—the evils
Of sensual sloth—produce ten thousand tyrants,
Whose delegated cruelty surpasses
The worst acts of one energetic master,
However harsh and hard in his own bearing.
BYRON—*Sardanapalus.* Act I. Sc. 2.

6
Tyranny
Is far the worst of treasons. Dost thou deem
None rebels except subjects? The prince who
Neglects or violates his trust is more
A brigand than the robber-chief.
BYRON—*The Two Foscari.* Act II. Sc. 1.

7
N'est-on jamais tyran qu'avec un diadème?
Is there no tyrant but the crowned one?
CHÉNIER—*Caius Gracchus.*

8
Tyran, descends du trône et fais place à ton maître.
Tyrant, step from the throne, and give place to thy master.
CORNEILLE—*Heraclius.* I. 2.

9
Tremblez, tyrans, vous êtes immortels.
Tremble, ye tyrants, for ye can not die.
DELILLE—*L'Immortalité de l'Âme.*

10
There is nothing more hostile to a city than a tyrant, under whom in the first and chiefest place, there are not laws in common, but one man, keeping the law himself to himself, has the sway, and this is no longer equal.
EURIPIDES—*Suppliants.* 429. Oxford trans. (Revised by BUCKLEY.)

11
Il n'appartient, qu'aux tyrans d'être toujours en crainte.
None but tyrants have any business to be afraid.
HARDOUIN DE PÉRÉFIXE. Attributed to HENRY IV.

12
'Twixt kings and tyrants there's this difference known:
Kings seek their subjects' good, tyrants their owne.
HERRICK—*Kings and Tyrants.*

13
Men are still men. The despot's wickedness
Comes of ill teaching, and of power's excess,—
Comes of the purple he from childhood wears,
Slaves would be tyrants if the chance were theirs.
VICTOR HUGO—*The Vanished City.*

14
Resistance to tyrants is obedience to God.
JEFFERSON. Found among his papers after his death.

15
Quid violentius aure tyranni?
What is more cruel than a tyrant's ear?
JUVENAL—*Satires.* IV. 86.

16
For how can tyrants safely govern home,
Unless abroad they purchase great alliance?
Henry VI. Pt. III. Act III. Sc. 3. L. 69.

17
This tyrant, whose sole name blisters our tongues,
Was once thought honest.
Macbeth. Act IV. Sc. 3. L. 12.

18
Bleed, bleed, poor country!
Great Tyranny! lay thou thy basis sure,
For goodness dares not check thee!
Macbeth. Act IV. Sc. 3. L. 31.

19
O nation miserable,
With an untitled tyrant bloody-scepter'd
When shalt thou see thy wholesome days again?
Macbeth. Act IV. Sc. 3. L. 103.

20
'Tis time to fear when tyrants seem to kiss.
Pericles. Act I. Sc. 2. L. 79.

21
I knew him tyrannous, and tyrants' fears
Decrease not, but grow faster than the years.
Pericles. Act I. Sc. 2. L. 84.

22
For what is he they follow? truly, gentlemen,
A bloody tyrant, and a homicide:
One rais'd in blood, and one in blood establish'd;
One that made means to come by what he hath,
And slaughter'd those that were the means to help him;
A base foul stone, made precious by the foil
Of England's chair, where he is falsely set;
One that hath ever been God's enemy.
Richard III. Act V. Sc. 3. L. 245.

23
Les habiles tyrans ne sont jamais punis.
Clever tyrants are never punished.
VOLTAIRE—*Mérope.* V. 5.

24
A company of tyrants is inaccessible to all seductions.
VOLTAIRE—*A Philosophical Dictionary. Tyranny.*

25
The sovereign is called a tyrant who knows no laws but his caprice.
VOLTAIRE—*A Philosophical Dictionary. Tyranny.*

U

UMBRELLA

1
We bear our shades about us; self-deprived
Of other screen, the thin umbrella spread,
And range an Indian waste without a tree.
COWPER—*Task.* Bk. I. L. 259.

2
Of doues I haue a dainty paire
Which, when you please to take the aier,
About your head shall gently houer,
Your cleere browe from the sunne to couer,
And with their nimble wings shall fan you
That neither cold nor heate shall tan you,
And like umbrellas, with their feathers
Sheeld you in all sorts of weathers.
MICHAEL DRAYTON—*Davis.*

3
Good housewives all the winter's rage despise,
Defended by the riding-hood's disguise;
Or, underneath the umbrella's oily shade,
Safe through the wet on clinking pattens tread,
Let Persian dames the umbrella's ribs display,
To guard their beauties from the sunny ray;
Or sweating slaves support the shady load,
When eastern monarchs show their state abroad;
Britain in winter only knows its aid,
To guard from chilling showers the walking maid.
GAY—*Trivia.* Bk. I. L. 209.

4
When my water-proof umbrella proved a sieve,
sieve, sieve,
When my shiny new umbrella proved a sieve.
ROSSITER JOHNSON—*A Rhyme of the Rain.*

5
The inseparable gold umbrella which in that country [Burma] as much denotes the grandee as the star or garter does in England.
J. W. PALMER—*Up and Down the Irrawadde.*

6
See, here's a shadow found; the human nature
Is made th' umbrella to the Deity,
To catch the sunbeams of thy just Creator;
Beneath this covert thou may'st safely lie.
QUARLES—*Emblems.* Bk. IV. 14.

7
It is the habitual carriage of the umbrella that is the stamp of Respectability. The umbrella has become the acknowledged index of social position. . . . Crusoe was rather a moralist than a pietist, and his leaf-umbrella is as fine an example of the civilized mind striving to express itself under adverse circumstances as we have ever met with.
STEVENSON—*Philosophy of Umbrellas.* Written in collaboration with J. W. FERRIER.

8
It is not for nothing, either, that the umbrella has become the very foremost badge of modern civilization—the Urim and Thummim of respectability. . . . So strongly do we feel on this point, indeed, that we are almost inclined to consider all who possess really well-conditioned umbrellas as worthy of the Franchise.
STEVENSON—*Philosophy of Umbrellas.*

9
Umbrellas, like faces, acquire a certain sympathy with the individual who carries them. . . . May it not be said of the bearers of these inappropriate umbrellas, that they go about the streets "with a lie in their right hand?" . . . Except in a very few cases of hypocrisy joined to a powerful intellect, men, not by nature, *umbrellarians,* have tried again and again to become so by art, and yet have failed—have expended their patrimony in the purchase of umbrella after umbrella, and yet have systematically lost them, and have finally, with contrite spirits and shrunken purses, given up their vain struggle, and relied on theft and borrowing for the remainder of their lives.
STEVENSON—*Philosophy of Umbrellas.*

10
The tucked-up sempstress walks with hasty
strides,
While streams run down her oil'd umbrella's
sides.
SWIFT—*Description of a City Shower.*

UNBELIEF

11
The fearful Unbelief is unbelief in yourself.
CARLYLE—*Sartor Resartus. The Everlasting No.* Bk. II. Ch. VII.

12
There is no strength in unbelief. Even the unbelief of what is false is no source of might. It is the truth shining from behind that gives the strength to disbelieve.
GEORGE MACDONALD—*The Marquis of Lossie.* Ch. XLII.

13
Unbelief is blind.
MILTON—*Comus.* L. 519.

14
I'm from Missouri; you must show me.
COL. WILLARD D. VANDIVER. See *Literary Digest*, Jan. 28, 1922. P. 42, where origin is discussed at length.

UNCERTAINTY

15
Quis scit, an adjiciant hodiernæ crastina summæ
Tempora di superi?
Who knows whether the gods will add to-morrow to the present hour?
HORACE—*Carmina.* IV. 7. 17.

16
Omnia sunt hominum tenui pendentia filo:
Et subito casu, quæ valuere, ruunt.
All human things hang on a slender thread: the strongest fall with a sudden crash.
OVID—*Epistolæ Ex Ponto.* IV. 3. 35.

17
Nothing is but what is not.
Macbeth. Act I. Sc. 3. L. 141.

18
This
I ever held worse than all certitude,
To know not what the worst ahead might be.
SWINBURNE—*Marino Faliero.* Act V.

19
Dum in dubio est animus, paulo momento huc illuc impellitur.
When the mind is in a state of uncertainty the smallest impulse directs it to either side.
TERENCE—*Andria.* I. 5. 32.

UNDERSTANDING (See KNOWLEDGE)

UNDERTAKERS

1
Ye undertakers, tell us,
'Midst all the gorgeous figures you exhibit,
Why is the principal conceal'd, for which
You make this mighty stir?
BLAIR—*The Grave*. L. 170.

2
There was a man bespake a thing,
Which when the owner home did bring,
He that made it did refuse it:
And he that brought it would not use it,
And he that hath it doth not know
Whether he hath it yea or no.
SIR JOHN DAVIES—*Riddle upon a Coffin.*

3
Why is the hearse with scutcheons blazon'd round,
And with the nodding plume of ostrich crown'd?
No; the dead know it not, nor profit gain;
It only serves to prove the living vain.
GAY—*Trivia*. Bk. III. L. 231.

4
Diaulus, lately a doctor, is now an undertaker; what he does as an undertaker, he used to do also as a doctor.
MARTIAL—*Epigrams*. Bk. I. Ep. 47.

5
There's a grim one-horse hearse in a jolly round trot;
To the churchyard a pauper is going I wot;
The road it is rough, and the hearse has no springs,
And hark to the dirge that the sad driver sings—
Rattle his bones over the stones,
He's only a pauper whom nobody owns.
THOMAS NOEL—*The Pauper's Drive.*

6
The houses that he makes last till doomsday.
Hamlet. Act V. Sc. 1. L. 66.

UNITY (See also GOVERNMENT)

7
When bad men combine, the good must associate; else they will fall, one by one, an unpitied sacrifice in a contemptible struggle.
BURKE—*Thoughts on the Cause of the Present Discontent.*

8
I never use the word "nation" in speaking of the United States. I always use the word "Union" or "Confederacy." We are not a nation but a *union*, a confederacy of equal and sovereign States.
J. C. CALHOUN—*To Oliver Dyer*. Jan. 1, 1849.

9
The Constitution in all its provisions looks to an indestructible union composed of indestructible States.
SALMON P. CHASE—*Decision in Texas vs. White*. See WERDEN'S *Private Life and Public Services of Salmon P. Chase*. P. 664.

10
Neque est ullum certius amicitiæ vinculum, quam consensus et societas consiliorum et voluntatum.

There is no more sure tie between friends than when they are united in their objects and wishes.
CICERO—*Oratio Pro Cnæo Plancio*. II.

11
Like two single gentlemen rolled into one.
GEO. COLMAN (the Younger)—*Broad Grins. Lodgings for Single Gentlemen.*
(See also SHERIDAN under GENTLEMAN)

12
Then join in hand, brave Americans all!
By uniting we stand, by dividing we fall.
JOHN DICKINSON—*The Liberty Song of* 1768.

13
When our two lives grew like two buds that kiss
At lightest thrill from the bee's swinging chime,
Because the one so near the other is.
GEORGE ELIOT—*Brother and Sister*. Pt. I. St. 1.

14
We must all hang together or assuredly we shall all hang separately.
BENJ. FRANKLIN. To JOHN HANCOCK. At Signing of the Declaration of Independence. July 4, 1776.

15
Entzwei' und gebiete! Tüchtig Wort,
Verein' und leite! Bess'rer Hort.
Divide and command, a wise maxim;
Unite and guide, a better.
GOETHE—*Sprüche in Reimen*. L. 516.

16
Was uns alle bändigt, das Gemeine.
The universal subjugator, the commonplace.
GOETHE—*Taschenbuch für Damen auf das Jahr* 1806.

17
Our Union is river, lake, ocean, and sky:
Man breaks not the medal, when God cuts the die!
Though darkened with sulphur, though cloven with steel,
The blue arch will brighten, the waters will heal!
HOLMES—*Brother Jonathan's Lament for Sister Caroline*. St. 7.

18
There with commutual zeal we both had strove
In acts of dear benevolence and love;
Brothers in peace, not rivals in command.
HOMER—*Odyssey*. Bk. IV. L. 241. POPE'S trans.

19
He that is not with me is against me.
Luke. XI. 23.

20
Then none was for a party;
Then all were for the state;
Then the great man helped the poor,
And the poor man loved the great:
Then lands were fairly portioned;
Then spoils were fairly sold:
The Romans were like brothers
In the brave days of old.
MACAULAY—*Lays of Ancient Rome. Horatius*. St. 32.

21
Oh, shame to men! devil with devil damn'd
Firm concord holds, men only disagree
Of creatures rational.
MILTON—*Paradise Lost*. Bk. II. L. 496.

22
The union of lakes—the union of lands—
The union of States none can sever—
The union of hearts—the union of hands—
And the flag of our Union for ever!
GEORGE P. MORRIS—*The Flag of Our Union.*

1
Behold how good and how pleasant it is for brethren to dwell together in unity.
Psalms. CXXXIII 1.

2
Concordia res parvæ crescunt, discordia maximæ dilabantur.
By union the smallest states thrive, by discord the greatest are destroyed.
SALLUST—*Jugurtha.* X.

3
Wir sind ein Volk, und einig wollen wir handeln.
We are one people and will act as one.
SCHILLER—*Wilhelm Tell.* II. 2. 258.

4
Seid einig—einig—einig.
Be united—united—united.
SCHILLER—*Wilhelm Tell.* IV. 2. 158.

5 So we grew together,
Like to a double cherry, seeming parted,
But yet a union in partition;
Two lovely berries moulded on one stem:
So, with two seeming bodies, but one heart;
Two of the first, like coats in heraldry,
Due but to one and crowned with one crest.
Midsummer Night's Dream. Act III. Sc. 2. L. 208.

6
Auxilia humilia firma consensus facit.
Union gives strength to the humble.
SYRUS—*Maxims.*

7
Their meetings made December June.
Their every parting was to die.
TENNYSON—*In Memoriam.* XCVII.

8
Quo res cunque cadant, unum et commune periculum,
Una salus ambobus erit.
Whatever may be the issue we shall share one common danger, one safety.
VERGIL—*Æneid.* II. 709.

9
Liberty and Union, now and forever, one and inseparable.
DANIEL WEBSTER—*Second Speech on Foote's Resolution.* Jan. 26, 1830.

10
One Country, one Constitution, one Destiny.
DANIEL WEBSTER—*Speech.* March 15, 1837.

UNKINDNESS

11
As "unkindness has no remedy at law," let its avoidance be with you a point of honor.
HOSEA BALLOU—*MS. Sermons.*

12
My lodging it is on the cold ground, and very hard is my fare,
But that which troubles me most, is the unkindness of my dear.
As it appeared in WILLIAM DAVENANT'S *Rivals,* an alteration of BEAUMONT AND FLETCHER'S *Two Noble Kinsmen.* Attributed by BOOSEY (publishers), to JOHN GAY.

13
Hard Unkindness' alter'd eye,
That mocks the tear it forced to flow.
GRAY—*Eton College.* St. 8.

14
Since trifles make the sum of human things,
And half our misery from our foibles springs;
Since life's best joys consist in peace and ease,
And though but few can serve, yet all may please;
Oh, let th' ungentle spirit learn from hence,
A small unkindness is a great offence.
HANNAH MORE—*Sensibility.*

15 She hath tied
Sharp-tooth'd unkindness, like a vulture here.
King Lear. Act II. Sc. 4. L. 136.

16 Unkindness may do much;
And his unkindness may defeat my life,
But never taint my love.
Othello. Act IV. Sc. 2. L. 158.

17
In nature there's no blemish but the mind;
None can be call'd deform'd but the unkind.
Twelfth Night. Act III. Sc. 4. L. 401.

V

VALENTINES

18
On paper curiously shaped
Scribblers to-day of every sort,
In verses Valentines yclep'd,
To Venus chime their annual court.
I too will swell the motley throng,
And greet the all auspicious day,
Whose privilege permits my song
My love thus secret to convey.
HENRY G. BOHN—*MS. From his Dictionary of Poetical Quotations. Valentines.*

19
Muse, bid the Morn awake!
Sad Winter now declines,
Each bird doth choose a mate;
This day's Saint Valentine's.
For that good bishop's sake
Get up and let us see
What beauty it shall be
That Fortune us assigns.
DRAYTON—*Additional Odes. To his Valentine.*

20
Oft have I heard both youths and virgins say,
Birds chuse their mates and couple too this day:
But by their flight I never can devine
When I shall couple with my valentine.
HERRICK—*To his Valentine, on St. Valentine's Day.*

21
No popular respect will I omit
To do the honour on this happy day,
When every loyal lover tasks his wit
His simple truth in studious rhymes to pay,
And to his mistress dear his hopes convey.
Rather thou knowest I would still outrun

All calendars with Love's whose date alway
Thy bright eyes govern better than the Sun,—
For with thy favour was my life begun,
And still I reckon on from smiles to smiles,
And not by summers, for I thrive on none
But those thy cheerful countenance compiles;
Oh! if it be to choose and call thee mine,
Love, thou art every day my Valentine!
HOOD—*Sonnet. For the 14th of February.*

1
Oh, cruel heart! ere these posthumous papers
Have met thine eyes, I shall be out of breath;
Those cruel eyes, like two funereal tapers,
Have only lighted me the way to death.
Perchance thou wilt extinguish them in vapours,
When I am gone, and green grass covereth
Thy lover, lost; but it will be in vain—
It will not bring the vital spark again.
HOOD—*A Valentine.*

2
Hail to thy returning festival, old Bishop Valentine! Great is thy name in the rubric, Thou venerable arch flamen of Hymen. * * * Like unto thee, assuredly, there is no other mitred father in the calendar.
LAMB—*Essays. Valentine's Day.*

3
Apollo has peeped through the shutter,
And awaken'd the witty and fair;
The boarding-school belle's in a flutter,
The twopenny post's in despair;
The breath of the morning is flinging
A magic on blossom and spray,
And cockneys and sparrows are singing
In chorus on Valentine's day.
PRAED—*Song for 14th of February.*

4
To-morrow is Saint Valentine's day,
All in the morning betime,
And I a maid at your window,
To be your Valentine.
Hamlet. Act IV. Sc. 5. L. 48.

5 Saint Valentine is past;
Begin these wood-birds but to couple now?
Midsummer Night's Dream. Act IV. Sc. 1. L. 144.

VALOR (See also BRAVERY, COURAGE)

6
But where life is more terrible than death, it is then the truest valour to dare to live.
SIR THOMAS BROWNE—*Religio Medici.* Pt. XLIV.

7
There is always safety in valor.
EMERSON—*English Traits. The Times.*

8
Valor consists in the power of self-recovery.
EMERSON—*Essays. Circles.*

9 A valiant man
Ought not to undergo, or tempt a danger,
But worthily, and by selected ways,
He undertakes with reason, not by chance.
His valor is the salt t' his other virtues,
They're all unseason'd without it.
BEN JONSON—*New Inn.* Act IV. Sc. 3.

10
Stimulos dedit æmula virtus.
He was spurred on by rival valor.
LUCAN—*Pharsalia.* I. 120.

11 In vain doth valour bleed,
While Avarice and Rapine share the land.
MILTON—*Sonnet. To the Lord General Fairfax.*

12 When valour preys on reason,
It eats the sword it fights with.
Antony and Cleopatra. Act III. Sc. 3. L. 199.

13
What valour were it, when a cur doth grin,
For one to thrust his hand between his teeth,
When he might spurn him with his foot, away?
Henry VI. Pt. III. Act I. Sc. 4. L. 56.

14
You are the hare of whom the proverb goes,
Whose valor plucks dead lions by the beard.
King John. Act II. Sc. 1. L. 137.

15 'Tis much he dares;
And, to that dauntless temper of his mind,
He hath a wisdom that doth guide his valour
To act in safety.
Macbeth. Act III. Sc. 1. L. 51.

16
He's truly valiant that can suffer wisely
The worst that man can breathe and make his wrongs
His outsides, to wear them like his raiment, carelessly;
And ne'er prefer his injuries to his heart.
To bring it into danger.
Timon of Athens. Act III. Sc. 5. L. 31.

17
My valor is certainly going!—it is sneaking off!—I feel it oozing out, as it were, at the palms of my hands.
SHERIDAN—*The Rivals.* Act V. Sc. 3.

18
Exigui numero, sed bello vivida virtus.
Of small number, but their valour quick for war.
VERGIL—*Æneid.* V. 754.

VALUE (See also WORTH)

19
That ye might learn in us not to think of men above that which is written.
I Corinthians. IV. 6. Quoted, "not to be wise above that which is written," by Prof. Scholefield *Hints for an Improved Translation of the New Testament.*

20
We ought not to treat living creatures like shoes or household belongings, which when worn with use we throw away.
PLUTARCH—*Life of Cato the Censor.*

21
A cynic, a man who knows the price of everything and the value of nothing.
OSCAR WILDE—*Lady Windermere's Fan.* Act III.

VANITY

22
It beareth the name of Vanity Fair, because the town where it is kept is "lighter than vanity."
BUNYAN—*Pilgrim's Progress.* Pt. I.

23
Oh, wad some power the giftie gie us
To see oursel's as ithers see us!
It wad frae monie a blunder free us,
And foolish notion.
BURNS—*To a Louse.*

1
Ecclesiastes said that "all is vanity,"
Most modern preachers say the same, or show it
By their examples of true Christianity:
In short, all know, or very soon may know it.
BYRON—*Don Juan.* Canto VII. St. 6.

2
Sooth'd with the sound, the king grew vain:
Fought all his battles o'er again;
And thrice he routed all his foes, and thrice he slew the slain.
DRYDEN—*Alexander's Feast.* L. 66.

3
Vanity of vanities, all is vanity.
Ecclesiastes. I. 2; XII. 8.

4
All is vanity and vexation of spirit.
Ecclesiastes. I. 14.

5
Vanity is as ill at ease under indifference as tenderness is under a love which it cannot return.
GEORGE ELIOT—*Daniel Deronda.* Bk. I. Ch. X.

6
How many saucy airs we meet,
From Temple Bar to Aldgate street!
GAY—*The Barley-Mow and Dunghill.* L. 1.

7
Vain? Let it be so! Nature was her teacher,
What if a lovely and unsistered creature
Loved her own harmless gift of pleasing feature.
HOLMES—*Iris, Her Book. The Professor at the Breakfast-Table.* X.

8
On parle peu quand la vanité ne fait pas parler.
We say little if not egged on by vanity.
LA ROCHEFOUCAULD—*Maximes.* 137.

9
Ce qui nous rend la vanité des autres insupportable, c'est qu'elle blesse la nôtre.
That which makes the vanity of others unbearable to us is that which wounds our own.
LA ROCHEFOUCAULD—*Maximes.* 389.

10
"Vanitas vanitatum" has rung in the ears
Of gentle and simple for thousands of years;
The wail still is heard, yet its notes never scare
Either simple or gentle from Vanity Fair.
FREDERICK LOCKER-LAMPSON—*Vanity Fair.*

11
What is your sex's earliest, latest care,
Your heart's supreme ambition? To be fair.
LORD LYTTLETON—*Advice to a Lady.* L. 17.

12
And not a vanity is given in vain.
POPE—*Essay on Man.* Ep. II. L. 290.

13
Here files of pins extend their shining rows,
Puffs, powders, patches, bibles, billet-doux.
POPE—*Rape of the Lock.* Canto I. L. 137.

14
Every man at his best state is altogether vanity.
Psalms. XXXIX. 5.

15
Surely men of low degree are vanity, and men of high degree are a lie: to be laid in the balance they are altogether lighter than vanity.
Psalms. LXII. 9.

16
Where doth the world thrust forth a vanity—
* * * * * *
That is not quickly buzz'd into his ears?
Richard II. Act II. Sc. 1. L. 24.

17
Light vanity, insatiate cormorant,
Consuming means, soon preys upon itself.
Richard II. Act II. Sc. 1. L. 38.

18
Hoy-day, what a sweep of vanity comes this way!
Timon of Athens. Act I. Sc. 2. L. 137.

19
Il est difficile d'estimer quelqu'un comme il veut l'être.
It is difficult to esteem a man as highly as he would wish.
VAUVENARGUES—*Reflexions.* LXVII.

20
Maud Muller looked and sighed: "Ah me!
That I the Judge's bride might be!
He would dress me up in silks so fine,
And praise and toast me at his wine."
WHITTIER—*Maud Muller.* L. 35.

21
Meek Nature's evening comment on the shows
That for oblivion take their daily birth
From all the fuming vanities of earth.
WORDSWORTH—*Sonnet. Sky. Prospect from the Plain of France.*

VARIETY (See also NOVELTY)

22
Amidst the soft variety I'm lost.
ADDISON—*Letter from Italy.* L. 100.

23
The earth was made so various, that the mind
Of desultory man, studious of change
And pleased with novelty, might be indulged.
COWPER—*The Task.* Bk. I. L. 506.

24
Variety's the very spice of life,
That gives it all its flavour.
COWPER—*The Task.* Bk. II. L. 606.
(See also PRIOR, RICHTER)

25
The variety of all things forms a pleasure.
EURIPIDES—*Orestes.* 234.

26
Variety's the source of joy below,
From whence still fresh-revolving pleasures flow,
In books and love the mind one end pursues,
And only change the expiring flame renews.
GAY—*Epistles. To Bernard Lintot, on a Miscellany of Poems.*

27
Countless the various species of mankind,
Countless the shades which sep'rate mind from mind;
No general object of desire is known,
Each has his will, and each pursues his own.
WM. GIFFORD—*Perseus.*

28
All concord's born of contraries.
BEN JONSON—*Cynthia's Revels.* Act V. Sc. 2.

29
Diversité, c'est ma devise.
Diversity, that is my motto.
LA FONTAINE—*Paté d'Anguille.*

1
Mille animos excipe mille modis.
Treat a thousand dispositions in a thousand ways.
OVID—*Ars Amatoria.* Bk. I. 756.

2
Variety alone gives joy;
The sweetest meats the soonest cloy.
PRIOR—*The Turtle and the Sparrow.* L. 234.
(See also COWPER)

3
Weil Verschiedenheit des Nichts mehr ergötzt, als Einerleiheit des Etwas.
For variety of mere nothings gives more pleasure than uniformity of something.
JEAN PAUL RICHTER—*Levana. Fragment V.* I. 100.
(See also COWPER)

4
When our old Pleasures die,
Some new One still is nigh;
Oh! fair Variety!
NICHOLAS ROWE—*Ode for the New Year.* (1717)

5
Omnis mutatio loci jucunda fiet.
Every change of place becomes a delight.
SENECA—*Epistles.* 28.

VENICE

6
I stood in Venice, on the Bridge of Sighs;
A palace and a prison on each hand;
I saw from out the wave her structures rise
As from the stroke of the enchanter's wand:
A thousand years their cloudy wings expand
Around me, and a dying glory smiles
O'er the far times, when many a subject land
Look'd to the wingèd Lion's marble piles,
Where Venice sate in state, throned on her hundred isles.
BYRON—*Childe Harold.* Canto IV. St. 1.

7
In Venice, Tasso's echoes are no more,
And silent rows the songless gondolier;
Her palaces are crumbling to the shore,
And music meets not always now the ear.
BYRON—*Childe Harold.* Canto IV. St. 3.

8
Venice once was dear,
The pleasant place of all festivity,
The revel of the earth, the masque of Italy.
BYRON—*Childe Harold.* Canto IV. St. 3.

9
White swan of cities, slumbering in thy nest
So wonderfully built among the reeds
Of the lagoon, that fences thee and feeds,
As sayeth thy old historian and thy guest!
LONGFELLOW—*Venice.*

10
The sylphs and ondines
And the sea-kings and queens
Long ago, long ago, on the waves built a city,
As lovely as seems
To some bard in his dreams,
The soul of his latest love-ditty.
OWEN MEREDITH—*Venice.*

11
Once did she hold the gorgeous East in fee,
And was the safeguard of the West.
WORDSWORTH—*Sonnet on the extinction of the Venetian Republic.*

VICE

12
De vitiis nostris scalam nobis facimus, si vitia ipsa calcamus.
We make a ladder for ourselves of our vices, if we trample those same vices underfoot.
ST. AUGUSTINE—*Sermon* 3. *De Ascensione.*
(See also LONGFELLOW)

13
Vitia temporis; vitia hominis.
Vices of the time; vices of the man.
BACON—*Humble Submission and Supplication to the Lords of Parliament.* (1621)

14
Vice gets more in this vicious world
Than piety.
BEAUMONT AND FLETCHER—*Love's Cure.* Act III. Sc. 1.

15
Vice itself lost half its evil, by losing all its grossness.
BURKE—*Reflections on the Revolution in France.*

16
To sanction Vice, and hunt Decorum down.
BYRON—*English Bards and Scotch Reviewers.* L. 621.

17
And lash the Vice and Follies of the Age.
SUSANNAH CENTLIVRE—*Prologue to The Man's Bewitched.*

18
Ne'er blush'd, unless, in spreading vice's snares,
She blunder'd on some virtue unawares.
CHURCHILL—*The Rosciad.* L. 137.

19
What maintains one vice would bring up two children.
FRANKLIN—*Poor Richard's Almanac.*

20
Omne animi vitium tanto conspectius in se
Crimen habet, quanto major qui peccat habetur.
Every vice makes its guilt the more conspicuous in proportion to the rank of the offender.
JUVENAL—*Satires.* VIII. 140.

21
We do not despise all those who have vices, but we despise all those who have not a single virtue.
LA ROCHEFOUCAULD—*Maxims.* No. 195.

22
A vice is a failure of desire.
GERALD STANLEY LEE—*Crowds.* Bk. IV. Ch. XIII.

23
Saint Augustine! well hast thou said,
That of our vices we can frame
A ladder, if we will but tread
Beneath our feet each deed of shame.
LONGFELLOW—*The Ladder of St. Augustine.* St. 1.
(See also AUGUSTINE, also LONGFELLOW under GROWTH)

24
Virtue, I grant you, is an empty boast;
But shall the dignity of vice be lost?
POPE—*Epilogue to Satires. Dialogue* I.

25
Vice is a monster of so frightful mien,
As to be hated needs but to be seen;

Yet seen too oft, familiar with her face,
We first endure, then pity, then embrace.
POPE—*Essay on Man.* Ep. II. L. 217.
(See also DRYDEN under TRUTH)

1
The heart resolves this matter in a trice,
"Men only feel the smart, but not the vice."
POPE—*Horace.* Bk. II. Ep. II. L. 216.

2
Hominum sunt ista [vitia], non temporum.
Those vices [luxury and neglect of decent manners] are vices of men, not of the times.
SENECA—*Epistles.* 97.

3
The gods are just, and of our pleasant vices
Make instruments to plague us.
King Lear. Act V. Sc. 3. L. 170. ("Scourge" for "plague" in quarto.)

4
There is no vice so simple but assumes
Some mark of virtue on his outward parts.
Merchant of Venice. Act III. Sc. 2. L. 81.

5
Vice repeated is like the wand'ring wind,
Blows dust in others' eyes, to spread itself.
Pericles. Act I. Sc. 1. L. 97.

6
O, what a mansion have those vices got
Which for their habitation chose out thee,
Where beauty's veil doth cover every blot,
And all things turn to fair that eyes can see!
Sonnet XCV.

VICTORY (See also SUCCESS)

7
Hannibal knows how to gain a victory, but not how to use it.
BARCA. To HANNIBAL, according to PLUTARCH.

8
Kings may be blest, but Tam was glorious,
O'er a' the ills o' life victorious.
BURNS—*Tam o' Shanter.*

9
Who thought he'd won
The field as certain as a gun.
BUTLER—*Hudibras.* Pt. I. Canto III. L. 11.
CERVANTES—*Don Quixote.* Pt. I. Bk. III. Ch. VII. DRYDEN—*Spanish Friar.* Act III. Sc. 2. (For "sure as a gun.")

10
Out spoke the victor then,
As he hail'd them o'er the wave,
Ye are brothers! ye are men!
And we conquer but to save;
So peace instead of death let us bring;
But yield, proud foe, thy fleet,
With the crews, at England's feet,
And make submission meet
To our King.
CAMPBELL—*The Battle of the Baltic.*

11
Not one of all the purple host
Who took the flag to-day
Can tell the definition
So clear of victory,
As he, defeated, dying,
On whose forbidden ear
The distant strains of triumph
Break agonized and clear.
EMILY DICKINSON—*Poems. Success.*

12
Our peace must be a peace of victors, not of the vanquished.
GEN. FOCH, as reported by G. WARD PRICE in the London *Daily Mail* (1919).

13
Victory is a thing of the will.
A favorite maxim of GEN. FOCH.

14
A Cadmean victory. (The conquerors suffer as much as the conquered.)
Proverb quoted by HERODOTUS. I. 66.
(See also PYRRHUS)

15
To the victors belong the spoils. (The spoils to the victors.)
As attributed to ANDREW JACKSON.
(See also MARCY)

16
From what far, heavenly height of hope
Didst thou descend to light our way,
Cleaving with flash of snowy robe
Time's dusky veil of twilight gray?
JULIA LARNED—*The Winged Victory.*

17
Peace must be framed on so equitable a basis, that the nations would not wish to disturb it . . . so that the confidence of the German people shall be put in the equity of their cause and not in the might of their armies.
LLOYD GEORGE—*Speech* at Glasgow. June 29, 1917.

18
Victrix causa Diis placuit, sed victa Catoni.
The victorious cause pleased the gods, but the victory pleased Cato.
LUCANUS—*Pharsalia.* 1. 118.

19
They see nothing wrong in the rule, that to the victors belong the spoils of the enemy.
W. L. MARCY—*Speech in the United States Senate.* (1832)
(See also JEFFERSON)

20
Who overcomes
By force, hath overcome but half his foe.
MILTON—*Paradise Lost.* Bk. I. L. 648.

21
There are some defeats more triumphant than victories.
MONTAIGNE—*Of Cannibals.* Ch. XXX.

22
Then should some cloud pass over
The brow of sire or lover,
Think 'tis the shade
By Victory made
Whose wings right o'er us hover!
MOORE—*Battle Song.*

23
Before this time tomorrow I shall have gained a peerage or Westminster Abbey.
NELSON. Before the Battle of the Nile.

24
Westminster Abbey, or Victory.
NELSON. In the battle off Cape Vincent, giving orders for boarding the San Josef. See SOUTHEY—*Life of Nelson.* Vol. I. Ch. IV.

25
We have met the enemy and they are ours.
OLIVER HAZARD PERRY—*Letter to Gen. Harrison after the Victory on Lake Erie.* Sept. 10, 1813.

1
Væ victis.
Woe to the vanquished!
PLAUTUS—*Pseudolus*. Act V. Also credited to LIVY. Became a proverbial saying when Rome was conquered by the Gauls under Brennus.

2
We conquered France, but felt our captive's charms,
Her arts victorious triumph'd o'er our arms.
POPE—*Horace*. Bk. II. Ep. I. L. 263.

3
But if
We have such another victory, we are undone.
Attributed to PYRRHUS by BACON—*Apothegms*. No. 193. PYRRHUS lost 3,500 men at the battle of Asculum B. C. 279. When congratulated on his victory he was reported to have made the reply quoted. Hence a "Pyrrhic Victory."
(See also HERODOTUS)

4
Heil dir im Siegeskranz.
Hail! Thou as victor crowned.
B. G. SCHUMACHER. Title and refrain of Prussian Nat. Hymn. From the original song by HEINRICH HARRIES. (1790)

5
Hail to the Chief who in triumph advances.
SCOTT—*Lady of the Lake*. Canto II. St. 19.

6
With dying hand, above his head,
He shook the fragment of his blade,
And shouted "Victory!—
Charge, Chester, charge! on, Stanley, on!"
Were the last words of Marmion.
SCOTT—*Marmion*. Canto VI. St. 32.

7
La victoire me suit, et tout suit la victoire.
Victory follows me, and all things follow victory.
SCUDÉRI—*L'Amour Tyrannique*.

8
Then with the losers let it sympathize;
For nothing can seem foul to those that win.
Henry IV. Pt. I. Act V. Sc. 1. L. 8.

9
To whom God will, there be the victory.
Henry VI. Pt. III. Act II. Sc. 5. L. 15.

10
Thus far our fortune keeps an upward course,
And we are grac'd with wreaths of victory.
Henry VI. Pt. III. Act V. Sc. 3. L. 1.

11
A victory is twice itself when the achiever brings home full numbers.
Much Ado About Nothing. Act I. Sc. 1. L. 8.

12
"But what good came of it at last?"
Quoth little Peterkin.
"Why, that I cannot tell," said he;
"But 'twas a famous victory."
SOUTHEY—*Battle of Blenheim*.

13
Victores victosque numquam solida fide coalescere.
Victor and vanquished never unite in substantial agreement.
TACITUS—*Annales*. Bk. II. 7.

14
Victoriam malle quam pacem.
To prefer victory to peace.
TACITUS—*Annales*. Bk. III. 60.

15
There is nothing so dreadful as a great victory—except a great defeat.
Quoted as WELLINGTON'S. EMERSON ascribes it to D'ARGENSON, as *reported by* GRIMM. See EMERSON—*Quotation and Originality*.

16
It must be a peace without victory. . . . Victory would mean peace forced upon the loser; a victor's terms imposed upon the vanquished. It would be accepted in humiliation, under duress, at an intolerable sacrifice, and would leave a sting, a resentment, a bitter memory upon which terms of peace would rest, not permanently, but only as upon quicksand. Only a peace between equals can last: only a peace, the very principle of which is equality, and a common participation in a common benefit.
WOODROW WILSON—*Address to the U. S. Senate*, Jan. 22, 1917.

VILLAINY

17
Calm, thinking villains, whom no faith could fix,
Of crooked counsels and dark politics.
POPE—*Temple of Fame*. L. 410.

18
O villainy! Ho! let the door be lock'd;
Treachery! seek it out.
Hamlet. Act V. Sc. 2. L. 322.

19
And thus I clothe my naked villainy
With old odd ends, stol'n out of holy writ,
And seem a saint, when most I play the devil.
Richard III. Act I. Sc. 3. L. 336.

20
Villain and he be many miles asunder.
Romeo and Juliet. Act III. Sc. 5. L. 82.

21
The learned pate
Ducks to the golden fool: all is oblique;
There's nothing level in our cursed natures,
But direct villainy.
Timon of Athens. Act IV. Sc. 3. L. 17.

VIOLETS

Viola

22
Early violets blue and white
Dying for their love of light.
EDWIN ARNOLD—*Almond Blossoms*.

23
Deep violets, you liken to
The kindest eyes that look on you,
Without a thought disloyal.
E. B. BROWNING—*A Flower in a Letter*.

24
Stars will blossom in the darkness,
Violets bloom beneath the snow.
JULIA C. R. DORR—*For a Silver Wedding*.

25
Again the violet of our early days
Drinks beauteous azure from the golden sun,
And kindles into fragrance at his blaze.
EBENEZER ELLIOTT—*Miscellaneous Poems. Spring*.

1
Cold blows the wind against the hill,
And cold upon the plain;
I sit me by the bank, until
The violets come again.
RICHARD GARNETT—*Violets.*

2
A vi'let on the meadow grew,
That no one saw, that no one knew,
It was a modest flower.
A shepherdess pass'd by that way—
Light-footed, pretty and so gay;
That way she came,
Softly warbling forth her lay.
GOETHE—*The Violet.* FREDERICK RICORD'S trans.

3
A blossom of returning light,
An April flower of sun and dew;
The earth and sky, the day and night
Are melted in her depth of blue!
DORA READ GOODALE—*Blue Violets.*

4
The modest, lowly violet
In leaves of tender green is set;
So rich she cannot hide from view,
But covers all the bank with blue.
DORA READ GOODALE—*Spring Scatters Far and Wide.*

5
The violets prattle and titter,
And gaze on the stars high above.
HEINE—*Book of Songs. Lyrical Interlude.* 9.

6
The eyes of spring, so azure,
Are peeping from the ground;
They are the darling violets,
That I in nosegays bound.
HEINE—*Book of Songs. New Spring.* 13.

7
Welcome, maids of honor,
You doe bring
In the spring,
And wait upon her.
HERRICK—*To Violets.*

8
The violet is a nun.
HOOD—*Flowers.*

9
We are violets blue,
For our sweetness found
Careless in the mossy shades,
Looking on the ground.
Love's dropp'd eyelids and a kiss,—
Such our breath and blueness is.
LEIGH HUNT—*Songs and Chorus of the Flowers. Violets.*

10
And shade the violets,
That they may bind the moss in leafy nets.
KEATS—*I Stood Tiptoe Upon a Little Hill.*

11
Violet! sweet violet!
Thine eyes are full of tears;
Are they wet
Even yet
With the thought of other years?
LOWELL—*Song.*

12
Winds wander, and dews drip earthward;
Rains fall, suns rise and set:
Earth whirls, and all but to prosper
A poor little violet.
LOWELL—*The Changeling.*

13
The violets were past their prime,
Yet their departing breath
Was sweeter, in the blast of death,
Than all the lavish fragrance of the time.
MONTGOMERY—*The Adventure of a Star.*

14
Hath the pearl less whiteness
Because of its birth?
Hath the violet less brightness
For growing near earth?
MOORE—*Desmond's Song.*

15
Steals timidly away,
Shrinking as violets do in summer's ray.
MOORE—*Lalla Rookh. Veiled Prophet of Khorassan.*

16
Surely as cometh the Winter, I know
There are Spring violets under the snow.
R. H. NEWELL (Orpheus C. Kerr) *Spring Violets under the Snow.*

17
The violet thinks, with her timid blue eye,
To pass for a blossom enchantingly shy.
FRANCES S. OSGOOD—*Garden Gossip.* St. 3.

18
The violets whisper from the shade
Which their own leaves have made:
Men scent our fragrance on the air,
Yet take no heed
Of humble lessons we would read.
CHRISTINA G. ROSSETTI—*"Consider the Lilies of the Field."* L. 13.

19
Who are the violets now
That strew the green lap of the new come spring.
Richard II. Act V. Sc. 2. L. 46.

20
The sweet sound,
That breathes upon a bank of violets,
Stealing and giving odour!
Twelfth Night. Act I. Sc. 1. L. 5.

21
Violets dim,
But sweeter than the lids of Juno's eyes.
Or Cytherea's breath.
Winter's Tale. Act IV. Sc. 4. L. 120.

22
And the violet lay dead while the odour flew
On the wings of the wind o'er the waters blue.
SHELLEY—*Music.*

23
Oh! faint delicious spring-time violet,
Thine odor like a key,
Turns noiselessly in memory's wards to let
A thought of sorrow free.
W. W. STORY—*The Violet.*

24
The smell of violets, hidden in the green,
Pour'd back into my empty soul and frame
The times when I remembered to have been
Joyful and free from blame.
TENNYSON—*Dream of Fair Women.* St. 20.

25
And from his ashes may be made
The violet of his native land.
TENNYSON—*In Memoriam.* XVIII.

1
And in my breast
Spring wakens too; and my regret
Becomes an April violet,
And buds and blossoms like the rest.
TENNYSON—*In Memoriam*. CXV.

2
A humble flower long time I pined
Upon the solitary plain,
And trembled at the angry wind,
And shrunk before the bitter rain.
And oh! 'twas in a blessed hour
A passing wanderer chanced to see,
And, pitying the lonely flower,
To stoop and gather me.
THACKERAY—*Song of the Violet.*

3
Banks that slope to the southern sky
Where languid violets love to lie.
SARAH HELEN WHITMAN—*Wood Walks in Spring*. L. 11.

4
The violets of five seasons reappear
And fade, unseen by any human eye.
WORDSWORTH—*Nutting.*

5
A violet by a mossy stone
Half hidden from the eye!
Fair as a star when only one
Is shining in the sky.
WORDSWORTH—*She Dwelt Among the Untrodden Ways.*

6
You violets that first appear,
By your pure purple mantles known,
Like the proud virgins of the year,
As if the spring were all your own—
What are you when the rose is blown?
SIR HENRY WOTTON—*To his Mistress the Queen of Bohemia.*

VIRTUE

7
Curse on his virtues! they've undone his country.
ADDISON—*Cato*. Act IV. Sc. 4.

8
If there's a power above us, (and that there is all nature cries aloud
Through all her works) he must delight in virtue.
ADDISON—*Cato*. Act V. Sc. 1.

9
Sweet are the slumbers of the virtuous man!
ADDISON—*Cato*. Act V. Sc. 4.

10
One's outlook is a part of his virtue.
AMOS BRONSON ALCOTT—*Concord Days. April Outlook.*

11
Virtue and sense are one; and, trust me, still
A faithless heart betrays the head unsound.
ARMSTRONG—*Art of Preserving Health*. Bk. IV. L. 265.

12
Virtue, the strength and beauty of the soul,
Is the best gift of Heaven: a happiness
That even above the smiles and frowns of fate
Exalts great Nature's favourites: a wealth
That ne'er encumbers, nor can be transferr'd.
ARMSTRONG—*Art of Preserving Health*. Bk. IV. L. 284.

13
Certainly virtue is like precious odours, most fragrant when they are incensed or crushed.
BACON—*Essays. Of Adversity.*

14
Virtue is like a rich stone, best plain set.
BACON—*Essays. Of Beauty.*

15
La vertu d'un cœur noble est la marque certaine.

Virtue alone is the unerring sign of a noble soul.
BOILEAU—*Satires*. V. 42.

16
Whilst shame keeps its watch, virtue is not wholly extinguished in the heart.
BURKE—*Reflections on the Revolution in France.*

17
Virtue is not malicious; wrong done her
Is righted even when men grant they err.
GEORGE CHAPMAN—*Monsieur D'Olive*. Act I. Sc. 1. L. 127.

18
Nam quæ voluptate, quasi mercede aliqua, ad officium impellitur, ea non est virtus sed fallax imitatio simulatioque virtutis.

That which leads us to the performance of duty by offering pleasure as its reward, is not virtue, but a deceptive copy and imitation of virtue.
CICERO—*Academici*. IV. 46.

19
Honor est præmium virtutis.
Honor is the reward of virtue.
CICERO—*Brutus*. LXXXI.
(See also PLAUTUS)

20
Virtute enim ipsa non tam multi præditi esse, quam videri volunt.

Fewer possess virtue, than those who wish us to believe that they possess it.
CICERO—*De Amicitia*. XXVI.

21
Nam ut quisque est vir optimus, ita difficillime esse alios improbos suspicatur.

The more virtuous any man is, the less easily does he suspect others to be vicious.
CICERO—*Epistolæ Ad Fratrem*. I. 1.

22
In virtute sunt multi adscensus.

In the approach to virtue there are many steps.
CICERO—*Oratio Pro Cnæo Plancio.* XXV.

23
Est haec sæculi labes quædam et macula virtuti invidere, velle ipsum florem dignitatis infringere.

It is the stain and disgrace of the age to envy virtue, and to be anxious to crush the very flower of dignity.
CICERO—*Gratio Pro Lucio Cornelio Balbo.* VI.

24
Virtue is a habit of the mind, consistent with nature and moderation and reason.
CICERO—*Rhetorical Invention*. Bk. II. Sc. LIII.

25
Ipsa quidem pretium virtus sibi.
Virtue is indeed its own reward.

CLAUDIANUS—*De Consulatu Malli. Theodorii Panegyris.* V. I.
(See also PLAUTUS)

1
Vile latens virtus.
Virtue when concealed is a worthless thing.
CLAUDIANUS—*De Quarto Consulatu Honorii Augusti Panegyris.* 222.

2
Well may your heart believe the truths I tell;
'Tis virtue makes the bliss, where'er we dwell.
COLLINS—*Eclogue I.* L. 5. *Selim.*

3
Is virtue a thing remote? I wish to be virtuous, and lo! virtue is at hand.
CONFUCIUS—*Analects.* Bk. I. Ch. IV.

4
Virtue is not left to stand alone. *He who practices it* will have neighbors.
CONFUCIUS—*Analects.* Bk. IV. Ch. XXV.

5
Toutes grandes vertus conviennent aux grands hommes.
All great virtues become great men.
CORNEILLE—*Notes de Corneille par La Rochefoucauld.*

6
The only amaranthine flower on earth
Is virtue.
COWPER—*Task.* Bk. III. L. 268.

7
And he by no uncommon lot
Was famed for virtues he had not.
COWPER—*To the Rev. William Bull.* L. 19.

8
Virtue alone is happiness below.
CRABBE—*The Borough.* Letter XVI.

9
Virtue was sufficient of herself for happiness.
DIOGENES LAERTIUS—*Plato.* XLII.
(See also PLAUTUS)

10
And virtue, though in rags, will keep me warm.
DRYDEN—*Imitation of Horace.* Bk. I. Ode XXIX. L. 87.

11
The only reward of virtue is virtue.
EMERSON—*Essays. Friendship.*

12
The virtue in most request is conformity. Self-reliance is its aversion. It loves not realities and creators, but names and customs.
EMERSON—*Essays. First Series. Self-Reliance.*

13
Shall ignorance of good and ill
Dare to direct the eternal will?
Seek virtue, and, of that possest,
To Providence resign the rest.
GAY—*The Father and Jupiter.*

14
Yet why should learning hope success at court?
Why should our patriots' virtues cause support?
Why to true merit should they have regard?
They know that virtue is its own reward.
GAY—*Epistle to Methuen.* L. 39.
(See also PLAUTUS)

15
Thus to relieve the wretched was his pride,
And e'en his failings lean'd to virtue's side.
GOLDSMITH—*The Deserted Village.* L. 163.

16
The virtuous nothing fear but life with shame,
And death's a pleasant road that leads to fame.
GEO. GRANVILLE (Lord Lansdowne). Verses written 1690. L. 47.

17
Only a sweet and virtuous soul,
Like season'd timber, never gives;
But though the whole world turn to coal,
Then chiefly lives.
HERBERT—*The Church. Vertue.*

18
Virtus repulsæ nescia sordidæ,
Intaminatis fulget honoribus;
Nec sumit aut ponit secures
Arbitrio popularis auræ.
Virtue knowing no base repulse, shines with untarnished honour; nor does she assume or resign her emblems of honour by the will of some popular breeze.
HORACE—*Carmina.* III. 2. 17.

19
Virtus, recludens immeritis mori
Cœlum, negata tentat iter via.
Virtue, opening heaven to those who do not deserve to die, makes her course by paths untried.
HORACE—*Carmina.* III. 2. 21.

20
Virtutem incolumem odimus,
Sublatam ex oculis quærimus.
We hate virtue when it is safe; when removed from our sight we diligently seek it.
HORACE—*Carmina.* III. 24. 31.

21
Mea virtute me involvo.
I wrap myself up in my virtue.
HORACE—*Carmina.* III. 29. 55.

22
Virtus est vitium fugere, et sapientia prima.
Virtue consists in avoiding vice, and is the highest wisdom.
HORACE—*Epistles.* I. 1. 41.

23
Vilius argentum est auro virtutibus aurum.
Silver is less valuable than gold, gold than virtue.
HORACE—*Epistles.* I. 1. 52.

24
Oderunt peccare boni virtutis amore.
The good hate sin because they love virtue.
HORACE—*Epistles.* I. 16. 52.

25
Virtue, dear friend, needs no defence,
The surest guard is innocence:
None knew, till guilt created fear,
What darts or poison'd arrows were.
HORACE—*Odes.* Bk. I. Ode XII. St. 1.
WENTWORTH DILLON'S trans.

26
Some of 'em [virtues] like extinct volcanoes, with a strong memory of fire and brimstone.
DOUGLAS JERROLD—*The Catspaw.* Act III. Sc. 1.

27
His virtues walked their narrow round,
Nor made a pause, nor left a void;
And sure th' Eternal Master found
The single talent well employed.
SAMUEL JOHNSON—*On the Death of Mr. Robert Lovett.*

1
Probitas laudatur et alget.
Virtue is praised and freezes.
JUVENAL—*Satires*. I. 74.

2
Nobilitas sola est atque unica virtus.
Virtue is the only and true nobility.
JUVENAL—*Satires*. VIII. 20.

3
Tanto major famæ sitis est quam
Virtutis: quis enim virtutem amplectitur ipsam
Præmia si tollas.
The thirst for fame is much greater than that for virtue; for who would embrace virtue itself if you take away its rewards?
JUVENAL—*Satires*. X. 140.

4
Semita certe
Tranquillæ per virtutem patet unica vitæ.
The only path to a tranquil life is through virtue.
JUVENAL—*Satires*. X. 363.

5
To be discontented with the divine discontent, and to be ashamed with the noble shame, is the very germ of the first upgrowth of all virtue.
CHAS. KINGSLEY—*Health and Education. The Science of Health.*

6
Our virtues are most frequently but vices disguised.
LA ROCHEFOUCAULD—*Maxims*. 179. (Ed. 1665) In 4th Ed. at head of *Reflexions*.

7
Virtue is an angel, but she is a blind one, and must ask of Knowledge to show her the pathway that leads to her goal.
HORACE MANN—*A Few Thoughts for a Young Man.*

8
God sure esteems the growth and completing of one virtuous person, more than the restraint of ten vicious.
MILTON—*Areopagitica. A Speech for the Liberty of Unlicensed Printing.*

9
Virtue could see to do what Virtue would
By her own radiant light, though sun and moon
Were in the flat sea sunk.
MILTON—*Comus*. L. 373.

10
Virtue may be assailed, but never hurt,
Surprised by unjust force, but not inthralled;
Yea, even that which mischief meant most harm
Shall in the happy trial prove most glory.
MILTON—*Comus*. L. 589.

11
Or, if Virtue feeble were,
Heaven itself would stoop to her.
MILTON—*Comus*. L. 1,022.

12
J'aime mieux un vice commode
Qu'une fatigante vertu.
I prefer an accommodating vice to an obstinate virtue.
MOLIÈRE—*Amphitryon*. I. 4.

13
La naissance n'est rien où la vertu n'est pas.
Birth is nothing where virtue is not.
MOLIÈRE—*Don Juan*. IV. 6.

14
Où la vertu va-t-elle se nicher?
Where does virtue go to lodge?
Exclamation of MOLIÈRE.

15
I find that the best virtue I have has in it some tincture of vice.
MONTAIGNE—*Essays. That we Taste Nothing Pure.*

16
Faut d'la vertu, pas trop n'en faut,
L'excès en tout est un défaut.
Some virtue is needed, but not too much.
Excess in anything is a defect.
MONVEL. From a comic opera. *Erreur d'un Moment.* Quoted by DESAUGIERS. See FOURNIER—*L'Esprit des Autres*. Ch. XXXV.

17
Judice te mercede caret, per seque petenda est
Externis virtus incomitata bonis.
In your judgment virtue requires no reward, and is to be sought for itself, unaccompanied by external benefits.
OVID—*Epistolæ ex Ponto*. Bk. II. 3. 35.
(See also PLAUTUS)

18
Virtutem videant, intabescantque relicta.
Let them (the wicked) see the beauty of virtue, and pine at having forsaken her.
PERSIUS—*Satires*. III. 38.

19
For virtue only finds eternal Fame.
PETRARCH—*The Triumph of Fame*. Pt. I. L. 183.

20
Virtus præmium est optimum.
Virtus omnibus rebus anteit profecto.
Libertas, salus, vita, res, parentes,
Patria et prognati tutantur, servantur;
Virtus omnia in se habet; omnia assunt bona, quom penes est virtus.
Virtue is the highest reward. Virtue truly goes before all things. Liberty, safety, life, property, parents, country and children are protected and preserved. Virtue has all things in herself; he who has virtue has all things that are good attending him.
PLAUTUS—*Amphitruo*. Act II. 2. 17.
(See also CICERO, CLAUDIANUS, DIOGENES, GAY, OVID, SILIUS)

21
Qui per virtutem peritat, non interit.
He who dies for virtue, does not perish.
PLAUTUS—*Captivi*. III. 5. 32.

22
Virtue may choose the high or low degree,
'Tis just alike to virtue, and to me;
Dwell in a monk, or light upon a king,
She's still the same belov'd, contented thing.
POPE—*Epilogue to Satires. Dialogue* I. L. 137.

23
But sometimes virtue starves while vice is fed.
What then? Is the reward of virtue bread?
POPE—*Essay on Man*. Ep. IV. L. 149.

24
The soul's calm sunshine and the heartfelt joy,
Is virtue's prize.
POPE—*Essay on Man*. Ep. IV. L. 168.

25
Know then this truth (enough for man to know)
"Virtue alone is happiness below."
POPE—*Essay on Man*. Ep. IV. L. 309.

1
Court-virtues bear, like gems, the highest rate,
Born where Heav'n's influence scarce can penetrate.
In life's low vale, the soil the virtues like,
They please as beauties, here as wonders strike.
POPE—*Moral Essays.* Ep. I. L. 141.

2
Virtue she finds too painful an endeavour,
Content to dwell in decencies forever.
POPE—*Moral Essays.* Ep. II. L. 163.

3
There is nothing that is meritorious but virtue and friendship; and indeed friendship itself is only a part of virtue.
POPE—*On his Death-Bed.* JOHNSON'S *Life of Pope.*

4
O let us still the secret joy partake,
To follow virtue even for virtue's sake.
POPE—*Temple of Fame.* L. 364.

5
Virtus, etiamsi quosdam impetus a natura sumit, tamen perficienda doctrina est.
Although virtue receives some of its excellencies from nature, yet it is perfected by education.
QUINTILIAN—*De Institutione Oratoria.* XII. 2. 1.

6
Nihil tam alte natura constituit quo virtus non possit eniti.
Nature has placed nothing so high that virtue can not reach it.
QUINTUS CURTIUS RUFUS—*De Rebus Gestis Alexandri Magni.* VII. 11. 10.

7
Divitiarum et formæ gloria fluxa atque fragilis; virtus clara æternaque habetur.
The glory of riches and of beauty is frail and transitory; virtue remains bright and eternal.
SALLUST—*Catilina.* I.

8
Marcet sine adversario virtus.
Virtue withers away if it has no opposition.
SENECA—*De Providentia.* II.

9
Virtus secundum naturam est; vitia inimica et infesta sunt.
Virtue is according to nature; vices are hostile and dangerous.
SENECA—*Epistles.* L.

10
To show virtue her own feature, scorn her own image, and the very age and body of the time his form and pressure.
Hamlet. Act III. Sc. 2. L. 25.

11
For in the fatness of these pursy times
Virtue itself of vice must pardon beg.
Hamlet. Act III. Sc. 4. L. 153.

12
Assume a virtue, if you have it not.
Hamlet. Act III. Sc. 4. L. 160.

13
My heart laments that virtue cannot live
Out of the teeth of emulation.
Julius Cæsar. Act II. Sc. 3. L. 13.

14
According to his virtue let us use him,
With all respect and rites of burial.
Julius Cæsar. Act V. Sc. 5. L. 76.

15
His virtues
Will plead like angels, trumpet-tongued, against
The deep damnation of his taking-off.
Macbeth. Act I. Sc. 7. L. 18.

16
Virtue is bold, and goodness never fearful.
Measure for Measure. Act III. Sc. 1. L. 215.

17
The trumpet of his own virtues.
Much Ado About Nothing. Act V. Sc. 2. L. 87.

18
I hold it ever,
Virtue and cunning were endowments greater
Than nobleness and riches: careless heirs
May the two latter darken and expend;
But immortality attends the former,
Making a man a god.
Pericles. Act III. Sc. 2. L. 27.

19
Virtue itself turns vice, being misapplied;
And vice sometimes by action dignified.
Romeo and Juliet. Act II. Sc. 3. L. 21.

20
Virtue that transgresses is but patched with sin; and sin that amends is but patched with virtue.
Twelfth Night. Act I. Sc. 5. L. 52.

21
Explorant adversa viros. Perque aspera dura
Nititur ad laudem virtus interrita clivo.
Adversity tries men; but virtue struggles after fame regardless of the adverse heights.
SILIUS ITALICUS—*Punica.* IV. 605.

22
Ipsa quidem virtus sibimet pulcherrima merces.
Virtue herself is her own fairest reward.
SILIUS ITALICUS—*Punica.* Bk. XIII. L. 663.
DRYDEN—*Tyrannic Love.* Act II. Sc. 3. HOME—*Douglas.* Act III. Sc. 1. L. 294. HENRY MOORE—*Cupid's Conflict.* PRIOR—*Ode in Imitation of Horace.* III. Ode 2. L. 146. PLATO—*Republic.*
(See also PLAUTUS)

23
Virtue often trips and falls on the sharp-edged rock of poverty.
EUGÈNE SUE.

24
Virtue, the greatest of all monarchies.
SWIFT—*Ode. To the Hon. Sir William Temple.*

25
Non tamen adeo virtutum sterile seculum, ut non et bona exempla prodiderit.
Yet the age was not so utterly destitute of virtues but that it produced some good examples.
TACITUS—*Annales.* Bk. I. 2.

26
Forgive what seem'd my sin in me;
What seem'd my worth since I began.
TENNYSON—*In Memoriam.* Introduction.
(See also YOUNG)

27
What, what is virtue, but repose of mind,
A pure ethereal calm, that knows no storm;
Above the reach of wild ambition's wind,

Above those passions that this world deform
And torture man.

THOMSON—*Castle of Indolence.* Canto I. St. 16.

1

Stat sua cuique dies; breve et irreparabile tempus
Omnibus est vitæ; set famam extendere factis
Hoc virtutis opus.

Every man has his appointed day; life is brief and irrevocable; but it is the work of virtue to extend our fame by our deeds.

VERGIL—*Æneid.* X. 467.

2

Virtue's a stronger guard than brass.

EDMUND WALLER—*Epigram Upon the Golden Medal.* L. 14.

3

Good company and good discourse are the very sinews of virtue.

IZAAK WALTON—*Compleat Angler.* Pt. I. Ch. II.

4

To Virtue's humblest son let none prefer
Vice, though descended from the conqueror.

YOUNG—*Love of Fame.* Satire I. L. 141.

5

Virtue alone outbuilds the pyramids:
Her monuments shall last, when Egypt's fall.

YOUNG—*Night Thoughts.* Night VI. L. 314.

6

His crimes forgive; forgive his virtues too.

YOUNG—*Night Thoughts.* Night IX. L. 2,290.

(See also TENNYSON)

VISIONS

7

Circa beatitudinem perfectam, quæ in Dei visione consistit.

Concerning perfect blessedness which consists in a vision of God.

THOMAS AQUINAS—*Summa Theologie.* Probably the origin of the phrase "beatific vision."

8

And like a passing thought, she fled
In light away.

BURNS—*The Vision.* Last lines.

9

The people's prayer, the glad diviner's theme!
The young men's vision, and the old men's dream!

DRYDEN—*Absalom and Achitophel.* Pt. I. L. 238.

10

So little distant dangers seem:
So we mistake the future's face,
Ey'd thro' Hope's deluding glass;
As yon summits soft and fair,
Clad in colours of the air,
Which to those who journey near,
Barren, brown, and rough appear.

DYER—*Gronger Hill.* L. 884.

11

Visions of glory, spare my aching sight!
Ye unborn ages, crowd not on my soul.

GRAY—*The Bard.* III. 1. L. 11.

12

I wonder if ever a song was sung but the singer's heart sang sweeter!
I wonder if ever a rhyme was rung but the thought surpassed the meter!
I wonder if ever a sculptor wrought till the cold stone echoed his ardent thought!
Or, if ever a painter with light and shade the dream of his inmost heart portrayed!

JAMES C. HARVEY—*Incompleteness.*

13

I have multiplied visions, and used similitudes.

Hosea. XII. 10.

14

Abou Ben Adhem (may his tribe increase!)
Awoke one night from a deep dream of peace,
And saw, within the moonlight in his room,
Making it rich, and like a lily in bloom,
An angel, writing in a book of gold;
Exceeding peace had made Ben Adhem bold,
And to the presence in the room he said—
"What writest thou?" The Vision raised its head,
And, with a look made all of sweet accord,
Answered, "The names of those who love the Lord."

LEIGH HUNT—*Abou Ben Adhem and the Angel.*

15

And it shall come to pass afterward, that I will pour out my Spirit upon all flesh; and your sons and your daughters shall prophesy, your old men shall dream dreams, your young men shall see visions.

Joel. II. 28. *Acts.* II. 17.

16

It is a dream, sweet child! a waking dream,
A blissful certainty, a vision bright,
Of that rare happiness, which even on earth
Heaven gives to those it loves.

LONGFELLOW—*Spanish Student.* Act III. Sc. 5.

17

An angel stood and met my gaze,
Through the low doorway of my tent;
The tent is struck, the vision stays;
I only know she came and went.

LOWELL—*She Came and Went.*

18

Gorgons, and Hydras, and Chimæras dire.

MILTON—*Paradise Lost.* Bk. II. L. 628.

19

O visions ill foreseen! Better had I
Liv'd ignorant of future, so had borne
My part of evil only.

MILTON—*Paradise Lost.* Bk. XI. L. 763.

20

My thoughts by night are often filled
With visions false as fair:
For in the past alone, I build
My castles in the air.

THOS. LOVE PEACOCK—*Castles in the Air.* St. 1.

21

Hence the fool's paradise, the statesman's scheme,
The air-built castle, and the golden dream,
The maid's romantic wish, the chemist's flame,
And poet's vision of eternal fame.

POPE—*Dunciad.* Bk. III. L. 9.

22

Where there is no vision, the people perish.

Proverbs. XXIX. 18.

23

Hence, dear delusion, sweet enchantment hence!

HORACE AND JAMES SMITH—*Rejected Addresses. An Address without a Phœnix. By "S. T. P."* (Not an imitation. Initials used to puzzle critics.)

1
Our revels now are ended. These, our actors,
As I foretold you, were all spirits, and
Are melted into air, into thin air;
And, like the baseless fabric of this vision,
The cloud-capped towers, the gorgeous palaces,
The solemn temples, the great globe itself,
Yea, all which it inherit, shall dissolve,
And, like this insubstantial pageant faded,
Leave not a rack behind.
Tempest. Act IV. Sc. 1. L. 148.

2
But shapes that come not at an earthly call,
Will not depart when mortal voices bid.
WORDSWORTH—*Dion.* V.

3
Fond man! the vision of a moment made!
Dream of a dream! and shadow of a shade!
YOUNG—*Paraphrase on Part of the Book of Job.* L. 187. Shadow of a shade is found in the prologue of *Nobody and Somebody*, a play acted by the servants of QUEEN ELIZABETH. Not the shadow of the shade of history said by PAUL BOURGET—*On Cœur de Femme.* P. 186. (Ed. 1890)
(See also FELLTHAM under WORLD)

VOICE

4
Her voice changed like a bird's:
There grew more of the music, and less of the words.
ROBERT BROWNING—*Flight of the Duchess.* St. 15.

5
The devil hath not, in all his quiver's choice,
An arrow for the heart like a sweet voice.
BYRON—*Don Juan.* Canto XV. St. 13.

6
His voice no touch of harmony admits,
Irregularly deep, and shrill by fits.
The two extremes appear like man and wife
Coupled together for the sake of strife.
CHURCHILL—*Rosciad.* L. 1,003.

7
He ceased: but left so charming on their ear
His voice, that listening still they seemed to hear.
HOMER—*Odyssey.* Bk. II. L. 414. POPE'S trans.
(See also MILTON, THOMSON)

8
The voice so sweet, the words so fair,
As some soft chime had stroked the air;
And though the sound had parted thence,
Still left an echo in the sense.
BEN JONSON—*Eupheme.* IV.

9
A still, small voice.
I Kings. XIX. 12.

10
Oh, there is something in that voice that reaches
The innermost recesses of my spirit!
LONGFELLOW—*Christus.* Pt. I. *The Divine Tragedy. The First Passover.* Pt. VI.

11
Thy voice
Is a celestial melody.
LONGFELLOW—*Masque of Pandora.* Pt. V.

12
Her silver voice
Is the rich music of a summer bird,
Heard in the still night, with its passionate cadence.
LONGFELLOW—*The Spirit of Poetry.* L. 55.

13
How sweetly sounds the voice of a good woman!
It is so seldom heard that, when it speaks,
It ravishes all senses.
MASSINGER—*The Old Law.* Act IV. Sc. 2. L. 34.

14
Vox clamantis in deserto.
The voice of one crying in the wilderness.
Matthew. III. 3; *Mark.* I. 3; *Luke.* III. 4; *John.* I. 23. (Vulgate.)

15
The Angel ended, and in Adam's ear
So charming left his voice, that he awhile
Thought him still speaking, still stood fix'd to hear.
MILTON—*Paradise Lost.* Bk. VIII. L. 1.
(See also HOMER)

16
A Locanian having plucked all the feathers off from a nightingale and seeing what a little body it had, "surely," quoth he, "thou art all voice and nothing else." (Vox et præterea nihil.)
PLUTARCH—*Laconic Apothegms.* Credited to LACON *Incert.* XIII, by LIPSIUS.
(See also SENECA)

17
Her voice was like the voice the stars
Had when they sang together.
DANTE GABRIEL ROSSETTI — *The Blessed Damozel.* St. 10.

18
A sweet voice, a little indistinct and muffled, which caresses and does not thrill; an utterance which glides on without emphasis, and lays stress only on what is deeply felt.
GEORGE SAND — *Handsome Lawrence.* Ch. III.

19
Vox nihil aliud quam ictus aer.
The voice is nothing but beaten air.
SENECA—*Naturalinum Quæstionum.* Bk. II. 29.
(See also PLUTARCH)

20
I thank you for your voices: thank you:
Your most sweet voices.
Coriolanus. Act II. Sc. 3. L. 179.

21
Her voice was ever soft,
Gentle and low, an excellent thing in woman.
King Lear. Act V. Sc. 3. L. 272.

22
But I will aggravate my voice so that I will roar you as gently as any sucking dove.
Midsummer Night's Dream. Act I. Sc. 2. L. 83.

23
And rolling far along the gloomy shores
The voice of days of old and days to be.
TENNYSON—*The Passing of Arthur.*

24
He ceased; but still their trembling ears retained
The deep vibrations of his witching song.
THOMSON—*Castle of Indolence.* Canto I. St. 20.
(See also HOMER)

1
Vox faucibus hæsit.
My voice stuck in my throat.
VERGIL—*Æneid.* II. 774; III. 48; IV. 280.

2
Two voices are there; one is of the sea,
One of the mountains: each a mighty Voice.
WORDSWORTH—*Thought of a Briton on the Subjugation of Switzerland.*

VOWS

3
Vow me no vows.
BEAUMONT AND FLETCHER — *Wit without Money.* Act IV. Sc. 4.

4
Better is it that thou shouldest not vow, than that thou shouldest vow and not pay.
Ecclesiastes. V. 5.

5
Oh, why should vows so fondly made,
Be broken ere the morrow,
To one who loves as never maid
Loved in this world of sorrow?
HOGG—*The Broken Heart.*

6
Vows with so much passion, swears with so much grace,
That 'tis a kind of Heaven to be deluded by him.
NATHANIEL LEE—*Rival Queens.* Act I. Sc. 1.

7
Ease would recant
Vows made in pain, as violent and void.
MILTON—*Paradise Lost.* Bk. IV. L. 96.

8
Let us embrace, and from this very moment
Vow an eternal misery together.
THOMAS OTWAY—*The Orphan.* Act IV. Sc. 1.
(See also FRERE under FRIENDSHIP)

9
Ay, springes to catch woodcocks. I do know
When the blood burns, how prodigal the soul
Lends the tongue vows.
Hamlet. Act I. Sc. 3. ("Lends" in quarto, "gives" in folio.)

W

WAR

(See also HEROES, NAVY, SOLDIERS)

10
It would be superfluous in me to point out to your Lordship that this is war.
CHARLES FRANCIS ADAMS—*Despatch to Earl Russell.* Sept. 5, 1863.

11
Both Regiments or none.
SAMUEL ADAMS—(*For the Boston Town Meeting.*) To Gov. Hutchinson, demanding the withdrawal of the British troops from Boston after March 5, 1776.

12
'Twas in Trafalgar's bay
The saucy Frenchmen lay.
SAMUEL JAMES ARNOLD—*Trafalgar Bay.*

13
My voice is still for war.
ADDISON—*Cato.* Act II. Sc. 1.

14
From hence, let fierce contending nations know
What dire effects from civil discord flow.
ADDISON—*Cato.* Act V. Sc. 4.

15
Fighting men are the city's fortress.
ALCÆUS—*Fragment.* XXII.

16
Fifty-four forty (54° 40′ N.), or fight.
WM. ALLEN—*In the U. S. Senate.* On the Oregon Boundary Question. (1844)

17
And by a prudent flight and cunning save
A life, which valour could not, from the grave.
A better buckler I can soon regain;
But who can get another life again?
ARCHILOCHUS—*Fragm.* VI. Quoted by PLUTARCH—*Customs of the Lacedæmonians.*
(See also BUTLER)

18
Let who will boast their courage in the field,
I find but little safety from my shield.
Nature's, not honour's, law we must obey:
This made me cast my useless shield away.
Another version of ARCHILOCHUS.

19
Instead of breaking that bridge, we should, if possible, provide another, that he may retire the sooner out of Europe.
ARISTIDES—Referring to the proposal to destroy XERXES' bridge of ships over the Hellespont. ("A bridge for a retreating army.") See PLUTARCH—*Life of Demosthenes.*
(See also RABELAIS)

20
If I am asked what we are fighting for, I can reply in two sentences. In the first place, to fulfil a solemn international obligation . . . an obligation of honor which no self-respecting man could possibly have repudiated. I say, secondly, we are fighting to vindicate the principle that small nationalities are not to be crushed in defiance of international good faith at the arbitrary will of a strong and overmastering Power.
PREMIER ASQUITH—*Statement,* to House of Commons, Declaration of War with Germany, August 4, 1914.

21
They shall not pass till the stars be darkened:
Two swords crossed in front of the Hun;
Never a groan but God has harkened,
Counting their cruelties one by one.
KATHERINE LEE BATES—*Crossed Swords.*
(See also BEGBIE, DIAZ, PETAIN, SHEPARD)

22
O great corrector of enormous times,
Shaker of o'er-rank states, thou grand decider
Of dusty and old titles, that healest with blood
The earth when it is sick, and curest the world
O' the pleurisy of people.
BEAUMONT AND FLETCHER—*The Two Noble Kinsmen.* Act V. Sc. 1.

1
All quiet along the Potomac they say
Except now and then a stray picket
Is shot as he walks on his beat, to and fro,
By a rifleman hid in the thicket.

ETHEL LYNN BEERS — *The Picket Guard.* Claimed by LAMAR FONTAINE.

2
All quiet along the Potomac.

Proverbial in 1861–62. Supposed to have originated with GEN. McCLELLAN.
(See also BRET HARTE)

3
She is a wall of brass;
You shall not pass! You shall not pass!
Spring up like Summer grass,
Surge at her, mass on mass,
Still shall you break like glass,
Splinter and break like shivered glass,
But pass?
You shall not pass!
Germans, you shall not, shall not pass!
God's hand has written on the wall of brass—
You shall not pass! You shall not pass!

HAROLD BEGBIE—*You Shall Not Pass.* In N. Y. *Tribune*, July 2, 1916.
(See also BATES)

4
Carry on, carry on, for the men and boys are gone,
But the furrow shan't lie fallow while the women carry on.

JANET BEGBIE—*Carry On.*

5
Gaily! gaily! close our ranks!
Arm! Advance!
Hope of France!
Gaily! gaily! close our ranks!
Onward! Onward! Gauls and Franks!

BÉRANGER—*Les Gaulois et François.* C. L. BETT's trans.

6
The inevitableness, the idealism, and the blessing of war, as an indispensable and stimulating law of development, must be repeatedly emphasized.

BERNHARDI — *Germany and the next War.* Ch. I.

7
War is a biological necessity of the first importance, a regulative element in the life of mankind which cannot be dispensed with. . . . But it is not only a biological law but a moral obligation and, as such, an indispensable factor in civilization.

BERNHARDI — *Germany and the next War.* Ch. I.

8
Our next war will be fought for the highest interests of our country and of mankind. This will invest it with importance in the world's history. "World power or downfall" will be our rallying cry.

BERNHARDI — *Germany and the next War.* Ch. VII.

9
We Germans have a far greater and more urgent duty towards civilization to perform than the Great Asiatic Power. We, like the Japanese, can only fulfil it by the sword.

BERNHARDI — *Germany and the next War.* Ch. XIII.

10
L'affaire Herzegovinienne ne vaut pas les os d'un fusilier poméranien.

The Herzegovina question is not worth the bones of a Pomeranian fusileer.

BISMARCK, (1875) during the struggle between the Christian provinces and Turkey, which led to the Russo-Turkish war. Another version is "The Eastern Question is not worth," etc. See also variation of same by BISMARCK under ART.

11
Lieber Spitzkugeln als Spitzreden.

Better pointed bullets than pointed speeches.

BISMARCK—*Speech*, (1850), relative to MANTEUFFEL's dealings with Austria during the insurrection of the People of Hesse-Cassel.
(See also GASCOIGNE)

12
Ich sehe in unserm Bundesverhältnisse ein Gebrechen Preussens, welches wir früher oder später ferro et igne werden heilen müssen.

I see in our relations with our alliance a fault of Prussia's, which we must cure sooner or later ferro et igne.

BISMARCK—*Letter* to BARON VON SCHLEINITZ. May 12, 1859.

13
[The great questions of the day] are not decided by speeches and majority votes, but by blood and iron.

BISMARCK—*Declaration to the Prussian House of Delegates.* Sept. 30, 1862. Same idea in SCHENKENDORF—*Das Eiserne Kreuz.*
(See also QUINTILIAN, SWINBURNE, also ARNDT under BRAVERY)

14
What a place to plunder!

FIELD MARSHAL VON BLÜCHER's comment on viewing London from St. Paul's, after the Peace Banquet at Oxford, 1814. Same idea in MALCOLM—*Sketches of Persia.* P. 232. THACKERAY—*Four Georges. George I*, says: "The bold old Reiter looked down from St. Paul's and sighed out, 'Was für Plunder!' The German women plundered; the German secretaries plundered; the German cooks and intendants plundered; even Mustapha and Mahomet, the German negroes, had a share of the booty." The German quoted would be correctly translated "what rubbish!" Blücher, therefore, has been either misquoted or mistranslated.

15
It is magnificent, but it is not war.

GENERAL PIERRE BOSQUET. On the Charge of the Light Brigade. Attributed also to MARSHAL CANROBERT.

16
He who did well in war just earns the right
To begin doing well in peace.

ROBERT BROWNING—*Luria.* Act II. L. 354.

17
The Government of the United States would be constrained to hold the Imperial German government to a strict accountability for such acts of their naval authorities.

W. J. BRYAN—To the German government, when Secretary of State. *European War Series of Depart. of State.* No. I. P. 54.

1

Lay down the axe; fling by the spade;
  Leave in its track the toiling plough;
The rifle and the bayonet-blade
  For arms like yours were fitter now;
And let the hands that ply the pen
  Quit the light task, and learn to wield
The horseman's crooked brand, and rein
  The charger on the battle-field.

BRYANT—*Our Country's Call.*

2

None of our soldiers would understand not being asked to do whatever is necessary to re-establish a situation which is humiliating to us and unacceptable to our country's honor.—We are going to counter-attack.

Credited to MAJOR-GEN. R. L. BULLARD, also to MAJOR-GEN. OMAR BUNDY, in reply to the French command to retire in the second battle of the Marne, 1918.

3

The American flag has been forced to retire. This is intolerable.

MAJOR-GEN. R. L. BULLARD, on leaving the Conference of French Generals, July 15, 1918. Expressing regret that he could not obey orders. He is called "The General of No Retreat." See N. Y. *Herald*, Nov. 3, 1919. (Editorial)

4

You are there, stay there.

MAJOR-GEN. R. L. BULLARD. Citation to American unit which captured Fay's Wood. See N. Y. *Herald*, Nov. 3, 1919. (Editorial)

5

If it were possible for members of different nationalities, with different language and customs, and an intellectual life of a different kind, to live side by side in one and the same state, without succumbing to the temptation of each trying to force his own nationality on the other, things would look a good deal more peaceful. But it is a law of life and development in history that where two national civilizations meet they fight for ascendancy. In the struggle between nationalities, one nation is the hammer and the other the anvil: one is the victor and the other the vanquished.

BERNHARD VON BÜLOW—*Imperial Germany.*

6

Justa bella quibus necessaria.

Wars are just to those to whom they are necessary.

Quoted by BURKE—*Reflections on the Revolution in France.*

7

"War," says Machiavel, "ought to be the only study of a prince"; and by a prince he means every sort of state, however constituted. "He ought," says this great political doctor, "to consider peace only as a breathing-time, which gives him leisure to contrive, and furnishes ability to execute military plans."

BURKE—*Vindication of Natural Society.* Vol. I. P. 15.

8

Scots, wha hae wi' Wallace bled;
Scots, wham Bruce has aften led,
Welcome to your gory bed,
  Or to victory!

BURNS—*Bruce to his Men at Bannockburn.*

9

Dieu est d'ordinaire pour les gros escadrons contre les petits.

God is generally for the big squadrons against the little ones.

BUSSY-RABUTIN—*Letter.* Oct. 18, 1677. Anticipated by TACITUS. Deus fortioribus adesse. (See also VOLTAIRE)

10

In all the trade of war, no feat
Is nobler than a brave retreat.

BUTLER—*Hudibras.* Pt. I. Canto III. L. 607.

11

For those that run away, and fly,
Take place at least o' th' enemy.

BUTLER—*Hudibras.* Pt. I. Canto III. L. 609.

12

There's but the twinkling of a star
Between a man of peace and war.

BUTLER—*Hudibras.* Pt. II. Canto III. L. 957.

13

For those that fly may fight again,
Which he can never do that's slain.

BUTLER—*Hudibras.* Pt. III. Canto III. L. 243.

14

For he who fights and runs away
May live to fight another day;
But he who is in battle slain
Can never rise and fight again.

BUTLER's lines misquoted by GOLDSMITH in a publication of NEWBERY, the publisher, *The Art of Poetry on a New Plan.* Vol. II. P. 147. The first lines appear in *Musarum Deliciæ.* Collection by SIR JOHN MENNIS and DR. JAMES SMITH. (1656) Accredited by some authorities to SUCKLING, but not confirmed by MENNIS.

(See also ARCHILOCHUS, DEMOSTHENES, ERASMUS, MENANDER, SATYRE, SCARRON, TERTULLIAN.)

Oft he that doth abide
  Is cause of his own paine,
But he that flieth in good tide
  Perhaps may fight again.

A Pleasant Satyre or Poesie. From the French. (About 1595)

15

Bloody wars at first began,
The artificial plague of man,
That from his own invention rise,
To scourge his own iniquities.

BUTLER—*Satire. Upon the Weakness and Misery of Man.* L. 105.

16

O proud was our army that morning
  That stood where the pine darkly towers,
When Sherman said—"Boys, you are weary,
  This day fair Savannah is ours."
Then sang we a song for our chieftain
  That echoed o'er river and lea,
And the stars on our banner shone brighter
  When Sherman marched down to the sea.

S. H. M. BYERS—*Sherman's March to the Sea.* Last stanza.

17

War, war is still the cry, "War even to the knife!"

BYRON—*Childe Harold.* Canto I St. 86.

1
And there was mounting in hot haste: the steed,
The mustering squadron, and the clattering car,
Went pouring forward with impetuous speed,
And swiftly forming in the ranks of war;
And the deep thunder peal on peal, afar
And near; the beat of the alarming drum
Roused up the soldier ere the morning star;
While throng'd the citizens with terror dumb,
Or whispering with white lips—"The foe! they come! they come!"

BYRON—*Childe Harold.* Canto III. St. 25.

2
Battle's magnificently stern array!

BYRON—*Childe Harold.* Canto III. St. 28.

3
The Assyrian came down like the wolf on the fold,
And his cohorts were gleaming in purple and gold.

BYRON—*Destruction of Sennacherib.*

4
Like the leaves of the forest when summer is green,
That host with their banners at sunset were seen;
Like the leaves of the forest when autumn hath blown,
That host on the morrow lay wither'd and strown!

BYRON—*Destruction of Sennacherib.*

5
Hand to hand, and foot to foot:
Nothing there, save death, was mute;
Stroke, and thrust, and flash, and cry
For quarter or for victory,
Mingle there with the volleying thunder.

BYRON—*Siege of Corinth.* St. 24.

6
Veni, vidi, vici.

I came, I saw, I conquered.

Attributed to JULIUS CÆSAR. PLUTARCH—*Life of Cæsar*, states it was spoken after the defeat of Pharnaces, at Zela in Pontus, B. C. 47, not the Expedition to Britain, B. C. 55. According to SUETONIUS—*Julius Cæsar.* 37, the words were not Cæsar's but were displayed before Cæsar's title, "non acta belli significantem, sicut ceteri, sed celeriter confecti notam." Not as being a record of the events of the war, as in other cases, but as an indication of the rapidity with which it was concluded. Ne insolens barbarus dicat, "Ueni, uidi, uici." Never shall insolent barbarian say "I came, I saw, I conquered." SENECA THE ELDER—*Suæsoria.* II. 22. BUECHMANN, quoting the above, suggests that Cæsar's words may be an adaptation of a proverb by APOSTOLIUS. XII. 58. (Or XIV, in Elzivir Ed. Leyden, 1653.)

(See also HENRY IV, SOBIESKI)

7
In bello parvis momentis magni casus intercedunt.

In war events of importance are the result of trivial causes.

CÆSAR—*Bellum Gallicum.* I. 21.

8
The combat deepens. On, ye brave,
Who rush to glory, or the grave!
Wave, Munich! all thy banners wave,
And charge with all thy chivalry.

CAMPBELL—*Hohenlinden.*

9
La Garde meurt, mais ne se rend pas.

The guard dies but does not surrender.

Attributed to LIEUT. GEN. PIERRE JACQUES, BARON DE CAMBRONNE, when called to surrender by COL. HUGH HALKETT. Cambronne disavowed the saying at a banquet at Nantes, 1835. The *London Times* on the Centenary of the battle of Waterloo published a letter, written at 11 P. M. on the evening of the battle, by CAPT. DIGBY MACKWORTH, of the 7th Fusiliers, A. D. C. to Gen. Hill. In it the phrase is quoted as already familiar. FOURNIER in *L'Esprit dans l'histoire*, pp. 412–15, ascribes it to a correspondent of the *Independant*, ROUGEMONT. It appeared there the next day, and afterwards in the *Journal General de France*, June 24. This seems also improbable in view of the above mentioned letter. See also VICTOR HUGO—*Les Miserables. Waterloo.*

10
War will never yield but to the principles of universal justice and love, and these have no sure root but in the religion of Jesus Christ.

WM. ELLERY CHANNING—*Lecture on War.* Sec. II.

11
O Chryste, it is a grief for me to telle,
How manie a noble erle and valrous knyghte
In fyghtynge for Kynge Harrold noblie fell,
Al sleyne on Hastyng's field in bloudie fyghte.

CHATTERTON—*Battle of Hastings.*

12
Bella suscipienda sunt ob eam causam, ut sine injuria in pace vivatur.

Wars are to be undertaken in order that it may be possible to live in peace without molestation.

CICERO—*De Officiis.* I. 11.

13
Parvi enim sunt foris arma, nisi est consilium domi.

An army abroad is of little use unless there are prudent counsels at home.

CICERO—*De Officiis.* I. 22.

14
Bellum autem ita suscipiatur, ut nihil aliud, nisi pax, quæsita videatur.

Let war be so carried on that no other object may seem to be sought but the acquisition of peace.

CICERO—*De Officiis.* I. 23.

15
Silent leges inter arma.

The law is silent during war.

CICERO—*Oratio Pro Annio Milone.* IV.

16
Pro aris et focis.

For your altars and your fires.

CICERO—*Oration for Roscius.* Ch. V. Also used by TIBERIUS GRACCHUS before this.

17
Nervi belli pecunia infinita.

Endless money forms the sinews of war.

CICERO—*Philippics.* V. 2. 5. LIBANIUS—*Orations.* XLVI. PHOTIUS—*Lex.* S. 5. RABELAIS—*Gargantua.* Bk. I. Ch. XXVI. ("Corn" for "money.")

(See also HULL, PLUTARCH, also BION under MONEY)

1
Well here's to the Maine, and I'm sorry for
Spain,
Said Kelly and Burke and Shea.
J. I. C. CLARKE—*The Fighting Race.*

2
We made war to the end—to the very end of the end.
CLEMENCEAU—*Message to American People.* Sept., 1918.

3
What voice did on my spirit fall,
Peschiera, when thy bridge I crossed?
"'Tis better to have fought and lost,
Than never to have fought at all."
ARTHUR H. CLOUGH—*Peschiera.*
(See also TENNYSON under LOVE)

4
War in fact is becoming contemptible, and ought to be put down by the great nations of Europe, just as we put down a vulgar mob.
MORTIMER COLLINS—*Thoughts in my Garden.* II. 243.

5
The flames of Moscow were the aurora of the liberty of the world.
BENJ. CONSTANT—*Esprit de Conquête.* Preface. (1813)

6
Hence jarring sectaries may learn
Their real interest to discern;
That brother should not war with brother,
And worry and devour each other.
COWPER—*The Nightingale and Glow-Worm.*

7
But war's a game, which, were their subjects wise,
Kings would not play at.
COWPER—*Task.* Bk. V. L. 187.

8
General Taylor never surrenders.
THOS. L. CRITTENDEN—*Reply to Gen. Santa Anna.* Buena Vista. Feb. 22, 1847.

9
We give up the fort when there's not a man left to defend it.
GENERAL CROGHAN. At Fort Stevenson. (1812)

10
From fear in every guise,
From sloth, from love of pelf,
By war's great sacrifice
The world redeems itself.
J. DAVIDSON—*War Song.*

11
Qui fugiebat, rusus prœliabitur.
The man who flies shall fight again.
DEMOSTHENES, on his flight at the battle of Chæronea, B.C. 338. Credited to him by TERTULLIAN—*De Fuga in Persecutione.* Sec. X. See CARDINAL NEWMAN—*Church of The Fathers.* P. 215. Same expression in ÆLIANUS. 1. 3. 4. 5. AULUS GELLIUS. Bk. XVII. 21. 32. NEPOS—*Thrasbulus.* Ch. II. JUSTINUS. 9. 6.
(See also BUTLER)

12
Di qui non si passa.
By here they shall not pass.
GENERAL DIAZ. Words inscribed on the Altar of Liberty temporarily erected at Madison Square, N. Y., on the authority of *Il Progresso Italiano.*

13
Non si passa, passereme noi.
The words ascribed to GENERAL DIAZ by the Italians at the battle of the Piave and Monta Grappa, June, 1918. These words are inscribed on the medals struck off for the heroes of this battle.
(See also BATES, PÉTAIN)

14
What argufies pride and ambition?
Soon or late death will take us in tow:
Each bullet has got its commission,
And when our time's come we must go.
CHARLES DIBDIN—*The Benevolent Tar.*
(See also GASCOIGNE)

15
A feat of chivalry, fiery with consummate courage, and bright with flashing vigor.
BENJ. DISRAELI. Of the Charge of the Light Brigade. In the House of Commons, Dec. 15, 1855.

16
Carry his body hence!
Kings must have slaves:
Kings climb to eminence
Over men's graves:
So this man's eye is dim;
Throw the earth over him!
HENRY AUSTIN DOBSON—*Before Sedan.*

17
They now to fight are gone;
Armor on armor shone;
Drum now to drum did groan,
To hear was wonder;
That with the cries they make,
The very earth did shake;
Trumpet to trumpet spake,
Thunder to thunder.
DRAYTON—*Ballad of Agincourt.* St. 8.
(See also TENNYSON)

18
War, he sung, is toil and trouble;
Honour but an empty bubble.
DRYDEN—*Alexander's Feast.* L. 99.

19
All delays are dangerous in war.
DRYDEN—*Tyrannic Love.* Act I. Sc. 1.

20
When 'tis an aven thing in th' prayin', may th' best man win . . . an' th' best man will win.
FINLEY PETER DUNNE—*Mr. Dooley in Peace and War. On Prayers for Victory.*

21
'Tis startin' a polis foorce to prevint war. . . . How'll they be ar-rmed? What a foolish question. They'll be ar-rmed with love, if coorse. Who'll pay thim? That's a financyal detail that can be arranged later on. What'll happen if wan iv th' rough-necks reaches f'r a gun? Don't bother me with thrifles.
FINLEY PETER DUNNE—*On Making a Will.* Mr. Dooley's version of W. J. BRYAN'S Speech. (1920)

22
There is no discharge in that war.
Ecclesiastes. VIII. 8.

23
By the rude bridge that arched the flood,
Their flag to April's breeze unfurl'd;
Here once the embattl'd farmers stood,

And fired the shot heard round the world.

EMERSON—*Hymn sung at the completion of the Concord Monument.*

1

That same man that renneth awaie
Maie fight again on other daie.

ERASMUS—*Apothegms.* Given as a saying of Demosthenes, and quoted as a "verse common in every body's mouth." Tr. by UDALL. (1542)

(See also BUTLER)

2

Ares (the God of War) hates those who hesitate.

EURIPIDES—*Heraclidæ.* 722.

3

Jellicoe has all the Nelsonic attributes except *one*—he is totally wanting in the great gift of insubordination.

LORD FISHER—*Letter to a Privy Councillor.* Dec. 27, 1916.

4

My right has been rolled up. My left has been driven back. My center has been smashed. I have ordered an advance from all directions.

Attributed to GEN. FOCH but authorship denied by him.

5

Then came the attack in the Amiens sector on August 8. That went well, too. The moment had arrived. I ordered General Humbert to attack in his turn. "No reserves." No matter. Allez-y (Get on with it) I tell Marshal Haig to attack, too. He's short of men also. Attack all the same. There we are advancing everywhere—the whole line! En avant! Hup!

GEN. FOCH. In an interview with G. WARD PRICE, correspondent of London *Daily Mail.* (1919)

6

All the same, the fundamental truths which govern that art are still unchangeable; just as the principles of mechanics must always govern architecture, whether the building be made of wood, stone, iron or concrete; just as the principles of harmony govern music of whatever kind. It is still necessary, then, to establish the principles of war.

GEN. FOCH—*Principles of War.* From the preface written for the post-bellum edition.

7

I am going on to the Rhine. If you oppose me, so much the worse for you, but whether you sign an armistice or not, I do not stop until I reach the Rhine.

GEN. FOCH to the Germans who came to ask for an armistice. As reported by G. WARD PRICE in the London *Daily Mail.* (1919)

8

Keep the home fires burning, while your hearts are yearning,
Tho' your lads are far away they dream of home.
There's a silver lining through the dark cloud shining;
Turn the dark cloud inside out till the boys come home.

MRS. LENA GUILBERT FORD. Theme suggested by IVOR NOVELLO, who wrote the music. Sung by the soldiers in the Great War.

9

There never was a good war or a bad peace.

BENJ. FRANKLIN—*Letter to Quincy.* Sept. 11, 1773.

10

Your flaming torch aloft we bear,
With burning heart an oath we swear
To keep the faith, to fight it through,
To crush the foe or sleep with you
In Flanders' fields.

C. B. GALBREATH. Answer to McCRAE's *In Flanders' Fields.*

11

When the red wrath perisheth, when the dulled swords fail,
These three who have walked with Death—these shall prevail.
Hell bade all its millions rise; Paradise sends three:
Pity, and Self-sacrifice, and Charity.

THEODOSIA GARRISON—*These shall Prevail.*

12

Sufficeth this to prove my theme withal,
That every bullet hath a lighting place.

GASCOIGNE—*Dulce Bellum Inexpertis.*

(See also BISMARCK, DIBDIN, SMOLLETT, WILLIAM III)

13

O, send Lewis Gordon hame
And the lad I maune name,
Though his back be at the wa'
Here's to him that's far awa'.
O, hon! my Highlandman,
O, my bonny Highlandman,
Weel would I my true love ken
Among ten thousand Highlandmen.

Accredited to GEDDES—*Lewis Gordon.* In *Scotch Songs and Ballads.*

(See also HAIG)

14

We have 500,000 reservists in America who would rise in arms against your government.

ZIMMERMANN to AMBASSADOR GERARD.

I told him that we had five hundred thousand and one lamp posts in America, and that was where the German reservists would find themselves if they tried any uprising.

AMBASSADOR GERARD'S answer. JAMES W. GERARD—*My Four Years in Germany.* P. 237.

15

It is an olde saw, he fighteth wele (well) that fleith faste.

Gesta Romanorum. Wolf and the Hare. 15th cent. *MS.*

(See also BUTLER)

16

Neither ridiculous shriekings for revenge by French chauvinists, nor the Englishmen's gnashing of teeth, nor the wild gestures of the Slavs will turn us from our aim of protecting and extending German influence all the world over.

Official secret report of the Germans, quoted in the *French Yellow Book.*

17

Ye living soldiers of the mighty war,
Once more from roaring cannon and the drums
And bugles blown at morn, the summons comes;
Forget the halting limb, each wound and scar:
Once more your Captain calls to you;
Come to his last review!

R. W. GILDER—*The Burial of Grant*

1
An attitude not only of defence, but defiance.
THOS. GILLESPIE — *The Mountain Storm.* "Defence not defiance" became the motto of the Volunteer Movement. (1859)

2
No terms except an unconditional and immediate surrender can be accepted. I propose to move immediately upon your works.
U. S. GRANT—*To Gen. S. B. Buckner.* Fort Donelson. Feb. 16, 1862.

3
I * * * purpose to fight it out on this line if it takes all summer.
U. S. GRANT—*Despatch from Spottsylvania Court House.* May 11, 1864.

4
The British army should be a projectile to be fired by the British navy.
VISCOUNT GREY. Quoted by LORD FISHER, in *Memories*, as "the splendid words of Sir Edward Grey."

5
Con disavvantaggio grande si fa la guerra con chi non ha che perdere.
We fight to great disadvantage when we fight with those who have nothing to lose.
GUICCIARDINI—*Storia d'Italia.*

6
Every position must be held to the last man. There must be no retirement. With our backs to the wall, and believing in the justice of our cause, each one of us must fight to the end.
FIELD MARSHAL HAIG. At the battle of Picardy. (1918) See also GEDDES. Song probably well known to Haig.

7
Yes; quaint and curious war is!
You shoot a fellow down
You'd treat if met where any bar is,
Or help to half-a-crown.
THOS. HARDY—*The Man he Killed.*

8
They were left in the lurch
For want of more wadding—He ran to the church—
* * * * * *
With his arms full of hymnbooks . . .
Rang his voice, "Put Watts into 'em—Boys, give 'em Watts."
BRET HARTE—*Caldwell of Springfield.*

9
An hour ago, a Star was falling.
A star? There's nothing strange in that.
No, nothing; but above the thicket,
Somehow it seemed to me that God
Somewhere had just relieved a picket.
BRET HARTE—*Relieving Guard.*
(See also BEERS)

10
Hark! I hear the tramp of thousands,
And of armèd men the hum;
Lo, a nation's hosts have gathered
Round the quick alarming drum—
Saying, Come,
Freemen, Come!
Ere your heritage be wasted,
Said the quick alarming drum.
BRET HARTE—*The Rèveille.*

11
Let the only walls the foe shall scale
Be ramparts of the dead!
PAUL H. HAYNE—*Vicksburg.*

12
My men never retire. They go forward or they die.
COL. WILLIAM HAYWARD to a French General who cried to him to retire his troops, the 369th Infantry, colored. See N. Y. *Herald.* Feb. 3, 1919. Attributed also to MAJOR BUNDY, but denied by him.

13
Napoleon healed through sword and fire the sick nation.
HEINE. See SCHERER—*History of German Literature.* II. 116.

14
Hang yourself, brave Crillon. We fought at Arques, and you were not there.
HENRY IV, to Crillon after a great victory. Sept. 20, 1597. Appeared in a note to VOLTAIRE's *Henriade.* VIII. 109.

15
Just for a word—"neutrality," a word which in war-time had so often been disregarded—just for a scrap of paper, Great Britain was going to make war on a kindred nation who desired nothing better than to be friends with her.
BETHMANN-HOLLWEG, German Chancellor, to SIR EDWARD GOSCHEN, British Ambassador, Aug. 4, 1914.
(See also LOYSON, and WILLIAM I. under GOVERNMENT)

16
Bleak are our shores with the blasts of December,
Fettered and chill is the rivulet's flow;
Throbbing and warm are the hearts that remember
Who was our friend when the world was our foe.
HOLMES—*Welcome to the Grand Duke Alexis,* Dec. 6, 1871. Referring to the fleet sent by Russia in Sept., 1863, an act with mixed motives, but for which we were grateful.

17
I war not with the dead.
HOMER—*Iliad.* Bk. VII. L. 485. POPE's trans. CHARLES V. *Of Luther.* Found in W. L. HERTSLET—*Der Treppenwitz der Weltgeschichte.*
(See also VERGIL)

18
Take thou thy arms and come with me,
For we must quit ourselves like men, and strive
To aid our cause, although we be but two.
Great is the strength of feeble arms combined,
And we can combat even with the brave.
HOMER—*Iliad.* Bk. XIII. L. 289. BRYANT's trans.

19
The chance of war
Is equal, and the slayer oft is slain.
HOMER—*Iliad.* Bk. XVIII. L. 388. BRYANT's trans.

20
Our business in the field of fight
Is not to question, but to prove our might.
HOMER—*Iliad.* Bk. XX. L. 304. POPE's trans.

1
It is not right to exult over slain men.
HOMER—*Odyssey*. XII. 412. Quoted by JOHN MORLEY in a speech during the Boer War. Also by JOHN BRIGHT in his speech on America, June 29, 1867. Compare ARCHILOCHUS—*Frag. Berk.* No. 64. (HILLER. No. 60. LIEBEL. No. 41.)
(See also VERGIL)

2
So ends the bloody business of the day.
HOMER—*Odyssey*. Bk. XXII. L. 516. POPE'S trans.

3
Nimirum hic ego sum.
Here indeed I am; this is my position.
HORACE—*Epistles*. Bk. I. 15. 42.
(See also LUTHER)

4
Postquam Discordia tetra
Belli ferratos postes portasque refregit.
When discord dreadful bursts her brazen bars,
And shatters locks to thunder forth her wars.
HORACE—*Satires*. I. 4. 60. Quoted. Original not known, thought to be from ENNIUS.

5
Ye who made war that your ships
Should lay to at the beck of no nation,
Make war now on Murder, that slips
The leash of her hounds of damnation;
Ye who remembered the Alamo,
Remember the Maine!
RICHARD HOVEY—*The Word of the Lord from Havana.*

6
Mine eyes have seen the glory of the coming of the Lord:
He is trampling out the vintage where the grapes of wrath are stored:
He hath loosed the fateful lightning of his terrible swift sword:
His truth is marching on.
JULIA WARD HOWE—*Battle Hymn of the Republic.*

7
L'Angleterre prit l'aigle, et l'Autriche l'aiglon.
The English took the eagle and Austrians the eaglet.
VICTOR HUGO. Napoleon adopted the lectern eagle for his imperial standard. His son was the eaglet.

8
Earth was the meadow, he the mower strong.
VICTOR HUGO—*La Légende des Siècles.*

9
The sinews of war are those two metals (gold and silver).
ARTHUR HULL to ROBERT CECIL, in a *Memorial*, Nov. 28, 1600. Same idea in FULLER'S *Holy State*. P. 125. (Ed. 1649)
(See also CICERO)

10
We don't want to fight, but by jingo if we do,
We've got the ships, we've got the men, we've got the money too.
We've fought the Bear before and while we're Britons true,
The Russians shall not have Constantinople.
G. W. HUNT. (Called "the Kipling of the Halls.") As sung by the "GREAT MCDERMOTT," in 1878 it made the term "Jingo" popular. "Jingo," first used as a political term of reproach, by GEORGE JACOB HOLYOAKE, in a letter to the London *Daily News*, March 13, 1878.
He . . . falls a-fighting it out of one hand into the other, tossing it this way and that; lets it run a little upon the line, then *tanutus, high jingo, come again.* Traced by the *Oxford Dict.* to JOHN EACHARD—*Grounds and Occasion of the Contempt of Clergy*. 1670. P. 34. See also OLDHAM—*Satires upon the Jesuits*. IV. (1679) "By Jingo" found in a trans. of RABELAIS—*Pantagruel*. Bk. IV. Ch. LV. Also in COWLEY—*Cutter of Coleman Street*, pub. 1663, performed, 1661. "By the living Jingo" in GOLDSMITH—*Vicar of Wakefield*. Ch. X.

11
The closeness of their intercourse [the intercourse of nations] will assuredly render war as absurd and impossible by-and-by, as it would be for Manchester to fight with Birmingham, or Holborn Hill with the Strand.
LEIGH HUNT—*Preface to Poems.*

12
Oh! if I were Queen of France, or, still better, Pope of Rome,
I would have no fighting men abroad and no weeping maids at home;
All the world should be at peace; or if kings must show their might,
Why, let them who make the quarrels be the only ones to fight.
CHARLES JEFFRIES—*Jeannette and Jeannot.*

13
He saith among the trumpets, Ha, ha; and he smelleth the battle afar off.
Job. XXXIX. 25.

14
The safety of the country is at stake. . . . We must let ourselves be killed on the spot rather than retreat. . . . No faltering can be tolerated today.
GENERAL JOFFRE—*Proclamation*. Sept. 6, 1914.

15
I have prayed in her fields of poppies,
I have laughed with the men who died—
But in all my ways and through all my days
Like a friend He walked beside.
I have seen a sight under Heaven
That only God understands,
In the battles' glare I have seen Christ there
With the Sword of God in His hand.
GORDON JOHNSTONE—*On Fields of Flanders.*
(See also WHITNALL)

16
The Philistines be upon thee, Samson.
Judges. XVI. 9.

17
The people arose as one man.
Judges. XX. 8.

18
Soon the men of the column began to see that though the scarlet line was slender, it was very rigid and exact.
KINGLAKE—*Invasion of the Crimea*. Vol. III. P. 455. The spruce beauty of the slender red line. KINGLAKE—*Invasion of the Crimea.* Vol. III. P. 248. Ed. 6.
(See also RUSSELL)

1
For agony and spoil
  Of nations beat to dust,
For poisoned air and tortured soil
  And cold, commanded lust,
And every secret woe
  The shuddering waters saw—
Willed and fulfilled by high and low—
  Let them relearn the Law.

KIPLING—*Justice.* (Oct. 24, 1918)

2
For heathen heart that puts her trust
  In reeking tube and iron shard—
All valiant dust that builds on dust,
  And guarding calls not Thee to guard—
For frantic boast and foolish word,
Thy mercy on Thy People, Lord!

KIPLING—*Recessional.*

3
You are ordered abroad as a soldier of the King to help our French comrades against the invasion of a common enemy. You have to perform a task which will need your courage, your energy, and your patience. Remember that the honor of the British Army depends on your individual conduct. It will be your duty not only to set an example of discipline and perfect steadiness under fire, but also to maintain the most friendly relations with those whom you are helping in this struggle. . . . Do your duty bravely. Fear God and honor the King.

KITCHENER—*A printed address to the British Expeditionary Force,* carried by the soldiers on the Continent.

4
Friendship itself prompts it (Government of the U. S.) to say to the Imperial Government (Germany) that repetition by the commanders of German naval vessels of acts in contravention of those rights (neutral) must be regarded by the Government of the United States, when they affect American citizens, as deliberately unfriendly.

Secretary of War LANSING. Reply to the German Lusitania Note. July 21, 1915.

5
There is no such thing as an inevitable war. If war comes it will be from failure of human wisdom.

BONAR LAW. Speech before the Great War.

6
I have always believed that success would be the inevitable result if the two services, the army and the navy, had fair play, and if we sent the right man to fill the right place.

AUSTIN H. LAYARD—*Speech in Parliament.* Jan. 15, 1855.

7
When Greeks joined Greeks, then was the tug of war!

NATHANIEL LEE—*The Rival Queens; or, Alexander the Great.* Act IV. Sc. 2.

8
Art, thou hast many infamies,
But not an infamy like this.
O snap the fife and still the drum
And show the monster as she is.

R. LE GALLIENNE—*The Illusion of War.*

9
O, God assist our side: at least, avoid assisting the enemy and leave the rest to me.

PRINCE LEOPOLD of ANHALT-DESSAU, according to CARLYLE—*Life of Frederick the Great.* Bk. XV. Ch. XIV.

10
The ballot is stronger than the bullet.

LINCOLN. (1856)

11
One month too late.

VON LINSINGEN'S remark when told of Italy's declaration of war against Austria in Great War.

12
To arms! to arms! ye brave!
  Th' avenging sword unsheathe,
March on! march on! all hearts resolved
  On victory or death!

JOSEPH ROUGET DE LISLE—*The Marseilles Hymn.* 7th stanza by Du Bois. See *Figaro,* Literary Supplement, Aug. 7, 1908.

13
At the Captain's mess, in the Banquet-hall,
Sat feasting the officers, one and all—
Like a sabre-blow, like the swing of a sail,
One raised his glass, held high to hail,
Sharp snapped like the stroke of a rudder's play,
Spoke three words only: "To the day!"

ERNEST LISSAUER—*Hassgesang gegen England.* (Song of Hate against England.)
(See also RICHMOND)

14
Ostendite modo bellum, pacem habebitis.
  You need only a show of war to have peace.

LIVY—*History.* VI. 18. 7. Same idea in DION CHRYSOSTOM—*De Regn. Orat.* I. SYRUS—*Maxims.* 465.

15
Justum est bellum, quibus necessarium; et pia arma, quibus nulla nisi in armis relinquitur opes.
  To those to whom war is necessary it is just; and a resort to arms is righteous in those to whom no means of assistance remain except by arms.

LIVY—*History.* Bk. IX. 1.

16
God has chosen little nations as the vessels by which He carries His choicest wines to the lips of humanity to rejoice their hearts, to exalt their vision, to strengthen their faith, and if we had stood by when two little nations (Belgium and Servia) were being crushed and broken by the brutal hands of barbarians, our shame would have rung down the everlasting ages.

LLOYD GEORGE—*Speech* at Queen's Hall. Sept., 1914.

17
The stern hand of Fate has scourged us to an elevation where we can see the everlasting things that matter for a nation—the great peaks we had forgotten, of Honour, Duty, Patriotism, and clad in glittering white, the pinnacles of Sacrifice, pointing like a rugged finger to Heaven. We shall descend into the valley again; but as long as the men and women of this generation last, they will carry in their hearts the image of these mighty peaks, whose foundations are not shaken, though Europe rock and sway in the convulsions of a great war.

LLOYD GEORGE—*Speech* at Queen's Hall. Sept., 1914.

1
Too late in moving here, too late in arriving there, too late in coming to this decision, too late in starting with enterprises, too late in preparing. In this war the footsteps of the allied forces have been dogged by the mocking specter of Too Late! and unless we quicken our movements, damnation will fall on the sacred cause for which so much gallant blood has flowed.

LLOYD GEORGE—*Speech*, in the House of Commons. Dec. 20, 1915.

2
The last £100,000,000 will win.

LLOYD GEORGE, when Chancellor of the Exchequer, at the beginning of the war. 1914. See *Everybody's Magazine*. Jan., 1918. P. 8.

3
Is it, O man, with such discordant noises,
With such accursed instruments as these,
Thou drownest Nature's sweet and kindly voices,
And jarrest the celestial harmonies?

LONGFELLOW—*Arsenal at Springfield*. St. 8.

4
Ultima ratio regum.
Last argument of kings. [Cannon.]

LOUIS XIV ordered this engraved on cannon. Removed by the National Assembly, Aug. 19, 1790. Found on cannon in Mantua. (1613) On Prussian guns of today. Motto for pieces of ordnance in use as early as 1613. BÜCHMANN—*Geflügelte Wörte*. Ultima razon de reges. (War.) The ultimate reason of kings. CALDERON. Don't forget your great guns, which are the most respectable arguments of the rights of kings. FREDERICK THE GREAT to his brother HENRY. April 21, 1759.

5
Ez fer war, I call it murder,—
Ther you hev it plain and flat;
I don't want to go no furder
Than my Testyment fer that.

LOWELL—*The Biglow Papers*. No. 1.

6
It don't seem hardly right, John,
When both my hands was full,
To stump me to a fight, John,
Your cousin, too, John Bull!
Ole Uncle S. sez he, "I guess
We know it now," sez he,
"The lion's paw is all the law,
According to J. B.,
That's fit for you an' me."

LOWELL—*The Biglow Papers*. *Jonathan to John*. St. 1.

7
We kind o' thought Christ went agin war an' pillage.

LOWELL—*The Biglow Papers*. No. 3.

8
Not but wut abstract war is horrid,
I sign to thet with all my heart,—
But civilysation *doos* git forrid
Sometimes, upon a powder-cart.

LOWELL—*Biglow Papers*. No. 7.

9
The Campbells are comin'.

ROBERT T. S. LOWELL—*The Relief of Lucknow*. Poem on same story written by HENRY MORFORD, ALEX. MACLAGAN.

10
Pourquoi cette trombe enflammée
Qui vient foudroyer l'univers?
Cet embrasement de l'enfer?
Ce tourbillonnement d'armées
Par mille milliers de milliers?
—C'est pour un chiffon de papier.
For what this whirlwind all aflame?
This thunderstroke of hellish ire,
Setting the universe afire?
While millions upon millions came
Into a very storm of war?
For a scrap of paper.

PÈRE HYACINTHE LOYSON—*Pour un Chiffon de Papier*. Trans. by EDWARD BRABROOK. In *Notes and Queries*, Jan. 6, 1917. P. 5.
(See also 335[8], 847[15])

11
Alta sedent civilis vulnera dextræ.
The wounds of civil war are deeply felt.

LUCAN—*Pharsalia*. I. 32.

12
Omnibus hostes
Reddite nos populis—civile avertite bellum.
Make us enemies of every people on earth, but prevent a civil war.

LUCAN—*Pharsalia*. II. 52.

13
Non tam portas intrare patentes
Quam fregisse juvat; nec tam patiente colono
Arva premi, quam si ferro populetur et igni;
Concessa pudet ire via.

The conqueror is not so much pleased by entering into open gates, as by forcing his way. He desires not the fields to be cultivated by the patient husbandman; he would have them laid waste by fire and sword. It would be his shame to go by a way already opened.

LUCAN—*Pharsalia*. II. 443.

14
'Aig [F.-M. Sir Douglas Haig] 'e don't say much; 'e don't, so to say, say nothin'; but what 'e don't say don't mean nothin', not 'arf. But when 'e do say something—my Gawd!

E. V. LUCAS—*Boswell of Baghdad*.

15
Here I stand. I can do no other. God help me. Amen.

MARTIN LUTHER. End of his speech at the Diet of Worms. April 18, 1521. Inscribed on his monument at Worms.
(See also HORACE, WILSON)

16
I beg that the small steamers . . . be spared if possible, or else sunk without a trace being left. (Spurlos versenkt.)

COUNT KARL VON LUXBURG, Chargé d'Affaires at Buenos Ayres. Telegram to the Berlin Foreign Office, May 19, 1917. Also same July 9, 1917, referring to Argentine ships. Cablegrams disclosed by Sec. Lansing as sent from the German Legation in Buenos Ayres by way of the Swedish Legation to Berlin.

If neutrals were destroyed so that they disappeared without leaving any trace, terror would soon keep seamen and travelers away from the danger zones.

PROF. OSWALD FLAMM in the Berlin *Woche*. Cited in N. Y. *Times*, May 15, 1917.

1
Oh! wherefore come ye forth in triumph from the North,
With your hands and your feet, and your raiment all red?
And wherefore doth your rout send forth a joyous shout?
And whence be the grapes of the wine-press which ye tread?
MACAULAY—*The Battle of Naseby.*

2
The essence of war is violence. Moderation in war is imbecility.
Attributed to LORD FISHER during the great War. Taken from MACAULAY'S *Essay on Lord Nugent's Memorials of Hampden.*

3
Take up our quarrel with the foe!
To you from failing hands we throw
The torch; be yours to hold it high.
If ye break faith with us who die
We shall not sleep, though poppies grow
In Flanders' fields.
JOHN MCCRAE—*In Flanders' Fields.* (*We shall not Sleep.*)
(See also GALBREATH, and MCCRAE under the topical heading POPPY)

4
Di qui nacque che tutti li profeti armati vinsero, e li disarmati rovinarono.
Hence it happened that all the armed prophets conquered, all the unarmed perished.
MACHIAVELLI—*Il Principe.* C. 6.

5
War in men's eyes shall be
A monster of iniquity
In the good time coming.
Nations shall not quarrel then,
To prove which is the stronger;
Nor slaughter men for glory's sake;—
Wait a little longer.
CHARLES MACKAY—*The Good Time Coming.*

6
We want no war of conquest. . . . War should never be entered upon until every agency of peace has failed.
WILLIAM MCKINLEY—*Inaugural Address.* Washington, March 4, 1897.
(See also WILSON)

7
The warpipes are pealing, "The Campbells are coming."
They are charging and cheering. O dinna ye hear it?
ALEXANDER MACLAGAN—*Jennie's Dream.*
(See also LOWELL)

8
There's some say that we wan, some say that they wan,
Some say that nane wan at a', man,
But one thing I'm sure that at Sheriff-Muir,
A battle there was which I saw, man.
And we ran and they ran, and they ran and we ran,
And we ran, and they ran awa', man.
MURDOCH MCLENNAN—*Sheriff-Muir.* (An indecisive battle, Nov. 13, 1715.)

9
J'y suis, et j'y reste.
Here I am and here I stay.
MACMAHON, before Malakoff. GABRIEL HANOTAUX, in *Contemporary France*, says that MacMahon denied this. MARQUIS DE CASTELLANE claimed the phrase in the *Revue Hebdomodaire*, May, 1908. Contradicted by *L'Éclair*, which quoted a letter by GEN. BIDDULPH to GERMAIN BAPST, in which GEN. BIDDULPH tells that MACMAHON said to him "Que j'y suis, et que j'y reste."

10
And, though the warrior's sun has set,
Its light shall linger round us yet,
Bright, radiant, blest.
DON JORGE MANRIQUE—*Coplas De Manrique.* Last lines. Trans. by LONGFELLOW.

11
Marlbrough s'en va-t-en guerre,
Mironton, mironton, mirontaine,
Marlbrough s'en va-t-en guerre,
Ne sait quand reviendra.
Marbrough (or Marlebrouck) *S'en va-t-en Guerre.* Old French Song. Attributed to Mme. de Sévigné. Found in *Rondes avec Jeux et Petites Chansons traditionnelles*, Pub. by AUGENER. Said to refer to Charles, Third Duke of Marlborough's unsuccessful expedition against Cherbourg or Malplaquet, probably the latter. (1709) See KING'S *Classical Quotations.* Air probably sung by the Crusaders of Godfrey de Bouillon, known in America "We won't go home until morning." Sung today in the East, tradition giving it that the ancestors of the Arabs learned it at the battle of Mansurah, April 5, 1250. The same appears in a Basque Pastorale; also in *Chansons de Geste.* Air known to the Egyptians.

12
And silence broods like spirit on the brae,
A glimmering moon begins, the moonlight runs
Over the grasses of the ancient way
Rutted this morning by the passing guns.
MASEFIELD—*August 14.* In *Philip the King.*

13
For a flying foe
Discreet and provident conquerors build up
A bridge of gold.
MASSINGER—*The Guardian.* Act I. Sc. 1.
(See also RABELAIS)

14
Some undone widow sits upon mine arm,
And takes away the use of it; and my sword,
Glued to my scabbard with wronged orphan's tears,
Will not be drawn.
MASSINGER—*New Way to Pay Old Debts.* Act V. Sc. 1.

15
Wars and rumours of wars.
Matthew. XXIV. 6.

16
Now deeper roll the maddening drums,
And the mingling host like ocean heaves:
While from the midst a horrid wailing comes,
And high above the fight the lonely bugle grieves.
GRANVILLE MELLEN—*The Lonely Bugle Grieves. Ode on the Celebration of Battle of Bunker Hill.* June 17, 1825. (Mellen is called the "Singer of one Song" from this Ode.)

1
A man that runs away may fight again.
MENANDER, after the battle of Chæronea. 338 B.C. In DIDOT—*Bib. Græca.* P. 91. Fragment appended to *Aristophanes.*
(See also BUTLER)

2
There is war in the skies!
OWEN MEREDITH (Lord Lytton)—*Lucile.* Pt. I. Canto IV. St. 12.

3
No war or battle sound
Was heard the world around.
MILTON—*Hymn of Christ's Nativity.* L. 31.

4 What though the field be lost?
All is not lost; the unconquerable will,
And study of revenge, immortal hate
And courage never to submit or yield,
And what is else not to be overcome.
MILTON—*Paradise Lost.* Bk. I. L. 105.

5 Heard so oft
In worst extremes, and on the perilous edge
Of battle.
MILTON—*Paradise Lost.* Bk. I. L. 275.

6
Th' imperial ensign, which, full high advanc'd,
Shone like a meteor, streaming to the wind.
With gems and golden lustre rich emblazed,
Seraphic arms and trophies.
MILTON—*Paradise Lost.* Bk. I. L. 536.
(See also COWLEY under HAIR, WEBSTER under FLAG)

7
My sentence is for open war.
MILTON—*Paradise Lost.* Bk. II. L. 51.

8 Others more mild,
Retreated in a silent valley, sing
With notes angelical to many a harp
Their own heroic deeds and hapless fall
By doom of battle.
MILTON—*Paradise Lost.* Bk. II. L. 546.

9 Black it stood as night,
Fierce as ten furies, terrible as hell,
And shook a dreadful dart.
MILTON—*Paradise Lost.* Bk. II. L. 670.

10
So frown'd the mighty combatants, that hell
Grew darker at their frown.
MILTON—*Paradise Lost.* Bk. II. L. 719.

11 Arms on armour clashing bray'd
Horrible discord, and the madding wheels
Of brazen chariots ray'd; dire was the noise
Of conflict.
MILTON—*Paradise Lost.* Bk. VI. L. 209.

12
To overcome in battle, and subdue
Nations, and bring home spoils with infinite
Man-slaughter, shall be held the highest pitch
Of human glory.
MILTON—*Paradise Lost.* Bk. XI. L. 691.

13
The brazen throat of war.
MILTON—*Paradise Lost.* Bk. XI. L. 713.

14
What boots it at one gate to make defence,
And at another to let in the foe?
MILTON—*Samson Agonistes.* L. 560.

15
In the wars of the European powers in matters relating to themselves we have never taken any part, nor does it comport with our policy so to do. It is only when our rights are invaded or seriously menaced that we resent injuries or make preparation for our defence.
JAMES MONROE—*Annual Message.* Dec. 2, 1823.

16
When after many battles past,
Both tir'd with blows, make peace at last,
What is it, after all, the people get?
Why! taxes, widows, wooden legs, and debt.
FRANCIS MOORE—*Almanac. Monthly Observations* for 1829. P. 23.

17
Thrilled ye ever with the story
How on stricken fields of glory
Men have stood beneath the murderous iron hail!
HENRY MORFORD—*Coming of the Bagpipes to Lucknow.* Poem on same story written by R. T. S. LOWELL and ALEX. MACLAGAN.

18
We had nae heed for the parish bell,
But still—when the bugle cried,
We went for you to Neuve Chapelle,
We went for you to the yetts o' Hell,
And there for you we died!
NEIL MUNRO—*Roving Lads.* (1915)

19
'Tis a principle of war that when you can use the lightning, 'tis better than cannon.
NAPOLEON I.

20
Providence is always on the side of the last reserve.
Attributed to NAPOLEON I.
(See also VOLTAIRE)

21
Baptism of fire.
NAPOLEON III in a letter to the EMPRESS EUGENIE after Saarbruecken. Referring to the experience of the Prince Imperial.

22
England expects every officer and man to do his duty this day.
NELSON—*Signal,* Oct. 21, 1805, to the fleet before the battle of Trafalgar. As reported in the *London Times,* Dec. 26, 1805. England expects that every man will do his duty. As reported by WILLIAM PRYCE CUNBY, First Lieut. of the Bellerophon. The claim is that Nelson gave the order "Nelson confides," which was changed to "England expects." See *Notes and Queries,* Series VI, IX, 261.283; also Nov. 4, 1905. P. 370.

23
For bragging time was over and fighting time was come.
HENRY NEWBOLT—*Hawke.*

24
A soldier of the Legion lay dying in Algiers;
There was lack of woman's nursing, there was dearth of woman's tears.
C. E. S. NORTON (Lady Stirling-Maxwell)—*Bingen on the Rhine.*

25
March to the battle-field,
The foe is now before us;

Each heart is Freedom's shield,
And heaven is shining o'er us.
B. E. O'Meara—*March to the Battle-Field.*

1
"Go, with a song of peace," said Fingal; "go, Ullin, to the king of swords. Tell him that we are mighty in war; that the ghosts of our foes are many."
Ossian—*Carthon.* L. 269.

2
Adjuvat in bello pacatæ ramus olivæ.
In war the olive branch of peace is of use.
Ovid—*Epistolæ Ex Ponto.* I. 1. 31.

3
There is a hill in Flanders,
Heaped with a thousand slain,
Where the shells fly night and noontide
And the ghosts that died in vain,
A little hill, a hard hill
To the souls that died in pain.
Everard Owen—*Three Hills.* (1915)

4
It is the object only of war that makes it honorable. And if there was ever a just war since the world began, it is this in which America is now engaged. * * *
We fight not to enslave, but to set a country free, and to make room upon the earth for honest men to live in.
Thomas Paine—*The Crisis.*
(See also Wilson)

5
These are the times that try men's souls. The Summer soldier and the sunshine patriot will, in this crisis, shrink from the service of their country, but he that stands it *now* deserves the love and thanks of man and woman. Tyranny, like Hell, is not easily conquered; yet we have this consolation with us, that the harder the conflict the more glorious the triumph. What we obtain too cheaply we esteem too lightly; it is dearness only that gives everything its value. Heaven knows how to put a proper price upon its goods; and it would be strange indeed if so celestial an article as *freedom* should not be highly rated.
Thomas Paine—*The Crisis.*

6
War even to the knife.
Palafox, the governor of Saragossa, when summoned to surrender by the French, who besieged that city in 1808. Generally quoted "At the point of the knife."

7
It cannot be made, it shall not be made, it will not be made; but if it were made there would be a war between France and England for the possession of Egypt.
Lord Palmerston—*Speech,* 1851, referring to the Suez Canal (an example of an indiscreet and unfulfilled prophecy).

8
Hell, Heaven or Hoboken by Christmas.
Attributed to General John Joseph Pershing. (1918)

9
Lafayette, we are here.
Col. C. E. Stanton.—*Speech,* July 4, 1917, delivered at Pipcus Cemetery, Paris. Wrongly attributed to Gen. John J. Pershing.

10
Infantry, Artillery, Aviation—all that we have—are yours to dispose of as you will. . . . I have come to say to you that the American people would be proud to be engaged in the greatest battle in history.
Gen. John Joseph Pershing to Gen. Foch, *Letter written from Office of the Commander-in-Chief, American Expeditionary Forces, in France.* March 28, 1918. See "Literary Digest History of World War," Vol. V. P. 43.

11
Ils ne passeront pas.
They shall not pass.
General Pétain. At the end of Feb., 1916, General de Castelnau was sent by General Joffre to decide whether Verdun should be abandoned or defended. He consulted with General Pétain, saying: "They (the Germans) must not pass." General Pétain said: "They shall not pass." In France the people credit it to General Joffre. See N. Y. *Times,* May 6, 1917. (See also Diaz)

12
From the Rio Grande's waters to the icy lakes of Maine,
Let all exult, for we have met the enemy again.
Beneath their stern old mountains we have met them in their pride;
And rolled from Buena Vista back the battle's bloody tide,
Where the enemy came surging swift like the Mississippi's flood,
And the Reaper, Death, with strong arms swung his sickle red with blood.
Santa Anna boasted loudly that before two hours were past
His Lancers through Saltillo should pursue us fierce and fast.
On comes his solid infantry, line marching after line.
Lo! their great standards in the sun like sheets of silver shine.
Gen. Albert Pike—*Battle of Buena Vista.*

13
If I were an American, as I am an Englishman, while a foreign troop was landed in my country I never would lay down my arms,—never! never! never!
William Pitt the Elder. Nov. 18, 1777.

14
He who first called money the sinews of the state seems to have said this with special reference to war.
Plutarch—*Life of Cleomenes.* 27.
(See also Cicero)

15
Sylla proceeded by persuasion, not by arms.
Plutarch—*Lysander and Sylla Compared.*

16
It is the province of kings to bring wars about; it is the province of God to end them.
Cardinal Pole—*To Henry VIII.*

17
She saw her sons with purple death expire,
Her sacred domes involved in rolling fire,
A dreadful series of intestine wars,
Inglorious triumphs and dishonest scars.
Pope—*Windsor Forest.* L. 323.

1
War its thousands slays,
Peace its ten thousands.
PORTEUS—*Death*. L. 178.

2
The waves
Of the mysterious death-river moaned;
The tramp, the shout, the fearful thunder-roar
Of red-breathed cannon, and the wailing cry
Of myriad victims, filled the air.
PRENTICE—*Lookout Mountain*. L. 16.

3
A man is known by the Company he joins.
Bad communication trenches corrupt good manners.
Never look a gift gun in the mouth.
A drop of oil in time saves time.
One swallow doesn't make a rum issue.
Where there's a war there's a way.
Proverbial sayings, popular in the Great War. Origin about 1917.

4
If this bill passes . . . as it will be the right of all, so it will be the duty of some, to prepare definitely for a separation, amicably if they can, violently if they must.
JOSIAH QUINCY—*Speech*. In Congress. Jan. 14, 1811, against the admission of Louisiana to the Union. Quoted by Henry Clay in Congress (1813), "Peaceably if we can, forcibly if we must."

5
Cœdes videtur significare sanguinem et ferrum.
(Slaughter) means blood and iron.
QUINTILIAN—*Declamationes*.
(See also BISMARCK)

6
Ouvrez toujours à vos ennemis toutes les portes et chemin, et plutot leur faites un pont d'argent, afin de les renvoyer.
Always open all gates and roads to your enemies, and rather make for them a bridge of silver, to get rid of them.
RABELAIS—*Gargantua*. Bk. I. Ch. XLIII. COUNT DE PITILLAN, according to GILLES CORROZET—*Les Divers Propos Memorables* (1571) uses the same phrase with "golden" bridge for "silver." The same suggestion was made by Aristides, referring to the proposal to destroy XERXES' bridge of ships over the Hellespont. ("A bridge for a retreating army.") See PLUTARCH—*Life of Demosthenes*. LOUIS II, BRANTOME—*Memoirs*. Vol. 1. II. P. 83. Also French trans. of THOMASI—*Life of Cæsar Borgia*. P. 64.
(See also MASSINGER, SCIPIO, AFRICANUS)

7
He that fights and runs away,
May turn and fight another day;
But he that is in battle slain,
Will never rise to fight again.
RAY—*History of the Rebellion*. P. 48. (1752)
(See also BUTLER)

8
And he gathered them together into a place called in the Hebrew tongue Armageddon.
Revelation. XVI. 16. Armageddon. Correct reading is Har-Magedon, signifying Mountain of Megiddo. Authorized version, City of Megiddo. Mount Megiddo possibly Mount Carmel. The plain of Megiddo lay at its foot. Scene of many battles.
(See also ROOSEVELT, WHITTIER)

9
Brother Jonathan sat by the kitchen fire,
Nursin' his foot on his knee.
"It's a turrible fight they're havin' out there,
But they can't git over to me."
And Jonathan jingled the coins in his han'
An' thanked the good God for the sea.
C. A. RICHMOND—*Brother Jonathan*.

10
Twelve mailed men sat drinking late,
The wine was red as blood.
Cried one, "How long then must we wait
Ere we shall thunder at the gate,
And crush the cursed brood?"
Twelve men of iron, drinking late,
Strike hands, and pledge a cup of hate:
"The Day!"
C. A. RICHMOND—*The Day*.
(See also LISSAUER)

11
The morning came, there stood the foe;
Stark eyed them as they stood;
Few words he spoke—'twas not a time
For moralizing mood:
"See there the enemy, my boys!
Now, strong in valor's might,
Beat them or Betty Stark will sleep
In widowhood to-night."
J. P. RODMEN—*Battle of Bennington*.

12
To you men who, in your turn, have come together to spend and be spent in the endless crusade against wrong; to you who face the future resolute and confident; to you who strive in a spirit of brotherhood for the betterment of our nation; to you who gird yourselves for this great new fight in the never-ending warfare for the good of mankind, I say in closing what I said in that speech in closing: "We stand at Armageddon and we battle for the Lord."
ROOSEVELT—*Speech*, at Chicago, Progressive Convention, Aug. 5, 1912, quoting from his speech in June.
(See also REVELATION)

13
Righteous Heaven,
In thy great day of vengeance! Blast the traitor
And his pernicious counsels, who, for wealth,
For pow'r, the pride of greatness, or revenge,
Would plunge his native land in civil wars.
NICHOLAS ROWE—*Jane Shore*. Act III. Sc. 1. L. 198.

14
War, the needy bankrupt's last resort.
ROWE—*Pharsalia*. Bk. I. 343.

15
He never would believe that Providence had sent a few men into the world, ready booted and spurred to ride, and millions ready saddled and bridled to be ridden.
RICHARD RUMBOLD. At his execution. (1685)
See MACAULAY—*History of England*. Ch. V.

16
[The Russians] dashed on towards that thin red line tipped with steel.
W. H. RUSSELL—*The British Expedition to the Crimea*. (Revised edition.) P. 187.
Also in his *Letters* to the London *Times*.

Oct. 25, 1854. Speaking of the 93rd Highlanders at Balaclava. Credit for authorship of "the thin red line" claimed by Russell in a letter printed in *Notes and Queries,* series 8. VII. P. 191.
(See also KINGLAKE)

1
Celuy qui fuit de bonne heure
Peut combattre derechef.
He who flies at the right time can fight again.
Satyre Menippée. (1594)
(See also BUTLER)

2
Qui fuit peut revenir aussi;
Qui meurt, il n'en est pas ainsi.
He who flies can also return; but it is not so with him who dies.
SCARRON.
(See also BUTLER)

3
Ein Schlachten war's, nicht eine Schlacht, zu nennen!
It was a slaughter rather than a battle.
SCHILLER—*Die Jungfrau von Orleans.* I. 9. 50.

4
Es ist hier wie in den alten Zeiten
Wo die Klinge noch alles thät bedeuten.
It is now as in the days of yore when the sword ruled all things.
SCHILLER—*Wallenstein's Lager.* VI. 140.

5
Hosti non solum dandam esse viam fugiendi verum etiam muniendam.
Give the enemy not only a road for flight, but also a means of defending it.
SCIPIO AFRICANUS, according to FRONTINUS—*Strateg.* IV. 7. 16.
(See also RABELAIS)

6
And the stern joy which warriors feel
In foemen worthy of their steel.
SCOTT—*Lady of the Lake.* Canto V. St. 10.

7
One blast upon his bugle horn
Were worth a thousand men.
SCOTT—*Lady of the Lake.* Canto VI. St. 18.
(See also THOMPSON)

8
In the lost battle,
Borne down by the flying.
Where mingles war's rattle
With groans of the dying.
SCOTT—*Marmion.* Canto III. St. 11.

9
"Charge, Chester, charge! On, Stanley, on!"
Were the last words of Marmion.
SCOTT—*Marmion.* Canto VI. St. 32.

10
Still from the sire the son shall hear
Of the stern strife, and carnage drear,
Of Flodden's fatal field,
When shiver'd was fair Scotland's spear,
And broken was her shield!
SCOTT—*Marmion.* Canto VI. St. 34.

11
Say to the seceded States: "Wayward sisters depart in peace."
WINFIELD SCOTT—*Letter addressed to* W. H. SEWARD. Washington, March 3, 1861. Quoted from this letter by HORACE GREELEY, and ascribed to him.

12
There was a stately drama writ
By the hand that peopled the earth and air,
And set the stars in the infinite,
And made night gorgeous and morning fair;
And all that had sense to reason knew
That bloody drama must be gone through.
Some sat and watched how the action veered—
Waited, profited, trembled, cheered—
We saw not clearly nor understood,
But yielding ourselves to the masterhand,
Each in his part as best he could,
We played it through as the author planned.
ALAN SEEGER—*The Hosts.*

13
It's easy to fight when everything's right
And you're mad with the thrill and the glory;
It's easy to cheer when victory's near,
And wallow in fields that are gory.
It's a different song when everything's wrong,
When you're feeling infernally mortal;
When it's ten against one, and hope there is none,
Buck up, little soldier, and chortle!
ROBERT W. SERVICE—*Carry On.*

14
When children's children shall talk of War as a madness that may not be;
When we thank our God for our grief today, and blazon from sea to sea
In the name of the Dead the banner of Peace . . . *that will be Victory.*
ROBERT W. SERVICE—*The Song of the Pacifist.*

15
Fortune is always on the side of the largest battalions.
MME. DE SÉVIGNÉ—*Letters.* 202.
(See also VOLTAIRE)

16
It is an irrepressible conflict between opposing and enduring forces.
WILLIAM H. SEWARD—*Speech. The Irrepressible Conflict.* Oct. 25, 1858.

17
And all the gods go with you! upon your sword
Sit laurel victory! and smooth success
Be strew'd before your feet!
Antony and Cleopatra. Act I. Sc. 3. L. 99.

18
All was lost,
But that the heavens fought.
Cymbeline. Act V. Sc. 3. L. 3.

19
Give me the cups;
And let the kettle to the trumpet speak,
The trumpet to the cannoneer without,
The cannons to heavens, the heavens to earth.
Hamlet. Act V. Sc. 2. L. 285.

20
It was great pity, so it was,
That villanous saltpetre should be digg'd
Out of the bowels of the harmless earth,
Which many a good tall fellow had destroy'd
So cowardly; and but for these vile guns
He would himself have been a soldier.
Henry IV. Pt. I. Act I. Sc. 3. L. 59.

21
We must have bloody noses and crack'd crowns,
And pass them current too. God's me, my horse!
Henry IV. Pt. I. Act II. Sc. 3. L. 96.

1

The fire-eyed maid of smoky war
All hot and bleeding will we offer them.
Henry IV. Pt. I. Act IV. Sc. 1. L. 114.

2

Tut, tut; good enough to toss; food for powder, food for powder; they'll fill a pit as well as better.
Henry IV. Pt. I. Act IV. Sc. 2. L. 71.

3

The arms are fair,
When the intent of bearing them is just.
Henry IV. Pt. I. Act V. Sc. 2. L. 88.

4

Our battle is more full of names than yours,
Our men more perfect in the use of arms,
Our armour all as strong, our cause the best;
Then reason will our hearts should be as good.
Henry IV. Pt. II. Act IV. Sc. 1. L. 154.

5

That I may truly say with the hook-nosed fellow of Rome, I came, I saw, and overcame.
Henry IV. Pt. II. Act IV. Sc. 3. L. 45.
(See also Cæsar)

6

Once more unto the breach, dear friends, once more;
Or close the wall up with our English dead.
Henry V. Act III. Sc. 1. L. 1.

7

From camp to camp through the foul womb of night
The hum of either army stilly sounds.
Henry V. Act IV. Chorus. L. 4.

8

The armourers, accomplishing the knights,
With busy hammers closing rivets up,
Give dreadful note of preparation.
Henry V. Act IV. Chorus. L. 12.
With clink of hammers closing rivets up.
Colley Cibber's altered version of *Richard III*. Act V. Sc. 3.

9

There are few die well that die in a battle.
Henry V. Act IV. Sc. 1. L. 148.

10

He which hath no stomach to this fight,
Let him depart; his passport shall be made.
Henry V. Act IV. Sc. 3. L. 35.

11

O war! thou son of hell,
Whom angry heavens do make their minister,
Throw in the frozen bosoms of our part
Hot coals of vengeance! Let no soldier fly.
He that is truly dedicate to war
Hath no self-love, nor he that loves himself.
Hath not essentially but by circumstance
The name of valour.
Henry VI. Pt. II. Act V. Sc. 2. L. 33.

12

It is war's prize to take all vantage.
Henry VI. Pt. III. Act I. Sc. 4. Same in Schiller—*Wallenstein's Tod*. Act I. Sc. 4.

13

Sound trumpets! let our bloody colours wave!
And either victory, or else a grave.
Henry VI. Pt. III. Act II. Sc. 2. L. 173.

14

They shall have wars and pay for their presumption.
Henry VI. Pt. III. Act IV. Sc. 1. L. 114.

15

Cæsar's spirit, ranging for revenge,
With Até by his side come hot from hell,
Shall in these confines with a monarch's voice
Cry "Havoc," and let slip the dogs of war.
Julius Cæsar. Act III. Sc. 1. L. 270.

16

The cannons have their bowels full of wrath,
And ready mounted are they to spit forth
Their iron indignation 'gainst your walls.
King John. Act II. Sc. 1. L. 210.

17

Now for the bare-pick'd bone of majesty
Doth dogged war bristle his angry crest
And snarleth in the gentle eyes of peace.
King John. Act IV. Sc. 3. L. 148.

18

Your breath first kindled the dead coal of wars
And brought in matter that should feed this fire;
And now 'tis far too huge to be blown out
With that same weak wind which enkindled it.
King John. Act V. Sc. 2. L. 83.

19

I drew this gallant head of war,
And cull'd these fiery spirits from the world,
To outlook conquest and to win renown
Even in the jaws of danger and of death.
King John. Act V. Sc. 2. L. 113.

20

When the hurly-burly's done,
When the battle's lost and won.
Macbeth. Act I. Sc. 1. L. 3.

21

Hang out our banners on the outward walls.
Macbeth. Act V. Sc. 5. L. 1.

22

Blow, wind! come, wrack!
At least we'll die with harness on our back.
Macbeth. Act V. Sc. 5. L. 51.

23

Lay on, Macduff,
And damn'd be him that first cries, "Hold, enough!"
Macbeth. Act V. Sc. 8. L. 33.

24

The bay-trees in our country all are wither'd
And meteors fright the fixed stars of heaven;
The pale-fac'd moon looks bloody on the earth
And lean-look'd prophets whisper fearful change;
Rich men look sad and ruffians dance and leap,
The one in fear to lose what they enjoy,
The other to enjoy by rage and war.
Richard II. Act II. Sc. 4. L. 8.

25

Let's march without the noise of threat'ning drum.
Richard II. Act III. Sc. 3. L. 51.

26

He is come to open
The purple testament of bleeding war.
Richard II. Act III. Sc. 3. L. 93.

27

Grim-visag'd war hath smoothed his wrinkled front.
Richard III. Act I. Sc. 1. L. 9.

28

Thus far into the bowels of the land
Have we march'd without impediment.
Richard III. Act V. Sc. 2. L. 3.

1
Conscience avaunt, *Richard's* himself again:
Hark! the shrill trumpet sounds, to horse, away,
My soul's in arms, and eager for the fray.
Richard III. Act V. Sc. 3. Altered by COLLEY CIBBER.

2
Put in their hands thy bruising irons of wrath,
That they may crush down with heavy fall
The usurping helmets of our adversaries.
Richard III. Act V. Sc. 3. L. 110.

3
Fight, gentlemen of England! fight, bold yeomen!
Draw, archers, draw your arrows to the head!
Spur your proud horses hard, and ride in blood;
Amaze the welkin with your broken staves!
Richard III. Act V. Sc. 3. L. 338.

4
Follow thy drum;
With man's blood paint the ground, gules, gules;
Religious canons, civil laws are cruel;
Then what should war be?
Timon of Athens. Act IV. Sc. 3. L. 58.

5
There was only one virtue, pugnacity; only one vice, pacifism. That is an essential condition of war.
BERNARD SHAW—*Heartbreak House: Preface. Madness in Court.*

6
In the arts of life man invents nothing; but in the arts of death he outdoes Nature herself, and produces by chemistry and machinery all the slaughter of plague, pestilence and famine.
BERNARD SHAW—*Man and Superman.*

7
They shall not pass, tho' battleline
May bend, and foe with foe combine,
Tho' death rain on them from the sky
Till every fighting man shall die,
France shall not yield to German Rhine.
ALICE M. SHEPARD—*They Shall Not Pass.*
(See also BATES)

8
Hold the Fort! I am coming.
GEN. W. T. SHERMAN—*Signalled to Gen. Corse.* Oct. 5, 1864.

9
War is Hell.
Attributed to GENERAL SHERMAN. (Not remembered by him.) JOHN KOOLBECK, of Harlem, Iowa, who was Aide de Camp to Gen. Winslow, testifies that after the battle of Vicksburg, 1861, Gen. Sherman was watching the crossing of the army across a pontoon bridge, at the river Pearl. Koolbeck distinctly heard him say: "War is Hell." See *Everybody's*. Oct., 1918. P. 71.
(See also ALEXANDER, VAN DYKE)

10
J'ai vécu.
I existed.
SIEYÈS, when asked what he did during the Reign of Terror. See MIGNET—*Notices Hist.* I. 81.

11
Sainte Jeanne went harvesting in France,
But ah! what found she there?
The little streams were running red,
And the torn fields were bare;
And all about the ruined towers
Where once her king was crowned,
The hurtling ploughs of war and death
Had scored the desolate ground.
MARION COUTHOUY SMITH—*Sainte Jeanne of France.*

12
Every shot has its commission, d'ye see? We must all die at one time, as the saying is.
SMOLLETT—*The Reprisal.* Act III. 8.
(See also GASCOIGNE)

13
I came, I saw, God overcame.
JOHN SOBIESKI—*to the Pope*, with the captured Mussulman standards.
(See also CÆSAR)

14
Terrible as an army with banners.
Song of Solomon. VI. 4 and 10.

15
Then more fierce
The conflict grew; the din of arms, the yell
Of savage rage, the shriek of agony,
The groan of death, commingled in one sound
Of undistinguish'd horrors.
SOUTHEY—*Madoc.* Pt. II. XV.

16
Either this or upon this. (Either bring this back or be brought back upon it.)
Said to be a Spartan mother's words to her son on giving him his shield.

17
War! war! war!
Heaven aid the right!
God move the hero's arm in the fearful fight!
God send the women sleep in the long, long night,
When the breasts on whose strength they leaned shall heave no more.
E. C. STEDMAN—*Alice of Monmouth.* VII.

18
The crystal-pointed tents from hill to hill.
E. C. STEDMAN—*Alice of Monmouth.* XI.

19
But, Virginians, don't do it, for I tell you that the flagon,
Filled with blood of Old Brown's offspring, was first poured by Southern hands;
And each drop from Old Brown's life-veins, like the red gore of the Dragon,
May spring up a vengeful Fury, hissing through your slave-worn lands:
And Old Brown,
Osawatomie Brown,
May trouble you worse than ever, when you've nailed his coffin down.
E. C. STEDMAN—*How Old Brown Took Harper's Ferry.* Written during Brown's Trial. Nov., 1859.

20
Hobbes clearly proves that every creature
Lives in a state of war by nature.
SWIFT—*Poetry. A Rhapsody.*

21
War, that mad game the world so loves to play.
SWIFT—*Ode to Sir Wm. Temple.*

22
Not with dreams, but with blood and with iron
Shall a nation be moulded to last.
SWINBURNE—*A Word for the Country.*
(See also BISMARCK)

1
Ratio et consilium propriæ ducis artes.
The proper qualities of a general are judgment and deliberation.
TACITUS—*Annales*. III. 20.

2
Miseram pacem vel bello bene mutari.
Even war is better than a wretched peace.
TACITUS—*Annales*. III. 44.

3
Deos fortioribus adesse.
The gods are on the side of the stronger.
TACITUS—*Annales*. IV. 17.
(See also VOLTAIRE)

4
We can start at once. We made preparations on the way.
COMMANDER JOSEPH K. TAUSSIG for the American Navy, to the British Admiral's query: "When will you be ready?" (1917) Erroneously attributed to ADMIRAL SIMS.

5
A little more grape, Captain Bragg.
Attributed to GENERAL TAYLOR at Buena Vista. Feb. 23, 1847.

6
Half a league, half a league,
Half a league onward,
All in the valley of Death
Rode the six hundred.
"Forward the Light Brigade!
Charge for the guns!" he said,
Into the valley of death
Rode the six hundred.
TENNYSON—*Charge of the Light Brigade*. St. 1.

7
Forward, the Light Brigade!
Was there a man dismayed?
Not tho' the soldier knew
Some one had blunder'd.
Theirs not to make reply,
Theirs not to reason why,
Theirs but to do and die.
Into the valley of death
Rode the six hundred.
TENNYSON—*Charge of the Light Brigade*. St. 2.

8
Cannon to right of them,
Cannon to left of them,
Cannon in front of them
Volley'd and thunder'd;
Stormed at with shot and shell,
Boldly they rode and well,
Into the jaws of Death,
Into the mouth of Hell
Rode the six hundred.
TENNYSON—*Charge of the Light Brigade*. St. 3. "Jaws of death" used by DU BARTAS—*Weekes and Workes*. Day I. Pt. IV. *Twelfth Night*. Act III. Sc. 4.
(See also DRAYTON)

9
The children born of thee are sword and fire,
Red ruin, and the breaking up of law.
TENNYSON—*Idylls of the King. Guinevere*. L. 423.

10
Omnia prius experiri verbis quam armis sapientem decet.
It becomes a wise man to try negotiation before arms.
TERENCE—*Eunuchus*. V. 1. 19.

11
Sed omissis quidem divinis exhortationibus illum magis Græcum versiculum secularis sententiæ sibi adhibent, "Qui fugiebat, rursus prœliabitur:" ut et rursus forsitan fugiat.
But overlooking the divine exhortations, they act rather upon that Greek verse of worldly significance, "He who flees will fight again," and that perhaps to betake himself again to flight.
TERTULLIAN—*De Fuga in Persecutione*. Ch. 10.
(See also BUTLER)

12
But what most showed the vanity of life
Was to behold the nations all on fire.
THOMSON—*Castle of Indolence*. Canto I. 55.

13
Ten good soldiers, wisely led,
Will beat a hundred without a head.
D. W. THOMPSON—*Paraphrase of Euripides*.
(See also SCOTT)

14
Fight the good fight of faith.
I Timothy. VI. 12.

15
A thousand touching traits testify to the sacred power of the love which a righteous war awakes in noble nations.
TREITSCHKE—*German History*. Vol. I. P. 482.

16
War is elevating, because the individual disappears before the great conception of the state. . . . What a perversion of morality to wish to abolish heroism among men!
TREITSCHKE—*Politics*. Vol. I. P. 74.

17
God will see to it that war always recurs as a drastic medicine for the human race.
TREITSCHKE—*Politics*. Vol. I. P. 76.

18
This is the soldier brave enough to tell
The glory-dazzled world that "war is hell."
HENRY VAN DYKE—*On the St. Gaudens' Statue of Gen. Sherman*.
(See also SHERMAN)

19
Arma virumque cano.
Arms and the man I sing.
VERGIL—*Æneid*. Bk. I. 1.

20
Una salus victis nullam sperare salutem.
The only safety for the conquered is to expect no safety.
VERGIL—*Æneid*. II. 354.

21
Dolus an virtus quis in hoste requirat?
Who asks whether the enemy were defeated by strategy or valor?
VERGIL—*Æneid*. II. 390.

22
Exigui numero, sed bello vivida virtus.
Small in number, but their valor tried in war, and glowing.
VERGIL—*Æneid*. V. 754.

23
Sævit amor ferri et scelerata insania belli.
The love of arms and the mad wickedness of war are raging.
VERGIL—*Æneid*. VII. 461.

1
Nullum cum victis certamen et æthere cassis.

Brave men ne'er warred with the dead and vanquished.

VERGIL—*Æneid*. XI. 104.
(See also HOMER)

2
On dit que Dieu est toujours pour les gros bataillons.

It is said that God is always on the side of the heaviest battalions.

VOLTAIRE—*Letter to M. le Riche*. Feb. 6, 1770. Also said by MARSHAL DE LA FERTÉ to ANNE OF AUSTRIA. See BOURSAULT—*Lettres Nouvelles*. P. 384. (Ed. 1698) Attributed to GENERAL MOREAU by ALISON; to GENERAL CHARLES LEE, by HAWTHORNE—*Life of Washington*.
(See also BUSSY-RABUTIN, NAPOLEON, SÉVIGNÉ, ZELLER)

3
On to Richmond.

FITZ-HENRY WARREN. Used as a standing headline in the N. Y. *Tribune*, by DANA, June–July, 1861, before the McDowell campaign.

4
A great and lasting war can never be supported on this principle [patriotism] alone. It must be aided by a prospect of interest, or some reward.

WASHINGTON—*Letter to John Banister*. Valley Forge, April 21, 1778.

5
To be prepared for war is one of the most effectual means of preserving peace.

WASHINGTON—*Speech to Both Houses of Congress*. Jan. 8, 1790.

6
We do not with God's name make wanton play;
We are not on such easy terms with Heaven;
But in Earth's hearing we can verily say,
"Our hands are pure; for peace, for peace we have striven,"
And not by Earth shall he be soon forgiven
Who lit the fire accurst that flames to-day.

SIR W. WATSON—*To the Troubler of the World*, Aug. 5, 1914.

7
They went to war against a preamble, they fought seven years against a declaration.

DANIEL WEBSTER—*Speech on the Presidential Protest*. May 17, 1834.

8
Up Guards and at 'em!

Attributed to WELLINGTON *during the Battle of Waterloo*. Denied by the Duke to Mr. Croker, in answer to a letter written March 14, 1852. "What I must have said, and possibly did say was, 'Stand up guards!' and then gave the order to attack." See J. W. CROKER'S *Memoirs*. P. 544. Also SIR HERBERT MAXWELL'S *Biography of Wellington*.

9
Nothing except a battle lost can be half so melancholy as a battle won.

WELLINGTON—*Despatch*. (1815)

10
The battle of Waterloo was won on the playing field of Eton.

Attributed to WELLINGTON. "The battle of Waterloo was won here," was said by the Duke of Wellington when present at a cricket match at Eton. PROF. W. SELWYN—*Waterloo, a Lay of Jubilee*. (Second Ed.)

11
The whole art of war consists in getting at what is on the other side of the hill.

DUKE OF WELLINGTON—*Saying*.

12
This new Katterfelto, his show to complete,
Means his boats should all sink as they pass by our fleet;
Then as under the ocean their course they steer right on,
They can pepper their foes from the bed of old Triton.

HENRY KIRKE WHITE—*The Wonderful Juggler*. Anticipating the submarine, in Napoleon's day.

13
Now we remember over here in Flanders,
(It isn't strange to think of You in Flanders!)
This hideous warfare seems to make things clear.
We never thought about You much in England,
But now that we are far away from England
We have no doubts, we know that You are here.

MRS. C. T. WHITNALL—*Christ in Flanders*. First appeared in the London *Spectator*. Later in the *Outlook*. July 26, 1916.
(See also JOHNSTONE)

14
We seemed to see our flag unfurled,
Our champion waiting in his place
For the last battle of the world,
The Armageddon of the race.

WHITTIER—*Rantoul*.
(See also REVELATION)

15
As long as war is regarded as wicked it will always have its fascinations. When it is looked upon as vulgar, it will cease to be popular.

OSCAR WILDE—*Intentions*.

16
I will die in the last ditch. (Dyke.)

WILLIAM OF ORANGE. HUME—*History of England*. Ch. XLIII.

17
Germany's greatness makes it impossible for her to do without the ocean, but the ocean also proves that even in the distance, and on its farther side, without Germany and the German Emperor, no great decision dare henceforth be taken.

WILLIAM II, the former German Emperor—*Speech*, July, 1900.

18
Our German Fatherland to which I hope will be granted . . . to become in the future as closely united, as powerful, and as authoritative as once the Roman world-empire was, and that, just as in the old times they said, "Civis romanus sum," hereafter, at some time in the future, they will say, "I am a German citizen."

WILLIAM II, the former German Emperor—*Speech*, in Oct., 1900.

19
Every bullet has its billet.

KING WILLIAM III, according to WESLEY—*Journal*, June 6, 1765. Also in Song by H.

R. BISHOP, sung in *The Circassian Bride.* Quoted by STERNE—*Tristram Shandy.* Vol. VIII. Ch. XIX.

(See also GASCOIGNE)

1
It's a long way to Tipperary, it's a long way to go;
It's a long way to Tipperary, to the sweetest girl I know!
Good-bye to Piccadilly, Farewell Leicester Square;
It's a long way to Tipperary, but my Heart's right there!

HARRY WILLIAMS AND JACK JUDGE—*It's a Long Way to Tipperary.* Popular in The Great War. Chorus claimed by Alice Smythe B. Jay. Written in 1908. See N. Y. *Times*, Sept. 20, 1907.

2
War is only a sort of dramatic representation, a sort of dramatic symbol of a thousand forms of duty. I fancy that it is just as hard to do your duty when men are sneering at you as when they are shooting at you.

WOODROW WILSON—*Speech.* Brooklyn Navy Yard, May 11, 1914.

3
You have laid upon me this double obligation: "we are relying upon you, Mr. President, to keep us out of war, but we are relying upon you, Mr. President, to keep the honor of the nation unstained."

WOODROW WILSON—*Speech.* At Cleveland, Jan. 29, 1916.

4
I am the friend of peace and mean to preserve it for America so long as I am able. . . . No course of my choosing or of theirs (nations at war) will lead to war. War can come only by the wilful acts and aggressions of others.

WOODROW WILSON—*Address to Congress.* Feb. 26, 1917.

5
It is a fearful thing to lead this great peaceful people into war, into the most terrible and disastrous of all wars, civilization itself seeming to be in the balance. But the right is more precious than peace, and we shall fight for the things which we have always carried nearest our hearts—for democracy, for the right of those who submit to authority to have a voice in their own governments, for the rights and liberties of small nations, for a universal dominion of right by such a concert of free peoples as shall bring peace and safety to all nations and make the world itself at last free.

WOODROW WILSON—*War Message to Congress.* April 2, 1917.

6
To such a task we can dedicate our lives and our fortunes, everything that we are and everything that we have, with the pride of those who know that the day has come when America is privileged to spend her blood and her might for the principles that gave her birth and happiness, and the peace which she has treasured. God helping her, she can do no other.

WOODROW WILSON—*War Message to Congress.* April 2, 1917.

(See also LUTHER, for last words)

7
It is not an army that we must train for war; it is a nation.

WOODROW WILSON—*Speech.* At dedication of a Red Cross Building, May 12, 1917.

8
They came with banner, spear, and shield;
And it was proved in Bosworth field,
Not long the Avenger was withstood—
Earth help'd him with the cry of blood.

WORDSWORTH—*Song at the Feast of Brougham Castle.* St. 3. Last line probably taken from JOHN BEAUMONT'S *Battle of Flodden Field.*

9
But Thy most dreaded instrument
In working out a pure intent,
Is man,—arrayed for mutual slaughter,—
Yea, Carnage is Thy daughter.

WORDSWORTH. Poems dedicated to *National Independence and Liberty.* Ode XLV. (1815) Suppressed in later editions.

But Man is thy most awful instrument,
In working out a pure intent;
Thou cloth'st the wicked in their dazzling mail,
And for thy righteous purpose they prevail.

Version in later editions.

10
As regards Providence, he cannot shake off the prejudice that in war, God is on the side of the big battalions, which at present are in the enemy's camp.

ZELLER—*Frederick the Great as Philosopher.* Referring to *Œuvres de Frederic.* XVIII. 186–188, the contents of a letter from FREDERICK to the DUCHESS OF GOTHA, about 1757. CARLYLE gives the date of the letter as May 8, 1760, in his *History of Frederick the Great.* II. Bk. XIX. Vol. V. P. 606.

(See also VOLTAIRE)

WASHINGTON

11
The defender of his country—the founder of liberty,
The friend of man,
History and tradition are explored in vain
For a parallel to his character.
In the annals of modern greatness
He stands alone;
And the noblest names of antiquity
Lose their lustre in his presence.
Born the benefactor of mankind,
He united all the greatness necessary
To an illustrious career.
Nature made him great,
He made himself virtuous.

Part of an Epitaph found on the back of a portrait of WASHINGTON, sent to the family from England. See WERNER'S *Readings.* No. 49. P. 77.

12
Simple and brave, his faith awoke
Ploughmen to struggle with their fate;
Armies won battles when he spoke,
And out of Chaos sprang the state.

ROBERT BRIDGES—*Washington.*

13
While Washington's a watchword, such as ne'er
Shall sink while there's an echo left to air.

BYRON—*Age of Bronze.* St. 5.

1
Where may the wearied eye repose,
When gazing on the Great;
Where neither guilty glory glows,
Nor despicable state?
Yes—one the first, the last, the best,
The Cincinnatus of the West
Whom envy dared not hate,
Bequeathed the name of Washington
To make man blush; there was but one.
BYRON—*Ode to Napoleon Buonaparte.* Referring to WASHINGTON.

2
There's a star in the West that shall never go down
Till the records of Valour decay,
We must worship its light though it is not our own,
For liberty burst in its ray.
Shall the name of a Washington ever be heard
By a freeman, and thrill not his breast?
Is there one out of bondage that hails not the word,
As a Bethlehem Star of the West?
ELIZA COOK—*There's a Star in the West.*

3
The character, the counsels, and example of our Washington * * * they will guide us through the doubts and difficulties that beset us; they will guide our children and our children's children in the paths of prosperity and peace, while America shall hold her place in the family of nations.
ED. EVERETT—*Speech. Washington Abroad and at Home.* July 5, 1858.

4
Here you would know, and enjoy, what posterity will say of Washington. For a thousand leagues have nearly the same effect with a thousand years.
BENJ. FRANKLIN—*Letter to Washington.* March 5, 1780.

5
O Washington! thrice glorious name,
What due rewards can man decree—
Empires are far below thy aim,
And scepters have no charms for thee;
Virtue alone has your regards,
And she must be your great reward.
PHILIP FRENEAU—*Washington's Arrival in Philadelphia.*

6
Since ancient Time began,
Ever on some great soul God laid an infinite burden—
The weight of all this world, the hopes of man,
Conflict and pain, and fame immortal are his guerdon.
R. W. GILDER—*Washington.* Speech at Trenton. Oct. 19, 1893.

7
Were an energetic and judicious system to be proposed with your signature it would be a circumstance highly honorable to your fame . . . and doubly entitle you to the glorious republican epithet,
The Father of your Country.
HENRY KNOX—*Letter to Washington.* March 19, 1787, urging that WASHINGTON attend the Philadelphia Convention. See FORD—*Washington's Writings.* Vol. XI. P. 123. (See also *Pennsylvania Packet*)

8
A nobleness to try for,
A name to live and die for.
GEORGE PARSONS LATHROP—*Name of Washington.*

9
First in war, first in peace, first in the hearts of his countrymen.
GEN. HENRY LEE—*Funeral Oration on Washington.*

10
First in war, first in peace, first in the hearts of his fellow citizens.
Resolution on Washington's Death. Prepared by GENERAL HENRY LEE and offered in the House of Representatives by JOHN MARSHALL.

11
This is the one hundred and tenth anniversary of the birthday of Washington. We are met to celebrate this day. Washington is the mightiest name on earth—long since mightiest in the cause of civil liberty; still mightiest in moral reformation. On that name an eulogy is expected. It can not be. To add brightness to the sun or glory to the name of Washington is alike impossible. Let none attempt it. In solemn awe pronounce the name and in its naked, deathless splendor leave it shining on.
LINCOLN—*Speech.* Feb. 22, 1842. Closing words. See *Sangamon Journal*, pub. at Springfield, Ill., Feb. 25, 1842. Entire speech was pub. in the *Sangamon Journal*, March 26, 1842. Copies on file in the Congressional Library.

12
The purely Great
Whose soul no siren passion could unsphere,
Thou nameless, now a power and mixed with fate.
LOWELL—*Under the old Elm.* The elm near Cambridge with the inscription "Under this tree, Washington first took command of the American Army, July 3, 1775."

13
Oh, Washington! thou hero, patriot sage,
Friend of all climes, and pride of every age!
THOMAS PAINE.

14
Every countenance seeked to say, "Long live George Washington, the Father of the People."
Pennsylvania Packet, April 21, 1789. After the election of Washington.

15
Our common Father and Deliverer, to whose prudence, wisdom and valour we owe our Peace, Liberty and Safety, now leads and directs in the great councils of the nation . . . and now we celebrate an independent Government—an original Constitution! an independent Legislature, at the head of which we this day celebrate The Father of his Country—We celebrate Washington! We celebrate an Independent Empire!
Pennsylvania Packet. July 9, 1789. P. 284. See ALBERT MATTHEWS' article in Colonial Society of Mass. Publications. *Transactions.* 1902-4. Vol. 8. P. 275-287 pub. 1906. In America the term was already familiar. GEORGE II was so-called by GOVERNOR BELCHER, Dec. 2, 1731. GEORGE III also, in a petition drawn up by the

Mass. House of Representatives June, 30, 1768. WINTHROP was styled thus by GOVERNOR HUTCHINSON. (1764) See *History of Mass.* I. 151.
(See also KNOX, also JUVENAL under PATRIOTISM)

1
His work well done, the leader stepped aside
Spurning a crown with more than kingly pride.
Content to wear the higher crown of worth,
While time endures, "First citizen of earth."
JAMES J. ROCHE—*Washington.*

2
'Twas his ambition, generous and great
A life to life's great end to consecrate.
SHELLEY—*Washington.*

3
While Washington hath left
His awful memory,
A light for after times.
SOUTHEY—*Ode written during the War with America.* (1814)

4
Washington—a fixed star in the firmament of great names, shining without twinkling or obscuration, with clear, beneficent light.
DANIEL WEBSTER.

5
That name was a power to rally a nation in the hour of thick-thronging public disasters and calamities; that name shone amid the storm of war, a beacon light to cheer and guide the country's friends; it flamed too like a meteor to repel her foes.
DANIEL WEBSTER—*Speech* at a public dinner. Feb. 22, 1832.

6
That name descending with all time, spreading over the whole earth, and uttered in all the languages belonging to all tribes and races of men, will forever be pronounced with affectionate gratitude by everyone in whose breast there shall arise an aspiration for human rights and liberty.
DANIEL WEBSTER—*Speech* at the Centennial Anniversary of WASHINGTON. Feb. 22, 1832.

7
America has furnished to the world the character of Washington! And if our American institutions had done nothing else, that alone would have entitled them to the respect of mankind.
DANIEL WEBSTER—*Completion of Bunker Hill Monument.* June 17, 1843. Vol. I. P. 105.

WATER

8
Still waters run no mills.
Quoted by AGLIONBY—*Life of Bickerstaff.* P. 5.

9
Pure water is the best of gifts that man to man can bring,
But who am I that I should have the best of anything?
Let princes revel at the pump, let peers with ponds make free,
Whisky, or wine, or even *beer* is good enough for me.
Anon. In the *Spectator*, July 31, 1920. Attributed to HON. G. W. E. RUSSELL, also to LORD NEAVES. Several versions given in *Notes and Queries.* Oct. 23, 1897.

10
Pouring oil on troubled water.
BEDE—*Historia Ecclesiastica.* Bk. III. Ch. XV. P. 142. (Hussey's Ed.) BEDE says he received the account from CYNEMUND, who heard it from UTTA. Found also in ST. BASIL—*Hexæm.* Hom. II. ERASMUS—*Adagia.* PLAUTUS—*Pœnulus.* V. IV. 66.
(See also BEDE under NAVIGATION)

11
A cup of cold Adam from the next purling stream.
TOM BROWN—*Works.* Vol. IV. P. 11.

12
The miller sees not all the water that goes by his mill.
BURTON—*Anatomy of Melancholy.* Pt. III. Sec. III. Memb. 4. Subsect. 1.
(See also TITUS ANDRONICUS)

13
Till taught by pain,
Men really know not what good water's worth;
If you had been in Turkey or in Spain,
Or with a famish'd boat's-crew had your berth,
Or in the desert heard the camel's bell,
You'd wish yourself where Truth is—in a well.
BYRON—*Don Juan.* Canto II. St. 84.

14
Water, water, everywhere,
And all the boards did shrink;
Water, water, everywhere,
Nor any drop to drink.
COLERIDGE—*Ancient Mariner.* Pt. II. St. 9.
(See also HOMER)

15
The world turns softly
Not to spill its lakes and rivers,
The water is held in its arms
And the sky is held in the water.
What is water,
That pours silver,
And can hold the sky?
HILDA CONKLING—*Water.*

16
Unstable as water, thou shalt not excel.
Genesis. XLIX. 4.

17
Water its living strength first shows,
When obstacles its course oppose.
GOETHE—*God, Soul, and World. Rhymed Distichs.*

18
And pines with thirst amidst a sea of waves.
HOMER—*The Odyssey.* Bk. XI. L. 722. POPE's trans.
(See also COLERIDGE)

19
Water is the mother of the vine,
The nurse and fountain of fecundity,
The adorner and refresher of the world.
CHAS. MACKAY—*The Dionysia.*

20
The rising world of waters dark and deep.
MILTON—*Paradise Lost.* Bk. III. L. 11.

21
I'm very fond of water:
It ever must delight
Each mother's son and daughter,—
When qualified aright.
LORD NEAVES—*I'm very fond of Water.*

1 Caducis
Percussu crebro saxa cavantur aquis.

Stones are hollowed out by the constant dropping of water.
OVID—*Epistolæ Ex Ponto*. II. 7. 39.

2
Est in aqua dulci non invidiosa voluptas.
There is no small pleasure in sweet water.
OVID—*Epistolæ Ex Ponto*. II. 7. 73.

3 Miserum est opus,
Igitur demum foderc puteum, ubi sitis fauces tedet.

It is wretched business to be digging a well just as thirst is mastering you.
PLAUTUS—*Mostellaria*. II. 1. 32.

4
A Rechabite poor Will must live,
And drink of Adam's ale.
PRIOR—*The Wandering Pilgrim*.

5
The noise of many waters.
Psalms. XCIII. 4.

6
As water spilt on the ground, which cannot be gathered up again.
II Samuel. XIV. 14.

7
Honest water, which ne'er left man in the mire.
Timon of Athens. Act I. Sc. 2. L. 59.

8
More water glideth by the mill
Than wots the miller of.
Titus Andronicus. Act II. Sc. 1. L. 85.
(See also BUTLER)

9
'Tis rushing now adown the spout,
And gushing out below,
Half frantic in its joyousness,
And wild in eager flow.
The earth is dried and parched with heat,
And it hath long'd to be
Released from out the selfish cloud,
To cool the thirsty tree.
ELIZABETH OAKES SMITH—*Water*.

10
And so never ending,
But always descending.
SOUTHEY—*The Cataract of Lodore*.

11
"How does the Water
Come down at Lodore?"
SOUTHEY—*The Cataract of Lodore*.

12 'Tis a little thing
To give a cup of water: yet its draught
Of cool refreshment, drain'd by feverish lips,
May give a thrill of pleasure to the frame
More exquisite than when nectarean juice
Renews the life of joy in happiest hours.
THOS. NOON TALFOURD—*Sonnet III*.

13
How dear to this heart are the scenes of my childhood,
When fond recollection presents them to view.
* * * * * *
The old oaken bucket, the iron-bound bucket,
The moss-covered bucket, which hung in the well.
SAMUEL WOODWORTH—*The Old Oaken Bucket*.

14
How sweet from the green mossy brim to receive it,
As, poised on the curb, it inclined to my lips!
Not a full blushing goblet could tempt me to leave it,
The brightest that beauty or revelry sips.
SAMUEL WOODWORTH—*The Old Oaken Bucket*.

WATER-LILY

Nymphæa

15
What loved little islands, twice seen in their lakes,
Can the wild water-lily restore.
CAMPBELL—*Field Flowers*.

16
The slender water-lily
Peeps dreamingly out of the lake;
The moon, oppress'd with love's sorrow,
Looks tenderly down for her sake.
HEINE—*Book of Songs*. *New Spring*. No. 15. St. 1.

17
Those virgin lilies, all the night
Bathing their beauties in the lake,
That they may rise more fresh and bright,
When their beloved sun's awake.
MOORE—*Lalla Rookh*. *Paradise and the Peri*.

18
Broad water-lilies lay tremulously,
And starry river-buds glimmered by,
And around them the soft stream did glide and dance
With a motion of sweet sound and radiance.
SHELLEY—*The Sensitive Plant*. Pt. I.

19
The water-lily starts and slides
Upon the level in little puffs of wind,
Tho' anchor'd to the bottom.
TENNYSON—*The Princess*. IV. L. 236.

20
Now folds the lily all her sweetness up,
And slips into the bosom of the lake;
So fold thyself, my dearest, thou, and slip
Into my bosom, and be lost in me.
TENNYSON—*The Princess*. VII. L. 171.

21
Swan flocks of lilies shoreward lying,
In sweetness, not in music, dying.
WHITTIER—*The Maids of Attitash*.

22
Rapaciously we gathered flowery spoils
From land and water; lilies of each hue,—
Golden and white, that float upon the waves,
And court the wind.
WORDSWORTH—*The Excursion*. Bk. IX. L. 540.

WEAKNESS

23
The cord breaketh at last by the weakest pull.
BACON—*On Seditions*. Quoted as a Spanish Proverb.

24
But the concessions of the weak are the concessions of fear.
BURKE—*Speech on the Conciliation of America*.

25
Amiable weakness.
HENRY FIELDING—*Tom Jones*. Bk. X. Ch. VIII. SHERIDAN—*School for Scandal*. Act V. Sc. 1.

1
Amiable weakness of human nature.
GIBBON—*Decline and Fall of the Roman Empire.* Ch. XIV.

2
Das sterbliche Geschlecht ist viel zu schwach
In ungewohnter Höhe nicht zu schwindeln.
The mortal race is far too weak not to grow dizzy on unwonted heights.
GOETHE—*Iphigenia auf Tauris.* I. 3. 98.

3
And the weak soul, within itself unbless'd,
Leans for all pleasure on another's breast.
GOLDSMITH—*The Traveller.* L. 271.

4
On affaiblit toujours tout ce qu'on exagère.
We always weaken whatever we exaggerate.
LA HARPE—*Mélanie.* I. 1.

5
Soft-heartedness, in times like these,
Shows sof'ness in the upper story!
LOWELL—*The Biglow Papers.* Second Series. No. 7.

6
If weakness may excuse,
What murderer, what traitor, parricide,
Incestuous, sacrilegious, but may plead it?
All wickedness is weakness; that plea, therefore,
With God or man will gain thee no remission.
MILTON—*Samson Agonistes.* L. 831.

7
Heaven forming each on other to depend,
A master, or a servant, or a friend,
Bids each on other for assistance call,
Till one man's weakness grows the strength of all.
POPE—*Essay on Man.* Ep. II. L. 249.

8
Fine by defect, and delicately weak.
POPE—*Moral Essays.* Ep. II. L. 43.

9
Even the weakest is thrust to the wall.
In SCOGIN'S *Tests.* (1540)
The weakest goeth to the wall.
Title of a play printed 1600, and 1618.
The weakest goes to the wall.
TUVILL—*Essays Morall.* (1609)

10
Weakness to be wroth with weakness! woman's pleasure, woman's pain—
Nature made them blinder motions bounded in a shallower brain.
TENNYSON—*Locksley Hall.* St. 75.

WEALTH (See also POSSESSION)

11
There are, while human miseries abound,
A thousand ways to waste superfluous wealth,
Without one fool or flatterer at your board,
Without one hour of sickness or disgust.
ARMSTRONG—*Art of Preserving Health.* Bk. II. L. 195.

12
I have mental joys and mental health,
Mental friends and mental wealth,
I've a wife that I love and that loves me;
I've all but riches bodily.
WM. BLAKE—*Mammon.*

13
Since all the riches of this world
May be gifts from the devil and earthly kings,
I should suspect that I worshipped the devil
If I thanked my God for worldly things.
WM. BLAKE—*Riches.*

14
But I have learned a thing or two; I know as sure as fate,
When we lock up our lives for wealth, the gold key comes too late.
WILL CARLETON—*The Ancient Miner's Story.*

15
Midas-eared Mammonism, double-barrelled Dilettantism, and their thousand adjuncts and corollaries, are *not* the Law by which God Almighty has appointed this His universe to go.
CARLYLE—*Past and Present.* Ch. VI.

16
Surplus wealth is a sacred trust which its possessor is bound to administer in his lifetime for the good of the community.
ANDREW CARNEGIE—*Gospel of Wealth.*

17
Las necedades del rico por sentencias pasan en el mundo.
The foolish sayings of the rich pass for wise saws in society.
CERVANTES—*Don Quixote.* II. 43.

18
Non esse cupidum, pecunia est; non esse emacem, vectigal est; contentum vero suis rebus esse, maximæ sunt, certissimæque divitiæ.
Not to be avaricious is money; not to be fond of buying is a revenue; but to be content with our own is the greatest and most certain wealth of all.
CICERO—*Paradoxa.* 6. 3.

19
Give no bounties: make equal laws: secure life and prosperity and you need not give alms.
EMERSON—*Wealth.*

20
Want is a growing giant whom the coat of Have was never large enough to cover.
EMERSON—*Wealth.*

21
If your Riches are yours, why don't you take them with you to t'other world?
BENJ. FRANKLIN—*Poor Richard.* (1751)

22
Who hath not heard the rich complain
Of surfeits, and corporeal pain?
He barr'd from every use of wealth,
Envies the ploughman's strength and health.
GAY—*Fables. The Cookmaid, Turnspit, and Ox.*

23
The ideal social state is not that in which each gets an equal amount of wealth, but in which each gets in proportion to his contribution to the general stock.
HENRY GEORGE—*Social Problems.* Ch. VI.

24
And to hie him home, at evening's close,
To sweet repast, and calm repose.
* * *
From toil he wins his spirits light,
From busy day the peaceful night;
Rich, from the very want of wealth,
In heaven's best treasures, peace and health.
GRAY—*Ode on the Pleasure Arising from Vicissitude.* L. 87. Last two lines said to have been added by the REV. WILLIAM MASON, Gray's biographer.

1
A little house well fill'd, a little land well till'd, and a little wife well will'd, are great riches.
Written in a copy of the *Grete Herbal*. (1516)
A little farm well tilled,
A little barn well filled,
A little wife well willed—
Give me, give me.
As adapted by JAMES HOOK in *The Soldier's Return*.

2
Dame Nature gave him comeliness and health,
And Fortune (for a passport) gave him wealth.
W. HARTE—*Eulogius*. 411.

3
For wealth, without contentment, climbs a hill,
To feel those tempests which fly over ditches.
HERBERT—*The Church Porch*. St. 19.

4
It cannot be repeated too often that the safety of great wealth with us lies in obedience to the new version of the Old World axiom—*Richesse oblige*.
HOLMES—*A Mortal Antipathy. Introduction*.

5
Base wealth preferring to eternal praise.
HOMER—*Iliad*. Bk. XXIII. L. 368. POPE'S trans.

6
These riches are possess'd, but not enjoy'd!
HOMER—*Odyssey*. Bk. IV. L. 118. POPE'S trans.

7
Know from the bounteous heavens all riches flow;
And what man gives, the gods by man bestow.
HOMER—*Odyssey*. Bk. XVIII. L. 26. POPE'S trans.

8
Imperat aut servit collecta pecunia cuique.
Riches either serve or govern the possessor.
HORACE—*Epistles*. I. 10. 47.

9
Omnis enim res,
Virtus, fama, decus, divina, humanaque pulchris
Divitiis parent.
For everything divine and human, virtue, fame, and honor, now obey the alluring influence of riches.
HORACE—*Satires*. II. 3. 94.

10
Et genus et virtus, nisi cum re, vilior alga est.
Noble descent and worth, unless united with wealth, are esteemed no more than seaweed.
HORACE—*Satires*. II. 5. 8.

11
And you prate of the wealth of nations, as if it were bought and sold,
The wealth of nations is men, not silk and cotton and gold.
RICHARD HOVEY—*Peace*.

12
We are not here to sell a parcel of boilers and vats, but the potentiality of growing rich beyond the dreams of avarice.
SAMUEL JOHNSON. Remark on the sale of Thrale's Brewery, 1781.
(See also MOORE)

13
Poor worms, they hiss at me, whilst I at home
Can be contented to applaud myself, * * *
with joy
To see how plump my bags are and my barns.
BEN JONSON—*Every Man Out of His Humour*. Act I. Sc. 1.

14
Private credit is wealth, public honour is security. The feather that adorns the royal bird supports his flight; strip him of his plumage, and you fix him to the earth.
JUNIUS—*Letter* 42. Jan. 30, 1771.

15
Rarus enim ferme sensus communis in illa
Fortuna.
Common sense among men of fortune is rare.
JUVENAL—*Satires*. VIII. 73.

16
Dives fieri qui vult
Et cito vult fieri.
He who wishes to become rich wishes to become so immediately.
JUVENAL—*Satires*. XIV. 176.

17
Facile est momento quo quis velit, cedere possessione magnæ fortunæ; facere et parare eam, difficile atque arduum est.
It is easy at any moment to resign the possession of a great fortune; to acquire it is difficult and arduous.
LIVY—*Annales*. XXIV. 22.

18
The rich man's son inherits cares;
The bank may break, the factory burn,
A breath may burst his bubble shares,
And soft, white hands could hardly earn
A living that would serve his turn.
LOWELL—*The Heritage*.

19
Our Lord commonly giveth Riches to such gross asses, to whom he affordeth nothing else that is good.
LUTHER—*Colloquies*. P. 90. (Ed. 1652)
(See also STEELE, SWIFT)

20
Infinite riches in a little room.
MARLOWE—*The Jew of Malta*. Act I. Sc. 1.

21
You often ask me, Priscus, what sort of person I should be, if I were to become suddenly rich and powerful. Who can determine what would be his future conduct? Tell me, if you were to become a lion, what sort of a lion would you be?
MARTIAL—*Epigrams*. Bk. XII. Ep. 92.

22
Those whom we strive to benefit
Dear to our hearts soon grow to be;
I love my Rich, and I admit
That they are very good to me.
Succor the poor, my sisters,—I
While heaven shall still vouchsafe me health
Will strive to share and mollify
The trials of abounding wealth.
EDWARD SANDFORD MARTIN—*A Little Brother of the Rich*.

23
The little sister of the Poor
* * * *
The Poor, and their concerns, she has

Monopolized, because of which
It falls to me to labor as
A Little Brother of the Rich.
EDWARD SANDFORD MARTIN—*A Little Brother of the Rich.*

1
But wealth is a great means of refinement; and it is a security for gentleness, since it removes disturbing anxieties.
IK MARVEL—*Reveries of a Bachelor. Over his Cigar.* III.

2
It is easier for a camel to go through the eye of a needle, than for a rich man to enter into the kingdom of God.
Matthew. XIX. 24.

3
Let none admire
That riches grow in hell; that soil may best
Deserve the precious bane.
MILTON—*Paradise Lost.* Bk. I. L. 690.

4
I am rich beyond the dreams of avarice.
EDWARD MOORE—*The Gamester.* Act II. Sc. 2.
(See also JOHNSON)

5
Opum furiata cupido.
The ungovernable passion for wealth.
OVID—*Fasti.* I. 211.

6
Effodiuntur opes irritamenta malorum.
Riches, the incentives to evil, are dug out of the earth.
OVID—*Metamorphoses.* I. 140.

7
Embarras des richesses
Embarrassment of riches.
Title of a French Comedy played at the Haymarket, London, Oct. 9, 1738. Trans. by OZELL.

8
Opes invisæ merito sunt forti viro,
Quia dives arca veram laudem intercipit.
Riches are deservedly despised by a man of honor, because a well-stored chest intercepts the truth.
PHÆDRUS—*Fables.* IV. 12. 1.

9
Nemini credo, qui large blandus est dives pauperi.
I trust no rich man who is officiously kind to a poor man.
PLAUTUS—*Aulularia.* II. 2. 30.

10
Get place and wealth, if possible, with grace;
If not, by any means get wealth and place.
POPE—*Epistles of Horace.* Ep. I. Bk. I. L. 103.

11
What riches give us let us then inquire:
Meat, fire, and clothes. What more? Meat, clothes, and fire.
Is this too little?
POPE—*Moral Essays.* Ep. III. L. 79.

12
Riches certainly make themselves wings.
Proverbs. XXIII. 5.

13
He that maketh haste to be rich shall not be innocent.
Proverbs. XXVIII. 20.

14
He heapeth up riches, and knoweth not who shall gather them.
Psalms. XXXIX. 6.

15
All gold and silver rather turn to dirt!
As 'tis no better reckon'd, but of those
Who worship dirty gods.
Cymbeline. Act III. Sc. 6. L. 54.

16
If thou art rich, thou art poor;
For, like an ass whose back with ingots bows,
Thou bear'st thy heavy riches but a journey,
And death unloads thee.
Measure for Measure. Act III. Sc. 1. L. 25.

17
O what a world of vile ill-favour'd faults
Looks handsome in three hundred pounds a year!
Merry Wives of Windsor. Act III. Sc. 4. L. 32.

18
Through life's dark road his sordid way he wends,
An incarnation of fat dividends.
SPRAGUE—*Curiosity.* St. 25.

19
No, he was no such charlatan—
Count de Hoboken Flash-in-the-Pan—
Full of gasconade and bravado,
But a regular, rich Don Rataplane,
Santa Claus de la Muscavado,
Senor Grandissimo Bastinado!
His was the rental of half Havana
And all Matanzas; and Santa Ana,
Rich as he was, could hardly hold
A candle to light the mines of gold
Our Cuban owned.
E. C. STEDMAN—*The Diamond Wedding.* St. 7.

20
The man is mechanically turned, and made for getting. . . . It was very prettily said that we may learn the little value of fortune by the persons on whom Heaven is pleased to bestow it.
STEELE—*Tatler, No.* 203.
(See also LUTHER)

21
If Heaven had looked upon riches to be a valuable thing, it would not have given them to such a scoundrel.
SWIFT—*Letter to Miss Vanhomrigh.* Aug. 12, 1720.
(See also LUTHER)

22
Repente dives nemo factus est bonus.
No good man ever became suddenly rich.
SYRUS—*Maxims.*

23
He that is proud of riches is a fool. For if he be exalted above his neighbors because he hath more gold, how much inferior is he to a gold mine!
JEREMY TAYLOR—*Holy Living. Of Humility.* Ch. II. Sc. 4.

24
Rich in good works.
I Timothy. VI. 18.

25
Can wealth give happiness? look round and see
What gay distress! what splendid misery!
Whatever fortunes lavishly can pour,
The mind annihilates, and calls for more.
YOUNG—*Love of Fame.* Satire V. L. 394.

1
Much learning shows how little mortals know;
Much wealth, how little worldlings can enjoy.
YOUNG—*Night Thoughts.* Night VI. L. 519.

WEEDS (See also TREES AND PLANTS)

2
Call us not weeds, we are flowers of the sea.
E. L. AVELINE—*The Mother's Fables.*

3
Great weeds do grow apace.
BEAUMONT AND FLETCHER — *The Coxcomb.* Act IV. Sc. 4.

4
Still must I on, for I am as a weed,
Flung from the rock, on Ocean's foam, to sail
Where'er the surge may sweep.
BYRON—*Childe Harold.* Canto III. St. 2.

5
An ill weed grows apace.
CHAPMAN—*An Humorous Day's Mirth.*
Evyl weed ys sone y growe.
Harl. MS. (1490)
(See also RICHARD III)

6
In the deep shadow of the porch
A slender bind-weed springs,
And climbs, like airy acrobat,
The trellises, and swings
And dances in the golden sun
In fairy loops and rings.
SUSAN COOLIDGE—*Bind-Weed.*

7
The wolfsbane I should dread.
HOOD—*Flowers.*

8
To win the secret of a weed's plain heart.
LOWELL—*Sonnet XXV.*

9
The richest soil, if uncultivated, produces the rankest weeds.
PLUTARCH—*Life of Caius Marcus Coriolanus.*

10
Nothing teems
But hateful docks, rough thistles, kecksies, burs,
Losing both beauty and utility.
Henry V. Act V. Sc. 2. L. 51.

11
Now 'tis the spring, and weeds are shallow-rooted;
Suffer them now, and they'll o'ergrow the garden
And choke the herbs for want of husbandry.
Henry VI. Act III. Sc. 1. L. 31.

12
I will go root away
The noisome weeds which without profit suck
The soil's fertility from wholesome flowers.
Richard II. Act III. Sc. 4. L. 37.

13
Small herbs have grace, great weeds do grow apace.
Richard III. Act II. Sc. 4.
(See also BEAUMONT)

14
The summer's flower is to the summer sweet,
Though to itself it only live and die,
But if that flower with base infection meet,
The basest weed outbraves his dignity;
For sweetest things turn sourest by their deeds;
Lilies that fester smell far worse than weeds.
Sonnet XCIV.

WEEPING (See TEARS)

WELCOME (See also GUESTS, HOSPITALITY)

15
'Tis sweet to hear the watch-dog's honest bark
Bay deep-mouth'd welcome as we draw near home;
'Tis sweet to know there is an eye will mark
Our coming, and look brighter when we come.
BYRON—*Don Juan.* Canto I. St. 123.

16
He enter'd in his house—his home no more,
For without hearts there is no home;—and felt
The solitude of passing his own door
Without a welcome.
BYRON—*Don Juan.* Canto III. St. 52.

17
Come in the evening, or come in the morning,
Come when you're looked for, or come without warning,
Kisses and welcome you'll find here before you,
And the oftener you come here the more I'll adore you.
THOMAS O. DAVIS—*The Welcome.*

18
Welcome, my old friend,
Welcome to a foreign fireside.
LONGFELLOW—*To an Old Danish Song-Book.*

19
Shall I meet other wayfarers at night?
Those who have gone before.
Then must I knock, or call when just in sight?
They will not keep you standing at that door.
CHRISTINA G. ROSSETTI—*Up Hill.*

20
Welcome as the flowers in May.
SCOTT—*Rob Roy.* Ch. VIII. JAMES HOWELL—*Proverbs.* CHARLES MACKLIN—*Love à la Mode.* Act I. Sc. 2.

21
Bid that welcome
Which comes to punish us, and we punish it
Seeming to bear it lightly.
Antony and Cleopatra. Act IV. Sc. 14. L. 136.

22
I hold your dainties cheap, sir, and your welcome dear.
Comedy of Errors. Act III. Sc. 1. L. 21.

23
A table full of welcome makes scarce one dainty dish.
Comedy of Errors. Act III. Sc. 1. L. 23.

24
Small cheer and great welcome makes a merry feast.
Comedy of Errors. Act III. Sc. 1. L. 26.

25
Sir, you are very welcome to our house:
It must appear in other ways than words,
Therefore I scant this breathing courtesy.
Merchant of Venice. Act V. Sc. 1. L. 139.

26
Trust me, sweet,
Out of this silence yet I pick'd a welcome.
Midsummer Night's Dream. Act V. Sc. 1. L. 99.

27
Welcome ever smiles,
And farewell goes out sighing.
Troilus and Cressida. Act III. Sc. 3. L. 168.

1
His worth is warrant for his welcome.
Two Gentlemen of Verona. Act II. Sc. 4. L. 102.

2
I reckon this always, that a man is never undone till he be hanged, nor never welcome to a place till some certain shot be paid and the hostess say "Welcome!"
Two Gentlemen of Verona. Act II. Sc. 5. L. 3.

WHIP-POOR-WILL

3
The moan of the whip-poor-will from the hillside; the boding cry of the tree-toad, that harbinger of storm; the dreary hooting of the screechowl.
IRVING—*Sketch Book. The Legend of Sleepy Hollow.*

4
Where deep and misty shadows float
In forest's depths is heard thy note.
Like a lost spirit, earthbound still,
Art thou, mysterious whip-poor-will.
MARIE LE BARON—*The Whip-Poor-Will.*

WICKEDNESS

5
There is a method in man's wickedness,
It grows up by degrees.
BEAUMONT AND FLETCHER—*A King and No King.* Act V. Sc. 4.

6
Animi labes nec diuturnitate vanescere nec omnibus ullis elui potest.
Mental stains can not be removed by time, nor washed away by any waters.
CICERO—*De Legibus.* II. 10.

7
All wickedness is but little to the wickedness of a woman.
Ecclesiasticus. XXV. 19.

8
The world loves a spice of wickedness.
LONGFELLOW—*Hyperion.* Ch. VII. Bk. I.

9
Destroy his fib, or sophistry—in vain!
The creature's at his dirty work again.
POPE—*Prologue to the Satires.* L. 91.

10
The wicked flee when no man pursueth; but the righteous are bold as a lion.
Proverbs. XXVIII. 1.

11
As saith the proverb of the Ancients,
Wickedness proceedeth from the wicked.
I Samuel. XXIV. 13. DAVID to SAUL. Said to be the oldest proverb on record.

12
Are you call'd forth from out a world of men,
To slay the innocent?
Richard III. Act I. Sc. 4. L. 186.

13
O cæca nocentum consilia!
O semper timidum scelus!
Oh, the blind counsels of the guilty!
Oh, how cowardly is wickedness always!
STATIUS—*Thebais.* II. 489.

14
'Cause I's wicked,—I is. I's mighty wicked, anyhow, I can't help it.
HARRIET BEECHER STOWE — *Uncle Tom's Cabin.* Ch. XX.

WIFE (See also HUSBAND, MATRIMONY)

15
She would rather be an old man's darling than a young man's warling.
HARRISON AINSWORTH—*Miser's Daughter.* Bk. III. Ch. XV. SWIFT — *Polite Conversation.* Dialog. I. Also in CAMDEN'S *Remaines.* P. 293. (Ed. 5.) *Ram Alley.* Act II. Sc. 1. *of* HAZLITT'S *Dodsley.*

16
Wives are young men's mistresses; companions for middle age; and old men's nurses.
BACON—*Of Marriage and Single Life.*

17
Now voe me I can zing on my business abrode:
Though the storm do beat down on my poll,
There's a wife brighten'd vire at the end of my road,
An' her love, voe the jaÿ o' my soul.
WILLIAM BARNES—*Don't Ceare.* St. 5.

18
And while the wicket falls behind
Her steps, I thought if I could find
A wife I need not blush to show
I've little further now to go.
WILLIAM BARNES—*Not Far to Go.*

19
My fond affection thou hast seen,
Then judge of my regret
To think more happy thou hadst been
If we had never met!

And has that thought been shared by thee?
Ah, no! that smiling cheek
Proves more unchanging love for me
Than labor'd words could speak.
THOS. HAYNES BAYLY—*To My Wife.*

20
Without thee I am all unblessed,
And wholly blessed in thee alone.
G. W. BETHUNE—*To My Wife.*

21
So bent on self-sanctifying,—
That she never thought of trying
To save her poor husband as well.
ROBERT BUCHANAN—*Fra Giacomo.*

22
In thy face have I seen the eternal.
BARON CHRISTIAN VON BUNSEN—*To his wife.* When dying at Bonn. (1860) Found in *Life of Baron Bunsen.* Vol. II. P. 389.

23
Were such the wife had fallen to my part,
I'd break her spirit, or I'd break her heart.
BURNS—*Henpecked Husband.*

24
She is a winsome wee thing,
She is a handsome wee thing,
She is a bonny wee thing,
This sweet wee wife o' mine.
BURNS—*My Wife's a Winsome Wee Thing.*

25
Be thou the rainbow to the storms of life!
The evening beam that smiles the clouds away
And tints to-morrow with prophetic ray!
BYRON—*The Bride of Abydos.* Canto II. St. 20.

26
Thy wife is a constellation of virtues; she's the moon, and thou art the man in the moon.
CONGREVE—*Love for Love.* Act II. Sc. 1.

1
What is there in the vale of life
Half so delightful as a wife,
When friendship, love, and peace combine
To stamp the marriage-bond divine?
COWPER—*Love Abused.*

2
Oh! 'tis a precious thing, when wives are dead,
To find such numbers who will serve instead:
And in whatever state a man be thrown,
'Tis that precisely they would wish their own.
CRABBE—*Tales. The Learned Boy.*

3
The wife was pretty, trifling, childish, weak;
She could not think, but would not cease to speak.
CRABBE—*Tales. Struggles of Conscience.*

4
The wife of thy bosom.
Deuteronomy. XIII. 6.

5
In every mess I find a friend,
In every port a wife.
CHARLES DIBDIN—*Jack in his Element.*
(See also GAY)

6
It's my old girl that advises. She has the head. But I never own to it before her. Discipline must be maintained.
DICKENS—*Bleak House.* Ch. XXVII.

7
You know I met you,
Kist you, and prest you close within my arms,
With all the tenderness of wifely love.
DRYDEN—*Amphitryon.* Act III. Sc. 1.

8
Flesh of thy flesh, nor yet bone of thy bone.
DU BARTAS—*Divine Weekes and Workes.* Fourth Day. Bk. II.

9
An undutiful Daughter will prove an unmanageable Wife.
BENJ. FRANKLIN—*Poor Richard.* (1752)

10
He knows little who will tell his wife all he knows.
FULLER—*Holy and Profane State.* Maxim VII. *The Good Husband.*

11
She commandeth her husband, in any equal matter, by constant obeying him.
FULLER—*Holy and Profane State. The Good Wife.* Bk. I. Maxim I. Ch. I.

12
One wife is too much for most husbands to bear,
But two at a time there's no mortal can bear.
GAY—*Beggar's Opera.* Act II. Sc. 2.

13
They'll tell thee, sailors, when away,
In every port a mistress find.
GAY—*Sweet William's Farewell.*
(See also DIBDIN)

14
Roy's wife of Aldivalloch,
Roy's wife of Aldivalloch,
Wat ye how she cheated me
As I cam o'er the braes of Balloch.
Attributed to MRS. GRANT, of Carron, but claimed for a shoemaker in Cabrach. (About 1727)

15
Now die the dream, or come the wife,
The past is not in vain,
For wholly as it was your life
Can never be again, my dear,
Can never be again.
HENLEY—*Echoes.* XIX.

16
Andromache! my soul's far better part.
HOMER—*Iliad.* Bk. VI. L. 624. POPE's trans.

17
A wife, domestic, good, and pure,
Like snail, should keep within her door;
But not, like snail, with silver track,
Place all her wealth upon her back.
W. W. HOW—*Good Wives.*
(See also BRITAINE under WOMAN)

18
Alas! another instance of the triumph of hope over experience.
SAMUEL JOHNSON. Referring to the second marriage of a friend who had been unfortunate in his first wife. Sir J. Hawkins's Collective Ed. of Johnson, 1787.

19
Being married to those sleepy-souled women is just like playing at cards for nothing: no passion is excited and the time is filled up. I do not, however, envy a fellow one of those honeysuckle wives for my part, as they are but creepers at best and commonly destroy the tree they so tenderly cling about.
SAMUEL JOHNSON—*Remark as Recorded by Mrs. Piozzi.*

20
He knew whose gentle hand was at the latch,
Before the door had given her to his eyes.
KEATS—*Isabella.* St. 3.

21
Sail forth into the sea of life,
O gentle, loving, trusting wife,
And safe from all adversity
Upon the bosom of that sea
Thy comings and thy goings be!
For gentleness and love and trust
Prevail o'er angry wave and gust;
And in the wreck of noble lives
Something immortal still survives.
LONGFELLOW—*Building of the Ship.* L. 368.

22
But thou dost make the very night itself
Brighter than day.
LONGFELLOW—*Christus. The Divine Tragedy. The First Passover.* Pt. III. L. 133.

23
Le ciel me prive d'une épouse qui ne m'a jamais donné d'autre chagrin que celui de sa mort.
Heaven deprives me of a wife who never caused me any other grief than that of her death.
LOUIS XIV.

24
How much the wife is dearer than the bride.
LORD LYTTLETON—*An Irregular Ode.*

25
O wretched is the dame, to whom the sound,
"Your lord will soon return," no pleasure brings.
MATURIN—*Bertram.* Act II. Sc. 5.

1
In the election of a wife, as in
A project of war, to err but once is
To be undone forever.
THOS. MIDDLETON—*Anything for a Quiet Life.* Act I. Sc. 1.

2 What thou bidd'st
Unargu'd I obey, so God ordains;
God is thy law, thou mine; to know no more
Is woman's happiest knowledge and her praise.
MILTON—*Paradise Lost.* Bk. IV. L. 635.

3 Awake,
My fairest, my espous'd, my latest found,
Heaven's last best gift, my ever new delight!
MILTON—*Paradise Lost.* Bk. V. L. 17.

4
For nothing lovelier can be found
In woman, than to study household good,
And good works in her husband to promote.
MILTON—*Paradise Lost.* Bk. IX. L. 232.

5 For what thou art is mine:
Our state cannot be sever'd; we are one,
One flesh; to lose thee were to lose myself.
MILTON—*Paradise Lost.* Bk. IX. L. 957.

6
Here were we fallen in a greate question of ye lawe whyther ye grey mare may be the better horse or not.
MORE—*The Dial.* Bk. II. Ch. V. The saying, "the grey mare is the better horse," is found in CAMDEN'S *Remains, Proverb concerning Britain.* (1605, reprint of 7th ed. 1870.) Also in *A Treatyse shewing and declaring the Pryde and Abuse of Women Now a Dayse.* (1550)

7
Giving honour unto the wife as unto the weaker vessel.
I Peter. III. 7.

8
Uxorem accepi, dote imperium vendidi.
I have taken a wife, I have sold my sovereignty for a dowry.
PLAUTUS—*Asinaria.* Act I. Sc. 1.

9
But what so pure, which envious tongues will spare?
Some wicked wits have libell'd all the fair.
With matchless impudence they style a wife
The dear-bought curse, and lawful plague of life;
A bosom-serpent, a domestic evil,
A night-invasion and a mid-day-devil.
Let not the wife these sland'rous words regard,
But curse the bones of ev'ry living bard.
POPE—*January and May.* L. 43.

10
All other goods by fortune's hand are given,
A wife is the peculiar gift of heaven.
POPE—*January and May. From Chaucer.* L. 51.

11
She who ne'er answers till a husband cools,
Or, if she rules him, never shews she rules;
Charms by accepting, by submitting sways,
Yet has her humour most when she obeys.
POPE—*Moral Essays.* Ep. II. L. 261.

12
The contentions of a wife *are* a continual dropping.
Proverbs. XIX. 13.

13
She looketh well to the ways of her household, and eateth not the bread of idleness.
Proverbs. XXXI. 27.

14
Fat, fair and forty.
SCOTT—*St. Ronan's Well.* Ch. VII. PRINCE REGENT'S *description of what a wife should be.* Found in an old song, *The One Horse Shay.* Sung by SAM COWELL in the sixties.
(See also TRENCH)

15 As for my wife,
I would you had her spirit in such another;
The third o' the world is yours; which with a snaffle
You may pace easy, but not such a wife.
Antony and Cleopatra. Act II. Sc. 2. L. 61.

16 O ye gods,
Render me worthy of this noble wife!
Julius Cæsar. Act II. Sc. 1. L. 303.

17
Happy in this, she is not yet so old
But she may learn; happier than this,
She is not bred so dull but she can learn;
Happiest of all is, that her gentle spirit
Commits itself to yours to be directed.
Merchant of Venice. Act III. Sc. 2. L. 162.

18
A light wife doth make a heavy husband.
Merchant of Venice. Act V. Sc. 1. L. 130.

19
I will be master of what is mine own;
She is my goods, my chattels; she is my house,
My household stuff, my field, my barn,
My horse, my ox, my ass, my anything;
And here she stands, touch her whoever dare.
Taming of the Shrew. Act III. Sc. 2. L. 231.

20 Why, man, she is mine own,
And I as rich in having such a jewel
As twenty seas, if all their sand were pearl,
The water nectar and the rocks pure gold.
Two Gentlemen of Verona. Act II. Sc. 4. L. 168.

21 Should all despair
That have revolted wives, the tenth of mankind
Would hang themselves.
Winter's Tale. Act I. Sc. 2. L. 198.

22
It is a woman's business to get married as soon as possible, and a man's to keep unmarried as long as he can.
BERNARD SHAW—*Man and Superman.*
(See also DISRAELI under MATRIMONY)

23
My dear, my better half.
SIR PHILIP SIDNEY—*Arcadia.* Bk. III.

24
Of earthly goods, the best is a good wife;
A bad, the bitterest curse of human life.
SIMONIDES.

25
Light household duties, ever more inwrought
With placid fancies of one trusting heart
That lives but in her smile, and turns

From life's cold seeming and the busy mart,
With tenderness, that heavenward ever yearns
To be refreshed where one pure altar burns.
Shut out from hence the mockery of life;
Thus liveth she content, the meek, fond, trusting wife.

ELIZABETH OAKES SMITH—*The Wife.*

1
Thou art mine, thou hast given thy word,
Close, close in my arms thou art clinging;
Alone for my ear thou art singing
A song which no stranger hath heard:
But afar from me yet, like a bird,
Thy soul in some region unstirr'd
On its mystical circuit is winging.

E. C. STEDMAN—*Stanzas for Music.*

2
Casta ad virum matrona parendo imperat.

A virtuous wife when she obeys her husband obtains the command over him.

SYRUS—*Maxims.*

3
When choosing a wife look down the social scale; when selecting a friend, look upwards.

TALMUD—*Yebamoth.* 63.

4
A love still burning upward, giving light
To read those laws; an accent very low
In blandishment, but a most silver flow
Of subtle-paced counsel in distress.
Right to the heart and brain, tho' undescried,
Winning its way with extreme gentleness
Thro' all the outworks of suspicious pride;
A courage to endure and to obey:
A hate of gossip parlance and of sway,
Crown'd Isabel, thro' all her placid life,
The queen of marriage, a most perfect wife.

TENNYSON—*Isabel.*

5
A fat, fair and fifty card-playing resident of the Crescent.

MRS. TRENCH—*Letter.* Feb. 18, 1816.
(See also SCOTT)

6
The world well tried—the sweetest thing in life
Is the unclouded welcome of a wife.

N. P. WILLIS—*Lady Jane.* Canto II. St. 11.

7
My winsome marrow.

WORDSWORTH — *Yarrow Revisited.* Quoting from "Busk ye, busk ye, my winsome marrow," an old song, *The Braes of Yarrow.*

WILL

8
A willing heart adds feather to the heel,
And makes the clown a winged Mercury.

JOANNA BAILLIE — *De Montfort.* Act III. Sc. 2.

9
He that will not when he may,
When he will he shall have nay.

BURTON—*Anatomy of Melancholy.* II. 2. 5. (Quoted). Also in *The Loyal Garland. Song 28.*
The fool that will not when he may,
He shall not when he wold.
Blow the Winds, Heigho! Northumbrian ballad. Percy's Relics. *Baffled Knight.*

10
He that complies against his will,
Is of his own opinion still,
Which he may adhere to, yet disown,
For reasons to himself best known.

BUTLER—*Hudibras.* Pt. III. Canto III. L. 547.

11
The commander of the forces of a large State may be carried off, but the will of even a common man cannot be taken from him.

CONFUCIUS—*Analects.* Bk. IX. Ch. XXV.

12
Barkis is willin'!

DICKENS—*David Copperfield.* Ch. I.

13
"When a man says he's willin'," said Mr. Barkis, "it's as much as to say, that man's a-waitin' for a answer."

DICKENS—*David Copperfield.* Ch. VIII.

14
There is nothing good or evil save in the will.

EPICTETUS.

15
Der Mensch kann was er soll; und wenn er sagt er kann nicht, so will er nicht.

A man can do what he ought to do; and when he says he cannot, it is because he will not.

FICHTE—*Letter.* (1791)

16
To deny the freedom of the will is to make morality impossible.

FROUDE—*Short Studies on Great Subjects. Calvinism.*

17
Aber wer fest auf dem Sinne beharrt, der bildet die Welt sich.

He who is firm in will molds the world to himself.

GOETHE—*Hermann und Dorothea.* IX. 303.

18
The only way of setting the will free is to deliver it from wilfulness.

J. C. AND A. W. HARE—*Guesses at Truth.*

19
The readinesse of doing doth expresse
No other but the doer's willingnesse.

HERRICK—*Hesperides. Readinesse.*

20
All theory is against the freedom of the will, all experience for it.

SAMUEL JOHNSON—*Boswell's Life.* (1778)

21
The star of the unconquered will,
He rises in my breast,
Serene, and resolute, and still,
And calm, and self-possessed.

LONGFELLOW—*The Light of Stars.* St. 7.

22
A boy's will is the wind's will.

LONGFELLOW—*My Lost Youth.*

23
Will without power is like children playing at soldiers.

Quoted by MACAULAY from *The Rovers.* Act IV. Found in *Poetry of the Anti-Jacobin.*

24
Tu si animum vicisti potius quam animus te est quod gaudias.

If you have overcome your inclination and not been overcome by it, you have reason to rejoice.

PLAUTUS—*Trinummus.* II. 9.

1
And binding nature fast in fate,
Left free the human will.
POPE—*The Universal Prayer*. St. 3.

2
I have known many who could not when they would, for they had not done it when they could.
RABELAIS—*Pantagruel*. Bk. III. Ch. XXVII.
(See also BURTON)

3
We sought therefore to amend our will, and not to suffer it through despite to languish long time in error.
SENECA—*Of Benefits*. Bk. V. Ch. XXV. Ep. 67.

4
My will enkindled by mine eyes and ears,
Two traded pilots 'twixt the dangerous shores
Of will and judgment.
Troilus and Cressida. Act II. Sc. 2. L. 63.

5
That what he will he does, and does so much
That proof is call'd impossibility.
Troilus and Cressida. Act V. Sc. 5. L. 28.

6
Our wills are ours, we know not how;
Our wills are ours, to make them thine.
TENNYSON—*In Memoriam. Introduction*. St. 4.

7
All
Life needs for life is possible to will.
TENNYSON—*Love and Duty*. L. 82.

WILLOW
Salix

8
I'll hang my harp on a willow tree.
JOHN, LORD ELPHINSTONE. Also credited to THOS. HAYNES BAYLY.

9
Willow, in thy breezy moan,
I can hear a deeper tone;
Through thy leaves come whispering low,
Faint sweet sounds of long ago—
Willow, sighing willow!
FELICIA D. HEMANS—*Willow Song*.

10
All a green willow, willow,
All a green willow is my garland.
JOHN HEYWOOD—*The Green Willow*.

11
The willow hangs with sheltering grace
And benediction o'er their sod,
And Nature, hushed, assures the soul
They rest in God.
CRAMMOND KENNEDY—*Greenwood Cemetery*.

12
Near the lake where drooped the willow,
Long time ago.
GEORGE P. MORRIS—*Near the Lake*.

13
We hanged our harps upon the willows in the midst thereof.
Psalms. CXXXVII. 2.

14
Know ye the willow-tree,
Whose grey leaves quiver,
Whispering gloomily
To yon pale river?

Lady, at even-tide
Wander not near it:
They say its branches hide
A sad, lost spirit!
THACKERAY—*The Willow-Tree*.

WIND (See also ZEPHYRS)

15
The hushed winds wail with feeble moan
Like infant charity.
JOANNA BAILLIE—*Orra*. Act III. Sc. 1. *The Chough and Crow*.

16
Blow, Boreas, foe to human kind!
Blow, blustering, freezing, piercing wind!
Blow, that thy force I may rehearse,
While all my thoughts congeal to verse!
JOHN BANCKS—*To Boreas*.
(See also STEVENS)

17
The faint old man shall lean his silver head
To feel thee; thou shalt kiss the child asleep,
And dry the moistened curls that overspread
His temples, while his breathing grows more deep.
BRYANT—*Evening Wind*. St. 4.

18
Where hast thou wandered, gentle gale, to find
The perfumes thou dost bring?
BRYANT—*May Evening*. St. 2.

19
Wind of the sunny south! oh, still delay
In the gay woods and in the golden air,
Like to a good old age released from care,
Journeying, in long serenity, away.
In such a bright, late quiet, would that I
Might wear out life like thee, mid bowers and brooks,
And, dearer yet, the sunshine of kind looks,
And music of kind voices ever nigh;
And when my last sand twinkled in the glass,
Pass silently from men as thou dost pass.
BRYANT—*October*. L. 5.

20
A breeze came wandering from the sky,
Light as the whispers of a dream;
He put the o'erhanging grasses by,
And softly stooped to kiss the stream,
The pretty stream, the flattered stream,
The shy, yet unreluctant stream.
BRYANT—*The Wind and Stream*.

21
As winds come whispering lightly from the West,
Kissing, not ruffling, the blue deep's serene.
BYRON—*Childe Harold*. Canto II. St. 70.

22
When the stormy winds do blow;
When the battle rages loud and long,
And the stormy winds do blow.
CAMPBELL—*Ye Mariners of England*.
(See also PARKER)

23
The wind is awake, pretty leaves, pretty leaves,
Heed not what he says, he deceives, he deceives;
Over and over
To the lowly clover
He has lisped the same love (and forgotten it, too).
He will be lisping and pledging to you.
JOHN VANCE CHENEY—*The way of it*.

24
The wind's in the east * * * I am always conscious of an uncomfortable sensation now and then when the wind is blowing in the east.
DICKENS—*Bleak House*. Ch. VI.
(See also ELIOT)

1
The winds that never moderation knew,
Afraid to blow too much, too faintly blew;
Or out of breath with joy, could not enlarge
Their straighten'd lungs or conscious of their charge.
DRYDEN—*Astræa Redux*. L. 242.

2
Perhaps the wind
Wails so in winter for the summer's dead,
And all sad sounds are nature's funeral cries
For what has been and is not.
GEORGE ELIOT—*The Spanish Gypsy*. Bk. I.

3
But certain winds will make men's temper bad.
GEORGE ELIOT—*The Spanish Gypsy*. Bk. I.
(See also DICKENS)

4
The wind moans, like a long wail from some despairing soul shut out in the awful storm!
W. H. GIBSON—*Pastoral Days. Winter.*

5
The wind, the wandering wind
Of the golden summer eves—
Whence is the thrilling magic
Of its tunes amongst the leaves?
Oh, is it from the waters,
Or from the long, tall grass?
Or is it from the hollow rocks
Through which its breathings pass?
FELICIA D. HEMANS—*The Wandering Wind.*

6
A little wind kindles, much puts out the fire.
HERBERT—*Jacula Prudentum.*

7
To a crazy ship all winds are contrary.
HERBERT—*Jacula Prudentum.*

8
An ill wind that bloweth no man good—
The blower of which blast is she.
JOHN HEYWOOD—*Idleness*. St. 5.
(See also HENRY IV, HENRY VI, TUSSER)

9
Madame, bear in mind
That princes govern all things—save the wind.
VICTOR HUGO—*The Infanta's Rose.*

10
He stayeth his rough wind in the day of the east wind.
Isaiah. XXVII. 8.

11
The wind bloweth where it listeth.
John. III. 8.

12
I hear the wind among the trees
Playing the celestial symphonies;
I see the branches downward bent,
Like keys of some great instrument.
LONGFELLOW—*A Day of Sunshine*. St. 3.

13
Chill airs and wintry winds! my ear
Has grown familiar with your song;
I hear it in the opening year,
I listen, and it cheers me long.
LONGFELLOW—*Woods in Winter*. St. 7.

14
It's a warm wind, the west wind, full of birds' cries;
I never hear the west wind but tears are in my eyes.
For it comes from the west lands, the old brown hills,
And April's in the West wind, and daffodils.
MASEFIELD—*The West Wind.*

15
The winds with wonder whist,
Smoothly the waters kisst.
MILTON—*Hymn on the Nativity*. St. 5.

16
While rocking winds are piping loud.
MILTON—*Il Penseroso*. L. 126.

17
When the gust hath blown his fill,
Ending on the rustling leaves,
With minute drops from off the eaves.
MILTON—*Il Penseroso*. L. 128.

18
Never does a wilder song
Steal the breezy lyre along,
When the wind in odors dying,
Wooes it with enamor'd sighing.
MOORE—*To Rosa.*

19
Loud wind, strong wind, sweeping o'er the mountains,
Fresh wind, free wind, blowing from the sea,
Pour forth thy vials like streams from airy mountains,
Draughts of life to me.
D. M. MULOCK—*North Wind.*

20
When the stormy winds do blow.
MARTIN PARKER—*Ye Gentlemen of England.*
(See also CAMPBELL)

21
Cum ventis litigare.
To strive with the winds.
PETRONIUS ARBITER. 83.

22
Who walketh upon the wings of the wind.
Psalms. CIV. 3.

23
And the South Wind—he was dressed
With a ribbon round his breast
That floated, flapped, and fluttered
In a riotous unrest
And a drapery of mist
From the shoulder to the wrist
Floating backward with the motion
Of the waving hand he kissed.
JAMES WHITCOMB RILEY—*The South Wind and the Sun.*

24
A young man who had been troubling society with impalpable doctrines of a new civilization which he called "the Kingdom of Heaven" had been put out of the way; and I can imagine that believer in material power murmuring as he went homeward, "it will all blow over now." Yes. The wind from the Kingdom of Heaven has blown over the world, and shall blow for centuries yet.
GEORGE W. RUSSELL—*The Economics of Ireland*. P. 23.

25
O the wind is a faun in the spring time
When the ways are green for the tread of the May!
List! hark his lay!
Whist! mark his play!
T-r-r-r-l!
Hear how gay!
CLINTON SCOLLARD—*The Wind.*

1
Take a straw and throw it up into the air, you may see by that which way the wind is.
JOHN SELDEN—*Table Talk. Libels.*

2
What wind blew you hither, Pistol?
Not the ill wind which blows no man to good.
Henry IV. Pt. II. Act V. Sc. 3. L. 89.
(See also HEYWOOD)

3
Ill blows the wind that profits nobody.
Henry VI. Pt. III. Act II. Sc. 5. L. 55.

4
O wild West Wind, thou breath of Autumn's being,
Thou, from whose unseen presence the leaves dead
Are driven, like ghosts from an enchanter fleeing,
Yellow, and black, and pale, and hectic red,
Pestilence-stricken multitudes.
SHELLEY—*Ode to the West Wind.* Pt. I.

5
O wind,
If Winter comes, can Spring be far behind?
SHELLEY—*Ode to the West Wind.* Pt. V.

6
Cease, rude Boreas! blustering railer!
G. A. STEVENS—*The Storm.*
(See also BANCKS)

7
There are, indeed, few merrier spectacles than that of many windmills bickering together in a fresh breeze over a woody country; their halting alacrity of movement, their pleasant business, making bread all day with uncouth gesticulation; their air, gigantically human, as of a creature half alive, put a spirit of romance into the tamest landscape.
STEVENSON—*Foreigner at Home.*

8
Emblem of man, who, after all his moaning
And strain of dire immeasurable strife,
Has yet this consolation, all atoning—
Life, as a windmill, grinds the bread of Life.
DE TABLEY—*The Windmill.*

9
Sweet and low, sweet and low,
Wind of the western sea,
Low, low, breathe and blow,
Wind of the western sea!
TENNYSON—*Princess.* Song. End of Pt. II.

10
A fresher Gale
Begins to wave the wood, and stir the stream,
Sweeping with shadowy gust the fields of corn;
While the Quail clamors for his running mate.
THOMSON—*Seasons. Summer.* L. 1,655.

11
Yet true it is as cow chews cud,
And trees at spring do yield forth bud,
Except wind stands as never it stood,
It is an ill wind turns none to good.
TUSSER—*Five Hundred Points of Good Husbandrie. Description of the Properties of Winds.* Ch. XII.
(See also HEYWOOD)

12
I dropped my pen; and listened to the wind
That sang of trees uptorn and vessels tost;
A midnight harmony and wholly lost
To the general sense of men by chains confined
Of business, care, or pleasure,—or resigned
To timely sleep.
WORDSWORTH—*Sonnet.* Composed while the author was engaged in writing a tract occasioned by the Convention of Cintra.

WINDFLOWER

Anemone

13
Or, bide thou where the poppy blows
With windflowers frail and fair.
BRYANT—*The Arctic Lover.*

14
The little windflower, whose just opened eye
Is blue as the spring heaven it gazes at.
BRYANT—*A Winter Piece.*

15
The starry, fragile windflower,
Poised above in airy grace,
Virgin white, suffused with blushes,
Shyly droops her lovely face.
ELAINE GOODALE—*The First Flowers.*

16
Thou lookest up with meek, confiding eye
Upon the clouded smile of April's face,
Unharmed though Winter stands uncertain by,
Eyeing with jealous glance each opening grace.
JONES VERY—*The Windflower.*

WINE AND SPIRITS (See also DRINKING)

17
I hang no ivie out to sell my wine;
The nectar of good wits will sell itself.
ALLOT—*England's Parnassus. Sonnet to the Reader.*
(See also LYLY, SYRUS)

18
Firm and erect the Caledonian stood;
Sound was his mutton, and his claret good;
"Let him drink port!" the English statesman cried:
He drank the poison, and his spirit died.
Anon. In DODD's *Epigrammatists.* (1870)

19
Old Simon the cellarer keeps a rare store
Of Malmsey and Malvoisie.
W. A. BELLAMY—*Simon the Cellarer.*

20
John Barleycorn was a hero bold,
Of noble enterprise,
For if you do but taste his blood,
'Twill make your courage rise,
Twill make a man forget his wo;
'Twill heighten all his joy.
BURNS—*John Barleycorn.* St. 13.

21
So Noah, when he anchor'd safe on
The mountain's top, his lofty haven,
And all the passengers he bore
Were on the new world set ashore,
He made it next his chief design
To plant and propagate a vine,
Which since has overwhelm'd and drown'd
Far greater numbers, on dry ground,
Of wretched mankind, one by one,
Than all the flood before had done.
BUTLER—*Satire Upon Drunkenness.* L. 105.

22
Few things surpass old wine; and they may preach
Who please, the more because they preach in vain,—

Let us have wine and women, mirth and laughter,
Sermons and soda-water the day after.
BYRON—*Don Juan*. Canto II. St. 178.

1
Which cheers the sad, revives the old, inspires
The young, makes Weariness forget his toil,
And Fear her danger; opens a new world
When this, the present, palls.
BYRON—*Sardanapalus*. Act I. Sc. 1.

2
Sweet is old wine in bottles, ale in barrels.
BYRON—*Sweet Things*. St. 5.

3
Sing! Who sings
To her who weareth a hundred rings?
Ah, who is this lady fine?
The Vine, boys, the Vine!
The mother of the mighty Wine,
A roamer is she
O'er wall and tree
And sometimes very good company.
BARRY CORNWALL—*A Bacchanalian Song*.

4 Ten thousand casks,
Forever dribbling out their base contents,
Touch'd by the Midas finger of the state,
Bleed gold for ministers to sport away.
Drink, and be mad then; 'tis your country bids!
COWPER—*The Task*. Bk. IV. L. 504.

5
The conscious water saw its God and blushed.
CRASHAW—*Translation of His Own Epigram on the Miracle of Cana. St. John's Gospel.* Ch. II.
(See also CRASHAW under MIRACLES)

6
"It wasn't the wine," murmured Mr. Snodgrass in a broken voice, "it was the salmon."
DICKENS—*Pickwick Papers*. Ch. VIII.

7
When asked what wines he liked to drink he replied, "That which belongs to another."
DIOGENES LAERTIUS — *Lives and Opinions of Eminent Philosophers. Diogenes.* VI. YONGE's trans.

8
Bring me wine, but wine which never grew
In the belly of the grape,
Or grew on vine whose tap-roots, reaching through
Under the Andes to the Cape,
Suffered no savor of the earth to escape.
EMERSON—*Bacchus*. St. 1.

9
From wine what sudden friendship springs?
GAY—*Fables*. Pt. II. Fable 6.

10
Let schoolmasters puzzle their brain,
With grammar, and nonsense, and learning;
Good liquor, I stoutly maintain,
Gives genius a better discerning.
GOLDSMITH—*She Stoops to Conquer*. Act I. Sc. 1. *Song*.

11
Call things by their right names * * * Glass of brandy and water! That is the current, but not the appropriate name; ask for *a glass of liquid fire and distilled damnation*.
ROBERT HALL. GREGORY'S *Life of Hall*. Vol. I. P. 59.

12
The wine in the bottle does not quench thirst.
HERBERT—*Jacula Prudentum*.

13
Wine makes all sorts of creatures at table.
HERBERT—*Jacula Prudentum*.

14
You cannot know wine by the barrel.
HERBERT—*Jacula Prudentum*.

15
Sparkling and bright, in liquid light,
Does the wine our goblets gleam in;
With hue as red as the rosy bed
Which a bee would choose to dream in.
CHARLES FENNO HOFFMAN—*Sparkling and Bright*.

16
And wine can of their wits the wise beguile,
Make the sage frolic, and the serious smile.
HOMER—*Odyssey*. Bk. XIV. L. 520. POPE'S trans.

17
Nunc vino pellite curas.
Now drown care in wine.
HORACE—*Carmina*. I. 7. 32.

18
Vino diffugiunt mordaces curæ.
By wine eating cares are put to flight.
Adapted from HORACE—*Carmina*. I. 18. 4; and 7. 31.

19
Quis post vina gravem militiam aut pauperiem crepat?
Who prates of war or want after his wine?
HORACE—*Carmina*. I. 18. 5.

20
Spes donare novas largus, amaraque
Curarum eluere efficax.
Mighty to inspire new hopes, and able to drown the bitterness of cares.
HORACE—*Carmina*. IV. 12. 19.

21
Fœcundi calices quem non fecere disertum.
Whom has not the inspiring bowl made eloquent.
HORACE—*Epistles*. I. 5. 19.

22
As for the brandy, "nothing extenuate"; and the water, put nought in in malice.
DOUGLAS JERROLD—*Jerrold's Wit. Shakespeare Grog*.

23
Claret is the liquor for boys; port for men; but he who aspires to be a hero must drink brandy.
SAMUEL JOHNSON—*Boswell's Life of Johnson*. (1779)

24
But that which most doth take my muse and me,
Is a pure cup of rich Canary wine,
Which is the mermaid's now, but shall be mine.
BEN JONSON—*Epigram* CI.

25
Wine it is the milk of Venus,
And the poet's horse accounted:
Ply it and you all are mounted.
BEN JONSON. From lines over the door of the "*Apollo*."
Wine to the poet is a wingéd steed:
Those who drink water come but little speed.
From the Greek Anthology.
(See also MOORE)

1
Dance and Provençal song and sunburnt mirth!
Oh for a beaker full of the warm South,
Full of the true, the blushful Hippocrene!
With beaded bubbles winking at the brim,
And purple-stained mouth.
KEATS—*Ode to a Nightingale.*

2
There is a devil in every berry of the grape.
The Koran.

3 Filled with the wine
Of the vine
Benign
That flames so red in Sansavine.
LONGFELLOW—*Hyperion.* Ch. VIII. (Quoted.)

4
When flowing cups pass swiftly round
With no allaying Thames.
RICHARD LOVELACE—*To Althea from Prison.* II.
(See also CORIOLANUS)

5
Things of greatest profit are set forth with least price. Where the wine is neat there needeth no ivie bush.
LYLY—*Euphues.* A. 3.
(See also ALLOT)

6
The produce of the vineyards has not failed everywhere, Ovidius. The heavy rains have been productive. Coranus made up a hundred jars by means of the water.
MARTIAL—*Epigrams.* Bk. IX. Ep. 98.

7
Bacchus, that first from out the purple grape,
Crushed the sweet poison of misused wine.
MILTON—*Comus.* II. 46.

8
If with water you fill up your glasses,
You'll never write anything wise;
For wine is the horse of Parnassus,
Which hurries a bard to the skies.
MOORE.
(See also JONSON)

9
O Roman punch! O potent Curaçoa!
O Maraschino! Maraschino O!
Delicious drams! Why have you not the art
To kill this gnawing Book-worm in my heart?
MOORE—*Twopenny Post Bag.* See Appendix, Letter VII.

10
Better be jocund with the fruitful Grape
Than sadden after none, or bitter fruit.
OMAR KHAYYAM—*Rubaiyat.* FITZGERALD'S trans. St. 54.

11
The Grape that can with Logic absolute
The Two-and-Seventy jarring Sects confute:
The sovereign Alchemist that in a trice
Life's leaden metal into Gold transmute.
OMAR KHAYYAM—*Rubaiyat.* FITZGERALD'S trans. St. 59.

12
Vina paract animos, faciuntque coloribus aptos:
Cura fugit multo diluiturque mero.
Wine stimulates the mind and makes it quick with heat; care flees and is dissolved in much drink.
OVID—*Ars Amatoria.* Bk. I. 237.

13
Magnum hoc vitium vino est,
Pedes captat primum; luctator dolosu est.
This is the great evil in wine, it first seizes the feet; it is a cunning wrestler.
PLAUTUS—*Pseudolus.* Act V. 1. 5.

14
It has become quite a common proverb that in wine there is truth.
PLINY the Elder—*Natural History.* Bk. XIV. Sec. XIV.

15
In proverbium cessit, sapientiam vino adumbrari.
It has passed into a proverb, that wisdom is overshadowed by wine.
PLINY the Elder—*Historia Naturalis.* XXIII. 23. 1.

16
Wine is a mocker, strong drink is raging.
Proverbs. XX. 1.

17
Look not thou upon the wine when it is red, when it giveth his colour in the cup; . . . at the last it biteth like a serpent, and stingeth like an adder.
Proverbs. XXIII. 31. 32.

18
Wine that maketh glad the heart of man.
Psalms. CIV. 15.

19
We care not for money, riches, nor wealth;
Old sack is our money, old sack is our wealth.
THOMAS RANDOLPH—*The Praise of Old Sack.*

20
Der Wein erfindet nichts, er schwatzt's nur aus.
Wine tells nothing, it only tattles.
SCHILLER—*Piccolomini.* IV. 7. 42.

21
Vinum incendit iram.
Wine kindles wrath.
SENECA—*De Ira.* Bk. II. 19.

22
A cup of hot wine with not a drop of allaying Tiber in 't.
Coriolanus. Act II. Sc. 1. L. 52.
(See also LOVELACE)

23
Give me a bowl of wine;
In this I bury all unkindness.
Julius Cæsar. Act IV. Sc. 3. L. 158.

24
O thou invisible spirit of wine, if thou hast no name to be known by, let us call thee devil!
Othello. Act II. Sc. 3. L. 283.

25
Come, come, good wine is a good familiar creature, if it be well used; exclaim no more against it.
Othello. Act II. Sc. 3. L. 313.

26 Give me a bowl of wine:
I have not that alacrity of spirit,
Nor cheer of mind, that I was wont to have.
Richard III. Act V. Sc. 3. L. 72.

27
Like the best wine, . . . that goeth down sweetly, causing the lips of those that are asleep to speak.
Song of Solomon. VII. 9.

1
Day and night my thoughts incline
To the blandishments of wine,
Jars were made to drain, I think;
Wine, I know, was made to drink.
R. H. STODDARD—*A Jar of Wine.*

2
You need not hang up the ivy branch over the wine that will sell.
SYRUS—*Maxim* 968.
(See also ALLOT)

3
When the wine's in, murder will out.
Talmud—Erubin 65.

4
Drink no longer water, but use a little wine for thy stomach's sake.
I Timothy. V. 23.

5
He has had a smack of every sort of wine, from humble port to Imperial Tokay.
REV. JAMES TOWNLEY—*High Life below Stairs.*

6
The hop for his profit I thus do exalt,
It strengtheneth drink, and it favoureth malt:
And being well brewed, long kept it will last,
And drawing abide—if you draw not too fast.
TUSSER—*Five Hundred Points of Good Husbandrie. A Lesson When and Where to Plant a Good Hop-Yard.* Ch. XLIII.

7
And must I wholly banish hence
These red and golden juices,
And pay my vows to Abstinence,
That pallidest of Muses?
WILLIAM WATSON—*To a Maiden who bade me shun Wine.*

WINTER

8
These Winter nights against my window-pane
Nature with busy pencil draws designs
Of ferns and blossoms and fine spray of pines,
Oak-leaf and acorn and fantastic vines,
Which she will make when summer comes again—
Quaint arabesques in argent, flat and cold,
Like curious Chinese etchings.
T. B. ALDRICH—*Frost-Work.*

9
O Winter! bar thine adamantine doors:
The north is thine; there hast thou built thy dark,
Deep-founded habitation. Shake not thy roofs,
Nor bend thy pillars with thine iron car.
WILLIAM BLAKE—*To Winter.*

10
When now, unsparing as the scourge of war,
Blasts follow blasts and groves dismantled roar;
Around their home the storm-pinched cattle lows,
No nourishment in frozen pasture grows;
Yet frozen pastures every morn resound
With fair abundance thund'ring to the ground.
BLOOMFIELD — *The Farmer's Boy. Winter.* St. 2.

11
Look! the massy trunks
Are cased in the pure crystal; each light spray,
Nodding and tinkling in the breath of heaven,
Is studded with its trembling water-drops,
That glimmer with an amethystine light.
BRYANT—*A Winter Piece.* L. 66.

12
Yet all how beautiful! Pillars of pearl
Propping the cliffs above, stalactites bright
From the ice roof depending; and beneath,
Grottoes and temples with their crystal spires
And gleaming columns radiant in the sun.
WM. HENRY BURLEIGH—*Winter.*

13
The tendinous part of the mind, so to speak, is more developed in winter; the fleshy, in summer. I should say winter had given the bone and sinew to literature, summer the tissues and the blood.
JOHN BURROUGHS—*The Snow-Walkers.*

14
The frost performs its secret ministry,
Unhelped by any wind.
COLERIDGE—*Frost at Midnight.* L. 1.

15
Every Fern is tucked and set,
'Neath coverlet,
Downy and soft and warm.
SUSAN COOLIDGE—*Time to Go.*

16
O Winter! ruler of the inverted year,
* * * *
I crown thee king of intimate delights,
Fireside enjoyments, home-born happiness,
And all the comforts that the lowly roof
Of undisturb'd Retirement, and the hours
Of long uninterrupted evening, know.
COWPER—*Task.* Bk. IV. L. 120.
(See also THOMSON)

17
On a lone winter evening, when the frost
Has wrought a silence.
KEATS—*On the Grasshopper and Cricket.*

18
His breath like silver arrows pierced the air,
The naked earth crouched shuddering at his feet,
His finger on all flowing waters sweet
Forbidding lay—motion nor sound was there:—
Nature was frozen dead,—and still and slow,
A winding sheet fell o'er her body fair,
Flaky and soft, from his wide wings of snow.
FRANCES ANNE KEMBLE—*Winter.* L. 9.

19
Every winter,
When the great sun has turned his face away,
The earth goes down into a vale of grief,
And fasts, and weeps, and shrouds herself in sables,
Leaving her wedding-garlands to decay—
Then leaps in spring to his returning kisses.
CHARLES KINGSLEY—*Saint's Tragedy.* Act III. Sc. 1.

20
Up rose the wild old winter-king,
And shook his beard of snow;
"I hear the first young hare-bell ring,
'Tis time for me to go!
Northward o'er the icy rocks,
Northward o'er the sea,
My daughter comes with sunny locks:
This land's too warm for me!"
LELAND—*Spring.*

21
But see, Orion sheds unwholesome dews;
Arise, the pines a noxious shade diffuse;
Sharp Boreas blows, and nature feels decay,
Time conquers all, and we must time obey.
POPE—*Ode to Winter.* L. 85.

1
Wintry boughs against a wintry sky;
Yet the sky is partly blue
And the clouds are partly bright.
Who can tell but sap is mounting high,
Out of sight,
Ready to burst through?
CHRISTINA G. ROSSETTI—*Spring signals to Winter.*

2
Here feel we but the penalty of Adam,
The seasons' difference, as the icy fang
And churlish chiding of the winter's wind,
Which, when it bites and blows upon my body,
Even till I shrink with cold, I smile and say,
"This is no flattery."
As You Like It. Act II. Sc. 1. L. 5.

3
Winter's not gone yet, if the wild-geese fly that way.
King Lear. Act II. Sc. 4. L. 46.

4
When icicles hang by the wall,
And Dick, the shepherd, blows his nail,
And Tom bears logs into the hall,
And milk comes frozen home in pail,
When blood is nipp'd and ways be foul,
Then nightly sings the staring owl,
Tu-whit;
Tu-who, a merry note,
While greasy Joan doth keel the pot.
Love's Labour's Lost. Act V. Sc. 2. L. 922.

5
In winter, when the dismal rain
Came down in slanting lines,
And Wind, that grand old harper, smote
His thunder-harp of pines.
ALEXANDER SMITH—*A Life Drama.* Sc. 2.

6
Lastly came Winter cloathed all in frize,
Chattering his teeth for cold that did him chill;
Whilst on his hoary beard his breath did freese,
And the dull drops, that from his purpled bill
As from a limebeck did adown distill:
In his right hand a tipped staffe he held,
With which his feeble steps he stayed still;
For he was faint with cold, and weak with eld;
That scarce his loosed limbes he hable was to weld.
SPENSER—*Faerie Queene.* Canto VII. *Legend of Constancie.* St. 31.

7
Under the snowdrifts the blossoms are sleeping,
Dreaming their dreams of sunshine and June,
Down in the hush of their quiet they're keeping
Trills from the throstle's wild summer-sung tune.
HARRIET PRESCOTT SPOFFORD—*Under the Snowdrifts.*

8
See, Winter comes, to rule the varied year,
Sullen and sad, with all his rising train;
Vapors, and Clouds, and Storms.
THOMSON—*Seasons. Winter.* L. 1.
(See also COWPER)

9
Through the hush'd air the whitening Shower descends,
At first thin wavering; till at last the Flakes
Fall broad, and wide, and fast, dimming the day
With a continual flow. The cherished Fields
Put on their winter-robe of purest white,
'Tis brightness all; save where the new Snow melts
Along the mazy current.
THOMSON—*Seasons. Winter.* L. 229.

10
Dread Winter spreads his latest glooms,
And reigns, tremendous, o'er the conquer'd Year.
How dead the vegetable kingdom lies!
How dumb the tuneful! Horror wide extends
His desolate domain.
THOMSON—*Seasons. Winter.* L. 1,024.

11
Make we here our camp of winter;
And, through sleet and snow,
Pitchy knot and beechen splinter
On our hearth shall glow.
Here, with mirth to lighten duty,
We shall lack alone
Woman's smile and girlhood's beauty,
Childhood's lisping tone.
WHITTIER—*Lumbermen.* St. 8.

12
What miracle of weird transforming
Is this wild work of frost and light,
This glimpse of glory infinite?
WHITTIER—*The Pageant.* St. 8.

13
Stern Winter loves a dirge-like sound.
WORDSWORTH—*On the Power of Sound.* St. 12.

WISDOM

14
To speak as the common people do, to think as wise men do.
ROGER ASCHAM—*Dedication to All the Gentlemen and Yeomen of England.*

15
A wise man is out of the reach of fortune.
SIR THOS. BROWNE—*Religio Medici.* Quoted as "That insolent paradox."
(See also JUVENAL)

16
The wisdom of our ancestors.
BURKE—*Observations on a Late Publication on the Present State of the Nation.* Vol. I. P. 516. Also in the Discussion on the Traitorous Correspondence Bill. (1793) CICERO—*De Legibus.* II. 2. 3. LORD ELDON—*On Sir Samuel Romilly's Bill.* 1815. SYDNEY SMITH—*Plymley's Letters.* Letter V. BACON said to be first user of the phrase. Ascribed also to SIR WILLIAM GRANT, in JENNINGS' *Anecdotal History of Parliament.*

17
But these are foolish things to all the wise,
And I love wisdom more than she loves me;
My tendency is to philosophise
On most things, from a tyrant to a tree;
But still the spouseless virgin *Knowledge* flies,
What are we? and whence come we? what shall be
Our *ultimate* existence? What's our present?
Are questions answerless, and yet incessant.
BYRON—*Don Juan.* Canto VI. St. 63.

18
Wise men learn more from fools than fools from the wise.
CATO. In PLUTARCH'S *Life of Cato.*
(See also TENNYSON)

1
Wisdom and goodness are twin-born, one heart
Must hold both sisters, never seen apart.
COWPER—*Expostulation*. L. 634.

2
Some people are more nice than wise.
COWPER—*Mutual Forbearance*.

3
But they whom truth and wisdom lead
Can gather honey from a weed.
COWPER—*Pine-Apple and Bee*. L. 35.

4
It seems the part of wisdom.
COWPER—*Task*. Bk. IV. L. 336.

5
Knowledge is proud that he has learn'd so much;
Wisdom is humble that he knows no more.
COWPER—*Task*. Bk. VI. L. 96.

6
Who are a little wise the best fools be.
DONNE—*The Triple Fool*.

7
In much wisdom is much grief.
Ecclesiastes. I. 18.

8
The words of the wise are as goads.
Ecclesiastes. XII. 11.

9
Man thinks
Brutes have no wisdom, since they know not his:
Can we divine their world?
GEORGE ELIOT—*The Spanish Gypsy*. Bk. II.

10
Nequicquam sapere sapientem, qui ipse sibi prodesse non quiret.
The wise man is wise in vain who cannot be wise to his own advantage.
ENNIUS. I. Quoted by CICERO—*De Officii*. 3. 15.

11
No one could be so wise as Thurlow looked.
CHARLES JAMES FOX. See CAMPBELL'S *Lives of the Lord Chancellors*. Vol. V. P. 661; also 551. Said also of WEBSTER.

12
Some are weather-wise, some are otherwise.
BENJ. FRANKLIN—*Poor Richard*. (1735)

13
Die Weisheit ist nur in der Wahrheit.
Wisdom is only found in truth.
GOETHE—*Sprüche in Prosa*. III.

14
Wisdom makes but a slow defence against trouble, though at last a sure one.
GOLDSMITH—*Vicar of Wakefield*. Ch. XXI.

15
The heart is wiser than the intellect.
J. G. HOLLAND—*Kathrina*. Pt. II. St. 9.

16
Chiefs who no more in bloody fights engage,
But, wise through time, and narrative with age,
In summer-days like grasshoppers rejoice,
A bloodless race, that send a feeble voice.
HOMER—*Iliad*. Bk. III. L. 199. POPE'S trans.

17
For never, never, wicked man was wise.
HOMER—*Odyssey*. Bk. II. L. 320. POPE'S trans.

18
In youth and beauty wisdom is but rare!
HOMER—*Odyssey*. Bk. VII. L. 379. POPE'S trans.

19
How prone to doubt, how cautious are the wise!
HOMER—*Odyssey*. Bk. XIII. L. 375. POPE'S trans.

20
Utiliumque sagax rerum et divina futuri.
Sagacious in making useful discoveries.
HORACE—*Ars Poetica*. 218.

21
Sapere aude.
Dare to be wise.
HORACE—*Epistles*. I. 2. 40.

22
Quis nam igitur liber? Sapiens qui sibi imperiosus.
Who then is free? The wise man who can govern himself.
HORACE—*Satires*. II. 7. 83.

23
He taketh the wise in their own craftiness.
Job. V. 13.

24
Wisdom shall die with you.
Job. XII. 2.

25
The price of wisdom is above rubies.
Job. XXVIII. 18.

26
Days should speak, and multitude of years should teach wisdom.
Job. XXXII. 7.

27
Great men are not always wise.
Job. XXXII. 9.

28
Away, thou strange justifier of thyself, to be wiser than thou wert, by the event.
BEN JONSON—*Silent Woman*. Act II. Sc. 2.
Wise after the event.
Quoted by SIR GEORGE STAUNTON in speech replying to SIR JAMES GRAHAM'S resolution condemning the Melbourne ministry, House of Commons, April 7, 1840. HOMER—*Iliad*. XVII. 32. HESIOD—*Works and Days*. V. 79 and 202. SOPHOCLES—*Antigone*. V. 1270; and 1350. FABIUS—*Liv.* XXII. 39. ERASMUS—*Epitome Chiliadum Adagiorum*. (Ed. 1528) P. 55; 295.

29
Victrix fortunæ sapientia.
Wisdom is the conqueror of fortune.
JUVENAL—*Satires*. XIII. 20.
(See also BROWNE)

30
Il est plus aisé d'être sage pour les autres, que pour soi-même.
It is easier to be wise for others than for ourselves.
LA ROCHEFOUCAULD—*Maximes*.

31
Ripe in wisdom was he, but patient, and simple, and childlike.
LONGFELLOW—*Evangeline*. Pt. I. III. L. 11.

32
Quisquis plus justo non sapit, ille sapit.
Whoever is not too wise is wise.
MARTIAL—*Epigrammata*. XIV. 10. 2.

1
Be wise;
Soar not too high to fall; but stoop to rise.
MASSINGER—*Duke of Milan.* Act I. Sc. 2. L. 45.
(See also WORDSWORTH)

2
Be ye therefore wise as serpents, and harmless as doves.
Matthew. X. 16.

3
Wisdom is justified of her children.
Matthew. XI. 19; *Luke.* VII. 35.

4
A little too wise they say do ne'er live long.
THOS. MIDDLETON—*The Phenix.* Act I. Sc. 1.

5
Though wisdom wake, suspicion sleeps
At wisdom's gate, and to simplicity
Resigns her charge, while goodness thinks no ill
Where no ill seems.
MILTON—*Paradise Lost.* Bk. III. L. 686.

6
But to know
That which before us lies in daily life,
Is the prime wisdom.
MILTON—*Paradise Lost.* Bk. VIII. L. 192.

7
Socrates * * *
Whom, well inspir'd, the oracle pronounc'd
Wisest of men.
MILTON—*Paradise Regained.* Bk. IV. L. 274.

8
Il est bon de frotter et limer notre cervelle contre celle d'autrui.
It is good to rub and polish our brain against that of others.
MONTAIGNE—*Essays.* Bk. I. Ch. XXIV.

9
The most manifest sign of wisdom is a continual cheerfulness: her state is like that of things in the regions above the moon, always clear and serene.
MONTAIGNE—*Essays.* Bk. I. Ch. XXV.

10
Le sage vit tant qu'il doibt, non pas tant qu'il peut.
A wise man sees as much as he ought, not as much as he can.
MONTAIGNE—*Essays.* Bk. II. Ch. III.

11
Qui aura esté une fois bien fol ne sera nulle aultre fois bien sage.
He who has once been very foolish will at no other time be very wise.
MONTAIGNE—*Essays.* Bk. III. Ch. VI.

12
Seven wise men on an old black settle,
Seven wise men of the Mermaid Inn,
Ringing blades of the one right metal,
What is the best that a blade can win?
ALFRED NOYES—*Tales of The Mermaid Tavern.* II.

13
Some men never spake a wise word, yet doe wisely; some on the other side doe never a wise deed, and yet speake wisely.
SIR THOMAS OVERBURY—*Crumms fal'n from King James Talk.* In *Works.*
(See also ROCHESTER under ROYALTY)

14
When swelling buds their od'rous foliage shed,
And gently harden into fruit, the wise
Spare not the little offsprings, if they grow
Redundant.
JOHN PHILIPS—*Cider.* Bk. I.

15
Feliciter sapit qui alieno periculo sapit.
He gains wisdom in a happy way, who gains it by another's experience.
PLAUTUS—*Mercator.* IV. 7. 40.

16
Nemo solus satis sapit.
No man is wise enough by himself.
PLAUTUS—*Miles Gloriosus.* III. 3. 12.

17
Nemo mortalium omnibus horis sapit.
No one is wise at all times.
PLINY the Elder—*Historia Naturalis.* VII. 41. 2.

18
Tell (for you can) what is it to be wise?
'Tis but to know how little can be known,
To see all other's faults, and feel our own.
POPE—*Essay on Man.* Ep. IV. L. 260.

19
Wisdom crieth without; she uttereth her voice in the street.
Proverbs. I. 20.

20
Wisdom is the principal thing; therefore get wisdom; and with all thy getting get understanding.
Proverbs. IV. 7.

21
Wisdom is better than rubies.
Proverbs. VIII. 11.

22
Be wisely worldly, but not worldly wise.
QUARLES—*Emblems.* Bk. II. Em. 2.

23
Ce n'est pas être sage
D'être plus sage qu'il ne le faut.
It is not wise to be wiser than is necessary.
QUINAULT—*Armide.*

24
Afin que ne semblons es Atheniens, qui ne consultoient jamais sinon après le cas faict.
So that we may not be like the Athenians, who never consulted except after the event done.
RABELAIS—*Pantagruel.* Ch. XXIV.

25
The power is yours, but not the sight;
You see not upon what you tread;
You have the ages for your guide,
But not the wisdom to be led.
EDWIN ARLINGTON ROBINSON—*Cassandra.*

26
Wouldst thou wisely, and with pleasure,
Pass the days of life's short measure,
From the slow one counsel take,
But a tool of him ne'er make;
Ne'er as friend the swift one know,
Nor the constant one as foe.
SCHILLER—*Proverbs of Confucius.* E. A. BOWRING's trans.

27
The Italian seemes wise, and is wise; the Spaniard seemes wise, and is a foole; the French

seemes a foole, and is wise; and the English seemes a foole and is a foole.

Quoted as a common proverb by THOS. SCOT, in *The Highwaies of God and the King*. P. 8. (1623)

1
Wisdom does not show itself so much in precept as in life—in a firmness of mind and mastery of appetite. It teaches us to do, as well as to talk; and to make our actions and words all of a color.

SENECA—*Epistles*. XX.

2
Nulli sapere casu obtigit.
No man was ever wise by chance.

SENECA—*Epistolæ Ad Lucilium*. LXXVI.

3
Melius in malis sapimus, secunda rectum auferunt.

We become wiser by adversity; prosperity destroys our appreciation of the right.

SENECA—*Epistolæ Ad Lucilium*. XCIV.

4
Full oft we see
Cold wisdom waiting on superfluous folly.

All's Well That Ends Well. Act I. Sc. 1. L. 115.

5
Wisdom and fortune combating together,
If that the former dare but what it can,
No chance may shake it.

Antony and Cleopatra. Act III. Sc. 13. L. 79.

6
Thou shouldst not have been old till thou hadst been wise.

King Lear. Act I. Sc. 5. L. 48.

7
To that dauntless temper of his mind,
He hath a wisdom that doth guide his valour
To act in safety.

Macbeth. Act III. Sc. 1. L. 52.

8
Well, God give them wisdom that have it; and those that are fools, let them use their talents.

Twelfth Night. Act I. Sc. 5. L. 14.

9
As for me, all I know is that I know nothing.

SOCRATES. In PLATO — *Phaedrus*. Sec. CCXXXV.

10
A short saying oft contains much wisdom.

SOPHOCLES—*Aletes*. Frag. 99.

11
Happy those
Who in the after-days shall live, when Time
Hath spoken, and the multitude of years
Taught wisdom to mankind!

SOUTHEY—*Joan of Arc*. Bk. I.

(See also JOB)

12
The doorstep to the temple of wisdom is a knowledge of our own ignorance.

SPURGEON—*Gleanings among the Sheaves. The First Lesson.*

13
By Wisdom wealth is won;
But riches purchased wisdom yet for none.

BAYARD TAYLOR—*The Wisdom of Ali*.

14
"The Prophet's words were true;
The mouth of Ali is the golden door
Of Wisdom."
When his friends to Ali bore
These words, he smiled and said: "And should they ask
The same until my dying day, the task
Were easy; for the stream from Wisdom's well,
Which God supplies, is inexhaustible."

BAYARD TAYLOR—*The Wisdom of Ali*.

15
'Tis held that sorrow makes us wise.

TENNYSON—*In Memoriam*. Pt. CVIII.

16
Nor is he the wisest man who never proved himself a fool.

TENNYSON—*Locksley Hall Sixty Years After*. St. 124.

17
Isthuc est sapere non quod ante pedes modo est
Videre sed etiam illa, quæ futura sunt
Prospicere.

True wisdom consists not in seeing what is immediately before our eyes, but in foreseeing what is to come.

TERENCE—*Adelphi*. III. 3. 32.

18
The children of this world are in their generation wiser than the children of light.

I Timothy. XVI. 8.

19
Wisdom alone is true ambition's aim
Wisdom the source of virtue, and of fame,
Obtained with labour, for mankind employed,
And then, when most you share it, best enjoyed.

W. WHITEHEAD—*On Nobility*.

20
Wisdom sits alone,
Topmost in heaven:—she is its light—its God;
And in the heart of man she sits as high—
Though grovelling eyes forget her oftentimes,
Seeing but this world's idols. The pure mind
Sees her forever: and in youth we come
Fill'd with her sainted ravishment, and kneel,
Worshipping God through her sweet altar fires,
And then is knowledge "good."

N. P. WILLIS—*The Scholar of Thibet. Ben Khorat*. Pt. II. L. 93.

21
Wisdom is the gray hair unto men, and an unspotted life is old age.

Wisdom of Solomon. IV. 8.

22
Wisdom is ofttimes nearer when we stoop
Than when we soar.

WORDSWORTH—*The Excursion*. Bk. III. L. 232.

(See also MASSINGER)

23
And he is oft the wisest man
Who is not wise at all.

WORDSWORTH—*The Oak and the Broom*.

24
On every thorn, delightful wisdom grows,
In every rill a sweet instruction flows.

YOUNG—*Love of Fame*. Satire I. L. 249.

25
Be wise to-day; 'tis madness to defer;
Next day the fatal precedent will plead;
Thus on, till wisdom is push'd out of life.

YOUNG—*Night Thoughts*. Night I. L. 390.

1
Wisdom, though richer than Peruvian mines,
And sweeter than the sweet ambrosial hive,
What is she, but the means of *happiness?*
That unobtain'd, than folly more a fool.
YOUNG—*Night Thoughts*. Night II. L. 496.

2
The man of wisdom is the man of years.
YOUNG—*Night Thoughts*. Night V. L. 775.

3
But wisdom, awful wisdom! which inspects,
Discerns, compares, weighs, separates, infers,
Seizes the right, and holds it to the last.
YOUNG—*Night Thoughts*. Night VIII. L. 1,253.

4
Teach me my days to number, and apply
My trembling heart to wisdom.
YOUNG—*Night Thoughts*. Night IX. L. 1,312.

WISHES

5
"Man wants but little here below
Nor wants that little long,"
'Tis not with me exactly so;
But 'tis so in the song.
My wants are many, and, if told,
Would muster many a score;
And were each wish a mint of gold,
I still should long for more.
JOHN QUINCY ADAMS—*The Wants of Man*. (See also GOLDSMITH)

6
Every wish
Is like a prayer—with God.
E. B. BROWNING—*Aurora Leigh*. Bk. II.

7
O, that I were where I would be,
Then would I be where I am not;
For where I am I would not be,
And where I would be I can not.
QUILLER COUCH. Quoted in *Ship of Stars*. Ch. XII.

8
If a man could half his wishes he would double his Troubles.
BENJ. FRANKLIN—*Poor Richard*. (1752)

9
Was man in der Jugend wünscht, hat man im Alter die Fülle.
What one has wished for in youth, in old age one has in abundance.
GOETHE—*Wahrheit und Dichtung*. Motto to Part II.

10
Man wants but little here below,
Nor wants that little long.
GOLDSMITH—*The Hermit*. St. 8.
(See also ADAMS, HOLMES, YOUNG)

11
And the evil wish is most evil to the wisher.
HESIOD—*Works and Days*. V. 264.

12
Little I ask; my wants are few;
I only wish a hut of stone
(A *very plain* brown stone will do),
That I may call my own;
And close at hand is such a one
In yonder street that fronts the sun.
HOLMES—*Contentment*.

13
With all thy sober charms possest,
Whose wishes never learnt to stray.
LANGHORNE—*Poems*. II. P. 123. (PARK'S Ed.)

14
I wish I knew the good of wishing.
HENRY S. LEIGH—*Wishing*.

15
You pursue, I fly; you fly, I pursue; such is my humor. What you wish, Dondymus, I do not wish, what you do not wish, I do.
MARTIAL—*Epigrams*. Bk. V. Ep. 83.

16
Vous l'avez voulu, vous l'avez voulu, George Dandin, vous l'avez voulu.
You have wished it so, you have wished it so, George Dandin, you have wished it so.
MOLIÈRE—*George Dandin*. Act I. Sc. 9.

17
Wert thou all that I wish thee, great, glorious and free,
First flower of the earth, and first gem of the sea.
MOORE—*Remember Thee*.

18
If I live to grow old, as I find I go down,
Let this be my fate in a country town;
May I have a warm house, with a stone at my gate,
And a cleanly young girl to rub my bald pate.
May I govern my passions with an absolute sway,
Grow wiser and better as my strength wears away,
Without gout or stone, by a gentle decay.
WALTER POPE—*The Old Man's Wish*. First appeared in *A Collection of Thirty-one Songs*. (1685)

19
Thy wish was father, Harry, to that thought:
I stay too long by thee, I weary thee.
Henry IV. Pt. II. Act IV. Sc. 5. L. 93.
Thy wish was father to that thought.
Idea found in ARRIAN—*Anabasis*. I. Ch. VII. ÆSCHYLUS—*Prometh. Vinct*. I. 928. ACHILLES TATIUS—*De Leucippes*. Bk. VI. 17. HELIODORUS. Bk. VIII. CÆSAR—*De Bello Gallico*. III. 18. QUINTILIAN—*Institutes*. Bk. VI. Ch. II. Sec. V. (Ed. BONNELL.) (1861)

20
Where nothing wants that want itself doth seek.
Love's Labour's Lost. Act IV. Sc. 3. L. 237.

21
I've often wished that I had clear,
For life, six hundred pounds a year,
A handsome house to lodge a friend,
A river at my garden's end,
A terrace walk, and half a rood
Of land, set out to plant a wood.
SWIFT—*Imitation of Horace*. Bk. II. Satire 6.

22
Quoniam id fieri quod vis non potest
Id velis quod possis.
As you can not do what you wish, you should wish what you can do.
TERENCE—*Andria*. II. 1. 6.

23
On ne peut désirer ce qu'on ne connaît pas.
We cannot wish for that we know not.
VOLTAIRE—*Zaïre*. I. 1.

1
Wishers and woulders be small householders.
Vulgaria Stambrigi. Pub. by WYNKYN DE WORDE. Early in the XVI. Cent.

2
What most we wish, with ease we fancy near.
YOUNG—*Love of Fame.* III.

3
Wishing, of all employments is the worst.
YOUNG—*Night Thoughts.* Night IV. L. 71.

4
He calls his wish, it comes; he sends it back,
And says he called another; that arrives,
Meets the same welcome; yet he still calls on;
Till one calls him, who varies not his call,
But holds him fast, in chains of darkness bound,
Till Nature dies, and judgment sets him free;
A freedom far less welcome than this chain.
YOUNG—*Night Thoughts.* Night IV. Lines near end.

5
Man wants but little, nor that little long;
How soon must he resign his very dust,
Which frugal nature lent him for an hour!
YOUNG—*Night Thoughts.* Night IV. L. 118.
(See also GOLDSMITH)

6
What folly can be ranker. Like our shadows,
Our wishes lengthen as our sun declines.
YOUNG—*Night Thoughts.* Night V. L. 661.

WIT

7
An ounce of wit is worth a pound of sorrow.
RICHARD BAXTER—*Of Self-Denial.*

8
Que les gens d'esprit sont bêtes.
What silly people wits are!
BEAUMARCHAIS—*Barbier de Séville.* I. 1.

9
Good wits will jump.
BUCKINGHAM—*The Chances.* Act IV. Sc. 1. JOHN BYROM—*The Winners.* L. 39. CERVANTES—*Don Quixote.* Pt. II. Ch. XXXVIII. STERNE—*Tristram Shandy.*

10
Aristotle said * * * melancholy men of all others are most witty.
BURTON—*Anatomy of Melancholy.* Pt. I. Sec. III. Memb. 1. Subsect. 3.

11
We grant, although he had much wit,
H' was very shy of using it,
As being loth to wear it out,
And therefore bore it not about;
Unless on holy days or so,
As men their best apparel do.
BUTLER—*Hudibras.* Pt. I. Canto I. L. 45.

12
Great wits and valours, like great states,
Do sometimes sink with their own weights.
BUTLER—*Hudibras.* Pt. II. Canto I. L. 269.

13
Votre esprit en donne aux autres.
Your wit makes others witty.
CATHERINE II—*Letter to Voltaire.*
(See also HENRY IV)

14
Don't put too fine a point to your wit for fear it should get blunted.
CERVANTES—*The Little Gypsy.*

15
I am a fool, I know it; and yet, Heaven help me, I'm poor enough to be a wit.
CONGREVE—*Love for Love.* Act I. Sc. 1.

16
His wit invites you by his looks to come,
But when you knock, it never is at home.
COWPER—*Conversation.* L. 303.
(See also POPE)

17
Wit, now and then, struck smartly, shows a spark.
COWPER—*Table Talk.* L. 665.

18
Great wits are sure to madness near allied,
And thin partitions do their bounds divide.
DRYDEN—*Absalom and Achitophel.* Pt. I. L. 163.
(See also BURNS under BLISS, and POPE under SENSE)

19
Ev'n wit's a burthen, when it talks too long.
DRYDEN—*Sixth Satire of Juvenal.* L. 573.

20
Wit will shine
Through the harsh cadence of a rugged line.
DRYDEN—*To the Memory of Mr. Oldham.*

21
Their heads sometimes so little that there is no room for wit; sometimes so long, that there is no wit for so much room.
FULLER—*The Holy and Profane States.* Bk. IV. Ch. XII. *Of Natural Fools.* Maxim I.

22
Mit wenig Witz und viel Behagen
Dreht jeder sich im engen Zirkeltanz
Wie junge Katzen mit dem Schwanz.
With little wit and ease to suit them,
They whirl in narrow circling trails,
Like kittens playing with their tails.
GOETHE—*Faust.* I. 5. 94.

23
As a wit, if not first, in the very first line.
GOLDSMITH—*Retaliation.* L. 96.

24
Les beaux esprits lernen einander durch dergleichen rencontre erkennen.
It is by such encounters that wits come to know each other.
ANDREAS GRYPHIUS—*Horribilicribfax.* Act IV. Sc. 7. VOLTAIRE—*Letter to Thieriot,* June 30, 1760, used the expression. See BÜCHMANN—*Geflügelte Worte.* Ed. 10. P. 123.
(See also HENRY IV)

25
Wit is the salt of conversation, not the food.
HAZLITT—*Lectures on the English Comic Writers.* Lecture I.

26
Wit's an unruly engine, wildly striking
Sometimes a friend, sometimes the engineer:
Hast thou the knack? pamper it not with liking;
But if thou want it, buy it not too deare
Many affecting wit beyond their power,
Have got to be a deare fool for an houre.
HERBERT—*Temple.* *Church Porch.* St. 41.

27
At our wittes end.
HEYWOOD—*Proverbs.* Pt. I. Ch. VIII. *Psalms* CVII. 27. ("Their wits.")

1
Wit is the clash and reconcilement of incongruities; the meeting of extremes round a corner.
LEIGH HUNT—*Wit and Humour.*

2
Wit, like money, bears an extra value when rung down immediately it is wanted. Men pay severely who require credit.
DOUGLAS JERROLD—*Specimens of Jerrold's Wit. Wit.*

3
This man [Chesterfield] I thought had been a lord among wits; but I find he is only a wit among lords.
SAMUEL JOHNSON—*Boswell's Life of Johnson.* (1754)
(See also POPE, TWELFTH NIGHT, also COWPER under FOLLY)

4
Je n'ai jamais d'esprit qu'au bas de l'escalier.
I never have wit until I am below stairs.
LA BRUYÈRE, according to J. J. ROUSSEAU. Esprit de l'escalier, backstair wit, is credited to M. DE TREVILLE by PIERRE NICOLE. For use of this phrase see *The King's English.* P. 32. Note.

5
He must be a dull Fellow indeed, whom neither Love, Malice, nor Necessity, can inspire with Wit.
LA BRUYÈRE—*The Characters or Manners of the Present Age.* Ch. IV.

6
A man does not please long when he has only one species of wit.
LA ROCHEFOUCAULD—*Maxims.* No. 438.

7
A small degree of wit, accompanied by good sense, is less tiresome in the long run than a great amount of wit without it.
LA ROCHEFOUCAULD—*Maxims.* No. 529.

8
On peut dire que son esprit brille aux dépens de sa mémoire.
One may say that his wit shines at the expense of his memory.
LE SAGE—*Gil Blas.* III. XI. Of Carlos Alonso de la Ventoleria.

9
Medio de fonte leporum
Surgit amari aliquid quod in ipsis floribus angat.
In the midst of the fountain of wit there arises something bitter, which stings in the very flowers.
LUCRETIUS. IV. 1133.
(See also MOORE, TENNYSON)

10
Mother Wit. (Nature's mother wit.)
MARLOWE—*Prologue to Tamerlaine the Great.* Pt. I. MIDDLETON—*Your five Gallants.* Act I. Sc. 1. DRYDEN—*Ode to St. Cecilia.* SPENSER—*Faerie Queene.* Bk. IV. Canto X. St. 21. *Taming of the Shrew.* Act II. Sc. 1.

11
Have you summoned your wits from wool-gathering?
THOS. MIDDLETON—*The Family of Love.* Act V. Sc. 3.

12
Nul n'aura de l'esprit, hors nous et nos amis.
No one shall have wit save we and our friends.
MOLIÈRE—*Les Femmes Savantes.* III. 2.

13
L'impromptu est justement la pierre de touche de l'esprit.
Repartee is precisely the touchstone of the man of wit.
MOLIÈRE—*Les Précieuses Ridicules.* X.

14
La raillerie est un discours en faveur de son esprit contre son bon naturel.
Raillery is a mode of speaking in favor of one's wit at the expense of one's better nature.
MONTESQUIEU—*Pensées Diverses.*

15
Whose wit, in the combat, as gentle as bright,
Ne'er carried a heart-stain away on its blade.
MOORE—*Lines on the Death of Sheridan.* St. 11.
(See also LUCRETIUS)

16
Wit is the most rascally, contemptible, beggarly thing on the face of the earth.
MURPHY—*The Apprentice.*

17
Sal Atticum.
Attic wit.
PLINY—*Natural History.* 31. 7. 41.

18
A wit with dunces, and a dunce with wits.
POPE—*Dunciad.* Bk. IV. L. 92.
(See also JOHNSON)

19
You beat your pate, and fancy wit will come;
Knock as you please, there's nobody at home.
POPE—*Epigram.* Last phrase in DICKENS—*Nicholas Nickleby.*
(See also COWPER)

20
For wit and judgment often are at strife,
Though meant each other's aid, like man and wife.
POPE—*Essay on Criticism.* L. 82.

21
So modest plainness sets off sprightly wit,
For works may have more wit than does 'em good,
As bodies perish through excess of blood.
POPE—*Essay on Criticism.* L. 302.

22
How the wit brightens! how the style refines!
POPE—*Essay on Criticism.* L. 421.

23
If faith itself has different dresses worn,
What wonder modes in wit should take their turn?
POPE—*Essay on Criticism.* L. 446.

24
True wit is nature to advantage dress'd,
What oft was thought, but ne'er so well expressed.
POPE—*Essay on Criticism.* Pt. II. L. 97.
Wit is that which has been often thought, but never before was well expressed.
As paraphrased by JOHNSON—*Life of Cowley.*

25
Some men's wit is like a dark lantern, which serves their own turn and guides them their own way, but is never known (according to the Scripture phrase) either to shine forth before men, or to glorify their Father in heaven.
POPE—*Thoughts on Various Subjects.*

1
Generally speaking there is more wit than talent in this world. Society swarms with witty people who lack talent.
De Rivarol—*On Mme. de Staël.*

2
Fine wits destroy themselves with their own plots, in meddling with great affairs of state.
John Selden—*Table Talk. Wit.*

3
You have a nimble wit; I think it was made of Atalanta's heels.
As You Like It. Act III. Sc. 2. L. 292.

4
Make the doors upon a woman's wit and it will out at the casement; shut that and 'twill out at the key-hole; stop that, 'twill fly with the smoke out at the chimney.
As You Like It. Act IV. Sc. 1. L. 162.

5
Since brevity is the soul of wit,
And tediousness the limbs and outward flourishes,
I will be brief.
Hamlet. Act II. Sc. 2. L. 90.
(See also Sophocles under Wisdom)

6
They have a plentiful lack of wit.
Hamlet. Act II. Sc. 2. L. 201.

7
I am not only witty in myself, but the cause that wit is in other men.
Henry IV. Pt. II. Act I. Sc. 2. L. 11.
(See also Catherine II, Gryphius, also Socrates under Goodness)

8
Rudeness is a sauce to his good wit,
Which gives men stomach to digest his words,
With better appetite.
Julius Cæsar. Act I. Sc. 2. L. 304.

9
His eye begets occasion for his wit;
For every object that the one doth catch,
The other turns to a mirth-moving jest.
Love's Labour's Lost. Act II. Sc. 1. L. 69.

10
Your wit's too hot, it speeds too fast, 'twill tire.
Love's Labour's Lost. Act II. Sc. 1. L. 120.

11
Great men may jest with saints; 'tis wit in them;
But, in the less, foul profanation.
Measure for Measure. Act II. Sc. 2. L. 127.

12
He doth, indeed, show some sparks that are like wit.
Much Ado About Nothing. Act II. Sc. 3. L. 193.

13
A good old man, sir: he will be talking, as they say, When the age is in, the wit is out.
Much Ado About Nothing. Act III. Sc. 5. L. 36.

14
Sir, your wit ambles well; it goes easily.
Much Ado About Nothing. Act V. Sc. 1. L. 159.

15
Thy wit is as quick as the greyhound's mouth; it catches.
Much Ado About Nothing. Act V. Sc. 2. L. 11.

16
To leave this keen encounter of our wits,
And fall somewhat into a slower method.
Richard III. Act I. Sc. 2. L. 115.

17
Thy wit is a very bitter sweeting: it is most sharp sauce.
Romeo and Juliet. Act II. Sc. 4. L. 87.

18
Look, he's winding up the watch of his wit; by and by it will strike.
Tempest. Act II. Sc. 1. L. 12.

19
Those wits that think they have thee, do very oft prove fools; and I, that am sure I lack thee, may pass for a wise man; for what says Quinapalus? "Better a witty fool than a foolish wit."
Twelfth Night. Act I. Sc. 5. L. 37.
(See also Johnson)

20
Man could direct his ways by plain reason, and support his life by tasteless food; but God has given us wit, and flavour, and brightness, and laughter, and perfumers, to enliven the days of man's pilgrimage, and to "charm his pained steps over the burning marle."
Sydney Smith—*Dangers and Advantages of Wit.*

21
Surprise is so essential an ingredient of wit that no wit will bear repetition;—at least the original electrical feeling produced by any piece of wit can never be renewed.
Sydney Smith—*Lectures on Moral Philosophy,* No. 10.

22
One wit, like a knuckle of ham in soup, gives a zest and flavour to the dish, but more than one serves only to spoil the pottage.
Smollett—*Humphrey Clinker.*

23
Wit consists in knowing the resemblance of things which differ, and the difference of things which are alike.
Madame de Staël—*Germany.* Pt. III. Ch. VIII.

24
It is having in some measure a sort of wit to know how to use the wit of others.
Stanislaus (King of Poland)—*Maxims and Moral Sentences.*

25
It is with wits as with razors, which are never so apt to cut those they are employed on as when they have lost their edge.
Swift—*Tale of a Tub: Author's Preface.*
(See also Young, also Montagu under Satire)

26
Too much wit makes the world rotten.
Tennyson—*Idylls of the King. The Last Tournament.*

27
And wit its honey lent, without the sting.
Tennyson—*To the Memory of Lord Talbot.*
(See also Lucretius)

28
He had too thoughtful a wit: like a penknife in too narrow a sheath, too sharp for his body.
Izaak Walton—*Life of George Herbert.* Reported as Herbert's saying about himself.

1
Nae wut without a portion o' impertinence.
JOHN WILSON—*Noctes Ambrosianæ.*

2
Though I am young, I scorn to flit
On the wings of borrowed wit.
GEORGE WITHER—*The Shepherd's Hunting.*

3
Against their wills what numbers ruin shun,
Purely through want of wit to be undone!
Nature has shown by making it so rare,
That wit's a jewel which we need not wear.
YOUNG—*Epistle to Mr. Pope.* Ep. II. L. 80.

4
As in smooth oil the razor best is whet,
So wit is by politeness sharpest set;
Their want of edge from their offence is seen,
Both pain us least when exquisitely keen.
YOUNG—*Love of Fame.* Satire II. L. 118.
(See also SWIFT)

WOE

5
An Iliad of woes.
DEMOSTHENES. 387. 12. DIODORUS SICULUS. DE QUINCEY—*Confessions of an Opium Eater.* Pt. II.

6
Waste brings woe, and sorrow hates despair.
ROBERT GREENE—*Sonnet.*

7
When one is past, another care we have;
Thus woe succeeds a woe, as wave a wave.
HERRICK—*Sorrows Succeed.*
(See also POPE, HAMLET, YOUNG)

8
And woe succeeds to woe.
HOMER—*Iliad.* Bk. XVI. L. 139. POPE'S trans.
(See also HERRICK)

9
Long exercised in woes.
HOMER—*Odyssey.* Bk. I. L. 2. POPE'S trans.

10
Woe unto you, . . . for ye pay tithe of mint and anise and cummin.
Matthew. XXIII. 23.

11
So perish all whose breast ne'er learned to glow
For other's good or melt at other's woe.
POPE—*Elegy to an Unfortunate Lady.* HOMER—*Odyssey.* Bk. XVIII. 269.

12
I was not always a man of woe.
SCOTT—*Lay of the Last Minstrel.* Canto II. St. 12.

13
One woe doth tread upon another's heel
So fast they follow.
Hamlet. Act IV. Sc. 7. L. 165.
(See also HERRICK)

14
All these woes shall serve
For sweet discourses in our time to come.
Romeo and Juliet—Act III. Sc. 5. L. 52.

15
Woes cluster; rare are solitary woes;
They love a train, they tread each other's heel.
YOUNG—*Night Thoughts.* Night III. L. 63.
(See also HERRICK)

WOMAN (See also COQUETRY, MATRIMONY, WIFE, WOOING)

16
Loveliest of women! heaven is in thy soul,
Beauty and virtue shine forever round thee,
Bright'ning each other! thou art all divine!
ADDISON—*Cato.* Act III. Sc. 2.

17
Divination seems heightened and raised to its highest power in woman.
AMOS BRONSON ALCOTT—*Concord Days. August. Woman.*

18
Oh the gladness of their gladness when they're glad,
And the sadness of their sadness when they're sad;
But the gladness of their gladness, and the sadness of their sadness,
Are as nothing to their badness when they're bad.
Anon.

19
Oh, the shrewdness of their shrewdness when they are shrewd,
And the rudeness of their rudeness when they're rude;
But the shrewdness of their shrewdness and the rudeness of their rudeness,
Are as nothing to their goodness when they're good.
Anon. Answer to preceding.

20
On one she smiled, and he was blest;
She smiles elsewhere—we make a din!
But 'twas not love which heaved her breast,
Fair child!—it was the bliss within.
MATTHEW ARNOLD—*Euphrosyne.*

21
Woman's love is writ in water,
Woman's faith is traced in sand.
AYTOUN—*Lays of Scottish Cavaliers. Prince Edward at Versailles.*

22
But woman's grief is like a summer storm,
Short as it violent is.
JOANNA BAILLIE—*Basil.* Act V. Sc. 3.

23
Not she with trait'rous kiss her Saviour stung,
Not she denied Him with unholy tongue;
She, while apostles shrank, could danger brave,
Last at His cross, and earliest at His grave.
EATON S. BARRETT—*Woman.* Pt. I. L. 141.
Not she with trait'rous kiss her Master stung,
Not she denied Him with unfaithful tongue;
She, when apostles fled, could danger brave,
Last at His cross, and earliest at His grave.
Version in ed. of 1810.

24
You see, dear, it is not true that woman was made from man's rib; she was really made from his funny bone.
BARRIE—*What Every Woman Knows.*
(See also DIXON)

25
Oh, woman, perfect woman! what distraction
Was meant to mankind when thou wast made a devil!
What an inviting hell invented.
BEAUMONT AND FLETCHER—*Comedy of Monsieur Thomas.* Act III. Sc. 1.

1
Then, my good girls, be more than women, wise:
At least be more than I was; and be sure
You credit anything the light gives life to
Before a man.
BEAUMONT AND FLETCHER—*Maid's Tragedy.* Act II. Sc. 2.

2
"And now, Madam," I addressed her, "we shall try who shall get the breeches.
WILLIAM BELOE—*Miscellanies.* (1795) Translation of a Latin story by ANTONIUS MUSA BRASSAVOLUS. (1540)
(See also BURTON)

3
Phidias made the statue of Venus at Elis with one foot upon the shell of a tortoise, to signify two great duties of a virtuous woman, which are to keep home and be silent.
W. DE BRITAINE—*Human Prudence.* (Ed. 1726) P. 134. Referred to by BURTON—*Anatomy of Melancholy.* Pt. III. Sec. III. Mem. 4. Subs. 2.
(See also DONNE, TAYLOR)

4
You forget too much
That every creature, female as the male,
Stands single in responsible act and thought,
As also in birth and death.
E. B. BROWNING—*Aurora Leigh.* Bk. II. L. 472.

5
A worthless woman! mere cold clay
As all false things are! but so fair,
She takes the breath of men away
Who gaze upon her unaware:
I would not play her larcenous tricks
To have her looks!
E. B. BROWNING—*Bianca among the Nightingales.* St. 12.

6
Thy daughters bright thy walks adorn,
Gay as the gilded summer sky,
Sweet as the dewy milk-white thorn,
Dear as the raptured thrill of joy.
BURNS—*Address to Edinburgh.*

7
Auld Nature swears, the lovely dears
Her noblest work she classes, O:
Her 'prentice hand she tried on man,
An' then she made the lasses, O.
BURNS—*Green Grow the Rashes.*
(See also CUPID'S WHIRLIGIG, LESSING)

8
Their tricks and craft hae put me daft,
They've ta'en me in, and a' that,
But clear your decks, and—Here's the sex!
I like the jads for a' that.
BURNS—*Jolly Beggars.*

9
It is a woman's reason to say I will do such a thing because I will.
BURROUGHS—*On Hosea.* Vol. IV. (1652)
(See also HILL, TAYLOR)

10
Women wear the breeches.
BURTON—*Anatomy of Melancholy. Democritus to the Reader.*
(See also BELOE)

11
The souls of women are so small,
That some believe they've none at all;
Or if they have, like cripples, still
They've but one faculty, the will.
BUTLER—*Miscellaneous Thoughts.*

12
Heart on her lips, and soul within her eyes,
Soft as her clime, and sunny as her skies.
BYRON—*Beppo.* St. 45.

13
Soft as the memory of buried love,
Pure as the prayer which childhood wafts above.
BYRON—*Bride of Abydos.* Canto I. St. 6.

14
The Niobe of nations! there she stands,
Childless and crownless, in her voiceless woe.
BYRON—*Childe Harold.* Canto IV. St. 79.

15
Her stature tall—I hate a dumpy woman.
BYRON—*Don Juan.* Canto I. St. 61.

16
A lady with her daughters or her nieces
Shine like a guinea and seven-shilling pieces.
BYRON—*Don Juan.* Canto III. St. 60.

17
I love the sex, and sometimes would reverse
The tyrant's wish, "that mankind only had
One neck, which he with one fell stroke might pierce;"
My wish is quite as wide, but not so bad,
And much more tender on the whole than fierce;
It being (not *now*, but only while a lad)
That womankind had but one rosy mouth,
To kiss them all at once, from North to South.
BYRON—*Don Juan.* Canto VI. St. 27.

18
I've seen your stormy seas and stormy women,
And pity lovers rather more than seamen.
BYRON—*Don Juan.* Canto VI. St. 53.

19
But she was a soft landscape of mild earth,
Where all was harmony, and calm, and quiet,
Luxuriant, budding; cheerful without mirth.
BYRON—*Don Juan.* Canto VI. St. 53.

20
What a strange thing is man! and what a stranger
Is woman! What a whirlwind is her head,
And what a whirlpool full of depth and danger
Is all the rest about her.
BYRON—*Don Juan.* Canto IX. St. 64.

21
And whether coldness, pride, or virtue dignify
A woman, so she's good, what does it signify?
BYRON—*Don Juan.* Canto XIV. St. 57.

22
She was his life,
The ocean to the river of his thoughts,
Which terminated all.
BYRON—*The Dream.* St. 2. "River of his Thought" from DANTE—*Purgatorio.* XIII. 88.
(See also LONGFELLOW)

23
Believe a woman or an epitaph,
Or any other thing that's false.
BYRON—*English Bards and Scotch Reviewers.*

24
The world was sad; the garden was a wild;
And man, the hermit, sigh'd—till woman smiled.
CAMPBELL—*Pleasures of Hope.* Pt. II. L. 37.

1
Of all the girls that are so smart,
There's none like pretty Sally.
HENRY CAREY—*Sally in our Alley.*
(See also SWIFT)

2
La muger que se determina á ser honrada entre un ejército de soldados lo puede ser.
The woman who is resolved to be respected can make herself so even amidst an army of soldiers.
CERVANTES—*La Gitanilla.*

3
Ther seyde oones a clerk in two vers, "what is bettre than Gold? Jaspre. What is bettre than Jaspre? Wisdom. And what is bettre than Wisdom? Womman. And what is bettre than a good Womman? No thyng."
CHAUCER—*Canterbury Tales. Melibeus.* L. 2,300.
(See also HARLEIAN MS.)

4
We shall find no fiend in hell can match the fury of a disappointed woman,—scorn'd! slighted! dismiss'd without a parting pang.
COLLEY CIBBER—*Love's Last Shift.* Act IV. Sc. 1.
(See also CONGREVE)

5
Heaven has no rage like love to hatred turned,
Nor hell a fury like a woman scorned.
CONGREVE—*The Mourning Bride.* Act III. Sc. 2.
(See also CIBBER, TUKE, VERGIL)

6
The sweetest noise on earth, a woman's tongue;
A string which hath no discord.
BARRY CORNWALL—*Rafaelle and Fornarina.* Sc. 2.

7
Her air, her manners, all who saw admired;
Courteous though coy, and gentle, though retired:
The joy of youth and health her eyes display'd,
And ease of heart her every look convey'd.
CRABBE—*Parish Register.* Pt. II.

8
Whoe'er she be,
That not impossible she,
That shall command my heart and me.
CRASHAW—*Wishes to his (Supposed) Mistress.*

9
Man was made when Nature was but an apprentice, but woman when she was a skilful mistress of her art.
Cupid's Whirligig. (1607)
(See also BURNS)

10
Were there no women, men might live like gods.
DEKKER—*Honest Whore.* Pt. I. Act III. Sc. 1.

11
There's no music when a woman is in the concert.
DEKKER—*Honest Whore.* Pt. II. Act IV. Sc. 3.

12
Les femmes ont toujours quelque arrière pensée.
Women always have some mental reservation.
DESTOUCHES—*Dissipateur.* V. 9.

13
But were it to my fancy given
To rate her charms, I'd call them heaven;
For though a mortal made of clay,
Angels must love Ann Hathaway;
She hath a way so to control,
To rapture the imprisoned soul,
And sweetest heaven on earth display,
That to be heaven Ann hath a way;
She hath a way,
Ann Hathaway,—
To be heaven's self Ann hath a way.
CHARLES DIBDIN—*A Love Dittie.* In his novel *Hannah Hewitt.* (1795) Often attributed to SHAKESPEARE.

14
But in some odd nook in Mrs. Todgers's breast, up a great many steps, and in a corner easy to be overlooked, there was a secret door, with "Woman" written on the spring, which, at a touch from Mercy's hand, had flown wide open, and admitted her for shelter.
DICKENS—*Martin Chuzzlewit.* Vol. II. Ch. XII.

15
She was not made out of his head, Sir,
To rule and to govern the man;
Nor was she made out of his feet, Sir,
By man to be trampled upon.
* * * * *
But she did come forth from his side, Sir,
His equal and partner to be;
And now they are coupled together,
She oft proves the top of the tree.
Ballads and Songs of the Peasantry of England. Collected by JAMES HENRY DIXON.
(See also BARRIE, HENRY, WESLEY)

16
Be then thine own home, and in thyself dwell;
Inn anywhere;
And seeing the snail, which everywhere doth roam,
Carrying his own home still, still is at home,
Follow (for he is easy-paced) this snail:
Be thine own palace, or the world's thy jail.
DONNE.
(See also BRITAINE, also HOW under WIFE)

17
And, like another Helen, fir'd another Troy.
DRYDEN—*Alexander's Feast.* L. 154.

18
For women with a mischief to their kind,
Pervert with bad advice our better mind.
DRYDEN—*Cock and Fox.* L. 555.

19
A woman's counsel brought us first to woe,
And made her man his paradise forego,
Where at heart's ease he liv'd; and might have been
As free from sorrow as he was from sin.
DRYDEN—*Cock and the Fox.* L. 557.

20
She hugg'd the offender, and forgave the offence;
Sex to the last.
DRYDEN—*Cymon and Iphigenia.* L. 367.

21
I am resolved to grow fat and look young till forty, and then slip out of the world with the first wrinkle and the reputation of five and twenty.
DRYDEN—*The Maiden Queen.* Act III. Sc. 1.

1
And that one hunting, which the devil design'd
For one fair female, lost him half the kind.
DRYDEN—*Theodore and Honoria.* L. 427.

2
What all your sex desire is Sovereignty.
DRYDEN—*Wife of Bath.*

3
Cherchez la femme.
Find the woman.
DUMAS—*Les Mohicans de Paris.* Vol. III. Ch. X. and elsewhere in the novel. Act III. Sc. 7. of the play. Probably from the Spanish. A common question of CHARPES. See *Revue des Deux Mondes.* XI. 822.
(See also JUVENAL, RICHARDSON, VERGIL)

4
Her lot is made for her by the love she accepts.
GEORGE ELIOT—*Felix Holt.* Ch. XLIII.

5
When greater perils men inviron,
Then women show a front of iron;
And, gentle in their manner, they
Do bold things in a quiet way.
THOMAS DUNN ENGLISH—*Betty Zane.*
(See also BUTLER under WAR)

6
There is no worse evil than a bad woman; and nothing has ever been produced better than a good one.
EURIPIDES—*Melanippe.*

7
Our sex still strikes an awe upon the brave,
And only cowards dare affront a woman.
FARQUHAR—*Constant Couple.* Act V. Sc. 1.

8
A woman friend! He that believes that weakness,
Steers in a stormy night without a compass.
FLETCHER—*Woman Pleased.* Act II. Sc. 1.

9
Woman, I tell you, is a microcosm; and rightly to rule her, requires as great talents as to govern a state.
SAMUEL FOOTE—*The Minor.*

10
Toute femme varie
Bien fol est qui s'y fie.
Woman is always fickle—foolish is he who trusts her.
FRANÇOIS I. Scratched with his ring on a window of Chambord Castle. (Quoted also "souvent femme.") See BRANTOME—*Œuvres.* VII. 395. Also *Le Livre des Proverbes Français,* by LE ROUX DE LINCY. I. V. 231. (Ed. 1859)
(See also OVERBURY, VERGIL)

11
Are women books? says Hodge, then would mine were
An Almanack, to change her every year.
BENJ. FRANKLIN—*Poor Richard.* Dec., 1737.

12
A cat has nine lives and a woman has nine cats' lives.
FULLER—*Gnomologia.*

13
'Tis a woman that seduces all mankind;
By her we first were taught the wheedling arts.
GAY—*The Beggar's Opera.* Act I. Sc. 1.

14
How happy could I be with either,
Were t'other dear charmer away!
But, while ye thus tease me together,
To neither a word will I say.
GAY—*The Beggar's Opera.* Act II. Sc. 2.

15
If the heart of a man is depressed with cares,
The mist is dispell'd when a woman appears.
GAY—*The Beggar's Opera.* Act II.

16
And when a lady's in the case,
You know all other things give place.
GAY—*Fables. The Hare and Many Friends.* L. 41.

17
Es ist doch den Mädchen wie angeboren, dass sie allem gefallen wollen, was nur Augen hat.
The desire to please everything having eyes seems inborn in maidens.
SALOMON GESSNER—*Evander und Alcima.* III. 1.

18
I am a woman—therefore I may not
Call to him, cry to him,
Fly to him,
Bid him delay not!
R. W. GILDER—*A Woman's Thought.*

19
Denn geht es zu des Bösen Haus
Das Weib hat tausend Schritt voraus.
When toward the Devil's House we tread,
Woman's a thousand steps ahead.
GOETHE—*Faust.* I. 21. 147.

20
Denn das Naturell der Frauen
Ist so nah mit Kunst verwandt.
For the nature of women is closely allied to art.
GOETHE—*Faust.* II. 1.

21
Das Ewig-Weibliche zieht uns hinan.
The eternal feminine doth draw us upward.
GOETHE—*Faust.* II. 5.
La Féminine Eternel
Nous attire au ciel.
French trans. of GOETHE by H. BLAZE DE BURY.

22
'Tis Lilith.
Who?
Adam's first wife is she.
Beware the lure within her lovely tresses,
The splendid sole adornment of her hair;
When she succeeds therewith a youth to snare,
Not soon again she frees him from her jesses.
GOETHE—*Faust.* Sc. 21. *Walpurgis Night.* BAYARD TAYLOR's trans.
(See also ROSSETTI)

23
Ein edler Mann wird durch ein gutes Wort
Der Frauen weit geführt.
A noble man is led far by woman's gentle words.
GOETHE—*Iphigenia auf Tauris.* I. 2. 162.

24
Der Umgang mit Frauen ist das Element guter Sitten.
The society of women is the foundation of good manners.
GOETHE—*Die Wahlverwandtschaften.* II. 5.

1
When lovely woman stoops to folly,
And finds too late that men betray,
What charm can soothe her melancholy?
What art can wash her guilt away?
GOLDSMITH—*Vicar of Wakefield.* Ch. XXIV.

2
Mankind, from Adam, have been women's fools;
Women, from Eve, have been the devil's tools:
Heaven might have spar'd one torment when we fell;
Not left us women, or not threatened hell.
GEO. GRANVILLE (Lord Lansdowne)—*She-Gallants.*

3
Vente quid levius? fulgur. Quid fulgure? flamma
Flamma quid? mulier. Quid mulier? nihil.
What is lighter than the wind? A feather.
What is lighter than a feather? fire.
What lighter than fire? a woman.
What lighter than a woman? Nothing.
Harleian MS. No. 3362. Folio 47.
(See also CHAUCER, also QUARLES under WORLD)

4
De wimmin, dey does de talkin' en de flyin', en de mens, dey does de walkin en de pryin', en betwixt en betweenst um, dey ain't much dat don't come out.
JOEL CHANDLER HARRIS—*Brother Rabbit and His Famous Foot.*

5
That the woman was made of a rib out of the side of Adam; not out of his feet to be trampled upon by him, but out of his side to be equal with him, under his arm to be protected, and near his heart to be loved.
MATTHEW HENRY—*Note on Genesis* II. 21 and 22. Also in CHAUCER—*Persones Tale.*
(See also DIXON)

6
First, then, a woman will, or won't,—depend on't;
If she will do't, she will; and there's an end on't.
But, if she won't, since safe and sound your trust is,
Fear is affront: and jealousy injustice.
AARON HILL—*Epilogue to Zara.*
(See also BURROUGHS)

7
Where is the man who has the power and skill
To stem the torrent of a woman's will?
For if she will, she will, you may depend on't;
And if she won't, she won't; so there's an end on't.
From the Pillar Erected on the Mount in the Dane John Field, Canterbury. *Examiner,* May 31, 1829.
(See also HILL)

8
Women may be whole oceans deeper than we are, but they are also a whole paradise better. She may have got us out of Eden, but as a compensation she makes the earth very pleasant.
JOHN OLIVER HOBBES — *The Ambassador.* Act III.

9
Man has his will,—but woman has her way.
HOLMES—*Autocrat of the Breakfast Table.* Prologue.

10
She moves a goddess, and she looks a queen.
HOMER—*Iliad.* Bk. III. L. 208. POPE'S trans.

11
O woman, woman, when to ill thy mind
Is bent, all hell contains no fouler fiend.
HOMER—*Odyssey.* Bk. XI. L. 531. POPE'S trans.

12
What mighty woes
To thy imperial race from woman rose.
HOMER—*Odyssey.* Bk. XI. L. 541. POPE'S trans.

13
But, alas! alas! for the woman's fate,
Who has from a mob to choose a mate!
'Tis a strange and painful mystery!
But the more the eggs the worse the hatch;
The more the fish, the worse the catch;
The more the sparks the worse the match;
Is a fact in woman's history.
HOOD—*Miss Kilmansegg. Her Courtship.* St. 7.

14
God in his harmony has equal ends
For cedar that resists and reed that bends;
For good it is a woman sometimes rules,
Holds in her hand the power, and manners, schools,
And laws, and mind; succeeding master proud,
With gentle voice and smiles she leads the crowd,
The somber human troop.
VICTOR HUGO—*Eviradnus.* V.

15
O woman! thou wert fashioned to beguile:
So have all sages said, all poets sung.
JEAN INGELOW—*The Four Bridges.* St. 68.

16
In that day seven women shall take hold of one man.
Isaiah. IV. 1.

17
Wretched, un-idea'd girls.
SAMUEL JOHNSON—*Boswell's Life of Johnson.* (1752)

18
I am very fond of the company of ladies. I like their beauty, I like their delicacy, I like their vivacity, and I like their *silence.*
SAMUEL JOHNSON. SEWARD'S *Johnsoniana.* 617.

19
Ladies, stock and tend your hive,
Trifle not at thirty-five;
For, howe'er we boast and strive,
Life declines from thirty-five;
He that ever hopes to thrive
Must begin by thirty-five.
SAMUEL JOHNSON—*To Mrs. Thrale, when Thirty-five.* L. 11.

20
One woman reads another's character
Without the tedious trouble of deciphering.
BEN JONSON—*New Inn.* Act IV.

21
And where she went, the flowers took thickest root,
As she had sow'd them with her odorous foot.
BEN JONSON—*The Sad Shepherd.* Act I. Sc. 1.

22
Nulla fere causa est in qua non femina litem moverit.
There's scarce a case comes on but you shall find
A woman's at the bottom.
JUVENAL—*Satires.* VI. 242.
(See also DUMAS)

1 Vindicta
Nemo magis gaudet, quam femina.
Revenge we find,
The abject pleasure of an abject mind
And hence so dear to poor weak woman kind.
JUVENAL—*Satires.* XIII. 191.

2
I met a lady in the meads
Full beautiful—a faery's child,
Her hair was long, her foot was light,
And her eyes were wild.
KEATS—*La Belle Dame sans Merci.*

3
When the Hymalayan peasant meets the he-bear in his pride,
He shouts to scare the monster, who will often turn aside.
But the she-bear thus accosted, rends the peasant tooth and nail,
For the female of the species is more deadly than the male.
KIPLING—*The Female of the Species.*

4
Ich hab' es immer gesagt: das Weib wollte die Natur zu ihrem Meisterstücke machen.
I have always said it—Nature meant woman to be her masterpiece.
LESSING—*Emilia Galotti.* V. 7.
(See also BURNS)

5
Was hätt ein Weiberkopf erdacht, das er
Nicht zu beschönen wüsste?
What could a woman's head contrive
Which it would not know how to excuse?
LESSING—*Nathan der Weise.* III.

6
The life of woman is full of woe,
Toiling on and on and on,
With breaking heart, and tearful eyes,
The secret longings that arise,
Which this world never satisfies!
Some more, some less, but of the whole
Not one quite happy, no, not one!
LONGFELLOW—*Christus. The Golden Legend.* Pt. II.

7
A Lady with a lamp shall stand
In the great history of the land,
A noble type of good,
Heroic womanhood.
LONGFELLOW—*Santa Filomena.* St. 10.
(See also MACDONALD)

8
Like a fair lily on a river floating
She floats upon the river of his thoughts.
LONGFELLOW—*Spanish Student.* Act II. Sc. 3. Idea taken from DANTE—*Purgatorio.* XIII. 88.
(See also BYRON, also DANTE under CONSCIENCE)

9
'Twas kin' o' kingdom-come to look
On sech a blessed cretur.
LOWELL—*Biglow Papers. Introduction to Second Series. The Courtin'.* St. 7.

10
Earth's noblest thing, a Woman perfected.
LOWELL—*Irene.* L. 62.

11
Parvula, pumilio, chariton mia tota merum sal.
A little, tiny, pretty, witty, charming darling she.
LUCRETIUS—*De Rerum Natura.* IV. 1158.

12
A cunning woman is a knavish fool.
LORD LYTTLETON—*Advice to a Lady.*

13
When all the medical officers have retired for the night, and silence and darkness have settled down upon those miles of prostrate sick, she [Florence Nightingale] may be observed alone, with a little lamp in her hand, making her solitary rounds.
MR. MACDONALD, on the staff of the London *Times*, in a letter to that paper when leaving Scutari. See *Pictorial History of the Russian War.* 1854–5–6. P. 310.
(See also LONGFELLOW)

14
Of all wild beasts on earth or in sea, the greatest is a woman.
MENANDER—*E Supposititio.* P. 182.

15
I expect that woman will be the last thing civilized by man.
MEREDITH—*Richard Feverel.* First page.

16
O woman, born first to believe us;
Yea, also born first to forget;
Born first to betray and deceive us,
Yet first to repent and regret.
JOAQUIN MILLER—*Charity.*

17
Too fair to worship, too divine to love.
MILMAN—*Apollo Belvidere.*

18
I always thought a tinge of blue
Improved a charming woman's stocking.
RICHARD MONCKTON MILNES—*Four Lovers.* II. *In Summer.*

19 My latest found,
Heaven's last best gift, my ever new delight!
MILTON—*Paradise Lost.* Bk. V. L. 18.

20
Grace was in all her steps, heaven in her eye,
In every gesture dignity and love.
MILTON—*Paradise Lost.* Bk. VIII. L. 488.

21 For nothing lovelier can be found
In woman, than to study household good.
MILTON—*Paradise Lost.* Bk. IX. L. 232.

22 Oh! why did God,
Creator wise, that peopled highest Heaven
With Spirits masculine, create at last
This novelty on Earth, this fair defect
Of Nature, and not fill the World at once
With men as Angels, without feminine.
MILTON—*Paradise Lost.* Bk. X. L. 888.

23
A bevy of fair women.
MILTON—*Paradise Lost.* Bk. XI. L. 582.

24
Disguise our bondage as we will,
'Tis woman, woman rules us still.
MOORE—*Sovereign Woman.* St. 4.

1
My only books
Were woman's looks,
And folly's all they've taught me.
MOORE—*The Time I've Lost in Wooing.*

2
The virtue of her lively looks
Excels the precious stone;
I wish to have none other books
To read or look upon.
Songs and Sonnets. (1557)

3
For if a young lady has that discretion and modesty, without which all knowledge is little worth, she will never make an ostentatious parade of it, because she will rather be intent on acquiring more, than on displaying what she has.
HANNAH MORE—*Essays on Various Subjects. Thoughts on Conversation.*

4
Queens you must always be: queens to your lovers; queens to your husbands and your sons; queens of higher mystery to the world beyond. . . . But, alas, you are too often idle and careless queens, grasping at majesty in the least things, while you abdicate it in the greatest.
D. M. MULOCK. Quoted from RUSKIN on the title page of *The Woman's Kingdom.*
(See also POPE)

5
A penniless lass wi' a lang pedigree.
LADY NAIRNE—*The Laird o' Cockpen.*

6
So I wonder a woman, the Mistress of Hearts,
Should ascend to aspire to be Master of Arts;
A Ministering Angel in Woman we see,
And an Angel need cover no other Degree.
LORD NEAVES—*O why should a Woman not get a Degree?*

7
Who trusts himself to women, or to waves,
Should never hazard what he fears to lose.
OLDMIXON—*Governor of Cyprus.*

8
What mighty ills have not been done by woman!
Who was't betray'd the Capitol? A woman;
Who lost Mark Antony the world? A woman;
Who was the cause of a long ten years' war,
And laid at last old Troy in ashes? Woman;
Destructive, damnable, deceitful woman!
THOMAS OTWAY—*The Orphan.* Act III. Sc. 1.

9
Who can describe
Women's hypocrisies! their subtle wiles,
Betraying smiles, feign'd tears, inconstancies!
Their painted outsides, and corrupted minds,
The sum of all their follies, and their falsehoods.
THOMAS OTWAY—*Orpheus.*

10
O woman! lovely woman! Nature made thee
To temper man: we had been brutes without you;
Angels are painted fair, to look like you:
There's in you all that we believe of Heaven,
Amazing brightness, purity, and truth,
Eternal joy, and everlasting love.
THOMAS OTWAY—*Venice Preserved.* Act I. Sc. 1.

11
Wit and woman are two frail things, and both the frailer by concurring.
THOMAS OVERBURY—*News from Court.* WEBSTER—*Devil's Law.* Act I. Sc. 2.
(See also FRANÇOIS I.)

12
Still an angel appear to each lover beside,
But still be a woman to you.
PARNELL—*When thy Beauty Appears.*

13
Ah, wasteful woman! she who may
On her sweet self set her own price,
Knowing man cannot choose but pay,
How has she cheapen'd Paradise!
How given for nought her priceless gift,
How spoil'd the bread and spill'd the wine,
Which, spent with due respective thrift,
Had made brutes men and men divine.
COVENTRY PATMORE—*The Angel in the House. Unthrift.* Bk. I. Canto III. 3.

14
To chase the clouds of life's tempestuous hours,
To strew its short but weary way with flow'rs,
New hopes to raise, new feelings to impart,
And pour celestial balsam on the heart;
For this to man was lovely woman giv'n,
The last, best work, the noblest gift of Heav'n.
THOMAS LOVE PEACOCK—*The Visions of Love.*

15
Those who always speak well of women do not know them sufficiently; those who always speak ill of them do not know them at all.
GUILLAUME PIGAULT-LEBRUN.

16
Nam multum loquaces merito omnes habemus,
Nec mutam profecto repertam ullam esse
Hodie dicunt mulierem ullo in seculo.
I know that we women are all justly accounted praters; they say in the present day that there never was in any age such a wonder to be found as a dumb woman.
PLAUTUS—*Aulularia.* II. 1. 5.

17
Multa sunt mulierum vitia, sed hoc e multis maximum,
Cum sibi nimis placent, nimisque operam dant ut placeant viris.
Women have many faults, but of the many this is the greatest, that they please themselves too much, and give too little attention to pleasing the men.
PLAUTUS—*Pœnulus.* V. 4. 33.

18
Mulieri nimio male facere melius est onus, quam bene.
A woman finds it much easier to do ill than well.
PLAUTUS—*Truculentus.* II. 5. 17.

19
Oh! say not woman's heart is bought
With vain and empty treasure.
* * * * *
Deep in her heart the passion glows;
She loves and loves forever.
ISAAC POCOCK. Song, in *The Heir of Vironi*, produced at Covent Garden, Feb. 27, 1817.

20
Our grandsire, Adam, ere of Eve possesst,
Alone, and e'en in Paradise unblest,
With mournful looks the blissful scenes survey'd,

And wander'd in the solitary shade.
The Maker saw, took pity, and bestow'd
Woman, the last, the best reserv'd of God.
POPE—*January and May*. L. 63.

1
Most women have no characters at all.
POPE—*Moral Essays*. Ep. II. L. 2.

2
Ladies, like variegated tulips, show
'Tis to their changes half their charms we owe.
POPE—*Moral Essays*. Ep. II. L. 41.

3
Offend her, and she knows not to forgive;
Oblige her, and she'll hate you while you live.
POPE—*Moral Essays*. Ep. II. L. 137.

4
Men some to business, some to pleasure take;
But every woman is at heart a rake;
Men some to quiet, some to public strife;
But every lady would be queen for life.
POPE—*Moral Essays*. Ep. II. L. 215.
(See also MULOCK)

5
O! bless'd with temper, whose unclouded ray
Can make to-morrow cheerful as to-day;
She who can own a sister's charms, or hear
Sighs for a daughter with unwounded ear;
She who ne'er answers till a husband cools,
Or, if she rules him, never shows she rules.
Charms by accepting, by submitting sways,
Yet has her humour most when she obeys.
POPE—*Moral Essays*. Ep. II. L. 257.

6
And mistress of herself, though china fall.
POPE—*Moral Essays*. Ep. II. L. 268.

7
Woman's at best a contradiction still.
POPE—*Moral Essays*. Ep. II. L. 270.

8
Give God thy broken heart, He whole will make it:
Give woman thy whole heart, and she will break it.
EDMUND PRESTWICH—*The Broken Heart*.

9
Be to her virtues very kind;
Be to her faults a little blind.
Let all her ways be unconfin'd;
And clap your padlock—on her mind.
PRIOR—*An English Padlock*.

10
The gray mare will prove the better horse.
PRIOR—*Epilogue to Lucius*. Last line. BUTLER—*Hudibras*. Pt. II. Canto L. L. 698. FIELDING—*The Grub Street Opera*. Act II. Sc. 4. *Pryde and Abuse of Women*. (1550) *The Marriage of True Wit and Science*. MACAULAY—*History of England*. Vol. I. Ch. III. Footnote suggests it arose from the preference generally given to the gray mares of Flanders over the finest coach horses of England. Proverb traced to Holland. (1546)

11
That if weak women went astray,
Their stars were more in fault than they.
PRIOR—*Hans Carvel*.

12
It is better to dwell in a corner of the housetop than with a brawling woman in a wide house.
Proverbs. XXI. 9.

13
Like to the falling of a star,
* * * *
Like to the damask rose you see,
Or like the blossom on the tree.
QUARLES—*Argalus and Parthenia*. Claimed by him but attributed to JOHN PHILLIPOT (Philpott) in Harleian MS. 3917. Folio 88 b., a fragment written about the time of James I. Credited to SIMON WASTELL (1629) by MACKAY, as it is appended to his *Microbiblion*. Said to be an imitation of an earlier poem by BISHOP HENRY KING.

14
If she undervalue me,
What care I how fair she be?
SIR WALTER RALEIGH.

15
If she seem not chaste to me,
What care I how chaste she be?
SIR WALTER RALEIGH. See BAYLEY'S *Life of Raleigh*.
(See also WITHER)

16
That, let us rail at women, scorn and flout 'em,
We may live with, but cannot live without 'em.
FREDERICK REYNOLDS — *My Grandfather's Will*. Act III.

17
Such a plot must have a woman in it.
RICHARDSON—*Sir Charles Grandison*. Vol. I. Letter 24.
(See also DUMAS)

18
A woman is the most inconsistent compound of obstinacy and self-sacrifice that I am acquainted with.
RICHTER—*Flower, Fruit, and Thorn Pieces*. Ch. V.

19
O wild, dark flower of woman,
Deep rose of my desire,
An Eastern wizard made you
Of earth and stars and fire.
C. G. D. ROBERTS—*The Rose of my Desire*.

20
Angels listen when she speaks;
She's my delight, all mankind's wonder;
But my jealous heart would break
Should we live one day asunder.
EARL OF ROCHESTER—*Song. My Dear Mistress has a Heart*. St. 2.

21
C'est chose qui moult me deplaist,
Quand poule parle et coq se taist.
It is a thing very displeasing to me when the hen speaks and the cock is silent.
Roman de la Rose. XIV. Cent.

22
Of Adam's first wife, Lilith, it is told
(The witch he loved before the gift of Eve)
That ere the snakes, her sweet tongue could deceive
And her enchanted hair was the first gold—
And still she sits, young while the earth is old
And, subtly of herself contemplative,
Draws men to watch the bright net she can weave,
Till heart and body and life are in its hold.
DANTE GABRIEL ROSSETTI—*Lilith*.
(See also GOETHE)

1
Toute fille lettrée restera fille toute sa vie, quand il n'y aura que des hommes sensés sur la terre.

Every blue-stocking will remain a spinster as long as there are sensible men on the earth.
ROUSSEAU—*Émile.* I. 5.

2
Une femme bel-esprit est le fléau de son mari, de ses enfants, de ses amis, de ses valets, de tout le monde.

A blue-stocking is the scourge of her husband, children, friends, servants, and every one.
ROUSSEAU—*Émile.* I. 5.

3
And one false step entirely damns her fame.
In vain with tears the loss she may deplore,
In vain look back on what she was before;
She sets like stars that fall, to rise no more.
ROWE—*Jane Shore.* Act I.

4
Ne l'onde solca, e ne l'arena semina,
E'l vago vento spera in rete accogliere
Chi sue speranze fonda in cor di femina.

He ploughs the waves, sows the sand, and hopes to gather the wind in a net, who places his hopes on the heart of woman.
SANNAZARO—*Ecloga Octava.* Plough the sands found in JUVENAL—*Satires.* VII. JEREMY TAYLOR—*Discourse on Liberty of Prophesying.* (1647) Introduction.

5
Such, Polly, are your sex—part truth, part fiction;
Some thought, much whim, and all a contradiction.
RICHARD SAVAGE—*To a Young Lady.*

6
Ehret die Frauen! sie flechten und weben
Himmlische Rosen in's irdische Leben.

Honor women! they entwine and weave heavenly roses in our earthly life.
SCHILLER—*Würde der Frauen.*

7
The weakness of their reasoning faculty also explains why women show more sympathy for the unfortunate than men; . . . and why, on the contrary, they are inferior to men as regards justice, and less honourable and conscientious.
SCHOPENHAUER—*On Women.*

8
Woman's faith, and woman's trust,
Write the characters in dust.
SCOTT—*Betrothed.* Ch. XX.

9
Widowed wife and wedded maid.
SCOTT—*Betrothed.* Last chapter.

10
O Woman! in our hours of ease,
Uncertain, coy, and hard to please,
And variable as the shade
By the light quivering aspen made;
When pain and anguish wring the brow,
A ministering angel thou!
SCOTT—*Marmion.* Canto VI. St. 30.

11
Age cannot wither her, nor custom stale
Her infinite variety.
Antony and Cleopatra. Act II. Sc. 2. L. 240.

12
If ladies be but young and fair,
They have the gift to know it.
As You Like It. Act II. Sc. 7. L. 37.

13
Run, run, Orlando: carve on every tree
The fair, the chaste, and unexpressive she.
As You Like It. Act III. Sc. 2. L. 9.

14
I thank God I am not a woman, to be touched with so many giddy offences as He hath generally taxed their whole sex withal.
As You Like It. Act III. Sc. 2. L. 366.

15
O most delicate fiend!
Who is't can read a woman?
Cymbeline. Act V. Sc. 5. L. 47.

16
Frailty, thy name is woman!—
A little month, or ere those shoes were old
With which she follow'd my poor father's body,
Like Niobe, all tears;—why she, even she,
* * * married with my uncle.
Hamlet. Act I. Sc. 2. L. 146.

17
And is not my hostess of the tavern a most sweet wench?
As the honey of Hybla, my old lad of the castle.
Henry IV. Pt. I. Act I. Sc. 2. L. 45.

18
'Tis beauty that doth oft make women proud;
But, God he knows, thy share thereof is small:
'Tis virtue that doth make them most admired;
The contrary doth make thee wondered at:
'Tis government that makes them seem divine.
Henry VI. Pt. III. Act I. Sc. 4. L. 128.

19
Her sighs will make a battery in his breast;
Her tears will pierce into a marble heart;
The tiger will be mild whiles she doth mourn;
And Nero will be tainted with remorse,
To hear and see her plaints.
Henry VI. Pt. III. Act III. Sc. 1. L. 37.

20
Two women plac'd together makes cold weather.
Henry VIII. Act I. Sc. 4. L. 22.

21
I grant I am a woman, but withal,
A woman that Lord Brutus took to wife:
I grant I am a woman; but withal
A woman well-reputed; Cato's daughter.
Julius Cæsar. Act II. Sc. 1. L. 292.

22
Ah me, how weak a thing
The heart of woman is!
Julius Cæsar. Act II. Sc. 4. L. 39

23
She in beauty, education, blood,
Holds hand with any princess of the world.
King John. Act II. Sc. 1. L. 493.

24
There was never yet fair woman but she made mouths in a glass.
King Lear. Act III. Sc. 2. L. 35.

25
A child of our grandmother Eve, a female; or, for thy more sweet understanding, a woman.
Love's Labour's Lost. Act I. Sc. 1. L. 266.

1
Fair ladies mask'd are roses in their bud:
Dismask'd, their damask sweet commixture shown,
Are angels veiling clouds, or roses blown.
Love's Labour's Lost. Act V. Sc. 2. L. 295.

2
Would it not grieve a woman to be overmaster'd with a piece of valiant dust? to make an account of her life to a cloud of wayward marl?
Much Ado About Nothing. Act II. Sc. 1. L. 63.

3
She speaks poniards, and every word stabs: if her breath were as terrible as her terminations, there were no living near her; she would infect to the north star.
Much Ado About Nothing. Act II. Sc. 1. L. 255.

4
One woman is fair, yet I am well; another is wise, yet I am well: another virtuous, yet I am well; but till all graces be in one woman, one woman shall not come in my grace.
Much Ado About Nothing. Act II. Sc. 3. L. 27.

5
A maid
That paragons description and wild fame;
One that excels the quirks of blazoning pens,
And in the essential vesture of creation
Does tire the ingener.
Othello. Act II. Sc. 1. L. 61.

6
You are pictures out of doors,
Bells in your parlours, wild-cats in your kitchens,
Saints in your injuries, devils being offended,
Players in your housewifery, and housewives in your beds.
Othello. Act II. Sc. 1. L. 110.

7
Have you not heard it said full oft,
A woman's nay doth stand for nought?
Passionate Pilgrim. L. 339.

8
Think you a little din can daunt mine ears?
Have I not in my time heard lions roar?
* * * * *
Have I not heard great ordnance in the field,
And heaven's artillery thunder in the skies?
* * * * * *
And do you tell me of a woman's tongue,
That gives not half so great a blow to hear
As will a chestnut in a farmer's fire?
Taming of the Shrew. Act I. Sc. 2. L. 200.

9
Why, then thou canst not break her to the lute?
Why, no; for she hath broke the lute to me.
Taming of the Shrew. Act II. Sc. 1. L. 148.

10
Say that she rail, why then I'll tell her plain
She sings as sweetly as a nightingale;
Say that she frown; I'll say she looks as clear
As morning roses newly wash'd with dew;
Say she be mute and will not speak a word;
Then I'll commend her volubility,
And say she uttereth piercing eloquence.
Taming of the Shrew. Act II. Sc. 1. L. 171.

11
A woman mov'd is like a fountain troubled,
Muddy, ill-seeming, thick, bereft of beauty.
Taming of the Shrew. Act V. Sc. 2. L. 142.

12
Why are our bodies soft and weak and smooth,
Unapt to toil and trouble in the world,
But that our soft conditions and our hearts
Should well agree with our external parts?
Taming of the Shrew. Act V. Sc. 2. L. 165.

13
Muse not that I thus suddenly proceed;
For what I will, I will, and there an end.
Two Gentlemen of Verona. Act I. Sc. 3. L. 64.

14
To be slow in words is a woman's only virtue.
Two Gentlemen of Verona. Act III. Sc. 1. L. 338.

15
If, one by one, you wedded all the world,
Or from the all that are took something good,
To make a perfect woman, she you kill'd
Would be unparallel'd.
Winter's Tale. Act V. Sc. 1. L. 13.

16
Women will love her that she is a woman
More worth than any man; men, that she is
The rarest of all women.
Winter's Tale. Act V. Sc. 1. L. 110.

17
In the beginning, said a Persian poet—Allah took a rose, a lily, a dove, a serpent, a little honey, a Dead Sea apple, and a handful of clay. When he looked at the amalgam—it was a woman.
WILLIAM SHARP. In the *Portfolio,* July, 1894. P. 6.

18
Woman reduces us all to the common denominator.
BERNARD SHAW—*Great Catherine.* Sc. 1.

19
The fickleness of the woman I love is only equalled by the infernal constancy of the women who love me.
BERNARD SHAW—*Philanderer.* Act II.

20
Woman's dearest delight is to wound Man's self-conceit, though Man's dearest delight is to gratify hers.
BERNARD SHAW—*Unsocial Socialist.* Ch. V.

21
You sometimes have to answer a woman according to her womanishness, just as you have to answer a fool according to his folly.
BERNARD SHAW — *Unsocial Socialist.* Ch. XVIII.

22
A lovely lady garmented in light.
SHELLEY—*The Witch of Atlas.* St. 5.

23
One moral's plain, * * * without more fuss;
Man's social happiness all rests on us:
Through all the drama—whether damn'd or not—
Love gilds the scene, and women guide the plot.
R. B. SHERIDAN—*The Rivals. Epilogue.*

24
She is her selfe of best things the collection.
SIR PHILIP SIDNEY—*The Arcadia. Thirsis and Dorus.*

25
Lor', but women's rum cattle to deal with, the first man found that to his cost,

And I reckon it's just through a woman the last man on earth'll be lost.
G. R. Sims—*Moll Jarvis o' Morley.*

1
What wilt not woman, gentle woman, dare
When strong affection stirs her spirit up?
Southey—*Madoc.* Pt. II. II.

2
He beheld his own rougher make softened into sweetness, and tempered with smiles; he saw a creature who had, as it were, Heaven's second thought in her formation.
Steele—*Christian Hero.* (Of Adam awaking, and first seeing Eve.)

3
She is pretty to walk with,
And witty to talk with,
And pleasant too, to think on.
Sir John Suckling—*Brennoralt.* Act II. Sc. 1.

4
Of all the girls that e'er was seen,
There's none so fine as Nelly.
Swift—*Ballad on Miss Nelly Bennet.*
(See also Carey)

5
Daphne knows, with equal ease,
How to vex and how to please;
But the folly of her sex
Makes her sole delight to vex.
Swift—*Daphne.*

6
Lose no time to contradict her,
Nor endeavour to convict her;
Only take this rule along,
Always to advise her wrong,
And reprove her when she's right;
She may then grow wise for spite.
Swift—*Daphne.*

7
O Woman, you are not merely the handiwork of God, but also of men; these are ever endowing you with beauty from their own hearts. . . . You are one-half woman and one-half dream.
Rabindranath Tagore—*Gardener.* 59.

8
Femmina è cosa garrula e fallace:
Vuole e disvuole, è folle uom chi sen fida,
Sì tra se volge.
Women have tongues of craft, and hearts of guile,
They will, they will not; fools that on them trust;
For in their speech is death, hell in their smile.
Tasso—*Gerusalemme.* XIX. 84.

9
All virtuous women, like tortoises, carry their house on their heads, and their chappel in their heart, and their danger in their eye, and their souls in their hands, and God in all their actions.
Jeremy Taylor—*Life of Christ.* Pt. I. II. 4.
(See also Britaine)

10
A woman's honor rests on manly love.
Esais Tegnèr—*Fridthjof's Saga.* Canto VIII.

11
For men at most differ as Heaven and Earth,
But women, worst and best, as Heaven and Hell.
Tennyson—*Idylls of the King. Merlin and Vivian.*

12
Airy, fairy Lilian.
Tennyson—*Lilian.*

13
Woman is the lesser man.
Tennyson—*Locksley Hall.* St. 76.

14
She with all the charm of woman,
She with all the breadth of man.
Tennyson—*Locksley Hall Sixty Years After.* L. 48.

15
Queen rose of the rosebud garden of girls.
Tennyson—*Maud.* Pt. I. XXII. St. 9.

16
With prudes for proctors, dowagers for deans,
And sweet girl-graduates in their golden hair.
Tennyson—*The Princess. Prologue.* L. 141.

17
A rosebud set with little wilful thorns,
And sweet as English air could make her, she.
Tennyson—*The Princess. Prologue.* L. 153

18 The woman is so hard
Upon the woman.
Tennyson—*The Princess.* VI.

19
For woman is not undeveloped man
But diverse; could we make her as the man
Sweet love were slain; his dearest bond is this
Not like to like but like in difference.
Tennyson—*The Princess.* VII.

20
Novi ingenium mulierum;
Nolunt ubi velis, ubi nolis cupiunt ultro.
I know the nature of women. When you will, they will not; when you will not, they come of their own accord.
Terence—*Eunuchus.* IV. 7. 42.

21
When I say that I know women, I mean that I know that I don't know them. Every single woman I ever knew is a puzzle to me, as I have no doubt she is to herself.
Thackeray—*Mr. Brown's Letters.*

22
Regard the society of women as a necessary unpleasantness of social life, and avoid it as much as possible.
Tolstoy—*Diary.*

23
Woman is more impressionable than man. Therefore in the Golden Age they were better than men. Now they are worse.
Tolstoy—*Diary.*

24
I think Nature hath lost the mould
Where she her shape did take;
Or else I doubt if Nature could
So fair a creature make.
A Praise of his Lady. In *Tottel's Miscellany.* (1557) The Earl of Surrey wrote similar lines, *A Praise of his Love.* (Before 1547)
(See also Ariosto under Man)

25
He is a fool who thinks by force or skill
To turn the current of a woman's will.
Sir Samuel Tuke—*Adventures of Five Hours.* Act V. Sc. 3. L. 483. Trans. from Calderon.
(See also Hill)

1
A slighted woman knows no bounds.
JOHN VANBRUGH—*The Mistake.* Pt. I. Act II. Sc. 1.
(See also CONGREVE)

2
Let our weakness be what it will, mankind will still be weaker; and whilst there is a world, 'tis woman that will govern it.
JOHN VANBRUGH—*Provoked Wife.* Act III.

3
Dux femina facti.
A woman was leader in the deed.
VERGIL—*Æneid.* I. 364.
(See also DUMAS)

4
Varium et mutabile semper,
Femina.
A woman is always changeable and capricious.
VERGIL—*Æneid.* IV. 569.
(See also FRANCIS I)

5
Furens quid fœmina possit.
That which an enraged woman can accomplish.
VERGIL—*Æneid.* V. 6.
(See also CONGREVE)

6
All the reasonings of men are not worth one sentiment of women.
VOLTAIRE.

7
Very learned women are to be found, in the same manner as female warriors; but they are seldom or ever inventors.
VOLTAIRE—*A Philosophical Dictionary. Women.*

8
"Woman" must ever be a woman's highest name,
And honors more than "Lady," if I know right.
WALTER VON DER VOGELWEIDE. Translated in the *Minnesinger of Germany. Woman and Lady.*

9
My wife is one of the best wimin on this Continent, altho' she isn't always gentle as a lamb with mint sauce.
ARTEMUS WARD—*A War Meeting.*

10
She is not old, she is not young,
The Woman with the Serpent's Tongue.
The haggard cheek, the hungering eye,
The poisoned words that wildly fly,
The famished face, the fevered hand—
Who slights the worthiest in the land,
Sneers at the just, contemns the brave,
And blackens goodness in its grave.
WILLIAM WATSON—*Woman with the Serpent's Tongue.*

11
What cannot a neat knave with a smooth tale
Make a woman believe?
JOHN WEBSTER—*Duchess of Malfi.* I. II.

12
Not from his head was woman took,
As made her husband to o'erlook;
Not from his feet, as one designed
The footstool of the stronger kind;
But fashioned for himself, a bride;
An equal, taken from his side.
CHARLES WESLEY—*Short Hymns on Select Passages of the Holy Scriptures.*
(See also DIXON)

13
There are only two kinds of women, the plain and the coloured.
OSCAR WILDE—*Dorian Gray.* Ch. III. Same in *Woman of no Importance.* Act III.

14
Oh! no one. No one in particular. A woman of no importance.
OSCAR WILDE—*Woman of No Importance.* Act I.

15
Shall I, wasting in despaire,
Dye because a woman's faire?
Or make pale my cheeks with care
Cause another's rosie are?
Be shee fairer than the day,
Or the flow'ry meads in May;
If she be not so to me,
What care I how faire shee be?
GEORGE WITHER—*Mistresse of Philarete.* PERCY—*Reliques.*
(See also RALEIGH)

16
A Creature not too bright or good
For human nature's daily food;
For transient sorrows, simple wiles,
Praise, blame, love, kisses, tears and smiles.
WORDSWORTH—*She was a Phantom of Delight.*

17
And now I see with eye serene,
The very pulse of the machine;
A Being breathing thoughtful breath,
A Traveller betwixt life and death;
The reason firm, the temperate will,
Endurance, foresight, strength, and skill.
WORDSWORTH—*She was a Phantom of Delight.*

18
A perfect Woman, nobly planned
To warn, to comfort, and command.
WORDSWORTH—*She was a Phantom of Delight.*

19
She was a Phantom of delight
When first she gleamed upon my sight;
A lovely Apparition, sent
To be a moment's ornament.
WORDSWORTH—*She was a Phantom of Delight.*

20
Shalt show us how divine a thing
A Woman may be made.
WORDSWORTH—*To a Young Lady. Dear Child of Nature.*

21
And beautiful as sweet!
And young as beautiful! and soft as young!
And gay as soft! and innocent as gay.
YOUNG—*Night Thoughts.* Night III. L. 81.

WONDERS

22
He shall have chariots easier than air,
That I will have invented; . . . And thyself,
That art the messenger, shalt ride before him
On a horse cut out of an entire diamond.
That shall be made to go with golden wheels,
I know not how yet.
BEAUMONT AND FLETCHER—*A King and No King.* Act V.

23
A schoolboy's tale, the wonder of an hour!
BYRON—*Childe Harold.* Canto II. St. 2.

1
Mira cano; sol occubuit;
Nox nulla secuta est.
Wonders I sing; the sun has set; no night has followed.
BURTON, quoting from a reference to a phrase of GIRALDUS GAMBRENSIS, found in CAMDEN—*Epigrammes.*

2
If a man proves too clearly and convincingly to himself . . . that a tiger is an optical illusion—well, he will find out he is wrong. The tiger will himself intervene in the discussion, in a manner which will be in every sense conclusive.
G. K. CHESTERTON.

3
The world will never starve for want of wonders; but only for want of wonder.
G. K. CHESTERTON—*Tremendous Trifles.*

4
We were young, we were merry, we were very, very wise,
And the door stood open at our feast,
When there passed us a woman with the West in her eyes,
And a man with his back to the East.
MARY E. COLERIDGE—*Unwelcome.*

5
"Never see . . . a dead post-boy, did you?" inquired Sam. . . . "No," rejoined Bob, "I never did." "No!" rejoined Sam triumphantly. "Nor never vill; and there's another thing that no man never see, and that's a dead donkey."
DICKENS—*Pickwick Papers.* Ch. LI.

6
Long stood the noble youth oppress'd with awe,
And stupid at the wondrous things he saw,
Surpassing common faith, transgressing nature's law.
DRYDEN—*Theodore and Honoria.* L. 217.

7
Men love to wonder and that is the seed of our science.
EMERSON—*Works and Days.*

8
This wonder lasted nine daies.
HEYWOOD—*Proverbs.* Pt. II. Ch. I. Nine days wonder. ROGER ASCHAM—*Scholemaster.* Title of book by KEMP. MASSINGER—*New Way to Pay Old Debts.* Act IV. Sc. 2.

9
The things that have been and shall be no more,
The things that are, and that hereafter shall be,
The things that might have been, and yet were not,
The fading twilight of joys departed.
LONGFELLOW — *Christus. Divine Tragedy. First Passover.* III. *Marriage in Cana.*

10
Wonder [said Socrates] is very much the affection of a philosopher; for there is no other beginning of philosophy than this.
PLATO—*Theætetus.* XXXII. CARY's trans.

11
Pretty! in amber to observe the forms
Of hairs, of straws, or dirt, or grubs, or worms!
The things, we know, are neither rich nor rare,
But wonder how the devil they got there.
POPE—*Prologue to the Satires.* L. 169.
(See also FLY, SPIDER)

12
Out of our reach the gods have laid
Of time to come th' event,
And laugh to see the fools afraid
Of what the knaves invent.
SIR C. SEDLEY—*Lycophron.*

13
O wonderful, wonderful, and most wonderful wonderful! and yet again wonderful, and after that, out of all hooping.
As You Like It. Act III. Sc. 2. L. 201.

14
O day and night, but this is wondrous strange.
Hamlet. Act I. Sc. 5. L. 164.
(See also OTHELLO)

15
Can such things be,
And overcome us like a summer's cloud,
Without our special wonder?
Macbeth. Act III. Sc. 4. L. 110.

16
Stones have been known to move and trees to speak.
Macbeth. Act III. Sc. 4. L. 123.

17
'Twas strange, 'twas passing strange;
'Twas pitiful, 'twas wondrous pitiful.
Othello. Act I. Sc. 3. L. 160.
(See also HAMLET)

18
There's something in a flying horse,
There's something in a huge balloon.
WORDSWORTH—*Peter Bell.* Prologue. St. 1.

19
We nothing know, but what is marvellous;
Yet what is marvellous, we can't believe.
YOUNG—*Night Thoughts.* Night VII.

20
Nothing but what astonishes is true.
YOUNG—*Night Thoughts.* Night IX.

WOODBINE

Lonicera

21
And stroke with listless hand
The woodbine through the window, till at last
I came to do it with a sort of love.
E. B. BROWNING—*Aurora Leigh.* Bk. I.

22
A filbert-hedge with wild-briar overtwined,
And clumps of woodbine taking the soft wind
Upon their summer thrones.
KEATS—*I Stood Tiptoe Upon a Little Hill.*

23
And the woodbine spices are wafted abroad,
And the musk of the rose is blown.
TENNYSON—*Maud.* Pt. XXII. St. I.

WOOING

24
Thrice happy's the wooing that's not long a-doing,
So much time is saved in the billing and cooing.
R. H. BARHAM—*Sir Rupert the Fearless.*
(See also BURTON)

25
Why don't the men propose, mamma?
Why don't the men propose?
THOMAS HAYNES BAYLY—*Songs and Ballads. Why Don't the Men Propose?*

1
'Yes,' I answered you last night;
'No,' this morning, sir, I say:
Colors seen by candle-light
Will not look the same by day.
E. B. BROWNING—*The Lady's "Yes."*

2
Alas! to seize the moment
When heart inclines to heart,
And press a suit with passion,
Is not a woman's part.

If man come not to gather
The roses where they stand,
They fade among their foliage,
They cannot seek his hand.
BRYANT—*Song*. Trans. from the Spanish of IGLESIAS.

3
Woo the fair one when around
Early birds are singing;
When o'er all the fragrant ground
Early herbs are springing:
When the brookside, bank, and grove
All with blossom laden,
Shine with beauty, breathe of love,
Woo the timid maiden.
BRYANT—*Love's Lessons*.

4
Duncan Gray cam here to woo,
Ha, ha, the wooing o't!
On blithe Yulenight when we were fou,
Ha, ha, the wooing o't!
Maggie coost her head fu' high,
Looked asklent and unco skeigh,
Gart poor Duncan stand abeigh:
Ha, ha! the wooing o't!
BURNS—*Duncan Gray*.

5
And let us mind, faint heart ne'er wan
A lady fair.
Wha does the utmost that he can
Will whyles do mair.
BURNS—*To Dr. Blacklock*.
(See also FLETCHER)

6
The landlady and Tam grew gracious
Wi' favours secret, sweet and precious.
BURNS—*Tam o'Shanter*. St. 7.

7
Blessed is the wooing
That is not long a-doing.
Quoted in BURTON—*Anatomy of Melancholy*.
(See also BARHAM)

8
How often in the summer-tide,
His graver business set aside,
Has stripling Will, the thoughtful-eyed
As to the pipe of Pan,
Stepped blithesomely with lover's pride
Across the fields to Anne.
RICHARD BURTON—*Across the Fields to Anne*.
(Referring to Shakespeare.)

9
He that will win his dame must do
As love does when he draws his bow;
With one hand thrust the lady from,
And with the other pull her home.
BUTLER—*Hudibras*. Pt. II. Canto I. L. 449.

10
She that with poetry is won,
Is but a desk to write upon;
And what men say of her they mean
No more than on the thing they lean.
BUTLER—*Hudibras*. Pt. II. Canto I. L. 591.

11
Do proper homage to thine idol's eyes;
But not too humbly, or she will despise
Thee and thy suit, though told in moving tropes:
Disguise even tenderness, if thou art wise.
BYRON—*Childe Harold*. Canto II. St. 34.

12
Not much he kens, I ween, of woman's breast,
Who thinks that wanton thing is won by sighs.
BYRON—*Childe Harold*. Canto II. St. 34.

13
'Tis an old lesson; time approves it true,
And those who know it best, deplore it most;
When all is won that all desire to woo,
The paltry prize is hardly worth the cost.
BYRON—*Childe Harold*. Canto II. St. 35.

14
And whispering, "I will ne'er consent"—consented.
BYRON—*Don Juan*. Canto I. St. 117.
(See also RALEIGH)

15
There is a tide in the affairs of women
Which, taken at the flood, leads—God knows where.
BYRON—*Don Juan*. Canto VI. St 2.

16
Some are soon bagg'd but some reject three dozen.
'Tis fine to see them scattering refusals
And wild dismay, o'er every angry cousin
(Friends of the party) who begin accusals,
Such as—"Unless Miss (Blank) meant to have chosen
Poor Frederick, why did she accord perusals
To his billets? *Why* waltz with him? Why, I pray,
Look *yes* last night, and yet say *No* to-day?"
BYRON—*Don Juan*. Canto XII. St. 34.

17
'Tis enough—
Who listens once will listen twice;
Her heart be sure is not of ice,
And one refusal no rebuff.
BYRON—*Mazeppa*. St. 6.

18
Better be courted and jilted
Than never be courted at all.
CAMPBELL—*The Jilted Nymph*.
(See also TENNYSON under LOVE)

19
Never wedding, ever wooing,
Still a lovelorn heart pursuing,
Read you not the wrong you're doing
In my cheek's pale hue?
All my life with sorrow strewing;
Wed or cease to woo.
CAMPBELL—*The Maid's Remonstrance*.

20
So mourn'd the dame of Ephesus her Love,
And thus the Soldier arm'd with Resolution
Told his soft Tale, and was a thriving Wooer.
COLLEY CIBBER—*Richard III*. (Altered). Act II. Sc. 1.

1
Faint heart hath been a common phrase, faire ladie never wives.
J. P. COLLIER'S *Reprint of The Rocke of Regard.* (1576) P. 122.
(See also FLETCHER)

2
And when with envy Time transported
Shall think to rob us of our joys,
You'll in your girls again be courted,
And I'll go wooing in my boys.
GILBERT COOPER, according to JOHN AIKIN, in *Collection of English Songs. Winifreda.* Claimed for him by WALTER THORNBURY—*Two Centuries of Song.* (1810) BISHOP PERCY assigns it a place in his *Reliques.* I. 326, (Ed. 1777), but its ancient origin is a fiction. Poem appeared in *Dodsley's Magazine* and in *Miscellaneous Poems by Several hands.* (1726)

3
"Chops and Tomata Sauce. Yours, Pickwick." Chops! Gracious heavens! and Tomata Sauce! Gentlemen, is the happiness of a sensitive and confiding female to be trifled away by such shallow artifices as these?
DICKENS—*Pickwick Papers.* Ch. XXXIV.

4
Ah, Foole! faint heart faire lady n'ere could win.
PHINEAS FLETCHER—*Brittain's Ida.* Canto V. St. 1. WM. ELLERTON—*George a-Greene.* Ballad written about 1569. *A Proper New Ballad in Praise of My Lady Marques.* (1569) Reprint Philobiblian So. 1867. P. 22. Early use in CAMDEN'S *Remaines.* (Ed. 1814) Originally published with SPENSER'S name on the title page.
(See also BURNS, COLLIER, also DRYDEN under BRAVERY)

5
Perhaps if you address the lady
Most politely, most politely,
Flatter and impress the lady
Most politely, most politely.
Humbly beg and humbly sue,
She may deign to look on you.
W. S. GILBERT—*Princess Ida.*

6
If doughty deeds my lady please,
Right soon I'll mount my steed,
And strong his arm and fast his seat,
That bears me from the meed.
Then tell me how to woo thee, love,
Oh, tell me how to woo thee
For thy dear sake, nae care I'll take
Though ne'er another trow me.
ROBERT GRAHAM—*Tell me how to woo Thee.*

7
I'll woo her as the lion woos his brides.
JOHN HOME—*Douglas.* Act I. Sc. 1.

8
The surest way to hit a woman's heart is to take aim kneeling.
DOUGLAS JERROLD—*Douglas Jerrold's Wit. The Way to a Woman's Heart.*

9
Follow a shadow, it still flies you,
Seem to fly, it will pursue:
So court a mistress, she denies you;
Let her alone, she will court you.
Say are not women truly, then,
Styled but the shadows of us men?
BEN JONSON—*The Forest. Song. That Women are but Men's Shadows.*

10
There be triple ways to take, of the eagle or the snake,
Or the way of a man with a maid.
KIPLING—*The Long Trail. L'Envoi to Departmental Ditties.*
(See also PROVERBS)

11
A fool there was and he made his prayer
(Even as you and I!)
To a rag and a bone and a hank of hair
(We called her the woman who did not care)
But the fool he called her his lady fair—
(Even as you and I!)
KIPLING—*The Vampire.*

12
If I am not worth the wooing, I surely am not worth the winning.
LONGFELLOW—*Courtship of Miles Standish.* Pt. III. L. 111.

13
Why don't you speak for yourself, John?
LONGFELLOW—*Courtship of Miles Standish.* III. Last line.

14
The nightingales among the sheltering boughs
Of populous many-nested trees
Shall teach me how to woo thee, and shall tell me
By what resistless charms or incantations
They won their mates.
LONGFELLOW—*The Masque of Pandora.* Pt. V. L. 62.

15
Come live in my heart and pay no rent.
LOVER—*Vourneen! when your days were bright.*

16
His heart kep' goin' pity-pat,
But hern went pity-Zekle.
LOWELL—*Introduction to The Biglow Papers.* Second series. *The Courtin'.* St. 15.

17
Whaur hae ye been a' day,
My boy Tammy?
I've been by burn and flowery brae,
Meadow green and mountain grey,
Courting of this young thing
Just come frae her mammy.
HECTOR MACNEILL—*Song.*

18
I will now court her in the conqueror's style;
"Come, see, and overcome."
MASSINGER—*Maid of Honour.* Act II. Sc. 1.

19
He kissed her cold corpse a thousand times o'er,
And called her his jewel though she was no more;
And he drank all the pison like a lovyer so brave,
And Villikins and Dinah lie buried in one grave.
HENRY MAYHEW condensed and interpolated the modern version in his *Wandering Minstrel.* The words of an old song given to him by the actor, MITCHELL, who sang it in 1831. The ballad is older than the age of Queen Elizabeth, according to G. A. SALA—*Autobiography.*

20
And every shepherd tells his tale
Under the hawthorn in the dale.
MILTON—*L'Allegro.* L. 67.

1
Her virtue and the conscience of her worth,
That would be woo'd, and not unsought be won.
MILTON—*Paradise Lost.* Bk. VIII. L. 502.

2
That you are in a terrible taking,
By all these sweet oglings I see;
But the fruit that can fall without shaking,
Indeed is too mellow for me.
LADY MARY WORTLEY MONTAGU—*Lines written for Lord William Hamilton.*

3
Let this great maxim be my virtue's guide:
In part she is to blame that has been tried;
He comes too near that comes to be denied.
LADY MARY WORTLEY MONTAGU—*The Lady's Resolve.* In *Works.* Vol. V. P. 104. Ed. 1803. Quoted from OVERBURY.
(See also OVERBURY)

4
If I speak to thee in friendship's name,
Thou think'st I speak too coldly;
If I mention Love's devoted flame,
Thou say'st I speak too boldly.
MOORE—*How Shall I Woo?*

5
'Tis sweet to think that where'er we rove
We are sure to find something blissful and dear;
And that when we're far from the lips we love,
We've but to make love to the lips we are near.
MOORE—*'Tis Sweet to Think.*

6
The time I've lost in wooing,
In watching and pursuing
The light that lies
In woman's eyes,
Has been my heart's undoing.
MOORE—*The Time I've Lost in Wooing.*

7
I sat with Doris, the Shepherd maiden;
Her crook was laden with wreathèd flowers;
I sat and wooed her through sunlight wheeling,
And shadows stealing for hours and hours.
ARTHUR JAMES MUNBY—*Pastoral.*

8
Ye shall know my breach of promise.
Numbers. XIV. 34.

9
In part to blame is she,
Which hath *without consent* bin only tride;
He comes *too neere*, that comes to be *denide.*
SIR THOS. OVERBURY—*A Wife.* St. 36.
(See also MONTAGU)

10
Ah, whither shall a maiden flee,
When a bold youth so swift pursues,
And siege of tenderest courtesy,
With hope perseverant, still renews!
COVENTRY PATMORE—*The Chase.*

11
They dream in courtship, but in wedlock wake.
POPE—*Wife of Bath.* L. 103.

12
The way of an eagle in the air; the way of a serpent upon a rock; the way of a ship in the midst of the sea; and the way of a man with a maid.
Proverbs. XXX. 19.
(See also KIPLING)

13
But in vain did she conjure him
To depart her presence so,
Having a thousand tongues t'allure him,
And but one to bid him go.
SIR WALTER RALEIGH—*Dulcina.* Attributed to BRYDGES, who edited Raleigh's poems.
(See also BYRON)

14
It was a happy age when a man might have wooed his wench with a pair of kid leather gloves, a silver thimble, or with a tawdry lace; but now a velvet gown, a chain of pearl, or a coach with four horses will scarcely serve the turn.
RICH—*My Lady's Looking Glass.*

15
Wooed, and married, and a',
Married, and wooed, and a'!
And was she nae very weel off
That was wooed, and married, and a'?
ALEX. ROSS—*Song.*

16
A pressing lover seldom wants success,
Whilst the respectful, like the Greek, sits down
And wastes a ten years' siege before one town.
NICHOLAS ROWE—*To the Inconstant. Epilogue.* L. 18.

17
Lightly from fair to fair he flew,
And loved to plead, lament, and sue,—
Suit lightly won, and short-lived pain,
For monarchs seldom sigh in vain.
SCOTT—*Marmion.* Canto V. St. 9.

18
A heaven on earth I have won by wooing thee.
All's Well That Ends Well. Act IV. Sc. 2. L. 66.

19
Most fair,
Will you vouchsafe to teach a soldier terms
Such as will enter at a lady's ear
And plead his love-suit to her gentle heart?
Henry V. Act V. Sc. 2. L. 98.

20
She's beautiful and therefore to be woo'd:
She is a woman, therefore to be won.
Henry VI. Pt. I. Act V. Sc. 3. L. 78.
(See also TITUS ANDRONICUS)

21
Be merry, and employ your chiefest thoughts
To courtship and such fair ostents of love
As shall conveniently become you there.
Merchant of Venice. Act II. Sc. 8. L. 43.

22
Wooing thee, I found thee of more value
Than stamps in gold or sums in sealed bags;
And 'tis the very riches of thyself
That now I aim at.
Merry Wives of Windsor. Act III. Sc. 4. L. 15.

23
We cannot fight for love, as men may do;
We should be woo'd and were not made to woo.
Midsummer Night's Dream. Act II. Sc. 1. L. 241.

24
Sigh no more, ladies, sigh no more,
Men were deceivers ever,
One foot in sea and one on shore;
To one thing constant never.
Much Ado About Nothing. Act II. Sc. 3. L. 64. Not in original folio. See also THOS. PERCY—*The Friar of Orders Gray.* ("Weep no more, Ladies.")

1
I was not born under a rhyming planet, nor I cannot woo in festival terms.
Much Ado About Nothing. Act V. Sc. 2. L. 40.

2
She wish'd she had not heard it, yet she wish'd
That heaven had made her such a man: she thank'd me,
And bade me, if I had a friend that lov'd her,
I should but teach him how to tell my story
And that would woo her.
Othello. Act I. Sc. 3. L. 162.

3
Was ever woman in this humour woo'd?
Was ever woman in this humour won?
Richard III. Act I. Sc. 2. L. 228.

4
O gentle Romeo,
If thou dost love, pronounce it faithfully.
Or if thou think'st I am too quickly won,
I'll frown and be perverse and say thee nay,
So thou wilt woo: but else, not for the world.
Romeo and Juliet. Act II. Sc. 2. L. 93.

5
She is a woman, therefore may be woo'd;
She is a woman, therefore may be won.
Titus Andronicus. Act II. Sc. 1. L. 82.
(See also Henry VI)

6
Women are angels, wooing:
Things won are done, joy's soul lies in the doing:
That she belov'd knows nought that knows not this:
Men prize the thing ungain'd more than it is.
Troilus and Cressida. Act I. Sc. 2. L. 312.

7
Win her with gifts, if she respect not words;
Dumb jewels often in their silent kind
More than quick words do move a woman's mind.
Two Gentlemen of Verona. Act III. Sc. 1. L. 89.

8
Never give her o'er;
For scorn at first makes after-love the more.
If she do frown, 'tis not in hate of you,
But rather to beget more love in you;
If she do chide, 'tis not to have you gone,
For why, the fools are mad if left alone.
Two Gentlemen of Verona. Act III. Sc. 1. L. 94.

9
Take no repulse, whatever she doth say;
For, "get you gone," she doth not mean, "away."
Flatter and praise, commend, extol their graces;
Though ne'er so black, say they have angels' faces.
That man that hath a tongue, I say, is no man,
If with his tongue he cannot win a woman.
Two Gentlemen of Verona. Act III. Sc. 1. L. 100.

10
Say that upon the altar of her beauty
You sacrifice your tears, your sighs, your heart:
Write till your ink be dry and with your tears
Moist it again, and frame some feeling line,
That may discover such integrity.
Two Gentlemen of Verona. Act III. Sc. 2. L. 73.

11
Bring therefore all the forces that ye may,
And lay incessant battery to her heart;
Playnts, prayers, vowes, truth, sorrow, and dismay;
Those engins can the proudest love convert:
And, if those fayle, fall down and dy before her;
So dying live, and living do adore her.
Spenser—*Amoretti and Epithalamion.* Sonnet XIV.

12
Full little knowest thou that hast not tried,
What hell it is in suing long to bide:
To loose good dayes, that might be better spent;
To waste long nights in pensive discontent;
To speed to-day, to be put back to-morrow;
To feed on hope, to pine with feare and sorrow.
Spenser—*Mother Hubberd's Tale.* L. 895.

13
Quiet, Robin, quiet!
You lovers are such clumsy summer-flies,
Forever buzzing at your lady's face.
Tennyson—*The Foresters.* Act IV. Sc. 1.

14
When Venus said "Spell no for me,"
"N-O," Dan Cupid wrote with glee,
And smiled at his success:
"Ah, child," said Venus, laughing low,
"We women do not spell it so,
We spell it Y-E-S."
Carolyn Wells—*The Spelling Lesson.*

WORDS

15
Words of truth and soberness.
Acts. XXVI. 25.

16
Words, as a Tartar's bow, do shoot back upon the understanding of the wisest, and mightily entangle and pervert the judgment.
Bacon—*Advancement of Learning.*
(See also Carleton, Dillon, Eliot, Heine, Menander)

17
Words of affection, howsoe'er express'd,
The latest spoken still are deem'd the best.
Joanna Baillie—*Address to Miss Agnes Baillie on her Birthday.* L. 126.

18
'Tis a word that's quickly spoken,
Which being restrained, a heart is broken.
Beaumont and Fletcher—*The Spanish Curate.* Act II. Sc. 5. *Song.*

19
'Twas he that ranged the words at random flung,
Pierced the fair pearls and them together strung.
Bidpai (Pilpay)—*Anvar-i Suhaili.* Eastwick's trans.
(See also Jones)

20
You have only, when before your glass, to keep pronouncing to yourself nimini-pimini; the lips cannot help taking their plie.
General Burgoyne—*The Heiress.* Act III. Sc. 2.

21
A very great part of the mischiefs that vex this world arises from words.
Burke—*Letter.* (About 1795)
(See also Dickens)

22
Boys flying kites haul in their white winged birds.
You can't do that way when you're flying words.
"Careful with fire," is good advice we know

"Careful with words," is ten times doubly so.
Thoughts unexpressed may sometimes fall back dead;
But God Himself can't kill them when they're said.

WILL CARLETON—*The First Settler's Story*. St. 21.
(See also BACON)

1
High Air-castles are cunningly built of Words, the Words well bedded also in good Logic-mortar; wherein, however, no Knowledge will come to lodge.

CARLYLE—*Sartor Resartus*. Bk. I. Ch. VIII.

2
The *Moral* is that gardeners pine,
Whene'er no pods adorn the vine.
Of all sad words experience gleans,
The saddest are: "It *might* have beans."
(I did not make this up myself:
'Twas in a book upon my shelf.
It's witty, but I don't deny
It's rather Whittier than I.)

GUY WETMORE CARRYL—*How Jack found that Beans may go back on a Chap*.
(See also WHITTIER)

3
Words writ in waters.

GEORGE CHAPMAN—*Revenge for Honour*. Act V. Sc. 2.

4
Words are but empty thanks.

COLLEY CIBBER—*Woman's Wit*. Act V.

5
Fair words butter no parsnips.

CLARKE—*Parœmiologia*. P. 12. (Ed. 1639) Quoted "soft words."

6
Mum's the word.

GEORGE COLMAN the Younger—*Battle of Hexham*. Act II. Sc. 1.

7
Without knowing *the force* of words, it is impossible to know men.

CONFUCIUS—*Analects*. Bk. XX. Ch. III

8
Words that weep, and tears that speak.

COWLEY—*The Prophet*. St. 2. L. 8.
(See also MALLET, also GRAY under THOUGHT)

9
Father is rather vulgar, my dear. The word Papa, besides, gives a pretty form to the lips. Papa, potatoes, poultry, prunes and prism are all very good words for the lips; especially prunes and prism.

DICKENS—*Little Dorrit*. Pt. II. Ch. V.
(See also BURGOYNE, GOLDSMITH)

10
But words once spoke can never be recall'd.

WENTWORTH DILLON—*Art of Poetry*. L. 442.
(See also BACON)

11
It used to be a common saying of Myson's that men ought not to seek for things in words, but for words in things; for that things are not made on account of words but that words are put together for the sake of things.

DIOGENES LAERTIUS—*Lives of the Philosophers*. Bk. I. *Myson*. Ch. III.

12
I trade both with the living and the dead for the enrichment of our native language.

DRYDEN — *Dedication to translation of The Æneid*.

13
And torture one poor word ten thousand ways.

DRYDEN—*Mac Flecknoe*. L. 208.

14
Let thy words be few.

Ecclesiastes. V. 2.

15
Let no man deceive you with vain words.

Ephesians. V. 6.

16
Our words have wings, but fly not where we would.

GEORGE ELIOT—*The Spanish Gypsy*. Bk. III.
(See also BACON)

17
What if my words
Were meant for deeds.

GEORGE ELIOT—*The Spanish Gypsy*. Bk. III.

18
An undisputed power
Of coining money from the rugged ore,
Nor less of coining words, is still confessed,
If with a legal public stamp impressed.

PHILIP FRANCIS—*Horace, Art of Poetry*.

19
New words and lately made shall credit claim
If from a Grecian source they gently stream.

PHILIP FRANCIS—*Horace, Art of Poetry*.

20
That blessed word Mesopotamia.

GARRICK tells of the power of GEORGE WHITEFIELD's voice, "he could make men either laugh or cry by pronouncing the word Mesopotamia." Related by FRANCIS JACOX. An old woman said she found great support in that comfortable word Mesopotamia. See BREWER's *Dictionary of Phrase and Fable*.

21
Der Worte sind genug gewechselt,
Lasst mich auch endlich Thaten sehn.
The words you've bandied are sufficient;
'Tis deeds that I prefer to see.

GOETHE—*Faust*. *Vorspiel auf dem Theater*. L. 214.

22
Gewöhnlich glaubt der Mensch, wenn er nur Worte hört,
Es müsse sich dabei doch auch was denken.
Man usually believes, if only words he hears,
That also with them goes material for thinking.

GOETHE—*Faust*. I. 6. 230.

23
Es macht das Volk sich auch mit Worten Lust.
The rabble also vent their rage in words.

GOETHE—*Torquato Tasso*. II. 2. 201.

24
At this every lady drew up her mouth as if going to pronounce the letter P.

GOLDSMITH—*Letter to Robt. Bryanton*. Sept., 1758.
(See also DICKENS)

25
If of all words of tongue and pen,
The saddest are, "It might have been,"
More sad are these we daily see,

"It is, but it hadn't ought to be."
BRET HARTE—*Mrs. Jenkins.*
(See also WHITTIER)

1
The arrow belongs not to the archer when it has once left the bow; the word no longer belongs to the speaker when it has once passed his lips, especially when it has been multiplied by the press.
HEINE—*Religion and Philosophy.* Preface. (1852)
(See also BACON)

2
Words and feathers the wind carries away.
HERBERT—*Jacula Prudentum.*

3
Words are women, deeds are men.
HERBERT—*Jacula Prudentum.*
(See also JOHNSON)

4
For words are wise men's counters—they do but reckon by them—but they are the money of fools.
THOMAS HOBBES—*The Leviathan.* Pt. I. Ch. IV. Sc. 15.

5
Words sweet as honey from his lips distill'd.
HOMER—*Iliad.* Bk. I. L. 332. POPE's trans.

6
Winged words.
HOMER—*Iliad.* Bk. XX. 331. POPE's trans.

7 Tristia mæstum
Vultum verba decent; iratum, plena minarum;
Ludentem, lasciva; severum, seria dictu.
Sorrowful words become the sorrowful; angry words suit the passionate; light words a playful expression; serious words suit the grave.
HORACE—*Ars Poetica.* 105.

8 Delere licebit
Quod non edideris; nescit vox missa reverti.
It will be practicable to blot written words which you do not publish; but the spoken word it is not possible to recall.
HORACE—*Ars Poetica.* 389. *Epistles.* I. 18. 71.

9
Words are the soul's ambassadors, who go
Abroad upon her errands to and fro.
J. HOWELL—*Of Words.*

10
How forcible are right words!
Job. VI. 25.

11
Who is this that darkeneth counsel by words without knowledge?
Job. XXXVIII. 2.

12
I am not yet so lost in lexicography, as to forget that words are the daughters of earth, and that things are the sons of heaven.
SAMUEL JOHNSON—*Preface to his Dictionary.* SIR WILLIAM JONES quotes the saying as proverbial in India ("deeds" for "sons"). Same used by SIR THOS. BODLEY—*Letter to his Librarian.* (1604)
(See also HERBERT, MADDEN)

13
To make dictionaries is dull work.
SAMUEL JOHNSON—*A Dictionary of the English Language. Dull.*

14
Like orient pearls at random strung.
SIR WILLIAM JONES. Trans. from the Persian of HAFIZ.
(See also BIDPAI)

15
The masterless man . . . afflicted with the magic of the necessary words. . . . Words that may become alive and walk up and down in the hearts of the hearers.
KIPLING—*Speech* at the Royal Academy Banquet, London. 1906.

16
We might have been—these are but common words,
And yet they make the sum of life's bewailing.
LETITIA E. LANDON—*Three Extracts from the Diary of a Week.*
(See also WHITTIER)

17
We should have a great many fewer disputes in the world if words were taken for what they are, the signs of our ideas only, and not for things themselves.
LOCKE—*Essay on the Human Understanding.* III. 10.

18
Speaking words of endearment where words of comfort availed not.
LONGFELLOW—*Evangeline.* Pt. I. V. L. 43.

19
My words are little jars
For you to take and put upon a shelf.
Their shapes are quaint and beautiful,
And they have many pleasant colours and lustres
To recommend them.
Also the scent from them fills the room
With sweetness of flowers and crushed grasses.
AMY LOWELL—*A Gift.*

20
There comes Emerson first, whose rich words, every one,
Are like gold nails in temples to hang trophies on.
LOWELL—*A Fable for Critics.*

21
Ein Wörtlein kann ihn fällen.
A single little word can strike him dead.
LUTHER. (Of the Pope.)

22
Some grave their wrongs on marble; He, more just,
Stooped down serene, and wrote them in the dust.
RICHARD R. MADDEN—*Poems on Sacred Subjects.*

23
Words are men's daughters, but God's sons are things.
SAMUEL MADDEN—*Boulter's Monument.* Said to have been inserted by Dr. Johnson.
(See also JOHNSON)

24
Words that weep, and strains that agonise.
DAVID MALLET (or Malloch)—*Amyntor and Theodora.* II. 306.

25
Strains that sigh and words that weep.
DAVID MALLET—*Funeral Hymn.* 23.
(See also GRAY under THOUGHT)

1
It is as easy to draw back a stone thrown with force from the hand, as to recall a word once spoken.
MENANDER—*Ex Incert. Comœd.* P. 216.
(See also BACON)

2
Words, however, are things; and the man who accords
To his language the license to outrage his soul,
Is controll'd by the words he disdains to control.
OWEN MEREDITH (Lord Lytton)—*Lucile.* Pt. I. Canto II. St. VI.

3
How many honest words have suffered corruption since Chaucer's days!
THOMAS MIDDLETON—*No Wit, No Help, Like a Woman's.* Act II. Sc. 1.

4
His words, * * * like so many nimble and airy servitors, trip about him at command.
MILTON—*Apology for Smectymnuus.*

5 With high words, that bore
Semblance of worth, not substance.
MILTON—*Paradise Lost.* Bk. I. 528.

6
Yet hold it more humane, more heav'nly, first,
By winning words to conquer willing hearts,
And make persuasion do the work of fear.
MILTON—*Paradise Regained.* Bk. I. L. 221.

7
And to bring in a new word by the head and shoulders, they leave out the old one.
MONTAIGNE—*Essays. Upon some Verses of Vergil.*

8
How many quarrels, and how important, has the doubt as to the meaning of this syllable "Hoc" produced for the world!
MONTAIGNE—*Essays.* Bk. II. Ch. XII. (Referring to the controversies on transubstantiation—"Hoc est corpus meum.")

9
Words repeated again have as another sound, so another sense.
MONTAIGNE—*Essays.* Bk. III. Ch. XII.

10
So spake those wary foes, fair friends in look,
And so in words great gifts they gave and took,
And had small profit, and small loss thereby.
WM. MORRIS—*Jason.* Bk. VIII. 379.

11
The word impossible is not in my dictionary.
NAPOLEON I.
(See also BULWER-LYTTON under FAILURE)

12
Things were first made, then words.
SIR T. OVERBURY—*A Wife.*

13
Hei mihi, quam facile est (quamvis hic contigit omnes),
Alterius lucta fortia verba loqui!
Ah me! how easy it is (how much all have experienced it) to indulge in brave words in another person's trouble.
OVID—*Ad Liviam.* 9.

14
Non opus est verbis, credite rebus.
There is no need of words; believe facts.
OVID—*Fasti.* II. 734.

15
Le monde se paye de paroles; peu approfondissement les choses.
The world is satisfied with words. Few appreciate the things beneath.
PASCAL—*Lettres Provinciales.* II.

16
In pertusum ingerimus dicta dolium, operam ludimus.
We are pouring our words into a sieve, and lose our labor.
PLAUTUS—*Pseudolus.* I. 3. 135.

17
Words will build no walls.
PLUTARCH—*Life of Pericles.* CRATINUS ridiculed the long wall PERICLES proposed to build.

18
Words are like leaves; and where they most abound,
Much fruit of sense beneath is rarely found.
POPE—*Essay on Criticism.* L. 309.

19
In words, as fashions, the same rule will hold:
Alike fantastic, if too new, or old:
Be not the first by whom the new are tried,
Nor yet the last to lay the old aside.
POPE—*Essay on Criticism.* L. 333.

20
Each word-catcher, that lives on syllables.
POPE—*Prologue to Satires,* 166.

21 They say * * *
That, putting all his words together,
'Tis three blue beans in one blue bladder.
PRIOR—*Alma.* Canto I. L. 26.

22
A word spoken in good season, how good is it!
Proverbs. XV. 23.

23
A word fitly spoken is like apples of gold in pictures of silver.
Proverbs. XXV. 11.

24
The words of his mouth were smoother than butter, but war was in his heart; his words were softer than oil, yet were they drawn swords.
Psalms. LV. 21.

25
Inanis verborum torrens.
An unmeaning torrent of words.
QUINTILIAN. 10. 7. 23.

26
Souvent d'un grand dessein un mot nous fait juger.
A single word often betrays a great design.
RACINE—*Athalie.* II. 6.

27
He that useth many words for the explaining any subject, doth, like the cuttle fish, hide himself for the most part in his own ink.
JOHN RAY—*On Creation.*

28
One of our defects as a nation is a tendency to use what have been called "weasel words." When a weasel sucks eggs the meat is sucked out of the egg. If you use a "weasel word" after another there is nothing left of the other.
ROOSEVELT—*Speech,* at St. Louis, May 31,

1916. "Weasel word" taken from a story by STEWART CHAPLIN in *Century Magazine*, June, 1900.

1

Satis eloquentiæ sapientiæ parum.
Enough words, little wisdom.
SALLUST—*Catilina*. V.
(See also TERENCE)

2

Schnell fertig ist die Jugend mit dem Wort.
Youth is too hasty with words.
SCHILLER—*Wallenstein's Tod*. II. 2. 99.

3

O! many a shaft, at random sent,
Finds mark the archer little meant!
And many a word, at random spoken,
May soothe or wound a heart that's broken!
SCOTT—*Lord of the Isles*. Canto V. St. 18.

4

Syllables govern the world.
JOHN SELDEN—*Table Talk*. *Power*.

5 What art thou? Have not I
An arm as big as thine? a heart as big?
Thy words, I grant, are bigger, for I wear not
My dagger in my mouth.
Cymbeline. Act IV. Sc. 2. L. 76.

6

What do you read, my lord?
Words, words, words.
Hamlet. Act II. Sc. 2. L. 193.
(See also TROILUS AND CRESSIDA)

7 Unpack my heart with words
And fall a-cursing, like a very drab.
Hamlet. Act II. Sc. 2. L. 614.

8

My words fly up, my thoughts remain below:
Words without thoughts never to heaven go.
Hamlet. Act III. Sc. 3. L. 97.

9

Familiar in his mouth as household words.
Henry V. Act IV. Sc. 3. L. 52.

10 'Tis well said again;
And 'tis a kind of good deed to say well:
And yet words are no deeds.
Henry VIII. Act III. Sc. 2. L. 152.

11

But yesterday the word of Cæsar might
Have stood against the world; now lies he there,
And none so poor to do him reverence.
Julius Cæsar. Act III. Sc. 2. L. 123.

12

Zounds! I was never so bethump'd with words
Since I first call'd my brother's father dad.
King John. Act II. Sc. 1. L. 466.

13

O they have lived long on the alms-basket of words. I marvel thy master hath not eaten thee for a word; for thou art not so long by the head as honorificabilitudinitatibus: thou art easier swallowed than a flap-dragon.
Love's Labour's Lost. Act V. Sc. 1. L. 42.
The word appears in BEAUMONT AND FLETCHER—*Mad Lover*. Act I. Also in *Complaynt of Scotland*, written before Shakespeare was born.

14

Taffeta phrases, silken terms precise,
Three-piled hyperboles, spruce affectation,
Figures pedantical.
Love's Labour's Lost. Act V. Sc. 2. L. 406.

15

Madam, you have bereft me of all words,
Only my blood speaks to you in my veins.
Merchant of Venice. Act III. Sc. 2. L. 177.

16

Here are a few of the unpleasant'st words
That ever blotted paper!
Merchant of Venice. Act III. Sc. 2. L. 254.

17

His very words are a fantastical banquet, just so many strange dishes.
Much Ado About Nothing. Act II. Sc. 3. L. 21.

18

But words are words; I never yet did hear
That the bruis'd heart was pierced through the ear.
Othello. Act I. Sc. 3. L. 218.

19

I know thou'rt full of love and honesty,
And weigh'st thy words before thou givest them breath.
Othello. Act III. Sc. 3. L. 118.

20

How long a time lies in one little word!
Four lagging winters and four wanton springs
End in a word: such is the breath of kings.
Richard II. Act I. Sc. 3. L. 213.

21

O, but they say the tongues of dying men
Enforce attention like deep harmony:
Where words are scarce, they are seldom spent in vain,
For they breathe truth that breathe their words in pain.
He that no more must say is listen'd more.
Richard II. Act II. Sc. 1. L. 5.

22

So all my best is dressing old words new.
Sonnet. LXXVI.

23

These words are razors to my wounded heart.
Titus Andronicus. Act I. Sc. 1. L. 314.

24

Words pay no debts, give her deeds.
Troilus and Cressida. Act III. Sc. 2. L. 58.

25

Words, words, mere words, no matter from the heart.
Troilus and Cressida. Act V. Sc. 3. L. 108.
(See also HAMLET)

26

Words are grown so false, I am loath to prove reason with them.
Twelfth Night. Act III. Sc. 1. L. 28.

27

A fine volley of words, gentlemen, and quickly shot off.
Two Gentlemen of Verona. Act II. Sc. 4. L. 33.

28 We know not what we do
When we speak words.
SHELLEY—*Rosalind and Helen*. L. 1,108.

29

Words are but holy as the deeds they cover
SHELLEY—*The Cenci*. Act II. Sc. 2.

1
The arts Babblative and Scriblative.
SOUTHEY—*Colloquies.*

2
The artillery of words.
SWIFT—*Ode to Sancroft.* L. 13.

3
But from sharp words and wits men pluck no fruit;
And gathering thorns they shake the tree at root;
For words divide and rend,
But silence is most noble till the end.
SWINBURNE—*Atalanta.*

4 I have not skill
From such a sharp and waspish word as "No"
To pluck the sting.
HENRY TAYLOR—*Philip Van Artevelde.* Act I. Sc. 2.

5
I sometimes hold it half a sin
To put in words the grief I feel;
For words, like Nature, half reveal
And half conceal the Soul within.
* * * * *
In words, like weeds, I'll wrap me o'er,
Like coarsest clothes against the cold;
But that large grief which these enfold
Is given in outline and no more.
TENNYSON—*In Memoriam.* V.

6
Dictum sapienti sat est.
A word to the wise is sufficient.
TERENCE—*Phormio.* III. 3. 8. PLAUTUS—*Persa.* Act IV. Sc. 7. Generally quoted "verbum sapienti satis est."
(See also SALLUST)

7
As the last bell struck, a peculiar sweet smile shone over his face, and he lifted up his head a little, and quickly said, "Adsum!" and fell back. It was the word we used at school, when names were called; and lo, he, whose heart was as that of a little child, had answered to his name, and stood in the presence of The Master.
THACKERAY—*Newcomes.* Bk. II. Ch. XLII.

8
Deep in my heart subsides the infrequent word,
And there dies slowly throbbing like a wounded bird.
FRANCIS THOMPSON—*Her Portrait.* St. 3.

9
Hold fast the form of sound words.
II Timothy. I. 13.

10
As shadows attend substances, so words follow upon things.
ARCHBP. TRENCH—*Study of Words.*

11
Dat inania verba,
Dat sine mente sonum.
He utters empty words, he utters sound without mind.
VERGIL—*Æneid.* 10. 639.

12
You [Pindar] who possessed the talent of speaking much without saying anything.
VOLTAIRE—*Sur la Carrousel de l'Impératrice de Russie.*

13
You phrase-tormenting fantastic chorus,
With strangest words at your beck and call.
SIR WM. WATSON—*Orgy on Parnassus.*

14
For of all sad words of tongue or pen,
The saddest are these: "It might have been!"
WHITTIER—*Maud Muller.* L. 105.
(See also LANDON)

15
Would you repeat that again, sir, for it soun's sae sonorous that the words droon the ideas?
JOHN WILSON—*Noctes Ambrosianiæ.* 27.

16
Three sleepless nights I passed in sounding on,
Through words and things, a dim and perilous way.
WORDSWORTH—*Borderer.* Act IV. Sc. 2.

17
Fair words enough a man shall find,
They be good cheap: they cost right nought,
Their substance is but only wind.
SIR THOS. WYATT—*Of Dissembling Words.*

WORK (See also LABOR)

18
Tools were made and born were hands,
Every farmer understands.
WM. BLAKE—*Proverbs.*

19
Hâtez-vous lentement; et, sans perdre courage,
Vingt fois sur le métier remettez votre ouvrage.
Hasten slowly, and without losing heart, put your work twenty times upon the anvil.
BOILEAU—*L'Art Poétique.* I. 171.

20
The dog that trots about finds a bone.
BORROW—*Bible in Spain.* Ch. XLVII. (Cited as a gipsy saying.)

21
The best verse hasn't been rhymed yet,
The best house hasn't been planned,
The highest peak hasn't been climbed yet,
The mightiest rivers aren't spanned;
Don't worry and fret, faint-hearted,
The chances have just begun
For the best jobs haven't been started,
The best work hasn't been done.
BERTON BRALEY—*No Chance.*

22 By the way,
The works of women are symbolical.
We sew, sew, prick our fingers, dull our sight,
Producing what? A pair of slippers, sir,
To put on when you're weary—or a stool
To tumble over and vex you * * * curse that stool!
Or else at best, a cushion where you lean
And sleep, and dream of something we are not,
But would be for your sake. Alas, alas!
This hurts most, this * * * that, after all, we are paid
The worth of our work, perhaps.
E. B. BROWNING—*Aurora Leigh.* Bk. I. L. 465.

23 Get leave to work
In this world,—'tis the best you get at all.
E. B. BROWNING—*Aurora Leigh.* Bk. III. L. 164.

1 Let no one till his death
Be called unhappy. Measure not the work
Until the day's out and the labour done.
E. B. BROWNING—*Aurora Leigh*. Bk. V. L. 78.

2 Free men freely work:
Whoever fears God, fears to sit at ease.
E. B. BROWNING—*Aurora Leigh*. Bk. VIII. L. 784.

3
And still be doing, never done.
BUTLER—*Hudibras*. Pt. I. Canto I. L. 204.

4
It is the first of all problems for a man to find out what kind of work he is to do in this universe.
CARLYLE—*Address at Edinburgh*. (1866)

5
Genuine Work alone, what thou workest faithfully, that is eternal, as the Almighty Founder and World-Builder himself.
CARLYLE—*Past and Present*. Bk. II. Ch. XVII.

6
All work, even cotton-spinning, is noble; work is alone noble.
CARLYLE—*Past and Present*. Bk. III. Ch. IV.

7
With hand on the spade and heart in the sky
Dress the ground and till it;
Turn in the little seed, brown and dry,
Turn out the golden millet.
Work, and your house shall be duly fed:
Work, and rest shall be won;
I hold that a man had better be dead
Than alive when his work is done.
ALICE CARY—*Work*.

8
Earned with the sweat of my brows.
CERVANTES—*Don Quixote*. Pt. I. Bk. I. Ch. 4.
(See also GENESIS)

9
Quanto mas que cada uno es hijo de sus obras.
The rather since every man is the son of his own works.
CERVANTES—*Don Quixote*. Bk. I. Ch. 4.

10
Each natural agent works but to this end,—
To render that it works on like itself.
GEORGE CHAPMAN—*Bussy d'Ambois*. Act III. Sc. 1.

11
Ther n' is no werkman whatever he be,
That may both werken wel and hastily.
This wol be done at leisure parfitly.
CHAUCER—*Canterbury Tales. The Merchantes Tale*. L. 585.
(See also HEYWOOD, SYRUS)

12
Nowher so besy a man as he ther was,
And yet he semed bisier than he was.
CHAUCER—*Canterbury Tales. Prologue*. L. 321.

13
Let us take to our hearts a lesson—
No lesson could braver be—
From the ways of the tapestry weavers
On the other side of the sea.
ANSON G. CHESTER—*Tapestry Weavers*.

14
Penelopæ telam retexens.
Unravelling the web of Penelope.
CICERO—*Acad. Quæst*. Bk. IV. 29. 95.
(See also HOMER)

15
All Nature seems at work, slugs leave their lair—
The bees are stirring—birds are on the wing—
And Winter, slumbering in the open air,
Wears on his smiling face a dream of Spring!
And I the while, the sole unbusy thing,
Nor honey make, nor pair, nor build, nor sing.
COLERIDGE—*Work Without Hope*. St. 1.

16
Every man's work shall be made manifest.
I Corinthians. III. 13.

17
Work thou for pleasure—paint or sing or carve
The thing thou lovest, though the body starve—
Who works for glory misses oft the goal;
Who works for money coins his very soul.
Work for the work's sake, then, and it may be
That these things shall be added unto thee.
KENYON COX—*Our Motto*.
(See also KIPLING)

18
Better to wear out than to rust out.
BISHOP CUMBERLAND, to one who urged him not to wear himself out with work. See HORNE—*Sermon on the Duty of Contending for the Truth*. BOSWELL—*Tour to the Hebrides*. P. 18. Note. Said by GEORGE WHITEFIELD, according to SOUTHEY—*Life of Wesley*. II. p. 170 (Ed. 1858)

19
The Lord had a job for me, but I had so much to do,
I said, "You get somebody else—or wait till I get through."
I don't know how the Lord came out, but He seemed to get along:
But I felt kinda sneakin' like, 'cause I know'd I done Him wrong.
One day I needed the Lord—needed Him myself—needed Him right away,
And He never answered me at all, but I could hear Him say
Down in my accusin' heart, "Nigger, I'se got too much to do,
You get somebody else or wait till I get through."
PAUL LAURENCE DUNBAR—*The Lord had a Job*.

20
All things are full of labour; man cannot utter it: the eye is not satisfied with seeing, nor the ear filled with hearing.
Ecclesiastes. I. 8.

21
The grinders cease because they are few.
Ecclesiastes. XII. 3.

22
All play and no work makes Jack a mere toy.
Quoted by MARIA EDGEWORTH—*Henry and Lucy*. Vol. II.

23
'Tis toil's reward, that sweetens industry,
As love inspires with strength the enraptur'd thrush.
EBENEZER ELLIOT—*Corn Law Rhymes*. No. 7.

24
Too busy with the crowded hour to fear to live or die.
EMERSON—*Quatrains. Nature*.

1
A woman's work, grave sirs, is never done.
Mr. Eusden—*Poem.* Spoken at a Cambridge Commencement.
(See also Honeywood)

2 Chacun son métier;
Les vaches seront bien gardées.
Each one to his own trade; then would the cows be well cared for.
Florian—*Le Vacher et le Garde-chasse.*

3
A ploughman on his legs is higher than a gentleman on his knees.
Franklin—*Poor Richard.* Preface. (1758)

4
Handle your tools without mittens.
Franklin—*Poor Richard.* Preface. (1758)

5
Plough deep while sluggards sleep.
Franklin—*Poor Richard.* Preface. (1758)

6
"Men work together," I told him from the heart,
"Whether they work together or apart."
Robert Frost—*Tuft of Flowers.*

7
In every rank, or great or small,
'Tis industry supports us all.
Gay—*Man, Cat, Dog, and Fly.* L. 63.

8
In the sweat of thy face shalt thou eat bread.
Genesis. III. 19.
(See also Cervantes)

9
So eine Arbeit wird eigentlich nie fertig; man muss sie für fertig erklären, wenn man nach Zeit und Umständen das Möglichste getan hat.
Properly speaking, such work is never finished; one must declare it so when, according to time and circumstances, one has done one's best.
Goethe—*Italienische Reise.* March 16, 1787.

10
He that well his warke beginneth
The rather a good ende he winneth.
Gower—*Confessio Amantis.*

11
A warke it ys as easie to be done
As tys to saye *Jacke! robys on.*
Halliwell—*Archæological Dictionary.* Quoted from an old Play. See Grose—*Classical Dictionary of the Vulgar tongue.* Hudson, the English singer, made popular the refrain, "Before ye could cry 'Jack Robinson.'"

12
Joy to the Toiler!—him that tills
The fields with Plenty crowned;
Him with the woodman's axe that thrills
The wilderness profound.
Benjamin Hathaway—*Songs of the Toiler.*

13
Haste makes waste.
Heywood—*Proverbs.* Pt. I. Ch. II.
(See also Chaucer)

14
The "value" or "worth" of a man is, as of all other things, his price; that is to say, so much as would be given for the use of his power.
Hobbes—*Leviathan.* Ch. X.

15
Light is the task when many share the toil.
Homer—*Iliad.* Bk. XII. L. 493. Bryant's trans.
(See also Martial, Patten)

16
The fiction pleased; our generous train complies,
Nor fraud mistrusts in virtue's fair disguise.
The work she plyed, but, studious of delay,
Each following night reversed the toils of day.
Homer—*Odyssey.* Bk. XXIV. L. 164. Pope's trans.
(See also Cicero)

17
When Darby saw the setting sun
He swung his scythe, and home he run,
Sat down, drank off his quart and said,
"My work is done, I'll go to bed."
"My work is done!" retorted Joan,
"My work is done! Your constant tone,
But hapless woman ne'er can say
'My work is done' till judgment day."
St. John Honeywood—*Darby and Joan.*
(See also Eusden)

18
Facito aliquid operis, ut semper te diabolus inveniat occupatum.
Keep doing some kind of work, that the devil may always find you employed.
St. Jerome.

19
I like work; it fascinates me. I can sit and look at it for hours. I love to keep it by me: the idea of getting rid of it nearly breaks my heart.
Jerome K. Jerome—*Three Men in a Boat.* Ch. XV.

20
Tho' we earn our bread, Tom,
By the dirty pen,
What we can we will be,
Honest Englishmen.
Do the work that's nearest
Though it's dull at whiles,
Helping, when we meet them,
Lame dogs over stiles.
Charles Kingsley—*Letter.* To Thomas Hughes (1856), inviting Hughes and Tom Taylor to go fishing. See *Memoirs of Kingsley*, by his wife. Ch. XV.

21
For men must work and women must weep,
And the sooner it's over the sooner to sleep,
And good-bye to the bar and its moaning.
Charles Kingsley—*Three Fishers.*
(See also Hamlet under World)

22
But till we are built like angels, with hammer and chisel and pen,
We will work for ourself and a woman, for ever and ever, Amen.
Kipling—*Imperial Rescript.*

23
The gull shall whistle in his wake, the blind wave break in fire.
He shall fulfill God's utmost will, unknowing His desire,
And he shall see old planets pass and alien stars arise,
And give the gale his reckless sail in shadow of new skies.

Strong lust of gear shall drive him out and hunger arm his hand,
To wring his food from a desert nude, his foothold from the sand.

KIPLING—*The Foreloper (Interloper)*. Pub. in *Century Magazine*, April, 1909. First pub. in London *Daily Telegraph*, Jan. 1, 1909. Title given as *Vortrekker* in his *Songs From Books*.

1
And only the Master shall praise us, and only the Master shall blame;
And no one shall work for money, and no one shall work for fame;
But each for the joy of the working, and each, in his separate star,
Shall draw the Thing as he sees It, for the God of Things as They Are!

KIPLING—*L'Envoi*. In *Seven Seas*.
(See also COX)

2
And the Sons of Mary smile and are blessed—they know the angels are on their side;
They know in them is the Grace confessed, and for them are the Mercies multiplied;
They sit at the Feet, they hear the Word, they see how truly the Promise runs;
They have cast their burden upon the Lord, and—the Lord He lays it on Martha's Sons!

KIPLING—*The Sons of Mary*.

3
Who first invented work, and bound the free
And holyday-rejoicing spirit down * * *
To that dry drudgery at the desk's dead wood? * * *
Sabbathless Satan!

LAMB—*Work*.

4
The finest eloquence is that which gets things done; the worst is that which delays them.

D. LLOYD GEORGE. At the *Conference of Paris*, Jan., 1919.

5
Unemployment, with its injustice for the man who seeks and thirsts for employment, who begs for labour and cannot get it, and who is punished for failure he is not responsible for by the starvation of his children—that torture is something that private enterprise ought to remedy for its own sake.

D. LLOYD GEORGE—*Speech*. Dec. 6, 1919.

6
Never idle a moment, but thrifty and thoughtful of others.

LONGFELLOW—*Courtship of Miles Standish*. Pt. VIII. L. 46.

7
No man is born into the world whose work
Is not born with him; there is always work,
And tools to work withal, for those who will;
And blessed are the horny hands of toil!

LOWELL—*A Glance Behind the Curtain*. L. 202.

Horny-handed sons of toil.

Popularized by DENIS KEARNEY (Big Denny), of San Francisco.

8
Divisum sic breve fiet opus.

Work divided is in that manner shortened.

MARTIAL—*Epigrams*. Bk. IV. 83. 8.
(See also HOMER)

9
Why do strong arms fatigue themselves with frivolous dumb-bells? To dig a vineyard is a worthier exercise for men.

MARTIAL—*Epigrams*. Bk. XIV. Ep. 49.

10
God be thank'd that the dead have left still
Good undone for the living to do—
Still some aim for the heart and the will
And the soul of a man to pursue.

OWEN MEREDITH (Lord Lytton)—*Epilogue*.

11
Man hath his daily work of body or mind
Appointed.

MILTON—*Paradise Lost*. Bk. IV. L. 618.

12
The work under our labour grows
Luxurious by restraint.

MILTON—*Paradise Lost*. Bk. IX. L. 208.

13
I am of nothing and to nothing tend,
On earth I nothing have and nothing claim,
Man's noblest works must have one common end,
And nothing crown the tablet of his name.

MOORE—*Ode upon Nothing*. Appeared in *Saturday Magazine* about 1836. Not in Collected Works.

14
The uselessness of men above sixty years of age and the incalculable benefit it would be in commercial, in political, and in professional life, if as a matter of course, men stopped work at this age.

WILLIAM OSLER—*Address*, at Johns Hopkins University, Feb. 22, 1905.

15
Study until twenty-five, investigation until forty, profession until sixty, at which age I would have him retired on a double allowance.

WILLIAM OSLER. The statement made by him which gave rise to the report that he had advised chloroform after sixty. Denied by him in *Medical Record*, March 4, 1905.

16
Many hands make light work.

WILLIAM PATTEN—*Expedition into Scotland*. (1547) In ARBER's Reprint of 1880.
(See also HOMER)

17
Nothing is impossible to industry.

PERIANDER of Corinth.

18
Ease and speed in doing a thing do not give the work lasting solidity or exactness of beauty.

PLUTARCH—*Life of Pericles*.

19
Man goeth forth unto his work and to his labour until the evening.

Psalms. CIV. 23.

20
When Adam dalfe and Eve spane
So spire if thou may spede,
Where was then the pride of man,
That nowe merres his mede?

RICHARD ROLLE DE HAMPOLE—*Early English Text Society Reprints*. No. 26. P. 79.

21
How bething the, gentliman,
How Adam dalf, and Eve span.

MS. of the Fifteenth Century. British Museum.

1
When Adam dolve, and Eve span,
Who was then the gentleman?

Lines used by JOHN BALL in *Wat Tyler's Rebellion*. See HUME—*History of England*. Vol. I. Ch. XVII. Note 8. So Adam reutte, und Eva span, Wer war da ein eddelman? (Old German saying.)
(See also GROBIANUS under ANCESTRY)

2
Der Mohr hat seine Arbeit gethan, der Mohr kann gehen.

The Moor has done his work, the Moor may go.

SCHILLER—*Fiesco*. III. 4.

3
Hard toil can roughen form and face,
And want can quench the eye's bright grace.

SCOTT—*Marmion*. Canto I. St. 28.

4
What work's, my countrymen, in hand? where go you
With bats and clubs? The matter? speak, I pray you.

Coriolanus. Act I. Sc. 1. L. 55.

5
Another lean, unwashed artificer.

King John. Act IV. Sc. 2. L. 201.

6
Why, universal plodding poisons up
The nimble spirits in the arteries,
As motion and long-during action tires
The sinewy vigour of the traveller.

Love's Labour's Lost. Act IV. Sc. 3. L. 305.

7
A man who has no office to go to—I don't care who he is—is a trial of which you can have no conception.

BERNARD SHAW—*Irrational Knot*. Ch. XVIII.

8
I am giving you examples of the fact that this creature man, who in his own selfish affairs is a coward to the backbone, will fight for an idea like a hero. . . . I tell you, gentlemen, if you can shew a man a piece of what he now calls God's work to do, and what he will later call by many new names, you can make him entirely reckless of the consequences to himself personally.

BERNARD SHAW—*Man and Superman*. Act III.

9
A day's work is a day's work, neither more nor less, and the man who does it needs a day's sustenance, a night's repose, and due leisure, whether he be painter or ploughman.

BERNARD SHAW—*Unsocial Socialist*. Ch. V.

10
How many a rustic Milton has passed by,
Stifling the speechless longings of his heart,
In unremitting drudgery and care!
How many a vulgar Cato has compelled
His energies, no longer tameless then,
To mould a pin, or fabricate a nail!

SHELLEY—*Queen Mab*. Pt. V. St. 9.

11
Nothing can be done at once hastily and prudently.

SYRUS—*Maxims*. 357.
(See also CHAUCER)

12
Ne laterum laves.

Do not wash bricks. (Waste your labor.)

TERENCE—*Phormio*. I. IV. 9. A Greek proverb.

13
A workman that needeth not to be ashamed.

II Timothy. II. 15.

14
Heaven is blessed with perfect rest but the blessing of earth is toil.

HENRY VAN DYKE—*Toiling of Felix*. Last line.

15
Le fruit du travail est le plus doux des plaisirs.

The fruit derived from labor is the sweetest of pleasures.

VAUVENARGUES—*Réflexions*. 200.

16
Too long, that some may rest,
Tired millions toil unblest.

WM. WATSON—*New National Anthem*.

17
But when dread Sloth, the Mother of Doom, steals in,
And reigns where Labour's glory was to serve,
Then is the day of crumbling not far off.

WM. WATSON—*The Mother of Doom*. August 28, 1919.

18
In books, or work, or healthful play.

ISAAC WATTS—*Divine Songs*. XX.

19
There will be little drudgery in this better ordered world. Natural power harnessed in machines will be the general drudge. What drudgery is inevitable will be done as a service and duty for a few years or months out of each life; it will not consume nor degrade the whole life of anyone.

H. G. WELLS—*Outline of History*. Ch. XLI. Par. 4.

20
Thine to work as well as pray,
Clearing thorny wrongs away;
Plucking up the weeds of sin,
Letting heaven's warm sunshine in.

WHITTIER—*The Curse of the Charter-Breakers*. St. 21.

WORLD (See also ACTING, LIFE, MAN)

21
The wrecks of matter, and the crush of worlds.

ADDISON—*Cato*. Act V. Sc. 1.

22
This restless world
Is full of chances, which by habit's power
To learn to bear is easier than to shun.

JOHN ARMSTRONG—*Art of Preserving Health*. Bk. II. L. 453.

23
Wandering between two worlds, one dead,
The other powerless to be born,
With nowhere yet to rest my head,
Like these, on earth I wait forlorn.

MATTHEW ARNOLD—*Stanzas from the Grande Chartreuse*.

24
Securus judicat orbis terrarum.

The verdict of the world is conclusive.

ST. AUGUSTINE—*Contra Epist. Parmen*. III. 24.

1
This world's a bubble.
Ascribed to BACON by THOMAS FARNABY. (1629) Appeared in his *Book of Epigrams;* and by JOSHUA SYLVESTER—*Panthea. Appendix.* (1630) See also *Wottonianæ.* P. 513. Attributed to BISHOP USHER. See *Miscellanes.* H. W. GENT. (1708)
(See also MOOR, QUARLES, WOTTON)

2
Earth took her shining station as a star,
In Heaven's dark hall, high up the crowd of worlds.
BAILEY—*Festus.* Sc. *The Centre.*

3
Dieu est le poète, les hommes ne sont que les acteurs. Ces grandes pièces qui se jouent sur la terre ont été composées dans le ciel.
God is the author, men are only the players. These grand pieces which are played upon earth have been composed in heaven.
BALZAC—*Socrate Chrétien.*
(See also DU BARTAS)

4
Fly away, pretty moth, to the shade
Of the leaf where you slumbered all day;
Be content with the moon and the stars, pretty moth,
And make use of your wings while you may.
* * * * * *
But tho' dreams of delight may have dazzled you quite,
They at last found it dangerous play;
Many things in this world that look bright, pretty moth,
Only dazzle to lead us astray.
THOS. HAYNES BAYLY—*Fly away, pretty Moth.*

5
Let the world slide.
BEAUMONT AND FLETCHER—*Wit Without Money.* Act V. Sc. 2. *Taming of the Shrew. Induction.* Sc. 1. L. 5. Also Sc. 2. L. 146. ("Slip" in folio.)
(See also HEYWOOD)

6
The world is like a board with holes in it, and the square men have got into the round holes, and the round into the square.
BISHOP BERKELEY, as quoted by *Punch.*
(See also SMITH)

7
Renounce the devil and all his works, the vain pomp and glory of the world.
Book of Common Prayer. Public Baptism of Infants.

8
The pomps and vanity of this wicked world.
Book of Common Prayer. Catechism.

9
He sees that this great roundabout,
The world, with all its motley rout,
Church, army, physic, law,
Its customs and its businesses,
Is no concern at all of his,
And says—what says he?—Caw.
VINCENT BOURNE—*The Jackdaw.* COWPER'S trans.

10
'Tis a very good world we live in
To spend, and to lend, and to give in;
But to beg, or to borrow, or ask for our own;
'Tis the very worst world that ever was known.
J. BROMFIELD. As given in *The Mirror,* under *The Gatherer.* Sept. 12, 1840. Quoted by IRVING in *Tales of a Traveller.* Prefixed to Pt. II. Another similar version attributed to EARL OF ROCHESTER.

11
This is the best world, that we live in,
To lend and to spend and to give in:
But to borrow, or beg, or to get a man's own,
It is the worst world that ever was known.
From *A Collection of Epigrams.* (1737)

12
The severe schools shall never laugh me out of the philosophy of Hermes, that this visible world is but a picture of the invisible, wherein as in a portrait, things are not truly, but in equivocal shapes, and as they counterfeit some real substance in that invisible fabric.
SIR THOMAS BROWNE—*Religio Medici.*
(See also JAMES)

13
In this bad, twisted, topsy-turvy world,
Where all the heaviest wrongs get uppermost.
E. B. BROWNING—*Aurora Leigh.* Bk. V. L. 981.

14
O world as God has made it! All is beauty.
ROBERT BROWNING—*Guardian Angel. A Picture at Fano.*

15
The wide world is all before us—
But a world without a friend.
BURNS—*Strathallan's Lament.*

16
I have not loved the world, nor the world me;
I have not flatter'd its rank breath, nor bow'd
To its idolatries a patient knee.
BYRON—*Childe Harold.* Canto III. St. 113.

17
Well, well, the world must turn upon its axis,
And all mankind turn with it, heads or tails,
And live and die, make love and pay our taxes,
And as the veering winds shift, shift our sails.
BYRON—*Don Juan.* Canto II. St. 4.

18
Such is the world. Understand it, despise it, love it; cheerfully hold on thy way through it, with thy eye on highest loadstars!
CARLYLE—*Essays. Count Cagliostro.* Last lines.

19
The true Sovereign of the world, who moulds the world like soft wax, according to his pleasure, is he who lovingly sees into the world.
CARLYLE—*Essays. Death of Goethe.*

20
Socrates, quidem, cum rogaretur cujatem se esse diceret, "Mundanum," inquit; totius enim mundi se incolam et civem arbitrabatur.
Socrates, indeed, when he was asked of what country he called himself, said, "Of the world;" for he considered himself an inhabitant and a citizen of the whole world.
CICERO—*Tusculanarum Disputationum.* Bk. V. 37. 108.
(See also DIOGENES, SENECA)

21
Such stuff the world is made of.
COWPER—*Hope.* L. 211.

1
'Tis pleasant, through the loopholes of retreat,
To peep at such a world; to see the stir
Of the Great Babel, and not feel the crowd.
COWPER—*Task*. Bk. IV. L. 88.

2
And for the few that only lend their ear,
That few is all the world.
SAMUEL DANIEL—*Musophilus*. St. 97.

3
Vien dietro a me, e lascia dir le genti.
Come, follow me, and leave the world to its babblings.
DANTE—*Purgatorio*. V. 13.

4
Quel est-il en effet? C'est un verre qui luit,
Qu'un souffle peut detruire, et qu'un souffle a produit.
What is it [the world], in fact? A glass which shines, which a breath can destroy, and which a breath has produced.
DE CAUX—*L'Horloge de Sable*. (1745) In D'ISRAELI'S *Curiosities of Literature. Imitations and Similarities.*
(See also GOLDSMITH)

5
I am a citizen of the world.
DIOGENES LAERTIUS.
(See also CICERO)

6
The world is a wheel, and it will all come round right.
BENJ. DISRAELI—*Endymion*. Ch. LXX.

7
Since every man who lives is born to die,
And none can boast sincere felicity,
With equal mind, what happens let us bear,
Nor joy nor grieve too much for things beyond our care.
Like pilgrims, to th' appointed place we tend;
The world's an inn, and death the journey's end.
DRYDEN—*Palamon and Arcite*. Bk. III. L. 2,159.
(See also HOWELL)

8
The world's a stage where God's omnipotence,
His justice, knowledge, love and providence,
Do act the parts.
DU BARTAS—*Divine Weekes and Workes. First Week. First Day.*

9
I take the world to be but as a stage,
Where net-maskt men doo play their personage.
DU BARTAS—*Divine Weekes and Workes. Dialogue Between Heraclitus and Democritus.*
The world is a stage; each plays his part, and receives his portion.
Found in WINSCHOOTEN'S *Seeman*. (1681) BOHN'S *Collection*, 1857. JUVENAL—*Satires*. III. 100. (Natio comœda est.)
(See also BALZAC, EDWARDS, HEYWOOD, MIDDLETON, MONTAIGNE, PETRONIUS, AS YOU LIKE IT, MERCHANT OF VENICE, TAGORE, also PALLADAS under LIFE)

10
But they will maintain the state of the world;
And all their desire is in the work of their craft.
Ecclesiasticus. XXXVIII. 34.

11
Pythagoras said that this world was like a stage,
Whereon many play their parts; the lookers-on the sage
Philosophers are, saith he, whose part is to learn
The manners of all nations, and the good from the bad to discern.
RICHARD EDWARDS—*Damon and Pythias.*
(See also DU BARTAS)

12
Good-bye, proud world! I'm going home;
Thou art not my friend; I am not thine.
EMERSON—*Good-bye, Proud World!* ("And I," in later Ed.)

13
Shall I speak truly what I now see below?
The World is all a carkass, smoak and vanity,
The shadow of a shadow, a play
And in one word, just Nothing.
OWEN FELLTHAM—*Resolves*. P. 316. (Ed. 1696) From the Latin said to have been left by LIPSIUS to be put on his grave.
(See also YOUNG under VISIONS)

14
Map me no maps, sir; my head is a map, a map of the whole world.
FIELDING—*Rape upon Rape*. Act I. Sc. 5.

15
Long ago a man of the world was defined as a man who in every serious crisis is invariably wrong.
Fortnightly Review. Armageddon—and After. Nov., 1914. P. 736.
(See also YOUNG)

16
Mais dons ce monde, il n'y a rien d'assure que le mort et les impots.
But in this world nothing is sure but death and taxes.
FRANKLIN—*Letter to M. Leroy*. (1789)

17
Eppur si muove. (Epur.)
But it does move.
GALILEO—*Before the Inquisition*. (1632) Questioned by KARL VON GEBLE; also by PROF. HEIS, who says it appeared first in the *Dictionnaire Historique*. Caen. (1789) GUISAR says it was printed in the *Lehrbuch der Geschichte*. Wurtzburg. (1774) Conceded to be apocryphal. Earliest appearance in ABBÉ IRAILH—*Querelles Litéraires.*

18
Il mondo è un bel libro, ma poco serve a chi non lo sa leggere.
The world is a beautiful book, but of little use to him who cannot read it.
GOLDONI—*Pamela*. I. 14.
(See also NOYES)

19
Ill fares the land, to hastening ills a prey,
Where wealth accumulates, and men decay;
Princes and Lords may flourish, or may fade—
A breath can make them, as a breath has made—
But a bold peasantry, their country's pride,
When once destroy'd can never be supplied.
GOLDSMITH—*Deserted Village*. L. 51.
(See also DE CAUX)

20
Creation's heir, the world, the world is mine!
GOLDSMITH—*Traveller*. L. 50.

21
Earth is but the frozen echo of the silent voice of God.
HAGEMAN—*Silence.*

1
Let the world slide, let the world go;
A fig for care and a fig for woe!
If I can't pay, why I can owe,
And death makes equal the high and low.
JOHN HEYWOOD—*Be Merry Friends.*
(See also BEAUMONT)

2
The world's a theatre, the earth a stage,
Which God and nature do with actors fill.
HEYWOOD—*Dramatic Works.* Vol. I. *The Author to His Book. Prefix to Apology for Actors.*
(See also DU BARTAS)

3
Nor is this lower world but a huge inn,
And men the rambling passengers.
JAMES HOWELL—*The Vote.* Poem prefixed to his *Familiar Letters.*
(See also DRYDEN)

4
There are two worlds; the world that we can measure with line and rule, and the world that we feel with our hearts and imaginations.
LEIGH HUNT—*Men, Women, and Books. Fiction and Matter of Fact.*

5
The nations are as a drop of a bucket.
Isaiah. XL. 15.

6
World without end.
Isaiah. XLV. 17.

7
The visible world is but man turned inside out that he may be revealed to himself.
HENRY JAMES (the Elder). From J. A. KELLOG—*Digest of the Philosophy of Henry James.*
(See also BROWNE, NOYES)

8
It takes all sorts of people to make a world.
DOUGLAS JERROLD—*Story of a Feather.* In *Punch.* Vol. V. P. 55.

9
I never have sought the world; the world was not to seek me.
SAMUEL JOHNSON—*Boswell's Life of Johnson.* (1783)

10
This world, where much is to be done and little to be known.
SAMUEL JOHNSON—*Prayers and Meditations. Against Inquisitive and Perplexing Thoughts.*

11
If there is one beast in all the loathsome fauna of civilization I hate and despise, it is a man of the world.
HENRY ARTHUR JONES—*The Liars.* Act I.
(See also YOUNG)

12
Upon the battle ground of heaven and hell
I palsied stand.
MARIE JOSEPHINE—*Rosa Mystica.* P. 231.

13
The world goes up and the world goes down,
And the sunshine follows the rain;
And yesterday's sneer and yesterday's frown
Can never come over again,
Sweet wife.
No, never come over again.
CHARLES KINGSLEY—*Dolcino to Margaret.*

14
For to admire an' for to see,
For to be'old this world so wide—
It never done no good to me,
But I can't drop it if I tried!
KIPLING—*For to Admire.* In *The Seven Seas.*

15
If all the world must see the world
As the world the world hath seen,
Then it were better for the world
That the world had never been.
LELAND—*The World and the World.*

16
It is an ugly world. Offend
Good people, how they wrangle,
The manners that they never mend,
The characters they mangle.
They eat, and drink, and scheme, and plod,
And go to church on Sunday—
And many are afraid of God—
And more of Mrs. Grundy.
FREDERICK LOCKER-LAMPSON—*The Jester's Plea.*

17
O what a glory doth this world put on
For him who, with a fervent heart, goes forth
Under the bright and glorious sky, and looks
On duties well performed, and days well spent!
LONGFELLOW—*Autumn.*

18
Glorious indeed is the world of God around us, but more glorious the world of God within us. There lies the Land of Song; there lies the poet's native land.
LONGFELLOW—*Hyperion.* Bk. I. Ch. VIII.

19
One day with life and heart,
Is more than time enough to find a world.
LOWELL—*Columbus.* Last lines.

20
Flammantia mœnia mundi.
The flaming ramparts of the world.
LUCRETIUS—*De Rerum Natura.* I. 73.

21 When the world dissolves,
And every creature shall be purified,
All places shall be hell that are not heaven.
MARLOWE—*Faustus.* L. 543.

22
The world in all doth but two nations bear,
The good, the bad, and these mixed everywhere.
MARVELL—*The Loyal Scot.*

23
This world is full of beauty, as other worlds above,
And if we did our duty, it might be as full of love.
GERALD MASSEY—*This World.*

24
The world's a stage on which all parts are played.
THOS. MIDDLETON—*A Game of Chess.* Act V. Sc. II.
(See also DU BARTAS)

25
Above the smoke and stir of this dim spot
Which men call Earth.
MILTON—*Comus.* L. 5.

26 Hanging in a golden chain
This pendent world, in bigness as a star
Of smallest magnitude close by the moon.
MILTON—*Paradise Lost.* Bk. II. L. 1,051.
(See also MEASURE FOR MEASURE)

1 A boundless continent,
Dark, waste, and wild, under the frown of night
Starless expos'd.

MILTON—*Paradise Lost*. Bk. III. L. 423.

2
Then stayed the fervid wheels, and in his hand
He took the golden compasses, prepared
In God's eternal store, to circumscribe
This universe and all created things:
One foot he centred, and the other turned
Round through the vast profundity obscure,
And said, "Thus far extend, thus far thy bounds,
This be thy just circumference, O World."

MILTON—*Paradise Lost*. Bk. VII. L. 224. God is like a skillful Geometrician. SIR THOMAS BROWNE—*Religio Medici*. Pt. I. Sect. XVI. Nature geometrizeth and observeth order in all things. SIR THOMAS BROWNE—*Garden of Cyrus*. Ch. III. The same idea appears in COMBER—*Companion to the Temple*. (Folio 1684) God acts the part of a Geometrician. . . . His government of the World is no less mathematically exact than His creation of it. (Quoting Plato) JOHN NORRIS—*Practical Discourses*. II. P. 228. (Ed. 1693) "God Geometrizes" is quoted as a traditional sentence used by Plato, in PLUTARCH—*Symposium*. By a carpenter mankind was created and made, and by a carpenter mete it was that man should be repaired. ERASMUS—*Paraphrase of St. Mark*. Folio 42.

3
The world was all before them, where to choose
Their place of rest, and Providence their guide.

MILTON—*Paradise Lost*. Bk. XII. L. 646.

4
Le monde n'est qu'une bransloire perenne.

The world is but a perpetual see-saw.

MONTAIGNE—*Essays*. Bk. III. Ch. II.

5
Is it not a noble farce wherein kings, republics, and emperors have for so many ages played their parts, and to which the vast universe serves for a theatre?

MONTAIGNE—*Of the Most Excellent Men*.
(See also DU BARTAS)

6
Or may I think when toss'd in trouble,
This world at best is but a bubble.

DR. MOOR. MS.
(See also BACON)

7
This world is all a fleeting show,
For man's illusion given;
The smiles of joy, the tears of woe,
Deceitful shine, deceitful flow,—
There's nothing true but Heaven.

MOORE—*This World is all a Fleeting Show*.
(See also KNOX under PRIDE)

8
This outer world is but the pictured scroll
Of worlds within the soul;
A colored chart, a blazoned missal-book,
Whereon who rightly look
May spell the splendors with their mortal eyes,
And steer to Paradise.

ALFRED NOYES—*The Two Worlds*.
(See also JAMES, also LONGFELLOW under NATURE)

9
Think, in this battered Caravanserai,
Whose Portals are alternate Night and Day,
How Sultán after Sultán with his Pomp
Abode his destined Hour, and went his way.

OMAR KHAYYAM—*Rubaiyat*. St. 17. FITZGERALD'S trans.

10
Love to his soul gave eyes; he knew things are not as they seem.
The dream is his real life: the world around him is the dream.

F. T. PALGRAVE—*Dream of Maxim Wledig*.

11
Quod fere totus mundus exerceat histrionem.

Almost the whole world are players.

PETRONIUS ARBITER—Adapted from Fragments. No. 10. (Ed. 1790) Over the door of Shakespeare's theatre, The Globe, Bankside, London, was a figure of Hercules; under this figure was the above quotation. It probably suggested "All the world's a stage."
(See also DU BARTAS)

12
They who grasp the world,
The Kingdom, and the power, and the glory,
Must pay with deepest misery of spirit,
Atoning unto God for a brief brightness.

STEPHEN PHILLIPS—*Herod*. Act III.

13
Alexander wept when he heard from Anaxarchus that there was an infinite number of worlds, and his friends asking him if any accident had befallen him he returned this answer: "Do you not think it is a matter worthy of lamentation that where there is such a vast multitude of them we have not yet conquered one?"

PLUTARCH—*On the Tranquillity of the Mind*. One world is not sufficient; he [Alexander the Great] fumes unhappy in the narrow bounds of this earth. Quoted from JUVENAL—*Satires*. X.

14
But as the world, harmoniously confused,
Where order in variety we see;
And where, tho' all things differ, all agree.

POPE—*Windsor Forest*.
(See also ROWLEY)

15
My soul, what's lighter than a feather? Wind.
Than wind? The fire. And what than fire? The mind.
What's lighter than the mind? A thought. Than thought?
This bubble world. What than this bubble? Nought.

QUARLES—*Emblems*. Bk. I. 4.
(See also BACON, also HARLEIAN MS. under WOMAN)

16
All nations and kindreds and people and tongues.

Revelation. VII. 9.

17
Le monde est le livre des femmes.

The world is woman's book.

ROUSSEAU.

18
The worlde bie diffraunce ys ynn orderr founde.

ROWLEY—*The Tournament*. Same idea in PASCAL—*Pensées*. BERNARDIN DE ST. PIERRE—

Etudes de la Nature. BURKE—*Reflections on the French Revolution.* HORACE—*Epistle* 12. LUCAN—*Pharsalia.* LONGINUS—*Remark on the Eloquence of Demosthenes.*
(See also POPE)

1
Es liebt die Welt, das Strahlende zu schwärzen
Und das Erhabne in den Staub zu ziehn.
The world delights to tarnish shining names,
And to trample the sublime in the dust.
SCHILLER—*Das Mädchen von Orleans.*

2
Denn nur vom Nutzen wird die Welt regiert.
For the world is ruled by interest alone.
SCHILLER—*Wallenstein's Tod.* I. 6. 37.

3
Non sum uni angulo natus; patria mea totus hic est mundus.
I am not born for one corner; the whole world is my native land.
SENECA—*Epistles.* 28.
(See also CICERO)

4
All the world's a stage,
And all the men and women merely players.
As You Like It. Act II. Sc. 7. L. 139.
(See also DU BARTAS)

5
This wide and universal theatre
Presents more woful pageants than the scene
Wherein we play in.
As You Like It. Act II. Sc. 7. L. 137.
(See also DU BARTAS)

6
How weary, stale, flat and unprofitable
Seem to me all the uses of this world!
Hamlet. Act I. Sc. 2. L. 133.

7
For some must watch, while some must sleep;
So runs the world away.
Hamlet. Act III. Sc. 2. L. 284.
(See also KINGSLEY under WORK)

8
Would I were dead! if God's good will were so:
For what is in this world but grief and woe?
Henry VI. Pt. III. Act II. Sc. 5. L. 19.

9
Mad world. Mad kings. Mad composition.
King John. Act II. Sc. 2. L. 561.
(See also TAYLOR)

10
The earth hath bubbles, as the water has,
And these are of them.
Macbeth. Act I. Sc. 4. L. 79.
(See also BACON)

11
To be imprisoned in the viewless winds
And blown with restless violence around about
The pendent world.
Measure for Measure. Act III. Sc. 1. L. 124.
(See also MILTON)

12
I hold the world but as the world, Gratiano:
A stage where every man must play a part.
Merchant of Venice. Act I. Sc. 1. L. 76.
(See also DU BARTAS)

13
Why, then, the world's mine oyster,
Which I with sword will open.
Merry Wives of Windsor. Act II. Sc. 2. L. 2.

14
The world is grown so bad,
That wrens make prey where eagles dare not perch.
Richard III. Act I. Sc. 3. L. 70.

15
You'll never have a quiet world till you knock the patriotism out of the human race.
BERNARD SHAW—*O'Flaherty, V. C.*

16
The world's great age begins anew,
The golden years return,
The earth doth like a snake renew
Her winter weeds outworn.
SHELLEY—*Hellas.* Last chorus.

17
Making a perpetual mansion of this poor baiting place.
SIR PHILIP SIDNEY—*Arcadia.* Same idea in MOORE—*Irish Melodies.* IRVING—*Bracebridge Hall.* Vol. I. P. 213. An adaptation of CICERO—*De Senectute.* 26; and SENECA—*Epistles.* 120.

18
If you choose to represent the various parts in life by holes upon a table, of different shapes,—some circular, some triangular, some square, some oblong,—and the persons acting these parts by bits of wood of similar shapes, we shall generally find that the triangular person has got into the square hole, the oblong into the triangular, and a square person has squeezed himself into the round hole. The officer and the office, the doer and the thing done, seldom fit so exactly that we can say they were almost made for each other.
SYDNEY SMITH—*Sketches of Moral Philosophy.* P. 309.
(See also BERKELEY)

19
O Earth! all bathed with blood and tears, yet never
Hast thou ceased putting forth thy fruit and flowers.
MADAME DE STAËL—*Corinne.* Bk. XIII. Ch. IV. L. E. L.'s trans.

20
This world surely is wide enough to hold both thee and me.
STERNE—*Tristram Shandy.* Bk. II. Ch. XII.

21
There was all the world and his wife.
SWIFT—*Polite Conversation.* Dialogue III. ANSTEY—*New Bath Guide.* P. 130. (1767)

22
In this playhouse of infinite forms I have had my play, and here have I caught sight of him that is formless.
RABINDRANATH TAGORE—*Gitanjali.* 96.
(See also DU BARTAS)

23
A mad world, my masters.
JOHN TAYLOR—*Western Voyage.* First line. MIDDLETON. Title of a play. (1608) NICHOLAS BRETON. Title of a pamphlet. (1603) Mundus furiosus. (a mad world) Inscription of a book by JANSENIUS—*Gallo-Belgicus.* (1596)
(See also KING JOHN)

24
So many worlds, so much to do,
So little done, such things to be.
TENNYSON—*In Memoriam.* Pt. LXXII. 1.

1
The world is a looking glass, and gives back to every man the reflection of his own face. Frown at it and it will in turn look sourly upon you; laugh at it and with it, and it is a jolly kind companion.

THACKERAY—*Vanity Fair.*

2
Even the linked fantasies, in whose blossomy twist
I swung the earth a trinket at my wrist.

FRANCIS THOMPSON—*Hound of Heaven.* L. 126.

3
Anchorite, who didst dwell
With all the world for cell!

FRANCIS THOMPSON—*To the Dead Cardinal of Westminster.* St. 5.

4
For, if the worlds
In worlds enclosed should on his senses burst * * *
He would abhorrent turn.

THOMSON—*Seasons. Summer.* L. 313.

5
Heed not the folk who sing or say
In sonnet sad or sermon chill,
"Alas, alack, and well-a-day!
This round world's but a bitter pill."
We too are sad and careful; still
We'd rather be alive than not.

GRAHAM R. TOMSON—*Ballade of the Optimist.*

6
Tout est pour le mieux dans le meilleur des mondes.

Everything is for the best in this best of possible worlds.

VOLTAIRE—*Candide.* I. (A hit against LEIBNITZ' Optimistic Doctrines.)

7
Leaving the old, both worlds at once they view,
That stand upon the threshold of the new.

WALLER—*Divine Poems. Works.* P. 316. (Ed. 1729)

8
This world is a comedy to those who think, a tragedy to those who feel.

HORACE WALPOLE—*Letter to Sir Horace Mann.* Dec. 31, 1769 and March 5, 1772.

9
If we suppose a sufficient righteousness and intelligence in men to produce presently, from the tremendous lessons of history, an effective will for a world peace—that is to say, an effective will for a world law under a world government—for in no other fashion is a secure world peace conceivable—in what manner may we expect things to move towards this end? . . . It is an educational task, and its very essence is to bring to the minds of all men everywhere, as a necessary basis for world cooperation, a new telling and interpretation, a common interpretation, of history.

H. G. WELLS—*Outline of History.* Ch. XLI. Par. 2.

10
What is this world? A net to snare the soule.

GEORGE WHETSTONE. In TOTTLE'S *Miscellany.* Erroneously attributed to GASCOIGNE.

11
I sound my barbaric yawp over the roofs of the world.

WALT WHITMAN—*Starting from Pawmano.* No. 52.

12
Was ist ihm nun die Welt? ein weiter leerer Raum,
Fortunen's Spielraum, frei ihr Rad herum zu rollen.

What is the world to him now? a vast and vacant space, for fortune's wheel to roll about at will.

WIELAND—*Oberon.* VIII. 20.

13
I have my beauty,—you your Art—
Nay, do not start:
One world was not enough for two
Like me and you.

OSCAR WILDE—*Her Voice.*

14
When the fretful stir
Unprofitable, and the fever of the world
Have hung upon the beatings of my heart.

WORDSWORTH—*Lines composed a few miles above Tintern Abbey.*

15
The world is too much with us; late and soon,
Getting and spending we lay waste our powers;
Little we see in Nature that is ours.

WORDSWORTH—*Miscellaneous Sonnets.* Pt. I. XXXIII.

16
The world's a bubble—and the life of man
Less than a span.
In his conception wretched, and from the womb
So to the tomb.
Nurst from the cradle, and brought up to years
With cares and fears.
Who then to frail mortality shall trust,
But limns in water, and but writes in dust.

WOTTON—*The World. Ode to Bacon.*

(See also BACON)

17
Man of the World (for such wouldst thou be called)—
And art thou proud of that inglorious style?

YOUNG—*Night Thoughts.* Night VIII. L. 8.

(See also FORTNIGHTLY, JONES)

18
They most the world enjoy who least admire.

YOUNG—*Night Thoughts.* Night VIII. L. 1,173.

19
Let not the cooings of the world allure thee:
Which of her lovers ever found her true?

YOUNG—*Night Thoughts.* Night VIII. L. 1,279.

WORLD PEACE

20
I am the last man in the world to say that the succor which is given us from America is not in itself something to rejoice at greatly. But I also say that I can see more in the knowledge that America is going to win a right to be at the conference table when the terms of peace are discussed. . . . It would have been a tragedy for mankind if America had not been there, and there with all her influence and power.

D. LLOYD GEORGE—*Speech,* at the Meeting of American Residents in London. April 12, 1917.

1
To Woodrow Wilson, the apparent failure, belongs the undying honor, which will grow with the growing centuries, of having saved the "little child that shall lead them yet." No other statesman but Wilson could have done it. And he did it.

GEN. JAN CHRISTIAN SMUTS—*Letter*. Jan. 8, 1921. Printed in N. Y. *Evening Post*, March 2, 1921.

2
It was the human spirit itself that failed at Paris. It is no use passing judgments and making scapegoats of this or that individual statesman or group of statesmen. Idealists make a great mistake in not facing the real facts sincerely and resolutely. They believe in the power of the spirit, in the goodness which is at the heart of things, in the triumph which is in store for the great moral ideals of the race. But this faith only too often leads to an optimism which is sadly and fatally at variance with actual results. It is the realist and not the idealist who is generally justified by events. We forget that the human spirit, the spirit of goodness and truth in the world, is still only an infant crying in the night, and that the struggle with darkness is as yet mostly an unequal struggle. . . . Paris proved this terrible truth once more. It was not Wilson who failed there, but humanity itself. It was not the statesmen that failed, so much as the spirit of the peoples behind them.

GEN. JAN CHRISTIAN SMUTS—*Letter*, Jan. 8, 1921. Printed in N. Y. *Evening Post*, March 2, 1921.

3
Rules of conduct which govern men in their relations to one another are being applied in an ever-increasing degree to nations. The battlefield as a place of settlement of disputes is gradually yielding to arbitral courts of justice.

WILLIAM HOWARD TAFT—*Dawn of World Peace*. In U. S. Bureau of Education Bulletin. No. 8. (1912)

4
The development of the doctrine of international arbitration, considered from the standpoint of its ultimate benefits to the human race, is the most vital movement of modern times. In its relation to the well-being of the men and women of this and ensuing generations, it exceeds in importance the proper solution of various economic problems which are constant themes of legislative discussion or enactment.

WILLIAM HOWARD TAFT—*Dawn of World Peace*. In U. S. Bureau of Education Bulletin. No. 8. (1912)

WORSHIP (See also RELIGION)

5
It is the Mass that matters.

AUGUSTINE BIRRELL—*What, Then, Did Happen at the Reformation?* Pub. in *Nineteenth Century*, April, 1896. Answered, July, 1896.

6
Ah, why
Should we, in the world's riper years, neglect
God's ancient sanctuaries, and adore
Only among the crowd and under roofs
That our frail hands have raised?

BRYANT—*A Forest Hymn*. L. 16.

7
He wales a portion with judicious care;
And "Let us worship God!" he says, with solemn air.

BURNS—*The Cotter's Saturday Night*. St. 12.

8
Isocrates adviseth Demonicus, when he came to a strange city, to worship by all means the gods of the place.

BURTON—*Anatomy of Melancholy*. Pt. III. Sec. IV. Memb. I. Subsec. 5.

(See also MONTAIGNE, also AMBROSE under ROME)

9
The heart ran o'er
With silent worship of the great of old!—
The dead, but sceptred sovereigns, who still rule
Our spirits from their urns.

BYRON—*Manfred*. Act III. Sc. 4.

10
Man always worships something; always he sees the Infinite shadowed forth in something finite; and indeed can and must so see it in any finite thing, once tempt him well to fix his eyes thereon.

CARLYLE—*Essays. Goethe's Works*.

11
And what greater calamity can fall upon a nation than the loss of worship.

EMERSON—*An Address*. July 15, 1838.

12
I don't like your way of conditioning and contracting with the saints. Do this and I'll do that! Here's one for t'other. Save me and I'll give you a taper or go on a pilgrimage.

ERASMUS—*The Shipwreck*.

13
What though the spicy breezes
Blow soft o'er Ceylon's isle;
Though every prospect pleases,
And only man is vile:
In vain with lavish kindness
The gifts of God are strown;
The heathen in his blindness
Bows down to wood and stone.

BISHOP HEBER—*From Greenland's Icy Mountains. Missionary Hymn*.

14
Ay, call it holy ground,
The soil where first they trod.
They have left unstained, what there they found—
Freedom to worship God.

FELICIA D. HEMANS—*The Landing of the Pilgrim Fathers*.

15
As the skull of the man grows broader, so do his creeds.
And his gods they are shaped in his image and mirror his needs.
And he clothes them with thunders and beauty,
He clothes them with music and fire,
Seeing not, as he bows by their altars,
That he worships his own desire.

D. R. P. MARQUIS (Don Marquis)—*The God-Maker, Man*.

16
For all of the creeds are false, and all of the creeds are true;
And low at the shrines where my brothers bow, there will I bow too;

For no form of a god, and no fashion
Man has made in his desperate passion,
But is worthy some worship of mine;
Not too hot with a gross belief,
Nor yet too cold with pride,
I will bow me down where my brothers bow,
Humble, but open eyed.
D. R. P. MARQUIS (Don Marquis)—*The God-Maker, Man.*
(See also MOORE)

1
Ev'n them who kept thy truth so pure of old,
When all our fathers worshipp'd stocks and stones.
MILTON—*On the Late Massacre in Piedmont.*

2 How often from the steep
Of echoing hill or thicket have we heard
Celestial voices to the midnight air,
Sole, or responsive each to other's note,
Singing their great Creator?
MILTON—*Paradise Lost.* Bk. IV. L. 680.

3
Every one's true worship was that which he found in use in the place where he chanced to be.
MONTAIGNE—*Apology for Raimond Sebond.* (Quoting Apollo.)
(See also BURTON)

4
Together kneeling, night and day,
Thou, for *my* sake, at Allah's shrine,
And I—at *any* God's for thine.
MOORE — *Lalla Rookh. Fire Worshippers.* Fourth Division. L. 309.
(See also MARQUIS)

5
So shall they build me altars in their zeal,
Where knaves shall minister, and fools shall kneel:
Where faith may mutter o'er her mystic spell,
Written in blood—and Bigotry may swell
The sail he spreads for Heav'n with blasts from hell!
MOORE—*Lalla Rookh. Veiled Prophet of Khorassan.*

6
Yet, if he would, man cannot live all to this world. If not religious, he will be superstitious. If he worship not the true God, he will have his idols.
THEODORE PARKER—*Critical and Miscellaneous Writings.* Essay I. *A Lesson for the Day.*

7 Stoop, boys: this gate
Instructs you how to adore the heavens and bows you
To morning's holy office.
Cymbeline. Act III. Sc. 3. L. 2.

8 Get a prayer-book in your hand,
And stand betwixt two churchmen.
Richard III. Act III. Sc. 7. L. 47.

WORTH

9
I care not twopence.
BEAUMONT AND FLETCHER—*Coxcomb.* Act V. Sc. 1. *Cupid's Revenge.* Act IV. Sc. 3.
(See also FOCH)

10
'Tis virtue, wit, and worth, and all
That men divine and sacred call;
For what is worth, in anything,
But so much money as 't will bring?
BUTLER—*Hudibras.* Pt. II. Canto I. L. 463.

11
This was the penn'worth of his thought.
BUTLER—*Hudibras.* Pt. II. Canto III.

12
Le jeu ne vaut pas la chandelle.
The game is not worth the candle.
French Proverb quoted by LORD CHESTERFIELD.

13
Nihil vulgare te dignum videri potest.
Nothing common can seem worthy of you.
CICERO to CÆSAR.

14
The two Great Unknowns, the two Illustrious Conjecturabilities! They are the best known unknown persons that have ever drawn breath upon the planet. (The Devil and Shakespeare.)
S. L. CLEMENS (MARK TWAIN)—*Shakespeare. Dead?* Ch. III.

15
You will always be fools! We shall never be gentlemen.
In the London *Times*, June 16, 1919. Quoted by LORD FISHER as a "classic" and as "the apposite words spoken by a German naval officer to his English confrère." LORD FISHER comments, "On the whole I think I prefer to be the fool—even as a matter of business."

16
Not worth twopence, (or I don't care twopence).
Favorite expression of MARSHAL FOCH. He is nicknamed "General Deux Sous" from this. WELLINGTON used "Not worth a twopenny dam." See WELLINGTON—*Dispatches.* Vol. I. Letter to his brother, the Governor-General. (The dam was a small Indian coin.)
(See also BEAUMONT)

17
He has paid dear, very dear, for his whistle.
BENJ. FRANKLIN—*The Whistle.*
(See also KING LEAR)

18
Too good for great things and too great for good.
FULLER—*Worthies.*

19
In native worth and honour clad.
Libretto of HAYDN'S *Creation.* Adapted from MILTON'S *Paradise Lost.* IV. 289. "God-like erect, with native honour-clad."

20
Of whom the world was not worthy.
Hebrews. XI. 38.

21 'Tis fortune gives us birth,
But Jove alone endues the soul with worth.
HOMER—*Iliad.* Bk. XX. L. 290. POPE'S trans.

22
This mournful truth is everywhere confess'd,
Slow rises worth by poverty depress'd.
SAMUEL JOHNSON—*London.* L. 175.

23
Il est plus facile de paraître digne des emplois qu'on n'a pas que de ceux que l'on exerce.
It is easier to appear worthy of a position one does not hold, than of the office which one fills.
LA ROCHEFOUCAULD—*Maximes.* 164.

1
An ounce of enterprise is worth a pound of privilege.
FREDERIC R. MARVIN—*Companionship of Books*. P. 318.

2
Mon verre n'est pas grand, mais je bois dans mon verre.
My glass is not large, but I drink from my glass.
ALFRED DE MUSSET.

3
Worth makes the man, and want of it the fellow;
The rest is all but leather and prunello.
POPE—*Essay on Man*. Epistle IV. 203.

4
I would that I were low laid in my grave;
I am not worth this coil that's made for me
King John. Act II. Sc. 1. L. 164.

5
I have been worth the whistle. O Goneril.
You are not worth the dust which the rude wind
Blows in your face.
King Lear. Act IV. Sc. 2. L. 27.
(See also FRANKLIN)

6
Let there be some more test made of my metal,
Before so noble and so great a figure
Be stamped upon it.
Measure for Measure. Act I. Sc. 1. L. 49.
(See also WYCHERLEY under MAN)

7
O, how thy worth with manners may I sing,
When thou art all the better part of me?
What can mine own praise to mine own self bring?
And what is't but mine own when I praise thee?
Sonnet XXXIX.

8
A pilot's part in calms cannot be spy'd,
In dangerous times true worth is only tri'd.
STIRLING—*Doomes-day. The Fifth Houre.*

9
It is a maxim, that those to whom everybody allows the second place have an undoubted title to the first.
SWIFT—*Tale of a Tub. Dedication.*

10
All human things
Of dearest value hang on slender strings.
EDMUND WALLER—*Miscellanies*. I. L. 163.

11
But though that place I never gain,
Herein lies comfort for my pain:
I will be worthy of it.
ELLA WHEELER WILCOX—*I Will be Worthy of It.*

12
It is easy enough to be prudent,
When nothing tempts you to stray;
When without or within no voice of sin
Is luring your soul away;
But it's only a negative virtue
Until it is tried by fire,
And the life that is worth the honor of earth,
Is the one that resists desire.
ELLA WHEELER WILCOX—*Worth While.*

13
Siempre acostumbra hacer el vulgo necio,
De le bueno y lo malo igual aprecio.
The foolish and vulgar are always accustomed to value equally the good and the bad.
YRIARTE—*Fables*. XXVIII.

WOUNDS

14
H' had got a hurt
O' th' inside of a deadlier sort.
BUTLER—*Hudibras*. Pt. I. Canto III. L. 309.

15
What deep wounds ever closed without a scar?
The hearts bleed longest, and but heal to wear
That which disfigures it.
BYRON—*Childe Harold*. Canto III. St. 84.

16
La blessure est pour vous, la douleur est pour moi.
The wound is for you, but the pain is for me.
CHARLES IX. to COLIGNY, who was fatally wounded in the massacre of St. Bartholomew's Day.

17
Tempore ducetur longo fortasse cicatrix;
Horrent admotas vulnera cruda manus.
A wound will perhaps become tolerable with length of time; but wounds which are raw shudder at the touch of the hands.
OVID—*Epistolæ Ex Ponto*. I. 3. 15.

18
Saucius ejurat pugnam gladiator, et idem
Immemor antiqui vulneris arma capit.
The wounded gladiator forswears all fighting, but soon forgetting his former wound resumes his arms.
OVID—*Epistolæ Ex Ponto*. I. 5. 37.

19
Thou hast wounded the spirit that loved thee
And cherish'd thine image for years;
Thou hast taught me at last to forget thee,
In secret, in silence, and tears.
MRS. DAVID PORTER—*Thou Hast Wounded the Spirit.*

20
Show you sweet Cæsar's wounds, poor, poor dumb mouths,
And bid them speak for me.
Julius Cæsar. Act III. Sc. 2. L. 229.

21
Safe in a ditch he bides,
With twenty trenched gashes on his head;
The least a death to nature.
Macbeth. Act III. Sc. 4. L. 26.

22
What wound did ever heal but by degrees?
Othello. Act II. Sc. 3. L. 377.

23
He in peace is wounded, not in war.
The Rape of Lucrece. L. 831.

24
He jests at scars that never felt a wound.
Romeo and Juliet. Act II. Sc. 2. L. 1.

25
The wound of peace is surety,
Surety secure.
Troilus and Cressida. Act II. Sc. 2. L. 14.

26
The private wound is deepest: O time most accurs'd
'Mongst all foes that a friend should be the worst.
Two Gentlemen of Verona. Act V. Sc. 4. L. 71.

27
Ah me! we wound where we never intended to strike; we create anger where we never meant

harm; and these thoughts are the thorns in our Cushion.
THACKERAY—*Roundabout Papers. The Thorn in the Cushion.*

1
I was wounded in the house of my friends.
Zechariah. XIII. 6.

WRATH (See ANGER)

WREN

2
And then the wren gan scippen and to daunce.
CHAUCER—*Court of Love.* L. 1372.

3
I took the wren's nest;—
Heaven forgive me!
Its merry architects so small
Had scarcely finished their wee hall,
That, empty still, and neat and fair,
Hung idly in the summer air.
D. M. MULOCK—*The Wren's Nest.*

4
For the poor wren,
The most diminutive of birds, will fight,
Her young ones in her nest, against the owl.
Macbeth. Act IV. Sc. 2. L. 9.

5
Thus the fable tells us, that the wren mounted as high as the eagle, by getting upon his back.
Tatler. No. 224.

6
Among the dwellings framed by birds
In field or forest with nice care,
Is none that with the little wren's
In snugness may compare.
WORDSWORTH—*A Wren's Nest.*

WRITING (See AUTHORSHIP JOURNALISM, PEN)

WRONGS (See also INJURY)

7
In the great right of an excessive wrong.
ROBERT BROWNING—*The Ring and the Book. The other Half—Rome.* L. 1,055.

8
Brother, brother; we are both in the wrong.
GAY—*Beggar's Opera.* Act II. Sc. 2.

9
Alas! how easily things go wrong!
A sigh too deep, or a kiss too long,
And then comes a mist and a weeping rain,
And life is never the same again.
GEORGE MACDONALD—*Phantastes. A Fairy Story.*

10
A man finds he has been wrong at every preceding stage of his career, only to deduce the astonishing conclusion that he is at last entirely right.
STEVENSON—*Crabbed Age.*

11
Once I guessed right,
And I got credit by't;
Thrice I guessed wrong,
And I kept my credit on.
Saying quoted by SWIFT. (1710)

12
Injuriarum remedium est oblivio.
The remedy for wrongs is to forget them.
SYRUS—*Maxims.*

13
Higher than the perfect song
For which love longeth,
Is the tender fear of wrong,
That never wrongeth.
BAYARD TAYLOR—*Improvisations.* Pt. V.

14
Wrongs unredressed, or insults unavenged.
WORDSWORTH—*The Excursion.* Bk. III. L. 377.

Y

YESTERDAY (See PAST)

YEW

Taxus

15
Careless, unsocial plant! that loves to dwell
'Midst skulls and coffins, epitaphs and worms:
Where light-heel'd ghosts and visionary shades,
Beneath the wan, cold Moon (as Fame reports)
Embodied, thick, perform their mystic rounds.
No other merriment, dull tree! is thine.
BLAIR—*The Grave.* L. 22.

16
For there no yew nor cypress spread their gloom
But roses blossom'd by each rustic tomb.
CAMPBELL—*Theodric.* L. 22.

17
Slips of yew
Sliver'd in the moon's eclipse.
Macbeth. Act IV. Sc. 1. L. 27.

18
Of vast circumference and gloom profound,
This solitary Tree! A living thing
Produced too slowly ever to decay;
Of form and aspect too magnificent
To be destroyed.
WORDSWORTH—*Yew-Trees.*

19
There is a Yew-tree, pride of Lorton Vale,
Which to this day stands single, in the midst
Of its own darkness, as it stood of yore.
WORDSWORTH—*Yew-Trees.*

YOUTH

20
Young men soon give and soon forget affronts;
Old age is slow in both.
ADDISON—*Cato.* Act II. Sc. 5.

21
Youth dreams a bliss on this side death.
It dreams a rest, if not more deep,
More grateful than this marble sleep;
It hears a voice within it tell:
Calm's not life's crown, though calm is well.
'Tis all perhaps which man acquires,
But 'tis not what our youth desires.
MATTHEW ARNOLD—*Youth and Calm.* L. 19.

1
Young men are fitter to invent than to judge; fitter for execution than for counsel; and fitter for new projects than for settled business.
BACON—*Of Youth and Age.*

2
I was between
A man and a boy, A hobble-de-hoy,
A fat, little, punchy concern of sixteen.
R. H. BARHAM—*Aunt Fanny.*
(See also TUSSER)

3
Smiling always with a never fading serenity of countenance, and flourishing in an immortal youth.
ISAAC BARROW—*Duty of Thanksgiving. Works.* Vol. I. P. 66.

4
Our youth we can have but to-day;
We may always find time to grow old.
BISHOP BERKELEY—*Can Love be Controlled by Advice?*

5
Young fellows will be young fellows.
BICKERSTAFF—*Love in a Village.* Act II. Sc. 2.

6
They shall not grow old, as we that are left grow old;
Age shall not weary them, nor the years condemn.
At the going down of the sun, and in the morning,
We will remember them.
LAURENCE BINYON—*For the Fallen.* Sept., 1915.

7
Blow out, you bugles, over the rich Dead!
There's none of these so lonely and poor of old,
But, dying, has made us rarer gifts than gold.
These laid the world away: poured out the red
Sweet wine of youth; gave up the years to be
Of work and joy, and that unhoped serene
That men call age, and those who would have been
Their sons, they gave their immortality.
RUPERT BROOKE—*The Dead.* (1914)

8
Every street has two sides, the shady side and the sunny. When two men shake hands and part, mark which of the two takes the sunny side; he will be the younger man of the two.
BULWER-LYTTON—*What Will He Do With It?* Bk. II. Heading of Ch. XV.

9
Ah! happy years! once more who would not be a boy!
BYRON—*Childe Harold.* Canto II. St. 23.

10
Her years
Were ripe, they might make six-and-twenty springs;
But there are forms which Time to touch forbears,
And turns aside his scythe to vulgar things.
BYRON—*Don Juan.* Canto V. St. 98.

11
And both were young, and one was beautiful.
BYRON—*The Dream.* St. 2.

12
Youth is to all the glad season of life; but often only by what it hopes, not by what it attains, or what it escapes.
CARLYLE—*Essays. Schiller.*

13
As I approve of a youth that has something of the old man in him, so I am no less pleased with an old man that has something of the youth. He that follows this rule may be old in body, but can never be so in mind.
CICERO—*Cato; or, An Essay on Old Age.*

14
Prima commendiato proficiscitur a modestia tum pietate in parentes, tum in suos benevolentia.
The chief recommendation [in a young man] is modesty, then dutiful conduct toward parents, then affection for kindred.
CICERO—*De Officiis.* II. 13.

15
Teneris, heu, lubrica moribus ætas!
Alas! the slippery nature of tender youth.
CLAUDIANUS—*De Raptu Proserpinæ.* III. 227.

16
Life went a-Maying
With Nature, Hope, and Poesy;
When I was young!
When I was young?—Ah, woful when!
COLERIDGE—*Youth and Age.*

17
A young Apollo, golden haired,
Stands dreaming on the verge of strife,
Magnificently unprepared
For the long littleness of life.
MRS. CORNFORD—*On Rupert Brooke.* (1915)

18
Be it a weakness, it deserves some praise,
We love the play-place of our early days;
The scene is touching, and the heart is stone,
That feels not at that sight, and feels at none.
COWPER—*Tirocinium.* L. 296.

19
Youth, what man's age is like to be, doth show;
We may our ends by our beginnings know.
SIR JOHN DENHAM—*Of Prudence.* L. 225.

20
Youth should watch joys and shoot them as they fly.
DRYDEN—*Aureng-Zebe.* Act III. Sc. 1.

21
Olympian bards who sung
Divine ideas below,
Which always find us young,
And always keep us so.
EMERSON—*Essays. The Poet.* Introduction.

22
Angelicus juvenis senibus satanizat in annis.
An angelic boyhood becomes a Satanic old age.
ERASMUS—*Fam. Coll.* Quoted as a proverb invented by Satan.

23
Si jeunesse savoit, si vieillesse pouvoit.
H. ÉTIENNE—*Les Premices.*
Si jeune savoit, et vieux pouvoit,
Jamais disette n'y auroit.
If youth but knew, and age were able,
Then poverty would be a fable.
Proverb of the Twelfth Century.

24
Youth holds no society with grief.
EURIPIDES. L. 73.

1
O happy unown'd youths! your limbs can bear
The scorching dog-star and the winter's air,
While the rich infant, nurs'd with care and pain,
Thirsts with each heat and coughs with every rain!
GAY—*Trivia*. Bk. II. L. 145.

2
Fair laughs the morn, and soft the zephyr blows,
While proudly rising o'er the azure realm
In gallant trim the gilded vessel goes,
Youth on the prow, and Pleasure at the helm.
GRAY—*Bard*. Pt. II. St. 2.

3
The insect-youth are on the wing,
Eager to taste the honied spring,
And float amid the liquid noon!
GRAY—*Ode on the Spring*. St. 3. L. 5.

4
Over the trackless past, somewhere,
Lie the lost days of our tropic youth,
Only regained by faith and prayer,
Only recalled by prayer and plaint,
Each lost day has its patron saint!
BRET HARTE—*Lost Galleon*. Last stanza.

5
There is a feeling of Eternity in youth which makes us amends for everything. To be young is to be as one of the Immortals.
HAZLITT—*Table Talk. The Feeling of Immortality in Youth.*

6
Ah, youth! forever dear, forever kind.
HOMER—*Iliad*. Bk. XIX. L. 303. POPE'S trans.

7
Youth! youth! how buoyant are thy hopes! they turn,
Like marigolds, toward the sunny side.
JEAN INGELOW—*The Four Bridges*. St. 56.

8
All the world's a mass of folly,
Youth is gay, age melancholy:
Youth is spending, age is thrifty,
Mad at twenty, cold at fifty;
Man is nought but folly's slave,
From the cradle to the grave.
W. H. IRELAND—*Modern Ship of Fools*. (*Of the Folly of all the World.*)

9
Towering in confidence of twenty-one.
SAMUEL JOHNSON—*Letter to Bennet Langton*. Jan., 1758.

10
When all the world is young, lad,
And all the trees are green;
And every goose a swan, lad,
And every lass a queen;
Then hey, for boot and horse, lad,
And round the world away;
Young blood must have its course, lad,
And every dog his day.
CHARLES KINGSLEY—*Water Babies*.

11
Our youth began with tears and sighs,
With seeking what we could not find;
We sought and knew not what we sought;
We marvel, now we look behind:
Life's more amusing than we thought.
ANDREW LANG—*Ballade of Middle Age*.

12
Flos juvenum (Flos juventutis).
The flower of the young men (the flower of youth).
LIVY. VIII. 8; XXXVII. 12.

13
Youth comes but once in a lifetime.
LONGFELLOW—*Hyperion*. Bk. II. Ch. X.

14
Standing with reluctant feet,
Where the brook and river meet,
Womanhood and childhood fleet!
LONGFELLOW—*Maidenhood*.

15
How beautiful is youth! how bright it gleams
With its illusions, aspirations, dreams!
Book of Beginnings, Story without End,
Each maid a heroine, and each man a friend!
LONGFELLOW—*Morituri Salutamus*. L. 66.

16
In its sublime audacity of faith,
"Be thou removed!" it to the mountain saith,
And with ambitious feet, secure and proud,
Ascends the ladder leaning on the cloud!
LONGFELLOW—*Morituri Salutamus*.

17
Youth, that pursuest with such eager pace
Thy even way,
Thou pantest on to win a mournful race:
Then stay! oh, stay!

Pause and luxuriate in thy sunny plain;
Loiter,—enjoy:
Once past, Thou never wilt come back again,
A second Boy.
RICHARD MONCKTON MILNES—*Carpe Diem*.

18
'Tis now the summer of your youth: time has not cropped the roses from your cheek, though sorrow long has washed them.
EDWARD MOORE—*The Gamester*. Act III. Sc. 4.

19
The smiles, the tears
Of boyhood's years,
The words of love then spoken.
MOORE—*Oft in the Stilly Night*.

20
Dissimiles hic vir, et ille puer.
How different from the present man was the youth of earlier days!
OVID—*Heroides*. IX. 24.

21
The atrocious crime of being a young man.
WILLIAM PITT to WALPOLE. *Boswell's Life of Johnson*. March 6, 1741.

22
When the brisk minor pants for twenty-one.
POPE—*Epistle I*. Bk. I. L. 38.

23
We think our fathers fools, so wise we grow;
Our wiser sons, no doubt, will think us so.
POPE—*Essay on Criticism*. Pt. II. L. 238.

24
De jeune hermite, vieil diable.
Of a young hermit, an old devil.
RABELAIS—*Pantagruel*. Quoted, as a "proverbe authentique."

25
My salad days;
When I was green in judgment.
Antony and Cleopatra. Act I. Sc. 5. L. 73.

1 The spirit of a youth
That means to be of note, begins betimes.
Antony and Cleopatra. Act IV. Sc. 4. L. 26.

2
The chariest maid is prodigal enough,
If she unmask her beauty to the moon;
Virtue itself 'scapes not calumnious strokes.
The canker galls the infants of the spring,
Too oft before their buttons be disclosed;
And in the morn and liquid dew of youth,
Contagious blastments are most imminent.
Hamlet. Act I. Sc. 3. L. 36. "Infants of the spring" found also in *Love's Labour's Lost.* Act I. Sc. 1. L. 100.

3 For youth no less becomes
The light and careless livery that it wears,
Than settled age his sables, and his weeds
Importing health and graveness.
Hamlet. Act IV. Sc. 7. L. 79.

4
Is in the very May-morn of his youth,
Ripe for exploits and mighty enterprises.
Henry V. Act I. Sc. 2. L. 120.

5
He that is more than a youth, is not for me, and he that is less than man, I am not for him.
Much Ado About Nothing. Act II. Sc. 1. L. 40.

6
Crabbed age and youth cannot live together;
Youth is full of pleasance, age is full of care;
Youth like summer morn, age like winter weather;
Youth like summer brave, age like winter bare.
Youth is full of sport, age's breath is short;
Youth is nimble, age is lame;
Youth is hot and bold, age is weak and cold;
Youth is wild, and age is tame.
Age, I do abhor thee; youth I do adore thee.
The Passionate Pilgrim. St. 12.

7
Thou art thy mother's glass, and she in thee
Calls back the lovely April of her prime:
So thou through windows of thine age shall see,
Despite of wrinkles this thy golden time.
Sonnet III.

8
Hail, blooming Youth!
May all your virtues with your years improve,
Till in consummate worth you shine the pride
Of these our days, and succeeding times
A bright example.
WM. SOMERVILLE—*The Chase.* Bk. III. L. 389.

9
Age may have one side, but assuredly Youth has the other. There is nothing more certain than that both are right, except perhaps that both are wrong.
STEVENSON—*Crabbed Age.*

10
For God's sake give me the young man who has brains enough to make a fool of himself.
STEVENSON—*Crabbed Age.*

11
Youth is wholly experimental.
STEVENSON—*To a Young Gentleman.*

12
Youth should be a savings-bank.
MADAME SWETCHINE.

13
What is that to him that reaps not harvest of his youthful joys,
Though the deep heart of existence beat forever like a boy's?
TENNYSON—*Locksley Hall.* St. 70.

14
What unjust judges fathers are, when in regard to us they hold
That even in our boyish days we ought in conduct to be old,
Nor taste at all the very things that youth and only youth requires;
They rule us by their present wants not by their past long-lost desires.
TERENCE—*The Self-Tormentor.* Act I. Sc. 3. F. W. RICORD's trans.

15
The next, keep under Sir Hobbard de Hoy:
The next, a man, no longer a boy.
TUSSER—*Hundred Points of Husbandry.*
(See also BARHAM)

16
Bliss was it in that dawn to be alive,
But to be young was very Heaven!
WORDSWORTH—*The Prelude.* Bk. XI.

17
A youth to whom was given
So much of earth, so much of heaven.
WORDSWORTH—*Ruth.*

18
Youth is not rich in time; it may be poor;
Part with it as with money, sparing; pay
No moment but in purchase of its worth,
And what it's worth, ask death-beds; they can tell.
YOUNG—*Night Thoughts.* Night II. L. 47.

YUKON

19
This is the law of the Yukon, that only the Strong shall survive;
That surely the Weak shall perish, and only the Fit survive.
Dissolute, damned and despairful, crippled and palsied and slain,
This is the Will of the Yukon,—Lo, how she makes it plain!
ROBERT W. SERVICE—*Law of the Yukon.*

20
There's a land where the mountains are nameless
And the rivers all run God knows where;
There are lives that are erring and aimless,
And deaths that just hang by a hair;
There are hardships that nobody reckons;
There are valleys unpeopled and still;
There's a land—oh, it beckons and beckons,
And I want to go back—and I will.
ROBERT W. SERVICE—*Spell of the Yukon.*

YVETTE (RIVER)

21
O lovely river of Yvette!
O darling river! like a bride,
Some dimpled, bashful, fair Lisette,
Thou goest to wed the Orge's tide.
O lovely river of Yvette!
O darling stream! on balanced wings
The wood-birds sang the chansonnette
That here a wandering poet sings.
LONGFELLOW—*To the River Yvette.* St. 5.

Z

ZEAL

1
There is no greater sign of a general decay of virtue in a nation, than a want of zeal in its inhabitants for the good of their country.
ADDISON—*Freeholder*. No. 5.

2
Zealous, yet modest.
BEATTIE—*The Minstrel*. Bk. I. St. 11.

3
Through zeal knowledge is gotten, through lack of zeal knowledge is lost; let a man who knows this double path of gain and loss thus place himself that knowledge may grow.
BUDDHA.

4
For zeal's a dreadful termagant,
That teaches saints to tear and cant.
BUTLER—*Hudibras*. Pt. III. Canto II. L. 673.

5
Awake, my soul! stretch every nerve,
And press with vigour on;
A heavenly race demands thy zeal,
And an immortal crown.
PHILIP DODDRIDGE—*Zeal and Vigour in the Christian Race*.

6
It is good to be zealously affected always in a good thing.
Galatians. IV. 18.

7
I remember a passage in Goldsmith's "Vicar of Wakefield," which he was afterwards fool enough to expunge: "I do not love a man who is zealous for nothing."
SAMUEL JOHNSON—*Boswell's Life of Johnson*. (1779)

8
Blinder Eifer schadet nur.
Blind zeal can only do harm.
LICHTWER—*Die Katzen und der Hausherr*.

9
A Spirit, zealous, as he seemed, to know
More of the Almighty's works, and chiefly Man,
God's latest image.
MILTON—*Paradise Lost*. Bk. IV. L. 565.

10
But his zeal
None seconded, as out of season judged,
Or singular and rash.
MILTON—*Paradise Lost*. Bk. V. L. 849.

11
But zeal moved thee;
To please thy gods thou didst it!
MILTON—*Samson Agonistes*. L. 895.

12
Zeal is very blind, or badly regulated, when it encroaches upon the rights of others.
PASQUIER QUESNEL.

13
Zeal then, not charity, became the guide.
POPE—*Essay on Man*. Ep. III. L. 261.

14
I have more zeal than wit.
POPE—*Imitations of Horace*. Bk. II. Satire VI. L. 56.

15
Poets heap virtues, painters gems, at will,
And show their zeal, and hide their want of skill.
POPE—*Moral Essays*. Ep. II. L. 185.

16
A zeal of God, but not according to knowledge.
Romans. X. 2.

17
My hat is in the ring.
ROOSEVELT. Said in Cleveland, when on his way to Columbus, Ohio, Feb. 21, 1912.

18
Der Freunde Eifer ist's, der mich
Zu Grunde richtet, nicht der Hass der Feinde.
The zeal of friends it is that razes me,
And not the hate of enemies.
SCHILLER—*Wallenstein's Tod*. III. 18. Last lines.

19
We do that in our zeal our calmer moment would be afraid to answer.
SCOTT—*Woodstock*. Heading of Ch. XVII.

20
If I had obeyed God, as I have obeyed him,
He would not have punished me.
SWAMWRA to the Governor of Basra when deposed by the Caliph. (675) See *Ibnu'l Athir*. Vol. III. P. 412. (Ed. Tomberg.)
(See also HENRY VIII under SERVICE)

21
Terms ill defined, and forms misunderstood,
And customs, when their reasons are unknown,
Have stirred up many zealous souls
To fight against imaginary giants.
TUPPER—*Proverbial Philosophy. Of Tolerance*.

22
Press bravely onward!—not in vain
Your generous trust in human kind;
The good which bloodshed could not gain
Your peaceful zeal shall find.
WHITTIER—*To the Reformers of England*.

ZEPHYRS (See also WIND)

23
Where the light wings of Zephyr, oppress'd with perfume,
Wax faint o'er the gardens of Gul in her bloom.
BYRON—*Bride of Abydos*. Canto I. St. 1.
(See also DYER)

24
Let Zephyr only breathe
And with her tresses play.
DRUMMOND—*Song. Phœbus, Arise*.

25
While the wanton Zephyr sings,
And in the vale perfumes his wings.
DYER—*Gronger Hill*.
(See also BYRON)

26
Fair laughs the morn, and soft the zephyr blows.
GRAY—*The Bard*. I. 2. L. 9.

27
And soon
Their hushing dances languished to a stand,
Like midnight leaves when, as the Zephyrs swoon,
All on their drooping stems they sink unfanned.
HOOD—*The Plea of the Midsummer Fairies*.

1
And on the balmy zephyrs tranquil rest
The silver clouds.
KEATS—*Posthumous Poems. Sonnets. Oh! How I Love on a Fair Summer's Eve.*

2
Soft is the strain when zephyr gently blows.
POPE—*Essay on Criticism.* Pt. II. L. 366.

3
Lull'd by soft zephyrs thro' the broken pane.
POPE—*Prologue to Satires.* L. 42.

4
And soften'd sounds along the waters die:
Smooth flow the waves, the zephyrs gently play.
POPE—*Rape of the Lock.* Canto II. L. 50.

5
Soft o'er the shrouds aerial whispers breathe,
That seemed but zephyrs to the train beneath.
POPE—*Rape of the Lock.* Canto II. L. 58.

6
The balmy zephyrs, silent since her death,
Lament the ceasing of a sweeter breath.
POPE—*Winter.* L. 45.

AUTHORS QUOTED IN THIS CYCLOPEDIA

With Places and Dates of Births and Deaths, and Brief Characterizations

NOTE.—The star (*) which precedes the names of some of the authors quoted indicates that they are cited too frequently to make it necessary to give the page folios on which quotations from their works will be found. Where the author is anonymous, the name of the volume or collection in which the quotation appears is cited. The following abbreviations are employed:

a, or ab.=about; b.=born; B.C.=Before Christ; c.=*circa* (about); d.=Dead or died; fl.=flourished; L.=Living or lived.

A

ABBOTT, WENONAH STEVENS, journalist, writer, lecturer, UNITED STATES, 1865–L. 736

ABD-EL-KADER, Arab chief. ALGERIA, 1807–1883 163

ABU 'L ALA, Arabian poet, died 977 440

ACHILLES TATIUS (or STATIUS), Alexandrian rhetorician, lived end of 5th Cent. and beginning of 6th Cent. 882

ADAM OF COBSHAM 355

ADAMS, CHARLES FRANCIS, lawyer, diplomat... UNITED STATES, 1807–1886 841

ADAMS, FRANKLIN PIERCE, journalist, humorist, writer, UNITED STATES, 1881–L. 801

ADAMS, JOHN, statesman, 2nd Pres. U. S., UNITED STATES, 1735–1826 329 330 368 584

ADAMS, JOHN QUINCY, 6th Pres. U. S., UNITED STATES, 1767–1848 106 163 588 618 634 882

ADAMS, SAMUEL, patriot and orator, UNITED STATES, 1722–1803 85 674 841

ADAMS, MRS. SARAH FLOWER, poet, ENGLAND, 1805–1848 315

ADAMS, THOMAS, clergyman of wit and learning.... ENGLAND, died before 1660 221

*ADDISON, JOSEPH, writer.. ENGLAND, 1672–1719

ADY, THOMAS, writer on witchcraft, ENGLAND, 1656(61)– 63

ÆMILIUS, PAULUS, Roman Consul, general, lived B.C. 216 291 486 705

ÆSCHINES, statesman and orator, GREECE, B.C. 389–314 522

ÆSCHYLUS, tragic poet.. GREECE, B.C. 525–456 12 34 163 182 208 244 289 350 364 397 434 518 550 564 566 631 647 735 762 780 882

AGESILAUS, "*The Great,*" king of Sparta.......... GREECE, B.C. 455–361. 557 705

AGLIONBY 862

AÏDÉ, CHARLES HAMILTON, French-English musician, composer, dramatist, novelist,.........1826–1906 413

AIKIN, LUCY, historian, writer, ENGLAND, 1781–1864 415

AINSWORTH, WM. HARRISON, novelist, ENGLAND, 1805–1882 561 868

AISÉE, MLLE., letter writer, daughter of Circassian chief, lived in FRANCE, 1694–1733 365

AKENSIDE, MARK, poet. ENGLAND, 1721–1770 43 383 434 487 700 815

AKERS, ELIZABETH, biographer, poet, UNITED STATES, 1832–1911 792

ALAMANNI, LUIGI, statesman, poet, ITALY, 1495–1556 233

ALANUS DE INSULUS. See INSULUS.

ALBERIC, MONK OF MONTE-CASSINO, FRANCE, 1140– 773

ALCÆUS, lyric poet, GREECE, flourished about B.C. 600 39 330 521 841

ALCIATUS, ANDREA, jurist, writer, ITALY, 1492–1550 312

ALCOTT, AMOS BRONSON, teacher and philosopher, UNITED STATES, 1799–1888 75 439 775 809 818 835 886

ALCUIN, abbot, scholar, reformer, friend of Charlemagne, ENGLAND, 735(?)–804 315 647

ALDRICH, JAMES, poet and journalist, UNITED STATES, 1810–1856 163

ALDRICH, THOMAS BAILEY, poet and prose writer. UNITED STATES, 1836–1907 54 57 139 161 163 184 201 210 246 379 457 501 554 568 572 615 655 716 769 780 787 877

ALDRIDGE (ALDRICH), HENRY, dean of Christchurch.. ENGLAND, 1647–1710 67 206

ALDRIDGE, IRA, negro tragedian, UNITED STATES, 1810–1867 261

ALDUS MANUTIUS, printer, scholar, ITALY, 1447–1515 85

ALESSANDRO, ALLEGRI, see ALLEGRI ALESSANDRO.

ALEXANDER THE GREAT, king of MACEDONIA, B.C. 356–323 113 600 615

ALEXANDER VI, pope, R. L. Borgia, b., SPAIN, 1430; d., ITALY, 1503. 333

ALEXANDER, MRS. CECIL FRANCES, poet....... GREAT BRITAIN, 1818–1895 114 337

ALEXANDER, PATRICK PROCTOR, author............ SCOTLAND, 1824– 716

ALEXANDER, WM., Earl of Stirling, poet, statesman, and courtier, SCOTLAND, ab. 1567–1640 163 423 710 920

ALEXIS GUILLAUME, Benedictine poet FRANCE, living 1506 506

BRYDGES, SIR SAMUEL, bibliographer, biographer, genealogist, ENGLAND, 1762–1837
313 901
BUCHANAN, GEORGE, scholar, historian, Latin poet. . SCOTLAND, 1506–1582 523
BUCHANAN, ROBERT, poet and novelist . . . . ENGLAND, 1841–1901
229 253 577 605 753 868
BÜCHMANN, GEORG, philologist, archælogist, classical scholar, compiler . . . . GERMANY, 1822–1884
706 844 850 883
BUCKINGHAM, GEORGE VILLIERS, DUKE OF, writer . . ENGLAND, 1627–1688
196 883
BUCKINGHAMSHIRE, DUKE OF, see SHEFFIELD, JOHN
BUCKSTONE, JOHN BALDWIN, comedian . . . . ENGLAND, 1802–1879
270 792
BUDDHA, or BOODDHA, Gotama, born near Kapilavastu, India, 568 B.C.; died near Kushinagara, Oudh, 488 B.C.; founder of Buddhism. 925
BUELL, MARY E. 416
BUFFON, G. L. L. DE, naturalist and philosopher . . . . FRANCE, 1707–1788
308 758
BUGEAUD, THOS. ROBERT, duc d'Isly, marshal of France, 1784–1849 725
BULFINCH, S. G., clergyman and writer . . . . . UNITED STATES, 1809–1870 238
BULLARD, MAJOR-GENERAL ROBERT LEE, distinguished in Great War . . . . UNITED STATES, 1861–L. 843
BULLEN, A. H., author and publisher, 1857–1920
97 470
BÜLOW, BERNARD, COUNT VON, statesman, chancellor . . . GERMANY, 1850– 843
*BULWER-LYTTON, EDWARD GEORGE (EARL LYTTON), novelist, ENGLAND, 1803–1873
BUNGAY, GEORGE W., journalist, ENGLAND, 1826–1892 723
BUNN, ALFRED, librettist, theatrical manager . . . . ENGLAND, 1796–1860
202 375 582
BUNNER, H. C., journalist and author, UNITED STATES, 1855–1896 23 39
BUNSEN, BARON CHRISTIAN, ambassador, scholar . . . . PRUSSIA, 1791–1860 868
BUNYAN, JOHN, author . . ENGLAND, 1628–1688
47 58 76 134 160 165 190 252 260 383 639 795 829
BURCHARD, SAMUEL D., clergyman, UNITED STATES, 1812–1891 610
BURDETTE, ROBERT JONES, humorist, lecturer . . . . UNITED STATES, 1844–1914 732
BÜRGER, G. A., poet . . . . GERMANY, 1748–1794
82 165
BURGESS, FRANK GELETT, humorist, writer and poet UNITED STATES, 1866–L.
97 145 286
BURGON, JOHN W., English clergyman, poet . . . . BURMA, 1819–1888 121
BURGOYNE, GEN. JOHN, soldier, dramatist . . . . GREAT BRITAIN, 1722–1792 902
BURGUILLOS, TOME, see VEGA, LOPE DE.
*BURKE, EDMUND, orator and statesman . . . . IRELAND, 1729–1797
BURLEIGH (BURGHLEY), WM. CECIL, LORD, statesman . . ENGLAND, 1520–1598 732
BURLEIGH, WILLIAM HENRY, poet, UNITED STATES, 1812–1871
18 218 877
BURMANN, PIETER, classical scholar, HOLLAND, 1668–1741 695
BURNAND, SIR FRANCIS COWLEY, humorist, novelist, editor of *Punch* . . . . ENGLAND, 1837–1917 465
BURNET, GILBERT, historian and prelate . . . . SCOTLAND, 1643–1715
430 661
BURNET, JAMES (LORD MONBODDO), lawyer . . . . SCOTLAND, 1714–1779 241
BURNETT, DANA, author, poet, UNITED STATES, 1888–L. 88
BURNS, JAMES DRUMMOND, poet, clergyman . . . . SCOTLAND, 1823–1864
388 792
*BURNS, ROBERT, poet . . SCOTLAND, 1759–1796
BURR, AARON, politician, UNITED STATES, 1756–1836 600
BURR, AMELIA JOSEPHINE, author, poet . . . . UNITED STATES, –L. 725
BURROUGHS, JEREMIAH, Congregational minister, writer, ENGLAND, 1599–1646 887
BURROUGHS, JOHN, naturalist, UNITED STATES, 1837–1921 243 877
BURTON, REV. HENRY, clergyman, writer . . . . ENGLAND, born 1840 415
BURTON, RICHARD EUGENE, poet, journalist, critic. UNITED STATES, 1861–L.
97 165 411 759 899
BURTON, SIR RICHARD FRANCIS, writer, traveler . . . . ENGLAND, 1821–1890 330
BURTON, LADY, wife of SIR RICHARD FRANCIS 420
*BURTON, ROBERT, writer, philosopher and humorist, ENGLAND, 1576–1640(39)
BURY, RICHARD DE, see AUNGERVILLE.
BUSHNELL, SAMUEL CLARKE, clergyman . . . . UNITED STATES, 1852– 801
BUSSY-RABUTIN, ROGER DE, officer and satirical writer . . . . . FRANCE, 1618–1693
474 615 843
BUTLER, MRS. FRANCES ANN KEMBLE, see KEMBLE.
BUTLER, JAMES, DUKE OF ORMONDE, royalist, soldier . . . ENGLAND, 1610–1688 753
BUTLER, JOSEPH, bishop . ENGLAND, 1692–1752
262 634 787
BUTLER, SAMUEL, philosopher, artist, archæologist, miscellaneous writer . . . . ENGLAND, 1835–1902 524
*BUTLER, SAMUEL, wit and poet, ENGLAND, 1612–1680
BUTLER, WILLIAM ALLEN, lawyer and poet . . . . UNITED STATES, 1825–1902 31
BUTTERWORTH, HEZEKIAH, writer, UNITED STATES, 1839–1905 127
BUTTS, MARY FRANCES, 1836 816
BYERS, SAM, H. M., author, soldier, UNITED STATES, 1838–L. 843
BYRD, or BIRD, WILLIAM, composer of church music and organist to Queen Elizabeth, ENGLAND, about 1540–1623 513
BYROM, JOHN, writer and poet, ENGLAND, 1691–1763
137 278 381 466 513 629 639 642 683 792 883
*BYRON, GEORGE GORDON NOEL, poet, ENGLAND, 1788–1824

C

CABLE, GEORGE WASHINGTON, novelist, lecturer . UNITED STATES, 1844–1925 54
CÆLIUS RHODIGINUS, see RHODIGINUS CÆLIUS.
CÆSAR, AUGUSTUS, see AUGUSTUS CÆSAR.
CÆSAR, CAIUS JULIUS, Roman general, statesman, writer, and orator, B.C. 100–44
66 129 267 289 430 534 844 882

E

EACHARD, JOHN, divine, teacher, 848
ENGLAND, 1636(?)–1697
EADMER (EDMER), eccles., historian, 647
biographer...ENGLAND, 1060(?)–1124(?)
EAST, REV. JOHN 316
EAST, REV. THOMAS 102
EASTWICK, EDWARD B., orientalist, 263
ENGLAND, 1814–1883
EATON, DORMAN B., lawyer, 817
UNITED STATES, 1823–1899
EBBSWORTH, JOS. W., ed. of ballads, 468
poet, miscel. writer,
ENGLAND, 1824–1908
EDDY, MRS. MARY BAKER GLOVER,
founder of Christian Science,
UNITED STATES, 1821–1910
196 316 513 706 819
EDGEWORTH, MARIA, author, 81 575 908
ENGLAND, 1767–1849
EDWARDS, AMELIA B., novelist, writer, 133
and Egyptologist..ENGLAND, 1831–1892
EDWARDS, RICHARD, dramatic poet, 297 913
ENGLAND, 1523–1566
EDWIN, JOHN, comedian. ENGLAND, 1749–1794
444
EEDES (EDES), RICHARD, Dean of 534
Worcester........ENGLAND, 1555–1604
EGAN, MAURICE FRANCIS, translator, 114
novelist, essayist, editor, diplomatist......UNITED STATES, 1852–1924
EGERTON PAPERS, (1552) 415
EGLINGTON, HUGH MONTGOMERIE, Earl of 141
statesman..GREAT BRITAIN, 1739–1819
ELDON, JOHN SCOTT (Earl of Eldon),
jurist............ENGLAND, 1751–1838
353 522 878
ELIOT, CHARLES W., educator, writer, 617
scholar.....UNITED STATES, 1834–1926
ELIOT, GEORGE, see CROSS, MARY ANN EVANS
ELIZABETH, Queen of England.....1533–1603
27 42 99 198 289 569 645
ELLENBOROUGH, EDWARD LAW, Lord 819
Chief Justice.....ENGLAND, 1750–1818
ELLERTON, WILLIAM, 900
ELLIOTT, EBENEZER, "*The Corn Law Rhymer*," poet....ENGLAND, 1781–1849
84 156 185 230 262 356 444 611
626 833 908
ELLIOTT, JANE, poet. ENGLAND, 1727–1805 279
ELLIS, SIR HENRY, antiquarian, librarian of British Museum, 532
ENGLAND, 1777–1869
ELLIS, MRS. SARAH STICKNEY, author, 297
ENGLAND, 1812–1872
ELLSWORTH, ERASTUS W., poet, 369
UNITED STATES, 1823–1902
ELPHINSTONE, JOHN, LORD, governor 872
of Madras and Bombay,
ENGLAND, 1807–1860
ELSTON, FRIAR, in reign of Henry 360
VIII
ELY, MRS. FOSTER, poet, 168
UNITED STATES, 20th Cent.
ELYOT, SIR THOMAS, diplomatist and 594 784
author.....ENGLAND, about 1499–1546
*EMERSON, RALPH WALDO, essayist
and poet....UNITED STATES, 1803–1882
EMMET, ROBERT, patriot. IRELAND, 1780–1803
230
EMMETT, DAN. DECATUR, song writer, 585
UNITED STATES, 1815–1904
ENGLAND'S PARNASSUS, a collection of 874
old English poets, compiler
given as ROBERT ALLOT (probably his father), registered Oct.
2, 1600; original in theBodleian
Library, Oxford, England.
ENGLEFIELD, SIR HENRY CHAS., antiquary............ENGLAND, 1752–1822 157
ENGLISH, THOMAS DUNN, poet and
writer......UNITED STATES, 1819–1902
494 506 811 889
ENNIUS, Roman epic poet, of Greek
origin....CALABRIA, about B.C. 239–169
83 187 230 354 364 667 848 879
EPICHARMUS, Dorian comic poet, 698
Pythagorean philosopher, B.C. 540(?)–450
EPICTETUS, philosopher......PHRYGIA, 60–120
120 288 303 327 596 643 668 871
ERASMUS, GERARD DIDIER, scholar,
philosopher, and writer,
HOLLAND, 1465–1536
35 113 140 199 239 247 252 271
293 312 338 346 435 445 493 497
542 636 647 670 705 706 754 777
794 819 846 862 879 915 918 922
ERSKINE, HENRY, Lord Advocate, orator, wit..........SCOTLAND, 1746–1817 674
ERSKINE, JOHN, divine, theologian, 804
SCOTLAND, 1721(?)–1803
ESSEX, ROBERT DEVEREUX, Earl of,
General, favorite of Queen
Elizabeth........ENGLAND, 1567–1601
658 726
ÉSTIENNE OR ÉTIENNE, HENRI, printer and scholar.....FRANCE, 1528–1598
468 644 922
EUCLID, geometer,
GREECE, alive during B.C. 323–283
435 641
EURIPIDES, tragic poet...GREECE, B.C. 48–406
6 121 168 289 306 311 312 316
364 396 445 468 506 559 586 645
650 670 671 675 724 775 788 796
816 825 830 846 889 922
EUSDEN, MRS. 909
EUSTATHIUS, archbishop of Thessalonica, classical commentator, –1198
110 220
EVANS, DR. ABEL, divine, poet, 230
ENGLAND, 1679–1737
EVERETT, DAVID, editor and writer, 573
UNITED STATES, 1769–1813
EVERETT, EDWARD, orator, scholar
and statesman,
UNITED STATES, 1794–1865
99 524 533 861
EVREMOND, CHARLES DE SAINT DENIS, littérateur, wit, and courtier...............FRANCE, 1613–1703 429
EWART, WILLIAM, scholar, politician, 126
ENGLAND, 1798–1869
EWER, W. N., poet.........pres. Cent. 295
EYTINGE, MARGARET, author 54

F

FABER, FREDERICK W., priest and
writer...........ENGLAND, 1815–1863
209 424 674 769 815
FABIUS 879
FAHNSTOCK, HARRIS C., financier, 181
UNITED STATES, 1835–1914
FAIRFAX, EDWARD, writer, 59
GREAT BRITAIN, 1580–1635
FAIRHOLT, FREDERICK WM., artist and 804
antiquary........ENGLAND, 1814–1866
FALCONER, WILLIAM, poet,
SCOTLAND, 1730–1769
398 704 765 770
FANE, JULIAN C. H., poet. ENGLAND, 1827–1870
89
FANSHAWE, CATHERINE M., author, 157 360
ENGLAND, 1765–1834
FARQUHAR, GEORGE, dramatist,
IRELAND, 1678–1707
4 142 308 522 532 536 585 642
712 755 889

FARRAR, FREDERICK WM., dean of St. Paul's, novelist, philologist, ecclesiastical writer..ENGLAND, 1831–1903
360 765
FAULKS, MRS. FREDERIC J. (THEODOSIA GARRISON), poet, UNITED STATES, 1874–L.
429 846
FAVART, CHAS. S., dramatist and writer............FRANCE, 1710–1792
392 683
FAWCETT, EDGAR, American-English novelist..................1847–1904 336
FAY, W. M. L., poet....ENGLAND, pres. cent.
168
FELLTHAM (FELTHAM), OWEN, moralist............ENGLAND, 1602(?)–1668
140 712 913
FÉNÉLON, FRANÇOIS, prelate and author..............FRANCE, 1651–1715
219 626 758
FENTON, ELIJAH, poet,...ENGLAND, 1683–1730
468
FERDINAND I., emperor of Germany, SPAIN, 1503–1564 415
FERGUSON, CHARLES, clergyman, lawyer, economist, writer, UNITED STATES, 1863–L. 218
FERGUSON, SAMUEL, poet.IRELAND, 1810–1886
71
FERGUSSON, JAMES, architect, SCOTLAND, 1808–1886 40
FERGUSSON, ROBERT, poet, SCOTLAND, 1750–1774 338
FERRIAR, JOHN, physician and writer, ENGLAND, 1761–1815 78
FERRIER, LOUIS, poet.....FRANCE, 1652–1721
262
FERTÉ, HENRI FRANÇOIS, MARSHAL DE LA............FRANCE, 1657–1703 859
FESSENDEN, WILLIAM P., U. S. Senator........UNITED STATES, 1806–1869 671
FEUERBACH, LUDWIG ANDREAS, philosopher and skeptic, GERMANY, 1804–1872 663
FICHTE, JOHANN GOTTLIEB, philosopher...........GERMANY, 1762–1814 871
FIELD, EUGENE, poet, humorist, lecturer.......UNITED STATES, 1850–1895
59 110 205 211 409 591 718
FIELD, NATHANIEL, actor, dramatist, ENGLAND, 1587–1633 641
FIELD, STEPHEN J., jurist, UNITED STATES, 1816–1899 431
FIELDING, HENRY, novelist, ENGLAND, 1707–1754
59 108 136 207 211 243 247 367
399 408 461 467 521 542 545 574
639 645 755 785 863 893 913
FIELDS, JAMES T., littérateur, UNITED STATES, 1817–1881
144 150 484 576
FILICAJA, VINCENZA DA, poet, ITALY, 1642–1707
402
FINCH, FRANCIS M., poet and lawyer, UNITED STATES, about 1828–1907 726
FIRDOUSI, FIRDOUSEE, or FIRDAUSI, ABOOL KÂSIM MANSOOR, Persian poet..KHORASSAN, about 940–1022 699
FIRMIN, GILES, physician, nonconformist..........ENGLAND, 1615–1697 362
FISHER OF KILVERSTONE, JOHN ARBUTHNOT, first sea Lord of Admiralty, writer....ENGLAND, 1841–1920
846 847 919
FITZGEFFREY (FITZJEFFREY), CHARLES, poet, clergyman, ENGLAND, 1575(?)–1638 585
FITZGERALD, EDWARD, poet and translator. (See also OMAR for his translations).....ENGLAND, 1809–1883 445
FLAMM, OSWALD, scientist, GERMANY, 1861–L. 850
FLATMAN, THOMAS, poet..ENGLAND, 1637–1688
168 174
FLAVEL, JOHN, logician...ENGLAND, 1596–1617
570
FLECKNOE, RICHARD, poet and dramatist........ENGLAND, died about 1680 708
FLEETWOOD, WILLIAM, bishop, theologian, scholar....ENGLAND, 1656–1723 221
FLEMING, ALICE 168
FLETCHER, ANDREW, Lord Innerpeffer, judge........SCOTLAND, –1650 48
FLETCHER, ANDREW, writer and orator..............SCOTLAND, 1653–1716 56
FLETCHER, GILES, poet, ENGLAND, about 1588–1623 655 772
FLETCHER, JOHN, dramatist, ENGLAND, 1576–1625
6 205 444 602 718 781 889
FLETCHER, PHINEAS, poet, ENGLAND, 1584–1650
31 481 624 772 900
FLEURY, MARIA DE, 415
FLORIAN, J. P. CLARIS DE, novelist and poet..........FRANCE, 1755–1794 909
FLORIO, JOHN, teacher, writer, translator..........ENGLAND, 1553(?)–1625 349
FLORUS, L. ANNÆUS, Roman historian, living in 125. 607
FLOWER, ROSWELL P., governor of New York..UNITED STATES, 1834–1899 817
FOCH, FERDINAND, Field Marshal, authority on military strategy, commander of allied forces in Great War........FRANCE, 1851–L.
832 846 919
FOLEY, JAMES WILLIAM, journalist, writer of sketches and verse, UNITED STATES, 1874–L. 402
FONTENELLE, BERNARD LE BOVIER DE, author............FRANCE, 1657–1757
283 674 819
FOOTE, SAMUEL, author and actor, ENGLAND, 1720–1777
24 524 889
FORD, JOHN, dramatist...ENGLAND, 1586–1640
373 468 497 505 639 776
FORD, MRS. LENA GILBERT, American poet, killed in London durdon during an air raid in the World War. 846
FORD (FORDE), THOMAS, author, ENGLAND, living 1660 474
FORDYCE, JAMES, author and divine, SCOTLAND, 1720–1796 316
FORMAN, SIMON, astrologer and physician.............ENGLAND, 1552–1611 124
FORSTER, JOHN, historian and biographer.............ENGLAND, 1812–1876 308
FORTESCUE, SIR JOHN, jurist, ENGLAND, died about 1476 641
FORTINGUERRA (CARTEROMACHUS), SCIPIONE, philologist. ITALY, 1466–1515 734
FORTUNATUS, Bishop of Poictiers, Latin poet........CENEDA, 530– 209
FOSS, SAM WALTER, poet, librarian, UNITED STATES, 1858–1911
22 81 108 379 380 570
FOSTER, HON. SIR GEORGE EULAS, minister of Trade and Commerce, writer, statesman, CANADA, 1847–L. 223
FOSTER, JOHN, clergyman, essayist, ENGLAND, 1770–1843 308
FOSTER, STEPHEN COLLINS, song writer......UNITED STATES, 1826–1864
199 773
FOTHERBY, MARTIN, bishop of Salisbury..........ENGLAND, 1549(?)–1619 535

G

GRAVINA, DOMINIC DA, historian, 125
ITALY, living 1330–1350
*GRAY, THOMAS, poet, prose writer, and scholar..........ENGLAND, 1716–1771
GREEK ANTHOLOGY.
277 321 322 360 361 694 875
GREELEY, HORACE, journalist,
UNITED STATES, 1811–1872
588 640 855
GREEN, ANNA KATHERINE, novelist, 207
UNITED STATES, 1846–L.
GREEN, MATTHEW, poet. ENGLAND, 1696–1737
32 168 245 549
GREENE, ALBERT G., poet, 32
UNITED STATES, 1802–1868
GREENE, EDWARD BARNABY, poet, 370
translator......ENGLAND, 1740(?)–1788
GREENE, GEORGE A., dramatist, 705
ENGLAND, time of Edward IV.
GREENE, ROBERT, dramatist,
ENGLAND, 1560–1592
65 134 142 185 248 262 317 379
404 469 514 639 886
GREFS 107
GREGORY I., "*The Great*," the Pope who reformed church service, 540(?)–604
26 424
GREGORY, JAMES, geometer, inventor, 392
scientist,........SCOTLAND, 1638–1675
GREGORY, NAZIENZEN (Gregorius Nazianzenus), "*The Theologian*," Greek father, pulpit orator.......................326–389 695
GREGORY VII., HILDEBRAND, POPE, 414
TUSCANY, about 1015–1085
GRELLET, ETIENNE DE, called STEPHEN when he joined the Quakers. Traveler and evangelist, 440
FRANCE, 1773–1855
GRESSET, JEAN B. L. DE, poet, 758
FRANCE, 1709–1777
GRESWELL 531
GRETE, HERBAL (1516) 865
GREVILLE, CHAS. CAVENDISH FULKE, 648
diarist...........ENGLAND, 1794–1865
GREVILLE, MRS. FRANCES, poet, 392
ENGLAND, 18th Cent.
GREY, EDWARD, viscount, diplomatist, 847
Sec. of State for foreign affairs 1905 to 1916......ENGLAND, 1862–L.
GRIFFIN, GERALD, novelist, poet, 507 636
dramatist.........IRELAND, 1803–1840
GRIMALD or GRIMOALD, NICHOLAS, 674
poet.......ENGLAND, died about 1563
GROBIANUS 24
GROTE, GEORGE, banker, historian, 491
GREAT BRITAIN, 1794–1871
GROTIUS, HUGO, father of International Law, theologian, historian............HOLLAND, 1583–1645 424
"GRÜN, ANASTASIUS," see AUERSPERG, ANTON ALEXANDER VON.
GRUNDY, SYDNEY, dramatist, 541
ENGLAND, 1848–1914
GRUTER, JAN, Flemish philologist, 1560–1627
231
GRYPHIUS, ANDREAS, poet, dramatist.............GERMANY, 1616–1664 883
GUARINI, GIAMBATTISTA, poet,
ITALY, 1537–1612
469 615
GUEST, EDGAR ALBERT, American humorist, poet, miscellaneous writer...........ENGLAND, 1881–L. 760
GUEVARA, ANTONIO, BISHOP. SPAIN, –1548
362
GUICHARD, CLAUDE DE, antiquary, 497
FRANCE, –1607
GUICCIARDINI, FRANCESCO, historian and dramatist.......ITALY, 1482–1540
239 387 753 760 847
GUIDO, RENI, painter 576
ITALY, 1575–1642
GUILBERT DE PIXÉRÉCOURT, R. C., 79
dramatist.........FRANCE, 1773–1844
GUINEY, LOUISE IMOGEN, poet, born 72 354
in U. S., lived later in England, –1920
GUITERMAN, ARTHUR, American poet,
AUSTRIA, 1871–L.
168 489
GUIZOT, FRANÇOIS PIERRE G., statesman, historian, eclectic philosopher ....FRANCE, 1787–1874
445 752
GURNEY, DOROTHY FRANCES, poet, living. 307
GUY DE FAUR, see PIBRAC.
GUYET, FRANÇOIS, scholar,
FRANCE, 1575–1655

H

HABINGTON, WILLIAM, poet,
ENGLAND, 1605–1645
140 521 684 749
HADRIAN or ADRIAN, HADRIANUS PUBLIUS, ÆLIUS, Roman emperor, 737
ITALY, 76–138
HADRIANUS, JULIUS 550
HAFIZ, MOHAMMED SHEMS-ED-DEEN,
poet.........PERSIA, about 1300–1388
59 262 469
HAGEMAN, SAMUEL MILLER, author, 913
UNITED STATES,
HAGENBACH, KARL RUDOLF, Protestant theologian, writer, 611
SWITZERLAND, 1831–1874
HAIG, SIR DOUGLAS, commander of British forces in France and Belgium.........SCOTLAND, 1861–L. 847
HAKEWELL, GEORGE, see HOKEWILL, GEORGE.
HALE, EDWARD EVERETT, author, 635
UNITED STATES, 1822–1909
HALE, LUCRETIA P., writer, 594
UNITED STATES, 1820–1900
HALE, SIR MATTHEW, judge, historian, 371
ENGLAND, 1609–1676
HALE, CAPTAIN NATHAN, patriot, 585
UNITED STATES, 1755–1776
HALE, SARAH J., author, 426 655
UNITED STATES, 1793–1879
HALES, JOHN, "*The Ever Memorable*," 31
scholar and divine...ENGLAND, 1584–1656
HALIBURTON, THOMAS CHANDLER, 120
author.......NOVA SCOTIA, 1797–1865
HALL, C. A. 346
HALL, JOSEPH, bishop and writer
ENGLAND, 1574–1656
169 338 345 566
HALL, ROBERT, minister and orator 49 875
ENGLAND, 1764–1831
HALLAM, HENRY, historian and critic, 85
ENGLAND, 1777–1859
HALLECK, FITZ-GREENE, poet,
UNITED STATES, 1790–1867
86 141 169 338 358 366 522 542
585
HALLIWELL, JAMES O., archeologist and author......ENGLAND, 1820–1889
32 396 725 757 909
HALPINE, CHARLES G., "*Miles O'Reilly*," American journalist, poet and humorist. IRELAND, 1829–1869 22 348 459
HAMILTON, ALEXANDER, statesman, orator, and general, 181 753
UNITED STATES, 1757–1804
HAMILTON, EUGENE LEE, see LEE-HAMILTON.
"HAMILTON, GAIL," see DODGE, MARY ABIGAIL.
HAMILTON, JOHN (LORD BELHAVEN), 570
statesman.......SCOTLAND, 1656–1708

I

J

K

L

M

N

POE, EDGAR ALLAN, poet and prose writer......UNITED STATES, 1809–1849
68 174 203 374 402 656 740 761 797
POINCARÉ, RAYMOND, Prime Minister and President of France, LORRAINE, 1860–L. 224
POLE, REGINALD, cardinal, Archbishop of Canterbury....ENGLAND, 1500–1558 853
POLIGNAC, MELCHIOR DE, cardinal, statesman, writer...FRANCE, 1661–1741
15 65 219 237
POLLARD, JOSEPHINE, poet, UNITED STATES, 1843–1892 291
POLLOK, ROBERT, religious poet, SCOTLAND, about 1798–1827
55 258 299 383 485 510 517 538 567 627 693 714 734 782
POLYBIUS, historian.....GREECE, B.C. 204–125
334
POMFRET, JOHN, poet....ENGLAND, 1667–1703
350 651 779
POMPADOUR, MME. JEAN A. P., Mistress of Louis XV...FRANCE, 1721–1764 305
POMPEY, CNEIUS, Roman general, triumvir.................. B.C. 106–48 767
POMPONIUS, LÆTUS JULIUS, antiquarian, historian.......ITALY, 1425–1497 338
POOR RICHARD'S ALMANAC, a collection of precepts, published by BENJAMIN FRANKLIN, under the assumed name of Richard Saunders (see FRANKLIN).
POOR ROBIN'S ALMANAC. This first appeared in 1663. Discontinued in 1828. 38
*POPE, ALEXANDER, poet and critic, ENGLAND, 1688–1744
POPE, WALTER, physician and writer..........ENGLAND, 1630–1714 581 882
POPHAM, SIR JOHN, Lord Chief Justice, ENGLAND, 1531(?)–1607 761
PORSON, RICHARD, Greek scholar, critic............ENGLAND, 1759–1808 42
PORTER, MRS. DAVID, UNITED STATES, 1790–1871 920
PORTER, HENRY, dramatist, ENGLAND, living 1599 638
PORTER, HORACE, general, UNITED STATES, 1837–1920 612
PORTER, WILLIAM SYDNEY (O. HENRY), journalist, story writer......UNITED STATES, 1862–1910
137 552
PORTEUS, BEILBY, bishop and writer, of prose and verse. ENGLAND, 1731–1808
115 174 450 534 854
POSIDIPPUS (POSEIDIPPOS), comic poet............living B.C. 289 571
POTTER, HENRY CODMAN, Protestant Episcopal bishop, UNITED STATES, 1835–1908 25 194
POUJOULAT, JEAN-JOSEPH-FRANÇOIS, writer............FRANCE, 1808–1880 486
POWELL, SIR JOHN, Judge. ENGLAND, 1633–1696
432
POWER OF ATHERSTONE 560
PRAED, WINTHROP MACKWORTH, poet, writer of *Vers de Société*, ENGLAND, 1802–1839
23 66 157 217 486 508 631 664 732 778 829
PRAYER OF PERSIAN DERVISH. 598
PRENTICE, GEORGE DENISON, poet, humorist, and journalist, UNITED STATES, 1802–1870
88 797 854
PRENTISS, ELIZABETH PAYSON, author, UNITED STATES, 1818–1878 719
PRESTON, HARRIET W., writer and translator, UNITED STATES, about 1843–1911 325
PRESTON, MARGARET J., poet, UNITED STATES, 1825–1897
19 368 458 463 575
PRESTWICH, EDMUND, poet and classical scholar...ENGLAND, living in 1651 893
PRIDEAUX, HUMPHREY, clergyman and Oriental scholar, ENGLAND, 1648–1724 644
PRIESTLY, DR. JOSEPH, philosopher, theologian, and the discoverer of oxygen.........ENGLAND, 1733–1804 198
*PRIOR, MATTHEW, poet and diplomatist...........ENGLAND, 1664–1721
PROCTER, ADELAIDE ANNE, poet, ENGLAND, 1825–1864
450 498 539 582 704 735 747 751 806
PROCTER, BRYAN WALLER, "*Barry Cornwall*," poet and author, ENGLAND, 1787–1874
215 347 378 439 566 574 598 622 694 764 793 875 888
PROCTER, EDNA DEAN, author, UNITED STATES, 1838–1923 210 381
PROPER NEW BALLAD IN PRAISE OF MY LADY MARQUES. (1569) 900
PROPERTIUS, SEXTUS, Roman elegiac poet...........UMBRIA, about B.C. 50
3 84 129 143 253 258 309 314 389 476 546 601
PROTAGORAS, GREEK sophist, philosopher.................. B.C. 490(?)–415(?) 491
"PROUT, FATHER," see MAHONY, FRANCIS.
PROVERBIAL SAYINGS CURRENT IN GREAT WAR 854
PROVERBS OR MANUAL OF WISDOM. Printed for Tabart & Co., LONDON (1804) 648
PROWSE, W. J., poet.....ENGLAND, 1836–1870
121
PRUDENTIUS, M. A. C., Spanish Roman, Christian poet, living in 348
411 751
PRUD'HOMME (SULLY), poet, FRANCE, 1839–1907 341
PRUDHON, CHAS. F. J., comedian, FRANCE, 1845–L. 616
PRYDE AND ABUSE OF WOMEN, (1550) 893
PRYNNE, WILLIAM, Puritan controversialist, jurist......ENGLAND, 1600–1669 415
PSEUDO-PHOCYL, 648
PSEUDO-SALLUST, name given to the spurious Sallust 291
PUBLIUS MIMUS 312
PUBLILIUS SYRUS, see SYRUS, PUBLILIUS
PUCCI, FRANCESCO, archdeacon, theological writer.........ITALY, 1540–1583 233
PULTENEY, WILLIAM, statesman and orator...........ENGLAND, 1684–1764 410
PUNCH, London 2 459 493 498 739 912
PURCELL, DANIEL, punster and wit, ENGLAND, about 1660–1718 404
PURCHAS, SAMUEL, editor, collector, traveler.........ENGLAND, 1577–1626 140
PUTTENHAM, poet, ENGLAND, 1520(?)–1601(?) 659
PYCHOWSKA, L. D. 353
PYPER, MARY, poet, SCOTLAND, 19th Cent. 233
PYRRHUS, king of Epirus......B.C. 318(?)–272
833
PYTHAGORAS, philosopher and mathematician..GREECE, about B.C. 582–500
154 242 613 627 694

Q

*QUARLES, FRANCIS, poet. ENGLAND, 1592–1644
QUERLON, ANNE GABRIEL M. DE, journalist, satiric writer, FRANCE, 1702–1780 293

T

THOMPSON, FRANCIS, poet, ENGLAND, about 1861–1907
3 27 33 53 56 62 63 204 239 250 320 349 412 458 482 530 557 565 576 579 580 614 681 733 739 744 767 769 800 907 917
THOMPSON, GEORGE M. P., reformer, anti-slavery advocate, statesman, orator......ENGLAND, 1804–1878 334
*THOMSON, JAMES, poet. SCOTLAND, 1700–1748
THOMSON, JAMES, poet..SCOTLAND, 1834–1882
121 399
THOREAU, HENRY DAVID, author and naturalist...UNITED STATES, 1817–1862
242 454 731 754 822
THORESBY, RALPH, antiquary, topographer...........ENGLAND, 1658–1725 423
THORNBURY, GEORGE W., writer, ENGLAND, 1828–1876 631
THORPE, ROSA H., poet, UNITED STATES, 1850– 68
THOUGHTS FOR THE CLOISTER AND CROWD..................... (1835) 569
THRALE, HESTER L., see PIOZZI, MME.
THUCYDIDES, Athenian historian, orator...............about B.C. 471–400
3 259 367 386 675 735 736
THURLOW, EDWARD (LORD), jurist and statesman........ENGLAND, 1732–1806
4 87 501 528 547
TIBERIUS, emperor of Rome...........ITALY, B.C. 42–A.D. 37 25 306 767
TIBULLUS, ALBIUS, elegiac poet, ITALY, about B.C. 54–18
160 179 203 226 243 378 483 652 671 677 712 731
TICKELL, THOMAS, poet and translator..............ENGLAND, 1686–1740
80 106 179 235 306 430
TIECK, LUDWIG, poet and novelist.........GERMANY, 1773–1853 93 483 492
TIGHE, MRS. MARY, poet. IRELAND, 1773–1810
458
TILLOTSON, JOHN, theologian, archbishop of Canterbury, ENGLAND, 1630–1694 320
TILTON, THEODORE, writer, poet, UNITED STATES, 1835–1907 282 800
TIMBERLY, C. H., editor. Living 1845. 235
TIMROD, HENRY, poet, UNITED STATES, 1829–1867 403
TINDAL, MATTHEW, jurist, deist, ENGLAND, 1657(?)–1733 570
TITUS, FLAVIUS SABINUS VESPASIANUS, Roman emperor who conquered Jerusalem........ 40–81 163
TITUS, SILLIUS (SILAS), politician, royalist........ENGLAND, 1623(?)–1704 535
TOBIN, JOHN, dramatist. ENGLAND, 1770–1804
33 146
TOLAND, JOHN, deistical writer, ENGLAND, 1669–1722 664
TOLSTOY, COUNT LEO, author, reformer............RUSSIA, 1828–1910 896
TOME BURGUILLOS, see VEGA.
TOMLINSON, RALPH 274
TOMSON, GRAHAM R., poet, UNITED STATES, 20th Cent. 917
TONSON, JACOB, publisher, ENGLAND, 1656(?)–1736 361
TOPLADY, AUGUSTUS M., divine, religious writer.....ENGLAND, 1740–1778 320
TOPSELL, EDWARD, divine, writer on religion and natural history, ENGLAND, –1638(?) 228
TORRENCE, FREDERIC RIDGELEY, librarian, editor, author, UNITED STATES, 1875–L. 419 483
TOTTEL, RICHARD, publisher, ENGLAND, died 1594
639 645 896 917
TOURNEUR, CYRIL, dramatist, poet, ENGLAND, c. 1575–1626 399
TOWNLEY, REV., JAMES, dramatist, ENGLAND, 1715–1778 702 877
TOWNSEND, MARY ASHLEY, poet, UNITED STATES, 1836–1901 179
TRAGEDY OF LOCRINE (1595), Shakespeare Apocrypha. 160
TRAPP, JOHN, divine, biblical commentator.........ENGLAND, 1601–1669 646
TRAPP, JOSEPH, clergyman, writer, ENGLAND, 1679–1747 436 437
TREATYSE SHOWING AND DECLARING PRYDE AND ABUSE OF WOMEN. (1550) 870 893
TREITSCHKE, LEO HEINRICH VON, militarist, writer..GERMANY, 1834–1896 858
TRENCH, MRS. MELESINA, author, poet.............IRELAND, 1768–1827 871
TRENCH, RICHARD CHENEVIX, ARCHBISHOP, philologist, theologian, and poet........ENGLAND, 1807–1886
81 191 253 312 320 454 583 907
TRIPTOLEMUS 665
TROLLOPE, ANTHONY, novelist, ENGLAND, 1815–1882 550
TROWBRIDGE, JOHN T., novelist, poet, and editor..UNITED STATES, 1827–1916
11 200 516 783
TRUE TRAGEDY OF RICHARD III (1594) 160 378
TRUE TRAGEDY OF RICHARDE, DUKE OF YORK (1600) 65 534
TRUMBULL, JOHN, lawyer and poet, UNITED STATES, 1750–1831
207 434 619 628 671 707
TUCKER, JOSIAH, political writer and clergyman.......ENGLAND, 1711–1799 225
TUCKER, MRS. MARY F., poet, 1837– 293
TUCKERMAN, HENRY THEODORE, critic, essayist, and poet, UNITED STATES, 1813–1871 483
TUKE, SIR SAMUEL, author, ENGLAND, 1610–1673 287 896
TUPPER, MARTIN FARQUHAR, poet, ENGLAND, 1810–1889
56 129 183 216 320 425 520 544 721 925
TURGOT, A. R. J., financier, publicist, FRANCE, 1727–1781 219
TURNER, CHARLES TENNYSON, divine and poet.........ENGLAND, 1808–1879
64 69 282 656
TURNER, SIR WILLIAM, Lord mayor of London..................living 1668 87
TURVEY, HILTON, novelist, 768
TUSSER, THOMAS, poet, ENGLAND, about 1527–1580
19 36 39 81 117 270 274 371 512 574 636 641 792 795 801 874 877 924
TWAIN, MARK, see CLEMENS, SAMUEL LANGHORNE.
TWEED, WILLIAM MARCY, Democratic politician and notorious criminal.........UNITED STATES, 1823–1878 613

U

UDALE, JOHN, ENGLAND, living 1598 572
UDALL, NICHOLAS, dramatist and Latin scholar.....ENGLAND, 1505–1556 34
UHLAND, lyric poet.....GERMANY, 1787–1862
746
UMBERTO I., King of Italy, 1844–1900 535
UNBELIEVER'S CREED, in *Connoisseur*, No. IX, March 28, 1754. 320
UNTERMEYER, LOUIS, poet, UNITED STATES, 1885–L. 366 557 628 629
USENER 751
USHER, JAMES, bishop, scholar, IRELAND, 1580–1656 912
USTERI, JOHANN MARTIN, poet, SWITZERLAND, 1763–1827 454

V

Valdarne 274
Valerius Maximus, Roman historian, living in 1st Cent. 206 351 671 709
Vanbrugh, Sir John, dramatist and architect...England, about 1666–1726 207 641 897
Van Buren, Martin, statesman and 8th Pres. of U. S., United States, 1782–1862 243
Vanderbilt, Wm. Henry, capitalist, railroad magnate, United States, 1821–1885 649
Vandiver, Col. Willard Duncan, naturalist, Congressman, United States, 1854–4 826
van Dyke, Henry, poet, writer, diplomat......United States, 1852–L. 23 29 361 371 380 762 768 858 911
Vandyke, Harry Stoe, writer of prose and verse...England, 1798–1828 271
Vardill, Anna Jane (Mrs. James Niven), writer... England, 1781–1852 687
Varro, Marcus Terentius, learned Latin author........Italy, B.C. 116–27 17 121 329 357 415 492
Vaughan, Henry, "*The Silurist*," physician, poet, and mystic, Wales, 1621–1693 117 271 345 389 440 629 656 721 790 814
Vaulabelle, Archille Tenaille de, journalist and statesman, France, 1799–1879 93
Vauvenargues, Luc de Clapier de, moralist..........France, 1715–1747 2 131 269 285 384 415 454 584 596 638 639 758 759 790 830 911
Vaux, Thomas, Lord, poet, England, 1510–1557 17
Vaux-de-Vire, earliest type of *Chanson Bachique* in France, of the middle or end of 16th Cent. First collected by Jean le Houx, an advocate of Vire. Said to have been written by Olivier Basselin, a poet and dyer. Probably a myth as he died about 1459 561
Vedder, David, poet...Scotland, 1790–1854 547
Vedic Funeral Rite 179
Vega, Carpio, Lope Felix de, "*Tome Burguillos*," poet and dramatist..................Spain, 1562–1635 806 807
Vegetius, author, fl. about 1450 591
Venning, Ralph, preacher, and writer......England, about 1620–1673 63 652
Vere, Sir Aubrey de, poet and dramatist..........Ireland, 1788–1846 155 250 329 385 509 581
Vere, Aubrey Thomas de, poet and prose writer.......Ireland, 1814–1902 483 721 736
Vere, Edward de (Earl of Oxford), poet and courtier, England, about 1540–1604 674
Vergennes, Chas. G. Comte de, statesman.........France, 1717–1787 815
Vergil, Polydore, ecclesiastic, historian, sent to England after Peter's Pence.........Italy, 1470–1550 639
*Vergil, Publius Virgilius Maro, Roman epic, didactic, and idyllic poet............Italy, B.C. 70–19
Vers sur la Mort, 12th Cent. 166
Very, Jones, poet and essayist, United States, 1813–1880 874
Vespasian, Titus Flavius, emperor of Rome.................Italy, 9–79 180 222
Vest, George, U. S. Senator, United States, 1830–1904 92 200
Veteran of Smokedom 805 806
Vicar of Bray, old song 683
Vicente, Gil, see Gil, Vicente.
Victor, Adam de, Saint, see St. Victor, Adam de.
Vida, Marco Girolamo, ecclesiastical Latin poet, writer .....1480(?)–1566 516
Viele, Herman Knickerbocker, poet, novelist, United States, 1866–1908 288 395
Vigée, J. B. E., littérateur, France, 1768–1820 697
Vigny, Alfred Victor, Comte de, writer, poet........France, 1799–1863 454
Villars, Claude Louis Hector de, general and marshal of France, France, 1653–1734 222
Villars, Mme. de. France, 18th Cent. 387
Villiers, Abbé de French writer, France, 1648–1728 631
Villiers, George, Duke of Buckingham, profligate, wit, poet, dramatist, statesman. England, 1628–1687 51 483
Villon, François, poet, France, about 1431–1484 163 235 723 778
Vincent de Beauvais (Bellovacensis), dominican.............–1264(?) 622
Vogelweide, Walther von der, minnesinger and lyric poet, Germany, about 1168–1230 559 897
Volney, Constantin François de Chassebœuf de, scholar, author and traveler...France, 1757–1820 687
*Voltaire, François Marie Arouet, historian, dramatist, critic, satirist, writer, and poet, France, 1694–1778
Volunteer Movement in England, (1859) 613 847
Voss, J. H., writer.....Germany, 1751–1826 473
Votivæ Angelicæ (1624) 105
Vulgaria Stambrigi (1510) 312 883
Vulgate, St. Jerome's Latin version of the Bible used as the authorized version by Roman Catholics.

W

Wace or Eustace, Robert, Anglo-Norman poet, Isle of Jersey, about 1124–1174 665
Wade, Joseph Augustine, musical composer......England, 1796(?)–1845 528
Wagner, Charles, writer, Alsace, 1851–1918 710
Walæus, Jan, anatomist. Holland, 1604–1649 308
Walcot, Johan, Lord Mayor of London.......................living 1402 390
Walker, Clement, Presbyterian leader, political writer, historian of independence, England, 1599(?)–1651 187
Walker, Katherine K. C., living 1864 642
Walker, William, schoolmaster, writer on grammar and rhetoric............England, 1623–1684 658
Wallace, Edgar, poet, war correspondent........England, 1875–L. 51 364
Wallace, Horace Binney, lawyer and writer.. United States, 1817–1852 619
Wallace, John Aikman 629
Wallace, William Ross, poet, United States, about 1819–1881 531 629

CONCORDANCE TO QUOTATIONS

INDEXES

1
I certainly think that the best book in the world would owe the most to a good index, and the worst book, if it had but a single good thought in it, might be kept alive by it.
HORACE BINNEY—*To S. Austin Allibone.*

2
So essential did I consider an index to be to every book, that I proposed to bring a bill into Parliament to deprive an author who publishes a book without an index of the privilege of copyright, and, moreover, to subject him for his offense to a pecuniary penalty.
LORD CAMPBELL—*Lives of the Chief Justices of England.* Preface to Vol. III.

3
An index is a necessary implement. * * * Without this, a large author is but a labyrinth without a clue to direct the readers within.
FULLER—*Worthies of England.*

4
The index tells us the contents of stories and directs to the particular chapters.
MASSINGER and FIELD—*Fatal Dowry.* Act IV. Sc. 1.

5
How index-learning turns no student pale,
Yet holds the eel of science by the tail.
POPE—*Dunciad.* Bk. I. L. 279.

6
That roars so loud and thunders in the index.
Hamlet. Act III. Sc. 4. L. 53.

7
And in such indexes, although small pricks
To their subsequent volumes, there is seen
The baby figure of the giant mass
Of things to come at large.
Troilus and Cressida. Act I. Sc. 3. L. 343.

CONCORDANCE TO QUOTATIONS

NOTE.—The indexed word is usually found in the phrase, indicated by its initial letter. When not found there it is to be understood that the phrase begins with the indexed word.

In general old spelling is not followed, but all words will be found under the correct form. This is the case with dialect, save when the spelling is so well known that the searcher would otherwise be misled. As the space allowed is often not adequate for a full phrase, unimportant words are omitted in order to convey the idea, although no word is changed.

The small black-faced figures that follow the page numbers indicate the numerical order of the quotation on the page.

A

C

D

see also Desire p. 189

E

F

G

L

M

N

O

P

Q

R

S

T

U

V

W

X

Y

Z